$44.50

McAinsh

June 26/79

43.75
50 postage + handling
25 insurance
44.50

HANDBOOK
OF
PSYCHOTHERAPY
AND
BEHAVIOR CHANGE

HANDBOOK
OF PSYCHOTHERAPY
AND
BEHAVIOR CHANGE:
AN EMPIRICAL ANALYSIS

Second Edition

SOL L. GARFIELD and ALLEN E. BERGIN, Editors,

Department of Psychology
Washington University

Values and Human Behavior Institute
Brigham Young University

JOHN WILEY & SONS

New York   **Chichester**   **Brisbane**   Toronto

Library of Congress Cataloging in Publication Data:

Handbook of psychotherapy and behavior change.

   First ed. (1971) edited by A. E. Bergin and
S. L. Garfield.
   Includes bibliographies and index.
    1.   Psychotherapy—Addresses, essays, lectures.
2.   Behavior therapy—Addresses, essays, lectures.
I.   Garfield, Sol Louis, 1918-   II.   Bergin,
Allen E., 1934-   III.   Bergin, Allen E., 1934-
Handbook of psychotherapy and behavior change. [DNLM:
1.   Behavior therapy.   2.   Psychotherapy. WM420.3
H236]
RC480.B376   1978   616.8'914   78-8526
ISBN 0-471-29178-1

Printed in the United States of America

10 9 8 7 6 5 4 3 2 1

CONTRIBUTORS

DIANE B. ARNKOFF
Department of Psychology
Pennsylvania State University
University Park, Pennsylvania

ALBERT BANDURA, Ph.D.
David Starr Jordan Professor of Social Science in
Psychology
Department of Psychology
Stanford University
Stanford, California

RICHARD L. BEDNAR, Ph.D.
Professor and Director
Clinical Training Program
University of Kentucky
Lexington, Kentucky

CURTIS L. BARRETT, Ph.D.
Associate Professor of Clinical Psychology
Department of Psychiatry
School of Medicine
University of Louisville
Louisville, Kentucky

AARON T. BECK, M.D.
Professor of Psychiatry
University of Pennsylvania
School of Medicine
Philadelphia, Pennsylvania

ALLEN E. BERGIN, Ph.D.
Professor of Psychology
Values and Human Behavior Institute
Brigham Young University
Provo, Utah

JAMES N. BUTCHER, Ph.D.
Professor of Psychology and Director of Graduate
Education in Clinical Psychology
University of Minnesota
Minneapolis, Minnesota

SOL L. GARFIELD, Ph.D.
Professor and Director
Clinical Psychology Program
Washington University
St. Louis, Missouri

JOHN M. GOTTMAN, Ph.D.
Associate Professor of Psychology
University of Illinois at Urbana-Champaign
Champaign, Illinois

ALAN S. GURMAN, Ph.D.
Associate Professor of Psychiatry and Director,
Outpatient Clinic
Department of Psychiatry
University of Wisconsin Medical School
Madison, Wisconsin

EDWARD HAMPE, Ph.D.
Associate Professor of Clinical Psychology
Department of Psychiatry
School of Medicine
University of Louisville
Louisville, Kentucky

STEVEN D. HOLLON, Ph.D.
Assistant Professor of Psychology
University of Minnesota
Minneapolis, Minnesota

KENNETH I. HOWARD, Ph.D.
Professor of Psychology
Northwestern University
Evanston, Illinois

LEONARD I. JACOBSON, Ph.D.
Professor of Psychology
University of Miami
Coral Gables, Florida

THEODORE J. KAUL, Ph.D.
Associate Professor of Psychology
Ohio State University
Columbus, Ohio

ALAN E. KAZDIN, Ph.D.
Professor of Psychology
Pennsylvania State University
University Park, Pennsylvania

DAVID P. KNISKERN, Psy. D.
Assistant Professor of Psychiatry
Department of Psychiatry
University of Cincinnati College of Medicine
Cincinnati, Ohio

MARY P. KOSS, Ph.D.
Assistant Professor of Psychology
Kent State University
Kent, Ohio

MICHAEL J. LAMBERT, Ph.D.
Associate Professor of Psychology
Brigham Young University
Provo, Utah

RAYMOND P. LORION, Ph.D.
Associate Professor of Psychology
Temple University
Philadelphia, Pennsylvania

LESTER LUBORSKY, Ph.D.
Professor of Psychology in Psychiatry
Hospital of the University of Pennsylvania
Philadelphia, Pennsylvania

MICHAEL J. MAHONEY, Ph.D.
Associate Professor of Psychology
Pennsylvania State University
University Park, Pennsylvania

HOWARD J. MARKMAN, Ph.D.
Assistant Professor of Psychology
Bowling Green State University
Bowling Green, Ohio

ISAAC M. MARKS, M.D.
Reader in Experimental Psychopathology
Consultant Psychiatrist, Institute of Psychiatry and
Bethlem/Maudsley Hospitals
University of London
London, England

RUTH G. MATARAZZO, Ph.D.
Professor of Medical Psychology
University of Oregon Medical School
Portland, Oregon

LOVICK MILLER, Ph.D.
Professor of Clinical Psychology
Department of Psychiatry
School of Medicine
University of Louisville
Louisville, Kentucky

LOUIS A. MORRIS, Ph.D.
Technical Information Specialist (Social Sciences)
Food and Drug Administration
Department of Health, Education, and Welfare
Rockville, Maryland

EDWARD J. MURRAY, Ph.D.
Professor of Psychology
University of Miami
Coral Gables, Florida

DAVID E. ORLINSKY, Ph.D.
Associate Professor of Psychology
Social Sciences Collegiate Division
University of Chicago
Chicago, Illinois

MORRIS B. PARLOFF, Ph.D.
Chief, Psychotherapy and Behavioral Intervention
Section
Clinical Research Branch
National Institute of Mental Health
Rockville, Maryland

TED ROSENTHAL, Ph.D.
Professor and Director of Clinical Training
Department of Psychology
Memphis State University and
Department of Psychiatry
University of Tennessee Center for the Health
Sciences
Memphis, Tennessee

ALAN O. ROSS, Ph.D.
Professor of Psychology
State University of New York at Stony Brook
Stony Brook, New York

GARY E. SCHWARTZ, Ph.D.
Associate Professor of Psychology
Yale University
New Haven, Connecticut

ARTHUR K. SHAPIRO, M.D.
Clinical Professor of Psychiatry
The Mount Sinai School of Medicine
New York, New York

DONALD P. SPENCE, Ph.D.
Professor of Psychiatry
Rutgers Medical School-CMDNJ
Piscataway, New Jersey

STANLEY R. STRONG, Ph.D.
Professor of Educational Psychology
University of Nebraska
Lincoln, Nebraska

HANS H. STRUPP, Ph.D.
Distinguished Professor of Psychology
Vanderbilt University
Nashville, Tennessee

IRENE ELKIN WASKOW, Ph. D.
Research Psychologist
Clinical Research Branch
National Institute of Mental Health
Rockville, Maryland

BARRY E. WOLFE, Ph.D.
Research Psychologist
Clinical Research Branch
National Institute of Mental Health
Rockville, Maryland

*This book is
affectionately dedicated
to Amy and Marian*

PREFACE

We were very pleased with the reception accorded the first edition of the *Handbook*. Our attempt to provide a comprehensive and critical appraisal of the empirical literature in the field of psychotherapy and behavior change was somewhat novel, and we had no way of knowing what the reaction might be. That the response was positive was personally gratifying for a number of reasons. Perhaps most important to us was the indication that research findings on psychotherapy were of interest to a diverse group of people who are involved with psychotherapy. The *Handbook* has been widely used in graduate training programs, which we hope has not only acquainted future psychotherapists with some of the research literature in the field, but has helped to instill in them an interest and respect for empirical research. The fact that the *Handbook* was also a selection of one of the professional book clubs and has had significant sales abroad demonstrates the interest among professionals in research on psychotherapy. This was a pleasant surprise, but one which, we hope, augurs well for the future improvement of psychotherapeutic services by means of research.

As we have been involved in preparing this second edition of the *Handbook,* we have been impressed with many developments, both positive and negative. On the positive side, there is evidence of a gradual increase in the quality of the research reported, a greater sophistication concerning research design and methodology, a greater awareness of the limitations of earlier research, and the application of research procedures to areas and types of psychotherapy and behavior change that were relatively undeveloped at the time of the first edition. More recent research has also reflected the increased interest in adapting therapeutic procedures to meet the needs for more efficient and effective services, as well as the needs of special groups in our society. Thus, the present edition contains new chapters on brief and crisis-oriented therapies, psychotherapy for the underprivileged, and behavior therapy for children. Other recent developments are reflected in new chapters on cognitive-behavioral therapy and marital and family therapy, as well as in the chapters that have appeared in *both* editions. For a variety of reasons, including our desire to keep the present volume at a manageable length, some chapters that appeared in the first edition have been excluded.

Another positive trend today is the greater interrelationship between diverse and competing theories of change. This is reflected in what appears to be a greater overlap or interrelationship among the different chapters in this revised volume. Several studies, for example, are relevant to the material reviewed in several of the chapters and it did not appear sensible to us to try to do away with this seeming overlap by requiring such studies to be restricted to only one chapter. We can hope that this trend signals a less parochial attitude toward procedures and research methods alike.

Although the above developments are most encouraging, there are also developments that are less positive. Certain hopes and enthusiasms expressed in the previous edition have not yet been realized, and a clear understanding of what variables help certain types of clients with certain kinds of problems is still to be ascertained. In recent years also, many "newer" therapies have mushroomed, all of which in various ways make strong claims for the efficacy of their procedures, but which, unfortunately, provide little or no empirical data in support of their claims. Obviously, in the absence of adequate research data, such therapies could not be included in the present volume. This, however, does not keep them from being popularized and offered to the public. There is also the problem of psychotherapeutic services being dispensed by individuals who have received training that varies widely in quality and quantity. In the long run, the efficacy or effectiveness of therapeutic procedures, as well as therapists, can only be appraised adequately by systematic research. At present, we have only made a beginning in this direction, but it is a beginning and progress is being made. We sincerely hope that this edition of the *Handbook* can be seen as one clear demonstration of this progress, and that in the years to come practice will be increasingly influenced by the findings secured from empirical research.

As was the case in the preparation of the first edition, the editors have found the preparation of the present volume to be a demanding but intellectually stimulating and rewarding experience. We have again been fortunate in securing the collaboration of knowledgeable and informed resear- chers in the area of psychotherapy and behavior change and take this opportunity to express our gratitude to our contributing authors and to our advisory editors for their cooperative efforts in our joint undertaking. We sincerely hope that this edition will be as well received as was the first.

Sol L. Garfield
Allen E. Bergin

ACKNOWLEDGMENTS

We are grateful to all of those who assisted the editors and contributors in completing this second edition of the *Handbook*. We acknowledge the help of individuals other than the consulting editors, who contributed by reviewing specific chapters for us. They are: Anthony Schuham, Kay Smith, M. Gawain Wells, Bert Cundick, Michael Lambert, Albert Bandura, John Paul Brady, and Aaron T. Beck. We particularly w : to express our thanks and deep appreciation to our secretaries, Marie McDonnell and Nancy Bergen, for their untiring efforts and devotion to this complex project, and to Ann Garfield who helped with the preparation of the subject index.

We also gratefully acknowledge the grant received by one of us (SLG) from the Special Research Fund of the Graduate School of Arts and Sciences of Washington University to help prepare the indexes for this volume.

Also we are grateful to the following editors, publishers, and publications for generously granting us permission to reproduce previously published materials:

American Psychological Association
American Psychiatric Association
Journal of Consulting Psychology
Journal of Abnormal Psychology
American Journal of Psychiatry
McGraw-Hill Book Company
Holt, Rinehart & Winston Publishers
International Journal of Psychiatry
University of Wisconsin Press

S.L.G.
A.E.B.

CONTENTS

PART I

BASIC METHODOLOGY AND ORIENTATION

1

PSYCHOTHERAPY RESEARCH AND PRACTICE: AN OVERVIEW[1]

HANS H. STRUPP

Vanderbilt University

A newcomer's first impression of modern psychotherapy is bound to be bewilderment: One observes a welter of theories and practices that seemingly have little in common (Harper, 1975); a mélange of practitioners whose philosophical leanings, training, and activities are grossly divergent; a wide range of persons who seek therapy for reasons that are often not very clear; an assortment of human unhappiness, malfunctions, and difficulties that are said to benefit from psychotherapy; a cacophony of claims and counterclaims that therapy is either highly effective or useless; a mixture of awe, fear, and puzzlement that greets the disclosure that someone is "in therapy." Perusal of the *New Yorker* or other magazines shows that therapists are a favorite target for jokes and caricatures.

What is psychotherapy? What does a psychotherapist do? How does he do it? What does psychotherapy accomplish? What are the risks?

Moreover, there are such troublesome questions as: What is the purpose of *research* in psychotherapy? What is its role and function? Who benefits from its findings—professional therapists, consumers (patients), the public at large? Why is research necessary in the first place?

WHAT IS PSYCHOTHERAPY?

Without attempting a formal definition, it may be said that psychotherapy is an interpersonal process designed to bring about modifications of feelings, cognitions, attitudes, and behavior which have proven troublesome to the person seeking help from a trained professional. There is considerable controversy whether and to what extent psychotherapy differs from other human relationships in which one person helps another to solve a personal problem; however, as ordinarily understood, the psychotherapist is a trained professional person who has acquired special skills.

Psychotherapy is practiced by members of numerous professions, including psychiatrists, clin-

[1] I have greatly benefited from comments and criticisms by Allen E. Bergin, Sol Garfield, Beverly Gomes-Schwartz, Suzanne Hadley, and Dianna Hartley. It is a pleasure to acknowledge their contributions.

ical psychologists, psychiatric social workers, and pastoral counselors. Psychoanalysts, who are usually members of one of these professions, are persons who have received specialized training in the treatment modality originated by Sigmund Freud; however, many psychotherapists employ psychoanalytic insights and techniques regardless of their professional affiliation.

Historically, psychotherapy has its roots in a wide variety of areas such as ancient medicine, religion, faith healing, and hypnotism. In the nineteenth century psychotherapy emerged as a prominent treatment for so-called nervous and mental diseases, and its practice became a medical art, restricted to psychiatrists. Around the middle of the current century many other professions gained entry into the field, which became broadened as a result of the growing demand for psychotherapeutic services, coupled with a redefinition of the earlier "disease model." Today the term psychotherapy is the generic term for psychological interventions designed to ameliorate emotional or behavioral problems of various kinds. Contemporary psychotherapy is characterized by a diversity of theoretical orientations (e.g., psychodynamic, client-centered, rational-emotive, Gestalt) and treatment modalities (individual, group, family, marital). Theories and techniques of behavior therapy, which have become prominent during the past few decades, are usually differentiated from psychotherapy although behavioral interventions are clearly psychological.

In broadest terms, psychotherapy is concerned with personality and behavior *change.* The patient who seeks help for a psychological problem desires change—he or she wants to feel or act differently, and the psychotherapist agrees to assist the patient in achieving this goal. The major issues in psychotherapy relate to *what* is to be changed and *how* change can be brought about. The first part of the question entails definition of the *problem* for which the patient is seeking help (depression, marital difficulties, shyness, nail biting, sexual dysfunctions, existential anxiety, etc.); the second pertains to the process and techniques by means of which change is effected (support, ventilation of feelings, interpretations, systematic desensitization, assertiveness training, etc.). Ideally, one would like to be

able to say that, given Problem X, the optimal approach is Technique Y. In practice, as the reader will discover, things are rarely so simple or straightforward; on the contrary, since human problems are extraordinarily complex, so are the issues facing the therapist who attempts to deal with these difficulties in therapeutic ways. For the same reason it is unlikely that there will ever be a single optimal approach to the solution of a psychological problem.

Psychotherapy is often described as a "treatment," and since medical terminology (patient, therapist, diagnosis, etiology, etc.) has traditionally been used, the analogy of a physician ministering to a passive patient readily springs to mind. By contrast, it is important to stress that psychotherapy, including the roles assumed by patient and therapist, has only a superficial resemblance to this model. More accurately, psychotherapy is a *collaborative* endeavor or a partnership, in which the patient, almost from the beginning, is expected to play an active part. In practice this means that patients must gradually become more autonomous, more self-directing, and more responsible for their feelings, beliefs, and actions. In order to feel better about themselves, their relationships with others, and their behavior, they must learn to make changes within themselves and in their environments that permit them to feel and act differently. The process of therapy is designed not to change patients but to help patients change themselves.

In this sense, psychotherapy is a learning process and the role of the therapist is analogous to that of a teacher or mentor. Psychotherapy is based on the assumption that feelings, cognitions, attitudes, and behavior are the product of a person's life experience—that is, they have been *learned.* If something has been learned, modification of the previous learning can occur. Where learning is impossible (for example, in conditions attributable to genetic or biochemical factors), psychotherapy has little to offer. Similarly, if the disturbance is solely due to factors in the person's social milieu (poverty, oppression, imprisonment) or if patients do not desire change on their own (referral by a court, school system, etc.), psychotherapists encounter great difficulties. Thus, psychotherapy works best if patients desire change of their own accord and are motivated to work toward it, if the environment in which they live tolerates the possibility of change, and if the inner obstacles to learning (defenses and rigidities of character) are not insurmountable.

It should be noted that no single definition of psychotherapy has found universal acceptance. Depending on the therapist's theoretical orientation and other factors, psychotherapy is seen by some as a "psychosocial treatment," by others as a special form of education, and by still others as a means of promoting personality growth and self-actualization—to cite but a few divergent views. Most therapists agree, however, that psychotherapy involves both a human relationship and techniques for bringing about personality and behavior change.

THE PATIENT

Perhaps the single most important characteristic of individuals who decide to consult a psychotherapist is that they are troubled. At times they may be unaware of the cause of their suffering and unhappiness; more often, they have identified a set of circumstances they view as accounting for their disturbance. Typically, they are dissatisfied with their life and complain of troublesome feelings (anxiety, depression, etc.) or they see difficulties with some aspect of their behavior (phobia, impulsiveness, etc.). Usually they have tried various means of combating their difficulties, without notable success. Not uncommonly, patients have previously consulted medical specialists who, sensing the involvement of emotional factors or out of a sense of futility, have referred the patient to a psychotherapist.

Prospective patients differ not only in the kinds of problems for which they seek help, but they show great variations in the degree of subjective distress they experience, the urgency with which they desire relief, and the eagerness with which they accept help once it is offered.

Further, they differ in their expectations of what a professional helper might do to bring about relief.

Virtually everyone has retained from childhood the hope of magical solutions, a wish that becomes intensified when a person experiences anxiety and distress. In addition, there are many unrealistic expectations of what psychotherapy can do. Such expectations occur not only among uneducated or unsophisticated patients, many of whom may simply lack information; they occur, perhaps in different forms and for different reasons, among individuals who, on the basis of their education or cultural experience, have heard or read a good deal about psychotherapy. At any rate, a prospective patient's expectations may have considerable bearing on his or her approach to psychotherapy and the evolving relationship with the therapist.

The patient typically wants to "feel better" or wants to "act differently." Often he or she wants to "stop" a pattern of behavior or wishes to shed inhibitions which "prevent" him or her from engaging in behavior he or she considers desirable. In most instances, the patient tends to complain of a lack of "will power" and feels more or less helpless. Alternatively, he or she tends to blame difficulties on the behavior of other persons in his or her life. Whatever the nature of the complaint, the patient generally measures the outcome of therapy by improvements in feelings and behavior.

From the therapist's standpoint, it is often not possible to bring about the changes to which the patient aspires, or at least not in the manner the patient desires. Frequently, it develops that while the patient ostensibly desires change of a certain kind, he or she is unwittingly committed to the maintenance of the status quo and actively opposes the change. For example, a patient may express a wish to become more assertive, while basically he or she is searching for a human relationship which allows him or her to be passive and dependent. The task of therapy is frequently to help the patient identify inner resistances to change and to deal therapeutically with these opposing forces. At other times, depending on the therapist's theoretical orientation, it may be possible to modify certain behaviors directly. In any case, the patient's problem is often not what it appears to be, and redefinitions of the problem as well as the goals of therapy may be indicated. As therapy proceeds, the patient typically experiences an increase in self-esteem and self-worth, regardless of the extent or nature of behavior change.

THE THERAPIST

The therapist attempts to be helpful to the patient or client. However, since there are considerable disagreements about the purpose of psychotherapy, the goals of treatment, and how therapeutic change is brought about, there is no consensus concerning the role and function of the therapist. Some therapists view their primary task as providing the patient with insight into his or her emotional conflicts; others seek to bring about a reorganization of the patient's cognitions and beliefs; still others work more directly toward behavior change in the hope that success experiences in one area will help the patient gain greater self-confidence, which in turn may enable him or her to tackle other problems in living. Most professionals agree that the therapist must acquire special skills, but for the reasons mentioned above there is less agreement on the nature of these skills or how to perfect them. Consequently, training programs for psychotherapists differ markedly in content, breadth, and duration. In the more recent past it has been asserted that "naturally helpful persons" (indigenous helpers, nonprofessionals, and paraprofessionals) may be as helpful as a professionally trained therapist.

Whatever the therapist's background or level of training, he or she cannot escape the necessity of (1) forming some notions or hypotheses about the patient's "problem" or difficulty, and (2) deciding what needs to be done to bring about an improvement in the patient's condition. In other words, therapists must first become diagnosticians before they engage in some activity they consider therapeutic. The latter usually entails verbal communications which occur in the context of a relationship which develops between patient and therapist. In this relationship the patient tends to express fears, hopes, and expectations, and looks to the therapist as a person who can provide relief from suffering. Some of the patient's expectations are realistic, but others, as already noted, are distorted and tinged with magic. The more the patient

is troubled, the greater is his or her tendency to imbue the therapist with superior powers, but in any case patients, almost by definition, view themselves as persons in need of outside help, which often means that they wish to be dependent on someone. Thus, unwittingly they tend to relate to the therapist as helpless children to a powerful and wise parent (transference). This tendency of many patients to turn the therapeutic relationship into a quasi parent-child relationship is of particular interest to psychodynamic therapists who essentially define the therapist as a specialist in transferences and how to resolve them. Other therapists, for example behavior therapists, while increasingly recognizing the importance of the therapeutic relationship (Wilson & Evans, 1977) regard it primarily as a vehicle for effecting behavioral or cognitive change; and, as already indicated, there are many other conceptions of the therapist's role.

In any event, it is clear that the therapist engages in a relationship with the patient and brings his or her personal influence to bear upon that relationship. Of course, both the patient's and therapist's personalities determine the character and quality of their interaction, but it is the therapist who defines the framework of the relationship and determines to a large extent how the relationship shall be used to achieve particular therapeutic ends. As we shall see, there is still a lively debate whether the therapist determines the outcome of therapy primarily by personal qualities or whether the outcome is primarily a function of the techniques employed by the therapist. We may find that both sets of variables contribute significantly but in varying combinations, depending of course in part on patient characteristics. But it is clear that the *personal qualities* of the therapist must be an important factor in the equation (see chapter by Parloff, Waskow, & Wolfe).

Finally, it is important to examine how the professional therapist differs from other helpful persons. Most significant perhaps is the proposition that the therapist creates a professional rather than a personal relationship with the patient. While the patient may be lonely and in need of a friend, the therapist does not view his or her task as fulfilling this need. Instead the goal is to facilitate the patient's interpersonal relationships with others and to help him or her cope more adaptively and effectively on his or her own. Consequently, the therapist seeks to avoid emotional involvement with the patient, a stance which is frequently contrary to the patient's wishes. On the other hand, this relative detachment allows the therapist to be more objective about the patient's difficulties. Even more important, it enables the patient to communicate more freely, since he or she does not need to be concerned about the therapist's personal reactions to material that ordinarily might evoke shame, fear, anger, and retaliation from others. As the patient can learn to trust the therapist and the safety of the therapeutic situation, he or she can often begin to tackle other troublesome problems in life. The professional therapist's stance of acceptance, respect, understanding, helpfulness, and warmth, coupled with deliberate efforts not to criticize, pass judgment, or react emotionally to provocations, creates a framework and an atmosphere unmatched by any other human relationship. How to create such a relationship and to turn it to maximal therapeutic advantage is the challenge facing the modern psychotherapist.

DOMAINS OF INQUIRY

Psychotherapy and Research
Psychotherapy has always been a very *practical* undertaking, growing out of the clinician's desire to help a suffering human being in the most effective, economical, efficient, and humane way. Psychotherapeutic techniques, accordingly, have always been "free inventions of the human spirit" and not blueprints created in the armchair or the laboratory. The clinician's first question has always been, "Does a treatment help?" Almost simultaneously, however, practitioners have devised theories to explain *why* a treatment works. Of course, a treatment or a set of therapeutic procedures may work when the theory is wrong; or, the theory may be reasonable, but the techniques may be inefficient or ineffective. The point to be made is that the individual practitioner has no sure way of answering these questions since he or she must necessarily rely on the clinical method, that is, naturalistic observation of a few cases. Furthermore, the history

of science amply demonstrates that humanity's capacity for self-deception is so great that misconceptions (e.g., the geocentric view of the universe) may persist for centuries.

As modern psychotherapy gained momentum and its practitioners grew in number, questions were raised relating to the quality of the outcome, the nature of the problems to which it might be applied, the relative effectiveness of different techniques, the adequacy of the underlying theoretical formulations, the training and qualifications of therapists, the possibility of harmful effects, and many other issues. From slow beginnings in the 1940s, research in psychotherapy has grown impressively in size and quality. As presented in this volume, it is a product of contemporary behavioral science, and as such it exemplifies the application of modern scientific methodology to the solution of important clinical and theoretical problems.

I shall next turn to a consideration of significant issues, which, along with others, will be discussed more fully in subsequent chapters of this *Handbook*.

The Problem of Therapy Outcome
The single most important problem overshadowing all others and placing them in perspective is the issue of effectiveness. As precise answers can be given to the question, "What kinds of therapeutic procedures will be helpful to particular patients under particular circumstances?" it will become possible to clarify the nature of the changes produced by *specific* treatment interventions and to delineate the variables that make a particular treatment effective or ineffective. (For a full discussion of this problem, see Strupp & Bergin, 1969, and Bergin & Strupp, 1972.)

It is apparent that the problem of psychotherapy outcome touches on many facets of human life, and that conceptions of mental health and illness cannot be considered apart from problems of philosophy, ethics, religion, and public policy. Inescapably we deal with human existence and humanity's place in the world, and ultimately we must confront questions of *value* (Strupp and Hadley, 1977). In the end, someone must make a judgment that a person's concern with duty is a virtue or a symptom of compulsiveness; that a decrement of 10 points on the Depression Scale of the MMPI in the 90—100 range is a greater or a lesser "improvement" than a like change between 50—60; that in one case we accept a patient's judgment that he or she feels "better" whereas in another we set it aside, calling it "flight into health," "reaction formation," "delusional," and so forth. These decisions can only be made by reference to the values society assigns to feelings, attitudes, and actions. These values are inherent in conceptions of mental health and illness as well as in clinical judgments based on one of these models.

One of the great stumbling blocks in psychotherapy research and practice has been a failure to realize the importance of values. While researchers have rightfully dealt with technical and methodological issues and made considerable gains in clarifying them, objective assessments and measurements have remained imperfect and imprecise. For example, it is a common finding (Garfield, Prager, & Bergin, 1971; chapter by Bergin & Lambert) that outcome assessments by patients, peers, independent clinicians, and therapists correlate only moderately. One may attribute this to the imperfection of the instruments and the fallibility of raters, but one should also be aware of the fact that raters bring different perspectives to bear and that the relative lack of correlation partially results from legitimate divergences in their vantage points.

Freud (1916) already saw the outcome issue as a practical one, and this may well be the best way to treat it. When all is said and done, there may be common sense agreement on what constitutes a mentally healthy, nonneurotic person. Knight (1941) postulated three major rubrics for considering therapeutic change which still seem eminently reasonable: (1) disappearance of presenting symptoms; (2) real improvement in mental functioning; and (3) improved reality adjustment. Most therapists and researchers, while they may disagree on criteria and operations for assessing these changes, would concur that therapeutic success should be demonstrable in the person's (1) feeling state (well-being), (2) social functioning (performance), and (3) personality organization (structure). The first is clearly the individual's subjective perspective, the second is that of society, including prevailing standards of conduct and "normality"; the third is the perspective of mental health profes-

sionals whose technical concepts (e.g., ego strength, impulse control) partake of information and standards derived from the preceding sources but which are ostensibly scientific, objective, and value free. As Strupp & Hadley (1977) have shown, few therapists or researchers have recognized these facts or taken the implications seriously. Therapists continue to assess treatment outcomes on the basis of global clinical impressions whereas researchers have assumed that quantitative indices can be interpreted as if they were thermometer readings; instead, values influence and suffuse every judgment of outcome.

Other reasons exist for rejecting the traditional question, "Is psychotherapy effective?" as neither appropriate nor potentially fruitful. It has become increasingly apparent that psychotherapy as currently practiced is not a unitary process nor is it applied to a unitary problem (Kiesler, 1966). Furthermore, therapists cannot be regarded as interchangeable units that deliver a standard treatment in uniform quantity or quality (see Parloff, Waskow, & Wolfe, this volume). Patients, depending on variables in their personality, education, intelligence, the nature of their emotional difficulties, motivation, and other variables, are differentially receptive to various forms of therapeutic influence (see Garfield, this volume). Finally, technique variables, since they are thoroughly intertwined with the person of the therapist, cannot be dealt with in isolation. Accordingly, the problem of therapeutic outcomes must be reformulated as a standard scientific question: What specific therapeutic interventions produce specific changes in specific patients under specific conditions?

There are, by now, clear indications that this formulation is being taken more seriously by contemporary researchers (e.g., Sloane et al., 1975), although as yet by few practicing therapists. There is a long-standing tradition among psychotherapists, exemplified in recent years by the practitioners of primal therapy (Janov, 1970), to view their respective approach as the answer to every problem presented by patients, with scant recognition that another technique might be more appropriate in a given case. (Freud's consistent refusal to view psychoanalysis as a panacea and his insistence upon carefully circumscribing its range of applicability stands as a notable exception.) It is fully apparent that neither therapists nor researchers can evade the necessity of working toward greater *specificity* in describing changes occurring in patients and evaluating the changes by reference to an explicit frame of values.

The foregoing considerations have important practical implications. For example, with increasing frequency insurance companies require practitioners to evaluate the outcome of treatment for which the patient or the therapist is being compensated. Predictably, greater specificity than a check mark on an insurance form that the patient has "improved" will be demanded in the future. There are similar concerns relating to evaluations of the effectiveness of a community mental health center or a therapy program which are often mandated by law. Both among the public and mental health professionals there continues to exist considerable lack of clarity about the outcomes that may be expected from psychotherapy and how to describe and evaluate them.

Research activity in the area of therapy outcomes, as a recent review (Gomes-Schwartz, Hadley, & Strupp, 1978) and the chapter by Bergin and Lambert demonstrate, has been voluminous and sustained. In the years since Eysenck (1952) charged that psychotherapy produces no greater changes in emotionally disturbed individuals than naturally occurring life experiences, researchers and clinicians alike have felt compelled to answer the challenge. Analyzing and synthesizing the data from 25 years of research on the efficacy of psychotherapy, Luborsky, Singer, and Luborsky (1975) have concluded that most forms of psychotherapy produce changes in a substantial proportion of patients—changes that are often, but not always, greater than those achieved by control patients who did not receive therapy. Other reviewers (e.g., Meltzoff & Kornreich, 1970) have reached similar conclusions. In an ingenious analysis, Smith and Glass (1977) demonstrated that across all types of therapy, patients, therapists, and outcome criteria, the average patient is better off than 75 percent of untreated individuals. The preponderance of the evidence, it has become clear, does not support Eysenck's pessimistic conclusion.

The literature also reflects increments in the number of studies that are methodologically sound

and clinically meaningful. Among the landmarks of outcome research are the investigations carried out at the University of Chicago Counseling Center with client-centered therapy (Rogers & Dymond, 1954); the Menninger Foundation Project (Kernberg et al., 1972); the Temple study in which treatment results from behavior therapy and psychotherapy were studied under controlled conditions (Sloane et al., 1975); the research by Paul (1966, 1967) and DiLoreto (1971). Some of the primary aims of these studies were to contrast variations in treatment and to investigate the impact of patient and therapist variables in determining outcomes. In addition, there have been a host of investigations of the impact of patient, therapist, and technique variables upon the *process* of psychotherapy. Detailed descriptions of these efforts are found in Chapters 6, 7, and 8 of this *Handbook*.

Patient Variables and the
Problem of Diagnosis

Therapy outcomes obviously depend to a significant extent on patient characteristics. From the moment they meet a patient, therapists seek to define the nature of the problem in need of treatment or amelioration. They become diagnosticians who attempt to identify a malfunction or a "problem" in order to take appropriate therapeutic steps. This requires an understanding of the vast array of *individual differences* among patients and how to deal with them. While seemingly simple, the problem is exceedingly fateful in its implications for therapy and research.

To illustrate, therapists and researchers have come to realize that a phobia, a depression, or an anxiety state in one patient is not identical to a seemingly comparable problem in another. Accordingly, it is hazardous for a variety of reasons to *categorize* or *type* patients on the basis of the presenting difficulty. Moreover, the utility of the classical diagnostic categories (hysteria, obsessive-compulsive neurosis, etc.) is very limited for either therapeutic practice or research. Other systems of classification (e.g., in terms of defensive styles or ego functions), while sometimes useful, have shortcomings of their own. The plain fact, long recognized by clinicians, is that patients differ on a host of dimensions—from intelligence, education, social class, and age, to such variables as psychological-mindedness, motivation for psychotherapy, organization of defenses, and rigidity of character.

Human personality, furthermore, is *organized* and personality organization often forms an integral part of the "therapeutic problem." For example, phobic patients tend to be generally shy, dependent, and anxious in many other situations (Andrews, 1966). In addition, temperament, genetic, social, and environmental factors of various kinds influence the patient's current disturbance. One must also recognize that the patient's life history, particularly interpersonal relationships in early childhood, may be crucially important for understanding and treating the current problem. The foregoing variables are typically intertwined in highly complex ways, resulting in a unique constellation.

Despite the uniqueness of individuals, there are commonalities in patients' "problems." People react in diverse yet limited ways to stresses and crises (e.g., bereavement, disappointments, rejection by important persons in their lives). Furthermore, despite individual variations, all members of our culture have had somewhat comparable childhood experiences. For example, most of us have learned early in our life that the expression of our impulses must be curbed in the interest of social living; that is, we have learned discipline and submission to authority. Since Americans, for example, have grown up in a relatively common culture, share the same language, and have common human desires, conflicts, and goals, others can understand our behavior and motives. For these reasons, as well as others, principles of personality functioning can be abstracted, and psychotherapy has the potential of becoming a scientific discipline. Sullivan's (1953) "one genus postulate" ("We are all much more simply human than otherwise") underscores the continuity of human experience regardless of ethnic differences or seemingly incomprehensible psychopathology.

In order to be maximally useful to a patient, the therapist must sort and integrate the large mass of information that becomes available through clinical interaction and evaluation, formulate the therapeutic problem in terms that are meaningful to both participants as well as to society, and institute ap-

propriate therapeutic procedures. In short, the psychotherapist and the therapy researcher must be sensitive diagnosticians, whose task far exceeds a one-time effort at pigeonholing individuals into diagnostic classes or categories.

The following implications and conclusions should be noted:

1. Formulating the therapeutic problem and achieving consensus among interested parties, both from the standpoint of clinical practice and of research, is a task of the greatest importance. It is also clear that progress in studying therapy outcomes, both within and across therapeutic approaches, will remain seriously hampered unless it becomes possible to deal more effectively with this problem.

2. Existing diagnostic schemes are helpful but inexact, as are theoretical formulations of patient problems simply in terms of presenting symptoms, difficulties, or "targets." The latter are often troublesome because they are the patient's (a layperson's) formulation of a problem which may not lend itself to therapy. In one case, patient and therapist may agree on the elimination of a phobia as the therapeutic goal. In another instance, however, the patient may state a vague or unrealistic target (like "becoming more popular" or "worrying less"). As therapy proceeds, the therapist may find it necessary to reformulate or sharpen the original target.

It has also become clear that in many instances it is insufficient to focus exclusively on one aspect of the patient's functioning (e.g., overt behavior *or* inner experience). Instead, estimates of the *totality* of the patient's personality functioning and performance on a number of dimensions must be obtained even when a specific area is targeted for change. It is gradually being recognized that in all forms of psychotherapy the patient will typically experience changes in self-identity and self-acceptance; that is, regardless of behavioral change, successful psychotherapy produces changes in the patient's *inner experience* (Strupp, Fox, & Lessler, 1969), a realization previously rejected but now often accepted by some behavior therapists (Wachtel, 1977).

3. Diagnosis is a process that calls for the exercise of significant clinical skills. It must be systematic, and it must lead to prognostic judgments that

can be translated into therapeutic operations as well as outcome evaluations.

4. The individual patient, his or her personality make-up and behavioral patterns, exert the single most important modulating effect on the therapist's total effort and therefore its effectiveness. Disregarding or giving short shrift to these variables is tantamount to developing tools without considering the material with which one intends to work.

As society has begun to recognize the importance of making psychotherapeutic services available to a broad spectrum of the population—not merely to its affluent members—the problem of defining and identifying those individuals who can (or cannot) benefit from particular forms of therapy has become increasingly pressing (see chapter by Lorion). With it has come the recognition that therapy must be tailored to the patient, his problem, and his needs rather than the reverse (Goldstein & Stein, 1976). This aim is reflected in research efforts to "socialize" patients prior to psychotherapy (Orne & Wender, 1968; Hoehn-Saric et al., 1964; Strupp & Bloxom, 1973), to increase their understanding of how therapy works, and to prepare them for therapy in other ways.

The study of patient characteristics in relation to therapeutic change, as Strupp & Bergin (1969) noted, has for the most part focused around one basic issue: How do patient variables influence and determine the immediate reaction to as well as the ultimate course of psychotherapy? The following question appears to be more significant: Which patient characteristics and problems are most amenable to which techniques conducted by which type of therapist in what type of setting? Thus, instead of the more common approach of trying to determine the kind of patient or initial status that will respond best to fairly heterogenous types of therapy, it is more important to devise specific therapies that will benefit particular kinds of patients. Although it seems obvious that differential initial status should lead to differential treatment, there have been few systematic efforts to deal with this problem.

Notable progress has been made in tackling more or less specific patient "problems"—chapters of this *Handbook* and a recent review (Gomes-Schwartz, Hadley, & Strupp, 1978) document continuing and persistent efforts, particularly by behavior therapists, in such areas as anxiety reactions, interpersonal problems (nonassertiveness, phobias, obsessive-compulsive disorders, depression, sexual dysfunctions, eating disorders, alcohol abuse, drug addiction, and smoking). However, there has as yet been insufficient refinement of patient variables that undoubtedly exert an important modulating effect on treatment outcomes. Such variables as initial state of disturbance, chronicity, motivation, expectations, socioeconomic status, age, or sex continue to receive ample attention from researchers. However, only modest advances have been made in assessing more elusive variables like coping ability, ego strength, or characterological rigidities which determine the patient's ability to become involved in, and profit from, a particular therapeutic regimen.

The Problem of Technique

Techniques are of course the core and *raison d'etre* of modern psychotherapy and, as previously noted, are usually anchored in a theory of psychopathology or maladaptive learning. Psychoanalysis has stressed the interpretation of resistances and transference phenomena as the principal curative factor, contrasting these operations with the "suggestions" of earlier hypnotists. Behavior therapy, to cite another example, has developed its own armamentarium of techniques, such as systematic desensitization, modeling (see chapter by Rosenthal & Bandura), aversive and operant conditioning (see chapter by Kazdin), training in self-regulation and self-control (see chapter by Mahoney & Arnkoff). In general, the proponents of all systems of psychotherapy credit their successes to more or less *specific* operations which are usually claimed to be uniquely effective. A corollary of this proposition is that a therapist is a professional who must receive systematic training in the application of the recommended techniques.

So far, it has not been possible to show that one technique is clearly superior to another, even under reasonably controlled conditions (e.g., Luborsky et al., 1975; Sloane et al., 1975). The commonly accepted finding that approximately two-thirds of neurotic patients who enter outpatient psychotherapy of whatever description show noticeable improvement (see the chapters by Garfield and Bergin & Lambert) likewise reinforces a skeptical attitude concerning the unique effectiveness of particular techniques. Finally, it often turns out that initial claims for a new technique cannot be sustained when the accumulating evidence is critically examined. The latter, for example, appears to be true of systematic desensitization in the treatment of phobias (see chapter by Marks).

An alternative hypothesis has been advanced (e.g., Frank, 1973) which asserts that psychotherapeutic change is predominantly a function of factors *common* to all therapeutic approaches. These factors are brought to bear in the human *relationship* between the patient and the healer. The proponents of this hypothesis hold that a person, defined by himself or others as a patient, suffers from demoralization and a sense of hopelessness. Consequently, any benign human influence is likely to boost his morale, which in turn is registered as "improvement" (see chapter by Shapiro & Morris). Primary ingredients of these common *nonspecific* factors include: understanding, respect, interest, encouragement, acceptance, forgiveness—in short, the kinds of human qualities that since times immemorial have been considered effective in buoying the human spirit.

Frank identifies another important common factor in all psychotherapies; that is, their tendency to operate in terms of a *conceptual scheme* and associated procedures which are thought to be beneficial. While the *contents* of the schemes and the procedures differ among therapies, they have common morale-building *functions.* They combat the patient's demoralization by providing an *explanation,* acceptable to both patient and therapist, for his or her hitherto inexplicable feelings and behavior. This process serves to remove the mystery from the patient's suffering and eventually to supplant it with hope.

Frank's formulation implies that training in and enthusiasm for a special theory and method may increase the effectiveness of therapists, in contrast to nonprofessional helpers who may lack belief in a coherent system or rationale.[2] This hypothesis also

underscores the continuity between faith healers, shamans, and modern psychotherapists. While the latter may operate on the basis of highly sophisticated scientific theories (by contemporary standards), the function of these theories may intrinsically be no different from the most primitive rationale undergirding a healer's efforts. In both instances "techniques" of whatever description are inseparable from the therapist's belief system, which in successful therapy is accepted and integrated by the patient. Some patients of course may be more receptive to, and thus more likely to benefit from, the therapist's manipulations than others.

Rogers (1957), from a different perspective, regards a set of "facilitative conditions" (i.e., accurate empathy, genuineness, and unconditional positive regard) as necessary *and* sufficient conditions for beneficial therapeutic change. Thus, both Rogers and Frank deemphasize the effectiveness of therapeutic techniques per se, and they elevate "relationship" factors to a position of preeminence.

Although the hypothesis of nonspecific factors may be correct, it is still possible that *some* technical operations may be superior to others with particular patients, particular problems, and under particular circumstances (Strupp, 1973). Such claims are made, for example, by therapists who are interested in the treatment of sexual dysfunctions (cf. Kaplan, 1974) and by behavior therapists who have tackled a wide range of behavior disorders (see chapter by Marks). As yet, many of these claims are untested, and a great deal of research needs to be done to document that specific techniques are uniquely effective.

In any event, it is clear that the problem has important ramifications for research and practice. For example, if further evidence can be adduced that techniques contribute less to good therapy outcomes than has been claimed, greater effort might have to be expended in selecting and training therapists who are able to provide the "nonspecific factors" mentioned earlier.[3] We also need far more information about the kinds of therapeutic services that may be safely performed

---

[2]On the other hand, a nonprofessional therapist may have a rationale, albeit commonsensical. For example, a college professor who functioned as an "alternative therapist" in the recent Vanderbilt project tended to insist that his patients (anxious, depressed and withdrawn male college students) suffered from "girl problems." He used this rationale quite effectively in his therapeutic interviews.

[3]This has been the thrust of a training developed by Truax & Carkhuff (1965) and Carkhuff (1969) which relies heavily on developing the therapist's empathy and related "interpersonal skills."

by individuals with relatively little formal training ("paraprofessionals") as well as the limits set by their lack of comprehensive training. In any case, there may be definite limitations to what techniques per se can accomplish (Frank, 1974), limits that are set both by patient characteristics (see preceding section) and therapist qualities, including level of training.

As Chapters 13–22 of this *Handbook* document, a wide variety of new techniques and modifications of traditional ones are being employed by therapists of diverse theoretical persuasions. Included here are the many varieties of individual and group therapy, family therapy, time-limited therapy and crisis intervention, behavioral techniques, the so-called "body" therapies which, in contrast to the "verbal" therapies, concentrate on the treatment of physical tensions, and "growth" therapies that emerged from the human potential movement. Most of the new or unusual treatments have yet to be subjected to empirical test. The permanence of the changes achieved by these treatments, in particular, is a subject that has received insufficient attention.

While there have been no major breakthroughs in our understanding of how psychotherapy works, there is no lack of evidence that various technical procedures—exemplified by such traditional techniques as interpretation, confrontation, and catharsis as well as the welter of behavior techniques—from systematic desensitization to cognitive behavior therapy, "multimodal approaches," modeling, covert sensitization and self-control procedures—yield beneficial results.

Experimental analyses of therapeutic techniques (as is true of psychotherapeutic interactions in general) are hampered by a host of methodological problems which have received ample attention over the years (e.g., Strupp & Bergin, 1969; Fiske et al., 1970; Paul, 1967, 1969). Among others, the problem of devising adequate control groups has been particularly troublesome and continues to defy elegant solutions. In recent years, the growing concerns with ethical issues relating in part to the protection of patients and subjects in research have often come into conflict with legitimate investigative efforts by researchers. Despite these difficulties, notable increases in researchers' expertise and sophistication have occurred.

The Person of the Therapist

As previously suggested, psychotherapy prominently involves the interaction of two or more *persons,* and the therapeutic influence is by no means restricted to the formal techniques a therapist may use. The patient, like the therapist, reacts to the other as a *total person,* hence both researchers and clinicians must become centrally concerned with the therapist as a human being. What has been said about enormous individual differences among patients applies of course with equal force to therapists. Indeed, it is difficult to fathom how in early psychoanalysis, as well as in a vast number of later research studies, therapists could ever have been treated as interchangeable units, presumably equal in skill and influence (Kiesler, 1966). Therapists, like patients, obviously differ on as many dimensions as one cares to mention—age, sex, cultural background, ethnic factors, level of professional experience, psychological sophistication, empathy, tact, social values, to name but a few. Any or all of these may have a significant bearing on the therapist's theoretical orientation, techniques, and the manner in which he or she interacts with and influences a given patient. There can be little doubt that the therapist's personality is a crucially important determinant of the therapeutic outcome.

The elusiveness of many therapist qualities has posed serious obstacles to research in this area. It is possible of course to specify human qualities a good therapist should possess (Holt & Luborsky, 1958) as well as those that may be harmful to patients (Strupp, Hadley, & Gomes-Schwartz, 1977). Because of the recent emphasis on the ancient medical principle "above all, do not harm," particular interest is currently being shown in those therapist qualities that may be detrimental to patients (see below and the discussion of negative effects in the chapter by Bergin & Lambert). At any rate, since therapists represent a combination of personality characteristics and qualities, it has been difficult to dissect strands in the therapist's total influence.

Among the therapist variables that have been subjected to quantitative research are: the therapist's personal adjustment (often measured by standard personality tests like the MMPI); the "facilitative conditions" already mentioned (warmth, empathy, and genuineness); therapist "types" (therapists [called Type "A"] who subordinate technique to a truly collaborative relationship with the patient appear to be especially effective with schizophrenic patients); therapists' cognitive styles; the therapist's level of professional experience (experienced therapists, as might be expected, generally tend to achieve better therapeutic results [cf. Meltzoff & Kornreich, 1970]); the therapist's professional status (professionals versus nonprofessionals or paraprofessionals); sex; age; socioeconomic status; ethnicity; and the therapist's social and cultural values. Effects of personality conflicts, needs, and attitudes of the therapist toward the patient have also been investigated in a variety of studies (see chapters by Parloff, Waskow & Wolfe, and Howard & Orlinsky).

Furthermore, patient personality characteristics demonstrably influence the therapist's effectiveness, which provides support for the conclusion that patients must be selected more carefully to match the therapist's capabilities. Finally, therapists appear to be differentially effective with particular patients (a preliminary finding of the recent Vanderbilt Psychotherapy Project). On the whole, however, it has proven difficult to isolate salient dimensions of the therapist's personality and to measure their impact.

It has frequently been mentioned that the effective therapist must be able to instill trust, confidence, hope, and to strengthen the patient's conviction in his or her own strength. Yet real as these variables undoubtedly are, they likewise have eluded quantification. It is becoming increasingly clear that *single* therapist variables, except perhaps for glaring defects in the therapist's personality, are not likely to provide the answers sought by researchers and clinicians; instead, a combination of therapist attributes appears to form an integrated Gestalt, to which the patient, other things being equal, responds positively, negatively, or neutrally. To have a therapeutic impact on the patient, the therapist's personality must have distinctive stimulus value or salience—he or she can never be an impersonal technician nor can he or she apply therapeutic techniques in a vacuum. At times, therapists must be capable of encouraging patients to explore a particular feeling, belief, attitude, etc.; at other times, they must wait patiently for the pa-

tient to arrive at his or her own solutions. They must be able to distinguish between the patient's neurotic and nonneurotic needs, and they must avoid getting entangled in the patient's neurotic maneuvers. Above all, they must make a careful assessment of how much help is needed, what kind of help is needed, and what obstacles prevent the patient from reaching a constructive solution. In short, the therapist must have a high level of personal maturity, as well as clinical sensitivity. Concerted efforts to specify these qualities may yield important clues to the question of what is ultimately effective in psychotherapy.

The Therapeutic Alliance

In recent years, some psychoanalytic theorists (e.g., Greenson, 1967; Langs, 1973, Menninger & Holtzman, 1973), have identified the relationship between patient and therapist as a major therapeutic force. As Freud developed the technique of psychoanalytic therapy, he recognized that the patient must become an active partner who collaborates with the therapist in his cure. Freud distinguished between the patient's "observing" and "experiencing ego," postulating that the former represents the reasonable and rational part of the patient's personality which forms an alliance and identifies with the therapist's efforts in analyzing the irrational (transferential) aspects of the patient's personality, the principal task of analytic therapy. Thus, the therapeutic relationship is composed of a "real" relationship (i.e., the relationship between two adults, one of whom desires therapeutic change) and a "transference" relationship (represented by continual but unwitting efforts on the patient's part to reenact his or her neurotic conflicts with the therapist).

To the extent that factors within the patient or the therapist interfere with the establishment of a productive therapeutic alliance, therapeutic progress will be retarded or even vitiated. Premature termination, or intractable dependency on the therapist are instances of such failures. It is also well known that patients who have relatively intact and strong egos have a better chance of succeeding in analytic therapy (Horwitz, 1974; Kernberg, 1976) and perhaps in other forms of therapy as well. Although empirical studies of the therapeutic alliance are as yet scarce (Hartley, 1978), preliminary support for the importance of this alliance comes from the Menninger project (Horwitz, 1974). Bordin (1974) has been an outspoken proponent of intensified research efforts in this area.

While superficially resembling any good human relationship (of the kind spoken of elsewhere in this chapter), the therapeutic alliance provides a unique starting point for the patient's growing *identification* with the therapist, a point stressed by the proponents of "object relations" theory (Fairbairn, 1952; Guntrip, 1971; Kernberg, 1976; Winnicott, 1968) who are spearheading advances in psychoanalytic theory. According to these authors, the "internalization" of the therapist as a "good object" is crucial for significant psychotherapeutic change. The present writer (Strupp, 1969, 1973), among others, has likewise stressed the importance of the patient's identification with the therapist which occurs in all forms of psychotherapy. Since the internalization of "bad objects" has made the patient "ill," therapy succeeds to the extent that the therapist can become a "good object." However, since the patient tends to remain loyal to the early objects of childhood, defending them against modification, therapy inevitably becomes a struggle. Even from this cursory sketch it is apparent that from this perspective the patient's amenability to therapy, that is, his or her ability to form a therapeutic alliance, is importantly influenced by his or her early relations with others.

Thus, the quality of the patient-therapist relationship and of the alliance as it manifests itself throughout the interaction appears to be a highly significant prognostic indicator of the forces working in favor of, or in opposition to, progress in therapy. Accordingly, it behooves researchers to scrutinize the therapeutic alliance as well as its determinants. Work along these lines, which is judged exceedingly promising, is currently being pursued by Luborsky (see chapter by Luborsky & Spence) and as part of the Vanderbilt Psychotherapy Project (Hartley, 1978.)

FUTURE DIRECTIONS

In conclusion, I wish to present some further observations about the status of psychotherapy research and its place in contemporary society.

Maturation of the Field

There are indications that research in psychotherapy is coming of age and that several developments warrant greater optimism about the future than voiced by Bergin and Strupp (1972) a few years ago. To illustrate:

Quality of research

The main requirements of good research—to describe with increasing stringency the nature of the therapeutic interventions, the kinds of patients whom a particular form of therapy is designed to benefit, and the changes expected from these interventions—are being taken more seriously. Journal editors and granting agencies, as well as researchers themselves, demand greater specificity which is rapidly becoming the hallmark of well-designed research. Although definitive studies are still difficult to find, researchers have developed a sure grasp for the design requirements of good research in the area, and it has become easier to predict whether a particular investigation is likely to yield meaningful answers. Indeed, one purpose of this book is to educate future researchers and clinicians to enable them to ask good questions about clinical practice and to formulate means for arriving at reasonable answers.

Persisting problems relate much less to questions of what needs to be done than to the logistics of doing it (e.g., recruiting adequate samples of a homogeneous patient population, obtaining the collaboration of clinic staffs, or meeting the requirements of committees for the protection of human subjects).

Research in the area is time-consuming, difficult, and expensive, but the cost is far less than that for research in the physical and biomedical sciences. Although governmental support of research in psychotherapy has decreased substantially over the last decade due to inflation (Brown, 1977), well-designed research continues to have a good chance of being supported, notably through the National Institute of Mental Health.

The desideratum of specificity of course has enormous practical implications because it will inevitably lead to more focused therapeutic strategies and provide sharper answers to the question of what psychotherapy can do for particular patients, at what cost, and over what periods of time.

Collaborative Research

While still not plentiful, collaborative research is on the increase, as exemplified by concerted efforts in the area of depression (Klerman, DiMascio, Weissman, Prusoff, & Paykel, 1974), which illustrate that researchers in psychotherapy and neighboring disciplines (e.g., psychopharmacology) can collaborate productively.

Rapprochement Between Researchers, Therapists, and Theoreticians

Researchers and clinicians are beginning to show greater tolerance toward each other, debates within and across theoretical systems are becoming more issue-oriented and less polemical (Garfield & Kurtz, 1976), and there appears to have occurred a general decline in ideological struggles. Dynamically oriented therapists have begun to recognize the utility of some behavioral techniques, and behavior therapists are becoming somewhat more attuned to psychodynamic factors (Wachtel, 1977). The latter-day popularity of cognitive factors and the growing literature on self-regulation and self-control by behavior therapists herald a move away from radical behaviorism and a growing concern with what occurs within the person (Mahoney, 1974; Meichenbaum, 1977; chapter by Mahoney & Arnkoff). With client-centered therapy on the decline, researchers and theoreticians within the psychodynamic and behavioral traditions are beginning to take a critical look at empirical data (Wachtel, 1977) in an effort to identify commonalities (as well as possible fundamental differences). The annual meetings of the Society for Psychotherapy Research, an interdisciplinary and nonideological organization, further exemplify the spirit of growing collaboration and open inquiry.

Problems and Issues

Among the problems facing therapists and researchers, the following continue to be in particular need of attention:

The Outcome Problem

As described in this chapter, the problem of outcome remains in a confused state. Because of its central importance for all research in the area, clarification is urgently needed. Critical questions include: (1) What kinds of specific changes are expected as a result of particular therapeutic interventions? (2) Who judges whether a given change is to be characterized as an improvement or as a negative effect—the patient, society, the therapist? (3) Is it reasonable to combine judgments derived from the foregoing domains, or should they be kept separate? (4) What instruments or measurement operations are adequate to assess changes? Across-the-board changes, as measured for example by the MMPI and other "inventories," or single indices like behavioral avoidance tests, increasingly emerge as inadequate. As elaborated by Strupp and Hadley (1977), the issues to be resolved are research tasks only in part. They also involve to a significant degree issues of researchers' beliefs, societal standards, and public policy—which in turn call for a thorough analysis of social values and the manner in which they enter into judgments of "mental health" and therapy change.

Techniques versus Nonspecific Factors

The issue of specific versus nonspecific factors in psychotherapy continues to be a topic of central theoretical and practical importance. There is as yet limited evidence that specific techniques are uniquely effective apart from "nonspecific factors"; indeed, earlier enthusiasm about the vaunted superiority of certain techniques (systematic desensitization) is giving way to more sober assessments as a growing body of literature is being critically examined (cf. chapter by Marks).

The Problem of Diagnosis

There is a great need to describe more adequately patient populations for whom particular forms of treatment are intended. The traditional diagnostic categories, as most researchers and therapists recognize, are woefully inadequate, but so are taxonomies based purely on behavioral indicators. So-called simple phobias in a presumed "normal" personality are rare, and it is increasingly being recognized that the person's total personality make-up (character) or social modes play a part in the presenting disorder. There are still only limited conceptual schemes for describing patients and their problems, a situation seriously impeding outcome assessments and treatment comparisons. In particular, we must develop better ways of assessing the totality of the patient's functioning—its strengths and weaknesses—within which descriptions of what constitutes a "problem" in need of therapeutic modification must take their place.

Thus, the time seems ripe for studies in which more sharply defined techniques are studied in relation to particular patient-therapist combinations, which again must be defined more stringently. Answers from such studies will not only shed light on the relative importance of particular techniques and particular combinations of personality factors, but they may also have important implications for optimal assignment (matching) of particular therapists to particular patients in clinics and other treatment centers.

Articulation of Techniques to Problems

Particularly within the domain of behavior therapy and to a lesser extent, within psychodynamic and cognitive therapies, there is a growing emphasis on developing more clearly definable techniques geared to the treatment of particular patient problems. Examples are biofeedback techniques for treatment of tension headaches and insomnia (chapter by Schwartz), brief psychodynamic psychotherapy geared to the resolution of "focal" problems (Malan, 1976; Sifneos, 1972), and the treatment of sexual dysfunctions by behavioral techniques (Kaplan, 1974). The claims put forward by the proponents of these approaches are in need of systematic study, together with an assessment of changes and their permanence. The chapters of this *Handbook* delineate in detail the current status of such efforts across a wide array of specific methods.

The Therapy Explosion and Society's Concerns

The enormous proliferation of therapies, training experiences, and assorted techniques for producing changes in mental and physiological functioning has affected, and will predictably continue to affect, practice and research in this area. From a form of medical treatment for "nervous and mental diseases" in the nineteenth century, psychotherapy in our time has become the primary secular religion, its goals ranging from heightened self-fulfillment, happiness, serenity, emotional and spiritual well-being (once called "peace of mind") to the traditional objectives of mitigating neurotic and psychotic disturbances.

Since "therapy" in the United States has captured the interest of a wide segment of the population (especially that of its more affluent members) and since various forms of therapy and "training" are offered to the public for a fee (thus inevitably becoming an "industry"), a host of questions have begun to be raised relating to quality control of services, professional ethics, and "truth in marketing" (see chapter by Marks). Another set of influences that will predictably shape psychotherapy research and practice is traceable to impending legislation for national health insurance, which will require mental health professionals to define more rigorously the nature of their professional services, the "condition" to be treated, outcome, and so forth. Finally, society's growing concern with malpractice in medicine is being extended to the practice of psychotherapy.

The Search for a Practical Treatment: Short-Term Psychotherapy

One of the serious criticisms leveled at Freud and the early psychoanalysts was the expense of their therapy, its length, and the sacrifices demanded of the patient as well as the therapist. Freud endeavored to respond to the challenge, and he foresaw a time at which the "pure gold" of psychoanalysis would be alloyed with other, more practical techniques. In our time the pressures for the development of forms of treatment that are effective, efficient, humane, and widely applicable have steadily mounted as society seeks solutions to its multifarious human problems. Various forms of behavior therapy have partly been a product of this challenge and have in turn contributed to the growing salience of behavioral treatments. Dynamically oriented therapists, despite some early significant contributions (Alexander and French, 1946), have been slow to respond, but as Butcher and Koss (Chapter 19) demonstrate, progress is being made and it is safe to predict that short-term psychotherapy will receive increasing attention from therapists and researchers in the coming years.

Reasons for this prognostication are not difficult to find:

1. Most forms of psychotherapy, whether or not they are specifically designated as "short-term," are in fact time-limited. It has long been known

(see chapter by Garfield) that in clinical practice the average length of therapy is only a few sessions. That is partly due to the realities of clinical practice (e.g., student therapists leaving a service when their rotation comes to an end) and partly due to mundane but potent factors (e.g., travel time to the clinic, women patients finding it difficult to secure baby sitters).

2. It has not been possible to adduce convincing evidence that long-term (intensive) psychotherapy produces therapeutic results that are impressively superior; on the contrary, time-limited psychotherapy appears to be as good as unlimited therapy (Luborsky et al., 1975). While there are undoubtedly cases in which prolonged therapeutic efforts are indicated (e.g., with persons who have experienced severe childhood traumas and serious emotional deprivations in their early life), for most patients unlimited psychotherapy is not practicable even if it is needed and if the resources were available, which frequently is not the case. Thus the professional community and society are forced, in the vast majority of instances, to settle for the achievement of more limited goals.

3. In terms of patients' expectations, resources, motivation, and reality considerations, it is essential to develop psychotherapies that yield significant returns in the shortest possible time and with the least expense. This does not mean that crisis intervention (e.g., 3 to 5 hours of therapy) should become the standard treatment, but it argues for the perfection of techniques that reach their maximum effectiveness in the course of approximately 20 to 40 hours.

4. Those traditional forms of psychotherapy that require painstaking and persistent self-exploration of the patient's feelings and neurotic patterns, followed by the gradual development of insights and improved adaptation, are increasingly being recognized as inappropriate to the needs of a great many individuals who enlist the services of a psychotherapist. From the standpoint of many therapists who are committed to the proposition that clients are best served when they are enabled to work through their neurotic problems at their own (usually slow) pace, this is regrettable. In many instances it may also be unrealistic to expect the therapist to intervene actively in the patient's life in the interest of providing "rapid" (which not

infrequently means magical) solutions. Nonetheless, we are on the threshold of what may be revolutionary change in therapeutic practice.

What might the future of short-term psychotherapy look like? The following recommendations (adapted from Garfield, 1977) are typical of contemporary views:

1. Short-term therapy should be the treatment of choice for practically all patients. On the basis of many reports (e.g., Harris, Kalis, & Freeman, 1963), about two-thirds of all patients will respond positively to such interventions; the remaining one-third can be continued if this seems indicated, referred elsewhere, or judged to be beyond currently available therapeutic efforts.

2. The goals of therapy should be the patient's—not the therapist's. (As noted earlier, such goals must of course be realistic and practicable.)

3. The therapist should take a much more active stance. In particular this means: The therapist must (a) set more modest goals in therapy; (b) take greater responsibility for becoming a "moving force" in the therapeutic encounter; (c) actively plan and implement interventions, as opposed to waiting for the gradual emergence of "problems" in the transference and their solution in that context; and (d) actively resist the temptation to broaden the therapeutic objectives once limited goals have been reached.

It is apparent that the preceding outline calls for a radical reorientation of the entire psychotherapeutic enterprise. Specifically, it demands (a) the development and testing of *techniques* purported to be uniquely effective; (b) the identification of *problems* and *patient* characteristics that lend themselves to short-term treatment (as well as those that do not); (c) concerted research efforts to determine the degree of permanence of therapeutic change (e.g., it is already known that many patients respond rapidly to almost any kind of therapeutic help although the changes may not be lasting); and (d) significant modifications in therapy training, philosophy, and practice. At the present time, few therapists (especially those trained in traditional therapy) are equipped to assume the role of an "active change agent" along the lines sketched above.

Finally, it is important to call attention to a potentially serious paradox faced by short-term psychotherapy (as well as other forms): A potentially successful candidate is expected to meet criteria (personality characteristics) which are precisely those that a good many applicants for therapeutic services do not possess. To illustrate, Sifneos (1972) and Malan (1976), among others, have asserted that candidates should have (a) the ability to recognize that symptoms are psychologically determined rather than external or situationally determined; (b) a tendency to introspect; (c) a willingness to participate actively in the treatment; (d) curiosity about themselves; (e) willingness to explore and change; (f) realistic expectations in the sense of not demanding instant relief; and (g) a willingness to make reasonable sacrifices. (It should be noted, however, that there are many other forms of short-therapy and crisis intervention, some of which are quite brief [7 to 20 sessions] and stipulate less stringent patient criteria.)

The foregoing paradox has given rise to the oft-repeated allegation that psychotherapy is most successful with those patients who need it the least. At the same time it is becoming increasingly apparent that a sizable segment of the population may not be able to profit from the forms of psychotherapy or behavior therapy that have been developed so far. Largely they are unable to participate actively and effectively in the therapeutic regimen, either because their ego resources are deficient or because their personality organization (character) presents serious resistances to therapy. From another perspective, this may underscore the inherent incompatiblity between the medical and the psychotherapeutic model in that psychotherapy basically demands the patient's active collaboration in the cure and it can do little for individuals who expect to be passively ministered to. Psychotherapy, in the final analysis, must lead to self-help.

Training of Therapists

In recent years, serious questions have been raised concerning the *quality of training* among psychotherapists (Chapter 23). Individuals practicing today typically show a wide diversity of backgrounds—some have extensive didactic training and a wealth of clinical experience whereas others are grossly deficient in formal preparation.

Training programs reflect widely divergent standards. While professional organizations such as the American Psychological Association and the American Psychiatric Association, among others, have formulated criteria, many individuals who call themselves therapists are ill-equipped to assume professional responsibilities. Certification and licensing laws now in effect in most states are a salutary development, but they are difficult to enforce and guarantee only minimal standards of competence. In addition to higher standards, research is needed to evaluate training programs and the competence of their graduates.

Psychotherapy's Growing Relevance

For all of these reasons research in psychotherapy is becoming increasingly "relevant." It is no longer the exclusive domain of a small cadre of scientists motivated by curiosity to understand fascinating human phenomena and forces, but is increasingly becoming an instrument of public policy and legislative efforts. Furthermore, since various forms of psychotherapy and behavior therapy ("psychosocial treatments") have staked a claim for viability and at least moderate effectiveness (especially vis-à-vis drugs, which are no longer seen as panaceas[4]), their refinement and development clearly falls within the public interest.

Need for Realism and Consumer Protection

Although exaggerated claims inevitably accompany the advent of new systems and techniques, serious workers in psychotherapy and behavior therapy have adopted a sober approach to the major problems that have been mentioned. Psychotherapy, assuredly, cannot be all things to all people, but if it can be some things to some people, there is no need for its proponents to feel defensive or ashamed. The task of the future is precisely to find out what it can do and for whom. As knowledge increases and appropriate standards of training are adopted, one may also anticipate

---

[4]It should not be concluded that psychotherapy has been shown to be superior to drugs or vice versa. Instead it appears that a *combination* of drug therapy and psychotherapy may be optimal in the treatment of schizophrenia (May, 1968) and depressions (Weissman et al., 1974). In common neurotic disturbances, drug therapy alone, on the other hand, has been unimpressive (see chapter by Hollon & Beck).

significant improvements in the quality of professional practice. Perhaps it is not entirely utopian to envisage the creation of an analogue to the Food and Drug Administration to protect the public from worthless or potentially damaging therapies. The mood of the times certainly points in that direction.

Negative Effects

Related to the foregoing is the rising interest in the problem of harmful (negative) effects from psychotherapy. Bergin (1966, 1971) was among the first to call attention to the fact that a certain percentage of patients in most outcome studies are described as "unimproved" or in a state of deterioration at the conclusion of therapy. This finding should have occasioned no surprise since psychotherapy, if it is a potent treatment, must be capable of producing harmful effects if applied inappropriately—to patients who are unsuited or by therapists who are inadequately trained, use improper techniques, or commit errors of judgment. However, for many years scant attention has been paid to the problem although there have been many scattered informal accounts by former patients who voiced disillusionment with their therapeutic experience. Strupp, Hadley, and Gomes-Schwartz (1977) in a recent study of the problem adduced evidence that there is now widespread concern about harm done during therapy within the professional community, whose members implicated a wide variety of factors that might be potential contributors to negative effects. Harmful effects from any treatment are obviously disquieting, particularly to a society that has become sensitive to consumer interests and is increasingly seeking to monitor the power and prerogatives it has extended to professional groups. Thus, we may anticipate further studies of the issue and more incisive analyses of variables within patients, therapists, and therapies which in particular combinations may result in serious harm. This domain is likely to provide an important and expanding role for psychotherapy researchers in the future.

Coda: Integration Between Research and Practice

In conclusion, I wish to offer a comment on the future relationships between practicing therapists and researchers. In the past, therapists have tended to regard researchers as unwelcome intruders who disrupted the sanctity of the patient-therapist relationship, produced findings of peripheral or trivial interest to the practitioner, and robbed a living human relationship of its excitement and vitality. To be sure, every scientific effort seeks to order, simplify, condense, and control. It is also true that practitioners cannot directly profit from statistical trends in their everyday dealings with patients; they must deal with the inevitable idiosyncrasies of every patient-therapist interaction (Strupp, 1960). The greater contribution of psychotherapy research may ultimately lie on a different plane: Researchers of the future, who must also be well-trained clinicians, must learn to work more closely with practicing therapists on vital issues encountered in everyday clinical work, subject these issues to experimental analysis and test, and provide clinicians with information they can use more readily. What is envisaged is a form of action research, originally proposed by Lewin (1947), in which research is brought to bear on a practical (clinical) problem; research findings are then promptly applied in the clinical setting; and their utility is again tested by means of research. Thus there results a continuous and productive feedback loop in which practice inspires research, and research provides information that is relevant to practice. For example, researchers may recommend to a clinic, on the basis of available research data relating to optimal matches between therapists and patients, that particular patients be assigned to particular therapists. The outcome of these dyads may then be studied and compared with random assignments; on the basis of these results, subsequent assignment procedures may then be modified in the light of the new information, at which point the process is repeated. This approach might also have important implications for the selection and training of young therapists. Obviously it would not replace more sustained research efforts along traditional lines, but it would be one means of bringing about a closer "working alliance" between therapists and researchers.

As responsible professionals, therapists must learn to think critically and scrutinize continually the quality of their professional activities and the "therapeutic product." This has always been the hallmark of a mature profession (Peterson, 1976).

As steps are taken in this direction, it is predictable that psychotherapy will become a better and more mature profession, meriting society's confidence and respect. Last, but not least, it will become a profession based on solid scientific knowledge.

REFERENCES

Alexander, F., & French, T. *Psychoanalytic therapy.* New York: Ronald Press, 1946.

Andrews, J. Psychotherapy of phobias. *Psychological Bulletin,* 1966, *66,* 455–480.

Bergin, A. E. Some implications of psychotherapy research for therapeutic practice. *Journal of Abnormal Psychology,* 1966, *77,* 235–246.

Bergin, A. E. The evaluation of therapeutic outcomes. In A. E. Bergin and S. Garfield (Eds.), *Handbook of psychotherapy and behavior change.* New York: John Wiley & Sons, 1971.

Bergin, A. E., & Strupp, H. H. *Changing frontiers in the science of psychotherapy.* Chicago: Aldine-Atherton, 1972.

Bordin, E. S. *Research strategies in psychotherapy.* New York: John Wiley & Sons, 1974.

Brown, B. S. The crisis in mental health research. *American Journal of Psychiatry,* 1977, *134,* 113–232.

Carkhuff, R. R. *Helping and human relations: A primer for lay and professional helpers.* Vol. 1. New York: Holt, Rinehart and Winston, 1969.

DiLoreto, A. O. *Comparative psychotherapy: An experimental analysis.* Chicago: Aldine-Atherton, 1971.

Eysenck, H. J. The effects of psychotherapy: An evaluation. *Journal of Consulting Psychology,* 1952, *16,* 319–324.

Fairbairn, R. *Object relations theory of the personality.* New York: Basic Books, 1952.

Fiske, D. W., Hunt, H. F., Luborsky, L., Orne, M. T., Parloff, M. B., Reiser, M. F., & Tuma, A. H. Planning of research on effectiveness of psychotherapy. *Archives of General Psychiatry,* 1970, *22,* 22–32.

Frank, J. D. *Persuasion and healing,* 2nd Ed. Baltimore: Johns Hopkins University Press, 1973.

Frank, J. D. Therapeutic components of psychotherapy. *Journal of Nervous and Mental Disease,* 1974, *159,* 325–342.

Freud, S. Analytic therapy (1916). In the *Standard Edition of the Complete Psychological Works of Sigmund Freud.* London: The Hogarth Press, 1963, Vol. 16, pp. 448–463.

Garfield, S. L. In H. Strupp (Chair), *Short-term psychotherapy for whom?* Symposium presented at the annual meeting of the Society for Psychotherapy Research, Madison, Wisconsin, 1977.

Garfield, S. L., & Kurtz, R. Clinical psychologists in the 1970s. *American Psychologist,* 1976, *31,* 1–9.

Garfield, S. L., Prager, R. A., & Bergin, A. E. Evaluating outcome in psychotherapy: A hardy perennial. *Journal of Consulting and Clinical Psychology,* 1971, *37,* 320–322.

Goldstein, A. P. & Stein, N. *Prescriptive Psychotherapies.* New York: Pergamon, 1976.

Gomes-Schwartz, B., Hadley, S. W., & Strupp, H. H Psychotherapy and behavior therapy. *Annual Review of Psychology.* Palo Alto: Annual Reviews, Inc., 1978.

Greenson, R. *The technique and practice of psychoanalysis.* New York: International University Press, 1967.

Guntrip, H. *Psychoanalytic theory, therapy, and the self.* New York: Basic Books, 1971.

Harper, R. A. *The new psychotherapies.* Englewood Cliffs, N.J.: Prentice-Hall, Inc., 1975.

Harris, M. R., Kalis, B., & Freeman, E. Precipitating stress: An approach to brief therapy. *American Journal of Psychotherapy,* 1963, *17,* 465–471.

Hartley, D. Therapeutic alliance and the success of brief individual psychotherapy. Unpublished doctoral dissertation. Vanderbilt University, Nashville, Tenn., 1978.

Hoehn-Saric, R., Frank, J. D., Imber, S. D., Nash, E. H., Stone, A. R., & Battle, C. C. Systematic preparation of patients for psychotherapy: I. Effects on therapy behavior and outcome. *Journal of Psychiatric Research,* 1964, *2,* 267–281.

Holt, R. R., & Luborsky, L. *Personality patterns of psychiatrists: A study in selection techniques.* Vol. 1. New York: Basic Books, 1958.

Horwitz, L. *Clinical prediction in psychotherapy.* New York: Jason Aronson, 1974.

Horwitz, L. *Internalization as a therapeutic process in psychotherapy and psychoanalysis.* Paper presented at the annual meeting of the Society for Psychotherapy Research, San Diego, June 1976.

Janov, A. *The primal scream: Primal therapy, the cure for neurosis.* New York: Putnam, 1970.

Kaplan, H. S. *The new sex therapy: Active treatment of sexual dynsfunctions.* New York: Brunner/Mazel, 1974.

Kornberg, O. F. Some methodological and strategic issues in psychotherapy research: Research implications of the Menninger Foundation's Psychotherapy Research Project. In R. L. Spitzer and D. F. Klein (Eds.), *Evaluation of psychological therapies.* Baltimore: Johns Hopkins University Press, 1976.

Kernberg, O. F., Burnstein, E. D., Coyne, L., Appelbaum, A., Horwitz, L., & Voth, H. Psychotherapy and psychoanalysis: Final report of the Menninger Foundation's psychotherapy research project. *Bulletin of the Menninger Clinic,* 1972, *36,* 1–276.

Kiesler, D. J. Some myths of psychotherapy research and the search for a paradigm. *Psychological Bulletin,* 1966, *65,* 110–136.

Kiesler, D. J. *The process of psychotherapy: Empirical foundations and systems of analysis.* Chicago: Aldine Publishing Company, 1973.

Klerman, G. L., DiMascio, A., Weissman, M. M., Prusoff, B., & Paykel, E. S. Treatment of depression by drugs and psychotherapy. *American Journal of Psychiatry,* 1974, *131,* 186–191.

Knight, R. P. Evaluation of the results of psychoanalytic therapy. *American Journal of Psychiatry,* 1941, *98,* 434–446.

Langs, R. *The technique of psychoanalytic psychotherapy.* New York: Jason Aronson, 1973.

Lewin, K. Frontiers in group dynamics: II. Channels of group life: Social planning and action research. *Human Relations*, 1947, *1*, 143–153.

Luborsky, L., Singer, B., and Luborsky, L. Comparative studies of psychotherapies: Is it true that "Everybody has won and all must have prizes?" *Archives of General Psychiatry*, 1975, *32*, 995–1008.

Mahoney, M. J. *Cognition and behavior modification.* Cambridge: Ballinger, 1974.

Malan, D. H. *Toward the validation of dynamic psychotherapy: A replication.* New York: Plenum, 1976.

May, P. R. *Treatment of schizophrenia.* New York: Science House, 1968.

Meichenbaum, D. (Ed.) *Cognitive behavior modification: An integrative approach.* Plenum, 1977.

Meltzoff, J., & Kornreich, M. *Research in psychotherapy.* New York: Atherton Press, Inc., 1970.

Menninger, K. A., & Holtzman, P. S. *Theory of psychoanalytic techniques.* 2nd Ed. New York: Basic Books, 1973.

Orne, M. T., & Wender, P. H. Anticipatory socialization for psychotherapy: Method and rationale. *American Journal of Psychiatry*, 1968, *124*, 1202–1212.

Paul, G. L. *Insight versus desensitization in psychotherapy: An experiment in anxiety reduction.* Stanford: Stanford University Press, 1966.

Paul, G. L. Strategy in outcome research in psychotherapy. *Journal of Consulting Psychology, 1967, 31,* 109–118.

Paul, G. L. Behavior modification research. Design and Tactics. In C. M. Franks (Ed.) *Behavior Therapy: Appraisal and Status,* New York: McGraw-Hill, 1969. Pp 29–62.

Peterson, D. R. Is psychology a profession? *American Psychologist*, August 1976, *31*, 553–560.

Rogers, C. R. The necessary and sufficient conditions of therapeutic personality change. *Journal of Consulting Psychology, 1957, 21,* 95–103.

Rogers, C. R., & Dymond, R. F. *Psychotherapy and personality change.* Chicago: University of Chicago Press, 1954.

Sifneos, D. *Short-term psychotherapy and emotional crisis.* Cambridge: Harvard University Press, 1972.

Sloane, R. B., Staples, F. R., Cristol, A. H., Yorkston, N. J., & Whipple, K. *Psychotherapy versus behavior therapy.* Cambridge: Harvard University Press, 1975.

Smith, M. L. & Glass, G. V. Meta-analysis of psychotherapy outcome studies. *American Psychologist, 1977, 132,* 752–760.

Strupp, H. H. Some comments on the future of research in psychotherapy. *Behavioral Science, 1960, 5,* 60–71.

Strupp, H. H. Toward a specification of teaching and learning in psychotherapy. *Archives of General Psychiatry, 1969, 21,* 203–212.

Strupp, H. H. Toward a reformulation of the psychotherapeutic influence. *International Journal of Psychiatry, 1973, 11,* 263–327.

Strupp, H. H., & Bergin, A. E. Some empirical and conceptual bases for coordinated research in psychotherapy. *International Journal of Psychiatry,* 1969, 7, 18–90.

Strupp, H. H., & Bloxom, A. L. Preparing lower-class patients for group psychotherapy: Development and evaluation of a role-induction film. *Journal of Consulting and Clinical Psychology, 1973, 41,* 373–384.

Strupp, H. H., Fox, R. E., & Lessler, K. *Patients view their psychotherapy.* Baltimore: Johns Hopkins Press, 1969.

Strupp, H. H., & Hadley, S. W. A tripartite model of mental health and therapeutic outcomes. *American Psychologist, 1977, 32,* 187–196.

Strupp, H. H., Hadley, S. W., and Gomes-Schwartz, B. *Psychotherapy for better or worse: An analysis of the problem of negative effects.* New York: Jason Aronson, 1977.

Sullivan, H. S. *Conceptions of modern psychiatry.* New York: W. W. Norton, 1953.

Truax, C. B., & Carkhuff, R. R. The experimental manipulation of therapeutic conditions. *Journal of Consulting Psychology, 1965, 29,* 119–124.

Wachtel, P. L. *Psychoanalysis and behavior therapy.* New York: Basic Books, 1977.

Weissman, M. M., Klerman, G. L., Paykel, E. S., Prusoff, B., & Hanson, B. Treatment effects on the social adjustment of depressed patients. *Archives of General Psychiatry, 1974, 30,* 771–778.

Wilson, G. T., & Evans, I. M. The therapist-client relationship in behavior therapy. In A. S. Gurman and A. M. Razin (Eds.), *Effective Psychotherapy: A Handbook of Research.* New York: Pergamon Press, 1978.

Winnicott, D. *The family and individual development.* London: Tavistock, 1978.

2

EXPERIMENTAL DESIGNS IN PSYCHOTHERAPY RESEARCH

JOHN GOTTMAN
HOWARD J. MARKMAN

University of Illinois
Bowling Green State University

INTRODUCTION

Any survey of research methods is inevitably tied to the nature of the research questions that are currently being posed by investigators, and these questions are in turn affected by the historical context through which they have evolved. Our understanding of research methodology would benefit from a review of the past hopes of its scholars and of our current hopes in an historical context. We would be doing a disservice if we did not assert at the outset that research design and statistical inference are not the fixed immutables we may long for; they are simply the logical tools of those who seek knowledge with an empirical base. Tools must be selected to do a job and invented to fit the research questions at hand. It therefore makes sense for a chapter on experimental design in psychotherapy research to begin with a review of the research questions that have been posed. There are three questions that have dominated research in

psychotherapy, and we will begin by considering these questions.

The First Question

The first question, "Is psychotherapy effective?" has always haunted us, and we need to make peace with this question in order to proceed. Eysenck's famous 1952 paper posed the initial challenge. He cited Denker's (1946) data (which came from insurance company files) which led Denker to conclude that 72 percent of the claimants suffering from psychoneurosis improved within two years with apparently little or no professional psychological treatment, while a 60 to 70 percent improvement rate was currently being reported by a variety of well-known psychiatric clinics. Denker used these results to conclude that psychoneurosis may run its own course in two years with or without psychological treatment. Certainly, the data from both sources, insurance files and therapists' reports of improvement, are highly questionable. The

23

Denker data were clearly not adequate to generate this conclusion; for example, to mention only one criticism leveled at Denker's conclusion, Cartwright (1955) suggested that the return to work of work disability claimants reflected a period of national economic recovery.

In a detailed criticism of Eysenck's work, Meltzoff and Kornreich (1970) pointed out that Eysenck consistently ignored data that disconfirmed his conclusions. For example, Eysenck (1960) fitted a curve to the Denker data of "spontaneous remission" and later Eysenck (1967) showed that the improvment rate data of Wallace and Whyte (1959) fit this curve. However, Eysenck used only part of the Wallace and Whyte data, and the part he did not use did not fit his exponential curve. Also, in 1960 Eysenck based his review on a small sample of studies. Meltzoff and Kornreich wrote,

Eysenck's appraisal of the effects of psychotherapy relied upon these four studies. In our review of the literature, however, we have found at least thirty controlled studies published in 1959 that were presumably available to Eysenck at the time. Eysenck's 1960 conclusions were based upon a small and unrepresentative sample of the available material. Five years later he again revised his review of the effects of psychotherapy (Eysenck, 1965) citing seven additional controlled studies for a total of eleven. His conclusions about the ineffectiveness of psychotherapy did not change, but new evidence was cited in favor of behavior therapy based on learning theory. (p. 73)

Meltozoff and Kornreich's thorough and thoughtful review addressed our first question on the effectiveness of psychotherapy. They separately reviewed 57 studies they considered methodologically adequate and 44 studies they considered questionable. Eighty-four percent of the adequate studies found positive effects of psychotherapy and 75 percent of the questionable studies found positive effects. They also concluded that,

In short, reviews of the literature that have con-

cluded that psychotherapy has, on the average, no demonstrable effect are based upon an incomplete survey of the existing body of research and insufficiently stringent appraisal of the data. (p. 177)

Glass and Smith (1976; Smith & Glass, 1977) recently conducted a "metastudy" on the effects of psychotherapy. They surveyed the outcome literature (including dissertations) and selected 375 controlled studies; each study became an element in their meta-study and was coded on a set of characteristics including estimates they made of effect size. Instead of simply counting studies with positive or null results, Glass and Smith calculated the mean difference on outcome measures between control and treatment groups divided by the standard deviation of the control group, which represents a considerable advance over tallying positive and null studies. Some 830 effect sizes were obtained from the 375 studies. Their work is a complex approach to comparing studies that vary widely in treatments, design, measures, therapist and client characteristics, and so on. Despite these complexities, Figure 2-1 presents their overall answer to our first question.
They wrote:

The average study showed a two-thirds (2/3) standard deviation superiority of the treated group over the control group. Thus, the average client receiving therapy was better off than seventy-five percent (75%) of the untreated controls. (p. 10)

They found only 12 percent of the effect sizes were negative and noted that, "if therapies of any type were ineffective and design and measurement flaws were immaterial, one would expect half the effect size measures to be negative." (p. 10)

The answer to our first question must therefore be "yes" if we have to choose between yes and no. However, since 1952 we have learned that the first question is really not as meaningful as it may at first seem; in fact, one important effect of Eysenck's 1952 paper challenging the effectiveness of psychotherapy was that it led us to reconsider the way we pose our research questions. In the last edition of this *Handbook,* Kiesler summarized his

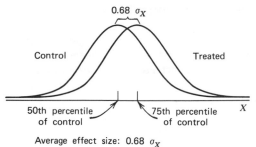

Figure 2-1 Results of Meta-analysis comparing changes in control and treated groups from 375 psychotherapy outcome studies. It can be seen that the average treated group showed about two-thirds standard deviation improvement over the average control group (Glass and Smith, 1976).

challenge of myths that assume that patients, therapists, and therapies are uniform concepts, and also in the last edition of the *Handbook,* Bergin reexamined Eysenck's work and subsequent work on therapeutic outcome, and challenged our notions of what a control group is; Bergin suggested that "spontaneous" recovery rates may be far lower than we have presumed. Many people in no-treatment control groups may seek help elsewhere and hence these groups are not control groups in the experimental sense. The first question has, therefore, become more specific and it has spawned new questions such as "What kinds of clients are we discussing?" and "How can we best measure improvement?" Bergin (1971) called interest in these questions evidence of "the need for specificity," and, although these questions have certainly not been answered, they have effectively altered the consciousness of the research enterprise. Outcome studies are more likely now than before 1952 to specify the target populations, to use a network of outcome measures, and to carefully describe the therapeutic interventions.

A question that is perhaps as persistent as the question of whether or not psychotherapy is effective is the question that has given birth to studies comparing therapies, a form of study that Glass and Smith called the Grand Prix study.

The Second Question
The second question haunting us is the Grand Prix question, namely, "What kind of therapy or therapeutic system is *the most effective?*" In their 1975 review of psychotherapy research, Bergin and Suinn referred to a study conducted by Sloane, Staples, Cristol, Yorkston, and Whipple (1975) as "probably the best comparative outcome study done to date" (p. 510). Let us examine this kind of study to understand its limitations.

Clients in the Sloane et al. study were matched on several variables and randomly assigned to behavior therapy, to short-term psychoanalytic therapy, or to a waiting list control group. The major outcome measures were pre- to posttest changes on a measure of target symptoms and measures of social and work adjustment. Results at the four-month posttest showed that the behavior therapy and the psychoanalytically oriented therapy groups had improved significantly more than the waiting list group on the measure of target symptoms change; however, there were no significant between-group differences on the measures of work and social adjustment. In general, across all measures used in the study, the four-month results showed that behavior therapy was about as effective as psychoanalytically oriented psychotherapy. How general is this result?"

Glass and Smith (1976) presented the Grand Prix results of their metastudy (See Table 2-1). Table 2-1 portrays the average effect sizes for 10 therapy types. Glass and Smith concluded that:

> *The first-place finisher in the therapy sweepstakes is systematic desensitization, the therapy which Joseph Wolpe based loosely on physiology and classical learning theory. (p. 14)*

Although in these results, types of therapy were not equated for type of problem, type of outcome measure, severity of the problem, duration of the treatment, and so on, Glass and Smith did statistically control for these factors in other analyses. They presented the results of a Shepard-Kruskal multidimensional scaling study that grouped therapies into two superclasses: behavioral therapies, and nonbehavioral therapies. The average effect size of the behavior superclass was $.8\sigma_X$ and the mean effect size for the nonbehavioral studies was $.6\sigma_X$. Furthermore, they concluded that,

TABLE 2.1   Grand Prix Results of Glass and Smith Metaanalysis

Therapy Type	Number of "Effect Sizes"	Average Effect Size (σx)	Approximate Standard Error of the Average (σx)
Psychodynamic	96	.59	.05
Adlerian	16	.71	.19
Eclectic	70	.48	.07
Transactional analysis	25	.58	.19
Rational emotive	35	.77	.13
Gestalt	8	.26	.09
Client-centered	94	.63	.08
Systematic desensitization	223	.91	.05
Implosion	45	.64	.09
Behavior modification	132	.76	.06

This difference in impact is not very large . . . the evaluators of behavioral superclass therapies waited an average of two months after therapy to measure its effects, whereas the post-assessment of the nonbehavioral therapies was made in the vicinity of five months, on the average. Furthermore, the reactivity or susceptibility to bias of the outcome measures was higher for the behavioral superclass than for the nonbehavioral superclass, i.e., the behavioral researchers showed a slightly greater tendency to rely on more subjective outcome measures. (p. 21)

When Glass and Smith statistically controlled for differences in experimental setting (e.g., experience of therapists, months after therapy of outcome assessment, type of outcome measure), the $.2\sigma_x$ difference between behavioral and nonbehavioral therapies was considerably reduced.

A hidden assumption in the Grand Prix study must be mentioned; namely, that we can adequately evaluate a therapeutic approach by pitting therapists with particular orientations against one another across a broad range of clients. In the Grand Prix study the therapists are like sluggers at bat who claim to be able to handle any ball that is pitched. The Grand Prix study thus assumes that it is unnecessary to systematically construct separate therapeutic programs for separate types of problems since any one therapy approach ought to enable the therapist to tailor the therapy for each individual client. There is thus some sense in which Grand Prix studies are generated by a traditional link between the client's behavior change and the behavior of the therapist. This link implies that the therapist in the Grand Prix study is like the modern gladiator of a therapeutic position. There is some reason to believe that therapists' behaviors and orientations are not important factors in accounting for effect size. In Glass and Smith's study Hays' omega-squared, which related the categorical variable "type of therapy" to the effect size, was .10 (i.e., only 10 percent of the variance was accounted for by type of therapy).* In this chapter we will argue that it may be necessary to upstage the therapist from the drama of behavior change if we are to learn about what conditions create change. We will continue this discussion when we address the next question. The focus on the therapists' behavior has also been responsible for the third important question of psychotherapy research.

The Third Question
The third question is, "What therapeutic processes lead to the most change?" and this question has

*These findings are debated by Gallo, Eysenck, Smith & Glass in *American Psychologist*, 1978, 515—519.

led to a form of psychotherapy study called the *process study*. Let us examine the history of the process study. The theme of the process study was well expressed by Bordin (1962) in the first of the three APA volumes on research in psychotherapy. Bordin wrote:

The key to the influence of psychotherapy on the patient is in his relationship with the therapist. Whenever psychotherapy is accepted as a significant enterprise, this statement is so widely subscribed to as to become trite. Virtually all efforts to theorize about psychotherapy are intended to describe and explain what attributes of the interactions between the therapist and the patient will account for whatever behavior change results. (p. 235)

This emphasis on the interaction between therapist and client did not diminish over the course of the three important APA volumes on research in psychotherapy. In the first volume we may observe work in progress based on attempts to score important dimensions of the therapist's behavior. For example, Bordin wrote:

To our ultimate frustration, we started with the assumption that warmth was a unitary variable which had a profound influence on personality change. Our data soon taught us that we were thinking too superficially. The first sign that something was wrong was provided by the too slender thread of agreement we found among independent observers. (p. 236)

The APA's second volume on research in psychotherapy recorded a move toward greater specificity, a move toward counting, coding, and categorizing specific episodes rather than relying on global ratings of the therapist's behavior (beginning with Strupp's thesis which used the Bales IPA system), and this volume also reflected the influence of social learning theory in Krasner's paper on "The therapist as a social reinforcement machine." This trend toward the greater specificity of process continued, and, in the third volume in 1968, therapist-patient interaction was analyzed in greater detail in Ekman and Friesen's paper on

nonverbal behavior, Mahl's paper on gesture and body movements, Laffal's paper on content analysis, and the Matarazzo, Weins, Matarazzo, and Saslow paper on speech and silence.

Process research was made possible by a breakthrough in the use of electronic recording in the late 1920s and early 1930s, initially pioneered by Earl F. Zinn and later by Carl Rogers. Kiesler's (1973) book on process variables, which is a valuable compendium of specific variables that have been used in the study of therapy process, pointed out the one common dilemma of the process researcher, namely, the data overload problem. Kiesler (1973) wrote about the Wisconsin schizophrenia study that "researchers possessed 1,204 hours of tape-recorded therapeutic interaction with twenty-eight patients" (p. 27). Reducing process data raises all the issues that process researchers confront in coding tapes, for example, the choice of a coding unit, issues in sampling, and the assessment of interobserver reliability.

In addition to the historical movement toward greater descriptive detail evident in the APA volumes, there was an additional crucial point raised by the third volume, namely the possibility of viewing the interaction between therapist and client as a *reciprocal* social influence process. This concept was implicit in the paper by Jaffe which proposed, using a Markov model of client and therapist talk, work that was continued so admirably in Jaffe and Feldstein's (1970) book *Rhythms of Dialogue*. Jaffe's paper suggested that by examining conditional probabilities between a client's speech and a therapist's speech it would be possible to quantify the notion of the reciprocity of social interaction. This idea was also raised by the Matarazzo et al. paper, which presented data on talk and interruptions over time for both therapist and patient. They concluded by writing:

We believe the various evidences (albeit mostly empirical and not theoretically based at this point) of "synchrony," "tracking," "modeling," and other forms of "reciprocal influence" demonstrated above for our seven therapy cases may hold just such promise for the student of "outcome" as well as for the investigator interested in the "process" involved in many other human-to-human communication and interaction networks. (p. 393)

Kiesler mentioned the issue of reciprocal influence, but only as a methodological problem in process studies. He wrote:

Let us assume that one finds a high positive correlation between therapists' accurate empathy behavior in therapy interviews and eventual successful outcome of patients. One would be tempted to conclude that therapists' high empathy leads to successful outcomes. But, it is equally plausible that some patient *factor is being used implicitly by the empathy raters as their cue of level of therapist empathy (since the patients' verbalizations are also present in the scoring and /or contextual unit), and that this patient variable is itself related to eventual successful outcome. (p. 40)*

Unfortunately, the implications of the concept of reciprocal influence have not yet been fully explored. There are two comments about the study of reciprocal influence in process and process/outcome research we would like to make; the first concerns the analysis of sequences and patterns of social interaction, and the other concerns the fundamental logic of process/outcome research. First, the kind of correlation Kiesler (1973) described has nothing to do with process notions of "reciprocity" in social interaction; Kiesler referred to the correlation *across* clients and therapists of rates of behaviors and not a correlation of a particular therapist's behavior with a particular client's behavior. The distinction is critical. Imagine two people that act purposely to make their behavior contingent. The contingency would mean that knowing the behavior of one person would allow us to reduce uncertainty in the behavior of the other person, or, stated another way, the conditional probabilities would exceed the unconditional probabilities. For example, suppose that knowing that a therapist has just been empathic (*EM*) will reduce uncertainty in our prediction of the client's self-disclosure (*SD*); this means that $p(SD/EM) > p(SD)$. For example, the client may self-disclose at an unconditional base rate of .05 (i.e., 5 percent

[5%] of the of the time), but the proportion of self-disclosure after an empathic response by the therapist may be .65. This concept of uncertainty reduction is now the generally accepted meaning of interpersonal connectedness used in other areas of research on social interaction (for example, see Lewis & Rosenblum, 1974). Kiesler's correlation does not describe contingent interaction *within* dyads but correlates base rates of behaviors *across* dyads. The process question, "How does a particular therapist's behavior affect the client?" is a within-dyad question. The comparison of conditional probability with unconditional across dyads may be made with a repeated measures analysis of variance where the two measures are conditional and unconditional probabilities. The comparison within one dyad suggested by Bakeman and Dabbs (1976) is a binomial test z-score, $z = (x - NP)/\sqrt{NPQ}$, where x = the observed joint frequency of the therapist's behavior used to predict the client's, P = the unconditional probability of the client's behavior), $Q = 1 - P$, and NPQ = the variance of the difference between predicted and observed. The value of N must be greater than 25, or NPQ greater than 9 (see Siegel, 1956, p. 40).

The issue of contingency and pattern within dyads points out a crucial flaw in process research. For example, Rogers (1957) proposed a kind of equation that a set of necessary and sufficient conditions that a therapist could provide would lead to client self-disclosure and exploration, which would then lead to change. The equation suggests a matter of pattern and timing; for example, the therapist's genuine empathy at the right time, perhaps following a client's fear or anger will lead the client to self-disclosure and then to self-exploration. However, the process study has operationalized the Rogers equation in terms of *rates* of these behaviors, and then searched for correlation across therapists and clients. Do rates adequately capture the process equation? Do we really presume that simply the more *frequently* a client self-discloses the better? The use of rates to operationalize process notions is an extremely crude swipe at what one might assume to be a reasonable process relationship.

The use of rates to operationalize process variables also involves the assumption that these rates characterize sessions and therapists, and that, in fact, it makes some sense to talk about therapists who provide the necessary and sufficient conditions. This assumption does not seem to have been supported. For example, Bergin and Suinn (1975) wrote:

> In analyzing four-minute segments as opposed to whole sessions, they [Mintz & Luborsky, 1971] discovered similar variables with much overlap in correlation except for the empathy variable, indicating the judgements of therapist empathy based on brief segments cannot be generalized to whole sessions! This finding is given strong support by Gurman's study (1973) in which three high-facilitative and three low-facilitative therapists were found to be extremely variable in empathy, etc., both within hours and between hours. These findings may invalidate much of this program of research. (p. 515)

Our second comment is that we have become accustomed to thinking of process variables as causing outcome variables, but that may be simply an artifact of when it is traditional to measure process (e.g., from tapes of therapy sessions) and outcome (pre, post, and followup). A recent paper of Matarazzo and Wiens (1977) reviewed two studies that related process measures to outcome and both studies found correlations. Their review suggested that those interviewers who talked more per utterance, used total silence (i.e., no response) less, spoke with a longer reaction time, and interrupted less frequently, were rated as higher in empathy than other therapists, and also that clients talked more with shorter reaction time with these therapists then with other therapists. Matarazzo and Wiens cited the Staples et al. (1976) study which found that for *both* behavior therapists and analytic therapists a better therapy outcome was associated with more patient talk time. Patients who changed most did not speak more frequently but for longer durations when they did talk. They also tended to react more rapidly to the therapist's comments. The result that the behaviors of successful therapists in either school (behavioral or psychoanalytic) may be similar suggests an additional problem with the Grand Prix study.

At first glance, the results reviewed by Matarazzo and Wiens appear to provide some support for the Rogers equation. However, *it is possible that process/outcome effects are bidirectional,* that is, that clients who are changing are likely to be more responsive to their therapists, and that those who are not changing will be less responsive. It may be easier for a therapist to maintain high levels of warmth and empathy with clients who are changing. Ordinary correlational research cannot test the validity of this causal model, since both process and outcome actually occur concurrently. To deal with this bidirectional problem, researchers can use time-series data to monitor change over time (as opposed to measuring change in a pre–post fashion) to separate the direction of influence between process and outcome measures.

Gottman (1973) described a method for analyzing the relationship between any two time series by studying concomitant variation called *transfer function* analysis. He wrote:

> Suppose that we have two time-series process, X_t called the input, and the response process, Y_t called the output. If X_t is a lead indicator of Y_t then Y_t ought to be predictable statistically from a weighted sum of the previous X_ts. If X_t leads Y_t by b time units, we ought to be able to predict Y_t from X_t, b units in advance. An equation to summarize this would be as follows:
>
> $$Y_t = V_0 X_{t-b} + V_1 X_{t-b-1} + \ldots + V_R X_{t-b-R} + N_t$$
>
> where N_t represents the lack of exact predictability of Y from X and is assumed to be a random variable independent of X.

> The analysis proceeds by defining a function called the cross-correlation *function as the correlation between the two time series lagged a number of time units,* k, k = 1,2,3, ... *Using this function, we can calculate best estimates for the vs in the equation above. The solution for these weights is analogous to the solution of a regression problem.* (p. 99)

An alternative solution was described by Hibbs (1974) which is a generalization of least squares regression analysis to the case of autocorrelated residuals. Both methods are ideally suited to the analysis of the relationship between outcome and process time series, and have the added advantage that they can be applied to single subjects. Time-series analyses are essential even with moderately autocorrelated data (Glass, Willson, & Gottman, 1975), and this is also true for time-series regression analysis (see Hibbs, 1974, pp. 257 and 266 for details).

The Need for Alternative Questions

This review of our three most prominent questions suggests to us that there is a need for a set of different questions in psychotherapy research that avoid the pitfalls of the three we have discussed. Furthermore, there is a need for a way to proceed with psychotherapy research that will make it possible for us to learn from our failures, so that the business of gathering data on the process and effectiveness of our interventions results in some improvement in our practices. Implicit in the way this last statement was phrased is the need for a way to proceed that will be useful to *both* the university scholar interested in psychotherapy research and the innovative clinical practitioner.

In the chapter on experimental design in the last edition of the *Handbook,* Kiesler (1971) distinguished between *Artisan* and *Scientist,* and, in part, he suggested that the research questions relevant to each are different. Kiesler made several recommendations in keeping with this distinction, although he did address both audiences. In effect, Kiesler suggested that the Artisans could ask research questions at what we like to think of as five specific "traffic flow points" in the treatment endeavor. These questions were:

1. *Candidates/Noncandidates:* How are those people who are candidates for the psychotherapy different from other patient groups or from nonpatient groups?

2. *Selected/Rejected:* How are the people selected for the psychotherapy different from the people not selected?

3. *Remainers/Dropouts:* How are people who drop out of the psychotherapy against professional advice different from those who remain in the therapy?

4. *Successful/Unsuccessful at Termination:* How are people who are successful at termination different from people who are not?

5. *Successful/Unsuccessful at Follow-up:* How are people who are successful at follow-up different from people who are not?

Kiesler also suggested that the Scientist can learn from the individual case study approach of the Artisan to increase the naturalness of the process under investigation and to reduce the confusion between process and outcome research. The distinction Kiesler made between Scientist and Artisan deserves further discussion. It led Kiesler to recommend a repeated-measures multifactorial, multivariate "Grid Model" for research in the psychotherapies. The grid was created by factorial combinations of: (a) homogeneous patient groups, (b) homogeneous therapist personality-attitude groups, (c) a range of patient behaviors, (d) a range of therapist behaviors, and all these facets were continued over time, from pretherapy to follow-up periods.

The present chapter will argue for the utility of notions that serve to blend the functions of Scientist and Artisan. We know that the distinction exists in our professional associations. We know that many "Artisans" have had far from uplifting experiences with the activity of scientific investigation. We also know that many "Scientists" have equally unpleasant associations to the practice of psychotherapy by "Artisans." The distinction may currently exist in our field, but it may not be useful for the progress of research in psychotherapy.

There are two key concepts that can be used to reduce the distinction between Artisan and Scientist. One concept is the notion of the *Intervention Program.* Certainly if an Intervention Program is to be maximally useful, it must be capable of being administered by a wide variety of therapeutic agents. Using the notion of an Intervention Program, some basic psychotherapy research questions can be restated as:

1. How shall the program be developed; that is, what should its *content* be?

2. How shall the program's content best be delivered?

3. What kinds of patients make what kinds of gains with this program?

With the *Program* as the focus of investigation, research questions involve assessing the program's benefits in relation to its costs, assessing the program's limitations, and engaging in the process of improving the program on the basis of information gained. The enterprise of psychotherapy research becomes an enterprise of program development and program evaluation. Process research becomes formative evaluation in which information about the functioning of the presumed active ingredients of the program feeds back to influence the program's operation. Outcome research becomes summative evaluation which may be used to assess the program's current limitations and possibly to improve its content. Research in psychotherapy thus becomes translated to the enterprises of *Program Development* and *Program Evaluation,* and these enterprises are interdependent.

Note that the settings for these enterprises may be treatment facilities or they may be university laboratories, or they may be both, and that those engaged in these enterprises are neither Artisans nor Scientists, but both. The semantic transformations involved in program development and program evaluation may make nontrivial modifications in psychotherapy research. An industrial counterpart of the emphasis on the program may help make this point.

Suppose that we were discussing the management of a chemical factory to produce a particular chemical. We could then apply the suggestions of Box and Draper (1969) that the operating procedures of that factory can evolve and improve as work progresses. In the Box and Draper model, an "evolutionary operations" (EVOP) committee in the factory generates several alternatives to standard operating procedure. These variants of the standard procedure are run alternately and compared using a sequential decision procedure (Wetherill, 1966) until it is clear that one variant is superior to the standard operating procedure. That variant then becomes the standard operating procedure, the EVOP committee meets again to generate a new set of variants, and the process continues. The EVOP committee may generate comparisons of theoretical interest or solely of practical utility. We are not suggesting that research in psychotherapy is the same as running a chemical factory, but that a shift in emphasis to the therapeutic program may make some aspects of the industrial EVOP strategy useful for the conduct of research in psychotherapy. Thus the first concept, the intervention program, generates semantic transformations which reconceptualize research questions in psychotherapy and also reduce the Scientist/Artisan distinction.

The second concept, which may reduce the distinction between Artisan and Scientist, is the notion of a *Program Development Model* (PDM) in psychotherapy as an alternative to the single, large, multifaceted, multivariate grid experiment suggested by Kiesler (1971). The resources required to conduct such a large-scale undertaking are out of bounds for most of us. It may seem that a chapter on experimental design should review a series of designs and suggest the best designs that control external and internal threats to validity (Campbell & Stanley, 1963). However, the concepts introduced by Campbell and Stanley were hardly intended as an automatic system for selecting research designs, nor were they intended as a substitute for systematic thinking. *No research effort can answer all or most of its questions with one grand factorial study. It is more feasible to consider a program of smaller studies, each of which deals with a specific set of research questions.* That is really the way most laboratories function, and it is also the way applied work may proceed. We gain confidence in our efforts through replication and extension over a series of studies, and not from the single, multifactorial study over time that controls all plausible rival hypotheses at once. Because there are different sets of research questions at different stages of program development and program evaluation, this chapter will discuss a range of design and analysis options at each stage of the Program Development Model (PDM).

An emphasis on the *Intervention Program* rather than on the behaviors of therapists will lead to a rephrasing of old research questions in terms of a different set of metaphors. Let us reason through the implications of using the language of a PDM. We must think of developing an Intervention Program for *a specific target population*. We must design the *content* of this program and select alternative *modes of delivery* of the content. The content of the program will determine the general nature of the variables we use to *evaluate the program.* This will make it possible to select a *measurement network of appropriate cost* to evaluate the program. We may begin by testing a *multicomponent delivery system.* If this system is effective in producing some change, we may ask the question "What kinds of people make what kinds of gains with this program?" Implicit in this question is the issue of long-term gains (which could be a question of the maintenance of initial gains, or the slow increment of an initial change process). Finally, we *systematically dismantle the program,* asking questions of *efficiency,* such as "What changes in content and delivery are necessary for specific target subgroups?" and "What is the best sequence of content and delivery?"

Figure 2-2 is a flowchart of this model that lists eight phases of research activity. We will discuss each of the eight phases of the Program Development Model (PDM) but it will be useful to begin by describing the evolution of this model in psychology since it has arisen from a Zeitgeist that has influenced many areas of psychological research. We hope that our readers will not be disturbed if we draw concepts from a variety of areas of psychology in addition to research in psychotherapy.

Historical Development of the Concepts of the PDM

The history of the Program Development Model (PDM) can be traced back to the study of intellectual competence. Butterfield (1978) pointed out that researchers who studied mentally retarded

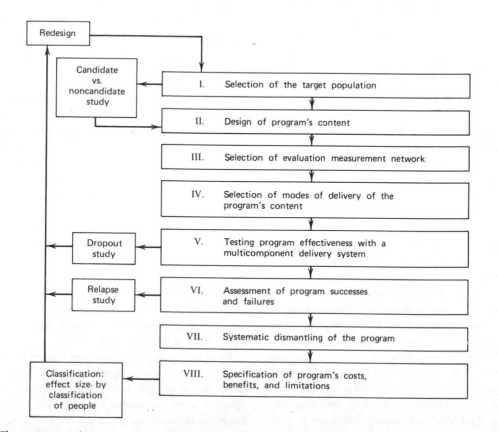

Figure 2-2   Schematic of the Program Development Model (PDM) for research in psychotherapy.

people have also simultaneously studied normal cognitive development. Often in the history of psychology an interest in abnormal functioning has led to the systematic study of normal functioning. Certainly early work on the growth and development of children was partly motivated by clinical interest stimulated by psychoanalysis. The intelligence testing movement begun by Binet and Simon was initially charged by the French Ministry of Education with identifying and helping slow learners. In Geneva, one tester, Jean Piaget, became intrigued by the kinds of errors normal children made on these cognitive tasks.

Research on discriminating between retarded and normal people led to questions of process, that is, an attempt to understand the precise nature of the response deficits of retarded people. For example, Ellis (1970) found that while the serial recall of normal subjects was markedly different from spaced to massed practice, the recall of retarded subjects in the two conditions was identical. Normal and retarded persons recalled accurately at terminal serial positions. Ellis inferred that the deficit was one of rehearsal rather than one of primary memory. This conclusion was an inference since rehearsal was not directly monitored by Ellis. Belmont and Butterfield (1969, 1971) then found that when normal and retarded people were given control over the presentation of items on a serial list, the normal people spent more time with the items than the retarded people, which is more direct confirmation of Ellis's conclusion.

Flavell, Beach, and Chinsky (1966) studied children's lip movements during a memory task and found out what children said to themselves as they prepared for a memory task. Using this knowledge, Flavell (1970) was able to obtain improved performance of children who did not recall accurately by eliciting verbalizations from these children. Flavell (1971) suggested that the problem was partly a problem of metamemory, of the executive functions of recall.

Based upon Flavell's work and work by Butterfield and his associates, Butterfield proposed an instructional strategy for validating a process explanation of deficient performance (Butterfield, 1976). He proposed that research engage in the following four steps:

1. Perform a process analysis on a particular task, within proficient and deficient groups.

2. Differentiate between groups with measures of processes that underlie performance within groups.

3. Teach deficient people to process as proficient ones, thereby raising their performance to the level of similarly instructed proficient performers, and,

4. Teach proficient people to process as deficient ones, thereby lowering their performance to the level of similarly instructed deficient performers.

This analysis of the distinction between competence and incompetence is remarkably similar to a suggestion made by Goldfried and D'Zurilla (1969) for program development in the area of social competence. They suggested that competence be conceptualized in terms of effective responses of the individual to specific life situations.[1] They suggested that: "In a general sense, a 'problematic situation' may be viewed as one which requires a solution to a problem or some decision for appropriate action" (p. 159). This definition was consistent with earlier suggestions made by Kanfer and Saslow (1969). However, Goldfried and D'Zurilla's definition of competence suggested that the responses selected by an individual fall somewhere on a continuum of effectiveness *for that particular situation*. Hence, their analysis of social competence suggested both the necessity of *empirically generating an item domain of problematic situations* and their analysis proposed that empirically generating a range of alternative responses in each situation will produce a *measure of competence for each situation*. The steps they proposed in program development were thus:

1. *Situational analysis*—obtaining the domain of problematic situations,

2. *Response enumeration*—obtaining the domain of response alternatives for each situation, and,

[1]This is a notion that Charlesworth (1978) is currently applying to an ethological study of intelligent behavior in children by observing children *in situ*.

3. *Response evaluation--scaling the responses on a dimension (or several dimensions) of effectiveness. This process leads directly to the development of measurement procedures.*

Perhaps the best methodological example of continued programmatic research using the PDM may be found in the work of McFall and his associates. McFall began by empirically generating a domain of more than 2000 problematic situations calling for assertive behavior (McFall & Marston, 1970). This list was then condensed to 80 non-redundant situations. Each situation included a *situational context,* an *interaction context,* and a *response demand.* For example:

You are standing in a ticket line outside of a theatre. You've been in line now for at least ten minutes, and it's getting pretty close to show time. You're still pretty far from the beginning of the line, and you're starting to wonder if there will be enough tickets left. There you are, waiting patiently, when two people walk up to the person in front of you and they begin talking. They're obviously all friends, and they're going to the same movie. You look quickly at your watch and notice that the show starts in just two minutes. Just then, one of the newcomers says to his friend in line:
Newcomer: *"Hey, the line is a mile long. How 'bout if we cut in here with you?"*
Person in Line: *"Sure, come on. A couple more won't make any difference."*
And as the two people squeeze in line between you and their friend, one of them looks at you and says:
Newcomer: *"Excuse me. You don't mind if we cut in, do you?"*
You Say: *(Response Demand).*

Based on their analysis of alternative responses in each situation, McFall and Marston (1970) developed and tested a semiautomated assertion training program using behavior rehearsal. Notice that the emphasis in this research was in the evaluation of a therapeutic *program,* and hence the evaluation minimized the research focus on the behaviors of the therapist. In fact, McFall and Marston utilized technicians as their therapists.

McFall and Lillesand (1971) found that a behavior rehearsal program with modeling and coaching was effective in producing change, compared to a control group on situations for which no training had been given, and on an extended interaction test. Covert rehearsal produced the greatest overall improvement. McFall and Twentyman (1973) then conducted four experiments, systematically dismantling the assertion training program. They found that symbolic modeling added little to the effects of rehearsal alone, or rehearsal plus coaching. This was true regardless of the type of assertive model used or the media used in presenting the models. There were also differences among the three modes of rehearsal used. The studies also found evidence of transfer of training effects.

McFall's work was subsequently extended to male psychiatric inpatients by Goldsmith and McFall (1975) who developed a general interpersonal skill training program; it was extended to returning Vietnam war veterans by Clark (1974); to lower income patients by Goldstein (1973); and to dating situations by Twentyman and McFall (1975) and Glass, Gottman, and Shmurak (1976). The work in social skills training has grown sizeable, and several reviews of this work are now in press (for example, Arkowitz, in press; Curran, 1977).

Although the work described above has been conducted primarily in the area of skill training, the PDM is not limited to this approach to behavior change. It is a general organizing scheme for research in psychotherapy.

The PDM is also represented by the work of Alexander and his associates. Alexander (1973) found differential patterns of defensiveness and supportiveness in families with and without a delinquent member. Klein, Alexander, and Parsons (1975) described four steps in program development and evaluation: (1) Identification of process discriminating target from nontarget groups, (2) modification of the process, (3) impact-outcome, which is a reduction of the problem in a secondary prevention sense, and (4) long-range impact, on primary prevention. Alexander and Parsons (1973) found significant reduction in recidivism for families with delinquent youth using their family therapy intervention program designed to modify the family's defensive and supportive interaction. Klein, Alexander, and Parsons (1975) found beneficial effects on the younger siblings of the identified youth in the treated families compared to no formal treatment or alternative treatments groups that did not specifically modify the process identified in the original Alexander (1973) study.

A similar format of program development and evaluation has been followed in marriage counseling by Weiss and his associates (Weiss, Birchler, & Vincent, 1974; Weiss, Hops, & Patterson, 1973). This work has produced promising results (see Jacobson & Martin, 1976). There is therefore a Zeitgeist that pervades intervention research in several areas of psychology, and this Zeitgeist can be articulated as the Program Development Model.

Upstaging the Therapist

The reader may have noticed that the historical discussion of the PDM above involved a conceptual focus on the problems of *clients* and in developing an intervention program based on understanding how our clients differ from those who adequately deal with similar problems. In this analysis there is a conspicuous absence of the therapist, and, to some extent the intention of the PDM is to turn intervention research toward a more descriptive understanding of our clients. This is an important point.

There is some sense in which research in psychotherapy has been traditionally linked to what therapists do. In fact, Kiesler (1971) wrote that factorial designs in which interaction effects are analyzed permit

> the ultimate answer to the crucial behavior modification question: which therapist behaviors produce what changes in what kinds of patients? (p. 63)

This would not be considered the crucial behavior modification question by a behavior therapist, and this phrasing of research questions suggests that our research designs must in some sense reflect the therapist's place in the spotlight. There is an implicit focus in our research on what

the therapist does, and transforming the old language of psychotherapy research to the language of the PDM will require a demystification of the therapist's behaviors. It ought to be our job as therapy researchers to discover low-cost conditions that produce change, and removing the therapist from the spotlight may facilitate that objective.

If we choose to generate therapy programs by focusing on what the therapist does, we must generate hypotheses about what we therapists think we do to facilitate change. For example, we may create a partial list such as that presented in Table 2-2 in which therapist behaviors are stated as ingredients of psychotherapy (see also Strupp, 1973). Or, we may attempt to discover how experienced therapists differ from inexperienced therapists (e.g., Pinsof, 1976) in an initial attempt to devise an effective therapeutic program.

It is natural for those of us who are engaged in clinical training to think of the client's change in terms of the activities of the therapist; however, the specification of therapist behaviors may facilitate the identification of hypotheses about "active ingredients" in the change process. These ingredients may then describe the therapy program, while the other ingredients may help specify an appropriate control group for the program evaluation phase of the PDM.

Correlation and Causation

It is customary for a chapter on experimental design to remind readers that correlational studies do not imply causal relationships, whereas well-controlled, planned intervention studies do. However, there are four reasons why this argument is misleading, even though it does contain some truth. First, we never demonstrate causal connection in any study; we merely eliminate some plausible rival hypotheses, with some degree of confidence, that militate against causal arguments.

Second, it is easy to forget that the correlation coefficient is simply one summary statistic for describing the relationship between two variables. Figure 2-3 illustrates ways in which the correlation coefficient may mislead a researcher who does not take the time to plot data. The correlation coefficient is merely an estimate of overall linear relationship between two variables. The message is

TABLE 2.2 Therapist Behaviors Stated as Ingredients of Psychotherapy

---

1. The therapist conveys an expectation that change is possible and likely to occur.
2. The therapist conveys a faith that *every* problem has a solution.
3. The therapist helps the client elaborate and specify the problems presented.
4. The therapist provides a new language system for organizing behavior and events. This may include a *relabeling* of what is "pathological," what is "healthy," (problems and goals), and perhaps etiology.
5. The therapist gives client normative data for client's experiences in therapy (e.g., "It is common to feel panicky at this point. We *expect* people to feel that way.").
6. The therapist provides ground rules (e.g., about fees, coming to sessions, number of sessions, calling if unable to come, homework, practice).
7. The therapist describes goals and methods for attaining goals.
8. The therapist structures situations that require approach instead of avoidance; therapist may also restructure situations so that it is more likely that approach behaviors will be rewarded naturally.
9. The therapist conveys the belief that positive consequences follow approach and negative consequences follow avoidance.
10. The therapist conveys an "experimental" norm:
    a. First *try* it
    b. *Then* evaluate it
    c. Then modify it
    d. Then try it again.
11. The therapist conveys the message that he or she cares about the client (he or she is listening, empathetic, supportive).
12. The therapist teaches alternative ways of behaving and thinking with consideration of step size (small enough to maximize likelihood of success), pacing (mostly at client's own pace), and feedback (specific).
13. The therapist restructures norms of social interaction in behavior setting of importance (e.g., changes consequences of specific behavior exchanges, and changes eliciting stimuli).
14. The therapist reinforces client for trying new behaviors, for sticking to programmed interventions, and for personalizing change within client's own style.
15. The therapist fades self out and insures that the client attributes change to self not to therapist, and provides for transfer of training.

---

clear—researchers should use visual displays of their data rather than relying on summary statistics alone; in other words, plot, plot, plot. Even when relationships between a set of variables are linear, and we have complete confidence in our correlation coefficients, we can use statistical techniques such as path analysis to explore the possibility of causal connection in nonexperimental data. These models are simple applications of partial correlation coefficients and regression analysis. For an introduction to these methods the reader is referred to Blalock (1961), Duncan (1975), and Heise (1975). An example or two may be helpful. If we have three variables x, y, and z, a causal model X Y Z would imply that the partial correlation $\rho_{yz \cdot x}$ that is, correlation between y and z controlling x is zero. The partial correlation is calculated as

$$\rho_{yz \cdot x} = \frac{\rho_{yz} - \rho_{yx} \, \rho_{zx}}{\sqrt{1 - \rho^2_{yz}} \ \sqrt{1 - \rho^2_{zx}}}$$

To be specific if x = therapist warmth, y = client self-disclosure, and z = client change, the causal model tests the initial causal impact of the therapist's warmth both in creating the conditions that facilitate change, and in creating client change itself. Cross-lagged panel correlation designs (for example, see Kenny, 1975) exemplify the application of path models when prior events ("causes") are linked to subsequent events ("effects").

To summarize, our second point about correlation and causation is that it is possible to statistically improve over correlations to make inferences about causal connection. In the simplest application of cross-lagged panel correlation, for example, two variables, X and Y are observed at times 1 and 2 which produces, across a set of subjects, two autocorrelations, $\rho_{x_1 x_2}$, $\rho_{y_1 y_2}$, and two cross-correlations, $\rho_{x_1 y_2}$ and $\rho_{y_1 x_2}$. The statement that X causes Y may be expressed by the direction of the cross-lagged differential $\rho_{x_1 y_2} - \rho_{y_1 x_2}$. Kenny (1975) wrote:

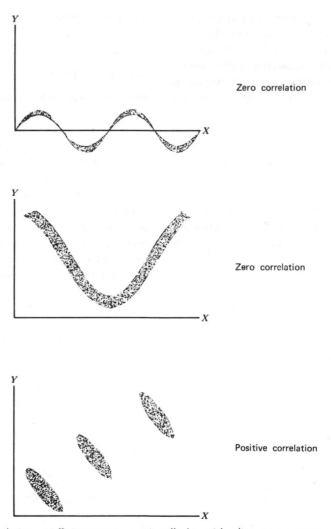

Figure 2-3   The correlation coefficient may occasionally be misleading as a summary of the relationship between two variables.

Campbell's original suggestion was that if X caused Y, then the cross-lagged differential would be positive, and if Y caused X, the differential would be negative. (p. 887)

The original suggestion has been considerably elaborated by the application of structural equations and factor analysis. Kenny (1975) discussed the use of cross-lagged panel correlation as a test for spuriousness; that is, that the causal association between X and Y is not due to the effects of a third variable, Z. For an application of cross-lagged panel correlation in program evaluation, see Jones (1974).

Our third point is that we often confuse *explanation* of a phenomenon with accounting for variance. It is important to note that we may in fact be able to account for all of the variance in a variable and still not understand the process of the relationship between those variables. For example, suppose we discovered that birth order accounted for 100 percent of the variance in a child's popularity with peers at school. We still would have no idea how the variable of birth order operates in any causal sense to produce the relationship with popularity with peers. We may, in fact, be able to *control* a dependent measure without understanding the process of control.

This brings us back to an earlier point, namely, the importance of *describing sequence*. We have pointed out that nearly all of our outcome and process measures that involve description of life events have been rates or relative frequency variables. Rates may at times be useful variables in discriminating between target and nontarget populations, but they do not help us understand how these populations are different. However, an attention to sequence does improve our sense of description, and, in fact, a sequential analysis of a series of events may get closer to what we mean intuitively when we speak of causal connection. To return to our birth order and peer popularity example, suppose we knew that the following sequences occur at home and in the school for first- and later-born children. When observed at home, first-born children prefer to be in the presence of their parents or an adult, while later-born children prefer to be alone or with peers; in a preschool classroom, when there is a squabble for possession of a toy, a later-born child is likely to act assertively, retaliate aggression, and then offer the other child a substitute toy, while the first-born child is likely to whine, flinch, look fearful, not to retaliate aggression but to tattle to the teacher, or to seek the company of a teacher's aide. Using a sociometric interview technique, suppose we find that a common reason children give in this nursery school for disliking some peers is that they "act like babies." These sequences begin to give us a description that gets at an *understanding* of the relationship between birth order and peer popularity. Yet we have done nothing to attempt to obtain change; we have experimentally controlled nothing. *Good sequential description is therefore useful for making causal inferences and for understanding variance accounted for in a relationship between variables.* Despite the fact that "understanding" is a subjective experience, our major point is that creating change is not the only way to understand causal connection. Consistent descriptions of sequences of events permit extremely convincing inferences about causal connection, and, furthermore, good description may lead to an informed intervention program. In the fictional birth order and popularity example, an obvious intervention is suggested for unpopular children by the description of differences in sequence.

STAGES OF THE PDM

Before we begin outlining the stages of the PDM, we wish to discuss a word that is often abused in the social sciences, namely, the word "theory." Personality "theories" are philosophies about the nature of humanity; "theories" of psychotherapy are equally far-ranging, broad conceptions about the ontogenesis of human nature, how it may malfunction, and how to change it. The word "theory" also sometimes refers to the set of predictions a researcher makes about a study before gathering data, and at other times "theory" refers to a mathematical model such as a path analysis among data already gathered.

The word "theory" has also been used to maintain the split between Artisan and Scientist. The Scientist presumably generates the theory, and the Artisan applies the theory in some setting where experimental control options are extremely limited. In this distinction it becomes clear that the Scientist is interested in Knowledge and the Artisan is interested in Doing Good Deeds. Campbell and Stanley (1963) succeeded in pointing out that experimental design options do exist that can be applied in nonlaboratory settings, and their work was partly intended to blur the Scientist/Artisan distinction. Lately the pendulum has swung too much the other way and some writers have suggested that any research in a naturalistic setting is more valuable than any controlled laboratory research. While we do not subscribe to this trend, we do believe that the word "theory" has been used as a vague criticism of something that is missing in research in applied settings, and we think that applied investigators ought to stop feeling inferior for being "atheoretical."

Let us suggest that the word "theory" does have a place in scientific investigation, and propose a sharper use of the word. In the history of physics we see three great scientists, Tycho Brahe, Johannes Kepler, and Isaac Newton, and the work of these three men embodies three separate phases of scientific investigation. Tycho Brahe made his contribution in summary description, by his endless observations of the motions of the stars and planets in the construction of charts. Johannes Kepler summarized Brahe's summary descriptions by identifying patterns in Brahe's charts such as the elliptical motion of the planets about the sun at a focus of the ellipse. Newton explained the patterns by proposing a few general principles that applied equally well to planets and projectiles. These three contributions are important in all scientific endeavor: (1) *summary description,* (2) *pattern identification,* and (3) *pattern explanation.* We suggest that the last stage be called "theory" and that the first two not be called theory. A mathematical model would thus not be a theory if it only describes the data, nor is it a theory if it reveals pattern in the data. Note also that all three aspects of the scientific enterprise are important; in fact, we are reminded of Newton's comment that if his vision was grand it was because he stood on the shoulders of giants. He referred to Kepler and Brahe. There is a sense in which we have not yet spawned our Brahes and Keplers, in which we have slighted the descriptive, hypothesis-generating phases of scientific investigation in favor of theory construction. We have paid the price in the creation of "theories" that are often little more than a collection of metaphors not solidly grounded in observable phenomena.

I. Selection of the Target Population

The selection of a target population is an activity that rarely receives systematic attention. In part this lack of attention is due to the notion of the therapist as a slugger at bat, that any psychotherapy system we consider ought to include some general theory of humanity, why humans are wrecked on the reefs of life, and how they can avoid the reefs and be guided to calmer, or at least more enjoyable waters. These implicit notions have made pseudoministers of many therapists and pseudotherapists of many ministers. They have also induced the false notion that psychotherapy is the application of psychological principles derived from laboratory investigation. Perhaps no one is more guilty of this latter fallacy than therapists who feel that they know all the laws of human behavior

and need only roll up their shirt sleeves to apply these laws to a particular clinical problem, and that most any problem will do. Both psychoanalysts and operant behavior modifiers historically have taken this position.

We must admit that we do not know the laws of human behavior. In most areas, in fact, we do not even have basic descriptive data about those aspects of human life that are most central to humans. For example, to name a few areas, we know very little about parent-infant interaction (Lewis & Rosenblum, 1974), about how children develop relationships with their peers (Hartup, 1970), about what friendship is like throughout the life span, about how social groups form, include people, exclude people, make decisions (Asher, Oden, & Gottman, 1977), about how families and marriages function and dysfunction (Riskin & Faunce, 1972; Jacob, 1975). We have created a social psychology based largely on the study of brief interactions between strangers, and a developmental psychology based largely on cognitive development. This is not intended to demean experimental psychology, but to suggest that therapy is not simply the application of well worked out experimental laboratory results in different settings. Well-conducted, informed applied undertakings may eventually make some theoretical contribution to experimental psychology.

Lack of care in selecting a target population may amount to a war on variance. The investigator may proceed by selecting that part of a population that is one or two standard deviations lower on some variable that seems to describe the target population. For example, O'Connor (1969, 1972) selected a group of isolated children by choosing those children who were observed to interact with their peers 8 percent of the time or less. There are no data to indicate that children who interact with their peers less than some specified rate are, in fact, at some psychological risk.

However, there are data that indicate that children who are unaccepted by their peers, using sociometric measures, are at risk (Cowen, Pederson, Babigian, Izzo, & Trost, 1973; Roff, Sells, & Golden, 1972). Gottman (1977) found that there was no relationship between the peer interaction measure of social isolation and the peer sociometric acceptance or rejection measures. The fact that the O'Connor measure of social isolation involves an observational measure has made the measure more credible to behaviorally oriented therapists. However, observational measures have to satisfy the same psychometric criteria of predictive validity required of any measurement procedure.

The selection of a target population must include some assessment of how the target population differs from people who would not be candidates for the program. This candidate/noncandidate study was suggested by Kiesler (1971) in the last edition of the *Handbook*. As an illustration of this type of study, Levenson and Gottman (in press) designed a situationally specific self-report measure of social competence in dating and assertion situations. The measures discriminated between clients who signed up for a dating skills or an assertion group and people who did not sign up. Also, the dating group clients reported more difficulty and incompetence on the dating subscale than the assertion group clients, and the assertion group clients reported more difficulty and incompetence on the assertion subscale than the dating group clients. Subsequent work showed that these scales were reliable, produced results parallel to those obtained from behavioral assessments of social competence in dating and assertion role plays, and measured differential improvement in a variety of eight-week intervention programs.

One final point concerns the decision to "screen" patients for specific kinds of therapy programs on *a-priori* grounds. We suggest that more is learned by not screening patients and carefully monitoring what kinds of patients make what kinds of gains from a particular program. For example, Masters & Johnson (1970) screened couples for sexual dysfunction therapy so that the only couples they treated were not psychotic or very neurotic, were happily married, communicated well, and were committed to the relationship. Their results are therefore of limited generality, and it is unfortunate that many subsequent research programs have followed similar screening procedures.

II. Design of the Content of the Program
This stage must proceed with an empirical study of competence, and by an investigation of the dimensions of competence and incompetence. Careful attention to the design of such a program will do away with the creation of psychotherapies through armchair speculations. We need to understand our clients. We need to understand the specific nature of performance discrepancies between competent and incompetent populations, in the general sense of performance discrepancy (Gottman & Leiblum, 1974).

We cannot overstate this case. For example, armchair therapy programs have been designed for socially isolated children that are not solidly grounded on the problems of children, nor on how children who are not isolated go about the task of making friends. Marriage counseling programs are designed without a knowledge about what nondistressed couples do to resolve marital conflict or enhance their own relationships. We must stop our design of interventions and admit to our ignorance. If we do not, we are unlikely to ever understand our clients.

We begin the process of designing the content of the intervention program by discovering the domain of situations that demand competent performance from our target population. A useful working hypothesis is that our clients are stuck at being able to solve some life problems. We need to begin by specifying these problems, by enumerating response alternatives, and by scaling these alternative responses on some dimensions of competence.

McFall and Marston (1970) generated a domain of problematic situations using a questionnaire; Goldsmith and McFall (1975) used interviews; Glass, Gottman, and Shmurak (1976) used both questionnaires and interviews: Alexander (1973) used observational methods, and Birchler, Weiss, and Vincent (1975) used observational methods and a behavioral checklist. All of these approaches have been used to provide convergent evidence of the validity of the problematic situation domain.

Gagné (1967) suggested a method called *task analysis* which can be helpful in identifying fundamental processes that distinguish competent performance from incompetent performance. A task analysis is a hypothetical specification of the components of competence. For example, suppose we wish to design an intervention program for school children who cannot perform long division. A task analysis of the skill of long division could identify the following subskills:

1. the ability to add,

2. the ability to subtract,

3. the ability to multiply,

4. the ability to use remainders, and

5. the ability to integrate these skills in a specified sequence.

Suppose we test the target population and discover that subgroups of our target population lack different skills. We could design the content of our intervention program according to this knowledge. We are also likely to find a subgroup of our target population who have all five skills, but whose attributional processes in response to initial failure feedback leads them to give up or to persist in a dysfunctional way (Dweck & Reppucci, 1973). This latter group has been identified, and intervention programs designed specifically to modify attributional processes have been effective with these children (Dweck, 1975).

Schwartz and Gottman (1976) conducted a task analysis study of assertive behavior. They found that most nonassertive subjects did not not differ from assertive subjects in their knowledge of what to say in assertion situations; they differed in their ability to actually deliver a competent response and in their cognitive self-statements. An intervention program for these subjects would contain content to modify these cognitive self-statements. Glass et al. (1976) found that such a cognitive self-statement modification program was more effective than a response acquisition program in producing change in shy males on dating situations, and that these differences were maintained in a six-month follow-up after treatment. The task analysis approach suggested by Gagné thus has potential for differentiating between target and nontarget populations on process dimensions similar to those suggested by Butterfield (1976).

The response evaluation phase suggested by Goldfried and D'Zurilla (1969) may proceed by using judges who are judged to be competent by some independent criterion (Goldsmith & McFall,

1975), or by field testing the responses. For example, McFall (in press) tested the effectiveness of a set of opening lines for initiating conversation delivered by confederates in public places. The lines were evaluated by the strangers the confederates approached.

III. Selection of Evaluation Measurement Network

Specification of the processes that discriminate between criterion and target populations will suggest a set of measurements for assessing therapeutic outcome. The selection of assessment measures should thus be tied to the specific nature of the therapy program. This is consistent with Bergin's (1971) statement "we feel quite strongly that researchers and therapists should begin to think more precisely in terms of the *kinds of change* rather than in terms of a general multiform change" (p. 247).

Glass and Smith (1976) conducted a "metastudy" on the results of 375 controlled psychotherapy outcome studies. Since many studies used more than one outcome measure, they obtained estimates of 833 effect sizes. The outcome measures were classified into 10 types, such as, "fear and anxiety reduction, self esteem, 'adjustment' [meaning freedom from debilitating symptoms that often require hospitalization], achievement in school or on the job, social relations, emotional-somatic problems, physiological stress measures, and so forth" (p. 10). Figure 2-4 shows their results for 688 measures in four categories. Glass and Smith wrote:

We see that 261 effect sizes from over 100 studies average about one standard deviation on measures of fear and anxiety reduction. Thus, the average treated client is better off than 83 percent of those untreated with respect to the alleviation of fear and anxiety.

The improvement in self-esteem is nearly as large. The effect sizes average nine-tenths of a standard deviation.

Improvement on variables in the "adjustment" outcome class averages considerably less, roughly six-tenths of a standard deviation. These outcome variables are very impressive

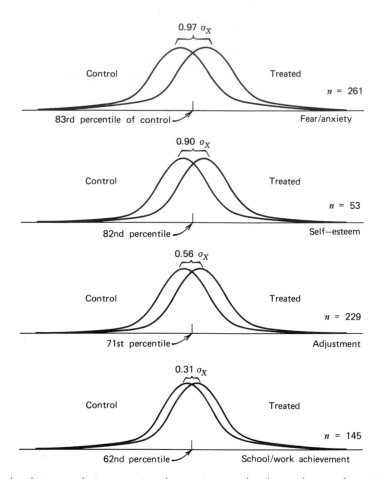

Figure 2-4   Results of Meta-analysis comparing changes in control and treated groups from 375 psychotherapy outcome studies on four types of outcome measures: fear/anxiety, self-esteem, adjustment, and school/work achievement (Glass and Smith, 1976).

measures of personal functioning and frequently involve indices of hospitalization for psychotic, alcoholic, or criminal episodes.

The average effect size for school or work achievement—most frequently grade point average—is smallest of the four outcome classes. (pp. 11–12)

These results may be used to argue that there is some continuum of psychotherapy effects that range from the more fragile self-report measures to the more stringent and less fakeable measures. However, that conclusion may be unwarranted on several grounds. It can be argued, and it is in the spirit of Glass and Smith's presentation to argue,

that each of these kinds of outcome measures is a legitimate domain for the assessment of psychotherapy programs, and a large variety of standardized assessment procedures may be appropriate to evaluate a specific effectiveness claim. McReynolds (1968, 1971, 1974) edited a three-volume work on recent developments in psychological assessment to which we refer the reader. The National Institute of Mental Health published a collection of papers in a volume called *Psychotherapy Change Measures* edited by Waskow and Parloff (1975). The papers in this volume are useful for those who are unacquainted with therapy outcome measures; the measures span a wide range of assessment procedures, therapeutic orientations, problems, and patient groups. Also, a "core battery" of measures was selected by a conference group to be applicable to a wide range of possible researchers. However, we feel that the "core battery" concept is a step backward in psychotherapy research for it continues to view therapy and change as uniform concepts. Change measures ought to be geared to what it is that a therapeutic program plans to accomplish; it makes as much sense to use the core battery to evaluate psychotherapy as it does to measure improvement in reading comprehension following treatment for sexual dysfunction. The reader is urged to apply common sense and logic in the selection of change measures.

The reader may suspect any therapy outcome results that use self-report measures. For example, anxiety and self-esteem are usually measured by self-report, even when anxiety is assessed by voluntary approach distance to a feared object. There is a general suspicion of the validity of self-report measures among researchers in psychotherapy, but we will argue that mounting evidence indicates that, under certain specific conditions, self-report measures can be highly valid. This digression will address itself to what may be a pseudo-controversy between behavioral and self-report measures.

Self-report measures have always been suspect by some psychologists and used by others. The psychoanalytic position's mistrust of reports subject to conscious censorship led Jung to develop the free association test and Rorschach to develop a projective measure based on what has been called the "X-ray hypothesis" of personality assessment (Murstein, 1963). While projective measures were being invented, Strong (1943) developed a vocational interest measure based entirely on conscious self-reports. In contrast to the analytic position, Rogerian theorists considered a client's self-report an accurate source of information about behavior, thoughts, and feelings. More recently, behaviorally oriented therapists have developed a mistrust of self-report measures in favor of direct observation of behavior. The critical question for this section on outcome measurement is not whether or not self-reports are better or worse than behavior observation measures, but under what condition both kinds of measures can best be used as outcome measures.

The Endler and Hunt anxiety (1966) and hostil-ity (1968) scales ask subjects to predict their physiological responses to a number of situations. For example, one item from the anxiety scale is, "You are about to give a speech before a class." The subject rates 14 possible reactions, such as "heart beats faster," on a five-point scale. D'Zurilla (1974) correlated scores on specific items and global anxiety scores with the number of times students spoke out in class. He found that the best prediction of the behavioral measure was anxiety scores on the public speaking item. Other situations and global anxiety trait measures showed lower correlations with speaking in class.

Research on assertion skill training has consistently found that changes on global measures of reported difficulty do not follow the same pattern as behavior observation measures across experimental and control groups; however, self-report measures based on reported difficulty (incompetence and discomfort) in a list of *specific* situations do follow the behavior observation pattern (McFall & Marston, 1970; McFall & Lillesand, 1971; McFall & Twentyman, 1973). Clark (1974), in a social skill training program with returning Vietnam war veterans found that clients' evaluation of the usefulness of the experimental and control treatments did not discriminate among groups; however, judges' ratings of tapes of a role-play assessment showed behavior changes only for the experimental group, and the situation specific assessments again followed the pattern of the behavioral measures.

The recommendation of situational specificity should probably be modified in two ways. First, subjects probably must be asked about situations in which they have had some experience; prediction of one's own behavior is likely to be worse in unfamiliar situations. Hence, Sherman, Wolosin, and Miller (unpublished) found that subjects underestimated their compliance rates to a situation in which they had to write a letter expressing counter-normative views. The subjects were not accurate predictors of their behavior in this situation. These investigators also found that the event of a self-prediction is a reactive measure that makes consistency with later observations of behavior more likely. Therefore, in an outcome study, self-predictions may introduce a pretesting confound into statements of external validity, and thus a

Solomon-four group design (Campbell & Stanley, 1963) would be recommended.

A second qualification of the situational specificity of self-report measures are two findings by Bem and Allen (1974). They found that the predictive utility of personality measures can be increased by asking the subject whether or not his or her behavior is consistent across situations. People who described themselves as more consistent showed higher cross-situational correlations than subjects who described themselves as less consistent.

Bem and Allen also suggested that it is important to be certain that subjects interpret the questions asked them in the same way the experimenter conceives of these questions. For example, for subjects to predict how "friendly" they would be in various situations, the subjects and the experimenters mus have the same conception of what it means to be friendly.

Endler and Hunt (1966) wrote that "validity of prediction is a function of the similarity of the test situation to which subjects are asked to report their responses, to the criterion situation" (p. 344). (See also Endler & Hunt, 1968.) Evidence for this conclusion continues to mount.

Moos (1969) compared the contribution of person, situation, and person by situation interaction variables derived from questionnaire and behavior measures. He found that there was great variability in the proportion of variance accounted for by each kind of variable depending on the questionnaire or behavior item. For example, items such as smoking were best predicted by person variables, while talking was best predicted by setting variables. The major point made by Moos and Endler and Hunt is that predictive validity is maximized by considering a person's specific response in a specific situation. This suggestion was also made by Goldfried and Kent (1972) and it continues to be supported by specific tests comparing the validity of specific values versus global self-report assessments to predict observations of behavior (for example, see Mellstrom, Cicala, & Zuckerman, 1976).

Mischel (1972) summarized studies that demonstrated that direct questions to subjects were generally better than or equal to more indirect methods of assessment. These studies and other studies and reviews by Mischel (Mischel & Bentler,

1965; Mischel, 1968) suggest that the predictive validity of subjects' *self-predictions* are usually only exceeded by actual behavior records. Mischel and Bentler (1965) also pointed out that the self-prediction should be to a situation as similar as possible to the criterion situation to which predictions are made. By "similar situations" Mischel (1968) meant situations that have similar role requirements, that is, situations that involve the same cognitive constructions of expected behavior. He also pointed out that predictions from self-report are likely to be poor when the subject is asked to make inferences about "global dispositions rather than providing a description of his specific reactions in response to specific situations" (p. 323).

Behavioral measures have enjoyed a honeymoon period in assessment as unquestionably the best, albeit the most expensive, method of assessment. Investigators should be aware that measures derived from observations must meet the same psychometric criteria as any other measures, and that not all approaches to behavior observation are equivalent in this regard. A number of issues have to be addressed by measures derived from observation.

Very few observational measures do not require observers to agree on some behavior classification or coding system. Exceptions to the use of humans as measuring instruments in observational research are the work of Jaffe and Feldstein (1970) and Haley (1964, 1967) on the patterns of talk and silence in conversations between strangers and in families, respectively. These investigators used an automated system for recording speech and silence. Although these variables are surprisingly rich sources of information, for a variety of reasons other investigators have been dissatisfied with simply observing talk and silence, and have used human observers. The use of human observers introduces a host of methodological problems.

Johnson and Bolstad (1973) recently reviewed problems in naturalistic observation such as reliability between observers, reliability drift, and reliability decay, many of which were investigated by Reid and his associates (for example, see Reid, 1970 and Taplin & Reid, 1973). At present, random spot checking of observer agreement must be included as a minimal strategy to maintain reliability. For an excellent review of the problems of reliability in observational research see Hollenbeck (1976). Mention must be made in this discussion of the extremely important recent work by Cronbach, Gleser, Nanda, and Rajaratnam (1972) on generalizability theory. Generalizability theory unifies the concepts of reliability and validity within the notion of the generalizability claim the researcher makes about a measurement instrument; for example, internal consistency reliability is a measure of generalization to an item domain; the total test score is a best estimate of universe true score (Nunnally, 1967); test-retest reliability is a generalization across occasions; intercoder reliability a generalization across coders, and so on. The general idea in generalizability theory is to partition the total variance in a study into those facets across which one wishes to generalize. For example, in assessing reliability across coders, the frequency of a particular code category is obtained by two independent coders across subjects. Good reliability means that the total variance in this repeated measures design is mostly attributable to variation across subjects and not coder variation or coder-by-subject interaction. Jones, Reid, and Patterson (1975) applied this approach to reliability to assess the reliability of their family interaction coding system for normal and deviant boys. Reliability is thus an assessment of the work one wishes the coding system to do; if it is to discriminate among families then it should obviously do that and not discriminate among coders. The generalizability claim is thus up to the researcher to specify. One implication of generalizability theory is that there is no such thing as *the reliability* of a measure; reliability is a function of the relevant generalizability claims.

Observer bias and the reactive effects of the observers' presence are nontrivial problems in behavior observation. There is also a problem with reliability on low-frequency events that have a high degree of salience to the investigation. To overcome such a problem it may be helpful to introduce the notion of the *Staged Naturalistic Event* which is a concept derived from ethological research. A staged naturalistic event is a field observation experiment in which the experimenter stages, in as unobtrusive a way as possible the low frequency event of interest. For example, Gottman

(submitted for publication) staged situations requiring socially unpopular and popular children to enter peer groups of varying sociometric compositions; McGrew (1972) studied the effects of a highly reduced play area on the aggressive behaviors of children toward their peers. In both studies the staged situation was accepted by the children as a natural event. The staging was set up in a manner consistent with the standard operating procedures in those settings.

Johnson and Bolstad (1973) pointed out that observational measures must also meet psychometric standards and they suggested the importance of demonstrating the convergent validity of an observational measure. As with any other measure, observational measures are psychometric tools that must work for the experimenter and give consistent results from study to study that are convergent with other indices. An excellent example of a line of research that has followed this convergent multimethod approach is the work of Weiss and his associates on the behavioral correlates of marital satisfaction (for example, see Birchler, Weiss, & Vincent, 1975).

An instructive counterexample is the work of O'Connor (1969, 1972) on social withdrawal in children. O'Connor used one behavioral measure of "withdrawal," the relative frequency of peer interaction. The construct of withdrawal was often referred to as "social isolation" in this work; these words implied that the child identified for intervention was a child who was shy, socially anxious, fearful of children, who would like to make friends, but did not know how. Subsequent research (Gottman, 1977) found that the children selected by the O'Connor criterion may be accepted and popular, rejected or not rejected, or disruptive or nondisruptive to the teacher. All kinds of children were included in the low-frequency interaction group. In short, the one measure used by O'Connor was insufficient to describe the construct he suggested. This line of research is also a good example of the bias behaviorally oriented researchers have in favor of behavioral measures, regardless of their demonstrated construct validity. Work using the O'Connor measure has ignored sociometric measures of social isolation despite their 40-year history, and their excellent track record in reliability and validity (for example, see Gronlund, 1959). Sociometric measures have demonstrated reliability indices second only to achievement tests, and validity indices second only to intelligence tests. Also, as we mentioned earlier in this chapter, recent evidence (Cowen et al., 1973; Roff et al., 1972) suggests that sociometric measures of peer acceptance are the best predictors from a wide class of possible predictors of later social functioning. Nonetheless, one reviewer for an applied behavioral journal recently rejected an intervention study using sociometric measures with the dismissal that all that was being assessed was "rating behavior."

There is some need to discuss the relationship between reliability and validity of behavioral observation measures. Waller and Leske (1973) made videotapes of a small children's reading group in which one target child's disruptive behavior was programmed to produce behavior to distract her peers. Initially the target child distracted the other child in 75 percent of the 20-second intervals, on each successive tape she reduced the number of distractible intervals by 5 percent per tape; the final tape contained 15 percent distractible intervals and 85 percent reading intervals. One group of observers were instructed to watch the tapes using a global nonspecific coding scheme and another group of observers used a more detailed coding scheme. Figure 2-5 presents the data obtained. There is generally less reliability between observers using the detailed scheme (called "objective observers" on the graph) than that obtained for the less detailed, more general observation

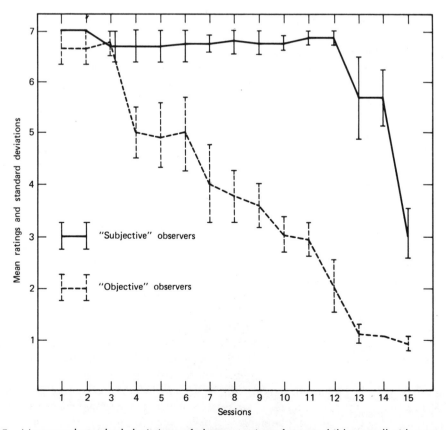

Figure 2-5 Means and standard deviations of observer rating of target child over all video tape sessions. (Adapted from R. G. Waller & G. Leske, accurate observer summary reports. *Journal of Nervous and Mental Disease*, 1973, **156.** © 1973 the Williams & Wilkins Co., Baltimore.)

scheme (called "subjective observers" on the graph). However, the less complex scheme was far less valid. These observers continued to see the initial level of disruptiveness until the thirteenth videotape, while the other observers correctly followed the preprogrammed pattern. There may thus be some sense in which favoring global systems which produce high levels of reliability may produce observations of low validity. We may need to concentrate on producing observational systems that optimize both reliability and validity rather than doing the job sequentially, that is, first insisting that reliability is arbitrarily in the 80 to 90 percent agreement range and then assessing validity.

One additional point needs to be made about self-report and behavioral measures. When we consider the cost of measurement, we are in what Glass and Smith (1976) called a Grand Prix situation—it is a race to see which is the better measure relative to cost. However, it may often be essential to use self-report data to *supplement* rather than replace observational data. Parke (1978) made this point in a discussion of research on parent-infant interaction. He wrote:

> One reason for the limited recognition of cognitive variables in current theoretical conceptualizations of parent-infant interaction is the failure to adequately distinguish between parental reports as objective measures of parental behavior and parental reports as indices of parental knowledge, attitudes, stereotypes and perceptions. These latter classes of variables are legitimate and important sources of data in their own right and are not easily derivable from observation alone. (p. 14)

Parke reviewed work that showed that if parents assume that infants are like kittens who cannot see for their first 10 days, these parents are unlikely to be very responsive to the infant's eye-to-eye contact or to provide much visual stimulation for the infant. Also, the parents' perceptions and evaluation of the infant's temperament and traits may modify the way they interact with the infant. This is a general point. We may benefit from studying the client's cognitive organization of salient events not as a *replacement* for behavioral data but as addi-

tional information to help us understand behavioral data. The two sources of knowledge in tandem may be invaluable (see also Mahoney, 1974). This suggestion is consistent with a recommendation of Bergin's (1971) in the last edition of the *Handbook*:

> Since "internal" and "external" criteria measure different human characteristics, since these characteristics are significant, since changes occur in both domains during therapy, and since important decisions regarding the value of different techniques continue to be based on the extent of change induced by them, we recommend that future studies include representative measures derived from this dichotomy. (p. 258)

IV. Selection of Modes of Delivery

Perhaps the greatest failing of any particular psychotherapy is its admonition to others that they should "Go and do likewise" when the sad truth is often that the components of the treatment program have not been adequately specified. Part of this failing can be understood historically in terms of the insulation of psychoanalytic institutes from the ravages of academic inquiry. Perhaps this pattern was set, in part, by Freud's 1934 reaction to receiving a set of reprints from Rosenzweig's first attempts to study repression. Freud wrote,

> I have examined your experimental studies for the verification of the psychoanalytic assertions with interest. I cannot put much value on these confirmations because the wealth of reliable observations on which these assertions rest make them independent of experimental verification. Still, it [experimental verification] can do no harm. (MacKinnon & Dukes, 1962, p. 103)

Psychotherapy research may have to give up something in specifying the mode of delivery of the program's content, but it will eventually gain in the potential for disconfirmation of cherished but yet unquestioned beliefs about the change process. As an example of this process, consider the italicized conclusions of Murray and Jacobson (1971) in the previous edition of the *Handbook* in their review of systematic desensitization research. They wrote:

Although the evidence on the nature of sys-
tematic desensitization is incomplete, there is
serious doubt as to whether it can be described
as a counterconditioning procedure. Neither
muscular relaxation, nor a progressive hierar-
chy, nor imaginal rehearsal seems essential. A
variety of techniques aimed at influencing be-
liefs seem to be of central importance in suc-
cessful desensitization. . . . (p. 727)

We are not suggesting that the reader accept Murray and Jacobson's conclusion. Certainly this issue
is the subject of considerable controversy. What we
do suggest, however, is that the fact that desensitization has specified its delivery components in a
step-by-step fashion makes it possible to eventually
test the claims desensitization programs make. We
can thus eventually rule out the usefulness of alternative approaches to the same problem.

For example, Glass and Smith (1976) were able
to compare 223 effect sizes in desensitization interventions with 45 effect sizes on implosion interventions. These two techniques usually consider similar problems. We do not suggest that studies can be
compared by a "voting" review of the literature
since some studies are far better methodologically
than others. However, Glass and Smith did manage some control over the quality of the studies
they considered. They found that the effect sizes of
systematic desensitization were .91 standard deviations over controls, whereas implosion effect sizes
were .64 of a standard deviation over controls, an
effect size similar to client-centered therapy (.63 of
a standard deviation), and greater than Gestalt
therapy (.26 of a standard deviation). When we
examine these results, we come away with a concrete comparison in the case of systematic desensitization and implosive therapy—the average effect size is markedly lower in the case of implosive
therapy. In many other Grand Prix comparisons
we are left puzzled partly because we have little
sense for the specific delivery components of the
therapy program.

Therefore, we argue that the specification of the
modes of delivery of a therapy program is essential.
When components can be combined in an additive
way, it is reasonable initially to combine them in
the hopes of producing a more powerful interven-

tion. Subsequent work dismantling the program
will make it possible to trim the program down. For
example, McFall (1976) found that response
playback was harmful to response acquisition in
the initial stages of training, but helpful later. He
also found that playback was more helpful to relatively more skillful unassertive subjects.

One point that should be made about the functioning of a multicomponent delivery system concerns *monitoring the intervention itself,* not simply
the expected outcomes of the intervention. If a
component of a program is designed to teach a
client something, then it would be extremely useful
to assess the extent to which that content was
learned. The degree to which the client learns what
is to be learned will affect the expected outcome.
Independent monitoring of the treatment processes
may also be viewed as valuable input for good
administrative decision making during the course
of the therapy program. Thus it may make mor‹
sense to specify the clients' continuing in therapy
until a particular process measure criterion level is
reached rather than equalizing the number of sessions each client receives. While this may introduce
a rival hypothesis about what accounts for
therapeutic effectiveness, this hypothesis is specific
and easily controlled. The point is that the researcher needs to know whether the components
of the program are doing the job they are supposed
to. It is good management as well as good research.

V. Testing the Program's Effectiveness
Perhaps the single most ignored dimension in
psychotherapy research is the dimension of Time.
We may trace this back historically to the agricul-
tural content of Fisher's work with analysis of variance. Time is automatically specified in agriculture
by the times to plant and the times to harvest.
However, there are not proper times to harvest in
areas of human change and the time to obtain a
posttest measure is entirely arbitrary.

Consider what we lose by ignoring the dimension of time. First, we lose information about the
form of change. Our effects may be gradual, or
they may be cyclic, or we may expect effects at
certain times and not others. As an example at this
point, consider the change curve that Glass,

Willson, and Gottman (1975) called the EVOP curve. Figure 2−6 illustrates the EVOP curve. Following the intervention, there is an initial decrement, followed by an eventual increment. We might expect such a curve when the intervention requires the unlearning of some behavior before the learning of a new behavior. It is similar to curves anecdotally reported in work on improving reading speed. At first the new reading methods cause a drop in reading comprehension, but as the new habits are learned, comprehension increases.

Let us assume for a moment that the EVOP curve is the fundamental change curve one would expect in psychotherapy research. Suppose further that four investigators took their posttests at the four different times depicted in Figure 2−6. Investigator 1, who took a posttest at Time 1, would show deterioration effects; investigator 2, who took a posttest at Time 2, would show no significant effects; investigator 3's effects would be marginally significant; and, investigator 4 would show a significant effect. The real situation is, of course, more complex but the point is that we are assuming that our clients' individual change curves balance out in such a way that we may entirely ignore the form of change.

Second, when we ignore time we lose the potential to conduct statistical investigations of change in single subjects. There has been adequate discus-

sion of the contribution made by single case studies (Davidson & Costello, 1969; Dukes, 1965; Kiesler, 1971; Lazarus & Davison, 1971). Lazarus and Davison (1971) listed six potential advantages of single case studies: (1) to cast doubt on a general theory, as in the study of the symptom substitution hypothesis; (2) to provide a heuristic device toward better-controlled research, as in the early clinical reports on desensitization, assertion, and sex therapy procedures; (3) to investigate rare but important phenomena, as in the study of chronic infantile vomiting (Lang & Melamed, 1969); (4) to apply principles and notions in new ways, as in Mary Cover Jones' classical work with little Peter (Jones, 1924); (6) to demonstrate a scientific point, as in the operant reversal design to demonstrate that a behavior is under the control of a particular reinforcer or set of stimuli; and (6) to place "meat on the 'theoretical skeleton' " (p. 207) by amplifying upon an experimental procedure in an applied setting (see Lazarus & Davison, 1971, p. 208).

Experimental Designs

Glass, Willson, and Gottman (1975) suggested that an annotated time series record can also be used to generate hypotheses about change interventions. We may, for example, have a client with tension headaches keep a personal journal as well as a rating of headache severity. Examination of events

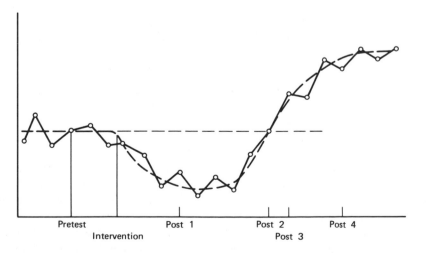

Figure 2-6 EVOP Curve (Glass, Willson, and Gottman, 1975.)

associated with peaks and valleys of the rating of headache severity may suggest a class of events related to onset, or maintenance of the headaches.

Glass et al. (1975) also presented a list of time-series designs that can be used with single subjects. Two useful additions to this literature for behavior modification are recent volumes by Hersen and Barlow (1976) and Kratochwill (1978). We will not review these volumes, but propose an additional function of single case research, and suggest two designs that may serve this function. This function of single case interventions we suggest in this phase of the PDM is simply *to pilot test the multicomponent intervention program*. For this purpose, we suggest the interrupted time series design diagrammed as:

$$0\ 0\ 0\ 0\ I\ 0\ 0\ 0\ 0$$

in which the 0's are a series of observations prior to and following the intervention program, I. Since this design does not control for rival hypotheses related to history (Campbell & Stanley, 1963), we suggest the *time-lagged control design,* first suggested again by Gottman, McFall, and Barnett (1969), but used earlier by Hilgard (1933) in a co-twin design (see Glass, Willson, & Gottman, 1975). This design is diagrammed as:

	Baseline		Period 1		Period 2
(R)	0 0 0 0	I	0 0 0 0		0 0 0 0
(R)	0 0 0 0		0 0 0 0	I	0 0 0 0

in which at least two subjects are required, one randomly assigned to receive the treatment at a later invited time, but to be observed throughout. This design provides untreated control data during Period 1, and an independent test of the replication of the intervention; this replication of the effect deals somewhat with rival hypotheses related to history.

Issues in the statistical testing of time-series data are reviewed in Gottman and Glass (1978) and analytic techniques are available for electronic computer (Glass et al., 1975). For some reason, whether or not one should use statistical methods to analyze interrupted time-series experiments, or just eyeball the data, has become a debated issue in applied behavior analysis. This issue is discussed in detail by Gottman and Glass (1978); the reader is also referred to Kazdin (1976). In general, it should be noted that experienced investigators are likely to err with the eyeball in both the direction of rejecting significant effects and accepting nonsignificant ones. Time-series models essentially transform time-series data so that the residuals are uncorrelated and so that *t*-tests for intervention effects are valid. Interrupted time-series techniques should not be considered a statistical slap on the wrist; time-series methods are an opportunity to investigate the form of effects over time. Gottman (1973) wrote:

> It may also be misleading to ignore the variable of time in follow-up research. Time-series designs do indeed offer an alternative when a traditional experimental design is not feasible. However, their most important contribution is that they offer a unique perspective on the assessment of interventions. Experimental designs in the Fisherian tradition may obfuscate important observations about the form of intervention effects across time. Simultaneous randomized designs have become so much the method of investigating treatment effects that behavioral scientists have lost sight of the fact that these designs were originally developed for use in evaluating agricultural field trials. Fisherian methodology was most appropriate for comparing agricultural treatments with respect to relative yields. The yields were crops which were harvested when ripe; it was irrelevant whether the crops grew slowly or rapidly. For social systems, however, there are no predetermined planting and harvesting times. Interventions with clients, institutions, communities, and societies do not merely have an "effect" but an "effect pattern" across time. The value of an intervention is not judged by whether the effect is observable at the fall harvest but whether the effect occurs immediately or is delayed, whether it increases or decays, whether it is temporarily or constantly superior to the effects of alterna-

tive interventions evaluated in a cost-benefit sense. The time-series designs provide a methodology appropriate to the complexity of the effects of interventions in human systems. (p. 95)

One point should be added, namely, that an interrupted time-series analysis makes it possible to specify a matrix called the *design matrix* which can provide a powerful test of specific hypotheses about the form of change over time. For example, Gottman and Glass (1978) showed how the design matrix can be used to test for an effect of menstruation on the subject's subsequent mood two days after the onset of vaginal bleeding, and to test for the increasing and then fading effects of a temporary gun-buyback program on homicides.

An important issue that must be addressed in this phase of the PDM is the selection of comparison groups.

Comparison Groups in Psychotherapy Research
We will begin our discussion of comparison groups by discussing the kinds of control groups that have been used in psychotherapy research and then discuss two alternatives for generating an appropriate comparison group.

Control groups in psychotherapy research
We will discuss five types of control groups that have been utilized in psychotherapy research: (1) a no contact—no treatment group; (2) a no treatment control group; (3) a waiting list control group; (4) an attention-placebo control group; and (5) other treatments as control groups.

No contact control groups. This type of control group requires collecting data on subjects without their knowledge so that there will be minimal experimental bias. Mitchell and Inhram (1970) collected measures of anxiety from an entire class and designated a subset of the class as a no-contact control group. The no contact group showed no improvement from pretest to a 14-week followup.

Paul's oft-cited (1966) comparison of systematic desensitization with insight therapy included a no contact group matched on personality, demographic, and anxiety measures. The no contact group was administered a test battery before pretreatment and at a six-week followup as part of a public speaking class. All of the other groups, including the waiting list control group, showed significantly more improvement than the no contact control group.

No treatment control groups. Bergin (1966) cited three studies (Frank, 1961; Gurin, Veroff, & Feld, 1960; Powers & Witmer, 1951) that found that subjects who do not receive psychotherapy frequently sought help elsewhere. Alternative sources of help included friends, clergy, relatives, and other professionals.

In Saslow and Peters' (1956) study 56 percent of their untreated clients showed some improvement. The Saslow and Peters study is one of the prime examples of the high rate of "spontaneous remission" of problems in untreated clients. However, the subjects in the Saslow and Peters' study were all accepted for treatment and then for some reason did not return. The authors cite that reasons for not returning are that these subjects lived too far from the clinic, refused therapy, were expected to manage without therapy, or the persons who did not respond to therapy. The Saslow and Peters' subjects are better considered as a dropout group than an untreated control.

Bergin's (1971) review of spontaneous recovery rates suggested that these rates may be considerably lower than the 67 percent figure suggested by Eysenck (1952). Excluding the Endicott and Endicott (1963) study whose rates were inflated by including slightly improved (Bergin, 1971, p. 241, Table 7.8), the average spontaneous recovery rate for neuroses was 22.46 percent. Bergin also pointed out that the term "spontaneous" is misleading. Gurin, Veroff, and Feld (1960) in a nationwide survey found that persons actively sought help for personal problems, and that the vast majority did not choose mental health professionals. Most people turned to professionals not in mental health (42 percent turned to clergymen, 29 percent to doctors, 6 percent to lawyers). Of the 2,460 people who said that they had at some time felt an "impending nervous breakdown," 29 percent used self-help, and 49 percent of the subjects who said they worried "all the time" used self-help. Although it is not clear what self-help means, one possibility is the use of self-help books available in any supermarket. In a seminar, the first author reviewed 70 of these books and found that these materials often control several of the 15 items listed in Table 2−1; they usually provide items 1, 2, 3, 4, 5, and 10 of Table 2−1 with the heaviest emphasis placed on providing a new language system for organizing behavior and events, including a relabeling of problems with such terms as "muddles" or "games" which are not as stigmatizing as more professional terms that describe abnormal behavior.

Agras, Chapin, and Oliveau (1972) reported a study that used an untreated control group in which some subjects were rated as phobic and did not receive therapy. The investigators identified potential subjects through an epidemiological survey and likely candidates for therapy were then interviewed by a psychologist in their homes. The interesting feature of this study is that subjects were selected from the initial large survey rather than being selected from a population that is seeking treatment.

Lambert (1976) pointed out that there is evidence that testing sessions or even one interview has therapeutic benefit to the clients, and thus the clients in a no treatment control group may be receiving some treatment. Some of the clients who were judged improved in the Saslow and Peters' study attributed their improvement to their initial interview. Other studies have shown that initial testing (Jurjevich, 1968) and initial contact (Wimberger & Millar, 1968) have positive effects on clients.

Therefore, subjects in no treatment control groups pose an important challenge to the treatment groups under investigation—they seek nonprofessional help, engage in self-help, and they view the assessments or interviews as help. If they change their behavior as much as the treatment group, it throws the therapy into question. However, we currently have no solid data about the extent to which these control subjects change their behavior.

Waiting list control groups. Waiting list control groups have several advantages over those

previously discussed: (1) waiting lists are a natural aspect of many clinics and thus form a natural control group, and (2) clients are more motivated to complete the postassessment by the guarantee of therapy. In fact, if therapy is scheduled for a specific time in the future, these subjects will constitute an *invited treatment* control group and may be less likely to seek help elsewhere during the waiting period.

Subotnik (1972) suggested that there are two subgroups of waiting list control subjects, those who will refuse therapy when it is offered, and those who will not. Grummon (1954) found that the waiting list clients who refused therapy had improved more during their wait than those who accepted therapy. Similar results were obtained by Endicott and Endicott (1963).

Attention-placebo control groups. This group may serve to control such factors as the frequency of contacts, and nonspecific factors such as expectation for improvement, and therapeutic interest (see items no. 1, 2, 5, 6, and 11 of Table 2−1). Paul's (1966) attention-placebo group improved more than the no treatment control and did not differ from the insight-oriented group. At the end of the two-year follow-up, the same pattern held.

Davison (1968) and Lang and Lazovik (1963) both used pseudotherapy groups as attention−placebo control groups and also found that these groups differed from untreated controls.

Borkovec and Nau (1972) found that some subjects in attention-placebo groups may question the credibility of the procedure. They found that ratings of credibility did differ in attention-placebo and therapy groups, and suggested that all groups in psychotherapy outcome studies include credibility ratings. However, Osarchuk and Goldfried (1975) did not replicate these findings.

Hampton (1973) argued that the goal of the attention-placebo group is to control expectancy effects and to engage the faith of the client in the placebo. He suggested that researchers measure the client's expectancy of a gain before or early in treatment to control for the effectiveness of placebo effects in both groups. This recommendation is consistent with our suggestion of monitoring the active ingredients or process variables of the therapy intervention.

Other treatment groups. These Grand Prix controls are so unclear as comparison groups that they can be useful only in a "value claims" sense that we shall discuss below.

Finally, we should add that dropouts from treatment, sometimes called "terminator controls" are inadequate as controls since there is some unknown selection factor operative in the termination, such as motivation for change, match with therapist, or dislike of the treatment program. It is, however, important to study dropouts since they can teach us some valuable things about the therapy program. For example, Shapiro and Budman (1973) studied clients from individual and family therapy who remained in treatment or terminated against professional advice. The pattern that emerged from their results was that clients in family therapy tended to appreciate an active therapist who presented a program with clearly articulated goals and direction, and that terminators disliked their therapists because the therapists were inactive, detached, uninvolved, and the therapy did not have a clear direction (See also Chapter 21).

The value claims approach

Another approach to the construction of comparison groups is called the "value claims" approach (Glass, personal communication).

In this approach, the researcher must make a statement that the therapy program is better than something else. The researcher thus sets up a unique Grand Prix, and this Grand Prix can have peculiarly local dimensions. For example, the value claim may be stated in terms of cost as, "This therapy program is more effective than Program X which costs about the same amount." Thus a sex therapy program can be compared to a two-week vacation of equal cost to the client in terms of how each option affects the marital satisfaction scores of couples with a sexual problem.

Or the therapy program that is highly staffed with professionals can be compared to the same program with a greater proportion of paraprofessionals. A demonstration of equal effectiveness could argue for expanding the population served at a smaller cost than duplicating the entire professional staff.

The value claims approach requires the researcher to make a creative claim about the value of the therapy program. The value claim then determines the comparison group.

The active ingredient approach

The active ingredient approach first requires the researcher to list all the main ingredients of the therapy program. Suppose, for example, that the components listed in Table 2–1 are selected as the major ingredients of the program, but the researcher feels that ingredients 8 and 9 are the active ingredients of the therapy. The comparison group would contain all the other 13 ingredients with ingredients 8 and 9 replaced with attention-placebo activities of listening, showing interest, and talking.

The active ingredient approach is similar to constructing a comparison group for a drug study with rats. The experimental group rats are picked up, given an injection of the drug appropriate to their body weight, and then placed in a maze with running time and number of errors recorded. The control procedure involves picking rats up, giving them an injection of saline solution, placing them in the maze, and recording running time and the number of errors.

In the active ingredient approach, the control group looks very much like the treatment group, except in a few specific features.

VI. Assessment of the Successes and Failures of the Program.

This phase of the PDM can include assessment of what kinds of people benefit from the program. At this point in program development and evaluation it would be useful to avoid screening clients. As we mentioned earlier in this chapter, screening cleints for sex counseling programs by Masters and Johnson (1970) and LoPiccolo and Lobitz (1973) limited their conclusions to distressed couples with only a single marital issue who have no other psychological problems. While this type of screening may be beneficial to avoid being discouraged during a program development phase, in Phase VI of the PDM we are very interested in the program's failures and successes, and learning to discriminate among them using salient characteristics that will improve the program's functioning. For this reason, the flowchart in Figure 2—2 contains an arrow to a "Redesign" box which feeds back to Stage II of the PDM.

We must expand resources during this stage of the PDM on following up dropouts, remainers, failures, and successes of the program. The issue of follow-up is essential in this activity.

One issue that should be addressed in an experimental design chapter is how long a follow-up period is sufficient. While this question in its general form is not likely to have a simple answer, the follow-up question speaks to our current models of the change process. Follow-up is usually discussed in connection with the *maintenance* of therapeutic gains, and with the redesign of extra-therapy environments to facilitate maintenance (for example, see Krasner, 1971). Hence, follow-up is confounded with the assessment of transfer of training. The model implicit in this confound is that a client is likely to make maximal changes in the therapeutic environment, and that after therapy, the pathogenic conditions have to fight remedies that are no longer continually being replenished by visits to the therapist. There may, however, be some clinical problems for which we can expect a different sort of change process, such as a gradual, or small step, change process, similar to those obtained in discrimination learning experiments.

There are a number of methodological considerations in planning a follow-up assessment. First, it is important to examine attrition in the follow-up by blocking follow-up subjects on pre-to-post gains, since it may be the case that only satisfied customers return for the follow-up assessments, which would militate against the conclusion that gains were maintained. More generally, the question is whether the follow-up subjects are representative of the treatment and comparison groups. Second, it is important to include the same measures taken at pre-and postassessment in the follow-up assessment.

Part of the usefulness of follow-up assessments are in the dismantling phase (Phase VII) of the PDM. One component of the program may be ineffective in producing change on its own, but in combination with another component may produce a program more effective in maintaining change. For example, self-monitoring has been relatively ineffective as a change strategy in weight loss (Mahoney, 1974) but it has been successful in maintaining loss (Hall et al., 1975). An important aspect of systematic dismantling of a program thus concerns the components of the program that are most useful in maintaining change.

One source of data that has been largely ignored in follow-up assessment is the group of patients that relapse. We may obtain extremely valuable information that would be useful in modifying the program's content if we could find patterns in relapse conditions. For example, Marlatt (personal communication) studied critical life events that preceded relapse in alcoholics. He found that there were two major kinds of events—social pressure to drink in which the client did not seem to know a socially graceful way of refusing one drink, and assertion situations in which the client was unable to obtain his rights (for example, an irate ex-wife denying visiting rights with children one weekend led to a binge). Marlatt also found that these clients had the cognitive set that one drink was the same as total failure and that cognition preceded a binge. This information can be valuable in adding social skill training and cognitive restructuring components to the therapy program.

There is need for a metastudy of the Glass and Smith type on effect size of various kinds of behavior problems as a function of a follow-up period after treatment. As a crude beginning toward this end, we reviewed literature in selected sources on three behavior problems. We selected one problem that is usually conceptualized as a "response increment" problem, where the therapeutic goal is increasing approach to a feared object; the problem selected was fear and the treatment selected was systematic desensitization. We selected one problem which is usually conceptualized as a "response decrement" problem, where the therapeutic goal is decreasing the frequency of some behavior; the problem selected was weight loss. We selected one "response acquisition" problem where the therapeutic goal is to create a new response in the client's repertoire; the problem selected was an assertion problem. We reviewed the following sources from 1970 to 1976; the *Annual Review of Psychology, Behavior Research and Therapy,* the *Journal of Abnormal Psychology,* the *Journal of Applied Behavior Analysis,* the *Journal of Consulting and Clinical Psychology* and the *Psychological Bulletin.* What follows is a crude beginning toward a systematic investigation of follow-up. It must be mentioned that tallying "overall patterns" of results will inevitably equate evidence from well-designed studies with evidence from poorer studies.

Of the 55 studies reviewed in systematic desensitization, 25 had follow-up measures, and the follow-up periods ranged from one month to four years; four studies had follow-up periods of less than six weeks, seven had periods of six weeks to six months, six had periods of six months to a year, and six had periods of one year or greater. The overall pattern of these results, based on both self-report and behavioral measures (when available), indicates that 14 studies maintained gains and six studies did not, while five studies could not be adequately evaluated for various methodological reasons. Of the remaining studies with follow-ups of six months or less, eight studies maintained gains and one did not; with follow-up periods greater than six months, eight studies maintained gains and three did not. In general, the effects for lasting gains are strong.[2] Similar results are obtained when the studies are compared separately by dependent variable (self-report or behavior).[3]

In the area of weight loss,[4] 29 studies were reviewed, and 26 of these reported follow-up measures, with the follow-up period ranging from four weeks to two years. Thirteen of these studies used follow-up periods of three months or less. Some studies show short-term gains but not long-term gains after a one- or two-year follow-up (Hall, 1972; Hall, 1973). Hall's (1972) review of weight loss studies concluded that studies with follow-ups less than 12 weeks show gains while studies with follow-ups of more than 12 weeks do not. Contrary to Hall, our review shows evidence that follow-up of six months duration still show lasting changes. Nearly all the studies we reviewed showed lasting gains. However, it must be pointed out that subjects vary widely on the criteria for being considered overweight, on the size of the significant effect, and on the pattern of change. This is one problem in which a time-series design would be ideal: Measurement is inexpensive and reliable and there would be considerable advantage to using each subject as his or her own control.

Thirteen studies in assertion training[5] were reviewed; of these, five had follow-ups ranging from two weeks to a year; of these five studies, four showed that the treatment group maintained gains, while one did not (Hedquist & Weinhold, 1970). However, in one of these studies there was no control group (Marzillier, Lambert, & Kellett, 1976) and in another (Galassi, Kostaka, & Galassi, 1975) there was some slippage on the behavioral measure. Since these two studies had the longest follow-up periods (six months and one year, respectively), the stability of change in this problem

---

[2]There is some evidence of inconsistency in maintained gains that varies with the measure used, but results do not consistently favor maintenance on one measure. For example, Krapfl and Nawas (1970) found maintenance on behavioral but not self-report measures on six-week follow-up, whereas Gillan and Rachman (1974) found the opposite pattern.

[3]The studies reviewed in systematic desensitization were Abrahms & Allen (1974), Allen & Desauliniers (1974), Baker, Cohen, & Saunders, (1973), Bandura (1969), Borkovec (1972), Boudewyns, & Wilson (1972), Cother (1970), Davison (1968), Donner (1970), Evans & Kellam (1973), Farmer & Wright (1971), Gillan & Rachman (1974), Graff (1971), Kraft (1970), Krapfl (1967), Krapfl & Nawas (1970), Lang & Lazovik (1965), Lazovik & Lang (1960), Lick (1975), Marks (1971), Marzillier, Lambert & Kellett (1976), Miller, Barrett, Hampe, & Noble (1972), Mitchell & Ingham (1970), Mylar (1972), Oliveau (1969), Paul (1966), Paul (1967), Rosen, Glasgow, & Barrera (1976).

[4]The studies reviewed in weight loss were Bellack, Rozensky, & Schwartz (1974), Bornstein & Sipprella (1973), Hall (1973), Hall & Hall (1974), Hall, Hall, Hanson & Borden (1974), Hall, Hall, Borden, & Hanson (1975), Harris & Hallbauer(1973), Jeffrey & Christensen (1972), Jeffrey (1974), Levitz & Stunkard (1974), Mahoney, Moura, & Wade (1973), Mahoney (1974), Manno & Marston (1972), McReynolds, Lutz, Paulsen, & Kohrs (1976), Romancyzk, Tracey, Wilson, & Thorpe (1973), Romanczyk (1974), Wollersheim (1970).

[5]The studies reviewed in assertion were Galassi, Kostka, & Galassi (1975), Hedquist & Weinhold (1970), Hersen, Eisler, & Miller (1973), Hersen, Eisler, Miller, Johnson, & Pinkston (1973), Kazdin (1974), Kazdin (1976).

area is still an open question. There is some evidence that lasting gains in response acquisition interventions are obtained by using a cognitive self-statement modification approach, at least for shy male subjects who know what to do in dating situations but for some reason do not perform competently (Glass, Gottman, & Shmurak, 1976).

Glass and Smith (1976) presented effect size regression equations for behavioral and nonbehavioral superclasses in which one of the independent variables was the number of months post-therapy at which outcome measures were taken. The regression coefficient for the behavioral therapies was .03 and −.02 for the nonbehavioral therapies, which is consistent with our conclusion of the maintenance of effects for behavioral interventions.

This review dramatizes the need for systematic investigation of follow-up patterns over varying times after treatment as a function of the target problem, the treatment program's components, and for different kinds of clients.

VII. Systematic Dismantling of the Program

The practical aspect of "dismantling" an intervention program means trying out versions of the program with and without certain content or delivery components in an effort to produce reasonable effect sizes with a reduction of the program's cost. A dismantling study in an applied context is thus an *efficiency* study. In a theoretical context, a dismantling study is of interest if the various components of the program represent different theoretical conceptions of change.

Examples of dismantling studies now abound. Eysenck and Beech's (1971) chapter on counter-conditioning methods in the last edition of the *Handbook* reviewed the Rachman (1965) study of spider phobia which compared four conditions—desensitization plus relaxation, desensitization alone, relaxation alone, and a no treatment control. Rachman found that relaxation and desensitization together gave the best results on avoidance scores.

Bandura (1971), in the last edition of the *Handbook* presented component analyses of modeling programs. He reviewed a study by Blanchard

(1969) of snake phobia. Blanchard compared modeling, modeling plus information, and modeling plus information plus participation to a control condition. Blanchard found that

> *Modeling accounted for approximately 60 percent of the behavior change, and 80 percent of the changes in attitudes and fear arousal; guided participation contributed the remaining increment. Informational influences, on the other hand, had no effect on any of the three response classes. In fact, the latter condition yielded the lowest scores on all three sets of dependent measures. Apparently, giving information to severely phobic people may, if anything, increase their fearfulness. (Bandura, 1971, p. 687).*

Since 1971, dismantling studies have been conducted on various social skill training approaches (for example, see Hersen, Eisler, Miller, Johnson, & Pinkston, 1973; and McFall & Twentyman, 1973, in assertion training; for reviews of dating skills training dismantling research see Arkowitz, in press; Curran, 1977). This research is beginning to analyze the specific contributions of each treatment component to the change effect. One caution that should be mentioned in systematic dismantling research is that because a component contributes to an effect does not automatically imply that the response deficit is specified by the component. For example, a coaching component could work because it teaches people how to respond, or because it makes the response more normative, or because it creates a cognitive change, or because it models a relaxed response, and so on. Theoretical understanding of the function a component serves is facilitated by a task analysis of the response deficit (Schwartz & Gottman, 1976).

VIII. Specification of Program's Cost, Benefits, and Limitations

Richard Price (personal communication) talks about a distinction between a "mastery" and a "mystery" approach to intervention. A mastery approach is one in which the researcher is out to demonstrate that the program being evaluated can master the problem it addresses. A mystery approach is one in which the research question is more complex, in which the interest is perhaps, "What kind of people make what kinds of specific gains in which specific settings with this program?"

The distinction is nontrivial in a major sense that two different attitudes are created in the mind of the investigator by these two approaches. The mastery investigator is likely to become angry at data that disconfirm the program's effectiveness and to be repulsed by a phenomenon that demonstrates itself to be complex.

The mystery investigator enjoys the data: Failure indicates that there is unexpected information in the phenomenon.

There is some sense in which it may be the case that most psychological models are simultaneously true in the sense that there are groups of people that fit each model. Different models may be true under different conditions. An example of this is a study by Notarius (1977) of emotional expression. Notarius examined male subjects' responses to stressful events (for example, the threat of shock, a sex change operation film, and a woman undressing) by coding facial expression changes and measuring physiological responses (GSR, heart-rate, respiration rate, and a hidden seat stabilometer). He was investigating a hydraulic model of emotional expression, that is, that emotional response would be expressed in *either* facial or physiological channels. This hydraulic model has obvious implications for a theory of psychosomatic illness. Notarius found that his subjects fit this model and that their response styles were stable in a free expression condition; he also found evidence for the expression of emotions in all channels under other instruction conditions. From the initial origins of psychoanalysis we see that Freud, Jung, and Adler developed different theories. However, it is important to note that they were working with entirely different patient groups, and that each theory makes the most sense in the context of the particular patient group from which it was developed.

The point is that program evaluation and theoretical experimentation in psychology need not be an all-or-none process. What is needed is some *classification of subjects on the basis of change processes.* An important book by Overall

and Klett (1972) presented a method called *linear typal analysis* for empirically generating clusters of people on the basis of their behavior in specific settings of concern. We will not discuss these analytic techniques here (see Gottman, 1978); however, the notions of classification are useful in this stage of the PDM in describing what kinds of people make what kinds of specific gains with the program. Bandura (1971) wrote,

Perhaps because psychological interventions rarely have immediate and spectacular consequences, a casual attitude has developed toward using untested techniques. New approaches are promoted enthusiastically, and it is not until the methods have been applied clinically for some time by a coterie of advocates that objective tests of efficacy are conducted, if at all. Usually the methods are unceremoniously retired by subsequent controlled studies or informal evaluation. Workers in psychotherapy have, therefore, come to view any new therapeutic approach as a passing fad. (p. 655)

The model proposed in this chapter is a research strategy that may help us at the outset to ground our investigation of psychotheapy on an empirical base, that may help us in learning from our failures, and successes, and, we hope, may make the enterprise of research a more exciting endeavor for both "Artisan" and "Scientist."

REFERENCES

Agras, W., Chapin, H., & Oliveau, D. The natural history of a phobia: Course and prognosis. *Archives of General Psychiatry,* 1972, *26,* 315–317.

Alexander, J. F. Defensive and supportive communication in normal and deviate families. *Journal of Consulting and Clinical Psychology,* 1973, *40,* 223–231.

Alexander, J. F., & Parsons, B. V. Short-term behavioral intervention with delinquent families: Impact on family process and recidivism. *Journal of Abnormal Psychology,* 1973, *51,* 219–233.

Arkowitz, H. The measurement and modification of minimal dating behavior. In M. Hersen, R. Eisler, & P. Miller (Eds), *Progress in behavior modification.* New York: Academic Press, in press.

Asher, S. R., Oden, S. L., & Gottman, J. M. Children's friendships in school settings. In L. G. Katz (Ed.),

Current topics in early childhood education. Vol. 1. Hillsdale, N. J.: Ablex Publishing Co., 1977.

Bakeman, R., & Dabbs, J. M., Jr. Social Interaction observed: Some approaches to the analysis of behavior streams. *Personality & Social Psychology Bulletin,* 1976, *2,* 335–345.

Bandura, A. Psychotherapy based upon modeling principles. In A. E. Bergin & S. L. Garfield, *Handbook of Psychotherapy and behavior change.* New York: John Wiley & Sons, 1971.

Belmont, J. M., & Butterfield, E. C. The relations of short-term memory to development and intelligence. In L. Lipsitt and H. Reese (Eds.), *Advances in child development and behavior.* Vol. 4. New York: Academic Press, 1969.

Bem, D., & Allen, S. On predicting some of the people some of the time: The search for cross-situational consistencies in behavior. *Psychological Review,* 1974, *81,* 6, 506–520.

Bergin, A. E. Some implications of psychotherapy research for therapeutic practice. *Journal of Abnormal Psychology,* 1966, *71,* 235–247.

Bergin, A. E. The evaluation of therapeutic outcomes. In A. E. Bergin and S. L. Garfield (Eds.), *Handbook of psychotherapy and behavior change.* New York: Wiley, 1971.

Bergin, A. E. & Suinn, R. M. Individual psychotherapy and behavior therapy. In M. R. Rosenzweig and L. W. Porter (Eds.), *Annual Review of Psychology, 1975.* Vol. 26. Palo Alto, Calif.: Annual Reviews, Inc., 1975.

Birchler, G. R., Weiss, R. C., & Vincent, J. P. Multimethod analysis of social reinforcement exchange between maritally distressed and nondistressed spouse and stranger dyads. *Journal of Personality and Social Psychology,* 1975, *31,* 349–360.

Bialock, H. M., Jr. Causal inferences in nonexperimental research. Chapel Hill, N.C.: University of North Carolina Press, 1961.

Blanchard, E. B. The relative contributions of modeling, informational influences, and physical contact in the extinction of phobic behavior. Doctoral dissertation. Stanford University, 1969.

Bordin, E. S. Inside the therapeutic hour. In E. A. Rubinstein and M. B. Parloff (Eds.), *Research in psychotherapy.* Vol. I. Washington, D.C.: American Psychological Association, 1962.

Borkovec, T., & Nau, S. Credibility of analogue therapy rationales. *Journal of Behavior Therapy and Experimental Psychiatry,* 1972, *3,* 257–260.

Box, G. E. P., & Draper, N. R. *Evolutionary operation: A method for increasing industrial productivity.* New York: Wiley, 1969.

Butterfield, E. C. On studying cognitive development. In G. P. Sackett (Ed.) *Observing Human Behavior,* Vol. 1. Baltimore, Md.: University Park Press, 1978.

Campbell, D. T., & Stanley, J. C. Experimental and quasi-experimental designs for research and teaching. In N. L. Gage (Ed.), *Handbook of research on teaching.* Chicago: Rand McNally, 1963.

Cartwright, D. S. Success in psychotherapy as a function of certain actuarial variables. *Journal of Consulting Psychology,* 1955, *19,* 357–363.

Charlesworth, W. R. Ethology: Its relevance for observational studies of human adaptation. In G. P. Sackett (Ed.) *Observing Human Behavior,* Vol. 1. Baltimore, Md.: University Park Press, 1978.

Clark, K. W. Evaluation of a group social skills training program with psychiatric inpatients: Training Viet Nam era veterans in assertion, heterosexual, and job interview skills. Doctoral dissertation, University of Wisconsin, 1974.

Cowen, E. L., & Pederson, A., Babigian, H., Izzo, L. D., & Trost, M. A. Long-term followup of early detected vulnerable children. *Journal of Consulting and Clinical Psychology,* 1973, *41,* 438–446.

Cronbach, L. J., Gleser, G. C., Nanda, H., & Rajaratnam, N. *The dependability of behavioral measurements.* New York: Wiley, 1972.

Curran, J. P. Skills training as an approach to the treatment of heterosexual-social anxiety: A review. *Psychological Bulletin,* 1977, *84,* 140–157.

Davison, G. Systematic desensitization as a counterconditioning process. *Journal of Abnormal Psychology,* 1968, *73,* 91–99.

Davidson, P. D., & Costello, C. G. (Eds.), *N = 1: Experimental studies of single cases.* New York: Van Nostrand Reinhold Company, 1969.

Denker, P. G. Results of treatment of psychoneuroses by the general practitioner—a follow-up of 500 cases. *New York State Journal of Medicine,* 1946, *46,* 2164–2166.

Dukes, W. F. N = 1. *Psychological Bulletin,* 1965, *64,* 74–79.

Duncan, O. D. *Introduction to structural equations models.* New York: Academic Press, 1975.

Dweck, C. S. The role of expectations and attributions in the alleviation of learned helplessness. *Journal of Personality and Social Psychology,* 1975, *31,* 674–685.

Dweck, C. S., & Reppucci, N. D. Learned helplessness and reinforcement responsibility in children. *Journal of Personality and Social Psychology,* 1973, *25,* 109–116.

D'Zurilla, T. J. Effects of behavioral influence techniques applied in group discussion on subsequent verbal participation. Unpublished doctoral dissertation, University of Illinois, 1964.

Ellis, N. R. Memory processes in retardates and normals. In N. R. Ellis (Ed.), *International review of research in mental retardation.* Vol. 4. New York: Academic Press, 1970.

Endicott, N., & Endicott, H. Improvement in untreated psychiatric patients. *Archives of General Psychiatry,* 1963, *9,* 575–585.

Endler, N. S., & Hunt, J. McV. Sources of behavioral variance as measured by the S-R inventory of anxiousness. *Psychological Bulletin,* 1966, *65,* 6, 336–346.

Endler, N. S., & Hunt, J. McV. S-R inventories of hostility and comparisons of the proportions of variance from persons responses, and situations for hostility and anxiousness. *Journal of Personality and Social Psychology,* 1968, *9,* 4, 309–315.

Eysenck, H. J. The effects of psychotherapy: An evaluation. *Journal of Consulting Psychology,* 1952, *16,* 319–324.

Eysenck, H. J. *Handbook of abnormal psychology.* London: Pitman, 1960.

Eysenck, H. J. New ways in psychotherapy. *Psychology Today,* 1967, *1,* 39–47.

Eysenck, H. J., & Beech, R. Counterconditioning and related methods. In A. E. Bergin and S. L. Garfield (Eds.), *Handbook of psychotherapy and behavior change.* New York: Wiley, 1971.

Flavell, J. H. Developmental studies in mediated memory. In H. Reese and L. Lipsitt (Eds.), *Advances in child development and behavior.* Vol. 5. New York: Academic Press, 1970.

Flavell, J. H. First discussant's comments: What is memory development the development of? *Human Development,* 1971, *14,* 272–278.

Flavell, J. H., Beach, D. R., & Chinsky, J. M. Spontaneous verbal rehearsal in memory task as a function of age. *Child Development,* 1966, *37,* 283–299.

Frank, J. *Persuasion and healing.* Baltimore: Johns Hopkins Press, 1961.

Gagné, R. M. Curriculum research and the promotion of learning. In R. E. Stake (Ed.), *AERA curriculum monograph series No. 1.* Chicago: Rand McNally, 1967.

Galassi, J., Kostka, M., & Galassi, M. Assertive training: A one-year follow-up. *Journal of Counseling Psychology,* 1975, *22,* 451–452.

Gillan, P., & Rachman, S. An experimental investigation of desensitization in phobic patients. *British Journal of Psychiatry,* 1974, *124,* 392–401.

Glass, C. R., Gottman, J. M., & Shmurak, S. S. Reshonse acquisition and cognitive self-statement modification approaches to dating skills training. *Journal of Counseling Psychology,* 1976, *23,* 520–526.

Glass, G. V., & Smith, M. L. Meta-analysis of psychotherapy outcome studies. Paper presented at meeting of the Society for Psychotherapy Research, June 1976, San Diego, California.

Glass, G. V., Willson, V. L., & Gottman, J. M. *Design and analysis of time-series experiments.* Boulder, Colo.: Colorado University Associated Press, 1975.

Goldfried, M. R., & D'Zurilla, T. J. A behavior-analytic model for assessing competence. In C. D. Spielberger (Ed.), *Current topics in clinical and community psychology.* Vol. 1. New York: Academic Press, 1969.

Goldfried, M. R., & Kent, R. N. Traditional versus behavioral personality assessment: A comparison of methodological and theoretical assumptions. *Psychological Bulletin,* 1972, *77,* 409–420.

Goldsmith, J. B., & McFall, R. M. Development and evaluation of an interpersonal skill training program for psychiatric inpatients. *Journal of Abnormal Psychology,* 1975, *84,* 51–58.

Goldstein, A. P. *Structured learning therapy: Toward a psychotherapy for the poor.* New York: Academic Press, 1973.

Gottman, J. M. N-of-one and N-of-two research in psychotherapy. *Psychological Bulletin,* 1973, *80,* 93–105.

Gottman, J. M. The effects of a modeling film on social isolation in preschool childen: A methodological investigation. *Journal of Abnormal Child Psychology,* 1977, *5,* 69–78.

Gottman, J. Nonsequential data analysis techniques in observational research. In Carl Haywood and Gene Sackett (Eds.), *Observing behavior, Vol. 2: Data collection and analysis methods.* Baltimore, Md.: University Park Press, 1978.

Gottman, J. M. Children's behavior when trying to enter a peer group. Submitted for publication.

Gottman, J. M., & Glass, G. V. Time-series analysis of interrupted time-series experiments. In T. Kratochwill (Ed.), *Strategies to evaluate change in single subject research.* New York: Academic Press, in press.

Gottman, J. M., & Leiblum, S. R. *How to do psychotherapy and how to evaluate it.* New York: Holt, Rinehart & Winston, 1974.

Gottman, J. M., McFall, R. M., & Barnett, J. T. Design and analysis of research using time series. *Psychological Bulletin,* 1969, *72,* 299–306.

Gronlund, N. E. *Sociometry in the classroom.* New York: Harper and Brothers, 1959.

Grummon, D. Personality change as a function of time in persons motivated for therapy. In C. Rogers & R. Dymond (Eds.), *Psychotherapy and personality change.* Chicago: University of Chicago Press, 1954

Gurin, G., Veroff, J., & Feld, S. *Americans view their mental health.* New York: Basic Books, 1960.

Haley, J. Research on family patterns: An instrument measurement. *Family Process,* 1964, *3,* 41–65.

Haley, J. Speech sequences of normal and abnormal families with two children present. *Family Process,* 1967, *6,* 81–97.

Hall, S. Self-control and therapist control in the behavioral treatment of overweight women. *Behavior Research and Therapy,* 1972, *10,* 59–68.

Hall, S. Behavioral treatment of obesity: A two-year follow-up. *Behavior Research and Therapy,* 1973, *11,* 647–648.

Hall, S., Hall, R., Borden, B., & Hanson, R. Follow-up strategies in the behavioral treatment of overweight. *Behavior Research and Therapy,* 1975, *13,* 167–172.

Hampton, P. Placebo treatment techniques in behavior therapy. *Behavior Therapy,* 1973, *4,* 481–482.

Hartup, W. W. Peer social organization. In P. Mussen (Ed.), *Manual of Child Psychology.* Vol. II. New York: Wiley, 1970.

Hedquist, F., & Weinhold, B. Behavioral group counseling with socially anxious and unassertive college students. *Journal of Counseling Psychology,* 1970, *17,* 237–242.

Heise, D. R. *Causal analysis.* New York: Wiley, 1975.

Hersen, M., & Barlow, D. H. *Single case experimental designs.* New York: Pergamon, 1976.

Hersen, M., Eisler, R. M., Miller, P. M., Johnson, M. B., & Pinkston, S. G. Effects of practice, instructions, and modeling on components of assertive behavior. *Behavior Research and Therapy,* 1973, *11,* 443–451.

Hibbs, D. A., Jr. Problems of statistical estimation and causal inference in time-series regression models. In H. A. Costner (Ed.), *Sociological methodology 1973–1974.* San Francisco: Jossey-Bass, 1974.

Hilgard, E. R. The effects of delayed practice on memory and motor performance studied by the method of co-twin control. *Genetic Psychology Monographs,* 1933, *6,* 67.

Hollenbeck, A. R. Problems of reliability in observational research. Paper presented at Lake Wilderness Conference on the Application of Observational-Ethological Methods to the Study of Mental Retardation, Washington, 1976.

Jacob, T. Family interaction in disturbed and normal families: A methodological and substantive review. *Psychological Bulletin,* 1975, *82,* 33–65.

Jacobson, N. S., & Martin, B. Behavioral marriage therapy: Current status. *Psychological Bulletin,* 1976, *83,* 540–556.

Jaffe, J., & Feldstein, S. *Rhythms of dialogue.* New York: Academic Press, 1970.

Johnson, S. M., & Bolstad, O. D. Methodological issues in naturalistic observation: Some problems and solutions for field research. In L. A. Hamerlynck, L. C. Handy, and E. J. Mash (Eds.), *Behavior change: Methodology, concepts, and practice.* Champaign, Ill.: Research Press, 1973.

Jones, M. C. The elimination of children's fears. *Journal of Experimental Psychology,* 1924, *7,* 382–390.

Jones, R. R. Design and analysis problems in program evaluation. In P. O. Davidson, F. W. Clark, and L. A. Hamerlynck (Eds.), *Evaluation of behavioral programs in community, residential and school settings: The Fifth Banff Research International Conference.* Champaign, Ill.: Research Press, 1974.

Jones, R. R., Reid, J. B., & Patterson, G. R. Naturalistic observation in clinical assessment. In P. McReynolds (Ed.), *Advances in psychological assessment.* Vol. 3. San Francisco: Jossey-Bass, 1975.

Jurjevich, R. Changes in psychiatric symptoms without psychotherapy. In E. Lesse (Ed.), *An evaluation of the results of the psychotherapies.* Springfield, Ill.: Charles C. Thomas, 1968.

Kanfer, F. H., & Saslow, G. Behavioral diagnosis. In C. M. Franks (Ed.), *Behavior therapy: Appraisal and status.* New York: McGraw-Hill, 1969.

Kazdin, A. Effects of covert modeling and model reinforcement on assertive behavior. *Journal of Abnormal Psychology,* 1974, *83,* 240–252.

Kazdin, A. Effects of covert modeling, multiple model and model reinforcement on assertive behavior. *Behavior Therapy,* 1976, *7,* 211–222.

Kenny, D. A. Cross-lagged panel correlation: A test for spuriousness. *Psychological Bulletin,* 1975, *82,* 887–903.

Kiesler, D. J. Experimental designs in psychotherapy research. In A. E. Bergin & S. L. Garfield (Eds.), *Handbook of psychotherapy and behavior change.* New York: Wiley, 1971.

Kiesler, D. J. *The process of psychotherapy.* Chicago: Aldine Publishing Company, 1973.

Klein, N., Alexander, J. F., & Parsons, B. V. Impact of family systems intervention on recidivisim and sibling delinquency: A study of primary prevention. Paper presented at the Annual Convention of the Western Psychological Association, Sacramento, April, 1975.

Krapfl, J. & Nawas, M. Differential ordering of stimulus presentation in systematic desensitization. *Journal of Abnormal Psychology,* 1970, *76,* 333–337.

Krasner, L. The operant approach in behavior therapy. In A. E. Bergin and S. L. Garfield *Handbook of psychotherapy and behavior change.* New York: Wiley, 1971.

Kratochwill, T. (Ed.). *Strategies to evaluate change in single subject research.* New York: Academic Press, in press.

Lambert, M. Spontaneous remission in adult neurotic disorders: A revision and summary. *Psychological Bulletin,* 1976, *83,* 1, 107–119.

Lang, P., & Lazovik, D. Experimental desensitization of a phobia. *Journal of Abnormal and Social Psychology,* 1963, *6,* 519–525.

Lang, P. J., & Melamed, B. G. Case report: Avoidance conditioning therapy of an infant with chronic ruminative vomiting. *Journal of Abnormal Psychology,* 1969, *74,* 1–8.

Lazarus, A. A., & Davison, G. C. Clinical innovation in research and practice. In A. E. Bergin and S. L. Garfield (Eds.), *Handbook of psychotherapy and behavior change.* New York: Wiley, 1971.

Lazovik, A., & Lang, P. A laboratory demonstration of systematic desensitization psychotherapy. *Journal of Psychological Studies,* 1960, *11,* 238–247.

Levenson, R. W., & Gottman, J. M. Toward the assessment of social competence. *Journal of Consulting and Clinical Psychology,* in press.

Lewis, M., & Rosenblum, L. A. (Eds.). *The effect of the infant on its caregiver.* New York: Wiley, 1974.

LoPiccolo, J. & Lobitz, W. C. Behavior therapy of sexual dysfunction. In L. C. Handy and E. J. Mash (Eds.), *Behavior change: The Fourth Banff Conference on behavior modification.* Champaign, Ill.: Research Press, 1973.

MacKinnon, D., & Dukes, W. F. Repression. In L. Postman (Ed.), *Psychology in the making.* New York: Knopf, 1962.

Mahoney, M. J. *Cognition and behavior modification.* Cambridge, Mass.: Ballinger Publishing Co. 1974.

Marziller, J., Lambert C., & Kellett, J. A controlled evaluation of systematic desensitization and social skills training for social inadequate psychiatric patients. *Behavior Research and Therapy,* 1976, *14,* 225–238.

Masters, W. H., & Johnson, V. *Human sexual inadequacy.* Boston: Little, Brown, 1970.

Matarazzo, J. D., & Wiens, A. N. Speech behavior as an objective correlate of empathy and outcome in interview and psychotherapy research: A review with implications for behavior modification. *Behavior Modification,* 1977, *1.*

Matarazzo, J. D., Wiens, A. N., Matarazzo, R. G., & Saslow, G. Speech and silence behavior in clinical psychotherapy and its laboratory correlates. In J. M. Shlien, H. F. Hunt, J. D. Matarazzo, and C. Savage. *Research in psychotherapy.* Vol. III. Washington, D.C.: American Psychological Association, 1968.

McFall, R. M. Analogue methods in behavioral assessment. Issues and prospects. In J. D. Cone and R. P. Hawkins (Eds.), *Behavioral assessment: New directions in clinical psychology.* New York: Brunner-Mazel, in press.

McFall, R. M., & Lillesand, D. B. Behavior rehearsal with modeling and coaching in assertion training. *Journal of Abnormal Psychology,* 1971, *77,* 313–323.

McFall, R. M., & Marston, A. R. An experimental investigation of behavioral rehearsal in assertive training. *Journal of Abnormal Psychology,* 1970, *76,* 295−303.

McFall, R. M., & Twentyman, C. T. Four experiments on the relative contributions of rehearsal, modeling, and coachings to assertion training. *Journal of Abnormal Psychology,* 1973, *81,* 199−218.

McGrew, W. C. *An ethological study of children's behavior.* New York: Academic Press, 1972.

McReynolds, P. (Ed.) *Advances in Psychological Assessment.* Vol. 1. Palo Alto, Calif.: Science and Behavior Books, 1968.

McReynolds, P. (Ed.) *Advances in Psychological Assessment.* Vol. 2. Palo Alto, Calif.: Science and Behavior Books, 1971.

McReynolds, P. (Ed.) *Advances in Psychological Assessment.* Vol. 3. San Francisco: Jossey-Bass, 1974.

Mellstrom, Jr., M., Cicala, G. A., & Zuckerman, M. General versus specific trait anxiety measures in the prediction of fear of snakes, heights, and darkness. *Journal of Consulting and Clinical Psychology,* 1976, *44,* 83−91.

Meltzoff, J., & Kornreich, M., *Research in psychology.* New York: Atherton Press, 1970.

Mintz, J., & Luborsky, L. Segments versus whole sessions: Which is the better unit for psychotherapy process research? *Journal of Abnormal Psychology,* 1971, *78,* 180−191.

Mischel, W. *Personality and assessment.* New York: Wiley, 1968.

Mischel, W. Direct versus indirect personality assessment: Evidence and implications. *Journal of Consulting and Clinical Psychology,* 1972, 433, 3, 319−324.

Mischel, W. & Bentler, P., The ability of persons to predict their own behavior. Unpublished manuscript, Stanford University, 1965.

Mitchell, K., & Ingham, R., The effects of general anxiety on group desensitization of test anxiety. *Behavior Research and Therapy,* 1970, *8,* 69−78.

Moos, R., Sources of variance in responses to questionnaires and behavior. *Journal of Abnormal Psychology,* 1969, *74,* 4, 405−412.

Murray, E. J., & Jacobson, L. I. The nature of learning in traditional and behavioral psychotherapy. In A. E. Bergin & S. L. Garfield (Eds.), *Handbook of psychotherapy and behavior change,* New York: Wiley, 1971.

Murstein, B. I. *Theory and research in projective techniques.* New York: Wiley, 1963.

Notarius, C. Effects of emotional expression on physiological response to stress. Doctoral dissertation, Indiana University, 1977.

Nunnally, J. C. *Psychometric theory.* New York: McGraw-Hill, 1967.

O'Connor, R. D. Modification of social withdrawal through symbolic modeling. *Journal of Applied Behavior Analysis,* 1969, *2,* 15−27.

O'Connor, R. D. Relative efficacy of modeling, shaping, and the combined procedures for modification of social withdrawal. *Journal of Abnormal Psychology,* 1972, *79,* 327−334.

Osarchuk, M., & Goldfried, M. A further examination of the credibility of therapy rationales. *Behavior Therapy,* 1975, *6,* 694−695.

Overall, J. E., & Klett, C. J. *Applied multivariate analysis.* New York: McGraw-Hill, 1972.

Parke, R. D. Parent-infant interaction: Progress, paradigms, and problems. In G. P. Sackett (Ed.), *Observing Human Behavior,* Vol. 1. Baltimore: University Park Press, 1978.

Paul, G. *Effects of insight, desensitization and attention placebo treatment of anxiety.* Stanford, California: Stanford University Press, 1966.

Pinsof, W. M. The effect of level of rated expertise on family therapist behavior during initial interviews: The development of a family therapist coding system. Paper presented at the Society for Psychotherapy Research Annual Convention, San Diego, June 1976.

Powers, E., & Witmer, H. *An experiment in the prevention of delinquency.* New York: Columbia University Press, 1951.

Rachman, S. Studies in desensitization. I. The separate effects of relaxation and desensitization. *Behavior Research and Therapy,* 1965, *3,* 245−252.

Reid, J. B. Reliability assessment of observational data: A possible methodological problem. *Child Development,* 1970, *41,* 1143−1150.

Riskin, J., & Faunce, E. E. An evaluative review of family interaction research. *Family Process,* 1972, *11,* 365−455.

Roff, M., Sells, B., & Golden, M. M. *Social adjustment and personality development in children.* Minneapolis: University of Minnesota Press, 1972.

Rogers, C. R. The necessary and sufficient conditions of therapeutic personality change. *Journal of Consulting Psychology,* 1957, *21,* 95−103.

Saslow, G., & Peters, A. A follow-up study of "untreated" patients with various behavior disorders. *Psychiatric Quarterly,* 1956, *30,* 283−302.

Schwartz, R. M., & Gottman, J. M. Toward a task analysis of assertive behavior. *Journal of Consulting and Clinical Psychology,* 1976, *44,* 910−920.

Shapiro, R. J., & Budman, S. H. Defection, termination, and continuation in family and individual therapy. *Family Process,* 1973, *12,* 55−68.

Sherman, J., Wolosin, R., & Miller, K. Three aspects of predictions of counter-normative behavior: Accuracy, self-other differences and effects on subsequent behavior. Unpublished manuscript, Indiana University, 1975.

Siegel, S. *Nonparametric Statistics for the Behavioral Sciences.* New York: McGraw-Hill, 1956.

Sloane, R. B., Staples, F. R., Cristol, A. H., Yorkston, N. J., & Whipple, K. *Psychotherapy versus behavior therapy.* Cambridge, Mass.: Harvard University Press, 1975.

Smith, M. L., & Glass, G. V. Meta-analysis of psychotherapy outcome studies. *American Psychologist,* 1977, *32,* 752−760.

Staples, F. R., Sloane, R. B., Whipple, K., Cristol, A. H., & Yorkston, N. J. Process and outcome in psychotherapy and behavior therapy. *Journal of Consulting and Clinical Psychology,* 1976, *44,* 340−350.

Strong, E. K., Jr. *Vocational interests of men and women.* Stanford, California: Stanford University Press, 1943.

Strupp, H. H. *Psychotherapy: Clinical research and theoretical issues.* New York: Jason Aronson, 1973.

Subotnik, L. Spontaneous remission: Fact or artifact? *Psychological Bulletin,* 1972, 77, 1, 32−48.

Taplin, P. S., & Reid, J. B. Effects of instructional set and experimenter influence on observer reliability. *Child Development,* 1973, 44, 547−554.

Twentyman, C. T., & McFall, R. M. Behavioral training of social skills in shy males. *Journal of Consulting and Clinical Psychology,* 1975, 43, 384−395.

Wallace, H. E. R., & Whyte, M. B. H. Natural history of the psychoneuroses. *British Medical Journal,* 1959, 1, 144−149.

Waller, R. G., & Leske, G. Accurate and inaccurate observer summary reports. *Journal of Nervous and Mental Disease,* 1973, 156, 386−394.

Waskow, I. E., & Parloff, M. B. (Eds.) *Psychotherapy change measures.* Rockville, Md.: National Institute of Mental Health, 1975.

Weiss, R. L., Birchler, G. R., & Vincent, J. P. Contractual models for negotiation training in marital dyads. *Journal of Marriage and Family,* 1974, 36, 321−331.

Weiss, R. L., Hops, H., & Patterson, G. R. A framework for conceptualizing marital conflict, a technology for altering it, some data for evaluating it. In L. A. Hamerlynck, L. C. Handy, and E. J. Mash (Eds.), *Behavior change: Methodology, concepts, and practice,* Champaign, Ill.: Research Press, 1973.

Wetherill, G. B. *Sequential methods in statistics.* London: Methuen & Company, Ltd., 1966.

Wimberger, H., & Millar, G. The psychotherapeutic effects of initial clinical contact on child psychiatric patients. In E. Lesse (Ed.), *An evaluation of the results of the psychotherapies,* Springfield, Ill.: Charles C. Thomas, 1968.

3

PSYCHOBIOLOGICAL FOUNDATIONS OF PSYCHOTHERAPY AND BEHAVIOR CHANGE

GARY E. SCHWARTZ

Yale University

INTRODUCTION

There has been a significant increase in interest among clinical psychologists in psychophysiological approaches to assessment and intervention. A recent survey of directors of APA approved programs in clinical psychology revealed that a substantial number of programs offer formal training in clinical psychophysiology (Feuerstein & Schwartz, 1977). Sixty-nine percent of respondents indicated that they currently provide training in clinical psychophysiology, while an additional 17 percent reported a desire to develop such training in the future. Feuerstein and Schwartz (1977) concluded that "the increased training in clinical psychophysiology is part of a broader trend reflecting the growing interest in psychobiological foundations of human behavior and its implications for clinical psychology and medicine."

The proliferation of terms linking the behavioral and biological sciences is both invigorating and confusing. There are now formal subdisciplines, journals and/or professional societies in biological anthropology, medical anthropology, sociobiology, medical sociology, biological psychology (psychobiology), medical psychology, health psychology, biological psychiatry, psychosomatic medicine, and behavioral medicine. Within psychology itself, psychophysiological research is finding its way into every major journal or area of research. However, I use "psychobiology" in the title, rather than psychophysiology, because psychobiology is a more general term encompassing all the biological sciences. Hence, within psychobiology are included psychophysiology (which traditionally refers to peripheral physiological effectors such as the skeletal muscle, cardiovascular and respiratory systems), psychoendocrinology (which traditionally refers to endocrine glands and their secretions), and psychoneurology (which refers specifically to the central nervous system). As will be shown below, different types of

63

psychotherapy, to varying degrees, involve different combinations or patterns of all of these three
major psychobiological components.

We are presently witnessing a revolution in our
thinking concerning the relationship between biology and behavior. This conceptual revolution has
profound implications for methods, theories, practice, and even licensing of psychotherapy and behavior change procedures. I do not use words such
as "profound" and "revolution" lightly. On the
contrary, this conclusion was forced upon me after
much reflection, and I set it forth here with some
trepidation. As Kuhn (1962) has so elegantly illustrated, science often goes through revolutions as
old paradigms are challenged and are ultimately
replaced by new ones. The psychobiology of
psychotherapy and behavior change is one expression of the present scientific revolution attempting
to integrate theories of mind and brain, behavior
and body (e.g., Schwartz & Shapiro 1976; 1978).

Not surprisingly, basic knowledge linking the
biological and behavioral sciences is advancing at a
more rapid rate than the systematic application of
this knowledge and consequent techniques to
psychotherapy and behavior change. However,
while specific applications may be lagging, changes
in concept or attitude need not fall so far behind.
This is evident, for example, in the biomedical
speciality closely associated with psychophysiology. According to Lipowski (1977),

> Psychosomatic medicine as a scientific discipline
> and an approach to medical practice has staged
> a spectacular come-back. After seeming to be
> dormant, if not extinct, for almost two decades,
> it is once more in the mainstream of contem-
> porary medicine and thought. The problem of
> assessing the relative contribution of psycholog-
> ical, biological and social factors to the de-
> velopment, course and outcome of physical and
> psychiatric disorders has regained a dominant
> position in both medicine and psychiatry. (p.
> 233)

Taking an even stronger position, Engel (1977)
has criticized the traditional medical model of disease as leaving "no room within its framework for
the social psychological and behavioral dimension
of illness," and has proposed a "biopsychosocial"
model which provides a "blueprint for research, a

framework for teaching, and a design for action in
the real world of health care" (p. 135).

The view of modern psychosomatic medicine as
a new attitude or conceptual orientation towards
biology and behavior is well stated by Leigh and
Reiser (1977):

> The modern concept of psychosomatic
> medicine is, therefore, not of a subspecialty of
> either medicine or psychiatry that treats defined
> psychosomatic illnesses, but rather of an at-
> titude that espouses a holistic medical practice,
> utilizing   up-to-date   psychiatric   and
> neurobiologic knowledge and concepts as well
> as principles and information gained from the
> social and behavioral sciences. (p. 238)

The new attitude regarding the psychobiology of
psychotherapy and behavior change is therefore
part of this broader evolving context linking behavioral factors to all health and all disease (e.g.,
Leigh & Reiser, 1977). The unique role of
psychology in this new, more global health care
conceptualization, might well encompass the determination of the biobehavioral mechanisms
whereby environmental and behavioral interventions lead to changes in a person's psychobiological state. The present chapter illustrates how
psychotherapeutic interventions involve the modification of psychobiological processes, be they expressed "verbally," "behaviorally," or "physiologically" (Lang, 1971; 1977a). I place these terms in
quotes because their separation into mental, behavioral, and physiological systems reflects the
fundamental problem that the new attitude discussed above is attempting to rectify. I will argue that
the traditional separation between psychology and
medicine is based on an underlying psychobiological property of the human brain which serves an
important function in the healthy individual, but
seriously impedes our understanding of the basic
processes themselves and therefore interferes with
the treatment of disorders (the brain self-regulation
paradox).

This chapter will present a selective overview of
this conceptual development as it relates to research on behavior change. My goal is not to provide a detailed review of the older literature on the
psychophysiology of psychotherapy and behavior
modification (since excellent reviews of this litera-

ture are available elsewhere, e.g., Lacey, 1959; Lang, 1971; Luborsky et al., 1975), but rather to illustrate present frontiers of theory and research so as to give the reader a conceptual framework by which to understand probable future developments in this area. Central concepts we will consider are those of (1) multiprocess patterning and emergent properties of complex systems, and (2) self-regulation and disregulation, two fundamental properties of feedback systems that provide a direct link between biology and behavior change.

PSYCHOBIOLOGY AS METHOD, MECHANISM, AND OUTCOME

There is a great deal of confusion over definition of terms and the use of concepts with regard to the application of psychophysiology to clinical psychology. It is helpful at the outset to consider three fundamental ways that psychophysiology is currently applied to clinical intervention, for this analysis serves the important dual purpose of illustrating the state of the art and the fundamentals of the new psychobiological attitude.

Psychophysiology as Method

Psychophysiology is sometimes defined in terms of its methods or procedures. Specifically, if one uses equipment to monitor physiological processes, one is practicing the techniques of psychophysiology. However, this definition of psychophysiology is both artificial and counterproductive, for it separates physiology from both behavior and neurology, and therefore creates disparate disciplines and theories.

Consider, for example, the measurement of eye movements. If a therapist asks a patient the following question: "Picture your father's face. What emotion strikes you?" and notes that the patient's eyes move to the left while reflecting on the answer, the eye movement is defined as "behavior" and is typically the province of psychology. It is defined as behavior because it was observed by the therapist using naturally provided biological apparatus (the therapist's eyes and brain). Studies of this sort would typically be published in psychology journals.

However, the therapist who wanted to obtain a more complete and accurate measure of eye movement would consider using modern procedures that extend these biological capacities for continuously monitoring and scoring signals of this sort. For example, he or she might consider placing electrodes on the outer corners of the eyes, amplifying the shifts in DC potential with the aid of modern bio-electronics, displaying the potential shifts on an oscilloscope screen or meter, and storing the signals on paper using a pen writing unit or on magnetic tape using an FM recorder. When employing these biomedical procedures, the therapist would no longer simply be recording behavior as a psychologist, but rather would be recording psychophysiological changes as a psychophysiologist. Note that although the theoretical questions might well be the same, the therapist's field and label could change simply because of the difference in method used.

Until very recently, psychophysiological methods required that some device be directly attached to the person's body. This was almost a defining characteristic of psychophysiology, and, parenthetically, was a defining characteristic of medicine involving the "laying on of hands" procedures of intervention. Thus, if the therapist monitoring eye movement chose instead to record the same activity using a video tape system, from a methodological point of view this would not traditionally be defined as psychophysiology.

I use the example of eye movement because it nicely illustrates the artificiality of defining a response as a behavior rather than a physiological response simply because of the method used. Although for convenience we speak of observational methods versus psychophysiological methods, this unfortunately promotes the dichotomy of therapists "seeing" responses as being "psychological" versus "measuring" them as "physiological." In the case of eye movement, or for that matter any response that is potentially observable by the traditional five senses, the classification of the activity as psychological versus physiological should not be based on the method used. Hence, it is artificial and counterproductive to define typing as a behavior when measured "behaviorally," and as a physiological variable when measured "physiologically" (e.g., using electromyographic procedures). Similarly, we can see that calling facial blushing a behavior when it is simply observed by the therapist, but a physiological change when measured by blood volume or skin temperature procedures, only leads to an artificial separation *of the same event.*

Consider facial exprsssion, which can be defined visually as a behavior. (Ekman & Friesen, 1975). The same facial behavior, however, can be monitored by placing electromyographic leads on the face and recording the underlying patterns of muscle activity that produce the patterns of skin movement observed by the naked eye (Schwartz et. al. 1976a, b). Is facial behavior now physiological, whereas before it was behavioral? Clearly, behavioral versus physiological determinations cannot and should not be made simply in terms of method. The fact that we do make these distinctions, and find it difficult to "see" human activity as both behavior and physiology *at the same time,* tells us something more about the nature of human information processing than it does about the behavior/biology in question.

I suggest that we should inhibit the natural temptation to define a psychobiological approach to psychotherapy and behavior change simply in terms of methods of procedure. Instead, as will be discussed in the next section, it is more parsimonious, and more integrative, to define psychophysiology in terms of underlying *mechanisms,* independent of the *methods* used to assess these mechanisms. From this point of view, one can "do" psychophysiology either with one's natural receptors, or one can extend the natural receptors with the aid of modern technology. Hence, when Ekman and Friesen (1976) presently classify facial expression patterns by *visually* labeling specific skin movements in terms of the underlying *muscle* changes, they are "doing" psychophysiology, even though they are not directly attaching electrodes to monitor the muscles. From this perspective, psychophysiology is not a method but rather a state of mind.

It is important to recognize that the technology is rapidly becoming available for monitoring certain physiological changes without attaching electrodes. For example, although it is currently popular to monitor surface skin temperature in specified regions using thermistors or thermocouples attached to the skin with tape, it is also possible, using infrared thermography equipment, to scan large regions of the skin or even the whole body from a distance. This equipment can be as unobtrusive as a hidden video camera, and it can generate visual displays reflecting complex patterns of skin temperature. Figure 3-1 shows a facial thermogram of a subject in an experiment comparing the effects of hearing a positive emotion tape (a person laughing) with a negative emotion tape (a person crying) (from Schwartz & Logue, in preparation). The results of this experiment indicated that facial temperature, particularly in the mouth and cheek regions, is warmer during happiness than sadness. What thermography equipment does is to extend our natural ability to react to changes in facial temperature, either visually (e.g., happy pregnant women tend to have warm, radiant faces) or kinesthetically (e.g., women tend to have colder noses than men).

It is likely that the technology of the future will

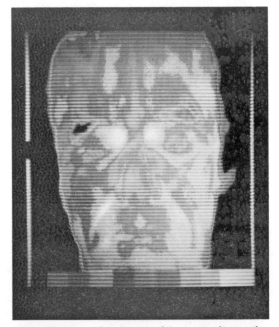

Figure 3-1. Thermographic recording of a human face. The color bar under the face reflects a 5°C range, with each color representing 0.5°C (from cooler to warmer). The recording illustrates how complex patterns of facial temperature are distributed across the face Laterality in facial temperature can be readily observed.

increase the capacity to monitor various parameters from a distance. These advances may include sensitive magnetometers for detecting brain waves and other biological processes involving magnetic shifts, and radiometric procedures (developed originally for radio telescopes) for monitoring neural and chemical activity from biological tissue at a distance. As this technology advances, the traditional distinction between behavioral observation and physiological monitoring in terms of "laying on of hands" will be eliminated, and the fallacy of defining activity as being either behavioral or physiological in terms of method will have become self-evident.

Since the publication of the first edition of the *Handbook of Psychotherapy and Behavior Change* (Bergin & Garfield, 1971), significant advances have been made in the development of procedures for monitoring human physiological activity. Some of the advances in method are derived from basic research. These include new indirect procedures for assessing blood pressure on a beat to beat basis via pulse propagation time, impedance procedures for assessing relatively local changes in brain blood flow, and procedures for monitoring cardiac output (and therefore determining peripheral resistance) using impedance cardiography. A basic introduction to physiological monitoring procedures, including references prior to 1970, are contained in the earlier chapter by Lang (1971). More recent reviews of psychophysiological techniques can be found in Lader (1975), Epstein (1976), and Kallman and Feuerstein (1977). An excellent introduction to psychophysiological methods and research is contained in *A Primer of Psychophysiology* by Hassett (1978).

A significant advancement in the use of physiological monitoring procedures in research and practice has occurred as a spinoff of the clinical biofeedback movement. In the process of developing instruments that were portable, safe, operable with minimal training, and useful in various environments, the biofeedback industry had provided novice researchers and clinicians with easy to use, affordable equipment. Also, a unique aspect of biofeedback instruments is that they are designed to provide immediate feedback to patients concerning their own physiological activity; in some of the more sophisticated devices, circuits are provided for obtaining summary information per unit period of time. Good quality biofeedback instrumentation today contains preamplifiers, amplifiers, filter circuits, various output displays, and data analysis procedures incorporating relevant components of digital computer processing. Although this development has helped to stimulate the current interest in clinical psychophysiology by making such recording easy and practical, it has also tended to promote misapplication of the methods and misinterpretation of the information by untrained individuals. As noted by Feuerstein and Schwartz (1977),

> With the ease in application of psychophysiological methods, a consequence of "portable psychophysiology" or the ubiquitous self-contained biofeedback unit, clinicians may move too rapidly and uncritically in areas of application. We must be fully aware of the problems and limitations as well as potentials the field presently offers. Quality academic-clinical training with a strong research foundation can provide this information and orientation. (p. 567)

Psychophysiology as Mechanism

Psychobiology in general, and psychophysiology in particular, should be defined in terms of underlying processes or mechanisms. Consider the eye movement example again. When the therapist simply observes a left eye movement in response to the spatial/emotional question posed to the patient, he or she would be defined as a psychologist, whereas if he or she monitors the same eye movement electrophysiologically, he or she would then be defined as a psychophysiologist. However, what would we call the therapist who went one step further and inferred from the left eye movement that the person had activated his or her right hemisphere while reflecting on the spatial/emotional question? (Schwartz, Davidson, & Maer, 1975). The discipline concerned with inferring neural functioning from observable behavior or from recorded biological activity (e.g., EEG records) is called neurology in the medical sciences, and in the behavioral sciences is called neuro-psychology. Here observable behavior is "seen" as the external manifestation of a functioning central nervous system, and in particular, of the brain.

Because human beings have a limited capacity for information processing (Neisser, 1967), it is understandable why the average person finds it extremely difficult to view a simple action occurring over time (such as the movement of the eye) as *simultaneously* being a behavior, a physiological change, *and* a peripheral expression of a complex pattern of neurophysiological changes in the central nervous system. Yet this is exactly the challenge facing researchers and clinicians concerned with integrating theories of "behavior" and "biology" as applied to clinical practice. From this psychophysiological perspective (or more appropriately, this psychoneurological perspective), there should not be a separation between behavioral, physiological, and neurological approaches to human activity. Instead, these approaches should be seen as reflecting different levels of analysis *of the same organism.*

From this perspective, it is inaccurate to talk about physiological *correlates* of behavior, since this implies that the physiology and behavior are separate. Similarly, it is inaccurate to talk about neural or endocrine correlates of behavior, since this too implies separation. Ideally, we should use terms such as physiological *components* or concomitants of behavior. However, this is not typically done. The reason, I submit, involves a fundamental characteristic of the brain and the human information processing system that contributes to the creation of the mind/body problem. This dualism in human experience interferes with our acceptance of the "psychobiology as mechanism" concept.

It is becoming increasingly recognized that the brain plays a central, integrative role in all behavior. Hence, behavioral development is neural development. A person learns through experience because the brain learns through experience. Thoughts and feelings, memories and wishes, skills and plans, involve the restructuring of the brain and its regulation of the bodily organs. Psychopathology, therefore, implies neuropathology, *regardless* of the specific cause. There may be

a lesion in certain portions of the nervous system caused by an external virus, or there may be a *functional* breakdown in certain neural systems due to psychosocial stresses (e.g., Whatmore & Kohli, 1974). It follows, then, that education is neuroeducation, and that psychotherapy is ultimately neurotherapy. Boldly stated, psychotherapy is ultimately a psychobiological process. Psychotherapy is ultimately biotherapy.

That such conclusions arouse feelings of discontent, if not anger, in the average reader attests to the resistance against accepting these conclusions. To argue against such strongly held convictions requires that we not only explain why the basic premise should be true, but also explain why it is so difficult to accept the premise in the first place. This leads us to consider the mind/body problem and its relevance to modern theories of psychobiology and behavior change.

The Brain Self-Regulation Paradox

If the brain is ultimately responsible for perception and for processing and regulating the peripheral organs, and hence all organismic behavior, it becomes fascinating to consider the fact that not only is the brain only partially aware of the feedback emanating from the various organs of the body, but the brain is also essentially incapable of consciously experiencing any of the feedback involved in regulating itself. This interesting dilemma involving the brain's lack of awareness of its own self-regulation I have termed the "brain self-regulation paradox." This problem has important implications for the genesis of the mind/body dichotomy, and hence its education may help to explain a part of the difficulty in holding a psychobiological perspective on psychotherapy and behavior change (Schwartz, 1977a).

Consider the simple act of moving one's hand. At a behavioral level, the moving of one's hand would be described in a global sense as a behavioral response that can be brought under self-control. However, at the next physiological level, it becomes clear that the act of moving one's hand actually involves the *coordination* and *patterning* of different combinations of muscles pulling on bone so as to result in a smooth flowing sequence of action. This psychophysiological analysis is still incomplete, however, since it does not go on to the next neural level. Clearly, the muscle patterning is not regulated by itself, but is actually controlled by patterns of peripheral neural activity which are ultimately coordinated by the brain. Thus, when one moves one's right hand, for example, one is actually regulating patterns of left hemispheric frontal and motor processes. Note that we have no conscious awareness that these are actually the processes initiating and controlling the action. We have no sensations of self-regulation *in our head*—rather the sensations are experienced *at the periphery*. In other words, we do not experience what systems are *doing* the controlling, but rather what peripheral end organs are *being* controlled.

The placement of the subjective experience at the periphery, and not in the central nervous system, has obvious evolutionary significance. In order for an organism to regulate itself in three-dimensional space, it must have the capacity to *localize* stimuli in three-dimensional space. As Powers (1973) has stated so beautifully, the brain and nervous system are designed to *construct* an experience of reality in three-dimensional space. Although the *source* of stimulation may be in the periphery, as will be elaborated below, it is *experienced* at the periphery because the *brain* puts it (back) there.

Studies of human brain stimulation have shown that the experience of one's hand in three-dimensional space can be produced by stimulating the appropriate sensory cortex in the brain (Penfield, 1975). Subjects do not report feeling that their brains are being stimulated—what they experience instead is the related "behavioral" consequence of the particular neural systems stimulated. In fact, the brain has no direct conscious feedback from itself—it can even be cut without any local feeling or discomfort. Hence, from a psychobiological perspective the experience of one's hand at the periphery is an "illusion," in that the localization of the subjective experience in the body is created (or recreated) by the nervous system. Imagine what would happen to an organism if *every time* it moved its limbs, it experienced sensations in the controller (the brain) rather than the effector organ being regulated (the body). The organism would not be able to effectively navigate in a three-

dimensional world. The brain's construction of three-dimensional space is a major accomplishment of a neural information processing system. Although this greatly helps the brain to process information and interact in a three-dimensional world, it consequently greatly hampers the brain's capacity to understand its own role in the very creation of these sensations.

This characteristic of the human nervous system (and probably of nervous systems of lower animals), has important implications for our understanding of both phantom limb phenomena and hallucinations. The tendency for the brain to "feel" that its limb is there, when actually it has been removed through injury or sugery, is typically described as an illusion that makes little biological sense. However, the perspective outlined here suggests that the phantom limb phenomenon uncovers a fundamental characteristic regarding the generation of subjective experience under normal circumstances. Such accidents of nature reveal a property of the brain that is contrary to common sense—meaning, from a psychobiological point of view, a phenomenon contrary to the way the brain is normally designed to understand its role in its own consciousness and self-regulation.

Hallucinations provide a similar example of this property of the nervous system. Hearing a voice outside of the body is, according to this analysis, a perceptual illusion created by the brain in order to accurately process an auditory stimulus in a real three-dimensional world. This perceptual illusion has obvious adaptive consequences when the brain is processing stimuli initially generated outside the body. However, when the brain fails in its ability to discriminate between neural patterns generated endogenously and those initiated by external stimuli, it will confuse internal and external sources of stimuli. The hallucinations of schizophrenic patients may reflect an initial breakdown in this natural mechanism of creating the experience of three-dimensional space.

The mechanism by which this biocognitive construction takes place is currently a mystery, although speculations have been offered regarding multilevel models potentially able to create such experiences (e.g., Powers, 1973). The fact that this problem has received so little attention up to now is consistent with the basic phenomenon itself! Since the brain has no direct experience that it is responsible for the creation of three-dimensional experience, it requires accidents of nature (e.g., phantom limbs, hallucinations) or the development of new technology (e.g., brain stimulation) to "see" beyond its own constraints.

The "brain self-regulation paradox" not only applies to the experience of body or environment in three-dimensional space, but also involves the experience of "mind" as well. Consider the simple act of imagining that one's right hand is moving, rather than actually trying to move one's hand. The healthy person can typically discriminate between the image and the action. Note, however, that it is terribly difficult to localize in the brain, body, or environment exactly where the image is. Also note that unlike actual physical movement, the creation of images allows far greater freedom to do things with one's hand (e.g., turning one's hand upside down and inside out in one's mind). To the extent that the generation of imagery also involves the regulation of patterns of neural processes, it becomes clear that the brain experiences the image, and not the neural pattern itself.

The capacity of the brain to discriminate between the perception (or generation) of bodily or environmental stimuli, and the generation of sensory or "mental" thoughts and images, is also a mystery whose mechanisms have yet to be described. However, although we do not know how such differentiations are made, it should be self-evident that it is highly adaptive for the nervous system to have evolved a means by which to make, and thereby to create, such internal discriminations. When this capacity to differentiate mind from body breaks down, psychopathological problems involving thought and action are said to be present. Note that the classic mind/body dichotomy, according to this hypothesis, reflects a functional property of the nervous system that has adaptive, survival characteristics. Its adaptive properties become maladaptive, however, when we try to fully accept the fact that the experience of both mind and body are emergent properties of neural patterning that cannot be directly experienced; that is, they are experienced separately from the brain even though they are actually created by the brain (Schwartz, 1975; John, 1976; Sperry, 1969).

The "brain self-regulation paradox" is of more than just philosophical interest. As stated above, I propose that this human structural problem may interfere with our capacity to develop an integrative, psychobiological view of human behavior and hence of behavioral intervention procedures. Consequently, it may have important implications for the way in which we conceptualize and conduct research.

The inability of the conscious brain to recognize and accept the fact of its own self-regulation is illustrated in biofeedback studies where visual and auditory feedback are presented for specific changes in brain wave activity (from Schwartz, 1977a). It has been found that subjects given biofeedback for occipital EEG alpha readily learned to control the predominance of their alpha, and especially to suppress alpha (reviewed in Beatty, 1977). Initially, this discovery was received with surprise and wonder, because the data implied that subjects could learn to directly control their brain waves. Before this experimental demonstration, since no one had actually observed a person regulating brain waves, the capacity for brain self-regulation was not generally recognized.

The second response to brain wave biofeedback studies was equally interesting. When the question was asked, "How were the subjects controlling their brain waves?" the explanations were given in terms of events that could be *consciously* perceived—they tensed their muscles, moved their eyes, generated arousing thoughts, or regulated their attention (Lynch & Paskewitz, 1971). But the conclusion that regulation of occipital EEG is associated, for example, with movements of the eye does not answer the fundamental question, "How do people control their eyes?" The answer should be that the *brain* regulates much of what the eye does, and the brain performs its regulation based on multiple sources of feedback impinging upon it at any one moment—including feedback from the eye itself (Gaarder, 1975). In the process of regulating its eyes, the brain changes its electrochemical configuration, which is expressed electrophysiologically in the EEG. In other words, eye movement and EEG are two different indices of the same thing—the brain's self-regulation.

The simplest procedure for determining what is regulating what is to examine closely the relative timing and sequencing of different events. If the brain is regulating itself, and if this regulation is expressed both electrophysiologically and behaviorally, then one would predict that EEG changes may precede the movement of the eye, even though the reverse is what is subjectively experienced. This more sophisticated approach to the assessment of brain self-regulation has yet to be found in the mainstream of biofeedback research.

Another example, more directly relevant to psychotherapy and behavior change, concerns research on the assessment and treatment of anxiety. As Lang (1971, 1977a) has repeatedly emphasized, anxiety as a construct involves multiple systems that are only loosely connected, and various systems can be differentially changed depending on the environmental conditions or behavioral treatments. Coming from a behavioral tradition, Lang dissects the human individual into three interactive systems: verbal, behavioral, and physiological. The question is, why does he choose this particular scheme for describing a person? The practical answer seems to be historical in nature, since these are the three different ways in which researchers have tended to assess a person in the past. However, this does not explain the rationale by which such a classification has evolved.

The point of view expressed in this chapter holds that verbal response, behavior, and physiology are *all* psychobiological processes, and separating them into these particular three categories confuses levels of analysis (from behavior to physiology and endocrinology to neurology). "Verbal" output is a psychobiological process which bases its activity to a large extent on conscious processes (both cognitive and somatic). "Behavioral" output is also a psychobiological process (which should more aptly be classified as *non*verbal behavior), which is not dependent on subjective experience. "Physiological" output is really the first level analysis of both verbal and nonverbal behavior. Saying that "physiology" often does not correlate with "behavior" implies that physiology and behavior are separate. It is accurate to say that certain behaviors do not covary with other behaviors, or certain physiological responses do not covary with other physiological responses, under specific conditions. Note, however, that saying the former, or saying the latter, is really saying the same thing.

I suggest that the split between verbal response, behavior, and physiology is intimately linked to the mind/body problem and the "brain self-regulation paradox." Classifying something as verbal versus behavioral is a modern language description for the distinction between mind (inferred from verbal behavior) and body (assessed by nonverbal or skeletal behavior). The additional separation of physiology and behavior is a reflection of the distinction between unconscious biological processes and the conscious, overt expressions of these processes. However, a psychobiological perspective of behavior requires that we consider all verbal and nonverbal behaviors as having physiological, endocrine, and neural components. As is suggested by the "brain self-regulation paradox," our problem in accepting the notion of mind and brain as one, or behavior and physiology as one, ultimately depends on the same issue: disconnecting the conscious experience of both mental and physical properties from their neural substrates.

Psychobiological Patterning and Emergent Property

Psychophysiology as mechanism is a concept that is being developed in various quarters. Testable hypotheses regarding the neural creation of conscious processes have recently been advanced (e.g., John, 1976; Sperry, 1977; Schwartz, 1977b). These theories argue that conscious processes are an emergent property of patterns of neural functioning. The biofeedback procedure is providing a new means by which to investigate the ways that complex patterns of response interact to produce unique psychobiological outcomes. This position has been recently illustrated by Schwartz (1977b).

Biofeedback research has begun to show that patterns of physiological response can be self-generated by the brain, producing unique cross-system interactions and perceptual gestalts that make up a significant component of human behavior and subjective experience (Schwartz, 1975). The concept of pattern here refers not simply to the isolated viewing of combinations of processes, but rather goes beyond the individual components making up the pattern to recognize the novel, interactive, or emergent property that patterns can acquire. Simply stated, the whole may have properties that are qualitatively and/or quantitatively different from the sum of its parts, yet it may be dependent upon the organization of its parts for its unique properties. This phenomenon is seen at all levels of physics and chemistry, and extends through biology and neuropsychology (Weiss, 1969). The term synergism is also used to describe patterning and emergent property, as recently elucidated in the comprehensive volume by Fuller (1975).

The concept of emergent property must be carefully considered in looking at patterning. In the area of consciousness, neuropsychologists speak of cell assemblies (Hebb, 1974), hyperneurons (John, 1976), holograms (Pribram, 1971), dynamic neural patterns (Sperry, 1969) or functional systems in the brain (Luria, 1973). In the area of emotion, the concept relating physiological patterning to emergent property has a long history, beginning with William James (1890), who described emotion as the brain's perception of patterns of visceral consequences of its action. More recently investigators such as Schachter and Singer (1962) have added biocognitive processes to visceral activity as an integral part of this pattern. Modern comprehensive theories like those of Tomkins (1962) and Izard (1971, 1977) suggest that the interaction of combinations of neurophysiological systems, including the processing of discrete patterns of postural and facial muscle activity, might be the neural mechanisms underlying the emergent experience of emotion.

Evidence for patterning of peripheral and central nervous system activity in human emotion and consciousness is evolving from two major research directions. One is an extension of traditional psychophysiology, where differential patterns of peripheral physiological and electrocortical responses are monitored while subjects engage in complex cognitive/affective tasks. For example, recent data from our laboratory have documented that cognitive/affective tasks can be meaningfully dissected into their underlying neuropsychological subcomponents, having predictable effects on the patterning of hemispheric activity (Schwartz, Davidson, & Maer, 1975). The data indicate that in right-handed subjects, verbal versus spatial cognitive processes differentially involve the left and

right hemispheres, respectively. In addition, the right hemisphere seems to play a special role in the nonverbal components of emotion. Consequently, questions involving both verbal (left hemisphere) and emotional (right hemisphere) processes (e.g., "What is the primary difference in the meanings of the words 'anger' and 'hate'?") accordingly elicit evidence of dual hemispheric activation. Questions that involve both spatial (right hemisphere) and emotional (right hemisphere) processes (e.g., "Picture your father's face—what emotion first strikes you?") elicit evidence of accentuated right hemisphere involvement.

The second research direction is more recent in origin and involves the use of biofeedback. At the simplest level, it has been pointed out that the self-regulation of patterns of responses can have different emergent properties from those observed when controlling individual functions alone (Schwartz, 1976). This basic observation provides the foundation for the hypothesis that it is possible to assess central and peripheral linkages between physiological responses and human behavior and consciousness by training subjects to voluntarily control patterns of visceral and motor responses (Schwartz, 1975; 1977b). This hypothesis is interesting in that it emerged somewhat unexpectedly in basic cardiovascular research concerned with the self-regulation of patterns of systolic blood pressure and heart rate. This research is reviewed in detail in Schwartz (1977b).

Additional experimental examples can be found emphasizing patterning of EEG changes in different psychobiological states. This research is directly influenced by modern neuropsychological models of human brain function. I particularly recommend The Working Brain (Luria, 1973), for an introduction to this perspective.

For example, based on the theory that the perception and regulation of visual processes involves the occipital cortex, whereas the perception and regulation of skeletal motor responses involves the sensory-motor cortex, Davidson, Schwartz, and Rothman (1976) conducted an experiment to determine whether attention to visual stimuli (light flashing) versus kinesthetic stimuli (tapping on the hand) would be associated with differential patterning of the EEG alpha in the visual versus sensory/

motor regions. Not only did they find evidence for such patterning, but subjects scoring high on a personality measure of capacity to be absorbed with one's attention (Tellegen & Atkinson, 1974) showed greater EEG patterning.

Based on these findings, a second experiment was performed in which subjects were asked to *imagine* a light flashing, a tapping sensation on the hand, or both occurring simultaneously, while EEG from the visual and sensory/motor regions were recorded (Davidson & Schwartz, 1978). The data indicated that when subjects self-generated the visual images, they generated significantly greater EEG activation over the visual cortex, whereas relative activation over the sensory/motor region was observed when they self-generated the kinesthetic images. Importantly, when subjects were requested to generate both types of images, relative activation in both cortical regions was observed. It might be noted that no subject in either experiment reported any knowledge or awareness that he or she was actually self-regulating these particular brain regions when controlling attention and imagery.

These data provide evidence for the association between the self-regulation of cognitive processes (attention and imagery) and the regulation of specific patterns of brain processes. The task of describing different psychotherapeutic procedures as modifying different patterns of neuropsychological systems is an important theoretical and practical challenge in the years ahead.

Lang (1977b) has recently suggested that for practical reasons images should be viewed as propositional structures that are essentially identical to the verbal instructions given to subjects. The following quote from Lang (1977b) states this position clearly and strongly: "To modify McLuhan's statement, 'the medium is the message,' the proposed research strategy affirms that *the message is the image*" (italics added). What Lang is saying is that to the extent that the subjects follow instructions, they are recreating the neural patterns suggested by the verbal instructions. If the medium is the image, then the medium is the neural pattern. Hence, verbal messages modulate brain self-regulation, while conscious processes are partial reflections of the environmental stimuli. From this perspective it directly follows that verbal therapy is

neurotherapy, even though we have no direct, conscious awareness that this is actually the case.

This view is similar to the early neurally based theory of Wolpe (1958, see Lang, 1977b) or the more modern neuropsychological theory of Whatmore and Kohli (1974, see Schwartz, 1977a). Lang (1977b) suggests that

> *While the neural image may be an ultimate reality, the practical utility of the concept is limited. Nevertheless, we should not be wholly dismayed. As it is not a knowledge of chemistry which guides the chef to a good bouillabaise, but knowing which fish to use and how to cook them, so in trying to understand the practical effect of desensitization, the primary task may not be facilitated by reductionism, but by a direct analysis of the information content of the image and the manner of its functional processing.*

It is here that a behavioral versus a psychobiological perspective on psychotherapy and behavior change part company. Although clearly the average chef need not know chemistry to cook a fish well, it is still possible, if not likely, that understanding the underlying chemistry will improve the trial and error means by which such cooking is approached and taught. As Weiss (1969) notes, the concept of emergent property has advanced every science that has embraced its tenets. The thesis of this chapter is that the methods, theory, teaching, and practice of behavioral intervention will be enhanced by developing integrated biobehavioral models. That this is no longer an article of faith is seen in modern advances in psychosomatic and behavioral medicine, and it seems only a matter of time until it will find its way successfully into the research and practice of psychotherapy and behavior change.

Examples of modern psychobiological theories having direct relevance to research in psychotherapy and behavior change include Galin's (1974) application of findings on lateralization of brain function to psychiatry, Izard's (1977) theory of differential emotions, and Hilgard's (1977) theory of hypnosis, neodissociation, and its psychobiological basis. We will return to such theories later in the chapter.

Psychophysiology as Outcome

The last definition of psychophysiology emphasizes a desired outcome or goal for therapy. These goals have traditionally been of two types. The first type emphasizes the concept of psychophysiological assessment of stress or emotion, and infers changes in emotion by observing "correlated" changes in physiology. This was the perspective of the older psychophysiological research on psychotherapy (reviewed in Lacey, 1959; Lang, 1971), and it continues to this day. The more modern extension of this approach is found in current research on behavior therapy, and in particular in the management of anxiety. As recently reviewed by Lang (1977a) there is still little agreement on a definition of anxiety, and therefore the separation of dependent measures into verbal, behavioral, and physiological categories becomes necessary.

However, viewing psychobiology in terms of mechanism points to the limitation in conceptualizing physiological variables as simple "correlates" of improvement in global psychological constructs such as anxiety. Instead, this view implies that biopsychological models of emotion include physiology as an integral component of the desired biobehavioral outcome. The challenge then becomes the development of theoretically meaningful and individually relevant physiological monitoring and quantification procedures for the particular problem at hand.

Davidson and Schwartz (1976) have suggested that the selection of specific physiological measures should be based on the underlying psychobiological processes in question. Haphazard recording of easily accessible physiological parameters in complex, often uncontrolled situations such as those found in traditional psychotherapy sessions will typically result in small associations between measures and in confusing results. Selection of the measures and procedures relevant to the particular psychobiological pattern of interest, and exposure of patients to selected environmental conditions likely to evoke the desired psychobiological response might prove to be a more fruitful strategy. The ultimate utility of the data obtained should be increased by examining patterns of response that

are directly relevant to particular psychosocial conditions.

The second approach to psychophysiology as outcome is derived historically from psychosomatic medicine and more recently has been elucidated in the emerging field of behavioral medicine. In the past, patients suffering from specific psychophysiological disorders such as hypertension or migraine might be monitored physiologically during various types of psychotherapy so that improvement in the physical symptoms might be inferred from physiological change. Recent research drawing on learning and cybernetic theory has provided a more direct and systematic model for behavioral treatment of various physical illnesses. The growth of biofeedback as an active behavioral intervention strategy has stimulated interest among clinical psychologists in psychophysiological outcome (Feuerstein & Schwartz, 1977).

The application of biofeedback and other behavioral procedures to the treatment of physical disorders is a lively and controversial field, and some of this research will be reviewed below. The important point here is to recognize that psychophysiology as outcome, of which biofeedback is a specific example, is an important but small component of a much broader trend toward considering the role of behavioral factors in health and illness. In fact, it has been proposed that the modern approach to psychosomatic medicine be relabeled behavioral medicine (Leigh & Reiser, 1977). A precise definition of behavioral medicine, illustrating its breadth of coverage and concern, was developed at the Yale Conference on Behavioral Medicine (see Schwartz & Weiss, 1977).

> *Behavioral medicine is the field concerned with the development of behavioral-science knowledge and techniques relevant to the understanding of physical health and illness and the application of this knowledge and these techniques to prevention, diagnosis, treatment and rehabilitation. Psychosis, neurosis and substance abuse are included only insofar as they contribute to physical disorders as an end point.*

Of course, from a psychobiological perspective, psychosis, neurosis, and substance abuse all involve the brain as a physical end point, and therefore fall within the purview of behavioral medicine. The perspective taken in this chapter is that a foundation for viewing psychophysiology as outcome should be derived from the perspective of psychobiology as mechanism. Specifically, this position holds that the extent to which the central nervous system is involved *functionally* in either "psychological" or "physical" disease is the extent to which psychosocial factors can play a role in the etiology and treatment of any disease. Interestingly, it is somewhat ironic that advances in the biological sciences currently provide the best justification for *behavioral* intervention in health and disease.

In addition to the chapters on psychophysiological methods referenced earlier, recent sources on psychophysiology as outcome include Birk (1973), Schwartz and Beatty (1977), Beatty and Legewie (1977), Gaarder and Montgomery (1977), and Williams and Gentry (1976).

PSYCHOBIOLOGICAL APPROACHES TO THEORY AND RESEARCH

The Brain as a Health Care System

Emphasizing the role of the brain in health and illness provides a foundation for developing a general system for conceptualizing etiology and treatment of disease. Figure 3-2 presents a highly simplified but conceptually useful way of linking environmental stimuli (State 1) to changes in the central nervous system (State 2) and their expression in the peripheral organ (Stage 3) (from Schwartz, 1977a). Of particular importance to the concept of the brain as a health care system is the existence of negative feedback systems (Stage 4) from the body back to the brain (State 2). It is the existence of these negative feedback loops that makes it possible for the brain to monitor the state of its peripheral organs and thereby to maintain stable functioning of the body (Cannon, 1932) and itself.

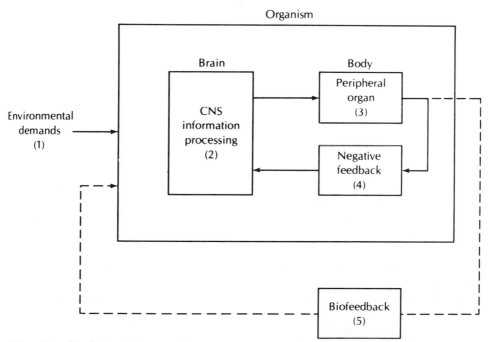

Figure 3-2. Simplified block diagram depicting (1) environmental demands influencing (2) the brain's regulation of its (3) peripheral organs, and (4) negative feedback from the periphery back to the brain. Disregulation can be initiated at each of these stages. Biofeedback (Stage 5) is a parallel feedback loop to State 4, detecting the activity of the peripheral organ (Stage 3) and converting it into environmental (Stage 1) input that can be used by the brain (Stage 2) to increase self-regulation (from Schwartz, 1977a).

When the environment (Stage 1) places demands on a person, the brain (Stage 2) performs the regulatory functions necessary to meet the specific demands. Depending on the nature of the environmental demand or stress, certain bodily systems (Stage 3) will be activated, while others may be simultaneously inhibited. However, if this process is sustained to the point where the tissue suffers deterioration or injury, the negative feedback loops (Stage 4) of the homeostatic mechanism will normally come into play, forcing the brain to modify its directives to aid the afflicted organ. Often these negative feedback loops lead to the experience of pain.

For example, if a person is eating a meal under stressful conditions, the stomach may be unable to function properly. Consequently, the stomach may generate negative feedback to the person's brain, which is experienced as a stomachache. This corrective signal should serve the important function of causing the brain to change its regulation in specific ways, such as to lead the person to slow down, change his or her environment or leave the environment, in order to allow digestion to occur more normally. The pain serves a second function in that it "teaches" the brain what it can and cannot do if the stomach is to work properly. The adaptive brain is one that can learn through its mistakes and develop the capacity to anticipate the needs of its organs.

This notion of the brain as a complex, multisystem/multiorgan health care system can be applied not only to understanding the health of the peripheral organs, but also to examining the functioning of various biocognitive systems within the brain itself. The healthy brain is one that can self-monitor its thoughts and images, and modify its behavior to meet specific information processing needs. Thus, if one is tired and having difficulty reading a chapter, the adaptive brain might take a rest, either by pursuing some other less demanding task, taking a nap, or meditating.

It is the existence of feedback loops, both within the brain and between the brain and body, that make it possible to have a self-regulating, and therefore self-correcting, biocybernetic health care system (Weiner, 1961). I find this psychobiological perspective useful because (1) it illustrates the role

of the central nervous system, and hence all neuropsychological processes, in health and disease, and (2) it places health care back in the hands (or more correctly, the brains) of individual persons. A major conclusion reached from the current research on biofeedback and self-regulation concerns the capacity for humans to learn to control various psychobiological processes with the addition of a new feedback loop (Stage 5 in Figure 2 Schwartz, 1977a). The "brain self-regulation paradox" helps alert us to the fact that, although we have very little direct awareness of these processes, we are continually regulating complex patterns of brain processes (and hence physiological processes) whenever we control our cognitions and external behavior. This realization provides the biological justification for placing primary responsibility for health care back within the individual person.

Disregulation and Psychobiological Disease

If feedback systems are essential for stable functioning and health care, then disruptions in feedback systems can lead to instability, disorder, and hence disease. I have termed this instability disregulation (Schwartz, 1977a).

Consider the stomach example again. Stimuli from the external environment (Stage 1) enter the brain (Stage 2) by means of sensory input (not shown) and the brain deals with this stimulation overtly by controlling its motor output (not shown). The stomach (Stage 3) is also regulated by the brain, and it can in turn influence the brain's regulation of itself through its negative feedback loop (Stage 4). However, the brain may fail to regulate itself effectively enough to meet the stomach's needs. The reasons for this can be quite varied, as they can occur at each of the four stages:

Stage 1: Environmental Demands

The stimuli from the external environment may be so demanding that the brain is forced to ignore negative feedback from the stomach. A person placed in an unavoidable stress situation must continue to act in certain ways despite the negative feedback that tells him or her to change the behavior. Many previous theories of psychosomatic disorders have emphasized this stage (see Graham, 1972).

Stage 2: Information Processing of the Central Nervous System (CNS)

The brain may be programmed, initially through genetics and subsequently through learning, to respond inappropriately to stimuli present in the external environment (or internal physiological environment). Thus, although the negative feedback from the abused organs may be present, the brain may be disinclined to respond in an appropriate fashion. In other words, the brain may select to act in ways that will lead it to ignore the corrective negative feedback or to use that feedback in ways that are deleterious to the well-being of the peripheral organ. The association between repression and psychosomatic disease is an illustration of this mechanism (e.g., Galin, 1974).

Stage 3: Peripheral Organ

The organ in question may itself be hypo- or hyperreactive to the neural stimulation coming from the brain. This is the literal translation of what sometimes has been called the "weak organ" theory of psychosomatic disorders. The weak organ concept can explain why, in response to the same environmental stress, different human organs ultimately become dysfunctional (Sternbach, 1966). It is possible that the brain cannot regulate itself to compensate for the altered negative feedback, or finds itself no longer capable of modifying the functioning of a diseased organ (regardless of the initial cause of the organ pathology).

Stage 4: Negative Feedback

Finally, it is possible that the negative feedback derived from the peripheral organ may itelf be inappropriate. In other words, it is possible for the protective negative feedback systems to themselves become less effective and in some cases to become inactivated. The extreme example of a lack of negative feedback is seen in people born without the normal system of detecting pain (Melzack, 1973). These people are constantly in danger of severely injuring themselves, for they lack the natural protective mechanisms for detecting and therefore coping with injury.

Although disregulation can occur at any of these four stages, the general consequences of disregulation are the same in each case. By responding inappropriately to negative feedback, the brain fails to maintain stable regulation of the organ in question, and disregulation (with its accompanying instability) occurs.

The concept of disregulation provides a possible framework for uncovering mechanisms that may underly any disorder mediated by the central nervous system. Not only can disregulation occur at each of the four stages in the system, but problems can occur simultaneously at multiple stages. In the extreme case, if (1) a person was exposed to a demanding situation in the environment that required continued adaptation (Stage 1), *and* (2) the brain processed the sensory information and reacted inappropriately due to genetic and/or learning deficiencies (Stage 2), *and* (3) the peripheral organ itself reacted inappropriately because of genetic or maturational deficiencies (Stage 3), *and* (4) the peripheral feedback mechanisms from this organ to the brain were also ineffective (Stage 4), this *pattern* of factors would increase the likelihood of the development of a specific psychosomatic disorder. Because the brain and body are composed of multisystems that must be coordinated in an integrated fashion, it becomes necessary to examine each of the components and then consider how they may combine to produce the final outcome that we call disease.

Although I have emphasized the psychophysiology as outcome aspect of self-regulation in health, and disregulation in illness, it should be recognized that this general perspective regarding psychobiology as mechanism has direct applications to disorders traditionally classified as psychological or psychiatric. For example, proponents of a modern model of repression have proposed that the tendency to be aware of little discomfort, even when underlying anxiety of physical illness is actually present, may reflect a "functional disconnection syndrome" in which the more verbal and conscious left hemisphere fails to accurately process the more spatial and emotional content generated by the right hemisphere (Galin, 1974). This functional disconnection of the left from the right hemisphere, according to the disregulation analysis, would lead to instability and disorder of processes involving the right hemisphere.

Another example concerns the effects of reducing the intensity or duration of anxiety on the tendency toward psychopathic behavior (e.g., Lykken, 1957). To the extent that anxiety is a psychobiological response system serving an adaptive feedback function that keeps antisocial behavior within certain constraints, then removing these constraints by whatever mechanism should result in disregulation of the relevant social behaviors.

Although previous attempts have been made to apply cybernetic theory to clinical psychology and psychiatry (e.g.,Ashby, 1954), this orientation has not received the attention it deserves (e.g., Powers, 1973). I find feedback concepts particularly useful because they are highly general, can be formulated in mathematical terms, and can be directly translated into biochemical, physiological, and behavioral levels of analysis. The central concepts of self-regulation and disregulation provide a psychobiological framework for viewing order and disorder, and hence provide a model for the correction of disease using various feedback oriented intervention procedures.

Biofeedback as a Central Component of All Biobehavioral Interventions

As shown in Figure 3-2, the biofeedback procedure can be seen as the creation of a new feedback loop between the body and brain, operating as an aid in self-regulation. This feedback loop can be used to help replace one that has been attenuated or injured, or can serve as an additional feedback loop for the purpose of increasing stability of the system.

Biofeedback has often been viewed as a psychophysiological procedure for directly modifying specific physiological dysfunctions (e.g., Shapiro & Surwit, 1976). However, there is a broader, more indirect concept of biofeedback emphasizing the use of biofeedback (a Stage 5 process) as a means of helping the patient to modify his or her environment (Stage 1) or cognitions and emotions (Stage 2) for the sake of physical health (Stage 3). In certain restricted applications of biofeedback, such as muscle rehabilitation in patients with strokes or other neuromuscular problems, the use

of biofeedback as a focused procedure for training a localized psychobiological skill makes theoretical and clinical sense (Basmajian, 1977). However, to the extent that the patient's disorder is maintained in part by problems at Stage 1 and 2, then theory and practice indicate that biofeedback should be used in a more indirect sense to foster appropriate Stage 1 and Stage 2 modifications for the sake of the peripheral organ's health.

As various writers have noted (e.g., Lazarus, 1975), feedback is a fundamental aspect of psychotherapy and behavior change. The therapist, in a real sense, is a provider of feedback concerning the patient's psychobiological state. Furthermore, ideally the therapist provides corrective feedback that will help the patient to change his or her environment (Stage 1) or behavior (mediated through Stage 2) for the sake of psychobiological health (combined Stages 2, 3, and 4). From this perspective the behavior therapist acts as a complex, psychobiologically based biofeedback system, since he or she monitors a patient's psychobiological state as a Stage 5 intervention. If one restricts the use of the psychophysiology to method, then the above argument is by definition wrong (since the therapist is not defined as a physiological device). However, if one adopts the definition of psychobiology as mechanism, then the psychotherapist is as much a psychobiological intervention system as the biofeedback device.

Of course, the therapist espousing a more traditional behavioral perspective could turn this perspective around and argue that biofeedback devices are essentially biomedical and behavior therapists. This, parenthetically, is the underlying rationale for classifying biofeedback as a behavior therapy rather than as a biological therapy. However, this chapter argues that both extreme positions are wrong. Biofeedback, in the general sense, is a psychobiological therapy having psychobiological consequences. From this perspective, the therapist who infers that a patient is embarrassed from a blush on the face and subsequently makes a suitable remark, is essentially practicing a psychobiologically oriented therapy, whether he or she is aware of this fact or not.

The strong form of this position is that all

therapy, be it behavioral, pharmacological or surgical involves biofeedback as a fundamental component. Consider various approaches to the treatment of hypertension (Shapiro et al., 1977). The most obvious form of biofeedback therapy is blood pressure biofeedback provided to the patient via a blood pressure monitoring system with the request that the patient use this feedback to lower blood pressure. The less obvious form of biofeedback therapy involves traditional psychotherapy, including psychoanalysis, where free association, insight, emotional expression, and support are provided with the goal of lowering blood pressure. Depending on the therapist, blood pressure might be taken at various phases of therapy to determine the efficacy of the psychotherapy.

Probably the least obvious form of biofeedback therapy for hypertension involves the use of drugs or surgery. Consider the typical sequence of events in drug therapy. A patient (he) first learns that he has high blood pressure because a nurse or doctor (she) takes his pressure and informs him (provides feedback, Stage 5) that the pressure is high. The physician then begins a set of interventions that necessitate *the patient's active, psychobiological cooperation in order for the procedures to effectively influence blood pressure.* For example, the patient must regularly take his medication, despite the negative side effects he may be experiencing, in order for lowered levels of blood pressure to be achieved and maintained. However, how does the doctor know whether or not the intervention is effective? The doctor might monitor the pressure in the office, or she also might have the patient or family members monitor pressure at work or at home, to determine the relative effectiveness. Depending on this feedback, the therapist will alter her interactions with the patient (e.g., provide other drugs) so as to ultimately stabilize the pressure.

Hence, in all forms of therapy, Stage 5 feedback processes play an essential role. What varies are the inputs or interventions that are being used to affect changes in the desired psychobiological system. Whether one succeeds in lowering pressure by removing environmental stresses (Stage 1), by changing the patient's perceptions or reactions to environmental stimuli (Stage 2), by giving drugs that *directly* affect the central (Stage 2) and/or

peripheral nervous system and organs (Stage 3), or by surgically changing the central nervous system (Stage 2), peripheral organs (Stage 3), or internal feedback mechanism (Stage 4), a complex psychobiological feedback loop system is required in order to assess and evaluate therapeutic outcome.

A major change triggered by research on biofeedback has been to emphasize more of the active monitoring, the carrying out of treatment programs, and the prevention of disease as the province and responsibility of the individual person. As noted earlier, biofeedback has provided an important demonstration of the potential for psychobiological self-regulation, and the recognition that Stage 1 and Stage 2 processes play a continual role in health and disease.

When I point out the fundamental role of feedback in all interventions I do not mean to imply that all interventions are the same. On the contrary, the remainder of this chapter is concerned with emphasizing the complexity of psychobiological mechanisms underlying different kinds of behavioral and biological interventions. The purpose of using a general construct such as feedback and concepts such as self-regulation and disregulation is to provide a foundation for placing behavioral and biological concepts under a common theoretical umbrella. This in turn provides a framework for viewing the tremendous complexities involved in analyzing complex patterns of psychobiological processes and their emergent interactions in different therapies.

Biological Concepts of Intervention and Their Evaluation

Before considering research on hypertension and anxiety as two areas that illustrate recent developments in the psychobiology of psychotherapy and behavior change, it is important to consider how questions of intervention and evaluation are approached in the biological sciences. In particular, since anxiety and hypertension are two problems which currently are treated by pharmacologic as well as behavioral procedures, it becomes imperative to consider a framework for comparing and contrasting these two major, and often competing, approaches to therapy.

Distinctions between behavioral and biological approaches to intervention, as discussed above, become blurred when one examines interventions in terms of underlying psychobiological mechanisms. As behavioral interventions find their way into medical practice, comparisons between different treatment modalities become particularly important. Although there is an obvious advantage in distinguishing between different forms of intervention in terms of *method* of administration, this should not imply that completely different theories should be required to understand their underlying *mechanisms*.

It turns out that an analysis of the logic underlying biological interventions is of value not only in developing a more integrative approach to intervention, but also because it uncovers sources of confusion between behavioral and biological approaches in usage of words that severely hamper communication and interdisciplinary research. An analysis of pharmacology reveals striking cases of such confusions (major examples listed in Table 3-1) and suggests the necessity for important clarifications that can improve biobehavioral research and practice (from Schwartz et al., 1978).

Consider, for example, the distinction between a chemical, a drug, and a medicine. A chemical refers to a compound that has a set of properties that can be studied independently of the material with which it interacts. Chemists typically study properties of chemicals, as well as basic chemical reactions. A chemical "becomes" a drug when it is administered to a biological substrate—for example, when it is given to a human. However, describing something as a drug does not necessarily imply that the drug has clinical value. Pharmacologists are chemists who study how chemicals act on biological systems. A drug only "becomes" a medicine when it is discovered that the actions or effects of the drug prove to have clinical value. The clinical values of drugs are typically studied by clinical pharmacologists, while their findings are utilized by physicians. Note that the properties that make something a "good" chemical need not be the same as those that make it a "good" drug. Furthermore, neither may be of importance in determining how "good" a medicine it is.

This classification scheme is of more than

TABLE 3-1 Terms Frequently Confused in the Literature on Pharmacological Intervention

Chemical, drug, medicine
action, effect
direct, indirect
response, reaction
effective, efficacy
main effects, side effects
specific, selectivity
modulation, modification
placebo effects, behavioral effects

semantic value. It emphasizes how the questions of interest will vary, depending on the goals of the investigator. Unfortunately, these distinctions are not used consistently, even within the biomedical community.

Consider a parallel scheme in the behavioral sciences. One can study the nature of a particular environment (e.g., a biofeedback laboratory) without considering its effects on the person. This sort of basic description, including the operation of the equipment and the nature of the environmental setting, or the instructions typically used, can be generated by various basic scientists in electronics and psychology. This is biofeedback as a "chemical." Biofeedback only becomes a "drug" when assessed for its effects on a person. These effects can be studied by basic scientists such as psychophysiologists.

However, biofeedback does not become a "medicine" until its "drug" effects are shown to have clinical value, as determined ultimately by clinicians in psychology and medicine. Blanchard and Young (1973), in their review of the biofeedback literature, concluded that statistically significant effects of biofeedback have been demonstrated, but clinically significant effects have yet to be established. In other words, the data that biofeedback has reliable "drug" effects is not in dispute—but its value as a "medicine" is still a question for future research.

Pharmacologists are careful to distinguish between action versus effect. The immediate or direct consequence of a drug is defined as that drug's action, while the term direct refers to the site of action. Hence, if blood pressure lowering is observed in response to a drug whose actual site of action is in the brain, it would be said that the changes in the relevant brain areas were a direct action of the drug, whereas the decrease in blood pressure was an effect of the drug. Effects, then, are indirect consequences of drugs. The terms direct and indirect refer to the precise description of the mechanisms of the drug. Immediate actions of the drug and consequential effects at various parts of the system distant from the site of action of the drug are thus carefully distinguished.

Within this framework, the results of behavioral interventions must always be seen as "indirect effects" and not "direct actions," since the direct action would actually be, for example, the immediate impact of the verbal instructions on the ears of the subject! Tremendous confusion is engendered when biomedically trained persons read behavioral literature in which statements such as "direct behavioral control over blood pressure" are used. From a biological point of view, an environmental stimulus can *never* "directly effect" a change in blood pressure—not only are the words contradictory when used together, but physiologically only the plumbing of the cardiovascular system itself can have a direct action on blood pressure. Even if blood pressure were raised, for example, by physically pressing on an artery, this would still be described as having an indirect effect on blood pressure(by means of a direct action on the skin, and through the skin, an indirect effect on the cardiovascular system). The terms indirect versus direct and action versus effect become useful for more precisely specifying what is influencing what in a complex psychobiological organism.

The definition of response in pharmacology is particularly interesting because response can refer to a particular action of a drug, a specific effect of a drug, or the entire set of actions and effects elicited by the drug. Hence, the term response must be specified in order to understand precisely what is being referred to. In the behavioral sciences, the word response is often used more casually. Some psychologists limit the use of the term only to observable behaviors, while others use the terms to refer to inferred, underlying subjective or physiological changes as well. From a psychobiological point of view, clarifying the use of

the word response by specifying its underlying components can be an important conceptual step.

Parenthetically, pharmacologists use the term reaction to refer to a response that is either countervailing to the main actions and effects of the drugs (in basic research), or one that has adverse qualities when used as a medicine (in clinical research). When behavioral scientists speak of the "reaction of their subjects to the instructions," the pharmacologist is likely to have the wrong impression about what is meant. Distinguishing between response and reaction helps to label components that are positive or negative.

Another often confused distinction refers to the dose at which a clinically effective response is observed versus the dose at which clinical efficacy is reached. In pharmacology, these terms are not synonymous—efficacy refers to the maximum response possible from *any* dose of the drug, whereas effectiveness can be reached at levels lower than the dosage needed to obtain a maximal effect. Translating this into behavioral terms, a "dose" of relaxation once a day for 15 minutes may be sufficient to be clinically effective in a given case, even though four hours of relaxation a day might achieve even larger effects approaching the efficacy of relaxation procedures.

One concept in pharmacology I find particularly valuable is the concept of selectivity. Selectivity refers to the fact that every drug elicits complex patterns or sets of actions and effects that comprise the total response. The degree of selectivity of a drug, then, is the precise delineation of the total number of actions and effects produced by the drug (both responses and reactions). No drug has ever been discovered that has a truly "specific" or single action and effect. Hence, the term selectivity applies to all drugs, since every drug produces a unique set or pattern of actions and effects.

The concept of selectivity points out the need to examine the total organismic response (and reaction) to any drug. In fact, every drug has its "main" effects and its "side" effects. However, what is defined as a main effect versus a side effect depends on the *particular interest* of the basic researcher (in the case of a drug) or clinician (in the case of a medicine). To the person taking marijuana to get "high," the psychological effect may be viewed as the main effect, while the simultaneous lowering of blood pressure would be viewed as a "side" effect. However, to the clinician interested in the possibility of using marijuana in the treatment of hypertension, the lowering of blood pressure becomes the main clinical effect of interest, while its "psychological" components might be viewed as a side effect.

Note that the term side effect does not necessarily mean adverse effect as is implied in common usage. All drugs, by definition, have side effects. Whether they are positive or negative depends on the judgment of the researcher or clinician. Thus, all drugs have side responses, and to varying degrees, side reactions.

The concept of selectivity is identical to the concept of patterning and multiresponse systems described earlier. Theoretically, no behavior technique is "specific" to the modification of one particular response. Instead, different treatments, to different degrees, influence different combinations of psychobiological systems. Although biofeedback for blood pressure may have more of a selective effect on the autonomic nervous system than progressive relaxation, neither treatment is "specific" to blood pressure. All have their psychobiological side effects. A comprehensive assessment of any behavioral treatment would ultimately involve the appropriate sampling of all major response systems in a person. This perspective in the behavior therapy literature is forcefully advocated by Lazarus (1973) in his concept of multimodality therapy.

One additional distinction of particular relevance to psychotherapy and behavior change concerns the distinction between modulation versus modification. Certain medicines modulate specific tissues leading to a set of actions and effects *so long as the medicine is present in the' system*. Such medicines do not directly modify the site of action, nor do they lead to modifications in effects. Medicines of this type must be taken chronically to maintain clinical effectiveness. However, other medicines do modify the system, either directly, through their source of action, or indirectly (e.g., by allowing or aiding an injured tissue to heal). In this case, subsequent removal of the medicine does not lead to a return of the symptom.

The distinction between modulation and modification has direct relevance to behavioral interven-

tion, even though the distinction is often blurred in the behavioral literature. Temporarily changing the environment of a patient (Stage 1) (e.g., by removing him from a stressful environment) may result in dramatic improvements, but these effects may only be modulations caused by the short-term change in the environment and not more permanent modifications either in the environment (Stage 1) or in the person (Stages 2 and 3). Hence, it should not be surprising that removing hypertensive patients from their stressful environments and placing them in quiet settings can lead to dramatic short-term gains, but minimal long term gains (Shapiro et al., 1977).

Since there is little reason to predict that significant modifications have been produced with this sort of behavioral intervention, it makes little sense to expect that such short-term gains will "transfer" back to the stressful environment. The corollary illustration in drug research would entail giving a drug that lowers blood pressure by acting on the periphery (Stage 3) to a person whose blood pressure is maintained in part by the effects of a stressful life situation (Stage 1). Since the drug is acting only on the periphery, and not on the actual source of stress to the system (in this case, the environment), it is naive to assume that if the person stops taking the drug, blood pressure will remain at lower levels.

A common term confused in both biology and psychology is the term placebo. As noted by Shapiro (1959, 1971), the term placebo initially came from the Latin word meaning "to please." By this definition, all treatments are, of course, undertaken to "please" the patient, be they methods derived from biology or psychology, and therefore all treatments are placebos!

However, as pharmacology evolved as a science, it became important in basic and clinical research to distinguish those effects associated with administrating a drug or medicine that were due to *direct actions* versus all other effects not attributable to the direct action of the drug. The former were labeled true drug or medicine actions and effects, the latter were labeled "nonspecific" and attributed to "placebo" responses.

The evolution of the double blind procedure was meant to help in the determination of whether the clinical effects of a medicine were due primarily to the direct actions of the drugs, or were contributed to by various actions and effects other than that direct action. The fact that these latter actions and effects might be very powerful, and could contribute importantly in an interactive sense to the final set of actions and effects observed, was not considered central to the interests of basic and clinical pharmacologists.

However, such "nonspecific" effects are the bread and butter of behavioral scientists. Note that by definition, *all* effects attributed to psychosocial variables are termed "placebo" effects. Hence, when a biomedical scientist says that relaxation or biofeedback procedures result in "placebo" effects, this is not necessarily a criticism. Instead, it may reflect the simple conclusion that the observed effects cannot be attributed to a direct action of a drug.

When behavioral scientists compare different behavioral treatments to a "placebo" control, they are using the term placebo in a different sense. Biomedical scientists, when adopting the strict definition of a pharmacologist, would be correct in arguing that all groups were showing "placebo" effects. On the other hand, behavioral sciences have the potential of being able to delineate and specify the underlying processes that contribute to the combination of uncontrolled psychosocial factors brought together under the global concept of a nonspecific placebo response.

Since the average biomedical scientist is not necessarily any more consistent in the use of terminology than the average behavioral scientist, serious miscommunication can arise through the use of seemingly simple terms such as placebo. From a psychobiological point of view, particularly one that emphasizes the development of a more common, consistent usage of concepts and terms, the demonstration of "placebo" effects in psychology and medicine provides some of the best uncontrolled evidence for the role of behavioral factors in health and illness.

Biobehavioral Phases of Clinical Research

In clinical psychology and psychiatry there is currently no consensual model for conceptualizing how clinical research should be approached and what phases justify what conclusions. However,

this in not the case for pharmacology, where advances in knowledge coupled with federal regulatory requirements have established a framework for conducting such research. When comparisons are to be made between various treatment methods, particularly when they cross disciplines (e.g., psychology versus pharmacology), some standard guidelines for comparison must be evolved (Shapiro et al., 1977). Drawing on the guidelines initially established for clinical pharmacology, we have argued that, given any treatment for which one wishes to define clinical effectiveness, methodology should be scrutinized to determine:

1. Rationale of the treatment, origins, and descriptions of the methods, and basic psychobiological effects.

2. Magnitude and duration of effects on the variables in question.

3. Methods, frequency, and intensity of administration.

4. Potential toxicity and side effects.

5. Therapeutic indications, including costs and relation to other therapies.

Although this set of effects has been established for certain pharmacologic treatments, I know of no single behavioral therapy that has been comprehensively analyzed and researched from this perspective. Pharmacology has established a set of phases by which such research should be conducted (shown in Table 3-2). Again, these phases or steps can readily be applied to any treatment modality (Shapiro et al., 1977). For drug therapies the following procedure is typically adopted.

Preclinical Phase

Here, the drug is developed by basic chemical and physiological research and tested in animals. The early researchers in behaviorally oriented therapies such as systematic desensitization (Wolpe, 1958) and to some extent biofeedback (Miller, 1969) considered this foundation essential.

Phase I Trials

Here, individual patients receive the drug to determine its basic physiological effect, its dose-response relationships, and its side effects. Again,

TABLE 3-2   Proposed Phases of Biobehavioral Clinical Research (Adopted from Research in Pharmacotherapy)

Preclinical Phase:	The intervention is developed by basic behavioral and biological research, and studied in animals.
Phase I Trials:	Individual patients receive the intervention to determine its basic psychobiological actions and effects, including side effects, and its dose-response relationships.
Phase II Trials:	Controlled comparisons of the intervention with other interventions in small groups of patients, with the goal of establishing the mechanisms of actions and effects, and further establishment of dose and toxicity.
Phase III Trials:	Broad scale clinical studies to establish the clinical value of intervention, essentially duplicating the circumstances that the intervention will be used in by the practicing therapist.
Phase IV Trials:	Follow-up evaluation in the field.

the literature on systematic desensitization began with such basic clinical trials (Wolpe, 1958), although precise parameters of administration were not well developed. The same applies to the initial clinical work in biofeedback (reviewed in Shapiro, Schwartz, & Tursky, 1972).

Phase II Trials

Here, controlled comparisons of the drug with placebo or other agents are conducted in small groups of patients, usually with double-blind techniques, and with further establishment of dose and toxicity. Phase II trials for systematic desensitization presently fill the research literature, and Phase II trials in biofeedback are just beginning to appear.

Phase III Trials

Here, broad clinical trials in large samples (e.g., thousands of subjects) are performed, essentially duplicating the circumstances used by the prescribing practitioner. Unlike drugs, which require Phase III trials before they can be classified as medicines, behavioral treatments have not required a rigorous Phase III demonstration to establish their true clinical value. Such studies require multihospital/ multiuniversity collaborations using a standard protocol, and demand large funding levels to support the personnel needed for assessment and follow-up.

There is currently a proposal before the Food and Drug Administration for the establishment of a Phase IV evaluation that attempts to replicate clinical effectiveness in the field after the drug has been released as a medicine. The clinical importance of this evaluation should not be questioned—the issues are more of a practical nature involving sources of funds and direction.

I describe this framework for evaluating drugs as medicines to illustrate the structure that already exists for establishing the clinical value of one type of intervention. The logic underlying this framework seems appropriate for any intervention. When interventions are viewed from the perspective of psychobiology as mechanism, we begin to appreciate the importance of applying an integrated biobehavioral approach to the analysis of holistic treatments. All treatments involve a combination of environmental and biological components, and the well-trained psychobiologically oriented clinical psychologist should be reasonably conversant with this general perspective. The same issue clearly applies to the future training of researchers and practitioners specializing in biomedical intervention procedures.

I should note that since the pharmacologic model emphasizes *sets or patterns* of actions and effects, both those elicited by the direct action of the drugs, and those generated by other factors (environmental, Stage 1, and personality, Stage 2), the general model provides a foundation for a comprehensive biobehavioral perspective. Add to this the notion of multi-drugs, or capsules, and we have a framework for considering techniques that combine biological and behavioral methods in the determination of the total psychobiological response to treatment.

EXAMPLES OF CURRENT PSYCHOBIOLOGICAL RESEARCH ON PSYCHOTHERAPY AND BEHAVIOR CHANGE

Psychobiology of Hypertension and Its Regulation

Behavioral approaches to the etiology and treatment of hypertension provide a framework for illustrating how psychophysiology as outcome can have implications for assessment and evaluation. Since hypertension is defined as the pathophysiological consequences of high blood pressure on the cardiovascular system, the measurement of blood pressure becomes an important outcome variable. Note that blood pressure has a direct action in causing pathological changes in the heart, kidney, and brain. However, hypertension is not defined as the presence of high blood pressure *per se,* but rather is seen in terms of the clinical consequences of the high blood pressure. This distinction is important because the ultimate clinical value of any treatment for hyptertension cannot be defined by the degree of blood pressure reduction *per se,* but rather by the extent to which a given decrease in blood pressure for a particular person leads to the improved status of the cardiovascular system. Since no behaviorally based study has yet demonstrated that blood pressure reductions are accompanied by physical improvement, it is not known whether such interventions have medical significance.

Hypertension is an excellent model system for examining the psychobiology of psychotherapy and behavior change, since changes in the patient's cognition and behavior are seen as important intermediary mechanisms by which decreases in blood pressure are produced. In fact, in an important article by Cohen and Obrist (1975), the authors document how skeletal/motor and cardiovascular responses (Stage 3 processes) are integrated at the level of the central nervous system (Stage 2). Therefore, changes in cognition and behavior *include* patterned changes in the cardiovascular system as a component. Neurophysiological models that link psychological and biological constructs provide the foundation for integrating the two approaches to intervention.

There have been a number of excellent reviews on behavioral approches to hypertension, including Shapiro, Mainardi, and Surwit (1977) and Miller and Dworkin (1977). A recent paper by Shapiro et al. (1977) has examined this literature from the perspective of phases of clinical pharmacologic research. They conclude that most of the research has not gone beyond Phase I demonstrations, while the few Phase II studies published to date have been relatively brief with small numbers of subjects per group.

An intriguing aspect of this literature is that experiments using the various behavioral approaches have tended to yield results indicating comparable reductions in blood pressure across different behaviorally oriented therapeutic modalities. Studies in which patients have been removed from stressful environments (Stage I modifications) have tended to result in large, short-term decreases in pressure. As noted previously, these approaches have involved modulations rather than modifications, so that the temporary nature of the reductions should not be surprising.

Early research on psychoanalytically oriented therapies emphasizing emotional expression and support have reported sizeable decreases in blood pressure in a proportion of patients. However, these early studies are of the Phase I variety, and it is impossible to determine from these uncontrolled interventions the mechanisms responsible for the observed decreases in pressure.

The recent research using blood pressure biofeedback has been more effective in (1) showing selective behavioral modulation of relevant cardiovascular responses and in (2) documenting transfer of training to environments outside of the laboratory. Given the role such studies have played in stimulating current interest in behavioral approaches to the treatment of hypertension, we will consider this research in more detail.

In the typical blood pressure biofeedback experiment, subjects are provided with visual or auditory feedback regarding the status of various components of their cardiovascular system. Some experiments have provided binary (yes/no) feedback for relative changes in systolic blood pressure, diastolic blood pressure, and/or heart rate at each heart beat using sophisticated physiological monitoring equipment. Some investigators have used complex computer displays to inform subjects and patients of their progress. Other studies have adopted portable blood pressure cuff instruments to provide simple, albeit inaccurate, feedback in the home. All these procedures, to varying degrees, have been shown to help people gain greater self-control over their blood pressure.

At the present time, neither the peripheral nor the central mechanisms involved in the self-regulation of blood pressure with biofeedback are known. Changes in muscle tension and respiration may be contributing factors but they are not the sole mechanisms of action. As shown in Figure 3-3, different procedures may yield decreases in blood pressure via different peripheral mechanisms. Differential control over heart rate and blood pressure

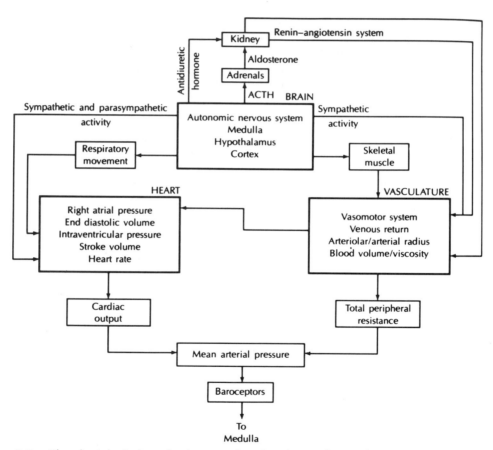

Figure 3-3.   The physiological mechanisms employed in the regulation of arterial blood pressure. The diagram oversimplifies the processes in order to provide a general overview of mechanisms most relevant to behavioral manipulation. Boxes labeled Heart, Brain, and Vasculature each contain a subset of relevant systems and functions. Although these are not necessarily temporally or functionally related in the order presented, the outside arrows indicate the site at which other systems exert their influence on the system described in the box. The reader should note the numerous and diverse pathways through which behavioral control over blood pressure could be exerted. For example, relaxation techniques acting on the musculature could have their main effect on the vasculature, producing a decrease in peripheral resistance. Yogic exercises emphasizing breath control might have their main effect on cardiac output by changing intraventricular pressure. Although the diagram suggests that a feedback approach including both cardiac and vasculature parameters would be most efficacious, it illustrates how verbal instruction acting on the cortex might also affect blood pressure (from Shapiro & Surwit, 1976).

can be achieved, depending on the specific type of biofeedback and the instructions used. For instance, in studies by Schwartz (1972, 1974) and Shapiro and colleagues (Shapiro et al., 1969; Shapiro, Tursky, & Schwartz, 1970a,b; Shapiro, Schwartz, & Tursky, 1972), normotensive subjects were taught to change either heart rate or systolic pressure, or both simultaneously by reinforcing different patterns of the two responses.

Importantly, patterned changes in blood pressure and heart rate can also occur if subjects are given specific instructions to control these functions, and they will draw on various cognitive and somatic strategies to produce more complex physiological patterns (Schwartz, 1977c). Since blood pressure is the outcome of the relation between cardiac output and peripheral resistance, then depending on the type of biofeedback and instructions used, changes in heart rate, stroke volume, and peripheral resistance may be differentially involved. In addition, it has been claimed that biofeedback for other potentially relevant physiological reponses such as muscle tension (electromyography), sweat gland activity (galvanic skin response), and skin temperature may also aid in the learned lowering of blood pressure (Patel, 1977).

In normotensive subjects, using binary feedback for relative decreases in systolic blood pressure, average declines of 5 to 17 mmHg within a single training session have been reported. Using biofeedback for diastolic blood pressure, the learned decreases have been smaller. In seven hypertensive subjects given multiple sessions of blood pressure biofeedback training, Benson et al. (1971) observed decreases within a typical session of only 5 mmHg on the average. However, the mean decline over 22 training sessions was 17.7 mmHg, ranging from 0 to 34mmHg.

In an excellent study, Kristt and Engel (1975) trained five hypertensive patients to both raise and lower systolic blood pressure; these subjects showed not only consistent within-session decreases of approximately 29 mmHg, but also a fall in systolic blood pressure baseline from 153 to 135 mmHg at a three-month follow-up. Furthermore, systolic pressure at home dropped 18 mmHg from the beginning of training, and the patients could voluntarily reduce systolic blood pressure at home

from 141 to 125 mmHg by means of the techniques learned in the laboratory.

In both of these studies involving hypertensive patients, blood pressure biofeedback tended to lead to the regulation of blood pressure without corresponding changes in heart rate. It is probable that one way of distinguishing between different techniques will be the examination of the extent to which different patterns of responses accompany observed decreases in pressure. In this way, differences in the selectivity of action of the differing methods can be uncovered.

Another related direction in which behavioral research on hypertension has expanded has involved the use of various types of relaxation and meditation training. Since the general efficacy of therapeutic results using different biofeedback and relaxation procedures appears comparable, some authors argue that simple relaxation procedures are less expensive, easier to use, and have broader clinical significance (e.g., they are more likely to be accompanied by decreases in the subjective experience of anxiety) than blood pressure biofeedback procedures (e.g., Benson, 1975). To the extent that high blood pressure reflects different combinations of cardiovascular response in different individuals, and to the extent that high blood pressure may be only one component of an even more complex psychobiological state (e.g., a subset of hypertensives may harbor excessive anger: see below), then a psychobiologically oriented multiprocess approach to treatment would suggest that the appropriate *combination* or *pattern* of Stage 1 and 2 interventions should be encouraged so as to produce maximal decreases in all the relevant systems. To the extent that certain relaxation procedures result in decreases in multiple processes and lead to the elicitation of a general, hypothalamic relaxation response (Benson, 1975), then such procedures should be followed with those hypertensive patients for whom heightened sympathetic activation is a problem.

Different relaxation procedures may engage different combinations of underlying psychobiological processes (Davidson & Schwartz, 1976). What is not generally recognized is that relaxation procedures currently employed in research on hypertension also involve the modulation or modification of complex patterns of underlying processes. For example, Benson (1975) approaches the induction of an integrated relaxation response by manipulating multiple components that contribute to disregulation. He requires that subjects sit in a quiet place, where there are few disturbing or distracting external stimuli (Stage 1). In addition, when subjects follow the instructions to sit quietly, they are reducing premotor and motor firing to the skeletal muscles (Stages 2 to 3). By attending to their breathing and by generating a nonstressful, simple auditory work (often called a mantra), they are eliminating other cognitions that normally would result in the continued elicitation of undesirable motor and visceral reactions (Davidson & Schwartz, 1976). By requiring subjects to turn their attention inward and to experience the pleasant sensations of the relaxed muscles and quiet breathing, Benson's procedure also accentuates the brain's recognition (Stage 2) of internal feedback (Stage 4) from the periphery (Stage 3). In this manner, a deceptively simple relaxation procedure may influence all four major stages where disregulation can occur.

There have been almost 10 years of concentrated research on biofeedback and relaxation procedures in the treatment of hypertension. Yet surprisingly little is known of the underlying psychobiological mechanisms involved in either the etiology or treatment of the disease. Since most researchers do not hold a comphrehensive psychobiological perspective regarding intervention procedures, the level of theoretical analysis tends to be limited. For example, when two different behavioral procedures are found to result in comparable decreases in blood pressure, the assumption is often made that the techniques are similar. Typically, however, little attempt is made to measure other relevant parameters so as to determine whether the selectivity or the pattern is actually the same.

Or, most studies simply measure blood pressure under resting conditions. Again, the assumption is made that if comparable decreases are observed, then the techniques must be equally effective for similar reasons. However, to the extent that biofeedback involves the learning of neuro-psychological skills that are more focused than those for relaxation training (e.g., Schwartz, 1975), then it is possible that under relevant stimulus conditions (e.g., stress) specific self-regulation differ-

ences may be uncovered suggesting that biofeedback is superior to general relaxation training in promoting selective response skill training. In an important study by DeGood and Adams (1976), this is precisely what was found.

Although most of the review articles mentioned above have hypothesized that *combinations* of biofeedback, relaxation, and other environmental, cognitive, and affective procedures are likely to be most effective in helping. patients with hypertension, there has been little research to date that systematically examines the interactions of these techniques. Furthermore, there has been little attention paid to the contribution of "placebo" effects (the role of positive experiences, redirection of attention, etc.) to the lowering of pressure. However, as noted by Miller and Dworkin (1977) and Schwartz (1977a), researchers are becoming more sophisticated in both experimental design and in psychobiological theories (e.g., hypertension as a complex disregulation disorder), and it is likely that major advances will be made in the Phase II development of this research.

The possibilities for doing creative research in this area are substantial. For example, recent evidence suggests that among patients with hypertension, a subgroup of patients have high plasma renin levels (Esler, et al; 1977). This subgroup tends to consist of patients for whom an overactive sympathetic nervous system is playing a major role in maintaining high blood pressure levels (as inferred from measures of norepinephrine in the blood, and by administration of drugs that block sympathetic control to the cardiovascular effector organs). Interestingly, this subgroup of "neurogenic" hypertensives tends to report evidence of suppressed hostility on various paper and pencil measures. Furthermore, these patients do not report more anxiety than the nonneurogenic hypertensive subjects.

These findings suggest that some of the old notions linking high blood pressure to suppressed or even repressed anger (Alexander, 1939) may apply to a subgroup of patients. Thus, for this particular subgroup of hypertensives, procedures aimed at assertive training and other behavioral methods of regulating anger may ultimately be relevant to the control of their high blood pressure. In an important experiment examining various behavioral approaches to the modification of the expression of anger in normotensive subjects, Novaco (1975) found that the technique of combining cognitive self-control procedures (modeled after Meichenbaum, 1974) with relaxation procedures led to the greatest improvement in expression of anger *and* the greatest decreases in blood pressure folowing an anger-provoking situation. Novaco suggests that the regulation of anger may play an important role in hypertension, and that behavioral approaches to the control of anger may be an important adjuct to treatment.

Since hypertensive patients are often medicated, it becomes imperative to consider the interaction of behavioral interventions with the medication. In fact, certain behavioral interventions may result in negative side effects, or side reactions, if not properly monitored. For example, some hypertensive patients are given propranolol (a sympathetic nervous system blocker). To the extent that relaxation procedures result in decreased sympathetic tone, the original dosage of propranolol could turn into an overdose. This potential difficulty also applies to diabetics who are taking insulin. In fact, unpublished case studies indicate that certain diabetic subjects may suffer insulin shock as a side effect of relaxation training.

A similar issue may apply to research on anxiety, although there has been relatively little cross-fertilization between behavioral and biomedical research on the regulation of anxiety. This difference probably reflects the fact that, historically, anxiety has been defined as a "psychological" problem whereas hypertension has been defined as a "medical" problem. Since the behavioral sciences have begun to make advances in the treatment of hypertension, the issue of behavioral versus pharmacologic treatment has become a major topic of concern. In this respect, research on hypertension provides a useful model for examining the interaction and integration of behavioral and biological approaches to comprehensive biobehavioral treatment.

Psychobiology of Anxiety and its Regulation

The topic of anxiety is a useful one for illustrating how research on psychophysiology as outcome employs physiological monitoring as an indirect assessment of desired change. I use anxiety as a primary example not only because of its long-standing position in clinical psychology and psychophysiology, but also because the study of anxiety has been sufficiently developed to provide a general conceptual framework for viewing the way in which a psychobiological approach to the assessment of change in any emotion, or pattern of emotions, may be approached in the future.

The concept of anxiety has played a central role in theories of personality (Lang, 1977a). Its assessment and regulation in therapy, therefore, is often seen as fundamental to the treatment of psychopathology and pathophysiology (Whatmore & Kohli, 1974). Unfortunately, there is little agreement regarding a definition of anxiety, and it is impossible to agree on a single measure of anxiety that could apply to all individuals. However, from a psychobiological perspective, the notion of a single measure of anxiety is ill-founded.

In an excellent review of the literature on the psychophysiology of anxiety, Lang (1977a) illustrates the way in which anxiety was first conceptualized as a subjective experience of fear and distress, and secondarily was defined as involving changes in behavior and physiology. Lang presents a detailed analysis of patterns of verbal, behavioral, and physiological "correlates" of anxiety, and he emphasizes how these various systems can be "discordant" with one another under certain conditions. In an important paper, Hodgson and Rachman (1974) illustrate how emotional desynchrony can occur, depending, for example, on the "level of demand" placed on the patient. They point to a study by Miller and Bernstein (1972) in which claustrophobics were asked to remain in a dark chamber while heart rate was recorded. Correlations between subjective anxiety, heart rate, and time in the chamber were relatively high (.42, .56) when subjects were under *no* pressure to remain in the situation longer than a period after which "you would usually want to leave the situation if it happened in your daily life." However, when under high demand to "control" their fear, correlations between responses dropped to zero.

The issue of discordance of multisystems has important implications for predicting therapeutic outcome. For example, Lang, Melamed, and Hart (1974) found that a subset of subjects who generated large cardiac responses during a period in which they were asked to imagine highly fearful scenes showed subsequent improvement in response to systematic desensitization. On the other hand, a subset of subjects who were discordant in their cardiac responses to the high imagery conditions (they generated small cardiac responses) showed little subsequent improvement to desensitization.

The phenomenon of synchrony and desynchrony deserves to be analyzed in terms of underlying psychobiological mechanisms. Unfortunately, many psychophysiologically oriented researchers do not take a more global psychobiological approach to therapy. They often do not discuss the possible underlying neural and endocrine mechanisms that are ultimately responsible for the observed effects. However, promising leads suggested by neuropsychology and psychopharmacology can stimulate more focused, psychobiologically meaningful research.

First, let us consider what a psychobiological definition of anxiety might be. Some researchers (e.g., Benson, 1975) view anxiety as synonymous with heightened sympathetic nervous system arousal mediated by the defense/alarm system of the hypothalamus. Postulating a particular neurophysiological functional system (Luria, 1973) has the advantage of allowing for differing intensities in expression of the *general* response. Furthermore, various degrees of association or disassociation can occur between the elicitation of this neural system response and (1) the perception and verbal labeling of the response, presumably performed by higher cortical structures and ultimately expressed by the left hemisphere (in the average right-handed subject) and/or (2) biobehavioral coping strategies mediated by the cortex and expressed in the periphery as patterns of skeletal behavior (muscle tension). Assessing the degree of synchrony between subsystems can reflect the extent to which the various subsystems are involved in the total, integrated response of anxiety.

We can hypothesize that were the total anxiety response present in a given individual, *all* the relevant functions making up the total psychobiological response would be seen as a synchronous pattern. The person would show sensory vigilance as he or she anxiously monitored the external environment, signs of fear and/or pain would show in facial expressions as reflected by patterns of facial muscle behavior, there would be evidence of behavioral tension and nervousness (as in the preparation for fight or flight), he or she would show the autonomic and endocrine components of the defense/alarm response, and the person would report various worries and concerns in terms of both verbal (left hemisphere) and visual (right hemisphere) biocognitions.

From this perspective, different degrees of desynchrony between various psychobiological components of the system could imply different underlying mechanisms. For example, if a person appeared overtly anxious (meaning that he or she showed signs of body and facial tension, the pattern reflecting a vigilant and possibly frightened posture and facial expression), it is likely that he or she would also show autonomic and endocrine changes (e.g., increases in heart rate and epinephrine). However, it is conceivable that an actor could generate the skeletal/motor pattern of anxiety without necessarily evoking the hypothalamically mediated defense/alarm component which would be expressed in the autonomic and endocrine systems. One can easily demonstrate this effect by voluntarily producing a fearful face and simultaneously measuring heart rate. The facial pattern may occur with little change in the autonomic nervous system.

The question of acting and the self-regulation of different components of the total psychobiological response has theoretical and clinical implications. For example, the method school of acting claims that the best way to experience, and hence to express, the total pattern of verbal, facial, postural, and vocal qualities of emotions is to (1) generate specific images that have elicited the particular emotion in the past and (2) voluntarily assume as much of the expressive pattern making up the total response as possible. The prediction is that the greater the number of systems brought into play, the stronger will be the experience of the emotion and the accuracy of the portrayal of the response. A related prediction would be that method actors should be better able to generate the autonomic concomitants of anxiety than actors simply trained to "go through the motions." Along these lines, Stern and Lewis (1968) demonstrated that method actors were more proficient at regulating their sweat gland responses with biofeedback than were actors who were not of the method school.

As described previously, psychobiological patterning and emergent property theory predicts that as more aspects of the peripheral expression of a given emotion are brought into play, the greater and more consistent will be the subjective experience of that emotion. Schwartz et al. (in Schwartz, 1977b) provided an initial test of this theory by training subjects to control combinations of heart rate and frontalis facial muscle activity using instructions and biofeedback. After each trial, subjects were requested to rate their subjective feelings of emotion using a modified form of Izard's Differential Emotion Scale (Izard, 1972). The results showed that not only could subjects control heart rate and frontalis muscle activity both relatively independently and in patterns, but they also reported experiencing the greatest anxiety when they were generating the *pattern* of high heart rate and high frontalis muscle tension. The intensity of subjective anxiety was therefore found to be higher for heart rate/frontalis pattern regulation than for the control of heart rate or frontalis tension alone.

That these results are not simply due to instructions or suggestions is shown by the fact that similar results were not obtained for the subjective rating of anger. The additive effect of high heart rate and high frontalis tension applied specifically to anxiety, and not to anger. Since frontalis muscle tension is more closely linked to the facial muscle pattern of the frightened face than to the facial muscle pattern of the angry face (Fair & Schwartz, 1977) the finding that high heart rate and high frontalis tension are more closely linked with fear than with anger makes some psychobiological sense. Also, since the typical subject does not know this particular piece of anatomical information, it seems unlikely that the results for anxiety were a function of simple demand characteristics generated inadvertently by the instructions and the task.

I have suggested that biofeedback can serve as an important tool for examining how combinations of different psychobiological systems interact and contribute to the emergent experience of emotion

and consciousness (Schwartz, 1976, 1977b). The importance of combining skeletal muscle *and* autonomic responses when evaluating these patterns needs to be underscored. When integrated emotional states occur spontaneously, they typically involve select combinations of motor and autonomic effectors (Stage 3). The challenge is to discover how these two major systems interact, both peripherally (Stage 3) and centrally (Stage 2) in the experience of emotion.

The need to be more explicit about a general psychobiological theory of emotion should also be underlined. Izard (1972) has proposed that emotional states such as anxiety and depression actually reflect complex patterns of underlying fundamental emotions. Izard suggests that anxiety is a complex pattern of emotions consisting of high fear, high distress, and some anger. Depression is also seen as a complex emotion, sharing with anxiety the emotions of fear and anger, but including sadness as well. Hence, anxiety and depression are seen to be linked to the extent that they share in common two or three underlying psychobiological patterns—they are seen to differ to the extent to which anxiety emphasizes fear while depression emphasizes sadness. It is curious that the massive research efforts on the psychology and biology of anxiety and its treatment have almost universally ignored the measurement of depression. A more comprehensive psychobiological perspective on emotion points to the inherent limitations of this state of affairs. Most researchers in the field of anxiety do not recognize that a "side" effect of various "anxiety-provoking" situations is the elicitation of "depression" as well, and that treatment programs for anxiety may have "side" effects of altering, to various degrees, symptoms of depression. A more sophisticated and comprehensive approach to the assessment of emotion, as suggested by the theories of Izard (1972, 1977), Ekman and Freisen (1975), and Tomkins (1962) could advance research in these areas substantially.

Returning to types of synchrony and desynchrony, if a person showed high skeletal/motor, autonomic and endocrine components of anxiety, but verbally reported little or no anxiety, this might imply at least two different mechanisms. One possibility might be that the person was lying, meaning that the demand charateristics in the environment were sufficiently strong (Stage 1) or were perceived to be strong enough (Stage 2) so as to lead the person to produce a verbal output that was consciously discordant with his or her own perceptions of thoughts and images (Stage 2) and his or her peripheral responses (Stages 3 and 4).

A second reason might be that the person has generated this pattern of anxiety because of an underlying biocognitive mechanism of denial or repression. In this case, a disregulated state would be especially evident since the person would not be accurately processing the state of his or her periphery, and hence could not appropriately self-regulate psychobiological systems for the sake of his or her health. This characteristic of the repressor is presumably what keeps the person from seeking help until the point at which damage or discomfort has occurred requiring serious medical or psychiatric attention.

Most of the current research on the psychophysiology of anxiety ignores this important pattern of psychobiological disassociation. Its importance, however, must be underscored (see Weinberger, Schwartz, & Davidson, 1977). For example, it applies to research on anxiety reduction since subjects may *report* decreases in anxiety for different reasons (implying different mechanisms). In fact, some techniques could conceivably, albeit inadvertently, lead persons to be less accurate in detecting the peripheral manifestations of their anxiety.

As Lazarus (1973), Lang (1971, 1977a), and others have suggested, different techniques may modify different components of anxiety. Although hypotheses of these investigators are primarily descriptive in orientation, they can readily be converted to a psychobiological framework. This kind of theorizing has value in that it can stimulate more focused research on different techniques as applied to different individuals under different conditions. The theory of Davidson and Schwartz (1976) illustrates how this perspective can be applied to the psychobiology of relaxation and related states.

Briefly stated, Davidson and Schwartz (1976) propose that different self-regulation therapies involve, to varying degrees, different patterns of psychobiological systems. Depending on which techniques are used, changes in different patterns of response should be observed. For example, if anxiety is broken down into the basic components of high- and low-cognitive versus somatic manifestations of anxiety, it is possible to draw predictions regarding which self-regulation practices should effect which psychobiological systems. This pattern of predictions is described in Table 3-3.

Stimulated by this analysis, a preliminary experiment was conducted to determine whether subjects who regularly practiced physical exercise (emphasizing skeletal muscle regulation) would show evidence of less somatic versus cognitive anxiety than subjects who regularly practiced meditation (a presumably cognitively oriented practice) (Schwartz, Davidson, & Goleman, 1978). The differential assessment of cognitive versus somatic anxiety was achieved by breaking down a global anxiety scale into specific items that tapped cognitive versus somatic perceptions. The purpose was to *separately* analyze the respective subscales as a

TABLE 3-3 Cognitive and somatic components of anxiety and associated activities hypothesized to reduce such anxiety. The activities in each of the cells maximally engage the system(s) in which anxiety is high. Thus, for example, both progressive relaxation and hatha yoga maximally engage the somatic system with little effect on the cognitive system while reading and watching television are hypothesized to have the opposite effect. Active sports are thought to maximally engage both modes while meditation is hypothesized to engage each of the two modes minimally. Table is adapted from Davidson and Schwartz, 1976.

| | | Somatic Anxiety | |
		Low	High
Cognitive anxiety	Low	Meditation	Progressive relaxation Hatha yoga
	High	Reading Watching television	Active sports

function of type of practice. The items used to tap cognitive and somatic components of sujectively experienced anxiety are presented in Table 3-4.

The results supported the basic hypothesis: meditators showed less cognitive and more somatic anxiety than a comparable group of exercisers. There was no significant difference between the groups on overall anxiety assessed globally. Note that these differences between groups would not have been found if simple global self-report measures had been used. Instead, a psychobiologically based orientation to mechanisms underlying different treatment procedures prompted the finer analysis of biologically relevant, subjectively based subscales leading to new findings.

Clearly, reliance on self-report scales alone to test these notions is at best incomplete, and at worst foolhardy. On the other hand, a psychobiological perspective can stimulate the development of better self-report scales, and can also lead to both the development of more relevant experimental designs and to the selection of more appropriate physiologically dependent variables (e.g., Schwartz, et al., 1976a,b).

This limited overview of research on the psychobiology of anxiety has attempted to indicate how a psychobiological approach to emotion and intervention is stimulating more focused and integrative research on the nature of anxiety and its regulation. I hope this general perspective illustrates how predictions such as "biofeedback training for lowering frontalis muscle activity should lead to general decreases in anxiety" are oversimplified and ultimately incorrect. I do not offer this as a criticism of research on biofeedback and anxiety *per se,* but rather as a criticism of behavioral (or biological) theories that look for single cause and effect relationships in the absence of a more complete psychobiological framework.

PERPETUATION OF DISEASE AND DISREGULATION THROUGH INAPPROPRIATE INTERVENTION

If it is to be useful, a model should be capable of not only integrating previously disparate data and phenomena, but also of uncovering new phenomena not previously recgnized or appreciated. In this final section, I would like to illus-

TABLE 3-4 Items Used to Create Subscales Tapping Cognitive and Somatic Components of Anxiety[a]

Cognitive Subscale	Somatic Subscale
1. I find it difficult to concentrate because of uncontrollable thoughts.	1. My heart beats faster.
2. I worry too much over something that doesn't really matter.	2. I feel jittery in my body.
3. I imagine terrifying scenes.	3. I get diarrhea.
4. I can't keep anxiety provoking pictures out of my mind.	4. I feel tense in my body.
5. Some unimportant thought runs through my mind and bothers me.	5. I nervously pace.
6. I feel that I am losing out on things because I can't make up my mind soon enough.	6. I become immobilized.
7. I can't keep anxiety provoking thoughts out of my mind.	7. I perspire.

[a](From Schwartz, Davidson and Goleman, 1978).

trate one such example stimulated by the psychobiology of disregulation (from Schwartz, 1977a). This novel, and somewhat disturbing, implication of the disregulation model questions the logic and the ultimate utility of the traditional medical model that ignores Stage 1 and 2 variables as important components of health and illness. The strict medical model implies the use of direct biological intervention (surgical or pharmacological) to correct injury or disease that results in tissue damage. The disregulation model predicts that because of incomplete diagnosis and treatment of disregulation, the strict medical model may inadvertently lead to its perpetuation—not only of bodily disease but of human social behavior as well.

The basic premise of the disregulation model is that the brain has primary responsibility for maintaining the health of itself and of its body, and that it succeeds in this task by altering or regulating itself to meet the needs of specific organs. Because the body, as any complex physical device, can only work effectively within certain tolerances, the brain must adjust itself to bring the disregulation back into balance.

As discussed previously, disregulation can be initiated and perpetuated at four stages. Often, the disregulation is initiated by exogenous stimulus demands (Stage 1) and the brain's response to them (Stage 2). If the brain is exposed to environmental conditions that ultimately lead to the breakdown of a given organ system (Stage 3) and a functional disorder develops, appropriate internal negative feedback loops are activated (Stage 4), many of which generate pain. This negative stimulus "drives" the brain to take corrective action. Even if the brain is busy attending to other stimuli and fails to recognize the breakdown of a given organ, at some point the organ will generate sufficient negative feedback (if the loop is intact) to redirect the brain. Anyone who has experienced a really strong stomachache caused by overeating or eating the wrong food knows well the power that negative feedback can have in commanding attention and altering subsequent behavior. Certain disorders like hypertension do not have a protective mechanism that activates conscious systems of pain and distress; such disorders are particularly difficult to treat through lack of immediate motivation for change (Schwartz, 1977a).

The fundamental question becomes one of the correct response of the brain to this internal stimulation. From a psychobiological perspective, the brain should either make modifications in the outside environment, leave the environment, or modify its interactions with the environment. Consequently, the intrinsic pain of the disturbed stomach keeps our behavior in check by forcing us to stop eating, or to not eat the dangerous food again.

However, for many sociological reasons, humanity is no longer content to follow its initial biological heritage. We may no longer feel competent to change either our environment or behavior—perhaps we no longer have the motivation. Because of our superior cortical structures and the consequent development of modern culture, humanity is no longer constrained to deal with disregulation by responding in the natural way. Instead, typical patients would rather not change their lifestyle or environment, the two factors (Stages 1 and 2) that together augment or cause the bodily dysfunction in the first place (Schwartz, 1973). Simply stated, humans choose instead to directly modify Stages 3 or 4, or both, by extrinsic biological intervention. According to the disregulation model, if the negative feedback mechanisms are removed artificially, the brain is freed to continue behaving in maladaptive ways that ultimately could be deleterious to survival and satisfaction. Lacking the stabilizing impact of negative regulation, the brain could go increasingly out of control.

Consider the simple stomachache. Modern society strongly reinforces the practice of taking drugs to eliminate stomachaches caused by the brain's disregulation. Antacid commercials of a few years ago exemplify this value system. For example, they depict an obese man stuffing himself with apple pies or spaghetti. When a functional stomachache follows, the obvious conclusion should be that the stomach and the rest of the body were not meant to be fed like that. The man's stomachache represents the biological feedback mechanism necessary to keep him from further abusing his body. Instead, what is communicated is "Eat—eat, and if you get a stomach ache, don't change your environment or behavior. Rather, eliminate the discomfort by taking a pill."

Or they depict a family at Christmas time, surrounded by crowds, trying with great difficulty to hold packages, rushing from counter to counter, continually inhibiting the resentment they feel at being bumped or otherwise offended. In the process, one member of the family develops a stomachache. The conclusion, according to the disregulation model, is that the stomach and the rest of the body were not meant to live like that. The person's stomachache represents the biological feedback mechanism necessary to keep him from further abusing his body. But this is not the message of the commercial. Instead, what is communicated is "Shop—shop, and if you get a stomachache, don't go home or change your behavior. Rather, eliminate the discomfort by popping a pill."

Simple antacids are a mild drug, and they do not always work. When they don't, other stronger medication is often prescribed to quell the pain. Then when the organ becomes so abused that an ulcer develops and internal bleeding occurs, does the person listen to his or her stomach and radically change his or her external environment and behavior? Often times no. What a person does instead is go to a surgeon for repair. Medicine is developing new and finer means of bypassing normal adaptive feedback mechanisms. A patient can have a vagotomy and totally eliminate the brain's ability to regulate the stomach neurally. And if the trend in modern medicine continues, people can look forward to the day when, if their stomachs continue to be an obstacle, they can simply go to their local surgeon and obtain an artificial stomach.

At that point the brain would no longer be constrained by the needs of a natural stomach. According to the disregulation model, this brain would be free to continue and even to expand upon the inappropriate disregulation initially causing the problem. The stomach is only one organ, however, whereas modern medicine is using the same strategy for all systems of the body. Modern culture often reinforces the idea that if the brain and body cannot cope with the external environment, they will simply have to undergo medical alteration to adjust. According to the disregulation model, this prospect, when carried to its extreme, would have serious consequences for the survival of the human species as we now know it.

The reader should not conclude that I am opposed to all biomedical interventions. On the contrary, a psychobiological perspective emphasizing self-regulation and disregulation helps to indicate under what specific conditions biomedical intervention is adaptive, not only in the short run, but more importantly in the long run. My point is that we should not come to the overly simplistic conclusion that the correction of Stages 3 and 4 of disregulation through biomedical interventions should be the *sole* approach to treatment. Instead, to keep the health and behavior of the human species intact, it may be necessary to accept the limitations and wisdom of the body as it is, even though this may require more active self-regulation on the part of our brains. A psychobiological perspective on biofeedback and behavioral medicine could play a role in this development.

SUMMARY AND CONCLUSIONS

This chapter has attempted to introduce the reader to a general psychobiological perspective of psychotherapy and behavior change. Since this perspective is by no means established or universally held, it must be viewed as speculative. It is not presented with the goal of providing a definite model for viewing psychotherapy as psychobiological therapy. Instead, it is presented with the intent of providing the reader with a framework for generating questions and speculations regarding directions that such a perspective may take in future research.

Miller (1975) has suggested a philosophy of science that should accompany future research in behavioral medicine. His proposal is that we should be "bold in what we try, but cautious in what we claim." Although the perspective presented in this chapter has been offered in a bold fashion, the reader will recognize that I have avoided drawing conclusions regarding the ultimate clinical value of particular behavioral interventions applied for a psychobiological purpose. Such conclusions are premature and can only be reached through future biobehavioral research.

Some of the concepts advanced in this chapter are deservedly controversial. The hypothesis that the psychobiology of the mind/body problem may be at the root of our difficulty in accepting an integrated, monistic, psychobiological perspective for interventions is one case in point. The thesis that all the brain is reponsible for creating an experience of mind and body that is separate from the brain, which leads to the "brain self-regulation paradox," will likely promote debate. So will the suggestion that biomedical interventions aimed at correcting problems initiated at Stages I and II may actually lead to increases in disregulation as an unexpected side effect of the treatment. On the other hand, it is probable that concepts of feedback, self-regulation, and disregulation emphasized in this chapter will continue to prove to be of value in psychobiological approaches to psychotherapy and behavior change, even though the examples presented in this chapter can only touch on the many complications involved in putting these ideas into practice. The concepts of multisystem patterning and emergent property may help to elucidate some of the conceptual and technical challenges facing researchers and clinicians.

We have examined psychophysiology as method, as mechanism, and as outcome, and I have illustrated how the view of psychobiology (broadly defined) as mechanism leads to the conclusion that all interventions involve behavioral and biological change, which ultimately are one and the same thing. If the reader has grasped the concept that viewing eye movements, for example, as behavior, physiology *and* neurology reflects different ways of viewing the *same* biobehavioral system, then it will have become clear how theories of intervention should not be based primarily on the specific methods used, but rather on similarities and differences in their underlying psychobiological mechanisms. The conclusion that all therapies involve biofeedback as a component is a direct extension of this principle.

I have described some of the components of the general pharmacologic model of drug intervention, and have pointed out some of the numerous instances where differences in language lead to miscommunication and counterproductive arguments between behavioral and biomedical scientists. The evolving field of behavioral medicine reflects an attempt to apply behavioral science knowledge and techniques to physical health and disease. To the extent that all disorders, both mental and physical, are ultimately seen as psychobiological, all medicine and all psychology must ultimately be seen as behavioral medicine. We are clearly a long way from reaching such a goal, but it is worth pursuing.

The revolution in conceptualizing health and disease may have far-reaching legal ramifications regarding who can practice what kinds of therapeutic techniques in what individuals and for what purpose. As it becomes more widely recognized that a "psychological" treatment like relaxation or modeling involves specific changes in peripheral organs that can have implications for health and illness, then therapists who use such techniques may be viewed as practicing "medicine." However, whether or not one classifies biofeedback, relaxation, psychotherapy (or for that matter, tennis lessons, education, or sailing instructions as medical treatments depends on one's definition of medical treatment. If medical treatment is defined in terms of *method,* which historically means the "laying on of hands," then all of the above would be excluded. However, if medical treatment is defined in terms of *outcome,* then the psychobiological approach outlined here illustrates how all environmental and human activities could ultimately fall into the medical treatment category. This issue is not simply one of semantics. It reflects a major, growing shift in paradigm (Kuhn, 1962), and we have only begun to recognize its many implications and ramifications.

REFERENCES

Alexander, F. Emotional factors in essential hypertension. *Psychosomatic Medicine,* 1939, *1,* 153–216.

Ashby, W. R. The application of cybernetics to psychiatry. *Journal of Mental Science,* 1954, Jan., *100* 114–124.

Basmajian, J. V. Learned control of single motor units. In G. E. Schwartz and J. Beatty (eds.) *Biofeedback: Theory and research.* New York: Academic Press, 1977.

Beatty, J. Learned control of alpha and theta frequency activity in the human electroencephalogram. In G. E. Schwartz and J. Beatty (Eds.) *Biofeedback: Theory and Research.* New York: Academic Press, 1977.

Beatty, J. & Legewie, H. *Biofeedback and behavior.* New

York: Plenum, 1977.

Benson, H. *The relaxation response.* New York: William Morrow, 1975.

Benson, H., Shapiro, D., Tursky, B., & Schwartz, G. E. Decreased systolic blood pressure through operant conditioning in patients with essential hypertension. *Science,* 1971, *173,* 740–742.

Bergin, A. E., & Garfield, S. L. (Eds.) *Handbook of psychotherapy and behavior change.* New York: Wiley, 1971.

Birk, L. (Ed.) *Biofeedback: Behavioral medicine.* New York: Grune and Stratton, 1973.

Blanchard, E. B., & Young, L. D. Self-control and cardiac functioning: A promise yet unfulfilled. *Psychological Bulletin, 1973, 79,* 145–163.

Cannon, W. B. *The wisdom of the body.* New York: W. W. Norton, 1932.

Cohen, D. H., & Obrist, P. A. Interactions between behavior and the cardiovascular system. *Circulation Research, 1975, 37,* 693–706.

Davidson, R. J., & Schwartz, G. E. The psychobiology of relaxation and related states: A multi-process theory. In D. I. Mostofsky (Ed.) *Behavior control and modification of physiological activity.* Englewood Cliffs, N. J.: Prentice-Hall, 1976.

Davidson, R. J., & Schwartz, G. E. Brain mechanisms subserving self-generated imagery: Electrophysiological specificity and patterning. *Psychophysiology,* 1978 in press.

Davidson, R. J., Schwartz, G. E., & Rothman, L. P. Attentional style and the self-regulation of mode-specific attention: An electroencephalographic study. *Journal of Abnormal Psychology, 1976, 85,* 611–621.

DeGood, D. E., & Adams, A. S. Control of cardiac response under aversive stimulation: Superiority of a heart-rate feedback condition. *Biofeedback and Self-Regulation, 1976, 1,* 373–386.

Ekman, P., & Friesen, W. *Unmasking the face.* Englewood Cliffs, N.J.: Prentice-Hall, 1975.

Ekman, P., & Friesen, W. Measuring facial movement. *Environmental Psychology and Non-Verbal Behavior, 1976, 1,* 56–75.

Engel, G. L. The need for a new medical model: A challenge for biomedicine. *Science, 1977, 196,* 129–136.

Epstein, L. H. Psychophysiological measurement in assessment. In M. Hersen and A. S. Bellack (Eds.) *Behavioral assessment: A practical handbook.* Oxford: Pergamon Press, 1976.

Esler, M., Julius, S., Zweifler, A., Randall, O., Harburg, E., Gardiner, H., & DeQuattro, V. Mild High-Renin Essential Hypertension: Neurogenic Human Hypertension? *The New England Journal of Medicine,* 1977, *296,* 405–411.

Fair, P., & Schwartz, G. E. Facial muscle patterning to affective imagery and the voluntary expression of emotion. *Psychophysiology,* 1977, *14,* 86 (abstract).

Feuerstein, M., & Schwartz, G. E. Training in clinical psychophysiology: Present trends and future goals. *American Psychologist, 1977, 32,* 560–568.

Fuller, R. B. *Synergetics.* New York: Macmillan, 1975.

Gaarder, K. R. *Eye movements, vision and behavior.* Washington, D. C.: Hemisphere Publishing Corporation, 1975.

Gaarder, K. R., & Montgomery, P. S. *Clinical biofeedback: A procedural manual.* Baltimore: Williams and Wilkins, 1977.

Galin, D. Implications of left-right cerebral lateralization for psychiatry: a neurophysiological context for unconscious processes. *Archives of General Psychiatry, 1974, 9,* 412–418.

Graham, D. T. Psychosomatic medicine. In N. S. Greenfield and R. A. Sternbach (Eds.). *Handbook of psychophysiology.* New York: Holt, Rinehart and Winston, 1972.

Hassett, J. *A primer of psychophysiology.* San Francisco: W. H. Freeman and Company, 1978.

Hebb, D. O. What psychology is about. *American Psychologist, 1974, 29,* 71–79.

Hilgard, E. *Divided consciousness.* New York: Wiley, 1977.

Hodgson, R., & Rachman, S. II. Desynchrony in measures of fear. *Behavior Research and Therapy, 1974, 12,* 319–326.

Izard, C. *The face of emotion.* New York: Appleton-Century-Crofts, 1971.

Izard, C. *Patterns of emotions.* New York: Academic Press, 1972.

Izard, C. *Human Emotions.* New York: Plenum, 1977.

James, W. *Principles of psychology.* New York: Holt, 1890.

John, E. R. A model of consciousness. In G. E. Schwartz and D. Shapiro (Eds.) *Consciousness and self-regulation: Advances in research. Volume I.* New York: Plenum, 1976.

Kallman, W. M., & Feuerstein, M. Psychophysiological procedures. In A. R. Ciminero, K. S. Calhoun, and H. E. Adams (Eds.) *The handbook of behavioral assessment.* New York: Wiley-Interscience, 1977.

Kristt, D. A., & Engel, B. T. Learned control of blood pressure in patients with high blood pressure. *Circulation, 1975, 51,* 370–378.

Kuhn, T. S. *The structure of scientific revolutions.* Chicago: University of Chicago Press, 1962.

Lacey, J. I. Psychophysiological approaches to the evaluation of psychotherapeutic process and outcome. In E. A. Rubinstein and M. B. Paroloff (Eds.) *Research in psychotherapy.* Volume I. Washington, D. C.: American Psychological Association, 1959.

Lader, M. *The psychophysiology of mental illness.* London and Boston: Routledge and Kegan-Paul, 1975.

Lang, P. J. The application of psychophysiological methods to the study of psychotherapy and behavior change. In A. E. Bergin and S. L. Garfield (Eds.) *Handbook of psychotherapy and behavior change.* New York: Wiley, 1971.

Lang, P. J. The psychophysiology of anxiety. In H. Akiskal (Ed.) *Psychiatric diagnosis: Exploration of biological criteria.* New York: Spectrum, 1977 in press. (a)

Lang, P. J. Imagery in therapy: An information processing analysis of fear. *Behavior Therapy, 1977, 8,* 862–886. (b)

Lang, P. J., Melamed, B. G., & Hart, J. H. Automating the desensitization procedure: A psychophysiological analysis of fear modification. In M. J. Kietzman

(Ed.) *Experimental approaches to psychopathology.* New York: Academic Press, 1974.

Lazarus, A. A. Multimodal behavior therapy: Treating the "basic id." *Journal of Nervous and Mental Disease,* 1973, *156,* 404–411.

Lazarus, R. S. A cognitively-oriented psychologist looks at biofeedback. *American Psychologist,* 1975, *30,* 553–561.

Leigh, H., & Reiser, M. F. Major trends in psychosomatic medicine: The psychiatrist's evolving role in medicine. *Annals of Internal Medicine,* 1977, *87,* 233–239.

Lipowski, Z. J. Psychosomatic medicine in the seventies: An overview. *The American Journal of Psychiatry,* 1977, *134,* 233–244.

Luborsky, L., Singer, B., & Luborsky, L. Comparative studies of psychotherapies: Is it true that "everyone has won and all must have prizes?" *Archives of General Psychiatry,* 1975, *32,* 995–1008.

Luria, A. R. *The working brain.* New York: Basic Books, 1973.

Lykken, D. T. A study of anxiety in the sociopathic personality. *Journal of Abnormal and Social Psychology,* 1957, *55,* 6–10.

Lynch, J. J., & Paskewitz, D. A. On the mechanisms of the feedback control of human brain wave activity. *Journal of Nervous and Mental Disease,* 1971, *3,* 205–207.

Meichenbaum, D. Therapist manual for cognitive behavior modification. Unpublished manuscript, University of Waterloo, Waterloo, Ontario, 1974.

Melzack, R. *The puzzle of pain.* New York: Basic Books, 1973.

Miller, B. V., & Bernstein, D. A. Instructional demand in a behavioral avoidance test for claustrophobic fears. *Journal of Abnormal Psychology,* 1972, *80,* 206–210.

Miller, N. E. Learning of visceral and glandular responses. *Science,* 1969, *163,* 434–445.

Miller, N. E. Behavioral medicine as a new frontier: Opportunities and dangers. In S. M. Weiss (Ed.) *Proceedings of the National Heart and Lung Institute Working Conference on Health Behavior: Bayse, Virginia, May 12–15, 1975.* (DHEW Pub. No. (NIH) 76–868). Washington, D. C.: U. S. Government Printing Office, 1975.

Miller, N. E., & Dworkin, B. R. Critical issues in therapeutic applications of biofeedback. In G. E. Schwartz and J. Beatty (Eds.) *Biofeedback: Theory and research.* New York: Academic Press, 1977.

Neisser, U. *Cognitive psychology.* New York: Appleton-Century-Crofts, 1967.

Novaco, R. W. *Anger control.* Lexington, Mass.: Lexington Books, D. C. Heath, 1975.

Patel, C. H. Biofeedback aided relaxation and meditation in the management of hypertension. *Biofeedback and Self-Regulation,* 1977, *2,* 1–41.

Penfield, W. *Mystery of the mind.* Princeton, N. J.: Princeton University Press, 1975.

Powers, W. T. *Behavior: The control of perception.* Chicago: Aldine, 1973.

Pribram, K. H. *Languages of the brain.* Englewood Cliffs, N. J.: Prentice-Hall, 1971.

Schachter, S., & Singer, J. E. Cognitive, social and physiological determinants of emotional state. *Psychological Review,* 1962, *69,* 379–399.

Schwartz, G. E. Voluntary control of human cardiovascular integration and differentiation through feedback and reward. *Science,* 1972, *175,* 90–93.

Schwartz, G. E. Biofeedback as therapy: Some theoretical and practical issues. *American Psychologist,* 1973, *28,* 666–672.

Schwartz, G. E. Toward a theory of voluntary control of response patterns in the cardiovascular system. In P. A. Obrist, A. H. Black, J. Brener, and L. V. DiCara (Eds.) *Cardiovascular psychophysiology.* Chicago: Aldine, 1974.

Schwartz, G. E. Biofeedback, self-regulation and the patterning of physiological processes. *American Scientist,* 1975, *63,* 314–324.

Schwartz, G. E. Self-regulation of response patterning: Implications for psychophysiological research and therapy. *Biofeedback and Self-Regulation,* 1976, *1,* 7–30.

Schwartz, G. E. Psychosomatic disorders and biofeedback: A psychobiological model of disregulation. In J. D. Maser and M. E. P. Seligman (Eds.) *Psychopathology: Experimental models.* San Francisco: W. H. Freeman and Company, 1977. (a)

Schwartz, G. E. Biofeedback and physiological patterning in human emotion and consciousness. In J. Beatty and H. Legewie (Eds.) *Biofeedback and behavior.* New York: Plenum, 1977. (b)

Schwartz, G. E. Biofeedback and patterning of autonomic and central processes: CNS- cardiovascular interactions. In G. E. Schwartz and J. Beatty (Eds.) *Biofeedback: Theory and research.* New York: Academic Press, 1977. (c)

Schwartz, G. E. and Beatty, J. (Eds.) *Biofeedback: Theory and research.* New York: Academic Press, 1977.

Schwartz, G. E., Davidson, R. J., & Goleman, D. Patterning of cognitive and somatic processes in the self-regulation of anxiety: Effects of meditation versus exercise. *Psychosomatic Medicine,* 1978 in press.

Schwartz, G. E., Davidson, R. J., & Maer, F. Right hemisphere lateralization for emotion in the human brain: Interaction with cognition. *Science,* 1975, *190,* 286–288.

Schwartz, G. E., Davidson, R. J., Weinberger, D. A., & Lenson, R. Voluntary control of patterns of facial muscle activity and heart rate: Effects on anxiety. Reported in G. E. Schwartz, Biofeedback and physiological patterning in human emotion and consciousness. In J. Beatty and H. Legewie (Eds.) *Biofeedback and behavior.* New York: Plenum, 1977.

Schwartz, G. E., Fair, P. L., Salt, P., Mandel, M., & Klerman, G. L. Facial muscle patterning to affective imagery in depressed and nondepressed subjects. *Science,* 1976, *192,* 489–491. (a)

Schwartz, G. E., Fair, P. L., Salt, P., Mandel, M. R. & Klerman, G. L. Facial expression and imagery in depression: An electromyographic study. *Psychosomatic Medicine,* 1976, *38,* 337–347. (b)

Schwartz, G. E., & Logue, L. Patterns of facial temperature during positive and negative emotions. In preparation.

Schwartz, G. E., Shapiro, A. P., Ferguson, D. C. E., Redmond, D. P., & Weiss, S. M. Behavioral and biological approaches to hypertension: An integrative analysis of theory and research. Submitted for publication, 1978.

Schwartz, G. E., & Shapiro, D. (Eds.) *Consciousness and self-regulation: Advances in research.* Vol. I. New York: Plenum, 1976.

Schwartz, G. E., & Shapiro, D. (Eds.) *Consciousness and self-regulation: Advances in research.* Vol. II. New York: Plenum, 1978.

Schwartz, G. E., & Weiss, S. M. *Proceedings of Yale Conference on Behavioral Medicine.* DHEW Publication No. (NIH) 78–1424, 1978.

Shapiro, A. K. The placebo effect in the history of medical treatment-implications for psychiatry. *American Journal of Psychiatry,* 1959, *116,* 298–304.

Shapiro, A. K. Placebo effects in medicine, psychotherapy and psychoanalysis. In A. E. Bergin and S. L. Garfield (Eds.) *Handbook of Psychotherapy and behavior change.* New York: Wiley, 1971.

Shapiro, A. P., Schwartz, G. E., Ferguson, D. C. E., Redmond, D. P., & Weiss, S. M. Behavioral methods in the treatment of hypertension: A review of their clinical status. *Annals of Internal Medicine,* 1977, *86,* 626–636.

Shapiro, D., Mainardi, J. A., & Surwit, R. S. Biofeedback and self-regulation in essential hypertension. In G. E. Schwartz and J. Beatty (Eds.) *Biofeedback: Theory and research.* New York: Academic Press, 1977.

Shapiro, D., Schwartz, G. E., & Tursky, B. Control of diastolic blood pressure in man by feedback and reinforcement. *Psychophysiology,* 1972, *9,* 296–304.

Shapiro, D., & Surwit, R. Learned control of physiological function and disease. In H. Leitenberg (Ed.) *Handbook of behavior modification and therapy.* Englewood Cliffs, N. J.: Prentice-Hall, 1976.

Shapiro, D., Tursky, B., Gershon, E., & Stern, M. Effects of feedback and reinforcement on the control of human systolic blood pressure. *Science,* 1969, *163,* 588–589.

Shapiro, D., Tursky, B., & Schwartz, G. E. Control of blood pressure in man by operant conditioning. *Circulation Research,* 1970, *26* (Suppl. 1), I-27-I-32. (a)

Shapiro, D., Tursky, B., & Schwartz, G. E. Differentiation of heart rate and blood pressure in man by operant conditioning. *Psychosomatic Medicine,* 1970, *32,* 417–423. (b)

Sperry, R. W. A modified concept of consciousness. *Psychological Review,* 1969, *76,* 532–536.

Sperry, R. W. Bridging science and values: A unifying view of mind and brain. *American Psychologist,* 1977, *32,* 237–245.

Stern, R. M., & Lewis, N. L. Ability of actors to control their GSRs and express emotions. *Psychophysiology,* 1968, *4,* 294–299.

Sternbach, R. A. *Principles of psychophysiology* New York: Academic Press, 1966.

Tellegen, A., & Atkinson, G. Openness to absorbing and self-altering experiences ("absorption"), a trait related to hypnotic susceptibility. *Journal of Abnormal Psychology,* 1974, *83,* 268–277.

Tomkins, S. S. *Affect, imagery, consciousness* (2 volumes). New York: Springer, 1962.

Weiss, P. A. The living system: Determinism stratified. In A. Koestler and J. R. Smythies (Eds.) *Beyond reductionism.* Boston: Beacon Press, 1969.

Whatmore, G. E. and Kohli, D. R. *The physiopathology and treatment of functional disorders.* New York: Grune and Stratton, 1974.

Weinberger, D., Schwartz, G. E., & Davidson, R. J. The psychophysiology of low anxiety: Interactions with repressive defensiveness. *Psychophysiology,* 1977, *14,* 87 (abstract).

Wiener, N. *Cybernetics: control and communication in the animal and the machine.* Cambridge, Mass.: M.I.T. University Press, 2nd. Ed., 1961.

Williams, R. B. Jr., & Gentry, W. D. *Behavioral approaches to medical treatment.* Cambridge, Mass.: Ballinger, 1977.

Wolpe, J. *Psychotherapy by reciprocal inhibition.* Stanford: Stanford University Press, 1958.

4

SOCIAL PSYCHOLOGICAL APPROACH TO PSYCHOTHERAPY RESEARCH[1]

STANLEY R. STRONG

University of Nebraska-Lincoln

APPROACH AND HISTORY

Psychotherapy can be viewed as a branch of applied social psychology. Psychotherapy is a setting for interpersonal influence, an area of study in social psychology. The major targets for change in psychotherapy are client behaviors in social interactions. How clients feel about themselves (vis-à-vis others), how effective they are in controlling themselves (in social interaction), and how effectively they control their environments (mostly other people) are aspects of behavior in social interaction, which is the major focus of social psychology.

The history of the application of social psychology to psychotherapy begins with Kurt Lewin (1948) as does experimental social psychology itself. Lewin's students have been foremost in generating concepts that are basic to psychotherapy, such as cognitive dissonance (Leon Festinger, 1957), social power (Darwin Cartwright, 1965), and causal attribution (Harold Kelley, 1967). Another student of Lewin's, Jerome Frank, entered the field of psychotherapy after completing several experiments on social persuasion with Lewin at Iowa (Frank, 1944a, 1944b, 1944c). Seventeen years later, Frank published his landmark book, *Persuasion and Healing* (Frank, 1961), which documented the contention that psychotherapy is a social persuasion and influence process.

Within a few years, several others were writing about the applicability of social psychological concepts to psychotherapy, especially of findings and

[1]I thank my friend and colleague Ronald Matross for his able support and contributions in conceptualizing this area of the discipline and identifying pertinent literature. I am grateful to him for his critique of the manuscript and suggestions for improvement. I also thank Deborah Seaburg for her assistance in assembling the literature and Cathrine Wambach for her help in conceptualizing the area. I am especially grateful to Carol Gersmehl for her skilled typing and editing of the manuscript in all its various forms. The manuscript was completed while at the University of Minnesota with the generous support of Student Life Studies and Planning.

concepts from Festinger's theory of cognitive dissonance. Arnold Goldstein published his studies on the influence of client expectancies on therapy (1962), and Allen Bergin completed the first "analogue" study applying persuasion and dissonance concepts to therapylike phenomena in his doctoral dissertation (1962). Leon Levy (1963) applied cognitive dissonance theory to psychological interpretation, the implications of which have not yet begun to be appreciated (Browning, 1966). In 1966 Goldstein introduced the extrapolating of concepts and findings of social psychology to psychotherapy and with Heller and Sechrest published an influential book which expanded his treatment of the subject (Goldstein, Heller, & Sechrest, 1966). A stimulus to the acceptance of these extrapolations was the growing success of extrapolations from the learning laboratory to behavior therapy (Lindsley, 1956; King, Armitage, & Tilton, 1960; Ayllon & Azrin, 1965). Especially influential were the studies on verbal conditioning which showed that, in interview-like settings, behavior could be purposively controlled by using concepts generated in experimental research (Kanfer, 1958; Krasner, 1958; Strong, 1964).

Strong's (1968) paper reasserted the influence-process view of therapy, and subsequent research in interview settings further linked the concepts of social psychology to therapy (Strong, 1971). Goldstein carried through a comprehensive effort to apply social psychology to therapy at Syracuse (Goldstein, 1971), and linkage research continues especially at Ohio State University (Lyle Schmidt and his colleagues), Baylor School of Medicine (Larry Beutler and his colleagues), and the University of Minnesota and the University of Nebraska (Strong, Matross, Dixon, and their colleagues). Other applications such as causal attribution theory are more recent (Strong, 1970; Kopel & Arkowitz, 1975) and are a major focus of this chapter.

In many respects the approach and format of this chapter are similar to that of Goldstein and Simonson (1971) in the first edition of the *Handbook*. When they prepared the chapter, research applying social psychological concepts to psychotherapy had just been begun. Much of their chapter reviewed research outside the psychotherapy literature and explored its applica-

tion to psychotherapy. In the seven years since then, more social psychologically oriented psychotherapy studies have been reported, but the number and diversity of these studies remains relatively small. Thus much of this chapter also focuses on major findings and approaches in social psychology and how they can be applied to psychotherapy. Specifically this chapter integrates and applies findings and concepts from the three theories in social psychology that have been dominant during the last 30 years: consistency theory, social power theory, and attribution theory.

GENERALIZING THEORY TO PRACTICE

Social psychology is a source of ideas about psychotherapy. Theories in social psychology are respositories of observed and hypothesized relationships among variables, and the question is how (and if) they apply to psychotherapy. To a limited extent, this is the problem of the external validity of experiments. Research is necessarily carried out in specific manifest situations. Experimental research is designed to test the adequacy of concepts or variables and their interrelationships as they apply to a specific setting. Positive results lend credence to theory (Aronson & Carlsmith, 1968, p. 21). Theory in turn carries concepts to new applications.

To determine if a theory has meaning for psychotherapy, we must conceptualize how the theory might apply to psychotherapy and test the resulting hypotheses in research in therapy or therapylike situations. Analogue studies that embody some of the characteristics of psychotherapy which are critical to the generalizability of concepts offer the advantage of high experimental control without interference in the delivery of psychological services, unlike similar research in ongoing psychotherapy. Once equipped with greater knowledge about the phenomena in question, the next step is direct study in psychotherapy. An integrated program of research that begins with analogue studies and systematically extends to ongoing psychotherapy, using both experimental and correlational methods, would be an ideal approach. Each research method has unique advantages and disadvantages. The adaptation and application of social psychological concepts to psychotherapy is advanced through the judicious intertwining of the advantages of each approach. The results of such research efforts are of interest to both social psychologists and clinicians. New methods and understandings result for clinicians, and for the social psychologist the adaptation is a strong test of the generality and utility of his theory.

The method described above generally has not been followed in research. Goldstein's (1971) programmatic analyses of therapist's attractiveness variables with clients is an exception and comes close to the suggested model of research. Goldstein and his colleagues systematically conducted studies in the laboratory and the field with college students and inpatients. They found distinct differences in how social attractiveness variables function in different circumstances.

A concern in analogue research and many of the studies reviewed here is the frequent reliance on deception to accomplish the manipulation of independent variables. To study social behavior in the laboratory, it is necessary to create a social reality for subjects, and often this reality is artificially created through deception. The use of deception in experiments is closely regulated by a code of ethics (American Psychological Association, 1973) and needs to be carefully monitored to prevent its unnecessary use and to prevent harmful effects on subjects. Although the use of deception in psychotherapy is not acceptable, the knowledge gained from experiments employing deception may be usefully applied in psychotherapy. Kopel and Arkowitz (1975) point out that the behavior principles derived in research of this kind go beyond the particular deception manipulation employed in the experiments. The application of the principles in psychotherapy can and should occur within the context of the client's needs and the therapist's sincere efforts to aid the client.

OBJECTIVES OF THERAPY

Social psychology and behavioral psychology have developed powerful ways to change people's behavior. But application of this knowledge requires a clear specification of what is to be changed. Although behavior therapy approaches have focused on specific targets of change, verbal insight psychotherapy approaches remain vague about change targets. This vagueness stems from an inadequate appreciation of the implications of the basic strategy for change of insight psychotherapy. This strategy for change is a two-step paradigm in which therapists' work with their clients changes clients in some way and clients use this change to make necessary changes in their broader lives. Clients are the agents of change in their lives, and therapists are like coaches that clients retain to help them do what they must. In this we find the assumption that people can control their behavior.

The assumption that people can exercise self-control is basic to psychotherapy. Psychotherapy is the business of helping people control themselves better and thus is based necessarily on understanding human behavior from the vantage point of persons as control agents. How do people control themselves and their environments? How can their control be improved? Unfortunately psychology as a base science for psychotherapy and counseling has been of little help to practitioners because it has concentrated on how environments control people rather than on how people control themselves and their environments. An increasing concern for self-control by some cognitive behavior therapists (Kanfer, 1975; Mahoney, 1974; Goldfried & Merbaum, 1973) promises to provide the practitioner with long-awaited help. Shapiro and Zifferblatt (1976, p. 519) have commented:

> A new paradigm of the person is emerging within the scientific community. This paradigm conceptualizes the healthy person as an individual who can pilot his or her own existential fate in the here-and-now environment, and who can have far greater self-regulatory control over his or her own body than heretofore imagined.

If we view psychotherapy as an intervention intended to strengthen the client's self-control, the targets of psychotherapy are the key elements of self-control. Unfortunately, our knowledge of these elements is minimal. Personal experience and the work of Bergin (1972), Kanfer (1973), Matross (1976), Miller, Galanter, and Pribram (1960), and Strong (1973b) suggest that the following key elements comprise a standard control sequence:

1. *Perception of Events*. What is perceived defines the range of opportunity for control. Distortion and ignorance mitigate against effective self-control.

2. *Processing Observations*. Processing observations has several components. "Are things as they should be" is a key evaluation and requires standards of judgment commonly known as values. Most of the troublesome affect clients experience comes from their e-valu-ation activities, and one of the key outcomes of psychotherapy is the convergence of the client's values to the therapist's values (Beutler, Johnson, Neville, Elkins, & Jobe, 1976; Pepinsky & Karst, 1964). Another key aspect of processing is determining the causes of the events observed, especially events judged as needing change. Insight-oriented psychotherapies surely derive their name from their emphasis on exploring and creating change in the client's perception of the causes of the events he has failed to control to his (or someone else's) satisfaction.

3. *Initiating Action*. Self-control is an active process and requires action to accomplish objectives. The clients must know how to accomplish their objectives, and the therapist teaches the clients skills in thinking, analysis, and interpersonal interaction. Action requires resolution to carry it through. Developing the motivation or will to carry out a change is critical to successful psychotherapy and is especially crucial for clients because their experience has been that, without the therapist's help, they have not been able to accomplish satisfactory self-control.

The three-step view of therapeutic processes suggests that the major psychotherapeutic targets are reduced distortion and ignorance in the client's perception of events, increased effectiveness in valuation and causal attribution in client's processing of observations, and increased skill and will to implement effective actions.

SOURCES OF CHANGE

Psychological Consistency

Several decades ago Porter (1950) emphasized that psychological counseling and psychotherapy take place inside the client. Strong and Matross (1973) elaborated this view and described therapy change as arising out of the interaction of psychological forces inside the client which the therapist affects with his or her remarks. The process that therapist remarks affect is the client's concern for psychological consistency. Persons strive for consistency among their actions, feelings, and thoughts, and this process of cognitive balance has been a major concern of social psychological research and theorizing (Aronson, 1969; Festinger, 1957; Heider, 1958; Osgood & Tannenbaum, 1955; Rokeach, 1973). The broadly replicated research finding is that if a person perceives himself to be in a psychologically inconsistent situation, for example, if he tells someone else something inconsistent with his own beliefs, he will change in some way. He may change his belief or attribute his actions to some compelling external pressures, or he may repent his action, seek restitution, and strive to avoid such actions in the future.

In his review of research generated by Festinger's theory of cognitive dissonance, Aronson (1969, pp. 26–30) suggested that the real source of change in most of the studies is not the inconsistency between two surface cognitions, such as "I told that fellow that the experiment was interesting, and he believed me" and "I was bored to tears in the experiment," but rather the significance of the two cognitions to the deeper beliefs of the person: his concept of the kind of person he is. The dynamic behind the incongruity of the two statements for the person is that, if they are both true, he is a liar, untrustworthy, and morally degenerate. If he does not hold this view of himself or does not want to, then he will need to operate on the two incongruent cognitions. An obvious response would be to attribute his actions to pressures in the experiment and from the experimenter, find the fellow he "misled" (sounds better doesn't it!) and make a clean breast of it. Experimenters prevent this mode of deflecting the threat to self-esteem. The subject could still attribute the act to the experimenter, but this would cast the experimenter, a scientist, in a morally degenerate position that most students find hard to believe. Also, experimenters have learned to make subjects in experiments of this kind feel responsible for choosing to lie to their fellows, and thus this mode of deflecting the threat flies in the face of their experience of having choice. The students are left with the choice of either deciding they are after all liars or that they overemphasized their boredom in the experiment. Perhaps there were some redeeming features in the experience that they had previously undervalued. And thus, when the students are asked after the experiment, their rating of enjoyment of the task has greatly increased.

Rokeach (1973) developed a hierarchical system of cognitions and actions and suggests that the concepts most resistant to change are the individual's self-concepts of competence and morality. He asserts that as a person elaborates these fulcrum or anvil concepts, the actions, attitudes, and values he perceives to be inconsistent with them will change. Rokeach posits that the perception of such inconsistency results in psychological discomfort (self-dissatisfaction, akin to cognitive dissonance) that continues to act on the person until the discrepancy is resolved. While Bem (1965, 1972) proposed a nonmotivational self-perception explanation for congruency effects, recent research (Brown, Klemp, & Leventhal, 1975; Pittman, 1975) demonstrates that at least some of the time psychological discomfort and arousal are present when inconsistencies are present. At this point, the congruency and self-perception views are interchangeable concepts when applied to the actor—they explain the same phenomena. The ultimate differential utility of the two concepts has yet to be determined.

Change in therapy arises out of the client's concern for consistency. The therapist's role is to induce discrepancy by identifying inconsistencies and bringing them to the client's awareness through reflections, interpretations, suggestions, instructions, and questions. Once the client accepts the therapist's assertions, the client's concern for consistency generates long-lasting, pervasive changes that eliminate the discrepancy.

Change resulting from therapists' remarks that help clients elaborate or realign basic values (self-concepts of competence and morality) can be dramatic. All of us are familiar with the pervasive, rapid changes emanating from religious conversion. Conversion is essentially adoption of a core value or morality system, and the changes in the person's living style result from the realignment to consistency of his thoughts, actions, and feelings. Rokeach and his colleagues have shown that elaboration of existing self-concepts leads to strong and lasting changes in behavior. For example, Rokeach and McLellan (1972) presented college students with data showing that persons concerned with civil rights valued both freedom and equality, while those against civil rights valued only freedom and "evidently care a great deal about their own freedom but are indifferent to others' freedom." This simple educational effort resulted in dramatic increases in the students' self-ratings of valuating equality and freedom and to higher levels of involvement in civil rights related efforts four months after the experiment. Other studies have shown changes in relation to racism (Rokeach & Cochrane, 1972), environmental issues (Hollen, 1972), locus of control (Hamid & Flay, 1974), and in values and effectiveness in teaching (Greenstein, 1976).

A basic component of psychotherapy is the therapist's belief that the client is a decent and worthy human being. Such acceptance and belief in the worth and morality of the client is embodied in "unconditional positive regard" and in the attribution method of persuasion (Gillis, 1974; Miller, Brickman, & Bolen, 1975; Strong, 1977). In this method the therapist attributes moral standards or values to the client (often in the face of contradictory evidence) that strengthen and elaborate the client's self-concept of worth and morality. The attribution of worth creates a basis or fulcrum from which change in the incongruous "surface" behavior is impelled. Realignment and elaboration of basic values and beliefs is fundamental to the efforts of psychotherapists, as is demonstrated by the convergence of client values onto therapist values referred to previously.

Change also arises from the therapists' remarks that bring into the client's awareness incongruencies among his thoughts, feelings, and actions, and with his (strengthening) self-concepts. The therapist's objective is to bring to the client's awareness existing incongruities by presenting new information and concepts, by creating "insight." An important source of incongruity in therapy results from the therapist's efforts to free client behaviors the client has not owned, behaviors he has attributed to external circumstances rather than to himself, for personal attribution. In the process of attributional change (discussed later), the client comes to view much of his symptomatic behavior as discrepant to his (emerging and strengthening) self-concepts and in need of change.

Therapist Power

The therapist's ability to influence the client arises from the client's perception that the therapist possesses resources that could help the client and the client's perception that he or she needs the help. The therapist uses his potential to influence the client to bring the client to accept as credible new information about himself and events in his life that the client subsequently uses to change himself (in search of consistency) and to change his environment.

Strong and Matross (1973) conceived of the ability to influence as therapist power, drawing on social power theory (Cartwright, 1965). Therapist power (P) is a function of the congruence ($\cong$) in the client's perception of therapist resources (R) and the client's perception of his needs (N) and can be symbolized as $P = f(R \cong N)$. Influence potential is controlled not by the existence of therapist resources but by the client's perception of the therapist's resources. Reputation and other sources of knowledge about the resources of therapists determine who will seek help from whom. One would hope that after contact, pertinent and accurate estimates of resources will result from therapeutic interaction. The therapist's ability to influence the client is also a direct function of the client's perception of his or her need for the therapist's resources. As a result, the client's dependency on the therapist is self-canceling. As therapy is successful and the client gains control of his problem, the need base of the therapist's influence power is eroded. The therapist's ability to influence has a specificity in the breadth of its effect because influence is limited to areas in which the client views himself as needing

help and perceives the therapist as possessing resources (Simons, Berkowitz & Moyer, 1970).

Dynamically, therapist power establishes the upper limit on the degree that the therapists can disagree with the clients' ideas and expect clients to accept their statements and points of view. The interaction of communicator credibility, opinion discrepancy, and opinion change is a basic topic in communication research (Hovland, Janis & Kelley, 1953; McGuire, 1969). One of the arts of therapy and a potentially fertile area of research is the ongoing relationship in the process of interaction between therapist power, interpretation discrepancy, and client acceptance or rejection of the therapist's views. Little research has been conducted on this process even though it was clearly described a decade ago (Levy, 1963).

The two major therapist power sources are credibility and attraction. Credibility arises out of clients' needs to solve problems and their perception of the therapist as knowledgeable of how to solve problems, such as the therapist's understanding of how problems are manifest in the clients' lives and the lack of ulterior motives to hurt rather than to help them. Attraction arises from clients' needs to have value consistency and their perception that the therapist has values similar to their own and thus is a source of testing value consistency. Attraction also arises from the clients' needs to be liked and accepted and the therapist's liking and acceptance of them. In addition, the therapists' physical attractiveness influences the clients' attraction to them.

The research reviewed below explores the credibility and attractiveness sources of therapist power. The review is restricted to studies intended to approximate psychotherapy and counseling settings. The vast number of studies in social psychology on communicator credibility, attractiveness, and attitude change are not reviewed here (see McGuire, 1969, for a review of the literature).

Credibility

Several studies have explored potential clients' perceptions of the resources of help-givers. Strong, Hendel, and Bratton (1971) asked college students to rate several campus help-givers and found that students viewed counselors as warm and friendly but less intellectual, analytic, cold, and critical than psychiatrists. Students viewed counselors as more appropriate for vocational-educational problems and psychiatrists as more appropriate for personal problems. Gelso and Karl (1974) replicated the study with more refined occupational categories and found that clinical and counseling psychologists were usually described in similar terms and were considered as appropriate for help with personal problems. College counselors, advisers, and high school counselors were thought of as less competent than persons with "psychologist" in their titles and as inappropriate for help with personal problems. Tinsley and Harris (1976) gave college students a questionnaire assessing their expectancies of counseling and found that the students expected to see experienced, genuine, expert, and accepting counselors they could trust. However, students' responses suggested that, should they need counseling help, their expectations for beneficial outcomes were modest.

In an effort to increase potential clients' perceptions of help-givers' resources, Gelso and McKensie (1973) presented information in short talks and written material to students in college dormitories about the appropriateness of seeking help for personal problems at counseling centers. They found that the talks and written material together increased the students' perception of the counseling center's appropriateness for personal problems but that the written information alone did not.

Several methods have been used to identify indicants of therapist resources for potential clients. Spiegel (1976), Atkinson and Carskaddon (1975), and Greenberg (1969) introduced therapists or counselors viewed by students in videotaped or audiotaped therapy excerpts as Ph.D.'s with extensive experience or as inexperienced graduate students. All three studies found that introducing the same interviewer with expert credentials as opposed to inexpert credentials resulted in the interviewer being rated as more expert, competent, and as someone the students would see for counseling with academic and personal problems. Atkinson and Carskaddon (1975) also found that students rated the interviewers as more knowledgeable about psychology when they used psychological jargon instead of concrete layman's language.

Schmidt and Strong (1970) asked college students to view videotaped excerpts of interviews of six interviewers with the same client-confederate, rate the expertness of the interviewers, and to indicate cues that they used of expertness and inexpertness. The following descriptions were generated from the students' cues and ratings.

The expert was attentive and interested in the subject. He looked at the subject; he leaned toward him and was responsive to the subject by his facial expressions, head nods, posture, and so on. He used hand gestures to emphasize his points. The inexpert was inattentive to the subject. He either did not look at the subject, or gave him a dead pan stare and was not reactive to him. He either did not use gestures, or his gestures were stiff, formal, and overdone. While the expert performed with an air of confidence, the inexpert was unsure, nervous, and lacked confidence.

The expert was organized and knew what he was doing. He structured the interview by suggesting possible topics and where the subject might begin. He described the task to the subject, and he explained that his own role in the interview was to facilitate the subject's discussions. The inexpert was confused and unsure of where to begin. He offered only minimal help to the subject and did not clarify his role in the interview. (Schmidt & Strong, 1970, p. 87).

Strong, Taylor, Bratton, and Loper's (1971) and Peoples and Dell's (1975) results support the suggestion running through the descriptions that a relaxed and responsive manner in the interview is related to perceptions of competence, expertness, and helpfulness.

Dell and Schmidt (1976) replicated the Schmidt and Strong (1970) study, using a wider range of observers and counselors. Their results were substantially in agreement with the earlier study. They found low to moderate correlations ($r = .23$ to $r = .43$) between expertness ratings and the performance of expert behavior as defined in the previous study. Importantly, they found larger correlations ($r = .36$ to $r = .75$) between perceived expertness and the students' willingness to refer close friends to the counselors. Although the Schmidt and Strong (1970) study found a negative relationship between rated expertness and the training and experience of the interviewers, Dell and Schmidt (1976) found no relationship at all, a still disquieting result. Because perceived expertness (credibility) determines willingness to accept influence, these studies suggest that, at least in the initial stages of contact, those who are trained to give help are no more successful in eliciting a willingness to be influenced than are those who are not so trained.

Strong and Schmidt (1970b), Kaul and Schmidt (1971), and Roll, Schmidt, and Kaul (1972) report similar studies of student judgments of videotaped interviews that explore perceptual cues of trustworthiness. These studies suggest that content acts such as superficial remarks, breaking confidences to others, and dishonest remarks affect students' ratings of trustworthiness in expected ways. The results of the latter two studies suggest that the counselor's manner, such as his gestures and facial expressions, is as influential on perceived trustworthiness as are content cues. Content and manner cues separately and together create significant differences in trustworthiness ratings for college students (Kaul & Schmidt, 1971; Strong & Schmidt, 1970a) and for white and black convicts (Roll, Schmidt & Kaul, 1972).

As a whole, these studies show that therapist credibility is an important variable in therapy. Potential clients have differential perceptions of the resources of various therapists for different problems, which probably affect who will seek help from whom. Gelso and McKensie (1973) show that these perceptions can be changed. Therapist behavior in the initial stages of therapy can affect clients' perception of the therapist's credibility.

Investigations of the relationship between credibility and change in therapylike settings were initiated by Bergin (1962), who obtained highly significant differences in attitude changes between high credibility and low credibility communicators on college students' rating of masculinity-feminity in an experiment purporting to measure various personality traits. Bergin's high credibility communicator was an experienced Ph.D. director of psychiatric assessment, situated in a well-furnished office, who used sophisticated clinical assessment tests which included physiological indicators to ar-

rive at his opinion. The low credibility communicator was a high school student who rated the subject in an experimental room in the basement of a campus building. Although these extremes do not exist in psychotherapy, the study demonstrated the impact of the therapist credibility power variable on influence.

Studies employing less extreme credential differences yield less extreme results. Binderman, Fretz, Scott, and Abrams (1972) introduced an interviewer to students as either an experienced Ph.D. psychologist or a beginning practicum student and found that college student subjects changed their personality ratings more toward the information presented in a test interpretation interview when they were interviewed by the expert than when they were interviewed by the inexpert. On the other hand, college students in Sprafkin's (1970) study changed their word meanings to that presented by an interviewer in a counselinglike one-interview analogue whether the interviewer was introduced as a Ph.D. or as an undergraduate student. Strong and Schmidt (1970a) found students changed their need for achievement self-ratings more in the direction advocated by an expert interviewer than an inexpert interviewer only when credentials (Ph.D. versus graduate student) and roles (expert versus inexpert) varied together. Neither credentials nor role alone created differences in opinion change. Strong and Schmidt (1970b) in an analogue test of the effects of untrustworthy content on credibility and influence in a one-interview analogue study obtained trustworthy rating differences but not opinion change differences.

Gutman and Haase (1972) tested the impact of credibility in a field experiment where students coming to counseling for routine test interpretation were interviewed by a psychologist who was introduced either as a Ph.D. member of the staff or as a graduate student in counseling training with the staff. The Ph.D. held his interview in a large, comfortable, prestigious room whereas the graduate student in training was relegated to a small, barren, windowless room. After the interviews, the students receiving the low prestige introduction to the interviewer reported on an opinion scale that they believed that they had learned more about their vocational interests and that the discussion had clarified their vocational goals more than did students receiving the high prestige introduction. On the other hand, the high prestige introduction students remembered more about what was presented in the interview than did the low prestige introduction students. Guttman and Haase's (1972) results support the power concept of credibility (the greater learning) and show predictable dissonance effects from seeing less prestigious interviewers (Tinsley & Harris, 1976).

Beutler, Johnson, Neville, Elkins, and Jobe (1976) asked patients in psychotherapy to describe the credibility of their therapist on a semantic differential scale after a mean of 16.5 therapy sessions. Ratings of therapists' credibility were found to be positively related to patients' self-rated improvement but not to changes in patients' attitudes toward significant areas of their lives. Changes in attitudes, while not related to ratings of improvement, were linearly and positively related to the initial discrepancy between the patient's pretherapy attitudes and the therapist's attitudes. Beutler's et al. (1976) results suggest that the credibility variable is operative in psychotherapy but they do not address the dynamic relationship between credibility and discrepancy in ongoing therapy. In a study of the ongoing process in therapy, Browning (1966) assigned 24 college student volunteers to either "high or low prestige therapists." The same therapist served in both conditions. After an initial interview devoted to orientation to therapy, each client received 24 interpretations spaced over two to four interviews. Browning found that a significantly greater number of large discrepancy interpretations were accepted by clients in the high prestige therapist condition than the low prestige therapist condition.

Credentials, especially a lack of them, can affect clients' acceptance of therapists' influence. This is especially true when inexpert credentials are combined with therapist behaviors that clients perceive as denoting inexpertness. Beutler's et al. (1976) research suggests that, in the psychotherapy clinic, the credibility of therapists may not vary sufficiently to account for differences in improvement but does vary sufficiently to be related to client satisfaction and perceived self-improvement. Apparently,

therapists tend to be perceived as sufficiently credible to make the discrepancy between clients' and therapists' attitudes the major variable in client change; this presumably has its effects through the discrepancies therapists' remarks generate in clients.

A variable not yet addressed in research is the effect of client need on credibility. The studies reviewed here held clients' (or client-surrogates') need for therapist resources constant and at rather minimal levels. Efforts to explore the impact of changes in need on seeking help and on responsiveness to therapist attempts to influence are clearly in order.

Attractiveness

Cash, Begley, McCown, and Weise (1975) have shown that physical attractiveness is related to potential clients' evaluations of the potential helpfulness of counselors. They asked college students to watch a videotape of a counselor describing himself. For one-half of the students, the counselor was cosmetically altered to be physically attractive, for the other half, the counselor was presented as unattractive. Two control groups of students heard the same descriptions on audiotape but did not see the counselor. When he was physically attractive, the counselor was rated as significantly more intelligent, friendly, assertive, trustworthy, competent, and more likely to produce a positive outcome than when he was physically unattractive. No significant differences were found between the two audio control groups who did not see the counselor.

Greenberg (1969) studied the effects of introductory information on a therapist's warmth and liking for the client on client's (or subject's) attraction to the therapist. Greenberg (1969) told college student subjects that the therapist they were about to hear in an audiotaped interview excerpt was warm or cold and found that the subjects rated themselves as more attracted to the therapist, more receptive to his influence, and more persuaded by his message when he was introduced as warm as opposed to cold. Goldstein (1971) found similar results in a similar study with psychiatric inpatients. Moving one step closer to therapy, Goldstein (1971) told college students in one study and psychiatric inpatients in another that the interviewer was warm or cold before they interacted with the interviewer in simulated counseling. Following an interview, college student subjects, but not psychiatric inpatients, rated the "warm" interviewer as more attractive than they rated the interviewer described as cold. Also in studies using simulated counseling interviews, Goldstein (1971) told college students (or psychiatric inpatients) that they were matched either with an interviewer who liked clients such as they or that no match on liking had been possible. Postinterview assessment of therapist attractiveness revealed that for neither group did the liking manipulation make a difference in perceived attractiveness of the interviewer. This series of studies suggests that "warm versus cold" preinterview introduction to therapists rather consistently affects attraction when subjects listen to therapists on tape but is less effective when subjects subsequently talk to the therapist.

The effects of perceived similarity on attraction have been studied by presenting similarity information before talking with therapists in simulated counseling interviews, therapist self-disclosures during simulated counseling interviews, and by matching on psychometric measures before therapy. Goldstein (1971) presented similarity information before simulated counseling interviews with college student subjects, as did Cheney (1975) with inmates serving sentences for public intoxication. In both studies, subjects were informed that the counselors to whom they would be talking had responded to an attitude inventory in either a highly similar or highly dissimilar fashion to their own responses. Postinterview assessments of the interviewer's attractiveness revealed that for neither college students nor the inmates was there a difference in attractiveness between the high and low similarity conditions. When using college student subjects watching videotapes, Spiegel (1976) also found that a preinterview manipulation of similarity was ineffective in producing differential attraction to the interviewer.

Murphy and his colleagues (Giannandrea & Murphy, 1973; Mann & Murphy, 1975; Murphy & Strong, 1972) explored the impact of counselor similarity self-disclosures on his perceived attractiveness in simulated counseling interviews. In the three studies, Murphy and colleagues varied the number of counselor self-disclosures during a short interview (for example, 0, 4, or 8 disclosures during 20 minutes). The findings of the studies were that an intermediate number of self-disclosures was maximally facilitative of client-surrogate self-disclosures, client-surrogate ratings of counselor empathy, regard, and congruence on the Barrett-Lennard Relationship Inventory (Mann & Murphy, 1975; Murphy & Strong, 1972) and client-surrogates' rate of returning for a second interview (Giannandrea & Murphy, 1973). Hoffman-Graff (1975) invited students concerned about their procrastination to an interview with expert counselors who, in the process of a structured 20-minute interview on aspects of the students' procrastination patterns, disclosed four times either experiences similar to the student's (i.e., procrastinating) or dissimilar experiences (always had completed assignments on time and other nonprocrastinating habits). She found that the students receiving the similar self-disclosures rated the interviewer as more attractive than students who received the dissimilar self-disclosures.

The above studies suggest that information on the warmth or similarity of a therapist before interview contact does not have much effect on clients' attraction to the therapist after the interview. However, the behavior of therapists in the interview, such as their self-disclosure (of similarity or dissimilarity) does affect client attraction to therapists after the interview.

Studies of the effect of client attraction to the therapist on the ability of the therapist to influence the client have obtained mixed and generally pessimistic results. Patton (1969) told student subjects that they would like or would not like an expert interviewer in a one-interview counseling simulation, and the counselors acted as if they liked or did not like the student in the interviews. He found that the subjects' ratings of attraction to the interviewers differed as expected and that attractive interviewers had somewhat more influence on students' opinions than did unattractive interviewers. Schmidt and Strong (1971) found no difference in the influence of counselors' opinions on students' self-ratings of achievement motivation between unattractive and attractive counselors in a one-interview counseling simulation, even though the attractiveness manipulation was very successful. In attractive roles, interviewers stated four times that they liked the same things the subject did and expressed liking for the subject in gestures and manner. In the unattractive role, the interviewers expressed four times dissimilar interests and attitudes and were cold and unresponsive to the subject. Sell (1974) in a similar study also failed to find significant differences in influence between interviewer attractive and unattractive roles. Strong and Dixon (1971) crossed attractive and unattractive interviewer role behavior with expert and inexpert interviewer introductions (experienced Ph.D. versus beginning graduate student) and also failed to find influence differences between attractive and unattractive role conditions with expert introductions. However, with inexpert introductions, the influence of interviewers when they played the attractive role was greater than when they portrayed the unattractive role both immediately after the interview and one week later. This result suggests that several of the other studies may have failed to show influence differences between attractive and unattractive communicators because of an overriding effect on the influence of the interviewers' perceived expertness.

Dell (1973) compared the effectiveness of sharply distinguished expert and attractive roles. His expert role exuded a task-oriented professionalism that included a high degree of structured questioning, evidenced a concern for complete information, had references to previous therapy or counseling experiences and training, and avoided overt warmth and responsiveness. His attractive role was defined by a high degree of warmth and responsiveness, with less structure and more emphasis on feelings and self-disclosures of similarities with the client. Following an experimental analogue interview, both roles were perceived as expected with the expert role rated as more expert and the attractive role rated as more attractive. The two roles were equally effective in inducing student subjects (self-identified procrastinators) to perform a behavioral action plan, although they tended to achieve most change when paired with an influence attempt compatible with the interviewer's role.

In psychotherapy, Goldstein (1971) studied the effects on attraction of similarity in interpersonal styles as tapped by Schutz's Firo B Scale. He administered the Firo B to pastoral counselors and psychiatric inpatients before the initiation of 12 weeks of counseling. Each counselor worked with a client who was highly compatible with him on the Firo B and one who was not compatible with him. The clients in high compatibility relationships rated their counselors as significantly more attractive than did clients in low compatibility relationships. Measures of behavior change on the ward, however, revealed no signficant differences between high and low similarity clients. In longer term psychotherapy, Beutler, Johnson, Neville, Elkins, and Jobe (1976) found that therapist outcome ratings were related positively to the similarity between patient and therapist before therapy, but only for therapists rated lower in credibility by their patients. On the other hand, patient attitude change was positively related to the degree of discrepancy between initial patient and therapist attitudes. Beutler's et al. (1976) results seem to be in line with other findings reveiewed here in that lower credibility therapists relied more on similarity attraction for influence whereas, overall, credibility and discrepancy were the major determinants of attitude change.

Attractiveness seems to have clear impact on change when credibility is low. High therapist credibility (expertness) seems to override attractiveness effects on client change. This finding seems to reinforce recent developments of peer counseling in that it suggests that attraction can function effectively as the therapist power base in the absence of credibility (expertness). However, change in psychotherapy requires the therapist to expose discrepancies in the client's behavior, and the potential for indirect dissimilar self-disclosure in the process of exposing discrepancies would seem to jeopardize perceived attractiveness and thus therapist effectiveness (Spiegel, 1976).

Inducing Discrepancy

Change in psychotherapy results from the application of therapist power to gain client acceptance of new information that is inconsistent with some existing client behavior (thoughts, feelings, or actions), and thus leads to change as the client reasserts congruity. For psychotherapy to have any effect on clients, therapists must introduce ideas discrepant from existing client ideas (Staines, 1969). Therapists introduce two kinds of information to clients. First, therapists bring to the client's awareness existing incongruencies among client behaviors and consequences of behaviors. The facts brought to the client's awareness may be aspects of events the client had not previously noticed, aspects he has distorted, denied, or repressed, or aspects he has attributed to external circumstances and thus not personally owned. The second kind of information the therapist presents that creates incongruency in the client is different standards for evaluating perceived events and different relationships and causal connections among event elements. This information can lead to changes in the client's processing of information, including different conceptions of his or her definition as a person. As the therapist makes the client aware of these ideas, the client experiences incongruity and changes. The effectiveness of the four methods of inducing descrepancy described below depends on: (1) the therapist's power or ability to have the client view the therapist's statements as credible, (2) the content in the life of the client to which the discrepancy inducing methods are applied, and (3) the artful abilities of the therapist to meaningfully and effectively combine the two.

Attribution Method

The attribution method operationalizes the therapist's belief in the client as a worthy, effective, and moral person. The therapist believes these are basic qualities of the client, attributes them to him, and evaluates and responds to the client's behavior in ways that communicate this belief to the client. The attribution method encompasses Rogers' (1959) unconditional positive regard and nonpossessive warmth.

Miller, Brickman, and Bolen (1975) devised a series of field experiments to contrast the effectiveness of the attribution method with other change methods and found that the attribution approach created a greater change that was maintained longer than the usual persuasion and reinforcement methods. For example, in one study a fifth

grade teacher commended her students in a variety of ways as being tidy and ecologically minded and anxious to do their part in maintaining order in their classroom. In another classroom, the teacher emphasized the disorderly state of the room and attempted to persuade the students to be more tidy. After several weeks of the campaign, the "attribution" treatment classroom was tidier than the "persuasion" classroom. More important, the attribution treatment classroom remained tidy after the treatment was discontinued while the "persuasion" classroom quickly returned to "normal."

In other experiments, Miller and colleagues worked with children who were having difficulties in math. When the teachers told the students that the students were able to do well and wanted to do well, the students improved and maintained their improvements. Children told that they must do better and study harder also improved but did not maintain the improvements after the treatment period. Miller and colleagues rationalized their results by contrasting the attributions of personal worth that the treatments implied. The attribution treatment assumed the students had the positive attitudes, ability, and desire to perform better than they were and that their poor performance represented deviations from their own values. The persuasion approach implied that the students were slovenly, had poor ability and poor desire, and must change. Change was consistent with the implied values in the attribution approach but inconsistent in the persuasion approach. Attribution treatment students maintained the changed behavior because it represented their personal values. Persuasion treatment subjects stopped complying when the environmental pressure maintaining compliance stopped.

The effect of the therapist's attribution of worth and dignity to the client in psychotherapy has not been directly assessed. Gillis (1974) and Strong (1977) discuss some applications of the method in therapy. Research on the relationship of unconditional positive regard and nonpossessive warmth are suggestive of its importance. In a laboratory study, Gross, Riemer, and Collins (1973) found that audience reactions indicating their belief that the subject-communicator was sincere and believed what he said, influenced the speaker's subsequent belief in the message he communicated. In therapy, the therapist's beliefs about what attitudes, values, and beliefs reflect the client's true personhood probably likewise affect what the client comes to believe about himself or herself. The attribution method is central to the effectiveness of psychotherapy as the client's basic self-concepts or beliefs determine what behavior is consistent or inconsistent and thus what behavior will change. As in the Miller, Brickman, and Bolen (1975) experiment, the therapist's firm belief in the worth of the client is discrepant with the client's flagging faith in himself and will thus cause the client discomfort— he is faced with the prospect of leaving therapy or coming to view himself as a person of worth.

Perspective

A factor in evaluation is the metric or comparison standards against which observations are judged. Ostrom (1970) labeled this the perspective aspect of attitudes and has shown in a series of studies that changes in the breadth of possible values or in the population of comparison leads to large changes in ratings of opinions and attitudes, even if the opinions and attitudes are not the content area of the persuasive communication (Ostrom, 1970; Steele & Ostrom, 1974; Upshaw, Ostrom & Ward, 1970). Ostrom has shown that it is not the content of attitudes or opinions that changes with perspective shifts but the ratings of the meaning of the content in light of the comparison group or perspective. Strong and Gray (1972) found that students' self-ratings of creativity were heavily influenced by comparisons with others in social settings and by the norms on psychological tests that a counselor presented. The Binderman, Fretz, Scott, and Abrams (1972) study, referred to previously, shows the same powerful effect of norms on the meaning of performance on psychological tests and the impact of test results on self-beliefs.

Hoffman-Graff (1975) found that although counselor similarity and dissimilarity self-disclosures affected clients' (students') attraction to counselors, the counselor self-disclosures also altered the students' self-ratings. Following the interviews, students receiving counselor similarity self-disclosures rated themselves as less procrastinating than they had before the interview, while those

receiving the dissimilar self-disclosures rated themselves as worse procrastinators than they had before the interview. Therapist self-disclosures provide social comparison data and thus increase or decrease patients' evaluations of themselves, the severity of their problems, the validity of their ideas, and even their self-esteem (Morse & Gergen, 1970). Burnstein and Vinokur (1975) suggested and found empirical support for the notion that changes in self-ratings that stemmed from perspective changes or social comparisons could be results of the recipient's self-persuasion in the process of deducing the rationales behind others' discrepant attitudes or opinions. These results suggest the role of deeper self-concept beliefs in the functioning of perspective changes.

Interpretation, Reflection, and Instruction

Staines (1969) argued that the impact of interpretation and reflection (empathy) in therapy is due to the discrepancy between the client's ideas and statements and those the therapist presents. Roger's (1959) description of empathy as dipping slightly deeper into the client's underlying feelings identifies the discrepancy value of the method. Harway, Dittman, Raush, Bordin, and Rigler (1955) developed a scale to measure the depth of interpretations that is based on the idea of discrepancy between client statements and therapist statements. Fisher (1956) found a correlation of $r = .87$ between the ratings of the discrepancy between therapists' responses and the clients' views of themselves and ratings of the same material for the depth of the therapist interpretation.

Interpretation focuses the client's attention on aspects of events and interrelationships the client has not previously examined and, when it is successful, leads to client acceptance of the views expressed and to client change (Levy, 1963; Browning, 1966). The relationship between discrepancy size and opinion change has been seriously addressed in communication research (McGuire, 1969) and in several therapy analogue studies (Bergin, 1962; Strong & Dixon, 1971). In general, "medium" sized discrepancies produce the greatest change. Small discrepancies often undertax the therapist's power to influence the client, and large discrepancies often overshoot it. Beutler,

Johnson, Neville, Elkins, and Jobe's (1976) finding that attitude change is positively and linearly related to the initial attitude discrepancies between clients and therapists suggests that the ongoing process of interpretataion and change in psychotherapy is limited ultimately to the discrepancy between therapist and client attitudes on relevant topics.

Research on the influence of the content of persuasive messages suggests, among other things, that interpretation and instruction strategies should thoroughly and adequately address rationales supporting the client's initial positions as well as those supporting the therapist's position (Hass & Linder, 1972; Jones & Brehm, 1970), and that they should be comprehensible (Eagly, 1974). Research on the content aspects of interpretation and other instruction efforts in psychotherapy is nascent (Hageseth & Schmidt, 1975; Levy, 1963).

Counter Attitudinal-forced Compliance

A way to induce discrepancy is to somehow lead the client to engage in an action that runs counter to his or her self-defeating beliefs and ineffective actions. Kelly's (1955) fixed role therapy flows from this principle, as well as Ellis' (1962) homework between therapy sessions and operant methods in behavior therapy. As we discuss in the rest of this chapter, the clients' perceptions of the circumstances under which they came to behave in the counter attitudinal way are crucial to the cognitive and long-term impact of the forced compliance performance. Kopel and Arkowitz (1975) lucidly discuss the implications of clients' perceptions of the circumstances surrounding forced compliance performance in behavior therapy. To ensure that performance will have the intended discrepancy-inducing and thus curative change-producing effects, clients need to perceive of themselves as having chosen to perform the acts and to perceive the acts as going against environmental rewards and costs, as having important consequences, and as flowing from their personal efforts. In the spirit of these considerations, Pliner, Hart, Kohl, and Saari (1974) and Zillman (1972) have shown that if minimal compliance or agreement can be achieved, the way is smoothed for larger action and attitude commitments. Once clients have opened themselves up by engaging in counter attitudinal ac-

tions, greater efforts can be induced based on clients' having agreed to perform the previous minimal actions. Client health usually results from a cumulation of many small steps. Actually, change for good or bad seldom occurs in any other way.

EQUIPPING CLIENTS FOR SELF-CONTROL

In the model of psychotherapy presented thus far, change occurs when a client encounters credible information discrepant with his beliefs, especially his core values or self-concept. If information is not discrepant or not credible, it will not produce change. A therapist initiates client change by introducing discrepant information to the client and lending it credibility through his or her behavior and characteristics. The therapist induces discrepancy and change for the purpose of helping the client achieve more effective self-control. A critical question is what information is useful to the client's efforts to increase the effectiveness of his self-control? Causal attribution theory addresses this question, and research results suggest the kinds of information needed to equip the client for effective self-control in psychotherapy. Much of the rest of the chapter explores the implications of attribution theory for psychotherapy.

Causal Attribution and Self-Control

The processes of control are to become informed, to determine discrepancy (variance) from a desired state, to diagnose the cause of the variance, and to act to control the variance (Strong, 1973b). Diagnosis of cause is key in the control sequence. The perceived cause of the variance becomes the change objective and determines the direction and form of controlling actions. Pragmatics has a great deal to do with effective self-control. Identified causes of important events must be modifiable to make control and change feasible. The actions or processes required to modify the identified causes must be within the capabilities of the person seeking control. Events whose causes are outside the capability of the person to modify are not amenable to his or her control.

It may seem that the controllability of events is a relatively simple matter to determine: their cause can or cannot be controlled. Actually, the cause of interpersonal and psychological events is not as straightforward as it may seem. Any event is chained to many other events temporally and spatially. Any event has many causes. The concept of cause is itself an abstraction that aids understanding and control of events (Strong, 1973a). A "cause" is an event that precedes the event of interest and that can be shown to have an invariant relationship to the event (Heider, 1958; Popper, 1961). If the cause can be prevented from occurring, the event of interest will not occur. If the cause does occur, the event of interest is inevitable. The concept of cause is conducive to control and prediction. Knowledge of chains of causes allows us to prevent or prepare for important events. It gives time to control.

Any event is preceded in time with as many other events as our discriminations allow us to identify, all of which could potentially qualify as causes. The event of interest could potentially be controlled by modifying any one of these causes. The key decision for persons attempting to control themselves and their environment is to identify a cause that they can modify to bring about desired change (Kelley, 1971a). In psychotherapy, insights that identify the causes persons can potentially control are essential to the helpfulness of psychotherapy to clients. Identifying uncontrollable causes may have some therapeutic value emotionally but cannot be a basis for client self-control.

The concept of attribution error in social psychology (Monson & Snyder, 1977) assumes that there is a correct attribution of cause. The correct causal explanation must describe the interaction of many cause factors and can be handled only by explanation at the level of the analysis of psychological forces operating in and on a person at a particular time, which is the field theory view Lewin (1935) urged decades ago. The problem for the person seeking self-control is to seize the cause that equips him to control the event of interest. The cause chosen is always a distortion of the complete causal picture. Both intuitive psychologists (persons) and sophisticated experimental and clinical psychologists commit errors in attribution that favor the tools for control at their disposal (Strong, 1975).

A key to successful psychotherapy is to lead clients to identify a cause of their problems that they can control. The cause must be something the person does in events that he could do differently, such as the way he perceives events, his thoughts, beliefs, or attitudes about and in the events, or his actions to others in events. These personal causes are amenable to the person's will and effort and, in turn, affect other events such as other people's behavior. Changes of these personal causes can create vast changes in the person's intrapsychic and interpersonal environments. Historical causes are not amenable to change; other persons' behavior and other external events are only indirectly amenable to change as a consequence of personal change, and certain personal causes such as inflexible abilities, traits, dispositions, and physical properties are not amenable to change: these causes are useless as causal focuses in psychotherapy, which is intended to enhance self-control.

Consequences of Causal Attribution

The importance of causal attribution lies in the directing effects of attributions on subsequent behavior, especially actions intended to control and emotional reactions. However, the effect of causal attribution on a person's control efforts has received little attention in research. It seems subjectively true and clinically obvious that what we see as the cause of an event we wish to change would heavily affect our next step. We would focus our attention on the causal element, determine how to control it, and act to control it. For example, the unfortunate event of my papers being blown off the desk leads me to scan for the cause. I quickly identify the open door, the open window, and the fan rotating at high speed as three possible agents causing the current of air that results in the disturbance to the papers. The rattling of the window leads me to believe it is the main culprit. I rise and slam the window shut. The papers settle down, and my attention returns to causal attribution.

Clinically, a distraught husband and wife in marriage counseling tell the counselor of their individual miseries. They describe their anger and resentment and each other's infuriating actions, which they have identified as causing their misery. Logically enough, they describe how they have attempted to control the other's actions through intimidation, isolation, assault, and punishment. As counseling proceeds, they increasingly grapple with their own attitudes of selfishness and pride as the causes of their misery. The change in attributed cause has redirected their control efforts (Strong, 1976, 1977).

The most provocative research on the impact of causal attribution on motivation and subsequent behavior is that of Weiner and his associates (Kukla, 1972; Weiner, Frieze, Kukla, Reed, Rest, & Rosenbaum, 1971; Weiner, Heckhausen, Meyer & Cook, 1972; Weiner & Kukla, 1970) and others in related studies (Dweck, 1975; Lefcourt, Hogg, Struthers & Holmes, 1975). Weiner and his associates studied achievement motivation, using the framework Heider (1958) proposed of performance as a function of ability, effort, task difficulty, and luck. Their point of view is that motivation to perform a task depends on the causes attributed to account for the outcomes of previous performances. Persons attributing success or failure to their own efforts (an internal and controllable cause) will be motivated to try to perform the task again, while those attributing failure to defects in ability or to task difficulty will not be motivated to try to perform a task again. Ability and task difficulty are invariant causal sources of either the person (ability) or the environment (task difficulty), and thus cannot be changed.

Dweck (1975) explored the effects of altering the attributed cause of failure on helpless children's reactions to failure. Dweck worked with 12 extremely helpless children, children whose behavior deteriorated badly in the face of failure. The children received training involving numerous trials on math problems on numerous sessions over 25 days. One half of the children experienced an "attribution" condition in which on 2 of the 15 tasks in each session they were programmed to fail, and the child was told that he or she should have tried harder. The other trials in the attribution condition were graded to insure success, as were all of the trials in the "success only" condition trials.

Following the treatment, Dweck found that the success only condition children still evidenced debilitating deterioration of performance following failure even though they had improved their performance during the training. On the other hand, the attribution condition children not only maintained their performance following failure, but in-

creased it. The children in the attribution condition voluntarily made statements emphasizing insufficient effort as the reason for failure. The other children continued to see failure as due to a lack of ability. These results are typical of the studies Wortman and Brehm (1975) reviewed on learned helplessness and psychological reactance. Results of a series of studies (Kukla, 1972; Riemer, 1975; Weiner & Kukla, 1970) suggest this same relationship between causal focus and motivation and support the proposition that individuals high in achievement motivation are more likely to take personal responsibility for success than individuals low in achievement motivation. These studies suggest that motivation to perform a task of any sort, including the work of self-change, depends on the person's viewing his or her own effort as responsible for the outcome. When the problem is seen as due to more permanent characteristics of the person, such as ability or personality traits, or of the environment, such as unchangeable others, he will not change but will revert to helplessness—the beginning state of many clients (Menapace & Doby, 1976).

Research on the effects of the source to which physiological arousal is attributed was stimulated by Schachter and Singer (1962) who suggested that the emotional impact of arousal depends on the source to which it is attributed. In a classic experiment they demonstrated that subjects identified the identical (drug-induced) physiological state as euphoria, anger, or emotionally neutral depending on the external cues that were provided about the source of arousal. The several studies that have explored the impact of attribution of arousal have shown that when a person is aroused and any of several explanations or sources of arousal are reasonable, the person's response to the arousal depends on the source to which he attributes the arousal (Calvert-Boyanowsky & Leventhal, 1975).

Storms and Nisbett (1970) demonstrated the impact of attributed cause on subsequent behavior in a study in which they led insomniacs to attribute their arousal at bedtime to an "arousal" pill (a placebo) taken as part of an experiment on dreaming. The persons attributing the arousal to the pill reported going to sleep significantly faster at night than those who, as part of the experiment, had received (placebo) pills that were described as having a calming effect. Storms and Nisbett reasoned that one of the contributing factors to insomnia was the person's emotional reaction (increased arousal) to emotionally toned cognitions to which the person attributed the initial arousal. The "arousal" pills provided a nonarousing explanation for the initial arousal, while the "calming" pills made the initial arousal even more alarming. Kellogg and Baron (1975) and Bootzin, Herman, and Nicassio (1976) were not able to reproduce Storms and Nisbett's findings, underlining the importance of the plausibility of information concerning the source of arousal (Calvert-Boyanowsky & Leventhal, 1975). Other studies have shown that subjects in experiments tolerate more shock and report less pain when their arousal is attributed to a "pill" (Nisbett & Schacter, 1966), and are more willing to risk electric shock for monetary reward when their arousal is attributed to white noise (Zimbardo, 1969) and other similar relationships (Dienstbier & Muntor, 1971; Loftis & Ross, 1974).

Pittman (1975) found that the source to which arousal is attributed strongly affects attitude change. Pittman exposed students to two sources of arousal: students chose to record a speech to be presented later advocating a position with which they did not agree, and they anticipated a second experiment entailing painful electric shock. He found that when the students were led to attribute their arousal to the speech (by a confederate), they changed their attitudes toward the speech position dramatically, whereas when they attributed their arousal to the upcoming shock, their attitudes toward the speech changed little. Pittman's results show the guiding effect of causal attribution on subsequent behavior, in this case attitude change. Greenberg and Frisch (1972) showed a similar directing effect of the motivation attributed to another for helping on subsequent attitudes toward the other and willingness to help the other.

In the control sequence, unexpected arousal should lead to information search, and the information search should terminate when a satisfactory cause of the arousal is identified. This reciprocal relationship between a satisfactory attribution and information searching is suggested by Girodo (1972). He exposed students to an 8-minute clip of the most gruesome and highly arousing scenes from the film "le Chien D' Andalou." He told some of the students that during the film they would be exposed to a gas from a nozzle in front of them that was basically harmless but that had side effects including increased breathing, heart rate, palpitation, and slight perspiration. Other students received the same exposure to the gas which he accurately described as compressed air. He said he was studying cognitive processes and that they would be asked about their reactions to the film. Students who received the "gas" explanation for their arousal reported significantly less arousal during the film than students who received no prior explanation for their arousal. The students who were given no explanation for their arousal attributed their arousal to the film and remembered significantly more of the details of the film than the "gas" students, suggesting that they were more sharply focused on the film, possibly searching for causes of their arousal.

These studies identify some of the effects of causal attribution on subsequent behavior. The cause attributed for an event affects actions, emotions, and attitudes. In psychotherapy, success in helping clients change their behavior is dependent on helping clients identify the causes for their difficulties that they can control or that facilitate their control. Research that explores the effects of causal attributions has only begun. Further research is needed to help therapists identify the causal attributions they should foster in their clients and the attributions they should seek to change.

Changing Causal Attributions in Psychotherapy

Changing the causes attributed for problems brought to therapy is a key task in equipping clients to control important events in their lives. The change occurs in the analysis of events in the client's life where the client is encouraged to elaborate and change his or her perception of the events and to reconsider the meanings of the elements in the events. Social psychological research on the process of attributing causes has identified many factors that have strong influence on the outcome of the process, and this research is reviewed here under the assumption that the processes identified in it operate in psychotherapy. This, however, may not be true. The research reviewed below focuses on how persons attribute causes for new events. In psychotherapy, clients face the task of changing their causal account from what they held when they entered therapy to another account that better equips them to control events. Psychotherapy as an attempt to change causal perceptions assumes that causal attributions are unstable and are alterable with new information. Only Dweck's (1975) and Storms and Nisbett's (1970) research assess this assumption. With these reservations in mind, nine possible sources of attribution change are reviewed that identify or suggest ways that causal attributions are or can be altered in psychotherapy.

Attention Focus

Causal attribution is an information processing activity and begins with information. The focus of attention determines what information is perceived and, therefore, limits potential attributions in that the cause must be constructed from what is observed (Arkin & Duval, 1975). Research results suggest that attention is focused by prior attributions, unexpected events, and perspective.

Prior attributions are the results of previous efforts to identify critical events and their causes. Control is enhanced if attention is focused on the elements of an event that has been identified by prior processing as crucial. Zadny and Gerard (1974) have shown that the intention an observer attributes to another focuses the observer's attention on the aspects of the other's activities that are relevant to the intention. In three experiments, Zadny and Gerard (1974) varied the intentions they informed student observers that actors had in skits the students observed, and found that students remembered more of the actions, events, and articles related to the intent they perceived the actors to have than did students who perceived different intents. The effect was found only when observers had been told the actors' intent before viewing the skits. Informing students of the actors' intent after they saw the skit did not result in selective identification, suggesting that the effect was due to selective attention during observation rather than selective recall.

Because of the channeling effect of prior attribu-

tions on attention and recall, it is likely that clients' recall of events is highly conditioned by their causal accounts of events. Reattribution of causes no doubt requires creative reconstruction of the events. Therapists need to help clients recall aspects of events they did not note earlier, as well as to introduce possible aspects of events clients do not recall to provide data for reattribution. As clients' perceptions of the causes of events begin to change, they can be expected to recall different aspects in current events. It seems likely (although Zadny and Gerard's data do not support it) that as clients begin to perceive new personal causes for past events, their recollection of the events and their role in them changes.

Unexpected events attract and focus observers' attention. Newtson (1973) found that after an unexpected event, the unit size of observation decreases and the finer units of observation lead to greater detailed recall and greater confidence in attributing causes in the events. Girodo (1973) found the same enhanced recall in his experiment described earlier. The effect of detailed observation of events on recall and on confidence of attribution seems basic to psychotherapists' interest in the details of their clients' lives. Detailed review surely enhances the therapist's attributions and may affect the client's retrospective reattribution of the causes of events in his life. Uncovering new and unexpected aspects of events should further encourage detailed examination of events.

Jones and Nisbett (1971) hypothesized that actors and observers describe events differently and attribute different causes for events because their perspective in events is different. To actors the dynamic aspects of events are in the environment around them. They attend to factors impinging on them, and effective control depends on accurate discrimination among the factors. For observers the same is true, except that actors are part of the observers' environment, and other persons are the most dynamic aspects of any observer's environment (De Charms, 1968). Because of the difference in perspective, Jones and Nisbett (1971) hypothesized that actors attribute more causal control to external factors while observers attribute more control to actors. This difference cuts through much of the attribution literature (Batson, 1975;

Cialdini, Braver & Lewis, 1974; Fontaine, 1975; Gurwitz & Panciera, 1975; Harvey, Harris & Barnes, 1975; Jones, Worchel, Goethals, & Grumet, 1971; Snyder & Jones, 1974; Stephan, 1975; Storms, 1973). For example, Gurwitz and Panciera (1975) randomly assigned students to either a teacher or student role. The teacher presented the student with anagrams and rewarded or punished the student for right or wrong answers according to a schedule that the experimenter determined. On posttests, students ascribed significantly more freedom to teachers in the situation than teachers ascribed to themselves, and students believed that teachers' performances in the anagram task were more informative of the teachers' usual behaviors than did teachers. On the other hand, teachers believed students' performances were more indicative of students' usual behavior than did students. Thus, both attributed more freedom and personal causation to the other as observers than they did to themselves as actors.

The attention focus of actors and observers can be reversed by reversing their perspectives. Storms (1973) showed actors (students) videotapes of themselves engaged in short conversations with others. He showed other students, who had previously observed the actors in the conversations, tapes taken from the actors' perspectives focused on the others. He found that both actors' and observers' attributions of situational or actor causes for the events in the interview were reversed by the reverse of perspective. Whereas immediately after the conversation, actors attributed more responsibility for the events in the interview to the situation and less to their own characteristics than did observers, after viewing the event from each other's perspectives, their causal attributions to the actor and to the situation reversed. Regan and Totten (1975) found that when observers of an actor in a get-acquainted conversation were instructed to observe the actor, they ascribed much responsibility for the events in the conversation to the actor's dispositions. When observers were instructed to empathize with the actor, they emphasized situational causes more than actor causes. Chaikin and Darley (1972) found powerful empathy or role-taking effects on perception of cause in a study where students, expecting to take different roles in

an event, arrived at different causal attributions after watching a film of the event.

These results suggest that one way of changing clients' views of the causes of events would be to ask them to look at the events from the perspectives of others who are involved in the events. Johnson (1971) has found role-taking especially effective in creating understanding of another's view of events, and some therapists use role-playing as a way of changing clients' views of their own role in events (Flowers, 1975).

Wicklund and his associates (Arkin & Duval, 1975; Duval & Wicklund, 1973; Wicklund, 1975; Wicklund & Duval, 1971) have shown that when actors (persons) are led to view themselves as objects of awareness, to focus more of their attention on themselves and their actions, their attributions to their own characteristics as causes of events increase. When actors' attentions are drawn away from themselves, actors attribute less causality to their own characteristics. Wicklund and Duval have also shown the same phenomenon for observers: observers' ascriptions of cause to an actor are dependent on the extent to which the observers focus on the actor as a dynamic aspect of events.

In psychotherapy, empathy allows the therapist to view events in the client's life from the client's perspective and thus to identify the elements to which the client attributes responsibility. Empathy allows the therapist to understand the client's causal system and equips the therapist with the information necessary to devise a treatment plan that is based on the client's psychological reality. Psychotherapy research suggests that the client's perception that the therapist understands the client's world as the client understands it increases the client's willingness to be influenced by the therapist (Truax & Mitchell, 1971).

Objective self-awareness is a vital part of psychotherapy. When a person focuses his attention on his role in events, he attributes considerable personal responsibility for the events to himself. Surely the therapist's attention to the client's feelings, thoughts, and actions in the events the client describes focuses the client's attention on himself and establishes a fertile situation for reattributing the causes of events to client variables. Role-taking, empathy, and objective self-awareness are powerful tools for inducing change in psychotherapy. Research is needed on how these tools can best be used to achieve purposive, positive change in the client's psychological reality and future behavior.

Concepts of Responsibility

A critical question in therapy is who or what is responsible for the client's problems. Fixing on one event as the cause of another event is a fiction supportable only for the raison d'etre of causal attribution—control (Strong, 1975). An event is always chained to many other events. For example, suppose that Sam, recently hired as a door-to-door salesman, rings a doorbell. Mary, a young mother, turns away from her baby whom she is bathing to answer the door. The baby turns her body and pitches off the unguarded sides of the bathinette onto the unpadded floor, lands on her head, and suffers a serious concussion. What or who is the cause of this terrible event? Sam's ringing of the doorbell may be the cause as this is the first event in the chain. Or perhaps the cause was the lack of sides on the bathinette, or the baby's own action, or the unpadded floor, or the fall pattern, which descended the head first.

The events are chained together, but they in turn each are chained historically to other events. Sam rang the bell at that time because his boss assigned him to that block and he finished his lunch early. He is a salesman because he is an alcoholic and couldn't hold his last job. Mary is inexperienced with babies and did not foresee the possible consequences of leaving her baby alone, just as the baby did not foresee the consequences of wiggling. But Mary has been forgetful and uneven in her care of her baby. Perhaps she resents the child's interference in her career plans and is unconsciously intending to eliminate this threat to her security. Mary's mother ignored her during much of her younger years and told her how uselsss she was, which now makes Mary's career very important to her. But why weren't there sides on the bathinette? The baby's father, Bill, was supposed to put them on months ago, but he hasn't managed it because he is at work all the time. Bill's work syndrome seems to be a result of his father's demands for excellence but may also be a symptom of Bill's dislike for Mary, or perhaps his resentment of Mary's attention being directed to their baby instead of to him.

Events are chained together temporally and spatially. Isolating the cause is a distortion that can help the attributer control events. Since each observer and actor has his own perspective to events, each may well differ in his causal attributions. Yet the process of attribution is the same. For each, the objective is to identify a cause that he can control. Because of this, the discussion of the determinants and consequences of attributed responsibility does not distinguish between studies of actors or of observers but assumes all of the findings are relevant to actors. Our concern is the client and his causal attributions: he or she is the actor and agent in therapy.

Given that seeing a single event as responsible for another event is a distortion of reality, we still observe that people do hold themselves and others responsible for acts. How is this done? Heider (1958) argued that people have invented the following five theories or concepts of responsibility to guide the determination of responsibility.

> *Global Association.* A person is responsible for an event if in some way he or she is associated with it. In our example, using this theory of responsibilty, the supervisor who hired Sam who rang the doorbell must share responsibility for the baby's accident, along with Sam, Mary, Bill, the baby, Bill and Mary's parents, and the manufacturer of the bathinette.
>
> *Extended Commission.* Persons are responsible for events their actions have in any way led to, whether the events could have been foreseen or not. In our example, Sam is definitely responsible for the accident because his actions led to it even though he definitely could not foresee the accident. All the other parties directly involved share responsibility according to this theory.
>
> *Careless Commission.* This theory of responsibility holds that persons are responsible for all the consequences of their actions that could have been foreseen—whether they were foreseen is irrelevant. This theory advocates judging people by what they do, not

by why they do them. The theory is harsh and unbending in that what one does is what one is. The theory is relied on to teach others, especially children, to become aware of the possible consequences of their actions and thus to encourage them to think first. With this theory there are no accidents. The theory would fix responsibility in our example on Bill and Mary. Both could have foreseen the consequence of their actions. They were careless.

Purposive Commission. Purposive commission requires that a person intend an effect in order to be responsible for it. The person must foresee the effect and commit the act in order to obtain the effect to be responsible for it. In our example, Mary is responsible for leaving her child in that she intended to leave the child and answer the doorbell. She did not foresee the accident and thus cannot be held responsible for it. Unconscious intentions come into play here. Did Mary unconsciously intend to injure her baby? Did Bill unconsciously intend to allow the possibility of injury, perhaps to punish Mary for not loving him?

Justified Commission. This theory holds that people are responsible for their actions and the effects of their actions only if there are no compelling external reasons for them to have committed the acts. I may intend to shock a college student in an experiment but, as experimenter, I have no choice but to carry out the prescriptions of the experiment. A college student may make a strong speech endorsing higher tuition, but she is not responsible for her action as she was paid $5 to do it. In the example, Mary may have unconsciously intended to injure her baby, but the shabby treatment her mother gave her exonerates Mary from responsibility for her act. Justification is a form of event chaining where the focus of control shifts from proximal events to the more distal events that caused the proximal events. In general, the guiding rule of thumb is that if most people would carry out the action given the circumstances (either situational or histori-

cal), then the person is not responsible but is justified in his action. A problem is determining what are justifying circumstances. What is justifying to some is not justifying to others.

Clinical experience and the research reviewed below suggest that most people hold a justified commission concept of responsibility. In therapy one of the key concerns is to free clients' behavior from justification so that their actions can be attributed to personal causes they can control. This objective could be achieved by removing a specific justification from a specific act or by altering the client's belief in justified commission. Many psychotherapy systems strongly emphasize personal responsibility for all acts, an existential point of view (Ellis, 1962; Mowrer, 1964; Strong, 1977). Alternatively, it should be noted that therapists could (and probably do) advocate different views of responsibility to achieve specific effects in their efforts to help clients. Exonerating clients from acts of the past or from current behavior reflecting past learnings could be accomplished by emphasizing the justified commission view or, as appropriate, the purposive commission view. Bringing clients to take responsibility for current behavior could be accomplished by discrediting the justified commission and purposive commission views of responsibility and emphasizing careless commission. Research is needed on the methods and effects of creating a shift in existential perspective in psychotherapy.

Alternatives and Prior Probabilities
A critical task in psychotherapy is to lead clients to perceive that they have a choice in how they behave, including their symptomatic behavior. Perceived choice is the basic determinant of personal responsibility and thus the exercise of self-control. Steiner (1970) referred to perceived choice as decision freedom, and several investigators have examined the determinants of decision freedom. A first requirement for the perception of choice is the perception of having alternatives (Harvey & Johnson, 1973). Having no alternatives justifies the person's actions and places responsibility for his or her actions on the circumstance that created the lack of choice. Studies have shown that a func-

tional equivalent of no alternatives is negative alternatives only, that is, alternatives none of which are attractive to the actor (Kruglanski & Cohen, 1974; Harvey & Harris, 1975). Wortman (1975) found that no knowledge of the consequences of alternatives is functionally equivalent to no alternatives. All of these conditions preclude the operation of the individual's dispositions and intentions in guiding his actions and thus leave his actions at the disposal of external forces.

Given at least one positive alternative, actors and observers perceive decision freedom to the extent that alternatives are equally attractive. Attractiveness is defined here as the desirability of the anticipated outcomes of alternatives. In general when one alternative is clearly more attractive than other alternatives, the individual is justified in choosing it because of the compelling nature of its outcome compared with the other alternatives (Ajzen, 1971; Harvey & Harris, 1975; Harvey & Johnston, 1973; Kruglanski & Cohen, 1973; Steiner, 1970; Steiner, Rotermund & Talaber, 1974; Trope & Burnstein, 1975). Persons attribute actions to personal causation only to the extent that the actions go against the expectations created by the perception of environmental forces. This is the essence of the counter attitudinal-forced compliance effects reviewed here.

Ajzen (1971) metricized the effect of prior probabilities on the information value of chosen alternatives in a study in which he asked college students to read a series of statements about individuals that listed action alternatives open to the individuals. He asked the students to indicate the probability that students would choose each of the alternatives, creating a prior probability for each action. He then asked different students to estimate the likelihood that the actor had each of several characteristics, given that he chose one or another of the alternatives of the given set of alternatives. Ajzen found that the amount of information a particular choice gave about the individual was an inverse function of the prior probability of the chosen alternative and a direct function of the prior probabilities of the unchosen alternatives. Only unexpected choices given alternatives of very different prior probabilities were useful, while any choice among equally probable alternatives generated

useful information. Trope and Burnstein (1975) report similar results. These results support Jones and Davis' (1965) theory of correspondent inferences. They hypothesized that observers attribute a personal cause (i.e., an intention) to account for actions to the extent the person is perceived to have selected from among available alternatives actions that are not accounted for by environmental pressures.

A therapist's task is to lead the client to perceive that he or she has (or had) alternatives to chosen behaviors (depression or the like). Directly or indirectly the therapist generates possible alternative actions given the circumstances and leads the client to consider them. The alternatives generated need to have positive qualities and must be realistic. The alternatives therapists generate often are what a person using the therapist's value system would do, for example, Ellis's (1962) rational man or Strong's (1977) responsibly loving person. Examining and changing the client's perception of the prior probabilities of chosen and unchosen alternatives will change the personal meaning of the event. Actions found to be selected from alternatives and not accounted for by external circumstances are available for interpretation as to their personal causes. The change in perceived prior probabilities arising from the generation of alternatives could either increase or decrease the client's perception of responsibility—the direction of change must rest on the therapist's judgment of what would be helpful to the client. Creating alternatives to generate perceived choice seems essential to successful psychotherapy and is an area requiring research attention.

Choice, Consequences, and Costs

Choice, consequences, and costs are major determinants of responsibility assignment for events given belief in the justified commission theory of responsibility. The theory posits that certain environmental "dispositions" compulse action such that the environmental disposition, not the actor, is seen as the final cause. Following orders, achieving financial rewards, avoiding harm, and growing up in poor neighborhoods, all identify external causal dispositions or forces, and if the observer believes that most people would comply with these external forces, a person's actions are justified, and he or she is not held personally responsible. In psychotherapy, identifying choice, consequences, and costs at variance with the client's initial perceptions should shift the client's perception of cause.

The most common method of studying the effects of justification is the counter attitudinal-forced compliance paradigm. With this method the effect of performance of a counter attitudinal act depends on whether the actor believes his performance was justified by external contingencies and on the negative consequences (or costs) of the act (Collins & Hoyt, 1972). For example, Hoyt, Henley, and Collins (1972) induced college students to write essays proposing that tooth brushing was unhelpful and damaging to the health. The experimenter told students in the high choice conditions that, while they were free to write essays either pro or anti tooth brushing, the experimenter had many pro statements and needed more "don't brush" arguments. The experimenter stressed the students' involvement in deciding to write the essays, their decision to help, and their choosing to help. The experimenter made no mention of choice or decision to students in the low choice conditions. Instead, the experimenter simply said, "What you are going to do is. . . ." Hoyt and colleagues found that students in the high choice conditions rated themselves more "anti" tooth brushing than those in the no choice conditions. The lack of choice served to justify the no choice students' actions and thus to remove their responsibility for their action. The effect of choice was most dramatic when the high choice subjects believed that their essays would have serious consequences (the essays would be used to convince school children not to brush their teeth, and they consequently would suffer more tooth decay). The effects of choice, consequences, and justification have been demonstrated in many other studies (Goethals & Cooper, 1972; Harvey & Mills, 1971; Heslin & Amo, 1972; Holmes & Strickland, 1970; Pallak, Sogin & Van Zante, 1974; Sherman, 1970b).

Although persons who feel they have a choice are more likely to maintain responsibility for their actions, several studies have shown that other external forces such as financial payment can remove responsibility by justifying the action. For example,

in a counter attitudinal study, Calder, Ross, and Insko (1973) led student subjects to tell other subjects that an experiment was interesting when it was terribly dull. Students who were led to believe that they had a choice in the matter and whose action had high consequences (they succeeded in convincing the next subject) rated their enjoyment of the experiment significantly higher than those who had no choice or low consequences. However, this effect was obtained only when the students received little reward for their act. When the high choice and consequences subjects received a large reward for their act (2 hours experimental credit versus 30 minutes), their rating of enjoyment of the task was significantly lowered. The reward or incentive served as a justification for the action, removing personal responsibility and the necessity for attitude change. On the other hand this study and others like it (Holmes & Strickland, 1970) have shown that when individuals feel they have no choice but to carry out an act, incentives (financial and otherwise) directly increase their rated enjoyment of the action. Thus, the effects of external rewards for an act on the actor depend on his perception of choice in carrying out the act. No choice leads to reinforcement effects, while perceived choice leads to justification effects (Collins & Hoyt, 1972).

In psychotherapy, clients often perceive that they have no choice but to behave as they do (be depressed, be angry with their spouse, and so on). Therapist enhancement of the perception of choice through the generation of alternatives is clearly needed. Once choice is perceived, the consequences of the action should be carefully elaborated. As clients come to view their behavior as having important consequences and costs to themselves and others, their concern for their behavior's personal meaning and for its control will increase, and the behavior will be fertile ground for interpretation. On the other hand, perceiving smaller consequences and costs of actions decreases personal responsibility and correspondent personal inferences. Surely, therapeutic change at times requires that clients decrease their perceived responsibility for events in order to decrease guilt and arousal to more manageable levels.

Rewards also affect perception of personal responsibility. Whereas costs and consequences affect perceived responsibility directly, rewards affect perceived responsibility inversely. Becoming aware of unseen or discounted rewards removes responsibility, but discounting rewards previously emphasized enhances perceived personal responsibility. It should be noted that when therapists lead clients to perceive that their actions were due to previously unseen or discounted rewards such as secondary gains, personal responsibility can be enhanced by showing that striving to obtain those rewards is unusual and not justified by the client's situation. The role of such causal "chaining" in therapy is discussed later. How these factors can be controlled in an interview and their impact in therapy are areas of needed research that have great potential for yielding practical help to therapists,

Rewards Achieved and Foregone
In the analysis of alternative actions, the positive consequences of the action chosen by the client and of the possible actions the therapist introduces are crucial to the intrinsic meaning of action to the client. In the studies discussed above, actions under the conditions of low justification plus important consequence (cost) led to attitude change in line with the action. Darley and Cooper (1972) reversed the usual forced compliance method and led college student subjects to choose not to write an essay counter to their beliefs (high schools should have enforced proper dress codes). By refusing, they also declined to receive a $1.50 (or $0.50) payment for their essays. Darley and Cooper (1972) found that all students strengthened their opposition to dress codes, and that the students who had been offered the higher incentive were significantly more opposed to dress codes and confident of their opinions than were students who refused the low incentive, or were the control (no reward) students.

Perceiving that one has chosen a course of action that goes against environmental constraints (has direct costs or foregoes rewards—opportunity costs) results in attitude change to support the choice. The action comes to be viewed as based on intrinsic motivation or interests. On the other hand, actions that are perceived as intrinsically valuable

are perceived as less intrinsically caused when external rewards occur that justify the actions. Benware and Deci (1975) asked college students to read essays expressing an attitude that they strongly endorsed (student control of university course offerings) to other students. One group of readers were paid $7.50 for their efforts; no mention of money was made to the other readers. Students who received payment for advocating their own personal views significantly decreased their allegiance to the views compared with the unpaid students. The negative impact of external justification on intrinsic motivation and performance has been demonstrated in the laboratory and in field settings (Deci, 1971, 1972; Uranowitz, 1975) and with children's liking for play objects (Lepper & Greene, 1975) and for games (Kruglanski, Alon & Lewis, 1972).

These studies show that, with the justified commission theory of responsibility, external justification moderates the relationship between actions and attitudes. Responsibility and attendant internal change increase when the person perceives that his or her actions are contrary to environmental forces. Responsibility and supporting internal beliefs and attitudes diminish when the person perceives that his or her actions are in line with justifying environmental forces. The critical word is *perceived*. Every action is attended with many and contradictory environmental forces, both real and imagined.

The therapist's role is to operate on the clients' perceptions of alternatives, consequences, costs, and rewards to facilitate clients' ability to control their actions. Many of the therapist's remarks will lead the client to perceive that he is personally responsible for his symptomatic behavior and will encourage the client to see symptoms as stemming from his attitudes, values, and motives—his self. This poses a severe dilemma because the client stands a good chance of becoming convinced that, as he is what he has done, he may as well give up. Bringing the client face to face with the personal implications of his or her symptomatic behavior will not serve therapeutic purposes unless it is seen as stemming from surface, controllable causes such as attitudes and beliefs that are at variance with his basic self-concept. The importance of the attribution method emerges here. If therapists do not strengthen the client's self-view as a worthy and basically good, ethical, wholesome person, attributional methods of analyses, instead of setting up the contradictions leading to conversion to health, will confirm the client's fears that he or she is after all hopelessly unworthy and unsavory. Therapy can indeed be for better or for worse (Bergin, 1963).

Unforeseen and Extreme Consequences

An outcome of event elaboration and analysis in therapy is that the client's behavior is found to have consequences he or she had not been aware of previously and that these unforeseen consequences are serious or extreme. In fact, clients will be in the unexpected position of taking responsibility for their symptomatic behavior as a consequence of lost justification. While the justified commission concept of responsibility clearly rejects the notion that a person is responsible for consequences of his actions he did not foresee, the results of research on the effect of unforeseen consequences on attitude change are uneven. Results of studies exploring the variables controlling the impact of the unforeseen on attitude change (Brehm & Jones, 1970; Cooper, 1971; Cooper & Brehm, 1971; Harris & Harvey, 1975; Harvey, Harris & Barnes, 1975; Pallak, Sogin & Van Zante, 1974; Sherman, 1970a) suggest that if an actor does not perceive she or he has a choice in undertaking an action, unexpected consequences have incentive effects only. The actor does not take responsibility for good or bad consequences. However, if an actor does perceive choice, the result of unforeseen consequences depends on whether the consequences are positive or negative, and whether the consequences appear to be results of the actor's efforts or of external circumstances. The effect of positive unforeseen consequences is to justify the action (Sherman, 1970a).

The effect of unforeseen negative consequences in the counter attitudinal-forced compliance situation is less straightforward. The results seem to depend on whether the subject students believe they created the unexpected circumstances or some external circumstances created them. Worchel and Brand (1972) and Pallak, Sogin, and Van Zante (1974) found that when students made decisions based on their own judgments that resulted in unforeseen negative consequences, they accepted responsibility for the consequences and experienced compensatory attitude changes. When the decisions were based on the experimenter's judgment, students did not accept responsibility for the unforeseen consequences and their attitudes reflected incentive effects only.

Kelley (1971a) implied that the more severe or extreme the consequences of an event, the more concerned an attributer would be to identify the cause (Harvey, Harris & Barnes, 1975). From the standpoint of effective control, events with severe consequences are compelling and urgent motivational forces. Causal attribution is a difficult task, and trivial events with unimportant consequences probably are not analyzed carefully and are often attributed to chance or accident. Important severe consequences, on the other hand, must be energetically investigated. Several studies have found that severe consequences are less likely to be attributed to chance than are mild consequences (Chaikin & Darley, 1972; Harvey, Harris & Barnes, 1975; Walster, 1966).

Although the pressure to find a controllable cause of severe consequence is understandably high, it is doubtful if severe consequences alone change the methods of determining causes. Failures to replicate Walster's (1966) finding that a driver was held more responsible for a severe accident than for a trivial one suggest that severity per se is not a factor in responsibility assignment but, instead, increases motivation to make some effective causal attribution (Shaver, 1970a, 1970b; Shaw & Skolnick, 1971). It is likely that severity leads actors and observers to analyze more carefully the conditions of choice and possible justifications. Differences in their perspectives on events suggest that their conclusions will be contradictory.

Unforeseen consequences or unappreciated severity of consequences have an energizing role in psychotherapy. The effect is large, since accepting personal responsibility for symptomatic behavior is an unforeseen consequence. By emphasizing the seriousness of the problems that the client's choice of symptomatic behavior has generated, the therapist increases the client's motivation and determination to find a workable cause and to do the hard work of changing. On the other hand, clients already too emotionally upset over their symptomatic behavior may be helped in effective problem solving by decreasing their perception of the severity of the consequences of their acts. The therapist's judgment and skill in the art of helping others is obviously crucial. The impact of unforeseen severe consequences depends on clients' concepts of responsibility, their perception of choice, and their perception of their personal creation of the consequence, all of which are amenable to therapist modification. Research is much needed to explore the intertwining of these processes in psychotherapy.

Consistency, Distinctiveness, and Consensus
Kelley (1967, 1971b) proposed that persons determine the cause of events by a kind of mental analysis of variance, where the attributer evaluates the event over time (consistency), stimuli (distinctiveness), and people (consensus), and that patterns of these three variables form "causal schemata" or templates that persons habitually use to reach causal inferences quickly and efficiently. McArthur (1972) and Orvis, Cunningham, and Kelley (1975) asked students to attribute causes for events in short vignettes in questionnaires and examined the impact of patterns of consistency, distinctiveness, and consensus information on their causal attributions. The dominant element of information in both studies was consistency over time. Inconsistent events were attributed to unstable circumstances but consistent events led to stable person or environment causal attributions. When the data patterns were incomplete, attributers assumed that the pattern described was consistent over time. When an event was thought of as consistent over time, it was seen as caused by the actor (person) if it was something the actor did with a variety of stimuli (low distinctiveness). If the action was unusual for the actor (highly distinctive), the event was attributed to some aspect of the stimulus (the environment).

Consensus information had an effect similar to but weaker than distinctiveness information. High consensus led to stimulus (environment) attribution and low consensus led to person (actor) attributions. Consensus is the justification variable and, considering the ambiguity of determining if an ex-

ternal pressure is compelling, the less powerful results for consensus are not surprising. Nisbett and Borgida (1975) found that consensus is not heavily relied on in making causal inferences. Attributers follow the "law of small numbers" (Tversky & Kahneman, 1971): the actions of one or two are readily taken as indicative of the justification value of external forces, while information of base rates in large populations is readily ignored.

Based on McArthur's (1972) and Orvis, Cunningham, and Kelley's (1975) results, the information required to change a client's causal attributions depends on the original inference. If the client believes his behavior is due to a special circumstance, event, or person, showing him a consistent pattern of similar actions over a wide spectrum of other persons or events would free the action for stable personal attribution. On the other hand, if the client views his action as personally caused, information that suggests he responds in that way only to a particular individual or circumstance, or that he has never behaved that way before or since, leads to external or circumstantial attribution. Following Nisbett and Borgida (1975), justification for an action and the consequent external causal inference is overcome by "uncovering" one alternative act the client could have performed that one or two others chose. Research on the purposive use of this kind of information in the interview has only begun (Strong & Matross, 1974; Matross, 1975) and is obviously needed.

Several studies have shown that knowledge of previous actions (high consistency and low distinctiveness) or of personal dispositions predisposing actions makes for rapid attribution of personal responsibility for similar current actions (Reisman & Schopler, 1973; Kruglanski & Cohen, 1973; Ross, Insko & Ross, 1971). While attributed dispositions based on past consistency make possible a rapid and confident causal accounting and predicting of actions, they also foster stereotyping and lock people into past relationships. For example, Regan, Straus, and Fazio (1974) found that observers quickly attributed the actions and consequences of actions of persons they observed as being personally caused or situationally determined (unstable), based on their prior liking or dislike for the actor. Positive, effective actions of liked actors were seen as caused by the actors, while their unpleasant and failing actions were seen as resulting from circumstances. When the observers disliked the persons, they attributed negative consequences of actions to the actor and positive consequences to unusual circumstances.

A client's previous causal attributions heavily affect his assumptions about and perceptions of events. The efficiency thus achieved mitigates against constructive changes and against the effectiveness of psychotherapy. In troubled relationships, past negative attributions mitigate against constructive changes in the relationship. Changing these causal attributions is the therapist's first order of business. This can be accomplished by generating alternatives to habitual client reactions through attacking the client's belief in the justified commission theory of responsibility, elaborating the consequences, costs, and rewards of client behavior, and by showing the client that while others do not respond to the other in the relationship as they do, the client responds to a variety of other people in the same way. Determining how the tools for change that have been identified in attribution research can be used for this task is a high priority for psychotherapy research.

Causal Chaining

Every event is woven into a fabric of other events such that determining *the* cause requires many assumptions. Any event seen as a cause of another event is caused by additional events. For example, I may decide that Bill wishes and intends to control Mary's actions, and his shouting at her is the method he has chosen for the job. But why does he wish to control Mary? Perhaps she is insulting and derogatory to him, and his reciprocal response attempts to restore equity in the relationship (Walster, Berscheid & Walster, 1976; Strong, 1977). On the other hand, Bill's intention surely stems from more lasting characteristics, perhaps, selfishness, pride, a need for dominance, or an inability to cope with unpredictable events. We may then inquire about the cause of these dispositions, and eventually we would examine Bill's developmental relationship with his parents. Thus Bill's behavior with Mary can be construed as chained to many internal and external causes that extend from the immediate to the deep and historical.

Brickman, Ryan, and Wortman (1975) initiated

research on the crucial phenomenon of causal chaining. They asked students to assign responsibility, control, and foreseeability to persons described as main parties in automobile accidents. In the description of the accidents, they systematically varied information of internal and external causes and immediate and more historical causes. For example, a car hitting a tree was attributed to either the driver taking his eyes off the road or a failure in the steering mechanism. For some subjects these immediate causes were then attributed to earlier causes. The driver took his eyes off the road because he was daydreaming or because a bystander waved at him to gain his attention. The steering failed because the driver, while warned that it urgently needed repair, had failed to see to it, or because a mechanic assembled the steering mechanism incorrectly.

When students responded to the immediate cause only, or to chains of consistent (internal or external) immediate and prior causes, Brickman, Ryan, and Wortman (1975) found that the internal causes led to much higher ascriptions of responsibility, control, and foreseeability than did the external causes. When the immediate and prior causes were of opposite kinds (internal immediate and external prior and vice versa), they found that responsibility, control, and foreseeability ratings corresponded to the prior cause. The influence of the opposite immediate cause was canceled.

Attributers appear to give more weight to the prior (deeper and more stable?) causes of behavior. Given that any event has multiple external and internal causes that are linked into history and "depth," what level of causal attribution in psychotherapy facilitates the most change with what problems? What effects do different levels of interpretation of cause have on the client, especially on the client's ability and motivation to change for the better? Although ability and motivation to change are maximized by attributions to immediate, personal causes, other therapeutic considerations such as workable level of arousal suggest that other levels of attribution have uses as well. A major difference between cognitive therapies (Beck, 1970; Ellis, 1962; Goldfried & Goldfried, 1975; Meichenbaum, 1975; Strong, 1977) and psychoanalytic therapies is that the cognitive therapies focus on immediate, effort-related, internal cause constructs, while Freudian therapies emphasize historical, deep, unchangeable cause constructs.

Effects Achieved and Foregone

Once a person's actions are judged to be his responsibility and thus an expression of his personal characteristics, what do his actions reveal about him? Content is deduced from what the person intended his actions to achieve and from a nomological inference system that identifies internal causes and their interrelationships (Levy, 1963). Jones and Davis (1965) hypothesized that an action's intention is deduced from the effects it achieves that rejected alternative actions would not achieve and, conversely, from the effects rejected alternatives would achieve that the action does not achieve. They hypothesize that the extremity and confidence of dispositional inferences would be greater the fewer the effects the chosen action attained and the more effects the rejected alternatives eliminated. Newtson (1974) systematically varied the number of effects unique to an actor's chosen and foregone actions in a vignette and asked students to indicate the degree various dispositions characterized the person. His results support the Jones and Davis hypothesis and suggest that attributer's judgments rely more heavily on effects unique to chosen alternatives than to rejected alternatives.

The content results of personal attribution have not been explored in attribution studies with few exceptions (Kelley & Stahelski, 1970; Miller, Brickman & Bolen, 1975). Attribution theory is process oriented, but the results of attribution processes are labels, entities, and interrelationships. A key challenge for psychotherapy research is to identify nomological systems that are effective in achieving changes in clients and equip clients for self-control.

SUMMARY

The concepts of how causal attribution is controlled that emerge from the reviewed social psychological research are a rich taxonomy for exploring and describing psychotherapy events. The possibility that purposive information display can facilitate planned changes in clients' thinking and subsequently their feeling and acting is tantalizing and urgently needs research. The concepts provide a level of description that facilitates the reexamination of psychotherapy to determine if the events described here can be identified in psychotherapy. The concepts should facilitate correlational research on relationships among measures of behavior change, the focus of attention, concepts of responsibility, perception of alternatives, perceived choice, costs, rewards and other consequences, chaining, and perception of consistency, distinctiveness, and consensus.

Especially needed are studies purposively exploring the processes described above under controlled circumstances in interviews that incorporate some of the attributes of psychotherapy. Experimental interview research with persons experiencing the minimal syndrome problems described previously would be promising. Although much of the research on these processes in social psychology has relied on deception to create the social reality necessary to study the processes in the laboratory, analogue studies as suggested here should need little deception to study the processes in interviews. The diversity of methods and frameworks used in the psychotherapeutic clinic is sufficiently broad to allow independent variable manipulation within the context of psychotherapeutic methods already in use. This kind of research should yield greater understanding of how to control information and how to purposively change causal attribution in interviews, and of the effects of these changes on client or client-surrogate behavior. Resulting increases in understanding will allow limited application in field experiments such as Paul's (1966) study, followed still later by full-scale applications in studies such as Sloane, Staples, Cristol, Yorkston, and Whipple (1975) report.

The purpose of the chapter has been to stimulate research on and thinking about psychotherapy from a social psychological perspective. The chapter has been organized around the model of psychotherapy shown in the Figure 4.1 and draws on three major theories in social psychology. Attribution theory suggests that clients do not con-

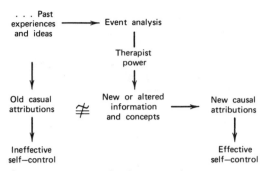

Figure 4-1. Psychotherapy change process model: New credible information from event analysis in psychotherapy which is incongruent ($\not\equiv$) with old causal attributions leads to changed attributions and effective self-control.

ceive of the causes of their problems in ways that enable them to control and change their behavior effectively. A task for the therapist is to induce clients to attribute their behavior to causes that will allow them to undertake effective action. Consistency theory suggests that the therapist induces the attribution change by introducing attributional information discrepant with the client's conception of events, role in them, and self-concept. The information is introduced in event analysis, the discussion and analysis of the events in the client's life. Social power theory suggests that the information presented in event analysis will not bring about inconsistency and, consequently, change unless it is viewed as discrepant and credible. The therapist's social or therapeutic power in his or her relationship with the client lends the information credibility. Therapeutic power arises from the client's perception that the therapist has valued resources that the client perceives himself to need.

While much has been learned about psychotherapy as a field of applied social psychology in the 17 years since Frank's (1961) book, the work has only begun. Conceptual development and research are needed on the self-control or self-regulation model that underlies the effectiveness of psychotherapy. Although sources of therapist power have been studied, research that views therapist influence as an emergent psychological force is needed, and examination of how the therapist's influence is best applied to induce discrepancy has not yet begun. The attribution

method that underlies constructive therapeutic change needs careful examination as well as the older but barely researched method of interpretation. Is the model of successful theapy as a conversion to health accurate? Research on attitude and value changes flowing from therapist influence is needed, in addition to a close study of the health value of different systems of values.

Psychotherapy as a field of applied social psychology is newly born. Time and serious conceptual and research efforts will determine its fruitfulness and longevity.

REFERENCES

Ajzen, I. Attribution of dispositions to an actor: Effects of perceived decision freedom and behavioral utilities. *Journal of Personality and Social Psychology,* 1971, *18,* 144–156.

American psychological Association. *Ethical principles in the conduct of research with human participants.* Washington, D.D.: Author, 1973.

Arkin, R. M., & Duval, S. Focus of attention and causal attributions of actors and observers. *Journal of Experimental Social Psychology,* 1975, *11,* 427–438.

Aronson, E. The theory of cognitive dissonance: A current perspective. In L. Berkowitz (Ed.), *Advances in experimental social psychology.* Vol. 4. New York: Academic Press, 1969.

Aronson, E., & Carlsmith, J. M. Experimentation in social psychology. In G. Lindzey and E. Aronson (Eds.), *The handbook of social psychology* (Vol. 2, 2nd ed.). Reading, Mass.: Addison-Wesley, 1968.

Atkinson, D. R., & Carskaddon, G. A prestigious introduction, psychological jargon, and perceived counselor credibility. *Journal of Counseling Psychology,* 1975, *22,* 180–186.

Ayllon, T., & Azrin, N. H. The measurement and reinforcement of behavior of psychotics. *Journal of Experimental Analysis of Behavior,* 1965, *8,* 357–383.

Batson, C. D. Attribution as a mediator of bias in helping. *Journal of Personality and Social Psychology,* 1975, *32,* 455–466.

Beck, A. T. Cognitive therapy: Nature and relation to behavior therapy. *Behavior Therapy,* 1970, *1,* 184–200.

Bem, D. J. An experimental analysis of self-persuasion. *Journal of Experimental Social Psychology,* 1965, *1,* 199–218.

Bem, D. J. Self-perception theory. In L. Berkowitz (Ed.), *Advances in experimental social psychology* Vol. 6, New York: Academic Press, 1972.

Benware, C., & Deci, E. L. Attitude change as a function of the inducement for espousing a proattitudinal communication. *Journal of Experimental Social Psychology,* 1975, *11,* 271–278.

Bergin, A. E. The effect of dissonant persuasive communications upon changes in a self-referring attitude. *Journal of Personality*, 1962, *30*, 423–438.

Bergin, A. E. The effects of psychotherapy: Negative results revisited. *Journal of Counseling Psychology*, 1963, *10*, 244–255.

Bergin, A. E. *Toward a theory of human agency.* Provo, Utah: Brigham Young University Press, 1972.

Beutler, L. E., Johnson, D. T., Neville, C. W., Jr., Elkins, D., & Jobe, A. M. Attitude similarity and therapist credibility as predictors of attitude change and improvement in psychotherapy. *Journal of Consulting and Clinical Psychology*, 1976, in press.

Binderman, R. M., Fretz, B. R., Scott, N. A., & Abrams, M. H. Effects of interpreter credibility and discrepancy level of results on responses to test results. *Journal of Counseling Psychology*, 1972, *19*, 399–403.

Bootzin, R. R., Herman, C. P., & Nicassio, P. The power of suggestion: Another examination of missattribution and insomnia. *Journal of Personality and Social Psychology*, 1976, *34*, 673–679.

Brehm, J. W., & Jones, R. A. The effect on dissonance of surprise consequences. *Journal of Experimental Social Psychology*, 1970, *6*, 420–431.

Brickman, P., Ryan, K., & Wortman, C. B. Causal chains: Attribution of responsibility as a function of immediate and prior causes. *Journal of Personality and Social Psychology*, 1975, *32*, 1060–1067.

Brown, D., Klemp, G., & Leventhal, H. Are evaluations inferred directly from overt actions? *Journal of Experimental Social Psychology*, 1975, *11*, 112–126.

Browning, G. J. An analysis of the effects of therapist prestige and levels of interpretation on client response in the initial phase of psychotherapy (Doctoral dissertation, University of Houston, 1966). *Dissertation Abstracts*, 1966, *26*, 4803.

Burnstein, E., & Vinokur, A. What a person thinks upon learning he has chosen differently from others: Nice evidence for the persuasive-arguments explanation of choice shifts. *Journal of Experimental Social Psychology*, 1975, *11*, 412–426.

Calder, B. J., Ross, M., & Insko, C. A. Attitude change and attitude attribution: Effects of incentive, choice, and consequences. *Journal of Personality and Social Psychology*, 1973, *25*, 84–99.

Calvert-Boyanowsky, J., & Leventhal, H. The role of information in attenuating behavioral responses to stress: A reinterpretation of the misattribution phenomenon. *Journal of Personality and Social Psychology*, 1975, *32*, 214–221.

Cartwright, D. Influence, leadership, control. In J. G. March (Ed.), *Handbook of organizations.* Chicago: Rand McNally, 1965.

Cash, T. F., Begley, P. J., McCown, D. A., & Weise, B. C. When counselors are heard but not seen: Initial impact of physical attractiveness. *Journal of Counseling Psychology*, 1975, *22*, 273–279.

Chaikin, A. L., & Darley, J. M. Victim or perpetrator?: Defensive attribution of responsibility and the need for order and justice. *Journal of Personality and Social Psychology*, 1972, *25*, 268–275.

Cheney, T. Attitude similarity, topic importance, and psychotherapeutic attraction. *Journal of Counseling Psychology*, 1975, *22*, 2–5.

Cialdini, R. B., Braver, S. L., & Lewis, S. K. Attributional bias and the easily persuaded other. *Journal of Personality and Social Psychology*, 1974, *20*, 631–637.

Collins, B. E., & Hoyt, M. F. Personal responsibility-for-consequences: An integration and extension of the "forced compliance" literature. *Journal of Experimental Social Psychology*, 1972, *8*, 558–593.

Cooper, J. Personal responsibility and dissonance: The role of foreseen consequences. *Journal of Personality and Social Psychology*, 1971, *18*, 354–363.

Cooper, J., & Brehm, J. W. Prechoice awareness of relative deprivation as a determinant of cognitive dissonance. *Journal of Experimental Social Psychology*, 1971, *7*, 571–581.

Darley, S. A., & Cooper, J. Cognitive consequences of forced noncompliance. *Journal of Personality and Social Psychology*, 1972, *24*, 321–326.

De Charms, R. *Personal causation: The internal affective determinants of behavior.* New York: Academic Press, 1968.

Deci, E. L. Effects of externally mediated rewards on intrinsic motivation. *Journal of Personality and Social Psychology*, 1971, *18*, 105–115.

Deci, E. L. Intrinsic motivation, extrinsic reinforcement, and inequity. *Journal of Personality and Social Psychology*, 1972, *22*, 113–120.

Dell, D. M. Counselor power base, influence attempt, and behavior change in counseling. *Journal of Counseling Psychology*, 1973, *20*, 399–405.

Dell, D. M., Schmidt, L. D. Behavioral cues to counselor expertness. *Journal of Counseling Psychology*, 1976, *23*, 197–201.

Dienstbier, R. A., & Muntor, P. O. Cheating as a function of the labeling of natural arousal. *Journal of Personality and Social Psychology*, 1971, *17*, 208–213.

Duval, S., & Wicklund, R. A. Effects of objective self-awareness on attribution of causality. *Journal of Experimental Social Psychology*, 1973, *9*, 17–31.

Dweck, C. S. The role of expectations and attributions in the alleviation of learned helplessness. *Journal of Personality and Social Psychology*, 1975, *31*, 674–685.

Eagly, A. H. Comprehensibility of persuasive arguments as a determinant of opinion change. *Journal of Personality and Social Psychology*, 1974, *29*, 758–773.

Ellis, D. *Reason and emotion in psychotherapy.* New York: Lyle Stuart, 1962.

Festinger, L. *A theory of cognitive dissonance.* Evanston, Ill.: Row, Peterson, 1957.

Fisher, S. Plausibility and depth of interpretation. *Journal of Consulting Psycholgy*, 1956, *20*, 249–256.

Flowers, J. V. Simulation and role playing methods. In F. H. Kanfer and A. P. Goldstein (Eds.), *Helping people change.* New York: Pergamon, 1975.

Fontaine, G. Causal attribution in simulated versus real situations: When are people logical, when are they not? *Journal of Personality and Social Psychology*, 1975, *32*, 1021–1029.

Frank, J. D. Experimental studies of personal pressure and resistance: I. Experimental production of resistance. *Journal of General Psychology*, 1944, *30*, 23–41. (a)

Frank, J. D. Experimental studies of personal pressure and resistance: II. Methods of overcoming resistance. *Journal of General Psychology*, 1944, *30*, 43–56. (b)

Frank, J. D. Experimental studies of personal pressure and resistance: III. Qualitative analysis of resistance behavior. *Journal of General Psychology*, 1944, *30*, 57–64. (c)

Frank, J. D. *Persuasion and healing.* Baltimore: Johns Hopkins, 1961.

Gelso, C. J., & Karl, N. J. Perceptions of "counselors" and other help-givers: What's in a label? *Journal of Counseling Psychology*, 1974, *21*, 243–247.

Gelso, C. J., & McKenzie, J. D. Effect of information on students' perceptions of counseling and their willingness to seek help. *Journal of Counseling Psychology*, 1973, *20*, 406–411.

Giannandrea, V., & Murphy, K. C. Similarity self-disclosure and return for a second interview. *Journal of Counseling Psychology*, 1973, *20*, 545–548.

Gillis, J. S. Social influence therapy: The therapist as manipulator. *Psychology Today*, 1974, *8*, 91–95.

Girodo, M. Film-induced arousal, information search, and the attribution process. *Journal of Personality and Social Psychology*, 1973, *25*, 357–360.

Goethals, G. R., & Cooper, J. Role of intention and postbehavioral consequence in the arousal of cognitive dissonance. *Journal of Personality and Social Psychology*, 1972, *23*, 293–301.

Goldfried, M. R., & Goldfried, A. P. Cognitive change methods. In F. H. Kanfer and A. P. Goldstein (Eds.), *Helping people change.* New York: Pergamon, 1975.

Goldfried, M. R., & Merbaum, M. (Eds.). *Behavior change through self-control.* New York: Holt, Rinehart & Winston, 1973.

Goldstein, A. P. *Therapist-patient expectancies in psychotherapy.* New York: Pergamon Press, 1962.

Goldstein, A. P. Psychotherapy research by extrapolation from social psychology. *Journal of Counseling Psychology*, 1966, *13*, 38–45.

Goldstein, A. P. *Psychotherapeutic attraction.* New York: Pergamon Press, 1971.

Goldstein, A. P., Heller, K., & Sechrest, L. B. *Psychotherapy and the psychology of behavior change.* New York: Wiley, 1966.

Goldstein, A. P., & Simonson, N. R. Social psychological approaches to psychotherapy research. In A. Bergin and S. Garfield (Eds.), *Handbook of psychotherapy and behavior change.* New York: Wiley, 1971.

Greenberg, M. S., & Frisch, D. M. Effect of intentionality on willingness to reciprocate a favor. *Journal of Experimental Social Psychology*, 1972, *8*, 99–111.

Greenberg, R. P. Effects of presession information on perception of the therapist and receptivity to influence in a psychotheapy analogue. *Journal of Consulting and Clinical Psychology*, 1969, *33*, 425–429.

Greenstein, T. Behavior change through value self-confrontation: A field experiment. *Journal of Personality and Social Psychology*, 1976, *34*, 254–262.

Gross, A. E., Riemer, B. S., & Collins, B. E. Audience reaction as a determinant of the speaker's self-persuasion. *Journal of Experimental Social Psychology*, 1973, *9*, 246–256.

Gurwitz, S. B., & Panciera, L. Attributions of freedom by actors and observers. *Journal of Personality and Social Psychology*, 1975, *32*, 531–539.

Guttman, M. A., & Haase, R. F. Effect of experimentally induced sets of high and low 'expertness' during brief vocational counseling. *Counselor Education and Supervision*, 1972, *11*, 171–178.

Hageseth, J. A., & Schmidt, L. D. Interviewee intelligence, explicitness of interviewer conclusions and attitude change in a counseling analogue. *Journal of Counseling Psychology*, 1975, *22*, 483–488.

Hamid, P. N., & Flay, B. R. Changes in locus of control as a function of value modification. *British Journal of Social and Clinical Psychology*, 1974, *13*, 143–150.

Harris, B., & Harvey, J. H. Self-attributed choice as a function of the consequence of a decision. *Journal of Personality and Social Psychology*, 1975, *31*, 1013–1019.

Harvey, J. H., & Harris, B. Determinants of perceived choice and the relationship between perceived choice and expectancy about feelings of internal control. *Journal of Personality and Social Psychology*, 1975, *31*, 101–106.

Harvey, J. H., Harris, B., & Barnes, R. D. Actor-observer differences in the perceptions of responsibility and freedom. *Journal of Personality and Social Psychology*, 1975, *32*, 22–28.

Harvey, J. H., & Johnston, S. Determinants of the perception of choice. *Journal of Experimental Social Psychology*, 1973, *9*, 164–179.

Harvey, J., & Mills, J. Effect of a difficult opportunity to revoke a counterattitudinal action upon attitude change. *Journal of Personality and Social Psychology*, 1971, *18*, 201–209.

Harway, N. I., Dittman, A. T., Raush, H. L., Bordin, E. S., & Rigler, D. The measurement of depth of interpretation. *Journal of Consulting Psychology*, 1955, *19*, 247–253.

Hass, R. G., & Linder, D. E. Counterargument availability and the effects of message structure on persuasion. *Journal of Personality and Social Psychology*, 1972, *23*, 219–233.

Heider, F. *The psychology of interpersonal relations.* New York: Wiley, 1958.

Heslin, R., & Amo, M. F. Detailed test of the reinforcement-dissonance controversy in the counter-attitudinal advocacy situation. Journal of Personality and Social Psychology, 1972, *23*, 234–242.

Hoffman-Graff, M. A. *Sex pairing and self-disclosure in counseling.* Unpublished doctoral dissertation, University of Minnesota, 1975.

Hollen, C. C. Value change, perceived instrumentality, and attitude change (Doctoral dissertation, Michigan State University, 1972). *Dissertation Abstracts International*, 1972, *33*, 899B.

Holmes, J. G., & Strickland, L. H. Choice freedom and confirmation of incentive expectancy as determinants of attitude change. *Journal of Personality and Social Psychology*, 1970, *14*, 39–45.

Hovland, C. I., Janis, I. L., & Kelley, H. H. *Communica-*

tion and persuasion: Psychological studies of opinion change. New Haven: Yale University Press, 1953.

Hoyt, M. F., Henley, M. D., & Collins, B. E. Studies in forced compliance: Confluence of choice and consequence on attitude change. Journal of Personality and Social Psychology, 1972, 23, 205–210.

Johnson, D. W. Role reversal: A summary and review of the research. International Journal of Group Tensions, 1971, 1, 318–334.

Jones, E. F., & Davis, K. E. From acts to dispositions: The attribution process in person perception. In L. Berkowitz (Ed.), Advances in experimental social psychology. Vol. 2. New York: Academic Press, 1965.

Jones, E. E., & Nisbett, R. E. The actor and the observer: Divergent perceptions of the causes of behavior. In E. E. Jones, D. E. Kanouse, H. H. Kelley, R. E. Nisbett, S. Valins, and B. Weiner (Eds.), Attribution: Perceiving the causes of behavior. Morristown, N. J.: General Learning Press, 1971.

Jones, E. E., Worchel, S., Goethals, G. R., & Grumet, J. F. Prior expectancy and behavioral extremity as determinants of attitude attribution. Journal of Experimental Social Psychology, 1971, 7, 59–80.

Jones, R. A., & Brehm, J. W. Persuasiveness of one- and two-sided communications as a function of awareness there are two sides. Journal of Experimental Social Psychology, 1970, 6, 47–56.

Kanfer, F. H. Verbal conditioning: reinforcement schedules and experimenter influence. Psychological Reports, 1958, 4, 443–452.

Kanfer, F. H. Self-regulation: Research, issues, and speculations. In M. R. Goldfried and M. Merbaum (Eds.), Behavior change through self-control. New York: Holt, Rinehart & Winston, 1973.

Kanfer, F. H. Self-management methods. In F. Kanfer and A. Goldstein (Eds.), Helping people change. New York: Pergamon, 1975.

Kaul, T. J., & Schmidt, L. D. Dimensions of interviewer trustworthiness. Journal of Counseling Psychology. 1971, 18, 542–548.

Kelley, H. H. Attribution theory in social psychology. In D. Levine (Ed.), Nebraska symposium on motivation, 1967. Lincoln: University of Nebraska Press, 1967.

Kelley, H. H. Attribution in social interaction. In E. E. Jones, D. E. Kanouse, H. H. Kelley, R. E. Nisbett, S. Valins, and B. Weiner (Eds.), Attribution: Perceiving the causes of behavior. Morristown, N. J.: General Learning Press, 1971a.

Kelley, H. H. Causal schemata and the attribution process. in E. E. Jones, D. E. Kanouse, H. H. Kelley, R. E. Nisbett, S. Valins, and B. Weiner (Eds.), Attribution: Perceiving the causes of behavior. Morristown, N. J.: General Learning Press, 1971b.

Kelley, H. H., & Stahelski, A. J. The inference of intentions from moves in the prisoner's dilemma game. Journal of Experimental Social Psychology, 1970, 6, 401–419.

Kellogg, R., & Baron, R. S. Attribution theory, insomnia, and the reverse placebo effect: A reversal of Storms and Nisbett's findings. Journal of Personality and Social Psychology, 1975, 32, 231–236.

Kelly, G. A. The psychology of personal constructs. Vol. 1. New York: W. W. Norton, 1955.

King, G. F., Armitage, S. G., & Tilton, J. R. A therapeutic approach to schizophrenics of extreme pathology: An operant-interpersonal method. Journal of Abnormal and Social Psychology, 1960, 61, 276–286.

Kopel, S., & Arkowitz, H. The role of attribution and self-perception in behavior change: Implications for behavior therapy. Genetic Psychology Monographs, 1975, 92, 175–212.

Krasner, L. Studies of the conditioning of verbal behavior. Psychological Bulletin, 1958, 55, 148–170.

Kruglanski, A. W., Alon, S., & Lewis, T. Retrospective misattribution and task enjoyment. Journal of Experimental Social Psychology, 1972, 8, 493–501.

Kruglanski, A. W., & Cohen, M. Attributed freedom and personal causation. Journal of Personality and Social Psychology, 1973, 26, 245–250.

Kruglanski, A. W., & Cohen, M. Attributing freedom in the decision context: Effects of the choice, alternatives, degree of commitment and predecision uncertainty. Journal of Personality and Social Psychology, 1974, 30, 178–187.

Kukla, A. Attributional determinants of achievement-related behavior. Journal of Personality and Social Psychology, 1972, 21, 166–174.

Lefcourt, H. M., Hogg, E., Struthers, S., & Holmes, C. Causal attributions as a function of locus of control, initial confidence, and performance outcomes. Journal of Personality and Social Psychology, 1975, 32, 391–397.

Lepper, M. R., & Greene, D. Turning play into work: Effects of adult surveillance and extrinsic rewards on children's intrinsic motivation. Journal of Personality and Social Psychology, 1975, 31, 479–486.

Levy, L. H. Psychological interpretation. New York: Holt, Rinehart & Winston, 1963.

Lewin, K. The conflict between Aristotelian and Galilean modes of thought in contemporary psychology. In K. Lewin (Ed.), A dynamic theory of personality. New York: McGraw-Hill, 1935.

Lewin, K. Resolving social conflicts. New York: Harper, 1948.

Lindsley, O. R. Operant conditioning methods applied to research in chronic schizophrenia. Psychiatric Research Reports, 1956, 5, 118–153.

Loftis, J., & Ross, L. Effects of misattribution of arousal upon the acquisition and extinction of a conditioned emotional response. Journal of Personality and Social Psychology, 1974, 30, 673–682.

Mahoney, M. J. Cognitive and behavior modification. Cambridge, Mass.: Ballinger Publishing Co., 1974.

Mann, B., & Murphy, K. C. Timing of self-disclosure, reciprocity of self-disclosure, and reactions to an initial interview. Journal of Counseling Psychology, 1975, 22, 304–308.

Matross, R. P. Socratic methods in counseling and psychotherapy. Unpublished doctoral dissertation, University of Minnesota, 1975.

Matross, R. P. TOTEL therapy: An outline. Counseling and Values, 1976, 21, 2–11.

McArthur, L. A. The how and what of why: Some determinants and consequences of causal attribution.

Journal of Personality and Social Psychology, 1972, *22*, 171—193.

McGuire, W. J. The nature of attitudes and attitude change. In G. Lindzey and E. Aronson (Eds.), *The handbook of social psychology* (Vol. 3, 2nd ed.). Reading, Mass.: Addison-Wesley, 1969.

Meichenbaum, D. Self-instructional methods. In F. H. Kanfer and A. P. Goldstein (Eds.), Helping people change. New York: Pergamon, 1975.

Menapace, R. H., & Doby, C. Causal attributions for success and failure for psychiatric rehabilitees and college students. *Journal of Personality and Social Psychology*, 1976, *34*, 447—454.

Miller, G. E. Galanter, E., & Pribram, K. *Plans and the structure of behavior.* New York: Holt, Rinehart & Winston, 1960.

Miller, R. L., Brickman, P., & Bolen, D. Attribution versus persuasion as a means for modifying behavior. *Journal of Personality and Social Psychology*, 1975, *31*, 430—441.

Monson, T. C., & Snyder, M. Actors, observers, and the attribution process: Toward a reconceptualization. *Journal of Experimental Social Psychology*, 1977, in press.

Morse, S., & Gergen, K. J. Social comparison, self-consistency, and the concept of self. *Journal of Personality and Social Psychology*, 1970, *16*, 148—156.

Mowrer, O. H. *The new group therapy.* Princeton, N. J.: Van Nostrand, 1964.

Murphy, K. C., & Strong, S. R. Some effects of similarity self-disclosure. *Journal of Counseling Psychology*, 1972, *19*, 121—124.

Newtson, D. Attribution and the unit of perception of ongoing behavior. *Journal of Personality and Social Psychology*, 1973, *28*, 28—38.

Newtson, D. Dispositional inference from effects of actions: Effects chosen and effects foregone. *Journal of Experimental Social Psychology*, 1974, *10*, 489—496.

Nisbett, R. E., & Borgida, E. Attribution and the psychology of prediction. *Journal of Personality and Social Psychology*, 1975, *32*, 932—943.

Nisbett, R., & Schachter, S. Cognitive manipulation of pain. *Journal of Experimental Social Psychology*, 1966, *2*, 227—236.

Orvis, B. R., Cunningham, J. D., & Kelley, H. H. A closer examination of causal inference.: The roles of consensus, distinctiveness, and consistency information. *Journal of Personality and Social Psychology*, 1975, *32*, 605—616.

Osgood, C. E., & Tannenbaum, P. H. The principles of congruity in the prediction of attitude change. *Psychological Review*, 1955, *62*, 42—55.

Ostrom, T. M. Perspective as a determinant of attitude change. *Journal of Experimental Social Psychology*, 1970, *6*, 280—292.

Pallak, M. S., Sogin, S. R., & Van Zante, A. Bad decisions: Effect of volition, locus of causality, and negative consequences on attitude change. *Journal of Personality and Social Psychology*, 1974, *30*, 217—227.

Patton, M. J. Attraction, discrepancy, and responses to psychological treatment. *Journal of Counseling Psychology*, 1969, *16*, 317—324.

Paul, G. *Insight vs. desensitization in psychotherapy.* Stanford: Stanford University Press, 1966.

Peoples, V. Y., & Dell, D. M. Black and white student preferences for counselor roles. *Journal of Counseling Psychology*, 1975, *22*, 529—534.

Pepinsky, H. B., & Karst, T. C. Convergency: a phenomenon in counseling and psychotherapy. *American Psychologist*, 1964, *19*, 333—338.

Pittman, T. S. Attribution of arousal as a mediator in dissonance reduction. *Journal of Experimental Social Psychology*, 1975, *11*, 53—63.

Pliner, P., Hart, H., Kohl, J., & Saari, D. Compliance without pressure: Some further data on the foot-in-the-door technique. *Journal of Experimental Social Psychology*, 1974, *10*, 17—22.

Popper, K. R. *The logic of scientific discovery.* New York: Science Editions, 1961.

Porter, E. H., Jr. *An introduction to therapeutic counseling.* Boston: Houghton, 1950.

Reisman, S. R., & Schopler, J. An analysis of the attribution process and an application to determinants of responsibility. *Journal of Personality and Social Psychology*, 1973, *25*, 361—368.

Regan, D. T., Straus, E., & Fazio, R. Liking and the attribution process. *Journal of Experimental Social Psychology*, 1974, *10*, 385—397.

Regan, D. T., & Totten, J. Empathy and attribution: Turning observers into actors. *Journal of Personality and Social Psychology*, 1975, *32*, 850—856.

Riemer, B. S. Influence of causal beliefs on affect and expectancy. *Journal of Personality and Social Psychology*, 1975, *31*, 1163—1167.

Rogers, C. R. Client-centered therapy. In S. Arieti (Ed.), *American handbook of psychiatry.* Vol. 3. New York: Basic Books, 1959.

Rokeach, M. *The nature of human values.* New York: Free Press, 1973.

Rokeach, M., & Cochrane, R. Self-confrontation and confrontation with another as determinants of long-term value change. *Journal of Applied Social Psychology*, 1972, *2*, 283—292.

Rokeach, M., & McLellan, D. D. Feedback of information about values of self and others as determinants of long-term cognitive and behavioral change. *Journal of Applied Social Psychology*, 1972, *2*, 236—251.

Roll, W. V., Schmidt, L. D., & Kaul, T. J. Perceived interviewer trustworthiness among black and white convicts. *Journal of Counseling Psychology*, 1972, *19*, 537—541.

Ross, M., Insko, C. A., & Ross, H. S. Self-Attribution of attitude. *Journal of Personality and Social Psychology*, 1971, *17*, 292—297.

Schachter, S., & Singer, J. Cognitive, social and physiological determinants of emotional state. *Psychological Review*, 1962, *69*, 379—399.

Schmidt, L. D., & Strong, S. R. "Expert" and "inexpert" counselors. *Journal of Counseling Psychology*, 1970, *17*, 115—118.

Schmidt, L. D., & Strong, S. R. Attractiveness and influence in counseling. *Journal of Counseling Psychology*, 1971, *18*, 348—351.

Sell, J. M. Effects of subject self-esteem, test performance feedback, and counselor attractiveness on influence in counseling. *Journal of Counseling Psychology*, 1974, *21*, 324–344.

Shapiro, D. H., Jr., & Zifferblatt, S. M. Zen meditation and behavioral self-control: Similarities, differences, and clincial applications. *American Psychologist*, 1976, *31*, 519–532.

Shaver, K. G. Defensive attribution: Effects of severity and relevance on the responsibility assigned for an accident. *Journal of Personality and Social Psychology*, 1970, *14*, 101–113. (a)

Shaver, K. G. Redress and conscientiousness in the attribution of responsibility for accidents. *Journal of Experimental Social Psychology*, 1970, *6*, 100–110. (b)

Shaw, J. I., & Skolnick, P. Attribution of responsibility for a happy accident. *Journal of Personality and Social Psychology*, 1971, *18*, 380–383.

Sherman, S. J. Attitudinal effects of unforeseen consequences. *Journal of Personality and Social Psychology*, 1970a, *16*, 510–520.

Sherman, S. J. Effects of choice and incentive on attitude change in a discrepant behavior situation. *Journal of Personality and Social Psychology*, 1970b, *15*, 245–252.

Simons, H. W., Berkowitz, N. N., & Moyer, R. J. Similarity, credibility, and attitude change: A review and a theory. *Psychological Bulletin*, 1970, *73*, 1–16.

Sloane, R. B., Staples, F. R., Cristol, A. H., Yorkston, N. J., & Whipple, K. *Psychotherapy versus behavior therapy*. Cambridge, Mass.: Harvard University Press, 1975.

Snyder, M., & Jones, E. E. Attitude attribution when behavior is constrained. *Journal of Experimental Social Psychology*, 1974, *10*, 585–600.

Spiegel, S. B. Expertness, similarity, and perceived counselor competence. *Journal of Counseling Psychology*, 1976, *23*, 436–441.

Sprafkin, R. P. Communicator expertness and changes in word meanings in psychological treatment. *Journal of Counseling Psychology*, 1970, *17*, 191–196.

Staines, G. L. A comparison of approaches to therapeutic communications. *Journal of Counseling Psychology*, 1969, *16*, 405–414.

Steele, C. M., & Ostrom, T. M. Perspective-mediated attitude change: When is indirect persuasion more effective than direct persuasion? *Journal of Personality and Social Psychology*, 1974, *29*, 737–741.

Steiner, I. D. Perceived freedom. In L. Berkowitz (Ed.), *Advances in experimental social psychology*, Vol. 5. New York: Academic Press, 1970.

Steiner, I. D., Rotermund, M., & Talaber, R. Attribution of choice to a decision maker. *Journal of Personality and Social Psychology*, 1974, *30*, 553–562.

Stephan, W. G. Actor vs observer: Attributions to behavior with positive or negative outcomes and empathy for the other role. *Journal of Experimental Social Psychology*, 1975, *11*, 205–214.

Storms, M. D. Videotape and the attribution process: Reversing actors' and observers' points of view. *Journal of Personality and Social Psychology*, 1973, *27*, 165–175.

Storms, M. D., & Nisbett, R. E. Insomnia and the attribution process. *Journal of Personality and Social Psychology*, 1970, *16*, 319–325.

Strong, S. R. Verbal conditioning and counseling research. *Personnel and Guidance Journal*, 1964, *42*, 660–669.

Strong, S. R. Counseling: An interpersonal influence process. *Journal of Counseling Psychology*, 1968, *15*, 215–224.

Strong, S. R. Causal attribution in counseling and psychotherapy. *Journal of Counseling Psychology*. 1970, *17*, 388–399.

Strong, S. R. Experimental laboratory research in counseling. *Journal of Counseling Psychology*, 1971, *18*, 106–110.

Strong, S. R. Systematic causality in counseling: Applications to theory, practice, and research. *Counseling and Values*, 1973a, *17*, 143–151.

Strong, S. R. A systems model of behaving organisms and persons: Implications to behavior change in counseling. *Office for Student Affairs Research Bulletin*, University of Minnesota, 1973b, *14* (1).

Strong, S. R. Pragmatic causal distortion in counseling. *British Journal of Guidance and Counselling*, 1975, *4*, 59–65.

Strong, S. R. Christian counseling. *Counseling and Values*, 1976, *20*, 151–160.

Strong, S. R. Christian counseling in action. *Counseling and Values*, 1977, *21*, 89–128.

Strong, S. R., & Dixon, D. N. Expertness, attractiveness, and influence in counseling. *Journal of Counseling Psychology*, 1971, *18*, 562–570.

Strong, S. R., & Gray, B. L. Social comparison, self-evaluation, and influence in counseling. *Journal of Counseling Psychology*, 1972, *19*, 178–183.

Strong, S. R., Hendel, D. D., & Bratton, J. C. College students' views of campus help-givers: Counselors, advisers, and psychiatrists. *Journal of Counseling Psychology*, 1971, *18*, 234–238.

Strong, S. R., & Matross, R. P. Change processes in counseling and psychotherapy. *Journal of Counseling Psychology*, 1973, *20*, 25–37.

Strong, S. R., & Matross, R. P. A study of attribution techniques in the interview. *Office for Student Affairs Research Bulletin*, University of Minnesota, 1974, *15* (2).

Strong, S. R., & Schmidt, L. D. Expertness and influence in counseling. *Journal of Counseling Psychology*, 1970a, *17*, 81–87.

Strong, S. R., & Schmidt, L. D. Trustworthiness and influence in counseling. *Journal of Counseling Psychology*, 1970b, *17*, 197–204.

Strong, S. R., Taylor, R. G., Bratton, J. C., & Loper, R. G. Nonverbal behavior and perceived counselor characteristics. *Journal of Counseling Psychology*, 1971, *18*, 554–561.

Tinsley, H. E., & Harris, D. J. Client expectations for counseling. *Journal of Counseling Psychology*, 1976, *23*, 173–177.

Trope, Y., & Burnstein, E. Processing the information contained in another's behavior. *Journal of Experimental Social Psychology*, 1975, *11*, 439–458.

Truax, C. B., & Mitchell, K. M. Research on certain therapist interpersonal skills in relation to process and outcome. In A. E. Bergin and S. L. Garfield (Eds.), *Handbook of psychotherapy and behavior change*. New York: Wiley, 1971.

Tversky, A., & Kahneman, D. Belief in the law of small numbers. *Psychological Bulletin,* 1971, *76,* 105–110.

Upshaw, H. S., Ostrom, T. M., & Ward, C. D. Content versus self-rating in attitude reserach. *Journal of Experimental Social Psychology,* 1970, *6,* 272–279.

Uranowitz, S. W. Helping and self-attributions: A field experiment. *Journal of Personality and Social Psychology,* 1975, *31,* 852–854.

Walster, E. Assignment of responsibility for an accident. *Journal of Personality and Social Psychology,* 1966, *3,* 73–79.

Walster, E., Berscheid, E., & Walster, G. W. New directions in equity research. In L. Berkowitz and E. Walster (Eds.), *Advances in experimental social psychology.* Vol. 9. New York: Academic Press, 1976.

Weiner, B., Frieze, I., Kukla, A., Reed, L., Rest, S., & Rosenbaum, R. M. Perceiving the causes of success and failure. In E. E. Jones, D. E. Kanouse, H. H. Kelley, R. E. Nisbett, S. Valins, and B. Weiner (Eds.), *Attribution: Perceiving the causes of behavior.* Morristown, N. J.: General Learning Press, 1971.

Weiner, B., Heckhausen, H., Meyer, W., & Cook, R. E. Causal ascriptions and achievement behavior: A conceptual analysis of effort and reanalysis of locus of control. *Journal of Personality and Social Psychology,* 1972, *21,* 239–248.

Weiner, B., & Kukla, A. An attributional analysis of achievement motivation. *Journal of Personality and Social Psychology,* 1970, *15,* 1–20.

Wicklund, R. A. Objective self-awareness. In L. Berkowitz (Ed.), *Advances in experimental social psychology.* Vol. 8. New York: Academic Press, 1975.

Wicklund, R. A., & Duval, S. Opinion change and performance facilitation as a result of objective self-awareness. *Journal of Experimental Social Psychology,* 1971, *7,* 319–342.

Worchel, S., & Brand, J. Role of responsibility and violated expectancy in the arousal of dissonance. *Journal of Personality and Social Psychology,* 1972, *22,* 87–97.

Wortman, C. B. Some determinants of perceived control. *Journal of Personality and Social Psychology,* 1975, *31,* 282–294.

Wortman, C. B., & Brehm, J. W. Responses to uncontrollable outcomes: An integration of reactance theory and the learned helplessness model. In L. Berkowitz (Ed.), *Advances in experimental social psychology,* Vol. 8. New York: Academic Press, 1975.

Zadny, J., & Gerard, H. B. Attributed intentions and informational selectivity. *Journal of Experimental Social Psychology,* 1974, *10,* 34–52.

Zillman, D. Rhetorical elicitation of agreement in persuasion. *Journal of Personality and Social Psychology,* 1972, *21,* 159–165.

Zimbardo, P. *The cognitive control of motivation.* Chicago: Scott, Foresman, 1969.

PART II

EVALUATION OF PROCESS AND OUTCOME IN PSYCHOTHERAPY AND BEHAVIOR CHANGE

5

THE EVALUATION OF THERAPEUTIC OUTCOMES

ALLEN E. BERGIN
MICHAEL J. LAMBERT

Brigham Young University

In this chapter we review studies on the effects of psychotherapy. We also discuss related issues such as the importance of spontaneous remission and deterioration effects in psychotherapy, conclusions that can be drawn from comparative studies, research designs which are promising for evaluating outcomes, and techniques for measuring therapeutic change.

As in the previous edition, we consider here the practice of traditional individual psychotherapies, for instance, the many variations of psychoanalytically oriented psychotherapy, various humanistic and relationship therapies, the client-centered approach, and eclectic mixtures of these and similar types of intervention. Although the scope of the discussion remains generally the same as it was in the previous edition, we have broadened our coverage to include brief descriptions of outcomes in behavioral, group, marital and family therapy, various fads, and with patients other than adult outpatient neurotics (i.e., children and psychotics).

A REASSESSMENT OF SELECTED OUTCOME STUDIES

Past reviews of the effects of psychotherapy have been hotly debated and highly influential. It is instructive and worthwhile to review studies of therapy outcome in the context of the controversy surrounding their implications for practice.

A crucial contributor to our more than two decades of debate has been the ambiguity of the data in question. This deficiency is best illustrated by reference to the Eysenck-Rachman surveys and reactions to them (Eysenck, 1952, 1960, 1965, 1966, 1967; Rachman, 1971, 1973). Every psychology undergraduate is now familiar with the fact that Eysenck purported to show that about two-thirds of all neurotics who enter psychotherapy improve substantially within two years and that an equal proportion of neurotics who never enter therapy improve within an equivalent period. Students are also familiar with the fact that the majority of therapy researchers disagree with these findings and interpretations. We show here why the nature of the data reviewed by Eysenck and Rachman makes it impossible to resolve this debate; why it is equally feasible to take any of the several positions that have been vigorously advocated in this connection; and finally, why the issue, as posed by them, has not led and cannot lead to further scientific progress.

The outpouring of praise and invective, and of claims and counterclaims, has been an extraordinary phenomenon (cf., Eysenck, 1954, 1955, 1961, 1964, 1972; Rachman, 1971, 1973; Luborsky, 1954, 1972; Cartwright, 1956; Rosenzweig, 1954; Strupp, 1963, 1964; De-Charms, Levy, & Wertheimer, 1954; Kiesler, 1966; Bergin, 1963, 1966, 1967a, 1967b, 1971; Strupp & Bergin, 1969b; Meltzoff & Kornreich, 1970; Truax & Carkhuff, 1967; Subotnik, 1972a; Bergin & Suinn, 1975; Malan, 1973a, Malan et al., 1975; Lambert, 1976). Although no longer crucial, the evidence presented and conclusions drawn by Eysenck and Rachman deserve to be reviewed before we consider more recent studies and contemporary issues.

Eysenck originally based his conclusions on the percentage of improvement in 8053 cases from 24 outcome studies. A review of these studies reveals the ambiguity of the original data. Different percentages of improvement may be derived, depending on what criteria and what method of tabulating the reviewer uses. It is clear that Eysenck imposed a set of criteria on the therapy data that yielded the lowest possible improvement rates while being more lenient with the spontaneous remission data. There is clearly nothing wrong with demanding rigor in evaluating therapy outcomes. It is a matter of opinion and style. Some of the writers during that period who examined the same studies arrived at conclusions that were similar to those of Eysenck; others did not (Miles, Barrabee & Finesinger, 1951a). However, the same standards should apply to both treated and untreated groups in order to eliminate bias. To clarify the situation, the studies reviewed by Eysenck (1952) were carefully re-reviewed, and the data from all of the 24 studies were retabulated to show how investigators with different biases can arrive at drastically different rates of improvement.

The analysis of these studies creates many difficulties that cannot be satisfactorily resolved. They include: (1) the lack of precisely comparable cases across studies, (2) the lack of equivalent criteria of outcome, (3) large variations in the amount of therapy received and in its quality, (4) differences in duration and thoroughness of follow-up, (5) variation in nature of onset and in duration of disturbance, and (6) (where comparable cases and outcome estimates appear to be used) imprecision of definitions of disorder and criteria for improvement to the extent of rendering their reliability questionable. Perhaps most troublesome of all is the fact that these early studies were not objective. There are usually no assessments of outcome made independently of the therapist's evaluations, and there are no checks on the reliability of the author's methods of tabulating the raw data.

To complicate matters further, it is frequently difficult to match the figures in the original reports with those in Eysenck's tables because: (1) the original tables themselves often include flaws such as incorrect addition and computation of percentages; (2) to examine the data on "neurotics," the only diagnostic group considered by Eysenck, one must extract figures from tables that include information on as many as 34 different diagnostic subtypes! Deciding which are to be included as "neurotic" is not simple, especially when nearly every author has a somewhat different set of categories; (3) to make matters worse, Eysenck made some errors in transferring the original figures to his own table; (4) the confusion created in this area is further multiplied by small matters such as Eysenck's stating that "psychopathic states" are *included* in his calcuations; whereas, his figures can be matched with the originals only when psychopaths are *excluded*. It seems logical to exclude them from a study of neuroses, but it required many hours of labor to discover that this had been done in the 1952 report; and (5) the ratings of outcome in different studies are based on different numbers of categories. Thus, in one study all cases may be categorized dichotomously as either improved or not improved, but in another study as many as six different degrees of improvement may be used. A reviewer is thus confronted with the difficult task of carefully comparing definitions of improvement and of then recasting data from the various reports into a more uniform set of categories to make percentages of improvement comparable across studies. This is sometimes made easier in articles where brief descriptions are given of each case, but too often it is impossible to differentiate "substantial" from "slight improvement." Eysenck has recast the data from the 24 studies he reviewed into his own system, and a new investigator must therefore cope with the double problem of interpreting the studies from his own viewpoint while also determining how Eysenck proceeded. One then usually winds up with three *different* views of the same case material (the original author's, Eysenck's, and one's own)—a fact that unfortunately reduces the objectivity and credibility of the information being summarized.

To provide an example of the complications involved in analyzing these studies and how interpretations of the data were derived, a representative study is discussed below.

The Berlin Psychoanalytic Institute

This report was published in 1930 by the Berlin Psychoanalytic Institute under the editorship of Sandor Rado, Otto Fenichel, and Carl Muller-Braunschweig, with Fenichel providing the statistical material. It was introduced with a foreword by Sigmund Freud.[1]

The report discloses that during its first 10 years the Institute had 1955 consultations, which led to the commencement of 721 analyses. Of these 721 cases, 363 had concluded treatment at the time of the report, 241 had terminated prematurely, and 117 were still in treatment. Of those who had completed treatment, 47 were considered uncured, 116 improved, 89 very much improved, and 111 were classified as cured.

The question at issue is: How shall the raw data be assembled to draw conclusions regarding the effects of treatment?

First, we agree with Eysenck that the focus should be on neuroses, broadly defined. This requires subtracting 47 cases from the 363 who completed treatment and 73 cases from among the 241 premature terminators.

[1]We thank Dr. E. Kunzler of the Psychosomatic Clinic of the University of Heidelberg for providing the report and Alice Mucha for graciously translating it.

Second, we must interpret Fenichel's defintions of degree of improvement. His criteria for success seem to be quite stringent. He states:

We were most particular in what was to be understood as "cured." Included were only such cases where success meant not merely the disappearance of symptoms but also the manifestation of analytically acceptable personality changes and, wherever possible, confirmative follow-up. This strictness of definition demands that most of the "very much improved" cases must, for all practical purposes, be closely coordinated with the "cured" ones. "Improved" cases are those who upon termination still lack in one aspect or another, including such cases as those which had to settle, for external reasons, with an only partially successful outcome. . . . (p. 19)

According to this definition, we would include the "improved" cases among those figured in the overall percent improved; and this is where Eysenck parts company. He uses a system of four categories: (1) Cured or Much Improved, (2) Improved, (3) Slightly Improved, and (4) Not Improved, Died, or Left Treatment. Cases in the first two categories are added to figure the *percent improved*. He classifies cases that Fenichel defined as "Improved" under "Slightly Improved," and they are thus excluded from the *percent improved*. A decision like this crucially affects the ultimate results, and it illustrates well how subjective bias is the only way of resolving ambiguities in the raw material. Our subjective bias in this instance is the opposite of Eysenck's and in conformity with Fenichel's description. Fenichel's definition of "Improved" seems substantial enough that cases so classified should be counted among the *percent improved*.

Another issue is whether premature dropouts are to be counted as failures. Eysenck believes they should be and so tabulates them, thus, significantly reducing the improvement rate. We doubt the validity of this view in that individuals drop out for numerous reasons, some of which have nothing to do with the therapy; and we consider it an unfair test of a method to count against it all cases where it was not fully applied.

Table 5-1 shows that differing attitudes regard-

TABLE 5-1 Results of Psychotherapy: Summary of Percent Cured, Much Improved, and Improved (Excluding Slightly Improved) by Differing Criteria

	Total N	A Eysenck Dropouts Included. Improved = Much Improved	B Bergin Dropouts Excluded. Improved = Moderately Improved or Better	C Alternative A—Dropouts Included. Improved = Moderately Improved or Better	D Alternative B (Knight 1941) Dropouts Excluded. Improved = Much Improved
Psychoanalysis					
1. Fenichel (1930)	484	39%	91% (287/316)	59%	59% (186/316)
2. Kessel and Hyman (1933)[a]	25	62%	68%	No dropouts reported	89% (16/18)
Hyman (1936)[b]	30		60% (18/30)		

#	Study	N				
3.	Jones (1936)[c] (London)	56	47%	68% (37/56)	No dropouts reported	47% (26/56)
4.	Alexander (1937)[d] (Chicago)	142	50%	69% (70/101)	49%	69% (70/101)
5.	Knight (1941) (Topeka)	41	67%	76% (28/37)	68%	76% (28/37)
	All cases	753[e]	44% (335/760)	83% (450/540)	60% (450/753)	62% (326/528)

[a]$N = 25$, not 34. Kessel and Hyman begin with 33, not the 34 that Eysenck states. Seven of these are psychotics and one is alcoholic; therefore, N for neuroses = 25.

[b]Follow-up of previous study, including some new cases (unreported by Eysenck).

[c]This report is based on 56 cases who completed more than 100 sessions at the London Clinic of Psychoanalysis between 1926 and 1936. They are, therefore, a highly selected group from among (1) the 738 patients who came to the clinic during this period and (2) the 176 who ultimately accepted treatment. Jones uses three categories of improvement: Cured, Improved, and Failed. Since there was no way to determine degree of improvement in the middle group, we simply divided them evenly between much improved and slightly improved to arrive at our percent *improved*. Neither Eysenck nor Knight's figures seem to follow logically from Jones' tables.

[d]Based on Knight's tables.

[e]Slight discrepancies between the original tables and Eysenck's compilation yields a total N of 753 here instead of Eysenck's 760.

ing each of the preceding points yield widely differing accounts of the effects of psychoanalysis as
practiced at the Berlin Institute between 1920 and
1930.

The figure of a 91 percent improvement rate
reported on line one of Table 5-1 may seem startling, but it is based on what we consider to be a
logical and reasonable interpretation of the information available. To arrive at this figure, (1) premature dropouts were eliminated from the sample, (2)
Fenichel's "Improved" cases were counted as improved, and (3) nonneurotics were eliminated from
the figures. Eysenck followed the opposite of (1)
and (2) to arrive at his 39 percent rate.

The "Alternative A" figure of 59 percent is arrived at by including all dropouts in the computation of the improved rate, while still counting
Fenichel's "Improved" as improved. The "Alternative B" rate, also 59 percent, is based directly on
Knight's reading of the same data. He excludes
dropouts but counts Fenichel's "Improved" as unimproved.[2]

The four divergent but equally reasonable tabulations of the Berlin Institute data, as summarized in
Table 5-1, clearly establish the point that there is
no valid way to assess the effects of psychoanalysis
from the information available. There is no clear
justification for choosing one interpretation over
another.

Although there were large discrepancies between our analysis and that of Eysenck with regard
to psychoanlaysis, our tabulations of the 19 studies
of eclectic therapies produced only modest differences. This was true even when later additional
studies reviewed by Eysenck (1966): (Powers &
Whitmer, 1951; Rogers & Dymond, 1954; Brill &
Beebe, 1955: Barron & Leary, 1955: Gliedman,
Nash, Imber, Stone, & Frank, 1958; Walker &
Kelly, 1960); and by Bergin (1971): (Bartlett,
1950; Bond & Braceland, 1937; Coriat, 1917;
Cowan & Combs, 1950; Friess & Nelson, 1942;
Kriegman & Wright, 1947; Lipkin, 1948, Wooten,

Armstrong & Lilley, 1935) were considered. These
early surveys indicate an improvement rate of 65
percent with a range from 42 to 87 percent.

These figures lead to the conclusion that on the
average about two-thirds of neurotics who enter
the broad spectrum of verbal psychotherapy, as
practiced over the last several decades, experience
improvement in their symptoms. These surveys do
not enlighten us much with regard to the effects of
psychotherapy. They simply lack information
specific enough to definitively interpret the meanings of the wide variations in percentages of improvement that they yield. This problem also
makes comparisons with spontaneous remission
rates difficult. No single rate takes into account the
responses of different diagnostic types nor the different populations served by specific clinics or
therapists. It appears to us that Eysenck has used
the ambiguity of these data to discredit
psychoanalysis—and to a lesser degree, verbal
psychotherapy—while suggesting that the behavioral therapies have a clear contribution to
make to neurotic problems.

Despite the limitations of these studies, the early
published evidence must be considered encouraging, though certainly not dramatic. Our more positive perspective, in contrast to Eysenck's rather
pessimistic view of the effectiveness of
psychotherapy, is also a function of further evidence. This evidence is provided by (1) additional
recent outcome studies, (2) evidence that spontaneous remission rates are well below Eysenck's
estimate, and (3) evidence that deterioration, diagnostic differences, and numerous other processes
complicate assessment of improvement rates.

Conclusions Drawn from Studies
Conducted Between 1953 and 1969

The earlier version of this chapter (Bergin, 1971)
summarized many additional outcome studies
drawn from a comprehensive bibliography of research in psychotherapy (Strupp & Bergin,
1969a). The data from 48 studies were presented
in tabular form. They were considered to be a representative sample of the studies published between 1953 and 1969. We present now a summary of conclusions from these studies. Some
readers will, however, want to review the more
detailed presentation given in the 1971 edition.

---

[2]Note that there are errors of addition in Knight's table
(e.g., number "apparently cured" should be 111 instead
of 101) and also similar errors in many of the articles
summarized by Eysenck. This type of problem has unnecessarily complicated interpretations of some of these
studies, and we have therefore attempted to make appropriate corrections when the data were retabulated.

1. The studies reported during this period generally did not specify the precise nature of treatment nor the limits of applicability. They were tests, for the most part, of whether therapy had any effect at all. It was hoped that in the 1970s there would be a decline in this type of broad study, which seemed to add so little to our knowledge. It is impossible to conclude very much from these inquiries except that psychotherapy "works."

2. While the precision and methodological sophistication of studies had improved markedly over time, the evidence continued to yield the general conclusion that psychotherapy, on the average, has at least modestly positive effects. Most studies did not seem to provide strong evidence, but the number showing positive results was clearly larger than chance.

3. There was a slight tendency for more adequately designed studies to yield more positive results.

4. It seemed clear from the empirical evidence that something potent or efficacious was operating in some portion of the therapy routinely offered; even though average effects were only moderately impressive when diverse cases, therapists, and change scores were lumped together.

5. There did not seem to be a relationship between duration of therapy and outcome.

6. There was no relationship between type of therapy and outcome.

7. Experienced therapists fared better than inexperienced therapists, and therefore it was recommended that future studies use experienced therapists to test for therapeutic effects.[3]

---

[3]Recently Auerbach and Johnson (1977) thoroughly reviewed the relationship between level of experience and psychotherapeutic effectiveness. Their conclusions were similar to Bergin's. However, their analysis clearly did *not* indicate that experience level was a powerful predictor of outcome. Accordingly, when considered alone and independently of other important therapist, patient, and technical factors, level of experience is only one of a few therapist qualities that can be shown to have a modest relationship to outcome. This suggests that it is important but not critical to study the effects of *experienced* therapists.

8. It was concluded that at least two important factors were operating which made the observed effect of therapy seem more limited: the fact that a portion of patients were made worse (deterioration effect), and the fact that a portion of neurotic patients improve without treatment (so-called "spontaneous remission" phenomena). We present an extensive discussion of these two important variables, at the conclusion of which we again consider the effects of psychotherapy by examining selected studies of treatment outcome.

SPONTANEOUS REMISSION

After 25 years and much debate, it is disheartening to find that there is still considerable controversy over the rate of improvement in neurotic disorders in the absence of formal treatment. This issue continues to be of major interest because spontaneous improvement is presumed to confound the success rates that are attributed to participation in psychotherapy. To what extent do rates of success in psychological treatments capitalize on the effects of unspecified extratherapeutic events or homeostatic mechanisms? Are there reliable "baseline" figures that represent improvement in neurotic patients who go untreated? These questions have stimulated considerable research and discussion.

Three recent articles are of considerable importance in determining which, if any, baselines are suitable. Bergin (1971), in his *Handbook* chapter in the first edition, gave an historical account of the controversy beginning with Eysenck's (1952) article, criticized the evidence presented, and reviewed 14 studies related to the issue. He argued that the available evidence was not in support of the two-thirds remission rate suggested by Eysenck and that a better estimate would be much lower. In fact, the median remission rate in the articles he cited is 30 percent! Rachman (1973) was very critical of the evidence suggested by Bergin, borrowing heavily from Eysenck and defending Eysenck's conclusions. He evaluated each of the 14 studies quoted by Bergin (1971), apparently accepting only two of them as evidence worth considering. He also cited 12 studies (several from Eysenck, 1952, 1967) and concluded that "in fact, the available evidence does not permit a revision of Eysenck's (1952) estimate of a gross spontaneous remission rate of approximately 65 percent of neurotic disorders over a two-year period" (1973, p. 819).

Lambert (1976) reviewed the articles quoted by Eysenck (1952), Bergin (1971), and Rachman (1973), plus several additional studies, and established yet another baseline. In the previous *Handbook* chapter and the article by Lambert (1976), the details of the controversy over a baseline figure are sufficiently dealt with. Instead of repeating an account of the deficiencies in past studies, we summarize here the evidence, such as it is, and state the conclusions that we believe are warranted by the data.

Tables 5-2 and 5-3 present figures from the research reports that are relevant to this topic. The data are presented in two tables to distinguish those studies that include subjects who had minimal treatment but not extensive psychotherapy from those studies that include subjects who were, for the most part, untreated. In addition, the studies in Table 5-2 are generally less sound methodologically than those that are presented in Table 5-3.

Inspection of Table 5-3 indicates a median spontaneous remission rate of 43 percent, with a range of 18 percent to 67 percent—far from the original estimate of two-thirds suggested by Eysenck (1952) and presently supported by Rachman (1973). This can be contrasted with the figure of 50 percent derived from the studies summarized in

TABLE 5-2   Studies of Minimal Treatment Outcome

Author	Sample Composition	N	Follow-up Period	Remission Rate
				(in percent)
Huddleson (1927)	Psychoneurosis	200	5 years	47
Curran (1937)	Mixed psychiatric	83	1–3 years	61
Landis (1937)	Psychoneurosis	119	—	72
Masserman et al. (1938)	Psychoneurosis	32	1 year	53
Denker (1946)	Psychoneurosis	500	2 years	72
Wheeler et al. (1950)	Anxiety neurosis	60	20 years	47
Miles et al. (1951b)	Anxiety neurosis	62	2–12 years	58
Shepherd & Grunberg (1957)	Psychoneurosis	—	3 years (?)	—
Hastings (1958)	Psychoneurosis	371	6–12 years	46
Ernst (1959)	Anxiety neurosis	31	24 years	45
Errera et al. (1963)	Phobic	47	23 years	21
Giel et al. (1964)	Psychoneurosis	100	5 years	71
Kringlen (1965)	Obsessional neurosis	91	5 years	19
Masterson (1967)	Mixed adolescent disorders	72	2½–5 years	38
Cremerius (1969)	Mixed neurosis/ somatic	371	11–30 years	8
Kedward (1969)	Psychoneurosis	422	3 years	73
Vorster (1966)	Psychoneurosis	65	0–3 years	65

Note: Dashes indicate data that are presented in such a way as to make it impossible to determine a specific figure.

TABLE 5-3 Spontaneous Remission Rates in Untreated Subjects

Author	Sample	N	Follow-up Period	Remission Rate
				(in percent)
Friess & Nelson	Psychoneurosis	70	5 years	29
(1942)	Psychoneurosis	66	5 years	35
Saslow & Peters	Psychoneurosis	83	1–6 years	37
(1956)				
Wallace & Whyte	Psychoneurosis	49	3 years	66
(1959)				
Cartwright & Vogel	Psychoneurosis (?)	22	1–6 months	55
(1960)				
Endicott & Endicott	Psychoneurosis	40	6 months	52
(1963)				
Paul (1967)	"Phobic"	30	2 years	18
Jurjevich (1968)	"Outpatients"	62	7 months	55
Schorer et al.	Psychoneurosis	55	2–8 years	65
(1968)				
Beiser (1971)	Neurotic/personality disorder	113	5 years	20–35
Agras et al.	Phobics	30	5 years	43
(1972)				
Malan et al.	Psychoneurosis	45	2–8 years	27–51
(1975)				
Subotnik (1972b)	Mixed	166	9–33 months	45
Shore & Massimo	Adolescent behavioral disorders	9	10 years	22
(1973)				
Sloane et al. (1975)	Neurotic personality disorder	11	1 year	48
Subotnik (1975)	"Emotionally disturbed"	59	3 years	50
Tyrer & Steinberg	Phobics	13	2 years	23
(1975)				
Noyes & Clancy (1976)	Anxiety	56	5 years	67

Table 5-2, which represents minimal treatment outcomes. *It can be noted that a two-thirds estimate is not only unrepresentative but is actually a most unrealistic figure for describing the spontaneous remission rate or even rates for minimal treatment outcomes.*

The figure of 43 percent represents another possible baseline estimate of spontaneous remission; however, like the others, it is an average figure that obscures considerable variation.

We have attempted, as Rachman (1973) did, to order spontaneous remission rates as a function of type of neurotic disorder and have concluded that at the present time such an ordering cannot be accomplished by reference to the research literature. It appears that anxiety and depressive neuroses have the highest spontaneous recovery rates, followed by hysterical, phobic, obsessive compulsive, and hypochondrical disorders; but no study has attempted to describe recovery rates by diagnostic classification while holding constant other important variables such as degree of disturbance, type of onset, and past history of disturbance. Our examination of the research evidence indicates large fluctuatioms in spontaneous improvement rates *within* various neurotic disorders such as phobias, obsessional neurosis, and the like. It is our impression that little will be gained by an ordering of remission rates until a revision in the classification system is accomplished.

We do have several conclusions that we believe are justified by our review of the studies relevant to the spontaneous remission issue.

1. The widely quoted and often accepted notion that two-thirds of neurotic patients will improve in two years without treatment is erroneous. The idea that psychological treatments (behavior or insight) must appreciably surpass this two-thirds rate is a position that is not supported by research data. Even if it were correct, psychotherapy would still show the advantage of two-thirds improvement in a much shorter time. Such evidence is sufficient to support practice, as is the case in many medical treatments.

2. Our estimate, which is based on a much wider accumulation of research data, does not yield a reliable figure for comparison with treatment groups. The evidence we reviewed indicates that rates vary from 0 percent to 90 percent at follow-up, and that very *low rates* of spontaneous remission *do not* necessarily mean that the course of treatment will be long and difficult and, therefore, do not invariably lead to low predictions of success with treatment. Also, high spontaneous recovery rates for a particular disorder do not always imply that patients referred for treatment will recover quickly.

3. Future researchers should pay more attention to the past history of their clients. It is apparent that some studies report results on mildly disturbed, acute cases; while others deal with a patient population that is chronic, having had their symptoms for decades before beginning psychotherapy. Variables

such as prior duration of disturbance, degree of disturbance, environmental stresses and supports, and the like, have a more powerful effect on the likelihood of remission than diagnostic label, at least within the broad classification category of the neuroses.

4. Past studies of spontaneous remission have yielded inflated improvement rates because a considerable number of wait-list and no-treatment subjects did receive psychotherapy or other special help. In addition, several reports (Malan, et al. 1975; Sloane et al., 1975) have indicated that a respectable number of these control subjects feel helped by a single assessment interview. Future studies should focus more attention on these confounding variables to determine the limits of their influence.

5. For future research it will be necessary to draw comparison groups from the treatment population under study. Given the present state of psychological knowledge, this appears to be the only way to insure a reasonable baseline for improvement in the absence of psychotherapy. Hopefully, we have seen an end to the oft quoted two-thirds remission rate as evidence that psychotherapy is not effective.[4]

What Is "Spontaneous"?

Despite the fact that spontaneous remission is less frequent than has been supposed, we are still confronted with the fact that some degree of "spontaneous" improvement occurs in disturbed persons who do not receive formal treatment. Indeed, the significant changes that occur in control groups have been major contributors to the negative findings in several well-designed studies of the effects of therapy (Powers & Whitmer, 1951; Barron & Leary, 1955; and Rogers, Gendlin, Kiesler, & Truax 1967). Although not always the case, this phenomenon underlines the existence of spontaneous personality changes. What is this mysterious process of spontaneous remission?

[4]For a more complete analysis of the data supporting these conclusions, see Lambert (1976).

This widely used explanatory concept is one of dubious value because it explains very little. It merely labels the existence of unknown processes as "spontaneous"; therefore, the concept has retarded scientific progress by seeming to make remission a consequence of events that are unresearchable. To say something is spontaneous is actually to argue that we do not know what is happening.

Thus, to identify some personality changes as being spontaneous is simply to acknowledge that some therapeutic processes occur "naturally"; that is, they occur outside the consulting room. Why do a portion of untreated subjects change? This is a fascinating question that bears directly on the issue of whether psychotherapy is a uniquely effective procedure for facilitating growth.

Previous reviews of relevant data (Bergin, 1963, 1966, 1971) suggest that the majority of people who experience psychological disturbance do *not* seek mental health professionals for treatment. Many of them obtain counsel, advice, and support from a variety of helping persons such as spouses, friends, teachers, physicians, and clergymen, who cannot be considered trained in these functions.

Evidence on this point is provided by Gurin, Veroff, and Feld (1960) in their nationwide interview survey conducted for the Joint Commission on Mental Illness and Health. They found that of those persons who actively sought help for personal problems, the vast majority contacted persons other than mental-health professionals, and that generally they were more satisfied with the help received than were those who chose psychiatrists and psychologists. Christensen and Magoon (1974) report a similar finding in a poll of college students who were asked to indicate the source of help for emotional concerns. Friends were listed first while psychiatrists were listed twelfth (out of twelve).

It is certainly conceivable that these data describe in part the process of spontaneous remission among persons not in therapy. Such change may therefore result from seeking and obtaining therapeutic help from nontherapists! To the extent that such assistance is effective, it may account for the change that occurs in control groups of disturbed persons who do not receive professional psychotherapy. Probably, these control subjects do not enjoy the pain of their disturbance while being detained as controls; hence, they seek relief elsewhere. Such a conclusion is further substantiated by Frank's finding (1973) that over a period of years approximately 50 percent of a group who had sought psychotherapy had also sought help from a variety of non-mental-health sources. He suggests that the continued positive change that occurred among them over a long period when they were *not* in therapy was the result of the effects of this nonprofessional "treatment." Gurin et al. commented on the significance of such phenomena (p. 341): "These findings underscore the crucial role that nonpsychiatric resources—particularly clergymen and physicians—play in the treatment process. They are the major therapeutic agents. . . ."

This type of analysis casts an entirely new light on the processes that ameliorate pathology. Perhaps psychotherapists are not unique. Perhaps selected helping persons in the "natural" social environment provide adequate or better coping conditions for neurosis than do trained mental health experts.

One example of a naturalistic therapy process comes from our experiences in conducting extensive personality assessments of normal persons for a governmental agency. During these evaluations we have occasionally noted an exceptionally effective person who has come from a chaotic and ordinarily pathology-inducing family life. A young college graduate illustrates this well. He came from an extremely disturbed home setting in which every member of his family except himself had been hospitalized for severe mental illness; and yet he had graduated from a renowned university with honors, had starred on the football team, and was unusually popular. During his government training he was held in the highest esteem by staff members and was rated as best liked and most likely to succeed by his peers.

In examining this young man's history we discovered that during his elementary school years he had essentially adopted a neighborhood family as his own and spent endless hours with them. Certain characteristics of this family appear most significant. They were a helping family in the sense that love emanated from them and was freely available to all. Of special significance for the fellow under consideration was his relationship with a boy in the family, a year older than he, who formed for him a positive role model with whom he closely identified and whom he followed to his considerable satisfaction.

An even more crucial factor was his relationship with the mother in this family, who became his guide, counselor, and chief source of emotional nurturance. His reports indicate that while this relationship was intense, it was not symbiotic, and seemed to foster his independence and self-development. This particular woman was apparently the prototypical mother and influenced more than one stray youth toward security, resilience, and accomplishment. It is difficult to deny the potent therapeutic impact of this woman, at least as it was portrayed by her protege's report. Although there are probably few like her, she represents a dimension of socially indigenous therapy that may be more significant than is usually recognized. Her home became a neighborhood gathering place. It might be characterized as an informal therapy agency, a kitchen clinic! Certainly, it makes the possibility of "spontaneous" remission more believable.

Is it unreasonable to suppose that people in distress have simply discovered potent change agents as they exist naturally in society and have put them to work with sufficient impact that they create changes equivalent to those appearing in psychotherapy? This is one possible explanation of spontaneous remission and of the fact that sometimes studies of therapy reveal no difference between experimentals and controls. The controls are getting better because they are getting help from persons untrained in formal psychotherapy, who practice a kind of natural therapy. It could be that these agents of personality integration are actually *more* effective *as a group* than trained therapists, for certain kinds of problems.

The rationale for such a conclusion is that these lay therapists are probably selected because their ability to form therapeutic relationships and to convey wise counsel is known by word of mouth. Professionals, on the other hand, may often be selected more for their academic credentials or professional political standing than for their ability to relate and to generate insights. In other words, the lay therapists may well be a more select group with

regard to the dimensions relevant to the actual work of therapy than are the professionals.

Strupp and Hadley (1978) tested this hypothesis by contrasting a group of five experienced and well-qualified psychotherapists with seven carefully selected college professors who were chosen for the study because of their natural helpfulness. The clients of both professional therapists and college teachers improved significantly more than the control subjects on a few outcome indices; yet they did not differ from each other on the variables considered in measuring therapeutic outcome.

A growing body of research supports the position that carefully selected, minimally trained persons can have substantial effects on the emotionally disturbed. The often quoted, although hardly flawless, reports by Poser (1966), as well as Carkhuff and Truax (1965), are examples of studies where nonprofessionals have demonstrated their usefulness. This seems to hold true across a variety of change agents and client populations (cf. Gruver, 1971; Berkowitz & Graziano, 1972; Johnson & Katz, 1973; Karlsruher, 1974; Siegel, 1973; O'Dell, 1974; Emrick & Lassen, 1977).

There has been an explosion of studies that focus on the value of minimally trained persons and contrast their performance with professional therapists (Knickerbocker & McGee, 1973; Levitz & Stunkard, 1974; Weinman, Kleiner, Yu, & Tillson, 1974). Another current trend in the United States is the growing number of self-help programs. People seeking help can obtain many kinds of self-directed change packages or kits that are mass produced (cf. Chamberlain, 1977; Rosen, Glasgow, & Carrera, 1976; Clark, 1973). These approaches raise serious ethical questions, not to mention their obvious implications for spontaneous remission. Future research will not only have to account for the benefits of nontechnical or so-called nonspecific factors, such as warmth and acceptance in self-help programs like Alcoholics and Neurotics Anonymous, but for a variety of learned technical procedures that may one day become common knowledge.

Even though the last 10 years has seen an increasing number of studies investigating the impact of nonprofessional change agents, few researchers have investigated the actual mechanisms that result in change via self-help programs.

The client-centered school has investigated the hypothesis that change is a question of a facilitative interpersonal climate and that the helpful conditions in therapy are the same as those offered outside of therapy. This very plausible explanation has yet to receive much empirical support. Reisman and Yamokoski (1974), for example, found that when friends discussed personal problems, empathic responses were infrequent; whereas they constituted the majority of responses for Rogerian therapists. Subjects in this analog study did not wish their friends or therapists to communicate "empathically" but rather with expository statements (e.g., advice).

It is interesting that in both this study and the one by Strupp and Hadley (1978) psychotherapists behaved differently than their counterparts, be it friend or nonprofessional therapist. Generally, therapists were seen as more accepting and gave more reflective remarks. Nonprofessionals gave more advice, asked more questions, and made more suggestions. These studies suggest the possibility that it is not the stylistic similarities between counseling and friendships that lead to the formation of a viable and helpful relationship.

The observation that a facilitative interpersonal climate may develop through a wide variety of behaviors has had important methodological implications. A growing number of researchers are stressing the importance of examining the quality of interpersonal relations across therapies and in family, marital, and friendship relationships with client perception measures. Lambert, DeJulio & Stein (1978) as well as Gurman (1977) have pointed out that the investigation of the power of variables such as client perceived empathy, warmth, and genuineness has been limited by "nonparticipant" judgments of the level of these qualities (i.e., standard rating scales and trained judges). The scales that are used to make these "nonparticipant" judgments may not generalize to therapies other than client-centered, and are possibly even more limited for assessing the nature and quality of friendships.

Barrett-Lennard (1973) has modified a therapy process scale (The Relationship Inventory) for use in a variety of situations, including parent-child, teacher-student, and marital relationships. A device such as this might prove useful in investigating the degree to which a person creates or discovers an interpersonal environment that is rich and supportive or barren and destructive.

A client perception measure such as the Barrett-Lennard Relationship Inventory has the advantage of assessing the *client's reported experience* instead of using some formalized way of measuring technically accurate therapist responses which are considered helpful. It characterizes the growing acceptance of the idea that much of what is of value in therapy is not unique but is rather available to a degree in the world outside of therapy. An important question then arises: Why do patients so often fail to take advantage of these naturally existing relationships? An answer suggested by Strupp (personal correspondence) is that their neurotic difficulties prevent them from using these resources. The purpose of psychotherapy is not exclusively to provide what can be obtained in the "ordinary" environment but to *enable* the patient to take advantage of what help there is, by removing the obstacles within the patient.

Another view of the important role of the environment in both causing and changing maladaptive behaviors has been elaborated on by Voth and Orth (1973). These authors, as part of the extensive Menninger Project, found environmental manipulation to be an often neglected part of treatment. In their clinical analysis they found that *decreasing the level or intensity of commitments to the environment resulted in symptomatic improvements.*

An inference of their study is that symptomatic changes in untreated cases could easily result if the patient is able to change the environment; or it changes, independent of their actions, in such a way that the "conflict trigger" is removed. Conflict trigger in this case refers, by and large, to stressful parental relationships and heterosexual relationships. In general, when they are the conflict trigger and the *client* breaks off such a relationship, temporary symptomatic improvement results.

It is evident that several factors may account for "spontaneous" remission phenomena, that these factors have therapeutic efficacy, that many of them may occur in psychotherapy as well as naturally, but that they are not necessarily unique to the formal therapy process. This means that subjects used in control groups or groups used to establish baseline percentages of improvement for comparisons with treatment cases are frequently not really controls at all! They are the recipients of formal, informal, and self-help procedures that are often enough identical or similar to psychotherapy that they cannot justifiably be used for this purpose (cf. Frank, 1959, for a discussion of controls in psychotherapy research).

Thus, we find that not only is the spontaneous remission rate lower than expected, but also that it is probably caused to a considerable degree by actual therapy or therapylike procedures. This certainly casts psychotherapy into a more promising position than has heretofore been considered, even though formal therapy should do better than informal therapy—which it does. This finding still does not mean that the general cross section of professional therapy is uniformly dramatic in its effects, but it does suggest once again that there are some important beneficial variables at work somewhere in the process.

Returning to the question of therapeutic effects, we can summarize the importance of the spontaneous remission data by contrasting the 43 percent spontaneous recovery rate with the 65 percent therapy improvement rate that is reported in gross studies of therapeutic improvement. The data, with all the difficulties they present for integration of knowledge, do lead us to the conclusion that, on the average, psychotherapy is better than no therapy, that above average therapy often yields excellent results, and that below average therapy may even be harmful, an outcome that we examine next.

DETERIORATION EFFECTS REVISITED

We have seriously considered the extent to which harmful consequences of seeking psychotherapy may have been a factor in tempering the reported effectiveness of psychological treatments. Our interest here stemmed both from research reports and from our belief that treatments which are capable of producing beneficial effects are capable of also producing harmful effects. Bergin (1966) pro-

posed the term *deterioration effect* to describe the general finding that a certain portion of psychotherapy patients were worse after treatment. Such an effect was suggested by the tendency for treated groups to show an increase in variance compared with control groups on outcome measures.

A diagram illustrating this phenomenon along with seven studies reported in 1966 was later reproduced by Bergin (1971) in the first edition of this *Handbook* with 23 additional studies that showed deterioration in a proportion of patients treated. Since then an even wider accumulation of research results has been assembled and interpreted. It shows that the "deterioration effect" is a significant problem in the area of psychotherapy, that it is not limited to individual psychotherapy, and that a delineation of mechanisms of negative change will be a significant step toward improving psychological services and our theoretical understanding of the process of change. In our more recent analysis of this problem, we focused on therapist-induced deterioration; but, of course, many negative effects from psychotherapy are not directly related to the person of the therapist (Lambert, Bergin, & Collins, 1977).

In this review of negative effects we ignore some important issues such as the degree to which psychological treatments are forms of social control (cf. Hurvitz, 1974) and the effects of labeling and diagnosis (cf. Doherty, 1975; Langer & Abelson, 1974; Bakker, 1975) as well as the popular idea that male therapists may have special negative effects on female clients (Brodsky & Holdroyd, 1975).

Deterioration implies an impairment of vigor, resilience, or usefulness from a previously higher state. Generally, it has been regarded as a worsening of the patient's symptomatic picture, the exaggeration of existing symptoms, or the development of new symptoms, as assessed before and after treatment. Hadley and Strupp (1976) have, in addition, suggested that the negative effects of therapy may include a sustained dependency on the therapist or therapy and the development of unrealistic expectations which result in patient activities that are beyond his or her capability. These may end in failure, guilt, self-contempt, and possibly contribute to disillusionment with therapy and a corresponding general loss of hope and disparagement about all helping endeavors. These latter possible negative effects are of course more subtle, and to them might be added the lack of significant improvement when it can be reasonably expected.

In the discussion that follows we summarize the evidence on the deterioration effect, elaborate on its prevalence and implications, discuss the vari-

ables and causal agents that seem to bring about this negative influence and, finally, make recommendations that are relevant to clinical practice and research.

Evidence of the Deterioration Effect

The deterioration effect can be easily conceptualized from an illustration. Figure 5-1 is an updated, revised representation of this phenomenon. It was suggested and revised on the basis of nine

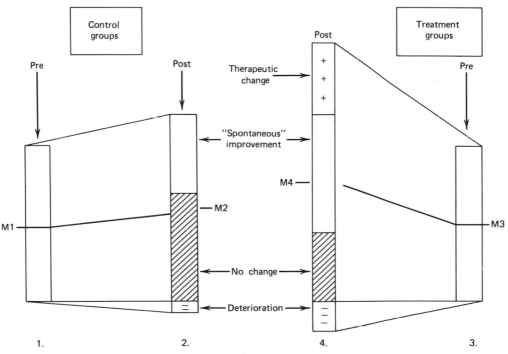

Figure 5-1 The diverse effects of psychotherapy: a schematic illustration of changes in pathology for control and treatment groups.

Bar 1	Distribution of test scores for disturbed control groups at beginning of studies.
Bar 2	Distribution of test scores for disturbed control group at end of study showing increased spread of scores due to "spontaneous" improvement and "spontaneous" deterioration.
Bar 3	Distribution of test scores for disturbed treatment group at beginning of therapy.
Bar 4	Distribution of test scores for disturbed treatment group at end of therapy showing increased spread of scores due to therapeutic change and therapist induced deterioration.
M1, M2 M3, M4	Median points, pre and post, which show greater change for therapy groups than control groups.
+NOTE:	Lengths of bars are approximations.

well-designed outcome studies and the repeated observation that outcome measures show patients to be both more and less disturbed than untreated control subjects. Current renderings, however, show that increased variance in posttest criterion scores of treated groups is not a necessary consequence of deterioration even though it occurs often. Therapy effects, including negative ones, can be distributed so as to show no change or even a restriction in variance. Figure 5-1 is therefore a convenient but not essential way of showing the diverse effects of therapy interventions as summarized across a large number of studies.

Table 5-4 summarizes the nine studies mentioned. It is felt that collectively these studies provide an empirical base for deterioration in psychotherapy even though individually there are weaknesses in each of them.

Other Empirical Evidence
In addition to the nine studies already discussed, the data base that supports the notion of a deterioration effect is much broader. This evidence is summarized elsewhere (Lambert, Bergin, & Collins, 1977) and includes more than 40 studies that add something to our knowledge of negative effects. Strupp, Hadley and Gomes-Schwartz (1977) have also comprehensively and critically evaluated this literature.

A recent study illustrates the presence of negative effects, assessed through a typical pretest-posttest design. Berzins, Bednar, and Severy (1975), in an analysis of 79 therapist-patient dyads and a variety of criteria from three sources; the therapist, patient, and a psychometrician, reported significant positive posttest changes for the treatment group as a whole. Through the use of typological analysis—a method of clustering the criteria—they found that all criterion sources agreed that 19 of the patients were improved while 11 showed a pattern of deterioration. This was agreed on by patient, therapist, and psychometrist. Eleven other patients showed differing patterns of agreement between the sources, with some criteria showing improvement and other criteria showing worsening. The remaining patients defied classification by this procedure.

The sufficiency of the *empirical* evidence for establishing prevalence and causation has been questioned by several writers (cf. Eysenck, 1967;

Braucht, 1970; May, 1971; Rachman, 1973). Strupp, Hadley, and Gomes-Schwartz (1977) while noting the shortcomings in the data do not question the presence and importance of negative effects. It is our view, after reviewing the empirical literature, that although there are many methodological shortcomings and ambiguities in the data, ample evidence exists that psychotherapy can and does cause harm to a portion of those it is intended to help. Many who have reviewed these data also support this view (Matarazzo, 1967; Malan, 1973a; Howard & Orlinsky, 1972; Frank, 1973; Korchin, 1976). This position is also supported by Hadley and Strupp (1976) in their survey of eminent clinicians and researchers. In response to the question: "Is there a problem of negative effects of psychotherapy?" there was a virtually unanimous "Yes" by the 70 experts who responded to the questionnaire. *It is our continuing belief that negative effects are widespread enough to influence the general evaluation of psychotherapy.* We hope that future research reports will examine this question more specifically and allow for more definitive conclusions about negative effects.

We now examine some important issues relating to therapy-induced deterioration.

How Widespread Is the Phenomenon?
Our examination of the empirical literature leads us to believe that deterioration can and does occur in a wide variety of patient populations with an equally wide variety of treatment techniques. It occurs in severely disturbed patients (Fairweather, Simon, Gebhard, Weingarten, Holland, Sanders, Stone, & Reahl, 1960); in predelinquent boys (Powers & Witmer, 1951); in normals (Lieberman, Yalom, & Miles, 1973); as well as in neurotic outpatients (Baron & Leary, 1955). It seems to be reported in studies that employed therapists who differ sharply in training and experience such as medical students (Uhlenhuth & Duncan, 1968); psychiatric residents (Gottschalk, Mayerson, Gottlieb, 1967); paraprofessionals (Carkhuff & Truax, 1965); social caseworkers (McCabe, 1967; Segal, 1972; Fischer, 1973); and combinations of experienced and inexperienced therapists (Fiefel & Eells, 1963; Rogers & Dymond, 1954).

The treatment techniques for which some deterioration can be identified are likewise very diverse and not limited to psychotherapy. Reports of

TABLE 5-4 Studies Demonstrating Both Deterioration and Positive Change as a Result of Psychotherapy

Authors	Date	Population	N	Therapy Type	Average Therapy Duration	Relevant Criteria
Powers & Witmer	1951	Predelinquent boys	325	Directed friendship: social work counseling	6 years	Test battery Delinquency data Adjustment ratings Case record
Rogers & Dymond	1954	Young adults	25	Client-centered	8 months	Q sort; behavior ratings
Barron & Leary	1955	Outpatient neurotics	42	Eclectic-analytic	8 months	MMPI
Mink & Isaksen	1959	Junior high school students	96	Client-centered (48) Directive-insight (48)	4 months	Calif. Test of Personality
Fairweather et al.	1960	Long-term psychotics; short-term psychotics	72	Eclectic-analytic	3–5 months	Q sort
Cartwright & Vogel	1960	Young adults	22	Client-centered	33 sessions	Q sort; TAT
Truax	1963	Hospitalized schizophrenics	16	Client-centered Eclectic, analytic	6 months 3½ years	Multiple tests and ward behavior
Volsky et al.	1965	College students	80	Eclectic, directive	3 sessions	Anxiety, defensiveness and problem-solving scales
Carkhuff & Truax	1965	Hospitalized psychotics	74	Lay client-centered	24 sessions	Ward behavior

psychotic episodes precipitated by ECT are not un-common (cf. Elmore & Sugarman, 1975). Ques-tions about psychosurgery have been raised, and deteriorative effects from drugs are not unknown (Shader & DiMascio, 1970). Some of these methods, in fact, may produce results that are de-structive enough to cause permanent negative be-havior change.

Fischer (1973) reviewed research on the effec-tiveness of professional casework. In this domain, controlled-outcome studies were sparse. However, of those reviewed, it was found that in just under 50 percent of the studies, clients who received casework services either deteriorated to a greater degree or improved at a slower rate than did con-trol subjects! These clients were troubled families or delinquents for the most part, and the criteria of improvement ranged from death rate to ratings of family functioning.

In the discussion that follows we elaborate more specifically on deterioration in various treatment modalities, but we mention here, in passing, that there is evidence of client worsening within all the major therapy systems, including behavioral, humanistic, psychoanalytic, and cognitive ap-proaches.

Do Deterioration Effects Vary with School?

One would hope that differing theories and ap-proaches to change would show marked tenden-cies for *differential* effects on patients and that these effects would be apparent in patient deterio-ration rates. This has not been borne out by the empirical evidence, although good comparative studies are rare. Despite this trend, our expectation is that some approaches may lead to greater de-terioration in some patients. Most of the data pre-sented thus far are based on traditional analytic, client-centered, and eclectic techniques. The re-sults of studies in these areas will be elaborated on when we consider therapist and technique vari-ables that lead to negative effects.

Unfortunately, systematic examination of nega-tive effects in behavior therapy studies has been limited. There is, however, reason to believe that therapy-induced deterioration occurs in misuses of techniques such as flooding, implosive therapy, and aversive and operant conditioning. Rachman

and Teasdale (1969) have discussed the tendency to "leave treatment" as a problem of considerable proportion in aversive conditioning. Marks (1971) has reported the development of significant de-pression in a proportion of phobic cases treated by desensitization. Bruch's (1974) report on the perils of behavior modification in treating anorexia ner-vosa and Blinder, Freeman and Stunkard's (1970) account of the possibility of suicide further confirm and extend our understanding of behavioral de-terioration effects.

Some case study material also implies that some patients being treated by behavior therapy (Palmer, 1970) get worse. Frequently this appears to be related to the focus on a specific symptom to the exclusion of more-difficult-to-define, internal feeling states that are significant to the patient. Ad-ditional evidence of relapse and symptom substitu-tion in cases of hysteria following the missapplica-tion of behavioral methods has been reported by Blanchard and Hersen (1976). Stuart and Lott (1972) also sound a warning on possible damaging effects of behavior contracting with delinquents: ". . . some Project families . . . show marked im-provement and others a moderate amount of de-terioration" (p. 167). We anticipate the day when there is an accumulation of evidence relating to deterioration in behavioral approaches so that indi-cations and contraindications for certain treatment methods can be supported. Current interest in be-havior therapy, as indicated by the many research reports appearing in recent years along with the decline of "miracle cures," makes this a likely pos-sibility.

The widespread concern about some behavioral technology certainly is reminiscent of the stir caused by T-groups but is clearly a source of greater concern to many. Portrayals of patients treated by these methods in books such as *A Clockwork Orange* have not done much for the public's expectations about behavioral methods. Their use in prisons has been criticized in connec-tion with their potential for harm as well as the violation of civil rights.

Objections to their use have been raised by humanistic practitioners such as Jourard (1973):

. . . There is a sense in which I regard efforts to foster change in another by environmental con-

trol or by shaping techniques or by any means that are not part of an authentic dialogue, as in some ways pernicious and mystifying and probably not good for the well-being and growth of the persons to whom these efforts are addressed, and probably not very enobling for the people who practice them. (p. 10)

Little in the way of comparative studies has been produced that allows comparison of differential negative effects in relation to the main schools of psychotherapy. It has been pointed out that viewing change from the point of view of theoretical orientation has not been productive because, among other reasons, professional orientation often tells us very little about what a therapist actually does in therapy.

From a researcher's point of view, traditional approaches like Psychoanalytic (Freud), Behavioral (Wolpe), Humanistic or Relationship (Rogers), and Cognitive (Kelly) therapies have generally shown positive effects, provided that they are implemented by a competent, experienced therapist. These therapies rest on a tradition of scholarship and research. It is probably their misapplication that creates most of the problems. Many other therapies derive from an antiintellectual tradition that spurns scholarly evidence and have the appearance of gimmickry, faddism, and the like. Some approaches, like Orgone therapy, Primal therapy, Rolfian massage, Scientology, Erhard Seminar Training, and much of the Encounter movement also rest on a questionable substantive base. Some of these methods appear to be designed for the general public instead of for a clinical population; however, the actual participants are frequently indiscriminable from psychotherapy clients, and one would expect misapplications to be easier and thus more frequent in these approaches.

Other approaches like Transactional Analysis and Reality Therapy derive from a more substantial history, but they can still be questioned from an empirical standpoint because their claims have not been verified experimentally, although it is conceivable that they might be. It is regrettable, however, that so many of these innovations are promoted prior to a reasonably objective test of their effects in the hands of a competent, well-adjusted therapist. This lack of outcome data on nearly all of them precludes any assessment of deterioration rates resulting from their use and, of course, equally precludes evaluation of possible improvement effects.

Do Deterioration Effects Vary with Treatment Modality?

Group Treatment

Despite the fact that experiential and laboratory groups have different purposes than traditional therapy and frequently exclude psychiatric patients, the parallels in outcome are obvious. These groups have stirred up more than their share of controversy. In fact, Gibb (1971) suggests that the concern about negative effects has been a barrier to innovation. Therefore, questions regarding negative effects have been more broadly examined than in most other treatment modalities. Some very interesting and helpful information has been discovered.

The controversy over casualties in experimental groups became apparent in the late 1960s. Campbell and Dunnette (1968) reviewed the research literature regarding the effectiveness of T-group experiences and alluded to several studies that showed some negative outcomes (e.g., Boyd & Ellis, 1962; Underwood, 1965). More recently, Hartley, Roback, and Abramowitz (1976) have specifically examined the empirical evidence on encounter groups with regard to the question of deterioration. Summarizing nine studies appearing since 1966, they report a large variation in estimated casualty rates across studies—from less than 1 percent to almost 50 percent. The median casualty rate was about 6 percent. These varying rates are a function of the casualty criteria employed, varying member characteristics, and perhaps the diverse nature of the treatments studied. For example, the definition of casualty ranged from "negative feelings about the experience" and "stressed enough to leave the workshop" to clinical judgment that a "psychotic reaction was precipitated or aggravated" in a T-group.

From the research literature it is difficult to identify deteriorative variables that relate specifically to this mode of "treatment." Lieberman, Yalom, and Miles (1973) indicate that generic labels identifying the groups they studied did not have differential process or outcome correlates. For example, one of the Gestalt groups evaluated was found to produce the most casualties, whereas another Gestalt group was among the most beneficial. Lieberman et al. (1973) were able to identify some group process variables that were related to negative effects. These variables include: the *encouragement of confrontation, expression of anger, rejection by group or leader,* and *feedback overload.* Others have stressed the potential negative consequences of *coercive group norms for participation,* and Lieberman et al. (1973) have also found some empirical support for this factor.

Continuing efforts need to be made in the area of group treatment in order to make more accurate predictions about casualties. Delineation of therapist and client variables, discussed in another section, will enable us to screen subjects for treatment and train group leaders more effectively. Further research is needed about facilitative group norms, optimal structure, and the interaction of these treatment variables with leader and participant variables. In general, we conclude that groups are usually less deleterious but, in some instances, can produce more deterioration than can individual psychotherapy.

Marital and Family Therapies

Gurman (1975) found evidence for deterioration in couples' therapy. His survey is summarized as follows:

1. Of 17 studies using a "worse" category, 8 (47 percent) found deterioration.

2. Deterioration rates in different types of marital therapy were: conjoint, 7 percent (48/702); concurrent, 5 percent (10/211); group, 8 percent (7/90); individual, 12 percent (26/224).

3. Stated otherwise, the deterioration rate for marital therapies where both spouses are involved in treatment in some way (conjoint, concurrent, group) is 6 percent (65/1003), or one-half that of individual therapy for marital problems; that is, 12 percent (26/224).

Although Gurman (1975) does not speculate at length about the reasons for this difference, *it does*

appear that treating the "relationship" rather than the "person" results in less deterioration.

4. The deterioration rate across all studies and all treatment types is 8 percent (N = 1638) but probably is higher (10 to 12 percent), since several studies have lumped "no change" and "worse" together and the 8 percent figure does not include them.

Conclusions are limited by the fact that no data were available on the level of deterioration in control couples and because the definition of deterioration in these studies was somewhat unclear.

Gurman and Kniskern (1976) also noted that of the family therapy studies which included a category for negative change, 33 percent or 5 of the 15 studies found evidence of negative effects. The deterioration rate seemed quite low (2.1 percent), and these authors suggested several reasons, including methodological ones, to account for these rates. In addition to the above results, the authors suggest that deterioration effects were found in both behavioral and nonbehavioral marital and family therapies, and that this *deterioration was not limited to the identified patient but was found in other family members as well.*

In these forms of treatment, the authors speculate that in addition to the usual reasons for deterioration, *the therapist's focus on emotionally loaded issues early in therapy,* and *the narrow focus on a single symptom,* may be among the unique, negative operations in marital and family therapies. (Also, see their chapter in this volume).

As yet, no one has studied the mechanisms of deterioration in marital or family therapy as it relates to the therapist and his techniques and their interaction with client characteristics. However, an interesting clinical report by Guttman (1973) has cautioned against the use of *conjoint family therapy with extremely anxious young patients* who are on the verge of decompensating or just recovering from an acute psychotic breakdown. The author presents four cases of deterioration that were linked to the process of family therapy. The approach used was one that assumed a capacity for insight and autonomous action; it was affectively oriented and not as directive as crisis-oriented techniques. It was felt that the deterioration in these adolescent patients resulted from facing unpleasant conflicts, mainly ambivalence toward their parents and concurrent dependency on them. This type of family therapy intervention was considered helpful with other patient groups but produced harmful consequences when "fragile" patients were treated. One is reminded here of the notion of a conflict trigger discussed previously and of the need for careful diagnosis in "active" psychotherapies.

What Client, Therapist, and Interactional Factors Lead to Deterioration?

Client Characteristics

Despite the lack of specificity in research reports, it is apparent that certain client variables correlate with negative change. Patient diagnosis and degree of disturbance are related variables that appear to be linked to deterioration. Indications are that more severely disturbed (psychotic) patients, as in Fairweather et al. (1960) and Feighner (1973); borderline patients, as in Horwitz (1974) and Weber, Elinson, and Moss (1965); or the initially most disturbed encounter group participants, as in Lieberman et al. (1973), are the most likely to experience negative outcomes. Berzins, Bednar and Severy (1975) also found that the patients who showed a consistent pattern of negative change were typified by a disproportionate number of schizophrenics and that other client characteristics were not significantly related to this pattern.

In the Yalom and Lieberman (1971) study, even further discussion of the characteristics of casualties took place. It was found that variables such as low involvement in the group, low levels of self-esteem, low positive self-concept, higher growth orientation, and greater anticipation or need for fulfillment, were positively related to deterioration. Likewise, casualties were more likely to use escape modes of coping and conversely to be less likely to use interpersonal skills in their ego defenses. As Yalom and Lieberman (1971) state:

The entire picture is a consistent one: individuals with generally less favorable mental health, with greater growth needs and higher anticipation for their group experiences, and yet who lacked self-esteem and the interpersonal skills to

operate effectively in the group situation were more likely to become casualties. (p. 27)

The data presented by Yalom and Lieberman (1971) are complemented by data gathered in the Menninger Foundation's Psychotherapy Research Project. Kernberg (1973) emphasized the relationship of Initial Ego Strength to outcome. This patient variable taps three separate qualities including: (1) integration of ego structure, (2) degree of deep, satisfying relations with others, and (3) symptom severity. Some very interesting conclusions regarding Initial Ego Strength, patient motivation, and anxiety tolerance are summarized here.

First, patients with low initial ego strength treated by therapists with high skill improved significantly more when the focus on transference was high. Kernberg writes: "A purely supportive approach that does not focus on the transference would be contraindicated in patients with significant ego weakness." It can be added that psychoanalytic treatment would also be contraindicated. Presumably, these clients cannot tolerate the regression inherent in psychoanalysis and do not develop a viable relationship in supportive treatment.

Like the work of Lieberman et al., Kernberg reports that *low quality of interpersonal relationships* was a prognostically poor sign; and that this, coupled with low initial anxiety tolerance and low motivation, yielded poor outcomes in psychoanalysis and supportive psychotherapies but better outcomes in supportive-expressive treatments.

In a further report of this project (Horwitz, 1974), the indications and contraindications for psychoanalytic treatment were spelled out in more detail. Of 22 cases who started out in psychoanalysis—and for whom the treatment was originally considered helpful—4 cases were dropped and shifted to a different treatment because it was felt that psychoanalysis was "too stressful" for the patient. Another 6 cases were considered by the research team to have been poorly selected for this type of treatment, and the suitability of 3 others was considered "questionable."

It would appear from this report that at least 10 of 22 patients originally considered suitable for psychoanalysis were eventually not so considered. Again, *ego weaknesses* were listed as the primary contraindiction. *Borderline personality organiza-tions* with potential for psychotic reactions plus a high proportion of patients with "predominant oral fixations' were among those considered hurt by the experience. All of the 13 cases where psychoanalysis was considered unsuitable or questionable demonstrated initial levels of *low frustration tolerance.*

Therapist Variables

Under the heading, "therapist variables," could be an endless list of factors that ultimately prove harmful to patients. Hadley and Strupp (1976) and Strupp, Hadley and Gomes-Schwartz (1977) listed 15 separate factors that lead to deterioration in the opinion of their panel of well-known psychotherapists.[5] In our analysis (Lambert, Bergin, & Collins, 1977), we limited ourselves to a few general categories suggested by research reports. They included: personal factors like race, gender, and the socioeconomic level of the therapist, the therapist's skills and attitudes as demonstrated in levels of empathy, warmth, and genuineness offered to clients, personality traits such as those measured by the A-B scales, and unconscious motivations as described by terms such as countertransference and pathogenesis.

Thus far, the results of studies examining many of these variables are inconclusive and do not allow for guidelines in practice.[6] It is hoped that future research will focus on the *specific mechanisms of injury such as interactional characteristics of the therapeutic encounter,* rather than on stable traits like level of experience, therapist sex, and the like which are not defined in terms of "process."

---

[5]For example, overly intense therapy, technical rigidity, misplaced focus, and dependency-fostering techniques were among the factors mentioned as being associated with negative effects.

[6]The interested reader might begin with the following list of studies: (1) Gender: Cartwright and Lerner (1963); Sines, Silver, and Lucero (1961); McNair, Lorr, and Callahan (1963); Mendelsohn and Geller (1967); Heilbrun (1971, 1973); Reiss (1973); Abramowitz et al. (1976); (2) Race: Sattler (1977); Banks (1972); Rogers and Dymond (1954); (3) Social Class: Mayer and Timms (1970); Wallach (1962); Heller, Myers, and Kline (1963); Snyder (1961); Schwartz and Abramowitz (1975); (4) Unconscious motivations: Singer and Luborsky (1977); Vandenbos and Karon (1971); (5) Therapist interpersonal skills: Truax and Carkhuff (1967); Truax and Mitchell (1971); Mitchell, Bozarth, and Krauft, (1977); Parloff, Waskow, and Wolfe (this volume).

A recent attempt to relate therapeutic effectiveness to an unconscious behavioral tendency of therapists has been examined by Vandenbos and Karon (1971) and Karon and Vandenbos (1972). Their basic hypothesis was that "pathogenic" therapists are those who consciously or unconsciously utilize dependent individuals (in this case, their clients) to satisfy the therapists' own personal needs; that is, pathogenic therapists will be more noxious and less clinically effective than therapists who put the legitimate needs of the client before their own needs.

Therapist pathogenesis was assessed via the TAT. "The results show that the patients of more benign therapists are functioning at higher levels after six months of treatment than are patients treated by more pathogenic therapists" (p. 116). These results, while interesting, have not as yet been replicated.

Another examination of mechanisms through which negative effects are transmitted was described by Yalom and Lieberman (1971). Each group leader in their study was rated both by participant questionnaires and by observer schedules. The participant and observer ratings were reduced to four basic dimensions of leader behavior: emotional stimuatlion, caring, meaning attribution, and executive functions. The leaders were then grouped into seven types: "Aggressive Stimulators," "Love Leaders," "Social Engineers," "Laissez-Faire," "Cool, Aggressive Stimulators," "High Structure," and "The Tape Leaders."

Although the data showed that characteristics of some participants made them more vulnerable to negative changes than others, the main finding was that the style of the group leader was the major cause of casualties. The most damaging style, "Aggressive Stimulator," was characterized by an intrusive, aggressive approach that involved considerable challenging and confronting of the group members. These leaders were impatient and authoritarian in approach, and they insisted on immediate self-disclosure, emotional expression, and attitude change. There were five leaders of this type, and all produced casualties except one (a total of nearly one-half of the most severe casualties). The one exception stated that he realized there were fragile persons in his group, so that he deviated from his usual style and "pulled his punches."

Another leader, whose group had three casualties, commented: ". . . it was a stubborn group, full of people 'too infantile to take responsibility for themselves and to form an adult contract' . . . 'I saw that most of the group didn't want to do anything so what I did was to just go ahead and have a good time for myself'" (Yalom & Lieberman, 1971, p. 28).

An example of a casualty resulting from one of the aggressive, confronting groups where the leader holds center stage in a charismatic manner was described by Yalom and Lieberman (1971, p. 24):

> . . . This subject was unequivocal in her evaluation of her group as a destructive experience. Her group, following the model and suggestions of the leader, was an intensely aggressive one which undertook to help this subject, a passive, gentle individual, to "get in touch with" her anger. Although the group attacked her in many ways, including a physical assault by one of the female members, she most of all remembers the leader's attack on her. At one point he cryptically remarked that she "was on the verge of schizophrenia." He would not elaborate on this statement and it echoed ominously within her for many months. For several months she remained extremely uncomfortable. She withdrew markedly from her family and friends, was depressed and insomniac; she was so obsessed with her leader's remark about schizophrenia that she dreaded going to bed because she knew her mind would focus on this point of terror. Often she lapsed into daydreams in which she relived, with a more satisfying ending, some event in the group. The only benefit of the experience, she said, was to help her appreciate how lonely she was; her discomfort has been so great, however, that she has been unable to make use of this knowledge. We consider this subject a severe and long-term casualty; at the interview eight months after the end of the group, she felt that she was gradually reintegrating herself but was not yet back to the point she was before the group began. Her negative experience was a function of aggres-

sive, intrusive leadership style which attempted to change her according to the leader's own values by battering down her characterologic defenses.

In another report from the vantage point of individual therapy, Ricks (1974) studied the adult status of a group of disturbed adolescent boys who had been seen by either of two therapists in a major child guidance clinic. Although the long-term outcomes of these two therapists were not different for less disturbed clients, there were striking differences in their therapeutic styles and outcomes with the more disturbed boys. The more successful therapist was labeled "supershrink" by one of the boys, and Ricks retains this label in describing his techniques versus those of therapist B whom Bergin and Suinn (1975) have called "pseudoshrink", most of whose cases became schizophrenic. For all cases in the sample, 55 percent were judged to have become schizophrenic in adulthood. However only 27 percent of supershrink's cases had such an outcome, whereas 84 percent of pseudoshrink's cases deteriorated to such a state. The caseloads of the two therapists were equal in degree of disturbance and other characteristics at the beginning of therapy.

In analyzing differences in therapist styles, it was found that therapist A devoted more time to those who were most disturbed while the less successful therapist B did the opposite. Therapist A also made more use of resources outside of the immediate therapy situation, was firm and direct with parents, supported movement toward autonomy, and facilitated problem solving in everyday life, all in the context of a strong therapeutic relationship. Ricks states:

> . . . A's supportive ego strengthening methods produced much more profound changes than the methods of Therapist B, who moved too precipitously into presumably deep material . . .
>
> The children considered here were already experiencing nearly intolerable degrees of anxiety, vulnerability, feelings of unreality, and isolated alienation. When the therapist increased those feelings, without being at the same time able to

*help the boy develop ways of coping with them,
he may well have played a part in the subsequent psychotic developments. Therapy may
lead one into health, but it may also be a part of
the complex process that ends up driving one
crazy. (p. 291)*

While therapist A rose to the occasion and devoted far more time, energy, and involvement to
the "sicker" boys, therapist B seemed to be
frightened by their pathology and withdrew from
them. The case notes reveal this strikingly in that B
frequently commented on the difficulties of cases
and seemed to become depressed when confronted with a particularly unpromising one.
Among many notes revealing this reaction is an
instance in which B ignored the hopeful elements
in a client's communication and emphasized the
depressed aspects: "I tell him my impression that
his spirit has been broken. . . ." Later, the therapist
noted that: "He is still very depressed and hardly
said anything to me at all. The case certainly has an
ominous aspect" (p. 282). The therapist was thus
caught up in the boy's depressed and hopeless feelings. He thereby reinforced the client's sense of
self-rejection and futility. Careful studies like this
give strong support to traditional clinical beliefs regarding the effects of therapist personality and
countertransference phenomena on outcomes.

The foregoing discussion of negative effects
makes it quite clear that psychotherapy is indeed
for better or worse. The documentation of negative
psychotherapy outcomes not only supports the
idea that the therapy experience has powerful consequences, but also should influence clinicians and
researchers to give earnest and immediate attention to the selection and training of therapists, as
well as to the role of licensing and continuing education policies which are adopted for practitioners.
The double-edged effects of treatments lead naturally toward a more complex view of
psychotherapy, and toward possible matching of
patient and therapist variables for optimal
psychotherapy outcomes. This may be important
because a given therapist may do well with certain
kinds of clients and poorly with others, as is shown
in the case of therapist B. This topic is discussed
further by Parloff, Waskow, and Wolfe in the present volume.

IS ONE KIND OF PSYCHOTHERAPY SUPERIOR TO ANOTHER IN PRODUCING POSITIVE OUTCOMES?

We have examined the outcome question in
psychotherapy, put it in a historical perspective,
and have indicated two sources of influence (spontaneous remission and the deterioration effect) that
have made outcomes in typical studies less than
remarkable. In the original *Handbook* chapter, Bergin was hopeful that when specific treatment procedures were investigated in conjunction with particular client problems, the results would be en-
lightening. One version of this question can be
viewed by examining outcomes in comparative
studies. Do practitioners who adhere to different
beliefs and practices produce differential outcomes?

Competing approaches to psychotherapy have
traditionally been pitted against one another. Presumably, the one shown to be most effective will
prove that position to be correct and will serve as a
demonstration that the "losers" should be persuaded to give up their views. Under the broad
question of "which treatment is more efficacious?"
are more meaningful and productive questions.
Which specific procedure obtains which results,
with which patients, in what amount of time, and
are these differential results equally enduring?
These more specific questions do not set up a *win-
lose* situation and, therefore, serve the more mature interests of inquiry.

Several past reviews have summarized the research on comparative studies. Meltzoff and Kornreich's (1970) is one such review. The authors list
as least 38 studies that they believe represent the
research relevant to the issue of differential outcome.

They summarize as follows:

*There is hardly any evidence that one tradi-
tional school of psychotherapy yields a better
outcome than another. In fact, the question has
hardly been put to a fair test. The whole issue
remains at the level of polemic, professional
public opinion, and whatever weight that can be
brought to bear by authoritative presentation of
illustrative cases. . . . there is no current evi-*

dence that one traditional method is more successful than another. . . . (p. 200)

Roback (1971), in a brief and overlapping review that considered outcomes in insight versus noninsight therapies, concluded there was no significant difference between behavior therapy and insight therapy outcomes. Lambert and Bergin (1973) and Bergin and Suinn (1975) contrasted the empirical evidence on outcomes of humanistic and behavioral approaches and, like Meltzoff and Kornreich (1970), concluded that neither had demonstrated a clear superiority but that behavioral techniques appeared to have the advantage with some restricted problems.

"Everyone has won and so all must have prizes," concluded the Dodo bird in *Alice in Wonderland;* and Luborsky, Singer, and Luborsky (1975) agreed that this verdict also applied to the various forms of psychotherapy that have been put to an empirical test. They published a detailed review of more than 100 comparative studies, some of which overlapped with the review of Meltzoff and Kornreich (1970). They presented data on comparisons between time-limited versus unlimited therapy, drugs versus psychotherapy (in numerous combinations), client-centered versus other psychotherapy, and behavior therapy versus other psychotherapy. This review is most relevant to our focus in this current chapter because it was similarly concerned with adult outpatients, patients instead of recruited subjects, and types of problems that excluded simple habit disorders.

Luborsky's conclusions were similar to those already mentioned: "Most comparative studies of different forms of psychotherapy found insignificant differences in proportions of patients who improved by the end of psychotherapy."

Beutler (1976) reexamined most of the comparative studies reviewed by Luborsky et al. (excluding drug studies), but added studies that used volunteer subjects and ones that had appeared since the Luborsky review. In all, 19 additional studies were reviewed, but 12 of them dealt with nonclinical subjects such as college volunteers. Beutler attempted to go beyond a summary of the implications of the empirical evidence by theorizing and drawing higher-level conclusions. These took the form of categorizing treatment approaches into

affective therapies, cognitive therapies, behavior therapies (classical conditioning), and behavior modification (operant learning), while categorizing symptoms into *habit patterns* and *adjustment patterns.* When thus classified, certain trends emerged that Beutler interpreted as allowing more differentiation and specification and, therefore, a revision of the Dodo bird verdict.

Among the conclusions derived from his analysis was the idea that behavior therapy and behavior modification are more effective than cognitive therapies in effecting change of habit patterns, whereas the treatments are at least equal in treating symptoms reflecting adjustment patterns, with the possibility that cognitive treatments may be more effective with patients who evidence this type of disturbance.

Kellner (1975) contrasted controlled outcome studies of various psychotherapeutic techniques, including behavioral ones, on psychosomatic disorders. The review was not exhaustive, with too few good studies to draw reliable conclusions. Although he did offer some tentative prescriptions, prescriptive conclusions cannot be drawn because too few studies identify client characteristics that are related to specific therapy procedures.

Goldstein and Stein (1976), in an ambitious endeavor, also attempted to go well beyond summarizing the results of comparative studies by listing diagnostic classifications, prescriptive psychotherapies, and the empirical evidence that supported one therapeutic approach as opposed to another.

In contrast to the other reviews quoted, these authors concentrated on single-group designs that studied treatment effects of a *single variable,* such as therapy technique on a *homogeneous sample* of subjects. Where possible, they reviewed more sophisticated studies with multiple group comparisons that included a no-treatment control group. Their review, like the others, deals mainly with adult individual psychotherapy. A summary from their report given here is based on six reports that applied a specific technique to patients diagnosed as having an obsessive-compulsive neurosis:

In summary, treatments such as paradoxical intention, "in vivo" desensitization, flooding, *that specifically focus on eliminating the sources of motivation that maintain an individual's compulsive rituals (e.g., guilt, anxiety) and also provide reinforced opportunities to engage in alternative, noncompulsive behaviors have been shown to be of therapeutic value with obsessive-compulsive neutotics. (p. 201)*

The work of Goldstein and Stein is indicative of the tendency of researchers to move in the direction of specificity (what works with whom) as well as a growing sensitivity to making the results of empirical research relevant to the practicing clinician; however, their effort demonstrates that this is still more of a hope than a reality.

Recent Outcome Studies

We now consider several recent outcome studies that were selected because they are exemplary of the outcome research conducted since this *Handbook* was first published. They also have a direct bearing on the question of differential effects to which we return following this analysis.

The Temple Study

This is probably the best comparative study of psychotherapy yet carried out (Sloane, Staples, Cristol, Yorkston, & Whipple, 1975). It involved more than 90 outpatients seen at the Temple University Health Sciences Center. Diagnostic and demographic information are reported in detail, and the study patients were typical of those usually seen clinically.

By diagnostic category, the majority (two-thirds) were judged neurotic, with the remaining patients (one-third) considered to have personality disorders. Patients, such as those with severe depression, who required medication were not included in the study.

Patients were assigned to short-term analytically oriented psychotherapy, behavior therapy, or to a minimal treatment wait list group. The groups receiving each treatment were matched with respect to sex and severity of symptoms but otherwise were randomly assigned to treatment groups.

The therapists in the study were six white males, five psychiatrists, and one clinical psychologist. Three were behavior therapists and three were psychoanalysts. All were considered good therapists by their peers and enjoyed excellent pro-

fessional reputations. They were: Herbert Freed, Arnold Lazarus, Michael Serber, Jay Urban, Raul Vispo, and Joseph Wolpe. A list of stipulative definitions for each treatment method was drawn up and agreed to by the therapists. Tape recordings of the fifth interview were made to provide an independent assessment of therapist activities.

Assessment procedures included standard psychological tests: MMPI; Eysenck Personality Inventory; California Psychological Inventory; the Target Symptoms Technique; the Structured and Scaled Interview to Assess Maladjustment; reports by informants who had known the patient for an average of 12 years, as well as ratings by the therapist, client, and an independent assessor.

Outcome was assessed after four months of treatment and again one year after commencing treatment. Both treatment groups as well as the waiting control improved significantly on target symptoms, but the behavior therapy and psychotherapy groups had improved significantly more than the wait-list group. There were no differences between behavior therapy and psychotherapy on any of the target symptoms as rated by an independent assessor, whose knowledge of the design was kept as blind as possible. On estimates of general functioning at work, in social situations, and the like, the groups also improved but did not differ from each other in amount of improvement. With respect to global outcome, the independent assessor rated 80 percent of the behavior therapy and psychotherapy groups as improved, whereas only 48 percent of the waiting controls were judged improved. On general adjustment, 93 percent of the group receiving behavior therapy were rated as significantly improved, whereas 77 percent of the psychotherapy and wait-list patients were rated as significantly improved.

All three groups maintained their improvement at follow-up. The general trend was for improvement to continue and for the patients in the wait-list group gradually to improve and to approach or equal the therapy groups. While this last finding supports the notion that therapy accelerates change that is otherwise going to occur in the absence of psychotherapy, it is confounded by the fact that only 8 of the original 30 wait-list subjects could be considered untreated during the eight months between treatment termination and follow-up.

The authors also note that the wait-list group might be most accurately considered a minimal treatment group. These clients made a public and personal commitment to recovery by their involvement in the original assessment (which involved more than 5½ hours). They had the opportunity of discussing their problems in depth with an experienced psychiatrist during the diagnostic interview. Some acknowledged that the reassurance and hope aroused by the interview were beneficial.

The analysis of tape recordings of the fifth interview indicated striking similarities and differences between these two small groups of therapists. The behavior therapists were more active and directive, and they talked more. The two groups were equal in warmth, but the *behavior therapists* received higher ratings on empathy and congruence as measured by the Truax scales! However, it should be pointed out that the Truax-type measures (both from independent judges and from patient perception) did not correlate with outcome. Interestingly, the two groups of therapists did not differ in number of interpretations made, although their interpretations were quite different in nature. This variable did not relate to the outcome of therapy.

No personality characteristics, specific symptomatology, demographic characteristics, or level of pathology were significantly related to successful outcome in either behavior therapy or psychotherapy patients. The only indication that one of the two treatments was more appropriate for specific patients was the finding that patients who were seen as having "acting-out" syndromes (on the MMPI) were considered to show more improvement with behavior therapy.

The authors suggest that this finding could mean that behavior therapy is more successful with a broader range of clients, or that psychotherapy works better than behavior therapy with some clients and worse than behavior therapy with other clients. Unfortunately, the data as presented do not allow us to test this possibility.

The Temple study is important for several reasons. It goes well beyond most past comparative studies and corrects for typical weaknesses. Among other strengths, this study: (1) matched subjects who were assigned to experimental and control groups on various important dimensions; (2) used real patients rather than volunteers who were recruited for the study; (3) studied the therapy of experienced therapists, equal in competence, who were committed to and valued the type of treatment they offered; (4) actually sampled portions of the therapies and evaluated them in terms of various process measures as well as the extent to which they were, in fact, representative of particular forms of therapy; (5) each treatment type was given in equal amounts and to the degree that one could presume that a reasonable amount of benefit might have occurred; and (6) outcome measures were varied and included those that would be expected to be especially appropriate for behavior therapy as well as outcomes that could be considered target goals for psychoanalytically oriented psychotherapy.

Among the limitations of this study were the following: (1) the follow-up data were of little value because patients and treatments were confounded by the time of the follow-up assessment (e.g., behavior therapy patients received psychotherapy, as did many control patients); (2) process observations were limited to a single interview; and, in the case of the Truax variables, to a single four-minute sample of this interview; (3) some of the process measures were not very relevant to clinical practice; and (4) the study focused on analytically oriented psychotherapy and behavior therapy as usually practiced, but did not add to our understanding of specific interventions with specific problems.

The DiLoreto Study

DiLoreto (1971) compared group treatments that employed systematic desensitization, rational emotive therapy, and client-centered therapy. The study involved 100 college student volunteers who reported high interpersonal anxiety and a desire for treatment. Twenty were assigned to each treatment group and an equal number was assigned to a placebo therapy group and a no-contact group, with approximately one-half of the students being introverts and one-half being extroverts.

All groups except the no-contact group were seen for 11 hours of therapy in group sessions consisting of five persons per group. The therapists were advanced graduate students who had experience in and commitment to each of the three main orientations. Evaluation included a multiple test battery and behavior observation ratings.

All three types of therapy were consistently superior to the control groups in outcome. Systematic desensitization was equally effective with introverts and extroverts, whereas the other treatments tended to be more effective with introverts. Although the study included elaborate experimental controls with 72 pages of statistical analyses, the results are somewhat limited by the nature of the subjects who were not from a clinical population, and by the limited experience of the therapists. In addition, commentators who represented the three schools of therapy each criticized the way in which their own therapy was conducted.

Even though this study is sometimes cited as demonstrating the superiority of behavior therapy, we do not believe that part of the evidence to be strong and, rather, believe that it supports the findings of the Temple study in that major differences in outcome as a result of different techniques were not evident.

The Pennsylvania Study.

Rush, Beck, Kovacs, and Hollon (1977) recently reported a study which investigated the effects of cognitive therapy on the symptomatic relief of depressive symptoms in a group of 41 outpatients.

The clients were carefully selected to include a homogeneous symptom pattern typical of neurotic depression. They were screened with the Beck Depression Inventory, Hamilton Rating Scale for Depression, and a clinical judgment consistent with a unipolar depressive syndrome. Patients who had a history of schizophrenia, drug dependence, character disorder, and the like, were excluded as well as patients who had a medical history that contraindicated the prescription of antidepressant medication or a prior history of a poor response to tricyclic antidepressants.

Patients were assigned to cognitive therapy (N = 19) or antidepressant treatment (N = 22) on a random basis prior to inclusion in the study. Therapists were, for the most part, inexperienced in psychotherapy but experienced in the use of

drugs with depression. The majority were psychiatric residents.

Treatment via cognitive therapy followed the training manual developed by Beck, Rush, and Kovacs (1977) and lasted for a maximum of twenty 50-minute sessions for 18 weeks, but averaged 15 sessions for 11 weeks. Drug treatment averaged 11 weeks in duration with one 20-minute session per week.

Results suggest that both procedures reduce the symptoms of depression; but the patient self-report, as measured by the Beck Depression Inventory, and clinician's judgment of improvement as rated by the Hamilton and Raskin scales, showed the cognitive therapy patients to be improved significantly more than the drug patients at termination and at three-month follow-up. This trend held up at the six-month follow-up but was not statistically significant. In addition, there was a tendency for drug patients to drop out of therapy early. When these dropouts are included in the analysis, cognitive therapy was superior to drug treatment at six months. In addition, 13 of 19 pharmacotherapy patients reentered treatment for depression, whereas only 3 of 19 psychotherapy patients sought additional treatment.

This study sharply contrasts with the typical finding of studies that compared psychotherapy with drugs for the relief of depression. In this literature (cf. Covi, Lipman, & Derogatis, 1974; Friedman, 1975; Klerman, Dimascio, Weissman, Prusoff, & Paykel, 1974) drugs or drugs plus psychotherapy have repeatedly been found to be superior to various forms of psychotherapy in the symptomatic relief of depression. However, the self-reports in this study could have been subject to experimenter demand effects, and the clinicians' judgments were neither blind nor unbiased. Controlled replication of this interesting report is therefore required prior to making any inferences about differential treatments for specific depressions.

The Arkansas Study and Related Studies of Therapist Conditions

Mitchell (1973) and Mitchell, Bozarth, and Krauft (1977) reported the results of a large-scale outcome study that aimed to examine the relationship of therapist empathy, warmth, and genuineness to client change. They studied therapy outcomes of 75 experienced therapists, one-half of whom were in private practice. The theoretical preference of this national sample of therapists was approximately one-third eclectic, one-third psychoanalytically oriented, with the remaining one-third being composed of other orientations, such as behavioral, existential, rational emotive, and client-centered. The therapists were a sample of only 5 percent of the number who were asked to participate.

The 120 clients were predominantly young, white, and lower middle class. Diagnostically they were judged to be schizophrenic (37 percent), or neurotic (29 percent), or other (34 percent). Forty-four percent of the clients were in therapy for at least six months while 22 percent were in therapy for only one to two months. The authors report that neither empathy nor warmth were related to client change. Minimally high levels of genuineness were found to have a modest relationship to client change.

In terms of global improvement as measured by the Current Adjustment Rating Scale, Social Ineffectiveness Scale, Psychiatric Status Scale, MMPI, and Self Ideal Q-sort, the authors report that 43 percent to 70 percent of the clients were judged as improved at treatment termination depending on the criterion under consideration. Although not an especially well-designed study, the results of the Arkansas project are representative of recent studies which attempt to test the client-centered hypothesis that facilitative therapist attitudes are necessary and sufficient conditions for client improvement.

Other recent studies that have tested this hypothesis but found no relationship between client improvement and therapist interpersonal skills include: Bergin and Jasper, 1969; Beutler, et al. (1972); Beutler, et al. (1973); Garfield and Bergin, 1971; Kurtz and Grummon, 1972; Mintz, Luborsky, and Auerbach, 1971; Mullen and Abeles, 1971; Sloane et al., 1975; Winborne and Rowe, 1972. Although it was once felt that this hypothesis had been clearly confirmed, it now appears that the relationship between these variables and outcome is more ambiguous than was once believed.

Mitchell, Bozarth, and Krauft (1977), Gurman (1977), and Lambert and DeJulio (1977), have reviewed much of the research literature related to the client-centered hypotheses, elaborated on their implications for training and practice, and have made recommendations for future research. Our review of this literature has led us to question the validity and general utility of the typically applied process measures, to point out the need for researchers to attend more carefully to methodological issues related to measuring therapy process, and to emphasize the need for more specificity in the hypotheses that are derived from client-centered theory. What is needed is a theoretical guide to understanding *client dynamics* in interaction with *therapist attitudes* (see Parloff et al. in this volume for an extended discussion and Lambert, De Julio and Stein, 1978).

The Menninger Study
Summarizing the results of the Menninger study (Kernberg, Burstein, Coyne, Applelbaum, Horwitz, & Voth, 1972; Voth & Orth, 1973) over the more than 20-year period since its inception in 1954 is a difficult task. The study included 42 adult outpatients and inpatients. The objective of the project was to investigate the relationship of personality change to patient, treatment, and situational variables. The patients were seen in psychoanalysis or psychoanalytically oriented psychotherapy by experienced therapists. Those in analysis were seen for an average of 835 hours, and those treated by psychotherapy for an average of 289 hours. Improvement in life adjustment appeared to occur on several concrete indicators such as work status and social functioning, although a number of patients did not seem to improve on these criteria, and some seemed to be worse. On the Health-Sickness Rating Scale, which was devised specifically for this study, the majority of patients improved, although there was no difference in improvement between those in psychoanalysis and those in analytic psychotherapy. The absolute amount of change from pre- to posttesting was apparently significant, although ordinary outcome data are not provided.

This naturalistic study provides an enormous number of correlations. They indicate that a high level of initial ego strength is correlated with positive change regardless of type of therapy—whether psychoanalysis, expressive psychotherapy, expressive-supportive psychotherapy, or only supportive psychotherapy. The feature of ego strength that was most predictive of outcome was the *quality of interpersonal relationships*. Patients with a low quality of interpersonal relationships tended to do poorly regardless of the type of therapy they received. Whereas *high* ego strength provides good prognosis for all types of treatment, psychoanalysis appears to produce the most improvement in such cases. Patients with low ego strength, when treated by therapists with high skill, improved significantly more when focus on the transference was high. Also, patients with ego weakness improved more when a supportive-expressive treatment was provided. Patients with severe ego weakness did better under an expressive approach that focused on the here and now of the transference and on the structuring of their life outside of treatment.

With respect to therapist skill, it was found that the patients of highly skilled therapists succeeded regardless of type of therapy, whereas the less-skilled therapists did better with expressive therapy, perhaps because expressive therapy implies a standardized technique and does not require as much flexibility and involvement by the therapist as supportive therapy.

A summary of the Kernberg et al. (1973a) report has been reprinted in the *International Journal of Psychiatry* with critiques by Malan (1973b), Greenson (1973), and May (1973), and a reply by Kernberg (1973b). Weaknesses noted include the fact that the researchers tested an enormous number of hypotheses on a very small number of patients; the fact that the ratings of therapist skill were *not* independent of knowledge of the therapists and their outcomes; and the fact that it is difficult to draw any strong conclusions about the general effectiveness of the treatment in the absence of an experimental design that includes control groups, and the like.

In our view, the study is commendable in its adherence to the clinical phenomena and its adaptation of clinical judgments to the needs of research. The correlation data have implications for the practice of psychoanalysis as well as related

methods, and do provide some basis for prescriptive psychotherapy. The results tend to confirm the widely held belief that appropriate transference resolution enhances outcome. The results, however, are not generally dramatic and cannot be shown to be better than the results of placebo therapy or other therapies. Therefore, the findings of this project are interesting but have not yet been demonstrated to have a profundity commensurate with the enormous investment of time, energy, and funds over a 20-year period.

The Tavistock Studies

Malan (1976a, 1976b) recently summarized the pioneering series of studies he and his colleagues have conducted at the Tavistock Clinic in London. In these naturalistic studies, series of 21 and 39 patients were treated with brief (10 to 40 sessions) psychoanalytically oriented psychotherapy. Among other purposes, the studies sought to discover whether brief treatment, which applied the same types of interpretations as full-scale analysis, could be as effective as traditional analysis with patients who varied considerably in degree of disturbance. Follow-up data were collected five to six years following treatment termination to determine whether changes induced by brief therapy would be enduring.

Although the results of these studies may be limited because of the research design employed, it appears that brief analytic treatment can be effective with some patients. The characteristics of those who were helped most by this treatment could not be clearly specified, but factors most highly related to positive outcome in both series of studies were (1) interpretive focusing on the transference/parent link, and (2) patient's motivation for change. In more general terms, positive outcome correlated with the process factor called "successful dynamic interaction," defined as a patient who wanted insight and accepted the interpretations of the therapist, especially with regard to the importance of early life relationships on current behavior patterns.

This finding is especially interesting in that it is similar to those reported from the Menninger study. Together, the two studies provide renewed support for the importance of transference and its resolution in personality change; but it is still unclear when and with whom this is especially effective, since many patients definitely improve without going through this process.

Another significant contribution of the Malan group will be discussed in detail later in this chapter. Briefly, it is the careful division of outcome criteria into those indicating symptomatic and dynamic criteria. By making a distinction of this kind and remaining close to the complex clinical material provided by the patients in their studies, these researchers were able to examine complex changes, yet summarize them in the form of simple ratings.

To summarize briefly, it seems fair to say that psychoanalysis and psychoanalytically oriented psychotherapy appear to be effective forms of treatment with some psychoneurotics and a variety of psychophysiological reactions. These therapies seem to be as effective in this regard as others. Because of the time required, its otherwise expensive nature, and its failure to show success exceeding other briefer forms of psychotherapy, psychoanalysis can hardly be considered the treatment of choice for particular clients or types of psychological disturbance. Despite this qualification, the research in this area has added considerably to an understanding of criterion issues, has reinforced the importance of dealing with certain topics in therapy, and has identified patient traits and characteristics that interact to produce both positive and negative outcomes.

The Vanderbilt Study

Strupp and his colleagues at Vanderbilt University (Strupp, 1977; Strupp & Hadley, 1978) contrasted the effectiveness of professionally trained expert therapists and a select group of college professors. This most interesting study examined process and outcome in therapy offered to 15 neurotic college students by five analytically or experientially oriented psychotherapists compared with "therapy" offered by seven nonprofessional college professors to 15 clients with similar disturbances. Outcomes for the two treatment groups were also contrasted with those attained by students who were assigned to either a minimal contact wait-list control group or a so-called silent control group of students from the college population who achieved similar MMPI profiles as the treatment subjects but who had not sought help for their problems.

Change was measured by the MMPI, patients'; therapists'; and clinicians' ratings of changes in target complaints, self-rated overall change, and experts' ratings on clinical scales of disturbance. Content analysis was done via the Vanderbilt Process Scale.

Although the results of this study were not completely analyzed and follow-ups were not finished at the time of this report, several tentative conclusions can be drawn from the preliminary and partial analysis of the data.

Comparisons of amount of change among groups revealed that:

1. There were no significant differences on any of the six measures based on the patient's own perspective.

2. Therapist measures, which apply to the two treated groups only, showed no significant differences between these two groups . . .

3. With respect to ratings made by the independent clinician, *there were no significant differences between the two treatment groups . . .*

Post hoc pairwise comparisons showed that both treated groups were significantly more improved than the control group on four of these six variables. On the remaining two variables, only the Therapist group was significantly more improved than the controls.

The foregoing preliminary results represent only a fraction of the analyses which will ultimately be performed; thus they must be interpreted and generalized with caution.

For all groups, inspection of the distributions revealed large within-group variances on many outcome criteria suggesting tremendous individual variability. Some individuals showed very marked improvement whereas others showed little change, and some even underwent deterioration. These findings suggest the need for examining the performance of individual patients with their respective therapists.

Analyses of process indicated that:

a. Professional therapists (Ts) (dichotomized into analytic and experientially-oriented groups) and alternate therapists (ATs) behaved quite differently in therapy. Therapists with analytic orientation tended to maintain distance between themselves and their patients . . . Experiential therapists offered friendlier more personal relationships . . . ATs were generally warm, supportive listeners who offered their patients specific suggestions about how they might change their lives. . . .

b. The positiveness of the patient's attitude toward therapy and his willingness to participate in the interaction did not vary as a function of the type of therapist he saw.

c. Examinations of the relationship between each of the three process dimensions . . . revealed that the degree to which the patient was actively and positively involved in the therapy interaction was the most consistent predictor of outcome . . . (Gomes-Schwartz, 1977).

d. Therapist activities positively related to good outcome on all measures were facilitation of communication, maintaining a current time focus, and talking about the patient's own experiences and feelings. . . .

e. Good outcome was associated with the therapist giving information, stating opinions, advising activities outside therapy, encouraging or approving certain behaviors, and talking about relationships other than the family. Poor outcome, on the other hand, was associated with more silence and with discussion of the past, especially past family relationships.

Definitive comment must await final data analyses and even replication of this report; but, at face value, these data are a significant challenge to professional treatment for these types of problems in male college students.

Summary of the Comparative Effects of Psychotherapy

After reviewing the comparative treatment and other outcome studies just highlighted, we have drawn the following conclusions.

1. Psychoanalytic/insight therapies, humanistic or client-centered psychotherapy, many behavioral therapy techniques and, to a lesser degree, cognitive therapies, rest on a reasonable empirical base. They do achieve results that are superior to no-treatment and to various placebo treatment procedures.

2. Generally, the above schools of therapy have been found to be about equally effective with the broad spectrum of outpatients to whom they are typically applied. The early dramatic results that overwhelmingly favored behavior therapy and its broad generalization are fading. This is probably because many positive results came from analogue studies instead of from clinical populations. As yet, the "Dodo bird" verdict suggested by Luborsky et al. (1975) and supported by Smith and Glass's meta-analysis of 375 outcome studies (1977) cannot be entirely rejected; however, we still face the problem of never having adequately measured the subtle intrapsychic changes that appear to occur in verbal psychotherapies. It is conceivable that sophisticated criteria of affective and cognitive changes would reveal differential consequences of different interventions; but, thus far, this has not been tested.

3. Although the foregoing are generally true, it seems clear that with circumscribed disorders, such as certain phobias, some sexual dysfunctions, and compulsions, certain technical operations can reliably bring about success. Even here, however, it appears that interpersonal and dynamic factors play an important part.

4. The above conclusions make the issue of efficiency more important than ever. If treatments are about equally effective, then length of treatment is crucial. Clearly, long-term psychotherapy is difficult to justify on the basis of research reports when they are compared with briefer treatment approaches, particularly as long as we evaluate symptomatic rather than dynamic criteria. The rate of change or the efficiency with which formal psychotherapy achieves change is also one of its important advan-

tages over the many change processes that occur under labels like "placebo" or "spontaneous remission."

This point is also a relevant counter to Eysenck's old argument that "2/3 of untreated neurotics improve over a two-year period." If we were to accept his two-thirds remission rate, the fact that his formula for computing spontaneous remission is based on a two-year period would still serve as positive, not negative, evidence for psychotherapy. Treatment effects of this magnitude are frequently obtained in six months or less in formal psychotherapy, a considerable evidence of therapy's efficiency/efficacy over no treatment.

5. Examining outcomes from the point of view of schools of therapy is still too general an approach to lead to many helpful conclusions. For the most part, school affiliation does not accurately describe therapeutic operations. There are probably systematic differences between types of therapy but these differences are not as clear-cut as the school designation implies. Future studies must go beyond lumping procedures under titles such as Gestalt, insight-oriented, and the like. These labels actually do very little to describe therapeutic operations and the process of therapy as practiced.

6. Increasing attempts are being made to merge traditional insight approaches with behavioral approaches (Feather & Rhoads, 1972; Kraft, 1971; Birk, 1974; Segraves & Smith, 1976; Wachtel, 1977), and this trend is even more apparent in the marriage of cognitive and behavioral methods. The trend toward a growing eclecticism has been documented by Garfield and Kurtz (1977) and raises many methodological issues for researchers who are conducting studies that presume to apply a specific procedure to a specific problem. The process of therapy will need to be monitored instead of simply defined by a title.

7. Few definitive studies on the question of specific treatments with specific problems have been reported. *The meager data that*

have been accumulated certainly cause us to question whether different techniques for different problems can be supported at present, with the possible exception of a few behavioral methods for specific problems.

CRITERION MEASUREMENT: TECHNIQUES AND ISSUES[7]

As much of the preceding discussion implies, advancements in our knowledge of how to facilitate behavior changes in those seeking treatment is dependent on our ability to assess the effects of treatment. Thus, we conclude this chapter with a discussion of measurement issues and recommendations for assessing psychotherapy outcomes.

Conclusion 1. Change is Multidimensional

It has proved far too simplistic to expect clients to show consistent and integrated improvement as a result of therapy. The now necessary and common practice of applying multiple criterion measures in research studies has made it obvious that multiple measures of even simple fears do not yield unitary results.

For example, we find in studies using multiple criterion measures (e.g., Ross & Proctor, 1973; Mylar & Clement, 1972; Wilson & Thomas, 1973) that a specific treatment used to reduce seemingly simple fears may result in a decrease in *behavioral avoidance* of the feared object while not affecting the self-reported *level of discomfort* associated with the feared object. Likewise, a *physiological indicator* of fear may show no change in response to a feared object as a result of treatment while improvement in *subjective self-report* will be marked.

This means that divergent processes are occurring in therapeutic change; that people themselves embody divergent dimensions or phenomena; and that divergent methods of criterion measurement must be used to match the divergency in human beings and in the change processes that occur within them. This confirms the notion that any assumptions of uniformity in client characteristics or

---

[7]Parts of this section are an expansion and updating of material that appeared in Strupp and Bergin (1969b) and Bergin and Strupp (1972).

in changes thereof are simply mythical (Kiesler, 1966, 1968).

Factor analyses of multiple change criteria used in complex psychotherapy outcome studies yield generally similar findings. *The main factors derived from these data tend to be closely associated with the measurement method or source of observation* used in collecting data *rather than being identified by some conceptual variable that would be expected to cut across techniques of measurement.* Among the most typical factors are (a) client self-evaluation, (b) therapist evaluation, (c) independent clinical judgment, (d) TAT or other fantasy evaluation, (e) indices of concrete overt behaviors, and (f) a miscellany of factors associated with specific instruments such as interest inventories, sentence completions, personality inventories (for example, subsets of MMPI and CPI scales) and the like (Cartwright, Kirtner, & Fiske, 1963; Gibson, Snyder & Ray, 1955; Forsyth & Fairweather, 1961; Nichols & Beck, 1960; Shore, Massimo, & Ricks, 1965).

Numerous other studies report interrcorrelations among two or more outcome measures; and, although the results sometimes appear to confirm the factor-analytic findings, they are highly variable and difficult to interpret cogently at the present time (Ends & Page, 1957; Parloff, Kelman, & Frank, 1954; Dietze, 1966, 1967; Paul, 1966; Shore, Massimo, & Mack, 1965; Shostrom & Knapp, 1966; & Knapp, 1965). A puzzling aspect of these studies is that significant correlations between different criteria occur consistently across studies in contradiction to the factor evidence, but they do not occur consistently within studies. Whether this is because of chance fluctuations in the diverse data or is the result of some more substantial factors, we are yet unable to determine.

It appears that outcome data may provide evidence about changes made by the individual *as well as the differing value orientations of the individuals providing outcome data* (Bergin, 1963; Strupp & Hadley, 1977).

A recent study by Berzins, Bednar, and Severy (1975), alluded to previously, addressed itself directly to the issue of consensus among criterion measures. The authors studied the relationship among outcome measures in 79 client-therapist dyads, using the MMPI, Psychiatric Status Schedule, and the Current Adjustment Rating Scale. Sources of outcome measurement involved the client, therapist, and trained outside observers. Data from all three sources and a variety of outcome measures showed generally positive outcomes for the treated group as a whole at termination. There was the usual lack of consensus between criterion measures.

Their primary thesis, however, was that problems of intersource consensus can be resolved through the application of alternatives to conventional methods of analysis. The principal components analysis showed four components: (1) changes in patients' experienced distress as reported by clients on a variety of measures; (2) changes in observable maladjustment as noted by psychometrist, client, and therapist (an instance of intersource agreement); (3) changes in impulse expression (an instance of intersource disagreement between psychometrist and therapist); and finally (4) changes in self-acceptance (another type of client perceived change). The practical implication of these findings is that a single criterion might suffice for measuring changes in observable maladjustment, while this practice would be misleading if "impulse control" were the outcome criterion. When outcome measures were partitioned into patient sources and other sources and analyzed with canonical analysis, further specification of areas of agreement between sources of outcome were identified. For example, considerable agreement between the patient and psychometrist regarding changes in psychoticism were found.

Analysis of homogeneous subgroups allowed for yet another examination of the data by focusing on patients who showed similar patterns of change according to all three sources. About half the sample of clients were clustered in this way in four homogeneous but distinct classes. The largest group of clients (19) showed improvement agreed on by all sources, with increased self-acceptance probably the most characteristic change. Eleven clients formed the second cluster with the *opposite pattern*—that of consensual deterioration. The last two cluster types were composed of six and five patients, and within each cluster a different pattern of criterion disagreement emerged.

This report, though not yet cross-validated, underscores the obvious complexity and wealth of knowledge that may be hidden from view by a limited analysis of data. This is further supported in a recent multivariate analysis by Mintz, Luborsky, and Cristoph (1979). Although these procedures require large sample sizes, they are promising.

Strupp and Hadley (1977) in a discussion of therapeutic outcomes emphasize the multiple effects of psychotherapy and the need for a conceptual model in evaluating the diverse changes that result from psychotherapy. They present a tripartite model which suggests that we view outcome from the vantage point of *society* (behavior), the *individual* himself (sense of well-being), and the *mental health professional* (theories of healthy mental functioning).

Strupp and Hadley further suggest that these three views be assessed simultaneously. The interested reader should consult their article for a discussion of the implications and meanings of changes in clients' well-being as assessed from each of these three points of view. They do an admirable job of dealing with the meanings that various discrepancies in functioning have for the assessment of outcome.

Recommendation 1.

(a) Major research effort should continue to be expended to more carefully delineate the *divergent* processes of change that take place as a result of the extant therapies. This may best be done by studying more extensively the relationships among client characteristics, change techniques, and the specific *kinds* of change that occur. (Garfield, Prager & Bergin, 1971a, 1971b; Fiske, 1971; Luborsky, 1971) We continue to believe quite strongly that researchers and therapists must study *kinds of change* instead of general multiform change. (b) A correlated activity would be the more rigorous and extensive development of *measures* for tapping different kinds of change. Some based directly on the factor analytic work would involve (1) more rigorous specification of the variables underlying clients', therapists', and others' ratings of outcome to determine whether differences between their ratings are spurious responses to different dimensions of the change process, or a function

of differing values (cf. Mintz, Auerbach, Luborsky, & Johnson, 1973); and (2) careful comparison of outcome factors such as thinking habits, overt behavior, physiological changes, and feeling states with the *process* of change, to detect and describe what is happening in these domains as a result of therapy.

Conclusion 2. Changes in Both Behavior and Internal States Are Important

Outcome studies should assess both changes in behavior and changes in internal states of experience. This issue emerges directly from the theoretical and technical controversies surrounding the confrontation between behavioral and more traditional therapies (Lambert & Bergin, 1973; Wachtel, 1977). Changes in overt behavior when targeted as criteria are currently very popular and, because they are more easily assessed, they are more impressive than phenomenological changes, though not necessarily more important. The problem of measuring experiential phenomena with adequacy and precision remains a crucial task for future research in criterion development. There is also a growing awareness of the inadequacies of behavioral assessment and the need for more systematic and thorough analysis of assessment procedures in this area (Ciminero, Calhoun & Adams, 1977).

The distinction between *dynamic* and *symptomatic* criteria has proved valuable in the interpretation of change data. Truax and Carkhuff (1967), for example, reviewed a number of studies of patient characteristics and patient change in which they found that certain apparent contradictions in outcome could be resolved by distinguishing between these two types of criteria. They point out, for example, that initial level of inner disturbance is positively correlated with outcome, whereas initial level of behavioral disturbance is negatively related to outcome.

Malan (1976b) and his associates have taken this concept one step further and devised what they call an assessment of internal or dynamic change as opposed to symptomatic or behavioral change. In their analysis, an assessment is made at treatment termination and follow-up to determine how the patient has handled situations that were initially predicted to be the cause of regression and symptom formation. That is, to be dynamically improved, the patient must increase his capacity to cope with *specific* stress-precipitating events. In their study, the spontaneous remission rate for untreated subjects was between 33 and 50 percent on dynamic criteria as opposed to 60 to 70 percent on symptomatic criteria.

From a somewhat different perspective, Cattell (1966) argues in favor of two major set of factors: source traits and surface traits. Source traits refer to the underlying source of behavior or symptoms and are rated by his 16-Personality-Factor Questionnaire. Surface traits refer to constellations of syndromes or symptoms like those that are measured by the MMPI. Factor-analytical studies also reflect this dichotomy when they derive factors representing self-evaluation or TAT factors and behavioral and other concrete factors based on post-therapy achievement or life functioning.

Recommendation 2.

Since "internal" and "external" criteria measure different human characteristics, since these characteristics are significant, since changes frequently occur in both domains during therapy, and since important decisions regarding the value of different techniques continue to be based on the extent of change induced by them, we recommended that future studies include representative measures derived from this dichotomy. Recommendations for specific measures are discussed later in this chapter. (b) We suggest further that therapy process measures be correlated with each of these kinds of criteria to determine more precisely how differing types of change are effected and whether single techniques have multiple effects. (c) We feel that energy might also be more vigorously devoted to specifying which type of client change is more crucial in a given case, thus laying the groundwork for eventually providing the kind of therapy that is most appropriate to the change desired.

Conclusion and Recommendation 3.
Traditional Personality Assessment
Seems Less Promising Than
"Situational" Measures

It is obvious that adequate outcome measurement in psychotherapy is dependent on the scientific status of personality measurement in general. Given the primitive and controversial nature of this field of inquiry, it is not surprising that difficulties arise when research in this area is *applied* to clinical phenomena.

Currently, there is considerable skepticism about the value of personality assessment. This skepticism comes from various quarters including: (a) the popularity of behavioral approaches and the corresponding lack of interest in standard assessment methods that lead to the assigning of people to diagnostic categories or in elaborating on internal dynamics; (b) the humanistically derived belief that the testing and diagnostic enterprise is itself an unhelpful way of relating to persons seeking help; and (c) the belief that personality tests do not work very well, and have unimpressive validity coefficients because they largely measure personality traits to the exclusion of situational variables (cf. Mischel, 1972, 1977).

Although we do not believe that traditional psychological tests should be abandoned, we are in sympathy with those who emphasize the need to assess situation-specific behaviors instead of global qualities, which are viewed as signs or indirect manifestations of important general tendencies (e.g., that human movement in Rorschach responding indicates creativity or impulse control). We believe that assessments that measure situation-specific behavior (e.g., social anxiety related to skill deficiency in heterosexual relationships) instead of general anxiety have proved to be of greater worth than traditional personality tests (especially projective tests) for the purposes of outcome research.

Therefore, future outcome research should attempt to employ, *among other criteria,* one or more of the following assessment procedures: (a) direct behavioral observation, either in vivo or in contrived situations, such as "role playing," and (b) self-report measures that are situation specific. These procedures are elaborated on in the next section. For a summary and critical review of some of the research in this area see Ciminero, Calhoun, and Adams (1977).

We can applaud and encourage the present variety of efforts underway to dimensionalize human behavior in meaningful ways. We suggest, however, that the ramifications of the widespread neurotic suffering which is erupting all about us today require both a sense of urgency and the need for more programmatic efforts.

Conclusion 4. Change Criteria Should Be Individualized

The possibility of tailoring change criteria to each individual in therapy is being mentioned with increasing frequency, and the idea offers intriguing alternatives for resolving several recalcitrant dilemmas in measuring change.

This notion strongly supports the development of a general trend toward *specific* rather than global improvement indices. Thus, if a person seeks help for severe depression and shows little evidence of pathological anxiety, we would emphasize changes in depression rather than changes in anxiety level or global psychological status. Taken together, the trends to specifiy and to individually tailor criteria offer a strong antidote to the vague and unimpressive conclusions so often reported in the outcome literature.

A procedure that is receiving widespread attention and increased use is Goal Attainment Scaling (GAS) (Kiresuk and Sherman, 1968). Goal Attainment Scaling requires that a number of mental health goals be set up prior to treatment by one or a combination of clinicians, client, and/or a committee assigned to the task. For each goal specified, a scale with a graded series of likely outcomes, ranging from least to most favorable, is devised. These goals are formulated and specified with enough precision that an unfamiliar observer can determine the point at which the patient is functioning at a given time. The procedure also allows for transformation of the overall goal attainment into a standardized score.

In using this method for the treatment of obesity, for example, one goal could be the specification and measurement of weight loss. A second goal could be reduction of depressive symptoms as measured by a scale from a standardized test such as the MMPI. The particular scale examined could be varied from patient to patient and, of course, other specific types of diverse measures from additional points of view could also be added. The value of a procedure like this becomes even more obvious when one reads examples of traditional research procedures which assume unidirectional changes to be valuable for all. Vosbeck, for

example (reported by Volsky, Magoon, Norman, & Hoyt, 1965) found that in using "grade-getting" and "degree-getting" behaviors as criteria for effectiveness of college counseling, counselors were often working "against" themselves by encouraging some individuals to seek alternatives to a college degree. In the same way, an increase in anxiety instead of a decrease could be the most beneficial goal of some therapy.

A similar procedure, the Problem-Oriented System (POS) (Weed, 1968; Klonoff & Cox, 1975), has also enjoyed widespread use in the evaluation of mental health services. Both procedures suffer from some of the same deficiencies: they are only frameworks for structuring the statement of goals, and neither assures that the individualized goals which are specified will be much more than poorly defined subjective decisions by patient or clinician. This leads to problems with setting-up goals, which are often not only difficult to state but are written at various levels of abstraction. GAS and POS therefore, add little to the improvement of evaluation procedures except a framework that is directed toward more individualized, behaviorally oriented, observable outcome indices on which there has been prior agreement by those concerned.

Recommendation 4

By giving all clients the same scales but considering movement in opposite directions for different clients' improvement, or by using diverse standardized measures tailored to the individual client, more precision can be brought into outcome studies. We encourage the continued use and diversification of methods to achieve this goal. We suggest that both old and new outcome studies might well be analyzed, using one or more of these techniques. We are impressed with the thought that the meager results of many studies may have been due to misapplications of the same criteria to different patients. This is apt to be especially true when personality questionnaires rather than global ratings or symptom ratings by clinicians have been the central outcome measure. It is entirely conceivable that significant therapeutic effects have been obscured by these blanket applications and that startling new findings await the creative researcher who refines criterion estimation so as to account for the divergent processes simultaneously occurring in groups of therapy cases. (b) We believe that the evidence presented under Conclusion 4, along with that presented in the first three conclusions, affirms the value of the trend noted toward the utilization of criteria specific to the change-induction technique, and to the specific target symptoms. We assume that this kind of precision can be applied in even the most complex cases by the use of multiple, but specifically applied, criteria; that the processes of change will thus be illuminated and the actual effects of psychotherapy will be more accurately assessed (Hammond & Stanfield, 1977).

Conclusion and Recommendation 5. A Standard Assessment Procedure Does Seem Desirable Though Not Yet Feasible

Waskow and Parloff (1975) published a report of their NIMH-sponsored attempt to recommend a battery of assessment devices that could form the core of assessment in psychotherapy outcome studies. A routinely given set of measures could go a long way toward coordinating and accelerating the advancement of knowledge about change endeavors. They were able to draw on the expertise of several well-known psychotherapy researchers and thereby to develop a standard test battery. This battery includes: Hopkins Symptom Checklist (Derogatis, Lipman, & Covi, 1973; Derogatis, Lipman, Rickles, Uhlenhuth, & Covi, 1974); Target Complaints (Battle et al., 1966); Psychiatric Status Schedule (Spitzer et al., 1967, 1970); MMPI (Dahlstrom, Welsh, & Dahlstrom, 1972); and either the Katz Adjustment Scales (Katz & Lyerly, 1963) or the Personal Adjustment and Role Skills Scales (Ellsworth, 1975).

Of course, much controversy is bound to develop over the appropriate devices to be included in such a battery, and at present it is not possible to reach agreement. Our impression of the recommendations of the Waskow/Parloff consultants is that they seem to recommend good measures that have wide, but not universal appeal, especially among behavioral researchers. The value of the battery as a whole, therefore, must await further research. We hope that a number of researchers studying diverse therapies will apply some common measures, and we feel some excitement in

anticipation of the results. Even so, diverse treatment samples, differences concerning valued directions of change, as well as theoretical and conceptual preferences, all make the possibility of an effectively applied, single core battery doubtful. Another possibility is that several core batteries could be developed and applied to treatment situations where appropriate.

Conclusion and Recommendation 6. Suggestions of Useful Techniques

The following discussion consists of brief commentaries on outcome criteria that have proved useful or appear promising. As previous conclusions and recommendations imply, we favor the use of multiple outcome measures. Given the lack of agreement among measures, we also favor the use of indices from a variety of viewpoints. In addition to giving a more complete picture of the change process, assessing change from diverse viewpoints prevents systematic bias and, therefore, unwarranted conclusions. To encourage this diversity we have organized outcome measures under headings that indicate their source: Patient Self-Report, Therapist Evaluation, Trained Outside Observer/Expert Observer Ratings, and Relevant Other Ratings.

Patient Self-Report

There is an abundance of measures calling on the client for an elaboration of his thoughts, beliefs, feelings, behaviors, and current status. Various measures are differentially subject to a host of biasing procedures (e.g., the "hello-goodbye" effect, social desirability, etc.). Most measures reported and summarized by Buros (1972) that are relevant to behavior change have potential as outcome measures. Those that seem most promising are described below.

1.*Minnesota Multiphasic Personality Inventory.* Among the traditional measures that have been used, certain MMPI scales repeatedly yield evidence that they are able to detect client change. Among the scales that appear to provide consistent validity as change indices are *D, Pt,* and *Sc* (Garfield, Prager, & Bergin, 1971). Scales that correlate with these, such as *Si, K,* and *Es,* also frequently manifest changes following psychotherapy. Anxiety scales derived from the MMPI, such as the

Taylor scale or the Welsh scale, also seem to be reasonable change indices, although they correlate highly with D and Pt. The sum of clinical scales has also been widely used and is of similar value (Dahlstrom & Welsh, 1960; Fulkerson & Barry, 1961). Although MMPI scales continue to be used frequently and thus have considerable merit for future work, the MMPI is often criticized as being an essentially outmoded instrument. This is in part for theoretical reasons having to do with the lack of clear meaning of the scales and the items comprising them, in part because of the strongly nosological orientation of the scales, and in part because the scales are not designed with specific types of therapeutic change in mind. Despite these defects, no other paper-pencil measure of psychopathology based on self-report offers anything better to the researcher.

2. *Patient Checklists.* Generally, checklists that have been used in psychotherapy research are of two types: (1) adjective checklists like that developed by Gough and Heilbrun and factored by Parker and Megargee (1967), which seem to identify client traits, needs, or dynamics; and (2) symptom checklists, such as the Hopkins Symptom Checklist (Derogatis et al., 1973) or the Symptoms Distress Checklist, which focuses more specifically on the symptomatic complaints of patients. These types of measures are easy to administer and appear to have value in assessing change. They are more sensitive than the MMPI, or at least they seem to change more readily than measures such as the MMPI. There is evidence that they are greatly affected by instructions during administration. There is also little evidence that they add significantly to what is measured by standardized self-report measures such as the MMPI.

3. *Self-Concept Measures.* Scales measuring self-esteem or self-acceptance continue to have strong influence in psychotherapy outcome research, as described particularly by Butler (1966) and by Truax and Carkhuff (1967) in reporting their series of studies. In addition to the original Q sort devised by Butler and Haigh (1954), several instruments have been devised that are reliable and valid. They include Dymond's Q Adjustment Score (1954), Van der Veen's Family Concept Q Sort (1965), Gergen and Morse's Self-Consistency Score (1967), Endler's adaptation of the Semantic Differential for self-descriptions (1961), the Tennessee Self-Concept Scale (Fitts, 1965), and various adaptations of Kelly's (1955) Role Construct Repertory Test. The intercorrelations of these measures is probably high, and it is difficult to select from them on bases other than personal predilection or popularity. The factor-analytic studies reported previously suggest that measures of this type add practically nothing to what is obtained from the MMPI or similar instruments, and vice versa. They are basically ways of reporting subjective distress, with the exception of the Kellian approach (Large, 1976).

4. *Self-Regulation Measures.* The currently popular trend of trying to effect changes in a person's self-control and self-regulation is resulting in the development of measures of this area of common difficulty among modern clinic populations. This domain has been inadequately tapped in the past and is one that is relevant to several of the newer therapies, for instance Reality Therapy (Glasser, 1965) and Integrity Therapy (Mowrer, 1968). Studies by Ricks, Umbarger, and Mack (1964) of temporal perspective in successfully treated delinquents are relevant here as are studies of delay of gratification (Mischel, 1966), long-range planning (Spivack & Levine, 1964), and general goal orientation. This dimension of patient change seems important, and measures of it are arising that have substance, partly because they derive from an area of general experimentation in psychology. Besides measures of values, such as Shostrom's (1963) Personal Orientation Inventory or the Ways to Live Test (Morris, 1956), there are many useful self-monitoring devices. They include timing devices, mechanical counters, self-monitoring cards, and specific uses for videotape equipment.

5. *Mood Scales.* Another intriguing type of measurement—which has not yet been explored very much in therapy research, with the exception of the Frank group in their role-induction interviews, placebo studies, and long-term follow-ups—is the analysis of moods. There is increasing evidence of a fairly substantial nature that moods can be reliably studied while retaining the experimental validity of the phenomenon. This is evidenced in the work of Wessman and Ricks (1966),

and in work using the Psychiatric Outpatient Mood Scale (POMS) (Lorr & McNair, 1966; McNair, Lorr & Droppleman, 1971). The wessman and Ricks volume, in particular, contains a variety of scales and also reveals a fact quite relevant to therapy research: that people can be reliably characterized by their mood levels and by the degree of stability or variability in these moods. Also, there tend to be quite different mood patterns across individuals. It has been noted by Frank et al. (1959) that moods (as measured by their Discomfort Scale) can be dramatically affected by brief encounters with diagnostic evaluators and initial interviewers. It might be that mood scales will eventually be a good way to evaluate what might be considered the superficial effects of placebo-related events.

6. *Posttherapy Questionnaires.* These "homemade" devices are frequently used in studies and serve the purpose of assessing client satisfaction and of providing gross evaluation of therapy effectiveness. For example, the Client Posttherapy Questionnaire was employed by Cartwright, Kirtner, and Fiske (1963) along with other outcome indices in their study. Strupp, Fox, and Lessler (1969) employed a similar device that asks questions about satisfaction with treatment, degree of change noted, and the like. These unstandardized instruments administered at the completion of treatment are simple, quick, and have high face validity. There is, however, no obvious evidence that they add much to what is measured by standardized instruments like the MMPI.

Therapist Evaluation

Interestingly enough, standardized procedures applied directly by the therapist are relatively few. Many of the instruments used by expert observers could, of course, be applied—with less credibility—by the therapist. These scales have the same virtues and deficiencies as do patient self-ratings. They seem to measure an independent factor in change, or perhaps simply a point-of-view is being measured. A venerable global outcome measure is the nine-point rating scale developed for the Rogers and Dymond project (1954). It is still in considerable use, and correlates so highly with other more complex and sophisticated therapist ratings (Cartwright et al., 1961 or the *Therapist Change Report,* Lorr, McNair, Michaux, & Raskin,

1962) that it may well be the measure of choice for this purpose. However, more specific behavioral ratings are becoming more widely used (see Gelder, Marks, & Wolff, 1967; and Spitzer's *Psychiatric Evaluation Form,* 1967). It is frequently hard for the therapist to provide ratings and methodologically sounder to get others to assess changes in client behavior.

The use of *Target Complaints* as a criterion of improvement continues (Battle, Imber, Hoehn-Saric, Stone, Nash, & Frank, 1966; Sloane et al., 1975) to be a viable method, although it is thought to be limited by the demand characteristics of the interview and considered by some to be superficial. A final device that looks promising but that to date has been used infrequently is the Interpersonal Behavior Inventory, developed by Lorr and McNair (1965). Its advantage is that its focus is on the behavior of the client; it can be filled out by the clinician in less than 15 minutes after four to six interviews with the client.

Expert "Trained Observers"

Judgments about the effects of psychotherapy can be obtained from experienced clinicians not involved in the treatment or by observers trained specifically on a particular device. The methods here are numerous. Among those that appear most promising are Timed Behavior Checklist for Performance Anxiety (Paul, 1966), Behavior Rating Category System used by Becker, Madsen, Arnold, and Thomas (1967), Behavioral Checklist of Interpersonal Anxiety (Diloreto, 1971), Analogue Procedures (Williams and Brown, 1974); Behavioral Assertiveness Test (Hersen, Eisler & Miller, 1973) and a host of frequency counts of specific behaviors performed in vivo or in simulated settings.

Several procedures have reached useful levels of development in standardizing interview evaluation. This approach has been carried out to rigorous dimensions by the Spitzer et al. (1967, 1970) group on the Psychiatric Status Schedule (PSS). This standardized interview covers factor-analytically-derived dimensions of mental status in addition to a broad spectrum of behavioral manifestation of psychopathology. Interjudge reliabilities are excellent, although much of the content is oriented toward inpatients, and initial experiments reveal modest validity data. The PSS is enjoying frequent use by researchers. Other scales developed by the group include the Psychiatric Evaluation Form and Current and Past Psychopathology Scales (Endicott & Spitzer, 1972a, 1972b).

Another similar procedure of considerable merit is the Structured and Scaled Interview to Assess Maladjustment. The interview is structured by an orderly series of questions that encourage the patient to describe different facets of adjustment in five areas: work-school, social-leisure, family, marriage, and sex. Within each area, nine types of maladjustment are assessed. Each type is considered to be a *behavioral deviation,* to show subjective *distress,* or to indicate *friction.* The information gained is rated on scales anchored by several definitions. The interviewer's set is consistently directed toward pathology and maladjustment in the area of social functioning, excluding inquiry into areas of physical health, thought disorder, and the like (see Gurland et al., 1972). This procedure has the advantage of being most appropriate for outpatient adults rather than hospitalized persons.

A device that continues to be applied frequently is the Current Adjustment Rating Scale (CARS) developed by Miles, Barrabee, and Finesinger (1951b). It consists of 14 nine-point Likert-type scales that require the respondent to evaluate the client's current functioning, various satisfactions, and social stimulus value. One advantage of this device is that it can be completed by an observer, the therapist, or a relative as well as by the patient.

The use of Indicators of Physiological Functioning have been employed with considerable success, especially with regard to anxiety and sexual arousal. However, there is at best only a modest relationship between self-report, behavioral, and physiological measures of anxiety. The use of a penile plethysmograph for measurement of penile erection in the treatment of male homosexuality has shown considerable promise (Yates, 1970) as have a number of related procedures.

Advocates of physiological measures have suggested that these devices provide objective and, therefore, "hard" data that are superior to self-report procedures. These methods at this point, however, are hardly infallible. Schwitzgebel and Rugh (1975) have indicated sufficiently large discrepancies in the quality and output of commercially available alpha feedback equipment that one should not be misled into thinking these devices provide "hard" data and are automatically superior to interviews and tests.

Evaluation by Relevant Others
Fiske (1975) categorizes methods that involve the report and evaluation of significant and/or relevant others in the patient's life. These assessments are generally of the kind that allow us to know something of the effects of treatment as perceived by family, friends, or peers, and in areas of living outside of the therapy relationship. This type of measure has been frequently employed to quantify the effects of T-groups on managerial staff by collecting peer ratings sometime after laboratory training (Miles, 1960). In addition, data such as factual records have been obtained and used in some studies (hospital discharge and readmission rates, parole violations, college grades, return to work, etc.). For a variety of reasons, these cannot be considered suitable criteria by themselves.

Considerable data on the Katz Adjustment Scale have been reported (Katz & Lyerly, 1963; Katz, Lowery, & Cole, 1967; Katz, Sanborn, & Gudeman, 1967); and this device, though quite lengthy, seems promising. As with other reports from relatives, and the like, it is wise to collect data from several informants and to use pooled judgments.

Ellsworth et al. (1968) and Duncan (1966) have also created standardized devices that can be used for this same purpose, although each has its unique disadvantages. Duncan's Reputation Test, for example, requires that the client be in a setting where peers have regular opportunities to observe each other's behavior. Measurement of the views of relevant others promises to be an area of appreciable future growth with the increasing use of marital and family therapies (cf. Weiss & Margolin, 1977).

SUMMARY AND IMPLICATIONS

In contrast to the chapter on this topic in the previous edition of the *Handbook,* wherein it was concluded that psychotherapy had an average effect that was modestly positive, recent outcome data look more favorable. A growing number of controlled outcome studies are analyzing a wide variety of therapies. These findings generally yield clearly positive results when compared with no-treatment, wait-list, and placebo or pseudotherapies. This may be the result of improvements in designs, but we believe that a major contributor to these newer findings is that more experienced and competent therapists have been used in recent studies. Our review of the empirical assessment of the broad range of verbal psychotherapies leads us to conclude that these methods are worthwhile when practiced by wise and stable therapists.

Clearly, some people profit considerably from their therapy experience; but it is disappointing to find that too often persons are not helped or are even hurt by inept applications of the very treatments that are intended to benefit them.

Although there is a growing body of knowledge that confirms the value of psychotherapy, differences in outcome between various forms of intervention are rare. Although behavior therapies, and their cognitive variations, sometimes show superior outcomes, this is by no means the general case. Even where it is the case, the criteria of change are often biased in the direction of being sensitive mainly to behavioral changes. Therefore, our hope that the study of specific treatments with specific problems would result in practically useful information has not been realized, with but few exceptions. Comparative studies do not encourage the notion that prescription in psychotherapy will be achieved soon.

Interpersonal and nonspecific or nontechnical factors still loom large as stimulators of patient improvement. It should come as no surprise that helping people to deal with inner conflicts, to form viable relationships, to become less threatened and defensive, or to engage in more productive behaviors can be greatly facilitated in an interpersonal relationship that is characterized by trust, warmth, acceptance, and human wisdom.

It appears that these personal factors are crucial ingredients even in the more technical therapies (cf. Gurman & Razin, 1977, for a comprehensive review of therapist factors in psychotherapy). This is not to say that techniques are irrelevant but that their power for change pales when compared with that of personal influence. Technique is crucial to

the extent that it provides a believable rationale and congenial modus operandi for the change agent and the client.

These considerations imply that psychotherapy is laden with nonspecific or placebo factors (Frank, 1973; Strupp, 1973); but these influences, when specified, may prove to be the essence of what provides therapeutic benefit. Instead of "controlling" for them in research designs by adopting a spurious parallel with medical placebos, we may be dismissing the active ingredients we are looking for.

Equally important is the evidence that client characteristics are strong predictors of outcome. We believe the hypothesis is supportable that the largest proportion of variation in therapy outcome is accounted for by preexisting client factors, such as motivation for change, and the like. Therapist personal factors account for the second largest proportion of change, with technique variables coming in a distant third. The importance of personal factors in change suggests that procedures that match or pair client and therapist characteristics promise to increase our understanding of how some patients improve and how others experience minimal change or even deterioration.

Future advances also will be assured as we examine more closely the outcomes of psychotherapy and the process of change simultaneously. Little progress will be made by undertaking additional studies of the gross effects of poorly described therapeutic interactions and procedures.

We assume that as the interpersonal dimensions of therapy interactions are more carefully examined, it will become possible to define more clearly which kinds of persons help which kinds of clients most effectively. Such evidence will reduce the importance placed on creating techniques and will increase the emphasis on therapist selection and interpersonal skill development. This also suggests that the role of the indigenous, nonprofessional helper will become more prominent, since beneficient personal qualities are widespread in the society at large.

We also hope that empirical tests will be conducted to examine the question of whether there are especially complex disorders that yield only to sophisticated, expert interventions as opposed to the simpler force of an especially humane interpersonal encounter. It will be equally valuable to know whether these interventions speed up the change process in comparison with nonprofessional helping. The special value of professional technical procedures would thus be confirmed or denied.

We cannot continue to assume that professional treatment involves uniquely therapeutic factors unless this can be demonstrated. Unfortunately, valid measurement of the subtle, but powerful, changes that often occur in therapy is rare. To the extent that we rely on gross, symptomatic indices, it will be difficult to show differences across therapies or between professional treatment and the effects of skilled amateurs such as in the Vanderbilt Study. It is therefore important to call, as we did in the last edition, for psychometric advances that will provide answers to basic questions which are otherwise unanswerable.

In conclusion, we continue to be optimistic that research is leading us toward becoming more and more helpful to the many suffering people who seek relief from psychological distress. There are few feelings more gratifying than the satisfaction of collaborating with the community of researchers and clinicians in an enterprise that may benefit those who need help.

REFERENCES

Abramowitz, S. I., Roback, H. B., Schwartz, J. M., Yasuna, A., Abramowitz, C. V., & Gomes, B. Sex bias in psychotherapy: A failure to confirm. *American Journal of Psychiatry*, 1976, 133, 706–709.

Agras, W. S., Chapin, H. N., & Oliveau, D. C. The natural history of phobia: Course and prognosis. *Archives of General Psychiatry*, 1972, 26, 315–317.

Alexander, F. *Five Year Report of the Chicago Institute for Psychoanalysis*, 1932–1937.

Auerbach, A. H., & Johnson, M. Research on the therapist's level of experience. In A. S. Gurman and A. M. Razin (Eds.); *The effective psychotherapist: A handbook;* New York: Pergamon Press, 1977.

Bakker, C. B. Why people don't change. *Psychotherapy: Theory Research and Practice*, 1975, 12, 164–172.

Banks, W. M. The differential effects of race and social class in helping. *Journal of Clinical Psychology*, 1972, 28, 90–92.

Barrett-Lennard, G. T. Relationship inventory: Experimental form OSS-42. Unpublished manuscript, Waterloo, Ontario: University of Waterloo, 1973.

Barron, F., & Leary, T. F. Changes in psychoneurotic patients with and without psychotherapy. *Journal of Consulting Psychology*, 1955, 19, 239–245.

Bartlett, M. R. A six-month follow-up of the effects of personal adjustment counseling of veterans, *Journal of Consulting Psychology*, 1950, 14, 393–394.

Battle, C. C., Imber, S. D., Hoehn-Saric, R., Stone, A. R., Nash, C., & Frank, J. D. Target complaints as criteria of improvement. *American Journal of Psychotherapy*, 1966, 20, 184–192.

Beck, A. T., Rush, A. J., & Kovacs, M. Individual treatment manual for cognitive/behavioral psychotherapy of depression. Unpublished manuscript, Philadelphia General Hospital, Philadelphia, 1977.

Becker, W. C., Madsen, C. H. Jr., Arnold, C. R., & Thomas, D. R. The contingent use of teacher attention and praise in reducing classroom behavior problems. *Journal of Special Education*, 1967, 1, 287–307.

Beiser, M. A psychiatric follow-up study of "normal" adults. *American Journal of Psychiatry*, 1971, 127, 40–48.

Bergin, A. E. The effects of psychotherapy: Negative results revisited. *Journal of Counseling Psychology*, 1963, 10, 244–250.

Bergin, A. E. Some implications of psychotherapy research for therapeutic practice. *Journal of Abnormal Psychology*, 1966, 71, 235–246.

Bergin, A. E. An empirical analysis of therapeutic issues. In D. Arbuckle (Ed.), *Counseling and psychotherapy: An overview*. New York: McGraw-Hill, 1967, 175–208. (a)

Bergin, A. E. Further comments on psychotherapy research and therapeutic practice. *International Journal of Psychiatry*, 1967, 3, 317–323. (b)

Bergin, A. E. The evaluation of therapeutic outcomes. In A. E. Bergin and S. L. Garfield (Eds.), *Handbook of psychotherapy and behavior change*. New York: Wiley, 1971.

Bergin, A. E., & Jasper, L. G. Correlates of empathy in psychotherapy: A replication. *Journal of Abnormal Psychology*, 1969, 74, 477–481.

Bergin, A. E., & Strupp, H. H. New directions in psychotherapy research. *Journal of Abnormal Psychology*, 1970, 75, 13–26.

Bergin, A. E., & Strupp, H. H. *Changing frontiers in the science of psychotherapy*. Chicago: Aldine-Atherton, 1972.

Bergin, A. E., & Suinn, R. M. Individual psychotherapy and behavior therapy. *Annual Review of Psychology*, 1975, 26, 509–556.

Berkowitz, B. P., & Graziano, A. M. Training parents as behavior therapists: A review. *Behavior Research and Therapy*, 1972, 10, 297–317.

Berzins, J. I., Bednar, R. L., & Severy, L. J. The problem of intersource consensus in measuring therapeutic outcomes: New data and multivariate perspectives. *Journal of Abnormal Psychology*, 1975, 84, 10–19.

Beutler, L. E. Psychotherapy: When what works with whom. Unpublished manuscript, Baylor College of Medicine, Houston, Texas, 1976.

Beutler, L. E., Johnson, D. T., Neville, C. W., Jr., & Workman, S. N. "Accurate empathy" and the A-B dichotomy. *Journal of Consulting and Clinical Psychology,* 1972, *38,* 372–375.

Beutler, L. E., Johnson, D. T., Neville, C. W., Workman, S. N., & Elkins, D. The A-B therapy type distinction, accurate empathy, nonpossessive warmth, and therapist genuineness in psychotherapy. *Journal of Abnormal Psychology,* 1973, *82,* 273–277.

Birk, L. Intensive group therapy: An effective behavioral-psychoanalytic method. *American Journal of Psychiatry,* 1974, *131,* 11–16.

Blanchard, E. B., & Hersen, M. Behavioral treatment of hysterical neurosis: Symptom substitution and symptom return reconsidered. *Psychiatry,* 1976, *39,* 118–129.

Blinder, B. J., Freeman, D. M. A., and Stunkard, A. J. Behavior therapy of anorexia nervosa: Effectiveness of activity as a reinforcer of weight gain. *American Journal of Psychiatry,* 1970, *126,* 77–82.

Bond, E. D., and Braceland, F. J. Prognosis in mental disease. *American Journal of Psychiatry,* 1937, *94,* 263–274.

Boyd, J. B., & Ellis, J. D. Findings of research into senior management seminars. *Toronto: Hydro-Electric Power Commission of Ontario,* 1962.

Braucht, G. N. The deterioration effect: A reply to Bergin. *Journal of Abnormal Psychology,* 1970, *75,* 293–299.

Brill, N. Q., & Beebe, G. W. A follow-up study of war neuroses. Washington, *V. A. Medical Monograph,* 1955.

Brodsky, A., & Holdroyd, J. Report of the task force on sex bias and sex role stereotyping in psychotherapeutic practice. *American Psychologist,* 1975, *30,* 1169–1175.

Bruch, H. Perils of behavior modification in anorexia nervosa. *Journal of the American Medical Association,* 1974, *230,* 1419–1422.

Buros, O. K. *The Seventh mental measurements yearbook.* Highland Park, N. J.: Gyphon Press, 1972.

Butler, J. M. Self-acceptance as a measure of outcome of psychotherapy. *British Journal of Social Psychiatry,* 1966, *1,* 51–62.

Butler, J. M., & Haigh, G. Changes in the relation between self-concepts and ideal concepts consequent upon client-centered counseling. In C. Rogers and R. Dymond (Eds.), *Psychotherapy and personality change.* Chicago: University of Chicago Press, 1954, 55–75.

Campbell, J. P., & Dunnette, M. D. Effectiveness of T-group experiences in managerial training and development. *Psychological Bulletin,* 1968, *70,* 73–104.

Carkhuff, R. R., & Truax, C. B. Lay mental health counseling: The effects of lay group counseling. *Journal of Consulting Psychology,* 1965, *29,* 426–431.

Cartwright, D. S. Effectiveness of psychotherapy: A critique of the spontaneous remission argument. *Journal of Counseling Psychology,* 1956, *20,* 403–404.

Cartwright, D. S., Kirtner, W. L., & Fiske, D. W. Method factors in changes associated with psychotherapy. *Journal of Abnormal and Social Psychology,* 1963, *66,* 164–175.

Cartwright, D. S., Robertson, R. J., Fiske, D. W., & Kirtner, W. L. Length of therapy in relation to outcome and change in personal integration. *Journal of Consulting Psychology,* 1961, *25,* 84–99.

Cartwright, R. D., & Lerner, B. Empathy, need to change, and improvement with psychotherapy. *Journal of Consulting Psychology,* 1963, *27,* 138–144.

Cartwright, R. D., & Vogel, J. L. A comparison of changes in psychoneurotic patients during matched periods of therapy and no therapy. *Journal of Consulting Psychology,* 1960, *24,* 121–127.

Cattell, R. B. Evaluating therapy as total personality change: Theory and available instruments. *American Journal of Psychotherapy,* 1966, *20,* 69–88.

Chamberlain, J. M. *Discover yourself by eliminating your own self-defeating behaviors.* Provo, Utah: Brigham Young University Press, 1977.

Christensen, K. C., & Magoon, T. M. Perceived hierarchy of help-giving sources for two categories of student problems. *Journal of Counseling Psychology,* 1974, *21,* 311–314.

Ciminero, A. R., Calhoun, K. S., & Adams, H. E. *Handbook of behavioral assessment.* New York: Wiley, 1977.

Clark, F. Self-administered desensitization. *Behavior Research and Therapy,* 1973, *11,* 335–338.

Coriat, I. H. Some statistical results of the psychoanalytic treatment of the psychoneuroses. *Psychoanalytic Review,* 1917, *4,* 209–216.

Covi, L., Lipman, R. S., & Derogatis, L. R. Drugs and group psychotherapy in neurotic depression. *American Journal of Psychiatry,* 1974, *131,* 191–198.

Cowen, E. L., & Combs, A. W. Follow-up of 32 cases treated by nondirective psychotherapy. *Journal of Abnormal and Social Psychology,* 1950, *45,* 232–258.

Cremerius, J. Spätschicksale unbehandelter Neurosen, *Die Berliner Arztekammer,* 1969, *12,* 389–392.

Curran, D. The problem of assessing psychiatric treatment. *Lancet,* 1937, *11,* 1005–1009.

Dahlstrom, W. G., & Welsh, G. S. Treatment. In W. Dahlstrom and G. Welsh (Eds.), *An MMPI handbook,* Minneapolis: University of Minnesota Press, 1960.

Dahlstrom, W. G., Welsh, G. A., & Dahlstrom, L. E. *An MMPI handbook: Volume I. Cinical applications.* (Rev. ed.) Minneapolis: University of Minnesota Press, 1972.

DeCharms, R., Levy, J., & Wertheimer, M. A note on attempted evaluations of psychotherapy. *Journal of Clinical Psychology,* 1954, *10,* 233–235.

Denker, P. G. Results of treatment of psychoneuroses by the general practitioner. *New York State Journal of Medicine,* 1946, *46,* 2164–2166.

Derogatis, L. R., Lipman, R. S., & Covi, L. SCL-90: An outpatient psychiatric rating scale (preliminary report). *Psychopharmacology Bulletin,* 1973, *9,* 13–27.

Derogatis, L. R., Lipman, R. S., Rickels, K., Uhlenhuth, E. H., & Covi, L. The Hopkins Symptom Checklist (HSCL): A measure of primary symptom dimensions. In P. Pichot (Ed.), *Psychological measurements in psychopharmacology: Modem problems in pharmacopsychiatry.* Basel, Switzerland: S. Karger, 1974, *7,* 79–110.

Dietze, D. Staff and patient criteria for judgments of improvement in mental health. *Psychological Reports,* 1966, *19,* 379–387.

Dietze, D. Consistency and change in judgement of criteria for mental health improvement. *Journal of Clinical Psychology,* 1967, *23,* 307–310.

DiLoreto, A. O. *Comparative psychotherapy: An experimental analysis.* Chicago: Aldine-Atherton, 1971.

Doherty, E. G. Labeling effects in psychiatric hospitalization: A study of diverging patterns of inpatient self-labeling processes. *Archives of General Psychiatry,* 1975, *32,* 562–568.

Duncan, C. B. A reputation test of personality integration. *Journal of Personality and Social Psychology,* 1966, *3,* 516–524.

Dymond, R. F. Adjustment changes over therapy from self-sorts. In C. R. Rogers and R. F. Dymond (Eds.), *Psychotherapy and personality change.* Chicago: University of Chicago Press, 1954.

Ellsworth, R. B. Consumer feedback in measuring the effectiveness of mental health programs. In E. L. Struening, and M. Guttentag, (Eds.), *Handbook of evaluation research.* Beverly Hills, Calif.: Sage Publications, 1975.

Ellsworth, R. B., Foster, L., Childers, B., Arthur, G., & Kroeker, D. Hospital and community adjustment as perceived by psychiatric patients, their families, and staff. *Journal of Consulting and Clinical Psychology Monograph Supplement,* 1968, *32,* (5), 1–41.

Elmore, J. L., & Sugarman, A. A. Precipitation of psychosis during electroshock therapy. *Diseases of the Nervous System,* 1975, *3,* 115–117.

Emrick, C. D., & Lassen, C. L. The non-professional therapeutic agent: Peers with similar problems. In A. S. Gurman and A. M. Razin (Eds.), *The effective psychotherapist: A handbook.* New York: Pergamon Press, 1977.

Endicott, N., & Endicott, J. 'Improvement' in untreated psychiatric patients. *Archives of General Psychiatry,* 1963, *9,* 575–585.

Endicott, J., & Spitzer, R. L. Current and Past Psychopathology Scales (CAPPS): Rationale, reliability and validity. *Archives of General Psychiatry,* 1972, *27,* 678–687. (a)

Endicott, J., & Spitzer, R. L. What! Another rating scale? The Psychiatric Evaluation Form. *Journal of Nervous and Mental Disease,* 1972, *154,* 88–104. (b)

Endler, N. S. Changes in meaning during psychotherapy as measured by the semantic differential. *Journal of Counseling Psychology,* 1961, *8,* 105–111.

Ends, E. J., & Page, C. W. Functional relationships among measures of anxiety, ego strength, and adjustment. *Journal of Clinical Psychology,* 1957, *13,* 148–150.

Ernst, K. Die prognose der neurosen. *Monograph Neurological Psychiatry, 85,* 1959.

Errera, P., & Coleman, J. V. A long-term follow-up study of neurotic phobic patients in a psychiatric clinic. *Journal of Nervous and Mental Disease,* 1963, *136,* 267–271.

Eysenck, H. J. The effects of psychotherapy: An evaluation. *Journal of Consulting Psychology,* 1952, *16,* 319–324.

Eysenck, H. J. A reply to Luborsky's note. *British Journal of Psychology,* 1954, *45,* 132–133.

Eysenck, H. J. The effects of psychotherapy: A reply. *Journal of Abnormal Psychology,* 1955, *50,* 147–148.

Eysenck, H. J. *Handbook of abnormal psychology.* London: Pitman, 1960.

Eysenck, H. J. The effects of psychotherapy. In H. J. Eysenck (Ed.), *Handbook of abnormal psychology.* New York: Basic Books, 1961.

Eysenck, H. J. The outcome problem in psychotherapy: A reply. *Psychotherapy,* 1964, *1,* 97–100.

Eysenck, H. J. The effects of psychotherapy. *International Journal of Psychiatry,* 1965, *1,* 97–178.

Eysenck, H. J. *The effects of psychotherapy.* New York: International Science Press, 1966.

Eysenck, H. J. The non professional psychotherapist. *International Journal of Psychiatry,* 1967, *3,* 150–153.

Eysenck, H. J. Note on "factors influencing the outcome of psychotherapy." *Psychological Bulletin,* 1972, *78,* 403–405.

Fairweather, G., Simon, R., Gebhard, M. E., Weingarten, E., Holland, J. L., Sanders, R., Stone, G. B., & Reahl, J. E. Relative effectiveness of psychotherapeutic programs: A multicriteria comparison of four programs for three different patient groups. *Psychological Monographs: General and Applied,* 1960, *74* (5, Whole No. 492).

Feather, B. W., & Rhodes, J. M. Psychodynamic behavior therapy. Theory and rationale. *Archives of General Psychiatry,* 1972, *26,* 496–511.

Feifel, H., & Eells, J. Patients and therapists assess the same psychotherapy. *Journal of Consulting Psychology,* 1963, *27,* 310–318.

Feighner, J. P., Brown, S. L., & Oliver, J. E. Electrosleep therapy. *Journal of Nervous and Mental Disease,* 1973, *157,* 121–128.

Fenichel, O. *Ten years of the Berlin Psychoanalytic Institute, 1920–1930.*

Fischer, J. Is casework effective? A review. *Social Work.* 1973, *1,* 5–20.

Fiske, D. W. The shaky evidence is slowly put together. *Journal of Consulting and Clinical Psychology,* 1971, *37,* 314–315.

Fiske, D. W. The use of significant others in assessing the outcome of psychotherapy. In I. E. Waskow and M. B. Parloff (Eds.), *Psychotherapy change measures.* Washington, D. C.: DHEW, 1975.

Fitts, W. F. *Tennessee self-concept scale manual.* Nashville: Counselor Recordings and Tests, 1965.

Forsyth, R., & Fairweather, G. W. Psychotherapeutic and other hospital treatment criteria. *Journal of Abnormal and Social Psychology,* 1961, *62,* 598–605.

Frank, J. D. Problems of controls in psychotherapy as exemplified by the psychotherapy research project of the Phipps Psychiatric Clinic. In E. A. Rubinstein and M. B. Parloff (Eds.), *Research in Psychotherapy.* Washington D. C.: American Psychological Association, 1959, *1,* 10–26.

Frank, J. D. *Persuasion and healing.* (2nd ed.) Baltimore: Johns Hopkins University Press, 1973.

Frank, J. D., Gliedman, L. H., Imber, S. D., Stone, A. R., & Nash, E. H. Patient's expectancies and relearning as factors determining improvement in psychotherapy. *American Journal of Psychiatry,* 1959, *115,* 961–968.

Friedman, A. S. Interaction of drug therapy with marital therapy in depressive patients. *Archives of General Psychiatry,* 1975, *32,* 619–637.

Friess, C., & Nelson, M. J. Psychoneurotics five years later. *American Journal of Medical Science,* 1942, *203,* 539–558.

Fulkerson, S. C., & Barry, J. R. Methodology and research on the prognostic use of psychological tests. *Psychological Bulletin,* 1961, *58,* 177–204.

Garfield, S. L., & Bergin, A. E. Therapeutic conditions and outcome. *Journal of Abnormal Psychology,* 1971, *77,* 108–114.

Garfield, S. L., & Kurtz, R. A study of eclectic views. *Journal of Consulting and Clinical Psychology,* 1977, *45,* 78–83.

Garfield, S. L., Prager, R. A., & Bergin, A. E. Evaluation of outcome in psychotherapy. *Journal of Consulting and Clinical Psychology,* 1971, *37,* 307–313. (a)

Garfield, S. L., Prager, R. A., & Bergin, A. E. Evaluating outcome in psychotherapy: A hardy perennial. *Journal of Consulting and Clinical Psychology,* 1971, *37,* 320–322. (b)

Gelder, M. G., Marks, I. M., & Wolff, H. H. Desensitization and psychotherapy in the treatment of phobic states: A controlled inquiry. *British Journal of Psychiatry,* 1967, *113,* 53–73.

Gergen, K. J., & Morse, S. J. Self-consistency: Measurement and validation. *Proceedings of the 75th Annual Convention of the American Psychological Association,* 1967, *2,* 207–208.

Gibb, J. R. The effects of human relations training. In A. E. Bergin and S. L. Garfield (Eds.), *Handbook of psychotherapy and behavior change.* New York: Wiley, 1971.

Gibson, R. L., Snyder, W. U., & Ray, W. S. A factor analysis of measures of change following client-centered psychotherapy. *Journal of Counseling Psychology,* 1955, *2,* 83–90.

Giel, R., Knox, R., & Carstairs, G. A five-year follow-up of 100 neurotic outpatients. *British Medical Journal,* 1964, *2,* 160–163.

Glasser, W. *Reality therapy.* New York: Harper and Row, 1965.

Gliedman, L. H., Nash, E. H., Imber, S. D., Stone, A. R., & Frank, J. D. Reduction of symptoms by pharmacologically inert substances and by short term psychotherapy. *A. M. A. Archives of Neurology and Psychiatry,* 1958, *79,* 345–355.

Goldstein, A. P., & Stein, N. *Prescriptive psychotherapies.* New York: Pergamon Press, 1976.

Gomes-Schwartz, B. "Psychotherapy process variables as predictors of outcome." Paper presented at the 8th Annual Meeting of the Society for Psychotherapy Research, Madison, Wisc., June 1977.

Gottschalk, L. A., Mayerson, P., & Gottlieb, A. A. Prediction and evaluation of outcome in an emergency brief psychotherapy clinic. *Journal of Nervous and Mental Disease,* 1967, *144,* 77–96.

Greenson, R. A critique of Kernberg's "summary and conclusions." *International Journal of Psychiatry,* 1973, *11,* 91–94.

Gruver, G. G. College students as therapeutic agents. *Psychological Bulletin,* 1971, *76,* 111–127.

Gurin, G., Veroff, J., & Feld, S. *Americans view their mental health.* New York: Basic Books, 1960.

Gurland, B. J., Yorkston, N. J., Stone, A. R. Frank, J. D., & Fleiss, J. L. The structured and scaled interview to assess maladjustment (SSIAM). *Archives of General Psychiatry,* 1972, *27,* 259–267.

Gurman, A. S. Evaluating the outcomes of marital therapy. In A. S. Gurman (chm.), Research in marital and family therapy. Workshop presented at the Sixth Annual Meeting of the Society for Psychotherapy Research, Boston, June 1975.

Gurman, A. S. The patient's perception of the therapeutic relationship. In A. S. Gurman & A. M. Razin (Eds.), *Effective Psychotherapy: A Handbook of Research.* New York: Pergamon Press, 1977. Pp. 503–543.

Gurman, A. S., & Kniskern, D. P. Deterioration in marital and family therapy: Empirical and conceptual issues. Paper presented at the Seventh Annual Meeting of the Society for Psychotherapy Research, San Diego, Calif. June 1976.

Gurman, A. S., & Razin, A. M. *Effective Psychotherapy: A Handbook of Research.* New York: Pergamon Press, 1977.

Guttman, H. A. A contraindiction for family therapy. The prepsychotic or post-psychotic young adult and his parents. *Archives of General Psychiatry,* 1973, *29,* 352–355.

Hadley, S. W., & Strupp, H. H. Contemporary views of negative effects in psychotherapy: An integrated account. *Archives of General Psychiatry,* 1976, *33,* 1291–1302.

Hammond, D. C., & Stanfield, K. *Multidimensional Psychotherapy.* Champaign, Illinois: IPAT, 1977.

Hartley, D., Roback, H. B., & Abramowitz, S. I. Deterioration effects in encounter groups. *American Psychologist,* 1976, *31,* 247–255.

Hastings, D. W. Follow-up results in psychiatric illness. *American Journal of Psychiatry,* 1958, *114,* 1057–1066.

Heilbrun, A. B. Female preference for therapist interview style as a function of "client" and therapist social role variables. *Journal of Counseling Psychology,* 1971, *18,* 285–291.

Heilbrun, A. B. History of self-disclosure in females and early defection from psychotherapy. *Journal of Counseling Psychology,* 1973, *20,* 250–257.

Heller, K., Myers, R. A., & Kline, L. Interviewer behavior as a function of standardized client roles. *Journal of Consulting Psychology,* 1963, *27,* 117–122.

Hersen, M., Eisler, R. M., & Miller, P. M. Effects of practice, instructions and modeling on components of assertive behavior. *Behavior Research and Therapy,* 1973, *2,* 443–451.

Horwitz, L. *Clinical prediction in psychotherapy.* New York: Jason Aronson, 1974.

Howard, K. I., & Orlinsky, D. E. Psychotherapeutic processes. *Annual Review of Psychology,* 1972, *23,* 615–668.

Huddleson, J. H. Psychotherapy in two hundred cases of psychoneurosis. *Military Surgeon,* 1927, *60,* 161–170.

Hurvitz, N. Manifest and latent functions in psychotherapy. *Journal of Consulting and Clinical*

Psychology, 1974, *42*, 301–302.

Hyman, H. T. The value of psychoanalysis as a therapeutic procedure. *Journal of the American Medical Association*, 1936, *107*, 326–329.

Johnson, C. A., & Katz, R. C. Using parents as change agents for their children: A review. *Journal of Child Psychology and Psychiatry*, 1973, *14*, 181–200.

Jones, E. Report of the clinic work (London Clinic of Psychoanalysis): 1926–1936.

Jourard, S. M. Changing personal worlds. *Cornell Journal of Social Relations*, 1973, *8*, 1–11.

Jurjevich, R. M. Changes in psychiatric symptoms without psychotherapy. In E. Lesse (Ed.), *An evaluation of the results of the psychotherapies*. Springfield, Ill.: Charles C. Thomas, 1968.

Karlsruher, A. E. The nonprofessional as a psychotherapeutic agent: A review of the empirical evidence pertaining to his effectiveness. *American Journal of Community Psychology*, 1974, *2*, 61–77.

Karon, B. P., & Vandenbos, G. R. The consequences of psychotherapy for schizophrenic patients. *Psychotherapy: Theory Research Practice*, 1972, *9*, 111–119.

Katz, M. M., & Lyerly, S. B. Methods for measuring adjustment and social behavior in the community: 1. Rationale, description, discriminative validity and scale development. *Psychological Reports*, 1963, *13* (4), 1503–1555.

Katz, M. M., Lowery, H. A., & Cole, J. O. Behavior patterns of schizophrenics in the community. In M. Lorr (Ed.), *Explorations in typing psychotics*. New York: Pergamon Press, 1967.

Katz, M. M., Sanborn, K. O., & Gudeman, H. Characterizing differences in psychopathology among ethnic groups in Hawaii. In F. Redlich (Ed.), *Social psychiatry*. Baltimore: Williams and Wilkins, 1969.

Kedward, H. The outcome of neurotic illness in the community. *Social Psychiatry*, 1969, *4*, 1–4.

Kellner, R. Psychotherapy in psychosomatic disorders: A survey of controlled outcome studies. *Archives of General Psychiatry*, 1975, *32*, 1021–1028.

Kelly, G. A. *The psychology of personal constructs*. New York: Norton, 1955.

Kernberg, O. F. Summary and conclusion of "psychotherapy and psychoanalysis: Final report of the Menninger Foundation's Psychotherapy Research Project." *International Journal of Psychiatry*, 1973, *11*, 62–77. (a)

Kernberg, O. F. Author's reply. *International Journal of Psychiatry*, 1973, *11*, 95–103. (b)

Kernberg, O. F., Burstein, E. D., Coyne, L., Appelbaum, A., Horwitz, L., & Voth, H. Psychotherapy and psychoanalysis: Final report of the Menninger Foundation's psychotherapy research project. *Bulletin of the Menninger Clinic*, 1972, *36*, 1–276.

Kessel, L., & Hyman, H. T. The value of psychoanalysis as a therapeutic procedure. *Journal of the American Medical Association*, 1933, *101*, 1612–1615.

Kiesler, D. J. Some myths of psychotherapy research and the search for a paradigm. *Psychological Bulletin*, 1966, *65*, 110–136.

Kiesler, D. J. A grid model for theory and research in the psychotherapies. In L. D. Eron (Ed.), *The relationship of theory and technique in psychotherapy*.

Chicago: Aldine, 1968.

Kiresuk, T. J., & Sherman, R. E. Goal attainment scaling: A general method for evaluating comprehensive community mental health programs. *Community Mental Health Journal*, 1968, *4*, 443–453.

Klerman, G. L., Dimascio, A., Weissman, M., Prusoff, B., & Paykel, E. S. Treatment of depression by drugs and psychotherapy. *American Journal of Psychiatry*, 1974, *131*, 186–191.

Klonoff, H., & Cox, B. A. Problem-oriented approach to analysis of treatment outcome. *American Journal of Psychiatry*, 1975, *132*, 836–841.

Knapp, R. R. Relationship of a measure of self-actualization to neuroticism and extraversion. *Journal of Consulting Psychology*, 1965, *29*, 168–172.

Knickerbocker, D. A., & McGee, R. K. Clinical effectiveness of non-professional and professional telephone workers in a crisis intervention center. In D. Lester, & G. Brockopp (Eds.), *Telephone therapy and crisis intervention*. Springfield, Ill.: Charles C. Thomas, 1973.

Knight, R. P. Evaluation of the results of psychoanalytic therapy. *American Journal of Psychiatry*, 1941, *98*, 434–446.

Korchin, S. J. *Modern clinical psychology: Principles of intervention in the clinic and community*. New York: Basic Books, 1976.

Kraft, T. A case of homosexuality treated by combined behavior therapy and psychotherapy: A total assessment. *Psychotherapy and psychosomatics*, 1971, *19*, 342–358.

Kriegman, G., & Wright, H. B. Brief psychotherapy with enuretics in the army. *American Journal of Psychiatry*, 1947, *104*, 254–258.

Kringlen, E. Obsessional neurosis: A long-term follow-up. *British Journal of Psychiatry*, 1965, *111*, 709–714.

Kurtz, R. R., & Grummon, D. L. Different approaches to the measurement of empathy and their relationship to therapy outcomes. *Journal of Consulting and Clinical Psychology*, 1972, *39*, 106–115.

Lambert, M. J. Spontaneous remission in adult neurotic disorders: A revision and summary. *Psychological Bulletin*, 1976, *83*, 107–119.

Lambert, M. J., & Bergin, A. E. Psychotherapeutic outcomes and issues related to behavioral and humanistic approaches. *Cornell Journal of Social Relations*, 1973, *8*, 47–61.

Lambert, M. J., Bergin, A. E., & Collins, J. L. Therapist-induced deterioration in psychotherapy. In A. S. Gurman and A. M. Razin (Eds.), *Effective Psychotherapy: A Handbook of Research*. New York: Pergamon Press, 1977. Pp. 452–481.

Lambert, M. J., & DeJulio, S. S. & Stein, D. M. Therapist interpersonal skills: Process, outcome, methodological considerations and recommendations for further research. *Psychological Bulletin*, 1978, *85*, 467–489.

Lambert, M. J., & DeJulio, S. S. Therapist interpersonal skills: Process, outcome, methodological considerations and recommendations for further research. Paper presented at the Seventh Annual Meeting of the Society for Psychotherapy Research, San Diego, Calif., June 1976.

Lambert, M. J., & DeJulio, S. S. Outcome research in Carkhuff's Human Resource Development Training

Programs: Where is the donut? *Counseling Psychologist,* 1977, *6,* 79–86.

Landis, C. A statistical evaluation of psychotherapeutic methods. In L. E. Hinsie (Ed.), *Concepts and problems of psychotherapy.* New York: Columbia University Press, 1937.

Langer, E. J., & Abelson, R. P. A patient by any other name . . .: Clinician group difference in labeling bias. *Journal of Consulting and Clinical Psychology,* 1974, *42,* 4–9.

Large, R. G. The use of the Role Contstruct Repertory Grid in studying changes during Psychotherapy. *Australian and New Zealand Journal of Psychiatry,* 1976, *10,* 315–320.

Levitz, L., & Stunkard, A. J. A therapeutic coalition for obesity: Behavior modification and patient self-help. *American Journal of Psychiatry,* 1974, *131,* 423–427.

Lieberman, M. A., Yalom, I. E., & Miles, M. B. *Encounter groups: First facts.* New York: Basic Books, 1973.

Lipkin, S. The client evaluates nondirective psychotherapy. *Journal of Consulting Psychology,* 1948, *12,* 137–146.

Lorr, M., & McNair, D. M. Expansion of the interpersonal behavioral circle. *Journal of Personality and Social Psychology,* 1965, *2,* 823–830.

Lorr, M., & McNair, D. M. Methods relating to evaluation of therapeutic outcome. In L. A. Gottschalk, and A. H. Auerbach (Eds.), *Methods of research in psychotherapy.* New York: Appleton Century-Crofts, 1966.

Lorr, M., McNair, D. M., Michaux, W. M., & Raskin, A. Frequency of treatment and change in psychotherapy. *Journal of Abnormal and Social Psychology,* 1962, *64,* 281–292.

Luborsky, L. A note on Eysenck's article, "The effects of psychotherapy: An evaluation." *British Journal of Psychology,* 1954, *45,* 129–131.

Luborsky, L. Perennial mystery of poor agreement among criteria for psychotherapy outcome. *Journal of Consulting and Clinical Psychology,* 1971, *37,* 316–319.

Luborsky, L. Another reply to Eysenck. *Psychological Bulletin,* 1972, *78,* 406–408.

Luborsky, L. Singer, B., & Luborsky, L. Comparative studies of psychotherapies. *Archives of General Psychiatry,* 1975, *32,* 995–1008.

Malan, D. H. The outcome problem in psychotherapy research: A historical review. *Archives of General Psychiatry,* 1973, *29,* 719–729. (a)

Malan, D. H. Science and psychotherapy. *International Journal of Psychiatry,* 1973, *11,* 87–90. (b)

Malan, D. H. *The Frontier of brief psychotherapy.* New York: Plenum Press, 1976. (a)

Malan, D. H. *Toward the validation of dynamic psychotherapy: A replication.* New York: Plenum Press, 1976. (b)

Malan, D. H., Heath, E. S., Bacal, H. A., & Balfour, F. H. G. Psychodynamic changes in untreated neurotic patients—II. Apparently genuine improvements. *Archives of General Psychiatry,* 1975, *32,* 110–126.

Marks, I. Phobic disorders four years after treatment: A prospective follow-up. *British Journal of Psychiatry,*
1971, *118,* 683–688.

Masserman, J. H., & Carmichael, H. T. Diagnosis and prognosis in psychiatry: With a follow-up study of the results of short-term general hospital therapy of psychiatric cases. *Journal of Mental Science,* 1938, *84,* 893–946.

Masterson, J. F., Jr. The symptomatic adolescent five years later: He didn't grow out of it. *American Journal of Psychiatry,* 1967, *123,* 1338–1345.

Matarazzo, J. D. Some psychotherapists make patients worse! *International Journal of Psychiatry,* 1967, *3,* 156–157.

May, P. R. A. For better or for worse? Psychotherapy and variance change: A critical review of the literature. *The Journal of Nervous and Mental Disease,* 1971, *152,* 184–192.

May, P. R. A. Research in psychotherapy and psychoanalysis. *International Journal of Psychiatry,* 1973, *11,* 78–86.

Mayer, J., & Timms, J. E. *The client speaks: Working class impression of casework.* London: Routledge and Kegan Paul, 1970.

McCabe, A. *The pursuit of promise.* New York: Community Service Society, 1967.

McNair, D. M. Lorr, M., & Callahan, D. M. Patient and therapist influences on quitting psychotherapy. *Journal of Consulting Psychology,* 1963, *27,* 10–17.

McNair, D. M., Lorr, M., & Doppleman, L. F. *Manual for the profile of mood states.* San Diego, Calif.: Educational and Industrial Testing Service, 1971.

Meltzoff, J., & Kornreich, M. *Research in psychotherapy.* New York: Atherton Press, 1970.

Mendelsohn, G. A., & Geller, M. H. Similarity, missed sessions, and early termination. *Journal of Counseling Psychology,* 1967, *14,* 210–215.

Miles, H., Barrabee, E. L., & Finesinger, J. E. Evaluation of psychotherapy. *Psychosomatic Medicine,* 1951, *13,* 83–105. (a)

Miles, H. H. W., Barrabee, E. L., & Finesinger, J. E. The problem of evaluation of psychotherapy: With a follow-up study of 62 cases of anxiety neurosis. *Journal of Nervous and Mental Disease,* 1951, *114,* 359–365. (b)

Miles, M. B. Human relations training: Process and outcomes. *Journal of Counseling Psychology,* 1960, *7,* 301–306.

Mink, O. G., & Isaksen, H. L. A comparison of effectiveness of nondirective therapy and clinical counseling in the junior high school. *School Counselor,* 1959, *6,* 12–14.

Mintz, J., Auerbach, A. H., Luborsky, L., & Johnson, M. Patient's, therapist's, and observers' views of psychotherapy: A "Rashomon" experience or a reasonable consensus. *British Journal of Psychology,* 1973, *46,* 83–89.

Mintz, J., Luborsky, L., & Auerbach, A. H. Dimensions of psychotherapy: A factor analytic study of ratings of psychotherapy sessions. *Journal of Consulting and Clinical Psychology,* 1971, *36,* 106–120.

Mintz, J., Luborsky, L., & Christoph. Measuring the outcomes of psychotherapy: Findings of the Penn. psychotherapy project. *Journal of Consulting and Clinical Psychology,* 1979, in press.

Mischel, W. Research and theory on delay of gratification. In B. A. Maher (Ed.), *Progress in experimental personality research*, New York: Academic Press, 1966, *3*, 85–132.

Mischel, W. Direct versus indirect personality assessment: Evidence and implications. *Journal of Consulting and Clinical Psychology*, 1972, *38*, 319–324.

Mischel, W. On the future of personality research. *American Psychologist*, 1977, *32*, 246–254.

Mitchell, K. M. Effective therapist interpersonal skills: The search goes on. Invited address, Michigan State University, East Lansing, Michigan, 1973.

Mitchell, K. M., Bozarth, J. D., & Krauft, C. C. A reappraisal of the therapeutic effectiveness of accurate empathy, nonpossessive warmth, and genuineness. In A. S. Gurman and A. M. Razin (Eds.), *Effective Psychotherapy: A Handbook of Research.* New York: Pergamon Press, 1977. Pp. 482–502.

Morris, C. *Varieties of human values.* Chicago: University of Chicago Press, 1956.

Mowrer, O. H. Loss and recovery of community: A guide to the theory and practice of integrity therapy. In G. M. Gazda (Ed.), *Theories and method of group psychotherapy and counseling.* Springfield, Ill.; Charles C. Thomas, 1968.

Mullen, J., & Abeles, N. Relationship of liking, empathy, and therapist's experience to outcome of therapy. *Journal of Counseling Psychology*, 1971, *18*, 39–43.

Mylar, J. L., & Clement, P. W. Prediction and comparison of outcome in systematic desensitization and implosion. *Behavior Research and Therapy*, 1972, *10*, 235–246.

Nichols, R. C., & Beck, K. W. Factors in psychotherapy change. *Journal of Consulting Psychology*, 1960, *24*, 388–399.

Noyes, R., & Clancy, J. Anxiety neurosis: A five-year follow-up. *Journal of Nervous and Mental Disease*, 1976, *162*, 200–205.

O'Dell, S. Training parents in behavior modification: A review. *Psychological Bulletin*, 1974, *81*, 418–433.

Palmer, J. O. *The psychological assessment of children.* New York: Wiley, 1970.

Parker, G. V. C., & Megargee, E. I. Factor analytic studies of the adjective check list. *Proceedings of the 75th Annual Convention of the American Psychological Association*, 1967, *2*, 211–212.

Parloff, M. B., Kelman, H. C., & Frank, J. D. Comfort, effectiveness and self-awareness as criteria of improvement in psychotherapy. *American Journal of Psychiatry*, 1954, *3*, 343–351.

Paul, G. L. *Effects of insight, desensitization, and attention placebo treatment of anxiety.* Stanford, Calif.: Stanford University Press, 1966.

Paul, G. L. Insight versus desensitization in psychotherapy two years after termination. *Journal of Consulting Psychology*, 1967, *31*, 333–348.

Poser, E. The effect of therapists' training on group therapeutic outcome. *Journal of Consulting Psychology*, 1966, *30*, 283–289.

Powers, E., & Witmer, H. *An experiment in the prevention of delinquency.* New York: Columbia University Press, 1951.

Rachman, S. *The Effects of Psychotherapy.* Oxford: Pergamon Press, 1971.

Rachman, S. The effects of psychological treatment. In H. Eysenck (Ed.), *Handbook of abnormal psychology.* New York: Basic Books, 1973.

Rachman, S., & Teasdale, J. *Aversion therapy and behavior disorders: An analysis.* Coral Gables, Fl.: University of Miami Press, 1969.

Reisman, J. M., & Yamokoski, T. Psychotherapy and friendship: An analysis of the communication of friends. *Journal of Counseling Psychology*, 1974, *21*, 269–273.

Reiss, B. F. Some causes and correlates of psychotherapy termination: A study of 500 cases. *International Mental Health Research Newsletter*, 1973, *15*, 4–7.

Ricks, D. F. Supershrink: Methods of a therapist judged successful on the basis of adult outcomes of adolescent patients. In D. F. Ricks, M. Roff, A. Thomas. (Eds.), *Life history research in psychopathology.* Minneapolis: University of Minnesota, 1974.

Ricks, D., Umbarger, C., & Mack, R. A. A measure of increased temporal perspective in successfully treated adolescent delinquent boys. *Journal of Abnormal and Social Psychology*, 1964, *69*, 685–689.

Roback, H. B. The comparative influence of insight and non-insight psychotherapies on therapeutic outcome: A review of the experimental literature. *Psychotherapy: Theory and Research Practice*, 1971, *8*, 23–25.

Rogers, C., & Dymond, R. *Psychotherapy and personality change.* Chicago: University of Chicago Press, 1954.

Rogers, C. R., Gendlin, E. T., Kiesler, D., & Truax, C. B. *The therapeutic relationship and its impact: A study of psychotherapy with schizophrenics.* Madison: University of Wisconsin Press, 1967.

Rosen, G. M., Glasgow, R. E., & Barrera, M., Jr. A controlled study to assess the clinical efficacy of totally self-administered systematic desensitization. *Journal of Consulting and Clinical Psychology*, 1976, *44*, 208–217.

Rosenzweig, S. A transevaluation of psychotherapy—a reply to Hans Eysenck. *Journal of Abnormal and Social Psychology*, 1954, *49*, 298–304.

Ross, S. M., & Proctor, S. Frequency and duration of hierarchy item exposure in a systematic desensitization analogue. *Behavior Research and Therapy*, 1973, *11*, 303–312.

Rush, A. J., Beck, A. T., Kovacs, J., & Hollon, S. Comparative efficacy of cognitive therapy and pharmacotherapy in the treatment of depressed outpatients. *Cognitive Therapy and Research*, 1977, *1*, 17–37.

Saslow, B., & Peters, A. Follow-up of "untreated" patients with behavior disorders. *Psychiatric Quarterly*, 1956, *30*, 283–302.

Sattler, J. M. The therapeutic relationship under varying conditions of race. In A. S. Gurman & A. M. Razin (Eds.), *The effective psychotherapist: A handbook.* New York: Pergamon Press, 1977.

Schorer, C., Lowinger, P., Sullivan, T., & Hartlaub, G. Improvement without treatment. *Diseases of the Nervous System*, 1968, *29*, 100–104.

Schwitzgebel, R. L., & Rugh, J. D. Of bread, circuses,

and alpha machines. *American Psychologist*, 1975, *30*, 363–370.

Shepherd, M., & Gruenberg, E. The age for neurosis. *Millbank Memorial Quarterly Bulletin*, 1957, *35*, 258–265.

Schwartz, J. M., & Abramowitz, S. I. Value-related effects on psychiatric judgment. *Archives of General Psychiatry*, 1975, *32*, 1525–1529.

Segal, S. P. Research on the outcome of social work therapeutic interventions: A review of the literature. *Journal of Health and Social Behavior*, 1972, *13*, 3–17.

Segraves, R. T., & Smith, R. C. Concurrent psychotherapy and behavior therapy: Treatment of psychoneurotic outpatients. *Archives of General Psychiatry*, 1976, *33*, 756–763.

Shader, R. I. & DiMascio, A. *Psychotropic drug side-effects: Clinical and Theoretical Perspectives.* Baltimore: Williams & Wilkins, 1970.

Shore, M. P., & Massimo, J. L. After ten years: A follow-up study of comprehensive vocationally oriented psychotherapy. *American Journal of Ortho-psychiatry*, 1973, *43*, 128–132.

Shore, M. F., Massimo, J. L., & Mack, R. The relationship between levels of guilt in thematic stories and un-socialized behavior. *The Journal of Projective Techniques and Personality Assessment*, 1964, *28*, 346–349.

Shore, M. F., Massimo, J. L., & Ricks, D. F. A factor analytic study of psychotherapeutic change in delinquent boys. *Journal of Clinical Psychology*, 1965, *21*, 208–212.

Shostrom, E. L. *Personal orientation inventory.* San Diego Calif.: Educational and Industrial Testing Service, 1963.

Shostrom, E. L., & Knapp, R. R. The relationship of a measure of self-actualization (POI) to a measure of pathology (MMPI) and to therapeutic growth. *American Journal of Psychotherapy*, 1966, *20*, 193–202.

Siegel, J. M. Mental health volunteers as change agents. *American Journal of Community Psychology*, 1973, *1*, 138–158.

Sines, L., Silver, R., & Lucero, R. The effect of therapeutic intervention by untrained "therapists." *Journal of Clinical Psychology*, 1961, *17*, 394–396.

Singer, B., & Luborsky, L. Countertransference: The status of clinical and quantitative research. In A. S. Gurman and A. M. Razin (Eds.), *Effective Psychotherapy: A Handbook of Research.* New York: Pergamon Press, 1977. Pp. 433–451.

Sloane, R. B., Staples, F. R., Cristol, A. H., Yorkston, N. J., & Whipple, K. *Short-term analytically oriented psychotherapy vs. behavior therapy.* Cambridge, Mass.: Harvard University Press, 1975.

Snyder, W. U. *The psychotherapy relationship.* New York: Macmillan, 1961.

Spitzer, R. L., Endicott, J., & Cohen, G. *The psychiatric status schedule: Technique for evaluating social and role functioning and mental status.* New York State Psychiatric Institute and Biometrics Research, New York, 1967.

Spitzer, R. L., Endicott, J., Fleiss, J. L., & Cohen, J. The psychiatric status schedule: A technique for evaluat-

ing psychopathology and impairment in role functioning. *Archives of General Psychiatry*, 1970, *23*, 41–55.

Spivack, G., & Levine, M. *Self-regulation in acting out and normal adolescents.* Devon, Pa: The Devereux Foundation, 1964.

Strupp, H. H. The outcome problem in psychotherapy revisited. *Psychotherapy*, 1963, *1*, 1–13.

Strupp, H. H. The outcome problem in psychotherapy: A rejoinder. *Psychotherapy*, 1964, *1*, 101.

Strupp, H. H. Specific vs. nonspecific factors in psychotherapy and the problem of control. In H. H. Strupp. *Psychotherapy: Clinical, Research and Theoretical Issues.* New York: Jason Aronson, 1973.

Strupp, H. H. The Vanderbilt psychotherapy process-outcome project. Paper presented at the 8th annual meeting, Society for Psychotherapy Research, Madison, Wisc., June 1977.

Strupp, H. H., & Bergin, A. E. *A bibliography of research in psychotherapy.* Washington, D. C.: National Instiute of Mental Health, 1969. (a)

Strupp, H. H., & Bergin, A. E. Some empirical and conceptual bases for coordinated research in psychotherapy: A critical review of issues, trends and evidence. *International Journal of Psychiatry*, 1969, *7*, 18–90 (b)

Strupp, H. H., & Hadley, S. W. A tripartite model of mental health and therapeutic outcomes: With special reference to negative effects in psychotherapy, *American Psychologist*, 1977, *32*, 187–196.

Strupp, H. H., & Hadley, S. W. Specific vs. nonspecific factors in psychotherapy: A controlled study of outcome. *Archives of General Psychiatry*, 1978.

Strupp, H. H., Fox, R. E., & Lessler, K. *Patients view their psychotherapy,* Baltimore: Johns Hopkins University Press, 1969.

Strupp, H. H., Hadley, S. W., & Gomes-Schwartz, B. *Psychotherapy for better or worse: An analysis of the problem of negative effects.* New York: Jason Aronson, 1977.

Stuart, R. B., & Lott, L. A. Behavioral contracting with delinquents: A cautionary note. *Journal of Behavioral Therapy and Experimental Psychiatry*, 1972, *3*, 161–169.

Subotnik, L. Spontaneous remission: Fact or artifact? *Psychological Bulletin*, 1972, *77*, 32–48. (a)

Subotnik, L. "Spontaneous remission" of deviant MMPI profiles among college students. *Journal of Consulting and Clinical Psychology*, 1972, *38*, 191–201. (b)

Subotnik, L. Spontaneous remission of emotional disorders in a general medical practice. *Journal of Nervous and Mental Disease*, 1975, *161*, 239–244.

Truax, C. B. Effective ingredients in psychotherapy: An approach to unraveling the patient-therapist interaction. *Journal of Counseling Psychology*, 1963, *10*, 256–263.

Truax, C. B., & Carkhuff, R. R. *Toward effective counseling and psychotherapy: Training and practice.* Chicago: Aldine, 1967.

Truax, C. B., & Mitchell, K. M. Research on certain therapist interpersonal skills in relation to process and outcome. In A. E. Bergin and S. L. Garfield

(Eds.), *Handbook of psychotherapy and behavior change.* New York: Wiley, 1971. Pp. 299–344.

Tyrer, P., & Steinberg, D. Symptomatic treatment of agoraphobia and social phobias: A follow-up study. *International Journal of Psychiatry,* 1975, *127,* 163–168.

Uhlenhuth, E. H., & Duncan, D. B. Subjective change in psychoneurotic outpatients with medical students I. The kind, amount, and course of change. Unpublished manuscript, Johns Hopkins University, 1968.

Underwood, W. J. Evaluation of laboratory method training. *Training Directors Journal,* 1965, *19,* 34–40.

Volsky, T., Jr., Magoon, T. J., Norman, W. T., & Hoyt, D. P. *The outcomes of counseling and psychotherapy.* Minneapolis: University of Minnesota Press, 1965.

Vandenbos, G. R., & Karon, B. P. Pathogenesis: A new therapist personality dimension related to therapeutic effectiveness. *Journal of Personality Assessment,* 1971, *35,* 252–260.

Van Der Veen, F. The parent's concept of the family unit and child adjustment. *Journal of Counseling Psychology,* 1965, *12,* 196–200.

Vorster, D. Psychotherapy and the results of psychotherapy. *South African Medical Journal,* 1966, *40,* 934–936.

Voth, H. M., & Orth, M. I I. *Psychotherapy and the role of the environment.* New York: Behavioral Press, 1973.

Wachtel, P. L. *Psychoanalysis and behavior therapy: Toward an integration.* New York: Basic Books, 1977.

Walker, R. G., & Kelley, F. E. Short term psychotherapy with hospitalized schizophrenic patients. *Acta Psychiatrica Neurologica Scandinavica,* 1960, *35,* 34–56.

Wallace, H., & Whyte, M. Natural history of psychoneurosis. *British Medical Journal,* 1959, *1,* 1–142.

Wallach, M. S. Therapists' patient preferences and their rleationship to two patient variables. *Journal of Clinical Psychology,* 1962, *18,* 497–501.

Waskow, I. E., & Parloff, M. B. *Psychotherapy change measures.* Washington, D. C.: DHEW, 1975.

Weber, J. J., Elinson, J., & Moss, L. M. The application of ego strength scales to psychoanalytic clinic records.

In G. S. Goldman and D. Shapiro (Eds.), *Developments in psychoanalysis at Columbia University: Proceedings of the 20th Anniversary Conference,* Columbia Psychoanalytic Clinic for Training and Research, New York, 1965.

Weed, L. I. Medical Records that Guide and Teach. *New England Journal of Medicine,* 1968, *278,* 593–657.

Weinman, B., Kleiner, R., Yu, J. H., & Tillson, V. A. Social treatment of the chronic psychotic patient in the community. *Journal of Community Psychology,* 1974, *2,* 358–365.

Weiss, R. L., & Margolin, G. *Assessment of marital conflict and accord.* In A. R. Ciminero, K. S. Calhoun, and H. E. Adams (Eds.), *Handbook of behavioral assessment.* New York: Wiley, 1977.

Wessman, A. E., & Ricks, D. F. *Mood and personality.* New York: Holt, Rinehart and Winston, 1966.

Wheeler, E. D., White, P. D., Reed, E. W., & Cohen, M. E. Neurocirculatory asthenia (anxiety neurosis, effort syndrome, neuroasthenia): A twenty-year follow-up study of one hundred and seventy-three patients. *Journal of the American Medical Association,* 1950, *142,* 878–889.

Williams, R. J., & Brown, R. A. Differences in baseline drinking behavior between New Zealand alcoholics and normal drinkers *Behavior Research and Therapy,* 1974, *12,* 287–294.

Wilson, G. T., & Thomas, M. G. W. Self- versus drug-produced relaxation and the effects of instructional set in standardized systematic desensitization. *Behavior Research and Therapy,* 1973, *11,* 279–288.

Winborn, B. B., & Rowe, W. Self-actualization and the communication of facilitative conditions—a replication. *Journal of Counseling Psychology,* 1972, *19,* 26–29.

Wooten, L. H., Armstrong, R. W., & Lilley, D. An investigation into the after-histories of discharged mental patients. *Journal of Mental Science,* 1935, *81,* 168–172.

Yalom, I. D., & Leiberman, M. A. A study of encounter group casualties. *Archives of General Psychiatry,* 1971, *25,* 16–30.

Yates, A. J. *Behavior therapy.* Wiley, New York: 1970.

6

RESEARCH ON CLIENT VARIABLES IN PSYCHOTHERAPY

SOL L. GARFIELD

Washington University

Whether our concern is research or practice, the client is clearly an important variable in psychotherapy and is the focus of many research investigations. In appraising the diverse material on this topic, I devote primary attention to the results of empirical research investigation. Clinical and theoretical discussions of psychotherapy, individual case studies, or descriptive accounts without supporting data, are generally bypassed.

In any conceptualization of the psychotherapeutic process, it is apparent that three main influences can be postulated: the client or patient, the therapist, and the resulting interaction of these two variables. Ideally, each of these variables should be studied in their natural interacting state and should be evaluated in relation to significant criteria of therapy. Unfortunately, the study of the interaction of patient and therapist variables in relation to specific outcome criteria has been a rarity (Beutler, 1973; Kiesler, 1966; Orlinsky & Howard, 1975; Paul, 1967; Saltzman, Luetgert, Roth, Creaser, & Howard, 1976).

A variety of studies have attempted to relate differing client attributes to selected variables. Among the client attributes have been social class variables, personality variables, diagnosis, age, sex, intelligence, and the like. These have been related to outcome, continuation in psychotherapy, therapy behavior, and similar variables. To the extent that some research findings are relatively stable and stand up under cross-validation with new samples, we have findings that appear to have definite relevance for clinical practice and theory. However, if research reports are weak methodologically or if there are conflicting findings in the literature, one must be cautious in the conclusions one derives from these data.

One problem in research on psychotherapy is a tendency to discuss and to view psychotherapy as if it were a unitary process. Many discussions refer generally to psychotherapy or psychotherapeutic treatment with little specification. With well over 100 different kinds of psychotherapy in existence, one cannot speak meaningfully of psychotherapy in general (Report of the Research Task Force of the National Institute of Mental Health, 1975). Although there has been a greater tendency recently to designate the therapeutic approach used in research studies, particularly in the case of behavioral and client-centered therapies, there are still instances where only crude designations have been used, with little attempt to describe the actual operations of psychotherapy.

Under these circumstances, it is not surprising that research on client variables may produce conflicting or inconsistent results. Although problems of this kind tend to limit the value or generalizability of much research, current research appears more cognizant of these difficulties. A careful review of past research, however, may indicate where we are at present, what findings appear to have some tenability and application, and the direction future research should take. The present chapter, therefore, focuses on empirical investigations in the field of psychotherapy that study client variables in relationship to some external criterion or outcome. Representative samples of the available research data are evaluated and some implications are indicated for practice and research.

THE SELECTION OF CLIENTS FOR PSYCHOTHERAPY

One interesting aspect of psychotherapy pertains to the kinds of people who voluntarily seek out psychotherapeutic treatment, those who are referred for psychotherapy, and those who are selected for psychotherapy. This is an intriguing problem with a number of implications for practice. Several kinds of data are available to help us appraise this matter, although they are admittedly incomplete. Most reports come from clinics and community surveys, and there is a dearth of information concerning clients who are treated by private practitioners. If we can hypothesize that there is a significant difference between those who go to low-cost clinics and those who receive long-term psychotherapy on a private basis (Udell & Hornstra, 1975), then it is apparent that the reported findings provide only a partial picture of who gets psychotherapy. Additional data on this problem would be of interest.

Frank (1974a) has suggested the importance of demoralization as a possible factor that causes people to seek out personal psychotherapy. Several studies have found that those individuals who

secured treatment exhibited more helplessness, social isolation, and a sense of failure or lack of worth than those who did not seek treatment (Galassi & Galassi, 1973; Kellner & Sheffield, 1973; Vaillant, 1972). In another study, a group of treated depressed patients were matched with an untreated group for degree of depression. The treated group was found to be more self-accusatory and helpless (Katz, 1970). Frank also believes that the most frequent symptoms of patients in psychotherapy, anxiety and depression, are expressions of the patients' feelings of demoralization. Not all patients who suffer from demoralization, however, necessarily seek out or accept psychotherapy when it is offered to them.

It is also apparent that not all individuals who apply for treatment receive psychotherapy. Coincidentally, not all individuals who are offered psychotherapy accept it. With regard to the latter, two reports indicate that approximately one-third of clients judged to be in need of psychotherapy, and to whom it was offered, refused such treatment (Garfield & Kurz, 1952; Rosenthal & Frank, 1958). In another investigation, 230 patients out of 603, or 38 percent, failed to return for treatment or disposition even though they were given a definite appointment (Weiss & Schaie, 1958). Marks (1978) also mentions that of several hundred patients who were offered behavioral treatment in his unit at the Maudsley Hospital from 1971 to 1974, 23 percent refused the treatment.

Several studies have investigated the possible factors or variables related to this rejection of therapy. Rosenthal and Frank (1958) found a significant relationship between acceptance on the part of the client and the client's income, and between acceptance and rated level of motivation. Level of education was related to acceptance only at a suggestive level of significance ($p < .10$). Yamamoto and Goin (1966) also reported a significant correlation between lower socioeconomic status and the failure of a client to keep his initial appointment. Thus, in these two studies, there is a suggestion of some relationship between socioeconomic variables and the acceptance of psychotherapy on the part of patients. In one other study in which 64 self-referred patients who failed to keep their first therapy appointment were compared with a comparable number of those who did, no differences were secured in terms of age, sex, or education (Noonan, 1973). However, a difference was noted between these groups of patients in the way they originally presented their problems. The pretherapy dropouts tended to state their problems in a vague and evasive manner, whereas the others varbalized more specific problems.

Two reports based on two different samples of referrals to the Psychiatric Outpatient Department of Boston City Hospital also indicate a large percentage of nonattenders for the initial appointment. In one study of 267 referrals, 42 percent did not keep their appointment (Raynes & Warren, 1971a), whereas in the other, 40 percent of 738 referrals did not attend (Raynes & Warren, 1971b). In the first report, it was also found that age and race were related to attendance. Blacks and those under 40 were significantly more likely to fail to keep their appointments. No data of this kind were reported in the second study (Raynes & Warren, 1971b), but there appeared to be a relationship between time on the waiting list and nonattendance.

Brandt (1964; Riess & Brandt, 1965) has challenged the finding that about one-third of those who apply to clinics for outpatient treatment reject psychotherapy, but his findings are not very convincing. In his first study, only two-thirds of the subjects were contacted and only one-half were willing to give complete data about whether they were receiving psychotherapy elsewhere. In a second study (Riess & Brandt, 1965), more than one-fourth of the applicants did not show up for intake, and another 10 percent withdrew from treatment. From that point on it is difficult to draw any firm conclusions from the published report. Nothing is said about the composition of the sample, and for many cases, insufficient data were obtained. Therefore, we have little reason to reject the notion that a sizable percentage of those who apply for outpatient treatment reject psychotherapy.

The problem of who is accepted for psychotherapy on the part of clinical personnel also has received attention from investigators. Schaffer and Myers (1954) found that social class status was positively related to acceptance for treatment. This finding, with minor variations, has also been reported in two other studies (Brill & Storrow, 1960; Cole, Branch, & Allison, 1962). A somewhat re-lated finding is also reported by Rosenthal and Frank (1958). They examined those patients who were specifically referred for psychotherapy from the total group who were seen at the Henry Phipps Clinic during a three-year period. Among other findings, they discovered a significant relationship between variables such as age, race, education, income, diagnosis and motivation, and referral for psychotherapy. Thus, in all four of these studies, which were carried out in a medical school complex, some relationship existed between social class variables and referral or acceptance for psychotherapy.

Similar findings have been reported in a study of a Veterans Administration (VA) Mental Hygiene Clinic (Bailey, Warshaw, & Eichler, 1959). As-signment to psychotherapy was reported to be re-lated to high socioeconomic status, intrapsychic complaints, age, expressed desire for psychotherapy, psychological test evaluation, and previous psychotherapy. Assignment to the psychosomatic clinic, on the other hand, was re-lated to low socioeconomic status, somatic complaints, lack of recommendation from the psychological test evaluation, and no previous psychotherapy.

Somewhat comparable findings are reported also in a study of a large urban mental health center (Lubin, Hornstra, Lewis, & Bechtel, 1973). Significant associations were found between variables such as education, occupation, age, race, and diagnosis, and the type of treatment initially accorded the patient. Patients with less than 12 years of education and with lower occupational ratings were assigned disproportionately more frequently to inpatient treatment, and less frequently to individual psychotherapy. The converse was true for those with some college education and higher occupational ratings. Race and age were also related to type of assignment, with blacks and those over 39 years of age being overrepresented in the inpatient service and underrepresented in individual psychotherapy. A study of a walk-in clinic also found a significant relationship between low socioeconomic status and the likelihood of receiving drugs rather than psychotherapy (Shader, 1970).

Some reference should be made also to another aspect of this problem. As pointed out by Hollingshead and Redlich (1958) in their classic study, different social classes appear to receive different kinds of treatment, with long-term psychoanalytic treatment being given mainly to middle and upper class clients. It is very likely that such individuals make up the largest proportion of those in private therapy. The results of the mental health survey reported by Ryan (1969) for the City of Boston would appear to support this view. For example, of those who are judged to be emotionally disturbed, less than 10 percent will apply for treatment at one of the outpatient psychiatric clinics in Boston—and of these individuals, less than one-half may be accepted for treatment. Less than one percent of those judged to be disturbed will be treated by psychiatrists in private practice, and these individuals appear to be a highly selected group. About two-thirds are females, four out of five have gone to college or are in college, "and occupations are generally consistent with education, reflecting a class level in the middle and upper ranges" (Ryan, 1969, p. 15).

A study of different kinds of clinics in New York City also indicates varying admission criteria related to social class variables (Lorenzen, 1967). These clinics had very different criteria with one, a psychoanalytic training clinic, being quite highly selective in terms of age, education, and relation to health professions. This particular clinic did not accept clients under 20 or over 34 years of age. The differences are also apparent in the widely different acceptance rates among the clinics. Two clinics accepted about 10 to 20 percent of applicants, whereas one clinic accepted 85 percent. Obviously, the kinds of problems and generalizations derived from such diverse samples of clients would also be expected to vary widely. Moreover, it appears likely that different approaches to therapy might be used in instances of this kind. The length of therapy did differ among the clinics and appeared to be related to the orientation of the clinic and its selectivity.

The interesting study by Kadushin (1969) provides similar findings and appears to have utilized many of the same clinics. Social class was considered to be the most important factor distinguishing the applicants to the various clinics. Furthermore, "the more closely affiliated a clinic is with the

orothodox psychoanalytic movement, the higher the social class of its applicants will be" (Kadushin, 1969, p. 51).

A somewhat similar analysis of social agencies has found that the more sophisticated an agency's therapeutic method is, and the more qualified its workers are, the more highly selected and higher in status is the population that it serves (Rudolph & Cumming, 1962). Furthermore, the higher the status of the agency, the less flexible are its methods of operation and the greater the tendency to label clients as unsuitable or unmotivated. Such agencies appear to emphasize their special procedures instead of focusing on the kind of social needs that require service.

Another interesting and related aspect of this problem pertains to the differential assignment of clients in terms of the different strata or hierarchy of therapists within a given clinical setting. Schaffer and Myers (1954) found a definite relationship between the rank of the therapist and the social class of the patients seen by him, with the senior staff members having more of the upper class patients. Although this finding was not supported in another study as far as psychiatrists and medical students were concerned, the psychiatric social workers, working largely with spouses of patients, had clients exclusively from the two lowest social classes (Cole, Branch, & Allison, 1962). Brill and Storrow (1960) also found no difference in the social class designations of the patients treated by medical students and psychiatric residents. Baker and Wagner (1966), however, reported that psychiatrists and psychiatric residents were more likely to be assigned upper class patients in a children's clinic, as compared with social workers who saw more lower class patients.

It is, of course, difficult to generalize from such limited and conflicting data, particularly when the personnel and clientele differ among clinics. Some clinics have an income ceiling for prospective clients, and individuals above that ceiling are referred to private practitioners. To the extent that many clinics utilize therapists in training, however, it is possible that the poorer clients receive the less experienced therapists.

It would appear, then, that many clinics have been somewhat selective in whom they accept for treatment, that this varies for the type of clinic, that selection is frequently related to social class criteria, and that the more expert the therapeutic staff, the more stringent are the procedures used for selection and acceptance of clients. Psychoanalytic or psychoanalytically oriented clinics that are looking for suitable candidates for their particular variants of psychotherapy, conceivably, use some degree of selectivity in deciding which clients are best suited for treatment, and generally these clients are the better educated, intelligent, verbal and "motivated" ones. On the other hand, this selectivity poses a problem for those who are seen as less desirable, or who appear to show less interest in psychotherapy. Because of increased attention to this and related problems in recent years, some innovative attempts have been made to provide services to lower class individuals and to adapt therapeutic procedures accordingly. Reference to this work is made later in this chapter and in more detail in Chapter 22.

RESEARCH PERTAINING TO CONTINUATION IN PSYCHOTHERAPY

As was mentioned previously, many persons who are actually offered psychotherapy appear to turn down this opportunity. A related problem encountered in clinic practice concerns those patients who do begin psychotherapy but who terminate their participation and drop out of therapy relatively early. Generally, such termination appears to be initiated by the client before there has been a mutual agreement that therapy has been completed. These discontinuers, premature terminators, or dropouts constitute a large percentage of those who begin therapy, and several studies have been carried out to evaluate this problem.

It may be worthwhile first to review briefly some representative findings on the nature of this problem. In Table 6-1, data are presented on the length of psychotherapy, expressed in terms of the number of interviews, for 560 patients seen at a VA Mental Hygiene Clinic (Garfield & Kurz, 1952). This group of patients consisted of all of those who had been offered and had accepted treatment at

TABLE 6-1   Length of Treatment

Number of Interviews	Number of Cases	Percentage of Cases
Less than 5	239	42.7
5 to 9	134	23.9
10 to 14	73	13.0
15 to 19	41	7.3
20 to 24	24	4.3
25 and over	49	8.8
Total	560	100.0

the clinic, and whose cases were officially closed at the time of the study. As the table shows, the median length of treatment was about 6 interviews, with approximately two-thirds of the cases receiving less than 10 interviews. By contrast, less than 9 percent of the patients came for 25 or more interviews, and only seven cases received more than 50 treatment interviews.

Although the data presented in Table 6-1 were published in the early 1950s and are the actual findings secured with the population of one clinic, they are typical of the kinds of results secured from a number of other clinics over a period of many years. Table 6-2 summarizes the findings of a representative number of investigations carried out in several types of clinics. As can be seen, a majority of the clinics have lost one-half of their therapy clients before the eighth interview. Although the median length of treatment varies from 3 to 12 interviews for the different clinics, there is a clustering around 6 interviews. While the methodology is not always clear or consistent among these studies, it can be emphasized that in those studies that excluded all those patients who were offered therapy but refused it, and included only actual therapy patients, the median number of interviews was between 5 and 6 (Garfield & Kurz, 1952; Schaffer & Myers, 1954; Kurland, 1956; Rosenthal & Frank, 1958).

In a study by Haddock and Mensh (1957) of two university student health services and one VA Mental Hygiene Clinic, similar findings were secured for the three separate settings. About two-thirds of the

TABLE 6-2   Median Number of Psychotherapy Interviews for Outpatient Clinics

Clinic	Median No. Interviews	Date	Source
VA Clinic, St. Louis	5	1948	Blackman
VA Clinic, Boston	10	1949	Adler, Valenstein, & Michaels
VA Clinic, Milwaukee	6	1952	Garfield & Kurz
VA Clinic, Baltimore	4	1956	Kurland
VA Clinic, Oakland	9	1958	Sullivan, Miller, & Smelser
VA Clinic, Chicago	3	1959	Affleck & Mednick
Psychiatric Clinics— General Hospitals, New York City	6	1949	NYC Commission on Mental Hygiene
Clinics in Four States plus VA Clinic, Denver	5 to 7	1960	Rogers
Yale University Clinic	4	1954	Schaffer & Myers
Henry Phipps Clinic	6	1958	Rosenthal & Frank
Nebraska Psychiatric Institute	12	1959	Garfield & Affleck
Nebraska Psychiatric Institute	8	1961	Affleck & Garfield
University of Oregon Clinic	4	1964	Brown & Kosterlitz
Ohio State University Clinic	4	1970	Dodd

patients were seen fewer than 5 hours, and only one patient in 20 was seen for more than 20 hours. Furthermore, more than one-half of the veterans and one-third of the students terminated treatment on their own without discussing it with the therapist. In another study of 400 clinic patients, 45 percent were seen for less than five interviews, with a majority simply discontinuing treatment (Gabby & Leavitt, 1970). Recent studies in three urban mental health centers have also revealed that 37 to 45 percent of adult outpatients terminate psychotherapy after the first or second session (Fiester & Rudestam, 1975). Another report from an inner-city mental health clinic indicates that only 57 percent of patients admitted to the clinic remained for four or more interviews (Craig & Huffine, 1976).

In addition, annual statistical reports for psychiatric clinics in the states of New York and Maryland indicate that the majority of patients are seen for less than five interviews (Gordon, 1965), and a study of comparable statistics for five other states show that a majority of patients have left treatment before the eighth interview (Rogers, 1960). Also of interest is the report of a large-scale survey published by the National Center for Health Statistics (1966). According to this study, 979,000 Americans consulted a psychiatrist during the 12-month period from July 1963 to June 1964. The average number of visits per person was 4.7. The latter figure thus approximates the findings already mentioned. Eiduson (1968), in a review of this problem, also concluded that "30 percent to 65 percent of all patients are dropouts in facilities representing every kind of psychiatric service." Furthermore, on the basis of limited evidence, it appears that those who terminate therapy early rarely go on to seek therapy elsewhere (Garfield, 1963a; Riess & Brandt, 1965).

On the basis of the data presented above, therefore, it is apparent that contrary to traditional expectations concerning length of therapy, most clinic clients remain in therapy for only a few interviews. In practically all of the clinics studied, this pattern was viewed as a problem and was not the result of a deliberately planned brief therapy. Rather, in most instances, the patient failed to return for a scheduled appointment.

It can be stated with confidence, therefore, that the finding of an unplanned and premature termination from psychotherapy on the part of many clients in traditional clinic settings has been a reasonably reliable one. The apparent rejection of psychotherapy by a number of those who appear to be in need of it has been a somewhat surprising and perplexing finding which, for a while, tended to be relatively ignored. However, after a steady output of research reports, the problem has been receiving increased attention in recent years. Before we examine some of the suggestions offered for remediation of this problem, however, let us review some of the findings secured in the attempt to find correlates and predictors of premature termination. The research to be reviewed can be categorized into a few broad groups: (1) social class and actuarial variables; (2) psychological test data; (3) expectancies and other variables.

Social Class and Actuarial Variables

As indicated previously, one group of variables that has been studied in relation to length of stay in psychotherapy concerns social class. Some investigations have simply used one of the well-known indices of social class, such as that of Hollingshead, whereas others have studied specific components such as education, income, occupation, and the like. Those who have used the former have generally found some relationship between length of stay and social class index. In one study, only 57.1 percent of lower class patients stayed beyond the fourth interview, whereas 88.9 percent of middle class patients went beyond the fourth interview (Imber, Nash, & Stone, 1955). In another study, about 12 percent of the two lower social class

groups, classified according to the Hollingshead classification, remained for more than 30 interviews as compared with 42 percent of those in the highest two social class groups (Cole, Branch, & Allison, 1962). Gibby, Stotsky, Hiler, and Miller (1954), using primarily occupational status as a measure of social class, also found that middle class patients remained in therapy longer than did lower class patients. Dodd (1970) reported that patients from the upper three social classes on the Hollingshead Index remained longer in treatment than those in the lower two classes, but the finding was not replicated on a smaller sample of 57 patients. Fiester and Rudestam (1975) also found a relationship between social class status on the Hollingshead Index and premature termination in one clinic but not in a hospital-based community health center.

Somewhat different findings were reported in a study by Albronda, Dean, and Starkweather (1964). Although they concluded that there was no significant relationship between social class and premature termination from therapy, they used four therapy sessions as the criterion of early termination. They also stated that "up to the eleventh interview . . . the upper class patients seemed to fare slightly better than the lower in terms of survival" (p. 282).

With regard to the more specific variables, for example, education, the findings, are slightly less consistent. Although most studies have reported a positive relationship between education and length of stay (Bailey, Warshaw, & Eicher, 1959; McNair, Lorr, & Callahan, 1963; Rosenthal & Frank, 1958; Rosenzweig & Folman, 1974; Rubinstein & Lorr, 1956; Sullivan, Miller, & Smelser, 1958), some have not (Garfield & Affleck, 1959; Pope, Geller, & Wilkinson, 1975; Weissman, Geanakapolos, & Prusoff, 1973). Part of this limited lack of agreement may be due to differences in the samples used, as well as the type of screening employed in selecting patients for psychotherapy. Where there are more rigorous standards for acceptance into treatment, the dropout rate tends to be less and the lower socioeconomic groups may be underrepresented. In some instances, the results may be influenced by other factors. In the study by Weissman et al. (1973), for example, 40 depressed patients received both casework and drugs. The low attrition rate and lack of difference between socioeconomic groups secured may have been influenced by the administration of medication, since other findings suggest that the giving of drugs may facilitate treatment continuation (Craig & Huffine, 1976; Dodd, 1970).

Two comments may be offered at this point. It is likely that education below a certain level may be a factor in continuation in therapy. For example, in the paper by Rosenthal and Frank (1958), the group that appeared to account for the significant findings obtained was the one with below ninth grade education. It also seems probable that educational level may be only one component of a larger factor or complex of factors that may include verbal ability, sophistication about psychotherapy, income, interest in receiving psychotherapy, and similar components. In any event, educational level, while not always related to length of stay, is found to have a significant relationship in most studies.

Before we discuss other actuarial variables, it is appropriate to comment about the very atypical findings secured in a study done at Tulane University (Lief, Lief, Warren, & Heath, 1961). At this clinic, in contrast to the typical findings already reported, only 6 percent of the clients dropped out before the sixth interview. The population of this clinic, however, was not typical of that found in most medical school clinics. Most unusual was the high educational level of the patients, which included a large number of medical students. Eighty-two percent of the patients had some college work and 49 percent also had completed some graduate work. The special characteristics of the sample would appear to account for the kinds of results secured.

Besides education, the most frequently studied actuarial variables examined in relation to length of stay have been sex, age, and diagnosis. Although income and occupation have also been evaluated, they have frequently been combined in estimates of social class.

The variable of sex has been investigated in several studies with most of the results showing no significant differences between males and females in terms of premature termination (Affleck & Gar-

field, 1961; Craig & Huffine, 1976; Frank, Gliedman, Imber, Nash, & Stone, 1957; Garfield & Affleck, 1959; Grotjahn, 1972; Koran & Costell, 1973). In four studies, males were found more frequently to be continuers in psychotherapy (Brown & Kosterlitz, 1964; Cartwright, 1955; Rosenthal & Frank, 1958; Weiss & Schaie, 1958). However, in the study by Cartwright (1955), only a small proportion of the total variance in length of therapy could be attributed to the sex of the patient. On the whole, and in contrast to a recent review of this topic (Baekeland & Lundwall, 1975), it does not appear that sex is an important predictor of continuation in psychotherapy (Garfield, 1977b).

A somewhat similar interpretation can be made for age of client. Although some therapists appear to show a preference for younger patients (Bailey, Warshaw, & Eichler, 1959), age does not appear to be an important variable, at least as far as continuation in psychotherapy is concerned (Affleck & Garfield, 1961; Cartwright, 1955; Frank et al., 1957; Garfield & Affleck, 1959; Rosenthal & Frank, 1958; Rubinstein & Lorr, 1956). In one study where age did statistically differentiate those continuing and discontinuing psychotherapy, the mean difference in age was less than two years (Sullivan, Miller, & Smelser, 1958).

Although perhaps not strictly an actuarial variable, psychiatric diagnosis has also been evaluated in terms of length of stay in outpatient psychotherapy. For the most part, in spite of the effort devoted to formulating a psychiatric diagnosis for patients, this classification appears to bear no significant relationship to continuation in outpatient psychotherapy in most studies (Affleck & Garfield, 1961; Bailey, Warshaw, & Eichler, 1959; Garfield & Affleck, 1959; Lief, Lief, Warren & Heath, 1961; Pope, Geller, & Wilkinson, 1975; Rosenthal & Frank, 1958). In one study, patients diagnosed as having anxiety or depressive reactions remained in treatment significantly longer than all others (Frank et al., 1957). In another study (Dodd, 1970), patients diagnosed as having either a psychotic or psychoneurotic reaction remained in treatment longer than those with other diagnoses. However, this finding was not replicated with a new sample of 57 patients. Craig and Huffine (1976) also reported that patients with a psychosis or personality disorder remained longer in therapy than did patients diagnosed as having a neurosis or transient situational disorder. However, they also found a relationship between length of stay and prescription of medication. Since psychotic patients almost always were prescribed medication, the results are questionable. On the whole, psychiatric or clinical diagnosis as such has not been shown to be related to continuation in psychotherapy.

Thus, our survey of research findings on continuation in psychotherapy indicates a likely relationship between social class and length of stay, some relationship of educational level, particularly an inverse one at the lower educational levels, and no clear relationship between length of stay and variables such as age, sex, and psychiatric diagnosis. It is possible, as mentioned previously, that findings of this kind may be related to other variables that may be important in conventional approaches to psychotherapy. A few studies have discussed this matter, and we briefly review some of the points presented.

In one study (Brill & Storrow, 1960), in which acceptance for psychotherapy was positively related to social class status, an attempt was made to evaluate "Psychological Mindedness" in relation to social class. Low social class was found to be significantly related to low estimated intelligence, a tendency to view the problem as physical rather than emotional, a desire for symptomatic relief, lack of understanding of the psychotherapeutic process, and lack of desire for psychotherapy. In addition, the intake interviewer had less positive feelings for lower class patients and considered them as less treatable by means of psychotherapy. In terms of the data already discussed, the last statement appears to have elements of a self-fulfilling prophecy. The findings, however, do suggest an interaction effect between attributes and expectations of lower class clients and attitudes of middle class therapists that may play a role in length of stay in psychotherapy.

In one other study, socioeconomic level was related to therapists' ratings of patient attractiveness, ease of establishing rapport and prognosis, each of which in turn was related to continuation in psychotherapy (Nash, Hoehn-Saric, Battle, Stone, Imber, & Frank, 1965). Another study investigated the relationship between values, social class, and duration of psychotherapy, and found a relationship between the interaction of social class and the discrepancy between patient and therapist values and continuation (Pettit, Pettit, & Welkowitz, 1974).

Other studies, to which we refer shortly, have investigated personality and other correlates of continuation in psychotherapy. Variables such as motivation, verbal ability, ability to introspect, and attitudes toward psychotherapy have been designated as being of importance in this regard. Although such attributes have not always been evaluated in relation to social class, as the study by Brill and Storrow (1960) showed, there may be some relationship between these two sets of variables.

A related aspect commented on by Hollingshead and Redlich (1958), as well as by others (Lerner & Fiske, 1973), is that therapists generally appear to prefer and be more comfortable with upper class clients, that is, with clients who talk their language and are more similar to them. Thus, while several writers have been critical of existing "insight oriented" psychotherapy for many lower class patients (Dean, 1958; Garfield, 1971; Rosenthal & Frank, 1958), and cite a need for experimentation with other forms of therapy, some appear to more tacitly accept psychotherapy as a treatment for middle and upper class clients (Hunt, 1960; Lief, Lief, Warren, & Heath, 1961). In fact, Lief et al. emphasized the need for selecting middle class patients "if we consider the needs of university clinics to train residents in insight therapy" (p. 208).

Another variable more recently investigated in relation to continuation in psychotherapy is that of race. Whereas race has tended to be correlated with social class status, it has also been studied separately and with reference to client-therapist interaction. One of the earlier studies of this type which looked at both social class and race was reported by Carkhuff and Pierce (1967). Four lay counselors with special training were selected to include one upper class white, one upper class Negro, one lower class white, and one lower class Negro, and each saw 16 patients distributed equally among the four classifications represented by the counselors in terms of a Latin-square design. Taped interview segments were rated according to "Depth of self-exploration in interpersonal process," a patient variable that has been positively correlated with outcome in psychotherapy. Race and social class of both patient and therapist were found to be significantly related to patient depth of self-exploration, and the interaction between patient and therapist variables was also significant. In general, "the patients most similar to the race and social class of the counselor involved tended to explore themselves most, while patients most dissimilar tended to explore themselves least" (p. 634).

Krebs (1971) conducted a study of all cases opened during a nine-month period in an adult outpatient service and analyzed the type of therapy assignment and number of appointments kept in terms of race and sex. It was found that a disproportionate number of black females were assigned to crisis-oriented brief therapy as compared with whites and black males. Black females also were reported to have missed a significantly larger number of appointments than were white males or females, or black males. Although the black females had a higher rate of hourly employment than their white counterparts, a factor of possible importance, those that missed a majority of their appointments did not differ on this variable from the black women who kept a majority of their appointments.

Another study appraised the differential attitudes of black and white families toward treatment in a child guidance clinic and secured somewhat equivocal findings (Warren, Jackson, Nugaris, & Farley, 1973). In terms of eight major categories of response based on 115 interview questions, there were no significant differences between the black and white patients. However, on selected items some significant differences were secured, with the white patients generally having a more favorable attitude toward therapy than the black patients. Although the length of therapy was longer for white patients, the difference was not significant.

In a relatively large-scale study of 17 community mental health clinics, black patients were found to attend significantly less sessions than whites and also to terminate therapy more frequently after the first session (Sue, McKinney, Allen, & Hall, 1974). There was a greater tendency for black patients in another study to see their therapists only briefly (Yamamoto, James, & Palley, 1968), and similar findings were reported in an additional investigation, which included a small number of nonwhites (Salzman, Shader, Scott, & Binstock, 1970). Rosenthal and Frank (1958) also reported that almost twice as many white patients as black patients remained for six therapy interviews. On the other hand, Weiss and Dlugokinski (1974) did not find race related to length of treatment for children, and at the Stanford University Mental Health Clinic, the termination rates of black students did not differ from those of other students (Gibbs, 1975).

Some additional investigations can be summarized briefly. In a study of precollege counseling, Ewing (1974) employed three experienced black counselors and eight experienced white counselors who each saw 13 black and 13 white students. Although the black students were more favorable to both groups of counselors than were white students, Ewing concluded that the racial similarity of client and counselor was not an important factor in this situation. Cimbolic (1972) studied black clients paired with white and black counselors and did not find any significant racial preference. In a study of preferences toward Mexican-American and Anglo-American psychotherapists by Acosta and Sheehan (1976), two groups of college students selected from these ethnic classifications both indicated a clear preference for the Anglo-American professional. Although none of these studies were concerned with continuation in therapy, their findings are indirectly of interest.

The overall picture is thus far from conclusive. While there appears to be a tendency for a more frequent early termination from psychotherapy by black clients than for whites, this is by no means a consistent pattern. This problem is also compounded by social class factors that generally have not been partialed out in most investigations. Those who are interested in this and related problems involving race as a variable in psychotherapy are referred to a comprehensive recent review by Sattler (1977).

The relationship reported between social class variables and continuation in psychotherapy thus may be a function of several variables acting independently or in interaction with each other. The attributes and expectations of the client clearly contribute one source of variance to this problem, while the personality and attitudes of the therapist contribute another. These variables, furthermore, may act singly or in combination. Although these are important and intriguing issues, let us put aside a further discussion of them and give our attention to some of the attempts that have been made to deal with the problems presented by the findings on premature termination of outpatient psychotherapy.

One type of response made to the problem of premature termination is that a more careful screening should take place before clients are assigned for psychotherapy. With the large demand for services, premature termination from psychotherapy has been viewed as a waste of professional manpower. This solution thus stresses the more careful selection of cases in terms of accepting those who may be seen as being more amenable to psychotherapy, and clearly places the blame for the problem on the "unsuitable client." In essence, such a view favors the more educated, intelligent, psychologically sophisticated, and less disturbed client as the preferred one for psychotherapy.

A second approach, which has received increasing attention in recent years, is that of providing some sort of pretherapy training to help prepare the client for psychotherapy (Heitler, 1976), or to help prepare the therapist for these kinds of difficulties. In some instances, this approach has called for a more active and flexible role on the part of the therapist (Baum & Felzer, 1964). This view, while focusing less blame or responsibility on the client, still does not basically question the efficacy of traditional approaches to psychotherapy. A somewhat related view, which takes cognizance of the differing expectations that clients may bring to therapy, emphasizes the need to consider the problem of expectations during the initial phase of treatment (Hoehn-Saric, Frank, Imber, Nash, Stone, & Battle, 1964; Overall & Aronson, 1962). In the study by Hoehn-Saric et al., for example, a "Role Induction Interview," based on the anticipatory socialization interview of Orne and Wender (1968), was

developed to give the patient appropriate expectations about certain aspects of psychotherapy in the hope that this would facilitate the process and outcome of therapy. The Role Induction Interview stressed four components: (1) a general exposition of psychotherapy, (2) the expected behavior of patient and therapist, (3) preparation for certain phenomena in therapy such as resistance, and (4) expectation for improvement within four months of treatment. The experimental group significantly exceeded the control group in this study on 6 of the 16 criterion measures used, including that of attendance at scheduled therapy sessions. The results thus suggest that attempts to prepare the patient for psychotherapy have an impact on his attendance and progress in therapy.

Attempts at "vicarious therapy pre-training" were also reported in several studies by Truax and his co-workers (Truax & Carkhuff, 1967; Truax & Wargo, 1969). They developed a 30-minute tape recording of excerpts of "good" therapy behavior, which allowed prospective clients to experience group psychotherapy prior to their own therapy. While this particular approach was not used by them with reference to the problem of continuation in psychotherapy, it apparently had a moderately beneficial effect on outcome. Two other studies with adult patients, however, did not secure any significant differences in premature termination as a result of therapy preparation (Sloane, Cristol, Pepernik, & Staples, 1970; Yalom, Houts, Newell, & Rand, 1967).

There have been several reports more recently of specific attempts to prepare lower class individuals for psychotherapy. Heitler (1973) utilized an "anticipatory socialization interview" based on the procedures of Orne and Wender (1968) with 48 inpatients in expressive group psychotherapy. Although no data on outcome or continuation are provided, the experimental group did exceed the control group on a number of process measures and therapists' ratings of patient participation in therapy. Strupp and Bloxom (1973) developed a role-induction film for lower class patients and compared its effectiveness with a role-induction interview and a control film with 122 patients with an average educational grade level of 10.8. Twelve weekly group therapy sessions were conducted.

Those patients receiving the role-induction film and the induction interview showed significantly more gains on a number of attitudinal and in-therapy measures, as well as indicating higher ratings of improvement. However, there were no differences between the groups on attendance, on therapists' ratings of improvement and on a symptom checklist.

In another study, lower class patients (Classes IV and V, Hollingshead Scale) in a walk-in clinic were assigned to one of four groups (Jacobs, Charles, Jacobs, Weinstein, & Mann, 1972). In one, the patient was given a brief preparatory interview; in another, the resident psychiatrist was given brief instruction in working with lower class patients; in a third, both patients and therapists were "prepared"; and the fourth was essentially a control group. Although the report is not completely clear, it appears that the dropout rate was not affected by the experimental treatment. However, more patients who were in the three preparation groups came for more than four sessions and were judged to be more improved than was true for the control group.

Still another attempt at some type of pretherapy training or instruction is reported in a study of 55 "low-prognosis" clients in connection with time-limited, client-centered psychotherapy (Warren & Rice, 1972). This training consisted of two parts and involved four half-hour sessions with someone other than the therapist. These sessions preceded the second, third, fifth, and eighth therapy sessions. The first part, labeled "stabilizing," was designed to encourage the client to discuss problems that he might be having with therapy or the therapist, and lasted from 5 to 10 minutes. The remaining time was spent in "structuring," which was an attempt to train the client to participate productively in the process of client-centered therapy. The experimental group had a significantly smaller amount of attrition than the control group.

Lastly, mention can be made of a study by Holmes and Urie (1975) in which one-half of a group of 88 children were given a therapy preparation interview, while the controls were given a social history interview. The prepared children dropped out significantly less than did the control children, but outcome ratings were not affected.

Even though the results are somewhat equivocal, attempted innovations of this kind appear to merit further investigation. In this regard, the following statement by Truax and Carkhuff (1967) appears pertinent: "If psychotherapy or counseling is indeed a process of learning and relearning, then the therapeutic process should allow for structuring what is to be learned, rather than depending on what amounts to 'incidental learning,' where the client does not have clearly in mind from the outset what it is he is supposed to learn" (p. 363). This, perhaps, may appear more readily applicable to learning theory approaches, although Truax and Carkhuff were client-centered therapists. Parrino (1971), in fact, found that relevant pretherapy information did facilitate the learning of approach responses to snakes in a study of individuals with snake phobias.

Finally, the implication of premature termination for some observers has been the need for modifications in conventional psychotherapies to better meet the needs of the dropouts from psychotherapy. Thus, from one point of view, these clients have been seen as undesirable clients or as failing to have the requisite attributes of candidates for psychotherapy; from another point of view, psychotherapy as practiced has been found wanting, and some changes in practice have been called for as a possible solution. Goldstein (1973), for example, has developed a structured learning therapy for the poor. These issues and the response to them with regard to disadvantaged groups have been examined also in a recent paper by Heitler (1976) and are discussed more fully in Chapter 22. We next review research that has investigated other types of variables in relation to continuation in psychotherapy.

Psychological Test Variables and Continuation in Psychotherapy

Psychologists showed considerable interests in past years in attempting to find predictive variables selected from psychological tests for assessing continuation in psychotherapy. This work was undoubtedly related to the emphasis on diagnostic testing in the postwar development of clinical psychology. Probably as a result of changes in professional activities and in the apparent limited utility of this work, there has been a noticeable decrease recently in publications relating psychological test variables and continuation in psychotherapy (Garfield, 1974).

Nevertheless, a variety of investigations which used many different tests and procedures were carried out in previous years. As has been pointed out, however, research in psychotherapy is beset by many difficulties. In addition to variations in psychotherapy, there are also sample differences, varying criteria for determining dropouts from therapy, different statistical analyses and approaches to the data, different uses of the same test, and variations in therapists and therapeutic settings. Such differences, of course, complicate the problem and make replications difficult. Let us, however, review some of the studies on psychological test variables and continuation in psychotherapy.

The Rorschach test is one technique which, because of its wide use in the past, has been investigated with regard to continuation in therapy. Overall, the findings have been contradictory. An early study by Rogers, Knauss, and Hammond (1951) secured negative results with a number of Rorschach scores. However, Kotkov and Meadow (1953) found that a weighted combination of three Rorschach scores (FC-CF, R and D%) was able to discriminate significantly those patients who continued for at least nine interviews. Auld and Eron (1953) attempted to replicate this study but secured negative results. They further analyzed each of the three Rorschach scores in relation to continuation and secured a significant relationship only with R (number of responses). Because of the possible correlation between R and intelligence, IQ was then partialed out and, with this, the significant relationship between R and continuation disappeared. In fact, on a sample of 23 patients, the correlation between IQ and continuation was .71.

Gibby, Stotsky, Miller, and Hiler (1953) also compared two groups of patients on various Rorschach scores and secured a number of significant findings. However, many of the separate scores were significantly correlated with R, and they used more extreme groups of subjects. The terminators had less than 6 sessions, whereas the continuers were those who remained for 20 or more sessions. These investigators then carried out another study (Gibby, Stotsky, Hiler, & Miller, 1954) as a follow-up of their first one. By utilizing

the method of discriminant function on the scores of 84 patients, they secured a formula that was then applied to 75 continuers and 110 terminators. However, in this study, they utilized 19 sessions or less to designate the group of terminators, a cutoff point that differs noticeably from those used in most other studies. In this investigation, a combination of three Rorschach scores were used (R and total K and M). When applied to the second sample, 67 percent of the patients were correctly categorized. However, if one computes a base rate for termination on the second sample, it is close to 60 percent. Thus the formula exceeds the base rate by only a small amount. Also, the formula is more predictive of terminators than it is of remainers. In fact, if the suggested cutoff score is used, it not only predicts 87 percent of the terminators correctly but it would keep out of therapy almost 63 percent of the remainers! It appeared also that R, or number of responses, alone would have also predicted continuation with an accuracy of 69 percent. Thus, as in most of these studies, the Rorschach variable that appeared to account for most of the variance was R, which correlates positively with IQ. When separate analyses were made for IQ and R in relation to continuation, the results were quite similar. Although the findings were not identical to those secured by Auld and Eron (1953), IQ seems to be as good or better a predictor than the best measure obtained from the Rorschach. Finally, it should be noted that social class also predicted continuation at a statistically significant level in this study. While correlations between IQ and social class were not reported, it would appear likely on the basis of other research that a positive relationship exists between these two variables.

Hiler (1958b) reported a separate investigation of the same samples of subjects that were used in the two preceding studies. This study evaluated the relationship of Wechsler-Bellevue IQ to continuation in outpatient psychotherapy. Terminators were defined as those quitting therapy within 5 sessions and remainers as those who continued for 20 or more sessions. Remainers secured an average IQ of 112, which was 10 points higher than the average IQ of the terminators.

Another comparable study in a VA outpatient clinic was reported by Affleck and Mednick (1959). They used a discriminant function of three

Rorschach variables, including R, to predict continuation after the third interview and cross validated their initial findings on another sample. While the measure used would have increased the accuracy of prediction 13 percent over the base rate, its practical value appears limited since terminators at the fourth and fifth interviews, labeled remainers in this study, would, of course, not have been predicted. It is interesting to note also that the discriminant functions reported by Kotkov and Meadow (1953) and Gibby et al. (1954), to which reference has already been made, approximated the base rates for terminators in the clinic studied by Affleck and Mednick.

Although interest in the Rorschach as a predictor of psychotherapy continuation appears to have clearly diminished, a situation not necessarily to be decried, one more recent study illustrates again some of the problems evident in this field of research (Whitely & Blaine, 1967). In this study an attempt was made to evaluate the Rorschach in relation to length of stay and outcome in psychotherapy for students at the Harvard University Health Service. Students who received short-term therapy (3 to 24 sessions) were compared with those who received long-term therapy (25 to 100 sessions). Nothing is said about the factors or decisions that led to length of therapy, and there is no indication of why some individuals received short-term therapy and others did not. Thus one cannot automatically assume that the former were terminators in the sense that this term has been used in most of the previous studies. Apart from other factors, it is not surprising, therefore, that most of the Rorschach measures reported on favorably in individual studies previously did not have much predictive validity in this study. The clients and the conditions were clearly different.

Other testing procedures besides the Rorschach have also been used as possible predictors of continuation in psychotherapy. Five scales of the Michigan Sentence Completion Test were found by Hiler (1959) to differentiate patients who remained less than 6 sessions from those who stayed in treatment for 20 or more sessions. The latter patients tended to be less evasive and more willing to reveal personal feelings, were more preoccupied with feelings of inadequacy, had stronger drives for achievement and status, and showed greater psychological sophistication. No data were given on the possible relationship of the attributes mentioned to social class or IQ, nor were the findings replicated.

Other tests and techniques also have been tried out in relation to continuation in psychotherapy. However, relatively little is to be gained in a review of single studies that have not been replicated. For example, Taulbee (1958), on the basis of selected MMPI and Rorschach variables, concluded that those who continue in therapy beyond the thrteenth interview are less defensive and more persistent, dependent, anxious, and introspective than are those who terminate early. These results, however, were not cross validated, and in another study no significant differences on the MMPI were found between continuers and terminators (Sullivan, Miller, & Smelser, 1958). The latter study was well designed, used three moderately large groups of subjects, and attempted two cross-validations of the findings secured with the initial sample of subjects, an important but rare event in clinical research. In this investigation, significant differences between the Stay and Non-Stay groups were found for several MMPI scales for each of the several groups of subjects studied. However, these scales were different for each of the groups studied, and not one single scale held up for even two of the groups. The authors concluded their report by emphasizing the necessity for cross-validation in studies of this type, a conclusion that is clearly supported by much of the research reported in this area.

Generally, investigations utilizing the MMPI, or scales derived from it, have not reported any consistent results with regard to continuation in psychotherapy. Wirt (1967) secured significant modest correlations between continuation and three MMPI scales for 24 female patients, but no such relationship was secured for 33 male subjects. The small sample and lack of replication obviously limit these findings. In the study and cross-validation by Dodd (1970), MMPI scores did not differentiate between continuers and remainers. Similarly, scores on the Barron Ego Strength Scale were not significantly different from continuers and remainers in group therapy, although the number of patients studied was small (Rosenzweig & Folman, 1974).

Imber, Frank, Gliedman, Nash, and Stone (1956) studied the relationship of suggestibility, as measured by the sway test, to length of stay in psychotherapy. They found that 77 percent of the swayers remained for 4 or more interviews, whereas 54 percent of the non-swayers terminated before the fourth interview. They also found that suggestibility and social class were practically independent of each other ($r=.16$). Here, it is again pertinent to point out the differences in the operational definition of remainers and terminators in the various studies mentioned, a problem that makes generalization difficult. Whereas Imber et al. define continuation in terms of 4 interviews, Hiler used 20 interviews. As indicated in Table 6.1, very different percentages of clinic populations are included when these diverse criteria are used. Obviously, with variation of this kind in the criterion variable, prediction will be difficult, if not impossible!

We can conclude this section with a reference to the previous research of Lorr and his colleagues. This research used relatively large samples of subjects at many VA outpatient clinics, and several replications were performed (Lorr, Katz, & Rubinstein, 1958; Rubinstein & Lorr, 1956). In the initial study, four short tests and questionnaires, referred to as the TR battery, were found to be predictive of length of stay. The tests, increased to five in the second study, included a shortened version of the Taylor Manifest Anxiety Scale, a 20-item F scale, a behavior disturbance scale, a 15-item vocabulary scale, and a brief self-rating scale. These instruments were selected on the basis of a double cross-validation on two random halves of a sample of 128 cases and were then further evaluated on two new samples of 115 cases each. Because of the particular distribution, those who stayed less than 7 weeks were compared with those who remained more than 26 weeks. It is interesting that none of the tests that were based on the scoring keys derived from the original cross-validation differentiated the two new samples, although the scores were consistently in the predicted direction. This is, of course, a perennial problem in psychological research but an important one, since findings based on the initial group studied become re-

ally significant only when they can be applied to other comparable groups. In this investigation, with two subsamples available, further analyses were done on one sample and then applied to the other. This did produce some statistically significant results. However, the multiple correlation of .67 for these test patterns shrank to .39 when one moved from the first subsample from which they were derived to the second subsample. In general, remainers were found to be more anxious, more self-dissatisfied, more willing to explore problems, more persistent and dependable, and less likely to have a history of antisocial acts.

The above study was cross-validated on another VA sample of 282 patients with somewhat comparable results (McNair, Lorr, & Callahan, 1963). The multiple R of the TR test battery was .44 as contrasted with .39 previously. Furthermore, although different criteria were used in selecting terminators in the two studies, the overall accuracy of prediction was about 15 percent higher than the sample base rates. These investigators thus replicated their findings several times, something that is rare in this area of research, and eventually came up with some stable results. Since this research is a model for other researchers to emulate, it is disheartening to have to refer next to a study that utilized three of the TR tests and found no significant relationship between predictions and continuation in therapy (Stern, Moore, & Gross, 1975). The latter investigators also took the view that previous research on termination confounded personality with social class variables and that the prediction of termination with the TR scale was based primarily on social class. Although these assertions, in my opinion, are not fully warranted (Garfield, 1977a), because of the limitations of space I will not comment on them here. It should be noted, however, that besides possible sample differences, patients were considered to be remainers "if they kept appointments for six consecutive sessions or if they missed only one of these sessions but had notified their therapist beforehand" (Stern et al., p. 342). Clearly, the definition of continuation differs considerably from that of the previous studies.

Sufficient studies have now been reviewed to acquaint the reader with this area of research. While conflicting and unreplicated findings have been frequent, the reasons for them should be apparent. The studies have utilized different definitions of early termination, the samples and methods of appraisal have differed, therapeutic conditions and frequency of therapy have not been consistent, comparable information on certain variables has not been available, and a number of similar types of difficulties have been encountered. Variations of this kind, of course, make reliable or clear-cut generalizations difficult. In contrast to the findings secured with psychological tests, social class variables appear to show a somewhat more consistent relationship to the phenomena being studied and are relatively easy to appraise.

Other psychological attributes that may or may not be related to social class have not given as consistent results, nor have they been systematically studied in relation to social class. One of the problems here is that personality variables discussed or studied in psychotherapy research are defined and measured differently in the various investigations. Thus, variables such as motivation or anxiety may be found to be related to continuation in some studies but not in others. For example, McNair et al. (1963) found therapists' ratings of motivation related to length of stay, but in three other studies ratings of motivation were not so related (Affleck & Garfield, 1961; Garfield, Affleck, & Muffley, 1963; Siegel & Fink, 1962). Similarly, Hiler (1958a) used Rorschach R as a measure of patient productivity and found it to be related in an interactive manner with therapist attributes and duration of stay. However, these findings tended not to be confirmed in two other investigations (Lorr, Katz, & Rubinstein, 1958; McNair et al., 1963). At the present time, therefore, one has relatively few reliable findings, and the results of unreplicated studies can only be viewed as suggestive.

Client Expectations and Other Variables in Relation to Continuation in Psychotherapy

Another area of investigation has been the relationship of the clients' expectancies concerning therapy to duration of stay. The client may have various expectations about being helped or about what will take place in therapy. If these are completely incongruent with what occurs, it is conceivable that the client may be dissatisfied and more inclined to withdraw.

Heine and Trosman (1960) conducted an investigation of the initial expectations of the doctor-patient interaction. Forty-six patients were given a questionnaire to tap attitudes toward psychiatric treatment, and the total group was dichotomized in terms of those still in treatment after six weeks. The two groups of patients did show some differences. The terminators tended to emphasize passive cooperation as a means of reaching their goal in treatment, and sought medicine or diagnostic information. The remainers, on the other hand, emphasized active collaboration and advice or help in changing behavior. These latter expectations were seen as being congruent with the expectations of the therapists. By contrast, the type of presenting complaint, whether somatic or emotional, or the degree of conviction that treatment would help, was unrelated to continuation.

In another study, patients who came for 12 or less interviews expressed some significantly different expectations of their therapists than did those who remained for 13 or more interviews (Heine, 1962). More terminators expected specific advice on their problems in the first therapy interview than did the continuers, and the latter more frequently expected a permissive attitude on the part of the therapist than did those who discontinued. In these respects, the continuers were more similar in their expectations to the therapists than were the discontinuers. In addition, patients who tended to leave therapy did not differentiate sharply the role of the psychiatrist (psychotherapist) from that of other medical experts.

In another study, 40 lower class patients were given a questionnaire to ascertain their expectations about therapy and were reevaluated after the first interview in terms of their perception of the interview (Overall & Aronson, 1962). The results indicated that these patients tended to expect a "medical-psychiatric" interview, with the therapist assuming an active supportive role. Furthermore, the patients whose expectations were generally least accurate in terms of therapist role were significantly less likely to return for treatment.

In a somewhat different type of study, Garfield and Wolpin (1963) evaluated the expectations of

70 patients referred for outpatient psychiatric treatment. The median level of education was 12 years, and none of the patients had had previous psychiatric treatment. In general, these patients indicated psychotherapy as the treatment of choice (88 percent), and a majority of them saw emotional factors as important in their difficulties. A majority also felt that an understanding of one's difficulties was significant and helpful in terms of their improvement. Thus the group as a whole seemed to display some positive attitudes and understanding of psychotherapy. However, more than one-third of them thought the therapy sessions would last 30 minutes or less, 73 percent anticipated some improvement by the fifth session, and 70 percent expected treatment to last 10 sessions or less. The latter expectations were clearly not congruent with those held by the therapists, but are not too discrepant from the median length of treatment reported by most clinics. In fact, one might even say that the clients were accurate in their expectations while the therapists were not!

It is also worth mentioning a related finding in a study of outpatient drug treatment for its potentially suggestive value for psychotherapy (Freedman, Engelhardt, Hankoff, Glick, Kaye, Buchwald, & Stark, 1958). In this study the doctors' notes of the initial interview were analyzed in terms of the warmth or detachment of the relationship provided by the therapist. Although the patients who dropped out of the therapy did not differ from those who remained in terms of the warmth of the doctor-patient relationship, when the type of relationship was matched with the patients' expectations about treatment, a significant interaction was found. Patients who denied mental illness *and* encountered a warm relationship tended to drop out, whereas the reverse was true with those patients who accepted their illness and were exposed to a warm relationship. This study also illustrates the importance of examining possible interactions between patient and therapist variables as compared with reliance solely on individual variables.

Although our focus here is on client variables or attributes, it should also be remembered that how the therapist perceives and regards the client may also affect the progress of therapy. If the therapist regards the client as unmotivated, overly defensive,

hostile, and difficult, it is conveivable that his attitudes may be communicated to the client and may influence his participation and continuation in psychotherapy. Some studies pertinent to this hypothesis are briefly alluded to here.

Heller and Goldstein (1961) conducted a study of client dependency and therapist expectancy as relationship maintaining variables in psychotherapy. They found a significant relationship between a measure of pretherapy client-therapist attraction on the part of the client and measures of dependency. They also secured a positive relationship between therapists' expectancy of client improvement at the fifth interview and client attraction. While the authors viewed their findings as offering partial support for the hypothesis that therapist expectations of change is a relationship-maintaining aspect of psychotherapy, no specific data on continuation are given. Although methodologically different, the studies of Garfield and Affleck (1961), and Affleck and Garfield (1961), are pertinent here. In the original study, ratings of therapeutic prognosis were found to be related to continuation in outpatient therapy. However, when this study was replicated on a new sample (Affleck & Garfield, 1961), the positive findings secured originally did not hold up. Again, it appears prudent to regard unreplicated findings as basically suggestive, and to withhold final judgments until the findings are replicated.

In one recent study, therapists' ratings at the end of the second session of group therapy on three factors were related significantly to continuation in therapy (Rosenzweig & Folman, 1974). These factors were the therapist's estimate of his ability to empathize with the client, his positive feelings toward the client, and his judgment of the client's ability to form a therapeutic relationship. In another study, the therapists' positive feelings toward clients and their positive prognoses for treatment were related to continuation, whereas ratings of psychopathology were not so related (Shapiro, 1974). The skill or experience of the therapist and how the therapist is perceived by the client may also play a role in continuation. Dodd (1970) found that medical students had a significantly higher rate of dropouts from psychotherapy with their patients than did psychiatric residents, and this finding was also cross validated on a new sample of 57 patients. Baekeland and Lundwall (1975) also report some relationship between therapist experience and continuation in psychotherapy in their review article, and a relationship between judged therapists' level of skill and continuation has been reported by Garfield et al. (1963). In this regard, it should also be mentioned that in a well-known study in which very experienced and nationally recognized therapists were used, there were no dropouts at the fourth interview, the point set for designating dropouts (Sloane, Staples, Cristol, Yorkston, & Whipple, 1975).

Some interesting findings have also been reported in a recent study that investigated certain aspects of the therapeutic relationship as they may pertain to both continuation and outcome in psychotherapy (Saltzman et al., 1976). The subjects in this study were 91 students who sought treatment at a university counseling center. Dropouts were defined as those who did not continue beyond the ninth interview. Both clients and therapists filled out forms pertaining to the treatment process after each of the first 10 interviews, and analyses were made of the responses to the first, third, and fifth interviews, the period during which most of the premature terminations occurred.

Several findings with regard to continuation are of interest. At the end of the first session, dropouts reported less anxiety than did the remainers. At the third and fifth sessions, dropouts were significantly lower than remainers on a number of dimensions pertaining to the relationship, such as the therapist's respect, confidence in the therapist, and involvement in therapy. In a complimentary fashion, dropouts were significantly lower than remainers on items completed by the therapists which pertained to the therapist's respect for the client and his own involvement in therapy. Thus, both clients' and therapists' views of the relationship early in therapy appeared to be related to continuation in therapy. However, therapist experience level and gender similarity of client-therapist pairs were not related to either continuation or outcome.

Two other kinds of results can be mentioned before concluding this section. In one investigation, 32 individuals who terminated after the first interview were compared with a like number who continued for additional interviews (the precise number is not given) (Proctor & Duehn, 1974). Stimulus-response congruence (whether the clinician's verbal responses acknowledged the content of the patient's preceding communication) and content congruence (the clinician's verbal statement being consistent with the patient's expectations concerning what was to be discussed) were the variables appraised. It was reported that the therapists were significantly more incongruent with defectors and that their verbal content was also significantly more irrelevant to the content expectations of the defectors.

The other interesting and somewhat serendipitous finding that is worth mentioning here has been noted in three studies. This is that patients who are asked to complete a test questionnaire or group of questionnaires prior to therapy, and who do in fact comply with this request, are more likely to continue in therapy than those who fail to complete the test. In one study, those patients completing he MMPI continued in therapy significantly longer than those who failed to do so (Wirt, 1967). In the second investigation, similar findings were secured with one sample of patients, but not with another smaller sample in an attempted replication (Dodd, 1970). In a third study, those patients who failed to complete a pretherapy packet of questionnaires dropped out of group therapy significantly more than those who completed the questionnaires (Koran & Costell, 1973). Does compliance with requests to complete questionnaires indicate a more general pattern of compliance or determination, or does it reflect greater motivation to cooperate in therapy? More data on this matter may help to clarify it.

Although the material just discussed is both interesting and plausible, it must be mentioned again that different samples of patients and therapists have been used in the various studies, as well as different procedures and criteria for defining continuation. In a similar manner, the meaning and definition of expectancies or expectations have also come under critical scrutiny in recent years (Wilkins, 1973). Since this latter problem has been investigated more extensively with regard to outcome in psychotherapy, we postpone further discussion of it until later.

In the light of what has been said, it would be of

interest to know the clients' own reasons for terminating their psychotherapy. One small follow-up study of 12 individuals who dropped out of psychotherapy before the seventh interview has been reported (Garfield, 1963a). Eleven of the 12 cases were contacted by a social worker and, among other questions, were asked why they discontinued psychotherapy. Six of the terminators gave as their reason some external difficulty, such as lack of transportation, no babysitter, and inability to get away from work. Of the remaining five, three were dissatisfied with the results of therapy or with the therapist, and two stated that they had improved. Although long-term studies with adequate samples have not been made, on the basis of this study and one other (Reiss & Brandt, 1965), it appears that very few of such terminators apply for therapy elsewhere after dropping out of therapy.

There are also two reports where dropouts from group therapy were asked their reasons for terminating from therapy. Although group therapy has some special features that distinguish it from individual psychotherapy, in the absence of other data, it is worth noting the results of these studies. Yalom (1966) was able to contact 26 of 35 dropouts and reported that there was rarely "a single cause for any patient's termination and often it was difficult to determine the major reason for the dropout" (p. 397). He grouped his responses into nine different categories, some of which dealt specifically with the group process. However, seven patients did indicate that they had a mistaken notion of therapy. A second smaller study of 9 of 15 dropouts also secured results that were similar to those of Yalom's in showing a diversity of reasons for termination (Koran & Costell, 1973).

In our review of a number of variables in relation to duration of stay in psychotherapy we have commented on some of the difficulties and complexities evident in securing reliable and generalizable results. Many findings do not appear to be confirmed when applied to new samples, and conditions from clinic to clinic and study to study vary. As a result, findings that have not been cross validated on new samples must be viewed as suggestive at best. Some potentially significant test variables also have not been very systematically explored. For example, in several of the studies

reviewed, IQ has appeared to show some relationship to length of stay in traditional outpatient psychotherapy (Affleck & Mednick, 1959; Auld & Eron, 1953; Gibby, Stotsky, Hiler, & Miller, 1954; Hiler, 1958b). However, in most of these studies, the analyses of IQ data have been secondary to other analyses and were carried out on a smaller number of subjects than was used in the main study. The intellectual level of the subject would appear to be of some significance for continuation in verbal psychotherapy as traditionally practiced, although its actual predictive value would depend to some extent on the client populations served. One would also expect to find a positive correlation between IQ and indices of social class.

Of the variables studied, those that pertain to social class appear to have the most consistent supporting evidence. However, although this relationship does have a fair amount of empirical support, the precise reasons advanced to explain this relationship must be viewed somewhat tentatively. Mutuality of expectations on the part of therapist and client is one hypothesis that seems plausible and has, at least, some empirical support. The matter of differing value systems and orientations among middle class therapists and lower class clients has been hypothesized as a possible explanation for the results secured (Myers & Schaffer, 1958), but systematic research on this has been limited (Lerner & Fiske, 1973).

Finally, it can be noted that most of the findings discussed thus far have pertained to "conventional" or "traditional" outpatient psychotherapy. The precise nature of the therapy offered is frequently not described in the reports. Occasionally, it is referred to as "dynamically oriented" or relationship therapy, but operational definitions are rarely, if ever, given. On the other hand, although the behavioral therapies have greatly increased in popularity in recent years, hardly any studies of attrition with this type of therapy have been published. One may speculate as to why this is true. Many reports of research on behavior therapy have indicated a relatively brief period of therapy, and this conceivably may negate or reduce the problem of attrition. A fair number of investigations have also utilized college students or other volunteers for specific studies of a particular problem, and it may be that considerable effort is exerted to keep subjects in a study until it is completed. To a certain extent, therefore, the individuals seen for treatment are given more explicit information concerning the therapy and the time it will take, and this may influence attrition. It is also conceivable that since many of the reports of behavior therapy are planned investigations of therapy outcome, little attention is focused on dropouts; rather, the emphasis is placed on filling the vacated slots in the different subject groups. Whatever the reasons, the matter of attrition in behavior therapy is either not a problem or has received little systematic study.

RESEARCH ON CLIENT VARIABLES AND OUTCOME IN PSYCHOTHERAPY

Although the problem of continuation in psychotherapy is of importance, it is, of course, secondary to the kind of outcome that is eventually secured. In fact, the assumption is usually made that a certain (frequently unspecified) amount of contact with a therapist must be made if progress in psychotherapy is to be attained. If a client discontinues therapy before the therapist believes there has been sufficient time to affect change, then such discontinuance directly influences and limits the amount of change to be expected. It is for this reason that early or premature termination on the part of the client is frequently viewed as a failure in psychotherapy, even though there has been practically no systematic research evaluating the outcome of therapy in such cases. Here, as elsewhere, various beliefs concerning psychotherapy are frequently held with relatively little attempt being made to secure research data to support or refute these beliefs. Thus, for example, while most investigators have tended to view the abrupt terminator as a failure in psychotherapy, some have viewed these individuals as post hoc successes with the belief that they must have changed for the better or they would have returned for psychotherapy (Garfield & Kurz, 1952).

With regard to length of psychotherapy, some investigators have reported a positive finding between the length of therapy and outcome (Lorr, McNair, Michaux, & Raskin, 1962; Bailey, Warshaw, & Eichler, 1959), whereas the findings in another study were less favorable (Nichols & Beck,

1960). Lorr (1962), in an early review of the limited data available, suggested that the "duration of treatment is a more influential parameter than sheer number of treatments." Luborsky, Chandler, Auerbach, Cohen, and Bachrach (1971) came to a more favorable conclusion concerning number of sessions and outcome, but pointed out that the problem is complex. What appears to be of possibly greater importance than length per se is how therapy is structured for the client and how the therapy meets his or her expectations. In two comparative reviews of brief time-limited therapy and unlimited therapy, essentially no differences in outcome between the two types of therapy have been secured (Luborsky, Singer, & Luborsky, 1975; Gurman & Kniskern, 1977).

Detailed evaluations of the outcome of early terminators, however, have not been made. In one follow-up study of 12 terminators and 12 remainders who had been studied more intensively for another purpose, both groups stated that they were getting along quite well and, if anything, the terminators gave more favorable reports (Garfield, 1963a). However, the follow-up was based on the self-reports of the clients and no before and after therapy measures were used. In contrast to this report, Yalom (1966) indicated that all but perhaps 3 of 35 dropouts from group therapy showed no improvement.

We can now proceed to the research that has been reported on client variables and outcome in psychotherapy. At the outset, something should be said about the difficulties evident in outcome research, even though they are discussed in other chapters of this volume. (See particularly Chapters 2 and 5.) Whereas the length of psychotherapy, as determined by the number of interviews, provides a reasonably clear and objective criterion for research investigation, when we turn our attention to outcome, we encounter a large number of variable and fallible criteria. Among the frequently used criteria for appraising outcome are therapists' judgments, clients' evaluations, ratings by judges, a variety of tests and questionnaires, behavioral tasks, and the like. This variety among the measures poses a number of difficulties in comparing the results of potential predictor variables among different studies. Several investigations, for example, have shown rather low agreement among different outcome criteria (Cartwright, Kirtner, & Fiske, 1963; Garfield, Prager, & Bergin, 1971; Horenstein, Houston, & Holmes, 1973; Keniston, Boltax, & Almond, 1971; Sloane et al., 1975). In some of these studies, it has also been shown that therapists' ratings of outcome tend to be more positive than other measures. In addition to these problems, there are also methodological issues concerning whether only global ratings of outcome are used, or whether difference scores, in terms of pre-post measures, or other procedures to take into account initial differences between clients have been used (Fiske, Hunt, Luborsky, Orne, Parloff, Reiser & Tuma, 1970; Luborsky et al., 1971). Consequently, it is exceedingly difficult and, at times, misleading to attempt to lump together studies that, among other things, have utilized different measures of outcome.

In addition to the problems encountered with outcome criteria, there are also variations in the type of therapy offered, variations in the training and competence of the therapists studied, and differences in the kinds of client samples treated. These types of problems, as we have already mentioned, not only place limitations on the value of any specific study but also present serious obstacles to the drawing of reliable and valid generalizations from the plethora of published studies. With this, then, as a caveat, let us now consider some representative studies. For convenience, the types of studies are again classified into a few broad categories.

Social Class and Other Demographic Variables

Although social class variables have received considerable attention in relation to matters such as assignment to psychotherapy and premature termination, they have not been studied with the same frequency with regard to outcome. In the extensive review of factors influencing outcome in psychotherapy by Luborsky et al., (1971), for example, only a relatively small number of such studies were mentioned. In general, other variables have received greater attention. Consequently, our discussion of social class variables and their relationship to outcome is brief.

In their review of five studies dealing with social class, Luborsky et al., (1971) essentially reported

no relationship between this variable and outcome. Two studies found no relationship (Brill & Storrow, 1960; Katz et al., 1958); two found a positive relationship (McNair, Lorr, Young, Roth, & Boyd, 1964; Rosenbaum, Friedlander, & Kaplan, 1956); and in one study of 35 patients, *lower* socioeconomic status was found to be associated with positive outcome in brief psychotherapy (Gottschalk, Mayerson, & Gottlieb, 1967). The study by Rosenbaum et al. (1956) which reported a negative relationship between social status and outcome has some deficiencies that make its findings questionable. First, "social strata" were "defined very simply, and probably too simply, as 'lower,' 'middle,' and 'upper.' No further description was provided" (p. 125). In addition, it appears that two of the three outcome groups had to be combined to obtain a significant chi-square.

Lorion (1973) in a general discussion of socioeconomic status and traditional treatment approaches also concluded that "while socioeconomic status appears to be a significant correlate of acceptance for, and duration of, individual psychotherapy, it does not relate to treatment outcome" (p. 263). Thus, two fairly recent reviews of this problem appear to come to quite similar conclusions. Besides those studies already mentioned, Rosenthal and Frank (1958); Cole, Branch, and Allison (1962); and Abronda, Dean, and Starkweather (1964) also did not find any relationship between social class and outcome in their investigations.

A few studies have also examined outcome in terms of the educational status of the client. While level of education generally is correlated with social class indices, the findings here tend to be more positive. Four studies have reported positive findings (Bloom, 1956; Hamburg, Bibring, Fisher, Stanton, Wallerstein, Weinstock, & Haggard, 1967; McNair, Lorr, Young, Roth, & Boyd, 1964; and Sullivan, Miller, & Smelser, 1958), whereas two found no significant results (Knapp, Levi, McCarter, Wermer, & Zetzel, 1960; Rosenbaum, et al., 1956). It should be noted, however, that in most of these studies therapists' ratings constituted the main criterion of outcome, in some the samples were small, and in Bloom's study, the criterion of poor outcome also included premature termination.

Several individuals have also discussed the matter of differential therapists' attitudes toward lower class patients and its potential importance for continuation in psychotherapy (Jones, 1974; Lorion, 1973, 1974; Lerner, 1972). However, few, if any, systematic studies have attempted to relate therapists' attitudes toward lower class patients and outcome in psychotherapy. In any event, the existing data do not indicate any strong relationship between social class and outcome, although there is a suggestion of a possible relationship between education and outcome.

A moderate number of studies have also examined variables such as age and sex in relation to outcome. In general, the results obtained are quite similar to those obtained in relation to premature termination. There do not appear to be any clear or obvious relationships between variables of this kind and outcome. Consequently, it does not appear worthwhile to list and review these studies in any detail. Instead I consider this area briefly, refer to the review by Luborsky et al. (1971), and then discuss some of the problems in this area of research.

It has generally been assumed that older people tend to be more rigid and fixed in their ways. Their patterns of behavior have a longer reinforcement history and supposedly their defenses and character structure are more resistant to change. We do know from more systematic studies that older subjects show some decline in mental functinting (Wechsler, 1958), and that they may not learn new skills as readily as younger individuals. Consequently, it could be presumed that they would be less favorable candidates for psychotherapy in terms of their potential for change. This, apparently, was Freud's view and, in my opinion, it has been an influential one. In a lecture delivered in 1904 and published the following year, Freud stated: "The age of patients has this importance in determining their fitness for psycho-analytic treatment, that, on the one hand, near or above the fifties the elasticity of the mental processes, on which the treatment depends, is as a rule lacking—old people are no longer educable—and, on the other hand, the mass of material to be dealt with would prolong the duration of treatment indefinitely" (Freud, 1950, pp. 258–259). Since the

writer of this chapter happens to be in his fifties, he may be incapable of scientific objectivity on this point. However, while I tend to agree with Freud that psychoanalysis of older individuals might take too long, I do not believe that there are research data to support the view that older clients are less desirable in terms of other psychotherapeutic approaches.

There is a problem pertaining to research on age and outcome, however, that does not exist with regard to the variable of sex. By and large, in the latter instance, all studies use the same criteria and subjects are classified into the same two categories: male and female. Age, however, is a different matter. It is a continuous variable and not a dichotomous one. Consequently, one cannot adequately draw conclusions from studies unles they have comparable groups of subjects. If one investigator has a group of patients that ranges in age from 20 to 40 years, and another has a sample that ranges in age from 30 to 60 years, it is difficult to draw any meaningful conclusions—and this appears to happen not infrequently in the investigations reported in this area.

In a tally of 11 studies made by Luborsky et al. (1971), 4 studies purportedly secured a positive relationship between age and outcome, 2 secured a negative relationship, and 5 secured no relationship. There appears to be some error in their listing the study by Zigler and Phillips (1961) as one of the positive studies. This study provides no data on age and outcome in psychotherapy but is, instead, an investigation of social competence and hospitalization. Thus this reduces the "positive" studies to 3. It should also be pointed out here that the positive findings as reported by Luborsky et al. actually represent a negative relationship between age and outcome in that younger subjects were considered to have the better outcome, and the reverse was true for the reported negative findings. Luborsky et al. (1971) concluded that "Older patients tend to have a slightly poorer prognosis" (p. 151), and noted also that in the two "negative" studies which found older patients to have a better outcome, the age range was restricted. We will now examine some of the studies that purport to have significant findings before concluding our discussion.

The study by Casner (1950), listed by Luborsky

et al., as showing significant results is, unfortunately, reported only in an abstract. It is a report of "personal adjustment counseling" on the 50 most improved and the 50 least improved veterans out of 159 referred for counseling. This categorization was determined by "the improvement ratings of judges who referred" these cases. Reliable differences were found for a number of variables favoring the successful cases, including "age under 30." In terms of the way the material was reported, I am not at all clear regarding what these comparisons entailed nor is any information given on the age range of the subjects or the statistical procedures and criteria used.

The report by Hamburg et al. (1967) is listed as showing that the age group 46 and above improved less. However, the data on which this report of psychoanalysis and psychotherapy are based leave much to be desired. Without going into detail, this report of 3019 rather highly selected patients from an unspecified population contains some ambiguous statements. In one section, it is stated that there was no significant relationship between "cure" and age. In another, it is stated that the age group 46 and above has a lower improvement rate than statistically expected. However, no data or elaboration are provided. The criterion of outcome was the judgment of individual analysts. Thus, although this study and the one by Casner (1950) are both considered to show a negative relationship between age and outcome, the two samples are quite divergent in terms of age.

Similar problems are apparent in two studies with very comparable age ranges. Knapp et al. (1960) reported a significant positive correlation with increasing age and outcome in 27 analytic patients, ages 20 to 40, whereas Seeman (1954) found no relationship in 23 cases ranging from 21 to 40 years of age who were receiving client-centered therapy. In the latter, the median age was used and the age of 28 put one in the "older" group.

In another "negative" study where older patients obtained better outcome, Conrad (1952) compared the 25 most successful cases with the 25 least successful. Thus, these are relatively extreme groups, although we are not informed about the population from which they are drawn. The mean age of the successful group was 32, the mean age of the other was 27. While this appears to be a large difference, no statistical tests are reported, and no age range is given. However, a statement is made that the "usual clinic patient was in his late twenties." It should be noted that the mean age of the two comparison groups was used here and no data on range of overlap were provided. In view of the variations in the different studies and the lack of any conclusive pattern of findings, I believe it is sounder to conclude that age has not been shown to be related to outcome.

It is not necessary to prolong this particular discussion, since hopefully the issues involved are clear. One should not discuss age in relation to outcome in the abstract, but instead should specify a particular age in relation to a particular therapy and with full awareness of the other potential factors that may play a possible role in outcome.

The prevailing evidence with regard to sex and outcome also appears to indicate that there is no clear relationship. Most of the studies show no differences in outcome. However, the problem, like other aspects of psychotherapy may be more complex. It is conceivable that there are possible interaction effects between the sex of the therapist and that of the client. If this is true, then focusing solely on one part of the equation would not provide meaningful answers. In any event, a few comments can be offered.

Most studies, as indicated, have reported no relationship between sex and outcome (Cartwright, 1955; Gaylin, 1966; Hamburg et al., 1967; Knapp, et al., 1960). Two have reported positive findings for women. In the study by Seeman (1954), this positive finding is based on 18 men and 11 women, a rather small number of clients. Furthermore, 16 of the clients were students at the University of Chicago, and all were middle class individuals who were above average in intelligence and education. The other study utilized 12 women and 15 men (Mintz, Luborsky, & Auerbach, 1971). Two different therapist rating scales were used as the criteria of outcome. One was a combined scale of judged success and patient satisfaction, while the other was a scale of "improvement." Significant results were secured with the first scale but not with the second. On the basis of these results, I believe one cannot make much of a case for sex being a significant variable in psychotherapy.

Personality and Test Variables Related to Outcome

A number of other studies also have been carried out in the search for variables that are predictive of or related to outcome in psychotherapy. A significant percentage of them deal with personality and test patterns of clients. Since different tests have been used in different combinations and with different interpretative schemes, it is frequently difficult to group them together or reach meaningful conclusions. Some typical studies are examined first, and then the research on a few techniques that have received a moderate amount of attention is reviewed and evaluated.

Several investigators, particularly earlier ones, have utilized projective techniques and batteries of psychological tests in a variety of ways. Rosenberg (1954), for example, examined the responses to the Wechsler-Bellevue Scale, the Rorschach, and a sentence completion test of 40 patients who received psychotherapy in a VA outpatient clinic. The protocols of the Rorschach and the sentence completion tests for one-half of each of the improved and unimproved groups of patients were then evaluated by two psychologists and rated in terms of 23 intellectual and personality variables. On 7 of these variables, as well as IQ, the two groups were significantly differentiated. The two raters were then informed of the variables that had differentiated the two groups of patients, and were asked to predict improvement in the remaining 20 patients. Each was able to make at least 15 correct predictions. It was concluded that the successful patient has superior intelligence, has the ability to produce associations easily, is not rigid, has a wide range of interests, is sensitive to his environment, feels deeply, exhibits a high energy level, and is free from bodily concerns. The use of clinical evaluations and predictions in this study, however, clearly limited its applicability to other situations that utilized other clinicians.

In another study, Roberts (1954) compared 11 Rorschach indices alleged to have prognostic signifiance for treatment with rather careful ratings of pre- and posttreatment status by three judges.

None of the measures was significantly related to the outcome criteria. A somewhat similar study was reported by Rogers and Hammond (1953). Fifty patients judged to be unimproved by their therapists were compared with 59 patients judged to be "slightly improved" or "improved." Ninety-nine Rorschach signs were used but failed to differentiate significantly between the two groups. Three types of clinical judgments of the Rorschach records also failed to differentiate the groups.

Barron (1953a) also attempted to secure some test correlates of response to psychotherapy in 33 outpatients, most of whom had weekly therapy sessions for six months. In part, he tried to replicate the earlier study of Harris and Christiansen (1946) by using a shortened form of the Wechsler-Bellevue Scale, the MMPI, and the Rorschach. He also added the Ethnocentrism Scale. Whereas Harris and Christiansen obtained positive results with their Rorschach Prognostic Index, Barron secured a correlation of .00 between it and ratings of judged improvement. In a similar fashion, whereas Harris and Christiansen found no relationship between improvement and intelligence test scores, Barron found a correlation of .46. Barron's total group had a higher mean IQ than the Harris and Christiansen group, with his unimproved group's mean IQ of 112 exceeding the mean of the total group used in the other study. Here again, subject differences in the two studies may account, at least in part, for the differences in findings, since all but 2 of the patients evaluated by Harris and Christiansen were hospitalized during therapy. However, there was some agreement between the two studies with reference to the MMPI, with unimproved patients securing higher scores on the Paranoid and Schizophrenia scales. Barron (1953a) concluded that "the patients who are most likely to get well are those who are not very sick in the first place," and in a later study reported that ego strength or degree of personality integration was positively related to outcome in psychotherapy (Barron, 1953b). Finally, Barron found that ethnocentrism was negatively related to change in psychotherapy.

Reference can also be made to a study by Gallagher (1954) of test indicators for prognosis in client-centered therapy. He compared a group of discontinuers with two groups judged to be the least successful and the most successful in therapy. He found no differences between the groups on the Elizur Roschach Anxiety Scale, Rorschach productivity, the Mooney Problem Check List, and the Barron Ego-Strength (ES) Scale, derived from the MMPI. The groups were differentiated on the Taylor Anxiety Scale, the Depression Scale of the MMPI, and on the number of words used by the subjects in summarizing their problems on the Mooney Check List. The findings were interpreted as supporting the hypothesis that success in client-centered therapy was positively related to the amount of overt stress and to verbal productivity shown on the pretherapy tests. It should be noted also that this group of clients differed considerably on the MMPI from those studied by Barron (1953a) and Harris and Christiansen (1946), particularly in having lower scores on the Pa and Sc scales, which were of some prognostic value in the other two studies. Furthermore, with reference to the positive predictive value of high MMPI Depression scores, just the opposite results were secured by Barron (1953a).

A five-year follow-up study by Stone, Frank, Nash, and Imber (1961) utilized a self-report scale that tapped five areas of symptomatology as a measure of initial disturbance and reported a significant association between greater initial disturbance and more positive outcome. Truax, Tunnell, Fine, and Wargo (1966) secured somewhat comparable results for group psychotherapy clients on four scales of the MMPI. Nevertheless, results in the opposite direction were secured by Kirtner and Cartwright (1958), who used clients' initial Thematic Apperception Test (TAT) protocols and an initial interview as a measure of initial disturbance. However, the two successful groups of clients here were composed of only four clients each. The report of the Wisconsin Project on a hospitalized group of psychotic patients also indicated a negative relationship between degree of disturbance and outcome in psychotherapy—high mental health ratings and a generally low level of manifest psychotic disturbance were positively related to outcome, as well as to ratings of therapist empathy (Rogers, Gendlin, Kiesler, & Truax, 1967). However, it should be pointed out that this group of rather chronic schizophrenic patients differs quite noticeably from most outpatient samples studied and, consequently, the degree of disturbance is also different, since it includes many types of thought disorders, instead of merely increased degree of personal distress.

In contrast to these studies, the one by Katz et al. (1958) with 232 outpatients in clinics of the Veterans Administration found no relationship between degree of disturbance and outcome. In this instance, degree of disturbance was based on four categories of diagnosis: psychoneurosis, psychosomatic disorders, character disorder, and psychosis. *Both* diagnoses and ratings of improvement were provided by the therapists. However, another study of 83 patients in a VA clinic using the MMPI found significant differences on a majority of the clinical scales, indicating "that those persons who are least equipped to meet life challenges are the ones who stand to gain least from psychotherapy" (Sullivan et al., 1958, p. 7). Despite this conclusion, essentially null results have been reported also in three other studies (Cartwright & Roth, 1957; Muench, 1958; Seeman, 1954).

After reviewing some of this literature, Truax and Carkhuff (1967) offered an hypothesis that patients with the greatest "felt disturbance" as measured by self-report measures and the least overt or behavioral disturbance are the ones who show the greatest therapeutic improvement. Although this is an interesting hypothesis, it has not been adequately confirmed, as the previous paragraphs indicate, nor have most studies distinguished between "felt disturbance" and overall degree of disturbance.

In a more recent study, the improved and unimproved patients were similar in initial ratings of "ego-weakness," but differed on manifest distress level as rated by nurses on the ward (Jacobs, Muller, Anderson, & Skinner, 1972). However, ratings of manifest distress level by therapists, other staff members, and patients were unrelated to outcome. Moreover, the results were confounded by the fact that the patients also received milieu therapy and medication, as well as psychotherapy.

Two important recent studies have also provided information on this topic. One is the comparative study of behavior therapy and analytically oriented psychotherapy by Sloane et al. (1975). In this study, the less disturbed patients, as measured by the MMPI, secured more positive outcome with analytically oriented psychotherapy. On the other hand, "behavior therapy was equally successful whether the patient had a high or low degree of pathology" (p. 176). In this instance, at least, the type of therapy appeared to be an important variable. It was also mentioned that for both groups, those patients who spoke in longer utterances showed significantly more improvement than those who spoke in shorter units.

The other study referred to is the 18-year research project that was carried out by the Menninger Foundation (Kernberg, Burstein, Coyne, Appelbaum, Horwitz, & Voth, 1972). This was an investigation of 21 patients who were selected for psychoanalysis and of 21 patients who received psychoanalytic psychotherapy. The specific finding of interest here is that clinical appraisals of ego strength were found to correlate positively with a measure of global improvement ($r = .35$). However, these investigators also emphasized that the appraisals of ego strength were relative to the population studied, basically a group of patients falling within the broad categories of neurosis and "borderline" conditions.

Space limitations permit only passing reference to some other recent studies of interest. Frank (1974b), in a review of 25 years of research, concludes "that the most important determinants of long-term improvement lie in the patient" (p. 339). In this regard, mention is made that symptoms of anxiety and depression improved the most, whereas poorer results were secured with somatic complaints. The presence of anxiety at the initiation of therapy has also been noted as a positive prognostic sign in other studies (Kernberg et al., 1972; Luborsky et al., 1971), although inconclusive studies have also been reported. The type and severity of anxiety must also be considered, as well as the stimuli that influence it. As Frank (1974b) states, "long-term prognosis largely depends on the strength of the person's coping capacities and the modifiability of the stress which leads him to seek help . . ." (p. 339). In other words, as indicated in another study also, patients who manifest anxiety in relation to their current situation or stress appear to secure better outcome (Smith, Sjöholm, & Niélzen, 1975).

Two recent studies of behavior therapy also deal with correlates of behavior change or outcome. In one study of participant modeling with snake phobics, "Neither initial attitudes toward snakes, severity of phobic-behavior, performance aroused fears, nor fear proneness correlated with degree of behavior change" (Bandura, Jeffrey, & Wright, 1974, p. 62). However, some measures of fear reduction taken after the initiation of therapy were predictive of subsequent behavioral change. The greater the fear decrements on the initially failed task and the less fear aroused by this task, the greater the degree of improvement.

In another study of 36 phobic patients, attempts were made to evaluate several predictor variables in relation to outcome with desensitization, flooding, and a control treatment (Mathews, Johnston, Shaw, & Gelder, 1974). Only two measures were significantly related to outcome at both termination and follow-up, and they both pertained to extroversion and traits related to it. However, severity of symptoms, high anxiety and neuroticism, low expectancy, and low rated motivation for treatment were not related to outcome. In general, "There was no evidence that by using the measures examined, patients could be individually allocated in advance to the treatment most likely to help them" (Mathews et al., 1974, p. 264). However, as in the previous study (Bandura et al., 1974), there was a greater reduction in measures of rated anxiety early in therapy by those who subsequently improved. It may be possible to predict subsequent outcome more accurately at a certain stage in therapy than at the very beginning, and this tentative lead is an interesting one that may be worth pursuing.

These reports reflect some of the problems evident in this type of research. Without belaboring the issue, it can be noted that sample differences, variations in how test responses or disturbances are evaluated and interpreted, different types of therapy, and possible differences in how clinical outcome is appraised are all apparent as potential problems in the studies just reviewed. Some of the measurement problems may be illustrated by reference to another study (Prager & Garfield, 1972). A number of indices of client disturbance were used, as well as six measures of outcome. In general, ratings of disturbance made at the beginning of therapy by clients, therapists, and supervisors were unrelated to the six measures of outcome used. However, initial disturbance as measured by the mean scale elevation of the MMPI, elevation of the neurotic triad of the MMPI, and a disturbance scale completed by the client were significantly and negatively correlated with various ratings of outcome provided by clients, therapists, and supervisors at the completion of therapy. Also, these latter measures of initial disturbance were not significantly related to three outcome measures based on differences in scores obtained at the beginning and termination of therapy. Thus, the finding that degree of initial or felt disturbance was negatively related to outcome was true for only certain indices of disturbance and certain criteria of outcome.

Two other observations made by Prager and Garfield (1972) are worth noting here. First, the studies that found that patients with higher levels of disturbance secured more positive results than those with less disturbance generally used the same instrument to measure both initial level of disturbance and outcome. Studies that reported a negative relationship between initial level of disturbance and outcome used an independent outcome measures, such as therapists' or judges' ratings. The problem of regression toward the mean could be a factor in the findings reported in the first set of studies. The second point is that initial level of disturbance is found to be inversely related to outcome primarily when global ratings of improvement, made at the termination of therapy, are used as the criteria of outcome. In these instances, the judgment of change involves the rater's *perception of change,* whereas actual difference scores require information relevant to the symptoms and feelings of the client at a particular time. It has also been reported that judgments of outcome, particularly by therapists, tend to be more favorable than other types of measures or ratings (Garfield, Prager, & Bergin, 1971; Horenstein, Houston, & Holmes, 1973).

Two scales of ego strength have also received a certain amount of attention with regard to outcome. The Barron ES Scale, already referred to, is one such measure. After Barron (1953b) had reported a positive relationship between scores on this scale and outcome, a number of essentially nonpositive results were reported (Fiske, Cartwright, & Kirtner, 1964; Gallagher, 1954; Getter & Sundland, 1962; Gottschalk, Fox, & Bates, 1973; Newmark, Finkelstein, & Frerking, 1974; Sullivan et al., 1958; Taulbee, 1958). It would appear, therefore, that the early promise of this scale has failed to be supported.

More positive results have been reported with the use of another index of ego strength derived from six components of the Rorschach test, the Rorschach Prognostic Rating Scale (RPRS) (Klopfer, Kirkner, Wisham, & Baker, 1951). Cartwright (1958) reported positive results with the RPRS and psychotherapy outcome in a study of 13 clients, and Johnson (1953) also reported similar results with 21 retardates in play therapy. Others reporting positive findings are Bloom (1956), Endicott and Endicott (1964), Kirkner, Wisham, and Giedt (1953), Mindess (1953), Newmark et al. (1974), and Sheehan, Frederick, Rosevear, and Spiegelman (1954). Studies that have secured negative findings, however, have been reported by Filmer-Bennett (1955), Fiske et al. (1964), and Lessing (1960). Thus, it appears that the positive findings occur more than twice as frequently as do the negative findings. The RPRS has been used also with several different kinds of therapy. In the study by Newmark et al. (1974), for example, significant differences in mean scores were secured between improved and unimproved subjects who received two different types of therapy: behavior modification and rational-emotive therapy. Nevertheless, some other considerations lessen its practical utility. The mean scores for various groups of subjects (judged to be improved or unimproved) show considerable variability; there is a noticeable overlap in scores between improved and unimproved clients; and the predictive norms provided by Klopfer et al. (1951) do not always appear applicable.

The criteria for judging improvement also vary considerably among the studies just cited and, consequently, there is a question of what is actually being predicted. For example, in the study by Mindess (1953), four therapists rated their patients *at the end of therapy* as to their status both at the beginning and end of therapy. The RPRS correlated positively with both sets of ratings, but no correlations were computed with the difference between the two sets of ratings. Thus the criteria were ratings of patient status made at the end of therapy and not of improvement. In the study by Johnson (1953), the criterion consisted of the therapist's judgment of "Improved" or "Unimproved" *and* teachers' judgments of improved social behavior. The therapist's judgment was based on her appraisal of "affective verbalization or projective play, insight and working through" (p. 321), which appear to be process variables rather than outcome criteria. Furthermore, how these judgments were combined with the evaluations of social behavior into one final determination of improvement is not specified in the report.

Similar concerns can be expressed with regard to some of the other studies. In Bloom's (1956), for example, the criterion was the patient's "therapeutic history." Those patients included in the "good" category contained some who were still in therapy, as well as others who had been terminated. The "poor" category included not only those who had shown no change but some who had dropped out of therapy. In the study by Sheehan et al. (1954) of 35 stutterers, the RPRS differentiated the most and least improved groups as judged by therapists' ratings of improvement, but bore no relationship to improvement in actual speech. Clearly, one has to be cautious in drawing conclusions.

Finally, as Frank (1967) has commented, the use of the RPRS in predicting outcome leads to a correct prediction in about two-thirds of the cases which, on the basis of some reported success rates in psychotherapy, might be predicted without utilizing any measures. Here, we have the old problem of base rates, which is frequently overlooked in this area of research. An effective predictor should exceed the base rates. The overall impression, therefore, is that whereas those with adequate ego strength or personality integration, as measured by the RPRS, appear to do better in psychotherapy than those with poor ego strength, prediction on this basis may not exceed the base rates for im-

provement. There are, however, other aspects of this problem that we will mention later.

In addition to the studies discussed above, are others that have reported both positive and negative findings with various scores or determinants from the Rorschach or other projective techniques. There is little purpose in either listing or reviewing these studies or in discussing the various types of test data that have been used. To the extent that studies have used idiosyncratic procedures, small subject samples, and questionable outcome criteria, and have not been replicated, they can be passed over. Illustrations of these problems have already been offered, and those who are interested in pursuing them further are referred elsewhere (Luborsky et al., 1971; Meltzoff & Kornreich, 1970). It seems preferable here to discuss and evaluate some of the generalizations and tentative conclusions drawn from previous reviews of research concerning the general personality resources of the client or his degree of disturbance in relation to outcome in psychotherapy.

One general statement which has been made is that the better integrated and less disturbed the individual is, the better the outcome in psychotherapy (Barron, 1953a; Garfield, 1971; Luborsky et al., 1971). Although there has been a certain acceptance of this view, there are also reports that fail to support it. Here, again, methodological problems must be considered. An important point stressed previously, and emphasized by Mintz (1972), pertains to how outcome is evaluated. As he demonstrated, global ratings of improvement made at the end of treatment tend to be very much influenced by the actual condition of the client at that time, *irrespective* of how the individual was at the beginning of therapy. Consequently, the person who functions at a relatively high level at the start and shows only slight change, is still rated as greatly improved as compared with someone who begins at a much lower level and, while progressing more, does not function terminally at the high level of the other client. In other words, it may be more correct to say that *clients who begin therapy at a high level of functioning terminate therapy at higher levels than those who begin at relatively low levels,* rather than that the former actually show the largest *gains* in psychotherapy. One issue here is that, in addition to the goal of positive change in psychotherapy, there is also an implicit goal of adequate functioning at the end of therapy. Consequently, an individual who gains more than another, but whose final level of adjustment is below that of the other on some norm, is considered less successful. For example, an individual whose IQ increased from 40 to 65 would show a greater gain than one who progressed from 110 to 120. However, he would still be regarded as mentally retarded, and if the goal were "normal" intelligence, his progress might be regarded as limited.

Another important problem concerns how personality functioning or psychopathology are defined or appraised. Severity of disturbance, for example, can be viewed in terms of clinical diagnosis (psychosis versus neurosis), intensity of discomfort or symptoms, duration of disturbance or chronicity, adjustment to current life situation, degree of impairment socially or occupationally, or in terms of scores on tests or rating scales. If a hypothetical personality construct such as ego strength, presumably reflecting personality integration and adjustment, is assessed by different techniques that show little relationship to each other, conflicting or confusing results are very likely to result. This situation is apparent in the results previously presented for the Barron ES Scale and the RPRS. Keeping these problems in mind may be helpful in trying to understand the variation in the findings that have been reported.

Before proceeding further, it is appropriate to comment on the findings and interpretation provided by Luborsky et al. (1971) in their detailed review of this area. In general, they conclude that the "Initially sicker patients do not improve as much with psychotherapy as the initially healthier do" (p. 149). In the first section of their review under the heading of "Degree of Initial Disturbance versus Adequacy of Functioning," 55 separate findings are listed (pps. 162–164). Of these, 31 are listed as showing a positive relationship between adequacy of adjustment and outcome, 1 is listed as negative, and 23 are listed as inconclusive or with nonsignificant results. Taken at face value, the positive findings appear to be the most frequent. It is also stated by these authors that be-

cause of the "poor statistical power of much of the research," the positive findings should be given more weight. Although there is a certain reasonableness to this argument, I am inclined to take a different view: that the quality of the research should determine the weight given to it. It should also be pointed out that in the review by Luborsky et al. (1971), some studies are listed more than once because comparisons were made with different predictive or outcome criteria. Since we have already reviewed many of the studies listed, we examine here only selected ones for the purposes of discussion.

In the review by Luborsky et al., (1971), only one study is listed as reporting that the more disturbed or disabled patients had the best response to psychotherapy, in this instance, brief psychotherapy (Gottschalk, et al., 1967). This finding was secured on 22 patients and was based on a Spearman rank order correlation of .35 between initial status on a rating scale and a difference score between ratings at pretreatment and posttreatment. A later study of 37 patients by the same senior investigator with the same assessment techniques, however, found that "the sicker patients are likely ($P < .01$) to have less improvement" (Gottschalk et al., 1973, p. 1110). In this instance, a negative correlation of $-.65$ was obtained between initial degree of disturbance and the same criterion of outcome used in the earlier study. Both studies secured significant findings, but in the opposite directions! In both studies, therapy was limited to six interviews and, in the second study, the *average* number of treatment sessions was 2.7 with the sessions ranging from 20 to 50 minutes in duration. One would have to be rather lacking in caution to generalize from these findings to psychotherapy in general.

Two findings are also listed by Luborsky et al. from a report by Luborsky (1962) on the Menninger psychotherapy project. One finding is a nonsignificant correlation of $-.18$ between initial ratings on the Health Sickness Rating (HSR) used in that project, and pre- and postdifferences on the HSR at termination. However, another finding from the same study is listed as positive—initial HSR correlated .71 with termination HSR and .54 with ratings of improvement. The issue here is which outcome measure best reflects change in psychotherapy, difference measures or final ratings? In this instance, the positive finding appears to reflect the relationship between initial and final status, rather than change due to psychotherapy.

A somewhat different problem is exemplified by the three separate listings of results, two positive and one inconclusive, from the study by Fiske et al. (1964). The inconclusive finding was with the RPRS and was noted in our previous discussion of that scale. The positive findings included a correlation of .24 between initial ratings and therapists' evaluation at termination, and a correlation of .23 between an initial TAT based estimate of adequacy and a residual change score on two MMPI scales. Here we have two rather low correlations, although significant at the .05 level, and different outcome criteria: that is, each of the two predictors only showed a significant correlation with one criterion of outcome (actually five were used). Although the three listings provided by Luborsky et al. (1971) convey a favorable two-to-one ratio of positive results, the authors of this study, themselves, concluded that their results were "distinctly unpromising."

My own evaluation of the research on client personal adjustment or integration in relation to outcome in psychotherapy leads me at this time to a more cautious and critical conclusion than I reached in my previous review (Garfield, 1971), and one that is similar to that expressed by Meltzoff and Kornreich (1970). A critical factor here is the criterion on which outcome is judged. If actual amount of change is the criterion, then I believe that the issue is moot and that several difficult methodological issues must be evaluated. Individuals who are near the top of the adjustment scale have a much smaller range of improvement open to them than do those who are much lower on the scale. Without a standardized measuring instrument with equal intervals, one also cannot compare amounts of change at different parts of the outcome scale. However, if the goal of therapy is some norm of personality functioning or adjustment, then it does seem tenable to say that those who begin therapy at higher levels generally finish at higher levels than those who begin at lower levels. However, one cannot validly state that those

who profit the most or show the most improvement are the ones who are the best adjusted at the beginning of therapy. They may be the most satisfied with therapy and their therapists may also find working with these clients most gratifying, but this is a different matter than amount of change.

Before we proceed to the next section, some mention should be made of intelligence in relation to outcome in psychotherapy. While most therapists would apparently prefer reasonably intelligent clients who also possess other virtues (Schofield, 1964), there have been reports of psychotherapy carried on successfully with individuals who were classified as mentally retarded (Garfield, 1963b). As far as I know, no minimum IQ has been shown convincingly to be required for successful performance in psychotherapy, although the type of therapy is a factor here. In psychoanalysis, where candidates apparently are rigorously screened, the majority are college graduates or better, and presumably of above average or superior intelligence (Hamburg et al., 1967; Siegel, 1962). At the other end of the pole, behavior therapists have apparently not been concerned with this matter. It is interesting, too, that two reviews of research on this topic appear to reach somewhat different conclusions.

In the review by Luborsky et al. (1971), 10 of 13 studies are listed as showing a positive relationship between intelligence and outcome in psychotherapy. Although some of these studies only indicate that a significant difference was obtained between improved and unimproved subjects, others list correlations ranging from .24 to .46. The study reporting the relatively high correlation of .46 is that of Barron's (1953a), which was discussed earlier. As noted, Barron's total group of patients had a relatively high mean IQ (117), with the unimproved group alone having a mean IQ of 112. If one were to attempt to apply these findings, he or she might presumably reject more than 75 percent of the population as psychotherapy candidates!

Meltzoff and Kornreich (1970), in their review, come up with a different tally. They mention seven studies as showing a positive relationship between IQ and outcome, and eight studies as indicating no relationship. One of the studies listed as positive by

Luborsky et al. (1971) is listed otherwise by them, since two different criteria are referred to by the different authors. Since Meltzoff and Kornreich's tally differs from that of Luborsky et al.'s, they reach a different conclusion and state that high intelligence is not a necessary condition for successful psychotherapy, even though it may be more important in some therapies than others.

What then might we conclude? If psychotherapy is a learning process or involves learning, as many believe, then some minimum amount of intelligence would seem to be required. As yet, no precise estimate of this has been clearly agreed upon. Most psychotherapists might also agree that other aspects of the individual besides sheer intellect are also of importance and, perhaps, of greater significance. If we were to take a correlation of around .30 as indicating the possible relationship of intelligence to outcome, intelligence would still account for less than 10 percent of the variance. For the time being, we shall have to maintain a flexible posture on this matter.

Client Expectations and Other Variables
in Relation to Outcome in
Psychotherapy
Another area of investigation that has received a fair amount of interest concerns the matter of the expectancies that the client has concerning psychotherapy. In previous years, this referred mainly to the expectations that the client had prior to initiating psychotherapy. More recently, particularly in studies of behavior therapy, there have also been attempts to manipulate experimentally certain specified expectancies. Recently, also, there has been somewhat of a controversy as to whether expectancies are potent influences in psychotherapy outcome or whether they actually exist. However, before we explore these problems, let us review some of the work in this area.

Frank and his colleagues were among the earliest to publish several papers pertaining to client expectancies and their relation to symptom change (Frank, 1959; Frank, Gliedman, Imber, Stone, & Nash, 1959; Rosenthal & Frank, 1956). Among other things, they asserted that the beliefs or expectancies about therapy which the patient brings to therapy may influence the results of therapy, and

that the greater the distress or need for relief, the greater the expectancy or likelihood of such relief. This received some support from other investigators. In one study, a group of control patients showed a significant correlation between their expected and perceived improvement (Goldstein, 1960), and other studies showed a positive relationship between expectancies of improvement in patients and their judged improvement (Lennard & Bernstein, 1960; Lipkin, 1954). Goldstein and Shipman (1961) also reported a positive relationship between expectancy and perceived symptom reduction, and also between expectancy and symptom intensity after the initial psychotherapeutic interview. However, in this study the relationship between expectancy and symptom reduction was a curvilinear one, that is, those patients with very high or very low expectancies for improvement showed the smallest symptom reduction. In another study (Friedman, 1963), a direct relationship between expectancy and symptom reduction was found in 43 patients after an initial evaluation interview. The symptoms associated with anxiety and depression were the ones most affected. Goldstein (1962) also published a comprehensive account of both therapist and patient expectancies.

Since these earlier writings, there has been a continuing output of studies. Because of the limitations of space and because there are several critical reviews available, our discussion of the available studies is exceedingly brief (Lick & Bootzin, 1975; Morgan, 1973; Wilkins, 1971, 1973).

Tollinton (1973), utilizing a variety of measures, found that initial expectations were significantly related to outcome in the early stages of treatment, but were "dissipated over time by the effects of neuroticism." In another study, Uhlenhuth and Duncan (1968) used symptom checklists, the MMPI, and subjects' ratings and reported that more favorable expectations were associated with improvement. Piper and Wogan (1970), however, did not find a relationship between prognostic expectancies and reported improvement. Negative results were also secured in another study where attempts were made to induce a positive expectancy for improvement within a treatment period of four weeks (Imber, Pande, Frank, Hoehn-Saric, Stone, & Wargo, 1970).

Although many of the studies appear to show some positive association between client expectancies and outcome, these investigations have received serious criticism (Perotti & Hopewell, 1976; Wilkins, 1973). Among the deficiencies noted have been the fact that expectancies have been inferred instead of being actually measured or appraised, and that most studies have relied on self-reports for measures of expectancies and of outcome. The matter of how the effects of expectancies are appraised appears to be a problem of importance. Wilson and Thomas (1973), for example, secured significant corelations between high expectancy ratings and self-report measures of outcome, but found no relationship between expectancy ratings and a behavioral measure of outcome.

Perhaps, in part because of the former criticism, a moderate number of studies have attempted to manipulate and measure the expectancies of the client. In contrast to the previous studies mentioned, which have been characterized as studies of "expectancy traits," the more recent investigations have focued on experimentally created "expectancy states" and have been mainly studies of behaviorally oriented therapy.

In his review of expectancy states and their effect on outcome, Wilkins (1973) lists six studies that showed positive results, eight that did not show these effects, and one that showed both effects. It is obvious from this kind of pattern that there are problems in this research and that no reliable conclusions can be drawn. A number of conceptual and methodological issues are discussed by Wilkins (1973), including how the expectancy instructions are given, whether the therapists were blind to the experimental conditions, confounding of measures of outcome with those of expectancy, and confounding of expectancy and feedback effects. Accordingly, he concludes that there is as yet insufficient evidence to support the construct of expectancy of therapeutic gain.

Another recent review of expectancy factors in the treatment of fears by Lick and Bootzin (1975) comes to a somewhat different conclusion and highlights additional problems. Some of the latter are rather complex and cannot be covered fully here. Among the points made by Lick and Bootzin (1975) is that most of the subjects that were used in the studies of systematic desensitization (SD) they reviewed were students who manifested relatively mild fears of small animals and who entered the studies to meet course requirements. They also emphasize the importance of the manner in which expectancies are created and assessed, as well as the importance of developing creditable placebo conditions for subjects in such studies. In addition, they state that although methodological problems in previous research "preclude firm empirical conclusions about the importance of therapeutic instruction in SD . . ., the available data do suggest that these influences are sizable" (Lick & Bootzin, 1975, p. 925). Reviewing many of these same studies, Perotti and Hopewell (1976) also conclude that expectancy effects are important in SD, but they differentiate two kinds of expectancies. Initial expectancy, which the client has at the beginning of therapy with regard to the probable success of treatment, and which has been the focus in most studies, they believe has little effect. However, the second type, which deals with beliefs the subject has during the treatment process that he is improving and is increasingly able to handle fear-provoking stimuli, is considered to be of some importance. A somewhat similar point is made by Lick and Bootzin (1975), who hypothesize that expectancy manipulation may motivate subjects more readily to test the reality conditions that could increase fear extinction and provide further reinforcement for improved behavior.

The possible importance of client expectancies for research on evaluating the effectiveness of SD and psychotherapy generally has been stressed recently in a thoughtful article by Kazdin and Wilcoxon (1976). Particular emphasis is placed on the importance of creating control conditions that are as potent in creating positive client expectancies for improvement as the experimental therapy being evaluated. Thus expectancies for therapeutic success are viewed as of some significance by these authors.

It would appear that the importance of client expectations as regards outcome in psychotherapy is still to be determined. In addition to the more recent distinction between expectancy traits and states, there is the issue of what different individuals mean when they employ the general term, "expectancy." In some instances, it has been used to designate the expectation a client has with regard to positive outcome or the therapeutic effectiveness of a particular therapist. In other instances, some of us have discussed the expectations clients have about the procedures in psychotherapy, the role of the therapist, the length of therapy, and the like (Garfield & Wolpin, 1963; Bent, Putnam, Kiesler, & Nowicki, 1975). If research is going to provide more light on this complex issue, it will have to be more specific in specifying the types of expectancies under investigation, as well as considering the possible interaction of different kinds of expectancies or of expectancies interacting with other variables. One recent study, for example, besides validating an expectancy manipulation on one group of subjects and then testing its effectiveness for behavioral effects with another group, also compared the effects of initial expectations concerning the helpfulness of psychotherapy, as well as those of an experimental manipulation (Lott & Murray, 1975). The results showed a positive effect for the expectancy manipulation but not for the initial expectancy. Although the measure of initial expectancy used leaves something to be desired, this type of design appears to offer more promise than more simplistic ones.

Another area of recent research has been concerned with the the frame of reference of the client in relation to type of therapy and outcome. In one study, two groups of clients were exposed to different forms of therapy designated as "relatively directive" and "relatively nondirective" (Abramowitz, Abramowitz, & Roback, 1974). The locus of control was measured by nine items from the Rotter I-E Scale (1966), and several scales were utilized to appraise outcome. Although the number of cases was small, the findings appeared to indicate that "externals" did better in the directive therapy, while "internals" did better with the nondirective therapy. In another, but different study, patients were rated on the basis of their symptoms or complaints as predominantly "externalizers" or "internalizers" (Stein & Beall, 1971). In this study, female externalizers showed significant negative association with various therapist ratings of change, but this was not true for male externalizers.

A study by Devine and Fernald (1973) on choice of therapy is somewhat related to the studies just mentioned. In this investigation 32 subjects with a fear of snakes viewed a videotape of four therapists who described and illustrated their particular methods of treatment. The four treatments were SD, an encounter approach, rational-emotive therapy, and a combination of modeling and behavioral rehearsal. The subjects then rated their preferences for the various therapies and were assigned to a preferred, nonpreferred, or random therapy. Although there was no significant difference between therapies, the difference between the preference conditions was significant. Subjects receiving a preferred treatment exhibited less fear of snakes than those receiving a nonpreferred or random therapy.

Other client characteristics have also been studied in relation to outcome in psychotherapy. Isaacs and Haggard (1966) found that high relatability, as appraised by the TAT, was related to improvement in psychotherapy. Patient attractiveness was also found to be related to outcome in a positive manner by another group of investigators (Nash, Hoehn-Saric, Battle, Stone, Imber, & Frank, 1965), although this relationship was not evident in a five-year follow-up study (Liberman, Frank, Hoehn-Saric, Stone, Imber, & Pande, 1972).

Somewhat related to the preceding papers are several studies that appraised the importance of patient likability for therapy process and outcome. Stoler (1963) reported that successful clients received significantly higher likability ratings based on taped therapy segments than did the less successful clients, and that the level of likability remained fairly constant from early to late interviews. A subsequent study carried out with schizophrenic patients instead of neurotics secured somewhat different findings (Tomlinson & Stoler, 1967). The less successful patients were better liked than the more successful ones.

In a study of psychiatric residents, Ehrlich and Bauer (1967) found that inexperienced therapists liked their patients less than did the relatively more experienced therapists; patients who were rated either extremely anxious or nonanxious were less well liked by their therapists; and patient prognosis was positively related to patient likability. Furthermore, patients who received low ratings in terms of likability were three times more likely to be placed on multiple drug regimes than were those who received high ratings. In addition, the therapists' ratings of change were positively correlated with such ratings. A positive correlation between the therapist's liking of the client and prognostic ratings of the client also has been reported (Garfield & Affleck, 1961), but more data are needed concerning the relationship of such ratings and objective criteria of outcome.

The matter of client-therapist similarity or complementarity has received research attention, although with rather conflicting results. Carson and Heine (1962) used the MMPI to compare therapists and clients, and reported that a curvilinear relationship existed between therapist-client similarity and rated improvement. Lichtenstein (1966), and Carson and Llewellyn (1966), however, failed to replicate these findings. Lesser (1961), utilizing a Q sort, found that similarity of self-concept between counselor and client was negatively related to therapeutic progress, whereas Levinson and Kitchener (1966), utilizing a different Q sort, secured more positive findings. Using the FIRO-B Scale, Sapolsky (1965) also reported a positive correlation between patient and doctor compatibility and outcome. On the other hand, Mendelsohn and Geller (1965), who used still another measure of compatibility, the Myers-Briggs Type Indicator, obtained a curvilinear relationship with outcome measures. In addition, some partial support for the importance of client-therapist complimentarity has been offered by Swenson (1967) for one personality dimension (dominance-submission) but not for another (love-hate).

More recently, Beutler, Jobe, and Elkins (1974) have reported that initial patient-therapist similarity and acceptability of attitudes were related more to patients' ratings of improvement than was attitude dissimilarity. On the other hand, Melnick (1972) found that greater patient identification with the therapist during therapy was moderately related to successful outcome. In a study of group therapy patients, McLachlan (1972) found that patients and therapists matched for conceptual level improved significantly on patients' ratings of im-

provement, but not on staff ratings of improvement. The conceptual levels of patients and therapists separately were not related to outcome. Berzins (1977) has also provided us with a comprehensive and critical review of the area of therapist-patient matching in psychotherapy. As he points out, although the idea of matching patients and therapists for the best therapeutic outcome is responded to favorably by clinicians and researchers alike, "there is at present no organized body of knowledge that could serve as an effective guide for implementing matching strategies . . ." (p. 222).

The problem of what kinds of personal attributes of clients are related to outcome in psychotherapy is clearly a complex one that is not readily answerable by the kinds of small-scale studies that have predominated in the past. The great variation among the variables under study limit replication and generalization, and the heterogeneity of the findings are difficult to synthesize. Nevertheless, we can state that patient variables such as social class, age, and sex do not appear to be predictive of outcome. The findings with regard to personality variables and disturbance are considerably more varied and difficult to interpret. Among the problems here are the constructs used, measuring devices, type of therapy, and outcome criteria. Each of these presents many difficulties for research, and little elaboration is required here. Although the personal qualities and expectations of the client appear to be of importance to most therapists, the more exact description of these qualities and their relationship to outcome in psychotherapy still awaits more definitive research. On the whole, the situation has not changed drastically since Fiske, Cartwright, and Kirtner (1964) stated, "It seems clear that there are reliable changes associated with psychotherapy but that none of our measures of initial status or initial assets accounts for any very appreciable proportion of the variance in such changes" (p. 425).

CONCLUSION AND IMPLICATIONS

We have now completed our survey of research pertaining to client variables in relation to issues such as acceptance for treatment, continuation in therapy, and outcome. As we note throughout the chapter, numerous conceptual and methodological problems make research and the drawing of conclusions in this area rather difficult. Admittedly, the problems are complex, and if we are to secure meaningful answers to our questions, we must change our research strategies. To the present reviewer, more comphreneisve, carefully planned, large-scale, and coordinated research efforts will be required in the future. A host of idiosyncratic studies of poorly defined populations with vaguely described therapies and exceedingly variable outcome criteria will not produce findings of any substance.

If we are to improve the practical value of our research efforts, then it will be necessary to include at least a few standard procedures that all researchers would adhere to if the results are to be in any way cumulative. For example, in terms of continuation, it would greatly facilitate comparisons if *all* studies reported the number of clients who *actually begin therapy* but voluntarily terminate before the sixth interview. Those who refuse therapy should be catalogued separately. The clients who continue beyond the fifth interview can be grouped into intervals of five interviews and the data can be readily presented (Table 6.1). Similar procedures can be followed with measures of outcome. While I believe that some measures of outcome should be clearly tailored to the problems of the individual client, it is important also to include some standard measures of initial client status and outcome. Although this latter point has been made by others (Fiske et al., 1970; Waskow & Parloff, 1975), it is something that has yet to be implemented. Perhaps a joint conference by the Society for Psychotherapy Research and the National Institute of Mental Health could provide the impetus for such a development. As it is, the task of attempting to interpret the current array of diverse procedures and findings is overwhelming. While each investigator has been free to pursue his own hypotheses with his own procedures, a tribute to our free society, the result is frequently chaotic. At one point in writing this chapter, I even felt that a small gain might accrue if we were to insist that all doctoral dissertations be viewed strictly as a learning experi-

ence and destroyed at the completion of the final oral.

Although the preceding comments may appear overly severe, I do not want to convey the impression that existing research has had no impact on practice. In spite of its limitations, it has. As indicated previously increased attention has been paid to the problem of premature termination, and various innovative attempts have been made to overcome this problem. The apparent lack of efficacy of traditional programs for the disadvantaged and other groups in our society has led to the creation of new programs for them (Goldstein, 1973; Shore & Massimo, 1973), as Chapter 22 also illustrates.

However, it also appears that many clinical settings are relatively unaffected by research findings. Part of this problem is undoubtedly related to the fact that many research studies are seen as being unrelated to the "real world" of clinical realities. Although this is certainly true to some extent, there are reports of modifications of traditional clinic procedures that have been at least partially influenced by research reports (Davids, 1975; Muench, 1965). Nevertheless, as indicated previously, we will have to improve the quality and significance of our research if it is to have a greater impact on practice.

Finally, I add a few closing statements regarding the matter of client variables and outcome research since this is of great importance. As I commented earlier, I have changed my own position concerning the view that those who do best in psychotherapy are those who initially are best adjusted. If the client's final status only is considered, then it does appear that those initially better off or less disturbed are at higher levels of adjustment at the termination of therapy. However, if actual amount of change is the criterion, then one cannot readily draw that conclusion. This, to me, is an issue that merits more intensive study, since it basically concerns the overall potency or efficacy of psychotherapy. We have far too often been satisfied with results that were significant at the .05 level of confidence when practical significance of those results was very weak indeed. It is time to focus more attention on the *actual amount of change* secured by means of psychotherapy and to appraise it realistically. If patients show a statistically significant change in ratings of outcome from a mean rating of 4 to a mean rating of 3.2 after therapy, or a significant change from a scaled score of 79 on an MMPI scale to a score of 70, what is the practical significance of those changes? Can the client actually function better in his life situation? In essence, *how much change* can we accomplish with individuals of varying levels and types of disturbance and what procedures work best with what types of clients? This is a basic issue to which we must direct more attention if we are to appraise more adequately the effectiveness of psychotherapy.

REFERENCES

Abramowitz, C. V., Abramowitz, S. I., Roback, H. B., & Jackson, C. Differential effectiveness of directive and nondirective group therapies as a function of client internal-external control. *Journal of Consulting and Clinical Psychology,* 1974, *42,* 849–853.

Acosta, F. X., & Sheehan, J. G. Preferences toward Mexican-American and Anglo-American Psychotherapists. *Journal of Consulting and Clinical Psychology,* 1976, *44,* 272–279.

Adler, M. H., Valenstein, A. F., & Michaels, J. J. A mental hygiene clinic. Its organization and operation. *Journal of Nervous & Mental Disease,* 1949, *110,* 518–533.

Affleck, D. C., & Garfield, S. L. Predictive judgments of therapists and duration of stay in psychotherapy. *Journal of Clinical Psychology,* 1961, *17,* 134–137.

Affleck, D. C., & Mednick, S. A. The use of the Rorschach Test in the prediction of the abrupt terminator in individual psychotherapy. *Journal of Consulting Psychology,* 1959, *23,* 125–128.

Albronda, H. F., Dean, R. L., & Starkweather, J. A. Social class and psychotherapy. *Archives of General Psychiatry,* 1964, *10,* 276–283.

Auld, F., Jr., & Eron, L. D. The use of Rorschach scores to predict whether patients will continue psychotherapy. *Journal of Consulting Psychology,* 1953, *17,* 104–109.

Baekeland, F., & Lundwall, L. Dropping out of treatment: A critical review. *Psychological Bulletin,* 1975, *82,* 738–783.

Bailey, M. A., Warshaw, L., & Eichler, R. M. A study of factors related to length of stay in psychotherapy. *Journal of Clinical Psychology,* 1959, *15,* 442–444.

Baker, J., & Wagner, N. Social class and treatment in a child psychiatry clinic. *Archives of General Psychiatry,* 1966, *14,* 129–133.

Bandura, A., Jeffrey, R. W., & Wright, C. L. Efficacy of participant modeling as a function of response induction aids. *Journal of Abnormal Psychology,* 1974, *83,* 56–64.

Barron, F. Some test correlates of response to

psychotherapy. *Journal of Consulting Psychology,* 1953, *17,* 235–241. (a)

Barron, F. An ego-strength scale which predicts response to psychotherapy. *Journal of Consulting Psychology,* 1953, *17,* 327–333. (b)

Baum, O. E., & Felzer, S. B. Activity in initial interviews with lower class patients. *Archives of General Psychiatry,* 1964, *10,* 345–353.

Bent, R. J., Putnam, D. G., Kiesler, D. J., & Nowicki, S., Jr. Expectancies and characteristics of outpatient clients applying for services at a community mental health facility. *Journal of Consulting and Clinical Psychology,* 1975, *43,* 280.

Berzins, J. I. Therapist-patient matching. In A. S. Gurman and A. M. Razin (Eds.), *Effective Psychotherapy: A Handbook of Research.* Elmsford, N. Y.: Pergamon Press, 1977.

Beutler, L. E. The therapy dyad: Yet another look at diagnostic assessment. *Journal of Personality Assessment,* 1973, *37,* 303–315.

Beutler, L. E., Jobe, A. M., & Elkins, D. Outcomes in group psychotherapy: Using persuasion theory to increase treatment efficiency. *Journal of Consulting and Clinical Psychology,* 1974, *42,* 547–553.

Blackman, N. Psychotherapy in a Veterans Administration mental hygiene clinic. *Psychiatric Quarterly,* 1948, *22,* 89–102.

Bloom, B. L. Prognostic significance of the underproductive Rorschach. *Journal of Projective Techniques,* 1956, *20,* 366–371.

Brandt, L. W. Rejection of psychotherapy? The discovery of unexpected numbers of pseudo-rejectors. *Archives of General Psychiatry,* 1964, *10,* 310–313.

Brill, N. Q., & Storrow, H. A. Social class and psychiatric treatment. *Archives of General Psychiatry,* 1960, *3,* 340–344.

Brown, J. S., & Kosterlitz, N. Selection and treatment of psychiatric outpatients. *Archives of General Psychiatry,* 1964, *11,* 425–438.

Carkhuff, R. R., & Pierce, R. Differential effects of therapist race and social class upon patient depth of self-exploration in the initial clinical interview. *Journal of Consulting Psychology,* 1967, *31,* 632–634.

Carson, R. C., & Heine, R. W. Similarity and success in therapeutic dyads. *Journal of Consulting Psychology,* 1962, *26,* 38–43.

Carson, R. C., & Llewellyn, C. E. Similarity in therapeutic dyads: A reevaluation. *Journal of Consulting Psychology,* 1966, *30,* 458.

Cartwright, D. S. Success in psychotherapy as a function of certain actuarial variables. *Journal of Consulting Psychology,* 1955, *19,* 357–363.

Cartwright, D. S., Kirtner, W. L., & Fiske, D. W. Method factors in changes associated with psychotherapy. *Journal of Abnormal and Social Psychology,* 1963, *66,* 164–175.

Cartwright, D. S., & Roth, I. Success and satisfaction in psychotherapy. *Journal of Clinical Psychology,* 1957, *13,* 20–26.

Cartwright, R. D. Predicting response to client-centered therapy with the Rorschach PR Scale. *Journal of Counseling Psychology,* 1958, *5,* 11–17.

Casner, D. Certain factors associated with success and failure in personal-adjustment counseling. *American Psychologist,* 1950, *5,* 348. (Abstract)

Cimbolic, P. Counselor race and experience effects on black clients. *Journal of Consulting and Clinical Psychology,* 1972, *39,* 328–332.

Cole, N. J., Branch, C. H., & Allison, R. B. Some relationships between social class and the practice of dynamic psychotherapy. *American Journal of Psychiatry,* 1962, *118,* 1004–1012.

Conrad, D. C. An empirical study of the concept of psychotherapeutic success. *Journal of Consulting Psychology,* 1952, *16,* 92–97.

Craig, T., & Huffine, C. Correlates of patient attendance in an inner-city mental health clinic. *The American Journal of Psychiatry,* 1976, *133,* 61–64.

Davids, A. Therapeutic approaches to children in residential treatment. Changes from the mid-1950s to the mid-1970s. *American Psychologist,* 1975, *30,* 809–814.

Dean, S. I. Treatment of the reluctant client. *American Psychologist,* 1958, 627–630.

Devine, D. A., & Fernald, P. S. Outcome effects of receiving a preferred, randomly assigned or non-preferred therapy. *Journal of Consulting and Clinical Psychology,* 1973, *41,* 104–107.

Dodd, J. A. A retrospective analysis of variables related to duration of treatment in a university psychiatric clinic. *Journal of Nervous and Mental Disease,* 1970, *151,* 75–85.

Ehrlich, H. J., & Bauer, M. L. Therapists' feelings toward patients and patient treatment and outcome. *Social Science and Medicine,* 1967, *1,* 283–292.

Eiduson, B. T. The two classes of information in psychiatry. *Archives of General Psychiatry,* 1968, *18,* 405–419.

Endicott, N. A., & Endicott, J. Prediction of improvement in treated and untreated patients using the Rorschach Prognostic Rating Scale. *Journal of Consulting Psychology,* 1964, *28,* 342–348.

Ewing, T. N. Racial similarity of client and counselor and client satisfaction with counseling. *Journal of Consulting Psychology,* 1974, *21,* 446–469.

Fiester, A. R., & Rudestam, K. E. A multivariate analysis of the early dropout process. *Journal of Consulting & Clinical Psychology,* 1975, *43,* 528–535.

Filmer-Bennett, G. The Rorschach as a means of predicting treatment outcome. *Journal of Consulting Psychology,* 1955, *19,* 331–334.

Fiske, D. W., Cartwright, D. S., & Kirtner, W. L. Are psychotherapeutic changes predictable? *Journal of Abnormal and Social Psychology,* 1964, *69,* 418–426.

Fiske, D. W., Hunt, H. F., Luborsky, L., Orne, M. T., Parloff, M. B., Reiser, M. F., & Tuma, A. H. Planning of research on effectiveness of psychotherapy. *Archives of General Psychiatry,* 1970, *22,* 22–32.

Frank, G. H. A review of research with measures of ego strength derived from the MMPI and the Rorschach. *Journal of General Psychology,* 1967, *77,* 183–206.

Frank, J. D. The dynamics of the psychotherapeutic relationship. *Psychiatry,* 1959, *22,* 17–39.

Frank, J. D. Psychotherapy: The restoration of morale. *American Journal of Psychiatry,* 1974, *131,* 271–274. (a)

Frank, J. D. Therapeutic components of psychotherapy. A 25-year progress report of research. *The Journal of Nervous and Mental Disease,* 1974, *159,* 325–342. (b)

Frank, J. D., Gliedman, L. H., Imber, S. D., Nash, E. H., Jr., & Stone, A. R. Why patients leave psychotherapy. *Archives of Neurology and Psychiatry,* 1957, *77,* 283–299.

Frank, J. D., Gliedman, L. H., Imber, S. D., Stone, A. R., & Nash, E. H. Patients' expectancies and relearning as factors determining improvement in psychotherapy. *American Journal of Psychiatry,* 1959, *115,* 961–968.

Freedman, N., Engelhardt, D. M., Hankoff, L. D., Glick, B. S., Kaye, H., Buchwald, J., & Stark, P. Drop-out from outpatient psychiatric treatment. *Archives of Neurology and Psychiatry,* 1958, *80,* 657–666.

Freud, S. On psychotherapy. In *Collected Papers.* Vol. 1. London: Hogarth Press and the Institute of Psycho-Analysis, 1950, pp. 249–263.

Freidman, H. J. Patient-expectancy and symptom reduction. *Archives of General Psychiatry,* 1963, *8,* 61–67.

Gabby, J. I., & Leavitt, A. Providing low cost psychotherapy to middle income patients. *Community Mental Health Journal,* 1970, *6,* 210–214.

Gallagher, J. J. Test indicators for therapy prognosis. *Journal of Consulting Psychology,* 1954, *18,* 409–413.

Galassi, J. P., & Galassi, M. D. Alienation in college students: A comparison of counseling seekers and nonseekers. *Journal of Counseling Psychology.* 1973, *20,* 44–49.

Garfield, S. L. A note on patients' reasons for terminating therapy. *Psychological Reports,* 1963, *13,* 38. (a)

Garfield, S. L. Abnormal behavior and mental deficiency. In N. R. Ellis (Ed.), *Handbook of mental deficiency.* New York: McGraw-Hill, 1963. (b)

Garfield, S. L. Research on client variables in psychotherapy. In A. E. Bergin and S. L. Garfield (Eds.), *Handbook of psychotherapy and behavior change.* New York: Wiley, 1971, 271–298.

Garfield, S. L. *Clinical psychology: The study of personality and behavior.* Chicago: Aldine Press, 1974.

Garfield, S. L. A note on the confounding of personality and social class characteristics in research on premature termination. *Journal of Consulting & Clinical Psychology,* 1977a, *45,* 483–485.

Garfield, S. L. Further comments on 'dropping out of treatment': A reply to Baekeland and Lundwall. *Psychological Bulletin,* 1977b, *84,* 306–308.

Garfield, S. L., & Affleck, D. C. An appraisal of duration of stay in outpatient psychotherapy. *Journal of Nervous and Mental Disease,* 1959, *129,* 492–498.

Garfield, S. L., & Affleck, D. C. Therapists' judgments concerning patients considered for psychotherapy. *Journal of Consulting Psychology,* 1961, *25,* 505–509.

Garfield, S. L., Affleck, D. C., & Muffley, R. A. A study of psychotherapy interaction and continuation in psychotherapy. *Journal of Clinical Psychology,* 1963, *19,* 473–478.

Garfield, S. L., & Kurz, M. Evaluation of treatment and related procedures in 1216 cases referred to a mental hygiene clinic. *Psychiatric Quarterly,* 1952, *26,* 414–424.

Garfield, S. L., Prager, R. A., & Bergin, A. E. Evaluation

of outcome in psychotherapy. *Journal of Consulting & Clinical Psychology,* 1971, *37,* 307–313.

Garfield, S. L., & Wolpin, M. Expectations regarding psychotherapy. *Journal of Nervous and Mental Disease,* 1963, *137,* 353–362.

Gaylin, N. Psychotherapy and psychological health: A Rorschach function and structure analysis. *Journal of Consulting Psychology,* 1966, *30,* 494–500.

Getter, H., & Sundland, D. M. The Barron ego-strength scale and psychotherapy outcome. *Journal of Consulting Psychology,* 1962, *26,* 195.

Gibby, R. G., Stotsky, B. A., Hiler, E. W., & Miller, D. R. Validation of Rorschach criteria for predicting duration of therapy. *Journal of Consulting Psychology,* 1954, *18,* 185–191.

Gibby, R. G., Stotsky, B. A., Miller, D. R., & Hiler, E. W. Prediction of duration of therapy from the Rorschach Test. *Journal of Consulting Psychology,* 1953, *17,* 348–354.

Gibbs, J. T., Use of mental health services by black students at a predominantly white university: A three-year study. *American Journal of Orthopsychiatry,* 1975, *45,* 430–445.

Goldstein, A. P. Patients' expectancies and non-specific therapy as a basis for (un)spontaneous remission. *Journal of Clinical Psychology,* 1960, *16,* 399–403.

Goldstein, A. P. *Therapist-patient expectancies in psychotherapy.* New York: Pergamon Press, 1962.

Goldstein, A. P. *Structured learning therapy: Toward a psychotherapy for the poor.* New York: Academic Press, 1973.

Goldstein, A. P., & Shipman, W. G. Patient expectancies, symptom reduction and aspects of initial psychotherapeutic interview. *Journal of Clinical Psychology,* 1961, *17,* 129–133.

Gordon, S. Are we seeing the right patients? Child guidance intake: The sacred cow. *American Journal of Orthopsychiatry,* 1965, *35,* 131–137.

Gottschalk, L. A., Fox, R. A., & Bates, D. E. A study of prediction and outcome of a mental health crisis clinic. *American Journal of Psychiatry,* 1973, *130,* 1107–1111.

Gottschalk, L. A., Mayerson, P., & Gottlieb, A. A. Prediction and evaluation of outcome in an emergency brief psychotherapy clinic. *Journal of Nervous and Mental Disease,* 1967, *144,* 77–96.

Grotjahn, M. Learning from dropout patients: A clinical view of patients who discontinued group psychotherapy. *International Journal of Group Psychotherapy,* 1972, *22,* 306–319.

Gurman, A. S., & Kniskern, D. P. Research on marital and family therapy. In S. L. Garfield and A. E. Bergin (Eds.), *Handbook of psychotherapy and behavior change. (2nd ed.)* New York: Wiley, 1978.

Haddock, J. N., & Mensh, I. N. Psychotherapeutic expectations in various clinic settings. *Psychological Reports,* 1957, , 109–112.

Hamburg, D. A., Bibring, G. L., Fisher, C., Stanton, A. H., Wallerstein, R. S., Weinstock, H. I., & Haggard, E. Report of Ad Hoc Committee on central fact-gathering data of the American Psychoanalytic Association. *Journal of the American Psychoanalytic Association,* 1967, *15,* 841–861.

Harris, R. E., & Christiansen, C. Prediction of response to brief psychotherapy. *Journal of Psychology,* 1946, *21,* 269–284.

Heine, R. W. (Ed.) *The student physician as psychotherapist.* Chicago: The University of Chicago Press, 1962.

Heine, R. W., & Trosman, H. Initial expectations of the doctor-patient interaction as a factor in continuance in psychotherapy. *Psychiatry,* 1960, *23,* 275–278.

Heitler, J. B. Preparation of lower-class patients for expressive group psychotherapy. *Journal of Consulting and Clinical Psychology,* 1973, *41,* 251–260.

Heitler, J. B. Preparatory techniques in initiating expressive psychotherapy with lower-class, unsophisticated patients. *Psychological Bulletin,* 1976, *83,* 339–352.

Heller, K., & Goldstein, A. P. Client dependency and therapist expectancy as relationship maintaining variables in psychotherapy. *Journal of Consulting Psychology,* 1961, *25,* 371–375.

Hiler, E. W. An analysis of patient-therapist compatibility. *Journal of Consulting Psychology,* 1958a, *22,* 341–347

Hiler, E. W. Wechsler-Bellevue Intelligence as a predictor of continuation in psychotherapy. *Journal of Clinical Psychology,* 1958b, *14,* 192–194.

Hiler, E. W. The sentence completion test as a predictor of continuation in psychotherapy. *Journal of Consulting Psychology,* 1959, *23,* 544–549.

Hoehn-Saric, R., Frank, J. D., Imber, S. D., Nash, E. H., Stone, A. R., & Battle, C.C. Systematic preparation of patients for psychotherapy. I. Effects on therapy behavior and outcome. *Journal of Psychiatric Research,* 1964, *2,* 267–281.

Hollingshead, A. B., & Redlich, F. C. *Social class and mental illness: A community study.* New York: Wiley, 1958.

Holmes, D. S., & Urie, R. G. Effects of preparing children for psychotherapy. *Journal of Consulting & Clinical Psychology,* 1975, *43,* 311–318.

Horenstein, D., Houston, B., & Holmes, D. Clients', Therapists' and Judges' evaluations of psychotherapy. *Journal of Counseling Psychology,* 1973, *20,* 149–153.

Hunt, R. G. Social class in mental illness: Some implications for clinical theory and practice. *American Journal of Psychiatry,* 1960, *116,* 1065–1069.

Imber, S. D., Frank, J. D., Gliedman, L. H., Nash, E. H., & Stone, A. R. Suggestibility, social class, and the acceptance of psychotherapy. *Journal of Clinical Psychology,* 1956, *12,* 341–344.

Imber, S. D., Nash, E. H., & Stone, A. R. Social class and duration of psychotherapy. *Journal of Clinical Psychology,* 1955, *11,* 281–284.

Imber, S. D., Pande, S. K., Frank, J. D., Hoehn-Saric, R., Stone, A. R., & Wargo, D. G. Time-focused role induction. *Journal of Nervous and Mental Disease,* 1970, *150,* 27–30.

Isaacs, K. S., & Haggard, E. A. Some methods used in the study of affect in psychotherapy. In L. A. Gottschalk and A. H. Auerbach (Eds.), *Methods of research in psychotherapy.* New York: Appleton-Century-Crofts, 1966.

Jacobs, D., Charles E., Jacobs, T., Weinstein, H., &

Mann, D. Preparation for treatment of the disadvantaged patient: Effects on disposition and outcome. *American Journal of Orthopsychiatry,* 1972, *42,* 666–674.

Jacobs, M. A., Muller, J. J., Anderson, J., & Skinner, J. C. Therapeutic expectations, premorbid adjustment, and manifest distress level as predictors of improvement in hospitalized patients. *Journal of Consulting and Clinical Psychology,* 1972, *39,* 455–461.

Johnson, E. Z. Klopfer's prognostic scale used with Raven's Progressive Matrices in play therapy prognosis. *Journal of Projective Techniques,* 1953, *17,* 320–326.

Jones, E. Social class and psychotherapy: A critical review of research. *Psychiatry,* 1974, *37,* 307–320.

Kadushin, C. *Why people go to psychiatrists.* New York: Atherton Press, 1969.

Katz, M. M. The classification of depression. In R. R. Fieve (Ed.), *Depression in the 1970's.* Amsterdam:Excerpta Medica, 1971, pp. 31–40.

Katz, M. M., Lorr, M., & Rubinstein, E. A. Remainer patients' attributes and their relation to subsequent improvement in psychotherapy. *Journal of Consulting Psychology,* 1958, *22,* 411–413.

Kazdin, A. E., & Wilcoxon, L. A. Systematic desensitization and nonspecific treatment effects: A methodological evaluation. *Psychological Bulletin,* 1976, *83,* 729–758.

Kellner, R., & Sheffield, B. F. The one-week prevalence of symptoms in neurotic patients and normals. *American Journal of Psychiatry,* 1973, *130,* 102–105.

Keniston, K., Boltax, S., & Almond, R. Multiple criteria of treatment outcome. *Journal of Psychiatry,* 1971, *8,* 107–118.

Kernberg, O. F., Burstein, E. D., Coyne, L., Appelbaum, A., Horwitz, L., & Voth, H. Psychotherapy and psychoanalysis: Final report of the Menninger Foundation's Psychotherapy Research Project. *Bulletin of the Menninger Clinic,* 1972, *36,* (Nos. 1/2).

Kiesler, D. J. Some myths of psychotherapy research and the search for a paradigm. *Psychological Bulletin,* 1966, *65,* 110–136.

Kirkner, F., Wisham, W., & Giedt, H. A report on the validity of the Rorschach prognosis rating scale. *Journal of Projective Techniques,* 1953, *17,* 465–470.

Kirtner, W. L., & Cartwright, D. S. Success and failure of client-centered therapy as a function of client personality variables. *Journal of Consulting Psychology,* 1958, *22,* 259–264.

Klopfer, B., Kirkner, F., Wisham, W., & Baker, G. Rorschach prognostic rating scale. *Journal of Projective Techniques,* 1951, *15,* 425–428.

Knapp, P. H., Levin, S., McCarter, R. H., Wermer, H., & Zetzel, E. Suitability for psychoanalysis: A review of 100 supervised analytic cases. *Psychoanalytic Quarterly,* 1960, *29,* 459–477.

Koran, L. M., & Costell, R. M. Early termination from group psychotherapy. *International Journal of Group Psychotherapy,* 1973, *23,* 346–359.

Kotkov, B., & Meadow, A. Rorschach criteria for predicting continuation in individual psychotherapy. *Journal of Consulting Psychology,* 1953, *17,* 16–20.

Krebs, R. L. Some effects of a white institution on black psychiatric outpatients. *American Journal of Orthopsychiatry,* 1971, *41,* 589–597.

Kurland, S. H. Length of treatment in a mental hygiene clinic. *Psychiatric Quarterly Supplement,* 1956, *30,* 83–90.

Lennard, H. L., & Bernstein, A. *The anatomy of psychotherapy. Systems of communication and expectation.* New York: Columbia University Press, 1960.

Lerner, B. *Therapy in the ghetto.* Baltimore: Johns Hopkins University Press, 1972.

Lerner, B., & Fiske, D. W. Client attributes and the eye of the beholder. *Journal of Consulting and Clinical Psychology,* 1973, *40,* 272–277.

Lesser, W. M. The relationship between counseling progress and empathic understanding. *Journal of Counseling Psychology,* 1961, *8,* 330–336.

Lessing, E. E. Prognostic value of the Rorschach in a child guidance clinic. *Journal of Projective Techniques,* 1960, *24,* 310–321.

Levinson, R., & Kitchener, H. Treatment of delinquents: Comparison of four methods for assigning inmates to counselors. *Journal of Consulting Psychology,* 1966, *30,* 364.

Liberman, B. L., Frank, J. D., Hoehn-Saric, R., Stone, A. R., Imber, S. D., & Pande, S. K. Patterns of change in treated psychoneurotic patients: A five-year follow-up investigation of the systematic preparation of patients for psychotherapy. *Journal of Consulting and Clinical Psychology,* 1972, *38,* 36–41.

Lichtenstein, E. Personality similarity and therapeutic success: A failure to replicate. *Journal of Consulting Psychology,* 1966, *30,* 282.

Lick, J., & Bootzin, R. Expectancy factors in the treatment of fear: Methodological and theoretical issues. *Psychological Bulletin,* 1975, *82,* 917–931.

Lief, H. L., Lief, V. F., Warren, C. O., & Heath, R. G. Low dropout rate in a psychiatric clinic. *Archives of General Psychiatry,* 1961, *5,* 200–211.

Lipkin, S. Clients' feelings and attitudes in relation to the outcome of client-centered therapy. *Psychological Monographs,* 1954, *68,* (Whole No. 372).

Lorenzen, I. J. Acceptance or rejection by psychiatric clinics. M. A. Essay, Columbia University, 1967.

Lorion, R. P. Socio-economic status and traditional treatment approaches reconsidered. *Psychological Bulletin,* 1973, *79,* 263–270.

Lorion, R. P. Patient and Therapist variables in the treatment of low-income patients. *Psychological Bulletin,* 1974, *81,* 344–354.

Lorr, M. Relation of treatment frequency and duration to psychotherapeutic outcome. In H. Strupp and L. Luborsky (Eds.), *Research in Psychotherapy,* Vol. 2. Washington, D. C.: American Psychological Association, 1962.

Lorr, M., Katz, M. M., & Rubinstein, E. A. The prediction of length of stay in psychotherapy. *Journal of Consulting Psychology,* 1958, *22,* 321–327.

Lorr, M., McNair, D. M., Michaux, W. W., & Raskin, A. Frequency of treatment & change in psychotherapy. *Journal of Abnormal and Social Psychology,* 1962, *64,* 281–292.

Lott, D. R., & Murray, E. J. The effect of expectancy manipulation on outcome in systematic desensitization. *Psychotherapy: Theory, Research & Practice,* 1975, *12,* 28–32.

Lubin, B., Hornstra, R. K., Lewis, R. V., & Bechtel, B. S. Correlates of initial treatment assignment in a community mental health center. *Archives of General Psychiatry,* 1973, *29,* 497–504.

Luborsky, L. The patient's personality and psychotherapeutic change. In H. H. Strupp and L. Luborsky (Eds.), *Research in Psychotherapy, Vol. 2.* Washington, D. C.: American Psychological Association, 1962.

Luborsky, L., Chandler, M., Auerbach, A. H., Cohen, J., & Bachrach, H. M. Factors influencing the outcome of psychotheraphy: A review of quantitative research. *Psychological Bulletin,* 1971, *75,* 145–185.

Luborsky, L., Singer, B., & Luborsky, L. Comparative studies of psychotherapies. Is it true that "Everyone has won and all must have prizes"? *Archives of General Psychiatry,* 1975, *32,* 995–1007.

Marks, I. Behavioral psychotherapy of adult neurosis. In S. L. Garfield & A. E. Bergin (Eds.), *Handbook of psychotherapy and behavior change. (2nd ed.)* New York: Wiley, 1978.

Mathews, A. M., Johnston, D. W., Shaw, P. M., & Gelder, M. G. Process variables and the prediction of outcome in behaviour therapy. *The British Journal of Psychiatry,* 1974, *125,* 256–264.

McLachlan, J. F. C. Benefit from group therapy as function of patient-therapist match on conceptual level. *Psychotherapy: Theory, Research & Practice,* 1972, *9,* 317–323.

McNair, D. M., Lorr, M., & Callahan, D. M. Patient and therapist influences on quitting psychotherapy. *Journal of Consulting Psychology,* 1963, *27,* 10–17.

McNair, D. M., Lorr, M., Young, H. H., Roth, I., & Boyd, R. W. A three-year follow-up of psychotherapy patients. *Journal of Clinical Psychology,* 1964, *20,* 258–264.

Melnick, B. Patient-therapist identification in relation to both patient and therapist variables and therapy outcome. *Journal of Consulting and Clinical Psychology,* 1972, *38,* 97–104.

Meltzoff, J. E., & Kornreich, M. *Research in psychotherapy.* New York: Atherton Press, 1970.

Mendelsohn, G. A., & Geller, M. H. Structure of client attitudes toward counseling and their relation to client-counselor similarity. *Journal of Consulting Psychology,* 1965, *29,* 63–72.

Mindess, M. Predicting patient's response to psychotherapy: A preliminary study designed to investigate the validity of the Rorschach Prognostic Rating Scale. *Journal of Projective Techniques,* 1953, *17,* 327–334.

Mintz, J. What is "success" in psychotherapy? *Journal of Abnormal Psychology,* 1972, *80,* 11–19.

Mintz, J., Luborsky, L., & Auerbach, A. H. Dimensions of psychotherapy: A factor-analytic study of ratings of psychotherapy sessions. *Journal of Consulting & Clinical Psychology,* 1971, *36,* 106–120.

Morgan, W. G. Nonnecessary conditions or useful procedures in desensitization: A reply to Wilkins. *Psychological Bulletin,* 1973, *79,* 373–375.

Muench, G. A. An investigation of the efficacy of time-limited psychotherapy. *Journal of Counseling Psychology,* 1965, *12,* 294–298.

Myers, J. K., & Schaffer, L. Social stratification and psychiatric practice: A study of an outpatient clinic. In E. G. Jaco (Ed.), *Patients, Physicians and Illness.* Glencoe, Ill.: The Free Press, 1958.

Nash, E. H., Hoehn-Saric, R., Battle, C. C., Stone, A. R., Imber, S. D., & Frank, J. D. Systematic preparation of patients for short-term psychotherapy. II. Relations to characteristics of patient, therapist, and the psychotherapeutic process. *Journal of Nervous and Mental Disease,* 1965, *140,* 374–383.

National Center for Health Statistics. *Characteristics of patients of selected types of medical specialists and practitioners: United States July 1963-June 1964.* Washington, D.C., Public Health Service Publication No. 1000, Series 10, No. 28, 1966.

Newmark, C. S., Finkelstein, M., & Frerking, R. A. Comparison of the predictive validity of two measures of psychotherapy prognosis. *Journal of Personality Assessment,* 1974, *38,* 144–148.

New York City Committee on Mental Hygiene of the State Charities Aid Association. *The functioning of psychiatric clinics in New York City.* New York, N.Y., 1949.

Nichols, R. C., & Beck, K. W. Factors in psychotherapy change. *Journal of Consulting Psychology,* 1960, *24,* 388–399.

Noonan, J. R. A follow-up of pretherapy dropouts. *Journal of Community Psychology,* 1973, *1,* 43–45.

Orlinsky, D. E., & Howard, K. I. *Varieties of psychotherapeutic experience.* New York: Teachers College Press, 1975.

Orne, M. T., & Wender, P. H. Anticipatory socialization for psychotherapy: Method and rationale. *American Journal of Psychiatry,* 1968, *124,* 1202–1212.

Overall, B., & Aronson, H. Expectations of psychotherapy in lower socioeconomic class patients. *American Journal of Orthopsychiatry,* 1962, *32,* 271–272.

Parrino, J. J. Effect of pretherapy information on learning in psychotherapy. *Journal of Abnormal Psychology,* 1971, *77,* 19–23.

Paul, G. L. Strategy of outcome research in psychotherapy. *Journal of Consulting Psychology,* 1967, *31,* 109–118.

Perotti, L. P., & Hopewell, C. A. Expectancy effects in psychotherapy and systematic desensitization: A review. Paper presented at the Seventh Annual Meeting of the Society for Psychotherapy research, June 18, 1976, San Diego, Calif.

Pettit, I., Pettit, T., & Welkowitz, J. Relationship between values, social class, and duration of psychotherapy. *Journal of Consulting & Clinical Psychology,* 1974, *42,* 482–490.

Piper, W. E., & Wogan, M. Placebo effects in psychotherapy: An extension of earlier findings. *Journal of Consulting & Clinical Psychology,* 1970, *34,* 447.

Pope, K. S., Geller, J. D., & Wilkinson, L. Fee assessment and outpatient psychotherapy. *Journal of Consulting & Clinical Psychology,* 1975, *43,* 835–841.

Prager, R. A., & Garfield, S. L. Client initial disturbance and outcome in psychotherapy. *Journal of Consult-*

ing & Clinical Psychology, 1972, 38, 112–117.

Proctor, E. K., & Duehn, W. D. Stimulus-response congruence and content relevance in the interactional control of premature discontinuance in treatment. Revised version of a paper presented at the Fifty-First Annual Meeting of the American Orthopsychiatric Association, April 12, 1974, San Francisco, Calif.

Raynes, A. E., & Warren, G. Some distinguishing features of patients failing to attend a psychiatric clinic after referral. American Journal of Orthopsychiatry, 1971a, 41, 581–589.

Raynes, A. E., & Warren, G. Some characteristics of "drop-outs" at first contact with a psychiatric clinic. Community Mental Health Journal, 1971b, 7, 144–151.

Report of the Research Task Force of the National Institute of Mental Health. Research in the Service of Mental Health. DHEW Publication No. (ADM) 75–236. Rockville, Md.: 1975.

Riess, B. F., & Brandt, L. W. What happens to applicants for psychotherapy? Community Mental Health Journal, 1965, 1, 175–180.

Roberts, L. K. The failure of some Rorschach indices to predict the outcome of psychotherapy. Journal of Consulting Psychology, 1954, 18, 96–98.

Rogers, C. R., Gendlin, E. T., Kiesler, D. J., & Truax, C. B. (Eds.), The therapeutic relationship and its impact. Madison.: University of Wisconsin Press, 1967.

Rogers, L. S. Drop-out rates and results in psychotherapy in government-aided mental hygiene clinics. Journal of Clinical Psychology, 1960, 16, 89–92.

Rogers, L. S., & Hammond, K. R. Prediction of the results of therapy by means of the Rorschach test. Journal of Consulting Psychology, 1953, 17, 8–15.

Rogers, L. S., Knauss, J., & Hammond, K. R. Predicting continuation in therapy by means of the Rorschach test. Journal of Consulting Psychology, 1951, 15, 368–371.

Rosenbaum, J., Friedlander, J., & Kaplan, S. Evaluation of results of psychotherapy. Psychosomatic Medicine, 1956, 18, 113–132.

Rosenberg, S. The relationship of certain personality factors to prognosis in psychotherapy. Journal of Clinical Psychology, 1954, 10, 341–345.

Rosenthal, D., & Frank, J. D. Psychotherapy and the placebo effect. Psychological Bulletin, 1956, 53, 294–302.

Rothal, D., & Frank, J. D. The fate of psychiatric clinic outpatients assigned to psychotherapy. Journal of Nervous & Mental Disease, 1958, 127, 330–343.

Rosenzweig, S. P., & Folman, R. Patient and therapist variables affecting premature termination in group psychotherapy. Psychotherapy: Theory, Research, & Practice, 1974, 11, 76–79.

Rotter, J. B. Generalized expectancies for internal versus external control of reinforcement. Psychological Monographs, 1966, 80, (1, Whole No. 609).

Rubinstein, E. A., & Lorr, M. A comparison of terminators and remainers in out-patient psychotherapy. Journal of Clinical Psychology, 1956, 12, 345–349.

Rudolph, C., & Cumming, J. Where are additional psychiatric services most needed? Social Work,

1962, 7, 15–20.

Ryan, W. (Ed.), Distress in the City. Cleveland: The Press of Case Western Reserve University, 1969.

Saltzman, C., Luetgert, M. J., Roth, C. H., Creaser, J., & Howard, L. Formation of a therapeutic relationship: Experiences during the initial phase of psychotherapy as predictors of treatment duration and outcome. Journal of Consulting and Clinical Psychology, 1976, 44, 546–555.

Salzman, C., Shader, R. I., Scott, D. A., & Binstock, W. Interviewer anger and patient dropout in walk-in clinic. Comprehensive Psychiatry, 1970, 11, 267–273.

Sapolsky, A. Relationship between patient doctor compatibility, mutual perception, and outcome of treatment. Journal of Abnormal Psychology, 1965, 70, 70–76.

Sattler, J. M. The effects of therapist-client racial similarity. In A. S. Gurman & A. M. Razin (Eds.), Effective Psychotherapy: A Handbook of Research. Elmsford, N.Y.: Pergamon Press, 1977.

Schaffer, L., & Myers, J. K. Psychotherapy and social stratification: An empirical study of practice in a psychiatric outpatient clinic. Psychiatry, 1954, 17, 83–93.

Schofield, W. Psychotherapy: The purchase of friendship. Englewood Cliffs, N.J.: Prentice-Hall, 1964.

Seeman, J. Counselor judgments of therapeutic process and outcome. In C. Rogers & R. F. Dymond (Eds), Psychotherapy and Personality Change. Chicago: University of Chicago Press, 1954.

Shader, R. I. The walk-in service: An experience in community care. In T. Rothman (Ed.), Changing patterns in psychiatric care. New York: Crown Publishers, 1970.

Shapiro, R. J. Therapist attitudes and premature termination in family and individual therapy. The Journal of Nervous & Mental Disease, 1974, 159, 101–107.

Sheehan, J. G., Frederick, C., Rosevear, W., & Spiegelman, M. A validity study of the Rorschach Prognostic Rating Scale. Journal of Projective Techniques, 1954, 18, 233–239.

Shore, M. F., & Massimo, J. L. After ten years: A follow-up study of comprehensive vocationally oriented psychotherapy. American Journal of Orthopsychiatry, 1973, 43, 128–132.

Siegel, N. H. Characteristics of patients in psychoanalysis. Journal of Nervous & Mental Disease, 1962, 135, 155–158.

Siegel, N., & Fink, M. Motivation for psychotherapy. Comprehensive Psychiatry, 1962, 3, 170–173.

Sloane, R. B., Cristol, A. H., Pepernik, M. C., & Staples, F. R. Role preparation and expectation of improvement in psychotherapy. Journal of Nervous & Mental Disease, 1970, 150, 18–26.

Sloane, R. B., Staples, F. R., Cristol, A. H., Yorkston, N.J., & Whipple, K. Psychotherapy versus behavior therapy. Cambridge, Mass.: Harvard University Press, 1975.

Smith, G. J.W., Sjöholm, L., & Nielzén, S. Individual factors affecting the improvement of anxiety during a therapeutic period of 1-1/2 to 2 years. Acta Psychiatrica Scandinavica, 1975, 52, 7–22.

Stein, K. B., & Beall, L. Externalizing-Internalizing symptoms and psychotherapeutic outcome.

Psychotherapy: Theory, Research & Practice, 1971, *8*, 269–272.

Stern, S. L., Moore, S. F., & Gross, S. J. Confounding of personality and social class characteristics in research on premature termination. *Journal of Consulting & Clinical Psychology*, 1975, *43*, 341–344.

Stoler, N. Client likability: A variable in the study of psychotherapy. *Journal of Consulting Psychology*, 1963, *27*, 175–178.

Stone, A. R., Frank, J. D., Nash, E. H., & Imber, S. D. An intensive five-year follow-up study of treated psychiatric outpatients. *Journal of Nervous & Mental Disease*, 1961, *133*, 410–422.

Strupp, H. H., & Bloxom, A. L. Preparing lower-class patients for group psychotherapy: Development and evaluation of a role-induction film. *Journal of Consulting & Clinical Psychology*, 1973, *41*, 373–384.

Sue, S., McKinney, H., Allen, D., & Hall, J. Delivery of community mental health services to black and white clients. *Journal of Consulting & Clinical Psychology*, 1974, *42*, 794–801.

Sullivan, P. L., Miller, C., & Smelzer, W. Factors in length of stay and progress in psychotherapy. *Journal of Consulting Psychology*, 1958, *22*, 1–9.

Swenson, C. H. Psychotherapy as a special case of dyadic interaction: Some suggestions for theory and research. *Psychotherapy: Theory, Research and Practice*, 1967, *4*, 7–13.

Taulbee, E. S. Relationship between certain personality variables and continuation in psychotherapy. *Journal of Consulting Psychology*, 1958, *22*, 83–89.

Tollinton, H. J. Initial expectations and outcome. *British Journal of Medical Psychology*, 1973, *46*, 251–257.

Tomlinson, R. M., & Stoler, N. The relationship between affective evaluation and ratings of therapy process and outcome in schizophrenics. *Psychotherapy: Theory, Research and Practice*, 1967, *4*, 14–18.

Truax, C. B., & Carkhuff, R. R. *Toward effective counseling and psychotherapy*. Chicago: Aldine Press, 1967.

Truax, C. B., Tunnell, B. T., Jr., Fine, H. L., & Wargo, D. G. The prediction of client outcome during group psychotherapy from measures of initial status. Unpublished manuscript, Arkansas Rehabilitation Research and Training Center, University of Arkansas, 1966.

Truax, C. B., & Wargo, D. G. Effects of vicarious therapy pretraining and alternate sessions on outcome in group psychotherapy with outpatients. *Journal of Consulting & Clinical Psychology*, 1969, *52*, 440–447.

Udell, B., & Hornstra, R. K. Good patients and bad therapeutic assets and liabilities. *Archives of General Psychiatry*, 1975, *32*, 1533–1537.

Uhlenhuth, E., & Duncan, D. Subjective change in psychoneurotic outpatients with medical student therapists. II. Some determinants of change. *Archives of General Psychiatry*, 1968, *18*, 532–540.

Vaillant, G. E. Why men seek psychotherapy. I: Results of a survey of college graduates. *American Journal of Psychiatry*, 1972, *129*, 645–651.

Warren, N. C., & Rice, L. Structure and stabilizing of psychotherapy for low-prognosis clients. *Journal of Consulting & Clinical Psychology*, 1972, *39*, 173–181.

Warren, R. C., Jackson, A. M., Nugaris, J., & Farley, G. K. Differential attitudes of black and white patients toward treatment in a child guidance clinic. *American Journal of Orthopsychiatry*, 1973, *43*, 384–393.

Waskow, I. E., & Parloff, M. B. (Eds.), *Psychotherapy Change Measures*. Washington, D.C.: DHEW Publication No. (ADM) 74-120, 1975.

Wechsler, D. *The measurement and appraisal of adult intelligence. (4th ed.)* Baltimore: Williams and Wilkins, 1958.

Weiss, S. L., & Dlugokinski, E. L. Parental expectations of psychotherapy. *Journal of Psychology*, *1974, 86*, 71–80.

Weiss, J., & Schaie, K. W. Factors in patient failure to return to clinic. *Diseases of the Nervous System*, 1958, *19*, 429–430.

Weissman, M. M., Geanakoplos, E., & Prusoff, B. Social class and attrition in depressed outpatients. *Social Casework*, 1973, *54*, 162–170.

Whitely, J. M., & Blaine, G. B., Jr. Rorschach in relation to outcome in psychotherapy with college students. *Journal of Consulting Psychology*, 1967, *31*, 595–599.

Wilkins, W. Desensitization: Social and cognitive factors underlying the effectiveness of Wolpe's procedure. *Psychological Bulletin*, 1971, *76*, 311–317.

Wilkins, W. Expectancy of therapeutic gain: An empirical and conceptual critique. *Journal of Consulting & Clinical Psychology*, 1973, *40*, 69–77.

Wilson, G. T., & Thomas, M. G. W. Self-versus drug-produced relaxation and the effects of instructional set in standardized systematic desensitization. *Behavior Research & Therapy*, 1973, *11*, 279–288.

Wirt, W. M. Psychotherapeutic persistence. *Journal of Consulting Psychology*, 1967, *31*, 429.

Yalom, I. D. A study of group therapy dropouts. *Archives of General Psychiatry*, 1966, *14*, 393–414.

Yalom, I. D., Houts, P. S., Newell, G., & Rand, K. H. Preparation of patients for group therapy. *Archives of General Psychiatry*, 1967, *17*, 416–427.

Yamamoto, J., & Goin, M. K. Social class factors relevant for psychiatric treatment. *Journal of Nervous & Mental Disease*, 1966, *142*, 332–339.

Yamamoto, J., James, Q. C., & Palley, N. Cultural problems in psychiatric therapy. *Archives of General Psychiatry*, 1968, *19*, 45–49.

Zigler, E. S., & Phillips, L. Social competence and outcome in psychiatric disorders. *Journal of Abnormal & Social Psychology*, 1961, *63*, 264–271.

7

RESEARCH ON THERAPIST VARIABLES IN RELATION TO PROCESS AND OUTCOME

MORRIS B. PARLOFF
IRENE ELKIN WASKOW
BARRY E. WOLFE

National Institute of Mental Health

INTRODUCTION

Students of psychosocial treatments generally agree that investigations of process and outcome ideally require attention to the intricate dynamic interactions among therapist, patient, techniques, and environments. For a variety of practical and heuristic reasons, researchers are usually content to conduct studies focused primarily on one or another of these interacting elements. This chapter is intended to offer a critical survey of the considerable body of research that places emphasis on psychotherapists' contributions. The researcher who elects to grant primacy to the therapist variable is faced with the problem of determining which characteristics, qualities, and activities of the therapist are most worthy of study. In the absence of adequate conceptual bases, the researcher would be faced with a plethora of so-called "objec-

tive" and "subjective" data of indeterminate significance for the task. To avoid this, the investigator, on the basis of theory, hypothesis, or conviction, selects some few variables as prepotent predictors of the outcome of the complex process of psychosocial treatment.

The investigator frequently acts as if he/she has identified a single or small set of readily measurable events or characteristics of the therapist that are so powerful that they consistently produce positive or negative effects regardless of the kind of patients or problems to be treated, the patient's and therapist's goals, the length of treatment, concurrent life events, or the particular sets of measures employed to assess outcome.

So great is the need to maintain the conviction of potency of selected variables, that even in the face of an accumulating body of nonsupporting evidence, researchers appear to persist in their be-

233

liefs. This chapter may be viewed, in part, as a tribute to the researchers' reluctance to relinquish any finding once it has been identified as "positive."

In this chapter we shall review and evaluate the major contributions of empirical studies that assess the association between a range of psychotherapist variables and the nature, degree, and durability of change in patients. For the most part, only those process studies will be included that pertain to therapist variables whose effects or association with patient outcome have been demonstrated.

In view of the vast amount of research that may be viewed as relevant to the topic of the therapist's impact on process and outcome, we have sampled rather than surveyed exhaustively the published literature. We have sought to base conclusions on the major convergences that emerge from sets of studies and have deemphasized inferences based on individual studies. This review draws on the scholarship of other reviewers and emphasizes areas of our agreement and disagreement with the interpretations and inferences they have offered. In selecting studies for inclusion we have given preference to those that report on the efforts of qualified therapists to treat bona fide clinical problems. Many studies based on the "treatment" or counseling of student volunteers, and many analogue studies involving pseudotherapists or pseudopatients have been omitted. Also omitted are reports dealing primarily with the impact of specific treatment techniques, schools of therapy, or professions.

This survey reviews studies published since the first edition of this volume; however, when this chapter discusses areas not previously reviewed, pertinent studies covering an earlier period are also included.

Studies appropriate to the purposes of this chapter appear to be classifiable under these major rubrics: (1) therapist variables independent of the patient: first, outside of the treatment setting—personality, mental health, sex, and level of experience; second, within the treatment setting—therapist styles, and therapist contributions to the therapeutic conditions; and (2) therapist and patient variables in combination but studied independent of the treatment setting: congruence of

therapist and patient expectations; matching of therapist and patient on demographic variables; similarity-dissimilarity on personality, cognitive dimensions, and values; therapist characteristics (A-B) matched with patient diagnoses; and matching on miscellaneous psychological variables.

Surprisingly, the category of studies dealing with experimental research on therapist and patient interactions within the treatment setting remains essentially null. Such studies as do exist have not yet related patient-therapist relationship dimensions to outcome (e.g., Gardner, 1964; Hill, Howard, & Orlinsky, 1970; Orlinksy & Howard, 1975; Orlinsky & Howard, 1977).

STUDIES OF THERAPIST INDEPENDENT OF PATIENTS

A number of investigators have attempted to identify some particular therapist characteristics as prepotent, independent of the particular patient with whom the psychotherapist interacts. This approach requires the following assumptions: (1) that those therapist characteristics identified outside of treatment remain stable and are manifested in the treatment setting independent of the patient, and (2) that the effect of the manifested therapist variable under study is constant for all patients.

The investigator who believes it is appropriate to focus on the therapist variable per se need not suppose that the therapist's behavior is somehow exempt from the rule that all behavior is determined or that the therapist is immune to patient influence. It may be assumed, instead, that the therapist's actions and reactions are schooled and bounded by his/her perceptions of what is required to further the therapeutic task. What may distinguish the trained therapist from the untutored is that the trained therapist does not react to the patient with either conventional social responses or with unbridled spontaneity but responds instead with disciplined, therapeutically motivated interventions that may come to appear spontaneous.

In sum, to the degree that the therapist is clear about the therapeutic task and is able to remain in "role," his/her behavior will be responsive to, but not controlled by, the patient or the setting. While sensitive and reactive to the individual patient and the environmental context, the therapist may function in what seems to be an independent and self-determined manner.

Outside of Treatment Setting

Four characteristics of the therapist are cited in the literature as significant independent of the treatment setting or the patients treated: personality, mental health, sex, and level of experience.

Personality

Whatever the form of psychotherapy or techniques originally intended, they are inevitably shaped and colored by the particular therapist who mediates them. The therapists' affinity for particular schools of psychosocial treatment, the techniques they find congenial, and their preferred assumptions regarding the nature and potential of human beings, all are influenced by their individual qualities and characteristics—personality, attitudes, beliefs, interests, values, and styles.

In recognizing the central role of the person of the therapist independent of techniques, training programs have made concerted efforts to minimize, utilize, or neutralize the impact of the therapist's individual characteristics. What the educator, clinician, and researcher seek to do about the therapist's personal influence depends on their view of the relative value of techniques of treatment and the personal characteristics of the purveyor of the techniques. Those who believe that psychological treatment is best viewed as a technology attempt to minimize the potential error introduced by the foibles and vicissitudes of the therapist's personality. Ideally, for such therapists, the training of the therapist should be sufficiently rigorous that when the powerful techniques are mastered, the idiosyncrasies of personality are submerged. However, to reduce the likelihood that untoward aspects of the therapist's personality might intrude in a countertherapeutic fashion, personal therapy for the prospective therapist is frequently recommended. Successful completion of a didactic analysis has long been a training requirement for the psychoanalyst. As we shall report later, the research evidence does not appear to support this sanguine view of the value to the patient of the personal therapy of the psychotherapist. The aim of training has been to increase the therapist's access to technical knowledge and skills unobstructed by emotional debris. The value placed on such qualities as personal adjustment, tact, integrity, and maturity did not imply that their existence ensured therapeutic success but that their absence hindered it.

In contrast to the classical analyst and the behavior therapist, who place a premium on technique, humanists and existentialists have placed primary value on the uniquely human qualities of the therapist as contributing to effective psychotherapy. In 1934 Jung wrote, "It is in fact largely immaterial what sort of techniques he uses, for the point is not the technique . . . the personality and attitude of the doctor are of supreme importance—whether he appreciates this fact or not . . . " (1964, pp. 159−160).

Independent of the particular weight placed on the human qualities of the therapist, there appears to be a consensus that all good therapists should share certain characteristics. The various prescriptions for the ideal psychotherapist have included a litany of virtues more suited perhaps to the most honored biblical figures than to any of their descendants. A partial listing of the qualities that at times have been advanced as those to which all prospective therapists should aspire includes: objectivity, honesty, capacity for relatedness, emotional freedom, security, integrity, humanity, commitment to the patient, intuitiveness, patience, perceptiveness, empathy, creativity, and imaginativeness (Krasner, 1962; Slavson, 1964; Swensen, 1971).

Although the view of the general healing qualities of the therapist persists, we know of no studies concerning the therapist characteristics conducted independent of the patient or class of patients, or independent of the therapist's activities within a treatment setting, which support this conviction. Indeed, there is much clinical literature cautioning that the therapist personality characteristics that appear suitable for effective work with particular classes of patients or problems—children, character disorders, psychotics, and so on—are more differential than general (e.g., Fromm-Reichmann,

1950; Sullivan, 1956). This appears to be supported by experimental studies (e.g., DiLoreto, 1971; Fairweather, Simon, Gebhard, Weingarten, Holland, Sanders, Stone, & Reahl, 1960). Studies of therapist personality as manifested in the treatment setting or in relation to his/her patients are reported in later sections of the chapter.

Mental Health

It is commonly believed that the more integrated and healthy the therapist, the greater likelihood that he/she will be useful. The corollary is also believed: the more disturbed the therapist, the more likelihood that the patient will be injured.

A study of therapists treating schizophrenics reported that the patients of therapists who scored high on a pathogenesis score derived from TAT responses, functioned at a lower level after six months of treatment than did patients treated by the healthier therapists (Vandenbos & Karon, 1971). Bergin (1966) found that those therapists who were more anxious, conflicted, defensive, or unhealthy were least likely to promote change in their patients. Garfield and Bergin (1971a) found that while few of their measures of therapists in training correlated with outcome, those therapists with elevated MMPI scores had less success than did those with less ominous scores. Therapists who were conflicted about accepting patients' expressions of hostility appeared to affect adversely the patients' progress in therapy (Bandura, Lipsher, & Miller, 1960).

In addition to the research that suggests that the therapist's psychopathology may inhibit effectiveness, there is a substantial body of evidence suggesting that the better the therapist's adjustment, the more useful he/she may be to his/her patients (Bandura et al., 1960; Cutler, 1958; Holt & Luborsky, 1958; Meltzoff & Kornreich, 1970; Rigler, 1957; Wogan, 1970). With the possible exception of a single study (Mihalick, 1970), the research evidence strongly suggests that the more evidence of psychological disorder in the therapist, the poorer the treatment results.

Whether the therapist who has undergone personal psychotherapy is more effective than colleagues who have not received such treatment has been the subject of some research, but the evidence is contradictory. Since neither the therapist's need for treatment nor the effectiveness of such treatment is reported in detail, the interpretation of these findings remains ambiguous. Claims for the utility of treatment of therapists are made by McNair, Lorr, Young, Roth, and Boyd (1964); while reports of its lack of utility have been presented by Holt and Luborsky (1958) and McNair, Lorr, and Callahan (1963). A particularly intriguing finding is that presented by Garfield and Bergin (1971a), who conclude epigrammatically that in the case of student therapists, "some therapy is worse than none and a lot is even worse than that." Because in some instances the therapists being studied were still in treatment, the full effects of treatment may not have been achieved. Garfield and Bergin also suggested that therapists in treatment may be too preoccupied with their own problems to attend effectively to the problems of others. They also referred to Strupp's finding that therapists who had personal therapy in the past were rated as more effective than those who had not. Thus, therapy for the therapist may be helpful; but if received concurrently with learning to practice therapy with patients, it may interfere with optimal therapist performance.

Sex

The demographic characteristics of therapists (race, sex, and socioeconomic status) have generally been studied in relationship to the corresponding characteristics of their patients; this body of research is discussed more fully later. A few researchers have also studied the effects of the sex of the therapist independent of the patients treated. Seven studies have investigated the relationship between therapist sex and outcome of therapy; in five of these, no differences were found attributable to this characteristic (Geer & Hurst, 1976; Grantham, 1973; Sullivan, Miller, & Smelser, 1958; Pardes, Papernik, & Winston, 1974; Scher, 1975).

Two studies reported differences in outcome related to the sex of the therapists. One of these (Mintz, O'Brien, & Luborsky, 1976) found higher rehospitalization rates for patients treated in a Community Mental Health Center by female as compared to male therapists. The sex of the therapist, however, was confounded with profession and patient sex since there were more female social workers and more female patients seen by female social workers. Thus the worst results—more rehospitalization—were found for female patients with female social workers. The female social workers, however, saw only two male patients. No differences because of therapist sex were found on adjustment scores at two-year follow-up for those patients not rehospitalized. It would be of interest to know whether the treatment given by female social workers differed in any ways—for example, intensity, duration, amount of medication—from that of the four male medical students and five male (out of six) psychiatrists. Kirshner, Hauser, and Genack (in press) concluded that female therapists were more effective than males, but this is based on only one (out of 11 possible) clearly significant difference, with higher scores for female therapists on clients' ratings of improvement in self-acceptance. Although there was a near-significant difference in favor of female therapists on satisfaction with treatment and although other differences do go in the predicted direction, we see the results as providing only weak evidence for the authors' conclusion. We also have reservations about the data base—questionnaires sent up to a year or more after therapy.

In one other study (Hill, 1975), clients of female counselors reported significantly more satisfaction after the second counseling interview, but this must be considered an interim "outcome" measure.

Thus, most of the studies reviewed do not show effects on outcome due to therapist sex, and a few show inconclusive results. Since the studies are few, many of the methodologies weak, and the populations varied, no firm conclusions can be drawn at this time on the effects of therapist sex on outcome of psychotherapy.

Level of Experience

One of the first characteristics usually considered in discussions of the factors influencing a therapist's effectiveness is the amount of experience that the therapist has had. As with any trained skill, it is generally assumed that experience must enhance the "expertness" with which the therapist plies his/her trade. With experience, the therapist learns about many different kinds of patients and gets feedback on what approaches seem to work best with them. Further, as Auerbach and Johnson (1977) point out, more experienced therapists are usually older, and often have integrated valuable life experiences with their philosophy about therapy. It seems likely, too, that with time therapists become more at ease, more confident, more flexible in their approach to patients. All these assumptions culminate in the final hypothesis that the therapist's level of experience should have a positive effect on the effectiveness of therapy. Auerbach and Johnson (1977), in their thorough review of this area, conclude that therapist experience is, in fact, related to the quality of the therapeutic relationship. The situation in regard to the effect of the therapist's experience on the outcome of therapy is, as we shall see, far less clear.

Although few studies have been designed for the specific purpose of studying the effects of therapist level of experience on the outcome of therapy, many researchers have included a test of the effects of experience in the analysis of their data. A common assumption in the field has been that these studies, by and large, support the conclusion that the therapist's experience is an important influence on the outcome of therapy.

Luborsky, Chandler, Auerbach, Cohen, and Bachrach (1971) list level of experience as one of only three therapist factors having a "noteworthy" relationship to outcome. This review cites 8 (out of 13) studies as showing a significant positive relationship between therapist experience and patient improvement. Bergin (1971) also concludes, from his fairly extensive review, that "outcomes differ significantly as a function of experience level" (p. 237). Although they raise many valid questions about individual studies and acknowledge that the handful of relevant findings do not produce a definitive picture, Meltzoff and Kornreich (1970) conclude that "The preponderant weight of evidence, nevertheless, is that experience *does* seem to make a difference" (pp. 272–273).

Auerbach and Johnson (1977), in what is probably the most comprehensive review of the area of therapist experience level, are more cautious in their conclusions. According to their count, only 5 out of 12 relevant studies demonstrated superior results for more experienced therapists, and even some of these have serious shortcomings. They conclude that "the view that experienced therapists achieve better results, while it may be true, does not find the unequivocal support that we expected" (p. 99). In comparing their conclusion to the more positive view of Bergin, Auerbach and Johnson point out that Bergin himself seems to have determined for each study whether the therapists involved were experienced or not, and related this to outcome results. Auerbach and Johnson, in contrast, considered only those studies that directly compared two or more levels of therapist experience. Since this approach controls for at least a few crucial variables (e.g., clinical setting, general patient population), while comparing results due to different levels of experience, it should lead to more valid conclusions.

We have reviewed the studies that were cited by Auerbach and Johnson (1977) and by Luborsky et al. (1971), and also several additional studies reported in the 1970s. We have taken the same general approach as that taken by Auerbach and Johnson, including only studies that make direct comparisons of two or more levels of experience. Although we may have missed studies with other focuses that include therapist experience level in their post-hoc analyses, we assume that we have included most or all of those that treated therapist experience level as a major variable.

We have not included studies of the relationship between therapist experience level and therapy process variables or therapist orientations and attitudes, which have been reviewed at length by Auerbach and Johnson (1977) and by Sundland (1977). Although Baekeland and Lundwall (1975) report that in six out of seven studies there was a positive relationship between therapist experience and length of patient stay in treatment, there is sufficient uncertainty about the relationship of length of treatment to outcome so that we have chosen not to include patient dropout rates or length of treatment as indicative of patient improvement. Further, we exclude studies using paraprofessional or lay counselors, since our focus is on level of experience of professionally trained therapists and counselors.

Since most researchers studying the effect of therapist level of experiences on outcome have not

designed their studies with this in mind, authors often report that patients were assigned in the usual or routine manner for a facility, or no mention is made of assignment procedures. Only one researcher (Barrett-Lennard, 1962) set out specifically (partly before and partly after the fact) to balance the groups of patients seeing more and less "expert" therapists. In other studies, there is no assurance that the two groups of patients seen by more and less experienced therapists are comparable. Whatever biases usually function in the assignment of patients are given full rein. And judging from some authors' post-hoc analyses, usually carried out in an effort to understand their results, such biases do exist. For example, Sullivan et al. (1958) found that more experienced therapists had been assigned patients with better prognoses, that is, higher educational and occupational status. Knapp, Levin, McCarter, Wermer, and Zetzel (1960) discovered that the five most difficult patients in their sample had all been assigned to analytic trainees as their first supervised cases. Myers and Auld (1955) also suggest that senior staff in their study may have selected patients with better prognoses. There may be inadvertent, as well as deliberate, biases functioning. Auerbach and Johnson (1977) report that in the University of Pennsylvania psychotherapy study (Luborsky, in preparation), although patients of more and less experienced therapists were equivalent in level of adjustment, more of the older patients tended to be seen by experienced therapists. Thus, researchers have attempted to explain a number of findings on the basis of differential selection of the patient populations seen by more experienced and less experienced therapists.

Another major difficulty in interpreting research findings in this area, and one that has been discussed by other reviewers (e.g., Auerbach & Johnson, 1977; Meltzoff & Kornreich, 1970), lies in the different definitions used of "therapist level of experience." In some studies, "inexperienced" therapists may have essentially no experience (e.g., Barrett-Lennard, 1962; Cartwright & Lerner, 1963; Cartwright & Vogel, 1960); experienced therapists may have very little experience (e.g., Cartwright & Lerner, 1963; Cartwright & Vogel, 1960; Sullivan et al., 1958); and the experience level of the different groups of therapists may not differ greatly (Cartwright & Vogel, 1960; Grigg, 1961).

These problems in definition lead to difficulties in interpreting negative as well as positive findings. If there is no difference due to experience level, is it simply because the two groups overlap too much in experience or inexperience?

Another problem in understanding the meaning of different therapist levels of experience stems from the possible confounding of experience with other variables. Chief among these is the training of the therapist. Many studies compare "staff" therapists to interns, residents, or others "in training" (e.g., Barrett-Lennard, 1962; Grigg, 1961; Myers & Auld, 1955). To get a pure test of experience, perhaps one has to compare two groups of therapists who have all completed their training, but who have had different amounts of experience. Even then, it is important to keep alert to other possible confounding variables—sex of therapist, type of training, age, completion of personal therapy, "traditional" attitudes, and so on.

One additional major methodological issue here is the measurement of outcome. The sole measure of outcome in a number of studies is the report of the therapist or counselor (Brown, 1970; Cartwright & Lerner, 1963; Katz, Lorr, & Rubinstein, 1958; Mindess, 1953; Myers & Auld, 1955); in two others, the only "outcome" measures analyzed are therapist ratings and length of treatment (Barrett-Lennard, 1962; Sullivan et al., 1958). Most other studies use patient or client ratings alone or together with therapist ratings. Only a very few study the differences between patients seen by more or less experienced therapists on psychological tests or inventories or ratings by independent clinical evaluators (Cartwright & Vogel, 1960; Fiske, Cartwright, & Kirtner, 1964; Luborsky, in preparation).

The use of therapist or counselor ratings as the sole indicator of outcome is a problem in any therapy research study, but it is a special problem when the focus is the effect of a therapist's experience on outcome. Several of the researchers in this area (e.g., Katz et al., 1958; Myers & Auld, 1955) have themselves acknowledged the difficulty of interpreting results based on these measures: how much, they ask, does a therapist's level of experi-

ence affect patients' actual outcome, and how much may it merely influence the way that the therapist rates outcome?

A related and often neglected question concerns the particular type of outcome selected. The therapist's experience may be less important, for example, in effecting symptom relief than in leading to increased self-awareness or to better interpersonal relations. Most researchers also do not ask whether the experience variable is more important for some patients than for others, although reviewers are beginning to do so (e.g., Auerbach & Johnson, 1977; Meltzoff & Kornreich, 1970). The one exception here consists of studies investigating the role of client sex in interaction with experience level (e.g., Hill, 1975; Kirshner et al., in press; Scher, 1975).

We have limited the studies included in this survey to those that assessed outcome on some measure other than therapist ratings, evidenced no obvious biases in patient assignment to more and less experienced therapists, and included a direct comparison of outcome assessments for patients seen by more and less experienced therapists. Finally, in assessing results, we have accepted as significant only findings that reach at least the .05 probability level.

Very few studies meet all of these requirements. Of these, Scher (1975) is the only one that reports clearly significant findings. In his counseling center population, clients of experienced therapists reported significantly greater symptom relief and greater satisfaction with therapy on three out of five measures. In addition, however, Scher reports a significant counselor experience/client sex interaction, in that greater client-rated symptom relief (on one item) and satisfaction (on one item) were reported by male clients seeing experienced counselors and female clients seeing inexperienced counselors. Thus, the results of this study are quite complex, suggesting that level of experience, though generally important, may have different effects in different counselor-client pairs.

Among other studies meeting the requirements, one reports positive findings for the effects of level of experience on clients' Q-Adjustment Scores and TAT Mental Health Rating (Cartwright & Vogel, 1960). However, it is difficult to tell from the authors' data analyses whether these findings are indeed significant. Interpretation of their results would have been facilitated by their use of an appropriate covariance analysis. We find the Cartwright and Vogel results suggestive but not compelling.

Of the studies meeting our requirements, nine found no significant differences due to therapist experience level. Four of these (Feifel & Eells, 1963; Fiske et al., 1964, and from the same study, Fiske & Goodman, 1965; Grigg, 1961; Luborsky, in preparation) have also been included among negative findings by other reviewers. One of these (Luborsky, in preparation) found that the patients of the more experienced therapists were older, and that older patients did not improve as much as younger. However, a subsequent analysis, covarying for patient age, still revealed no significant differences due to experience level (Auerbach, personal communication).

Three of the nine are more recent studies. Kirshner et al. (in press), investigating effects of patient and therapist sex as well as therapist experience level, also report no main effect for therapist experience. Third-order interactions are reported on 3 out of 11 patient improvement and satisfaction measures, but only two of these are significant by our standards. Lerner (1972) reports no differences between her 8 experienced (minimum of 5 years of experience and having seen at least 50 clients) and 7 inexperienced (psychologist and social work trainees) therapists. Sloane, Staples, Cristol, Yorkston, and Whipple (1975) also report no difference on outcome due to three experience levels (two therapists per level). Their two least experienced therapists, however, had seen 250 or 300 patients, which makes them more experienced than many of the "experienced" therapists in other studies.

Two other recent studies that found no general effects of experience level on "outcome" used measures based on patients' ratings of particular therapy sessions, which might also be considered process measures (Hill, 1975; Orlinksy & Howard, 1975).

Our conclusions are even more pessimistic than those of Auerbach and Johnson. This may be due partly to our exclusion of studies that used therapist's ratings as the only indices of outcome (Barrett-Lennard, 1962; Brown, 1970; Cartwright & Lerner, 1963; Katz et al., 1958; Myers & Auld, 1955) and partly to our inclusion of several more recent studies with null findings (Kirshner et al., in press; Lerner, 1972; Sloane et al., 1975; and Orlinsky & Howard, 1975).[1]

The most important statement that we have to make in summing up our impressions of the literature on the influence of the therapist's level of experience on outcome is this: the body of data available is not sound enough to permit us to draw any firm conclusions. Reviewing and rereviewing past studies, tallying their results, and belaboring their inadequacies seems to us to have become a pointless endeavor. Although researchers have become more sophisticated over time, old research does not improve with age. Time would be better spent now in designing systematic, prospective research studies that will yield interpretable data.

The studies should meet minimal requirements: First, the groups of patients seeing more and less experienced therapists should be as equivalent as possible. Second, the experience level should be stringently defined at a clinically "high level" and should clearly differentiate the contrasted therapists. Experience also should not be confused with "expertness." Both more and less experienced groups should have completed comparable amounts of training, and should be equated as far as possible on relevant variables aside from experience level. Additionally, it may be important to specify the amount of experience that the therapist has had with particular patient populations, as was done by Lerner (1972) with regard to lower-class and psychotic patients. Both Meltzoff and Kornreich (1970) and Auerbach and Johnson (1977) also suggest that it may be important to consider possible differential effects of experience on different patient populations—for example, the need for an experienced therapist may vary for patients of different levels of disturbance.

Outcome measures should include not only the

---

[1] It is possible that we might have had a slightly more optimistic conclusion if we had included findings on dropouts and length of therapy, as did Meltzoff and Kornreich (1970). Until such studies provide us with more information about the actual outcomes for early and later terminators, however, we do not feel there is an adequate basis to consider "dropping out" or early termination as an unequivocal indication of "poor outcome."

therapist's assessments, but also assessments by the patient, an independent clinical evaluator, and, ideally, significant others in the patient's life.

Within the Treatment Setting

Early in the history of psychotherapy research, the investigator, by choice or necessity, was limited to using data secured outside of the sacrosanct psychotherapy chamber. With the relaxation of the therapist's Heisenbergian concerns and the improvements in technology, the researcher has been free not only to enter the mysterious black box but to prowl about with unholstered tape recorder and camera. One of the consequences was that the investigator ran the risk of being inundated by masses of "raw data." Some investigators have responded by attempting to simplify their task and focusing attention primarily on the therapists' rather than the patients' in-treatment activities.

In the section that follows, two major kinds of therapist functioning within the treatment setting are discussed: a brief overview of therapist styles, and an extended discussion of the research dealing with therapists as creators and purveyors of the "necessary and sufficient" therapeutic conditions.

Therapist Styles

The term *style* is applied in its broadest sense to the manner or mode of the therapist's expression and communication patterns independent of the content of such expression. The researcher's emphasis on stylistic variables suggests the conviction that the forms of expressive and instrumental communication are not simply the epiphenomena of interaction but are as important as—or perhaps even more important than—what is said.

Style includes a range of dimensions: (1) *nonlexical properties of speech,* such as inflection, fluency, stress, contours, loudness, pitch (Mahl, 1963; Boomer, 1978; Pittenger, Hockett, & Danehy, 1960) and activity level (Matarazzo, Wiens, Matarazzo, & Saslow, 1968); (2) *lexical aspects,* such as infrequently used words (Jaffe & Feldstein, 1970); (3) *kinesics*—body movements and gestures (Birdwhistell, 1963; Dittmann, 1972; Fretz, 1966); (4) *techniques/schools,* that is, the therapist qualities that are sometimes merged with techniques and schools, for example, directed focus, traditional supportive, cognitive/goal emphasis (Rice, Gurman, & Razin, 1974); directive, non-

directive (Sundland & Barker, 1962); (5) *connotative meanings* inferred from the verbal and nonverbal patterns: Some inferences pertain directly to the characterization of the therapist, such as "stimulating"—combining expressive voice quality, a focus on inner exploration, and use of fresh connotative language (Rice, 1965); charismatic, laissez-faire, impersonal, and so on (Lieberman, Yalom, & Miles, 1973); or authoritarian, understanding, accepting (Lorr & McNair, 1966).

By far the preponderance of research that purports to deal with therapist style is concerned with process rather than outcome. In accordance with the stated purpose of this chapter, we have limited ourselves to considering only those studies that have attempted to assess the impact of therapist style on patient change—positive or negative.

Of the various categories of styles, only "connotative meanings" based on broad patterns of verbal and nonverbal behaviors have provided noteworthy evidence of impact on patient outcome, although considerable research has been conducted on the other categories.

We know of no body of literature that reports that sheer amount of therapist activity or the nature and properties of therapist speech or body movements are powerfully related to patient outcome. Pope's recent review of the extensive literature on therapist activity level concludes, "There is no evidence here to justify the view that the long-term goals of psychotherapy are necessarily better served by high therapist activity. Rather the evidence points only to lesser strain, and the easier flow of communication with high rather than low therapist verbal activity" (Pope, 1977, p. 371).

The question of the relationship of therapist styles to techniques and behaviors advocated by particular schools is beyond the scope of this chapter. However, it may be sufficient to note that no compelling evidence has yet been presented that particular techniques or psychotherapy approaches are uniquely potent independent of the patient or problem being treated. Similarly, the therapist's professed therapy orientation has not been found to be related to outcome of therapy (Sundland, 1977).

One of the most promising approaches to developing an index of style that relates to outcome has been developed by Lieberman, Yalom, and

Miles (1973). They approached the analysis of style by attempting to categorize encounter group leaders' manner of relating to students in their groups. Although the encounter groups did not have explicit therapeutic intent, the research is included here as illustrative of a method.

Lieberman et al. (1973) used several observational schedules to study the activities of pairs of eminent group leaders who identified their approaches as representative of gestalt, psychodrama, Synanon, transactional analysis, T-groups, psychoanalysis, marathon, eclectic marathon, and personal growth. Intercorrelations of the various assessment data yielded four basic behavioral clusters: (1) emotional stimulation, (2) caring, (3) meaning-attribution (interpreting patients' feelings and behavior), and (4) executive function (p. 234).

An analysis of the relationship of these four basic dimensions of leader behavior to the authors' battery of outcome measures suggested that the ideal leadership style involved moderate stimulation, high caring, high meaning-attribution, and moderate executive function (p. 240). In contrast, the data indicated that factors that might contribute to less effective leadership were either very low or very high stimulation, low caring, little meaning-attribution, and too little or too much executive function. The actual group leaders in the study manifested various combinations of these dimensions, some more effective than others. "It appears that the two central functions, without which leaders rarely were successful, are sufficient Caring and Meaning-Attribution" (p. 241).

With the exception of the two gestalt leaders, the patterns of behavioral dimensions of the leaders varied more in terms of the individual than in terms of their orientations.

An analysis of the leaders' profiles permitted the identification of six leadership types: A. Energizers, B. Providers, C. Social Engineers, D. Impersonals, E. Laissez-Faires, F. Managers. The leadership type associated with the greatest positive change and the least negative change was Type-B Providers: high caring and meaning-attribution; moderate stimulation and executive function (i.e., the "ideal" pattern). The other results are mixed, depending on how one interprets the outcome measures, but there was some indication of both high casualties

and considerable positive change (combination of high and moderate) among the Type A-Energizers: intense emotional stimulation; moderate to high executive function; most charismatic. These were the only leaders (Type-A) who were strongly attached to a belief system and to a founder.

These results are limited by the varying interpretations that can be given to the outcome measures, the different numbers of participants in each of the final style categories, insufficient follow-up data, and, of course, by the fact that the groups were encounter groups of students and not therapy groups of patients. Further, since they concern group leadership, the results can only hint at similar types of studies that might be attempted in individual psychotherapy.

Therapist Contributions to the Therapeutic Conditions

Although a number of the studies included here purport to deal with the "therapeutic relationship," they are, in fact, concerned primarily with what the therapist does—or, more accurately, is described as doing —vis-à-vis his or her patients. Such research does not attempt to describe or to study the complexities of the reciprocal interactions and accommodations that may occur between therapist and patient.

The largest body of literature in this area has been produced by a relatively small coterie of energetic researchers whose conceptions and instrumentation were derived from the client-centered and humanistic orientation. In recognition of the enormous influence that this research has had on the field of psychotherapy research, if not the practice of psychotherapy, we will review here, in some detail, the past and current status of this work.

An entire generation of psychologists has been influenced by the idea that the necessary and sufficient conditions for effective psychotherapy are simply these: that the patient perceives the therapist to be "genuine," and that the patient believes the therapist to be experiencing some minimal degree of empathy and warmth toward him/her over a sustained but unspecified period of time.

A seeming agreement exists among different schools of therapy regarding the usefulness of establishing positive relationships with one's patients. However, the role and weight assigned to the therapist-patient relationship differs markedly between the psychodynamically or behaviorally oriented therapists on the one hand and the client-centered (humanistically oriented) therapists on the other.

The psychodynamically and the behaviorally oriented therapist generally accept the importance of the prerequisite therapeutic relationship. Although Freud stressed the importance of the development and analysis of transference as the sine qua non of analytic treatment, he drew a careful distinction between "transference" and the necessary "working alliance" (1910). He believed that the working alliance was based on the patient's recognition that the therapist was understanding and well disposed toward him/her. Freud later stressed that the therapist should provide conditions whereby the patient could experience warm and positive feelings toward him, on the grounds that such feelings effected successful results in psychoanalysis as in all other remedial methods (Freud, 1912).

The importance of the therapeutic relationship as a basis for permitting the work of analysis to proceed is also endorsed by most of the neo-Freudian therapists (Alexander, 1948; Horney, 1950; and Sullivan, 1953). Similarly, behavior therapists have always acknowledged the value of some aspects of the therapist-patient relationship, particularly those behaviors that communicate that "all that the patient says is accepted without question or criticism. He is given the feeling that the therapist is unreservedly on his side. This happens not because the therapist is expressly trying to appear sympathetic, but as a natural outcome of a completely nonmoralizing objective approach to the behavior of human organisms" (Wolpe, 1958, p. 106).

Gelder, Marks, and Wolff, (1967) noted that in the course of desensitization used in the treatment of phobic states, transference relationships build up even though not encouraged or interpreted in the traditional manner. They found that the positive aspect of the transference was useful as a means of engaging the cooperation of the patient.

In behavior therapy the relationship not only is

seen as enabling the patient to participate in the therapeutic process (Wachtel, 1977), but also is described as a means of heightening the therapist's ability to influence the patient toward therapeutic ends (Goldstein, 1973; Goldstein, Heller, & Sechrest, 1966), and as a source for modeling and reinforcement of new behavior (Shoben, 1949).

In brief, all schools of psychotherapy appear to be in accord that a positive relationship between patient and therapist is a necessary precondition for any form of psychotherapy. But Rogers went far beyond this agreement when he introduced the startling hypothesis that only six conditions, taken in combination, were "necessary and sufficient" to produce "constructive personality change" (Rogers, 1957, 1967, 1975). Three of the conditions referred to specific "attitudinal characteristics" of the therapist—genuineness, unconditional positive regard, and empathy; a fourth condition required that the patient perceive these therapist attitudinal characteristics. The remaining two conditions are apparently so self-evident that they have dropped out of subsequent discussions of the necessary-and-sufficient-conditions hypothesis: (1) the patient and therapist must be in psychological contact, that is, each must be aware of the presence of the other, and (2) the client must be in a state of "Incongruence, being vulnerable or anxious" (Rogers, 1957, p. 96).

The core conditions required of the therapist were elaborated as follows: (1) Genuineness—"the therapist should be, within the confines of this relationship, a congruent, genuine, integrated person . . . within the relationship he is freely and deeply himself, with his actual experience accurately represented by his awareness of himself"[2] (Rogers, 1957, p. 97). (2) Unconditional positive regard—"To the extent that the therapist finds himself experiencing a warm acceptance of each aspect of the client's experience as being a part of that client, he is experiencing unconditional positive regard"

---

[2]Rogers' use of the term *genuineness* is not synonymous with the terms *transparency* and *self-disclosure*. In his view, the therapist's awareness of his/her own feelings enables him/her to decide when it is appropriate to reveal such feelings to the patient. The therapist can ". . . choose to express attitudes which are strong and persistent, or not to express them at this time if that seems highly inappropriate" (Rogers, 1970, p. 53).

(p. 98). (3) Empathy—"the therapist is experiencing an accurate, empathic understanding of the client's awareness of his own experience. To sense the client's private world as if it were your own, but without ever losing the 'as if' quality—this is em-. pathy . . ." (p. 98). The final requirement, and the most critical one, concerned the client's perception of the therapist's attitude: "the client perceives, to a minimal degree, the acceptance and empathy which the therapist experiences for him. Unless some communication of these attitudes has been achieved, then such attitudes do not exist in the relationship as far as the client is concerned and the therapeutic process could not, by our hypothesis, be initiated" (p. 99).

Rogers further emphasized that these conditions were necessary and sufficient independent of the professional qualifications and training of the therapist, and independent of the type of client, or the diagnosis. Moreover, Rogers wrote that psychotherapy is not a "special kind of relationship, different in kind from all others which occur in everyday life" (p. 101).

By implication, he dismissed any notion that the techniques of the various therapies were important other than as vehicles for achieving one or another of these conditions. Consistent with this formulation, he abandoned the view that the nondirective therapy technique of "reflecting feelings" had any unique or specific therapeutic impact; instead, he proposed that like such techniques as free association, analysis of transference, and suggestion, it was simply a mechanism for communicating the therapist's sensitive empathy and unconditional positive regard.

Finally, in order to provide a straightforward and operationally defined criterion for the acceptance or rejection of the hypothesis, he stated: "If one or more of these conditions is not present, constructive personality change will not occur" (1957, p. 100).

In sum, Rogers set forth a hypothesis of remarkable specificity. His aim was to provoke research that, in the course of testing his extraordinary hypothesis, would help advance the field. He hoped that research would ultimately succeed in identifying the elements critical to the therapeutic process. He challenged some of the most treasured beliefs of therapists regarding the role of techniques and training. The hypothesis, while stemming from the client-centered orientation and experience, was not confined to it. It addressed the therapeutic process per se.

What has been the response to this courageous and well-intentioned challenge to the field? The psychoanalytically oriented clinicians and researchers responded as one—one who is not paying attention. Most analytically oriented research has been content to investigate psychodynamic formulations dealing with psychological process independent of outcome. Relevant clinical observations have also cast doubt on the universal applicability of the principle that the greater the degree of genuineness, empathy, and warmth, the greater the benefit to all patients. It has been noted, for example, that schizophrenic patients may be more harmed than helped by a therapist's premature display of warmth, and that an excessively empathic statement may provoke anxiety and defensiveness in some neurotic patients (Frank, 1973; Garduk & Haggard, 1972; Howard & Orlinsky, 1972; Speisman, 1959).

Although behavior therapists (with some notable exceptions, e.g., Alexander, Barton, Schiavo, & Parsons, 1976) have increasingly acknowledged that aspects of the therapist's relationship with the patient limit or enhance the potency of particular techniques, the notion that the relationship may act as the necessary and sufficient condition for effective behavior therapy has never been seriously entertained. However, it appears to have been implied by Murray and Jacobson (1971) in their analysis of the active agents in systematic desensitization.

A more respectful reception has been accorded the Rogerian hypothesis within the school of client-centered therapy. A small group of investigators developed scales to measure the three basic therapist conditions and other related aspects of therapist behaviors (Barrett-Lennard, 1962; Halkides, 1958; Truax, 1970; Truax & Carkhuff, 1967). A formidable number of studies have been published, each purporting to show that therapist effectiveness is a function of the ability to extend to the patient a relationship perceived as high on the dimensions of genuineness, nonpossessive warmth, and accurate empathy. Most of these studies, however, dealt with judges' rather than patients' perceptions of the therapists.

The importance of these findings was further underlined by the suggestion that patients who are exposed to therapists who fail to provide these three conditions to an adequate degree do not simply show little or no change, but get worse, that is, "deteriorate" (Truax & Carkhuff, 1967; Truax & Mitchell, 1971). This claim appeared to give considerable support to an attractive hypothesis highlighted by Bergin (1963)—that the seemingly unimpressive data concerning the effectiveness of psychotherapy were due primarily to the fact that patient change occurred in psychotherapy in two opposite directions, with the direction depending on the therapist's qualities. Bergin suggested that the positive effects of one group of therapists might be cancelled out by the negative effects of another group when the two are considered as a single group (Bergin, 1963).

The initial results of research efforts based on Rogers' hypothesis were, with few exceptions, exhilarating. They suggested that the field of psychotherapy research had achieved a major breakthrough. The prediction of therapeutic effectiveness might become a fairly simple matter of describing therapist behaviors on a few scales. The focus of research could then shift to investigating those variables that appeared to facilitate or inhibit the development of the prerequisite and sufficient therapeutic conditions.

Based on their thorough review and analysis of the pertinent literature up to 1970, Truax and Mitchell (1971) offered the following conclusions:

These studies taken together suggest that therapists or counselors who are accurately empathic, nonpossessively warm in attitude, and genuine are indeed effective. Also, these findings seem to hold with a wide variety of therapists and counselors, regardless of their training or theoretic orientation, and with a wide variety of clients or patients, including college underachievers, juvenile delinquents, hospitalized schizophrenics, college counselors, mild to severe outpatient neurotics, and the mixed variety of hospitalized patients. Further,

the evidence suggests that these findings hold in a variety of therapeutic contexts and in both individual and group psychotherapy or counseling. (p. 310)

This conclusion suggests that Truax and Mitchell (1971) believed that there was clear evidence for the altered hypothesis that the therapists who *are* accurately empathic, warm, and genuine (rather than simply so perceived by their patients) provide the necessary and sufficient conditions for effective treatment, independent of kind of problem or school of therapy.

As indicated, these authors also concluded "that low levels of accurate empathy, nonpossessive warmth and genuineness are important factors leading to deterioration" (p. 313).

The Truax and Mitchell (1971) review not only concluded that the evidence was directly supportive of Rogers' basic hypothesis, but pointed out a new and unanticipated confirmation implicit in the tendency for patients who receive low levels of the three prerequisite conditions not simply to fail to improve, but to become clinically worse. This looked like powerful confirmation indeed.

This overall assessment of research evidence available to them, however, seems somewhat injudicious, for they failed to give sufficient weight to the obvious inconsistencies among the reports they cited. In addition, some of the research included in their survey has been seriously questioned by Chinsky and Rappaport (1970), Rachman (1973) and Blackwood (1975), among others.

An illustration of one of the more troublesome disparities among research reports is found in the early publications of the basic work emanating from the Wisconsin Psychotherapy Project (Rogers, Gendlin, Kiesler, & Truax, 1967). For example, Truax and Carkhuff's (1967) report of the project does not coincide with that of Van der Veen (1967) or with that of Kiesler, Klein, Mathieu, and Schoeninger (1967). Because this issue has been adequately discussed by Bordin (1974), we shall not dwell on it here.

Truax and Mitchell also deemphasized findings that did not coincide with those predicted by Rogers' hypothesis. For example, one element of the hypothesis clearly stated that if one or more of the therapeutic conditions is not present, constructive personality change will not occur. The evidence does not appear to support this prediction.

For example, a study of 40 hospitalized chronic schizophrenics treated in group therapy revealed that patients who received *low* levels of "genuineness" showed a uniform tendency toward greater improvement than those receiving high levels of genuineness (Truax, Carkhuff, & Kodman, 1965). A group of investigators studying individual therapy with outpatients found that *"nonpossessive warmth"* was negatively related to outcome (Truax, Wargo, Frank, Imber, Battle, Hoehn-Saric, Nash, & Stone, 1966a, 1966b). In contrast to previous reports, this study found that there was little evidence of absolute deterioration associated with low therapeutic relationship conditions. Although Truax and Mitchell did recognize these and other exceptions (1971, Figs. 9.1 to 9.4, pp. 311–313), they tended to minimize their importance.

Bergin and Jasper (1969) used a global outcome rating to describe changes and the Truax accurate empathy scale to describe the therapeutic relationship. No significant correlation was found between the empathy scores of the therapists and the rated outcome of patients ($r = .05$).

Thus, evidence had appeared that seemed to challenge the original hypothesis that high scores on accurate empathy, warmth, and genuineness combined are prerequisite for positive change. Similarly, the Truax and Mitchell conclusion that low ratings on these dimensions tend to be correlated with deterioration was not supported. To accommodate these erratic findings, Truax and Carkhuff (1967) had earlier proposed a new principle: "when any two therapeutic conditions are sufficiently high, positive patient or client change will occur" (p. 91).

One possible source of such inconsistent findings appears to have been consistently overlooked, namely, that the measures of outcome differed from study to study. One of the best-established facts in the field of psychotherapy is the repeated finding that different measures of even the same criterion fail to show high correlations (e.g., Berzins, Bednar, & Severy, 1975; Cartwright, Kirtner, & Fiske, 1963; Fiske, 1975; Fiske, Cartwright, & Kirtner, 1964; Kelman & Parloff, 1957; Parloff, Kelman, & Frank, 1954; Strupp & Hadley, 1977).

Different measures are not interchangeable. Each measure may have its own pattern of relationships (Fiske, Cartwright, & Kirtner, 1964; Goldstein, 1960).

These and other authors have also documented the fact that different criteria may not correlate highly. The particular outcome criteria used by the therapist, patient, diagnostician, and those who know the patient as he/she functions at home, at work, or at play may differ considerably. Such discrepancies in criteria and measures limit the comparability of findings among studies.

In testing the therapeutic conditions hypothesis, considerable attention has been directed at specifying the nature of each of the prerequisite conditions and its measurement. While the degree to which such efforts have been successful may be justifiably challenged, what is of more immediate interest here is the fact that no comparable attempt has been made to specify the nature or dimensions of outcome to be effected by these therapeutic conditions. Outcome, unfortunately, is another of psychotherapy's nonparsimonious variables.

In fairness to Truax and Mitchell it should be noted that they do specifically note several qualifications to their final summary. For example, they acknowledge that: "techniques that are specific to certain kinds of patients and psychotherapy goals can be quite potent in the hands of the therapist who is inherently helpful and who offers high levels of empathic understanding, warmth, genuineness, potency, immediacy, and who confronts his patients in a constructive manner" (p. 341).

One serious question raised regarding their survey concerns the inclusion of research that based the ratings of the therapeutic conditions on the judgments of individuals other than the patients. This practice appears to overlook Rogers' effort to distinguish between the fact of therapist empathy, warmth, and genuineness and the patient's perception of these attitudes. (The issue of what is an appropriate source of such ratings is amplified later.)

The basic problems have not been significantly ameliorated in the more recent research reports, nor are the conclusions less equivocal. In 1973 Mitchell published a reanalysis (Mitchell, Bozarth, Truax, & Krauft, 1973) of the original 14 studies in the earlier Truax and Mitchell (1971) review. The revision revealed greater evidence of inconsistency between the so-called facilitative conditions and patient outcome. For example, of the 109 possible relationships tested between accurate empathy and outcome, 24 were significantly positive; of 108 correlations between warmth and outcome, 34 were significantly positive; and of 88 correlations between genuineness and outcome, 26 were statistically significant—however, six of these were significantly negative. The latter finding is of particular interest since therapist genuineness has been described as a prerequisite condition if the patient is to give credibility to the other two therapist conditions (Truax & Mitchell, 1971).

A review of the recent literature on the therapeutic effectiveness of accurate empathy, nonpossessive warmth, and genuineness led Mitchell, Bozarth, and Krauft (1977) to conclude that there is conflicting evidence regarding the existence of any direct relationship between such interpersonal skills and outcome. Although a number of studies suggest that one or more of the interpersonal dimensions are related to positive outcome (e.g., Cairns, 1972; Minsel, Bommert, Bastine, Langer, Nickel, & Tausch, 1971; Truax, 1970; Truax & Wittmer, 1971; Truax, Wittmer, & Wargo, 1971), other investigators have reported that there was little or no evidence of such an association (e.g., Beutler, Johnson, Neville, & Workman, 1972; Beutler, Johnson, Neville, Workman, & Elkins, 1973; Garfield & Bergin, 1971b; Kurtz & Grummon, 1972; Mintz, Luborsky, & Auerbach, 1971; Mullen & Abeles, 1971; Sloane, Staples, Cristol, Yorkston, & Whipple, 1975; Mitchell, Bozarth, Truax, & Krauft, 1973).

Mitchell, Bozarth, and Krauft (1977) conclude: "The recent evidence, although equivocal, does seem to suggest that empathy, warmth, and genuineness are related in some way to client change but that their potency and generalizability are not as great as once thought" (1977, p. 481). In our view this modest conclusion, derived primarily from studies in which independent judges rated therapy tape excerpts, need not be altered by the recent report by Gurman (1977), who concluded on the basis of a review of patient-perceived "therapeutic conditions" that *"there exists substantial, if not overwhelming, evidence in support of the hypothesized relationship between patient-*

perceived therapeutic conditions and outcome in individual psychotherapy counseling" (p. 521; italics Gurman's).[3] As we shall discuss later, the significance of Gurman's findings may be attenuated by methodological problems.

One of the major implications of the original hypothesis was that the training of therapists did not require professional backgrounds and should emphasize the development of the three therapeutic attitudes, which were subsequently termed "therapist skills." It must be noted in passing that there appears to be a lack of agreement among investigators as to whether they are dealing with therapist attitudes that are manifested in the treatment setting, or with therapist traits, skills, techniques, and language styles, or with the global apperception of the therapist as a "good guy."

Serious efforts have been made, particularly by Carkhuff and his associates, to train therapists, counselors, and nonprofessional helpers to develop the necessary and sufficient "therapist skills." Carkhuff's version of the therapeutic conditions was incorporated into a training format identified as the "Human Resources Training Program" or "Systematic Human Relations Training." On the basis of his experience in training "helpers" to work with students, adult and juvenile offenders, emotionally disturbed, minority groups and hardcore unemployed, he concluded that the clients of therapists who had been trained showed greater improvement than did the clients of untrained helpers. In support of these conclusions, Carkhuff cited 30 studies (1972). Empirical support for the effectiveness of such training in enhancing patient outcome has been increasingly challenged (Gormally & Hill, 1974).

Lambert and DeJulio (1976) undertook a careful review of these studies and offered the following conclusions:

The studies reported and relied upon by Carkhuff and his students have failed to specify the

___

[3]Interestingly, a review of 11 comparable studies of group psychotherapy failed to provide similar support (Gurman, 1977). It seems plausible that group psychotherapy, which places considerable emphasis on the importance of patient-patient relationships as well as patient-therapist relationships, might attentuate the association between therapist behaviors and patient improvement.

nature of treatment; its components seem to vary from one study to the next; control groups of a comparative type are frequently missing; and when present have not been equivalent in expectation, motivation, contact time, leader skill, or enthusiasm. A major weakness of most of these studies is their use of measures of empathy, respect, etc., which are not a new situation from training. Subjects have been aware of the criterion for evaluation and have not shown their learning to be practically important or broadly generalized. (p. 25)

An independent review of this area by Mitchell et al. (1977) concluded that while there appears to be some indirect evidence that trainees who achieve minimally facilitative levels have clients who improve more than the clients of less facilitative therapists, there are no studies "which directly test the contention that special training programs increase levels of skills and that such trainees have clients who, in turn, significnatly improve" (p. 493).

The evidence for the hypothesis that the conditions of accurate empathy, warmth, and genuineness represent the necessary and sufficient conditions for positive change in patients independent of the school of therapy is similarly in doubt. Perhaps the most relevant study to test the generalizability of the conditions across therapy approaches is that of Mitchell et al. (1973). This large-scale study involved 75 therapists treating 120 patients for periods ranging from six months to more than two years. Only seven percent of the therapists described themselves as adherents of the client-centered approach. The overall effectiveness of treatment was rated as "moderate" by the investigators. Improvement rates ranged from 43 percent to 71 percent on representative global measures. Only two percent of the patients showed any signs of deterioration. The predicted relationship between outcome and rater-judged levels of accurate empathy or warmth was not found. However, "minimal levels of genuineness were related modestly to outcome" (Mitchell et al., 1977, p. 483). Other studies involving non-client-centered therapists similarly found a lack of support for the hypothesis (e.g., Garfield & Bergin, 1971b; Bergin & Jasper, 1969; Sloane et al., 1975).

A related study by Mintz, Luborsky, and Auerbach (1971) is of special interest for it represents a relatively rare attempt to investigate simultaneously the associations between outcome and a variety of therapist modes of relating to patients. Mintz et al. (1971) studied the treatment of 30 nonpsychotic patients by 15 experienced therapists of psychoanalytic and eclectic orientations. Factor analyses of judges' ratings of a number of process variables over a period of sixty therapy sessions identified three distinct therapeutic modes: (1) optimal empathic relationship; (2) directive; and (3) interpretive with receptive patients. This study found that if therapy was described as high in optimal empathic relationship, a mode that appears to incorporate the conditions of empathy, warmth, and unconditional positive regard, "the outcome rating by the therapist was higher if it was also seen as not Directive; if the therapy was seen as high Directive therapy, outcome was higher when it was also seen as low in Optimal Empathy Relationship" (p. 119).

In response to the fact that the more recent studies have failed to support the initial enthusiastic claims for validity of the basic hypothesis concerning the necessary and sufficient therapeutic conditions, increased effort has been devoted to trying to reconcile the apparent discrepancies. Prominent among such analyses have been attempts to identify flaws and limitations in the nonconfirmatory studies. We shall discuss two of the most frequently cited objections: (a) failure to provide the prerequisite minimal levels of therapeutic conditions, and (b) the use of different sources of ratings.

Levels of "facilitative" conditions.   An explanation that has often been offered for the lack of significant associations between facilitative conditions and patient outcome is the failure of newer studies to provide an absolute, high level of the facilitative conditions (Mitchell, Bozarth, & Krauft, 1977).

Truax and Mitchell (1971), in their original review of 14 studies, reported that patients who had manifested higher levels of change on a variety of outcome measures had been provided with "*high* levels of nonpossessive warmth, genuineness, and accurate empathic understanding," and that patients who "exhibited deterioration in personality and behavioral functioning" had been offered" *relatively low levels* of these interpersonal skills" (p. 302; emphasis added). These conclusions suggest the existence of some clearly enunciated, absolute levels of interpersonal skills that are the basic minimum of facilitative conditions.

There is little evidence that any of the researchers—early or late—were, in fact, preoccupied with the notion of an absolute minimum standard. Truax and Wargo (1966) described their procedure as follows:

> *The mean value of the three research scales for each case was examined and the therapy patients then divided at the closest significant gap in level of conditions so as to divide the treated group into halves. (p. 509)*

There are, however, some bases for inferring guidelines for such standards. Truax and Carkhuff (1967) had suggested that scores of 2.5 on the 5-point warmth and genuineness scales and 3.5 to 4.0 on the 9-point empathy scale might represent minimum levels. Similarly, Carkhuff (1969) appears to suggest that the minimally facilitative therapist must function at 3.0 and above on each of his 5-point scales.

Contrary to the impression given by Truax and Mitchell (1971), a number of the early studies failed to indicate on what basis therapists had been classified as either high or low facilitators. Studies that did indicate the numerical scores did not all attain the criterion levels suggested by either Truax or Carkhuff for minimally facilitative conditions. "Indeed, several of the 'higher groups' mean scores were only slightly above 2.0" (Mitchell, Bozarth, & Krauft, 1977, p. 496).

At least two recent studies do exceed the minimum levels of "facilitative" conditions, yet fail to provide support for the hypothesis that absolutely high levels of facilitative conditions are significantly associated with improvement (Kurtz & Grummon, 1972; Sloane et al., 1975). Of interest, too, is the evidence regarding the observation that relatively low levels of facilitative conditions may be associated with negative or deterioration effects (Truax & Mitchell, 1971, p. 313). There can be no disputing the fact that relatively low facilitative conditions were adequately represented in many of the

more recent studies. The "deterioration effect," presumably, could undergo appropriate testing. Confirmation of this phenomenon, however, is no less difficult to find in the post-1970 studies than confirmation of the effects of high facilitative conditions. As previously indicated, in Mitchell et al.'s large-scale study (1973), only two percent of 120 patients could reasonably be classified as showing negative effects, despite relatively low levels of therapeutic conditions.

In brief, it appears that the absence of high levels of therapeutic conditions does not preclude client/patient benefit nor predict negative effects.

The issue of therapist conditions is also complicated by the fact that a therapist's "levels" may vary with the length of the therapy unit assessed (Mintz & Luborsky, 1971); the point in therapy (Beutler, Johnson, Neville, & Workman, 1973; Gurman, 1973); and the particular patient (Mitchell et al., 1973).

In our view, research favoring the position that the therapist's levels of functioning are influenced by the patient (Houts, MacIntosh, & Moos, 1969; Moos & MacIntosh, 1970; Van der Veen, 1965) seems more credible clinically than studies purporting to show that the therapist, independent of the patient, determines the level of the therapeutic conditions (Truax, 1963; Truax & Carkhuff, 1967).

It must be concluded that the unqualified claim that "high" levels (absolute or relative) of accurate empathy, warmth, and genuineness (independent of the source of rating or the nature of the instrument) represent the "necessary and sufficient" conditions for effective therapy (independent of the outcome measures or criterion) is not supported.

Sources of ratings.   As mentioned previously, Rogers has consistently held that an appropriate test of his formulation regarding the necessary and sufficient conditions for effective therapy requires that the patient be the source of the judgment of the levels of therapeutic conditions offered (1957, 1967, 1975). Nevertheless, much of the subsequent research in this area has been based on the ratings of judges other than the patient. This disparity has been cited as one possible reason that support for the original hypothesis has been equivocal.

Two justifications for using judges other than the

patient have been given: (1) judges can adequately represent the viewpoint of the patient, and (2) judges' ratings are better predictors of outcome than patients' ratings. The literature fails to provide firm support for the first of these contentions and rather convincingly disconfirms the second.

If independent judges could function as surrogates for patients, this would have wide appeal to many clinicians and researchers, who feel that involving the patient in research may be an offensive intrusion that might alter or interfere with the normal processes of psychotherapy.

The early findings that judges' ratings may effectively represent patients' perceptions of therapist-offered conditions (Kiesler, Mathieu, & Klein, 1967) have not appeared to generalize to other studies. Subsequent attempts to compare the judgments of therapist behavior as made by clients, judges, and therapists have failed to demonstrate consistent agreement among these sources (e.g., Hansen, Moore, & Carkhuff, 1968; Bozarth & Grace, 1970; Fish, 1970; Kurtz & Grummon, 1972; Mitchell et al., 1973). The ratings of patients tend to be consistently higher than those of the nonparticipant judges, so that the assumption that judges' ratings may be used as adequate representations of the patients' perceptions seems unwarranted.

A number of authors have attempted to explain the disagreement between patients' and nonparticipant judges' ratings by attributing it to the different sets of data available to patients and judges (e.g., Mehrabian & Ferris, 1967; Chinsky & Rappaport, 1970; Rappaport & Chinsky, 1972). Judges are usually limited to a relatively small sample of audiotape excerpts of the overall treatment period. In contrast, the patient has available the full context of his/her interaction with the therapist, including all the interactive richness of the nonverbal as well as the verbal cues. Some impressive examples of the interaction of the verbal and nonverbal variables are reported by Haase and Tepper (1972), who found in an analogue study that verbal responses were rated as much more empathic when eye contact was present.

Patients and nonparticipant judges also may place different weight on available information. For example, Fish (1970) found that judges tended to

assign higher empathy ratings to certain verbal styles of therapists, while patients gave higher empathy ratings to older therapists.

The patients and judges also use quite different instruments. The judges most frequently used Truax and Carkhuff's (1967) or Carkhuff's modified scale (1969) rating empathy, warmth, and genuineness. The client typically used the Barrett-Lennard Relationship Inventory (Barrett-Lennard, 1962) or the Truax Relationship Scale (Truax & Carkhuff, 1967). Further, while judges are frequently carefully trained in the use of their scales, the client is not.

The second major justification for the use of nonpatient rather than patient ratings is that judges' ratings are better predictors of outcome. Confirmation of such a finding would be of considerable theoretical interest, but it would tend to undermine the original Rogers thesis. The position of Truax and Carkhuff (1967) and Carkhuff and Burstein (1970)—that patients distort their perceptions of their therapist and misinterpret therapists' interventions—is consistent with the views of psychodynamically oriented clinicians. However, the decision to dismiss the patient as a credible source of data regarding *his or her own perceptions* is to misconstrue the very essence of the concept of the "necessary and sufficient" therapeutic conditions. Patients, like any judge, may wittingly or unwittingly distort the reports of their perceptions, in response to their understanding of the task. To insist, however, on the advantage of using the ratings of objective judges suggests that the power of the "actual" behaviors of the therapist will operate on a subliminal or "subception" basis independent of the patient's own awareness of the therapist's interventions.

Gurman's (1977) recent review of studies that related the outcome of individual psychotherapy to patients' ratings of their therapists' attitudes and behaviors toward them may be reassuring to those who have feared that patients' ratings of therapist activities were poor predictors of therapeutic change. Of the 22 patient-based studies surveyed, only one (Lesser, 1961) failed to show that patients' perceptions of their therapists were related to judgments of outcome. (It was duly noted that Lesser's research, unfortunately, represented the only study in this corpus that had appropriately corrected for the levels of initial scores in the analysis of pre- to post-change scores.) As indicated previously, Gurman interpreted his survey as offering "substantial . . . evidence in support of the hypothesized relationship between patient-perceived therapeutic conditions and outcome . . ." (p. 521). The reader is cautioned that Gurman's review was not aimed at testing the Rogerian hypothesis and therefore a number of the studies surveyed do not provide relevant measures of the hypothesized conditions of accurate empathy, warmth, and genuineness. Nevertheless, there is a serious circularity in a number of these studies that involved patients' ratings of therapist conditions as well as therapeutic outcome.

Many of the studies used measures only tangentially related to the postulated prerequisite therapeutic conditions. For example, Board (1959) focused on the patient's feelings of liking and being liked by the therapist; Feifel and Eells (1963) reported that the patients predominantly thought that what had helped them was "the opportunity to talk over problems"; Libo (1957) derived a "therapist attraction" score on the basis of the patient's responses to a projective technique; Grigg and Goodstein (1957) had patients complete a questionnaire describing such therapist behaviors as activity level, working closely, listening, and so on; Sapolsky (1965) had patients complete a semantic differential scale; and Ryan and Gizynski (1971) conducted post-therapy interviews to determine the patients' confidence in and liking for their therapists.

In at least 11 of the 21 supportive studies the outcome criteria were provided in whole, or in part, by the patients' own assessment of their therapeutic outcome. These assessments were then correlated with the patients' perceptions of their therapists (Board, 1959; Cain, 1973; Feifel & Eells, 1963; Grigg & Goodstein, 1957; Hill, 1974; Libo, 1957; Lorr, 1965; McClanahan, 1974; McNally, 1973; Ryan & Gizynski, 1971; Tausch, Sander, Bastine, & Friese, 1970). Since the patient's ratings of therapist and outcome are likely to be reflections of the patient's overall satisfaction with the therapy, and therefore highly interrelated, the usefulness of these studies as independent tests of the facilitative

conditions hypothesis must further be questioned.

This concern is underscored by the inclusion of studies that are clearly retrospective reports by the patient. Whether the patients' perceptions of the therapists were, indeed, instrumental in effecting the "favorable" outcome or whether the favorable assessment influenced the patients' recall of their therapists' characteristics cannot be determined (e.g., Board, 1959; Feifel & Eells, 1963; Grigg & Goodstein, 1957; Ryan & Gizynski, 1971; Strupp, Fox, & Lessler, 1969).

As we indicated, the aim of the effort to test the therapeutic conditions hypothesis is not simply to establish further that the therapist's activities are related to the outcome of the therapy, but rather to test whether three specific conditions are the *"necessary and sufficient"* conditions for all successful therapeutic efforts independent of problems to be treated, the techniques employed, the school of therapy to which the therapist subscribes, and so on. From our skeptical vantage point, support for the hypothesis would require a rather formidable array of consistent evidence based on expert treatment of a wide range of patients. Such evidence has not been forthcoming.

The pace of the search for the single set of therapist variables that will account for all patient change—positive in its presence and negative in its absence—has slowed perceptibly. Most reviewers of the large body of studies in this area are now content to acknowledge that after some 20 years of effort the evidence for the therapeutic conditions hypothesis is not persuasive. The associations found are modest and suggest that a more complex association exists between outcome and therapist "skills" than originally hypothesized.

Increasingly, researchers of process and outcome of psychosocial interventions have accepted the wisdom of pursuing a more complex model. The importance of the "therapeutic relationship" is not dismissed but is included as one of a number of important factors to be considered. The formulations of Frank (1973) are illustrative of this approach. He has concluded that all psychotherapists, independent of school, provide their patients with a common set of "nonspecific" elements: an emotionally charged relationship with a helping person, the opportunity to use the therapist's personal qualities to strengthen the patient's expectations of help, a plausible explanation of the causes of the patient's distress, techniques and procedures based on a rationale acceptable to the patient, and some experience of success with new ways of behaving and feeling.

The field is moving, albeit slowly, away from the linear strategy and toward studying a broader range of therapist activities as they interact with differentiated patient groups under a variety of specified treatment conditions. Even such early advocates as Mitchell and his associates have now concluded that "Therapist orientation, type of client, and type of therapy as well as a host of more specific variables, must be taken into account" (Mitchell et al., 1977, p. 496). We hope that the Gurman review of the literature reporting that the patients' perceptions of the therapists' efforts do correlate with outcome will not rekindle the belief that a simple solution may yet be found to the complex problem of increasing the effectiveness of psychosocial treatment with a broad range of patients and problems.

We share with Rogers the conviction that the importance of his hypothesis lies not simply in whether it is supported or disconfirmed, but rather in the possibility that it might stimulate research that would produce new and more refined understanding of the therapist's role in relation to the process and outcome of psychotherapy. In this endeavor Rogers' efforts have been rewarded.

STUDIES OF THERAPIST AND PATIENT VARIABLES IN COMBINATION

The effort by researchers to discover combinations of therapists and patients that are predictive of positive therapeutic outcome is usually traced to the work of Whitehorn and Betz (1954, 1957, 1960). Since their investigations with the A-B Scale, which was designed to differentiate therapists in terms of their ability to work well with schizophrenic patients, a sizable number of studies have been conducted in an effort to discover maximal matches of patients and therapists.

Such a research strategy assumes that felicitous combinations of therapists and patients might be formed on the basis of some general, characterological tendencies of the participants, which are independent of the treatment setting but which, nevertheless, make their inevitable appearance throughout the course of therapy. The meshing of these characteristics is then presumed to lead to the enhancement of positive therapeutic changes in the patient. By inference, it is also presumed that an inappropriate "match" of therapist and patient may block or limit the therapist's effectiveness with that particular patient.

The idea of therapist-patient matching, however, is one with very uncertain conceptual boundaries. In its broadest meaning, it suggests only that certain therapist-patient combinations are better than others. It gives no immediate hint regarding which dimensions are most suitable for matching or whether it is better for the participants to be very much alike or very different on a particular dimension.

The first set of such studies to be reviewed here includes those on the effect of *congruence of the therapy participants' expectations regarding therapy* on the outcome of therapy. For a variety of reasons, patients and therapists often come together with very different expectations concerning therapy. We review not only studies attempting to measure the effects of such differences, but also those that have attempted to achieve expectancy congruence between the participants before therapy begins.

Studies in which such *demographic variables* as *race, social class,* and *sex* have served as a basis for exploring optimal therapist-patient combinations are also considered. These studies reflect the assumption that demographic differences imply substantial differences in cultural and socialization experiences that may impede the development and maintenance of therapeutic rapport. Often such differences in socialization shape differing expectations and attitudes about one's environment; consequently, the studies on congruence of expectations overlap with studies in which the participants differ demographically.

A substantial number of studies have concerned the predictive ability of matching therapy dyads in terms of similarity on a wide range of psychological factors—*personality factors, cognitive factors,* and *values.* In these studies, varying degrees of similarity-dissimilarity have been plumbed in the hope of discovering a basis in the personalities, cognitive styles, or values of the therapy participants for maximizing the probability of a successful therapeutic experience.

Under personality factors, we consider a variety of personality instruments that have been used as the basis for defining similar and dissimilar dyads, including the Minnesota Multiphasic Personality Inventory (MMPI), the Myer-Briggs Type Indicator (MBTI), the Fundamental Interpersonal Relations Orientation Scale (FIRO-B), the A-B Scale, and some miscellaneous instruments. Four different cognitive variables have been employed in therapist-patient matching studies. Very little systematic research has been conducted in terms of the similarity of the values of patients and therapists.

In the last section, we review a few efforts to match the therapy participants systematically in terms of *multiple, miscellaneous psychological variables.*

Congruence of Therapist and Patient Expectations

Studies of the relationship between the congruence of therapist and patient expectations and therapy outcome have been grounded in the intuitively appealing assumption that insofar as the therapy participants are not at cross-purposes regarding the nature of psychotherapy, progress should be enhanced. Widely discrepant expectations, in fact, may make the establishment of a truly therapeutic alliance painfully difficult. On the other hand, if the therapy participants share the same expectations regarding therapy, it has been assumed that the patient is more likely to continue in therapy and derive benefit from it.

With these assumptions in mind, researchers have tackled the question of how important shared expectations are for the eventual outcome of psychotherapy. They have approached the problem in three separate ways. Some studies have *experimentally* established congruent and incongruent therapeutic dyads before the inception of therapy and then compared them posttherapy in

terms of the number of patients in each type of dyad who benefited from the therapy. "*Naturalistic*" studies have assessed the expectations of patients at the outset and then performed post-hoc correlational analyses on the groups of patients who showed positive and negative changes in the outcome of therapy. A third group, "*preparation*" studies, employed patient preparation programs in an effort to *induce* congruence between the expectations of therapists and patients regarding their respective roles in therapy; then congruent and incongruent dyads were compared in terms of changes on particular outcome variables.

Altogether, there have been 12 studies[4] that explored the possible relationship between congruence of therapist-patient expectations and therapy outcome. Three of these studies, it should be noted, treated "remaining in therapy" as an outcome variable (Heine & Trosman, 1960; Overall & Aronson, 1963; Warren & Rice, 1972). The remaining nine studies included a variety of measures of patient improvement as the major dependent variables.

As a group, the experimental and naturalistic studies reveal virtually no relationship between congruence of expectations and patient improvement (Goin, Yamamoto, & Silverman, 1965; Goldstein, 1960; Martin, Sterne & Hunter, 1976; Mendelsohn, 1968). Congruence of expectations, however, does seem to affect the dropout rate by encouraging patients to remain in therapy (Heine & Trosman, 1960; Overall & Aronson, 1963; Warren & Rice, 1972).

The "preparation" studies have not only reduced the attrition rate, but also show a much stronger effect on patient improvement than the experimental or naturalistic studies (Hoehn-Saric, Frank, Imber, Nash, Stone, & Battle, 1964; Jacobs, Charles, Jacobs, Weinstein, & Mann, 1972; Sloane, Cristol, Pepernik, & Staples, 1970; Strupp & Bloxom, 1973; Truax & Wargo, 1969).

Only two studies were of the *experimental* type

---

[4]Several studies were exclusively concerned with the impact of congruence of expectations on the process of psychotherapy. Since our primary concern is therapy outcome, we will not review these here (Clemes & D'Andrea, 1965; Heitler, 1973; Lennard & Bernstein, 1960; Yalom, Houts, Newell, & Rand, 1967).

(i.e., employed a pre-therapy matching design). Mendelsohn (1968) examined the role expectations of both therapists and patients and found no relationship between congruence of expectations and therapy outcome. This study, however, was concerned with psychological counseling that lasted only two or three sessions.

In a more recent study, Martin, Sterne, and Hunter (1976) assessed the effects on patient improvement of congruence of expectations that therapists will be nurturant or critical. No differences were found between congruent and noncongruent expectation dyads for each of the two dimensions taken alone. An interaction effect was found, however, for a small portion of the sample.

The naturalistic studies also provide little evidence that congruence of expectations is an important factor for patient improvement. Goin et al. (1965) found no differences in terms of therapist ratings of improvement between patients who sought advice and received it and those who sought advice and did not receive it. They did find, however, that significantly more patients felt satisfied with treatment if their treatment was congruent with their expectations.

Goldstein (1960) studied congruence of therapist and patient expectations regarding how much patients will change as a result of therapy. He found no relationship at all between patient-perceived change and congruence of therapists' and patients' initial expectations of improvement.

Despite the lack of evidence for a relationship between congruence of therapist-patient expectations and patient improvement, some efforts have been made to increase such congruence by specific preparation programs. Such an approach appeared consistent with clinical observations that if patients understood the therapists' assumptions they seemed better able to participate in treatment. Many of these programs have been directed at lower and working class patients to reduce the high frequency with which they drop out of the psychotherapy that they have been offered.

Although these programs have been labeled "patient socialization programs" or programs for the preparation of patients for therapy, they may also be seen as programs to induce expectancy congruence between patient and therapist. Orne

and Wender (1968) developed an "anticipatory socialization interview," which is an individual clinical interview designed to provide an explicit discussion of treatment rationale, the roles of the participants, and the likely vicissitudes of the therapy experience, such as the occurrence of resistance and negative transference. The authors use this interview with all of their patients, but they thought it might be especially helpful with patients who may be quite unfamiliar with what actually takes place in therapy, and may, therefore, not understand how mere "talking" can help them. Their work has stimulated a number of studies that have assessed the value of this and similar preparatory procedures.

In his review of preparatory programs designed specifically for lower class and "unsophisticated" patients, Heitler (1976) concluded that a variety of such techniques held promise "for facilitating a therapeutic alliance in expressive psychotherapy with unsophisticated patients from any social class and that these techniques may be particularly useful with lower class populations . . ." (p. 350). Lorion's (1974) review of essentially the same literature concurs with Heitler's conclusions. In Lorion's view, pretreatment preparation helps make therapy less mysterious and more comfortable for low-income patients.

The five outcome studies that have been conducted in the area of induced congruence of therapist and patient expectations indicate that there is a consistent, modestly positive relationship between patient preparation and patient improvement (Hoehn-Saric et al., 1964; Jacobs et al., 1972; Sloane et al., 1970; Strupp & Bloxom, 1973; Truax & Wargo, 1969).

Four of the above studies "prepared" only the patient for psychotherapy in an effort to induce congruence of expectations between the therapy participants. The study by Jacobs et al. (1972) represents a significant departure from this paternalistic strategy. They prepared both the patients and the psychiatric resident therapists. Patients received a modification of the role induction interview. Residents received an orientation from the Chief Resident that focused on the difficulties that lower-income patients may experience in exploring their feelings, in accepting a psychological explanation of their disorder, and in tolerating delay in receiving help.

Of the "prepared" patients seen by "prepared" residents, 67 percent improved as compared to only 37 percent in the condition in which neither participant had been prepared. About 50 percent of the patients improved in the two conditions where only one participant was prepared. Consequently, a fairly substantial gain was obtained in terms of the number of patients improved as an apparent result of the preparation of both therapy participants.

The results of these studies suggest that regardless of the type of induction procedure employed (i.e., interview, tape-recording, or film), some orientation as to the nature of psychotherapy will involve the patients more in their treatment, encourage them to remain, and help them to achieve more improvement. Orienting therapists toward their patients may further enhance patient improvement.

Demographic Variables

Race, social class, and sex frequently have been deemed important *patient* variables in psychotherapy research, but are less often considered potentially important *therapist* variables.

Recent interest in these characteristics of the therapist has been stimulated by a trend in social criticism that has questioned the fairness and the adequacy of the treatment provided by mental health institutions in general, and psychotherapists in particular, for black people, members of lower socioeconomic groups, and women. Basically, two questions have been generated: (1) Do biases and stereotypes held by therapists about such patients result in their inadequate treatment? (2) Does an absence of shared experiences and values interfere with the therapist's ability to establish rapport and to treat these patients effectively?

We will review the relevant research in each of these areas separately and then draw some general conclusions. Although we deal with race and social class as separate research variables, they are often confounded in studies, and certainly in practice, since blacks constitute a large relative proportion of lower-class patient samples, as they do of the lower class in society at large. Very few researchers have attempted to look systematically at the interactions of race, social class, and sex.

Race

In the last few years, there have been a number of reviews of the effects of the race of the therapist (or counselor), and/or racial matching of the therapy pair, on the process and outcome of psychotherapy (Gardner, 1971; Harrison, 1975; Griffith, 1977; Sattler, 1970, 1977). In describing the history of this area, Griffith (1977) points out that the possible role of racial differences in therapy was discussed in the early period of interracial therapy following World War II, but that the literature devoted to the topic quickly declined during the "integration era" of the 1950s. The last decade—and especially the last five years—has seen a renewed interest in the subject, evidenced not only by theoretical and clinical writings about race and psychotherapy, but also by a number of research studies. This renewed interest is attributed by Griffith to the increased number of black patients and therapists in the mental health system, and the questions they have raised about the importance of race in psychotherapy. Certainly the general rise in Black Consciousness during the 1960s and 1970s has also played a role in the increased concern about racial factors in therapy.

The most frequent question raised is whether a white therapist can effectively help a black patient. Several writers have discussed the problems (and occasionally the possible advantages) that may be present in white therapist/black client relationships, and in other racial pairings, such as black therapist/black client and black therapist/white client (e.g., Gardner, 1971; Jackson, 1973a; Griffith, 1977). Researchers have also addressed the issue of race in counseling and psychotherapy—a sufficient number so that at least three reviewers have recently surveyed research findings (Harrison, 1975; Griffith, 1977; Sattler, 1977).

A majority of the studies examining the effects of counselor or therapist race on the process or outcome of counseling or psychotherapy have utilized nonpatient (usually college student) "clients," most of them seen for only a single interview (Banks, 1972; Banks, Berenson, & Carkhuff, 1967; Cimbolic, 1972; Bryson & Cody, 1973; Grantham,

1973; Ewing, 1974; Gardner, 1972; Carkhuff & Pierce, 1967). The studies have necessarily been largely limited to measures of the process of that interview, although several researchers have included such "outcome" measures as clients' ratings of therapist effectiveness (Cimbolic, 1972), client satisfaction (Grantham, 1973), and clients' views of the helpfulness of the counseling (Ewing, 1974). A few also asked clients whether they would be willing to return for more counseling (e.g., Banks et al., 1967; Cimbolic, 1972; Ewing, 1974).

Only one study (Carkhuff & Pierce, 1967) based on a single-interview situation utilized a patient population. They report significant main effects due to patient and therapist race and social class. They also report a significant patient-by-therapist interaction but do not present findings regarding interaction of patient and therapist race except to say that "*in general,* the patients most similar to the race and social class of the counselor involved *tended* to explore themselves most, while patients most dissimilar tended to explore themselves least" (pp. 633–634; italics added). This study is often cited as evidence for the effects of racial and social class matching, but since the authors do not present means or tests of multiple comparisons, these results are difficult to evaluate. The study's relevance is also questionable because of the use of lay counselors and the reliance on a single interview. The interpretation of the study is further limited by its assumption that patient depth of self-exploration is significantly related to therapy outcome.

Reviewers have come to different conclusions regarding the single-interview analogue studies of counselor and client race. Griffith (1977), while pointing out their shortcomings, nevertheless cites some of them as the major evidence for his conclusion that "the limited research literature does support clinical observations that racial differences have a somewhat negative effect upon psychotherapy . . . racial similarity led to greater self-disclosure and higher ratings of rapport with the therapist" (p. 33). Sattler, on the other hand, states that "the therapist's race is for the most part not a significant variable in affecting the performance and reactions in these types of non-clinical initial interviews" (p. 39). The differences in their conclusions seem to be based on: (a) the inclusion

in Sattler's review of a number of additional studies demonstrating no difference (or even differences in the reverse direction) due to racial matching (e.g., Bryson & Cody, 1973; Ewing, 1974); (b) Griffith's reliance on a very few studies even though he acknowledged their inadequacies; and (c) the different weights they place on the importance of self-exploration measures.

Regardless of the direction of the conclusions, we question the relevance of these single-interview, nontherapy analogues to what actually transpires in psychotherapy. Jones (1977) has recently questioned the generalizability of any of these results, especially in the light of his own finding of the changes on a number of process measures between the first and subsequent therapy sessions.

Three additional studies that utilized nonpatient populations did include more than one counseling session. In two of these (Heffernon & Bruehl, 1971; Owen, 1970), there were no differences in outcome ratings for school children seen in group settings by black or white therapists. There are numerous difficulties with both studies, but most important is the fact that in neither of them were there significant changes on outcome measures for *any* of the groups. In the third study (Williams, 1974), no differences were found in trust and self-disclosure ratings of black students seen either by white professional counselors or by black college student counselors who had only ten hours of training in facilitative skills in counseling. The authors conclude that their finding supports the position that race of the therapist is not a crucial variable, since the white counselors did as well as the black. One might interpret the results in just the reverse fashion: it is impressive that the black peer counselors with so little training could do as well as the white professional counselors. There is no evidence on how much their effectiveness was actually due to race, to similarities in age and life situation, or perhaps even to differences in sex of the counselors. It is not clear, in fact, that they *were* effective, since there was no control group.

Is there any evidence of differences in outcome for patients treated by therapists of their own race and patients treated by therapists of another race? Are white therapists as effective as black therapists in treating black patients? Sattler (1977) cites a number of studies in his generally positive review of the benefits derived by black patients from seeing white therapists. Most of these, however, fail to include a comparison group of black patients seen by black therapists. Lerner (1972), for example, reports on treatment of black and white patients, including a large proportion of lower-class and severely disturbed individuals, by white therapists in an outpatient mental health center. She presents statistical and clinical evidence that white therapists can be equally helpful to black or white lower-class disturbed patients.

Two studies (Goldberg, 1973; Winston, Pardes, & Papernik, 1972) report more improvement in black than in white patients seen by white therapists. Goldberg (1973) found that predominantly lower social class black (but not white) women seen at mental health clinics reported fewer problems following treatment than when they began. The black women, however, also reported more problems pretreatment. Winston et al. (1972) used a global clinical rating scale to assess the functioning of patients treated in individual psychotherapy by white therapists in an inpatient milieu setting. They found that black patients did better than white during their hospitalization and that these differences tended to persist at a one-year follow-up. The authors discuss the difficulty of separating out the effects of the individual therapy from the rest of the treatment program, and point out that most of the nursing staff was black—a significant fact, in the light of the role that nurses play in a patient's treatment.

Warren, Jackson, Nugaris, and Farley (1973) conducted structured interviews with black and white parents in families treated by white therapists in a child guidance clinic. Although this study has been cited (e.g., Griffith, 1977) as showing that black patients perceived therapy as significantly less beneficial than did white patients, the actual findings are less clear. No significant differences were found on eight general categories, including perceived helpfulness of the therapist, though the differences were all in the expected direction. "Significance" was obtained only by a test of the differential of certain selected items. Less equivocal is the finding that 40 percent of the subjects felt that

the therapy had been hampered by the white therapists' failure to understand the patient and by their lack of contact with black people.

The fact that almost no studies have been reported of "real" therapy comparing black and white therapists seriously limits the inferences to be drawn from this literature. In all likelihood, this limitation is due primarily to the shortage of black mental health professionals in many clinical settings. At present, we find only two studies including black therapists, and one of them is an older, impressionistic study.

Jones (1977) has recently completed an exploratory study on the effects of therapist and client race on the process and "short-term outcome" of dynamic, insight-oriented therapy. Black and white female "neurotic" patients were matched on age and education, and therapists were asked to collect data on the first ten sessions of the open-ended treatment. There were no significant differences among the four racial matchings on outcome ratings made by therapists on patients. With N's of three or four per cell it is difficult to conclude much from these findings, but Jones points out that there were not even any trends to suggest better outcome of black clients with black therapists. Differences were found, however, on a number of process measures, suggesting some racial influence. Jones suggests that the lack of significant findings on outcome may have been due partly to the predominance in his patient sample of young, fairly well-educated women (a "good prognosis" group), and partly to self-selection effects in the white therapist volunteers, who were less likely to be biased.

Phillips' impressionistic study (1960) compared the relative effectiveness of black and white therapists with a group of black male students described as disruptive in classes, tardy, uncooperative, and so on. White counselors were clearly less effective than black counselors with these students. It was also reported that the white counselors appeared to have little grasp of how to relate to these black clients.

The Phillips study may illustrate some of the oft-cited complaints that even well-intentioned white therapists may not be very useful to their black patients because of lack of experience with the background and subculture of this population. Clinical writers suggest that it is critical for the effective treatment of black patients that the therapist be able to understand and empathize with their culture, values, and problems. Without such understanding, for example, white therapists may inaccurately label adaptive behavior as pathological.

An interesting example of the effect of experience with a black population comes from the study by Heffernon and Bruehl (1971). Black eighth-grade boys were asked, before their fifth counseling session, whether they preferred to go to counseling or to the school library. All the boys seeing black counselors chose counseling, but only 11 of 23 seeing white counselors did. However, all the boys seeing a particular white counselor chose counseling. He was the only white counselor with substantial previous experience with this black ghetto population.

Another issue has been the role played by the biases and stereotypes about blacks that the white therapist has learned and may still hold. A few researchers have attempted to document the existence of such stereotypes about blacks and other minorities. Bloombaum, Yamamoto, and James (1968) concluded on the basis of structured interviews with 16 practicing therapists that nearly a quarter of their responses about various minority groups were culturually stereotypic, and that over 75 percent of the reponses indicated the presence of at least subltle stereotypes. Yamamoto, James, Bloombaum, and Hattem (1967), looking at what is apparently the same population of white therapists, found that therapists scoring higher on a measure of ethnocentricity were less likely to see their black clients six or more times than they were to see their white clients that often. The lower-scoring therapists, on the other hand, saw proportionately as many black clients as whites six or more times.

The therapist's attitudes may also in part be responsible for the lower attendance and the higher dropout rates that have sometimes been reported for black patients (e.g., Krebs, 1971; Raynes & Warren, 1971; Sue, McKinney, Allen, & Hall, 1974; Rosenthal & Frank, 1958). Krebs (1971), in a post-hoc analysis, also suggests a relationship between the white therapist's failure to discuss racial

issues in the first few sessions and black lower attendance.

It is probable that research that depends on the participation of self-selected therapists may inadvertently underrepresent the prevalence of racial biases that may continue to exist among the population of therapists. Subtle effects of biases may be difficult for the researcher to identify. Such research may require more precise and sophisticated measures of process and outcome than are generally used.

This review of the research on race of the therapist does not provide much definitive information about the effects of race per se or of intra and interracial matching on the outcome of therapy. Although there may be some benefits to communication and to feelings of satisfaction in same-race pairs in a single-interview situations, and some short-term process differences in actual therapy, there are almost no findings with regard to outcome. Several studies suggest that white therapists can be of help to black patients. Whether white therapists are as helpful as or more helpful than black therapists cannot, however, be inferred, since these studies included no control or comparison groups.

More systematic research is needed on the effects of various racial pairings on the outcome of therapy—research that includes such important variables as sex and social class. What are probably even more important than studies of therapist race, however, are studies of the effects of different therapist attitudes toward and understanding of people with backgrounds and experiences different from their own. Future research on interracial therapy should also investigate the effects of specific therapeutic approaches, such as the early discussion of racial issues.

Social Class
Most studies dealing with the social class of patients have reported that lower-class individuals are less likely than those in the middle or upper classes to be accepted for treatment, are less likely to be assigned to intensive psychotherapy, and are more likely to drop out of therapy early.[5] For those who

---

[5]"Social class" has generally been defined in this literature in terms of the Hollingshead Two-Factor Index of

remain in treatment, however, there does not seem to be much evidence of differences in outcome.

Various explanations have been offered for these differences in treatment statistics. Some explanations focus on the lower-class patient: expectations, motivation, manner of dealing with psychological issues, and real-life problems that may make it difficult to attend sessions. Others focus on present treatment approaches and question their appropriateness and relevance for lower-class patients. Emerging from questions about the relevance of current approaches are many new techniques and modifications of traditional approaches (see, e.g., Goldstein, 1973; Gould, 1967; Lorion, 1974; Riessman, Cohen, & Pearl, 1964). All these issues are discussed fully by Garfield and Lorion in Chapters 6 and 22 in this volume (for other reviews see Garfield, 1971; Jones, 1974; Lorion, 1973, 1974; Meltzoff & Kornreich, 1970).

Our primary interest here is in the role of the therapist in the treatment of patients of different social classes. There has been very little research on the influence of the social class background of therapists, and on other therapist characteristics, attitudes, and biases that might be related to the social class treatment differences.

A major emphasis by writers in this area (e.g., Hollingshead & Redlich, 1958; Schaffer & Myers, 1954; Rosenthal & Frank, 1958; Lorion, 1974) has been on the middle-class values and biases of many mental health professionals. Middle-class therapists, it is said (with some support from research), prefer to work with patients like themselves, who share their values and speak their language, with whom they are comfortable and feel they can communicate, and whom they consider "good candidates" for insight therapy.

Some writers have suggested that middle and

upper-class therapists may not be able to gain rapport, to understand and empathize with lower-class patients, or to communicate effectively with them. This has implications for the number of therapists who might be of help to lower-class patients, for most practicing therapists must, by reason of their educational and professional status, be classified as upper-middle or upper class. We do not include here paraprofessionals or lay therapists.

It has also been suggested that perhaps it is not the present social class of the therapist that is relevant, but rather his or her social class of origin. Here the assumption is made that therapists who have had backgrounds and experiences similar to those of their lower-class patients would be more responsive to them, more able to understand them, and thus more able to help them in therapy. According to Henry, Sims, and Spray (1971), there may be a considerable number of therapists who originally came from lower-middle or lower-class backgrounds (about 48 percent of their total sample). Only 6 percent, however, came from Class V, the class of patients who have most often been rejected for treatment (Schaffer & Myers, 1954; Cole, Branch, & Allison, 1962).

There have been two studies that have been concerned with the social class of origin of the therapist. Kandel (1966) studied the issue of therapist and patient social class in a hospital setting in which each patient was assigned to a psychiatric resident who could choose whether to include psychotherapy in his treatment plan. Therapists whose own social class origins were "lower" class (III and IV) saw approximately equal proportions of each class of patients in therapy. Therapists of higher class origins (I and II), however, chose to undertake therapy with 100 percent of their Class I patients, and only 65 percent of their Class V patients. Mitchell and Namenek (1970) found in a large study of psychiatrists and psychologists throughout the United States, that therapists reporting themselves as having lower social class origins also tended more often to report that their "typical" patients were of lower socioeconomic status than did therapists of middle or upper social class origins. Both of these studies suggest, then, that therapists of lower-class origins may more often choose to do therapy with lower-

---

Social Position, based on occupational and educational status. Occasionally, individual measures of education, occupation, or income are used. It is not clear whether different measure are interchangeable and what information may be lost in a composite. There are also questions about the possible out-datedness of Hollingshead's occupational scale. Furthermore, authors in this area of research usually group patients in Classes II and III into "upper" class and Classes IV and V into "lower" class. Lorion (1973) argues for the need to differentiate between Class IV and Class V patients.

class patients (or in the case of Mitchell and Namenek, to be chosen by them). However, these studies investigate only the socioeconomic levels of the participants in therapy, and not whether therapy is more or less successful with particular social class pairings.

The Carkhuff and Pierce study (1967) described in the section on race found significant differences on depth of self-exploration associated with the present social class as well as the race of both the lay counselors and the patients.

There have not yet been any studies, to our knowledge, that investigate the effects of social class similarity of the patient and the therapist on the *outcome* of therapy. It is recognized that not all individuals of lower-class backgrounds have shared similar experiences and values, nor need it be assumed that they can communicate particularly well with each other. However, it seems reasonable to expect that the shared knowledge and experiences that membership in comparable social classes implies might aid communication and rapport and thereby facilitate therapeutic change.

Some therapists, regardless of their own class backgrounds, may be more helpful with lower-class patients than other therapists. Although there has been a fair amount written on this topic, there is little relevant systematic research. In a study by Terestman, Miller, and Weber (1974), therapists who were more successful in treating blue-collar workers were also rated as being more skillful by their teachers. These therapists were considered particularly good at identifying and actively dealing with issues related to class and race differences between themselves and their patients. This is similar to Krebs's (1971) suggestion that therapists seemed to be more successful at keeping black patients in treatment if they dealt with racial issues in the first few sessions. Baum, Felzer, D'Zmura, and Schumaker (1966) found that therapists who had more clinical experience (not necessarily psychiatric) had lower dropout rates with lower-class patients. Their impression was that these therapists were also more secure, more task-oriented, and more flexible, using a broad spectrum of therapeutic approaches. There is clearly a need for systematic research on these clinical impressions.

One study in the psychopharmacology literature

(Howard, Rickels, Mock, Lipman, Covi, & Bauman, 1970) is particularly relevant here. Psychotropic drug (or placebo) administration was accompanied by three 20- to 30-minute supportive sessions. Patients were predominantly lower-class (88% IV or V). Three experienced psychiatrists who had relatively low dropout rates were compared to three others with relatively high dropout rates. Their behavior in initial sessions was observed and rated by other experienced clinicians. The therapists with low dropout rates were seen as more actively involved with their patients and as making more efforts to involve the patients in the treatment process—for example, they were rated significantly higher on using the patient's name, vocal and facial animation, verbal activity, patient-oriented body position, seeming personable, seeming to like patient and to feel comfortable. They were also rated higher on providing interview structure, that is, supportive, interpretative, and focused on both history and current situations. Some of the differences are significant because of the large N's, but the differences are quite small in absolute terms; nevertheless, they present interesting leads concerning therapists' behaviors that might be related to lower-class patients' remaining in treatment. We do not know whether they are related to outcome for those patients who do remain, nor whether the behaviors can be taught. It is the authors' impression that the two therapists with the highest dropout rates "were unable or unwilling to modify their therapeutic styles, expressed by passivity, sitting back, and waiting for the patient to initiate verbal contact" (p. 109).

Some clinical writers have focused on the need to train therapists to use more flexible, active styles with lower-class patients—styles compatible with those behaviors observed in the Howard, Rickels et al. study. Baum and Felzer (1964), reporting on an attempt to train therapists to work more effectively with lower-class patients, also recommended more active reaching out to the patients. Their training focused on both sensitizing the residents to the special needs and expectations of lower-class patients and encouraging them to deal more with their own expectations and resistance. They report that 65 percent of their Class IV and Class V patients continued through 6 or more sessions, a figure that is probably fairly high, although they cite no comparison figures in their setting. Bernard (1965) outlines various ways in which a therapist might be more actively involved early in therapy, and points out the difficulty that many traditionally oriented therapists have in operating in a situation where there are fewer guidelines, a need for greater flexibility, and the possibility of greater "psychic exposure."

As previously noted, it is widely believed that middle-class therapists prefer middle-class patients over lower-class patients. Gottschalk, Mayerson, and Gottlieb (1967), in a study of brief crisis-oriented therapy, did indeed find that their therapists liked Class II and III better than Class IV and V patients. However, therapist liking was not related to outcome; in fact, the lower-class patients in this study changed significantly more on a Psychiatric Morbidity Scale than did upper-class patients. The authors suggest that therapist liking may not be an important variable when treatment is oriented toward specific short-term goals.

The suggestion that therapist attitudes may not be important in specific goal-oriented approaches is buttressed by Sloane et al.'s (1975) finding that therapist liking of the patient was related to outcome for their psychodynamically oriented treatment condition, but not for behavior therapy. Another very interesting finding in the Sloane et al. study was a significant relationship between income level and improvement (on target symptoms) in the psychotherapy condition, with high income patients improving more, and no relationship between income and improvement in the behavior therapy group. Sloane et al. report greater changes for the psychotherapy than for the wait-list patients; however, the means suggest that this finding is entirely due to the higher income group! The behavior therapy group, on the other hand, shows more improvement than wait-list patients for both higher and lower income groups. (This does not hold true for groupings in terms of education, again raising questions about the usual lumping of education and occupation in deriving social class measures.) Thus, in two of the approaches that have been specifically suggested for working with lower-class patients (Lorion, 1974)—brief crisis-oriented therapy and behavior therapy—therapist

attitudes may not play quite as heavy a role as they appear to do in traditional psychodynamically oriented psychotherapy.

There has been some concern voiced, however (Bernard, 1965; Lerner, 1972), that in our effort to try new approaches more relevant for lower social class populations, we do not end up by creating two separate systems of therapy, one for lower-class and one for upper-class patients. It is important to recognize differences among patients in both these groups and to find treatments that meet patients' specific needs. It is also important that we continue to be concerned about therapists' attitudes and styles, and how these affect therapy outcome. Lerner's research (1972, 1973) suggests that one particular therapist attitude, a commitment to democratic values, may be an important factor in enabling a therapist to work successfully with lower-class, severely disturbed patients, using a modified psychoanalytically oriented approach. It is also important to remember that in her study, whose results suggest considerable improvement for lower-class patients, many of the therapists had specifically chosen to work with lower-class, severely disturbed patients and were optimistic about being able to help them.

It may also be important here—as with race—that the therapist have adequate knowledge about the life styles, values, and beliefs of the patients he or she treats.

Thus there may be certain basic characteristics, values, and attitudes of therapists, other than their own social class origins, which may make them good "risks" or good "candidates" for treating lower-class patients. By learning more about these characteristics and what effects they have on the process and outcome of therapy, we may increase our general knowledge of the mechanisms involved in psychotherapeutic change, not just for lower-class people, but for all patients.

Sex

Questions have increasingly been raised in the last few years about the adequacy of treatment for women patients. Unlike the situation in regard to race and social class, there are no indications that women are less frequently accepted for treatment, that they are not assigned to individual therapy, or that they drop out early. If anything, the indications are just the opposite, and it is generally stated that (male) therapists *prefer* to treat women—especially white, middle-class women. One group of researchers (Abramowitz, Roback, Schwartz, Yasuna, Abramowitz, & Gomes, 1976) has, in fact, suggested that the *longer* period of time that women were seen in therapy by male psychology trainees in their study might have been more in the service of the trainee than the patient. The questions that have been raised in terms of inadequacies and biases in treatment have concerned the treatment women *do* receive, often for interminable time periods.

A number of mental health professionals have joined members of the Women's Movement in raising questions about psychotherapy as it is "traditionally" practiced. The main emphasis of their argument has been that mental health institutions and practitioners often, themselves, perpetuate sex-role stereotypes and thus may harm rather than help their patients by training them to conform to narrowly defined roles and adjust to unhealthy life situations. The focus of these criticisms has generally been on traditional psychoanalytically oriented therapists, the vast majority of whom are men.

Writers in this area have ranged widely in their views about the importance of the sex of the therapist. Some (e.g., Chesler, 1971) doubt that any male therapist, growing up in this society, could be helpful to a woman. Other writers sympathetic with the feminist perspective suggest that while some male therapists may be useful, in today's society it may be particularly advantageous for a woman patient to be treated by a woman therapist, who may serve as a role model, facilitate expression of feelings, and communicate understanding and empathy (e.g., Brodsky, 1973; Kronsky, 1971). That there may be particular circumstances when a female rather than a male therapist is the more appropriate choice is pointed out by Rawlings and Carter (1977) and by Carter (1971). The possible advantages to a given patient of having male and female therapists at different times, or together as co-therapists, are suggested by Fodor (1974a, 1974b); Lazarus (1974); Rice and Rice (1973). However, Barrett, Berg, Eaton,

and Pomeroy (1974) warn that such co-therapist pairs might simply reinforce stereotypes of male-female relationships.

This focus on the importance of the sex of the therapist in psychotherapy with women has led to a number of recent studies. We have reviewed the five available studies on the effects of therapist-patient sex-matching on the outcome of therapy, a few particularly relevant studies on process, and two studies on alternative approaches to therapy with women, and we agree with previous reviewers (e.g., Meltzoff & Kornreich, 1970; Tanney & Birk, 1976; Johnson, 1977) that few conclusions can be drawn at this time.

Scher (1975) found no significant interactions due to client and counselor sex on client and counselor ratings of symptom relief and satisfaction with treatment. Persons, Persons, and Newmark (1974), using undergraduate peers as therapists, reported that females are more responsive to female therapists and males to male therapists in terms of helpful characteristics that they listed following therapy.

Geer and Hurst (1976), in one of the few behavior therapy studies in this area, report a significant therapist sex/patient sex interaction, following systematic desensitization of test anxiety. They reported that a male counselor did better with female subjects than a female counselor did, and the female counselor seemed to do much better with males than females. However, their interpretation of their statistical analysis is questionable, and since there was only one counselor of each sex, no generalization regarding the effect of sex-pairing is warranted.

Although Kirshner et al. (in press) report two significant triple-order interactions among patient sex, therapist sex, and therapist experience, the findings appear to be little more than could be expected by chance. Cartwright and Lerner (1963), two of the earliest researchers to concern themselves with sex-matching, reported greater improvement (on a composite of four therapist ratings) for same-sex pairs in which the therapist is experienced and opposite-sex pairs in which the therapist is inexperienced.

There are also a few studies that used "intermediate" outcome measures—for example, satisfaction with particular therapy sessions. Hill's

(1975) counseling center clients who saw female counselors reported more satisfaction after the second interview than did clients who were treated by male counselors; however, there were no significant interactions due to sex-matching on this variable. Orlinksy and Howard, (Howard, Orlinsky, & Hill, 1970; Orlinsky & Howard, 1975, 1976) found that female outpatients seen by female therapists reported feeling more satisfaction across a number of interviews and had more "helpful experiences" than did women seen by male therapists. Categorizing these patients in terms of age and marital and parental status, Orlinsky and Howard (1976) found that the major impact of therapist sex was on the young and unattached, and on the depressed women patients; for these groups, the experience with women therapists seemed most supportive and satisfying.

Three researchers have reported effects due to therapist sex or sex-matching on patient expression of feelings and self-disclosure or self-exploration. Conclusions are difficult to draw since results reported include higher scores on one or another of these variables for same-sex dyads (Hill, 1975), for opposite-sex dyads (Brooks, 1974), and for dyads containing a female as client or counselor (Fuller, 1963; Brooks, 1974). Interpretations are further complicated by interactions with counselor experience (Hill, 1975; Fuller, 1963) and perceived status (Brooks, 1974). In addition, the Brooks study is limited by its nonpatient sample and the fact that the significant effects were found only in the first three minutes of the interview.

All of these studies had been carried out in clinical settings using fairly traditional therapy approaches. One of the consequences of the feminist critiques of such traditional treatment has been the development of alternative approaches and suggestions for the modification of existing techniques. Alternatives included feminist therapy (see Marecek and Kravetz, 1977), counseling centers to handle crises unique to women, and self-help groups (Glaser, 1976). Some writers have also viewed consciousness-raising groups as alternatives to therapy (see Kirsch, 1974; Kravetz, 1976). In addition, a number of women therapists have described modifications of existing techniques, including behavioral (Fodor, 1974a; Jakubowski,

1977) and psychoanalytically oriented (Kronsky, 1971; Menaker, 1974), for dealing with specific problems of women.

Research is just beginning on these approaches, especially in the area of assertiveness training for women (e.g., Wolfe & Fodor, in press; Linehan, Goldfried, & Goldfried, 1977). Linehan et al. (1977) investigated the effects of sex of therapist on the outcome of assertiveness training for women. Women volunteering for assertiveness training were screened for lack of assertiveness and were then randomly assigned to a number of treatment and control groups, half to a male therapist and half to a female therapist. The authors found no significant effects due to the sex of the therapist on any of their outcome measures. They suggest that any effects of therapist bias may have been obscured by the predetermined goal of facilitating assertive behavior.

One further study has relevance to issues raised by the Women's Movement. Johnson (1976), in an exploratory study, compared outcomes for women being seen in the Philadelphia Feminist Therapy Collective with women in the same age and educational range being seen in a more traditional clinic or private practice setting (Luborsky, in preparation). No significant differences were found between the two groups on severity of pretreatment complaints, degree of target complaint change, and satisfaction with therapy. Feminist therapy clients were seen in groups, by female therapists, for an average of four months; patients in the other setting were seen individually, by male therapists, in traditional psychodynamically oriented treatment, for an average of 10 months. Johnson emphasizes that the short-term group therapy in the collective setting appeared as effective, as evaluated by the clients, as the lengthier individual therapy in the clinic or private practice setting.

A major problem in many of the studies that have looked at the role played by therapist sex is that most of them were not originally designed with this variable in mind and are therefore fraught with such inadequacies as lack of random assignment, confounding with other variables, inadequate attention to relevant outcome measures, and so on.

Because there are so many problems inherent in

most of the studies investigating effects of sex-matching on both the process and outcome of psychotherapy, it is difficult to make any simple summary statement. There is very little evidence to support any conclusions of the effects of same-sex versus opposite-sex pairs on outcome. Turning to process, results on expression of feelings and self-disclosure are complicated by interactions with experience level, status of "therapist," and so on. One interesting hint, based on an analysis in one study (Orlinksy & Howard, 1976) and the client populations used in two others (Persons et al., 1974; Hill, 1975), is that it may primarily be young female patients who find that working with female therapists enables them to express more feelings and to experience more satisfaction with therapy.

As in the areas of race and social class, it may well be the attitudes and values of the therapist that are of primary importance rather than his or her sex per se (Waskow, 1976). A number of authors (e.g., Rice & Rice, 1973; Kronsky, 1971; Jackson, 1973b) have stressed the need for greater general sensitivity on the part of therapists to sex-role issues and the need for therapists to acquire more knowledge about the psychology of women and the role of social and environmental factors in women's problems. Several (Stevens, 1971; Brodsky, 1977; Barrett et al., 1974) emphasize the importance of having therapists make explicit their own values in this area.

Although there has been a fair amount of research on clinicians' concepts of mental health for men and women and sex-role attitudes (Neulinger, Stein, Schillinger, & Welkowitz, 1970; Broverman, Broverman, Clarkson, Rosenkrantz, & Vogel, 1970; Fabrikant, 1974; Stricker, 1977; Brown & Hellinger, 1975; Maslin & Davis, 1975), there have not, to our knowledge, been any studies of the impact of sex-role attitudes on the outcome of therapy.

The effects of therapist sex-role attitudes may not be found on some of the standard measures used to evaluate outcome. Klein (1976) has outlined some of the sexist biases present in these measures. Furthermore, some of the influences of sex-role attitudes might not be manifest at termination, but may become evident later. For example, relatively "biased" and "nonbiased" therapists might effectuate the same amount of symptom relief and "satisfaction" in the short run, but the effects of a therapist's encouraging autonomy and role choices in a woman and enhancing her basic sense of self-esteem may become clearer as time passes and new stresses emerge. This perspective suggests the need for relevant outcome measures and for an adequate follow-up period in future studies in this area.

Summary of Demographic Variables

Our survey of the literature relevant to the issue of matching patient and therapist according to race, social class, and sex permits us to draw no firm conclusions about the influence of such matching on the outcome of psychotherapy. This is due largely to the paucity of research systematically investigating the effects of such matching on the *outcome* of therapy.

Research does suggest that the attitudes and biases of the therapist—for example, in regard to blacks, lower-class people, and women—may be more important than the demographic variables themselves. Evidence on this issue, while never clear-cut, has become increasingly difficult to secure because of the growing public awareness of and concern with these questions and the desire of therapists to portray themselves as free of bias. Perhaps the most fruitful research procedure is the investigation of therapists' actual behavior in the therapy situation rather than their answers to questionnaires.

There are intimations that the therapist's experience with a particular population may be very important. It is not clear, however, whether experience alone necessarily counteracts initial biases, especially those that are interwoven with theories of psychopathology.

Researchers and commentators have recommended that the therapist should have more specific knowledge about the particular group of patients with whom he or she is working. Specific suggestions have stressed the potential usefulness of obtaining concrete information about various subcultures in our society and about the psychology of women, as well as increasing the therapist's sensitivity to and awareness of these issues. Perhaps future research should include measures of a therapist's sensitivity and knowledge relevant to the particular patient population being studied.

The importance of a therapist's dealing early in therapy with issues of the therapist-patient differences has also been stressed by clinicians, and has been hinted at by researchers' post-hoc analyses of data. This seems related to another theme that has emerged in some of the studies: the desirability of therapist flexibility and active participation in therapy.

There have been several suggestions in the literature on both social class and sex that the attitudes and demographic characteristics of the therapist may not play as large a role in therapeutic approaches that are brief and behaviorally or crisis oriented, and in which goals are clearly defined in the beginning.

Finally, there are some suggestions that therapist demographic characteristics and attitudes may be particularly salient for certain subpopulations, for example, for young female patients in the case of the sex of the therapist.

One of the major difficulties in drawing conclusions from the research in this area is the lack of studies specifically designed to investigate the effects of these variables. It is important that design of future studies assure comparable populations assigned to therapists with different characteristics and/or attitudes. Analyses of outcome data must also take into account the possibility of biased samples resulting from selective assignments and differential dropout rates.

Other problems relate to the issue of outcome evaluation itself, and the fact that outcome measures are rarely chosen for their relevance to the hypotheses that are being tested. The fact that the effects of these variables are sometimes found on process measures but not on outcome measures may also be related to the crudeness of the outcome measurements that are often employed.

Similarity, Dissimilarity, and Compatibility

In the broadest sense, all matching research implies that one is attempting to discover combinations of therapists and patients of an optimal degree of similarity and dissimilarity on a wide array of psychological dimensions that will enhance the probability of positive therapeutic changes in the patients. The difficulty of the task resides in the detective work required for discovering that "magic" amount of similarity, dissimilarity, and compatibility as well as the appropriate dimensions on which obtaining similarity is most crucial for enhancing positive therapeutic change. Researchers have particularly focused on three broad dimensions in their studies of similarity: personality factors, cognitive factors, and values. In each area, the same kinds of arguments are offered by various investigators to defend their view of the requisite amount of similarity for enhancing therapy outcome.

Some have argued that substantial similarity is required for the therapist to be able to empathize with and understand the concerns of the patient. Others say dissimilarity is required to heighten the therapist's objectivity. Still others propose a curvilinear relationship between similarity and outcome. In this view, a positive therapeutic outcome requires enough similarity so that the therapist can adequately "tune in" to the problems of the patient, but not so much that the therapist overidentifies with the patient. Finally, there are those who argue that an optimal combination of therapist and patient may not require them to possess similar characteristics, but that whatever differences do exist between them must be compatible ones. To make the issue even more complex, the compatibility argument often includes the notion that it may encompass similarity between the therapy participants on some dimensions and dissimilarity on others.

Research in the similarity area has employed a vast array of personality instruments, four separate cognitive variables, and one or two efforts at establishing optimal combinations of therapists and patients on the basis of values. In reviewing these studies, we consider the A-B Scale separately because of the extensive body of research associated with it. We also consider two studies that have applied factor analysis to matching on multiple variables.

Personality Factors

To the degree that the personality of the therapist contributes significantly to therapy outcome, it does not operate in a vacuum. The therapist's personality interacts with that of the patient. The interaction of their personalities affects the way in which treatment is administered as well as the receptivity of the patient to the treatment. The question arises, therefore, as to what combination of personalities fosters positive therapeutic change, and what combinations hinder it.

To date, the research evidence gathered on this issue proffers us little precise information. The disparity in results is partly traceable to the varied methodologies employed in the "similarity" studies, and these methodologies reveal, as well, differing degrees of scientific adequacy.

Personality similarity has been established in these studies on the basis of several personality instruments. Different results have been obtained not only with different instruments, but also with the same instrument scored in different ways (e.g., MMPI). Further, the results are based on differing measures of outcome, including a composite measure of patient and therapist ratings, supervisor's ratings of patient progress, patient ratings only, therapist ratings only, and independent ratings of therapist's notes of the therapy sessions. The findings are just as variable. Some investigators have found positive relationships between therapist-patient similarity and outcome; others have found a negative relationship. Still others found no relationship at all between similarity and improvement.

The MMPI studies began with a positive finding that could not be replicated. Carson and Heine (1962) studied five groups of dyads, made up of medical students and outpatients, representing decreasing degrees of MMPI profile similarity. They found a curvilinear relationship between degree of similarity of MMPI profiles (shape alone considered) and successful outcome. Dyads of medium similarity had the best therapeutic outcomes as measured by a composite measure of patient satisfaction, therapist judgment, symptomatic relief, and ratings of work adjustment and interpersonal relations.

Using a very similar methodology, Lichtenstein (1966) was unable to replicate the finding. Carson also tried to replicate his own finding (Carson & Llewellyn, 1966) but was unsuccessful. He concluded that failure to replicate was probably due to the crudeness of both the similarity measures and the outcome measures used.

Wogan (1970) matched therapist and patient on pre-therapy factor scores derived from selected MMPI scales. In general, he found that therapist-patient similarity was a detriment to therapy, decreasing both the patient's rating of progress and his or her liking for the therapist.

Swensen (1967) scored the MMPI profiles of both participants to determine their respective placements on the Dominance and Love quadrants of the Leary (1957) Interpersonal Circle. He found that improvement proportions were higher when dyad members were complementary on the DOM dimension (therapist dominant, patient submissive, or vice versa) and similar on the LOV dimension.

Another instrument that has been employed in a number of similarity studies is the Myer-Briggs Type Indicator (MBTI). This instrument is based on the Jungian theroy of psychological types and it measures perceptual tendencies on four bi-polar scales (judgment vs. perception, sensation vs. intuition, thinking vs. feeling, extraversion vs. introversion).

The few studies that have employed the MBTI found limited evidence of a relationship between therapist-client similarity and remaining in therapy. When similarity was considered in relation to improvment, virtually no relationship was found (Mendelsohn & Geller, 1963, 1965, 1967).

Studies using other personality measures seem to show that dissimilarity may be more important for patient improvement than similarity (Bare, 1967; Lesser, 1961).

As indicated, one viewpoint holds that an optimal combination of therapist and patient may not require them to possess similar personality traits; what may be essential, however, is that whatever differences exist between the participants should be compatible ones. This assumption underlies another group of studies that have attempted to discover predictive optimal combinations of therapists and patients on the basis of interpersonal compatibility. In these studies, the Fundamental Interpersonal Relations Orientation Scale (FIRO-B) was used to form the therapeutic dyads.

The FIRO-B studies reveal a very modest relationship—for female patients only—between interpersonal compatibility and therapeutic improvement (Gassner, 1970; Mendelsohn & Rankin, 1969; Sapolsky, 1965). Since Gassner's (1970) patients did not improve, the issue of the relationship between compatible dyads and patient improvement became moot. Mendelsohn and Rankin (1969) found a relationship between compatibility and outcome only for those dyads containing female clients. Sapolsky (1965) developed compatibility dyads with three psychiatric residents and 25 female inpatients. The overall index of compatibility (K index) was related to supervisor's ratings of patient improvement. The results are made problematic, however, by problems with the K index. As Berzins (1977) points out, two of the three scales can take on only positive values while the third scale (Originator compatibility) can have both positive and negative values. Consequently, the K index includes scales of noncomparable units.

It has yet to be demonstrated that forming combinations of therapists and patients on the basis of similar or compatible personal or interpersonal traits produces a significant influence on therapeutic outcome. Although widely varying methodologies of various degrees of scientific adequacy have been employed in these studies, and quite divergent personality characteristics have served as the basis for forming therapist-patient combinations, weak relationships between similarity and compatibility variables and therapy outcome prevail. If there is any merit at all to the notion that personality similarity or compatibility may enhance outcome, the relationships are quite complex.

Therapist Characteristics Matched with Patient Diagnosis: The A-B Scale

One of the best-known and most tantalizing efforts to match therapists and patients on the basis of the therapist's personality has been the use of the Whitehorn and Betz A-B Scale. Whitehorn and Betz differentiated the Phipps Clinic therapists working with schizophrenic patients, labeling those who were most successful with such patients as "A's" and those least successful as "B's." In preliminary attempts to discern the personality and style differences between the two groups, Whitehorn and Betz described the A's in part as characterized by active, personal participation and the ability to establish a trusted relationship. The

B's were in part characterized by passive permissiveness, the use of interpretation, and an instructional style (Whitehorn & Betz, 1957, 1960).

Whitehorn and Betz subsequently reported that the A's and B's responded to the Strong Vocational Interest Blank (SVIB) with significantly different patterns on four career scales (Whitehorn & Betz, 1960). The A's were interested in the occupations of Lawyer and Certified Public Accountant and not interested in those of Printer and Mathematics/Physical Science Teacher; for B's the pattern of career interests was reversed. After some refinement of the data, Whitehorn and Betz derived a 23-item scale from the SVIB (Whitehorn & Betz, 1960; Betz, 1962). The most striking generalization from this scale was that A's tended to reject manual and mechanical activities, and to show some interest in manifesting leadership, and that B's were interested in manual and mechanical activities.

In 1962, a study by McNair, Callahan, and Lorr seemed to expand the original findings, suggesting that with outpatients in VA clinics, B therapists apparently had better results than A's. Although the exact diagnostic breakdown in this study was not known, about 80 percent of the patients treated in such clinics are usually described as neurotics. These findings led to the development of the "interaction hypothesis," that is, A therapists were best with schizophrenics and B therapists with neurotics. A-therapists paired with schizophrenic or schizoid patients, and B-therapists paired with neurotic patients have been referred to as complementary (or "compatible") dyads. Although many studies of the interaction hypothesis assumed that complementary dyads were more therapeutic than "incompatible" dyads, McNair et al. were much more conservative about the implications of their 1962 study.

Nevertheless, their work launched numerous A-B interaction studies of questionable methodological soundness. Frequently, such studies failed to take into account other therapist qualities that might override the A-B properties. Much of the research used analogue studies whose findings cannot be assumed to generalize to the clinical setting. Further, institutional orientations might emphasize attitudes that would influence therapists' responses to the A-B scales or might affect evaluations of outcome. As increased reliance was placed on drug therapy of schizophrenics, the possibility also arose that the potency of drug effects would outweigh the impact of therapist A-B factors. Finally, it is possible that changes in society have changed the meaning of the responses to the various items.

A series of reviews attempted to sort out the seemingly contradictory and inconsistent data. Carson's 1967 survey considered the typology as "a possible critical variable," but acknowledged the conflicting findings. Razin (1971) pointed out methodological flaws and discouraged further correlational personological studies, but felt that the clinical studies of the effect of A-B differences on outcome were still worth pursuing. He also formulated the description of A's to include such qualities as openness to unusual perceptions, flexibility, ability to communicate to schizoid patients, and acceptance of bizarre behavior and experiences.

Chartier's (1971) review focused on analogue studies, and although he was more critical than Razin, he reached similar conclusions. His general feeling was that analogue studies had extrapolated from "tenuous assumptions" (Chartier, 1971, p. 31), but he did recommend continued clinical studies of the A-B interaction effect.

A 1974 review by May was even more skeptical, basing some of its conclusions on a close examination of the original Whitehorn and Betz data. May pointed to several factors that rendered the A-B differences in the original studies less clear-cut than reported, such as the possibility of bias in the evaluation of outcome, a possibility of contamination of psychotherapy effects by insulin shock effects, the incorrect classification of some of the therapists, and the disappearance of differences between A's and B's in 5-year outcome follow-up (May, 1974).

Stephens, Shaffer, and Zlotowitz (1975) constructed a new and improved A-B Scale, but their results with even this refined instrument were less than impressive. They concluded that although under certain circumstances male therapists' A-B scores may be related to short-term improvement, there is little evidence that "high scoring therapists" (A's) are more likely to have a favorable long-range impact on schizophrenics.

In his most recent review, Razin (1977) gives a detailed analysis of A-B research of the late 1960s and early 1970s in the areas of outcome, process, and personality research, examining both clinical studies and analogue research. The research has become increasingly rigorous and increasingly disappointing, with inpatients yielding almost no support for the interaction hypothesis, outpatients yielding weak support under special circumstances, and process studies providing conflicting findings.

In those studies most germane to the use of A-B as a basis for matching therapists and inpatients, there is virtually none that shows A-B differences or "interaction hypothesis" effects with inpatients. A recent rigorous study not available for Razin's review (Tuma, May, Yale, & Forsythe, 1978) concluded that the A-B dimension made no significant contribution to the effective treatment of schizophrenics, whether by psychotherapy, psychotherapy plus drugs, or drugs alone.

Of the A-B studies on outpatients reported by Razin, four showed no A-B differences in outcome. Three found support for B effectiveness, but the findings were limited in statistical magnitude or generalizability.

Thus, a wide range of research over the past decade on the A-B variable reveals very little support for the hypothesis that the A-B Scale has utility in predicting long-term outcome, and there is inconsistent and weak support for the possibility that the A-B Scale might predict short-term outcome. Nevertheless, research in this area continues.

One of the more imaginative efforts is the as yet unpublished work of Dent, who has argued that the A-B Scale is not a true scale and should be called an A-B Predictor. He found correlations of items within particular A-B scales, and identified these as "A-B Clusters." Dent postulated that some of the clusters might have different *meanings* for different groups (*multisemantic*), and that other clusters might have a common meaning for personality (*manifest scale*). Dent thought that a predictor containing both multisemantic and manifest clusters might reverse its meaning across various groups of subjects. Studies based on his hypothesis indicated that for psychiatrists as a whole the "A-B Predictor" tends to have little meaning—that whatever meaning it has for hospital psychiatrists ("somatically" oriented) tends to be reversed for nonhospital psychiatrists ("psychosocially" oriented). Subsequently, Dent devised his own predictors and scales, and the predictor that he derived for therapists treating neurotics did predict success in a replication study with delinquent neurotics. He also obtained some evidence of validity of a predictor for the treatment of schizophrenia without drugs. However, it is premature to draw conclusions about the utility of these new predictors pending further testing.

Cognitive Similarity

The rationale for matching therapists and patients on cognitive variables rests upon the assumption that successful communication between two persons is dependent on a similarity in the cognitive dimensions employed by each to describe their experiences (Carr, 1970). The five studies reviewed here are difficult to compare, for they consider four different cognitive variables as the basis for matching therapeutic dyads, measured by different instruments. Three of the studies indicate that cognitive similarity is important for positive therapeutic outcome (Carr, 1970; McLachlan, 1972, 1974), while the other two suggest that cognitive *dissimilarity* enhances outcome (Landfield, 1971; Edwards & Edgerly, 1970).

Carr (1970) hypothesized that compatibility between therapist and patient in terms of level of conceptual differentiation (measured by his own Interpersonal Discrimination Test) would enhance outcome. In his study of neurotic patients treated by fourth-year medical students, he found that patients whose initial differentiation scores were closer to those of their therapists showed more improvement than patients whose initial differentiation scores were more discrepant from their therapists.

In McLachlan's study (1972), five therapists conducted group therapy with 11 groups made up of 8 to 13 alcoholic inpatients. Groups were formed (for the purpose of statistical analysis) on the basis of conceptual levels (CL), measured by scoring free responses to six topics contained in the Paragraph Completion Test. Patients with high CL congruence with their therapists showed better patient-rated improvement scores than did those in incongruent pairings. No differences between the

groups, however, were found in terms of therapist and co-therapist ratings of patient improvement.

In a follow-up study of the same patients, McLachlan (1974) found that 70 percent of the patients who were matched to their therapist in terms of conceptual level continued to be abstinent a year after treatment. Of the mismatched patients, 50 percent were similarly abstinent a year later.

Edwards and Edgerly (1970) studied the relationship of cognitive congruence to outcome of brief counseling. Cognitively congruent dyads were established by means of ratings of 12 concepts on scales drawn from the Evaluative dimension of the Semantic Differential. High, medium, and low congruence groups were formed. Outcome was measured by patient change scores on the Evaluative dimension and on the Dymond Adjustment Index. The results suggested that patients in the low congruence dyads changed the most. Unfortunately, the confounding of level of congruence with particular therapists made the interpretation of these findings difficult.

Landfield (1971) conducted an extensive study of therapist-patient similarity in personal constructs which was grounded in the theoretical assumptions of George Kelly's personal construct theory. Eight therapists (seven males) and the college clinic patients they worked with were given the Role Construct Repertory Test to assess personal constructs. The research findings suggest that therapy outcomes were better when there was initial dissimilarity in the content of the constructs of the therapy participants, when their constructs converged during the course of therapy, and when patients shifted their conception of their present "selves" toward their therapists' "ideal selves." Therapist-patient initial similarity in content of personal constructs tended, surprisingly, to evoke negative evaluations of the patients by the therapists. The results seem to suggest that in addition to some minimal degree of shared perspective, therapeutic communication and perhaps successful outcome require initial differences in the participants' content of constructs.

Thus, the results in the five studies indicate that *similarity* on two structural variables—"conceptual differentiation" and "conceptual level"—seems to enhance therapy outcome, while *dissimilarity* on the other two, cognitive content variables—"cognitive congruence" and "personal constructs"—seems related to improvement. The question arises as to whether there is any connection between the two variables for which similarity is important for outcome, and between the two variables for which dissimilarity is important for outcome.

Interestingly, the study by Carr and the studies by McLachlan consider cognitive variables that emphasize differentiation of cognitive structure. This is a notion not unlike cognitive complexity. Some support for the linking of these two variables comes from the fact that Carr's Interpersonal Discrimination Test correlates substantially with McLachlan's CL level (Carr, 1965). Both variables focus on the *complexity of perception* as measured by the number of discriminations or alternatives that are perceived in the environment. McLachlan's high CL person shows substantial autonomy and is one who perceives numerous alternatives, while Carr's highly differentiated person is one who perceives a great number of interpersonal discriminations. It may well be that *similarity in the complexity of cognitive structure* facilitates communication for therapist and patient by allowing participants to consider the patient's problems, as well as their potential solution, at similar levels of complexity. By contrast, incongruent pairings on cognitive complexity variables conjoin two individuals who are literally on different "wavelengths" (Posthuma & Carr, 1975).

The studies of Edwards and Edgerly (1970) and Landfield (1971), although not free of methodological problems, indicate that content-based dissimilarity may produce better therapeutic outcomes than similarity.

Dissimilarity in cognitive content may well be the motive force for change in therapy. The different perspective of the therapist may serve to clarify the perspective of the patient while providing a reference point for the directions in which the patient needs to change. Support for this hypothesis is given by the findings in the Landfield study (1971) that showed positive therapy outcome related to a convergence of the constructs of therapy participants, particularly when patients shifted their conception of themselves to conform with the therapists' "ideal selves."

The results of these few studies suggest that outcome in therapy may be enhanced if therapy participants are cognitively similar concerning the level of differentiation in their constructs, but dissimilar with respect to the content of these constructs. This hypothesis, however, requires systematic research exploration.

Similarity in Values

The significance of values for psychotherapy has been researched empirically for the last two decades. Although the actual number of studies is not large, these studies have served to challenge the myth that psychotherapy is a value-free enterprise. The early studies tended to show not only that therapists communicate their values to patients, but also that therapists' and observers' judgments of patients' improvement in psychotherapy are correlated with the extent to which patients appear to adopt the values of their therapists and perhaps of the mental health community (Parloff, Goldstein, & Iflund, 1960; Parloff, Iflund, & Goldstein, 1957; Rosenthal, 1955).

This "convergence of values" phenomenon, which has been found in other studies as well (Beutler, Pollack, & Jobe, 1977; Petoney, 1966; Welkowitz, Cohen, & Ortmeyer, 1967), is much like the "convergence of constructs" found to be important in the cognitive dissimilarity studies. The findings in both these areas suggest that treatment is experienced as effective when the therapy participants begin with somewhat differing perspectives but close the gap as therapy progresses. The significance of the similarity-dissimilarity bi-polarity for therapy may be that both are necessary at different points in the therapy.

No studies are available in which similar and dissimilar therapy dyads were established on the basis of values at the beginning of therapy and subsequently related to therapy outcome. A few studies have conducted a post-hoc analysis of the relationship of value similarity and patient improvement. Beutler, Johnson, Neville, Elkins, and Jobe (1975) found no relationship between attitude similarity between therapist and patient and patient improvement. Pettit, Pettit, and Welkowitz (1974) found that complementarity of values (patients submissive to authority matched with therapists high in autonomy) was related to lower-income patients' remaining in therapy. No data are available regarding therapy outcome.

This paucity of empirical research on value similarity and therapy outcome belies the importance of the hypothesis that relates to the two dimensions. Values seem to be an inherent part of the therapy process and therefore appear to be necessarily affected by the outcome of therapy. Understanding the particular relationships that link the values of therapist and patient seems to us a priority area of research.

Matching on Multiple, Miscellaneous Psychological Variables

In an effort to obtain greater methodological rigor and precision, two investigators have applied the methods of factor analysis to the problem of therapist-patient matching. By such means, these investigators hope to derive a prediction equation(s) that by including the weighted combination of the most relevant variables for matching patients and therapists will be able to enhance the probability of a successful therapy outcome. These variables have included a vast array of psychological and personality variables. In these studies, however, only the methodology—as opposed to the results—is generalizable. As the investigators of both studies point out, this emerges from the fact that both the development of the prediction equations and their experimental validation took place in a single institutional setting.

Dougherty (1976) combined therapists and patients on 11 psychological variables derived from the Omnibus Personality Inventory, the Personal Orientation Inventory, MMPI, FIRO-B (and F) and the Differential Emotion Scale. In addition patients were given the Tendency Toward Psychosis Scale, while therapists were given the Therapist Orientation Inventory and the A-B Scale.

After five prediction equations were obtained and cross-validated, they were experimentally validated on six groups of therapeutic dyads: one experimental group for which optimal outcome was predicted, a second experimental group for which minimal therapeutic gain was predicted, and two control groups each for both the optimal and minimal match groups that controlled for patient type and therapist type. The mean differences in outcome, as measured by therapist satisfaction ratings, in the comparision of the minimal matched group both with its own control groups and with the optimally matched group, were significant. The clinical significance of these findings suggested that these prediction equations were only moderately helpful in developing optimal matches of therapists and patients.

The most extensive effort at systematic matching of therapists and patients was conducted by Berzins (1974, 1977)—the Indiana Matching Project. The project represents a four-year effort to develop a formula for combining therapists and patients in a college clinic that specializes in short-term, crisis-intervention oriented psychotherapy. Measures were obtained on four interpersonal roles that patients typically adopt in their interactions (avoidance of others; turning against self; dependency on others; turning toward others and self), through factor analytic and rational procedures. These procedures yielded eight patient predictor scores addressing the four roles. Pre-therapy assessment of these variables was conducted on 751 (391 males, 360 females) patients. Therapist predictor scores for the ten therapists (six men) were derived from their responses to the Personality Research Form. These predictor scores focused on relatively stable personality characteristics that included impulse expression, ambition, acceptance, dominance, caution, and abasement.

Patients were randomly assigned to the ten project therapists. Over the course of the study each project therapist saw between 29 and 145 patients (mean = 75.1) for at least three weeks. After the last therapy session, therapist and patient completed 13 short post-therapy rating scales (seven therapist ratings and six patient ratings). The ratings were intercorrelated and factor analyzed.

In general, the outcome-enhancing pairs appeared to be those that provided a complementarity of therapist and patient needs. The pairs that seemed most facilitative of positive therapy outcome included submissive, inhibited, passive patients with dominant, expressive, structure-offering therapists and occasionally vice versa. This generalization is qualified, however, by an interesting sex difference. With respect to the role orientation of turning toward others and self, the finding on complementarity applied to the dyads containing the male patients, whereas the dyads consisting of female patients with male therapists showed that *similarity of needs* facilitated outcome (Berzins, 1977).

The Indiana Matching Project represents a practical demonstration of the feasibility of developing an effective matching scheme that, once in operation, can be used by nonprofessionals to assign patients to therapists. Assignment by this means, however, can be made problematical by the researchers' efforts to match poor therapists with suitable patients. For example, the "rejecting" therapist cannot be "utilized" but only "neutralized." It was found that rejecting therapists performed "better" with male patients who were low rather than high on measures of interpersonal anxiety. It had previously been found that patients showing "low interpersonal anxiety" typically showed little benefit from treatment offered by any Indiana clinic therapist. Therefore, Berzins argues, even if "rejecting" therapists generally obtain lower levels of improvement than accepting therapists, their future performance should be *less poor* when their patients are low in interpersonal anxiety. This kind of assignment may tend to reduce the harmful effects of the inadequate therapist, but it does not do much for the patient who characteristically seems to benefit least from the clinic's efforts.

Although the number of such studies is as yet too small to judge their value adequately, the Berzins study strongly suggests that factor analysis as applied to the matching problem may have great practical as well as theoretical significance. The implications for staff selection and training are clear.

Overview of Therapist-Patient Matching

To summarize the second major section of the chapter, the area of matching in which the most positive findings have been obtained concerns the patient preparation programs that essentially in-

duce congruence in the therapy role expectations of the participants. Some positive relationships between induced congruence of expectations and changes on some measures of therapy outcome were found in all five outcome studies reviewed. Despite the variety of methodologies, the studies do suggest that some orientation of the patient to the nature of therapy—and perhaps, of the therapist to the special needs of the patient—tends to enhance the course and outcome of psychotherapy.

The positive findings in the area of cognitive similarity also give promise that this may be a fruitful area in which to attempt the matching of therapists and patients for psychodynamic therapy. The results indicate the possible importance of differentiating between cognitive content and cognitive structure in any hypotheses regarding an optimal degree of similarity between therapist and patient.

The substantial body of literature on the use of various personality factors as a basis for matching therapists and patients has thus far yielded a parade of weak and frequently tortuous findings. Yet, the findings are such that one can neither totally part with the matching hypothesis nor be assured that it represents a fruitful area of research.

Experimental studies in the area of value similarity are virtually nonexistent. The naturalistic studies in this area suggest a "convergence" phenomenon, which relates positive therapeutic change to patients' adopting the values of their therapists. Perhaps an optimal degree of intial dissimilarity in values between the participants may represent one basis for matching.

In the demographic areas, there are also very few experimental outcome studies relating matched and unmatched dyads to therapy outcome. From the strict perspective of matching, whether therapist-patient combinations predictive of positive outcome can be formed on the basis of race, social class, or sex is still a relatively untested issue. However, there is reason to believe that a crucial variable in the demographic areas is not whether patients are treated by a same-race, same-class, or same-sex therapist, but rather whether the attitudes and experiences of therapists are such that they allow therapists to establish rapport and empathize with patients and facilitate their therapy.

The two studies that have applied factor analytic techniques to the problem of matching provide some positive findings but none that can be generalized beyond the particular research setting. The results of the Berzins study in particular suggest that matching on multiple psychological variables may be an aid in the running of a mental health clinic.

CONCLUSIONS

The therapist variables most frequently selected by the researcher for study are, unfortunately, such simplistic, global concepts as to cause this field to suffer from possibly terminal vagueness. Therapist variables categorized as personality, mental health, experience, sex, race, socioeconomic status, and so on, can be usefully related to specific treatment goals only at a gross probabilistic level. The actual therapeutically relevant mechanisms that may be embedded in these molar concepts remain obscure.

Since the research problems associated with each class of studies reviewed have been detailed earlier, they will not be repeated here; however, we wish to emphasize that serious research problems inhere in studies that have attempted to relate patient change—mediate or ultimate—to selected therapist characteristics or qualities. The specified therapist variables inevitably are confounded with other uncontrolled therapist characteristics, with unspecified patient characteristics, and with the therapist's idiosyncratic adaptation of treatment techniques. With these caveats in mind the following capsule summary of findings is offered.

Therapist variables considered independent of the patient
- Although no outcome effects are clearly attributable to therapist personality characteristics, therapist's emotional problems may interfere with effective treatment.
- The contribution of personal psychotherapy to the enhancement of the therapist's usefulness remains undemonstrated.
- The effect of the therapist's sex as a main effect on outcome is unconfirmed.
- Evidence that the level of therapist experience is a determinant of outcome is surprisingly weak and not adequately tested.
- Process studies of diversely defined therapist stylistic variables remain difficult to interpret. Studies relating outcome to therapist "in-treatment" styles are in an exploratory stage.
- Evidence for the hypothesis that judged accurate empathy, warmth, and genuineness of the therapist represent the "necessary and sufficient" conditions of effective treatment has become increasingly clouded. Many investigators concede that more complex relationships exist among therapist, patients, and techniques.

Therapist and patient variables combined
- The congruence of therapist and patient expectations regarding outcome appears unrelated to actual effectiveness but may lessen the dropout rate.
- Adequate preparation of the patient for psychosocial treatment may enhance treatment outcome.
- The interactive roles of therapist and patient on variables of race, social class, and sex have not been adequately tested.
- The effect of demographic variables and therapist attitudes may play a lesser role in brief crisis-oriented therapies and in behaviorally oriented therapies than in long-term psychodynamically oriented treatments.
- Only suggestive evidence is found for the usefulness of establishing compatible therapist-patient dyads on the basis of personality dimensions, and it is not clear which dimensions are most important for effective compatibility.
- The value of the A-B Scale as a predictor of outcome has been increasingly questioned; nonetheless, efforts to refine the scale continue.
- "Matching" of therapist and patient on cognitive dimensions may offer some promise for improving treatment effectiveness.

- The effects of therapist-patient value similarities have not been experimentally tested; however, post-hoc studies suggest that judgment of patient improvement is related to increased convergence between patient and therapist values.
- Factor analytic techniques for deriving empirically based matching of patient and therapist in a given treatment setting may permit more effective use of treatment staff.

Acknowledgments

The authors acknowledge with gratitude the assistance of Judy Simons, Dona Kelly, Irma Einheber, and Mary Martin in the preparation of this chapter. Special thanks go to Gloria Parloff for her invaluable and relentless editorial assistance, and to Lisa Fredman for her meticulous bibliographic assistance.

REFERENCES

Abramowitz, S. I., Roback, H. B., Schwartz, J. M., Yasuna, A., Abramowitz, C. V., & Gomes, B. Sex bias in psychotherapy: A failure to confirm. *American Journal of Psychiatry,* 1976, *133,* 706–709.

Alexander, F. *Fundamentals of psychoanalysis.* New York: W. W. Norton, 1948.

Alexander, J. F., Barton, C., Schiavo, R. S., & Parsons, B. V. Systems-behavioral intervention with families of delinquents: Therapist characteristics, family behavior and outcome. *Journal of Consulting and Clinical Psychology,* 1976, *44,* 656–664.

Auerbach, A. H., & Johnson, M. Research on the therapist's level of experience. In A. S. Gurman & A. M. Razin (Eds.), *Effective psychotherapy: A handbook of research.* New York: Pergamon Press, 1977.

Baekland, F., & Lundwall, L. Dropping out of treatment: A critical review. *Psychological Bulletin,* 1975, *82,* 738–783.

Bandura, A., Lipsher, D., & Miller, P. E. Psychotherapists' approach-avoidance reactions to patients' expressions of hostility. *Journal of Consulting Psychology,* 1960, *24,* 1–8.

Banks, G., Berenson, B. G., & Carkhuff, R. R. The effects of counselor race and training upon counseling process with Negro clients in initial interviews. *Journal of Clinical Psychology,* 1967, *23,* 70–72.

Banks, W. M. The differential effects of race and social class in helping. *Journal of Clinical Psychology,* 1972, *28,* 90–92.

Bare, C. E. Relationship of counselor personality and counselor-client similarity to selected counseling success criteria. *Journal of Counseling Psychology,* 1967, *14,* 419–425.

Barrett, C. J., Berg, P. I., Eaton, E. M., & Pomeroy, E. L. Implications of women's liberation and the future of psychotherapy. *Psychotherapy: Theory, Research and Practice,* 1974, *11,* 11–15.

Barrett-Lennard, G. T. Dimensions of therapist response as causal factors in therapeutic change. *Psychological Monographs,* 1962, *76* (43, Whole No. 562).

Baum, O. E., & Felzer, S. B. Activity in initial interviews with lower-class patients. *Archives of General Psychiatry,* 1964, *10,* 345–353.

Baum, O. E., Felzer, S. B., D'Zmura, T. L., & Schumaker, E. Psychotherapy, dropouts, and lower socioeconomic patients. *American Journal of Orthopsychiatry,* 1966, *36,* 629–635.

Bergin, A. E. The effects of psychotherapy: Negative results revisited. *Journal of Counseling Psychology,* 1963, *10,* 244–250.

Bergin, A. E. Some implications of psychotherapy research for therapeutic practice. *Journal of Abnormal Psychology,* 1966, *71,* 235–246.

Bergin, A. E. The evaluation of therapeutic outcomes. In A. E. Bergin and S. L. Garfield (Eds.), *Handbook of psychotherapy and behavior change: An empirical analysis.* New York: Wiley, 1971.

Bergin, A. E., & Jasper, L. G. Correlates of empathy in psychotherapy: A replication. *Journal of Abnormal Psychology,* 1969, *74,* 477–481.

Bernard, V. W. Some principles of dynamic psychiatry in relation to poverty. *American Journal of Psychiatry,* 1965, *122,* 254–267.

Berzins, J. I. *Matching patients with therapists: Conceptual, empirical, and pragmatic perspectives.* Paper presented at fifth annual meeting of the Society for Psychotherapy Research, Denver, Colorado, June 1974.

Berzins, J. I. Therapist-patient matching. In A. S. Gurman and A. M. Razin (Eds.), *Effective psychotherapy: A handbook of research.* New York: Pergamon Press, 1977.

Berzins, J. I., Bednar, R. L., & Severy, L. J. The problem of intersource consensus in measuring therapeutic outcomes: New data and multivariate perspectives. *Journal of Abnormal Psychology,* 1975, *84,* 10–19.

Betz, B. J. Experiences in research in psychotherapy with schizophrenic patients. In H. H. Strupp and L. Luborsky (Eds.), *Research in psychotherapy* (Vol. 2). Washington, D.C.: American Psychological Association, 1962.

Beutler, L. E., Johnson, D. T., Neville, C. W., Jr., Elkins, D., & Jobe, A. M. Attitude similarity and therapist credibility as predictors of attitude change and improvement in psychotherapy. *Journal of Consulting and Clinical Psychology,* 1975, *43,* 90–91.

Beutler, L. E., Johnson, D. T., Neville, C. W., Jr., & Workman, S. N. "Accurate empathy" and the A-B dichotomy. *Journal of Consulting and Clinical Psychology,* 1972, *38,* 372–375.

Beutler, L. E., Johnson, D. T., Neville, C. W., Jr., & Workman, S. N. Some sources of variance in "accurate empathy" ratings. *Journal of Consulting and Clinical Psychology,* 1973, *40,* 167–169.

Beutler, L. E., Johnson, D. T., Neville, C. W., Jr., Workman, S. N., & Elkins, D. The A-B therapy-type distinction, accurate empathy, non-possessive warmth, and therapist genuineness in psychotherapy. *Journal of Abnormal Psychology*, 1973, *82*, 273–277.

Beutler, L. E., Pollack, S., & Jobe, A. *On "accepting" patients vs. "accepting" therapists*. Paper presented at the ninth annual meeting of the Society for Psychotherapy Research, Madison, Wisconsin, June 1977.

Birdwhistell, R. *Introduction to kinesics*. Louisville, Ky.: University of Louisville Press, 1963.

Blackwood, G. L., Jr. *Accurate empathy: Critique of a construct*. Unpublished manuscript, Vanderbilt University, May 1975.

Bloombaum, M., Yamamoto, J., & James, Q. Cultural stereotyping among psychotherapists. *Journal of Consulting and Clinical Psychology*, 1968, *32*, 99.

Board, F. A. Patients' and physicians' judgments of outcome of psychotherapy in an outpatient clinic. *Archives of General Psychiatry*, 1959, *1*, 185–196.

Boomer, D. S. The phonemic clause: Speech unit in human communication. In A. W. Siegman and S. Feldstein (Eds.), *Nonverbal behavior and communication*. Hillsdale, N.J.: Erlbaum, 1978.

Bordin, E. S. *Research strategies in psychotherapy*. New York: Wiley, 1974.

Bozarth, J. D., & Grace, D. P. Objective ratings and client perception of therapeutic conditions with university counseling center clients. *Journal of Clinical Psychology*, 1970, *26*, 117–118.

Brodsky, A. M. The consciousness-raising group as a model for therapy with women. *Psychotherapy: Theory, Research and Practice*, 1973, *10*, 24–29.

Brodsky, A. M. Therapeutic aspects of consciousness-raising groups. In E. I. Rawlings and D. K. Carter (Eds.), *Psychotherapy for women*. Springfield, Ill.: Charles C. Thomas, 1977.

Brooks, L. Interactive effects of sex and status on self-disclosure. *Journal of Counseling Psychology*, 1974, *21*, 469–474.

Broverman, I. K., Broverman, D. M., Clarkson, F. E., Rosenkrantz, P. S., & Vogel, S. R. Sex-role stereotypes and clinical judgments of mental health. *Journal of Consulting and Clinical Psychology*, 1970, *34*, 1–7.

Brown, C. R., & Hellinger, M. L. Therapists' attitudes toward women. *Social Work*, 1975, *20*, 266–270.

Brown, R. D. Experienced and inexperienced counselors' first impressions of clients and case outcomes: Are first impressions lasting? *Journal of Counseling Psychology*, 1970, *17*, 550–558.

Bryson, S., & Cody, J. Relationship of race and level of understanding between counselor and client. *Journal of Counseling Psychology*, 1973, *20*, 495–498.

Cain, D. J. The therapist's and client's perceptions of therapeutic conditions in relation to perceived interview outcome. *Dissertation Abstracts International*, 1973, *33* (12–B), 6071.

Cairns, K. V. *Desensitization and relationship quality*. Unpublished master's thesis, University of Calgary, 1972.

Carkhuff, R. R. *Helping and human relations*. New York: Holt, Rinehart and Winston, 1969.

Carkhuff, R. R. The development of systematic human resource development models. *Counseling*

Psychologist, 1972, *3*, 4–10.

Carkhuff, R. R., & Burstein, J. Objective therapist and client ratings of therapist-offered facilitative conditions of moderate to low functioning therapists. *Journal of Clinical Psychology*, 1970, *26*, 394–395.

Carkhuff, R. R., & Pierce, R. Differential effects of therapist race and social class upon patient depth of self-exploration in the initial clinical interview. *Journal of Consulting Psychology*, 1967, *31*, 632–634.

Carr, J. E. The role of conceptual organization in interpersonal discrimination. *Journal of Psychology*, 1965, *59*, 159–176.

Carr, J. E. Differentiation similarity of patient and therapist and the outcome of psychotherapy. *Journal of Abnormal Psychology*, 1970, *76*, 361–369.

Carson, R. C. A and B therapist "types": A possible critical variable in psychotherapy. *Journal of Nervous and Mental Disease*, 1967, *144*, 47–54.

Carson, R. C., & Heine, R. W. Similarity and success in therapeutic dyads. *Journal of Consulting Psychology*, 1962, *26*, 38–43.

Carson, R. C., & Llewellyn, C. E. Similarity in therapeutic dyads. *Journal of Consulting Psychology*, 1966, *30*, 458.

Carter, C. A. Advantages of being a woman therapist. *Psychotherapy: Theory, Research and Practice*, 1971, *8*, 297–300.

Cartwright, D. S., Kirtner, W. L., & Fiske, D. W. Method factors in changes associated with psychotherapy. *Journal of Abnormal and Social Psychology*, 1963, *66*, 164–175.

Cartwright, R. D., & Lerner, B. Empathy, need to change, and improvement with psychotherapy. *Journal of Consulting Psychology*, 1963, *27*, 138–144.

Cartwright, R. D., & Vogel, J. L. A comparison of changes in psychoneurotic patients during matched periods of therapy and no therapy. *Journal of Consulting Psychology*, 1960, *24*, 121–127.

Chartier, G. M. A-B therapist variable: Real or imagined? *Psychological Bulletin*, 1971, *75*, 22–23.

Chesler, P. Marriage and psychotherapy. In J. Agel (Ed.), *The radical therapist: The radical therapist collective*. New York: Ballantine Books, 1971.

Chinsky, J. M., & Rappaport, J. Brief critique of meaning and reliability of "accurate empathy" ratings. *Psychological Bulletin*, 1970, *73*, 379–382.

Cimbolic, P. Counselor race and experience effects on black clients. *Journal of Consulting and Clinical Psychology*, 1972, *39*, 328–332.

Clemes, S., & D'Andrea, V. J. Patients' anxiety as a function of expectation and degree of initial interview ambiguity. *Journal of Consulting Psychology*, 1965, *29*, 397–404.

Cole, N. J., Branch, C. H., & Allison, R. B. Some relationships between social class and the practice of dynamic psychotherapy. *American Journal of Psychiatry*, 1962, *118*, 1004–1012.

Cutler, R. L. Countertransference effects in psychotherapy. *Journal of Consulting Psychology*, 1958, *22*, 349–356.

Dent, J. K. *Dimensions of the psycho-social therapies as revealed by the personalities of effective therapists.*

Unpublished manuscript, 1977.

DiLoreto, A. O. *Comparative psychotherapy, an experimental analysis.* Chicago: Aldine-Atherton, 1971.

Dittmann, A. T. *Interpersonal messages of emotion.* New York: Springer, 1972.

Dougherty, F. E. Patient-therapist matching for prediction of optimal and minimal therapeutic outcome. *Journal of Consulting and Clinical Psychology,* 1976, *44,* 889–897.

Edwards, B. C., & Edgerly, J. W. Effects of counselor-client congruence on counseling outcome in brief counseling. *Journal of Counseling Psychology,* 1970, *17,* 313–318.

Ewing, T. N. Racial similarity of client and counselor and client satisfaction with counseling. *Journal of Counseling Psychology,* 1974, *21,* 446–449.

Fabrikant, B. The psychotherapist and the female patient: Perceptions, misperceptions, and change. In V. Franks and V. Burtle (Eds.), *Women in therapy: New psychotherapies for a changing society.* New York: Brunner/Mazel, 1974.

Fairweather, G., Simon, R., Gebhard, M. E., Weingarten, E., Holland, J. L., Sanders, R., Stone, G. B., & Reahl, J. E. Relative effectiveness of psychotherapeutic programs. A multicriteria comparison of four programs for three different patient groups. *Psychological Monographs: General and Applied,* 1960, *74,* (5, Whole No. 492).

Feifel, H., & Eells, J. Patients and therapists assess the same psychotherapy. *Journal of Consulting Psychology,* 1963, *27,* 310–318.

Fish, J. M. Empathy and the reported emotional experiences of beginning psychotherapists. *Journal of Consulting and Clinical Psychology,* 1970, *35,* 64–69.

Fiske, D. W. A source of data is not a measuring instrument. *Journal of Abnormal Psychology,* 1975, *84,* 20–23.

Fiske, D. W., Cartwright, D. S., & Kirtner, W. L. Are psychotherapeutic changes predictable? *Journal of Abnormal Psychology,* 1964, *69,* 418–426.

Fiske, D. W., & Goodman, G. The post therapy period. *Journal of Abnormal Psychology,* 1965, *70,* 169–179.

Fodor, I. E. Sex role conflict and symptom foundation in women: Can behavior therapy help? *Psychotherapy: Theory, Research and Practice,* 1974a, *11,* 22–29.

Fodor, I. E. The phobic syndrome in women: Implications for treatment. In V. Franks and V. Burtle (Eds.), *Women in therapy: New psychotherapies for a changing society.* New York: Brunner/Mazel, 1974b.

Frank, J. D. *Persuasion and healing: A comparative study of psychotherapy.* (Rev. ed.) Baltimore: Johns Hopkins University Press, 1973.

Fretz, B. R. Postural movements in a counseling dyad. *Journal of Counseling Psychology,* 1966, *13,* 335–343.

Freud, S. The future prospects of psychoanalytic therapy (1910). *Standard Edition, 11,* 139–151. London: Hogarth Press, 1957.

Freud, S. Recommendations for physicians on the psycho-analytic method for treatment (1912).

Standard Edition, 12, 109–120. London: Hogarth Press, 1957.

Fromm-Reichmann, F. *Principles of intensive psychotherapy.* Chicago: University of Chicago Press, 1950.

Fuller, F. F. Influence of sex of counselor and of client on client expressions of feeling. *Journal of Counseling Psychology,* 1963, *10,* 34–40.

Gardner, G. G. The psychotherapeutic relationship. *Psychological Bulletin,* 1964, *61,* 426–437.

Gardner, L. M. The therapeutic relationship under varying conditions of race. *Psychotherapy: Theory, Research and Practice,* 1971, *8,* 78–87.

Gardner, W. E. The differential effects of race, education, and experience in helping. *Journal of Clinical Psychology,* 1972, *28,* 87–89.

Garduk, E. L., & Haggard, E. A. The immediate effects on patients of psychoanalytic interpretations. *Psychological Issues,* 1972, *7,* (4, Monograph 28).

Garfield, S. L. Research on client variables in psychotherapy. In A. E. Bergin and S. L. Garfield, *Handbook of psychotherapy and behavior change.* New York: Wiley, 1971.

Garfield, S. L., & Bergin, A. E. Personal therapy, outcome and some therapist variables. *Psychotherapy: Theory, Research and Practice,* 1971a, *8,* 251–253.

Garfield, S. L., & Bergin, A. E. Therapeutic conditions and outcome. *Journal of Abnormal Psychology,* 1971b, *77,* 108–114.

Gassner, S. M. Relationship between patient-therapist compatibility and treatment effectiveness. *Journal of Consulting and Clinical Psychology,* 1970, *34,* 408–414.

Geer, C. A., & Hurst, J. C. Counselor-subject sex variables in systematic desensitization. *Journal of Counseling Psychology,* 1976, *23,* 296–301.

Gelder, M. G., Marks, I. M., & Wolff, H. N. Desensitization and psychotherapy in the treatment of phobic states: A controlled inquiry. *British Journal of Psychiatry,* 1967, *113,* 53–75.

Glaser, K. Women's self-help groups as an alternative to therapy. *Psychotherapy: Theory, Research and Practice,* 1976, *13,* 77–81.

Goin, M. K., Yamamoto, J., & Silverman, J. Therapy congruent with class-linked expectations. *Archives of General Psychiatry,* 1965, *13,* 133–137.

Goldberg, M. *The black female client, the white psychotherapist: An evaluation of therapy through clients' retrospective reports.* Doctoral dissertation, California School of Professional Psychology, San Francisco, 1972. *Dissertation Abstracts International,* 1973, *33,* 3302B. (University Microfilms No. 72–33. 287).

Goldstein, A. P. Therapist and client expectation of personality change in psychotherapy. *Journal of Counseling Psychology,* 1960, *7,* 180–184.

Goldstein, A. P. *Structured learning therapy.* New York: Pergamon Press, 1973.

Goldstein, A. P., Heller, K., and Sechrest, L. B. *Psychotherapy and the psychology of behavior change.* New York: Wiley, 1966.

Gormally, J., & Hill, C. E. Guidelines for research on Carkhuff's model. *Journal of Counseling Psychol-*

ogy, 1974, *21*, 539–547.

Gottschalk, L. A., Mayerson, P., & Gottlieb, A. A. Prediction and evaluation of outcome in an emergency brief psychotherapy clinic. *Journal of Nervous and Mental Disease*, 1967, *144*, 77–96.

Gould, R. E. Dr. Strangeclass: Or how I stopped worrying about the theory and began treating the blue-collar worker. *American Journal of Orthopsychiatry*, 1967, *37*, 78–86.

Grantham, R. J. Effects of counselor sex, race, and language style on black students in initial interviews. *Journal of Counseling Psychology*, 1973, *20*, 553–559.

Griffith, M. S. The influence of race on the psychotherapeutic relationship. *Psychiatry*, 1977, *40*, 27–40.

Grigg, A. E. Client response to counselors at different levels of experience. *Journal of Counseling Psychology*, 1961, *8*, 217–222.

Grigg, A. E., & Goodstein, L. D. The use of clients as judges of the counselor's performance. *Journal of Counseling Psychology*, 1957, *4*, 31–36.

Gurman, A. S. Instability of therapeutic conditions in psychotherapy. *Journal of Counseling Psychology*, 1973, *20*, 16–24.

Gurman, A. S. The patient's perception of the therapeutic relationship. In A. S. Gurman and A. M. Razin (Eds.), *Effective psychotherapy: A handbook of research*. New York: Pergamon Press, 1977.

Haase, R. F., & Tepper, D. T., Jr. Nonverbal components of empathic communication. *Journal of Counseling Psychology*, 1972, *19*, 417–424.

Halkides, G. An investigation of therapeutic success as a function of four variables. Unpublished doctoral dissertation, University of Chicago, 1958.

Hansen, J. C., Moore, G. D., & Carkhuff, R. R. The differential relationships of objective and client perceptions of counseling. *Journal of Clinical Psychology*, 1968, *24*, 244–246.

Harrison, I. K. Race as a counselor-client variable in counseling and psychotherapy: A review of the research. *The Counseling Psychologist*, 1975, *5*, 124–133.

Heffernon, A., & Bruehl, D. Some effects of race of inexperienced lay counselors on black junior high school students. *Journal of School Psychology*, 1971, *9*, 35–37.

Heine, R. W., & Trosman, H. Initial expectations of the doctor-patient interaction as a factor in continuance in psychotherapy. *Psychiatry*, 1960, *23*, 275–278.

Heitler, J. B. Preparation of lower-class patients for expressive group psychotherapy. *Journal of Consulting and Clinical Psychology*, 1973, *41*, 251–260.

Heitler, J. B. Preparatory techniques in initiating expressive psychotherapy with lower-class, unsophisticated patients. *Psychological Bulletin*, 1976, *83*, 339–352.

Henry, W. E., Sims, J. H., & Spray, S. L. *The fifth profession*. San Francisco: Jossey-Bass, 1971.

Hill, C. E. A comparison of the perceptions of a therapy session by clients, therapists, and objective judges. *JSAS Catalog of Selected Documents in Psychology*, 1974, *4*, 16 (Ms. No. 564).

Hill, C. E. Sex of client and sex and experience level of counselor. *Journal of Counseling Psychology*, 1975, *22*, 6–11.

Hill, J. A., Howard, K. I., & Orlinsky, D. E. The therapist's experience of psychotherapy. Some dimensions and determinants. *Multivariate Behavioral Research*, 1970, *5*, 435–451.

Hoehn-Saric, R., Frank, J., Imber, S., Nash, E., Stone, A., & Battle, C. Systematic preparation of patients for psychotherapy: I. Effects of therapy behavior and outcome. *Journal of Psychiatric Research*, 1964, *2*, 267–281.

Hollingshead, A. B., & Redlich, F. C. *Social class and mental illness*. New York: Wiley, 1958.

Holt, R. R., & Luborsky, L. *Personality patterns of psychiatrists*, Vol. 1. New York: Basic Books, 1958.

Horney, K. *Neurosis and human growth*. New York: W. W. Norton, 1950.

Houts, D. S., MacIntosh, S., & Moos, R. H. Patient-therapist interdependence: Cognitive and behavioral. *Journal of Consulting and Clinical Psychology*, 1969, *33*. 40–45.

Howard, K. I., Orlinsky, D. E. & Hill, J. A. Patients' satisfaction in psychotherapy as a function of patient-therapist pairing. *Psychotherapy: Theory, Research and Practice*, 1970, *7*, 130–134.

Howard, K. I., & Orlinsky, D. E. Psychotherapeutic processes. *Annual Review of Psychology*, 1972, *23*, 615–668.

Howard, K., Rickels, K., Mock, J. E., Lipman, R. S., Covi, L., & Bauman, N. C. Therapeutic style and attrition rate from psychiatric drug treatment. *Journal of Nervous and Mental Disease*, 1970, *150*, 102–110.

Jackson, A. M. Psychotherapy: Factors associated with the race of the therapist. *Psychotherapy: Theory, Research and Practice*, 1973a, *10*, 273–277.

Jackson, A. M. Problems experienced by female therapists in establishing an alliance. *Psychiatric Annals*, 1973b, *3*, 6–9.

Jacobs, D., Charles, E., Jacobs, T., Weinstein, H., & Mann, D. Preparation for treatment of the disadvantaged patient: Effects on disposition and outcome. *American Journal of Orthopsychiatry*, 1972, *42*, 666–674.

Jaffe, J., & Feldstein, S. *Rhythms of dialogue*. New York: Academic Press, 1970.

Jakubowski, P. A. Self-assertion training procedures for women. In E. I. Rawlings and D. K. Carter (Eds.), *Psychotherapy for women*. Springfield, Ill.: Charles C. Thomas, 1977.

Johnson, M. An approach to feminist therapy. *Psychotherapy: Theory, Research and Practice*, 1976, *13*, 72–76.

Johnson, M. Influence of counselor gender and of client gender and effect on counselor response. Unpublished doctoral dissertation, University of Pennsylvania, 1977.

Jones, E. E. Social class and psychotherapy: A critical review of research. *Psychiatry*, 1974, *37*, 307–329.

Jones, E. E. The effects of race on psychotherapy process and outcome: An exploratory investigation. Submitted for publication in *Psychotherapy: Theory, Research and Practice*, 1977.

Jung, C. G. The state of psychotherapy today (1934). *Collected Works, Vol. 10, Civilization in transition*.

Princeton, N.J.: Princeton University Press, 1964, pp. 157–173.

Kandel, D. B. Status homophily, social context, and participation in psychotherapy. *American Journal of Sociology,* 1966, *71,* 640–650.

Katz, M. M., Lorr, M., & Rubinstein, E. A. Remainer patient attributes and their relation to subsequent improvement in psychotherapy. *Journal of Consulting Psychology,* 1958, *22,* 411–413.

Kelman, H. C., & Parloff, M. B. Interrelations among three criteria of improvement in group therapy: comfort, effectiveness, and self-awareness. *Journal of Abnormal and Social Psychology,* 1957, *54,* 281–288.

Kiesler, D. J., Klein, M. H., Mathieu, P. L., & Schoeninger, D. Constructive personality change for therapy and control patients. In C. R. Rogers (Ed.), *The therapeutic relationship and its impact: A study of psychotherapy with schizophrenics.* Madison: University of Wisconsin Press, 1967.

Kiesler, D. J., Mathieu, P. L., & Klein, M. H. Measurement of conditions and process variables. In C. R. Rogers (Ed.), *The therapeutic relationship and its impact: A study of psychotherapy with schizophrenics.* Madison: University of Wisconsin Press, 1967.

Kirsh, B. Consciousness-raising groups as therapy. In V. Franks and V. Burtle (Eds.), *Women in therapy.* New York: Brunner/Mazel, 1974.

Kirshner, L. A., Hauser, S. T., & Genack, A. Effects of gender on short-term psychotherapy. *Psychotherapy: Theory, Research and Practice,* in press.

Klein, M. H. Feminist concepts of therapy outcome. *Psychotherapy: Theory, Research and Practice,* 1976, *13,* 89–95.

Knapp, P. H., Levin, S., McCarter, R. H., Wermer, H., & Zetzel, E. Suitability for psychoanalysis: A review of one hundred supervised analytic cases. *Psychoanalytic Quarterly,* 1960, *29,* 459–477.

Krasner, L. The therapist as a social reinforcement machine. In H. H. Strupp and L. Luborsky (Eds.), *Research in psychotherapy,* Vol. 2. Washington, D.C.: American Psychological Association, 1962.

Kravetz, D. F. Consciousness-raising groups and group psychotherapy: Alternative mental health resources for women. *Psychotherapy: Theory, Research and Practice,* 1976, *13,* 66–71.

Krebs, R. L. Some effects of a white institution on black psychiatric outpatients. *American Journal of Orthopsychiatry,* 1971, *41,* 589–596.

Kronsky, B. J. Feminism and psychotherapy. *Journal of Contemporary Psychotherapy,* 1971, *3,* 89–98.

Kurtz, R. R., & Grummon, D. L. Different approaches in the measurement of therapist empathy and their relationship to therapy outcomes. *Journal of Consulting and Clinical Psychology,* 1972, *39,* 106–115.

Lambert, M. J., & DeJulio, S. S. *Outcome research in Carkhuff's human resource development training programs: Where is the donut?* Paper presented at eighth annual meeting of the Society for Psychotherapy Research, San Diego, California, June 1976.

Landfield, A. W. *Personal construct systems in psychotherapy.* Chicago: Rand McNally, 1971.

Lazarus, A. A. Women in behavior therapy. In V. Franks and V. Burtle (Eds.), *Women in therapy: New psychotherapies for a changing society.* New York: Brunner/Mazel, 1974.

Leary, T. *Interpersonal diagnosis of personality.* New York: Ronald Press, 1957.

Lennard, H. L., & Bernstein, A. *The anatomy of psychotherapy: Systems of communication and expectation.* New York: Columbia University Press, 1960.

Lerner, B. *Therapy in the ghetto: Political impotence and personal disintegration.* Baltimore: Johns Hopkins University Press, 1972.

Lerner, B. Democratic values and therapeutic efficacy: A construct validity study. *Journal of Abnormal Psychology,* 1973, *82,* 491–498.

Lesser, W. M. The relationship between counseling progress and empathic understanding. *Journal of Counseling Psychology,* 1961, *8,* 330–336.

Libo, L. M. The projective expression of patient-therapist attraction. *Journal of Clinical Psychology,* 1957, *13,* 33–36.

Lichtenstein, E. Personality similarity and therapeutic success. A failure to replicate. *Journal of Consulting Psychology,* 1966, *30,* 282.

Lieberman, M. A., Yalom, I. D., & Miles, M. B. *Encounter groups: First facts.* New York: Basic Books, 1973.

Linehan, M. L., Goldfried, M. R., & Goldfried, A. P. Assertion therapy: Skill training or cognitive restructuring. Submitted for publication to *Journal of Consulting and Clinical Psychology,* 1977.

Lorion, R. P. Socioeconomic status and traditional treatment approaches reconsidered. *Psychological Bulletin,* 1973, *79,* 263–270.

Lorion, R. P. Patient and therapist variables in the treatment of low-income patients. *Psychological Bulletin,* 1974, *81,* 344–354.

Lorr, M. Client perceptions of therapists. *Journal of Consulting Psychology,* 1965, *29,* 146–149.

Lorr, M., & McNair, D. M. Methods relating to evaluation of therapeutic outcome. In L. A. Gottschalk and A. Auerbach (Eds.), *Methods of research in psychotherapy.* New York: Appleton-Century-Crofts, 1966.

Luborsky, L. Who benefits from psychotherapy? In preparation, 1977. (Described in A. H. Auerbach and M. Johnson, Research on the therapist's level of experience. In A. S. Gurman and A. M. Razin (Eds.), *Effective psychotherapy: A handbook of research.* New York: Pergamon Press, 1977.)

Luborsky, L., Chandler, M., Auerbach, A. H., Cohen, J., & Bachrach, H. M. Factors influencing the outcome of psychotherapy. *Psychological Bulletin,* 1971, *75,* 145–185.

Mahl, G. F. The lexical and linguistic levels in the expression of the emotions. In P. H. Knapp (Ed.), *Expression of the emotions in man.* New York: International Universities Press, 1963.

Marecek, J., & Kravetz, D. Women and mental health: A review of feminist change efforts. *Psychiatry,* 1977, *40,* 323–329.

Martin, P. J., Sterne, A. L., & Hunter, M. L. Share and share alike: Mutuality of expectations and satisfaction with therapy. *Journal of Clinical Psychology,*

1976, 32, 677–683.

Maslin, A. & Davis, J. L. Sex-role stereotyping as a factor in mental health standards among counselors-in-training. Journal of Counseling Psychology, 1975, 22, 87–91.

Matarazzo, J. D., Wiens, A. N., Matarazzo, R. G., & Saslow, G. Speech and silence behavior in clinical psychotherapy and its laboratory correlates. In J. M. Shlien (Ed.), Research in psychotherapy. Washington, D.C.: American Psychological Association, 1968.

May, P. R. A Brave New World revisited: Alphas, Betas, and treatment outcome. Comprehensive Psychiatry, 1974, 15, 1–17.

McClanahan, L. D, A comparison of counseling techniques and attitudes with client evaluations of the counseling relationship. Doctoral dissertation, Ohio University. Dissertation Abstracts International, 1974, 34 (9–A), 5637.

McLachlan, J. C. Benefit from group therapy as a function of patient-therapist match on conceptual level. Psychotherapy: Theory, Research and Practice, 1972, 9, 317–323.

McLachlan, J. C. Therapy strategies, personality orientation and recovery from alcoholism. Canadian Psychiatric Association Journal, 1974, 19, 25–30.

McNair, D. M., Callahan, D. M., & Lorr, M. Therapist "type" and patient response to psychotherapy. Journal of Consulting Psychology, 1962, 26, 425–429.

McNair, D. M., Lorr, M., & Callahan, D. M. Patient and therapist influences on quitting psychotherapy. Journal of Consulting Psychology, 1963, 27, 10–17.

McNair, D. M., Lorr, M., Young, H. H., Roth, I., & Boyd, R. W. A three-year follow-up of psychotherapy patients. Journal of Clinical Psychology, 1964, 20, 258–264.

McNally, H. A. An investigation of selected counselor and client characteristics as possible predictors of counseling effectiveness. Dissertation Abstracts International, 1973, 33, (12–A), 6672–6673.

Mehrabian, A., & Ferris, S. R. Inference of attitudes from nonverbal communication in two channels, Journal of Consulting and Clinical Psychology, 1967, 31, 248–252.

Meltzoff, J., & Kornreich, M. Research in psychotherapy. New York: Atherton Press, 1970.

Menaker, E. The therapy of women in the light of psychoanalytic theory and the emergence of a new view. In V. Franks and V. Burtle (Eds.), Women in therapy. New York: Brunner/Mazel, 1974.

Mendelsohn, G. A. Client-counselor compatiblity and the effectiveness of counseling. Unpublished manuscript, University of California, Berkeley, 1968.

Mendelsohn, G. A., & Geller, M. H. Effects of counselor-client similarity on the outcome of counseling. Journal of Counseling Psychology, 1963, 10, 71–77.

Mendelsohn, G. A., & Geller, M. H. Structure of client attitudes toward counseling and their relation to client-counselor similarity. Journal of Consulting and Clinical Psychology, 1965, 29, 63–72.

Mendelsohn, G. A., & Geller, M. H. Similarity, missed sessions, and early termination. Journal of Counseling Psychology, 1967, 14, 210–215.

Mendelsohn, G. A., & Rankin, N. O. Client-counselor compatibility and the outcome of counseling. Journal of Abnormal Psychology, 1969, 74, 157–163.

Mihalick, R. E. Values in psychotherapy. Dissertation Abstracts International, 1970, 30, 4377.

Mindess, H. Predicting patients' responses to psychotherapy: A preliminary study designed to investigate the validity of the "Rorschach Prognostic Rating Scale." Journal of Projective Techniques, 1953, 17, 327–334.

Minsel, W., Bommert, H., Bastine, R., Langer, I., Nickel, H., & Tausch, R. Weitere untersuchung der auswirkung und prozess klienten-zentrieter gespraschstherapie zeitsch R.F. Klinische Psychologie, 1971, 1, 232–250.

Mintz, J., & Luborsky, L. Segments vs. whole sessions: Which is the better unit for psychotherapy research? Journal of Abnormal Psychology, 1971, 78, 180–191.

Mintz, J., Luborsky, L., & Auerbach, A. H. Dimensions of psychotherapy: A factor-analytic study of ratings of psychotherapy sessions. Journal of Consulting and Clinical Psychology, 1971, 36, 106–120.

Mintz, J., O'Brien, C. P., & Luborsky, L. Predicting the outcome of psychotherapy for schizophrenics. Archives of General Psychiatry, 1976, 33, 1183–1186.

Mitchell, K. M., Bozarth, J, D., & Krauft, C. C. A reappraisal of the therapeutic effectiveness of accurate empathy, nonpossessive warmth, and genuineness. In A. S. Gurman and A. M. Razin (Eds.), Effective psychotherapy: A handbook of research. New York: Pergamon Press, 1977.

Mitchell, K. M., Bozarth, J. D., Truax, C. B., & Krauft, C. C. Antecedents to psychotherapeutic outcome. NIMH Grant Report (12306). Arkansas Rehabilitation Research and Training Center. University of Arkansas/Arkansas Rehabilitation Services, Hot Springs, Arkansas, March 1973.

Mitchell, K. M., & Namenek, T. M. A comparison of therapist and client social class. Professional Psychology, 1970, 1, 225–230.

Moos, R. H., & MacIntosh, S. Multivariate study of the patient-therapist system: A replication and extension. Journal of Consulting and Clinical Psychology, 1970, 35, 298–307.

Mullen, J., & Abeles, N. Relationship of liking, empathy, and therapist's experience to outcome of therapy. Journal of Counseling Psychology, 1971, 18, 39–43.

Murray, E. J., & Jacobson, L. I. The nature of learning in traditional and behavioral psychotherapy. In A. E. Bergin & S. L. Garfield (Eds.), Handbook of psychotherapy and behavior change. New York: Wiley, 1971.

Myers, J. K., & Auld, F. Some variables related to outcome of psychotherapy. Journal of Clinical Psychology, 1955, 11, 51–54.

Neulinger, J., Stein, M. I., Schillinger, M., & Welkowitz, J. Perceptions of the optimally integrated person as a function of therapists' characteristics. Perception and Motor Skills, 1970, 30, 375–384.

Orlinsky, D. E., & Howard, K. I. Varieties of

psychotherapeutic experience: Multivariate analyses of patients' and therapists' reports. New York: Teachers College Press, 1975.

Orlinsky, D. E., & Howard, K. I. The effects of sex of therapist on the therapeutic experiences of women. Psychotherapy: Theory, Research and Practice, 1976, 13, 82–88.

Orlinsky, D. E., & Howard, K. I. The therapist's experience of psychotherapy. In A. S. Gurman and A. M. Razin (Eds.), Effective psychotherapy: A handbook of research. New York: Pergamon Press, 1977.

Orne, M. T., & Wender, P. H. Anticipatory socialization for psychotherapy: Method and rationale. American Journal of Psychiatry, 1968, 124, 1202–1212.

Overall, P., & Aronson, H. Expectations of psychotherapy in patients of lower socioeconomic class. American Journal of Orthopsychiatry, 1963, 33, 421–430.

Owen, I. Adlerian counseling in racially mixed groups of elementary school children. Individual Psychologist, 1970, 7, 53–58.

Pardes, H., Papernik, D. S., & Winston, A. Field differentiation in inpatient psychotherapy. Archives of General Psychiatry, 1974, 31, 311–315.

Parloff, M. B., Goldstein, N., & Iflund, B. Communication of values and therapeutic change. Archives of General Psychiatry, 1960, 2, 300–304.

Parloff, M. B., Iflund, B., & Goldstein, N. Communication of "therapy values" between therapist and schizophrenic patients. Paper presented at the American Psychiatric Association annual meeting, Chicago, May 1957.

Parloff, M. B., Kelman, H. C., & Frank, J. D. Comfort, effectiveness, and self-awareness as criteria of improvement in psychotherapy. American Journal of Psychiatry, 1954, 111, 343–351.

Persons, R. W., Persons, M. K., & Newmark, I. Perceived helpful therapists' characteristics, client improvements, and sex of therapist and client. Psychotherapy: Theory, Research and Practice, 1974, 11, 63–65.

Petoney, P. Value change in psychotherapy. Human Relations, 1966, 19, 39–45.

Pettit, I. B., Pettit, T. F., & Walkowitz, J. Relationship between values, social class, and duration of psychotherapy. Journal of Consulting and Clinical Psychology, 1974, 42, 482–490.

Phillips, W. B. Counseling Negro pupils: An educational dilemma. Journal of Negro Education, 1960 29, 504–507.

Pittenger, R. E., Hockett, C. F., & Danehy, J. J. The first five minutes: A sample of microscopic interview analysis. Ithaca, N.Y.: Paul Matineau, 1960.

Pope, B. Research on therapeutic style. In A. S. Gurman and A. M. Razin (Eds.), Effective psychotherapy: A handbook of research. New York: Pergamon Press, 1977.

Posthuma, A. B., & Carr, J. E. Differentiation matching in psychotherapy. Canadian Psychological Review, 1975, 16, 35–43.

Rachman, S. J. The effects of psychological treatment. In H. Eysenck (Ed.), Handbook of abnormal psychology. New York: Basic Books, 1973.

Rappaport, J., & Chinsky, J. M. Accurate empathy: Con-

fusion of a construct. Psychological Bulletin, 1972, 77, 400–404.

Rawlings, E. I., & Carter, D. K. Feminist and nonsexist psychotherapy. In E. I. Rawlings and D. K. Carter (Eds.), Psychotherapy for women. Springfield, Ill.: Charles C. Thomas, 1977.

Raynes, A. E., & Warren, G. Some distinguishing features of patients failing to attend a psychiatric clinic after referral. American Journal of Orthopsychiatry, 1971, 41, 581–588.

Razin, A. A-B variable in psychotherapy: A critical review. Psychological Bulletin, 1971, 75, 1–22.

Razin, A. M. The A-B variable: Still promising after twenty years? In A. S. Gurman and A. M. Razin (Eds.), Effective psychotherapy: A handbook of research. New York: Pergamon Press, 1977.

Rice, L. N. Therapist's style of participation and case outcome. Journal of Consulting Psychology, 1965, 29, 155–160.

Rice, D. G., Gurman, A. S., & Gazin, A. M. Therapist sex, "style," and theoretical orientation. Journal of Nervous and Mental Disease, 1974, 159, 413–421.

Rice, J. K., & Rice, D. G. Implications of the women's liberation movement for psychotherapy. American Journal of Psychiatry, 1973, 130, 191–196.

Riessman, F., Cohen, J., & Pearl, A. (Eds.). Mental health of the poor. Glencoe, Ill.: The Free Press of Glencoe, 1964.

Rigler, D. Some determinants of therapist behavior. Unpublished doctoral thesis, University of Michigan, 1957.

Rogers, C. R. The necessary and sufficient conditions of therapeutic personality change. Journal of Consulting Psychology, 1957, 21, 95–103.

Rogers, C. R. On encounter groups. New York: Harper & Row, 1970.

Rogers, C. R. Empathic: An appreciated way of being. Counseling Psychologist, 1975, 5, 2–10.

Rogers, C. R., Gendlin, G. T., Kiesler, D. V., & Truax, C. B. The therapeutic relationship and its impact: A study of psychotherapy with schizophrenics. Madison: University of Wisconsin Press, 1967.

Rosenthal, D. Changes in some moral values following psychotherapy. Journal of Consulting Psychology, 1955, 19, 431–436.

Rosenthal, D., & Frank, J. D. The fate of psychiatric clinic outpatients assigned to psychotherapy. Journal of Nervous and Mental Disease, 1958, 127, 330–343.

Ryan, V., & Gizynski, M. Behavior therapy in retrospect: Patients' feelings about their behavior therapists. Journal of Consulting and Clinical Psychology, 1971, 37, 1–9.

Sapolsky, A. Relationship between patient-doctor compatibility, mutual perception, and outcome of treatment. Journal of Abnormal Psychology, 1965, 70, 70–76.

Sattler, J. M. Racial "experimenter effects" in experimentation, testing, interviewing, and psychotherapy. Psychological Bulletin, 1970, 73, 137–160.

Sattler, J. M. The effects of therapist-client racial similarity. In A. S. Gurman and A. M. Razin (Eds.), Effective psychotherapy: A handbook of research. New York: Pergamon Press, 1977.

Schaffer, L., & Myers, J. K. Psychotherapy and social

stratification. *Psychiatry,* 1954, *17,* 83–93.

Scher, M. Verbal activity, sex, counselor experience, and success in counseling. *Journal of Counseling Psychology,* 1975, *22,* 97–101.

Shoben, E. J., Jr. Psychotherapy as a problem of learning theory. *Psychological Bulletin,* 1949, *46,* 366–392.

Slavson, S. R. *A textbook in analytic group psychotherapy.* New York: International Universities Press, 1964.

Sloane, R. B., Cristol, A. H., Pepernik, M. C., & Staples, F. R. Role preparation and expectation of improvement in psychotherapy. *Journal of Nervous and Mental Disease,* 1970, *150,* 18–26.

Sloane, R. B., Staples, F. R., Cristol, A. H., Yorkston, N. J., & Whipple, K. *Short-term analytically oriented psychotherapy vs. behavior therapy.* Cambridge, Mass.: Harvard University Press, 1975.

Speisman, J. C. Depth of interpretation and verbal resistance in psychotherapy. *Journal of Consulting Psychology,* 1959, *23,* 93–99.

Stephens, J. H., Shaffer, J. W., & Zlotowitz, H. I. An optimum A-B scale of psychotherapist effectiveness. *Journal of Nervous and Mental Disease,* 1975, *160,* 267–281.

Stevens, B. The psychotherapist and women's liberation. *Social Work,* 1971, *16,* 12–18.

Stricker, G. Implication of research for psychotherapeutic treatment of women. *American Psychologist,* 1977, *32,* 14–22.

Strupp, H., & Bloxom, A. Preparing lower class patients for group psychotherapy: Development and evaluation of a role-induction film. *Journal of Consulting and Clinical Psychology,* 1973, *41,* 373–384.

Strupp, H. H., Fox, R. E., & Lessler, K. *Patients view their psychotherapy.* Baltimore: Johns Hopkins University Press, 1969.

Strupp, H. H., & Hadley, S. W. A tripartite model of mental health and therapeutic outcomes: With special reference to negative effects in psychotherapy. *American Psychologist,* 1977, *32,* 187–196.

Sue, S., McKinney, H., Allen D., & Hall, J. Delivery of community mental health services to black and white clients. *Journal of Consulting and Clinical Psychology,* 1974, *42,* 794–801.

Sullivan, H. S. *Conceptions of modern psychiatry.* New York: W. W. Norton, 1953.

Sullivan, H. S. *Clinical studies in psychiatry.* New York: W. W. Norton, 1956.

Sullivan, P. L., Miller, C., & Smelser, W. Factors in length of stay and progress in psychotherapy. *Journal of Consulting Psychology,* 1958, *1,* 1–9.

Sundland, D. M. Theoretical orientations of psychotherapists. In A. S. Gurman and A. M. Razin (Eds.), *Effective psychotherapy: A handbook of research.* New York: Pergamon Press, 1977.

Sundland, D. M., & Barker, E. N. The orientation of psychotherapists. *Journal of Consulting Psychology,* 1962, *26,* 201–212.

Swensen, C. H. Psychotherapy as a special case of dyadic interaction: Some suggestions for theory and research. *Psychotherapy: Theory, Research and Practice,* 1967, *4,* 7–13.

Swensen, C. H. Commitment and the personality of the successful therapist. *Psychotherapy: Theory, Re-search and Practice,* 1971, *8,* 31–36.

Tanney, M. F., & Birk, J. M. Women counselors for women clients? A review of the research. *The Counseling Psychologist,* 1976, *6,* 28–31.

Tausch, R., Sander, K., Bastine, R., & Friese, H. Variaben und ergebnisse bei client–centered psychotherapie mit alternierenden psychotherapeuten. *Sonderdruck aus Psychologische Rundschau,* 1970, *21,* 29–37.

Terestman, N., Miller, J. D., & Weber, J. J. Blue-collar patients at a psychoanalytic clinic. *American Journal of Psychiatry,* 1974, *131,* 261–266.

Truax, C. B. Effective ingredients in psychotherapy: An approach to unraveling the patient-therapist interaction. *Journal of Counseling Psychology,* 1963, *10,* 256–263.

Truax, C. B. Effects of client-centered psychotherapy with schizophrenic patients: Nine-year pretherapy and nine-year post-therapy hospitalization. *Journal of Consulting and Clinical Psychology,* 1970, *35,* 417–422.

Truax, C. B., & Carkhuff, R. R. *Toward effective counseling and psychotherapy: Training and practice.* Chicago: Aldine, 1967.

Truax, C. B., Carkhuff, R. R., & Kodman, F., Jr. Relationships between therapist-offered conditions and patient change in group psychotherapy. *Journal of Clinical Psychology,* 1965, *21,* 327–329.

Truax, C. B., & Mitchell, K. M. Research on certain therapist interpersonal skills in relation to process and outcome. In A. E. Bergin and S. L. Garfield (Eds.), *Handbook of psychotherapy and behavior change: An empirical analysis.* New York: Wiley, 1971.

Truax, C. B., & Wargo, D. G. Psychotherapeutic encounters that change behavior for better or for worse. *American Journal of Psychotherapy,* 1966, *20,* 499–520.

Truax, C. B., & Wargo, D. G. Effects of vicarious therapy pretraining and alternate sessions on outcome in group psychotherapy with outpatients. *Journal of Consulting and Clinical Psychology,* 1969, *33,* 440–447.

Truax, C. B., Wargo, D. G., Frank, J. D., Imber, S. D., Battle, C. C., Hoehn-Saric, R., Nash, E. H., & Stone, A. R. Therapist's contribution to accurate empathy, nonpossessive warmth and genuineness in psychotherapy. *Journal of Clinical Psychology,* 1966a, *22,* 331–334.

Truax, C. B., Wargo, D. G., Frank, J. D., Imber, S. D., Battle, C. C., Hoehn-Saric, R., Nash, E. H., & Stone, A. R. Therapist empathy, genuineness, and warmth and patient therapeutic outcome. *Journal of Consulting Psychology,* 1966b, *30,* 395–401.

Truax, C. B., & Wittmer, J. The effects of therapist focus on patient anxiety source and the interaction with the therapist level of accurate empathy. *Journal of Clinical Psychology,* 1971, *27,* 297–299.

Truax, C. B., Wittmer, J., & Wargo, D. G. Effects of the therapeutic conditions of accurate empathy, nonpossessive warmth, and genuineness on hospitalized mental patients during group therapy. *Journal of Clinical Psychology,* 1971, *27,* 137–142.

Tuma, A. H., May, P. R. A., Yale, C., & Forsythe, A. B. Therapist charactistics and the outcome of treatment in schizophrenics. *Archives of General Psychiatry,* 1978, *35,* 81–85.

Vandenbos, G. R., & Karon, B. P. Pathogenesis: A new therapist personality dimension related to therapeutic effectiveness. *Journal of Personality Assessment,* 1971, *35,* 252–260.

Van der Veen, F. Effects of the therapist and the patient on each other's therapeutic behavior. *Journal of Consulting Psychology,* 1965, *29,* 19–26.

Van der Veen, F. Basic elements in process of psychotherapy: A research study. *Journal of Consulting and Clinical Psychology,* 1967, *31,* 295–303.

Wachtel, P. L. *Psychoanalysis and behavior therapy.* New York: Basic Books, 1977.

Warren, R. C., Jackson, A. M., Nugaris, J., & Farley, G. K. Differential attitudes of black and white patients toward treatment in a child guidance clinic. *American Journal of Orthopsychiatry,* 1973, *43,* 384–393.

Warren, N., & Rice, L. Structuring and stabilizing of psychotherapy for low-prognosis clients. *Journal of Consulting and Clinical Psychology,* 1972, *39,* 173–181.

Waskow, I. E. Summary of discussion following workshop (Workshop on research on psychotherapy with women). *Psychotherapy: Theory, Research and Practice,* 1976, *13,* 96–98.

Welkowitz, J., Cohen, J., & Ortmeyer, D. Value system similarity: Investigation of patient-therapist dyads. *Journal of Consulting Psychology,* 1967, *31,* 48–55.

Whitehorn, J. C., & Betz, B. J. A study of psychotherapeutic relationships between physicians and schizophrenic patients. *American Journal of Psychiatry,* 1954, *111,* 321–331.

Whitehorn, J. C., & Betz, B. J. A study of psychotherapeutic relationships between physicians and schizophrenic patients when insulin is combined with psychotherapy and when psychotherapy is used alone. *American Journal of Psychiatry,* 1957, *113,* 901–910.

Whitehorn, J. C., & Betz, B. J. Further studies of the doctor as a crucial variable in the outcome of treatment with schizophrenic patients. *American Journal of Psychiatry,* 1960, *117,* 215–223.

Williams, B. M. Trust and self-disclosure among black college students. *Journal of Counseling Psychology,* 1974, *21,* 522–525.

Winston, A., Pardes, H., Papernik, D. S. Inpatient treatment of blacks and whites. *Archives of General Psychiatry,* 1972, *26,* 405–409.

Wogan, M. Effect of therapist-patient personality variables on therapeutic outcome. *Journal of Consulting and Clinical Psychology,* 1970, *35,* 356–361.

Wolfe, J. L., & Fodor, I. G. A comparison of three approaches to modifying assertive behavior in women: Modeling-plus-behavior researsal, modeling-plus-behavior rehearsal-plus-rational therapy and consciousness raising. *Behavior Therapy,* in press.

Wolpe, J. *Psychotherapy by reciprocal inhibition.* Stanford, Calif.: Stanford University Press, 1958.

Yalom, I., Houts, P., Newell, G., & Rand, K. Preparation of patients for group therapy: A controlled study. *Archives of General Psychiatry,* 1967, *17,* 416–427.

Yamamoto, J., James, Q. C., Bloombaum, M., & Hattem, J. Social factors in patient selection. *American Journal of Psychiatry,* 1967, *124,* 84–90.

8

THE RELATION OF PROCESS TO OUTCOME IN PSYCHOTHERAPY

DAVID E. ORLINSKY

University of Chicago and Institute for Juvenile Research

KENNETH I. HOWARD

Northwestern University and Institute for Juvenile Research

CONCEPTUAL FOUNDATIONS

The Current State of Research

Extraordinary diversity in concepts and methods, in types of instrumentation and of data collected, in problems attempted and in criteria accepted for their resolution characterizes the state of research activity that Thomas Kuhn (1962) described as "pre-paradigmatic." The difficulties encountered in this earliest stage of science arise not from the absence of a model for research, but from the multiplicity of basic models dividing the allegiances of researchers. Each paradigm-contender offers a different definition of the nature of the phenomena to be studied, the significant problems in the field, and the rules to be followed in establishing evidence and in drawing conclusions.

Those who enter the field tend to work within one or another of these competing orientations, according to personal preference and the historical accidents of their training and work environs. Some feel obliged to devote a great deal of time and energy to weighty preliminaries, defining and defending first principles. Others, impelled to more practical measures, limit themselves to dealing with the most readily observable (though not necessarily the most meaningful) aspects of phenomena. Accordingly, debate over general theoretical or methodological issues, and also a more or less haphazard accumulation of empirical findings, tend to account for much of the effort that is expended. Under these circumstances little cumulative scientific progress is made, notwithstanding the impressive achievements of scattered individuals.

Kuhn cites the state of research in physical optics prior to Newton as one example of the pre-paradigmatic phase in scientific development:

No period between remote antiquity and the end of the seventeenth century exhibited a single generally accepted view about the nature of light. Instead, there were a number of competing schools and sub-schools, most of them espousing one variant or another of Epicurean, Aristotelian, or Platonic theory. . . . Each of the corresponding schools derived strength from its relation to some particular metaphysic, and each emphasized, as paradigmatic observations, the particular cluster of optical phenomena that its own theory could do most to explain. . . . Being able to take no common body of belief for granted, each writer on physical optics felt forced to build his field anew from its foundations. In doing so, his choice of supporting observation and experiment was relatively free, for there was no standard set of methods or of phenomena that every optical writer felt forced to employ and explain. (1962, pp. 12–13)

Although we cannot set out to prove it in detail, it seems to us that only minor changes of name in the foregoing passage would be needed for it to be an accurate description of research in psychotherapy today. Our purpose in pointing to the pre-paradigmatic state of our field is not to level criticism, or to suggest that a real solution to the problem can be negotiated by a representative panel of experts. Our purpose is simply to acknowledge, at the outset, that we operate under certain historical constraints, and to note that our review and summary of research on the relation of psychotherapeutic process to outcome must in some way grapple with these constraints.

The extraordinary diversity that we find in psychotherapy research parallels (and to a large extent is the product of) the amazing variety of conceptualizations and procedures that define the clinical practice of psychotherapy. There are, to name a few: psychoanalytic and neo-analytic therapies; behaviorist and neo-behaviorist therapies; cognitive, emotive, and body therapies; verbal, activity, and play therapies; individual, group, and family therapies; as well as combinations, permutations, eclectic integrations, and idiosyncratic syntheses. Among them all, there is no standard definition of what occurs in, or is distinctive of, therapeutic *process;* no consensus

about the intended effects of therapy, or the criteria of therapeutic *outcome;* hence, no agreement concerning the selection and measurement of meaningful process and outcome *variables.*

What strategies are available to us in dealing with this situation? One recourse is simply to accept the situation as it is, and to produce a catalogue of the studies that have been done to date. This is a legitimate response in so far as it offers the reader a useful bibliographic tool and a critical overview of the field. As an alternative, we might adopt one or another of the competing theoretical viewpoints and try to offer a systematic integration of the findings that are most relevant to its practitioners and their problems.

A third alternative, "reframing" the problem (Watzlawick, Weakland, and Fisch, 1974), would entail neither a retreat from theory nor the limitation of scope to a single theoretical perspective. The strategy of "reframing" takes the problem out of the customary context in which it has proven intractable, and places it in a fresh conceptual context where it can be approached in a potentially more productive fashion. So far as research on psychotherapy is concerned, we believe that this can best be done by avoiding the use of *clinical* theory in defining the significant variables and in formulating the fundamental problems of the field. In the spirit of Frank (1961) and Goldstein, Heller, and Sechrest (1966), we propose to view psychotherapeutic process and outcome in a broader, nonclinical perspective.

A Generic Definition of Psychotherapy

To begin, we need a general definition of psychotherapy to set reasonable boundaries on the field of inquiry without excluding any of the specific practices, findings, or perspectives that have been significant in clinical work. For the present task, such a definition can be formulated as follows: *Psychotherapy is (1) a relation among persons, engaged in by (2) one or more individuals defined as needing special assistance to (3) improve their functioning as persons, together with (4) one or more individuals defined as able to render such special help.* Part (1) broaches the matter of therapeutic process in the broadest terms, and part (3) suggests the terms in which we shall deal with therapeutic outcome. Parts (2) and (4) specify the minimal conditions of participation in therapy as patient or as therapist, and need little further elaboration here.

Categories of Therapeutic Process

The part of our definition that is relevant to therapeutic process simply states that "Psychotherapy is a relation among persons." The implication is that therapeutic process can be viewed in terms that apply to all social relationships. A conceptual scheme developed at this level of generality would provide a frame of reference that is descriptively inclusive and *not* restricted to any particular clinical perspective. The framework that we present here is an elaboration of one that we have previously used to review research on psychotherapeutic process (Howard and Orlinsky, 1972).

We shall distinguish four major facets of process in social relationships: *co-oriented activity; concurrent experience; dramatic interpretation;* and *regular association.* "Co-oriented activity" emphasizes the behavioral, interactional aspect of social relations. "Concurrent experience" denotes the phenomenological, perceptual dimension of social events. "Dramatic interpretation" indicates the symbolic formulations of meaning and value that are made and communicated by participants in a relationship. "Regular association" refers to the normative, prescriptive patterns of relatedness that bind the participants to the relationship.

Each of the facets highlights one aspect of process in social relationships, and can be further differentiated analytically to provide a detailed framework for empirical observation. That direction leads toward a systematically defined (and, from a clinical viewpoint, theoretically neutral) descriptive language, whose development we shall explore in reviewing process-outcome research. Each of the facets, however, also represents one of four interrelated aspects of social process considered as a whole, and these aspects can be conceptually synthesized to provide a comprehensive, integrative view of what happens in a relationship. We shall move in that direction when we attempt an interpretive overview of process-outcome research. Because the framework that underlies this

review forms an integral part of it, we shall devote some preliminary remarks to its conceptual derivation.

The framework is dialectically derived through a sequence of binary distinctions, starting with a single concept and then having two, four, eight, and so on. Each distinction polarizes the concept prior to it into two complementary facets, each of which is further divided, and so on (as shown in Figure 8-1).

The first, most general concept that we take as our starting point is the idea of the *social field* constituted by an actual face-to-face encounter. This may be polarized into two slightly more specific (but also more abstract) complementary ideas: the *interpersonal process* or organized system of events taking place in the social field; and the *functional context* or background against which the process is observed as something distinct. The distinguishing principle is the contrast between "figure" and "ground" that is familiar in the gestalt theory of perception as a phenomenon arising through the simple act of focusing attention.

The second distinction is drawn in terms of the scope of observation: the microscopic or molecular versus the macroscopic or molar. This distinction is applied to each of the two prior ideas, process and context, with the following results. The events comprising *interpersonal process* are distinguished into those molecular, relatively circumscribed, short-term occurrences that, at any given moment, make up what is "going on" in the encounter—as contrasted to those molar, less immediately noticeable but in the long-term quite palpable changes that emerge cumulatively from a series of encounters. We call the first aspect of process the *occurring involvement,* and the second aspect the *emerging relation.* Words, deeds, feelings, thoughts and so on flow between and within the participants in a relationship, comprising the momentarily *occurring involvement.* Yet through these, over successive encounters, molar processes are discernible that transform the *emerging relation* from one of acquaintance (for example) to one of familiarity, from familiarity to friendship, and so on. *Involvement* and *relation* are integral aspects of interpersonal process, differing only in the scope of the observations that are made.

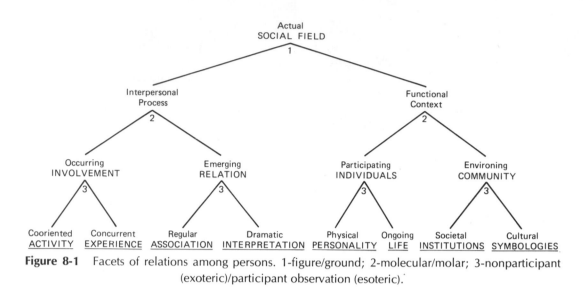

Figure 8-1   Facets of relations among persons. 1-figure/ground; 2-molecular/molar; 3-nonparticipant (exoteric)/participant observation (esoteric).

Distinguishing *functional context* by the same molecular versus molar principle, we find ourselves dealing with psychological and psychophysiological functions, on one hand, and with sociocultural functions on the other. The former are embodied in each of the *participating individuals;* the latter, in the *environing community* in which their encounters take place.

The third principle of distinction is the observational perspective assumed by the researcher. The choice here is between nonparticipant observation, in which the researcher views events from the outside, as it were, and participant observation, in which the perspective is that of the insider. Traditional epistemology treats the nonparticipant perspective as the "objective," and supposedly the more valid viewpoint, especially where a consensus of nonparticipant observers can be obtained. So far as we are concerned, however, participant and nonparticipant observation are just two perspectives from which events can be viewed, each of which brings to light some features that the other obscures (Orlinsky and Howard, 1975).

In applying this distinction, we find that the non-participant observation of *occurring involvement* highlights the behavioral or interactive aspect of relations among persons; and, taking this view, we see involvement as *co-oriented activity.* Participant observation, on the other hand, shows the occurring involvement in terms of the participants' perceptions, that is, phenomenologically. This second,

complementary aspect is embodied in their *concurrent experiences.* From this standpoint, behavior and experience are subsumed under the more general concept of involvement as interdependent polarities of molecular process.

The distinction between nonparticipant and participant observational perspectives also applies to the molar aspect of *interpersonal process,* that is, to the *emerging relation.* Viewed from the outside or nonparticipant perspective, the *emerging relation* is mainly a matter of *regular association* between participating individuals. "Regularity" has the dual implication of recurrence and of regulation. Association takes form through the recurrent contacts of individuals, and that form is established through the generation of, and adherence to, rules or norms. The rules applicable to each person in the relation define his or her role; taken together, these rules (along with the rules for enforcing them) define the role system as a basic aspect of interpersonal process. With respect to our present concerns, we note that the definition and operation of patient and therapist roles, together with the normative definition of the situation, constitute a major facet of psychotherapeutic process.

Another common meaning of the word "relation" indicates the narration or telling of a story. This meaning becomes significant in *interpersonal process* when the *emerging relation* is viewed from the perspective of the participant observer. A relationship is, among other things, a *dramatic in-*

terpretation: a meaningful tale that is being spoken and acted out by the participants as an improvisational play that they themselves construct, review, and appreciate in light of the ideal schemata of plot and character suggested by the surrounding culture. This dramatistic aspect of *interpersonal process* has been emphasized by social psychologists in the "symbolic interactionist" tradition (e.g., Burke, 1965; Goffman, 1967).

Thus far we have distinguished four coordinate categories of social process. The distinctions through which these facets have been derived pertain to the cognitive focus, scope, and perspective of the observer. Further distinctions can be made within each facet, to progressively delimit conceptual categories until a level of specificity is attained that corresponds to empirical variables. These are introduced as we consider the results of process-outcome studies.

Categories of Therapeutic Outcome

Therapeutic outcome, viewed as a descriptive problem, pertains to one phase of a broader two-phase flow that is traceable between an *interpersonal process* and its *functional context.* Prior contextual conditions (i.e., characteristics of the *participating individuals* or the *environing community*) that influence activity, experience, dramatic interpretation, or association constitute the "functional inputs" or determinants of therapeutic process. Subsequent states of the *participating individuals* and the *environing community* that have been influenced by activity, experience, dramatic interpretation, and association constitute the "functional outputs" or consequences of therapeutic process. The study of outcome belongs to this latter phase, but requires further specification of which consequences should be subjected to evaluation.

Progress in this direction can be made by applying the third principle of binary distinction introduced above. Viewed from the exoteric perspective of the nonparticipant observer, the *participating individual* may be thought of as an objectively embodied, palpably active *physical personality.* Viewed from the complementary esoteric perspective of the participant observer, the same individual appears as the existential subject or protagonist, coauthor, and more or less comprehending witness of an *ongoing life.*

The same principle, applied to the concept of *environing community,* leads to a differentiation between *societal institutions* (exoteric aspect) and *cultural symbologies* (esoteric aspect). This is essentially the idea introduced by Talcott Parsons (Parsons and Shils, 1951) and generally used by sociologists and anthropologists to distinguish "social system" from "cultural system."

Bringing the discussion back to the specific context of psychotherapy, we are thus led to consider the personal functioning and the personality development of the participants (patients and therapists). We are also led to consider the respective life situations and intersecting life courses of patients and therapists as another aspect of the functional context of psychotherapy. We recognize the institutional organization and societal tradition of psychotherapy as a meaningful aspect of the functional context (Kadushin, 1969; Roman and Trice, 1974). Similarly, we are accustomed to a variety of symbolic orientations to therapy in our own cultural tradition, and recognize these as significant contexts of therapeutic process.

The working definition of psychotherapy proposed earlier permits us to narrow the area of context that is relevant to outcome assessment still further. The definition states that therapy is engaged in by patients to "improve their functioning as persons." This implies that the impact of therapy on its institutional and cultural environment, however significant in its own right, has no direct bearing on the evaluation of therapeutic outcome. The effect of psychotherapy in stimulating theory and research in psychology, the social sciences, and philosophy; its manifold influence on the creative arts and letters; its impact on popular thought and imagination—all are quite beside the point when it comes to judging therapeutic effectiveness with individual patients. Also extraneous is the influence of therapeutic process on the therapist, which can be excluded here without denying that therapy may have interesting consequences for the public and private lives of psychotherapists (Henry, Sims, and Spray, 1973).

For practical purposes, psychotherapeutic outcome focuses on positively or negatively evaluated changes in the life and personality of the patient. The systematic relationship of the patient's life and personality to the facets of psychotherapeutic process is presented schematically in Table 8-1. The rows of the table represent progressively delimited facets of process to be used in organizing the findings of our survey. We shall report sequentially on Therapy as Activity, Therapy as Experience, Therapy as Dramatic Interpretation, and Therapy as Association. Because a major goal of this chapter is to introduce and test the heuristic value of a scheme for the coordinated study of therapeutic process, our treatment of process is conceptually far more refined than our treatment of outcome. Obviously it is desirable to present both with the same degree of conceptual differentiation (Table 8-1 suggests the form that this might take), but to do so would require a careful substantive analysis of all of the outcome measures employed in psychotherapy research—a task that is clearly beyond the scope of this chapter.

The Scope and Limitations of the Review

To be included in our survey, a study had to report *empirical relationships* (positive, negative, or null) between *actually measured process* and *actually measured outcome* variables in *actual cases of psychotherapy*. We have tried to be inclusive in our survey of relevant research, partly through reliance on the prior scholarship of others. For the period preceding 1970, we use as a base the several excellent works that appeared at about that time: the distinguished first edition of this *Handbook* (Bergin and Garfield, 1971); the monumental report by Meltzoff and Kornreich (1970); the important review by Luborsky, Chandler, Auerbach, Cohen, and Bachrach (1971); and our own previous coverage of the years 1969 to 1971 (Howard and Orlinsky, 1972). We have also used the more recent works by Bordin (1974), Bergin and Suinn (1975), Yalom (1975), and Lieberman (1976). For the period January 1972 through June 1976, we surveyed the *Psychological Abstracts* and independently reviewed all the empirical literature relating aspects of therapeutic process to outcome.[1]

Following our criteria for inclusion, analogue studies were omitted, along with studies using subjects who were not patients in the sense of seeking

[1]We gratefully acknowledge the diligent and intelligent assistance of Ms. Linda Marks in this phase of our work.

to improve their personal functioning in some respect. We also excluded studies that merely reported therapeutic outcome without relating it in some fashion to the process facets of activity, experience, dramatic interpretation, or association. Similarly, studies of the influence of patient and/or therapist characteristics on outcome were excluded as being input-output rather than process-outcome research. Studies of changes in patient personality or life situation that are concommitants of therapeutic outcome were excluded, again, as output-outcome research rather than process-outcome research. And, of course, studies of the influence of certain aspects of therapeutic process on other aspects of process (e.g., depth of interpretation on patient resistance) were excluded as not bearing directly on independent measures of therapeutic outcome. Studies of behavioral therapies are reviewed elsewhere in this volume.

Other limitations apply to quality. The process-outcome studies we have reviewed are plagued with problems that threaten the internal and external validity of their results, and interpretive formulations based on them. One could with little difficulty disqualify any single study as seriously flawed in one way or another, and therefore feel justified in discounting the reported findings. That approach allows the reviewer much opportunity for the venting of spleen and the proving of unimpeachable purity, but would have the unfortunate effect of leaving little to say when it comes to assembling the facts. If that is the case, of course, it is arguable that little need or ought to be said. Readers who find this restrictive stance sympathetic are advised to regard all of the substantive statements in this chapter as exceedingly tentative, and to consider only that research quality has gradually improved over the years before deciding to abandon the field altogether.

Despite its manifold temptations, and despite frequent "uncharitable mutterings" (Glass and Smith, 1976) against researchers, dissertation sponsors, and journal editors, we have not taken that harsh approach. Being researchers ourselves we are temperamentally more hopeful and, like the optimistic brother in the old joke, could not help feeling that "there must be a horse in there somewhere." If study after flawed study seemed to point

TABLE 8-1 The Relation of Process Facets to Therapeutic Outcome

Facets of Interpersonal Process			Outcome Categories			
			Patient's Physical Personality		Patient's Ongoing Life	
			Personality Functioning	Personality Development	Life Situation	Life Course
Occurring *Involvement*	Therapy as *Activity*	Individual	Therapist behavior			
			Patient behavior			
		Joint	Behavioral interaction			
	Therapy as *Experience*	Individual	Patient perception			
			Therapist perception			
		Joint	Conjoint experience			
Emerging *Relation*	Therapy as *Dramatic Interpretation*	Individual	Patient message			
			Therapist message			
		Joint	Symbolic interaction			
	Therapy as *Association*	Individual	Patient prescription			
			Therapist prescription			
		Joint	Normative organization			

significantly in the same general direction, we could not help believing that somewhere in all that variance there must be a reliable real effect. We strongly agree with Glass and Smith (1976) that "Too many attempts to integrate research restrict variation in both outcomes and situational variables by arbitrarily discarding studies which fail to meet picayune design requirements or by eliminating studies that employ [process or] outcome measures the reviewer dislikes. Such approaches are wasteful of significant data that, though ambiguous when they stand alone, can be informative when viewed in the context of dozens of other studies."

We do not, however, wish to encourage readers

to approach research—as one supposedly does poetry—with a "willing suspension of disbelief." A scientific attitude, on the contrary, calls for the willing suspension of credulity, even in the face of a well-founded desire for knowledge. The careful reader will notice two practices, in particular, that tend to bias our review in favor of a fuller, more positive picture of process-outcome research than might otherwise be obtained. We treat all outcome measures as if they were equivalent, and we count studies that used multiple outcome measures as showing positive findings if there was a statistically significant association of process with at least one major outcome variable. These are not desirable practices, but in the present pre-paradigmatic stage of research they are defensible defects. We are still trying to move from a global, intuitive formulation of isolated variables toward a more analytical, systematic definition of empirical constructs. Accordingly, we concentrate here on the careful analysis of therapeutic process, and regard that as the most enduring contribution of this review. Despite the excellent survey of outcome measures recently provided by leading workers in the field (Waskow and Parloff, 1975), a systematic substantive analysis of outcome remains to be done. Until that has been accomplished, it is feasible to argue with Glass and Smith (1976) that "All outcome measures [are] more or less related to 'well-being' and so at a general level are comparable." On the side of stringency, we note that we do not dwell on statistically insignificant ($p > .05$) trends or on unreplicated findings, nor do we count only "significant" findings without mentioning reported null results as well. With these strictures in mind, we turn to our survey of empirical research.

THERAPY AS ACTIVITY

The *occurring involvement* in the therapeutic process, viewed externally from the perspective of the nonparticipant observer, is conceived as a system of activity. This activity may be treated "objectively" in the sense that it can be made meaningful to the observer without recourse or reference to the meaning that it has for the participating actors. Process-outcome studies of therapy as an activity

system have focused primarily on certain aspects of *therapist behavior* and of *patient behavior,* and to a much smaller extent on characteristics of the *behavioral interaction.*

Therapist Behavior and Therapeutic Outcome

An individual's activity in a social situation is generally differentiated for analytic purposes into task behavior and interpersonal behavior. The category of task behavior refers to the specific content or agenda imposed by the individual's role, as it is realized in his or her role performance. Task behavior includes instrumental activities, which might be described as tactical "moves" made in regard to the individual's goals in the involvement, and communicative activities whose function is to transmit information. Interpersonal behavior, on the other hand, refers to the individual's style or manner in orienting to co-participants in the involvement. One aspect of interpersonal behavior is the individual's "approach" or "attitude" toward others. A complementary aspect is the individual's demeanor or self-presentation in the situation.

Therapist Instrumental Activity

The therapist's instrumental activity is usually conceptualized as clinical technique, and a number of studies comparing therapeutic outcome for different techniques have been reported in the research literature. Recently Luborsky, Singer, and Luborsky (1975) and Glass and Smith (1976) have independently reviewed this literature and have found the differences in therapeutic efficacy to be relatively marginal. Unfortunately, most of these studies simply identify the clinical techniques under comparison by reference to the therapist's professed orientation, without monitoring actual in-session therapist behavior. The danger of assuming that there is a close correspondecne between professed orientation and actual behavior, or that methods of practice are as distinctive as the labels associated with them, is made clear by a recent study that compared behavioral and analytic therapies. Sloane, Staples, Cristol, Yorkston, and Whipple (1975) monitored various aspects of behavior in both analytic and behavioral therapists, and found similarities and differences that would not have been anticipated on the basis of professed orientation. For example, behavior therapists and analytic therapists used "interpretation" to approximately the same extent, and behavior therapists were rated as more "empathic" than analytic therapists. Since our aim here is to focus particularly on Therapy as Activity, we shall restrict ourselves to those process-outcome studies in which actual therapist behaviors were observed.

Given these limitations, there are surprisingly few studies that relate therapists' instrumental techniques to therapeutic outcome. These generally indicate that, in typical segments of treatment process, active and positive participation by the therapist is linked to successful outcome. Thus, "leading" behavior (Ashby, Ford, Guerney, and Guerney, 1957), confrontation (Johnson, 1971; Mainord, Burk, and Collins, 1965; Truax and Wittmer, 1973), praise (Rogers, 1973), and direct approval (Sloane et al., 1975) were all associated with positive therapeutic outcome. Baker (1960), however, found no significant differences in the effect of "leading" versus "reflective" techniques, and Nagy (1973) found confrontation to be unrelated to outcome in a study of short-term therapy.

A more differentiated study of the interaction between therapist technique and patient characteristics (Abramowitz, Abramowitz, Roback, and Jackson, 1974) found that patients at a college counseling center who were oriented to an external locus of control had better outcomes in highly structured or "directive" group therapy, whereas patients who were oriented to an internal locus of control had better outcomes in unstructured or "nondirective" groups. This finding makes good clinical sense, and suggests an important qualification to the position implied by the previously cited studies. However, some doubt was cast on the generality of this finding by another study using marathon groups with institutionalized drug addicts (Kilmann and Howell, 1974) in which no interaction was found between locus of control and therapist structuring in relation to therapeutic outcome.

Contrasting the impact of typical insight-oriented "moves" (e.g., interpretation, reflection of feeling, advice) with therapist techniques that aim to increase the patient's direct emotional participation (e.g., role playing, repetition of affect laden phrases, and expressive movements such as striking a couch), Nichols (1974) obtained evidence that marginally favored emotive techniques in brief individual therapy with students seen at a university counseling center. Semon and Goldstein (1957) had previously compared therapist interventions in group therapy with hospitalized schizophrenics, aimed either at promoting patient interaction or promoting insight into underlying motivations, but observed no significant differences in patients' hospital adjustment.

On the negative side, therapist behavior associated with comparatively poorer outcomes was described in different studies as emphasizing "reflection" (Ashby et al., 1957), clarifying and interpretive statements (Sloane et al., 1975), and evaluative—presumably critical or judgmental—statements (Truax, 1970a).

A technical procedure that is not directly a function of therapist behavior, but is nevertheless sometimes utilized by therapists as an alternative means of fostering self-awareness in patients is audio or video feedback. So far, studies of this technique have produced mixed results regarding therapeutic outcome (Bailey, 1970; Kaswan and Love, 1969; Paredes, Gottheil, Tausig, and Cornelison, 1969).

Although active and positive therapist participation seems to be therapeutically productive, and certain kinds of therapist behavior may be deleterious, the studies reviewed in this section provide little solid information regarding the direction of causal influence. For example, it seems quite plausible that patients who are making good progress in therapy may elicit more positive responsiveness and praise from their therapists. Ordinary correlational analysis would not discriminate between this case and the obverse case in which therapist instrumental behavior leads to positive outcome. This is an area in which true experiments (Campbell and Stanley, 1966)—experiments in which therapist instrumental activities are systematically varied—or models for the causal analysis of nonexperimental data (e.g., Howard, Krause, and Orlinsky, 1969) might be employed.

Therapist Communicative Activity
The therapist's messages to the patient are conveyed by means of activities such as speech and

gesture. Logically, the meaning content of the messages are distinct from the media and channels of message transmission. Signal production and other specifically nonsymbolic aspects of communication (e.g., quantity of verbalization, vocal quality, and format characteristics such as use of questions vs. use of statements) define the sphere of communicative activity.

Several studies have attempted to relate therapists' communicative activities to outcome, with generally disappointing results. Various measures of the amount and rate of therapist speech showed no relationship to therapeutic outcome in a study reported by Barrington (1961). Essentially the same results were obtained for amount of therapist verbal activity by Scher (1975) and by Sloane et al. (1975), although evidence to the contrary regarding length of therapist response was reported by Truax (1970b). The degree of therapist control over message flow, as measured by Lennard and Bernstein (1969) categories, was also found to be unrelated to therapeutic outcome (Sloane et al., 1975)

The most promising work on therapists' communicative activity is that reported by Rice (1965), who focused on voice quality and the freshness of words and word combinations. She found that an expressive vocal style and use of fresh and vivid language by therapists were associated with positive patient change, whereas an "artificial" voice quality and stereotypic language were associated with poorer outcomes. These features of expressive behavior verge on interpersonal style or orientation, to which we turn next.

Therapist Interpersonal Behavior
Interpersonal behavior denotes the individual's orientation or manner of relating to coparticipants in a social situation, as distinct from the specific content or quantity of words and deeds that are exchanged. It is a matter of the "atmosphere" or "spirit" in which the therapeutic work is done. An example will serve to clarify the distinction in respect to therapist behavior. The technique of confrontation (an instrumental task behavior) might be utilized in a friendly and sympathetic way, or in an aggressive impersonal fashion, or even in a hostile-competitive mode. The interpersonal aspect

of behavior complements and qualifies the task aspect, and ideally the two should be studied in conjunction if the relative impact of each on therapeutic outcome is to be determined.

One of the most familiar and widely utilized schemes for studying interpersonal behavior is that developed by Leary and his associates (Freedman, Leary, Ossorio, and Coffee, 1951; Leary, 1957): a circular ordering of descriptors constructed around the orthogonal axes of attachment (acceptance-rejection, affection-hostility, warmth-coldness) and power (dominance-dependence, assertiveness-submissiveness, directiveness-compliance). Only Crowder (1971, 1972) has employed this scheme in a process-outcome study. Sampling segments from early, middle, and late phases in the course of treatment, he found that therapists in both successful and unsuccessful cases were most frequently "supportive-interpretive" (i.e., warm and somewhat assertive) in their interpersonal behavior, as one might expect from the "helping" character of the therapist role. Neverthless, therapists in cases with favorable outcomes were found to be significantly more "supportive-interpretive," less "hostile-competitive" and less "passive-resistant" *late* in therapy, and relatively more "hostile-competitive" and less "passive-resistant" (i.e., perhaps more challenging) *early* in treatment, than were therapists in unsuccessful cases. These findings tend to reinforce the impression about the therapeutic value of active and positive participation by the therapist given by studies of therapist task behavior, but the same methodological caution concerning the drawing of causal inferences applies here as well.

A great many studies that bear on therapist interpersonal behavior have been done to test the theory of "facilitative conditions" articulated by Rogers (1957). Therapist empathy, unconditional positive regard, and self-congruence or genuineness are conceptually complex variables, as Kiesler (1973) has observed, and they have been measured in various ways. Some measures, such as Barrett-Lennard's (1959) Relationship Inventory, are based on patient or therapist perceptions of the "facilitative conditions," and provide an insider's perspective on the occurring involvement that belongs to the facet of Therapy as Experience. The main alternative measurement instruments are the scales developed by Truax and his associates (Truax and Carkhuff, 1967) based on ratings of recorded process segments by nonparticipant observers, but of these only the scale for "nonpossessive warmth" (unconditional positive regard) unambiguously belongs in the conceptual domain of interpersonal behavior. A close reading of the rating scales suggests, for instance, that the concept of "genuineness" might be translated by the terms "sincerity" and "presence," which from our perspective would place it in the sphere of Therapy as Dramatic Interpretation. The concept of "accurate empathy" is even more ambiguous: insofar as it implies a correct understanding of the patient's message *and* a response from the therapist referring to the viewpoint and couched in the phrases of the patient's statement, then it too is a matter of symbolic communication or Therapy as Dramatic Interpretation. However, insofar as these things imply that the therapist takes the patient's implicit meaning very seriously and treats it with the careful attention that something very important deserves, then "accurate empathy" also belongs with "nonpossessive warmth" in the domain of interpersonal behavior, as a sign of deep respect. The combination of empathy and positive regard would place the therapist in the accepting-receptive quadrant of the Leary circumplex, and define a particular manner of relating to the patient. With these considerations in mind, we shall review the evidence from process-outcome research regarding nonparticipant ratings of warmth and empathy here, returning to similar ratings of genuineness and empathy in treating Therapy as Dramatic Interpretation; participant ratings of these "conditions" are considered in terms of Therapy as Experience. For a more extended critique of theoretical and methodological issues involved in research on "facilitative conditions," especially with reference to Rogers' hypothesis that they constitute necessary and sufficient conditions for client improvement, see the chapter by Parloff, Waskow, and Wolfe (this volume).

Since the original study by Halkides (1958) in which a positive relationship was found between therapist warmth, empathy, and therapeutic outcome, a great deal of research has been devoted to

this topic. Truax and Mitchell (1971), reviewing their own and others' work published prior to 1970, cited eleven process-outcome studies on nonpossessive warmth and thirteen on accurate empathy. Our own search added another twelve studies on warmth (Donofrio, 1969; Truax, 1970c; Truax, Wargo, and Volksdorf, 1970; Truax, Wittmer, and Wargo, 1971; Garfield and Bergin, 1971; Melnick and Pierce, 1971; Mullen and Abeles, 1971; McNally, 1973; Mitchell, Bozarth, Truax, and Krauft, 1973; Truax, Altman, Wright, and Mitchell, 1973; Schauble and Pierce, 1974; Sloane et al., 1975) and twenty-two on empathy (the twelve above, plus Bergin and Jasper, 1969; Tausch, Eppel, Fittkau, and Minsel, 1969; Tausch, Sander, Bastine, and Friese, 1970; Truax, 1970b; Truax, and Wittmer, 1971a; Mintz, Luborsky, and Auerbach, 1971; Kurtz and Grummon, 1972; Minsel, Bommert, Bastine, Langer, Nickel, and Tausch, 1971; Beutler, Johnson, Neville, and Workman, 1972; Nagy, 1973). Approximately two-thirds of the twenty-three studies of warmth, and a similar percentage of the thirty-five studies of empathy show a significant positive association between the externally rated aspects of therapist interpersonal behavior and therapeutic outcome; the remaining one-third show mostly null results, with significant negative correlations the rare exception (e.g., Truax, Wargo, Frank, Imber, Battle, Hoehn-Saric, Nash, and Stone, 1966, with regard to therapist warmth).

Taken at face value, these results lead to the conclusion that warmth and empathy are highly desirable qualities of therapist behavior. A simple tally gives no insight into the uneven quality and methodological problems of this body of research (for this, see Parloff et al., this volume), but it does seem to make two points fairly clear: (1) the results are far too variable to support the hypothesis that warmth and empathy are necessary and sufficient conditions of good outcome; (2) if they do not by themselves guarantee a good outcome, their presence probably adds significantly to the mix of beneficial therapeutic ingredients, and almost surely does no harm. That these factors interact differentially with other aspects of therapist style is suggested by Mintz et al. (1971), who found that an "optimal empathic relationship" was positively related to outcome only when therapist directiveness was minimal, while directiveness was positively associated with outcome when empathic warmth was low. If generally true, this would help to explain why students of nondirective Rogerian therapy have mainly found positive results, while those studying more heterogeneous therapies have tended to get null findings (e.g., Garfield and Bergin, 1971; Mitchell et al., 1973; Sloane et al., 1975). Even without the evident convergence of studies, it is plausible to assume that a minimal level of nonpossessive warmth and empathy is important, since an exceedingly exploitative, rejecting, and insensitive therapist is likely to benefit no one.

Patient Behavior and Therapeutic Outcome

The patient's behavior in therapy may also be thought of in terms of task behavior and interpersonal behavior, although process-outcome studies of the latter outnumber the former. This is probably due to the fact that therapeutic techniques are usually thought of as aspects of therapist behavior, but not patient behavior. Studies of patient task behavior focus on communicative rather than instrumental activities, although there is no obvious reason why patients should not also be seen as making tactical "moves" in pursuit of their own strategic goals vis-à-vis therapists.

Patient Communicative Activity

Four studies report evidence on the association of therapeutic outcome with the quantity and patterning of patients' speech and silence. Smith, Bassin, and Froehlich (1960) found no relation between outcome in group therapy and the amount of time that patients talked during their sessions. Scher (1975) also found no relation between outcome in individual therapy and the proportion of time that patients talked in typical segments. Sloane et al. (1975), however, reported a positive association between outcome in individual analytically oriented therapy and the total amount of time that the patient spoke during the fifth interview. This association actually resulted from the fact that successful patients "did not speak more often but rather spoke in longer blocks when they did speak" (p. 193). In a convergent vein, Cook (1964) found that successful patients tended to be silent for

longer periods within typical session segments, and a similar trend was noted by Sloane et al. (1975). Taken together, these studies would appear to imply that more successful patients take the time to think about what it is they want to say, and then have more to say about it.

Two other studies suggest that certain formal characteristics of the patient's language differentiate between better and poorer therapeutic outcomes. Barrington (1961) found that patients using more sophisticated words (larger number of syllables per word) in the first two sessions tended to have a more positive outcome. Moreover, Roshal (1953) reported an increasing variety in word usage (as measured by the type-token ratio) over the course of treatment for successful patients in individual therapy.

Voice quality is another aspect of patient communicative activity that has been studied in relation to therapeutic outcome. Butler, Rice, and Wagstaff (1962, 1963) rated segments of initial interviews and found that patients who were successful in client-centered therapy spoke with more vocal "energy," "openness," and "expressiveness" than less successful patients. In general, more aspects of patients' than of therapists' communicative behavior seem to be associated with therapeutic outcome. This is probably due to a greater variabliity among patients than among therapists, since therapists tend to be trained in particular patterns of task behavior.

Patient Interpersonal Behavior

One aspect of interpersonal style is affective expressiveness, the degree and quality of feeling that is displayed in an interaction. Regarding quantity of affective expression, Nichols (1974) reported that sucessful outcome in a brief cathartic therapy designed to intensify emotional discharge was significantly correlated with patient expressiveness, with the "high dischargers" showing more positive change than the "low dischargers." Cabral, Best, and Paton (1975), however, found no relation between amounts of abreaction and outcome among patients in an exploratory study of two therapy groups.

In the more typical therapeutic procedure, quality of affect expressed was also found to be related to outcome. Truax (1971) gave evidence that patients in group therapy who were better able to express negative feelings tended to have better outcomes. Mintz et al. (1971), studying tapes of early sessions in individual therapy, also found that patients who expressed hostility were more successful. One of the findings reported by Crowder (1971, 1972) lends support to the results of Mintz et al. Crowder noted that more sucessful patients were significantly more "hostile-competitive" in behavioral orientation in the early phase of treatment. He also found that more successful patients were less "passive-resistant" in early and middle phases of treatment, suggesting that they were in general more assertive in expressing feeling attitudes to the therapist. Successful patients were also found to be significantly more "support-seeking" during the same early and middle phases, implying an interesting balance of assertiveness and ingratiation.

Studies in which patient likeability was rated by nonparticipant judges may also be thought of as a function of the patient's interpersonal behavior, insofar as patients who show more ingratiating (support-seeking) behavior are likely to be rated by judges as more likeable. (Therapist perceptions of patient likeability, though perhaps not unrelated empirically, would be considered as an aspect of therapist experience.) If this interpretation is allowed, then Stoler's (1963, 1966) reports of a positive association between patient likeability and outcome reinforce Crowder's finding concerning support-seeking behavior. This is somewhat qualified by Prager's (1971) result indicating that rated likeability was greater in more successful patients only in the latter phase of treatment, a finding running counter to Crowder's (1971, 1972) failure to find differences between successful and unsuccessful cases in terms of patient interpersonal behavior during the last third of treatment sessions. Even with these inconsistencies, however, patient interpersonal behavior so far seems to be a promising area of exploration.

Behavioral Interaction and Therapeutic Outcome

Therapeutic activities thus far have been viewed only as functions of individual participants, that is, the therapist and the patient. The mutual fit and patterning of individual activities, however, also constitute an important aspect of Therapy as Activity, and these emergent patterns of behavioral interaction between patient and therapist have received some attention in the research literature.

The same distinctions that we have drawn in dealing with individual behavior reappear at the level of the behavioral interaction. The convergence of the patient's and the therapist's task behaviors defines the substantive thrust of the interaction, both in terms of their instrumental acivities (strategic exchange) and in terms of their communicative activities (communicative exchange). Similarly, a certain stylistic balance arises through the interaction of the patient's and the therapist's interpersonal behaviors.

Surprisingly, we have found no process-outcome studies focusing on the substantive thrust of interactive behavior in therapy considered in terms of strategic exchange, and only one that related outcome to the amount of communicational flow. Coons (1957), obtained significantly higher percentages of patient improvement in therapy groups that had high proportions of patient-patient interaction, as contrasted to therapy groups with minimal peer interaction. We did, however, find three process-outcome studies concerning the stylistic balance of the behavioral transaction. In one, Parloff (1961) assessed the quality of patient-therapist relationship between each patient and the therapist in three therapy groups, and found that the degree to which the relationship converged on Fiedler's (1950) "ideal therapeutic relationship" was significantly correlated in the expected direction with therapeutic outcome. In another study of group therapy, Cabral et al. (1975) had observers rate characteristics of group response to each patient, finding that an accepting (warm and permissive) group atmosphere was positively associated with patient change. Frequency of group attention to patient remarks was not related to outcome, however. In the third study, Dietzel and Abeles (1975) used the Leary circumplex to determine the complementarity between patient and therapist interpersonal behavior during three phases of individual treatment. They found no difference between more and less successful cases in the initial and final phases of treatment, but did observe that successful patient-therapist pairs were significantly lower in complementarity during the middle phase.

This suggests that a period of disequilibrium—perhaps through the therapist's refusal to meet patient expectations—may be a critical factor in the successful induction of therapeutic change, once a solid complementarity has been initially established.

Summarizing studies of Therapy as Activity, our cumulative impression is that in cases with better therapeutic outcome, nonparticipant observers note that therapists exhibit active and positive instrumental task behavior, and are warm and respectful toward patients in their interpersonal behavior. In these more successful cases, nonparticipant observers also note that patients' use of speech (communicative activity) is relatively deliberate, sophisticated and vocally expressive, and the patients relate to their therapists with likeable, support-seeking but also assertive interpersonal behavior. The studies done thus far suggest that the positive quality of the relational bond, as exemplified in the reciprocal interpersonal behaviors of the participants, is more clearly related to patient improvement than are any of the particular treatment techniques used by therapists.

THERAPY AS EXPERIENCE

The facet of experience highlights the *occurring involvement* in the therapeutic process as it is viewed internally from the perspective of the participant observer. Participants in therapy must report or record their perceptions in some way for these to be treated as data, but once reports are given they can be treated with the same methodological objectivity as any other data (see Orlinsky and Howard, 1975, for an extended discussion of this issue). It is also important to note that reports of their experiences by participants may include their perceptions of others and of the social and physical milieu, and are not limited to perceptions of self.

Patient Experience and Therapeutic Outcome

The individual's perception in a social situation is generally divided in a shifting, fluid way between self-awareness and a typically more salient awareness of the "object world" that is comprised of co-participating persons and the current situation in

which they are mutually involved. Two things may differentiate psychotherapy from most other social situations, so far as the patient's perception is concerned. First, the therapist is likely to be an unusually influential focus of awareness for the patient, expecially in individual therapy where the therapist is virtually the sole occupant of the patient's "object world." Second, the patient's own self-perceptions are likely to be brought more forcefully into the foreground of awareness than in most other social situations. Both of these factors should heighten sensitivity to the impact of the experiential aspects of the relationship on the patient.

Patient Self-Perceptions

Just as the individual's perception generally is divided between "self" and "other," so the individual's self-perception is in turn typically divided between the externalization of self in conduct and appearance (i.e., the "public" or outward manifestations of self) and the internal milieu of feeling and identity (i.e., the "private" or inward manifestations of self). Regarding the externalization of self, we have found no process-outcome studies involving the patient's self-perception of appearance (e.g., attractiveness) and, more surprisingly, only a few involving the patient's self-perception of his or her own participation.

In most therapies the patient's participation consists of engagement in a specialized sort of conversation. A recent study by Saltzman, Luetgart, Roth, Creaser and Howard (1976) of patients' (and therapists') perceptions of therapeutic process produced two findings that are pertinent to this conversation. One was that clients at a university student counseling service who perceived themselves as expressing their thoughts and feelings with greater "openness" early in treatment (third session) had significantly better outcomes than clients who perceived themselves as less open in talking with their therapists. Complementing this, clients who felt that they had a better "understanding" of what their therapists were trying to communicate to them also had significantly better outcomes than their less comprehending cohorts. The attainment of self-understanding through honest encounters with others, and the opportunity for emotional catharsis and self-expression, were also instrumental qualities of participation in group psychotherapy stressed by successfully terminated patients (Yalom, Tinklenburg, and Gilula, 1975).

In addition to qualities of instrumental participation, another aspect of instrumentality that is salient in perceptions of conduct is goal attainment. Not surprisingly, Saltzman et al. (1976) found that the client's sense of "movement" or progress in solving problems, even as early as the third session, was significantly and positively related to client improvement (as judged by the therapist at termination). This finding is reinforced by Tovian's (1977) analysis of our own data (118 female outpatients in individual therapy), which indicated that "experienced benefit" and the attainment of catharsis, encouragement, and a sense of mastery and insight by patients in their therapy sessions were predictive of patient improvement at termination.

Relational aspects of participation are also salient in the individual's perception of his or her own externalization of self, in this case taking the form of the patient's awareness of relating to the therapist. Tovian (1977) found that patients who saw themselves as acting in an "accepting" (i.e., friendly, attentive, agreeing) manner toward their therapists were more likely to be rated as improved. A complementary finding was reported by Lorr and McNair (1964), whose data indicated that patients perceiving themselves as acting in a "hostile-controlling" manner had significantly poorer outcomes than others.

The same two studies give information on a related aspect of patients' self-perception of their conduct toward their therapists. Lorr and McNair (1964) reported no significant association between outcome and patient self-perceptions as relating in a "dependent" or in a "controlling-resistive" manner toward their therapists, but indicated that patients who viewed themselves as "actively involved" were significantly more improved. Tovian (1977) also found that patients who reported acting in a "structuring" (i.e., actively initiating) manner with their therapists had better outcomes. Considering the differences in patient population (Lorr's all male V.A. patients vs. our own all female urban clinic patients), the convergence in findings is reassuring.

A few findings are available on patients' internal self-experience. In terms of patients' sense of role-identity, for example, Saltzman et al. (1976) found a tendency toward better self-rated outcome among patients who felt a greater sense of "responsibility" for solving their own problems and changing their own behavior, as compared with those who put the responsibility for this more on their therapists. Again, Jeske (1973) found that patients in group psychotherapy who more often "identified" with the experiences reported by other patients tended to have more favorable outcomes than those who felt less identified. These findings suggest that the patient's experience of active and positive involvement is predictive of good outcome in diverse forms of psychotherapy.

The realm of feeling tends to be perceived as perhaps the inner-most core of self-experience. Among thirty-some patient feelings routinely surveyed in our data on patient self-perception, Tovian (1977) found two clusters to be significantly associated with improvement: feeling "relieved" (relieved, grateful, pleased, hopeful) and "confident" (confident, relaxed, likeable). Saltzman et al. (1976) found that the patient's awareness of having emotional reactions focused on the therapist distinguished significantly between more and less improved patients, while awareness of feelings not focused on the therapist (i.e., hostility, anxiety, depression) was unrelated to outcome. In this vein, Board (1959) found a relation between the patient's feeling of liking for the therapist and outcome. Also, in an exploratory study of group therapy, Cabral et al. (1975) noted a consistent relationship between outcome and patients' perceptions of intense emotional expression. More research in this area of patient self-experience seems indicated by the few findings accumulated thus far.

Patient Perceptions of the Therapist

As in the case of self-perception, it seems natural to distinguish between the patient's view of the therapist's self-externalization (i.e., appearance and conduct) and the therapist's seemingly "inherent" attributes as an individual. We have found no process-outcome studies dealing with therapist appearance, and as regards the patient's perception of the therapist's conduct, we found that all of the relevant studies concentrated on the therapist's relational or interpersonal participation.

The emphasis on the patient's perception of the

therapist's manner of relating is a direct result of the Rogerian concern with warmth, empathy, and genuineness, as formulated in Barrett-Lennard's "Relationship Inventory" and Truax's "Relationship Questionnaire." Unlike the original Halkides (1958) study and the subsequent development of behavioral scales by Truax and his colleagues, Barrett-Lennard drew on the perceptions of the participants themselves. That is why some of the research concerning "therapist-offered conditions" was reviewed in our section on Therapy as Activity, and some here in the section on Therapy as Experience. Studies that have compared ratings of these conditions from the nonparticipant and participant perspectives (e.g., Bozarth and Grace, 1970; Caracena and Vicory, 1969; Carkhuff and Burstein, 1970; Fish, 1970; Kurtz and Grummon, 1972; McNally, 1973; Mitchell et al., 1973) tend to show little correlation between the perspectives, and in terms of our own scheme we find no reason to assume that warmth, empathy, and genuineness rated by nonparticipant observers are conceptually equivalent to warmth, empathy, and genuineness rated by patients and/or therapists. If our scheme is sound in this respect, there should be no reason to expect that correlations between nonparticipant and participant perspectives on occurring involvement (i.e., between "activity" and "experience") would be on the same order as reliability coefficients, or that failure to find such high correlations impugns the validity of the scales.

The therapist's relational participation, as perceived by the patient, can be treated for convenience in terms of value contact and status contact. A great many studies focus on the patient's experience of the therapist's value contact in relation to outcome. This includes perceptions of the therapist's nonpossessive warmth, positive regard, acceptance, positive valuing, and respect. Although fine distinctions might be drawn among these constructs, it seems to us that their commonality must outweigh the nuances of difference. Moreover, the evidence of thirteen studies, ranging in temporal focus from the idealized "moment" of process to the whole course of treatment, is unanimous in indicating that the patient's perception of the therapist's manner as affirming the patient's value is positively and significantly as-

sociated with good therapeutic outcome (Board, 1959; Barrett-Lennard, 1962; Strupp, Wallach and Wogan, 1964; Lorr, 1965; Feitel, 1968; Cain, 1973; McNally, 1973; Mitchell et al., 1973; McClanahan, 1974; Sloane et al., 1975; Bent, Putnam, and Kiesler, 1976; Martin and Sterne, 1976; Saltzman et al., 1976). Given the diversity of samples, measurement instruments, and analytical strategies represented by these studies, the convergence of findings seems especially impressive. Further confirmation comes from two of the studies (Lorr, 1965; Martin and Sterne, 1976) which found that patient perception of the therapist's manner as "critical-hostile" was significantly and negatively associated with therapeutic outcome. The consistency of results using patients' perceptions of therapist warmth (in conformance with Rogers', 1957, original hypothesis) may be contrasted with studies based on ratings of nonparticipant observers. Those studies using client outcome ratings are, of course, vulnerable to halo effects, but that cannot explain all of the findings. Although it would be implausible to reduce therapeutic efficacy to mere benevolence of manner—correlations are not exceptionally high, and do not prove a causal relationship—it would also seem foolish to discount the patient's sense of affirmation by the therapist as one probable ingredient of productive therapeutic experience.

Less attention has been given to patient perceptions of the status contact implicit in the therapist's manner in connection with outcome. Lorr (1965), however, found that patients who saw their therapists as "independence-encouraging" had significantly better outcomes than others, while those who viewed their therapists as "authoritarian" in manner had significantly poorer outcomes. Using the same instrument more than a decade later, and with a rather different type of patient and treatment setting, Martin and Sterne (1976) were able to confirm the positive association of outcome with patients' perceptions of their therapists as "independence-encouraging," but found no association between outcome and "authoritarian" manner.

Perceptions of the therapist's relational participation inevitably overlap to some extent with perceptions of the therapist's "inherent" attributes as an individual. The two are, however, separable in experience, as indicated by the fact that we sometimes feel an individual's actions are "out of character," that is, the qualities attributed to his or her conduct are incongruent with the qualities attributed to the person. The individual's perceived attributes are discriminable, further, into role attributes (characteristics as performer of a given role) and personal attributes (general human qualities). Among the perceived role attributes of the therapist is his or her therapeutic skill or ability, and chief among the skills that have been studied in relation to outcome is the therapist's empathy or empathic understanding.

Fifteen studies present evidence on the relation of outcome to the patient's perception of the therapist as empathically understanding. Focusing on the idealized average "moment" of process, Lesser (1961), Barrett-Lennard (1962), Lorr (1965), Feitel (1968), and Cain (1973) found significant associations between perceived empathic understanding and patient improvement. Studying the early phase of treatment (generally within the first six sessions), Kurtz and Grummon (1972), McNally (1973), McClanahan (1974), Saltzman et al. (1976), and Tovian (1977) all found patient perception of therapist empathy to be a significant predictor of good outcome, although Mitchell et al. (1973) did not. Finally, in considering process over the course of therapy, Sapolsky (1965) and Martin and Sterne (1976) found positive relations between patient perceived understanding and patient improvement, while Sloane et al. (1975) found only a consistent but nonsignificant trend in the same direction. Kalfas (1974) reported no significant association between level of perceived empathy and outcome, but did note a significant association between outcome and variability in patient's ratings over time (the less consistent the rating of therapist empathy, the poorer the outcome). Generally, these studies support the notion that the sense of being understood by one's therapist is a fairly consistent feature of beneficial therapy as experienced by patients.

Other aspects of perceived therapeutic skill are reflected in the patient's experience of the therapist as "helpful" (Tovian, 1977), as "competent and committed to help" (Saltzman et al., 1976), as

"credible" (Beutler, Johnson, Neville, Elkins, and Jobe, 1975), as "confident" and able to induce positive expectations of treatment (Ryan and Gizynski, 1971)—all of which were found to be positively related to therapeutic outcome. Tovian (1977) also found that patients who saw their therapists as feeling "uncertain" (apprehensive, perplexed, unsure) tended to have significantly poorer outcomes.

In addition to responding to the therapist's apparent skillfulness, patients also react to their sense of the therapist's personal investment in his role functioning. Strupp, Wallach, and Wogan (1964), for example, found that patients' retrospective perceptions of their therapists as really "interested" over the course of treatment was positively associated with good outcome. Using the Strupp inventory, Bent et al. (1976) found that patients who perceived their therapists as "active" and "involved" also had significantly better outcomes. Patients, on the other hand, who saw their therapists early in treatment as feeling "detached" (bored, detached, tired, and distracted)—like those seen as feeling "uncertain"—tended to deteriorate rather than improve in therapy (Tovian, 1977). Another sign of perceived therapist investment that was positively linked to good outcome was the patient's experience of the therapist as being "satisfied" (Ryan and Gizynski, 1971). Finally, a study by Horenstein (1974) suggests that perceived therapist qualities are not simply related as such to outcome, but are also influential as confirmations or disappointments of prior expectaions—with the confirmative perceptions positively associated with patient improvement. The same principle is illustrated in reverse in a study by Hayward (1974), who found that only clients who expected low self-disclosure from therapists showed more improvement with therapists whom they saw as high in self-disclosure.

The core portion of the patient's perception of the therapist is composed of personal attributes—the sort of person that the therapist seems to be, as distinct from the skill or investment that he or she manifests in the therapist role. One variable in this area that has been studied is the patient's perception of the therapist's genuineness or self-congruence, which Barrett-Lennard (1962), Cain

(1973), McNally (1973), Mitchell et al. (1973), and McClanahan (1974) found to be positively related to outcome, but which Sloane et at. (1975) found to show only a consistent but nonsignificant positive trend. In addition to this aspect of the therapist's personal presence, the patient's sense of the therapist as "likeable" has also been found to be positively associated with outcome (Lipkin, 1954; Board, 1959; Bent et al., 1976).

Patient Perceptions of the Therapeutic Relationship

Aside from the co-participating individuals, perceptions of the "object world" also include awareness of the physical and social milieu in which they are active. We found no studies that examined the influence of patients' (or therapists') perceptions of their physical milieu on outcome, but there are a few studies that focus on the therapeutic relationship *per se* (in individual therapy) or the group process *per se* (in group therapy) and thus give information about the perceived social milieu.

Sapolsky (1965) reported that female inpatients who saw their therapists as similar to themselves in self-image, and who attributed a corresponding sense of similarity to their therapists, were judged as significantly more improved at discharge by clinical supervisors. Looking at a different aspect of relationship, Saltzman et al. (1976) found that patients who viewed their therapy as highly different from other social relationships, and reported that it was an active focus of their thoughts and feelings outside of actual sessions, were more likely than others to improve. Tovian (1977) also found that patients high on an experience dimension called "erotic transference communication" (feeling erotized affection toward the therapist, seeing the therapist as feeling intimate, and talking together about the relationship) tended to improve significantly more than others, while those patients who strongly experienced a dimension called "confrontation with a cold, domineering therapist" tended to deteriorate in treatment. This emphasis on the quality of the perceived emotional bond in dyadic relationships echoes the emphasis on patients' perceptions of group cohesion and emotional support as a correlate of outcome in therapeutic groups. Dickoff and Lakin (1963), Kapp, Gleser, Bressen-

den, Emerson, Winget, and Kashdan (1964), Yalom, Houts, Zimerbag, and Rand (1967), and Cabral et al. (1975) all report that patients who improve more in group psychotherapy perceive a warm, accepting atmosphere more often than those who fare less well. With the exception of Yalom et al., who sampled patient perceptions of group cohesiveness in the sixth and twelfth sessions of ongoing groups, these data derive from retrospective reflections on the course of treatment.

Therapist Experience and Therapeutic Outcome

Process-outcome research utilizing the therapist's perceptions of process has focused primarily on the therapist's view of the patient, secondarily on the therapist's self-experience, and to a very slight extent on perceived qualities of their relationship.

Therapist Perceptions of the Patient

The therapist's view of the patient can be differentiated into perceptions of the patient's self-externalization in appearance and conduct, and the patient's attributes as a co-participant in therapy. We found no process-outcome studies involving the therapist's perception of the patient's appearance, but several studies have examined various aspects of patients' participation as seen by their therapists.

The patient's instrumental participation includes both role engagement and goal attainment, related in the therapist's view to the "means" and "ends" (respectively) of the patient's conduct. Certain qualities of patient role engagement, as observed by therapists, have been associated significantly with therapeutic outcome. Gendlin, Jenney, and Shlien (1960), for example, found that therapist reports of clients' movement from talking about to experiencing feelings, were positively associated with improvement in individual client-centered therapy. Roether and Peters (1972), studying 64 sex offenders in group therapy, found that therapist perceptions of patients' expression of hostility was positively related to outcome. A complementary finding reported by Strupp, Wallach, Jenkins, and Wogan (1963) was a moderate but significant negative correlation between outcome and therapists' retrospective perceptions of patient defensiveness. Other aspects of patient role participation perceived by therapists, however, seemed un-related to therapeutic outcome. Gendlin et al. (1960), replicating Seeman (1954), found no as-sociation between outcome and therapists' impres-sions of patients' talking about therapy, the therapist, or the present. Therapists' perceptions of their patients' "understanding," as rated after the third session (Saltzman et al., 1976) were positively but marginally related to outcome; another study (Sloane et al., 1975), however, after four months found no significant relationship between therapist estimates of patient understanding and outcome. These preliminary and scattered results suggest that therapist awareness of patients' freedom in experiencing feelings is predictive of good therapeutic outcome, and also suggest that further research attention to this area would be quite worthwhile.

Only two studies give data relevant to therapist perceptions of patient ongoing goal attainment in relation to eventual outcome, and their findings are somewhat in conflict. Saltzman et al. (1976) found that therapist ratings of patient "movement" or progress in problem resolution, judged from the third session, were unrelated to outcome. Malan (1976), on the other hand, found that therapists' intercurrent impressions that therapy was "going well" did positively relate to eventual outcome in brief psychotherapy. Closer attention to the time frame in which this sort of observation is made in future studies may help to resolve the apparent difference.

Therapists' perceptions of patient relational par-ticipation, as reflected in their impressions of pa-tient cooperation, approval, and critical behavior, were found by Sloane et al. (1975) to be unrelated to outcome. Given the relative prominence of rela-tional participation as a predictor of outcome from other observational standpoints, it is surprising to find that so little research attention has been given to this area in dealing with the therapist's experi-ence of the patient in psychotherapy.

A number of process-outcome studies focus on the patient's "inherent" attributes rather than the patient's self-externalization in conduct as a target of therapist perceptions. These attributes may be divided into role attributes and personal attributes, and within the former category into attributes of

role investment and role ability. The therapist's perception of the patient's motivation is one role investment variable examined in several process-outcome studies. Prager (1971) did not find therapists' ratings of patient motivation in the early phase of treatment to be related to outcome. Malan (1976), however, found that therapists' impres-sions of high initial motivation in their patients pre-dicted success in brief therapy, and Strupp et al. (1963) reported that therapists' retrospective as-sessments of patient motivation were positively as-sociated with good case outcome. Another indica-tion of patient role investment studied from the therapist's viewpoint by Saltzman et al. (1976) was patient "responsibility," or self-reliance in problem solving in therapy, which was significantly and posi-tively related to outcome. The therapist's view of the patient's sense of the therapy relationship as unique and paradigmatic among the patient's so-cial involvements (which we would take as a qual-itative feature of role investment) was also reported to be positively associated with outcome by Gendlin et al. (1960). The previously noted nega-tive relation between outcome and therapist-perceived patient defensiveness (Strupp et al., 1963) also reflects on the nature of role invest-ment, and adds to the impression that a complex blend of quantitative and qualitative aspects of pa-tient role investment (as perceived by therapists) is probably significantly associated with therapeutic outcome.

A scattering of variables bearing on the therapist's impression of the patient's skill or ability in the patient role have been included in some process-outcome studies. Prager (1971), for example, found therapists' early estimates of pa-tients' ability to form a good therapeutic relation-ship to be unrelated to outcome. Similarly, Sloane et al. (1975) reported that the therapist's impres-sion of the patient's suitability for therapy was unre-lated to outcome, as was the therapist's sense of the patient's judgment of how good the therapist was.

Therapist ratings of patient prognosis seem per-tinent to both the role attributes and the personal attributes of the patient, as these strike the therapist. Of the three process-outcome studies that included this variable, Prager (1971) found no association between improvement and good prognosis in the early phase of therapy, while Saltzman et al. (1976) found a significant positive association between outcome and prognosis rated in the third session, and Strupp et al. (1963) found that therapists' retrospective assessments of patient prognosis also correlated positively with outcome. On a closely related issue, Prager (1971) also found no relation between outcome and therapists' early impressions of the degree of patient disturbance. Further study obviously is needed to clarify these mixed results.

Client likeability, as seen by therapists, is the personal attribute variable most often included in process-outcome studies. Gottschalk, Mayerson, and Gottlieb (1967), studying extremely short-term emergency therapy, found no relationship between likeability (therapist liking) and outcome. Prager (1971), again, found no association between outcome and client likeability as rated by therapists early in treatment, but did find a significant positive correlation at termination—suggesting an increasing sense of liking toward more successful clients over the course of treatment, and the usual problem about direction of causal influence. Strupp et al. (1964), Ryan and Gizynski (1971), and Sloane et al. (1975), all reported significant positive associations between outcome and terminal or retrospective therapist assessments of client likeability, but offer no answer to whether the more likeable clients improve, or the more successful clients are better liked by their therapists. Brown (1970), at least, found likeability in the first session significantly and positively related to subsequent outcome, but this is qualified by the aforementioned failure of Gottshalk et al. and of Prager to obtain similar early findings. There thus remains a presumption of some connection between client likeability and therapeutic outcome, as well as a puzzle as to precisely what that connection is.

Sloane et al. (1975) assessed how "interesting" a person the patient seemed to the therapist, but found no relation between degree of interest and outcome. One would think that therapists' perceptions of their patients' personal attributes would have been a more central concern for psychotherapy researchers than seems to have been the case. Simple curiosity demands more,

and more finely differentiated, exploration of these personal attributes in relation to outcome.

Therapist Self-Perceptions

Although the therapist is not the focus of therapeutic concern, and may enter his or her own awareness most often in a subsidiary way, there is much clinical lore and some research (e.g., Howard, Orlinsky, and Hill, 1969; Orlinsky and Howard, 1975) to suggest that the therapist's self-perceptions are an especially interesting aspect of therapeutic process. We have found a few process-outcome studies in the literature that have an explicit look at the therapist's self-experience, both through self-externalization and through internalized feeling and reflection.

Two studies focused on therapists' awareness of their instrumental participation with patients, and both reported positive findings in relation to outcome. Ryan and Gizynski (1971) found in behaviorally oriented treatment that therapists of more improved clients were more likely to report after treatment that they had deliberately fostered positive expectations. Malan (1976), studying brief psychoanalytically oriented treatment, reviewed therapists' reports of their interpretive interventions and found "that directed interpretations, i.e., those that do refer to actual people, give strong positive correlations with outcome" (p. 237). Transference interpretations, which point out similarities between patient reactions toward the therapist and earlier familial relations, were particularly emphasized in this respect, while "undirected" (impersonal) interpretations were found to be negatively related to patient improvement. The success of these two exploratory studies should encourage others to investigate therapists' perceptions of their techniques with patients.

Therapists' awareness of their interpersonal or relational participation has also been the subject of process-outcome studies. Strupp et al. (1964) found a cluster of variables indicative of therapists' experience of "warmth" in relating to patients to be positively associated with therapeutic outcome. Studying the early phase of treatment, Mitchell et al. (1973) found therapists' ratings of their own nonpossessive warmth, and Saltzman et al. (1976) found therapist perceptions of their own respect and acceptance, to be significantly predictive of subsequent measures of improvement. Cain (1973) and McNally (1973), however, both failed to obtain significant relations between therapists' perceptions of their own behavior and treatment outcome.

The therapist's sense of inner involvement in therapy can be thought of as a complementary blending of situational role identity and personal identity. Among the process-outcome studies surveyed, greater interest seems to have focused on the therapist's self-experience in terms of skill and investment in the therapist role. A chief feature of the therapist's sense of skillfulness is his or her understanding of the patient's communications, but therapists' ratings of their own empathic sensitivity have not been found to correlate with outcome (Kurtz and Grummon, 1972; Cain, 1973; McNally, 1973), or to do so only very modestly (Mitchell et al., 1973; Saltzman et al., 1973).

Regarding the therapist's sense of role investment, Rosenthal and Levine (1970) found that for brief individual therapy with children, at least, poor therapist motivation for the procedure was associated with poorer therapeutic outcome. Saltzman et al. (1976), however, did not find any relation between patient improvement and the therapist's sense of "involvement" or sense of "emotional availability," defined in terms of concern and attentiveness. The two studies are not highly similar, but since there are no others bearing on this point the issue concerning the impact of therapist's self-perceived motivation is left in some doubt.

A qualitative aspect of therapist role investment is reflected in the degree of transparency or self-disclosure assumed by the therapist, which parallels to some extent the patient's perception of therapist genuineness and authenticity. Two process-outcome studies dealt with this variable, again with mixed results. Saltzman et al. (1976) found a modest positive correlation between outcome and self-perceived therapist openness early in therapy; Hayward (1974), however, found no evidence of association between client improvement and therapist ratings of self-disclosure. Cain (1973), Mitchell et al. (1973), and McNally (1973) also found no significant relationship between

therapists' self-rated genuineness and outcome. It may, of course, be no easier for therapists than for others to admit to being phony and defensive.

An individual's personal identity in a social situation is typically revealed most forcefully, if not always most clearly, by the feelings that are aroused in the course of interaction. One process-outcome study (Saltzman et al., 1976) provides some data on therapists' self-perceived affect in therapy: feeling focused on the patient (in an early session) bore no significant relation to subsequent outcome, but more general therapist depression in that session was significantly and negatively related to patient problem resolution. This is an area that has barely been opened to research.

Therapist Perceptions of the Therapeutic Relationship

Two studies of the therapeutic relationship have focused on therapist perceptions of similarity to their patients. Sapolsky (1965), studying female patients with male and female therapists, found little evidence of difference in outcome between dyads high and low in therapist-perceived similarity. Cartwright and Lerner (1963), however, found a complex interaction between outcome, similarity, and the sexual composition of dyads, which might account for Sapolsky's null finding. Cartwright and Lerner also found no significant overall association between outcome and initial accuracy, but found a significant positive association between therapist accuracy and client improvement by termination—suggesting a process of improving accuracy of therapist perception in successful cases (and progressive misperception in poorer outcomes) over the course of treatment.

Conjoint Experience and Therapeutic Outcome

Conjoint experience is the term that we apply to the patterns that emerge when the perceptions of various participants in a situation are compared. Sometimes the pattern is simply one of agreement or discrepancy; sometimes an emergent pattern is revealed that could not have been predicted from anyone's individual experience (Orlinsky and Howard, 1975). A pattern of conjoint experience among participant observations of occurring involvement is logically analogous to a pattern of behavioral interaction among nonparticipant ob-servations. One finding that might be placed here is the positive relation between outcome in group psychotherapy and a patient's general popularity early in treatment, determined sociometrically by the consensus of individual members' perceptions reported by Yalom et al. (1967).

Summarizing studies of Therapy as Experience, the following composite portrait may be sketched from the convergence of findings that relate various patient perceptions to therapeutic outcome. In more successful cases, patients experience a sense of progress in instrumental participation, and see themselves taking active initiative, though being basically accepting in relating to their therapists. They view their therapists' manner of relating in strongly complementary terms, stressing the at-titudes of affirmation and encouragement to inde-pendence that they perceive in their therapists' in-terpersonal participation. The therapeutic relation-ship itself is seen as an intimate, warm, emotionally absorbing involvement. Patients who improve more also describe their therapists as more compe-tent and confident (vs. uncertain) and more per-sonally committed or involved (vs. detached) in their roles as professional helpers, and, not surpris-ingly, more likeable as individuals. In contrast to these varied findings, only one aspect of therapist experience has thus far been clearly related to pa-tient improvement. In those cases with better therapeutic outcome, therapists viewed themselves as relatively more accepting and affirmative in their interpersonal participation. This, at least, adds the therapists' testimony to the association of outcome with these relational qualities already attested by the perceptions of patients and by nonparticipant observers of Therapy as Activity.

THERAPY AS DRAMATIC INTERPRETATION

Dramatic Interpretation refers to the construal and communication of meaning by the participants in a relationship. It is a symbolic issue of mutual com-prehension and orientation spun progressively in the course of communication, a web of interpenet-rating perspectives that is established and sustained through the participants' use of a common com-municative code. Through this joint process of Dramatic Interpretation, the *emerging relation* comes to have a "purpose" and a "history," an acknowledged scope of explicit reference and a vague penumbra of quietly disregarded implica-tions. Moreover, insofar as a relationship is viewed as a symbolic interaction, it manifests a miniature cultural system of its own—an "esoteric" set of beliefs and values that is transparent to its creators and translucent to initiates, but opaque to external observers who have not mastered the symbolic code or attended sufficiently to understand its idiomatic usage (Berger and Luckman, 1967).

Concretely, Dramatic Interpretation consists of the interplay of lines of dialogue and of significant gestures and expressions between actors, together with the qualifications and emphases suggested by the nuances of their renditions. In studying this facet of the psychotherapeutic relationship, interest focuses on what patients and therapists say and convey to each other, explicitly and implicitly: on the stories that are enacted, told, and critically dis-cussed during therapy sessions. It is not the means of transmission (i.e., communicative activity), but the meaning of the messages transmitted that is our primary concern in this section. In what follows, we review studies of *patient messages, therapist mes-sages,* and their *symbolic interaction,* as these bear on the outcome of psychotherapy.

Patient Messages and Therapeutic Outcome

The message transmitted by an actor may be characterized with respect to both its matter and manner, that is, what it is about and how it is stated. The content, of course, may be complex, and is usually capable of alternative forms of ex-pression. Marsden (1971) provided an extensive review of the methods that have been used to analyze communications in psychotherapy, and has documented the great difficulty of devising quantifiable categories capable of capturing their richness and subtlety. One thing that has struck us particularly in reviewing process-outcome studies is the frequency with which these coding schemes seem to confound the content and stylistic aspects of messages.

The great majority of process-outcome studies

of patient messages focus on whether and how the patient talks about his or her personal life and self, and the cumulative impression they convey is that patients who talk about themselves in a concrete way, with feeling, tend to be more successful in therapy than do those who focus "objectively" and generally on external circumstances.

Early studies in this area include those of Blau (1950), who found that an index of positive self-attitudes expressed by patients during treatment was indicative of subsequent successful outcome; Vargas (1954), who found increasing self-awareness in patients to be similarly predictive; and Rosenman (1955), who found greater increase in reported positive actions toward self and others among patients who improved more in treatment.

Kirtner and Cartwright (1958) examined patient communications in the first session of client-centered therapy, and were able to differentiate successful from unsuccessful cases: those who immediately dealt with "feelings in relationship problems" were invariably judged successful at termination; those who spoke of their problems as basically external to themselves were nearly always judged unsuccessful; while of those who vacillated between these two extremes, about half were successful and half unsuccessful. Although there are many doubtful features to this study, its findings are generally supported by Truax and Wittmer (1971b), who found that use of personal rather than nonpersonal references by patients was associated with positive outcome. Schauble and Pierce (1974) also reported that good outcome was associated with initially higher and progressively increasing levels of clients' internal rather than external viewing of problems, and commitment to change (manifested in clients' directly confronting their problems and feelings). The same was found by these authors to be true for clients' willingness to "own" their feelings, which reinforces Braaten's (1961) earlier finding that increasing expression of self-referent feelings in therapy characterized clients who had better treatment outcomes.

Almost all the aforemention studies were influenced by the client-centered theory of psychotherapy. The trend of interests represented in them was formalized by Carl Rogers in 1957 as a "process conception" of therapeutic change, and was subsequently formulated into several quantitative measures that came to be known as the "process scales." These were: "experiencing," or immediate exploration of self and personal involvements in a responsive way; "personal constructs," or flexibility of interpretive attitudes; "manner of problem expression," or the patient's degree of acknowledged contribution to his or her own problems; and "manner of relating," or degree of collaborative involvement. A number of studies were conducted using these "process scales" during the 1960s, and eventual interest focused especially on the "experiencing scale" whose development was strongly influenced by the thought of Eugene Gendlin. Since the "experiencing scale" and the other three are rather highly intercorrelated (Tomlinson, 1967), we shall review these process-outcome studies as a group.

Of the ten studies that focused on "process" or "experiencing" level, nine found significant positive correlations with good therapeutic outcome (Walker, Rablen, and Rogers, 1960; Kirtner, Cartwright, Robertson, and Fiske, 1961; Tomlinson and Hart, 1962; Stoler, 1963; Tomlinson and Stoler, 1967; van der Veen, 1967; Kiesler, Mathieu, and Klein, 1967; Gendlin, Beebe, Cassens, Klein, and Oberlander, 1968; Kiesler, 1971b); while only one has failed to yield a significant association (Tomlinson, 1967). The results are somewhat less decisive with respect to *increase* in "experiencing" and "process" levels: four studies report a significant positive relation with outcome (Tomlinson and Hart, 1962; Tomlinson, 1967; Kiesler et al., 1967; Gendlin et al., 1968), although the obtained relation seems far from simple; two studies failed to find a significant positive association (van der Veen, 1967; Kiesler, 1971b). It seems fair to conclude that, in client-centered therapy at least, high levels of "process" functioning and especially "experiencing" in patient communications are consistently predictive of good therapeutic outcome.

A somewhat different scale, developed by Truax and called "depth of self-exploration," has been used in a few process-outcome studies with less impressive results. Three studies showed some significant positive associations between outcome and clients' depth of self-exploration (Truax and Wargo, 1969; Mitchell et al., 1973; Schauble and Pierce, 1974), while three others did not (Truax et al., 1970; Prager, 1971; Sloane et al., 1975).

The only *negative* relationship between outcome and patients' thematic emphasis on self-expression that we know of was reported by Strassberg, Roback, Anchor, and Abramowitz (1975) in a study of group psychotherapy of hospitalized schizophrenics. They found higher rates of self-disclosure in the group contributions of patients who did less well in treatment. This study, perhaps, suggests some of the limiting conditions that apply to the general consensus of other findings.

One of the classic content measures developed for the analysis of message *affect* was the Discomfort-Relief Quotient (DRQ) which had some early applications in therapy research (Mowrer, Hunt, and Kogan, 1953; Mowrer, 1953). Scrutiny of research reports on the DRQ, however, shows no substantive process-outcome data beyond a few illustrative and inconclusive case histories. A more recent study by Mintz et al. (1971)—using other measures—did find that expressed hostility and low distress among women in the early sessions of individual therapy were significantly predictive of good therapeutic outcome. Truax (1971) obtained a similar finding for group psychotherapy. The apparent importance of expressed hostility for good therapy outcome suggests that further research attention to the specific affective content of patient messages would be rewarding.

A small number of process-outcome studies have focused on the cognitive structure rather than the content manifested in patient messages, with some interesting results. Most intriguing is the finding of a relatively strong negative correlation between therapeutic outcome and the "rationality" of patient messages. Patients whose communications were judged to be less integrated, logical, relevant, coherent, concrete, rational, realistic, and systematic in the fifth session of individual outpatient psychotherapy improved more than patients who exerted more intellectual self-control (Wargo, Millis, and Hendricks, 1971). This finding may represent one tail of a curvilinear relationship, since extremes of patient irrationality are probably as unproductive in therapy as extremes of patient rationality. In another study bearing on cognitive structure, Schauble and Pierce (1974) found that higher and increasing levels of cognitive differentiation of problems, feelings, and concerns expressed by patients were significantly associated with better outcomes. That there is an optimum mode of cognitive orientation was also suggested by the earlier findings of Butler, Rice, and Wagstaff (1962, 1963) concerning the relation of good therapeutic outcome to an expressive stance among patients that appeared equally divided between objective analysis and subjective reaction.

Therapist Messages and Therapeutic Outcome

Process-outcome studies of therapist messages have focused on a scatter of variables pertaining to message content, and on a single major variable (genuineness or self-congruence) that we view as an exemplification of message style.

Most of the studies of message content examine the thematic emphases found in therapists' statements. In an exploratory study of very short-term therapy, Nagy (1973) found that clients of therapists whose messages were high in "personally relevant concreteness" did significantly better in treatment. This accords with Malan's (1976) earlier cited finding concerning personally "directed" versus "undirected" interpretations. Similarly, Rice (1965) found significantly more improvement in clients of therapists whose comments were directed to their immediate inner experience. Mitchell (1971) found no significant relationship between outcome and the therapist's immediate references to the external situation (i.e., the therapist and the therapeutic relationship), suggesting that the valuable part of the here-and-now emphasis is in dealing with the patient's focal feelings and concerns, whatever they refer to. This impression is supported by Truax and Wittmer's (1971a) report that client improvement is positively associated with therapists' messages that focus on the client's anxiety source, and these authors' later report (1973) that the same was true for therapists' messages that focus on the client's defense mechanisms.

Evidence in therapists' messages of a sense of responsibility to facilitate client self-exploration and growth was found to be positively related to therapeutic outcome by Pierce and Schauble (1970). This message of positive concern and active involvement from the therapist reinforces the cumulative impression about these process elements derived from research in the process facets of activity and experience.

Therapist self-disclosure was the focus of a process-outcome study by Dickinson (1969), who found this variable to be unrelated to client improvement in individual psychotherapy, but significantly and positively related to improvement in group psychotherapy with schizophrenic patients. Taken together with the negative correlation between outcome and patient self-disclosure reported above (Strassberg et al., 1975) in group therapy with such patients, Dickinson's finding implies that reversal of the traditional allocation of self-disclosure between patient and therapist roles may be indicated for this type of patient and treatment.

The cognitive structure implicit in therapists' messages has been related to therapeutic outcome in two studies. Rice (1965) found a significant negative association between the client's improvement and the therapist's "observing" orientation, exemplified by the therapist's analyzing the patient's self as an object. Wargo et al. (1971) found a significant negative correlation between client improvement and the "rationality" of therapist messages. One way of phrasing the implication of these studies is that therapists are better advised to pursue the logic of feeling than the logic of fact.

The stylistic feature of therapist messages that has been most intensively studied is the Rogerian variable of genuineness or self-congruence. Usually this is treated together with empathy and unconditional positive regard as one of the therapist-offered "facilitative conditions," but our examination of the actual scales in use has led us to incorporate these separately into our conceptual scheme. Therapist genuineness seems decisively a matter of meaning: that the therapist "really means" what he or she says; that the total communicative flow from the therapist is consistent with and confirms the verbal portion of the message; that the style adds appropriate rather than qualifying nuances to the content.

The results of twenty studies on therapist genuineness seem fairly consistent, despite considerable variation in subjects, designs, and quality of execution (see Parloff et al., this volume, for a methodological critique). Six studies showed null or marginally mixed results (Truax, Carkhuff, and Kodman, 1965; Donofrio, 1969; Truax, 1970c; Garfield and Bergin, 1971; Mitchell et al., 1973; Sloane et al., 1975), while fourteen others found a significant positive association between therapist self-congruence and outcome (Truax, 1963; Truax, 1966; Truax et al., 1966; Truax and Wargo, 1967a; Truax and Wargo, 1967b; Hansen, Moore, and Carkhuff, 1968; Truax and Wargo, 1969; Truax et al., 1970; Truax et al., 1971; Melnick and Pierce, 1971; Nagy, 1973; Truax et al., 1973; McNally, 1973; Schauble and Pierce, 1974). Cumulatively, these studies seem to warrant the conclusion that therapist genuineness is at least innocuous, is generally predictive of good outcome, and at most may indeed be a causal element in promoting client improvement. Beyond a reasonable minimum, however, it is probably neither a necessary nor a sufficient condition of therapeutic benefit.

Symbolic Interaction and Therapeutic Outcome

The communication of meaning in relationships is, by definition, a bilateral act, yet almost all the process-outcome studies of Therapy as Dramatic Interpretation have focused separately on either patients' or therapists' messages. Consequently, there is little mention in this section that has not already been referred to. Listening to moments of interactive dialogue in four therapeutic groups. Abramowitz and Jackson (1974) found no significant relation between outcome and thematic emphasis on the here-and-now versus the there-and-then. This accords with the similar findings from different perspectives and treatment modes by Gendlin et al. (1960) and by Mitchell (1971), as noted above. Also, in their study of cognitive orientation in patient and therapist messages, Wargo et al. (1971) found that "rationality" viewed additively as a function of the joint symbolic interaction was negatively correlated with patient improvement.

The most important block of studies with relevance to charateristics of the symbolic interaction that arises from the interplay of patient and therapist messages is concerned with the variable called "accurate empathy." This is usually thought of as a therapist-offered rather than as an interactive condition of treatment; but, as we have said before, it seems to us that empathy is quite a complex construct. On the one hand, it denotes therapist interpersonal behavior that is attentive and deeply respectful toward the patient; on the other hand, it implies a significant attunement or resonance of meanings between the patient's and the therapist's messages. It is with regard to the latter that we recall here the convergence of findings indicating a positive association between empathy and therapeutic outcome.

Summarizing process-outcome research concerning Therapy as Dramatic Interpretation, we would say that successful cases are likely to be those in which the patients talk about themselves and their personal lives in a concrete, responsive, and not too "rational" way; in which the therapists direct their comments to their clients' immediate inner experiences, feelings, and operations, in a genuine or self-congruent fashion; and in which a high degree of shared meaning and mutual attunement of symbolic perspectives is attained in the relationship.

THERAPY AS ASSOCIATION

If Dramatic Interpretation can be described metaphorically as the "soul" of a relationship, then it would not be at all unfair to call Regular Association its living body. Regular Association is the body of a relationship in two senses: through recurrent contacts among participants, the physical presence and temporal continuity of the relationship are established; and, through normative regulation, the skeleton or structural design, the musculature or potential activity, and the organs or specialized functions of the relationship are determined. A relationship is born when its participants begin to associate with one another, grows as the pattern of the association evolves, and survives only so long as they continue to have contact.

Following the general scheme that we are using

to organize process-outcome studies, we would deal with this facet first in terms of the individual categories—that is, patient and therapist—and then in terms of the characteristics emergent in their combination. We dealt with therapist behavior, patient behavior, and behavioral interaction; patient experience, therapist experience, and conjoint experience; patient messages, therapist messages, and symbolic interaction. The parallel treatment of Therapy as Association would lead to reviewing process-outcome research in terms of *patient prescriptions* (i.e., normative claims), *therapist prescriptions,* and the *normative organization* resulting from the negotiation of these two sets of claims. The problem with this procedure is that there are no process-outcome studies to review under the headings of patient prescriptions and therapist prescriptions.

Generally the normative organization of therapeutic process is unilaterally determined by the therapist's prescription, with the patient's negotiative options reduced to acceptance or refusal of the therapist's terms (when treatment is voluntary). If the therapist allows it, there may be some negotiation over fees, hours, and frequency of visits. If the patient wills it, a covert resistance against the arrangement can be maintained. The therapist's authority as a socially sanctioned specialist is further reinforced by the power imbalance that is created by the patient's state of need and the relative supply and demand for therapeutic services. Thus, we pass directly to normative organization.

Normative Organization and Therapeutic Outcome

Normative organization reflects the consensus of prescriptive intentions among participants in a relationship or group, formed in proportion to their relative power, and enforced to protect their mutual if not always equal interests. The social system aspect of interpersonal process, thus formed, may be viewed differentially as a social structure and as a situational structure channelling and constraining the flow of interaction, experience, and symbolic interpretation. The social structure resolves the enduring reciprocal claims of participants into a role system and establishes the general rules governing formation of collectivities. The situational structure, on the other hand, determines the appropriate scene or setting (location, decore, costumes, props) and the appropriate schedule or timing (e.g., frequency, duration, incidence, continuity) of the association. Process-outcome studies were found in three of these categories, to which we now turn.

The Therapeutic Role System

One aspect of the role system that has received some sustained attention in process-outcome research concerns the training of new recruits to the patient role. We have found nine studies that relate "role induction" or "vicarious pre-training" to therapeutic outcome, with very promising results. Two (Hoehn- Saric, Frank, Imber, Nash, Stone, and Battle, 1964; Sloane, Cristol, Pepernik, and Staples, 1970) found a significant advantage at termination of relatively brief individual therapy (four months) for patients who received "role induction" interviews prior to treatment. In studies of group therapy, Truax and Carkhuff (1965) found "vicarious pre-training" effective for hospitalized patients; Truax and Wargo (1969) obtained similar results with neurotic outpatients; and Strupp and Bloxom (1973) reported positive findings with lower-class patients, using both interview and film as contrasting modes of preparation. Another study of lower-class patients (Jacobs, Charles, Jacobs, Weinstein, and Mann, 1972) found increased percentages of successful outcome when therapists were oriented to the special needs of this population in advance of treatment, when patients were given an orientation to therapy, and especially when both patient and therapist were given prior role preparation. Similarly, Warren and Rice (1972), using different procedures, found that special training in "productive client behavior" given in the early phase of treatment was effective with patients in individual client-centered therapy who had been initially rated for poor prognosis. One limitation of pre-training was reported by Truax et al. (1970), who found no significant enhancement of outcome when role induction procedures were used with institutionalized juvenile delinquents. A different type of limitation emerged in the five year follow-up done by Liberman, Frank, Hoehn-Saric,

Stone, Imber, and Pande (1972) of the patients originally studied by Hoehn-Saric et al. At that later point there were no significant differences in long-term improvement between patients who had received "role induction" training and those who had not. Even if such procedures have a circumscribed effect, however, their apparent benefits in different types of therapy with different types of client would seem to justify the effort they require.

Fee payment is another aspect of the therapeutic role system that has been studied in relation to outcome. Fees are the membership dues that clients are obliged to pay as the price of participating in the therapeutic role system, and process-outcome studies have focused on the question as to whether patients who pay their own dues get more benefits from their membership. Evidence reported by Rosenbaum, Friedlander, and Kaplan (1956) indicated that fee paying clients did improve significantly more than nonpaying clients at an outpatient clinic, and a positive relation between outcome and fee payment was also found by Goodman(1960). However, a recent study by Pope, Geller, and Wilknson (1975) of a large number of clinic patients in five closely related fee categories found no significant differences in improvement between these categories. Further study of this issue, perhaps with attention to patient income and third-party payment, seems warranted by the practical importance and social timeliness of the topic.

Relations among reciprocal roles may be characterized in terms of normative task-allocation and standards of social etiquette, that is, the "business" and the "amenities" obligatory for participants vis-à-vis each other. Studies of psychotherapy have concentrated on task definition and allocation more than etiquette—although Goffman's (1961, 1967) essays offer some fascinating insights into the importance of the latter. Under the heading of therapeutic task definition and task allocation we place all those studies that compare the relative effectiveness of different treatment procedures (e.g., psychoanalytic vs. client-centered therapy) without measuring some facets of the actual therapeutic process. The information that can be recovered from such "black box" designs pertains (loosely) only to the prescriptive writings of the leading clinical authorities (e.g., Freud and Rogers) about how treatment *should* be done. Lomont, Golmer, Spector, and Skinner (1969), for example, compared brief insight-oriented group therapy with brief group assertion training for nonpsychotic psychiatric inpatients, and found the latter treatment produced better outcomes. Kilmann and Auerbach (1974) compared marathon therapy groups of institutionalized female addicts directed by a therapist to follow a program of planned exercises, with similar groups where the therapist declined responsibility for group direction, finding increases in patient anxiety in the former treatment and decreases in anxiety in the latter treatment. The difference between treatments in these cases is specified only in normative task definitions, and in many studies of this sort even the normative specifications given are rather vague. It is not enough, in our opinion, that "everyone knows" the difference between behavior therapy and psychotherapy (Sloane et al., 1975), or between client-centered, rational-emotive and systematic desensitization therapies (DiLoreto, 1971); it is essential to provide detailed specifications and observations of the actual processes, as these authors have wisely done. Luborsky et al. (1975) and Glass and Smith (1976) recently reviewed comparative studies of psychotherapies, including some of the sort referred to here, and for the most part found few significant differences in outcome.

An interesting variant on studies of normative role definition was one that focused on patient-therapist consensus concerning in-therapy behavior. Schonfield et al. (1969) found a significant relation between patient improvement and increasing *consensus* over the course of brief (15 session) individual psychotherapy. The direction of causal influence, of course, remains to be determined, but the sophisticated thought reflected in the study is appreciated.

The Therapeutic Collectivity

Besides specifying what patient and therapist should do and how they should deal with one another, social structural norms also specify the appropriate size and composition of their meetings. The main types of therapeutic collectivity involve one patient and one therapist ("individual"

therapy) or several unrelated patients and one or two therapists ("group" therapy), but current practice sometimes entails the meetings of several related patients and one or two therapists ("family" therapy), a single patient and two therapists ("multiple" therapy), and other variations.

Almost all the process-outcome studies of therapeutic collectivity have addressed themselves to the relative efficacy of "group" versus "individual" therapy—and the great majority of these have shown no significant differences in outcome (Peck, 1949; Thorley and Craske, 1950; Haimowitz and Haimowitz, 1952; Barron and Leary, 1955; Imber, Frank, Nash, Stone, and Gliedman, 1957, and subsequent reports in that series, e.g., Frank, Gliedman, Imber, Stone, and Nash, 1959, and Stone, Frank, Nash, and Imber, 1961; Slawson, 1965; Boe, Gocka, and Kogan, 1966; Covi, Lipman, and Derogatis, 1974; Herz, Spitzer, Gibbon, Greenspan, and Reibel, 1974; Newcomer and Morrison, 1974). A few studies have found group therapy significantly better than individual therapy (Pearl, 1955; Mordock, Ellis and Greenstone, 1969; Ravid, 1969; O'Brien, Hamm, and Ray, 1972), and two others found the combination of group and individual therapy superior to individual therapy alone (Conrad, 1952; Baehr, 1954). On the other hand, patients in individual therapy sometimes had better outcomes than patients who were only given group therapy (Baehr, 1954; Gelder, Marks, and Wolff, 1967).

In a study of multiple therapy using male and female co-therapists, Reiner (1973) found individual treatment slightly superior to multiple therapy for a sample of undergraduate female patients.

The general impression fostered by these studies is that the size of the therapeutic collectivity, in itself, has a negligible effect on therapeutic outcome. In a sense this can be taken as favorable to group therapy, since it produces equivalent results more economically. Yet it still seems plausible that some sorts of patients, or some sorts of problems, might be treated more effectively on an individual basis, while for others group therapy of some kind would be the treatment of choice. Ravid (1969), for example, found that patients who had already received a good deal of individual therapy, but who still needed further treatment, did better to have group therapy than to have still more individual therapy. Further studies of this issue only seem warranted if they investigate the possibilities of interaction between size of therapeutic collectivity and other input or process factors.

One interesting study that addressed itself to the issue of group composition rather than size *per se* found that therapeutic groups for boys that included a number of normal well-adjusted peers were more effective than therapeutic groups made up of patients only (Hilgard, Straight, and Moore, 1969). This, of course, does not necessarily imply that well-adjusted peers are, by themselves, sufficient therapeutic agents (Goodman, 1972).

Temporal Aspects of Therapeutic Association
Psychotherapy is a highly scheduled form of association. It occurs at certain predetermined times, for a certain amount of time each time, and continues at recurrent intervals for a length of time lasting anywhere from weeks to years. A great many process-outcome studies have included temporal factors as variables, if for no other reason than the simplicity with which they can be measured. These studies may be distinguished according to their focus on contractually specified time factors or on contingently determined temporal aspects of association.

Time is an essential element in the normative organization of therapeutic contracts, and two principal contractual variations have received much research attention. One variation is the use of time-limited versus time-unlimited contracts, the former fixing a predetermined number of sessions for the course of treatment and the latter continuing until one or both parties decides to terminate. Often these studies confound this contractual stipulation with the overall length of treatment, yet the studies either show no difference or tend to favor time-limited association. Shlien (1957), for example, found no significant difference in outcome between time-limited and unlimited cases of individual client-centered therapy, and in a second study Henry and Shlien (1958) obtained similar results when comparing brief time-limited with long time-unlimited therapy. Pascal and Zax (1956) had also reported no difference in outcome between pa-

tients given brief supportive therapy and others given longer, more "ideal" courses of treatment. Shlien, Mosak, and Dreikurs (1962) extended these findings in a comparison that found no superiority of time-unlimited over time-limited treatment for Adlerian as well as client-centered types of psychotherapy. Three more recent studies have even found time-limited therapy to be significantly superior to time-unlimited therapy (Muench, 1965; Reid and Schyne, 1969; Munro and Bach, 1975). On the basis of research to date, therefore, time-limited therapeutic contracts appear to be no worse, and in some cases definitely better, than time-unlimited arrangements (even when time-limited courses of treatment are briefer). Before translating these important findings into clinical practice, however, one would want to see a few studies explore such questions as whether types of patient, or other factors such as therapist motivation, do not interact significantly with limited versus unlimited contracts in producing more or less favorable outcomes.

A second variation in the temporal organization of therapeutic contracts that has been studied intensively is the relative frequency with which sessions are scheduled. Of the sixteen published reports, only one study indicated a negative association between frequency and outcome (Graham, 1958), finding that adult psychotics in outpatient therapy did less well on a twice-weekly than on a once-weekly regimen. Beyond this the results are somewhat ambiguous, with about half the reports indicating no significant association between therapeutic outcome and session frequency, while the other half suggest some degree of advantage for relatively more intensive schedules.

The following report no significant relation between outcome and session frequency: Rosenbaum et al., 1956; Zirkle, 1961; Lorr, McNair, Michaux, and Raskin, 1962; Kaufman, Frank, Freind, Heims, and Weiss, 1962; Heilbrunn, 1966; Heinicke, 1969; Van Slambrouck, 1973; Kernberg, Bernstein, Coyne, Applebaum, Horwitz, and Voth, 1972. Heilbrunn and Kernberg et al., compared psychoanalytically oriented therapy with full psychoanalysis. Kaufman et al. studied schizophrenic children, and Heinicke compared his own child therapy clients in outpatient treatment.

Lorr et al. studied a large number of V. A. clinic patients after four and eight months of therapy, while Zirkle studied very brief contacts with schizophrenic inpatients (five minutes five times per week vs. one twenty-five minute session per week). McNair and Lorr (1960) also found no significant relation between outcome and therapists' judgments of the suitability of their patients' treatment schedules.

The results cited above are qualified by positive findings in other studies that related treatment frequency to outcome. Graham (1958) reported that neurotic adults in outpatient therapy on a twice-weekly schedule had significantly better outcomes than those seen once-weekly. Ends and Page (1959) found significantly more improvement in alcoholic patients who were seen in group therapy twice-weekly than those attending once-weekly group sessions. Imber et al. (1957) and Frank et al. (1959), reporting on a Phipps Clinic Study, found once-weekly sessions of individual therapy or of group therapy superior to a minimal treatment group of patients who were seen for half an hour every two weeks; but Stone et al. (1961) found these differences in outcome did not persist at a five year follow-up assessment. Dreiblatt and Weatherley (1965) found some evidence favorable to six brief contacts as contrasted with three brief contacts weekly with psychiatric inpatients. Cappon (1964), reviewing records on 160 of his own patients, found that those seen less than once a week had poorer outcomes than clients who had been seen at least once-weekly, but found no consistent differences between those seen once-weekly and those seen more frequently.

One of the more intriguing twists taken by this highly varied series of studies is the possibility that session frequency may have a delayed effect on therapeutic outcome. Thus, while Lorr et al. (1962) found no association between schedule and outcome in their V.A. outpatients after four and eight months of treatment, McNair, Lorr, Young, Roth, and Boyd (1964) did find a significant positive association in these same patients after one and three years. A similar finding was obtained by Heinicke (1969) in a smaller study of young boys in analytic therapy; whereas those seen four times per week had no advantage at termination over others seen once-weekly, there did seem to be a significant

positive difference between them at follow-up. Considering the finding of Stone et al. (1961), this delayed effect may be a function of absolute level as well as relative frequency of treatment contact.

The studies reviewed are quite varied, and of varied quality, but the overall impression that remains is that, with the potentially important exception cited by Graham (1958), there is generally no harm and potentially some real advantage in relatively more intensive (e.g., twice-weekly) schedules, although no clear-cut advantage in very intensive (e.g., everyday) schedules. The practical problem left by so general and tentative a conclusion, of course, is that cost per case doubles and case load is reduced by half as session frequency doubles. One would want to see more highly differentiated cost-benefit analyses of session frequency before using this body of findings as a sanction for something other than a moderate therapy schedule.

A third type of contractual variation in scheduling concerns session duration. An exploratory study bearing on this issue by Ross, McReynolds, and Berzins (1974) compared patients in a 17 hour marathon group with patients seen in daily two hour group sessions over a two week period, and found that patients in both time formats showed comparable reductions on the MMPI "neurotic triad."

There are also time factors in psychotherapy that are not usually specified in the contractual arrangements made by patients and therapists. One such factor is the delay imposed on patients before therapy sessions actually begin. We found three studies devoted to this issue, and their results are impressively consistent. Gordon and Cartwright (1954) found significantly poorer outcomes in clients who accepted a 60 day waitlist delay, and Roth, Rhudick, Shaskan, Slobin, Wilkinson, and Young (1964) obtained similar results in patients delayed 28 days before therapy was begun. Finally, Uhlenhuth and Duncan (1968) reported a significant negative correlation between therapeutic outcome and the length of time elapsed between intake evaluation and the start of treatment. The message to the therapist appears to be that, however frequently patients are seen, they should be seen as promptly as possible.

The largest single mass of process-outcome research findings that has been accumulated deals with the relation of outcome to the total amount of therapy received. The simple question is, does more mean better? The answer, however, appears to be more complicated than the question. Amount of therapy has been measured both by the duration of therapy, that is, the time elapsed from initiation to termination, and by the number of sessions included in the total course of treatment. Drawing mainly on the reviews of Luborsky et al. (1971) and of Meltzoff and Kornreich (1970), and adding the studies that we found in our own search of more recent literature, we have compiled the following tabulation of results.

Of 33 studies dealing with number of sessions, *positive relations* were found between amount of therapy and outcome in 20 (Bartlett, 1950; Mensh and Golden, 1951; Garfield and Kurz, 1952; Seeman, 1954; Dana, 1954; Myers and Auld, 1955; Tolman and Mayer, 1957; Standal and van der Veen, 1957; Graham, 1958; Feldman, Lorr, and Russell, 1958; Garfield and Affleck, 1959; Nichols and Beck, 1960; Cabeen and Coleman, 1961, 1962; Cartwright, Robertson, Fiske, and Kirtner, 1961; Getter and Sundland, 1962; Lorr et al., 1962; Fiske, Cartwright, and Kirtner, 1964; McNair et al., 1964; Cappon, 1964; Malan, 1976); *no significant relations were found in seven* (Pascal and Zax, 1956; Dorfman, 1958; Cartwright and Lerner, 1963; Heilbrunn, 1966; Errera, McKee, Smith, and Gruber, 1967; Kernberg et al., 1972; Nichols, 1974; Mitchell et al., 1973; Glass and Smith, 1976); while *curvilinear relations* were reported in six (Miles, Barrabee, and Finesinger, 1951; Cartwright, 1955; Taylor, 1956; Rosenthal and Frank, 1958; Pruit, 1963; Johnson, 1965). Of 22 studies dealing with time in treatment, twelve reported *positive relations* of outcome with duration (Conrad, 1952; Dymond, Grummon, and Seeman, 1956; Tolman and Mayer, 1957; Sullivan, Miller, and Smelser, 1958; Bailey, Warshaw, and Eichler, 1959; Cartwright et al., 1961; Lorr et al., 1962; Fiske et al., 1964; O'Connor, Daniels, Flood, Carush, Moses, and Stern, 1964; Rosenthal and Levine, 1970; Garfield, Prager, and Bergin, 1971; Astrachan, Brauer, Harrow, and Schwartz, 1974); nine found *no significant relation* (Rosenbaum et al., 1956; Grigg and Goodstein, 1957; Frank et al., 1959; Kaufman et al., 1962; Lorr and

McNair, 1964; McNair et al., 1964; Gelder and Marks, 1966; Kernberg et al., 1972; Mitchell et al., 1973); while a *negative relation* was reported in one (Muench, 1965). Obviously, a substantial majority of these studies found some significant positive association between amount of treatment and therapeutic benefit. The balance in favor of this finding is clearer when number of sessions rather than total duration is used, suggesting that time *per se* is less a "healing" factor than the absolute amount of therapeutic contact. This lends a bit of support to the notion that a more intensive schedule of contacts may be desirable, if only because the therapeutic outcome may be more quickly attained. This, however, is hardly to be counted as a sure thing, since, besides methodological deficiencies, a significant minority of studies showed no association between outcome and amount of therapy, while another group of studies indicated the existence of a curvilinear relation. Those studies add another bit of confusion, though, since some indicate an early period of success followed by a "failure zone" and another period of successful outcome beyond that (e.g., Cartwright, 1955), while other studies indicate a positive relation up to a certain optimum followed by an increasingly negative relation between number of sessions and outcome (e.g., Rosenthal and Frank, 1958). The erratic association between treatment length and outcome is, of course, due in part to major differences in the studies compared, but it no doubt also simply betokens the fact that purely quantitative variations in the course of therapy (e.g., number of sessions) are secondary to more important qualitative variations in therapeutic process (e.g., treatment intensity). More of a good thing is better than less of it; more of a bad thing is worse; and there may very well be a point of diminishing returns in any therapeutic relationship beyond which only negligible (or even retrogressive) results are attainable.

Summarizing process-outcome studies of Therapy as Association, we find convergence bearing on two social structural aspects of normative organization: there is evidence that educating patients for *effective role performance* is worthwhile; there is no evidence that the *size* of the collectivity in itself is a major factor in therapeutic outcome. Concerning temporal aspects of therapy (situational structure), research to date suggests that time-limited contracts and session schedules of moderate frequency are on balance more beneficial than unlimited and infrequent sessions; delay in seeing patients who have requested therapy seems definitely undesirable; and, for unlimited contracts at least, a positive relation has been found between amount of treatment and therapeutic outcome. Contractual term, session schedule, and amount of treatment generally have been confounded rather than systematically varied, so that any conclusions regarding these issues must be tentative.

SYNTHESIS AND CRITIQUE

We have brought together an abstract conceptual scheme and a large, variegated body of empirical research. It may be said that the scheme has been imposed on the research data, since the studies reviewed were not originally conceived in terms of it; but the data, equally, have been assimilated with little strain or omission into the schematic structure. Both the scheme and the research have been affected as a result of this interaction. The scheme has been further refined and concretized in the attempt to incorporate and digest diverse specific process-outcome findings. At the same time, this scattered and heretofore somewhat disorderly area of research has been transformed into the beginnings of a connected, if still unevenly textured, body of knowledge. The results are subject to important critical strictures, but let us summarize them briefly before considering the critical problems that remain in process-outcome research.

The Status of the Conceptual Scheme

The conceptual scheme was developed in the first part of this chapter to the point at which four facets of process and four facets of context had been differentiated (Figure 8-1). No further distinctions were made beyond this point in the area of context, but several have been introduced in dealing with the separate facets of process. These descriptive specifications are summarized in Figures 8-2 through 8-5. (Categories used to mark subsections

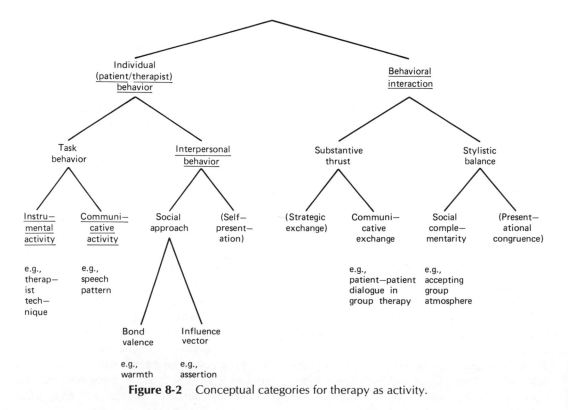

Figure 8-2 Conceptual categories for therapy as activity.

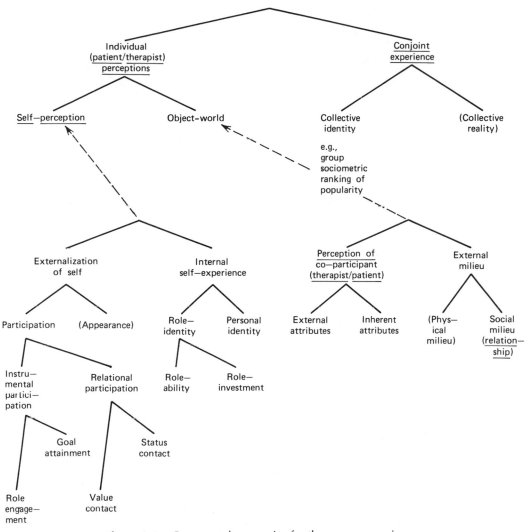

Figure 8-3   Conceptual categories for therapy as experience.

of the text are underlined in the figures; those for which no process-outcome findings were cited are enclosed in parentheses; the rest were all mentioned in organizing and reporting research results.) Proceeding from top to bottom, the first distinction drawn in each of the four facets was between process viewed as a function of individual participants (e.g., patient or therapist behavior) and process viewed as a function of their joint participation (e.g., behavioral interaction). Other distinctions were drawn as needed.

The most obvious thing to be noted in comparing these figures is how unevenly they were differentiated in response to the research. Generally, more categories were needed to encompass individually analyzed variables than jointly defined variables, with the exception of Therapy as Association. The conceptual categories for Therapy as Experience were the most highly differentiated of all in dealing with the individual level of analysis (patient and therapist perceptions). Apparently it is easier for researchers to formulate variables in terms of their own perceptions of psychotherapy as a basis for inquiring into the experiences of patients and therapists.

The principal challenge at this point is to further

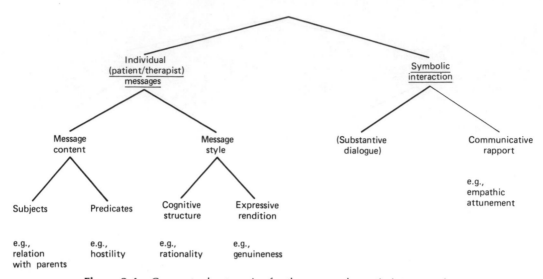

Figure 8-4   Conceptual categories for therapy as dramatic interpretation.

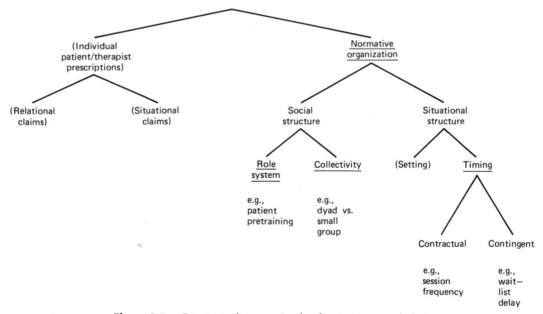

Figure 8-5   Conceptual categories for therapy as association.

differentiate the contextual facets so as to produce a more refined analysis of input and output (including outcome) variables. Another direction to work in is the differentiation of joint process analysis to the same level of refinement as individual process analysis, and to bring both to the point of concreteness where empirical measurement operations are naturally suggested. Although the number of categories expands exponentially, the process of refinement at every stage remains the simplest possible dialectical procedure of binary distinction.

An Empirically Grounded Impression of Effective Psychotherapy

The ultimate goal of all the effort expended in this chapter, and of all the research reviewed in it, is to develop an empirically grounded picture of effective psychotherapy, and to determine the beneficial ingredients in therapeutic process. An overall, if tentative, impression of what has been learned about psychotherapy can be developed by rereading the summaries provided for the sections on Therapy as Activity, Experience, Dramatic Interpretation, and Association. We offer the formulation that follows as our own interpretive synthesis of these summaries.

Effective psychotherapy, as an *interpersonal*[2] *process,* is distinguished most consistently by the positive quality of the bond that develops between its participants. Whether it occurs in a dyadic relationship or in a primary group, the bond among participants in beneficial therapy is marked by a high degree of cohesiveness. This is shown in various ways.

There is an intense and effective investment of energy in relationship roles, evident both in the patient's self-expressive emotional attachment to the therapist (or to the group), and in the therapist's active collaboration through whichever techniques he or she feels most capable and confident in using. (Techniques in themselves have not yet been shown to have a consistently powerful differential effect on therapeutic outcome, but without some technique that feels right and good the therapist cannot very well participate actively and confidently in the treatment. One must, of course, allow that a technique that feels right and good to one therapist may feel indifferent or even quite wrong to another.)

A second element associated with cohesiveness of the social bond in beneficial psychotherapy is the good personal contact, the solid grounding in one another, that is made by the participants. This personal contact is characterized by mutual comfortableness and trust, a lack of defensiveness on both sides, seen in the patient's spontaneity and the therapist's genuineness; and also by a strong and sensitive rapport, a sense of being on the same wavelength, that arises through empathic resonance and reciprocal understanding.

There is, finally an expansive mutual good will mobilized between participants in beneficial psychotherapy—a strong sense of affirmation that is not merely acceptance but also acceptance and

encouragement of independence, that can be challenging as well as supportive out of concern and respect for the other person's basic interests and autonomy. This safe, stimulating, but supportive atmosphere balances and makes tolerable the direct expression of deeply painful, frightening, and abrasive sentiments—sentiments that might be (and probably have been) overwhelming in other, less resiliently cohesive relationships. (It is a fair guess that something akin to this is at the core of effective psychotherapy, whether one prefers to think of it in terms of "growth facilitating conditions," "positive transference" and "working through," "corrective emotional experience," "reciprocal inhibition" due to the generalized relaxing influence of the therapeutic bond, "modeling," or "positive reinforcement" for the emission of adaptive interpersonal and self-directed responses.)

Effective investment of energy, good personal contact, and mutual affirmation stand out as three aspects of the cohesiveness that seems to mark the beneficial therapeutic bond. Some may be inclined to feel concerned that this formulation emphasizes so-called nonspecific factors, that is, processes that are not unique to the psychotherapeutic relationship. Perhaps it is just a "purchase of friendship" after all? Or a purchase of parenthood, for that matter? Probably there is nothing beneficial (or harmful) in psychotherapy that cannot also be found in some other type of relationship. It is well to remember that psychotherapy is only one form of relationship to which people turn for help in improving their personal functioning, and is generally resorted to only when the help normally available on the basis of reciprocity through the individual's kinship and friendship networks is either qualitatively or quantitatively insufficient to meet the need. Psychotherapy at its best provides a "purer culture" of help—less admixed with the helper's own needs, more intense, more extensive, more penetrating—but may not be basically different from the help that can be found in less specialized "caring" relationships.

The impression of beneficial therapy has been sketched in idealized terms. Therapy may also be ineffective, and it may be harmful. Ineffective therapy, which makes little positive or negative impact on the patient's personal functioning, might be characterized in the terms we have been using as

---

[2]*Interpersonal process,* in our sense, includes Experience as well as Activity, etc., and thus includes aspects of therapy that may be viewed by others as intrapersonal.

follows: little effective investment of energy from the patient (role training might help this), or from the therapist; poor personal contact (mutual discomfort and mistrust, or lack of rapport) between them; and an atmosphere of limited or conditional affirmation, or plain indifference. Therapeutic relationships that produce deterioration, on the other hand, might be characterized by poor personal contact, by fairly intense but misdirected or inappropriate investment of energy, and by an atmosphere of negation or subtle exploitation.

Here we venture into the tempting but formidable area of substantive theorizing, which takes us beyond the scope and limitations of this chapter. The steps leading from reports of specific variables to schematic categories, from categories to each of the section summaries, and from those summaries to this impressionistic interpretaion, have each involved a small enough jump in level of conceptual generality to let the reader follow apace. To do a proper job of substantive theorizing, however, we should have to retrace our steps and carefully explicate the summary (and somewhat metaphorical) terms "effective investment of energy," "good personal contact," and "mutual affirmation." We should have to show what each of these mean in terms of concrete observational categories, and suggest appropriate measures to serve as category indices, in order to avoid generating still another "clinical" theory. The advantage of grounding a theoretical impression of psychotherapy explicitly in empirical research rather than intuitively in personal experience would be lost. However, the ground of empirical research that we have surveyed is not yet really firm enough to support the weight of much substantive theory. Before advancing further in that direction, process-outcome studies must be subjected to critical analysis to assess how much credence may be safely placed in their results.

A Critique of Process-Outcome Research

To facilitate the growth of research in this field, we have tried to be accepting, empathic, concrete, and constructively interpretive in our treatment of the assembled studies. Sensing that we have built a good working alliance, we shall be more confronting of their aggregate weaknesses in the pages that remain. There are five basic problems in

psychotherapy research that we call to the attention of those who work in this field: the "descriptive specificity" problem; the "fair sample" problem; the "causal inference" problem; the "outcome evaluation" problem; and the "prescriptive utility" problem.

Descriptive Specificity

One of the persistent problems that we encountered in reading the report of a process-outcome study was the feeling that we never knew enough about what was investigated. We really didn't know very much about what was done or what happened, nor did we generally know very much about the people who were involved, the circumstances of their lives, or the conditions under which their contacts with one another took place. Part of the difficulty was that typically only a few parameters of the event were provided; another part of it was that even those variables reported were vaguely conceived and/or inadequately described. We were given labels for treatments, a few words or phrases for operational variables, and stereotypes for personnel, then a quick ritual dash through the data (basic data were rarely reported in independently analyzable form) to the all-important probability levels. This was much less true in studies that relied heavily on case reports (e.g. Malan, 1976), but those were usually minimally quantified and unsystematic in their coverage. Lack of diligence was only partially to blame, for this is one instance of what it means to be at a pre-paradigmatic stage of scientific development.

The real problem is that no one yet has persuasively shown us what the basic elements are that must be taken into account. The abhorrent vacuum has consequently been filled with "uniformity myths" (Kiesler, 1966), which though long noted and decried have not yet effectively been displaced. Assuredly there are a multiplicity of basic input, process, and output parameters whose description is fundamental to knowing what a study actually entailed. This implies that intensive multivariate designs, mapping one set of variables on to another, are essential to the further advancement of process-outcome research. But what are these basic parameters of process and contextual input and output? We have tried to point in the direction of an answer with respect to therapeutic process at least, though we obviously have not gone far enough to find it. What is needed is a comprehensive list of input, process, and output factors that makes sense and is subscribed to by most of the people working in the field—no matter what their theoretical predilections might be—so that their efforts may become mutually intelligible and their results comparable and cumulative. The sooner someone arranges this little matter, the better off we shall all be and much indebted for the favor.

Fair Samples

One of the impressive results of this survey is what is not to be seen or summarized—the empty spaces in the conceptual scheme that represent variables not studied. Those unfilled categories were not so hard to think of, nor do they seem so remote from common experience. The information gaps exist primarily because the people who did the research were not sufficiently interested. The sort of thing that gets studied (sometimes the result of the study, too) is naturally influenced by the theoretical or ideological concerns of the researcher. Psychoanalytically oriented researchers study such things as interpretation, transference, and ego strength; Rogerian researchers study empathy, positive regard, and self-congruence. The problem arises from the fact that not everyone does psychotherapy research, nor do those who do so represent the full range of viewpoints and special interests in the field. Psychotherapy research has been done mainly by investigators in academic settings, and (with the exclusion of behavioral therapies) these have mainly represented the more "respectable" Freudian and Rogerian orientations. It can hardly come as a great surprise that the general impression of beneficial therapy gleaned from process-outcome findings shows more than a passing resemblance to (the relatively more frequently studied) client-centered therapy, as well as a few similarities to psychoanalytically oriented therapy.

The samples of patients, therapists, and treatment settings are as unrepresentative as the sample of therapies studied. Patients included in research generally are (1) students attending sessions at a university counseling center, (2) service-connected males in treatment at V.A. clinics, (3) lower middle class urban residents, predominantly female, seen in psychiatry department outpatient clinics, and (4) inpatients at university-affiliated or V.A. psychiatric hospitals. Therapists who are studied generally are psychology interns or psychiatric residents in training at the above-mentioned settings. Well-heeled (and well-healed?) patients treated in private practice by the best recommended and most experienced therapists are never (or hardly ever) studied, and patients at the opposite end of the social spectrum are all too rarely studied (e.g., Lerner, 1972). Together they may very well constitute the majority of therapy cases, but since we have few relevant studies of them they have not influenced our picture of the process-outcome relationship.

Research has been done by academics and students in training centers on a limited variety of patients treated with a limited range of academically respectable therapies. We do not mean to sound ungrateful; without their efforts, there would be no research to interpret or criticize. It is difficult and frequently unrewarding work—and that, alas, is the source of another sample bias. There has been an understandable tendency at various research centers (including our own) to create data banks of therapy cases that are repeatedly subjected to empirical analysis. As a consequence, series of separately published studies are carried out that are not truly independent inquiries, nor are their connections with other studies of the same cases always made explicit. Clearly a greater effort must be made to extend the data base of process-outcome studies if a fairer picture of what is beneficial or harmful in therapy is to be obtained.

Causal Inference

The core problem of psychotherapy research is the determination of causal relations between sets of process and outcome variables. To what extent, and in what ways, are changes in the patient's personality and life the consequences of events that occur in psychotherapy? This link, after all, must be established before psychotherapy can rightfully be given praise or blame for a patient's fate. As of the present moment, such a causal attribution is supported mainly be circumstantial evidence, practical assumptions, and intuition.

The usual inductive method for determining the causal dependence of one set of variables on another is the experiment, but clinical psychotherapy has proven a peculiarly difficult subject for true experiments. Random assignment of patients to different therapies and therapists is usually precluded or hedged by a sense of clinical responsibility to provide what one believes to be the best available treatment for the patient. The additional difficulty of designing a meaningful control group has long been acknowledged. Furthermore, it is virtually impossible to randomly assign therapists to different treatments or process conditions, since questions of role-skill and role-investment are usually essential.

As a result we are limited to conclusions that certain process variables are associated with certain outcome variables at acceptable levels of statistical significance. If the process variables are assessed at the same time that outcome ratings are made (i.e., retrospectively or at termination), one can only say that certain features of process are *indicative* of good or poor outcome. If a substantial period of time has elapsed between assessment of process and rating of outcome, then one can say that certain features of process are *predictive* of good or poor outcome. The latter is certainly useful knowledge, but it still falls short of the desired conclusion that certain features of process are *productive* of good or poor outcome.

The need is to find some way of discounting plausible alternative explanations of therapeutic outcome. These alternative explanations generally attribute outcome to concommitant contextual factors (rather than to therapeutic processes *per se*) such as: an endogenous depression whose relief is attributable to passage into the benign phase of its cycle; an anxiety state whose abatement is attributable to the resolution by others of a critical life situation; an existential funk whose amelioration is attributable to the "windfall profit" of narcissistic pleasure that accrues from suddenly falling in love or being selected for a new position. Such contextual factors may be the common cause of changes in therapeutic process and in outcome, making the indicative or predictive correlation of process with outcome a causally spurious one.

The "treatment effectiveness" hypothesis does not require that contextual inputs exert negligible influence on outcome. High levels of "ego strength" or of "experiencing" in patients (inputs)

probably do not by themselves cause patients to improve, but probably do enable patients to make good personal contact and effective investments of energy in psychotherapeutic relationships (process). Most probably there is a complex chain of interacting input and process factors that determine the eventual outcome of therapy, and what is needed to diminish reasonable doubts are very fine-grained studies of the interplay of input with process factors, focusing on the cumulation of small incremental outputs into an evaluatable "outcome." If a cohesive therapy session can make a chronically depressed, unassertive, self-deprecatory individual feel buoyantly expansive and act self-assertively for a short time after, will repeated dosage in an increasingly cohesive therapeutic relationship gradually change that individual's stance vis-à-vis himself, and lead him to make positive changes in his life?

There will have to be rather substantial alterations of research design to get data that are responsive to such questions. Repeated measurement of a comprehensive set of relatively short-term variations in the patient's life and personality, together with multivariate session-by-session assessment of therapeutic process, would be needed over a relatively long period of time. Prime interest would focus not on the statistical significance levels of intercorrelations, but on the size (percentage of variance—see Howard, Orlinsky, and Perilstein, 1976, for an example) and temporal cross-lagging of effects. Since large randomly selected patient samples would be impractical, the generality and limits of results would have to be determined by systematic replication with diversified samples. This approach to the causal problem may only result in establishing that changes in a patient's life or personality are *probable* consequences of certain therapeutic processes—but we think that is not bad, is better than we have, and is the best we are likely to obtain.

Outcome Evaluation

The judgment of psychotherapeutic outcome is a complex procedure involving two distinct steps often confounded in practice. The *description* of the changes that are probably consequences of participation in psychotherapy is only the first step.

Logically the second step is an *evaluation* of these changes with reference to explicit value standards. No one would argue that change in itself is the desired end of therapeutic involvement. Change may be for better or worse, or it may be indifferent. Improvement and deterioration are the important terms in outcome evaluation.

The assessment of outcome has been liable to three sorts of confusion. An important and common one is the confounding of descriptive and evaluative stages of judgment that occurs when patients, or therapists, or other raters are asked to make global evaluations of improvement. Readers (and the researcher) are simply at a loss to know what was being evaluated, since the particular referents of judgment are left unspecified. The procedure is little more than an opinion survey, whose results are possibly interesting but of very low information value.

A second confusion enters into outcome evaluation by a failure to recognize that patients vary considerably in the level of personal functioning that is being aimed at. Roughly speaking there are three levels of personal functioning against which an individual may be judged: the minimal level of adequate age-appropriate behavior tolerated in members of the commufity, short of which the individual is stigmatized is grossly deviant or "abnormal"; the average expectable level of functioning in the community, short of which the individual may be viewed by self and others as experiencing unnecessarily and undesirably low levels of personal comfort and social effectiveness; and the maximum level conceivably attainable by a person, short of which the individual departs significantly from the culturally defined character-ideal. Obviously some patients start therapy at a level that other patients may aspire to but never attain; and a ceiling-effect may constrain judgments of benefit even when ratings are made relative to the patient's initial level of functioning. Are units of "gain" comparable across these conditions?

A third confusion in outcome evaluation stems from the fact that there are always various *value standards* that can be applied in assessing change, and various "parties" with legitimate but potentially conflicting interests in the outcome of treatment. Krause and Howard (1976) have recently explored the problems arising from this multiplicity of value perspectives, and the reader is referred to their discussion.

Prescriptive Utility

Finally, it should be kept in mind that there are inevitably practical as well as theoretical issues at stake in process-outcome research. The audience for research findings ultimately extends beyond the small community of investigators to include practicing therapists and current or prospective patients. There is a reasonable expectation that process-outcome studies should be able to tell therapists how to utilize their resources most effectively, and (from the standpoint of consumer advocacy) tell patients how to maximize their chances of gaining therapeutic benefits. To do this, however, it is necessary to translate research findings into the languages of patient and therapist *perception*. Much worthwhile knowledge can be acquired through the use of nonparticipant observation, but unless it is couched in terms of phenomena that are perceptible to therapists and patients that knowledge will be of little use to them. Practical prescriptive recommendations must be formulated in terms of Therapy as Experience. Research on Therapy as Activity, Association, and Dramatic Interpretation is essential to our theoretical understanding, but research on the varieties of psychotherapeutic experience, and their interrelatedness with these other facets, will remain the critical link between scientific inquiry and clinical application.

REFERENCES

Abramowitz, C. V., Abramowitz, S. I., Roback, H. B., & Jackson, C. Differential effectiveness of directive and nondirective group therapies as a function of client internal-external control. *Journal of Consulting and Clinical Psychology,* 1974, *42,* 849–853.

Abramowitz, S. I., & Jackson, C. Comparative effectiveness of there-and-then versus here-and-now therapist interpretations in group psychotherapy. *Journal of Counseling Psychology,* 1974, *21,* 288–293.

Ashby, J. D., Ford, D. H., Guerney, B. B., & Guerney, L. F. Effects on clients of a reflective and a leading type of therapy. *Psychological Monographs,* 1957, 71:24.

Astrachan, B. M., Brauer, L., Harrow, M., & Schwartz, C. Symptomatic outcome in schizophrenia. *Archives of*

General Psychiatry, 1974, *31,* 155–160.

Baehr, G. O. The comparative effectiveness of individual psychotherapy, group psychotherapy, and a combination of these methods. *Journal of Consulting Psychology,* 1954, *18,* 179–183.

Bailey, K. G. Audiotape self-confrontation in group psychotherapy. *Psychological Reports,* 1970, *27,* 439–444.

Bailey, M. A., Warshaw, L., & Eichler, R. M. A study of factors related to length of stay in psychotherapy. *Journal of Clinical Psychology,* 1959, *15,* 442–444.

Baker, E. The differential effects of two psychotherapeutic approaches on client perception. *Journal of Counseling Psychology,* 1960, *7,* 46–50.

Barrett-Lennard, G. T. Dimensions of perceived therapist response related to therapeutic change. Unpublished doctoral dissertation, University of Chicago, 1959.

Barrett-Lennard, G. T. Dimensions of therapist response as causal factors in therapeutic change. *Psychological Monographs,* 1962, *76* (43, Whole No. 562).

Barrington, B. Prediction from counselor behavior of client perception and of case outcome. *Journal of Counseling Psychology,* 1961, *8,* 37–42.

Barron, F. & Leary, T. F. Changes in psychoneurotic patients with and without psychotherapy. *Journal of Consulting Psychology,* 1955, *19,* 239–245.

Bartlett, M. R. A six-month follow-up of the effects of personal adjustment counseling of veterans. *Journal of Consulting Psychology,* 1950, *14,* 393–394.

Bent, R. J., Putnam, D. G., & Kiesler, D. J. Correlates of successful and unsuccessful psychotherapy. *Journal of Consulting and Clinical Psychology,* 1976, *44,* 149.

Berger, P. L., & Luckmann, T. *The social construction of reality.* Garden City, New York: Doubleday and Company, Inc., 1967.

Bergin, A. E., & Garfield, S. L. (Eds.) *Handbook of psychotherapy and behavior change: An empirical analysis.* New York: Wiley, 1971.

Bergin, A. E., & Jasper, L. G. Correlates of empathy in psychotherapy: A replication. *Journal of Abnormal Psychology,* 1969, *74,* 477–481.

Bergin, A. E., & Suinn, R. M. Individual psychotherapy and behavior therapy. *Annual Review of Psychology,* 1975, *26,* 509–556.

Beutler, L. E., Johnson, D. T., Neville, C. W., Elkins, D., & Jobe, A. M. Attitude similarity and therapist credibility as predictors of attitude change and improvement in psychotherapy. *Journal of Consulting and Clinical Psychology,* 1975, *43,* 90–91.

Beutler, L. E., Johnson, D. T., Neville, C. W., & Workman, S. N. "Accurate empathy" and the AB dichotomy. *Journal of Consulting and Clinical Psychology,* 1972, *38,* 372–375

Blau, T. H. Report on a method of predicting success in psychotherapy. *Journal of Clinical Psychology,* 1950, *6,* 405–406.

Board, F. Patients' and physicians' judgments of outcome of psychotherapy in an outpatient clinic. *Archives of General Psychiatry,* 1959, *1,* 185–196.

Boe, E., Gocka, E. F., & Kogan. W. S. The effect of group psychotherapy on interpersonal perceptions of psychiatric patients. *Multivariate Behavioral Research,* 1966, *1,* 177–187.

Bordin, E. S. *Research strategies in psychotherapy.* New York: Wiley, 1974.

Bozarth, J. D., & Grace, D. P. Objective ratings and client perceptions of therapeutic conditions with university counseling center clients. *Journal of Clinical Psychology,* 1970, *26,* 117–118.

Braaten, L. J. The movement from non-self to self in client-centered psychotherapy. *Journal of Counseling Psychology,* 1961, *8,* 20–24.

Brown, R. D. Experienced and inexperienced counselors' first impressions of clients and case outcomes: Are first impressions lasting? *Journal of Counseling Psychology,* 1970, *17,* 550–558.

Burke, K. *Permanence and change: An anatomy of purpose.* Indianapolis: Bobbs-Merrill, 1965.

Butler, J. M., Rice, L. N., & Wagstaff, A. K. On the naturalistic definition of variables: An analogue of clinical analysis. In H. H. Strupp & L. L. Luborsky (Eds.), *Research in psychotherapy, Vol. 2.* Washington, D. C.: American Psychological Association, 1962.

Butler, J. M., Rice, L. N., & Wagstaff, A. K. *Quantitative naturalistic research.* Englewood Cliffs, N. J.: Prentice-Hall, 1963.

Cabeen, C. W., & Coleman, J. C. Group therapy with sex offenders: Description and evaluation of group therapy program in an institutional setting. *Journal of Clinical Psychology,* 1961, *17,* 122–129.

Cabeen, C. W. & Coleman, J. C. The selection of sex-offender patients for group psychotherapy. *International Journal of Group Psychotherapy,* 1962, *12,* 326–334.

Cabral, R. J., Best, J., & Paton, A. Patients' and observers' assessments of process and outcome in group therapy: A follow-up study. *The American Journal of Psychiatry,* 1975, *132,* 1052–1054.

Cain, D. J. The therapist's and client's perceptions of therapeutic conditions in relation to perceived interview outcome. *Dissertation Abstracts International,* 1973, *33,* 12-B, 6071.

Campbell, D. T. & Stanley, J. C. *Experimental and quasiexperimental designs for research.* Chicago: Rand McNally, 1966.

Cappon, D. Results of psychotherapy. *British Journal of Psychiatry,* 1964, *110,* 35–45.

Caracena, P. F., & Vicory, J. R. Correlates of phenomenological and judged empathy. *Journal of Counseling Psychology,* 1969, *16,* 510–515.

Carkhuff, R. R., & Burstein, J. W. Objective therapist and client ratings of therapist-offered facilitative conditions of moderate to low functioning therapists. *Journal of Clinical Psychology,* 1970, *26,* 394–395.

Cartwright, D. S. Success in psychotherapy as a function of certain actuarial variables. *Journal of Consulting Psychology,* 1955, *19,* 357–363.

Cartwright, D. S., Robertson, R. J., Fiske, D. W., & Kirtner, W. L. Length of therapy in relation to outcome and change in personal integration. *Journal of Consulting Psychology,* 1961, *25,* 84–88.

Cartwright, R. D., & Lerner, B. Empathy, need to change, and improvement in psychotherapy. *Jour-*

nal of Consulting Psychology, 1963, 27, 138–144.

Conrad, D. C. An empirical study of the concept of psychotherapeutic success. Journal of Consulting Psychology, 1952, 16, 92–97.

Cook, J. J. Silence in psychotherapy. Journal of Counseling Psychology, 1964, 11 42–46.

Coons, W. H. Interaction and insight in group psychotherapy. Canadian Journal of Psychology, 1957, 11, 1–8.

Covi, L., Lipman, R. S., & Derogatis, L. R. Drugs and group psychotherapy in neurotic depression. American Journal of Psychiatry, 1974, 131, 191–198.

Crowder, J. E. Transference, transference dissipation, and identification in successful vs. unsuccessful psychotherapy. Dissertation Abstracts International, 1971, 31, 6894B.

Crowder, J. E. Relationship between therapist and client interpersonal behaviors and psychotherapy outcome. Journal of Counseling Psychology, 1972, 19, 68–75.

Dana, R. H. The effects of attitudes towards authority on psychotherapy. Journal of Clinical Psychology, 1954, 10, 350–353.

Dickenson, W. A. Therapist self-disclosure as a variable in psychotherapeutic process and outcome. Dissertation Abstracts International, 1969, 30, 2434B.

Dickoff, H., & Lakin, M. Patients' views of group psychotherapy: Retrospections and interpretations. International Journal of Group Psychotherapy, 1963, 13, 61–73.

Dietzel, C. S., & Abeles, N. Client-therapist complementarity and therapeutic outcome. Journal of Counseling Psychology, 1975, 22, 264–272.

DiLoreto, A. O. Comparative psychotherapy: An experimental analysis. Chicago: Aldine-Atherton, Inc., 1971.

Donofrio, D. S. The effect of therapist variables on parents and their children as a function of work with parent counseling groups. Dissertation Abstracts International, 1969, 30, 2904B.

Dorfman, E. Personality outcomes of client-centered child therapy. Psychological Monographs, 1958, 72, Whole No. 456.

Dreiblatt, I. S., & Weatherley, D. A. An evaluation of the efficacy of brief-contact therapy with hospitalized psychiatric patients. Journal of Consulting Psychology, 1965, 29, 513–519.

Dymond, R. R., Grummon, D. L., & Seeman, J. Patterns of perceived interpersonal relations. Sociometry, 1956, 19, 166–177.

Ends, E. J., & Page, C. W. Group psychotherapy and concomitant psychological change. Psychological Monographs, 1959, 73, Whole No. 480.

Errera, P., McKee, B., Smith, D., & Gruber, R. Length of psychotherapy: Studies done in a university community psychiatric clinic. Archives of General Psychiatry, 1967, 17, 454–458.

Feitel, B. Feeling understood as a function of a variety of therapist activities. Unpublished doctoral dissertation, Teachers' College, Columbia University, 1968.

Feldman, R., Lorr, M., & Russell, S. B. A mental hygiene clinic case survey. Journal of Clinical Psychology, 1958, 14, 245–250.

Fiedler, F. E. The concept of an ideal therapeutic relationship. Journal of Consulting Psychology, 1950, 14, 239–245.

Fish, J. M. Empathy and the reported emotional experiences of beginning psychotherapists. Journal of Consulting and Clinical Psychology, 1970, 35, 64–69.

Fiske, D. W., Cartwright, D. S., & Kirtner, W. L. Are psychotherapeutic changes predictable? Journal of Abnormal and Social Psychology, 1964, 69, 418–426.

Frank, J. D. Persuasion and healing. Baltimore: John Hopkins University Press, 1961.

Frank, J. D., Gliedman, L. H., Imber, S. D., Stone, A. R., & Nash, E. H. Patients' expectancies and relearning as factors determining improvement in psychotherapy. American Journal of Psychiatry, 1959, 115, 961–968.

Freedman, M. B., Leary, T. F., Ossorio, A. B., & Coffee, H. S. The interpersonal dimension of personality. Journal of Personality, 1951, 20, 143–161.

Garfield, S., & Affleck, D. C. An appraisal of duration of stay in outpatient psychotherapy. Journal of Nervous and Mental Disease, 1959, 129, 492–498.

Garfield, S. L., & Bergin, A. E. Therapeutic conditions and outcome. Journal of Abnormal Psychology, 1971, 77, 108–114.

Garfield, S. L., & Kurz, M. Evaluation of treatment and related procedures in 1,216 cases referred to a mental hygiene clinic. Psychiatric Quarterly, 1952, 26, 414–424.

Garfield, S. L., Prager, R. A., & Bergin, A. E. Evaluation of outcome in psychotherapy. Journal of Consulting and Clinical Psychology, 1971, 37, 307–313.

Gelder, M. G., & Marks, I. M. Severe agoraphobia: A controlled prospective trial of behavior therapy. British Journal of Psychiatry, 1966, 112, 309–319.

Gelder, M. G., Marks, I. M., & Wolff, H. H. Desensitization and psychotherapy in the treatment of phobic states: A controlled inquiry. British Journal of Psychiatry, 1967, 113, 53–73.

Gendlin, E. T., Beebe, J., Cassens, J., Klein, M. H., & Oberlander, M. Focusing ability in psychotherapy, personality and creativity. In J. M. Shlien, H. F. Hunt, J. D. Matarazzo, and C. Savage (Eds.), Research in psychotherapy. Vol. 3. Washington, D. C.: American Psychological Association, 1968.

Gendlin, E. T., Jenney, R., & Shlien, J. Counselor ratings of process and outcome in client-centered therapy. Journal of Clinical Psychology, 1960, 16, 210–213.

Getter, H., & Sundland, D. M. The Barron ego strength scale and psychotherapy outcome. Journal of Consulting Psychology, 1962, 26, 195.

Glass, G. V., & Smith, M. L. Meta-analysis of psychotherapy outcome studies. Paper presented at the Society for Psychotherapy Research, San Diego, 1976.

Goffman, E. Asylums. Garden City, N. Y.: Anchor Books, 1961.

Goffman, E. The nature of deference and demeanor. In Interaction ritual. Garden City, N. Y.: Anchor Books, 1967.

Goldstein, A. P., Heller, K., & Sechrest, L. B.

Psychotherapy and the psychology of behavior change. New York: Wiley, 1966.

Goodman, G. *Companionship therapy.* San Francisco: Jossey-Bass Inc., 1972.

Goodman, N. Are there differences between fee and non-fee cases? *Social Work,* 1960, *5,* 46–52.

Gordon, T., & Cartwright, D. S. The effect of psychotherapy on certain attitudes toward others. In C. Rogers and R. F. Dymond (Eds.), *Psychotherapy and personality change.* Chicago: University of Chicago Press, 1954.

Gottschalk, L. A., Mayerson, P., & Gottlieb, A. A. Prediction and evaluation of outcome in an emergency brief psychotherapy clinic. *Journal of Nervous and Mental Disease,* 1967, *144,* 77–96.

Graham, S. R. Patient evaluation of the effectiveness of limited psychoanalytically oriented psychotherapy. *Psychological Reports,* 1958, *4,* 231–234.

Grigg, A. E., & Goodstein, L. D. Use of clients as judges of counselors' performance. *Journal of Counseling Psychology,* 1957, *4,* 31–36.

Haimowitz, N. R., & Haimowitz, M. L. Personality changes in client-centered therapy. In W. Wolff & J. A. Precher (Eds.), *Success in psychotherapy.* New York: Grune & Stratton, Inc., 1952.

Halkides, G. An investigation of four therapist variables. Unpublished doctoral dissertation, University of Chicago, 1958.

Hansen, J. C., Moore, G. D., & Carkhuff, R. R. The differential relationship of objective and client perceptions of counseling. *Journal of Clinical Psychology,* 1968, *24,* 244–246.

Hayward, R. H. Process and outcome consequences of therapist self-disclosure. *Dissertation Abstracts International,* 1974, *34,* 6210B–6211B.

Heilbrunn, G. Results with psychoanalytic therapy and professional commitment. *American Journal of Psychotherapy,* 1966, *20,* 89–99.

Heinicke, C. M. Frequency of psychotherapeutic sessions as a factor affecting outcome: Analysis of clinical ratings and test results. *Journal of Abnormal Psychology,* 1969, *74,* 553–560.

Henry, W. E., & Shlien, J. Affective complexity and psychotherapy: Some comparisons of time-limited and unlimited treatment. *Journal of Projective Techniques,* 1958, *22,* 153–162.

Henry, W. E., Sims, J. H., & Spray, S. L. *Public and private lives of psychotherapists.* San Francisco: Jossey-Bass, 1973.

Herz, M. I., Spitzer, R. L., Gibbon, M., Greenspan, K., & Reibel, S. Individual versus group aftercare treatment. *American Journal of Psychiatry,* 1974, *131,* 808–812.

Hilgard, J. R., Straight, D. C., & Moore, U. S. Better adjusted peers as resources in group therapy with adolescents. *Journal of Psychology,* 1969, *73,* 75–100.

Hoehn-Saric, R., Frank, J. D., Imber, S. D., Nash, E. H., Stone, A. R., & Battle, C. C. Systematic preparation of patients for psychotherapy: I. Effects on therapy behavior and outcome. *Journal of Psychiatric Research,* 1964, *2,* 267–281.

Horenstein, D. The effects of confirmation or disconfirmation of client expectations upon subsequent

psychotherapy. *Dissertation Abstracts International,* 1974, *34,* 6211B.

Howard, K. I., Krause, M. S., & Orlinsky, D. E. Direction of affective influence in psychotherapy. *Journal of Consulting and Clinical Psychology,* 1969, *33,* 614–620.

Howard, K. I., & Orlinsky, D. E. Psychotherapeutic processes. *Annual Review of Psychology,* 1972, *23,* 615–668.

Howard, K. I., Orlinsky, D. E., & Hill, J. A. The therapist's feelings in the therapeutic process. *Journal of Clinical Psychology,* 1969, *25,* 83–93.

Howard, K. I., Orlinsky, D. E. & Perilstein, J. Contribution of therapists to patients' experiences in psychotherapy: A components of variance model for analyzing process data. *Journal of Consulting and Clinical Psychology,* 1976, *44,* 520–526.

Imber, S. D., Frank, J. D., Nash, E. H., Stone, A. R., & Gliedman, L. H. Improvement and amount of therapeutic contact: An alternative to the use of no-treatment controls in psychotherapy. *Journal of Consulting Psychology,* 1957, *21,* 309–315.

Jacobs, D., Charles, E., Jacobs, T., Weinstein, H., & Mann, D. Preparation for psychotherapy of the disadvantaged patient. *American Journal of Orthopsychiatry,* 1972, *42,* 666–674.

Jeske, J. O. Identification and therapeutic effectiveness in group therapy. *Journal of Counseling Psychology,* 1973, *20,* 528–530.

Johnson, D. J. The effect of confrontation in counseling. *Dissertation Abstracts International,* 1971, *32,* 180A.

Johnson, R. W. Number of interviews, diagnosis and success of counseling. *Journal of Counseling Psychology,* 1965, *12,* 248–251.

Kadushin, C. *Why people go to psychiatrists.* New York: Atherton, 1969.

Kalfas, N. S. Client-perceived therapist empathy as a correlate of outcome. *Dissertation Abstracts International,* 1974, *34,* 5633A.

Kapp, F. T., Gleser, G., Bressenden, A., Emerson, R., Winget, J., & Kashdan, B. Group participation and self-perceived personality change. *Journal of Nervous and Mental Disease,* 1964, *139,* 255–265.

Kaswan, J., & Love, L. R. Confrontation as a method of psychological intervention. *Journal of Nervous and Mental Disease,* 1969, *148,* 224–237.

Kaufman, I., Frank, T., Freind, J., Heims, L. W., & Weiss, R. Success and failure in the treatment of childhood schizophrenia. *American Journal of Psychiatry,* 1962, *118,* 909–913.

Kernberg, O. F., Bernstein, C. S., Coyne, R., Appelbaum, D. A., Horwitz, H., & Voth, T. J. Psychotherapy and psychoanalysis: Final report of the Menninger Foundation's psychotherapy research project. *Bulletin of the Menninger Clinic,* 1972, *36,* 1–276.

Kiesler, D. J. Some myths of psychotherapy research and the search for a paradigm. *Psychological Bulletin,* 1966, *65,* 110–136.

Kiesler, D. J. Experimental designs in psychotherapy research. In A. E. Bergin & S. L. Garfield (Eds.), *Handbook of psychotherapy and behavior change: An empirical analysis.* New York: Wiley, 1971a.

Kiesler, D. J. Patient experiencing and successful outcome in individual psychotherapy of schizophrenics and psychoneurotics. *Journal of Consulting and Clinical Psychology,* 1971b, *37,* 370–385.

Kiesler, D. J. *The process of psychotherapy: Empirical foundations and systems of analysis.* Chicago: Aldine Publishing Co., 1973.

Kiesler, D. J., Mathieu, P., & Klein, M. H. Process movement in therapy and sampling interviews. In C. R. Rogers et al. (Eds.), *The therapeutic relationship and its impact: A study of psychotherapy with schizophrenics.* Madison: University of Wisconsin Press, 1967.

Kilmann, P. R., & Auerbach, S. M. Effects of marathon group therapy on trait and state anxiety. *Journal of Consuting and Clinical Psychology,* 1974, *42,* 607–612.

Kilmann, P. R., & Howell, R. J. Effects of structure of marathon group therapy and locus of control on therapeutic outcome. *Journal of Consulting and Clinical Psychology,* 1974, *42,* 912.

Kirtner, W. L. & Cartwright, D. S. Success and failure in client-centered therapy as a function of initial in-therapy behavior. *Journal of Consulting Psychology,* 1958, *22,* 329–333.

Kirtner, W. L., Cartwright, D. S., Robertson, R. J., & Fiske, D. W. Length of therapy in relation to outcome and change in personal integration. *Journal of Consulting Psychology,* 1961, *25,* 84–88.

Krause, M. S. & Howard, K. I. Program evaluation in the public interest: A new research methodology. *Community Mental Health Journal,* 1976, *12,* 291–300.

Kuhn, T. *The structure of scientific revolutions.* Chicago: University of Chicago Press, 1962.

Kurtz, R. R., & Grummon, D. L. Different approaches to the measurement of therapist empathy and their relationship to therapy outcomes. *Journal of Consulting and Clinical Psychology,* 1972, *39,* 106–115.

Leary, T. *Interpersonal diagnosis of personality.* New York: Ronald Press, 1957.

Lennard, H. L., & Bernstein, A. *Patterns in human interaction.* San Francisco: Jossey-Bass, 1969.

Lerner, B. *Therapy in the ghetto.* Baltimore: John Hopkins University Press, 1972.

Lesser, W. M. The relationship between counseling progress and empathic understanding. *Journal of Counseling Psychology,* 1961, *8,* 330–336.

Liberman, B. L., Frank, J. D., Hoehn-Saric, R., Stone, A. R., Imber, S. D., & Pande, S. K. Patterns of change in treated psychoneurotic patients: A five-year follow-up investigation of the systematic preparation of patients for psychotherapy. *Journal of Consulting and Clinical Psychology,* 1972, *38,* 36–41.

Lieberman, M. A. Change induction in small groups. *Annual Review of Psychology,* 1976, *27,* 217–250.

Lipkin, S. Clients' feelings and attitudes in relation to the outcome of client-centered therapy. *Psychological Monographs,* 1954, *68*(1, Whole No. 372).

Lomont, J. F., Gilner, F. H., Spector, N. J., & Skinner, K. K. Group assertion training and group insight therapies. *Psychological Reports,* 1969, *25,* 463–470.

Lorr, M. Client perceptions of theapists: A study of the therapeutic relation. *Journal of Consulting Psychology,* 1965, *29,* 146–149.

Lorr, M., & McNair, D. M. The interview relationship in therapy. *Journal of Nervous and Mental Disease,* 1964, *139,* 328–331.

Lorr, M., McNair, D., Michaux, W., & Raskin, A. Frequency of treatment and change in psychotherapy. *Journal of Abnormal and Social Psychology,* 1962, *64,* 281–292.

Luborsky, L., Chandler, M., Auerbach, A. H., Cohen, J., & Bachrach, H. M. Factors influencing the outcome of psychotherapy: A review of quantitative research. *Psychological Bulletin,* 1971, *75,* 145–185.

Luborsky, L., Singer, B., & Luborsky, L. Comparative studies of psychotherapies. *Archives of General Psychiatry,* 1975, *32,* 995–1008.

Mainord, W. A., Burk, H. W., & Collins, L. G. Confrontation versus diversion in group therapy with chronic schizophrenics as measured by a "positive incident" criterion. *Journal of Clinical Psychology,* 1965, *21,* 222–225.

Malan, D. H. *Toward the validation of dynamic psychotherapy.* London: Plenum Medical Book Company, 1976.

Marsden, G. Content analysis studies of psychotherapy: 1954 through 1968. In A. E. Bergin and S. L. Garfield (Eds.), *Handbook of psychotherapy and behavior change: An empirical analysis.* New York: Wiley, Inc., 1971.

Martin, P. J., & Sterne, A. L. Post-hospital adjustment as related to therapists' in-therapy behavior. *Psychotherapy: Theory, Research and Practice,* 1976, *13,* 267–273.

McClanahan, L. D. Comparison of counseling techniques and attitudes with client evaluations of the counseling relationship. *Dissertation Abstracts International.* 1974, *34,* 9–A, 5637.

McNair, D. M., & Lorr, M. Therapists' judgements of appropriateness of psychotherapy frequency schedules. *Journal of Consulting Psychology,* 1960, *24,* 500–506.

McNair, D. M., Lorr, M., Young, H. H., Roth, I., & Boyd, R. W. A three-year follow-up of psychotherapy patients. *Journal of Clinical Psychology,* 1964, *20,* 258–264.

McNally, H. A. An investigation of selected counselor and client characteristics as possible predictors of counseling effectiveness. *Dissertation Abstracts International,* 1973, *33,* 12–A, 6672–6673.

Melnick, B., & Pierce, R. M. Client evaluation of therapist strength and positive-negative evaluation as related to client dynamics, objective ratings of competence and outcome. *Journal of Clinical Psychology,* 1971, *27,* 408–410.

Meltzoff, J., & Kornreich, M. *Research in Psychotherapy.* New York: Atherton Press, Inc., 1970.

Mensh, I., & Golden, J. Factors in psychotherapeutic success. *Journal of the Missouri State Medical Association,* 1951, *48,* 180–184.

Miles, H. W., Barrabee, E. L., & Finesinger, J. E. Evaluation of psychotherapy, with a follow-up of 62 cases of anxiety neuroses. *Psychosomatic Medicine,* 1951, *13,* 83–105.

Minsel, W., Bommert, H., Bastine, R., Langer, I., Nickel,

H., & Tausch, R. Weitere untersuchung der aufwir-kung und prozess klienten-zentrieter ges-prachstherapie. *Zeitschrift fur Klinische Psychologie,* 1971, *1,* 232–250.

Mintz, J., Luborsky, L., & Auerbach, A. Dimensions of psychotherapy: A factor-analytic study of ratings of psychotherapy sessions. *Journal of Consulting and Clinical Psychology,* 1971, *36,* 106–120.

Mitchell, K., Bozarth, J., Truax, C., & Krauft, C. *Antecedents to psychotherapeutic outcome.* Arkansas Rehabilitation Research and Training Center, University of Arkansas, 1973 (NIMH Final Report, MH 12306).

Mitchell, R. M. Relationship between therapist response to therapist-relevant client expressions and therapy process and client outcome. *Dissertation Abstracts International,* 1971, *32,* 1853B.

Mordock, J. B., Ellis, M. H., & Greenstone, J. L. The effect of group and individual therapy on sociometric choice of disturbed institutionalized adolescents. *International Journal of Group Psychotherapy,* 1969, *19,* 510–517.

Mowrer, O. H. Changes in verbal behavior during psychotherapy. In O. H. Mowrer (Ed.), *Psychotherapy: Theory and research.* New York: Ronald Press, 1953.

Mowrer, O. H., Hunt, J. McV., & Kogan, L. Further studies utilizing the discomfort-relief quotient. In O. H. Mowrer (Ed.), *Psychotherapy: Theory and research.* New York: Ronald Press, 1953.

Muench, G. A. An investigation of the efficacy of time-limited psychotherapy. *Journal of Counseling Psychology,* 1965, *12,* 294–298.

Muller, J., & Abeles, N. Relationship of liking, empathy, and therapist's experience to outcome of therapy. *Journal of Counseling Psychology,* 1971, *18,* 39–43.

Munro, J. N., & Bach, T. R. Effect of time-limited counseling on client change. *Journal of Counseling Psychology,* 1975, *22,* 395–398.

Myers, J. K., & Auld, F. Some variables related to outcome of psychotherapy. *Journal of Clinical Psychology,* 1955, *11,* 51–54.

Nagy, T. F. Therpist level of functioning and change in clients' quantifiable anxiety level and verbal behavior. *Dissertation Abstracts International,* 1973, *34,* 878B–879B.

Newcomer, B. L., & Morrison, T. L. Play therapy with institutionalized mentally retarded children. *American Journal of Mental Deficiency,* 1974, *78,* 727–733.

Nichols, M. P. Outcome of brief cathartic psychotherapy. *Journal of Consulting and Clinical Psychology,* 1974, *42,* 403–410.

Nichols, R. C., & Beck, K. W. Factors in psychotherapy change. *Journal of Consulting Psychology,* 1960, *24,* 388–399.

O'Brien, C., Hamm, K., & Ray, B. Group vs. individual psychotherapy with schizophrenics: A controlled outcome study. *Archives of General Psychiatry,* 1972, *27,* 474–478.

O'Connor, J. F., Daniels, G., Flood, C., Karush, A., Moses, L., & Stern, L. O. An evaluation of the effectiveness of psychotherapy in the treatment of ulcerative colitis. *Annals of Internal Medicine,* 1964, *60,* 587–602.

Orlinsky, D. E., & Howard, K. I. *Varieties of psychotherapeutic experience.* New York: Teachers College Press, 1975.

Paredes, A., Cottheil, E., Tausig, T. N., & Cornelison, F. S. Behavioral changes as a function of repeated self-observation. *Journal of Nervous and Mental Disease,* 1969, *148,* 287–299.

Parloff, M. B. Therapist-patient relationships and outcome of psychotherapy. *Journal of Consulting Psychology,* 1961, *25,* 29–38.

Parson, T., & Shils, E. (Eds.) *Toward a general theory of action.* Cambridge: Harvard University Press, 1951.

Pascal, G. R., & Zax, M. Psychotherapeutics: Success or failure? *Journal of Consulting Psychology,* 1956, *20,* 325–331.

Pearl, D. Psychotherapy and ethnocentrism. *Journal of Abnormal and Social Psychology,* 1955, *50,* 227–229.

Peck, R. E. Comparison of adjunct group therapy with individual psychotherapy. *Archives of Neurological Psychiatry,* 1949, *62,* 173–177.

Pierce, R. M., & Schauble, P. G. A note on the role of facilitative responsibility in the therapeutic relationship. *Journal of Clinical Psychology,* 1970, *26,* 250–252.

Pope, K. S., Geller, J. D., & Wilkinson, L. Fee assessment and outpatient psychotherapy. *Journal of Consulting and Clinical Psychology,* 1975, *43,* 835–841.

Prager, R. A. The relationship of certain client characteristics to therapist-offered conditions and therapeutic outcome. *Dissertation Abstracts International,* 1971, *31,* 5634B–5635B.

Pruit, W. A. Satiation effect in vocationally oriented group therapy as determined by the Palo Alto Group Psychotherapy Scale. *Group Psychotherapy,* 1963, *16,* 55–58.

Ravid, R. Effect of group therapy on long term individual patients. *Dissertation Abstracts International,* 1969, *30,* 2427B.

Reid, W. J., & Schyne, A. W. *Brief and extended casework.* New York: Columbia University Press, 1969.

Reiner, C. A. Multiple and individual therapy: A comparative study of client outcome, attitudes, and discussion of the two treatment modalities. *Dissertation Abstracts International,* 1973, *34,* 5206B–5207B.

Rice, L. N. Therapist's style of participation and case outcome. *Journal of Consulting Psychology,* 1965, *29,* 155–160.

Roether, H. A., & Peters, J. J. Cohesiveness and hostility in group psychotherapy. *American Journal of Psychiatry,* 1972, *128,* 1014–1017.

Rogers, C. R. The necessary and sufficient conditions of therapeutic personality change. *Journal of Consulting Psychology,* 1957, *21,* 95–103.

Rogers, H. B. M. Therapists' verbalization and outcome in monitored play therapy. *Dissertation Abstracts International,* 1973, *34,* 424B.

Roman, P. M., & Trice, H. M. (Eds.) *The sociology of psychotherapy.* New York: Jasen Aronson, 1974.

Rosenbaum, M., Friedlander, J., & Kaplan, S. Evaluation of results of psychotherapy. *Psychosomatic*

Medicine, 1956, *18,* 113–132.

Rosenman, S. Changes in the representation of self, other and interrelationship in client-centered therapy. *Journal of Counseling Psychology,* 1955, *2,* 271–278.

Rosenthal, D., & Frank, J. D. The fate of psychiatric clinic outpatients assigned to psychotherapy. *Journal of Nervous and Mental Disease,* 1958, *127,* 330–343.

Rosenthal, A. J., & Levine, S. V. Brief psychotherapy with children: A preliminary report. *The American Journal of Psychiatry,* 1970, *127,* 646–651.

Roshal, J. G. The type-token ratio as a measure of changes in behavior variability during psychotherapy. In W. U. Snyder (Ed.), *Group report of a program of research in psychotherapy.* State College, Pa.: Pennsylvania State College Press, 1953.

Ross, W. F., McReynolds, W. T., & Berzins, J. I. Effectiveness of marathon group psychotherapy with hospitalized female narcotics addicts. *Psychological Reports,* 1974, *34,* 611–616.

Roth, I., Rhudick, P. J., Shaskan, D. A., Slobin, M. S. Wilkinson, A. E., & Young, H. Long-term effects on psychotherapy of initial treatment conditions. *Journal of Psychiatric Research,* 1964, *2,* 283–297.

Ryan, V. L., & Gizynski, M. N. Behavior therapy in retrospect: Patients' feelings about their behavior therapies. *Journal of Consulting and Clinical Psychology,* 1971, *37,* 1–9.

Saltzman, C., Luetgert, M. J., Roth, C. H., Creaser, J., & Howard, L. Formation of a therapeutic relationship: Experiences during the initial phase of psychotherapy as predictors of treatment duration and outcome. *Journal of Consulting and Clinical Psychology,* 1976, *44,* 546–555.

Sapolsky, A. Relationship between patient-doctor compatibility, mutual perceptions, and outcome of treatment. *Journal of Abnormal Psychology,* 1965, *70,* 70–76.

Schauble, P. G., & Pierce, R. M. Client in-therapy behavior: A therapist guide to progress. *Psychotherapy: Theory, Research and Practice,* 1974, *11,* 229–234.

Scher, M. Verbal activity, sex, counselor experience, and success in counseling. *Journal of Counseling Psychology,* 1975, *22,* 97–101.

Schonfield, J., Stone, A. R., Hoehn-Saric, R., Imber, S. D., & Pande, S. K. Patient therapist convergence and measures of improvement in short-term psychotherapy. *Psychotherapy: Theory, Research and Practice,* 1969, *6,* 267–271.

Seeman, J. Counselor judgments of therapeutic process and outcome. In C. Rogers and R. F. Dymond (Eds.), *Psychotherapy and personality change.* Chicago: University of Chicago Press, 1954.

Semon, R. G., & Goldstein, N. The effectiveness of group psychotherapy with chronic schizophrenic patients and an evaluation of different therapeutic methods. *Journal of Consulting Psychology,* 1957, *21,* 317–322.

Shlien, J. M. Time-limited psychotherapy: An experimental investigation of practical values and theoretical implications. *Journal of Counseling Psychology,* 1957, *4,* 318–322.

Shlien, J. M., Mosak, H. H., & Dreikurs, R. Effects of time limits: A comparison of two psychotherapies. *Journal of Counseling Psychology,* 1962, *9,* 31–34.

Slawson, P. F. Psychodrama as a treatment for hospitalized patients: A controlled study. *American Journal of Psychiatry,* 1965, *122,* 530–533.

Sloane, R. B., Cristol, A. H., Pepernik, L., & Staples, F. R. Role preparation and expectation of improvement in psychotherapy. *Journal of Nervous and Mental Disease,* 1970, *150,* 18–26.

Sloane, R. B., Staples, F. R., Cristol, A. H., Yorkston, N. J., & Whipple, K. *Psychotherapy versus behavior therapy.* Cambridge: Harvard University Press, 1975.

Smith, A. B., Bassin, A., & Froehlich, A. Changes in attitudes and degree of verbal participation in group therapy with adult offenders. *Journal of Consulting Psychology,* 1960, *24,* 247–249.

Standahl, S. W., & van der Veen, F. Length of therapy in relation to counselor estimates of personal integration and other case variables. *Journal of Consulting Psychology,* 1957, *21,* 1–9.

Stoler, N. Client likeability: A variable in the study of psychotherapy. *Journal of Consulting Psychology,* 1963, *27,* 175–178.

Stoler, N. *The relationship of patient likability and the A-B psychiatric resident types.* (Doctoral dissertation, University of Michigan) Ann Arbor, Mich.: University Microfilms, 1966.

Stone, A. R., Frank, J. D., Nash, E. H., & Imber, S. D. An intensive five-year follow-up study of treated psychiatric outpatients. *Journal of Nervous and Mental Disease,* 1961, *133,* 410–422.

Stassberg, D. S., Roback, H. B., Anchor, K. N., & Abramowitz, S. I. Self-disclosure in group therapy with schizophrenics. *Archives of General Psychiatry,* 1975, *32,* 1259–1261.

Strupp, H. H., & Bloxom, A. Preparation of lower class patients for group psychotherapy. *Journal of Consulting and Clinical Psychology,* 1973, *41,* 373–384.

Strupp, H. H., Wallach, M. S., Jenkins, J. W., & Wogan, M. Psychotherapists' assessments of former patients. *Journal of Nervous and Mental Disease,* 1963, *137,* 222–230.

Strupp, H. H., Wallach, M. L., & Wogan, M. The psychotherapy experience in retrospect: A questionnaire survey of former patients and their therapists. *Psychological Monographs,* 1964, *78:*11.

Sullivan, P. L., Miller, C., & Smelser, W. Factors in length of stay and progress in psychotherapy. *Journal of Consulting Psychology,* 1958, *22,* 1–9.

Tausch, R., Eppel, H., Fittkau, B., & Minsel, W. Variablen und zusammenhange in der gesprachspsychotherapie. *Zeitschrift fur Psychologie,* 1969, *176,* 93–102.

Tausch, R., Sander, K., Bastine, R., & Friese, H. Variablen und ergebnisse bei client-centered psychotherapie mit alternierenden psychotherapeuten. *Sonderdruck aus Psychologische Rundschau,* 1970, *21,* 29–37.

Taylor, J. W. Relationships of success and length in psychotherapy. *Journal of Consulting Psychology,* 1956, *20,* 332.

Thorley, A. S., & Craske, N. Comparison and estimate of group and individual methods of treatment. *British Medical Journal,* 1950, *1,* 97–100.

Tolman, R. S., & Mayer, M. M. Who returns to the clinic for more therapy? *Mental Hygeine,* 1957, *41,* 497–506.

Tomlinson, T. M. The therapeutic process as related to outcome. In C. R. Rogers et al. (Eds.) *The therapeutic relationship and its impact: A study of psychotherapy with schizophrenics.* Madison: University of Wisconsin Press, 1967.

Tomlinson, T. M., & Hart, J. T. Jr. A validation study of the process scale. *Journal of Consulting Psychology,* 1962, *26,* 74–78.

Tomlinson, T. M., & Stoler, N. The relationship between affective evaluation and ratings of therapy process and outcome with schizophrenics. *Psychotherapy: Theory, Research and Practice,* 1967, *4,* 14–18.

Tovian, S. M. Patient experiences and psychotherapy outcome. Unpublished doctoral dissertation Northwestern University, 1977

Truax, C. B. Effective ingredients in psychotherapy: An approach to unraveling the patient-therapist interaction. *Journal of Counseling Psychology,* 1963, *10,* 256–263.

Truax, C. B. Therapist empathy, warmth, and genuineness and patient personality change in group psychotherapy: A comparison between interaction unit measures, time sample measures, and patient perception measures. *Journal of Clinical Psychology,* 1966, *22,* 225–229.

Truax, C. B. Therapist's evaluative statements and patient outcome in psychotherapy. *Journal of Clinical Psychology,* 1970a, *26,* 536–538.

Truax, C. B. Length of therapist response, accurate empathy and patient improvement. *Journal of Clinical Psychology,* 1970b, 26, 539–541.

Truax, C. B. Effects of client-centered psychotherapy with schizophrenic patients: Nine years pretherapy and nine years posttherapy hospitalization. *Journal of Consulting and Clinical Psychology,* 1970c, *35,* 417–422.

Truax, C. B. Degree of negative transference occurring in group psychotherapy and client outcome in juvenile delinquents. *Journal of Clinical Psychology,* 1971, *27,* 132–136.

Truax, C. B., Altman, H., Wright, L., & Mitchell, K. M. Effects of therapeutic conditions in child therapy. *Journal of Community Psychology,* 1973, *1,* 313–318.

Truax, C. B., & Carkhuff R. R. The experimental manipulation of therapeutic conditions. *Journal of Consulting Psychology,* 1965, *29,* 119–124.

Truax, C. B., & Carkhuff, R. R. *Toward effective counseling and psychotherapy.* Chicago: Aldine, 1967.

Truax, C. B., Carkhuff, R. R., & Kodman, F. Jr. Relationships between therapist-offered conditions and patient change in group psychotherapy. *Journal of Clinical Psychology,* 1965, *21,* 327–329.

Truax, C. B., & Mitchell, K. M. Research on certain therapist interpersonal skills in relation to process and outcome. In A. E. Bergin and S. L. Garfield (Eds.) *Handbook of psychotherapy and behavior change: An empirical analysis.* New York: John Wiley & Sons, Inc., 1971.

Truax, C. B., & Wargo, D. G. Antecedents to outcome in group psychotherapy with juvenile delinquents: Effects of therapeutic conditions, alternate sessions, vicarious therapy pre-training and client self-exploration. Unpublished manuscript, Arkansas Rehabilitation Research and Training Center, University of Arkansas, 1967a.

Truax, C. B., & Wargo, D. G. Antecedents to outcome in group psychotherapy with hospitalized mental patients: Effects of therapeutic conditions, alternate sessions, vicarious therapy pre-training and patient self-exploration. Unpublished manuscript, Arkansas Rehabilitation Research and Training Center, University of Arkansas, 1967b.

Truax, C. B., & Wargo, D. G. Effects of vicarious therapy pre-training and alternate sessions on outcome in group psychotherapy with outpatients. *Journal of Consulting and Clinical Psychology,* 1969, *33,* 440–447.

Truax, C. B., Wargo, D. G., Frank, J. D., Imber, S. D., Battle, C. C., Hoehn-Saric, R., Nash, E. H., & Stone, A. R. Therapist empathy, genuineness, and warmth and patient therapeutic outcome. *Journal of Consulting Psychology,* 1966, *30,* 395–401.

Truax, C. B., Wargo, D. G., & Volksdorf, N. R. Antecedents to outcome in group counseling with institutionalized juvenile delinquents: Effects of therapeutic conditions, patient self-exploration, alternate sessions, and vicarious therapy pretraining. *Journal of Abnormal Psychology,* 1970, *76,* 235–242.

Truax, C. B., & Wittmer, J. Effects of therapist focus on patient anxiety source and the interaction with the therapist's level of accurate empathy. *Journal of Clinical Psychology,* 1971, *27,* 297–299 (a).

Truax, C. B., & Wittmer, J. Patient non-personal reference during psychotherapy and therapeutic outcome. *Journal of Clinical Psychology,* 1971, *27,* 300–302. (b)

Truax, C. B., & Wittmer, J. The degree of the therapist's focus on defense mechanisms and the effect on therapeutic outcome with institutionalized juvenile delinquents. *Journal of Community Psychology,* 1973, *1,* 201–203.

Truax, C. B., Wittmer, J., & Wargo, D. G. Effects of the therapeutic conditions of accurate empathy, non-possessive warmth, and genuineness on hospitalized mental patients during group therapy. *Journal of Clinical Psychology,* 1971, *27,* 137–142.

Uhlenhuth, E., & Duncan, D. Subjective change in psychoneurotic outpatients with medical student therapists. II. Some determinants of change. *Archives of General Psychiatry,* 1968, *18,* 532–540.

van der Veen, F. Basic elements in the process of psychotherapy. *Journal of Consulting Psychology,* 1967, *31,* 295–301.

Van Slambrouck, S. Relation of structural parameters to treatment outcome. *Dissertation Abstracts International,* 1973, *33,* 5528B.

Vargas, M. J. Changes in self-awareness during client-centered therapy. In C. R. Rogers and R. F. Dymond (Eds.) *Psychotherapy and personality change.* Chicago: University of Chicago Press, 1954.

Walker, A., Rablen, R. A., & Rogers, C. R. Development of a scale to measure process change in psychotherapy. *Journal of Clinical Psychology,* 1960, *16,* 79–85.

Wargo, D. G., Millis, W. E., & Hendricks, N. G. Patient rational verbal behavior as an antecedent to outcome in psychotherapy. *Psychotherapy: Theory, Research and Practice,* 1971, *8,* 199–201.

Warren, N. C., & Rice, L. N. Structuring and stabilizing psychotherapy for low-prognosis clients. *Journal of Consulting and Clinical psychology,* 1972, *39,* 173–181.

Waskow, I. E. & Parloff, M. B. (Eds.) *Psychotherapy change measures.* Rockville, Md.: National Institute of Mental Health, 1975,

Watzlawick, P., Weakland, J., & Fisch, R. *Change.* New York: Norton, 1974.

Yalom, I. D. *The theory and practice of group psychotherapy.* New York: Basic Books, Inc., 1975.

Yalom, I. D., Houts, P. S., Zimerberg, S. M., & Rand, K. H. Prediction of improvement in group therapy. *Archives of General Psychiatry,* 1967, *17,* 159–168.

Yalom, I. D., Tinklenburg, J., & Gilula, M. Curative factors in group therapy. Unpublished paper, 1975.

Zirkle, G. A. Five-minute psychotherapy. *American Journal of Psychiatry,* 1961, *118,* 544–546.

9

QUANTITATIVE RESEARCH ON PSYCHOANALYTIC THERAPY*

LESTER LUBORSKY

University of Pennsylvania

DONALD P. SPENCE

Rutgers Medical School-CMDNJ

Quantitative psychoanalytic research remains little known. Rare is the psychoanalyst who knows of any of these studies, and even rarer is the psychoanalyst whose practice has been altered by them. Our aim is to bring this research area out of obscurity and guide it by reviewing what has been done and what needs to be done.

Our review takes as its domain the attempts at quantitative research that rest on at least two articles of faith: (1) respect for the clinical theory of psychoanalysis and for the conditions of psychoanalytic treatment; (2) an appreciation of

the twin needs of science: to reduce diversity to simplicity, and to state observations in objective language (see Rapoport, 1968). We will use the word "quantitative" as a general term to refer to any use of controlled observation beyond the usual form of clinical observation.

The focus of our review will be on research on psychoanalytic treatment itself, not on psychoanalytically oriented psychotherapy. Even though psychoanalytically oriented psychotherapy is a form of psychotherapy commonly practiced in the United States, it includes a much wider range of techniques than does psychoanalytic treatment. Psychoanalytic treatment is a relatively clearly defined—if not widely practiced—treatment modality. It is an intensive treatment—three to five years of four to five sessions a week—in which the patient reclines and tries to say whatever comes to

*This investigation was supported by United States Public Health Service Grant MH-15442 and Research Scientist Award MH-40710 (to Dr. Luborsky). We thank Arthur Auerbach, Helene Peterson, Harold Sampson, Leonard Horowitz, and Henry Bachrach for their assistance and advice, and Marjorie Cohen who assisted in manuscript preparation.

mind (free association), while the analyst responds interpretively, with particular reliance on the concepts of transference and resistance.

No one has surveyed this tiny area in toto. The studies to be reviewed here are scattered in the literature, and we cannot claim to have achieved our aim of an exhaustive review. The best general review of psychoanalytic research on psychoanalytic treatment is by Wallerstein and Sampson (1971). Schlessinger, Pollock, Sabshin, Sadow and Gedo (1966) have dealt with psychoanalytic contributions to psychotherapy research, but most of these studies are nonquantitative—of the 29 references, only two report quantitative studies (Alexander, French and Pollock, 1968; Knapp, 1963). Only a small percentage of the articles appearing in the two most widely read psychoanalytic journals, the *Journal of the American Psychoanalytic Association,* and the *International Journal of Psychoanalysis,* discuss quantitative psychoanalytic research. The annual *Psychoanalysis and Contemporary Science* and the new journal *Psychoanalysis and Contemporary Thought* has a higher percentage. Of all the psychological journals, *Psychological Issues* has had the best balance of clinical and quantitative psychoanalytic studies. The most popular topic among those interested in psychoanalytic research has been the broad issue of the *problems* of conducting research in psychoanalysis. The articles on this topic are often more impressive than the research itself! These occasionally contain some references to quantitative studies of psychoanalytic treatment and are written by outstanding theoreticians and researchers (such as Benjamin, 1950; Brenman, Kubie, Murray, Kris, & Gill, 1947; Engel, 1968; Escalona, 1952; Frenkel-Brunswik, 1954; Freud, 1913; Glover, 1952, 1955; Hartmann, 1958, 1959; Hartmann, Kris, & Lowenstein, 1953; G. Klein, 1949; Kris, 1947; Kubie, 1952; Lustman, 1963; Pfeffer, 1961; Pumpian-Mindlin, 1952; Ramzy, 1963; Rapaport, 1959; Rapoport, 1968; Sargent, 1961; Shakow, 1960; Waelder, 1962; Wallerstein, 1966; Wallerstein & Sampson, 1971).

Our chapter is organized around the main questions asked about psychoanalytic treatment. These turn out to be similar to those asked about any form of psychotherapy: (1) the kinds of patients who are most suited to it; (2) the kinds of therapists who are most suited to perform it; (3) the types of changes (outcomes) that are accomplished by it; and (4) the nature of the process the patient and therapist go through during it. To further the growth of research on the process of psychoanalytic treatment, we have included an enlarged section (as compared with the version of this chapter written seven years ago) on the locations, collaborations, and findings from the various primary data banks of psychoanalytic sessions. Finally, we will offer some conclusions about the main implications of all of this for psychoanalytic practice and research.

RESEARCH ON QUALITIES OF MOST SUITABLE PATIENTS

A large research literature concerns the question of "analyzability"—the type of patient who is most suitable for psychoanalytic treatment (reviewed by Bachrach & Leaff, in press). It largely supports the common working assumption that patients for psychoanalysis should be in the neurotic range. They might start with symptoms that cause them considerable suffering, but should have considerable psychological-mindedness and capacity for insight.

In general, the analytic patient ought to have more personality assets than the patient for other forms of psychotherapy. This conclusion has been verified in a general way by a study done in 1952 of all patients in psychotherapy in the Department of Adult Psychiatry of the Menninger Foundation at that time (Luborsky, 1962a). Obvious differences were found in the initial state of patients who were receiving different forms of psychotherapy. On the 100-point "Health-Sickness Rating Scale" (see Luborsky, 1962a, 1975; Luborsky & Bachrach, 1974), the patients receiving psychoanalysis began significantly higher, that is, healthier (51.4), than the patients receiving expressive psychotherapy (38.2) or supportive psychotherapy (36.7). (These treatment modalities have been briefly defined by Wallerstein et al., 1956.) The differences between these scores merely confirm that patients are, in fact, referred for treatment differentially on the basis of their degree of health or sickness, among other considerations. The same impression of mental health is given by the findings of Aronson and Weintraub (1968b) and Weintraub and Aronson (1968) on the social background and vital statistics of patients who go into analysis. For example, only 8 percent of their patient group were vocationally incapacitated while 37 percent were already operating optimally in their work at the beginning of treatment.

Only five quantitative studies have been reported on psychoanalytic patients in which an aspect of the patient's initial state was related to the outcome of the treatment. Three of these five dealt with small groups of patients. These are H. Klein (1960, 30 patients); Knapp, Levin, McCarter, Wermer, and Zetzel (1960, 27 patients); and the Menninger study (Wallerstein, Robbins, Sargent, & Luborsky, 1956, Kernberg et al., 1972, 21 patients in psychoanalytic treatment and 21 in psychoanalytically oriented psychotherapies). The fourth, a large mail survey (Hamburg, Bibring, Fisher, Stanton, Wallerstein, & Haggard, 1967), covered approximately 3000 patients on whom therapists filled out initial and final questionnaires. The fifth was a retrospective study of 183 patients in psychoanalytic treatment (Sashin, Eldred, & VanAmerongen, 1975).

Findings from these five studies are similar to those of 166 studies relating initial factors to outcome of treatment by any form of psychotherapy (Luborsky, Chandler, Auerbach, Cohen, & Bachrach, 1971). The similarity was not only in terms of the types of predictors but also in the modest level of prediction success achieved by any of these initial characteristics. Such a modest level was found both for the psychotherapy studies (Luborsky et al., 1971) as well as in three large-scale multivariate prediction studies (Luborsky, Mintz, Auerbach, & associates, in preparation.

In the psychotherapy studies (Luborsky et al., 1971) patients with the best initial personality functioning tended to show the best results from treatment in 13 studies; in 13 other studies the relationship did not reach significance. None of the studies showed a significant negative relationship between initial level and treatment outcome. It is hard to discern why the relationship reached significance in some studies and not in others. In some cases (such as H. Klein, 1960) the range of dysfunction is relatively small (they were all analytic patients),

which would limit the possibility of a significant relationship. Yet other samples (e.g., Knapp et al., 1960) also included analytic patients but showed a significant relationship. In the large survey (Hamburg et al., 1967), the patients were much more diverse; those with the poorest general personality functioning tended to do most poorly in treatment. Of those patients who were initially diagnosed as "schizophrenic," fewer were judged to be improved at the end of those treatments which had been judged by the analyst to have been completed.

In the Hamburg et al. study (1967), the patients who were judged to be anxious initially improved more than the patients without initial anxiety. This is consistent with the Menninger study finding (Luborsky, 1962b) that patients with higher initial anxiety made more gains in treatment, a finding that applied to those patients who started treatment above 50 on the Health-Sickness Rating Scale which includes mainly *the patients who were in psychoanalytic treatment*. Knapp et al. (1960) found, however, that obsessional patients did better ($p < .02$) than other diagnostic groups. Hysterics did very well, or very badly, depending on the experience level of the therapist.

Hamburg et al. (1967) reported that younger patients did better than older patients and the 46-and-older group had a lower improvement rate than expected by chance ($p < .05$). Knapp et al. (1960) also found that younger patients did better even though the age range was only 20 to 40.

In the psychotherapy research studies (Luborsky et al., 1971), higher educational level was a good prognostic sign. Hamburg et al. (1967) found the same, but Knapp et al. (1960) found no relationship—possibly because the educational level of the whole sample was high.

In the psychotherapy research (Luborsky et al., 1971), similarity between patient and psychotherapist (such as on values or social class) tended to be prognostically favorable. That may be the meaning of the finding of Hamburg et al. (1967) that patients in the professional ranks or patients who are psychiatrists or analytic candidates are more likely to complete psychoanalytic treatment than the general population. (There are, of course, some obvious other factors that contribute to the completion behavior of candidates, such as the completion of treatment being pre-requisite for completion of training.)

Hamburg et al. (1967) and H. Klein (1960) found no relationship between having had previous treatment and the outcome of the present treatment. Hamburg et al. (1967) and Knapp et al. (1960) did not find that the patient's sex made any difference in the outcome of treatment.[1]

The Menninger Foundation Psychotherapy Research Project (Kernberg et al., 1972) looked at patient qualities that predict good psychotherapy outcome. The best predictors were patient anxiety (correlation of .50 with global improvement) and patient ego-strength (.35 with global improvement).

A Human Relations Scale was developed as part of a study of short-term treatment (Gottschalk, Mayerson, & Gottlieb, 1967). The patient talks freely for about five minutes about a dramatic experience he or she has been through. The scale was based on a prediction derived from psychoanalytic theory that patients with initially better "object relationships" as shown in these experiences should fare better in psychotherapy and in psychoanalysis. Isaacs and Haggard (1966) offer the similar concept of *relatability*, which in client-centered as well as psychoanalytically oriented settings proved to be a way to predict improvement. Relatability refers to a hierarchy of levels in a person's capacity for object relations. Relatability is determined from a measure of the object relations depicted in the patient's TAT.

Conclusion 1
Some quantitative reseach has been conducted on the relation of the initial qualities of the patient to the outcome of the treatment. If we take significant results in at least two studies as a basic require-

---

[1]Another questionnaire study (Aronson and Weintraub, 1968a) has been made of 127 patients of 28 analysts, but the information represents patients at any point in analysis rather than at the beginning and end of analysis. Findings were: (1) the initial diagnostic state showed no significant relationship to gains from the treatment, although there was a nonsignificant tendency for the borderline patients to become worse with analysis more often than patients with other diagnostic classifications; (2) a steady increase in improvement occurred the longer the patients remained in analysis. (Luborsky et al., 1971, reported the same finding in 20 of 23 psychotherapy studies.)

ment, we emerge with four positive initial qualities: (1) better general personality functioning (or absence of severe psychopathology such as schizophrenia); (2) younger age; (3) stronger anxiety; and (4) higher educational level. Strong anxiety is an especially positive predictor in patients with good general personality functioning.

Conclusion 2
These positive findings are similar to those based on other forms of psychotherapy (as established in the studies reviewed by Luborsky et al., 1971; Luborsky et al., in preparation) both in terms of which initial qualities of patients are predictive as well as the modest levels of prediction success achieved by initial evaluations.

RESEARCH ON DESIRABLE QUALITIES FOR PSYCHOANALYTIC THERAPISTS

More is demanded of psychoanalysts than of therapists who perform other types of psychotherapy, according to a survey of the clinical lore (see Holt & Luborsky, 1958, Vol. 2, Table 15.2) In this study opinions were elicited by interview from 55 training analysts. Although the list of qualities mentioned was long—approximately 90—there was much agreement about the more important ones (but bear in mind that the analysts themselves generated the opinions). A number of other sources were also included in the survey: published references on requisites for psychiatry, psychoanalysis, psychotherapy, and clinical psychology (p. 369, Vol. 2) and another collection of expert opinion (Ellis, 1955a, 1955b). A summary was provided (Holt & Luborsky, 1958, Vol, 2, p. 392 ff.) on the agreement among various sources of *opinion* about personality requisites for psychiatric residents, psychiatrists, psychotherapists, and psychoanalysts; and, in the same table, of *research findings* about psychiatric residents. One way to extract the essence of the very long list in the table is to single out those qualities that are requisite for psychoanalysis in the opinions of the experts, *and* are also shown to be valuable in the research findings on psychiatric residents. *By this dual criterion, the following requisites emerge: intelligence; empathy; verbal facility; objectivity;*

capacity for growth; flexibility; self-objectivity; interest in psychiatry; and self-confidence and security. One general conclusion from this huge survey is that although more is demanded of the psychoanalyst than of other therapists, the degree of overlap between the requisites for different types of therapists (psychiatric residents, psychiatrists, psychotherapists, and psychoanalysts) is impressive.

Quantitative research on qualities of psychoanalysts is, however, almost nonexistent, nor is there very much known about necessary qualities of other kinds of psychotherapists despite the fine summary by Gurman and Razin (1977). Relatively less is known about requisite qualities of therapists than about requisite qualities of patients (Luborsky et al., 1971). The only qualities of the therapist on which studies agree are the experience level of the therapist and certain major similarities between therapist and patient (for example, in values and orientation to people).

Available quantitative research tends to focus on psychiatric residents in training or psychoanalytic candidates in training—not finished practitioners. It has been found that supervisors' judgments of "competence as a therapist" correlate highly with their judgments of "competence as a future analyst" (Holt & Luborsky, 1958). The same correlation appears in the judgments of psychiatric residents by their peers—residents who are considered "good psychotherapists" are also considered to be "good potential psychoanalysts." Psychoanalysts who were retrospectively described by their analysts as having superior skills as analysts were considered to have been healthier to begin with, to have changed more in the course of their analysis, and to have had a more successful analysis.

H. Klein (1965, p. 82 ff.) has completed the only study in which estimates of a psychoanalyst's competence by supervisors were related to the success of the treatment of actual patients. She reports that for three groups of psychoanalysts in training— judged by supervisors as "superior," "above average," or "below average"—judged competence of the analyst and degree of success of analyses were related (e.g., $r = .37, p < .01$). For 66 patients, 63 percent of the patients treated by analysts of superior skills showed substantial improvement, but only 39 percent of the patients treated by

below-average analysts showed comparable improvement. The limitation here is that the same supervisor who evaluated the analyst's competence also estimated the success of the treatment; one view could be colored by the other. However, an independently applied scale estimating dependency was applied to the content of the patient's record at the beginning and end of treatment: for 40 percent of the superior analysts more than one-half of their patients improved on the dependency scale, while for only 20 percent of the "below-average" analysts was there comparable improvement in their patients.

Conclusion 1
Almost no quantitative studies have been made of the personality qualities of the psychoanalyst.

Conclusion 2
What little research of this type exists concerns supervisors' opinions of analytic candidates. These results indicate considerable similarity between the qualities that are requisite for psychoanalysts and those that are requisite for psychotherapists of a psychoanalytically oriented, insight-giving type. One opinion is that "healthier" analysts (in the sense of objectivity, self-confidence, and the like) will be of more help to their patients.

Conclusion 3
One quantitative study (H. Klein, 1965) does imply that the supervisor's estimate of skill of the student psychoanalyst is related to the benefits derived by the patient.

RESEARCH ON THE OUTCOME OF PSYCHOANALYTIC TREATMENT

Most of the studies fall into one of two main groups: simple studies in which the critical conditions are unspecified, and complex studies with more explicit conditions.

1. The simple outcome studies—a large, familiar group—have been with us for a long time. They typically report that a relatively unspecified kind of treatment has produced such-and-such a percentage of cures, partially improved patients, and patients who are unchanged or got worse.

The Berlin Psychoanalytic Institute outcome

data of 1920–1930 are probably the earliest of such reports (Fenichel, 1930). A host of other such outcome reports have appeared, such as Alexander (1937); Duhrssen and Jorswieck (1965); Glover, Fenichel, Strachey, Bergler, Nunberg, & Bibring (1937); Graham (1958, 1960); Knight (1941); Lorand and Console (1958); Nunberg (1954); Oberndorf (1950, 1953); and Schjelderup (1955). One of the latest is an analysis of clinical cases over 11 years at the Clinic of the Southern California Psychoanalytic Institute (Feldman, 1968). Ninety-nine patients were accepted during that period. According to a simple improvement scale rated by the therapist, about two-thirds of the patients treated by psychoanalysis seemed to improve. This figure is, unsurprisingly, similar to the results of other studies of treatment by psychoanalysis or any other form of psychotherapy. *Two-thirds* has long been thought to be the magical improvement figure, although the range is wider than has been assumed (Bergin, 1971).

The best-known summary of this type of outcome study is by Eysenck (1952, 1961). His main conclusion, which is easy to miss (and many readers miss it), is that *there is no good evidence* that any type of psychotherapy—psychoanalysis or any such form of treatment—does any good. What most readers conclude, however, is that he *shows* that psychotherapy does no good. Not much light and a lot of heat have come from Eysenck's review. There is ample documentation of the major defects in Eysenck's summarization of data (Duhrssen and Jorswieck, 1962, 1965; Luborsky, 1954; Rosenzweig, 1954; Strupp, 1963; Bergin, 1971.)

2. As already noted, several complex outcome studies exist (Hamburg et al., 1967; H. Klein, 1960; Knapp et al., 1960; the Menninger Study by Wallerstein et al., 1956, Kernberg, Burstein, Coyne, Appelbaum, Horwitz, & Voth, 1972). These deal mainly with types of change that presumably occur as a result of psychoanalytic treatment. They do not report percentages of "cure," because such data are difficult to interpret in the absence of reasonable comparison groups.

The Menninger Foundation Psychotherapy Research Study is undoubtedly the most intensive study to date of the changes that occur during long-term psychotherapy and psychoanalysis (Kernberg et al., 1972). Psychological tests and interviews were done at three points in time: initially, at termination, and two years after treatment was completed. At each of those times not only was the patient studied, but near-relatives and occasionally the patient's employer were interviewed. Not only was the therapist interviewed, but also the therapist's supervisor, if one was available. This report would have been more valuable if the authors, in addition to reporting the predictors of improvement, had stated what percentage of patients showed varying degrees of improvement.

The report by Hamburg et al. (1967) is certainly the most ambitious *survey* study of psychoanalysis. Very little in the final report, however, deals with the nature of the changes that occurred in psychoanalysis because of uncertainty about the adequacy of the questionnaire method.

3. Comparative studies of the outcome of psychoanalysis versus other psychotherapies would be very desirable, but at present hardly any reasonably controlled ones exist (Luborsky, Singer, and Luborsky, 1975). Eysenck (1952, 1961) tried to make some comparison of treatment results by combining the percentages of many outcome studies, but his figures were derived from the simple or unspecified type of outcome studies. Eysenck offered this result: psychoanalytically treated patients improved to the extent of 44 percent; eclectically treated, 64 percent; and those treated only custodially or by general practitioners, 72 percent. Since Eysenck only presents *outcome* percentages and nothing about initial level is given, conclusions are hard to draw. The outcome figures may have much to do with the level of the patient's expectation from treatment, or different standards and criteria of improvement, or they may have to do with the obvious differences in the initial state of the patients who received the different forms of treatment. As we noted earlier, patients who have received different forms of treatment tend to have started out with very different levels of mental health.

Cartwright (1966) has contributed the only controlled comparative study in the entire literature, comparing psychoanalysis and client-centered therapy for the kinds of changes that take place. She used two pairs of matched patients—two compulsive males and two anxious-hysteric females (a very small sample, needless to say)—and four therapists; two of them client-centered and two psychoanalysts. One male patient and one female received psychoanalytic therapy, and one male patient and one female received client-centered therapy. The segment of the treatment used was 40 sessions (very short for psychoanalytic treatment). Cartwright found that the degree of experiencing and level of self-observation reached by matched patients were independent of professed style of therapy (that is, they were similar in the two types of treatment). There are, of course, obvious limits to this study.

It would be interesting to see what similarities would appear if measures that are supposed to be unique to psychoanalysis were applied to both the client-centered and psychoanalytic treatment samples. Some dimensions of change are crucial for psychoanalysis in terms of the emphasis of its theory of change, and therefore ought to receive a great deal of attention in outcome studies of psychoanalysis or in comparative studies. These are (according to Luborsky & Schimek, 1964): (1) anxiety level and anxiety tolerance; (2) insight; (3) transference resolution or mastery; (4) regression in the service of the ego; and (5) neutralization of thinking.

Follow-Up by a Second Analyst

In a series of papers (1959, 1961, 1963), Pfeffer described a method for assessing the outcome of an analysis which captures the important clinical material and, at the same time, puts it in a form that can be conveniently studied and rated by many groups of judges.[2] In his procedure, the terminated patient is interviewed by a second analyst some months or years after the conclusion of treatment. The interviews take place once a week for four or five visits while the patient is sitting up. Despite the difference in mode of treatment and in the treating doctor, the patient very quickly recovered many of the important themes and feelings experienced during the original analysis. The patient dealt with the follow-up study as if it were a continuation of

---

[2]Judgments are made about the quality of the original analysis by comparing the patient's present functioning and his or her version of the outcome of the treatment with that of the treating analyst.

the original analysis, and typically experienced an upsurge of some of the preanalytic symptoms. Some of the original transference feelings were also briefly revived, together with some of the patient's characteristic defenses.

Norman, Blacker, Oremland and Barrett (1976) applied the method to a new set of five former analytic patients, all of whom had successfully concluded treatment, and observed many of the same phenomena noted by Pfeffer—striking parallels between the original analytic experience and the follow-up interview. The follow-up also provided the patient with some new insights. Similar findings were reported by Schlessinger and Robbins (1975).

The Pfeffer method has already contributed by (1) providing a valuable follow-up method for psychoanalysis; (2) showing the continuities in the analytic and postanalytic experience; and (3) demonstrating the readiness with which the analytic experience is revived even in successfully treated patients. Several further types of studies should be done with it. First, one might examine the extent to which a recently completed analysis was revived in the follow-up as compared with a more dated analysis. Secondly, one could examine precisely the degree to which the core relationship theme is revived in the follow-up interviews as compared with the analysis itself, and whether the overlap in thematic content between the follow-up and the original analysis depends on the correspondence between treating and follow-up analysts in their technique and personality. Thirdly, one could inquire whether the extent of overlap was related to the success of the treatment. Finally, the Pfeffer method is especially suited to computer-assisted studies, such as the establishment of long-term trends in linguistic and paralinguistic features.

Conclusion 1

Simple, unspecified outcome studies of psychoanalysis have not been useful, even toward their main aim of showing the efficacy of the treatment.

Conclusion 2

As compared with the simple studies, the better-specified studies have more to say about the nature of the treatment and what changes occur in the course of psychoanalysis. Some evidence was found that patients increase their level of experiencing and self-observation (Cartwright, 1966). The Menninger Project (Kernberg et al., 1972) found that patients show global improvement, resolution of the transference, and increase in ego-strength. We must still *assume* that psychoanalysis is especially beneficial in achieving its stated aim of characterological change, in addition to a lessening of symptoms. Much more needs to be done to see whether, in fact, resolution of the transference occurs in successful treatment or whether mastery of the still evident transference is a more applicable concept (Luborsky, 1977a; see Research on Transference, p. 343).

Conclusion 3

Controlled comparisons of psychoanalytic with other forms of treatment are almost nonexistent. The review by Luborsky, Singer, and Luborsky (1975) of all comparative studies of *psychotherapies* shows that (1) because proper studies of this type are difficult, there are also relatively few of them. The implication of this conclusion is obvious: it is impossible to say that one type of psychotherapy is better than another. (2) For those comparisons for which a sufficient number of studies exist, there is usually a nonsignificant difference in percentage of patients improving with each treatment (with only a couple of nonimpressive exceptions). One strong implication is that treatment effects are mainly a product of nonspecific factors that those treatments have in common. (3) No good studies exist dealing with differences in the *quality* of the outcomes. For example, two types of treatments may yield the same percentage of patients benefiting but differ drastically in the quality of insight they aim for and achieve. Comparisons with other analytic approaches might be especially valuable, for example, approaches such as Malan (1976) in which the therapeutic effort consists of a concentrated short-term treatment experience focused on interpretation of the transference. This is where research is very much needed.

Parloff's (1968) conclusion is fitting: "Like beauty, therapeutic effectiveness is in the eye of the beholder. No form of psychotherapy has ever been initiated without a claim that it has unique therapeutic advantages, and no form of psychotherapy has ever been abandoned because of its failure to live up to these claims." Engel (1968) makes the same point: "No one has yet devised a scientifically valid means of testing the results of any form of psychotherapy" (p. 203). Guidelines for doing treatment comparisons have been formulated by a committee of the National Institute of Mental Health (Fiske, Hunt, Luborsky, Orne, Parloff, Reiser, & Tuma, 1970). These include necessity for multiple criteria, control over case assignments to each therapist, and establishment of the expectation level of the patient and therapist at the initiation of the treatment.

RESEARCH ON THE PROCESS OF PSYCHOANALYTIC TREATMENT

The aim of most studies of the process of treatment is to find aspects that change from the beginning to the end, and to see how these are related to the main psychoanalytic concepts of change. Most research falls into the following categories: The adequacy of the patient's productions (meaningfulness, productivity, experiencing, and associative freedom); treatment techniques (especially accuracy of interpretation); transference and countertransference; emergence and decline of symptoms during treatment; and systematic reexamination of the theory of psychoanalytic change.

Adequacy of Patient's Productions During Psychoanalysis

Meaningfulness

Isaacs and Haggard (1966) have shown that psychologists, psychoanalysts, and social workers can substantially agree on the meaningfulness of the patient's statements. Furthermore, when 20 therapist-judges were asked independently to rate each of 50 patient-statements for nine characteristics and a factor analysis of their ratings was performed, the following three factors were mainly correlated with meaningfulness: (a) the extent of the patient's concern with self and his or her problems; (b) the patient's concern with the ability to relate to others; and (c) the patient's current motivational state. In further studies, the authors explored the relationship of meaningfulness of patient's statements to interventions by the therapist. Patients were more likely to give meaningful material when the therapist's intervention contained affective words—that is, when the therapist deals with affective material, the patient follows suit. These results hold, whatever the therapist's therapeutic orientation. They suggest that when the therapist, regardless of orientation, responds to the patient's affect, he or she is likely to elicit a more meaningful response containing affective verbalization, fewer and longer responses, and a greater number of spontaneous returns to the content of the intervention after a set time interval.

Productivity of the Patient During the Sessions

Simon (1967) worked with the concept of analytic productivity. This is one of a number of concepts that have been explored by means of tape recordings of a psychoanalytic patient (*Patient A*).[3] Clinicians were asked to judge which of a number of sessions were ones in which the patient was most productive. At that stage the clinicians were using whatever standards they would use ordinarily in judging patients' productivity. From these judgments Simon developed the Patient Productivity Rating Scale (PPRS), consisting of five main levels of analytic productivity. For example, minimal productivity was characterized by a fair amount of silence, an absence of reflectiveness, an absence of psychological-mindedness and few, if any, connecting links between different segments of material. In samples of high productivity, the patient attempted to link past and present, attempted to understand painful material, and maintained the dual position of reporting associations while observing oneself in the process. Simon and his group have carried out four studies using this scale; intrajudge reliabilities have ranged in significance from $p<.01$ to $p<.001$, which suggests that the rating scale can be consistently applied to short (3 to 6 min.) therapy segments.

Spence (1969b) took 15 segments that had been clinically rated and submitted them to a computer-based analysis of variables including

ratio of long words to total words, ratio of qualifiers to total words, and ratio of reflectors to total words. Qualifiers included such words as "but," "perhaps," "probably," and the like; reflectors included such words as "because," "as," "if," "make sense," and the like. The best predictor, by a wide margin, proved to be reflectors/total words—it correlated .80 with the ratings of the judges ($p < .001$). In a further step, Spence selected 12 additional samples, rated them on the reflector ratio, and had them rated by two sets of judges. On the new sample, the correlations between reflector ratio and clinical rating (using the PPRS) were .59 in one set of judges ($p < .05$) and .71 in the other set ($p <.01$). These new values are encouragingly high. Whether the same predictor will work with another patient remains to be seen; at the least, the reflectors *seem* to overlap with the dimensions of meaningfulness (see above) and experiencing (see below), as we had anticipated.

Experiencing

More work has been devoted to the concept of experiencing than any other process variable, beginning with the work of Gendlin (1961). It is based on verbal behavior in the course of treatment and taps the patient's capacity to both (1) feel deeply and immediately, and also (2) to be aware of and reflective about this feeling. Patients would get low scores if they were remote from their feelings and unable to understand their implicit meanings. Defined this way, the concept begins to sound very similar to "the split in the ego," frequently described in the psychoanalytic literature as essential for good patient performance, a state in which the patient's attention is alternately involved in experience and in reporting or reflecting on it.

Experiencing has been shown by Rogers and others to predict the outcome of treatment, even when based on only a four-minute segment of the patient's speech (Kirtner, Cartwright, Robertson, & Fiske, 1961; Rogers, 1959; Tomlinson, 1967; Tomlinson & Hart, 1962; Walker, Rablen, & Rogers, 1966). It can be rated reliably (Klein, Mathieu, Gendlin, & Kiesler, 1970), although occasionally the reliabilities are only moderate; for example, in Auerbach and Luborsky (1968; the

---

[3]The designation *Patient A* is used in the interest of uniformity—as noted under Data Banks. *Patient A* was the data base in several studies.

only study in which an entire session was used as the basis for rating experiencing) the agreement between judges was .42, significant at the .01 level but low in terms of one's hopes for a reliability measure.

Meaningfulness, productivity, and experiencing (and also the quality to be described next, associative freedom) sound as if they have much in common although very little information exists about their interrelationships. The only such study in which experiencing is included and in which entire sessions have been judged is Mintz, Luborsky, and Auerbach (1971). In that study of 60 sessions, 110 variables were rated, a high percentage of which were therapist variables. Factor analysis yielded four main variables, one of which—the intensive-interpretive mode factor—included the intercorrelated variables: of experiencing, receptiveness, and empathy for therapist. Apparently experiencing is facilitated in the context of the therapist's use of interpretation.

Associative Freedom

Free association—the mental set to say the thoughts one is thinking—is the traditional set suggested to patients in psychoanalysis at the beginning of the treatment. Individual differences in the ability of patients to follow this instruction must be large, and the treatment process must also free the patient to allow more genuine free association. One would assume that the ability of the patient to free-associate could be assessed by clinical judges. This does not happen to be known and would, in itself, make an interesting study. It has not been demonstrated to what extent the mental set of free association can be taught, and to what extent it changes from the beginning to the end of treatment.

Even though free association has a central place in psychoanalytic treatment, psychotherapy researchers and personality researchers of all kinds have largely neglected it as a medium of an object of research (Janis, 1958), although a few beginnings at quantitative investigation have recently been made. Colby (1960) systematically varied some external conditions that might influence the content and quality of free associations. He found,

for example, that when a (male) observer was present, as compared to a condition in which subjects talked to a tape recorder, the number of personyms (references to people) increased with particular emphasis on male personyms. He also found that "causal correlatives inputs" (that is, interpretations) resulted in significantly greater amounts of free association and a greater percentage of references to relevant people and topics (Colby, 1961). Strupp (1968) and Bordin (1966) have also investigated some factors that influence free association, and Bellak (in Spence, 1967) has developed a conceptual model.

Associative freedom might also be related to other aspects of free association conceived of as a state of consciousness. A large literature has grown up over the years on free association as a state of consciousness, compared with dreaming, hypnosis, reverie, and other states (see Gill & Brenman, 1959).

Several steps might be taken to further the study of associative freedom (as was suggested in the 1971 version of this chapter): (1) a rating by clinicians of associative freedom followed by examination of the sessions to determine the kinds of qualities that seem to go along with the clinical judgment; (2) a comparison of qualities of free-association sessions at the beginning and end of psychoanalytic treatment; (3) an intercorrelation, in a multivariate analysis, of associative freedom with such other concepts as experiencing and productivity; and (4) a rating of dimensions of states of consciousness in a sample of psychoanalytic sessions to see how these dimensions correspond to clinical judgments of associative freedom.

Conclusion

Quantitative studies have been made of four main concepts that conceptualize the patient's adequacy of production during psychoanalytic treatment: meaningfulness, productivity, experiencing, and associative freedom. Of these, associative freedom has figured least in the quantitative research. Productivity has been explored by means of computer systems. One of its aspects, "reflective statements," suggests that it has much in common with experiencing. There is much need now for a multivariate study in which the same data are judged according to each of the four concepts, to determine the extent of overlap.

Therapeutic Techniques

Variety Versus Uniformity in Therapeutic Techniques

Even though the underlying therapeutic technique of psychoanalytic treatment is clearly stated (for example, Bibring, 1954), there is much variety in the ways the "basic rules" are applied by different analysts, although psychoanalysis is probably a more uniform mode than other psychotherapies. To many analysts, the technique appeared to be so well specified that it came as something of a surprise to find (as in the old Vienna Seminar, A. Freud, 1954) that techniques differed and that the content they chose to focus on differed, even when they were discussing the same patients and had available the same data about the patients. Glover (1955) was apparently the first to investigate the problem systematically; in 1940 he sent out questionnaires to the members of the British Psychoanalytic Association. Marked differences in technique were revealed by analysts' written responses to the questionnaire; much less is known about what was actually done. When the question is one of subscribing to views about preferred treatment techniques, agreement is probably higher than it would be if actual sessions were examined and classified in terms of technique, but the latter study has not been done. A well-known set of studies by Fiedler (1950a, 1950b, 1951) *implies* that experienced therapists, regardless of the kind of psychotherapy they perform, are in considerable agreement about ideal therapeutic relationships, and are in more agreement than are beginners.

On the other hand, inexperienced therapists of any particular school probably adhere more than experienced therapists to what they consider to be the techniques of their school and, within any one school, they would be more similar to one another than would be experienced therapists. A few quantitative studies support this view (Fey, 1958; Strupp, 1955, 1960).

Conclusion

There is likely to be much variation in technique from analyst to analyst, and this variation probably increases with experience.

Accuracy of Interpretations and Empathy

According to many writers on the technique of psychoanalysis, the crucial technique is interpretation. The other techniques, listed (for example, by Bibring, 1954) as suggestive, abreactive, manipulative, and clarifying, are to some extent preparation for interpretation. Bibring classifies a psychotherapeutic technique as "any purposive, more or less typified, verbal or nonverbal behavior on the part of the therapist, which intends to affect the patient in the direction of the (intermediary or final) goals of the treatment." Psychoanalysis is thought to be distinguished from other psychotherapies in the proportion of these techniques, especially in its emphasis on interpretation. As Bibring says, "Insight through *interpretation* is the supreme agent in the hierarchy of therapeutic principles characteristic of analysis." Kubie (1952) places the same stress on interpretation: "Analysis stands or falls by the validity of its specific interpretations in specific instances." Kubie discusses the validity of interpretations and the inherent difficulties of demonstrating their truth: "Sometimes it is possible to show that presenting the patient with the hypothesis which is called technically an 'interpretation' may produce profound psychological changes, from which, in turn, we can deduce fresh hypotheses. None of this, however, has that directness as evidence which science requires." Kubie would look for evidence of the accuracy of interpretations mainly in the patient's further free associations. In essence, he suggests that our only tests of an interpretation's validity come "(1) from the patient's associations to it, which may confirm, correct, or reject; (2) from alterations of symptoms; and finally but only rarely; (3) through our ability to predict future behavior." A philosopher has recently clarified the difficulty in judging the truth of interpretations (Farrell, 1964). He presents a sample from a session with a 16-year-old boy and then takes certain statements of the therapist, examines them for their truth or falsity, and considers the criteria for acceptance of their truth as (1) whether the patient accepts the statement; (2) whether it fits with the rest of what he says; and (3) whether the implied meaning is the usual implied meaning for other patients. He concludes with an obvious but frequently overlooked point: that one reason why our search for criteria of the truth of an interpretation is so frustrating is that such interpretations are not primarily declarative or hypothesis-stating in character. Their chief function seems to be instrumental; that is, many of the therapist's statements are intended to get the patient to recognize and talk about feelings and to make him or her more relaxed and outgoing.

In view of the centrality of interpretation to analytic technique, quantitative research on this topic would be welcome. Some studies have been on depth of interpretation (such as Speisman, 1959), and Gill and his colleagues have concentrated on studying the consequence of certain kinds of interpretation. Paul and Gill (unpublished) deal with the obvious first question: Can "goodness" of an interpretation be recognized by independent judges? The answer is that it can, with a remarkable degree of agreement. Judges listened to tape recordings of short segments of the patient's production followed by statements by the analyst, and then rated the "goodness" of each interpretation. An unexpected puzzle came to light when it was found that agreement among judges on the goodness of an interpretation was virtually as great when the patient's prior statement was not included! Obviously, the judges were basing their judgments on what the analyst said, *not* on what the patient said. Apparently there exists a conception of good interpretations so that judges can agree upon them. (It would have been helpful to also judge *accuracy of interpretation* to see whether the same results would obtain.) This is not an isolated finding, however. Those who have worked on an allied concept, the therapist's empathy, turned up something that seems to be identical: judges' ratings of empathy in a therapist statement are also not influenced by what the patient has just said (Truax, 1966). Truax concluded that "the findings support the original hypothesis suggesting that there is no significant degree of con-

tamination of the measurement of therapist behavior (on accurate empathy and nonpossessive warmth) by knowledge of the patient behavior." Thus, the puzzle remains.

The difference between the therapist's "capacity to make accurate interpretations" and "empathy" may be merely one of language. Analysts tend to use the former term, but all therapists (including analysts) use the concept of empathy. It is the client-centered therapists who are best known for their research on empathy. The best known of these scales is *accurate empathy* (Truax, 1961; Truax, Wargo, Frank, Imber, Battle, Hoehn-Saric, Nash, & Stone, 1966; Rogers, Gendlin, Kiesler, & Truax, 1967). A similar but simpler scale is by Raskin (1965); another slight revision of the Truax Accurate Empathy scale is the Bergin-Solomon revision (Truax and Carkhuff, 1967, p.59). Bachrach's (1965, 1968) *conjunctive empathy* scale is more influenced by psychoanalytic thinking; it is similar to Schafer's (1959) concept of *generative empathy* as well as to Truax's concept of *accurate empathy*. The Raskin, Truax, and Bachrach scales when applied to the same sample intercorrelate highly (Bachrach, Mintz, & Luborsky, 1971). For a psychoanalytically oriented treated sample, empathy and skill as judged both from tapes and by supervisors' ratings were highly intercorrelated (Bachrach, Luborsky, & Mechanick, 1974). Bachrach (1976) in fact suggests that what is being measured in empathy measures based on brief segments of sessions is a broad evaluative dimension, "goodness of psychotherapy," and for that reason primarily does not depend on hearing the patients' communications.

Most of these empathy scales show moderate reliability when applied to four-minute segments (for example, for "accurate empathy" for three judges, .63 intraclass; .36 average correlation; Rogers et al., 1967, p. 149). In applying the Raskin version of the empathy scale to entire psychotherapy sessions rather than to four-minute segments, Auerbach and Luborsky (1958) found that agreement between two professional judges was only .51 (significant at less than the .01, but low for an interjudge reliability).

Empathy sometimes predicts the outcome of psychotherapy (Truax, 1963; Truax et al., 1966).

However, Bergin and Jasper (1969), and Mitchell, Bozarth, Truax, and Krauft (1973) did not achieve significant results. The therapist's empathy might instead be rated by the patient directly as in the Barrett-Lennard inventory (1962); such measures of empathy correlated significantly with outcome in three out of four studies (Luborsky, et al., 1971).

A number of researchers (e.g., Bachrach, 1968) have investigated the factors associated with empathy. Bachrach found a high correlation between adaptive regression in the therapist (as estimated from the Holt Primary Process Manual for the Rorschach, Holt, 1964), and empathy as scored by his own Conjunctive Empathy Scale. Some evidence indicates that the therapist's personality, training, and experience, and qualities of the patient, all influence the level of the therapist's empathy (Truax & Carkhuff, 1967; Bergin & Solomon, 1969). Bergin and Jasper (1969) similarly found that therapists' depression and anxiety, as scored on the D and Pt scales of the MMPI, correlate negatively with their empathy in actual psychotherapy. This is clearly consistent with the common supposition that the more healthy and integrated the therapist, the greater his or her therapeutic effectiveness; specifically, the less his or her depression and anxiety, the more the therapist can accurately hear what the patient is saying.

A series of experiments on psychological and psychophysiological correlates of empathy has been carried out by Spence and his group. These studies support Freud's view that free-floating attention facilitates empathy; for example, mild distraction can facilitate the taking in of certain kinds of information. In one study (Spence and Greif, 1970) Ss' attention was monitored as they listened to a passage of *double-entendres*. Depending on whether S attended to the manifest or latent content, parts of the passage (e.g., "and so they went back and forth") could be heard either as an argument or as a seduction. Hearing the passage in a sexual way (i.e., hearing latent content) was correlated with paying less attention to the passage and more attention to a secondary task.

It seems that sensitivity to latent content was increased by "listening away"—not paying full attention to the stimulus material. In a second study (Spence & Lugo, 1972), Ss listened to excerpts from a therapy protocol and attempted to predict when a stomach pain would be reported. (The data was derived from Luborsky, 1953; see below, "Symptom Context Methods."). Two groups of Ss, as they listened, were distracted by two types of pacing tasks. A third group was not distracted. Ss in the slow/fast distraction condition made more correct predictions of the stomach symptom than Ss in the no-distraction and Ss in the fast/low distraction condition. A certain degree and kind of distraction appears to facilitate clinical sensitivity.

Conclusion 1
More research needs to be done on accuracy of interpretation. When that research is completed, it probably will show that a therapist's accuracy of interpretation is similar to his or her empathy.

Conclusion 2
Judges can agree moderately well on the therapist's empathy (with coefficients of .4 to .6, depending on the type of reliability).

Conclusion 3
Empathy in some studies is a good predictor of the outcome of psychotherapy. In other studies, it fails to predict significantly. It would be valuable to be able to distinguish the conditions that are responsible for its predictive power.

Conclusion 4
Both accurate interpretations and empathy are probably shown most by the therapists who are most "healthy," that is, least disturbed by anxiety or depression during the session.

Conclusion 5
The fact that judgments of goodness of an interpretation or empathy can be made reliably without knowledge of the patient's prior statements implies that the concept itself needs further clarification.

Conclusion 6
"Free-floating attention" or certain kinds of mild distraction appear to facilitate understanding of latent content.

Research on Transference
Quantitative research on the patient's transference response to the analyst is slight, even though clinicians have placed transference at the core of what

needs to change in effective psychoanalytic treatment. The classical definition of transference is the expression of attitudes and behavior from early conflictual relationships with significant people in the current relationship with the analyst. Much of the quantitative research is seriously qualified by its tenuous relation to the classical concept.

1. Transference in group therapy was investigated by Chance (1952). Transference was defined in terms of the similarity between the patient's description of his or her "significant parent" and his or her description of the psychotherapist. This is a limited definition which may not correspond to the clinical phenomenon of transference. The research is cited since it remains a question of interest to try to relate this quantitative definition to assessments of transference based on the classical definition.

2. In some of Fiedler's experiments (such as Fiedler and Senior, 1952), transference was supposed to have been measured by a comparison of the patient's description of the ideal person and his or her prediction of the psychotherapist's self-description with similar measures filled out by the therapist. The same criticism would apply: transference may not be measurable in this way.

3. Apfelbaum (1958) required the patient to fill out a special Q-sort in terms of expectations about the therapist he or she would be assigned (although the therapist had not yet been introduced). The Q-sort was administered again at the end of treatment. The patients were grouped according to the kinds of expectations described in their Q-sorts. Three clusters were found: Cluster A (therapist will give nurturance); Cluster B (therapist will be a model); Cluster C (therapist will be a critic). It is interesting that each of these "transference" expectations tended to be maintained to the end of treatment—there is a substantial test-retest reliability of the Q-sort, despite psychotherapy as an intervening condition. The fact that "transference" expectations about the therapist tended to remain constant indicates that some stable attitude was being measured. Whether it was an aspect of transference remains to be seen.

A problem in all three studies is that transference is reduced to a cluster of items in a questionnaire. To refine the concept further and to give better validity information, samples of each patient's

therapy might be extracted to clinically determine the transference pattern and relate it to the three clusters. Unfortunately, none of these studies was concerned with psychoanalytic treatment—a further qualification.

4. The Menninger Foundation study of psychotherapy and psychoanalysis (Wallerstein et al., 1956) included an estimate of transference, made initially by two clinicians working together and at termination by several other clinicians working together. The estimate of transference was a discursive, free description. A large and detailed file of interviews and test reports was available at both points from which to make the estimates, but the manner of conceptualizing the transference was left up to the judges.

5. The Analytic Research Group of the Institute of the Pennsylvania Hospital has taken the concept of transference as its research focus and is basing its studies on tape recordings of psychoanalytic sessions. All their work so far has involved ratings of *amount* rather than *type* of transference. In their first study (Luborsky, Graff, Pulver, & Curtis, 1973) of one psychoanalytic patient, 30 five-minute segments were judged on amount of transference and related variables. There was a low positive correlation among judges when the judgment was based on the amount of transference expressed in relation to each object (person) referred to in the transcript. Lower, Escoll, Little and Ottenberg (1973) compared the high-transference with the low-transference segments and found high-transference segments had markedly more affect, which was probably an important basis for the clinicians' judgments of transference. Eight psychoanalysts in the group rated 23 transference-related concepts on the same segments and considerable agreement was found for each of the eight psychoanalyst's factor space (Luborsky, Crabtree, Curtis, Ruff, & Mintz, 1975). In one study, ratings were made of transference and resistance, using a therapy session checksheet at the end of each session during the psychoanalytic treatment of four patients (Graff and Luborsky, 1977). The two relatively more improved patients ultimately showed a pattern of increasing transference with resistance either staying the same or decreasing; the two relatively unimproved patients showed no such difference between the levels of

transference and resistance. These results raise questions about the commonly held concept of resolution of transference during psychoanalysis as implying eradication of transference. Instead of being removed in a successful analysis, the transference patterns very likely move more and more into the focus of attention of both the patient and the analyst.

6. A new method has been constructed for measuring a concept that may be more closely allied to what is meant by the clinical concept of transference than any so far (except Gill & Hoffman, 1976). It has been designated the Core Conflictual Relationship Theme Method (Luborsky, 1977a). The data for deriving the new concept came from the 10 most improved and the 10 least improved of the 73 patients in psychoanalytically oriented psychotherapy in the Penn Psychotherapy Project (Luborsky, 1976). Entire sessions were not considered to be necessary for judging the core relationship theme, but rather only the "relationship episodes" within two early and two late sessions for each patient. A "relationship episode" is that part of the session in which the patient presents an example of his or her interaction with significant people: father, mother, brother, sister, friends, therapist, and so forth. These relationship episodes (marked off within the first 20 minutes of each session) were given to clinical judges with the instruction to find the theme that is the most pervasive in the most relationship episodes. Considerable agreement was shown from inspection of the data by different clinical judges in identifying the same single main theme for each patient. That same theme was identifiable both in the early sessions and in the late sessions. The later sessions for both improvers and nonimprovers showed a deepening in affectual involvement in terms of the core relationship theme, but only the improvers showed evidences of some mastery of the theme. It seems very likely that the core relationship theme of each patient is close to what is meant by the clinical concept of transference; however, a systematic study is necessary to show the similarity. The principal impediment to such a study is the need for a classification system for identifying the clinically derived transference patterns.

7. More recently, Gill and Hoffman (1976) have devised scoring categories for kinds of interventions, measured their reliability in a small sample of sessions randomly selected from different analytic cases, and are applying them to a more extended set of sessions. The work is based on the theory that transference manifestations are more frequent than is usually recognized, that they can be present in a wide variety of latent transformations, and that they can be effectively interpreted quite early in treatment, even in the face of a positive therapeutic alliance. Gill and Hoffman believe that Freud is often misunderstood as warning against early transference interpretation.

Building on this general formulation, Gill and his group are comparing (1) the effects of a correctly executed transference interpretation with (2) the effect of not making the interpretation despite the presence of interpretable material. These comparisons will be carried out on early, middle, and later portions of a case. Particular interest is focused on the early sessions because it is often argued that premature interpretation may interrupt the flow of material and interfere with the development of the therapeutic alliance. Data on this question should provide new clinical knowledge that can be of help to the practicing analyst.

Conclusion 1

Several quantitative research methods have been developed with the aim of capturing behavior that might be labeled *transference*. The quantitative studies have not yet been adequately related to clinical conceptions of transference. It is, therefore, difficult to know whether the clinical and quantitative measures are estimating the same thing.

Conclusion 2

Clinical conceptions of transference are much in need of classifications that will lend themselves to quantification. These classifications (e.g., Gill & Hoffman, 1976) in turn should be related to the quantitative methods described.

Research on Countertransference Attitudes

As classically defined, countertransference is a subtle source of interference in treatment (see for example, Greenson, 1967, p. 348): The patient comes to represent for the analyst a person from his or her past onto whom past feelings and wishes

are projected, analogous to the patient's transference relationship with the analyst. Several attempts have been made to study therapist countertransference by quantitative approaches; a few
samples of these will be described and then their
conclusions will be compared with those derived
from the more numerous and older clinical contributions.

1. One of the most systematic attempts was part
of the Menninger Foundation's Psychotherapy
Project. At termination of treatment, the evaluation
group tried to discern the degree to which the
therapist's countertransference attitudes had interfered with the treatment (according to a schedule
of questions described in Luborsky, Fabian, Hall,
Ticho, & Ticho, 1958). The evaluation group
found that it was difficult to rate countertransference, even from the large amount of information
available after two posttreatment interviews with
the therapist, after reading the therapist's process
notes for the entire treatment, after interviewing the
patient, and even after interviewing the supervisor
of the treatment. The supervisor most often had
some clues about countertransference, but only
when it obtruded in a form detrimental to the
treatment.

2. Franz Alexander (unpublished research) introduced a useful methodological variation; he
provided the therapist with a key that could be
pressed the moment he or she wanted to record
the time of a personal reaction to be described at
the end of the session. By this means, the therapist
could prevent some reactions from being forgotten,
but could do nothing about reactions that took
place outside of awareness—the bulk of countertransference responses.

3. Paul Bergman, when he was a member of the
NIMH Psychotherapy Research Project, recorded
his introspections after therapeutic sessions. Some
of these data are available in Bergman (1966).
From the methods of Alexander and Bergman, a
design could be worked out in which the therapist
notes when, in a session, he or she has some introspections about mental operations, including countertransference attitudes. If he or she is taking
notes, the therapist can record these introspections,
although at the risk of distraction in the conduct of
the treatment. A further drawback is that the actual

countertransference reaction often needs to be
pointed out by a third person.

4. When the *therapist's* view of the transaction in
a psychotherapy session differs markedly from the
view of the *patient* or of *outside observers,* one
might find countertransference activity to be the
responsible agent. This possibility was considered
in the "triple-view" study (Mintz, Auerbach,
Luborsky, & Johnson, 1973), but no conclusion
could be drawn. Even when large differences in
perception of the psychotherapy occur, it is hard to
discover from the therapist the nature of the countertransference problem that *may* be responsible.

5. The larger and older clinical contributions
have been reviewed and contrasted with the smaller and newer quantitative research on countertransference by Singer and Luborsky (1978). The
quantitative research has dealt with mainly conscious attitudes, although a few researchers have
tried to investigate unconscious conflicts (e.g.,
Bandura et al., 1960; Cutler, 1958). Mostly the
quantitative research uses the broader definition of
countertransference, which includes all
personality-based responses of the analyst to the
patient, rather than the more restricted classical definition of countertransference (see above).

Conclusion 1

There has not been enough overlap between the
quantitative and clinical research on countertransference. The quantitative approach has
tended to be more superficial and to use the most
general definition of countertransference while the
clinical research more often restricts itself to the
classical definition. Finally, the two approaches differ in a major premise: For the classical literature,
countertransference is considered to be an intrinsic
phenomenon in psychoanalysis; for the quantitative research, the aim has been mainly to find evidence for its existence and then to find methods to
analyze the phenomenon.

Conclusion 2

The two types of research have some congruence
in their conclusions: Both agree on the position that
uncontrolled countertransference has a poor effect
on the treatment and both agree that countertransference is often communicated through
peripheral cues such as the tone of voice and other

nonverbal means (as observed by Sherman, 1965).

Conclusion 3

The quantitative research provides new insight into the real stimulus value of the patient (Singer & Luborsky, 1978). In evaluating countertransference reactions, it is important to determine the proportions of contribution from the patient and from the conflicts of the therapist as well as the degree to which it is chronic or transient. More than the clinical literature implies, the patient has marked and predictable influence upon the therapist. Moreover, when the therapist endeavors to avoid certain conflictual topics, there is often a direct relationship to the frequency with which these topics are expressed by the patient.

Research on Therapist's Attitudes

Therapist's attitudes include such attitudes as warmth, acceptance, neutrality, objectivity, affective distance, and the therapist's conveying the impression that he or she can help the patient. These may well be crucial attitudes. However, little controlled and quantitative psychoanalytic research has appeared, although there is impressive related client-centered psychotherapy research (e.g., Barrett-Lennard, 1962). One proposed content analysis method to capture the therapists' behaviors that facilitate or inhibit the patient's experiencing of a helping relationship has recently been developed (Luborsky, 1976).

Research on the Context for Symptom Formation in Psychoanalytic Sessions

A different kind of process research has been developed, aimed at providing controlled methods for examining the context in sessions when recurrent symptoms or behaviors appear. Since psychoanalytic sessions were, after all, the data from which psychoanalytic concepts were generated, it seems natural to go back to sessions to reexamine these concepts, particularly those related to symptom formation (as put forward by Freud, 1926).

One method has been to isolate certain segments of the therapy process in which a critical event occurred. Often the event is the outbreak of a recurrent symptom (as in Luborsky, 1964, 1967).

These segments are then matched with segments of therapy from the same patient, in which the critical event did *not* occur. The two sets of events—critical and control—are then (1) rated on scales to see on which variables they differ; (2) rated by clinicians who are asked to discriminate critical from control segments; and/or (3) subjected to computer-based content analysis to determine which words distinguish critical from control.

The matching procedure owes a heavy debt to a study of changes in state of consciousness by Brenman, Gill, and Knight (1952). A landmark in quantitative naturalistic research, it was one of the first studies to organize the raw material of therapeutic sessions (in this case, hypnotherapy) according to a clearly defined behavioral "benchmark"—in this case, the spontaneous statement by the patient that he was "going deeper" (into hypnosis). Critical segments containing this statement were matched with control segments from the same patient. The main finding was a shift in the impulse-defense balance just before the experience.

Since the method facilitates systematic studies of the conditions that lead to the formation of symptoms, Luborsky and Auerbach (1969) used this pairing method with three symptomatic behaviors: stomach pain, headache, and momentary forgetting. In the case of the first two, a patient reported that his stomach was bothering him, or, another patient, that he was having a headache; critical segments were matched with control segments from the same patient. One set of findings will illustrate the fruits of the method on the stomach-pain data (derived from Luborsky, 1953). Luborsky and another judge rated the critical and control stomach segments on 18 categories and found significant discrimination for *both* independent judges on three: concern over loss of supplies, anxiety, and helplessness (all present to a greater extent in the critical segments). These findings were used in a subsequent study in which three judges rated 24 matched pairs of sentences, first by "intuition" and then with the clue that the critical member of each pair was higher in "concern about supplies with a helpless feeling about being able to obtain them." With no clues, the rating outcome was only chance; rating with the additional clues, two of the three judges did significantly better than chance.

In a further study of the same data, Spence (1969b) used categories from the Harvard Need Affiliation dictionary (Stone, Dunphy, Smith, & Ogilvie, 1966) together with three categories based on Luborsky's three discriminating clues and the two words "down" and "up," chosen by another independent clinical rater as potentially differentiating labels. A computer-based content analysis scanned the critical and control segments for frequencies of all categories; the resulting tabs were then inserted into a multiple-regression program with symptom or no symptom as the criterion. The words "up" and "down" were the best predictors, and accounted for about 25 percent of the variance (the up-down dimension has also proved valuable for other psychosomatic symptoms, [e.g., Fisher & Greenberg, 1977]); three categories from the Need Affiliation dictionary accounted for another 25 percent. The two words plus the three categories correlated .70 with the criterion of symptom or no symptom. It should be noted that Luborsky's rated categories (as translated into the word categories by Spence) did not appear among the best five predictors.

Clearly, a rationale is needed for the selection of categories. Luborsky, starting with a set of 18 variables, settled on three that seemed reasonably discriminating; the addition of categories from the Need Affiliation dictionary displaced Luborsky's; and the additional clinical rater, adding the two words, "up" and "down," displaced all the rest. (Note that the final clinician, working only on hunch, wins this round.) A further set of categories might conceivably displace the two magic words; the process has, in theory, no limits, because we have not agreed on a minimal set of categories to use in this kind of rating.

Similar work has been done on samples matched according to momentary forgetting in order to find the conditions during psychoanalysis and psychotherapy which lead to this memory dysfunction (Luborsky, 1964, 1967). In this case, the patient has a thought in mind and then loses it. The typical comment runs as follows: "I just had a thought (pause) but I forget what I was going to say . . . Oh, this was it!" The target thought may or may not be permanently forgotten. Luborsky rated 37 pairs of critical and control segments on 12 categories (overlapping in some degree with the 18 categories used in the stomach-symptom research). Some categories that discriminated critical from control segments were: new attitude or behavior; difficulty with attention; guilt; and lack of control or competence.

The benchmark of momentary forgetting is a particularly good choice for this kind of research because it occurs naturally in the course of treatment (although not frequently; Luborsky [1964, 1967] noted 69 instances in 2079 sessions, and a lesser frequency in a later sample [Luborsky, Sackeim, and Christoph, in press]). It also stands a good chance of being reported. In contrast, stomach pain and headache are not necessarily part of the flow of ideas, and hence the reporting of them is confounded by the state of the transference. Another comparison was, therefore, tried of a symptom that does not require self-report; that is, petit-mal epileptic attacks (Luborsky, Docherty, Todd, Knapp, Mirsky, & Gottschalk, 1975). These are signaled by a three-cycle-per-second spike and wave on the EEG. For a patient in psychotherapy significant differences were found for critical versus control segments, especially on helplessness and helplessness-related variables.

Conclusion 1

The symptom-context methods have shown their worth for analyzing psychoanalytic sessions to reexamine psychoanalytic concepts in a controlled way. The methods have been used especially for understanding the conditions leading to the formation of symptoms in the course of psychoanalysis but they can be applied to any recurrent behavior, such as the context in which the analyst chooses to make transference interpretations.

Conclusion 2

Five intensive case studies are now available on which the symptom-context analyses have been performed (petit-mal attacks, Luborsky et al., 1975; *Patient A* with momentary forgetting, Luborsky and Mintz, 1975; migraine headaches, Luborsky and Auerbach, 1969; stomach pain, Luborsky and Auerbach, 1969; precipitous shifts in depression, Luborsky, Singer, and Hartke, in preparation). Across-patient analyses showed that for all five patients' helplessness, a concept considered by Freud (1926) as central to his theory of symptom formation, was discriminating.

Conclusion 3

Three main factors are especially crucial in explaining the momentary forgetting symptom during psychotherapy and psychoanalysis (and probably apply as well to other symptoms): (1) a significantly increased level of cognitive disturbance before the appearance of the symptom; (2) increased involvement in the relationship with the analyst; (3) activation of a recurrent patient-specific main theme at the time of the symptom formation.

Research on Therapeutic Trends

Another approach that also starts with the raw clinical material might be called *trend analysis* and can be illustrated by a recent study by Spence (1973) using material from *Patient A*. As noted in more detail below, the patient investigated had been in analysis for seven months when treatment was unexpectedly terminated; five months later treatment was resumed with another analyst who, as it turned out, was five months pregnant. The pregnancy may have signaled the danger of another interruption; the patient alerted by the first interruption and by related occurrences in her life history, was understandably sensitive to something similar happening again. In the fifth hour with the second analyst, the patient asked her if she were pregnant. Taking this segment as the target segment, Spence investigated the preceding four hours to determine whether the target segment had been anticipated in earlier hours and, if a trend did exist, what form it took. The trend analysis made use of specially developed categories of words and phrases that were related to pregnancy: motherhood, separation, childbirth, hospitalization, and the like. Added to the content categories was a set of formal categories related to patient productivity, described above in relation to Simon's work. Frequencies of each category were plotted over time (after dividing each hour into quarters to enlarge the data base) and fitted to a number of different curves. The data analysis relied heavily on the work of Stone et al. (1966); the modified computer programs are described in Spence (1969a).

Early findings show that a strong trend occurred within each hour, starting low and reaching a peak when the hour ended. This trend was repeated in each of the five hours.

Pregnancy associates did not increase progressively over time. What linear change there was took place within each hour. But a larger change did occur across hours, although it was quite irregular. Associations about pregnancy started high, began to fall, recovered, and then fell again. The moment of confrontation (asking the therapist if she were pregnant) occurred just after the second peak. The shape of the function suggests that the patient may have been aware at the start that the therapist was pregnant but was unable to ask the question until the relationship had stabilized, until her anxiety had diminished, or until her ambivalence about resuming treatment had been clarified—these and other possibilities can be resolved only by further study. The irregular function may also reflect the early state of treatment; five hours taken during a later period might show more continuity over time.

More generally, the trends themselves—and the critical units—may change as the stage of treatment changes. In the early phases, we might concentrate on the single hour; later in therapy, when we can assume a certain continuity, we can look for trends over larger blocks of time. An interesting question arises here: At what point in the course of treatment will a trend run over a weekend? . . . over a week's holiday? . . . over a summer vacation?

A final word about the method. It lends itself to computer-based content analysis, an obvious boon to reliability. On the other hand, it is restricted by the categories used. Urgently needed is a standard set of analytic categories that can be applied to a wide variety of clinical samples; the work of Dahl (1972; discussed below) may help fill this gap.

Research on an Alternate Theory of the Process of Psychoanalytic Treatment

Harold Sampson and Joseph Weiss head a large research group that has been testing a revised psychoanalytic theory of therapy. Their theory, which has been developed largely by Weiss (1967), attributes to the patient much more motivation for mastery and much more capacity to work for mastery than other psychoanalytic theories. Weiss (1971) and Sampson (1976) assume that the patient's chief *motivation,* both conscious and unconscious, is to solve his or her problems, and that his or her chief *activity,* both conscious and unconscious, is working to solve them. Moreover, they assume that patients wish to solve problems in a fundamental way by making conscious, and mastering, the conflicts which underlie them, and that patients work throughout their treatment to reach this goal. Patients are able to do this kind of work unconsciously because they exert at least a crude control over unconscious mental life. They are able unconsciously to regulate behavior by thinking about what they would like to do, deciding on a course of action, making plans for doing it, and carrying out plans. The concept of unconscious decision making distinguishes the Weiss-Sampson hypotheses from other commonly held hypotheses. For example, in the traditional psychoanalytic theory there is no unconscious decision making, and conscious decisions are conceptualized largely as epiphenomena, determined dynamically by a play of forces.

The Weiss-Sampson hypotheses also assume that patients are able to lift their defenses, and that they do so—and bring warded-off mental contents to expression or awareness—when they unconsciously decide that they could safely do so. Patients work to bring these contents forth by creating a relationship with the therapist that makes it safe for them to bring them forth. Much of the patients' work to create such a relationship is carried out by testing the analyst. The analyst, according to Weiss and Sampson, may best help patients by inferring their unconscious plan of work and helping them to carry it out.

The Weiss-Sampson group has investigated several of their hypotheses in a series of interrelated studies on the case of Mrs. C *(Patient C).* These studies include:

1. The research group made a formal prediction, based on study of the first 10 sessions of the case of Mrs. C., that the patient would be able to tolerate warded-off feelings of closeness with others, including warded-off feelings of sexual pleasure with her husband, *only* when she developed greater capacity to fight with others (disagree, criticize, blame).

This case-specific prediction was based on the general hypothesis of Weiss and Sampson that formerly warded-off mental contents ordinarily emerge during treatment when a patient judges that he or she can express or experience them safely.

Horowitz, Sampson, Siegelman, Wolfson, & Weiss (1975) tested this prediction by devising a reliable procedure for identifying all instances in the first 100 treatment hours in which the patient blamed, criticized, or disagreed with others. These instances were typed on cards, and sorted by independent judges on a scale of the explicitness and directness with which the behavior was expressed. A parallel procedure was applied to behaviors expressing closeness and sexual responsiveness. They found: (1) that Mrs. C. became more direct and more overt in her expressions of *both* fighting and closeness during the first 100 hours; and (2) that, as predicted, changes in fighting *preceded* changes in closeness. They took this finding as supportive of the idea that a patient regulates the emergence of warded-off contents on the basis of judgments that it would be safe to experience them.

Note that in this case the data consist of statements by the patient (about her feelings and behavior) that may or may not correspond to her actual outside behavior.

2. If the patient was becoming more able to fight overtly and to be close overtly, how did these changes come about? Were they related, for example, to increasing insight? In the prediction study described above, the research group had stated that Mrs. C.'s difficulties in fighting were based on unconscious omnipotent fantasies of hurting others. The group investigated whether Mrs. C. gained insight into these conflicts while she was reporting that she was becoming more overtly aggressive in her behavior.

Cynthia Johnson (unpublished) devised a rating scale to assess how much insight the patient had into her conflicts about omnipotence. At a relatively low level of insight, for example, Mrs. C. was only aware of vague feelings of irrational responsibility for other people, but did not know why she felt that way. At a higher stage of insight she became aware of fears of hurting the other person;

and at a still higher stage of insight she began to differentiate between thoughts and actions and to assess the realistic consequences of her actions. The items comprising the scale were randomly sorted before being judged. They were then reassembled into the original time sequence. They found that the patient gradually developed insight into these initially unconscious conflicts during the first 100 hours.

3. Had Mrs. C. gained insight because the analyst interpreted this conflict to her? To answer this question, Marla Isaacs and Jan Drucker (in preparation) selected all the analyst's comments in the first 100 hours of the case of Mrs. C. Those comments related to conflicts over omnipotence were rated on a scale that paralleled that used by Johnson to rate the patient. When the two sets of findings were compared, it was found that the patient reached each successive stage of insight before the analyst made any interpretations at that stage. This finding implies, as Weiss and Sampson have proposed, that a patient has the motivation and the capacity to make an unconscious conflict conscious and to gain insight into it, and therefore may even be able to do so on some occasions without interpretive help by the analyst.

4. How do the analyst's interventions help the patient? In a pilot study on the case of Mrs. C., Joseph Caston (unpublished data) found that interventions by the analyst that were congruent with the patient's "unconscious plan" (as this was formulated by the research group on the basis of their study of the first 10 hours of the case) led to an immediate increase in the patient's boldness and insight, while interventions incongruent with Mrs. C.'s unconscious plan tended to lead to an immediate decrease in her boldness and insight.

5. In another study of how the analyst's behavior influences the course of therapy, Silberschatz (1977) compared the Weiss-Sampson theory directly against the traditional psychoanalytic theory. The traditional theory assumes that when a patient makes a transference demand and the therapist does not satisfy the demand, the patient is unconsciously frustrated, the unconscious transference wish is intensified, and the wish may press toward consciousness, mobilizing anxiety and defenses. In contrast, Weiss and Sampson assume

that when a patient makes a transference demand, this constiutes a "test" of the analyst, and that when the analyst does not satisfy the demand, this often constitutes a "passing" of the test. If the analyst passes the test, the patient will feel reassured, and will often proceed with increased boldness, and diminished anxiety, to explore previously warded-off material.

Silberschatz developed a method to compare the predictions of the two theories against empirical observation in the case of Mrs. C. His results (1977) confirm the predictions of the theory advanced by Weiss and Sampson. When the patient's transference demands were not satisfied, the patient did not become frustrated, anxious, or conflictful, but instead proceeded with diminished anxiety to explore her problems.

Research on Speech Dysfluencies

Speech measures applied to psychotherapy sessions provide a reliable dependent measure of shifts in patients' emotional states. After the ground-breaking work of Dollard and Mowrer (1953), and Mowrer, Hunt, and Kogan (1953) on the "discomfort-relief quotient," researchers from several schools of psychotherapy, but especially from a psychoanalytic orientation, have tried this and similar methods (Weintraub & Aronson, 1963, 1964, 1965, 1967, 1969, 1974). Mahl's (1956, 1959) speech disturbance measure has been used in many studies and generally supported the thesis that it reflects the waxing and waning of anxiety (Kasl & Mahl, 1958, 1965). Luborsky's Cognitive Disturbance measure (unpublished manuscript) showed a buildup of "cognitive disturbance" before certain symptoms, e.g., momentary forgetting (Luborsky, 1973; Luborsky, Sackeim and Christoph in press, and petit-mal epileptic attacks [Luborsky et al., 1975]). A measure that combines features of the Mahl and Luborsky measures was developed by Horowitz and referred to as a "discomfort quotient" (Horowitz, Sampson, Siegelman, Wolfson, & Weiss, 1975). Research with the discomfort quotient suggests that when the therapist is neutral at the time a previously warded-off content appears, the patient's discomfort drops.

DEALING WITH THE "PRIMARY DATA" OF PSYCHOANALYSIS

Problems of Recording Primary Data

Haggard, Hiken, and Isaacs (1965), together with a number of other researchers (Bergman, 1966; Carmichael, 1966; English, 1966; Erickson, 1966; Jackson, 1966) have reviewed the effects of recording and filming on the process of therapy. These reviews indicate that one records or films at one's peril if one is not aware of the variety of meanings attributed by the patient to the act of recording or filming. One must deal with them as with any other aspect of the relationship that is introduced by the therapist. The peril comes from trying to ignore the meanings of this aspect of the relationship. With an awareness of the possible meanings and impact of the research, it is possible to maintain a workable treatment relationship, and the paraphernalia of the research and the very existence of the research become another problem in the treatment, to be dealt with along with such issues as the therapist's treatment technique, style of setting fees, and so forth.

In all of these tape-recorded treatments, special care must be taken to ensure confidentiality. It is also helpful to both patient and therapist that any research using the tapes be done *after* the treatment is completed, rather than concurrently.

Finally, there is the definition of "primary data." Is the primary data the words of the patient alone, based on a transcript of a tape recording, or something more? Clearly, the recording may be complete but neglect key information that is in the mind of the analyst. It may be important to get the analyst's introspections and account of what he or she believes happened in the course of each session. Not only is it true that the analyst can give a reasonably faithful account of what happened in each session when he or she records this immediately at the end of the session, but the summary may be a tremendously valuable shortcut to the essence of the treatment interaction (Wolfson & Sampson, 1976). Obtaining the introspections of the analyst can therefore be considered an important aspect of the primary data (and this was done by Franz Alexander, Paul Bergman, Merton Gill, and Hartvig Dahl).

Problems of Agreement in Evaluating Primary data

Mintz, Luborsky, & Auerbach (1971) have factor-analyzed the ratings on 60 sessions by three judges and have identified four groupings (factors) that seem to be the main dimensions that a judge tends to listen to when rating psychotherapy sessions. These are (1) optimal therapeutic behavior; (2) therapist directiveness; (3) patient health versus sickness; and (4) therapist interpretiveness. The problem of agreement of judges seems directly tied to the problem of the category being judged. If a judge is asked to attend to one of the four "natural" categories listed above, his or her reliability with the next judge will probably be much higher than if he or she is asked to listen to an "unnatural category." Bellak and Smith (1956), for example, found only moderate agreement among judges listening to psychoanalytic sessions; possibly they were being asked to focus on "unnatural" categories. Similarly, Auerbach and Luborsky (1968) found only moderate agreement among three judges using many variables to rate psychotherapy and psychoanalytic sessions; inspection of the variables might show that when "natural" factors were represented, agreement tended to be higher.

Agreement in rating *amount* of transference was modest although significant (Luborsky, et al., 1973; Luborsky, et al., 1975; Lower, et al., 1973). However, a promising possibility for agreement exists in rating *type* of transference as in the "core conflictual relationship theme method" (Luborsky, 1977a).

Something like a *Rashomon* experience occurred when agreement was sought across different independent points of view of the same sessions that is, by patient, therapist, and clinical judge (Mintz et al., 1973).

Data Banks of Psychoanalytic Treatment Records

Although in this section 11 data banks are described, there is still a paucity of good primary data—data accumulated during actual analytic sessions. Ideally, two conditions should be met: The case should be clearly defined as analytic, meeting whatever criteria of process and outcome a panel of judges might determine; and the data should be recorded, transcribed, and indexed so as to maximize accessibility. Of the three patients who have been most relied upon as specimen cases, that is, *Patient A, Patient B,* and *Patient C* (to be referred to especially in this section), *Patient C* comes closest to meeting the criteria. It is a completely recorded five-year psychoanalysis, fully supervised, with process notes by the analyst. It is, therefore, most acceptable to other analysts as a treatment specimen. It is clearly superior to the Zinn case, of 1933 which was the first ever recorded (Carmichael, 1966) and to the Bergman case (1966) with their many inconsistencies in technique.

Dahl–Downstate Medical Center, SUNY
An extensive series of computer-based studies have been in progress at Downstate, some for many years. The initial work was based on *Patient A* (Gill, Simon, Fink, Endicott, & Paul, 1968; and Dahl, 1972), and more recently on *Patient C*. The case material lends itself naturally to the detailed analysis of such questions as how specific interpretations and interventions influence subsequent material, how key memories change over time, and how symptoms change with respect to interpretations. The raw text of the recordings will eventually be processed by computer, using such systems as those developed by Stone et al. (1966), Iker and Harway (1965), and Spence (1969a).

Dahl has completed a dictionary of high-frequency words gathered from 15 sessions each, from 15 recorded cases. The data are useful for both within and across case analyses. Some of the categories are organized around such basic psychoanalytic concepts as positive transference, resistance, different kinds of defenses, and the like. By applying the special analytic dictionary to the computer-based transcripts, it may be possible to summarize the material in terms of critical psychoanalytic concepts and in this way generate a profile of the key themes of the case.

University of Ulm, Department of Psychotherapy
The aim of the group under the direction of H. Thomae and H. Kaechele is to solve the problems of computerized measurement in psychoanalytic treatment. In one study of an anxiety-prone patient clinical ratings were made of 55 sessions sampled from 650 sessions. Three dimensions were found: castration anxiety, separation, and aggression. With these three dimensions as criteria, an attempt was made to try to predict them from 16 of the 60 known category frequencies. Multiple correlations were extremely high (.7 to .9). It appears they are able to predict some of the complex ratings by a machine scoring process. The group is continuing the study of automatic classification of sessions. For example, by using the computer-based judgments, it was possible to cross-validate the ratings on a second sample of statements from the same patient (Kaechele et al., 1975, 1976.)

Columbia Psychoanalytic Clinic
What must be by far the largest number of *written* records of psychoanalytic treatment has been gathered since 1959 at the Columbia University Psychoanalytic Clinic for Training and Research. The records include both psychoanalysis and psychoanalytically oriented psychotherapy of low-fee patients by psychiatrists in psychoanalytic training. Weber et al. (1966) have reported some results of the treatment of 1348 of these patients, 588 of whom were in psychoanalysis and 760 in psychotherapy. Within the limits imposed by written records (see Wolfson & Sampson, 1976, for an optimistic evaluation of these limits), the group does careful and sophisticated research. They are aided by computer analyses of the many types of information comparing the patient at the beginning and the end of treatment. An example of this sophistication is their way of dealing with the fact that patients are assigned to the two types of treatment on a nonrandom basis, and it is necessary to distinguish between the effects of selection and the effects of the type of treatment. One of their solutions was to compare groups of patients of the same diagnosis and same initial severity of discomfort. They found, for example, that in the group with "more severe" dysfunction at the beginning of treatment, patients diagnosed as "neurotic personality" showed a higher proportion of improvement in analysis than in psychotherapy. Although there was a net improvement in both forms of treatment of borderline and psychotic patients, this group got

worse more often in analysis. Psychoanalysis, therefore, appears to be the treatment of choice for the neurotic personality but *not* for the borderline or psychotic patient. (Compare the earlier discussion of "Most Suitable Patient Qualities").

Gill–University of Illinois Medical Center

In 1964, Gill and his colleagues began to acquire recordings from an analytic case (Patient A) and began a systematic study of some aspects of the process. The case began with seven months of analysis which was temporarily interrupted. After a short interval, a second analyst resumed the treatment and the recordings continued. After some 566 sessions, the analysis ended and was shifted briefly to dynamic psychotherapy. Although not a complete analytic case, it still lends itself to the study of such questions as: How does change in the analyst affect the quality of the transference and the nature of the interaction? Can the decision to shift from psychoanalysis to psychotherapy be anticipated by some of the earlier material?

Patient A has been the subject of several published studies. Dahl (1972) reduced the first 363 sessions to six factors by means of a Topic Index. Process notes from each session were scored on the Topic Index of 53 variables. Dahl factored the Topic Index over all sessions and reduced them to six factors which accounted for 73 percent of the variance. Simon used some of the full transcripts to develop his Patient Productivity Rating Scale. Spence (1973) took the first five hours with the second analyst (who happened to be pregnant) and looked in detail at changes over time with respect to themes related to pregnancy. Luborsky and Mintz (1975) used some sessions for an analysis of momentary forgetting.

During recent years Gill, and Gill and Hoffman (1976) have developed the concept of "latent transference" and ways of estimating it. This appears to be an important addition to the usually explicit or direct transference. Their thesis is that the more the analyst deals with the latent transference, the better the outcome of treatment will be.

Rochester Project on the Computer Analysis of Content

A group at the University of Rochester has focused on devising methods for efficient data reduction of psychoanalytic sessions. Segments of a complete, successful tape-recorded analysis (carried out by Gordon Pleune) have been analyzed by a special computer-based factor analytic method. Successive five-minute segments of the treatment are scored for the frequency of individual words; intercorrelations among a selected set of words are then factored. The factors appear to represent meaning clusters that are central for the patient. These meaning clusters seem to be largely independent of the words selected—beginning with a different set of the patient's words tends to yield similar meaning clusters. These clusters make clinical sense; that is, they correspond to the central themes of the protocol. The method is distinctive in that it does not depend on a set of external categories, but proceeds from within; this feature has been playfully labeled UHH, or *untouched by human hands* (Harway & Iker, 1964, 1966; Iker & Harway, 1965).

Analytic Research Group of the Institute of the Pennsylvania Hospital

This group is composed of 10 experienced psychoanalysts who also share a research background. It has been meeting regularly since 1968, in an effort to plan basic research in the process and outcome of the psychoanalytic method (Graff & Crabtree, 1972). The project is focused on studies of process, although information will also be available about the initial state of the patient and the outcome of the treatment. The target sample is a set of tape recordings of 30 psychoanalytic patients who have been in treatment for 50 sessions or more, and another set of 30 patients who terminated before the fiftieth session.

The process research consists of two parts. In *phase 1,* patients not in the target sample were studied in an attempt to formulate promising hypotheses about the concept of transference. In *phase 2,* the hypotheses were applied to the target sample (a summary of the research is included in the section on transference.)

All of the studies so far are in *phase 1.* The first studies were based on the Rochester Project case (see this page, Data Banks, and pages 344 and 345, under Transference Studies). Recently, the immediate impacts of transference interpretations were investigated using 16 transference interpretations selected from each of three patients, *Patient A, Patient B,* and *Patient C* (Luborsky, Bachrach, Graff, Pulver, and Christoph, in preparation). It was discovered, for example, that the level of immediate beneficial impacts of the interpretations were in keeping with the level of the beneficial impact of the total treatment as independently established at its termination.

The Therapeutic Process Study (Mount Zion Hospital and San Francisco Psychoanalytic Institute)

The work of this group has been described earlier under "Research on an Alternate Theory of the Process of Psychoanalytic Treatment." The group's work represents a systematic testing of concepts in the classical theory of psychoanalytic change. Some of the thinking of the group is described in Sampson and Wallerstein (1972) and Sampson, Weiss, Mlodnosky, & Hause (1972). The group has mainly examined transcripts or process notes from two patients. In one early study with *Patient B,* Horowitz et al. (1975) studied the emergence of warded-off content over the course of the first 100 sessions. Themes were identified that emerged for the first time between sessions 41 and 100. Twenty clinicians read process notes of the first 10 sessions and judged which of the new themes had previously been warded off. Judges' ratings were found to be highly reliable. Several related findings supported the view that these reliably judged contents had been warded off, for example, the content produced discomfort when it first emerged.

University of Illinois School of Medicine, Psychotherapy Film Laboratory

David Shakow started one of the earliest film laboratories for psychotherapy and psychoanalysis at the University of Illinois, originally with Ray Sternberg and Hugh Carmichael, and continued by Elizabeth Tower, Morris Sklansky, Arthur Miller, Kenneth Isaacs, and Ernest Haggard. Some of their recent work is referred to above under "Relatability and Meaningfulness"; other work includes a systematic study of levels of meaning in the patient's and therapist's statements (Sklansky, Isaacs, Levitov, & Haggard, 1966), and the context for

interpretation versus noninterpretation interventions (Garduk & Haggard, 1972).

National Instiute of Mental Health Filmed Therapy Project

Although the NIMH project started by David Shakow concerns psychotherapy and not psychoanalytic treatment, it deserves mention here because it is one of the few available samples of film and sound recording; the quality of the sound is exceptionally good (Bergman, 1966). The patient, a woman in her early 40s was seen by an experienced psychoanalyst, Paul Bergman, for four years and three months—a total of 632 sessions. The treatment was originally analytic, but for various reasons was changed to psychotherapy soon after it started. Possibly, selected segments of this case would be undistinguishable from certain segments of the analytic cases mentioned elsewhere; at any rate, such a comparison would throw light on features that differentiate the two kinds of treatment. This kind of comparison might also be carried out by means of a computer-based category-listing procedure.

Some initial research and some preliminary observations on this case are described by Cohen and Cohen (1961); some studies of body movement in this case have been described by Dittmann (1962).

The Hampstead Index (The Hampstead Clinic)

In the Hampstead Index, aspects of psychoanalytic treatment are classified according to a long list of rubrics and in the form of a card index that can be used for research in psychoanalysis. Each typed card contains a piece of "material"—a so-called "unit of observation" and a reference to the page in the patient's case notes from which it was extracted, or which it summarizes. It also contains the name of the patient and related data (Sandler, 1962).

The method represents a form of concept development that stands, in its degree of rigor, somewhere between unaided clinical research and quantitative research. It has much in common with the method used by Freud, but it has advantages over the usual clinical research, in that (1) it is easier to find patients who fit a certain category, and (2) it is easier to refine psychoanalytic terms because the terms refer to specific patients. The index differs from some other collections of data described in this section in that its contents are not primary data, but the therapist's observations of the therapy process. In this sense, it has much in common with Dahl's collection of process notes, discussed earlier.

One of the serious defects of the index also characterizes some aspects of the Menninger Foundation's Psychotherapy Research Project (Wallerstein et al., 1956): when a therapist is interviewed about his or her experience with a patient, the data are transmitted from the therapist to the research interviewer; the research interviewer does not have access to the actual way in which the patient and therapist interacted. It is obviously better to have the research interviewer *also* witness some of the patient-therapist interaction. Furthermore, the index is especially vulnerable to varieties of usage of the same terms.

Menninger Foundation Psychotherapy Research Project

By far the largest and oldest of the quantitative therapy projects is the Menninger Project, which began in its present form in 1954. (A smaller committee had been working since 1949.) Although not a source of raw data from treatment (since no session recordings were made), it deserves mention here as a source of significant research methods. Particularly important was a procedure developed by Sargent (see Sargent, 1961; Sargent, Horwitz, Wallerstein, & Appelbaum, 1968) for making predictions about the course and outcome of treatment. Her method calls for specifying three aspects of each prediction: the *if*-clause (if a certain condition pertains), the *then*-clause (the prediction), and the *because*-assumption (the reasoning behind the prediction). A second useful method suggested by Sargent is the paired comparison procedure for the comparison of one treatment with another. A third innovation is the application of Guttman's facet analysis and multidimensional scaleogram analysis to psychotherapy and psychoanalytic data. Facet design is a way to choose items to be included and to develop new concepts. It starts with a "mapping sentence" defining the sets or facets to be studied. One result of the Menninger facet analysis was that

the many complex variables on patients in treatments could be described by only 16 basic sets of elements which could be presented by geometrical representation. The Menninger project also has a special position because of the intensive clinical and diagnostic test assessments of the patient before, just after, and two years after termination of treatment. The main final reports are Kernberg, et al., (1972), Voth and Orth (1973), and Horwitz (1974).

The last of these (Horwitz, 1974) presents the results of the intensive pre- and post-test evaluations of each of the 42 patients. The curative process is examined for each of the patients. Three major findings are presented in the conclusions which significantly contributed to a revised view of the theory of change: (1) Therapeutic alliance: the patient must possess and then expand and internalize a disposition to see the therapist as a helpful person. (2) The stable effect of supportive psychotherapy: the results showed the ability of supportive psychotherapy to effect substantial improvement; these are treatments in which the therapeutic work included little or no uncovering or interpreting of transference. (3) The supportive aspects of expressive treatment: the researchers were impressed with the power of the therapeutic relationship, even in those instances where the designation of the treatment was expressive. These three observations led to an emphasis on the importance of *internalization* of the therapeutic alliance which is a contribution of the book to a reformulation of the psychoanalytic theory of change.

PSYCHOANALYTIC TREATMENT ANALOGUES

The treatment situation is too complex to be understood in analogue form; each case and each session differ along a number of dimensions hard to specify in advance. For this reason, Freud was probably right in his pessimistic evaluation of one of the early analogue studies. Asked to comment on Saul Rosenzweig's analogue study of repression, Freud replied, "I have examined your experimental studies for the verification of the psychoanalytic assertions with interest. I cannot put much value on these confirmations because the wealth of reliable observations on which these assertions rest make them independent of experimental verification. Still, it can do no harm." (Quoted in MacKinnon & Dukes, 1962). The laboratory experimenter must show that he or she is dealing with the same phenomenon that has been observed clinically, and this is an all-but-impossible requirement. Nevertheless, despite flaws, a number of analogue studies deserve mention at this point.

The analogue studies are of two main kinds: those dealing primarily with verifying psychoanalytic concepts and those dealing especially with the attempt to reproduce in the laboratory conditions that pertain during treatment. It is the second, of course, that we are primarily concerned with although the first does have some relevance. Sears (1943a, 1943b) comprehensively reviewed "objective studies of psychoanalytic concepts." Madison's review (1956) was primarily concerned with repression, Kline (1972) was a comprehensive review of both kinds of studies, Holmes (1974) dealt with phenomena related to memory and self-deception; the most recent and comprehensive of all is that of Fisher and Greenberg (1977). Although these studies have had little influence on clinicians, mainly because they are thought to be not close enough to the clinical phenomena to represent a test of them, some recent work—notably by Sackeim and Gur (in press)—has been able to answer objections about its cogency for clinical concepts.

Analogues to phenomena that occur in psychoanalysis—such as free-association sessions—have been investigated by a number of researchers, including Colby (1960, 1961), Bordin (1966), and Keet (1948). The last study has been reviewed by Hilgard (1952). The Keet approach entails the "induction" of a so-called mild neurosis in the laboratory. Different treatment methods can then be compared with respect to their ability to "cure" the neurosis. It seems like a good approach, but there has been difficulty in replicating the finding that the interpretive technique was superior in recovering forgotten material. Several attempts to replicate it have failed because of difficulty in establishing the artificial neurotic illness (see Merrill, 1952, for one unsuccessful attempt.)

SUMMARY AND IMPLICATIONS FOR PSYCHOANALYTIC PRACTICE AND RESEARCH

The same main questions are being asked about psychoanalytic treatment that have been asked about other forms of treatment: What kinds of patients are most suited to it? What kinds of therapists are most suited to perform it? What types of outcomes are accomplished by it? What process do patient and therapist go through in doing it? It will be interesting to see what convergence develops among the findings from psychoanalysis and from other forms of treatment.

As in all scientific fields, the research style has become more quantitative and controlled. We have listed some evidence that psychoanalysis, too, is beginning to follow the trend. Psychoanalysis is now showing signs of setting up a base of quantitative research to support it—note especially (under section "Primary Data Banks") the number of process studies under way.

In the seven years since the first version of this chapter was written, what is most new? These six areas especially: (1) The Mount Zion research testing an alternate theory of the process of psychoanalytic treatment. (2) Much more research on transference: The work of the Analytic Research Group of the Institute of the Pennsylvania Hospital; the scoring systems for transference by Gill and Hoffman; the core conflictual relationship theme method. (3) The Menninger Foundation Psychotherapy Research Project has completed its two-decade study with several massive final reports. These are contributions especially to knowledge of the kinds of changes that occur in psychotherapy and psychoanalysis, as well as the degree to which the changes can be predicted. (4) Improvements in computer methods for analyzing content of sessions by Dahl (1972) and Spence (1969a). (5) Further developments of methods for reexamining the theories of symptom formation. (6) The primary data banks for transcribed psychoanalytic cases are richer than they were.

We began the review with the observation that quantitative psychoanalytic therapy research has been consigned to a limbo in relation to its import to clinical practice. Does it deserve it? The answer at this point is a qualified "yes." At times in reviewing the literature we were reminded of an experimenter who put an ad in a paper for a "reliable, vigorous young man for an important, decision-making job." Among the applicants was a spry, superannuated man who was obviously not qualified for the job. The interviewer asked him why he had applied. The old man answered, "Young man, I just came here to let you know that on *me, you can't rely." Quantitative research on psychoanalytic therapy presents itself, so far, as an unreliable support to clinical practice. Far more is known now through clinical wisdom than is known through quantitative, objective studies.* Much of what is contributed by the quantitative literature represents a cumbersome, roundabout way of showing the clinician what he or she already "knows"—see, for example, Waelder (1962). (Quantitative research on psychoanalytic treatment is not, however, in a position different from quantitative research on other therapies [except for the behavior therapies] with respect to the lack of impact on practice—see Luborsky, 1969).

Still, some general conclusions can be drawn. As this review of quantitative research shows, *areas exist in which guidance could be given to practice:* (1) Some studies confirm clinical impressions about the selection of patients who are most suitable for psychoanalytic treatment, although a high level of prediction success based on these patient qualities seems unlikely. (2) In the selection of psychoanalysts, certain healthy qualities might be worth seeking, such as objectivity, self-confidence, and security. (3) Some progress is now being made in research on the process of psychoanalytic treatment, and it has, therefore, been given correspondingly more space in this review. Some of the findings about the qualities of the patient's productions (whether labeled *productivity, meaningfulness, experiencing,* or *associative freedom*) have been explored. One of the core aspects of productivity was found to be *the patient's reflective statements.* For the therapist's interpretive behavior, some of the studies of the psychoanalytic process (such as Spence & Greif, 1970) stress the *efficacy of the clinical concept of "listening away" as a way to sharpen one's hearing of what the patient is saying.* (4) The studies of the Mount Zion group have implications for the technique of psychoanalytic

treatment; for example, interpretations that are consistent with the "unconscious plan" seem to be more effective; the neutrality of the analyst's response at the time unconscious contents emerge, appears to have an important beneficial effect, and for a patient with high motivation and capacity for insight, the patient may on some occasions proceed in gaining insight without interpretive help.

In this review we have restricted ourselves to *quantitative* psychoanalytic research on psychoanalytic treatment because psychoanalysis needs a better balance between clinical wisdom alone and clinical wisdom combined with more controlled methods. From its inception, psychoanalysis has elicited strong responses— either favorable or unfavorable—not neutral ones. Controversy persists today, although the main basis for criticism has *shifted.* Formerly it was aimed at the question of unconscious contents; now, the insufficiency of controlled research to support the concepts has come under attack. Occasionally a preference for a simpler theory of psychotherapy has been voiced. For example, some exponents of behavior therapy emphasize the *sufficiency* of learning theory explanations; psychoanalysis needs evidence from controlled research to justify its particular views.

The research with analogues of psychoanalytic concepts, so common in the past few decades, has not been useful—mainly because it has not been possible to create real analogues to critical clinical situations. This failure may stem, in part, from the fact that many concepts need clarification to be useful in quantitative studies, but it may also stem from the fact that a substantial part of quantitative psychoanalytic treatment research has been—and still is—carried out by nonanalysts. When Rapaport (1959) said, "Psychoanalysis will use methods and concepts from other sciences, but results will be achieved by the sweat of our own brow," he may have meant that few nonanalysts have the motivation or know-how to carry out the research properly. Our review shows that many nonanalysts have sweated over these issues, especially by trying to create experimental analogues of concepts, but too often have missed their essence. As our review also shows, the attention of research psychoanalysts has turned instead to fashioning controlled methods for dealing with the data from the psychoanalytic situation.

Researchers on psychoanalytic treatment have begun to conquer the difficulties of amassing sufficient primary data for proper research, and more will become available. Several recorded analyses and symptom-context protocols are now available as specimens for examination by researchers of various viewpoints (see "Primary Data Banks").

The battle to introduce the tape recorder into the analytic session is just about won, and fully recorded cases are potentially avaiable. But just as this is happening, it is becoming clear that much more data is needed; that the *spoken* interchange, no matter how faithfully recorded, is incomplete, and that the full context of an utterance—including, at the least, both the therapist's and the patient's surrounding intentions and feelings—are necessary before its meaning can be fully understood. In this way we can begin to appreciate the full range of meanings in any utterance, and do justice to one of our most prized principles—overdetermination.

Thus the issue is no longer whether process notes are sufficient (see below for more on this point); it has moved to the question of whether even audio recordings capture enough of the hour to be representative specimens of the analytic reality. The problem can be illustrated by looking at the issue of intention. The statement "You have been silent now for some time," when made by the analyst, is more than an observation; it is usually spoken with the aim of prompting the patient to speak. A full specification of that intention will not appear in the transcript, and although it may be supplied by the sophisticated reader, it may not occur to all readers with the same degree of force. Thus different readings of the same text are more than likely to occur, increasing the unreliability of ratings and adding noise to any study of process. And the problem stems from the fact that this intention does not reside in the primary data base.

If full transcripts are fallible, process notes are even more defective. Despite their usefulness as an index of the full session and, when combined, as an index of the full treatment (Wolfson & Sampson, 1976), they should be treated with extreme caution. The following objections can be listed: (1) *Theoretical bias.* Process notes are written by an analyst who has been trained to look for certain units of behavior, and combine them according to specific rules. The analyst cannot help but filter the raw stuff of the session through some kind of framework, and produce observations that, to at least a partial extent, suit the theory. Thus process notes will tend to be insensitive to events not predicted by theory, and will not capture units that are justified by some other set of principles. (2) *Surface structure ignored.* The specific language of the patient is necessarily ignored in favor of a description of the main underlying themes. But the specific language may contain a wealth of unconscious material. Just as slips of the tongue are the most obvious examples of unconscious derivatives, other kinds of word choice may be equally at the mercy of unconscious forces; the slip may survive the process notes but the more subtle changes will probably not be noticed. The same argument applies to the therapist's comments. (3) *Countertransference.* Process notes, because they are written by the analyst, tend to be insensitive to countertransference problems. (4) *Critical units.* Although they are fairly sensitive to large units of material (e.g., memories of father and mother—see Wolfson & Sampson, 1976), there is no evidence to show that process notes capture the specific wording employed by the patient, or that they are sensitive to subunits within these larger themes. And although they are sensitive to repetition (see Wolfson & Sampson, 1976), there is no evidence that process notes are sensitive to specific changes in wording over time, changes that often indicate subtle shifts in attitude or emphasis.

On the other hand, process notes contain something of the analyst's perspective, which is acutely missing from the recorded transcript. Unfortunately, this all-important context is not even sampled, with the result that we hear more about excitement over new discoveries than we do about boredom with repetitious and unproductive hours. We do not have a continuous record of his or her state of mind to lay alongside the full record of the spoken transcript. Some way must be found, now that the tape recording has been accepted, to go the next step and make public the patient's and therapist's associational contexts.

More is known now about concepts that can be judged from the psychoanalytic sessions or can be coded for computer manipulation. Much more needs to be done in this area, but a start has been made. Some specific evidence for the revitalization of psychoanalytic concepts is to be found in the creation of reliable rating scales for certain concepts applicable to psychoanalytic and psychoanalytically oriented psychotherapy (Auerbach & Luborsky, 1968; Mintz et al., 1971; Mintz & Luborsky, 1970). Computer programs are being created for many analytic concepts (Spence, 1969a and b; Dahl, 1972).

There has also been a trend among analytic theoreticians toward a theoretical sharpening of psychoanalytic concepts by separating them into main components for which measures might more readily be developed. Such refined concepts should be more reliable and, therefore, more amenable than earlier formulations for use in controlled studies. We have already described the control mastery theory of Weiss (1971) and Sampson (1976). Holt's work on bound versus free cathexis (1962) and on energy concepts (1967) is another example of this development. Other reformulations have been attempted that bring together psychoanalysis and information and learning theory—see, for example, the work of Peterfreund and Schwartz (1971), Greenspan (1975) and Wachtel (1977). Many of Rapaport's (1959) contributions were attempts to simplify and clarify psychoanalytic concepts with a view toward using them in quantitative research, as he had begun to do a few years before his untimely death.

Organizational research backing has increased in the past decade. The formation of the Society for Psychotherapy Research, a multidisciplinary international organization of all types of psychotherapy researchers, is evidence of organizational research. Some psychoanalytic organizations, troubled by the lack of research, have taken action. The American Psychoanalytic Association conducted an intensive examination of its research and education practices (see Goodman, 1977) and at its December 1975 meeting, approval was given for a psychoanalytic research foundation to be funded by governmental and private sources. The American Academy of Psychoanalysis has also de-

veloped a research department. Albert Stunkard, its recent chairman, relied upon a procedure in which a trained cohort of psychoanalysts have agreed to take part in research efforts. Two studies using the cohorts have so far appeared: one on homosexuals versus heterosexuals for which each analyst provided information on a patient in psychoanalysis who was a homosexual and one who was not (Bieber, Dain, Dince, Drellich, Grand, Gundlach, Kremer, Rifkin, Wilber, & Bieber, 1961); and another one on obese patients versus normals in which a patient in psychoanalysis who was obese was compared with a matched one who was not (Rand & Stunkard, 1977). Finally, there is increased interest in psychoanalytic process research in this country and abroad. Some of the process research groups listed in our first review have stayed with their work long enough to have cross-collaborated with other process research projects, especially in sharing the same data, and are doing studies of the psychoanalytic treatment process.

HISTORICAL CODA

It is fitting to end the chapter by putting the problem of quantitative research in historical perspective.

The main fruits of quantitative psychoanalytic research can be found in advances in method. Only a few "discoveries" have added to the store of clinical wisdom; few, if any, quantitative research findings have changed the style or outcome of psychoanalytic practice. In this respect, psychoanalysis is in the position of any new science. Changes in method must, of necessity, precede changes in content; much more work needs to be done simply to understand in some systematic way what the analyst does, how interpretations work, how transference can manifest itself, and how insight is acquired.

Psychoanalysts, like other psychotherapists, literally *do not know* how they achieve their results, although they have searched longer and deeper than others and possess a unique store of clinical wisdom. They have learned their craft from a long line of practitioners schooled in a master-apprentice relationship; the rules are taught more by example than by explanation. More work must be done in a naturalistic way (and here is where recordings are valuable) but guided by specific hypotheses to understand what makes a good therapist good. Observation by means of videotape is particularly important because certain aspects of the therapeutic process take place outside of the patient's and therapist's awareness, and therefore one cannot simply ask the therapist what he or she does.

Despite its rather prosaic nature, a systematic naturalistic inventory of the analytic process is long overdue. The field has skipped from the initial insight of Freud to high-flown metapsychological formulations; now it must step back and fill in the middle ground before any substantial progress can be made.

Our position can be thought of generationally: Freud, the discoverer and innovator, was the first generation; those he assembled around him, the disseminators, expounders, and teachers of his views were the second generation, and we who are filling in the middle ground by controlled observations and testing of the theory are in the third generation. It is now our turn to contribute in the terms that suit our times.

REFERENCES

Alexander, F. *Five-year report of the Chicago Institute for Psychoanalysis—1932–1937.* Chicago: Institute for Psychoanalysis, 1937.

Alexander, F., French, T., & Pollock, G. *Psychosomatic specificity.* Vol. 1. Chicago: University of Chicago Press, 1968.

Apfelbaum, B. *Dimensions of transference in psychotherapy.* Berkeley: University of California Press, 1958.

Aronson, H., & Weintraub, W. Patient changes during classical psychoanalysis as a function of initial status and duration of treatment. *Psychiatry,* 1968a, *31,* 369–379.

Aronson, H., & Weintraub, W. Social background of the patient in classical psychoanalysis. *Journal of Nervous and Mental Disease,* 1968b, *146,* 91–97.

Auerbach, A. H., & Luborsky, L. Accuracy of judgments of psychotherapy and the nature of the "good hour." In J. Shlien, H. F. Hunt, J. P. Matarazzo, and C. Savage (Eds.) *Research in psychotherapy,* Vol. 3. Washington, D. C.: American Psychological Association, 1968, pp. 155–168.

Bachrach, H. The Conjunctive Empathy Scale. Doctoral Dissertation, University of Chicago, 1966.

Bachrach, H. Adaptive regression, empathy, and psychotherapy. *Psychotherapy: Theory, Research and Practice,* 1968, *5,* 203–209.

Bachrach, H. Empathy: We know what we mean, but what do we measure? *Archives of General Psychiatry,* 1976, *33,* 35–38.

Bachrach, H., & Leaff, L. Analyzability: A systematic review of the clinical and quantitative literature. *Journal of the American Psychoanalytic Association,* in press.

Bachrach, H., Luborsky, L., & Mechanick, P. G. The correspondence between judgments of empathy and other sensitivity measures. *British Journal of Medical Psychology,* 1974, *47,* 337–340.

Bachrach, H., Mintz, J., & Luborsky, L. On rating empathy and other psychotherapy variables: An experience with the effects of training. *Journal of Consulting and Clinical Psychology,* 1971, *36:*445.

Bandura, A. Psychotherapists' anxiety level, self-insight, and psychotherapeutic competence. *Journal of Abnormal and Social Psychology,* 1956, *52,* 333–337.

Bandura, A., Lipsher, D. H., & Miller, P. E. Psychotherapists' approach-avoidance reactions to patients' expression of hostility. *Journal of Consulting Psychology,* 1960, *24,* 1–8.

Barrett-Lennard, G. T. Dimensions of therapist response as causal factors in therapeutic change. *Psychological Monographs,* 1962, *76* (43, Whole No. 562).

Bellak, L., & Smith, M. B. An experimental exploration of the psychoanalytic process. *Psychoanalytic Quarterly,* 1956, *25,* 385–414.

Benjamin, J. Methodological considerations in the validation and elaboration of psychoanalytical personality theory. (Approaches to a dynamic theory of development.) *American Journal of Orthopsychiatry,* 1950, *20,* 139–156.

Bergin, A. E. The evaluation of therapeutic outcomes. In A. E. Bergin and S. L. Garfield (Eds.), *Handbook of Psychotherapy and Behavior Change: An empirical analysis.* New York: John Wiley & Sons, Inc., 1971, pp. 217–270.

Bergin, A. E., & Jasper, L. G. Correlates of empathy in psychotherapy: A replication. *Journal of Abnormal Psychology,* 1969, *74,* 447–481.

Bergin, A. E., & Solomon, S. Personality and performance correlates of empathic understanding in psychotherapy. In T. Tomlinson and J. Hart, (Eds.), *New directions in client-centered therapy.* Boston: Houghton-Mifflin, 1969, pp. 223–236.

Bergman, P. An experiment in filmed psychotherapy. In L. A. Gottschalk and A. H. Auerbach (Eds.) *Methods of research in psychotherapy.* New York: Appleton-Century-Crofts, 1966, pp. 35–49.

Bibring, E. Psychoanalysis and the dynamic psychotherapies. *Journal of the American Psychoanalytic Association,* 1954, *2,* 745–770.

Bieber, I., Dain, J. H., Dince, P. R., Drellich, M. G., Grand, H. G., Gundlach, R. L., Kremer, M. W., Rifkin, A. H., Wilbur, C. B., & Bieber, T. B. *Homosexuality, A Psychoanalytic Study of Male Homosexuals.* New York: Basic Books, 1961.

Bordin, E. S. Free association: An experimental analogue of the psychoanalytic situation. In L. A. Gottschalk and A. H. Auerbach (Eds.), *Methods of research in psychotherapy.* New York: Appleton-Century-Crofts, 1966, pp. 189–208.

Brenman, M., Gill, M., & Knight, R. P. Spontaneous fluctuations in depth of hypnosis and their implication for ego function. *International Journal of Psychoanalysis,* 1952, *33,* 22–33.

Brenman, M., Kubie, L., Murray, H. A., Kris, E., & Gill, M. Problems in clinical research. *American Journal of Orthopsychiatry,* 1947, *17,* 196–230.

Carmichael, H. Sound-film recording of psychoanalytic therapy: A therapist's experiences and reactions. In L. A. Gottschalk and A. H. Auerbach (Eds.), *Methods of research in psychotherapy.* New York: Appleton-Century-Crofts, 1966, pp. 50–59.

Cartwright, R. A comparison of the response to psychoanalytic and client-centered psychotherapy. In L. A. Gottschalk and A. H. Auerbach (Eds.), *Methods of research in psychotherapy.* New York: Appleton-Century-Crofts, 1966, pp. 517–529.

Chance, E. The study of transference in group therapy. *International Journal of Group Psychotherapy.* 1952, *2,* 40–53.

Cohen, R. A., & Cohen, M. B. Research in psychotherapy: A preliminary report. *Psychiatry,* 1961, *24,* 46–61.

Colby, K. M. Experiment on the effects of an observer's presence on the imago system during psychoanalytic free association. *Behavioral Science,* 1960, *5,* 216–232.

Colby, K. M. On the greater amplifying power of causal-correlative over interrogative inputs on free association in an experimental analytic situation. *Journal of Nervous and Mental Disease,* 1961, *133,* 233–239.

Cutler, R. L. Countertransference effects in psychotherapy. *Journal of Consulting Psychology,* 1958, *22,* 349–356.

Dahl, H. A quantitative study of a psychoanalysis. In R. Holt and E. Peterfreund (Eds). *Psychoanalysis and Contemporary Science,* Vol. 1. New York: Macmillan, 1972, pp. 237–257.

Dittmann, A. T. The relationship between body movements and moods in interviews. *Journal of Consulting Psychology,* 1962, *26,* 480.

Dollard, J., & Mowrer, O. A method of measuring tension in written documents. In O. H. Mowrer (Ed.), *Psychotherapy: Theory and Research.* New York: Ronald Press, 1953, pp. 235–256.

Duhrssen, A., & Jorswieck, E. Zur korrektur von Eysenck's Berichterstattung uber psychoanalitische behandlungsergebnisse. *Acta Psychotherapy,* 1962, *19,* 329–342.

Duhrssen, A., & Jorswieck, E. Ein Empirischstatistische Untersuchung zur Leistungsfahigkeit psychoanalytischer behandlung. (An empirical-statistical investigation into the efficacy of psychoanalytic therapy.) *Nervenarzt,* 1965, *36,* 166–169.

Eissler, K. *Medical orthodoxy and the future of psychoanalysis.* New York: International Universities Press, 1965.

Ellis, A. Psychotherapy techniques for use with psychotics. *American Journal of Psychotherapy,* 1955a, *9,* 452–476.

Ellis, A. New approaches to psychotherapy techniques. *Journal of Clinical Psychology, Monograph Supplement II,* 1955b, 208–260.

Engel, G. L. Some obstacles to the development of research in psychoanalysis. (With discussions and closing comments by David Beres, Mark Kanzer, Robert S. Wallerstein, and Elizabeth R. Zetzel.) *Journal of the American Psychoanalytic Association,* 1968, *16,* 195–229.

English, O. S. Subjective reaction to being filmed. In L. A. Gottschalk and A. H. Auerbach (Eds.), *Methods of research in psychotherapy.* New York: Appleton-Century-Crofts, 1966, p. 60.

Erickson, M. The experience of interviewing in the presence of observers. In L. A. Gottschalk and A. H. Auerbach (Eds.), *Methods of research in psychotherapy.* New York: Apppleton-Century-Crofts, 1966, pp. 61–63.

Escalona, S. Problems in psychoanalytic research. *International Journal of Psychoanalysis,* 1952, *33,* 11–21.

Eysenck, H. The effects of psychotherapy: An evaluation. *Journal of Consulting Psychology,* 1952, *16,* 319–324.

Eysenck, H. The effects of psychotherapy. In H. Eysenck (Ed.), *Handbook of abnormal psychology.* New York: Basic Books, 1961, pp. 697–725.

Farrell, B. The criteria for a psychoanalytic interpretation. In D. F. Gustafson (Ed.), *Essays in philosophical psychology.* Garden City: Doubleday, 1964, pp. 299–323.

Feldman, F. Results of psychoanalysis in clinic case assignments. *Journal of the American Psychoanalytic Association,* 1968, *16,* 274–300.

Fenichel, O. Statisticher bericht uber die therapeutische tatigkeit, 1920–1930. In *Zehn Jahre Berliner Psychoanalytisches Institut.* Vienna: Internationale Psychoanalytischer Verlag, 1930, pp. 13–19.

Fey, W. F. Doctrine and experience: their influence upon the psychotherapist. *Journal of Consulting Psychology,* 1958, *22,* 403–409.

Fiedler, F. The concept of an ideal relationship. *Journal of Consulting Psychology,* 1950a, *14,* 239–245.

Fiedler, F. A. comparison of therapeutic relationships in psychoanalytic, nondirective and Adlerian therapy. *Journal of Consulting Psychology,* 1950b, *14,* 426–445.

Fiedler, F. Factor analyses of psychoanalytic, nondirective, and Adlerian therapeutic relationships. *Journal of Consulting Psychology,* 1951, *15,* 32–38.

Fiedler, F., & Senior, K. An exploratory study of unconscious feeling reactions in 15 patient-therapist pairs. *Journal of Abnormal and Social Psychology,* 1952, *47,* 446–453.

Fisher, S. and Greenberg, R. *The scientific credibility of Freud's theories and therapy.* New York: Basic Books, Inc., 1977.

Fiske, D. W., Hunt, H. F., Luborsky, L., Orne, M. T., Parloff, M. B., Reiser, M. F., and Tuma, H. Planning of research on effectiveness of psychotherapy. (Report of a workshop sponsored by the Clinical Projects Research Review Committee, National Institute of Mental Health, November, 1968.) *Archives of General Psychiatry,* 1970, *22,* 22–32.

Frenkel-Brunswik, E. Psychoanalysis and the unity of science. *Proceedings of the American Academy of Arts and Sciences,* 1954, 80.

Freud, Anna. The widening scope of indications for psychoanalysis: Discussion. *Journal of the American Psychoanalytic Association,* 1954, *2,* 607−620.

Freud, S. (1913). The claims of psychoanalysis to the interest of the nonpsychological sciences (*Standard Edition*). Vol. 13. London: Hogarth Press, 1955.

Freud, S. (1926). Inhibitions, symptoms, and anxiety *(Standard Edition).* Vol. 20. London: Hogarth Press, 1959.

Garduk, E. L., & Haggard, E. A. Immediate effects on patients of psychoanalytic interpretations. *Psychological Issues, 8,* No. 4, Monograph 28, 1972.

Gendlin, E. T. Experiencing: A variable in the process of psychotherapeutic change. *American Journal of Psychotherapy,* 1961, *15,* 233−245.

Gill, M., & Brenman, M. *Hypnosis and related states: Psychoanalytic studies in regression.* New York: International Universities Press, 1959.

Gill, M., & Hoffman, I. Paper delivered to Mid-Winter meeting of the American Psychoanalytic Association, George Klein Forum, 1976, on definitions and scoring of latent and related transference behaviors in psychoanalytic sessions.

Gill, M., Simon, J., Fink, G., Endicott, N. A., & Paul, I. H. Studies in audio-recorded psychoanalysis. I. General considerations. *Journal of the American Psychoanalytic Association,* 1968, *16,* 230−244.

Glover, E. Research methods in psychoanalysis. *International Journal of Psychoanalysis,* 1952, *33,* 403−409.

Glover, E. Common technical practices: A questionnaire research (1940). In E. Glover, *The technique of psychoanalysis.* New York: International Universities Press, 1955, pp. 261−350.

Glover, E., Fenichel, O., Strachey, J., Bergler, E., Nunberg, N., & Bibring, E. Symposium on the theory of the therapeutic results of psychoanalysis. *International Journal of Psychoanalysis,* 1937, *18,* 125−189.

Goodman, S. *Psychoanalytic education and research: The current situation and future possibilities.* New York: International Universities Press, 1977.

Gottschalk, L., Mayerson, P. and Gottlieb, A. Prediction and evaluation of outcome in an emergency brief psychotherapy clinic. *Journal of Nervous and Mental Disease,* 1967, *144,* 77−96.

Graff, H., & Crabtree, L. Vicissitudes in the development of a psychoanalytic research group. *Journal of the American Psychoanalytic Association,* 1972, *20,* 820−830.

Graff, H., & Luborsky, L. Long-term trends in transference and resistance: A quantitative analytic method applied to four psychoanalyses. *Journal of the American Psychoanalytic Association,* 1977, *25,* 471−490.

Graham, S. R. Patient evaluation of the effectiveness of limited psychoanalytically oriented psychotherapy. *Psychological Reports,* 1958, *4,* 231−234.

Graham, S. R. The effects of psychoanalytically oriented psychotherapy on levels of frequency and satisfaction in sexual activity. *Journal of Clinical Psychology,* 1960, *16,* 94−95.

Greenspan, S. A consideration of some learning variables in the context of psychoanalytic theory. *Psychological Issues, 9,* Monograph 33, 1975.

Greenson, R. R. *The technique and practice of psychoanalysis.* Vol. 1. New York: International Universities Press, 1967.

Group for Advancement of Psychiatry (GAP) Committee Report: Knapp, P. (Chrmn.), Brosin, H., Meyer, E., Offenkrantz, W., Robbins, L., Scheflen, A., Shands, H., Tower, L., and Luborsky, L. (Consultant). *Psychotherapy and the dual research tradition.* American Psychiatric Association, 1970.

Gurman, A. and A. Razin (Eds.), *Effective Psychotherapy: A Handbook of Research.* New York: Pergamon Publishing Co., 1977.

Haggard, E. A., Hiken, J. R., & Isaacs, K. S. Some effects of recording and filming on the psychotherapeutic process. *Psychiatry,* 1965, *28,* 169−191.

Hamburg, D., Bibring, G., Fisher, C., Stanton, A., Wallerstein, R., & Haggard, E. Report of *ad hoc* committee on central fact-gathering data of the American Psychoanalytic Association. *Journal of the American Psychoanalytic Association,* 1967, *15,* 841−861.

Hartmann, H. Comments on the scientific aspects of psychoanalysis. *The Psychoanalytic Study of the Child,* 1958, *13,* 127−146.

Hartmann, H. Psychoanalysis as a scientific theory. In S. Hook (Ed.), *Psychoanalysis, scientific method, and philosophy.* New York: New York University Press, 1959.

Hartmann, H., Kris, E., & Loewenstein, R. The function of theory in psychoanalysis. In R. Loewenstein, (Ed.), *Drives, affects, and behavior.* New York: International Universities Press, 1953.

Harway, N. I., & Iker, H. P. Computer analysis of content in psychotherapy. *Psychological Reports,* 1964, *14,* 720−722.

Harway, N. I., & Iker, H. P. Objective content analysis of psychotherapy by computer. In K. Enslein (Ed.), *Data acquisition and processing in biology and medicine.* Vol. 4. New York: Pergamon Press, 1966.

Hilgard, E. Experimental approaches to psychoanalysis. In E. Pumpian-Mindlin (Ed.), *Psychoanalysis as science.* Stanford: Stanford University Press, 1952, pp. 3−45.

Holmes, D. S. Investigations of repression: Differential recall of material experimentally or naturally associated with ego threat. *Psychological Bulletin,* 1974, *81,* 632−653.

Holt, R. R. A critical examination of Freud's concept of bound versus free cathexis. *Journal of the American Psychoanalytic Association,* 1962, *10,* 475−525.

Holt, R. R. A manual for scoring primary process manifestations in Rorschach test responses. New York University, 1964. (Unpublished manuscript, ninth draft.)

Holt, R. R. Beyond vitalism and mechanism: Freud's concept of psychic energy. In B. Wolman (Ed.), *Historical roots.* New York: Harper & Row, 1967.

Holt, R. R., & Luborsky, L. *Personality patterns of psychiatrists: A study in selection techniques.* Vol. 1. New York: Basic Books, 1958; Vol. II. Topeka: The Menninger Foundation, 1958.

Horowitz, L. M., Sampson, H., Siegelman, E. Y.,

Wolfson, A. W., & Weiss, J. On the identification of warded-off mental contents. *Journal of Abnormal Psychology*, 1975, *84*, 545–558.

Horwitz, L. *Clinical Prediction in Psychotherapy*. New York: Jason Aronson, 1974.

Iker, H. P., & Harway, N. I. A computer approach towards the analysis of content. *Behavioral Science*, 1965, *10*, 173–183.

Isaacs, K., & Haggard, E. Some methods used in the study of affect in psychotherapy. In L. A. Gottschalk and A. H. Auerbach (Eds.), *Methods of research in psychotherapy*. New York: Appleton-Century-Crofts, 1966, pp. 226–239.

Jackson, D. Filming of psychotherapeutic sessions as a personal experience. In L. A. Gottschalk and A. H. Auerbach (Eds.), *Methods of research in psychotherapy*. New York: Appleton-Century-Crofts, 1966, pp. 64–65.

Janis, I. L. The psychoanalytic interview as an observational method. In G. Lindzey (Ed.), *Assessment of human motives*. New York: Rinehart, 1958, pp. 149–182.

Kaechele, H., Gruenzig, H.-J., & Mergenthaler, E. Psychoanalytic Process Research with Computer-Aided Content Analysis. In S. Dragi (Ed.), The Pisa Conference on Content-Analysis, (in preparation).

Kaechele, H., Thomae, H., & Schaumburg, C. Veranderungen des Sprachinhaltes in einem psychoanalyticischen Proze B. Schweizer Archiv for Neurologie. *Neurochirurgie and Psychiatrie*, 1975, *116*: 197–228. (Changes of verbal content during a psychoanalytic process.)

Kasl, S. V., & Mahl, G. F. Experimentally induced anxiety and speech disturbances. *American Psychologist*, 1958, *13*, 349.

Kasl, S. V., & Mahl, G. F. Disturbance and hesitation in speech. *Journal of Personality and Social Psychology*, 1965, *1*, 425–433.

Keet, C. D. Two verbal techniques in a miniature counseling situation. *Psychological Monographs*, 1948, 62 (Whole No. 294).

Kernberg, O., Burstein, E., Coyne, L., Appelbaum, A., Horwitz, L., & Voth, H. Psychotherapy and psychoanalysis: Final report of the Menninger Foundations's Psychotherapy Research Project. *Bulletin of the Menninger Clinic*, 1972, *36*, 1–275.

Kirtner, W. L., Cartwright, D. S., Robertson, R. J., & Fiske, D. W. Length of therapy in relation to outcome and change in personal integration. *Journal of Consulting Psychology*, 1961, *25*, 84–88.

Klein, G. A clinical perspective for personality research. *Journal of Abnormal and Social Psychology*, 1949, *44*, 42–50.

Klein, H. A study of changes occurring in patients during and after psychoanalytic treatment. In P. H. Hoch and J. Zubin (Eds.), *Current approaches to psychoanalysis: Proceedings of the 48th annual meeting of the American Psychopathological Association*. New York: Grune & Stratton, 1960, pp. 151–175.

Klein, H. *Psychoanalysts in training: Selection and evaluation*. New York: Columbia University College of Physicians and Surgeons, 1965, p. 82 ff.

Klein, M., Mathieu, P. L., Gendlin, E. T., & Kiesler, D. J.

The experiencing scale: A research and training manual. Madison: University of Wisconsin (Bureau of Audio-Visual Instruction), 1970.

Kline, P. *Fact and fantasy in Freudian theory*. London: Methuen, 1972.

Knapp, P. H. Short-term psychoanalytic and psychosomatic predictions. *Journal of the American Psychoanalytic Association*, 1963, *11*, 245–280.

Knapp, P. H., Levin, S., McCarter, R. H., Wermer, H., & Zetzel, E. Suitability for psychoanalysis: A review of 100 supervised analytic cases. *Psychoanalytic Quarterly*, 1960, *29*, 459–477.

Knight, R. P. Evaluation of the results of psychoanalytic therapy. *American Journal of Psychiatry*, 1941, *98*, 434–446.

Kris, E. The nature of psychoanalytic propositions and their validation. In S. Hook and M. Konwitz (Eds.), *Freedom and experience*. Ithaca: Cornell University Press, 1947.

Kubie, L. Problems and techniques of psychoanalytic validation and progress. In E. Pumpian-Mindlin (Ed.), *Psychoanalysis as science*. Stanford: Stanford University Press, 1952, pp. 74–89.

Lorand, S., & Console, W. A. Therapeutic results in psychoanalytic treatment without fee. *International Journal of Psychoanalysis*, 1958, *39*, 59–64.

Lower, R., Escoll, P., Little R., & Ottenberg, B. P. An experimental examination of transference. *Archives of General Psychiatry*, 1973, *29*, 738–741.

Luborsky, L. Repeated intra-individual measurements *(P technique)* in understanding symptom structure and psychotherapeutic change. In O. H. Mowrer (Ed.), *Psychotherapy: theory and research*. New York: Ronald Press, 1953, Chapter 14.

Luborsky, L. A note an Eysenck's article, "The effects of psychotherapy: An evaluation." *British Journal of Psychology*, 1954, *45*, 129–131.

Luborsky, L. Clinicians' judgments of mental health: A proposed scale. *Archives of General Psychiatry*, 1962a, *7*, 407–417.

Luborsky, L. The patient's personality and psychotherapeutic change. In H. Strupp and L. Luborsky (Eds.), *Research in psychotherapy*. Vol. 2. Washington, D. C.: American Psychological Association, 1962b, pp. 115–133.

Luborsky, L. A psychoanalytic research on momentary forgetting during free association. *Bulletin of the Philadelphia Association for Psychoanalysis*, 1964, *14*, 119–137.

Luborsky, L. Momentary forgetting during psychotherapy and psychoanalysis: A theory and research method. In R. R. Holt (Ed.), *Motives and thought: Psychoanalytic essays in honor of David Rapaport. Psychological Issues*, 5, Nos. 2–3, Monograph 18/19, 1967, pp. 177–217.

Luborsky, L. Research cannot yet influence clinical practice. (An evaluation of Strupp and Bergin's "Some empirical and conceptual bases for coordinated research in psychotherapy: A critical review of issues, trends, and evidence.") *International Journal of Psychiatry*, 1969, 7 (3), 135–140.

Luborksy, L. Forgetting and remembering (momentary forgetting) during psychotherapy: A new sample. In M. Mayman (Ed.), *Psychoanalytic Research: Three* approaches to the experimental study of subliminal processes. *Psychological issues, 8,* No. 2, Monograph 30, 1973, pp. 29–55.

Luborsky, L. The Health-Sickness Rating Scale: Sample cases and rating forms. *Bulletin of the Menninger Clinic, 1975, 35,* 448–480.

Luborsky, L. Helping alliances in psychotherapy: The groundwork for a study of their relationship to its outcome. In J. L. Claghorn (Ed.), *Successful psychotherapy.* New York: Brunner/Mazel, 1976, pp. 92–111.

Luborsky, L. Measuring a pervasive psychic structure in psychotherapy: The core conflictual relationship theme. In N. Freedman (Ed.), *Communicative structures and psychic structures.* New York: Plenum Press, 1977a.

Luborsky, L. Curative factors in psychoanalytic and psychodynamic psychotherapies. In J. P. Brady, J. Mendels, M. Orne, and W. Rieger (Eds.), *Psychiatry: Areas of promise and advancement.* New York: Spectrum, 1977b

Luborsky, L., & Auerbach, A. H. The symptom-context method: Quantitative studies of symptom formation in psychotherapy. *Journal of the American Psychoanalytic Association,* 1969, *17,* 68–99.

Luborsky, L., & Bachrach, H. Factors influencing clinicians' judgments of mental health: Eighteen experiences with the Health-Sickness Rating Scale. *Archives of General Psychiatry, 1974, 31,* 292–299.

Luborsky, L., Bachrach, H., Graff, H., Pulver, S., & Christoph, P. Preconditions and consequences of transference interpretations: A clinical-quantitative investigation. (In preparation).

Luborsky, L., Chandler, M., Auerbach, A. H., Cohen, J., & Bachrach, H. M. Factors influencing the outcome of psychotherapy: A review of quantitative research. *Psychological Bulletin, 1971, 75,* 145–185.

Luborsky, L., Crabtree, L., Curtis, H., Ruff, G., & Mintz, J. The concept "space" of transference for eight psychoanalysts. *British Journal Med. Psychology,* 1975a, *48,* 65–70.

Luborsky, L., Docherty, J., Todd, T., Knapp, P., Mirsky, A., & Gottschalk, L. A context analysis of psychological states prior to petit-mal seizures. *Journal of Nervous and Mental Disease, 160,* 1975b, 282–298.

Luborsky, L., Fabian, M., Hall, B. H., Ticho, E., & Ticho, G. Treatment variables. *Bulletin of the Menninger Clinic, 1958, 22,* 126–147.

Luborsky, L., Graff, H., Pulver, S., & Curtis, H. A clinical-quantitative examination of consensus on the concept of transference. *Archives of General Psychiatry, 1973, 29,* 69–75.

Luborsky, L., & Mintz, J. What sets off momentary forgetting during a psychoanalysis? Methods of investigating symptom-onset conditions. In L. Goldberger and V. Rosen (Eds.), *Psychoanalysis and contemporary Science.* Vol. 3. International Universities Press, 1975c, pp. 233–268.

Luborsky, L., Mintz, J., Auerbach, A. H., & associates. Are outcomes of psychotherapy predictable?—Results of the Penn Psychotherapy Project. (In preparation).

Luborsky, L., Mintz, J., & associates. *Psychotherapy:*

Who Benefits and How? (Book in preparation).

Luborsky, L., Sackeim, H., & Christoph, P. The state conducive to momentary forgetting, In J. Kihlstrom and E. J. Evans (Eds.), *Functional disorders of memory.* Lawrence Erlbaum Assoc., in press, 1977.

Luborsky, L., & Schimek, J. Psychoanalytic theories of therapeutic and developmental change: Implications for assessment. In P. Worchel and D. Byrne (Eds.), *Personality change.* New York: Wiley, 1964, pp. 73–99.

Luborsky, L., Singer, B., & Hartke, J. Shifts in depressive mood during psychotherapy: Which concepts of depression fit the context of Mr. Q's shifts? (In preparation.)

Luborsky, L., Singer, B., & Luborsky, L. Comparative studies of psychotherapies: Is it true that "Everybody has won and all must have prizes?" *Archives of General Psychiatry,* 1975d, *32,* 995–1008.

Lustman, S. L. Some issues in contemporary psychoanalytic research. *The psychoanalytic study of the child, 1963, 18,* 51–74.

MacKinnon, D. & Dukes, W. F. Repression. In L. Postman (Ed.), *Psychology in the making.* New York: Knopf, 1962, pp. 662–744.

Madison, P. Freud's repression concept. *International Journal of Psychoanalysis, 1956, 37,* 75–81.

Mahl, G. F. Disturbances and silences in patient's speech in psychotherapy. *Journal of Abnormal and Social Psychology, 1956, 53,* 1–15.

Mahl, G. F. Exploring emotional states by content analysis. In I. de S. Pool (Ed.), *Trends in content analysis.* Urbana: University of Illinois Press, 1959, 89–130.

Malan, D. *Towards the Validation of a Dynamic Psychotherapy.* New York: Plenum Press, 1976.

Meehl, P. E. Some methodological reflections on the difficulties of psychoanalytic research. In M. Mayman (Ed.), *Psychological Issues, 8,* Monograph 30, 1973, pp. 104–117.

Merrill, R. M. On Keet's study, "Two verbal techniques in a miniature counseling situation." *Journal of Abnormal and Social Psychology,* 1952, *47,* 722.

Mintz, J., Auerbach, A., Luborsky, L., & Johnson, M. Patient's, therapist's, and observers' views of psychotherapy: A "Rashomon" experience or a reasonable consensus? *British Journal of Medical Psychology, 1973, 46,* 83–89.

Mintz, J., & Luborsky, L. *P-technique* factor analysis in psychotherapy research: An illustration of a method. *Psychotherapy, 1970, 7,* 13–18.

Mintz, J., Luborsky, L., & Auerbach, A. H. Dimensions of psychotherapy: A factor analytic study of ratings of psychotherapy sessions. *Journal of Consulting and Clinical Psychology, 1971, 36,* 106–120.

Mitchell, K., Bozarth, J., Truax, C., & Krauft, C. Antecedents to psychotherapeutic change. An NIMH Final Report, MH 12306, March 1973.

Mowrer, O., Hunt, J. McV., & Kogan, L. Further studies utilizing the discomfort-relief quotient. In O. H. Mowrer (Ed.), *Psychotherapy: Theory and Research.* New York: Ronald Press, 1953, pp. 257–295.

Norman, H. P., Blacker, K. H., Oremland, J. D., & Barrett, W. G. The fate of the transference neurosis after termination of a satisfactory analysis. *Journal of the American Psychoanalytic Association,* 1976, *24,* 471–498.

Nunberg, H. Evaluation of the results of psychoanalytic treatment. *International Journal of Psychoanalysis,* 1954, *35,* 2–7.

Oberndorft, C. P. Unsatisfactory results of psychoanalytic therapy. *Psychoanalytic Quarterly,* 1950, *19,* 393–407.

Oberndorf, C. P. Results to be effected with psychoanalysis. *AMA Archives of Neurology and Psychiatry,* 1953, *69,* 655 (Society Transactions).

Parloff, M. Analytic group psychotherapy. In J. Marmor (Ed.), *Modern Psychoanalysis.* New York: Basic Books, 1968, pp. 492–531.

Paul, I. A., & Gill, M. M. Responses to exact and inexact interpretations. (Unpublished paper.)

Peterfreund, E., & Schwartz, J. Information Systems and Psychoanalysis: An Evolutionary Biological Approach to Psychoanalysis. *Psychological Issues, 7,* Monograph 25 and 26, 1971.

Pfeffer, A. Z. A procedure for evaluating the results of psychoanalysis: A preliminary report. *Journal of the American Psychoanalytic Association,* 1959, *7,* 418–444.

Pfeffer, A. Z. Panel report: Research in psychoanalysis. *Journal of the American Psychoanalytic Association,* 1961, *9,* 562–570.

Pfeffer, A. Z. Follow-up study of a satisfactory analysis. *Journal of the American Psychoanalytic Association,* 1961, *9,* 698–718.

Pfeffer, A. Z. The meaning of the analyst after analysis—a contribution to the theory of therapeutic results. *Journal of the American Psychoanalytic Association,* 1963, *11,* 229–244.

Pumpian-Mindlin, E. The position of psychoanalysis in relation to the biological and social sciences. In E. Pumpian-Mindlin (Ed.), *Psychoanalysis as science.* Stanford: Stanford University Press, 1952, pp. 125–158.

Ramzy, I. Research aspects of psychoanalysis. *Psychoanalytic Quarterly,* 1963, *32,* 58–76.

Rand, C., & Stunkard, A. J. Psychoanalysis and obesity. *Journal of American Academy of Psychoanalysis,* 1977, *5,* 459–499.

Rapaport, D. The structure of psychoanalytic theory—A systematizing attempt. In S. Koch (Ed.), *Psychology: A Study of a Science,* Vol. 3. New York: McGraw-Hill, 1959, pp. 55–183.

Rapoport, A. Psychoanalysis as science. *Bulletin of the Menninger Clinic,* 1968, *32,* 1–20.

Raskin, N. J. The psychotherapy research project of the American Academy of Psychotherapists. *American Psychologist,* 1965, *20,* 547 (Abstract).

Rogers, C. R. A tentative scale for the measurement of process in psychotherapy. In L. Rubinstein and M. Parloff (Eds.), *Research in psychotherapy.* Vol. 1. Washington, D. C.: American Psychological Association, 1959, pp. 96–107.

Rogers, C. R., Gendlin, E. T., Kiesler, D. J., & Truax, C. B. *The therapeutic relationship and its impact: A study of psychotherapy with schizophrenics.* Madison: University of Wisconsin Press, 1967, p. 555 ff.

Rosenzweig, S. A transvaluation of psychotherapy—a reply to Hans Eysenck. *Journal of Abnormal and Social Psychology,* 1954, *49,* 298–304.

Sackeim, H., & Gur, R. Self-deception, self-confrontation, and consciousness. In G. E. Schwartz and D. Shapiro (Eds.), *Consciousness and Self-Regulation, Advances in Research.* Vol. II. New York: Plenum Press, 1978.

Sampson, H. A critique of certain traditional concepts in the psychoanalytic theory of therapy. *Bulletin of the Menninger Clinic,* 1976, *40,* 255–262. ·

Sampson, H., & Wallerstein, R. S. New research directions: Comment from a psychoanalytic perspective. In H. Strupp and A. E. Bergin (Eds.), *Changing frontiers in the science of psychotherapy.* Chicago: Aldine-Atherton, 1972, pp. 444–446.

Sampson, H., Weiss, J., Mlodnosky, L., & Hause, E. Defense analysis and the emergence of warded-off mental contents: An empirical study. *Archives of General Psychiatry,* 1972, *26,* 524–532.

Sandler, J. Research in psychoanalysis. The Hampstead Clinic as an instrument of psychoanalytic research. *International Journal of Psychoanalysis,* 1962, *43,* 287–291.

Sargent, H. D. Intrapsychic change: Methodological problems in psychotherapy research. *Psychiatry,* 1961, *24,* 93–108.

Sargent, H. D., Horwitz, L., Wallerstein, R., & Appelbaum, A. Prediction in psychotherapy research: A method for the transformation of clinical judgments into testable hypotheses. *Psychological Issues, 4,* No. 1, Monograph 21, 1968.

Sashin, J., Eldred, S., & VanAmerongen, S. A search for predictive factors in institute supervised cases: A retrospective study of 183 cases from 1959–1966 at the Boston Psychonanalytic Society and Institute. *International Journal of Psychoanalysis,* 1975, *56,* 343–359.

Schafer, R. Generative empathy in the treatment situation. *Psychoanalytic Quarterly,* 1959, *28,* 342–373.

Schafer, R. *A new language for psychoanalysis.* New Haven: Yale University Press, 1976.

Schjelderup, H. Lasting effects of psychoanalytic treatment. *Psychiatry,* 1955, *18,* 109–133.

Schlessinger, N., Pollock, G. H., Sabshin, M., Sadow, L., & Gedo, J. E. Psychoanalytic contributions to psychotherapy research. In L. A. Gottschalk and A. H. Auerbach (Eds.), *Methods of research in psychotherapy.* New York: Appleton-Century-Crofts, 1966, pp. 334–360.

Schlessinger, N., & Robbins, F. Assessment and follow-up in psychoanalysis. *Journal of the American Psychoanalytic Association,* 1974, *22,* 542–567.

Schlessinger, N., & Robbins, F. The psychoanalytic process: Recurrent patterns of conflict and changes in ego. *Journal of the American Psychoanalytic Association,* 1975, *23,* 761–782.

Sears, R. R. *Survey of objective studies of psychoanalytic concepts.* New York: Social Science Research Council, 1943a.

Sears, R. R. Experimental analyses of psychoanalytic phenomena. In J. McV. Hunt (Ed.), *Fundamentals of personality and behavior disorders.* New York: Ronald Press, 1943b.

Seitz, P. F. D. The consensus problem in psychoanalytic research. In L. A. Gottschalk and A. H. Auerbach (Eds.), *Methods of research in psychotherapy.* New York: Appleton-Century-Crofts, 1966, pp. 209–225.

Shakow, D. The recorded psychoanalytic interview as an objective approach in research psychoanalysis. *Psychoanalytic Quarterly,* 1960, *29,* 82–97.

Sherman, M. Peripheral cues and the invisible counter-transference. *American Journal of Psychotherapy,* 1965, *19,* 280–292.

Shlien, J., Mosak, H., & Dreikurs, R. Effective time limits: A comparison of client-centered and Adlerian psychotherapy. *American Psychologist,* 1960, *15,* 415 (Abstract).

Silberschatz, G. The effects of the analyst's neutrality on the patient's feelings and behavior in the psychoanalytic situation. Doctoral Dissertation, New York University, 1977.

Simon, J., Fink, G., & Endicott, N. A. *Journal of the Hillside Hospital, 16,* Nos. 3 and 4, 1967.

Singer, B., & Luborsky, L. Countertransference: The status of clinical vs. quantitative research. In A. Gurman and A. Razin (Eds.) *Effective Psychotherapy: A Handbook of Research.* New York: Pergamon, 1978.

Sklansky, M. A., Isaacs, K. S., Lovitov, E. S., & Haggard, E. A. Verbal interaction and levels of meaning in psychotherapy. *Archives of General Psychiatry,* 1966, *14,* 158–170.

Speisman, J. Depth of interpretation and verbal resistance in psychotherapy. *Journal of Consulting Psychology,* 1959, *23,* 93–99.

Spence, D. P. (Ed.), *The broad scope of psychoanalysis—selected papers of Leopold Bellak.* New York: Grune & Stratton, 1967.

Spence, D. P. PL/1 programs for content analysis. *Behavioral Science,* 1969a, *14,* 432–433.

Spence, D. P. Computer measurement of process and content in psychoanalysis. *Transactions of the New York Academy of Science,* 1969b, *31,* 828–841.

Spence, D. P. Tracing a thought stream by computer. In B. B. Rubinstein (Ed.), *Psychoanalysis and contemporary science,* Vol. II. New York: Macmillan, 1973.

Spence, D. P., & Greif, B. An experimental study of listening between the lines. *Journal of Nervous and Mental Disease,* 1970, *151,* 179–186.

Spence, D. P., & Lugo, M. The role of verbal clues in clinical listening. In R. R. Holt and E. Peterfreund (Eds.), *Psychoanalysis and contemporary science,* Vol. 1. New York: International Universities Press, 1972.

Stone, J. P., Dunphy, D. C., Smith, M. S., & Ogilvie, D. M. *The general inquirer.* Cambridge: M.I.T. Press, 1966.

Strupp, H. H. Psychotherapeutic technique, professional affiliation, and experience level. *Journal of Consulting Psychology,* 1955, *19,* 97–102.

Strupp, H. H. *Psychotherapists in action: Exploration of the therapist's contribution to the treatment process.* New York: Grune & Stratton, 1960.

Strupp, H. H. Psychotherapy revisited: The problem of outcome. *Psychotherapy,* 1963, *1,* 1–13.

Strupp, H. H. Psychoanalytic therapy of the individual. In

J. Marmor (Ed.), *Modern psychoanalysis: New direction and perspectives.* New York: Basic Books, 1968, pp. 293–342.

Tomlinson, T. M. The therapeutic process as related to outcome. In C. R. Rogers (Ed.), *The therapeutic relationship and its impact.* Madison: University of Wisconsin Press, 1967.

Tomlinson, T. M., & Hart, J. T. A validation of the process scale. *Journal of Consulting Psychology,* 1962, *26,* 74–78.

Truax, C. B. A scale for the measurement of accurate empathy. *Psychiatric Institute Bulletin, Wisconsin Psychiatric Institute, University of Wisconsin,* 1961, *1,* No. 12.

Truax, C. B. Effective ingredients in psychotherapy: An approach to unravelling the patient-therapist interaction. *Journal of Counseling Psychology,* 1963, *3,* 256–263.

Truax, C. B. Influence of patient-statements on judgments of therapist-statements during psychotherapy. *Journal of Clinical Psychology,* 1966, *22,* 335–337.

Truax, C. B., & Carkhuff, R. R. *Toward effective counseling in psychotherapy.* Chicago: Aldine, 1967.

Truax, C. B., Wargo, D. G., Frank, J. D., Imber, S. D., Battle, C. C., Hoehn-Saric, R., Nash, E., & Stone, A. Therapist empathy, genuineness, and warmth and patient therapeutic outcome. *Journal of Consulting Psychology,* 1966, *30,* 394–401.

Voth, H., & Orth, M. *Psychotherapy and the role of the environment.* New York: Behavioral Publications, 1973, pp. 1–354.

Wachtel, P. *Psychoanalysis and behavior therapy.* New York: Basic Books, Inc., 1977.

Waelder, R. Psychoanalysis, scientific method and philosophy. *Journal of the American Psychoanalytic Association,* 1962, *10,* 617–637.

Walker, A., Rablen, R. A., & Rogers, C. R. Development of a scale to measure process change in psychotherapy. *Journal of Clinical Psychology,* 1966, *16,* 183–225.

Wallerstein, R. The current state of psychotherapy: Theory, practice, and research. *Journal of the American Psychoanalytic Association,* 1966, *14,* 183–225.

Wallerstein, R., Robbins, L., Sargent, H., & Luborsky, L. The psychotherapy research project of the Menninger Foundation. *Bulletin of the Menninger Clinic,* 1956, *20,* 221–280.

Wallerstein, R. S., & Sampson, H. Issues in research in the psychoanalytic process. *International Journal of Psychoanalysis,* 1971, *52,* 11–50.

Weber, J., Elinson, J., & Moss, L. M. The application of electronic machine techniques to psychoanalytic clinic records. Reprinted from *Excerpta Medica, International Congress Series* #150: Proceedings of the World Congress of Psychiatry, Madrid, Sept. 1966, pp. 2317–2320.

Weintraub, W., & Aronson, H. The application of verbal behavior analysis to the study of psychological defense mechanisms: Methodology and preliminary report. *Journal of Nervous and Mental Disease,* 1963, *134,* 169–181.

Weintraub, W., & Aronson, H. The application of verbal

behavior analysis to the study of psychological defense mechanisms. II. Speech pattern associated
with impulsive behavior. *Journal of Nervous and
Mental Disease,* 1964, *139,* 75–82.

Weintraub, W., & Aronson, H. The application of verbal
behavior analysis to the study of psychological defense mechanisms. III. Speech pattern associated
with delusional behavior. *Journal of Nervous and
Mental Disease,* 1965, *141,* 172–179.

Weintraub, W., & Aronson, H. The application of verbal
behavior analysis to the study of psychological defense mechanisms. IV. Speech pattern associated
with depressive behavior. *Journal of Nervous and
Mental Disease,* 1967, *144,* 22–28.

Weintraub, W., & Aronson, H. A survey of patients in
classical psychoanalysis: Some vital statistics. *Journal of Nervous and Mental Disease,* 1968, *146,*
98–102.

Weintraub, W., & Aronson, H. Application of verbal behavior analysis to the study of psychological defense
mechanisms. V. Speech pattern associated with
overeating. *Archives of General Psychiatry,* 1969,
21, 739–744.

Weintraub, W., & Aronson, H. Verbal behavior analysis
and psychological defense mechanisms. VI. Speech
pattern associated with compulsive behavior. *Archives of General Psychiatry,* 1974, *30,* 297–300.

Weiss, J. The integration of defenses. *International Journal of Psychoanalysis,* 1967, *48,* 520–524.

Weiss, J. The emergence of new themes: A contribution
to the psycho-analytic theory of therapy. *International Journal of Psychoanalysis,* 1971, *52,*
459–467.

Wolfson, A., & Sampson, H. A comparison of process-
notes and tape recordings: Implications for therapy
research. *Archives of General Psychiatry,* 1976, *33,*
558–563.

10

THE PLACEBO EFFECT IN MEDICAL AND PSYCHOLOGICAL THERAPIES

ARTHUR K. SHAPIRO

The Mount Sinai School of Medicine

LOUIS A. MORRIS

Food and Drug Administration

INTRODUCTION

Placebo effect research provides both an historic and methodological perspective of psychotherapy and behavior change. Psychotherapy is commonly believed to be a modern treatment based on scientific principles while the placebo effect is believed to be a superstitious response to a sugar pill. Yet, the placebo effect may have greater implications for psychotherapy than any other form of treatment because both psychotherapy and the placebo effect function primarily through psychological mechanisms.

The concept of the placebo effect is generally

This article was written in part by Louis Morris in his private capacity. No official support or endorsement by the Food and Drug Administration is intended or should be inferred.

not popular among therapists and researchers. Physicians tend to deny their own use of placebos and assume that other physicians use placebos more often than themselves (Hofling, 1955; Shapiro & Struening, 1974). In research, placebo effects are viewed as experimental artifacts (McGuire, 1969). These artifacts are ignored or are sought to be controlled or eliminated from ongoing research. Very rarely does the placebo effect undergo empirical scrutiny as a research topic in its own right.

However, the placebo effect is an important component and perhaps the entire basis for the existence, popularity, and effectiveness of numerous methods of psychotherapy. The thesis of this chapter is that much can be learned about psychotherapy from study of the placebo effect. Attention to the placebo effect may help differentiate the meaningful specific influences from the nonspecific factors in psychotherapy. A true understanding of the specific components of psychotherapy can only occur when the components of the placebo effect are also understood (Gliedman, Nash, Imber, Stone, & Frank, 1958).

These considerations led to the search for generalizations and hypotheses about all methods of therapy. Although various mechanisms and processes have been proposed as explanations of the placebo effect, empirical support for an adequate theory is absent. Hypotheses and conclusions about psychotherapy and the placebo effect will be derived from review of prescientific and modern treatment, and the placebogenic factors contributed by the patient, situation, physician, and their interrelationships. Selected theoretical concepts, drawn primarily from the social, clinical, and experimental psychological literature, will be utilized to explain placebo effects. Only those concepts that can be applied to psychotherapy and behavior change will be focused on in this review.

PRESCIENTIFIC MEDICINE

Psychological factors, always important in medicine, were recognized as early as the period of Hipprocrates. Galen estimated that 60 percent of patients had symptoms of emotional rather than physical origin. This figure is close to the contemporary estimate of 50 to 80 percent. Despite Galen's and Hippocrates' acumen, few if any of the drugs used by the physicians of their day caused pharmacologically induced therapeutic change. Treatment was primitive, unscientific, largely ineffective, and often shocking and dangerous (Shapiro, 1959, 1960a).

Patients took almost every known organic and inorganic substance—crocodile dung, teeth of swine, hooves of asses, spermatic fluid of frogs, eunuch fat, fly specks, lozenges of dried vipers, powder of precious stones, bricks, furs, feathers, hair, human perspiration, oil of ants, earthworms, wolves, spiders, moss scraped from the skull of a victim of violent death, and so on. Blood from every animal was prepared and administered in every way, and was used to treat every conceivable

symptom and disease. Almost all human and animal excretions were used.

Some famous treatments used for centuries include the Royal Touch, Egyptian mummy, unicorn horn, bezoar stone, and mandrake. Theriac contained 37 to 63 ingredients; mattioli contained 230 ingredients and required several months to concoct. Galen's elaborate pharmacopoeia, all worthless, contained 820 substances. Medical reasoning was primitive: Lung of fox, a long-winded animal, was given to consumptives. Fat of bear, a hirsute animal, was prescribed for baldness. Mistletoe, a plant that grows on the oak that cannot fall, was specific for the falling sickness (Lehmann & Knight, 1961). A wound was treated by sympathetic powder that was applied to the inflicting implement. Throughout medical history patients were purged, puked, poisoned, punctured, cut, cupped, blistered, bled, leached, heated, frozen, sweated, and shocked (Garrison, 1921; Haggard, 1929, 1933, 1934; Major, 1955; Shapiro, 1959, 1960a).

Although medicine has held a place in the finest scientific, religious, cultural, and ethical traditions throughout history, one may wonder how physicians maintained their position of honor and respect. Useful drugs or procedures were applied infrequently and were usually forgotten by succeeding generations. For thousands of years physicians prescribed what we now know were useless and often dangerous medications. This would have been impossible were it not for the fact that physicians did help their patients.

Today we know that the effectiveness of these procedures and medications was due to psychological factors often referred to as the placebo effect. Since almost all medications until recently were placebos, the history of medical treatment can be characterized largely as the history of the placebo effect.

The first major contribution to the end of Galenism and to the beginning of scientific medical treatment is often attributed to Sydenham in the seventeenth century. He is erroneously credited with demonstrating that cinchona bark (which contains quinine) was specific only for fevers of malarial origin, and not for all febrile infections (Duran-Reynals, 1946; Forrer, 1964a). Cinchona bark often has been thought of as the first drug that was not a placebo, because previously there had been no way to distinguish between placebo and nonplacebo. But the placebo effect flourished as the norm of medical treatment even after the beginning of modern scientific medicine seven or eight decades ago (Shapiro, 1959, 1960a).

These considerations have led to the famous admonition: *Treat as many patients as possible with the new remedies while they still have the power to heal.*

DEFINITION OF PLACEBO

The history of the placebo begins with the Hebrew Bible. The first word of Psalm 166:9 is "Ethalech," which was translated into the Latin Bible as "placebo." The word "placebo" is derived from the verb "placere," meaning "to please" (Murray, 1933). "Placebo" entered the English language in the twelfth century by becoming the name commonly given to vespers for the dead, a custom that is no longer followed and whose meaning is now obscure (*The Catholic Encyclopedia,* 1911).

"Placebo" took on a secular meaning in the fourteenth century and its connotations gradually became derisive during the next several centuries. The word was used to describe a servile flatterer, sycophant, toady, and parasite. The usage derives from disparagement of the professional mourners who were paid to "sing placebos" at the bier of the deceased, a role originally assigned to the family.

Few people realize that medical dictionaries have limited their definitions of the placebo to inert or inactive drugs only during the last three decades (Blakiston's *New Gould Medical Dictionary,* 1949). The original that appeared in the 1785 edition of *Motherby's New Medical Dictionary* (1795) was: "A commonplace method or medicine."

This original definition was misquoted as a "commonplace method *of* medicine." This error in the etymology of placebo has influenced the meaning attributed to the word. The distinction between "of" or "or" is important, since the former limits the definition to medicine, whereas the latter includes methods *and* medicines. Although the original definition included all therapies, as drugs be-

came more important in medical theory and practice, the term became limited to pharmacologic interventions. This continued until 1949 when medical dictionaries, partly owing to their perpetuation of early errors, began to limit the definition to inert substances. Such interpretation has influenced the thinking of many physicians and nonphysicians, who conceive of placebos only as inert drugs. Recently, as treatments have changed and psychotherapy has become more prominent, definitions of placebo have expanded and now are more like the original definition that appeared in 1785.

Our proposed definition, which we believe fulfills historic and heuristic criteria, follows:

A *placebo* is defined as any therapy or component of therapy that is deliberately used for its nonspecific, psychological, or psychophysiological effect, or that is used for its presumed specific effect, but is without specific activity for the condition being treated.

A *placebo,* when used as a control in experimental studies, is defined as a substance or procedure that is without specific activity for the condition being evaluated.

The *placebo effect* is defined as the psychological or psychophysiological effect produced by placebos.

There are several important features of this definition. There are no assumptions made about the intent of the therapist to issue placebo therapy. The therapist may knowingly give placebo treatment. Conversely, he or she may administer placebos in the belief that they are specific and active but by *objective evaluation* the therapy does not have specific activity for the condition under treatment. There are also no assumptions made about the effects of therapy. Placebos may have positive, negative, or no effect. Placebos may or may not induce side effects.

Implicit in this definition is the assumption that active treatments may contain placebo components. Even with specific therapies results are apt to be due to the combination of both placebo and nonplacebo effects. Treatments that are devoid of active, specific components are known as pure placebos, whereas therapies that contain nonplacebo components are called impure placebos (Leslie, 1954). Treatments that have specific components but exert their effects primarily through nonspecific mechanisms are considered placebo therapies. The relative contribution of placebo components in any therapeutic process is likely to decrease as more becomes known about the cause and cure of the condition, and as therapies more directly and specifically affect the maladaptive or disease entity.

The key concept in defining placebo is that of "specific activity." In nonpsychological therapies, specific activity is often equated with nonpsychological mechanisms of action. When the specific activity of a treatment is psychological, this method of separating specific from nonspecific activity is no longer applicable. Therefore, a more general definition of specific activity is necessary. Specific activity is the therapeutic influence attributable solely to the contents or processes of the therapies rendered. The criterion for specific activity (and therefore the placebo effect) should be based on scientifically controlled studies. In behavior therapy, some investigators have utilized "active placebo" control groups whereby some aspects of the therapy affect behavior but those aspects differ from the theoretically relevant ingredients of concern to the investigator (Kazdin & Wilcoxon, 1976).

This definition does not mention the mechanism of placebo action, although it implies that psychological factors are important determinants. The placebo effect is a multidetermined phenomenon influenced by many different factors and processes. Some of these factors are considered in subsequent sections. However, the issue is left open in our current definition because placebogenic factors are not yet well understood or documented.

Although this definition may prove to be too inclusive, for heuristic reasons it would be premature to make specific exclusions at this time. It is likely that various placebogenic factors will be isolated in the future. When enough is known about the placebo effect so that its effects can be predicted, the definition will no longer be needed, except in lexicons of obsolete terms. This is something to consider for the future.

MODERN MEDICINE

Modern medicine no longer relies chiefly on placebo effects. Today, there are an increasing number of specific and predictable drugs, devices, and procedures. However, as long as individuals are aware that they are receiving treatment, psychological factors cannot be excluded. Of course, if the dosage of a drug is high enough all patients will react with toxicity and even death, regardless of psychological factors. However, the predictability of toxicity is of little consequence because toxic dosages are rarely prescribed. Normal dosages are within the range in which placebo effects are important.

Claims about the importance of placebo effect to modern medicine range from ". . . the most effective [drug] . . . to be developed by the pharmaceutical laboratories . . ." (Zimbardo, 1969) to ". . . they are small treatments for small illnesses . . ." (Hamilton, 1968). Although, placebo effects are more prominent with certain conditions and treatments than others, the placebo effect remains an important element in modern medicine. Placebo effects have been demonstrated in dentistry (Shipman, Greene, & Laskin, 1974; Valins, Adelson, Weiner, & Goldstein, 1971), podiatry (Morris, Shangold, & Greenberg, 1975), optometry (Carter & Allen, 1973) and in every aspect of modern medical treatment including biofeedback (Miller, 1974; Stroebel & Glueck, 1973), acupuncture (Chaves & Barber, 1973; Gaw, Chang, & Shaw, 1975; Kroger, 1973), cancer treatment (Klopfer, 1957), surgery (Diamond, Kittle, & Crockett, 1960), and electroconvulsive therapy (ECT) (Guido & Jones, 1961; Marshall & Izard, 1974). Placebos have been demonstrated to be addictive (Vinar, 1960), to mimic the effects of active drugs (Lasagna, Laties, & Dohan, 1958), to reverse the action of potent drugs (Hagens, Doering, Ashley, Clarke, & Wolf, 1957; Wolf, 1959), and to have direct effects on bodily organs (Sternbach, 1964; Wolf, 1950) and on organic illnesses (Shapiro, 1963).

Recent interest in the placebo effect of medical treatment has also fostered the development of clinical methodology to control placebo effects in therapeutic studies. General appreciation of the placebo influence is perhaps the main reason for the growth and acceptance of controlled clinical studies. In psychotherapy research, the placebo has become synonymous with the search for the appropriate control group against which therapies are compared.[1]

PROBLEMS OF RESEARCH

In reviewing placebo effect research, one is struck by the conflicting findings and failure to replicate. These inconsistent results occur partly because of the diversity of subject populations (ranging from college students to clinic patients to subhuman species), testing environments (from experimental laboratories to hospital clinics), degree and types of illnesses (from normals to organically ill to maladjusted), range of treatments (from surgery to biofeedback) and methods of measurement (from subjective self report measures to objective indicies of physiological change).

However, replication is infrequent even when seemingly identical procedures are used on highly similar populations (Bootzin, Herman, & Nicassco, 1976; Storms & Nisbett, 1970; Kellogg & Baron, 1975; Lipman, 1966). When the same subjects are given identical placebo stimuli in different environments, the response is inconsistent (Wolf, Doering, Clark, & Hagans, 1957; Liberman, 1964; Frank, 1968). The inconsistency of reaction could lead to the conclusion that the placebo effect is a random factor. A more likely conclusion, however, is that the placebo effect is not caused by a unitary process. Placebo effects are probably the result of a complex combination of many different variables and modes of action.

Identification and integration of all the different variables and processes affecting placebo reaction will await many more years of investigation. However, as placebo processes become identified and explained, they also gain the potential to become nonplacebo therapies. For example, operant con-

ditioning, which may be a basis of the placebo effect, is now itself used as a specific therapeutic tool.

Unfortunately, explanations for the placebo effect are more often the result of ex post facto theorizing than empirical study. It is noteworthy that the recent motivation prompting interest in the placebo effect is the desire to improve research methodology (Honigfeld, 1964a, 1964b). The main methodological tenet from placebo effect research is that comparisons cannot be made in a vacuum. The only "facts" are derived on a relative basis and valid judgments about the effectiveness of any therapy can be made only by comparison to the appropriate control group (Boring, 1968).

Much of the theorizing about the placebo effect is based on the responses of control groups that were retrospectively interpreted but rarely tested prospectively. Explanations are more often based on the theories of the investigator than on study results. However, empirical study has suggested different variables and processes of placebo action. The contribution of any single element will likely depend on a multitude of factors. Variables that have not received full empirical confirmation cannot be dismissed at the present time, because if they were, there would be little left to report.

PATIENT VARIABLES

The Placebo Reactor

Although retrospective analyses indicate that the placebo effect was the cause of the success of many medical treatments, it is only since the middle 1950s that the placebo effect has become a research topic in its own right (Shapiro, 1960a). The observation that some subjects reacted to placebos while others did not fostered the hypothesis that reaction to placebos was an enduring patient characteristic.

There are two important features of the placebo reactor hypothesis. First, to validate this assumption, there must be a consistency of reaction across several placebo administrations. This is necessary to demonstrate that some enduring trait of the individual receiving treatment, rather than a transient factor, causes the placebo reaction. Second, if placebo reaction is an enduring characteristic of the individual receiving therapy, demographic and

[1]Borkovec; 1973; Borkovec & Nau, 1972; Boudewyns & Borkovec; 1974; Cutela, Flannery, & Hanley, 1974; Foreyt & Hagen, 1973; Haynes, Woodward, Moran & Alexander, 1974; Marshall, Boutilier, & Minnes, 1974; McReynolds, Barnes, Brooks, & Rehagen, 1973; Nau, Caputo, & Borkovec, 1974; Tori & Worell, 1973; Young, Rimm, & Kennedy, 1973.

personality traits may be isolated to identify the placebo reactor. Once identified, placebo reactors could benefit from placebo therapies that do not have the adverse effects of active treatments (Evans, 1974); they could be systematically excluded from therapy evaluations, thereby increasing the sensitivity and power of these studies (Ainsle, Jones, & Stiefel, 1965; Lasagna, Mosteller, von Felsinger, & Beecher, 1954; Linn, 1959); and placebo reactions might serve as a diagnostic aid (Bush, 1974).

Early placebo researchers reported support for the consistency assumption. Beecher (1955) reviewed 15 studies of 1082 patients, which evaluated placebo effectivenesss in varying subject populations and conditions. He reported an average placebo effect of "35.2 ± 2.2 percent." Beecher's figures are often quoted[2] as an indication of the high degree of consistency of placebo reaction. However, almost totally overlooked is the fact that Beecher's measure of variability, "±2.2 percent," was not a range or standard deviation, but a standard error of the mean (the standard deviation divided by the square root of the summed number of items). More recent reviews have shown that placebo effects vary from 0 to almost 100 percent among different populations, disease and treatment conditions (Hass, Fink, & Hartflider, 1963; Parkhouse, 1963; Shapiro, 1964a).

It is important to recognize that even if the percentage of individuals who react to placebos is consistent, the consistency assumption would remain unproven. The placebo reactor hypothesis predicts that the same individuals react to placebos over time and varying environmental conditions. Studies of placebo reactions over time (Frank, 1968; Wolf et al., 1957), and for various conditions (Liberman, 1964), find inconsistent placebo reactions. Even investigators, who previously favored the placebo reactor model, now reject it (Lasagna, 1972; Liberman, 1966).

These data do not support the model of a consistent placebo reactor. However, it is possible that there are enduring patient characteristics that, together with other factors, might predict placebo reaction. If individuals do not consistently react to placebos, traits cannot be considered strong correlates of placebo reaction. It is possible that no definitive traits exist. However, a more accepted view is that certain traits may predispose some individuals to react to placebos but that a multitude of other factors also determine placebo effect (Campbell & Rosenbaum, 1967; Fisher, 1967; Gelfand, Gelfand, & Randin, 1965; Honigfeld, 1964a; Lasagna, 1972; Liberman, 1964). Two types of predispositions have been hypothesized: general predispositions that exert their influence in various environments and specific predispositions that become associated with placebo reactivity only in certain situations (Fisher, Cole, Rickels, & Uhlenhuth, 1964; Liberman, 1961).

The difficulty of relating personality and demographic variables to the placebo effect is demonstrated by a study of Shapiro, Mike, Barton, & Shapiro (1973). Fifty-five variables, which previous literature indicated might predict placebo response, were analyzed for their relationship to the placebo effect. The placebo effect was measured by four different self-report indices; change in symptomatology, global rating of overall change, the occurrence of side effects, and total score based on a combination of these three measures. Stepwise discriminant analyses showed that for each method of scoring the placebo effect, 85 percent of the patients could be correctly classified as to the type of placebo reaction (positive, negative, or neutral) by utilizing all 55 variables as predictors. However, the relative importance of each variable as a predictor was highly dependent on the method of scoring placebo reaction. Only four predictor variables were common to the first (and therefore most important) 25 predictors chosen in each of the four discriminant analyses: the MMPI variables of depression, hypochrondriasis and repression, and the duration of current illness as measured by a demographic scale.

Demographic Variables

Some studies have reported that females have more placebo reactions than males (Abramson, Jarvik, Levine, Kaufman, & Hirsch, 1955;

---

[2]Benson & Epstein, 1975; Blackwell, Bloomfield, & Buncher, 1972; Bourne, 1971; Brodeur; 1965; Carter & Allen, 1973; Davidson, 1960; Evans, 1969; Gliedman, Gantt, & Teitelbaum, 1957; Kurland, 1957; Lehmann, 1964; Lesse, 1964.

Beecher, 1955; Gliedman et al., 1958; O'Brien, 1954; Rickels, 1965), some that males react more than females (Goldberg, Schooler, Davidson, & Kaye, 1966), while other studies have found no difference between the sexes (Batterman & Lower, 1968; Bishop & Gallant, 1966; Black, 1966, Lasagna, et al., 1954; Samuels & Edison, 1961; Tibbets & Hawkins, 1956). These conflicting results would seem to rule out patient sex as generally predisposing a placebo reaction. However, Aletky and Carlin (1975) have suggested that the method of measuring placebo reaction and pertinant sex role expectations may function as intervening variables that mitigate placebo effects. In some studies, young age correlated positively with placebo effects (Gliedman et al., 1958; Kurland, 1958; Shapiro, Wilensky, & Struening, 1968; Tibbets & Hawkins, 1956); in others it correlated negatively (Lasagna et al., 1954; O'Brien, 1954), or did not correlate either positively or negatively (Abramson et al., 1955; Black, 1966; Fischer & Dlin, 1956; Hankoff, Engelhardt, & Freedman, 1966; Isaacs, 1959; Knowles & Lucas, 1960; Roberts & Hamilton, 1958; Stukat, 1958).

Like the sex variable, it is unlikely that age is a general predisposing factor for placebo reaction. Even when sex and age are conjointly examined, additional factors regarding the context in which therapy is administered, must be taken into account to explain results (Raskin, 1974).

Placebo effect have been associated with lower verbal IQ in one study (Rickels & Downing, 1965) but not in two others (Grimes, 1948; Shapiro et al., 1968). One study found lower educational level to predict placebo response (Gliedman et al., 1958), one study found higher educational level associated with placebo response (Moertel, Taylor, Roth, & Tyce, 1976), and several others found no significant effect of education (Downing & Rickels, 1973; Isaacs, 1959; Rickels & Downing, 1962; Rickels, Downing, & Howard, 1971; Samuels & Edisen, 1961).

Blacks have been reported to have greater placebo effects than whites in four studies (Batterman & Lower, 1968; Goldberg et al., 1966; Rickels, Gordan, Jenkins, Perloff, Sachs, & Stepansky, 1970; Samuels & Edisen, 1961). However, in one published (Shapiro et al., 1973) and

three unpublished studies (Shapiro, Struening, Shapiro, Morris, & Raab, in preparation) race was unrelated to placebo reaction. These latter studies differed from the former in that the clinics treated primarily middle-class rather than lower-class patients. Any conclusions relating race to placebo reaction must be considered as extremely tentative in light of the multitude of confounding factors such as differential diagnoses and limited sampling of social classes.

Personality Variables

Suggestibility

The most extensively investigated factor in the study of the placebo effect is the concept of suggestion. This approach is important because of the presummed common components in tests of suggestibility and the placebo effect. Over the years, the meaning of the term "suggestibility" has expanded to include many diverse phenomena, including the placebo effect (Beecher, 1968, Sturpp, Levenson, Manuck, Snell, Hinrichsen, & Boyd, 1974). Although the plausible expectation that tests of suggestibility would correlate with the placebo effect has received partial substantiation (Duke, 1964; Hornsby, Bishop, & Gallant, 1967; McGlashan, Evans, & Orne, 1969; Steinbook, Jones, & Ainsle, 1965), overall, it has not been consistency supported (Bentler, O'Hare, & Kransner, 1963; Butler, Gaines, & Lenox, 1976; Duke, 1962; Evans, 1967; Frank, Gliedman, Imber, Nash, & Stone, 1967; Gliedman et al., 1968; Grimes, 1948; Stukat, 1958).

One possible explanation for this inconsistant relationship is that the placebo stimulus is not the same as that of a test of suggestibility. Barber and Calvery (1964) have shown that responses to a suggestibility test vary greatly depending upon whether the suggestions are introduced as a test of "gullibility" or "imagination." Placebos are commonly associated with therapeutic stimuli whereas tests of suggestibility are associated with laboratory experiments. Patient motivations and their interpretation of stimuli may vary greatly depending whether tests are administered in the context of experiments or therapies (Shapiro, 1960, 1964, 1968). Therefore, the relationship of suggestibility to placebo reaction is moderated by variables such as expectations and the meaning attributed to stimuli by patients (Wolf, 1959).

Acquiescence and Social Desirability

The basis of the placebo effect is often conceptualized as due to a response style characteristic. People who tend to comply with questionnaire items regardless of content, or who answer questions in a socially desirable manner, are considered likely positive placebo reactors.

Reports relating traits such as social desirability, response bias, acquiescence, and "yea saying" to placebo reaction have appeared in the literature (Fisher & Fisher, 1963; Gelfand et al., 1965; Pichot & Perse, 1968). However, this relationship has not been consistently substantiated (Bank, 1969; Fast & Fisher, 1971; Linton & Langs, 1962; McNair, Kahn, Dropleman, & Fisher, 1968; Shapiro et al., 1973; Raskin, Boothe, Schulterbrandt, Reatig, & Odle, 1973).

At best, traits such as social desirability and acquiescence can be considered weak correlates of placebo reaction. The influence of these traits might be more substantial when placebo effects are measured by self-report paper-and-pencil tests. It seems unlikely that a response can be totally dissociated from the content of the questionnaire material (Rogers, 1974; Rorer, 1965; Taylor, Carithers, & Coyne, 1976). Therefore, the importance of these personality variables in any particular study may be highly reliant on the specific questions used to measure the trait and the placebo effect.

Dependency

The concept of dependency involves both emotional and perceptual components. Clinical folklore suggests the association between emotional dependency and placebo reaction. However, the only measure of emotional dependency that has been related to the placebo effect is based upon projective techniques used in a study by Lasagna et al. (1954). This study cannot be considered as offering adequate support for the relationship between emotional dependency and placebo reaction because of the low reliability of projective techniques and other methodological shortcomings. Questionnaire measures of emotional dependency fail to indicate any significant relationship (Campbell & Rosenbaum, 1967; Sharp, 1965). The related concept of external locus of control is similiarly uncorrelated with the placebo effect (Bradsma, 1973).

The perceptual measure of field dependency, hypothesized as related to placebo reaction, has not been confirmed by empirical study (Bradsma, 1973; Dinnerstein & Halm, 1970; Freund, Krupp, Goodenough, & Preston, 1972; Shapiro et al., in preparation).

Introversion-Extraversion

Both introversion and extraversion have been related to placebo reaction. The rationale relating introversion to placebo response is based on learning theory. The placebo effect is viewed as a generalization from other situations. Introverts, having greater speed of conditioning, should acquire placebo responses more readily and lose them less readily than extraverts (Trouton, 1957). Although by no means unanimous (Shapiro et al., in press), some empirical data support this relationship (Luoto, 1964; Morison, Woodmansey, & Young, 1961; Thorn, 1962).

The postulated relationship between extraversion and the placebo effect is based on extraverts' greater reliance on external factors. Knowles and Lucas (1960) have suggested that extraverts may be more apt to attribute relatively normal changes in behavior or physiological state to the action of an external agent such as a placebo. Support for this relationship is found in several studies (Black, 1966; Campbell & Rosenbaum, 1967; Gartner, 1961; Knowles & Lucas, 1960), but again, unconfirmed in a study of Shapiro et al. (in preparation).

Research supporting the relationship between the placebo effect and both of these opposite traits highlights the complicated association between personality and the placebo effect. It suggests the possibility of different pathways for placebo effects. The inherent contradiction of both introversion and extraversion being related to placebo reaction also suggests that this relationship may be artifactual. These results warrant further study utlizing reliable and valid measures of introversion-extraversion and the placebo effect.

Psychopathology

Placebo reactions are common in patients diagnosed as normal, neurotic, or psychotic. Conflicting results have been reported for an association between placebo effects and a general trait of neuroticism (Gartner, 1961; Luoto, 1964; Knowles & Lucas, 1960). Different methods of measuring placebo reaction make it impossible to directly compare the susceptibility of normals, neurotics, and psychotics to placebo effects. However, the range of measurements suggest that the nature and intensity of placebo reactions are greater for the psychotic. Hysteria, prone to suggestion effects, would seem likely to be related to placebo reactivity. However, several studies have failed to support this relationship (Gartner, 1961; Kornetsky & Humphries, 1957; Muller, 1965; Shapiro et al., 1973).

Shapiro et al. (1968) reported that placebo effects range from 18 to 67 percent for various diagnostic categories. The most frequently cited symptoms associated with placebo reactions are emotionality, depression, and anxiety (Lasagna et al., 1954; Pichot & Perse, 1968; Rickels & Downing, 1967; Shapiro, 1959, 1960a, 1968; Shapiro et al., 1973; Shipman et al., 1974; Sharp, 1965; Thorn, 1962). Manifest, unelaborated anxiety is frequently associated with placebo reaction. Beecher (1960) in anesthiology, Castiglioni (1946) in history and Parsons (1951) in sociology believe that suggestibility increases with increased stress. In proper amounts, anxiety also facilitates learning and focuses attention. Anxiety is considered a favorable prognostic sign in psychotherapy, insulin treatment, and lobotomy. However, careful evaluation of the importance of anxiety in studies of the placebo effect reveal somewhat inconsistent effects and weak correlations (Shapiro et al., in preparation). More carefully conceived and executed studies are required to substantiate this relationship and possibly elucidate the type of anxiety that may be associated with placebo reactions.

SITUATIONAL VARIABLES

The situation in which therapy is administered is an important determinant of its effectiveness. Judg-ments about the need for therapy and interpretation of a therapy's effectiveness are both highly reliant on situational factors. For example, Beecher (1956) found that the same type of wound caused vastly different reports of pain depending on whether the patient received the wound from surgery or in a war. Soldiers reported much less pain and need for analgesia, presumedly because the wound was a signal to them that they might be sent home.

Situational factors are especially important when placebo effects are measured by subjective reports, such as mood change (Schachter & Singer, 1962; Lyerly, Ross, Krugman, & Clyde, 1964), pain threshold (Clark 1969; Feather, Chapman, & Fisher, 1972; Davison & Valins, 1969), and the achievement of a marijuana (placebo) "high" (Ademec, 1973; Becker, 1974; Carlin, Bakker, Halperin, & Post, 1972; Carlin, Post, Bakker, & Halperin, 1974; Lennard, Epstein, Bernstein, & Ranson, 1971). Situational factors are conceived as providing an integral component of any emotional response. According to Schachter and Singer's (1962) theory of emotion, individuals interpret their own reactions by means of situational cues. The rendering of therapy provides a potent environmental cue.

In addition to interacting with bodily state changes, situational cues can influence the "milieu" in which therapy is given. Some of the situational variables that affect placebo reactions are staff attitudes, type of population under study, the setting, the treatment procedure, and other miscellaneous factors. Therapist variables, which constiute a major set of situational factors, will be discussed in a separate section.

Staff

Staff attitudes, expectations, biases, conflicts, and harmony can influence placebo effects.[3] Negative staff attitudes can reduce the effectiveness of active medication (Sabshin & Ramot, 1956). The effect

[3]Baker & Thorpe, 1957; Eissen, Sabshin, & Heath, 1959; Goldstein, 1962; Hofling, 1955; Linn, 1959; Mezaros & Galagher, 1958, Rathod, 1958; Shapiro, 1960a; Stanton & Schwartz, 1954; Volgyesi, 1954; Von Mehring & King, 1957.

of a placebo can be reduced from 70 to 25 percent if the negative attitude toward placebo injections by a nurse are communicated to the patient (Volgyesi, 1954). In another study, patients treated with placebos improved more than those on tranquilizers, a result the authors attributed to the bias of the nurses against psychochemotherapy and for habit-training psychotherapy (Baker & Thorpe, 1957). Nurses were observed crushing, dissolving, and tasting the tablets in order to distinguish placebo from active agents. Such attempts to identify drugs in controlled research have been reported in other studies (Fischer & Dlin, 1956).

Staff attitudes and behavior, such as displaying interest and optimism can influence patient behavior—for example, the disturbed behavior of patients has been attributed to staff conflicts (Rathod, 1958; Linn, 1959; Shottstaedt, Pinsky, Mackler, & Wolf, 1959; Stanton & Schwartz, 1954).

Setting
The setting within which treatments are administered offers a multitude of potential therapeutic stimuli for patients (Gelfand, Ullmann, & Krasner, 1963; Nash, Frank, Imber, & Stone, 1964; Barber, 1960). Patients sometimes improve without therapy, simply because they are placed in a therapeutic milieu (Goldstein, 1960; Goldstein & Shipman, 1961). The importance of the milieu is demonstrated in a study by Park and Covi (1965) in which patients were given placebos and told that the administered drugs were sugar pills. Despite this disclosure, all of the 14 patients who took the placebos improved. Although some patients thought that the drug contained active medication, the majority believed that they were helped by the placebo, the doctor, or themselves.

Changes can occur in patients after institution of research, which are unrelated to the contents or type of research activity. This process is similiar to the "Hawthorne Effect" observed in industrial psychology in which workers increased productivity because of the heightened interest, increased attention, and social stimulation of the research atmosphere rather than because of the variables manipulated by the researchers. In therapeutic situations this "milieu effect" can produce improvement in 80 percent of patients (Rashkis &

Smarr, 1957). The bias introduced by research can influence clinical and experimental results in any number of ways (Rosenthal & Rosnow, 1969; Grosz & Grossman, 1968; Rosnow & Aiken, 1973).

The setting, because of its inherent "therapeutic" stimulus value, is a potent placebo variable. Direct comparisons of placebo response in different settings leaves no doubt that the setting can induce placebo effects and affect treatment outcome in many ways (Rickels, Downing, & Downing, 1966; Rickels, Catell, Weiss, Gray, Yee, Mallin, & Aaronson, 1966).

Population
A change in study setting may also change the nature of the population being measured. Lipman (1966) reported that an identical research protocol yielded opposite results when medical clinic patients were compared to psychiatric clinic patients. Differences in placebo reaction between private patients and clinic patients have also been noted (Rickels & Macafee, 1966; Heshbacker, Rickels, Gordon, Gray, Meckelburg, Weise, & Vandervort, 1970; Downing & Rickels, 1973).

Clinical patients and experimental subjects display vastly different response to placebo analgesia. Beecher (1960) found that about 35 percent of patients reported substantial pain relief from placebos but that only about 3 percent of experimental subjects reported substantial relief. Evans (1969), in a review of 14 other experimental studies, found average placebo relief to be about 16 percent, still well below the figure reported by Beecher for clinic patients. It is likely that factors such as individual needs, motivations and anxiety levels (Davison & Valins, 1969; Buss & Portnoy, 1967), the role of the "patient" versus that of the "subject" (Rosnow & Aiken, 1973; Silverman, 1968), and the norms for each situation (Orne, 1970) contribute to these findings.

Subjects used for clinical or experimental studies of the placebo effect are often volunteers. The ability to generalize results to nonvolunteer subjects is questionable (Rosenthal & Rosnow, 1975).

Treatment Procedure
Although clinical folklore gives the impression that the best placebo treatments have an element of

mysticism and cause a bit of discomfort, the empirical evidence is scanty (Honigfeld, 1964b). Patients do not react uniformly to different treatment procedures (Wolf 1959). Morison et al. (1961) and Traut and Passarelli (1957) found placebo injections to have greater efficacy then oral drugs, but another study found no difference (Goldman, Witton, & Scherier, 1965). Reactions to size, color, and shape of tablets or capsules vary (*JAMA*, 1955; Leslie, 1954; Schapira, McClelland, Griffiths, & Newells, 1970).

The efficacy of various placebo treatments may ultimately depend on the treatment modality that serves as the appropriate stimulus for each patient. One group of individuals may react best to a drug stimulus, another to psychotherapy or psychoanalysis, and another to biofeedback, behavior modification, or acupuncture, for example. Four studies by the authors (Shapiro et al., in preparation) revealed a consistent relationship between the desire for psychochemotherapy and positive response to medication placebo.

Miscellaneous Factors

Factors external to the administered therapy may cause changes that are misattributed to the influence of the therapy. Some of these external factors are; preexisting symptoms (Bushfield, Sneller, & Capra 1962; Schulterbrandt, Raskin, & Reatig, 1974; Green, 1964), spontaneous remissions (Lesse, 1964, 1966), the influence of group pressures and reactions of other patients (Knowles & Lucas, 1960; Letemendia & Harris, 1959; Morrison & Walters, 1972; Schachter & Singer, 1962) significant life events (Lipman, Hammer, Bernades, Park, & Cole, 1965; Davidson, 1960) and the process of filling out questionnaires (Glaser & Whittow, 1954).

Placebo reactivity is related to type of referral (Hankoff, Engelhardt, Freedman, Mann, & Margolis, 1960). Untreated patients may be favorably influenced by treated patients (Craig & Coren, 1974; Meszaros & Gallagher, 1958). The taste of a pill can influence placebo reaction (Baker & Thorpe, 1957). The type of bodily or behavioral reaction, and whether it is expected or unexpected, can affect the degree of placebo response (Morris & O'Neal, 1975).

There are many other factors, not fully explored, that probably influence placebo effects. Some situational variables that may influence placebo response include the cost of treatment, type and size of practice, reputation of the therapist, atmosphere of the office (informal or intimate, busy or unhurried, supporting or rejecting, etc.), use of therapeutic adjuncts such as nurses or aids to administer treatments, reinforcing directions with written information sheets or audiovisual aids, and so on.

PHYSICIAN VARIABLES

Although the relationship between physician and patient has been recognized throughout history as an important determinant of response to medical treatment, the responsibility of the patient has always been emphasized. However, therapeutic evaluations indicate that physician characteristics constiute a crucial variable in therapy. The great bulk of evidence supporting the role of the physician in therapy is derived from studies completed in the 1950 and 1960s. Although reaffirmed in more modern evaluations (Luborsky, Singer, & Singer, 1975), this potentially fruitful area has not become a major research topic for prospective research.

The study of the physician's contribution to placebo and therapeutic effects is referred to as iatroplacebogenics—physician-caused placebo effects. Iatroplacebogenics can be direct or indirect. The former refers to placebo effects produced by the physician's attitude to the patient, to the treatment procedure, and to the treatment results. Indirect iatroplacebogenics, a much more subtle mechanism, occurs when the patient misinterprets the physician's intent, and experiences the physician's interest in a therapy or procedure as a personal interest.

Direct Iatroplacebogenics

Attitude to Patient

Attitude to patient refers to the therapist's interest, warmth, friendliness, liking, sympathy, empathy, neutrality, lack of interest, rejection, and hostility. Its general importance is indicated by a survey that cited the physician's personal interest—not his or her competence—as the main determinant of whether patients like their doctors (Polansky & Kounin, 1956).

Psychotherapy. The most impressive evidence supporting iatroplacebogenics in psychotherapy is furnished by a recent critical review by Luborsky, Singer, and Luborsky (1975). Methodologically sound comparative studies of several types of psychotherapy were examined. The review indicated a "tie score effect"; a high percentage of patients receiving any of the psychotherapies tended to improve, but none of the psychotherapies emerged as clearly superior to the others. Luborsky et al. concluded that the most potent explanation for this tie score effect was that improvement was related to the existence of the patient-therapist relationship common to all forms of psychotherapy.

The psychotherapist's interest in the patient is associated with the likelihood of acceptance of treatment (Brill & Storrow, 1963; Lowinger & Dobie, 1963, 1964), fewer dropouts (Freedman, Engelhardt, Hankoff, Glick, Kaye, Buchwald, & Stark, 1958; Hiller, 1958; Lowinger & Dobie, 1964; McNair, Lorr, & Callahan, 1963; Nash, Frank, Gliedman, Imber, & Stone, 1957), fewer complaints by patients (Nash et al., 1964), and successful outcome of treatment.[4]

Extensive research by Goldstein on the importance of patient-physician expectations in therapy indicates that the therapist's favorable feelings to the patient are related to the therapist's expectation of improvement and the patient's attraction to the therapist (Heller & Goldstein, 1961; Garfield & Affleck, 1960) and influence the obtained improvement (Goldstein, 1962).

Strupp has demonstrated in many studies that the therapist's liking or disliking of the patient is associated with the therapist's evaluation of the patient's personality, motivation, maturity, insight,

anxiety, clinical status, diagnosis, treatment goals, proposed techniques, improvement expected, and mutual beliefs of patient and therapist.[5]

The frequent observation, although inadequately studied, that therapists are often more successful when they begin their careers than when they have become more experienced, may be related to greater interest of the novice in the patient.[6] Liking or not liking of patients may be a better explanation for reported cases of countertransference cures (Barchilon, 1958; Kolb & Montgomery, 1958), for failures in therapy (Ends & Page, 1957), and for the suggestibility of patients in psychoanalysis (Fisher, 1953).

Support for the positive association between physician attitude toward the patient and patient's therapeutic improvement is offered by a recent study (Shaprio, Struening, Shapiro, & Barten, 1976). Physicians were asked to rate patients in terms of likability, attractiveness, and how good a patient for treatment they appeared to be. Each of these three variables was strongly correlated with physician's rating of patient improvement.

Psychochemotherapy. Interest in the patient is related to successful treatment with antidepressants (Sheard, 1963) and minor tranquilizers (Uhlenhuth, Canter, Neustadt, & Payson, 1959; Rickels, Baum, Taylor, & Raab, 1964), as well as to the type of LSD response (Malitz, 1963) and drug acceptance by patients (Raskin, 1961).

General. The interest of the investigator affects surgery in dogs (Wolf, 1962), gastric acid secretion (Engel, Reichsman, & Segal, 1956), metabolic changes (Schottstaedt et al., 1956), laboratory procedures (Kaplan, 1956), and galvanic skin responses (Dittes, 1957). It has been described as a crucial variable for successful psychotherapy in

---

[4]Heine, 1959; Seeman, 1954; Blaine & McArthur, 1958; Board, 1959; Snyder & Snyder, 1961; Parloff, 1961; Cartwright & Lerner, 1963; Stoler, 1963; Strupp et al, 1964; Battle, Imber, Hoehn-Sarac, Stone, Nash, & Frank, 1966; Gendlin, 1966; Truax & Wargo (1966) summarized 14 additional studies that attributed successful treatment largely to the warmth or empathy of the therapist.

[5]Strupp et al., 1964; Strupp, 1958a, 1958b, 1958c, 1959, 1960a, 1960b, Strupp & Williams, 1960; Wallach and Strupp, 1960; Strupp & Wallach, 1965.

[6]Lowinger & Dobie, 1964; Truax & Wargo, 1966; Strupp, 1958c; Strupp & Williams, 1960; Ginsburg & Arrington, 1948; Brill, Koegler, Epstein, & Forgy, 1964; Berman, 1949; Kubie, 1956; Glover, cited by Kubie, 1956; Grinker, 1958; Barchilon, 1959; Frank, 1961; Cole, Branch, & Allison, 1962; Karno, 1965.

summaries reported at national research conferences on psychotherapy (Parloff & Rubinstein, 1959; Strupp & Luborsky, 1962); as the cornerstone of Rogerian client-centered therapy (Rogers, 1951, 1957a, b, 1961); and as important in behavior therapy, psychotherapy and psychoanalysis,[7] the placebo effect,[8] hypnosis (Barber, 1962), the success of shamans (Frank, 1961; Kiev, 1964) and quacks (Masserman, 1963), and the saving of derelicts by the Salvation Army (Feldman, 1956).

Attitude to Treatment

Recent research has established that the physician's attitude toward treatment—such as faith, belief, enthusiasm, conviction, commitment, optimism, positive and negative expectations, skepticism, disbelief, and pessimism—is a nonspecific factor in most therapies.

Psychochemotherapy. Feldman (1956) was the first to present data supporting the idea that the success of drug therapy varied with the enthusiasm of the doctor. He reported similar findings in a follow-up study, and observed that unsuccessful therapists had a greater commitment to psychoanalysis than to psychochemotherapy (Feldman, 1963).

These findings were confirmed in a study by Uhlenhuth et al. (1959), which indicated that only the interested and enthusiastic physician obtained significant improvement with active drugs compared with placebos, while the uninterested and unenthusiastic physician showed no differences in improvement, whether active or inactive drugs were used. An important implication of this study is that the therapist's interest may be a necessary prerequisite for the success of some treatments. These results have been confirmed in subsequent studies (Fisher et al., 1964; Rickels et al., 1964a; Rickels, Boren, & Stuart, 1964; Rickels & Catell, 1969; Uhlenhuth, Rickels, Fisher, Park, Lipman, & Mock, 1966).

Interest in drug treatment has been associated with successful treatment of depressed patients (Haefner, Sacks, & Mason, 1960; Sheard, 1963), schizophrenics and hospitalized patients (Honigfeld, 1962; Pearlin, 1962; Tuma & May, 1969), and depressed patients on placebo (Honigfeld, 1963). Negative attitudes toward drug treatment are associated with less favorable results.[9] Similar finding have been reported in the treatment of patients with bleeding ulcers (Volgyesi, 1954), as well as those treated by hypnosis (Orne, 1959; Troffer & Tart, 1964).

Psychotherapy. A relationship between the psychotherapist's interest in treatment and successful outcome has been described in studies of brief psychotherapy (Frank, 1965) and in studies of psychiatrists (Board, 1959; Frank, 1965) or medical students (Frank, 1961; Ginsburg & Arringron, 1948; Goldstein & Shipman, 1961). The psychotherapist's interest in the treatment has also been associated with the likelihood of patients remaining in psychotherapy (Heine & Trossman, 1960; McNair et al., 1963) and was cited as important in the summary report of the first Research Conference on Psychotherapy (Rubinstein & Parloff, 1959). Optimistic therapists rate their patients more improved than do pessimistic therapists (Rickels et al., 1964b; Rubinstein & Parloff, 1959).

Indirect evidence of a relationship between the therapist's interest in psychotherapy and success of treatment appears in the work of Strupp and Goldstein. Their work indicates that the therapist's

---

[7]Parloff, 1961; Strupp, 1960a, 1960b; Strupp & Williams 1960; Snyder, 1946; Fiedler, 1950; Ginsburg & Arrington, 1948; Barchilon, 1958; Frank, 1961; Cole, Branch, & Allison, 1962; Karno, 1965; Krasner, Ullman, & Fisher, 1964; Snyder, 1958; Greenachre, 1953; Ferenczi, cited by Greenachre, 1953; Fenichel, 1954; Braaty, 1954; Ellis, 1955; Breuer & Freud, 1957; Frank, Gliedman, Imber, Nash, & Stone, 1957; Frank, 1958, Frank, cited in Rubenstein & Parloff, 1959; Masserman, 1957, 1963; Meerloo, 1963; Berman, 1949; Heine & Trossman, 1960; White, 1961; Hobbs, 1962; Lesse, 1962, 1964, Voth, Herbert, & Orth, 1962; Luborsky, 1962, Hammett, 1965; Paul, 1963, Jaspers, 1965.

[8]Honigfeld, 1963; Lesse, 1964; Rickels et al., 1964a; Shapiro, A.P., 1959; Shapiro, A.K., 1959, 1960a, 1963, 1964a, 1964c, 1964f, 1968; Wolf, 1962.

[9]Baker & Thorpe, 1957; Eissen, Sabshin & Heath, 1959; Fisher et al., 1964; Feldman, 1963; Haefner et al., 1960; Honigfeld, 1962; Pearlin, 1962; Rickels et al., 1964b, Sabshin & Ramot, 1956; Uhlenhuth et al., 1959, Uhlenhuth et al, 1966.

evaluation of the patient's suitability for psychotherapy determines the therapist's interest in treatment (Strupp, 1960a). This correlates with the mutual attraction of therapist and patient and with the positive evaluation of the patient and the patient's success in therapy (Goldstein, 1962; Strupp, 1960a, b; Strupp, Wallach, & Wogan, 1964; Wallach & Strupp, 1960).

Unfortunately, in all of the studies cited, it is difficult to differentiate between the therapist's interest in the patient and the therapist's interest in treatment. Several studies suggest, however, that interest in treatment is primary and leads to a secondary interest in the patient. For example: a patient's motivation for therapy influences the therapist's estimation of prognosis and capacity to like the patient (Strupp, 1969a, b; Strupp & Wallach, 1965; Strupp & Williams, 1960). Some therapists dislike patients solely on technical grounds (Strupp, 1960b) or because they are more severely disturbed (Wallach & Strupp, 1960). Patients who complete studies are liked more than dropouts (Rickels et al., 1964a). The therapist's prognostic expectations relate to patient's attraction to the therapist (Heller & Goldstein, 1961). The therapist's evaluation of prognosis, capacity for insight, liking, empathizing, and eagerness to accept the patient vary with the patient's motivation for therapy (Wallach & Strupp, 1960). Retaining patients for psychotherapy appears to be more directly associated with the therapist's interest in treatment than with his or her interest in the patient (McNair et al., 1963). Experimenters may become more likable, personal, and interested in subjects if early data returns are favorable (Rosenthal, 1963a).

The observation about the success of younger therapists was previously related to their having more positive feelings toward patients than do older therapists. Neophytes may also be excessively enthusiastic (Frank, 1961) and optimistic (Strupp, 1960b) about the effectiveness of treatment because of their need for reassurance (Strupp, 1960b; Frank, 1961; Lesse, 1964), whereas the needs of experienced therapists shift from curing to understanding (Barchilon, 1958). The observation that some therapists are more successful with certain patients may be related to the therapist's interest in particular problems or types of patients.[10]

The profit motive has been conspicuously unexplored and may be a significant determinant of the therapist's interest in the treatment, patient, and results (Chodoff, 1964; Davids, 1964; Foreman, 1964; Kubie, 1964; Lesse, 1962; Mowrer, 1963; Ubell, 1964).

General. Finally, the therapist's interest in treatment is frequently cited as important in placebogensis,[11] general medical treatment (Honigfeld, 1964b; Houston, 1938; Janet, 1924; Lord, 1950; Shapiro, A. P., 1955, 1959; Shapiro, A. P., Myers, Reiser, & Ferris, 1954), insulin coma treatment (Shapiro, 1960a), hypnosis (Orne, 1959, 1962, 1970; Troffer & Tart, 1964), and the success of shamans (Eliode, 1964; Ellenberger, 1956; Kiev, 1962, 1964).

Attitude to Results

Attitude toward results refers to data distortion caused by random observer effects and by intentional or unintentional observer bias (Rosenthal, 1966; Rosenthal & Halas, 1962). Data distortion or unintended observer bias are probably more extensive than frauds and intended effects (Humphrey, 1963; Rosenthal, 1966, 1969).

Rosenthal's technique of demonstrating that "experimenters obtain the results they want or expect" is illustrated in a study of rat learning (Rosenthal, 1966; Rosenthal & Fode, 1963). Experimenters were told that their rats had been specially bred for either brightness or dullness, al-

[10]McNair et al., 1963; Snyder & Snyder, 1961; Goldstein, 1962; Strupp, 1960b; Heine & Trossman, 1960; Jaspers, 1965, Fenichel, 1945; Karpman, 1949; Oberndorf, Greenachre, & Kubie, 1953; Wolberg, 1954; Thompson, 1956; Alexander, 1958; Frank, 1959; Engel et al., 1956; Kubie, 1964.

[11]Frank 1961; Lesse, 1962, 1964; Weatherall, 1962, Shapiro, 1959, 1960a, 1960b, 1963, 1964c, 1964d, 1964f, 1968; Baker & Thorpe, 1957; Frank, 1959, Janet, 1924, 1925; Tibbetts & Hawkins, 1956; Wolf, 1959; British Medican Journal, 1961; Kelly, 1962; Liberman, 1961; Honigfeld, 1964b.

though rats in both groups were from the same genetically pure strain. The results indicated that experimenters obtained significantly better learning from rats they considered bright than did experimenters who believed that their rats were dull.

This is not an isolated study. Similar results have been obtained in more than 90 experiments involving rat, planaria, and human subjects (Rosenthal, 1963a, 1964, 1966, 1969; Rosenthal & Halas, 1962; Rosenthal, Persinger, Mulry, Vikan-Kline, & Grothe, 1964; Rosenthal, Persinger, Vikan-Kline, & Fode 1963a).

Sources of experimenter bias include the experimenter's hypotheses (Rosenthal, 1963a), expectation (Rosenthal, 1964; Shuller & McNamara, 1976), motivation (Rosenthal et al., 1964), and prestige (Rosenthal et al., 1963a; Rosenthal et al., 1964). Other factors are instances of cheating (Rosenthal, 1966; Rosenthal, Friedman, Johnson, Fode, Shill, White, & Vikan-Kline, 1964), early data returns (Rosenthal, Kohn, Greenfield, & Carota, 1965; Rosenthal, Persinger, Vikan-Kline, & Fode, 1963b), nonspecific factors in pre-data-gathering interaction (greeting, seating and instructing), (Rosenthal, Fode, Vikan-Kline, & Persinger, 1964), verbal conditioning (Rosenthal et al., 1963a; Rosenthal et al., 1964), visual and verbal cues (Rosenthal et al., 1964c), experimenter and subject physical, demographic and personality characteristics (Chapman, Chapman, & Brelje, 1969; Eisman & Huber, 1970; Rosenthal & Fode, 1963; Rosenthal & Lawson, 1963, Rosenthal et al., 1963a; Schultz & Hartup, 1967).

Rosenthal concluded that human beings engage in highly effective and influencial unintended communication with one another. This communication is so subtle that casual observation is unlikely to reveal the nature of the process (Heine, 1950; Rosenthal, 1963, 1966, 1969; Rosenthal et al., 1964).

Similar findings have been reported both in clinical psychology (Kent, O'Leary, Diament, & Dietz, 1974; Masling, 1959, 1960, 1965; Rosenthal, 1964) and experimental psychology (Friedlander, 1964; Krasner, Knowles, & Ullmann, 1965; Krasner, Ullmann, & Fisher, 1964; McGuigan, 1963; Orne, 1962, 1970; Rosenthal, 1966, 1969);

the placebo effect,[12] psychochemotherapy;[13] psychotherapy;[14] psychoanalysis;[15] clinical and experimental hypnosis (Barber, 1962, 1965a, 1965b; Orne, 1959, 1962; Troffer & Tart, 1964); and clinical medicine (Friedman, Kurland, & Rosenthal, 1965; Garland, 1960; Shapiro, A. P., 1955, 1959; Williams, & McGee, 1962).

The prestige of the investigator, physician, or healer influences clinical and experimental results,[16] and has always been one of the common denominators in "bandwagon effects" in science (Kety, 1961), the success of quacks (Frank, 1961) and shamans (Eliode, 1964; Kiev, 1962; Shapiro, 1964d), the placebo effect (Lesse, 1962; Liberman, 1961; Shapiro, 1959, 1960a, 1960b, 1963, 1964c, 1964d, 1964f), and other healing techniques (Greenachre, 1953; Jaspers, 1965).

During the last decade, physicians and investigators have become increasingly aware of their bias. Bias is so pervasive that some investigators have suggested that clinical judgments may be less informative about patients than the therapists who make them (Grosz & Grossman, 1964). Bias explains why uncontrolled studies report success more frequently than controlled studies (Foulds, 1958; Fox, 1961). Attempts to minimize bias have led to increased use of statistics, placebos, double-blind procedures, independent assessment teams (Guy, Gross, & Dennis, 1967), and other controls.

---

[12]Shapiro, 1959, 1960a, 1960b, 1963, 1964d, 1964f, 1964c, 1968; Baker & Thorpe, 1957; Kelley, 1962; Letermendia & Harris, 1959; Wilson & Huby, 1961; Wilson, 1962a, 1962b; Joyce, 1962.

[13]Shapiro, 1959, 1964d, 1964f; Feldman, 1956, 1963; Sabshin & Ramot, 1956; Baker & Thorpe, 1957, Eissen et al., 1959; Letermendia & Harris, 1959; Wilson & Huby, 1961; Wilson, 1962a, 1962b; Uhr & Miller, 1960; Foreman, 1964.

[14]Garfield & Alleck, 1960; Strupp, 1960b; Wallach & Strupp, 1960; Shapiro, 1964c, 1968; Ward, 1964, Rezikoff & Toomey, 1959, Cutler, 1958; Endicott, 1962; Grosz & Grossman, 1964; Gill & Brenman, 1948.

[15]Krasner, 1962; Greenachre, 1953; Ward, 1964; Rosenthal, 1963b; Gill & Brenman, 1948; Burrow, 1927; Schmidberg, 1958; Glover, 1952; Kubie, 1953; Ehrenwald, 1958; Marmor, 1962; Sullivan, 1936–37.

[16]Kahn, 1957; Karno, 1965; Ullman & McFarland, 1957; Friedman, Kurland, & Rosenthal, 1965; Masserman, 1957; Meerloo, 1963; Rosenthal, Persinger, Mulry, Vikan-Kline, & Groth, 1964; Krasner, Knowles & Ullmann, 1965; Reiser, Reeves, & Armington.

Whereas controlled studies appeared infrequently in the medical literature before 1950, today they are the norm (Karch & Lasagna, 1974; Shapiro, 1960a, 1963, 1968; Waife & Shapiro, A.P., 1959).

Recognition of the subtlety and omnipresence of these effects has led some investigators to believe that objective experiments are illusory (Feldman, 1963; Grenier, 1962; Kelly, 1962; Kety, 1961; Rosenthal, 1966; Rosenthal et al., 1964). It has prompted suggestions that every experiment be done by an enthusiast and skeptic and that the investigator's bias about expected results be specified in the paper. Various suggestions have been made about how to make methodology more rigorous and foolproof.[17] Consistant with these conclusions is the recent demonstration by Barber and Silver (1968) of a Rosenthal "effect" on Rosenthal's procedures.

Observer bias may be related to the therapist's need for results. Therapeutic failure would be cognitively dissonant (Board, 1959; Davids, 1964; Lesse, 1962; Sullivan, 1936–1937; Ubell, 1964; Wolens, 1962). For example, unsuccessful cases may not be remembered and failures may be forgotten. Patients who are expected to be failures may be disliked and their treatment potentials may be negatively evaluated. In addition, investigators tend to be selective in their review of pertinent literature and they may assimilate and misrepresent their summary of the literature while omitting important details that are inconsistent with their views (Berkowitz, 1971). This latter effect, plus the tendency of journals to publish only positive results, tends to perpetuate the popularity of ineffective therapies (Russell, 1974).

Therapists may subtlely and unknowingly communicate information to patients, such as hypotheses, expectations, attitudes, cultural values, and so on.[18] The returned communication is then regarded as an independent confirmation of the therapist's theory (Frank, 1961; Gendlin, 1966). This increases the credulity and suggestibility of both. Bias influences the selection of patients, prognostic expectations, evaluation of insight potentiality, likability, warmth, the obtainment, perception, and remembering of raw data, and the interpretation and presentation of results.

Interest in results stimulates the need and activity to achieve them. It changes the therapist's behavior and interacts with his or her interest in the treatment and patient (Goldstein, 1966). The therapist is more interested in the treatment and the patient, gives more time and help, and shows more warmth and concern. The patient responds to the therapist with warmth and improvement. This relationship is reinforcing and circular. All these factors, and various interactions and secondary effects, result in real or imagined treatment success.

An inescapable conclusion is that the therapist's interest in the patient, treatment, and results is related to success in treatment and placebo effects. Research clearly supports the generality of the phenomena. The evidence includes many clinical studies of many patients with varying diagnoses and backgrounds, and treated with different methods by many therapists with diverse orientations and experience. The generality of the evidence is supported by similar findings in clinical and experimental psychology, psychiatry, and medicine.

A second conclusion is that there is complex interaction among the variables of therapists' interest in the patient, the treatment, and the ultimate results. The explanation of how those factors influence results is not clear. It is also not clear which factors are primary or secondary, or how these factors interrelate, and cause and effect one another.

---

[17]Goldstein, 1962; Rosenthal, 1963b, 1964; Rosenthal, Persinger, Mulry, Viken-Kline, & Grothe, 1964; Masling, 1959, 1960; Friedman, Kurland, & Rosenthal, 1965; Masserman, 1957; Barber, 1962, 1965b; Feldman, 1963; Troffer & Tart, 1964; Orne, 1962; Ward, 1964; Reznikoff & Toomey, 1959; McGuigan, 1963; Greiner, 1962; Endicott, 1962; Barber & Calvery, 1964; Kety, 1961; Shapiro, 1960a, 1961, 1963, 1964a, 1964b, 1968.

[18]Strupp, 1959, 1960b; Strupp & Wallach 1965; Strupp, Wallach & Wogan, 1964; Goldstein, 1962; Snyder, 1946; Karno, 1965; Rosenthal, 1963b; Rosenthal, Persinger, Mulry, Vikan-Kline, & Grothe, 1964; Krasner, 1962; Lesse, 1964; Alexander, 1958, 1963; Gill & Brenman, 1948; Marmor, 1962; Sheard, 1963; Snow & Rickels, 1965; Frank, 1961; Rosenthal, 1966.

For example, a therapist may be interested in the treatment of a patient, expect success, and then like the patient. The patient may react to the therapist with similar feelings and stimulate the therapist with more interest in the patient, greater enthusiasm for treatment, and increased expectation of favorable results. All these factors may contribute to the final success of therapy.

Understanding of the complex interactions of the therapist's interest in the patient, treatment, and results requires more than retrospective speculation. Careful prospective studies are necessary to determine the relevance and primacy of these factors for placebogenesis and therapeutic effects.

Indirect Iatroplacebogenics

The physician's interest in his or her treatment and patient is a necessary component of almost every specific therapy, has a synergistic effect with most therapies, and often produces psychological or placebo effects in and of itself. Although the concept of direct iatroplacebogenesis has been demonstrated in many studies, another probably more subtle and extensive process, indirect iatroplacebogenesis, has not been considered adequately in the literature (Berman, 1949; Board, 1959; Frank, 1961; Glover, 1931; Greenachre, 1953; Honigfeld, 1964b; Rosenthal, 1963b).

Medical History

Medical history is characterized by a succession of prestigious physicians with compelling intellectual and emotional investments in various therapeutic theories and practices. These are frequently elaborate, detailed, expensive, time consuming, fashionable, esoteric, and dangerous. The majority were later judged to be ineffective (Shapiro, 1959, 1960a). A common factor in these therapies is the interest of the physicians.

The greater a physician's interest in a theory of therapy, particularly if he or she has innovated it, or if he or she is a recent convert, the more effective that therapy will be. This may occur because the patient displaces the interest from the therapy to himself or herself and experiences the physician's interest in treatment as a personal one. Many psychological factors arise in the patient-physician relationship. Hopes, expectations, fantasies, fears, feelings of guilt and inadequacy, and so on, become involved in the relationship and treatment. For example, if a patient has ego-alien impulses and fantasies, an interest on the part of the physician, to whom transference has developed, can decrease superego pressures, conflicts, and eventually symptoms. The patient may simply feel that if a physicain is interested, then he or she is not worthless.

The physician may be neutral or minimally interested in the patient. However, the physician's commitment to a treatment modality may produce an intense interest in the results of therapy. The patient may experience the physician's interest as an interest in himself or herself. In addition, the physician's interest in his or her treatment may enable the physician to tolerate or be unaffected by the personal idiosyncracies of the patient. The patient may expect criticism or rejection and be surprised or reassured when the physician responds with interest. In other words, some treatments, although ostensibly directed at the patient, may unknowingly affect the physician, and then mediate psychological change in the patient. The effectiveness of these treatments would be primarily due to the process of indirect iatroplacebogenesis.

Pharmacotherapy

Once fashionable insulin coma treatment is increasingly thought of as a complex placebo treatment (Shapiro, 1960a). The interest of the staff, necessitated by the dangers during treatment, may provide part of the explanation for its effectiveness. Patients were selectively chosen for this treatment and were a therapeutic elite. The treatment was expensive, fashionable, elaborate, time consuming, esoteric, dangerous, and patients required considerable attention during and after treatment.

A physician with an interest in psychochemotherapy usually has considerable knowledge about such treatment. He or she will be interested in the symptoms and the differential response of the patient to various drugs and will be careful to observe side effects, especially those that may be dangerous. The physician may encourage the patient to call at any time if side effects develop.

A new therapy whose indications, contraindications, and side effects are not fully evaluated will elicit even more interest and promote a greater intellectual and emotional investment of the physician. This may partially explain the reports of almost universal effectiveness accompanying the introduction of new therapies (Shapiro, 1959, 1960a, 1960b, 1963, 1964c, 1964d, 1964f, 1968).

Indirect iatroplacebogeneics can be illustrated by the following clinical case:

A 31-year-old married woman with a chronic borderline condition was referred to a psychiatrist for psychochemotherapy because of her inability to awaken in time for psychotherapy sessions. The underlying reason was probably that she could not be tolerated by whomever served as her therapist. She was the source of constant irritation, with excessive oral and dependent needs, and her behavior caused everyone to reject her. She had almost always reacted adversely to medication. The psychiatrist knew that he would have no greater success than others in changing the patient's masochistic pattern of thwarting attempts to help her. The psychiatrist decided to use a treatment he had never dared to try before, since there was no alternative. In addition, he wanted first to reassure himself that she was not highly sensitive to the effects of medicine.

She was put on an elaborate schedule of three different placebos totaling 12 tablets. Two hours after the patient left, she called stating that all the tablets had fallen out of their boxes and were mixed up in her handbag.

She returned the following week, and in a rash of words described her horrendous experience. She cautiously took only half the dosage at bedtime and on awakening. Immediately after the morning dosage she was nauseated, dizzy, groggy, experienced feelings of unreality, became markedly depressed, sleepy, and began to cry. This lasted six days. Needless to say, the patient discontinued the medication. The doctor followed her associations carefully, recorded much of the interview, and at an appropriate moment told her that she had taken placebos. At first she had no idea what a placebo was. Then she insisted that it was impossible for placebos to have caused her symptoms. Only after the doctor offered to swallow the remaining tablets was she convinced.

Somewhat anxious about using this procedure, the physician became even more so when the patient exclaimed that if medicine didn't work, she had no alternative but to kill herself. Reassuring her that this was not necessary, the therapist told the patient that the procedure was used to determine that her symptoms were caused by powerful psychological factors, not by the medication. The doctor acknowledged that the side effects were not imaginary, but insisted that they could not be serious. It was emphasized that the subtle beneficial effects of the medication could not possibly compete with her overwhelming psychological reaction. For treatment to be successful she must take the prescribed dosage of medication despite the development of side effects. If these did occur, she could always call her doctor. Although serious side effects were unlikely, should any develop, he would be able to differentiate between the serious and nonserious.

The patient seemed to accept the explanation, but needed time to get over the effects of the previous week.

Several months later, she called for an appointment. Treatment was begun with antidepressant medication. No calls were received during that week. At the next session that patient was improved, reporting only reliable side effects of the medication. One week later she said that she did not know if she had received placebos or not, but had no side effects. The nurse checked and found that the patient had been given placebos by mistake. The active medication was then resumed.

Many explanations for the patient's remarkable response are possible: that the physician was strong, authoritative, and could not be manipulated; the patient felt safe, with less need to discharge anxiety through masochistic development of side effects; the confrontation improved reality testing; and so on.

Although many explanations are possible, indirect iatroplacebogenesis is probably the best explanation. The psychiatrist was intellectually and emotionally interested in the placebo phenomenon, negative placebo responses, and the innovation of a treatment procedure. Management was elaborative, detailed, time consuming, esoteric, dangerous, fashionable, and potentially expensive.

In other words, interest in the phenomenon was responsible for the doctor's not reacting to the patient's masochism with distance, lack of interest, hopelessness, and rejection. This experience was unique for the patient who was a specialist at courting rejection. Under the usual circumstances of the patient-physician relationship, the doctor might have reacted to the patient's masochism with anxiety, guilt, distance, lack of interest, hopelessness, and possible rejection.

To view the method that was used as having an effect only on the patient would be misleading. Its effect on the doctor probably had an effect on the patient. The underlying mechanism is the indirect interest of the physician in the patient. The mechanism of indirect iatroplacebogenesis is formulated as treatment directed at the patient, but unknowingly having effects on the physician which, in turn, mediates psychological change in the patient.

This formualtion was confirmed in an interview three years later. The patient, markedly improved, was asked about the effect of the placebo procedure and what helped her get well. She said that the effect of those "clever" placebos made her feel that the doctor was really "trying to help . . . really interested and concerned," whereas physicians previously "were too busy . . . uninterested" and "would only give her boxes of pills." The patient said she was "able to have faith in the clinic and the doctors," which enabled her to take medication and finally improve.

Psychotherapy and Psychoanalysis
How would this formulation apply to intensive psychotherapy? Psychotherapy shares with other therapies many placebogenic factors (Shapiro, 1964a, 1964b, 1968). It is a new method with considerable emotional, intellectual, and financial investment by prestigious practitioners. It is elaborate, fashionable, esoteric, and sometimes dangerous.

Many clinicials agree with this formulation, but might limit its applicability to therapies other than their own. For example, insight-oriented psychotherapists might say that the goal of other

therapies was limited to reduction of symptoms through nonspecific factors or unresolved transference. The goal of psychotherapy is a reorganization of character; it is achieved through insight into unconscious processes, defense mechanisms, character traits, and a resolution of the transference neurosis. The therapist is characterized as a mirror-like, objective, uninvolved technican with minimum direct interest in the patient and results (Hammet, 1965; Loenwald, 1960; Murphy, 1958; Strupp, 1960b). Although the concept of the mirrorlike therapist is a formulation of the naive past and increasingly regarded as fiction rather than fact,[19] nevertheless the insight-oriented psychotherapist communicates less old-fashioned, naive, and simple interest in the patient than does the nonsight-oriented therapist. Direct interest in the treatment or technique, however, may be greater than in other therapies and lead to indirect iatroplacebogenesis.

Classical psychoanalysis, a good example of a therapy with minimal direct interest in the patient and maximal interest in the treatment, can illustrate the mechanism of indirect iatroplacebogenesis, as well as clarify the problem of suggestion in psychoanalysis that was referred to by Freud as inadequately understood (Freud, 1948).

Acceptance for treatment by a prestigious physician has long been regarded as reassuring to patients. Because of the technical emphasis on suitability for psychoanalysis, many patients interpret acceptance for such treatment as evidence of intellectual capacity, insight potentiality, favorable prognosis, and not being seriously ill (Bergman, 1958; Boring, 1964; Scharaf & Levinson, 1964; Schmideberg, 1958).

The careful selection of patients for psychoanalysis involves many criteria that maximize response to therapy (Eyesenck, 1965;

[19]Lowinger & Dobie, 1963, 1964; Snyder & Snyder, 1961; Strupp, 1961; Strupp, 1958c, 1959, 1960b; Strupp & Williams, 1960; Wallach & Strupp, 1960; Berman, 1949; Frank, 1961; Krasner, 1962; Meerloo, 1963; Hobbs, 1962; Hammett, 1965; Karpman, 1949; Oberndorf, Greenachre & Kubie, 1953; Wolberg, 1954; Alexander, 1958; Schmideberg, 1939; Gill & Brenman, 1948, Hatterer, 1965; Glover, 1955; Wolff, 1956; Miller, 1949; Szasz & Nemiroff, 1963; Alexander, 1963; Jackson & Haley, 1963; Stein, 1966.

Glover, 1952; Hatterer, 1965). The criteria for selection has changed since Freud first treated patients who were diagnosed as hysteric, and recently rediagnosed as psychotic or having severe character disorders (Zetzel, 1965). Patients are now the least ill of any group, and have comparatively favorable prognoses even without therapy. The criteria for selection may have evolved during the past 60 years into an empirical recognition of those patients most likely to respond to psychoanalytic treatment and perhaps to any appropriate treatment (Burrow, 1927; Eyesenck, 1965; Frank, Gliedman, Imber, Nash, & Stone, 1957; Hatterer, 1965; Hobbs, 1962; Luborsky, 1962; Meehl, 1965; Zetzel, 1965).

Patients who meet the criteria for psychotherapy or psychoanalysis frequently have sociocultural expectations, backgrounds and interests that are similar to their therapists.[20] Cultural mutuality, as noted previously, is related to the therapist's interest in the patient, treatment results and the success of treatment (Cole, Branch, & Allison, 1962; Frank, 1961; Goldstein, 1962; Gumpert, 1963, Heine & Trossman, 1960; Lesse, 1964). The patient's ability to pay a large fee for a long time is a prerequisite for treatment and the therapist's interest (Chodoff, 1964; Hatterer, 1965; Kubie, 1964; Mowrer, 1963).

Patients may be more educated, creative, intelligent, informed, accomplished, successful, and wealthier than the treating psychiatrist. Such patients would reject simple reassurance, persuasion, reeducation, support, and other culturally inappropriate placebo techniques. Only an unapproachable and prestigious physician, who was a master of esoteric dynamic theory, which was not easily understood by the uninitiated, would be able to engender the magic and mystery (one-upmanship) (Haley, 1953) necessary for placebo responses. As Schmideberg (1939), put it, drugs are a placebo for some patients; psychoanalysis for

[20]Lowinger & Dobie, 1963, 1964; Snyder & Snyder, 1961; Strupp, 1960a; Frank, 1961; Cole, Branch, & Allison, 1962; Rickels, Baum, Taylor, & Raab, 1964; Frank, Gliedman, Imber, Nash, & Stone, 1957; Heine & Trossman, 1960; Hobbs, 1962; Lesse, 1962; Luorsky, 1962; Burrow, 1927; Goldstein, 1966; Eysenck, 1965; Hatterer, 1965; Zetzel, 1965; Meehl, 1955; Schaffer & Myers, 1954; Hollingshead & Redlich, 1958; Wood, Rokusin, & Morse, 1965.

others (Fenichel, 1954; Jaspers, 1965; Kiev, 1962; Levenson, 1958). In the previous version of this chapter (Shapiro, 1971) a psychoanalytic case history was discussed to demonstrate that psychoanalysis is potentially susceptible to many placebogenic and iatroplacebogenic effects.

Many psychoanalysts believe that analytic treatment is differentiated from other therapies because it has specific, nonplacebo, and nonsuggestive effects. This review suggests the contrary position that it may have extensive, potent, and subtle placebo effects on patients for whom the treatment is appropriate (Bailey, 1965; Frank, 1961; Glover, 1955; Goldstein, 1966; Hatterer, 1965; Kiev, 1964; Rachman, 1963; Schmideberg, 1939).

The concept of iatroplacebogenesis is supported by its general applicability to many therapies. Iatroplacebogenesis is more important in some forms of therapy than others. It does not preclude concomitant specific effects, such as insights in psychotherapy or pharmaceutical effects in drug therapy. It may function as a prerequisite or catalyst for therapies that involve psychological factors or interpersonal relationships; see, for example, the evidence that specific effects occur in psychochemotherapy when the iatroplacebogenic atmosphere is favorable.

Many of these placebogenic and iatroplacebogenic influences are major but unacknowledged factors in the clinical practice and therapeutic claims of behaviorally oriented therapists (Russell, 1974; Shapiro, 1976; Shapiro, Bruun, & Sweet, in press). The existence of these same placebogenic factors and themes in disparate therapies such as psychoanalysis and behavior therapy (as well as biofeedback, megavitamin, acupuncture treatment, and innumerable other newly introduced and to-be-introduced therapies) is testimony to the inevitability, reoccurrence, and power of the placebo effect in the past, present, and the future history of clinical therapies.

NEGATIVE PLACEBO EFFECTS

An early, curious finding of placebo effect research was that placebos caused negative as well as desired or positive therapeutic reactions. Negative placebo effects are defined as the occurrence of side effects or as the worsening of symptomatology following placebo administration. It is important to separate these two definitions since the origin and significance of negative placebo effects may differ depending on the definition utilized.

Placebo-Induced Side Effects

The findings that side effects often followed ingestion of placebos has contributed to the mystique and potency attributed to placebos (Beecher, 1955). Early studies reported placebo side effects such as vomiting, headaches, dizziness, dry mouth, drowsiness, and nervousness (Brown, 1948; Diehl, 1933). Recent studies have confirmed the frequency of these placebo-induced side effects (Dhune, Agshikart, & Dimiz, 1975; Gowdery, Hamilton, & Philip, 1967; Hass, Fink, & Hartleider, 1963; Pogge, 1963).

The frequency and types of placebo side effects varies among studies. Pogge (1963) tabulated the results of 67 studies and found that 817 of 3549 patients (23 percent) reported at least one side effect following placebo treatment. The type of side effect was related to the type of active medication or disease entity under study. For example, nausea was more frequently reported with antispasmodic placebos and drowsiness with tranquilizer placebos. Many other studies have described the variety and extensiveness of placebo-induced side effects.

Placebo-induced side effects can occur in several ways. Some placebo side effects may be symptoms of the original disease. Even with active medications there may be a misinterpretation of the cause of a side effect. Many of the side effects of antidepressant medication are also symptoms of depression (Busfield, Schneller, & Capra, 1962; Schulterbrandt, Raskin, & Reatig, 1974).

Some placebo-induced side effects may be the result of becoming more sensitive to and aware of bodily reactions. Reidenberg and Lowenthal (1968), in a survey of healthy subjects not taking medication, found that only 19 percent did not experience any of the 25 symptoms inquired about in the last two days. Had they been taking medication, these symptoms would have likely been called side effects.

In two studies, the number of side effects was similar in subjects taking placebos and control subjects not given a placebo (Glaser & Whittow, 1954; Shapiro, Chassen, Morris, & Frick, 1974). However, the type of side effects were different. Patients on placebos tended to report somatic side effects (e.g., headache) while those not on placebo tended to report cognitive or affective side effects (e.g., inability to concentrate) (Linton & Langs, 1962; Shapiro et al., 1974). The environmental set induced by taking medication may, therefore, influence patients to interpret and "label" their bodily reactions in somatic terms (e.g., headache) rather than cognitive-affective terms (e.g., tension).

Some placebo-induced side effects may be considered a patient's indirect communication of dissatisfaction with treatment. High scores on a scale measuring indirect hostility positively correlated with placebo side effects (Downing & Rickels, 1967). Placebo side effects are more frequently reported by clinic patients compared to private practice patients (Rickels et al., 1964b). Two studies found that placebo-induced side effects were correlated with increased clinical symptomatology (Keup, 1971; Rickels, 1964). However, another study found that placebo side effects were common for improved patients as well as those reporting a worsening of symptoms (Shapiro et al., 1973). Thus, side effects may facilitate improvement in some patients, possibly by the communication that a treatment is working (Kast & Loesch, 1961).

Placebos and the Worsening of Symptoms

Eight to 48 percent of patients given placebos in various studies report their condition to be worsened (Keup, 1971; Morison et al., 1961; Shapiro, et al., 1968; Wolf & Pinsky, 1954). Although several mechanisms have been proposed to explain this type of negative placebo effect, the most frequently cited explanation is the "violation of expectation."

Therapist instructions lead patients to have expectations about the effects of their therapy (Knapp & Knapp, 1973; Morris & O'Neal, 1975). Patients may interpret unfulfilled expectations about therapy as an indication that their symptoms were worse than originally thought. For conditions like insomnia, worry may cause an exacerbation of symptoms (Mitler, Guilleminault, Orem, Zarcone, & Dement, 1975; Storms & Nisbett, 1970). This type of "boomerang" in which the suggestion of improvement leads to worsening of an illness may be associated with factors such as "overselling" the efficacy of treatment (Valins, Adelson, Goldstein, & Weiner, 1971; Uhlenhuth et al., 1966) and patient inexperience with the treatment or the disease (Rickels, Baum, Raab, Taylor, & Moore, 1965; Rickels, Lipman, & Raab, 1966).

These considerations suggest that overall there are three types of placebo effects: a positive placebo effect defined as therapeutic improvement, a neutral placebo effect defined as the absence of change, and a negative placebo effect defined as a worsening of presenting symptomatology. Placebo-induced side effects are associated with both positive and negative placebo reactions (Shapiro et al., 1968). Therefore, placebo-induced side effects should not necessarily be labeled as negative placebo reactions. They should be considered as another aspect of placebo phenomenology and studied as a separate but related area (Struening, Shapiro, & Shapiro, in preparation).

CONCEPTS OF PLACEBOGENESIS

The method(s) by which placebos cause placebo effects is unknown. However, many processes have been advanced to explain placebo effects. Although there is little empirical verification for these processes, it is important to hypothesize processes of placebogenesis to organize and integrate the various relationships and predisposing factors associated with the placebo effect.

Three general themes serve to group the various placebogenic processes or mechanisms: social influence effects, expectancy effects, and evaluation effects.

Social Influence Effects
The role of the physician in society is unique. He or she performs and combines functions that have always been important to people—those of healer, priest, and scientist. These attributes facilitate the tendency of patients to view the physician as a socially powerful individual. Similarly, the experimenter's social power has been dramatically documented by Milgram's studies in which subjects were pressured into delivering potentially dangerous electric shocks to unseen victims (Milgram, 1963). Thus, therapists and investigators may contribute placebogenic influences by means of rewards and punishments or by their ability to deliver persuasive arguments. Placebo effects may also be attributable to normative role demands or the patients' and subjects' own suggestibility.

The patient-physician relationship gives rise to special transference and countertransference interactions. Several investigators have conceived of the placebo effect as due to this transference-countertransference relationship. Finally, the interest of the therapist in a patient may have a primary effect on reducing patient guilt thereby contributing to patients' improvement.

Suggestion
Suggestibility is the most often cited mechanism of placebo action. Several investigators have assumed that the placebo effect is merely a variation of the suggestibility response (Beecher, 1968; Strupp, Levenson, Manuck, Snell, Hinrichsen, & Boyd, 1974; Trouton, 1957). Although the process of suggestibility has not been well defined, factor analytic studies have demonstrated two major components. Primary suggestibility involves bodily responses to direct suggestions while secondary suggestibility is heavily loaded on items stressing the gullibility of subjects (Eyesenck & Furneaux, 1945; Evans, 1967). Both of these components are applicable to placebo effects. However, Trouton (1957) and Tibbetts and Hawkins (1956) considered secondary suggestibility more important in the genesis of placebo effects becuase both secondary suggestibility and the placebo effect involved "attitudes" whereas primary suggestibility involved "aptitudes."

Tests of suggestibility have been used as successful predictors of hypnosis. Unfortunately the hope that tests of suggestibility would predict response to placebo has not received empirical support.

Evans (1967) has suggested that a "therapeutic element" is necessary for suggestibility to correlate with the placebo effect. Shapiro (1964c) has hypothesized that differences in stimulus value of a test of suggestibility (which involves laboratory procedures) and a placebo test (which utilizes a clinical setting) may account for the lack of association. In a study by Frank et al. (1957) tests of suggestibility administered in a clinical setting were positively correlated with placebo reaction. It seems likely that if both placebo and suggestibility procedures are viewed as therapy, rather than one as a treatment and the other as a gullibility test, results would have greater concordance (Barber & Calvery, 1964).

Persuasion

Following the general model advanced by Hovland, Janis, and Kelley (1953), Liberman (1961) conceptualized the placebo effect as a function of the persuasive influence of a therapist who is perceived by the patient as expert and trustworthy. In addition, certain personality characteristics may predispose patients to placebo reactions. Some of the characteristics are related to placebo reaction only under certain circumstances while other traits are not situation bound. Finally, the observed placebo effect is measured both as a "true" response reflecting actual therapeutic change and as an "artifactual" response such as a faked or spontaneous change.

Both suggestibility and persuasion are general models of social influence. The persuasibility model views the placebo reactor as a rational individual rather than a gullible patient. The power of the physician's arguments, rather than the yielding of the patient, is stressed.

Transference

In the suggestion and persuasion paradigms, no distinction is made between the therapeutic and nontherapeutic environments. In the transference model, the placebo response is viewed as an outgrowth of the patient-therapist relationship. Although transference-type relationships may occur in experiments, they are apt to be qualitatively different from ones that could occur with a therapist. A classical definition of transference is that feelings, such as love, hatred, trust, and distrust, which the patient attached to significant persons in the past, are unknowingly displaced onto the therapist. Positive placebo effects stem from a positive transference caused by satisfactory early experiences

with parents or parent surrogates, or by individuals who expect succor and comfort from the therapist despite unsatisfactory early relationships. A patient's dependent relationship on the therapist may be made acceptable by the placebo, which presents a socially permissible vehicle for patient's regressions (Kast & Loesch, 1959). Negative placebo effects can result from a patient's unsatisfactory transference relationship with the therapist, and the doctor's countertransference relationship with the patient. Patients' hostility may be manifested by the report of negative side effects (Downing & Rickels, 1967). Dramatic symptom relief may be the manifestation of a positive transference relationship.

The transference paradigm views the patient as an active communicator who has established a special relationship with the therapist. Placebo effects are patient communications that have symbolic meaning and may predict ultimate treatment response.

Role Demands

Pressures to behave in certain prescribed manners are inherent in the role of a patient or experimental subject. In a clinical situation, positive placebo reactions may reflect the role of a "good patient." A patient who reacts positively would justify the therapist's initial concern and subsequent interest, care, and attention (Goldstein, Rosnow, Goodstadt, & Suls, 1972).

The subject may pick up subtle cues in an experimental trial (Rosenthal & Rosnow, 1969), integrate hints from the experimental procedure to guess the true nature of the experimental hypothesis (Orne, 1970), or model his or her behavior after the experimenter (Chaves, & Barber, 1974). Subjects may then behave in a fashion that will confirm the hypothesis. Even under postexperimental questioning, subjects may not divulge their awareness of the true hypothesis in an attempt to satisfy the experimenter.

Mutual or congruent therapist-patient role expectations can have a positive effect on treatment outcome, whereas discrepant role expectancies can lead to the failure of treatment (Goldstein, 1962). In addition to the therapist, other patients may communicate normative influences about proper behavior in particular situations (Schachter & Singer, 1962; Craig & Coren, 1975).

Operant Conditioning

High esteem for both the experimenter and therapist characterizes the experimental and therapeutic atmosphere and increases the potential of the therapist or experimenter to deliver rewards and punishments. Therefore, by both intended and unintended means, operant conditioning principles may shape subject and patient responses (Bourne, 1971; Frank, 1968; Gelfand, Ullmann, & Krasner, 1963; Kurland, 1957).

Buckalew (1972) demonstrated that reinforcements may increase placebo responding, independent of and in addition to the effects of suggestion. Conditioning by experimenters and therapists influences and reinforces simple behaviors as well as attitudes and complicated behaviors (Krasner, Ullmann, & Fisher, 1964). Operant conditioning may directly influence physiological responding (Byerly, 1976; Miller, 1974) or indirectly by cultivating arousal states that heighten patient's influenceability (Gliedman, Gantt, & Teitelbaum, 1957).

Guilt Reduction

The primary and direct effect of the therapist's interest in the patient is probably on guilt. Guilt is universal, and has been an important part of religion, philosophy, literature, and psychology throughout recorded history (Black, 1966; London, Schulman, & Black, 1966). It is involved in every system of psychopathology, clinically apparent in all patients with psychological and physical illness, and detected in nonpatients as well.[21] Guilt is manifested by or associated with many common feelings such as worthlessness, inadequacy, inferiority, impotence, depression, conflict between inner and outer behavior and shame about inner impulses and past behavior. Fantasies are often perceived as ego-alien experiences, not shared by other people. Inner sensitivity to irrationality stimulates fear and defense against insanity and loss of control, which cannot be fully examined without help from another person.

The prestigious heritage of the priest, scientist, and physician is represented in our culture by the psychotherapist (Frank, 1959, 1961; Jaspers, 1965; Kiev, 1964). To the physician are attributed omniscience, onmipotence, integrity, dedication, and esoteric knowledge (Schmideberg, 1939). Society's sanction of this role makes the physician an even more pretigious figure.[22]

Illness is usually stressful (Kiev, 1964). Familiar cues for integration decrease; ambiguity and stimulus hunger increase (Heine, 1950; Frank, 1969, 1961; Krasner, 1962, Kiev, 1964; Ward, 1964; Schmideberg, 1939); and regressive fantasies (Fisher, 1953), guilt (Frank, 1961; Glover, 1931), anxiety,[23] depression (Frank, 1961; Shapiro, 1963, 1964c, d, f, 1968), and dependency (Frank, 1961; Zuckerman & Grosz, 1958; Jakubszak & Walter, 1959) are stimulated: all these factors that have been cited as correlates of suggestibility and the placebo effect.[24]

The favorable feelings of the therapist have been associated with the increased expression of affect by patients (Fiedler, 1953; Frank, 1961), which may further decrease guilt through catharsis. It is also related to increased suggestibility, conditioning, and learning in patients. Patients become suggestible and are inordinately reassured by the interest of the prestigious therapist (Strupp et al., 1964; Frank, 1961; Brown, 1929; Schmideberg, 1939; Sargant, 1957; Estes, 1948; Sherif & Haney, 1952). Powerful therapeutic forces have now been set into motion. Guilt, anxiety, and discomfort are reduced, hope is mobilized and previ-

[21]Strupp, 1960b; Kahn, 1957; Fenichel, 1954; Hobbs, 1962; Kiev, 1962, 1964; Mowrer, 1963; Elliode, 1964; De Grazia, 1952; Rogers, 1956; Ripley & Jackson, 1959; Jersild & Lazard, 1962; Haley, 1963; Sargant, 1957; Mowrer, 1961; Murphy, 1964; La Barre, 1964.

[22]Heine, 1950; Frank, 1961; Fenichel, 1954; Lesse, 1964; Jaspers, 1965; Kiev, 1962, 1964; Ellenberger, 1956; Gumpert, 1963; Scharaf & Lerinson, 1964.

[23]Goldstein, 1962; Krasner, 1962; Kiev, 1962, 1964; Ellenberger, 1956; Estes, 1948; Sherif & Haney, 1952; Dibner, 1958; Walters, Marshall, & Shooter, 1960; Walters & Ray, 1960; Walters & Quinn, 1960; Walters & Parke, 1964.

[24]Strupp, Wallach, & Wogan, 1964; Goldstein, 1962; Barchilon, 1958; Frank, 1959, 1961; Krasner, 1962; Brown, 1929; Schmideberg, 1939; Kiev, 1962; Eliode, 1964; Sargant, 1957; Dibner, 1958; Walters, Marshall, & Shooter, 1960; Walters & Ray, 1960; Walters & Quinn, 1960; Borodin, 1955.

ously impaired assets can better be utilized (Frank, 1961; Estes, 1948). Spontaneous remission, as well as favorable environmental and other changes, have a greater chance of occurring, and are more easily stimulated, integrated, and utilized because of the favorable psychological state of the patient. These changes may be attributed to therapy, increasing the suggestibility of therapist and patient. At the same time, the therapist's interest is associated with increased understanding of the patient's behavior. These nonspecific therapeutic factors may now interact with the specific effects of various therapies.

Another possible mechanism is that interest in the patient leads to or coexists with an interest in the treatment.

An intense interest in treatment by a prestigious therapist mobilizes the patient's hope and optimism. The patient can depend on the therapist's integrity and competence, and be supported by the belief that he or she will be helped. The more intense the belief of the therapist in the patient's treatment, the more impressed will be the patient and the greater his or her belief. The patient may translate the therapist's belief: if the doctor is sure he or she can help me, I can rely on him or her to be helped (Frank, 1961; Kiev, 1964; Bergman, 1958; Menninger, 1959).

The therapist's interest in the patient's treatment also has an effect on guilt. A patient is reassured when problems are treated as symptoms of illness and not shameful character traits (Strupp et al., 1964; Snyder, 1946; Frank, 1961), or when or she learns that fears of losing control, insanity, and pathological uniqueness are unrealistic fantasies. Reassurance may occur in treatment with drugs and psychotherapy, in uncovering and repressive therapies, and whether or not direct reassurance is given.

The patient is in a highly suggestible state, as previously described, and may react to the therapist's interest with more hope and optimism than is warranted or realistic. Guilt and anxiety decrease and may interact with other therapeutic factors such as spontaneous remission, environmental changes, better utilization of resources, and other previously described factors. Finally, the therapist's interest in treatment may interact with his or her interest in the patient and in the results of treatment, and all of these factors may now interact with the potential specific effect of many therapies.

Support for the generation of guilt reduction from these factors and processes as well as the importance of guilt reduction to therapeutic and placebo effects requires empirical verification. Similarly, concepts such as operant conditioning, transference, suggestion, and persuasion are only hypothetically related to placebo reaction.

Expectancy Effects

Along with establishing special relationships with their patients, experimenters and therapists, by both intended and unintended means, communicate expectations about the effects of administered treatments. If the therapist does not explicitly supply these expectations, the patients may search for "cues" or rely on their own ideas and values (Morris & O'Neal, 1975; Sternbach, 1966).

Patients and subjects may also enter therapy or an experiment with preconceived notions derived from past experience or what has been learned from others. Although there is some research indicating that patients' general attitudes about chemotherapy may predict improvement on medication (Honigfeld, 1963; Sheard, 1964), this finding is inconsistent (Glick, 1968; Gorham & Sherman, 1961). Patients' attitudes may contribute to the therapeutic milieu. The more favorable the patient and staff attitudes in the milieu, the greater the "therapeutic potential" (Honigfeld, 1963).

Although general attitudes are weak correlates of placebo response, "specific attitudes" (i.e., expectations) seem to be better predictors of the placebo effect (Goldstein, 1960; Goldstein & Shipman, 1961; Hill, Belleville, & Wikler, 1957; Morris & O'Neal, 1974; Uhlenhuth et al., 1966). Attitudes and expectancies are thought to be important, nonspecific aspects of psychotherapy (Nash et al., 1964).

Expectations are formed and modified by patients' or subjects' previous experience with a specific treatment. Studies of the nonspecific effects of marijuana intoxication indicate that familiarity with the active drug increases subsequent placebo response (Carlin et al., 1974; Jones, 1971). Other studies suggest that previous experience may tend to decrease placebo reaction (Rickels, Lipman, & Raab, 1966; Snyder, Schultz, & Jones, 1974; Valins et al., 1971). The finding that previous experience with a treatment can both increase or decrease placebo reaction supports the contention that placebo effects can occur through any number of pathways. Differences in procedures, populations studied, or any number of variables could possibly account for these conflicting results.

There are at least four ways expectations contribute to placebogenesis: by classical conditioning, by "cognitive dissonance," by influencing the internal standard against which therapeutic effects are evaluated, and by affecting the hope and faith of an individual about the therapist and therapy.

The importance of expectations in drug therapy is highlighted by the findings that normal behavioral responses to active drugs are not found when patients are not told the nature of the drug they are administered (Lyerly et al., 1964; Penick & Hinkle, 1964) and physiological responses are decreased by inappropriate expectations (Penick & Fisher, 1965).

Classical Conditioning

When expectations are produced by prior temporal association, classical conditioning is believed to be a prime determinant of the placebo effect. The earliest demonstration of classically conditioned placebo effects was by Pavlov himself (Pavlov, 1927). Dogs who were initially injected with morphine reacted with salivation, nausea, and emesis. After repeated injections, the dogs displayed the same reactions to being prepared for the injection as they did to the initial injection. This conditioned placebo response was more complete and less dependent on the organism's motivational state than other forms of classical conditioning (Grant, 1964).

Classical conditioned reactions to drugs have been demonstrated in animals (Hernstein, 1962; Pickins & Crowder, 1967; Altman, 1971) and humans (Knowles, 1963). The finding that physiological reactions to drugs may occur quicker than when induced by a pharmacological mechanism has also been attributed to classical conditioning (Petrie, 1960; Stanley & Schrosberg, 1953).

Cognitive Dissonance

The anticipation that a therapy will produce a physiological effect can lead to the occurrence of that effect (Wolf, 1950). Cognitive dissonance has been advanced as a motivational mechanism that can account for psychologically caused changes in bodily states (Totman, 1976; Zimbardo, 1969).

When two beliefs are in a dissonant relationship (i.e., they are the logical converse of one another), there is believed to be a generalized (arousing) drive state within the individual to resolve this dissonance (Festinger, 1957; Pallak & Pittman, 1972; Waterman 1969; Zana & Cooper 1974). To resolve the aversive qualities of dissonance, individuals may be forced to change the attitude or belief that offers the "least resistance" to change. If attitutes or beliefs are strongly held, physiological functioning may be changed to achieve a state of cognitive consonance. Although the experimental demonstrations of dissonance produced physiological changes have been limited to pain endurance (Zimbardo, 1969), it is possible to envision more generalized application. An individual's belief in a prestigious therapist's dictum that certain events will occur ("my doctor said this therapy will make me feel better") or in the power of a therapy ("only very sick people fail to improve with psychotherapy") may be strongly entrenched. If the individual does not start to feel better, a state of dissonance will evolve. Beliefs that restore consonance such as "the doctor lied" or "the doctor did not know what he was talking about" may not be acceptable in the individual's value system. To achieve consonance, a dissonance caused placebo effect may be induced.

Internal Standards

Evaluation of a therapy is relative since an identical therapeutic outcome could be judged a success or a failure based solely on the criterion utilized. Therapies are evaluated in experiments by comparison with appropriate control groups. The criterion for the individual receiving treatment, however, is based on an internal standard. Expectations play a role in determining both the level and strength of this standard.

The placebo effect can be affected by instructions given by therapists that are conveyed by different therapists' attitudes (Uhlenhuth et al., 1959), or by explicity assigned roles (Uhlenhuth et al., 1966). An interesting finding is that unfilled therapeutic promises may backfire and lead to clinical worsening (Valins et al., 1971; Storms & Nisbett, 1970). Similarly, if patients' expectations about treatment are highly discrepant with the initial perceptions, they may prematurely drop out of treatment (Rickels & Anderson, 1967).

A second factor that influences the strength of an internal standard is the previous experience of the patient with the disease or therapy. Patients highly familiar with a therapy or a disease are apt to have more realistic expectations and, therefore, better standards of comparison. Rickels, Lipman, & Raab (1966) reviewed data indicating that a longer duration of illness and history of taking medication were both negatively correlated with placebo reaction. Data from studies utilizing the same patients in multiple treatments support the conclusion that once having experienced a satisfactory response, patients develop and employ this frame of reference to evaluate subsequent treatments (Adam, Adamson, Brezinova, & Oswald, 1976; Haertzen, 1969; Galanter, Stillman, Wyatt, Vaughn, Weingartner, & Nurnberg, 1974; Rickels, Lipman, & Raab, 1966). Accurate expectations, supplied by giving greater detail about the physical sensations one will experience can reduce the distress of painful stimuli (Johnson, 1973).

Hope

Expectations combined with desire are the essential ingredients of hope. Frank (1961) has argued persuasively for the importance of hope in psychotherapy and placebo effects. Hope is viewed as an integration of physiological arousal with certain cognitions. The cognitive component of hope involves envisioning a favorable change in one's life situation, usually in relation to one's actions or an anticipated environmental event.

Anticipations about therapy begin before the individual labels himself or herself a patient and are reformulated at the initial and subsequent stages of therapy (Goldstein, 1962). Hope is an essential element in the motivation of goals (Stotland, 1969). Frank (1963) views hope as directly related to the reduction of anxiety, depression, and other symptoms.

The importance of faith is reflected in the fact that one of the major, best-educated religious groups in the United States denies the rational efficacy of any treatment or medicine, and attributes all therapeutic benefits to faith. Faith, frequently denoted by terms such as trust, confidence, and the strength of a belief, might augment the influence of expectations on the placebo effect.

Evaluation Effects

A third process that influences placebo effects is derived from attempts to evaluate the placebo response. Patients may modify subjective reports or change their behavior because of the knowledge that they are being monitored. A more subtle mechanism occurs when patients are asked to report an emotion or attitude, and they rely on salient cues to "label" their response. Bodily states or behavioral responses may be interpreted in the context of the measurement situation. Misattribution is another process that influences placebo responses. The knowledge that therapy has been rendered constiutes a major environmental cue to both the patient and the therapist. A change in a patient's status may be misattributed to the therapy when it is actually caused by some other situational factor.

Response Artifacts

The assessment of therapeutic effects can distort the data (Webb, Campbell, Schwartz, & Sechrest, 1966; Nelson, Lipinski, & Black, 1975; Roberts & Renzaglia, 1965). Since there is so much variance in tests used to estimate the placebo effect (Shapiro et al., 1973), the reliability and validity of placebo effect measures is generally unknown. What investigators call placebo effects may actually be patients' response bias.

Response bias may be caused by inherent design problems of self-rating scales. In filling out questionnaires, patients may lie, fake, or tend to present themselves in a favorable light (Dahlstrom & Welsh, 1960). They may be thoughtless, overly generous, or tend to consistantly give themselves the benefit of the doubt (Jones & Sigall, 1971). They may consistently rate all aspects of a stimulus "good or "bad" without proper discrimination (O'Neal & Mills, 1969). They may generally tend to give socially desirable responses (Marlowe & Crowne, 1964; Edwards, 1957). Apprehension by patients about being evaluated can prompt a biased response (Rosenberg, 1969) or response bias can be stimulated by a desire to please or impress therapists (Tedeschi, Schlenker, & Bonoma, 1970).

Labeling

It is assumed that emotions can be validly measured by asking patients to reflect on their inner state. However, Schachter and Singer (1962) have hypothesized that an emotion is the result of a bodily state change that is "labeled" by means of appropriate environmental cues. The same change in bodily state can result in an angry or euphoric emotion, depending on the context in which the change occurs.

When a patient is asked to rate "how he or she feels," he or she may be uncertain about the nature and extent of his or her feelings. A most potent environmental cue is the fact that a therapy has recently been adminstered. The therapeutic milieu may lead the patient to "label" an ambiguous bodily state with "positive" words that reflect a therapeutic outcome.

The particular labels an individual chooses are apt to be dependent on the type of therapy rendered. Shapiro et al., (1974) administered drug-placebo and control-placebo therapies to psychiatric outpatients. The control placebo was conveyed by asking patients to sit in a quiet room for an hour and rate how their symptoms spontaneously varied. The number of side effects reported by patients did not differ between the two groups. However, patients who received the drug placebos tended to describe their side effects as somatic, such as "headache" and "stomach pain," whereas the control-placebo patients tended to use cognitive-affective labels such as "upset" or "feeling sorry for self."

In addition to environmental factors, previous experience with the particular therapy or similar therapies may supply appropriate labels in ambiguous situations (Linn, 1959). Becker (1953), has theorized that the experience of a marijuana induced "high" is dependent on an individual learning to label the bodily reactions that consitute this reaction.

An interesting phenomenon related to the labeling process is that any change in bodily arousal stimulates the need to explain the cause of the arousal. Individuals search the environmental for appropriate explanations (Barefoot & Straub, 1971; Girodo, 1973; Goldstein, Fink, & Mettee, 1972; Valins, 1966). If an adequate explanation does not exist, perceptions may be distorted to account for the arousal (Wilkins, 1971). The arousal associated with the uncertainty of the initial aspects of therapy may be "labeled" with terms that denote therapeutic success.

Misattribution

The basic premise of attribution theory is that people seek to know the causes of behavior, even their own behavior. However, sometimes mistakes are made and people misattribute the causes of behavior. (Jones, Kanouse, Kelley, Nisbett, Valins, & Weiner, 1972). Positive placebo effects may occur when the cause of a change in bodily state or behavioral response is erroneously attributed to the therapy rather than the actual cause such as some other environmental factor (Morris & O'Neal, 1974; Valins & Nisbett, 1971). The explanatory potential for misattribution as a mechanism for placebo effects is highlighted by a study by Schorer, Lowinger, Sullivan, and Hartlaub (1968). Sixty-four percent of a group of patients awaiting psychotherapy stated that their status had improved, even though they had not received treatment. Had these patients received psychotherapy it is likely that they would have attributed the improvement to their treatment.

According to attribution theory, individuals seek not only to assign reasons for observed changes, but also seek to fully explain why these changes occurred (Kruganski, 1975). If expected bodily state or behavioral changes do not occur, patients may experience a negative placebo effect. The negative placebo effect can occur when patient expectations about therapeutic results are overly optmistic (Hoenh-Saric, Liberman, Imber, Stone, Frank, & Ribich, 1974; Valins et al., 1971) or when patients assume that the cause of a therapy's failure is the severity of their illness (Storms & Nisbett, 1970).

Medication placebos have been used to manipulate the perceived cause for a reaction. By inducing people to falsely ascribe autonomic changes to the action of a placebo, fear of impending shocks can be diminished (Nisbett & Schachter, 1966), snake phobia can be reduced (Valins & Ray, 1967) discomfort from cigarette withdrawal can be reduced (Barefoot & Girodo, 1972), insomniacs may fall asleep sooner (Storms & Nisbett, 1970), cognitive dissonance can be decreased (Zanna & Cooper, 1974), and anxiety from watching an upsetting film can be lessened (Girodo, 1973).

More recent studies have shown that the misattribution process may have severe limitations in therapeutic situations (Bootzin, Hermin, & Nicassio, 1976; Calvert-Boyanowski & Leventhal, in press; Kellogg & Baron, 1975; Hoehn-Saric et al., 1974; Singerman, Borkovec & Baron, 1976). Further study of the applicability of attribution theory to the placebo reaction is warrented.

CONCLUSION

Therapy is impaired if physicians are unaware of placebo effects. Therapeutic effects are attributed to specific procedures that, unknown to the physician, are caused by nonspecific or placebo effects. The therapist's credulity about the efficacy and specificity of the procedure are exaggerated, and it encourages the use of one procedure or technique for all patients. Therapists who rely on one technique are unable to treat many patients; some may be hurt because of inappropriate treatment (Jasper, 1965; Ward, 1964), and specific indications for a therapeutic procedure are obfuscated. Awareness of placebo effects enable clinicians to better evaluate the effects of therapy, contribute to the development of more flexible and appropriate procedures, and make therapy more comprehensive, resourceful, and effective.

The recognition that these factors contribute to the treatment process improve studies by investigators and may help clarify unsolved problems of the specificity of many therapies.

It is important to remember that much of this chapter is based on review of retrospective data. Careful prospective studies are necessary for clarification of the primacy, relevancy and validity of these concepts.

The history of both physiologic and psychologic treatment is largely the history of the placebo effect; those who forget the past are destined to repeat it. Garrison observed that "whenever many different remedies are used for a disease, it usually means that we know little about treating the dis-

ease, which is also true of a [remedy] when it is vaunted as a panacea or cure-all for many diseases" (Garrison, 1921).

If we keep those thoughts in mind, we may avoid the problem that the complier of the Paris Pharmacologia insightfully observed a century ago: "What pledge can be afforded that the boasted remedies of the present day will not be like their predecessors, fall into disrepute, and in their turn serve only as a humiliating memorial of the credulity and infatuation of the physicians who recommended and prescribed them" (Haggard, 1934).

REFERENCES

Abramson, H. A., Jarvik, M. E., Levine, A., Kaufman, M. R., & Hirsch, M. W. Lysergic acid diethylamide (LSD-25). The effects produced by substitution of tap water placebo. *Journal of Psychology*, 1955, *40*, 367–383.

Adam, K., Adamson, L., Brezinova, V., & Oswald, I. Do placebos alter sleep? *British Medical Journal*, 1976, *1*, 195–196.

Ademec, C. Extra-pharmacological factors in marijuana intoxication. Paper presented at 81st American Psychological Association, Montreal, 1973.

Ainslie, J. D., Jones, M. B., & Stiefel, J. R. Practical drug evaluation method. *Archives of General Psychiatry*, 1965, *12*, 368–373.

Aletky, P. J., & Carlin, A. S. Sex differences and placebo effects: Motivation as an intervening variable. *Journal of Consulting and Clinical Psychology*, 1974, *43*, 278.

Alexander, F. The dynamics of psychotherapy in the light of learning theory. *American Journal of Psychiatry*, 1963, *120*, 441–449.

Alexander, F. Unexplored areas in psychoanalytic theory and treatment. *Behavioral Science*, 1958, *3*, 293–316.

Bailey, P. *Sigmund the unserene*. Springfield, Ill.: Charles C Thomas, 1965.

Baker, A. A., & Thrope, J. G. Placebo response. *AMA Archives of Neurology and Psychiatry*, 1957, *78*, 57–60.

Bank, S. P. *An investigation of the placebo effect*. Dissertation Abstracts, 1969, *29* (7-B), 2626.

Barber, T. X. "Hypnosis," analgesia and the placebo effect. *Journal of the American Medical Association*, 1960, *172*, 680–683.

Barber, T. X. Experimental controls and the phenomena of "hypnosis." A critique of hypnotic research methodology. *Journal of Nervous and Mental Disease*, 1962, *134*, 493–505.

Barber, T. X. Physiological effects of "hypnotic suggestions." A critical review of recent research. *Psychological Bulletin*, 1965, *63*, 201–222(a).

Barber, T. X. Experimental analysis of "hypnotic" behavior. A review of recent empirical findings. *Journal of Abnormal Psychology*, 1965, *70*, 132–154(b).

Barber, T. X., & Calvery, D. S. The definition of the situation as a variable affecting "hypnotic like" suggestibility. *Journal of Clinical Psychology*, 1964, *20*, 438–440.

Barber, T. X., & Silver, M. J. Fact, fiction and the experimenter bias effect. *Psychological Bulletin in Monograph Supplement*, 1968, *70*, 1–29.

Barchilon, J. On countertransference "cures." *Journal of the American Psychoanalytic Association*, 1958, *6*, 222.

Barefoot, J. C., & Girodo, M. The misattribution of smoking cessation symptoms. *Canadian Journal of Behavioral Science*, 1972, *4*, 358–363.

Barefoot, J. C., & Straub, R. B. Opportunity for information search on the effect of false heart rate feedback. *Journal of Personality and Social Psychology*, 1971, *17*, 154–157.

Batterman, R. C., & Lower, W. R. Placebo responsiveness—influence of previous therapy. *Current Therapeutic Research*, 1968, *10*, 136–143.

Battle, C. C., Imber, S. D., Hoen-Saric, R., Stone, A. R., Nash, E. R., & Frank, J. D. Target complaints as criteria of improvement. *American Journal of Psychotherapy*, 1966, *1*, 184–192.

Becker, H. S. Becoming a marijuana user. *American Journal of Sociology*, 1953, *59*, 235–242.

Becker, H. S. Consciousness, power and drug effects. *Journal of Psychedelic Drugs*, 1974, *6*, 67–76.

Beecher, H. K. The powerful placebo. *Journal of the American Medical Association*, 1955, *159*, 1602–1606.

Beecher, H. K. Relationship of significance of wound to pain experienced. *Journal of the American Medical Association*, 1956, *161*, 1609–1613.

Beecher, H. K. Increased stress and effectiveness of placebos and "active" drugs. *Science*, 1960, *132*, 91–92.

Beecher, H. K. Placebo effects of situations, attitudes and drugs: A quantitative study of suggestibility. In K. Rickels (Ed.). *Nonspecific Factors of Drug Therapy*. Springfield, Ill.: Charles C Thomas, 1968.

Benson, H., & Epstein, M. D. The placebo effect: A neglected asset in the care of patients. *Journal of the American Medical Association*, 1975, *232*, 1225–1227.

Bergman, P. The role of faith in psychotherapy. *Bulletin of the Menninger Clinic*, 1958, *22*, 92–103.

Berkowitz, L. Reporting of the experiment: A case study in leveling, sharpening and assimilation. *Journal of Experimental Social Psychology*, 1971, *7*, 237–243.

Berman, L. Countertransferences and attitudes of the analyst in the therapeutic process. *Psychiatry*, 1949, *12*, 159–166.

Bishop, M., & Gallant, D. Observations of placebo response in chronic schizophrenic patients. *Archives of General Psychiatry*, 1966, *14*, 497–503.

Black, A. A. Factors predisposing to placebo response in new outpatients with anxiety states. *British Journal of Psychiatry*, 1966, *112*, 487, 557–562.

Blackwell, B., Bloomfield, S. S., & Buncher, C. R. Dem-

onstration to medical students of placebo responses and non-drug factors. *Lancet*, 1972, *1*, 1279–1282.

Blaine, G. B., & McArthur, C. L. What happened in therapy as seen by the patient and his psychiatrist. *Journal of Nervous and Mental Diseases*, 1958, *127*, 678–681.

Blakiston New Gould medical dictionary. (1st ed.) Philadelphia: 1949.

Board, F. A. Patient's and physician's judgments of outcome of psychotherapy in an outpatient clinic. *AMA Archives of General Psychiatry*, 1959, *1*, 185–196.

Bootzin, R. R., Herman, P. C., & Nicassio, P. The power of suggestion: Another examination of misattribution and insomnia. *Journal of Personality and Social Psychology*, 1976, *34*, 673–679.

Boring, E. G. Cognitive dissonance: Its use in science. *Science*, 1964, *145*, 680–685.

Boring, E. G. Perspective: Artifact and Control. In R. Rosenthal & R. L. Rosnow (Eds.), *Artifact in behavioral research*. New York: Academic Press, 1969.

Borkovec, T. D. The role of expectancy and physiological feedback in fear research: A review with special reference to subject characteristics. *Behavior Therapy*, 1973, *4*, 491–505.

Borkovec, T. D., & Nau, S. D. Credibility of analogue therapy rationales. *Journal of Behavior Therapy and Experimental Psychiatry*, 1972, *3*, 257–260.

Borodin, E. S. Ambiguity as a therapeutic variable. *Journal of Consulting Psychology*, 1955, *19*, 9–15.

Boudewyns, P. A., & Borkovec, T. D. *Credibility of psychotherapy and placebo therapy rationales*. Newsletter for research on mental health and behavioral sciences, 1974, *16*, 15–18.

Bourne, H. R. The placebo—a poorly understood and neglected therapeutic agent. *Rational Drug Therapy*, 1971, *11*, 1–6.

Braaty, T. Fundamentals of psychoanalytic technique. New York: Wiley, 1954.

Brandsma, J. M. Effects of personality and placebo-instructional sets on psychophysiological responding. *Catalog of Selected Documents in Psychology*, 1973, *3*, 78.

Breuer, J., & Freud, S. *Studies on hysteria*. New York: Basic Books, 1957.

Brill, N. Q., Koegler, R. R., Epstein, L. J., & Forgy, E. W. Controlled study of psychiatric outpatients treatment. *Archives of General Psychiatry*, 1964, *10*, 581–595.

Brill, N. Q., & Storrow, H. W. Prognostic factors in psychotherapy. *Journal of the American Medical Association*, 1963, *183*, 913–916.

British Medical Journal. Placebos. 1961, *1*, 43–44.

Brodeur, D. W. A short history of placebos. *Journal of the American Pharmaceutical Association*, 1965, *NS5*, 662–663.

Brown, S. Side reactions in pyribenzamine medication. *Proceedings of the Society for Experimental Biology and Medicine*. 1948, *67*, 373–374.

Brown, W. *Science and personlity*. New Haven: Yale University Press, 1929.

Buckalew, L. An analysis of experimental components in a placebo effect. *The Psychological Record*, 1972, *22*, 113–119.

Burrow, T. *The social basis of consciousness.* New York: Harcourt, Brace & Co., 1927.

Busfield, B., Schneller, P., & Capra, D. Depressive symptom or side effect? A comparative study of symptoms during pre-treatment and treatment of patients on three antidepressant medications. *Journal of Nervous and Mental Disease,* 1962, *134,* 339–345.

Bush, P. The placebo effect. *Journal of the American Pharmaceutical Association,* 1974, *NS14,* 671–674.

Buss, A. H., & Portnoy, N. W. Pain tolerance and group identification. *Journal of Personality and Social Psychology,* 1967, *16,* 106–108.

Byerly, H. Explaining and exploiting the placebo effect. *Perspectives in Biology and Medicine,* 1976, *3,* 423–435.

Calvert-Boyanowsky, J., & Leventhal, H. The role of information in attenuating behavioral response to stress: A reinterpretation of the misattribution phenomenon. *Journal of Personality and Social Psychology,* in press.

Campbell, J., & Rosenbaum, P. Placebo effect and symptom relief in psychotherapy. *Archives of General Psychiatry,* 1967, *16,* 364–368.

Carlin, A. S., Bakker, C. B., Halpern, L., & Post, R. D. Social facilitation of marijuana intoxication: Impact of social set on pharmacological activity. *Journal of Abnormal Psychology,* 1972, *80,* 132–140.

Carlin, A. S., Post, R. D., Bakker, C. B., & Halpern, L. M. The role of modeling and previous experience in the facilitation of marijuana intoxication. *Journal of Nervous and Mental Disease,* 1974, *159,* 275–281.

Carter, D., & Allen, D. Evaluation of the placebo effect in optometry. *American Journal of Optometry and Archives of the American Academy of Optometry,* 1973, *50,* 94–104.

Castiglioni, A. *Adventures of the mind.* New York: Alfred A. Knopf, 1946.

The Catholic encyclopedia. New York: Gilmary Society, *2, 7, 8,* 1911.

Cartwright, R. D., & Lerner, B. Empathy, need to change and improvement with psychotherapy. *Journal of Consulting Psychology,* 1963, *27,* 138–144.

Cautela, J. R., Flannery, R. B., & Hanley, S. Covert modeling: An experimental test. *Behavior Therapy,* 1974, *5,* 494–502.

Chapman, L. J., Chapman, J. P., & Brelje, T. Influence of the experimenter on pupillary dilatation to sexually provocative pictures. *Journal of Abnormal Psychology,* 1969, *74,* 396–400.

Chaves, J. F., & Barber, T. X. Acupuncture analysis: A six factor theory. *Human Behavior,* 1973, *2,* 48–63.

Chaves, J. F., & Barber, T. X. Cognitive strategies. experimenter modeling and expectation in the attenuation of pain. *Journal of Abnormal Psychology,* 1974, *83,* 356–363.

Chodoff, P. Psychoanalysis and fees. *Comprehensive Psychiatry,* 1964, *5,* 137–145.

Clark, W. Sensory-decision theory analysis of the placebo effect on the criterion for pain and thermal sensitivity (d'). *Journal of Abnormal Psychology,* 1969, *74,* 363–371.

Cole, N., Branch, C., & Allison, R. Some relationships between social class and the practice of dynamic psychotherapy. *American Journal of Psychiatry,* 1962, *118,* 1004–1012.

Craig, K. D., & Coren, S. Signal detection analyses of social modeling influences on pain expressions. *Journal of Psychosomatic Research,* 1975, *19,* 105–112.

Cutler, R. Countertransference effects in psychotherapy. *Journal of Consulting Psychology,* 1958, *22,* 349–356.

Dahlstrom, W. G., & Welsh, G. S. *An MMPI handbook: A guide to use in clinical practice and research.* Minneapolis: University of Minnesota Press, 1960.

Davids, A. The relationship of cognitive-dissonance theory to an aspect of psychotherapeutic practice. *American Psychologist,* 1964, *19,* 329–332.

Davidson, A. Placebos, pills and physicians. *Canadian Medical Association Journal,* 1960, *83,* 1310–1313.

Davison, G. C., & Valins, D. Maintenance of self-attributed and drug-attributed behavior change. *Journal of Personality and Social Psychology,* 1969, *11,* 25–33.

De Grazia, D. *Errors in psychotherapy.* New York: Doubleday and Co., 1952.

Dhume, V. G., Agshikar, N. V., & Dimiz, R. S. Placebo induced side effects in healthy volunteers. *The Clinician,* 1975, 39, 289–291.

Dibner, A. S. Ambiguity and anxiety. *Journal of Abnormal and Social Psychology,* 1958, *56,* 165–174.

Diehl, H. Medical treatment of the common cold. *Journal of the American Medical Association,* 1933, *101,* 2042–2049.

Dimond, E. G., Kittle, C. F., & Cockett, J. E. Comparison of internal mammary artery ligation and sham operation for angina pectoris. *The American Journal of Cardiology,* 1960, *4,* 483–486.

Dinnerstein, A. J., & Halm, J. Modification of placebo effects by means of drugs. *Journal of Abnormal Psychology,* 1970, *75,* 308–314.

Dittes, J. E. GSR as a measure of patient's reaction to therapist's permissiveness. *Journal of Abnormal and Social Psychology,* 1957, *18,* 263–277.

Downing, R. and Rickels, K. Self report of hostility and the incidence of side reactions in neurotic outpatients treated with tranquilizing drugs and placebo. *Journal of Consulting Psychology,* 1967, *31,* 71–76.

Downing, R. W. and Rickels, K. Predictors of response to amitriptyline and placebo in three outpatient treatment settings. *Journal of Nervous and Mental Diseases,* 1973, *156,* 109–129.

Duran-Reynals, M. L. *The Fever Bark Tree.* New York: Doubleday and Co., 1964.

Edwards, A. L. The relationship between the judged desirability of a tract and the probability that tract will be endorsed. *Journal of Applied Psychology,* 1953, *37,* 90–93.

Ehrenwald, K. J. Doctrinal compliance in psychotherapy and problems of scientific methodology. In H. H. Masserman & J. I. Moreno (Eds.) *Progress in psychotherapy.* New York: Grune and Stratton, 1958.

Eisenman, R., & Huber, H. Creativity, insolence and attractiveness of female experimenters. *Perceptual and Motor Skills,* 1970, *30,* 515–520.

Eissen, S. B., Sabshin, M., & Heath, H. A comparison of the effects of investigators' and therapists' attitudes in the evaluation of tranquilizers prescribed to hospital patients. *Journal of Nervous and Mental Diseases,* 1959, *128,* 256–261.

Eliode, M. *Shamanism.* New York: Random House, 1964.

Ellenberger, H. The ancestry of dynamics of psychotherapy. *Bulletin of the Menninger Clinic,* 1956, *20,* 288–290.

Ellis, A. Psychotherapy techniques for use with psychotics. *American Journal of Psychotherapy,* 1955, *9,* 452–476.

Endicott, N. A. The problems of controls in the evaluation of psychotherapy. *Comparative Psychiatry,* 1962, *3,* 37–46.

Endo, E. J., & Page, C. W. A study of three types of group psychotherapy with hospitalized malinebriates. *American Journal of Studies of Alcoholism,* 1957, *18,* 263–377.

Engel, G. L., Reichsman, F., & Segal, H. L. A study of an infant with a gastric fistula. *Psychosomatic Medicine,* 1956, *18,* 374–398.

Estes, G. G. Concerning the therapeutic relationship in the dynamics of cure. *Journal of Consulting Psychology,* 1948, *12,* 76–81.

Evans, F. The power of a sugar pill. *Psychology Today,* 1974, *4,* 55–59.

Evans, F. J. Social psychological and pharmacological factors in pain perceptions. Paper presented at the American Psychological Association, Washington, D. C., 1969.

Evans, F. S. Suggestibility in the normal waking state. *Psychological Bulletin,* 1967, *67,* 114–129.

Eyesenck, H. J., & Furneaux, W. D. Primary and secondary suggestibility: An experimental and statistical study. *Journal of Experimental Psychology,* 1945, *35,* 485–503.

Fast, G. and Fisher, S. The role of body attitudes and acquiescence in epinephrine and placebo effects. *Psychosomatic Medicine,* 1971, *33,* 63–84.

Feather, B., Chapman, C., & Fisher, S. The effect of placebo on the perception of painful radient heat stimuli. *Psychosomatic Medicine,* 1972, *34,* 290–294.

Feldman, P. E. The personal element in psychiatric research. *American Journal of Psychology,* 1956, *113,* 52–59.

Feldman, P. E. Non-drug parameters of psychopharmacotherapy. The role of the physician. In M. Rinkel (Ed.), *Specific and non-specific factors in psychopharmacology.* New York: Philosphical Library, 1963.

Fenichel, O. *The psychoanalytic theory of neurosis.* New York: W. W. Norton 1945.

Fenichel, O. *Brief psychotherapy in the collected papers of Otto Fenichel.* New York: W. W. Norton, 1954.

Festinger, L. *A theory of cognitive dissonance.* Stanford: Stanford University Press, 1957.

Fiedler, F. E. A comparison of therapeutic relationships in psychoanalytic non-directive and Adlerian therapy. *Journal of Consulting Psychology,* 1950, *14,* 436–445.

Fiedler, F. E. Quantitative studies on the role of therapists' feelings toward their patients. In O. H. Mowrer (Ed.), *Psychotherapy theory and research.* New York: Ronald Press, 1953.

Fischer, H. K., & Dlin, B. M. the dynamics of placebo therapy: A clinical study. *American Journal of Medical Science,* 1956, *232,* 504–512.

Fisher, C. The transference meaning of giving suggestions. *Journal of the American Psychoanalytic Association,* 1953, *1,* 406–437.

Fisher, S. The placebo reactor: Thesis, antihesis, synthesis and hypothesis. *Diseases of the Nervous System,* 1967, *29,* 510–515.

Fisher, S., Cole, J. O., Rickels, K., & Uhlenhuth, E. H. Drug-set interaction: The effects of expectations on drug response in outpatients. In P. B. Bradley, F. Flugel, & P. Hoch (Eds.), *Neuropsychopharmacologia.* New York: Eisevier Publishing Co., 1964.

Fisher, S., & Fisher, R. L. Placebo response and acquiescence. *Psychopharmacologia,* 1963, *4,* 298–301.

Foreman, M. E. On cognitive dissonance as motivation toward successful therapy. *American Psychologist,* 1964, *19,* 777–782.

Foreyt, J. P., & Hagen, R. L. Covert sensitization: Conditioning or suggestion? *Journal of Abnormal Psychology,* 1973, *82,* 17–23.

Foulds, G. Psychoanalytic research in psychiatry. *Journal of Mental Science,* 1958, *104,* 259–267.

Fox, B. The investigation of the effects of psychiatric treatment. *Journal of Mental Science,* 1961, *107,* 493–502.

Frank, J. D. Some effects of expectancy and influence in psychotherapy. In J. H. Masserman & J. I. Moreno (Eds.). Volume III. *Progress in psychotherapy.* New York: Grune and Stratton, 1958.

Frank, J. D. The dynamics of the psychotherapeutic relationship, determinants and effects of the therapist's influence. *Journal of the Study of Interpersonal Process,* 1959, *22,* 17–39.

Frank, J. D. *Persuasion and healing.* Baltimore: Johns Hopkins Press, 1961.

Frank, J. D. Discussion of papers by H. J. Eyesenck, The effects of psychotherapy. *International Journal of Psychotherapy,* 1965, *1,* 150–152.

Frank, J. D. The role of hope in psychotherapy. *International Journal of Psychiatry,* 1968, *5,* 383–395.

Frank, J. D., Gliedman, L. H., Imber, S. D., Nash, E. J., & Stone, A. R. Why patients leave psychotherapy. *Archives of Neurology and Psychiatry,* 1957, *77,* 283–299.

Freedman, R., Engelhardt, D. M., Hankoff, L. D., Glick, B. S., Kaye, H., Buchwald, J., & Stark, P. Drop-out from outpatient psychiatric treatment. *Archives of Neurology and Psychiatry,* 1958, *80,* 657–666.

Freud, S. *Group psychotherapy and the analysis of the ego.* London: Hogarth Press, 1948.

Freund, J., Krupp, G., Goodenough, D., & Preston, L. The doctor-patient relationship and drug effect. *Clinical Pharmacology and Therapeutics,* 1972, *13,* 172–180.

Friedlander, F. Type I and type II bias comment. *American Psychologist,* 1964, *19,* 198–199.

Friedman, N., Kurland, D., & Rosenthal, R. Experimenter

behavior as an unintended determinant of experimental results. *Journal of Projective Techniques and Personality Assessment,* 1965, *29,* 479–490.

Galanter, M., Stillman, R., Wyatt, R. S., Vaughn, T. B., Weingartner, H., & Nurnberg, F. L. Marijuana and social behavior, a controlled study. *Archives of General Psychiatry,* 1974, *30,* 518–521.

Garfield, S. L., & Affleck, D. C. Therapists' judgments concerning patients considering psychotherapy. *American Psychologist,* 1960, *13,* 414.

Garland, L. H. The problem of observer error. *Bulletin of the New York Academy of Medicine,* 1960, *36,* 569–584.

Garrison, F. H. *An introduction to the history of medicine.* Philadelphia, Pa: W. B. Saunders, 1921.

Gartner, M. A. Selected personality difference between placebo reactors and nonreactors. Journal of the American Osteopathic Association, 1961, *60,* 377–378.

Gaw, A. C., Chang, L. W., & Shaw, L. Efficacy of acupuncture on osteoarthritic pain: A controlled, double blind study. *New England Journal of Medicine,* 1975, *293,* 375–378.

Gelfand, D. M., Gelfand, S., & Rardin, M. W. Some personality variables associated the placebo responsivity. *Psychological Reports,* 1965, *17,* 555–562.

Gelfand, S., Ullmann, L., and Kracnor, L. The placebo response: An experimental approach. *Journal of Nervous and Mental Disease,* 1963, *136,* 379–387.

Gendlin, E. T. Research in psychotherapy with schizophrenic patients and the nature of that "illness." *American Journal of Psychotherapy,* 1966, *20,* 4–16.

Gill, M. G., & Brenman, M. Research in psychotherapy. *American Journal of Orthopsychiatry,* 1948, *18,* 100–110.

Ginsburg, S. W., & Arrington, W. Aspects of psychiatric clinic practice. *American Journal of Orthopsychiatry,* 1948, *18,* 322–333.

Girodo, M. Film induced arousal, information search and the attribution process. *Journal of Personality and Social Psychology,* 1973, *25,* 357–360.

Glaser, E., & Whittow, G. Experimental errors in clinical trials. *Clinical Science,* 1954, *13,* 199–210.

Glick, B. S. Attitude toward drug and clinical outcome. *American Journal of Psychiatry,* 1968, *124,* 37–39.

Gliedman, L. H., Gantt, W. H. and Teitelbaum, H. A. Some implications of conditional reflex for placebo research. *American Journal of Psychiatry,* 1957, *113,* 1103–1107.

Gliedman, C. H., Nash, E. H., Imber, S. D., Stone A. R., & Frank, J. D. Reduction of symptoms by pharmacology and short term psychotherapy. *Archives of Neurology and Psychiatry,* 1958, *79,* 345–351.

Glover, E. The therapeutic effect of inexact interpretation: A contribution to theory of suggestion. *International Journal of Psychoanalysis,* 1931, *12,* 397–412.

Glover, E. Research methods, in psychoanalysis. *International Journal of Psychoanalysis,* 1952, *23,* 403–412.

Glover, E. *The technique of psychoanalysis.* New York: International Universities Press, 1955.

Goldberg, S. C., Schooler, N. R., Davidson, E. M., & Kayce, M. M. Sex and race differences in response to drug treatment among schizophrenics. *Psychopharmacologia,* 1966, *9,* 31–47.

Goldman, A. R., Whitton, K., & Scherer, J. M. The drug ritual, verbal instruction and schizophrenics' word activity levels. *Journal of Nervous and Mental Diseases,* 1965, *140,* 272–279.

Goldstein, A. P. Patient expectancies and nonspecific therapy as a basis for (un)spontaneous remission. *Journal of Clinical Psychology,* 1960, *16,* 399–403.

Goldstein, A. P. *Therapist-patient expectancies in psychotherapy.* New York: Pergamon Press, 1962.

Goldstein, A. P. Psychotherapy research by extrapolation from social psychology. *Journal of Consulting Psychology,* 1966, *13,* 38–46.

Goldstein, A. P., & Shipman, W. G. Patient expectancies, symptom reduction and aspects of the initial psychotherapeutic interview. *Journal of Clinical Psychology,* 1961, *17,* 129–133.

Goldstein, D., Fink, D., & Mettee, D. R. Cognition of arousal and actual arousal as determinants of emotion. *Journal of Personality and Social Psychology,* 1972, *21, 41*–51.

Goldstein, J. H., Rosnow, R. L., Goodstodt, B. E., & Suls, J. M. The "good subject" in verbal operant conditioning research. *Journal of Experimental Research in Personality,* 1972, *6,* 29–33.

Gorham, D. R., & Sherman, L. J. The relation of attitude toward medication to treatment outcomes in chemotherapy. *American Journal of Psychiatry,* 1961, *117,* 830–832.

Grant, D. L. Classical and operant conditioning. In A. W. Melton (Ed.), *Categories of human learning.* New York: Academic Press, 1964.

Green, D. Pre-existing conditions, placebo reactions and "side effects." *Annals of Internal Medicine,* 1964, *60,* 255–265.

Greenachre, P. Symposium on the evaluation of therapeutic results. In C. P. Obendorf, P. Greenachre and L. Kubie (Eds.). *International Journal of Psychoanalysis,* 1953, *29,* 8–32.

Greiner, T. Subjective bias of the clinical pharmacologist. *Journal of the American Medical Association,* 1962, *181,* 120–121.

Grimes, F. V. *An experimental analyses of the nature of suggestibility and its relation to other psychological factors.* Washington, D. C.: Catholic University Press, 1948.

Grinker, R. R. Discussion of article by W. Bromberg, An analysis of therapeutic usefulness. *American Journal of Psychiatry,* 1958, *114,* 725–732.

Grosz, H. J., & Grossman, K. G. The sources of observer variation and bias in clinical judgments: I. The item of psychiatric history. *Journal of Nervous and Mental Diseases,* 1964, *138,* 105–113.

Growdey, C. W., Hamilton, J. T., & Philip, R. B. A controlled clinical trial using placebos in normal subjects: A teaching exercise. *Canadian Medical Association Journal,* 1967, *96,* 1317–1322.

Guido, J. A., & Jones, J. "Placebo" (simulation) electroconvulsive therapy. *American Journal of Psychiatry,* 1961, *117,* 838–839.

Gumpert, G. Witch-doctor "psychiatrist" Smith, Kline and French *Psychological Reports,* 1963, *9,* 2–8.

Guy, W., Gross, M., & Dennis, H. An alternative to the double blind procedure. *American Journal of Psychiatry,* 1967, *123,* 1505–1512.

Haefner, D. P., Sacks, J. M., & Mason, A. S. Physicians' attitudes toward chemotherapy as a factor in psychiatric patients' responses to medication. *Journal of Nervous and Mental Diseases,* 1960, *131,* 64–69.

Haertzen, C. A. Contract effect on subjective experience in drug experiments. *Psychological Reports,* 1969, *24,* 69–70.

Hagens, J. A., Doering, C. R., Ashley, F. W., Clark, M. L., & Wolf, S. The therapeutic experiment: Observations on the meaning of controls and on the biologic variation resulting from the treatment situation. *Journal of Laboratory and Clinical Medicine,* 1957, *49,* 282–285.

Haggard, H. W. *Devils, drugs and doctors.* New York: Harper & Row, 1929.

Haggard, H. W. *Mystery, magic and medicine.* New York: Doubleday, Doran and Co., Inc., 1933.

Haggard, H. W. *The doctor in history.* New Haven: Yale University Press, 1934.

Haley, J. *Strategies of psychotherapy.* New York: Grune and Stratton, 1963.

Halkides, G. *An experimental study of four conditions necessary for therapeutic change.* Unpublished doctoral dissertation. University of Chicago, 1958.

Hamilton, M. Cited by K. Rickels in, Critique. *Non-specific factors in drug therapy,* K. Rickels (Ed.). Springfield, Ill.: Charles C Thomas, 1968.

Hammet, V. B. P. A consideration of psychoanalysis in relation to psychiatry generally circa, 1965. *American Journal of Psychiatry,* 1965, *122,* 42–54.

Hankoff, L. D., Engelhardt, D. M., & Freedman, N. Placebo response in schizophrenic outpatients. *Archives of General Psychiatry,* 1960, *2,* 43–52.

Hankoff, L. D., Engelhardt, D. M., Freedman, N., Mann, D., & Margolis, R. Denial of illness in schizophrenic outpatients. Effects of psychopharmacological treatment. *AMA Archives of General Psychiatry,* 1960, *3,* 657–664.

Hass, H., Fink, H., & Hartflider, G. Das placebo problem . . . Translation of selected parts. *Psychopharmacology Service Center Bulletin,* 1963, *2,* 1–65.

Hatterer, I. J. *The artist in society.* New York: Grove Press, 1965.

Haynes, S. N., Woodward, S., Moran, R., & Alexander, P. Relaxation treatment in insomnia. *Behavior Therapy,* 1974, *5,* 555–558.

Heine, R. W. *A comparison of patients' reports on psychotherapy experience with psychoanaltyic, nondirective and Adlerian therapists.* Unpublished doctoral dissertation. University of Chicago, 1950.

Heine, R. W., & Trossman, H. Initial expectations of the doctor-patient interaction as a factor in continuance of psychotherapy. *Psychological Journal of the Study of Interpersonal Processes,* 1960, *23,* 275–278.

Heller, K., & Goldstein, A. P. Client dependency and therapist expectancy as relationship maintaining variables in psychotherapy. *Journal of Consulting Psychology,* 1961, *25,* 371–375.

Hernnstein, R. Placebo effect in the rat. *Science,* 1962, *138,* 677–678.

Heshbacker, P. T., Rickels, K., Gordon, P. E. Gray, G., Meckelburg, R., Weise, C. C., & Vandervort, W. J. Setting, patient and doctor effects on drug response in neurotic patients. I. Differential attribution, dosage deviation and side reaction responses to treatment. *Psychopharmacologia,* 1970, *18,* 180–208.

Hill, H. E., Belleville, R. E., & Wikler, A. Motivational determinants in modification of behavior by morphine and phenobarbital. *AMA Archives of Neurology and Psychiatry,* 1957, *77,* 28–35.

Hiller, F. W. An analysis of patient-therapist compatibility. *Journal of Consulting Psychology,* 1958, *22,* 341–353.

Hobbs, N. Sources of gain in psychotherapy. *American Psychologist,* 1962, *17,* 741–747.

Hoehn-Sarc, R., Liberman, B., Imber, S., Stone, A. R., Frank, J. D., & Ribich, F. D. Attitude change and attribution of arousal in psychotherapy. *Journal of Nervous and Mental Diseases,* 1974, *159,* 234–243.

Hofling, C. K. The place of placebos in medical practice. *GP,* 1955, *11,* 103–107.

Hollingshead, A. B., & Redlich, F. C. *Social class and mental illness.* New York: Wiley, 1958.

Honigfeld, G. Relationships among physicians' attitudes on response to drugs. *Psychological Reports,* 1962, *2,* 683–690.

Honigfeld, G. Physician and patient attitudes as factors influencing the placebo response in depression. *Diseases of the Nervous System.,* 1963, *16,* 343–347.

Honigfeld, G. Non-specific factors in treatment. I. Review of placebo reactions and placebo reactors. *Diseases of the Nervous System,* 1964, *25,* 145–156.

Honigfeld, G. Non-specific factors in treatment. II. Review of social-psychological factors. *Diseases of the Nervous System,* 1964, *25,* 225–239.

Houston, W. R. The doctor himself as a therapeutic agent. *Annals of Internal Medicine,* 1938, *8,* 1416–1425.

Hovland, C. I., Janis, I. L., & Kelley, H. H. *Communication and persuasion: Psychological studies of opinion change.* New Haven: Yale University Press, 1953.

Humphrey, H. H. Interagency coordination in drug research and regulation. Hearing before the Subcommittee on Reorganization and International Organizations of the Committee on Government Operations. United States Senate, Bureau of Medicine of the Food and Drug Administration, 1963.

Isaacs, M. L. *Personality dimensions associated with positive placebo reaction, Washington D.C.:* Catholic University Press, *1959.*

Jackson, D. D., & Haley, J. Transference revisited. *Journal of Nervous and Mental Diseases,* 1963, *137,* 363–371.

Jakubszak, L. F., & Walters, R. H. Suggestibility as dependency behavior. *Journal of Abnormal and Social Psychology,* 1959, *50,* 102–107.

Janet, P. *Principles of Psychotherapy.* New York: The Macmillian Co., 1924.

Jaspers, K. *The nature of psychotherapy.* Chicago, Ill.: University of Chicago Press, 1965.

Jersild, A. T., & Lazar, E. A. *The meaning of psychotherapy in the teacher's life and work.* New

York: Bureau of Publications. Teachers College, Columbia University, 1962.

Johnson, J. E. Effects of accurate expectations about sensations on the sensory and discomfort components of pain. *Journal of Personality and Social Psychology,* 1973, *27,* 261–275.

Jones, E. E., Kanouse, D. E., Kelley, H. H., Nisbett, R. E., Valins, S., & Weiner, B. *Attribution: Perceiving the causes of behavior.* Morristown, N. J.: General Learning Press, 1972.

Jones, E. E., & Sigall, H. The bogus pipeline. A new paradigm for measuring affect and attitude. *Psychological Bulletin,* 1971, *76,* 349–364.

Journal of the American Medical Association. Placebos. (Editorial.) 1955, *159,* 780–781.

Joyce, C. R. B. Difference between physicians as revealed by clinical trials. *Proceedings of the Royal Society of Medicine,* 1962, *55,* 776–778.

Kahn, R. K. *Therapist discomfort in two psychotherapies.* Unpublished doctoral dissertation. Pennsylvania State University, 1957.

Kaplan, S. M. Laboratory procedures as an emotional stress. *Journal of the American Medical Association,* 1956, *161,* 677–688.

Karch, F., & Lasagna, L. *Adverse Drug Reactions in the United States: An analysis of the scope of the problem and recommendation for future approaches.* Washington, D.C.: Medicine in the public interest, 1974.

Karno, M. Communication reinforcement and "insight"—the problem of psychotherapeutic effect. *American Journal of Psychotherapy,* 1965, *19,* 467–479.

Karpman, B. Objective psychotherapy. *Journal of Clinical Psychology,* 1949, *5,* 1–154.

Kast, E. C., & Loesch, J. A contribution to the methodology of clinical appraisal of drug action. *Psychosomatic Medicine,* 1959, *11,* 228–234.

Kast, E. C., & Loesch, J. Influence of the doctor-patient relationship on drug action. *Illinois Medical Journal,* 1961, *119,* 390–393.

Kazdin, A. E., & Wilcoxon, L. A. Systematic densitization and non-specific treatment effects: A methodological evaluation. *Psychological Bulletin,* 1976, *83,* 729–758.

Kellogg, R., & Baron, R. S. Attribution theory, insomnia and the reverse placebo effect: A reversal of Storm's and Nisbett's findings. *Journal of Personality and Social Psychology,* 1975, *32,* 231–236.

Kelley, M. The tempestuous winds of fashion in medicine. *Archives in Internal Medicine,* 1962, *110,* 287–298.

Kent, R. N., O'Leary, K. D., Diament, C., & Dietz, A. Expectation bias in observational evaluation of therapeutic change. *Journal of Clinical and Consulting Psychology,* 1974, *42,* 774–780.

Kety, S. The academic lecture, the heuristic aspect of psychiatry. *American Journal of Psychiatry,* 1961, *118,* 363–397.

Kiev, A. The psychotherapeutic aspects of primitive medicine. *Human Organizations,* 1962, *21,* 25–29.

Kiev, A. The study of folk psychiatry. In A. Kiev (Ed.), *Magic, faith and healing.* London: Collier-Macmillian, Ltd., 1964.

Klopfer, B. Psychological variables in human cancer.

Journal of Projective Techniques, 1957, *21,* 331.

Knapp, D. E., & Knapp, D. A. Drug use: A guide to research utilizing a process model and social psychology. *Catalog of Selected Documents in Psychology,* 1973, *3,* 53.

Knowles, J. Conditioning and the placebo effect: The effects of decaffeinated coffee on simple reaction time in habitual coffee drinkers. *Behavior Research Therapy,* 1963, *1,* 151–157.

Knowles, J. B., & Lucas, C. J. Experimental studies of the placebo response. *Journal of Medical Science,* 1960, *106,* 231–240.

Kolb, L. C., & Montgomery, J. An explanation for transference cure: Its occurrence in psychoanalysis and psychotherapy. *American Journal of Psychiatry,* 1958, *115,* 414–420.

Kornetsky, C., & Humphries, O. Relationship between effects of a number of centrally acting drugs and personality. *AMA Archives of Neurology and Psychiatry,* 1957, *77,* 325–327.

Krasner, L. Therapist as a social reinforcement machine. In H. L. Strupp and L. Luborsky (Eds.), *Research in psychotherapy,* Washington, D.C.: American Psychological Association, 1962.

Krasner, L., Knowles, J. B., & Ullman, L. P. Effect of verbal conditioning of attitudes on subsequent motor performance. *Journal of Personality and Social Psychology,* 1965, *1,* 407–412.

Krasner, L., Ullman, L. P., & Fisher, D. Changes in performance as related to verbal conditioning of attitudes toward the examiner. *Perceptual and Motor Skills,* 1964, *19,* 811–816.

Kroger, W. S. Acupunctural analgesia: Its explanations by conditioning theory, autogenic training and hypnosis. *American Journal of Psychiatry,* 1973, *130,* 855–860.

Kruganski, A. W. The endogenous-exogenous partition in attribution theory. *Psychological Review,* 1975, *82,* 387–406.

Kubie, L. Symposium on the evaluation of therapeutic results. *International Journal of Psychoanalysis,* 1953, *29,* 33–46.

Kubie, L. Some unsolved problems of psychoanalytic therapy. In F. Fromm-Reichman and J. Moreno (Eds.), *Progress in psychotherapy.* New York: Grune and Stratton, 1956.

Kubie, L. The changing economics of psychotherapeutic practice. *Journal of Nervous and Mental Diseases,* 1964, *139,* 311–312.

Kurland, A. A. The drug placebo—its psychodynamic and conditioned reflex action. *Behavioral Science,* 1957, *2,* 101–110.

Kurland, A. A. The placebo. In J. H. Masserman and I. I. Moreno (Eds.), *Progress in psychotherapy, Volume 3.* New York: Grune and Stratton, 1958.

LaBarre, W. Confessions as cathartic therapy in American Indian tribes. In A. Kiev (Ed.), *Magic, faith and healing.* London: Collier-Macmillian, 1964.

Lasagna, L. The impact of scientific models on clinical psychopharmacology: A pharmacologist's view. *Seminars in Psychiatry,* 1972, *4,* 271–282.

Lasagna, L., Laties, V. G., & Dohan, J. L. Further studies on the "pharmacology" of placebo administration. *Journal of Clinical Investigation,* 1958, *37,* 533–537.

Lasagna, L., Mosteller, F., Von Felsinger, J., and Beecher, H. A study of the placebo response. *American Journal of Medicine,* 1954, *16,* 770–779.

Lehman, H. E. The placebo response and the double-blind study. In P. Hoch and J. Zubin (Eds.), *Evaluation of psychiatric treatment.* New York: Grune and Stratton, 1964.

Lehmann, H. E., & Knight, D. A. Measurement of changes in human behavior under the effects of psychotropic drugs. *Neuropsychopharmacology,* 1961, *2,* 291–303.

Lennard, H., Epstein, L., Bernstein, A., & Ransom, D. Mystification in the judgment of drug effects. *Mystification and Drug Misuse.* Jossey-Bass: San Francisco, 1971.

Leslie, A. Ethics and practice of placebo therapy. *American Journal of Medicine,* 1954, *16,* 854–862.

Lesse, S. Placebo reactions in psychotherapy. *Diseases of the Nervous System,* 1962, *23,* 313–319.

Lesse, S. Placebo reactions and spontaneous rhythms. *American Journal of Psychotherapy,* 1964, *18,* 99–115.

Lesse, S. Pre-therapeutic remissions and exacerbations. In proceedings of the 5th Congress of Neuropsychopharmacologia. Washington, D.C., 1966, 1156–1158.

Letemendia, F. J., & Harris, A. D. The influence of side effects on the reporting of symptoms. *Psychopharmacologia,* 1959, *1,* 39–47.

Levenson, D. J. The psychotherapist's contribution to the patient's treatment caree. In H. H. Strupp and L. Luborsky (Eds.), *Research in psychotherapy.* Washington, D.C.: American Psychological Association, 1962.

Liberman, R. An analysis of the placebo phenomenon. *Journal of Chronic Diseases,* 1961, *15,* 761–783.

Liberman, R. An experimental study of the placebo response under three different situations of pain. *Journal of Psychiatric Research,* 1964, *2,* 233–246.

Liberman, R. P. The elusive placebo reactor. In proceedings of the 5th Congress of Neuropsychopharmacologica, Washington, D.C., 1966.

Linn, E. L. Drug therapy, milieu change and release from a mental hospital. *Archives of Neurology and Psychiatry,* 1959, *81,* 785–794.

Linton, H. B., & Langs, R. J. Placebo reactions in a study of LSD (LSD-25). *Archives of General Psychiatry,* 1962, *6,* 364–383.

Lipman, R. S. Differential results of pharmacotherapy in clinics following an identical protocol. Proceedings of the 5th International Congress of Neuropsychopharmacologica, Washington, D.C., 1966.

Loenwald, H. W. On the therapeutic action of psychoanalysis. *International Journal of Psychoanalysis,* 1960, *41,* 1–18.

London, P. Schulman, R., & Black, M. Religious guilt and ethical standards. *Journal of Social Psychology,* 1966, *63,* 145–159.

Lord, E. Experimentally induced variations in Rorschach performance. *Psychological Monographs,* 1950, *64,* (10 Whole No. 316).

Lowinger, P. and Dobie, S. The attitudes and emotions of the psychiatrist in the initial interview. Paper presented at the Association for the Advancement of Psychotherapy. St. Louis, Missouri, 1963.

Lowinger, P., & Dobie, S. Psychiatrist variable in the process of interview and treatment. *Nature,* 1964, *201,* 1246–1247.

Luborsky, L. In H. H. Strupp and L. Luborsky (Eds.), *Research in psychotherapy.* Washington, D.C.: American Psychological Association, 1962.

Luborsky, L., Singer, B., & Luborsky, L. Comparative studies of psychotherapy. *Archives of General Psychiatry,* 1975, *32,* 995–1008.

Luoto, K. Personality and placebo effects upon timing behavior. *Journal of Abnormal and Social Psychology,* *68,* 54–61.

Lyerly, S., Ross, S., Krugman, A., & Clyde, D. Drugs and placebos: The effects of instructions upon performance and mood under amphetamine sulfate and chloral hydrate. *Journal of Abnormal and Social Psychology,* 1964, *68,* 321–327.

Major, R. H. *Classic descriptions of disease.* Springfield, Ill.: Charles C Thomas, 1955.

Malitz, S. Variables and drug effectiveness. In M. Rinkel (Ed.), *Specific and non-specific factors in psychopharmacology.* New York: Philosophical Library, 1963.

Marlowe, D., & Crowne, D. P. Social desirability and response to perceived situational demands. *Journal of Consulting Psychology,* 1961, *25,* 109–115.

Marmor, J. Psychoanalytic therapy as an education process: Common denominators in the therapeutic approaches of different psychoanalytic "schools." In J. H. Masserman (Ed.), *Science and Psychoanalysis,* Volume 5. New York: Grune and Stratton, 1962.

Marshall, A. G., & Izard, C. E. Cerebral Electrotherapeutic treatment of depression. *Journal of Consulting and Clinical Psychology,* 1974, *42,* 93–97.

Marshall, W. C., Boutilier, J., & Minnes, P. The modification of phobic behavior by covert reinforcement. *Behavior Therapy,* 1974, *5,* 469–480.

Masling, T. The effects of warm and cold interaction on the administration and scoring of an intelligence test. *Journal of Consulting Psychology,* 1959, *23,* 336–341.

Masling, T. The influence of situational and interpersonal variables in projective testing. *Psychological Bulletin,* 1960, *57,* 66–85.

Masling, T. Differential indoctrination of examiners and Roschach responses. *Journal of Consulting Psychology,* 1965, *29,* 198–201.

Masserman, J. H. Evolution vs. "revolution" in psychotherapy: A biodynamic integration. *Behavioral Science,* 1957, *2,* 89–100.

Masserman, J. H. Humanitarian psychiatry. *Bulletin of New York Academy of Medicine,* 1963, *39,* 533–544.

McGuigan, J. F. The experimenter: A neglected stimulus object. *Psychological Bulletin,* 1963, *60,* 421–428.

McGuire, W. J. Suspiciousness of the experimenter's intent. In R. Rosenthal and R. L. Rosnow (Eds.), *Artifact in behavioral research.* New York: Academic Press, 1969.

McMair, D., Kahn, R., Droppleman, L., & Fisher, S. Patient acquiescence and drug effects. In K. Rickels (Ed.), *Non-specific factors in drug therapy.*

Springfield: Illinois: Charles C. Thomas, 1968.

McNair, D. M., Lorr, M., & Callahan, D. M. Patient and therapist influences on quitting psychotherapy. *Journal of Consulting Psychology, 1963, 27,* 10–23.

McReynolds, W. T., Barnes, A. R., Brooks, S., & Rehagen, N. J. The role of attention-placebo influences in the efficacy of systematic desensitization. *Journal of Consulting and Clinical Psychology, 1973, 41,* 86–92.

Meehl, P. E. Psychotherapy. *Annual Review of Psychology, 1955, 6,* 357–378.

Meerloo, J.A.M. The essence of mental cure. *American Journal of Psychotherapy, 1963, 12, 2–63.*

Menninger, K. The academic lecture, hope. *American Journal of Psychiatry, 1959, 115,* 481–491.

Meszaros, A. F., & Gallagher, D. L. Measuring indirect effects of treatment on chronic warts. *Diseases of the Nervous System, 1958, 19,* 167–172.

Milgram, S. Behavioral study of obedience. *Journal of Abnormal and Social Psychology, 1963, 67,* 371–378.

Miller, H. F. "Acceptance" and related attributes as demonstrated in psychotherapeutic interviews. *Journal of Clinical Psychology, 1949, 5,* 83–87.

Miller, N. E. Biofeedback: Evaluation of a new technique. *New England Journal of Medicine, 1974, 290,* 684–685.

Mitler, M. M., Guilleminault, C., Orem, J., Zarcone, V. P., & Dement, W. C. Sleeplessness, sleep attacks and things that go wrong in the night. *Psychology Today, 1975, 12,* 45–50.

Moertel, C. G., Taylor, W. F., Roth, A., & Tyce, F.A.J. Who responds to sugar pills? *Mayo Clinic Proceedings, 1976, 51,* 96–100.

Morison, R. A. H., Woodmansey, A., & Young, A. J. Placebo response in an arthritis trial. *Annals of Rheumatic Diseases, 1961, 20,* 179–185.

Morris, L. A., & O'Neal, E. Drug name familiarity and the placebo effect. *Journal of Clinical Psychology, 1974, 30,* 280–282.

Morris, L. A., & O'Neal, E. C. Judgments about a drug's effectiveness: The role of expectations and outcomes. *Drugs in Health Care, 1975, 2,* 179–186.

Morris, L. A., Shangold, J., & Greenberg, F. The placebo effect on podiatry. *Journal of the American Podiatry Association, 1975, 65,* 662–664.

Morrison, B., & Walters, S. The placebo effect: I. Situational anxiety and model behavior. *Psychonomic Science, 1972, 27,* 80–82.

Motherby, G. *A new medical dictionary or general repository of physics.* (4th ed.) London: J. Johnson, 1795.

Mowrer, O. *The crisis in psychiatry and religion.* New York: Van Nostrand, 1961.

Mowrer, O. Payment or repayment? The problem of private practice. *American Psychologist, 1963, 18,* 577–580.

Muller, B. P. Personality of placebo reactors and nonreactors. *Diseases of the Nervous System, 1965, 26,* 58–61.

Murphy, W. R. A comparison of psychoanalysis with the dynamic psychotherapies. *Journal of Nervous and Mental Disease, 1958, 126,* 441–450.

Murphy, J. M. Psychotherapeutic aspects of shaminism on St. Lawrence Island, Alaska. In A. Kiev (Ed.), *Magic, faith and healing.* London: Collier-Macmillian, 1964.

Murray, J. H. *A new English dictionary on historic principles.* Oxford: Claredon Press, 1933.

Nash, F. H., Frank, J. D., Gliedman, L. D., Imber, S. D., & Stone, A. R. Some factors related to patients remaining in group therapy. *International Journal of Group Psychotherapy, 1957, 7,* 264–276

Nash, F. H., Frank, J. D., Imber, S. D., & Stone, A. R. Selected effects of inert medication on psychiatric outpatients. *American Journal of Psychotherapy, 1964, 18, 33–48.*

Nau, S. D., Caputo, J. A., & Borkovec, T. D. The relationship between and credibility of therapy and simulated therapeutic effects. *Journal of Behavior Therapy and Experimental Psychiatry, 1974, 5,* 129–133.

Nelson, R. O., Lipinski, D. P., & Black J. L. The effects of expectancy on the reactivity of self recording. *Behavior Therapy, 1975, 6,* 337–349.

Nisbett, R. E., & Schachter, S. Cognitive manipulation of pain. *Journal of Experimental Social Psychology, 1966, 2,* 227–236.

Oberndorf, C. P., Greenachre, P., & Kubie, L. Symposium on the evaluation of therapeutic results. *International Journal of Psychoanalysis, 1953, 29,* 13–19.

O'Brien, D. M. Is liver a "tonic"? A short study of injecting placebos. *British Medical Journal, 1954, 7,* 136–137.

O'Neal, E. and Mills, J. The influence of anticipated choice on the halo effect. *Journal of Experimental Social Psychology, 1969, 5,* 347–351.

Orne, M. The nature of hypnosis. Artifact and essence. *Journal of Abnormal and Social Psychology, 1959, 58,* 277–299.

Orne, M. T. On the social psychology of the psychological experiment: With particular reference to demand characteristics and their implications. *American Psychologist, 1962, 17,* 776–783.

Orne, M. T. Hypnosis, motivation and the ecological validity of the Psychological experiment. In W. J. Arnold and M. M. Page (Eds.), *Nebraska symposium on motivation.* Lincoln: University of Nebraska Press, 1970.

Pallak, M. S., & Pittman, T. S. General motivational effects of dissonance arousal. *Journal of Personality and Social Psychology, 1972, 21,* 349–358.

Park, L. C., & Covi, L. Non-blind placebo trial. *Archives of General Psychiatry, 1965, 12,* 336–345.

Parkhouse, J. Placebo reactor. *Nature, 1963, 199,* 308–310.

Parloff, M. B. Therapist-patient relationships and outcome of psychotherapy. *Journal of Consulting Psychology, 1962, 25,* 29–38.

Parloff, M. B. and Rubinstein, E. A. Summary of research problems in psychotherapy conference, 1958. In E. A. Rubinstein and M. B. Parloff (Eds.), *Research in psychotherapy,* Washington, D.C.: American Psychological Association, 1958.

Parsons, T. *The social system.* The Free Press: Glencoe, Ill. 1951.

Paul, L. The operations of psychotherapy. *Comprehensive Psychiatry*, 1963, *4*, 281–290.

Pavlov, I. P. *Conditioned reflexes* (Trans. G. V. Anrep). London: Oxford University Press, 1927. Reprinted New York: Dover Press, 1960.

Pearlin, L. J. The values of enthusiasm for drugs in a mental hospital. *Journal of Interpersonal Processes*, 1962, *25*, 170–179.

Penick, S. B. and Fisher, S. Drug set interaction: Psychological and physiological effects of epinephrine under differential expectations. *Psychosomatic Medicine*, 1965, *27*, 177–182.

Penick, S. B., & Hinkle, L. E. Effect of expectation on response to phenmetrazine. *Psychosomatic Medicine*, 1964, *26*, 369–373.

Petrie, A. Some psychological aspects of pain relief and suffering. *Annals of the New York Academy of Science*, 1960, *86*, 13–27.

Pichot, P., & Perse, J. Placebo effects as response set. In K. Rickels (Ed.), *Non-specific Factors in Drug Therapy*. Springfield, Ill.: Charles C Thomas, 1968.

Pickens, R., & Crowder, W. Effects of CS-US interval on conditioning of drug response, with assessment of speed of conditioning. *Psychopharmacologia*, 1967, *11*, 88–94.

Pihl, R. O., & Altman, J. An experimental analysis of the placebo effect. *Journal of Clinical Pharmacology and New Drugs*, 1971, *11*, 91–95.

Pogge, R. The toxic placebo. *Medical Times*, 1963, *91*, 773–778.

Polansky, N., & Kounin, J. Client's reactions to initial interviews. *Human Relations*, 1956, *9*, 237–242.

Rachman, S. *Critical essays on psychoanalysis.* New York: The Macmillian Co., 1963.

Raskin, A. A comparison of acceptors and resistors of drug treatment as an adjunct to psychotherapy. *Journal of Consulting Psychology*, 1961, *25*, 366–379.

Rashkis, H. A., & Smarr, E. R. Drug and milieu effects with chronic schizophrenics. *Archives of Neurology and Psychiatry*, 1957, *78*, 89–94.

Raskin, A. Age-sex differences in response to antidepressant drugs. *Journal of Nervous and Mental Diseases*, 1974, *159*, 120–130.

Raskin, A., Boothe, H., Schulterbrandt, J., Reatig, N. & Odle, D. A model for drug use with depressed patients. *Journal of Nervous and Mental Diseases*, 1973, *186*, 130–142.

Rathod, N. H. Tranquilizers and patients' environment. *Lancet*, 1958, *1*, 611–613.

Reidenberg, M. & Lowenthal, D. Adverse nondrug reactions. *New England Journal of Medicine*, 1968, *279*, 678–679.

Reisner, M. F., Reeves, R. B., & Armington, J. Effects of variations in laboratory procedure and experimenter upon ballistocardiogram, blood pressure and heart rate in healthy young men. *Psychosomatic Medicine*, 1955, *27*, 185–199.

Reznikoff, M., & Toomey, L. C. *Evaluation of changes associated with psychiatric treatment.* Springifield, Ill.: Charles C Thomas, 1959.

Rickels, K. Placebo reactions and drop-outs in anxious and depressed patients visiting psychopharmacology clinics. In P. B. Bradley & P. Hoch (Eds.), *Neuropsychopharmacology*, Vol. 3. Amsterdam: Elsevier Publishing Co., 1964.

Rickels, K. Some comments on non-drug factors in psychiatric drug therapy. *Psychosomatics*, 1965, *6*, 303–309.

Rickels, K., & Anderson, F. L. Attrited and completed lower socioeconomic class clinic patients in psychiatric drug therapy. *Comprehensive Psychiatry*, 1967, *8*, 90–99.

Rickels, K., Baum, M. C., Raab, E., Taylor, W., & Moore, E. A psychopharmacological evaluation of chlordiazexpoxide, LA-1, and placebo carried out with anxious, neurotic medical clinic patients. *Medical Times*, 1965, *93*, 238–245.

Rickels, K., Baum, N. C., Taylor W., & Raab, E. Humanism in clinical research. *Psychosomatics*, 1964, *5*, 315–316(a).

Rickels, K., Boren, R., & Stuart, H. Controlled psychopharmacological research in general practice: A contribution to the methodology of clinical drug evaluation. *Journal of New Drugs*, 1964, *4*, 138–148(b).

Rickels, K., & Cattell, R. B. Drug and placebo responses as a function of doctor and patient type. In R. A. May & J. Wittenborn (Eds.), *Psychotropic drug response*. Springfield, Ill.: Charles C Thomas, 1969.

Rickels, K., Cattell, R. B., Weise, C., Gray, B., Yee, R., Mallin, A., & Aaronson, H. G. Controlled psychopharmacological research in private psychiatric practice. *Psychopharmacologia*, 1966, *9*, 288–306.

Rickels, K., & Downing, R. Verbal ability (intelligence) and improvement in drug therapy of neurotic patients. *Journal of New Drugs*, 1965, *5*, 303–307.

Rickels, K., & Downing, R. Drug and placebo-treated neurotic outpatients. *Archives of General Psychiatry*, 1967, *16*, 369–372.

Rickels, K., Downing, R., & Downing, M. Personality differences between somatically and psychologically oriented neurotic patients. *Journal of Nervous and Mental Diseases*, 1966, *42*, 10–18.

Rickels, K., Downing, R. W., & Howard, K. Predictors of chlordiazepoxide response in anxiety. *Clinical Pharmacology and Therapeutics*, 1971, *12*, 263–273.

Rickels, K., Gordon, P. E., Jenkins, B. W., Perloff, M., Sachs, T., & Stepansky, W. Drug treatment in depressive illness, (amitriptyline and chlorodiazepoxide in two neurotic populations). *Diseases of the Nervous System*, 1970, *31*, 30–42.

Rickels, K., Lipman, R., & Raab, E. Previous medication, duration of illness and placebo response. *Journal of Nervous and Mental Diseases*, 1966, *142*, 548–554.

Rickels, K., & Macafee, A. Placebo responses in four neurotic patient populations. In proceedings of the 5th Congress of Neuropsychopharmacologia, Washington, D.C., 1966.

Ripley, H. S., & Jackson, J. K. Therapeutic factors in Alcoholics Anonymous. *American Journal of Psychology*, 1959, *116*, 44–50.

Roberts, R. R. & Renzaglia, G. A. The influence of tape recording on counseling. *Journal of Counseling Psychology*, 1965, *12*, 10–16.

Roberts, J. M., & Hamilton, M. Treatment of anxiety states. *Journal of Mental Science,* 1958, *104,* 1052–1068.

Rogers, C. R. *Client-centered therapy.* Boston, Mass.: Houghton Mifflin, 1951.

Rogers, C. R. Client-centered therapy: A current view. In F. Fromm-Reichman & J. L. Mareno (Eds.), *Progress in psychotherapy.* New York: Grune and Stratton, 1956.

Rogers, C. R. The necessary and sufficient conditions of therapeutic personality change. *Journal of Consulting Psychology,* 1957, *21,* 95–103(a).

Rogers, C. R. A therapist's view of the good life. *Humanist,* 1957, *17,* 291–300(b).

Rogers, C. R. *On becoming a person.* Boston, Mass.: Houghton Mifflin, 1961.

Rogers, T. B. An analysis of two central sates underlying responding to personality items: The self-referent decision and response selection. *Journal of Research in Personality,* 1974, *8,* 128–138.

Rorer, L. G. The great response-style myth. *Psychological Bulletin,* 1965, *63,* 129–156.

Rosenberg, M. J. The conditions and consequences of evaluation apprehension. In R. Rosenthal & R. L. Rosnow (Eds.), *Artifact in behavioral research.* New York: Academic Press, 1969.

Rosenthal, R. On the social psychology of the psychological experiment: The experimenter's hypothesis as unintended determinant of experimental results. *American Scientist,* 1963, *51,* 268–283(a).

Rosenthal, R. Experimental modeling effects as determinants of subjects' responses. *Journal of Projection and Personality Assessment,* 1963, *27,* 467–471(b).

Rosenthal, R. Experimenter outcome orientation and the results of the psychological experiment. *Psychological Bulletin,* 1964, *61,* 405–412.

Rosenthal, R. *Experimenter effects in behavioral research.* New York: Appleton-Century-Crofts, 1966.

Rosenthal, R. Interpersonal expectations: Effects of the experimenter's hypothesis. In R. Rosenthal & R. L. Rosnow (Eds.), *Artifact in behavioral research.* New York: Academic Press, 1969.

Rosenthal, R. and Fode, K. L. The effect of experimenter bias on the performance of the albino rat. *Behavioral Science,* 1963, *8,* 183–189.

Rosenthal, R., Fode, K. L., Vikan-Kline, L. L., & Persinger, G. W. Verbal conditioning: Mediator of experiment, expectancy effects. *Psychological Reports,* 1964, *114,* 71–74.

Rosenthal, L. R., Friedman, C. J., Johnson, C. A., Fode, K., Schill, T., White, R. C., & Viken, L. L. Variables affecting experimenter bias in a group situation. *Genetic Psychology Monographs,* 1964, *70,* 271–296(c).

Rosenthal, R., & Halas, E. S. Experimenter effect in the study of invertebrate behavior. *Psychological Reports,* 1962, *11,* 251–256.

Rosenthal, R., Kohn, P., Greenfield, P. M., & Carota, N. Experimenter hypothesis-confirmation and mood as determinants of experimental results. *Perceptual and Motor Skills,* 1965, *20,* 1237–1252.

Rosenthal, R., & Lawson, F. A. A longitudinal study of the effects of experimenter bias on the operant learning of laboratory rats. *Journal of Psychiatric Research,* 1963, *2,* 61–72.

Rosenthal, R., Persinger, G. W., Mulry, R. G., Vikan-Kline, L., & Grothe, M. Emphasis on experimental procedure, sex of subjects and the biasing effect of experimental hypotheses. *Journal of Projective Techniques,* 1964, *128,* 470–473.

Rosenthal, R., Persinger, G. W., Vikan-Kline, L., & Fode, K. L. The effect of experimenter outcome-bias and subject set on awareness in verbal conditioning experiments. *Journal of Verbal Learning Behavior* 1963, *2,* 275, 283(a).

Rosenthal, R., Persinger, G. W., Vikan-Kline, L., & Fode, K. L. The effect of early data returns on data subsequently obtained by outcome-bias experimenters. *Sociometry,* 1963, *26,* 487–498(b).

Rosenthal, R., & Rosnow, R. L. *Artifact in Behavioral Research.* New York: Academic Press, 1969.

Rosenthal, R., & Rosnow, R. L. *The Volunteer Subject.* New York: Wiley, 1975.

Rosnow, R. L., & Aiken L. S. Mediation of artifacts in behavioral research. *Journal of Experimental Social Psychology,* 1973, *9,* 181–201.

Rubinstein, E. A., & Parloff, M. B. *Research in psychotherapy.* Washington, D.C.: American Psychological Association, 1959.

Russell, E. W. The power of behavioral control: A critique of behavior modification methods. *Journal of Clinical Psychology,* 1974, *30,* 111–136.

Sabshin, M., & Ramot, J. Pharmacotherapeutic evaluation and the psychiatrist setting. *Archives of Neurology and Psychiatry,* 1956, *75,* 362–370.

Samuels, A. S., & Edisen, C. B. A study of the psychiatric effects of placebo. *The Journal of the Louisana State Medical Society,* 1961, *113,* 114–117.

Sargant, W. *Battle for the mind.* New York: Doubleday and Co., 1957.

Schachter, S., & Singer, J. E. Cognitive, social and physiological determinants of emotional state. *Psychological Review,* 1962, *69,* 379–399.

Schaffer, I., & Myers, J. K. Psychotherapy and social stratification. *Psychiatry,* 1954, *17,* 83–93.

Schapira, K., McClelland, H. A., Griffith, N. R., & Newells, D. J. Study on the effects of tablet colour in the treatment of anxiety states. *British Medical Journal,* 1970, *2,* 446–449.

Scharaf, M. R., & Levenson, D. J. The quest for ominpotence in professional training. *Psychiatry,* 1964, *27,* 135–149.

Schmideberg, M. Values and goals in psychotherapy. *The Psychiatric Quarterly,* 1958, *32,* 333–365.

Schmideberg, M. The role of suggestion in analytic therapy. *Psychoanalytic Review,* 1939, *26,* 223.

Schorer, C., Lowinger, P., Sullivan, T., & Hartlaub, G. H. Improvement without treatment. *Diseases of the Nervous System,* 1968, *29,* 100–104.

Schottstaedt, W. W., Pinsky, R. H., Mackler, P., & Wolf, S. Prestige and social interactions on a metabolic ward. *Psychosomatic Medicine,* 1959, *21,* 132–148.

Schulterbrandt, J. G., Raskin, A., & Reatig, N. True and apparent side effects in a controlled trial of chloropromazine and imipramine in depression. *Psychopharmacologia,* 1974, *38,* 303–317.

Schultz, T. R., & Hartup, W. H. Performance under social reinforcement as a function of masculinity-feminity of experimenter and subject. *Journal of Personality and Social Psychology,* 1967, *6,* 337–341.

Seeman, J. Counselor judgments of therapeutic process and outcome. In C. R. Rogers & R. F. Dymond (Eds.), *Psychotherapy and personality change.* Chicago: University of Chicago Press, 1954.

Shapiro, A. K. The placebo effect in the history of medical treatment: Implications for psychiatry. *The American Journal of Psychiatry,* 1959, *116,* 298–304.

Shapiro, A. K. A contribution to the history of the placebo effect. *Behavioral Science,* 1960, *5,* 109–135(a).

Shapiro, A. K. Attitudes toward the use of placebo in treatment. *Journal of Nervous and Mental Diseases,* 1960, *130,* 200–211(b).

Shapiro, A. K. Feasibility of "browsing" double blind studies. *Diseases of the Nervous System,* 1961, *32,* 223–225.

Shapiro, A. K. Psychological aspects of medication. In H. I. Lief, V. E. Lief, & N. R. Lief (Eds.), *The psychological basis of medical practice.* New York: Harper & Row, 1963.

Shapiro, A. K. A historic and heuristic definition of the placebo. *Psychiatry,* 1964, *27,* 52–58(a).

Shapiro, A. K. Rejoinder. *Psychiatry,* 1964, *27,* 178–179(b).

Shapiro, A. K. Factors contributing to the placebo effect. *American Journal of Psychotherapy,* 1964, *18,* 73–88(c).

Shapiro, A. K. Etiological factors in placebo effect. *Journal of the American Medical Association,* 1964, *187,* 712–714(d).

Shapiro, A. K. Placebogenics and iatroplacebogenics. *Medical Times,* 1964, *92,* 1037–1047(f).

Shapiro, A. K. The placebo response. In J. G. Howells (Ed.), *Modern perspectives in world psychiatry.* Edinburgh: Oliver and Boyd, 1968.

Shapiro, A. K. Placebo effects in medicine, psychotherapy and psychoanalysis. In A. E. Bergin & S. L. Garfield (Eds.), *Handbook of psychotherapy and behavior change: Empirical Analysis.* New York: Wiley, 1971.

Shapiro, A. K. The behavior therapies: Therapeutic breakthrough or latest fad? *American Journal of Psychiatry,* 1976, *133,* 154–159.

Shapiro, A. K., Chassen, J., Morris, L. A., & Frick, R. Placebo induced side effects. *Journal of Operational Psychiatry,* 1974, *6,* 43–46.

Shapiro, A. K., Mike, V., Barton, H., & Shapiro, E. Study of the placebo effect with a self-administered test. *Comprehensive Psychiatry,* 1973, *14,* 535–548.

Shapiro, A. K., Shapiro, E., Bruun, R., & Sweet, R. *Gilles de la Tourettes' Syndrome.* New York: Raven Press, in press.

Shapiro, A. K., & Struening, E. A comparison of the attitudes of a sample of physicians about the effectiveness of their treatment and the treatment of other physicians. *Journal of Psychiatric Research,* 1974, *10,* 217–229.

Shapiro, A. K., Struening, E., Shapiro, E., & Barten, H. Prognostic correlates of psychotherapy in psychiatric outpatients. *American Journal of Psychiatry,* 1976, *133,* 802–808.

Shapiro, A. K., Struening, E. L., Shapiro, E., Morris, L. A., & Raab, G. *Placebology.* In preparation.

Shapiro, A. K., Wilensky, H., & Struening, E. L. Study of the placebo effect with a placebo test. *Comprehensive Psychiatry,* 1968, *9,* 118–137.

Shapiro, A. P. Influence of emotional factors in evaluation of hypotensive drugs. *Psychosomatic Medicine,* 1955, *17,* 291.

Shapiro, A. P. The investigator himself. In S. O. Waife & A. P. Shapiro (Eds.). *Clinical evaluation of new drugs.* New York: Paul B. Haeber, 1959.

Shapiro, A. P., Myers, T. Reiser, M. F., & Ferris, E. B. Comparison of blood pressure response to veriloid and to the doctor. *Psychosomatic Medicine* 1954, *16,* 478–488.

Sharp, H. C. Identifying placebo reactors. *Journal of Psychology,* 1965, *60,* 205–212.

Sheard, M. H. The influence of doctor's attitude on the patient response to antidepressant medication. *Journal of Nervous and Mental Diseases,* 1963, *136,* 555–560.

Sherif, M., & Haney, O. J. A study in eye functioning, elimination of stable audiographs in individuals with group silentness. *Sociometry,* 1952, *16,* 272–305.

Shipman, W. G., Greene, C. S., & Laskin, D. M. Correlation of placebo responses and personality characteristists in myofacial pain-dysfunction (MPD) patients. *Journal of Psychosomatic Research,* 1974, *18,* 475–483.

Shuller, D. Y., & McNamara, J. R. Expectancy factors in behavioral observation. *Behavior Therapy,* 1976, *7,* 519–527.

Silverman, I. Role related behavioral of subjects in laboratory studies of attitude change. *Journal of Personality and Social Psychology,* 1968, *8,* 343–348.

Singerman, K. S., Borkovec, T. D., & Baron, R. S. Failure of a "misattribution therapy" manipulation with a clinically relevant target behavior. *Behavior Therapy,* 1976, *7,* 306–313.

Snow, L. H. & Rickels, K. Use of direct observations in the teaching and learning of psychotherapy. *American Journal of Psychotherapy,* 1965, *19,* 487–491.

Snyder, M., Schluz, R., & Jones, E. Expectancy and apparent duration as determinants of fatigue. *Journal of Personality and Social Psychology,* 1974, *29,* 429–434.

Snyder, W. U. In E. A. Rubinstein & M. B. Parloff (Eds.), *Research in psychotherapy.* Washington, D.C.: American Psychological Association, 1958.

Snyder, W. U. "Warmth" in non-directive counseling. *Journal of Abnormal and Social Psychology,* 1946, *41,* 491–495.

Snyder, W. U.,& Snyder, B. J. *The psychotherapy relationship.* New York: Macmillan Co., 1961.

Stanton, A. H., & Schwartz, M. S. *The mental hospital.* New York: Basic Books, 1954.

Stanley, W. C., & Schlosberg, H. The psychophysical effects of tea. *Journal of Psychology,* 1953, *36,* 435–448.

Stein, M. H. A consideration of psychoanalysis in relation to psychiatry. *American Journal of Psychiatry,* 1966, *122,* 830–833.

Sternbach, R. A. The effects of instructional sets on autonomic responsivity. *Psychophysiology,* 1964, *1,* 67–72.

Sternbach, R. A. *Principles of psychophysiology.* New York: Academic Press, 1966.

Stoler, N. Client likeability: A variable in the study of psychotherapy. *Journal of Consulting Psychology,* 1963, *27,* 175–178.

Storms, M. D., & Nisbett, R. E. Insomnia and attribution process. *Journal of Personality and Social Psychology,* 1970, *2,* 319–328.

Stotland, E. *The psychology of hope.* San Francisco: Jossey-Bass, 1969.

Stroebel, C. F., & Glueck, B. C. Biofeedback treatment in medicine and psychiatry: An ultimate placebo? *Seminars in Psychiatry,* 1973, *5,* 379–393.

Struening, E. L., Shapiro, A K., & Shapiro, E. *Reliability and validity of a placebo test.* In preparation.

Strupp, H. H. The performance of psychiatrists and psychologists in a therapeutic interview. *Journal of Clinical Psychology,* 1958a, *19,* 219–226.

Strupp, H. H. The performance of psychoanalytic and client-centered therapists in an initial interview. *Journal of Consulting Psychology,* 1958b, *22,* 265–272.

Strupp, H. H. The psychotherapist's contribution to the treatment process. *Behavioral Science,* 1958c, *3,* 34–67.

Strupp, H. H. The psychotherapist's contribution to the treatment process. *Psychiatry,* 1959, *22,* 349–362.

Strupp, H. H. Nature of psychotherapist's contribution to treatment process. *AMA Archives of General Psychistry,* 1960, *2,* 434–440.

Strupp, H. H. *Psychotherapists in action.* New York: Grune and Stratton, 1960b.

Strupp, H. J., Levenson, R. W., Manuck, S. B., Snell, J. D., Hinrichsen, J. J., & Boyd, S. Effects of suggestion on total respiratory resistance in mild asthmatics. *Journal of Psychosomatic Research,* 1974, *18,* 337–346.

Strupp, H. H., & Luborsky, L. *Research in Psychotherapy.* Washington, D.C.: American Psychological Association, 1962.

Strupp, H. H., & Wallach, M. S. A further study of psychiatrists' responses in quasi-therapy situations. *Behavioral Science,* 1965, *10,* 113–120.

Strupp, H. H., Wallach, M. S., & Wogan, M. The psychotherapy experience in retrospect: A questionnaire survey of former patients and their therapists. *Psychological Monographs,* 1964, *78,* 1–45.

Strupp, H. H., & Williams, J. V. Some determinants of clinical evaluations of different psychiatrists. *AMA Archives of General Psychiatry,* 1960, *2,* 434–440.

Stukat, H. H. *Suggestibility: A factorial and experimental analysis.* Stockholm: Almqvist and Wiksell, 1958.

Sullivan, H. S. A note on the implications of psychiatry, the study of interpersonal relations for investigators in the social sciences. *American Journal of Sociology,* 1936–1937, 2, 848–861.

Szasz, T. S., & Nemiroff, R. A. A questionnaire study of psychoanalytic practices and opinions. *Journal of Nervous and Mental Diseases.* 1963, *137,* 209–221.

Taylor, J. B., Carithers, M., & Coyne, L. MMPI perfor-

mance, response set and the "self-concept hypothesis" *Journal of Consulting and Clinical Psychology,* 1976, *44,* 351–362.

Tedeschi, J. T., Schlenker, B. R., & Bonoma, T. V. Cognitive dissonance: Private ratiocination or public spectacle. *American Psychologist,* 1971, *26,* 685–695.

Thompson, C. The role of the analyst and personality in therapy. *American Journal of Psychotherapy,* 1956, *10,* 347–359.

Thorn, W. A. The placebo reactor. *Australian Journal of Pharmacy,* 1962, *43,* 1035–1037.

Tibbetts, R. W., & Hawkins, J. R. The placebo response. *Journal of Mental Science,* 1956, *102,* 60–66.

Tori, C., & Worell, L. Reduction of human avoidant behavior: A comparison of counter conditioning, expectancy and cognitive information approaches. *Journal of Consulting and Clinical Psychology,* 1973, *41,* 269–278.

Totman, R. Cognitive dissonance and placebo response: The effect of differential justification for undergoing dummy injections. *European Journal of Social Psychology,* 1976, *5,* 441–456.

Traut, E. F., & Passarelli, E. W. Placebos in the treatment of rheumatoid arthritis and other rheumatic conditions. *Annuals of Rheumatic Diseases,* 1957, *16,* 18–21.

Troffer, S. A., & Tart, C. T. *Experimenter bias in hypnotist performance.* Laboratory of Human Development: Stanford University, California, 1964. (abstract).

Trouton, D. S. Placebos and their psychological effect. *Journal of Mental Science,* 1957, *103,* 344–354.

Truax, C. B., & Wargo, D. G. Psychotherapeutic encounters that change behavior for better or for worse. *American Journal of Psychotherapy,* 1966, *20,* 499–521.

Tuma, A. H., & May, P. R. A. The effect of therapist attitude on outcome of drug treatment and other therapies in schizophrenia. In P. R. A. May & J. Wittenborn (Eds.), *Psychotropic drug response.* Springfeld, Ill.: Charles C Thomas, 1969.

Ubell, E. *Efforts to measure psychotherapy success.* New York: Herald Tribune, 1964.

Uhlenhuth, E. H., Canter, A., Neustadt, J. O., & Payson, H. E. The symptomatic relief of anxiety with meprobamate, phenobarbital and placebo. *American Journal of Psychiatry,* 1959, *115,* 905–910.

Uhlenhuth, E. H., Rickels, K., Fisher, S., Park, L. C., Lipman, R. S., & Mock, J. Drug, doctor's verbal attitudes and clinical setting in the symptomatic response to pharmacotherapy. *Psychopharmacologia,* 1966, *9,* 392–418.

Uhr, L., Miller, J. G. *Drugs and Behavior.* New York: Wiley, 1960.

Ullman, L. P., & McFarland, R. L. Productivity as a variable in TAT protocols: A methodological study. *Journal of Projective Techniques,* 1957, *21,* 80–87.

Valins, S. Cognitive effects of false heart rate feedback. *Journal of Personality and Social Psychology,* 1966, *4,* 400–408.

Valins, S., Adelson, R., Goldstein, J., & Weiner, M. The negative placebo effect-consequences of overselling a treatment. Paper presented at the International Association of Dental Research, 1971.

Valins, S., & Nisbett, R. E. Attribution processes in the development and treatment of emotional disorders: In E. Jones, D. E. Kanouse, H. H. Kelly, R. E. Nisbett, S. Valins, & B. Weiner (Eds.), *Attribution: Perceiving the causes of behavior.* New York: General Learning Press, 1971.

Valins, S., & Ray, A. A. Effects of cognitive desentization on avoidance behavior. *Journal of Personality and Social Psychology,* 1967, 7, 345–350.

Vinar, O. Dependence on a placebo: A case report. *British Journal of Psychiatry,* 1969, *115,* 1189–1190.

Volgyesi, F. A. "School for patients" hypnosis-therapy and psychoprophylaxis. *British Journal of Medical Hypnotism,* 1954, 5, 8–16.

VonMehring, Ó., & King, S. R. *Renovating the Mental Patient.* New York: Russell Sage Foundation, 1957.

Voth, V. M., Herbert, M. C., & Orth, M. H. Situational variables in the assessment of psychoanalytic results. *Bulletin of the Menninger Clinic,* 1962, *26,* 73–81.

Waife, S. O., & Shapiro, A. P. *The clinical evaluation of new drugs.* New York: Hoeber, 1959.

Wallach, M. S., & Strupp, H. H. Psychotherapists' clinical judgments and attitudes toward patients. *Journal of Consulting Psychology,* 1960, *24,* 316–323.

Waterman, C. K. The facilitating and interfering effects of cognitive dissonance 'on simple and complex paired associated learning tasks. *Journal of Experimental Social Psychology,* 1969, 5, 31–42.

Walters, R. H., Marshall, W. E., & Shooter, J. R. Anxiety, isolation and susceptibility to social influence. *Journal of Personality,* 1960, *28,* 518–529.

Walters, R. H., & Parke, R. D. Emotional arousal, isolation and discrimination learning in children. *Journal of Experimental Psychology,* 1964, *1,* 163–173.

Walters, R. H., & Quinn, M. J. The effects of social and sensory deprivations on autokinetic judgments. *Journal of Personality,* 1960, *28,* 210–219.

Walters, R. H., & Ray, E. Anxiety, isolation and reinforcement effectiveness. *Journal of Personality,* 1960, *28,* 358–367.

Ward, C. H. Psychotherapy research: Dilemmas and directions. *Archives of General Psychiatry,* 1964, *10,* 596–662.

Weatherall, M. Tranquilizers. *British Medical Journal,* 1962, *1,* 1219–1224.

Webb, E. J., Campbell, D. T., Schwartz, R. D., & Sechrest, L. *Unobtrusive Measures: Nonreactive research in the social sciences.* Chicago, Ill.: Rand McNally, 1966.

White, R. B. Recent developments in psychoanalytic research. *Diseases of the Nervous System,* 1961, *22,* 2–15.

Wilkins, W. Perceptual distortion to account for arousal. *Journal of Abnormal Psychology,* 1971, *78,* 252–257.

Williams, M., & McGee, T. The bias of the drug administration in judgments of the effects of psychopharmacological agents. *Journal of Nervous and Mental Diseases,* 1962, *135,* 569–573.

Wilson, W. M. Suggestion and the placebo: An analysis of bias in clinical trials. In C. A. Keels & F. Smith (Eds.), *UFAW symposium: The assessment of pain in man and animals.* London: E & S. Livington, Ltd., 1962(a).

Wilson, W. M. An analysis of factors contributing to placebo responses *Proceedings of the Royal Society of Medicine,* 1962, *55,* 780–785(b).

Wilson, C. W. M., & Huby, P. M. An assessment of the responses to drugs acting on the central nervous system. *Clinical Pharmacology and Therapeutics,* 1961, *2,* 587–598.

Wolberg, I. R. *The technique of psychotherapy.* New York: Grune and Stratton, 1954.

Wolens, E. Responsibility for raw data. *American Psychologist,* 1962, *17,* 657–658.

Wolf, S. Effects of suggestion and conditioning on the action of chemical agents in human subjects—The pharmacology of placebos. *Journal Clinical Investigation,* 1950, *29,* 100–109.

Wolf, S. The pharmacology of placebos. *Pharmacology Review,* 1959, *11,* 689–704.

Wolf, S. Placebos: Problems and pitfalls. *Clinical Pharmacology and Therapeutics,* 1962, *3,* 254–257.

Wolf, S., & Pinsky, R. Effects of placebo administration and occurence on toxic reactors. *Journal of the American Medical Association,* 1954, *155,* 339–341.

Wolff, W. *Contemporary psychotherapists examine themselves.* Chicago, Ill.: Charles C Thomas, 1956.

Wood, E. C., Rokusin, J. M., & Morse, E. Resident psychiatrist in the admitting office. *Archives of General Psychiatry,* 1965, *13,* 54–61.

Young, E. R., Rimm, D. C., & Kennedy, T. D. An experimental investigation of modeling and verbal reinforcement in the modification of assertive behavior. *Behavior Research and Therapy,* 1973, *11,* 317–319.

Zanna, M. P., & Cooper, J. Dissonance and the pill: An attributional approach to studying the arousal properties of dissonance. *Journal of Personality and Social Psychology,* 1974, *29,* 703–709.

Zetzel, E. R. The effects of psychotherapy. *International Journal of Psychiatry,* 1965, *1,* 144–150.

Zimbardo, P. G. *The cognitive control of motivation.* Glenville, Ill.: Scott Foresman & Co., 1969.

Zuckerman, M., & Grosz, H. J. Suggestibility and dependency. *Journal of Consulting Psychology,* 1958, *22,* 328–336.

11

RESEARCH ON CHILD PSYCHOTHERAPY

CURTIS L. BARRETT
I. EDWARD HAMPE
LOVICK C. MILLER

University of Louisville

In this chapter we review research on child psychotherapy to date, summarize some of the implications of that research, and indicate the directions we believe future child psychotherapy research should take. The research on which we report excludes behavior modification with children, family therapy where the child is the identified patient, and programs such as Re-Ed. These forms of intervention with disturbed children are discussed elsewhere in this volume (see chapter 15 by Ross and Chapter 21 by Gurman & Kniskurn). For the present writers' views on behavior modification techniques with children, the reader is referred to Rie (1971, pp. 374–386). We also excluded from this review most single case studies and work that describes technique which is not clearly based on research.

The worth of any presentation of the kind given here is limited by the research method that is its base. Some work, while perhaps having merit for other purposes, is excluded, and the bibliography is not exhaustive but selective. For readers who wish a comprehensive bibliography we recommend the two that we have used to supplement our own: Klein (1973) and Berlin (1976).

We intend what we present to be useful not only to the student of psychotherapy but also to the practitioner. Gardner (1953) noted the need of child psychiatric *clinics* for research oriented as well as training and service oriented personnel. Like Gardner, we see the ideal child psychotherapy researcher as one who has "passable competence in psychotherapy" and is therefore aware of the types of studies that would be useful to the practicing clinician.

Finally, our introductory remarks would be incomplete if we failed to follow a custom among persons who deal with the problems of children, that is, to lament the lack of resources directed toward dealing with the behavior disorders of children. Levitt (1971) pointed to the few pages of the *Annual Review of Psychology* dealing with psychotherapy for children. In retrospect, more significant evidence was available by assessing the percentage of the first edition of this volume that addressed psychotherapy or behavior change with children. Unfortunately, the situation is worse than even these data can show. Adams (1975) has documented that even when substantial amounts of money are earmarked for the treatment of children, much of that money is used to support work with adults who happen also to have children. As Adams puts it:

> Children are the parapeople—the recipients of paraservices, assigned to paraprofessionals and always reached indirectly, through parents, through teachers, through pediatricians, through courts, through anyone except children themselves—children's services are frequently token services, sham services or, at best, indirect services and "paraservices." (p.18)

Tabulation of services rendered for children reflected what Adams (1975) termed "a premium on indirectness":

> . . . the services for children valued most highly are those which are most indirect, such as educational and preventive work or consultation not with children but with adults who, in turn, do have direct contacts with children. Indirect work is justified by virtue of the fact that therapy for adults is chalked up as a service for children, adopting the logic that what makes for happier marital pairs will ultimately benefit any children they may bring up. . . . [one official said, quite uncritically] Every center tries to consult with schools even if they do nothing else for children (p. 26)

The results of our review show clearly that child psychotherapy research is no match in quantity or quality for that with adults. Nor have we found comparable attempts to grapple with the significant issues that face both research areas. Strupp and Bergin (1969), for example, specifically excluded child psychotherapy research from their review. Similarly, Luborsky, Chandler, Auerbach, Cohen,

and Bachrach (1971) discussed factors influencing the outcome of *adult* psychotherapy. For the most part, child psychotherapy research continues to be what Gardner described it to be nearly 25 years ago: "the product of evening, weekend and vacation period labor," which is, in effect, tacked on to service and training.

It is reasonable to ask why child psychotherapy research is in its present state. As we will learn, a research *attitude* was characteristic of those who pioneered mental health services for children, but the product of their efforts has been limited. During the last 15 years, it appears to us, that systematic investigation of child psychotherapy has been supplanted by programatic development and a general drop in interest in the specific variables that cause and ameliorate emotional disorders. The field has been lying fallow for a period of time, but let us describe its evolution and present status.

CHILD PSYCHOTHERAPY RESEARCH IN THE CHILD GUIDANCE MOVEMENT

For much of its history, child psychotherapy and related research were primarily identified with the child guidance clinic movement. Rie (1971, pp. 1—47) has described the development of this movement in the context of the larger mental hygiene approach advocated by Adolph Meyer and others in the first decade of this century. The growth rate of clinics was tremendous as the following description by Rie (1971) illustrates:

> From fewer than a half dozen in 1917, and perhaps ten in 1921, there were more than eighty by 1931. (Stevenson and Smith 1934). Kanner (1957) reports that there were more than 500 on this continent by 1930. The number of clinics continued to increase in the 1930's and 1940's until by 1946, it was estimated that there were 285 clinics, exclusively for children, and 350 serving children and adults had been established. (Deutch, 1949)

Early in the Child Guidance movement two important traditions were established. First, the tri-disciplinary collaboration of psychiatry, psychology, and social work was set, and it continues to be found in child guidance clinics today. Second, the early clinics emphasized what today would be called program evaluation and thereby produced what constitutes most of the significant research on child psychotherapy. For example, Healy, Bronner, Baylor, and Murphy (1929) stressed the need for the evaluation of programs designed to modify children's behavior:[1]

> We have consistently stressed that a great deal of work that goes under the name of social service and is initiated by people of humane tendencies is continued mainly because of the momentum it has achieved rather than because it is thought that results are being accomplished. Curiously little evaluation of achievement is typical of much of the social service work that is now being called on; many social agencies, not of a critical turn of mind, show no apparent interest in the results of their labors. . . . In the present survey of the facts we stand squarely for measurement of achivement according to objective standards, even though we acknowledge some vulnerability in the standards such as there always will be in dealing with human beings. (p. 5)

Evaluation certainly occurred. The research of the 1930s is remarkable for its detail and its attention to demographic variables. There is no better example of the research of this period than that of Helen Leland Witmer and her students (Witmer and Students, 1933). They studied 299 closed cases. Data were collected in great detail on the patient (e.g., age, sex, IQ), the family (e.g., siblings, parents, father's role) and the treatment received (e.g., dates of contact, treatment plan, reason for closing). Among their findings were that 75 cases (25 percent) were closed as "successfully ad-

justed," 154 cases (51 percent) were closed as "partially adjusted," and 61 (20 percent) were "unimproved." Thus, it appears that treatment results were positive in three-fourths of all cases.

By 1935 Witmer was able to report on the comparative effectiveness of child guidance clinics (Witmer, 1935). Outcome, as judged by raters, was placed in one of five categories:

> A. Original problems have disappeared and no new problems have appeared.

> B. The problem for which the child was referred has very definitely improved though some traces of them may remain.

> C. Some problem still exists, sufficiently marked to handicap the child in his adjustment at school, at home and with peers. Further treatment is indicated but there is no emergency.

> D. The child shows definite behavior or personality problems (no or very little improvement). New problems may have appeared: real need for further treatment. Definitely maladjusted in the three spheres: home, friends, school or work.

> E. The problems are more severe than when he was referred or during treatment. New problems have probably appeared. Adjustment is unsatisfactory in all three spheres.

Four child guidance clinics that "differed in set up and general working methods" were compared.[2] The range of the settings is illustrated by noting that the Judge Baker Guidance Center (Boston) and Guy's Hospital (London) were included. Table 11-1 shows the results for children with IQ's of 70 or above. At this point it appeared that substantial benefit was gained by children in diverse settings who presented varied problems and received a heterogeneous array of intervention procedures. Indeed, the chances for some improvement approached 8 in 10.

The confidence and optimism of child psychotherapists remained until the mid 1950s, al-

---

[1]Note that the aim of "modifying behavior" was clearly stated in this work. The term psychotherapy was used to mean one specific form of intervention. They noted that psychotherapy is often unsuccessful if the old environment is unchanged and that most success is gained in their clinics by "those who appreciate the great value of changing the individual's own mental attitude as well as his external conditions." (p. 21)

[2]Actually the study permitted comparison across 13 settings, since an earlier portion reported on the results of 13 diagnostic types, each in a different setting.

TABLE 11-1   Results from Four Child Guidance Clinics

Clinic	Cases	A, B, or C	D or E
Judge Baker Guidance Center, Boston	56	47(84%)	9(16%)
Institute for Child Guidance, New York	190	136(72%)	54(28%)
Minneapolis Child Guidance Clinic	39	30(76%)	9(23%)
Guy's Hospital, London	53	41(78%)	12(22%)

[a]After Witmer 1935. The original tables gave the results for A and A2 or B and then collapsed A, B, and C. The present authors found $X^2 = 3.61$, $df = 3$, $p > .30$ for this matrix, indicating that there was little difference in outcome across settings.

though little additional investigation was done. Then Levitt (1957, 1963; Levitt, Beiser, & Robertson, 1959), following Eysenck's (1952) lead began a series of studies that evaluated the results of child psychotherapy. Initially Levitt (1957) reported on 18 studies of psychotherapy with results measured at close of treatment and 17 that reported results at follow-up. His data are presented in Table 11-2 and 11-3. The mean percentage of "partial" or "much" improvement across all studies was 67.05 percent. "Much" improvement was shown in an average of 34.54 percent of all cases and "partial" improvement was shown in 32.51 percent. Thus, about one-third of all cases were "unimproved" at close of treatment.

Analysis of the results at follow-up showed that, on the average, slightly more cases showed "much" or "partial" improvement, that is, 78.22 percent as compared with 67.05 percent. It is not possible to make a direct comparison of these data, since different cases were often involved. We can say that Levitt found that for cases evaluated at close, 67.05 percent had improved, and for cases evaluated at follow-up, 78.22 percent were improved. The studies that he analyzed included a wide variety of patients, varied follow-up periods, diverse settings and treatments, and other variations that make them a heterogeneous lot. Nevertheless, the analysis provided some estimate of the results of intervention with children.

More significant than his study of the results of psychotherapy with children was Levitt's resurrection of a question raised earlier by Witmer and Keller (1942). Namely, he asked what the *baseline* for improvement was for children who were determined to be in need of treatment but who did

not receive it (defectors). The figure that Levitt reported was 72.5 percent which, if accurate, is no different from the recovery rate with treatment— the data that previously had spurred optimism! Thus it is important that we examine more carefully his basis for using a baseline of 72.5 percent in evaluating child psychotherapy research.

Levitt (1957) based his percentage figure on the results of two studies: Witmer and Keller (1942) and Lehrman et al. (1949). The first of these studies was concerned with a sample of 50 children matched to the sample in an investigation conducted by Shirley, Baum, and Polsky (1940). At follow-up, 8 to 13 years after being examined at the Worcester clinic, 24 children were rated "successful," 15 were rated "improved," and 11 "unimproved." Collapsing the "successful" and the "improved" categories, we arrive at a 78 percent baseline or base rate. A number of factors make this figure questionable as Witmer and Keller noted. First, 30 percent of the cases came from the court and 20 percent from physicians. At the time, both of these sources requested only diagnostic service, suggesting that the children were not seriously impaired. If so, they were hardly a representative sample of disturbed children on which to form an "improvement" actuary. Furthermore, it is not reasonable to assume that "no intervention" occurred, since all families were evaluated and recommendations were made (even though only 14 of 34 cases followed the recommendations). Our own research suggests that the diagnostic process itself constitutes an intense short-term therapeutic process, particularly with young mildly disturbed acute phobic children (Miller, Barrett, Hampe, & Noble, 1972).

TABLE 11-2 Levitt's (1957) Summary of Results of Psychotherapy with Children at Close

Levitt's Ref. No.	Study	N	Much Improved	Partially Improved	Unimproved	Percent Improved
(11)	Cohen & Davis (1934)	57	16	18 12	8 3	80.7
(26)	Hubbard & Adams (1936)	100	13	18 42	26 1	73.0
(28)	Irgens (1936)	70	12	29 19	10	85.7
(44)	Ried & Hagan (1952)	250	54	82 46	68	72.8
(34)	Lehrman, Sirluck, Black & Glick (1949)	196	76	52	68	65.3
(31)	Lamore (1941)	50	15	18	17	66.0
(10)	Christianson, Gates & Fay (1934)	126	25	54	47	62.7
(53)	Witmer et al. (1933)	290	75	154	61	79.0
(2)	Barbour (1951)	814	207	398	209	74.3
(43)	Newell (1934)	72	26	31	15	79.2
(33)	Lee & Kenworthy (1929)	196	93	61	42	78.6
(6)	Brown (1947)	27	5	11	11	59.3
(9)	Carpenter (1939)	31	13	8	10	67.7
(8)	Canaday (1940)	23	2	9	12	47.8
(7)	Burlingham (1931)	75	35	22	18	76.0
(1)	Albright (1938)	80	31	21	28	65.0
(35)	Maas et al. (1955)	522	225		297	43.1
(13)	Cunningham, Westerman & Fischoff (1955)	420	251		169	59.8
	All cases	3399	1174	1105	1120	67.05
	Percent	100.00	34.54	32.51	32.95	

Witmer and Keller argue that their data are best accounted for by assessing the age of the child at the time of follow-up. That is, "the inherent capacity to grow and mature tends to assert itself over obstacles, so that even many of the unsuccessfully treated eventually attain social stability" (p. 85) This would support the view that the effect of child guidance is to hasten improvement. Unfortunately, the research design did not permit a full test of this hypothesis.

To summarize, there is reason to question the selection of Witmer and Keller's outcome for "diagnostic" cases as a baseline for improvement without psychotherapy. Moreover, there is reason to question whether it is best to classify the reported intervention strategies as "psychotherapy."

The second referent point for Levitt's baseline is the work of Lehrman et al. (1949), a landmark study in child psychotherapy research in which a total of 366 children (264 boys, 102 girls) were observed and evaluated for a period of six weeks. Most of the work was done by a social worker but psychological and psychiatric assistance were also available "when necessary." The children, ranging in age from 3 to 20 years, included those with primary behavior disorders (59.8 percent), psychoneurosis (24.6 percent), psychopathic personality (6.3 percent), other disorders (severe, 7.4 percent) and 1.9 percent who showed no psychiatric disorder. From this group, 196 were accepted for treatment. They received no less than 5 "client interviews" and in 75 percent of the cases more than 30 such interviews. Treatment was based on psychoanalytic principles (termed "transference analysis") and "frequent" use was made of adjunctive facilities, for example, volunteer department, psychiatrically oriented camps. Treatment was conducted by a supervised social worker and coordinated by a team under the direction of a psychiatrist. Thus it would appear that "treatment" in this study approached a fairly rigorous definition of "child psychotherapy."

TABLE 11-3　Levitt's (1957) Summary of Results of Psychotherapy with Children at Follow-up

Levitt's Ref. No.	Study	Interval (Years)	N	Much Improved	Partially Improved		Unimproved		Percent Improved
(33)	Lee & Kenworthy (1929)	1–5	197	49	55	39	38	16	72.6
(5)	Browne (1931)	2	33	8	11	7	6	1	78.8
(11)	Cohen & Davis (1934)	2–3	57	25	17	6	6	3	84.2
(52)[a]	Witmer (1935)	1–10	366	81	78	106	101		72.4
(28)	Irgens (1936)	2–3	70	21	30	13	6		91.4
(51)	Walcott (1931)	5–8	17	7	3		4	3	58.8
(34)	Lehrman, Sirluck, Black & Glick (1949)	1	196	99	46		51		74.0
(41)	Morris, Soroker & Burress (1954)	16–27	34	22	11		1		97.1
(2)	Barbour (1951)	1–20	705	358	225		122		82.7
(4)	Bronner (1944)	5–18	650	355	181		114		82.5
(36)	Mayberly & Struge (1939)	3–15	484	111	264		109		77.5
(19)	Feton & Wallace (1938)	1–4	732	179	398		155		78.8
(13)	Cunningham, Westerman & Fischoff (1955)	5	359	228	80		51		85.8
(21)	Gollander (1944)	1–2	25	6	12		7		72.0
(42)	Moses (1944)	1–2	25	10	6		9		64.0
(35)	Maas (1955)	½–1½	191	82			109		42.9
(23)	Healy, Bronner & Baylor (1929)	1–20	78	71			7		91.0
	All cases	4.8[b]	4219	1712	1588		919		78.22
	Percent		100.0						

[a]Data based on 13 studies originally reported in (42); results of 8 of these are included here.
[b]Estimated average follow-up interval per case.

The control group consisted of 110 children from the 366 observed children. All of them had been considered to need treatment, to be appropriate for the agency, and not to have had treatment at another service. An additional 60 children entered treatment but were referred elsewhere.

At one-year follow-up, outcome was classified as "Success," "Partial Success," or "Failure" on the basis of a final clinical rating procedure that is acceptably similar to Witmer's (1935) as described above. Unfortunately the exact procedure for obtaining ratings is not reported in a way that would permit replication. Numerous other variables were assessed (e.g., age, sex) which will not be considered.

Table 11-4 gives the outcome, at one-year follow-up, for the two groups. Our analysis confirms the authors' report of statistically significant differences between the distribution of cases in categories and that expected by chance. It would

appear that this result stems mainly from there being a better quality of improvement in the treatment group than that found in the control group, since the number of failures appear about equal. In view of the controversy about the effectiveness of psychotherapy with children, it is interesting that Lehrman et al. conclude that their study

. . . leaves no doubt about the fact that the children in the Jewish Board of Guardians Treatment Group fared better in the community a year after closing than the children in the Jewish Board of Guardians Control Group.

A certain irony exists in the fact that the outcome for the control group, shown to be inferior to the outcome for the treated group, would later be used to demonstrate the ineffectiveness of child psychotherapy.

As with Witmer and Keller's study, additional

TABLE 11-4 Adjustment at One-Year Follow-Up[a]

	Success	Partial	Failure	
Treated	99	46	51	196
Control	35	42	33	110
	134	88	84	306

[a]After Lehrman et al., 1949.

analyses by Lehrman et al. raise questions about whether the treatment and control groups that they used were comparable. For example, while children in the control group were reported to be clearly in need of treatment, they also were somewhat less disturbed and had more adequate parents. Possibly the latter fact accounts for their terminating treatment. After six weeks observation or up to five interviews more of involvement with the clinic, the parents decided to attempt to handle the problem themselves.

Whatever the technical drawbacks of their study, and Lehrman et al. (1949) clearly recognized them, we must still conclude that Levitt (1957) selected an excellent study from which to select a base-rate. Unless one is willing to argue that the observation period of six weeks can be equated with that *plus* 30 or more psychoanalytically oriented interviews and adjunctive intervention, the baseline of 70 percent improvement for "untreated" children must be accepted as a reasonable one.

Response to the general argument and results of Levitt was not quick in coming. Heinicke and Goldman (1960) reviewed much the same literature as had Levitt and concluded that there were 17 studies "similar enough to warrant pooling." The dimensions of similarity that they used were: (1) an eclectic psychotherapy was used, (2) there was a follow-up study and (3) at least three measures of outcome were used. Even so, 7 of the of the 17 studies were rejected for various reasons such as use of a restricted sample of children, for example, delinquents. On the basis of 10 studies, Heinicke and Goldman (1960) concluded that a mean of 57 percent of children treated showed successful adjustment, 24 percent showed partial

adjustment, and no improvement was shown by 18 percent. By combining the first two categories, a mean percentage of 81 percent improved is obtained. In effect, Heinicke and Goldman selected studies that showed psychotherapy with children to be effective and sidestepped Levitt's central issue: the high rate of improvement for untreated children. Having come to the conclusion that treatment was effective, they called for a shift in research emphasis away from outcome and toward process. They called for addressing the question: What changes can we observe in a certain kind of child or family that can be attributed to involvement in a certain kind of therapeutic interaction.

A second response to Levitt's position was made by Hood-Williams (1960). His arguments included one that we alluded to above, that it is difficult to establish an appropriate baseline for improvement of untreated controls. But Hood-Williams also noted an effect of the date of study on outcome. That is, high success rates in clinics were associated with treatment conducted during the period 1931 to 1932. Low success rates were associated with treatment after 1940. He suggested that the later lowered success rates might be due to an increased case load of "deep-seated cases of disturbances requiring extensive psychotherapy and less with minor cases that could be treated by manipulation of the environment." At this point Hood-Williams concluded that "the question 'How effective is psychotherapy with children?' is still unanswered."

A third major response in the controversy was made by Halpern (1968). His was less a reworking of older studies and comparison with more recent ones than an attempt to address a number of critical issues. First, Halpern noted that the results for treated, diagnosed, and untreated children are highly varied. Second, he raised the question of what to measure or control. Should studies focus on time, intensity of the therapeutic experience, specific diagnostic categories, readily identified subgroups, or some other issue altogether? Finally, Halpern raised a familiar issue from the child development literature. Would more be learned if a longitudinal instead of a sampling (cross-sectional) approach were taken? Clearly this raises familiar complex issues. As Halpern points out, "Comparisons with control groups may not be helpful unless children are matched for comparable maturational gradients (Thomas et al., 1960), neurophysiological functioning (Knobloch et al., 1956), and psychosocial criteria (Furman et al., 1965; Passamanick et al., 1956)."

The Levitt camp was certainly neither silent nor inactive as the controversy over the effectiveness of child psychotherapy developed. They produced two significant papers that buttress their original findings and attempt to meet some of the more sigificant methodological criticisms. Levitt, Beiser, and Robertson (1959) studied the effectiveness of treatment as provided through the Institute for Juvenile Research, Chicago. The methodology was quite similar to that of Lehrman et al. (1949), and it is sound work. They demonstrated that treatment defectors, as a group, do not differ from treatment groups on 61 diagnostic variables, in severity of symptoms or motivation for treatment (Levitt, 1957b). Moreover, they demonstrated that judges could not predict from the clinical records of children who would be defectors (Levitt, 1958).

In design, Levitt et al. (1959) departed from the single sample case, that is, comparing their treatment results to a baseline, and chose to compare results for 327 treated children and 142 controls. Outcome variables included objective psychological tests, parent's opinions and evaluation, the child's statements about himself and his feelings, and "clinical judgments of the child by interviewers in the data collection situation."

They found no statistically significant differences between the outcomes for treated children and their defector controls. They did, however, question the appropriateness in their design of labeling 5 interviews as "treatment." This caution seemed prudent since, in the reference experiment (Lehrman et al., 1949), 5 treatment interviews *after* six weeks of observation placed children in the "treated" group. Therefore, the data were reevaluated with treatment redefined as 10 interviews. This resulted in a reduction of the treated group by 27 males and 18 females with a total of 192 cases remaining. The average number of interviews was increased from 18 to 26 per case. No change in the findings resulted from this reanalysis. That is, there was no outcome difference at follow-up between treated and untreated children.

Despite the obvious strengths of the study, Levitt et al. (1959) approached their findings with considerable caution. They noted that for 35.5 percent of the cases in the experimental group, treatment was done by students and more than 50 percent were "in the hands of individuals with one year of experience or less." Furthermore, as an assessment of psychotherapy *with children,* the study is deficient in that the child alone was the focus of treatment in only one-tenth of the cases and the *mother* was the only family member treated in more that 40 percent of all cases. Thus, in more than one-half of all cases that might be offered as evidence for the lack of effectiveness of *psychotherapy with children,* the child himself was not "treated"! One might wonder what the response would be to the presentation of results of psychotherapy outcome with adults when the *child* alone was seen. After all, reducing the child's symptoms could possibly reduce a parent's anxiety.

In addition to conducting his own original research as a check on the results indicated by evaluation of previous studies, Levitt (1963) responded to the comments by Eisenberg and Gruenbert (1961), Heinicke (1960) and Hood-Williams (1960). He defended the use of "defectors" as controls and addressed the question of whether therapy results are independent of diagnostic categories. His diagnostic categories were: psychotic children; special symptoms (tics, school phobia); delinquency, aggressive behaviors, antisocial acting out; analogs of adult neurosis; and, the largest group, which represented a mix of "general or unclassified child guidance cases" (p. 48).

Results from 22 evaluation studies were categorized in the now-familiar way: "much improved," "partly improved," and "unimproved." A total of 1741 cases were categorized by this method. The results indicate the robustness of the figure for percentage improved across studies. When applied to cases other than psychotic and aggressive children, the percent improved was 68.3 percent. Analysis of the three outcome categories by five diagnostic categories matrix with X^2 shows a significant deviation from expectancy ($p < .01$). Levitt next eliminated the two categories that provided the greatest variation (acting out, special symptoms) and then the resulting matrix did not yield a significant X^2 value. Some may take exception to eliminating psychotic and acting out children in arriving at the overall percent "improved" and eliminating children with acting out and special symptoms to test the independence of outcome and diagnostic category. Therefore, we have reanalyzed Levitt's data to determine whether outcome and diagnostic category are independent in the sample that generates a percent improved of 68.3 percent. Table 11-5 is a rearranged presentation of Levitt's (1963) Table 1.

The results of the reanalysis are quite interesting. A X^2 value of 119.17 ($df=4$, $p<.05$) was obtained from the 3 x 3 matrix indicating significant deviation of outcome from what would be expected by chance. In our opinion further statistical tests of these data would not be appropriate, since no comparisons were planned a priori. But we note that for neuroses there are fewer children in the "much improved" category but the same does not hold true for either the partially improved or unimproved categories. Quite the opposite occurred for the special symptoms group where more children are found to be "much improved" and there were fewer "partially improved." For the "mixed" category, which accounts for by far the most cases, a third pattern is found. There were fewer "much

improved" and about the expected number of "partially improved" and "unimproved" cases.

If these results are examined in light of clinical experience and conventional wisdom they appear to make sense. What many consider to be the treatments of choice for the neuroses—psychoanalytic-depth individual therapy or behavior therapy—have not been available in Child Guidance Clinics so the maximum benefit was not achieved. The special symptoms category includes such troublesome disorders as tics and enuresis which, by their specific noxious qualities, may tend to motivate parents to continue treatment until a good response is achieved. The "mixed" category, although accounting for the majority of cases, by its nature lacks specificity and, therefore, would be unlikely to lead to the development of specific treatment approaches. Obviously a formal test of this explanation of Levitt's results is needed.

At this point, it should be clear that we have chosen to take an historical point of view in tracing the controversy over the outcome of psychotherapy with children. In doing so we have essentially duplicated the efforts of other reviewers and we obtained similar results. That is, we have chosen to accept the methodology of some studies rather than others, to agree with the logic of some investigations and not with others, to raise issues and critique conclusions, and so forth. In looking at

TABLE 11-5 Summary of Levitt's (1963) Evaluation Data From 22 Studies

Type of Disorder	No. of Studies	Much Improved		Partially Improved		Unimproved		Total	
		N	%	N	%	N	%	N	Overall Improved
Neurosis[a]	3	34	15	107	46	89	39	230	61
Special symptoms[a]	5	114	54	49	23	50	23	213	77
Mixed[a]	6	138	20	337	48	222	32	697	68
Acting out	5	108	31	84	24	157	45	349	55
Psychosis	5	62	25	102	40	88	35	252	65
Totals	24	456	26.2	679	39.0	606	34.8	1741	(65.2)

[a]X^2 analysis performed on these data (see text).
  $X^2 = 119$; $df = 4$, $p < .05$

the literature we have found our share of studies that we felt should not have been excluded and we assume that someone else might find others. One example of an overlooked study that we like will suffice to make the point.

Martens and Russ (1932) published an evaluation of the clinical program in Berkeley, California. Treatment was conducted by a "behavior clinic team" consisting of a psychiatrist (part-time), a pediatrician (part-time volunteer), a full-time psychologist, and four half-time visiting counselors. This study is remarkable because "treatment" seldom included formal psychotherapy. Instead it emphasized the sorts of environmental manipulation reported in child guidance clinics as adjuncts to a clinic-based treatment plan, for example, "Shortly after his first visit Willard was transferred to a class the teacher of which was a most understanding woman" (p. 19). Interpersonal influence procedures by the clinic team included, for example, "more or less regular visits to the counselor's office" or, in response to a sex offense by a 14-year old boy, "Willard and the doctor had a frank talk."

A total of 250 problem children were identified by the principals and teachers. Of these 113 were selected to receive "every aid toward adjustment that the clinical program offered" (p. 31). Four of the selected children could not be matched to a control group and were dropped, leaving a total of 109 children in the experimental group. Two control groups were used. The first, called the nonproblem control, included children who were not identified as in need of treatment but who matched a child in the experimental group in age, sex, grade, intelligence, and school. In 82 percent of all cases the experimental and nonproblem control children also had the same teacher. The second control group, called problem control, was selected from the 137 remaining of the originally identified 250 problem children. These 50 problem children received no clinical attention either because of limited clinical time or lack of cooperation by parents. The investigators could not closely match the problem control children to the experimental and nonproblem controls but attempted to select 50 children who presented behavior difficulties most similar in number and type to those in the experimental group.

The dependent variable was a 44-item checklist covering the following major categories: irregularity of attendance, disobedience, lack of application, dishonesty, damage to property, cruelty, profanity, emotional instability, sex difficulty, and personal cleanliness. The checklist was completed by all teachers who had contact with the children and a composite judgment was derived.

At the two year follow-up, 81 of the children in the experimental group and 85 of those in nonproblem control were available for evaluation. The results indicated that while the experimental group continued to have more behavioral disorder than the nonproblem control, the former showed a significant *decrease* in its mean score and the latter showed a significant *increase* in its mean score. The mean score for the 50 children in the Problem Control Group showed a nonsignificant decrease in their overt problem behavior. Marten and Russ also evaluated results at follow-up for the children who were in the experimental group and actually received the treatment. The total N of 81 included 20 who were not treated. Their behavior problem mean scores tended to remain close to the initial level while mean scores for the actually treated children decreased.

At this time what can we take the results reviewed in this section to mean? Having conducted our own analysis of the evidence usually cited for the effectiveness of child psychotherapy and having considered the results of reviews by others, we conclude that there is probably little to be gained by again reworking the data. We should, however, acknowledge the sophistication of that early work and the fact that nearly all of the issues of today were recognized by those investigators. The charge of Healy, Bronner, Baylor, and Murphy (1929) to conduct evaluative research on the effectiveness of what we do with humane intent would be equally valid today.

OTHER STUDIES OF CHILD PSYCHOTHERAPY

Aside from child guidance practice the most researched form of therapy with children is play therapy. Play therapy, of course, is not a single technique but refers to the therapeutic use of play within a theoretical system. Early applications were based in psychoanalytic theory but the majority of systematic investigation has occurred with non-directive therapy.

Snyder (1945; Landisberg & Snyder, 1946) was among the first to investigate the nature of non-directive play therapy and chose to focus on process rather than outcome. On the basis of four cases, which generated 5751 analyzable statements, Landisberg and Snyder (1946) concluded that there were processes and therapist behaviors that defined nondirective play therapy. For example, they found that therapists were nondirective, that the therapist made only 40 percent of the responses, and that the nondirective response "reflection of feeling" preceded 57 percent of all client responses. Negative feelings remained relatively constant (around 30 percent). Outcome data, in the form of anecdotal reports, showed that three of the four children were making good adjustments.

Fleming and Snyder (1947) investigated social and personal changes following nondirective *group* play therapy. Children were not "patients" in the technical sense but were residents of a children's home. Four boys and three girls, each of whom ranked among the most "disturbed" in their cottages, were selected. Verbatim records were made of their therapy during half-hour periods per week for six weeks. Outcome was measured using a personality test, a sociometric instrument and a "guess who" technique (e.g., "Guess who brags a lot?"). Results were compared with those for untreated boys and girls. Significant improvement following treatment was found for girls but no significant change occurred in the boys. Of course, the small numbers involved require that any conclusions from the research be quite tentative. For example, most of the change in the girls' scores came from the change in one girl. The others showed little change.

Following Axline's (1947) lead, Bills (1950a) applied nondirective play therapy with "retarded readers." Eight children whose reading scores and age were discrepant served as experimental subjects. A comparison group consisted of 10 children in the same class who did not receive therapy. Actually the therapy and nontherapy groups differed significantly and no direct statistical tests could be made (e.g., average IQ in the therapy group was 130; for the nontherapy group, 95). On the basis of Gray Oral Reading Test scores, all eight of the therapy group children were found to have made gains. Ratings of the adjustment of the children were less consistent. Three judges rated five children who had been seen by at least two of three raters as maladjusted as having "gained in emotional adjustment." Two judges rated another child as better and two children were judged not to have gained. Thus, of the eight children six (75 percent) gained and two did not. These seem to be familiar figures despite the presenting disorder, method of research, and treatment technique.

Bills (1950b) next tested the hypothesis that nondirective play therapy would *not* benefit retarded readers who showed no maladjustment; that is, "children who had a primary reading disorder." Eight third grade children, who showed reading retardation of 6 to 34 months (mean, 21 months), were selected as well adjusted on the basis of the California Test of Personality, Rorschach and Thematic Apperception Test records. For the group the average IQ was 112 as compared with 110 for the remainder of the class. Results showed that unlike the maladjusted retarded readers, the well adjusted children who were retarded in reading did not make significant gains. Thus there was some evidence to suggest that nondirective therapy relieved a secondary but not a primary reading disorder.

Seeman and Edwards (1954) asked whether a "therapeutic" approach to teaching would accomplish much the same changes in reading gain and adjustment. A "teacher-therapist" interacted with an experimental group for 67 sessions over four months. A matched control group received regular classroom procedures. Thus the independent variable was an intervention procedure that called for providing "an open, permissive, understanding atmosphere which could encourage explanation and expression by the children" (p. 452). Art materials, games, puzzles, and so forth were available to the children for the period.

The results showed that the experimental group made significant gains in reading compared with the control group. There was a trend toward better adjustment scores on one of the two measures but this did not reach statistical significance. It should be noted, however, that unlike children in Bills' study, the children in neither group began with a reading disorder.

Studies of play therapy reflected three shifts in emphasis. First, the methodology increasingly utilized a comparison or control group (two-sample case) instead of the one-sample case or base rate design that was described earlier. Second, the trend was away from clinical judgment of "improved" or "successful" and toward psychometric or sociometric criteria. Finally, studies tended not to use the typical clinic sample. Instead, children who were judged maladjusted by an instiution (school, orphanage) but not referred by parents served as subjects. This meant that the intervention took place and was evaluated in, for example, the school situation.

An excellent example of this trend is a study by Cox (1953). Two groups of nine children were matched for age, sex, residential placement within an orphanage, adjustment, and sociometric measures. The treatment group received Axline-style nondirective play therapy for nine weeks while the control group experienced a comparable "rest" period. Significant improvement was shown for children in the treatment group.

Process seemed to continue to be the focus of most research on play therapy. Moustakas and Schlalock (1955) analyzed therapist-child interaction in play therapy. Subjects were 10 four-year-old nursery school children classified as "without emotional problems" (3F, 2M) and four boys and a girl rated as having "emotional problems sufficient to impair personal and social relations in the nursery school" (p. 144). Two of the 10 children were seen for one 40 minute play session: the remainder were seen for two such sessions. The scope of the investigation is immediately apparent when the data available from these few sessions are assessed: 4610 observations for group A and 4934 for the disturbed group! Space does not permit a full report of the results. But we will note (1) that the two groups were more *alike* than different in their interactions and (2) that where "problem" children were different it was more in the time spent in noninteractive play that did not involve the therapist.

Nearly 20 years after the Moustakas and Schlalock attempt to measure process in nondirective play therapy, Wright, Truax, and Mitchell (1972) investigated the possibility of obtaining reliable process ratings during child psychotherapy of an unspecified sort. Trained raters were presented video tape segments from each of two therapy interviews. The following Truax and Carkuff variables were rated: accurate empathy, nonpossessive warmth, and genuineness. Therapists included four Ph.D. clinical child psychologists, six third year psychiatry residents, and six clinical psychology trainees. Statistically significant but low interrater reliabilities were obtained. This suggests that with further development process ratings of child psychotherapy might become practicable and useful. However, it would be worth knowing in advance whether these variables are more reliable in experienced (and possibly more consistent) child psychotherapists and then whether their presence predicts outcome.

The next important study along this line is that of Dorfman (1958). The therapy group consisted of 17 children of at least normal intelligence (12M, 5F) whose teachers and principal believed them to be maladjusted. The children ranged in age from 9 to 12 years, and their parents consented to the treatment. Control children were matched for age and sex and were not therapy candidates. Thus they would not fall into the "defector" category described earlier but instead would function as a "normal" comparison group. Treatment was conducted once weekly (twice weekly for one student) in the school and Axline's guidelines were followed. Ratings of "success" were made by the therapist and seem to us to be too subjective to be considered here. Further, the results of the experiment are quite complex and it is not correct to say unequivocally, as have Seeman, Barry, and Ellinwood (1964), that "(her) results indicated significant positive changes associated with therapy" (p. 64). Dorfman herself states best the limitations on generalizations from her study.

We have noted statistically significant therapy changes on both Rogers and Sentences tests, but this does not guarantee practical significance, which depends upon the size of the change of relation to the amount of effort expanded in bringing it about. . . .

On the Rogers Test the average Total Score improvement during therapy is 5.88 points which is 14% of the mean pre-therapy score of 41.46. But the SD of pre-therapy scores is 9.72 points so that the mean therapy change represents less than 1 SD (p 15).

Similar limitations applied to change as assessed by the projective techniques. Thus, Dorfman's final conclusion is: "Owing to the absence of behavioral data, we do not know whether test improvements reflect actual changes in life adjustments" (p. 18).

Seeman, Barry and Ellinwood (1964), in a study that was similar to Dorfman's (1958), theorized that play therapy might be effective in modifying aggressive disorders. This disorder, as was noted earlier, has consistently presented difficulties for child psychotherapy and other methods of intervention. Subjects were third graders from a predominantly upper middle class school in a large city. Treatment, for a median length of 37 weekly sessions, took place in a clinical facility and not in the school. Posttherapy teachers gave all children in the "aggressive" group scores that were lower than for the class average. These results are encouraging and suggest the possibility that fairly young, aggressive children might respond to a permissive rather than to a controlling/structured therapeutic approach.

Recent Studies of Child Psychotherapy
Toward the end of their response to Levitt's finding on the effects of child psychotherapy, Heinicke and Goldman (1960) alluded to an extensive project of research underway at the Reiss-Davis Clinic. The results of that project have been reported (Heinicke 1965, 1969) and a summary of research findings, their implications, and recommendations for further research are available (Heinicke & Strassman, 1975).

Heinicke and Strassman (1975) note that the decade and a half between their response to Levitt and their present work showed little progress in child psychotherapy research. In their view a few studies have demonstrated the direction that research should take. First, they call for abandon-

ment of the question "does child psychotherapy work?" and imply that the current question in adult psychotherapy be adopted, that is, "what therapy, under what condition, for which patients with which disorder yields results?" Thus they cite research on vocationally oriented psychotherapy with delinquents, using a control group, as one study achieving measurable and theoretically meaningful results (Shore & Massimo, 1973). Second, they urge systematic attention to the developmental status of the child along the lines suggested by Anna Freud (1962). Third, they suggest the investigation of limited but theoretically meaningful variables such as the psychotherapy equivalent of "dosage," that is, frequency of sessions and duration of treatment (Heinecke, 1969). Fourth, they recommend systematic attention to "parental impact," age, variations in therapist characteristics, and so forth. Finally, they recommend recently developed methods and instruments that permit more specific outcome assessment (e.g., Peterson-Quay Behavior Problem Check List).

Heinecke and Strassman (1975) and Heinecke (1969) detail the results of a study in which psychotherapy "dosage" was shown to affect outcome. Subjects were carefully matched and assigned randomly to psychoanalytic child psychotherapy for either once or four times per week. Outcome measures included (1) *clinical data* (factor scores based on 46 clinical ratings: level of ego integration, extent of ego flexibility, capacity for peer relations, extent of self-reliance), and (2) data related to the presenting learning disorder (reading achievement). No control group for these nine-year-old patients was used. Instead, they were determined not to have responded to extensive previous educational efforts pretreatment. Results for both the clinical and the presenting disorder favored the more intensively treated group at follow-up. Further, a second study replicated the findings under conditions where a child was seen once per week for a year and then shifted to four times per week.

Clearly, Heinecke (1969) has completed a project that demonstrates a more positive effect for intensive, long-term analytically oriented child psychotherapy than for less intensive therapy of this type. It is possible to criticize the study on the basis of its small sample or for the absence of a control group. But on the other hand Heinecke's use of a baseline period is similar to commonly used behavior therapy methodology. The study is strengthened by use of ratings from an independent clinician although we are not assured that the rater was "blind" to the independent variable. Finally, the use of both one and two year follow-up evaluations is impressive.

Our own attempts to study the effects of child therapies bear some similarities to Heinecke's approach. We chose what appeared at the outset to be a specific childhood disorder (phobic reactions) to which we applied what appeared to be clearly different forms of intervention; psychotherapy, systematic desensitization, and waiting list control (Miller, Barrett, Hampe, & Noble, 1972). Other features of the study included: the use of an appropriate control group; stratified random assignment of children to time limited therapy; use of a representative clinical sample with a range in age, severity of disorder, degree of disturbance, intelligence, socioeconomic status, and variety of phobic object; use of same-sex therapists who differed in age and experience; identical assessment of children at pre-, post- and follow-up of treatment; control of initial values by covariance; replication of primary evaluator's ratings by an independent rater; and treating parents and child ethically without sacrificing research standards. Of all of these research design demands the most difficult to apply was randomly assigning children. This meant that even severely phobic children from this clinical sample who presented symptoms such as panic-induced flight from home or school, marked depression, suicidal ideation, or anorexia stood an equal probability of assignment to control.

We evaluated a total of 148 children referred as phobic. Fifty-three were rejected as not phobic because their symptoms cleared or because they failed to meet the project criteria. Eighty-six were accepted for treatment and, of these, 67 were full participants (5 decided against treatment after being accepted, 10 served as pilot subjects, and 4 dropped out). For the psychotherapy and systematic desensitization groups a total of 24 treatment sessions at the rate of 3 per week (8 weeks) were

provided. Follow-up for these groups occurred at 14 weeks, 1 year, and 2 years (Hampe, Noble, Miller, & Barrett, 1973). Children in the waiting list control (WLC) group were reevaluated at the same time as treated children. Treatment was offered at the end of 14 weeks to WLC children.

Multiple outcome measures were used. Parents and the independent clinician (Primary Evaluator, PE) rated the severity of the target phobia. In making the ratings the PE had available data from his own interview; a school behavior checklist completed by the teacher (Miller, 1972); a completed Louisville Behavior Check List (Miller, 1967); a Child's Fear Thermometer (Walk, 1956); a Louisville Fear Survey Schedule (Miller, Barrett, Hampe, & Noble, 1972); five consecutive days of report by parents; and a behavioral fear test.

We draw no simple conclusions from this study. Based on one criterion measure, the Primary Evaluator's ratings of severity, children showed a significant reduction of phobia across time. However, a 2 (therapists) by 3 (treatments) repeated measures analysis of covariance, using pretreatment score as the covariate, showed no effect of treatment or of therapist. On the other hand, *parent* ratings showed an effect of *treatment* but no effect of therapist. Treatments did not differ but both differed from the results for WLC (control). Similar findings were shown for the fear scale of the LBCL and for the LFSC, both of which were completed by parents. Age of the child was shown to influence results. That is, the rate of success for younger children (6 to 10 years) who were treated was 23 of 24 (96 percent) and for WLC the rate was 8 of 14 (57 percent). For older phobic children the success rate with treatment was 9 of 20 (45 percent) and for WLC 4 of 9 (45 percent). Sex, IQ, socioeconomic status and chronicity were unrelated to outcome. Children of parents rated highly motivated were more likely to succeed than were those of low motivated parents.

Follow-up two years after the six weeks follow-up evaluation was possible for 62 of the original 67 children. Results indicated that an attempt to evaluate a "treatment" effect at that point was not meaningful. Children who were successes at the end of treatment tended to remain successes, while failures (60 percent of whom had obtained additional formal treament) showed dramatic decrease in primary symptoms in the first year and con-tinued to improve through the second year. Thus, at the end of two years only 7 percent of a sample selected as presenting clinical levels of phobia still had severe phobia.

It is tempting to focus on the temporal factor in attempting to make sense of our results. However, "time" as a factor conceals more than it reveals. We know that 60 percent of the children who were still phobic after treatment sought further formal treatment. From anecdoctal evidence we know that many sought guidance from schools, churches, and "inherently helping persons." We also know that major family changes occurred but cell frequencies were too small to permit analysis.

A second conclusion from Miller et al. (1972) is the critical importance of the control group. The design called for random assignment of children to treatment, therapist, and control conditions. When faced with a child, his/her family and, for example, a school setting that were under severe stress, it was sorely tempting to exercise clinical judgment and to do what we thought would help the most even if the subject were lost to the study. Referral sources were often confused when they observed a moderately disturbed child quickly accepted for treatment and a severely disturbed child placed on a waiting list. But the results of the study vindicate the decision to hold to the original design. Having done so we can be certain that the improvement rate shown by the WLC was not due to the bias of assigning less disturbed children to it.

The importance of the age factor suggests that it be assessed in a manner that is more sophisticated than our simple device of splitting the groups into "younger (6 to 10)" and "older (11+)." One such attempt is reported by Heinicke and Strassman (1975). They used the Developmental Profile (Freud, 1962) which distinguishes diagnostic guidelines that are meaningful within a psychoanalytic framework: for example, pathologi-cal formulations that are transitory and by-products of developmental strain versus those that represent arrested development and pervasive regressions as evidenced in infantilisms, borderline states, delin-quency, or psychosis (Heinicke & Strassman, 1975, p. 562).

If we compare Heinicke (1969) and Miller et al. (1972) we note differences in treatment type, length and frequency of treatment, and in the dis-order that was treated. However, both studies show continued progress across time if a disorder persists. Clearly, improvement in our subjects can-not be attributed to intense psychotherapy inter-vention like that provided by Heinicke but for the same age group results were comparable. If the age factor holds for learning disorders, as it does for phobia, older children should present a more strin-gent test of the effectiveness of intensive psychotherapy.

RELEVANCE OF LIFE HISTORY RESEARCH FOR RESEARCH ON CHILD PSYCHOTHERAPY

Life history research is concerned with changes that take place in people over *extended* periods of time. The most comprehensive treatment of the area is given in three volumes edited by Merril Roff, David Ricks and others (Roff & Ricks, 1970; Roff, Robins, & Pollack, 1972; Ricks, Thomas, & Roff, 1974). These volumes illustrate the varied perspec-tives that have been adopted in attempting to un-derstand the psychopathology that psychotherapy is used to treat. An obvious overlap of psychotherapy research and life history research occurs when one studies the lives of persons for whom an intervention (e.g., psychotherapy, drugs) was made. Whereas this is not "outcome" in the same sense used in a two year follow-up of psychotherapy, it is the only meaningful outcome design if one requires that intervention demon-strate "lasting effects that have real, long term life significance" (Ricks, Thomas, & Roff, 1974, p. 275).

One study from the life history research litera-ture that is relevant to child psychotherapy re-search is Ricks (1974). He determined the adult status of 28 comparable, severely disturbed boys who received psychotherapy from one of two therapists. Each therapist was highly experienced in working with boys in their clinic and worked in about the same period in the clinic's history. Out-come for the two therapists was as follows (Ricks, 1974, p. 280).

	Therapist A	Therapist B
Chronic schizophrenic	0	3
Released schizophrenic	4	8
Socially inadequate	5	2
Socially adequate	6	0
	15	13

A X^2 analysis, when the outcomes were classified as "schizophrenic" and "nonschizophrenic" indicated that the difference was not attributable to chance.

Further analysis of records indicated considerable differences in the way the therapists allotted their time. The mean hours spent, classified by outcome for the boys, was as follows (Ricks, 1974, p. 281).

	Therapist A	Therapist B
Chronic schizophrenic	—	9
Released schizophrenic	38	19
Socially inadequate	25	24
Socially adequate	13	—

This indicates that Therapist A concentrated his intervention on the boys who needed it the most. (Ricks suggests that the cynic might conclude that the more time with Therapist A, the worse the outcome).

Therapist A was known by the children in the residence operated by his center as "Supershrink." Further examination of case records indicated other differences between the psychotherapy and other interventions conducted by Supershrink and those of Therapist B.

1. Therapist B precipitated termination by overloading an already tenuous relationship with too much anxiety-arousing or depression-arousing interpretation.

2. Supershrink more frequently used outside resources such as camps and temporary group placement. He carefully worked out in therapy the meaning of the placements.

3. Supershrink was firm and direct in working with parents. He met with them and the boy to correct destructive misinformation that the boys were given and to improve the parent-child relationship.

4. Supershrink aimed at developing the boy's sense of autonomy.

5. Supershrink used the therapy relationship to provide the boy with an anchor in reality. He responded to the full range of feelings and was a long-term resource in the boys life, for example, remembered with letters, visits. Therapist B, on the other hand, "tended to take a distant, cognitive attitude toward expressions of feeling. He also seemed selective in the feelings that he did respond to. Unless there were expressions of depressions or anxiety, he seemed to believe that nothing was going on in therapy" (Ricks, p. 287).

6. Supershrink worked toward helping the boys reach solutions to problems of real life, for example, vocational ambitions and possibilities. He promoted competence. Therapist B tended to judge the good therapy hour as one that produced material of deep psychodynamic interest.

The dramatic differences in outcome for the boys 20 years after therapy should not obscure the fact that psychotherapy was but one of many events in the lives of these boys. No simple cause-effect statement is possible. But the therapeutic strategies and tactics that appear to have been effective for Supershrink need to be assessed for their effectiveness in the hands of other therapists. Further, incorporation of the long-term follow-up characteristic of life history research would permit a better assessment of the positive and negative effects of intervention in children's lives.

A second contribution of life history research to child psychotherapy research is our increased knowledge about the natural course of childhood disturbances. Earlier we noted that phobic children who had been referred for treatment tended to be nonphobic after about two years. Those who were treatment failures usually continued to seek help of various sorts until the problem was resolved.

Robins (1966) investigated the adult status of 524 predominately white Child Guidance patients 30 years after their treatment. Outcome was compared with that for 100 nonpatients of the same sex, age, race, intelligence and neighborhood. As adults, expatients showed more psychiatric disorder than did nonpatients. Early descriptions of antisocial behavior (sociopathic personality) tended to predict chronic problems of this nature although other psychiatric disorders (e.g., schizophrenia, hysteria) were found. The neuroses and affective disorders were not found more in expatients than in nonpatients.

Similar results were found for black school boys who showed antisocial disorders (Robins, Murphy, Woodruff, & King, 1971). Having an antisocial personality as an adult was strongly related to having displayed antisocial behavior as a child. Further, antisocial blacks were at great risk for early, violent death.

Another group that has been the focus of life history research has been the shy, withdrawn child. The most significant of this work has been connected with the Southwestern Medical School and its affiliates. Morris, Soroker, and Burruss (1954) followed up 34 persons (24M, 10F) classified as "internal reactors," who had been diagnosed but not treated by the Dallas Child Guidance Clinic 16 to 27 years earlier. On the whole such children, as adults, were doing well. Between the 34 evaluated and another 20 for whom partial information was available, only two were "sick." The majority (two-thirds) were satisfactorily adjusted and most of the others were at least "marginally adjusted" by the authors' criteria.

In a second study of the withdrawn child the incidence of schizophrenia was assessed (Michael, Morris, & Soroker, 1955). Follow-up occurred 24 to 47 years after being seen on a consultation or diagnostic basis: none had had continuous treatment. Of some 164 children classified as "introverts" only one was found to have been diagnosed schizophrenic and none had other diagnoses. Among ambiverts the incidence of schizophrenia was 6 of 174 and there were six other diagnoses. Of 268 extroverts, three were diagnosed schizophrenic and eight had other diagnoses. This would indicate, again, differential prognosis and a different baseline for children considered to be shy or withdrawn and those labeled antisocial. In a third study, Michael (1955) checked the incidence of criminal behavior among introverted children. Those who had a record of delinquent behavior before being seen at the Child Guidance Clinic were dropped from the study. The results indicated that of 165 introverts, eight (5 percent) showed an incidence of delinquency or crime. For extroverts the number was 57 (25 percent) and for 162 ambiverts it was 18 (11 percent). Thus, significantly fewer introverts than ambiverts or extroverts were involved in crime or delinquency.

The developing area of life history research holds some promise as a source of guidance for development of technique in child psychotherapy and for allocation of effort. The area also can provide data on base rates for improvement for specific disorders, for example, the antisocial. Further, the life history perspectives "show that intervention can be interpreted in a more comprehensive and systematic way than it has been in the past" (Ricks, Thomas, & Roff, 1974, p. viii).

SUMMARY AND CONCLUSIONS

It is relatively simple to review and to organize the literature on child psychotherapy although one inevitably runs the risk of neglecting or overlooking articles that others see as crucial. It is quite another matter to address the question, "what does it all mean?" But that is the task that we turn to now.

1. Our first conclusion regards the controversy stirred up by Levitt (1957, 1963, 1971). We have found little reason to fault his methodology or his conclusions although, like other researchers, we recognize certain limitations. But Levitt, too, recognized limitations. If one chooses to apply a single sample case design and needs a base rate Levitt's expected frequency, across groups, is as good as any and better than most. Investigators should recognize what they are up against, however. Assume 100 treated and 100 control cases to be rated simply "improved" or "unimproved." Using Levitt's

expected frequency of about 70 percent, what improvement rate would yield a χ^2 value significant at $p < .05$? An improvement rate of 80 percent would yield $\chi^2 = 2.66$, $df = 1$, $p < .10$. If 85 percent of the treated group were improved, $\chi^2 = 10.96$, $df = 1$, $p < .05$. Thus with 100 treated subjects, between 80 and 85 percent would have to be improved in order to exceed the baseline rate of Levitt. If the investigator were to have 50 treated and 50 untreated patients, with the same baseline, an improvement rate of 85 percent (43) would not be significantly different from the baseline (35 of 50 improved). This is not to say "don't even try." Instead, we emphasize the limited power of such research designs to find effects when they are there. Investigators who do not carefully attend to the research design issue may find the results obscured by what we call "macrovariables." These are unanticipated variables that account for large amounts of variance and preclude showing other effects. An example is the age variable discussed in the Miller et al. (1972) study. Outcome for phobic children depended more on their age than on any other factor, including therapist experience and degree of disturbance.

2. Our second conclusion is that there probably is little more to be gained by further reworking of the outcome data of the 30s. Having recently done it ourselves we are convinced that no one has done it exhaustively and no one is likely to do so. It is best to recognize the merits of the early work, the significant changes in our culture, patterns of diagnoses and concepts of mental illness that have occurred, and go on.

3. Third, we concur with Heinicke and Strassman (1975) that the question "Does psychotherapy work?" is one that has been abandoned in adult psychotherapy research. Today's question should be "Which set of procedures is effective when applied to what kind of patients with which sets of problems and practiced by which sort of therapists?" Shifting to the more appropriate question in

no way simplifies our task; indeed, it complicates it.

4. Fourth, from the earliest child psychotherapy reserach to the present it has been clear that response to treatment is a function of the diagnostic category. This finding needs further systematic attention since our classification procedures are quite crude. In our own research we attempted to study effects of therapy or control procedures on a specific set of disorders. In the process, we were forced to study the disorder per se and to develop instruments to define and measure it. We doubt that there is any disorder of childhood that would not lead to the same behavior on the part of the investigator. Simply put, we are in need of a better system for classifying childhood disorders.

5. Fifth, child psychotherapy research has not controlled for the developmental stage of the child. Age, corrected for maturation/developmental level, is a significant variable and must be better defined and controlled.

6. Sixth, the definition of child psychotherapy to a much greater degree than that of adult psychotherapy, must take into account the developmental level of the child and the systems with which he or she must interface.

7. Seventh, it is necessary that a taxonomy of child therapy procedures that add to Frank's (1963) "general factor" be established. We must ask whether it makes sense to adapt an undefined set of intervention procedures to the range of disorders that present themselves to us. *Why* should play therapy be effective with learning disorders or reading difficulties? *Why* should "general child guidance treatment" be expected to treat neurotic, mixed, or special symptoms?

8. Eighth, we conclude that great progress has been made in developing dependent variables that may be sensitive to changes in child psychopathology. Despite the fact that NIMH, in its wisdom, chose not to sponsor a parallel, for child therapy research, of its project on psychotherapy change measures

(Waskow & Parloff, 1975), progress has been made. Miller (1967, 1972) has developed the Louisville Behavior Check List and the School Behavior Check List to the point that they adequately measure psychopathology as assessed by the parent and the teacher. Fearful children can be assessed by the Louisville Fear Survey for Children. Heinicke (1969), using a psychoanalytic framework, has developed reliable rating scales. Thus, there is good reason to believe that child psychotherapy research in the future can be at least partly replicable across settings.

9. Finally, we conclude that child psychotherapy research has suffered for lack of a model that specified its task. As a field, child psychotherapy is part of a larger field that involves parenting, child advocacy, development, education, preparation for citizenship, and so forth. It cannot long stand independent of the evaluation of the family and of the larger society.

SOME ENDURING ISSUES

As we view the child psychotherapy research from a historical perspective we are first struck by its discontinuity. Beginning in the 1920s and continuing until the early 1960s there were vigorous attempts by many investigators to study the effect of child therapy, parent counseling, or a combination of both. From the early 1960s until now relatively little outcome research has been done. This sudden reduction appears to us to have occurred for two reasons. First, there was a dramatic change in the culture in the early sixties embodied in the *Zeitgeist* of the Great Society. Politicians, community leaders, and mental health professionals shifted their attention from the systematic study of individuals to action programs. Time, money, and energy were poured into community mental health centers, early intervention programs, primary prevention, child advocacy, and public policy. Mental health professionals went about building institutions and developing programs to deal with disturbed children rather than tackling the question of the

effectiveness of child psychotherapy. The literature of the mid-sixties and the seventies reflects this preoccupation. A look at the table of contents of *Child Clinical Psychology* (Williams & Gordon, 1974) or of any of the annual reviews of child development and child psychiatry will suffice to make the point.

A second reason for the sudden slowdown in systematic research in child therapy, we think, is that child clinicians experienced no aversive consequences as a result of Levitt's conclusion that the effectiveness of child psychotherapy had not been demonstrated. Their equanimity in the face of Levitt's statement has to be contrasted with the anger and anxiety of adult clinicians toward the work of Eysenck. His study rocked the adult mental health establishment, many of whose members responded by designing and executing quality outcome research. Others moved toward research with the new behavioral therapies. As a result, evidence for effectiveness of psychotherapy and other interventions with adults is much better than it was. (Meltzoff & Kornreich, 1970; Malan, 1973; Sloane, 1975).

Levitt's article did not prompt the same response from child clinicians. There were several attempts to rework the literature that Levitt reviewed, and to try to ameliorate his general conclusion, but there was no massive surge of higher quality outcome research. Instead many child clinicians turned their attention toward other modalities, such as behavior therapy and family therapy, and to building the institutions and programs of the Great Society. In short, Levitt's final critique came along at a time when other options were becoming available to the child clinician and the spirit of the times pushed child clinicians toward those options and not toward developing research that would build on Levitt's work. Those who wanted to do child psychotherapy did so. Parents continued to bring their children to child guidance clinics and someone had to see them.

It appears to us that the emphasis on institutions and programs is decreasing and that there is a resurgence of interest in individuals and their differences (c.f. Hogan, DeSoto, & Solano, 1977). Perhaps the time is right for a renewed commitment to systematic outcome research on child psychotherapy. If so, then the literature reviewed here provides new researchers with one very critical lesson: If we resort to macrovariable research (e.g., combining all kinds of diagnostic categories, patients being seen by therapists with a wide variety of personal styles, each making all kinds of interventions, and then assessing outcome in some gross fashion like improved, partially improved, unimproved) we will continue to demonstrate that 70 percent of disturbed children improve with psychotherapy or with time alone. Our first step, therefore, must be that of refining our measures in at least four critical areas: the child and his or her disorder, the therapist and his or her personality, intervention techniques, and outcome measures. Some suggestions based on our own struggles include the following.

The Child and the Disorder

At least four factors need to be controlled: age, intelligence, type of onset, and severity of disorder. Age is, of course, easy to determine but, as we commented above, a more sophisticated developmental assessment is needed. So is intelligence. The chronicity of the condition would appear to be easy to assess, but it isn't. How, for example, do you quantify a school phobic reaction in a 13 year old that was present for three weeks in the first grade, then disappeared only to resurface for a time in the fourth grade, only to disappear again and reappear in the seventh grade? Depending on your viewpoint, this condition could be called acute or chronic. We need some standard way of quantifying chronicity in order to facilitate cross-study comparisons. A potentially useful instrument is the Onset of Symptomatology Scale, developed by Gossett, Meeks, Barnhart & Phillips (1976).

Another major stumbling block to conducting effective psychotherapy research is that of equating for "severity of illness." All of the critiques of Levitt's original review raised this valid issue, stating that in the absence of any standard way to measure severity of disturbance, comparisons across outcome studies are meaningless. Most studies used only unidimensional ratings (e.g., mildly disturbed, moderately disturbed, severely disturbed) with the rating points left unreferenced.

Yet we know that clinicians can make reliable judgments on "severity of disturbance." In a study by Coddington and Offord (1967) four psychiatrists obtained an overall interrater reliability of .90 when judging severity of disturbance of 21 children on a six point linear scale.

In research with phobic children we conceived of severity as the product of the intensity of the child's distress and the extensity of the phobia's effect on the child's life. Each dimension was rated on a seven point scale, and each point was referenced, albeit subjectively. This way of conceptualizing severity resulted in ratings that had high interrater reliability and they made good clinical sense. For example, a phobia of high intensity but no extensity has relatively little clinical interest while phobias that are moderately high on both dimensions are clearly important clinically.

McConville and Purohit (1973) have suggested that severity subsumes one other dimension—community tolerance for the problem. In their study they rated community tolerance on a five point scale, with each point carefully referenced. Interrater reliability was good.

It has since occured to us that severity involves one other component—probability that the disorder can be successfully treated. We have not yet developed a method for rating this dimension. Again, though, these four variables as components of severity of disturbance seem to make good clinical sense. A severe disorder is subjectively distressing; it is not circumscribed but invades many facets of a person's life; it is not tolerated by the community; and it is resistant to treatment.

The Therapist and His or Her Personality

There have been many studies concerning the relationship of therapist characteristics and the outcome of psychotherapy, almost all of which have been with adults (c.f. Meltzoff & Kornreich, 1970). There is reasonable consensus that warmth, genuiness, empathy, level of experience, and freedom from neurotic difficulties all promote successful outcome, while the discipline of the therapist and his or her having had personal therapy are unrelated to outcome. The research findings are not uniform with respect to the contributions to outcome of the therapist's age, gender, race, religion and social class, although there is an emerging belief that there is a curvilinear relationship between these variables and outcome. Therapeutic communication is most likely to transpire between people who are neither too much alike nor too different from each other (e.g., Carson & Heine, 1962).

These generic variables must certainly apply to child therapists in much the same fashion as they apply to adult clinicians. It is difficult, for example, to imagine an effective child therapist who is not warm, genuine, and empathetic. Beyond this point, however, we do not know as precisely as we should the characteristics of a Supershrink. Ricks (1974), of course, made a significant attempt to answer a part of this question. His research strategy is worth emulation.

The Intervention Techniques

It would seem redundant to state that reciprocal inhibition therapy and play therapy are two different techniques. To a large extent, though, the activities conducted under these two names are quite similar, so much so that in our own research we found it possible and profitable to describe a generic set of procedures that we found ourselves using no matter which kind of treatment we were doing (Miller, Barrett, & Hampe, 1974). Moreover, these common procedures probably accounted for the fact that we obtained no differential treatment effect. One treatment *was* the other. Therefore, it appears to us that the first step is that of discovering and describing those procedures that are common to nearly all child treatments and assessing their impact. Once the impact of these procedures is known, we can determine whether those maneuvers that are exclusive to one type of therapy add anything beyond the "G" variables.

The Measurement of Outcome

Everyone is agreed that the unstructured, undimensional judgments of improved, partially improved, and unimproved made by only the patient's therapist will not produce meaningful data. Of the many refinements of therapy outcome, one of the most appealing to us is that which has been advocated by Strupp and Hadley (1977). Theirs is a comprehensive and relativistic approach, in that they take into account the vantage points of those who evaluate change and the values of those who occupy each vantage point. They identify three major "interested parties" who are concerned with

evaluating human functioning: (1) society (including significant persons in the patient's life) (2) the individual patient, and (3) the mental health professional. Society, they note, is concerned primarily with the maintainence of an orderly world. Hence, society and its representatives tend to define mental health in terms of behavioral stability, predictability, and conformity to the social code. The individual, however, is most likely to focus on a subjective sense of well-being. There are, as we all know, very few people in treatment who are content with themselves, and it is generally a feeling of discomfort that motivates a person toward treatment. This facet of Strupp and Hadley's model will need to be modified in order to be used with children because many children who are brought for treatment are firm in stating that they are subjectively comfortable.

Last, mental health professionals who engage in child psychotherapy typically view an individual's functioning in terms of the structure and dynamics of the child's personality. The richness of his or her ego structures, the balance between drives and defenses, and the person's generalized orientation toward the self and others, are of interest.

The upshot is that "the same individual may simultaneously be judged as mentally healthy or mentally ill and correspondingly, his therapeutic experience may be judged as positive or negative depending on who is evaluating the patient" (p. 196). Judgments of therapy outcome from only one perspective based on only one set of criteria cannot, therefore, be compared with a judgment from another perspective based on another set of criteria. Strupp and Hadley go on to note that "a truly adequate, comprehensive picture of an individual's mental health is possible only if the three facets of functioning—behavior, affect and inferred psychological structure—are evaluated and integrated (p. 196).

Our thinking leads us to conclude that the issue of perspective is complicated by the fact that none of the three viewpoints has *exclusive* use of its principal viewpoint. For example, while society is primarily concerned with stability, responsibility, and conformity, at least the empathetic members of society wish the patient a sense of well-being and a solid but evolving personality structure. Moreover, a majority of patients want not only a sense of well-being but also an integrated personality and at least a moderate ability to respect society's conventions. Therapists do indeed value intrapsychic integrity, but they also want their patients to have a sense of well being and an ability to behave in moderately conforming responsible and courageous fashion. Hence, each interested party needs an opportunity to evaluate the person from all three viewpoints. What is needed, therefore, is an instrument or set of instruments that can be used by the patient, the therapist, and by significant representatives of society (generally peers and parents, teachers of the child). When used, the instrument should tap behavior, affect, and psychological functioning in all of its normal and deviant varieties.

This is quite an order, especially when one realizes that, for example, 5 year olds, 10 year olds, and 15 year olds will each require instruments that are tailored to their developmental levels. Obviously the field cannot wait on the development of perfect instruments. As a criterion to aim for, however, it makes good conceptual and intuitive sense.

The last of the enduring issues for child psychotherapy research is one that we mentioned in our introductory comments. Namely, child psychotherapy as a field must resist the trend toward making children parapeople who receive paraservice based on results from pararesearch. This will not be easy in light of current trends in the family and behavioral therapies that we too endorse. There will be a new wave of child psychotherapy research, whatever it is called, and it can allow us to improve the quality of our work. This potential ability to contribute will be based largely on the contributions of researchers whose work is reviewed here. These people cared. They wanted to know how well they were doing in their therapeutic work and, to the best of their ability, they found out. They taught us much. What is needed now is another group of researchers who care with equal intensity.

REFERENCES

Adams, P. L. Children and para-services of the Community Mental Health Centers. *Journal of the American Academy of Child Psychiatry*, 1975, *14*, (1), 18–31.

Albright, S., & Gambrell, H. Personality traits as criteria for the psychiatric treatment of adolescents. *Smith College Studies in Social Work*, 1938, *9*, 1–26.

Axline, V. M. *Play Therapy*. Boston: Houghton-Mifflin, 1947.

Barbour, R. F. Selected surveys prepared for the inter-clinic conference. In J. F. Davidson (Chair), *Follow-up on child guidance cases* (ninth edition). Inter-conference, London, 1951, 49–59.

Berlin, I. N. *Bibliography of Child Psychiatry*. New York: Human Sciences Press (Behavioral Publications, Inc.), 1976.

Bills, R. E. Nondirective play therapy with retarded readers. *Journal of Consulting Psychology*, 1950a, *14*, 140–149.

Bills, R. E. Play therapy with well adjusted retarded readers. *Journal of Consulting Psychology*, 1950b, *14*, 246–249.

Bronner, A. F. Treatment and what happened afterward. *American Journal of Orthopsychiatry*, 1944, *14*, 28–35.

Brown, J. L. The follow-up procedure of an intermittent child guidance clinic. Unpublished master's thesis, Smith College, 1931.

Brown, M. Adolescents treatable by a family agency. *Smith College Studies in Social Work*, 1947, *18*, 37–67.

Burlington, S. A quantitative analysis of psychiatric social treatment carried out in seventy-five cases at the Instiute for Juvenile Research. Unpublished master's thesis, Smith College, 1931.

Canaday, L. J. A way of predicting the probable outcome of treatment of young children who run away. Unpublished master's thesis, Smith College, 1940.

Carpenter, J. A. Some factors relating to the method and outcome of case work treatment with the adolescent girl when the girl herself is the focus of treatment. Unpublished master's thesis, Smith College, 1939.

Carson, R. C., & Heine, R. W. Similarity and success in therapeutic dyads. *Journal of Consulting Psychology*, 1962, *26*, 38–43.

Christianson, E., Gates, M., & Coleman, F. A survey of the intake of a mental hygiene clinic with special reference to the outcome of treatment. *Smith College Studies in Social Work*, 1934, *5*, 211–212.

Coddington, R. D., & Offord, D. R. Psychiatrists' reliability in judging ego function. *Archives of General Psychiatry*, 1967, *16*, 48–55.

Cohen, M., & Davis, E. Factors related to the outcome of treatment in a child guidance clinic. *Smith College Studies in Social Work*, 1934, *5*, 212–214.

Cox, P. N. Sociometric status and individual adjustment before and after play therapy. *The Journal of Abnormal and Social Psychology*, 1953, *48*, 354–356.

Cunningham, J. M., Westerman, H., & Fischoff, J. A follow-up of children seen in a psychiatric clinic for children. Paper read at American Orthopsychiatric Association, Chicago, March 1955.

Deutch, A. *The mentally ill in America*. New York: Columbia University Press, 1949.

Dorfman, E. Personality outcomes of client-centered child therapy. *Psychological Monographs: General and Applied*, 1958, *72* (3 whole No. 456).

Eisenberg, L., & Gruenber, E. M. The current status of

secondary prevention in child psychiatry. *American Journal of Orthopsychiatry*, 1961, *31*, 355–377.

Eysenck, H. J. The effects of psychotherapy: An evaluation. *Journal of Consulting Psychology*, 1952, *16*, 319–324.

Fenton, N., & Wallace, R. Child Guidance in California communities: Follow-up study of bureau cases. *Journal of Juvenile Research*, 1938, *22*, 43–60.

Fleming, L., & Snyder, W. U. Social and personal changes following nondirective group play therapy. *American Journal of Orthopsychiatry*, 1947, *17*, 101–116.

Frank, J. D. *Persuasion and healing.* Baltimore: The Johns Hopkins Press, 1963.

Freud, A. Assessment of childhood disturbances. *Psychoanalytic Study of the Child*, 1962, *17*, 149–158.

Furman, S. S., Sweat, L. G., & Crocetti, G. M. Social class factors in the flow of children to outpatient psychiatric facilities. *American Journal of Public Health*, 1965, *55*, 385.

Gardner, G. Evaluation of therapeutic results in child guidance programs. *Association for Research in Nervous Diseases*, 1953, *31*, 131–150.

Gollander, B. A study of over inhibited and unsocialized children III: later adjustment. Unpublished master's thesis, Smith College, 1944.

Gossett, J. T., Meeks, J. E., Barnhart, F. D., & Phillips, V. A. Follow-up of Adolescents treated in a psychiatric hospital: the onset of symptomatology scale. *Adolescence*, 1976, *11*, 195–211.

Gurman, A. & Kniskern, D. P. Research on marital and family therapy: Progress, perspective and prospect. Chapter 21, this volume.

Halpern, W. I. Do children benefit from psychotherapy? A review of the literature on follow-up studies. *Bulletin of the Rochester Mental Health Center*, 1968, *1*, 4–12.

Hampe, I. E., Noble, H., Miller, L. C., & Barrett, C. L. Phobic children one and two years posttreatment. *Journal of Abnormal Psychology*, 1973, *82*, 446–453.

Healy, W., Bronner, A., Baylor, E., & Murphy, J. P. *Reconstructing behavior in youth.* New York: Alfred A. Knopf, 1929.

Heinicke, C. M. Frequency of psychotherapeutic session as a factor affecting the child's developmental status. *The Psychoanalytic Study of the Child*, 1965, *XX*, 42–98.

Heinicke, C. M. Frequency of psychotherapeutic session as a factor affecting outcome: analysis of clinical ratings and test results. *Journal of Abnormal Psychology*, 1969, *74*(5), 533–560.

Heinicke, C. M., & Goldman, A. Research on psychotherapy with children: A review and suggestions for further study. *American Journal of Orthopsychiatry*, 1960, *30*(3).

Heinicke, C. M., & Strassman, L. H. Toward more effective research on child psychotherapy. *American Academy of Child Psychiatry*, 1975, 561–588.

Hogan, R., DeSoto, C., & Solano, C. Traits, tests and personality research. *American Psychologist*, 1977, *32*, 255–264.

Hood-Williams, J. The results of psychotherapy with children. *Journal of Consulting Psychology*, 1960, *24*,

84–88.

Hubbard, R. M., & Adams, C. Factors affecting the success of child guidance treatment. *American Journal of Orthopsychiatry*, 1936, *6*, 81–102.

Irgens, E. M. Must parents' attitudes become modified in order to bring about adjustment in problem children? *Smith College Studies in Social Work*, 1936, *7*, 17–45.

Kanner, L. *Child Psychiatry.* Springfield, Ill.: Charles C. Thomas, 1957.

Klein, Z. E. *Research in the child psychiatric and guidance clinics: Supplementary bibliography 11 (1972)* Department of Psychiatry. University of Chicago, 1973. (Includes Series 1971, 1923–70; 1972, through 1971).

Knobloch, H., Rider, R. V., Hasper, P., & Passamanick, B. Neuropsychiatric sequellae of prematurity: a longitudinal study. *Journal of American Medical Association*, 1956, *161*, 581.

LaMore, M. T. An evaluation of a state hospital child guidance clinic. *Smith College Studies in Social Work*, 1941, *12*, 137–164.

Landisberg, S. & Snyder, W. N. Non-directive play therapy. *Journal of Clinical Psychology*, 1946, *2*(3).

Lee, P. R. & Kenworthy, M. E. *Mental hygiene and social work.* New York: Commonwealth Fund, 1929.

Lehrman, L. J., Sirluck, H., Black, B. J., Glick, S. J., et al. Success and failure of treatment of children in the Child Guidance Clinics of the Jewish Board of Guardians. *Research Monograph*, 1949, No. 1.

Levitt, E. E. Research on psychotherapy with children. In A. E. Bergin and S. Garfield, *Handbook of psychotherapy and behavior change.* New York: Wiley, 1971, Pp. 474–493.

Levitt, E. E. The results of psychotherapy with children: An evaluation. *Journal of Consulting Psychology*, 1957, *21*, 186–189.

Levitt, E. E. A comparative judgmental study of "defection" from treatment at a child guidance clinic. *Journal of Clinical Psychology*, 1958, *14*, 429–432.

Levitt, E. E., Beiser, H. R., & Robertson, R. E. A follow-up evaluation of cases treated at a community child guidance clinic. *American Journal of Psychiatry*, 1959, *29*, 337–347.

Levitt, E. E. Psychotherapy with children: A further evaluation. *Behavior Research and Therapy*, 1963, *60*, 326–329.

Luborsky, L., Chandler, M., Auerbach, A. H., Cohen, J., & Bachrach, H. M. Factors influencing the outcome of psychotherapy: a review of quantitative research. *Psychological Bulletin*, 1971, *75*(3), 145–185.

McConville, B. J., & Purohit, A. P. Classifying Confusion: a study of results in a multidisciplinary children's center. *American Journal of Orthopsychiatry*, 1973, *43*(3).

Maas, H. S., et al. Socio-cultural factors in psychiatric services for children: a collaborative study in the New York and San Francisco metropolitan areas. *Smith College Studies in Social Work*, 1955, *25*, 1–90.

Malan, D. H. The outcome problem in psychotherapy research: A historical review. *Archives of General Psychiatry*, 1973, *29*, 719–729.

Martens, E. J., & Russ, H. Adjustment of behavior problems of school children: a description of the clinical program in Berkeley, California. *Bulletin,* 1932, No. 18, Office of Education. (Available from Superintendent of Documents, U.S. Government Printing Office, Washington, D.C.)

Mayberly, A., & Struge, B. After results of child guidance. *British Medical Journal,* 1939, *1,* 1130–1134.

Meltzoff, J., & Kornreich, M. *Research in psychotherapy.* New York: Atherton, 1970.

Michael, C. M. Relative incidence of criminal behavior in long-term follow-up studies of shy children. *Dallas Medical Journal,* January 1957, 22–26.

Michael, C. M., Morris, D. P., & Soroker, E. Follow-up studies of shy, withdrawn children II: Relative incidence of schizophrenia. *American Journal of Orthopsychiatry,* 1957, *27,* 331–337.

Miller, L. C. Louisville Behavior Check List for males, 6–12 years of age. *Psychological Reports,* 1967, *21,* 885–896.

Miller, L. C., Barrett, C. L., Hampe, E., & Noble, H. Comparison of reciprocal inhibition, psychotherapy and waiting list control for phobic children. *Journal of Abnormal Psychology,* 1972, *79*(3), 269–279.

Miller, L. C. School Behavior Check List: An inventory of deviant behavior for elementary school children. *Journal of Consulting and Clinical Psychology,* 1972, *38,* 134–144.

Morris, D. P., Soroker, E., & Burruss, G. Follow-up studies of shy, withdrawn children 1: Evaluation of later adjustment. *American Journal of Orthopsychiatry,* 1954, *24,* 743–754.

Moses, J. A study of overinhibited and unsocialized children Part IV: The later adjustment of unsocialized aggressive children. Unpublished master's thesis, Smith College, 1944.

Moustakas, C. E., & Schlalock, H. D. An analysis of therapist child interaction in play therapy. *Child Development,* 1955, *26*(2), 143–157.

Newell, N. W. The methods of child guidance adapted to a public school system. *Mental Hygiene New York,* 1934, *18,* 362–373.

Oneal, P., & Robins, L. The relation of childhood behavior problems to adult psychiatric status: a 30-year follow-up of 150 subjects. *American Journal of Psychiatry,* 1958, *115,* 385–391.

Passamanick, B., Knobloch, H., & Lilienfield, A. M. Socio-economic status and some precursors of neuropsychiatric disorder. *American Journal of Orthopsychiatry,* 1956, *26,* 594.

Ricks, D., Thomas, A., & Roff, M. (Eds.) *Life history research in psychopathology.* Vol 3. Minneapolis: The University of Minnesota Press, 1974.

Rie, H. E. (Ed.) *Perspectives in Child Psychopathology.* Chicago: Aldine-Atherton, 1971.

Ried, J. H., & Hagan, H. R. *Residential care of emotionally disturbed children.* New York: Child Welfare League of America, 1952.

Robins, L. N. *Deviant children grown up: A sociological and psychiatric study of sociopathic personality.* Baltimore: Williams and Wilkins, 1966.

Robins, L. N., Murphy, G. E., Woodruff, R., & King, L. J. Adult psychiatric status of Black school boys. *Archives of General Psychiatry,* 1971, *24,* 338–345.

Roff, M. & Ricks, D. (Eds.) *Life history research in psychopathology.* Minneapolis: The University of Minnesota Press, 1970.

Roff, M., Robins, L. N., & Pollack, M. (Eds.) *Life history research in psychopathology.* Vol. 2. Minneapolis: University of Minnesota Press, 1972.

Ross, A. Behavior therapy with children. Chapter 15, this volume.

Seeman, J., Barry, E., & Ellinwood, C. Interpersonal assessment of play therapy outcome. *Psychotherapy: Theory, Research and Practice,* 1964, *1,* 64–66.

Seeman, J., & Edwards, B. A therapeutic approach to reading difficulties. *Journal of Consulting Psychology,* 1954, *18,* 451–453.

Shirley, M., Baum, B., & Polsky, S. Outgrowing childhood's problems: A Follow-up of child guidance patients. *Smith College Studies of Social Work,* 1940, *XI,* 31–60.

Shore, M. F., & Massimo, J. L. After ten years: A follow-up study of comprehensive vocationally oriented psychotherapy. *American Journal of Orthopsychiatry,* 1973, *43,* 128–132.

Sloane, R. B. *Psychotherapy versus behavior therapy.* Cambridge: Harvard University Press, 1975.

Snyder, W. V. Investigation of Non-directive Psychotherapy. *Journal of Genetic Psychology,* 1945, *33,* 193–223.

Stevenson, G. S., & Smith, G. *Child Guidance Clinics: a quarter century of development.* New York: Commonwealth Fund, 1934.

Strupp, H. H., & Bergin, A. E. Some empirical and conceptual issues for coordinated research in psychotherapy: A critical review of issues, trends and evidence. *International Journal of Psychiatry,* 1969, *7,* 18–90.

Strupp, H. H., & Hadley, S. W. A tripartite model of mental health and therapeutic outcomes: With special reference to negative effects in psychotherapy. *American Psychologist,* 1977, *32,* 187–196.

Thomas, A., Chess, S., Birch, H. G., & Hertzig, M. A longitudinal study of primary reaction patterns in childhood. *Comprehensive Psychiatry,* 1960, *1,* 103.

Walcott, E. A study of the present adjustment made by solitary children who had withdrawn into an imaginary world. Unpublished master's thesis, Smith College, 1938.

Walk, R. D. Self ratings of fear in a fear invoking situation. *Journal of Abnormal and Social Psychology,* 1956, *52,* 171–178.

Waskow, I. E., and Parloff, M. B. (Eds.) *Psychotherapy change measures.* DHEW Publication No. (ADM) 74-120 (Supt. Doc. Stock No. 1724-00397), 1975.

Williams, G. J., & Gordon, S. (Eds.) *Clinical child psychology.* New York: Behavioral Publications, 1974.

Witmer, H. L. A comparison of treatment results in various types of child guidance clinics. *American Journal of Orthopsychiatry,* 1935, *5,* 351–360.

Witmer, H. L., & Keller, J. Outgrowing childhood problems: a study of the value of child guidance treatment. *Smith College Studies in Social Work,* 1942, *13,* 74–90.

Witmer, H. L., and Students. The outcome of treatment in a child guidance clinic. *Smith College Studies in*

Social Work, 1933, *3,* 339–399.

Wright, D. M., Moelis, I., & Pollack, L. J. The outcome of individual psychotherapy: increments at follow-up. *Journal of Child Psychology and Psychiatry,* 1976, *17,* 275–285.

Wright, L., Truax, C. B., & Mitchell, K. M. Reliability of process ratings of psychotherapy with children. *Journal of Clinical Psychology,* 1972, *28,* 232–234.

12

PSYCHOTHERAPY AND DRUG THERAPY: COMPARISON AND COMBINATIONS

STEVEN D. HOLLON
AARON T. BECK

University of Pennsylvania

This chapter focuses on the relationships between psychotherapy and drug therapy. Both approaches to treatment are widely used in current clinical practice and frequently combined in a pragmatic fashion. Little empirical evidence exists to guide the clinician in choosing between or in combining the two in any systematic fashion.

Two basic questions can be asked; the first comparative, the second combinative.

1. Can one type of treatment (or combination of treatments) be said to be superior to the other?

2. What are the consequences of combining the two types of treatment?

Each of these questions is best answered in relation to specific types of patients. Diagnostic groupings provide a useful means of categorization, but are only one way of dividing relevant patient sam-ples. A host of other patient variables—age, intelligence, social class, sex, and so forth—may prove important. Reviews are available of the relationships between patient variables and either psychotherapy (Garfield, 1971; Luborsky, Chandler, Auerbach, Cohen, & Bachrach, 1971) or drug therapy (Rickels, 1968).

These questions are by no means easy to answer. Outcome studies are notoriously difficult to control. Studies of this type deal with issues of importance to the participants involved. Ethical considerations, control over extraneous sources of variance, and the maintenance of the initial design integrity become vital concerns. Dealing with people in clinical settings not only ensures that the procedures have an impact on the patient involved, but also decreases the likelihood of producing tightly controlled, clearly interpretable conclusions. The investment of subjects in outcomes and the relative lack of control over important variables are difficulties shared by the studies in ongoing program evaluation and social experimentation (Riecken & Boruch, 1974). The discussion to follow draws on theoretical and methodological considerations from that literature.

While any outcome study is difficult to execute, studies involving both psychotherapies and drug therapies present special problems of their own. Double-blind methodologies are generally difficult to achieve, necessary control conditions multiply geometrically, differential biasing factors frequently operate, and statistical analyses require considerable caution. Comparing two potentially active treatment approaches, particularly two approaches so manifestly different as psychotherapy and drug therapy, necessitates special care in interpreting results and formulating conclusions.

The review is divided into two sections. The first section focuses on defining the boundaries of the comparative literature and reviewing the methodological, logical, and practical problems inherent in studies of this kind. The second section is devoted to a review of the existing comparative literature. This section is organized in accordance with the diagnostic group or target population studied. Summaries of existing findings and suggestions for future research are presented.

PREVIOUS REVIEWS

Previous reviews (Uhlenhuth, Lipman, & Covi, 1969; May, 1971; Luborsky, Singer, & Luborsky, 1975) have attempted to draw conclusions regarding the relative efficacy of drugs and psychotherapy. Box scores are provided to facilitate this process. For example, Uhlenhuth and colleagues concluded that: "Combined treatment usually offers no greater benefit than pharmacotherapy alone. Combined treatment, however, usually does offer greater benefit than psychotherapy alone" (p. 60). May (1971) concurred for hospitalized psychotic patients, but deferred judgment when neurotic or borderline patients were concerned. Luborsky and colleagues listed a preponderance of outcomes favoring combined treatments over either drugs or psychotherapy alone. Combined treatments showed a greater relative advantage over

psychotherapy alone than over drugs alone. Further, when drugs alone were specifically compared with psychotherapy alone, the drugs appeared to be superior. The authors did, however, suggest that the types of patients studied and the types and lengths of psychotherapies utilized may have prevented demonstrating psychotherapy effects.

In the review to follow, we have been forced to eschew any conclusions that are not linked to specific treatments in specific diagnostic categories. It is important to guard against the tacit acceptance of any of the uniformity myths (Kiesler, 1966). Not everything that comes in a capsule is a drug, and not everything that occurs between a professional and a client is psychotherapy. Box scores approaches can too easily obscure effective treatments for select patient groups by inadvertently "hiding" them in a forest of noneffective approaches.

We concur with May's (1974) recommendation that readers must turn to the literature in areas of interest. Evidence gathered on a shaky methodological basis is like bad advice; its inadequacy becomes apparent only after it has been acted upon. None of the studies to be reviewed can be considered definitive, although several are quite informative. Overall, the comparative literature appears to be still in its formative stages. Some tentative conclusions can be drawn, but only after clearly recognizing the perils and pitfalls inherent in research in this area.

PSYCHOTHERAPY DEFINED

May (1971) restricted his review to what he termed "formal" psychotherapy, which he defined as a "specific personal individualized intervention over and above the management and administrative therapeutic contact that is necessary for the treatment of all psychiatric patients" (p. 497). We have included the various behavior therapies specifically excluded by May. Several studies have recently been added to the literature focusing specifically on interventions based on learning models.

It has become increasingly difficult to separate the use of interventions drawing on behavioral procedures or learning models from what can be fairly considered formal psychotherapy. A number of recent works have focused on approaches to therapy that combine aspects of formal psychotherapy and newer cognitive or learning models (cf. Beck, 1976; Kaplan, 1974; Lazarus, 1976). Similarly, a variety of studies focusing on sociological or social casework approaches to therapy have also been included when their intent was to provide more than simple administrative contact with the patients.

PHARMACOTHERAPY DEFINED

We have restricted our review to those presumably psychoactive medications currently used to modify, ameliorate, or suppress various psychiatric or behavioral phenomena. In several instances, we have included studies dealing with medications not currently available in this country. Specifically excluded are medications used solely to facilitate abreaction (the release of tension through the expression of an emotion-laden repressed experience), hallucinogens designed to "expand consciousness," or pharmacological agents administered solely to induce coma or convulsions. Similarly excluded are drugs used solely to induce more rapid relaxation responses during desensitization (Mawson, 1970; Yorkston, Sergeant, & Rachman, 1968) or used in combination with conditioning therapies to facilitate exposure to fearful situations (Hafner & Marks, 1976; Marks, Viswanathan, Lipsedge, & Gardner, 1972). Finally, the review excludes all nonpharmacological somatic therapies, for example, electroconvulsive therapy.

Medications currently available can be placed in several general categories on the basis of major usage and chemical similarity (Appleton, 1976). Major categories include: the drugs used in the treatment of depression (the tricyclics, the monoamine oxidase inhibitors (MAOIs), the stimulants, and more recently, lithium); the major tranquilizers used in the treatment of the schizophrenias (the phenothiazines, butyrophenones, thioxanthenes, oxiondoles, and rauwolfia alkaloids); the minor tranquilizers used in anxiety states (chlordiazepoxide, meprobamate, and diazepam); and a variety of miscellaneous medications.

Studies Considered: True Experiments

Our review emphasizes controlled comparative studies that can be considered true experiments, or their quasi-experimental equivalents. In true experiments (Campbell, 1957), assignment to different conditions is made on a random basis. Significance tests are used to rule out sampling error as a cause for any observed differences between the experimental conditions.

When random assignment is not used, biased assignment and a variety of interactions between biased assignment and other factors become plausible alternatives to concluding that the treatments were different. Campbell and Stanley (1963) discuss a variety of quasi-experimental designs. These designs approximate the control provided by the true experiment by systematically building in ways of ruling out various plausible rival explanations for observed effects. We have limited our review to those studies that were initially designed to be true experiments or their quasi-experimental equivalents.

The adequacy of the randomization for providing initially equivalent groups is related to the size of the sample drawn; small samples are more likely to be influenced by extreme values or the vagaries of sampling. Similarly, differential attrition can reduce a true experiment to a quasi-experiment. Pretests designed to assess the initial equivalence of the groups formed and research strategies geared to ruling out plausible rival hypotheses are recommended.

It is important to distinguish between the adequacy of the design and the adequacy of its execution. We have set rather stringent criteria for inclusion in our review, excluding one study included by Luborsky and colleagues in their review (Luborsky et al., 1975) which did not use random assignment (Overall & Tupin, 1969). Nonetheless, some of the studies included in our review failed to meet minimum standards for interpretability due to difficulties encountered during their execution. Problems encountered frequently included high levels of attrition, absence of checks on the compliance with protocol, uncontrolled lengths of treatment, failure to control extraneous sources of treatment, and inadequate sample sizes and statistical analyses.

POSSIBLE DRUG AND PSYCHOTHERAPY INTERACTION: OUTCOMES

Klerman (1975) and Uhlenhuth and colleagues in Baltimore (Uhlenhuth et al., 1969) have presented a variety of models suggesting possible interactions between drugs and psychotherapy when administered in combination. Figure 12-1, adapted from the Baltimore group's article, displays four possible patterns that could result from combining two separate treatments, A and B. Results are described in terms of a single measure, or outcome; for example, a scale score on specific symptoms, years out of hospital, or overall improvement. Different treatments may have different loci of action, so that a number of possible outcomes may result from a single drug-psychotherapy combination.

Additivity (1) results when the separate effects of both treatments operate on the phenomena of interest in a straightforward, noninteractive fashion. The total amount of change is roughly equivalent to the sum of the impact of each treatment separately.

Potentiation (2), or *synergism* in Klerman's (1975) taxonomy, represents an impact greater than the sum of the two parts. This outcome repre-

sents an interaction between some aspect of the two treatments that accelerates the observed effects of either alone.

Either of the two previous outcomes reflects "desirable" outcome; advocates of combinative treatments generally hope to improve their results over either treatment alone. An everyday example comes from drug advertisements which suggest that drugs help make patients "amenable" to psychotherapy, or cases in which the therapeutic relationship may be useful in insuring compliance to a drug regimen.

Inhibition (3) represents a negative interaction; the observed effects of the combination are less than the effects of either alone. *Reciprocation* (4a and 4b) reflects more complex relationships; the combination of the two treatments produces effects similar to either the greater or the lesser of the two treatments. In the first instance (4a), the reciprocation might be related to a ceiling effect (where only a finite amount of improvement is possible), the absence of any addition or interaction of the lesser on the greater, or the occurrence of a complex interaction resulting in a fortuitously equivalent outcome. In the second instance (4b), the joint action of the two does not exceed that of the lesser.

Inhibition or reciprocation represent "negative" outcomes. Radical critics of either drugs or psychotherapy often warn against combinations on exactly such grounds. For example, drugs may be felt to affect a patient's view of himself or herself or

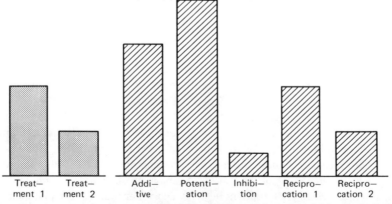

Figure 12-1   Possible drug-psychotherapy interactions. (Adapted from E.H. Uhlenhuth, R.S. Lipman, & L. Covi, Combined pharmacotherapy and psychotherapy: Controlled studies. *Journal of Nervous and Mental Disease, 1969, 148,* p. 60 © 1969 The Williams & Wilkins Co., Baltimore.)

of the therapeutic relationship, to reduce motivation for treatment, or to be seen as meeting infantile needs. Conversely, critics of psychotherapy may charge that combinations including psychotherapy may, at best, add nothing over drugs other than expense, or, at worst, may lead to undesirable and unnecessary complications, such as increased dependency or regression.

When any combination is administered, a wide variety of possible phenomena may be affected. Thus, Klerman and colleagues (Klerman, DiMascio, Weissman, Prusoff, & Paykel, 1974; Weissman, Klerman, Paykel, Prusoff, & Hanson, 1974) reported that the effects of combining a tricyclic antidepressant with interpersonally oriented social casework differed depending on the outcome observed. Within a single study, the drug alone seemed to prevent clinical relapse in terms of depressive symptoms as well as drugs and psychotherapy combined and better than psychotherapy alone. Conversely, psychotherapy alone and drug plus psychotherapy were equally effective in improving interpersonal relationships, while drugs alone had little impact on this phenomenon. A. S. Friedman (1975) found a similar pattern of results. Tricyclics alone or in combination with marital therapy reduced acute depression; while marital therapy, alone or in combination, had little effect on depression measures but showed positive effects on measures of marital satisfaction.

In such cases, when different treatments appear to have different foci, combinations may prove desirable despite the absence of any beneficial effect on any single measure. Similarly, combinative treatments may prove desirable when it is difficult to predict in advance to which treatment an individual might respond.

MECHANISMS OF INTERACTION

The preceding section listed a number of possible outcomes that might be obtained when drugs and psychotherapies are combined. In this section, a number of mechanisms that might mediate such outcomes are considered. Most of these mechanisms are drawn from clinically or theoretically based speculations. May (1971) and Klerman

(1975) provide additional reviews of these and related phenomena.

Klerman (1975) discussed a variety of phenomena representing what he termed "negative placebo" effects: negative effects of pill-taking on psychotherapy processes. Changes in the attitudes and behaviors of either the patient or the therapist are possible examples, as well as undesirable changes in the therapeutic relationship. Either participant may come to rely on the medication to produce change or might ascribe "magical" properties to the idea of medication. Patients might become dependent on the act of taking medications or accept a more passive stance toward therapy. The prescribing professional might adopt a more authoritarian stance than indicated. Subtle distortions in the transference and countertransference have been hypothesized.

Several mechanisms based on specific pharmacological mechanisms have also been postulated. The effective reduction of acute distress might well reduce a patient's motivation for treatment, leading to premature termination or lack of attention during therapy. For some schools of psychotherapy, reducing acute symptoms might be expected to prematurely alter defenses before "real" conflicts are resolved. Behavior theorists have expressed concern about state-dependent learning. Here, therapeutic gains achieved under the influence of some kind of drug (e.g., exposure to a fearful situation when tranquilized) disappear as the drug wears off.

Conversely, drugs might have positive effects on psychotherapy, for either nonspecific or pharmacologically mediated reasons. Positive placebo effects—the mobilization of hope, an increase in confidence, for example—are as likely as negative effects. Active medications may facilitate psychotherapy by reducing acute symptoms and making the patient accessible to verbal or conditioning therapies. Similarly, drugs might shore up ego or reality-testing functions.

Psychotherapy, on the other hand, may influence chemotherapy in a variety of ways. Klerman (1975) noted that considerably less attention has been paid to these mechanisms than those presumed to underlie the effects of drugs in psychotherapy. A chief concern involves the possibility that psychotherapy may prove symptomatically disruptive, focusing on conflicts best left undisturbed. Similarly, an undue reliance on psychotherapy may lead to the patient's failure to adhere to a medication regimen or the therapist's failure to work actively enough to ensure regimen compliance. Conversely, the quality of the psychotherapeutic relationship may facilitate regimen compliance.

The potential nature of the mechanism can have important implications for the design of the comparative study. Clearly, a design in which all patients believed they were receiving medications (either placebo or active drug) would detect only those mechanisms related to the pharmacological properties of the medications. Conversely, a design in which all patients believed they were entering into a psychotherapeutic relationship (whether nonspecific control or theoretically relevant procedures) would detect only those mechanisms related to the "active" components of the psychotherapy. Designs that compare active treatments with control conditions that do not attempt to provide nonspecific expectations (i.e., waiting-list, assessment only) allow the mechanisms discussed to emerge, but do not allow a differentiation between those based on nonspecific versus specific treatment components.

Full cell designs in which individual patients are exposed to active treatment, nonspecific control, and no treatment conditions (along any single treatment dimension) have been relatively rare. Only three studies in the literature (Lorr, McNair, & Weinstein, 1962; Lorr, McNair, Weinstein, Michaux, & Raskin, 1961; and the joint Klerman et al., 1974, Weissman et al., 1974 studies) included treatments cells in which psychotherapy was combined with three levels of medication: active drug, nonspecific (placebo) control, and no pill. In no study was active medication crossed with three levels of psychotherapy: active treatment, nonspecific control, and no psychotherapy. Seventeen of 20 studies combining psychotherapy with some level of medication used active-drug versus placebo combinations. Here, none of the potential mechanisms based on the act of pill-taking could differ across groups. The remaining three studies (Gorham, Pokorny, & Moseley, 1964; May, 1968; and Karon and Vanderbos, 1970; 1972) all com-

pared psychotherapy plus active medication with psychotherapy alone (no pill). Further, all three involved schizophrenic populations, so that the results obtained regarding interactions were generalizable only to a circumscribed, albeit important, group of potential patients.

The situation appears reversed for mechanisms involving combinations of active drugs with "levels" of psychotherapy. As noted, no study combined active medication with active psychotherapy, nonspecific control, and no psychotherapy conditions. Only three of the 19 reported comparisons involved drug plus active psychotherapy versus drug plus nonspecific control (Covi, Lipman, Derogatis, Smith, & Pattison, 1974; Friedman, A. S., 1975; Zitrin, Klein, Lindemann, Tobak, Rock, Kaplan, & Ganz, 1976). In each case, the nonspecific control was actually an alternative form of psychotherapy (group versus individual, marital versus individual, and behavioral versus traditional, respectively) believed to be less effective by the researchers involved. Similarly, the remaining 16 studies generally appeared to involve drug plus psychotherapy versus drug alone comparisons. Here, it is not clear from many of the reports exactly how much time and energy was invested in conducting the "active" psychotherapies. Further, it is not clear that the drug plus no psychotherapy conditions were perceived as involving "no psychotherapy" by the patients. Our impression is that contact with a prescribing physician is frequently construed as a psychotherapy session by patients, even if no formal "contact" is agreed upon. Classification into specific versus nonspecific versus no psychotherapies is far more problematic than classification into active drug versus nonspecific placebo versus no pill medication conditions.

The issue is that some of the questions asked in the comparative literature simply cannot be answered on the basis of existing data, particularly those questions relating to the mechanisms underlying obtained interactions. The state of the literature is such that questions related to the outcomes of specific combinations for specific populations can be handled more adequately than questions as to why those outcomes were obtained. If comparative research is to begin to address itself to more sophisticated questions, it will need to give more attention to research designs specifically relevant to these theoretical issues.

METHODOLOGICAL CONSIDERATIONS: OVERVIEW

A number of reviews of the methodological problems involved in conducting evaluative outcome research are available (cf. Bergin, 1971; Fiske, Hunt, Luborsky, Orne, Parloff, Reiser, & Tuma, 1970; Kiesler, 1966, 1971; Meltzoff & Kornreich, 1970).[1] The following section will focus on a variety of factors that are either unique, or of special relevance, to comparative studies. Comparing two potentially active treatments, particularly two such disparate approaches as psychotherapy and pharmacotherapy, can create special problems not specifically encountered in single treatment outcome studies. The reader is referred to a listing of some of those factors by Pokorny and Klett (1966).

Conclusions based on inadequately designed studies are more likely to be accepted in the comparative literature than in the single treatment outcome studies. First, the greater number of actual comparisons made increases the possibility of accepting a finding due to chance alone. Second, design inadequacies may prevent demonstrating treatment efficacy for one modality but not the other. In this instance, the joint occurrence of significant and nonsignificant findings in the same design may incorrectly increase the confidence with which the null hypothesis (that a given treatment has no effect) is accepted. Further, such a study is more likely to be published than one in which a single treatment was found not to differ from a single control, since some group difference was obtained.

The validity of the conclusions drawn from any design can be evaluated in several ways. Campbell and colleagues (Campbell, 1957; Campbell & Stanley, 1963; Cook & Campbell, 1975) have distinguished between the *internal, external, statistical conclusion,* and *construct validities* of conclusions drawn on the basis of experimental data. *Internal*

validity refers to the correctness with which observed effects are attributed to the experimental manipulation. *External validity* refers to the populations and situations to which the observed effects can legitimately be generalized. *Statistical conclusion validity* refers to the likelihood that the design and analyses used would have detected a real effect if one had existed. Finally, *construct validity* refers to the correctness with which the researcher identifies or labels the actual causal element in the experimental manipulation.

Several threats to the validity of the conclusions that can be drawn are unique or have special relevance to comparative studies. These threats include differential attrition (internal validity), differential selection (external validity), and inadequate statistical analyses (statistical conclusion validity).

BIASING VIA DIFFERENTIAL ATTRITION

Few problems create greater difficulties in an otherwise well-conducted study than differential attrition (Lasky, 1962). Attrition, by definition, is not under experimental control. When subjects discontinue treatment for different reasons in the different experimental conditions, the adequacy of the random assignment to conditions is undermined. Observed differences between groups cannot be clearly attributed to the experimental manipulation.

Several strategies can be followed, none of them wholly adequate. Replacing dropouts only accelerates any attrition process related to subject characteristics. Various end point analysis strategies involve collecting as much data as possible at all scheduled assessment points. Combined with efforts to elicit reasons for dropping out and multiple data analyses, these strategies may permit reasonable conclusions to be salvaged.

BIASING VIA DIFFERENTIAL SELECTION

A closely related phenomenon is that of differential selection; biasing the conclusion of a comparative study by the way in which the initial sample is selected. The danger is primarily to the external validity of the results since selection generally occurs prior to assignment to treatment.

[1]A "Check-list of Issues in Designs for Research on the Effectiveness of Psychotherapy," based on Fiske, et al. 1970, is available from Fiske. This checklist might well prove helpful to investigators in designing a prospective study.

An example here should suffice to demonstrate the phenomenon. In our own work (Rush, Beck, Kovacs, & Hollon, 1977), we conducted a comparison of imipramine hydrochloride and cognitive therapy for the treatment of outpatient depressives. One criterion for exclusion from the study was a prior history of nonresponse to an "adequate" trial on any tricyclic antidepressant. Our concern was with the ethics of assigning someone with a history of nonresponse to a medication to that treatment cell. We were specifically excluding exactly those people most likely to "fail" to respond to one of the treatments but not the other. People with long histories of failure in prior psychotherapies were accepted since the psychotherapy was a novel one. Since our plan was to compare the two groups' mean scores on a series of outcome measures, the "dice" were in effect loaded against the psychotherapy. Only the combination of a relatively low rate of tricyclic "nonresponders" and the superiority of the cognitive therapy group prevented real problems in interpretation. Had the number of people excluded been large and had the drug proven superior to psychotherapy we would have been forced to limit the generality of our results to a different population than we had intended. Instead of talking about the relative merit of drugs and cognitive therapy for outpatient depressives, we would have been talking about the *relative* merits of imipramine and cognitive therapy for outpatient depressives excluding those known not to respond to drugs.

BIASING VIA INADEQUATE STATISTICAL ANALYSES

For a variety of reasons, any analysis should incorporate direct treatment cell comparison; any differing treatment conditions (e.g., active drug versus drug plus psychotherapy versus pill-placebo versus pill-placebo plus psychotherapy) which are applied to individual patients should, at some point, be directly compared. When direct cell comparisons or tests for interactions are not made, the researcher runs at least two risks.

First, a treatment may be effective without being robust. Relying on tests of main effects, in which cells involving the active treatment alone are pooled with cells combining the active treatment with other manipulations (e.g., attention-controls or pill-placebos,) risks misattributing interaction effects to the "active" treatment alone.

Second, without direct treatment cell comparison, interpreting significant main effects may prove misleading. For example, finding a significant main effect for one active treatment and not the other does not indicate that the first treatment is superior to the second. The observed main effects can be interpreted only in relation to the respective control conditions. One control condition may have a greater impact than the other (e.g., pill-placebo may be associated with more symptom relief than brief supportive contact). A direct comparison between patients receiving one active treatment versus patients receiving only the other active treatment would be required to document the superiority of one treatment over the other.

REVIEW OF THE COMPARATIVE OUTCOME LITERATURE

The remainder of this chapter focuses on existing comparative studies across a variety of psychopathological categories. Studies which (1) contain at least one presumably active psychotherapy and at least one presumably psychoactive drug, and (2) employ a "true" experimental design (or a quasi-experimental equivalent), are included. Studies involving one treatment modality only or which use nonequivalent groups are excluded. Similarly, analogue studies, naturalistic studies, and reports based solely on uncontrolled clinical observations are also excluded.

Studies meeting these criteria are listed in Table 12-1. The studies are grouped in terms of major areas of psychopathology treated. Comparative studies can be found in each of the following areas: the major affective disorders (depression and mania), the anxiety states, the phobic conditions, the schizophrenias, and childhood disorders.

By and large, the comparative studies have followed the establishment of the efficacy of a pharmacological agent. The emergence of the major tranquilizers in the early 1950s was followed by the increase in comparative studies in the schizo-phrenias; the establishment of the tricyclic antide-pressants and lithium have spurred the comparative studies in the affective disorders in the seventies. In general, there has been a progressive emphasis on meticulously screened, diagnostically homogene-ous patient samples, an emphasis reflected in the organization of the review to follow.

The Major Affective Disorders

The major affective disorders include those phenomena classically characterized as involving a primary mood disorder, either depression or mania or both. As noted, there has been a marked in-crease in interest in comparative treatment studies in these disorders.

A variety of typologies and/or categories within the affective disorders have been suggested (see Beck, 1967 for a review). One important distinc-tion appears to lie between individuals who show show a history of only depressive episodes (unipo-lar) verus individuals who show a history of manic episodes either with or without depressions (bipo-lar). Unipolars and bipolars may differ in terms of etiology, manifest symptomatology, clinical course, and treatment response (Winokur, 1973; Wood-ruff, Goodwin & Guze, 1974). Family histories of bipolar episodes (Kupfer, Pickar, Himmelhoch, & Detre, 1975), the presence of fixed delusions (Glassman, Kantor, & Shostak, 1975), and the presence of schizo-affective features (Kasanin, 1933) are additional factors that appear to have important implications. A classificatory system based on these dimensions (Feighner, Robins, Guze, Woodruff, Winokur, & Munoz, 1972; Spitzer, Endicott, & Robins, 1975) has been widely used by researchers in this area.

At this point, it appears that the various antidep-ressant and antimanic drugs represent the current treatments of choice for the bulk of the affective disorders. The following sections review the current state of the literature in terms of single modality treatments.

Drugs in Depression

A large number of carefully controlled, double-blind studies evaluating drug-drug and drug-control treatments in the unipolar depressions are available. Morris and Beck (1974) reviewed 146 studies involving marketed antidepressants. Only studies that met the following criteria were in-cluded: (1) the use of a control group, (2) random assignment to treatment, and (3) double-blind re-search design. The various tricyclics were found to be superior to placebo in 61 of 83 reported studies. No study reported a superiority for placebo over active drug. The MAO inhibitors were found to be more effective than placebo in 8 of 13 studies. While some evidence points to the efficacy of lithium in controlling acute episodes of depression (in both unipolars and bipolars) (Mendels, 1973, 1976) and acute episodes of mania, it appears that the tricyclics or MAOI's are at least as effective in acute depression (APA Task Force, 1975). Lithium appears to be uniquely effective in controlling acute mania, although the major tranquilizers may also prove to be of use.

Davis (1976) reviews data suggesting that the various medications either prevent or reduce the occurrence of clinical relapse. The tricyclics appear effective in unipolar samples, while lithium appears useful in both unipolar and bipolar samples. Nonetheless, relapse rates in bipolar samples may still average up to 55 percent over a several year period even with maintenance medication (Prien & Caffey, 1974).

Psychotherapy in Depression

Few studies have compared either behavioral or traditional psychotherapies with control groups in actual clinical populations. As opposed to the vast array of drug-control outcome studies, we are un-aware of any therapy study involving only tradi-tional psychotherapy versus control comparison in the treatment of depression.

Recent interest in both cognitive and behavioral treatment interventions have spurred investigations of nonpharmacological approaches to depression. Lewinsohn and colleagues (Lewinsohn, 1974) have pioneered the development of behavioral in-terventions. Both Shaw (1977) and Taylor and Marshall (1977) have demonstrated the superior-ity of behavioral interventions over nondirective or waiting list controls in subclinical populations, al-though in both cases, cognitive or cognitive-behavioral approaches proved to be the most ef-fective interventions. Similarly, studies by Gioe

TABLE 12-1   Comparative Studies: 1955—

Key (Cells)*
1. CDP—Drug and Psychotherapy Combination
2. D —Drug Only
3. P —Psychotherapy Only
4. Dp —Drug and Psychotherapy Control (or brief psychotherapy)
5. Pd —Psychotherapy and Drug Control (i.e. placebo)
6. d —Drug Control (i.e. placebo)
7. p —Psychotherapy Control (i.e. contact control)
8. cdp —Drug Control and Psychotherapy Control Combination
9. N.T.—No Treatment (could involve milieu, waiting list, etc.)
10. ( ) —other type of treatment or combination

Study	Sample	Cells	Psychotherapy	Drug	Criteria	Time	Results	Comments
Daneman, 1961	Depressives: outpatients n = 195	1. CDP 5. Pd	Psychoanalytically oriented Individual Single therapist (experienced) 1 to 2 hours per week	Imipramine Hydrochloride (50-200 mg./day)	Global Rating of Improvement (by author/ therapist)	2 months (extended to 3 months)	CDP > Pd	Single therapist (also served as sole rater) Uncontrolled use of adjunctive drugs and psychotherapy contacts
Covi et al. 1974	Depressives: outpatients n = 149 *Females only	1. CDP (a) 1. CDP (b) 4. Dp (a) 4. Dp (b) 5. Pd 8. cdp	Psychoanalytically oriented Group Two therapists (experienced) 1 hour per week	a. Imipramine (100-200 mg/day) b. Diazepam	*Self-report* SCL-90 POMS *Clinician ratings*	16 weeks	CDP (a) = Dp(a) CDP (a) > Pd Dp (a) > Pd Pd = cdp	Only two therapists High attrition (47%)

Study	Sample	Groups	Treatment	Drug	Measures	Duration	Results	Comments
Friedman, 1975	Depressives: outpatients; n = 196; *All married	1. CDP; 4. Dp; 5. Pd; 8. cdp	P = Conjoint marital therapy (1 hr/wk); p = Individual brief supportive psychotherapy (30 min./2 wks.); Experienced therapists	Amitriptyline hydrochloride (100–200 mg./day)	*Self-report* HSCL 2 measures marital adjustment; *Clinician ratings* HRS & BPRS Global improvement	12 weeks	Not reported as cell comparison: Drug > placebo, on symptom measures Marital>supportive on marital measures	Raters not blind to treatment Cell comparisons not reported Patients receiving marital therapy did better on marital measures
Rush et al., 1977	Depressives: outpatients; n = 41	3. P; 4. Dp	P=Cognitive therapy (2 hr/wk); p=Brief supportive therapy (15 min./wk.); Individual; Inexperienced Therapists (18)	Imipramine hydrochloride (100–250 mg./day)	*Self-report* BDI; *Therapists ratings* Raskin; *Clinician ratings* HRS-D	12 weeks	P > Dp	Raters not blind to treatment Dropout greater in Dp (results analyzed with and without dropouts)
Klerman et al., 1974 Weissman et al., 1974	*Maintenance* Depressives: outpatients; n = 150; *Females only	1. CDP; 2. D; 3. P; 5. Pd; 6. d; 9. N.T.	Interpersonal social casework (1 hr/wk) Individual; Experienced therapists (2)	Amitriptyline (100–200 mg./day)	*Relapse* (Clinician rating on Raskin); KAS— Self & sign. other report of social skill	8 months	Not reported as cell comparisons: Drug>no drug Psychotherapy=no psychotherapy Combined= drug>psychotherapy: on relapse	Two therapists Only patients who responded to drug included in trial Psychotherapy pts. did better on measures of interpersonal functioning

TABLE 12-1 (continued)

Study	Sample	Cells	Psychotherapy	Drug	Criteria	Time	Results	Comments
Davenport et al., 1975	*Maintenance* Bipolar manics: outpatients n = 23 *All married	1. CDP 4. D	Conjoint couples counseling (1 hr/wk) Group sessions Therapist experience unknown (2)	Lithium (dosage schedule not specified)	Relapse Marital stability Clinicians ratings of interpersonal phenomena	2 to 10 years	CDP = D on relapse CDP>D (?) on marital stability and rating	Assignment suspect Low sample sizes: not clear what outcome would have been on relapse measure Uncontrolled length of time between assessments
Gibbs et al., 1957	Mixed: Inpatients and outpatients (neurotic = 69% psychotic = 31%) n = 39	1. CDP(a) 1. CDP(b) 5. Pd	Short-term supportive (1 hr./wk.) Experienced therapists(2)	a. Chlorpromazine (75–125 mg./day) b. Chlorpromazine (150–450 mg./day)	*Self-report* MMPI *Therapist ratings* Malamud Rating Scale	8 weeks	No differences	Ratings not blind (done by therapist) Psychotics differentially distributed across groups

448

Study	Sample	Code	Therapy	Drug	Measures	Duration	Results	Comments
Lorr et al., 1961	Mixed: Outpatients (neurotic= 57% psychotic= 16% other= 27%) n = 180 *Males only	1. CDP(a) 1. CDP(b) 1. CDP(c) 3. P 5. Pd	Unspecified nature (1 hr/wk) Individual Experienced therapists (?) (n = 122)	a. Chlorpromazine (100 mg./day) b. Meprobamate (1600 mg. per day) c. Phenobarbital (2 grains per day)	*Self-rating* Anxiety Hostility Discomfort *Therapist ratings* Anxiety Hostility Discomfort	12 weeks	No differences	Attrition high (50%): did not differ across cells
Lorr et al., 1962	Mixed: Outpatients (neurotic= 42% psychotic= 18% other= 40%) n = 150 *Males only	1. CDP 2. D 3. P 5. Pd 9. N.T.	Unspecified intensive (1 hr./wk.) Individual Experienced therapists	Chlordiazepoxide (20–80 mg./day)	*Self-rating* Variety of symptom areas *Therapist ratings* Variety of symptom ratings	4 weeks	*Patient:* No differences *Therapists:* CDP > D CDP > P D > P Pd > P	Attrition high (46%): did not differ across cells *Psychotherapy plus placebo equal to Drug plus psychotherapy, better than psychotherapy alone
Brill et al., 1964	Anxiety states: Outpatients	3. P 4. Dp(a) 4. Dp(b) 4. Dp(c) 8. cdp 9. N.T.	Insight oriented (1 hr./wk.) Individual Inexperienced therapists	a. Meprobamate b. Phenobarbital sodium c. Prochlorperazine	*Symptom ratings* Patient Sign. other Therapist	5 to 12 months	Dp(a) = P > N.T. No Differences between Active Treatment	Attrition high (46%)
Koegler and Brill, 1967	n = 299							Length of treatment uncontrolled

TABLE 12-1 (continued)

Study	Sample	Cells	Psychotherapy	Drug	Criteria	Time	Results	Comments
Rickels et al., 1966	Anxiety: Outpatients n = 114	1. CDP 5. Pd	Unspecified nature (private practice) Individual Experienced therapists (n = 5)	Meprobamate (1600 mg/day)	*Self-report* IPAT verbal anxiety IPAT anxiety IPAT regression Global Improvement *Therapist rating* Clyde Mood Scale Global Improvement	6 weeks	CDP > Pd on most measures	Moderate attrition (16%) Not all Pd got placebo Assessed adequacy of "double-blind" Assessed therapist expectations (biases)
Hesbacher et al., 1970	Anxiety: Outpatient n = 147	1. CDP(a) 1. CDP(b) 5. Pd	Unspecified nature (private practice) Individual Experienced therapists (5)	a. Diazepam (10 mg/day) b. Phenobarbital (150 mg/day)	*Self-report* SCL *Therapist rating* Emotional Somatic Global *Behavioral* Attrition	4 weeks	No differences (at 4 wks.) (at 2 wks. CDPa > CDPb=Pd)	Moderate attrition (18%) Minority of patients (36%) received either "guidance" or no psychotherapy rather than psychotherapy

Study	Population	Groups	Treatment	Drug	Measures	Duration	Results	Comments
Podobnikar, 1971	Anxiety: Outpatient n = 38 *Includes some children	1. CDP 5. Pd	Analytically oriented psychotherapy (1 hr./wk. or 1 hr./2 wks.) Individual Experienced therapists (1)	Chlordiaxopoxide (20—30 mg./day)	*Therapist ratings* Anxiety/depression Fatigue "Hyperaggressiveness" Anxiety/tension	1 to 4½ months	CDP > Pd	Single therapist (also sole assessor) Length of treatment not controlled
Lipsedge et al., 1973	Phobia: Outpatient	1. CDP(a) 1. CDP(b) 2. D 5. Pd(a) 5. Pd(b) 6. d	a. Drug-assisted behavior therapy (30 min./week) b. Standard behavior therapy (30 min./week) Individual Experienced therapists	Iproniazid (25—50 mg/day)	*Self-report* Anxiety Avoidance *Clinician ratings* Anxiety Avoidance	8 weeks	No significant differences between active treatments. All active treatments > placebo.	Moderate Attrition (15%) (with replacement) Groups not comparable at beginning (CDP(b) and Pd(b) less symptomatic: had received 6 hr. relaxation training before pretest)

TABLE 12-1 (continued)

Study	Sample	Cells	Psychotherapy	Drug	Criteria	Time	Results	Comments
Solyon et al., 1973	Phobia: Outpatient n = 50	3. P(a) 3. P(b) 3. P(c) 4. Dp 8. cdp	a. Systematic desensitization (1 hr./wk.) b. Aversion relief (1 hr/wk) c. Flooding (1 hr/wk) Individual Experienced therapists	Phenelzine (45 mg./day)	*Self-report* Phobic avoidance Social maladjustment Wolpe-Lange FSS *Clinician rating* IPAT	3 months	Pa=Pb=Pc= Dp > cdp	Actually two separate samples combined Authors report drugs "faster," but no data Follow-up indicates improvement more likely to be maintained in behavior therapy cells
Zitrin et al., 1976	Phobia: Outpatient n = 62	1. CDP(a) 1. CDP(b) 5. Pd(b)	a. Supportive psychotherapy (1 hr/wk) b. Behavior therapy (1 hr/wk)	Imipramine (150–300 mg./day)	*Clinician* Global Improvement	26 weeks	For agoraphobics CDP(a) = CDP(b) > Pd(b)	Excluded known imipramine nonresponders

452

Study	Sample	Conditions	Therapy	Drug	Measures	Duration	Results	Comments
Cowden et al., 1955	Schizophrenia: inpatient (chronic) n = 32 *Males only	1. CDP 2. D 5. Pd 9. N.T.	Dynamically oriented but reality oriented) (3 hrs./week) Group sessions Experienced therapist (1) Inexperienced therapist (1)	Reserpine (1—8 mg./day)	*Therapist rating* Lorr Multi-dimensional Rating Scale *Attendant Rating Scale* Behavioral measures (number of disruptions)	8 months	No between group differences	Ratings not blind Not clear that assignment was random Single treatment group Only two therapists Reserpine no longer utilized
Cowden et al., 1956	Schizophrenia: Inpatient (chronic) n = 24 *Males only	1. CDP 2. D 9. N.T.	Dynamically oriented (but reality oriented) (3 hrs./wk.) Group sessions Experienced(1) and inexperienced therapists	Chlorpromazine (75—600 mg./day)	Attendant ratings Behavior measures	4 months	CDP = D > N.T.	Ratings not blind Not clear that assignment was random Single therapy group Only two therapists

TABLE 12-1 (continued)

Study	Sample	Cells	Psychotherapy	Drug	Criteria	Time	Results	Comments
King, 1958	Schizophrenia: Inpatient (chronic) n = 95 *Males only	1. CDP 2. D 9. N.T. 10. P(REST) —— REST: Regressive electroconvulsive shock therapy 10. (REST)	Unspecified nature (combined with REST) Group sessions Experienced therapist (1)/author	Chlorpromazine (300 mg./day)	Therapist ratings Malamud Rating Scale	6 months	CDP = D > N.T. =P (REST) > (REST)	Psychotherapy only confounded w/REST 2 patients died from REST (Regressive electroconvulsive shock therapy) Only one therapist Only one treatment group Therapist did ratings, not blind
Evangelakis, 1961	Schizophrenia: Inpatient (chronic) n = 100 *Females only	1. CDP (plus adj.) 1. CDP 2. D (plus adj.) 2. D 5. Pd (plus adj.)	Unspecified nature (2 hrs./wk.) Group sessions Therapists unspecified	Trifluoperazine (up to 50 mg./day)	Discharge from hospital/or to open ward	4 to 18 months	CDP (plus adj.) = D (plus adj.) > CDP=D >Pd (plus adj.)	No statistical analyses presented Not clear patients randomly assigned

Study	Sample	Groups	Therapy	Drug	Measure	Duration	Results	Comments
King, 1963	Schizophrenia: Inpatient (chronic) n = 40 *Females only	1. CDP 2. D	Unspecified nature (?) Group sessions Experienced therapists (3)	Chlorpromazine (300 mg./day)	Discharge	12 months	No differences CDP = D	Only one group
Honigfeld et al., 1965	Schizophrenia: Inpatient (chronic) n = 308 *Males only *All between 54–74 yrs.	1. CDP(a) 1. CDP(b) 1. CDP(c) 2. D(a) 2. D(b) 2. D(c) 5. Pd 6. d	Social interactions (2 hr/wk) Group sessions Inexperienced therapists (n=?)	a. Acetophenazine (up to 240 mg./day) b. Imipramine (up to 300 mg./day) c. Trifluoperazine (up to 24 mg./day)	*Clinician ratings* IMPS *Nurses ratings* NOSIE	24 weeks	Drugs A vs. C > drug D vs. placebo Group > no group (on some measures of adjustment)	Attrition low (10%) Actual amount of drug reported Cell comparisons not conducted
Grinspoon et al., 1968	Schizophrenia: Inpatient (chronic) n = 20 *Males only	1. CDP 5. Pd	Psychoanalytically oriented Individual Experienced therapists	Thioridazine (300–800 mg./day)	*Clinician rating* Hospital adjustment scale	24 months	CDP > Pd	

TABLE 12-1 (continued)

Study	Sample	Cells	Psychotherapy	Drug	Criteria	Time	Results	Comments
Gorham et al., 1964	Schizophrenia: Inpatient (recent admissions) n = 150	1. CDP 2. D 3. P	Unspecified nature (3 hrs./wk.) Group sessions Experienced therapists	Thioridazine (500 mg./day)	Physician's ratings Therapist ratings Nurses ratings Clinician's ratings	12 weeks	CDP=D > P	Study involved nine different treatment centers Attrition rates not reported = dropouts replaced
May and Tuma, 1964, 1965 May, 1968	Schizophrenia: Inpatient (first admissions) n = 228	1. CDP 2. D 3. P 9. N.T. 10. (ECT)	Psychoanalytically oriented: ego supportive (2 hr/wk) Individual Inexperienced therapists	Stelazine (10–120 mg./day)	Discharge Nurses ratings Therapist's ratings Clinician's ratings		CDP=D > P = N.T.	Confounds treatment with dormitory Less drug used in CDP than Drug only

Study	Sample	Design	Treatment	Measures	Duration	Results	Comments
Shader et al., 1969	Schizophrenia: Inpatient (acute) $n = 41$	1. CDP(a) 1. CDP(b) 5. Pd	Unspecified nature Frequency (?) Inexperienced therapists ($n = ?$)	a. Thioridazine (300–900 mg./day) b. Haloperidol (4–12 mg/day)	*Nurses ratings* (HRS) hospital adjustment behavior disturbance index (BDI) *Clinician's rating* (IMPS)	8 weeks	CDP(a) > CDP(b) = Pd
Karon & Vanderbos, 1970	Schizophrenia: Inpatient (first admissions) $n = 36$	1. CDP(a) 2. D 3. P(b)	a. "Ego oriented" Psychoanalytically oriented Individual Experienced therapist Inexperienced therapist b. "Active psychoanalytically oriented Individual Experienced therapist Inexperienced therapist	Clinician ratings Length of hospitalization Battery of intellectual tests Projective tests	20 months	P(b)=CDP(a) > D Experienced therapists> Inexperienced therapists	Confounds treatment site with treatment type Differing levels of drugs given in combination than drug only Assignment to therapist type (experienced vs. inexperienced) not random

TABLE 12-1 (continued)

Study	Sample	Cells	Psychotherapy	Drug	Criteria	Time	Results	Comments
Paul et al., 1972	Maintenance schizophrenia: Inpatients (chronic) $n = 52$	1. CDP(a) 1. CDP(b) 5. Pd(a) 5. Pd(b)	a. Milieu therapy b. Social-learning therapy	Variety of psychotropic drugs: (Low dosage maintenance drugs)	Nurses ratings Observers ratings Clinicians ratings	17 weeks	No differences between groups: all groups improved	Heterogeneity of drugs, all low dosage No attrition
Claghorn et al., 1974	Maintenance schizophrenia: Outpatient (recently discharged) (first admissions) $n = 49$	1. CDP(a) 1. CDP(b) 2. D(a) 2. D(b)	Structured, problem-solving focus (1 hr./wk.) Group sessions Experienced therapist	a. Chloropromazine (up to 300 mg./day) b. Thiothixene (up to 30 mg./day)	*Clinician rating* BPRS *Testing* Interpersonal diagnosis *Personality Battery* (MMPI Interpersonal checklist (TAT)	6 months	(Some changes on measures, not clear about meaning)	No clear statements made relating measures of change to desirability of change

Study	Sample	Codes	Psychotherapy	Drug	Outcome Measures	Duration	Results	Comment
Hogarty, et al., 1973, 1974, 1974	Maintenance schizophrenia: Outpatient	1. CDP 2. D 5. Pd 6. d	Major role therapy (social casework & vocational rehabilitation counseling) (minimum 1 hr./month: no maximum) Individual Experienced therapists(?)	Chlorpromazine (minimum 100 mg./day, no maximum)	"Time in Community"	24 months	CDP=D > Pd = P *[see comment: cell means no: presented] *(Reanalysis, p. 482, suggests CDP > D	Reanalysis (p. 482) suggests that CPD > D on "Relapse" as dichotomous variable (authors conclude that this interaction did not replicate across clinic sites)
Gittleman-Klein, et al., 1976	Childhood Disorders: hyperkinesis n = 34	1. CDP 2. D 5. Pd	Behavior therapy (token system) Individual	Methylphenidate (10–60 mg/day)	Clinician ratings Observers ratings Teachers ratings Parents ratings	8 weeks	CDP=D > Pd	Preliminary report, additional subjects being run Raters blind only to drug-placebo comparison

(1975), Morris (1975), Schmickley (1976) and Shipley and Fazio (1973), suggested the efficacy of cognitive therapy in a variety of populations. Finally, Fuchs and Rehm (1977) have demonstrated the utility of interventions based on a self-control model.

Overall, no evidence is available to support the efficacy of traditional psychotherapies in depression. Some evidence exists suggesting the potential efficacy of behavioral or cognitive interventions in depression. Finally, we are unaware of any controlled study evaluating any psychotherapy in bipolar patients.

Comparative Studies in Unipolar Depressives

Daneman (1961)

Daneman (1961) reported an early double-blind comparison of an antidepressant (imipramine hydrochloride) plus psychotherapy versus a placebo plus psychotherapy. A total of 195 patients were assigned randomly to the two conditions. The majority (159) were diagnosed as neurotic depressive reactions, a minority (32) as psychotic depressive reactions, and the remainder (4) as showing depressions in organic brain syndromes. Patients were seen in an outpatient, private office practice setting.

The length of treatment depended on individual progress, but in most cases lasted from 30 to 90 days. Psychotherapy consisted of 45 minute sessions of psychoanalytically oriented psychotherapy, one to two times per week. Ratings were made by the author (who also served as the sole therapist) on a series of symptom rating scales. The results were reported in terms of global judgments of improvement.

After one month, 79 percent of the drug-psychotherapy patients were in "full remission" versus 7 percent of the placebo-psychotherapy patients. At two months, the comparable figures stood at 87 percent for the drug and psychotherapy group versus 10 percent for the placebo plus psychotherapy group. Both differences were significant.

The results indicated the clear superiority of the combination of active drug (imipramine hydrochloride) plus psychoanalytically oriented psychotherapy over the combination of pill-placebo plus psychoanalytically oriented psychotherapy. It seems that combining drugs and psychotherapy proved relatively effective.

Several comments are necessary. First, the internal validity of the study is open to question: the author noted that adjunctive therapies (family interviews, phenothiazines, and other medications) were provided in an uncontrolled fashion. Further, attrition was high: 14 percent at the one-month reevaluation and 49 percent at the two-month revaluation. The use of a single therapist severely restricted the generality of the findings. Similarly, the absence of a psychotherapy only (no pill) cell could lead to misinterpreting a negative interaction between psychotherapy and pill-placebo as indicating psychotherapy ineffectiveness. Nonetheless, it is, of course, quite possible that the type of psychotherapy utilized was simply ineffective in this population.

Johns Hopkins Group (Covi et al., 1974)

The Johns Hopkins Group, in the first of three NIMH collaborative studies, randomly assigned 218 depressed female outpatients between the ages of 20 and 50 to one of six cells in a 3 x 2 factorial design. The three levels of medications were (1) imipramine hydrochloride (100 to 200 mg/day), (2) diazepam (10 to 20 mg/day), and (3) pill-placebo. The two levels of psychotherapy were (1) weekly psychodynamically oriented group psychotherapy (high contact), and (2) biweekly 20-minute individual sessions (low contact). All therapy was conducted by one of two experienced clinicians. Active treatment extended over 16 weeks. All patients were symptomatically depressed at the start of treatment as defined by a rating of seven or above on the 15-point Raskin Depression Scale (Raskin, Schulterbrandt, Reating, & McKeon, 1970). Patients who did not maintain that level of depression over a two-week placebo "washout" period were excluded from the study.

All patients completed a battery of self-report measures including the Hopkins Symptom Checklist (SCL-90) (Derogatis, Lipman, & Covi, 1973) and the Psychiatric Outpatient Mood Scale (POMS) (McNair, & Lorr, 1964), both of which yield scores for depressive symptoms. Further, all patients were rated on a seven point global improvement scale by a research clinician.

The results generally supported the efficacy of imipramine over either diazepam or placebo. There was no evidence of any advantage for group therapy over the biweekly brief supportive sessions. Further, there was no indication of any beneficial interaction effect; group therapy did not facilitate the impact of imipramine on acute symptom levels.

Differential attrition represented the major threat to the internal validity of the study; the higher dropout rate in the placebo groups versus the two active drugs approached significance. Overall, attrition was high. Twenty percent of the initial sample failed to survive the placebo "washout" period, while another 32 percent of those surviving did not complete the 16 weeks of active treatment. Overall, 47 percent of the sample screened into the study failed to complete the treatment protocol. It is not possible to determine whether dropouts represent remissions, treatment failures, or excessive side effects, for example. Presuming that the results were internally valid and not attributable to differential attrition, the exact nature of the sample completing might have been quite different from those accepted into treatment.

Clearly, psychodynamically oriented group psychotherapy conducted on a weekly basis over 16 weeks failed to have any effect on depressive symptoms relative to brief biweekly supportive sessions. Again, psychotherapy was always administered with a pill, whether active drug or inert placebo. Strictly speaking, the lack of effect may well not generalize to psychotherapy of this type alone. Still, the data are not encouraging for advocates of this type of psychotherapy. There is no indication of any beneficial effect of psychotherapy, either in combination with placebo or active medication.

Philadelphia Psychiatric Center (A. S. Friedman, 1975)

A. S. Friedman conducted a second NIMH collaborative study, focusing on acute symptomatology in outpatient depressives. One hundred and ninety-six male and female outpatients, all married, all rated at seven or above on the 15-point Raskin Depression Scale, and all screened to exclude other psychiatric symptoms, were randomly assigned to one of four cells.

The four cells were (1) drug (amitriptyline) and psychotherapy (marital therapy), (2) drug (amitriptyline) and minimal contact individual therapy, (3) pill-placebo and marital therapy, and (4) pill-placebo and minimal contact individual therapy. Maximum doses of amitriptyline ranged from 100 to 200 mg/per day. Marital therapy involved one-hour sessions conducted once per week; spouses were specifically included, and additional family members were occasionally included.

All patients were assessed on a variety of measures, some relevant to depressive symptoms, some measuring marital adjustment. Patient self-report measures included a variant of the Hopkins Symptom Checklist (including a subscale for depression) and two marital adjustment measures. Physician ratings included a combined version of the Hamilton Depression Scale (Hamilton, 1960) plus the Brief Psychiatric Rating Scale (Overall & Gorham, 1962) and a six-point global improvement scale. Raters were not blind. Each rating was composed of the averaged scores of the treating clinician and an independent clinician.

The results indicated that the active drug was associated with a variety of changes in current symptomatology relative to placebo. The active drug was superior to placebo on 36 of 203 comparisons, whereas marital therapy produced positive changes on 20 of 203 comparisons.[2] It is important to note that the results were reported in terms of the number of significant comparisons, rather than via post hoc comparisons of individual cell means on the respective variables. It is not clear exactly how the average patients in the respective cells compared with one another. The author notes that the drug produced more rapid symptom reduction than marital therapy, but here the analyses were based on indirect comparisons of main effects rather than on direct comparisons of the respective treatment cells.

[2] A total of 10 comparisons would be expected to be significant on the basis of chance alone. Further, many of the comparisons were drawn from the repeated administrations of the same scales increasing the likelihood of significant differences based on chance alone.

Where interactions occurred, they tended to favor the combination treatment over either active treatment alone. However, the total number of significant interactions (11 of 203 comparisons) was equal to what would have been expected on the basis of chance alone. In general, patients receiving active drugs tended to do better on symptom measures while patients receiving marital therapy did better on marital adjustment measures. Even though no actual interaction on any single measure was found, patients receiving the combination showed the benefits of each active treatment alone on the respective types of measures.

The author concluded that marital therapy was superior to minimal contact psychotherapy in terms of reducing depressive symptomatology, but it is not clear that the data support this interpretation. Finding a near chance number of significant differences on a large number of discrete item comparisons hardly supports the efficacy of one treatment over another. It is not clear why the respective treatment cells were not compared on total scale scores, the typical way of analyzing the outcome measures utilized in this study. The way in which the data were analyzed resulted in far too much ambiguity; conclusions suggesting the efficacy of marital therapy on depressive symptoms appear based on only a small subset of the relevant scale items. These results could easily be attributed to chance alone.

The internal validity of the study appears sound, although the use of raters not blind to treatment conditions is troublesome. Obviously, the results are generalizable only to married depressives.

The statistical conclusion validity of the report is suspect. The absence of individual cell comparison makes the evaluation of the results difficult. Counting the number of times the respective active treatments prove significantly better than their respective controls does not serve as an adequate comparison of the two active treatments. It is quite possible for one active treatment cell to be significantly different from its control cell, while a second active treatment cell may not differ significantly from the other control. The experimenter has not adequately ruled out random sampling differences as a rival alternative to treatment effects associated with the second treatment, nor has he or she ruled

out the possibility that one control is more effective than the other. Counting comparisons made against different baselines is a hazardous procedure. Discovering a pattern on 20 or 20,000 different variables does not "prove" the superiority of treatment one over treatment two; it simply fails to rule out a plausible rival hypothesis a greater number of times. Specific treatment cell comparisons would have provided a more appropriate analyses.

Again, all patients received some pill, whether active medication or placebo. The absence of any no-pill conditions prevented the evaluation of placebo-psychotherapy interactions.

Boston-New Haven Collaborative Project
(Klerman et al., 1974; Weissman et al., 1974)
The final study in the NIMH collaborative study involved two separate reports made on data collected in the same research project. The focus was on the prevention of relapse following active treatment. Two hundred and seventy-eight depressed females were given a four to six week trial on amitriptyline (100 to 200 mg daily). Patients were selected on the basis of a score of 7 or above on the Raskin Depression Scale and the diagnosis of primary affective illness.

One hundred and fifty patients showing at least a 50 percent reduction in depressive symptomatology, as measured by the Raskin, were then screened into the actual study. It is important to note that only those patients responding to the drug trial entered the subject pool. The patients were then randomly assigned to one of six cells for what was, essentially, maintenance treatment.

Three levels of chemotherapy, (1) amitriptyline, (2) placebo, and (3) no pill, were crossed with two levels of psychotherapy, (1) weekly individual supportive therapy with an experienced social worker versus (2) minimal contact for assessment and medication purposes only. Patients were randomly assigned to treatment. Ratings were made by independent clinicians in a double-blind design.[3] The maintenance treatment lasted for eight months, or

---

[3]It is not clear how adequately the double-blind was maintained. Drug and placebo patients can frequently be discriminated from no pill patients on the basis of observable side-effects.

until clinical relapse, as defined by a return to symptom levels required for study entrance, lasting at least one month.

Results were reported in terms of Raskin-defined symptomatic relapse (Klerman, et al., 1974) and social adjustment, as measured by the Social Adjustment Scale (Weissman et al., 1974). The latter study reported results for only the 106 patients "surviving" the full eight-month period without relapse.

The results indicated a significant main effect for amitriptyline over placebo and no-pill conditions. No similar main effect for high contact psychotherapy over minimal contact was evident. High contact psychotherapy did have a significant effect on indices of social adjustment, but only after six to eight months. No significant effect was noted for amitriptyline on social adjustment. There was no evidence of any interaction between active drug and high contact psychotherapy on either dependent measure alone. The different loci of the two main effects was interpreted as suggesting that a combined treatment approach possessed greater value by virtue of producing a broader spectrum of changes (Weissman, et al., 1974).

Overall, the study demonstrated adequate internal validity, with the possible exception of biasing due to selective attrition. Forty-four subjects (29.3 percent) failed to complete the eight-month maintenance study; 33 because of clinical relapse (22 percent) and 11 for other reasons (7.3 percent). Relapse, of course, served as a major dependent variable in its own right.

The external validity of the results is restricted by the nature of the population studied. It is important to note that the sample consisted solely of depressed women who had already shown a significant remission during a four- to six-week course of tricyclic therapy.

Further, a question can be raised as to whether the design represented a reasonable comparison of drug and psychotherapy. The sample selection proceedures may well have biased the sample against the psychotherapy by including only probable drug responders.

Finally, no tests for interaction (or individual cell means comparisons) were conducted, since the authors considered the cell sizes (n=25) to be in-

adequate (Weissman, 1976). Figure 12-2 presents the probability of relapse, as calculated by the life-table analyses used by the authors (Klerman et al., 1974), as a function of treatment cell. The relapse rates for the various cells were: (1) drug plus psychotherapy, 12.5 percent, (2) drug only, 12.0 percent, (3) psychotherapy plus placebo, 28.0 percent, (4) placebo alone, 30.8 percent, (5) psychotherapy alone, 16.7 percent, and (6) no-pill, no psychotherapy, 36.0 percent. Visual inspection suggests the presence of a negative placebo-psychotherapy interaction. Although the active medication was clearly effective in preventing relapse in known drug responders, it is not at all clear that psychotherapy alone (when not combined with pill-placebo) was not.

The psychotherapy did appear to have a beneficial effect on social adjustment. While the combination of drugs and psychotherapy may have produced positive effects on both depressive symptomatology and social adjustment, there was no evidence of positive interaction (either additivity or potentiation) on either phenomenon.

University of Pennsylvania (Rush et al., 1977)
Finally, our own research suggested that at least one psychotherapeutic approach, cognitive therapy, may be a more effective, short-term inter-

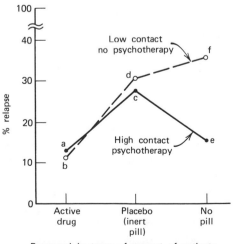

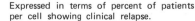
Expressed in terms of percent of patients per cell showing clinical relapse.

Figure 12-2   Relevant cell means for Klerman et al. (1974).

vention in unipolar depressions than tricyclic medications. Forty-one male and female outpatient depressives, all nonpsychotic, were randomly assigned to either drug (imipramine) or psychotherapy (cognitive therapy). Dosage levels for imipramine ranged from 150 to 250 mg per day. Treatment lasted for an average of 12 weeks, with a maximum of 20 one-hour psychotherapy visits and 12 weekly drug visits.

All patients completed the Beck Depression Inventory (Beck, Ward, Mendelson, Mock, & Erbaugh, 1961). In addition, all patients were rated on the Hamilton Rating Scale for Depression (Hamilton, 1960), and for anxiety (Hamilton, 1959). Ratings were made by independent clinicians not blind to treatment assignment.

Although both groups showed significant preposttreatment changes across all depression and anxiety measures, the results indicated that the cognitive therapy produced significantly greater reduction in depressive symptomatology than imipramine. Drop-out rates were also significantly higher in the drug treatment group. Fifteen of 19 cognitive therapy completers showed a clinical remission; 5 of the 14 drug completers showed a similar remission.

The internal valdity of the study appeared adequate. Although the use of blind clinical judges would have been better, both clinician ratings and self-report measures of depressive sumptoms supported the superiority of cognitive therapy. Attrition in the drug group was high: 36 percent of the patients assigned dropped out versus only 5.7 percent of the cognitive group. None of the drug group dropouts showed any significant clinical improvement; six of eight subsequently reentered treatment.

In this study, the drug served as an active treatment comparison group. This strategy involved a real risk; an effective antidepressant such as imipramine will generate a response rate that is difficult to improve upon. In this instance, however, cognitive therapy did prove superior to drug therapy. Further controlled studies will be required to control for such nonspecific factors as expectation or therapeutic attention. However, no other nonmedication treatment has, to our knowledge, been found to be effective in treating depressives in an outpatient setting.

Comparative Studies in Bipolar Depressives

Bipolar Depressives (Davenport, Ebert, Adland, Goodwin, 1975)

Davenport and colleagues provided a comparison between drugs alone and drugs plus psychotherapy in the maintenance treatment of individuals exhibiting a bipolar affective illness, manic type. A total of 65 married patients, all previously hospitalized at the National Instiute for Mental Health (NIMH) for major manic episodes, were followed after discharge from the hospital.

Three groups were formed: (1) lithium carbonate prophylaxis plus conjoint couples group, at NIMH ($n = 12$), (2) lithium carbonate prophylaxis alone, at NIMH ($n = 11$), and (3) community care (in the patients' home community). Patients in this third group were not randomly assigned to treatment, nor was it clear that their treatment was carefully monitored or their medication carefully maintained.

Couples group met weekly for one hour. Two actual groups were conducted. Group membership ranged from 12 to 14 months. All patients were asymptomatic at the start of the study. No information was provided regarding medication dosages or regimen details.

Patients were followed for periods ranging from one to ten years. It is not clear whether the two medication groups differed in lengh of time in follow-up. Major outcome variables involved (1) relapse, defined as rehospitalization, (2) marital failure, (3) rating of social functioning, (4) family interaction, and (5) mental status. No rehospitalizations or marital failures occurred in the drug plus psychotherapy group, while two rehospitalizations and five marital failures occurred in the lithium only group. The groups did not differ significantly in terms of rehospitalization but did suggest a trend in terms of marital failures.[4] The groups also differed in the ratings of family interaction, with the combination treatment proving superior.

The actual measure of symptom return did not document any differences between the two groups, although the only two relapses that did occur oc-

---

[4]Our analysis of the data using a Fisher's exact probability test yielded a probability of $p = .08$, one-tailed.

currred in the drug-only cell. It appeared that the combination treatment might have been superior to drug-only in terms of its effect on a second phenomenon of interest, marital stability and/or family interactions.

These data are of interest for two reasons. First, they represent the only comparative trial of which we are aware which involves diagnosed bipolar patients. Second, they tend to suggest that a variety of psychotherapy may have an impact on non-symptomatic phenomena in bipolar patients, given that the patients were asymptomatic at the time the treatment was received. It is difficult to draw conclusions regarding the impact of either the combination or the drug-only treatment on symptom phenomena, given the small sample sizes.

Summary

The results of the drug and psychotherapy comparisons, in general, support the efficacy of tricyclic antidepressants in reducing depressive symptomatology. Cognitive therapy (Rush et al., 1977) was the only psychotherapy found to have an unambiguous impact on depressive symptoms and the only psychotherapy found to be superior to active medication. The more traditional psychotherapies, individual analytically oriented therapy (Daneman, 1961), group analytically oriented therapy (Covi et al., 1974), marital therapy (Friedman, A. S., 1975), and individual interpersonally oriented therapy with a social worker (Klerman et al., 1974; Weissman et al., 1974), appeared to have no discernable impact on depressive symptoms. Both marital therapy (Friedman, 1975) and individual psychotherapy with a social worker (Weissman et al., 1974) had beneficial effects on phenomena other than depression. Couples group therapy may have had a positive effect on marital and social interaction but not affective symptoms in bipolar depressives (Davenport et al., 1975).

Little evidence exists regarding either positive or negative interactions between drugs and psychotherapy on depressive symptoms. It may be that, with the exception of the cognitive therapy, the other therapeutic approaches simply had no independent effect to add. Further, the combination of drugs and psychotherapy may have joint, but independent, impacts on different phenomena;

depressive symptoms and marital or interpersonal adjustment, respectively. Cognitive therapy, the therapeutic approach that compared most favorably with drugs, was not combined with medication.

At present, there seems to be no contraindication to combining drugs and psychotherapy, although there is little empirical basis for this conclusion. It is important to note that psychotherapy was rarely offered without also prescribing some pill, whether an active medication or a placebo. Only the Boston-New Haven study included both pill-placebo and no pill conditions. The data in that study suggest some interesting interactions. However, none of the individual cell comparisons was significant.

On the whole, the several studies reviewed compared drugs and psychotherapies more adequately than they evaluated the interactions of the two. Tricyclic antidepressants continued to demonstrate their efficacy; of the psychotherapies, only cognitive therapy appeared to reduce depressive symptomatology. There was some evidence that combining drugs with psychotherapy may broaden the spectrum of the phenomena affected. Although there was no evidence for any negative drug and psychotherapy interactions, there was a suggestion of a negative placebo-psychotherapy interaction. This concern remains, at this time, purely speculative, and will require further confirmation.

Psychoneurotic Patient Samples: Anxiety States and Phobias

Introduction

The following review is divided into three sections. First, three early comparative studies involving mixed psychoneurotic and psychotic samples are reviewed. Second, four comparative studies involving relatively pure psychoneurotic samples in outpatient settings are reviewed. The final group of studies focus primarily on phobic conditions. The three studies select relatively homogeneous patient groups centered around specific target complaints. Further, the three are noteworthy in that they employ behavior therapies. They reflect two major trends in the comparative literature: toward greater sample homogeneity and toward increasing use of short-term, behavioral, or cognitive therapies aimed at specific target phenomena.

Psychoneurotics (Mixed Daignosis)

Inpatient Sample (Gibbs, Wilkins, & Lautergach, 1957)

Gibbs and colleagues conducted the earliest comparative study involving a predominantly, but not exclusively, psychoneurotic sample. As noted in Table 12-1, 39 male and female inpatients were randomly assigned to either (1) low dose chlorpromazine plus psychotherapy, (2) high dose chlorpromazine plus psychotherapy, or (3) pill-placebo plus psychotherapy.

The results, consisting of ratings on the Revised Malamud Rating Scale (Malamud & Sands, 1947); scores on the Wechsler-Bellevue Adult Intelligence Scale (WAIS), and scores on the Minnesota Multiphasic Personality Inventory (MMPI), were inconsistent and largely inconsequential. The study is of interest primarily for historical reasons. The heterogenetiy of the samples, the initial noncomparability of the groups, the unspecified nature of the psychotherapy, the use of a major ataraxic with a predominantly psychoneurotic population, and the absence of any real group differences all combined to prevent drawing any meaningful conclusions regarding drug and psychotherapy combinations.

Veterans Administration Cooperative Study I: Psychoneurotics (Mixed Diagnosis): Outpatients (Lorr et al., 1961)

Lorr and colleagues conducted an early trial of various medications combined with psychotherapy in a Veterans Administration setting. Three hundred and eight male outpatients (16 percent psychotic, 57 percent neurotic, and 27 percent psychosomatic), were randomly assigned to one of five cells: (1) psychotherapy plus meprobamate (1600 mg/day), (2) psychotherapy plus chlorpromazine (100 mg/day), (3) psychotherapy plus phenobarbital (2 grains/day), (4) psychotherapy plus placebo, and (5) psychotherapy alone.

Both patients and therapists made a variety of ratings. On the whole, group differences did not emerge, at either eight or twelve weeks. Overall, the study basically showed few treatment differences. Other changes were confined to within group pretest-posttest changes only; the individual treatment cells did not actually differ from one another.

Veterans Administration Cooperative Study II: Psychoneurotics (Mixed Diagnosis): Outpatients (Lorr et al., 1962)

Lorr and colleagues conducted a second Veterans Administration collaborative study involving various combinations of drug (chlordiazepoxide) and psychotherapy. One hundred fifty of an initial 280 male outpatients were randomly assigned to one of six cells; (1) psychotherapy plus chlordiazepoxide, (2) chlordiazepoxide only, (3) psychotherapy plus placebo, (4) placebo only, (5) psychotherapy only, and (6) waiting list control.

Overall, the results offer some support for the efficacy of combined drug and psychotherapy over psychotherapy plus placebo or psychotherapy alone. The group differences are, however, limited to the therapist ratings only; patient self-reports indicated no differences. Individual cell comparisons were not adequately presented; it is impossible to directly compare the various cells with one another. The authors do present tables listing the number of within-group, pre-post changes that were significant. However, this form of presentation does not allow an adequate evaluation of treatment (cell) comparisons.

Summary

The three studies just reviewed yielded little information regarding drug and psychotherapy combinations and comparisons. Of the three, only the second Veterans Administration study produced any significant results. In general, the heterogeneity of the samples, absence of analysis by diagnostic types, brevity and nonspecificity of the psychotherapies, and high attrition rates combined to limit the potential contribution of these studies.

Psychoneurotic Samples

Female Psychoneurotic Outpatients (Brill, Koegler, Epstein, & Forgy, 1964; Koegler & Brill, 1967)

The first of the relatively homogeneous sample studies of female outpatient neurotics was conducted by Brill and colleagues at the UCLA Neuropsychiatric Institute. The sample included patients diagnosed as psychoneurotic, psychosomatic, borderline schizophrenic states, and as having personality disorders. None were actually psychotic or severely depressed.

Patients were randomly assigned to one of six cells: (1) meprobamate plus brief supportive therapy, (2) phenobarbital sodium plus brief supportive psychotherapy, (3) prochlorperazine (a major tranquilizer) plus brief psychotherapy, (4) pill-placebo plus brief supportive psychotherapy, (5) individual insight oriented psychotherapy (weekly, 50 minute sessions), and (6) a no-treatment waiting list control group. Treatment lasted up to 12 months, but averaged five months per patient. It was not clear how the decision to terminate was actually made. All treatment was conducted by relatively inexperienced psychiatric residents.

Dependent measures were obtained from ratings made on a variety of symptoms and levels of functioning by therapists, patients, and some significant other for each patient. Each patient was also tested on the Minnesota Multiphasic Personality Inventory. Finally, each patient was interviewed by a social worker, with the resultant recent life histories then rated by an independent social worker on levels of functioning.

The results obtained indicate few group differences in terms of therapist ratings. The insight-oriented psychotherapy group was rated by therapists as being higher on "ability to work effectively" and higher on "understanding of self." Twenty-four other comparisons failed to indicate any group differences. Waiting list patients were not included in these ratings.

Patient ratings revealed a larger number of group differences. One or more of the active treatment groups proved significantly more improved, relative to the waiting list control, on 9 of 13 different ratings. In each instance, the group receiving meprobamate plus brief supportive psychotherapy ranked first, although they were tied by other groups in several instances. There were differences between active treatment groups on seven of the 13 ratings (excluding the waiting list control group).

It is not clear whether the meprobamate plus brief supportive psychotherapy group differed significantly from the insight-oriented psychotherapy group on any of the measures. On most ratings, the insight-oriented psychotherapy group tied for first or ranked second on the various ratings. The authors' major finding was the absence of any marked differences between their five treatment groups. All five groups showed improvement while the waiting list group did not.

Overall, there seems to be no particular advantage for either the various medications (particularly the meprobamate) paired with brief supportive psychotherapy or the insight-oriented psychotherapy. The study represents a purely comparative study with drug (plus minimal contact) being compared with insight-oriented psychotherapy. No particular advantage emerged for either. No effort was made to investigate the effects of combining the two modalities.

Rickels, Cattell, Weise, Gray, Yee, Mullin, and Aaronson (1966)

Rickels and colleagues provided a methodologically sound, if somwhat limited, comparative study in the comparison of drug plus psychotherapy versus placebo plus psychotherapy. The brief duration of the trial and the nature of the measures combined to suggest that the trial bordered on being only a drug-placebo comparison.

One hundred fourteen psychoneurotic outpatients were assigned to one of two conditions: (1) meprobamate (1600 mg/day) and individual psychotherapy, or (2) pill-placebo and individual psychotherapy. Attrition was notably low, only nine patients from each cell failed to complete treatment. Active treatment lasted six weeks. The actual type of psychotherapy conducted was not specified in the report. All patients were assessed before treatment, and at two, four, and six weeks.

Meprobamate plus psychotherapy proved superior to placebo plus psychotherapy on patient reports of improvement, global ratings (by both patient and therapist), two subscales of the Clyde Mood Scale, and the Ego Scale of the IPAT verbal battery. In general, the more objective self-report measures, IPAT O-A anxiety and regression batteries failed to show any treatment differences.

Overall, the results demonstrated the superiority of the combination of meprobamate plus psychotherapy over pill-placebo plus psychotherapy. Methodologically, the study appears to be quite sound in terms of its internal validity. It is difficult to evaluate the external validity of the study. The use of real patients being treated by practicing, experienced clinicians is noteworthy. However, the brevity of the treatment and the lack of detail regarding the type of psychotherapy used make generalization of the results difficult.

Hesbacher, Rickels, Hutchinson, Raab, Sablosky, Whalen, and Phillips (1970)

Hesbacher and colleagues conducted a controlled combinative trial involving anxious psychoneurotic outpatients. Within a context of a larger study, 147 patients were assigned to one of three conditions: (1) diazepam (10 mg/day), (2) phenobarbital (150 mg/day), and (3) placebo. Some patients in all cells received psychotherapy of an unspecified nature.

The authors reported significant advantages on the Hopkins Symptom Checklist (Williams, Lipman, Rickels, Covi, Uhlenhuth, & Mattsson, 1968) for the diazepam and psychotherapy combination over either the phenobarbital plus psychotherapy or the placebo plus psychotherapy cells at two weeks. At four weeks, however, there were no differences between the groups.

Strictly speaking, the study meets the definition of a comparative study, but the focus was clearly on drug differences at the expense of the impact of psychotherapy. The psychotherapy modality was hardly discussed in the body of the report, and only some patients in each cell received psychotherapy.

The results indicate that the combination of diazepam and psychotherapy may, at two weeks, provide some advantage over the other two combinations, including pill placebo and psychotherapy. The absence of any such differences at four weeks makes it difficult to draw any firm conclusions.

Psychoneurotic Outpatients (Podobnikar, 1971)

Podobnikar presented a controlled, double-blind study involving psychoneurotic patients drawn from his own private practice. All assessments and all therapy sessions were conducted by the author.

Thirty-eight male and female outpatients were randomly assigned to one of two conditions: (1) chlordiazepoxide hydrochloride (20–30 mg/day) plus analytically oriented psychotherapy, or (2) pill-placebo plus analytically oriented psy-

chotherapy. Treatment lasted from one to four and one-half months. Therapy sessions were held either weekly or bimonthly.

Ratings were made by the author on four-point scales on each of the following areas: (1) anxiety-tension, (2) anxiety-depression, (3) fatigue, and (4) "neurotic hyperaggressiveness." Both groups showed a general improvement on the measures, while the active drug plus psychotherapy group proved significantly superior to the placebo plus psychotherapy group on all measures.

The use of a single therapist severely limited the generality of the results. In addition, it is not clear whether the two groups were equated for length of time in treatment. As the results stand, they indicate the greater efficacy of the combined treatment. However, the limitations of the study reduce confidence in these conclusions.

Summary

The four studies just reviewed provide little useful data regarding drug and psychotherapy combinations and comparisons in relatively homogeneous psychoneurotic populations. As shown in Table 12-1, three of the four studies found significant advnatages for the combination of drugs plus psychotherapy over psychotherapy alone. However, in each case, the psychotherapy condition patients were also given a placebo. It is not clear that placebo plus psychotherapy can be regarded as the equivalent of psychotherapy alone, particularly since, from the patient's point of view, he or she may well be receiving an active medication. In two of the three studies (Rickels et al., 1966; Hesbacher et al., 1970), the brevity of the treatment (four weeks) and the lack of attention paid to describing the actual operations of the psychotherapy raise serious questions as to the representativeness of the modality. Further, in the Hesbacher study, the advantages for the combined treatment over placebo plus psychotherapy was seen only at the first assessment (two weeks) and had dissipated by the end of the study (four weeks). Finally, the third study showing an advantage for the combination treatment (Podobnikar, 1971) was based on a trial conducted solely by a single therapist, a strategy severely limiting the generality of the findings.

The remaining study (Brill et al., 1964; Koegler & Brill, 1967) was the only study to directly compare drug (with brief supportive psychotherapy) versus psychotherapy with no placebo. No significant differences were found between the two modalities.

Overall, the comparative literature regarding the use of drugs and psychotherapy in psychoneurotic populations appears to have little actual information to offer. Drug and psychotherapy combinations proved significantly better than psychotherapy "alone" in four to six comparisons, but in three of those four studies the results were suspect (see above). Drug plus psychotherapy was compared with drug alone in only one study (Lorr et al., 1962). No significant differences were found. Drug "alone" and psychotherapy "alone" were compared in two studies. Again, no significant differences were found in either case.

The strategy of operationalizing psychotherapy "alone" as placebo plus psychotherapy (four studies) without also including a no pill psychotherapy group is viewed as a major problem. Only the second Veterans Administration study (Lorr et al., 1962) appears to adequately speak to the significant comparative questions, although, again, the brevity of the study (four weeks) presents problems. The comparative literature in the area of psychoneurotic patients can only be regarded at this time as being inconclusive.

Phobic Conditions

Over the last several years, a series of studies have appeared comparing the efficacy of drug and psychotherapy in the treatment of phobic conditions. The studies represent the increasing trend toward sample homogeneity; the populations treated here would have formed part of the larger group defined as "psychoneurotic" in early comparative studies. Secondly, each of the studies has used antidepressant agents, either the monoamine oxidase inhibitors or tricyclic antidepressants. Finally, each of the studies involved the use of behavioral therapies.

Several studies have pointed to the potential efficacy of various antidepressant agents in the treatment of phobic conditions. Both monoamine oxidase inhibitors (MAOI's) (Tyrer, Candy, & Kelly, 1973) and imipramine, a tricyclic (Klein, 1964, 1967) have proven effective when compared to pill-placebos. Similarly, the efficacy of various behavioral interventions has been well established (cf. Marks, 1969, 1976; Wolpe, 1958; see also Chapters 13–18 in this volume). Additionally, several studies have dealt with intravenous barbiturate or tranquilizer assisted desensitization (Friedman, D., 1966; Hafner & Marks, 1976; Marks et al., 1972; Mawson, 1970; Yorkston et al., 1968). These studies suggest that drug assisted desensitization may, under certain conditions, prove more effective or at least more rapid, than conventional relaxation training plus desensitization. These studies were not included in the review to follow, since the drugs alone would not be used in the absence of the behavioral treatment.

Agoraphobia (Lipsedge, Hajioff, Huggins, Napier, Pearce, Pike, and Rich, 1973)

Lipsedge and colleagues presented a controlled trial comparing two types of systematic desensitization and a monoamine oxidase inhibitor (MAOI) in the treatment of severe agoraphobia. The sample consisted of male and female outpatients, all unable to leave their homes unaccompanied.

A total of 71 patients were randomly assigned to one of six conditions in a 3×2 factorial design. The three levels of behavior therapy consisted of (1) methohexitone-assisted systematic desensitization, (2) standard systematic desensitization with relaxation training, and (3) no systematic desensitization. These were crossed with either (1) iproniazid (25–50 mg t.d.s.), or (2) inert pill-placebo. Methohexitone sodium was used during the actual systematic desensitization treatment to facilitate relaxation. Both types of systematic desensitization involved exposure to evoked images related to anxiety-soothing situations. Treatment sessions lasted 30 minutes and were conducted weekly over an eight-week period. Patients in the standard systematic desensitization groups received an average of six one-hour relaxation training sessions prior to actual treatment.

Ratings on two five-point scales were made by the patients and by an independent clinician blind to group assignment. One scale rated the degree of anxiety when traveling alone; the second rated the degree of avoidance. Ratings were made before treatment and at the end of two months. All patients were interviewed two years later by a social worker.

The two standard desensitization groups began treatment with significantly lower scores on the ratings than the methohexitone-assisted desensitization groups. These initial differences might have reflected the effects of the six hours of relaxation training or they might have reflected the failure of randomization in small samples.

Eleven of the original 71 patients discontinued treatment and were replaced. Nine of the eleven dropouts were from the three placebo cells, three from each of the cells, giving a significantly higher attrition rate across the pooled placebo groups relative to the pooled iproniazid cells, X^2 (1) = 3.88, $p<.05$. The patients dropping out most frequently cited lack of progress as the reason for discontinuing. Dropouts were replaced, a questionable procedure since the effect would be to accelerate the potential for biasing the sample via selective attrition.

The main effect for drug versus placebo was significant on the clinicians ratings of anxiety, but not on patient's ratings of anxiety, or on clinician's or patient's ratings of avoidance. The main effect for the type of desensitization, as determined by clinician's ratings of anxiety, was nonsignificant but indicated a trend in favor of methohexitone-assisted desensitization.

Comparisons between the six actual treatment cells (the most appropriate statistical comparison for generalization to actual clinical practice), indicated that all five active treatment approaches were superior to placebo-no desensitization in terms of patient's ratings of anxiety. The combinations of drug with methohexitone-assisted desensitization, placebo with methohexitone-assisted desensitization, and drug without desensitization proved superior to placebo alone on patient's ratings of avoidance. No other treatment cell comparisons were significant.

The study generated some evidence that any of the three treatment approaches, drug plus methohexitone-assisted desensitization, drug alone, or methohexitone-assisted desensitization alone, were superior to pill-placebo in the treatment of severe agoraphobia. No significant difference emerged between these treatment cells. Standard systematic desensitization, either with active drug or placebo, was demonstrably superior to placebo alone on only one of four measures (ver-

sus two of four for the other active treatment groups).

Mixed Agoraphobias and Other Specific Phobic Conditions (Solyon, Heseltine, McClure, Solyon, Ledrige, and Steinberg 1973)

Solyon and colleagues reported a controlled comparison between behavior therapy and phenelzine in the treatment of phobic conditions. The study actually involved two separate studies, with data pooled in a single report. The initial sample consisted of 20 phobic patients, including both agoraphobias and patients with specific phobias. Patients were randomly assigned to either (1) aversion relief, a behavioral technique involving the counter-conditioning of specific anxiety stimuli by the contingent relief from electric shocks delivered to the finger, or (2) standard systematic desensitization. The second sample consisted of 30 patients, again including both agoraphobics and patients with specific phobias. Patients here were randomly assigned to one of three conditions: (1) deconditioning via "flooding," (2) phenelzine (45 mg/day), a monoamine oxidase inhibitor not currently available in this country, combined with brief supportive psychotherapy, and (3) a pill-placebo combined with brief supportive psychotherapy. The type of phobia (agoraphobia versus specific phobia) was counterbalanced across treatment cells.

Patients in the three behavior therapy conditions received a total of 12 hours of therapy. None of the therapies was conducted *in vivo*. Patients in the two pill conditions also received supportive psychotherapy consisting of six biweekly one-hour sessions. The exact nature of the supportive therapy was not specified. Active treatment lasted 12 weeks in all conditions.

All patients completed a battery of self-report measures, including rating of their phobias on a 0–4 point scale. The patients were also rated on the same scale by one of two research psychiatrists. The Wolpe-Lang Fear Survey Schedule (Wolpe & Lang, 1964) provided a third measure of the phobias.

All groups showed significant decreases in symptomatology on psychiatrist's ratings; the anxiety relief, flooding, and phenelzine-brief psychotherapy groups showed significant decreases on the Fear Survey Schedule, while only the phenelzine-brief psychotherapy group reported a significant decrease on self-ratings. The anxiety relief and phenelzine brief-psychotherapy groups showed greater reductions than the placebo-brief psychotherapy group on two of three measures; flooding was superior to placebo-brief psychotherapy on one measure.

The author noted that the phenelzine-brief psychotherapy had a more rapid impact and seemed to have a greater "cost efficiency" than the behavior therapy groups. Since only pre post measures are reported, it is difficult to determine exactly how the more rapid impact was detected. Excluding the placebo plus supportive psychotherapy treatment cell, none of the other treatment cells differed from one another.

The authors note that the patients treated with one of the three behavior therapies showed a 10 percent relapse rate over a two-year period. In the drug plus supportive psychotherapy cell, six of the ten patients discontinued their medication after treatment ended; all six showed a clinical relapse. It is not clear how relapse was determined during the follow-up.

Overall, the study appeared to be reasonably well conducted. The use of two separate samples presents problems, but the absence of significant differences on pretest rules out sampling bias as a rival hypotheses. It is not clear whether the drug or placebo groups can be considered "pill only" treatments; in each case, they were combined with six hours of supportive psychotherapy. Clearly, active drug plus supportive psychotherapy patients showed more improvement than placebo plus supportive psychotherapy. The three behavioral treatments also appeared more effective than placebo plus supportive psychotherapy and no different than drug plus supportive psychotherapy. For summary purposes, it appears that either the combination of drug plus supportive psychotherapy or a behavioral treatment is superior to placebo plus supportive psychotherapy in treating phobic conditions.

Phobias: Agoraphobias versus Specific Phobias (Zitrin et al., 1976)

Zitrin and colleagues reported a comparative trial involving behavior therapy and imipramine in the treatment of agoraphobia and phobic neurosis.

Klein and colleagues (Klein & Fink, 1962; Klein, 1964) and others (Kelly, Guirguis, Frommer, Mitchell-Heggs, & Sargent, 1970; Tyrer et al., 1973) have explored the use of various antidepressants (tricyclics or MAO inhibitors) in the treatment of the panic attack component of agoraphobia. The authors contend that agoraphobics tend to differ from more traditional phobic neurotics: the former tend to experience both spontaneous panic and anticipatory anxiety, while the latter experience only the anticipatory anxiety related to the specific phobic objects. The spontaneous panic attacks are generally absent from patients showing phobic neurosis, although extreme anxiety may occur in specific situations. In the Klein studies cited, the antidepressants were effective in decreasing the panic attacks; but persuasion, direction, and supportive psychotherapy were required to overcome the related anticipatory anxiety and avoidance behaviors.

The Zitrin and Klein study, currently still in progress, involved separating phobics into three groups: agoraphobics, (specified) phobic neurotics, and mixed phobics. The last group was composed largely of patients showing spontaneous panic attacks but no travel restrictions. To date, 62 patients had completed 26 weeks of treatment. Patients from each of the three diagnostic groups were assigned to one of three treatment cells: (1) behavior therapy plus imipramine, (2) behavior therapy plus placebo, and (3) supportive therapy plus imipramine. Behavior therapy consisted of yoga-like relaxation training, followed by systematic desensitization, occasional in vivo desensitization, and occasional assertive training. Supportive therapy involved the use of a nonjudgmental, accepting, emphatic therapeutic setting to facilitate the understanding of anxieties, defenses, and interpersonal relationships. Imipramine was administered in dosages between 150 and 300 mg/day.

Each patient was assessed at admission and at intervals up until termination, with a five-year follow-up planned. Measures were completed by the patient, the therapist, and an independent evaluator. All raters were blind to medication between the two behavior therapy cells, but not to type of therapy, or membership in the imipramine-supportive therapy group. Measures included a variety of rating scales; results were reported, to date, only in terms of global improvement. It is not clear exactly how the various assessment procedures were used to determine the final criterion reported: overall "improvement." Data for agoraphobics and mixed phobics were pooled, since treatment responses for these two groups were found to be identical.

Agoraphobic and mixed phobic patients receiving imipramine (combining drug and behavior therapy with drug and supportive therapy cells) were reported to have improved more than patients receiving placebo plus behavior therapy. Comparing only the behavior therapy groups, those patients receiving imipramine did better than those receiving placebo. When those patients receiving imipramine, but differing in therapy type, were compared (behavior therapy versus supportive therapy), no differences were observed. Unfortunately, the authors did not compare behavior therapy-placebo with supportive-therapy directly, but rather combined all imipramine patients to demonstrate superiority over placebo patients. This comparison, of course, confounds the efficacy of imipramine plus supportive psychotherapy with the efficacy of imipramine plus behavior therapy.

Results for the phobic neurosis patients were generally inconclusive, although this may be more a function of the fact that fewer patients here had completed the study at the time of report. The evaluator rated phobic neurosis patients receiving behavior therapy plus imipramine as being more improved than phobic neurosis patients receiving behavior therapy and placebo. The therapists rated behavior therapy (drug or placebo) patients as more improved than patients receiving supportive therapy and imipramine.

The authors drew several tentative conclusions: (1) that imipramine was uniquely effective for preventing spontaneous panic attacks, facilitating improvement for agoraphobics but not specific phobic neurotics; (2) that either behavior therapy or supportive therapy was equally effective in agoraphobics once the panic attacks are controlled by imipramine; and (3) that imipramine was not particularly effective in phobic neuroses, where panic attacks were not a prominent feature. For phobic neurotics, psychotherapy alone was seen as sufficient.

Unfortunately, the design utilized did not permit a full exploration of these hypotheses, although the data were highly suggestive. Behavior therapy plus placebo was equated with behavior therapy, discounting any possible differences between the two procedures. Future use of a behavior therapy only group appears indicated. Secondly, the data as reported did not compare behavior therapy versus imipramine; significant differences here in favor of the imipramine group would be necessary to support the author's interpretations. It is not appropriate to collapse across all imipramine patients (including those also receiving behavior therapy) in order to document the efficacy of imipramine "alone." Such a strategy overlooks the possibility that treatment effects could be due to the interaction between drug (imipramine) and behavior therapy rather than to the effects of imipramine alone (or in combination with supportive psychotherapy).

Again, we must point out the necessity of making clean statistical comparisons. If the possibility of an interaction exists, it should be explored using appropriate statistical techniques. The failings rarely lie in the application of statistics, per se, so much as in the logic of the design and/or the logic of the ways in which data are combined. The preliminary report described a useful study that can answer three, but only three, questions: (1) how does behavior therapy plus imipramine compare to behavior therapy plus placebo? (2) how does behavior therapy plus imipramine compare with supportive therapy plus imipramine? and (3) how does behavior therapy plus placebo compare with supportive therapy plus imipramine? It is not clear from the present report exactly how each of these qeustions has been answered.

Overall, the data indicated that either of two drug and psychotherapy comparisons might be superior to placebo plus behavior therapy alone in the treatment of agoraphobia. It is not clear whether that advantage applies to both combinations or only one or the other. No clear advantage emerged for the specific phobic neurotics.

Phobic Conditions: Summary
The three studies just reviewed provide relatively inconclusive data pertaining to drug and

psychotherapy combinations or comparisons. Lipsedge and colleagues (Lipsedge et al., 1973) found no differences between combined drug and behavior therapy, behavior therapy plus placebo, and drug alone, although all appeared superior to placebo alone in agoraphobics. Since all patients received some type of pill, only those interactions involving specific medication effects could manifest themselves in this design.

Solyon and colleagues (Solyon et al., 1973) found essentially no difference between a variety of behavior therapies versus an active drug plus supportive psychotherapy, although, again, the active therapy treatments out-performed placebo plus supportive therapy. Here, the drug plus supportive psychotherapy is best considered a combination treatment, since it is impossible to separate the possible effects of the active medication from the possible effects of a drug and supportive psychotherapy interaction.

Finally, the Zitrin study (Zitrin et al., 1976) suggests that either of two combination treatments (drug plus behavior therapy or drug plus supportive therapy) was superior to the combination of placebo plus behavior therapy for agoraphobic, but not specific phobic, conditions. However, the design used and the ways in which the data were analyzed make the conclusions tentative.

The Schizophrenic Conditions

Two advances in the early 1950s altered therapeutic approaches to the schizophrenic disorders. First was the emergence of the major tranquilizers, particularly the phenothiazines. During the same time period, fundamental changes were occurring in the type of inpatient milieu and alternative care strategies available. May (1976) noted that the type of milieu available may well play a major role in the treatment process.

Several factors are of concern in evaluating the comparative outcome literature in the schizophrenias. Chief among these are sample selection procedures. Frequently in this literature, samples are specified along the acute-chronic continuum. Acute episodes are marked by a relatively rapid onset of symptoms prior to the initiation of treatment. Chronic conditions generally imply a longer-term period of illness, greater stability of symptomatology, and greater personality deterioration.

Whether the sample consists of in- or outpatients, is, of course, a significant factor. Clearly, milieu factors are of greater importance in terms of the amount of "treatment" in inpatient samples than in outpatient samples. Further, it may be important to discriminate between patients with recent first hospitalizations and those with long, continuous or frequent, repeated, hospitalizations.

May (1976) noted that a failure in comparative studies in this area frequently involves the inability of the research team to control other treatments. Particularly in studies involving inpatient samples, where the patients are exposed to a variety of professional and nonprofessional treatment staffs, the possibility of treatment contamination becomes a major factor.

Finally, considerable controversy exists regarding exactly how outcome should be measured. It is not always clear whether high readmission rates reflect treatment failures in keeping patients in the community or treatment successes in moving marginal patients out of the hospital. Real controversy exists as to whether the goal of treatment is or should be a restitution of premorbid levels of functioning, a change in underlying personality or thought processes, or a change in tractability (May, 1976).

Evaluation of the Noncomparative Outcome Literature

Several comprehensive reviews of the drug control outcome literature are available (Cole & Davis, 1969; Appleton & Davis, 1973; May, 1975). Cole and Davis noted that of 130 controlled drug-placebo comparisons, 106 favored active medication. The bulk of the studies not favoring active medication suffer from serious methodological difficulties and/or strikingly low dosage levels. There appears to be overwhelming evidence documenting the efficacy of the various antipsychotic drugs.

The picture emerging from the psychotherapy versus control literature is far more ambiguous (May, 1975). In general, the results tended to suggest that little of the variance was accounted for by the psychotherapies. Where differences did emerge, they tended to favor goal-directed, reality-oriented treatment modalities.

Review of the Comparative Outcome Studies

Table 12-1 lists 14 studies conforming with our definition of comparative studies. In general, they support the notion that psychotherapy may or may not serve as a useful adjunct to drug therapy; but that drug therapy is clearly indicated. Three basic divisions can be made; chronic versus relatively nonchronic patient samples, impatient versus outpatient samples, and active treatment versus maintenance studies. None of the active treatment studies were conducted with outpatient samples.

Chronic Schizophrenic Inpatients: Reserpine (Cowden, Zax, & Sproles, 1955, 1956)

Cowden and colleagues at the Gulfport Mississippi Veterans Administration reported a comparative trial involving reserpine and group psychotherapy in the management of chronic schizophrenic inpatients.

The four groups were: (1) group psychotherapy plus drug, (2) group psychotherapy plus placebo, (3)drug only, and (4) continued custodial care. The group therapy consisted of three one-hour sessions per week, conducted by an experienced psychologist and a psychology trainee. Therapy was primarily supportive and reality-oriented, although the guiding philosophy was psychodynamic. Ratings on the Lorr Multidimensional scales, on-ward behavior indices, and transfer to open ward rates failed to show any group differences. Since reserpine is no longer used in this population, the study is primarily of historical interest.

Chronic Schizophrenic Inpatients: Chlorpromazine (Cowden, Zax, Hague, & Finney, 1956)

Cowden and colleagues reported a second comparative trial in the same clinical setting at the Gulfport, Mississippi Veterans Administration Hospital, in this case involving a major ataraxic, chlorpromazine. Twenty-four chronic withdrawn inpatient schizophrenics were assigned to one of three groups; (1) drug and group psychotherapy, (2) drug only, and (3) continued custodial care.

All patients were rated by ward attendants on an 11-point behavior scale; in addition, records were kept of the number of wet packs administered, the number of collateral electroconvulsive shock administrations (ECT), the number of disciplinary reports received, and the number of on-ward fights. The data indicated the clear superiority of the drug with group therapy and the drug only cells over the continued care control cell on attendant ratings. The combined treatment cell showed a trend toward greater improvement than the drug only group, but the trend did not reach significance. The results were, for the most part, reflected in the measures regarding disruptive behavior.

Unfortunately, the uncontrolled application of ECT to all groups undermined the confidence with which the results can be interpreted. This confounding factor points to the clear necessity of controlling for additional treatments; patients in the combined treatment cell received fewer ECT treatments than drug only patients.

Chronic Schizophrenic Inpatients (King, 1958)

King presented an early comparative trial involving chronic male schizophrenic inpatients. Ninety-five patients were blocked into matched groups of five, then randomly assigned from within the matched quintets to one of five treatment conditions. All patients had spent from eight to 35 years in an inpatient setting.

Treatment groups included: (1) no-treatment control: general ward milieu, (2) REST: regressive electroshock therapy, (3) REST, followed by group psychotherapy, (4) chlorpromazine (300 mg/day), and (5) chlorpromazine (300 mg/day) and group psychotherapy. Group sessions of an unspecified nature were conducted once per week by the author.

Ratings on the Malamud Rating Scale (Malamud & Sands, 1947) indicated the superiority of either drug and group therapy or drug only over the other three treatments. The REST plus group therapy and no treatment groups did not differ, while the REST group only was significantly worse than all others.

Chronic Psychotic Inpatients (Female) (Evangelakis, 1961)

Evangelakis presented an early comparative trial involving trifluoperazine versus group psychotherapy and adjunctive therapy with a mixed group of clinic inpatients. One hundred female inpatients were matched on a variety of factors and assigned to one of five treatment groups. It was not possible to determine whether assignment was random with respect to unmatched variables.

Patients were assigned to one of five treatments: (1) pill-placebo plus on-ward group therapy and off-ward adjunctive therapies, (2) drug only, (3) drug plus on-ward group therapy, (4) drug plus off-ward adjunctive therapy, and (5) drug plus on-ward group therapy and off-ward adjunctive therapy.

The drug utilized was trifluoperazine, administered either intramuscularly or orally in doses up to 50 mg daily. The exact nature of the twice weekly on-ward group therapy was not specified, nor was the experience level of the therapists indicated. Adjunctive therapy involved the availability of recreational, social, vocational, and educational facilities and activities. Treatment lasted from four to eighteen months.

The results indicated the superiority of each of the three drug and group therapy and/or adjunctive therapy combinations over either the drug alone cell or the placebo plus group therapies plus adjunctive therapy cell. Criteria utilized were movement statistics; categories at the termination of treatment in descending order of "value" were (1) discharged, (2) trial visit, (3) placement in sheltered environment, (4) unchanged, and (5) worse. Unfortunately, the author did not present any statistical analyses of the data. Our own chi square analyses of the data indicated nonsignificant differences between the drug and group therapy plus adjunctive therapy and the drug plus adjunctive therapies, with significant differences between these two and the other three groups. Drug plus group therapy was not significantly better than drug alone, while both were significantly better than psychotherapy.

The results demonstrate the efficacy of drugs in this type of chronic inpatient population; they further point to the potential efficacy of combination treatments. The unspecified nature of the group therapy leaves the question open as to the actual efficacy of the therapy. The adjunctive therapy sounds very similar to what is typically described as milieu therapy by current standards. It appears that group psychotherapy added little over either adjunctive therapy or drug therapy. The drugs alone were clearly effective, while the drugs in combination with adjunctive therapy, either with or without group therapy, proved most effective.

Chronic Schizophrenic Inpatients, Females (King, 1963)

King reported a second controlled comparative trial involving chronic female schizophrenics. Forty matched patients were randomly assigned to one of two groups: (1) chlorpromazine plus group psychotherapy versus (2) chlorpromazine alone. Treatment was continued over a one-year period.

The nature of the group therapy was not specified. The chlorpromazine was administered in doses up to 300 mg a day. Discharge from the hospital, determined by administrators other than the therapists, served as the outcome criterion.

The data indicated no significant differences between the groups. It appeared that the combined treatment added nothing over the drug alone. It was not possible to determine the extent to which either treatment was effective, since no base rates for discharge or comparison groups were provided.

VA Cooperative Project in a Geriatric Population (Honigfeld, Rosenblum, Blumenthal, Lambert, & Roberts 1965)

Honigfeld and colleagues provided a large multi-center collaborative study involving male geriatric schizophrenics. A total of 308 chronic inpatient male schizophrenics, all between 54 and 74 years of age, were randomly assigned to one of eight treatment cells. Three active medications were administered either in combination with group social therapy or alone. The drugs used were: (1) acetophenazine (a phenothiazine), up to 240 mg/day, (2) trifluoperazine (a phenothiazine), up to 24 mg/day, and (3) imipramine (an antidepressant), up to 300 mg/day. Twice-weekly group social therapy plus pill-placebo and pill-placebo alone constiuted the remaining two cells.

The results on a variety of ratings indicated a superiority for both phenothiazines over either imipramine or placebo on seven of seventeen possible ratings, including conceptual disorganization, excitement, and manifest psychosis. Group sessions were associated with greater improvement on ratings of motor disturbance (IMPS) and irritability, cooperation, and personal neatness (NOSIE).

The authors concluded that the phenothiazines were particularly useful in these populations, while group social therapy served as a useful additional agent. Tests for cell differences were not conducted. In general, the active phenothiazines seemed effective on several measures, including those related to manifest symptomatology. The group sessions appeared to have an impact on several variables related to on-ward behavior.

Chronic Schizophrenic Inpatients: Males (Grinspoon, Ewalt, & Shader, 1967, 1968a, 1968b)

Grinspoon and colleagues reported a long-term controlled comparison of intensive individual psychotherapy plus placebo versus intensive individual psychotherapy plus an active phenothiazine (thioridazine). Twenty male chronic schizophrenic inpatients were transferred to a specially administered inpatient setting and randomly assigned to one of two cells: (1) psychotherapy plus placebo, or (2) psychotherapy plus drug.

Patients in the drug cell received between 300 and 800 mg of thioridazine per day. Active medication was begun at week 13, following 12 weeks of uniform placebo administration. Drug cell patients were switched back to placebo at week 83 and back again to placebo at week 95. Medication and ratings were made on a double-blind basis. All patients received intense individual psychodynamic psychotherapy with an experienced clinician.

Patients were rated at regular intervals on the Hospital Adjustment Index (a measure of functioning in the hospital environment) and the Behavioral Disturbance Index. Ratings were made by ward attendants and nursing personnel, respectively.

On both measures, the combination of drugs plus psychotherapy was clearly superior to placebo plus psychotherapy. The authors concluded that intensive psychotherapy had little, if any, effect in chronic schizophrenia, while the combination of drugs plus psychotherapy appeared to be beneficial.

Summary

The seven studies just reviewed provided data suggesting that drugs are relatively effective in chronic inpatient populations. Psychotherapy, as practiced in these studies, appeared to be of little benefit. Drug and psychotherapy combinations appeared to add little over drugs alone. The lack of rigor in the designs and the various methodological flaws discussed undermined confidence in these conclusions.

It is interesting that adjunctive activities appeared to enhance either drugs alone or drug plus psychotherapy (Evangelakis, 1961). Similarly, the group sessions provided the geriatric inpatients (Honigfeld et al., 1965) bore little resemblance to traditional psychotherapy, but did seem to have some impact. While drug therapy is gnerally indicated in this population, varieties of activity-oriented learned experiences or milieu may well have proven beneficial.

New or Recent Admissions Samples

The following four studies reported on schizophrenic samples with relatively acute symptom onsets. It is frequently difficult to determine whether this refers simply to recency of hospitalization in an ongoing disorder, recency of recurrence in a disorder in remission, or to the first episode of a disorder requiring hospitalization.

Schizophrenic Inpatients (Males: Veterans Administration Colloborative Study: (Gorham et al., 1964)

Gorham and colleagues presented a large nine-center collaborative Veterans Administration Hospital study comparing drugs, psychotherapy, and a combination treatment with male schizophrenic inpatients. A total of 150 patients were assigned to one of three treatments: (1) drug only, (2) group psychotherapy only, (3) combined drug and group psychotherapy. It was impossible to determine from the report whether assignment was random.

The drug utilized was thioridazine, in doses ranging from 300 to 500 mg/day. It is not known whether the different cells received equivalent dosages. The psychotherapy involved 36 sessions of group psychotherapy, all conducted by experienced clinicians. The type of therapy varied across centers, but, in general, involved the exploration of personal history material and an emphasis on the development of significant interpersonal processes.

Patients were assessed on a variety of measures (see Table 12-1). The results demonstrated an impressive consistency across measures. In almost all cases, the drug only and drug plus group psychotherapy groups were equivalent to one another and superior to the psychotherapy only group.

Overall, the results were impressive and, when combined with the results of the Schizophrenia Research Project (reported below), strongly suggested the efficacy of the major ataraxics and the relative inefficacy of psychotherapies with recent admission inpatient schizophrenics. Several points were, however, troublesome, including the ambiguity in the initial assignment, the absence of reported attrition rates, and the absence of actual documentation regarding drug dosages or (in other cases) the amount of psychotherapy received. These considerations underscore the importance of reporting all relevant data and describing, in detail, all experimental procedures.

First Admission Schizophrenics: Schizophrenia Research Project (May and Tuma, 1964, 1965; May, 1968)

May and colleagues presented a major comparative trial involving inpatient schizophrenics. Two hundred twenty-eight schizophrenic patients both male and female ranging in age from 16 to 45, were randomly assigned to one of five treatment conditions. All patients were "first admission" schizophrenics with no evidence of brain damage, epilepsy, or drug addiction. Further, patients were selected to represent the mid-range of prognosis; those patients expected to require prolonged hospitalization and those showing a rapid remission (release in 18 days or under) were excluded prior to assignment to treatment.

Patients accepted were assigned to one of five experimental inpatient wards where they received one of the following treatments: (1) milieu alone (control), (2) electroconvulsive therapy (ECT), (3) psychotherapy alone, (4) drugs, (5) psychotherapy plus drugs. Treatment was conducted by psychiatric residents ranging from six months and six years of experience. Psychotherapy involved an average of 2 hours per week until the patient was released or adjudged a treatment failure. Time in psychotherapy ranged from 7 to 87 hours, with an average of 49 hours per patient. Therapy was de-

scribed as psychoanalytically oriented, "ego-supportive," and reality-oriented, with a minimum of interpretation.

The predominant medication was stelazine, although a few patients received chlorpromazine as well. Drug dosages were fixed by the individual therapist and his or her superiors, but ranged from 10 to 120 mg/day. The total amount of medication received was somewhat higher for the drug only group than for the drug plus psychotherapy group.

A variety of criteria were utilized, including release rate, nurses' ratings, therapists' ratings, ratings by independent clinicians, and objective self-report indices. This resulted in a total of 34 dependent measures. None of the measures indicated any significant ($p<.05$) interactions between drugs and psychotherapy, and only seven of the 34 indicated even a nonsignificant trend ($.05<p<.25$).

In general, the data indicated a clear ordering of means, with drugs or drugs plus psychotherapy showing the best response. ECT showed an intermediate response, and the psychotherapy alone and milieu alone showed the least response. The authors concluded that psychotherapy alone is not the treatment of choice for hospitalized schizophrenics. They further concluded that drugs alone provide the preferred modality, since it was as effective as the combination of drugs and psychotherapy while being less expensive.

In general, the project maintained high levels of internal validity. The only design flaws of consequence involved the confounding of treatment type with living quarters, the absence of clearly stated criteria for defining a patient as a treatment failure, and the flexible dosage schedule that allowed the drug plus psychotherapy group to receive less medication than the drug only group. Since dosage schedules were in part determined by symptom levels, the lower levels of prescribed medication may have reflected a greater response to the combination. Whenever the combination of drugs and psychotherapy is compared with either alone, it would have been useful to have had the levels of each component in the combined therapy equal to the levels of either component above.

The main finding, that psychotherapy alone tends to be a poor treatment choice was buttressed by the results of a five-year, posthospitalization following of the cohort (May, Tuma, & Dixon, 1976). Results indicated that patients treated with psychotherapy alone fared significantly worse in terms of subsequent relapses after discharge than patients in the three other treatment groups: drugs, drugs and psychotherapy, and ECT.

Overall, the project was well designed and executed. The main conclusions: (1) that psychotherapy alone had little effect, and (2) that psychotherapy added little when added to drugs, appear justified for the type of therapy utilized and the type of patient treated.

Massachusetts Mental Health Center (Shader, Grinspoon, Ewalt, & Zahn, 1969)

Shader and colleagues provided a comparative trial involving acute male schizophrenics and utilizing inexperienced therapists in an inpatient setting. Forty-one new admissions schizophrenics were randomly assigned to one of three treatment cells: (1) thioridazine plus individual psychotherapy, (2) haloperidol plus individual psychotherapy, and (3) placebo plus individual psychotherapy. Drug dosages were not specified.

Treatment covered an eight-week period. Ratings were made by nursing personnel on the BDI (Behavioral Disturbance Index) and by independent clinicians on the IMPS. In general, the results indicated the superiority of the thioridazine plus psychotherapy combination over either of the other two treatments.

The study appeared to maintain adequate internal validity. Little time or attention was devoted to the description of the psychotherapy used. The relevant comparisons here were between active medication plus psychotherapy versus placebo plus psychotherapy. The cell differences indicated that the specific pharmacological component accounted for the bulk of the patient improvement.

Michigan State Psychotherapy Project (Karon & Vanderbos, 1970, 1972)

The Michigan State Psychotherapy Project involved a controlled comparison of drugs and psychotherapy in the treatment of hospitalized schizophrenic patients. Thirty-six patients were randomly assigned to one of three modalities: (1) "active" psychoanalytically oriented psychotherapy without drugs, (2) "ego-oriented" psychoanalytically oriented psychotherapy with phenothiazine (100 to 600 mg of thorazine/day), or (3) phenothiazine alone (300–1600 mg of thorazine/day). The authors specifically criticized the May and Tuma Schizophrenia Research Project (1964, 1965) because in that project the psychotherapists involved were basically inexperienced. In the Michigan State Project, patients were treated by either experienced or inexperienced therapists.

All patients were assessed at the beginning of treatment, and again at 6, 12 and 20 months (end of treatment). Each assessment included a battery of intelligence tests, Rorschach, Thematic Apperception Test, and a clinical status interview. Scoring was done from protocols or tapes by judges blind to treatment assignment. Discharge from the hospital served as an additional outcome measure. Patients were frequently discharged from the hospital, but continued in treatment on an outpatient basis.

The authors reported significant differences favoring the two groups receiving psychotherapy (one being the combined drug and psychotherapy) over the drug only group on global clinical ratings, length of hospital stay, and three of four measures of intellectual ability. No differences were evident on the fourth intellective measure and the two projective tests (Rorschach and TAT). In breaking down the groups into five cells (each of the two psychotherapy groups divided into experienced and inexperienced therapists) the authors concluded that experience is a factor that interacts with medication. Patients treated by experienced therapists without medication tended to show less formal thought disorder and more days out of the hospital; those working with inexperienced therapists tended to spend more time out of the hospital if on medication than if not, but in either case, they retained their indications of "thought disorders."

These data are clearly discrepant from the main trend of the literature in drug-psychotherapy outcome studies in schizophrenia. May and Tuma (1970) responded to the preliminary reports with a critique of the methodology employed in the Michigan project. Among the discrepancies, the authors noted that:

1. The design utilized prevented clearly attributing group differences to drugs, type of

psychotherapy, unique personality characteristics of the therapists, experience, or other factors.

2. Patients in the "drug only" group were transferred to another hospital if they failed to show a rapid improvement. They remained in the assessment pool. This procedure clearly confounds hospital milieu with "psychotherapy alone" versus "drug alone" comparisons.

3. Assignment to inexperienced versus experienced therapist was not made on a random basis. Splitting a single cell into two cells for comparative purposes undermines the initial randomization.

4. Finally, several patients refused retesting and were assigned "100 percent error" scores on the intellective tests. This procedure inevitably resulted in an underestimation of intellective capacities, confounding motivational with intellectual deficits. Most refusal occurred among patients of inexperienced therapists.

We are inclined to agree with May and Tuma that design and methodological problems preclude drawing firm conclusions. Confounding the transfer of nonresponding patients with "drug only" treatment presents a threat to the internal validity of the study. At this point, the rest of the literature so clearly runs contrary to the Michigan Project results that any evidence would need to be impeccable to command attention. Supporting evidence, suggesting the superiority of experienced therapists, working either with or without drugs, does not appear to be currently available in other studies. The relative success of the "psychotherapy only" cell appears to be based on reasonably adequate methodology. The study does represent the only indication of which we are aware of any support for the efficacy of psychotherapy in this population.

Summary: Recent Admission Samples.
The results of the four studies reviewed with recent admission schizophrenic inpatients appear relatively solid. Three of four studies (Gorham et al., 1964; May, 1968; Shader et al., 1969), including

one with experienced therapists, found drugs alone both superior to psychotherapy (with or without placebo) and equivalent to the drug plus psychotherapy combination. The Michigan State data (Karon & Vanderbos, 1972) seemed to suggest that an experienced therapist using a specific approach may have better results than drugs alone. However, a number of methodological problems reduce confidence in that conclusion. Replication in more tightly controlled designs appears indicated here before the variables of therapist experience and therapy type can be accepted as determining outcome in this population.

The May (1968) study appeard particularly sound. Our only concern here is that subtle interactions between psychotherapy and drugs may have been present but not documented; while the drug only and drug plus psychotherapy groups did not differ in outcome, the combination treatment group received less overall medication. Future research might well be addressed to just such a subtle interaction.

Maintenance Therapies for Schizophrenics
The studies reviewed considered the comparative impact of drugs, psychotherapy, and drug plus psychotherapy combinations on current manifestations of the schizophrenic syndrome; that is, patients were either hospitalized at the beginning of the study or were presenting for treatment. The section to follow considers the comparative effectiveness of drugs and psychotherapy on issues of prevention; does maintenance therapy prevent (or retard) the reemergence of new episodes?

Follow-up studies are, generally, uncontrolled (May, Tuma, & Dixon, 1976). The maintenance studies, reported below, in general ask a different question and ask it in a more controlled fashion. Figure 12-3 presents the parameters of the three types of designs. The maintenance comparative study is, essentially, a controlled clinical comparison that takes groups of patients roughly equal on current psychopathological phenomena and asks which treatments are differentially effective in keeping them well.

The issues related to internal validity are as critical here as in the active comparative trials, and methodological rigor should be as important a con-

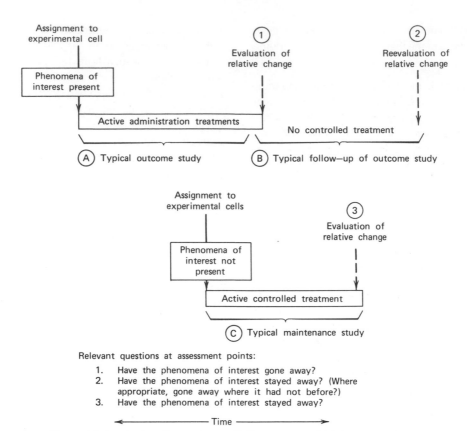

Figure 12-3   Active Comparisons, Follow-ups, and Maintenance Designs.

sideration here as in any other well-designed outcome study. The issues of external validity are especially complex, since the initial pool of patients that the investigator has to work with is frequently defined by the prior history of treatment response.

Davis (1975) reviewed the existing maintenance treatment literature in the area of the schizophrenias. He concluded that the maintenance antipsychotic medications are effective in preventing relapse in patients at risk. An earlier review by Tobias and MacDonald (1974) had concluded that, on the whole, the existing maintenance literature was marred by frequently repeated design errors that negated any clear conclusions. Specifically, these flaws included: (1) the breakdown of double-blind methodologies, (2) differential attrition resulting in the loss of integrity of the initially randomized groups, (3) biased assessment, especially where different criteria were applied to define relapse between drug and placebo cells, and (4)

limitations in design and analysis. The two reviews have sparked a lively exchange between the authors (Davis, Gosenfeld, & Tsai, 1976; MacDonald & Tobias, 1976), which may lead to an upgrading of methodological procedures. We are inclined to agree with the substance of both reviews, if not the conclusions. The data reviewed by Davis are vast and, in at least the more adequately controlled studies, we believe compelling for the populations actually studied. The design limitations pointed to by Tobias and MacDonald are indeed problems. However, in most instances they could hardly account for the magnitude of the medication-placebo differences noted; and, in many other instances, would be expected to obscure differences.

Abrupt Drug Withdrawal (Paul, Tobias, & Holly, 1972)

Paul and colleagues provided a test of hypotheses related to abrupt drug-withdrawal in a clinical inpatient population. Paul's patients carried a hospital diagnosis of schizophrenia, although the authors specificially questioned the adequacy of the diagnostic procedures.

Fifty-two hospitalized male and female inpatients, all with two or more years of continuous hospitalization, were assigned to one of four treatment cells in a 2/2 factorial design. The two levels of the drug factor involved (1) continued maintenance medication versus (2) abrupt substiution of an inert placebo. These conditions were crossed with two levels of social-environmental treatment programs: (1) milieu therapy versus (2) social-learning therapy. Both focused on training various social skills, the former via group pressure and principles, the latter via means of a token economy. All patients had been transferred to one of the two identical treatment units prior to the beginning of the study, confounding unit of residence with type of social-environmental treatment.

Patients in the two maintenance medication cells were continued on the types of medications they had been receiving during their ongoing hospitalizations. These medications included phenothiazines, butyrophenones, tricyclic antidepressants, phenothiazines and tricyclic combinations, and barbiturates.

All patients were assessed on a battery of observational and structured interview measures both before and after treatment. Assessments were carried out over a 17-week medication withdrawal period.

The results indicated an absence of effects associated with drug withdrawal. Continued drug versus placebo groups did not differ on any of the major measures. Withdrawal of medication was not associated with any increase in symptomatology or biazarre behavior. All groups evidenced a statistically significant change in patient behavior. None of the differences between milieu and social learning programs achieved significance.

Overall, the results suggest that abrupt withdrawal from low-dose maintenance medications did not seem to be associated with negative consequences. Positive behavioral changes were found across all groups, with some indication that changes occurred more rapidly for placebo than drug cells.

The study seems to be quite sound methodologically. No attrition occurred, measures appeared carefully taken, and the program seemed tightly run. It is unfortunate that all patients received one of the two active social-environmental training programs, since change in the patients cannot clearly be attributed to either program. It would have been more convincing to have been able to have demonstrated group differences across subjects at posttest, than to have simply reported within-group changes for all cells. While it is unlikely that this population changed drastically as a result of the passage of 17 weeks, it is always possible that scales and raters did. Raters may be blind to treatment assignment, but may not always be blind to pretest-posttest status.

Nonetheless, the study is of considerable interest. The conclusions drawn by the authors suggest that low-dose maintenance medications may be at best superfluous, or, at worst, contraidicated, where active social-retraining programs are available.

Outpatient Maintenance (Hogarty, Goldberg, & the Collaborative Study Group, 1973; Hogarty, Goldberg, Schooler, & the Collaborative Study Group, 1974; Hogarty, Goldberg, Schooler, & Ulrich, & the Collaborative Study Group, 1974) Hogarty and colleagues presented a series of reports based on a long-term maintenance study involving outpatient schizophrenics. Each of 374 recently discharged schizophrenic patients was randomly assigned to one of four treatment cells: (1) placebo only, (2) sociotherapy plus placebo, (3) drug only, and (4) drug plus sociotherapy.

The sociotherapy used was Major Role Therapy, a sociotherapy consisting of intensive individual social casework and vocational rehabilitation counseling. Protocol called for a minimum of one contact per month, but no maximum. The drug utilized was chlorpromazine with a minimum dose of 100 mg/day, but no maximum. All patients were started on chlorpromazine (regardless of cell), then switched to placebo at two months in the relevant cells.

Relapse served as the primary dependent variable in two of the three reports (Hogarty, et al., 1973; Hogarty, Goldberg, Schooler, & Ulrich,

1974). Relapse here was defined as clinical deterioration of such magnitude that hospitalization seemed imminent. Roughly 75 percent of those defined as "relapsed" by a project psychiatrist were subsequently hospitalized.

The results related to relapse clearly favored the drug, whether administered alone or in combination with sociotherapy. Sociotherapy showed a small but significant effect when all patients were compared at 12 months, but no significant effect at 24 months. The combination of drugs and sociotherapy was not reported to be associated with any significant effect on relapse.

It is important to note that their data reflected "time in the community," a continuous variable appropriate for analysis of variance. The authors also presented the percent of patients per cell relapsing, but provided no analysis of these data. Briefly, the four cells showed the following relapse percentages: (1) placebo only, 80 percent, (2) sociotherapy plus placebo, 80 percent, (3) drug only, 52 percent and (4) sociotherapy plus drug, 36 percent. Although based on incomplete data (relapse rates and initial sample sizes), our own reanalysis of the data suggests that the combination of drug plus sociotherapy appeared to be associated with significantly lower cumulative relapse rates than drug alone (our estimated chi-square was associated with a probability of $p < .001$).

The authors noted this apparent interaction, but concluded that it represented an effect apparent at only one of their three participant clinics (Goldberg, Schooler, Hogarty, & Roper, 1977; Hogarty & Ulrich, 1977). Although apparently internally valid (the interaction did appear real), they questioned the external validity (generalizability) of the interaction, since it is not clear whether the finding holds only for subtypes of patients, or some therapists, or some clinics, and so forth. Our opinion is that an internally valid finding still has credibility even though the parameters of its generalizability are difficult to specify. Internal and external validity are both important considerations; any real treatment effect in this population deserves, we feel, further exploration. Serendipitous findings which are difficult to explain can prove to be important in the process of matching patients to treatments or in developing innovative approaches to treatment.

Claghorn, Johnstone, Cook, and Itschner (1974)
Claghorn and colleagues present a controlled maintenance trial in schizophrenic outpatients in remission. Forty-nine males and females were selected following their first hospital admission.

Patients were assigned to one of four cells: (1) chlorpromazine alone, (2) chlorpromazine plus group psychotherapy, (3) thiothixene alone, and (4) thiothixene plus group psychotherapy. Chlorpromazine was administered in doses up to 300 mg/day; thiothixene in doses up to 30 mg/day. Group therapy involved an emphasis on structured problem solving, focusing on problems and tasks of daily living. Patients from both cells met as a single therapy group on a weekly basis. Treatment lasted for six months.

All patients were assessed on a battery of scales including the Brief Psychiatric Rating Scale (rated by a psychiatrist) and the Inter-personal Diagnosis of Personality battery (IDP) (Leary, 1957), consisting of the MMPI, the Interpersonal Checklist, and the Thematic Apperception Test.

The data indicated few, if any, cell differences. The IDP battery indicated some cell changes; patients receiving both drug and group tended to rate themselves as less dominant and less affiliative at the level of "conscious self-perceptions" (presumably the Interpersonal Checklist), while rating themselves as more dominant on a preconscious level (presumably the TAT data).

Overall, the study did suggest some differences between psychotherapy and no psychotherapy conditions (when both are combined with drugs), but the clinical relevance of these differences is not clear. There were no significant treatment group differences on the primary symptom measure, the BPRS, nor any reported treatment effects on relapse or the maintenance of remission variables.

Summary: Maintenance Therapies for Schizophrenics

The results here appear inconsistent. One study (Paul et al., 1972) appeared to suggest that low dosage maintenance drug therapy adds little to drug plus psychotherapy combinations. A second (Hogarty et al., 1973) suggested that drugs help maintain schizophrenics in remission in the community, while social role therapy has little impact on relapse variables, although there was some evidence to suggest an interesting interaction at one participating clinic. The third study (Claghorn et al., 1974) appeared to add little interpretatable data.

This may well prove an interesting area for future research. It is not clear how the samples studied in the first two studies compared; it may well be that producing change in "hard core" chronic hospitalized patients is a totally different matter from preventing relapse in an outpatient population starting out in fairly good remission. The former population may have had trouble becoming more symptomatic, even with drug withdrawal. While this interpretation is purely speculative, it is likely that the populations and the respective targets differed across the two relevant studies.

Overall Summary: Schizophrenias
The efficacy of drugs in the schizophrenias seems well established. Psychotherapy alone, by and large, compared poorly with drug alone or drug plus psychotherapy combinations, although the data are more numerous for new or recent admissions than for chronic inpatients. One study (Karon & Vanderbos, 1972) suggested that therapist experience was a critical variable, but at least two others (Grinspoon et al., 1968 a & b; Gorham et al., 1964) suggested that it was not.

Comparative maintenance therapy studies are few in number. Such data as exist are contradictory, although this may be due to sample and target differences.

Comparative studies focusing on mechanisms of interaction and more restricted target questions appear indicated. The current literature suggests that traditional psychotherapy has little impact, either alone or in combination with drugs. All but two of the studies were conducted with inpatient populations; most used relatively inexperienced therapists, and few utilized more structured psychotherapy approaches. Future comparative research might well address itself to whether psychotherapy and drug combinations offer any advantage over drugs alone when these variables are explored.

Childhood Disorders: Hyperkinesis
The hyperkinetic syndrome in children is classically described as consisting of motor hyperactivity, impulsively, poor frustration tolerance, poor concent-

ration, distractibility, and immaturity and/or aggressiveness. Short-term pharmacology has long been recognized as an effective intervention in the management of these disorders. Preferred medications include the stimulants, either dextroamphetamine or methylphenidate, the major tranquilizers (especially chlorpromazine), and, more recently, imipramine.

Empirical evidence is available supporting the efficacy of either drug or behavioral approaches (Rosenbaum, O'Leary, & Jacob, 1975; O'Leary, Pelham, Rosenbaum, & Price, 1976). The exact modes of action for each remain unclear (Gittelman-Klein & Klein, 1975). It remains to be determined whether drugs and behavior therapies will facilitate, inhibit, or not interact at all with one another.

Three studies currently available compare drugs, behavior therapies, and drug-therapy combinations in the management of the hyperkinetic syndrome. Two are not considered to be adequate comparative clinical trials; Sprague and colleagues (Sprague, Christensen, & Werry, 1974) because treatment groups differed significantly before treatment on the primary dependent measure, and Christensen (1975) because of the low drug dosages utilized (average dose, 11.7 mg methylphenidate). The third study (Gittleman-Klein, Klein, Abikoff, Katz, Gloisten, & Kates, 1976), consists of a preliminary report of an ongoing drug and behavior therapy comparative trial.

Hyperkinesis (Gittleman-Klein et al., 1976)
To date, 36 children between the ages of six and twelve showing a hyperkinetic reaction have been treated in one of three treatment conditions: (1) drug only (methylphenidate, 10 to 60 mg/day), (2) behavior therapy plus drug, and (3) behavior therapy plus placebo. The behavioral program emphasized behavior modification based on reinforcement principles.

Attrition was relatively low, with only two of the 36 failing to complete the program. One child developed a severe medication reaction; the second was withdrawn from the medication by a parent.

All children were assessed by a variety of means: classroom teachers ratings on the Conners' Teacher Rating Scale (Conners, 1969), observation of in class behavior by trained raters, and ratings by parents, teachers, and a research psychiatrist of global symptom status.

The results demonstrated a consistent pattern of treatment results. All treatments were associated with significant pre-post improvement on all measures, but, in almost all ratings, the combination of drugs and behavior therapy or drugs alone proved superior to behavior therapy plus placebo. The combination of drug and behavior therapy did not differ significantly from the drug only group, although in general, mean scores were more "improved." Only the mother's ratings of global improvement failed to show any significant group effects.

While no untreated or placebo-only group was included to provide a no-treatment baseline, the authors suggested that the significant pre-post changes could be accepted as reflecting the efficacy of all three treatments. The authors cited other studies (e.g., O'Leary et al., 1976) in which little, or no change was noted in placebo controls.

The between-groups comparisons appear valid, both internally and externally. The population was one of considerable clinical interest and the treatments consistent with current clinical practice. Of particular interest was the finding that children receiving the combination treatment compared favorably at the end of treatment to a sample of normal children; it is helpful to see an attempt made to compare treatment outcomes with normative data.

Summary

It appears that the one adequately controlled comparative study in the area documents the superiority of either drug combined with behavior therapy or drug alone over behavior therapy plus placebo in the treatment of hyperkinesis. All three treatments appeared to be effective. The absence of a behavior therapy only group (without pill-placebo) was seen as the only factor that limited full interpretation of the results.

CONCLUSIONS

Considered as a whole, the studies reviewed appear to have generated little consistent information.

There appears to be little evidence against combining drugs and psychotherapies; however, there was little opportunity for negative interactions, if they occur in nature, to emerge. Most hypothesized negative interactions involve the psychological impact of pill-taking. In 31 studies reviewed, 23 involved psychotherapy "alone" treatment cells. In 14 of these studies, the psychotherapy "alone" was actually a psychotherapy plus pill-placebo treatment. Since the studies were run on a double-blind basis, this means that patients believed they were receiving medication. Psychologically mediated negative interactions could not be detected in these designs, even if they did occur. Eleven of the 14 studies found the combination of psychotherapy plus active medication superior to the combination of psychotherapy plus placebo. The remaining three studies found no difference, but also found none in any other comparisons. There are at least two ways of interpreting these data: (1) drugs plus psychotherapy combinations are superior to psychotherapy (disregarding the use of placebos, as most box scores do); or (2) if you are going to prescribe a placebo, you might as well prescribe an active drug.

Seven studies utilized a psychotherapy without pill placebo. The outcomes here were less conclusive and, perhaps, more encouraging to advocates of psychotherapy. In two cases, both involving recent admission schizophrenics (Gorham et al., 1964; May, 1968) the psychotherapy alone conditions fared worse than either drug alone or drug and psychotherapy combinations. In a third study with a similar population(Karon & Vanderbos, 1972) the psychotherapy may have fared as well or better than either drugs alone or drugs plus psychotherapy, although conclusions here are open to question. In a fourth study (Gibbs et al., 1957), no differences were found in any study comparison. A fifth study (Brill et al., 1964) found no difference between drugs plus brief supportive psychotherapy versus psychotherapy alone, but found both superior to no treatment. A sixth study (Solyom, et al., 1973) found either active drug or a variety of behavioral (psychotherapy alone) interventions superior to pill-placebo plus supportive psychotherapy in phobias. Finally, our own research (Rush et al., 1977) has found psychotherapy alone superior to drug plus brief supportive psychotherapy in outpatient depressives.

Three studies involve both psychotherapy alone and psychotherapy plus pill-placebo comparisons. Here, negative interactions based on pill-taking could be detected, if any actually existed. One study (Lorr et al., 1961) found no differences between any treatment comparisons. A second (Lorr et al., 1962) found the psychotherapy plus placebo superior to psychotherapy alone, but after only four weeks of treatment and only on therapist (and not patient self-report) measures. The third (Klerman et al., 1974; Weissman et al., 1974) used an analysis which precluded meaningful cell comparisons. Plotting cell differences (Figure 12-2) gives the appearance of a negative interaction between pill-placebo and psychotherapy, although none of the cell comparisons reached significance.

It is not at all clear whether psychotherapy had any positive or negative effects on medication regimens. In no instance did the combination of drugs plus psychotherapy perform worse than drug alone. Four studies (Friedman, A. S., 1975; Klerman et al., 1974; Davenport et al., 1975; Hogarty et al., 1973) suggested that drugs may have different foci of action than psychotherapy; the combination of the two may have proven beneficial because each procedure produced changes on different phenomena.

Finally, it should be noted that several of the mechanisms of interaction might be expected to appear as either patient attrition or symptom substitution. If drugs reduce motivation (and if that is bad), dropout rates might prove to be the outcome variable of interest. If psychotherapy interferes with the motivation for enduring medication side effects, the effort necessary for working through negative feelings about pill-taking might not be expended. Here, differential regimen compliance rates might be the variable of greatest interest, not symptom measures.

Overall, we are inclined to agree with earlier reviews that stress the absence of negative drug and psychotherapy interactions in the comparative literature. We would simply point out that the bulk of the comparative studies have not been designed to explore those questions. A design similar to that used by the Boston-New Haven study (Klerman et al., 1974), with drug plus psychotherapy, placebo plus psychotherapy, and psychotherapy only (with adequate cell sizes) would be necessary to adequately test for the effects of drugs on psychotherapy. Conversely, drugs would need to be combined with various levels of specific psychotherapies, nonspecific factors, and no-psychotherapy contracts. Several cautions appear indicated:

1. The effects of drugs, psychotherapies, and drug plus psychotherapy combinations should be evaluated in relation to specific diagnostic groups, target problems, and patient types. Conclusions appear to hold, for example, for inpatient schizophrenics that do not hold for outpatient psychoneurotics.

2. In most cases, we probably know less about drug and psychotherapy combinations than is desirable. Certainly, most of the speculations regarding the mechanisms underlying interactions have been inadequately evaluated, if they have been evaluated at all.

3. The comparative literature consists of studies covering a broad range of design adequacy and methodological rigor. No single study was definitive in any area, although several were quite well designed. By and large, however, the bulk of the studies contain a variety of methodological flaws and restrictions on generality that undermine confidence in conclusions drawn.

4. Specific treatments, designed, or found in prior research, to focus on specific targets, appear to produce the best results. This holds across therapy type, whether drug or psychotherapy. Combinations frequently reflect the separate foci of treatment effects.

5. Any manipulation might be expected to have some impact on a patient, at least until proven otherwise. The practice of equating psychotherapy and drug control procedure with psychotherapy alone, or conversely, drug plus psychotherapy control with drug alone, appears unjustified.

Given the above cautions, several conclusions can be drawn:

1. The efficacy of drugs appears most firmly established in the schizophrenias and the affective disorders.

2. The relative ineffectiveness of psychotherapies (of the types used) seems most apparent in the schizophrenias. Drug plus psychotherapy combinations appear to add little over drug alone in controlling manifest symptomatology, but may facilitate behavior change (Paul et al., 1972) or interpersonal functioning (Hogarty et al., 1973).

3. The impact of psychotherapy on the affective disorders appears to depend on the type of psychotherapy utilized. Cognitive therapy appears superior to drug alone in one study, while other approaches appear to have little impact on manifest depressive symptomatology.

4. The relative impact of drugs and/or psychotherapies on psychoneurotic disorders also appears open to question. Several of the studies were little more than drug versus placebo comparisons in samples receiving ongoing, but brief, psychotherapy. Much more meaningful work could be done in this area.

5. Research in the area of the phobias is relatively recent and quite promising. Data to date suggest that appropriate medications may prove to be a necessary, but not sufficient, component of treatment in agoraphobia, which has proven particularly resistant to single modality treatments. Specific phobias still appear to be the province of various behavior therapies, although some interesting work is being done with drug-assisted desensitization or *in vivo* exposure.

6. Research in the area of one of the childhood disorders (hyperkinesis) appears promising, although it appears to be too early to draw any firm conclusions.

Overall, the comparative literature appears to be in its infancy. Most data to date are based largely on designs that can only address questions of outcome: what works best with which patient. The logic of the designs have precluded the exploration of the mechanics of interaction, while methodological inadequacies have vitiated the conclusions regarding comparative outcome that can be drawn. The use of cumulative box scores based largely on frequency counts risks minimizing the contribution of those studies, usually the more recent, which most adequately address questions of clinical and theoretical interest. Similarly, such counts may obscure the emergence of newer, more powerful treatments targeted at specific phenomena or at more rigorously defined populations.

The comparative trial might best be conceptualized as an evaluation of two or more treatment packages. A variety of factors are likely to be represented whenever any medication is administered or whenever any psychotherapy is attempted. Rarely does the control over independent variables within the treatment package even begin to approach the rigor obtainable within a precisely controlled laboratory setting. Conceptualizing such studies as attempts to assess *value* (what works best), as is done in the literature on program evaluation, may prove to be a useful methodological approach. Efforts to establish the mechanisms of interaction may require more rigorously controlled designs and, perhaps, might best follow studies that establish the value of the combinations.

REFERENCES

American Psychiatric Association Task Force. The current status of lithium therapy: Report of an APA Task Force. *American Journal of Psychiatry,* 1975, *132,* 997–1001.

Appleton, W. S. Third psychoactive drug usage guide. *Diseases of the Nervous System,* 1976, *37,* 39–51.

Appleton, W. S., & Davis, J. M. *Practical clinical psychopharmacology.* New York: Medcom Press, 1973.

Beck, A. T. *Depression: Clinical, experimental, and theoretical aspects.* New York: Harper and Row, 1967. (Republished as *Depression: Causes and Treatment.* Philadelphia: University of Pennsylvania Press, 1972.)

Beck, A. T. *Cognitive therapy and the emotional disor-*

ders. New York: International Universities Press, 1976.

Beck, A. T., Ward, C. H., Mendelson, M., Mock, J. E., & Erbaugh, J. K. An inventory for measuring depression. *Archives of General Psychiatry*, 1961, *4*, 561–571.

Bergin, A. E. The evaluation of therapeutic outcomes. In A. E. Bergin & S. L. Garfield (Eds.), *Handbook of Psychotherapy and behavior change*. New York: Wiley, 1971.

Brill, N. Q., Koegler, R. R., Epstein, L. J., & Forgy, E. W. Controlled study of psychiatric outpatient treatment. *Archives of General Psychiatry*, 1964, *10*, 581–585.

Campbell, D. T. Factors relevant to the validity of experiments in social settings. *Psychological Bulletin*, 1957, *54*, 297–312.

Campbell, D. T., & Stanley, J. C. *Experimental and quasi-experimental designs for research*. Chicago: Rand McNally, 1963.

Christensen, D. E. Effects of combining methylphenidate and a classroom token system in modifying hyperactive behavior. *American Journal of Mental Deficiency*, 1975, *80*, 266–276.

Claghorn, J. L., Johnstone, E. E., Cook, T. H., & Itschner, L. Group therapy and maintenance treatment of schizophrenics. *Archives of General Psychiatry*, 1974, *31*, 361–365.

Cole, J. O., & Davis, J. M. Anti-psychotic drugs. In L. Bellak & L. Loeb (Eds.), *The schizophrenic syndrome*. New York: Grune & Stratton, 1969.

Conners, C. K. A teacher rating scale for use in drug studies with children. *American Journal of Psychiatry*, 1969, *126*, 152–156.

Cook, T. D., & Campbell, D. T. The design and conduct of quasi-experiments and true experiments in field settings. In M. D. Dunnette (Ed.) *Handbook of industrial and organizational research*. Chicago: Rand McNally, 1975.

Covi, L., Lipman, R. S., Derogatis, L. R., Smith, J. E., & Pattison, J. H. Drugs and group psychotherapy in neurotic depression. *American Journal of Psychiatry*, 1974, *131*, 191–198.

Cowden, R. C., Zax, M., Hague, J. R., & Finney, R. C. Chlorpromazine: Alone and as an adjunct to group psychotherapy in the treatment of psychiatric patients. *American Journal of Psychiatry*, 1956, *112*, 898–902.

Cowden, R. C., Zax, M., & Sproles, J. A. Reserpine alone and as an adjunct to psychotherapy in the treatment of schizophrenia. *Archives of Neurological Psychiatry*, 1955, *74*, 518–522.

Cowden, R. C., Zax, M., & Sproles, J. A. Group psychotherapy in conjunction with a physical treatment. *Journal of Clinical Psychology*, 1956, *12*, 53–56.

Daneman, E. A. Imipramine in office management of depressive reactions (a double-blind study). *Diseases of the Nervous System*, 1961, *22*, 213–217.

Davenport, Y. B., Ebert, M. H., Adland, M. L., & Goodwin, F. K. Lithium prophylaxis: The married couples group. Unpublished manuscript,1975.

Davis, J. M. Overview: Maintenance therapy in psychiatry: I. Schizophrenia. *American Journal of Psychiatry*, 1975, *132*, 1237–1245.

Davis, J. M. Overview: Maintenance therapy in psychiatry: II. affective disorders. *American Journal of Psychiatry*, 1976, *133*, 1–14.

Davis, J. M., Gosenfeld, L., & Tsai, C. C. Maintenance antipsychotic drugs do prevent relapse: A reply to Tobias and MacDonald. *Psychological Bulletin*, 1976, *83*, 431–447.

Derogatis, L. R., Lipman, R. S., & Covi, L. SCL-90: An outpatient psychiatric rating scale—preliminary report. *Psychopharmacology Bulletin*, 1973, *9*, 13–28.

Evangelakis, M. G. De-institutionalization of patients (the triad of trifluoperazine-group-psychotherapy-adjunctive therapy). *Diseases of the Nervous System*, 1961, *22*, 26–32.

Feighner, J. P., Robins, E., Guze, S. B., Woodruff, R. A., Winokur, G., & Munoz, R. Diagnostic criteria for use in psychiatric research. *Archives of General Psychiatry*, 1972, *26*, 57–63.

Fiske, D. W., Hunt, H. F., Luborsky, L., Orne, M. T., Parloff, M. B., Reiser, M. F., & Tuma, A. H. Planning of research on effectiveness of psychotherapy. *Archives of General Psychiatry*, 1970, *22*, 22–32.

Friedman, A. S. Interaction of drug therapy with marital therapy in depressive patients. *Archives of General Psychiatry*, 1975, *32*, 619–637.

Friedman, D. A new technique for the systematic desensitization of phobic symptoms. *Behavior Research and Therapy*, 1966, *4*, 139–140.

Fuchs, C. Z., & Rehm, L. P. A self-control behavior therapy program for depression. *Journal of Consulting and Clinical Psychology*, 1977, *45*, 206–215.

Garfield, S. L. Research on client variables in psychotherapy. In A. E. Bergin, &. S. L. Garfield (Eds.), *Handbook of psychotherapy and behavior change*. New York: Wiley, 1971.

Gibbs, J. J., Wilkins, B., & Lauterbach, C. G. A controlled clinical psychiatric study of chlorpromazine. *Journal of Clinical and Experimental Psychopathology*, 1957, *18*, 269–283.

Gioe, V. J. Cognitive modification and positive group experience as a treatment for depression. Unpublished doctoral dissertation, Temple University, 1975.

Gittleman-Klein, R., & Klein, D. F. Are behavioral and psychometric changes related in methylphenidate-treated children: *International Journal of Mental Health*, 1975, *4*, 182–198.

Gittleman-Klein, R., Klein, D. F., Abikoff, H., Katz, S., Gloisten, M. C., & Kates, W. Relative efficacy of methylphenidate and behavior modification in hyperkinetic children: An interum report. Unpublished manuscript, 1976.

Glassman, A., Kantor, S., & Shostak, M. Depression, delusions, and drug response. *American Journal of Psychiatry*, 1975, *132*, 716–719.

Goldberg, S. C., Schooler, N. R., Hogarty, G. E., & Roper, M. Prediction of relapse in schizophrenia outpatients treated by drugs and sociotherapy, *Archives of General Psychiatry*, 1977, *34*, 171–188.

Gorham, D. R., Pokorny, A. D., & Moseley, E. C. Effects

of a phenothiazine and/or group psychotherapy with schizophrenics. *Diseases of the Nervous System*, 1964, *25*, 77–86.

Grinspoon, L., Ewalt, J. R., & Shader, R. Long-term treatment of chronic schizophrenia: A preliminary report. *International Journal of Psychiatry*, 1967, *4*, 116–128.

Grinspoon, L., Ewalt, J. R., & Shader, R. Psychotherapy and pharmacotherapy in chronic schizophrenia. *American Journal of Psychiatry*, 1968, *134*, 1645–1652. (a)

Grinspoon, L., Ewalt, J. R., & Shader, R. *Schizophrenia: Pharmacotherapy and psychotherapy*. Baltimore: Williams and Wilkins, 1968. (b)

Hafner, J., & Marks, I. Exposure *in vivo* of agoraphobics: Contributions of diazepam, group exposure and anxiety evocation. *Psychological Medicine*, 1976, *6*, 71–88.

Hamilton, M. The assessment of anxiety states by rating. *British Journal of Medical Psychology*, 1959, *32*, 50–55.

Hamilton, M. A rating scale for depression. *Journal of Neurology, Neurosurgery, and Psychiatry*, 1960, *23*, 56–61.

Hesbacher, P. T., Rickels, K., Hutchison, J., Raab, E., Sablosky, L., Whalen, E. M., & Phillips, F. J. Setting, patient, and doctor effects on drug response in neurotic patients: II. Differential improvement. *Psychopharmacologia*, 1970, *18*, 209–226.

Hogarty, G. E., Goldberg, S. C., & the Collaborative Study Group. Drug and sociotherapy in the aftercare of schizophrenic patients. *Archives of General Psychiatry*, 1973, *28*, 54–64.

Hogarty, G. E., Goldberg, S. C., Schooler, N. R., & the Collaborative Study Group. Drug and sociotherapy in the aftercare of schizophrenic patients. III. Adjustment of nonrelapsed patients. *Archives of General Psychiatry*, 1974, *31*, 609–618.

Hogarty, G. E., Goldberg, S. C., Schooler, N. R., Ulrich, R. F., & the Collaborative Study Group. Drug and sociotherapy in the aftercare of schizophrenic patients. II. Two-year relapse rates. *Archives of General Psychiatry*, 1974, *31*, 603–608.

Hogarty, G. E., & Ulrich, R. F. Temporal effects of drug and placebo in delaying relapse in schizophrenic outpatients. *Archives of General Psychiatry*, 1977, *34*, 297–304.

Honigfeld, G., Rosenblum, M. P., Blumenthal, I. J., Lambert, H. L., & Roberts, A. J. Behavioral improvement in older schizophrenic patients: Drug and social therapies. *Journal of the American Geriatric Society*, 1965, *13*, 57–72.

Kaplan, H. S. *The new sex therapy*. New York: Brunner/Mazel, 1974.

Karon, B. P., & Vanderbos, G. R. Experience, medication and the effectivensss of psychotherapy with schizophrenics. *British Journal of Psychiatry*, 1970, *116*, 427–428.

Karon, B. P., & Vanderbos, G. R. The consequences of psychotherapy for schizophrenic patients. *Psychotherapy: Theory, Research, and Practice*, 1972, *9*, 111–119.

Kasanin, J. Acute schizo-affective psychoses. *American Journal of Psychiatry*, 1933, *13*, 97–126.

Kelly, D., Guirguis, W., Frommer, E., Mitchell-Heggs, N., & Sargent, W. Treatment of phobic states with antidepressants. *British Journal of Psychiatry*, 1970, *116*, 387–398.

Kiesler, D. J. Some myths of psychotherapy research and the search for a paradigm. *Psychological Bulletin*, 1966, *65*, 110–136.

Kiesler, D. J. Experimental design in psychotherapy research. In A. E. Bergin & S. L. Garfield (Eds.) *Handbook of psychotherapy and behavior change*. New York: Wiley, 1971.

King, P. D. Regressive ECT, chlorpromazine and group therapy in the treatment of hospitalized chronic schizophrenics. *American Journal of Psychiatry*, 1958, *115*, 354–357.

King, P. D. Controlled study of group psychotherapy in schizophrenics receiving chlorpromazine. *Psychiatry Digest*, 1963, *24*, 21–26.

Klein, D. F. Delineation of two drug-responsive anxiety syndromes. *Psychopharmacologia*, 1964, *5*, 397–408.

Klein, D. F. Importance of psychiatric diagnosis in prediction of clinical drug effects. *Archives of General Psychiatry*, 1967, *16*, 118–126.

Klein, D. F., & Fink, M. Psychiatric reaction patterns to imipramine. *American Journal of Psychiatry*, 1962, *119*, 432–438.

Klerman, G. L. Combining drugs and psychotherapy in the treatment of depression. In M. Greenblatt (Ed.) *Drugs in combination with other therapies*, New York: Grune & Stratton, 1974.

Klerman, G. L., DiMascio, A., Weissman, M., Prusoff, B., & Paykel, E. S. Treatment of depression by drugs and psychotherapy. *American Journal of Psychiatry*, 1974, *131*, 186–191.

Klerman, G. L. Psychoneurosis: Integrating pharmacotherapy and psychotherapy. Paper presented at the Symposium on Effective Psychotherapy, Texas Research Instiute of Mental Science, Houston, Texas, 1975.

Koegler, R. R., & Brill, N. Q. *Treatment of psychiatric outpatients*. New York: Appleton-Century-Crofts, 1967.

Kupfer, D. J., Pickar, D., Himmelhoch, J. M., & Detre, T. P. Are there two types of unipolar depressions? *Archives of General Psychiatry*, 1975, *32*, 866–871.

Lasky, J. J. The problem of sample attrition in controlled treatment trials. *Journal of Nervous and Mental Diseases*, 1962, *35*, 332–338.

Lazarus, A. A. *Multimodal behavior therapy*. New York: Springer, 1976.

Leary, T. F. *Interpersonal diagnosis of personality: A functional theory and methodology for personality evaluation*. New York: Ronald Press, 1957.

Lewishohn, P. M. A behavioral approach to depression. In R. M. Friedman, & M. M. Katz (Eds.) *The psychology of depression: Contemporary theory and research*. Washington, D. C.: V. H. Winston, 1974.

Lipsedge, M. S., Hajioff, J., Huggins, P., Napier, L., Pearce, J., Pike, D. J., & Rich, M. The management of severe agoraphobia: A comparison of iproniazid and systematic desensitization. *Psychopharmacol-*

gia, 1973, 32, 67–80.

Lorr, M., McNair, D. M., & Weinstein, G. J. Early effects of cloridiazepoxide (Librium) used with psychotherapy. *Journal of Psychiatric Research*, 1962, 1, 257–270.

Lorr, M., McNair D. M., Weinstein, G. J., Michaux, W. W., & Raskin, A. Meprobamate and chlorpromazine in psychotherapy: Some effects on anxiety and hostility of outpatients. *Archives of General Psychiatry*, 1961, 4, 381–389.

Luborsky, L., Chandler, M., Auerbach, A., Cohen, J., & Bachrach, H. M. Factors influencing the outcome of psychotherapy: A review of quantitative research. *Psychological Bulletin*, 1971, 75, 145–185.

Luborsky, L., Singer, B., & Luborsky, L. Comparative studies of psychotherapies. Is it true that "Everyone has won and all must have prizes"? *Archives of General Psychiatry*, 1975, 32, 995–1008.

MacDonald, M. L., & Tobias, L. L. Withdrawal causes relapse? Our response. *Psychological Bulletin*, 1976, 83, 448–451.

Malamud, W., & Sands, S. A Revision of the psychiatric rating scale. American *Journal of Psychiatry*, 1947, 104, 231–237.

Marks, I. M. *Fears and phobias*. New York: Academic Press, 1969.

Marks, I. M. "Psychopharmacology": The use of drugs combined with psychological treatment. In R. L. Spitzer and D. F. Klein (Eds.) *Evaluation of psychological therapies*. Baltimore: The Johns Hopkins University Press, 1976.

Marks, I. M., Viswanathan, R., Lipsedge, M. S., & Gardner, K. Enhanced relief of phobias by flooding during waning diazepam effect. *British Journal of Psychiatry*, 1972, 121, 493–505.

Mawson, A. B. Methohexitone-assisted desensitization in treatment of phobias. *Lancet*, 1970, 1, 1084–1086.

May, P. R. A. *Treatment of schizophrenia*. New York: Science House, 1968.

May, P. R. A. Psychotherapy and ataraxic drugs. In A. E. Bergin and S. L. Garfield (Eds.) *Handbook of psychotherapy and behavior change*. New York: Wiley, 1971.

May, P. R. A. Treatment of schizophrenia: I. A critique of reviews of the literature. *Comprehensive Psychiatry*, 1974, 15, 179–185.

May, P. R. A. Schizophrenia: Overview of treatment methods. In A. M. Friedman, H. I. Kaplan, & B. J. Sadock (Eds.) *Comprehensive Textbook of Psychiatry-II*. Baltimore: Williams and Wilkins, 1975.

May, P. R. A. Pharmacotherapy of schizophrenia in relation to alternative treatment methods. In G. Sedvall, B. Uvnas, &. Y. Zotterman, (Eds.) *Anti-psychotic drugs: pharmacodynamics and pharmacokinetics*. Oxford: Pergamon Press, 1976.

May, P. R. A., & Tuma, A. H. The effect of psychotherapy and stelazine on length of hospital stay, release rate and supplemental treatment of schizophrenic patients. *Journal of Nervous and Mental Diseases*, 1964, 139, 362–369.

May, P. R. A., & Tuma, A. H. Treatment of schizophrenia. *British Journal of Psychiatry*, 1965, 3, 503–510.

May, P. R. A., & Tuma, A. H. Methodological problems in psychotherapy research: Observations on the Karon-Vanderbos study of psychotherapy and drugs in schizophrenia. *British Journal of Psychiatry*, 1970, 117, 569–570.

May, P. R. A., Tuma, A. H., & Dixon, W. J. Schizophrenia-a follow-up study of results of treatment. I. *Archives of General Psychiatry*, 1976, 33, 474–478.

McNair, D. M., & Lorr, M. An analysis of mood in neurotics. *Journal of Abnormal Social Psychology*, 1964, 69, 620–627.

Meltzoff, J., & Kornreich, M. *Research in psychotherapy*. New York: Atherton Press, 1970.

Mendels, J. Lithium and depression. In S. Gershon & B. Shopsin (Eds.) *Lithium. Its role in psychiatric research and treatment*. New York: Plenum Press, 1973.

Mendels, J. Lithium in the treatment of depression. *American Journal of Psychiatry*, 1976, 133, 373–378.

Morris, J. B., & Beck, A. T. The efficacy of antidepressant drugs. *Archives of General Psychiatry*, 1974, 30, 667–674.

Morris, N. E. A group self-instruction method for the treatment of depressed outpatients. Unpublished doctoral dissertation, University of Toronto, 1975.

O'Leary, K. D., Pelham, W. E., Rosenbaum, A., & Price, G. H. Behavioral treatment of hyperkinetic children: An experimental evaluation of its usefulness. *Clinical Pediatrics*, 1976, 15, 274–279.

Overall, J. E., & Gorham, D. R. The brief psychiatric rating scale. *Psychological Reports*, 1962, 10, 799–812.

Overall, J. E., & Tupin, J. P. Investigation of clinical outcome in a doctor's choice treatment setting. *Diseases of the Nervous System*, 1969, 30, 305–313.

Paul, G. L., Tobias, L. L., & Holly, B. L. Maintenance psychotropic drugs in the presence of active treatment programs: A "triple-blind" withdrawal study. *Archives of General Psychiatry*, 1972, 27, 106–115.

Podobnikar, I. G. Implementation of psychotherapy by Librium in a pioneering rural-industrial psychiatric practice. *Psychosomatics*, 1971, 12, 205–209.

Pokorny, A. D., & Klett, C. J. Comparison of psychiatric treatments: Problems and pitfalls. *Diseases of the Nervous System*, 1966, 27, 648–652.

Prien, R. F., & Caffey, E. M. Lithium prophylaxis: A critical review. *Comprehensive Psychiatry*, 1974, 15, 357–363.

Raskin, A., Schulterbrandt, J. G., Reating, N., & McKeon, J. J. Differential response to chlorpromazine, imipramine, and placebo: A study of subgroups of hospitalized depressed patients. *Archives of General Psychiatry*, 1970, 23, 164–173.

Rickels, K. *Non-specific factors in drug therapy*. Springfield, Ill.: Charles C. Thomas, 1968.

Rickels, K., Cattell, R. B., Weise, C., Gray, B., Yee, R., Mullin, A., & Aaronson, H. G. Controlled psychopharmacological research in private psychiatric practice. *Psychopharmacologia*, 1966, 9, 288–306.

Riecken, H. W., & Boruch, R. F. *Social experimentation. A method for planning and evaluating social intervention.* New York: Academic Press, 1974.

Rosenbaum, A., O'Leary, K. D., & Jacob, R. G. Behavioral intervention with hyperactive children: Group consequences as a supplement to individual contingencies. *Behavior Therapy,* 1975, *6,* 315–323.

Rush, A. J., Beck, A. T., Kovacs, M., & Hollon, S. D. Comparative efficacy of cognitive therapy and pharmacotherapy in the treatment of depressed outpatients. *Cognitive Therapy and Research,* 1977, *1,* 17–37.

Schmickley, V. G. The effects of cognitive-behavior modification upon depressed outpatients. Unpublished doctoral dissertation, Michigan State University, 1976.

Shader, R. I., Grinspoon, L., Ewalt, J. R., & Zahn, D. A. Drug responses in schizophrenia. In D. V. S. Sankar (Ed.) *Schizophrenia: Current concepts and research.* Hicksville, N. Y.: PJD Publications, 1969.

Shaw, B. F. A comparison of cognitive therapy and behavior therapy in the treatment of depression. *Journal of Consulting and Clinical Psychology,* 1977, *45,* 543–551.

Shipley, C. R., & Fazio, A. F. Pilot study of a treatment for psychological depression. *Journal of Abnormal Psychology,* 1973, *82,* 372–376.

Solyon, L., Heseltine, G. F. D., McClure, D. J., & Solyon, C., Ledridge, B., & Steinberg, G. Behavior therapy versus drug therapy in the treatment of phobic neurosis. *Canadian Psychiatric Association Journal,* 1973, *18,* 25–31.

Spitzer, R. L., Endicott, J., & Robins, E. Research diagnostic criteria (RDC) for a selected group of functional disorders. Unpublished manuscript, Biometrics Research, New York State Psychiatric Instiute, 1975.

Sprague, R. L., Christensen, D. E., & Werry, J. S. Experimental psychology and stimulant drugs. In C. K. Conners (Ed.) *Clinical use of stimulant drugs in children.* The Hague: Exerpta Medica, 1974.

Taylor, F. G., & Marshall, W. L. A cognitive-behavioral therapy for depression. *Cognitive Therapy and Research,* 1977, *1,* 59–72.

Tobias, L. L., & MacDonald, M. L. Withdrawal of maintenance drugs with long-term hospitalized patients: A critical review. *Psychological Bulletin,* 1974, *81,* 107–125.

Tyrer, P. J., Candy, J., & Kelly, D. H. W. Phenelzine in phobic anxiety: A controlled trial. *Psychological Medicine,* 1973, *3,* 120–124.

Uhlenhuth, E. H., Lipman, R. S., & Covi, L. Combined pharmacotherapy and psychotherapy: Controlled studies. *Journal of Nervous and Mental Disease,* 1969, *148,* 52–64.

Weissman, M. Personal Communication, 1976.

Weissman, M., Klerman, G. L., Paykel, E. S., Prusoff, B., & Hanson, B. Treatment effects on the social adjustment of depressed patients. *Archives of General Psychiatry,* 1974, *30,* 771–778.

Williams, H. V., Lipman, R. S. Rickels, K., Covi, L., Uhlenhuth, E. H., & Mattsson, N. B. Replication of symptom distress factors in anxious neurotic outpatients. *Multivariate Behavior Research,* 1968, *3,* 199–212.

Winokur, G. The types of affective disorders. *Journal of Nervous and Mental Disorders,* 1973, *156,* 82–96.

Wolpe, J. *Psychotherapy by reciprocal inhibition.* Stanford, Calif: Stanford University Press, 1958.

Wolpe, J., & Lang, P. J. A fear survey schedule for use in behavior therapy. *Behavior Research and Therapy,* 1964, *2,* 27–30.

Woodruff, R. A., Goodwin, D. W., & Guze, S. B. *Psychiatric diagnosis.* New York: Oxford Universities Press, 1974.

Yorkston, N., Sergeant, H., & Rachman, S. Methohexitone relaxation for desensitizing agoraphobic patients. *Lancet,* 1968, *2,* 651–653.

Zitrin, C. M., Klein, D. F., Lindemann, C., Tobak, P. Rock, M., Kaplan, J. H., & Ganz, V. H. Comparisons of short-term treatment regimens in phobic patients. In R. L. Spitzer and D. F. Klein (Eds.) *Evaluation of psychological therapies.* Baltimore: Johns Hopkins University Press, 1976.

PART III

ANALYSES OF DEVELOPMENTS IN THE BEHAVIOR THERAPIES

13

BEHAVIORAL PSYCHOTHERAPY OF ADULT NEUROSIS

ISAAC MARKS

University of London

INTRODUCTION

A mere 10 years ago it was customary for behavioral psychotherapists to draw their main theoretical inspiration from laboratory experiments on animals and human volunteers. Useful as these are, the spate of controlled work in patients is producing a clinical discipline that stands in its own right. It is evolving its own models of more immediate relevance to patients than are analogue experiments in human volunteers or in animals. The dialectic will continue between clinical and more basic fields, each cross-fertilizing the other, but sophisticated clinicians of the future will need to be increasingly steeped in the literature of clinical experiments, which will be the final arbiter of clinical practice with neurosis. For this reason this chapter will concentrate on work done in patients. The vast literature concerning analogue experiments in volunteers will only be touched on briefly. Much of it has already been reviewed in detail elsewhere (e.g., Kazdin & Wilcoxon, 1976; Marks, 1975 & 1978) and is of questionable relevance to severe clinical problems (Rosen, 1975).

Limitations of Analogue Studies
Analogue studies involve volunteers, usually students, who happen to have a problem for which they would not normally seek professional aid. In the past the problem was usually mild fear, say, of snakes, although recent experiments have also concerned mild social and sexual difficulties. The intensity of the problem in these studies varies widely. Some select only those few who are most handicapped out of a large screened population, while others take almost all comers, most of whom have trivial or no difficulties. Students represent but a small section of the general population; that is, intelligent, middle-class, generally white students. Except where seriously disabled subjects are studied, only limited clinical conclusions can be drawn from such a sample.

Differences Between Volunteer and Voluntary Clinic Populations
As an example, volunteers who are not sufficiently distressed by a fear to seek treatment until sought out by a keen experimenter differ in important respects from voluntary psychiatric patients with se-

vere phobias or obsessions (Marks, 1976, p. 75) although specific phobic patients often resemble volunteers with fears, those with complex agoraphobic and obsessive-compulsive syndromes differ markedly. Not only are their phobias likely to be more intense and extensive, but commonly associated problems like free floating anxiety and disruptive social relationships confound treatment programs. In some patients their presenting psychopathology is the least of their difficulties. A phobia or obsession can simply be a respectable admission ticket for treatment of some other problem like frigidity, loneliness, or depression. Specific phobics may present for treatment because they happen to be depressed at that particular time and not because of their long-standing phobia. Similarly, homosexual men who seek help in changing their orientation tend to have other neurotic problems and in that respect resemble other neurotics more than nonclinical homosexuals (Feldman, 1973).

The difference between clinic and other populations is emphasized by the findings of Lieberman and Gardner (1976). They gave questionnaires to large samples of prospective clients at psychiatric clinics, growth centers, and a National Training Laboratory, and compared scores among these populations and with a normative sample obtained from Uhlenhueth. The questionnaires concerned (1) life stress, based on the scale of Holmes and Rahe (2) neurotic symptoms, based on the Hopkins symptom checklist, and (3) intensity of motivation for help to deal with life problems, solve personal hangups or get relief from troublesome feelings. The results were unequivocal (Table 13-1). Clinic patients were significantly more disturbed than the other populations, having more life stress and neurotic symptoms, and more intense need for help. These disturbances complicate treatment programs much more for clinical populations than for analogue volunteers, so results from the latter cannot be assumed to apply to the former.

There are, of course, good reasons why controlled studies have been carried out so much more often with volunteers than in patients. Obviously, it is easier to study a captive volunteer student population with clearcut isolated difficulties than it is to mount controlled treatment trials of psychiatric pa-

tients who have complicated problems. Furthermore, volunteer studies are usually completed in a much shorter time, especially if adequate follow-up is omitted as is, sadly, the usual case. Historically, many psychology training centers developed divorced from psychiatric clinics, making it difficult for psychologists to have access to severely disturbed populations.

Progress in treating severe pathology would accelerate if more workers dealt with the sobering realities of clinical settings. Badly needed are more investigations on populations of disturbed patients selected for homogeneity of problem, using closely defined techniques with follow-up of at least three to six months to ensure that the outcome effects being discussed are stable. Such studies are naturally expensive in time, effort, and money but their results are more useful for clinicians who are the ultimate consumers of such research. Fortunately, the false dichotomy of being *either* a researcher *or* a clinician is breaking down, and more examples are appearing of that hybrid breed, the research-clinician. From these a body of knowledge is accumulating about patient populations which has direct clinical significance, whereas volunteer experiments are more relevant to normal psychology. In a real sense analogue and clinical experiments belong to different universes of discourse which only come together at a few points. Even at these points, analogue studies often have weaknesses in their design that reduce the strength of their implications.

Design Problems

These make the results of many analogue studies difficult to interpret.

Outcome measures.   A recurrent weakness in fear experiments is a failure to measure sufficient aspects of fear behavior, with a slavish reliance on behavioral avoidance tests at one or two points in time. Such tests in an experimental situation are often but a poor guide to performance in the more natural situations which are the key focus of interest for clinicians. Even crippled patients not uncommonly succeed in touching the feared stimulus in an experimental test, even though afterwards they continue to avoid as much as usual in a

TABLE 13.1 Differences among Four Populations According to Agency from which They Seek Help.[A]

	(n)	Variables		
		Life Stress (high score = high stress)	Neurotic Symptoms (high score = many symptoms)	Motivation for Help (lowest score wants least help)
Normative		5.6	9.8	—
National training laboratory	(128)	7.6	19.0	2.30
Growth center	(656)	9.4	23.3	2.07
Psychiatric clinic	(150)	12.4	36.8	1.29

[A] On every variable differences between each population are significant ($p < .01$) based on data from Lieberman and Gardner, 1976.

natural situation (Hand, Lamontagne, & Marks, 1974.

Follow-up. Another defect in many analogue studies is the absence of reasonable followup. Ephemeral effects are of little interest to clinicians whose interest is in stable change. In volunteer studies often but a few minutes or at most weeks elapse before testing, whereas reasonable stability of changes can be judged only after a minimum followup of six months, at which time measures are needed of several modalities of behavior. The importance of follow-up is emphasized by findings that schizophrenics lost their gains during 16 months followup after social skills training (Falloon Lindley, McDonald, & Marks, 1978), while transsexuals uniformly relapsed by two years after electric aversion (Marks, Gelder, & Bancroft, 1970).

Control groups. A common misconception in analogue studies concerns the role of control groups. The term control simply implies a contrasting condition without the treatment variable under consideration. It does not necessarily mean an untreated or placebo group. What constitutes an adequate control group for one question is inappropriate for another. If the problem under examination is the role of relaxation, only two groups need to be contrasted, one with and one without relaxation. If the point at issue is the duration of

exposure, then a minimum of two groups of varying durations are required. Untreated control groups are useful for answering questions about the role of therapeutic set, while placebo control groups help understanding of the part played by such factors as therapist's attention and therapeutic commitment by the client. Wait-list controls are given the expectancy of not improving if they are promised treatment at the end of the wait-list period, unless they are specifically told that their problem might well clear up without treatment, especially if they try to devise their own solutions to their problems. In an experiment on duration of exposure it would be meaningful to sacrifice a no treatment control group for an extra group with a different duration of exposure, thus enabling more to be learned about that key variable, rather than about a factor that is peripheral for us in that particular experiment.

Limitations of any design. Perhaps the hardest lesson for a research student to learn is that each experimental design can only answer very few questions, and selection of a particular design automatically precludes answering most other issues. Progress is necessarily slow with our current logic of experimentation, and no revolution in this state of affairs is in sight. The more the number of contrasting conditions that there are in an experiment, each designed to answer a specific question about a therapeutic ingredient, the more detailed the conclusions that might be possible from the study concerned. However, this makes the research more cumbersome and difficult to finish. The number of contrasted conditions possible is severely limited by practical considerations.

Lack of phenomenological perspective. A final shortcoming in much analogue work is failure to appreciate the usual features of the clinical problems being simulated. Without this knowledge little perspective is possible on the value of treatment interventions. At this point it is therefore necessary to define the clinical focus of this chapter, which concerns adult neurosis.

Definition of Neurosis

The term neurosis dates back to William Cullen, former professor of medicine in Edinburgh, who coined the term in 1769 to denote "a general affection of the nervous system" (Knopff, 1971). Neuroses were one of his four main subdivisions of diseases, the other three categories being pyrexia, cachexia, motions and sensations of the nervous system. It included today's neurological, psychosomatic, neurotic and psychotic disorders.

Toward the end of the nineteenth century, "neurosis" came to describe psychiatric disorders that are not organic, psychotic, or psychopathic in nature. This broad meaning of neurosis is still commonly employed today and denotes any repetitive maladaptive behavior, especially in the interpersonal context, characterized by conflict and pain; it is the basis for the definition of neurosis in the World Health Organization's International Glossary. A narrower definition of neurosis indicates well-defined specific neurotic syndromes. It was introduced by Freud as the triad of hysteria, obsessive-compulsive neurosis, and anxiety neurosis (Freud, 1892, 1894, and 1895). Anxiety neurosis was further subdivided when the phobic disorders were split from them (Marks, 1969). This narrower meaning now also includes problems such as certain forms of depression, occupational cramps, and sometimes sexual neuroses associated with anxiety, such as frigidity (anorgasmia and vaginismus) and impotence of various kinds.

In its broad sense neurosis includes mild trans-ient depression and anxiety often labeled "affective disorders." These constitute perennial features of the human condition and form the bulk of all psychiatric consultations in general practice (Shepherd, Cooper, Kalton & Brown, 1966). The natural course of this vast bulk of distress is not clear, although many of these may be short-lived (Goldberg & Blackwell, 1970), possibly with a tendency to relapse into further transient episodes. Neurosis in this sense is common in developing as well as in industrialized countries (summarized by Marks, 1973). These mild neuroses can respond to minimum counseling, whether given by a general practitioner (Johnstone & Goldberg, 1976) or a social worker (Cooper, Harwin, Depla, & Shepherd, 1975). There is no evidence as yet that behavioral psychotherapy is particularly useful for such conditions.

In contrast, behavioral psychotherapy has a vital part to play in the management of selected neurosis in its narrower sense. Well-defined neurotic syndromes are much less common than mild affective disorders, though their incidence in the general population is largely unknown. Severely disabling phobias are only present in 2.2 percent of the normal population (Agras Chapin, & Oliveau, 1972). The prevalence of other neurotic syndromes in the community remains to be determined, although Cooper (1972) noted in London general practices that specific neurotic problems, such as phobias, obsessions, and hypochondriasis, were found in only 2.8 percent of patients consulting a general practitioner with a psychiatric problem, the latter constituting 47 percent of all G.P. consultations.

An Operational Framework for Therapeutic Influences

Behavioral treatments of adult neurotics can be seen to occur within a dual process framework (Marks, 1976) (Figure 13-1). First the patient needs to be *motivated* to seek and complete treatment. Many influences will affect this process, including the patient's own commitment to change, social pressure on the patient to improve, that vague element called suggestion, and the credibility of the therapist. Of 300 patients in the author's unit who were offered behavioral treatment in 1971–1974,

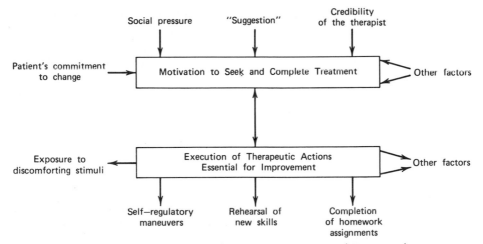

Figure 13-1 Therapeutic Influences: An Operational Framework.

23 percent refused it, a refusal rate which compares well with that of many other treatments.[1] In such cases treatment fails at the motivational stage—the patient fails to swallow the psychological pill so to speak. However, most behavioral treatments are, in fact, acceptable to adult neurotic patients.

The second process involves the patient's *execution* of therapeutic actions essential for improvement, for example, a few hours exposure to a phobic stimulus, or a complex interaction with other people in a social training program. When execution of these actions is satisfactory, the failure rate is very low in phobic and obessive-compulsive patients.

This framework helps us make sense of much psychotherapeutic data that would otherwise be puzzling. Motivation increases the likelihood of treatment adherence, which is a pervasive problem in all forms of treatment (Blackwell, 1976) . That triad of genuineness, empathy, and warmth (cf. chapter by Parloff et al.) which is said to have

a significant if slight effect in facilitating psychotherapy could be seen to act as a motivating or energizing variable. The same might apply to so-called operant variables like praise for progress.

The motivational domain also accommodates Bandura's (1977) suggestion that "psychological procedures, whatever their form, alter the level and strength of self efficacy . . . expectations of personal efficacy determine whether coping behavior will be initiated, how much effort will be expanded, and how long it will be sustained in the face of obstacles and aversive experiences." Self-regulatory approaches of all kinds depend on the patient wanting to carry them out with the appropriate diligence and detail.

In contrast, a patient's dealing with a phobia by exposure to the feared stimulus would be part of the executive aspect of the therapeutic process. Other examples of executive actions include a patient's behavior rehearsal of a new skill which has just been modeled for him or her, or the use of covert sensitizing imagery to dispel temptation to engage in behavior he or she wishes to discard.

Both motivating and executing factors are crucial. An effective treatment is of little use if patients cannot be motivated to carry it out. However, there is no point in a highly motivated patient religiously carrying out inert procedures; for example, obsessive-compulsives who diligently carry out re-

[1]For example, of 384 patients referred for psychotherapy, 35 percent failed to accept it (Rosenthal & Frank, 1958); of 768 patients offered outpatient treatment in a mental hygiene clinic 27 percent refused it (Garfield & Kurz, 1952), while 23 percent failed to keep their first appointment in a psychiatric outpatient clinic (Yamamoto & Goin, 1966).

laxation exercises do not lose their rituals as a result (Marks, Hodgson, & Rachman, 1975; Roper, Rachman & Marks, 1975).

The dual process framework also makes sense of the fact that patients with good previous personality and social adjustment do better with a wide variety of treatments (Garfield, 1971; Luborsky, Chandler, Auerbach, Cohen, & Bachrach, 1971).[2] This issue is not about initial level of criterion (target problem) dysfunction, but concerns level of *social* disability. This point was recognised long ago in the biblical adage "to him that hath it shall be given even more." Such patients have "more going for them" and more assets to capitalize on in the first place. In other words, they are better executives. However, they may also be better motivated to seek and complete treatment, and have a more supportive social network to help them do so. Their relatives are probably more likely to act as cotherapists when needed and less likely to obstruct treatment. This is a general aspect of treatment adherence. Patients are more likely to take prescribed medication when a helpful partner is available to monitor their program (Blackwell, 1976).

PHOBIC AND OBSESSIVE-COMPULSIVE DISORDERS

The Therapeutic Principle of Exposure to the Evoking Stimulus

The principle of exposure involves relief from phobias and compulsions by the individual's continued contact with those situations that *evoke* discomfort (the evoking stimuli, ES) until it subsides (Marks, 1977).

Most behavioral approaches to the treatment of anxiety syndromes like phobic and obsessive-compulsive disorders employ the common principle of *exposure* to the ES. What at first sight seem to be widely different forms of fear reduction—for example, desensitization in fantasy, flooding *in vivo*, cognitive rehearsal, modeling, and operant condition—all appear to be ways of exposing the patient to the frightening situation until he or she

[2]For a more extended and different view of this matter, see Chapter 6.

gets used to it. This process could also be called adaptation, extinction, or habituation.

A guide to the numerous variants of exposure appears in Marks (1975, 1977). Desensitisation contains within it the principle of exposure. The method involves repeated brief approach to the phobic situation in fantasy or in vivo, with a 'counteracting' response such as relaxation during and between approaches (Wolpe, 1958). *Flooding* involves rapid prolonged approach into the phobic situation in fantasy or *in vivo* (Marks, 1972). *Operant shaping* or conditioning of fear reactions describes systematic reward of the subject's steady approach toward the frightening situation; it is obvious that during operant treatment the therapist does not shape the fear away from the phobic object but toward it (Crowe Marks, Agras, & Leitenberg, 1972). The same applies to *modeling* in fear reduction. Here the therapist approaches the ES in front of the patient, and then encourages the patient to do the same (Bandura, 1971). In symbolic modeling the patient sees approach to the feared situation in a film.

Procedures such as *cognitive rehearsal* (Hart, 1966) and *self-regulation* (Meichenbaum, 1978) usually involve the subject picturing the discomforting situation and then devising some means of dealing with the resultant anxiety. *Paradoxical intention* (Frankl, 1975) is like exposure in vivo in that subjects are asked to expose themselves to precisely those situations they fear, for example, someone afraid of fainting is asked to deliberately try to faint. With *aversion relief,* shocks are associated with the termination of brief periods of exposure to phobic objects or fantasies (Solyom, Heseltine, McClure, Ledwidge, & Kenny, 1971).

Response prevention may be yet another example of treatment that finally works through exposure; for example, a compulsive washer may be asked to "contaminate" himself with the dirt that usually evokes his washing, but then to refrain from washing, thus maintaining his exposure to the ES of the discomfort he experiences with dirt (Marks et al., 1975).

Relief by exposure to the stressful situation is important not only for phobias and obsessions, but also for social deficits and sexual problems, although here it is bound up with training in interpersonal and other skills. In social skills training and in sexual retraining programs, of which Masters and Johnson pioneered one form, patients are required to rehearse appropriate behavior repeatedly in their problem situation until they lose their discomfort and acquire the requisite fluency of performance. The exposure principle does not explain why improvement occurs under therapeutic conditions but indicates *the strategy which the psychotherapist needs to follow. Clinicians need to search for the ES—those cues that trigger phobias and rituals—and to persuade the patient to come into contact with these cues until he or she is comfortable in their presence.* The noxious stimulus may be a troublesome fantasy, a feeling of insecurity, a shopping expedition, or sexual contact.

Once situations repeatedly produce discomfort, as in phobias and obsessions, then sufferers usually lose this discomfort by agreeing to remain exposed to those situations until they feel better about them. Exposure is a similar concept to extinction. "Extinction" simply means that the response ceases to occur, without explaining why. Similarly the concept of exposure simply holds that given enough contact with the provoking situation, the phobic or obsessive person ceases to respond with avoidance, distress or rituals. Unlike extinction, exposure assumes merely that the discomfort has been acquired, not necessarily conditioned.

A crucial theoretic question is why in general exposure treatments produce habituation of patients to the ES, the noxious stimuli that evoke discomfort, rather than sensitize them to those cues. Sensitization in therapy is rare, though it occurred in about 3 percent of a series of the author's cases, despite their fulfilment of criteria for predicted success, i.e. adequate motivation, absence of serious depression, no attempts to escape in fantasy or reality during exposure, and adequate duration of the treatment.

Unfortunately, we do not know what causes such sensitization, a reaction that has important theoretical implications. The problem is why these few fail to improve at all, and not a problem of relapse, which is a different but a less serious issue. Why should exposure to trauma sometimes produce phobias and at other times cure them? Which sets of conditions predict a traumatic or curative

outcome must still be delineated. This is a central issue in learning theory which remains to be resolved. It is relevant not only to treatment, but also to the etiology of psychopathology. Illumination of the relevant conditions would better explain how stimuli come to be perceived as noxious in the first place, why one man's meat is another man's poison.

There are two other shortcomings of the exposure model of fear-reduction. First, some phobic, obsessive-compulsive, and other forms of anxiety improve with antidepressant drugs in the absence of exposure (Tyres, Candy, & Kelly, 1973). Second, without any exposure to the specific phobic stimulus, anxiety sometimes remits after the abreaction of intense emotion, for example, fear that is irrelevant to the phobic stimulus (Watson & Marks, 1971), anger (Marks, 1965), or other feelings.

A tempting explanation for the value of irrelevant fear might be that it teaches the patient a form of coping. This is a widening of the exposure hypothesis. It states that the patient benefits from exposure to relevant fear as he or she would to unpleasant emotions in general. This concept is related to that of stress immunization and training in coping procedures. It raises the possibility of preventing disorders by appropriate procedures in childhood and later periods. The idea was not new in ancient Sparta and amounts to the teaching of stoicism. This form of coping can increase the tolerance of ischaemic pain in the forearm induced by a pressure cuff on the arm (Meichenbaum, 1978), or prolong the time students can keep a hand immersed in iced water (Wooley, Epps, & Blackwell, 1975). The question is to what extent stress immunization can be generalized, when it should be applied, in what way, for how long, and at what ages. The conditions leading to adaptive behavior involve many processes that are still unknown. Those that have been explored are now reviewed.

Arousal Level During Exposure
Low Arousal. Wolpe suggested that relaxation and other procedures are necessary to "reciprocally inhibit" the patient's anxiety during contact with the phobic stimulus in order that improvement

can follow. This idea triggered a great deal of investigation on relaxation. These concern several questions:

1. Does muscle relaxation reduce anxiety at rest? Marks (1975) reviewed evidence that although differential instructions can influence levels of background activity, this effect is uncertain, and the value of prolonging muscular relaxation training beyond a few brief instructions is unconvincing.

2. Does relaxation decrease initial or repeated responses to neutral and to stressful situations? This too is still unproved (Marks, 1975). Evidence so far confirms Mathews' (1971) conclusion that "no direct evidence has been found for one of the central postulates of reciprocal inhibition theory that relaxation reduces or prevents autonomic anxiety responses associated with phobic imagery."

3. Does relaxation affect outcome by the end of treatment and follow-up? This is the crucial clinical question. Of 20 controlled studies on the subject which the author has encountered from 1969 onward, 17 found no lasting value in trained muscular relaxation being added to exposure to the phobic stimulus, whether in fantasy, *in vivo,* or in the course of counseling techniques (Marks, 1975, p. 88, and Sue, 1975). Most of these studies were in volunteers. Neither of those done in patients supported the value of relaxation (Benjamin, Marks, & Huson, 1972; Gillan & Rachman, 1974).

Two studies employed psychophysiological measures to see whether relaxation had occurred. In an analogue report about rat fearful students during rat slide presentation (Waters, McDonald, & Koresco, 1972) desensitization subjects showed less skin conductance, though not heart rate activity, than the nonrelaxation controls, yet both groups improved similarly in avoidance, GSR and heart rate. Low arousal during treatment was thus not associated with better outcome.

The second controlled experiment to employ a

psychophysiological measure of relaxation comes from Benjamin et al. (1972) with eight chronic phobic patients. These patients imagined phobic images up a hierarchy while they were either relaxed or in a neutral affective state. The hypothesis of reciprocal inhibition predicts that relaxed subjects will feel less anxiety to phobic images during treatment and have a superior outcome in reduction of fear.

Experimental manipulation was successful in producing two significantly differentiable conditions. During treatment sessions relaxed patients had significantly less skin conductance activity between phobic images than did patients who had not been relaxed, that is, they were less aroused. However, in conflict with prediction from a reciprocal inhibition model, decreased arousal between images during treatment did not correlate with decreased anxiety during phobic imagery, either during or after treatment. Relaxation did not increase the speed with which patients lost their fears during sessions, nor did it increase improvement by the end of treatment. During sessions subjective anxiety and heart rate diminished at the same rate whether the phobic images were visualized during a state of relaxation (desensitization) or neutral affect (exposure). After the end of each treatment condition the reduction in phobias was similar.

This result was replicated by Gillan and Rachman (1974) who found comparable outcomes in phobic patients after treatment by desensitization in fantasy with (group SD) and without (group H) accompanying training in muscular relaxation (left half of Figure 13-2, contrast SD—desensitization and group H—hierarchies). Training in muscular relaxation can thus be omitted without affecting results adversely.

4. As regards relaxation without exposure, several controlled studies in obsessive-compulsive patients have found this to have no significant effect on outcome of rituals, although exposure *in vivo* with response prevention but no relaxation did reduce rituals significantly/(see Fig. 5 later, based on Marks et al., 1975). In children who were afraid of dentists, relaxation without exposure had no therapeutic effect, whereas im-

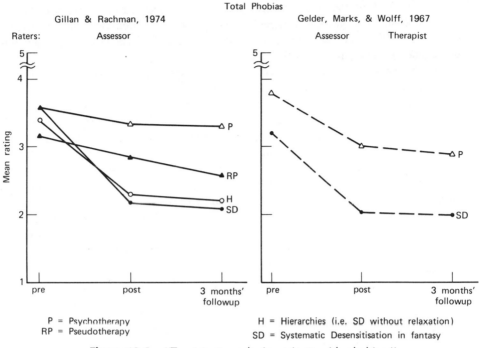

Figure 13-2 "Treatment results in patients with phobias."

aginal exposure led to some improvement (Rezin and Mathews, 1976). One controlled analogue study did find relaxation without exposure to reduce anxiety as much as systematic desensitization. This is the 'cue controlled relaxation' of test anxious students reported by Russell, Miller, and June (1975) but follow-up was only one week after the final session, so no data is available about durable effects. Furthermore, Marchetti, McGlynn, and Patterson, (1977) found no therapeutic benefit from cue-controlled relaxation in test anxious students.

The overwhelming controlled evidence is that to achieve lasting reduction in fears or rituals systematic training in muscular relaxation is redundant and timewasting. Therapeutic time is better spent on straightforward exposure to the stimuli that evoke discomfort or rituals, using any strategy to help the subject remain in their presence and manage the resultant feelings. More needs to be known about the effects on fear reduction of simple instructional sets (as opposed to systematic training) to relax or

tense up during exposure, and of autogenic training and meditation. As most phobic and obsessive-compulsive patients obtain durable improvement in 3 to 20 sessions of exposure treatment, such adjuvants would be clinically useful only if they produced tangible extra improvement without prolonging treatment time.

High arousal. A view opposite to that of reciprocal inhibition is Stampfl's notion of implosion (1967). This holds that for improvement to occur, anxiety must be maximally aroused during exposure until the patient is so exhausted that he cannot experience any more emotion. The evidence for this concept is based on uncontrolled clinical evidence (reviewed by Marks, 1972) and can be paraphrased from Stampfl's comment about one obsessive-compulsive handwasher: "He who has lived in a cesspool for a few days (in his mind) will not worry later about a bit of dirt on his hands."

The question is whether the deliberate evocation of anxiety adds to the therapeutic effect of exposure. In several studies outcome has not correlated with anxiety level during treatment sessions

(Johnstone et al., 1976; Mathews, 1976; Marks, Boulougouris, & Marset, 1971; Watson & Marks, 1971; Stern & Marks, 1973). A more direct test of this point was made by Hafner and Marks (1976). Chronic agoraphobic patients were exposed continuously for three hours a day over four days to their real phobic situations; for example, they were asked to shop in crowded supermarkets or ride in subway trains until they felt better about being in these situations. In a high anxiety condition the therapist commented on how bad the patients looked and mentioned all the catastrophes that might befall them in these situations. In a low-anxiety condition the therapist was reassuring, although he or she could not eliminate all anxiety. The experimental manipulation produced two significantly differentiable treatment conditions, with patients experiencing significantly more discomfort during exposure in the high anxiety conditions. However, this produced no difference in outcome on any measure. Up to six months follow-up low-anxiety patients improved at the same speed and to the same extent as high-anxiety patients. Thus anxiety did not facilitate improvement during exposure.

Further evidence that high arousal is not especially helpful comes from a second controlled experiment by Hafner and Marks (1976). In a double-blind study chronic agoraphobics were exposed in groups to their real phobic situations. Patients receiving diazepam reported less discomfort during exposure than did patients receiving placebo, yet they improved at the same rate as placebo patients, all maintaining their improvement to 6 months follow-up.

Evidence that arousal level does not affect outcome during fantasy (as opposed to in vivo) exposure comes from the study reported by Gelder, Bancroft, Gath, Johnston and Mathews, (1973) and Mathews, Johnston, Shaw, and Gelder (1974). Here 36 mixed agoraphobic and other chronic phobic patients were assigned randomly to one of three weekly treatments as outpatients, each lasting 15 sessions, the first three of which were history taking, the next eight fantasy treatment, and the last four in vivo treatment. The three treatment conditions were mainly differentiated on the basis of the eight fantasy sessions: (1) "Nonspecific con-

trol" patients were asked to use their phobic imagery as a basis for free-associative psychotherapy; (2) desensitization in fantasy subjects had muscular relaxation with hierarchy images; (3) flooding in fantasy used relevant cues without dynamic content.

Figure 13-3 shows that the two fantasy-exposure conditions, whether in low arousal as in desensitization, or high arousal as in flooding, improved equally, and significantly more than did the control condition. Some of this improvement occurred only during the final in vivo phase (compare Figures 13-3 a and b). Arousal level was thus not especially important. The study also illustrates that the superior improvement of the desensitization and flooding conditions is not due to "nonspecific support" as the control group that also had these improved significantly less.

It is thus clear that phobias and obsessions improve with exposure treatment, but it is not crucial whether patients are relaxed, neutral, or anxious during such exposure. It is possible that the anxiety level at the end of the session is important; for example, it might be more useful to end on a "good note" than while the patient is still anxious, but this is a difficult point to test experimentally without confusing the variable of duration of exposure. Nevertheless it is of such practical importance that experiments should be done to obtain evidence to guide clinicians.

In vivo Versus Fantasy Exposure

Although many have compared fantasy with live exposure indirectly, conclusions are usually difficult because of confounding influences such as duration and gradient of exposure, or accompanying relaxation, praise, or modeling (Marks, 1975 and 1977). Two analogue studies have compared live with fantasy exposure without such confounding variables (LoPiccolo, 1969; Sherman, 1972). Both found exposure in vivo to be far more rapidly effective than exposure in fantasy. Further comparison of in vivo with fantasy exposure is possible in a third analogue study, this time of Bandura, Blanchard and Ritter, (1969). Although the authors interpreted their outcome as demonstrating the effect of modeling, in fact the study argues more powerfully for the role of in vivo exposure as the agent of

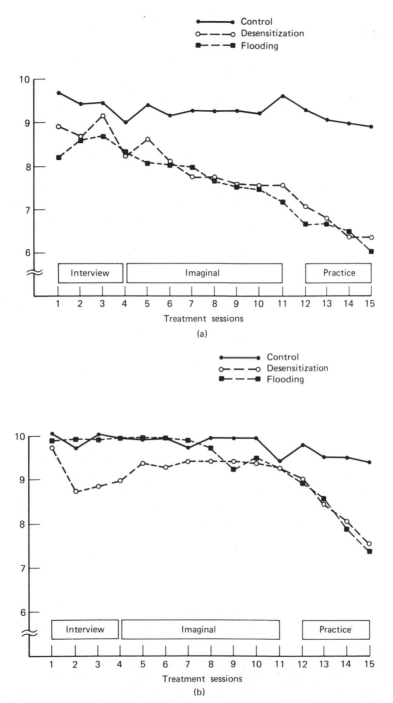

Figure 13-3 (a) Mean scores for anxiety "when thinking about" phobic situations for each treatment group. (b) Mean scores of anxiety estimated for phobic situations 'in real life' for each treatment group (Mathews et al., 1970).

change, since of the two groups that both had modeling, that which also had live exposure did much better, while a "symbolic modeling" condition did no better than desensitization in fantasy without modeling.

In patients, the value of prolonged live exposure was suggested by uncontrolled studies of Watson, Gaind, and Marks. 1971, and Gaind, Watson, and Marks, 1971, in ten patients with specific phobias who improved after two to three afternoons of treatment over an average of six hours each. In a subsequent study of agoraphobics (Stern & Marks, 1973) taped fantasy exposure had no effect when measured immediately posttreatment, although prolonged in vivo exposure had a significant effect when measured three days later. However, the differing times of outcome measure confounded effects and the crossover design employed precluded conclusions about long term effects over follow-up. Furthermore taped fantasy exposure might be less effective than that given by a live therapist. A final problem was that an invariant order of fantasy followed by in vivo exposure precluded the teasing out of any order effect.

The order effect was controlled in a replication study by Rabavilas, Boulougouris & Stefanis, (1976) in 12 compulsive ritualizers. These workers also employed a Latin square design to compare long and short exposure in fantasy and in vivo, but this time the order of fantasy versus in vivo exposure was balanced. In vivo exposure produced significantly more reduction of rituals than did fantasy exposure. However, again the crossover design did not allow comments about follow-up effects beyond three days after treatment.

A systematic comparison of exposure in vivo and in fantasy in agoraphobics was made by Emmelkamp and Wessels (1975). Patients had four 90-minute sessions, three times weekly of (1) exposure in vivo or (2) combined flooding in fantasy for 45 minutes followed immediately by exposure in vivo for 45 minutes. After the 4 sessions significantly more benefit occurred in the prolonged exposure in vivo condition. Next best was the combined fantasy and in vivo condition, and the least effective was the pure fantasy condition. Thereafter all patients had eight 90-minute sessions of graded self-exposure in vivo, with patients being accom-

panied by therapists in the first two of these sessions. After this additional in vivo practice, further significant improvement occurred to one-month follow-up.

Yet another comparison in agoraphobics was by Watson, Mullett, and Pillay (1973) who found that group exposure in vivo was significantly superior to taped group exposure in fantasy. Outcome was measured immediately after treatment and the crossover design precluded conclusions about long term effects.

Systematic comparison of imaginal with in vivo exposure was reported by Mathews, Whitehead, Hackmann, Julier, Bancroft, and Gath (1976) and Johnstone et al. (1976). They assigned 36 agoraphobic women randomly to three therapists for treatment in 16 weekly 90-minute sessions in one of three conditions: (1) exposure in vivo only or (2) 45 minutes imaginal followed by 45 minutes in vivo exposure or (3) eight sessions of imaginal exposure followed by eight sessions of in vivo exposure. Patients were instructed to practice agreed phobic items at home before the next treatment appointment and to record these in daily diary forms. These were discussed at the start of each treatment visit. Agoraphobic patients went out on an average once a day.

No significant difference was found between the imaginal and the in vivo exposure conditions on clinical scales, neither after 8 or 16 sessions, nor at one, three, or six months follow-up. As in the study by Emmelkamp and Wessels, preceding exposure in fantasy did not potentiate exposure in vivo immediately afterward.

The contradiction of results from this study and those of Emmelkamp and Wessels might be explained by one important difference between the two studies. Unlike Emmelkamp and Wessels, Mathews et al. gave strong instructions to patients to practice self-exposure between sessions and to record this in special diaries. This might have obscured differences resulting from the weekly sessions of therapist-assisted exposure. Treatment was also more frequent with Emmelkamp and Wessels—thrice rather than once weekly—which left less time between sessions for an effect to develop from uninstructed self-exposure. The discrepancy between the two studies raises the possibility that an important aspect of treatment is self-exposure, and that all therapist-assisted strategies such as desensitization or flooding in fantasy or prolonged exposure *in vivo* are simply ways of persuading the patient to expose himself or herself to the ES, the stimulus which evokes discomfort.

Apart from the study reported by Mathews et al. and Johnstone et al., evidence in volunteers and in patients suggests that *in vivo is more potent than fantasy exposure,* although the point remains to be clinched with appropriate controls for self-directed as opposed to therapist-aided exposure, and with follow-up of at least six months.

Duration of Exposure

A large literature suggests in animals and in volunteers (Marks, 1975 pp. 30–84, and 1977) that in general long exposure is more effective than short exposure in terms of duration of sessions. There are two controlled studies of this issue in neurotic patients. One is by Stern and Marks (1973) who found in a Latin square design that two hours of continuous exposure in vivo was significantly better than four interrupted half hours in one afternoon. In contrast, long fantasy exposure was not better than short fantasy exposure, but this was given by tape recorder rather than by a live therapist. Rabavilas et al. (1976) in obsessive-compulsive ritualizers also found that long was better than short *in vivo* exposure, in this case 80 minutes versus four separate periods of 20 minutes.

Duration of exposure is presumably important because it gives certain unidentified processes more time to work while exposure is going on. For example, it might give people time to develop self-regulatory strategies to control their own emotions or to reach critical levels of habituation that may be necessary for lasting change to occur. The latter is implied in the question "Is it best to end on a good note?" We have no answer as yet.

Modeling During Exposure

The act of modeling denotes observation of somebody else performing behavior that one is subsequently required to perform oneself. We can also imagine (? observe) ourselves performing behavior in fantasy. This is cognitive or role rehearsal, sometimes also termed "self-modeling," but to be meaningful 'modeling' should connote observation of

somebody else, not of oneself. What is modeled needs to be distinguished from the act of observation itself. The term "modeling" is often used as though it were synonymous with exposure. Distinction between these two concepts is easy to miss but has practical import, and so requires elaboration.

It is perfectly possible to model meaningful therapeutic procedures that contain no exposure to the ES, whether direct, vicarious, or symbolic. Examples of therapeutic procedures that can be modeled yet usually contain no significant component of exposure include relaxation, hypnosis, and analytic psychotherapy. Many therapists and patients regard these procedures as meaningful treatments, though little fear reduction occurs with any of them when focus on the ES is omitted (e.g., for patients see Gelder, Marks, & Wolff, 1967; Gillan & Rachman, 1974; Marks et al., 1975; Roper et al., 1975; for fearful volunteers see the analogue controls reviewed by Marks, 1975, pp. 80–82). Perhaps these procedures have therapeutic value for nonfearful problems, but that is not our present concern. Just as modeling procedures can omit exposure, so exposure approaches commonly omit modeling, that is, patients approach the ES in treatment without anybody first showing them how to do it. In fact patients often say "It's no use watching *you* doing it (touching the phobic object). I know you can do it, I want to learn to do it *myself.*" Exposure treatments without modeling usually lead to fear-reduction.

One meaningful treatment can omit both exposure and modeling, yet lead to fear reduction in some depressed phobics and obsessives. This is the administration of antidepressant drugs (see p. 469). If rigorous testing bears out such clinical anecdote, this will make it necessary to modify the exposure hypothesis of fear reduction, but need not detain us here.

From many experiments we can conclude that *interactional exposure without modeling produces fear reduction, but modeling without interactional exposure does not.* Interactional exposure implies approach to the ES in some form and is a critical variable; in contrast, modeling is at best a modifying variable in the management of phobias and obsessions. Modeling of required behavior has a major role in transmitting information for the acquisition of complex new skills and in motivating patients to do things they might otherwise not (see Chapter by Rosenthal and Bandura in this volume). However, the value of modeling per se, over and above exposure to the ES, has *not* been established for the reduction of fear in most patients, though some do say that watching the therapist approach the ES first makes it easier for them. This point is not trivial, as it affects clinical practice.[3]

For the reduction of phobias and obsessions, clinical practice is moving towards patients managing as much of their own treatment program as possible, that is, toward increasing self-exposure and decreasing therapist-assisted exposure. How far this process can go remains to be seen, but the more that treatment can be self-managed, the more economic it is likely to be, and the cost of treatment is an increasingly important consideration in the delivery of health care. What has this to do with modeling? In therapist-assisted exposure it is easy enough for the therapist to model approach to the ES. In contrast, it is often time-consuming or even impossible to arrange a model for patients carrying out self-exposure homework. The question is whether it is worth troubling to arrange a model, for example from the family. So far the answer is no. The evidence is that the value of observing a model approaching the ES is little greater than the value of a patient doing the same without seeing someone else do so first, whether directly, vicariously, or symbolically.

The value of pure modeling without exposure could only be inferred from one of two types of study, Type 1 where exposure to the ES is performed with and without modeling, but with otherwise similar durations and types of exposure, or Type 2 where the modeling is contrasted of exposure and nonexposure conditions. In anxiety-reduction studies, so-called "modeling" nearly always involves the client observing a model entering the fear situation, which constitutes vicarious exposure of the client to that situation, and this exposure is not usually adequately controlled in the nonmodeling groups. The influences of modeling and of exposure are thus confounded, as mentioned

earlier for Bandura et al. (1969) in a Type 1 study. In that study symbolic modeling had no greater effect than desensitization in fantasy without modeling.

Modeling and interactional exposure are also confounded in the Type 1 study by Bandura, Grusec, and Menlove, (1967). Dog phobic children either (1) saw a peer model approach a dog or (2) passively observed the dog without approach or a model. The children in the "modeling" condition had both modeling and vicarious exposure of approach to and interaction with a live dog; in contrast, children in the nonmodeling condition had neither, only passive exposure to a dog at a distance without attempts at approaching or interacting with it. The exposure was for three minutes per session in each of 8 sessions. In a "modeling" experiment by Lewis (1974) the subjects who did best had the longest periods of exposure to swimming.

In a further Type 1 study (Bandura, Adams, & Beyer, 1978) adult snake phobics either had (1) *in vivo* exposure with modeling, followed by *in vivo* exposure alone ("self-directed mastery"), or (2) vicarious exposure by watching a model, but without subsequent self-directed exposure, or (3) no treatment. The order of efficacy was that which would be predicted by the exposure hypothesis, that is, (1) was best and (2) next best. Bandura et al. found that self-rating of likelihood of executing behavioral tasks predicted subsequent performance, and suggested this meant improvement was a function of "expectations of self-efficacy." An alternative interpretation is that ratings of "self-efficacy" are largely a measure of fearful attitude, a dependent rather than an independent variable, which changes as a consequence of interactional exposure. This interpretation could be tested by repeating the experiment using measures of subjective fear and attitude, as well as expectations of self-efficacy.

Where the exposure variable has been controlled, modeling adds little. There are several Type 1 examples. Patients with compulsive rituals improved similarly whether exposure *in vivo* included or excluded modeling (Hodgson, Rachman & Marks, 1972; Marks et al., 1975). Nonassertive students improved significantly in social behavior

---

[3]For a different view of modeling see the chapter by Rosenthal & Bandura.

after behavior rehearsal without modeling, and adding videotape modeling did not enhance the outcome (McFall & Twentyman, 1973). Another Type 1 experiment on socially anxious students illustrates that the effect of live exposure and practice in the natural setting can override not only modeling but even role rehearsal and exposure in treatment settings (Royce & Arkowitz, 1977). Volunteer students who wished to feel more comfortable with friends were assigned at random to (1) 12 practice meetings, twice weekly, with a different same sex partner selected for them each week, (2) the same plus six 1½ hour sessions of social skills training, including modeling and role rehearsal of coping with discomforting friendship situations, tailored to individuals' needs, (3) a minimum treatment control, including six counseling sessions, but no practice, modeling or role rehearsal, (4) delayed treatment control, (5) no treatment control. Results showed that groups 1 and 2 which both had exposure-practice, did equally well, and significantly better than control groups up to three months follow-up, maintaining and generalizing this improvement to 15 month follow-up. Group 2, which had 9 hours of additional modeling, role rehearsal, and exposure in the treatment setting, did no better than group 1. Therapist time for group 1 was negligible, being limited to giving information on which person to meet for interaction on each of the six weeks. One caveat about this study is that the subjects were fairly socially skilled to begin with, and we do not know how a "pure homework" approach would suit more disturbed patients.

So far we have seen that fear reduction in "modeling" experiments can usually be attributed to the confounding presence of exposure, and that modeling contributes little beyond this. Type 2 experiments have been no more encouraging about the value of modeling when exposure is omitted, demonstrating that the mere act of observing a therapeutic model is not enough to improve phobias and obsessions. In a Type 2 experiment in obsessive-compulsive patients Roper et al. (1975) showed that modeling of relaxation after the therapist did not reduce rituals, whereas watching the therapist expose herself to contaminating situations had a significant effect; modeling with live participation (exposure) conferred the most

benefits of all, as is usual in experiments in this area (see Figure 13-6). That modeling without exposure is not helpful is emphasized in a further Type 2 study by Emmelkamp and Emmelkamp-Benner (1975); watching a filmed model discussing treatment in general, without exposure, was not therapeutic for agoraphobics.

Further experiments by Kazdin (1973; 1974a, b, and c; 1975) shed additional light on this issue. His subjects had snake fears or social inhibitions and were treated by fantasied scenes. Most of these experiments included a control scene, in which subjects imagined the phobic situation but without approaching or interacting with it, for example, the snake merely sticking its head up out of the cage, or the model was present in a social context where an assertive response was appropriate, but made no such response. In contrast, the "modeling" conditions depicted interaction of models with the relevant ES. "Modeling" conditions did better than the controls, who did not improve over the treatment time used of 30 minutes, which is less than in most successful studies of exposure in fantasy.

The results of Kazdin's work argue not for the effect of pure modeling but for that of varied *interactional* exposure rather than monotonous static exposure. By interactional exposure is meant exposure to varied facets of the ES while the patient is approaching it in some way. *Interaction with the ES need involve no modeling whatsoever.* Subjects can improve very well by *self*-exposure to the ES without watching anyone; for example, a dog phobic might herself approach a dog without anyone else nearby, or she can imagine herself doing so. In most experiments Kazdin's control subjects did not interact with the ES, whereas "modeling" groups visualized interaction. This suggests that the operative ingredient might be interaction with the phobic stimulus, with or without modeling. This idea is supported by further results from Kazdin (1974b). Subjects who imagined themselves coping with the snake without a model did as well as those who imagined a model doing the same, suggesting that what is important is less the model, or even exposure per se, than what is done with the phobic stimulus. This itself might explain why a coping model is better than a mastery model, as in this experiment. The explanation has little to do with the kind of modeling, but rather with the kind of exposure.

The point is lent extra weight from work by Thase and Moss (1976). They replicated the finding of Kazdin (1974) that volunteers who imagined themselves approaching a snake in fantasy reduced snake avoidance as much as those who imagined a model doing so. Furthermore, as with Bandura et al. (1969), modeling of *in vivo* exposure (guided participation) yielded the greatest improvement. In other words, when observation is kept constant, the variable that affects improvement is the presence and type of exposure. In contrast, when exposure is kept constant and modeling (observation of someone else) is varied, then outcome is not affected.

In other experiments of Kazdin (1975) in nonassertive volunteers, scenes of four models being assertive did better than one model until four months follow-up. It is obvious that four models produce a greater variety of interactional exposure experiences. Such variety is therapeutic, and can be obtained equally well without a model. Similarly, in a second experiment of Kazdin (1974c) on timid volunteers, a modeling condition was said to yield better results than a no-modeling one until three months follow-up. However, here modeling was confounded with role-rehearsal, which includes a form of interactional exposure. The appropriate control to see the effect of pure modeling would have been subjects imagining *themselves* rather than a model being assertive, along the lines of the experiment by Kazdin (1974b).

In brief, the important point is to unravel *which type of exposure has the most therapeutic effect,*[4] regardless of whether modeling is present or not. The value of pure modeling (i.e., observation of a therapist carrying out a supposedly therapeutic action) independent of exposure is not proven for fear reduction. In practice, however, little time is lost by the therapist demonstrating how to approach the ES, provided the patient himself does it in real life afterward. The role of pure modeling would be of practical importance if research eventually showed that self-exposure homework was as good as therapist-assisted exposure. In that case, self-exposure homework might become the most economic treatment, and modeling would be time-consuming to arrange unless done by the family; the latter would only be worthwhile if modeled interactional exposure was clearly better than interactional exposure alone. To provide guidelines for clinicians it is necessary to clear up this issue by further experiments.

In experiments in this area it is important always to specify in advance whether interactional rather than static exposure is occurring, to avoid circularity of reasoning. Theoretically the notion of interactional exposure is related to that of coping or dealing with the problem situation, an issue outside the scope of this section, but one in which circular reasoning can hamper progress.

Bandura (personal communication) remarked that though a group of individuals may improve as a whole with exposure, individuals vary in their outcome after the same amount of exposure. This is, of course, true, as it is for outcome to any treatment, be it modeling of exposure, medication, faithhealing, or whatever. The question is whether the variation is so wide as to make statements about group levels meaningless. This is not the case. As already noted similar exposure treatments lead repeatedly to predictable group levels of improvement, and muscular relaxation without exposure leads to predictable lack of group response. Inevitably there is some individual variation within groups, but our main concern is with the population as a whole.

Group Exposure in vivo

Prolonged exposure *in vivo* in groups can save time and possibly enhance potency through social cohesion. There have been four studies of such groups in agoraphobics. The first was by Hand et al. (1974) who treated 24 chronic agoraphobics in groups of 4 to 5 patients each in two balanced conditions with high and low social cohesion. Over one week each patient had three four-hour sessions of group exposure *in vivo*. There was one session per day lasting four continuous hours, interrupted midday for a half-hour lunch break. Outcome of all groups was at least as good as from

[4]This is similar to Bandura's comment (personal communication) that "the issue of interest is . . . how transactions with fearful stimuli effect changes in behavior."

previous trials with individual patients. Patients from cohesive and noncohesive groups improved similarly on phobic scales three days after treatment. Cohesive groups had fewer dropouts during treatment, and slightly increased their improvement between three and four months followup. Patients as a whole improved significantly in work, leisure, and social adjustment despite several exacerbations of preexisting marital and personality problems. Another value of group exposure was the social "spin-off" of an unplanned contribution of social skills and assertive training. This presumably resulted from the rehearsal of social behavior which occurred naturally during group treatment.

A second study also found that group exposure was effective in agoraphobics (Hafner & Marks, 1976). Fifty-seven chronic agoraphobic patients were assigned at random to group or individual exposure in vivo for comparable lengths of time. Group treatment was along the lines of Hand et al., but with moderate social cohesion. It included a total of 12 hours of exposure in vivo in groups of four to seven patients over four days in a two-week period. Three hours of exposure in vivo was given on each treatment day. Anxiety management instructions were like those given by Hand et al. Forty one patients completed group exposure in one of two diazepam conditions and also a placebo condition. Twelve patients completed individual exposure of similar duration, but in the presence of the therapist rather than a group.

Improvement from group exposure was comparable to that obtained by Hand et al; it was maintained to six months follow-up but did not increase during this time, thus resembling the outcome in Hand et al.'s noncohesive groups. There was a consistent trend for individually treated patients to improve slightly less than group-treated patients but this was only significant on nonphobic measures like general anxiety, leisure activities, and the number of visits to hospital requested by patients during follow-up.

Other workers also found significant improvement from group exposure in vivo of agoraphobics (Watson, Mullett, & Pillay, 1973). A fourth study to find group exposure of value for agoraphobics was by Teasdale, Walsh, Lancashire, and Mathews, (1977). They tried to replicate the high group cohesion condition of Hand et al. (1974), using comparable conditions of treatment and measurement. The amount of group cohesion turned out to be midway between the high and low cohesive groups of Hand et al. The immediate effects of treatment were similar to those found in the studies of Hand et al. and Hafner and Marks. As with patients from the Hafner and Marks' moderately cohesive groups, improvement was maintained at six months follow-up, but did not actually increase during that time.

Group versus Individual Exposure
Of the three studies just mentioned, the only one which contrasted group with individual exposure in vivo and included follow-up was that of Hafner and Marks (1976). In that study outcome was only slightly better after group than after individual exposure. Another comparison of group with individual exposure in vivo is that of Butollo and Mittelstaedt (1977). Their population consisted of specific phobias, not agoraphobics, and contained volunteers as well as patients. A further difference is that the clients within groups had different phobias from one another, while in the preceding studies groups were homogenous with respect to agoraphobia. These workers treated 30 outpatients in 11 sessions over four months. The groups (each $n = 5$ or 6) met monthly after the end of treatment and discussed progress. Individually treated subjects actually did slightly better than group-treated clients to the end of two months follow-up, but they had rather more in vivo exposure than group-treated subjects because group treatment included some nonexposure discussion.

In summary, the saving of therapist's time gives a clear advantage to group over individual exposure in vivo, even though the results are comparable. The five studies just cited of group exposure in vivo agree on the clinical usefulness of this approach. Whether high social cohesion actually enhances the process is a matter for further replication.

Home-Based Exposure
No systematic comparison has yet been made of treatment of agoraphobics at home rather than in clinics. An uncontrolled report on home based

treatment comes from Mathews, Teasdale, Munby, Johnston, and Shaw, (1977). They treated 12 married women living with husbands who agreed to cooperate as cotherapists in treatment. Patients and spouses were given a detailed manual emphasizing the selection of target behaviors and treatment, the importance of regular graded self-exposure during the use of tranquilizers, and the management of panic. The couple were visited at home by the therapist six times over four weeks and only in the first week was there therapist-assisted exposure. Other sessions were spent on the progress of the patient and spouse on the self-exposure homework program, which was recorded in a detailed diary kept by the patient. The patients improved to the same extent during this program as in previous studies at Oxford, but in less time than previously used by Oxford workers, though in comparable time to that spent by nurse-therapists treating agoraphobics in hospital-based Maudsley training programs (Marks, Hallam, Philpott, & Connolly, 1977). This uncontrolled study of Mathews et al. leaves unanswered the role of the spouse, of the instruction manual, and of practice in the home situation. Nevertheless, it raises the question whether self-exposure homework might not be an economic form of treatment for agoraphobics.

Most of the controlled studies of Emmelkamp and co-workers employed treatment which was home-based, though they did not examine this particular issue. (Emmelkamp & Ultee, 1974; Everaerd, Rijken, & Emmelkamp, 1973; Emmelkamp, 1974; Emmelkamp & Wessels, 1975). Patients improved in all these studies.

Biofeedback During Exposure in vivo
Little controlled work has appeared on this topic in patients. One phobic patient of the author's expressed the main issue in the course of true feedback of heart rate during exposure *in vivo*. When praised because her true heart rate slowed after prolonged exposure, she simply retorted, "Yes, I know my heart is beating more slowly, but that does not help me—it's what I feel up in my head that is important." The problem is whether true biofeedback can promote therapeutic advance.

Two experiments by Nunes and Marks (1975, 1976) examined this issue during rapid exposure *in vivo* of specific phobic patients. The first experiment in 10 patients found that pulse rates were significantly reduced over half-hour exposure periods containing visual feedback of pulse rate plus instructions to lower it, compared to half-hour controlled exposure periods without such feedback. However, enhanced decline in heart rate did not affect the rate of decline in subjective anxiety during the two-hour session of treatment.

The second study was a partial replication with three improvements: (1) Epochs of instructions to reduce heart rate without feedback were added (2) An hour's training with feedback was added before treatment. (3) The effect was measured on respiratory rate and skin conductance as well as on heartrate and subjective anxiety.

As in the first experiment, 10 specific phobic patients, all women, were treated by exposure *in vivo* during a mean of two sessions in a balanced design. Patients improved as expected, and short-term results replicated those of the first study that self-control of heart rate with the aid of biofeedback significantly reduced heart rate during treatment but this did not hasten reduction of subjective anxiety nor of respiratory rate or skin conductance responses. An hour's pretreatment training in self-control of heart rate with the aid of biofeedback did not enhance the effects. Mere instructions to lower heart rate without feedback did significantly lower the rate during treatment, but the addition of heart rate feedback to instructions further and significantly augmented the decline in heart rate.

These studies emphasize that barring a few exceptions that do not concern anxiety syndromes, biofeedback has so far been of more theoretical than clinical value. Both physiology and behavior can be easier to influence than subjective feelings.

Psychotropic Drugs During Exposure
Until recently the actions of drugs and of behavioral treatments have tended to be examined in isolation from one another. However, the possibility of interactional effects leads to the need for study of their value when used in combination as well as separately.

Oral drugs.   So far three classes of oral drug have been studied—so-called "antidepressants," sedatives, and beta-blockers. These labels may not be a guide to the way the drugs act in anxiety syndromes.

In phobias, antidepressants like tricyclics (imipramine), (Klein, 1964; Gittelman-Klein & Klein, 1971; Zitrin et al., 1976) and monoamine oxidase inhibitors (MAOIs), (e.g., phenelzine—Tyrer et al., 1973; Tyrer & Steinberg, 1975; Solyom, Heseltine, McClure, Solyom, Ledwidge, & Steinberg, 1973 and Solyom, Lapierre, Solyom, & Smyth, 1974; iproniazid, (Lipsedge, Hajioff, Huggings, Napier, Pearce, Pike, & Rich, 1973) have produced significantly more benefit than placebo, though the improvement is not large, the effect is not of an obvious antidepressant kind and there is a high relapse rate folllowing drug withdrawal. In obsessive-compulsives uncontrolled claims have been made for the value of clomipramine (Capstick, 1971).

In many of these studies systematic variation was of the drug rather than the behavioral treatment and it was not clear how much improvement could be attributed to uncontrolled variables such as instructions to carry out self-exposure homework. Obvious questions to answer include the class of drug that may be relevant, the dose and duration of drug needed, whether the drug acts by potentiating exposure to the ES (whether therapist-assisted or self-directed) and if so how, and whether the instructions about homework-exposure make a difference while the patient is taking the drugs.

One of the few published studies of "antidepressants" to manipulate both drug and behavioral treatments is that of Lipsedge et al. (1973). In this study 60 severely agoraphobic outpatients were assigned at random to one of six groups in a 2 x 3 factorial design. The drug comparison was of iproniazid (a MAOI) versus placebo. In one condition patients had desensitization in fantasy. All patients were encouraged to carry out a daily home program of graded exposure and to keep a daily diary of these activities, and were praised for improvement. Dosage of iproniazid was up to 150 mg daily over eight weeks. While still on medication at the end of treatment, iproniazid patients showed significantly more improvement than placebo patients on anxiety but not on avoidance. Withdrawal of iproniazid was followed by frequent relapse. Given the same self-exposure homework, phobias were more improved on iproniazid than on placebo but this effect was not enhanced by the addition of desensitization in fantasy.

Outcome with beta-adrenergic blockers has not been especially encouraging. Ullrich, Crombach, and Peikert (1974) compared alprenolol with placebo during exposure in vivo in 32 agoraphobics. Alprenolol patients reduced their autonomic symptoms significantly more than did placebo patients up to six months follow-up, but avoidance was not affected (Ullrich, Ullrich, & Peikert, 1974). In another study of 23 agoraphobics the beta blocker propanolol reduced panics during group exposure in vivo, but this did not help outcome—placebo patients actually had fewer phobias and other problems over three months follow-up (Hafner & Milton, 1978). Similar findings were reported in a small third study of beta-blockers, this time oxprenolol in specific phobics (Gaind, 1976). Although drug patients again felt more comfortable during exposure in vivo, improvement was less with oxprenolol than with placebo.

Several controlled studies have examined the role of the sedative diazepam during exposure in vivo of phobics. In four agoraphobic inpatients, Johnston and Gath (1973) contrasted the effect of 20 mg of oral diazepam with placebo and with the presence of a dummy syrup to which patients attributed drug effects. Treatment was on three consecutive days a week for four weeks, for a total of 12 sessions, in an incomplete Latin square design. Exposure was for 45 minutes in fantasy followed by 60 minutes in vivo. Outcome was measured the day after each treatment block and the crossover design did not allow assessment to follow up effects. Exposure treatment was more effective when given together with diazepam. Improvement was unaffected by the patients' attribution of the effects to a dummy syrup.

A larger and earlier crossover design was by Marks, Viswanathan, and Lipsedge, (1972) in 18 specific phobics. Oral diazepam or placebo was given double blind during individual exposure in vivo lasting two hours. Two days after treatment fear was reduced significantly more shortly after exposure was given during the waning psychotropic phase of diazepam than during placebo. Exposure during the peak psychotropic phase of diazepam was intermediate in its effect. There was no evidence of state dependence with diazepam in moderate dosage (0.1 mg per kg) and no relationship between outcome and blood levels of diazepam, which varied greatly between individuals but was constant within the same individuals over different occasions. Subjective anxiety was rather similar during exposure with or without diazepam, though patients in the waning diazepam phase allowed slightly earlier direct contact with the phobic object during exposure *in vivo*.

The outcome of this study suggested that phobics might be treated better by exposure *in vivo* which began several hours, not immediately, after oral sedation and continued for several hours while psychotropic effects were declining A variant of this idea was tried by Hafner and Marks (1976) but differences in the experimental design might affect conclusions which can be drawn. They assigned 42 agoraphobic outpatients randomly to treatment in one of three conditions of exposure *in vivo* given in four sessions over two weeks. Each session of exposure was 3½ hours beginning ½ hour after 0.1 mg per kg of oral diazepam in the "peak" condition, or 3½ hours after diazepam in the "waning" condition, or following similar time intervals after placebo in a third condition.

An important difference from the previous study was that exposure *in vivo* was given to groups of six patients at a time, not individually. Each group of six contained two patients in each of the two diazepam and one placebo conditions. Another difference from the previous study was that this was a parallel design without crossover so that follow up effects could be studied. A final difference was that patients here were agoraphobic, not specific phobics.

Outcome two days after treatment showed only a slight nonsignificant trend for superiority of phobic reduction in the waning diazepam group, and this difference disappeared totally by one, three and six month follow-up. Phobias of patients in all three conditions improved significantly, and maintained their gains to the six month follow-up. Diazepam reduced subjective anxiety significantly but only slightly during exposure to the phobic situation and in moderate dosage may be less anxiolytic in its action than has hitherto been supposed. An attempt was made to monitor the

psychotropic effect of diazepam by measuring flicker fusion thresholds. These did not discriminate in any way between drug and placebo conditions. Serum drug levels were not measured.

The pace of exposure *in vivo* was set by the groups as a whole and was not tailored to any one person, unlike the situation with individual exposure in the preceding study by Marks et al. (1972). Every group of patients in the Hafner and Marks study contained subjects in waning and peak diazepam and in the placebo conditions. If diazepam works at all, it might be by allowing a more rapid pace of exposure to the phobic situation. As the speed of a convoy is that of its slowest ship, diazepam patients *may* have been held back by placebo patients. In specific phobics diazepam was found to yield no advantage over placebo when the amount of exposure was controlled (Mathews, 1976); patients were exposed to their predetermined worst situation for an hour, though they were not encouraged to do as much as possible, a variable that requires further enquiry.

Yet another possibility is that diazepam might affect specific phobics and agoraphobics differently; the two studies (Marks et al., 1972; Hafner & Marks, 1976) differed with respect to these populations. The pace of exposure and the type of population need to be paid more attention in future studies in this area. Meanwhile, data so far indicate that small doses of diazepam do not aid outcome at follow-up, though they can have a slight anxiolytic effect during exposure.

Intravenous drugs. Compared to oral medication intravenous drugs carry two disadvantages. They can be dangerous and usually require the presence of a doctor at the patient's side during treatment. This is an important consideration at a time when therapy is being given increasingly by nonmedical personnel. There is little evidence as yet that intravenous is better than oral administration of drugs during behavioral treatment, apart from instilling a sense of potency in the doctor.

Intravenous thiopental was studied by Husain (1971), who contrasted its effects with that of a saline infusion in patients with agoraphobia or social phobia. Patients had either flooding or desensitization in fantasy assisted either by thiopental or saline intravenously. Thiopental facilitated flooding but made no difference to desensitization in fantasy. The design involved crossover of treatments, which precludes conclusions about persistence of effects during follow-up.

Another intravenous barbiturate, methohexitone, is often recommended as an adjuvant to desensitization in fantasy. Three studies have examined this with some kind of control, but none has yet included the crucial control for the effect of a mere injection, for example of saline. Yorkston, Sergeant, and Rachman (1968) found discouraging results in severe agoraphobics. In less severe phobics, Mawson (1970) noted that intravenous methohexitone significantly enhanced the value of desensitization compared to that of muscular relaxation without an injection. This was a crossover design that did not allow assessment of follow-up beyond a few days. In another study of severe agoraphobia, Lipsedge et al. (1973) reported that methohexitone desensitization in fantasy reduced phobias more than did desensitization with simple muscular relaxation, but again there was no saline injection control.

Another sedative, propanidid, has been used intravenously during exposure in vivo of agoraphobics (Hudson, Tobin, & Gaind, 1972), and the tricyclic clomipramine has been used intravenously in obsessives (Capstick, 1971; Rack, 1971). All these were uncontrolled.

In brief, the value of intravenous drugs used in combination with psychological treatment has yet to be substantiated from experimental evidence; this combination carries distinct disadvantages compared to oral drugs of the same class.

Outcome Issues

There are now several studies of phobic and obsessive-compulsive patients which found that exposure treatments produced significant improvement in phobias or compulsions up to the latest two to four year follow-ups available. These results can be obtained with real-life exposure after 1 to 30 sessions. The last hundred patients treated in the author's unit by nurse-therapists in 1974 to 1976 required a mean of 11 treatment sessions. More complex problems with wider ramifications require longer treatment. However, chronicity of illness is not especially important; even long-

standing problems can be relieved, sometimes with surprisingly brief treatment.

The longest follow-up of phobics after controlled comparisons of behavioral treatment is for four years (Marks, 1971). The behavioral treatment used here was an early form of exposure treatment, namely desensitization in fantasy, in which patients are relaxed and asked to repeatedly imagine themselves gradually approaching the object that causes them fear. Phobic images were visualized only for a few seconds at a time, and the subject was asked to relax between images. In an early trial by Gelder, Marks, and Wolff (1967), desensitisation reduced phobias significantly and more rapidly than did dynamic psychotherapy (Figure 13-4). A defect in these studies was that raters were not "blind." Patients who did not improve with psychotherapy were given desensitization in fantasy, which then reduced their phobias (Gelder & Marks, 1968). The superiority of desensitization was gradually eroded as other patients improved over the years, but subjects receiving desensitization improved earlier and with much less treatment, and maintained their improvement at four-year follow-up. Similar improvement was maintained four years after desensitization in fantasy and after hypnotic suggestions of benefit (Marks, Gelder, & Edwards, 1968).

These results were replicated up to three months follow-up by Gillan and Rachman (1974) in a similar group of phobic patients. They found that desensitization in fantasy was superior to dynamic psychotherapy for the relief of phobias and that improvement continued to three months followup. The amount of improvement was comparable to that obtained in the earlier investigation (Figure 13-2).

Desensitization in fantasy turns out to be a slow, inefficient form of treatment. As we have seen, relaxation training is not necessary while exposure *in vivo* seems more useful than exposure in fantasy. Several clinical studies in phobics found that improvement after exposure *in vivo* continued during follow-up to six months (Mathews et al., 1976; Teasdale et al., 1977; Hand et al., 1974; Hafner & Marks, 1976) and to 1 year (Marks et al., 1977; Ginsberg & Marks, 1977).

For compulsive rituals there are now at least three follow-up studies of two years or longer

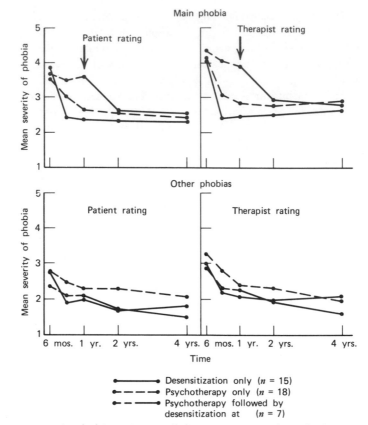

Figure 13-4   Improvement in phobic patients will desensitization and psychotherapy. [Based on material from Gelder and associates (1967), Gelder and Marks (1968), and Marks (1971).]

showing durable improvement in compulsive rituals after comparable exposure *in vivo*. In an uncontrolled study reported as it evolved in several papers, Meyer and his colleagues (Meyer, 1966; Meyer & Levy, 1971; Levy & Meyer, 1971; Meyer, Levy, & Schnurer, 1974) treated 10 compulsive ritualizers by interrupting the rituals and bringing patients into contact with those situations that triggered the rituals. Treatment involved 24 hours supervision by nurses to prevent the patient ritualizing. To stop this, patients were engaged in other activities, discussion, cajoling and, rarely, mild physical restraint with their agreement. Almost total prevention of rituals was achieved. Continuous supervision was continued for one to four weeks, during which the patient was gradually exposed to situations that had previously evoked rituals (e.g., dust, lavatories) and was again prevented from carrying these out. Supervision was then gradually de-

creased until the patient was finally totally unsupervised but occasionally observed. At two years follow-up, of the original 10 patients six were much improved in their rituals, two improved and two unchanged.

In a later report, a coworker with Meyer, Robertson (1975) noted that in a comparison in 13 patients of 24 hours versus 1 hour daily response prevention, similar results were obtained up to 18 months follow-up, with no advantage for continuous supervision. At follow-up all patients were improved in their rituals, 11 a great deal.

Comparable improvement in chronic ritualizers after exposure *in vivo* was found by Marks et al. (1975) in a partially controlled series of pilot studies. Weaknesses in the pilot design were the absence of blind raters, small numbers in several experimental cells, and the fact that only two of the cells were randomly assigned. Altogether 20 patients were treated who had chronic obsessive-compulsive rituals that were evoked by identifiable stimuli in their environment. The response prevention which accompanied exposure in vivo was purely self-imposed, not supervised. There were five comparison conditions, including a relaxation and four exposure in vivo conditions. In all five conditions treatment took 15 sessions over three weeks as inpatients, sessions lasting 50 minutes. The first 10 patients had (1) relaxation without modeling followed by random assignment to (2) slow exposure in vivo from the bottom of the hierarchy with modeling or (3) rapid exposure in vivo at the top of the hierarchy without modeling. Five subsequent patients had relaxation condition (1) followed by (4) rapid exposure in vivo at the top of the hieararchy without modeling. Five subsequent patients had relaxation condition (1) followed by (4) rapid exposure in vivo at the top of the hierarchy with modeling. A final five patients were added (condition 5) who had three weeks of rapid exposure at the top with modeling, but without the preceding relaxation phase. After the six week experimental period (three weeks in condition 5), patients were followed up, some having booster sessions when necessary, usually in the first few months. Overall, patients had a mean of 23 sessions of in vivo exposure.

Results showed that the 15 patients who received three weeks of relaxation did not improve after it on any measures of obsessive-compulsive phenomena, even though relaxation produced significant improvement in self-rated depression (Figure 13-5) and depersonalization. Patients enjoyed relaxation, but it did their compulsions no good. In contrast, treatment by three weeks exposure in vivo improved the compulsions significantly more than did relaxation. The five patients who had exposure without preceding relaxation improved as much as the 15 whose exposure followed relaxation. Modeling did not significantly enhance the effect of exposure.

Improvement was maintained at 24 month follow-up. Of the 20 patients, 14 responded very well, 1 moderately well, and 5 only slightly or not at all. Six patients were ritual free. Some improved patients still experienced problems in resisting rituals and dealing with obsessive thoughts. All pa-tients who were much improved after three weeks of treatment by exposure remained so at two year follow-up, as did all 12 patients who were much improved at six months follow-up. Interestingly the overall level of moderate depression and anxiety was unchanged by the improvement in rituals. The improvement obtained was replicated in a further series of patients treated by Roper et al. (1975; see Figure 13-6).

A third study to find improvement in compulsive rituals at two year follow-up after exposure in vivo comes from Boulougouris (1977). He followed up the 12 patients reported by Rabavilas et al. (1976), plus three more, over a mean of 2.8 years. Patient characteristics and measures were similar to those reported by Marks et al. (1975). Outcome was also comparable, including the fact that there was further improvement during long-term follow-up (Figure 13-7).

Several uncontrolled studies have found similar treatment to yield comparable impressive outcome after follow-up to a mean of one year. Twenty-nine patients were treated by nurse-therapists during Maudsley training programs in a mean of 20 sessions of treatment. Up to the one year follow-up available, significant improvement was obtained in rituals and in work adjustment comparable to that obtained by Marks et al. in 1975 (Marks et al., 1977 and Marks, Bird, & Lindley, 1978). In an unpublished series from New York, Anderson treated 15 chronic ritualizers in a mean of 14 sessions. He followed them up for a mean of one year, when eight were much improved in their rituals, four slightly to moderately improved, while three were unchanged. In another series (Foa and Goldstein, 1978) 23 ritualizers and checkers improved greatly up to a mean follow-up of 15 months after treatment, which involved two weeks intensive inpatient treatment by exposure in vivo and continuously supervised response prevention, followed by monitoring sessions in outpatients.

Yet another follow-up, this time to six months after exposure in vivo, comes from Roper et al. (1975). This was a controlled study of 10 chronic obsessive-compulsive ritualizers who were assigned at random to one of two conditions of inpatient treatment over six weeks, divided into two three week blocks of 15 sessions. In the initial three

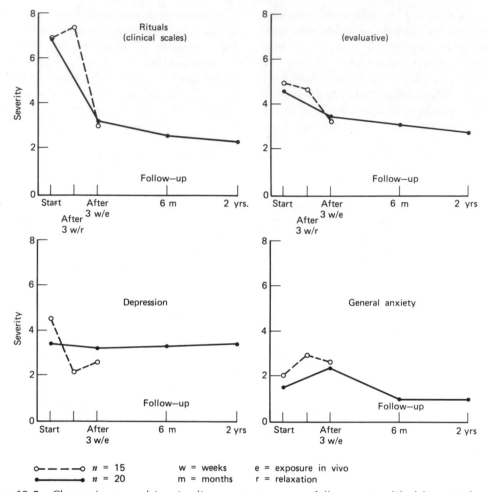

Figure 13-5   Change in compulsive ritualizers up to two years follow-up (modified from Marks et al., 1975).

week block, one condition was (1) *modeling of relaxation* during which the therapist modeled re- laxation exercises *without* exposure to the con- taminating or ritual-evoking situations, and asked the patients to carry out similar relaxation exer- cises. Patients in this condition hardly changed in their rituals; merely observing the therapist carrying out a "therapeutic" exercise was therefore not helpful.

The contrasting condition in the first three-week block was (2) *passive modeling of exposure;* that is, patients passively observed the therapist engaging in anticompulsive behavior like deliberately con- taminating herself or making things untidy. Com- pulsions of patients in this passive exposure condi-

tion improved significantly more than in the passive relaxation condition, even though modeling (ob- servation of the therapist carrying out supposedly therapeutic exercises) was present equally in both conditions.

After the first three weeks, all 10 patients crossed over to three weeks of participant modeling of ex- posure in which the patients themselves were re- quired to engage in compulsive behavior in the way the therapist had demonstrated. Patients were now also given instructions for self-imposed re- sponse prevention between treatment, which in- structions had not been given in the first three weeks. This confounds interpretation of the finding that participant modeling of exposure was significantly superior to both modeling of relaxation and to passive modeling of exposure. As patients in the three conditions had similar amounts of modeling, differences between the three conditions can be attributed to differences in the amount and type of exposure given, and the accompaning instructions for response prevention. Patients maintained their improvement to the last follow-up available, six months after treatment (Figure 13-6.) Mean number of exposure sessions was 23, the same as in the series of Marks et al. 1975.

In brief there is now good evidence from several series of patients treated with exposure *in vivo* by different professionals in three independent centres

(two in London and one in Greece) that improvement in compulsive rituals is maintained up to third year of follow-up so far available (Meyer et al., 1974; Marks et al., 1975; Boulougouris, 1977). New York, Philadelphia, and London workers found the same to one year follow-up (Anderson, unpublished; Foa and Goldstein, 1978; Marks et al., 1977). Gratifying as the improvement usually is after exposure *in vivo*, the active ingredients need to be further refined. Practical issues in management are dealt with elsewhere (Marks, 1977).

Obsessive thoughts without rituals. Outcome of treatment here is less predictably satisfac-

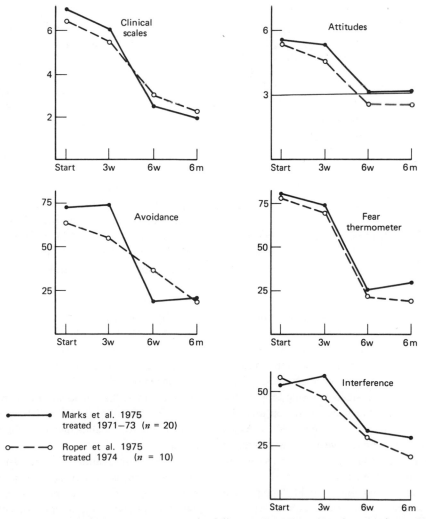

Figure 13-6 Comparison of outcome to 6 months follow-up in two series of compulsive ritualizers.

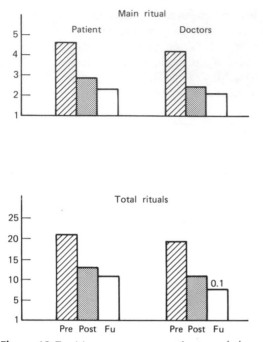

Figure 13-7 Mean scores on patients and doctors ratings on main and total obsessions before treatment, after treatment, and at follow-up. [Paper to EABT, Spetsae, Greece, Sept. 1976. In J.C. Boulougouris & A. Rabavilas (Eds.) *Studies in Phobic and Obsessive-Compulsive Disorders.* Pergamon, 1977.]

tory than it is with ritualizers. Several procedures have been used that include some exposure to the undesirable thoughts. One such is thought-stopping (Stern, 1970; Kumar & Wilkinson, 1971; Yamagami, 1971). In this procedure the patient is relaxed and asked to think of the obsessive thought. The therapist shouts "stop" and makes a sudden noise at the same time. The patient is then told to shout "stop" himself to dispel the thought, and then to whisper, and eventually to employ a subvocal command. Instead of saying 'stop' to the obsessive thoughts, the patient can stop them by shocking himself from a portable shockbox. As yet another alternative, he can wear an elastic band on his wrist and snap it sharply onto his skin to disrupt the thoughts (Mahoney, 1971).

It could be argued that thought-stopping is a form of exposure to obsessive thoughts in repeated brief sequences, rather like with desensitization in

fantasy. Whether the relaxation or the aversive component that often accompanies thought-stopping is in fact essential is debatable.

Thought-stopping could be construed as an exercise in self-regulation or coping whereby the patient learns to control his or her own thoughts. In a controlled trial (Stern, Lipsedge, & Marks, 1973) 4 out of 11 patients improved more by learning to stop neutral thoughts than by stopping obsessive thoughts. This argues for the acquisition of a coping set, not specific extinction of the obsessive ideas. A subsequent series of six patients treated in the author's unit by thought-stopping yielded variable results, and the same has been true in a further five ruminators treated by Emmelkamp (1976, personal communication). The value of thought-stopping is thus unpredictable.

Thought-stopping procedures all aim to interrupt the undesirable thoughts repeatedly. This by itself could be the operative mechanism. An argument against this idea, however, is that sometimes the opposite technique of prolonged exposure in fantasy, or lengthy writing about the obsessive thoughts, can also help patients.

An intriguing combination of thought-stopping with role-play was reported by Rosen and Schnapp (1974). Though anecdotal, it merits attention. The problems was the husband's rumination about his wife's past affair, with distrust of outside interaction. In the presence of his wife the patient was asked to describe aloud an obsessive train of thought about her affair, and to cross-examine her about ambiguities in her alibis. When the couple were deeply engrossed in this process, one of the two therapists shouted "stop" without warning, then the patient was asked to shout "stop." As he learned to do this the wife was asked to do the same whenever he cross-examined her. After three sessions of rehearsing this, four sessions more were given of family therapy to improve communication skills. Treatment stopped after 12 sessions and improvement was maintained to eight months followup.

None of the treatments of obsessive thoughts, be they exposure in fantasy, thought stopping or any of their variants is as predictably effective as exposure in vivo is for compulsive ritualisers who cooperate in treatment.

Operational Model for the Treatment of Phobias and Obsessions

Let us briefly return to the model outlined earlier and in Figure 13-1 and see how it applies to phobic-obsessive disorders. Motivational issues decide whether patients will ask for help in the first place, and the therapist can heighten their motivation up to a point by playing hard to get, obtaining the patient's clear commitment to carry out those actions necessary for improvement to occur (with a written contract to be signed by waiverers) and involvement of significant others as co-therapists where possible. Motivation might be further increased through modeling by the therapist and others, and by treatment in a group and in the family setting.

Nevertheless, however high a patient's motivation might be, he or she must in addition carry out certain executive factors that are usually essential before improvement can take place. These involve the patient's exposure to the ES until tolerance develops, and most behavioral forms of fear-reduction are variants on this theme. During the exposure, arousal level is not especially important, but long durations are preferable, and *in vivo* is more efficient than fantasy exposure. Exposure itself might be acting by unwittingly forcing the patient to develop their own coping (self-management) strategies in the face of discomfort, but this explanation is hard to test and liable to become circular. Psychotropic drugs, if they turn out to be useful, could theoretically act both by heightening motivation (e.g., through decreasing concomitant depression) and by facilitating executive actions (e.g., by directly speeding up habituation during exposure).

SEXUAL DISORDERS

Sexual Dysfunction

Sexual dysfunction is a common presenting problem in the clinic, though better data are needed about its detailed prevalence in the community. Nonorganic sexual dysfunction is often regarded as a form of neurosis in the broad sense. When sexual dysfunction has always been present it is termed primary and when it begins after an initial period of normal function it is labeled secondary. Failures of sexual function are often associated with sexual anxiety, fear, or digust, and other complications like social skills deficits. In the male sexual dysfunction can take the form of *premature ejaculation* and *failure of erection* (erectile impotence), which often occur together, and the rarer condition of *ejaculatory failure* (incompetence) despite adequate and prolonged erection. In the female "frigidity" ranges from extreme *sexual phobias* (where a woman cannot bear to be touched anywhere on her body) to more localised *vaginismus* where anxiety and spasm occur only on attempted penetration. Either of these might be sufficiently severe to result in nonconsumation of a marriage. Severe vaginismus and nonconsummation can coexist with normal orgasm through mutual masturbation. The least severe form of "frigidity" is *anorgasmia,* where coitus may actually be pleasurable but orgasm is unobtainable.

The first step in the behavioral management of failed sexual function is adequate delineation of the difficulty. Organic causes, including drugs, need to be excluded. Psychological causes include marital dysharmony, severe depression and, occasionally, traumatic sexual experiences. Where clearcut causes are present these must be dealt with in their own right. Special attention is needed to the interpersonal aspects of therapy, and it can be far from easy to disentangle the contribution of sexual and of interpersonal problems to marital discord in a given case.

Where the problem is sexual dysfunction, the treatment approach which automatically springs to mind is that pioneered by Masters and Johnston (1970) and developed into several variants by later workers (e.g., Annon, 1974; LoPiccolo, 1975; Bancroft, 1975; Evereard, Lambers, van der Bout, & Schacht, 1977). The approach has many behavioral components which boil down to the reduction of anxiety and the training of sexual skills in a graduated program in which the couple is treated together. A good discussion of the behavioral components of a sexual skills training program is given by LoPiccolo (1975):

1. The couple is told that they have mutual responsibility for the problem and even where

only one partner has the obvious difficulty the other might be told "Had you responded differently he/she could have overcome the problem."

2. Appropriate information and education in sexual matters is given.

3. Relevant sexual attitudes are modified as appropriate

4. Performance anxieties are decreased by regular graded practice and by decreasing demand, for example, by paradoxical instructions not to have intercourse or an erection, and so on.

5. Communication in sexual skill is increased by a variety of maneuvers, for example, (i) share sexual fantasies, erotic literature, and movies, (ii) show one another masturbatory techniques (iii) provision of information with feedback.

6. Destructive life styles and sex roles have to be changed, and time has to be made for privacy for sex, which has to be given a high priority during treatment.

7. Graded steps are prescribed for specific items of sexual behavior which have to be carried out as homework. The couple gradually progresses from less to more difficult tasks, the gradient of difficulty not necessarily being a simple function of increasing intimacy. Tasks include (i) pleasuring exercises, of which sensate focus is one variant, the sexual partners learning to caress one another in the nude, (ii) a ban on performance demands such as pressures to have an erection, orgasm, or coitus, (iii) a written homework diary recording each step of sexual behavior performed, (iv) sometimes a deposit made at the start which is forfeited to charity if the couple does not attend regularly or do homework adequately.

8. Particular problems require specific techniques of management.
   (i) *Problems in men:* for *premature ejaculation* the squeeze or pause technique is recommended to be carried out by the wife or by the husband. This involves lengthy penile stimulation (usually manually, but can be orally), stopping immediately before ejaculation is imminent (pause). The wife can if desired further inhibit ejaculation by squeezing the base of the glans penis between her fingers (squeeze). When the urge to ejaculate has passed, penile stimulation is resumed. Once penile stimulation can continue for 10 to 15 minutes without urges to ejaculate developing the same technique is applied during coitus. An alternative maneuvre to inhibit ejaculation is sharp pulling down of the scrotum. For *erectile failure* stimulation from the wife is recommended, including teasing while the penis is flaccid. For *ejaculatory failure* super stimulation is recommended, sometimes with a vibrator. Another technique reported to be useful for inducing emission is for the wife to cup and press the scrotum against the perineum with her hand.
   (ii) *Problems in women: Anorgasmia.* For primary anorgasmia, where the wife has never experienced an organism, LoPiccolo recommends a program of graduated directed self-masturbation, together with the use of a vibrator, involvement of the husband, and role-play by the wife with her husband of grossly exaggerated orgasm. For secondary anorgasmia these maneuvres may be useful together with marital counseling. For vaginismus graded vaginal dilators can be inserted by the doctor, the wife, and the husband. Alternatively graded insertion of small and then larger fingers can be practiced in digital dilation exercises which include contraction of the vaginal muscles to achieve voluntary control.

While the results reported by Masters and Johnson for their original version of a sexual skills training program were encouraging, their series was uncontrolled and many factors in the complicated package of treatment could have contributed to their results. Their couples pay fees and are treated in a special clinic far from home in a honeymoon setting. Problems are sometimes encountered in the transfer of treatment gains from the clinic to the home. An expensive male plus female therapist combination is also used for each couple.

Since Masters and Johnson made sex therapy respectable, sex clinics proliferated well before controlled research on the subject, but it is an old observation that clinical practice correlates imperfectly with its scientific base. Only recently have controlled clinical experiments been launched, most still being unpublished. A brief review of these follows, though definitive appraisal of several must await final publication of the studies.

Controlled Behavioral Studies of Sexual Dysfunction

There are several controlled studies of sexual skills training programs that find behavioral methods to be of value in the treatment of sexual and marital disorders. Most of these are still unpublished, and final evaluation will often require more detail. In a study reported by Bancroft (1975/6) and by Mathews et al. (1976), 36 couples were randomly assigned to one of three behavioral treatments each of which was given by one or by two therapists. In half the couples the presenting patient was the man and in half it was the woman. The first treatment condition consisted of systematic desensitization in fantasy plus counseling focused on the reduction of anxiety. The second condition used a modification of the Masters and Johnson approach with direct practice aimed at the growth of sexual responding, plus counseling. The third condition (postal Masters and Johnson) was similar to the second, being directed practice along Masters and Johnson lines, but with only minimal counseling and therapist contact, most of it being via mailed instruction sheets. There were 12 weekly sessions, or weekly postal contact for the third condition. The first 2 sessions consisted of similar assessment for each condition, and the last 10 sessions differed according to the group assigned. Ratings were by an independent assessor and by the therapist before and after treatment and at four months follow-up.

Results found that the desensitization condition did worst and the directed practice condition with counseling did best on therapist ratings of female sexual enjoyment and on increase in coital frequency (but p only $< .1$). Two therapists did *slightly* better than one therapist ($p < .1$) only with directed practice plus counseling.

In a later study Bancroft (1976) found that women with sexual dysfunction improved significantly more when a behavioral approach was combined with a small dose of testosterone rather than of diazepam, and that this superiority continued to six months follow-up even after the testosterone had been discontinued. This was a double blind comparison of testosterone with diazepam, there being a mean of 12 weekly treatment sessions, plus written manuals to take home.

Three controlled studies by a Dutch research group are so far incomplete (Everaerd et al. 1977a and Everaerd, Stufkens-Veerman, Van der Bout, Hofman, Sijben-Schrier, & Schacht, 1977b, and Schacht, van Vloten, Mol, & Everaerd, 1977). The first is in 48 couples where the woman had sexual dysfunction, usually anorgasmia (Schacht et al., 1977). They were randomly divided into four conditions (each $11 = 12$). Here a behavioral Masters and Johnson approach was contrasted with desensitization in fantasy and with a third condition combining both. Treatment was twice weekly to a total of 12 sessions. The three treated conditions showed no significant differences from one another but were significantly better than a waitlist control. At six month follow-up treatment gains are maintained on the 23 of 36 patients available.

In a second study by Everaerd et al. of 42 couples where the wife had anorgasmia, a mean of 15 sessions of behavioral Masters and Johnson was compared with a mean of 17 sessions of communication training. Treatment sessions were twice weekly. At one and six months follow-up significantly greater sexual satisfaction was reported by both sexes after the behavioural approach. After sex therapy couples who had originally been satisfied with their marriage improved in their general as well as their sexual relationship, while those initially unhappy in their marriage improved slightly in their general adjustment but did not gain in their sexual relationship. From his results Everaerd (1976) concluded that specific work directed at the sexual problem seemed more effective than communication training.

In the third study by Everaerd and his colleagues, this time into erectile impotence and premature ejaculation, a behavioral Masters and Johnson approach twice a week was compared with desensitization twice a week, for a mean of 23 treatment sessions. At incomplete six months follow-up so far the behavioral Masters and Johnson had better results than desensitization.

Results from this third study accord with those of Kockott, Dittmar, and Nusselt, (1975) in 25 men with a minimum of six months history of erectile impotence. All had a partner. They were assigned at random into three groups, matched for age, primary or secondary impotence, intelligence, and neuroticism. One group had 14 sessions of desensitization in fantasy, another had "routine therapy" four times at intervals of three to five weeks and the third group was placed on a waiting list. Outcome was not encouraging in any of the groups, with no change in five patients in each of the two treatment groups or in seven of the waitlist group. Subsequent to this Kockott used a behavioral Masters and Johnson approach in similar patients; preliminary follow-up data indicate results are superior to those obtained with desensitization in fantasy (Kockott, 1976).

Female "sexual anxiety" was treated in a controlled study by Husted (1972, cited by Annon, 1974). There was a control group (unspecified) and four desensitization conditions (1) imaginal, with sexual communication training (2) imaginal alone (3) in vivo with sexual communication training (4) in vivo alone. All four groups showed significantly greater decrease in sexual anxiety and a significantly greater increase in coital frequency, noncoital responsiveness, and ratings of improvement on posttreatment and follow-up measures as compared to the control group. Treatment groups did not differ except for the unusual finding that significantly fewer sessions were required by the imaginal compared with the in vivo conditions.

Another study of anorgasmia is by Munjack, Cristol, Goldstein, Phillips, Goldberg, and Whipple (1976). This was partially controlled in that 22 anorgasmic women (12 primary) most with happy marriages, were assigned at random to 20 weekly sessions of behavioral treatment, or to 10 weeks on a waitlist with the expectation of treatment subsequently, after which these patients also had behavioral treatment. Treatment was given by one therapist and included the usual components of a sexual skills training program. The patient was seen alone without the husband about 75% of the time.

Results were only reported in terms of significant change from pretreatment to posttreatment and followup, and no direct comparisons are reported between the treatments. Moreover, results of the wait list patients are reported at the 10 weeks point when they began treatment, whereas changes of treated patients are reported after 20 weeks. Treated patients improved significantly in sexual feelings while wait list patients showed little change. Up to nine month followup women with secondary anorgasmia did significantly better than those with primary anorgasmia. In several of the latter women marital problems emerged during treatment.

Design problems confound the comparison of treatment with waitlist patients who were measured after a shorter time (10 vs. 20 weeks), having no therapist contact and presumably no expectation of improvement while on the waitlist because they expected treatment at the end of 10 weeks. Furthermore, significant statistical differences between the two groups are not reported, only change within each group. Nevertheless, it is of interest how much better outcome was in secondary than in primary anorgasmia. There were twice more treatment sessions (20 vs. 10) than in the study by Crowe (1976).

A large controlled investigation of sexual dysfunction (Obler, 1973) selected 64 volunteer students (60% male) out of 235 referred from university clinics on the basis of Manifest Anxiety Scale scores and interviews. These students were all well motivated and intelligent. They were divided into three matched groups: (1) desensitization for 45 minutes weekly over 15 weeks; (2) traditional group therapy 1½ hours weekly over 10 weeks; and (3) no treatment. The researcher carried out all treatment. Desensitization included not only hierarchy images facilitated by seeing sexual films and slides, but also four sessions of assertive training and role play of sex-related social situations.

Results showed significant increases in the success/experience ratio for the desensitized group, and for females over the nontreatment control and for males over both other groups. The GSR and heart rate decreased more in the desensitized group. Desensitized subjects also showed significantly more gains than both other groups on scales measuring specific sexual stress, and more gains than the no-treatment control on the Manifest Anxiety Scale. Eighty percent of the desensitized subjects became "sexually functional" and at 18-month follow-up no regression was found. Some improvement was also found in the other two groups. The author commented on the value of graphic aids for the presentation of hierarchy images.

A problem in interpreting results of this study is that Obler's desensitization included role rehearsal methods which might have contributed even more to the effect than the desensitization in fantasy. Another difficulty is that sexual dysfunction includes a wide range of disorders. No data are given which can separate premature ejaculation from erectile impotence, nonconsummation of marriage, vaginismus, or anorgasmia (or whether these were primary or secondary). Furthermore, volunteer student populations are not necessarily comparable to more broad spectrum clinic populations. Phobic patients are usually more disturbed and difficult to treat than phobic volunteers, especially students (Olley & McAllister, 1974), and the same might apply to persons with sexual problems. The report is too compressed to allow assessment of the seriousness of the sexual problems treated and the follow-up data are inadequate. There is also a lingering possibility that the volunteer population had a subcultural disbelief in traditional group treatment, or a strong belief in desensitization, since two volunteers refused to have group treatment instead of desensitization.

Two controlled studies of the value of videotaped material in the treatment of sex dysfunction are summarized by Annon (1974) and Annon and Robinson (1976) though definitive assessment must await their publication in detail. Wincze and Caird (1973) compared the relative effectiveness of desensitization in fantasy, video desensitization, and an untreated control condition. Subjects were 21 women complaining of sexual frigidity. In the video desensitization procedure subjects had a pool of 140 four-minute scenes of heterosexual behavior from which to create appropriate hierarchies. Both experimental groups received identical treatment except that in the video group hierarchy scenes were presented via videotapes. Both experimental groups showed significant decreases in heterosexual anxiety immediately after treatment.

However, at follow-up, the video treated group reported more improvement in sexual relations than the group exposed to standard desensitization.

Robinson (1974) assessed the effects of a videotape treatment program for orgasmic dysfunction. The tapes depicted a male therapist talking to a role-playing couple where the woman was anorgasmic. Apart from an untreated control group there were two video conditions. In video series A the therapist presented a wide range of sexual information to the modeling couple. In video series B information was limited to the area of self-stimulation and was accompanied by specific therapeutic suggestions to the women. Twenty-three couples were randomly assigned to one of three conditions (1) viewing first series A and then series B (2) viewing the series B only (3) wait-list control. No suggestions were given to clients to follow what was modeled on the tapes. They were merely asked to "view the video tapes."

Results indicated that both videotape conditions (i.e., A + B, or B only) promoted more positive attitudes toward self-stimulation, and increased its frequency. The frequency of orgasm increased more reliably for those women who had experienced orgasm before. The more global attitude changes which client subjects showed after exposure to three hours of videotaped sexual material had little relationship to subsequent self-stimulation. Significant behavior change only occurred after exposure to the B series, which involved limited information *and* specific suggestions directly related to the client's problem area.

An especially careful controlled trial with 18 month followup is that of Crowe (1976). It differs from studies just reviewed in that just over half the couples presented with marital problems, and only the remainder had dominant sexual difficulties. Nevertheless, overall outcome of sexual adjustment is relevant. Fourty-two couples who had marital or sexual difficulties were assigned at random to one of three conjoint approaches, yielding 14 couples for each condition (1) *directive* operant-interpersonal treatment along the lines of Stuart (1969), including behavioral contracting as well as a behavioral Masters and Johnson approach for sexual difficulties where these were present; (2) *interpretative* treatment was given along group analytic lines; and (3) the *support* condition had neither directive advice nor interpretations, only routine support.

Couples in all three conditions had 10 hour-long sessions of treatment weekly except for seven couples (two directive, three interpretative, two supportive) who had only five sessions. There was only *one* therapist per couple. Thirty-seven of the 42 couples were treated by Crowe himself, and the other five were treated by two other therapists.

Sessions were tape recorded and blind raters listening to these were able to differentiate accurately between the three treatments in 78% of cases. Although the content of the sessions was mainly "nonspecific" in all three treatments, there were important differences consistent with the experimental manipulations. Of all comments sampled, the proportion that were directive comments was, respectively, 43% and 10% in the directive and interpretative conditions. Conversely, the proportion of all comments that were interpretative were respectively 6% and 36% in the directive and interpretative conditions.

After treatment 72% of couples improved. The best outcome was in the directive condition, with significant improvement on all measures, including those of sexual adjustment. Compared with the support condition, outcome from directive therapy was significantly superior after treatment and up to 18 months follow-up on sexual, marital, and general adjustment, on target problems, and on the couple's evaluation of the contribution of treatment to their improvement. The interpretative condition was superior to support only at follow-up, and then only on marital adjustment and global ratings. The support condition was never superior to the directive one, and was superior to interpretative therapy on only one measure at one point.

In brief, the Crowe study showed that sexual, marital, and general maladjustment was improved significantly more by a directive operant-interpersonal approach which included sexual skills training where appropriate for sexual difficulties. Interpretative and especially support conditions did less well up to 18 months follow-up. The long follow-up is crucial as short-term honeymoon effects can occur after many treatments. Prolonged follow-up is essential to decide the cost-effectiveness of an approach.

General Issues

Results of early controlled studies of sexual skills training programs are encouraging (e.g., Everaerd et al., 1977a & b; Schacht et al., 1977; Crowe, 1976; Robinson, 1974; Husted, 1972) though they remain to be published in definitive form, and much work is still in progress. While the program packages seem valuable, the utility of particular components is less clear, and there are many practical problems. Often brief advice and therapy suffices without need for prolonged programs (Annon, 1974; Annon & Robinson, 1976).

Two therapists versus one.   An important issue is whether two therapists are better than one for a given couple. Although it is customary for many clinics to employ two therapists the results have to be very much better than those of one therapist to justify the procedure on economic grounds, as using two therapists instead of one doubles the cost of treatment. While the use of two therapists enables experienced therapists to teach inexperienced cotherapists how to impart sexual skills, this does not justify it as a routine clinical rather than teaching procedure. Bancroft (1976) found a slight advantage for using two therapists, but this did not seem enough to compensate for the extra expense. Crowe, who has the longest follow-up so far, obtained his superior behavioral results using only one therapist. For couples therapy in general there is no clear justification for the use of two therapists rather than one (Gurman, 1975; Stuart, 1975), except possibly for couples treated in groups (Gurman, 1975).

Couple or individual treatment?   Another issue that remains to be clairfied is whether treatment of the couple together rather than separately is indeed useful. While the former makes clinical sense and seems to save time, there is no hard data to back up this view.

Group treatment of sexual dysfunction offers further hope of saving therapists' time, but the issue is complex. The advantages of behavioral group treatment were described by Leiblum, Rosen, and Pierce (1975) as being decreased costs, provision of group support and encouragement, and a sense of having common problems. The disadvantages were feelings of embarrassment, difficulty in providing sufficient individual tailoring to treatment for a couple's needs, and proper pacing of homework exercises for individuals at different stages of goal attainment.

Kaplan, Kohl, Pomeroy, Offit, and Hogan (1974) reported four couples where the male had premature ejaculation who were treated in a group with advice about the pause and squeeze method. There were six 45-minute sessions, and therapist time averaged 1½ hours per couple. Two couples reported success by the end of treatment and by four months follow-up all couples reported much improvement.

More heterogeneous "sexual enhancement" groups for couples were reported by LoPiccolo (1975), McGovern, Kirkpatrick, and LoPiccolo (1976) and Leiblum et al. (1975). The group of Leiblum et al. contained five couples aged 25 to 45. All except one had a reasonable marriage. There were 10 sessions once weekly, with follow-up six weeks later. During the sessions the couples saw slides describing genitals, were taught to record sexual behavior on special forms, and learned about sensate focus. At subsequent sessions they reported on their homework, discussed each other's sexual problems and were given homework like body massage, including the genitals after session 3. Therafter they discussed masturbation, saw sexual films, and were taught further sexual skills, with a final review at session 10. Five of the six couples improved to some extent, though one maritally disturbed couple did not.

Group treatment of couples with sexual dysfunction is worth exploring further, if only because of its potential economic advantages at a time when there is an escalating demand for treatment of sexual dysfunction with few facilities to give it.

Instructional aids of a wide variety seem useful. Books, diagrams, and anatomical models can all help desensitize couples and provide information. The work cited earlier by Robinson and by Wincze and Caird argue for the value of suitable video film material. The value of books as instructional aids is noted in uncontrolled work by Greist (personal communication). He and his coauthors gave their manual (Kass, Strauss, Weill, Greist, Chiles, & Thurrell, 1976) to volunteer couples with sexual problems. Of the first 20 couples using it, most made progress, and about half attained the goals they set themselves, which usually included mutual orgasm through coitus.

Frequency of treatment sessions merits more research. Unpublished data from LoPiccolo and from Bancroft and Mathews indicate monthly sessions can be as effective as more frequent treatment. One factor affecting optimum frequency is the opportunity couples might have for practicing their sexual exercises at home, between sessions with the therapist. This might be but once or twice a week for those with low libido or poor housing. Much of sexual skills training is in essence a set of interviews during which the therapist prescribes home exercises for the couple, monitors the result, and then makes further suggestions.

Moral and Interpersonal Issues.   In the treatment of any problem a therapist acts on implicit or explicit moral judgments. These include the patients' right to have treatment, the therapist's right to help them change, and which treatment methods may be used. These issues inevitably color the management of sexual disorders, for example, can and should couples be treated who have no stable commitment to one another? Is genital pleasure as realistic and acceptable an aim as "loving union"? Can surrogates be used? These problems are outside the scope of this chapter, but some are discussed by Sollod & Kaplan (1977, p. 140–152).

Sexual Deviation

Sexual deviants seek help from clinicians less often than do sufferers from sexual dysfunction. Exhibitionism is perhaps the commonest sexual deviation seen in the clinic in Britain and many other countries. Homosexuals seem to seek help less since the change in the law in some western countries. Transsexualism is very rare. Homosexuality apart, the great majority of sexual deviants are males, and very few reports of females are to be found in the literature (Kinsey, Pomeroy, & Martin, 1953).

Persistent homosexuality is the commonest sexual deviation in the community, occurring in about 4% of adult males, and in rather fewer women (Kinsey, Pomeroy, & Martin, 1948 and 1953). It is fortunate for therapists that most homosexuals do not seek to change their orientation because clinics would otherwise be overwhelmed. Exhibitionists only come when difficulties, usually legal, arise from their activities. The features of clients who present for treatment of sexual problems at clinics are not necessarily the same as those of untreated people with similar sexual behavior. Siegelman (1972a & b) found that nonclinical male and female homosexuals who answered a questionnaire were as well adjusted as comparable heterosexuals. Within the male homosexuals, masculine were better adjusted than feminine homosexuals. Homosexuals who seek help in changing their orientation tend to have other neurotic problems and in that respect resemble other neurotics more than nonclinical homosexuals (Feldman, 1973). Differences between clinical and nonclinical populations need to be borne in mind in management.

Sexual deviants are attracted by an unusual sexual object or mode of sexual stimulation. This attraction has to be reduced before the client can be considered improved. Sexual deviations do not necessarily correlate with the presence of heterophobia, and although improvement in fears of heterosexuality can sometimes lead to resolution of sexual deviance as well, this is by no means the rule. Treatment thus requires decrease of the deviant attraction, and where necessary, reduction of heterophobia and increase of heterosexual skills. The field has been reviewed by Bancroft (1974) and Marks (1976).

Psychological treatments of sexual deviations have a memorable history, and in the 1890s Schrenck-Notzing in Germany devised a program of desensitization *in vivo* for homosexuals (see Bancroft, 1970b). In 1935 Max wrote his pioneering account of electric aversion in homosexuals, but such treatment was only taken up again systematically a generation later. Many other methods have developed and are evolving further. Unfortunately, controlled investigations are the exception, not the rule. More systematic work is required using refined techniques in well selected homogenous populations of deviants with adequate follow-up of a year or more.

Decreasing Deviant Behavior

This usually involves some kind of aversion. *Aversion therapy* can take many forms. The aversive stimulus can be paired with any type of deviant cue, including fantasies, photographs, slides, narratives, or real life situations. The timing of the aversive stimulus can vary from the moment of contact with the deviant cue (either immediate or delayed) to only after erections or other signs of arousal appear to the deviant cues. The aversive stimulus can be given once or many times, regardless of the patient's behavior, or terminating only when the deviant behavior or erection ceases. Reinforcement can be partial or complete. Aversion can be paired with relief stimuli (usually heterosexual) at the moment the aversive stimulus ceases.

Many aversive stimuli have been used. *Chemical* aversion was used widely until a few years ago but has fallen into disfavor because, compared with electric aversion, it is more cumbersome, less precise, and potentially dangerous. In addition, fewer trials are possible, it cannot be self-administered, and it must be given in a medical setting. *Electric* aversion has been studied more than any other form. It has been given by classical conditioning, avoidance conditioning, backward conditioning, and aversion relief.

Covert sensitization is often used. This form of aversion utilizes the patient's fantasies as noxious stimuli instead of an external agent such as injection or shock (Cautela & Wisocki, 1971; Davison, 1968; Barlow, Leitenberg, & Agras, 1969; Harbert, Barlow, Hersen, & Austin 1973; and Callahan & Leitenberg, 1973). The patient is asked to imagine himself engaging in the undesired behavior. When this is achieved he is asked at the same time to imagine a noxious scene such as vomiting, anxiety-provocation (Kolvin, 1967) or shame (Curtis & Presley, 1972). A small controlled study of covert sensitization was made by Barlow, Agras, Leitenberg, Callahan, and Moore (1972) in four male homosexuals. Results suggested that overall instructions and patient expectations played but a minor role in covert sensitization in the short term. The long term effects of covert sensitization remain to be demonstrated in a controlled fashion. To the extent that subjects learn to summon up their own noxious fantasies when they have deviant temptations, the method can be regarded as a form of self-regulation.

A pilot aversive method is *smell sensitization* in which deviant stimuli are paired with real unpleasant smells like ammonia or ammonium sulphide (Colson, 1972) or valeric acid (Maletzky, 1973). This is a form of chemical aversion, but noxious inhalations are more practicable than injections. Another pilot technique is *shame aversion,* in which the patient is required to perform the deviant act in front of other people, the aversion coming from embarrassment (Serber, 1970, 1972; Reitz & Keil, 1971). *Aversive tickling* (Greene & Hoats, 1971) has not been reported in sexual deviations, nor has *scoline apnea.* An *elastic band worn around the wrist* can be held taut and snapped back suddenly to sting the skin as effectively as any shock apparatus. It is simple, and the patient can use it as a "self-regulator" or "thought-stopper" as well as an aversive stimulus. In recent years in the author's unit electric aversion has been used steadily less and replaced by methods like covert sensitization or an elastic band on the wrist. These methods require no equipment, can be readily self-induced and can be combined with other aspects of a self-management program.

Controlled Studies of Aversion in Sexual Deviance. These were summarized by Marks (1976). Little difference was found between the efficacy of chemical or electrical methods (McConaghy, 1969) or between different forms of electric aversion (Feldman & MacCulloch, 1971; Bancroft, 1970a & b; McConaghy & Barr, 1973). Compared to nonaversive methods, electric aversion was not superior to desensitization (Bancroft, 1970), but was to placebo conditioning (Birk, Huddleston, Miller, & Cohler, 1971), brief "psychotherapy" (Feldman & MacCulooch, 1971), self-regulation and muscular relaxation (Rooth & Marks, 1974). Barlow and Agras (1973) found that covert sensitization was significantly superior to repeated deviant imagery alone. Significant differences in all these studies referred to decrease in deviance, not to increase in heterosexuality. All concerned homosexuality, except Rooth and Marks, which involved exhibitionism. All were parallel designs with follow-up except Barlow et al. who had a repeated measures design and Rooth and Marks who used an incomplete Latin square. Both the latter allowed interpretation only of short term effects between procedures. None except Bancroft paid much attention to de-

creasing heterosexual anxiety and increasing heterosexual skills.

General Issues in Aversion Therapy
The unpleasantness of aversion therapy varies greatly depending on its mode of administration. Perceived aversiveness increases with strength of shock and greater delay before its receipt (Franzini, 1970). There is no evidence that extreme unpleasantness is important. Tanner (1973) compared a 5 mA strength of shock with self-selected strength (average 3−4.5 mA) in 26 male homosexuals having aversion treatment. The 5 mA group improved slightly more, but had a higher dropout rate. Marks and Gelder (1967) used just enough shock to overcome the pleasure that patients experienced from deviant stimuli; the aim was not to produce suffering but to abolish pleasure. The patients of Hallam, Rachman, and Falkowski (1972) rated electric aversion as less unpleasant than a dental visit. Aversion can thus be given humanely in a manner that is acceptable to most patients. Obviously, however, if more pleasant treatments can be found that are equally effective these should replace aversive methods.

Although the evidence does suggest that aversion decreases deviance more than several other methods, it is not absolutely conclusive, and the overall effects are not startlingly large even when significant. There is also evidence that aversion to deviant stimuli can increase heterosexual erections and desires in the short term (Bancroft, 1970a & b) but the mechanism and durability of this effect is obscure. An agreed prognostic factor is the favorable effect of some prior heterosexual interest. This was one determinant of subsequent heterosexual behavior in the series of Feldman and MacCulloch (1971), Bancroft (1970a & b), Marks et al. (1970), and Rooth and Marks (1973).

Aversion is commonly described as a "conditioning" treatment, but evidence that it works *mainly* by setting up conditioned anxiety responses is unimpressive (McConaghy & Barr, 1973; Bancroft, 1970a & b; Hallam & Rachman, 1972; Marks et al., 1970). Lasting conditioned anxiety is exceptional during aversion. Hallam et al. (1972) demonstrated increases in heart rate to deviant fantasies after successful aversion, but in another study Hallam and Rachman (1972) reported that such increases were also found to alcoholic stimuli in alcoholics who improved both with aversion and with nonaversive procedures. The usual response of patients who improve after aversion is to report, not anxiety, but indifference to their formerly attractive stimuli (Marks et al., 1970; Hallam et al., 1972). On semantic differential scales, attitudes to deviant objects usually change from being attractive to simply neutral rather than aversive (Bancroft, 1970b; Marks et al., 1970, 1977). The paradox is that, although aversion therapy works, it produces changes that are neutralizing rather than aversive.

Far from anxiety being associated with improvement to aversion, the opposite was found by Marks et al. (1970) and by Bancroft (1970a & b). Outcome at follow-up in transvestites and fetishists after aversion was significantly *negatively* correlated with anxiety scores for "myself" after three days aversion and for "electric shocks" on admission, and with devalued scores on admission for "other people with the same trouble as me." Morgenstern, Pearce, & Rees (1965) found that of transvestites treated by apomorphine aversion those who were less anxious and less introverted on admission did best. Similarly, Feldman and MacCulloch (1971) found the best prognosis in homosexuals with stable personalities who were least neurotic. In general, therefore, aversion seems to work best in patients with higher self-esteem and less anxiety before and during treatment.

The importance of an *aversive* stimulus is suggested by the results of Birk et al. (1971) in which a placebo conditioning procedure produced inferior results. However, this does not argue for *conditioning* processes—only a noncontingent shock control could prove this, and has not yet been reported in sexual deviants. The fact that backward conditioning has produced as good results as forward conditioning (McConaghy & Barr, 1973) argues against conventional conditioning mechanisms. That the precise form of aversion is not important indicates that the mechanisms of change are still poorly understood. Morgenstern et al. (1965) found that outcome to apomorphine aversion did not correlate with classical eyeblink conditioning; they thought that outcome did correlate with instrumental verbal conditioning, though

Rachman and Teasdale (1969, p. 162) questioned this conclusion. McConaghy and Barr (1973) found that outcome to electric aversion did not correlate with "classical appetitive conditioning" (erection to green triangles seen before male slides) although it did correlate with "classical aversive conditioning" (G.S.R. to tone before male slides). In the absence of a general factor of conditionability across stimulus-response systems, it is less useful to think in terms of general conditionability than to attend to the precise S-R systems involved. The concepts of stimulus prepotency (Marks, 1969 & 1972) and of species preparedness for some S-R connections rather than others (Seligman & Hager, 1972) suggest ideas for developing more powerful therapeutic tools. As an example, electric shock is an unnatural stimulus to connect with sexual responses. In contrast, smell might well be more potent, and a trial of smell versus covert sensitization and versus electric aversion in sexual deviations is overdue. Other stimuli such as apnea to scoline injections are less acceptable ethically.

During aversion treatment attitudes, erections, and behavior tend to change in parallel, although the usual sequence is not clear and may depend on the way in which aversion is applied; for example, aversion to erections may produce decrement in those before change in attitude, and vice versa.

Non Aversive Methods

Fading.   Here the deviant stimuli are gradually shifted toward a more conventional heterosexual content during periods of sexual arousal (*see* Marks, 1976, pp. 285–7). It can be executed purely in fantasy (Bancroft, 1971; Gold & Neufeld, 1965) or using slides (Beech, Watts, & Poole, 1971; Barlow & Agras, 1973).

Self-regulation.   With this method the precise conditions are defined under which self-control is deficient and the client is then trained to control impulses by interrupting the response chain; for example, by switching thoughts. Bergin (1969) described the treatment of a male and female homosexual with this method. Both patients did well until 10 to 12 months followup.

The only controlled trial of self regulation to date is that of Rooth and Marks (1974). The crossover design employed precluded statements about long-term effects. Self-regulation had a significant short-term effect but less so than electric aversion. The method required the patient and therapist to discuss the most recent exhibitionistic urges; data were obtained from a time sheet and daily self-regulation form. Choice points were identified and, where faced with alternative moves, the patient was instructed to take any action less likely to lead to exposure. Possible future situations were rehearsed and responded to; for example, one patient would get resentful when he felt unfairly treated at work or at home and would then plan to expose over the next few days. He was instructed to challenge such resentful or other moods and to articulate the covert decision to expose which was made at this point. Many patients disguised their decision to expose by pretending they wanted to go out for a walk or to go fishing. During self-regulation they became more aware of their exposure plans. As the patient moved toward a potential exposure situation (e.g., park or train) he had to become aware of the situation and its danger, and execute alternative behavior that would decrease the likelihood of exposure, for example, walk away from young girls, or if he could not do so, look at a shop window or read a newspaper, or memorize verse, solve crossword puzzles, think of his family, or look at a photograph of his children, or think of a policeman coming. The latter is a form of covert sensitization.

On that measure which improved most with self-regulation, the effect was significantly greater when it was preceded by electric aversion. The possibility of treatment combining both methods thus arises. One patient said that he felt unable to apply self-regulation when exhibitionistic urges were very strong, but used self-regulation successfully after their strength had been reduced by electric aversion. Self-administered aversion can be given by an elastic wrist band or by a portable shock box carried in one's pocket, and then constitutes a form of self-regulation.

Increasing Heterosexuality

Where deviants have clear heterosexual anxiety, reduction of this alone can sometimes lead to decrease in deviance, but we have no clear guidelines when to focus on reducing deviance and when on increasing heterosexuality. Where a sexual partner is available the usual sexual skills training employed for sex dysfunction can be used as described earlier. Social skills training may be necessary to help the patient obtain a partner. Deviant sexual arousal can also be paired with heterosexual arousal, as in "fading and shaping" or in "orgasmic conditioning." The latter describes masturbatory fantasies being systematically guided into heterosexual paths just before orgasm. In summary, behavioral forms of treatment are useful for sexual deviants, especially in reducing their deviant urges. However, more controlled work with follow-up is needed. Recent emphasis has shifted from external aversive to more self-regulatory methods, with patients learning to be their own case manager, using self-aversive methods when needed.

Transsexualism: Poor Behavioral Results versus One Triumph of Faithhealing

Transsexuals have a gender identity opposite to their anatomical sex. Behavioral methods to help this problem have so far been unencouraging. Marks et al. (1970) followed up 24 sexual deviants for two years after treatment and found that though 12 transvestites and fetishists and 5 sadomasochists maintained their improvement over two years, the 7 male transsexuals made little improvement by the end of treatment, and lost this completely by follow-up. Barlow, Abel, and Blanchard (1977) described limited improvement in 3 male transsexuals after massive prolonged behavioral programs over nearly a year; this improvement was maintained over three and five years in the 2 patients where follow-up was possible.

In contrast, Barlow, Abel, and Blanchard (1977b) reported dramatic and complete cure over 2½ years follow-up in a lifelong, 21-year-old transsexual (John) after one two to three hour session of "exorcism" by a physician faithhealer, and a "booster" of 15 minutes a few weeks later with a different faithhealer. This case is so well documented and raises such fundamental questions about psychotherapy that it requires discussion in detail. John had taken estrogens and developed breasts over the previous five years, been living as a woman (Judy) over the previous year, taken out a driver's license in a woman's name, and prepared his employer for his impending sex change through surgery. His feminine manner and attitude was rated in the transsexualism clinic during the year before surgery was planned.

Just before surgery John kept a promise to his employer (a woman owner of a fast food restaurant whom he had known for some years) to visit a physician of the same fundamental Protestant faith as his employer. This was foreign to that of John, who was raised as a Southern Baptist but was not religious. The physician examined John physically and said he could live quite well as a woman, but the real problem was possession by evil spirits. There followed two to three hours of exhortation and prayer, laying of the physician's hands on John's head and shoulders, and several faints by the patient. The physician exorcised 22 spirits which he called by name as they left John's body. During and after the session John experienced repeated waves of God's love come over him, and felt physically drained. In a letter to the authors, the physician confirmed this account, noting that he showed John his life was a fake, that Jesus could redeem him, and that a standard prescription of Scripture readings caused the spirit of the woman in John to disappear.

Immediately after the session John announced he was a man, discarded his female clothes, put on male clothes (hiding his breasts as best he could), and had his hair cut short in masculine style. In the next two weeks some feminine feelings recurred. He accompanied his employer to another faithhealer where the miracles he saw renewed his faith. After John waited 3½ hours in line the healer prayed and laid his hands on John for 10 or 15 minutes. The patient fainted twice, and as he stood to step off the platform down into the audience he "realized that his breasts were gone."

At follow-up there was no residual breast enlargement, though it is not clear when the breasts shrank. Some sexual thoughts of men disappeared after a few months. By 2½ years followup the patient had dated 10 girls, including one stable relationship, and looked forward to marriage. He reported sexual arousal to these girls, but did not masturbate nor consider coitus, and refused penile measurement to the viewing of erotic slides as his minister thought the viewing of nude males might

again allow the Devil access to his soul. John worked normally, and had been promoted. During a few hours of faithhealing he had acquired a complete repertoire of normal masculine behavior and a lasting masculine gender identity. Measures of these in the seven months before faithhealing and the 2½ years of followup fully bore out these changes.

Miracle cures of this kind are rarely described and measured so reliably, though they have occurred with apparently irreversible cancer as they have with behavioral problems. The speed and durability of these faithhealing cures leaves behavioral and other forms of psychotherapy far behind in terms of cost-effectiveness. The problem is repeatibility. In an ideal world maybe we could set up efficient faithhealing clinics for behavior change, but we don't know how to produce these results regularly and reliably. We are not likely to be funded in research toward this endeavor, perhaps rightly so because present knowledge does not help us design precise experiments in the area, or even tell us which questions are worthwhile. In the author's view the patient John offers us a tantalizing glimpse of immense possibilities for rapid behavioral change given so far unknown conditions. One of our tasks is to discover these conditions. When it works, faithhealing has a power far surpassing existing psychotherapy technology. The order of magnitude of this difference is like that between nuclear and more conventional explosives. But we have not yet harnessed nuclear power satisfactorily, and our understanding of faith and religious processes is far more primitive than our knowledge of subatomic particles. Given a prepared mind, however, some paths into this labyrinth might be laid down. The important point is for hard-nosed experimenters to be alive to these possibilities, while retaining their methological rigor.

OTHER NEUROTIC CONDITIONS

Mixed Neurosis

Controlled study of mixed neurotic patients are rare. A large controlled comparison of behavioral and psychodynamic psychotherapy was published by Sloane, Staples, Cristol, Yorkston, and Whipple

(1975). Though also reported elsewhere in this volume it is relevant to the theme of this chapter. They treated 94 mixed neurotic outpatients. These comprised 57 with anxiety states, 26 with personality disorders, and the remainder with a mixture of neurotic problems. Patients were assigned at random to treatment by experienced behavioral or psychoanalytic therapists, or they were placed on a four month wait list while remaining able to telephone a psychiatrist for help if need be, and being called at intervals by an assistant to assure them they were not forgotten. Each kind of treatment condition was given by one of three therapists for a mean of 14 sessions. Ratings were mainly blind, and in two-thirds of cases came from informants as well.

At four month follow-up patients from all three conditions improved significantly on target problems; both treatment groups improved significantly more than the wait list control group. Only behavioral patients improved significantly on work adjustment. By one year follow-up most wait list patients had also received treatment. There were now no significant differences between the three groups, though behavioral patients showed a trend for more improvement on target problems than did wait list patients. Improvement was maintained to two years follow-up. Those patients whose target problems improved also showed improvement in other measures of adjustment. Symptom substitution was not found..

Although there were few significant differences between the groups on measures of *outcome,* there were interesting differences in *process* variables in a direction opposite to what might have been anticipated. Behavior therapists were significantly more empathic and self-congruent and made more interpersonal contact with their patients than did psychoanlytic therapists (these variables did not correlate with outcome). Not surprisingly, more talking was done by patients during psychoanalytic sessions and by therapists during behavioral sessions. In both treatment conditions patients who spoke longer improved more. Behavioral therapists were more directive and informative. It is thought-provoking that psychoanalytic treated patients did better where they had received fewer "clarifications and interpretations" or were more liked by their therapists. The latter finding has often been reported elsewhere as well.

The interest of this careful study lies mainly in its process variables. Not surprisingly, few measures of outcome showed significant differences between the three treatment conditions, though the trend was for treated patients to do better than wait list patients and for patients who had "acting out" disorders on the MMPI to do better with a behavioral approach. As most behavioral treatments have been shown to exert their effect by specific procedures for particular forms of behavioral disorder, a broad approach for a mixed bag of difficulties loaded the dice against finding significant differences, as in fact occurred. Furthermore the wait list patients had far less therapist contact, and little expectation of improvement, merely marking time until they could receive treatment; thus even the limited superiority of the treated groups could be due to simple therapist contact, rather than to the behavioral or psychoanalytic content of the sessions. The indifferent (though statistically significant) results emphasize the importance of selecting suitable patients for behavioral psychotherapy. Most of the patients in the study of Sloane et al. had anxiety states and personality disorders. As yet these have not been shown to respond especially well to behavioral and not other treatment, despite extensive claims for anxiety-management-training in volunteers (reviewed by Marks, 1978).

Neurotic Depression

Much is written about the behavioral theory and treatment of depression. Depression is so common and serious as to constitute a major public health problem and several antidepressant drugs have a well established place in their treatment. Drugs have three disadvantages: (1) Improvement from them often takes several weeks to start; (2) drugs have side effects, though most patients tolerate these well; (3) some patients are not helped by drugs. When helpful, antidepressant drugs commonly need to be continued for many months or even for years, suggesting they are damping down the depressive process until it remits naturally, rather than curing the problem. On the other hand, several effective antidepressants are cheap, and little time is needed to prescribe and supervise them.

To be more useful than drugs, behavioral approaches have either (1) to be cheaper than drugs for the same amount of improvement, or (2) to produce greater improvement alone or in combination with drugs, or (3) to help sufferers who do not respond to drugs or do not take them because of side effects. As yet, present behavioral approaches are not specially promising for the management of severe depression.

One idea which has been advanced is that the state known as "learned helplessness" in animals and in humans constitutes a paradigm for clinical depression (Seligman, 1977). However, it has not so far been shown that learned helplessness is associated with the concomitants of serious clinical depression such as guilt, nihilism, suicidal ideas, anorexia, and insomnia lasting at least several weeks. At the moment the common features which have been demonstrated are *brief* blue mood, decreased reaction time and problem-solving ability, and distortion of skill expectancy. Furthermore, these deficits might well be present in many psychiatric states other than depression, and this remains to be tested. Because A and B share certain features C does not prove their commonality. Element C might also be present in D through Z. Seligman has commented (personal communication) that "model airplanes do not need to make transatlantic flights, they only need to embody the essence of flying in an airplane." Clinicians might reply that model airplanes cannot fly the Atlantic, and until they do they have little practical significance, as with so many other models.

Because learned helplessness diminishes after experience of mastery or success, these have been suggested as a treatment for clinical depression. However, success or mastery experiences have so far only been shown to be associated with transient improvement in mood and have not been demonstrated to be useful for severe and lasting clinical depression. Furthermore, in phobics and obsessives who improve with exposure treatments that provide many mastery experiences, the tendency to depressive spells remains unchanged (Marks, 1971; Marks et al., 1975). Although it is possible that to reduce depression the mastery experiences need to be in specific areas linked to that depression, this remains to be demonstrated. Until the learned helplessness model can be shown either to produce or to alleviate clinical depression its relevance remains dubious. It may be more relevant perhaps to states of chronic apathy such as those found in certain deprived children.

There are occasional case reports of behavioral approaches producing worthwhile results in isolated cases, for example, by contingency management (Liberman & Ruskin, 1971; Lewinsohn, 1975). A rash of controlled studies is appearing of cognitive, behavioral, and combined approaches in neurotic depression. They are summarized in Table 13-2. The results are sobering.

Five studies were on patients. In only one was uncontaminated comparison with controls possible at follow-up (Rush, Beck, Kovacs, & Hollow, 1977), and here there were no significant differences from drugs at follow-up, even though drugs were given for a shorter time (three months) than is customary with many clinicians, and the drug group had far less therapist contact. Harpin (1977) found no difference in depression between a cognitive-behavioral and a wait list condition even at the end of treatment. The other two studies had no follow-up.

Two studies were on volunteers. These compared the controls with treated groups only at the end of treatment, never at follow-up. The cognitive group of Taylor and Marshall showed some relapse of depression on the Hamilton Scale at one month follow-up (their fig. 2).

The largest clinical study to date is that of Rush et al. and this deserves more detailed consideration. Forty-one unipolar severely depressed outpatients were assigned randomly to individual treatment with either cognitive behavior therapy or imipramine 250 mg. daily. Treatment sessions were given weekly to a total of 12 for the drug group and a mean of 15 for cognitive behavioral treatment. Cognitive sessions lasted 50 minutes and drug sessions only 20 minutes, so that the cognitive group had a total of 750 minutes therapist time compared with only 210 minutes time for the drug-treated group.

By the end of treatment both groups improved significantly in depression, but cognitive behavior therapy produced significantly superior results on self-report and *non*-blind therapist and assessor ratings, and had fewer dropouts. At follow-up both groups maintained most of their improvement on self-ratings on the Beck Depression Inventory, though the cognitive group had lost some of their gains. However, differences were no longer significant between patients who completed cognitive or imipramine therapy ($p < .06$ at three months and $< .23$ at six months), although significantly more drug patients had asked for retreatment. This is of little consequence, as imipramine is cheap and requires negligible therapist time for maintenance. A weakness in the design was that imipramine was terminated after 11 weeks and not continued during follow-up, whereas many clinicians see the need to continue such medication for a longer period, though with minimal therapist contact. The point is emphasized by Beck's comment (personal communication) that patients improved again on retreatment.

If all patients *including dropouts* are included, the cognitive therapy group had significantly lower scores at three month follow-up than the drug group ($p < .01$). Including dropouts before drugs could act is not a fair trial of drugs, although it does raise the issue of treatment acceptability. In general tricyclic drugs have high acceptability. Where they do not, psychological treatments are worth considering. However, it should be remembered that treatment adherence can be increased by simple measures like involving relatives as co-therapists to give the drug (Blackwell, 1976), and keeping a diary of tablets taken. This is worth a try before giving up drugs, unless the side effects are serious.

Another flaw in the design of Rush et al. (1977) is that duration of therapist contact was far longer in the cognitive than in the imipramine patients. It is thus not clear whether the temporarily superior results of cognitive therapy were due to the specifically "cognitive" component of the treatment, or to the substantial directive therapist contact given to "cognitive" patients. Spending 350% more therapists' time can only be justified if the results are outstandingly and lastingly better than conventional treatment with tricyclics. This was hardly the case here. Patients were taken into this trial where they surpassed a score of 20 on the Beck Depression Inventory, whose maximum is given as 40 in Figure 2 of Rush et al. At six months follow-up the

mean score had decreased from 31 pretreatment to 8 for cognitive, and 12 for imipramine patients, a difference well within chance limits ($p < .23$), nor seems clinically worthwhile considering the much greater investment of time in cognitive patients. Rush et al. mention several further but unpublished studies concerning the value of cognitive therapy for depression. It remains to be seen whether their designs allow more optimistic conclusions.

At the moment behavioral or cognitive methods can hardly be recommended as a routine for neurotic depression. However, there is a case for helping patients with their social problems where such are present, in addition to giving them antidepressant medication. Klerman, Dimascio, Weissman, Prusoff, and Paykel (1974) found that depressed women who had already improved on amitriptyline maintained this improvement more in the next year of follow-up if they continued their medication, and improved in their social adjustment where they had casework. Outcome was best where they had both.

Also relevant is the finding that three potentially remedial features are associated with vulnerability of working class women to depression: lack of an intimate confidant, rearing of three or more small children unaided, and lack of employment (Harris, 1976). Help with such issues might be therapeutic.

Behavioral methods may have a contribution to make in helping patients solve life's difficulties, but it would be a pity if premature enthusiasm for "cognitive behavior therapy" raised unjustified hopes. More realistic would be careful exploration of the respective roles of antidepressant medication and various problem-solving approaches, separately and combined.

Stammering:
Stammering is sometimes regarded as neurotic behavior. It is usually the domain of the speech therapist, but speech control techniques have recently been adopted by behaviorists. Varied assemblies of procedures have been used, and the critical components are not yet clear, nor have adequate controlled trials with followup been done. The methods have been reviewed by Azrin and Nunn (1974) and by Burns and Brady (1977). The latter take about 20 sessions. In the first 8

TABLE 13-2 Depression: Controlled Studies of Behavioral and/or Cognitive Treatments

		N per Cell	Features of Population	No. of Sessions	Comparison Groups P=psychotherapy C=cognitive therapy B=behavior therapy W=waitlist v=versus	Follow-up (FU)	Comments
Outpatients							
Harpin	1978	6	chronic, mod/severely depressed; previous failure to respond to drugs	10	CB v W	6 months	no change for either group on depression. C + B improved on social adjustment. No control for therapist contact. No comparison possible at FU
Morris	1975	13	women only	6	C self-instruction v insight P v experiential P v W	0	C best at end of treatment, but no FU
Rush et al.	1977	20	chronic, severely depressed	15 for CB, 12 for drug	CB v imipramine	6 months	CB significantly better only at end of treatment, not at FU. CB had 350% > therapist contact

	Year						
Schmickley	1976	11	women only	4	CB only, reversal design	0	improvement decreased after reversal. No FU.
Shaw	1977	8	self-referred or from student Health Service	8	C v B v non-directive v W	1 month	blind raters. CB best at end of treatment; At FU, C=B, but no comparison with controls
Volunteers							
Gioe	1975	10	mild depression	?	C v positive group experience v both v control	?0	combined group did best; no change in self-concept. No FU
Taylor & Marshall	1977	7	not on drugs; depression "not less than two weeks duration"	6	C v B v CB combined v W	5 weeks	CB did best at end of treatment, but no comparison with W at FU

sessions they train the patient to be fluent with the aid of a desk metronome in the office and in the home. Speech rate is increased by gradually increasing the metronome rate and pacing longer units of speech to each of the metronome's beats. The target is a normal speech rate of 100 to 160 words per minute at home. During sessions 8 to 15 the desk metronome is replaced by a miniaturized electronic metronome that can be worn behind the ear in all treatment and practice situations. During this phase of generalization of fluent speech patients may have intense anxiety in certain feared situations and these can be overcome by graduated exposure methods. Finally in sessions 15 to 20 patients are gradually weaned from the metronome, starting with speaking situations where they have the least difficulty. Sometimes it is useful for them to pace their speech for a while to the beats of an imagined metronome.

When stutterers have great difficulty initiating speech Burns and Brady use an ancillary method called airflow, or easy onset. Speech is initiated only toward the end of an easy expiration of air, the first syllable is stretched in a smooth flowing movement blending imperceptibly with exhalation, and speech is slow. The airflow method helps blocks in getting ready to speak, whereas metronome-conditioned speech retraining focuses on the maintenance of adequate speech. Although good fluency can often be quickly achieved, many weeks and months of diligent daily practice are required before the airflow approach becomes an automatic part of normal speech. A home coach—a parent or spouse—is useful to provide feedback about correct daily practice at home. A coaching form can be kept which records the daily duration of practice, adequacy of breathing technique, stretching of the first syllable, rate of speaking and grouping of words.

In several double-blind studies reviewed by Burns and Brady, haloperidol was said to be significantly better than placebo in the treatment of stuttering. They use this drug in low doses (0.5 mg once or twice daily) in conjunction with speech retraining programs.

A variant of the airflow technique was described by Azrin and Nunn (1974) with encouraging results in fewer sessions than those of Burns and Brady. In the author's unit, using this method nurse-therapists taught stammerers to speak reasonably in a few sessions. Patients learned to breathe with the diaphragm rather than the chest, to speak only during exhalation with the diaphragm, and to practice this repeatedly in increasingly difficult and anxiety-provoking situations. This method can be taught in a group, with improvement continuing to 3 month follow-up in the author's unit.

Tics and Spasms.

Whether these are neuroses is debatable, as is the applicability of behavioral methods. However, Azrin and Nunn (1973) reported encouraging results by a habit reversal technique in which patients were required to perform the opposite movements to those involved in the tic whenever the tic came on, and nurse-therapists have applied this method successfully in several cases in the author's unit. R. Liberman reports the same (personal communication). Occupational spasms like writer's cramp can also be treated by this approach. Definitive evaluation requires more controlled study with long-term follow-up.

COST-EFFECTIVENESS AND ETHICS

Cost Effectiveness Considerations

As the effectiveness of behavioral psychotherapy comes to be recognized for certain conditions, demand for treatment of those conditions increases far more rapidly than the supply of therapists. Given limited therapeutic resources, increasing demands impose rationing by long waiting lists. Every patient taken on for treatment denies it to another who has to wait. Under this constraint, therapists can help many more patients by concentrating their scarce time on sufferers more likely to show tangible improvement with treatment. Obviously a certain proportion of a nation's resources needs to be devoted also to palliation as opposed to cure, to long-term as opposed to brief treatment, and to some patients who require massive therapeutic investment for limited improvement, in contrast to many who can benefit greatly with inexpensive interventions. Deciding the balance is a decision for the political arena and outside the scope of this chapter. However, it is worth examining some of the economic consequences of successful brief treatment of selected phobics and obsessives by behavioral psychotherapy. To this end, a pilot cost-benefit analysis was made of the costs and benefits of behavioral psychotherapy given by nurse-therapists for selected neurotic problems (Ginsberg & Marks, 1977).

A study of this kind necessarily bristles with assumptions. The first is that most patients who can benefit from brief behavioral treatment simply cannot get it. This assumption is borne out by the embarrassing surplus of suitable patients who come for behavioral treatment wherever nurse-therapists are made available in hospitals or in general practice settings. Many of these patients have previously had other forms of treatment, presumably without lasting benefit. How many were previously totally untreated is not known; only careful epidemiological research can indicate the size of the untreated pool in the community and such remains to be done. Yet other assumptions concern what should be included as costs and benefits, and the duration of benefits after behavioral treatment; this last rests upon outcome data cited earlier in this chapter. A final assumption is that untreated phobics do not improve (see final paragraph of this section).

Cost-benefit figures were based on the treatment of 42 neurotics (36 phobic, 3 obsessive-compulsive and 3 sexual disorders) whose mean duration of disorder was 12 years. They completed exposure treatment with nurse-therapists in a mean of 9 sessions (16 hours). Outcome of phobias was measured on a variant of the Gelder-Marks scale, whose interrater reliability was .91 (Marks et al., 1977). Reduction of phobias in patients treated by nurse-therapists was at least as good as that obtained on Gelder-Marks type scales in comparable patients who had exposure treatments from psychologists and psychiatrists in Britain and Canada. Significant improvement of the 42 patients also occurred on a fear survey schedule, free-floating anxiety, general neurotic symptoms on mood and work adjustment (Marks et al., 1977). These gains were not included in the economic calculations, as they could not be monetarized.

The cost-effectiveness calculations concerned

the year before and after treatment. Results found that monetary benefits after treatment largely resulted from three factors: reduced use of health care resources after treatment compared to before, less time taken off work, saved extra expenses to patients and their families formerly incurred through being ill. The internal rate of return became worthwhile when treatment benefits (improvement) continued beyond 2 years. For benefits lasting 3 years the internal rate of return was 39% per annum, reducing to 17% if the benefit of increased housework by patients was valued at 0 (Figure 13-8). To pass the 10% criterion used for British government projects benefits needed to continue at least 2¼ years when housework was included and 2¾ years when it was excluded. Were duration of benefits to last less than two years then the internal rate of return would become negative; that is, treatment could not be justified on purely economic grounds. This highlights the importance of long durations of follow-up in psychotherapy.

Given the reasonable assumption (see pp. 513-17) that benefits last for at least 3 years, the pilot study thus found that the purely monetary benefits of behavioral psychotherapy by nurse-therapists for selected neurotic patients produced a reasonable rate of return. Calculations for this study left aside the numerous psychiatric and human benefits that treatment generated to patients and their families. Intangible benefits like reduction in distress are still difficult to value and the cost benefit analysis treated the substantial decrease in suffering as having a value of 0 dollars.

The study emphasizes the importance of trying to maintain patients functioning in the community after the active phase of treatment has ended. After behavioral psychotherapy most patients do not need further treatment, though a selected minority do, and for them duration of improvement might be prolonged, perhaps indefinitely, if there were periodic brief reviews of progress of patients at risk, for example, phobics and obsessive-compulsives with a history of mood swings. Maintenance need not generally take more than a few hours a year, and could save the need for expensive readmission or other intensive retreatment. Follow-up servicing for selected patients could be productive, as a small

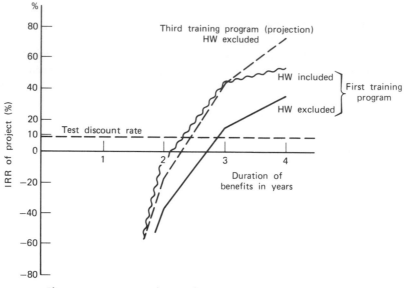

Figure 13-8   Internal rate of return (IRR), HW = housework.

therapeutic expenditure in terms of time and other resources might prolong benefits well beyond the three years at which the internal rate of return shows an unequivocal gain for money spent on treatment. Calculations from the pilot study showed that if 4 hours of posttreatment servicing annually per patient prolonged benefits from 2¾ to 4 years then the internal rate of return (excluding benefits from housework) would increase from 10 to 16 percent.

Ideally the cost-benefit study should have been controlled by randomly assigning patients to treatment and to no treatment. This was not feasible at the time. It is unlikely that the patient would have improved over the study period without treatment, as Agras et al. (1972) found that untreated agoraphobics did not improve over 5 years follow-up, and patients in the cost benefit study had been ill already for a mean of 12 years. The widely quoted two-thirds spontaneous remission rate for neurosis is a myth concerning a mixed bag of many types of problems, is highly questionable even then (see Cooper, Gelder, & Marks, 1965) and is inapplicable to a population consisting mainly of chronic phobics and obsessive compulsives. A cost-benefit study of different problems, sexual disorders, for examples might yield very different results from one in phobics. For a start, the

natural history might differ, as well as the economic consequences of the disorder and its remedy.

Honesty Towards the Consumer: A Psychotherapeutic Ethic.

As we have seen, behavioral psychotherapy is an effective treatment for certain neurotic syndromes such as chronic phobic and obsessive-compulsive disorders, and probably for some forms of sexual dysfunction. Indeed, so strong is the controlled clinical evidence for the value of certain behavioral methods in these conditions that some might question the ethics of giving other approaches of dubious efficacy for these syndromes. Eyebrows might be similarly raised by the withholding of antidepressant drugs or ECT for severe depression or phenothiazines for florid schizophrenia. Annon and Robinson (1976) opined "that it is now unethical to involve clients (with sexual dysfunction) in an expensive, long-term treatment program of any type without first trying to resolve their problem from within a brief therapy approach," the latter being behavioral in orientation.

Where the patient defines the goal of treatment as the reduction of phobias, obsessive-compulsive rituals, or sexual dysfunction, then it could be argued that inert or expensive procedures are unethical. However, if such patients are told clearly that the aim of, say, psychoanalysis, or an encounter group experience is the growth of "personality" or "self-awareness," and that the specific problems are *not* likely to improve as a result, then the ethics cannot be questioned. At the present time, many psychotherapists do not customarily specify to patients what they can and cannot expect to gain from treatment.

The time has come where our knowledge of treatment effects is sufficiently sound to be able to offer certain patients an informed choice. As an example, a compulsive ritualizer might be told that with up to 20 sessions of behavioral exposure *in vivo* he or she has a good chance of losing most of the compulsive rituals though wider aspects of his personality function will not be touched; Alternatively the patient could have intensive psychotherapy aimed at heightening self-awareness but in all likelihood leaving him or her with the same rituals as before. It is then up to the patient, the consumer, to decide according to what he or she wants to get out of treatment.

SUMMARY AND CONCLUSIONS

Behavioral psychotherapy of adult neurosis can be construed as operating within a dual process framework. First the patient needs to be motivated to seek and complete treatment. Second, during treatment he or she needs to execute those actions that are essential for improvement to occur. Treatment failure can result from lack of motivation leading to inadequate execution of therapeutic maneuvres. However, well-motivated patients do not improve from diligent execution of inert procedures. Some actions are more useful than others. Effective executive actions lead to patients learning to manage their hitherto undesirable emotions in those settings that trigger them, to monitor relevant events, and to devise strategies for dealing with snags. But it is too trite merely to say that behavioral treatments are exercises in the acquisition of self-control. To be meaningful the detailed chain of events required must be specified, and many more links have to be worked out before we can reach a reasonable theory of behavioral control.

Most behavioral approaches for phobic and obsessive-compulsive syndromes employ the common principle of exposure. This principle is also an integral part of social and sexual skills training programs, although these train new skills as well as reduce anxiety. The principle of exposure involves relief from anxiety by the individuals' continued contact with those situations that evoke discomfort (the evoking stimuli, ES). Clinicians need to search for those cues that trigger anxiety and to confront the patient, given his or her agreement, with these cues. Such exposure leads to eventual decrease in anxiety in most patients, but the mechanisms mediating this process are still far from clear. A crucial theoretical task for the future is separation of those parameters that lead exposure to be sensitizing from those that produce tolerance and improvement. Research in this field could thus illuminate both etiology and treatment.

The arousal level during exposure has not affected the rate of improvement. From controlled studies it is not crucial whether patients are relaxed, neutral, or anxious during exposure to the fantasied or real ES. In contrast, duration of exposure does seem important. Longer sessions of exposure *in vivo* were superior to shorter sessions in 2 controlled studies, one in agoraphobics and the other in compulsive ritualizers. Modeling is not a crucial determinant of improvement, though it may facilitate exposure in a minority.

In agoraphobics as well as specific phobics exposure *in vivo* has been successfully carried out in groups. Group exposure yields results comparable to those of individual exposure in vivo, and saves much therapist time. Treatment of agoraphobics can also be based on excursions from the patient's home rather than from the clinic. It is possible that ultimately behavioral treatments of anxiety act by persuading patients to exposure themselves to the ES outside treatment sessions. It remains to be seen how much therapist-assisted exposure, which constitutes the bulk of behavioral approaches to anxiety reduction, contributes anything beyond self-directed "exposure homework."

Biofeedback during exposure *in vivo* has been examined in two controlled investigations of specific phobics. While instructions to lower the heart rate with the aid of biofeedback does significantly lower the heart rate during exposure, this has not enhanced the reduction of subjective anxiety, skin conductance, or heart rate. Instructions to lower heart rate without feedback can have a significant effect alone, though this is augmented when feedback is added. At the present time biofeedback has little clinical value and requires unnecessary equipment, although research may in time lead to its being of more use in the clinic. That day has not yet come.

At a time when the demand for effective behavioral treatment outstrips the availability of therapists, cost-effectiveness considerations become important. A pilot study found that nurse-therapists' treatment of neurotics (mainly phobics and compulsives) yielded a worthwhile internal rate of return, given the reasonable assumption that benefits lasted three years. Benefits flowed mainly from reduced posttreatment use of health resources, reduced time of patients and relatives lost from work, and fewer expenses due to illness. Economics can be expected to dictate policy increasingly in the delivery of behavioral and other forms of psychotherapy.

The contribution of psychotropic drugs to behavioral treatment of phobics and obsessives is not yet clear. In controlled studies diazepam during exposure *in vivo* produced conflicting results. Beta blockers have not been of lasting value. A significant but limited effect was found in phobics from so-called "antidepressants," including both monoamineoxidaze inhibitors and tricyclics; relapse was common on stopping the drugs.

Several controlled trials with phobic and obsessive-compulsive patients have found exposure treatments to produce significant reduction in the phobias and rituals in 1 to 30 sessions. This improvement has been greater than with nonexposure treatments and lasts up to the two to four year follow-ups available. Such results have been obtained independently by several centers in different countries. Desensitization in fantasy can be regarded as a weak and slow form of exposure. Exposure *in vivo* appears more potent. Relaxation is an inert and redundant procedure for reducing phobias and rituals, both by itself, or in combination with exposure treatments. Time is much better spent concentrating on exposure.

Sexual dysfunction has recently been shown to respond to a "behavioral Masters and Johnson" approach. Several controlled studies have found this approach superior to contrasting methods, with one follow-up showing improvement up to 18 months later. Good results have been obtained using one rather than two therapists per couple. This questions whether the doubling of expense by use of two therapists is justified by the marginal gains in outcome it produced in the only controlled study of this issue. Early experiments with group treatments of couples with sexual dysfunction have been encouraging.

Behavioral methods are also useful for reducing a variety of sexual deviations. Recent emphasis has moved away from the patient passively being averted by the therapist toward devising his or her own self-management program, including self-administered aversion when necessary.

Although neurotic depression has been treated by a "cognitive-behavioral" approach designed to give the patient "success" or "mastery" experiences, it is much too early to know the value of this approach. Although useful results have been obtained using speech retraining, breathing exercises, and "habit reversal" in stammerers and in tic-queurs, these pilot reports need replication with long-term follow-up.

Clinical behavioral psychotherapy has recently developed its own experimental base separate from the study of animals and volunteers, although these three areas cross-fertilize one another. Evidence is lacking that behavioral psychotherapy has much to offer the commonest mild diffuse neuroses such as transient depression and anxiety. It has a crucial role, however, for defined neurotic syndromes like phobic and obsessive-compulsive disorders, and plays an important part in the management of social skills deficits, sexual dysfunction, and sexual deviation.

Many questions remain unanswered, but these indications are based on controlled evidence. This leads to a clear psychotherapeutic ethic. Honesty toward consumers, in this instance patients with such neuroses, dictates that they should be given an informed choice of treatments knowing their effects, for example, up to 20 sessions of behavioral treatment for the reduction of compulsive rituals without major personality change, or some other approach less likely to diminish rituals, but perhaps having other effects.

In conclusion, behavioral psychotherapy is now the treatment of choice in several defined neurotic syndromes that make up perhaps 10 percent of all psychiatric outpatients. Improvement continues over several years follow-up and can spill over into nontargeted areas. Trained nurses can do these treatments as well as other professionals, and yield worthwhile results in cost-benefit terms. The role of drugs with behavioral treatments of neurosis awaits definition from further research (see also Chapter 12). Indiscriminate use of behavioral treatments for *all* neurotic patients can lead to much wasted effort. The most efficient use of behavioral treatment in neurosis comes from selection of suitable patients who are responsive to appropriate approaches in a reasonably short time. The potency of some behavioral methods also gives them a theoretical application as tools of experimental psychopathology which can illuminate mechanisms maintaining behavior. In mapping out the many possibilities for behavior change, our geography needs to include the startling but rare and unpredictable cures effected by religious healers.

REFERENCES

Agras, W S., Chapin, N., & Oliveau, D. C. The natural history of phobia: course and prognosis. *Archives of General Psychiatry,* 1972, *26,* 315–317.

Annon, J. S. *The behavioral treatment of sexual problems.* Vol. 1: Brief therapy, 1974. Kapiolani Health Services, 1319 Punahoa Street, Honolulu, Hawaii, 96814. Enabling Systems Inc.

Annon, J. S., & Robinson, C. H. The use of vicarious learning in the treatment of sexual concerns. Unpublished, 1976.

Azrin, N. H., & Nunn, R. G. Habit reversal: a method of eliminating nervous habits and tics. *Behavior Research and Therapy,* 1973, *11,* 619–628.

Azrin, N. H., & Nunn, R. G. A rapid method of eliminating stuttering by a regulated breathing approach. *Behavior Research and Therapy,* 1974, *12,* 279–286.

Bancroft, J. H. J. A comparative study of two forms of behaviour therapy in the modification of homosexual interest. M.D. Thesis, University of Cambridge, 1970a.

Bancroft, J. H. J. A comparative study of aversion and desensitisation in the treatment of homosexuality. Chapter in: Burns, L. E. & Worsley, J. H. (Eds) *Behaviour therapy in the 1970's.* 1970b, Bristol: Wright.

Bancroft, J. H. J. The application of psychophysiological measures to the assessment and modification of sexual behavior. *Behavior Research and Therapy,* 1971, *9,* 119–130.

Bancroft, J. H. J. *Deviant sexual behaviour: Modification and assessment.* Oxford: Clarendon, 1974.

Bancroft, J. H. J. The treatment of marital sexual problems: Comparison of 3 methods. Paper to International Academy of Sex Research, Stonybrook, N.Y. 1975.

Bancroft, J. H. J. Issues in sex therapy. Paper to EABT, Spetsae, Greece, Sept. 1976.

Bandura, A. Psychotherapy based upon modeling principles. In A. E. Bergin & S. L. Garfield (Eds.). *Handbook of Psychotherapy,* New York: Wiley, 1971.

Bandura, A. Self-efficacy: Towards a unifying theory of behavioral change. *Psychological Review,* 1977, *84,* 191–215.

Bandura, A., Adams, N. E., & Beyer, J. Cognitive processes mediating behavior change. Unpublished manuscript, Stanford University, 1977.

Bandura, A., Blanchard, E. B., & Ritter, B. Relative efficacy of desensitisation and modeling approaches for inducing behavioral, affective and attitudinal changes. *Journal of Personality and Social Psychology,* 1969, *13,* 173.

Bandura, A., Grusec, J. E., & Menlove, F. L. Vicarious extinction of avoidance behavior. *Journal of Personality and Social Psychology,* 1967, *5,* 16.

Barlow, D. H., Abel, G. G., & Blanchard, E. B. Gender identity change in transsexuals: followup and replications. 1977a, in preparation.

Barlow, D. H., Abel, G. G., & Blanchard, E. B. Gender identity change in transsexuals: an exorcism. *Archives of Sexual Behavior,* 1977b, *6,* 387–395.

Barlow, D. H., & Agras, W. S. Fading to increase heterosexual responsiveness in homosexuals. *Journal of Applied Behavior Analysis,* 1973, *6,* 355–366.

Barlow, D. H., Agras, W. S., Leitenberg, H., Callahan, E. F., & Moore, R. C. The contribution of therapeutic instruction to covert sensitization. *Behavior Research and Therapy,* 1972, *10,* 411–5.

Barlow, D. H., Leitenberg, H., & Agras, W. S. The experimental control of sexual deviation through manipulation of the noxious scene in covert sensitisation. *Journal of Abnormal Psychology,* 1969, *74,* 596–601.

Beech, H. R., Watts, F., & Poole, A. D. Classical conditioning of sexual deviation: a preliminary role. *Behavior Therapy,* 1971, *2,* 400–402.

Benjamin, S., Marks, I. M., & Huson, J. Active muscular relaxation in desensitization of phobic patients. *Psychological Medicine,* 1972, *2,* 381.

Bergin, A. E. A technique for improving desensitization via warmth, empathy and emotional reexperiencing of hierarchy events. In R. D. Rubin, C. M. Franks and A. A. Lazarus (Eds.) *Proceedings of the Association for Advancement of the Behavioral Therapies.* New York: Academic Press, 1969.

Birk, L., Huddleston, W., Miller, E., & Cohler, B. Avoidance conditioning for homosexuality. *Archives of General Psychiatry,* 1971, *25,* 314–323.

Blackwell, B. Treatment adherence. *British Journal of*

Psychiatry, 1976, *129,* 513–531.

Boulougouris, J. C. Variables affecting the behaviour of obsessive-compulsive patients treated by flooding. Paper to EABT Spetsae, Greece, Sept. 1976. In Boulougouris, J. C., and Rabavilas, A. (Eds). *Studies in phobic and obsessive-compulsive disorders.* Oxford: Pergamon, 1977.

Brady, J. P. Metronome-conditioned speech retraining for stuttering. *Behavior Therapy,* 1971, *2,* 129–150.

Burns, D., & Brady, J. P. The treatment of stuttering. Chapter in Goldstein, A. and Foa, E. B. (eds). *Handbook of behavioral interventions.* New York: Wiley, 1977.

Butollo, W. & Mittalstaedt, L. Systematic combination of treatment components for severe phobic disorders. Paper to EABT, Spetsae, Greece, Sept. 1976. In Boulougouris, J. C. & Rabavilas, A. (Eds). *Studies in phobic and obsessive-compusive disorders.* Oxford: Pergamon, 1977.

Callahan, E. F. & Leitenberg, H. Aversion therapy for sexual deviation: contingent shock and covert sensitisation. *Journal of Abnormal Psychology,* 1973, *81,* 60–73.

Capstick, N. Anafranil in obsessional states—a followup study. Paper presented at the Fifth World Congress of Psychiatry, Mexico, 1971.

Cautela, J. R. & Wisocki, P. A. The use of male and female therapists in the treatment of homosexual behavior. Chapter in Rubin, R. & Franks, C. (Eds). *Advances in behavior therapy,* New York: Academic Press, 1969.

Colson, C. E. Olfactory aversion therapy for homosexual behavior. *Journal of Behavior Therapy and Experimental Psychiatry,* 1972, *3,* 1–3.

Cooper, B. Clinical and social aspects of chronic neurosis. *Proceedings of the Royal Society of Medicine,* 1972, *65,* 509.

Cooper, J. C., Gelder, M. G., & Marks, I. M. Results of behaviour therapy in 77 psychiatric patients. *British Medical Journal,* 1965, *3,* 1222.

Cooper, B., Harwin, B. G., Depla, C. & Shepherd, M. Mental Health Care in the community: an evaluative study. *Psychol. Med.,* 1975, *5,* 372–380.

Crowe, M. J. Evaluation of conjoint marital therapy. D. M. dissertation, University of Oxford, 1976.

Crowe, M. J., Marks, I. M., Agras, W. S., & Leitenberg, H. Time limited desensitisation, implosion and shaping for phobic patients: A crossover study. *Behavior Research and Therapy,* 1972, *10,* 319–328.

Curtis, R. H., & Presley, A. S. The extinction of homosexual behavior by covert sensitization: a case study. *Behavior Research and Therapy,* 1972, *10,* 81–84.

Davison, G. C. Elimination of a sadistic fantasy by a client-centered counter-conditioning technique. *Journal of Abnormal Psychology,* 1968, *73,* 84–9.

Emmelkamp, P. M. G. Self-observation in the treatment of agoraphobia. *Behavior Research and Therapy,* 1974, *12,* 229.

Emmelkamp, P. M. G., & Emmelkamp-Benner, A. Effects of historically portrayed modeling and group treatment on self-observation: a comparison with agoraphobics. *Behavior Research and Therapy,* 1975, *13,* 135.

Emmelkamp, P. M. G., & Ultee, K. A. A comparison of "successive approximation" and "self-observation" in the treatment of agoraphobia. *Behavior Therapy,* 1974, *5,* 606.

Emmelkamp, P. M. G., & Wessels, H. Flooding in imagination v. flooding in vivo. A comparison with agoraphobics. *Behavior Research and Therapy,* 1975, *13,* 7.

Everaerd, W. T. Paper to Annual Meeting of EABT., Greece, Sept. 1976.

Everaerd, W., Lambers, K., van der Bout, J., & Schacht, H. II. A comparative analysis of sex therapy and communication training in the treatment of female sexual dysfunction. 1977a, awaiting publication.

Everaerd, W. T., Rijken, H. M., & Emmelkamp, P. M. G. A comparison of "flooding" and successive approximation in the treatment of agoraphobia. *Behavior Research and Therapy,* 1973, *11,* 105.

Everaerd, W., Stufkens-Veerman, I., Van der Bout, J., Hofman, A., Sijben-Schrier, M., & Schacht, H. III. A comparative analysis of an adaptation of Masters and Johnson and systematic desensitization methods in the treatment of male sexual dysfunction. 1977b, awaiting publication.

Falloon, I. R. H., Lindley P., McDonald, R., & Marks, I. M. Social skills training of outpatient groups: a controlled study of rehearsal and homework. *British Journal of Psychiatry,* 1978, *131,* 599–609.

Feldman, M. P. Abnormal sexual behaviour in males. Chapter in Eysenck, H. J. (Ed.) *Handbook of Abnormal psychology,* 2nd Ed. London: Pitman, 1973.

Feldman, M. P. & MacCulloch, M. J. *Homosexual behaviour: Therapy and assessment,* Oxford: Pergamon, 1971.

Foa, E. B. & Goldstein, A. Continuous exposure and complete response prevention treatment of obsessive-compulsive neurosis. Behavior Therapy, 1978, In press.

Franzini, L. R. Magnitude estimations of the aversiveness of the interval preceding shock. *Journal of Experimental Psychology,* 1970, *84,* 526–8.

Frankl, V. E. Paradoxical intention and dereflection: Chapter in Arieti, S. (Ed.) New Dimensions in Psychiatry: A world view. New York: Wiley, 1975.

Freud, S. On the psychical mechanism of hysterical phenomena, pp. 24–6. In *Collected Works,* Vol. I. Hogarth Press and Institute of Psychoanalysis. 1892.

Freud, S. The justification for detaching from neurasthenia a particular syndrome: The anxiety neurosis, pp. 78–106. In *Collected Works,* Vol. I. Hogarth Press and Institute of Psychoanalysis, 1894.

Freud, S. A reply to criticisms on the anxiety neurosis, pp. 107–127. In *Collected Works,* Vol. 1. Hogarth Press and Institute of Psychoanalysis, 1895.

Gaind, R., Watson, J. P., & Marks, I. M. Some approaches to the treatment of phobic disorders. *Proceedings of the Royal Society of Medicine,* 1971, *64,* 1118.

Gaind, R. The role of beta blockers in behaviour therapy. Paper to European Association of Behaviour Therapy, Greece, Sept. 1976.

Garfield, S. Research on client variables in psychotherapy. In A. B. Bergin and S. L. Garfield

(Eds.) *Handbook of psychotherapy and behavior change,* Chappter 8, New York: Wiley, 1971.

Garfield, S. L., & Kurz, M. Evaluation of treatment and related procedures in 1216 cases referred to a mental hygiene clinic. *Psychiatric Quarterly,* 1952, *26,* 414–424.

Gelder, M. G., & Marks, I. M. A crossover study of desensitisation in phobias. *British Journal of Psychiatry,* 1968, *114,* 323–328.

Gelder, M. G., Marks, I. M. & Wolff, H. Desensitisation and psychotherapy in phobic states: a controlled enquiry. *British Journal of Psychiatry,* 1967, *113,* 53.

Gelder, M. G., Bancroft, J. H. J., Gath, D. H., Johnston, D. W., Mathews, A. M. & Shaw, P. M. Specific and non specific factors in behavior therapy. *British Journal of Psychiatry,* 1973, *123,* 445.

Gillan, P. & Rachman, S. An experimental investigation of behavior therapy in phobic patients. *British Journal of Psychiatry,* 1974, *124,* 392.

Ginsberg, G. & Marks, I. M. Cost and benefits of behavioural psychotherapy: a pilot study of neurotics treated by nurse-therapists. 1977, *Psychological Medicine, 7,* 685–700.

Gioe, V. J. Cognitive modification and positive group experiences as a treatment for depression. Ph.D. dissertation, Temple University, 1975.

Gittelman-Klein, R. & Klein, D. F. Controlled imipramine treatment of school phobia. *Archives of General Psychiatry,* 1971, *25,* 204.

Gold, S. & Neufeld, I. L. A learning approach to the treatment of homosexuality. *Behavior Research and Therapy,* 1965, *2,* 201–4.

Goldberg, D. P. & Blackwell, B. Psychiatric illness in general practice. A detailed study using a new method of case identification. *British Medical Journal,* 1970, *2,* 439.

Greene, R. J. & Hoarts, D. L. Aversive tickling: a simple conditioning technique. *Behavior Therapy,* 1971, *2,* 389–393.

Gurman, A. S. Implications of marital therapy research. Chap. 22 in Gurman, A S. & Rice, D. G. (Eds.). *Couples in conflict,* 1975, New York: Jason Aronson.

Hafner, J., & Marks, I. M. Exposure in vivo of agoraphobics: the contributions of diazepam, group exposure and anxiety evocation. *Psychological Medicine,* 1976, *6,* 71–88.

Hafner, J., & Milton, F. The influence of propanolol on the exposure in vivo of agoraphobics. Unpublished, 1978.

Hallam, R., Rachman, S., & Falkowski, W. Subjective, attitudinal and physiological effects on electrical aversion therapy. *Behavior, Research and Therapy,* 1972, *10,* 171–180.

Hand, I., Lamontagne, Y., & Marks, I. M. Group exposure (flooding) in vivo for agoraphobics. *British Journal of Psychiatry,* 1974, *124,* 588.

Harbert, T. L., Barlow, D. H., Hersen, M., & Austin, J. B. Measurement and modification of incestuous behavior: a case study. *Psychological Reports,* 1973.

Harpin, E. A psychosocial treatment of depression. Ph.D. dissertation. Department of Psychology, State Univ. of New York. 1978.

Harris, T. Social factors in neurosis, with special reference to depression. Chapter in Van Praag, H. M. *Research in neurosis.* Bohn, Schellema & Holkenna, Utrecht. 1976.

Hart, J. D. Fear reduction as a function of the assumption and success of a therapeutic role. Unpublished master's thesis. Univ. of Wisconsin, 1966.

Hodgson, R., Rachman, S., & Marks, I. M. The treatment of chronic obsessive-compulsive neurosis: followup and further findings. *Behavior Research and Therapy,* 1972, *10,* 181–189.

Hudson, B. L., Tobin, J. C., & Gaind, R. Followup of a group of agoraphobic patients. Paper presented at the Second Annual Conference of Psychiatry, Mexico, 1972.

Husain, M. Z. Desensitization and flooding (implosion) in treatment of phobias. *American Journal of Psychiatry,* 1971, *127,* 1509–1514.

Husted, J. R. The effect of method of systematic desensitization and presence of sexual communication in the treatment of female sexual anxiety by counterconditioning. Ph.D. dissertation UCLA. Dissertation Abstracts International 1972, No. 72–20, 446. (Cited by Annon, 1974.)

Johnston, D., & Gath, D. Arousal levels and attribution effects in diazepam-assisted flooding. *British Journal of Psychiatry,* 1973, *122,* 463–466.

Johnston, D., Lancashire, M., Mathews, A. M., Munby, M., Shaw, P. M. & Gelder, M. G. Imaginal flooding and exposure to real phobic situations: changes during treatment. *British Journal of Psychiatry,* 1976, *129,* 372.

Johnstone, A., & Goldberg, D. Psychiatric screening in general practice. *Lancet,* 1976, *1,* 605–608.

Kaplan, H. S., Kohl, R. N., Pomeroy, W. B., Offit, A. R., & Hogan, B. Group treatment of premature ejaculation. *Archives of Sexual Behavior,* 1974, *3,* 443–452.

Kass, D., Stauss, F. F., Weill, E., Greist, J. H., Chiles, J. A., & Thurrell, R. J. *Sex therapy at home,* New York: Simon and Schuster, 1976.

Kazdin, A. E. Covert modeling and the reduction of avoidance behavior. *Journal of Abnormal Psychology,* 1973, *81,* 87.

Kazdin, A. E. Covert modeling, model similarity, and reduction of avoidance behavior. *Behavior Therapy,* 1974a, *5,* 325.

Kazdin, A. E. The effect of model identity and fear-relevant similarity on covert modeling. *Behavior Therapy,* 1974b, *5,* 624.

Kazdin, A. E. Effects of covert-modeling and model reinforcement on assertive behavior. *Journal of Abnormal Psychology,* 1974c, *83,* 240.

Kazdin, A. E. Covert modeling, imagery assessment and assertive behavior. *Journal of Consulting and Clinical Psychology,* 1975, *34,* 716.

Kazdin, A. E., & Wilcoxon, L. A. Systematic desensitization and nonspecific treatment effects: a methodological evaluation. *Psychological Bulletin,* 1976, *83,* 229–258.

Kinsey, A. C., Pomeroy, W. B., & Martin, C. E. *Sexual behaviour in the human male.* Philadelphia: W. B. Saunders, 1948.

Kinsey, A. C., Pomeroy, W. B., & Martin, C. E. Sexual behavior in the human female. Philadelphia: W. B. Saunders, 1953.

Klein, D. F. Delineation of two drug-responsive anxiety syndromes. *Psychopharmacologia*, 1964, *5*, 397.

Klerman, G. L., Dimascio, A., Weissman, M., Prusoff, B., & Paykel, E. S. Treatment of depression by drugs and psychotherapy. *American Journal of Psychiatry*, 1974, *131*, 2.

Kockott, G. Behaviour therapy for sexual inadequacy. Paper to EABT, Greece, Sept. 1976.

Kockott, G., Dittmar, F., & Nusselt, L. Systematic desensitisation of erectile impotence: a controlled study. *Archives of Sexual Behavior*, 1975, *4*, 493.

Kolvin, I. "Aversive imagery" treatment in adolescents. *Behavior Research and Therapy*, 1967, *5*, 245–9.

Knopff, W. F. History of the term "neurosis." Paper to Fifth World Congress of Psychiatry, Mexico, 1971.

Kumar, K., & Wilkinson, J. C. M. Thought-stopping: a useful treatment in phobias of "internal stimuli." *British Journal of Psychiatry*, 119, 305, 1971.

Leiblum, S. R., Rosen, R. C., & Pierce, D. The group treatment format: mixed sexual dysfunctions. *Archives of Sexual Behavior*, 1975, *5*, 313–322.

Lewis, S. A comparison of behavior therapy techniques in the reduction of fearful avoidance behavior. *Behavior Therapy*, 1974, *5*, 648.

Lewinsohn, P. M. The behavioral study of treatment of depression. Chapter in Hersen, R., et al. (Eds.) *Progress in behavior modification*, Vol. I. p. 19–64, New York: Academic, 1975.

Levy, R. & Meyer, V. Ritual prevention in obsessional patients. *Proceedings of the Royal Society of Medicine*, 1971, *64*, 1115.

Lieberman, M. A., & Gardner, J. R. Institutional alternative to psychotherapy. *Archives of General Psychiatry*, 1976, *33*, 157–162.

Liberman, R., & Ruskin, D. E. Depression: a behavioral formulation. *Archives of General Psychiatry*, 1971, *24*, 515–523.

Lipsedge, M. S. Therapeutic approaches to compulsive rituals: a pilot study. M. Phil. dissertation, University of London, 1975.

Lipsedge, M., Hajioff, J., Huggings, P., Napier, L., Pearce, J., Pike, D. J., and Rich, M. The management of severe agoraphobia: a comparison of iproniazid and systematic desensitization. *Psychopharmacologia*, 1973, *32*, 67.

LoPiccolo, J. Effective components of systematic desensitization. Unpublished doctoral dissertation, Yale University, 1969.

LoPiccolo, J. Direct treatment of sexual dysfunction. Chapter in Money, J. & Musaph, H. (Eds.) *Handbook of sexology* Amsterdam: ASP Biological and Medical Press, 1975.

LoPiccolo, J. A program for enhancing the sexual relationship of normal couples. *The Counseling Psychologist*, 1975, *5*, 41–46.

Luborsky, L., Chandler, M., Auerbach, A. H., Cohen, J., & Bachrach, H. M. Factors influencing the outcome of psychotherapy: a review of quantitative research. *Psychological Bulletin*, 1971, *75*, 145–185.

McConaghy, N. Subjective and penile plethysmograph responses following aversion-relief and apomorphine aversion therapy for homosexual impulses. *British Journal of Psychiatry*, 1969, *1*, 151–3.

McConaghy, N., & Barr, R. F. Classical, avoidance and backward conditioning treatments of homosexual-

ity. *British Journal of Psychiatry*, 1973, *122*, 151–162.

McFall, R. M., & Twentyman, C. T. Four experiments on the relative contributions of rehearsal, modeling, and coaching to assertion training. *Journal of Abnormal Psychology*, 1973, *81*, 199.

McGovern, K., Kirkpatrick, C., & LoPiccolo, J. A behavioral group treatment program for sexually dysfunctional couples. *Journal of Marriage and Family Counseling*, Oct. 1976, 397–404.

Mahoney, M. J. The self-management of covert behavior. A case study. *Behavior Therapy*, 1971, *2*, 575.

Maletzky, R. M. "Assissted" covert sensitisation: a preliminary report. *Behavior Therapy*, 1973, *4*, 117–9.

Marchetti, A., McGlynn, F. D., & Patterson, A. S. Effects of cue-controlled relaxation, a placebo treatment, and no treatment on changes in self-reported and psychophysiological indices of test anxiety among college students. *Behavior Modification*, 1977, *1*, 47–72.

Marks, I. M. *Patterns of meaning in psychiatric patients.* Maudsley Monograph No. 13. Oxford: Oxford University Press, 1965.

Marks, I. M. *Fears and phobias.* Heinemann Medical and Academic Press, 1969.

Marks, I. M. Phobic disorders 4 years after treatment. *British Journal of Psychiatry*, 1971, *118*, 683–8.

Marks, I. M. Flooding (implosion) and related treatments: Chapter 6 in Agras, W. S. (Ed.) *Behavior modification: Principles and clinical applications.* Boston: Little, Brown, 1972.

Marks, I. M. Research in neurosis: a selective review. 1. Causes and courses. *Psychological Medicine*, 1973, *3*, 436.

Marks, I. M. Behavioral treatments of phobic and obsessive-compulsive disorders: a critical appraisal. Chapter in Hersen R. et al. (Eds.) *Progress in behavior modification*, Vol. I. New York: Academic Press, 1975.

Marks, I. M. The current status of behavioral psychotherapy: theory and practice. *American Journal of Psychiatry*, 1976, *133*, 253.

Marks, I. M. "Psycholopharmacology": The use of drugs combined with psychological treatment. Chapter in Evaluation of Psychological Therapies. Spitzer, R. L., & Klein, D. F. (Eds) *Proceedings of the 64th Annual Meeting of the APA,* Baltimore: Johns Hopkins Univ. Press, 1976b.

Marks, I. M. Exposure Treatments. Chapter in Agras, S. (Ed) *Behavior modification* 2nd Ed. Boston: Little, Brown, 1978.

Marks, I. M. Phobias and obsessions. Chapter in Maser, J. & Seligman, M. (Eds.) *Experimental psychopathology.* New York: Wiley, 1977.

Marks, I. M., Bird, J., & Lindley, P. Behavioural nurse therapists. *Behavioural Psychotherapy*, 1978, *6*, 25–36.

Marks, I. M., Boulougouris, J., & Marset, P. Flooding vs. desensitization in phobic disorders. *British Journal of Psychiatry*, 1971, *119*, 353.

Marks, I. M. & Gelder, M. G. Transvestism and fetishism: A clinical and psychological change during faradic aversion. *British Journal of Psychiatry*, 1967, *113*, 711–739.

Marks, I. M., Gelder, M. G., & Edwards, J. G. A controlled trial of hypnosis and desensitisation for phobias. *British Journal of Psychiatry*, 1968, *114*, 1263.

Marks, I. M., Gelder, M. G., & Bancroft, J. H. J. Sexual deviants two years after aversion. *British Journal of Psychiatry*, 1970, *117*, 173–185.

Marks, I. M., Hallam, R. S., Philpott, R., & Connolly, J. *Behavioural psychotherapy for neurosis: An advanced clinical role for nurses.* Book for Research Series of Royal College of Nursing, 1977. Cavendish Square, London, W. 1.

Marks, I. M., Hodgson, R., & Rachman, S. Treatment of chronic obsessive-compulsive neurosis by in vivo exposure: a two year followup and issues in treatment. *British Journal of Psychiatry*, 1975, *127*, 349.

Marks, I. M., Viswanathan, R., & Lipsedge, M. S. Enhanced extinction of fear by flooding during waning diazepam effect. *British Journal of Psychiatry*, 1972, *121*, 493.

Mathews, A. M. Psychophysiological approaches to the investigation of desensitization and allied procedures. *Psychological Bulletin*, 1971, *76*, 73.

Mathews, A. M. Behavioural treatment of agoraphobia: New findings and new problems. Paper to EABT, Greece, Sept. In Boulougouris, J. & Rabavilas, A. (Eds). *Phobias and obsessions.* Oxford: Pergamon, in press.

Mathews, A. M., Johnston, D. W., Shaw, P. M., & Gelder, M. G. Process variables and the prediction of outcome in behaviour therapy. *British Journal of Psychiatry*, 1974, *125*, 256–264.

Masters, W., & Johnson, V. *Human sexual inadequacy.* Boston: Little, Brown, 1970.

Mathews, A. M., Johnston D. W., Lancashire, M., Munby, D., Shaw, P.M. & Gelder, M. G. Imaginal flooding and exposure to real phobic situations: Treatment outcome with agoraphobic patients. *British Journal of Psychiatry*, 1976b, *129*, 362–371.

Mathews, A. M., Teasdale, J., Munby, M., Johnston, D., & Shaw, P. A home based treatment programme for agoraphobics. *British Journal of Psychiatry*, 1977.

Mathews, A. M., Whitehead, A., Hackmann, A., Julier, D., Bancroft, J., Gath, D. & Shaw, P. The behavioural treatment of sexual inadequacy: a comparative study. *Behavior Research and Therapy*, 1976, *14*, 427.

Mawson, A. N. Methohexitone-assisted desensitization in the treatment of phobias. *Lancet*, 1970, *1*, 1084–1086.

Meichenbaum, D. *Cognitive behavior modification.* New York: Plenum, 1978.

Meyer, V. Modification of expectations in cases with obsessional rituals. *Behavior Research and Therapy*, 1966, *4*, 273.

Meyer, V., & Levy, R. Treatment of obsessive-compulsive neurosis. *Proceedings of the Royal Society of Medicine*, 1971, *64*, 1115.

Meyer, V., Levy, R., & Schnurer, A. The behavioural treatment of obsessive-compulsive disorders. Chapter 10, p. 233–258 in Beech, H. R. (Ed.) *Obsessional states.* London: Methuen, 1974.

Morgenstern, F. S., Pearce, J. F., & Rees, W L. Predicting the outcome of behaviour therapy by psychological tests. *Behavior Reseach and Therapy*, 1965, *2*, 191–200.

Morris, N. E. A group self-instruction method for the treatment of depressed outpatients. Ph.D. dissertation. Univ. of Toronto, 1975.

Munjack, D., Cristol, A., Goldstein, A., Phillips, D., Goldberg, A., Whipple, K. Staples, F., & Kanno, P. Behavioural treatment of orgasmic dysfunction: a controlled study. *British Journal of Psychiatry*, 1976, *129*, 497–502.

Nunes, J., & Marks, I. M. Feedback of true heart rate during exposure in vivo. *Archives of General Psychiatry*, 1975, *32*, 933–936.

Nunes, J., & Marks, I. M. Feedback of true heart rate during exposure in vivo. Partial replication with methodological improvement. *Archives of General Psychiatry*, 1976, *33*, 1346.

Obler, M. Systematic desensitization in sexual disorders. *Journal of Behavior Therapy and Experimental Psychiatry*, 1973, *4*, 93–101.

Olley, M., & McAllister, H. Some psychometric reflections on the status of phobic illness. *Psychological Medicine*, 1974.

Rabavilas, A. D., Boulougouris, J. C., & Stefanis, C. Duration of flooding session in the treatment of obsessive-compulsive patients. *Behavior Research and Therapy*, 1976, *14*, 349–355.

Rachman, S. & Teasdale, J. *Aversion therapy.* Oxford: Pergamon, 1969.

Rack, P. H. Intravenous anafranil and obsessional states. Paper presented at the Fifth World Congress of Psychiatry, Mexico, 1971.

Reitz, W. E., & Keil, W. E. Behavioral treatment of an exhibitionist. *Journal of Behavior Therapy and Experimental Psychiatry*, 1971, *2*, 67–69.

Rezin, V. A., & Mathews, A. M. Imaginal exposure with dental phobics. Paper to BABP Annual Meeting, Exeter, July, 1976.

Robertson, J. A. Role of response prevention in treatment of obsessive-compulsive disorders. Paper to Soc. for Psychotherapy Res. London, July, 1975.

Robinson, C. H. The effects of observational learning on sexual behaviors and attitudes in orgasmic dysfunctional women. Doctoral dissertation, Univ. of Hawaii, 1974 (cited by Annon and Robinson, 1976) Dissertation Abstracts International 1975, 35 (9-B) Univ. Microfilms, No. 75–5040, 221.

Rooth, F. G., & Marks, I. M. Aversion, Self-regulation and relaxation in the treatment of exhibitionism. *Archives of Sexual Behavior*, 1974, *3*, 227–248.

Roper, G., Rachman, S. & Marks, I. Passive and participant modelling in exposure treatment of obsessive-compulsive neurotics. *Behavior Research and Therapy*, 1975, *13*, 271.

Rosen, G. M. Is it really necessary to use mildly phobic analogue subjects? *Behavior Therapy*, 1975, *6*, 68–71.

Rosen, R. C. & Schapp, B. J. The use of a specific behavioral technique (thought stopping) in the context of conjoint couples therapy: A case report. *Behavior Therapy*, 1974, *5*, 261–4.

Rosenthal, D., & Frank, J. D. The fate of psychiatric clinic outpatients assigned to psychotherapy. *Journal of Nervous and Mental Disease*, 1959, *127*, 330–343.

Royce, W. S. & Arkowitz, H. Multimodel evaluation of in

vivo practice as treatment for social isolation, 1977, awaiting publication.

Rush, A. J., Beck, A. T., Kovacs, M., Hollon, S. Comparative efficacy of cognitive theory and pharmacotherapy in the treatment of depressed outpatients. *Cognitive Therapy, 1,* 1977, *1,* 17–37.

Russell, R. K., Miller, D. E. & June, L. N. Group cue-controlled relaxation in the treatment of test anxiety. *Behavior Therapy,* 1975, *5,* 572.

Schacht, H., van Vloten, A., Mol, H., Everaerd, W. I. A comparative analysis of an adaptation of Masters and Johnson and systematic desensitisation methods in the treatment of female sexual dysfunction. 1977, awaiting publication.

Schmickley, V. G., & Johnson, R. G. Cognitive Therapy and Research. I. A self-managed cognitive-behavioral treatment for depression. 1977.

Seligman, M. Chapter in Maser, J. and Seligman, M. (Eds.) *Psychopathology.* San Francisco: W. H. Freeman & Co., 1977.

Seligman, M., & Hager, J. *Biological boundaries of learning.* New York: Appleton-Century-Crofts, 1972.

Serber, M. Shame aversion therapy. *Behavior Therapy and Experimental Psychiatry,* 1970, *1,* 219–221.

Serber, M. Shame aversion therapy with and without heterosexual training. In *Advances in behavior therapy.* New York: Academic Press, 1972.

Shaw, B. F. A comparison of cognitive therapy and behavior therapy in the treatment of depression. *Journal of Consulting and Clinical Psychology.* 1977, *45,* 543–51.

Shepherd, M., Cooper, B., Kalton, G. W., & Brown, A. C. *Psychiatric illness in general practice,* Oxford University Press, London: 1966.

Sherman, A. R. Real life exposure as a primary therapeutic factor in desensitisation treatment of fear. *Journal of Abnormal Psychology, 79,* 19, 1972.

Siegelman, M. Adjustment of male homosexuals and heterosexuals. *Archives of Sexual Behavior,* 1972a, *2,* 9–25.

Siegelman, M. Adjustment of homosexual and heterosexual women. *British Journal of Psychiatry,* 1972b, *120,* 477–481.

Sloane, R. B., Staples, F. R., Cristol, A. H., Yorkston, N.J., Whipple, K., *Psychotherapy versus behaviour therapy.* Cambridge, Mass. and London: Harvard University Press, 1975.

Sollod, R. N. & Kaplan, H. S. The new sex therapy: an integration of behavioral psychodynamic and interpersonal approaches. In Claghorn, J. L. (Ed). *Successful psychotherapy.* New York: Brunner Mazel. 1977.

Solyom, L., Heseltine, C. F. O., McClure, D. J., Ledwidge, B., & Kenny, F. Comparative study of aversion relief and systematic desensitisation in the treatment of phobias. *British Journal of Psychiatry,* 1971, *119,* 299–303.

Solyom, L., Heseltine, C. F. O., McClure, D. J., Solyom, C., Ledwidge, B., & Steinberg, G. Behaviour therapy versus drug therapy in the treatment of phobic neurosis. *Canadian Psychological Association Journal,* 1973, *18,* 25.

Solyom, L., Lapierre, Y. D. Solyom, C., & Smyth, D. The interaction of phenelzine and exposure to the phobic situation in the treatment of phobias. Paper to Canad. Psychiat. Assoc. Meeting, Ottawa, 1974.

Stampfl, T. G. Implosive therapy: the theory, the subhuman analogue, the strategy and the technique. Part I, the theory. In Armitage, S. G. (Ed.) *Behavior modification techniques in the treatment of emotional disorders,* Battle Creek, Mich.: V.A. Publication, 1967, pp. 22–37.

Stern, R. S. Treatment of a case of obsessional neurosis using thought-stopping technique. *British Journal of Psychiatry, 117,* 441, 1970.

Stern, R. S., Lipsedge, M. S., & Marks, I. M. Thought-stopping of neutral and obsessive thoughts: a controlled trial. *Behavior Research and Therapy,* 1973, *11,* 659.

Stern, R. S., & Marks, I. M. A comparison of brief and prolonged flooding in agoraphobics. *Archives of General Psychiatry,* 1973, *28,* 210.

Stuart, R. B. Operant interpersonal treatment for marital discord. *Journal of Consulting Clinical Psychologists,* 1969, *33,* 675–682.

Stuart, R. B. Behavioral remedies for marital ills. Chap. 12 in Gurman, A. S., & Rice, D. G. (Eds). *Couples in conflict,* New York: Jason Aronson, 1975.

Sue, D. The effect of duration of exposure on systematic desensitization and extinction. *Behavior Research and Therapy,* 1975, *15,* 55.

Tanner, B. A. Shock intensity and fear of shock in the modification of homosexual behaviour in males by avoidance learning. *Behavior Research and Therapy,* 1973a, *11,* 213–8.

Taylor, F. G., & Marshall, W. L. A cognitive behavioral therapy for depression. *Cognitive Therapy & Research, 1,* March 1977.

Teasdale, J. D., Walsh, P. A., Lancashire, M., & Mathews, A.M. Group exposure for agoraphobics: a replication study. *British Journal of Psychiatry,* 1977, *130,* 186.

Thase, M. E. & Moss, M. J. The relative efficacy of covert modeling procedures and guided participant modeling. *Journal of Behavior Therapy and Experimental Psychiatry,* 1976, *7,* 7–12.

Tyrer, P. J., Candy, J., & Kelly, D. H S. Phenelzine in phobic anxiety: a controlled trial. *Psychological Medicine,* 1973, *3,* 120.

Tyrer, P., & Steinberg, D. Symptomatic treatment of agoraphobia and social phobias: a followup study. *British Journal of Psychiatry,* 1975, *127,* 163–8.

Ullrich, R., Ullrich, R., Crombach, G., & Peikert, V. Alpha and beta blockers in flooding in vivo of agoraphobia. Unpublished manuscript. 1974.

Waters, W. F., McDonald, D. G., & Koresko, R. L. Psychophysiological responses during analogue desensitization and non-relaxation control procedures. *Behavior Research and Therapy,* 1972, *10,* 381.

Watson, J. P., Gaind, R., & Marks, I. M. Prolonged exposure: a rapid treatment for phobias. *British Medical Journal,* 1971, *1,* 13.

Watson, J. P., & Marks, I. Relevant vs. irrelevant flooding in the treatment of phobias. *Behavior Therapy,* 1971, *2,* 275.

Watson, J. P., Mullett, G. E., & Pillay, H. The effects of prolonged exposure to phobic situations upon agoraphobic patients treated in groups. *Behavior*

Research and Therapy, 1973, *11,* 531.

Wincze, J. P., & Caird, W. K. A comparison of systematic desensitization and video desensitization in the treatment of sexual frigidity. AABT meeting in Miami, Dec. 1973 (cited by Annon and Robinson, 1976).

Wolpe, J. *Psychotherapy by reciprocal inhibition.* Stanford: Stanford University Press, 1958.

Wooley, S. C., Epps, B., & Blackwell, B. Pain tolerance in chronic illness behavior. *Psychosomatic Medicine,* 1975, *37,* 1. (Jan–Feb).

Yamagami, T. The treatment of an obsession by thought stopping. *Journal of Behavior Therapy and Experimental Psychiatry,* 1971, *2,* 233.

Yamamoto, J. & Goin, M. K. Social class factors relevant for psychiatric treatment. *Journal of Nervous and Mental Diseases,* 1966, *142,* 332–9.

Yorkston, N., Sergeant, H. & Rachman, S. Methohexitone relaxation for desensitizing agoraphobic patients. *Lancet,* 1968, *2,* 651–653.

Zitrin, C. Unpublished manuscript 1976.

14

THE APPLICATION OF OPERANT TECHNIQUES IN TREATMENT, REHABILITATION, AND EDUCATION

ALAN E. KAZDIN[1]

The Pennsylvania State University

A major area within behavior modification is the application of techniques derived from operant conditioning. A wide range of therapeutic procedures has been developed from such principles as reinforcement, extinction, punishment, stimulus control, and others. For any given principle or empirically established relation between antecedent and consequent events and behavior, several behavior-change procedures can be generated. For example, procedures based upon positive reinforcement can vary greatly depending on the reinforcer selected, antecedent events with which the response consequences are associated, who administers the reinforcer or determines the criterion for reinforcement, and various parameters of reinforcement such as magnitude, schedule, and quality of the reinforcer. Operant conditioning techniques that are used for therapeutic purposes have been described and illustrated in other

[1]This chapter was completed while the author was a Fellow at the Center for Advanced Study in the Behavioral Sciences.

sources (e.g., Gelfand & Hartmann, 1975; Kazdin, 1975a; Sulzer & Mayer, 1972).

Aside from a set of techniques, the operant approach embraces specific methodological characteristics such as the focus on individual subjects, assessment and modification of clearly defined overt behaviors that can be reliably recorded, and an emphasis on antecedent and consequent events to change behavior. The experimental approach embraced by the application of operant techniques is referred to as "applied behavior analysis" and has been described elsewhere (Baer, Wolf, & Risley, 1968; Kazdin, 1978b; Risley, 1970). More than a specific set of techniques and experimental stance, the operant approach consists of a conceptualization of behavior and its treatment. Krasner (1971) has outlined the view of abnormal behavior from the standpoint of operant conditioning and highlighted some of the major historical developments that led to contemporary applications.

The application of operant techniques in treatment, rehabilitation, and education has proliferated in recent years. This proliferation can be attested to in several ways. First, recent compendia and annual reviews that encompass the entire domain of behavior modification (e.g., Franks & Wilson, 1977; Hersen, Eisler, & Miller, 1977) and operant techniques or applied behavior analysis (e.g., Brigham & Catania, 1977; Leitenberg, 1976; Ramp & Semb, 1975) document the recent advances with select techniques and applications. Second, within the last several years, the application of operant techniques and methods has increased in diverse disciplines including psychiatry, clinical psychology, education, special education, mental retardation, and others, as shown by journal publications in each of these areas (Kazdin, 1975c). Finally, the range of settings, populations, and target problems to which operant techniques are applied has extended remarkably (Kazdin, 1975b).

The growth of operant techniques in the last few years militates against a complete review of the research, treatment accomplishments, techniques, and trends in a single chapter. This chapter provides a status report of contemporary applied behavior analysis plus an overview of the accomplishments of operant techniques with diverse populations, reviews of recent trends and advances, and a discussion of select issues that remain to be adequately resolved. In addition, operant techniques are critically evaluated across several dimensions and compared with alternative treatment techniques. Finally, the chapter addresses legal issues that affect the application and implementation of operant techniques in applied settings.

AN OVERVIEW OF MAJOR ACCOMPLISHMENTS IN TREATMENT, REHABILITATION, AND EDUCATION

This section provides an overview of treatment accomplishments with various populations and across several behaviors. The populations discussed include psychiatric patients, the mentally retarded, individuals in classroom settings, children in institutional settings, delinquents, adult offenders, drug addicts, alcoholics, medical patients, and outpatient applicants.

The research that is reviewed, with few exceptions, consists of experimental work that has met the usual methodological desiderata of applied behavior analysis. Hence, the investigations typically include assessment of overt behavior, although global measures may be included as well. Also, the interventions usually are evaluated experimentally either in intrasubject replication, or less commonly, between-group designs. In addition, the interventions usually are carefully described so that treatment effects can be replicated. Thus, the relation between behavior and environmental events with which it is associated are specified.

The vast amount of research on the therapeutic application of operant techniques across diverse populations and target behaviors precludes scrutiny of the methodological adequacy or unresolved issues of individual investigations in the present chapter. Hence, the overview provided in this section is largely uncritical. Of course, presenting the accomplishments of operant research is not meant to obscure criticisms of the literature. Indeed, the literature reviewed in the present section will be critically evaluated later in the chapter.

Psychiatric Patients

Operant techniques have been applied widely with psychiatric patients (see Gripp & Magaro, 1974; Kazdin, 1975d for reviews). In most applications, token economies are implemented on a ward where patients can earn tokens (e.g., points, coins, tickets) for specific target behaviors (e.g., self-care, attending occupational therapy) and spend them for various backup events in the setting (e.g., items at a canteen, extra ground privileges).

General Wardwide Programs

The majority of reinforcement programs for psychiatric patients have emphasized adaptive behaviors in the hospital such as self-care, performing jobs on and off the ward, attending and participating in activities, taking medication, cleaning one's room, and so on. This focus characterized early ward programs in the field and has continued through the present (Kazdin, 1977c). The evidence shows very clearly that general ward behaviors can be readily altered. Altering routine ward behaviors has been considered useful in overcoming maladaptive and dependent behaviors associated with institutionalization. Perhaps of greater interest, reinforcing behaviors such as housekeeping, grooming, attending occupational therapy, and social behaviors has reduced such behaviors or states as screaming, depression, and overt ritualistic and compulsive mannerisms associated with hallucinations (Anderson & Alpert, 1974; Hersen, Eisler, Alford, & Agras, 1973; O'Brien & Azrin, 1972). Many other improvements are made when adaptive behaviors are altered including increases in cooperativeness on the ward, communication skills, social interaction, mood states, reductions in ratings of psychoticism, and less reliance on medication (Maley, Feldman, & Ruskin, 1973; Shean & Zeidberg, 1971).

Perhaps, the most general measure of improvement, and probably the one most amenable to the influence of nontreatment variables, is discharge and subsequent readmission. Programs focusing on general ward behaviors usually show increased patient discharge and lower readmission rates than custodial care (e.g., Hollingsworth & Foreyt, 1975; Rybolt, 1975). The extent to which changes in these measures can be unambiguously attributed to the contingencies often is unclear because implementing the program may reflect an overall change in hospital philosophy with respect to discharge (Gripp & Magaro, 1974; Kazdin & Bootzin, 1972).

Symptomatic Behaviors

Several programs have focused directly on therapeutically significant behaviors. In many programs, delusional, paranoid, or irrational verbalizations have been altered by reinforcing coherent and/or punishing incoherent verbalizations (e.g., Kazdin, 1971; Patterson & Teigen, 1973; Wincze, Leitenberg, & Agras, 1972). For example, Liberman, Teigen, Patterson, and Baker (1973) provided and terminated social interaction with delusional chronic paranoid schizophrenics contingent on their speech. Delusional speech terminated interaction with staff whereas protracted rational speech earned evening chats with a therapist. In a multiple-baseline design across patients, the social contingencies were shown to increase the duration of rational speech. Other behaviors have been altered such as episodes of excessive crying, aggres-

sive and violent acts, and compulsive handwashing (see Kazdin, 1975d, 1977c; Stahl & Leitenberg, 1976).

Social Behaviors

To overcome social withdrawal, several programs have developed behaviors ranging from simple greeting responses to peer social interaction. In some programs, verbalizations in the context of group sessions have been increased by providing social or token reinforcement for conversation (e.g., Liberman, 1972; Tracey, Briddell, & Wilson, 1974). In other programs, patients have received contingent attention, tokens, or money for such behaviors as talking to, working or playing with, or being in close proximity to another individual (Leitenberg, Wincze, Butz, Callahan, & Agras, 1970; Wallace & Davis, 1974). For example, Doty (1975) provided psychiatric patients with money contingent upon their social behaviors on the ward (e.g., proximity to others and social interaction). Social behaviors increased on the ward and transferred to group discussion sessions where no specific contingencies were invoked. Social behaviors reinforced in the context of specific treatment sessions have been shown to transfer to the ward (e.g., Bennett & Maley, 1973).

Other Behaviors

A wide range of other behaviors have been altered such as performing academic tasks, assisting the staff, making eye contact with a therapist, violating ward rules, losing weight, and others. A few areas seem particularly interesting and relevant to the patient's hospital treatment. For example, Parrino, George, and Daniels (1971) decreased pill-taking by withdrawing tokens for PRN (pro re nata) medication, i.e., those pills delivered "as needed." Over a 20-week period, there was a substantial reduction in the use of medication. Another area that affects the patient's hospital stay is the role that they take in their own treatment. Several self-help behaviors have been altered such as making suggestions for ward practices and management, making group decisions, and submitting treatment proposals that are likely to lead to discharge (e.g., Greenberg, Scott, Pisa, & Friesen, 1975; O'Brien, Azrin, & Hensen, 1969; Olson & Greenberg,

1972). Thus, increasingly patients are given greater control over their own fate in the hospital.

The Mentally Retarded

Operant techniques have been widely applied to the mentally retarded (see Birnbrauer, 1976; Gardner, 1971; Kazdin, 1977c, 1978a; Thompson & Grabowski, 1972 for reviews).The range of behaviors is especially great because of the different levels of retardation focused on in diverse settings ranging from institutions and day-care facilities to sheltered workshops and special classrooms.

Ward and Self-Care Behaviors

Operant programs have focused on self-care behaviors related to institutional life including getting up, grooming, attending activities, exercising, and tooth brushing, similar to many programs with psychiatric patients (see Kazdin, 1977c). For the retarded, extensive attention has been given to developing fundamental skills such as toileting, self-feeding, and dressing.

Certainly, the area that has received the greatest attention and notoriety has been toilet training. Although several investigators have effectively trained toileting skills, Azrin and Foxx (1974; Foxx & Azrin, 1973) have developed a treatment "package" that has been particularly effective. The package is comprised of several techniques including frequent and immediate reinforcement of dry pants and for urinating correctly, a large number of trials to practice appropriate toileting, imitation and manual guidance to help initiate behaviors, symbolic rehearsal of the desired behavior, and other techniques. The procedure has effectively eliminated toileting accidents both with institutionalized retarded as well as "normal" children in a relatively brief period of time (e.g., in less than a day [Azrin & Foxx, 1974]). Follow-up data suggest that the gains are maintained several months after treatment (Foxx & Azrin, 1973).

Self-stimulatory and Bizarre Behaviors

Self-stimulatory behaviors such as rocking, head weaving, and hand gestures or self-destructive acts such as headbanging, face slapping, and biting frequently are performed by the retarded. An extensive literature is available showing that operant techniques significantly reduce self-stimulatory behaviors (e.g., Forehand & Baumeister, 1976; Frankel & Simmons, 1976; Smolev, 1971). Electric shock has been especially effective in reducing these behaviors, although alternative procedures have been successful as well. Providing reinforcing consequences for not engaging in self-stimulation or especially requiring individuals to perform specific effortful behaviors contingent upon self-stimulation (i.e., positive practice) have been effective. For example, Azrin, Kaplan, and Foxx (1973) reduced self-stimulatory behaviors (e.g., rocking, head weaving) in severely and profoundly retarded adults with positive practice (requiring and manually guiding extensive rehearsal of behaviors incompatible with self-stimulation contingent upon the response) and reinforcement for incompatible behaviors. The combined practice and reinforcement procedures rapidly reduced self-stimulation to almost zero.

In addition to self-stimulatory behaviors, various bizarre behaviors have been suppressed. For example, Foxx (1976) used overcorrection to eliminate public disrobing (stripping) in two profoundly retarded adults. Requiring the residents to wear extra clothing and to help others with their grooming and dressing needs, contingent on disrobing, eliminated this behavior within two weeks. Other bizarre or disruptive behaviors have been suppressed in the retarded including exhibitionism (Lutzker, 1974), sprawling on the floor (Azrin & Wesolowski, 1975), agitated behaviors such as screaming and crying (Webster & Azrin, 1973), and eating trash and excrement (Foxx & Martin, 1975), to mention a few examples. In many reports, follow-up data indicate that the suppressed behaviors do not return.

Verbal Behavior and Language Acquisition

Diverse forms of verbal behavior have been altered including receptive and productive language, topographical features of speech, speech content, and inappropriate speech. The behavior focused on depends on the age and initial skill level of the client. For example, with the severely retarded, language behaviors may consist of verbally identifying various stimuli such as letters and numbers and asking simple questions (e.g., Twardosz &

Baer, 1973). With moderately retarded clients, the focus may be on developing correct subject-verb agreement in speech (e.g., Lutzker & Sherman, 1974). With borderline retardates, the focus may be on verbalizations about specific topics such as current events (e.g., Keilitz, Tucker, & Horner, 1973). In many studies, idiosyncratic aspects of speech are altered. For example, Jackson and Wallace (1974) reinforced increases in voice volume with tokens in a mildly retarded child who spoke almost inaudibly. Wheeler and Sulzer (1970) developed appropriate sentences in a boy who omitted articles and auxiliary verbs when speaking. An important focus that has received attention is the responsiveness of retardates to the language of others. Various studies have developed responsiveness to instructions or instruction-following behavior (e.g., Frisch & Schumaker, 1974; Gladstone & Sherman, 1975; Whitman, Zakaras, & Chardos, 1971). For example, Kazdin and Erickson (1975) provided food and physical prompts (guidance) to severely and profoundly retarded adolescents and adults for following instructions in a cooperative play task. In a multiple-baseline design across residents, the procedures were shown to markedly enhance instruction following. Developing responsiveness to instructions is an important focus with individuals who have severe response deficits. Once verbal control over behavior is established, it may facilitate the acquisition of other behaviors.

Social Behaviors

Relatively few operant programs have focused on social behaviors with the retarded. Some studies have altered greeting responses. For example, Stokes, Baer, and Jackson (1974) developed handwaving of severely or profoundly retarded children. Responses, initially prompted by the experimenter, were reinforced with food, verbal approval, and physical pats of approval. In other reports, with higher level retardates, peer interaction has been altered. For example, Kazdin and Polster (1973) increased the frequency that two male adult borderline retardates conversed with their peers in a sheltered workshop setting by delivering tokens for conversing. Knapczyk and Yoppi (1975) increased play behaviors of five institutionalized educably retarded children. Points and praise were delivered for initiating either cooperative or competitive play.

Work-Related Behaviors

Programs frequently focus on aspects of work in an attempt to develop community job placements. In many programs, trainable retardates receive praise, or more commonly tokens, for increasing productivity and accuracy of task completion (see Kazdin, 1977c). For example, Welch and Gist (1974) reported a comprehensive program where retardates received tokens for completing jobs in a day-treatment facility. As the clients improved in their performance, they were allowed to advance to a job that entailed greater responsibility and prestige within the faciility. The eventual goal was to place individuals at the highest level of responsibility into community work. Initial results suggested that the program was successful, although the effects could not be unambiguously attributed to the reinforcement contingencies.

Test Performance

A major determinant of child placement into educational and rehabilitation settings is performance on standardized psychological tests. Interestingly, some studies have shown that the incentive conditions during test administration influence performance. For example, trainable retardates as well as children of "average" intelligence improved on readiness or intelligence tests under conditions of token or food reinforcement (Ayllon & Kelly, 1972, Exp. 1 & 2; Edlund, 1972). Altering the conditions of test administration, of course, alters the interpretation that can be made of the test results. Thus, perhaps of greater interest is the use of tests administered under standard conditions. Ayllon and Kelly (1972, Exp. 3) showed that trainable retardates who participated in a reinforcement program for academic responses showed superior performance on the Metropolitan Readiness Test to control subjects who were not exposed to the special program.

Individuals in Classroom Settings

Operant techniques have been applied more extensively in the classroom than in any other setting (Kazdin, 1975b). The focus on the setting in which the progrm has been conducted rather than the population is justified here in part because of the similarity of the programs. Reinforcement programs have been established in the classroom with diverse populations (e.g., "normal" children, retardates, delinquents), educational levels (e.g., preschool, highschool, and college), and settings (e.g., classes in hospitals, special education and adjustment classes).

Disruptive and Inattentive Behavior

The majority of programs have focused upon classroom deportment at the elementary school level. The goals are to increase attentiveness to the lesson and to decrease disruptive behavior such as being out of one's seat, talking without permission, fighting, disturbing someone else, not complying with instructions, complaining, and so on. The delivery of praise and tokens for appropriate deportment has been shown to dramatically alter behavior in a plethora of studies (Drabman, 1976; Kazdin, 1975a; O'Leary & O'Leary, 1972).

In most programs, the assumption has been that increasing attentive or study behavior will enhance academic performance. With high levels of disruption, some amount of appropriate deportment might be a precondition for academic progress. However, most studies have focused on mildly disruptive classes where eliminating disruptions often does not increase academic performance (e.g., Ferritor, Buckholdt, Hamblin, & Smith, 1972; Harris & Sherman, 1974). Operant techniques might be training individuals to be quiet in class as an end in itself without any clear implications for progress in academic areas (Winett & Winkler, 1972). Fortunately, research increasingly has focused upon academic behaviors directly rather than upon deportment alone (Kazdin, 1975b).

Academic Behaviors

A major impetus for focusing on academic behaviors is the finding that academic performance is not necessarily changed when deportment is improved. Perhaps more impressive is the finding that deportment often is improved when students receive reinforcing consequences for their academic performance (e.g., Ayllon, Layman, & Burke, 1972; Ayllon & Roberts, 1972; Marholin, Steinman, McInnis, & Heads, 1975).

A wide range of academic behaviors have been altered with operant techniques including reading, writing, arithmetic, and spelling, completing in-class and homework assignments, developing vocabulary, and others. Many behaviors represent complex response classes. For example, to develop creative writing, elementary school students have received tokens for specific compositional skills such as using different adjectives, action verbs, novel sentence beginnings, and new and different words (e.g., Brigham, Graubard, & Stans, 1972; Glover & Gary, 1976; Maloney & Hopkins, 1973). Alteration of specific compositional skills is related to subjective judgments of composition quality.

Programs that focus on academic performance in the classroom have shown promising gains in student performance. Several studies have shown that students participating in such programs increase on achievement test performance (e.g., Stanford Achievement Test, Wide Range Achievement Test) relative to untreated controls (e.g., Bushell, 1974; Clark, Lachowicz, & Wolf, 1968; Kaufman & O'Leary, 1972; Kent & O'Leary, 1976). Some studies have reported changes in tested intelligence (e.g., Wechsler Intelligence Scale for Children) (Mulligan, Kaplan, & Reppucci, 1973; Sachs, 1971). However, in most of the above studies, the use of operant techniques specifically has not been demonstrated to account for the improvements. Methodological artifacts (e.g., differential regression among treatment and control groups) and the inability to conduct true experiments (e.g., nonrandom assignment of subjects) has led to some interpretive problems.

Operant techniques have been incorporated into college level teaching in a method referred to as the Personalized System of Instruction (PSI), developed by F. S. Keller (1968; Ryan, 1972). PSI refers to a way of structuring a course so that specific contingencies are devised toward course completion. The features include allowing the students to complete course requirements at their own rate, dividing the course content into units, providing exams over each unit, allowing repeated examination until mastery over the content is achieved, providing immediate feedback for performance, and others. Self-paced courses have included a number of variations on the original procedure. Research shows that instructional systems based upon the Keller method or its variations often result in higher levels of mastery and retention of course material relative to traditional course formats.

Other Behaviors

Specific behaviors have been studied in the classroom aside from deportment and academic performance and include developing instructional control over behavior, developing speech for children with articulation problems, and increasing participation in activities. Social behaviors have received attention as well. For example, Sacks, Moxley, and Walls (1975) reinforced social interaction (with cards that made pictures) of three withdrawn preschoolers. The cards were delivered for entering and remaining in a group and talking to adults or other children. In an especially interesting program, Hauserman, Walen, and Behling (1973) reinforced interracial social interaction in a first grade classroom. To socially integrate black children in the predominantly white classroom, students received tokens and praise for selecting a "new friend" during lunch. Although interracial combinations were not specified as the desired response, these increased during the reinforcement phase and temporarily transferred to a free-play period after lunch.

Children in Institutional Settings

Most applications of operant techniques with children have altered attentive or academic behavior in the classroom. Severely disordered behavior often is treated in institutional settings. Institutionalized children diagnosed as autistic or hyperactive have been treated with operant techniques. Autistic or schizophrenic children have been treated with operant techniques to develop a wide range of behaviors.[2] Most reports have focused on eliminating self-destructive behaviors

[2]A distinction often is made between autism and childhood schizophrenia. Behavior modifiers have not adhered to this distinction in designing treatment programs, and often discuss the clients according to the diagnosis previously made and given to them in advance of their appearance to the behavior modifier. Many authors have used these terms interchangeably. Since the main focus is on the behaviors altered, the distinction will not be made here.

where electric shock has produced rapid and durable effects. Positive behaviors have been developed with autistic children including imitating others, responding to instructions, contacting and seeking out adults, language and speech, play, social interaction, and basic academic skills.

The work of Lovaas and his colleagues has been programmatic in developing treatment programs for autistic children (Lovaas & Bucher, 1974). In Lovaas' program, children receive treatment daily for several hours during which various procedures are used and different behaviors are altered. The techniques include reinforcement with such events as food and praise, extinction including withdrawal of attention, punishment, and negative reinforcement such as presenting and withdrawing shock. Changes in specific behaviors such as self-destructive behavior and the development of receptive and productive speech have been well documented in Lovaas' program. Aside from these changes, tested intelligence and social competence have improved as a result of treatment.

Follow-up data from one to four years after treating autistic children indicated that whether gains were maintained depended on the subsequent care the children received after leaving the program (Lovaas, Koegel, Simmons, & Long, 1973). Children who returned to their parents, who had been trained to utilize behavior modification in the home, retained their behavioral gains and, indeed, improved. In contrast, children who were placed in a state hospital lost most of what they had gained. Their psychotic behaviors such as echolalia and self-stimulation returned, whereas their appropriate verbal and social behaviors were lost. When some of the children in this latter group were returned to Lovaas for treatment, their appropriate behavior increased and psychotic behavior decreased. These gains, however, were lost again when the children were returned to institutional life.

Hyperactive children also have been treated with operant techniques. The behaviors that serve as a focus of treatment vary depending in part on the setting in which behaviors are assessed such as the home, school, or institution. The behaviors usually include gross motor acts such as running around, being out of one's seat, constantly moving, aggressing against others, and failing to attend to a task. Reinforcement techniques have developed incompatible behaviors such as working on school assignments or sitting still. For example, Ayllon, Layman, and Kandel (1975) decreased gross motor behaviors, disruptive noise, and similar behaviors and increased academic performance in hyperactive children. Similarly, Christensen (1975) decreased in-seat activity of hyperactive institutionalized retarded children in a classroom by providing token reinforcement for completing assignments, paying attention, and working. (As reviewed later, evidence suggests that reinforcement techniques are a viable alternative to drug treatment for hyperactive children.)

An extremely wide range of behaviors with children have been altered with operant techniques. Problems with feeding, toileting, and disruptive behavior such as tantrums have received particular attention. Many of these behaviors are altered in institutional settings as with the retarded, at school, or in the home and are addressed in other sections.

Predelinquents and Delinquents

Operant techniques have been applied for several years with delinquent youths (see Braukmann & Fixsen, 1975; Burchard & Harig, 1976; Davidson & Seidman, 1974 for reviews). Although programs focus on eliminating specific antisocial behaviors, positive skills and prosocial behaviors such as academic performance, vocational skills, and appropriate interaction usually serve as the primary focus.

Before describing the specific behaviors focused on, it is important to mention the accomplishments of Achievement Place, a home-style facility for predelinquent youths in Kansas. The program at Achievement Place is distinguished because it has undergone very careful experimentation to isolate effective treatment procedures. The program, which includes separate facilities for males and females, relies heavily on a token economy. Diverse behaviors have been increased such as room cleaning, watching daily newscasts, saving money, articulating correctly, studying school assignments, conversing, accepting criticism without aggressing, and others. Behaviors that have been decreased include aggressive statements or threats, use of poor grammar, tardiness in returning home to the

facility, and going to bed late (see Burchard & Harig, 1976; Kazdin, 1977c for reviews). These and other behaviors have been shown to change as a function of carefully controlled and evaluated interventions. Many of the interventions involve innovative procedures such as using peers as contingency managers, allowing a semi-self-government where youths determine consequences for behavior by consensus, and group contingencies.

Aside from the plethora of specific behaviors altered, more global measures reflect the program's accomplishments as well. Participation in Achievement Place has been shown to result in improved achievement orientation, personal feelings of mastery, and self-concept (Eitzen, 1975). Perhaps of greater interest are the follow-up data. Up to two years after individuals graduated from Achievement Place, these youths showed fewer contacts with police and the courts, committed fewer acts that resulted in readjudication, and had slightly higher grades than individuals who had attended traditional institutional treatment or originally had been placed on probation (Fixsen, Phillips, Phillips, & Wolf, 1976). The nonrandom assignment of subjects across these treatment modalities weakens the specific conclusions about treatment.

Antisocial Behavior

Despite the obvious importance of antisocial acts, these usually have not served as the primary focus of treatment. Initially, problematic behaviors that are encompassed by delinquency often are of a relatively low frequency (e.g., homicide, car theft) and cannot be readily monitored or incorporated into treatment. Also, elimination of inappropriate behaviors does not ensure that appropriate behaviors will be performed in their place. For these reasons, many programs have developed particular competencies.

A few studies have reported altering specific problematic delinquent behaviors. For example, Burchard and Tyler (1965) reduced disruptive behavior (e.g., breaking and entering, glue sniffing, property damage) in an institutionalized adolescent by isolating the boy for disruptive behaviors and providing tokens for periods of appropriate behavior. Additional research also has shown that antisocial behaviors such as physical and verbal assault, fighting, lying, cheating, and so on in delinquent youths can be effectively suppressed with time out from reinforcement and loss of tokens (Burchard & Harig, 1976).

Academic Behaviors

Several programs with delinquents have emphasized academic behaviors in institutional settings. Two well-known projects were initiated at the National Training School for Boys in Washington, D. C. These projects, referred to as CASE (Contingencies Applicable for Special Education) I and II, were token economies where individuals could earn tokens for completion of academic tasks and select social behaviors (Cohen & Filipczak, 1971). The effects of the CASE programs were demonstrated on standard achievement tests as well as reduced recidivism rates (i.e., return to incarceration) relative to federal juvenile parole releases for at least a few years after treatment. However, the precise effects of the program are difficult to evaluate due to several methodological problems (e.g., selection of the original group, attrition) (see Burchard & Harig, 1976).

Preventive programs have been designed for junior high school students whose behavioral patterns (e.g., drop in grade levels, truancy, runaway from home) suggest a high probability of later delinquent activities. In a program referred to as Programming Interpersonal Curricula for Adolescents (PICA), students attend a special day program as well as continue regular school (Cohen, 1972; Filipczak & Cohen, 1972). Performance on self-instructional material on academic topics and social interaction are reinforced with points exchangeable for money and recreational opportunities. Gains in school, overall IQ and grades, and decreases in suspensions from school and discipline instances at school have been the suggested results of this program. Several other reports have shown that academic behaviors such as answering questions related to daily news, reading proficiency, work comprehension, or in-class performance in the institution can be altered with reinforcing consequences. In some applications, individuals receive reinforcing consequences at the treatment facility

for their performance at their regular schools (e.g., Harris, Finfrock, Giles, Hart, & Tsosie, 1976; Kirigin, Phillips, Fixsen, & Wolf, 1972).

Social Skills

Developing positive social interaction has received relatively little attention. Research at Achievement Place has demonstrated that social skills are amenable to change with operant procedures. In one report, delinquent girls were trained to accept criticism and negative feedback from others without reacting aggressively or arguing (Timbers, Timbers, Fixsen, Phillips, & Wolf, 1973). Positive responses were developed such as making eye contact and acknowledging others and negative behaviors were eliminated such as throwing things, pouting, frowning, and stamping one's feet. Token reinforcement, praise, and loss of tokens were combined with verbal prompts and role playing. In a similar demonstration, conversational skills were taught to predelinquent girls at Achievement Place (Minkin, Braukmann, Minkin, Timbers, Timbers, Fixsen, Phillips, & Wolf, 1976). The girls were taught to ask questions during conversation and to provide positive feedback and approval. Instructions, modeling, practice, feedback, and token reinforcement were used to develop these behaviors in conversations with adults.

Adult Offenders

Recent programs in prison settings have utilized operant techniques (see Kennedy, 1976; Milan & McKee, 1974 for reviews). Some prison programs have been controversial in part because of the reliance on aversive conditions and techniques that infringe the rights of the prisoners (see Subcommittee on Constitutional Rights, 1974). In general, programs have developed adaptive behaviors within the prison rather than preparing inmates for release.

One program that received widespread attention was referred to as START (Special Treatment and Rehabilitative Training) (Federal Bureau of Prisons, 1972). The program was designed to segregate severely aggressive and resistive prisoners and to develop adaptive behaviors so they could return to normal *prison* life. The program evolved over the few years it was in effect. At its most complex state, it consisted of a multilevel system that relied on earning basic privileges (e.g., opportunity to shower, exercise, or shave) for compliance with rules (e.g., refraining from making threats to staff, not fighting). Increased performance demands and access to privileges were associated with higher levels of advancement in the program. The outcome data showed that the program did not successfully return individuals to the usual prison environment. Indeed, the program was surrounded by controversy and litigation because of the infringements of the rights of the inmates (cf. Subcommittee on Constitutional Rights, 1974). With litigation pending, the program was voluntarily terminated.

Other prison programs have used operant techniques to develop self-care behaviors, work, academic performance, participation in rehabilitative activities, and keeping up on current events. For example, in one maximum security institution for young offenders, youths earned tokens and activities for engaging in academic tasks such as working on programmed materials. Other behaviors such as getting up on time, making one's bed, and performing maintenance jobs also were incorporated into the incentive system (Milan & McKee, 1976; Milan, Wood, Williams, Rogers, Hampton, & McKee, 1974). Token reinforcement was more effective in increasing self-care behaviors than was praise and feedback for performance, or coercive and aversive control procedures commonly relied upon in prisons (e.g., intimidation, threats, extra work). Reinforcement contingencies also increased study behavior during leisure time and academic performance. Although changes within the program were marked, follow-up data did not indicate significant reductions in recidivism rates relative to controls who received traditional prison treatment (Jenkins, Witherspoon, DeVine, de Valera, Muller, Barton, & McKee, 1974).

Programs also have been implemented for inmates who reside in a correctional hospital. In these programs, inmates usually receive tokens for adaptive behaviors on the ward (e.g., Lawson, Greene, Richardson, McClure, & Padina, 1971). The military has used reinforcement techniques with "delinquent soldiers" whose behaviors are diagnosed as character disorders because they violate military rules and have a history of difficulty with the law. Individuals are hospitalized and parti- cipate in a ward reinforcement system similar to the usual programs for psychiatric patients (Boren & Colman, 1970; Colman & Baker, 1969). Interestingly, follow-up data have suggested that participation in the program is associated with higher rates of completing one's tour of duty than if no treatment is provided (Colman & Baker, 1969).

Drug Addicts and Alcoholics

Operant techniques for drug addicts and alcoholics have been applied on an outpatient and inpatient basis (see Götestam, Melin, & Öst, 1976; Miller & Eisler, 1976 for reviews). Institutional programs for drug addicts and alcoholics very much resemble the wardwide programs for psychiatric patients because privileges or tokens are delivered for self-care behaviors, attending activities, working on the ward, and similar responses. In some programs, specific behaviors pertaining to the addictive behavior itself serves as a major part of the contingencies. For example, Eriksson, Götestam, Melin, and Öst (1975) subtracted points as part of a larger token program when drug addicts in the hospital showed drug traces in their urine. The contingency, evaluated in an ABAB design, was associated with a reduction in drug traces. Similarly, Cohen and her colleagues have controlled drinking of alcoholics by providing reinforcers such as tokens or the privilege of living under "enriched" hospital conditions for drinking moderately or for complete abstinence (Cohen, Liebson, & Faillace, 1971, Cohen, Liebson, Faillace, & Speers, 1971). Few results are available on the long-term effects of institutional reinforcement programs on addictive behaviors. One reinforcement program showed a higher percentage of drug-free patients at a one-year follow-up than for a group of nonrandomly assigned controls (Melin & Gotestam, 1973).

Medical Patients

Recently, medical applications of behavioral techniques, an area referred to as behavioral medicine, have proliferated. In these applications, diverse procedures extending beyond the confines of operant techniques are applied to patients who suffer medical or psychosomatic disorders (see Katz & Zlutnick, 1974; Knapp & Peterson, 1976 for reviews). The techniques often are used in conjunction with medical treatments. For example, one of the more carefully studied problems is the reduction of pain behaviors in patients who are medicated for chronic pain. Behaviors such as time out of one's bed, grimacing, moaning, verbal complaints, walking in a guarded or protective manner, reclining or sitting to ease pain, and relying on medication have been altered by contigency management in the hospital or in the patient's everyday interactions with relatives. Pain behaviors are altered by reinforcing activity and physical exercise, and by decreasing attention and delivery of medication based on the expression of pain (e.g., Fordyce, Fowler, Lehman, DeLateur, Sand, & Trieschmann, 1973).

Many of the demonstrations in behavioral medicine are case applications and the role of specific interventions in changing behavior cannot be determined. Yet, several well-controlled experiments have revealed the role of operant consequences in controlling medically related problems. For example, Zlutnick, Mayville, and Moffat (1975) controlled epileptic seizures in five children and adolescents by interrupting preseizure behaviors with aversive consequences such as loud reprimands and physical shaking or by reinforcing nonseizure behavior with food and praise. In separate ABAB designs, the interventions were shown to account for reductions in the number of seizures. Follow-up data to several months showed sustained effects of treatment. As another illustration, Wolf, Birnbrauer, Lawler, and Williams (1970) demonstrated the role of response consequences in controlling vomiting of a nine-year old retarded girl. The girl frequently vomited in class, which typically resulted in her return to the residence hall. In an ABA design, the consequences associated with vomiting (release to the hall or remaining in class) were shown to increase and decrease (respectively) the frequency of vomiting.

The range of medical symptoms treated with operant techniques is broad and includes asthmatic attacks, spasmodic torticollis, ruminations, constipation, dermatitis, drooling, and posture. Behavioral techniques also are used to help maintain adherence to medical treatment regimens. For example, contingencies in the hospital or natural environment have been designed to ensure that patients take fluids, adhere to their medication

schedule, and exercise or use prosthetic devices, such as crutches or wheelchairs (Knapp & Peterson, 1976).

An area of research sometimes included in behavioral medicine is biofeedback, which has been used clinically to alter cardiovascular disorders, headaches, seizures, and similar problems. Feedback is provided based on specific physiological responses (e.g., heart rate, body temperature). Occasionally, incentives are provided when the client meets criterion levels of responding (see Blanchard & Young, 1974).[3] (See Chapter 3.)

Outpatient Populations

Operant techniques have been extended to outpatient treatment in several ways. It is useful to discuss these in terms of outpatient behavior therapy and interventions in the natural environment. In outpatient behavior therapy, individuals come to therapy for treatment where the interventions are designed, described, and implemented. The therapist plays a major role in actually administering the contingencies. With interventions in the natural environment, the program is designed and agreed to in therapy but is carried out by someone in everyday contact with the client (e.g., parent or spouse) in the usual living situation.

Outpatient Therapy

In outpatient therapy, the therapist provides reinforcing and punishing consequences based on the client's performance. For example, Ross (1974) devised an effective contingency contract for a woman who was a chronic nailbiter. The contract specified that her nails had to remain at an acceptable length and increase in length over time to avoid losing money that she had provided at the inception of treatment. Failure to meet the requirements led to a fine that consisted of sending precompleted money orders to an organization she regarded as repugnant. In other outpatient applications, reinforcing or punishing consequences have

---

[3]Biofeedback has been used to treat diverse disorders such as hypertension,, cardiac arrhythmias, headaches, and others. Although biofeedback utilizes operant principles, its history extends beyond operant conditioning. Biofeedback usually is viewed as an independent area of research rather than a specialty of operant conditioning (Shapiro & Surwit, 1976) and will not be detailed in this chapter.

been provided in the treatment sessions to control such behaviors as overeating, cigarette smoking, alcohol consumption, and drug abuse (e.g., Abrahms & Allen, 1974; Boudin, 1972; Mahoney, Moura, & Wade, 1973; Miler, 1972).

When the therapist delivers consequences for client performance, usually this is restricted to individual therapy sessions. There are exceptions when the therapist administers consequences in the natural environment. For example, Miller, Hersen, Eisler, and Watts (1974) provided token reinforcement to an adult male treated for excessive alcohol consumption on an outpatient basis. Alcohol consumption was assessed through blood/alcohol concentration randomly twice each week. The individual was phoned at different times and immediately visited by someone to conduct assessment. The client received coupon booklets redeemable for items at the hospital commissary for the absences of alcohol traces in his blood. Blood concentrations of alcohol changed as a function of the reinforcement contingency, as shown in an ABAB design.

Interventions in the Natural Environment with Children and Adolescents

Operant programs in the natural environment are implemented and managed by someone in the client's everyday living situation. Many of these applications have been conducted in the home where parents implement incentive systems for their children to increase completion of chores, cooperative behavior, compliance with requests, school attendance, and to reduce idiosyncratic bizarre and self-stimulatory behaviors, acts of destruction, and fighting (e.g., Christopherson, Arnold, Hill, & Quilitch, 1972; Frasier & Williams, 1973).

Patterson and his colleagues have developed treatment programs for families of children with severe conduct disorders at home and at school (e.g., stealing, running away, setting fires, fighting) (see Patterson, 1971). Parents are trained to conduct programs in their homes after reading materials on the subject, identifying target behaviors, collecting data, and other exercises. The parents use token systems, contingency contracts, and similar procedures to alter individually tailored problematic be-

haviors. At school, the teachers also reinforce appropriate classroom behavior and social interaction. Deviant child behavior decreases with training and falls within the level of deviant behavior of children who are not identified as behavior problems (e.g., Patterson, 1974).

Kent and O'Leary (1976) provided conduct problem children with behavioral programs in the home and at school. The program consisted of providing reinforcement for academic and appropriate classroom behavior at school and reinforcement for appropriate behavior and extinction or loss of privileges for inappropriate behavior at home. At the end of treatment, classroom data showed higher levels of appropriate behavior of the treated children than no-treatment control children. At a six month follow-up, nontreated subjects had improved sufficiently to eliminate many of the differences between treatment and no-treatment subjects. However, treated children continued to show higher grades and achievement test performance.

Many applications are administered in the community rather than restricted to the home. Interestingly, reinforcement programs have been implemented by therapists who interact with the clients in the natural environment. For example, Fo and O'Donnell (1974) developed a large-scale reinforcement program in the community for youths with behavior and academic problems. Adults from the community were trained to serve as therapists and then designed interventions to alter behaviors such as truancy, fighting, not completing homework. The adults met with the clients individually, engaged in various activities, and provided social and or monetary reinforcement as an incentive for engaging in the desired responses. Select behaviors such as truancy were shown to decrease. Follow-up data indicated that some clients had increased in their deviant behavior whereas others decreased, as defined by contact with the courts (Fo & O'Donnell, 1975).

Interventions in the Natural Environment with Adults

Operant programs have been used in the natural environment with adults. Many of the reports with adults have been case studies rather than experimental evaluations. Typically, spouses, relatives, and friends are trained to implement contingencies in the home. In some reports, spouses have been trained to manage incentive systems to treat marital discord. For example, Stuart (1969) reported home-base incentive systems for couples with severe marital conflict. For engaging in conversation with their wives, husbands received tokens that could be exchanged for physical affection, as individually determined for each couple. Although the program was not experimentally evaluated, follow-up assessment up to one year indicated increased marital satisfaction and frequency of sexual contact between spouses.

Designing contingency contracts has been an effective procedure to alter behaviors in the natural environment. For example, Miller (1972) utilized a contingency contract between a husband and wife to control the husband's excessive drinking. Excessive drinking was controlled by having the husband pay money to the wife for exceeding a moderate daily drinking criterion. Money was paid by the wife to the husband for nagging and disapproving comments for drinking. Drinking gradually decreased with some days of abstinence and maintained at an acceptable level at a six-month followup.

Major Accomplishments: General Comments

The above overview illustrates the range of populations studied with operant techniques. The review of populations was not exhaustive. Indeed, programs have been applied to additional populations such as geriatric residents (e.g., Sachs, 1975), stutterers (e.g., Ingham, Andrews, & Winkler, 1972), aphasics (e.g., Ayers, Potter, & McDearmon, 1975), and others. These latter applications are no less important but represent areas that are less frequently reported in the literature than the major areas reviewed. Among the major areas reviewed, operant techniques have been most frequently conducted with children and adolescents and with the mentally retarded. Classrooms and institutions or hospitals are the settings that are reported most frequently as employing operant techniques. Finally, the behaviors focused on most frequently are academic behaviors of children and general man-

agement or problematic behaviors across all populations (Kazdin, 1975b). Current research indicates that the focus of operant techniques is changing. The diversity of settings in which programs are implemented is increasing along with the range of behaviors focused upon.[4]

RECENT TRENDS AND ADVANCES IN OPERANT PROGRAMS

Over several years of applications, operant programs have changed in a variety of ways. As alluded to earlier, the focus of programs have changed somewhat in terms of the settings, populations, and behaviors studied (Kazdin, 1975b). In addition to these changes, several specific research areas have received increased attention. Of the many topics that might be discussed, four appear particularly salient. These include using peers to administer contingencies, developing self-reinforcement programs, training behavior-change agents, and developing a technology to maintain behavior.

Peer Administration of the Contingencies

Administration of the contingencies refers to who selects the criteria for providing consequences or who actually delivers the consequences. While the majority of programs use staff, aides, teachers, and parents to implement contingencies, this is changing somewhat. Frequently, peers are involved in administering the contingencies.

The use of peers as reinforcing agents has been investigated extensively in the program for predelinquents at Achievement Place. For example, boys at the facility served as therapists for their peers who made articulation errors (Bailey, Timbers, Phillips, & Wolf, 1971). Boys judged the adequacy of pronunciation, provided or withdrew

[4]A major development is the application of operant techniques to alter community relevant behaviors including energy conservation, littering, use of mass transit, recycling of waste material, job procurement and on-the-job performance, racial integration, and community self-help behaviors. Applications of operant techniques for socially and environmentally relevant behaviors extend beyond the therapeutic application of operant techniques and the scope of the present chapter (see Kazdin, 1977a).

points, and received points based on the behavior of the clients. In another demonstration, a managerial system was studied in which one boy provided or withdrew points to develop specific behaviors in his peers (e.g., cleaning the bathroom). The manager selected peers to do the cleaning and rewarded or fined them based on his judgment of the job. The manager earned or lost points based on how well the job was completed. The peer-managed system markedly improved performance (e.g., Phillips, 1968; Phillips, Phillips, Wolf, & Fixsen, 1973). In many classroom programs, peers are trained to attend to appropriate behavior in target subjects who engage in disruptive behavior and to ignore inappropriate behavior. Several studies have shown that peers can administer effective contingencies in the classroom to control deportment and academic behaviors (e.g., Axelrod, Hall, & Maxwell, 1972; Solomon & Wahler, 1973).

While peers may be used directly to administer the contingencies, they may be incorporated indirectly as well. In many reinforcement programs, the contingencies are designed so that peers monitor and provide consequences for their own behavior. Group contingencies provide one means of accomplishing this (Hayes, 1976). With some group contingencies, reinforcing or punishing consequences are delivered to each individual based on the performance of the group as whole. In these programs, peers have been reported to assist each other and even occasionally threaten punishment to promote desirable performance. A related way to structure the contingency is to have individuals share in the reinforcing consequences. If one client participates in a reinforcement program, the consequences (s)he earns may be divided among the peers. When peers earn on the basis of the performance of one or a few clients, they tend to actively support appropriate behavior of the target subject. Also, for many clients, earning reinforcers for one's peers is more effective than earning for oneself (e.g., Kazdin & Geesey, 1977; Rosenbaum, O'Leary, & Jacob, 1975).

There are potential advantages that recommend involving peers in the administration of the contingencies. First, sometimes stimulus control exerted by the staff is a problem in programs where

only the staff administer consequences (Kazdin, 1973b). Clients perform the behavior only in the presence of the staff. When peers administer the contingencies, broader stimulus control is likely to result. Indeed, behaviors developed by peers appear to be maintained after the contingencies are withdrawn (Johnston & Johnston, 1972; Stokes & Baer, 1976). Second, staff may not readily detect many behaviors (e.g., stealing) they wish to change. Third, for some clients, consequences provided by peers might differ in their efficacy from similar events administered by staff. Finally, if peers administer reinforcing and punishing consequences to each other, social interaction might increase which may be a therapeutic goal in its own right (Abrams, Hines, Pollack, Ross, Stubbs, & Polyot, 1974).

Self-Administration of the Contingencies

A relatively recent development in operant conditioning applications is the self-administration of contingencies. Usually, clients are trained to deliver reinforcing or punishing consequences to themselves, referred to as self-reinforcement and self-punishment, respectively. Applications of self-reinforcement, the more commonly used procedure, can include two different operations. First, the client can determine the response requirements for delivering the reinforcer or how much of the reinforcer (e.g., tokens) should be delivered (self-determined reinforcement). Second, the individual can deliver the reinforcers to him or herself even if someone else has determined the criteria (self-administered reinforcement). Self-reinforcement is best achieved when the individual can determine and self-administer the consequences. This minimizes the external constraints on the contingency.

Several studies, conducted primarily in the classroom, have shown that when individuals self-reward, their behavior improves (see Jones, Nelson, & Kazdin, 1977). For example, Glynn and Thomas (1974) permitted elementary school students to self-determine and self-administer points (checkmarks) for on-task behavior. Intermittent tape-recorded signals ("beeps") cued the children to place a check on their cards if they considered themselves to be attending to the task at that time of the signal. Self-delivered points (exchangeable for free time) increased on-task behavior.

Several investigations have shown that self-administered and externally-administered consequences are equally effective in changing behavior (e.g., Felixbrod & O'Leary, 1974; Frederiksen & Frederiksen, 1975). Some of the comparisons often confound sequence effects, delay between behavior and the receipt of reinforcers, and uncontrolled and unmonitored teacher behavior with the interventions. As might be expected, teacher-administered reinforcement sometimes is more effective than student-administered reinforcement because students become lenient and reinforce noncontingently (e.g., Santogrossi, O'Leary, Romanczyk, & Kaufman, 1973). To combat leniency, Drabman, Spitalnik, and O'Leary (1973) developed accurate self-evaluation and delivery of reinforcers by providing reinforcing consequences from the teacher for accuracy in self-ratings of behavior. By checking the students intermittently, contingent self-reinforcement was maintained.

Aside from self-determining and self-administering tokens, clients have been involved in their own programs in other ways such as self-recording attentive behavior, inappropriate or disruptive behavior, and completing academic assignments (Kazdin, 1974). Self-observation has been investigated extensively in its own right as a behavior-change technique.

Overall, self-administration of consequences appears to be a viable treatment option. Research suggests that some means are required to ensure that individuals can easily evaluate whether the appropriate response has occurred and whether the consequences are delivered contingently. Whether individuals can administer consequences to control their own behavior without explicitly programmed consequences for adherence to or violation of the contingency beyond brief periods is unclear (Anderson & Alpert, 1974; Drabman et al., 1973).

An advantage of allowing self-reward as an adjunct to the program is that stimulus control over the target behavior may be broadened beyond a few staff-monitored situations. Also, self-administration of the contingencies may play a role in maintaining behavior. If the client self-administers the contingencies, the program may be continued over time and across settings.

Training Behavior-Change Agents

Although peer- and self-administered contingencies are used increasingly in operant programs, most programs still are conducted by traditional behavior-change agents (e.g., parents, teachers, aides). A major research issue is training individuals in contact with the clients to effectively implement the contingencies. The success of an intervention program often is a function of how well the contingencies are implemented.

The concerns over the behavior of the individuals who serve as behavior-change agents is twofold. Initially, individuals in the natural environment may inadvertently develop or contribute to the deviant behaviors they wish to alter. Subtle reinforcing contingencies often are operative where bizarre behavior patterns are attended to and gradually shaped to increasing levels of severity (Patterson & Reid, 1970). Training individuals in contact with the client or potential client must sensitize them to the operation of operant principles in everyday interactions. Second, individuals who administer a behavior-change program frequently do not conduct the program with the consistency required to effect behavior change.

Training individuals to conduct behavioral programs in institutions, classrooms, and the natural environment has been a topic of extensive research (Yen & McIntire, 1976). A plethora of training techniques have been used (Kazdin, 1976a; Kazdin & Moyer, 1976). Typically, instructional techniques are employed whereby individuals receive didactic training, workshops, and extensive discussions of behavioral techniques and their implementation. With few exceptions, instructional techniques effect little or no behavior change of individuals who are in contact with the clients (e.g., Gardner, 1972; Nay, 1975).

Occasionally training is completed in simulated situations where behavior-change agents are exposed to models who perform the desired behaviors. This sometimes is supplemented with role playing where the individual can alternately take the role of the client whose behavior is to be changed and the behavior-change agent. Modeling and role-playing techniques have effectively altered responses of behavior-change agents (e.g., Cash & Evans, 1975; Ringer, 1973).

Training conducted in the actual situation in which behavior is to be changed appears to be effective in altering behavior. In many programs, behavior-change agents receive feedback and social or token reinforcement for their performance in relation to the clients (e.g., Pomerleau, Bobrove, & Smith, 1973; Watson, 1976). For example, Bricker, Morgan, and Grabowski (1972) provided feedback to attendants for their performance on the ward with mentally retarded residents. While staff viewed themselves on tape, they received praise and trading stamps from the project director contingent on interacting with the residents. This procedure increased interaction on the ward.

Although token reinforcement systems relying on money, trading stamps or points redeemable for various events are very effective in altering staff behavior, praise and attention often are sufficient. For example, Cossairt, Hall, and Hopkins (1973) found that praise from an experimenter contingent on teacher behavior increased teacher praise in the classroom. Moreover, students dramatically increased in study behavior although they were not focused on directly. Perhaps more dramatic examples of praise on the behavior of staff are those cases where the clients themselves develop behavior in the behavior-change agent. For example, Graubard and his colleagues trained special education students to provide reinforcing and punishing consequences to their teachers (Graubard, Rosenberg, & Miller, 1974). To develop positive teacher interactions, the students reinforced teacher responses by smiling, making eye contact, sitting up straight, and making comments such as "I work so much better when you praise me." To discourage negative teacher contacts, students made statements such as "It's hard for me to do good work when you're cross with me." Positive teacher contacts increased with the student delivery of social consequences for teacher behavior.

A problem in developing behavior of individuals in contact with the client is that their behavior is not maintained once training is completed. The behavior reverts to baseline levels as soon as training and extrinsic consequences for performance are terminated (see Kazdin, 1976a). The problem for behavior-change agents is that the existing system in which the agents may function do not actively support the desired behaviors. For example, the rewards of being an effective teacher (e.g., student change) apparently are too remote from the actual teacher behaviors to sustain teacher performance. More immediate consequences are needed to maintain teacher behavior, perhaps from superiors or from the students.

Developing a Technology to Maintain Behavior Changes

There is little question that behavior changes have been effected across diverse populations and settings as a result of operant programs. Establishing an effective method of behavior change leaves a major question unanswered, namely, whether the changes are maintained once the contingencies are terminated and the client leaves the treatment setting. One aspect of this question, referred to as response maintenance or resistance to extinction, is concerned with maintenance of behavior after the contingencies are withdrawn. Another aspect of this question, referred to as transfer of training, is concerned with the extension of behavior from the situation in which the program has been in effect to another situation in which there has been no program. Transfer of training obviously is important because a concern of most treatments is that behavior change achieved in one setting (e.g., the hospital or classroom) extends to other settings (e.g., community or home).

Although several studies have shown that behaviors are maintained after reinforcement or punishment contingencies are withdrawn in various treatment and educational settings, these are in the minority. Typically, behaviors revert to or approach preintervention levels once the contingencies are withdrawn (see Kazdin, 1975a, 1977c; Marholin, Siegel, & Phillips, 1976; Stokes & Baer, 1977 for reviews). Similarly, with few exceptions, the bulk of the evidence suggests that behavior changes effected during a program do not transfer to settings where the contingencies have not been in effect.

Various investigators have recommended developing behaviors that are likely to be maintained by the natural environment (Ayllon & Azrin, 1968; Baer & Wolf, 1970). Baer and Wolf (1970) raised the notion of a "behavioral trap" to refer to the environmental support systems (e.g., peer praise or attention) that are likely to result from altering a specific child behavior. Once a behavior is developed, perhaps through contrived reinforcers, it may enter into a "trap" which controls its subsequent performance. For example, once social interaction is increased, it may be "trapped" into a social matrix that supports subsequent interaction.

Although the general recommendation appears sound and select instances from the literature suggest that behaviors occasionally are trapped and maintained (e.g., Berkowitz, Sherry, & Davis, 1971), this strategy has not proven particularly useful in most operant programs. Many behaviors that would be expected to be sustained (e.g., eating skills, reading, social interaction) are not maintained invariably or even usually once a program is terminated (see Kazdin, 1977c). Specific procedures usually need to be employed to achieve response maintenance and transfer. Preliminary evidence suggests several procedures that can develop durable behavior changes. The present section only highlights major techniques (see Kazdin, 1977c; Marholin et al., 1976; Stokes & Baer, 1977 for extended discussions).

Substituting One Program for Another

One way to develop maintenance and transfer is to substitute one behavior-change program for another. Initially, a program can be developed based upon contrived reinforcers and eventually shifted to more naturally-occurring events. For example, training relatives to continue a variation of the treatment contingencies maintains behavior after the individual leaves the treatment setting (e.g., Kallman, Hersen, & O'Toole, 1975; Lovaas et al., 1973).

Actually, substituting one program for another is not a maintenance or transfer strategy. The new program that replaces the initial one still constitutes control over the contingencies of the client's behaviors. Yet, substituting one program for another is relevant to the issue of maintenance and transfer when all of the contingencies are finally withdrawn. For example, Walker, Hops, and Johnson (1975,

Exp. 1) altered the behavior of "highly deviant" children placed in a special education classroom. When the children returned to their regular classes, some of them received a program that substituted more natural reinforcers (grades, praise) in place of the token program to which they had been initially exposed. As expected, these children maintained their behaviors in their regular classes to a greater extent than did those who returned to the classroom with no program in effect. More importantly, when all contingencies were finally withdrawn, the children who had received the substitute program in their regular class maintained gains demonstrated in the original treatment program up to four months of follow-up. This study suggests that implementing programs across settings and types of reinforcing events ultimately may facilitate maintenance and transfer.

Fading the Contingencies

Behavior can be maintained by gradually removing or fading the contingencies before the program is completely withdrawn. In many reinforcement programs, clients traverse through various levels or tiers that make greater performance demands and provide stronger incentives. At higher levels, the contingencies are gradually withdrawn so that eventually an individual receives the reinforcers without specific contingencies to control behavior.

One way to fade the contingencies has been to decrease the number of clients in a group situation whose behaviors are monitored and to decrease the opportunities to receive reinforcers. For example, in a classroom program students self-reinforced for appropriate behavior (Turkewitz, O'Leary, & Ironsmith, 1975). The reinforcers children received depended on their accuracy of observations. The checks made by the teacher and eventually the opportunity to exchange points for back-up events were gradually decreased. The program was completely withdrawn while the children continued their appropriate behavior at a high level.

Expanding Stimulus Control

One way of conceptualizing the failure of behavior to be maintained and to transfer to new settings is based on the notion of stimulus control. Clients readily discriminate between conditions in which the contingencies are in effect from those in which they are not. Several studies have systematically expanded the range of stimuli that control behavior during training to achieve response maintenance and transfer. For example, Emshoff, Redd, and Davidson (1976) used praise and points (exchangeable for money) to develop positive interpersonal comments with delinquent adolescents. Some clients were trained under varied stimulus conditions across activities (e.g., during games and discussions), trainers, locations in the facility, and time of the day. Clients who received training under varied stimulus conditions rather than under constant conditions showed greater positive comments under diverse conditions of generalization such as when reinforcers were delivered noncontingently, when a new trainer was introduced, and when the activity and setting all varied. Also, these clients showed greater maintenance of behavior three weeks after training was terminated than those trained under constant conditions. Other studies have shown that when behavior is developed in the presence of a limited range of cues it may not generalize. However, developing behavior in the presence of a select sample of new stimuli leads to transfer of the behavior across a broad range of stimuli (see Kazdin, 1977c; Stokes & Baer, 1977 for reviews).

Scheduling Intermittent Reinforcement

Intermittent reinforcement has been used to maintain behavior in two ways. One use is to continue the delivery of the reinforcing consequences to maintain behavior at a high level. Essentially, the reinforcing consequences are still administered but on a lean schedule without loss of behavior gains (e.g., Phillips, Phillips, Fixsen, & Wolf, 1971). A second use of intermittent reinforcement is to fade the contingencies so that all programmed consequences are eliminated entirely. For example, Kale, Kaye, Whelan, and Hopkins (1968) developed greeting responses in psychiatric patients with cigarettes and praise as the reinforcer. As greetings increased, the reinforcers were provided on an increasingly lean variable ratio schedule until the consequences were no longer provided. Yet, behavior was maintained at its reinforced level even up to the three-month follow-up period.

Intermittent reinforcement may be useful only in forestalling extinction temporarily or in facilitating the transfer of control from reinforcers specifically programmed in the setting to those that might naturally follow the target behavior. At present, the long-term effects of intermittent reinforcement on maintenance have not been extensively explored.

Delaying Reinforcer Delivery

Behavior also might be maintained by increasing the delay between the target behavior and delivery of the reinforcer. Essentially, behavior can be developed with immediate reinforcement. As the response stabilizes, the consequences can be delayed increasingly until they are not presented at all. While this method of ensuring maintenance has not been widely studied, suggestive evidence has been provided. For example, Greenwood, Hops, Delquadri, and Guild (1974) demonstrated that increasing the delay between appropriate classroom behaviors and reinforcing consequences led to maintenance of behavior up to approximately three weeks after the program had been terminated completely. The specific role of the delay procedure on maintenance was not assessed.

Self-Control Techniques

Maintenance and transfer of behavior might be enhanced if the clients themselves could be trained to control their own behaviors. A self-administered program would never have to be withdrawn or be restricted to one setting. Various self-control techniques have been used to help the client control behavior.

As noted earlier, self-reinforcement programs have received increased attention in recent years. In most programs, clients receive some external consequences from others (e.g., teachers, therapist) for maintaining the self-reinforcement contingency. If external consequences are not provided, the client may begin to relax the standards for self-reinforcement and reward noncontingently. Individuals can be trained to self-reinforce accurately without becoming lenient. With such training, individuals do maintain standards for self-reinforcement and their behaviors are sustained at high levels (Drabman et al., 1973). Actually, few studies have looked at the long-term effects of self-reinforcement as a maintenance strategy. Existing studies have shown only that individuals can continue to self-reinforce without any external contingencies for periods no greater than about two weeks (e.g., Drabman et al., 1973; Turkewitz et al., 1975). Longer follow-up periods where the client has complete control over the contingency free from specific externally-controlled reinforcement contingencies have not been tested.

Self-instruction training is a technique that appears to show promise both for response maintenance and transfer of training. In self-instruction training, clients are taught to provide themselves with suggestions and directives how to perform behavior. For example, Meichenbaum and Goodman (1971) trained impulsive and hyperactive children to work methodically on various tasks (e.g., coloring, copying). The children were trained to "talk to themselves" first aloud and then covertly to perform the tasks in a deliberate fashion. The experimenter modeled the self-instructional statements and reinforced use of these by the client. Gains made in training were maintained up to one month of follow-up assessment. Other studies with such populations as psychiatric patients have shown that self-instruction leads to maintenance of behavior and transfer of the response across new situations and behaviors (Meichenbaum, 1973), although there are exceptions (e.g., Robin, Armel, & O'Leary, 1975). (See also Chapter 18.)

General Comments

The discussion of separate procedures to develop response maintenance and transfer of training implies that select procedures are used in an exclusive fashion. The techniques are not mutually exclusive. They often are combined to increase the likelihood that behaviors will be maintained. While studies have demonstrated that individual procedures mentioned above can lead to maintenance and transfer, many studies combine the procedures. For example, Jones and Kazdin (1975) developed response maintenance of appropriate classroom behavior in a special education class of retarded children by substituting naturally-occurring reinforcers (peer praise and attention) in place of tokens, increasing the delay between token earnings and back-up reinforcer exchange, and in general, fading the contingencies. Behaviors continued to be main-

tained up to 12 weeks after all contingencies were terminated. Similarly, Ayllon and Kelly (1974) restored speech in a mute retarded child. After the behavior was established, reinforcement was scheduled intermittently, natural reinforcers were substituted for candy, and stimulus control over behavior was expanded. A follow-up one year after training had been terminated indicated that behavior was maintained. Overall, research suggests that behavior changes achieved with operant techniques need not be ephemeral and can be made to extend over time and situations.

CRITICAL EVALUATION OF OPERANT PROGRAMS IN APPLIED SETTINGS

Along with the examination of the impressive accomplishments and recent trends, it is important to evaluate possible limitations of current research and outline select areas for future investigation. The evaluation encompasses several areas including the therapeutic focus of operant programs, the variables that contribute to behavior change, and the relative efficacy of operant versus other techniques. A final area of evaluation is the extent to which operant interventions have achieved clinically important changes in behavior.

Therapeutic Focus

Target Behaviors
One criticism of the operant approach that might be made is the target behaviors studied. Considerable attention has focused upon responses that may be more convenient rather than of clear therapeutic significance. If a naive observer were asked to infer the problems of select treatment populations, the defining characteristics of the populations might well be distorted. A naive observer might infer that psychiatric patients are individuals whose main problems are a failure to bathe, dress, and groom themselves, to get up on time, and to attend activities punctually. The plethora of investigations that have focused on self-care would not make this inference unjust. Similar inferences might be made of other populations. Delinquents might be construed as individuals whose difficulties lay in cleaning their rooms,

watching the news, or attending activities on time. Prisoners might be construed as individuals who merely lack education and self-care skills. Finally, children and adolescents might be seen as individuals who do not remain in their seats at school.

Although this characterization of operant programs is hyperbolic, there is some basis for the general point. Most programs seem to focus on managing the clients (e.g., patients, students) by merely altering behaviors adaptive to the setting. Classroom programs most obviously reflect this point because they have emphasized deportment despite the fact that improved deportment does not necessarily enhance academic performance (Winett & Winkler, 1972). Moreover, in many classrooms deportment is not uncontrollable or even necessarily in need of intervention. As a general point, many programs have altered behaviors that are not clearly related to the problems or priorities usually ascribed to the treated population.

Although the focus of much research can be criticized, it would be misleading to imply that significant behaviors of therapeutic or educational import have been overlooked. As discussed earlier, diverse behaviors related to rehabilitating psychiatric patients, retardates, delinquents, and others have been altered. Moreover, follow-up data support the efficacy of operant interventions on global measures of obvious social concern. For example, programs with adjudicated delinquents have reduced recidivism rates (e.g., Alexander & Parsons, 1973; Fixsen et al., 1976). Yet, there are many cases where follow-up data reveal that treatment has little or no effect on important measures (e.g., Jenkins et al., 1974). Across all treatment populations, greater attention might be given to those behaviors that are likely to ensure adequate functioning in extratreatment settings.

Settings

Criticism of the behaviors focused on may be related to the settings in which programs usually are conducted. Operant programs often are implemented in facilities that themselves may interfere with therapeutic change. Programs in psychiatric hospitals, prisons, special education classes, and other settings may alter behaviors in situations where the problem behavior does not ordinarily occur. For example, if a psychiatric patient is not adjusting to community life, removal and treatment in a noncommunity setting may fail to resolve this problem unless training somehow eventually is conducted in the community (Kazdin, 1976b).

The criticism against programs in various treatment settings cannot be directed at operant programs alone. As new treatments develop, they tend to be integrated into existing facilities even when these facilities may violate some of the principles upon which the treatments are based. The settings may foster the behaviors that operant programs are designed to ameliorate. For example, most programs with psychiatric patients merely try to overcome the debilitating behaviors that develop from being hospitalized and receiving custodial care.

The thrust of the criticism is not that operant programs have been conducted in institutional environments. Indeed, with few exceptions, alternative settings have not been available. The criticism is that investigators have implicitly endorsed current institutional structure by designing programs for management purposes and perhaps have failed to stress the inadequacy of institutional structure based on various principles of behavior modification.

Behavioral programs not only endorse institutional settings but may *rely* on their inadequacies to effect change. For example, the deprivation states of many individuals in the setting make the usual reinforcers quite effective in altering behavior. Certainly, a legitimate question is whether an operant program would be as effective if the setting normally did not restrict access to various reinforcing events. The efficacy of reinforcement programs seems to depend on an institution ordinarily not providing a large number of reinforcers or access to those that are available on a limited basis. The notion that operant programs may depend on inadequacies of existing treatment practices can be illustrated in educational programs. In some programs, leaving school early is used as a reinforcer and staying after school as an aversive consequence (Harris & Sherman, 1973). The efficacy of these contingencies depends on the aversiveness of school per se. Perhaps an appropriate focus would be to alter the valence of school so that spending time at school is a reward. It might be that the aversiveness of school in part accounts for many of the problems for which operant programs are designed to ameliorate.

Some of the problems of operant programs may result from focusing on behaviors in institutional settings rather than in the natural environment. For example, achieving response maintenance and transfer may result from the stimulus control achieved by particular settings. Developing behavior in the natural environment whenever possible would seem to be a much more desirable focus. For many clients, it is the natural environment that sustains the problem behavior and may continue to foster the problem unless it is altered.

Populations

Little criticism would seem appropriately placed against the populations focused on with operant techniques because of the wide range of clients studied. Yet, questions can be raised about the appropriateness of the focus. The obvious clients for operant programs are those individuals who are to be treated, rehabilitated, or educated. In many instances, the behavior of individuals who influence the clients such as parents, teachers, prison guards, aides, and so on, may be a more appropriate focus than the behavior of the clients. For example, focusing on student behavior in a classroom may be less ideal than focusing on teacher behavior. If the teacher's behavior is altered, these changes are directly reflected in student performance (Kazdin & Moyer, 1976). If the behaviors of the teacher are not focused on directly, it is unlikely that the student behavior changes will be maintained.

Training individuals to implement operant techniques usually has transient effects unless change is encouraged within the system that these individuals operate. "System" here refers to the complex hierarchy of individuals who constitute a treatment or education program. To ensure performance at any given level of staff, accountability needs to be built into the system. Thus, specific achievements (behaviors) at any level (e.g., students, teachers) need to be followed with contingent consequences from a higher level (e.g., teachers, principals). The

behavioral approach has recognized the importance of changing systems in which programs occur but had made relatively few inroads in this area (Harshbarger & Maley, 1974).

General Comments

The above discussion raises questions about the focus of many operant programs. Programs that alter circumscribed behaviors adaptive to the treatment setting do not provide an adequate test of what can be accomplished clinically. Developing behaviors that enhance functioning in the community for populations who eventually are released from the treatment setting remains to be exploited.

Critical evaluation of operant techniques in light of an idealized form of treatment ignores the context of contemporary treatment research. At present, no other form of treatment seems to have been applied so widely across behaviors, settings, and populations, at least among those techniques that have been empirically validated. Hence, the criticisms of the previous discussion suggest areas where research is needed rather than dismiss the existing accomplishments. Several avenues of research seem to be implied by the above criticism including investigation of the relationship between behaviors developed in treatment settings and subsequent community adjustment, the long-term effects of treatment, whether training relatives enhances long-term adjustment, whether programs in nontreatment settings can replace institutionalization for some clients, and whether systems and settings in which many clients receive treatment should be restructured. These areas address larger questions about treatment and whether it effects clinically important and durable changes.

Variables Contributing to the Effects of Reinforcement Programs

Operant programs often consist of the simultaneous manipulation of several variables to effect change. These might include instructions about the contingencies, praise provided for performance, modeling influences, and others. In most reinforcement programs, investigators refer to the effectiveness of the contingency as the source of behavior change. Yet other variables than the contingency may account for behavior change. The present discussion examines variables that commonly vary in reinforcement programs. For purposes of discussion, token reinforcement programs are examined because of their widespread application and their clear use of techniques and procedures that can be readily separated from the specific contingencies.

Instructions

Instructions to the clients are manipulations that are used to prompt behavior or to describe behavior and the consequences associated with it. The importance of instructions in behavior change was suggested by Ayllon and Azrin (1964) who showed that providing reinforcing consequences to psychiatric patients for picking up eating utensils with their meals did not change behavior until the patients were given instructions stating the contingency. Other applied studies have shown that a contingency may not change behavior until instructions are provided stating the requirements to earn the reinforcer (e.g., Herman & Tramontana, 1971), although there are exceptions (e.g., Kazdin, 1973c).

The effects of instructions might depend in part on whether the clients have the target response in their repertoire. When clients do not perform the response initially, their improvements may be accounted for by instructions on how to perform the response or by the acquisition of information rather than by reinforcement per se. For example, Suchotliff, Greaves, Stecker, and Berke (1970) markedly improved grooming behaviors of psychiatric patients by providing instructions on how to perform the response. When tokens were provided later, further changes were not obtained. In many programs, instructions to perform a given behavior are not sufficient without additional incentives (e.g., Greenwood et al., 1975). Occasionally, instructions stating that behavior is contingent upon a particular behavior combined with the noncontingent delivery of reinforcers may increase that behavior (Kazdin, 1973c). In general, instructions appear to play an important role in operant programs. The extent to which providing consequences for behavior contributes to change over and above directives to perform well or information about the behavior usually is not evaluated.

Social Reinforcement

Praise, attention, and approval often serve as the manipulation to effect behavior change. Although social reinforcement is effective in changing behavior in its own right, several studies have shown that token reinforcement is more effective than the delivery of social consequences alone (Kazdin & Polster, 1973; Walker, Hops, & Fiegenbaum, 1976; Zifferblatt, 1972). Typically, social and token reinforcement are combined so that the separate and combined effects of these procedures are not determined.

The failure to assess the contribution of social consequences to behavior change limits the conclusions that can be drawn about the controlling variables in any given study. Social consequences may vary systematically with some other intervention that is assumed to be the source of behavior change. For example, research has shown that when psychiatric aides and teachers administer a token economy, they decrease their use of discipline in the form of reprimands and disapproval, attend less to inappropriate behavior, and increase in overall contact with the clients and in attention and approval to appropriate behavior (e.g., Breyer & Allen, 1975; Mandelker, Brigham, & Bushell, 1970; Parrino et al., 1971; Trudel, Boisvert, Maruca, & Leroux, 1974). The effects of token economies in part might be attributed to the complex behaviors altered in the staff over and above the delivery of tokens.

Modeling Influences

For operant programs in a group situation, behavior changes in the clients may in part be attributed to modeling effects. Clients frequently observe that others receive reinforcing consequences. Parameters important to promote modeling (e.g., observing multiple models and models who are similar to oneself) normally are present in programs in group settings such as a ward or classroom.

In many studies, investigators have found that providing reinforcing or punishing consequences for one client leads to systematic behavior change in other clients whose behavior has not been directly reinforced (e.g., Broden, Bruce, Mitchell, Carter, & Hall, 1970; Kazdin, 1973a, 1977d; Kazdin, Silverman, & Sittler, 1975; Kounin, 1970).

These results suggest that vicarious effects contribute to reinforcement and punishment programs even when they are not usually evaluated. The extent to which behavior change in reinforcement programs depend on vicarious effects is not clear. Research might concentrate on separating the direct effects of reinforcement from the vicarious effects of observing others. If vicarious effects play a crucial role, they could be programmed more systematically than they normally are.

Subject and Demographic Variables

A relatively unexplored set of factors that may contribute to the effects of operant techniques are subject and demographic variables. These variables refer to characteristics of the population that may interact with the effects of contingency manipulations. There is a paucity of research investigating subject variables so that relatively few affirmative statements can be provided. In the available studies, sex, age, intelligence, patient diagnosis, and years of institutionalization are not consistently related to efficacy of reinforcement programs with psychotic patients. For example, psychiatric patients who are more educated and less withdrawn have been more likely to gain from ward-wide operant programs (Atthowe & Krasner, 1968; Ayllon & Azrin, 1968; Golub, 1969). Length of hospitalization has been positively or negatively related and unrelated to treatment outcome in separate studies (Allen & Magaro, 1971; Golub, 1969; Panek, 1969). Psychiatric diagnosis also has not been consistently related to responsiveness to operant programs (Ayllon & Azrin, 1965). Overall, while some studies have reported relationships between subject variables and success in the program, the evidence is contradictory.

In general, the prevailing assumption of operant techniques is that they are applicable across (virtually) all populations. Even if a given subject variable might interact with the reinforcement contingencies in altering behavior, this effect might only be a function of specific features of the program. Nevertheless, the role of subject variables in operant programs needs to be explored. Although it is unlikely that programs will be completely effective with some clients or ineffective with others, specific questions might be addressed by looking at subject variables. Finer program recommendations might be made if select subject variables interact with the efficacy of different manipulations such as the type of contingencies used, the reinforcers likely to be effective, the ideal parameters of reinforcer delivery, and similar program options.

General Comments

Research on the components of reinforcement and punishment programs needs to examine carefully the contribution of particular components to behavior change. Some research suggests that various procedures produce additive effects. For example, Walker et al. (1976, Exp. 1) found that sequentially introducing social reinforcement, token reinforcement, and response cost (loss of tokens) led to gradual improvements in classroom behavior. Each element contributed to behavior change and the extent of behavior change associated with different components could be examined. Many other components of operant programs need to be evaluated in an analytic fashion. The analysis of components and various procedures might provide a way of deciding the precise treatment plan that will be most likely to change behavior.

Comparison of Reinforcement Programs with Other Treatment Techniques

Operant techniques have been compared with several different treatment interventions. The most systematic body of information has compared reinforcement programs such as the token economy with other techniques, usually for institutionalized populations. This research will be reviewed briefly here to address the relative efficacy of operant techniques and other procedures. In general, there is a paucity of comparative studies across all operant techniques. This may stem from the usual requirement that between-group designs are best suited for comparisons of different treatments. Operant research has tended to eschew the use of between-group designs in general relative to intrasubject-replication comparisons (cf. Kazdin, 1976c, 1977b). Yet, a sufficient number of studies have been reported to address some general questions.

Reinforcement Programs versus Standard or Routine Treatment

Many studies have compared reinforcement programs with nonspecific interventions that constitute routine programs such as custodial ward treatment in a psychiatric hospital. Typically, patients in the reinforcement program receive tokens for engaging in self-care, social behaviors, activities, work, and other behaviors adaptive on the ward. A relatively consistent finding has been that patients on a ward with a reinforcement program show superior performance to control patients on such measures as ratings of psychotic symptoms and cognitive disturbance, cooperativeness, communication skills, social interaction, participation in activities, time out of the hospital, reduction in the use of medication, responsiveness to instructions, increased discharge rates, and similar gains (see Kazdin, 1975d).

Although the above results are impressive, it is not surprising that a reinforcement program, or perhaps almost any specific treatment, improves appropriate performance relative to custodial care. Custodial care might be more analogous to a no-treatment control group than to another treatment. All sorts of practices including even a change in hospital wards or a move to improved physical facilities improve performance in psychiatric patients (DeVries, 1968; Higgs, 1970).

More convincing evidence for operant techniques might be culled from settings where standard treatments constitute active program interventions. For example, reinforcement programs in the classroom are compared with traditional educational methods that involve the use of special curricula, delivery of grades, teacher feedback, reprimands, approval, and so on. In many cases, reinforcement programs merely systematize existing procedures so that consequences follow performance more frequently, regularly, immediately. Of course, in most classroom programs evaluated in intrasubject designs, "baseline" periods constitute traditional educational practices and are less effective than are reinforcement programs. In between-group comparisons, the results have been similar. For example, Rollins, McCandless, Thompson, and Brassell (1974) compared 16 inner city school classes that received a token reinforcement program with 14 classes that did not.

Reinforcement classes were superior on measures of on-task and disruptive behavior, intelligence, and reading and math achievement relative to control classes. Here again, the superiority of a token reinforcement program comes as no surprise. Many of the consequences in the classroom are not systematically programmed. Even when they are, some of the consequences used such as grades are not as effective as tokens backed by other reinforcers (McLaughlin & Malaby, 1975).

Reinforcement Programs versus Other Specific Treatments

Studies have compared reinforcement programs with other specific practices such as insight therapy and milieu treatment. For example, in a hospital setting, Hartlage (1970) showed that traditional "insight-oriented" therapy was less effective than was reinforcement (social, activities, and consumables) for adaptive responses in the hospital, as measured by hospital adjustment and therapist ratings. In contrast, Marks, Sonoda, and Shalock (1968) showed no differences between reinforcement programs and relationship therapy, across several measures of adjustment, mental efficiency, language skills, and others. Unfortunately, the unclear criteria for administering reinforcement raises questions about the implementation of that program.

Other studies in psychiatric hospitals have shown that reinforcement programs are superior to milieu therapy and milieu plus group therapy on measures such as attending activities in the hospital and taking passes out of the hospital (Olson & Greenberg, 1972). However, adding components of milieu therapy to token reinforcement programs (e.g., providing incentives for group decision making) is superior to a reinforcement program alone in increasing the time that individuals spend out of the hospital (Greenberg et al., 1975).

Not all comparative studies have been completed in hospital settings. For example, Fo and O'Donnell (1974) compared different community treatments where individuals recruited from the community treated behavior problem adolescents. Social or token reinforcement for individually determined appropriate behaviors decreased school truancy rates and various other problems (e.g., fighting, staying out late) to a greater extent than did relationship therapy and no-treatment control conditions. Similarly, Alexander and Parsons (1973) showed that using reinforcement techniques to develop positive family communication and specific behaviors was superior to client-centered and psychodynamic treatments in altering family interaction of delinquent youths. More importantly, six to eight month follow-up data revealed that the reinforcement program was associated with lower recidivism (i.e., rereferral to the courts) than were the other treatments.

It is unlikely that one form of treatment is superior to another per se but that different treatments may achieve different effects. This was supported by Jesness (1975) who found that transactional analysis and reinforcement techniques were differently effective in altering the performance of delinquent youths. Behavioral measures tended to reflect greater gains of the reinforcement program whereas self-report and attitudinal measures tended to favor transactional analysis.

Reinforcement Programs versus Pharmacotherapy

Studies comparing reinforcement programs with pharmacotherapy, a specific treatment technique, warrant mention in their own right. These studies are of particular interest because reinforcement programs and drugs often are used to manage problem behavior. Comparative studies have assessed treatment effects with hyperactive children who engage in such behaviors as gross motor movements, disruptive noise, and disturbing others. For example, in a classroom program, Ayllon et al. (1975) demonstrated that Ritalin (methylphenidate) and reinforcement were equally effective in controlling hyperactive behaviors of the three youths. However, the drug impeded academic performance whereas the reinforcement program accelerated it.

Other studies have demonstrated that the hyperactive and aggressive behaviors of children and adults are better controlled with reinforcement techniques than with Ritalin (e.g., Christensen, 1975) or Thorazine (chlorpromazine) (e.g., McConahey, Thompson, & Zimmerman, 1977). In some studies, the effects of reinforcement pro-

grams are enhanced by drugs (e.g., Christensen & Sprague, 1973), although this is not always the case (e.g., Paul, Tobias, & Holly, 1972).

General Comments

Comparative studies have suggested that reinforcement programs are superior to routine treatments as well as to diverse specific procedures. The conclusions must be made cautiously from this literature because of the methodological requirements for comparative research and the difficulty in ruling out alternative hypotheses as rival explanations of the results. In several comparative studies, treatment has been confounded with variables such as a change in setting (e.g., Birky, Chambliss, & Wasden, 1971), selection of special staff to administer the reinforcement program (e.g., Gripp & Magaro, 1974), initial differences in client disorders (Shean & Zeidberg, 1971), and selection of subjects on the basis of consent regarding particular aspects of treatment (Christensen & Sprague, 1973). Many investigations are quasi-experiments in which select features such as nonrandom assignment of subjects to conditions interferes with the conclusions that can be drawn. Such evaluations are admirable and informative in any case. The paucity and methodological problems of comparative studies apply widely across techniques rather than to behavioral techniques in particular. Thus, even the small and tentative literature favoring reinforcement techniques provides a promising evaluation.

Evaluating the Effects of Operant Programs

Two criteria have been suggested for evaluating the effects of operant interventions. These include an experimental criterion in which the causal relation between treatment and behavior change is assessed and a therapeutic criterion in which the clinical or social importance of behavior change is evaluated (Risley, 1970). The clinical value of change raises important questions regarding the significance of the behaviors that are changed and the magnitude of the behavior change achieved. The importance of the target behaviors selected for operant interventions has been evaluated above. An important issue remaining to be discussed pertains to the importance or clinical significance of the behavior changes that are achieved. This refers to the extent to which the change in behavior has some bearing on the client's functioning in everyday life. Unfortunately, applied work has not specified the criteria to determine whether change in behavior is of applied significance. Statistical evaluation, of course, is not the appropriate tool because even a major change in behavior in the statistical sense may be of no clinical consequence (cf. Kazdin, 1976c).

Recent work has attempted to assess the importance of behavior change through *social validation,* that is, determining the validity or utility of the change in the client's social situation (Wolf, 1976). Validation of treatment effects has been assessed either by showing that the effect of treatment has brought the client's behavior within the range of acceptable levels of behavior evinced by his or her peers or leads others in the environment to evaluate behavior more favorably. For example, Patterson (1974) demonstrated that behavioral interventions with conduct problem boys at home and at school changed deviant behaviors and that these chages at follow-up brought the behavior of the treated boys within the range of nondeviant control subjects (i.e., peers). At least for the target behaviors selected, the clients presumably were no longer distinct as a problem group. In some studies, the criterion of normative levels of performance has not been met. For example, Walker, Mattson, and Buckley (1971) found that a reinforcement program for elementary students increased attentiveness but performance was still below normative data for nonproblem classmates of the target subjects.

Aside from showing the extent to which behavior change brings the client to the level of some normative groups, social validation also has relied on the opinions of individuals not associated with treatment to judge the importance of behavior change. For example, Maloney and Hopkins (1973) have shown that increases in specific writing responses in elementary school children were associated with increased ratings of creativity of compositions by independent judges. In studies with delinquents, programs have developed conversational skills by reinforcing specific behaviors such as asking questions, providing feedback to the other individual in the conversation, and volunteering information. These changes are associated with increases in the ratings of general conversational ability, politeness, and cooperativeness by independent judges (Maloney, Harper, Brauckmann, Fixsen, Phillips, & Wolf, 1976; Minkin et al., 1976).

The above studies provide a small sample of the types of steps that have been taken to assess the importance of the change effected with operant techniques. Relatively few studies have attempted to assess the importance of clinical change either within operant techniques or indeed for other techniques as well. Certainly this is an area that warrants examination. In the evaluation of therapy techniques in general, the relative efficacy of various techniques may be insignificant if the best procedure does not even approach achieving clinically important changes (see Kazdin, 1977e).

Although it is important to clinically validate procedures used for treatment purposes, this area will be beset with problems of its own. Comparing the behavior of individuals with one's nondeviant peers raises various issues. In some cases, it will be difficult to identify an appropriate comparative group of nondeviant peers and the criteria for clinical improvement might either be too stringent or perhaps impossible to achieve. In the case of rating behaviors, this too will require additional work. Rated behavioral improvements are subject to various artifacts and may not necessarily reflect behavior change of the client. Nevertheless, social validation of behavior change warrants additional work across treatment modalities.

LEGAL ISSUES RAISED BY CONDUCTING OPERANT PROGRAMS

Developing a technology of behavior change has made salient the potential conflict between the rights and values of individuals and society. The conflict is especially pronounced in cases where individual freedoms are guaranteed by the United States Constitution and the state intervenes and restricts freedom in the name of treatment or rehabilitation. Legal questions have been prominent with institutionalized populations who are involuntarily confined. Until recently, the courts have assumed a "hands off" policy in which institutions were assumed to be the best judge of the type of treatment and the conditions of its administration (Martin, 1975; Wexler, 1973). A change in this attitude has brought legal decisions with far-reaching implications for treatment programs. The present discussion provides an overview of major issues and legal decisions in the United States that pertain directly to implementing reinforcement and punishment programs. Extended discussions of these issues are provided in several other sources (e.g., Budd & Baer, 1976; Friedman, 1975; Kassirer, 1974; Martin, 1975; Stolz, 1976; Wexler, 1975a, 1975b).

Contingent Consequences and Environmental Restraint

Reinforcement programs in institutional settings use various events and amenities in the setting as reinforcers. For example, with psychiatric patients, basic items such as comfortable living quarters, private space, a bed (rather than a cot), ground privileges, recreational activities, and similar amenities often are incorporated into a reinforcement program to develop patient behavior. Recently the courts have ruled on whether basic amenities can be withheld from institutionalized populations and deliverd contingently upon behavior. A landmark decision was *Wyatt v. Stickney* which addressed several features regarding institutional treatment of psychiatric patients and the mentally retarded. One aspect of this decision specified that patients are entitled by *right* to various items and activities that sometimes are used as reinforcing events. The court specified that patients are entitled to a comfortable bed, a balanced meal, a place for personal belongings, opportunities to attend religious services, to interact with the opposite sex, to be outdoors frequently, to receive visitors, and so on. With other populations such as institutionalized delinquents, the courts have ruled that similar events are to be provided to the clients by right (*Morales v. Turman*).

These rulings have obvious implications for operant programs. In reinforcement programs, many amenities have been viewed as *privileges* (i.e., benefits enjoyed by individuals who earn them) and not *rights* (i.e., events to which any client has just claim). The rulings require the noncontingent presentation of many amenities that would otherwise be delivered contingently. There are exceptions, of course. In special cases, the individual can waive his or her right and receive a given event contingently or the state may intervene in behalf of individuals considered incompetent to make such a decision (Friedman, 1975). However, the above decisions require most programs to identify and provide reinforcing events not already available in the situation.

Rulings that patients have a right to various events in the environment is part of a broader right. This right is that the environment to which an individual is committed should be the "least restrictive alternative" of confinement (Ennis & Friedman, 1973). The individual is entitled to the least restrictive conditioins to achieve the purpose of confinement so that the interests of the public (confining someone of potential danger) and the individual (personal liberty) are balanced. This doctrine was first enumerated in the case of *Lake v. Cameron* which held that a psychiatric patient could be confined only if less drastic but suitable alternatives could not be found (see also *Covington v. Harris; Lessard v. Schmidt*).

This doctrine could be extended to behavioral programs that restrict conditions of the client. Outside of obviously restrictive conditions such as physical restraint and possibly other punishment techniques, maintaining individuals on closed wards, withholding some events until specific behaviors are performed, limiting social interaction, or even controlling behavior with contingencies, may involve restrictive conditions. Current evidence does not overwhelmingly support long-term gains of psychological or behavioral treatment. The lack of evidence may increase the difficulty of justifying restrictions placed on clients as part of treatment.

Use of Aversive Techniques

Operant techniques rely heavily on positive reinforcement and to a much lesser extent on aversive stimuli as part of punishment and negative reinforcement contingencies. Of course, aversive consequences have been used in treatment and penology long before behavior modification. Thus, the courts have a lengthy history of addressing those punishments that can be used and the conditions of administration required to protect rights of patients and inmates.

In dealing with punishing consequences used in behavior modification, distinctions need to be made of the precise procedures used. Understandably, the courts' views of punishment have varied across different procedures.[5] Treatment programs frequently include time out from reinforcement or the removal of an individual from sources of reinforcement for a brief period. In time out, individuals may be taken out of the situation and placed in seclusion, usually for only a few minutes. Courts have intervened in cases where seclusion is used as a form of punishment. Some rulings have specified that extended periods of seclusion cannot be used, and that the client must have access to food, lighting, and other basic humane conditions. Perhaps more interestingly, the courts have ruled that individuals have a right to be free from isolation (*Wyatt v. Stickney*).

Occasionally, the courts have distinguished types of isolation and seclusion that may be used as punishment and have allowed for brief time out periods under close professional supervision for target behaviors such as those leading to physical harm or property destruction (*Morales v. Turman; Wyatt v. Stickney*). In other cases, this distinction has not been made and isolation for clients such as retardates have been ruled out (*New York State Association for Retarded Children v. Rockefeller*). Clear and consistent guidelines are not available for the use of time out. Indeed, in some cases contradictory recommendations could be inferred. For example, time out as brief period of isolation can be used but not seclusion. Yet, seclusion is sometimes defined by the courts as placing an individual in a locked room. Occasionally, this is what behavior modifiers refer to as time out.

Electric shock as a punishing stimulus is used

relatively infrequently for such behaviors as self-destruction. The courts have provided clear restrictions in the use of shock. For example, the *Wyatt v. Stickney* decision specified that for retarded clients, shock could only be used in extraordinary circumstances, such as self-destructive behavior that is likely to inflict physical damage. Moreover, the decision specified that shock could only be applied after alternative procedures have been tried, after obtaining approval from a committee on human rights, with informed consent from the client or a relative, and under direct order of the institution's superintendent. It is understandable that shock should be so carefully restricted by the courts in part because of the danger of misuse and the implications for cruel and unusual punishment and because of the traditional misuse of electroconvulsive shock for many patients.

Although behavior modifiers usually do not use drugs as punishers in applied settings, occasionally drugs have been delivered contingently to suppress behavior. The most well publicized program of this type was at a prison facility in Vacaville, California. Aggressive behaviors of the inmates were followed with injections of a drug (succinylcholine) that inhibits respiration and apparently gives the experience of suffocation and drowning. The courts have recognized that drug treatment of this type may constitute cruel and unusual punishment (*Knecht v. Gillman*). This decision specified carefully monitored conditions under which drugs might be used such as supervision by a physician, written consent of the client, the opportunity to withdraw consent, and others. In other cases, the courts have ruled simply that drugs cannot be used as punishment (*Wyatt v. Stickney*).

The courts have not addressed some specific forms of punishment that are used as part of operant techniques. The most notable procedure is overcorrection, which consists of correcting the environmental effects of an inappropriate behavior and extensively rehearsing the correct forms of appropriate behavior (e.g., Foxx & Azrin, 1972). For example, an individual who throws things might be punished by being made to pick up the things thrown (i.e., correcting the environmental effects) and by straightening other areas beyond those disrupted by the original act (i.e., rehearsing correct

---

[5]There are specific practices that constitute punishment as that term is commonly rather than technically used. For example, physically restraining individuals or using corporal punishment have been used in traditional treatment and criminal practices. However, these techniques are not part of accepted and widely practiced operant techniques. Thus, the rulings for these practices will not be reviewed here.

behaviors). Response cost, a punishment procedure usually conducted by withdrawing tokens contingent on behavior (Kazdin, 1972), also has not been specifically ruled upon by the courts. Both overcorrection and response cost are used relatively commonly in the literature and probably constitute mild forms of punishment from the standpoint of the courts. Independently of the specific procedures used, the major issue in the use of aversive procedures appears to be obtaining the consent of the client or a guardian or relative if the resident is not able to give consent. The issue of informed consent transcends the use of aversive techniques and is addressed below in a separate section.

Selection of Target Behaviors

Most behaviors focused on in operant programs have not raised legal questions. Indeed, operant techniques usually are used to accomplish traditional goals (e.g., to reduce psychiatric symptoms, to increase academic performance). An exception to this pertains to the use of psychiatric patients to work on jobs that maintain the institution. Using patients to complete hospital work without providing payment is widespread practice independently of behavior modification programs (Ennis & Friedman, 1973), although it has been incorporated into several token economies in the hospital (Kazdin, 1977c). One concern about using patients to perform hospital work is that their contribution to the hospital may compete with the therapeutic goal of discharge.

The courts have intervened to ensure that patients are not exploited. An important decision ruled that patient work that is laborsaving for the institution with no therapeutic value may be unconstitutional because it entails involuntary servitude (Jobson v. Henne). The Wyatt v. Stickney decision extended this by noting that work that maintained the hospital whether or not deemed therapeutic could only be performed if minimum wages were provided. The court specified that other incentives (e.g., privileges, release from the hospital) could not be contingent on work performance. The court noted some exceptions to the rule against involuntary work which included select tasks of clear therapeutic value (e.g., vocational

training) and personal tasks (e.g., making one's own bed). Although the above decisions apply to a single type of behavior, the widespread use of hospital work in reinforcement programs makes the decision have far-reaching consequences.

Right to Treatment

The client's right to treatment is directed to institutionalized individuals who are involuntarily confined (Birnbaum, 1960). If an individual's freedom is denied through confinement to treatment, some treatment must be given that might return him or her to the community. In a landmark decision (Rouse v. Cameron), the court ruled on a case where a patient was committed to a mental hospital after determining he was not guilty (of carrying a weapon) for reasons of insanity. His hospitalization exceeded the period that criminal conviction would have brought. He attempted to obtain release alleging that he received no psychiatric treatment. The eventual ruling in the case was that a patient committed to a hospital has a right to receive adequate treatment. Adequate treatment need not necessarily cure the patient but only be a bona fide attempt to do so in light of existing knowledge. In general, the courts cannot determine whether treatment is the optimal one but only whether it is reasonable in view of the patient's circumstances.

Extensions of the right to treatment have asserted that patients cannot be confined without treatment if they present no danger to themselves or others (Donaldson v. O'Connor). Confinement without treatment is tantamount to unlawful imprisonment (Renelli v. Department of Mental Hygiene). The right to treatment has been extended to sexual psychopaths, drug addicts, and juveniles. Guaranteeing a right to "adequate treatment" raises a host of problems such as defining the basic terms, determining the methods by which the adequacy will be assessed for a given patient, and others. Currently, the courts appear to be more concerned with providing some specific treatment intervention than the effects of that intervention on behavior.

Refusal of Treatment

Although the individual may have right to treatment, both the means and ends of treatment might conflict with individual rights. Thus, legal decisions have provided precedent for an individual's right to refuse treatment. There are some apparent inconsistencies in this area. In many cases, the courts have rejected the claims made by the clients who have attempted to refuse treatment (e.g., such as being required to receive drug or medical treatment) because treatment may entail some sacrifice of individual liberty (*Haynes v. Harris; Peek v. Ciccone*). In other cases, patients have been able to refuse treatments, such as taking drugs in conflict with religious beliefs, or as part of aversion therapy, or receiving electroshock (*New York City Health and Hospital Corporation v. Stein; Winters v. Miller*). In general, the decision to override a patient's right depends on balancing the interests of the individual and society. Personal rights are most likely to be overridden when there is some immediate danger the state wishes to protect (see Martin, 1975).

The assignment of individuals to treatment may raise issues of due process. A prominent case in point was raised in litigation against the START program, mentioned earlier, where intractible prisoners were transferred to a special facility to participate in a behavioral program (*Clonce v. Richardson*). Although the program terminated while litigation was pending, the court ruled that transfer to the prison involved a major change in the prisoners' conditions of confinement and upheld the challenge of the inmates that the transfer to the facility violated due process of law.

Informed Consent

Many of the problems raised by implementing programs with confined individuals can be alleviated if consent is provided about restrictions imposed by interventions. Although informed consent would seem to protect against infringing upon individual client rights, there are many ambiguities about the nature of consent and how it can and should be obtained (Kassirer, 1974).

Consent includes at least three elements, namely, competence, knowledge, and voluntariness (Friedman, 1975; Martin, 1975; Wexler, 1973). Competence refers to the individual's ability to make a well-reasoned decision, to understand the nature of the choice presented, and to meaningfully give consent. Many individuals exposed to

behavior modification programs (e.g., some psychiatric patients, children, retardates) need others to act in their behalf and provide consent. Even where consent has been obtained, it is unclear whether patients were competent and understood what they had provided. For example, Palmer and Wohl(1972) queried patients who signed voluntary admission forms, thereby admitting themselves to a psychiatric hospital. Sixty percent of the patients were unable to recall signing the form within 10 days after admission; 33 percent did not recall the content of the form or could not recall it accurately. Some of the patients even denied signing the form. These results raise questions either about the competence of the patients or the procedures used to secure consent.

Knowledge, the second element of consent, refers to understanding the nature of treatment, the alternatives available, and potential benefits and risks involved. This may be a difficult condition to meet given that so little is known about many available treatments. Voluntariness, the third element of consent, refers to the notion that the individual must agree to participate in the treatment. Moreover, agreement must not be given under duress. It is difficult to ensure that decisions are made without duress. In prisons and psychiatric hospitals, inmates may feel compelled to participate in treatment programs because of the anticipated long-term gains from favorable evaluation of staff and administrators who play important and decisive roles in their release.

Voluntary consent may not be possible for involuntarily confined individuals because the environment may be inherently coercive, that is, because privileges and release may depend on the individual's cooperativeness. This conclusion was reached in a landmark decision of *Kaimowitz v. Michigan Department of Mental Health* where psychosurgery was to be used to control aggressive behavior of a psychiatric patient. Even though the patient gave consent, the court ruled that truly voluntary and informed consent was not possible. The involuntary status of the patient militated against voluntary consent. Also, the nature of the intervention (i.e., a dangerous and irreversible treatment) and lack of information about its benefits and risks militated against informed consent. The treatment was regarded as unconstitutional independently of the patient's consent.

The *Kaimowitz* decision could have far-reaching implications. In the extreme, it could mean that patients confined involuntarily are never in a position to give voluntary consent because of their status. Wexler (1975a, 1975b) has challenged the notion that patients committed involuntarily are necessarily coerced by their status in the institution. If the lure of release is regarded as inherently coercive, all therapy for involuntarily institutionalized persons would be coercive despite their desire or consent.

The issue of consent raises several problems for treatment in general as well as for operant techniques. Even if clients give consent for a particular treatment, they may withdraw consent at will (*Knecht v. Gillman*). For example, in a reinforcement program a patient may waive the right for various events such as ground privileges and adequate sleeping quarters. These events, with the patient's initial consent, can be delivered contingently. Yet, if the patient does not earn these events at some point in the program, he or she may withdraw consent then and terminate the program. Withdrawing consent, of course, may be easier than performing the target behaviors upon which the events were contingent (Wexler, 1975b). Thus, from the standpoint of implementing effective programs, consent does not guarantee that contingencies will be adequately applied.

Protection of Client Rights

The guidelines provided by the courts have begun to outline individual rights, especially for residents who are involuntarily committed. The conditions that will safeguard individual rights are incomplete and will require additional litigation and legislation. Other recommendations for deciding individual treatment regimens have been provided. For example, Kittrie (1971) has proposed a *Therapeutic Bill of Rights* to serve as guidelines for treatment. These guidelines include the notion that no person should be compelled to undergo treatment except for the defense of society, that there is an inviolable right to be free of excessive forms of modification, that no social sanctions can be invoked unless the person shows a clear and present danger through truly harmful behavior, that an involuntary patient shall have the right to receive treatment, that any compulsory treatment be the least required to protect society, that committed individuals have access to counsel and the right to petition the courts for relief, and others.

Rights such as these incorporate many of the doctrines and decisions of the courts (e.g., least restrictive alternative). Yet they are quite general and may not be sufficiently concrete to deal with specific treatment cases. For example, to say that an individual has a right to treatment does not specify what constitutes treatment. Is treatment any intervention that a professional so labels or one that has in fact produced change? Many procedures currently considered to be therapeutic and advanced by professionals have little supporting evidence. In general, abstract guidelines might not be sufficient to protect client rights.

Another proposal is that the relationship of the client and the therapist or institution be conceptualized as a contractual agreement (Schwitzgebel, 1975). Patients and therapists could negotiate the conditions of treatment. The contract could make explicit the goals, methods, risks, and benefits of treatment, insofar as these are known. The contract may not necessarily guarantee therapeutic outcome but it would increase the accountability of treatment and practitioners. Also, by formulating treatment as a contract, the client may have some legal power to sue for breach of contract or to be compensated for injury. Perhaps one of the greatest advantages of a contract from the standpoint of patient rights is that it could specify the conditions for cure or sufficient improvement to obtain release from confinement.

An illustration of a contractual arrangement in treatment was provided by Ayllon and Skuban (1973) who treated an eight-year-old boy who engaged in tantrums and negativistic behavior. The boy was trained to comply with instructions and not engage in tantrums in a wide range of situations in everyday life. Prior to treatment, a contractual arrangement was made specifying that treatment outcome would be evaluated by testing the boy's compliance in a special session attended by the parents, therapist, and some other person. Criteria were set regarding the percentage of commands complied with and the amount of tantrums allowed to conclude that treatment had been successful. Interestingly, success of treatment partially determined whether a portion of the therapist's fee would have to be paid by the parents.

Although the idea of a contractual arrangement during treatment is attractive, it is unclear whether it would adequately protect a patient. The differences in status, power, and information about treatment as well as the involuntary status of the patient may limit the legitimacy of the contract. For the contract to be upheld by the courts, the usual conditions of informed consent (i.e., competence, knowledge, voluntariness) may have to be met (Friedman, 1975).

Guidelines for using behavior modification procedures and for protecting client rights have been developed by various states and professional organizations. One of the better-known proposals was developed in Florida in response to a program that engaged in several abuses for treatment of retarded, delinquent, and disturbed boys. The abuses, many of which were inappropriately labeled behavior modification, included severe physical punishment, forced sexual acts, deprivation, and other procedures.

These abuses led to formation of a Task Force to develop guidelines based on psychological and legal principles against which subsequent programs could be evaluated. The guidelines included recommendations pertaining to competence, informed consent, and the least restrictive alternative doctrine (Friedman, 1975; Wexler, 1975a). Also, the guidelines proposed development of review committees to oversee any proposed treatment program. The committees could include experts in behavior modification, legal counsel, lay individuals interested in the client population, and others. Essentially, the review committee would represent civil liberties of the clients as well as judge the adequacy of treatment from different perspectives.

A leveled system was recommended to evaluate how intrusive treatment is to the client. More intrusive procedures would require greater scrutiny by advocacy and review panels. At an initial level, neither the target behaviors nor the techniques used to alter them would be viewed as interfering with the rights of the client (e.g., developing language or self-help skills with praise). At a higher level, more intrusive procedures might be used (e.g., such as time out) for behaviors in the previous level. At the final level, both the behaviors studied and the interventions used might be controversial such as using shock to alter patterns of sexual behavior. The review process would focus on interventions at the higher levels to ensure that the client's rights were maximally protected in cases where clear guidelines for change and the use of intrusive treatments were recommended.

Generally, the precise methods that can best protect patient rights remain to be determined. Recent litigation has increased sensitivity of individuals responsible for designing and implementing treatment to the rights of their clients. This by itself probably has reduced the likelihood of using controversial and intrusive techniques. Additional specific guidelines will be implemented to ensure that formal means of evaluating treatment and protecting clients is provided.

General Comments

Recent legal decisions have raised the question whether select techniques will continue to exist at all or in the form that has been commonly used. Litigation already has altered the legality of specific features that have been commonly employed such as the contingent delivery of various events in institutional settings, alteration of select target behaviors, and so on. Also, a liberal interpretation of the general policies such as the least restrictive alternative doctrine could limit the application of contingencies with involuntarily confined populations in general. Although specific features of operant techniques may change, it is unlikely that they will be applied less widely. Operant techniques, particularly variations of positive reinforcement, are firmly entrenched in areas where relatively few legal questions arise such as in programs in the classroom where traditional goals (e.g., academic accomplishment) are accelerated. In areas where litigation does apply, it is likely to exert positive influences toward the advancement of operant techniques. Some changes are evident in programs that have developed innovative events as reinforcers rather than use amenities to which institutionalized populations are entitled by right.

On a more general level, the legal issues increasingly bring into public awareness the importance of demonstrably effective treatment strategies. Although behavioral techniques are undergoing scrutiny, so may all techniques. The basis for using a given technique increasingly may be challenged. The challenges of the courts partially stress the accountability of treatment. This could well prove to be the strength of the behavioral approach to treatment in general because both the goals of treatment and the means to achieve these goals are explicit.

CONCLUSION

Operant techniques have been applied widely across target populations, behaviors, and settings. An overwhelming amount of experimental evidence has been amassed establishing the efficacy of operant techniques with clinical populations. Perhaps one of the most impressive features of operant techniques is their adaptability to diverse populations differing widely in characteristics. The flexibility of the approach is an advantage when designing programs across populations that usually are thought to require drastically different techniques or even with a given population where individual differences need to be considered. Operant techniques provide a general framework for altering behavior and designing contingencies and leave unspecified several variables to incorporate specific characteristics of the population.

When viewed against other techniques, operant techniques appear to have made major advances. The extent of empirical validation of operant techniques across a wide range of applications is not approached by other psychological treatment methods. Thus, relative to other approaches operant techniques fare well. When viewed against ultimate treatment goals, operant techniques need to be evaluated much more critically. Operant techniques by no means have solved the problems in diverse areas of treatment, rehabilitation, and education. For example, operant techniques do not routinely return patients to the community with no further signs of psychopathology or social deficits, or improve the diagnostic status of educably retarded children so that their performance completely falls within the range of normal performance, or eliminate postconfinement crime of prisoners. Of course, the difficulty in evaluating treatment stems from the ambiguity in the possible gains that can be achieved. It is important to mention this otherwise obvious point to explain the zeal with which many operant programs are implemented and reported. The enthusiasm evident in the literature reflects excitement over progress achieved rather than celebration after completion of the tasks set for the mental-health professions.

Commenting on the progress of operant techniques should not imply that most of the issues with this approach are resolved. Perhaps, the major issue is developing strategies to ensure that changes made during operant programs are maintained and transfer to extratreatment settings. The technology of behavior change is much more advanced than is the technology of maintaining behavior and ensuring its transfer. The literature suggests that the procedures used to change behavior differ from those used to maintain that change. Now that the technology of change is reasonably well researched, increased attention is focused on the technology of maintenance and transfer. Sufficient advances have been made already to regard the development of such a technology as inevitable and not as a mere promissory note.

This chapter has emphasized the substantive advances made in applied operant research as well as areas that warrant further investigation. Although the substantive issues and questions are of primary consideration in evaluating the state of the art, it is important to emphasize the methodological stance of the operant approach in treatment. The major characteristic of the approach is the reliance on experimental evaluation of treatment effects. The commitment to empirical demonstration as a means of evaluating treatment is more characteristic of applied behavior analysis than is the strict derivation of techniques from operant conditioning. It is this experimental stance that is likely to foster continued gains in treating the populations reviewed in the present chapter.

REFERENCES

Abrahms, J. L., & Allen, G. J. Comparative effectiveness of situational programming, financial pay-offs, and group pressure in weight reduction. *Behavior Therapy,* 1974, *5,* 391–400.

Abrams, L., Hines, D., Pollack, D., Ross, M., Stubbs, D. A., & Polyot, C. J. Transferrable tokens: Increasing social interaction in a token economy. *Psychological Reports,* 1974, *35,* 447–452.

Alexander, J. F., & Parsons, B. V. Short-term behavioral intervention with delinquent families: Impact on family process and recidivism. *Journal of Abnormal Psychology,* 1973, *81,* 219–225.

Allen, D. J., & Magaro, P. A. Measures of change in token-economy programs. *Behaviour Research and Therapy,* 1971, *9,* 311–318.

Anderson, L. T., & Alpert, M. Operant anlysis of hallucination frequency in a hospitalized schizophrenic. *Journal of Behavior Therapy and Experimental Psychiatry,* 1974, *5,* 13–18.

Atthowe, J. M., Jr., & Krasner, L. Preliminary report on the application of contingent reinforcement procedures (token economy) on a "chronic" psychiatric ward. *Journal of Abnormal Psychology,* 1968, *73,* 37–43.

Axelrod, S., Hall, R. V., & Maxwell, A. Use of peer attention to increase study behavior. *Behavior Therapy, 1972. 3,* 349–351.

Ayers, S. K. B., Potter, R. E., & McDearmon, J. R. Using reinforcement therapy and precision teaching techniques with adult aphasics. *Journal of Behavior Therapy and Experimental Psychiatry,* 1975, *6,* 301–305.

Ayllon, T., & Azrin, N. H. Reinforcement and instructions with mental patients. *Journal of the Experimental Analysis of Behavior,* 1964, *7,* 327–331.

Ayllon, R., & Azrin, N. H. The measurement and reinforcement of behavior of psychotics. *Journal of the Experimental Analysis of Behavior,* 1965, *8,* 356–383.

Ayllon, R., & Azrin, N. H. *The token economy: A motivational system for therapy and rehabilitation.* New York: Appleton-Century-Crofts, 1968.

Ayllon, T., & Kelly, K. Effects of reinforcement on standardized test performance. *Journal of Applied Behavior Analysis,* 1972, *5,* 477–484.

Ayllon, T., & Kelly, K. Reinstating verbal behavior in a functionally mute retardate. *Professional Psychology,* 1974, *5,* 385–393.

Ayllon, T., Layman, D., & Burke, S. Disruptive behavior and reinforcement of academic performance. *Psychological Record,* 1972, *22,* 315–323.

Ayllon, T., Layman, D., & Kandel, H. J. A behavioral-educational alternative to drug control of hyperactive children. *Journal of Applied Behavior Analysis,* 1975, *8,* 137–146.

Ayllon, T., & Skuban, W. Accountability in psychotherapy: A test case. *Journal of Behavior Therapy and Experimental Psychiatry,* 1973, *4,* 19–30.

Azrin, N. H., & Foxx, R. M. *Toilet training in less than a day.* New York: Simon & Schuster, 1974.

Azrin, N. H., Kaplan, S. J., & Foxx, R. M. Autism reversal: Eliminating stereotyped self-stimulation of retarded individuals. *American Journal of Mental Deficiency,* 1973, *78,* 241–248.

Azrin, N. H. & Wesolowski, M. D. The use of positive practice to eliminate persistent floor sprawling by profoundly retarded persons. *Behavior Therapy,* 1975, *6,* 627–631.

Baer, D. M., & Wolf, M. M. The entry into natural communities of reinforcement: In R. Ulrich, T. Stachnik, & J. Mabry (Eds.), *Control of human behavior, Vol. 2.* Glenview, Illinois: Scott, Foresman and Company, 1970.

Baer, D. M., Wolf, M. M., & Risley, T. R. Some current dimensions of applied behavior analysis. *Journal of Applied Behavior Analysis,* 1968, *1,* 91–97.

Bailey, J. S., Timbers, G. D., Phillips, E. L., & Wolf, M. M. Modification of articulation errors of pre-delinquents by their peers. *Journal of Applied Behavior Analysis,* 1971, *4,* 265–281.

Bennett, P. S., & Maley, R. S. Modification of interactive behaviors in chronic mental patients. *Journal of Applied Behavior Analysis,* 1973, *6,* 609–620.

Berkowitz, S., Sherry, P. J., & Davis, B. A. Teaching self-feeding skills to profound retardates using reinforcement and fading procedures. *Behavior Therapy,* 1971, *2,* 62–67.

Birky, H. J., Chambliss, J. E., & Wasden, R. A comparison of residents discharged from a token economy and two traditional psychiatric programs. *Behavior Therapy,* 1971, *2,* 46–51.

Birnbaum, M. The right to treatment. *American Bar Association Journal,* 1960, *10,* 499–505.

Birnbrauer, J. S. Mental retardation. In H. Leitenberg (Ed.), *Handbook of behavior modification and behavior therapy.* Englewood Cliffs, N. J.: Prentice-Hall, 1976.

Blanchard, E. B., & Young, L. D. Clinical applications of biofeedback. *Archives of General Psychiatry,* 1974, *30,* 573–589.

Boren, J. J., & Colman, A. D. Some experiments on reinforcement principles with a psychiatric ward for delinquent soldiers. *Journal of Applied Behavior Analysis,* 1970, *3,* 29–37.

Boudin, H. M. Contingency contracting as a therapeutic tool in the deceleration of amphetamine use. *Behavior Therapy,* 1972, *3,* 604–608.

Braukmann, C. J., & Fixsen, D. L. Behavior modification with delinquents. In M. Hersen, R. M. Eisler, and P. M. Miller (Eds.), *Progress in behavior modification,* Vol. 1. New York: Academic Press, 1975.

Breyer, N. L., & Allen, G. J. Effects of implementing a token economy on teacher attending behavior. *Journal of Applied Behavior Analysis,* 1975, *8,* 373–380.

Bricker, W. A., Morgan, D. G., & Grabowski, J. G. Development and maintenance of a behavior modification repertoire of cottage attendants through T. V.

feedback. *American Journal of Mental Deficiency,* 1972, *77,* 128–136.

Brigham, T. A., & Catania, A. C. *The Handbook of applied behavior research: Social and instructional processes.* New York: Irvington Press/Halstead Press, in press.

Brigham, T. S., Graubard, P. S., & Stans, A. Analysis of the effects of sequential reinforcement contingencies on aspects of composition. *Journal of Applied Behavior Analysis,* 1972, *5,* 421–429.

Broden, M., Bruce, C., Mitchell, M. A., Carter, V., & Hall, R. V. Effects of teacher attention on attending behavior of two boys at adjacent desks. *Journal of Applied Behavior Analysis,* 1970, *3,* 199–203.

Budd, K. S., & Baer, D. M. Behavior modification and the law: Implications of recent judicial decisions. *Journal of Psychiatry and Law,* 1976, *4,* 171–244.

Burchard, J. D., & Harig, P. T. Behavior modification and juvenile delinquency. In H. Leitenberg (Ed.), *Handbook of behavior modification and behavior therapy.* Englewood Cliffs, N. J. :Prentice-Hall, 1976.

Burchard, J. D., & Tyler, V. O. The modification of delinquent behaviour through operant conditioning. *Behaviour Research and Therapy,* 1965, *2,* 245–250.

Bushell, D., Jr. The design of classroom contingencies. In F. S. Keller & E. Ribes-Inesta (Eds.), *Behavior modification: Applications to education.* New York: Academic Press, 1974.

Cash, W. M., & Evans, I. M. Training pre-school children to modify their retarded siblings' behavior. *Journal of Behavior Therapy and Experimental Psychiatry,* 1975, *6,* 13–16.

Christensen, C. E. Effects of combining methylphenidate and a classroom token system in modifying hyperactive behavior. *American Journal of Mental Deficiency,* 1975, *80,* 266–276.

Christensen, D. E., & Sprague, R. L. Reduction of hyperactive behavior by conditioning procedures alone and combined with methylphenidate (Ritalin) *Behaviour Research and Therapy,* 1973, *11,* 331–334.

Christopherson, E. R., Arnold, C. M., Hill, D. W., & Quilitch, H. R. The home point system: Token reinforcement procedures for application by parents of children with behavior problems. *Journal of Applied Behavior Analysis,* 1972, *5,* 485–497.

Clark, M., Lachowicz, J., & Wolf, M. M. A pilot basic education program for school dropouts incorporating a token reinforcement system. *Behaviour Research and Therapy,* 1968, *8,* 183–188.

Clonce v. Richardson, 379 F Supp. 338 (W. D. Mo. 1974).

Cohen, H. L. Programming alternatives to punishment: The design of competence through consequences. In S. W. Bijou & S. Ribes-Inesta (Eds.), *Behavior modification: Issues and extensions.* New York: Academic Press, 1972.

Cohen, H. L., & Filipszak, J. *A new learning environment.* SanFrancisco: Jossey-Bass, 1971.

Cohen, M., Liebson, I. A., & Faillace, L. A. The role of reinforcement contingencies in chronic alcoholism: An experimental analysis of one case. *Behaviour Research and Therapy,* 1971, *9,* 375–379.

Cohen, M., Liebson, I. A., Faillace, L. A., & Speers, W. Alcoholism: Controlled drinking and inventives for abstinence. *Psychological Reports, 1971, 28,* 575–580.

Colman, A. D., & Boren, J. J. An information system for measuring patient behavior and its use by staff. *Journal of Applied Behavior Analysis,* 1969, *2,* 207–214.

Cossairt, A., Hall, R. V., & Hopkins, B. L. The effects of experimenter's instructions, feedback, and praise on teacher praise and student attending behavior. *Journal of Applied Behavior Analysis,* 1973, *6,* 89–100.

Covington v. Harris, 419 F. 2d. 617 (D. C. 1969).

Davidson, W. S., II, & Seidman, E. Studies of behavior modification and juvenile delinquency: A review, methodological critique, and social perspective. *Psychological Bulletin,* 1972, *81,* 998–1011.

DeVries, D. L. Effects of environmental change and of participation on the behavior of mental patients. *Journal of Consulting and Clinical Psychology,* 1968, *32,* 532–536.

Donaldson V. O'Connor, 493 F. 2d. 507 (5th Cir. 1974).

Doty, D. W. Role playing and incentives in the modification of the social interaction of chronic psychiatric patients. *Journal of Consulting and Clinical Psychology,* 1975, *43,* 676–682.

Drabman, R. S. Behavior modification in the classroom. In W. E. Craighead, A. E. Kazdin, & M. J. Mahoney (Eds.), *Behavior modification: Principles, issues, and applications.* Boston: Houghton Mifflin, 1976.

Drabman, R. S., Spitalnik, R., & O'Leary, K. D. Teaching self-control to disruptive children. *Journal of Abnormal Psychology,* 1973, *82,* 10–16.

Edlund, C. V. The effect on the test behavior of children, as reflected in the IQ scores, when reinforced after each correct response. *Journal of Applied Behavior Analysis,* 1972, *5,* 317–319.

Eitzen, D. S. The effects of behavior modification on the attitudes of delinquents. *Behaviour Research and Therapy,* 1975, *13,* 295–299.

Emshoff, J. G., Redd, W. H., & Davidson, W. S. Generalization training and the transfer of treatment effects with delinquent adolescents. *Journal of Behavior Therapy and Experimental Psychiatry,* in press.

Ennis, B. J., & Friedman, P. R. (Eds.), *Legal rights of the mentally handicapped,* Vol. 1 and 2. Practicing Law Institute, The Mental Health Law Project, 1973.

Eriksson, J. H., Gotestam, K. G., Melin, L., & Öst, L. A token economy treatment of drug addiction. *Behaviour Research and Therapy,* 1975, *13,* 113–125.

Federal Bureau of Prisons. START—Revised program. Washington, D. C.:1972.

Felixbrod, J. J., & O'Leary, K. D. Self-determination of academic standards by children: Toward freedom from external control. *Journal of Educational Psychology,* 1974, *66,* 845–850.

Ferritor, D. E., Buckholdt, D., Hamblin, R. L., & Smith, L. The noneffects of contingent reinforcement for attending behavior on work accomplished. *Journal of Applied Behavior Analysis,* 1972, *5,* 7–17.

Filipczak, J., & Cohen, H. L. The Case II contingency

system and where it is going. Paper presented at the American Psychological Association, Honolulu, Hawaii, September, 1972.

Fixsen, D. L., Phillips, E. L., Phillips, E. A., & Wolf, M. M. The teaching-family model of group home treatment. In W. E. Craighead, A. E. Kazdin, & M. J. Mahoney (Eds.), *Behavior modification: Principles, issues, and applications.* Boston: Houghton Mifflin, 1976.

Fo, W. S. O., & O'Donnell, C. R. The buddy system: Relationship and contingency conditions in a community intervention program for youth with non-professionals as behavior change agents. *Journal of Consulting and Clinical Psychology,* 1974, *42,* 163–169.

Fo, W. S. O., & O'Donnell, C. R. The buddy system: Effect of community intervention on delinquent offenses. *Behavior Therapy,* 1975, *6,* 522–524.

Fordyce, W. E., Fowler, R. S., Lehmann, J. F., DeLateur, B. J., Sand, P. L., & Trieschmann, R. B. Operant conditioning in the treatment of chronic pain. *Archives of Physical Medicine and Rehabilitation,* 1973, *54,* 399–408.

Forehand, R., & Baumeister, A. A. Deceleration of aberrant behavior among retarded individuals. In M. Hersen, R. M. Eisler, & P. M. Miller (Eds.) *Progress in behavior modification.* Vol. 2. New York: Academic Press, 1976.

Foxx, R. M. The use of overcorrection to eliminate the public disrobing (stripping) of retarded women. *Behaviour Research and Therapy,* 1976, *14,* 53–61.

Foxx, R. M., & Azrin, N. H. Restitution: A method of eliminating aggressive-disruptive behavior of retarded and brain damaged patients. *Behaviour Research and Therapy,* 1972, *10,* 15–27.

Foxx, R. M., & Azrin, N. H. *Toilet training the retarded: A rapid program for day and night time independent toileting.* Champaign, Ill.: Research Press, 1973.

Foxx, R. M., & Martin, E. D. Treatment of scavenging behavior (coprophagy and pica) by overcorrection. *Behaviour Research and Therapy,* 1975, *13,* 153–162.

Frankel, R., & Simmons, J. Q. Self-injurious behavior in schizophrenic and retarded children. *American Journal of Mental Deficiency,* 1976, *80,* 512–522.

Franks, C. M., & Wilson, G. T. (Eds.), *Annual review of behavior therapy theory and practice, Volume 5.* New York: Brunner/Mazel, 1977.

Frasier, J. R., & Williams, B. R. The application of multiple contingencies to rocking behavior in a non-retarded child. *Journal of Behavior Therapy and Experimental Psychiatry,* 1973, *4,* 289–291.

Frederiksen, L. W., & Frederiksen, C. B. Teacher-determined and self-determined token reinforcement in a special education classroom. *Behavior Therapy,* 1975, *6,* 310–314.

Friedman, P. R. Legal regulation of applied behavior analysis in mental institutions and prisons. *Arizona Law Review,* 1975, *17,* 39–104.

Frisch, S. A., & Schumaker, J. B. Training generalized receptive propositions in retarded children. *Journal of Applied Behavior Analysis,* 1974, *7,* 611–621.

Gardner, J. M. Teaching behavior modification to non-professionals. *Journal of Applied Behavior Analysis,* 1972, *5,* 517–521.

Gardner, W. I. *Behavior modification in mental retardation.* Chicago: Aldine, 1971.

Gelfand, D. M., & Hartmann, D. P. *Child behavior analysis and therapy.* New York: Pergamon, 1975.

Gladstone, B. W., & Sherman, J. A. Developing generalized behavior-modification skills in high-school students working with retarded children. *Journal of Applied Behavior Analysis,* 1975, *8,* 169–180.

Glover, J. & Gary, A. L. Procedures to increase some aspects of creativity. *Journal of Applied Behavior Analysis,* 1976, *9,* 79–84.

Glynn, E. L., & Thomas, J. D. Effect of cueing on self-control of classroom behavior. *Journal of Applied Behavior Analysis,* 1974, *7,* 299–306.

Golub, C. M. The influence of various demographic variables on the participation of Veterans Administration Day Treatment Center patients in a token economy. Unpublished Doctoral Dissertation, University of Minnesota, 1969.

Götestam, K. G., Melin, L., & Öst, L. Behavioral techniques in the treatment of drug abuse: An evaluative review. *Addictive Behaviors,* 1976, *1,* 205–225.

Graubard, P. S., Rosenberg, H., & Miller, M. B. Student applications of behavior modification to teachers and environments or ecological approaches to social deviancy. In R. Ulrich, T. Stachnik, & J. Mabry (Eds.), *Control of human behavior,* Vol. 3. Glenview, Ill.: Scott, Foresman and Company, 1974.

Greenberg, D. J., Scott, S. B., Pisa, A., & Friesen, D. D. Beyond the token economy: A comparison of two contingency programs. *Journal of Consulting and Clinical Psychology,* 1975, *43,* 498–503.

Greenwood, C. R., Hops, H., Delquadri, J., & Guild, J. Group contingencies for group consequences in classroom management: A further analysis: *Journal of Applied Behavior Analysis,* 1974, *7,* 413–425.

Gripp, R. F., & Magaro, P. A. The token economy program in the psychiatric hospital: A review and analysis. *Behaviour Research and Therapy,* 1974, *12,* 205–228.

Harris, V. W., Finfrock, S. R., Giles, D. K., Hart, B. M., & Tsosie, P. C. The use of home-based consequences to modify the classroom behavior of institutionalized delinquent youth. *Journal of Applied Behavior Analysis,* in press.

Harris, V. W., & Sherman, J. A. Use and analysis of the "Good Behavior Game" to reduce disruptive classroom behavior. *Journal of Applied Behavior Analysis,* 1973, *6,* 405–417.

Harris, V. W.' & Sherman, J. A. Homework assignments, consequences, and classroom performance in social studies and mathematics. *Journal of Applied Behavior Analysis,* 1974, *7,* 505–519.

Harshbarger, D., & Maley, R. F. (Eds.), *Behavior analysis and systems analysis: An integrative approach to mental health programs.* Kalamazoo, Mich.: Behaviordelia, 1974.

Hauserman, N., Walen, S. R., & Behling, M. Reinforced racial integration in the first grade: A study in generalization. *Journal of Applied Behavior*

Analysis, 1973, *6,* 193–200.

Hayes, L. A. The use of group contingencies for behavioral control: A review. *Psychological Bulletin,* 1976, *83,* 628–648.

Haynes v. Harris, 344 F. 2d 463 (8th Cir. 1965).

Herman, S., & Tramontana, J. Instructions and group versus individual reinforcement in modifying disruptive group behavior. *Journal of Applied Behavior Analysis,* 1971, *4,* 113–119.

Hersen, M., Eisler, R. M., Alford, G. S., & Agras, W. S., Effects of token economy on neurotic depression: An experimental analysis. *Behavior Therapy,* 1973, *4,* 392–397.

Hersen, M., Eisler, R. M., & Miller, P. M. (Eds.), *Progress in behavior modification,* Vol. 4. New York: Academic Press, 1977.

Higgs, W. J. Effects of gross environmental change upon behavior of schizophrenics: A cautionary note. *Journal of Abnormal Psychology,* 1970, *76,* 421–422.

Hollingsworth, R., & Foreyt, J. P. Community adjustment of released token economy patients. *Journal of Behavior Therapy and Experimental Psychiatry,* 1975, *6,* 271–274.

Ingham, R. J., Andrews, G., & Winkler, R. Stuttering: A comparative evaluation of the shortterm effectiveness of four treatment techniques. *Journal of Communication Disorders,* 1972, *5,* 91–117.

Jackson, D. A., & Wallace, R. F. The modification and generalization of voice loudness in a fifteen-year-old retarded girl. *Journal of Applied Behavior Analysis,* 1974, *7,* 461–471.

Jenkins, W. O., Witherspoon, A. D., DeVine, M. D., de-Valera, E. K., Muller, J. B., Barton, M. C., & McKee, J. M. The post-prison analysis of criminal behavior and longitudinal follow-up evaluation of institutional treatment. A report on the Experimental Manpower Laboratory for Corrections, February, 1974.

Jesness, C. F. Comparative effectiveness of behavior modification and transactional analysis programs for delinquents. *Journal of Consulting and Clinical Psychology,* 1975, *43,* 758–779.

Jobson v. Henne, 355 F. 2d 129 (2d Cir. 1966), Cited in 61 Calif. L. Rev. at 91.

Johnston, J. M., & Johnston, G. T. Modification of consonant speech-sound articulation in young children. *Journal of Applied Behavior Analysis,* 1972, *5,* 233–246.

Jones, R. T., & Kazdin, A. E. Progamming response maintenance after withdrawing token reinforcement. *Behavior Therapy,* 1975, *6,* 153–164.

Jones, R. T., Nelson, R. E., & Kazdin, A. E. The role of external variables in self-reinforcement: A review. *Behavior Modification,* 1977, *1,* 147–178.

Kaimowitz v. Michigan Department of Mental Health, 42 U. S. L. Week 2063 (Mich. Cir. Ct., Wayne Cty., 1973).

Kale, R. J., Kaye, J. H., Whelan, P. A., & Hopkins, B. L. The effects of reinforcement on the modification, maintenance, and generalization of social responses of mental patients. *Journal of Applied Behavior Analysis,* 1968, *1,* 307–314.

Kallman, W. H., Hersen, M., & O'Toole, D. H. The use of social reinforcement in a case of conversion reaction. *Behavior Therapy,* 1975, *6,* 411–413.

Kassirer, L. B. Behavior modification for patients and prisoners: Constitutional ramifications of enforced therapy. *Journal of Psychiatry and Law,* 1974, *2,* 245–302.

Katz, R. C., & Zlutnick, S. *Behavioral therapy and health care: Principles and applications.* New York: Pergamon, 1974.

Kaufman, K. F., & O'Leary, K. D. Reward, cost and self-evaluation procedures for disruptive adolescents in a psychiatric hospital. *Journal of Applied Behavior Analysis,* 1972, *5,* 293–309.

Kazdin, A. E. The effect of response cost in suppressing behavior in a pre-psychotic retardate. *Journal of Behavior Therapy and Experimental Psychiatry,* 1971, *2,* 137–140.

Kazdin, A. E. Response cost: The removal of conditioned reinforcers for therapeutic change. *Behavior Therapy,* 1972, *3,* 533–546.

Kazdin, A. E. The effect of vicarious reinforcement on attentive behavior in the classroom *Journal of Applied Behavior Analysis,* 1973a, *6,* 71–78.

Kazdin, A. E. Issues in behavior modification with mentally retarded persons. *American Journal of Mental Deficiency,* 1973b, *78,* 134–140.

Kazdin, A. E. Role of instructions and reinforcement in behavior changes in token reinforcement programs. *Journal of Educational Psychology,* 1973c, *64,* 63–71.

Kazdin, A. E. Self-monitoring and behavior change. In M. J. Mahoney & C. E. Thoresen (Eds.), *Self-control: Power to the person.* Monterey, Calif.: Brooks Cole, 1974,

Kazdin, A. E. *Behavior modification in applied settings.* Homewood, Ill.: Dorsey Press, 1975a.

Kazdin, A. E. Characteristics and trends in applied behavior analysis. *Journal of Applied Behavior Analysis,* 1975b, *8,* 332.

Kazdin, A. E. The impact of applied behavior analysis on diverse areas of research. *Journal of Applied Behavior Analysis,* 1975c, *8,* 213–229.

Kazdin, A. E. Recent advances in token economy research. In M. Hersen, R. M. Eisler, & P. M. Miller (Eds.), *Progress in behavior modification,* Vol. 1. New York: Academic Press, 1975d.

Kazdin, A. E. Implementing token programs: The use of staff and patients for maximizing change. In R. L. Patterson (Ed.), *Maintaining effective token economies.* Springfield, Ill.: Charles C. Thomas, 1976a.

Kazdin, A. E. The modification of "schizophrenic" behavior. In P. A. Magaro (Ed.), *The construction of madness: Emerging conceptions and interventions into the psychotic process.* New York: Pergamon, 1976b.

Kazdin, A. E. Statistical analyses for single-case experimental designs. In M. Hersen & D. Barlow, *Single-case experimental designs: Strategies for studying behavior change.* New York: Pergamon, 1976c.

Kazdin, A. E. Extensions of reinforcement techniques to socially and environmentally relevant behaviors. In M. Hersen, R. M. Eisler, & P. M. Miller (Eds.), *Prog-*

ress in behavior modification, Vol. 4. New York: Academic Press, 1977a.

Kazdin, A. E. Methodology of applied behavior analysis. In T. A. Brigham & A. C. Catania (Eds.), The handbook of applied behavior research: Social and instructional processes. New York: Irvington Press/Halstead Press, 1977b.

Kazdin, A. E. The token economy: A review and evaluation. New York: Plenum Press, 1977c.

Kazdin, A. E. Vicarious reinforcement and direction of behavior change in the classroom. Behavior Therapy, 1977d, 8, 57–63.

Kazdin, A. E. Assessing the clinical or applied importance of behavior change through social validation. Behavior Modification, 1977e, 1, 427–452.

Kazdin, A. E. Behavior modification in mental retardation. In J. T. Neisworth & R. M. Smith (Eds.), Retardation: Issues, assessment and intervention. New York: McGraw-Hill, 1978a.

Kazdin, A. E. History of behavior modification: Experimental foundations of contemporary research. Baltimore: University Park Press, 1978b.

Kazdin, A. E., & Bootzin, R. R. The token economy: An evaluative review. Journal of Applied Behavior Analysis, 1972, 5, 343–372.

Kazdin, A. E., & Erickson, L. M. Developing responsiveness to instructions in severely and profoundly retarded residents. Journal of Behavior Therapy and Experimental Psychiatry, 1975, 6, 17–21.

Kazdin, A. E., & Geesey, S. Simultaneous-treatment design comparisons of the effects of earning reinforcers for one's peers versus for oneself. Behavior Therapy, 1977, 8, 682–693.

Kazdin, A. E., & Moyer, W. Training teachers to use behavior modification. In S. Yen & R. McIntire (Eds.), Teaching behavior modification. Kalamazoo, Mich.: Behaviordelia, 1976.

Kazdin, A. E., & Polster, R. Intermittent token reinforcement and response maintenance in extinction. Behavior Therapy, 1973, 4, 386–391.

Kazdin, A. E., Silverman, N. A., & Sittler, J. L. The use of prompts to enhance vicarious effects of nonverbal approval. Journal of Applied Behavior Analysis, 1975, 8, 279–286.

Keilitz, I., Tucker, D. J., & Horner, R. D. Increasing mentally retarded adolescents' verbalizations about current events. Journal of Applied Behavior Analysis, 1973, 6, 621–630.

Keller, F. S. "Good-bye teacher . . ." Journal of Applied Behavior Analysis, 1968, 1, 79–89.

Kent, R. N., & O'Leary, K. D. A controlled evaluation of behavior modification with conduct problem children. Journal of Consulting and Clinical Psychology, 1976, 44, 586–596.

Kirigin, K. A., Phillips, E. L., Fixsen, D. L., & Wolf, M. M. Modification of the homework behavior and academic performance of pre-delinquents with home-based reinforcement. Paper read at the American Psychological Association, Honolulu, Hawaii, 1972.

Kittrie, N. N. The right to be different: Deviance and enforced therapy. Baltimore, Md.: The Johns Hopkins Press, 1971.

Knapczyk, D. R., & Yoppi, J. O. Development of cooperative and competive play responses in developmentally disabled children. American Journal of Mental Deficiency, 1975, 80, 245–255.

Knapp, T. J., & Peterson, L. W. Behavior management in medical and nursing practice. In W. E. Craighead, A. E. Kazdin, & M. J. Mahoney (Eds.), Behavior modification: Principles, issues, and applications. Boston: Houghton Mifflin, 1976.

Knecht v. Gillman, 488 f. 2d 1136, 1139 (8th Cir. 1973).

Kounin, J. S. Discipline and group management in classrooms. New York: Holt, Rinehart & Winston, 1970.

Krasner, L. The operant approach in behavior therapy. In A. E. Bergin & S. L. Garfield (Eds.), Handbook of psychotherapy and behavior change: An empirical analysis. New York: Wiley, 1971.

Lake v. Cameron, 364 f. 2d. 657 (D. C. 1966).

Lawson, R. B., Greene, R. T., Richardson, J. S., McClure, G., & Padina, R. J. Token economy program in a maximum security correctional hospital. Journal of Nervous and Mental Diseases, 1971, 152, 199–205.

Leitenberg, H. (Ed.), Handbook of behavior modification and behavior therapy. Englewood Cliffs, N. J.: Prentice-Hall, 1976.

Leitenberg, H., Wincze, J., Butz, R., Callahan, E., & Agras, W. Comparison of the effect of instructions and reinforcement in the treatment of a neurotic avoidance response: A single case experiment. Journal of Behavior Therapy and Experimental Psychiatry, 1970, 1, 53–58.

Lessard v. Schmidt, 349 F. Supp. 1078 (E. D. Wisc. 1972).

Liberman, R. P. Reinforcement of social interaction in a group of chronic mental patients. In R. D. Rubin, H. Fensterheim, J. D. Henderson, & L. P. Ullmann (Eds.), Advances in behavior therapy. New York: Academic Press, 1972.

Liberman, R. P., Teigen, J., Patterson, R., & Baker, V. Reducing delusional speech in chronic, paranoid schizophrenics. Journal of Applied Behavior Analysis, 1973, 6, 57–64.

Litow, L., & Pumroy, D. K. A brief review of classroom group-oriented contingencies. Journal of Applied Behavior Analysis, 1975, 8, 341–347.

Lovaas, O. I., & Bucher, B. D. (Eds.), Perspectives in behavior modification with deviant children. Englewood Cliffs, New Jersey: Prentice-Hall, 1974.

Lovaas, O. I., Koegel, R., Simmons, J. Q., & Long, J. S. Some generalization and follow-up measures on autistic children in behavior therapy. Journal of Applied Behavior Analysis, 1973, 6, 131–166.

Lovaas, O. I., & Simmons, J. Q. Manipulation of self-destruction in three retarded children. Journal of Applied Behavior Analysis, 1969, 2, 143–157.

Lutzker, J. R. Social reinforcement control of exhibitionism in a profoundly mentally retarded adult. Mental Retardation, 1974, 12, 46–47.

Lutzker, J. R., & Sherman, J. Producing generative sentence usage by imitation and reinforcement procedures. Journal of Applied Behavior Analysis, 1974, 7, 447–460.

Mahoney, M. J., Moura, N. G., & Wade, T. C. The relative efficacy of self-reward, self-punishment, and self-monitoring techniques for weight loss. *Journal of Consulting and Clinical Psychology,* 1973, *40,* 404–407.

Maley, R. F., Feldman, G. L., & Ruskin, R. S. Evaluation of patient improvement in a token economy treatment program. *Journal of Abnormal Psychology,* 1973, *82,* 141–144.

Maloney, D. M., Harper, T. M., Braukmann, C. J., Fixsen, D. L., Phillips, E. L., Wolf, M. M. Teaching conversation-related skills to pre-delinquent girls. *Journal of Applied Behavior Analysis,* 1976, *9,* 371.

Maloney, K. B., & Hopkins, B. L. The modification of sentence structure and its relationship to subjective judgments of creativity in writing. *Journal of Applied Behavior Analysis,* 1973, *6,* 425–433.

Mandelker, A. V., Brigham, T. A., & Bushell, D. The effects of token procedures on a teacher's social contacts with her students. *Journal of Applied Behavior Analysis,* 1970, *3,* 169–174.

Marholin, D., II, Siegel, L. J., & Phillips, D. Treatment and transfer: A search for empirical procedures. In M. Hersen, R. M. Eisler, & P. M. Miller (Eds.), *Progress in behavior modification,* Vol. 3. New York: Academic Press, 1976.

Marholin, D. II, Steinman, W. M., McInnis, E. T., & Heads, T. B. The effect of a teacher's presence on the classroom behavior of conduct-problem children. *Journal of Abnormal Child Psychology,* 1975, *3,* 11–25.

Marks, J., Sonoda, B., & Schalock, R. Reinforcement vs. relationship therapy for schizophrenics. *Journal of Abnormal Psychology,* 1968, *73,* 397–402.

Martin, R. *Legal challenges to behavior modification: Trends in schools, corrections and mental health.* Champaign, Ill.: Research Press, 1975.

McConahey, O. L., Thompson, T., & Zimmerman, R. A token system for retarded women: Behavior therapy, drug administration, and their combination. In T. Thompson & J. Grabowski (Eds.), *Behavior modification of the mentally retarded,* (Second Edition). New York: Oxford University Press, 1977.

McLaughlin, T. F., & Malaby, J. E. The effects of various token reinforcement contingencies on assignment completion and accuracy during variable and fixed token exchange schedules. *Canadian Journal of Behavioral Science,* 1975, *7,* 411–419.

Meichenbaum, D. H. Cognitive factors in behavior modification: Modifying what clients say to themselves. In R. D. Rubin, J. P. Brady & J. D. Henderson (Eds.), *Advances in behavior therapy,* Vol. 4. New York: Academic Press, 1973.

Meichenbaum, D. H., & Goodman, J. Training impulsive children to talk to themselves: A means of developing self-control. *Journal of Abnormal Psychology,* 1971, *77,* 115–126.

Melin, G. L., & Gotestam, K. G. A contingency management program on a drug-free unit for intravenous amphetamine addicts. *Journal of Behavior Therapy and Experimental Psychiatry,* 1973, *4,* 331–337.

Milan, M. A., & McKee, J. M. The cellblock token economy: Token reinforcement procedures in a maximum security correctional institution for adult male felons. *Journal of Applied Behavior Analysis,* 1976, *9,* 253–275.

Milan, M. A., Wood, L. F., Williams, R. L., Rogers, J. G., Hampton, L. R., & McKee, J. M. *Applied behavior analysis and the Important Adult Felon Project I: The cellblock token economy.* Elmore, Ala.: Rehabilitation Research Foundation, 1974.

Miller, P. M. The use of behavioral contracting in the treatment of alcoholism: A case report. *Behavior Therapy,* 1972, *3,* 593–596.

Miller, P. M., & Eisler, R. M. Alcohol and drug abuse. In W. E. Craighead, A. E. Kazdin, & M. J. Mahoney (Eds.), *Behavior modification: Principles, issues, and applications.* Boston: Houghton Mifflin, 1976.

Miller, P. M., Hersen, M., Eisler, R. M., & Watts, J. G. Contingent reinforcement of lowered blood/alcohol levels in an outpatient chronic alcoholic. *Behaviour Research and Therapy,* 1974, *12,* 261–263.

Minkin, N., Braukmann, C. J., Minkin, B. L., Timbers, G. D., Timbers, B. J., Fixsen, D. L., Phillips, E. L., & Wolf, M. M. The social validation and training of conversational skills. *Journal of Applied Behavior Analysis,* 1976, *9,* 127–139.

Morales v. Turman, 383 F. Supp. 53 (E. D. Tex. 1974).

Mulligan, W., Kaplan, R. D., & Reppucci, N. D. Changes in cognitive variables among behavior problem elementary school boys treated in a token economy special classroom. In R. D. Rubin, J. P. Brady, & J. D. Henderson (Eds.), *Advances in behavior therapy,* Vol. 4. New York: Academic Press, 1973.

Nay, W. R. A systematic comparison of instructional techniques for parents. *Behavior Therapy,* 1975, *6,* 14–21.

New York City Health and Hospital Corporation v. Stein, 335 N. Y. S. 2d 461 (Sup. Ct. 1972).

New York State Association for Retarded Children v. Rockefeller, 357 F. Supp. 752 (EDNY 1973).

O'Brien, F., & Azrin, N. H. Symptom reduction by functional displacement in a token economy: A case study. *Journal of Behavior Therapy and Experimental Psychiatry,* 1972, *3,* 205–207.

O'Brien, F., Azrin, N. H., & Henson, K. Increased communications of chronic mental patients by reinforcement and response priming. *Journal of Applied Behavior Analysis,* 1969, *2,* 23–29.

O'Leary, K. D., & O'Leary, S. G. (Eds.), *Classroom management: The successful use of behavior modification.* New York: Pergamon, 1972.

Olson, R. P., & Greenberg, D. J. Effects of contingency-contracting and decision-making groups with chronic mental patients. *Journal of Consulting and Clinical Psychology,* 1972, *38,* 376–383.

Palmer, A. B., & Wohl, J. Voluntary-admission forms: Does the patient know what he's signing? *Hospital and Community Psychiatry,* 1972, *23,* 250–252.

Parrino, J. J., George, L., & Daniels, A. C. Token control of pill-taking behavior in a psychiatric ward. *Journal of Behavior Therapy and Experimental Psychiatry,* 1971, *2,* 181–185.

Patterson, G. R. Behavioral intervention procedures in the classroom and in the home. In A. E. Bergin & S.

L. Garfield (Eds.), *Handbook of psychotherapy and behavior change: An empirical analysis.* New York: Wiley, 1971.

Patterson, G. R. Interventions for boys with conduct problems: Multiple settings, treatments, and criteria. *Journal of Consulting and Clinical Psychology,* 1974, *42,* 471–481.

Patterson, G. R., & Reid, J. B. Reciprocity and coercion: Two facets of social systems. In C. Neuringer & J. L. Michael (Eds.), *Behavior modification in clinical psychology.* New York: Appleton-Centruy-Crofts, 1970.

Patterson, R., & Teigen, J. Conditioning and post-hospital generalization of nondelusional responses in a chronic psychotic patient. *Journal of Applied Behavior Analysis,* 1973, *6,* 65–70.

Paul, G. L. Chronic mental patient: Current status—future directions. *Psychological Bulletin,* 1969. *71,* 81–84.

Paul, G. L., Tobias, L. T., & Holly, B. L. Maintenance psychotropic drugs with chronic mental patients in the presence of active treatment programs: A "triple-blind" withdrawal study. *Archives of General Psychiatry,* 1972, *27,* 106–115.

Peek v. Ciccone, 288 F. Supp. 329 (E. D. Mo. 1968).

Phillips, E. L., Phillips, E. A., Fixsen, D. L., & Wolf, M. M. Achievement Place: Modification of the behaviors of pre-delinquent boys within a token economy. *Journal of Applied Behavior Analysis,* 1971, *4,* 45–59.

Phillips, E. L., Phillips, E. A., Wolf, M. M., & Fixsen, D. L. Achievement Place: Development of the elected manager system. *Journal of Applied Behavior Analysis,* 1973, *6,* 541–561.

Pomerleau, O. F., Bobrove, P. H., & Smith, R. H. Rewarding psychiatric aides for he behavioral improvement of assigned patients. *Journal of Applied Behavior Analysis,* 1973, *6,* 383–390.

Ramp, E., & Semb, G. (Eds.), *Behavior analysis: Areas of research and application.* Englewood Cliffs, N. J.: Prentice-Hall, 1975.

Renelli v. Department of Mental Hygiene, 340 N. Y. S. 2d 498 (Sup. Ct. 1973).

Ringer, V. M. The use of a "token helper" in the management of classroom behavior problems and in teacher training. *Journal of Applied Behavior Analysis,* 1973, *6,* 671–677.

Risley, T. R. Behavior modification: An experimental-therapeutic endeavor. In L. A. Hammerlynck, P. O. Davidson, & L. E. Acker (Eds.), *Behavior modification and ideal mental health services.* Calgary, Alberta, Canada: University of Calgary Press, 1970.

Robin, A. L., Armel, S., & O'Leary, K. D. The effects of self-instruction on writing deficiencies. *Behavior Therapy,* 1975, *6,* 178–187.

Rollins, H. A., McCandless, B. R., Thompson, M., & Brassell, W. R. Project success environment: An extended application of contingency management in inner-city schools. *Journal of Educational Psychology,* 1974, *66,* 167–178.

Rosenbaum, A., O'Leary, K. D., & Jacob, R. G. Behavioral intervention with hyperactive children: Group consequences as a supplement to individual contingencies. *Behavior Therapy,* 1975, *6,* 315–323.

Ross, J. A. The use of contingency contracting in control-ling adult nailbiting. *Journal of Behavior Therapy and Experimental Psychiatry,* 1974, *5,* 105–106.

Rouse v. Cameron, 373 F. 2d 451 (D. C. Cir. 1966).

Ryan, B. A. *Keller's Personalized System of Instruction: An appraisal.* Washington, D. C.: American Psychological Association, 1972.

Rybolt, G. A. Token reinforcement therapy with chronic psychiatric patients: A three-year evaluation. *Journal of Behavior Therapy and Experimental Psychiatry,* 1975, *6,* 188–191.

Sachs, D. A. WISC changes as an evaluative procedure within a token economy. *American Journal of Mental Deficiency,* 1971, *76,* 230–234.

Sachs, D. A. Behavioral techniques,in a residential nursing home facility. *Journal of Behavior Therapy and Experimental Psychiatry,* 1975, *6,* 123–127.

Sacks, A. S., Moxley, R. A., Jr., & Walls, R. T. Increasing social interaction of preschool children with "mixies." *Psychology in the Schools,* 1975, *12,* 74–79.

Santogrossi, D. A., O'Leary, K. D., Romanczyk, R. G., & Kaufman, K. F. Self-evaluation by adolescents in a psychiatric hospital school token program. *Journal of Applied Behavior Analysis,* 1973, *6,* 277–287.

Schwitzgebel, R. K. A contractual model for the protection of the rights of institutionalized mental patients. *American Psychologist,* 1975, *8,* 815–820.

Shapiro, D., & Surwit, R. S. Learned control of physiological function and disease. In H. Leitenberg (Ed.), *Handbook of behavior modification and behavior therapy.* Englewood Cliffs, N. J.: Prentice-Hall, 1976.

Shean, J. D., & Zeidberg, Z. Token reinforcement therapy: A comparison of matched groups. *Journal of Behavior Therapy and Experimental Psychiatry,* 1971, *2,* 95–105.

Smolev, S. R. Use of operant techniques for the modification of self-injurious behavior. *American Journal of Mental Deficiency,* 1971, *76,* 295–305.

Solomon, R. W., & Wahler, R. G. Peer reinforcement control of classroom problem behavior. *Journal of Applied Behavior Analysis,* 1973, *6,* 49–56.

Stahl, J. R., & Leitenberg, H. Behavioral treatment of the chronic mental hospital patient. In H. Leitenberg (Ed.), *Handbook of behavior modification and behavior therapy.* Englewood Cliffs, N. J.: Prentice-Hall, 1976.

Stokes, T. F., & Baer, D. M. Preschool peers as mutual generalization-facilitating agents. *Behavior Therapy,* 1976, *7,* 549–556.

Stokes, T. F., & Baer, D. M. An implicit technology of generalization. *Journal of Applied Behavior Analysis,* 1977, *10,* 349–367.

Stokes, T. F., Baer, D. M., & Jackson, R. L. Programming the generalization of a greeting response in four retarded children. *Journal of Applied Behavior Analysis,* 1974, *7,* 599–610.

Stolz, S. B. Ethical issues in behavior modification. In G. Bermant & H. Kelman (Eds.), *Ethics of Social Intervention.* Washington, D.C.: Hemisphere, in press.

Stuart, R. B. Token reinforcement in marital treatment. In R. D. Rubin & C. M. Franks (Eds.), *Advances in behavior therapy, 1968.* New York: Academic Press, 1969.

Subcommittee on Constitutional Rights, Committee of

the Judiciary, United States Senate, Ninety-Third Congress, *Individual rights and the federal role in behavior modification*. Washington, D. C.: U. S. Government Printing Office, 1974.

Suchotliff, L., Greaves, S., Stecker, H., & Berke, R. Critical variables in the token economy. *Proceedings of the 78th Annual Convention of the American Psychological Association*, 1970, *5*, 517–518.

Sulzer, B., & Mayer, G. R. *Behavior modification procedures for school personnel*. Hinsdale, Ill.: Dryden, 1972.

Thompson, T., & Grabowski, J. (Eds.), *Behavior modification of the mentally retarded*. New York: Oxford University Press, 1972.

Timbers, G. D., Timbers, B. J., Fixsen, D. L., Phillips, E. L., & Wolf, M. M. Achievement Place for predelinquent girls: Modification of inappropriate emotional behaviors with token reinforcement and instructional procedures. Paper read at the American Psychological Association, Montreal, Canada, 1973.

Tracey, D. A., Briddell, D. W., & Wilson, G. T. Generalization of verbal conditioning to verbal and nonverbal behavior: Group therapy with chronic psychiatric patients. *Journal of Applied Behavior Analysis*, 1974, *7*, 391–402.

Trudel, G., Boisvert, J., Maruca, F., & Leroux, P. Unprogrammed reinforcement of patients' behaviors in wards with and without token economy. *Journal of Behavior Therapy and Experimental Psychiatry*, 1974, *5*, 147–149.

Turkewitz, H., O'Leary, K. D., & Ironsmith, M. Generalization and maintenance of appropriate behavior through self-control. *Journal of Consulting and Clinical Psychology*, 1975, *43*, 577–583.

Twardosz, S., & Baer, D. M. Training two severely retarded adolescents to ask questions. *Journal of Applied Behavior Analysis*, 1973, *6*, 655–661.

Walker, H. M., Hops, H., & Fiegenbaum, E. Deviant classroom behavior as a function of combinations of social and token reinforcement and cost contingency. *Behavior Therapy*, 1976, *7*, 76–88.

Walker, H. M., Hops, H., & Johnson, S. M. Generalization and maintenance of classroom treatment effects. *Behavior Therapy*, 1975, *6*, 188–200.

Walker, H. M., Mattson, R. H., & Buckley, N. K. The functional analysis of behavior within an experimental class setting. In W. C. Becker (Ed.), *An empirical basis for change in education*. Chicago: Science Research Associates, 1971.

Wallace, C. J., & Davis, J. R. Effects of information and reinforcement on the conversational behavior of chronic psychiatric patient dyads. *Journal of Consulting and Clinical Psychology*, 1974, *42*, 656–662.

Watson, L. S. Shaping and maintaining behavior modification skills in staff using contingent reinforcement techniques. In R. L. Patterson (Ed.), *Maintaining effective token economies*. Springfield, Ill.: Charles C. Thomas, 1976.

Webster, D. R., & Azrin, N. H. Required relaxation: A method of inhibiting agitative-disruptive behavior of retardates. *Behaviour Research and Therapy*, 1973, *11*, 67–78.

Welch, M. W., & Gist, J. W. *The open token economy system: A handbook for a behavioral approach to rehabilitation*. Springfield, Ill.: Charles C. Thomas, 1974.

Wexler, D. B. Token and taboo: Behavior modification, token economies, and the law. *California Law Review*, 1973, *61*, 81–109.

Wexler, D. B. Behavior modification and other behavior change procedures: The emerging law and the proposed Florida guidelines. *Criminal Law Bulletin*, 1975a, *11*, 600–616.

Wexler, D. B. Reflections on the legal regulation of behavior modification in institutional settings. *Arizona Law Review*, 1975b, *17*, 132–143.

Whitman, T. L., Zakaras, M., & Chardos, S. Effects of reinforcement and guidance procedures on instruction-following behavior of severely retarded children. *Journal of Applied Behavior Analysis*, 1971, *4*, 283–290.

Wincze, J. P., Leitenberg, H., & Agras, W. S. The effects of token reinforcement and feedback on the delusional verbal behavior of chronic paranoid schizophrenics. *Journal of Applied Behavior Analysis*, 1972, *5*, 247–262.

Winett, R. A., & Winkler, R. C. Current behavior modification in the classroom: Be still, be quiet, be docile. *Journal of Applied Behavior Analysis*, 1972, *5*, 499–504.

Winters v. Miller, 446 F. 2d 65 (2d Cir. 1970), reversing 306 F. Supp. 1158 (E. D. N. Y. 1969), cert. denied 404 U. S. 985, 92 S. Ct. 450. 30l. Ed. 2d 369.

Wolf, M. M. Social validity: The case for subjective measurement or how applied behavior analysis is finding its heart. Paper presented at the American Psychological Association, Washington, D. C., September, 1976.

Wolf, M., Birnbrauer, J., Lawler, J., & Williams, T. The operant extinction, reinstatement, and re-extinction of vomiting behavior in a retarded child. In R. Ulrich, T. Stachnik, & J. Mabry (Eds.), *Control of human behavior: From cure to prevention*, Vol. 2. Glenview, Ill.: Scott, Foresman, & Company, 1970.

Wyatt v. Stickney, 344 F. Supp. 373, 344 F. Supp. 387 (M. D. Ala. 1972) affirmed sub nom. Wyatt v. Aderholt, 503 F. 2d. 1305 (5th Cir. 1974).

Yen, S., & McIntire, R. W. (Eds.), *Teaching behavior modification*. Kalamazoo, Mich.: Behaviordelia, 1976.

Zifferblatt, S. M. The effectiveness of modes and schedules of reinforcement on work and social behavior in occupational therapy. *Behavior Therapy*, 1972, *3*, 567–578.

Zlutnick, S., Mayville, W. J., & Moffat, S. Modification of seizure disorders: The interruption of behavioral chains. *Journal of Applied Behavior Analysis*, 1975, *8*, 1–12.

15

BEHAVIOR THERAPY WITH CHILDREN

ALAN O. ROSS

State University of New York at Stony Brook

INTRODUCTION

Behavior therapy is best viewed as an orientation to clinical problems. It is an orientation that seeks to relate therapeutic intervention to knowledge derived from psychological research and insists on objective definitions and measurable procedures, thus permitting an evaluation of outcome. A corollary of this orientation is the assumption that psychological disorders are forms of behavior that have been acquired or modified through the lawful operation of psychological principles of development, learning, perception, cognition, and social interaction and that the application of these principles can be used to bring about therapeutic change. From this standpoint, it can be said that behavior therapy is the application of psychology to the alleviation of psychological distress. It should be emphasized that behavior therapy is thus not defined in terms of any specific technique or theory; that it is not identifiable with any one person or "school"; and that it is an open-ended, self-correcting, and thus constantly changing field of endeavor.

Not unlike other approaches to therapy, behavior therapy counts among its advocates people who would define it in such a way as to exclude any method that is not based on either operant or respondent conditioning principles. Others would demand that behavior therapists limit their conceptualizations to overt behavior and eschew such mediating events as physiological arousal states or cognitive processes. Such arbitrary orthodoxy places unnecessary restrictions on those who seek to expand the effectiveness of behavioral approaches by the application of empirically derived psychological principles which have, as yet, not found application in the therapeutic realm. The touchstone of a behavioral technique is whether it has objective, observable referents that permit one to put its validity to empirical test; not whether it fits neatly into the procrustean bed of one theory or another.

When behavior therapy first came upon the clinical scene in the 1950s it occasioned considerable opposition on the part of therapists and writers who had been trained in the approaches to treatment then dominant. In reaction to this opposition, the early pioneers of behavior therapy spoke and wrote in rather arrogant and aggressive terms, at times making hyperbolic predictions regarding the effectiveness of their form of treatment.

At this point, with the early attacks from traditionally oriented therapists abated and behavioral approaches quite widely accepted in even some of the most orthodox institutions, behavior therapists have entered a period of consolidation and circumspect exploration of new approaches. In a sense, the field has grown beyond its stage of missionary zeal and embarked upon a mature self-scrutiny that a securely established endeavor can afford. One now finds an increasing number of reports on research projects that explored the parameters of therapeutic methods and examined the conditions under which treatment-produced gains can be enhanced and maintained. There are promising publications whose authors reason that other therapeutic approaches cannot be completely wrong and who seek to discover the "active ingredient" of these approaches in hopes of incorporating them among their own procedures (Goldfried & Davison, 1976).

This review of the current status of child behavior therapy will be organized around the various problems and disorders of children that come to the attention of therapists, not around the techniques these therapists may use. The emphasis in behavior therapy should be on the conceptualization of problems and not on specific techniques. Besides, most clinical situations call not for one, but for a combination of methods. Discussion of specific treatment techniques will thus appear in the context of disorders to which they have been applied. This form of organizing the topic results in some repetition since the same methods have to be cited under several rubrics. To limit this redundancy, some of the theoretical bases and technical aspects of each method will be presented in detail only when they are first mentioned.

Psychological disorders will be grouped in two major categories: behavior deficits and behavior excesses. In the former the therapeutic task is to establish and increase desired behaviors; in the latter, it is to reduce and eliminate undesirable behaviors. That these are not mutually exclusive approaches should be apparent for, where the therapeutic goal is the elimination of undesirable or maladaptive behaviors, it is the therapist's concurrent task to see to it that the child acquires desirable, adaptive behaviors in their stead.

The Importance of Assessment.

The first and essential step in any attempt to intervene in a child's problems must be a careful assessment of the situation. It is highly irresponsible, if not unethical, for a therapist to attempt to treat a presumed problem without first thoroughly studying the problem. This point bears stressing because behavior therapy with its well-defined, easily taught procedures, lends itself to "treatment packages" that can be blindly applied even by the nonspecialist.

Assessment cannot be limited to obtaining second-hand information from the child's parents or teachers, nor to merely observing the child. Assessment must take the totality of the child's current life situation into consideration. Behavior is often situation-specific so that a child who is a problem at school may be a model child at home. Or a child who is a problem at home may be perfectly well-behaved in the therapist's consulting room. A study by Lobitz and Johnson (1975) demonstrated that different sources of reports about a child will give different descriptions of the child's behavior. Whereas parent attitudes toward the child discriminated most reliably between deviant and normal children, such attitudes often lacked validity in that they failed to correlate with direct observations of child behavior. The authors' recommendation that one go beyond parental reports in assessing children's disorders should stand as an important admonition, particularly to those who would provide behavioral prescriptions for intervention solely on the basis of parents' complaints.

Not only must careful assessment precede any intervention, but once intervention has begun, concurrent assessment must continue. In fact, the responsible therapist pursues assessment beyond the termination of treatment in order to ascertain through periodic follow-up that the change brought about during treatment is maintained and continues in the desired direction. The importance of on-going evaluations of treatment programs was underscored in a publication by Herbert and others

(Herbert, Pinkston, Hayden, Sajwaj, Pinkston, Cordua, & Jackson, 1973) which reports on the adverse effects on several children of two parent-training projects where mothers of young children had been taught to use a simple method of differentially attending to their children as a means of enhancing desirable and reducing undesirable behaviors.

As is the case in all therapeutic interventions, there is the inevitable question in behavior therapy whether improvements reflected in assessment conducted before and after treatment can be attributed to the effectiveness of that treatment. Particularly with children, whose behavior undergoes changes in the course of development, the possibility exists that problems for which their parents seek help might disappear in the course of time even if no treatment were undertaken. We know very little about the natural history of the psychological disorders of children. The phobias of young children, for example, may dissipate spontaneously over time, but, as Hampe, Noble, Miller, and Barrett (1973) concluded from their follow-up study, treatment appears to hasten this process. A similar finding was reported by Kent and O'Leary (1976). They found in their follow-up study on behavior therapy with conduct problem children that the treated children showed a significantly greater improvement than untreated controls. Nine months later, however, the controls' behavior had improved to a point where the behavioral differences between the groups were no longer significant, although the grades and achievement test scores of the treated children remained significantly higher. In reading reports on treatment outcome in the following pages, the *post hoc, ergo propter hoc* issue should always be kept in mind.

THE TREATMENT OF BEHAVIOR DEFICITS

Social Skill Deficits

In the process of their development most children acquire various social skills that the people around them consider age and gender appropriate. Although the expectations may vary somewhat from one sociocultural group to another, there is a general consensus as to what is "normal" for a child of a given age and sex. When a child deviates from this expectation, intervention is often sought, and whether this be called teaching, or training, or therapy, it involves helping the child acquire the skills the environment considers essential. It is in the acquisition of such skills that the principles of reinforcement have found their most frequent application.

This is not the place to explicate the details of reinforcement theory. Suffice it to stress the basic assumption that behavior is a function of its consequences and to review the definitions of the most frequently used terms. For a more detailed treatment of this topic, the reader should turn to one of many sources, such as Craighead, Kazdin, and Mahoney (1976).

If behavior is a function of its consequences, it is essential that one examine the consequences and to see what effect they have on the preceding behavior. Conversely, one should study behavior that is of interest in terms of the consequences it usually evokes from the environment. The systematic study of the relationship has become known as a *functional analysis of behavior*.

The consequences of a particular response is defined in terms of the fate of the response on future occasions. If the response is more likely to occur after it had been followed by a particular consequence, that is, if the response has been strengthened, the consequence is viewed as a reinforcement. If the response is less likely to occur after it had been followed by a particular consequence, that is, if the response has been weakened, the consequence is viewed as punishment. It is well to stress that the definition of reinforcement and of punishment depends on their effect on the *preceding* response on a *succeeding* occasion. One cannot speak of universal reinforcers or punishers but must, on each occasion and with every child, determine the effect a given consequence has on specific behavior. Nor must one make a priori assumptions about a particular consequence being either a reward or a punishment for, often in quite paradoxical fashion, a presumed reward turns out to be a punisher and what was thought to be a punishment turns out to strengthen a response, thus being a reinforcement.

Reinforcement and punishment can be subdivided on the basis of whether they entail the response-contingent application or removal of an event (stimulus). When reinforcement involves the application of a stimulus (as is the case when we give a child a reward), we speak of it as *positive reinforcement*. When it involves the removal of a stimulus (as in the cessation of nagging), we speak of *negative reinforcement*. Note that negative reinforcement is *not* the same as punishment! Punishment can also take two forms. One involves the delivery of a stimulus or event, in which case we call it *punishment by application* in order to differentiate it from the situation where a stimulus is removed (as in the case of deprivation of a privilege) which we call *punishment by removal*. The latter has come to be called *time-out from positive reinforcement* but since this has the effect of reducing the frequency of the behavior for which it is a consequence, it is more appropriately called and viewed as a form of punishment.

There are thus four possible consequences to any given act or response; positive reinforcement, negative reinforcement, punishment by application, and punishment by removal. A fifth possibility must also be mentioned. It is that nothing happens as a consequence of the response, as is the case when a child's behavior is totally ignored. In that event, the response will also be weakened and we speak of this process as *extinction*.

While behavior therapists who work in the framework of reinforcement theory find it convenient to use the terminology of the operant conditioning laboratory, it must be recognized that the realities of the clinic, home, or school often preclude the literal adoption of laboratory methods. An experimental psychologist in a soundproof laboratory who wishes to use an extinction schedule can arrange that absolutely nothing happens in consequence to a subject's response. If a teacher in a classroom decides to ignore a child's disruptive behavior, one might call this process "extinction" but it would be folly to assume that the child receives absolutely no reaction on the part of the environment in consequence of the disruption. Similarly, studies in behavior therapy often speak of a baseline measure when the frequency of the target behavior is recorded prior to initiating intervention. In an operant conditioning laboratory

a lengthy period is often devoted to baseline recording and the independent variable is introduced only when a truly stable baseline that meets a previously determined criterion has been established. The records kept by a behavior therapist for a few pretreatment days rarely have the rigor of the laboratory and the stability of these so-called baseline measures often leaves much to be desired. A parent seeking help with a child's behavior problem is not likely to agree to weeks or months of record keeping prior to therapy simply for the sake of obtaining a convincing baseline measure.

With these considerations in mind we can now turn to some examples of the application of operant principles in the development of social skills. One such application, involving the use of positive reinforcement, can be found in the oft-cited demonstration by Allen, Hart, Buell, Harris, and Wolf (1964). A four-year-old attending nursery school spent almost no time with the other children although she interacted freely with adults. A functional analysis revealed that adult attention served as a positive reinforcer for this girl, identified as "Ann." On this basis it was decided to introduce a reversal of contingencies. The teachers were to attend to this girl only when she interacted with other children, not when she was alone or with an adult. Since there was little or no social interaction with children in the girl's repertoire at first, any approximation of it, such as standing near another child, was reinforced by teacher attention. Soon, Ann began to play with groups of children more frequently and for longer periods. Reinforcement now took the form of statements directed not at Ann as an individual but as a participant in the group. After six days during which this procedure was systematically followed, Ann was interacting with other children some 65 percent of the time, while she sought adult contact only approximately 15 percent of the time; an almost complete reversal from the preintervention baseline period.

In order to demonstrate that manipulating adult attention had indeed been responsible for the change in the child's behavior, the contingencies for giving attention were reversed to the original state for the next five days. Under these conditions, Ann's previous behavior pattern immediately reappeared. She averaged less than 20 percent in interaction with children and about 40 percent in interaction with adults. At this point the previously successful contingencies were reinstated.

The carefully maintained records for the next nine days showed Ann again playing with children 60 percent of the time and seeking inateraction with adults only about 25 percent of the time. Teachers now began to relax the systematic fashion in which attention had been given and withheld, so that Ann's schedule of reinforcement became intermittent and more like that operating for the other children in the class. When spot-checks of her behavior were made 6, 13, 15, and 26 days later, the record showed that the pattern of interacting primarily with other children and minimally with adults had been maintained.

This case not only illustrates the often demonstrated effectiveness of contingent adult attention as a reinforcer for child behavior (Drabman, 1976) but it also shows the use of behavior-shaping by successive approximations of desired behavior. The case further exemplifies the application of an ABAB design in which a period during which baseline measures are taken is followed by a period during which the changed contingencies are in effect. This, in turn, is followed by a reversal to the original contingencies with a subsequent reinstitution of the approach whose effectiveness has now received support. In cases where a study is limited to one individual, as in the typical clinical situation, and where no control group can be used this and similar designs can be powerful tools for conducting research.

Before leaving the case of Ann it is worth pointing out that the approach used to help her learn to interact with other children had been specifically designed for her. Prior to the intervention, observations had revealed that she was neither severely withdrawn or frightened; that she had a varied and well-developed repertoire of skills that drew the interested attention of adults but failed to attract the companionship of children. Furthermore, it had been ascertained that adult attention served as a source of positive reinforcement for this child so that the use of attention for bringing about a behavior change represented an individualization of the approach. Other children who do not interact with their peers may do so because they are afraid of them, or they may have no skills from which to generalize, or they may be reinforced not by adult attention but by physical contact, or trinkets, or food. Only a systematic and individualized approach based on careful observations and explicit recording can hope to succeed in helping a child achieve a desired behavioral goal. This point is too often ignored by people who think that an indiscriminate handing out of M&M candies represents an authentic operant program of behavior change.

Inappropriate Gender Behavior

Another problem that can be construed as a deficit in social skills is the case of the child who does not engage in gender-appropriate behavior. Gender behavior disturbances, sometimes labeled childhood cross-gender identity problems, may be accompanied by verbalizations to the effect that the child wishes he or she were of the opposite sex, dressing in wearing apparel appropriate for the opposite sex, and displaying mannerisms and speech patterns stereotypically associated with the opposite sex.

As is the case with other behavior disorders, this problem might be construed as reflecting an excess of inappropriate behavior or a deficit of appropriate behaviors. As with bedwetting, where one might debate whether the problem is excessive micturition in the wrong place or deficient control over the urethral sphincter, the issue of classification can be settled by asking which direction therapeutic intervention must take; the teaching of responses not in the child's repertoire or the reduction of responses that occur with excessive frequency or intensity. In the case of gender identity problems, the therapeutic task is not to work on the suppression or elimination of the cross-gender behavior (which would leave the child without gender-appropriate responses). The task is, instead, to teach gender-appropriate responses so that these can replace the responses that the social environment deems inappropriate. This is the therapeutic approach taken by Rekers who, alone or in collaboration, has done extensive research in this area (Rekers, 1975; Rekers & Lovaas, 1974; Rekers, Lovaas, & Low, 1975).

Before presenting a representative study of the effect of behavior therapy on inappropriate gender behavior, a word must be said about research using a single-subject design. For those to whom research means experimental and control groups, measures of variance and central tendency, correlation coefficients and tests of significance, the details of an investigation that used a single subject may seem more like a clinical case study than a research report. Originated in the operant laboratory, the intrasubject design is eminently suited for research in the clinic where homogeneous populations, matched control groups, uniformity of procedures, and other desiderata of good experiments are often impossible to obtain. At the same time, only a treatment approach that permits the systematic application of objectively defined procedures lends itself to a single-subject methodology. Behavior therapy based on operant procedures is thus often evaluated in this fashion. The following report is presented in some detail not only because it exemplifies the $N = 1$ design but also because it emphasizes a number of important points about the application of behavioral principles in child therapy. These will be highlighted later.

A boy, age eight years, eight months, identified as "Carl," was treated by Rekers, Lovaas, and Low (1975) with the aim of having masculine sex-typed behaviors replace a full repertoire of feminine behaviors. He had pronounced feminine inflection and content in his speech and made excessively female gestures. He was unassertive with his peers, preferred to play with girls and girls' toys, and often stated that he preferred to be viewed as a girl. His male peers called him "sissy" and "queer" and ostracized him, leading to increasing social isolation, ridicule, and chronic unhappiness.

Because Carl's problem was not situation-specific but generalized over home and school and was also seen in the clinic, and since it, further, involved a variety of discrete behaviors, his case lent itself to a multiple-baseline intrasubject design across stimulus environments and across behavior. Such a design, as Gelfand and Hartmann (1975) have pointed out, is a means for testing the effectiveness of an intervention when the typical ABAB reversal design cannot be used. In a clinic case, such as Carl's, one would obviously not wish to have him revert to the feminine behaviors after masculine behavior patterns had been established,

simply for the sake of demonstrating that the specific intervention method was indeed the critical independent variable.

Carl was treated in one environment at a time. This permitted the assessment of the generalization of treatment effects across clinic, home, and school. In each of these settings trained observers recorded clearly specified behaviors and in the home the mother, who had been trained in the use of a behavior checklist, contributed an independent set of data. The observational categories were highly concrete and objective. Feminine-gesture mannerisms, for example, subsumed eight specific behaviors, such as feminine gait which was defined as "walking with a rhythmic side-to-side movement of the torso and hips, while extending the arms away from the sides of the body or with the elbow(s) flexed such that an angle formed by the forearm and upper arm is less than 90 degrees" (p. 102). Such specificity of objective target behaviors is an essential of behavior therapy. Vague targets, such as "effeminate behavior," "insecurity," or "paying attention" do not lend themselves to systematic intervention.

The target for treatment in the clinic was Carl's sex-typed verbal behavior. After gathering baseline data on masculine and feminine speech content during six story-telling sessions, the therapist introduced differential social reinforcement. Statements or questions with masculine or neutral content were followed by expressions of positive interest, while references to feminine topics resulted in withdrawal of attention on the part of the therapist. This contingency remained in effect for three sessions during which feminine speech content decreased from an initial level of 21 percent to a mean of 2.5 percent. A brief reversal of contingencies demonstrated that the therapeutic intervention had indeed been responsible for the change in behavior since the feminine speech content immediately returned to 20.5 percent. Masculine speech content mirrored the frequency of feminine content in that it increased to 12 percent from an initial level of 6 percent and fell to 9 percent when the original baseline condition was reinstated. A noteworthy response generalization was also observed in that the boy's feminine inflections showed a decrease although no reinforcement contingencies had been specifically applied to that be-havior. On the other hand, there was no stimulus generalization of the treatment effect to other set-tings. In the home and in the school, feminine speech content and inflections continued without change. At this point, treatment was shifted to the home situation.

Carl's mother was taught to administer a be-havior modification program based on a system of token reinforcements. The boy could initially earn blue tokens for masculine play with his brother. After two weeks on that contingency, he was given red tokens whenever he engaged in feminine ges-tures. Red tokens represented a response-cost condition in that a red token would cancel a blue token when these tokens came to be exchanged for back-up reinforcers (candy, TV time, etc.). In line with the multiple baseline design, work on a new behavior (e.g., feminine speeech content and voice inflections) was only begun after the target of the previous contingency condition had shown a clear change in frequency. In the course of these sessions, the data showed an increase in Carl's masculine play with his brother and a decrease in feminine gestures, feminine speech content, feminine voice inflection, and playing with his sis-ter. Again, however, the treatment effect remained specific to the setting in which treatment had taken place, the home. There was no generalization to the school situation.

Accordingly, treatment was extended to the school, where the teacher was trained to apply a response-cost procedure to Carl's disobedient "brat" behaviors. This system entailed having Carl automatically receive 10 points at the beginning of each school day. From this "account" he would lose one point each time he created a class distur-bance, bossed another child, behaved rudely to the teacher, or teased another child. When these prob-lem behaviors had decreased, the system was ex-tended to cover feminine-gesture mannerisms as well. The effectiveness of these interventions was once more demonstrated although they again did not generalize from the classroom in which they had been used. When, in line with routine school procedures, Carl's class was moved to a different classroom and teacher, his pretreatment behaviors reemerged until the contingencies were reinstated

by the new teacher. At that point the positive ef-fects of the intervention were manifested im-mediately.

Formal treatment extended over a total of 15 months at which point the explicit token-economy contingencies were discontinued. Reports from var-ious sources, including an independent evaluation by two clinical psychologists who administered a battery of personality tests and interviews, con-firmed that Carl's previous feminine behaviors had markedly declined to only rare instances and that there was no remaining evidence of a cross-gender identification. He had developed a masculine interest pattern and major improvements were ob-served in his overall social and emotional adjust-ment. When he was transferred to a different school in order to get away from his prior repuation as a "sissy and queer," the new teacher considered him to be as well-adjusted and well accepted as any other child in her class.

In view of the fact that Carl had a major lack of gender-appropriate social skills, there now fol-lowed an additional 15-months period designed to teach him games and sports, considered approp-riate for boys in our society. Since he lacked a stable relationship with his new stepfather, a young male undertook to establish a buddy relationship with the boy. A year later, a follow-up revealed that the therapeutic gains continued to maintain stabil-ity in this, now 12 years, 2 months old boy.

As we said earlier, this study emphasizes several important points about child behavior therapy. One is the critical issue of the generalization of treatment effects. Many maladaptive child be-haviors are limited to one setting; the child who is disruptive in the school may be a very conforming child at home and vice versa. In these cases, treat-ment can focus on the setting where the problem behavior takes place and once this behavior has been changed in the desired direction, the case can be closed. Many other problem behaviors, on the other hand, manifest themselves in a variety of set-tings. Such was the case with Carl, whose difficul-ties were not situation-specific but had generalized over home and school and even to a novel setting, the clinic. Here it is not enough to work on the problem in a single setting. Helping Carl emit more gender-appropriate behaviors in the clinic clearly had no effect on his behavior in home and school. The therapist thus had to make explicit plans for enhancing the generalization of the treatment effect, implementing this, in part, by instituting interventions in each relevant setting. When one views the situational variables as having significant control over behavior, it stands to reason that behavior change plans must take these variables into consideration.

The second important point about behavior therapy illustrated by Carl's case involves the participation of the parents (in this instance, the mother) in the treatment plan. Treatment has little chance for being effective if it is restricted to the intermittent contact between the professional therapist and the client. The traditional 50-minute session, once a week, can hardly be expected to carry the burden of changing behavior during the remaining 10,000 minutes in the week. Behavior therapists often involve in the treatment of children significant other persons who are in contact with the child in day-to-day living, such as teachers and parents. Involvement of such auxiliary therapists cannot be done casually, such as by handing a parent one of the several good manuals on behavior change (e.g., Patterson & Gullion, 1968). As was the case with Carl's mother, the auxiliary therapist must be taught to discriminate the behaviors to be changed, to observe and record these behaviors, and to manage the reinforcement contingencies in a consistent and systematic fashion. Many child behavior therapists find that their time is spent more effectively and efficiently in training and working with auxiliary therapists than in face-to-face contact with the child. It stands to reason that the same principles of learning that form the basis of the intervention with the child should also be employed in the training of the auxiliary therapist. Since success is a powerful reinforcer for parents and teachers, it is well to select as the first target of intervention one of the child's behaviors that has high probability of responding quickly to a therapeutic regimen.

The third point illustrated by the treatment of Carl is the importance of making explicit efforts to strengthen desired responses and to teach responses that are not in a child's repertoire when one undertakes to reduce the frequency of undesired responses. It was, for example, not enough to ignore Carl's feminine speech content thus hoping to have these responses become extinguished. The therapist systematically attended to and thus reinforced the desired verbalizations. Similarly, after Carl had ceased his interest in feminine play and companionship, he was helped to acquire masculine interests and skills which facilitated his interaction with same-sex peers.

Lastly, the case of Carl serves to highlight a therapeutic phenomenon about which we know relatively little. It is that certain discrete responses seem to belong to response clusters so that, when one of these responses is modified, others in the same cluster also undergo change. In Carl's case, clinic treatment had been targeted on the *content* of his speech; his feminine voice inflection was recorded by an observer but no contingency was applied to it. Nonetheless, the record showed that the increase in masculine speech content and the concomitant decrease in feminine speech content were accompanied by a marked decrease in feminine voice inflections. Content and inflection thus seem to belong to a cluster so that response generalization is facilitated. Although most child behavior problems consist of many discrete and different responses, it is not necessary to establish explicit treatment procedures for each of these. Work on one often generalizes to others but at this point we do not know how to identify these "key" responses and the clusters are often difficult to recognize. This issue represents a crucial agenda for behavior therapy research.

In speaking of the value of involving a child's parents and teachers in the treatment process, we made the point that such auxiliary therapists can be so effective because they are with the child for so much more time than any therapist can ever hope to be. There is, of course, someone who can be said to be with a child all of the time and that is the child who is the client. Treatment could probably achieve maximum effectiveness and efficiency if the child could be taught to be his or her own therapist. Steps in this direction are being taken by therapists who are studying techniques of behavioral self-control (Spates & Kanfer, 1977).

Varni and Rekers (1975) reported work with a six-year-old boy who, not unlike Carl, had gender identity problems. After they had been able to demonstrate that this boy's gender typed behavior could be modified by social reinforcement delivered by the child's parents, they taught him to monitor his own masculine play, using a wrist-counter to record his own responses. This training was accomplished in the clinic where a special device ("Bug-in-the-ear") permitted the transmission of verbal instructions through a minature FM receiver that is worn like a wireless hearing-aid. As is often the case when people begin to make an explicit record of their own behavior (Broden, Hall, & Mitts, 1971), the child's masculine play increased in reactance to the self-monitoring. This reactive effect diminished over time and the child was then instructed to give himself a small piece of candy for each point recorded on the wrist-counter. Assessment, using a reversal design, demonstrated that this reinforcement condition produced exclusive masculine play. Unlike reinforcement delivered by the parents, where the effect had remained highly situation specific, self-monitoring combined with self-reinforcement was shown to generalize across activities.

It is too early to tell whether this form of treatment of gender problems in young boys has a long-range effect, whether, in particular, these children will engage in gender-appropriate social behavior as adolescents and young adults. Nor do we yet know whether masculine behavior can be maintained when the self-monitoring with self-reinforcement introduced by Varni and Rekers (1975) is faded out, but these methods are intriguing in the promise they hold for maximizing the services which can be rendered by the relatively few professionally trained therapists.

Academic Skill Deficits

Academic performance in such areas as reading, spelling, and arithmetic has been improved and increased by the application of the principles of reinforcement in numerous instances. Staats was one of the first to conceptualize reading performance as an operant response and to use operant principles in a systematic fashion to help children with reading difficulties (Staats, Minke, Finley, Wolf, & Brooks, 1964; Staats & Butterfield, 1965; Staats, Minke, Goodwin, & Landeen, 1967; Ryback & Staats, 1970).

The usual procedure in working with children who have a deficit in one of the academic skills is to establish a token program where defined units of correct responses are immediately followed by a token reinforcer, such as checkmarks or plastic disks, which can later be traded for prizes or privileges of the child's own choosing. As is the case in other operant learning situations, the token thus serves as both informational feedback on the accuracy of the response and as incentive.

The reinforcers are at first delivered on a continuous or near-continuous schedule and are then "thinned out" so as to be delivered as infrequently as once for every 30 correct responses (Sibley, 1967). The individualization of procedures possible with this approach is one of its major attractions and probably an important source of its effectiveness. Sibley (1967) found that poorer, less persevering readers perform best under low ratios of reinforcement (FR 2, that is, one reinforcement for every two responses) while for better readers a higher fixed ratio (FR 30) was more effective. A flexible schedule of reinforcements was also used by Hewett, Mayhew, and Rabb (1967), who taught basic reading skills to mentally retarded, neurologically impaired, emotionally disturbed, and autistic children. For the first three lessons reinforcement was continuous; one unit of reinforcement being delivered for every correct response. After this, a child had to make five correct responses before earning reinforcement (FR 5). Eventually this was further thinned to an FR 10 schedule and finally to FR 200, structured to include a delay of the back-up reinforcement until the end of the session. The ultimate aim of these approaches is, of course, to help the child reach a point where reading is its own reward so that the extrinsic reinforcers, which serve as a crutch for those who do not find reading an intrinsically reinforcing activity, can be eliminated altogether.

Basic operant principles are easy to teach so that they can be applied by relatively untrained individuals. Ryback and Staats (1970) used the reading-disabled children's own parents as therapy technicians in a highly effective program of remedial reading. Drass and Jones (1971) taught learning-disabled children to serve as tutors for their learning-disabled peers. Heiman, Fischer, and Ross (1973) used college students as tutors in a seven-month program of individual tutoring based on operant principles in which the children's reading performance improved an average of 1.2 years on standardized reading tests.

Working with normal second grade children and using arithmetic as their target, Felixbrod and O'Leary (1973) demonstrated that reinforcement contingencies determined by the children themselves are as effective as contingencies that are imposed externally. An earlier study by Lovitt and Curtiss (1969), who had worked with a single child in a class for children with behavior disorders, had shown that a higher rate of academic performance could be obtained when the child managed his or her own contingencies than when the teacher imposed the performance standards. This effect was not observed in the Felixbrod and O'Leary (1973) study nor in the work of Glynn (1970). It appears that the effect of self-imposed standards differs depending on whether they are used for a group of children in a classroom setting or for one child who is working in a group. When Glynn and Thomas (1974) sought to implement a self-control procedure in classroom management, they found that a high and stable effect could be obtained only through the addition of a cueing procedure that specified reinforceable behaviors. Although there is much attraction in finding ways to have children participate in a behavior change procedure through self-assessment, self-recording, self-determination of criteria, and self-administration of reinforcements, considerable work remains to be done before the parameters of these approaches can be considered fully known.

Not only are there many variables in the delivery of reinforcement, the very nature of reinforcement also plays a role in the effectiveness of a program. Thus, Dalton, Rubino, and Hislop (1973) have demonstrated that token reinforcement is superior to verbal praise in producing improvement in the academic performance of retarded children. In practice it is probably best to combine the delivery of tokens with praise statements (Ryback and Staats, 1970) since the latter can be continued when the more artificial contingencies are eliminated. This prepares the child for a situation more like that encountered in the natural environment.

The pairing of a tangible reinforcer with a social reinforcer is an effective way of seeing to it that the social praise statements acquire reinforcement properties for a child to whom praise is initially meaningless (Lovaas, Freitag, Kinder, Rubenstein, Schaeffer, & Simmons, 1966). Zigler and Balla (1972) have shown that different children respond to social reinforcement in different ways, depending on such factors as age (younger children are more responsive than older children), intellectual status (retarded are more responsive than normals), and the retarded child's history prior to institutionalization. Greater responsiveness to social reinforcement was found among retarded children who received few visits from relatives and who had greater deprivation prior to institutionalization. These findings should serve to remind one that no reinforcer can be deemed universally effective and that one must establish in each and every case which consequences strengthen and which weaken the preceding response since reinforcement can only be defined in terms of this function. In addition, the Zigler and Balla (1972) study highlights the fact that a social reinforcement, like any other reinforcer, is subject to the effects of deprivation and satiation, calling for the ongoing monitoring of reinforcer effectiveness even after the effectiveness of a given reinforcer has been established for a particular child.

When one seeks to help children who are deficient in reading, it is important to select an outcome criterion that is relevant to the ultimate goal of obtaining meaning from written material. The ability to make a correct verbal response to the stimulus of a written word (word calling) is not an adequate outcome measure, nor is it sufficient to demonstrate that a child's sight vocabulary has increased or that the rate and accuracy of oral reading of single words or passages have improved. As Lahey, McNees, and Brown (1973) have pointed out, a primary purpose of reading instruction is to teach individuals to answer accurately questions about passages they have read; that is, to demonstrate comprehension. These investigators worked with two sixth-grade children whose reading for comprehension was tested to be two years below grade level. By a procedure that involved the reinforcement, by praise and coins, of correct answers to questions about the content of what they had read, Lahey and his colleagues (1973) succeeded in bringing the comprehension of these children to the level of children whose comprehension was grade-appropriate.

Language Deficits

Operant approaches to the development of responses that are missing in a child's repertoire require the reinforcement of a response from which the desired behavior can be shaped. When a child is mute and the treatment goal is the development of language, the therapist must find a response that has a functional relationship to language. Starting with any vocalization one should be able to shape the production of words by reinforcing successive approximations to speech. When a child is able to imitate, the therapist can model simple words which, when imitated, can then be reinforced. Where a child does not imitate, as in a case described by Hewett (1965), the first step in treatment may have to be training in imitation. Children with early infantile autism and other profoundly disturbed children often engage in echolalia which, though noncommunicative speech, is speech nonetheless. Risley and Wolf (1967) used such speech as a starting point for establishing functional speech. A study of echolalia by Carr, Schreibman, and Lovaas (1975) has since disclosed that echoing a question may be a response the child emits when faced with a verbal stimulus that he or she cannot comprehend. When such a child is taught an appropriate response to the question, the echolalic response to this stimulus disappears. Beginning a language training program by reinforcing an echolalic response may thus not be the most efficient way in which to proceed.

When a child already possesses a rudimentary repertoire of speech it is possible to expand on this by operant techniques (Wheeler & Sulzer, 1970). Here, as in other programs of intervention, it is important to ascertain that the new responses learned in the treatment setting generalize to the child's nontreatment environment (Keeley, Shemberg, & Carbonell, 1976). Such generalization should not be left to chance but built into the treatment procedures. One way to accomplish this is by systematically reinforcing speech under a variety of conditions (Risley & Wolf, 1967). Ferster (1967) pointed to the distinction between arbitrary and natural reinforcers, where the former bear no intrinsic relationship to the response (as candy to saying one's name) while the latter are the normally expected consequences to a given response (as an answer to "Hello, how are you?"). While operant methods for establishing language usually have to begin with arbitrary reinforcers because these may be the only stimuli with reinforcing properties, once a child has acquired a small language repertoire, the natural (social) consequences of speech usually come into play and, by serving to reinforce speech in a variety of settings, aid in establishing generalization of the advances the child has made in the therapeutic setting. Thus, the boy described by Hewett (1965) who was initially trained on candy and light, eventually encountered people who sought him out for verbal interactions that not only maintained but enlarged his newly acquired speaking vocabulary.

A study that demonstrated teaching of the use of compound sentences to describe novel stimuli was reported by Stevens-Long, Schwarz, and Bliss (1976) who worked with a six-year-old autistic boy. This child's speech consisted almost entirely of two-word phrases and echolalia. He was trained to repond to pictures depicting two or more people in various activities. At first he was reinforced for any verbal response to the pictures, later he was taught to use simple sentences to describe the pictures. Finally, he learned to use the connective "and" between two of these sentences. Training procedures included imitative prompts. That is, when the boy failed to respond or produced an incorrect response, the experimenter would model the correct response for him. He was differentially reinforced (with food and verbal praise) only when he produced or reproduced two correct sentences relevant to a picture (e.g., "The boy is reading and the teacher is putting the book away"). When he did not produce a correct response or failed to imitate the teacher's prompt, the training card was placed face down on the table and the teacher turned away for 10 seconds. The authors refer to this as a time-out procedure.

Once this boy had reached the point where he produced correct, unprompted compound sentences 91 percent of the time, he was tested for generalization of what he had learned on the training pictures. This was done by the use of probe trials; pictures that had not been used as training stimuli. To these, the boy had to produce a complete, grammatically correct, and semantically relevant sentence in order to have the response counted as correct. At the end of a total of 31 half-hour training sessions, this child responded correctly to these novel stimuli in 70 percent of the trials. What is more, his teacher reported that he had begun describing everyday objects and events using compound sentences in classroom and playground conversation. The authors' conclusion that operant procedures can be used to teach the productive use of compound sentence forms to speech-deficient children would seem to be justified.

Deficits in Attending Behavior

The teaching of academic and language skills is closely related to teaching the child to attend to the stimuli that the teacher is presenting and to which the child is supposed to learn an appropriate response. Investigators working with learning-disabled children (Douglas, 1972; Ross, 1976) generally agree that one of the common characteristics of these children is a difficulty in attention, possibly resulting from a lag in the development of the capacity to sustain selective attention. Systematic efforts to enhance the attending behavior of learning disabled children have shown promise of making instruction in remedial reading more effective (Heiman, Fischer, & Ross, 1973).

Hyperactivity, impulsivity, limited attention span, and learning disability are frequently confounded, and different investigators have addressed different aspects of this problem cluster. Some have chosen to focus on reducing hyperactivity by differentially reinforcing periods of sitting still and attending to the task at hand (Patterson, Jones, Whittier, & Wright, 1965). Others (Palkes, Stewart, & Kahana, 1968) have taught impulsive children to "stop, look, listen, and think" before giving an answer or responding to a task. An often cited study by Meichenbaum and Goodman (1971) explored whether one can train impulsive children to improve their performance by giving them instruction in self-guidance. The use of live or film-mediated models (Ridberg, Parke, & Hetherington, 1971) has proved effective in such self-instruction train-

ing. In these studies, the effectiveness of the interventions was usually evaluated on tests designed to measure impulsive responding, such as Kagan's (1965) Matching Familiar Figures test. Such tests show that children can be taught to slow their response times and increase the accuracy of their responses. Important as such laboratory studies are in enhancing understanding of the variables that play a role in the problems of such children, the crucial question whether such methods improve academic performance is only rarely investigated. A notable exception is the work of Egeland (1974) who reports significant improvements on a test of reading comprehension in a group of "impulsive children" whom he had taught a response strategy.

The notion of a response strategy has important implications for work with learning-disabled children (Torgesen, 1975). It does not seem to be enough to teach a child to "pay attention" or to stop before responding. One must also teach children what one wants them to pay attention to or what they are to do while they stop between question and answer. Egeland (1974) had two experimental groups. One was trained to wait 10 to 15 seconds before responding ("think about your answer and take your time"). The other group was given a set of rules and basic strategies for attacking the training tasks. These rules were designed to enhance attention to the relevant features of the stimuli, to induce them to examine alternatives, to break the alternatives down into component parts, to look for similarities and differences, and to eliminate alternatives until only the correct one remained. One group was thus trained to delay their responses while the other was taught what to do during the delay. While the performance of both groups on the Matching Familiar Figures test improved after a four-week training period, only the group that had been taught the strategies had maintained this improvement two months later and only that group scored significantly higher on a test of reading comprehension administered five months after completion of the training.

Behavioral methods that have been used to help individual children improve attending behavior have also been applied in classroom settings with groups of so-called hyperactive and disruptive children. This work is discussed in Chapter 14.

Norm-violating Behavior

The norm-violating behavior of the child who, when apprehended and processed through the judicial system comes to be labeled a juvenile delinquent is here construed as resulting from a behavioral deficit. If the focus is on a failure to have learned the ability to postpone immediate (and often unlawful) gratification and the lack of socially endorsed skills which might open ways of alternate forms of gratification, or if one postulates that the norm-violator has not learned to discriminate between acceptable and unacceptable behavior, the logical treatment becomes a teaching of these controls, skills, or discriminations; not a punishment for disapproved actions.

This formualtion not only shifts the treatment of delinquency from a punitive to a constructive base with youth who have been apprehended and adjudicated delinquent (Cohen & Filipczak, 1971), it also facilitates a preventive approach with children who are considered to be "pre-delinquent" (Reid & Hendricks, 1973). In such preventive work the aim is to teach constructive social skills as alternatives to such behavior as aggression, noncompliance, and stealing. This has been done by increasing the mutual reinforcement among the members of the child's own family (Alexander & Parsons, 1973), by a system of behavioral contracting (Stuart, 1971), or by having the child live within a behaviorally oriented, family-style program with specially trained "teaching parents" (Phillips, 1968; Phillips, Phillips, Fixsen, & Wolf, 1971).

Achievement Place

The home-style rehabilitation setting based on operant principles and directed by a trained staff was pioneered by Phillips (1968) in a program that has come to be known as Achievement Place. As mentioned in the preceding chapter, this has served as a model for numerous other family-style homes in various communities. It is the premise of these programs that delinquent behavior is the product of inadequate social learning experiences so that the development of appropriate behavior becomes the goal of intervention. Accordingly, a structured, systematic program is established that is aimed at teaching such social skills as how to make an introduction, academic skills like how to study and do homework, self-care skills in such areas as meal preparation and personal hygiene, and prevocational skills designed to permit a young person to find work in the community. The typical resident in such a group home is of junior high school age, about three to four years below grade level on academic achievement tests, whose trouble with the law has resulted in being adjudicated delinquent. Referral is usually by the juvenile court. Length of stay is nine to twelve months.

The details of an Achievement Place program have been described by Phillips, Phillips, Fixsen, and Wolf (1971) who speak of it as based on a token economy. The boys earn points which are established as reinforcers for specified desired behavior. These points can be converted into a variety of privileges such as the use of tools, telephoning, snacks, or an allowance. Initially, behavior is heavily reinforced in a daily point system. This is later faded to a weekly point system, and ultimately, the boys progress to a merit system in which all privileges are free and reinforcement for desirable behavior takes the form of praise, approval, and affection. Behavior is carefully monitored throughout and after four successful weeks on the merit system, a boy is advanced to the homeward bound system in which he returns to his own home while spending occasional nights at Achievement Place for disucssion of any problems he may be having at home. This return to the boy's own home is coordinated through regular meetings between his parents and the program staff. These meetings too are discontinued once the boy's behavior is problem free.

The original Achievement Place program in Lawrence, Kansas, has been the site of numerous studies assessing both the specific aspects of the endeavor, such as the reliability of self-reporting (Fixsen, Phillips, & Wolf, 1972), the efficacy of self-government (Fixsen, Phillips, & Wolf, 1973), and its overall effectiveness (Fixsen, Phillips, Phillips, & Wolf, 1972). To assess the latter, a comparison was conducted between 16 boys whom the court had committed to Achievement Place, 15 boys who had been sent to a state institution, housing about 250 youths, and 13 boys who had been placed on probation. Although it must be stressed that the boys had not been assigned to these three groups at random, such measures as school attendance, police and court contacts, and academic performance revealed the superiority of the Achievement Place program over the other two dispositions. The reduction in recidivism rate, usually the outcome measure deemed most relevant in the rehabilitation and correction field, is particularly impressive. Within the first twelve months, 6 percent of the Achievement Place boys, 13 percent of the state school boys, and 31 percent of the boys on probation had committed some delinquent act that led to their being readjudicated by the court and placed in an institution. By the end of 24 months following their release, the cumulative totals of readjudicated youths was 19 percent for Achievement Place, 53 percent for the state institution, and 54 percent for those on probation.

Behavioral Contracting.
If one accepts the premise that behavior is a function of its consequences, it becomes essential that one examine the consequences of behavior one wishes to change. In the day-to-day interactions of children with their parents and teachers, desirable behavior is all too often taken for granted, so that few if any consequences are forthcoming, whereas undesirable behavior, by the demand characteristics inherent in such behavior, elicits all sorts of consequences. An obvious way of trying to increase desirable behaviors is to make sure that such behaviors are the occasion for positive social consequences, and since social behavior involves the interaction between two or more people, all partners in such interactions should experience such positive consequences. It is this thinking that led Stuart (1971) to introduce behavioral contracting as a means of assuring the scheduled exchange of positive reinforcement between the members of a delinquent child's family.

The incidence of positive interchanges between a delinquent child and his or her family is usually quite low; many of the interactions revolve around the child's undesirable behavior. For this reason Stuart (1971) recommends the assignment of responsibilities and duties to various members of the family for which each can receive previously agreed-upon privileges. It should be obvious that

such a systematizing of family interactions, which has highly artificial overtones, is appropriately used in families in need of help and would make little sense for those whose interactions are generally positive and constructive.

As the word *contract* implies, it involves a reciprocity to which all parties have agreed. Like other contracts it can be renegotiated in order to insure its viability, and it specifies sanctions for violations of its provisions. The actual contract is often supplemented by involving the child's school in the treatment program or, as in the case described by Stuart (1971), by seeking support from other institutions in the community.

The obstacles to assigning delinquent children at random to treatment and control groups (juvenile court judges do not readily fit their decisions to an experimental design) make the evaluation of interventions such as Achievement Place or behavioral contracting quite difficult. Comparing a group of children who had contingency contracting treatment with a group whose families declined such treatment, a not altogether satisfactory control group, Stuart and Tripodi (1973) reported better school attendance and academic performance for the contingency group.

Deficient Sphincter Control
The incontinence of urine and feces, labeled enuresis and encopresis, respectively, is fruitfully conceptualized as a behavioral deficit since intervention must take the form of teaching the child two related responses. One is to inhibit (delay) elimination, the other is to urinate or defecate in the place society has designated as "proper."

The problem most frequently encountered in the area of sphincter control is bedwetting. Its frequency, the relative ease with which it can be treated by methods based on a conditioning paradigm, and the objective criteria for determining outcome, have made bedwetting the object of a number of well-controlled investigations (Baker, 1967; DeLeon & Mandell, 1966; DeLeon & Sacks, 1972; Finley, Besserman, Bennett, Clapp, & Finley, 1973; Lovibond, 1964; Novick, 1966). Most of these studies involve the use of the bell-and-pad method developed by Mowrer and Mowrer (1938) in which an alarm rings at the onset of urination and the child is instructed to go to the toilet to finish elimination.

Treatment by bell and pad was originally conceptualized as the application of respondent conditioning principles but it is probable that operant learning is also involved inasmuch as even the original Mowrer method included rewards for improvement and dry nights (Ross, 1972). Collins (1973) has shown the importance of the contiguous pairing of bladder cues with the alarm signal which induces sphincter contraction and/or awakening. James and Foreman (1973) highlighted the contribution to treatment outcome made by the adult who participates in the procedure by instructing the child, getting him or her out of bed, and demonstrating the setting and resetting of the alarm system.

Outcome studies of Mowrer-type treatment of nocturnal enuresis have generally been highly favorable. DeLeon and Mandell (1966) demonstrated its superiority over methods based on psychodynamic formulations, and a follow-up of their treated cases by DeLeon and Sacks (1972), conducted four years later, showed that 81 percent had not wet the bed during the year prior to the follow-up phone contact. Baker (1967) had earlier demonstrated that successful treatment of bedwetting by conditioning procedures is frequently accompanied by improvements in the child's behavior in other (untreated) areas and that there is no evidence for either symptom substitution or negative side effects. The relapse rate after initial treatment, which is reported to range between 20 and 30 percent, may well represent the extinction of an acquired response. This would suggest that treatment on an intermittent basis, with the alarm system operating on some nights and not on others, should make the stay-dry response more resistant to extinction. Indeed, this was demonstrated by Finley et al. (1973) who compared continuous, intermittent, and "placebo" methods of treating bedwetting.

Another method of approaching the treatment of bedwetting from a behavioral point of view is to teach the child sphincter control during the waking state. Once this is accomplished, the response appears to generalize to the night when the child is asleep. Paschalis, Kimmel, and Kimmel (1972), having found that bedwetting children have a higher rate of urination during the day than children who can sleep through the night staying dry, had parents teach bladder control to their own child. After only two hours of training, the parents held daily sessions in which the child was rewarded for holding urine for two to three minutes longer than the day before, up to a total of 45 minutes. Treatment lasted from 15 to 20 days and when the child had succeeded in staying dry at night for one week, he or she was rewarded with a previously selected gift. Followup was conducted three months later and showed that of the 31 children, none of whom had ever previously had a dry night, 15 were competely dry and 8 had improved significantly.

The highly successful, rapid toilet training procedure introduced by Foxx and Azrin (1973a) and detailed in Azrin and Foxx (1974) entails having the child drink a lot of fluids in order to increase the frequency of the need to urinate, thus massing the trials during which voiding in the toilet can be reinforced. For young children who are to be toilet trained in the course of normal socialization, this can be structured as a game and positive outcome is usually achieved in one day. Azrin, Sneed, and Foxx (1974) report that this method can also be used to help older children with problems of bedwetting.

A novel aspect of these toilet training procedures is what Foxx and Azrin (1973a) call positive practice or overcorrection (Foxx & Azrin, 1973b). This consists of a period of practicing the correct response whenever the changeworthy response has been emitted. Thus, after the child has wet himself or herself, the trainer indicates his or her disapproval and then requires the child to practice going to the toilet or potty-chair from various locations in the house for a total of ten rapidly conducted trials. During each trial, the child goes to the appropriate place, lowers his or her pants, sits for about two seconds, stands up, raises the pants and then moves to another location from where the procedure is repeated. Foxx and Azrin (1973a) consider this an educative experience but they also recognize that the effort involved gives the procedure the aspects of punishment.

Although there are numerous studies of behavioral approaches to enuresis, such work on the problem of encopresis is relatively rare. Gelber and Meyer (1965) presented a case report where a 14-year-old encopretic boy was hospitalized in order to gain contingency control. Once in the hospital, the privilege of leaving the ward was used as the positive consequence for appropriate toilet behavior while restriction to the ward was used as the punisher for soiling. This operant method is reported to have brought the problem under control. Similar approaches to encopresis and stool retention were reported by Edelman (1971)and Tomlinson (1970) but the absence of required experimental controls makes it impossible to conclude that the reinforcement contingencies were indeed responsible for the improvement. The fact that such controls are extremely difficult to use— even a reversal design would be highly controversial—does not mitigate the fact that the burden of proof rests with those who claim to know what was responsible for the laudable improvement of their treated cases.

In a brief discussion of the neurophysiology of bowel control Young (1973) pointed out that the encopretic children he treated "had no perception of the gastro-ileal or gastro-colic reflexes and could exercise no control over their bowel actions" (p. 501). He treated these children with a mild laxative and then had them sit on the toilet for 10 minutes following food intake 20 to 30 minutes previously. When a bowel movement occurred, the parents rewarded the child with praise. This treatment was successful within a mean of 7 months for 22 of the 24 children in the series. While Young (1973) fails to report whether the children had attained perception of the reflexes involved in bowel control, it does appear that sphincter pressure can be brought under operant control. This was shown in a case report by Kohlenberg (1973) who treated a 13-year-old encopretic boy. By inserting a fluid-filled balloon into the boy's rectum in order to be able to measure the pressure exerted by the anal sphincter and reinforcing increases in this pressure, this investigator found that pressure changes were a function of the reinforce-

ment schedule in effect. When a child is unaware of colonic pressures and sphincter tonus, such external feedback may facilitate learning to bring the necessary responses under control.

Hyperactivity

Problems in deficient motility control may lead to a child being labeled hyperactive. Although often found in conjunction with learning disabilities, hyperactivity should be viewed as a separate target for intervention because helping a child overcome a learning disability does not automatically reduce hyperactivity. Nor, for that matter, will helping a child sit still automatically improve academic performance, whether the motility is reduced by chemical or behavioral means (Sroufe & Stewart, 1973).

One of the earliest demonstrations of the systematic application of behavioral principles to the modification of hyperactivity was presented by Patterson, Jones, Whittier, and Wright (1965) who treated a 10-year-old brain-injured, retarded boy, attending a special school for physically handicapped children. By making the delivery of reinforcement contingent on brief periods during which "nonattending behavior" was absent, these investigators were able to reduce this boy's hyperactivity while that of a control child remained the same. In this study an observer had to indicate to the child via a radio signal when he had earned a reinforcement and at the end of the session the number of such signals was translated into pieces of candy that the boy could share with the other children in class. The boy's peers thus probably served as a further source of reinforcement. The fact that the peer group is an important factor in the behavior of the individual child has led other investigators to use group contingencies (Hall, Lund, & Jackson, 1968), time-out (Kubany, Bloch, & Sloggett, 1971), and various classroom token economies (O'Leary, Becker, Evans, & Saudargas, 1969), which are discussed in Chapter 14.

A promising method of working with hyperactive and impulsive children entails verbally mediated self-control training, based on the pioneering study by Meichenbaum and Goodman (1969). A treatment "package" using self-instruction has been described by Bornstein and Quevillon (1976) who worked with three overactive preschool boys in a Head Start program. These four-year-old children were described as highly distractible and disruptive, unable to follow directions, inattentive, and aggressive. The target of intervention was on-task behavior; that is, performing prescribed and accepted classroom activities. Off-task behaviors, the only other category observers were asked to record, included movement about the room, playing with toys, shouting, fighting, kicking, and leaving the classroom without permission. During the baseline period which occupied the first eight days of the investigation, the mean rates of on-task behavior of the three boys ranged from 10.0 to 14.6 percent. Following two hours of training in self-instruction, on-task behavior increased immediately as reflected in means ranging from 70.8 to 82.3 percent. On one of two follow-up observations, held 22½ weeks after treatment, the on-task behavior of the three boys remained at 77, 68, and 67 percent, respectively.

These results, and particularly the remarkable maintenance data, warrant a more detailed presentation of the self-instruction training. As described by Bornstein and Quevillon (1976), the procedure entailed a massed self-instruction session for each child, lasting for two hours. The experimenter first modeled the task for the child while talking aloud to himself. The verbalizations were of four types: Questions about the task ("What does the teacher want me to do?"); answers to these questions ("Oh, that's right, I'm supposed to copy that picture"); self-instructions that guide through the task ("OK, first I draw a line here . . . "); and self-reinforcement ("How about that, I really did that one well"). On many of the tasks the experimenter purposely made mistakes and then corrected himself, thus preparing the child for taking occasional difficulties in his stride. Following such a modeling display, the child was asked to perform the task while the experimenter verbalized the guiding statements. Finally, the child was instructed to make the statements himself, while working on the task with reinforcement (initially candy, later praise) dispensed for both the self-instruction and for correct performance.

The self-instruction training was sequentially administered in a multiple-baseline design across subjects. This design controlled for expectancy effects and such potential nonspecific effects as attention and experience with the stimulus material. Its use lends considerable confidence to the reliability of the results and the effectiveness of the treatment package. Which of the various parts of this program might be the crucial ingredient must, of course, await further research.

THE TREATMENT OF BEHAVIOR EXCESSES

Excessive Avoidance Behavior

Fears and phobias, here viewed as finding expression in excessive avoidance responses that must be reduced if the child is to be helped, have been the target of behaviorally based treatment from as far back as 1924 when Mary Cover Jones worked with the classical case known as Peter. Jones (1924) applied the principles of respondent conditioning in pairing the presentation of a fear-arousing stimulus with a stimulus assumed to be eliciting a fear incompatible response. By carefully grading the exposure to these stimuli in such a manner that the strength of the elicited fear was always less than the strength of the incompatible response, Jones succeeded in bringing Peter to the point where the previously fear-arousing object (a rabbit) had become a source of apparent pleasure.

Because fear is an internal state that can only be inferred from observing such behavior as avoidance or escape responses, the treatment of fears calls for a number of assumptions that raise a variety of theoretical issues. Among these are whether pleasure, as in Peter's case, or relaxation, as in the work of Wolpe (1958), or positive emotions as those presumably aroused by "emotive imagery" (Lazarus & Abramovitz, 1965) are indeed substituting for fear as implied by the term counterconditioning. The implication of the more frequently used expression, systematic desensitization, would have it that the client is gradually acquiring fear-incompatible approach responses as a result of systematically graded exposure to the feared object. Yet again, as Davison and Wilson (1973) have pointed out, it is not at all clear whether this is indeed the critical ingredient in this form of treatment. What is fairly certain is that principles other than those derived from classical conditioning come into play when therapists help clients overcome their fears. Cognitive factors (what the children say to themselves) and social reinforcement (the implicit or explicit approval of the therapist) are undoubtedly involved. This being the case, and since theoretical niceties are of little concern to the practicing clinician, many therapists systematically combine gradual exposure to feared stimuli with explicit reinforcement for approach responses (e.g., Lazarus, Davison, & Polefka, 1965) while the research of others (Kanfer, Karoly, & Newman, 1975) suggests that teaching fearful children to make statements such as, "I am a brave girl; I can take care of myself in the dark" can help them overcome fear of the dark.

Another method of treating fear of the dark by young children involves reinforced practice (Leitenberg & Callahan, 1973). Here, fearful children are instructed to remain in a darkened room for initially brief, then gradually lengthening periods of time. Reinforcement is contingent on the increases in exposure, that is, for measured progress. Yet again, exposure and positive reinforcement are not the only ingredients in this treatment. The instructions given to the children are designed to arouse expectations of gradual success and the graphically depicted progress provides potentially important feedback.

The effectiveness of treating children's fears and phobias by various forms of desensitization depends greatly on the child's ability to follow instructions. Approaches that call for representation of the feared object in imagery, as Wolpe's therapy by reciprocal inhibition (1958), or those where the child must imagine himself or herself as a fearless driver of a racing car (Lazarus & Abramovitz, 1965) may be of limited usefulness. When Miller, Barrett, Hampe, and Noble (1972) compared children treated by reciprocal inhibition or psychotherapy with waiting list controls they found both forms of treatment to be effective but no more effective than no treatment at all. On the basis of a follow-up one and two years later (Hampe, Noble, Miller, & Barrett, 1973) they concluded that young children's phobias tend to "go away by themselves" but that treatment hastens recovery.

The most successful (and best researched) method of treating children's fears is to expose them to fearless models. This approach was explored by Bandura, Grusec, and Menlove (1967) who speak of the procedure as vicarious extinction of avoidance behavior. In a study demonstrating the effectiveness of vicarious extinction of children's fears of dogs, Bandura et al. (1967) had a group of children observe a fearless four-year-old boy model progressively closer approach behavior to a dog. These children had first been given a pretest involving 14 tasks that required coming into increasingly more intimate contact with the dog. The same test was repeated after eight 10-minute treatment sessions and revealed a marked increase in fearless behavior. Follow-up assessment, one month later, revealed that these approach responses were maintained.

The use of four different experimental groups permitted Bandura et al. (1967) to draw several other conclusions. Thus, they showed that mere exposure of fearful children to a dog in the positive context of a birthday party, which might be deemed a form of desensitization, or participation in such a party where no dog was present did little to increase approach responses. On the other hand, modeling in a positive context and modeling alone had very similar constructive effect although, in terms of the follow-up, the group of children who had observed the model in the party context earned the highest approach scores.

The use of live models in a so-called in vivo treatment situation requires a good deal of stage managing on the part of the therapist who must have access to an appropriate model and (in the case of dog phobias) a cooperative animal. In terms of the practical application of this procedure it is thus encouraging to know that vicarious extinction of fears can also be accomplished when fearful children observe several models whose approach behavior is displayed in a film (Bandura and Menlove, 1968). The similarity of the model to the observing child, especially with respect to age, is an important variable in the effectiveness of vicarious extinction procedures (Kornhaber & Schroeder, 1975). Another dimension of similarity would seem to be fearfulness itself. A fearful child observing a fearless child sees a model who is different on an important dimension. This may be why such children who, after all, see fearless peers around them all the time have not long ago lost their fears. Most of the successful modeling precedures thus display a model who is initially hesitant about approaching the feared object and only gradually increases contact with it. In fact, a film designed to reduce children's fears of dentists (Adelson, Liebert, Poulos, & Herskovitz, 1972) shows two children, one fearless, the other ostensibly fearful, where the latter gradually comes to display less and less fear.

The effectiveness of modeling procedures has also been demonstrated with nursery school children who exhibited shyness, that is, excessive social withdrawal (O'Connor, 1969, 1972). A film portraying 11 scenes of young children in progressively more active interaction was shown to a group of socially withdrawn children while a matched control group viewed a film about dolphins. On the modeling film, a female narrator talked about what the children were doing and of the fun they were having. Behavior observations carried out in the classroom immediately after the showing of the film revealed the effectiveness of the modeling film in that the children who had been exposed to it now displayed more social assertiveness than the children in the control group. In fact, on blind behavior ratings, the intially shy children were indistinguishable from their socially normal classmates. O'Connor (1972) was also able to show that the effects of modeling lasted at least over a three-week follow-up period, with treated children's peer-interaction scores remaining at normal levels. On the other hand, Keller and Carlson (1974) report that the effect of film-mediated modeling for children with low levels of social responsiveness was maintained over a similar period of time for only some of their subjects. It may be that maintenance of the positive effects of modeling depends on the child having opportunities to practice the newly facilitated response pattern under conditions where they receive positive reinforcement, particulary from their peers, for interacting with other children. (see also Chapter 16).

School Phobia.

School refusal, based on an excessive fear of school, usually called *school phobia*, is a phenomenon of considerable magnitude not only because of its high incidence among the school-age population but also because a child who is unable to attend school is disabled in the principal role society has assigned to its children. Kennedy (1965) differentiates between Type I school phobia, characterized by acute onset in the early grades, and Type II, where the problem is of more chronic nature, thus found primarily among older children. He demonstrated that Type I cases can be treated very effectively by insistence on immediate return to school, coupled with a structured inverview with the parents and a brief interview with the child. Parents are instructed to praise the child for attending school for at least 30 minutes on the first day and to celebrate full return to school, which was usually accomplished on the third day of treatment. This rapid treatment was successful in all of the 60 cases treated over a 12-year period and follow-ups found no recurrence of the problem, nor the development of other difficulties. The approach pioneered by Kennedy (1965) calls for good professional relations between the clinic, the school, and local physicians since rapid referral and cooperation is an essential aspect of the treatment method. One should also note that good communication between well-adjusted parents who can easily understand the treatment rationale are among the defining characteristics of Type I phobias. When these conditions are not met, as is the case in Type II school phobias, other approaches to treatment may well be required.

One such approach is *in vivo* desensitization, as used by Garvey and Hegrenes (1966). They helped a 10-year-old school phobic boy return to school by having him make closer and closer approaches to school over a period of 20 days. At first this approach was in the company of the therapist, then the boy's father went with the child, and finally the school principal took over. Although this approach has many of the characteristics of respondent counterconditioning, it should be noted that the implicit and explicit approval of increasing success on the part of the adults serves to reinforce and strengthen approach responses in the direction of the school. It is unlikely that a clinical treatment program can be conceptualized solely in terms of a single conditioning paradigm and the effective ingredients of such a program remain to be isolated by carefully controlled research.

In many cases of school phobia, remaining away from school is reinforced not only by the inherent fear avoidance but also by the positive reinforcement entailed in staying home. Therapists who approach these cases from an operant point of view, thus seek to decrease the reinforcements available to the child by staying at home, while arranging contingencies in such a way that successive approximations to returning to school and school attendance itself receives positive reinforcement (Hersen, 1970). This technique of differential reinforcement (DRO), though taking more time than Kennedy's rapid treatment, is less stressful than forced return to school. A follow-up over a period of nine months (Ayllon, Smith, & Rogers, 1970) found it to have lasting effect and no untoward consequences. With appropriate instructions, the child's parents can do most of the actual treatment by managing the necessary contingencies once these have been identified through careful assessment on the part of the professional therapist (Tahmasian & McReynolds, 1971).

Overeating

Excessive food intake resulting in obesity has been successfully treated through a program of parental training and contingency contracting (Aragona, Cassady, & Drabman, 1975). These investigators worked with a group of 15 girls between the ages of 5 and 10 whom both their physicians and parents considered to be overweight.

After the parents and their child had together decided on a weight-loss goal of between one and two pounds per week, the family would deposit a small sum of money with the therapist. This deposit was to be forfeited if the family unilaterally dropped out of the program. Failure to attend weekly sessions, failure to bring completed charts and graphs to the meeting, and failure of the child's losing the predetermined amount of weight all resulted in response-cost, a forfeiture of money in the deposit account. The children in one of the experimental groups also received reinforcement for negotiated daily calorie-intake reduction and weight loss.

At the end of the 12-week treatment period, the children in the experimental groups had lost sig-

nificantly more weight than those in the control group. A follow-up eight weeks later, revealed that the response-cost plus reinforcement group was still significantly below the controls while the response-cost-only group had regained some of the lost weight. At follow-up 31 weeks after termination of treatment, the effect was no longer statistically significant though the response-cost plus reinforcement group showed a trend toward slower weight gain.

Like other time-limited experimental studies of treatment effect, where the length of treatment is more often dictated by the length of an academic semester than by the needs of the clients, the work of Aragona, Cassady and Drabman (1975) is dogged by the problem of maintenance. Dramatic treatment effects are often demonstrated at the end of a treatment program and these effects are usually maintained for a relatively brief period of follow-up. When the effect is evaluated some six to twelve months later, however, the results are often disappointing (Keeley, Shemberg, & Carbonell, 1976).

It may well be that this problem with maintenance is an artifact of the way in which many of these outcome studies are conducted. In order to exercise rigorous experimental control, investigators decide to treat all cases for the same length of time, following this with a set period of no contact at the end of which follow-up data are gathered. When one treats each case until the records of that case show that treatment has been effective, then gradually fades treatment contact while making certain that the progress is continued and giving "booster" sessions when needed, later follow-up usually demonstrates that the treatment effect is maintained (e.g., Hampe, Noble, Miller, & Barrett, 1973; O'Leary, Turkewitz, & Taffel, 1973; Patterson, 1974; Rekers, Lovaas, & Low, 1974).

Self-injurious Behavior

Profoundly disturbed children, such as those labeled schizophrenic or autistic, at times engage in behavior that inflicts injury on themselves. As described by Bachman (1972), such behavior often consists of repetitive head-banging, face-slapping, scratching, or biting of various body parts. Some of these children thus produce serious damage to themselves, such as blindness, concussions, or large, bleeding lesions. The drastic nature of this behavior has led to equally drastic attempts to control it, including physical restraint and deep sedation. An early functional analysis of this behavior by Lovaas, Freitag, Gold, and Kassorla (1965) led to the conclusion that for the children they studied self-injurious behavior was being maintained by the reinforcement inherent in the solicitous social attention that is almost invariably the consequence of such actions. Withholding this attention in an attempt to have self-injurious behavior undergo extinction is obviously not feasible, particularly in view of the fact that a response put on an extinction schedule will, at first, show a marked increase in frequency and /or intensity. For this reason behavior therapists sought rapid response suppression by introducing aversive stimulation (punishment) as a consequence for instances of self-injurious behavior (Lovaas et al., 1965; Tate & Baroff, 1966).

The use of punishment in the treatment of children, particularly where such punishment entails the administration of an electric shock, should be tolerated only when all other known forms of intervention fail to work and where the child's health or safety is at stake. Further, as Bachman (1972) has stressed, suppression of the dangerous response through punishment must always be accompanied by explicit efforts to establish desirable alternative responses through positive reinforcement. It should also be stressed that therapists who are working with less profoundly disturbed children can introduce negative consequences for undesirable behavior that are less drastic than the infliction of physical pain, such as the time-out procedures used by Wolf, Risley, and Mees (1964) and by Risley (1968) who found that tantrums, self-slapping, throwing of eye-glasses, and dangerous climbing on furniture responded to this form of intervention.

While self-injurious behavior is limited to profoundly disturbed, psychotic children, self-stimulation is a more frequently encountered phenomenon, particularly among retarded, blind, and moderately autistic children. This behavior consists of repetitive, stereotyped rocking, hand-flapping, head-twisting, or mouthing objects or body parts. Because these actions interfere with the acquisition of more adaptive behaviors, including social skills, therapists must seek to eliminate them as a part of comprehensive treatment plans. Bucher and Lovaas (1968) reported that a firm slap on the child's thigh would suppress self-stimulatory behavior that disrupted language training sessions. More recently, Foxx and Azrin (1973) introduced positive practice overcorrection for the elimination of such behavior which has no apparent functional effect on the environment.

As discussed by Foxx and Azrin (1973), positive practice overcorrection requires the child to engage in intensive practice of an overly correct form of relevant, appropriate behavior. Among the children who served as subjects in a study of the effectiveness of positive practice overcorrection was an eight-year-old severely retarded girl who constantly weaved her head in a wide arc from side to side and a seven-year-old autistic boy who almost continuously engaged in hand-clapping. For both children positive practice overcorrection consisted of teaching them to move the body parts in question only for functional reasons, that is, only when instructed to do so. Thus, any time the head-weaving began the child was given functional movement training for five minutes. The teacher would first restrain the child's head with her hands and instruct her verbally and by manual prompts to move the head up or down or to hold it straight. The child was required to hold her head in the indicated position for 15 seconds at the end of which another instruction was given.

For hand-clapping the procedure was similar. The child would be instructed to move his hands in one of five positions: above his head, straight out in front of him, into his pockets, held together, or held behind his back. Again, the teacher would pair verbal instructions with manual guidance, the latter being gradually faded out as the responses were brought under verbal control. The child would be required to hold his hands in the indicated position for 15 seconds and then another instruction would follow. When overcorrection had reduced the self-stimulatory behavior to a near-zero frequency, a verbal warning procedure was introduced with overcorrection used only if the child failed to stop the nonfunctional behavior.

In the first of two studies, Foxx and Azrin (1973) compared the effectiveness of overcorrection for object or hand-mouthing with reinforcement for incompatible behaviors, physical punishment (slaps), and painting a distasteful solution on the child's hand. For both of the children studied, whose frequency for mouthing had been over 100 times per hour, overcorrection proved to be the most effective method of intervention, reducing the self-stimulatory mouthings to zero. The second study investigated whether the effect of overcorrection for hand or object-mouthing, head-weaving, and hand-clapping could be maintained through the school day and over a period of up to five months. During the initial (baseline) period the four children in this study were self-stimulating over 80 percent of the time. When overcorrection was introduced this behavior decreased by half or more within four days, and fell to a near-zero level within 10 days. After this, self-stimulation virtually ceased and this state could be maintained by the verbal warning ("stop") usually available from adults in a child's environment. The positive effect of the overcorrection had also been carried over into the children's behavior at home after the parents had been instructed in how to use the procedure for a brief period of time.

Foxx and Azrin (1973) view the effectiveness of their procedure as based on the fact that it achieves several objectives at the same time. Among these are the immediate interruption of self-stimulatory behavior by the teacher's intervention; the annoying consequences for the self-stimulation that result from the physical effort required to practice the overcorrection while being manually guided by the teacher; the learning of socially acceptable and instruction-responsive movements with limbs previously used for self-stimulation; and the availability of positive reinforcement for outward-directed activities that are available to the child once the self-stimulation has ceased.

Aggressive and Disruptive Behavior

Aggression in the form of physical attacks on other people appears to be another of the behaviors that are maintained by their consequences. As Patterson, Littman, and Bricker (1967) demonstrated, aggressive behavior increases in frequency when the target of the aggression yields to the aggressor, thus providing a positive consequence for the aggressive act. In the case of children, the peer group is an important source of these positive consequences (Solomon & Wahler, 1973). Attempts to modify aggressive behavior must therefore entail a withdrawal of this source of reinforcement. The most feasible method for doing this is the response-contingent removal of the child who emits aggressive or disruptive behavior from the peer group; the method known as time-out.

Since time-out has the function of reducing the frequency of a response, it is a form of punishment; an aversive event that is introduced when response reduction is desired (Leitenberg, 1965; Kanfer & Phillips, 1970). When time-out is used in the treatment of children it entails the *brief* removal of the child from the opportunity to obtain reinforcement, including the social reinforcement that may be forthcoming from peer attention. Response-contingent social isolation is thus also a form of time-out (Drabman & Spitalnik, 1973). While many of the parameters of time-out procedures when used with children remain to be investigated (MacDonough & Forehand, 1973), we have fairly convincing evidence that brief periods of time-out are far more effective than long periods of punitive confinement (Burchard & Tyler, 1965) and that some schedules of intermittent use of time-out may be as effective as its application on a continuous schedule where every instance of undesirable behavior is followed by this form of punishment (Clark, Rowbury, Baer, & Baer, 1973).

Another negative consequence that can be introduced contingent on aggressive behavior is the loss of a reinforcer, the so-called response cost contingency (Kaufman & O'Leary, 1972). Here the child is either given a supply of reinforcers, usually tokens, from which "fines" are subtracted contingent on the behavior to be reduced or the fines are charged against tokens previously earned in reinforcement for desired behavior. In either case, the response cost results in fewer tokens available to the child when these are to be traded for back-up reinforcers.

A response cost system was used by Burchard and Barrera (1972) and, in combination with contingent social isolation, it was effective in reducing various forms of aggression by institutionalized male delinquents below baseline levels. With that group time out of 30-minutes duration proved more effective than shorter periods. However, with younger, retarded children Repp and Deitz (1974) demonstrated that a period as brief as 30-second time-out, combined with the differential positive reinforcement of other behavior, can reduce both aggressive and self-injurious behavior.

When time-out is used in classroom settings as a device for reducing disruptive behavior it usually entails physically removing the child from the group. In working with individual children, the teacher's or therapist's turning away from the child, thus withdrawing his or her attention, appears to be an effective negative consequence. Pinkston, Reese, Leblanc, and Baer (1973) demonstrated the role of contingent teacher attention in maintaining a preschool child's aggressive behavior to peers. When the teacher ignored the child's aggression and attended instead to the target of the aggression, this behavior decreased to an acceptable rate.

Disruptive behavior in the classroom has been modified by the contingent use of teacher attention (Madsen, Becker, & Thomas, 1968), by having the teacher deliver soft instead of loud reprimands (O'Leary, Kaufman, Kass, & Drabman, 1970), and by the contingent delivery of tokens or points that are later exchanged for back-up reinforcers (Patterson, 1974). These back-up reinforcers can take the form of natural consequences, such as additional recess time or movies that all children in the classroom can share, or they can be individualized by a cooperative program involving school and home where the child receives back-ups at home for points earned in the classroom (Ayllon, Garber, & Pisor, 1975). The application of positive practice, similar in principle to the overcorrection used to treat self-injurious or self-stimulatory behavior (Foxx & Azrin, 1973) has also been found effective in eliminating classroom disturbances (Azrin & Powers, 1975). Since all of these methods require participation, hence cooperation by the classroom teacher, recent explorations of self-management by the students are particularly promising. Drabman, Spitalnik, and O'Leary (1973) demonstrated that children can be trained to monitor their own behavior within the context of a token program

while Bolstad and Johnson (1972) have shown that when children are given control over dispensing reinforcers to themselves, based on self-collected behavior data, disruptive classroom behavior can be reduced.

Involving parents in the treatment of their own children has both practical and theoretical advantages. Pactical because this approach reduces the amount of time professionally trained therapists need to spend on a case; theoretical because the effect of treatment taking place in the environment where the child lives does not depend on the generalization from one setting to another, as would have to be the case where treatment is conducted in a clinic.

Patterson (1974) summarized the outcome of treatment programs for boys with conduct problems which he and his colleagues had conducted over a period of 4½ years. In all 27 cases treatment had consisted in training the child's parents to implement the treatment plan. For 14 of the cases, treatment also took place in the classroom. Criteria of treatment effectiveness were based on direct observations made in the children's homes and classrooms before, during, and after the intervention as well as on daily reports obtained from the parents.

The treatment procedure for the home consisted of giving the parents at least one month of training. This included learning social-learning principles from a programmed text, learning to observe and record child behavior, participating in a parent training group where appropriate techniques were taught by modeling and role playing, and learning to construct behavioral contracts that specified contingencies for a list of problem behaviors.

The treatment procedures for the classroom included an initial use of observers who would signal the child when he or she was engaging in nondisruptive, work-oriented behavior that earned points and back-up reinforcers. Later a school-home program was initiated in which the child would bring a work card from school on the basis of which the parents delivered previously contracted consequences. As the disruptive behavior came under control and the program ran smoothly, its administration was turned over to the classroom teacher.

Patterson (1974) reports that both sets of procedures, the home as well as the classroom-based intervention, were "moderately successful in producing reductions in noxious behaviors in the settings for which they were designed" (p. 479). On follow-up 12 months after termination of treatment the total deviant behavior in the home was in the "normal" range. The same was true for appropriate classroom behavior when it was checked four to six months after termination of the program. Patterson's conclusion regarding the success of the program is tempered by the fact that for half of the families there was an increase in noxious behavior immediately following termination so that what he terms a "booster shot" of about two hours of additional work was needed in order to assure maintenance of the progress that had been achieved while intervention was in effect. In addition, it appears that this form of treatment is differentially effective, depending on certain family background variables. Thus, the most difficult cases to treat were father-absent families of lower social class where the mother perceived herself as unable to cope with the multitude of crises impinging on her. As others have observed (Berkowitz & Graziano, 1972; Forehand & Atkeson, 1977; O'Dell, 1974), parent training appears to be effective but attention must now be directed toward enhancing this effectiveness by isolating the components contributing to the success.

PROBLEMS, CRITICISM, AND CONTROVERSIES

Recent years have seen an ever-increasing amount of research on child behavior therapy. Some of this is of high quality, some is open to criticism. The most frequent shortcoming is the brief period over which treated cases are followed to ascertain whether the treatment effect is maintained. Even when follow-up does extend over a relatively long period of time it often entails no more than a telephone interview with the child's parents. While the logistical problems are admittedly of considerable magnitude, we will remain in relative ignorance about the effectiveness of our treatment until objective measures are applied over three or four years. The fact that researchers using other treatment approaches have no good follow-up data either can hardly serve as a reason not to correct our own deficiencies.

A related weakness in behavior therapy research is that many studies are unrepresentative analogues of clinical treatment procedures. Selecting children who have only one problem and having relatively inexperienced graduate students give all of them the same, time-limited treatment tells us little about the effect or effectiveness of treatment of the complex, multiple problems with which children are brought to service-oriented community clinics where they are seen by experienced professional clinicians. It may be that where the abbreviated analogue is effective, real-life treatment is even more effective but we cannot know that until the necessary research has been conducted.

One of the problems facing the experimenter wishing to evaluate outcome of child therapy is the criterion to be used. Investigators have repeatedly found that parents tend to evaluate treatment outcome more positively than either the therapists (O'Leary, Turkewitz, & Taffel, 1973) or independent observers (Eyberg & Johnson, 1974; Patterson, 1974). While parental judgment of the severity of a problem usually serves as the basis for initiating treatment, that judgment at or after termination of treatment may well be influenced by factors other than child behavior itself (Walter & Gilmore, 1973; Johnson & Christensen, 1975). Yet, since parents' view of the child's behavior will, in itself, influence that behavior, it is certainly important to assess their opinion. On the other hand, as Eyberg and Johnson (1974) observed, evaluation of treatment outcome must include more than parental judgment.

Another issue in the behavioral treatment of children, which so often takes place in the home or the school and involves important modifications of the relevant environment, is the effect of the intervention on the siblings or classmates of the targeted child. Parents and teachers often ask how they can reinforce the behavior of one child when the other children who observe this do not receive similar consequences for their behavior. The obvious answer to this is that everyone's behavior should get the recognition it deserves. In addition, the use of group contingencies or the sharing of back-up reinforcers with peers can readily prevent untoward reactions by other children. In fact, even when such precautions are not taken, the behavior of nontargeted children often changes in a positive direction (Arnold, Levine, & Patterson, 1975; Christy, 1975; Drabman & Lahey, 1974).

Other objections to the use of tangible reinforcers, including the assertion that one should not have to reinforce a child "for doing his moral duty," that an activity should be intrinsically reinforcing and not require an extrinsic reward, and that positive reinforcement is a form of bribery, have been effectively dealt with in considerable detail in an article by O'Leary, Poulos, and Devine (1972). Objections of this nature are usually based on a failure to understand the principles of reinforcement or to appreciate the fact that extrinsic reinforcers are being used *because* the particular behavior had not acquired intrinsic reinforcement value for that child. It would be sheer folly to deliver extrinsic, tangible reinforcement to a child who is already engaging in desirable behavior "for its own sake." If one did this, one should not be surprised to find that this unnecessary intervention disrupts the already established behavior.

Winett and Winkler (1972) took issue with the use of behavior modification in classroom settings by pointing out that the changeworthy behavior is consistently defined as behavior that interferes with order, quiet, and decorum. The value system of those who seek to change the behavior of children does play a role in the choice of the goal of intervention. Both professionals and the general public must thus be alert to the potential misuse of techniques that are effective in controlling behavior. Yet, as O'Leary (1972) stressed in his rejoinder to the Winett and Winkler article, the goal of classroom intervention is not "be still, be quiet, be docile" but the creation of an environment that is conducive to learning. It is an empirical question whether children, particularly disturbed children or learning-disabled children, learn best in structured or in unstructured classrooms.

FUTURE DIRECTIONS

In the first paragraph of this chapter we stressed that behavior therapy is an open-ended, self-correcting, thus constantly changing field of endeavor. Where is this change leading? It is always hazardous to attempt predictions of the future, but there are several observable trends from which one can venture a few extrapolations.

One of these trends is the introduction into "behavior" therapy of concepts and constructs from the studies of cognitive processes (Meichenbaum & Goodman, 1971) and perception (Ross, 1976). (See chapter 18.) One can expect that this trend will continue and that concepts from developmental, social, and physiological psychology will come to find application in endeavors aimed at helping children with psychological problems.

It has been recognized for some time that a focus on the treatment of psychological problems is but an attempt to set right something that has gone wrong. Ultimately, we should be able to see to it that things do not go wrong in the first place; that is, we should be able to prevent psychological problems before they arise. One direction such efforts will probably take is to develop methods of early detection or prediction of problems, so that preventive strategies can be instituted. The work of Cowen in the Rochester Primary Mental Health Project (Cowen, Trost, Lorion, Dorr, Izzo, & Isaacson, 1975) is at the frontier of that direction.

Parent training has been one of the recent developments in the field of child behavior therapy. This entails the use of parents as therapeutic agents in the treatment of their own children. Although considerably more work needs to be done in this area, it is not unreasonable to assume that the field will move beyond this and begin training potential parents in empirically based child rearing methods. If this could be done successfully, training for parenthood would be another means of contributing to the prevention of psychological problems.

Yet another direction in which the field appears to be moving is the development of methods by which the individual child can learn to manage his or her own behavior. Various forms of self-monitoring, self-instruction, self-evaluation, and self-reinforcement in children's learning are becoming the focus of psychological research (Spates & Kanfer, 1976). Such behavioral self-control (Thoreson & Mahoney, 1974) has much to recommend it, not only because it is another way of maximizing the scarce professional resources but also because it addresses the troublesome ethical issue that is involved in the imposition of control by one person over another. While our behavior is constantly controlled by factors in our environment, the greater the individual's role in arranging this environment, the less is the potential for the abuse of behavior control methods by others. The extent to which we are willing to place the means of self-control into the hands of our children represents a real challenge to our society.

REFERENCES

Adelson, R., Liebert, R. M., Poulos, R. W., & Herskovitz, A. A modeling film to reduce children's fear of dental treatment. *International Association for Dental Research Abstracts*, March 1971, p. 114.

Alexander, J. F., & Parsons, B. V. Short-term behavioral intervention with delinquent families: Impact on family process and recidivism. *Journal of Abnormal Psychology*, 1973, *81*, 219–225.

Allen, K. E., Hart, B. M., Buell, J. S., Harris, F. R., & Wolf, M. M. Effects of social reinforcement on isolate behavior of a nursery school child. *Child Development*, 1964, *35*, 511–518.

Aragona, J., Cassady, J., & Drabman, R. S. Treating overweight children through parental training and contingency contracting. *Journal of Applied Behavior Analysis*, 1975, *8*, 269–278.

Arnold, J. E., Levine, A. G., & Patterson, G. R. Changes in sibling behavior following family intervention. *Journal of Consulting and Clinical Psychology*, 1975, *43*, 683–688.

Ayllon, T., Garber, S., & Pisor, K. The elimination of discipline problems through a combined school-home motivational system. *Behavior Therapy*, 1975, *6*, 616–626.

Ayllon, T., Smith, D., & Rogers, M. Behavioral management of school phobia. *Journal of Behavior Therapy and Experimental Psychiatry*, 1970, *1*, 125–138.

Azrin, N. H., & Foxx, R. M. *Toilet training in less than a day*. New York: Simon & Schuster, 1974.

Azrin, N. H., & Powers, M. A. Eliminating classroom disturbances of emotionally disturbed children by positive practice procedures. *Behavior Therapy*, 1975, *6*, 525–534.

Azrin, N. H., Sneed, T. J., & Foxx, R. M. Dry-bed training: Rapid elimination of childhood enuresis. *Behavior Research and Therapy*, 1974, *12*, 147–156.

Bachman, J. A. Self-injurious behavior: A behavioral analysis. *Journal of Abnormal Psychology*, 1972, *80*, 211–224.

Baker, B. L. Symptom treatment and symptom substitution in enuresis. *Journal of Abnormal Psychology*, 1969, *74*, 42–49.

Bandura, A., Grusec, J. E., & Menlove, F. L. Vicarious extinction of avoidance behavior. *Journal of Personality and Social Psychology*, 1967, *5*, 16–23.

Bandura, A., & Menlove, F. L. Factors determining vicarious extinction of avoidance behavior through symbolic modeling. *Journal of Personality and Social Psychology*, 1968, *8*, 99–108.

Berkowitz, B. P., & Graziano, A. M. Training parents as behavior therapists: A review. *Behavior Research and Therapy*, 1972, *10*, 297–317.

Bolstad, P. D., & Johnson, S. M. Self-regulation in the modification of disruptive behavior. *Journal of Applied Behavior Analysis*, 1972, *5*, 443–454.

Bornstein, P. H., & Quevillon, R. P. The effects of a self-instructional package on overactive preschool boys. *Journal of Applied Behavior Analysis*, 1976, *9*, 179–188.

Broden, M., Hall, R. V., & Mitts, B. The effect of self-recording on the classroom behavior of two eighth-grade students. *Journal of Applied Behavior Analysis*, 1971, *4*, 191–199.

Bucher, B., & Lovaas, O. I. Use of aversive stimulation in behavior modification. In M. R. Jones (Ed.), *Miami symposium on the prediction of behavior 1967: Aversive stimulation*. Coral Gables: University of Miami Press, 1968, pp. 77–145.

Burchard, J., & Barerra, F. An analysis of time-out and response cost in a programmed environment. *Journal of Applied Behavior Analysis*, 1972, *5*, 271–282.

Burchard, J., & Tyler, V., Jr. The modification of delinquent behavior through operant conditioning. *Behavior Research and Therapy*, 1965, *2*, 245–250.

Carr, E. G., Schreibman, L., & Lovaas, O. I. Control of echolalic speech in psychotic children. *Journal of Abnormal Child Psychology*, 1975, *3*, 331–351.

Christy, P. R. Does use of tangible rewards with individual children affect peer observers? *Journal of Applied Behavior Analysis*, 1975, *8*, 187–196.

Clark, H. B., Rowbury, T., Baer, A. M., & Baer, D. M. Timeout as a punishing stimulus in continuous and intermittent schedules. *Journal of Applied Behavior Analysis*, 1973, *6*, 443–455.

Cohen, H. L., & Filipczak, J. *A new learning environment*. San Francisco: Jossey Bass, 1971.

Collins, R. W. Importance of the bladder-cue buzzer contingency in the conditioning treatment for enuresis. *Journal of Abnormal Psychology*, 1973, *82*, 299–308.

Cowen, E. L., Trost, M. A., Lorion, R. P., Dorr, D., Izzo, L. D., & Isaacson, R. V. *New ways in school mental health: Early detection and prevention of school maladaptation*. New York: Human Sciences, Inc., 1975.

Craighead, W. E., Kazdin, A. E., & Mahoney, M. J. *Behavior modification: Principles, issues, and applications*. Boston: Houghton Mifflin, 1976.

Dalton, A. J., Rubino, C. A., & Hislop, M. W. Some effects of token rewards on school achievement of children with Down's syndrome. *Journal of Applied Behavior Analysis*, 1973, *6*, 251–259.

Davison, G. C., & Wilson, G. T. Processes of fear-reduction in systematic desensitization: Cognitive and social reinforcement factors in humans. *Behavior Therapy*, 1973, *4*, 1–21.

DeLeon, G., & Mandell, W. A comparison of conditioning and psychotherapy in the treatment of functional enuresis. *Journal of Clinical Psychology*, 1966, *22*, 326–330.

DeLeon, G., & Sacks, S. Conditioning functional enuresis: A four year follow-up. *Journal of Consulting and Clinical Psychology*, 1972, *39*, 299–300.

Douglas, V. I. Stop, look and listen: The problem of sustained attention and impulse control in hyperactive and normal children. *Canadian Journal of Behavioral Science*, 1972, *4*, 259–281.

Drabman, R. S. Behavior modification in the classroom. In W. E. Craighead, A. E. Kazdin, and M. J. Mahoney (Eds.), *Behavior modification: Principles, issues, and applications*. Boston: Houghton Mifflin, 1976, pp. 227–242.

Drabman, R. S., & Lahey, B. B. Feedback in classroom behavior modification: Effects on the target and her classmates. *Journal of Applied Behavior Analysis*, 1974, *7*, 591–598.

Drabman, R., & Spitalnik, R. Social isolation as a punishment procedure: A controlled study. *Journal of Experimental Child Psychology*, 1973, *16*, 236–249.

Drabman, R. S., Spitalnik, R., & O'Leary, K. D. Teaching self-control to disruptive children. *Journal of Abnormal Psychology*, 1973, *82*, 10–16.

Drass, S. D., & Jones, R. L. Learning disabled children as behavior modifiers. *Journal of Learning Disabilities*, 1971, *4*, 418–425.

Edelman, R. I. Operant conditioning treatment of encopresis. *Journal of Behavior Therapy and Experimental Psychiatry*, 1971, *2*, 71–73.

Egeland, B. Teaching children to discriminate letters of the alphabet through errorless discrimination training. *Journal of Reading Behavior*, 1974, *6*, 142–150.

Eyberg, S. M., & Johnson, S. M. Multiple assessment of behavior modification with families: Effects of contingency contracting and order of treated problems. *Journal of Consulting and Clinical Psychology*, 1974, *42*, 594–606.

Felixbrod, J. J., & O'Leary, K. D. Effects of reinforcement on children's academic behavior as a function of self-determined and externally imposed contingencies. *Journal of Applied Behavior Analysis*, 1973, *6*, 241–250.

Ferster, C. B. Arbitrary and natural reinforcement. *Psychological Record*, 1967, *17*, 341–347.

Finley, W. W., Besserman, R. L., Bennett, L. F., Clapp, R. K., & Finley, P. M. The effect of continuous, intermittent, and "placebo" reinforcement on the effectiveness of the conditioning treatment for enuresis notcurna. *Behavior Research and Therapy*, 1973, *11*, 289–297.

Fixsen, D. L., Phillips, E. L., Phillips, E. A., & Wolf, M. M. The teaching-family model of group home treatment. Paper presented at the meeting of the American Psychological Association, Honolulu, Hawaii, September, 1972.

Fixsen, D. L., Phillips, E. L., & Wolf, M. M. Achievement Place: The reliability of self-reporting and peer-reporting and their effects on behavior. *Journal of Applied Behavior Analysis*, 1972, *5*, 19–30.

Fixsen, D. L., Phillips, E. L., & Wolf, M. M. Achievement Place: Experiments in self-government with pre-delinquents. *Journal of Applied Behavior Analysis*, 1973, *6*, 31–47.

Forehand, R., & Atkeson, B. M. Generality of treatment effects with parents as therapists: A review of assessment and implementation procedures. *Behavior Therapy*, 1977, *8*, 575–593.

Foxx, R. M., & Azrin, N. H. Dry pants: A rapid method of toilet training children. *Behavior Research and Therapy*, 1973a, *11*, 435–442.

Foxx, R. M., & Azrin, N. H. The elimination of autistic self-stimulatory behavior by overcorrection. *Journal of Applied Behavior Analysis*, 1973b, *6*, 1–14.

Garvey, W. P., & Hegrenes, J. R. Desensitization techniques in the treatment of school phobia. *American Journal of Orthopsychiatry*, 1966, *36*, 147–152.

Gelber, H., & Meyer, V. Behaviour therapy and encopresis: The complexities involved in treatment. *Behavior Research and Therapy*, 1965, *2*, 227–231.

Gelfand, D. M., & Hartmann, D. P. *Child behavior analysis and therapy*. New York: Pergamon, 1975.

Glynn, E. L. Classroom applications of self-determined reinforcement. *Journal of Applied Behavior Analysis*, 1970, *3*, 123–132.

Glynn, E. L., & Thomas, J. D. Effect of cueing on self-control of classroom behavior. *Journal of Applied Behavior Analysis*, 1974, *7*, 299–306.

Goldfried, M. R., & Davison, G. C. *Clinical behavior therapy*. New York: Holt, Rinehart & Winston, 1976.

Hall, R. V., Lund, D., & Jackson, D. Effects of teacher attention on study behavior. *Journal of Applied Behavior Analysis*, 1968, *1*, 1–12.

Hampe, E., Noble, H., Miller, L. C., & Barrett, C. L. Phobic children one and two years posttreatment. *Journal of Abnormal Psychology*, 1973, *82*, 446–453.

Heiman, J. R., Fischer, M. J., & Ross, A. O. A supplementary behavioral program to improve deficient reading performance. *Journal of Abnormal Child Psychology*, 1973, *1*, 390–399.

Herbert, E. W., Pinkston, E. M., Hayden, M. L., Sajwaj, T. E., Pinkston, S., Cordua, G., & Jackson, C. Adverse effects of differential parental attention. *Journal of Applied Behavior Analysis*, 1973, *6*, 15–30.

Hersen, M. Behavior modification approach to a school-phobic case. *Journal of Clinical Psychology*, 1970, *20*, 395–402.

Hewett, F. M. Teaching speech to an autistic child through operant conditioning. *American Journal of Orthopsychiatry*, 1965, *35*, 927–936.

Hewett, F. M., Mayhew, D., & Rabb, E. An experimental reading program for neurologically impaired, mentally retarded, and severely emotionally disturbed children. *American Journal of Orthopsychiatry*, 1967, *37*, 35–48.

James, L. E., & Foreman, M. E. A-B status of behavior therapy technicians as related to success of Mowrer's conditioning treatment for enuresis. *Journal of Consulting and Clinical Psychology*, 1973, *41*, 224–229.

Johnson, S. M., & Christensen, A. Multiple criteria follow-up of behavior modification with families. *Journal of Abnormal Child Psychology*, 1975, *3*, 135–154.

Jones, M. C. A laboratory study of fear: The case of Peter. *Pediatrics Seminar*, 1924, *31*, 308–315.

Kagan, J. Reflection-impulsivity and reading ability in primary grade children. *Child Development*, 1965, *36*, 609–628.

Kanfer, F. H., Karoly, P., & Newman, A. Reduction of children's fear of the dark by competence-related and situational threat-related verbal cues. *Journal of Consulting and Clinical Psychology*, 1975, *43*, 251–258.

Kanfer, F. H., & Phillips, J. S. *Learning foundations of behavior therapy*. New York: Wiley, 1970.

Kaufman, K. F., & O'Leary, K. D. Reward, cost, and self-evaluation procedures for disruptive adolescents in a psychiatric hospital school. *Journal of Applied Behavior Analysis*, 1972, *5*, 293–309.

Keeley, S. M., Shemberg, K. M., & Carbonell, J. Operant clinical intervention: Behavior management or beyond? Where are the data? *Behavior Therapy*, 1976, *7*, 292–305.

Keller, M. F.; & Carlson, P. M. The use of symbolic modeling to promote social skills in preschool children with low levels of social responsiveness. *Child Development*, 1974, *45*, 912–919.

Kennedy, W. A. School phobia: Rapid treatment of fifty cases. *Journal of Abnormal Psychology*, 1965, *70*, 285–289.

Kent, R. N., & O'Leary, K. D. A controlled evaluation of behavior modification with conduct problem children. *Journal of Consulting and Clinical Psychology*, 1976, *44*, 586–596.

Kohlenberg, R. J. Operant conditioning of human anal sphincter pressure. *Journal of Applied Behavior Analysis*, 1973, *6*, 201–208.

Kornhaber, R. C., & Schroeder, H. E. Importance of model similarity on extinction of avoidance behavior in children. *Journal of Consulting and Clinical Psychology*, 1975, *43*, 601–607.

Kubany, E., Bloch, L., & Sloggett, B. The good behavior clock: Reinforcement/timeout procedure for reducing disruptive classroom behavior. *Journal of Behavior Therapy and Experimental Psychiatry*, 1971, *2*, 173–174.

Lahey, B. B., McNees, M. P., & Brown, C. C. Modification of deficits in reading for comprehension. *Journal of Applied Behavior Analysis*, 1973, *6*, 475–480.

Lazarus, A. A., & Abramovitz, A. The use of "emotive imagery" in the treatment of children's phobias. In L. P. Ullmann and L. Krasner (Eds.), *Case studies in behavior modification*. New York: Holt, 1965, pp. 300–304.

Lazarus, A. A., Davison, G. C. & Polefka, D. A. Classical and operant factors in the treatment of a school phobia. *Journal of Abnormal Psychology*, 1965, *70*, 225–229.

Leitenberg, H. Is time-out from positive reinforcement an aversive event? *Psychological Bulletin*, 1965, *64*, 428–441.

Leitenberg, H., & Callahan, E. J. Reinforced practice and reduction of different kinds of fears in adults and children. *Behavior Research and Therapy*, 1973, *11*, 19–30.

Lobitz, G. K., & Johnson, S. M. Normal versus deviant children: A multimethod comparison. *Journal of Abnormal Child Psychology*, 1975, *3*, 353–374.

Lovaas, O. I., Freitag, G., Gold, V. J., & Kassorla, I. C. Experimental studies in childhood schizophrenia: Analysis of self-destructive behavior. *Journal of Experimental Child Psychology*, 1965, *2*, 67–84.

Lovaas, O. I., Freitag, G., Kinder, M. I., Rubenstein, B. D., Schaeffer, B., & Simmons, J. Q. Establishment of social reinforcers in two schizophrenic children on the basis of food. *Journal of Experimental Child Psychology*, 1966, *4*, 109–125.

Lovibond, S. H. *Conditioning and enuresis*. Oxford: Pergamon Press, 1964.

Lovitt, T. C., & Curtiss, K. A. Academic response rate as a function of teacher- and self-imposed contingencies. *Journal of Applied Behavior Analysis*, 1969, *2*, 49–53.

MacDonough, T. S., & Forehand, R. Response-contingent time out: Important parameters in behavior modification with children. *Journal of Behavior Therapy and Experimental Psychiatry*, 1973, *4*, 231–236.

Madsen, C. H., Becker, W. C., & Thomas, D. R. Rules, praise, and ignoring: Elements of elementary classroom control. *Journal of Applied Behavior Analysis*, 1968, *1*, 139–150.

Meichenbaum, D. H., & Goodman, J. Training impulsive children to talk to themselves: A means of developing self-control. *Journal of Abnormal Psychology*, 1971, *77*, 115–126.

Miller, L. C., Barrett, C. L., Hampe, E., & Noble, H. Comparison of reciprocal inhibition, psychotherapy, and waiting list control for phobic children. *Journal of Abnormal Psychology*, 1972, *79*, 269–279.

Mowrer, O. H., & Mowrer, W. M. Enuresis—a method for its study and treatment. *American Journal of Orthopsychiatry*, 1938, *8*, 436–459.

Novick, J. Symptomatic treatment of acquired and persistent enuresis. *Journal of Abnormal Psychology*, 1966, *71*, 363–368.

O'Connor, R. D. Modification of social withdrawal through symbolic modeling. *Journal of Applied Behavior Analysis*, 1969, *2*, 15–22.

O'Connor, R. D. Relative efficacy of modeling, shaping, and the combined procedures for modification of social withdrawal. *Journal of Abnormal Psychology*, 1972, *79*, 327–334.

O'Dell, S. Training parents in behavior modification: A review. *Psychological Bulletin*, 1974, *81*, 418–433.

O'Leary, K. D. Behavior modification in the classroom: A rejoinder to Winett and Winkler. *Journal of Applied Behavior Analysis*, 1972, *5*, 505–511.

O'Leary, K. D., Becker, W. C., Evans, M. B., & Saudargas, R. A. A token reinforcement program in a public school: A replication and systematic analysis. *Journal of Applied Behavior Analysis*, 1969, *2*, 3–13.

O'Leary, K. D., Kaufman, K. F., Kass, R. E., & Drabman, R. The effects of loud and soft reprimands on the behavior of disruptive children. *Exceptional Children*, 1970, *37*, 145–155.

O'Leary, K. D., Poulos, R. W., & Devine, V. T. Tangible reinforcers: Bonuses or bribes? *Journal of Consulting and Clinical Psychology*, 1972, *38*, 1–8.

O'Leary, K. D., Turkewitz, H., & Taffel, S. J. Parent and therapist evaluation of behavior therapy in a child psychological clinic. *Journal of Consulting and Clinical Psychology*, 1973, *41*, 279–283.

Palkes, H., Stewart, M., & Kahana, B. Porteus maze performance of hyperactive boys after training in self-directed verbal commands. *Child Development*, 1968, *39*, 817–829.

Paschalis, A. P., Kimmel, H. D., & Kimmel, E. Further study of diurnal instrumental conditioning in the treatment of enuresis nocturna. *Journal of Behavior Therapy and Experimental Psychiatry*, 1972, *3*, 253–256.

Patterson, G. R. Interventions for boys with conduct problems: Multiple settings, treatments, and criteria. *Journal of Consulting and Clinical Psychology*, 1974, *42*, 471–481.

Patterson, G. R., & Gullion, M. E. *Living with children: New methods for parents and teachers*. Champaign, Ill.: Research Press, 1968.

Patterson, G. R., Jones, R., Whittier, J., & Wright, M. A. A behavior modification technique for the hyperactive child. *Behavior Research and Therapy*, 1965, *2*, 217–226.

Patterson, G. R., Littman, R. A., & Bricker, W. Assertive behavior in children: A step toward a theory of aggression. *Monographs of the Society for Research in Child Development*, 1967, 32, 5 (Whole #113).

Phillips, E. L. Achievement Place: Token reinforcement procedures in a home-style rehabilitation setting for "pre-delinquent" boys. *Journal of Applied Behavior Analysis*, 1968, *1*, 213–223.

Phillips, E. L., Phillips, E. A., Fixsen, D. L., & Wolf, M. M. Achievement Place: Modification of the behaviors of pre-delinquent boys within a token economy. *Journal of Applied Behavior Analysis*, 1971, *4*, 45–59.

Pinkston, E. M., Reese, N. M., LeBlanc, J. M., & Baer, D. M. Independent control of a preschool child's aggression and peer interaction by contingent teacher attention. *Journal of Applied Behavior Analysis*, 1973, *6*, 115–124.

Reid, J. B., & Hendricks, A. F. Preliminary analysis of the effectiveness of direct home intervention for the treatment of predelinquent boys who steal. In L. A. Hamerlynck, L. C. Handy and E. J. Mash (Eds.), *Behavior change: Methodology, concepts, and practice*. Champaign, Illinois: Research Press, 1973, pp. 209–220.

Rekers, G. A. Stimulus control over sex-typed play in cross-gender identified boys. *Journal of Experimental Child Psychology*, 1975, *20*, 136–148.

Rekers, G. A., & Lovaas, O. I. Behavioral treatment of deviant sex-role behaviors in a male child. *Journal of Applied Behavior Analysis*, 1974, *7*, 173–190.

Rekers, G. A., Lovaas, O. I., & Low, B. The behavioral treatment of a "transsexual" preadolescent boy. *Journal of Abnormal Child Psychology*, 1975, *2*, 99–116.

Repp, A. C., & Deitz, S. M. Reducing aggressive and self-injurious behavior of institutionalized retarded children through reinforcement of other behaviors. *Journal of Applied Behavior Analysis*, 1974, *7*, 313–325.

Ridberg, E. H., Parke, R. D., & Hetherington, E. M. Modification of impulsive and reflective cognitive styles through observation of film-mediated models. *Developmental Psychology*, 1971, *5*, 369–377.

Risley, T. R. The effects and side effects of punishing the autistic behaviors of a deviant child. *Journal of Applied Behavior Analysis*, 1968, *1*, 21–34.

Risley, T., & Wolf, M. Establishing functional speech in echolalic children. *Behavior Research and Therapy*, 1967, *5*, 73–88.

Ross, A. O. Behavior therapy. In H. C. Quay and J. S. Werry (Eds.), *Psychopathological disorders of childhood*. New York: Wiley, 1972, pp. 273–315.

Ross, A. O. *Psychological disorders of children: A behavioral approach to theory, research, and therapy*. New York: McGraw-Hill, 1974.

Ross, A. O. *Psychological aspects of learning disabilities and reading disorders*. New York: McGraw-Hill, 1976.

Ryback, D., & Staats, A. W. Parents as behavior therapy-technicians in treating reading deficits (dyslexia). *Journal of Behavior Therapy and Experimental Psychiatry*, 1970, *1*, 109–119.

Sibley, S. A. Reading rate and accuracy of retarded readers as a function of fixed-ratio schedules of conditioned reinforcement. *Dissertation Abstracts*, 1967, *27*, 4134–4135.

Solomon, R. W., & Wahler, R. G. Peer reinforcement control of classroom problem behavior. *Journal of Applied Behavior Analysis*, 1973, *6*, 49–56.

Spates, C. R., & Kanfer, F. H. Self-monitoring, self-evaluation and self-reinforcement in children's learning: A test of a multi-stage self-regulation model. *Behavior Therapy*, 1977, *8*, 9–16.

Sroufe, L. A., & Stewart, M. A. Treating problem children with stimulant drugs. *New England Journal of Medicine*, 1973, *289*, 407–413.

Staats, A. W., & Butterfield, W. H. Treatment of nonreading in a culturally deprived juvenile delinquent: An application of reinforcement principles. *Child Development*, 1965, *36*, 925–942.

Staats, A. W., Minke, K. A., Finley, J. R., Wolf, M. M., & Brooks, L. O. A. Reinforcer system and experimental procedure for the laboratory study of reading acquisition. *Child Development*, 1964, *35*, 209–231.

Staats, A. W., Minke, K. A., Goodwin, W., & Landeen, J. Cognitive behavior modification: "Motivated learning" reading treatment with sub-professional therapy-technicians. *Behaviour Research and Therapy*, 1967, *5*, 283–299.

Stevens-Long, J., Schwarz, J. L., & Bliss, D. The acquisition and generalization of compound sentence structure in an autistic child. *Behavior Therapy*, 1976, *7*, 397–404.

Stuart, R. B. Behavioral contracting within the families of delinquents. *Journal of Behavior Therapy and Experimental Psychiatry*, 1971, *2*, 1–11.

Stuart, R. B., & Tripodi, T. T. Experimental evaluation of three time-constrained behavioral treatments for pre-delinquents and delinquents. In R. B. Rubin, J. P. Brady, and J. D. Henderson (Eds.), *Advances in Behavior Therapy*, Vol. 4, New York: Academic Press, 1973, pp. 1–12.

Tahmasian, J., & McReynolds, W. Use of parents as behavioral engineers in the treatment of a school-phobic girl. *Journal of Counseling Psychology*,

1971, *18*, 225–228.

Tate, B. G., & Baroff, G. S. Aversive control of self-injurious behavior in a psychotic boy. *Behaviour Research and Therapy,* 1966, *4*, 281–287.

Thoresen, C. E., & Mahoney, M. J. *Behavioral self-control.* New York: Holt, Rinehart & Winston, 1974.

Tomlinson, A. The treatment of bowel retention by operant procedures: A case study. *Journal of Behavior Therapy and Experimental Psychiatry,* 1970, *1*, 83–85.

Torgesen, J. K. The role of non-specific factors in the task performance of learning disabled children: A theoretical assessment. Report #65, Developmental Program, Department of Psychology, University of Michigan, Ann Arbor, Michigan, 1975.

Varni, J. W., & Rekers, G. A. Behavioral self-control treatment of "cross-gender identity" behaviors. Paper presented at the 9th Annual Convention of the Association for Advancement of Behavior Therapy, San Francisco, December 1975.

Walter, H., & Gilmore, S. K. Placebo versus social learning effects in parent training procedures designed to alter the behaviours of aggressive boys. *Behaviour Research and Therapy,* 1973, *4*, 361–377.

Wheeler, A. J., & Sulzer, B. Operant training and generalization of a verbal response form in a speech deficient child. *Journal of Applied Behavior Analysis,* 1970, *3*, 139–147.

Winett, R. A., & Winkler, R. C. Current behavior modification in the classroom: Be still, be quiet, be docile. *Journal of Applied Behavior Analysis,* 1972, *5*, 499–504.

Wolf, M. M., Risley, T., & Mees, H. L. Application of operant conditioning procedures to the behaviour problems of an autistic child. *Behaviour Research and Therapy,* 1964, *1*, 305–312.

Wolpe, J. *Psychotherapy by reciprocal inhibition.* Stanford: Stanford University Press, 1958.

Young, G. C. The treatment of childhood encopresis by conditioned gastro-ileal reflex training. *Behaviour Research and Therapy,* 1973, *11*, 499–503.

Zigler, E., & Balla, D. Developmental course of responsiveness to social reinforcement in normal children and institutionalized retardates. *Developmental Psychology,* 1972, *6*, 66–73.

16

PSYCHOLOGICAL MODELING: THEORY AND PRACTICE

TED L. ROSENTHAL

Memphis State University

ALBERT BANDURA

Stanford University

Whatever their conceptualization or techniques, psychological treatment approaches have the common goal of restoring clients to realistic and effective social living. From antiquity on, the decisive impact of social example on human conduct has been acknowledged. Greco-Roman and medieval thinkers practiced what they preached. They assigned a major part to learning from appropriate live and symbolic models in raising the next generation, and developing or refining complex skills in adults (Bahn & Bahn, 1970; Clark, 1957). Applied intuitively, modeling techniques were seen as obvious tools to guide, redirect, and educate people. Until recently, however, observational methods remained dormant; they were largely ignored by practitioners and researchers alike. Among historical bases for that neglect, two stand out: one was the dictum firmly held by peripheralistic Behaviorism that all stable learning required the person to perform overt activities directly. In that view, social exemplars were subordinate to first-hand trial and error practice, which alone could establish new behavior (Miller & Dollard, 1941; Skinner, 1953). An overt practice bias narrowed the preceived relevance of modeling to literal, motoric imitation of movements. Since most vicarious benefits are regulated by the symbolic extraction and covert processing of meaningful information, there was a paradigm clash. The restoration of interest in observational learning demanded evidence that would challenge doctrinaire, overt practice accounts of learning. More recent research using observational paradigms confirms that observation creates acquisition. As well as motor acts, the most diverse linguistic, conceptual, and generalizable competencies can be developed or restored by vicarious means (Bandura, 1977a; Rosenthal, 1976).

Another obstacle to clinical use of therapeutic modeling stemmed from the intrapsychic premises and interview approaches of the verbal psychotherapies. Ironically, those leanings may derive from Freud's having too readily adopted then-fashionable beliefs about the organization of mental life, based on associationism. If mental contents are joined by associative bonds, it seems sensible to seek the sources of psychological dysfunctions by analyzing patients' free verbalizations as clues to inaccessible determinants. Experimental psychology, preoccupied with overt molecular acts, was little help. It offered few vivid analogies to clinicians facing clients' inept and self-defeating conduct. Many therapeutic concerns seemed too remote from the research laboratory and its typically infrahuman clientele. Rarely meeting on common ground, researchers studied simple behavior while therapists modeled sympathetic listening and interpretative statements or actions—withholding practical guidance lest clients' self-corrective tendencies and spontaneous insights become tainted.

INFORMATION AND GUIDANCE PROVIDED BY SOCIAL EXEMPLARS

Since the first edition of this handbook, there has been enormous progress. Research on information processing and conceptual learning has advanced a view of people as active problem-solvers whose assumptions and cognitive plans guide overt behavior. Between the first sensory registration of input cues and their eventual use in living, current research discloses organized complexity in their symbolic representation, transformation into memory codes, and refinement as viable mnemonic maps (Estes, 1975). Applied study has shown the value of systematic guidance for aiding clients. Of present concern, a burgeoning literature confirms the value of modeling treatments for redressing deficits in social and cognitive skills, and for helping to remove defensive avoidant behavior. With their promise amply documented, modeling therapies now pose questions of how to best refine techniques, to join them with other guidance methods for stronger composite programs, and to

adapt them for prevention and other new purposes. In addition to the therapeutic applications, social learning approaches provide means for increasing our understanding of the relationship between cognition and behavior. Since social learning principles allow a host of applications, their potentialities are better grasped and developed from a conceptual framework.

Some Main Roles Served by Models

Other people are salient and powerful models, but not the only ones. Seeing an object fall over a crumbling cliff-edge can alert us to the danger. We use the events witnessed and our inferences about their meaning as useful information to guide expectations and conduct, here, to avoid the precipice. Functionally, a model is any stimulus array so organized that an observer can extract and act on the main information conveyed by environmental events without needing to first perform overtly. Guidance thus stems from cognitive activities by the observer, rather than from direct terminal responding and its feedback consequences. In this view, modeling arrays may involve human actors who can be live, filmed, audiotaped, or depicted by sketches. Displays may instead contain impersonal cues both animate and static. Even then, observers may endow neutral stimuli with social properties, depending on context. For example, viewers infer various social meanings from the motions of geometric figures, based on the spatial topography and temporal sequencing of the moving forms (Bassili, 1976).

Many helpful displays are wholly impersonal, such as roadmaps, naval charts, or training films in which mechanical components move into proper order for repair and assembly. No doubt social models are most relevant clinically and have nearly always been used in therapy studies. Nonetheless, organizing events into systematic programs as with *in vivo* task hierarchies, or observing the correct terminal patterns created earlier by an unseen model, also conveys useful guidance to observers (Alford & Rosenthal, 1973; Robert, White, & Rosenthal, 1975). Studying an antipasto platter arranged by a deft cook would be a homely example. Diverse senses—vision, audition, olfaction—can transmit modeling cues. In therapeutic applications, displays may contain various combinations of illustrative versus summary or narrative guidance. It is convenient to locate these format options along a heuristic continuum. At one imaginary pole, all content would be taught by demonstration or exemplification; the total display would contain exemplary instances with no orienting statements, summary rules, or interpretive guidance. At the other pole, all content would take the form of instructions or narrative summation devoid of demonstrations. There is little reason to endorse either extreme as a possible strategy. Instructions seem most efficient when content is relatively familiar and already known in part. But most often some synthesis of formats will yield the most clarity and impact. There is little research on the optimal balance between exemplary and narrative guidance for defined change programs or types of clients. That realm remains a topic for the future.

One can see that modeling may encompass a very wide span of modes and content formats, even though human performers who illustrate adaptive coping efforts are usual for clinical purposes. Also, effective modeling rarely comprises a skein of disjoined actions or statements. As a rule, one does not rely on exemplifications devoid of background rationales, goal implications, or supplements that enable clients to relate modeling episodes to concrete problems in their own lives. Meaningful guidance occurs in situational aids and explanations. The models behave in a comprehensible fashion to assist observers' understanding and retention. The client's values are taken into account. Otherwise, treatment aids may be dismissed because they affront, or conflict with observers' belief systems. Exemplary performances usually depict meaningful solutions to relevant problems, often portraying the naturalistic consequences to be expected if clients adopt the modeled styles of behavior. Much helpful guidance is carried under natural circumstances with contextual supports.

Modeling influences can produce four separable kinds of effects in observers. Each class of effects has important features for the planning and implementation of therapy.

1. Observational Learning Effects

First, observers can acquire new patterns of be-havior and coping strategies that were not present in their repertoires, or were unavailable in an integrated, usable form. Such *observational learning effects* are shown most clearly when models exhibit novel response patterns that observers have not yet learned to execute. After observation, clients are able to adopt and implement these new solutions in substantially identical form.

Complex patterns of behavior are conveyed as integrated sequences; their meaningful regularities and functional essentials are preserved. This occurs when new action compounds are exemplified, and also when response elements that already exist in the repertoire are organized anew to follow guidelines or principles grasped through observation. Many discrete acts, response sequences, and cognitive elements already exist as products of maturation, instrumental conditioning, and prior observational learning. Modeling exposures serve an instructional role. They teach new components and guide the recombination of other elements. For example, although the color and form dimensions of stimuli may be familiar, arranging them to satisfy a new abstract rule sets demands that learners cannot meet unaided. After modeling exposures, adults and adolescents could apply a concept that was totally unavailable before (Rosenthal & Kellogg, 1973). They had learned new ways to classify familiar objects and gained new facility with a symbolic principle. Many modeling effects in therapy are analogous, as when submissive clients become more assertive with interaction partners.

Some writers doubt if behavior formed by unique recombinations of elements already available represents new learning, because the components exist in subjects' repertoires. From that stance, no new musical composition can occur; have not Bach, Beethoven, and Brahms already used most chords? Indeed, Beethoven would not deserve credit for new symphonies, since he merely rearranged a few existing notes. A pianist who masters a demanding concerto would have learned nothing new since the intricate finger movements were present in his or her repertoire; and an "original" novel would demand neologisms, rather than social language. In fact, after childhood very few components of thought or conduct are totally virginal. Yet the assembly of parts into new wholes may be greatly original. Any behavior array having very low or zero probability of occurrence under appropriate stimulus conditions qualifies as a new response. Most novel molar activities are composed of common behavioral elements.

A great virtue of social learning techniques is their integrative capabilities. Integrated molar solutions are grasped largely intact. Observers can comprehend the interrelationships among components and the principles guiding modeled events. They acquire and can utilize organized, schematic representations of modeled configurations. Often, symbolic elaboration of the events portrayed prepares learners to cope with generalized problems, remote from the concrete details of the exemplars. They devise and can report symbolic rationales that map the key meaning of silent demonstrations (Rosenthal & Zimmerman, 1976). Like knowledge drawn from any other source, vicariously derived information is actively codified by observers as best they can. With well-structured exemplifications, people usually extract much knowledge useful in future conduct. They gain a coherent view of what needs to be done and how to proceed. Then, overt practice and corrective feedback can further refine new skills. Errors in executing component acts, in sequencing elements, or judging informative cues are put right. Guided, and later independent, performance helps stabilize competence and assures learners of their mastery. Their path is smoothed because vicarious guidance equips them for much or most coping before direct practice begins.

In contrast, acquisition prospects were gloomier until recently. It was widely assumed that new response patterns were acquired by gradual shaping through selective reinforcement of trial and error attempts. Discrete responses were slowly shaped and chained by stepwise progression in a laborious sequence. Often avoiding cognitive structuring, or even verbal prompts, the successive approximations paradigm was tedious, if not costly, for learner and teacher alike. Fortunately for survival and efficiency, most naturalistic learning does not take this tedious path. At home, in school, on the playing field, and on the job the novice learns from the precedents and guidance of those with expertise. Moreover, research confirms that observational learning is valuable for countless activities; they span a myriad of cognitive, affective, and be-

havioral domains (Bandura, 1977a; Rosenthal, 1976).

2. Inhibitory and Disinhibitory Effects

A second main function of modeling influences is to strengthen or to weaken inhibitions of responses that are available in observers' repertoires (Bandura, 1971). The impact of modeling on behavioral restraints largely depends on (1) the rewarding or punishing outcomes produced by models' deeds, (2) observers' inferences that similar or unlike consequences would result from emulating the conduct witnessed, and (3) observers' judgments of their ability to enact the modeled behavior.

Inhibitory effects occur when observers either reduce performing the modeled class of behavior, or generally curtail their rate of response as the result of negative consequences perceived. Clinical modeling rarely seeks to create inhibitions. Yet for some cases, such applications may be warranted. If the behavior is seriously harmful to self or society, inhibitory modeling might aid to reduce the noxious conduct while more functional alternatives are developed.

Disinhibitory effects are evident when observers increase production of formerly inhibited acts after models perform them without any adverse results. Disinhibitory effects are common in clinical modeling designed to reduce fears. Observing another approach, cope with, and master situations that scare clients can vicariously enhance expectations of personal effectiveness and thus reduce fear reactions in observers. With inhibitory avoidance reduced, clients gain optimism and are more apt to undertake direct approaches to threats that formerly were too fearsome. Then, successful overt encounters further reinforce a sense of self-efficacy, allowing the persons to favorably reassess their ability to manage the task. Judgments of one's own efficacy are major determinants of overt performance that mediate confident approach or timorous avoidance in the future (Bandura, 1977b). Research illustrating the foregoing points is reviewed later.

It is important that clients do not perceive modeling displays as coercive pressures. If they make new approaches to avoid shame or embarrassment, overt disinhibition may be bought at the price of covert distress. In that case, they may judge themselves as too weak or faint-hearted to initiate future approaches. Thus, in structuring trial encounters, it is important to minimize feedback that confirms self-appraisals of incompetence.

3. Response Facilitation Effects

The behavior of others can also serve as discriminative cues or priming stimuli. Perceiving others perform facilitates observers' production of the same general class of responses, which already exist in their repertoires. Response facilitation effects are distinguished from observational learning and disinhibition because (1) no new responses are acquired, and (2) disinhibitory processes are not involved because the activity is socially acceptable and not encumbered by restraints. Countless examples occur in everyday interactions. If one guest recounts her vacation experiences, others join in and share theirs. One laugh in a room often provokes others. Subtle configurations of behavior can be elicited by modeling. Thus, demonstrating the reaction patterns characteristic of a hypnotized person cues performance equal to standard hypnotic induction (Comins, Fullam, & Barber, 1975). As priming cues, response facilitators are related to set effects. By sensitive use of facilitative exemplars, learners might be aided to become skillful conversationalists or interaction partners. Indeed, a therapist's style and pacing may provide social cues that alter clients' coping and self-reactions for better or worse. Teaching clients and therapists to exemplify social cues that bring out the best in other people's repertoires seems a plausible goal. Since the social activities that people engage in at any moment are partly regulated by the behavior of others, the response-eliciting and cueing function of modeling influences operates continually in all social situations.

4. Cognitive Standards for self-regulation

Most routine behavior is governed by our past experience in the form of adaptation levels and judgmental standards. We seldom react to situations as unique. We are guided by expectations from related events that are categorized and interpreted as similar. Even perceptual cues are scanned in relation to standards. Once perceived, new information is compared to former inputs that act as meaningful decision-making guidelines (Banks, Clark, & Lucy, 1975). Such frames of reference prepare us to handle current and future demands. If conditions shift, refractory standards can disrupt harmonious adjustment. When people suffer serious illness, like stroke, they typically revise their levels of aspiration downward so that expectations remain in tune with capabilities (Levine & Zigler, 1975). Rigid self-demands would bring the patient chronic disappointment or worse. But the hard-driving achiever will at first lack guidelines for matching aspirations to lowered physical capacity. Usually, as people begin to recognize key features of a situation, they relate them to prior analogues and act accordingly. However, in many cases people lack clear standards for conduct or opinion. Tasks and issues suddenly change or are too novel to apply guidelines from our repertoires. Value judgments must be made but criteria are lacking. There is no handy way to weigh the worth of alternative deeds because the significance of action outcomes is ambiguous. At such times one typically dispels uncertainty by adopting the norms enacted or endorsed by others as evaluative criteria. The fourth main function served by models is providing standards to judge the adequacy and appropriateness of performance under ambiguous or greatly altered conditions.

Modeling influences affect self-regulation standards in many spheres. When novices have to assess their own progress, they may prove extremely self-critical from lack of reference criteria. After exposure to their instructors' more favorable judgments about the same accomplishments, learners' self-evaluations became more realistic (Watts, 1973). A model's choice of performance goals, and what amount of self-reward is fair for meeting them, can instate similar standards in observers even when the exemplary self-demands are stringent (Bandura, 1976b). Indeed, when payment is deferred, viewing the pledges made by others can lead observers to promise enormous donations; the magnitude of pledge increased proportional to modeled standards, with little sign of incredulity or "boomerang" effects (White, 1975).

Modeled standards can alter observers' expectancies and inner states with surprising vigor. Perhaps most striking has been the vicarious alteration of pain thresholds. Exposure to models who are tolerant of shocks lead observers to accept more shocks, and of stronger intensity—without showing any greater autonomic response than groups given less pain. They also rate the shock experiences as less noxious than controls. Observing a model who is intolerant to pain has reverse effects (Craig, Best, & Ward, 1975; Craig & Neidermayer, 1974).

Such data suggest treatment applications worth exploring. Clients whose dysphoria involves unrealistic discontent with their own situations relative to others', and people who devalue their self-worth and deprive themselves of attainable joys because of excessively stringent levels of aspiration, might benefit from appropriate modeling.

Although one can distinguish the foregoing main effects of modeling influences, they often interact. Thus, new social competences may rest on a combination of newly learned social skills, reduced inhibitions about self-expression, social facilitation of preexisting patterns, and the adoption of more realistic standards for judging one's own social performance. In specific cases, classifying the relevant modeling process may be rather arbitrary, since changes are multiply determined.

Determinants of Vicarious Influence

Several interrelated subprocesses jointly control how modeled information is comprehended and utilized by observers. When these components are properly implemented, powerful therapeutic changes can be predictably achieved. Neglect of any subprocess may retard or neutralize the entire treatment plan. Hence, analysis of the subsystems aids both for designing modeling applications and for analyzing procedures that fail to produce their intended effects. Also, recent basic research on the component processes is expanding knowledge rapidly, and revising psychological conceptions of human potentialities. In part, divergence between social learning principles and the operant or nonmediational associative positions stem from these new developments.

Attentional processes.

Presenting a modeling display does not assure that learners will perceive it. They must be able to register the sensory events as coherent input. When stimuli appear chaotic, are too fast, too weak, or carry too many cues simultaneously, observers may fail to discriminate the relevant aspects. Distractions from competing contextual events and other interference have similar effects. If observers actively attend to and register sense impressions, they still must be able to decipher them. Both semantic and judgmental acts are involved. Even in the earliest phases of processing cues presented by tachistoscope, familiar stimuli have greater meaning and dominate more equivocal ones. The semantic influence on "peripheral" scanning events is shown by differences in apparent duration and recognizability among more and less familiar stimuli viewed for fractions of a second (Avant & Lyman, 1975). This occurs although perceptual capacity is surprisingly robust as the number of factors to be detected increases (Rosenthal, White, & Alford, 1974; Shiffrin, McKay, & Shaffer, 1976). Thus, stimulus meanings affect sensory recognition, which is the gateway to short-term memory.

The contents of short-term memory decay very quickly unless stabilized by cognitive transformations. Even in this brief stage, multiple distinct coding systems, built up from past experience, seem available for various types of sensory input (Posner, 1973). More important, it is then that selective attention determines which content will earn priority and which will be promptly lost. Judgmental processes operate to filter key from negligible gist. With auditory cues, for example, the observer attempts to segregate ongoing events worthy of attention from others to be ignored; even so, the structure of the rejected cues can interfere with differential attention (Bregman & Rudnicky, 1975).

For the molar input sequences typical in therapeutic modeling, judicious selective attention is critical. Three different types of attention loss are plausible. If a modeling display seems boring or has little personal relevance, observers may disattend and scanning grows perfunctory (Kanfer, Karoly, & Newman, 1974). A second hazard involves client-produced covert interference, often mediated by states of excess arousal. A display may be too upsetting for clients. It may trigger their helpless and hopeless self-definition, remind them that they will soon need to attempt the fearsome acts depicted, or encourage deeds that violate strongly entrenched values. At such times, observers may redirect attention to competing cognitions and functionally attentuate the modeling influences (Bandura & Rosenthal, 1966; Spiegler & Liebert, 1973). In that event, one needs to present the threat level more gradually by interpolating easier tasks or protective supplements. When values clash, one must assure that clients approve of treatment's aims. They should be active participants in selecting the direction of change. Sometimes one may work to change values, but the clients should decide the nature of the change.

An alternative kind of covert arousal problem is best seen in some acute psychotics whose attention is dominated by private events. There, excessive self preoccupation or emotionality disrupts attentiveness to external events. Strong excitation from any source can disrupt cognitive functioning and prevent the processing of new guidance information. Acute affective disorders are an example. It is largely futile to attempt symbolic ministrations while individuals are mired in despondent agitation or are in the thrall of manic excitements. Fortunately, there have been major recent advances in biological psychiatry for reducing acute arousal (e.g., Akiskal & McKinney, 1973; Fieve, 1973). Once extreme disequilibria are corrected, psychosocial techniques can begin profitably. Clients can be taught new adaptive strategies and helped to rectify the problems they often create by rash decisions, made when their functioning deteriorated.

A third hurdle for attentional processes involves the client's skill at monitoring and interpreting modeled events to extract their meaning. Attending to relevant information and avoiding distractors is an essential step in effective observational learning. However, sheer duration of attention is less crucial than discerning focus on key meaning components. Judicious observation covaries more strongly with learning than does gross amount of attention time (Yussen, 1974). To assure that clients perceive the crux of modeling routines, and interpret the information properly, one can ask people to describe what they have learned. Omissions or misconceptions can then be corrected by repeating modeled segments, by additional displays, by explanatory summaries, or by discussing guidelines for future conduct.

Retention Processes

Once discriminated, input is soon lost if not recast in more durable form. Modeled information must be represented and encoded in a framework. Such symbolic codes must be available when needed for the response information to be used. Mnemonic systems organize knowledge to aid retrieval.

The representation of information involves complementary but recursive steps, depending on its form and meaning, which jointly dictate how cues are sorted and cognized (Schvaneveldt, Meyer, & Becker, 1976). For example, judgments of an arrow as pointing up or down are faster if "up" arrows are high in their surround and if "down" arrows are low, that is, when the semantic thrust of *up* direction and *high* position are congruent (Clark & Brownell, 1975). Both with verbal and nonverbal input, interactions between form and meaning are typical. Verbal material is often learned better if people attach pictorial (iconic) images while representing it. Many verbal learning studies find that constructing internal images aids memory, whether input is brief or lengthy (e.g., Bower, 1972; Pressley, 1976). It is still too soon to gauge the relative merits of iconic, motor, and verbal imagery as representation modes. Results will depend on task demands, on content's meaning and patterning, and on learners' skills. Verbal symbols support the lion's share of knowledge in daily life, but it is often hard to separate mediating systems. Verbal and pictorial items can interfere equally with iconic scanning, cautioning against a sharp dichotomy (Chow & Murdock, 1976). For difficult content, retention and subjective interest rise if graphic aids are used to represent verbal abstractions (Rigney & Lutz, 1976; White & Rosenthal, 1974). What seems clear is that learning results from cognitive processes and not sheer contiguity or classically conditioned bonds (Bandura & Jeffery, 1973; Langevin & Martin, 1975, Rosenthal & White, 1972). Thus, people perform intricate transformations on mental analogs of spatial inputs (Bundesen & Larsen, 1975; Cooper & Shephard, 1975). Color categories are represented by structural analogies (Rosch, 1975). Stimuli are flexibly encoded (Hawkins, Reicher, Rogers, & Peterson, 1976). A first representation may undergo multiple recodings before grouping it into higher-order units, and the microsegment's form can interact with molar organization (Spoehr & Smith, 1975).

Thus, modeled inputs are represented in diverse modes and frameworks. Imaginal and verbal mediators are prominent, but the format of cues does not fix the format of storage. Modeled events elicit visual images of serial acts and context stimuli; these can be held as inconic codes that maintain core features. Likewise, observers encode displays into condensed, summary verbal symbols. The same central processes operate in learning from overt experience. In both cases, acquisition stems from symbolic transformations of external information. Except for minimizing errors and backtracking, modeling surveys most cues perceived by performers. In both enactive and vicarious experience, the ongoing input can be too long or detailed for isomorphic storage. Some elements are promptly dismissed as irrelevant. Others are interpreted and revised into meaningful forms. Even when tasks invite rote learning, people redefine them and seek understanding (Bower, 1974; Goldberg, 1974; Rosenthal, White, & Rosenthal, 1975). Also, in both overt and vicarious learning, the representations of novel data will not long endure unless the learner evolves suitable memory codes.

Reductive memory codes maintain modeled events far better than isomorphic imagery. People who devise capsule labels to summarize complex demonstrations retain far more than those who seek to remember by duplicating the cue sequences as imaginal or verbal copies (Gerst, 1971). Memory codes may differ in form from their referents. Bandura and Jeffery (1973) taught one group to code modeled acts into number keys, and another to use a letter code. Both coding groups proved comparable, but surpassed observers who tried to improvise mnemonics. After delay, the systematic coders retained far more than the impromptu groups, which recalled little. Thus, retrieval depends on the power and availability of symbolic transforms to preserve information. Narrative and iconic facsimiles can lose data if not condensed but arbitrary codes will be forgotten unless tied to meaningful guidelines. Pictures, metaphors, analogies, and other salient illustrations bridge novel and familiar information, making it easier to store and retrieve new mediators (Royer & Cable, 1976). If observers first reduce modeled sequences

to codes, and then devise intelligible acronyms to facilitate recall of the codes, they retain much more than people who use either component strategy alone (Bandura, Jeffery, & Bachicha, 1974). After delay, retrieval covaried closely with availability of the prior codes that the dual strategy preserved best. Hence, higher-order symbols, like other mediators, depend on organizing frameworks.

External organization involves the patterning and tempo of stimuli; this may differ from the subjective organization that learners covertly apply to the events. Input arrangements interact with people's expectations and organizing styles. Memory and transfer improve when overt and covert structures harmonize. Natural patterns, forming good gestalts that mesh with past rubrics, are easier to encode and store (Bell & Handel, 1976). Haphazard sequences create weaker conceptual learning and transfer than orderly displays, but maximum external structure may not optimize storage and retrieval (Rosenthal & Zimmerman, 1973; 1976). Some degree of uncertainty can prompt learners to think, and strive harder than with overly programed tasks. Cognitive challenge can deflect distracting influences.

The component processes of memory and retrieval are not rigid. Modeling new cognitive strategies and styles can alter processing habits (Zimmerman & Rosenthal, 1974). Momentary cognitive organization hinges on many factors like subjective priorities, cue salience, social demands, and which solution strategy is chosen. The familiarity and spatial configuration of inputs may interact to shift processing tactics (Ambler & Proctor, 1976). Readers actively parse and code to fit task goals. Asked to recall sentences, people read to emphasize syntactic structures (e.g., phrase boundaries); but if asked to comprehend prose, subjects instead dwell on key semantic units (Aaronson & Scarborough, 1976). Mnemonic strategies thus govern how knowledge is approached and cognized.

No magic is needed to improve covert processing by clients or students. Apt organizing schemes and memory aids can be demonstrated, their regularities distilled by discourse, and their correct use assured by practice and corrective feedback. To learn a new language, one group was taught to connect each foreign word with a familiar English word that shared a common sound, and then to visualize the pair interacting. This cognitive rehearsal technique produced better language acquisition than having learners covertly pair words as contiguous associates (Raugh & Atkinson, 1975). Modeling results are very similar. Observers who adopt organized retention schemes outperform peers who use associative rehearsal, or who lack mnemonic codes (Bandura & Jeffery, 1973; Bandura, Jeffery, & Bachicha, 1974).

Motoric Reproduction Processes.
The third main determinant of modeling effects is motor reproduction competence. Some tasks require combining familiar, easy movements to enact very abstract plans; chess is an example. Symbolic representations and codes guide motor execution in those undertakings. Jeffery (1976) had observers watch a model assemble more and less complex sturctures. Then, learners rehearsed cognitively, or motorically with the building pieces, or had composite practice. On both structures, all symbolic organization and rehearsal surpassed purely motor practice, whose results were matched by unrehearsed controls. The outcome was unchanged after a week's delay. For such cases, once an abstract model is acquired, motor enactment is routine unless learners have physical deficits.

For other tasks, goal plans are simple but motor components demand great finess, for example, hurling the javelin or discus. In such feats, response integration depends on proprioceptive and equilibratory cues, not readily conveyed by the distal senses that inform observers. Athletes report planning and rehearsing symbolically upcoming performances (Mahoney, 1974). Such organized imagery is not perceived by spectators, although the strategy could be taught. Thus, modeling takes a smaller role in the refinement of motor skills governed by movement-contingent feedback. Apt demonstrations confine overt trials to plausible bounds; augmented feedback of learners' errors though videotaped replays aid future attempts. But overt practice and its movement effects are essential for proficiency.

Many tasks join subtle strategies with intricate motor acts, as ballet or violin recitals. Efficiency rises if concept elements are first modeled, and then motor practice given for implementation. In Jeffery's (1976) study, symbolic-then-motor rehearsal led to somewhat faster performance than the reverse sequence. Since so many intricate deeds are guided by central representation, organized solution patterns aid clients. Then, complementary motor practice can refine component movements and molar response integration.

Motivation and Incentive Processes.
The last main subprocess underlying modeling outcomes concerns motivational or reinforcement effects. Persons may attend to modeled activities, grasp their meaning, code the gist into durable symbols, retain the guidance in accessible form, and have the response competence to execute it adeptly. Yet, they will rarely perform behavior if they face unfavorable incentive conditions or expect negative sanctions for so acting. In such cases, providing positive incentives can promptly elicit overt enactment of observational learning (Bandura, 1965). Judgments about response consequences do not just dictate what acts to perform and when. Incentive expectations also steer acquisition by prompting selective attention, deliberate coding, and active rehearsal if the modeled patterns promise high utilitarian value (Masters, Gordon, & Clark, 1976).

Reward operations do not stamp in the behavior that precedes them, or assure better performance. Incentives have informative effects and, like other sources of information, are symbolized and weighted before they can guide action (Bandura, 1977a). Thus, depressives may have acquired deficits in aiming deeds at future rewards (Miller & Seligman, 1975). Cognizing response-reward contingencies often controls patients' behavior more strongly than applying reinforcers (Resick, Forehand, & Peed, 1974). If people accept task goals, and are not deterred by negative expectations, the offer or delivery of rewards may have little or no effect (Zimmerman & Rosenthal, 1974). Under special conditions, rewards may do harm. Communal incentives can prompt threats that further handicap laggards (Axelrod, 1973). When people are rewarded for undertaking activities irrespective of quality of performance, the rewards may lower elective persistence (Lepper & Greene, 1975; Ross, 1976). If tasks are redefined as toil, performance and demeanor can suffer (Garbarino,

1975). Such anomalies may occur if attention fixates on incentive features, arousing consummatory sets that detract from instrumental activity.

In any case, rewards bear no absolute valence. Like other events they are weighed in reference to one's adaptation level. Contextual factors that provide standards for comparison, and social equity norms defining fair play, also decide the net worth of a reinforcer. Scarce or plentiful supply, and what partners earn for equivalent performance, will alter the value of raises and praise alike. Satisfaction with a given outcome is relative to others' payoffs and changes when attributed to skill versus chance (Brickman, 1975). Likewise, self-chosen reward schedules motivate stronger response than externally imposed wages in some task settings, but not others (Bandura, 1976b; Weiner & Dubanoski, 1975).

At times, no amount of structured guidance will sustain behavioral involvement unless inducements are provided (Miller, Hersen, & Eisler, 1974). But often rewards are the only source of feedback supplied. Then, performance gains mediated by informative value of reward may be attributed to incentive control. When informative and incentive functions of rewards are separated, clients may learn as well without tangible payoffs (Rosenthal & Kellogg, 1973), and cognitive supports can far exceed reinforcer effects (Zimmerman & Rosenthal, 1974). Such data, and the relativity of valence, should caution therapists against overreliance on incentive inducements. In most cases, far more than needing token points or weekend passes to reward specific performances, people whose lives seem a hopeless morass need (1) cognitive guides that depict their obstacles and options accurately, (2) solution routes that lead in attainable steps from their current status to a more effective level of functioning, and (3) the cognitive and social skills to implement such plans. The subprocesses governing modeled phenomena provide categories to identify deficits, and to suggest apt correctives by modeling and other procedures.

Guided Practice and Corrective Feedback.
Demonstrations and instructions are fine means to impart informative rules and to illustrate their use. Therapy does not end when clients grasp

exemplary principles or solutions. They need help to apply knowledge until they gain secure mastery in diverse situations, to assure transfer skills and to confirm positive self-expectations. Just as modeling prevents gross flaws in approach, and reduces trial-and-error fumblings, so does guided practice. Before coping unaided, clients usually need guided practice with corrective feedback and encouragement. Errors are promply corrected and not allowed to grow habitual or to alter clients' lives detrimentally. A problem with interview insights, even when cogent, is that people are not then aided to devise or execute applications. Clients may ignore them, or translate meanings into rash or clumsy acts that foster new stresses. Structured plans and rehearsal are called for. Typically, combining modeling with guided practice exceeds each method alone (Bandura, 1977b; Zimmerman & Rosenthal, 1974). Feedback can boost cognitive rehearsal, which is better than passive information-processing (Diamond, Steadman, Harada, & Rosenthal, 1975).

Further, therapists' corrective feedback and guidance aid clients' self-regulation on later independent attempts. With many hierarchical skills to integrate, neglecting early mishaps invites steep cumulative costs. So does inattention to personal factors. One does not promote more tolerant self-conceptions, nor inspire respect, by modeling stern fixation on technical milestones. Time gaps between developing and using new skills can long delay gratifications. Unless faith and trust in the therapist can bridge such strains, clients may exit before the fruits of a superbly conceived program grow visible.

REMOVING FEARS AND INHIBITIONS THROUGH MODELING

Modeling techniques can reduce fears and overt avoidance in diverse phobias and related conditions. Once clients are willing to undertake formerly inhibited acts, graded exposures can diminish remaining doubts and instill the benefits of firsthand mastery.

Conditions Maintaining Avoidance
It was once axiomatic that traumatic learning created defensive, "neurotic" conduct. Noxious

events gave associated cues the capacity to elicit autonomic arousal which, in turn, was reduced by instrumental activities that kept one from the locus of fear. By stimulus generalization, anxiety spread on multiple dimensions to related events. By response generalization, avoidant acts fanned out from conduct originally punished to related behavior. This dual-process theory, hinging on physiological arousal and peripheral regulation, has been questioned on grounds discussed elsewhere (Bandura, 1977a; Rachman, 1976). First, much fear learning occurs from observation and not direct experience (Bandura, Blanchard, & Ritter, 1969; Bandura & Menlove, 1968; Fazio, 1972; Rachman, 1974). Second, anxiety and overt avoidance are not strongly linked (Orenstein & Carr, 1975; Riccio & Silvestri, 1973); changes in one system need not alter the other (Black, 1965; Schroeder & Rich, 1976). Third, surgical removal of autonomic feedback capability in animals has little effect on the acquisition of avoidance behavior. Maintenance of avoidance behavior is even less dependent on autonomic feedback (Rescorla & Solomon, 1967). Such cognitive regulators as expectations, social reactions, and situational clues are major influences on emotion (Calvert-Boyanowsky & Leventhal, 1975; Rogers & Deckner, 1975). Since central events can activate and maintain bodily arousal, affective labeling, and defensive strategems, avoidance rests largely on semantic cues and symbolic inferences.

Thus, a family resemblance exists between the information-processing operations discussed earlier and the variables that maintain avoidance. The perceived locus of dangers will depend on what cues are selectively attended to and coded as threats, and on categorical similarities in form, function, or meaning that extend avoidance from initial instances to generalized classes. Sensitization effects—that is, weak response until several aversive exposures to a stimulus class have cumulative impact—may perhaps require grouping the inputs as allied.[1]

People dwell on danger cues in order to fend them off. But in so doing, they rehearse worries and prepare escapes that validate and vivify the threats. Sharp distinctions are made among stimuli never encountered, which are often considered as the worst because multiple negative aspects logically demand additive effects. Clients envision their failures, panics, embarrassment, and physical distress. Such cognitive practice can raise autonomic arousal, further validating the avoidance and confirming self-appraisals of weakness or incompetence to cope with the avoided. Also, repeated rehearsal of anticipatory dangers can spur positive feedback cycles that magnify arousal (Eysenck, 1976).

Relearning that cognized threats are less formidable, and habituating to them, are precluded by active efforts to prevent contact. Corrective feedback is ruled out by avoidance. Negative perceptions, and beliefs that one cannot manage certain endeavors, may go unchallenged. If parents, peers, or spouses will not accept the defensive behavior, they may reduce the pattern by coaxing, coercing, and otherwise prompting approach. But if they defer to, encourage, or themselves share the avoidance tendencies, they may support it by special concessions to clients' limitations. Such sympathetic attention to the sufferer, easing of duties, and excuses to escape demands peripheral to the defensive pattern, can further reward avoidance. At times, truly aversive or hazardous fates are thus averted. Far more often, secondary gains are trivial compared to the impoverished experience, self-critical evaluation, social stigma, and convoluted detours imposed by avoidance behavior. In any case, the therapy task is to restore competence and a sense of personal mastery in dealing with feared events.

Vicarious Procedures

Because defensive behavior is largely maintained by cognitive preparations to ward off anticipated dangers, fear reduction depends on changing the

---

[1]Given the volume and complexity of informational traffic, some errors in grouping and retrieving information within and between classes is inevitable. Slips of the pen or tongue may hinge on extracting items, not entirely on the conceptual focus, from overlapping categories. So may wit, for example, James Joyce's quip about youthful sexuality, "When we were jung and easily freudened." Cognitive slippage sometimes ascribed to "unconscious" phenomena may stem from similar causes, especially when intense arousal burdens subtle symbolic tuning mechanisms.

covert meanings that regulate response to overt events. When safe, successful approach steps are directly enacted, threatening stimuli are progressively redefined as harmless by performers. Events once construed as aversive become neutral (e.g., heights, small animals), or are viewed as means to satisfactions (e.g., driving, swimming, social interaction). Much of the information created by direct approach is available to observers who witness models engage in feared acts, or who cognitively practice equivalent symbolic facsimiles. Through observation, clients can rehearse symbolically the feared activities that share many features of direct approach. Such efforts are steps enroute to eventual performance, and weaken the customary inhibitory pattern. Clients can also provide themselves with positive feedback, similar to what is derived from overt action. For fear extinction to occur in any therapy, cognitive regulators must be altered. External danger is trivial compared to dire symbolic representations and their defensive effects. The physical features of writhing snakes, dark rooms, and steep mountain trails remain constant before and after treatment. Fear is eliminated when the perception, meaning, and anticipatory sets triggered by environmental events no longer signify threat. The nominal source of disinhibiting feedback counts far less than its impact on client's cognitive processes. New information may stem from direct contacts, observation of models' direct contacts, or purely imaginal rehearsal of contacts. But the locus of extinction is symbolic in each case. What changes is the predictive value of environmental events—their subjective meaning and judgments about their implications for action. When vicarious exposures lower avoidance enough that clients will attempt overt coping, direct experiences create further positive feedback until confident mastery is achieved.

Overt Modeling.
Fearful observers profit from viewing others perform threatening activities. Much research shows that observing live or filmed models can extinguish timorous conduct and affect, partly or totally, depending on the intensity of clients' avoidant behavior. Instead of hoping for insights to transfer from consulting room to real life, or awaiting spon-

taneous encounters to elicit approach, the therapist fosters response enactment by structured demonstrations. With phobic children, live and filmed modeling in which peers interacted calmly with feared objects brought similar gains (Bandura, Grusec, & Menlove, 1967; Bandura & Menlove, 1968). Restored approach competence transferred to new test situations and was maintained in follow-up tests. Socially anxious, withdrawn toddlers viewed a film of peers who first watched and then gradually took part in enjoyable group activities. The observers later increased their level of interpersonal interaction, unlike matched controls who remained isolates (O'Connor, 1969). Next, contingent reward for social participation was contrasted with filmed modeling. Whether given rewards or not, the groups having the benefit of modeling commenced interaction faster, and maintained sociability at follow-up. The rewarded group reverted to withdrawal, interacting at the level of untreated, control isolates (O'Connor, 1972).

Adults and adolescents presenting various inhibitions have benefitted from similar overt modeling. Vicarious extinction of fears, and behavioral disinhibition, have been found with severe animal phobias (e.g., Bandura & Barab, 1973; Bandura, Blanchard, & Ritter, 1969; Blanchard, 1970), with examination anxiety (e.g., Jaffe & Carlson, 1972; Mann, 1972), with compulsive rituals (Rachman, Hodgson, & Marks, 1971), and with sexual underresponsiveness (Wincze & Caird, 1976). Other examples of overt modeling producing vicarious gains are given below, in studies comparing alternative modeling treatments. Recent trends suggest that modeling is being included in multicomponent, composite programs to successfully remove inhibitions, such as phobic reactions to air travel (Denholtz & Mann, 1975) and social communication (Wright, 1976).

Covert and Symbolic Alternatives.
If reduction in fears and inhibitions depends on the cognitive formulations and preparatory responses that people generate toward external events (rather than on automatic control by peripheral cues), symbolic counterparts of overt experiences should produce many of the same effects. In principle, if equivalent meanings result from direct, observed,

and imagined approach sequences, there should be no outcome differences among the alternative modes of exposure. Particular guidance formats may diverge in the vividness, plausibility, and clarity of the information they impart. Some messages will have greater impact than others. The organization of content, its personal appeal, and client characteristics may favor one mode over another. However, when variant forms of treatment have similar symbolic effects, clients should benefit equally despite differences in the vehicles conveying the information. Thus, cognitively visualizing a modeling episode, or properly interpreting directions that specify similar covert approach steps, should have consequences akin to scrutinizing a model's behavioral portrayals.

In fact, with cognitively sophisticated college samples, covertly imagining models enact approach scenarios has had salutary results. For example, Kazdin (1973, 1974a, 1974b) instructed snake-fearful students to imagine people engaging in progressive contacts with serpents. Approach behavior increased and fearfulness declined after the cognitive modeling. Differences in the status and demeanor of the symbolic models produced outcomes that paralleled those from comparable variations used with overt modeling. Similar covert modeling benefits have been obtained with socially timid, submissive clients. Those who visualized models deal forcefully with interpersonal situations reduced inhibitions more than untreated controls. When the performers and the response consequences for social expressiveness were varied in imagination, differential treatment outcomes were found (Kazdin, 1974c, 1975, 1976). A group that imagined modeled acts earning reward elaborated the content of scenes more than did a no reward condition, but qualitative nuances of imagery failed to alter extinction (Kazdin, 1976).

In direct comparisons to date, overt and covert therapeutic modeling arrays have yielded equivalent benefits with college samples. Cautela, Flannery, and Hanely (1974) report that imaginal modeling and observing live modeling produce comparable results, although the latter treatment reduced fear and achieved terminal performances more effectively. Functional equivalence of methods was found among women afraid to resist infringements of their rights. Although all conditions made gains, viewing overt demonstrations of protecting personal interests was no better than a group that imagined the same modeling scenes, or another group that imagined the scenes recast as individually tailored episodes (Rosenthal & Reese, 1976). Students proved readily able to represent cognitively the content of modeling scenarios in both foregoing studies.

Obviously, further confirmation that cognitive modeling compares favorably with overt demonstrations would argue for the covert technique on utilitarian grounds. Reliance on images is simpler and more efficient than are behavioral demonstrations. Also, difficult to arrange resources like access to airplanes, public speaking practice forums, or remote locales, could be reserved for direct mastery trials after vicarious extinction has made its contribution. Several boundary constraints on covert modeling need further checking. If clients' symbolic facility is poor, imagined activities may lack fidelity compared to overt demonstration. Thus, young children (Rosenthal & Zimmerman, 1972) and retardates (Forehand & Yoder, 1974; Rosenthal & Kellogg, 1973) have processed actual examples better than symbolic facsimiles. Likewise, many activities may be too intricate for people to address in fantasy (consider the skein of conditional rejoinders needed to aptly handle a stressful employment interview), or may be too threatening for very avoidant clients to represent accurately early in treatment. Such instances invite fantasy errors in adept enactment, but are also the cases where distortions seem hardest for therapists to monitor, detect, and rectify promptly. Hence, research is needed to clarify the problems and client characteristics that admit or discourage the use of covert modeling techniques. However, clinical evidence that overt and symbolic demonstrations can promote similar changes sheds light on how therapeutic outcomes are mediated.

Source of Information and Functional Redundancy

Observationally achieved gains illustrate that overt response is not required to diminish fear and avoidance. Covert modeling gains illustrate that useful guidance can be extracted from multiple informative channels. This further suggests that common central mechanisms underlie many externally distinctive brands of therapy. Therapist-defined procedures count less than client-defined meanings to determine functional similarities and differences among alternative methods. Not that procedural permuations are trivial—or that research comparing specific format variations is contraindicated! But until there is better understanding of the variables that control how clients interpret, and act on, therapeutic influences, it will not be surprising if plausible variations in method foster negligible outcome differences. For example, there is reason to doubt that the best organized task will necessarily surpass structuring that forces learners to make some active efforts to organize things for themselves (e.g., Battig, 1972). Moreover, the ordering of training sequences has complex effects on learning and transfer, depending on the specific task procedures (Rosenthal & Zimmerman, 1973, 1976). Thus, exclusive focus on presenting complaints need not be the optimal strategy for constructing modeling displays. Some groups of phobic clients only witnessed modeled episodes based on their respective problems. Other groups instead received one-third as many exposures drawn from handicaps, and on the remaining trials viewed approach scenes not of major concern to them. Yet both content variations produced equal vicarious extinction of the target complaints (Linehan, Rosenthal, Kelley, & Theobald, in press). Such data exemplify the conceptual gap between intuitively plausible expectations and symbolic processes that govern behavioral progress. Sometimes variations in the sequencing of component steps will lead observers to adopt divergent standards. Those, in turn, can produce complex treatment outcomes that depend on which modeling variables are selected for study or are ignored (Feist & Rosenthal, 1973).

Related to the therapy impact of specific event structures is the puzzle of untangling causation if multiple interventions share common meanings. The assets and shortcomings of a treatment element will hinge not only on its virtues, but on the context in which it is introduced and its effects measured. The guidance value of a procedure administered by itself will differ from its worth if assessed relative to other options, redundant in information, which accompany, precede, or follow it. For example, clinical studies find that a first intervention usually promotes more change than procedures that follow afterward (Boulougouris, Marks, & Marset, 1971; Watson & Marks, 1971). This probably occurs because all the variance shared by related precedures will be preempted by the initially applied method. It will create the changes that could largely be prompted by any of its functional counterparts, thereby imposing a ceiling effect on their common contributions: later procedures that provide redundant information will only add appreciably if they also control variance not highly correlated with the common factor. Such primacy effects are especially likely in crossover designs, and when a narrowly defined element is placed after, or added to, another technique. In that case, operations that are helpful by themselves may appear weak, even though inverting the sequence of procedures might qualify or reverse the results (Blanchard, 1970; McFall & Twentyman, 1973; Mann, 1972). To prevent misleading conclusions, perhaps the simplest expedient would be to routinely counterbalance serial position among related procedures. But this will pose problems when the organization of treatment procedures is governed by logical, stylistic, or pragmatic constraints.

The issues discussed above are often neglected or misunderstood. For example, Marks' chapter in this handbook dwells on the element of exposure to threats in modeling therapies to reduce fear. No meaningful treatment of fearful behavior, whatever its form, can be applied devoid of exposure—whether it is direct, vicarious, or symbolic—to what people fear. Since it is impossible for a treatment to be directed at a void, the notion of exposure reduces to the simple observation that reduction of fearful behavior requires some commerce with fear-relevant stimuli. One can, of course, have fearful people engage in activities in which they are provided with no opportunities to interact with feared objects, to observe others do so, or to confront what they fear in imaginal representation. Such a procedure would be regarded as a handy control condition but a nonsensical treatment.

Both acquisitional modeling and disinhibitory

modeling serve as ways of transmitting information, but they alter behavior though different types of information. Acquisitional modeling informs observers on how response elements are synthesized into new patterns. From observing others, one forms a conception of how new behavior patterns are performed and on later occasions the symbolic construction serves as a guide for action. Disinhibitory modeling operates through the information it conveys about personal efficacy and the consequences of approach responses. Contrary to Marks, the term modeling has never been used as synonymous with exposure. Disinhibitory modeling has always been explicitly defined in terms of observing actions performed toward threatening objects *without any untoward consequences to the model* (Bandura, 1969).

Experiments can be performed to demonstrate that modeling nonsensical and irrelevant behaviors involving no commerce with threats does not reduce fearful behavior. Marks cites several studies of this type. The findings of such studies say more about the irrelevance of the research than about the effectiveness or processes of disinhibitory modeling. The substantial evidence already reviewed demonstrates that modeling provides an effective mode for transmitting information about personal efficacy and the likely consequences of approach responses. Such information reduces fear. Control conditions expressly designed to assess the effects of exposure to threatening objects show that exposure alone has negligible effects (Bandura, Grusec, & Menlove, 1967; Kazdin, 1973, 1974a, 1975).

The judgments expressed by Marks regarding disinhibitory modeling rest heavily on arbitrary relabeling of treatments. For example, two versions of modeling in which subjects observe either themselves or others successfully executing approach responses are transformed into "modeling" versus "nonmodeling" categories. Since the two versions yield comparable results, the arbitrary dichotomy is interpreted to show that modeling has no effects. The data, however, merely affirm that similar modeling treatments (visualizing approach responses without adverse consequences) produce similar outcomes. In other examples, modeling is arbitrarily wedded to irrelevant activities but divorced from relevant performances. In treating clients who are

obsessed over dirt contamination, seeing a therapist relax is designated as modeling, whereas observing a therapist engage in soiling activites is labeled as "the therapist expose(s) herself to contaminating situations." Since observing irrelevances (e.g., relaxation or hearing former clients describe variable improvements) does not change obsessions or agoraphobias, modeling is again judged unhelpful. Other judgments of comparative efficacy are derived from studies of redundant treatments that confound order of administration or include modeling as unrecognized elements in the alternative formats. Arbitrary analytic practices create confusions, spurious disputes, and trivialize substantive issues of importance.

The issue of interest is not whether a viable treatment does or does not include exposure, but rather the form the transactions with the threats take, the information derived from those transactions, and the mechanisms by which the transactions produce changes in behavior. The descriptive concept of "interactional exposure" has no explanatory value and little predictive utility. No one would argue with the notion that duration of commerce with feared stimuli is a variable that can affect behavioral change. However, when one examines this conception for more specific predictions, it yields little.

According to Marks, approach to feared objects is the critical ingredient in interactional exposure. Actually, it is not the interactional exposure but the effects of interaction that form the critical factor in reducing fears and defensive behavior. Interactional exposures that produce injurious consequences create and reinforce fears and inhibitions; interactions that result in personal mastery and beneficial outcomes eliminate fears and inhibitions.

Gross variations in amount of exposure to threats without adverse consequences will ordinarily produce some differences at the group level. That is, participants who deal with threats for five hours will, *as a group,* usually achieve greater change than those who are treated for one hour. But "exposure" is of no value either in explaining or in predicting the wide variations in behavioral changes exhibited by clients who have received the same amount of exposure. Regardless of whether the treatment involves desensitization, flooding, rational emotiveness, cognitive restructuring, or any other method one might wish to insert, the standard finding is marked variation in behavior under the same duration of treatment. Nor is exposure of much help in predicting changes in behavior achieved through different forms of treatment. Enactive mastery produces substantially better results, in much shorter periods of exposure, than does symbolic mastery (Bandura, 1977b; Bandura, Blanchard, & Ritter, 1969). Although enactive and imaginal formats both involve "interactional exposure," it is the modality through which self-efficacy and outcome information is conveyed, not exposure, that is the useful predictor. Exposure is best considered as a quantitative variable (e.g., the amount of time spent confronting threatening stimuli if therapies diverge in this respect) and not as an explanatory construct, or as a categorical basis to distinguish among treatment strategies.

Research conducted within the social learning framework, to be reviewed later, lends substantial validity to the theory that psychological influences alter defensive behavior by enhancing the level and strength of perceived self-efficacy (Bandura, 1977b). By encompassing all modalities through which efficacy information is conveyed (i.e., enactive, vicarious, exhortative, and emotive), this conceptualization provides a common theoretical framework for explaining and predicting behavioral changes accompanying diverse modes of treatment. Thus, efficacy expectations predict with high accuracy variations in improvement between and within treatments, and even the rate of improvement during the course of treatment.

Marks suggests that self-efficacy may reflect a "fearful attitude." As we have previously noted, the findings of different lines of research lend little support to the view that fear regulates defensive behavior. Fear and avoidance are not closely related. Both are effects of some other cause. In the social learning theory of anxiety, it is mainly perceived lack of efficacy for managing potentially aversive situations that makes them fearsome. People are afraid of things they cannot cope with, but they do not find them fearsome if they believe they can manage them. A weak sense of efficacy can thus produce both fear and defensive behavior. Empirical tests support the view that perceived self-

efficacy mediates fear (Bandura & Adams, 1977). High self-efficacy is associated with weak anticipatory fear and low fear arousal during performance of threatening activities.

Attributes of Models.

People are more likely to process and implement information transmitted by social sources who compel attention (Grusec & Skubiski, 1970; Yussen, 1974), who deserve trust (Beutler, Johnson, Neville, Elkins, & Jobe, 1975; McGarry & West, 1975; Raw, 1976), who appear realistic reference figures to compare with oneself (Brown, Brown, & Danielson, 1975; Festinger, 1954, Kanfer, Karoly, & Newman, 1974), who depict consensus in a sample of individuals (Bandura & Menlove, 1968; Kazdin, 1975, 1976), and whose conduct offers plausible standards to guide observers' aspirations (Bandura, 1976b; Kazdin, 1974b; Rosenthal & White, 1972; Thelen & Kirkland, 1976). In essence, models' impact will be positive functions of their *relevance* and *credibility* for observers.

However, the specific operations that determine models' impact will vary with context, and depend on clients' inferences and standards of comparison. Coping models, who begin by sharing some of clients' fears or failings but progressively gain poise and confidence, typically surpass mastery models, who start with faultless expertise (Meichenbaum, 1971; Kazdin, 1973, 1974b). A coping model first mirrors clients' own woes (more relevance), but also, people who overcome handicaps and shift toward success earn positive social judgments (Levine, Ranelli, & Valle, 1974). Exceptions occur if coping models display excessive distress, social distance from observers, or both.

To the extent that coping models facilitate boldness in others, the effects are probably achieved by increasing expectations of personal efficacy rather than by the modeled fearfulness. It is possible to capitalize on the benefits of model similarity without temporarily exacerbating fear arousal by exposure to frightened models. The similarity can be presented historically by depicting the skilled model as a person who had previously suffered similar fears that were successfully eliminated through treatment. In this type of approach, which is a common rehabilitation practice among self-help groups, model mastery of problems is portrayed historically rather than enacted currently.

Within limits, model-client similarity (e.g., in age, sex, or needs) improves vicarious outcomes (Kazdin, 1974a; Kornhaber & Schroeder, 1975; Thelen, Dollinger, & Roberts, 1975). Such results suggest that peers who have solved, or share, common problems are effective tutors. Some efforts to test peer systems have worked well (e.g., Fremouw & Harmatz, 1975; Nelson, Worrell, & Polsgrove, 1973) and invite further extensions (Rosenthal, 1976), yet, diversity in social exemplars is helpful. Progress is greater if clients observe multiple models performing the feared activities (Bandura & Menlove, 1968; Marburg, Houston, & Holmes, 1976) and also when models occupy a range of positions relative to the client's status (Kazdin, 1975, 1976).

In contrast, models' personality styles have had negligible effects (Bandura, Blanchard, & Ritter, 1969; Mann & Rosenthal, 1969), unless harsh or otherwise inappropriate (Vernon, 1974). A warm, nurturant model elicited more incidental emulation by chronic psychotics, but no better task progress than a neutral model (Chartier & Ainley, 1974). In treatment with neurotics, warm, and neutral model roles proved equal, but both surpassed a cold model group that gained no more than untreated controls (Goldstein, Martens, Hubben, Van Belle, Schaaf, Wiersma, & Goedhart, 1973). Because models are usually perceived as assistants to the therapist, who is (or should be) warm and supportive, clients will extend trust to models if not clearly unmerited. Thus, models' personal traits seem less critical than how well their aptitudes and behavior provide cogent guidelines.

When models grossly depart from plausible conduct (Vernon, 1974), clients are more likely to define therapuetic influences in ways not intended by therapists. Because therapists' social influence will depend on their credibility, and can count more in treatment than permutations of method (Russell, Armstrong, & Patel, 1976), the clients' viewpoint must be taken into account. Ambiguity or doubt can raise people's vulnerability to threats even if degree of perceived similarity to the model has no effect (Brown, 1974). The situational set or definition that clients adopt can greatly alter what the influences signify, and lead to different results, despite constancy in modeled performance. Thus, observers who empathized with their model reacted quite unlike others who took a detached, onlooker role (Aderman, Brehm, & Katz, 1974; Regan & Totten, 1975). As with the loose coupling between fearful affect and avoidant acts, the linkage between modeled events and observer response depends on the stance, interpretation, and expectancies that patients adopt.

Common Features in Variant Symbolic Procedures.

Similar information and meaningful inferences can be drawn from many permutations of input. Hence, it is not surprising if symbolic modeling produces much the same results as related guidance techniques bearing other labels like systematic desensitization, role-playing, and flooding. Nominal format differences may prompt contrasting brandnames that emphasize superficial distinctions but obscure basic commonalities. Ordinarily, all such methods share a number of important treatment features that overlap substantially in form, organization, substance, and functional consequences. These common aspects include: (1) *situational settings and goals.* Clients enter treatment with the aim of changing certain patterns of behavior. (2) *Encounters with beneficial feedback.* Clients observe, imagine, or simulate restored contact with threats, and gain appropriate performance skills, by symbolic rehearsal with corrective guidance under protected conditions. (3) *Organized presentation formats.* The treatment procedures are directed at actively developing or restoring competence, using orderly sequences of steps clients can grasp. Whether for symbolic, simulate, or actual practice, the essential components of the desired behavior are mapped and transmitted coherently, usually in graded stepwise progression. Therapists often supply guiding rationales to explain why treatment elements will assist the client. (4) *Inferential parallels for self-directed efforts.* Whatever the specific treatment procedures, similar core implications are conveyed: to increase contacts with the formerly avoided, to speak up for oneself, to converse with companions in ways that are mutually interesting, to negotiate compromises with partners about budgeting, sexual conduct, childcare, and so on. All these features, and (5) *social influence* exerted by the therapist, occur in most behavioral psychotherapies. As with other types of information, a range of social sources and influence formats can lead to comparable molar effects (Simpson, Rosenthal, Daniel, & White, in press).

Sometimes, the special hallmark of one therapy is equally applicable to variant brands. For example, implosion rests on a strategy of presenting high intensity fantasy items at the outset. Within limits, this may be an efficient technique (e.g., Boudewyns, 1975; Emberle, Rehm, & McBurney, 1975), because stringent instances create judgmental displacement of the remaining items (i.e., "contrast effects"). After visualizing a jeering, hostile audience, clients will by contrast weight public speeches under usual clasroom conditions as relatively innocuous, even if the more dramatic trappings of implosion fail to enhance progress (White, Rosenthal, & Gerber, 1975). However, the perceived contrast produced by intense items as standards are not specific to the implosion method. The same strategy can be adapted to desensitization hierarchies (as flooding), to modeled episodes, or to role-playing routines.

The difference between self and another as actor can be important, especially on overt trials where one's own poise is far more relevant than a stranger's. With symbolic trials, frightened clients may at times find it more plausible if a model meets the peak challenges than if they try to visualize themselves coping with terrifying events. However, videotaped models were no better than desensitization scenes for removing spider fears (Denney & Sullivan, 1976). Observing a performer overcome social inhibitions, imagining a model perform instead, and imagining oneself as the actor can produce the same changes (Rosenthal & Reese, 1976). Further, in actual clinical practice, many therapists elaborate desensitization items to generalize their content, increase their vividness, and expand clients' perception of sustained, correct participation. Under such conditions, desensitization and symbolic modeling may not only yield indistinguishable benefits, but may involve substantially identical cognitive events. Research comparing direct with vicarious desensitization of test anxious students has found equivalent results whether observers watched videotapes or treatment given to live peers, and whether clients were treated individually or in groups (Denney, 1974; Mann & Rosenthal, 1969).

Although various studies (e.g., Borkovec, Kaloupek, & Slama, 1975) have confirmed the value of relaxation training, its inclusion or exclusion has not greatly altered comparative outcomes. Relaxation does not enhance the effects achieved by live modeling (Bandura, Grusec, & Menlove, 1967) or symbolic modeling (Bandura, Blanchard, & Ritter, 1968). Vicarious desensitization gains were unchanged if the relaxation component was omitted, and whether or not observers actively copied the model's responses (Mann, 1972). In a test with small animal fears, symbolic modeling progress rose by slender margins if supplemented by relaxation (Denney & Sullivan, 1976).

Likewise, when modeled and role-played simulations were combined, improvement has been somewhat better than, or just equal to, desensitization, depending on which response measures are examined (e.g., Curran & Gilbert, 1975; Marzillier, Lambert, & Kellett, 1976). Similar marginal differences were found in comparisons between symbolic modeling and flooding (Rachman, Marks, & Hodgson, 1973). But adding versus omitting a modeling tape (Emmelkamp & Emmelkamp-Benner, 1975), or terminal response demonstrations (McFall & Twentyman, 1973), had no effect when largely redundant with other guidance procedures that were also given. Sometimes, related but competing procedures overlap in major themes, yet vary in so many details, that crediting an advantage to one or another approach becomes arbitrary (e.g., Lira, Nay, McCollough, & Etkin, 1975; McFall & Twentyman, 1973). However, when alternative methods provide distinct sources of influence, combining procedures will typically surpass each separate component. Videotaped playback of self-modeled behavior added to narrative commentaries was far more useful than the purely verbal feedback alone (Edelson & Seidman, 1975). Opposed response-prevention methods both improved when either was joined with modeling (Boersma, Den Hengst, Dekker, & Emmelkamp, 1976). If we had some means to compute the coefficients of overlap among alternative methods, they might facilitate selecting elements for composite programs rationally. A simple, pragmatic hypothesis is proposed: unless procedures are structurally incompatible (e.g., imaginal flooding and desensitization), the less covariation between two effective treatments, the better their combination, and vice versa.

In related spheres, contingent and noncontingent covert (imagined) reward and fantasy exposure without reward were equally helpful but all exceeded an attention-placebo control group (Hurley, 1976). This again illustrates the weakness of incentive prompts if clients grasp treatment meanings and concur with their implications. Pitted against each other, contingent praise assisted much less than precise feedback for overcoming phobic avoidance (Leitenberg, Agras, Allen, Butz, & Edwards, 1975). Under naturalistic conditions, people's ability to benefit from new experience depends on being able to discriminate their performance by assessing its strengths and failings, and to apply that information to guide future efforts constructively. Thus, monetary loss or gain contingent on stuttering acts had trivial impact compared with training to use self-observation and recording as feedback devices (Lanyon & Barocas, 1975).

Equivocal at first blush, all the foregoing data taken together provide further evidence for the importance of human information-processing. Comparing covert, filmed, and live symbolic modeling, or any of those with desensitization, flooding, or simulated role-plays, one finds roughly equal outcomes. Those, in turn, reflect the functional overlap of information provided by the methods as well as commonalities in the mediating events that underlie client changes. What does appear to make a major difference is whether treatment is confined to facsimile conditions or, instead, is moved out into the natural contexts and provides clients with practiced skills to deal effectively with the problems they face in daily living.

Participant Modeling

"Nothing succeeds like success." Folk wisdom (The proof of the pudding . . .") has long asserted the hazards of extrapolating from the potential to the achieved. Clients who observe others or im-

agine themselves renewing contact with avoided situations must still put simulated progress to actual test. People often doubt that they can "really" tolerate enclosed spaces or mount steep heights unless actual trials confirm restored ability. Desensitization clients sometimes worry that fantasied advances will be refuted when they ultimately face what they fear (Karoly, 1974). Only direct confrontation, if performed adequately, can fully remove such concerns. Even taking a few overt contacts in stride may leave lingering doubts. Clients need evidence of some sustained mastery with a range of real instances before they can firmly accept that success in first encounters was not a fluke. Treatment is incomplete until clients are confident they will be able to perform adeptly on future occasions, when alone and unaided (Röper & Rachman, 1976).

Contrary to the widely accepted view that all forms of treatment are equally effective (Luborsky, Singer, & Luborsky, 1975), some treatment approaches are decidedly more powerful than others. Most of the behavioral treatments developed in recent years have been implemented either through performance or by symbolic procedures. Regardless of the methods involved, results of comparative studies attest to the superiority of performance-based treatments (Bandura, 1977b). Performance desensitization produces substantially greater behavioral change than does symbolic desensitization (LoPicollo, 1970; Sherman, 1972; Strahley, 1966). Real encounters with threats are superior to imagined exposure (Emmelkamp & Wessels, 1975; Stern & Marks, 1973; Rabavilas, Boulougouris & Stefanis, 1976; Watson, Mullet, & Pillay, 1973). Participant modeling, which uses successful performance as the primary vehicle of change, is much more effective than modeling alone (Bandura, Blanchard, & Ritter, 1969; Blanchard, 1970; Lewis, 1974; Ritter, 1969; Röper, Rachman, & Marks, 1975), symbolic desensitization (Bandura, Blanchard, & Ritter, 1969; Litvak, 1969), and cognitive modeling (Thase & Moss, 1976). Further, clients who only make partial improvement after facsimile contacts promptly attain complete recoveries when subsequently administered modeling with guided participation (Bandura, Blanchard, & Ritter, 1969; Thase & Moss, 1976).

Participant modeling programs eliminate separation in time or context between demonstrations and guided practice elements. Clients and therapists work at a graded hierarchy of tasks that eventually leads to mastery of feared activities. At each step the therapist exemplifies the relevant activity while the client observes, then accompanies the client during performance until the client gains enough skill and self-assurance to attempt the task alone. Once clients can handle formerly threatening situations on their own with relative comfort, more difficult tasks are introduced. The same stategy is applied until the hardest steps are eventually completed. At that stage, further independent practice is supplied until clients have mastered several different instances by themselves, and expect they can tackle successfully any plausible future encounters (Bandura, Jeffery, & Gajdos, 1975). Treatment continues as long as needed for clients to confirm overt competence and a strong sense of personal efficacy.

A number of technical features allow therapy to commence in the natural setting. First, the presence of the therapist is a source of comfort and support (Epley, 1974). Even in a simplified situation, clients accompanied by the therapist are able to approach feared stimuli more closely than those who performed while the therapist, only a few feet distant, watched (Feist & Rosenthal, 1973). Second, pains are taken to reduce the client's inhibitions and distress during overt attempts by means of diversified response induction aids (Bandura, Jeffery, & Wright, 1974). Even profoundly inhibited acts can usually be elicited if their form, context, or duration is modified to match clients' tolerance. Initially, claustrophobics might endure confinement for just seconds, with intervals gradually lengthening until minutes and later hours can be tolerated. Verbal or physical reassurance from the therapist can reduce avoidance and arousal during early trials, before clients are willing to attempt the subtask on their own (Ritter, 1968, 1969).

The severity and type of problem will determine the specific performance aids that may be required. A program to remove driving inhibitions might start with brief trips on secluded streets in minimal traffic, advance to longer drives on more active routes with scattered traffic, and culminate in lengthy ex-

cursions on crowded freeways under difficult weather conditions. The same dimensional principles are applied to graduating and structuring the components of active practice tasks. Some data suggest that stepwise increase in task difficulty has advantages over immediately facing the client with intensely demanding performances (Boersma, Den Hengst, & Emmelkamp, 1976; Emmelkamp, 1974), but this will depend on the severity of clients' handicaps and the range of situations spanned in the hierarchy (Kirsch, Wolpin, & Knutson, 1975; Rankin, 1976). Clients who abandon appealing careers, or deny themselves many social and recreational rewards because of incapacitating fears and inhibitions, will not likely achieve high competence without first mastering intermediate challenges, especially when skill deficits as well as inhibitions must be overcome.

In any case, treatment planning is constrained by the specific activities the client will or will not undertake (Rosenthal, 1976). Clients' attempting or refusing to perform a given task sets the limits on the momentary content of treatment. Therefore, various behavior supports are provided to facilitate coping efforts. protective devices can be introduced and progressively faded out. Contact with feared animals can be prompted if their movements are first restrained, and if clients wear protective gear. Peering down from windy rooftops or sheer cliffs is eased if safety lines secure the client to firm anchorings. Other performance aids designed to overcome fearful avoidance during overt practice are illustrated elsewhere (Bandura, Jeffery, & Wright, 1974; Rosenthal, 1976).

When participant modeling is used to redress skill deficits, added kinds of behavior supports may be valuable. Thorough assessments that delineate concrete facets of interpersonal conflict will prepare the clinicians to deliver cogent guidance and feedback (e.g., Thomas, Walters, & O'Flaherty, 1974). Then, various cueing devices can be used to prompt appropriate behavior during complex social interactions (Carter & Thomas, 1973; Weathers & Liberman, 1973). Demonstrating self-regulatory strategies and providing cognitive mnemonics can guide conduct and help keep clients' attention from straying into futile or self-defeating channels. Unless information processing activities are properly guided, an intervention may have variable or harmful effects (Kauffman, La Fleur, Hallahan, & Chanes, 1975). Many natural categories for representing events do not reflect a reasoned weighting of instances, but instead rely on subjective prototypes that can distort or ignore intended meanings (Rachman & Seligman, 1976, Rosch, 1975).

The advantages of performance aids for *inducing* requisite behavior should not be confused with their limitations for *maintaining* behavior. Put most simply, the more aids used to assure performance, the more that treatment departs from the real life conditions clients must eventually manage unaided. Once clients can endure participation, the supports are faded out until competence is sustained without any aids. Unless people end by attributing their gains to enhanced personal resources, they have reason to doubt the significance of progress and its predictive value for future challenges. One cannot assume that the more protective devices the better. When participant modeling outcomes were compared for clients given few, more, or many inductive aids, the minimally aided gained much less than both other groups, but maximally aided did not surpass moderately aided treatment. Yet the most extreme, refractory cases later profited from added therapy with unlimited response induction aids (Bandura, Jeffery, & Wright, 1974). In practice, therapists will use however many aids are needed to assure early successful performance, but will then withdraw supports as clients become skilled at the activities. At that point, independent practice in various situations is added to instill mastery. Providing opportunities for self-directed accomplishments after the desired behavior has been established further increases the level and generality of change and enhances perceived self-efficacy (Bandura, Jeffery, & Gajdos, 1975).

A Common Cognitive Mechanism of Operation.

Bandura (1977b) has proposed a theory to account for changes produced by alternative treatments that differ in external form. According to this theory, psychological procedures, whatever their format, serve as ways of creating and strengthening expectations of personal effectiveness. Expectations of efficacy affect people's choice of activities and behavioral settings, how hard they strive, and how long their attempts will persist despite barriers, adverse feedback, or other response costs.

Expectations of personal efficacy stem from four main sources of information. Performance accomplishments provide the most influential efficacy information because such information is based on personal mastery experiences. The other sources include the vicarious experiences of observing others cope and succeed; verbal persuasion, exhortation, and allied types of social influence; and states of physiological arousal from which people judge their level of anxiety and vulnerability to stress. A number of factors influence the cognitive processing of efficacy information arising from enactive, vicarious, exhortative, and emotive sources. Thus, for example, cognitive appraisals of the difficulty level of the tasks will affect the impact of performance accomplishments on perceived self-efficacy. To succeed at easy tasks provides no new information for altering one's sense of self-efficacy, whereas mastery of challenging tasks conveys salient evidence of enhanced competence. Momentary setbacks or advances count less than the conclusions clients draw from sequences of events. People who stumble and fail, but detect relative progress, may enhance self-judged efficacy more than those who succeed but interpret their efforts as deteriorating or stuck on a plateau compared to prior attempts. Perceived self-efficacy refers to people's conviction that they can engage in and successfully execute given deeds, not to short-run payoffs the behavior may earn. Obviously, although confident about their ability to perform, people withhold actions that are judged too costly or against their best interests.

Empirical tests of this theory (Bandura & Adams, 1977; Bandura, Adams, & Beyer, 1977) confirm that different treatment approaches alter expectations of personal efficacy, and the more dependable the source of efficacy information, the greater the changes in self-efficacy. Thus, treatments based on performance accomplishments through the aid of participant modeling produce higher, stronger, and more generalized expectations of personal efficacy than vicarious experiencès alone, or elimination of emotional arousal through systematic desensitization. Behavioral changes correspond closely to level of self-efficacy regardless of the mode of treatment. The higher the mastery expectations, the greater the likelihood that clients will cope successfully with threatening situations. The relationship is most precisely revealed by microanalysis of the congruence between self-efficacy and performance at the level of individual tasks. This measure is obtained by recording whether or not clients consider themselves capable of performing the various tasks and computing the percent of accurate correspondence between efficacy judgment and actual performance. Self-efficacy was an accurate predictor of performance in 89 percent of the behavioral tasks for participant modeling, in 86 percent of the tasks for mastery expectations instated by modeling alone, and in 89 percent of the tasks for increases in self-efficacy produced by desensitization treatment. When clients are tested at periodic intervals during the course of treatment, self-efficacy predicts with a high degree of accuracy how much the individuals will change in their behavior after receiving limited amounts of treatment.

In general, the efficacy analysis is able to account for performance variations both between and within therapeutic modes, and to predict behavioral approach on specific tasks during the course of treatment and after it is completed. The foregoing theory integrates the results of heterogeneous treatment approaches. It proposes a common cognitive mechanism that regulates overt behavior, and provides an explanatory framework for the impact of behavioral psychotherapies in general. Most of the treatment isssues, already reviewed and to be discussed, gain coherence when viewed in these terms.

DEVELOPING SOCIAL SKILLS THROUGH MODELING

Personal problems often intermesh skill deficits with behavioral inhibitions. For inhibited ability, guided performance seems the intervention of choice. But to acquire new competence, observational methods offer special advantages (Bandura, 1976a). Development of skills would be exceed-

ingly laborious, not to mention perilous, if learning were based solely on trial-and-error experiences without the guidance of models who exemplify the effective patterns. Shifting the balance between deficit and avoidance should alter the respective merits of exemplary and enactive options. In most complex problems, composite programs that include multiple forms of guidance serve clients best.

Profound Deficits

Major deficits arise if people have never acquired generalizable competencies, or if their living conditions have so encumbered once-learned behavior that it remains functionally void. When clients lack the rudiments of coping ability, demonstration is a key tool to instate skill. Modeling can convey needed information faster and better than other methods that rely on rewarding self-generated fragments of requisite patterns.

If a client cannot perform any segment of the appropriate activity, the first goal is eliciting some molecule of action to build on. Gross deficits are found in autistic children, who may only enact bizarre and self-injurious conduct, or in regressed, chronic psychotics who remain largely mute, in stupor, and unresponsive. For such cases, modeling first drew notice when operant researchers could not evoke rewardable acts unless imitiative prompts combining modeling, guided performance, and reinforcement of progress were supplied. The basic strategy is much the same in treating adults (e.g., Sherman, 1965) and autistic children (Lovaas & Newsom, 1976; Risley & Wolf, 1967). The therapist first gains control over the child's attending behavior. Complex behavior is gradually elaborated by modeling the activities in small steps of increasing difficulty. If the child fails to respond, verbal and manual aids are used to facilitate the behavior. Response induction aids are gradually withdrawn and reinforcement for prompted behavior is later withheld to counteract passive responding. As is typical, acquisition begins slowly but accelerates with continued participant modeling. After desired behavior is established, children are taught to generalize their new capabilities by rewarding appropriate responsiveness in a variety of settings toward a variety of people.

Sometimes vastly prolonged treatment is needed before the first few instances of a response class are modeled. Once those responses gain meaning, progress is much faster and far exceeds waiting until impaired clients spontaneously emit rewardable acts. It is of interest that the more abstract the skill, the more exemplification has aided learning (Lovaas, Freitas, Nelson, & Whalen, 1967). Children whose parents continue the therapeutic practices maintain or expand skills at long-term follow-ups. If put in milieux that neglect sustained guidance, conduct reverts but relearning is fairly rapid (Lovaas, Kogel, Simmons, & Stevens, 1973).

Essentially the same principles and techniques apply to institutionalized retardates. Prompted demonstrations provide effective guidance to correct gross skill deficits. Robust gains are confirmed across variations in age, type of behavior, and putative nosology (Azrin, Gottlieb, Hughart, Wesolowski, & Rahn, 1975; Baer, Peterson, & Sherman, 1967; Bernal, Jacobson, & Lopez, 1975). Consistent with the findings of disinhibition through multiple modeling, seriously retarded clients generalized far better if taught by multiple than by single models (Marburg, Houston, & Holmes, 1976). When deficits are less severe, competence develops further and faster.

Verbal Expressiveness

Faithful carrier-waves do not censor the message they bear: Ample research finds modeling helpful to promote more vivid affect and more intimate discourse during interviews. Prior reviews (e.g., Marlatt, 1972; Rosenthal, 1976) summarize much of this evidence; current studies continue the tradition. Often, subjects first observe exemplary self-revelations via alternative modeling formats whose impact is then tested in an interview. Thus, an "expert" model evoked more self-disclosure than a peer (Doster & McAllister, 1973), but positive versus negative content led to equal candor (Doster & Brooks, 1974). Compared to controls, audiotaped strangers raised frank self-references, but less than filmed models (Stone & Stebbins, 1975) or the interviewer's live examples (Davis & Skinner, 1974). Yet as taped models, another person described as a "colleague" surpassed the interviewer and verbally describing self-disclosure proved weak unless examplary tapes were added (McAllister & Kiesler, 1975). Demonstration was more

helpful when joined to longer sets of specific instructions than when briefer, global directions were supplied (Stone & Gotlib, 1975). Varying time and narrative versus exemplary guidance, longer demonstrations aided most, but short directions exceeded scanty illustrations (McGuire, Thelen, & Amolsch, 1975). Demonstration, instructions, and rehearsal were compared to enhance empathic talk; strongest by itself, demonstration was bolstered if either other method was added (Stone & Vance, 1976). In pactice, mode of conveying information should count less than ability to discern relevant cues, and to organize them into cogent classes (Hersen & Eisler, 1976; Hersen, Eisler, & Miller, 1974).

Although caution is needed in judging when and how to stimulate intimate disclosures (Shimkunas, 1972), exemplary frankness can promote clinical gains. Exemplary disclosures raised intimate talk but also suspicion in nonpsychotics, and elevated delusions and autism in psychotics. Self-modeled practice before conversation reduced inept statements more than monitoring by self or other during conversation (Cavior & Marabotto, 1976). Resistive, involuntary counselees were more communicative after peer demonstrations (Smith & Lewis, 1974), as were asocial clients given modeling aids (Gutrude, Goldstein, & Hunter, 1973). Contrasts between coping and mastery models expressing positive versus neutral affect did not alter skill judged in simulated job interviews; but psychotics' self-rated arousal was less with coping than mastery models (Bruch, 1975). A starkly constricted man grew and remained more animated after his therapist exemplified spontaneity for just one session (Wexler & Butler, 1976). Modeling, role-playing, and rehearsal were given to reorient stilted clients; their social behavior, as rated by friends, improved significantly (Cabush & Edwards, 1976). In all, modeling options seem promising tools to rectify constricted, rigid styles of personal conduct.

Assertiveness.

People who cannot behave assertively and express their legitimate rights will suffer considerable aversive control by others. Their satisfactions in living and self-regard may be chronically meager. Fortunately, modeling can rectify submissive patterns in samples ranging from timid students (McFall & Lillesand, 1971; Rathus, 1973) to hospitalized psychotics (Goldstein et al., 1973; Hersen & Bellack, 1976a). Earlier work is capsuled elsewhere (Hersen & Eisler, 1976; Rosenthal, 1976). Typically, demonstrations, instructions, prompting, and role-playing are joined to simulated or actual practice. Exemplary plus narrative guidance surpasses either method alone (Hersen, Eisler, & Miller, 1974; Hersen, Eisler, Miller, Johnson, & Pinkston, 1973). Such composite guidance has created stable long-term gains (Galassi, Kostka, & Galassi, 1975). To date, structured rehearsal of assertiveness in natural situations is skimpy. That lack may explain many failures on new, transfer demands (McFall & Lillesand, 1971; McFall & Twentyman, 1973; Rosenthal & Reese, 1976; Young, Rimm, & Kennedy, 1973).

To *assess* severity, handling social situations requiring assertiveness may tax clients more than responding to simulated situations presented on autiotape (Galassi & Galassi, 1976). But content medium counts less in promoting change. Audio and videotapes proved equal (McFall & Twentyman, 1973); covert modeling works well, especially if multiple models are visualized (Kazdin, 1975, 1976); and imagining self or other perform was as good as a live peer (Rosenthal & Reese, 1976). Incentive inducements hinge on their cognitive effects (cf., Moore, Mischel, & Zeiss, 1976). Praising clients' practice did not boost gains (Young, Rimm, & Kennedy, 1973). Yet if assertive fantasy models earn reward, progress improves (Kazdin, 1974c, 1976) because clients elaborate on favorable performances more (Kazdin, 1975).

Assertive guidance as a behavioral aid, or supplement, can facilitate changes in other problems like inept social behavior (Hallam, 1974) and sexual difficulties (Stevenson & Wolpe, 1960; Yulis, 1976). The treatment strategy can bring enduring advances, and is helpful when applied to related complaints. Its ultimate potential needs testing in formats that assure sustained practice of assertiveness in the natural environment (Bandura, 1973).

Social Competencies

Perhaps the most prevalent and critical adjustment problems stem from deficits or deviance in relating to others. Whether deprived of opportunity, or handicapped by dysfunctional development, clients' prospects for adept relearning are hopeful. Although still an infant realm, treatments based on social learning principles have made strides in promoting cognitive and social skills.

Withdrawal.

A combination of modeling, repeated role-playing, and feedback was compared with desensitization to assist socially inadequate outpatients. Both methods increased social contacts relative to non-treated controls, but composite guidance produced a wider range of new interpersonal behavior than did desensitization (Marzillier, Lambert, & Kellett, 1976). Videotaped or narrated behavioral guides, plus rehearsal, were given to elicit appropriate social conduct from psychotics who averaged over 20 years in hospitals. Each modeling format surpassed an attention-placebo group, with no differences based on treatment medium (Jaffe & Carlson, 1976). Social gains achieved through demonstrations, instructions, and feedback transfer to new situations and are maintained over time (Bellack, Hersen, & Turner, 1977).

In a milestone study, Goldsmith and McFall (1975) devised and validated a treatment program in a hospital setting. First, they carefully assessed interpersonal deficits on comparable wards to locate exemplary coping behavior, and to specify principles for later guidance. Then a new sample was assigned to skill development, pseudotherapy, or assessment-only conditions (balanced for schizophrenic and neurotic or character disorders). Treatment spanned the following explicit sequence: (1) narrative description; (2) coaching on principles of effective conduct; (3) observing competent styles of behavior demonstrated; (4) review of the prior content; (5) check on clients' understanding, and willingness to role-play; (6) simulated rehearsal; followed by (7) audio-taped playback, first judged by client and then by the therapist. The guided group exceeded the controls on simulated role-playing, in self-reported change, and in a structured situational test. The treated group also achieved slightly lower readmission rates. These gains held across diagnoses, although just three hours' guidance was supplied! Such data confirm the utility of their strategy. It is hard to gauge how psychotics treated for three hours compared in severity with some chronic schizophrenics who, for example, required 20 to 30 sessions (Edelstein & Eisler, 1976; Hersen & Bellack, 1976b). To what extent did briefer treatment rest on more efficient therapy, on less deviant participants, or both? Growth of systematic programs will magnify the need for shared and valid criteria of social skills, to allow comparisons among studies.

Marital and Dating Problems.

Efforts have begun to devise methods for assessing dating skills. Peer-ratings, self-reports, and speech during verbally simulated interactions separated high from low male daters, but tests in natural situations did not (Arkowitz, Lichtenstein, McGovern, & Hines, 1975). Distinct patterns were later found in women, who mainly lacked familiarity with social guidelines, while poor self-appraisals most hampered men (Glasgow & Arkowitz, 1975). Diverse composites of role-playing, demonstration, coaching, and group feedback have aided shy males; grasping generalizable dating strategies seems more crucial than rehearsing discrete acts (Curran, Gilbert, & Little, 1976; Macdonald, Lindquist, Kramer, McGrath, & Rhyne, 1975; McGovern, Arkowitz, & Gilmore, 1975; Twentyman & McFall, 1975). Thus, desensitization was as good as repeating modeled responses (Curran, 1975). When instructions and group discussion clarified events, skill development surpassed desensitization (Curran & Gilbert, 1975). Likewise, fear of dating was reduced best if simulated practice was joined to role-playing and feedback by partners, but adding desensitization brought no extra gain (Bander, Steinke, Allen, & Mosher, 1975).

Analogous guidance can resolve spouse discord. Demonstrations taught dyadic feedback rules to couples with faulty interaction styles, who then showed clear progress (McLean, Ogston, & Grauer, 1973). Modeling and discussion followed by structured home practice with feedback improved spouse communication (Ely, Guerney, & Stover, 1973). Exemplary modeling to clarify reciprocal reward patterns aided a reinforcement-oriented marital skills approach (Azrin, Naster, & Jones, 1973). An ambitious stepwise program spanned four stages: (1) identifying dyadic conflicts and strengths; (2) role-playing with feedback to improve joint efforts; (3) contracting to negotiate

compromises, assisted by therapist demonstrations and bargaining rules; and (4) implementing prior learning and agreements. The couples made rapid gains on several measures, and continued feedback might have aided still further (Tsoi-Hoshmand, 1976). Symbolic modeling has also helped in programs to enhance sexual competence (Obler, 1973; Serber, 1974). As skill dimensions in conjugal dysharmony are better specified, a host of vicarious applications should have treatment value (Jacobson & Martin, 1976).

The foregoing research suggests that many social competencies are best taught by programs organized along the following lines: (1) the learning task is structured in an orderly, stepwise sequence to effectively communicate the needed skill guidance. (2) Generalizable rules of effective conduct are explained and demonstrated, and clients' understanding is checked to permit clarification if necessary. (3) Guided simulated practice is provided with feedback that rewards clients' successes and corrects their errors. (4) Once the desired behavior has been established, less structured opportunities for self-directed accomplishments are given so that people can authenticate a sense of personal efficacy. (5) During this transition to independent mastery, consultation and feedback by the therapist can further enhance provisional gains. (6) As a final step, clients test their newly acquired skills in the natural environment, at first under conditions likely to produce favorable results, and then in more demanding situations. (7) Transfer performance assignments are progressively adjusted to clients' capabilities at the given time, to enhance and reward their developing competence.

Cognitive and Self-Control Competencies

The evidence so far reviewed suggests this trend: As requisite skills grow more abstract or demand conditional judgments, guidance in strategic principles gains value, but repetition of discrete acts loses efficiency. Much human endeavor depends on the plans that govern the organization of already available component behavior. Problem-solving rules, self-regulatory standards, and habit change regimens that clients execute on their own are examples. A comprehensive discussion of this realm is given in Mahoney and Arnkoff's chapter of this handbook. Our analysis, instead, concentrates on the vicarious elements in symbolic control.

Problem-solving.

Substantial research, elesewhere reviewed (Rosenthal, 1976; in press; Zimmerman & Rosenthal, 1974), confirms that modeling techniques are prime channels to convey abstract rules. Demonstrations can, for instance, transmit difficult principles (White & Rosenthal, 1974), subtle decision criteria (Macri, 1976), and elaborate concepts far better than instructions (Tumblin, Gholson, Rosenthal, & Kelley, 1977) or overt practice options, with excellent transfer despite major changes in physical cues (Rosenthal & Zimmerman, 1976). If learners' prior repertoires are limited, or the content highly novel, exemplary methods excel. Regardless of their level of ability, children acquire a new concept far better taught by example than by narration (Rosenthal, in press; Rosenthal & Kellogg, 1973). Conceptual progress is often best if information is exemplified and a summation of its guiding principles also given. Vicarious techniques are hence among the methods of choice to teach abstract competence. In applied settings, modeling becomes a versatile tool to convey new strategies and guidelines for living.

Although viewing treatment as problem-solving is hardly new (D'Zurilla & Goldfried, 1971), programmatic research is limited. Isolated papers, however, span a wide range of preliminary applications. Those run from role reversals between therapist and clients to prompt their devising new solutions for old problems (Alperson, 1976), to using peer norms as performance standards that helped depressives on anagrams tasks (Klein, Fencil-Morse, & Seligman, 1976). Test-anxious learners usually validate the Yerkes-Dodson law by scoring less well on abstract tests than calmer peers. Yet anxious students solved puzzles as well as normals if a model both demonstrated solutions and commented on guidelines to be followed (Sarason, 1973); they surpassed normals on a memory task if shown a coping model who acknowledged test fears but shared tactics to abate emotionality (Sarason, 1975). Modeling boosted clients' questions to aid personal problem solving, and videotaped feedback of own efforts most in-

creased judicious queries (Arnkoff & Stewart, 1975). A modeling tape, used to orient clients about vocational guidance, led to more solicitation of career data than did control methods (Fisher, Reardon, & Burck, 1976). Exemplifying a painful act reduced pain for people taught a cognitive coping plan, but raised distress for unguided observers (Chaves & Barber, 1974). The lion's share of benefit in a program to lower alcoholism resulted from combining videotaped playback of own drunkeness with guidance to discern and control blood alcohol level; behavioral counseling (demonstrations, role-playing, and social feedback), alcohol education, and competing response practice to setting cues further enhanced outcomes (Volger, Compton, & Weissbach, 1975). Academic guidance (by study manuals, cognitive and participant modeling, and programmed instruction) plus desensitization for test worries best aided students with scholastic problems (Mitchell, Hall, & Piatkowska, 1975). Guided group discussions that illustrated rationales to explain fear helped phobics more than desensitization (Wein, Nelson, & Odom, 1975). The foregoing medley of problem-solving themes invites further recitals.

Self-regulation.

The ultimate therapy goal is to replace handicaps with effective conduct, independently guided and maintained. Research on means to give clients control over changes, by altering covert regulators, is moving forward. Since laboratory studies clarified the processes by which people acquire standards of self-reward through modeling (Bandura, 1971, 1976b) the realm has burgeoned. Standards displayed by others may alter observers' phenomenology and deeds in subtle ways (Coyne, 1976; McGarry & West, 1975; Piliavin, Piliavin, & Rodin, 1975; White, 1975). Modeled standards also modify the satisfactions and future goal aspirations people extract from performance attainments (Fry, 1976; Masters & Christy, 1974; Masters, Gordon, & Clark, 1976) as well as the impact of therapy procedures (Rosenthal, Hung, & Kelley, 1977; White, Rosenthal, & Gerber, 1975).

The growth of treatments combining cognitive modeling with self-instructions has been an especially interesting development. First proposed by

Meichenbaum (1973), and kin to other cognitive behavior therapies (Beck, 1976; Goldfried, Decenteceo, & Weinberg, 1974), this approach combines recursive cycles of demonstration, cognitive modeling of action strategies, guided practice, and self-rehearsal planning to resolve problems in stepwise fashion. During treatment, the locus of guidance by external displays is faded into covert ultimate self-regulation. Thus, hospitalized schizophrenics moved from serial progress in conceptual tasks and reasoning, to mastering social communication skills (Meichenbaum & Cameron, 1974; Meyers, Mercatoris, & Sirota, 1976). Similar programs have helped shy people become more openly expressive (Cabush & Edwards, 1976), have aided hyperaggressive youngsters to develop self-control, (Goodwin & Mahoney, 1975) and to improve their cognitive functioning by adopting reflective styles of behavior (Bender, 1976; Debus, 1976). The content of self-directions and the event-structure of therapy dictate precise outcomes. Omitting a guiding rationale can impair results (Bender, 1976). As noted earlier, the more abstract the self-regulatory skill, the less that teaching by acutal toil on component acts seems to offer; in contrast, guides to strategic, executive principles grow more valuable. This is probably because repeating fairly simple elements is a poor means to recode and integrate information, but reviewing summary rules or cognitive strategies is efficient. Time and future data will tell best. From such investigations into modeling of cognitive processes, and self-directed, symbolic regulation, we will learn better how to organize, sequence, and combine elements of information that vary in difficulty and abstractness.

POTENTIAL DIRECTIONS

The bulk of the literature, already discussed, suggests that vicarious guidance has come of age to alleviate dysfunctional fears and inhibitions and to teach new competence. A shift from retrospect to prospect is eased by recalling that a growing family of information-producing and social influence tools can generate similar molar outcomes and cognitive mediators. Separate routes may differ in speed of clinical gain, or have special merits for defined tasks and samples, but still reach the same goal. Also, methods may interact well or poorly if conjoined, but rarely will one procedure yield outcomes as good as with an array of tools. Not sheer utility but cost criteria—reckoned in time, staff, "side-effects," attrition, and success rates—will decide whether and which modeling procedures are called for, and how diverse techniques should be hybridized. We can only hope that the best is yet to come.

Education and Preventative Possibilities

Educating parents or teachers to manage conduct problems in their children offers several advantages beyond savings in staff time. Since the model mediating change is a natural member of the milieu, access is automatic, gains from improved practices can extend to other children not initially referred, and the adult's prior role in creating deviance can be altered without stigma as part of lessons. Modeling aids are prominent in many such guidance programs. Benefits have come to families with aggressive and autistic children (Glogower & Sloop, 1976; Lovaas & Newsom, 1976; Patterson & Reid, 1973). Children improve more, because parents learn better, from a performance composite (including demonstration and role-playing) than from "reflective" counseling (Tavormina, 1975). Positive changes at home, designed to help a particular child, can generalize to other kin. Siblings not specifically treated as clients reduced their rates of deviant conduct, and maintained progress after new modeling patterns were instated (Arnold, Levine, & Patterson, 1975). Reciprocally, sibs (Laviguer, 1976) and parents who excel as learners (Butler, 1976) become ideal models to teach the less adept. Mothers' videotaped demonstrations surpassed several other parent education methods, such as lectures (Nay, 1975). There is evidence that social deficiencies characterize children who later become schizophrenic (Watt & Lubensky, 1976), and that derogatory self-reactions underlie much chronic maladjustment (e.g., Meichenbaum & Cameron, 1974). Given such data, various kinds of hazardous naturalistic modeling deserve concern, including: (1) withdrawn, or grossly aberrant parental interaction styles; (2) chronic patterns of demeaning negative feedback from adults to child;

and (3) excessive, deviant, or niggardly self-reinforcement by parents that may transmit harmful frames of reference across generations. There are substantial benefits to warding off developmental casualties as early as possible. Outreach projects are one solution. College students, serving as visiting models, were able to improve the parenting skills of mothers from disadvantaged backgrounds (Goodman, 1975).

With teachers, exemplary group guidance via modeling and role-playing led to better grasp of behavior principles than a manual; more important, student conduct was more improved in classrooms taught by the guided modeling group than by teachers given other methods (McKeown, Adams, & Forehand, 1975). Similar outcomes emerged in comparisons of counselor education programs (Eskedal, 1975). Such results argue that courses on advanced topics (White & Rosenthal, 1974), or social skills (Springer, Springer, & Aaronson, 1975), should adopt exemplary formats rather than lectures. Modeling applications to schoolroom pedagogy remain largely unexplored. Videotaped demonstration has primed observers to seek career information (Fisher, Reardon, & Burck, 1976). Disadvantaged adults in a basic education course watched coping models advance in study skills and attitudes favorable toward schooling; these observers showed better test grades, attendance, and eventual continuance of studies than did control classmates (Kunce, Bruch, & Thelen, 1974).

Preventative health offers great possibilities. Videotaped modeling of people undergoing dental procedures plus relaxation enabled more dental phobics to successfully complete dental treatment than did desensitization (Shaw & Thoresen, 1974). Shown to youngsters facing surgery, films of coping peer models reduced fear arousal both before and after surgical operations, and prevented the rise in home adjustment problems found for unprepared controls (Melamed & Siegel, 1975). Many of the above examples lend themselves to mass media formats, but the potential of televised education and prophylaxis remains scarcely tapped. In a rare exploration, weekly programs on local public television sought to teach self-control techniques, with some evidence that unselected viewers profited (Mikulas, 1976).

In an innovative program of research, Maccoby and Farquhar (1975) have successfully used mass media procedures on a community-wide basis to inform the public on how personal habits (e.g., dietary habits, smoking, overeating, exercise) affect the risk of premature heart disease and to change longstanding risk-related behaviors. Multi-media campaigns are used to create interest in the health program; instructional manuals and personal influence relying on modeling, guided practice, and reinforcing feedback are used to change habits injurious to health. Medical examinations of people selected from the community reveal that media influences produce significant reduction in risk-related behavior. Personal guidance in conjunction with mass media achieves more extensive and rapid changes than the media alone. Results of this exemplary project illustrate how personal habits conducive to health can be promoted on a community-wide basis with minimum involvement of health professionals.

Applications to Communal and Residential Settings

For some people, extent of deficit or the nature of their deviance thwarts early return to fully independent living as a proximate treatment goal. Lack of adequate resources, irreversible handicaps based on physical debility, social abandonment by family and friends, or legal sanctions facing the person require that treatment must maximize clients' potentialities within circumscribed or institutional boundaries. Often, those narrower aims can later be refocused toward wider horizons. But sometimes client and therapist must seek to optimize coping under sheltered conditions. In such cases, social learning principles offer a gamut of stratagems that have yet to be harnessed at large.

Programs designed to help social offenders develop broadly useful skills that enable them to participate successfully in the larger society face related problems. They must overcome distrustful reactions if new aspirations and styles of living are to be developed in the confined milieu. They must also bridge between a restricted treatment setting and the freer environment in which beneficial changes will need to be maintained. Often, staff may be viewed with distrust. In contrast, peers who have advanced in a program, and have achieved positive changes, are much harder to dismiss as exemplars. Their testimony and precedents will carry more weight. Few models seem as plausible or relevant as people who have shared but overcome clients' own problems. This is critical if a client rejects staff members as reference figures because they appear too remote in age, education, status, ethnicity, and so on, for suitable comparisons with self, or are perceived as outsiders, lacking vivid conversance with the client's burdens and viewpoint. Although positive interaction styles can raise staff credibility and influence (Jesness, 1975), delinquents may gain more from constructive peer modeling. Even brief videotapes have some favorable impact (Thelen, Fry, Dollinger, & Paul, 1976). If youngsters observe advanced peers in the same milieu demonstrate prosocial changes, more pervasive gains may follow (Eitzen, 1975). Graduates from a reeducation program have helped newer arrivals by exemplifying functional skills (Silver, 1976).

Transitions from confined settings to more natural milieux can be harder to accomplish than provisional change in protected contexts. Maintenance and transfer of gains cannot be left to the vagaries of fate without inviting recidivism (Fairweather, Sanders, Maynard, & Cressler, 1969; Hill, Hops, & Johnson, 1975; Lovaas, Koegel, Simmons, & Stevens, 1973). Peer role models can develop self-presentation and practical judgment skills. For example, practice in group discussion, decision-making, and planning was introduced. Once begun, mutual modeling, feedback, and choice of solutions aided hospitalized clients; they improved their social interactions and spent more time working in the community or at home than did people given a conventional token economy program (Greenberg, Scott, Pisa, & Friesen, 1975). Even teaching humble skills like how to shop, to cook, or to sustain audible conversations, can boost family acceptance of a deviant member compared with unguided visits at home or in the hospital (O'Brien & Azrin, 1973). Sometimes, modeling can defuse communal crises to prevent the spread of fears and of symptoms by group exemplification and consensual validation (Shelton, 1973). More often, modeling principles can help dischargees or other clients with common plights to regain meaningful community roles.

Transition programs are starting to be tested. In one, guided planning assisted unemployed clients find jobs, using a clublike setting. There, clients shared information, skills, and social support while seeking employment. Their families and friends were enlisted to supply leads for jobs. Mutual modeling and feedback prompted job-seeking efforts, guided members to improve their dress and grooming, and helped them organize career resumes. Demonstrations and role-playing prepared clients before employment interviews. Compared to matched controls, the club members found jobs much more often, started work sooner, and earned significantly higher salaries (Azrin, Flores, & Kaplan, 1975).

Programs of these sorts are called for to harvest the progress that can start during institutional treatment. In a longitudinal scheme, new recruits would receive guidance from proficient models, including advanced or graduate peers, as well as vocational and social skill consultants. Clients would witness a stepwise structure that exemplifies and rewards progressive levels of competence. As people achieve beneficial changes, they would be called on as tutors for neophytes, and the best models could eventually win staff positions. Upon discharge, the client would move to a transition phase where realistic needs and problems were met through group support, feedback, and cooperation, and by modeled guidance as needed, until clients earned stable and useful roles in the community. This strategy fosters multiple benefits; it helps assure relevant models; incoming clients can see the milieu strive to promote and reward progress toward independent success, not passive compliance for institutional convenience; group efforts and resources are used to ease transition stresses on each member; and jobs are created for dischargees in which their background invites hiring, not stigma. It should be possible to devise and implement sequential rehabilitation programs that capitalize on the foregoing social system guidelines. Such projects promise to more fully realize the educative and therapeutic potentialities of modeling influences.

Conclusion

The above potentialities encourage wider sociocultural horizons for social learning approaches, and imply optimism about people's capacity for change. In a real sense, the current and future directions of psychological modeling mirror those in our discipline generally. From peripheralistic focus on observable acts, one sees reorientation toward symbolic processes and social guidelines that regulate overt acts. From chain-link views of causation examplified by the S-R metaphor, we are moving toward more explanatory prototypes whereby personal meanings and thought integrate diverse information to arrive at observable patterns of behavior. Our view of reality is changing from exclusively experimenter-defined to largely person-constructed. We are devising new research paradigms to open up the "black box" and are finding predictive and explanatory contents within. New frontiers for vicarious processes and applications depend on progress toward improved understanding of human organization and intricacy. Let us hope these developments bring better models of mankind to serve observers—both in the role of clients and as interpreters of human nature.

REFERENCES

Aaronson, A., & Scarborough, H. S. Performance theories for sentence coding: Some quantitative evidence. *Journal of Experimental Psychology: Human Perception and Performance,* 1976, *2,* 56–70.

Aderman, D., Brehm, S. S., & Katz, L. B. Empathic observation of an innocent victim: The just world revisited. *Journal of Personality and Social Psychology,* 1974, *29,* 342–347.

Akiskal, H. S., & McKinney, W. T. Depressive disorders: Toward a unified hypothesis. *Science,* 1973, *182,* 20–29.

Alford, G. S., & Rosenthal, T. L. Process and products of modeling in observational concept attainment. *Child Development,* 1973, *44,* 714–720.

Alperson, J. R. Gone with the wind: Role reversed desensitization for a wind phobic client. *Behavior Therapy,* 1976, *7,* 405–407.

Ambler, B. A., & Proctor, J. D. The familiarity effect for single-letter pairs. *Journal of Experimental Psychology: Human Perception and Performance,* 1976, *2,* 222–234.

Arkowitz, H., Lichtenstein, E., McGovern, K., & Hines, P. The behavioral assessment of social competence. *Behavior Therapy,* 1975, *6,* 3–13.

Arnkoff, D. B., & Stewart, J. The effectiveness of modeling and videotape feedback on personal problem solving. *Behaviour Research and Therapy,* 1975, *13,* 127–133.

Arnold, J. E., Levine, A. G., & Patterson, G. R. Changes in sibling behavior following family intervention. *Journal of Consulting and Clinical Psychology,* 1975, *43,* 683–688.

Avant, L. L., & Lyman, P. J. Stimulus familiarity modifies perceived duration in prerecognition visual processing. *Journal of Experimental Psychology: Human Perception and Performance,* 1975, *1,* 205–213.

Axelrod, S. Comparison of individual and group contingencies in two special classes. *Behavior Therapy,* 1973, *4,* 83–90.

Azrin, N. H., Flores, T., & Kaplan, S. J. Job-finding club: A group-assisted program for obtaining employment. *Behaviour Research and Therapy,* 1975, *13,* 17–27.

Azrin, N. H., Gottlieb, L., Hughart, L., Wesolowski, M. D., & Rahn, T. Eliminating self-injurious behavior by educative procedures. *Behaviour Research and Therapy,* 1975, *13,* 101–111.

Azrin, N. H., Naster, B. J., & Jones, R. Reciprocity counseling: A rapid learning-based procedure for marital counseling. *Behaviour Research and Therapy,* 1973, *11,* 365–382.

Baer, D. M., Peterson, R. F., & Sherman, J. A. The development of imitation by reinforcing behavioral similarity to a model. *Journal of Experimental Analysis of Behavior,* 1967, *10,* 405–416.

Bahn, E., & Bahn, M. L. *A history of oral interpretation.* Minneapolis, Minn.: Burgess, 1970.

Bander, K. W., Steinke, G. V., Allen, G. J., & Mosher, D. L. Evaluation of three dating-specific approaches for heterosexual dating anxiety. *Journal of Consulting and Clinical Psychology,* 1975, *43,* 259–265.

Bandura, A. Influence of model's reinforcement contingencies on the acquisition of imitative responses. *Journal of Personality and Social Psychology,* 1965, *1,* 589–595.

Bandura, A. *Principles of behavior modification.* New York: Holt, Rinehart & Winston, 1969.

Bandura, A. Vicarious and self-reinforcement processes. In R. Glaser (Ed.), *The nature of reinforcement.* New York: Academic Press, 1971. Pp. 228–278.

Bandura, A. *Aggression: A social learning analysis.* Englewood Cliffs, N.J.: Prentice-Hall, 1973.

Bandura, A. Social learning perspective on behavior change. In A. Burton (Ed.), *What makes behavior change possible?* New York: Brunner/Mazel, 1976a. Pp. 34–57.

Bandura, A. Self-reinforcement: Theoretical and methodological considerations. *Behaviorism,* 1976b, *4,* 135–155.

Bandura, A. *Social learning theory.* Englewood Cliffs, N.J.: Prentice-Hall, 1977a.

Bandura, A. Self-efficacy: Towards a unifying theory of behavioral change. *Psychological Review,* 1977b, *84,* 191–215.

Bandura, A., & Adams, N. E. Analysis of self-efficacy theory of behavioral change. Unpublished manuscript, Stanford University, 1977.

Bandura, A., Adams, N. E., & Beyer, J. Cognitive processes mediating behavioral change. *Journal of Personality and Social Psychology,* 1977, *35,* in press.

Bandura, A., & Barab, P. G. Processes governing disinhibitory effects through symbolic modeling. *Journal of Abnormal Psychology,* 1973, *82,* 1–9.

Bandura, A., Blanchard, E. B., & Ritter, B. The relative

efficacy of desensitization and modeling approaches for inducing behavioral, affective, and attitudinal change. *Journal of Personality and Social Psychology*, 1969, *13*, 173–199.

Bandura, A., Grusec, J. E., & Menlove, F. L. Vicarious extinction of avoidance behavior. *Journal of Personality and Social Psychology*, 1967, *5*, 449–455.

Bandura, A., & Jeffery, R. W. Role of symbolic coding and rehearsal processes in observational learning. *Journal of Personality and Social Psychology*, 1973, *26*, 122–130.

Bandura, A., Jeffery, R. W., & Bachicha, D. L. Analysis of memory codes and cumulative rehearsal in observational learning. *Journal of Research in Personality*, 1974, *7*, 295–305.

Bandura, A., Jeffery, R. W., & Gajdos, E. Generalizing change through participant modeling with self-directed mastery. *Behaviour Research and Therapy*, 1975, *13*, 141–152.

Bandura, A., Jeffery, R. W., & Wright, C. L. Efficacy of participant modeling as a function of response induction aids. *Journal of Abnormal Psychology*, 1974, *83*, 56–64.

Bandura, A., & Menlove, F. L. Factors determining vicarious extinction of avoidance behavior through symbolic modeling. *Journal of Personality and Social Psychology*, 1968, *8*, 99–108.

Bandura, A., & Rosenthal, T. L. Vicarious classical conditioning as a function of arousal level. *Journal of Personality and Social Psychology*, 1966, *3*, 54–62.

Banks, W. P., Clark, H. H., & Lucy, P. The locus of the semantic congruity effect in comparative judgments. *Journal of Experimental Psychology: Human Perception and Performance*, 1975, *1*, 35–47.

Bassili, J. N. Temporal and spatial contingencies in the perception of social events. *Journal of Personality and Social Psychology*, 1976, *33*, 680–685.

Battig, W. F. Intratask interference as a source of facilitation in transfer and retention. In R. G. Thompson and J. F. Voss (Eds.), *Topics in learning and performance*. New York: Academic Press, 1972.

Beck, A. T. *Cognitive therapy and the emotional disorders*. New York: International Universities Press, 1976.

Bell, H. H., & Handel, S. The role of pattern goodness in the reproduction of backward masked patterns. *Journal of Experimental Psychology: Human Perception and Performance*, 1976, *2*, 139–150.

Bellack, A. S., Hersen, M., & Turner, S. M. Generalization effects of social skills training in chronic schizophrenics: An experimental analysis. *Behaviour Research and Therapy*, 1976, *14*, 391–398.

Bender, N. N. Self-verbalization versus tutor verbalization in modifying impulsivity. *Journal of Educational Psychology*, 1976, *68*, 347–354.

Bernal, G. Jacobson, L. I., & Lopez, G. N. Do the effects of behavior modification endure? *Behaviour Research and Therapy*, 1975, *13*, 61–64.

Beutler, L. E., Johnson, D. T., Neville, C. W., Elkins, D., & Jobe, A. M. Attitude similarity and therapist credibility as predictors of attitude change and improvement in psychotherapy. *Journal of Consulting and Clinical Psychology*, 1975, *43*, 90–91.

Black, A. H. Cardiac conditioning in curarized dogs: The relationship between heart rate and skeletal behavior. In W. F. Prokasy (Ed.), *Classical conditioning: A symposium*. New York: Appleton-Century-Crofts, 1965. Pp. 20–47.

Blanchard, E. B. The relative contributions of modeling, information influences, and physical contact in the extinction of phobic behavior. *Journal of Abnormal Psychology*, 1970, *76*, 55–61.

Boersma, K., Den Hengst, S., Dekker, J., & Emmelkamp. P. M. G. Exposure and response prevention in the natural environment: A comparison with obsessive-compulsive patients. *Behaviour Research and Therapy*, 1976, *14*, 19–24.

Borkovec, T. D., Kaloupek, D. G., & Slama, K. M. The facilitative effect of muscle tension-release in the relaxation treatment of sleep disturbance. *Behavior Therapy*, 1975, *6*, 301–309.

Boudewyns, P. A. Implosive therapy and desensitization therapy with inpatients: A five year follow-up. *Journal of Abnormal Psychology*, 1975, *84*, 159–160.

Boulougouris, J. C., Marks, I. M., & Marset, P. Superiority of flooding (implosion) to desensitization for reducing pathological fear. *Behaviour Research and Therapy*, 1971, *9*, 7–16.

Bower, G. H. Mental imagery and associative learning. In L. Gregg (Ed.), *Cognition in learning and memory*. New York: Wiley, 1972. Pp. 5.–88.

Bower, G. H. Selective facilitation and interference in retention of prose. *Journal of Educational Psychology*, 1974, *66*, 1–8.

Bregman, A. S., & Rudnicky, A. I. Auditory segregation: Stream or streams? *Journal of Experimental Psychology: Human Perception and Performance*, 1975, *1*, 263–267.

Brickman, P. Adaptation level determinants of satisfaction with equal and unequal outcome distributions in skill and chance situations. *Journal of Personality and Social Psychology*, 1975, *32*, 191–198.

Brown, I. Effects of perceived similarity on vicarious emotional conditioning. *Behaviour Research and Therapy*, 1974, *12*, 165–173.

Brown, R. D., Brown, L. A., & Davidson, J. E. Instructional treatments, presenter types, and learner characteristics as significant variants in instructional television for adults. *Journal of Educational Psychology*, 1975, *67*, 391–404.

Bruch, M. A. Influence of model characteristics on psychiatric inpatients' interview anxiety. *Journal of Abnormal Psychology*, 1975, *84*, 290–294.

Bundesen, C., & Larsen, A. Visual transformation of size. *Journal of Experimental Psychology: Human Perception and Performance*, 1975, *1*, 214–220.

Butler, J. F. The toilet training success of parents after reading *Toilet training in less than a day*. *Behavior Therapy*, 1976, *7*, 185–191.

Cabush, D. W., & Edwards, K. J. Training clients to help themselves: Outcome effects of training college student clients in facilitative self-responding. *Journal of Counseling Psychology*, 1976, *23*, 34–39.

Calvert-Boyanowsky, J., & Leventhal, H. The role of information in attenuating behavioral responses to stress: A reinterpretation of the misattribution phenomenon. *Journal of Personality and Social Psychology*, 1975, *32*, 214–221.

Carter, R. D., & Thomas, E. J. A case application of a

signaling system (SAM) to the assessment and modification of selected problems of marital communication. *Behavior Therapy,* 1973, *4,* 629–645.

Cautela, J. R., Flannery, R. B., & Hanley, S. Covert modeling: An experimental test. *Behavior Therapy,* 1974, *5,* 494–502.

Cavior, N., & Marabotto, C. M. Monitoring verbal behaviors in a dyadic interaction. *Journal of Consulting and Clinical Psychology* 1976, *44,* 68–76.

Chartier, G. M., & Ainley, C. Effects of model warmth on imitation learning in adult chronic psychotics. *Journal of Abnormal Psychology,* 1974, *83,* 680–682.

Chaves, J. F., & Barber, T. X. Cognitive strategies, experimenter modeling, and expectation in the attenuation of pain. *Journal of Abnormal Psychology,* 1974, *83,* 356–363.

Chow, S. L., & Murdock, B. B. Concurrent memory load and the rate of readout from iconic memory. *Journal of Experiemntal Psychology: Human Perception and Performance,* 1976, *2,* 179–190.

Clark, D. L. *Rhetoric in Greco-Roman education.* New York: Columbia University Press, 1957.

Clark, H. H., & Brownell, H. H. Judging up and down. *Journal of Experimental Psychology: Human Perception and Performance,* 1975, *1,* 339–352.

Comins, J. R., Fullam, F., & Barber, T. X. Effects of experimenter modeling, demands for honesty, and initial level of suggestibility on response to "hypnotic" suggestions. *Journal of Consulting and Clinical Psychology,* 1975, *43,* 668–675.

Cooper, L. A., & Shepard, R. N. Mental transformations in the identification of left and right hands. *Journal of Experimental Psychology: Human Perception and Performance,* 1975, *1,* 48–56.

Coyne, J. C. Depression and the response of others. *Journal of Abnormal psychology,* 1976, *85,* 186–193.

Craig, K. D., Best, H., & Ward, L. M. Social modeling influences on psychophysical judgments of electrical stimulation. *Journal of Abnormal Psychology,* 1975, *84,* 366–373.

Craig, K. D., & Neidermayer, H. Autonomic correlates of pain thresholds influenced by social modeling. *Journal of Personality and Social Psychology,* 1974, *29,* 246–252.

Curran, J. P. Social skills training and systematic desensitization in reducing dating anxiety. *Behaviour Research and Therapy,* 1975, *13,* 65–68.

Curran, J. P., & Gilbert, F. S. A test of the relative effectiveness of a systematic desensitization program and an interpersonal skills training program with date anxious subjects. *Behavior Theapy,* 1975, *6,* 510–521.

Curran, J. P., Gilbert, F. S., & Little, L. M. A comparison between behavioral replication training and sensitivity training approaches to heterosexual dating anxiety. *Journal of Counseling Psychology,* 1976, *23,* 190–196.

Davis, J. D., & Skinner, A. E. Reciprocity of self-disclosure in interviews: Modeling or social exchange. *Journal of Personality and Social Psychology,* 1974, *29,* 779–784.

Debus, R. L. Observational learning of reflective strategies by impulsive children. Unpublished manuscript, University of Sydney, 1976.

Denholtz, M. S., & Mann, E. T. An automated audiovisual treatment of phobias administered by non-professionals. *Journal of Behavior Therapy and Experimental Psychiatry,* 1975, *6,* 111–115.

Denney, D. R. Active, passive, and vicarious desensitization. *Journal of Counseling Psychology,* 1974, *21,* 369–375.

Denney, D. R., & Sullivan, B. J. Desensitization and modeling treatments of spider fear using two types of scenes. *Journal of Consulting and Clinical Psychology,* 1976, *44,* 573–579.

Diamond, M. J., Steadman, C., Harada, D., & Rosenthal, J. The use of direct instructions to modify hypnotic performance: The effects of programmed learning procedures. *Journal of Abnormal Psychology,* 1975, *84,* 109–113.

Doster, J. A., & Brooks, S. J. Interviewer disclosure modeling, information revealed, and interviewee verbal behavior. *Journal of Consulting and Clinical Psychology,* 1974, *42,* 420–426.

Doster, J. A., & McAllister, A. Effect of modeling and model status on verbal behavior in an interview. *Journal of Consulting and Clinical Psychology,* 1973, *40,* 240–243.

D'Zurilla, T. J., & Goldfried, M. R. Problem solving and behavior modification. *Journal of Abnormal Psychology,* 1971, *78,* 107–126.

Edelson, R. I., & Seidman, E. Use of videotaped feedback in altering interpersonal perceptions of married couples: A therapy analogue. *Journal of Consulting and Clinical Psychology,* 1975, *43,* 244–250.

Edelstein, B. A., & Eisler, R. M. Effects of modeling and modeling with instructions and feedback on the behavioral components of social skills. *Behavior Therapy,* 1976, *7,* 382–389.

Eitzen, D. S. The effects of behavior modification on the attitudes of delinquents. *Behaviour Research and Therapy,* 1975, *13,* 295–299.

Ely, A. L., Guerney, B. G., & Stover, L. Efficacy of the training phase of conjugal therapy. *Psychotherapy: Theory, Research, and Practice,* 1973, *10,* 201–207.

Emberle, T. M., Rehm, L. P., & McBurney, D. H. Fear decrement to anxiety hierarchy items—effects of stimulus intensity. *Behaviour Research and Therapy,* 1975, *13,* 225–261.

Emmelkamp, P. M. G. Self-observation versus flooding in the treatment of agoraphobia. *Behaviour Research and Therapy,* 1974, *12,* 229–237.

Emmelkamp, P. M. G., & Emmelkamp-Benner, A. Effects of historically portrayed modeling and group treatment of self-observation: A comparison with agoraphobics. *Behaviour Research and Therapy,* 1975, *13,* 135–139.

Emmelkamp, P. M. G., & Wessels, H. Flooding in imagination vs flooding in vivo: A comparison with agoraphobics. *Behaviour Research and Therapy,* 1975, *13,* 7–15.

Epley, S. W. Reduction of the behavioral effects of aversive stimulation by the presence of companions. *Psychological Bulletin,* 1974, *81,* 271–283.

Eskedal, G. A. Symbolic role modeling and cognitive learning in the training of counselors. *Journal of Counseling Psychology,* 1975, *22,* 152–155.

Estes, W. K. (Ed.). *Handbook of learning and cognitive*

processes (Vol. 1 & 2). Hillsdale, N.J.: Lawrence Erlbaum Associates, 1975.

Eysenck, H. J. The learning theory model of neurosis—a new approach. Behaviour Research and Therapy, 1976, 14, 251–267.

Fairweather, G. W., Sanders, D. H., Maynard, H., & Cressler, D. L. Community life for the mentally ill: An alternative to institutional care. Chicago: Aldine, 1969.

Fazio, A. F. Implosive therapy with semiclinical phobias. Journal of Abnormal Psychology, 1972, 80, 183–188.

Feist, J. R., & Rosenthal, T. L. Serpent versus surrogate and other deteriminants of runway fear differences. Behaviour Research and Therapy, 1973, 11, 483–489.

Festinger, L. A theory of social comparison processes. Human Relations, 1954, 7, 117–140.

Fieve, R. R. Overview of therapeutic and prophylactic trials with lithium in psychiatric patients. In S. Gerhson and B. Shopsin (Eds.), Lithium—its role in psychiatric research and treatment. New York: Plenum Press, 1973. Pp. 317–350.

Fisher, T. J., Reardon, R. C., & Burck, H. D. Increasing information-seeking behavior with a model-reinforced videotape. Journal of Counseling Psychology, 1976, 23, 234–238.

Forehand, R. & Yoder, P. Acquisition and transfer of conceptual learning by normals and retardates: The effects of modeling, verbal cues, and reinforcement. Behaviour Research and Therapy, 1974, 12, 199–204.

Fremouw, W. J., & Harmatz, M. G. A helper model for behavioral treatment of speech anxiety. Journal of Consulting and Clinical Psychology, 1975, 43, 652–660.

Fry, P. S. Success, failure, and self-assessment ratings. Journal of Consulting and Clinical psychology, 1976, 44, 413–419.

Galassi, J. P., & Galassi, M. D. The effects of role playing variations on the assessment of assertive behavior. Behavior Therapy, 1976, 7, 343–347.

Galassi, J. P., Kostka, M. D., & Galassi, M. D. Assertive training: A one year follow-up. Journal of Counseling Psychology, 1975, 451–452.

Garbarino, J. The impact of anticipated reward upon cross-age tutoring. Journal of Personality and Social Psychology, 1975, 32, 421–428.

Gerst, M. S. Symbolic coding processes in observational learning. Journal of Personality and Social Psychology, 1971, 19, 7–17.

Glasgow, R. E., & Arkowitz, H. The behavioral assessment of male and female social competence in dyadic heterosexual interaction. Behavior Therapy, 1975, 6, 488–498.

Glogower, F., & Sloop, E. W. Two strategies of group training of parents as effective behavior modifyers. Behavior Therapy, 1976, 7, 177–184.

Goldberg, F. Effects of imagery on learning incidental material in the classroom. Journal of Educational Psychology, 1974, 66, 233–237.

Goldfried, M. R., Decenteceo, E. T., & Weinberg, L. Systematic rational restructuring as a self-control technique. Behavior Therapy, 1974, 5, 247–254.

Goldsmith, J. B., & McFall, R. M. Development and

evaluation of an interpersonal skill-training program for psychiatric inpatients. Journal of Abnormal Psychology, 1975, 84, 51–58.

Goldstein, A. P., Martens, D., Hubben, J., Van Belle, H. A., Schaaf, W., Wiersma, H., & Goedhart, A. The use of modeling to increase independent behavior. Behaviour Research and Therapy, 1973, 11, 31–42.

Goodman, E. O. Modeling: A method of parent education. The family coordinator, 1975, 24, 7–11.

Goodwin, S. E., & Mahoney, M. J. Modification of aggression through modeling: An experimental probe. Journal of Behavior Therapy and Experimental Psychiatry, 1975, 6, 200–202.

Greenberg, D. J., Scott, S. B., Pisa, A., & Friesen, D. D. Beyond the token economy: A comparison of two contingency programs. Journal of Consulting and Clinical Psychology, 1975, 43, 498–503.

Grusec, J. E., & Skubiski, S. L. Model nurturance, demand characteristics of the modeling experiment, and altruism. Journal of Personality and Social Psychology, 1970, 14, 352–359.

Gutrude, M. E., Goldstein, A. P., & Hunter, G. F. The use of modeling and role playing to increase social interaction among asocial psychiatric patients. Journal of Consulting and Clinical Psychology, 1973, 40, 408–415.

Hallam, R. S. Extinction of ruminations: A case study. Behavior Therapy, 1974, 5, 565–568.

Hawkins, H. L., Reicher, G. M., Rogers, M., & Peterson, L. Flexible coding in word recognition. Journal of Experimental Psychology: Human Perception and Performance, 1976, 2, 380–385.

Hersen, M., & Bellack, A. S. Social skills training for chronic psychiatric patients: Rationale, research findings, and future directions. Comprehensive Psychiatry, 1976a, 17, 559–580.

Hersen, M., & Bellack, A. S. A multiple-baseline analysis of social-skills training in chronic schizophrenics. Journal of Applied Behavior Analysis, 1976b, 9, 239–245.

Hersen, M., & Eisler, R. M. Social skills training. In W. E. Craighead, A. E. Kazdin, and M. J. Mahoney (Eds.), Behavior modification: Principles, issues, and applications. Boston: Houghton-Mifflin, 1976. Pp. 361–375.

Hersen, M., Eisler, R. M., & Miller, P. M. An experimental analysis of generalization in assertive training. Behaviour Research and Therapy, 1974, 12, 295–310.

Hersen, M., Eisler, R. M., Miller, P. M., Johnson, M. B., & Pinkston, S. G. Effects of practice, instructions, and modeling on components of assertive behavior. Behaviour Research and Therapy, 1973, 11, 443–451.

Hill, M. W., Hops, H., & Johnson, S. M. Generalization and maintenance of classroom treatment effects. Behavior Therapy, 1975, 6, 188–200.

Hurley, A. D. Covert reinforcement: The contribution of the reinforcing stimulus to treatment outcome. Behavior Therapy, 1976, 7, 374–378.

Jacobson, N. S., & Martin, B. Behavioral marriage therapy: current status. Psychological Bulletin, 1976, 83, 540–556.

Jaffe, P. G., & Carlson, P. M. Modeling therapy for test

anxiety: The role of model affect and consequences. *Behaviour Research and Therapy*, 1972, *10*, 329–339.

Jaffe, P. G., & Carlson, P. M. Relative efficacy of modeling and instructions in eliciting social behavior from chronic psychiatric patients. *Journal of Consulting and Clinical Psychology*, 1976, *44*, 200–207.

Jeffery, R. W. The influence of symbolic and motor rehearsal in observational learning. *Journal of Research in Personality*, 1976, *10*, 116–127.

Jesness, C. F. Comparative effectiveness of behavior modification and transactional analysis programs for delinquents. *Journal of Consulting and Clinical Psychology*, 1975, *43*, 758–779.

Kanfer, F. H., Karoly, P., & Newman, A. Source of feedback, observational learning, and attitude change. *Journal of Personality and Social Psychology*, 1974, *29*, 30–38.

Karoly, P. Multicomponent behavioral treatment of fear of flying: A case report. *Behavior Therapy*, 1974, *5*, 265–270.

Kauffman, J. M., LaFleur, N. K., Hallahan, D. P., & Chanes, C. M. Imitation as a consequence for children's behavior: Two experimental case studies. *Behavior Therapy*, 1975, *6*, 535–542.

Kazdin, A. E. Covert modeling and the reduction of avoidance behavior. *Journal of Abnormal Psychology*, 1973, *81*, 87–95.

Kazdin, A. E. Covert modeling, model similarity, and reduction of avoidance behavior. *Behavior Therapy*, 1974a, *5*, 325–340.

Kazdin, A. E. The effect of model identity and fear-relevant similarity on covert modeling. *Behavior Therapy*, 1974b, *5*, 624–635.

Kazdin, A. E. Effects of covert modeling and model reinforcement on assertive behavior. *Journal of Abnormal Psychology*, 1974c, *83*, 240–252.

Kazdin, A. E. Covert modeling, imagery assessment, and assertive behavior. *Journal of Consulting and Clinical Psychology*, 1975, *43*, 716–724.

Kazdin, A. E. Effects of covert modeling, multiple models, and model reinforcement on assertive behavior. *Behavior Therapy*, 1976, *7*, 211–222.

Kirsch, I., Wolpin, M., & Knutson, J. L. Comparison of *in vivo* methods for rapid reduction of "stage fright" in the college classroom: A field experiment. *Behavior Therapy*, 1975, *6*, 165–171.

Klein, D. C., Fencil-Morse, E., & Seligman, M. E. P. Learned helplessness, depression, and the attribution of failure. *Journal of Personality and Social Psychology*, 1976, *33*, 508–516.

Kornhaber, R. C., & Schroeder, H. E. Importance of model similarity on extinction of avoidance behavior in children. *Journal of Consulting and Clinical Psychology*, 1975, *43*, 601–607.

Kunce, J. T., Bruch, M. A., & Thelen, M. H. Vicarious induction of academic achievement in disadvantaged adults. *Journal of Counseling Psychology*, 1974, *21*, 507–510.

Langevin, R., & Martin, M. Can erotic responses be classically conditioned? *Behavior Therapy*, 1975, *6*, 350–355.

Lanyon, R. I., & Barocas, V. S. Effects of contingent events on stuttering and fluency. *Journal of Consulting and Clinical Psychology*, 1975, *43*, 786–793.

Lavigneur, H. The use of siblings as an adjunct to the treatment of children in the home with parents as therapists. *Behavior Therapy*, 1976, *7*, 602–613.

Leitenberg, H., Agras, W. S., Allen, R., Butz, R., & Edwards, J. Feedback and therapist praise during treatment of phobias. *Journal of Consulting and Clinical Psychology*, 1975, *43*, 396–404.

Lepper, M. R., & Greene, D. Turning play into work: Effects of adult surveillance and extrinsic rewards on children's intrinsic motivation. *Journal of Personality and Social Psychology*, 1975, *31*, 479–486.

Levine, J. M., Ranelli, C. J., & Valle, R. S. Self-evaluation and reaction to a shifting other. *Journal of Personality and Social Psychology*, 1974, *29*, 637–643.

Levine, J., & Zigler, E. Denial and self-image in stroke, lung cancer, and heart disease patients. *Journal of Consulting and Clinical Psychology*, 1975, *43*, 751–757.

Lewis, S. A comparsion of behavior therapy techniques in the reduction of fearful avoidance behavior. *Behavior Therapy*, 1974, *5*, 648–655.

Linehan, K. S., Rosenthal, T. L., Kelley, J. E., & Theobald, D. E. Homogeneity and heterogeneity of problem class in modeling treatment of fears. *Behaviour Research and Therapy*, in press.

Lira, F. T., Nay, W. R., McCollough, J. P., & Etkin, M. W. Relative effects of modeling and role playing in the treatment of avoidance behaviors. *Journal of Consulting and Clinical Psychology*, 1975, *43*, 608–618.

Litvak, S. B. A comparison of two brief group behavior therapy techniques on the reduction of avoidance behavior. *The Psychological Record*, 1969, *19*, 329–334.

LoPiccalo, J. Effective components of systematic desensitization. *Dissertation Abstracts International*, 1970, *31*, (3-b), 1543.

Lovaas, O. I., Freitas, L., Nelson, K., & Whalen, C. The establishment of imitation and its use for the development of complex behavior in schizophrenic children. *Behaviour Research and Therapy*, 1967, *5*, 171–181.

Lovaas, O. I., Koegel, R., Simmons, J. Q., & Stevens, J. Some generalization and follow-up measures on autistic children in behavior therapy. *Journal of Applied Behavior Analysis*, 1973, *6*, 131–166.

Lovaas, O. I., & Newsom, S. C. Behavior modification with psychotic children. In H. Leitenberg (Ed.), *Handobook of behavior modification and behavior therapy*. Englewood Cliffs, N.J.: Prentice-Hall, 1976. Pp. 303–360.

Luborsky, L., Singer, B., & Luborsky, L. Comparative studies of psychotherapies: Is it true that "everyone has won and all must have prizes"? *Archives of General Psychiatry*, 1975, *32*, 995–1008.

Maccoby, N., & Farquhar, J. W. Communication for health: unselling heart disease. *Journal of Communication*, 1975, *25*, 114–126.

MacDonald, M. L., Lindquist, C. U., Kramer, J. A., McGrath, R. A., & Rhyne, L. L. Social skills training: Behavior rehearsal in groups on dating skills. *Journal of Counseling Psychology*, 1975, *22*, 224–230.

Macri, I. Scope of modeling array in concept attainment. Unpublished M. A. thesis, University of Arizona, Tucson, Az., 1976.

Mahoney, M. J. *Cognition and behavior modification*. Cambridge, Mass.: Ballinger, 1974.

Mann, J. Vicarious desensitization of test anxiety through observation of videotaped treatment. *Journal of Counseling Psychology*, 1972, *19*, 1–7.

Mann, J., & Rosenthal, T. L. Vicarious and direct counterconditioning of test anxiety through individual and group desensitization. *Behaviour Research and Therapy*, 1969, *7*, 359–367.

Marburg, C. C., Houston, B. K., & Holmes, D. S. Influence of multiple models on the behavior of institutionalized retarded children: Increased generalization to other models and other behaviors. *Journal of Consulting and Clinical Psychology*, 1976, *44*, 514–519.

Marlatt, G. A. Task structure and the experimental modification of verbal behavior. *Psychological Bulletin*, 1972, *78*, 335–350.

Marzillier, J. S., Lambert, C., & Kellett, J. A controlled evaluation of systematic desensitization and social skills training for socially inadequate psychiatric patients. *Behaviour Research and Therapy*, 1976, *14*, 225–238.

Masters, J. C., & Christy, M. D. Achievement standards for contingent self-reinforcement: Effects of task length and task difficulty. *Child Development*, 1974, *45*, 6–13.

Masters, J. C., Gordon, F. R., & Clark, L. V. Effects of self-dispensed and externally dispensed model consequences on acquisition, spontaneous and oppositional imitation, and long-term retention. *Journal of Personality and Social Psychology*, 1976, *33*, 421–430.

McAllister, A., & Kiesler, D. J. Interviewee disclosure as a function of interpersonal trust, task modeling, and interviewer self-disclosure. *Journal of Consulting and Clinical Psychology*, 1975, *43*, 428.

McFall, R. M., & Lillesand, D. B. Behavioral rehearsal with modeling and coaching in assertion training. *Journal of Abnormal Psychology*, 1971, *77*, 313–323.

McFall, R. M., & Twentyman, C. T. Four experiments on the relative contributions of rehearsal, modeling, and coaching to assertion training. *Journal of Abnormal Psychology*, 1973, *81*, 199–218.

McGarry, M. S., & West, S. G. Stigma among the stigmatized: Resident mobility, communication ability, and physical appearance as predictors of staff-resident interactions. *Journal of Abnormal Psychology*, 1975, *84*, 399–405.

McGovern, K. B., Arkowitz, H., & Gilmore, S. K. The evaluation of social skills training programs for college dating inhibitions. *Journal of Counseling Psychology*, 1975, *22*, 505–512.

McGuire, D., Thelen, M. A., & Amolsch, T. Interview self-disclosure as a function of length of modeling and descriptive instructions. *Journal of Consulting and Clinical Psychology*, 1975, *43*, 356–362.

McKeown, D., Jr., Adams, H. E., & Forehand, R. Generalization to the classroom of principles of behavior modification taught to teachers. *Behaviour Research and Therapy*, 1975, *13*, 85–92.

McLean, P. D., Ogston, K., & Grauer, L. A behavioral approach to the treatment of depression. *Journal of Behavior Therapy and Experimental Psychiatry*, 1973, *4*, 323–330.

Meichenbaum, D. Examination of model characteristics in reducing avoidance behavior. *Journal of Personality and Social Psychology*, 1971, *17*, 298–307.

Meichenbaum, D. Cognitive factors in behavior modification: Modifying what clients say to themselves. In C. M. Franks and G. T. Wilson (Eds.), *Annual review of behavior therapy: Theory and practice*. New York: Brunner-Mazel, 1973. Pp. 416–431.

Meichenbaum, D., & Cameron, R. Training schizophrenics to talk to themselves: A means of developing attentional controls. In M. J. Mahoney and C. E. Thoresen (Eds.), *Self-control: Power to the person*. Monterey, Calif.: Brooks-Cole, 1974. Pp. 263–290.

Melamed, B. G., & Siegel, L. J. Reduction of anxiety in children facing hospitalization and surgery by use of filmed models. *Journal of Consulting and Clinical Psychology*, 1975, *43*, 511–521.

Meyers, A., Mercatoris, M., & Sirota, A. Use of covert self-instruction for the elimination of psychotic speech. *Journal of Consulting and Clinical Psychology*, 1976, *44*, 480–482.

Mikulas, W. L. A televised self-control clinic. *Behavior Therapy*, 1976, *7*, 564–566.

Miller, N. E., & Dollard, J. *Social learning and imitation*. New Haven: Yale University Press, 1941.

Miller, P. M., Hersen, M., & Eisler, R. M. Relative effectiveness of instructions, agreements, and reinforcement in behavioral contracts with alcoholics. *Journal of Abnormal Psychology*, 1974, *83*, 548–553.

Miller, W. R., & Seligman, M. E. P. Depression and learned helplessness in man. *Journal of Abnormal Psychology*, 1975, *84*, 228–238.

Mitchell, K. R., Hall, R. F., & Piatkowska, O. E. A group program for the treatment of failing college students. *Behavior Therapy*, 1975, *6*, 324–336.

Moore, B., Mischel, W., & Zeiss, A. Comparative effects of the reward stimulus and its cognitive representation in voluntary delay. *Journal of Personality and Social Psychology*, 1976, *34*, 419–424.

Nay, W. R. A systematic comparison of instructional techniques for parents. *Behavior Therapy*, 1975, *6*, 14–21.

Nelson, C. M., Worrell, J., & Polsgrove, L. Behaviorally disordered peers as contingency managers. *Behavior Therapy*, 1973, *4*, 270–276.

Obler, M. Systematic desensitization in sexual disorders. *Journal of Behavior Therapy and Experimental Psychiatry*, 1973, *4*, 93–101.

O'Brien, F., & Azrin, N. H. Interaction priming: A method of reinstating patient-family relationships. *Behaviour Research and Therapy*, 1973, *11*, 133–136.

O'Connor, R. D. Modification of social withdrawal through symbolic modeling. *Journal of Applied Behavior Analysis*, 1969, *2*, 15–22.

O'Connor, R. D. Relative efficacy of modeling, shaping, and the combined procedures for modification of social withdrawal. *Journal of Abnormal Psychology*, 1972, *79*, 327–334.

Orenstein, H., & Carr, J. Implosion therapy by tape-recording. *Behaviour Research and Therapy*, 1975, *13*, 177–182.

Patterson, G. R., & Reid, J. B. Intervention for families of aggressive boys: A replication study. *Behaviour Re-*

search and Therapy, 1973, 11, 383–394.

Piliavin, I. M., Piliavin, J. A., & Rodin, J. Costs, diffusion, and the stigmatized victim. Journal of Personality and Social Psychology, 1975, 32, 429–438.

Posner, M. I. Coordination of internal codes. In W. G. Chase (Ed.), Visual information processing. New York: Academic Press, 1973.

Pressley, G. M. Mental imagery helps eight-year-olds remember what they read. Journal of Educational Psychology, 1976, 68, 355.

Rabavilas, A. D., Boulougouris, J. C., & Stefanis, C. Duration of flooding sessions in the treatment of obsessive-compulsive patients. Behaviour Research and Therapy, 1976, 14, 349–355.

Rachman, S. The meanings of fear. Harmondsworth, Middlesex, England: Penguin, 1974.

Rachman, S. The passing of the two-stage theory of fear and avoidance: Fresh possibilities. Behaviour Research and Therapy, 1976, 14, 125–131.

Rachman, S., Hodgson, R., & Marks, I. M. Treatment of chronic obsessive-compulsive neurosis. Behaviour Research and Therapy, 1971, 9, 237–247.

Rachman, S., Marks, I. M., & Hodgson, R. The treatment of obsessive-compulsive neurotics by modelling and flooding in vivo. Behaviour Research and Therapy, 1973, 11, 463–471.

Rachman, S., & Seligman, M. E. P. Unprepared phobias: Be prepared. Behaviour Research and Therapy, 1976, 14, 333–338.

Rankin, H. Are models necessary? Behaviour Research and Therapy, 1976, 14, 181–183.

Rathus, S. A. Instigation of assertive behavior through videotape-mediated assertive models and directed practice. Behaviour Research and Therapy, 1973, 11, 57–65.

Raugh, M. R., & Atkinson, R. C. A mnemonic method for learning a second-language vocabulary. Journal of Eductional Psychology, 1975, 67, 1–16.

Raw, M. Persuading people to stop smoking. Behaviour Research and Therapy, 1976, 14, 97–101.

Regan, D. T., & Totten, J. Empathy and attribution: Turning observers into actors. Journal of Personality and Social Psychology, 1975, 32, 850–856.

Rescorla, R. A., & Solomon, R. L. Two-process learning theory: Relationships between Pavlovian conditioning and instrumental learning. Psychological Review, 1967, 74, 151–182.

Resick, P. A., Forehand, R., & Peed, S. Prestatement of contingencies: The effects on acquisition and maintenance of behavior. Behavior Therapy, 1974, 5, 642–647.

Riccio, D. C., & Silvestri, R. Extinction of avoidance behavior and the problem of residual fear. Behaviour Research and Therapy, 1973, 11, 1–9.

Rigney, J. W., & Lutz, K. A. Effect of graphic analogies in chemistry on learning and attitude. Journal of Educational Psychology, 1976, 68, 305–311.

Risley, T. R., & Wolf, M. M. Establishing functional speech in echolalic children. Behaviour Research and Therapy, 1967, 5, 73–88.

Ritter, B. The group treatment of children's snake phobias, using vicarious and contact desensitization procedures. Behaviour Research and Therapy, 1968, 6, 1–6.

Ritter, B. The use of contact desensitization, demonstration-plus-participation, and demonstration alone in the treatment of acrophobia. Behaviour Research and Therapy, 1969, 7, 157–164.

Robert, M., White, G. M., & Rosenthal, T. L. Format for exposure and complexity of array in observational rule attainment. Psychological Reports, 1975, 37, 999–1007.

Rogers, R. W., & Deckner, C. W. Effects of fear appeals and physiological arousal upon emotion, attitudes, and cigarette smoking. Journal of Personality and Social Psychology, 1975, 32, 222–230.

Roper, G., & Rachman, S. Obsessional-compulsive checking: Experimental replication and development. Behaviour research and Therapy, 1976, 14, 25–32.

Roper, G., Rachman, S., & Marks, I. Passive and participant modeling in exposure treatment of obsessive-compulsive neurotics. Behaviour Research and Therapy, 1975, 13, 271–279.

Rosch, E. The nature of mental codes for color categories. Journal of Experimental Psychology: Human Perception and Performance, 1975, 1, 303–322.

Rosenthal, R. H., White, G. M., & Rosenthal, T. L. Probability matching through direct and vicarious experience. Psychological Reports, 1975, 36, 883–889.

Rosenthal, T. L. Modeling therapies. In M. Hersen, R. M. Eisler, and P. M. Miller (Eds), Progress in behavior modification, Vol. 2. New York: Academic Press, 1976. Pp. 53–97.

Rosenthal, T. L. Learning by observation, vicarious and self-reinforcement processes. In H. Zeier (Ed.), The psychology of the twentieth century, Vol. 5. Zurich: Kindler Verlag, in press.

Rosenthal, T. L., Hung, J. H., & Kelley, J. E. Therapeutic social influence: Sternly strike while the iron is hot. Behaviour Research and Therapy, 1977, 15, 253–260.

Rosenthal, T. L., & Kellogg, J. S. Demonstration versus instructions in concept attainment by mental retardates. Behaviour Research and Therapy, 1973, 11, 299–302.

Rosenthal, T. L., & Reese, S. L. The effects of covert and overt modeling on assertive behavior. Behaviour Research and Therapy, 1976, 14, 463–469.

Rosenthal, T. L., & White, G. M. Initial probability, rehearsal, and constraint in associative class selection. Journal of Experimental Child Psychology, 1972, 13, 261–274.

Rosenthal, T. L., White, G. M., & Alford, G. S. Some memory effects with sequential impoverished visual stimuli. Perceptual and Motor Skills, 1974, 38, 1115–1120.

Rosenthal, T. L., & Zimmerman, B. J. Modeling by exemplification and instruction in training conservation. Developmental Psychology, 1972, 6, 393–401.

Rosenthal, T. L., & Zimmerman, B. J. Organization, observation, and guided practice in concept attainment and generalization. Child Development, 1973, 44, 606–613.

Rosenthal, T. L., & Zimmerman, B. J. Organization and

stability of transfer in vicarious concept attainment. *Child Development,* 1976, *47,* 110–117.

Ross, M. The self-perception of intrinsic motivation. In J. H. Harvey, W. J. Ickes, and R. F. Kidd (Eds.), *New directions in attribution research.* Hillsdale, N.J.: Lawrence Erlbaum Associates, 1976.

Royer, J. M., & Cable, G. W. Illustrations, analogies, and facilitative transfer in prose learning. *Journal of Educational Psychology,* 1976, *68,* 205–209.

Russell, M. A. H., Armstrong, E., & Patel, U. A. Temporal contiguity in electric aversion therapy for smoking. *Behaviour Research and Therapy,* 1976, *14,* 103–123.

Sarason, I. G. Test anxiety and cognitive modeling. *Journal of Pesonality and Social Psychology,* 1973, *28,* 58–61.

Sarason, I. G. Test anxiety and the self-disclosing coping model. *Journal of Consulting and Clinical Psychology,* 1975, *43,* 148–153.

Schroeder, H. E., & Rich, A. R. The process of fear reduction through systematic desensitization. *Journal of Consulting and Clinical Psychology,* 1976, *44,* 191–199.

Schvaneveldt, R. W., Meyer, D. E., & Becker, C. A. Lexical ambiguity, semantic context, and visual word recognition. *Journal of Experimental Psychology: Human Perception and Performance,* 1976, *2,* 243–256.

Serber, M. Videotape feedback in the treatment of couples with sexual dysfunction. *Archives of Sexual Behavior,* 1974, *3,* 377–380.

Shaw, D. W., & Thoresen, C. E. Effects of modeling and desensitization in reducing dental phobia. *Journal of Counseling Psychology,* 1974, *21,* 415–420.

Shelton, J. L. Murder strikes and panic follows—can behavior modification help? *Behavior Therapy,* 1973, *4,* 706–708.

Sherman, A. R. Real-life exposure as a primary therapeutic factor in desensitization of fear. *Journal of Abnormal Psychology,* 1972, *79,* 19–28.

Sherman, J. A. Use of reinforcement and imitation to reinstate verbal behavior in mute psychotics. *Journal of Abnormal Psychology,* 1965, *70,* 155–164.

Shiffrin, R. M., McKay, D. P., & Shaffer, W. O. Attending to forty-nine spatial positions at once. *Journal of Experimental Psychology: Human Perception and Performance,* 1976, *2,* 14–22.

Shimkunas, A. Demand for intimate self-disclosure and pathological verbalizations in schizophrenia. *Journal of Abnormal Psychology,* 1972, *80,* 197–205.

Silver, S. N. Outpatient treatment for sexual offenders. *Social Work,* 1976, *21,* 134–140.

Simpson, C. J., Rosenthal, T. L., Daniel, T. C., & White, G. M. Social influence variations in evaluating managed and unmanaged forest areas. *Journal of Applied psychology,* in press.

Skinner, B. F. *Science and human behavior.* New York: Macmillan, 1953.

Smith, J. A., & Lewis, W. A. Effect of videotaped models on the communications of college students in counseling. *Journal of Counseling Psychology,* 1974, *21,* 78–80.

Spiegler, M. D., & Liebert, R. M. Imitation as a function of response commonality, serial order, and vicarious punishment. *Journal of Experimental Child Psychology,* 1973, *15,* 116–124.

Spoehr, K. T., & Smith, E. E. The role of orthographic and phonotactic rules in perceiving letter patterns. *Journal of Experimental Psychology: Human Perception and Performance,* 1975, *1,* 21–34.

Springer, J., Springer, S., & Aaronson, B. An approach to teaching a course on dating behavior. *The family coordinator,* 1975, *24,* 13–19.

Stern, R., & Marks, I. Brief and prolonged flooding: A comparison in agoraphobic patients. *Archives of General Psychiatry,* 1973, *28,* 270–276.

Stevenson, I., & Wolpe, J. Recovery from sexual deviations through overcoming of non-sexual neurotic responses. *American Journal of Psychiatry,* 1960, *116,* 737–742.

Stone, G. L., & Gotlib, I. Effect of instructions and modeling on self-disclosure. *Journal of Counseling Psychology,* 1975, *22,* 288–293.

Stone, G. L., & Stebbins, L. W. Effect of differential pretraining on client self-disclosure. *Journal of Counseling Psychology,* 1975, *22,* 17–20.

Stone, G. L., & Vance, A. Instructions, modeling, and rehearsal: Implications for training. *Journal of Counseling Psychology,* 1976, *23,* 272–279.

Strahley, D. F. Systematic desensitization and counterphobic treatment of an irrational fear of snakes. *Dissertation Abstracts,* 1966, *27,* 973B.

Tavormina, J. B. Relative effectiveness of behavioral and reflective group counseling with parents of mentally retarded children. *Journal of Consulting and Clinical Psychology,* 1975, *43,* 22–31.

Thase, M. E., & Moss, M. K. The relative efficacy of covert modeling procedures and guided participant modeling in the reduction of avoidance behavior. *Journal of Behavior Therapy and Experimental Psychiatry,* 1976, *7,* 7–12.

Thelen, M. H., Dollinger, S. J., & Roberts, M. C. On being imitated; its effects on attraction and reciprocal imitation. *Journal of Personality and Social Psychology,* 1975, *31,* 467–472.

Thelen, M. H., Fry, R. A., Dollinger, S. J., & Paul, S. C. Use of videotaped models to improve the interpersonal adjustment of delinquents. *Journal of Consulting and Clinical Psychology,* 1976, *44,* 492.

Thelen, M. H., & Kirkland, K. D. On status and being imitated: Effects on reciprocal imitation and attraction. *Journal of Personality and Social Psychology,* 1976, *33,* 691–697.

Thomas, E. J., Walters, C. L., & O'Flaherty, K. A verbal problem checklist for use in assessing family verbal behavior. *Behavior Therapy,* 1974, *5,* 235–246.

Tsoi-Hoshmand, L. Marital therapy: An integrative behavioral-learning model. *Journal of Marriage and Family Counseling,* 1976, *2,* 170–191.

Tumblin, A., Gholson, B., Rosenthal, T. L., & Kelley, J. E. Vicarious acquisition and problem-solving strategies: Four training conditions. Unpublished manuscript, Memphis State University, 1977.

Twentyman, C. T., & McFall, R. M. Behavioral training of social skills in shy males. *Journal of Consulting and Clinical Psychology,* 1975, *43,* 384–395.

Vernon, D. T. A. Modeling and birth order in responses to painful stimuli. *Journal of Personality and Social*

Psychology, 1974, *29*, 794−799.

Vogler, R. E., Compton, J. V., & Weissbach, T. A. Integrated behavior change techniques for alcoholics. *Journal of Consulting and Clinical Psychology*, 1975, *43*, 233−243.

Watson, J. P., & Marks, I. M. Relevant and irrelevant fear in flooding: A crossover study of phobic patients. *Behavior Therapy*, 1971, *2*, 275−293.

Watson, J. P., Mullet, G. E., & Pillay, H. The effects of prolonged exposure to phobic situations upon agoraphobic patients treated in groups. *Behaviour Research and Therapy*, 1973, *11*, 531−545.

Watt, N. F., & Lubensky, A. W. Childhood roots of schizophrenia. *Journal of Consulting and Clinical Psychology*, 1976, *44*, 363−375.

Watts, M. W. Behavior modeling and self-devaluation with video self-confrontation. *Journal of Educational Psychology*, 1973, *64*, 212−215.

Weathers, L., & Liberman, R. The porta-prompter—a new electronic prompting and feedback device: A technical note. *Behavior Therapy*, 1973, *4*, 703−705.

Wein, K. S., Nelson, R. O., & Odom, J. V. The relative contributions of reattribution and verbal extinction to the effectiveness of cognitive restructuring. *Behavior Therapy*, 1975, *6*, 459−474.

Weiner, H. R., & Dubanoski, R. A. Resistence to extinction as a function of self- or externally-determined schedules of reinforcement. *Journal of Personality and Social Psychology*, 1975, *31*, 905−910.

Wexler, D. A., & Butler, J. M. Therapist modification of client expressiveness in client-centered therapy. *Journal of Consulting and Clinical Psychology*, 1976, *44*, 261−265.

White, G. M. Contextual determinants of opinion judgments: Field experimental probes of judgmental relativity boundary conditions. *Journal of Personality and Social Psychology*, 1975, *32*, 1047−1054.

White, G. M., & Rosenthal, T. L. Demonstration and lecture in information transmission: A field experiment. *Journal of Experimental Education*, 1974, *43*, 90−96.

White, G. M., Rosenthal, T. L., & Gerber, K. Anchoring effects in judging hierarchy items. Poster session presented at the Association for the Advancement of Behavior Therapy Convention, San Francisco, December, 1975.

Wincze, J. P., & Caird, W. K. The effects of systematic desensitization and video desensitization in the treatment of essential sexual dysfunction in women. *Behavior Therapy*, 1976, *7*, 335−342.

Wright, J. C. A comparison of systematic desensitization and social skill acquistion in the modification of a social fear. *Behavior Therapy*, 1976, *7*, 205−210.

Young, E. R., Rimm, D. C., & Kennedy, T. D. An experimental investigation of modeling and verbal reinforcement in the modification of assertive behavior. *Behaviour Research and Therapy*, 1973, *11*, 317−319.

Yulis, S. Generalization of therapeutic gain in the treatment of premature ejaculation. *Behavior Therapy*, 1976, *7*, 355−358.

Yussen, S. R. Determinants of visual attention and recall in observational learning by preschoolers and second graders. *Developmental Psychology*, 1974, *10*, 93−100.

Zimmerman, B. J., & Rosenthal, T. L. Observational learning of rule-governed behavior by children. *Psychological Bulletin*, 1974, *81*, 29−42.

PART IV

LEARNING, COGNITIVE, AND SELF-CONTROL PROCESSES IN PSYCHOTHERAPY AND BEHAVIOR CHANGE

17

COGNITION AND LEARNING IN TRADITIONAL AND BEHAVIORAL THERAPY

EDWARD J. MURRAY
LEONARD I. JACOBSON

University of Miami

This chapter is an attempt to integrate conceptually the methods used in traditional and behavioral therapy within the context of a modern view of the learning process. Over the last few decades profound changes have taken place in the area of learning that have important implications for understanding all forms of psychotherapy. These changes include a cognitive view of the learning process itself and a greater integration of cognitive processes with emotion, personality, and social interaction.

To begin, it should be appreciated that all forms of therapy involve learning, broadly defined. Sometimes it is difficult to see the learning aspect because of a confusing vocabulary of growth, motivation, lifting of repressions, freeing of energy, personality reorganization, and so on. Yet a close analysis of the meaning behind the metaphors indicates that learning in the sense of cognitive, emotional, and behavioral changes usually is intended (Ford and Urban, 1963).

Psychoanalytic theory, for example, actually includes a primitive learning theory in which gratifications produce attachments, traumas produce fixations, and so on (Hilgard & Bower, 1966). Treatment is a new learning situation. In fact, Freud described psychoanalysis as ". . . a re-education in overcoming internal resistances" (1904, 1950, p.262). Later, Alexander and French (1946) suggested that the essence of psychotherapy was a "corrective emotional experience," both in therapy and real life. Nevertheless, these implicit learning ideas were not formalized, nor did the psychology of learning have much impact on psychotherapy for a long time.

Historically, the first formal attempts to apply learning concepts to psychotherapy came in the decade following World War II (Dollard & Miller, 1950; Mowrer, 1950; Murray, 1954; Rotter, 1954; Shoben, 1949). Dollard and Miller, for example, reinterpreted psychoanalytic psychotherapy in learning terms such as reinforcement, generalization, and extinction. A significant aspect of their effort was that they found it necessary to postulate many additional processes, such as mediated discrimination and generalization, verbal labels and cue-producing responses, and approach-avoidance conflict on the symbolic level, in order to account for the higher mental processes that were involved in the phenomena they were attempting to explain. In addition, they made a number of assumptions about learned social responses in order to account for the social aspects of the patient's difficulties and the transference relationship between the patient and therapist.

Initially, the application of learning concepts to psychotherapy received a cool reception from most dynamically oriented psychologists and clinicians. In reviewing Dollard and Miller's book, Rapaport (1953) took the position that most theories of learning had not really developed to the point where they could deal with many clinical problems. In spite of the fact that Dollard and Miller went beyond the theories of their day, Rapaport felt that they did not come to grips with ego functions or with social and cultural factors. Actually, traditional therapists from nearly all schools of thought, neoanalytic, interpersonal, client-centered, existential, and humanistic, tended to reject the application of formal learning theories to psychotherapy.

The major objections to the theories of learning that were available in the early 1950s were that they did not adequately account for the importance of cognitive, personality, and social variables. Most therapists objected to the behavioristic exclusion of consciousness from scientific consideration, the causal model that assumes that behavior is fully determined by environmental events, and the reliance on the mechanistic conditioning model of learning. Therapists could not reconcile their own experiences with the view of the human being suggested by many learning theorists, particularly the extreme behaviorists (Skinner, 1953).

Since the early 1950s the application of learning principles to therapy has become identified with behavior therapy and behavior modification (Eysenck, 1960; Krasner & Ullmann, 1965; Wolpe, 1958). The behavioral approach has been characterized by the development of new techniques and the application of learning principles to a variety of clinical problems. The behavioral approach has had a vitalizing effect on the whole therapy field. At the same time, the behavioral approach was based on the learning theories available in the early 1950s. Classical conditioning, operant conditioning, and associational learning have been emphasized. The behavioral approaches tended to avoid consideration of cognitive and social aspects of the therapeutic situation. The approach was based on the behavioristic tenets of excluding consciousness, environmental causality, and mechanistic conditioning.

At first the behavioral approach appeared justified pragmatically. It was widely believed that Eysenck (1960) had provided powerful evidence against the efficacy of traditional psychotherapy, while evidence of the positive effects of the behavioral approach seemed to emerge on all sides. The situation seems different now. The Eysenck analysis has been challenged effectively by Bergin (1971). Some of the positive effects of behavior therapy turned out to be short-lived and limited. Recent evidence suggests that there is relatively little difference in effectiveness in a wide variety of therapeutic techniques (Bergin & Suinn, 1975). Although the whole issue of therapy outcome is complex and unresolved, the abandonment of traditional techniques in favor of behavioral techniques on the basis of efficacy does not seem justified at this time.

The theoretical basis for behavior therapy has also been challenged. Some time ago, Breger and McGaugh (1966) pointed out that the conditioning model did not really account for the complex cognitive and social variables operating in behavior therapy. Locke (1971) has pointed out that the methods developed by Wolpe violate the basic premises of behaviorism. Wolpe uses introspective methods to assess and test various aspects of consciousness such as thinking, feeling, and imagining, as well as asking the client to control them. Locke says that therapy with human beings necessarily involves dealing with conscious processes, whether acknowledged or not. He suggests that it was psychology's scientific defensiveness that made the study of mental processes unfashionable.

The crumbling of both theoretical and empirical justifications has led to a time of self-doubt in the behavioral therapy group. In fact, some have called for an abandonment of theory and the institution of a completely empirical attack on practical problems (London, 1972). We do not mourn the passing of the ideological flavor of the behavioral movement, but a completely empirical approach has its own limitations. An alternative is the development of better scientific theories tied in with both empirical research and clinical practice.

Since the 1950s, major changes have occurred in the area of learning that have major implications for psychotherapy and behavior therapy. The changes include an abandonment of the basic behaviorist model with its exclusion of consciousness, direct environmental causation, and the mechanistic conditioning process. What is taking its place is a cognitive model in which the human being is viewed as an information processing organism, capable of symbolization and thought, self-controlling and controlling the environment. Cognitive, personality, and social variables are considered fundamental parameters of the learning process.

Therefore, an interesting situation has emerged. Clinicians have in recent years shown considerable interest in applications of the psychology of learning. At the same time, learning researchers have become more and more impressed with the importance of many of the variables that have been of traditional importance to clinicians. This convergence may result in the development of an increasingly powerful and exciting psychology in which human behavior with all its ramifications can become an active area of scientific investigation.

In this chapter we will discuss this developing convergence of clinical and learning psychology. We will begin by reviewing research indicating the increased emphasis on cognitive, personality, and social interaction variables as fundamental parameters of human learning. We will then view both traditional and behavioral therapy in terms of these same factors and conclude by applying our analysis directly to some of the problems and controversies in psychotherapy and behavior modification research and practice. We hope to demonstrate that all three areas—learning, traditional

psychotherapy, and behavioral therapy—are moving closer together because it is being recognized that they deal with many of the same problems and processes.

COGNITION AND LEARNING

Classical Conditioning

There is, perhaps, no other concept that has had as profound an effect on psychological thought as the idea of conditioning. In his original experimental work, Pavlov started with existing, inborn reflexes, such as salivation to a food stimulus. Then he associated a previously neutral stimulus, such as a tone, with the food stimulus. In Pavlov's thinking, the association of the two stimuli produced a new neural connection between the tone and the salivary response, a conditioned reflex (Pavlov, 1927, 1960). The importance of this simple demonstration is that it provided the first coherent theory, as well as a useful vocabulary, for the explanation of acquired behavior far beyond the laboratory situation. Watson (1925), in particular, made the conditioned reflex the key concept in his behavioristic analysis of habit, emotion, language, thought, and personality.

A half a century of research on classical conditioning has changed markedly the conception that we have as to the basic processes that are involved. To begin with, not all stimuli are equally conditionable; some are more prepotent, suggesting innate factors. Most important, perhaps, is that in both appetitive and aversive animal conditioning, the conditioned response turns out to be different from the unconditioned response, sometimes dramatically so. The conditioned response seems to be more of a preparation for the unconditioned stimulus and the conditioned stimulus a signal for it. Furthermore, the contingency between the conditioned stimulus and the unconditioned stimulus can be learned without an overt response occurring, sometimes on the basis of observation alone. Motivational and emotional factors are also involved. Although it is not usually emphasized, even Pavlov knew that he had to keep his dogs hungry to get salivary conditioning (McGuigan & Lumsden, 1973; Schneiderman, 1973).

In the light of all of this research on classical conditioning, the basic explanation in terms of the formation of a new neural connection between the conditioned stimulus and the response has been abandoned gradually. If any connection is to be assumed, it is between the two stimuli. Even when "connection" is used in this sense, an extremely limited conception of the mammalian brain and its learning capacities is implied. An alternative conception is that the animal in the classical conditioning situation is being provided with information that is processed and stored in memory, while response selection is based on the requirements of the situation, the available repertoire, and the anticipated consequences. The classical conditioning of both skeletal and autonomic responses can be viewed in this cognitive framework.

When the classical conditioning procedure is applied to human subjects, it becomes clear that more is involved than forming a new stimulus-response connection. The subject is not a passive recipient of stimui, but is actively interpreting the situation. The subject can be seen as perceiving and storing information instead of having a response conditioned. The subject can even do this vicariously by observing someone else in a conditioning procedure. Furthermore, the human subject may voluntarily produce or inhibit the conditioned response. In short, human behavior in a classical conditioning situation depends on a number of personal, social, and cognitive variables (McGuigan & Lumsden, 1973; Prokasy, 1965).

Some researchers have applied classical conditioning procedures to complex human situations and interpreted the results in terms of a conditioning process without taking into account the personal, social, and cognitive processes involved. For example, Staats and Staats (1957, 1958) reported the classical conditioning of meaning and attitudes in a complex deception experiment. Under the guise of learning two lists of words simultaneously, nonsense syllables were presented visually and evaluative words were presented verbally. Certain nonsense syllables were paired with positive evaluative words and others with negative ones. Later the nonsense syllables were rated for affec-

tive tone. The results were interpreted as showing a classical conditioning process. However, subsequent research showed that the results could be accounted for by the degree to which the subjects were aware of the contingencies between the nonsense syllables and the evaluative words as well as their awareness of the demand characteristics of the study and their willingness to comply with the demands (Insko & Oakes, 1966; Page, 1969).

The implication of all of this is that when we place a human being in a classical conditioning procedure, we can not circumvent the complex cognitive processes in operation. It is possible to present simple stimuli and observe discrete responses while ignoring everything else. But the subject is actively engaged in trying to understand the situation and in deciding what he or she wants to do about it. An adequate account of the phenomena must include these mediating processes and the interpersonal context in which they occur. Furthermore, if we give up the conditioning explanatory model, we can think up new and more effective methods of presenting information and motivating behavior change. The field of social psychology, in particular, offers a vast array of procedures for changing meaning, values, attitudes, and behavior that go way beyond anything suggested by simple classical conditioning (Goldstein, Heller, & Sechrest, 1966).

Operant Conditioning

A whole approach to the study and understanding of behavior has been developed from the principles of operant conditioning (Skinner, 1953). Reinforcement contingencies are said to explain not only much of animal behavior, but also human behavior of the most complex personal and social kinds. Furthermore, the explanation of behavior does not require consideration of internal events that are seen as no more than links in a causal chain. Now there is little doubt on anyone's part that rewards and punishments are of great importance in our lives. The issue, at this point, is how we can best construe the role of reinforcement and relate it to other psychological processes.

In formulating the Law of Effect, Thorndike's thinking was not too far from Pavlov's in conceiving of learning as consisting of neural connections between stimuli and responses that could be strengthened or weakened by outcome (Hilgard & Bower, 1966). Although Skinner (1938) made a clear distinction between classical and operant conditioning in terms of procedure, the basic concept of a reflex was originally applied to both. The underlying model, whether stated in neurological or functional terms, is that behavior can be explicated by linear relationships between overt responses and environmental stimuli. Reinforcement is assumed to operate directly on preceding responses without reference to mediating processes.

The concept of reinforcement so central to the operant conditioning approach has not been consistently supported by research on animal learning. Bolles (1972) summarizes a number of studies in which behavior appears superficially to be under reinforcement control but is actually a species-specific food-getting or defensive reaction. The animals learn to expect a reinforcement and then show species-specific behavior. In fact, the concept of reinforcement can be replaced by that of incentive motivation. An animal learns expectancies or contingencies between stimuli and between responses and stimuli. Whether a response is performed or not depends on motivational factors. Therefore, even on the animal level, learning theorists are turning toward a model that stresses the mediating processes of cognition and motivation.

The application of operant conditioning to human behavior is even more problematic. There is an increasing mass of data inexplicable by the conditioning model, as shown in the recent comprehensive review by Horton and Turnage (1976). One good example is verbal conditioning, an important process in the early application of learning theory to psychotherapy. In the original demonstration of verbal conditioning, Greenspoon (1962) found that subjects instructed to say random words aloud would increase the frequency of a given class to which the experimenter responded with an unobtrusive "mmm-hmm.' The pattern of results looked like typical conditioning and extinction curves.

The most controversial aspect of the Greenspoon effect was the claim that the subject was unaware of what the experimenter was doing. There-

fore, the effect looked like an automatic, unconscious conditioning procedure with great possibilities as a powerful tool for behavior control. Historically, verbal conditioning was introduced during an era when the possibilities of brainwashing, subliminal perception, and other involuntary methods of behavior control were being explored and were creating considerable concern.

In any case, the first controversy concerned the role of awareness in verbal conditioning. Awareness was defined as a verbal report by the subject indicating that he or she recognizes that the presentation of the reinforcing stimulus is contingent on the emission of specific responses by him or her. In the early studies, just a few open-ended questions were asked at the end of the study, with little awareness being reported. However, as the postexperimental interviews became more detailed and sophisticated, it was found that awareness was closely related to verbal conditioning. In fact, the best evidence indicates that only subjects aware of the correct response-reinforcement contingency demonstrate acquisition and extinction of verbal behavior; unaware subjects do not condition (Dulany, 1962; Jacobson, 1969; Spielberger & DeNike, 1966).

The role of awareness has also been demonstrated in the operant conditioning of nonverbal responses. Paul, Eriksen, and Humphreys (1962) placed subjects in a heat-humidity chamber in which the temperature was 105° F and the humidty was 85 percent. A 10 second draft of cool air was used as the reinforcer. The investigators then systematically reinforced various motor responses. Conditioning was found only for subjects who were able to verbalize the relationship between their responses and the reinforcer. In fact, it is difficult to find impressive evidence of human learning of any kind without awareness.

It would seem, then, that the crucial process in verbal conditioning, as well as in other forms of human learning, is the communication of information. The protracted process of response shaping and extinction is not necessarily the most efficient means of communicating information to a mature, intact human subject. In fact, observing another subject in a verbal conditioning study may be sufficient for learning. Such vicarious learning may even be more efficient that direct learning (Kanfer & Phillips, 1970). Under some conditions, direct instructions to the subject may be the most effective way of increasing or decreasing verbal responses (Merbaum & Lukens, 1968).

The way the subject processes the information given to him or her will also influence what happens in an operant conditioning situation. For example, if a subject believes he or she is being reinforced on one schedule, such as fixed ratio, but is actually being reinforced on another, such as fixed-interval, the subject may behave in accordance with beliefs instead of in accordance with the real contingencies (Baron, Kaufman, & Stauber, 1969). So, too, the effects of operant conditioning and extinction may depend on whether the subject attributes the occurrence of reinforcement to his or her own skill and efforts or to some outside agency or mere chance. (Rotter, Liverant, & Crowne, 1961). In other words, the subject is not only responding to reinforcement, but also to his or her interpretation of what that reinforcement means.

Verbal conditioning is a complex social situation; the transmission of information is not the only thing involved. After becoming aware of the response-reinforcement contingency, the subject must also become demand aware; this means that the subject realizes that he or she is expected to emit the reinforced responses (Dulany, 1968; Page, 1972). Even after the subject becomes contingency aware and demand aware, he or she has to be motivated to comply with the situational demands. Personality variables would be expected to be related to such compliance. In one study, Alegre and Murray (1974) found that verbal conditioning was related to Rotter's measure of locus of control. External locus of control subjects not only conditioned better, but stated that they had intended to cooperate.

Finally, very complex human motives may be involved in the verbal conditioning situation. Some subjects seem to comply and others seem to be negative. The critical motive for both of these behaviors seems to be evaluation apprehension. Kingsbury, Stevens, and Murray (1975) led some subjects to believe that the verbal conditioning task was a test of intelligence. These subjects conditioned much faster than control subjects. The slowest subjects to condition were those who were

led to believe that the verbal conditioning procedure was a revealing adjustment test. Both experimental procedures made the subjects apprehensive about being evaluated, but led to different coping strategies.

Therefore, both animal and human research raise serious questions about the adequacy of operant conditioning as an explanatory concept for complex learning situations. The subject seems to be learning expectancies, or acquiring information, about environmental contingencies and response consequences. The actual performance of responses depends on a number of personality, motivational, and situational factors.

Complex Human Learning

In addition to classical and operant conditioning, the traditional learning approach in psychology included a variety of tasks involving verbal learning, memory, and motor performance. This work was based on the fundamental concept of association, actually very similar to the processes assumed in conditioning. If two psychological events are associated, one elicits the other, and they are said to be connected or bonded (McGeoch, 1942).

In this traditional view of human learning the person was assumed to associate passively verbal stimuli and responses. Introspection and intervening processes were minimized. In fact, the process was considered "simple rote learning." However, when one of these classical tasks, such as paired associate learning, is examined closely, it is clearly neither simple nor rote, and it is probably not even true learning (Jacobson, Elenewski, & Lordahl, 1968).

In verbal learning experiments, subjects appear to be active, thinking, and motivated. The newer emphasis is on organizational processes, hypothesis testing, imagery, information processing, coping strategies, and other intervening processes based largely on computer analogs. The model that seems to be replacing the associational one is a cognitive, information-processing one. Based on a computer analog, the new model stresses the flow of information through stages of perception, encoding, short-term memory, long-term storage, retrieval, and outputs of various kinds. Learning consists not just of linking stimuli and responses, but of placing the information provided by the antecedent or consequent stimulus in a hierarchically organized network of information. The new information can be simply stored or might produce a cognitive reorganization at lower or even higher parts of the network. Behavior is governed by rules governing many situations instead of by an aggregation of links. Language, meaning, and context become very important (Horton & Turnage, 1976).

In psychology, the landmark book outlining the full implications of the cognitive approach was *Plans and the Structure of Behavior* (Miller, Galanter, & Pribram, 1960). Many psychologists began to see the possibility of a scientific model of people that did justice to the complexity of human thought, feeling, and behavior. The computer model provided a palpable basis for mental phenomena. The idea of programming made purposiveness concrete. Hierarchical organization and reorganization suggested new ways of looking at learning and problem solving. Finally, the central role of language in all aspects of human life was dramatized.

A second major force in the emergence of cognition was the developmental work of Piaget (Flavell, 1963). The seminal work of Piaget opened up the field of cognitive development. The method provided a way of studying the interaction of the organism and environment on intellectual, moral, and social development. Piaget suggested mental structures as ways of organizing experience and regulating behavior. Finally, the developing child was viewed as an active information-seeking and processing organism instead of as a passive receptacle for environmental inputs.

The widespread implications of the cognitive approach can be illustrated by a recent textbook by Lindsay and Norman (1972). Information-processing concepts are applied to brain functioning, perception, memory, language, learning, cognitive development, problem solving, decision making, social interaction, and motivation. Information processing is not just another topic in psychology; it is a new way of looking at the entire spectrum of human functioning.

Social learning theories have paralleled the development of the cognitive approach in human learning. These theories were developed largely by psychologists who had applied, clinical interests in the kind of learning that goes on in real social situations. They were convinced that psychopathology and psychotherapy involved learning processes, but they were dissatisfied with existing theories of learning, which seemed distant from the phenomena of greatest interest in social behavior.

One of the first of these social learning approaches was Miller and Dollard's *Social Learning and Imitation* (1941). Miller and Dollard worked within a conditioning framework. However, learning processes from the animal laboratory were modified and broadened to include acquired drives and rewards, learned cue-producing responses, language and reasoning, imitative learning, and cultural influences in learning. The book was ahead of its time in emphasizing "higher mental processes" such as attention, symbolization, mediated transfer, and foresight. In fact, Miller and Dollard suggest higher-order habits, such as grammar, that govern the manner in which other responses are combined.

A second social learning theorist is Julian Rotter (Rotter, 1954; Rotter, Chance, & Phares, 1972). Rotter's social learning theory is clearly cognitive, deriving from the tradition of field theory in psychology. One of the basic concepts is reinforcement, but reinforcement is used more in the incentive sense than in a conditioning one. Reinforcement values for a particular person are related to broad categories of needs such as status, dependency, dominance, independence, affect, and physical comfort. The second basic concept is expectancy, which is the subjective probability of a given behavior leading to a particular reinforcement. Expectancies may be very specific to a given situation, but people are assumed to have generalized expectancies that are brought into a specific situation. Such generalized expectancies include interpersonal trust and internal versus external control of reinforcement. Finally, behavior is defined in a very comprehensive way to include cognitive activities such as planning, reclassifying, rationalizing, and repressing.

The social learning theory proposed by Bandura (1969, 1974, 1977) has been particularly influential in recent years. Bandura clearly rejects the conception of learning in which behavior is automatically shaped by environmental forces. Behavioral consequences provide information and motivate the person, but behavioral outcome depends on intervening thought processes. Information is acquired, stored, and retrieved. Bandura's work on vicarious learning constitutes some of the strongest evidence against the response conditioning view of how reinforcement works. Bandura also has emphasized self-control processes that often transcend direct environmental control. For example, people internalize standards of behavior and reinforce themselves independently of external reinforcement. Bandura's approach leads to a sophisticated view of social interaction that includes reciprocal control, contractual arrangements, and moral principles.

Recently, Bandura (1977) proposed a theory of self-efficacy to explain changes in several modes of treatment. He suggests that the key to therapeutic change is the person's expectations of his or her own efficacy in specific situations. Expectations are based on information that can be provided from several sources. These sources include the person's own performance, vicarious experience, verbal persuasion, and emotional arousal. These sources of information are involved in a variety of traditional and behavioral therapeutic techniques.

In summary, complex human learning is no longer viewed as based on association or conditioning processes. Instead, a cognitive theory has emerged that is based on the information-processing models derived from the computer model. In addition, more clinically oriented social learning theorists have developed similar cognitive models, but with greater emphasis on motivational and personality aspects.

Emotion and Cognition

Conceptions of learning have important implications for the understanding of emotional reactions, which are of special significance in personality and psychotherapy. The traditional learning approach views an emotion, such as anxiety, as an autonomic response that is classically conditioned to environmental stimuli and that tends to disrupt ongoing behavior. The organism may learn to avoid the conditioned stimulus as if it were like the original pain or fear stimulus on which it was based. The autonomic state itself may produce aversive stimuli that function as a drive for learning new avoidance responses. The sort of treatment suggested by this concept of emotional learning is to stamp out the emotional response by extinction or by a pharmacological intervention.

The cognitive approach to emotion emphasizes the appraisal, not necessarily conscious, of the situation as a mediator between the environmental stimulus and the emotional response (Murray, 1964). The emotional response is not viewed as abnormal or disorganizing in itself, but as part of the adaptation to a situation that is judged to require a preparation for action of some kind. Thus, the perception of a person approaching is followed by a cognitive appraisal of the person as, in the simplest example, friend or foe. The bodily arousal reaction, experienced as a tendency to approach or avoid, constitutes the emotion proper. Therefore, the mediating cognitions are critical in understanding emotion.

The cognitive appraisal of a situation depends on the information available to the person, contextual as well as immediately relevant, and the characteristic way the person processes that information and deals with it. Thus, it is possible to alter a person's emotional reaction to a seemingly threatening stimulus by providing a benign interpretation of the event. An extinction procedure may be the simplest way of doing this, but more complex methods involving persuasion, vicarious experiences, and other communications may be more important in altering the appraisal of socially and symbolically threatening situations. Long-term personality factors, such as the tendency to appraise every setback as a catastrophe, may have to be dealt with to produce signigicant emotional change.

In addition to the appraisal of an environmental threat, the appraisal of the person's own ability to cope with the threat determines the emotional reaction. We risk death every day that we drive on a highway, but we do not react emotionally because we believe that we can cope with the situation. Even on the animal level, the autonomic arousal of a rat in a fear situation declines as an avoidance response is learned. Thus, the self-efficacy type of cognition described by Bandura (1977) plays a crucial role in emotional reactions. Both situational and personality factors would be expected to influence the appraisal of one's efficacy in a particular problem area.

There is little reason to believe that each emotion, as experienced by the person, consists of a discrete autonomic or bodily reaction. The bodily measures of emotion show too much variability and overlap for that. At the same time, a completely uniform arousal in all emotional states does not seem to exist. In fact, the broad energization once attributed to drive states is not consistent with observations of motives such as the motive to sleep after sleep deprivation. Murray (1965) has suggested that bodily arousal be viewed as a preparatory part of the response process instead of as an integral part of the motive or emotion. That is, the particular pattern of bodily arousal is determined by the appraisal of the response requirements of the anticipated situation. The situation may be judged as requiring increased or decreased autonomic arousal, tension in certain muscle groups but not in others, a feezing reaction or random activity, and so on. Although innate processes may also play a part in emotional reactions, the present analysis highlights the role of the cognitive appraisal of the response requirements in the situation.

Finally, the bodily arousal itself provides feedback information that must be appraised by the person. In some cases, the feedback is consistent with the other information the person has and poses no problem. In other cases, such as the Schachter type of situation, the person has no adequate explanation for the bodily arousal experienced and seeks additional information from the environment. The cases in which bodily reactions of various types are misinterpreted, such as the patient who viewed an instance of impotence as evidence of latent homosexuality, are of special clinical significance. A reattribution of this bodily symptom to performance anxiety led to improvement.

In summary, emotions need not be viewed as simple conditioned autonomic reactions. Emotions involve a complex sequence of environmental and bodily events mediated by cognitive appraisals of the situation, the person's ability to cope with the situation, and the feedback from the person's bodily reactions. The cognitive appraisals can be influenced by information from several sources with a consequent effect on the bodily reactions and experienced emotions. Bodily reactions can be viewed as preparatory for anticipated behavioral demands. In general, there is an intimate reciprocal relationship between cognitive processes and bodily reactions in emotion.

TRADITIONAL THERAPY

We turn now to an examination of traditional psychotherapy, particularly the psychoanalytic and client-centered forms of therapy. We will review data that indicate that initial expectations of help may lead to the reduction of emotional distress, that approach-avoidance behavior during therapy may be related to changes in expectations, and that the therapist influences such changes by his or her interventions. Psychotherapy will be viewed as a complex cognitive, emotional, and behavioral learning process operating within an interpersonal context.

Expectancy and Emotional Distress

Typically, the person who enters psychotherapy voluntarily is suffering emotionally as a result of unsatisfactory human relationships and low self-esteem. Most forms of psychopathology may be viewed primarily as unsuccessful patterns of interaction with significant others that interfere with the continuity and stability of important relationships. These interactions may be regarded as unsatisfactory by the patient, the significant others, or both. One of these unsuccessful interactions for the patient is the development of acute emotional distress (Murray, 1963; Murray, 1964).

As we discussed earlier, the modern approach to emotions stresses the cognitive appraisal of the situation that the person finds himself or herself in (Murray, 1964; Arnold, 1970). The clinical study of anxiety and depression also points to cognition as the key factor in emotional distress (Beck, 1976). The patient believes that he or she is helpless to cope with the present situation or that the future is hopeless. If anything changes the basic appraisal of the person, there should be a change in the emotional reaction.

In going to a psychotherapist, the patient hopes to get relief from the emotional distress and to improve self-esteem. In a comprehensive analysis of psychotherapy, Frank (1973) says that the demoralized patient does get relief from someone who offers hope of improvement. In a primitive society that someone may be a witch doctor or, among the less well-educated in our own society, a faith healer. The common elements are that a socially sanctioned healer, usually meeting in a special place, provides a therapeutic task, all justified by a belief system accepted by the patient. In our society, the physician plays that role for both physical and emotional distress by using medication. The medication depends largely on a placebo effect in reducing anxiety, depression, and related physical symptoms. The psychotherapist also plays the role of healer for emotional distress in some parts of our society, so that entering therapy arouses hopeful feelings.

With the arousal of hope, there is a decrease in the symptoms of emotional distress and demoralization. The process of anxiety reduction has been studied with a content analysis procedure by Murray (1956, 1964, 1968b). The initial reduction in anxiety was shown in content measures of recorded psychotherapy interviews. During the first few interviews, the measures showed a decline in physical complaints and intellectual defenses (Murray, 1954) and psychotic symptoms (Murray, 1962). Since little specific therapeutic activity had taken place, these dramatic reductions were probably due to the arousal of hope.

The expectancy effect is common to many forms of therapy and to primitive forms of healing. It is tempting to attribute the initial reduction of emotional distress to one's own brand of therapy. However, there is increasing evidence of expectancy of improvement as a nonspecific therapeutic factor. Research needs to be designed to distinguish between factors that are specific to the particular therapy being used and the nonspecific ones. We will illustrate this problem with a study on encounter groups, currently a popular form of therapy.

Encounter groups seem to arouse even more enthusiasm and expectation of favorable outcome than individual therapy. In one of the few controlled studies in this area, McCardel and Murray (1974) studied nonspecific factors in several types of groups. One was a highly structured, exercise-oriented group; one was a basic encounter group along the lines suggested by Rogers; and another was mixed. All of these groups showed favorable changes in comparison to an "at home" control group. However, an "on site" control group was led to believe that they were also in an encounter experience. Actually, they only engaged in recreational activities. Nevertheless, the "on site" control group did just as well as the therapy groups. The general expectancy of favorable change and group enthusiasm were enough to produce changes that looked like personal growth.

The importance of expectancy factors in the improvement of patients during the initial stages of therapy is not only of theoretical importance. Traditional psychotherapy has always been most effective with verbal, intelligent patients from the middle and upper socioeconomic classes. These patients seem to have the right expectations about psychotherapy, presumably because they have learned, in both formal and informal situations, that their problems have a psychological basis that can be helped by psychotherapy. On the other hand, lower-class patients do not share these beliefs. Recent research, however, has shown that lower-class patients can be taught these expectations through the use of preparatory interviews, dramatic movies, and other educational means. When the role expectations of patient and therapist are more congruent, lower-class patients remain in therapy long enough for other therapeutic processes to operate (Heitler, 1976).

Approach-Avoidance Behavior

Subsequent to the initial reduction of symptoms due to expectations of help, traditional psychotherapy appears to move into a more complex phase. The new phase involves discussing the disturbing interpersonal problems with which the person needs help. Discussing these problems is often difficult and may at times lead to an intensification of symptoms. These events have been described in terms of conflicting approach-avoidance behavior (Murray, 1964; Murray, 1968a).

In one psychoanalytically oriented case, for example, the patient, a young college student, had many hostile feelings about his family, who tended to dominate him (Murray, 1954). Content categories were used to provide quantitative measures of the events in the case and are presented in Figure 17-1. Initially, the discussion in therapy consisted of defensive content, mostly physical complaints and intellectualization. Although, presumably, the patient wanted to approach and discuss his hostile feelings about his domineering family, he avoided doing so because the topic was emotionally disturbing and embarrassing to reveal to the therapist. The defensive content was a way of avoiding the painful areas. The initial decline in defenses, shown in Figure 17-1, was probably due to the expectation of help and increasing trust in the therapist. Following this decline, there was an increase in hostility that represented an approach to significant feelings about the family. Hours 4 to 8 show an alternation between approach and avoidance that is usually referred to as conflict oscillation. By the end of therapy, the hostile feelings associated with the family were being discussed openly and consistently.

In a study of direct analysis (Murray, 1962) it was shown that comparable categories of psychotic symptoms and family problems also seemed to reflect an approach-avoidance conflict. There was an initial reduction in the psychotic symptom category and then an alternation of family problems and psychotic symptoms. An important implication of these findings is that the psychotic symptoms in this schizophrenic patient functioned in about the same way as the neurotic defenses in the patient discussed previously.

In the original analyses of the cases just described, the defensive behavior and symptoms were thought to be motivated by anxiety. It was assumed that anxiety was being extinguished over the course of therapy, but there was no direct evidence of either anxiety or extinction. A more direct demonstration of an extinction process in a patient treated with psychoanalytic psychotherapy was presented by Dittes (1957a). A continuous measure of galvanic skin response (GSR) was made during the therapy sessions. The content of the patient's speech was scored for "embarrassing sexual statements." Over the course of therapy, the GSR reaction to embarassing sexual statements decreased in a manner very similar to anxiety extinction curves in other situations. In a related study, Dittes (1957b) showed that GSR measures for the hour as a whole were related to the judged permissiveness of the remarks and general attitudes of the therapist.

Although a simple extinction explanation seems adequate to explain the data mentioned so far, there are complications that require additional analysis. For example, there does not appear to be a steady reduction in emotional distress throughout therapy. In one successful case, Murray, Auld, and White (1954) showed that tension ratings remained high over the course of treatment. The patient went into different aspects of her problems, and each one produced a good deal of tension. In this case, the patient was progressing into more and more significant areas, but without a corresponding increase in tension. The college student previously described also discussed different aspects of his family problems at about the same level of tension. However, he first talked about the most significant person, his mother, then about his aunt, then other people, and finally about his mother again. The pattern in this case was described in terms of displacement (Murray & Berkun, 1955). In both cases the patient shifted from one problem

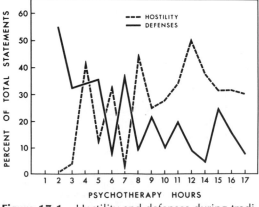

Figure 17-1 Hostility and defenses during traditional psychotherapy. (After Murray, 1954.)

area to another, keeping the tension level about the same.

In analyzing comparable phenomena in the area of systematic desensitization, Bandura (1977) offers a cognitive alternative to the anxiety extinction process. He points out that emotional arousal is not well correlated with defensive behavior. If the behavior avoids the threat, there is no need for arousal. If the defense fails, the emotional arousal intensifies. The key to defensive behavior is the patient's appraisal of the threat. If the patient changes expectations of being able to cope with the threat, the defensive behavior is no longer necessary. Mastery of one problem area increases the expectation of being able to cope with other problems, even more threatening ones. In the case of systematic desensitization, Bandura found that subjects' judgments of their own efficacy predicted how well they would do on more difficult tasks. Although there is no direct evidence of these cognitive processes operating in the present cases, it would not be inconsistent with the facts to assume that the patients' expectations about how the therapist would react and how they themselves would cope were important in their behavior.

The Role of the Therapist

There is general agreement that the relationship between the therapist and the patient is of central importance in psychotherapy. The therapeutic relationship may be crucial in changing belief systems. Changes may occur in the therapeutic relationship that lead to changes in the real-life situation of the patient.

Specifically, how does the therapist influence the patient? It was mentioned earlier that the reduction of the GSR to embarassing sexual statements in one case was related to the permissive attitudes of the therapist. The permissive behavior of the therapist may be viewed as a reinforcer. Approval and disapproval have been demonstrated in both cases mentioned in the previous section—one treated by psychoanalytically oriented psychotherapy (Murray, 1954) and the other by direct analysis (Murray, 1962). Approval and disapproval seem to have reinforcing and punishing effects.

All therapists react, implicitly or explicitly, to the verbalizations of the patient. In this sense, a truly

nondirective therapy, as originally described by Rogers (1942), does not seem possible. In order to test this hypothesis, Murray (1956) applied a content analysis system to a verbatim nondirective case published by Rogers (1942). Inspection of the results showed that one group of categories (primarily "independence") was approved and another group (including "dependence," "sexual material," and "defenses") was disapproved. It was predicted that verbal behavior related to the approval categories would increase and that verbal behavior related to the disapproved ones would decrease. Figure 17-2 indicates that these predictions were confirmed. These results suggest that therapist approval and disapproval function as rewards and punishments. Furthermore, reinforcement may be applied systematically and differentially, even in Rogerian therapy.

Recently, Truax (1966) has essentially replicated Murray's findings. Rogers (1951) assumes that the client learns a great deal about himself or herself and relations with others in client-centered therapy. This learning is supposed to result from the creation by the therapist of certain general therapeutic conditions, such as empathic understanding and unconditional positive regard. In a case treated by Rogers, Truax showed that therapeutic conditions were not uniformly distributed, but were systematically related to certain client categories. Thus, for example, the therapist was more empathic and

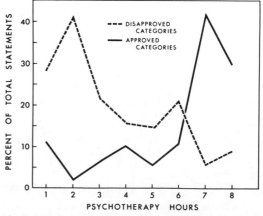

Figure 17-2 The effects of subtle approval and disapproval in nondirective psychotherapy. (After Murray, 1956.)

positive when the client showed evidence of insight, discrimination learning, and expressive style similar to that of the therapist. Furthermore, these reinforced categories increased in frequency during the course of therapy.

Several studies have shown that therapist responses of many kinds may be divided into those approaching a given topic and those avoiding it. Approach is assumed to function as a positive reinforcer and avoidance as a punishment. Bandura, Lipsher, and Miller (1960) found that within a therapy hour patients continued to express hostility following an approach response on the part of the therapist. However, a therapist avoidance response was likely to result in dropping the topic. Winder, Ahmad, Bandura, and Rau (1962) replicated this finding and found a similar effect for therapist approach and avoidance for a dependency category. Caracena (1965) also found evidence for this effect.

Winder et al. (1962) demonstrated the importance of therapist approach-avoidance in the therapeutic relationship. Approach and avoidance had short-term reinforcing effects, and they were also related to whether patients continued or terminated therapy. Patients whose therapists reacted to patient dependency with approach more than with avoidance tended to remain in therapy; patients whose therapists avoided dependency more than they approached it tended to terminate therapy. This effect was most marked when the dependency was directed toward the therapist. Although there are a number of interactions here, it would appear that some therapists foster a dependent relationship and thereby retain some patients whom they might otherwise lose.

What determines the use of approach or avoidance of important topics on the part of the therapist? At least two factors have been demonstrated. The first factor is the personality of the therapist, specifically his or her anxiety in various areas. Bandura (1956) has shown that therapeutic effectiveness is related to the therapist's anxiety in the areas of dependency, hostility, and sex. Subsequently, Bandura et al. (1960) showed that therapists' anxiety level in the hostility area predicted whether they would approach or avoid the expression of hostility by the patient. As Winder et al. (1962) point out, a similar prediction could be

made also for dependency anxiety. The second variable is training. Bohn (1967) demonstrated that student therapists became less directive in their responses to tape recordings with increased training.

Although the approach-avoidance behavior of the therapist has clear effects on the behavior of the patient, the mode of operation is probably not that of operant conditioning (Varble, 1968; Murray, 1968c). Caracena (1965) has suggested that the approach and avoidance responses he observed in therapy functioned as informational cues instead of as reinforcing stimuli. Along this line, Murray (1956) presented data suggesting that the patient in the Rogers case was aware of the pattern of approval and disapproval. Twenty naive students were asked to read Hour 6, the critical session just before the major increase in the approved categories. On a questionnaire, the students indicated, in their own words, that the patient was trying to choose between independence and dependence. Nearly all of the students indicated that they thought that the therapist wanted the patient to choose independence. Furthermore, they felt that the therapist communicated his views in a subtle and indirect way.

The way the therapist influences the patient in psychotherapy seems consistent with a cognitive view. The verbal reinforcement can be seen as having informational and incentive properties, as has been found to be true in verbal conditioning studies. As the patient learns how to predict the therapists reactions, expectancies are changed and progress is made. There is no reason why the patient cannot learn a good deal by observing the therapist. Bandura (1961) suggests that in conventional psychotherapy the patient observes incidental cues involving the therapist's beliefs and values, which the patient may adopt for his or her own. Strupp (1969) also emphasizes learning by imitation and identification in psychotherapy. The therapist may be seen as an ideal of mastery and competence that the patient may emulate. Vicarious learning is clearly related to the quality of the therapeutic relationship.

Cognitive Learning
There is some reluctance to see cognitive changes as of central importance in psychotherapy. Cognition seems too much like intellectualization to

many therapists, who place a premium on emotional expression, particularly on some sort of anger catharsis. There is some evidence that such an expression is helpful in reducing destructiveness in interpersonal relations (Nichols, 1974). However, what is often overlooked in such therapeutic observations is that the expression of feeling is intimately tied up with cognitive changes. In an experimental study, Green and Murray (1975) compared several methods of reducing hostility in college students whose self-esteem had been threatened. The expression of hostility produced only a nonsignificant reduction in hostility, as did a simple cognitive reinterpretation by the attacker. But a combination of the expression of hostility and the cognitive reinterpretation produced a significant reduction in hostility. In therapies that emphasize emotional expression, there is usually a good deal of reinterpretation provided or encouraged by the therapist. As Frank (1973) suggests, cognitive change may be easier to accomplish during a period of emotional arousal.

According to Frank (1973), the cognitive learning that is of most importance concerns the "assumptive world" of the person. Presumably, everyone has a complex set of beliefs, values, and expectations that are essential to successful adaptation to the world. A realistic and internally consistent assumptive system may be an important factor in maintaining reliable and satisfactory relations with others, while an inaccurate and internally conflicted assumptive system may lead to frustration and failure.

After the reduction of symptoms and the establishment of a relationship, the therapist begins a number of maneuvers to change the "assumptive world" of the patient. However, this cognitive learning is not a simple matter of presenting information in a didactic manner. In applying research findings on attitude change to psychotherapy, Johnson and Matross (1975) mention the importance of first building trust and decreasing defensiveness before attempting serious modification of a person's attitudes and beliefs. Since Freud's day, it has been known that it is necessary to deal with the patient's resistance to changes in beliefs and behavior.

Psychoanalytic forms of psychotherapy can be viewed in cognitive terms. For example, Peterfreund and Schwartz (1971) suggest replacing psychoanalytic language with information-processing language. They describe the person as governed by a hierarchically organized set of programs that processes information and makes decisions in branching tree fashion. Motivation, awareness, and defense can be construed as special programming and processing functions. A cognitive learning theory is included that suggests that psychoanalytic therapy involves reprogramming and changes in the hierarchical organization. They also suggest that psychoanalysis requires so much repetition and working through and is so long and difficult because reprogramming and hierarchical restructuring of the person's conceptions of major areas in life may be necessary.

Cognitive processes have also been emphasized in current thinking in the client-centered group (Wexler & Rice, 1974). The therapist may have to intervene at several points to help the client's information processing; this may include helping the client process information that was previously out of the client's awareness. Of the therapeutic triad of empathy, warmth, and congruence, empathy is emerging as the most important and may involve the therapist functioning as a surrogate information processor for the client. Personal experience is created by cognitive processes, so that the goal of increased experience is enhanced by the proper flow of information.

Upon close examination, many of the humanistic therapies can be cast within a cognitive language. In some cases, the therapy already has a cognitive flavor. For example, Raimy (1975), in tracing the development of his own cognitive therapy, finds that many early theorists, non-Freudian analysts, and even Gestalt therapists held some version of the "misconception" hypothesis as essential to understanding psychopathology and psychotherapy. The most notable of these early cognitivists was Alfred Adler. Adler believed that the neurotic person had unrealistic and often antisocial goals, such as wanting to be superior to all others or to dominate others. In his therapy, Adler would attempt to change the patient's belief that he or she had to attain such goals, and he would try to encourage more socially productive ideas. In fact,

Adler may be viewed as the forerunner of many modern cognitive therapists, such as Albert Ellis, Julian Rotter, George Kelly, Eric Berne, and Aaron Beck.

What are the new beliefs that a patient learns in traditional therapy? According to Strupp (1969), the patient learns the following sorts of lessons. First, the patient learns that the world is not as bad and frightening as he or she believed and that he or she can cope with the tensions and frustrations that are experienced. Second, the patient has to change immature expectations of others; he or she must demand less, delay gratification, and learn to compromise. Third, the patient has to change his or her strategies of getting along with other people, because they do not work and may be self-defeating. These include decreasing maneuvers such as ingratiation, negativism, and vindictiveness while increasing honesty, cooperation, and responsibility. In general, the lessons to be learned amount to giving up immature beliefs and strategies in favor of more mature, realistic, and responsible patterns.

BEHAVIORAL THERAPY

In this section we will consider the nature of the cognitive learning processes involved in three of the better known behavioral techniques— systematic desensitization, operant therapy, and aversion therapy. Although these behavioral techniques are explicitly based on learning theory, they tend to be derived from older and simplistic versions of learning theory that do not reflect the changes described in the first section of this chapter. Typically, the learning that occurs is attributed to classical conditioning or simple reinforcement effects. Nevertheless, as we will show, research has begun to make it more and more clear that the learning that occurrs in the behavioral therapies involves complex cognitive, emotional, and motivational changes operating within a social context.

Systematic Desensitization
Systematic desensitization is a procedure developed by Wolpe (1958) to treat anxiety responses, particularly the relatively localized fears invloved in phobias. Typically the patient is taught deep muscular relaxation. Then he or she is asked to imagine a graded series of scenes that are relevant to the phobia. Progress along this hierarchy is halted whenever the patient experiences anxiety. According to Wolpe, systematic desensitization is based on the principle of counterconditioning. The fearful stimulus is presented while the patient is relaxed. Since muscular relaxation is incompatible with the autonomic responses involved in fear, the relaxation is conditioned to the imaginal stimulus. The progressive hierarchy is important to insure that the imagined stimulus does not elicit the anxiety response in spite of the relaxation. Although systematic desensitization appears to be an effective method for reducing certain kinds of fear, a controversy exists over the theoretical explanation of these effects.

In our earlier review, we took the position that the counterconditioning explanation of systematic desensitization was inadequate for a number of reasons. To begin with, the evidence at that time raised doubts as to the necessity of the basic components of systematic desensitization such as relaxation and imagery for successful fear reduction. The research since that time has made the counterconditioning position difficult to defend. No single component seems essential, including relaxation, imagery, their pairing, a progressive hierarchy, spaced trials, low anxiety levels, and relevant autonomic changes. Yates (1975) concludes that since none of the components are necessary, systematic desensitization is left with only its smile.

Systematic desensitization is actually a complex social transaction involving changes in the beliefs and attitudes of the person going through the process. In recent years, research has demonstrated that the subject in the typical social psychological experiment is an active participant trying to understand the procedure and its implications for his or her self-evaluation (Jung, 1971). So, too, the outcome of systematic desensitization is influenced by explicit instructional sets, implicit demands, and reactive dependent measures, including behavioral ones (Bernstein & Neitzel, 1973; Rosen, 1976). Furthermore, successful systematic desensitization seems to be accompanied by much broader positive changes in the person's self-concept (Ryan, Krall, & Hodges, 1976). A dramatic illustration of the interpersonal nature of the systematic desensitization procedure was the finding that "warm" therapists were more successful than "cold" ones (Morris & Suckerman, 1974a). Even with an automated version of systematic desensitization, the "warmth" of the taped voice giving instructions was related to outcome (Morris & Suckerman, 1974b).

The most important aspect of the social situation in which systematic desensitization is presented is the extent to which it communicates an expectation of therapeutic gain. A social influence process of this sort offers an alternative to the counterconditioning explanation of successful outcome. There are several methods of communicating expectancies. Several studies have shown that a more favorable outcome is obtained when systematic desensitization is presented as a treatment to reduce fear instead of as a nontherapeutic experiment on fear (Lick & Bootzin, 1975). On the other hand, most studies that have presented systematic desensitization as a treatment and then attempted to induce positive or negative expectancies by means of instructions have *not* shown expectancy effects. However, several authors (Lick & Bootzin, 1975; Rosen, 1976; Wilkins, 1973) have pointed out that the validity and credibility of these expectancy manipulations have to be established, preferably independently of the outcome measure. Lott and Murray (1975) did a study in which they independently validated an expectancy manipulation involving a placebo medication and then demonstrated an effect of the manipulation on outcome with systematic desensitization. In general, the expectancy manipulations that actually influence the beliefs of the person have an effect on outcome.

Although expectancy manipulations seem to enhance the effects of systematic desensitization, some positive treatment effects may appear even under conditions of low manipulated expectancy. This residual effect could be due to a counterconditioning process that operates beyond expectancy. On the other hand, the procedure of systematic desensitization itself may arouse an expectation of therapeutic gain implicitly because of the scientific rationale, the pleasant relaxation, and the inherent credibility of the whole enterprise. Therefore, manipulating expectancy would face a lower limit of

creditability. The inherent expectancy effect can be evaluated by a different design—a comparison of systematic desensitization with a control procedure that arouses the same expectancy of therapeutic gain but without any of the counterconditioning elements that are analogous to a medical placebo.

A number of expectancy control procedures have been used in research on systematic desensitization. One of the earliest was a "pseudotherapy" procedure consisting of imagining neutral scenes and discussing nonanxiety-rousing topics (Lang, Lazovik, & Reynolds, 1965). Another was Paul's (1966) "attention-placebo" control involving a placebo medication and a signal detection task. Most of the early studies showed that systematic desensitization was more effective than these control procedures, thus supporting the counterconditioning position. However, more recently it has been shown that these control procedures are much less credible and believable than systematic desensitization (Borkovec & Nau, 1972; McGlynn & McDonell, 1974). In order to evaluate the expectancy of gain aspect of systematic desensitization, it is necessary to compare it with a control procedure that has been demonstrated to arouse the same degree of expectancy of gain.

When systematic desensitization is compared with a control that has been demonstrated clearly to be of equal credibility, such as "dissonance enhancement" (McReynolds, Barnes, Brooks, & Rehagen, 1973) or "subliminal T-scope therapy" (Lick, 1975), systematic desensitization is no more effective than the control. In reviewing this body of research, Lick and Bootzin (1975) conclude that expectancy variables are important in systematic desensitization. They even characterize systematic desensitization as a procedure that is especially effective in arousing therapeutic expectancies. In another review, Kazdin and Wilcoxon (1976) take the more conservative position that nonspecific factors such as expectancy of therapeutic gain cannot be ruled out in accounting for the effects of systematic desensitization. In any case, it is difficult to see how anyone could now defend a counterconditioning interpretation of systematic desensitization. Instead, it appears to be a means of convincing the phobic person that his or her fears can be reduced and brought under control.

In our original analysis of systematic desensitization, we concluded that the chief mechanism for the reduction of fear was that the person comes to believe that he or she can cope with the situation. We also suggested that other methods, such as implosive therapy, vicarious desensitization, and progressive relaxation, reduce fears largely through a change in the person's belief in his or her ability to cope with the situation. Generally, these methods implicitly communicate the hope of being able to cope instead of teaching specific coping skills.

Recently, in his self-efficacy work, ,Bandura (1977) has taken a similar position. Desensitization procedures involving actual performance, vicarious experience, fantasy procedures, or physiological feedback all provide information that may influence the person's sense of efficacy or mastery. In comparing enactive and vicarious desensitization, it was found that expectations of self-efficacy were more predictive of future performance than actual previous performance.

Goldfried (1971) has reconceptualized systematic desensitization as a procedure for developing self-control instead of a passive desensitization. He suggests that clients learn to reinterpret their bodily cues, to use relaxation as an active mastery technique, and to develop self-confidence in being able to cope. Goldfried then went on to develop a procedure that placed emphasis on using relaxation to cope with anxiety-arousing situations in imagination and real life. This new coping form of desensitization was shown to be more effective than ordinary systematic desensitization (Goldfried & Trier, 1974). Meichenbaum (1972) used a similar coping form of desensitization in combination with a cognitive procedure involving the substitution of positive self-statements for anxiety-arousing ones. He found this new combination superior to regular systematic desensitization. Since these new procedures involve elements of standard systematic desensitization along with coping instructions, it is not clear how much of the effect is due to cognitive changes.

In a comparison of systematic desensitization and cognitive modification, Holroyd (1976) eliminated the desensitization and relaxation elements from Meichenbaum's procedure. Holroyd compared group desensitization, group cognitive modification, and an equally credible placebo group in the reduction of severe test anxiety in college stu-

dents. Cognitive modification involved the identification of anxiety-arousing self-statements, a gentle challenging of their validity, and the construction of alternative anxiety coping self-statements. The cognitive modification procedure was clearly superior to systematic desensitization in a laboratory test situation and in grade point average. Systematic desensitization was essentially equivalent lo the pseudotherapy control.

Systematic desensitization, then, seems to involve three major cognitive processes. First, the impressive treatment package arouses a general hope of favorable outcome that results in improved performance in the fearful situation. This improvement is no greater than a pseudotherapy procedure and may be attributed to the expectancy-placebo effect. Second, systematic desensitization, as well as other forms of desensitization, may influence the person's sense of mastery of self-efficacy as progress is made in the procedure itself. Third, the procedure may inadvertantly lead some of the clients to use relaxation or positive self-statements as active coping techniques in the fearful situation. If this coping is increased deliberately, a greater improvement is obtained. Finally, the relaxation and other hangovers from systematic desensitization can be completely eliminated in a highly effective cognitive coping procedure. Systematic desensitization is now giving way to more explicitly cognitive modification procedures in the reduction of fearful behavior.

Operant Therapy

The basic principle of conditioning responses through the use of reinforcement contingencies has been applied to a variety of problems, but particularly to the problems of children in the home, school, and institution and to the problems of patients in psychiatric hospitals (O'Leary & Wilson, 1975). In the case of children in the home, the emphasis recently has been on parent training; most of the institutional work has involved some system of tokens or points. Individual case reports often show dramatic changes, such as the reduction of tantrums by teaching the mother to ignore negative behavior and reward positive behavior (Bernal, Duryee, Pruett, & Burns, 1968).

The overall pattern of results from operant programs tends to be positive according to recent reviews (Davidson & Seidman, 1974; Erickson, 1975; Margolies, 1977; O'Dell, 1974; O'Leary & Drabman, 1971). Yet there is a great deal of concern in these sympathetic reviews for the scientific adequacy of the research that has been done. For example, the heavy reliance on simple AB or ABAB designs has made it difficult to tell what aspect of the usually complex interventions is actually effective or to rule out alternative explanations such as demand characteristics or observer bias. As Davidson and Seidman (1974) say: "The important variables have been selected a priori and any others systematically left out of investigative efforts. There is no real sense of an effort toward discovery, rather only the application of a conceptually closed paradigm to a new content area" (p. 1008).

When some comparison can be made with other methods of intervention, the positive effects of operant therapy do not appear unique. For example, Erickson (1975) points out that while token economy programs are often successful in improving the adjustment of mental hospital patients, similar results are reported for a wide variety of group, milieu, and community interventions using techniques ranging from lectures to beer parties. In one of the few controlled studies, reinforcement and relationship therapies had almost identical effects on the social and cognitive functioning of patients (Marks, Sonoda, & Schalock, 1968). So, too, the impressive results of behavioral programs for delinquents (Davidson and Seidman, 1974) are duplicated by a variety of action programs for multi-problem, hard-core, inner-city youth (Cowen, 1973). Finally, reflective methods of parent counseling may be useful as well as behavioral methods (Tavormina, 1974). In other words, there may be some general, nonspecific factors inherent in all interventions that may account for some of the positive outcome of operant therapy.

Two of the very few studies that deal directly with nonspecific factors in operant therapy concern interventions in disturbed family interactions. In the first, Azrin, Naster, and Jones (1973) had marital couples go through a "placebo" catharsis period before a behavioral reciprocity treatment. No improvement was shown until the behavioral treatment was introduced. Jacobson and Martin (1976) point out the obvious shortcomings of this study,

particularly the fact that the placebo treatment was never demonstrated to be a credible procedure and did not include nonspecific elements of the behavioral treatment, such as the daily exchange of happiness ratings that constituted the dependent measure. In another study, Walter and Gilmore (1973) compared a social learning procedure for training parents of aggressive boys with a placebo procedure of leaderless group discussions involving parents with similar boys. Although both groups of parents had positive expectations and reported general improvement, only the boys in the behavioral program actually decreased aggression. In this study the placebo procedure dealt only with the parents and not with the disturbed parent-child interaction. To evaluate the necessity of the reinforcement procedures thoroughly, it is necessary to introduce alternative procedures in the marital interaction or the parent-child interaction. For example, the provision of information may be effective, as in the exchange of happiness ratings just mentioned or the public monitoring of a child's behavior. More powerful procedures might include improving communication, changing perceptions through role reversal, and parent effectiveness training.

Operant therapy programs are complex interventions that involve much more than the specific contingencies. In reading the well-known program at the National Training School for Boys, described by Cohen and Filipczak (1971), for example, it is clear that the staff developed warm, positive relationships with the boys in which they communicated real concern and respect. The contingencies operate within this positive social context as to the ultimate goal of the program. The role of these contextual factors has simply not been evaluated in any systematic fashion. Incidental observations do suggest that if the participants do not perceive the intent of the program as being in their long-term best interests, the program may fail.

The role of specific conditioning contingencies in operant therapy has not been studied as systematically as it has in systematic desensitization and aversion therapy. Nevertheless, distinguished operant therapists have begun to raise questions about the adequacy of the operant formulation. For example, Wahler (1975), in an article entitled "The decline and fall of the 'operant conditioning' therapies," cites not only examples of the failure of operant procedures but also of puzzling positive "side effects." Positive changes in the reinforced class of responses can be accompanied by positive changes in another class with no detectable common environmental stimuli. A phenomenon similar to behavioral contrast can be observed in which a child improves in one setting but gets worse in another. O'Leary and Drabman (1971) discuss how tenuous the tie is between laboratory studies of schedules of reinforcement and superficially similar prodcedures in naturalistic settings. There is no compelling reason to conceptualize the very real effects of rewards and incentives in terms of operant conditioning.

One of the most persistent problems in operant therapy has been the difficulty in getting behavioral changes that have been achieved in the training situation to generalize across time and situations (O'Leary & Wilson, 1975). Actually, it is puzzling as to why behavior modifiers expect such generalization. If environmental contingencies are all that affect behavior, a given bit of reinforced behavior should continue in the same situation or in a similar situation only if environmental contingencies continue as during training. True generalization occurs only the first time a response is made in a new situation. After that the contingencies that are actually operating should take over or, if no reinforcement is available, a discrimination should be built up. Yet operant behavior modifiers do expect generalization.

A related issue is that of "fading out" tangible reinforcers or tokens after some change has occurred. For example, tokens are used to get a child to sit still; they are then gradually eliminated in favor of the teacher's praise O'Leary & Drabman, 1971). Often the behavior does persist after the fading out. Why? One explanation is that the teacher's praise becomes secondarily reinforcing; however, pure secondary reinforcement tends to be transitory. Another explanation is that the tangible and token rewards can be eliminated because "natural" reinforcements in the situation can take over. But why did they not work earlier? Perhaps the tangible rewards function to focus the child's attention. Still another explanation is that the tangi-

ble or token system functions to provide feedback or information to the child about how to get rewards (Davidson and Seidman, 1974). Of course, these are cognitive explanations and not conditioning ones. The procedures of operant conditioning may be ways of demonstrating to people what the rules of the game are in that social situation. One would expect "generalization" of such rules only to other social situations to which they are believed to apply.

But do people function according to direct environmental contingencies in most social situations? Would a delinquent brought under such control be a welcome member of society? O'Leary and Drabman (1971) caution against the heavy use of tokens with children lest they begin to model themselves after the teacher and become "manipulative." This is also the basis for some of the objections to token systems as "bribes" (O'Leary, Poulos, & Devine, 1972). Gagnon and Davison (1976) criticize the use of token economies with mental hospital patients as duplicating the outside market economy that originally may have had something to do with their downfall. These patients may be learning a way of dealing with other people that is not acceptable in most human relationships.

In the ordinary world, one's behavior is not under the control of immediate environmental contingencies in the sense implied by operant theorists. Long-term goals, rules of conduct, general beliefs, and symbolic rewards play a more significant role. People are expected to control themselves and assume personal responsibility. In fact, many behavior modifiers are moving in the direction of teaching people self-control through methods such as self-observation, self-reward, and self-guiding principles (Thoresen & Mahoney, 1974).

In order to be really successful, a behavior modification program has to go beyond the control of behavior through immediate environmental contingencies. One of the best-known operant therapy programs is Achievement Place (Phillips, Phillips, Fixsen, & Wolf, 1971). A "point system" with many innovations was developed to control the behavior of institutionalized predelinquent boys. The points were earned by good behavior and could be exchanged for various tangible reinforcers. The program has been successful in changing the academic and social behavior of the boys. Yet the staff realizes that the outside world does not operate in such a systematic way, and they have devised a merit system. After a boy does well on the point system, he may be promoted to the "merit system," where privileges are free but social reinforcement is important. Finally, ,he may be promoted to a "homeward-bound system," which is even less tied to immediate consequences. Therefore, the total program puts a premium on self-control and personal responsibility.

The sequence of training systems in Achievement Place bears a remarkable similarity to current conceptions of stages of moral development in adolescense (Kohlberg & Gilligan, 1972). Upon entry predelinquent boys show at best a Stage 1 pattern of responding only to punishment and coercive power. The point system seems to advance the boys to Stage 2, which involves instrumental hedonism and concrete reciprocity, in the tradition of the marketplace. The merit system seems based on a Stage 3 conventional morality of pleasing others and gaining approval. The homeward-bound system is like conventional Stage 4 in accepting authority and the social order. It is not clear whether further moral development might take place.

The sequence of programs at Achievement Place is developmentally sound in that moral development, like cognitive development, is thought to require passing through an invariant sequence of stages. Achievement Place starts where the boys are at morally and does not skip stages. A more lofty program might eschew the marketplace morality of the point system in an effort to produce a Stage 6 philosopher. Such a program could fail if progress must be through an invariant sequence of stages.

How does Achievement Place foster moral development? A simple operant conditioning explanation seems inadequate. It is true that rewards operate at each stage, but the nature of these rewards changes from the avoidance of punishment, to tangible reinforcers, to social praise and, finally, to internal, symbolic self-rewards. Conditioning theory offers no real explanation for this progression. Why do the boys not simply stay at Stage 2 with their tangible rewards? Obviously a great deal of research must be done on this process.

Nevertheless, we would like to suggest that the answer will involve the positive relationship between the staff and the boys that provides a basis for the acceptance of the moral ideology of the staff by the boys.

The procedures used in operant therapy generally do produce changes in behavior. It is unlikely, however, that these changes can be explained in terms of operant conditioning. The operant procedures involve many complex social and cognitive processes, as do other treatment programs. The important changes that occur are not simple, behavioral responses to environmental contingencies. Instead, these operant procedures may be a vehicle for more fundamental changes in cognitive and moral development. A greater understanding of these developmental processes could result in an improved use of operant techniques with better results and fewer problems in generalization and maintainance of behavioral change.

Aversion Therapy

Although aversion therapy is among the oldest of the behavioral techniques, it is still the most controversial (Rachman & Teasdale, 1969). Aversion therapy includes a variety of specific techniques based on both classical and instrumental conditioning paradigms, and it is sometimes combined with other behavioral techniques. Typically, aversion therapy is used to eliminate various types of approach behavior such as alcoholism and other addictions, various forms of sexual behavior, smoking, overeating, and some forms of obsessive-compulsive responding.

An historically important case described by Raymond (1956) illustrates the dramatic results that sometimes occur and the basis for the marked ambivalence toward aversion therapy on the part of many clinicians. The patient was a fetishist who had attacked baby carriages and handbags since the age of 10 years. Traditional therapy had failed, and the patient had been arrested for a recent attack. The aversion treatment consisted of many pairings of handbags, baby carriages, and photographs of these objects with an injection of a drug that produced nausea and vomiting in a grueling, week-long, day and night marathon. The treatment was repeated several times with excellent results.

Although dramatic results such as those in

Raymond's fetishist are sometimes reported, the effects of aversion therapy are highly variable and often disappointing (Franks & Wilson, 1973; O'Leary & Wilson, 1975). Thus, for example, Davidson (1974) concludes that the positive results of aversive conditioning with alcoholics tends to disappear when appropriate control groups are employed. Aversive techniques frequently result in an immediate decrease in the problematic behavior, such as smoking, but follow-up studies show an almost complete relapse (Yates, 1975). There is a real question as to how far any changes generalize from laboratory-like training situations. Actually, a host of methodological inadequacies make the evaluation of aversion therapy outcome quite difficult, as is illustrated by Callner's (1975) review of the behavioral treatment of drug abuse.

There is reason to believe that the positive results that are sometimes found with aversion therapy can be attributed, at least in part, to nonspecific therapeutic factors. Yates (1975) reviewed studies showing that procedures introduced as controls, such as group therapy, transactional analysis, and nonspecific group discussion, often were as effective as aversion therapy in reducing smoking on a short-term basis. McFall and Hammen (1971) went on to devise a nonspecific placebo treatment, involving instructional demands and self-monitoring, that was also effective in reducing smoking. Similar results have been found with alchoholism (Davidson, 1974). For example, Miller, Herson, Eisler, and Hemphill (1973) found no difference among alcoholics treated with electrical aversion therapy, a minimal shock control procedure, and group therapy. They attribute their results to the expectations and demands in the situation. The role of nonspecific factors has not been tested as extensively in the applications of aversion therapy to other problems.

In a slightly different approach to understanding aversion therapy, several studies have tested the necessity for specific conditioning contingencies using the type of controls traditional in the conditioning literature (O'Leary & Wilson, 1975). For example, Vogler, Lunde, Johnson, and Martin (1970), using electrical aversion with alcoholics, were unable to show significant differences among groups treated with the real conditioning procedure and groups given pseudoconditioning (random

shock) or sham conditioning (no shock). In a study of smoking, Carlin and Armstrong (1968) found no differences among aversive classical conditioning, pseudoconditioning (shock paired with irrelevant stimuli), and sham conditioning (subjects thought they were getting subliminal shock). Even more dramatic results were found by Conway (1977), with subthreshold shock sometimes more effective than the real aversion conditioning. In a study that seems to run counter to most of the evidence, Birk, Huddleston, Miller, and Cohler (1971) found a stronger effect from electrical aversion than from an elaborate placebo "associate conditioning" procedure with homosexuals desiring treatment. However, the differences between the groups disappeared on follow-up. It is difficult to evaluate this study; all of the patients were in long-term group therapy before, during, and after the conditioning period.

In an important study on the mechanisms involved in electrical aversion therapy, Hallam, Rachman, and Falkowski (1972) measured autonomic reactions to the conditioned stimulus before and after conditioning. The patients were chronic alcoholics, and the conditioned stimuli were alcohol-related slides. There was no evidence that the patients developed conditioned skin resistance or heart rate responses. Instead, successful patients in both the experimental and control groups developed a more negative attitude toward the slides. Those developing the negative attitude also showed some increase in heart rate responses. This physiological effect was not due to aversion therapy, since it occurred in the control group as well as in the experimental group. Instead, changing attitudes of patients responding to the general hospital program may have mediated the autonomic response to alcohol relevant slides. The authors suggest that their results pose problems for a conditioning theory of aversion therapy, and they tend to favor a cognitive explanation.

Of course, some behaviorists believe that cognitive processes consist of covert responses subject to the same rules of classical and operant conditioning as overt responses. Cautela's (1967) method of covert sensitization is based on this conceptualization. The person, for example, imagines smoking and then becoming nauseous. Although it is not clear whether covert sensitization is any more effective than regular aversion therapy, it is somewhat more appealing on ethical grounds (O'Leary & Wilson, 1975). In any case, several studies have tested the conditioning basis for the effects of covert sensitization. Results with the treatment of alcoholism, obesity, and smoking indicate that backward conditioning or reversed contingency controls are as effective as covert sensitization (Ashem & Donner, 1966; Barrett & Sachs, 1974; Sachs & Ingram, 1972). Furthermore, in a well-designed study of smoking, covert sensitization was found to be no more effective than an attention-placebo control or a self-control suggestion procedure (Sipich, Russell, & Tobias, 1974). Obviously, more is involved than covert conditioning.

The empirical evidence suggests that the beneficial results that sometimes occur with aversion therapy may be more accurately attributed to cognitive processes than to a conditioning process, either classical or operant. In considering the current status of aversion therapy, two of its most distinguished proponents, Franks and Wilson (1973) conclude that the conditioning procedures involved in aversion therapy probably operate through cognitive processes instead of directly on the behavioral response. In fact, Franks and Wilson state that conditioned aversion reactions cannot be developed " . . . without the client's deliberate, conscious cooperation" (1975, pp. 586–587).

What cognitive processes are involved in aversion therapy? First, aversion therapy and the conviction of the therapist offer hope to a patient strongly motivated to gain control over an undesired pattern of behavior. Second, if the aversive stimulation does result in stopping the behavior, even temporarily, it serves as a demonstration to the patient that he or she can exercise self-control. As Ratcliff and Steins' (1968) neurodermatitis patient put it, he " . . . never thought he had enough will power to resist an urge to scratch" (p.398). As Cautela (1967) suggests, demonstrations of this sort help the person to develop feelings of self-mastery. Thus aversion therapy may result in important changes in beliefs about the self.

Actually, aversion therapy as an exclusive treatment for problematic behavior is giving way to more comprehensive behavioral methods with a decidedly cognitive flavor (O'Leary & Wilson,

1975). For example, a multifaceted approach to sexual difficulties has been proposed in which aversion therapy is minimized or eliminated. The new approach includes increasing desired sexual behavior in a positive fashion through anxiety reduction, developing appropriate social skills, and changing thought patterns. The treatment for obesity and smoking has also recently involved multifaceted programs emphasizing self-control techniques such as self-monitoring and self-rewards, often in the context of a treatment contract that puts a good deal of the responsibility on the patient. Finally , a behavioral treatment for alcoholism now may involve a comprehensive community program providing social relationships, artificial families, and job training. Individual approaches include the correction of irrational cognitions, fear reduction, and the teaching of self-control strategies.

In summary, aversion therapy, even when successful, does not appear to operate through classical or operant conditioning processes. Instead, the aversion therapy procedure is a complex social interaction that arouses hope of success, produces changes in self-perception, and requires the active participation of the patient. Most recently aversion therapy has been giving way to a more comprehensive behavioral approach involving cognitive and social changes.

CONCLUSIONS

A major change in conceptions of learning has been taking place in psychology. The newer thinking emphasizes cognitive, emotional, and social processes in the learning process. The conditioning model is being replaced by an information-processing model. These new modes of thinking about learning and behavior change are beginning to have an impact on thought in the psychotherapy area. Traditional therapists, who were largely unreceptive to early applications of learning theory, are much more receptive to the cognitive learning approach. Behavioral therapists are more and more reformulating their techniques in cognitive and social learning terms instead of in conditioning terms. Therefore, traditional therapy and behavioral therapy have many features and goals in common. For example, in their study of psychotherapy versus behavior therapy, Sloane, Staples, Cristol, Yorkston, and Whipple (1975) conclude that, although psychotherapists were more concerned with feelings and behavior therapists with behavior, both groups wanted both feelings and behavior changed as long-range goals.

The first basic process to be seen in all therapeutic techniques is arousal of *expectations of help*. All forms of therapy seem to rely to some extent on a psychological placebo effect. The demoralized individual comes to therapy; almost anything offered will arouse some expectations of help, and morale will improve. These effects have been demonstrated in dynamic, humanistic, and behavioral treatments. In some cases, such as systematic desensitization, the entire therapeutic effect may be accounted for by expectancy. Today, it is essential that a new treatment be compared against a credible placebo control before making claims as to efficacy. But expectancy should not be considered a nuisance factor that obscures real therapeutic processes. A realistic expectancy of favorable therapeutic outcome is as important to better living as a realistic expectancy of business success is to economic growth in a society. A variety of procedures could be used to heighten a realistic expectancy of improvement.

The second cognitive change involves correction of *nonadaptive beliefs about the world*. Psychoanalytic therapies often involve corrective emotional experiences with a permissive therapist who is not punitive about sexual thoughts, for example. More confrontive techniques may be used by the humanistic therapists. Group methods are particularly potent in teaching a person about the feelings behind the social facade of others. Behavioral techniques may change the beliefs of the person about feared stimuli. Operant and modeling techniques may teach the person something about how the contingencies in the real world operate. Finally, there is much more incidental informational learning going on in therapy than is usually appreciated. More creative efforts could be made to assess the common misconceptions people have about the world and develop dramatic, emotionally involved educational methods to change these be-liefs. It is clear that important emotional changes follow the correction of erroneous beliefs about the world.

The third area is developing *competencies in dealing with social living*. In addition to being more realistic about the world, it is necessary to find ways of dealing with the world effectively. In dynamic therapy, the therapist often functions as an effective model. In group situations, feedback is available to help the person learn how to handle various situations. Behavioral methods of modeling, feedback, and reinforcement are used to develop skills such as assertiveness for use in social living. These procedures involve learning new responses and new attitudes. That is, a woman may know how to be assertive, but she may not feel justified in behaving in that way. The development of competencies assumes that therapists know what works in the world. A good deal of basic research must to be done on social competence so that therapists really know what competencies should be developed.

The next area is *beliefs about the self*. Perhaps the most pervasive nonspecific factor in all therapy is the acceptance of the person as a worthwhile human being by the therapist. Traditional therapists are quite explicit about the importance of the empathetic relationship in fostering positive changes in self-concept. In dealing positively with socially undesirable behavior, behavior therapists also communicate a basic acceptance. Techniques of self-control imply that the person can control himself or herself. Cognitive therapists deal directly with the thoughts and assumptions the person makes about himself or herself. As the person's beliefs are altered, he or she begins to have better self-esteem, to develop personal maturity, and to accept responsibility.

These changes interact with one another. The arousal of hope makes the person willing to go along with therapeutic tasks. The trust in the therapist may enable the person to examine beliefs about the world. Increased self-esteem may encourage the person to try out more competent behavior and, conversely, competent performance may increase self-esteem. Therapy operates on a complex cognitive, emotional, and social system of human behavior.

Clearly, in spite of the underlying similarities described above, traditional and behavioral therapies use different techniques. Even within each school a great variety of techniques are used. However, a new trend is to combine techniques from all sources for the benefit of the client. Beck (1976), starting from a dynamic background, has developed a treatment package that combines cognitive and behavioral techniques. Starting from a behavioral background, Lazarus (1976) has developed a multimodal approach that uses techniques from all schools of thought. The task for clinical research is to discover how the myriad of techniques can be fit together to alter the complex cognitive, emotional, and social functioning that is involved in social living and personal development.

REFERENCES

Allegre, C., & Murray, E. J. Locus of control, behavioral intention, and verbal conditioning. *Journal of Personality,* 1974, *42,* 668–681.

Alexander, F., & French, T. M. *Psychoanalytic therapy.* New York: Ronald, 1946.

Arnold, M. (Ed.) *Feelings and emotions.* New York: Academic Press, 1970.

Ashem, B., & Donner, L. Covert sensitization with alcoholics: A controlled replication. *Behavior Research and Therapy,* 1968, *6,* 7–12.

Azrin, N. H., Naster, B. J., & Jones, R. Reciprocity counseling: A rapid learning-based procedure for marital counseling. *Behavior Research and Therapy,* 1973, *11,* 365–382.

Bandura, A. Psychotherapist's anxiety level, self-insight, and psychotherapeutic competence. *Journal of Abnormal and Social Psychology.* 1956, *52,* 333–337.

Bandura, A. Psychotherapy as a learning process. *Psychological Bulletin.* 1961, *58,* 143–159.

Bandura, A. *Principles of behavior modification.* New York: Holt, Rinehart, and Winston, 1969.

Bandura, A. Behavior theory and the models of man. *American Psychologist,* 1974, *29,* 859–869.

Bandura, A. Self-efficacy: Towards a unifying theory of behavioral change. *Psychological Review,* 1977, *84,* 191–215.

Bandura, A., Lipsher, D. H., & Miller, P. E. Psychotherapists' approach-avoidance reactions to patients' expressions of hostility. *Journal of Consulting Psychology,* 1960, *24,* 1–8.

Baron, A., Kaufman, A., & Stauber, K. A. Effects of instructions and reinforcement-feedback on human operant behavior maintained by fixed-interval reinforcement. *Journal of the Experimental Analysis of Behavior,* 1969, *12,* 701–712.

Barret, T. J., & Sachs, L. B. Test of the classical conditioning explanation of covert sensitization. *Psychological Reports,* 1974, *34,* 1312–1314.

Beck, A. T. *Cognitive therapy and the emotional disorders.* New York: International Universities, 1976.

Bergin, A. E. The evaluation of theraputic outcomes. In A. E. Bergin and S. L. Garfield (Eds.) , *Handbook of psychotherapy and behavior change.* New York: Wiley, 1971.

Bergin, A. E., & Suinn, R. M. Individual therapy and behavior therapy. In M. R. Rosenzweig and L. W. Porter (Eds.), *Annual review of psychology.* Palo Alto, Calif.: Annual Reviews, 1975.

Bernal, M. E., Duryee, J. S., Pruett, H. L., & Burns, B. J. Behavior modification and the brat syndrome. *Journal of Consulting and Clinical Psychology,* 1968, *32,* 447–455.

Bernstein, D. A., & Nietzel, M. T. Procedural variations in behavioral avoidance tests. *Journal of Consulting and Clinical Psychology,* 1973, *41,* 165–174.

Birk, L., Huddleston, W., Miller, E., & Cohler, B. Avoidance conditioning for homosexuality. *Archives of General Psychology,* 1971, *25,* 314–325.

Bohn, M. J. Therapist responses to hostility and dependency as a function of training. *Journal of Consulting Psychology,* 1967, *31,* 195–198.

Bolles, R. C. Reinforcement, expectancy, and learning. *Psychological Review,* 1972, *79,* 394–409.

Borkovec, T. D., & Nau, S. D. Credibility of analogue therapy rationales. *Journal of Behavior Therapy and Experimental Psychiatry.* 1972, *3,* 257–260.

Breger, L, & McGaugh, J. L. Learning theory and behavior therapy: A reply to Rachman and Eysenck. *Psychological Bulletin,* 1966, *65,* 170–173.

Callner, D. A. Behavioral treatment approaches to drug abuse: A critical review of the research. *Psychological Bulletin,* 1975, *82,* 143–164.

Caracena, P. F. Elicitation of dependency expressions in the initial stage of psychotherapy. *Journal of Counseling Psychology,* 1965, *12,* 268–274.

Carlin, A. S., & Armstrong, N. E. "Aversive conditioning": Learning or dissonance reduction. *Journal of Consulting and Clinical Psychology,* 1968, *32,* 674–678.

Cautela, J. R. Covert sensitization. *Psychological Reports,* 1967, *20,* 459–468.

Cohen, H. L., & Filipczak, J. *A new learning environment.* San Francisco: Jossey-Bass, 1971

Conway, J. B. Behavioral self-control of smoking through aversive conditioning and self-management. *Journal of Consulting and Clinical Psychology,* 1977, *45,* 348–357.

Cowen, E. J. Social and community interventions. In P. H. Mussen and M. R. Rosenzweig (Eds.), *Annual review of psychology.* Palo Alto, Calif.: Annual Reviews. 1973.

Davidson, W. S. Studies of aversive conditioning for alcoholics: A critical review of theory and research methodology. *Psychological Bulletin,* 1974, *81,* 571–581.

Davidson, W. S. and Seidman, E. N. Studies of behavior modification and juvenile delinquency: a review, metholologidal critique, and social perspective. *Psychological Bulletin,* 1974, *81,* 998–1011.

Dittes, J. E. Extinction during psychotherapy of GSR accompanying "embarrassing" statements. *Journal of Abnormal and Social Psychology,* 1957a, *54,* 187–191.

Dittes, J. E. Galvanic skin response as a measure of patient's reaction to therapist's permissiveness. *Journal of Abnormal and Social Psychology,* 1957b, *55,* 295–303.

Dollard, J., & Miller, N. E. *Personality and psychotherapy.* New York: McGraw-Hill, 1950.

Dulany, D. E. Awareness, rules, and propositional control: a confrontation with S-R behavior theory. Chap. 13 in T. R. Dixon & D. L. Horton (Eds.), *Verbal behavior and general behavior theory.* Englewood Cliffs, N. J.; Prentice-Hall, 1968.

Erickson, R. C. Outcome studies in mental hospitals: A review. *Psychological Bulletin,* 1975, *82,* 519–540.

Eysenck, H. (Ed.) *Behavior therapy and the neuroses.* New York: Pergamon, 1960.

Flavell, J. H. *The developmental psychology of Jean Piaget.* Princeton, N. J.: Van Nostrand, 1963.

Ford, D. H., & Urban, H. B. *Systems of psychotherapy.* New York: Wiley, 1963.

Frank, J. D. *Persuasion and healing.* Baltimore: Johns Hopkins, 1973.

Franks, C. M., & Wilson, G. T. (Eds.) *Annual review of behavior therapy: Theory and practice.* New York: Brunner-Mazel, 1973.

Franks, C. M., & Wilson, C. T. (Eds.) *Annual review of behavior therapy: Theory and practice.* New York: Brunner-Mazel, 1975.

Freud, S. [On psychotherapy, 1904.] Chapter in S. Freud *Collected Papers I.* (J. Riviere, ed. and trans.). London: Hogarth, 1950.

Gagnon, J. H., & Davison, G. C. Asylums, the token economy, and the metrics of mental life. *Behavior Therapy,* 1976, *7,* 528–534.

Goldfried, M. R. Systematic desensitization as training in self-control. *Journal of Consulting and Clinical Psychology,* 1971, *37,* 228–234.

Goldfried, M. R., & Trier, C. S. Effectiveness of relaxation as an active coping skill. *Journal of Abnormal Psychology,* 1974, *83,* 348–355.

Goldstein, A. P., Heller, K., & Sechrest, L. B. *Psychotherapy and the psychology of behavior change.* New York: Wiley, 1966.

Green, R. A., & Murray, E. J. Expression of feeling and cognitive reinterpretation in the reduction of hostile aggression. *Journal of Consulting and Clinical Psychology,* 1975, *43,* 375–383.

Greenspoon, J. Verbal conditioning and clinical psychology. In A. J. Bachrach (Ed.), *Experimental foundations of clinical psychology.* New York: Basic Books, 1962, Pp. 510–553.

Hallam, R., Rachman, S., & Falkowski, W. Subjective, attitudinal and physiological effects of electrical aversion therapy. *Behaviour Research and Therapy,* 1972, *10,* 1–13.

Heitler, J. B. Preparatory techniques in initiating expressive psychotherapy with lower-class, unsophisticated patients. *Psychological Bulletin,* 1976, *83,* 339–352.

Hilgard, E. R. & Bower, G. *Theories of Learning* (3rd ed.). New York: Appleton-Century-Crofts, 1966.

Holroyd, K. Cognition and desensitization in the group treatment of test anxiety. *Journal of Consulting and Clinical Psychology,* 1976, *44,* 991–1001.

Horton, D. L., & Turnage, T. W. *Human learning.* Englewood Cliffs, N. J.: Prentice-Hall, 1976.

Insko, C. A., & Oakes, W. F. Awareness and the "conditioning" of attitudes. *Journal of Personality and Social Psychology,* 1966, *4,* 487–496.

Jacobson, L. I. The effects of awareness, problem solving ability, and task difficulty on the acquisition and extinction of verbal behavior. *Journal of Experimental Research in Personality,* 1969, *3,* 206–213.

Jacobson, L. I., Elenewski, J. J., & Lordahl, D. S. The relationship between rote learning and mediated and nonmediated concept learning. *Psychonomic Science,* 1968, *10,* 342–348.

Jacobson, N. S., & Martin, B. Behavioral marriage therapy: Current status. *Psychological Bulletin,* 1976, *83,* 540–556.

Johnson, D. W., & Matross, R. P. Attitude modification methods. In F. H. Kanfer and A. P. Goldstein (Eds.), *Helping people change.* New York: Pergamon, 1975.

Jung, J. *The experimenter's dilemma.* New York: Harper & Row, 1971.

Kanfer, F. H., & Phillips, J. S. *Learning foundations of behavior therapy.* New York: Wiley, 1970.

Kazdin, A. E., & Wilcoxon, L. A. Systematic desensitization and nonspecific treatment effects: A methodological evaluation. *Psychological Bulletin,* 1976, *83,* 729–758.

Kingsbury, S. J., Stevens, D. P., & Murray, E. J. Evaluation apprehension in verbal conditioning: A test of four subject effects models. *Journal of Personality and Social Psychology,* 1975, *32,* 271–277.

Kohlberg, L., & Gilligan, C. The adolescent as a philosopher: The discovery of the self in a post conventional world. In J. Kagan and R. Coles (Eds.), *Twelve to sixteen: Early adolescence.* New York: W. W. Norton, 1972.

Krasner, L. & Ullmann, L. P. (Eds.) *Research in behavior modification* New York: Holt, Rinehart & Winston, 1965.

Lang, P. J., Lazovik, A. D., & Reynolds, D. J. Desensitization, suggestibility, and pseudotherapy, *Journal of Abnormal Psychology,* 1965, *70,* 395–402.

Lazarus, A. A. *Multi-modal behavior therapy.* New York: Springer, 1976.

Lick, J. Expectancy, false galvanic skin response feedback, and systematic desensitization in the modification of phobic behavior. *Journal of Consulting and Clinical Psychology,* 1975, *43,* 557–567.

Lick, J., & Bootzin, R. Expectancy factors in the treatment of fear: Methodological and theoretical issues. *Psychological Bulletin,* 1975, *82,* 917–931.

Lindsay, P. H., & Norman, D. A. *Human information processing.* New York: Academic Press, 1972.

Locke, E. A. Is "behavior therapy" behavioristic? (An analysis of Wolpe's psychotherapeutic methods). *Psychological Bulletin,* 1971, *76,* 318–327.

London, P. The end of ideology in behavior modification. *American Psychologist,* 1972, *27,* 913–920.

Lott, D. R., & Murray, E. J. The effect of expectancy manipulation on outcome in systematic desensitization. *Psychotherapy: Theory, Research, and Practice,* 1975, *12,* 28–32.

Margolies, P. J. Behavioral approaches to the treatment of early infantile autism: A review. *Psychological Bulletin,* 1977, *84,* 249–264.

Marks, J., Sonoda, B., & Schalock, R. Reinforcement

versus relationship therapy for schizophrenics. *Journal of Abnormal Psychology*, 1968, *73*, 397–402.

McCardel, J., & Murray, E. J. Nonspecific factors in weekend encounter groups. *Journal of Consulting and Clinical Psychology*, 1974, *42*, 337–345.

McFall, R. M., & Hammen, C. L. Motivation, structure, and self-monitoring: Role of nonspecific factors in smoking reduction. *Journal of Consulting and Clinical Psychology*, 1971, *37*, 80–86.

McGeoch, J. A. *The psychology of human learning.* New York: Longmans, Green, 1942.

McGlynn, F. D., & McDonell, R. M. Subjective ratings of credibility following brief exposure to desensitization and pseudotherapy. *Behavior Research and Therapy*, 1974, *12*, 141–146.

McGuigan, F. J. & Lumsden, D. B. (Eds.) *Contemporary approaches to conditioning and learning.* New York: Wiley, 1973.

McReynolds, W. T., Barnes, A. R., Brooks, S., & Rehagen, N. J. The role of attention-placebo influences in the efficacy of systematic desensitization. *Journal of Consulting and Clinical Psychology*, 1973, *41*, 86–92.

Meichenbaum, D. Cognitive modification of test anxious college students. *Journal of Consulting and Clinical Psychology*, 1972, *39*, 370–380.

Merbaum, M., & Lukens, H. C. Effects of instructions, elicitations, and reinforcements in the manipulation of affective behavior. *Journal of Abnormal Psychology*, 1968, *73*, 376–380.

Miller, G. A., Galanter, E., & Pribram, K. N. *Plans and the structure of behavior.* New York: Holt, Rinehart and Winston, 1960.

Miller, N. E., & Dollard, J. *Social learning and imitation.* New Haven, Conn.: Yale University, 1941.

Miller P. M., ,Hersen, M., Eisler, R. M., & Hemphill, D. P. Electrical aversion therapy with alcoholics: An analogue study. *Behavior Research and Therapy*, 1973, *11*, 491–497.

Morris, R. J., & Suckerman, K. R. The importance of the therapeutic relationship in systematic desensitization. *Journal of Consulting and Clinical Psychology*, 1974a, *42*, 148.

Morris, R. J. & Suckerman, K. R. Therapist warmth as a factor in automated desensitization. *Journal of Consulting and Clinical Psychology*, 1974b, *42*, 244–250.

Mowrer, O. H. *Learning theory and personality dynamics.* New York: Ronald, 1950.

Murray, E. J. A case study in a behavioral analysis of psychotherapy. *Journal of Abnormal and Social Psychology*, 1954, *29*, 305–310.

Murray, E. J. A content-analysis method for studying psychotherapy. *Psychological Monographs*, 1956, *70*, (13), Whole No. 420.

Murray, E. J. Direct analysis from the viewpoint of learning theory. *Journal of Consulting Psychology*, 1962, *26*, 226–231.

Murray, E. J. Learning theory and psychotherapy: Biotropic versus sociotropic approaches. *Journal of Counseling Psychology*, 1963, *10*, 250–255.

Murray, E. J. Sociotropic-learning approach to psychotherapy. In P. Worchel and D. Byrne (Eds.), *Personality change.* New York: Wiley, 1964. Pp. 249–288.

Murray, E. J. *Motivation and emotion.* Englewood Cliffs, N. J.: Prentice-Hall, 1964.

Murray, E. J. *Sleep, dreams, and arousal.* New York Appleton-Century-Crofts, 1965.

Murray, E. J. Conflict: Psychological aspects. *International Encyclopedia of the Social Sciences.* New York: Crowell, Collier, and MacMillan, 1968a. Pp. 220–226.

Murray, E. J. Social learning, personality change, and psychotherapy. In H. H. Gregory (Ed.), *Learning theory and stuttering therapy.* Evanston, Ill.: Northwestern University, 1968b. Pp. 21–51.

Murray, E. J. Verbal reinforcement in psychotherapy. *Journal of Consulting and Clinical Psychology*, 1968c, *32*, 243–246.

Murray, E. J., Auld, F., & White, A. M. A psychotherapy case showing progress by no decrease in the discomfort-relief quotient. *Journal of Consulting Psychology*, 1954, *18*, 349–353.

Murray, E. J. & Berkun, M. M. Displacement as a function of conflict. *Journal of Abnormal and Social Psychology*, 1955, *51*, 47–56.

Nichols, M. P. Outcome of brief cathartic psychotherapy. *Journal of Consulting and Clinical Psychology*, 1974, *42*, 403–410.

O'Dell, S. Training parents in behavior modification: A review. *Psychological Bulletin*, 1974, *81*, 418–433.

O'Leary, K. D., & Drabman, R. Token reinforcement programs in the classroom: A review. *Psychological Bulletin*, 1971, *75*, 379–398.

O'Leary, K. D., Poulos, R. W., & Devine, V. T. Tangible reinforcers: Bonuses or bribes. *Journal of Consulting and Clinical Psychology*, 1972, *38*, 1–8.

O'Leary, K. D., & Wilson, G. T. *Behavior therapy: Application and outcome.* Englewood Cliffs, N. J.: Prentice-Hall, 1975.

Page, M. M. Demand characteristics and the verbal operant conditioning experiment. *Journal of Personality and Social Psychology*, 1972, *23*, 372–378.

Page, M. M. Social psychology of a classical conditioning experiment. *Journal of Personality and Social Psychology*, 1969, *11*, 177–186.

Paul, G. L. *Insight vs. desensitization in psychotherapy.* Stanford, Calif.: Stanford University Press, 1966.

Paul, G., Eriksen, C. W., & Humphreys, L. G. Use of temperature stress with cool air reinforcement for human operant conditioning. *Journal of Experimental Psychology*, 1962, *64*, 329–335.

Pavlov, I. P. *Conditioned reflexes* (1927) New York: Dover, 1960.

Peterfreund, E., & Schwartz, J. T. *Information, systems, and psychoanalysis.* New York: International Universities, 1971.

Phillips, E. L., Phillips, E. A., Fixsen, D. L., & Wolf, M. M. Achievement place: Modification of the behaviors of pre-delinquent boys within a token economy. *Journal of Applied Behavior Analysis*, 1971, *4*, 45–59.

Prokasy, W. F. (Ed.), *Classical conditioning,* New York: Appleton-Century-Crofts, 1965.

Rachman, S., & Teasdale, J. *Aversion therapy and behaviour disorders: An analysis.* Coral Gables, Fla.: University of Miami, 1969.

Raimy, V. *Misunderstandings of the self*. San Francisco: Jossey-Bass, 1975.

Rapaport, D. A critique of Dollard and Miller's "Personality and Psychotherapy." *American Journal of Orthopsychiatry*, 1953, *23*, 204–208.

Ratcliff, R. G., & Stein, N. H. Treatment of neurodermatitis by behavior therapy: A case study. *Behavior Research and Therapy*, 1968, *6*, 396–399.

Raymond, M. Case of fetishism treated by aversion therapy. *British Medical Journal*, 1956, *2*, 854–856.

Rogers, C. R. *Counseling and psychotherapy*. Boston: Houghton Mifflin, 1942.

Rogers, C. R. *Client-centered Therapy*. Cambridge, Mass.: Riverside Press, 1951.

Rosen, G. M. Subjects' initial therapeutic expectancies and subjects' awareness of therapeutic goals in systematic desensitization: A review. *Behavior Therapy*, 1976, *7*, 14–27.

Rotter, J. B. *Social learning and clinical psychology*. Englewood Cliffs, N. J.: Prentice-Hall, 1954.

Rotter, J. B., Chance, J. E., & Phares, E. J. *Applications of a social learning theory of personality*. New York: Holt, Rinehart and Winston, 1972.

Rotter, J. B., Liverant, S., & Crowne, D. P. The growth and extinction of expectancies in chance controlled and skilled tasks. *Journal of Psychology*, 1961, *52*, 161–177.

Ryan, V. L., Krall, C. A., & Hodges, W. F. Self-concept change in behavior modification. *Journal of Consulting and Clinical Psychology*, 1976, *44*, 638–645.

Sachs, B., & Ingram G. Covert sensitization as a treatment for weight control. *Psychological Reports*, 1972, *30*, 971–974.

Schneiderman, N. *Classical (Pavlovian) conditioning*. Morristown, N. J.:General Learning Press, 1973.

Shoben, E. J. Psychotherapy as a problem in learning theory. *Psychological Bulletin*, 1949, *46*, 366–393.

Sipich, J. F., Russell, R. K., & Tobias, L. L. A comparison of covert sensitization and "nonspecific" treatment in the modification of smoking behavior. *Journal of Behavior Therapy and Experimental Psychiatry*, 1974, *5*, 201–203.

Skinner, B. F. *The behavior of organisms*. New York: Appleton-Century, 1938.

Skinner, B. F. *Science and human behavior*. New York: MacMillan, 1953.

Sloane, R. B., Staples, F. R., Cristol, A. H., Yorkston, N. J., & Whipple, K. *Psychotherapy versus behavior therapy*. Cambridge, Mass.: Harvard University, 1975.

Spielberger, C. D., & DeNike, L. D. Descriptive behaviorism versus cognitive theory in verbal operant conditioning. *Psychological Review*, 1966, *73*, 306–326.

Staats, C. K., & Staats, A. W. Meaning established by classical conditioning. *Journal of Experimental Psychology*, 1957, *54*, 74–80.

Staats, A. W., & Staats, C. K. Attitudes established by classical conditioning. *Journal of Abnormal and Social Psychology*, 1958, *57*, 37–40.

Strupp, N. N. Towards a specification of teaching and learning in pscychotherapy. *Archives of General Psychiatry*, 1969, *21*, 203–212.

Tavormina, J. B. Basic models of parent counseling: A critical review. *Psychological Bulletin*, 1974, *81*, 827–835.

Thoresen, C. E., & Mahoney, M. J. *Behavioral self-control*. New York: Holt, Rinehart and Winston, 1974.

Truax, C. B. Reinforcement and nonreinforcement in Rogerian psychotherapy. *Journal of Abnormal Psychology*, 1966, *71*, 1–9.

Varble, D. L. Relationship between the therapists' approach-avoidance reactions to hostility and client behavior in therapy. *Journal of Consulting and Clinical Psychology*, 1968, *32*, 237–242.

Vogler, R. E., Lunde, S. E., Johnson, G. R., & Martin, P. L. Electrical aversion conditioning with chronic alcoholics. *Journal of Consulting and Clinical Psychology*, 1970, *34*, 302–307.

Wahler, R. G. The decline and fall of the "operant conditioning" therapies. Presidential Address, Southeastern Association for the Advancement of Behavior Therapy, Atlanta, 1975.

Walter, H. I., & Gilmore, S. K. Placebo versus social learning effects in parent training procedures designed to alter the behavior of aggressive boys. *Behavior Therapy*, 1973, *4*, 361–377.

Watson, J. B. *Behaviorism*. New York: W. W. Norton, 1925.

Wexler, D. A., & Rice, L. N. (Eds.) *Innovations in client-centered therapy*. New York: Wiley, 1974.

Wilkins, W. Expectancy of therapeutic gain: An empirical and conceptual critique. *Journal of Consulting and Clinical Psychology*, 1973, *40*, 69–77.

Winder, C. L., Ahmad, F. Z., Bandura, A. & Rau, L. C. Dependency of patients, psychotherapists' responses, and aspects of psychotherapy. *Journal of Consulting Psychology*, 1962, *26*, 129–134.

Wolpe, J. *Psychotherapy by reciprocal inhibition*. Stanford, Calif: Stanford University Press, 1958.

Yates, A. J. *Theory and practice in behavior therapy*. New York: Wiley, 1975.

18

COGNITIVE AND SELF-CONTROL THERAPIES

MICHAEL J. MAHONEY
DIANE B. ARNKOFF

The Pennsylvania State University

One of the most recent and perhaps surprising developments in clinical psychology has been the emergence of fundamentally cognitive therapies within the boundaries of behavior therapy. This development was not, however, an isolated and solely internal occurrence. The boundaries between behavioral and nonbehavioral therapies have become more and more permeable over the last decade, and conceptual flexibility seems to be the most popular trend in contemporary clinical psychology (Garfield & Kurtz, 1976). It is nevertheless ironic to view such strange bedfellows as cognitive psychology and behavior modification easing into a cautious rapprochement. Although there have been a few outspoken critics of such a merger, the more typical response has been one of enthusiasm and fervid research. There are already several dozen books devoted to the area and two new journals (*Biofeedback and Self-Regulation* and *Cognitive Therapy and Research*) serving to disseminate a mushrooming literature. In this chapter we will review the historical development of what might be termed "cognitive learning perspec-

tives." Our review will include some of the major therapeutic procedures that are associated with these hybrids and a survey of their current empirical status.

HISTORY OF THE COGNITIVE-BEHAVIORAL INTERFACE

In 1964 Sigmund Koch was predicting the imminent demise of behaviorism. His comments were hardly those of a bereaved mourner.

> *I would be happy to say that what we have been hearing could be characterized as the death rattle of behaviorism, but this would be a rather more dignified statement than I should like to sponsor, because death is, at least, a dignified process. (p. 162)*

If behaviorism was indeed moribund in 1964, one must marvel at its awesome recovery. Despite continuing criticism, behavioristic approaches have survived their fragile childhood and stormy adolescence. They can no longer be dismissed as a short-lived fad, and their growing popularity must be viewed as indisputable regardless of one's ideological preferences (Mahoney, Kazdin, & Lesswing, 1974).

While they have unquestionably survived, it is equally clear that the behavioral theories and therapies of today are substantially different from those popular a decade ago. This ability to change may, in fact, be partly responsible for behaviorism's hearty perseverance. Bandura (1969) talks about the various "generations" of behavior modifiers and how each has contributed to today's technology. In the late 1950s and early 1960s, operant conditioners ventured from their animal laboratories and into institutions and school systems. There—often with painstaking effort—they tried to duplicate exactly their experimental procedures with human subjects. Emphasis was placed on immediate and tangible reward or punishment and a minimization of "extraneous artifacts" such as instructions. Although these early efforts were often very successful, it was not until the mid-1960s that behavior therapy (or behavior modification) could be considered a serious contender for a position of respect in clinical psychology and psychiatry.

This acceptability may have been greatly enhanced by the popularization of desensitization in the treatment of fear and avoidance patterns. Behaviorism now had something to offer the practitioner who dealt with nonpsychotic adults. Behavior therapists of this era were adamant in defending the behavioral foundations of a procedure that is extensively reliant on mental imagery. With the popularization and empirical scrutiny of desensitization there also came a liberalization of prior operant conditioning technologies. The emphasis on immediate and somewhat mechanical consequences was gradually replaced by one that incorporated instructions, modeling, and the substitution of verbal praise for prior tangible rewards.

Most relevant to our current discussion, however, was the emergence of behavioristic interest in the phenomenon of self-control. Although Skinner had devoted an entire chapter to this topic in *Science and Human Behavior* (1953), very little

applied interest was discernible until the mid-1960s. Ferster, Nurnberger, and Levitt (1962) outlined a behavioristic approach to weight control that later formed the basis of Stuart's (1967) pioneering work in this area. In 1965 Goldiamond reported the successful self-application of behavior change principles by several of his clients. Meanwhile, a host of laboratory studies on self-regulatory processes were being conducted by Kanfer (1970b) and Bandura (1969, 1971).

The emergence of self-control as a topic of behavioristic research must be considered a significant and perhaps revolutionary development. Prior to this, the prevalent and explicit assumption of behaviorists was one of *environmental determinism* (i.e., that the forces shaping a person's life lie primarily in the external environment). In fact, the longstanding debate between behaviorists and humanists was basically focused on "internalism" versus "externalism" (Matson, 1973). With the exception of several staunch supporters of strict environmental determinism, behavioral research on self-control also ushered in the acceptance of a *reciprocal determinism* that emphasized complex and continuous causal interaction between the organism and its environment (Bandura, 1969, 1971; Thoresen & Mahoney, 1974). The human organism was no longer viewed as a passive product of environmental influence, but as an active participant in his or her own complex development. Although this philosophy of interactionism was hardly new to other quarters of psychology, it was a truly revolutionary one in behavioral circles. Attesting to its revolutionary nature have been the numerous debates and arguments spawned by such a viewpoint (Bandura, 1976; Catania, 1975; Goldiamond, 1976; Mahoney, 1976c; Rachlin, 1974; Stuart, 1972). In stimulating controversy it also stimulated further scrutiny, and the concepts of choice, freedom, and countercontrol soon became topics receiving increased behavioristic attention (Davison, 1973; Mahoney, 1974a; Skinner, 1971, 1974).

The concept of reciprocal determinism constituted only half of the revolution begun in the mid-1960s, however. The other half was comprised of a reappraisal of the radical behavioristic neglect of "private events." In 1965 one of Skinner's former students, Lloyd Homme, published a brief position paper on "coverants, the operants of the mind." In it he argued that human thoughts could be functionally analyzed and modified by simply extrapolating the principles of behavior change. Homme argued that these private events were not wholly unobservable if one acknowledges that they can be scrutinized by their owner (i.e., the person experiencing them). Indeed, he pointed out that the conventional neglect of private events by behaviorists was tantamount to endorsing the mentalistic dualism that they so strongly criticized. Homme went on to outline a sample technology of *coverant control* that involved programmed exercises in the cueing and reinforcement of specific thoughts.

Soon after Homme's paper there came a host of articles and case studies on *covert conditioning*—the application of conditioning principles to covert events. Some of the earliest of these emanated from Cautela (1966, 1967), whose technique of "covert sensitization" (an imagery-based aversion procedure) was rapidly incorporated into the behavior therapist's practical armament. Covert conditioning constituted a significant development in the trend toward a cognitive-behavioral interface. For the first time in decades, behaviorists were openly and actively scrutinizing their subjects' self-reported thoughts, feelings, and images. Not only were these formerly banished phenomena now welcomed as the *targets* of clinical concern, but they were also employed as a *means* toward inducing other behavior change. Not surprisingly, when behaviorism made this tardy move into the black box, it brought with it the accoutrements of its stimulus-response tradition. The processes and procedures of laboratory conditioning were soon imposed on human thought processes, and mediation came to be viewed as a chain of covert stimuli and responses. Besides some very serious conceptual problems, this conditioning model of cognition soon faced empirical embarrassments, and the time was ripe for yet another theoretical leap (Mahoney, 1974a).

At this point our historical survey must leave its neat chronological theme, which has been so far restricted to behaviorists. As mentioned earlier, the development of a cognitive-behavioral hybrid can-

not be solely attributed to changes within the domain of behavioristic psychology. Outside that domain, the entire field was undergoing a veritable cognitive revolution (Dember, 1974). One could document these developments in almost any subspeciality of mental health. Since our primary focus is clinical psychology, we will restrict our brief historiography to that domain. There were, of course, the quasicognitive traditions of psychoanalysis and existential-gestalt therapy. By and large, however, these were considered too "foreign" to most behavior therapists and there was relatively little interstimulation. The seeds of a cognitive-behavioral interface were often sown by the behaviorists themselves (in their weaker moments, no doubt) and by a handful of hard-to-classify clinical scientists who left a lasting impact on the field. Kelly (1955), Rotter (1954), and Beck (1963) are three examples of early cognitive-learning cultivators whose influence is very apparent in contemporary work. Through their research, theories, and the impact they had on students, these three may have been the founding fathers of our current trend. To their influence must be added that of Albert Ellis, a prolific and persuasive writer whose forceful emphasis on cognition did much to bring clients' belief systems into the forefront of clinical psychology (Ellis, 1962). Ellis had, of course, been anticipated by several "thought management" writers who had made "positive thinking" a household word (Bain, 1928; Carnegie, 1948; Coué, 1922; Maltz, 1960; Peale, 1960), who were themselves anticipated by DuBois' 1904 writings on the role of "incorrect ideas" in psychological distress. In many ways, Ellis shared the cool academic reception given to these Madison Avenue trade writers. However, as his rational-emotive therapy (RET) gained in lay popularity, it soon demanded more serious respect. By 1976, RET claimed a greater professional following than Carl Rogers' client-centered approach (Garfield & Kurtz, 1976).

While these cognitive and social learning theorists were offering models and procedures for clinical adoption, behavior therapists were expanding their own internal horizons. Following the covert conditioning revolution of the mid-1960s there came an explicit shift to cognitive and information-processing models of behavior change. This revolutionary development was ushered in by Bandura's (1969) classic text, *Principles of Behavior Modification*. While emphasizing the role of behavioral *procedures* in effective psychotherapy, Bandura argued that the basic *processes* of behavior change involve central (cognitive-symbolic) mechanisms. Drawing on literatures ranging from awareness to vicarious learning, he documented his assertions with an encyclopedic mass of evidence. While still digesting Bandura's contentions, behavior therapists were faced with parallel embracements of cognition by influential figures such as Estes (1971), Lazarus (1971), Goldfried (1971), Kanfer (1971), and Mischel (1973). Explicit invitations to a cognitive-behavioral merger were soon legion (Beck, 1970a; Blackwood, 1970, 1972; Ellis, 1969, 1973; Meichenbaum, 1972b).

Within a very short period of time cognitive terms and themes became a major aspect of behavioral research. Thus, earlier conditioning analyses of self-control began to be replaced by more mediational accounts, and behavior therapists began exploring the relevance of social and cognitive psychology for their clinical endeavors. The traditionally restrictive format of behavior therapy began to evolve into a broader, coping skills paradigm emphasizing problem-solving training (D'Zurilla & Goldfried, 1971; Mahoney, 1977b; Mahoney & Mahoney, 1976a, 1976b; Spivack & Shure, 1974). Attribution theory began to play a significant part in clinical conceptualizations (Bem, 1970; Kopel & Arkowitz, 1975; Lefcourt, 1976; Rotter, Chance, & Phares, 1972) and developmental research on self-verbalization spawned a variety of clinical treatment procedures (Meichenbaum, 1974, 1977). Early animal research on learned helplessness began to blend into a cognitive theory of depression (Seligman, 1975), and the role of cognition in psychopathology was given more expansive credit (Beck, 1970a, 1970b, 1971, 1976). As behavior therapy became more cognitive, of course, its differentiation from other conceptual approaches became correspondingly less distinct (Raimy, 1975).

At the present time the cognitive learning perspective continues to be a relatively diversified amalgam of principles and procedures that have yet to be formalized into a monolithic system or model. While apparently sharing some basic assumptions (Mahoney, 1977c), proponents of these perspectives range widely in their specific emphases and procedures. Among their commonalities seem to be the following.

1. Humans develop adaptive and maladaptive behavior and affective patterns through cognitive processes (selective attention, symbolic coding, etc.).

2. These cognitive *processes* can be functionally activated by *procedures* that are generally isomorphic with those of the human learning laboratory (although there may be other procedures which activate the cognitive processes as well).

3. The resultant task of the therapist is that of a diagnostician-educator who assesses maladaptive cognitive processes and subsequently arranges learning experiences that will alter cognitions and the behavior and affect patterns with which they correlate.

Depending on the extremity of a given theorist's perspective, varying degrees of credit may be awarded to maladaptive cognitive processes. Some, for example, may go so far as to argue that psychopathology is "nothing but" irrational thinking. Our perspective would argue an important— but hardly an exclusive—role for cognition in deviant behavior. Given the inseparability of environmental, biological, and phenomenological processes, a debate on the priority of these elements would not seem promising. However, even in their current informal state, cognitive learning perspectives face a number of problems and potential problems from conceptual to procedural. Before exploring some of those problems, it might be worthwhile to examine the actual content and format of the cognitive and self-control therapies. This will provide a background against which to place our critical evaluation.

Since we have used a chronological format in introducing these various therapies, such a strategy may be helpful in structuring our review of the literature. Thus, in the sections that follow, we will address each of the major therapies roughly as they emerged in the aforementioned chronology. At the conclusion of this historical survey, we will return to a summary evaluation of the problems and promise of contemporary systems.

BEHAVIORAL SELF-CONTROL

Although the phenomenon of self-control had long interested psychologists of all persuasions, relatively little research had been devoted to it prior to the 1960s. This may have been partly due to the tautologous practice of equating self-control with terms such as "willpower" and "ego strength." A person was said to be capable of difficult self-regulatory tasks *because* he or she possessed willpower. When asked to defend the attribution of willpower, however, the theorist would often invoke the to-be-explained behavior and end up with a deceptive and uninformative analytic truth. With the advent of behavioral interest in self-control—sparked by Skinner's still classic 1953 chapter—there came the demand for clearer definitions and a functional analysis of controlling influences. Self-control became something a person *does* instead of something he or she *has*. Thus, Thoresen and Mahoney (1974) suggested that:

> *A person displays self-control when, in the relative absence of immediate external constraints, he engages in a behavior whose previous probability has been less than that of alternatively available behaviors. (p. 12)*

Unfortunately, neither this definition nor any of its rivals entirely clarifies the issue. How does one assess, for example, "the relative absence of immediate external constraints?" Does "previous probability" refer to an interval of seconds, days, or years? How does one determine the "availability" of alternate responses?

The problem of defining "self-control" takes on different dimensions if approached from the perspective of the labeler instead of that of the labeled behavior. For the most part, self-control lies in the eye of the beholder (i.e., it is an attribution of the observer more than a characteristic of the behavior). This viewpoint leads to the question of

what criteria are used by observers to ascribe the label "self-control" to a person or performance. Even a cursory inspection reveals some interesting features of situations in which the term "self-control" is employed. First, there are no apparent topographical differences between self-control and non-self-control responses. The context and history of a given behavior are the primary factors that determine whether it is labeled "self-control." A heavy smoker who decides to quit and declines a cigarette offer may be described as showing self-control. A nonsmoker would not earn the label for the same performance. Likewise, if he or she had been abstinent for 10 years, the ex-smoker would be unlikely to receive self-control credit for the effort.

A second issue has to do with the conspicuousness of current controlling factors. It is only in situations in which the controlling variables are inconspicuous that we attribute self-control. A lonely jogger sparks our admiration and respect. If the jogger is wearing a khaki uniform and is surrounded by other army recruits, however, we do not see the physical exertion as being "self-determined." It is also noteworthy that we seem to reserve the label of self-control for socially acceptable acts in which there is clear intent of self-improvement. The masochist, for example, is seldom lauded for self-imposed pain.

Finally, there is an intriguing regularity in the patterns that are often discussed in self-control terms. To date, virtually all of those patterns have been characterized by what might be called a *reversing consequence gradient*. That is, the consequences of the behavior may be initially positive but eventually negative, or vice-versa. Undesired (decelerative) target behaviors, for example, often have immediately pleasant effects that camouflage more negative delayed consequences (addictions, overeating, etc.). Desirable (accelerative) targets, on the other hand, are often characterized by immediately aversive consequences but long-range positive benefits (physical exercise, financial thrift, etc.). One of the goals of effective self-control training would seem to be the alteration of this reversing gradient, with particular emphasis on making the delayed consequences of an action more salient or immediate.

The relationship between self-control patterns and the much-revered "law of effect" has stimulated considerable discussion. Many individuals (and a few behaviorists) have viewed self-control phenomena as some sort of violation of general learning principles. They seem to equate it with a free will clause in which a person can rise above normal causal chains. The theory and evidence in the area, however, suggest that self-regulatory patterns are complex molecular events that must be analyzed in molar perspective. Skinner (1953) pointed out the important distinction between the *self-controlled response* (e.g., smoking) and the *self-controlling response* (e.g., self-punishment). Theoretically, both are accountable to the same general principles. If the self-controlling responses are not adequately motivated, they should not maintain. The validity of this prediction has yet to be challenged by research with humans, and it has been consistently illustrated in a series of animal analogs to self-control (Bandura & Mahoney, 1974; Bandura, Mahoney, & Dirks, 1976; Colotla, McArthur, & Casanueva, in press; Mahoney & Bandura, 1972; Mahoney, Bandura, Dirks, & Wright, 1974). However, given the currently shaky status of long-revered principles such as the "law of effect" and the "conditioning" basis of learning, this compatability may not be altogether reassuring (Bolles, 1972; Brewer, 1974; McKeachie, 1974).

Early research on self-control techniques was primarily divided into four areas (Mahoney, 1972): (1) stimulus control, (2) self-monitoring, (3) self-reward, and (4) self-punishment. Since several of these have spawned sizable literatures of their own, it would be impossible to review them in detail here. Such a review is available elsewhere (Thoresen & Mahoney, 1974). Instead, we will summarize the major findings and offer a selective updating of the 1974 review. Other overviews of the field may be found in Goldfried and Merbaum (1973), Mahoney and Thoresen (1974), and Kanfer (1976).

Stimulus Control

As the name implies, stimulus control techniques rely on the cueing function of environmental events. One of the most prolific areas in early animal research focused on the role of discriminative

stimuli in response patterning. Pigeons, for example, can be trained to peck a disc in the presence of a green light and to avoid pecking it when a red light is present. Humans show the same discrimination when those lights are placed near a traffic intersection. In these situations, the various stimuli function to preview or predict the consequences of different behaviors. However, in acquiring this discriminative function, they also appear to gain other properties that can influence response patterns. For example, after a behavior has been repeatedly reinforced in the presence of a stimulus, presentation of the stimulus alone will increase the likelihood of the behavior. In a sense, the *stimulus* has gained *control* over the response.

This principle was adopted by early self-control researchers in their extrapolation of a conditioning model to human problems. Ferster, Nurnberger, and Levitt (1962), for example, analyzed human eating patterns in terms of their controlling stimuli and made specific suggestions for altering maladaptive sequences. The obese individual was told to restrict his or her eating to very limited situations and times (e.g., a particular place in the kitchen) so as to minimize the number of domestic cues associated with food. If an easy chair had been a frequent site of previous snacking, it may have acquired properties by which simple sight of the chair might elicit hunger pangs. The basic strategy in stimulus control is one of progressively reducing (or eliminating) the cues associated with undesirable behaviors and the simultaneous expansion of stimuli that correlate with more adaptive responses.

Although Ferster and his colleagues were not very successful in their attempts to utilize this procedure, their approach formed the basic strategy of Stuart's (1967) classic study on the behavioral control of overeating. With unprecedented consistency, Stuart's clients lost 26 to 47 pounds. His brief report sparked a veritable avalanche of studies on the behavioral treatment of obesity—an area that can now claim relatively dense documentation (Stunkard & Mahoney, 1976). Unfortunately, many of these studies suffer from serious methodological limitations, and their underlying assumptions have often escaped critical scrutiny (Mahoney, 1975, 1976a). Even considering these shortcomings, however, there can be little doubt that behavioral techniques have been superior to more traditional methods of weight management. Since traditional methods have been appallingly poor, the fact that behavioral techniques are *more* effective does not insure that they are therefore *very* effective. Although they have unquestionably improved our clinical power in this domain, there is still much variance in responsiveness to treatment and considerable room for therapeutic refinement.

More pertinent to our present discussion is the fact that subsequent research on stimulus control strategies in weight loss has suggested that they may be an important therapeutic component, but not a sufficient one. Except where they have been supplemented by other therapeutic strategies, stimulus control techniques have not been consistently powerful. Applications to areas other than obesity have included study habits (Beneke & Harris, 1972; McReynolds & Church, 1973; Richards, 1975), smoking (Bernard & Efran, 1972), and even marital problems (Goldiamond, 1965). However, in each of the extant studies, stimulus control procedures have been combined with several others so that their independent therapeutic power cannot be estimated. Moreover, many of the published applications of stimulus control have been uncontrolled case studies and therefore leave open the question of relative superiority over no-treatment or attention-placebo conditions. We must therefore conclude that—although stimulus control procedures have been frequent elements in successful self-control applications—their singular contribution has yet to be adequately assessed.

Self-Monitoring

The strategy of recording one's habits probably began well before Benjamin Franklin's famous "personal virtue" diary. Nevertheless, self-observation did not receive controlled empirical attention until after the advent of behavioral experimentation on self-control phenomena. It is interesting to note that various strategies of self-recording were first introduced as "control" procedures in experiments directed at other issues. When self-monitoring came into its own as a research topic, it soon became obvious that this *assessment* procedure was often a reactive *treatment*

strategy. Early studies suggested that the act of recording a behavior often had a dramatic influence on the frequency of the behavior. It seemed that self-control researchers were faced with a human analog to the Heisenberg (uncertainty) principle in physics (i.e., that the act of measuring a phenomenon might itself influence the phenomenon). Unfortunately, the reactive effects of self-monitoring were not consistent across subjects or studies, and a variety of factors were often left uncontrolled in the early research (Kanfer, 1970a; Kazdin, 1974f). To make matters more complicated, there was the difficult issue of assessing the reliability of subjects' self-reports. As of 1974, the following tentative generalizations were offered (Thoresen & Mahoney, p. 63).

1. Individuals are not "naturally" accurate self-observers. Training in the discrimination and recording of a behavior is essential. Such training may be enhanced by modeling, immediate accuracy feedback, systematic reinforcement, and graduated transfer of recording responsibilities (external to self).

2. The accuracy of self-recorded data varies dramatically across subjects, situations, behaviors, and recording systems. Discrete behaviors and simple self-recording systems appear to enhance self-monitoring accuracy.

3. As a measurement device, self-observation represents a crucial preliminary stage in successful self-regulation. The individual may need accurate data on both his or her own behavior and relevant controlling influences before an effective self-change program can be developed.

4. As a treatment technique, the effects of self-observation are often variable and short-lived. Unless supplemented by additional behavior change influences (e.g., social reinforcement), self-monitoring does not offer promise in the long-term maintenance of effortful behavior.

5. The use of explicit goals may or may not enhance the effects of self-observation, depending on the nature of the behavior and the goals adopted.

A sizable body of research has been published since the above generalizations were offered (Nelson, 1976). With a few minor exceptions, however, the foregoing generalizations appear to remain reasonably consistent with more recent studies and applications of self-monitoring (Bellack, 1976; Boren & Jagodzinski, 1975; Bristol & Sloane, 1974; Cavior & Marabotto, 1976; Emmelkamp, 1974; Emmelkamp & Ultee, 1974; Epstein & Peterson, 1973; Epstein, Webster, & Miller, 1975; Frederiksen, Epstein, & Kosevsky, 1975; Hoon, 1976; Horan, Hoffman, & Macri, 1974; Katz, Thomas, & Williamson, 1976; Kazdin, 1974e; Knapczyk & Livingston, 1973; Layne, Rickard, Jones, & Lyman, 1976; Lipinski, Black, Nelson, & Ciminero, 1975; Lipinski & Nelson, 1974; McKenzie & Rushall, 1974; Nelson, Lipinski, & Black, 1976; Richards, in press; Richards, McReynolds, Holt, & Sexton, 1976; Romanczyk, 1974; Rozensky, 1974; Seymour & Stokes, 1976; Sieck & McFall, 1976; Sobell & Sobell, 1973; Vargas & Adesso, 1976; Zimmerman & Levitt, 1975).

Some of the issues that remain to be clarified in this area deal with the dual-purpose role of self-monitoring in clinical applications. When used primarily for its therapeutic effects, self-monitoring has shown limited and variable success. What are the paramenters of that variability—subjects, target behaviors, recording systems? Do they vary for socially approved versus socially condemned actions (e.g., physical exercise versus alcoholism)? How does one insure that a client will, in fact, self-monitor? This latter question shades into the second role of this procedure, assessment. Theoretically, a client has uniquely comprehensive access to his or her own behavior in the sense that it can never occur without the client being present. Reliable and valid self-observations could offer invaluable information to the therapist. But how is one to know whether a client's self-reports are accurate? If therapist praise and counseling decisions are based solely on self-report, what is to prevent changes in these reports with no corresponding changes in their referents? Do occasional "honesty" checks elevate self-monitoring accuracy? What grounds have we for assuming that an external observer's records are always the best (most valid) criterion?

The need for answers to these and other questions is pressing because of the widespread (and expanding) use of self-monitoring procedures in clinical psychology. Therapists ranging widely in focus and theoretical orientation have begun to rely more heavily on the clinical information provided by participant observation (Shelton & Ackerman, 1974). It is commendable that research has begun to clarify some of the complex factors that influence human self-observation. Likewise, it is imperative that we recognize the currently staggering ratio of ignorance to knowledge and the need to intensify our empirical efforts in this area.

Self-Reward

One of the most heavily researched procedures of behavioral self-control is self-reinforcement—the self-presentation of rewards contingent on performance of some desired response. This strategy is a direct extrapolation from laboratory research on operant conditioning, with the nontrivial exception that the experimenter and subject share the same identity. The use of self-reward in clinical counseling situations was preceded by several years of laboratory research (Bandura, 1969, 1971; Kanfer, 1970b). In these preliminary studies it was shown that subjects—when given control over their own reinforcing consequences—will often match prior external reinforcement schedules, and their response rates are frequently comparable to those of individuals who remain on external reinforcement. Bandura's social learning approach emphasized the role of models in the acquisition of self-reinforcement patterns and in the adoption of varying personal performance standards. Of particular interest in these early studies was the finding that subjects often imposed very stringent requirements on their performance despite the opportunity to reward themselves noncontingently. Moreover, there were some data to suggest that individuals who had been trained to monitor and reward their own performances not only compared well with externally reinforced subjects, but actually surpassed the latter during extinction phases (when all reward opportunities were removed).

Kanfer's (1970b, 1971) early work led him to postulate a three-phase model of self-regulation. According to this model, a person must first self-monitor his or her performance. This focus of attention is often instigated by an event that marks a deviation from homeostasis or normal functioning.

Self-monitoring is followed by a phase of *self-evaluation,* in which the person compares his or her monitored performance to goals or standards based on prior learning. If the performance matches or exceeds those goals, *self-reinforcement* may occur. A substandard performance may elicit self-criticism or an attempt to repeat (and improve) the performance.

The implications of these hypotheses and early laboratory findings were soon to receive attention from applied researchers. Rehm and Marston (1968), for example, compared self-reinforcement to a nonspecific (placebo) therapy and no treatment in the alleviation of heterosexual anxieties among male college students. The self-reinforcement subjects displayed significantly better improvement according to self-reports of both anxiety and actual behavioral performance. These improvements were maintained over a 7 to 9 month follow up. Within a short time there were several studies reporting similar positive results with self-reinforcement in the classroom. Extrapolations to clinical populations were next to arrive, and a number of experimental and case studies reported the successful use of self-reward with depressives and obese individuals. These preliminary investigations have now been refined and expanded to even broader clinical populations. Ongoing research and several heuristic case studies suggest that self-reinforcement has been relatively consistent in yielding positive outcomes (Ballard & Glynn, 1975; Bass, 1972; Bellack, 1976; Bellack, Glanz, & Simon, 1976; Brigham et al., 1976; Burns & Powers, 1975; Cross & Cooper, 1976; Drabman, Spitalnik, & O'Leary, 1973; Felixbrod & O'Leary, 1973; Frederiksen & Frederiksen, 1975; Frederiksen & Miller, 1976; Glynn & Thomas, 1974; Glynn, Thomas, & Shee, 1973; Greiner & Karoly, 1976; Gulanick, Woodburn, & Rimm, 1975; Helland, Paluck, & Klein, 1976; Karoly & Kanfer, 1974; Mahoney, 1974b; Masters & Mokros, 1974; Masters & Santrock, 1976; McLaughlin & Malaby, 1974; McReynolds & Church, 1973; Reschly, 1973; Rozensky & Bellack, 1974; Rozensky & Bellack, 1976; Santogrossi, O'Leary, Romanczyk, & Kaufman, 1973; Spates & Kanfer, 1977; Speidel, 1974; Thomas, 1976).

Unfortunately, despite this abundance of research demonstrating the effectiveness of self-reward procedures, very little progress has been made in isolating the relative contribution of component processes. For example, a molecular analysis suggests that any given instance of self-reinforcement probably involves (1) beliefs and expectancies regarding the probable success of this procedure, (2) self-deprivation of freely available rewards, (3) self-monitoring of a targeted performance, (4) evaluation of that performance relative to some adopted goal or standards, (5) cognitive and affective self-reactions, and (6) the act of presenting oneself with a tangible reward. Recent workers have begun to question the importance of tangible self-reinforcement and have speculated that training in positive self-evaluations (self-praise) may be sufficient. Other workers have focused on the distinction between presenting oneself with a reward and determining one's own contingencies. In classroom applications, for example, it is possible for a teacher to select performance contingencies but to ask the student to administer his or her own rewards. Preliminary research has suggested that the mechanical act of self-consequation may be less important than the opportunity to select and alter one's performance contingencies. Likewise, there have been few attempts to evaluate critically the importance of demand characteristics and therapeutic expectancies in self-reinforcement applications. These and other issues offer ample targets for continuing research in this area.

Self-Punishment

Self-punishment is defined as a procedure in which the person optionally self-administers some aversive stimulus (or self-removes a positive stimulus) contingent on the occurrence of some undesired response. It again represents a relatively straightforward extrapolation from animal experimentation. In contrast to the prolific research on self-reinforcement, however, there have been relatively few studies addressed to self-punishment. This sparsity of research may be partly due to the meager success reported in initial self-punishment applications. As with almost any clinical procedure, there are a handful of case studies claiming the success of techniques such as the self-presentation of electric shock contingent on cigarette smoking (Thoresen & Mahoney, 1974). However, in studies incorporating placebo, self-monitoring, or no-treatment control groups, self-punishment techniques have not demonstrated any respectable degree of consistency in response suppression (Keutzer, 1968; Lichtenstein & Keutzer, 1969; Ober, 1968; Weingartner, 1971; Wilson, Leaf, & Nathan, 1975).

One of the problems with aversive self-regulatory procedures is the paradoxical dilemma of using a stimulus that is aversive enough to be suppressive but not too aversive to jeopardize its self-employment. Laboratory research on self-punishment has suggested that this procedure is less favorably viewed by subjects and less consistently applied than would be the case if it were externally administered. Unless there is a forthcoming change in the trend of these findings, it would appear that self-administered punishment may hold comparatively less promise than alternative self-regulatory techniques.

Before concluding our remarks on this area, mention should be made of the research that has been conducted on the patterns of pain endurance and resistance to temptation. These two patterns are often considered self-regulatory in that they involve voluntary continuation of a painful stimulus or postponement of a reward. In the case of pain tolerance, a number of studies have suggested that factors such as cognitive distractions, pleasant imagery, and performance contracts may substantially enhance a person's ability to tolerate painful stimulation (see Thoresen & Mahoney, 1974; also see Berger & Kanfer, 1975; Grimm & Kanfer, 1976; Horan, 1973; Kanfer & Seidner, 1973; Levendusky & Pankrantz, 1975; Spanos, Horton, & Chaves, 1975). Likewise, research on delay of gratification and resistance to temptation has identified several strategies—again predominantly cognitive—that seem to facilitate abilities in these areas (Kanfer, 1976; Mischel, 1973).

Current Issues in Self-Control
Despite their relatively late arrival on the scene of empirical scrutiny, self-control strategies have enjoyed a tremendous amount of research attention in the last decade. As is often the case with good research, however, the result of all this intense scrutiny can be couched more comfortably in the form of questions instead of answers. First, we may

ask for a comprehensive model of human self-regulation. There are several contemporary contenders for this honor, and each has spawned a respectable group of evaluative studies. At this point however, the selection of a "most likely to succeed" would seem premature. Until each model has received the technical scrutiny it deserves, a confident endorsement is hardly in order. Of particular note to this chapter, however, is the fact that each of the major theoretical contenders invoke cognitive processes in their explanation of self-control. This cognitive convergence is also reflected in current procedural shifts—away from the early operant self-control procedures involving primarily tangible reinforcement (e.g., self-presentation of tokens) and toward more symbolic self-regulatory activities (e.g., covert self-praise or imaginal anticipation of delayed consequences). Given the extent to which the "cognitive revolution" has pervaded our models and procedures, let us hope that it is a constructive shift.

Besides the need for an adequate model of self-control, researchers in this area face many technical issues that bear on specific self-regulatory procedures. What are the parameters of reliable self-monitoring? Under what circumstances is this strategy reactive? Are there some clinical situations in which self-monitoring would be contraindicated? Do stimulus control strategies significantly contribute to the effectiveness of some self-regulatory therapies? What are the active therapeutic components in self-reinforcement and self-punishment? To what extent do demand characteristics and expectancies (both client and therapist) contribute to the effects of all of the above?

Despite the voluminous literature on self-control, our knowledge has been unfortunately hampered by methodological problems. Attention-placebo control groups, for example, have been glaringly absent in this area, as have groups that would control for the reactive effects of testing. The potential influence of experimenter bias and demand characteristics remain to be examined in self-regulatory research. Likewise, many independent variables have been poorly specified—a fact that may help to account for some of the variability reported on the effects of self-monitoring. Uncontrolled case studies—which served a valuable heuristic function a decade ago—continue to earn journal space that would have been more efficiently reserved for controlled group studies. When these methodological problems are added to the general tendency to publish only positive results (Mahoney, 1976b), an accurate understanding of self-regulatory phenomena seems less than imminent.

When conceptual and methodological problems are resolved, the self-control researcher must still face issues such as follow-through and maintenance. The development of effective self-regulatory procedures is of little value if these procedures are not implemented and maintained by clients. What are the most effective methods for teaching self-control? Should component skills be graduated and taught piecemeal, or would a broader approach be superior? How does one deal with "unmotivated" clients? If motivation is modifiable, what are the ethical issues raised by such interventions? Are self-control therapies actually more cost-efficient than alternate forms of counseling? These questions should seem familiar, because they represent the perennial issues that face any therapeutic endeavor. Which therapy is effective for whom, under what circumstances, by which criterion, and at what cost? If research in self-control continues at its present pace, we can at least look forward to a sharper awareness of the questions to be answered at the close of another decade.

COVERT CONDITIONING

Although it is admittedly arbitrary to separate research on behavioral self-control from that dealing with covert conditioning, it is also true that the latter formed a critical link between earlier behavior therapies and the more recent cognitive learning hybrids. In this section we will briefly survey the empirical status of attempts to apply a conditioning model to private events. Our discussion will encompass five basic covert conditioning procedures: (1) covert counterconditioning, (2) thought stopping, (3) coverant control, (4) covert sensitization, and (5) other covert conditioning techniques. A summary evaluation of the covert conditioning model will then be presented.

Covert Counterconditioning

Although Wolpe (1958, 1976) has been adamant in minimizing the role of cognitive processes in systematic desensitization, there can be little doubt that this procedure has traditionally relied on mental imagery. In its most typical form, desensitization requires that a client be relaxed as he or she is asked to *imagine* progressively more aversive scenes or performances. The fact that this procedure relies on covert conditioning assumptions is clear in Wolpe's description of it as a "conditioning therapy."

It is not our purpose here to review the sizable literature on systematic desensitization. There seems to be little debate about *whether* this clinical procedure is effective. However, one could devote an entire volume to the theories and hypotheses about *why* it is effective. Extinction, counterconditioning, attribution, placebo effects, cognitive reappraisal—all have been proposed as contending explanations (Bandura, 1969; Davison & Wilson, 1973; Kazdin & Wilcoxon, 1976). With the exception of Wolpe's reciprocal inhibition hypothesis, none has been conclusively eliminated from the competition. The point is simply that a very popular and ostensibly effective behavior therapy procedure has relied on covert events (images) and processes for almost two decades. Notwithstanding the occasional attempts to minimize cognitive considerations, one wonders whether this extensive preoccupation with clients' symbolic processes may not have at least contributed to behavior therapists' increasing interest in private events.

Thought Stopping

As its name implies, "thought stopping" is a procedure designed to terminate unwanted cognitions. One of the earliest references to it dates back to Alexander Bain's (1928) *Thought Control in Everyday Life*. It was later adopted by behavior therapists and became one of their standard clinical procedures (Wolpe, 1958, 1969). In essence, thought stopping involves several practice sessions in which a client with ruminative problems is asked to intentionally think about his or her undesired cognitions. During a first trial—when the client is thought to be deeply immersed in ruminations—

the therapist shouts "STOP!" This often produces a startle response along with termination of the undesired cognition. Using this demonstration as a rationale, the client is instructed to practice the sequence himself or herself. That is, the client is told to engage in ruminations and then loudly shout "STOP!" The self-presented shout eventually becomes covert, and the client is instructed to use the command whenever ruminations become a problem.

Unlike some other behavior therapy techniques, thought stopping is a procedure that lacks even a remote analog in animal experimentation. It is, in fact, more similar to the popular lay solution for many behavioral problems (i.e., simply telling the person to "stop it"). Its derivation and theoretical status must, however, be considered secondary to its clinical effectiveness. Unfortunately, the latter has yet to be demonstrated. Although there had been almost two dozen case studies reported by 1974, only two group studies had been published (Mahoney, 1974a). One of these combined thought stopping with another procedure (Rimm, Saunders, & Westel, 1975) and the second, in addition to suffering from serious methodological problems, failed to demonstrate any substantial promise for the technique (Wisocki & Rooney, 1974). Studies reported since that time have not necessitated revision of the statement that thought stopping is a procedure that has little to support it other than tradition (Hackmann & Mclean, 1975). Despite the fact that this procedure has been practiced by behavior therapists for over two decades, there has yet to be a single controlled group study demonstrating its effectiveness.

Coverant Control

In his classic 1965 article, Homme suggested a procedure called "coverant control." The term "coverant" is an abbreviation of "covert operant." Homme suggested that individuals be trained to alter maladaptive thought chains by arranging to reinforce more appropriate alternate cognitions. This required a somewhat complicated sequence in which the person first rehearsed a negative coverant, then a positive one, and finally engaged in some rewarding activity. The negative coverant was demanded by the fact that Homme's proce-

dure was primarily aimed at decelerative (undesired) target behaviors. Thus, a reforming smoker might be asked to respond to smoking urges first with a negative coverant (e.g., "smoking causes cancer"). This would be immediately followed by a positive coverant (i.e., one emphasizing an incompatible response, such as "I'll save money by not smoking"). Finally, to reward these two covert calisthenics, the person would be told to reinforce himself or herself with some pleasant activity.

With due respect for its role as a historical landmark, coverant control therapy is plagued by both conceptual and empirical problems (Mahoney, 1974a). Among the former is its tacit assumption of *automaticity* (i.e., that reinforcing events automatically strengthen whatever responses preceded them). The literature of experimental and cognitive psychology suggest that the human organism is more discriminating than would be predicted by the automaticity assumption. One cannot simply rehearse a skill before meals and expect the meals to strengthen them automatically. Although regular events such as meals may help to structure the rehearsal of assignments, it is not clear that their function is one of consequating instead of cueing responses. Aside from its conceptual problems, coverant control is a strong competitor with thought stopping for the dubious honor of "weakest empirical status" among behavior therapy techniques. In the case of coverant control, however, this weakness derives as much from poor clinical outcomes as from the absence of controlled research. Evaluation of a technique requires that one distinguish among nonexistent data, data that are rendered ambiguous by poor methodology, and experimentally sound data that suggest a weak clinical procedure (Mahoney, 1974a). All three of these can be cited in the case of coverant control. Although subsequent studies have helped to clarify some of the issues in this area, they have not suggested much clinical promise for this covert conditioning strategy (Epstein & Hersen, 1974; Horan, 1974; Horan et al., 1975; Horan, Smyers, Dorfman, & Jenkins, 1975; Zimmerman, 1975).

Covert Sensitization

Probably the most popular covert conditioning technique is "covert sensitization," an aversion therapy endorsed by Cautela (1966, 1967, 1971a, 1973). Cautela has been a prolific and influential contributor to behavior therapy and must be credited with stimulating much of the early interest in covert conditioning. The basic strategy in covert sensitization is to associate imaginally some undesired behavior with unpleasant consequences. Cautela has likened the procedure to both classical (respondent) conditioning and operant punishment. In any case, the clinical use of covert sensitization involves having a client first imagine some maladaptive habit and then imagine very negative consequences. To reduce an obese client's consumption of sweets, for example, a scene such as the following might be used.

> I want you to imagine you've just had your main meal and you are about to eat your dessert, which is apple pie. As you are about to reach for the fork, you get a funny feeling in the pit of your stomach. You start to feel queasy, nauseous and sick all over. As you touch the fork, you can feel some food particles inching up your throat. You're just about to vomit. As you put the fork into the pie, the food comes up into your mouth. You try to keep your mouth closed because you are afraid that you'll spit the food out all over the place. You bring the piece of pie to your mouth. As you're about to open your mouth, you puke; you vomit all over your hands, the fork, over the pie. It goes all over the table, over the other people's food. Your eyes are watering. Snot mucus is all over your mouth and nose. Your hands feel sticky. There is an awful smell. As you look at this mess you just can't help but vomit again and again until just watery stuff is coming out. Everybody is looking at you with a shocked expression. You turn away from the food and immediately start to feel better. You run out of the room, and as you run out, you feel better and better. You wash and clean yourself up and it feels wonderful. (Cautela, 1967, p. 462).

Nauseating imagery has been the most frequently employed, and many clients do report that these vivid scenarios have emetic properties. However, the question is whether this procedure can claim support from controlled outcome research. There is a host of clinical case studies that offer very limited evaluative information. Group studies addressed to alcoholism, smoking, and obesity have generally lent little support to the efficacy of covert sensitization (see Mahoney, 1974a; also see Hedberg & Campbell, 1974; Wilson & Tracey, 1976).

Several studies have recently attempted to evaluate the contribution of experimental demand characteristics and therapeutic expectancy in those few instances in which covert sensitization appeared to surpass no treatment. Sachs and Ingram (1972) and Ashem and Donner (1968), for example, found that *reversing* the covert sensitization procedure did not appear to reduce its effectiveness. That is, it does not appear to make any difference whether the imagined aversive event precedes or follows the target behavior. These data challenge the notion that a direct conditioning analogue is appropriate. Likewise, Foreyt and Hagen (1973) reported that using positive imagery was just as effective as using nauseating scenes. Davidson and Denney (1976) found that a placebo control group was more effective than covert sensitization in the treatment of nailbiting. Similarly negative results were reported when attention-placebo procedures were compared to covert sensitization in the treatment of obesity (Diament & Wilson, 1975; Elliott & Denney, 1975) and smoking (Sipich, Russell, & Tobias, 1974). When viewed against the strong tendency to publish only positive outcome studies in psychology (Mahoney, 1976b), these negative and placebo equivalence reports must be given serious consideration.

A handful of single-subject experimental studies have suggested the possibility that covert sensitization may hold some promise in the treatment of selected sexual disorders (Mahoney, 1974a). Until these are replicated and supplemented with more adequate experimental designs, however, we must remain cautious and conservative in our conclusions. At the present time, one can only state that covert sensitization has not shown any consistent or impressive effectiveness as a therapeutic procedure. On the basis of the available evidence, it cannot be said that this technique is ineffective—but only that its effectiveness has yet to be demonstrated. Continuing research in this area will hopefully offer some valuable and overdue clarification.

Other Covert Conditioning Techniques

Although covert sensitization has been the dominant procedure in this area, behavior therapists have recently witnessed a dramatic proliferation of covert conditioning techniques. Extrapolating each of the standard behavior modification procedures, Cautela and his colleagues have virtually exhausted the hypothesized isomorphism between laboratory conditioning and covertized techniques. Thus, there are now invitations to *covert reinforcement* (positive and negative), *covert extinction, covert modeling,* and *covert response cost* (Cautela, 1970a, 1970b, 1971a, 1971b, 1973; Cautela, Flannery, & Hanley, 1974; Haney & Euse, 1976; Scott & Rosenstiel, 1975). The clinical promise of these various procedures has yet to be unequivocally demonstrated (Mahoney, 1974a). With the possible exception of covert modeling—which we will discuss under cognitive therapies—the few laboratory and clinical outcome studies on these supplementary techniques (1) have been methodologically limited, (2) have shown only meager effectiveness, or (3) have suggssted that the processes involved can hardly be said to conform to traditional conditioning assumptions (Bajtelsmit & Gershman, 1976; Berecz, 1976; Blanchard & Draper, 1973; Daniels, 1976; Hurley, 1976; Ladouceur, 1974; Marshall, Boutilier, & Minnes, 1974).

The foregoing studies not only challenge many of the conceptual aspects of covert conditioning, but they present an empirical picture that is less than exciting. At the risk of oversimplification, we must conclude that covert conditioning techniques are hardly the straightforward laboratory analogs they claim to be and have generally shown relatively modest clinical promise. Where successful applications have been reported, methodological inadequacies have often prevented unequivocal attribution of credit. Likewise, there seems to be a consistent tendency for the better controlled studies to find covert conditioning techniques little more effective than attention-placebo controls.

This pessimistic conclusion should not be interpreted as a blanket pronouncement of ineffectiveness or a recommendation to terminate clinical research in this area. On the contrary, what seems to be most urgent is accelerated research with greater

care in the control and assessment of therapeutic process and outcome (Kazdin, 1977). Whatever the verdict of that research, we should bear in mind the valuable historical role played by the covert conditioning perspective. This approach ushered in a revolutionary interest in private events among behavior therapists and laid the groundwork for a functional rapprochement of scientific methodology and intimate experience. Likewise, it is possible that the covert conditioning therapies may be heuristic even if they turn out to be inadequate. That is, a clearer understanding of their failure to demonstrate clinical promise might suggest ways of refining these and other therapeutic procedures. Does the fact that covert conditioning techniques rely primarily on *imagery* implicate the latter as a less promising medium of clinical intervention? The cognitive therapies, which we will soon discuss, rely more heavily on covert *verbal* (language-based) mechanisms. However, as we will see, research on more recent cognitive procedures that emphasize visual imagery suggest that the use of imagery per se is not responsible for the relatively poor showing of covert conditioning techniques. Is it some dimension of the *content* of imagery (e.g., realistic versus unrealistic scenes)? These are only a few of the issues whose examination might expand the potential contribution of covert conditioning techniques to our ongoing refinement of clinical methods.

COGNITIVE LEARNING THERAPIES

As mentioned in our introduction, the cognitive learning therapies are a loose aggregate of procedures that share a few fundamental assumptions but that vary widely in their theoretical parentage and technical operations. One can readily detect contributions from cybernetics and information processing, social psychology, perception, developmental psychology, biofeedback, and decision theory. In keeping with its chronological theme, our review will follow a rough historical format in addressing the three major divisions of current cognitive learning therapies: (1) cognitive restructuring, (2) coping skills therapies, and (3) problem-solving therapies. A rough classification schema is offered in Table 18-1. Representative references for each of the various therapies are also presented. It should be noted that Table 18-1 does not include reference to works that were instrumental in encouraging cognitive therapies but that have either failed to outline a distinctive therapeutic protocol (e.g., Frank, 1961; Rotter, 1954) or have failed to muster any substantial practice (e.g., Kelly, 1955). It also excludes the therapies that presume cognitive change mechanisms but that do not focus on cognitive components per se (e.g., participant modeling). Finally, it need hardly be pointed out that the therapies classified in Table 18-1 do not exhaust the clinical approaches that deal with some aspect of cognition, coping skills, or problem solving. Indeed, in at least one sense, cognitive learning therapists would argue that *all* forms of counseling—intentionally or otherwise—are attempts to assess and therapeutically alter clients' perceptions of themselves and their worlds (Raimy, 1975). The distinguishing feature of cognitive learning therapies is their simultaneous endorsement of the importance of cognitive *processes* and the functional promise of experimentally developed (and often behavioristic) *procedures*. As mentioned earlier, the increasing permeability between behavioral and nonbehavioral perspectives may soon make even this distinction anachronistic.

Because of space limitations, our survey will deal only with empirical research on the effectiveness of the various cognitive therapies. An equally large literature has addressed the role of cognition in human adjustment (Beck, 1976; Ellis, in press; Mahoney, 1974a, in press). Of particular interest are the recent suggestions of possible cognitive influence in hyperactivity, alcoholism, obesity, depression, and avoidance patterns (cf. Kazdin & Wilcoxon, 1976; Polivy & Herman, 1976; Rehm, in press; Whalen & Henker, 1976; Wilson & Lawson, 1976; Wooley, 1972). Likewise, Bandura's (in press) recent theory of "self-efficacy" offers a stimulating and heuristic model of cognitive processes in adjustment. Such models and basic research offer valuable supplements and suggestions to therapeutic efforts, but our primary focus in this chapter will be on demonstrated clinical outcome.

Cognitive Restructuring

Perhaps the best known of the cognitive therapies is rational-emotive therapy (RET), developed primarily by Ellis (1962). Although RET has historically been the most dominant and visible therapy of this genre, its monopoly seems to have been substantially reduced by more recent innovations. As we will see in a moment, the newer cognitive therapies pose less of a challenge to the ideology of RET than they do to its procedural features and its restrictiveness. That is, most of the therapies in this area accept Ellis' assumption that maladaptive feelings are often caused by maladaptive thoughts. At

TABLE 18-1 Contemporary Cognitive Learning Therapies

Cognitive Restructuring	Coping Skills Therapies	Problem Solving Therapies
Rational-emotive therapy (RET) (Ellis, 1962)	Covert modeling (Cautela, 1971; Kazdin, 1973)	Behavioral problem solving (D'Zurilla & Goldfried, 1971)
Self-instruction (Meichenbaum, 1974)	Coping skills training (Goldfried, 1971)	Problem-solving therapy (Spivack & Shure, 1974; Spivack, Platt, & Shure, 1976)
Cognitive therapy (Beck, 1970, 1976)	Anxiety management training (Suinn & Richardson, 1971)	Personal science (Mahoney, 1974a, 1977b)
	Stress inoculation (Meichenbaum, 1975)	

issue, however, are questions such as (1) whether rationality and adaptiveness are always isomorphic, (2) whether RET is too restrictively focused on emotion-laden disorders (versus, for example, those more accurately described as skills deficiencies), and (3) whether RET's rather curt and didactic approach is the most cost-efficient method for altering maladaptive thought patterns.

One of the features of RET that has stimulated some criticism from other cognitive therapists has been its insistence that "certain core irrational ideas . . . are at the root of most emotional disturbance" (Ellis, 1970). These irrational ideas are:

1. That it is a dire necessity for an adult to be loved by everyone for everything he or she does.

2. That certain acts are awful or wicked, and that people who perform such acts should be severely punished.

3. That is is horrible when things are not the way one would like them to be.

4. That human misery is externally caused and is forced on one by outside people and events.

5. That if something is or may be dangerous or fearsome one should be terribly upset about it.

6. That it is easier to avoid than to face life difficulties.

7. That one needs something greater than oneself on which to rely.

8. That one should be thoroughly competent, intelligent, and achieving in all possible respects.

9. That because something once strongly affected one's life, it should indefinitely affect it.

10. That one must have certain and perfect control over things.

11. That human happiness can be achieved by inertia and inaction.

12 That one has virtually no control over one's emotions and that one cannot help feeling certain things.

According to Ellis, one or more of these irrational ideas are usually responsible for a person's distress. In fact, with true phenomenological flavor, Ellis argues that it is the *idea* and not the reality that is upsetting. This is illustrated in his A-B-C analysis of maladaptive arousal. "A" refers to some real-life experience (e.g., the loss of a loved one). "B" symbolizes the thoughts that (irrationally) ensue (e.g., "This is horrible; I can't go on living"). "C," the emotional distress, is said to be caused by one's perception of an event instead of by the event per se. It is the task of the rational-emotive therapist, of course, to help the client to discriminate and alter these maladaptive cognitions.

A component analysis of rational-emotive therapy suggests that this clinical approach often includes:

1. Direct instruction and persuasion toward the basic RET premise (i.e., that irrational thoughts play an important role in subjective distress).

2. Recommendations to monitor one's thought patterns.

3. Modeling of a rationalistic evaluation and modification of personal thought patterns.

4. Candid feedback (positive and negative) on reported changes in thinking patterns and self-evaluation.

5. Performance assignments and rehearsal tasks to improve discrimination and evaluation of performance-relevant cognitions.

Although RET has become a more and more popular therapy over the last decade, this popularity can hardly be attributed to the strength of its empirical support. Until very recently, there were only a handful of controlled experimental evaluations of RET, and these offered only modest support for its clinical efficacy (Mahoney, 1974a). Thus, Ellis's (in press) statement that the data supporting RET are "immense, almost awesome" is more than slightly generous. There is substantial evidence for the role of cognition in some patterns of stress reaction, but specific processes and relationships remain to be clarified (Rogers & Craighead, in press). Outcome studies on RET have been sparse, and much of the controlled research in this area followed the introduction of variants of cognitive restructuring—self-instructional training and Beck's (1970a, 1976) cognitive therapy.

Self-instructional training is a therapeutic approach that derives partly from RET heritage, but that adds other features stemming from areas such as children's development of covert speech (Luria, 1961; Vygotsky, 1962). There is now a sizable body of literature demonstrating that the nature of one's "self-talk" (private monologs) can dramatically influence one's performance of widely varying tasks. The extension of this research to a variety of clinical disorders was spearheaded by Donald Meichenbaum and his colleagues (Meichenbaum, 1974, 1977). In one of their early studies, for example, they showed that training speech anxious clients to discriminate and alter maladaptive thought patterns resulted in significant improvements over attention-placebo and no-treatment control groups (Meichenbaum, Gilmore, & Fedoravicius, 1971). Similarly promising results were reported in applications of self-instructional training to impulsive children, institutionalized schizophrenics, test-anxious students, and creativity development (Meichenbaum, 1972a, 1975, 1977; Meichenbaum & Cameron, 1973), and their results have been extended by other workers (Glass, Gottman, & Shmurak, 1976; Holroyd, 1976; Masters & Santrock, 1976). The generalizability of some of these results has been questioned, however, in one study that failed to replicate Meichenbaum and Cameron's (1973) findings with schizophrenics (Margolis & Shemberg, 1976).

The differences between orthodox RET and self-instructional training are perhaps more difficult to enumerate than their similarities. Both emphasize the importance of self-statements and thought patterns in adaptive and maladaptive behavior. However, there are important differences in technique and focus. Where Ellis tends to focus on his set of "core irrational ideas," Meichenbaum et al. have seemed to be more interested in idiosyncratic thought patterns. The latter have also de-voted more attention to the role of graduated practice in their cognitive training package. In addition, self-instructional training presents a somewhat more heterogeneous package that contains elements of desensitization, modeling, and behavior rehearsal. Of particular note is the fact that this approach emphasizes practical coping skills for dealing with problematic situations. Although the major emphasis of RET is the *destruction* of maladaptive beliefs, self-instructional training supplants this with a *constructive* phase of skills development. Where RET highlights the *rationality* of a thought—believing that rationality is synonymous with adaptiveness—self-instructional training places more emphasis on its adaptiveness and its constructive alternatives. Thus, while RET posits differences in the thoughts of normal and distressed persons, a self-instructional therapist would place more emphasis on an individual's methods of coping with those thoughts (Meichenbaum, personal communication). In other words, it is not the content or incidence of irrational beliefs that differentiates normal and distressed persons—it is their learned means of coping with these beliefs.

A third approach to cognitive restructuring is that developed by Beck (1970a, 1976), which he has termed "cognitive therapy." Working independently of Ellis, Beck was early struck by the pervasiveness of irrational thoughts and fantasies in depression (Beck, 1963). His subsequent clinical research led him to postulate patterns of irrational cognitions that are common to various clinical syndromes (Beck, 1976). Processes such as selective attention, magnification, and arbitrary (illogical) inference are said to result in cognitive schema that vary in their general themes. Thus, for each of the neurotic disorders Beck suggests distinctive ideational contents. (See listing, p. 706).

As in RET and self-instructional training, the goals of the cognitive therapist are fundamentally those of helping the client to (1) discover and detect maladaptive cognitions, (2) recognize their deleterious impact, and (3) supplant them with more appropriate and adaptive thought patterns. These steps are specifically acknowledged by Beck (1976) in his elucidation of the principles of cognitive therapy. According to him, the successful client

Disorder	Cognitive Content
1. Depression	1. Thoughts centering on the experience of *loss* along with the "cognitive triad": (a) a devaluation of self, (b) a negative view of life experiences, and (c) a pessimistic view of the future
2. Anxiety	2. Thoughts of danger predominate
3. Paranoia	3. Thoughts focus on interference and intrusion by other people
4. Obsession	4. Thoughts generally focus on doubts (e.g., about a past performance or a future capacity)

must pass through stages in correcting faulty conceptions and self-signals.

> *First, he has to become aware of what he is thinking. Second, he needs to recognize what thoughts are awry. Then he has to substitute accurate for inaccurate judgments. Finally, he needs feedback to inform him whether his changes are correct (p. 217).*

There are many subtle differences between Beck's cognitive therapy and RET. For example, Beck's techniques, in contrast to Ellis's straightforward didacticism, emphasize a structuring of the therapeutic interaction so that the client discovers for himself or herself those thoughts that are inaccurate. This "Socratic dialogue" is different from nondirective reflection and very different from Ellis's strategy of direct confrontation. In cognitive therapy, the client is led to make personal discoveries by a tactful progression of questions. In addition to identifying maladaptive cognitions, the client is encouraged to improve personal methods of hypothesis testing. It is noteworthy that many of the "personal experiments" encouraged in cognitive therapy require active behavioral performance—a component that seems to be present in many of the most effective forms of psychotherapy (Mahoney, 1977c).

Despite these differences, there are many similarities between Beck's cognitive therapy and RET. At the risk of oversimplification one might even argue that RET, self-instructional training, and Beck's cognitive therapy all employ somewhat divergent *procedures* aimed at the same general *effects*: more adaptive thought patterns. Experimental studies have yet to explore many of the parameters that are presumed by these theorists to be operative.

The processes and optimal procedures of cognitive restructuring remain to be elucidated, but we are now at least beginning to see some well-controlled demonstrations of positive therapeutic outcome. Whatever the mechanisms involved, preliminary studies in this area suggest that these therapies may well be worth more energetic cultivation. Although ranging widely in their internal and external validity, an increasing number of studies has documented the potential efficacy of these therapies (Bender, 1976; Bornstein & Quevillon, 1976; Cabush & Edwards, 1976; Denney, 1975; Goldfried & Sobocinski, 1975; Goodwin & Mahoney, 1975; Keller, Croake, & Brooking, 1975; Levendusky & Pankrantz. 1975; Moleski & Tosi, 1976; Novaco, 1975, 1976; Reeves, 1976; Rush et al., 1977; Rush, Khatami, & Beck, 1975; Sanchez-Craig, 1976; Spanos, Horton, & Chaves, 1975; Taylor & Marshall, 1977; Thorpe, 1975; Thorpe, Amatu, Blakely, & Burns, 1976; Wein, Nelson, & Odom, 1975).

Since many of these studies have not included a legitimate (equally credible) attention-placebo comparison group, the contribution of factors such as rationale and therapist demand characteristics cannot be determined. As Shapiro (1971) has pointed out, it is not unusual for a new therapeutic procedure to enjoy striking successes during its professional honeymoon. Whether cognitive restructuring will remain a fertile and productive approach can only be evaluated in the years to come. It is ironic, however, that should their initial success be ultimately attributed to "placebo effects," one must be prepared for the reaction that the latter are cognitively mediated. The cognitive therapist must be careful here not to insulate himself or herself against component falsification. That is, the fact that placebo effects may well be mediated by cognitive processes does not invalidate a demonstration that the alleged ingredients of a therapy may not be the active ones.

Our review has surveyed the three major representatives of cognitive restructuring. Omission of approaches such as Kelly's (1955) fixed role therapy, Lazarus' (1973) basic id therapy, and attribution therapy (Kopel & Arkowitz, 1975) stem partly from limitations of space and from the fact that these perspectives—while making valuable contributions to the cognitive learning interface— have not yet been as heuristic or visible either in clinical practice or in controlled outcome research.

Coping Skills Therapies

The coping skills therapies are a more heterogeneous collection of procedures that overlap with both cognitive restructuring and the problem-solving approaches that will be discussed next. The distinguishing feature of these intermediate strategies seems to be their emphasis on helping the client to develop a repertoire of skills that will facilitate adaptation in a variety of stress situations. These skills include the self-instructional procedures examined earlier along with supplementary skills such as relaxation training, meditation, self-distraction, and preperformance rehearsal. For example, the technique of *covert modeling* (Cautela, 1971a) enables clients to rehearse mentally target performances prior to their real-life attempt. Although Cautela classifies covert modeling as a covert conditioning technique, we have here included it as a cognitive therapy primarily because its underlying mechanisms have been presented as being parallel to those of vicarious learning. Since the latter is generally considered to be a cognitive and not a conditioning process (Bandura, 1969, 1971), it seems more reasonable to classify its covert analog as a cognitive therapy. Likewise, although this procedure is a relative newcomer to behavior therapy, it has long been a popular strategy with hypnotists and sport psychologists. Numerous studies with athletes have suggested that this procedure often yields beneficial effects (Corbin, 1972), and imagery procedures have hardly been foreign to other therapeutic approaches (Singer, 1974). Preliminary research with selected clinical problems has supported the efficacy of covert modeling in the treatment of disorders such as phobias and unassertiveness (Kazdin, 1973, 1974a, 1974b, 1974c,

1974d, 1976; Meichenbaum, 1971; Rosenthal & Reese, 1976) but has questioned its equivalence to actual motoric rehearsal (Thase & Moss, 1976). Thus, one tentative possibility might be the use of these cognitive rehearsal strategies when overt practice is unfeasible (Kazdin, 1977).

An intriguing subissue that has emerged from covert modeling research has been the distinction between *coping* and *mastery* modeling (Spiegler et al., 1969). The mastery model is one who demonstrates a flawless performance without any sign of hesitation, emotional distress, or self-doubt. The coping model, on the other hand, displays initial performance anxieties, makes mistakes, and generally shows all the signs of an apprehensive apprentice. In keeping with therapeutic goals, however, the coping model perseveres and demonstrates strategies for controlling and coping with these diverse obstacles. Several studies have suggested that the coping model may be a more effective one and that the display of relevant stress-regulating strategies may be a valuable therapeutic component (Kazdin, 1973, 1974a, 1974b; Meichenbaum, 1971; Sarason, 1975). If these findings survive replication, they could have far-reaching implications for the role of some degree of therapist self-disclosure in psychotherapy. The coping/mastery distinction is unquestionably deserving of further empirical scrutiny (Bruch, 1976).

Other coping skills therapies include Goldfried's (1971) modification of standard systematic desensitization procedures. Contrary to Wolpe's (1958, 1969) recommendation that the client be told to immediately terminate any image that induces anxiety, Goldfried recommended that clients be encouraged to maintain the image, cope with the anxiety, and learn to relax it away. Theoretically, this strategy would result in a more generalizable skill, since the client would be learning to regulate his or her own physiological arousal instead of simply relaxing to one specific stimulus theme. This is similar to an argument offered by Sipprelle (1967). Preliminary studies have supported the promise of this recommendation (Bornstein & Sipprelle, 1973a, 1973b; Chang-Liang & Denney, 1976; Deffenbacker & Snyder, 1976; Goldfried & Trier, 1974; Kelly & Curran, 1976; Mendonca & Siess, 1976; Speigler et al., 1976), but the data are still far from adequate. In addition to its emphasis on relaxation as a general coping strategy, this procedure has encouraged the use of multiple-theme hierarchies to insure that clients' coping skills would generalize to a wide range of arousal situations. Similar operations are employed by Suinn and Richardson (1971) in their *anxiety management training* and by Meichenbaum (1975) in the technique called *stress inoculation*. The common denominator of these various procedures seems to be their attempt to *induce* stress (through imagery, electric shock, etc.) and then to train clients in effective coping strategies. Controlled outcome studies are too sparse to warrant a confident evaluation of the coping skills therapies. Their clinical promise has begun to receive respectable documentation, however, and it is perhaps indicated to some degree by the optimistic results now being reported with other cognitive therapies. The coping skills approach shares many parallels with rational psychotherapies and with some of the more recent problem-solving perspectives. We have already seen the beginnings of a respectable documentation for the former. Let us therefore turn our attention to the latter.

Problem-Solving Therapies

Although the phenomenon of problem solving has long been of interest to experimental and cognitive psychologists, its relevance to clinical concerns has only recently been explored. The need for that exploration was first noted in behavioral quarters by D'Zurilla and Goldfried (1971).

> Much of what we view clinically as "abnormal behavior" or "emotional disturbance" may be viewed as ineffective behavior and its consequences, in which the individual is unable to resolve certain situational problems in his life and his inadequate attempts to do so are having undesirable effects, such as anxiety, depression, and the creation of additional problems. (p. 107)

Despite their timely article, however, there was no immediate response on the part of applied behavioral researchers.

Much of the credit for the recent growth of problem-solving therapies must be given to Spivack and his colleagues. In a series of studies on preschoolers, emotionally disturbed children, adolescents, and institutionalized psychiatric patients, Spivack et al. reported two important findings: (1) they encountered differences in the problem-solving skills of "normal" and "deviant" populations, and (2) they reported preliminary success in several projects in which "deviant" subjects were given systematic training in personal problem solving (Platt, Scura, & Hannon, 1973; Platt & Spivack, 1972a, 1972b, 1973, 1974; Shure & Spivack, 1972; Shure, Spivack, & Jaeger, 1971; Siegel & Spivack, 1976; Spivack & Shure, 1974; Spivack, Platt, & Shure, 1976). Of particular note was the finding that individuals labeled "emotionally disturbed" were often significantly inferior to normal peers in the sheer number of possible solutions that they perceived in hypothetical problem situations. In addition to this apparent deficiency in their ability to generate options, however, was the fact that the solutions they did suggest were often antisocial (e.g., physically aggressive) and they frequently had very inaccurate expectancies about the probable consequences of different options.

Supplementing the research of Spivack and his colleagues have been a number of studies addressing the clinical promise of a personal problem-solving approach. Thus, Kifer et al. (1974) reported that instruction and practice of problem-solving skills were beneficial in helping predelinquent youths to negotiate conflict situations. Similarly, positive results were reported by Blechman in her work with families (Blechman, 1974; Blechman, Olson, & Hellman, 1976; Blechman et al., 1976). Indeed, Vincent, Weiss, and Birchler (1976) extended the earlier Spivack results by showing differences in the problem-solving patterns within conflictual versus nonconflictual marriages. Arnkoff and Stewart (1975) reported that modeling and videotape feedback may facilitate processes such as information gathering in personal problem solving. These results are congruent with the earlier success reported by Sarason and his colleagues in the use of modeling to teach problem-solving skills to delinquents (Sarason, 1968; Sarason & Ganzer, 1969a, 1969b, 1973). Additional data bearing on the clinical promise of this strategy have been reported by Evans and

Cody (1969), MacPherson, Candee, and Hohman (1974), Stone, Hinds, and Schmidt (1975), Coche and Flick (1975), Mendonca and Siess (1976), Jacobson (1977), and Coche and Douglas (in press).

Likewise, a number of clinical practitioners have included problem-solving training in successful treatment packages (Haley, 1976; Weiss, Hops, & Patterson, 1973). In their work with obese adults, for example, Mahoney and Mahoney (1976a, 1976b) have used an apprenticeship format in which clients develop progressively more complex problem-solving skills. Personal problems are likened to the research scientist's problems, and the same skills are deemed beneficial. Thus, in this "personal science" approach to adjustment (Mahoney, 1977b), subskills are integrated into a basic seven-step sequence that can be represented by the mnemonic SCIENCE.

S   Specify general problem.
C   Collect information.
I   Identify causes or patterns.
E   Examine options.
N   Narrow options and experiment.
C   Compare data.
E   Extend, revise, or replace.

In the various stages of problem solving the client develops skills such as self-monitoring, means-ends thinking, evaluation of probable consequences, rehearsal of possible options, and so on. For example, a client might define his or her problem as obesity. Information collected through a behavioral diary might help to identify potential causes (e.g., late evening snacking and sedentary life-style). Possible solutions would then be considered and one would be tested in a personal experiment. If the solution proved helpful, it might be continued and expanded; otherwise, a reappraisal and alternate solution would be sought. This general strategy has been effectively used with obese individuals (Mahoney et al., 1977).

The potential promise of the foregoing approaches merits extended comment. Among the cognitive learning therapies, it is our opinion that the problem-solving perspectives may ultimately yield the most encouraging clinical results. This is partly due to the fact that—as a broader clinical endeavor—they encompass both the cognitive restructuring and the coping skills therapies (not to mention a wide range of other "noncognitive" perspectives). With the problem-solving approaches, clients are not only taught specific coping skills, but also the more general strategies of assessment, problem definition, and so on. In a sense, the therapist is sharing years of professional training by making the client an apprentice in therapy—a student of effective self-regulation.

Despite its broad therapeutic goals, however, this approach allows substantial room for the uniqueness of individual clients. In fact, the core feature of problem solving as a therapeutic approach would seem to be *pragmatism*—its focus on helping the individual to discover and implement whatever adjustment strategies are effective in a given situation. An empirical eclecticism is explicitly encouraged. Moreover, it might be argued that the problem-solving therapies add substantial humanism to their empirical commitment. If one were to summarize the most common indictments against contemporary psychotherapies, they would probably include:

1. *Ineffectiveness,* particularly as defined by the client.

2. *Poor generalization* to problems and situations outside those specifically addressed by the therapy.

3. *Poor maintenance* over time.

4. *Poor cost-efficiency* as measured by both monetary and personal effort standards.

5. *Ethical dilemmas* in which the client's rights and responsibilities are not respected.

If the problem-solving therapies continue to demonstrate therapeutic power, they may pose one of the most promising hybrids in clinical science. Reviewing the above five categories, one can see that these therapies are specifically geared toward personal effectiveness. Clients are taught to evaluate changes in their behavior and to adjust their self-directive efforts according to their own individual progress. Because they emphasize broad coping skills, the problem-solving therapies may also fare much better in the realms of generalization and maintenance. To the extent that clients can learn personal adjustment skills that will enhance their independent ability to cope and grow with a changing environment, the issue of cost-efficiency may likewise diminish as an indictment. Finally, since the problem-solving therapies not only condone—but require—the active and responsible participation of the client in therapeutic decisions and actions, they may offer a welcome option with regard to contemporary issues on the ethics of psychotherapy. There are, of course, clients and disorders that may not be suited to this broader therapeutic perspective, but its feasibility would seem to merit serious examination.

SUMMARY

Let us briefly review our evaluation of the various self-control and cognitive therapies. Our survey has taken us from the relatively behavioristic strategies of self-regulation, through the transitional waters of covert conditioning, and into the more recent developments that share both cognitive and behavioristic heritage. Although the *conceptualization* of self-control processes has changed substantially, the *efficacy* of at least some of the self-regulatory procedures has not been seriously challenged. Self-reinforcement, for example, seems to have demonstrated relatively consistent effects across a wide range of subjects and behaviors. The effects of self-monitoring are more variable, and further research is needed to elucidate the parameters of its influence. Evidence on stimulus control and self-punishment remain relatively sparse, although there are preliminary indications that the latter may hold limited promise as a clinical procedure.

In the realm of covert conditioning we found a high ratio of theory to evidence, with a variety of extrapolation problems and theoretical dilemmas. Thought stopping, coverant control, and covert sensitization have been popular therapeutic strategies whose clinical effectiveness remain to be adequately assessed. The state of the art might be summarized as follows.

1. There is relatively little research on the processes and effects of covert conditioning therapies.

2. What research does exist is generally poor in either internal or external validity.

3. Those few studies with more adequate experimental methodologies have generally lent little support to the clinical promise of covert conditioning therapies.

The situation is somewhat brighter in the area of cognitive learning therapies (but this evaluation should be filtered through the realization that the authors would classify themselves in this category). After a relatively slow start in terms of empirical assessment, the cognitive restructuring therapies are now beginning to muster growing support in clinical outcome research. This is also the case with the coping skills therapies, but the data here are still too sparse to allow more than a cautious demand for more research. The problem-solving therapies fare somewhat better, although their therapeutic power can hardly be said to rest on an extensive empirical footing. Thus, in keeping with a longstanding tradition in clinical psychology, the contemporary cognitive learning therapist might be said to be engaging in "the art of applying a science which does not yet exist" (Meehl, 1960). The data are promising but preliminary; the techniques are diversified and unrefined. Depending on whether one leans toward optimism or pessimism, this state of affairs may signal an exciting new path in clinical science or yet another addition to our diversity of impotence.

ISSUES AND IMPLICATIONS

The cognitive learning perspective faces problems other than its youth, however. We will here briefly survey some of those problems, along with the potential promise of this bipartisan hybrid. Our discussion will focus on six broad issues: (1) the problem of reconciling cognitive psychology and behaviorism; (2) basic conceptual problems surrounding the terms and models employed by cognitive behaviorists; (3) methodological problems faced by researchers in this area; (4) the question of balance between procedure and process research; (5) the promise of a cognitive learning perspective in terms of prevention; and (6) the implications of that perspective for the training of therapists.

Reconciliation of the Odd Couple

As we mentioned earlier, one of the most ironic and intriguing aspects of the cognitive-learning trend has been its integration of two formerly bitter rivals. In fact, some would consider a "cognitive behaviorism" self-contradictory due to the basic tenets outlined by John B. Watson. However, as has been outlined elsewhere (Mahoney, 1974a), one must distinguish among several brands of behaviorism. Of particular relevance to the present discussion is the distinction between *metaphysical* (or "radical") and *methodological* behaviorism. The former makes strong allegations about exclusive physicalism (usually in reference to the mind-body problem); methodological behaviorism is characterized by an emphasis on the importance of objectivity and experimental rigor in the analysis of behavior.

There have, of course, been more than a few lively discussions of the compatability of cognitive and behavioral ideologies. Skinner (1974) and Rachlin (In press), for example, have criticized such a merger on the ground that science can deal only with publicly observable events and that mediational accounts of behavior are problematic *because* they are inferential. These arguments fare poorly when one acknowledges that science *never* deals with directly observable phenomena. The doctrine of immaculate perception (naive realism) has long been abandoned by philosophers of science, and the practice of controlled inference forms the backbone on all scientific disciplines. It is ironic that in mimicking the rigor of the physical sciences, many behaviorists have overlooked the abundance of inference in these disciplines. The fact that subatomic particles must always be inferred has not presented serious problems for nuclear physicists. Behaviorists need not face a question of *whether* to infer in their analyses of behavior—such inferences are unavoidable. The question is *which* inferences add to our predictive or explanatory power.

The inadequacies of a nonmediational model need not be reiterated here (Bandura, 1969; Mahoney, 1974a). Suffice it to say that the evidence for cognitive processes in human learning seems nothing short of overwhelming (Brewer, 1974). This is not, however, to say that the cognitive models now in existence are faultless. Despite their relative recency, it is clear that contemporary mediational theories are not yet adequate to the complexities of human adaptation. Our choice between mediational and nonmediational models is therefore relative, not absolute. The strengths and weaknesses of a cognitive learning perspective must be weighed against those of a conditioning model. It is our opinion that this contest is won handily by the cognitive contender, but this evaluation is again couched in the acknowledgment that there are many problems facing cognitive-behavioral researchers. Indeed, we would argue that the empirical skills of the methodological behaviorist are sorely needed in exploring this new perspective.

Conceptual Problems

Some of the most basic problems facing researchers in this area deal with conceptual and terminological issues. For example, what is a "cognition?" Is it an event? A process? Is it restricted to the central nervous system? Most research and theory has focused on covert visual experiences (e.g., visual images) and covert linguistic (auditory) experiences (e.g., thoughts). Are there other forms of cognition? Indeed, can these two forms be reliably distinguished? Are there any isomorphisms between modality of stimulus input and the neurological mechanisms of cognition (e.g., do a visual image and a visual perception excite the same neurons)? How do cognitions relate to emotions (and vice-versa)?

The lack of unequivocal definitions for basic terms is not, of course, an exception in psychology. Behaviorists have long been embarrassed by the formal inadequacy of such terms as "stimulus," "response," and "learning." This shared culpability does not legitimate the shortcomings of the cognitive theorist, nor should it avert efforts to resolve and refine terminological issues. It does, however, place in perspective the magnitude and uniqueness of this one deficiency. An additional conceptual problem to be faced by cognitive researchers is the role of the therapeutic relationship in the cognitive learning therapies. An emphasis on the therapeutic interaction can be found in many contemporary quarters (Bandler & Grinder, 1975; Frank, 1961; Haley, 1963; Luborsky, Singer, & Luborsky, 1975; Strupp, 1973). The rising interest in placebo effects and so-called nonspecific factors also suggests the need to examine the therapeutic relationship. It is imperative that cognitive therapists attempt to delineate fully the components of their therapy, including the role of the relationship between client and therapist. In other words, cognitive therapists need to know what they are actually doing with their clients, not just what they think they are doing. Furthermore, empirical exploration of the components of therapeutic change can lead to powerful refinement of treatment techniques.

As suggested by this issue of the exploration of therapeutic process, the most telling conceptual criticism of cognitive learning perspectives may be their lack of formal theoretical models. It is difficult to evaluate a perspective critically when its specific hypotheses and predictions are not clearly delineated. Although flexibility and informality may be adaptive features in the early gestation of a model, its later growth and refinement require the more focused scrutiny that can only be provided in the context of a formal paradigm. Some rudimentary assumptions have begun to emerge, but more specific and comprehensive models are sorely needed. As has been repeatedly demonstrated in the history of science, formalization of a perspective is often the first step in its critical scrutiny—and ultimately its rejection (Kuhn, 1962; Mahoney, 1976b). As it stimulates more sophisticated research, it exposes its own inadequacies and makes way for a newer paradigm. If the cognitive learning perspective is, indeed, an emerging paradigm in clinical science, its adherents should be prepared for its inevitable concession to a future contender. Such is the way of science, but we can hardly hope to grow if we are unwilling to change.

Methodological Problems

Many of the methodological problems invoked by cognitive research have been discussed in other contexts (Mahoney, 1974a, 1977a; Paivio, 1975; Reese, 1971). The importance of anchored inferences and operational definitions, for example, hardly needs reiteration. Two of the most important problems here, however, warrant brief review. First, there is the ever-present danger of tautology. In the evaluation of hypotheses that include cognitive terms, researchers must be careful to *define* the term independently of their hypothesis *evaluation*.

For example, consider the hypothesis that "self-critical thoughts produce negative affect." In evaluating this assertion one might experimentally manipulate the occurrence of self-critical thoughts (e.g., through instructions) and look for systematic differences in measures of negative affect (self-report, physiology, etc.). A tautology would arise, however, if indices of negative affect were used to infer the presence of self-critical thoughts. This would yield a circular (analytic) truth totally devoid of empirical information. For any hypothesis of the form "when condition X exists, outcome Y will follow," tautology can be avoided by insuring that the outcome measures (Y) are not used in the ascertainment of the antecedent condition (X). In cognitive hypotheses, this often means that the presence of a cognitive variable must be defined independently of its hypothesized effects (e.g., through the stimuli presented or on the basis of some other performance, such as a self-report).

The second major methodological problem facing cognitive researchers is the temptation to relax experimental standards in the name of "confirming" their paradigm. This is apparent in two common practices: (1) the acceptance of weak inference (e.g., correlational) methodologies as if they were stronger in their implications, and (2) the tendency to emphasize selectively those studies that support the paradigm and to discredit or ignore those that do not. The first practice can be seen in studies reporting cognitive differences between intact subject groups (mental patients and normals, obese and nonobese persons, etc.). Although these differences may be heuristic in suggesting factors deserving experimental scrutiny, they cannot demonstrate any causal role for the factors in question. More detrimental, however, may be the "confirmatory bias" evident among cognitive-behavioral researchers. The tendency to publish and cite selectively positive results is hardly an exclusive feature of cognitive behaviorists, however. Scientists seem to share this general penchant for "confirmation" despite the logical superiority of disconfirmatory reasoning (Mahoney, 1976b). Cognitive behaviorists may point to a long line of precedents for their illogical actions, but this does not reduce the epistemological costs of these practices. Given their familiarity with some of the fallibilities of human cognitive processes, let us hope that proponents of a cognitive learning approach will work toward setting some new precedents.

The Question of Balance

A related problem is the looming risk of an over-zealous adoption of the cognitive therapies (Mahoney, 1977a). It is not uncommon for researchers and practitioners to offer an uncritical welcome to the most recent therapeutic messiah. Likewise, as Bandura (1969) has pointed out, we must guard against the tendency to confuse therapeutic *procedures* with therapeutic *processes*. The cognitive therapist may invoke cognitive processes as the primary mechanisms of human adaptation, but he or she should not overlook the fact that those processes are linked to specifiable intervention procedures. It is imperative that researchers and practitioners communicate what they did to produce therapeutic changes, not what they presumed to have occurred inside the client's head. In this sense, at least, the term "cognitive therapy" may be misleading in that it conjures up the image of a cognition being repaired. Cognitive processes are presumably the underlying mechanisms of therapeutic behavior change, but they are not ends in and of themselves. To the extent that studying cognitions enhances our refinement of procedures that lead to more consistent or cost-efficient clinical improvements, then their ideological dues are paid. At the present time, it would appear that some of the procedures developed by behavior therapists are among the most effective in activating the cognitive processes that seem to precede therapeutic improvement. The cognitive therapist should bear in mind, however, that the merits of a cognitive approach must ultimately be translated into procedures and must be decided by empirical arbiters. If today's venture into cognitive models does not result in the improvement of tomorrow's therapies, we must be prepared to abandon the venture.

Preventive Promise

On the more positive side, let us look at some of the implications of a cognitive learning perspective for timely issues such as the prevention of behavior disorders. Although chronological studies have not yet been reported, applications of cognitive and self-control therapies to schoolchildren have yielded exciting preliminary results. What would happen if these exploratory efforts were expanded into a large-scale empirical trial in which personal problem solving became a standard part of the educational curriculum? Would the incidence of maladjustment be reduced if coping skills were taught at both the elementary and secondary school levels? Moreover, what would be the effects of changing society's view of therapy—moving away from the conventional stigma (where "therapy" connotes "pathology") and toward a more liberal view in which counseling is seen as an educational instead of a curative enterprise? Would tomorrow's children feel more responsible and prepared if they had received a structured apprenticeship in problem solving? These and other fantasies have yet to be examined, but they may at least offer some seductive promises to researchers and practitioners. With continuing efforts such as those described earlier (Spivack & Shure, 1974), we may soon be in a better position to evaluate their practical merit.

Therapist Training

We have thus far explored a number of problems and issues that face the contemporary cognitive learning theorist. The preliminary issues are (1) *whether* the cognitive therapies work, and (2) if they do, *why*. As confidence in the power and processes of these therapies increases we can turn our attention to the issue of their dissemination. If the cognitive learning therapies survive critical empirical scrutiny, what would be the implications for therapist training?

Our review has suggested that the cognitive learning therapies may present a unique challenge to the clinical scientist. For the first time in recent history, we are faced with an approach that combines an appreciation of intimate experience with an acknowledgment of external determinants and, more important, an appreciation of the awesomely complex interaction between these two. To these must be added a recognition of the clinical relevance of factors ranging from the microbiological to the cultural (Mahoney, 1974a). The "compleat" cognitive learning therapist may therefore require a broad interdisciplinary training. He or she may need an understanding of the biochemical factors that interact with adaptation, and an appreciation for the societal and cultural forces that shape human lives. In addition to the basic principles of human learning, the therapist may require a more sophisticated knowledge of information processing and the processes of human knowing. Finally, the therapist may need to appreciate that his or her role is that of an intervener, an agent of persuasive change who must rely on basic communicative procedures.

The beginnings of this interdisciplinary diversification are already apparent in some quarters (Wexler, 1976). Likewise, we have recently seen the collaborative efforts of behavior therapists and sociologists in assessing cultural factors in clinical dysfunction (e.g., Gagnon & Davison, 1976). Cognitive and clinical psychologists are beginning to speak to one another, and it is probably only a matter of time before the cognitive learning therapists will recognize their possible compatibility with the "communication therapies" (Bandler & Grinder, 1975; Haley, 1968, 1976; Ruesch, 1961). All in all, there seems to be a clear convergence toward divergence. In pursuing this more comprehensive approach to human adjustment, the cognitive learning therapist is faced with a substantial challenge—the challenge of diversifying his or her knowledge while simultaneously integrating that knowledge into practical intervention skills. An eclectic breadth of vision will need to be blended with a sensitive empiricism, and trite debates over first causes will have to give way to more constructive dialectics. In short, the psychotherapist of the future may well be forced to adopt a perspective that is broad in its conceptualization, pragmatic in its technology, and summarily more befitting the complexity of its subject matter.

REFERENCES

Arnkoff, D. B., & Stewart, J. The effectiveness of modeling and videotape feedback on personal problem solving. *Behaviour Research and Therapy*, 1975, *13*, 127–133.

Ashem, B., & Donner, L. Covert sensitization with alcoholics: A controlled replication. *Behaviour Research and Therapy*, 1968, *6*, 7–12.

Bain, J. A. *Thought control in everyday life*. New York: Funk & Wagnalls, 1928.

Bajtelsmit, J. W., & Gershman, L. Covert positive reinforcement: Efficacy and conceptualization. *Journal of Behavior Therapy and Experimental Psychiatry*, 1976, *7*, 207–212.

Ballard, K. D., & Glynn, T. Behavioral self-management in story writing with elementary school children. *Journal of Applied Behavior Analysis*, 1975, *8*, 387–398.

Bandler, R., & Grinder, J. *The structure of magic*. Palo Alto, Calif.: Science and Behavior Books, 1975.

Bandura, A. *Principles of behavior modification*. New York: Holt, Rinehart and Winston, 1969.

Bandura, A. Vicarious and self-reinforcement processes. In R. Glaser (Ed.), *The nature of reinforcement*. New York: Academic Press, 1971. Pp. 228–278.

Bandura, A. Self-reinforcement: Theoretical and methodological considerations. *Behaviorism*, 1976, *4*, 135–155.

Bandura, A. Self-efficacy: Toward a unifying theory of behavioral change. *Psychological Review*, in press.

Bandura, A., & Mahoney, M. J. Maintenance and transfer of self-reinforcement functions. *Behaviour Research and Therapy*, 1974, *12*, 89–98.

Bandura, A., Mahoney, M. J., & Dirks, S. J. Discriminative activation and maintenance of contingent self-reinforcement. *Behaviour Research and Therapy*, 1976, *14*, 1–6.

Bass, B. A. Reinforcement history as a determinant of self-reinforcement. *Journal of Psychology*, 1972, *81*, 195–203.

Beck, A. T. Thinking and depression, I. Idiosyncratic content and cognitive distortions. *Archives of General Psychiatry*, 1963, *9*, 324–333.

Beck, A. T. Cognitive therapy: Nature and relation to behavior therapy. *Behavior Therapy*, 1970a, *1*, 184–200.

Beck, A. T. Role of fantasies in psychotherapy and psychopathology. *Journal of Nervous and Mental Disease*, 1970b, *150*, 3–17.

Beck, A. T. Cognition, affect, and psychopathology. *Archives of General Psychiatry*, 1971, *24*, 495–500.

Beck, A. T. *Cognitive therapy and the emotional disorders*. New York: International Universities Press, 1976.

Bellack, A. S. A comparison of self-reinforcement and self-monitoring in a weight reduction program. *Behavior Therapy*, 1976, *7*, 68–75.

Bellack, A. S., Glanz, L. M., & Simon, R. Self-reinforcement style and covert imagery in the treatment of obesity. *Journal of Consulting and Clinical Psychology*, 1976, *44*, 490–491.

Bem, D. J. *Beliefs, attitudes, and human affairs*. Monterey, Calif.: Brooks/Cole, 1970.

Bender, N. N. Self-verbalization versus tutor verbalization in modifying impulsivity. *Journal of Educational Psychology*, 1976, *68*, 347–354.

Beneke, W. M., & Harris, M. B. Teaching self-control of study behavior. *Behaviour Research and Therapy*, 1972, *10*, 35–41.

Berecz, J. Treatment of smoking with cognitive conditioning therapy: A self-administered aversion. *Behavior Therapy*, 1976, *7*, 641–648.

Berger, S., & Kanfer, F. H. Self-control: Effects of training and presentation delays of competing responses on tolerance of noxious stimulation. *Psychological Reports*, 1975, *37*, 1312–1314.

Bernard, H. S., & Efran, J. S. Eliminating versus reducing smoking using pocket timers. *Behaviour Research and Therapy*, 1972, *10*, 399–401.

Blackwood, R. The operant conditioning of verbally mediated self-control in the classroom. *Journal of School Psychology*, 1970, *8*, 257–258.

Blackwood, R. *Mediated self-control: An operant model of rational behavior*. Akron, Ohio: Exordium Press, 1972.

Blanchard, E., & Draper, D. O. Treatment of a rodent phobia by covert reinforcement: A single subject experiment. *Behavior Therapy*, 1973, *4*, 559–564.

Blechman, E. A. The family contract game: A tool to teach interpersonal problem solving. *Family Coordinator*, 1974, *23*, 269–281.

Blechman, E. A., Olson, D. H. L., & Hellman, I. D. Stimulus control over family problem-solving behavior: The family contract game. *Behavior Therapy*, 1976, *7*, 686–692.

Blechman, E. A., Olson, D. H. L., Schornagel, C. Y., Halsdorf, M., & Turner, A. J. The family contract game: Technique and case study. *Journal of Consulting and Clinical Psychology*, 1976, *44*, 449–455.

Bolles, R. C. Reinforcement, expectancy, and learning. *Psychological Review*, 1972, *79*, 394–409.

Boren, J. J., & Jagodzinski, M. G. The impermanence of data-recording behavior. *Journal of Behavior Therapy and Experimental Psychiatry*, 1975, *6*, 359–360.

Bornstein, P. H., & Quevillon, R. P. The effects of a self-instructional package on overactive preschool boys. *Journal of Applied Behavior Analysis*, 1976, *9*, 179–188.

Bornstein, P. H., & Sipprelle, C. N. Group treatment of obesity by induced anxiety. *Behaviour Research and Therapy*, 1973a, *11*, 339–342.

Bornstein, P. H., & Sipprelle, C. N. Induced anxiety in the treatment of obesity: A preliminary case report. *Behavior Therapy*, 1973b, *4*, 141–143.

Brewer, W. F. There is no convincing evidence for operant or classical conditioning in adult humans. In W. B. Weimer and D. S. Palermo (Eds.), *Cognition and the symbolic processes*. Hillsdale, N.J.: Lawrence Erlbaum Associates, 1974. Pp. 1–42.

Brigham, T. A., Hawkins, R., Scott, J. W., & McLaughlin, T. F. (Eds.) *Behavior analysis in education: Self-control and reading*. Dubuque, Ia.: Kendall/Hunt Publishing Co., 1976.

Bristol, M. M., & Sloane, H. N. Effects of contingency contracting on study rate and test performance. *Journal of Applied Behavior Analysis*, 1974, *7*, 271–285.

Bruch, M. A. Coping model treatments: Unresolved issues and needed research. *Behavior Therapy*, 1976, *7*, 711–713.

Burns, D. J., & Powers, R. B. Choice and self-control in children: A test of Rachlin's model. *Bulletin of the Psychonomic Society*, 1975, *5*, 156–158.

Cabush, D., & Edwards, K. Training clients to help themselves: Outcome effects of training college student clients in faciliatative self-responding. *Journal of Counseling Psychology*, 1976, *23*, 34–39.

Carnegie, D. *How to stop worrying and start living*. New York: Simon & Schuster, 1948.

Catania, A. C. The myth of self-reinforcement. *Behaviorism*, 1975, *3*, 192–199.

Cautela, J. R. Treatment of compulsive behavior by covert sensitization. *Psychological Record*, 1966, *16*, 33–41.

Cautela, J. R. Covert sensitization. *Psychological Reports*, 1967, *20*, 459–468.

Cautela, J. R. Covert negative reinforcement. *Journal of Behavior Therapy and Experimental Psychiatry*, 1970a, *1*, 273–278.

Cautela, J. R. Covert reinforcement. *Behavior Therapy*, 1970b, *1*, 33–50.

Cautela, J. R. Covert conditioning. In A. Jacobs and L. B. Sachs (Eds.), *The psychology of private events: Perspectives on covert response systems*. New York: Academic Press, 1971a.

Cautela, J. R. Covert extinction. *Behavior Therapy*, 1971b, *2*, 192–200.

Cautela, J. R. Covert processes and behavior modification. *Journal of Nervous and Mental Disease*, 1973, *157*, 27–36.

Cautela, J. R., Flannery, R. B., & Hanley, E. Covert modeling: An experimental test. *Behavior Therapy*, 1974, *5*, 494–502.

Cavior, N., & Marabotto, C. M. Monitoring verbal behaviors in a dyadic interaction. *Journal of Consulting and Clinical Psychology*, 1976, *44*, 68–76.

Chang-Liang, R., & Denney, D. R. Applied relaxation as training in self-control. *Journal of Counseling Psychology*, 1976, *23*, 183–189.

Coche, E., & Douglas, A. A. Therapeutic effects of problem-solving training and play-reading groups. *Journal of Clinical Psychology*, in press.

Coche, E., & Flick, A. Problem-solving training groups for hospitalized psychiatric patients. *Journal of Psychology*, 1975, *91*, 19–29.

Colotla, V. A., McArthur, D., & Casanueva, H. Autoshaping and "self-control" in the dove and the pigeon. *Revista Latinoamericana de Psicologia*, in press.

Corbin, C. B. Mental practice. In W. P. Morgan (Ed.), *Ergogenic aids and muscular performance*. New York: Academic Press, 1972. Pp. 93–118.

Coué, E. *The practice of autosuggestion*. New York: Doubleday, 1922.

Cross, D. E., & Cooper, E. B. Self- versus investigator-administered presumed fluency reinforcing stimuli. *Journal of Speech and Hearing Research*, 1976, *19*, 241–246.

Daniels, L. K. Effects of covert reinforcement on reading attitude with reinforcing scenes of varying intensity. *Perceptual and Motor Skills*, 1976, *42*, 810.

Davidson, A., & Denney, D. R. Covert sensitization and information in the reduction of nailbiting. *Behavior Therapy*, 1976, *7*, 512–518.

Davison, G. C. Counter-control in behavior modification. In L. A. Hamerlynck, L. C. Handy, and E. J. Mash (Eds.), *Behavior change: Methodology, concepts and practice*. Champaign, Ill.: Research Press, 1973.

Davison, G. C., & Wilson, G. T. Processes of fear-reduction in systematic desensitization: Cognitive and social reinforcement factors in humans. *Behavior Therapy*, 1973, *4*, 1–21.

Deffenbacker, J. L., & Snyder, A. L. Relaxation as self-control in the treatment of test and other anxieties. *Psychological Reports*, 1976, *39*, 379–385.

Dember, W. N. Motivation and the cognitive revolution. *American Psychologist*, 1974, *29*, 161–168.

Denney, D. The effects of exemplary and cognitive models and self-rehearsal on children's interrogative strategies. *Journal of Experimental Child Psychology*, 1975, *19*, 476–488.

Diament, C., & Wilson, G. T. An experimental investigation of the effects of covert sensitization in an analogue eating situation. *Behavior Therapy*, 1975, *6*, 499–509.

Drabman, R. S., Spitalnik, R., & O'Leary, K. D. Teaching self-control to disruptive children. *Journal of Abnormal Psychology*, 1973, *82*, 10–16.

Dubois, P. C. *The psychic treatment of nervous disorders.* 1904. New York: Funk & Wagnalls, 1909.

D'Zurilla, T. J., & Goldfried, M. R. Problem solving and behavior modification. *Journal of Abnormal Psychology*, 1971, *78*, 107–126.

Elliott, C. H., & Denney, D. R. Weight control through covert sensitization and false feedback. *Journal of Consulting and Clinical Psychology*, 1975, *43*, 842–850.

Ellis, A. *Reason and emotion in psychotherapy.* New York: Stuart, 1962.

Ellis, A. A cognitive approach to behavior therapy. *International Journal of Psychotherapy*, 1969, *8*, 896–900.

Ellis, A. *The essence of rational psychotherapy: A comprehensive approach to treatment.* New York: Institute for Rational Living, 1970.

Ellis, A. Are cognitive behavior therapy and rational therapy synonymous? *Rational Living*, 1973, *8*, 8–11.

Ellis, A. Rational-emotive therapy: Research data that supports the clinical and personality hypotheses of RET and other modes of cognitive-behavior therapy. *Counseling Psychologist*, in press.

Emmelkamp, P. M. G. Self-observation versus flooding in the treatment of agoraphobia. *Behavior Research and Therapy*, 1974, *12*, 229–237.

Emmelkamp, P. M. G., & Ultee, K. A. A comparison of "successive approximation" and "self-observation" in the treatment of agoraphobia. *Behavior Therapy*, 1974, *5*, 606–613.

Epstein, L. H., & Hersen, M. A. A multiple baseline analysis of coverant control. *Journal of Behavior Therapy and Experimental Psychiatry*, 1974, *5*, 7–12.

Epstein, L. H., & Peterson, G. L. Differential conditioning using covert stimuli. *Behavior Therapy*, 1973, *4*, 96–99.

Epstein, L. H., Webster, J. S., & Miller, P. M. Accuracy and controlling effects of self-monitoring as a function of concurrent responding and reinforcement. *Behavior Therapy*, 1975, *6*, 654–666.

Estes, W. K. Reward in human learning: Theoretical issues and strategic choice points. In R. Glaser (Ed.), *The nature of reinforcement.* New York: Academic Press, 1971. Pp. 16–36.

Evans, J. R., & Cody, J. J. Transfer of decision-making skills learned in a counseling-like setting to similar and dissimilar situations. *Journal of Counseling Psychology*, 1969, *16*, 427–432.

Felixbrod, J. J., & O'Leary, K. D. Effects of reinforcement on children's academic behavior as a function of self-determined and externally imposed contingencies. *Journal of Applied Behavior Analysis*, 1973, *6*, 241–250.

Ferster, C. B., Nurnberger, J. I., & Levitt, E. B. The control of eating. *Journal of Mathetics*, 1962, *1*, 87–109.

Foreyt, J. P., & Hagen, R. L. Covert sensitization: Conditioning or suggestion? *Journal of Abnormal Psychology*, 1973, *82*, 17–23.

Frank, J. D. *Persuasion and healing* Baltimore: Johns Hopkins Press, 1961.

Frederiksen, L. W., Epstein, L. H., & Kosevsky, B. P. Reliability and controlling effects of three procedures for self-monitoring smoking. *Psychological Record*, 1975, *25*, 255–264.

Frederiksen, L. W., & Frederiksen, C. B. Teacher-determined and self-determined token reinforcement in a special education classroom. *Behavior Therapy*, 1975, *6*, 310–314.

Frederiksen, L. W., & Miller, P. M. Peer-determined and self-determined reinforcement in group therapy with alcoholics. *Behaviour Research and Therapy*, 1976, *14*, 385–388.

Gagnon, J. H., & Davison, G. C. Asylums, the token economy, and the metrics of mental life. *Behavior Therapy*, 1976, *7*, 528–534.

Garfield, S. L., & Kurtz, R. Clinical psychologists in the 1970's. *American Psychologist*, 1976, *31*, 1–9.

Glass, C. R., Gottman, J. M., & Shmurak, S. H. Response-acquisition and cognitive self-statement modification approaches to dating-skills training. *Journal of Counseling Psychology*, 1976, *23*, 520–526.

Glynn, E. L., & Thomas, J. D. Effect of cueing on self-control of classroom behavior. *Journal of Applied Behavior Analysis*, 1974, *7*, 299–306.

Glynn, E. L., Thomas, J. D., & Shee, S. M. Behavioral self-control of on-task behavior in an elementary classroom. *Journal of Applied Behavior Analysis*, 1973, *6*, 105–113.

Goldfried, M. R. Systematic desensitization as training in self-control. *Journal of Consulting and Clinical Psychology*, 1971, *37*, 228–234.

Goldfried, M. R., & Merbaum, M. (Eds.) *Behavior change through self-control.* New York: Holt, Rinehart and Winston, 1973.

Goldfried, M. R., & Sobocinski, D. Effect of irrational beliefs on emotional arousal. *Journal of Consulting and Clinical Psychology*, 1975, *43*, 504–510.

Goldfried, M. R., & Trier, C. S. Effectiveness of relaxation as an active coping skill. *Journal of Abnormal Psychology*, 1974, *83*, 348–355.

Goldiamond, I. Self-control procedures in personal behavior problems. *Psychological Reports*, 1965, *17*, 851–868.

Goldiamond, I. Self-reinforcement. *Journal of Applied Behavior Analysis*, 1976, *9*, 509–514.

Goodwin, S., & Mahoney, M. J. Modification of aggression via modeling: An experimental probe. *Journal of Behavior Therapy and Experimental Psychiatry,* 1975, *6,* 200–202.

Greiner, J. M., & Karoly, P. Effects of self-control training on study activity and academic performance: An analysis of self-monitoring, self-reward, and systematic planning components. *Journal of Counseling Psychology,* 1976, *23,* 495–502.

Grimm, L., & Kanfer, F. H. Tolerance of aversive stimulation. *Behavior Therapy,* 1976, *7,* 593–601.

Gulanick, N., Woodburn, L. T., & Rimm, D. C. Weight gain through self-control procedures. *Journal of Consulting and Clinical Psychology,* 1975, *43,* 536–539.

Hackmann, A., & McLean, C. A comparison of flooding and thought stopping in the treatment of obsessional neurosis. *Behaviour Research and Therapy,* 1975, *13,* 263–269.

Haley, J. *Strategies of psychotherapy.* New York: Grune & Stratton, 1963.

Haley, J. *Uncommon therapy.* New York: Grune & Stratton, 1968.

Haley, J. *Problem solving therapy.* San Francisco: Jossey-Bass, 1976.

Haney, J. N., & Euse, F. J. Skin conductance and heart rate responses to neutral, positive and negative imagery: Implications for covert behavior therapy procedures. *Behavior Therapy,* 1976, *7,* 494–503.

Hedberg, A. G., & Campbell, L. A comparison of four behavioral treatments of alcoholism. *Journal of Behavior Therapy and Experimental Psychiatry,* 1974, *5,* 251–256.

Helland, C. D., Paluck, R. J., & Klein, M. A comparison of self- and external reinforcement with the trainable mentally retarded. *Mental Retardation,* 1976, *14,* 22–23.

Holroyd, K. A. Cognition and desensitization in the group treatment of test anxiety. *Journal of Consulting and Clinical Psychology,* 1976, *44,* 991–1001.

Homme, L. E. Perspectives in psychology: XXIV. Control of coverants, the operants of the mind. *Psychological Record,* 1965, *15,* 501–511.

Hoon, P. W. Effects of self-monitoring and self-recording on ecological acts. *Psychological Reports,* 1976, *38,* 1285–1286.

Horan, J. J. "In vivo" emotive imagery: A technique for reducing childbirth anxiety and discomfort. *Psychological Reports,* 1973, *32,* 1328.

Horan, J. J. Negative coverant probability: An analogue study. *Behaviour Research and Therapy,* 1974, *12,* 265–266.

Horan, J. J., Baker, S. B., Hoffman, A. M., & Shute, R. E. Weight loss through variations in the coverant control paradigm. *Journal of Consulting and Clinical Psychology,* 1975, *43,* 68–72.

Horan, J. J., Hoffman, A. M., & Macri, M. Self-control of chronic nailbiting. *Journal of Behavior Therapy and Experimental Psychiatry,* 1974, *5,* 307–309.

Horan, J. J., Smyers, R. E., Dorfman, D. L., & Jenkins, W. W. Two analogue attempts to harness the negative coverant effect. *Behaviour Research and Therapy,* 1975, *13,* 183–184.

Hurley, A. D. Covert reinforcement: The contribution of the reinforcing stimulus to treatment outcome. *Behavior Therapy,* 1976, *7,* 374–378.

Jacobson, N. S. Problem solving and contingency contracting in the treatment of marital discord. *Journal of Consulting and Clinical Psychology,* 1977, *45,* 92–100.

Kanfer, F. H. Self-monitoring: Methodological limitations and clinical applications. *Journal of Consulting and Clinical Psychology,* 1970a, *35,* 148–152.

Kanfer, F. H. Self-regulation: Research, issues and speculations. In C. Neuringer and J. L. Michael (Eds.), *Behavior modification in clinical psychology.* New York: Appleton-Century-Crofts, 1970b. Pp. 178–220.

Kanfer, F. H. The maintenance of behavior by self-generated stimuli and reinforcement. In A. Jacobs and L. B. Sachs (Eds.), *The psychology of private events: Perspectives on covert response systems.* New York: Academic Press, 1971. Pp. 39–59.

Kanfer F. H. The many faces of self-control, or behavior modification changes its focus. Paper presented at the Eighth International Banff Conference, March 1976.

Kanfer, F. H., & Seidner, M. L. Self-control: Factors enhancing tolerance of noxious stimulation. *Journal of Personality and Social Psychology,* 1973, *25,* 381–389.

Karoly, P., & Kanfer, F. H. Situational and historical determinants of self-reinforcement. *Behavior Therapy,* 1974, *5,* 381–390.

Katz, R. C., Thomas, S. L., & Williamson, P. Effects of self-monitoring as a function of its expected benefits and incompatible response training. *Psychological Record,* 1976, *26,* 533–540.

Kazdin, A. E. Covert modeling and the reduction of avoidance behavior. *Journal of Abnormal Psychology,* 1973, *81,* 87–95.

Kazdin, A. E. Comparative effects of some variations of covert modeling. *Journal of Behavior Therapy and Experimental Psychiatry,* 1974a, *5,* 225–231.

Kazdin, A. E. Covert modeling, model similarity, and reduction of avoidance behavior. *Behavior Therapy,* 1974b, *5,* 325–340.

Kazdin, A. E. The effect of model identity and fear-relevant similarity on covert modeling. *Behavior Therapy,* 1974c, *5,* 624–635.

Kazdin, A. E. Effects of covert modeling and modeling reinforcement on assertive behavior. *Journal of Abnormal Psychology,* 1974d, *83,* 240–252.

Kazdin, A. E. Reactive self-monitoring: The effects of response desirability, goal setting, and feedback. *Journal of Consulting and Clinical Psychology,* 1974e. *42,* 704–716.

Kazdin, A. E. Self-monitoring and behavior change. In M. J. Mahoney and C. E. Thoresen (Eds.), *Self-control: Power to the person.* Monterey, Calif.: BrookssCole, 1974f. Pp. 218–246.

Kazdin, A. E. Effects of covert modeling, multiple models, and model reinforcement on assertive behavior. *Behavior Therapy,* 1976, *7,* 211–222.

Kazdin, A. E. Research issues in covert conditioning. *Cognitive Therapy and Research,* 1977, *1,* 45–58.

Kazdin, A. E., & Wilcoxon, L. Systematic desensitization and nonspecific treatment effects: A methodological evaluation. *Psychological Bulletin,* 1976, *83,* 729–758.

Keller, J., Croake, J., & Brooking, J. Effects of a program in rational thinking on anxieties in older persons.

Journal of Counseling Psychology, 1975, *22,* 54–57.

Kelly, A. H., & Curran, J. P. Comparison of a self-control approach and an emotional coping approach to the treatment of obesity. *Journal of Consulting and Clinical Psychology,* 1976, *44,* 683.

Kelly, G. A. *The psychology of personal constructs.* New York: Norton, 1955.

Keutzer, C. S. Behavior modification of smoking: The experimental investigation of diverse techniques. *Behaviour Research and Therapy,* 1968, *6,* 137–157.

Kifer, R. E., Lewis, M. A., Green, D. R., & Phillips, E. L. Training predelinquent youths and their parents to negotiate conflict situations. *Journal of Applied Behavior Analysis,* 1974, *7,* 357–364.

Knapczyk, D. R., & Livingston, G. Self-recording and student teaching supervision: Variables within a token economy structure. *Journal of Applied Behavioral Analysis,* 1973, *6,* 481–486.

Koch, S. Psychology and emerging conceptions of knowledge as unitary. In T. W. Wann (Ed.), *Behaviorism and phenomenology.* Chicago: University of Chicago Press, 1964. Pp. 1–41.

Kopel, S., & Arkowitz, H. The role of attribution and self-perception in behavior change: Implications for behavior therapy. *Genetic Psychology Monographs,* 1975, *92,* 175–212.

Kuhn, T. S. *The structure of scientific revolutions.* Chicago: University of Chicago Press, 1962.

Ladouceur, R. An experimental test of the learning paradigm of covert positive reinforcement in deconditioning anxiety. *Journal of Behavior Therapy and Experimental Psychiatry,* 1974, *5,* 3–6.

Layne, C. C., Rickard, H. C., Jones, M. T., & Lyman, R. D. Accuracy of self-monitoring on a variable ratio schedule of observer verification. *Behavior Therapy,* 1976, *7,* 481–488.

Lazarus, A. A. *Behavior therapy and beyond.* New York: McGraw-Hill, 1971.

Lazarus, A. A. Multimodal behavior therapy: Treating the basic id. *Journal of Nervous and Mental Disease,* 1973, *156,* 404–411.

Lefcourt, H. M. *Locus of control.* Hillsdale, N.J.: Lawrence Erlbaum Associates, 1976.

Levendusky, P., & Pankrantz, L. Self-control techniques as an alternative to pain medication. *Journal of Abnormal Psychology,* 1975, *84,* 165–168.

Lichtenstein, E., & Keutzer, C. S. Experimental investigation of diverse techniques to modify smoking: A follow-up report. *Behaviour Research and Therapy,* 1969, *7,* 139–140.

Lipinski, D. P., Black, J. L., Nelson, R. O., & Ciminero, A. R. Influence of motivational variables on the reactivity and reliability of self-recording. *Journal of Consulting and Clinical Psychology,* 1975, *43,* 637–646.

Lipinski, D., & Nelson, R. The reactivity and unreliability of self-recording. *Journal of Consulting and Clinical Psychology,* 1974, *42,* 118–123.

Luborsky, L., Singer, B., & Luborsky, L. Comparative studies of psychotherapies: Is it true that "Everyone has won and all must have prizes"? *Archives of General Psychiatry,* 1975, *32,* 995–1008.

Luria, A. *The role of speech in the regulation of normal and abnormal behavior.* New York: Liveright, 1961.

MacPherson, E. M., Candee, B. L., & Hohman, R. J. A comparison of three methods for eliminating disruptive lunchroom behavior. *Journal of Applied Behavior Analysis,* 1974, *7,* 287–297.

Mahoney, K., Rogers, T., Straw, M., & Mahoney, M. J. Human obesity: Assessment and treatment. Unpublished manuscript, Pennsylvania State University, 1977.

Mahoney, M. J. Research issues in self-management. *Behavior Therapy,* 1972, *3,* 45–63.

Mahoney, M. J. *Cognition and behavior modification.* Cambridge, Mass.: Ballinger, 1974a.

Mahoney, M. J. Self-reward and self-monitoring techniques for weight control. *Behavior Therapy,* 1974b, *5,* 48–57.

Mahoney, M. J. The obese eating style: Bites, beliefs, and behavior modification. *Addictive Behaviors,* 1975, *1,* 47–53.

Mahoney, M. J. The behavioral treatment of obesity: A reconnaissance. *Biofeedback and Self-Regulation,* 1976a, *1,* 127–133.

Mahoney, M. J. *Scientist as subject: The psychological imperative.* Cambridge, Mass.: Ballinger, 1976b.

Mahoney, M. J. Terminal terminology: A self-regulated response to Goldiamond. *Journal of Applied Behavior Analysis,* 1976c, *9,* 515–517

Mahoney, M. J. Cognitive therapy and research: A question of questions. *Cognitive Therapy and Research,* 1977a, *1,* 5–16.

Mahoney, M. J. Personal science: A cognitive learning therapy. In A. Ellis and R. Grieger (Eds.), *Handbook of rational psychotherapy.* New York: Springer, 1977b.

Mahoney, M. J. Reflections on the cognitive learning trend in psychotherapy. *American Psychologist,* 1977c, *32,* 5–13.

Mahoney, M. J., & Bandura, A. Self-reinforcement in pigeons. *Learning and Motivation,* 1972, *3,* 293–303.

Mahoney, M. J., Bandura, A., Dirks, S. J., & Wright, C. L. Relative preference for external and self-controlled reinforcement in monkeys. *Behaviour Research and Therapy,* 1974, *12,* 157–164.

Mahoney, M. J., Kazdin, A. E., & Lesswing, N. J. Behavior modification: Delusion or deliverance? In C. M. Franks and G. T. Wilson (Eds.), *Annual review of behavior therapy theory and practice.* Vol. 2. New York: Brunner/Mazel, 1974. Pp. 11–40.

Mahoney, M. J., & Mahoney, K. *Permanent weight control.* New York: W. W. Norton, 1976a.

Mahoney, M. J., & Mahoney, K. Treatment of obesity: A clinical exploration. In B. J. Williams, S. Martin, and J. P. Foreyt (Eds.), *Obesity: Behavioral approaches to dietary management.* New York: Brunner/Mazel, 1976b. Pp. 30–39.

Mahoney, M. J., & Thoresen, C. E. (Eds.), *Self-control: Power to the person.* Monterey, Calif.: Brooks/Cole, 1974.

Maltz, M. *Psycho-cybernetics.* Englewood Cliffs, N.J.: Prentice-Hall, 1960.

Margolis, R. B., & Shemberg, K. M. Cognitive self-instruction in process and reactive schizophrenics: A failure to replicate. *Behavior Therapy,* 1976, *7,* 668–671.

Marshall, W. L., Boutilier, J., & Minnes, P. The modification of phobic behavior by covert reinforcement. *Behavior Therapy,* 1974, *5,* 469–480.

Masters, J. C., & Mokros, J. R. Self-reinforcement processes in children. In H. Reese (Ed.), *Advances in child development and behavior.* Vol. 9. New York: Academic Press, 1974.

Masters, J. C., & Santrock, J. W. Studies in the self-regulation of behavior: Effects of contingent cognitive and affective events. *Developmental Psychology,* 1976, *12,* 334–348.

Matson, F. W. (Ed.), *Without/within: Behaviorism and humanism.* Monterey, Calif.: Brooks/Cole, 1973.

McKeachie, W. J. The decline and fall of the laws of learning. *Educational Researcher,* 1974, *3,* 7–11.

McKenzie, T. L., & Rushall, B. S. Effects of self-recording on attendance and performance in a competitive swimming training environment. *Journal of Applied Behavior Analysis,* 1974, *7,* 199–206.

McLaughlin, T. F., & Malaby, J. E. Increasing and maintaining assignment completion with teacher and pupil controlled individual contingency programs: Three case studies. *Psychology,* 1974, *11,* 1–7.

McReynolds, W. T., & Church, A. Self-control, study skills development, and counseling approaches to the improvement of study behavior. *Behaviour Research and Therapy,* 1973, *11,* 233–235.

Meehl, P. E. The cognitive activity of the clinician. *American Psychologist,* 1960, *15,* 19–27.

Meichenbaum, D. Examination of model characteristics in reducing avoidance behavior. *Journal of Personality and Social Psychology,* 1971, *17,* 298–307.

Meichenbaum, D. Cognitive modification of test anxious college students. *Journal of Consulting and Clinical Psychology,* 1972a, *39,* 370–380.

Meichenbaum, D. Ways of modifying what clients say to themselves: A marriage of behavior therapies and rational-emotive therapy. *Rational Living,* 1972b, *7,* 23–27.

Meichenbaum, D. *Cognitive behavior modification.* Morristown, N.J.: General Learning Press, 1974.

Meichenbaum, D. A self-instructional approach to stress management: A proposal for stress inoculation training. In I. Sarason and C. D. Spielberger (Eds.), *Stress and anxiety.* Vol. 2. New York: Wiley, 1975. Pp. 227–263.

Meichenbaum, D. *Cognitive behavior modification.* New York: Plenum, 1977.

Meichenbaum, D., & Cameron, R. Training schizophrenics to talk to themselves: A means of developing attentional controls. *Behavior Therapy,* 1973, *4,* 515–534.

Meichenbaum, D., Gilmore, J., & Fedoravicius, A. Group insight vs. group desensitization in treating speech anxiety. *Journal of Consulting and Clinical Psychology,* 1971, *36,* 410–421.

Mendonca, J. D., & Siess, T. F. Counseling for indecisiveness: Problem-solving and anxiety-management training. *Journal of Counseling Psychology,* 1976, *23,* 339–347.

Mischel, W. Toward a cognitive social learning reconceptualization of personality. *Psychological Review,* 1973, *80,* 252–283.

Moleski, R., & Tosi, D. J. Comparative psychotherapy: Rational-emotive therapy versus systematic desensitization in the treatment of stuttering. *Journal of Consulting and Clinical Psychology,* 1976, *44,* 309–311.

Nelson, R. O. Self-monitoring: Procedures and methodological issues. In J. D. Cone and R. P. Hawkins (Eds.), *Behavioral assessment: New directions in clinical psychology.* New York: Brunner/Mazel, 1976.

Nelson, R. O., Lipinski, D. P., & Black, J. L. The relative reactivity of external observations and self-monitoring. *Behavior Therapy,* 1976, *7,* 314–321.

Novaco, R. W. *Anger control: The development and evaluation of an experimental treatment.* Lexington, Mass.: D. C. Heath, 1975.

Novaco, R. W. Treatment of chronic anger through cognitive and relaxation controls. *Journal of Consulting and Clinical Psychology,* 1976, *44,* 681.

Ober, D. C. Modification of smoking behavior. *Journal of Consulting and Clinical Psychology,* 1968, *32,* 543–549.

Paivio, A. Neomentalism. *Canadian Journal of Psychology,* 1975, *29,* 263–291.

Peale, N. V. *The power of positive thinking.* Englewood Cliffs, N.J.: Prentice-Hall, 1960.

Platt, J., Scura, W. C., & Hannon, J. R. Problem-solving thinking of youthful incarcerated heroin addicts. *Journal of Community Psychology,* 1973, *1,* 278–281.

Platt, J., & Spivack, G. Problem-solving thinking of psychiatric patients. *Journal of Consulting and Clinical Psychology,* 1972a, *39,* 148–151.

Platt, J., & Spivack, G. Social competence and effective problem-solving thinking in psychiatric patients. *Journal of Clinical Psychology,* 1972b, *28,* 3–5.

Platt, J., & Spivack, G. Studies in problem-solving thinking of psychiatric patients: I. Patient-control differences; II. Factorial structure of problem-solving thinking. *Proceedings of the 81st Annual Convention of the American Psychological Association,* 1973, *8,* 463–464.

Platt, J., & Spivack, G. Means of solving real-life problems: I. Psychiatric patients versus controls, and cross-cultural comparisons of normal females. *Journal of Community Psychology,* 1974, *2,* 45–48.

Polivy, J., & Herman, C. P. Effects of alcohol on eating behavior: Influence of mood and perceived intoxication. *Journal of Abnormal Psychology,* 1976, *85,* 601–606.

Rachlin, H. Self control. *Behaviorism,* 1974, *2,* 94–107.

Rachlin, H. Reinforcing and punishing thoughts. *Behavior Therapy,* in press.

Raimy, V. *Misunderstandings of the self.* San Francisco: Jossey-Bass, 1975.

Reese, H. W. The study of covert verbal and nonverbal mediation. In A. Jacobs & L. B. Sachs (Eds.), *The psychology of private events: Perspectives on covert response systems.* New York: Academic Press, 1971. Pp. 17–38.

Reeves, J. L. EMG-biofeedback reduction of tension headache: A cognitive skills-training approach. *Biofeedback and Self-Regulation,* 1976, *1,* 217–225.

Rehm, L. P. A self-control model of depression. *Behavior Therapy,* in press.

Rehm, L. P., & Marston, A. R. Reduction of social anxiety

through modification of self-reinforcement: An instigation therapy technique. *Journal of Consulting and Clinical Psychology,* 1968, *32,* 565–574.

Reschly, D. J. Consistency of self-reinforcement rates over different tasks, and sex, task success, and ability as determinants of rates of self-reinforcement. *Psychological Record,* 1973, *23,* 237–242.

Richards, C. S. Behavior modification of studying through study skills advice and self-control procedures. *Journal of Counseling Psychology,* 1975, *22,* 431–436.

Richards, C. S. Assessment and behavior modification via self-monitoring. An overview and a bibliography. *JSAS Journal of Selected Documents in Psychology,* in press.

Richards, C. S., McReynolds, W. T., Holt, S., & Sexton, T. The effects of information feedback and self-administered consequences on self-monitoring study behavior. *Journal of Counseling Psychology,* 1976, *23,* 316–321.

Rimm, D. C., Saunders, W. D., & Westel, W. Thought stopping and covert assertion in the treatment of snake phobics. *Journal of Consulting and Clinical Psychology,* 1975, *43,* 92–93.

Rogers, T., & Craighead, W. E. Physiological responses to self-statements: The effects of statement valence and discrepancy. *Cognitive Therapy and Research,* in press.

Romanczyk, R. G. Self-monitoring in the treatment of obesity: Parameters of reactivity. *Behavior Therapy,* 1974, *5,* 531–540.

Rosenthal, T. L., & Reese, S. L. The effects of covert and overt modeling on assertive behavior. *Behaviour Research and Therapy,* 1976, *14,* 463–470.

Rotter, J. B. *Social learning and clinical psychology.* Englewood Cliffs, N.J.: Prentice-Hall, 1954.

Rotter, J. B., Chance, J. E., & Phares, E. J. (Eds.) *Applications of a social learning theory of personality.* New York: Holt, Rinehart and Winston, 1972.

Rozensky, R. H. The effect of timing of self-monitoring behavior on reducing cigarette consumption. *Journal of Behavior Therapy and Experimental Psychiatry,* 1974, *5,* 301–303.

Rozensky, R. H., & Bellack, A. S. Behavior change and individual differences in self-control. *Behaviour Research and Therapy,* 1974, *12,* 267–268.

Rozensky, R. H., & Bellack, A. S. Individual differences in self-reinforcement style and performance in self- and therapist-controlled weight reduction programs. *Behaviour Research and Therapy,* 1976, *14,* 357–365.

Ruesch, J. *Therapeutic communication.* New York: W. W. Norton, 1961.

Rush, A. J., Beck, A. T., Kovacs, M., & Hollon, S. Comparative efficacy of cognitive therapy and pharmacotherapy in the treatment of depressed outpatients. *Cognitive Therapy and Research,* 1977, *1,* 17–37.

Rush, A. J., Khatami, M., & Beck, A. T. Cognitive and behavior therapy in chronic depression. *Behavior Therapy,* 1975, *6,* 398–404.

Sachs, L. B., & Ingram, G. L. Covert sensitization as a treatment for weight control. *Psychological Reports,* 1972, *30,* 971–974.

Sanchez-Craig, M. Cognitive and behavioral coping strategies in the reappraisal of stressful social situations. *Journal of Counseling Psychology,* 1976, *23,* 7–12.

Santogrossi, D. A., O'Leary, K. D., Romanczyk, R. G., & Kaufman, K. F. Self-evaluation by adolescents in a psychiatric school token program. *Journal of Applied Behavior Analysis,* 1973, *6,* 277–287.

Sarason, I. G. Verbal learning, modeling, and juvenile delinquency. *American Psychologist,* 1968, *23,* 254–266.

Sarason, I. Test anxiety and the self-disclosing coping model. *Journal of Consulting and Clinical Psychology,* 1975, *43,* 148–153.

Sarason, I. G., & Ganzer, V. J. Developing appropriate social behaviors of juvenile delinquents. In J. D. Krumboltz and C. E. Thoresen (Eds.), *Behavioral counseling.* New York: Holt, Rinehart and Winston, 1969a.

Sarason, I. G., & Ganzer, V. J. Social influence techniques in clinical and community psychology. In C. D. Spielberger (Ed.), *Current topics in clinical and community psychology.* New York: Academic Press, 1969b.

Sarason, I. G., & Ganzer, V. J. Modeling and group discussion in the rehabilitation of juvenile delinquents. *Journal of Counseling Psychology,* 1973, *20,* 442–449.

Scott, D. S., & Rosenstiel, A. K. Covert positive reinforcement studies: Review, critique, and guidelines. *Psychotherapy: Theory, Research and Practice,* 1975, *12,* 374–384.

Seligman, M. E. P. *Helplessness.* San Francisco: W. H. Freeman, 1975.

Seymour, F. W., & Stokes, T. F. Self-recording in training girls to increase work and evoke staff praise in an institution for offenders. *Journal of Applied Behavior Analysis,* 1976, *9,* 41–54.

Shapiro, A. K. Placebo effects in medicine, psychotherapy, and psychoanalysis. In A. E. Bergin and S. L. Garfield (Eds.), *Handbook of psychotherapy and behavior change.* New York: Wiley, 1971. Pp. 439–473.

Shelton, J. L., & Ackerman, J. M. *Homework in counseling and psychotherapy.* Springfield, Ill.: Charles C. Thomas, 1974.

Shure, M., & Spivack, G. Means-ends thinking, adjustment and social class among elementary school-aged children. *Journal of Consulting and Clinical Psychology,* 1972, *38,* 348–353.

Shure, M., Spivack, G., & Jaeger, M. Problem-solving thinking and adjustment among disadvantaged pre-school chidren. *Child Development,* 1971, *42,* 1791–1803.

Siegel, J. M., & Spivack, G. A new therapy program for chronic patients. *Behavior Therapy,* 1976, *7,* 129–130.

Sieck, W. A., & McFall, R. M. Some determinants of self-monitoring effects. *Journal of Consulting and Clinical Psychology,* 1976, *44,* 958–965.

Singer, J. L. *Imagery and daydream methods in psychotherapy and behavior modification.* New York: Academic Press, 1974.

Sipich, J. F., Russell, R. K., & Tobias, L. L. A comparison

of covert sensitization and "nonspecific" treatment in the modification of smoking behavior. *Journal of Behavior Therapy and Experimental Psychiatry,* 1974, *5,* 201–203.

Sipprelle, C. N. Induced anxiety. *Psychotherapy: Theory, Research and Practice,* 1967, *4,* 36–40.

Skinner, B. F. *Science and human behavior.* New York: Macmillan, 1953.

Skinner, B. F. *Beyond freedom and dignity.* New York: Alfred A. Knopf, 1971.

Skinner, B. F. *About behaviorism.* New York: Alfred A. Knopf, 1974.

Sobell, L. C., & Sobell, M. B. A self-feedback technique to monitor drinking behavior in alcoholics. *Behaviour Research and Therapy,* 1973, *11,* 237–238.

Spanos, N., Horton, C., & Chaves, J. The effect of two cognitive strategies on pain threshold. *Journal of Abnormal Psychology,* 1975, *84,* 677–682.

Spates, C. R., & Kanfer, F. H. Self-monitoring, self-evaluation, and self-reinforcement in children's learning: A test of a multistage self-regulation model. *Behavior Therapy,* 1977, *8,* 1–8.

Speidel, G. E. Motivating effect of contingent self-reward. *Journal of Experimental Psychology,* 1974, *102,* 528–530.

Spiegler, M. D., Cooley, E. J., Marshall, G. J., Prince, H. T., & Puckett, S. P. A self-control versus a counterconditioning paradigm for systematic desensitization: An experimental comparison. *Journal of Counseling Psychology,* 1976, *23,* 83–86.

Spiegler, M. D., Liebert, R. M., McMains, M. J., & Fernandez, L. E. Experimental development of a modeling treatment to extinguish persistent avoidance behavior. In R. D. Rubin and C. M. Franks (Eds.), *Advances in behavior therapy.* New York: Academic Press, 1969. Pp. 45–51.

Spivack, G., Platt, J. J., & Shure, M. D. *The problem-solving approach to adjustment.* San Francisco: Jossey-Bass, 1976.

Spivack, G., & Shure, M. B. *Social adjustment of young children: A cognitive approach to solving real-life problems.* San Francisco: Jossey-Bass, 1974.

Stone, G. L., Hinds, W. C., & Schmidt, G. Teaching mental health behaviors to elementary school children. *Professional Psychology,* 1975, *6,* 34–40.

Strupp, H. H. On the basic ingredients of psychotherapy. *Journal of Consulting and Clinical Psychology,* 1973, *41,* 1–8.

Stuart, R. B. Behavioral control of overeating. *Behaviour Research and Therapy,* 1967, *5,* 357–365.

Stuart, R. B. Situational versus self-control. In R. D. Rubin, H. Fensterheim, J. D. Henderson, and L. P. Ullmann (Eds.), *Advances in behavior therapy.* New York: Academic Press, 1972. Pp. 129–146.

Stunkard, A. J., & Mahoney, M. J. Behavioral treatment of the eating disorders. In H. Leitenberg (Ed.), *Handbook of behavior modification.* New York: Appleton-Century-Crofts, 1976.

Suinn, R. M., & Richardson, F. Anxiety management training: A nonspecific behavior therapy program for anxiety control. *Behavior Therapy,* 1971, *2,* 498–510.

Taylor, F. G., & Marshall, W. L. A cognitive-behavioral

therapy for depression. *Cognitive Therapy and Research,* in press.

Thase, M. E., & Moss, M. K. The relative efficacy of covert modeling procedures and guided participant modeling on the reduction of avoidance behavior. *Journal of Behavior Therapy and Experimental Psychiatry,* 1976, *7,* 7–12.

Thomas, J. D. Accuracy of self-assessment of on-task behavior by elementary school children. *Journal of Applied Behavior Analysis,* 1976, *9,* 209–210.

Thoresen, C. E., & Mahoney, M. J. *Behavioral self-control.* New York: Holt, Rinehart and Winston, 1974.

Thorpe, G. L. Desensitization, behavior rehearsal, self-instructional training and placebo effects on assertive-refusal behavior. *European Journal of Behavioural Analysis and Modification,* 1975, *1,* 30–44.

Thorpe, G. L., Amatu, H. I., Blakey, R. S., & Burns, L. E. Contributions of overt instructional rehearsal and "specific insight" to the effectiveness of self-instructional training: A preliminary study. *Behavior Therapy,* 1976, *7,* 504–511.

Vargas, J. M., & Adesso, V. J. A comparison of aversion therapies for nailbiting behavior. *Behavior Therapy,* 1976, *7,* 322–329.

Vincent, J. P., Weiss, R. L., & Birchler, G. R. A behavioral analysis of problem solving in distressed and nondistressed married and stranger dyads. *Behavior Therapy,* 1975, *6,* 475–487.

Vygotsky, L. S. *Thought and language.* Cambridge, Mass.: M.I.T. Press, 1962.

Wein, K. S., Nelson, R. O., & Odom, J. V. The relative contributions of reattribution and verbal extinction to the effectiveness of cognitive restructuring. *Behavior Therapy,* 1975, *6,* 459–474.

Weingartner, A. H. Self-administered aversive stimulation with hallucinating hospitalized schizophrenics. *Journal of Consulting and Clinical Psychology,* 1971, *36,* 422–429.

Weiss, R. L., Hops, H., & Patterson, G. R. A framework for conceptualizing marital conflict: A technology for altering it, some data for evaluating it. In L. A. Hamerlynck, L. C. Handy, and E. J. Mash (Eds.), *Behavior change: Methodology, concepts, and practice.* Champaign,, Ill.: Research Press, 1973. Pp. 309–342.

Wexler, M. The behavioral sciences in medical education. *American Psychologist,* 1976, *31,* 275–283.

Whalen, C. K., & Henker, B. Psychostimulants and children: A review and analysis. *Psychological Bulletin,* 1976, *83,* 1113–1130.

Wilson, G. T., & Lawson, D. M. Expectancies, alcohol, and sexual arousal in male social drinkers. *Journal of Abnormal Psychology,* 1976, *85,* 587–594.

Wilson, G. T., Leaf, R. C., & Nathan, P. E. The aversive control of excessive alcohol consumption by chronic alcoholics in the laboratory setting. *Journal of Applied Behavior Analysis,* 1975, *8,* 13–26.

Wilson, G. T., & Tracey, D. A. An experimental analysis of aversive imagery versus electrical aversive conditioning in the treatment of chronic alcoholics. *Behaviour Research and Therapy,* 1976, *14,* 41–52.

Wisocki, P. A., & Rooney, E. J. A comparison of thought

stopping and covert sensitization techniques in the treatment of smoking: A brief report. *Psychological Record,* 1974, *24,* 191–192.

Wolpe, J. *Psychotherapy by reciprocal inhibition.* Stanford, Calif.: Stanford University Press, 1958.

Wolpe, J. *The practice of behavior therapy.* New York: Pergamon, 1969.

Wolpe, J. Behavior therapy and its malcontents—II. Multimodal eclecticism, cognitive exclusivism and "exposure" empiricism. *Journal of Behavior Therapy and Experimental Psychiatry,* 1976, *7,* 109–116.

Wooley, S. C. Physiologic versus cognitive factors in short term food regulation in the obese and nonobese. *Psychosomatic Medicine,* 1972, *34,* 62–68.

Zimmerman, J. If it's what's inside that counts, why not count it? I: Self-recording of feelings and treatment by "self-implosion." *Psychological Record,* 1975, *25,* 3–16.

Zimmerman, J., & Levitt, E. E. Why not give your client a counter: A survey of what happened when we did. *Behaviour Research and Therapy,* 1975, *13,* 333–338.

PART V

APPRAISALS OF GROUP AND INNOVATIVE APPROACHES IN PSYCHOTHERAPY AND BEHAVIOR CHANGE

19

RESEARCH ON BRIEF AND CRISIS-ORIENTED THERAPIES[1]

JAMES N. BUTCHER

University of Minnesota

MARY P. KOSS

Kent State University

Many psychotherapeutic contacts, whether or not they initially were planned to be, turn out to be brief ones. A recent large-scale survey of 979,000 patients in some type of psychiatric treatment found an average of 4.7 contacts with therapist (National Center for Health Statistics reported in Lorion, 1974). These results coincide with the findings of earlier studies that high percentages of patients terminate in the first six to eight sessions. (Rogers, 1960: over 50 percent; Rubenstein & Lorr, 1956: 30 to 60 percent. Also see the discussion by Garfield in Chapter 6.)

The fact that the course of psychotherapy is often brief is no doubt partly due to premature termination of long-range therapeutic contacts (Rosenthal & Frank, 1958), but it is also true that

many individuals seek psychological help with the expectation that the treatment will be a brief experience (Garfield, 1971). This may particularly be the case with persons from lower socioeconomic or lower educational strata (Lorion, 1974). In recent years, the rapid growth of crisis clinics has been spurred by the desire of professionals to offer low-cost therapy for "disenfranchised" or underprivileged people. This has resulted in the greater utilization of brief treatment methods to reach more persons who need help. In more traditional mental health centers brief psychotherapeutic approaches have become more widely employed, since many practitioners have realized that numerous patients come to mental health resources seeking specific and focal problem resolution and not always for general personality "overhauls," as has been too often assumed.

This chapter will provide an overview of the con-

[1]We thank Drs. A. Jack Hafner, Gloria Leon, Zigfrids Stelmachers, and Stanley Strong for their comments on an earlier version of this chapter.

725

temporary practice of brief psychotherapy and will examine the existing research evidence on the effectiveness of brief psychotherapy. In the overview, we will look at historical developments that have influenced brief psychotherapy methods and delineate a variety of approaches to brief therapy. The characteristics common to brief psychotherapy will be described in order to give the reader a comparative picture of the issues relevant to brief psychotherapy. The process by which psychotherapeutic change is brought about in short-term treatment will be discussed. The research literature supporting the hypothetical change processes will be reviewed. Later in the chapter, we will examine the research literature on the relative effectiveness of brief treatment methods as compared to long-term psychotherapy. Evidence for the efficacy of brief psychotherapy to produce desired outcome will also be presented.

SOME HISTORICAL ANTECEDENTS

During the early days of psychoanalysis, the treatment period was often quite brief. However, as analytic treatment became more involved with transference interpretation and less involved with focal symptom relief, the course of treatment concomitantly became more prolonged (Malan, 1963). Some early efforts were made by a few psychoanalytic theorists to reverse the trend and shorten psychoanalysis. Ferenczi (1920) attempted to keep analysis short by assigning a more active, directive role to the analyst. Alexander and French (1946) conducted studies in an effort to abbreviate analytic treatment. They believed that neurotic adjustment had become a problem for a larger proportion of the population than could be treated by traditional psychoanalysis. Thus, they adapted techniques from psychoanalysis that would "give rational aid to all those who show early signs of maladjustment." They pointed out that psychodynamic principles could be used for therapeutic effect, regardless of the length of treatment.

Much of the impetus for short-term treatment came as a result of emergencies. In periods of great stress in which many individuals experience psychological "breakdowns," available treatment re-

sources and traditional therapeutic techniques have not been sufficient to handle the problems. During World War II, when a large number of soldiers developed stress-related neuroses, short-term treatment programs were designed to provide treatment as soon as possible after the initial breakdown had occurred. This early form of crisis intervention was aimed at stress reduction, symptom relief, and prevention of further breakdown by helping the individual to restore self-esteem and avoid further retreat into maladjustment (Grinker & Spiegel, 1944a and b, 1945; Kardiner, 1941).

Another important development in emergency brief psychotherapy was initiated by Lindemann. As a result of his work with families of victims of the Coconut Grove nightclub fire in 1943, Lindemann (1944) published his classic study on crisis intervention. He delineated phases of grief work through which people must go to free themselves from the deceased and readjust to the environment without the deceased person. Lindemann's contribution to understanding bereavement and the grieving process and his demonstration that people can be helped to work through grief established the efficacy of crisis intervention therapy. Lindemann also formulated one of the basic elements of crisis therapy—that behavior in crisis is unique, it is related to the crisis itself and not to premorbid personality. Lindemann and his associates (Caplan, 1961) have developed a theory of transitional pathology that is associated with crisis states; the theory underlies many modern crisis therapy approaches.

Another more recent development contributing to the thrust of briefer psychotherapies was the free clinic movement of the 1960s (Glasscote, Raybin, Reifler, & Kane, 1975). During this period, there was a great deal of social upheaval created by political countercultural activities, widely accessible drugs, and changing moral standards. These factors resulted in many individuals experiencing both situational and personal turmoil, which often resulted in their needing psychological help. At the same time, there was widespread mistrust of "traditional" institutions; thus, many people were without acceptable treatment resources. The feeling of being disenfranchised by society and thereby isolated from traditional mental health resources resulted in the development of counterculture "rap" centers, drop-in clinics, and other alternative agencies to meet the needs of people with problems. The antiestablishment reaction accompanying the counterculture movement produced a great diversity in free clinics.

The free clinics provided a nonestablishment staff who shared the values and spoke the language of the "disenfranchised." Many of these clinics provided limited services such as drug, draft, or abortion counseling by nonprofessional volunteers. There also were many clinics operated by volunteer professionals that provided more or less "traditional" counseling in a nontraditional setting (Butcher & Maudal, 1976).

Another important historical development in brief treatment has been the use of behavioral techniques in the modification of behavior. The brief treatment of behavioral problems using learning-based principles has a long, although somewhat sporadic, history. Early demonstration of "unlearning" by Watson and Rayner (1920) is a classic one. Even though the mainstream of psychological treatment mostly ignored the beneficial effects of behavioral therapy until more recently (Wolpe, 1952), there have been, for some time, working "behaviorists" in the treatment realm (Holmes, 1936; Jones, 1931; Terhune, 1949).

Considering behavioral therapy as a brief therapy may be questioned, since behavioral treatment, in fact, may be fairly long-term or may not fit well in the "psycho-" prefix often preceding the word therapy. However, we consider many behavioral techniques to be such integral parts of effective brief therapy as to require their presentation in the historical context. The directive nature of brief psychotherapy that will be discussed later makes behavioral procedures, language, and "habits" of checking the effectiveness of an intervention essential ingredients to a short-term treatment contract.

SYSTEMS OF BRIEF AND CRISIS-ORIENTED PSYCHOTHERAPY

Approaches to brief psychotherapy can be classified as psychodynamically oriented, crisis-oriented, behavioral, and other miscellaneous verbal psychotherapies. The following discussion includes therapeutic approaches designed for the one-to-one, individual outpatient psychotherapy of nonpsychotic adults with any type of behavioral problem. We have excluded from consideration group treatment, family therapy, marital counseling, and telephone approaches to psychotherapy and inpatient programs. Auerbach and Kilmann (1977) have reviewed several facets of crisis intervention not covered in this chapter. Some of these treatment approaches are covered in other chapters of this textbook. Because the focus of this volume is on empirical research findings, our presentation in this section is brief. However, a guide to the published clinical literature is provided for the benefit of readers who wish to read further about the available techniques.

Psychodynamically Oriented Techniques

Pychodynamically oriented insight approaches to brief psychotherapy are most numerous (see Table 19-1). The goals of these systems include developing at least limited psychogenetic understanding of the focal problem. Interpretations are still the major therapeutic technique, but they are usually slightly modified for the short-term situation. Interpretations are designed to be integrative instead of regressive. They focus on present circumstances, not on childhood experiences (Sarvis, Dewees, & Johnson, 1958). Positive transference is generally thought to be essential to the success of therapy. Interpretations of negative transference may be made, but allowing a transference neurosis to develop is often considered undesirable. Discussions of psychodynamically oriented techniques include: Alexander and French (1946), "Psychoanalytic Therapy"; Ansbacher (1972), "Adlerian Psychotherapy"; Balint, Ornstein, and Balint (1972), "Focal Psychotherapy"; Bellak and Small (1965); Burdon (1963); Deutsch (1949), "Applied Psychoanalysis"; Ferenczi (1920), "Active Psychoanalytic Technique"; Gillmann (1965); Gutheil (1944); Hoch (1965); Lewin (1966); Malan (1963, 1976a, 1976b); Mann (1973), "Time-Limited Psychotherapy"; McGuire (1965a, 1965b), "Short-Term Insight Psychotherapy"; Merril and Cary (1975); Semrad, Binstock, and White (1966); Sifneos (1972), "Anxiety Provoking Psychotherapy"; and Wolberg (1965).

TABLE 19-1 Approaches to Brief and Crisis-Oriented Psychotherapies

Psychodynamically Oriented	Brief Behavioral	Crisis-Oriented	Miscellaneous
Alexander and French (1946) (psychoanalytic therapy)	Gelder et al. (1967)	A. General support	A. Hypnotherapy
Ansbacher (1972) (Adlerian psychotherapy)	Hogan (1966, 1967) (implosive therapy)	Coleman (1960) (dynamically oriented supportive psychotherapy)	Frankel (1973)
Balint et al. (1972) (focal psychotherapy)	Lantz and Werk (1976) (short-term casework)	Coleman and Zwerling (1959)	London (1947)
Bellak and Small (1965)	Levis and Carrera (1967)	Sifneos (1972) (anxiety suppressive therapy)	Stein (1972, 1975)
Burdon (1963)	Mitchell and Orr (1974) (massed desensitization)	B. Generic crisis intervention	Wolberg (1965)
Deutsch (1949) (applied psychoanalysis)	Phillips and Weiner (1966)	Caplan (1964)	B. Cathartic psychotherapy
Ferenczi (1920, 1951) (active psychoanalytic technique)	Reid (1975) (task-centered casework)	Lindemann (1965)	Nichols (1974)
Gillman (1965)	Robinson et al. (1975)	C. Individual crisis intervention	Nichols and Reifler (1973)
Gutheil (1944)	Suinn et al. (1970) (accelerated massed desensitization)	Butcher and Maudal (1976) (crisis therapy)	C. Confrontation
Heiberg et al. (1975)		Harris et al. (1963) (precipitating stress approach)	Garner (1970)
Hoch (1965)		Hoffman and Remmel (1975)	D. Logotherapy/paradoxical intention
Lewin (1966)		Jacobson et al. (1968)	Buda (1972)
Malan (1963, 1976a, 1976b)		Levy (1966)	Frankl (1960)
Mann (1973) (time-limited psychotherapy)		Sifneos (1972) (crisis support therapy)	
McGuire (1965a, 1965b) (short-term insight psychotherapy)		Waltzer et al. (1963)	
Merrill and Cary (1975)			
Semrad et al. (1966)			
Sifneos (1972) (anxiety-provoking psychotherapy)			
Wolberg (1965) (short-term psychotherapy)			

Brief Behavior Therapies

The classification of behavior therapies as brief therapies is not, by any means, a snug fit (see Table 19-1). Most behavioral techniques are not specifically described as "brief," although many can be completed within the time limits of brief psychotherapy. For example, Wolpe's (1952) series of 70 cases were seen for 4 to 125 interviews. Reviews of behavioral techniques are available (Bergin & Suinn, 1975; Lazarus, 1971). Behaviorally oriented clinicians who have experimented with especially brief modifications of traditional behavior techniques include: Hogan (1966, 1967); Levis and Carrera (1967), "Implosive Therapy"; Gelder, Marks, and Wolff (1967); Mitchell and Orr (1974), "Massed Desensitization"; and Suinn, Edie, and Spinelli (1970), "Accelerated Massed Desensitization." These modified approaches to desensitization include fewer but longer sessions.

Logotherapy and paradoxical intention (Buda, 1972; Frankl, 1960) have been categorized by Phillips and Weiner (1966) as behavior therapies. Paradoxical intention is a technique for teaching a patient to deal with anticipatory fear situations. Whenever patients feel anticipatory anxiety about a potential terrible outcome, they are asked to visualize that it has already happened.

Task-centered casework (Reid, 1975) includes many behavioral techniques. In this approach, tasks to be worked on in therapy are developed collaboratively. A task (or goal) may state the general direction of action ("become more assertive") or may specify the exact behavior ("ask for a raise"). Specific techniques for accomplishing the tasks include modeling, rehearsal, and guided practice.

Crisis-oriented Therapies

Jacobson, Strickler, and Morley (1968) describe four levels of crisis intervention, all of which are effective with certain types of clients. The first level is environmental manipulation, where the helper serves as a referral source. The second level, general support, involves active listening without threatening or challenging. Approaches to supportive crisis therapy have been described by Sifneos (1972), "Anxiety Suppressive Therapy"; Coleman (1960); and Coleman and Zwerling (1959), "Dynamically Oriented Supportive Psycho-therapy"). In the third level, the generic approach, a particular crisis is believed to have a similar meaning to most affected individuals, regardless of their personality dynamics. Generic crisis intervention requires that the helper have a thorough knowledge of techniques that are particularly helpful in resolving specific crises. This approach is well described by Caplan (1964) and Klein and Lindemann (1961). The fourth level is labeled the individual approach and stresses understanding the personality dynamics of patients and helping them to develop an understanding of why the present situation developed into a "crisis." Characteristic of individual approaches to crisis intervention are: Butcher and Maudal (1976), "Crisis Therapy"; Harris, Kalis, and Freeman (1963); Hoffman and Remmel (1975), "Precipitating Stress Approach"; Jacobson et al. (1965); Levy (1966); and Sifneos (1972), "Crisis Support Therapy."

Miscellaneous Brief Verbal Therapies

Several clinicians (Frankel, 1973; London, 1947; Stein, 1972, 1975; Wolberg, 1965) have discussed the value of hypnosis, hypnoanalysis, and narcoanalysis as techniques of brief therapy. Hypnosis is usually used as a treatment for a "target symptom" (Wolberg, 1965) in conjunction with other techniques, but occasionally recovery can be effected solely through the use of hypnosis. Wolberg (1965) states, however, that symptoms that serve an important purpose in the psychological economy may resist influence.

Brief cathartic psychotherapy emphasizes emotional catharsis (Bierenbaum, Nichols, & Schwartz, 1976; Nichols, 1974; Nichols & Reifler, 1973). Techniques include role playing, repetition of affect-laden phrases, and expressive movements such as striking the couch. These procedures are designed to intensify the emotional tone of the sessions and to promote affective discharge. The confrontation problem-solving technique (Garner, 1970) is a short-session psychotherapy designed for use by nonpsychiatrically trained physicians.

COMMON TECHNICAL CHARACTERISTICS OF CRISIS-ORIENTED AND BRIEF PSYCHOTHERAPY SYSTEMS

It is useful to compare the various psychotherapy systems in terms of the structure of the psychotherapy session and the techniques employed. A survey of brief and crisis-oriented approaches to psychotherapy reveals a core of technical points considered essential by most practitioners of short-term treatment. We will present a summary of the extensive clinical literature on the following important common technical characteristics: utilization of time; limitation of goals; focus of sessions; activity of the therapist; use of assessment; flexibility of therapeutic roles; timing of the intervention; therapeutic use of catharsis; characteristics of the therapeutic relationship; and criteria for patient selection. No attempt will be made to summarize in detail all the studies or issues on each of these variables, since entire books could (and have) been devoted to the topics. We will provide a general summary of the characteristics at the end of the section.

The factors to be discussed here have received wide attention in the clinical literature. In the section following this condensed summary of clinical techniques, there will be a discussion of relevant research on some process variables in brief psychotherapy. Additional information concerning some of the "common characteristics" will be discussed further in that section.

Time Factors

Time is one of the major variables differentiating brief approaches from other forms of psychotherapy. Consequently, most brief therapists have been careful to define the maximum number of therapeutic interviews they consider "brief" and to discuss the meaning and effect of the short time limit on the progress of therapy. Alexander and French (1946) felt that brief therapy should be limited to 40 sessions, but they often concluded their own cases in as few as three sessions. Today, most practitioners agree that 25 sessions is the upper limit of "brief" therapy, with as many clinicians recommending courses of treatment lasting from one to six sessions as the longer 10 to 25 session treatment. Crisis-oriented therapists follow Lindemann's (1944) conceptualization of crisis as a time-limited phenomenon that is resolved one way or another in 6 weeks. Thus, most crisis-oriented psychotherapy is very brief (see Table 19-2).

Slightly longer therapy durations may occur in focal psychotherapy (Balint, Ornstein, & Balint, 1972; Malan, 1963; 1976a, 1976b), which usually averages 10 to 40 sessions and anxiety-provoking psychotherapy (Sifneos, 1972), which lasts 2 to 12 months. Leeman and Mulvey (1975) report procedures that require 3 to 7 months of therapy.

Many therapists recommend telling the patient during the first session that the therapy will be short and time limited (see Table 19-2). Informing patients of the time limits accomplishes two therapeutic goals. It encourages patient optimism through the therapist's confidence that improvement is possible in a relatively short time, and definite time limits give the therapy the added structure of having a definite beginning, middle, and end.

Most practitioners adhere to the standard 45 to 60 minute hour and the 1-week interval, although there is variability. Sessions of 10 to 20 minutes have been advocated by Barten (1965); Cattell, MacKinnon, and Forster (1963); Garner (1970); Koegler (1966); and Koegler and Cannon (1966). Short sessions are used most frequently where service demands are great, such as in the military, or where supportive goals are the object of the therapy. Bierenbaum, Nichols, and Schwartz (1976) compared three schedules of therapy: 1 hour per week, ½ hour twice a week, and 2 hours every other week. They reported that the 1-hour condition resulted in the most emotional catharsis, the most client satisfaction, and greatest reduction in target symptom severity. The ½-hour condition resulted in the most anxiety reduction. The authors suggest that 1-hour durations may be most appropriate for expressive techniques and ½-hour durations for supportive therapy. Crisis-oriented approaches, particularly, may use variable session lengths (Levy, 1966). The initial session may be long in order to obtain all necessary information and allow for the emotional ventilation that may occur at this stage of crisis. Later sessions might then be shorter.

Roth, Berenbaum, and Garfield (1969) and Muench and Schumacher (1968) describe two drastic departures from standard practice. Roth, Berenbaum and Garfield (1969) published a case report on a man treated with client-centered techniques in one 10-hour session. Immediate feedback from the patient and therapist and 6 months' follow-up data were favorable. Muench and

Schumacher (1968) studied "rotational time-limited psychotherapy," in which college student clients were given 12 interviews: six with one therapist and two each with three different therapists. Their data indicated that students felt it beneficial to discuss their problems with different therapists who inevitably had slightly different points of view.

Wolberg (1965) makes an important observation about the practice of short-term psychotherapy. He notes that integrating changed self-concepts into behavior is often a lengthy process. The long-term therapist observes these changes during the "working through" period. The brief therapist must discharge a patient before the changes are complete and may consequently be vulnerable to occasional feelings of dissatisfaction with the results of therapy. Very long follow-up data (Frank, 1974) seem to support Wolberg's contention that patients continue to improve and change for years after a brief therapy course.

Limited Goals

The time limitations of brief psychotherapy make many of the goals of traditional psychotherapy such as extensive personality reconstruction or dynamic insight into psychogenetic origins of behavior impossible. Brief psychotherapy requires that "therapeutic perfectionism" (Malan, 1963) and "prejudices of depth" (Wolberg, 1965) be abandoned.

Ursano and Dressler (1974) found that the focal nature of brief psychotherapy was actually the essential difference between brief and long-term psychotherapy rather than the traditional idea that brief therapy was more supportive and long-term therapy was more explorative. Most short-term psychotherapists strive to accomplish one or more of the following goals: *removal or amelioration of the patient's most disabling symptoms as rapidly as possible* (see Table 19-2); *prompt reestablishment of the patient's previous emotional equilibrium;* and *development of the patient's understanding of the current disturbance and increased coping ability in the future.*

The patient frequently brings to therapy an idea of the symptoms he or she would most like to alleviate. Most clinicians suggest that the patient have a major input in choosing the goals for a limited therapy.

Sarvis, Dewees, and Johnson (1958) suggest that many psychotherapists have adopted the infectious disease model of psychotherapy. In this view, disturbing behaviors are seen as diseases and psychotherapeutic techniques are seen as a specific and permanent cure (like antibiotics) that will transform the patient into a completely healthy individual for the rest of his or her life. They emphasize that adaptive coping is a lifelong process and psychotherapy can only hope to increase a patient's coping skills. Wolberg (1965) discusses the potential of short-term psychotherapy to guide patients in the right direction and help them begin the process of self-study that is necessary to cope with the inevitable problems that arise after therapy has ended.

Focused Interviewing and Present Centeredness

The goals of brief therapy can be accomplished most effectively if therapeutic attention is carefully focused on thorough exploration of a primary problem area (see Table 19-2). Most often the focus is a current problem in the patient's life. Small (1971) believes that "Achievement and maintenance of a focus can be regarded as the single most important technical aspect of brief psychotherapy. . . ." (p. 121). The focus should be determined as early in the course of therapy as possible. Wolberg (1965) and Malan (1963) suggest that the focus be determined in the first interview and communicated to the client as part of the description of the terms and structure of the therapy. After the first session the patient's verbalizations are kept centered on the problem area that is the focus through skillful use of selected attention (Malan, 1963) and benign neglect (Pumpian-Mindlin, 1953). Childhood memories, dreams, or transference interpretations may all have a place in brief therapy, but only if they are directly related to the focus (Wolberg, 1965). Malan (1976b) further noted in the recent follow-up study of brief and analytic therapy: "Those cases will tend to be successful who present a focus early and have the motivation to work through it. This will tend to lead to short, successful therapy" (p. 203).

TABLE 19-2 Common Technical Characteristics of Crisis-Oriented and Brief Psychotherapy Systems

Time Factors	Selection of Patients	Goals of Therapy	Technical Factors
A. One to Six session procedures Bellak and Small (1965) Coleman (1960) Coleman and Zwerling (1959) Frankel (1973) Greenblatt et al. (1963) Harris et al. (1963) Howard (1965) Jacobson et al. (1965) Koegler and Cannon (1966) Levy (1966) Miller (1968) Rosenthal (1965) Saul (1951) Socarides (1954) Spoerl (1975) Stein et al. 1967 B. Up to 25 session procedures Ansbacher (1972) Barten (1965) Bonime (1953) Burdon (1963) Jacobs et al. (1968) Lindemann (1944) Mann (1973) McGuire (1965a,b) Meyer et al. (1967) Schoenberg and Carr (1963) Seitz (1953) Shlein et al. (1962) Sifneos (1972) Stewart (1972)	A. Behavioral problems of acute onset Alexander and French (1946) Bellak and Small (1965) Berliner (1941) Gottschalk et al. (1967) Hoch (1965) McGuire (1965) Straker (1966) Visher (1959) Wolberg (1965) B. Previously good adjustment Gillman (1965) Harris and Christiansen (1946) McGuire (1965) Pumpian-Mindlin (1953) Sifneos (1972) Straker (1966) Visher (1959) C. Good ability to relate Berliner (1941) Gottschalk et al. (1967) Malan (1963) McGuire (1965) Pumpian-Mindlin (1953) Sifneos (1972) Visher (1959) D. Lower-class membership Hunt (1966) Imber et al. (1956) Jacobson (1965) Lief et al. (1961)	A. Removal or amelioration of most disabling symptom Bellak and Small (1965) Greenblatt et al. (1963) Grinker and Spiegel (1944) Hoch (1965) Lester (1968) Malan (1963, 1976a, 1976b) Normand et al. (1963) Parad (1967) Waltzer et al. (1963) Wolberg (1965) B. Prompt reestablishment of equilibrium Coleman (1960) Coleman and Zwerling (1959) Harris et al. (1963) Jacobson (1965) Kris (1960) Normand et al. (1963) Waltzer et al. (1963) Wolberg (1965) C. Develop understanding of current disturbance Bellak (1960) Burdon (1963) Frank (1966) Harris et al. (1963) Malan (1963, 1976a, 1976b) Sifneos (1972) Wolberg (1965) D. Patient should choose goals	A. Prompt intervention Bellak and Small (1965) Harris et al. (1963) Jacobson et al. (1965) Rosenthal (1965) Small (1972) B. Early assessment Barten (1969) Bellak and Small (1965) Butcher and Maudal (1976) Fenichel (1954) Grinker (1942) Klein and Lindemann (1959) Morley (1965) Sifneos (1972) Small (1972) C. Allow for ventilation Alexander and French (1946) Baker (1947) Butcher and Maudal (1976) Erlich and Phillips (1963) Frank (1974) Lindemann (1944) Mann (1973) Semrad et al. (1966) Small (1972) Wolberg (1965) Wolpe and Lazarus (1966) D. Focus on primary problem Ansbacher (1972) Balint et al. (1972) Bellak and Small (1965)

Stone (1951)
Straker (1966)
Terhune (1960)

C. Up to 40 sessions
Balint et al. (1972)
Leeman and Mulvey (1975)
Malan (1963, 1976a, 1976b)
Sifneos (1972)

D. Recommend specific communication of time limits
Ansbacher (1972)
Ferenczi (1920)
Haskel et al. (1969)
Levy (1966)
Malan (1963)
Mann (1973)
Muench (1965)
Phillips and Johnston (1954)
Sarvis et al. (1958)
Seitz (1953)
Shlein et al. (1962)
Small (1971)
Stekel (1950)
Straker (1966)

Lorion (1973, 1974)
Normand et al. (1963)
Rosenthal and Frank (1958)
Strassi and Messer (1976)

E. Marginally adjusted or severely limited
Barten (1971)
Parad (1967)
Wolberg (1965)

Bellak and Small (1965)
Rosenbaum (1964)
Wolberg (1965)

Bonstedt (1970)
Gillman (1964)
Harris et al. (1963)
Haskell et al. (1969)
Koegler (1966)
Malan (1963, 1975, 1976)
Mann (1973)
Phillips and Weiner (1966)
Semrad et al. (1966)
Small (1972)
Stekel (1950)
Wolberg (1965)

E. Use of active techniques
Avnet (1965)
Barten (1971)
Baum and Felzer (1964)
Bellak and Small (1965)
Bonstedt (1970)
Burdon (1963)
Butcher and Maudal (1976)
Ferenczi (1920)
Gillman (1965)
Gross (1968)
Hoch (1965)
Lester (1968)
Malan (1963, 1976a, 1976b)
Mann (1973)
McGuire (1965a,b)
Merrill and Cary (1975)
Perlman (1975)
Sarvis et al. (1958)

F. Flexible choice of specific techniques
Alexander and French (1946)
Errera et al. (1967)
Hoch (1965)

TABLE 19-2 (continued)

Time Factors	Selection of Patients	Goals of Therapy	Technical Factors
			Malan (1963)
			Mann (1973)
			Small (1972)
			Stein et al. (1967)
			Wayne (1966)
			Wolberg (1965)
			G. Use of persuasion, suggestion, formulation of plans of action, factual information
			Baker (1947)
			Barten (1965)
			Bellak and Small (1965)
			Butcher and Maudal (1976)
			Gelb and Ullman (1967)
			Mann (1973)
			Saul (1951)
			Sifneos (1972)
			Small (1971)
			Stein et al. (1967)
			Visher (1959)
			Wolberg (1965)
			H. Develop positive expectancies
			Aldrich (1968)
			Ansbacher (1972)
			Baum and Felzer (1964)
			Bellak and Small (1965)
			Bonstedt (1970)
			Butcher and Maudal (1976)
			Frank (1974)
			Lick and Bootzin (1975)
			Sifneos (1972)

Small (1972)
Wolberg (1965)
I. Foster positive transference
Bellak and Small (1965)
Malan (1963, 1976a, 1976b)
Sifneos (1972)
Small (1972)
Wolberg (1965)

Activity and Directiveness

Maintaining a focus requires that the therapist participate more actively in the therapeutic process than is characteristic of many long-term approaches. Generally, being "active" means talking more, directing more conversation when necessary, actively exploring areas of interest, offering support and guidance, and formulating plans of action for the patient to follow. Wolberg (1965) notes that passivity is "anathema" in short-term therapy. Many clinicians have described their approaches as "active." A more active therapeutic style is reported to be especially helpful with lower-class patients.

Suggestion, persuasion, and formulating plans of action for patients are recommended by several therapists. Gelb and Ullman (1967) summarize: "The well-trained therapist can on the basis of brief exploration guide the patient towards methods of behavior and interaction different from his customary mode, and thus lead him into new forms of experience which will result in a more satisfactory and productive life."

Wolberg's (1965) stress on helping the patient develop an adaptive life philosophy clearly implies a didactic element in his therapeutic work. Strupp's (1957) interesting multidimensional analysis of the verbatim transcripts of the entire therapeutic course of a patient successfully treated by Wolberg in nine sessions verifies the role of direct guidance in Wolberg's procedures. Strupp categorized every therapist's verbalization in each session into several categories: clarification, direct guidance, exploration, interpretation, minimal activity, and miscellaneous. Direct guidance was the second most frequent therapeutic activity consistently throughout the sessions. McGuire and Sifneos (1970) also employ didactic methods to teach problem-solving methods.

Sloane, Staples, Cristol, Yorkston, and Whipple (1975) showed that short-term therapists with a behavioral approach were significantly more directive in therapy than psychoanalytically oriented therapists.

Rapid, Early Assessment

There is virtually no disagreement in the literature that brief psychotherapy requires some exploration and information gathering during the first session.

However, the assessment must go beyond simple psychiatric classification, since diagnosis has no clear-cut relationship to choice of treatment technique. Small (1971) noted that "Intervention cannot be made a matter of chance, hence more likely to lengthen rather than shorten the process" (p. 73). Several authors have stressed the need for early assessment (see Table 19-1). The focus of assessment differs among therapists. Many crisis-oriented therapists strive for a full understanding of the precipitating event of the crisis and the dynamic meaning of the crisis situation in the history of the patient [Harris, Kalis, & Freeman, 1963; Jacobson et al., 1965; Sifneos, 1972 (crisis support therapy)].

Small (1972) provided a tentative guide for a psychodynamic formulation for brief therapy assessment. He suggests exploring the complaint, the precipitating cause of the symptoms, antecedent analogues of present behavior, the meanings of the symptoms, and the strengths and weaknesses of the ego system. Sifneos (1972) focuses on understanding unresolved emotional conflicts. Wolberg (1965) provides a procedure for the initial interview. He attempts to develop a "working understanding of the patient's psychodynamics and an understanding of his neurotic patterns." In addition, he attempts to gauge the degree of homeostatic imbalance as indicated by anxiety and its equivalents, the mechanisms of defense that are being used, the amount of self-esteem, dependence-independence, the character of interpersonal relationships, and the disintegrative potential.

Therapeutic Flexibility

Brief and crisis-oriented psychotherapies serve a wide range of patients: anxious, depressed, suicidal, excited, panicky, delirious, psychotic, assaultive, or antisocial. Meeting the needs of these diverse problems requires a variety of therapeutic techniques. The therapist who adheres to one school of psychotherapy and one set of techniques could not function well in a brief therapy setting. Alexander and French (1946) conclude that flexibility of the therapist in adapting interventions to meet the requirements of the individual is the primary technical principle in shortening psychotherapy. Wolberg (1965) suggests that the techniques used in short-term psychotherapy may come from psychiatry, psychoanalysis, psychology, or sociology.

Promptness of Intervention

Both crisis-oriented and brief therapists strive to provide treatment to a patient as early as possible after the initial request, and they discourage the use of intake interviewers different from the future therapist or lengthy psychometric assessment before therapy has been started.

Most formulations of crisis situations (Caplan, 1961; Lindemann, 1944) stress the time-limited nature of these disequilibriums and the heightened susceptibility to intervention during the crisis period. Most crisis intervention centers try to offer an appointment within 24 hours, and many are open 24 hours a day. Bellak and Small (1965) report attempts to reach out immediately to people in disaster through the use of mobile counseling units. Wolkon (1972) found that better outcome occurred in a group of patients who were given immediate crisis therapy than in a group asked to wait several days for an appointment.

Much of the impetus for providing brief forms of therapy stems from the desire to be responsive to a greater range of patients and to cut down the waiting list at clinics. In addition, the emphasis in brief therapy on current life problems suggests the necessity of offering the therapy when a patient has problems and is motivated to work on them.

Ventilation

All major approaches to brief and crisis-oriented psychotherapy recognize the value of allowing the patient to ventilate emotional tension (see Table 19-2). Most therapists seek to create a therapeutic environment in which the patient feels accepted and safe and in which he or she can express feelings and experience catharsis spontaneously and naturally. A small number of therapists (Nichols, 1974; Nichols & Reifler, 1973; Stampfl & Levis, 1967) deliberately attempt to elicit strong emotions to facilitate tension release.

Therapeutic Relationship

Bergin and Suinn (1975) noted that a therapeutic relationship is a prerequisite to progress in any school of psychotherapy. The time constraints of short-term psychotherapy require the therapist's ability to develop a working relationship rather quickly.

Many brief therapists mention the critical role that hope and expectation of recovery play in developing the therapeutic relationship. Lick and Bootzin (1975) reviewed the literature on the importance of the subject's expectation of therapeutic gain in facilitating fear reduction. They concluded that expectancy variables are important change mediators in the densensitization of fear. Most brief therapists recommend developing a confident attitude and communicating this hope to the patient. Malan (1963) feels that the therapist's enthusiasm has a critical effect on therapeutic outcome. He notes that many young therapists experience several brief, dramatic "cures" early in their careers that they are unable to duplicate in later years. Waning enthusiasm for one's therapeutic techniques may account for this phenomenon.

Malan (1976b), in his replication of the early study, again concluded that therapist enthusiasm and involvement in the therapy was an important element in successful therapy.

Psychoanalytically oriented therapists often discuss the importance of positive transference to the success of brief psychotherapy (see Table 19-2). Positive transference feelings of warmth, liking for the therapist, trust, admiration, and confidence are often considered unrealistic in long-term therapy and are interpreted as such. They are considered necessary for success in the time-limited situation, however.

Selection of Patients

After an extensive investigation into the relative effectiveness of specific procedures in short-term analytic and behavior therapy, Staples, Sloane, Whipple, Cristol, and Yorkston (1976) concluded that little could be said about specific interventions as being harmful or beneficial. Instead, they concluded that successful treatment "may be more a function of the patient than any specific therapeutic procedures." Saltzman et al. (1976) reported that the determinants of the therapeutic relationship included the patient, the therapist, and their interaction. These conclusions highlight the importance of patient selection. Some dissenting evidence has been reported. Schonfield, Stone, Hoehn-Saric, Imber, and Pande (1969) found a mutual adjustment process (between patient and therapist) in short-term therapy and found that individual patient characteristics did not affect the process of adaptation in any way.

Short-term psychotherapy has been attempted with virtually every diagnostic group of patients (Small, 1971). In spite of this diversity, there does seem to be some consensus about the *most suitable* types of patients. Wolberg (1965) believes that any patient thought suitable for psychotherapy should first be tried in short-term treatment. Perhaps this recommendation is analogous to the medical practice of instituting less radical procedures before more drastic ones. Gillman (1965) considers regressive long-term therapy to be a disservice to any patient who views his or her functioning prior to the current problem as satisfactory. Barten (1971) believes that long-term therapy is equally as unsuitable for chronic, long-term processes as it is for adjustment problems of recent origin, crises, and uncomplicated anxiety and depression. Parad (1966) once suggested that crisis intervention may be most valid for the very strong or very weak.

The following types of patients are considered to be best suited to brief techniques (see Table 19-2 for references).

1. Those in whom the behavioral problem is of acute onset.   A number of therapists have pointed to recent onset as an important selection criterion for brief therapy (see Table 19-2). There is some evidence that recent onset is *not* a sufficient condition for therapeutic improvement. Malan (1976b), following up patients treated in brief analytic therapy, found that a subsample of young patients with recent onset of symptoms was particularly difficult to treat. These patients with acute phobic symptoms did not respond well to brief analytic therapy, but we conjecture that these same patients might have responded better to behavioral treatment. Consequently, we do not think this is necessarily a failure in the "recent onset" hypothesis of patient selection for brief therapy.

2. Those whose previous adjustment has been good.   White, Fichtenbaum, and Dollard (1969) found that patients initially in better mental health are more likely to improve than less healthy patients. Sloane et al. (1975) found that psychotherapy was more effective with patients with lower MMPI-measured psychopathology. The review of factors influencing therapeutic outcome by Luborsky, Chandler, Auerbach, Cohen, and Bachrach (1971) concluded that virtually all the studies to that date showed that the healthier the patient is to begin with, the better the outcome. The conclusion that the initially more disturbed patients have poorer outcomes has been questioned by several investigators. Methodological differences may account for the differences in conclusions. Studies that utilize global ratings of improvement may favor the conclusion that "healthy" patients improve more than the more disturbed patients. Mintz (1972) showed that global ratings at the end of treatment tend to be influenced by the actual condition at the time the measure was taken, regardless of the patient's initial level of adjustment. When difference scores are used to evaluate improvement, persons with higher initial disturbance may improve most in terms of having higher gain scores, but still be considered less well adjusted than patients with initially better adjustment but lower gain scores according to global ratings at the end of treatment. (For a more detailed discussion of this problem, see Garfield, Chapter 6.) This is an important consideration for brief psychotherapy, since patients with relatively poor initial adjustment may be referred for short-term, limited goals treatment. There is enough research evidence and clinical lore to support the use of brief directive therapy with fairly disturbed patients when the goals are concrete and kept within reach of the patient (Butcher & Maudal, 1976). Malan (1976b) found that "the nature of psychopathology and duration of symptoms did not influence outcome." He thus concluded that "some severe and chronic conditions can respond to brief therapy."

3. Those with a good ability to relate.   Staples and Sloane (1970) studied the relationship between speech patterns and empathic ability and patient responsiveness to approval and disapproval. They concluded that "individual differences in the capacity to respond to cues provided by a therapist may be an important source of variation in patients' therapeutic potential" (p. 104). Nash, Hoehn-Saric, Battle, Stone, Imber, and Frank (1965) concluded that "attractiveness," an impressionistic judgment of suitability for psychotherapy made by an initial interviewer, was significantly related to outcome. Attractive patients were younger and better educated than unattractive patients and also participated in a better therapeutic relationship.

4. *Those with high initial motivation.* Many therapists have recorded the importance of high initial motivation for successful therapy. Malan (1976b) considered that initial motivation was a more important patient characteristic than any other included in their studies. However, their correlations of initial motivation with rated outcome were nonsignificant.

Motivation for therapeutic change is a complex variable that has not been adequately studied. There has been no delineation of patient motivational attributes that would provide practical guidelines for therapists to determine, in advance, if patients want change or can profit from verbal therapeutic interaction.

Brief therapy is thought to be more appropriate than long-term therapy for lower-class clients (Imber et al., 1970; Jacobson, 1965; Lorion, 1973, 1974; Normand et al., 1963). Frank, Gliedman, Imber, Nash, and Stone (1957) found that lower-class patients leave therapy sooner than other patients, although Meyer et al. (1967) did not find that race, sex, socioeconomic status, marital status, diagnosis, duration of symptoms, or history of parental loss related to completion of the therapy. A more complete review of these pre-1970 studies can be found in Garfield (1971).

Since the cost of long-term treatment is generally prohibitive for many patients and brief treatment methods are effective for many types of patients and problems, brief treatment is a highly desirable treatment option for lower-socioeconomic-class patients. The tactics followed by brief therapists (directiveness, concrete goal orientation, etc.) are both acceptable to lower-class patients and, in many instances, an expected helping mode.

In a recent study of characteristics of patients referred for brief versus long-term psychotherapy, Ursano and Bressler (1974) found no differences in age, sex, race, marital status, education, or source of referral between patients referred for the two types of psychotherapy. However, they found a number of factors that were associated with referral to brief therapy: patients with a recent onset of illness (6 months) tended to be referred for brief therapy; clinicians who had treated a number of cases with brief methods also tended to refer more patients for brief treatment; patients in brief therapy were more often diagnosed "situational"; patients tended to have less severe problems; and patients tended not to require medication.

Patients who have been mentioned as being definitely unsuitable for short-term therapy are those who desire personality reconstruction, are deeply dependent, act out persistently, or are unrestrainably anxious (Wolberg, 1965). Castelnuovo-Tedesco (1966) noted that brief treatment does not work if the patient is outspokenly self-centered, passive-dependent, masochistic, or self-destructive. Frank (1974) excluded patients with less than fifth-grade education, organic-toxic illness, mental deficiency, or psychosis. Warren and Rice (1972) found that low-prognosis patients could be kept in therapy longer with extra therapy training sessions; however, they found that there was no particular advantage when the patient "merely stays in therapy somewhat beyond the attrition cutoff point."

Summary and Evaluation of Common Characteristics of Brief Therapies

An extensive array of studies and opinions on what constitutes brief psychotherapy has been presented in this section. This material provided a glimpse of these views and a guide to the published literature. Can a unitary view of the basic elements or main theme of what constitutes brief psychotherapy be gleaned from these studies? It is clear from examining this literature that there are many brief therapies with different foci, structures, goals, tactics, and probably outcomes. However, certain elements characterize most brief therapy approaches. Most therapists structure brief treatment as about 6 to 10 sessions of 50 minutes in length once a week. Most therapists inform the patient of the time limitations in advance and expect that the focused and limited goals will be achieved in that period. Generally, therapists limit therapeutic goals within attainable reach. Goals such as amelioration of the most disabling symptoms, reestablishment of a previous level of functioning, and development of some understanding of current disturbance to increase coping ability are adopted. Most brief therapy sessions are usually centered around concrete content and are focused on the "here and now" instead of early life events.

In order to maintain direction and organization of the sessions, the therapist tends to be both active and direct in relating to the patient. Most theorists believe that effective brief therapy requires a highly experienced therapist who can keep the therapeutic goals in sight and not get bogged down in content that is irrelevant to the agreed-on goals. The necessity of early, rapid assessment in brief therapy underscores the importance of having an experienced therapist. It is important for the therapist to be able to gather relevant information and develop a working formulation during the early sessions. This assessment must provide an understanding of the extent of the patient's problem, the critical nature of the present situation, and the personal resources the patient might have that could be called into play to increase their coping skills. Most short-term therapeutic approaches consider flexibility in the therapist's role an essential element in abbreviating therapy. Many brief therapeutic approaches are aimed at prompt early intervention at the onset of symptoms or during an experienced crisis. Certainly one of the attractive features of short-term therapy programs is the potential of providing therapeutic contact to more patients. Reaching patients with prompt assistance at an early point in their crisis can aid in resolving immediate problems and prevent more serious or chronic pathology that may require more lengthy treatment at a later date.

The development of a therapeutic relationship is an important element in short-term therapy as it is in any form of psychotherapy. With the constraints imposed by the time limitation, the short-term therapist is often caught between sometimes mutually antagonistic roles—"relating-understanding" (developing a relationship) and "directive-confronting." The success of directive intervention generally depends on the patient's acceptance of the competence, authority, and benevolence of the therapist. This receptive attitude in patients is highly related to the strength and quality of the therapeutic relationship. Thus, it is important for short-term therapists to be aware of and foster the development of a therapeutic relationship. It is an important ingredient in all approaches to brief therapeutic intervention.

Selecting the appropriate patients for brief treatment is an important consideration. Patients who have had a good premorbid adjustment and an acute onset of symptoms are considered by many to be better candidates for short-term therapy than more severely disturbed patients. However, recent evidence, both clinical and research, suggests that some short-term therapeutic interventions might be highly successful with more severely disturbed patients. Patients who have a good ability to relate are also considered to be better candidates for brief therapy than those who have difficulty forming relationships.

IMPORTANT PROCESS VARIABLES IN BRIEF PSYCHOTHERAPY

What are the factors in brief psychotherapy that contribute to change in the patient? Much of the existing literature on psychotherapy research relates to this question, since there is a great degree of commonality among all forms of psychotherapy, brief or long-term. Many theorists have noted the common therapeutic processes such as the nature of the patient-therapist relationship and various formal aspects of the therapeutic relationship such as the patient's expectations of receiving help or the amount and type of activity by the therapist. Consequently, it is not possible to review here all the factors that are important to short-term psychotherapy. There are relevant reviews elsewhere in this volume that summarize more extensively and focally these broader process variables. This section examines several factors that are perhaps more salient in the short-term psychotherapies. This review is limited to variables that, for the most part, have been subjected to objective empirical investigation instead of to the more abundant clinical literature.

It is important to reiterate the great lack of sound empirical research in the delineation of process variables in brief psychotherapies. This scarcity highlights a general deficit in psychotherapy research, since brief psychotherapy lends itself particularly well to psychotherapy research. Frank (1974) noted that the staff at Johns Hopkins utilized time-limited, short-term therapy in their research into the psychotherapeutic process, since "it is not feasible to do controlled experiments otherwise." There are a number of reasons why psychothrapy researchers might choose short-term therapy for evaluating the outcome or studying various psychotherapy processes.

1. Most of the variables and processes are similar or identical to those in long-term therapy. Consequently, variables important to long-term psychotherapeutic change might be studied more easily in a short-term therapy situation.

2. The short-term contact provides a greater opportunity to control extraneous influences in a research design.

3. Logistically, arranging and monitoring numbers of patients, therapists, assistants, and the like, is a more manageable task over a short period of time than over longer times.

4. Since treatment is generally goal-oriented and focused, the criteria for improvement can be kept more clearly in sight than in other less focused therapies. Thus, the criteria required for sound outcome and process research are easier to define.

5. The important questions that can only be answered by adequate follow-up study can be more readily approached in the context of short-term therapeutic contacts.

In this section we will review several factors that are important to brief contact therapy and have been the focus of recent research investigations.

Transference

The therapeutic relationship is an important element in the brief psychotherapies, just as in long-term therapy, in spite of the defined limit on the treatment and the more directive focus in brief therapy. Malan (1973) has made a strong case for the importance of the "transference" in the outcome of brief psychotherapy. The necessity of focusing on the therapeutic relationship in psycho-

logical treatment is not a new discovery. Analytically oriented, brief therapists have traditionally maintained the importance of utilizing positive transference. In fact, critics of short-term therapy have referred to positive outcome in brief treatment as "transference cures." Whittington (1962) noted that "Certainly, transference in pure culture does not appear in such psychotherapy (brief); the brevity of the process, active interaction between therapist and patient, focus on current reality problems, all tend to obscure and distort transference" (p. 504).

Malan (1976b) reported that undirected interpretations were negatively correlated with outcome, while interpretations about the transference relationship were positively related to outcome. He considers this evidence (from the 1963 and the 1976 studies) to support strongly analytically oriented therapy, since analyzing the transference relationship is considered the most important ingredient of analytically oriented therapy whether it is time unlimited or brief in duration. Although this study attempted to shed light on the important relationship between interpretative statements and outcome, the methodological problems pervading this study warn against firm conclusions. There are several problems with the ratings used in the study. Since the same persons rated both outcome and the nature of the interpretations, the ratings are not independent. Moreover, the interpretation ratings were not made from verbatim transcripts but from incomplete summaries of the therapy. This unfortunate situation allows for an alternate explanatory hypothesis to be cited: that the therapists recalled only interpretations that "fit" with the psychoanalytic method. Consequently, there may be a study bias adversely influencing the findings.

The nature of the therapeutic relationship has been the focus of other studies. Nash, Hoehn-Saric, Battle, Stone, Imber, and Frank (1965) reported that therapists who offered the best therapeutic relationship (defined by ratings of taped treatment interviews) produced more successful therapeutic outcomes. Saltzman, Luetgert, Roth, Creaser, and Howard (1976) studied the formation of a psychotherapeutic relationship. They obtained therapist and client reports on several relationship dimensions after each of the initial

10 sessions of therapy. Dropouts and remainers in therapy were significantly different on a number of relationship dimensions: anxiety, respect, understanding, openness, security, uniqueness, continuity, and movement. However, comparisons only of remainers in therapy (3 months versus 6 months versus 1 year) revealed few significant differences. The authors conclude that "Thus, as early as the first session, there is evidence that the viability of the therapeutic relationship rests not only on the qualities or experiences of the individual participants but also on the pattern of interaction between them" (p. 553).

Malan (1963) noted that therapist involvement in the therapy was an important consideration. He noted that therapists often produce dramatically successful "cures" in their early treatment cases when they are enthusiastic about the method. In the 1976 replication study, Malan (1976b) again concluded that therapist enthusiasm was an important ingredient in the relationship and consequently to the success of the therapy.

The therapeutic relationship, per se, has not been considered as important to success in behaviorally oriented approaches. However, the recent study by Sloane et al. (1975), comparing the effectiveness of analytically versus behaviorally oriented, short-term therapy, showed that in a 2-year follow-up in which patients rated the factors in their therapy that they considered important to their improvement, the personality of the therapist was ranked first by patients in both therapy approaches. The authors point out that "Similarly a behavior therapist might be surprised that in the eyes of his successful patient most of the factors important to his success involve the patient-therapist relationship" (p. 207).

The development of congruence in the therapeutic relationship has been examined to determine its bearing on outcome. Schonfield et al. (1969) studied the development of "congruent" attitudes between patients and therapists in a 15-session brief psychotherapy. They found that patients who were more congruent with therapist attitudes considered themselves more improved than lower "congruent" patients. The patient's changed attitudes may result from viewing things more like the therapist, or the findings may have resulted from the therapist becoming more "congruent" or

accepting of the patient's behavior. However, there was no relationship between therapist ratings of improvement and therapist-patient congruence. Also, no relationship was found between congruence scores and reduction of target symptoms.

Sloane et al. (1975) found that patients who were liked by their therapists improved most. However, therapist liking of patient was not related to improvement in short-term behavioral therapy. Frank (1974), in summarizing research conducted over 25 years, concluded that "The quality of the therapeutic interaction, to which patient, therapist and therapeutic method contribute, is probably the major determinant of short-term therapeutic response" (p. 338).

Role of Interpretation

Most short-term therapists consider directiveness and interpretation, if not straightforward advice-giving, as the key change-producing behaviors on the part of the therapist (Butcher & Maudal, 1976). Malan (1973, 1976b) noted that interpretation, especially with regard to the transference, is an important factor in good therapeutic outcome. Whittington (1962), on the other hand, provides several cases illustrating that verbal interpretations are not always the chief modality of dealing with transference manifestations. He considers the brief therapy process to be an "active interaction" in which the therapist thwarts the gratification of transference expectations by actively resisting being cast in the transference role. The empirical literature showing the effectiveness of direct interpretation is not abundant. White, Fichtenbaum, and Dollard (1969) studied the "messages" communicated to patients in brief psychotherapy and related these verbal interpretations (and behavioral messages) to rated improvements in adjustment.

Patients who indicated in follow-up that they had learned better verbally what the therapists taught were more likely to have improved adjustment. Also, patients who reported that they had behaviorally learned what the therapists taught were more likely to have improved in mental health. Insight alone was not found to be sufficient to produce improved adjustment in all areas (e.g., sexual adjustment). However, "behavioral learning" was associated with improved adjustment.

The amount of time utilized in interpretation,

advice-giving, and the like, is important in brief psychotherapy. The amount of patient verbalization in relation to therapist's communication may be related to successful treatment outcome. Staples and Sloane (1970) found that the more the patient talks relative to the therapist, the greater the improvement. Also, the longer the duration of the patient's "average" speech in therapy, the greater the improvement. Sloane et al. (1975) found that patients who spoke more in psychotherapy improved more than those who spoke less. However, the improvement rate between patients who talked more and those who talked less in behavior therapy was not as marked, although patients in behavior therapy who spoke in longer utterances did show greater improvement.

Sloane et al. (1975) reported one "paradoxical" finding: "Patients whose psychotherapists used fewer clarifying and interpretative statements showed greater improvement than those whose therapists used more." [Malan (1976b) also noted a negative correlation between number of interpretations and positive outcome.] This finding suggests that the more the therapists attempted to interpret or clarify problems by giving the patient information related to his or her problem, the less successful the treatment was. One possible explanation of this finding is that therapeutic interpretation is not valuable. However, there are other, more likely explanations. It could be that the more "difficult" patients call forth more heroic therapeutic efforts that find the therapists becoming more and more "interpretative" when therapy is not progressing well.

Depth of exploration in therapy dictates the kinds of interpretation that are made in a session. It seems that there may be no great differences in the extent of exploration between various approaches to therapy. Interpretations offered by behavior therapists were found to be as related to past history and dynamics as those of analytically oriented therapists (Sloane et al., 1975).

Interpretation is an essential element in all forms of brief psychotherapy. The nature, amount, and "level" of interpretation may vary somewhat, depending on the approach; some therapists (e.g., analytically oriented) focus on earlier life events and others (e.g., rational emotive) focus more on present relationships. Although a few studies have been directed at examining the ways in which interpretative remarks by the therapist are received and processed, the actual and complete anatomy of the interpretation process has not been well defined. More research needs to be directed toward therapeutic interpretation—the major tool with which therapists attempt to bring about change in patients.

Patient Expectation of Receiving Help

The beneficial effects of psychotherapy have been considered heightened by the patient's expectation of improvement. An examination of psychotherapy processes is not complete without discussing the importance of hope and expectation on therapeutic issues (Frank, 1974). The influence of patient expectation on positive therapeutic outcome has become recognized as an important factor to control for in any psychotherapy outcome study. Patient expectation conditions (e.g., placebo groups) generally show greater improvement than noncontact control conditions (DiLoreto, 1971; Frank, 1974; Sloane et al., 1975). Patient expectation of success may be a more important factor in short-term than in long-term therapy, since the immediate mobilization of patient's resources is usually encouraged.

Regarding studies of placebo effects, Frank (1974) noted that these findings support the assumption that the short-term symptomatic effects of both psychotherapy and placebo depend on their mobilization of the patient's hopes for relief. He pointed out that "the main conclusion to be drawn from studies on the placebo effect is that its simplicity is only apparent." He considers a more promising approach to be the direct experimental manipulation of expectations about psychotherapy.

Several studies have been reported in which patients were prepared for psychotherapy in order to enhance the positive effects of the patient's expectation. Hoehn-Saric et al. (1964) studied the effects of a "role induction interview" on behavior in therapy and therapeutic outcome. They concluded that patients receiving role preparation showed more appropriate behavior and had better outcomes than patients who failed to receive the role induction interview. The same conclusions were reported by Sloane, Cristol, Pepernick, and Staples

(1970). More recently, Heitler (1973) demonstrated that a preparatory interview prior to group psychotherapy effectively prepared patients for group therapy. The study showed that prepared patients had lower latencies for voluntary participation, tended to communicate more (more frequently and spend more time communicating), initiated more communications, and engaged in more self-explanatory behavior. Strupp and Bloxom (1973) found that role induction interviews and the use of a role induction film significantly increased the patient's motivation to begin group sessions, effected favorable change in the patient's understanding of the therapy process and his or her role in it, raised the patient's and therapist's expectations of improvement, and increased the patient's "attractiveness" to the therapist.

Warren and Rice (1972) used four "extra" ½-hour sessions by an investigator (not the therapist) to prepare the low-prognosis patient for continued participation in the therapy. These sessions trained the patient to use the therapy. The experimental, extra therapy sessions were successful in keeping low-prognosis patients in therapy longer. Heitler (1976) summarized the literature on the effectiveness of preparatory techniques to prepare patients for psychotherapy.

> While further research is needed, it is clear that a variety of preparatory techniques hold promise for facilitating a therapeutic alliance in expressive psychotherapy with unsophisticated patients from any social class, and that these techniques may be particularly useful with lower class patient populations, in which unsophisticated and potentially counter-productive role expectations seem to be more prevalent. (p. 350)

These procedures for preparing patients for psychotherapy may have particular value in short-term therapy programs, since brief therapy is perhaps the only viable psychological treatment for lower-class patients. Imber, Pande, Frank, Hoehn-Saric, Stone, and Wargo (1970) attempted to influence therapeutic outcome by inducing a "hope for improvement." Neurotic patients were given mock physiological tests. Half of them were

informed that the tests "revealed" that they would experience improvement by the fourth week of therapy. Outcome measures showed no differences between the experimental group and control group at the 4-week point or at the termination of therapy. The authors concluded that patients' expectations are not easily manipulated.

Not all patient expectations improve the likelihood of therapeutic success, however. Hornstra, Lubin, Lewis, and Willis (1972) surveyed 611 consecutive applicants (and 443 relatives) to a community health center. They found that there were unrealistic expectations of services in this predominantly lower-class population. The patients studied indicated a desire for quick symptom relief and services that would require a minimum commitment on their part. Only 16.7 percent of the sample felt that regularly scheduled appointments to talk about their problems would be helpful. Most people wanted medication and occasional advice. Lorion (1974) discussed problems associated with providing psychological treatment for lower socioeconomic classes. It appears that lower-class patients have unrealistic ideas about therapy. The effects of negative expectations have not been as widely studied as positive expectation effects and placebos.

Wilkins (1973) warns that utilizing the construct "expectancy of therapeutic gain" to account for positive therapeutic change is circular and unjustified. He concludes:

> It appears from the literature reviewed that the construct "expectancy of therapeutic gain" emerged prematurely and without the empirical support necessary to establish its validity. As yet, all of the variables contributing to therapeutic improvement are not known. Unable to identify all of these variables, psychotherapy researchers and theorists seem to have classified them under the rubric "expectancy effects" and then have attributed causality to this rubric in order to "explain" the therapeutic improvement which has not otherwise been accounted for. (p. 75)

Wilkins encourages researchers to "relinquish expectancy of therapeutic gain as an explanatory construct and focus research efforts more directly on the functional relationships between observable events and improvement in psychotherapy" (p. 76).

Expectation of receiving help is an important consideration for any type of psychotherapy, but perhaps especially so for brief therapy, since the time constraints require that treatment sessions be fast moving and oriented toward achieving agreed-on goals. Negative expectations induce fatalistic attitudes into the treatment and are difficult to overcome in the limited sessions available. Most of the research literature supports the view that expectancy of receiving help is associated with improvement in therapy. The exact conditions under which this "guaranteed" improvement takes place has not been fully determined, although research in several areas has been supportive of the expectancy viewpoint. It has also been pointed out that expectancy effects are not easily manipulated. It is clear that the final word on this matter has not been written and that future research will need to focus on producing less ambiguous results. The detrimental effects of negative expectations have not been sufficiently explored. Future studies might profitably develop research designs that encompass the range of expectancy effects. More information on negative attitudes that precede and occur in ongoing therapy might aid in clarifying the influence of expectation upon therapeutic outcome.

Amenability to Change under Heightened Emotional Arousal

Short-term therapy, especially crisis therapy, is often conducted while the patient is experiencing intense emotional feelings. This may be more the case in brief therapy than long-term treatment because:

1. The directive (sometimes confrontive) nature of the brief therapy often provokes strong feelings in the patient.

2. The time limitation on the therapy keeps the sessions at a higher pitch.

3. The type of patients often seen in short-term therapy are frequently individuals who seek therapy immediately following crisis.

An area of research important to the understanding of brief psychotherapy involves the study of attitude change under heightened emotional arousal. Frank (1974) studied the effects of emotional arousal on patient susceptibility to focal attitude change in therapy. Ether was used to produce emotional arousal. Patients were then interviewed about their emotionally charged experiences and were given suggestions concerning the preselected "focal concept" when they were emotionally aroused. The patients changed in the direction of the therapists' suggestions. It is not known whether demand characteristics, placebo, or arousal produced the shift.

Another experiment by Hoehn-Saric et al. (1972), which controlled for the placebo effect and demand characteristics in the experiment, found that focal concepts showed more lability and shifted more in the high-arousal group of patients than the low-arousal group. But the results were less dramatic and more transient than in the first experiment.

One additional experiment (Frank, 1974) attempted to shift a patient's attitudes about a focal concept important to him under an adrenalin arousal condition. The effects were less than previous studies showed, but still yielded confirmation that emotional arousal (without the confusion associated with the ether studies) generally results in greater suceptibility to therapists' persuasive communications.

Saltzman et al. (1976) found that individuals who drop out of therapy in the early sessions are those who experience relatively lower levels of anxiety. In their review of the relationship between affect and change in therapy, Luborsky et al. (1971) concluded that "almost any affect is better than no affect," and patients who are anxious or depressed at the beginning of therapy are the ones more likely to benefit from therapy.

We have observed a reluctance on the part of beginning therapists to pick up on emotionally charged material, thereby deferring or frustrating the patients' emotional experience in therapy. One recent study of brief emotive psychotherapy (Bierenbaum et al., 1976) found that experienced therapists produced more emotional catharsis than less experienced therapists.

The heightened state of arousal resulting from

the patient having just recently experienced an emotional crisis may make the patient particularly amenable to directive intervention. Some crisis clinics that offer drop-in counseling services perhaps see patients who are more "keyed up" for change than therapeutic institutions that require that the patient arrange to be in the office at 9:00 A.M. every Thursday, sometimes a week or more after the important crisis took place. Reports on interventions with patients under heightened states of arousal at crisis clinics from the clinical literature have supported the effectiveness of intervention immediately following crises (Butcher & Maudal, 1976). However, research into the process lags behind. Little empirical research exists either comparing whether the heightened state of arousal is more prominent in crisis clinics or examining the actual effectiveness of interventions under these conditions.

Process of Therapeutic Change in Crises

Little empirical research on individual change in crisis-oriented therapy or crisis intervention (see distinction in Butcher & Maudal, 1976) is available. A great deal has been written about the time-bound and self-limiting nature of crises, but research evidence for this is unclear. Halpern (1973, 1975) constructed a crisis scale consisting of 60 items from the MMPI. Factor analysis of these items suggest that there is a group of traits that characterizes all crises. There is some evidence (Gottschalk et al., 1967; Green et al., 1975) to indicate that crises are not necessarily one-time events that happen to people, but that some individuals have more crises than others.

The idea of "transitional pathology" affecting the individual in crisis has received only preliminary conceptual attention and little research inquiry. Dressler (1976) presented some survey data on the types of life events that led to emergency hospitalization in a series of patients. Interpersonal difficulties (arguments, insults, separation) were the precipitating stress in 75 percent of the cases. He reported that the actual event was often over-evaluated or distorted by the patient.

The actual processes by which various crisis interventions bring about desired individual changes have not received enough attention to enable an evaluation of them. It is not known whether they differ from other short-term therapeutic change processes.

In general, with the exception of a few studies, very little research effort has been directed toward examining the theoretical model underlying crisis intervention strategies. The lack of empirical justification has not, however, interfered with the rapid growth of clinical services in the field.

Time Limitation

Several writers have noted that the patient's awareness that therapeutic time is limited speeds up the therapeutic change process. Mann (1973) presents a view, based on clinical experience, that time limitation is an important aspect of the short-term contract in that when the full extent of the therapy is known in advance, the patient has an opportunity to work through the termination. The therapy has a beginning, a middle, and an end, and the patient and therapist, knowing this, will be able to deal with problems associated with each therapy phase.

Time limitation, itself, may be an important ingredient for producing change in short-term treatment. Frank (1959a) found out that there is some evidence that patients respond more promptly to treatment when they know in advance that the therapy is limited. Shlien, Mosak, and Dreikurs (1962) compared time-limited, client-centered therapy (18 sessions) with unlimited client-centered therapy (averaging 37 sessions), using the results of an 80-item self-ideal Q-sort. Results for patients in time-limited therapy were similar to patients in long-term therapy. For both groups, it was noted that improvement in therapy took place early in treatment and then reached a plateau. Wattie (1973) compared the relative effectiveness of a planned short-term therapy (eight sessions) to an unlimited service. Van der Veen family Q-sort ratings and therapist improvement ratings were used as criterion measures. The results indicated that the two approaches were equally effective.

There is some indication that regular sessions of at least 1 hour in duration is important for enhancing intense emotional experience. Bierenbaum et al. (1976) studied the relationship of length and frequency of brief psychotherapy sessions on emotional catharsis. They found that patients seen for weekly 1-hour sessions experienced more catharsis and reported more improvement than patients seen for ½-hour sessions twice weekly or patients seen for 2 hours every 2 weeks. They conclude that within a specific time frame, emotional catharsis can lead to certain positive outcomes in brief emotive therapy. However, patients receiving more frequent sessions, ½ hour per week, improved most on personality tests, regardless of the amount of emotional experience produced. Bierenbaum et al. (1976) suggest that the successful treatment occurring in this time frame was more supportive in nature rather than confrontive and more cathartic.

Muench and Schumacher (1968) studied time limitation on psychotherapy in a program of rotating therapists. They found that there were no significant differences between rotational therapy and normal time-limited psychotherapy on three psychodiagnostic instruments, the MMPI, the Mooney Problem Check List, and the Rotter Incomplete Sentence Test.

Roth et al. (1969) published a note on a time-limited therapy case that was conducted in one 10-hour session. They concluded that this approach maximizes the development of the therapeutic relationship and allows for a great deal of therapeutic interaction. Patient response was highly favorable to this approach.

Is there a unique contribution to therapeutic outcome that lies in the time constraints inherent in brief psychotherapy? Does the time limitation itself result in a process that differs from long-term therapy and produce relatively greater patient improvement in a telescoped time span? Many clinical theorists who expound the brief therapeutic attitude believe so. Brief therapy is not just abbreviated long-term therapy; it is a separate, unique treatment modality.

Research into the processes of brief psychotherapy resulting from the time constraints has not demonstrated an empirical foundation for these beliefs. Actually, the influence of time constraints on the attitudes of the patient, pace of the sessions, or relative effectiveness of the therapy has not been studied enough to generate even tentative conclusions. More research into the specific effects of time limitation is needed before the widely held clinical assumption can be supported.

There is some evidence to suggest that behaviorally oriented, short-term therapy may be better received as a brief therapeutic contact than more dynamic approaches. Sloane et al.'s (1975) 2-year follow-up study of patients who had been treated in either short-term analytic therapy or behavior therapy found that none of the behavior therapy patients complained of the brevity of treatment; however, four out of the nine psychotherapy failures complained about the briefness of treatment. They concluded that behavioral methods are probably better suited to brief treatment because even if it has not succeeded at 4 months, patients feel treatment has been given more of a fair trial and feel less frustrated when therapy is terminated.

Directiveness

The review of the clinical literature presented in an earlier section noted that one of the elements common to most brief psychotherapies is directiveness on the part of the therapist. Strupp (1973) pointed out that change in therapy is due, to a great extent, to skilled management or manipulation by the therapist in the context of an emotionally charged affectional relationship. He wrote that "There is no such thing as 'nonmanipulative' or 'nondirective' psychotherapy if one is seriously interested in personality and behavior change, except insofar as a 'good' relationship in and of itself exerts a palliative influence" (p. 7). However, therapists who follow different approaches differ in the amount of directiveness. Patterson, Levene, and Breger (1971) compared brief behavior therapy with brief analytic therapy in a program using inexperienced therapists. Semantic differential ratings containing 17 adjective pairs were obtained from the therapists at the end of the project. They found that behavior therapy was seen as more active, more directive, simpler, and faster than brief analytic therapy. Rusk and Gerner (1972) found that the therapists of "successful" patients talked for significatly less time in the first third and significatly more in the last third of the interview than therapists of unsuccessful cases.

Sloane et al. (1975) utilized the Lennard and Bernstein Scale to measure the degree of therapist control over the content of the therapeutic interaction. They found that behavior therapists exerted more control over the content of the therapy than analytic psychotherapists did. The psychotherapists used more comments designed to encourage the patient to follow a topic that the patient initiated. The psychotherapists initiated fewer new topics than behavior therapists. In this study, behavior therapists also prescribed more courses of action for the patient than the analytically oriented therapists did.

However, Sloane et al. (1975) reported that patients who had been seen in analytic therapy and behavior therapy at a 2-year follow-up felt that their therapy was important because their therapists (regardless of orientation) had given them encouragement, advice, and reassurance.

Regardless of therapeutic orientation, most brief therapists are directive in their approach to patients. This approach is adopted in order to make more efficient use of time and to keep the session content on track. In many instances, it is the therapeutic role that the patient, who seeks brief treatment, expects. The specific effects of therapist communications on patient behavior or on therapeutic outcome have not been widely studied. Future process research studies might profitably focus on delineation of various types of therapist communications and their power to influence patients' behavior. Some research along these lines is discussed in Chapter 4 by Strong.

Behavioral Practice

As important as the goal directedness of short-term psychotherapy is the therapists' frequent encouragement of the patients to change their behavior in order to alleviate their problem situation. Actively encouraging a patient to try out new roles, seek alternative behaviors, etc. is an important part of brief therapy, regardless of the therapeutic orientation of the therapist. This is important in order to enable patients to make changes in their present stress-producing situation and, more important, to help them develop confidence that they can master the problems that surround them.

Frank (1974) considers enhancement of the patient's sense of mastery or control over themselves and their situations to be one of the most important features of short-term treatment. He pointed out that "The therapist can heighten the beneficial effect of successes by praise and ameliorate the demoralizing effects of failures by indicating that they

have not reduced his respect for the patient." (p. 335)

A study by Liberman, Imber, Stone, Hoehn-Saric, and Frank (reported in Frank, 1974) showed that patients whose behavioral changes were resulting from their own efforts at mastery maintained their progress longer than patients whose changes in treatment were a function of placebo. Both conditions produced change initially. As noted above, patients who improved most in adjustment were those who showed "behavioral learning" and not just having insight (White, et al., 1969).

In the Sloane, et al. study (1975) comparing the effectiveness of short-term analytic versus behavior therapy, it was expected that patients would view the behavioral therapist as directive, and encouraging the patient to try out new behaviors. However, a somewhat unexpected result was found in the follow-up study with regard to the patient's view of the analytic therapist's behavior. The patient considered the psychotherapist's behavior of "encouraging him to practice facing the things that bother him" to be one of the most important things in the therapy.

Available research evidence supports the widely held view among brief therapists that concrete implementation of new roles or behaviors is an important and effective process in brief treatment approaches.

In this section we have reviewed research studies that focus on processes common to most brief psychotherapy approaches. It has been pointed out that many processes in brief therapy are similar enough to those in long-term therapy (e.g., transference, role of interpretation, and expectancy effects) that they might be studied more easily in short-term context. We noted, however, that there is a paucity of clear findings in many areas of process research in brief therapy despite the fact that this treatment modality lends itself particularly well to empirical research compared with other types of psychotherapy.

From the studies reviewed in this section, we arrived at several tentative conclusions that might serve as guides to further empirical research. We noted that "transference," although differing in nature from that described in long-term analytic therapy, is nevertheless an important element in brief psychotherapy. This appears to be the case even when the short-term therapeutic relationship in brief psychotherapy and the ways in which it is used to induce patient change have not been delineated.

Directive interpretation is an essential change-producing behavior for the therapist in brief therapy. A number of studies have focused on the effects of interpretation. However, a great deal more work needs to be done on the actual procedures of direct interpretation and their impact on the patient's feelings, attitudes, and subsequent behaviors.

Much has been written about the important effect that the expectation of receiving help has on therapeutic success. Although some controversy still exists about the power of expectancy, most investigators accept the view that the patient's pretherapy attitudes have an important bearing on the therapy itself. Further research spelling out the role of both positive and negative expectancy effects is recommended.

An important process in many brief therapy or crisis intervention contacts involves the patient's amenability to change under heightened emotional arousal. Research in this area has only begun to suggest the processes involved. Future research could profitably be directed toward specifying the kinds of situations, therapeutic operations, and so on, that are important to positive behavioral change under different emotional states.

Many brief therapists consider the time constraints imposed on the therapy to be an important factor in the therapy itself. The therapist and the patients in brief therapy, recognizing the time-bound nature of the treatment, work together to produce a change-oriented treatment environment that is a unique therapeutic modality. Research on the nature and effects of time limitation does not clearly support this view. More evidence is required before the clinical impression that time constraints themselves are an essential therapeutic ingredient is confirmed.

OUTCOME RESEARCH IN BRIEF PSYCHOTHERAPY

The outcome research literature on brief and crisis-oriented psychotherapy addresses three main questions: "Does brief psychotherapy result in pa-

tient improvement?" "How does the improvement produced by brief psychotherapy compare to that produced by long-term methods?" "Is one short-term approach superior to another?" Unfortunately, many studies fail to meet the qualifications for good outcome research discussed by Malan (1973), Luborsky et al. (1971), Fiske, Hunt, Luborsky, Orne, Parloff, Teiser, and Tuma (1970), and Meltzoff and Kornreich (1970). Thus, much of the published research does not unequivocally answer these questions.

Patient and Therapist Ratings of Outcome

Patient and therapist ratings of therapy outcome are noted to be biased sources of information on the outcome of psychotherapy. Therapists often report more positive change in patients than any other source (Frank, Gleidman, Imber, Stone, & Nash, 1959; Levene et al., 1972; Sloane et al., 1975). It would be unusual for outcome studies based on patient and therapist ratings to report negative findings, and positive reports are not particularly instructive. In spite of the obvious shortcomings of such a design, numerous studies attesting to the efficacy of short-term methods are of this type.

Most of these studies (Haskell, Pugatch, & McNair, 1969; Malan, 1973; Rosenbaum, Friedlander, & Kaplan, 1956; Sifneos, 1972; Stewart, 1972; Straker, 1966) report improvement in approximately 70 percent of the cases. Avnet (1965a and b) followed up a large group of patients and found that 81 percent of the patients and 76 percent of the therapists felt there had been some degree of improvement. Baxter and Beaulieu (1976) followed up 41 patients who had completed a short-term, outpatient therapy contract. The 23 patients who completed the follow-up material had significantly lower scores on all of the MMPI clinical scales and reported significantly less depression and anxiety. A high percentage of patients studied (79.1 percent) reported that they felt much better as compared to when they came for services.

Objective Measures of Outcome

Studies employing measures of outcome (standardized interview procedures, symptom ratings, observer ratings of improvement, objective tests, etc.) and employing untreated control groups for comparison are much more useful but are also more scarce. In general, these studies produce evidence suggestive of a high degree of improvement in treated as well as in minimal contact groups. (see Table 19-3.) The largest differential in status is seen immediately upon termination of therapy, when the treated groups are generally found to be significantly more improved than the untreated groups. These differences disappear on long-term follow-up.

Frank et al. (1959) treated patients in individual therapy, group therapy, or minimal contact therapy for 6 months. Therapists were psychiatric residents. Data gathered immediately after therapy ended indicated that 67 percent of the patients had improved and 30 percent were deteriorated in observer-rated social effectiveness. The short-term individual therapy patients improved significantly in social effectiveness from their pretherapy baseline, but the minimal contact and group therapy patients did not. All three groups showed a drop in self-rated discomfort, and all improved more than patients who dropped out of therapy during the first month. Continued negatively accelerated improvement was seen in all groups at the 5-year follow-up (Stone, Frank, Nash, & Imber, 1961). At this point, 97 percent of the patients were rated improved in social effectiveness, and there were no significant differences among any groups. The follow-up data were complicated by the patients' behavior after the period of formal short-term treatment had ended. Fully two-thirds remained in therapy for a year, and one-third were still in therapy at the end of 2 years. Thus, these data become less relevant with the increased time interval as a specific demonstration of the performance of brief therapy methods.

Sloane et al. (1975) report on the results of 4 months of psychotherapy (PT) or behavior therapy (BT) conducted by highly experienced therapists. Patients were typical "complex neurotics" who were matched on demographic variables and severity of symptoms but were otherwise randomly assigned to the treatment groups and to a minimal contact wait list (WL) group. At the posttherapy testing, all three groups had improved, as reflected in a decrease of rated target symptom severity, but the two treated groups had improved more than the WL group ($p < .01$). Decrease in anxiety was

noted in 53 percent WL, 66 percent BT, and 63 percent PT patients. Improvements in work adequacy (BT $p < .001$, PT and WL $p < .10$) and social adjustment (BT $p < .05$, WL $p < .01$) were also seen. Follow-ups at 1 year and 2 years were complicated by patients who were receiving further therapy. However, the total amount of additional therapy received by these patients still keeps them within the range of short-term therapy. Generally, improvement was seen to continue in treated as well as in the untreated group, with the WL group gradually approaching the BT and PT patients. However, since some WL patients also received psychotherapy, the results are unclear with respect to change during the follow-up period.

The conclusions of Frank et al. (1959) and Sloane et al. (1975) are remarkably similar, in spite of the fact that they were completed 16 years apart and one employed nationally known, experienced therapists while the other used psychiatric residents. Both report positive changes in the minimal contact group that are present at therapy termination but are generally significantly lower than those seen in the treated cases. Change continues in both treated and untreated groups and reaches about the same level at follow-up 1 to 5 years later. Frank et al. (1959) have suggested that these changes in the minimal contact group result from the positive expectations of change that can be engendered by even minute expressions of professional concern. Kellner and Sheffield (1971) performed a study that suggested that these positive expectations can lead to more symptom reduction than resulted from 6 hours of intense sessions involving drug-mediated abreaction and interpretative psychotherapy designed as "placebo" therapy.

Early reduction in the level of anxiety and depression in both treated and untreated groups is seen in both Sloane et al. (1975) and Frank et al. (1959) and is also reported by Haskell et al. (1969). The reduction of discomfort is greatest in the treated groups, but is significant in the minimal contact group as well. Changes in somatic distress, work adequacy, and social adjustment seem to develop more slowly.

Bergin and Suinn (1975) conclude that the results of the Sloane et al. (1975) study suggest that the main effect psychotherapy is to accelerate change instead of to produce change that would

TABLE 19-3   Outcome studies of brief and crisis-oriented therapies

A. Therapist- or patient-rated outcome

    1. Avnet (65) — Follow-up of Group Health subscribers showed that 81 percent of 801 patients and 76 percent of 740 therapists saw "some improvement" after brief therapy

    2. Baxter & Beaulieu (76) — Self-ratings of 41 patients indicated that 79.1 percent felt they were improved

    3. Haskell et al. (69) — Psychiatric residents rated 71 percent of 43 patients "slightly improved" or more after brief therapy

    4. Malan (63) — Positive outcome was reported in 21 cases treated with focal therapy by experienced therapists

    5. Rosenbaum et al. (56)

    6. Sifneos (72) — Therapist rated improvement was found in 58 to 91 percent of 21 patients on various outcome criteria

    7. Stewart (72) — Therapists rated 80 percent of 20 patients improved

    8. Straker (66)

B. Outcome studies utilizing objective criteria

    1. Frank et al. (59)
       Imber et al (58)
       Stone et al. (61) — Short-term treatment was found to be significantly more effective than group or minimal contact treatment in increasing social effectiveness but not in reducing discomfort. No significant differences between treated and untreated groups were seen at 5-year follow-up

    2. Sloane et al. (75)
       Sloane et al. (76)
       Staples et al. (76) — Significant differences between treated patients and wait list controls existed at therapy termination on various outcome criteria. Differences were smaller and becoming nonsignificant by 1-year follow-up

C. Long-term versus short-term treatment

    1. Henry and Shlien (58)
       Shlien (57)
       Shlien et al. (62)
       Shlien (64) — Patients treated for 37 sessions and 18 sessions showed equivalent improvement. Both showed more improvement than no contact and minimal contact controls

    2. Muench (65) — Patients in two short-term treatments (3 to 7 sessions and 8 to 19 sessions) improved more than those in long-term treatment (20+ interviews)

TABLE 19.3 *(continued)*

3. Pascal and Zax (56)	Brief psychotherapy, supportive therapy, and "ideal" long-term therapy were found to produce equivalent results
D. Comparative outcome studies	
1. Argyle et al. (74)	
2. Levene et al. (72) Patterson et al. (71)	Patients treated with behavioral techniques rated themselves more improved than those receiving four other approaches, but therapist and observer ratings or outcome were equivalent for all approaches
3. Moleski and Tosi (76)	Rational procedures were found superior to traditional psychotherapy in reducing stuttering
4. Nichols (74) Nichols and Reifler (73)	Brief psychotherapy produced greater decrease in MMPI elevation than cathartic techniques
5. Nigl (76)	
6. Paul (66, 67)	Desensitization was more effective than insight-oriented or placebo treatment in reducing public speaking anxiety in college students
7. Rockwell et al. (76	
8. Sloane et al. (75, 76)	Brief dynamic or brief behavioral therapy was applied to complex neurotics by highly experienced therapists. The few significant differences that emerged favored behavior therapy
E. Crisis therapy outcome	
1. Berzins et al. (72)	Brief crisis-oriented therapy outcome was not related to the A-B therapist dimension
2. Gottschalk et al. (67)	Crisis treatment by psychiatric residents resulted in 85 percent improved, 8 percent deteriorated on the psychiatric morbidity scale. Treatment dropouts were used as controls
3. Gottschalk et al. (73)	Patients treated an average of 2.7 sessions in crisis therapy failed to demonstrate greater gains than a minimal contact group

TABLE 19.3 *(continued)*

4. Green et al. (75)	Immediate follow-up of 77 crisis patients indicated 78.8 percent improved and 15.6 percent worse
5. Maris and Connor (73)	One-year follow-up of 99 patients seen in crisis therapy indicated 60 percent were improved
6. Williams (76)	Crisis intervention failed to reduce the number of physical problems among treated relatives of a sudden death victim as compared to untreated relatives
F. Brief behavioral therapy	
1. Crowe et al. (72)	No significant differences on a symptom rating scale were found among desensitization, implosion, and shaping treatments of phobic patients. Untreated phobics were controls
2. Hogan (66, 67) Levis and Carrera (67)	Implosive therapy was reported effective as a short-term treatment of phobias in psychotics and outpatients
3. Mitchell and Orr (74) Richardson and Suinn (74)	Standard and short-term massed desensitization were found equally effective in reducing heterosexual anxiety
4. Zitrin et al. (76)	

not occur without therapy. Thus, psychotherapy may spare patients months of considerable pain and suffering. The results of these studies have also been interpreted as suggesting that the most significant determinants of change lie not in the therapeutic relationship or in the therapeutic techniques, but in the patient. Stone et al. (1961) conclude that therapeutic success depends on the patient's ability to communicate difficulties to the therapist. Gottschalk, Fox, and Bates (1973) feel that the *patient's* past history of interactions and current ability to form close human relationships may be the significant determinants of outcome.

Long-term Versus Short-term Psychotherapy

Shlien (1957), Henry and Shlien (1958), Shlien, Mosak, and Dreikurs (1962), and Shlien (1964) studied the effects of time limits on Adlerian and client-centered therapy outcome. All therapy was conducted by experienced therapists. At follow-up the self-ideal correlations on the Butler-Haigh Q-sort for patients treated by time-unlimited client-centered, time-limited client-centered, and time-limited Adlerian therapy were all significantly different ($p < .01$) from the no-contact "normals" and the minimal contact group. There were no significant differences among any of the treated groups. Shlien et al. (1962) concluded that the time-limited methodology is not only as *effective* as unlimited therapy, but is also twice as *efficient*.

Muench (1965) reported a similar study of counseling center clients treated by experienced therapists. Unfortunately, the outcome measures employed in this study make it difficult to compare it with previous results. Muench's findings are generally supportive of Shlien et al. (1962). Pascal and Zax (1956) reported that "ideal" long-term treatment, brief supportive therapy, and environmental manipulation were not significantly different from each other in the level of change produced.

Luborsky, Singer, and Luborsky (1975) reviewed a number of studies comparing the results obtained by long-term and short-term methods and concluded that:

> *Since Otto Rank, treatments that are structured at the outset as time-limited have been thought by some practitioners to be as good as the more usual time-unlimited treatment. The eight available controlled comparative studies are mostly (five out of eight) consistent with this view in that there is no significant difference between the two. (p. 1001)*

In the research studies that are available, only one study (Henry and Shlien, 1958) showed short-term treatment less effective then time-unlimited treatment. Thus, in addition to being more efficient in terms of professional time required, brief therapy appears to be as effective with respect to measurable results.

A further group of studies that purport to relate to the efficacy of brief therapy methods are mainly from the 1950s and early 1960s. These studies correlated the amount of change seen in a patient to the number of sessions of therapy he or she had received [e.g., Getter & Sundland (1962); Graham (1958); Lorr, McNair, Michaux, & Raskin (1964)]. Luborsky et al. (1971) summarized these findings.

> *In 20 of 22 studies of essentially time unlimited treatment the length of treatment was positively related to outcome; the longer the duration of treatment or the more sessions, the better the outcome! It is tempting to conclude—and it may*

> *be an accurate conclusion—that if psychotherapy is a good thing, the more the better. Other interpretations however, may also fit: a) Patients who are getting what they need stay, those who are not drop out sooner. b) Therapists may overestimate positive change in patients who have been in therapy longer. A complementary trend may also operate— therapists often assume some minimal number of sessions are needed before real change can occur, so that early dropouts tend to get poor outcome ratings. (p. 154)*

The interpretation provided by Luborsky et al. is a sound one. Garfield, Prager, and Bergin (1971) found that length of therapy was significantly associated with ratings of change by clients, therapists, and supervisors. However, length of therapy was not correlated with other outcome measures, such as self-report inventories given before and after therapy.

The studies reviewed by Luborsky et al. (1971) utilized time-unlimited therapeutic techniques that differ in critical aspects of activity, directiveness, focus, type of interpretation, and the like, from brief methods. For example, initial history taking in unlimited therapy may require several sessions. It is an unfair comparison to conclude that a patient who drops out after three history-taking sessions preliminary to long-term therapy has received "brief psychotherapy." Parad and Parad (1968) pointed out the difference between planned and unplanned short-term therapy. The only justified comparison is between long-term therapy and planned short-term therapy utilizing methods found to be most successful under time constraints. Thus, this group of studies is not directly relevant to the question of the relative efficacy of brief and long-term psychotherapy. In a further study (Levene et al., 1972) the outcome of psychoanalytic brief therapy, brief behavioral therapy, brief Jungian therapy, brief group therapy, and an intake control group were compared. Therapists were inexperienced at therapy. Outcome was rated by student, patient, and a telephone interviewer at a 12-month follow-up. No differences in global outcome rating were found among the approaches. The global statement of "improved" or "unimproved" on the official record showed that approximately 50 percent of the patients in brief therapy improved, while 41 percent of the minimal contact control sample were rated improved.

Weitz, Abramowitz, Steger, Calabria, Conable, and Yarus (1975) related the number of sessions of psychotherapy to client-rated improvement in areas such as specific problems, grades, decision making, and self-respect. Of those attending two to five sessions, 45.7 percent felt they had been helped on a specific problem, 28.6 percent had improved decision making, and 25.7 percent felt they had enhanced self-respect. The comparable figures among the long-term group (20+ sessions) were 70.7 percent, 46.6 percent, and 50.0 percent. There were some suggestions of a "failure zone" between sessions 6 to 10 during which time clients showed less improvement in self-esteem than did clients who dropped out of therapy in two to five sessions. However, this study is subject to many of the criticisms cited above.

Comparative Outcome Studies

Six recent studies have examined the comparative outcome of different approaches to brief psychotherapy (DiLoreto, 1971; Levene, Breger, & Patterson, 1972; Nichols and Reifler 1973; Nichols, 1974; Patterson et al., 1971; Paul, 1966, 1967; Sloane et al., 1975, 1976). Patterson et al. (1971) compared behavior therapy with short-term therapy using inexperienced therapists. They did not include a no-treatment control group. They found that unselected patients in brief behavior therapy, treated by inexperienced therapists, rate themselves more improved immediately following therapy than patients treated in brief psychotherapy. Ratings by therapists and independent judges show differences in the same direction, but at borderline significance. The authors point out that brief behavior therapy may be learned more readily than brief psychotherapy.

The Sloane et al. (1975) study pitted three psychodynamically oriented therapists against three behavioral therapists. All therapists were highly experienced. Outcome measures included the Structured and Scaled Interview to Assess Maladjustment (SSIAM), global ratings of improvement, patient and therapist ratings of improvement, anxiety and depression ratings, ratings of target symptom severity (an idiographic measure), and objective inventories. All ratings were made by persons who did not know what type of treatment a patient had received. The results indicated few significant differences between the approaches. All the significant results, however, favored behavior therapy. For example, at 4 months patients treated by behavior therapy were rated significantly improved in work adjustment, social adequacy, and target symptoms. The patients treated by psychotherapy were improved on target symptoms and work adjustment ($p < .10$) only. At the 1-year follow-up, behavior therapy patients were rated significantly lower in target symptom severity than psychotherapy patients ($p < .05$). Sloane et al. (1975) concluded that behavior therapy seems to produce change slightly sooner and produces more focused change.

Paul (1966, 1967) also compared behavior therapy to psychotherapy in a widely cited study. It is of less relevance here because the subjects were college students with public speaking anxiety who were recruits, not volunteer help seekers. Nevertheless, as an analogue study, it was carefully designed and well executed. The results are suggestive of superiority of behavioral methods, but many critics feel that this reflects the narrow type of problem with which Paul worked.

DiLoreto (1971) compared systematic desensitization, Ellis' rational therapy, and Roger's client-centered therapy. However, he utilized inexperienced graduate student therapists and provided the treatment in groups. Thus, the findings, although supportive of the Sloane et al. (1975) study, are not directly generalizable. Nichols and Reifler (1973) and Nichols (1974) compared brief cathartic therapy and traditional insight-oriented dynamic psychotherapy. Experienced therapists were especially trained in the emotive style of psychotherapy and, in the study, the same therapists offered treatment to both cathartic and traditional groups. The traditional group was the only one to show significant reduction in pathology on the MMPI ($p < .05$), which was the only standard outcome measure employed. Moleski and Tosi (1976) compared the relative effectiveness of Ellis' rational therapy and systematic desensitization in the treatment of stuttering. After eight treatment sessions, the patients in rational therapy showed more improvement than patients in systematic desensitization. Both treated groups showed fewer disfluencies than an untreated control group.

Overall, there is little support for a statement of significant superiority for any of the diverse approaches to brief psychotherapy examined to date. Studies comparing the effectiveness of different brief treatment approaches have not produced unambiguous results. In some instances relatively inexperienced therapists have been used, and in others the techniques have been applied in nonclinical situations (volunteer college students). Thus, methodological limitations do not allow stable conclusions at this point. It will be important for future research to incorporate more sound features into the research design and include experimental replication of studies in order to obtain a clearer picture of the relative effectiveness of the different methods as applied to clearly defined populations.

Outcome of Crisis-Oriented Psychotherapy

A serious methodological problem in outcome studies of crisis intervention is the mobility of the population resulting in loss of sample. Lowry, Wintrob, Borwick, Garmaise, and King (1971) reported that nearly half of their follow-up sample could not be fully interviewed because they died, moved, or had given false names. Preliminary indications suggested that this unreachable group contained more physically ill people, more alcoholics, and more people in trouble with the police.

A second factor adversely influencing sound outcome research in crisis therapy is the difficulty of sample specification. Crisis intervention techniques are recommended for any client in crisis, regardless of his or her typical adjustment and situational pressures. Such heterogeneity, unless fully described, causes problems in comparing studies. For example, Jacobson et al. (1965) reported diagnostic impressions of 721 patients who visited Benjamin Rush Center between 1962 and 1963. Their population included 16.5 percent transient situational disorders, 28.2 percent personality disorders, 31.6 percent psychoneurotic disorders, 18.7 percent psychotic disorders, and 5 percent others

(brain disorders, mental retardation, etc.). Clearly, this is a more disturbed population than that seen in many other forms of psychotherapy.

Gottschalk, Mayerson, and Gottleib (1967) reported two examinations of the effectiveness of emergency psychotherapy in the treatment of acutely disturbed psychiatric patients. Patients were treated by psychiatric residents. Assessment was carried out by a separate evaluation team. For the treated group who completed therapy, 85 percent showed definite improvement (greater than a one-point reduction in their rating on a five-point psychiatric morbidity scale). No change was seen in 9 percent and 6 percent became worse. Data on dropout patients were presented as a comparison group: 57 percent improved, 14 percent showed no change, and 29 percent became worse. Follow-up 3 to 7 months later indicated that 81 percent of the treated patients were still improved, 16 percent were the same as their initial assessment, and 3 percent were worse, as compared to 40 percent improved, 40 percent unchanged, and 20 percent worse among dropouts.

A second study (Gottschalk et al., 1973) involved patients randomly assigned to immediate intervention or to a wait list group. Ratings were made by a research team. The treated patients received an average of 2.7 sessions over a 6-week period in addition to two evaluation sessions that both the treated and untreated groups received. The psychiatric morbidity rating was most predictive of outcome. Patients initially rated high in severity of symptoms improved the least. However, no significant differences in amount of improvement were seen between the treated and untreated groups. One wonders whether the differential in amount of professional contact given the experimental versus the control group was great enough to reveal any differences, or if the two evaluation sessions had some effect on the untreated group.

Maris and Connor (1973) evaluated the efficacy of a crisis service. Two hundred consecutive patients were tested and treated. One year later, 99 of the 200 patients responded to a request to come for a follow-up interview. "Getting better" was defined as receiving a higher score on the self-esteem bar and a lower score on a depression scale. By these criteria, 60 percent of the patients were improved. One-third were found to have received some form of psychotherapy during the year's time. At follow-up the percentage of patients reporting "no chief complaints" was 19 percent up from the initial 2 percent ($p < .0001$). The percentage of patients reporting "no major problems in the last week" was 42 percent up from 3 percent ($p < .0001$). Maris and Connor also reported what they labeled "some disturbing changes." The number of patients reporting "unusual fears" doubled (6 to 12 percent) and financial problems were listed as major by an additional 8 percent (up from 2 percent). Overall, 23 categories were examined. Thirteen of these showed a 5 percent or greater change from initial evaluation to follow-up. Of these changes, eight were in the direction of less reported symptoms at follow-up and five were in the direction of greater symptoms. Maris and Connor concluded that crisis intervention may "exchange one set of symptoms for another" (p. 319). This conclusion seems tenuous in the absence of appropriate statistics indicating to what extent these observed symptom increases reflect sampling fluctuation. However, these phenomena certainly warrant further study.

Berzins, Ross, and Friedman (1972) studied outcome of brief therapy in a crisis-oriented therapy situation and found that outcome as reported by patient evaluation was not associated with therapist being either an A-type or B-type therapist.

Green, Gleser, Stone, and Seifert (1975) presented extensive data on the interrelations of diverse measures of crisis intervention outcome and concluded that symptom relief rating is the most appropriate. The patients were 77 outpatients who were experiencing acute stress reactions; they were chosen for participation in brief crisis-oriented psychotherapy for six sessions or less. Therapists were second- and third-year residents. Patients were evaluated by a research team. Immediately after the course of therapy, an average of 78.8 percent were improved, 5.6 percent were unchanged, and 15.6 percent were worse on a self-rating symptom checklist. On the Hamilton Depression Rating Scale filled out by the observer, 76 percent were improved, 14 percent unchanged, and 10 percent were worse. This rater also filed out the Psychiatric Evaluation Form, which indicated that 58 percent of the patients had improved, 36

percent were unchanged, and 6 percent were worse. Global ratings of improvement made by the therapist indicated that 95 percent of the patients had improved. However, only 74 percent of the patients rated themselves as changed. Some patients actually reported more and more severe symptoms after therapy.

The data of several studies suggest a deterioration among patients of crisis services (Gottschalk et al., 1967; Green et al., 1975). Deterioration has also been noted among patients receiving brief psychotherapy (Frank et al., 1959), but Sloane et al. (1975) found none in their brief therapy patients. The major difference between studies finding deterioration and those not reporting it was experience level of therapists.

Deterioration or negative effects from psychotherapy have been receiving a great deal of attention recently. Bergin (1963, 1971), Hadley and Strupp (1976), and Strupp, Hadley, and Gomes-Schwartz (1977) have pointed out the importance of evaluating negative outcomes in psychotherapy. Iatrogenic factors may be a particularly important element in brief psychotherapy. The relatively more direct involvement of the therapist may make brief therapy particularly vulnerable to therapeutically induced negative change. It has been widely noted that the success of brief therapy depends on the experience level of the therapist. When inexperienced or unqualified therapists utilize brief therapy techniques, there may be a greater likelihood that negative or unwanted patient reactions will result. The relatively fast pace and the need for prompt therapist intervention may result in premature or incorrect "therapeutic" action. The important area of patient and situational assessment may not receive the required attention under the imposed time pressures of brief therapy. Another factor that deserves further consideration and research is the fact that the brevity of the intervention and the difficulty or lack of follow-up may not provide the therapist with sufficient time to observe the effects (either positive or negative) of the interventions. This potential problem highlights the importance of therapeutic follow-up of brief psychotherapy.

Outcome research in crisis-oriented psychotherapy is one of the most difficult undertakings. The patients receiving treatment in crisis settings are extremely heterogeneous and defy classification into neat research designs. In addition, this population as a whole tends to be quite transient and difficult to locate in follow-up. Consequently, the research literature is scarce and generally flawed. Studies of outcome of crisis intervention therapy, of course, also suffer from the same problem inherent in other outcome studies (e.g., differential results depending on the type of patients used and outcome measures employed).

Outcome of Brief Behavioral Therapy
Several papers offer data on the outcome of behavioral techniques (Bergin & Suinn, 1975; Lazarus, 1971; Wolpe & Lazarus, 1966), and this research is covered elsewhere in this book. Several behavioral therapists have specifically examined procedures with potential for producing gains in short periods of time. The most notable are the therapists who are exploring implosive therapy (Hogan, 1967; Levis & Carrera, 1967) and short-term, massed desensitization (Mitchell & Orr, 1974; Richardson & Suinn, 1974). Mitchell and Orr (1974) were unable to demonstrate significant differences between standard desensitization (two 90-minute relaxation sessions and four desensitization sessions) and short-term, massed desensitization (two 90-minute relaxation sessions and two desensitization sessions). Both procedures were reported "effective" in reducing heterosexual anxiety. None of these studies have tackled the important question of the performance of specific behavioral techniques in standard clinical situations.

Crowe, Marks, Agras, and Leitenberg (1972) attempted to examine the comparative effects of desensitization, implosion, and shaping on 14 clinic patients with phobias. Each patient had a main phobia and minor ones. The minor phobias, were untreated and served as a control against which to evaluate progress on the treated phobia. Treatment was administered by one experienced therapist, and evaluation was done by an independent rater. Each subject received all three procedures in a randomized order with a rest period in between. All treatment courses were four sessions long. Regardless of the type of treatment, the third treatment was always less effective and the second treatment most effective. No significant differences were found among the procedures on the

symptom rating scales. Desensitization was found to be ineffective on in vivo tests of phobia mastery, but it resulted in more improvement of the untreated control phobia than the focal phobia. Crowe et al. suggest that the treatment duration used here is too brief for maximum effectiveness of desensitization.

SUMMARY AND CONCLUSIONS

Many psychotherapeutic contacts, whether by plan or by premature termination, are brief, lasting less than eight sessions. In recent years, partly because of situational emergencies and partly because of design, brief psychotherapy has become a treatment of choice. Short-term therapies have been developed to deal with focal problem types or with specific patient populations. Comparative studies of brief and unlimited therapies show essentially no differences in results. Consequently, brief therapy results in a great saving of available clinical time and can reach more people in need of treatment. It is quite likely that brief therapies will be more widely utilized in the future if government health plans and private insurance companies cover the costs of psychotherapy. Such insurance coverage would likely be limited to relatively few sessions; this falls within the "short-term range."

We examined a number of short-term therapeutic approaches and noted that they could be classified into three broad orientations: psychoanalytic, behavioral, and crisis intervention therapy. A great deal has been written about these brief treatment approaches. In this review, we noted that despite somewhat different theoretical assumptions and treatment strategies, there are several technical characteristics that most brief treatments have in common. Among these are:

1. Management of temporal limitation therapeutically.

2. Limitation of therapeutic goals.

3. Centering the therapeutic content in the present.

4. Directive management of the sessions by the therapist.

5. Rapid, early assessment.

6. Flexibility on the part of the therapist (effectiveness often calls for more experienced therapist).

7. Promptness of intervention, since there may not be a next session.

8. Ventilation or catharsis, an important part of most approaches.

9. A quickly established interpersonal relationship from which to obtain therapeutic leverage.

10. Appropriate selection of patients, since not all patients can profit from a brief therapeutic contact.

The process variables that are important to short-term therapy were reviewed. In this section, more attention was paid to the empirical research literature than to the clinical domain in order to ascertain what scientific basis has been established for the processes that we "know" clinically are important to bringing about behavioral change in patients. We found, as so many others before us, that hard facts are scarce, largely because such processes are exceedingly difficult to carve up into objectively measurable quantities. The published literature is scarce and often inconclusive on these issues.

The importance of the therapeutic relationship in short-term treatment has been studied. Even in behaviorally oriented approaches, where the relationship has been minimized, "transference" or some focus on the patient-therapist relationship has been shown to be an important variable. Although the quality of the therapeutic relationship is considered by many to be the major determinant in therapeutic change, the operations through which this is brought about have not been objectively delineated.

Most short-term therapies place a great emphasis on interpretation—usually directive in nature. The effectiveness of directive interpretation such as confrontation or advice giving has not been clearly demonstrated. Since brief psychotherapies rely on directiveness and activity on the part of the therapist to keep sessions moving at a productive pace, it behooves psychotherapy researchers to demonstrate that therapist activity and directiveness are superior technical operations to more "passive" therapeutic approaches.

The role of "expectation of receiving help" has received a great deal of attention in short-term therapy research. Substantial evidence suggests that the patient's expectation of receiving help is an important factor in therapeutic gain. However, it is clear that psychotherapy researchers cannot rest with the feeling that the task is complete. Expectancy is simply another variable to study, not an explanatory concept. More clearly focused studies on expectancy effects need to be conducted to clarify the role that patient (and therapist) expectation has on therapeutic outcome.

An interesting line of research that may have particular bearing on brief and crisis-oriented therapies involves attitude change under conditions of heightened emotional arousal. Many patients in brief treatment settings are in crisis or are experiencing a heightened emotional state due to the confrontive or directive nature of the interview. Research designs that take these factors into account might be utilized to throw additional light on this variable. To date, however, crisis intervention research has focused more on descriptive surveys than on important processes involved in the treatment itself.

The role of time limitation and the uses to which temporal awareness is put is thought to be important in brief psychotherapy. Research studies have pointed to the importance of time limitation in brief therapy for keeping the patient tuned in to the need for rapid goal attainment. The effectiveness of time limitation over unlimited therapy for bringing about change has not been clearly shown in research. We believe that there is a lower limit on the amount of time a therapist can spend with a patient and demonstrate any therapeutic gain at all. Some theorists in the crisis intervention area suggest that one or two sessions may be profitable. However, time limitation has not been studied sufficiently as a variable itself to allow firm conclusions on the relationship of time allocation to therapeutic gain.

The research on outcome of brief psychotherapy has been plagued with difficulty. The inclusion of "real" control groups in empirical studies has not been resolved in any of the studies reported. Most outcome studies that have reported substantial improvement rates may still be considered to be a replication of the Hawthorne effect—demonstrating that almost anything done to a patient results in measured improvement, as long as the patient knows you are thinking of and checking on him or her every so often. Comparisons of various psychological treatments may now be the only ethical way to approach controlled investigations.

The outcome research literature on brief and emergency-oriented therapies suggests that these techniques produce positive change. Behavioral techniques seem to produce change fastest, but they can be ineffective and unacceptable to patients over very brief durations. Patients followed up over very long time periods tend to show gradual improvement for several years after treatment. The major value of brief psychotherapy may be that it helps to accelerate positive change in the patient. There is evidence that short-term or crisis-oriented therapies may produce psychological deterioration in the patient, especially where inexperienced therapists are employed.

One of the main problems with the existing outcome studies involves the failure to utilize clear control groups and not specifying the actual procedures used in brief therapy or crisis intervention. In addition to being a clearly viable clinical treatment option, short-term psychotherapy has been shown to have value as a long-term therapy analogue and as a format for studying, with some precision, the effectiveness of specific intervention techniques on specific problems. The similarity of many psychotherapeutic processes and some encouraging outcome studies suggest that research on brief psychotherapy may throw light on psychotherapy generally. We are impressed with the need for more sophisticated research designs and more attention to rigor through clearer specification of techniques in future studies. We believe that research on brief treatments holds an important key to the study of process and outcome in psychotherapy.

REFERENCES

Adler, K. A. Techniques that shorten psychotherapy illustrated with five cases. *Journal of Individual Psychology*, 1972, *28*, 155–168.

Aldrich, C. K. Brief psychotherapy: A reappraisal of some theoretical assumptions. *American Journal of Psychiatry*, 1968, *125*, 585–592.

Alexander, F., & French, T. M. *Psychoanalytic therapy: Principles and applications*. New York: Ronald Press, 1946.

Ansbacher, H. L. Adlerian psychology: The tradition of brief psychotherapy. *Journal of Individual Psychology*, 1972, *28*, 137–151.

Appelbaum, S. A. Parkinson's law in psychotherapy. *International Journal of Psychoanalytic Psychotherapy*, 1975, *4*, 426–436.

Argyle, M., Bryant, B., & Trower, P. Social skills training and psychotherapy: A comparative study. *Psychological Medicine*, 1974, *4* (4), 435–443.

Auerbach, S. M., & Kilmann, P. R. Crisis intervention: A review of outcome research. *Psychological Bulletin*, 1977, *84*, 1189–1217.

Avnet, H. H. How effective is short-term therapy. In L. R. Wolberg (Ed.), *Short-term psychotherapy*. New York: Grune and Stratton, 1965a.

Avnet, H. H. Short-term treatment under auspices of a medical insurance plan. *American Journal of Psychiatry*, 1965b, *122*, 147–151.

Baker, E. Brief psychotherapy. *Journal of the Medical Society of New Jersey*, 1947, *44*, 260–261.

Balint, M., Ornstein, P., & Balint, E. *Focal psychotherapy*. London: Tavistock Publications, 1972.

Barten, H. H. The 15-minute hour: Brief therapy in a military setting. *American Journal of Psychiatry*, 1965, *122*, 565–567.

Barten, H. H. The coming of age of the brief psychotherapies. In L. Bellack and H. H. Barten (Eds.), *Progress in community mental health*. Vol. I. New York: Grune and Stratton, 1969.

Barten, H. H. *Brief therapies*. New York: Behavioral Publications, 1971.

Barten, H. H. Comment on "Adlerian psychology: The tradition of brief psychotherapy." *Journal of Individual Psychology*, 1972, *28*, 152–153.

Baum, O. E., & Felzer, S. B. Activity in initial interviews with lower-class patients. *Archives of General Psychiatry*, 1964, *10*, 345–353.

Baxter, J. W., & Beaulieu, D. E. Impact of short-term, individual psychotherapy: looking for change. Unpublished manuscript, 1976.

Bellak, L. A general hospital as a focus of community psychiatry. A trouble shooting clinic combines important functions as part of hospital's service. *Journal of the American Medical Association*, 1960, *174*, 2214–2217.

Bellak, L., & Small, L. *Emergency psychotherapy and brief psychotherapy*. New York: Grune and Stratton, 1965.

Bergin, A. E. The effects of psychotherapy: Negative results revisited. *Journal of Counseling Psychology*, 1963, *10*, 244–250.

Bergin, A. E. The evaluation of therapeutic outcomes. In A. E. Bergin and S. L. Garfield (Eds.), *Handbook of psychotherapy and behavior change*. New York: John Wiley, 1971.

Bergin, A. E., & Strupp, H. H. *Changing frontiers in the science of psychotherapy*. Chicago: Aldine, 1972.

Bergin, A. E., & Suinn, R. M. Individual psychotherapy

and behavior therapy. *Annual Review of Psychology*, 1975, *26*, 509–555.

Berliner, B. Short psychoanalytic psychotherapy: Its possibilities and its limitations. *Bulletin of the Menninger Clinic*, 1941, *5*, 204.

Berzins, J. I., Ross, W. F., & Friedman, W. H. A-B therapist distinction, patient diagnosis, and outcome of brief psychotherapy in a college clinic. *Journal of Consulting and Clinical Psychology*, 1972, *38*, 231–237.

Bierenbaum, H., Nichols, M. P., & Schwartz, A. J. Effects of varying session length and frequency in brief emotive psychotherapy. *Journal of Consulting and Clinical Psychology*, 1976, *44*, 790–798.

Bonime, W. Some principles of brief psychotherapy. *Psychiatric Quarterly*, 1953, *27*, 1–18.

Bonstedt, T. Crisis intervention or early access brief therapy? *Diseases of the Nervous System*, 1970, *31*, 783–787.

Buda, B. Utilization of resistance and paradox communication in short-term psychotherapy. *Psychotherapy and Psychosomatics*, 1972, *20*, 200–211.

Burdon, A. P. Principles of brief psychotherapy. *Journal of the Louisiana Medical Society*, 1963, *115*, 374–378.

Butcher, J. N., & Maudal, G. R. Crisis intervention. In I. B. Weiner (Ed.), *Clinical methods in psychology*. New York: John Wiley, 1976.

Caplan, G. *An approach to community mental health*. New York: Grune and Stratton, 1961.

Caplan, G. *Principles of preventive psychiatry*. New York: Basic Books, 1964.

Castelnuovo-Tedesco, P. Brief psychotherapeutic treatment of depressive reactions. In G. J. Wayne and R. R. Koegler (Eds.), *Emergency psychiatry and brief therapy*. Boston: Little, Brown, 1966.

Cattell, J. P., MacKinnon, R. A., & Forster, E. Limited goal therapy in a psychiatric clinic. *American Journal of Psychiatry*, 1963, *120*, 255–260.

Coleman, M. D. Methods of psychotherapy: Emergency psychotherapy. In J. H. Masserman and J. L. Moreno (Eds.), *Progress in psychotherapy*. New York: Grune and Stratton, 1960.

Coleman, M. D., & Zwerling, I. The psychiatric emergency clinic: A flexible way of meeting community mental health needs. *American Journal of Psychiatry*, 1959, *115*, 980–984.

Crowe, M. J., Marks, L. M., Agras, S. W., & Leitenberg, H. Time-limited desensitization, implosion and shaping for phobic patients. *Behaviour Research and Therapy*, 1972, *10*, 319–328.

Deutsch, F. *Applied psychoanalysis: Selected lectures on psychotherapy*. New York: Grune and Stratton, 1949.

DiLoreto, A. O. *Comparative psychotherapy: An experimental analysis*. Chicago: Aldine-Atherton, 1971.

Dodd, J. A retrospective analysis of variables related to duration of treatment in a university psychiatric clinic. *Journal of Nervous and Mental Disease*, 1970, *151*, 75–84.

Dressler, D. M. Life stress and emotional crisis: The idiosyncratic interpretation of life events. *Comprehensive Psychiatry*, 1976, *17*, 549–568.

Erlich, R. E., & Phillips, P. B. Short-term psychotherapy of the aviator. *Aerospace Medicine*, 1963, *43*, 1046–1047.

Errera, P., McKee, B., Smith, D. C., & Gruber, R. Length of psychotherapy. *Archives of General Psychiatry*, 1967, *17*, 454–458.

Fenichel, O. Brief psychotherapy. In H. Fenichel and D. Rapaport (Eds.), *The collected papers of Otto Fenichel*. New York: W. W. Norton, 1954.

Ferenczi, S. *Further contribution to the theory and technique of psychoanalysis*. 1920 (Trans. J. Suttie). London: Hogarth, 1950.

Ferenczi, S. (Ed.) The further development of an active therapy in psychoanalysis. In *Further contribution to the theory and techniques of psychoanalysis*. New York: Basic Books, 1951.

Fiske, D. W., Hunt, H. F., Luborsky, L., Orne, M. T., Parloff, M. B., Reiser, M. F., & Tuma, A. H. The planning of research on effectiveness of psychotherapy. *Archives of General Psychiatry*, 1970, *22*, 22–32.

Frank, J. D. The dynamics of the psychotherapeutic relationship. *Psychiatry*, 1959a, *22*, 17–39.

Frank, J. D. Problems of controls in psychotherapy as exemplified by the Psychotherapy Research Project of the Phipps Psychiatric Clinic. In E. A. Rubinstein and M. B. Parloff (Eds.), *Research in psychotherapy*, Vol. II, 10–26. Washington, D.C.: American Psychological Association, 1959b.

Frank, J. D. Treatment of the focal symptom: An adaptional approach. *American Journal of Psychotherapy*, 1966, *20*, 564–575.

Frank, J. D. Therapeutic components of psychotherapy: A 25-year progress report of research. *Journal of Nervous and Mental Disease*, 1974, *159*, 325–342.

Frank, J. D., Gliedman, L. H., Imber, S. D., Nash, E. H., & Stone, A. R. Why patients leave psychotherapy. *Archives of Neurological Psychiatry*, 1957, *77*, 283–299.

Frank, J. D., Gliedman, L. H., Imber, S. D., Stone, A. R., & Nash, E. H. Patients' expectancies and relearning as factors determining improvement in psychotherapy. *American Journal of Psychiatry*, 1959, *115*, 961–968.

Frankel, F. H. The effects of brief hypnotherapy in a series of psychosomatic problems. *Psychotherapy and Psychosomatics*, 1973, *22*, 269–275.

Frankl, V. E. Paradoxical intention: A logotherapeutic technique. *American Journal of Psychotherapy*, 1960, *14*, 520–535.

Garfield, S. L. Research on client variables in psychotherapy. In A. E. Bergin and S. L. Garfield (Eds.), *Handbook of psychotherapy and behavior change*. New York: John Wiley, 1971.

Garfield, S. L. Research on client variables in psychotherapy. In S. L. Garfield and A. E. Bergin (Eds.), *Handbook of psychotherapy*. (Rev. ed.) New York: John Wiley, 1978.

Garfield, S. L., Prager, R. A., & Bergin, A. E. Evaluation of outcome in psychotherapy. *Journal of Consulting and Clinical Psychology*, 1971, *37*, 307–313.

Garner, H. H. *Psychotherapy: Confrontation problem solving techniques*. St. Louis: W. H. Green, 1970.

Gelb, L. A., & Ullman, M. As reported anon., in "Instant psychotherapy offered at an outpatient psychiatric clinic." *Frontiers of Hospital Psychiatry*, 1967, *4*, 14.

Gelder, M. G., Marks, I. M., & Wolff, H. H. Desensitization and psychotherapy in the treatment of phobic states: A controlled inquiry. *British Journal of Psychiatry*, 1967, *113*, 53–73.

Getter, H., & Sundland, D. M. The Barron ego strength scale and psychotherapy outcome. *Journal of Consulting Psychology*, 1962, *26*, 195.

Gillman, R. D. Brief psychotherapy: A psychoanalytic view. *American Journal of Psychiatry*, 1965, *122*, 601–611.

Glasscote, R. M., Raybin, J. B., Reifler, C. B., & Kane, A. W. *The alternate services: Their role in mental health.* Washington, D.C.: American Psychiatric Service, 1975.

Gordon, T., & Cartwright, D. S. The effect of psychotherapy on certain attitudes toward others. In C. Rogers and R. F. Dymond (Eds.), *Psychotherapy and personality change.* Chicago: University of Chicago Press, 1954.

Gottschalk, L. A., Fox, R. A., & Bates, D. E. A study of prediction and outcome in a mental health crisis clinic. *American Journal of Psychiatry*, 1973, *130*, 1107–1111.

Gottschalk, L. A., Mayerson, P., & Gottlieb, A. A. Prediction and evaluation of outcome in an emergency brief psychotherapy clinic. *Journal of Nervous and Mental Disease*, 1967, *144*, 77–96.

Graham, S. R. Patient evaluation of the effectiveness of limited psychoanalytically oriented psychotherapy. *Psychological Reports*, 1958, *4*, 231–234.

Green, B. L., Gleser, G. C., Stone, W. N., & Seifert, R. F. Relationships among diverse measures of psychotherapy outcome. *Journal of Consulting and Clinical Psychology*, 1975, *43*, 689–699.

Greenblatt, M., Moore, R., & Albert, R. *The prevention of hospitalization: Report on the Community Extension Service of the Massachusetts Mental Health Center, Boston, Massachusetts.* New York: Grune and Stratton, 1963.

Grinker, R. R., & Spiegel, J. P. Brief psychotherapy in war neuroses. *Psychosomatic Medicine*, 1944a, *6*, 123–131.

Grinker, R. R., & Spiegel, J. P. *Management of neuropsychiatric casualties in the zone of combat. Manual of military neuropsychiatry.* Philadelphia: W. B. Saunders, 1944b.

Grinker, R. R., & Spiegel, J. P. *Men under stress.* Philadelphia: Blakiston, 1945.

Gross, R. B. Supportive therapy for the depressed college student. *Psychotherapy: Theory, Research and Practice*, 1968, *5*, 262–267.

Gutheil, E. A. Psychoanalysis and brief psychotherapy. *Journal of Clinical Psychopathology*, 1944, *6*, 207–230.

Hadley, S. W., & Strupp, H. H. Contemporary views of negative effects in psychotherapy. *Archives of General Psychiatry*, 1976, *33*, 1291–1302.

Haley, J. Control in brief psychotherapy. *Archives of General Psychiatry*, 1961, *4*, 139–153.

Halpern, H. Crisis theory. *Community Mental Health Journal*, 1973, *9*, 342–349.

Halpern, H. The crisis scale. *Community Mental Health Journal*, 1975, *11* (3), 295–300.

Harris, M. R., Kalis, B. L., & Freeman, E. H. Precipitating stress: An approach to brief therapy. *American Journal of Psychotherapy*, 1963, *17*, 465–471.

Harris, R. E., & Christiansen, C. Predictions of response to brief psychotherapy. *Journal of Psychology*, 1946, *21*, 269–284.

Haskell, D., Pugatch, D., & McNair, D. M. Time-limited psychotherapy for whom? *Archives of General Psychiatry*, 1969, *21*, 546–552.

Heiberg, A., Sørensen, T., & Olafsen, O. Short-term dynamic psychotherapy: Three models of treatment. *Psychotherapy and Psychosomatics*, 1975, *26*, 229–236.

Heitler, J. B. Preparation of lower-class patients for expressive group psychotherapy. *Journal of Consulting and Clinical Psychology*, 1973, *41*, 251–260.

Heitler, J. B. Preparatory techniques in initiating expressive psychotherapy in lower-class unsophisticated patients. *Psychological Bulletin*, 1976, *83*, 339–352.

Henry, W. E., & Shlien, J. Affective complexity and psychotherapy: Some comparisons of time limited and unlimited treatment. *Journal of Projective Techniques*, 1958, *22*, 153–162.

Hoch, P. H. Short-term versus long-term therapy. In L. R. Wolberg (Ed.), *Short-term psychotherapy.* New York: Grune and Stratton, 1965.

Hoehn-Saric, R., Frank, J. D., & Gurland, B. L. Focused attitude change in neurotic patients. *Journal of Nervous and Mental Disease*, 1968, *147*, 124–133.

Hoehn-Saric, R., Frank, J. D., Imber, S. D., Nash, E. H., Stone, A. R., & Battle, C. C. Systematic preparation of patients for psychotherapy. I. Effects of therapy behavior and outcome. *Journal of Psychiatric Research*, 1964, *2*, 267–281.

Hoehn-Saric, R., Liberman, R., Imber, S. D., Stone, A. R., Pande, S. K., & Frank, J. D. Arousal and attitude change in neurotic patients. *Archives of General Psychiatry*, 1972, *26*, 51–56.

Hoehn-Saric, R., Liberman, B., Imber, S. D., Stone, A. R., Frank, J. D., & Ribich, F. D. Attitude change and attribution of arousal in psychotherapy. *Journal of Nervous and Mental Disease*, 1974, *159*, 234–244.

Hoffman, D. L., & Remmel, M. L. Uncovering the precipitant in crisis intervention. *Social Casework*, 1975, *56*, 259–267.

Hogan, R. A. Implosive therapy in the short-term treatment of psychotics. *Psychotherapy: Theory, Research and Practice*, 1966, *3*, 25–32.

Hogan, R. A. Preliminary report of the extinction of learned fears via short-term implosive therapy. *Journal of Abnormal Psychology*, 1967, *72*, 106–109.

Holmes, F. B. An experimental investigation of a method of overcoming children's fears. *Child Development*, 1936, *7*, 6–30.

Hornstra, R., Lubin, B., Lewis, R., & Willis, B. Worlds apart: Patients and professionals. *Archives of General Psychiatry*, 1972, *27*, 553–557.

Howard, H. S. Of "gimmicks and gadgets" in brief psychotherapy. *Delaware Medical Journal*, 1965, *37*, 265–267.

Hunt, R. G. Social class and mental illness: Some implications for clinical theory and practice. *American Journal of Psychiatry*, 1960, *116*, 1065–1069.

Imber, S. D., Frank, J. D., Gliedman, L. H., Nash, E. H., & Stone, A. R. Suggestibility, social class and the acceptance of psychotherapy. *Journal of Clinical Psychology,* 1956, *12,* 341–344.

Imber, S. D., Nash, E. H., Hoehn-Saric, R., Stone, A. R., & Frank, J. D. A ten year follow-up study of treated psychiatric outpatients. In S. Lesse (Ed.), *An evaluation of the results of the psychotherapies.* Springfield, Ill.: Charles C Thomas, 1968.

Imber, S. D., Pande, S. K., Frank, J. D., Hoehn-Saric, R., Stone, A. R., & Wargo, D. G. Time-focused role induction. *Journal of Nervous and Mental Disease,* 1970, *150,* 27–30.

Jacobs, M. A., Muller, J. J., Eisman, H. D., Knitzer, J., & Spilkan, A. The assessment of change in distress level and styles of adaptation as a function of psychotherapy. *Journal of Nervous and Mental Disease,* 1968, *145,* 392–404.

Jacobson, G. F. Crisis theory and treatment strategy: Some sociocultural and psychodynamic considerations. *Journal of Nervous and Mental Disease,* 1965, *141,* 209–218.

Jacobson, G. F. Some psychoanalytic considerations regarding crisis therapy. *Psychoanalytic Review,* 1967, *54,* 649–654.

Jacobson, G. F. The briefest psychiatric encounter. *Archives of General Psychiatry,* 1968, *18,* 718–724.

Jacobson, G. F., Strickler, M., & Morley, W. E. Generic and individual approaches to crisis intervention. *American Journal of Public Health,* 1968, *58,* 339–343.

Jacobson, G. F., Wilner, D. M., Morley, W., Schneider, S., Strickler, M., & Sommer, G. The scope and practice of an early-access brief treatment psychiatric center. *American Journal of Psychiatry,* 1965, *121,* 1176–1182.

Jones, H. E. The conditioning of overemotional responses. *Journal of Educational Psychology,* 1931, *22,* 127–130.

Kardener, S. H. A methodologic approach to crisis therapy. *American Journal of Psychiatry,* 1975, *29,* 4–13.

Kardiner, A. *The traumatic neurosis of war.* New York: Hoeber, 1941.

Kellner, R., & Sheffield, B. F. The relief of distress following attendance at a clinic. *British Journal of Psychiatry,* 1971, *118,* 195–198.

Klein, D., & Lindemann, E. Preventive intervention in individual and family crisis situations. In G. Caplan (Ed.), *Prevention of mental disorders in children.* New York: Basic Books, Inc., 1961.

Koegler, R. R. Brief-contact therapy and drugs in outpatient treatment. In G. J. Wayne and R. R. Koegler (Eds.), *Emergency psychiatry and brief therapy.* Boston: Little, Brown, 1966.

Koegler, R. R., & Cannon, J. A. Treatment for the many. In G. J. Wayne and R. R. Koegler (Eds.), *Emergency psychiatry and brief therapy.* Boston: Little, Brown, 1966.

Kris, E. B. Intensive short-term treatment in a day care facility for the prevention of rehospitalization of patients in the community showing recurrence of psychotic symptoms. *Psychiatric Quarterly,* 1960, *34,* 83–88.

Lantz, J. F., & Werk, K. Short-term casework: A rational emotive approach. *Child Welfare,* 1976, *55,* 29–38.

Lazarus, A. A. *Behavior therapy and beyond.* New York: McGraw-Hill, 1971.

Leeman, C. P., & Mulvey, C. H. Brief psychotherapy of the dependent personality: Specific techniques. *Psychotherapy and Psychosomatics,* 1975, *25,* 36–42.

Lester, E. P. Brief psychotherapies in child psychiatry. *Canadian Psychiatric Association Journal,* 1968, *13,* 301–309.

Levene, H., Breger, L., & Patterson, V. A training and research program in brief psychotherapy. *American Journal of Psychotherapy,* 1972, *26,* 90–100.

Levis, D. J., & Carrera, R. N. Effects of ten hours of implosive therapy in the treatment of outpatients: A preliminary report. *Journal of Abnormal Psychology,* 1967, *72,* 504–508.

Levy, R. A. How to conduct 6 session crisis oriented psychotherapy. *Hospital and Community Psychiatry,* 1966, *17,* 340–343.

Levy, R. A. As reported anon., in "How to conduct 6-session crisis-oriented psychotherapy." *Frontiers of Hospital Psychiatry,* 1967, *4,* 9.

Lewin, K. A method of brief psychotherapy. *Psychiatric Quarterly,* 1966, *40,* 482–489.

Liberman, B. I., Imber, S. D., Stone, A. R., Hoehn-Saric, R., & Frank, J. D. Mastery: Prescriptive treatment and maintenance of change in psychotherapy. Cited in J. D. Frank, Therapeutic components of psychotherapy. *Journal of Nervous and Mental Disease,* 1974, *159,* 325–342.

Lick, J. R., & Bootzin, R. R. Expectancy, demand characteristics, and contact desensitization in behavior change. *Behavior Therapy,* 1970, *1,* 176–183.

Lick, J. R., & Bootzin, R. R. Expectancy factors in the treatment of fear: Methodological and theoretical issues. *Psychological Bulletin,* 1975, *82,* 917–931.

Lief, H. I., Lief, U. F., Warren, C. O., & Heath, R. C. Low dropout rate in a psychiatric clinic. *Archives of General Psychiatry,* 1961, *5,* 200–211.

Lindemann, E. Symptomatology and management of acute grief. *American Journal of Psychiatry,* 1944, *101,* 141–148.

Lindemann, E. Symptomatology and management of acute grief. In H. J. Parad (Ed.), *Crisis intervention.* New York: Family Service Association of America, 1965.

London, L. S. Hypnosis, hypno-analysis and narco-analysis. *American Journal of Psychotherapy,* 1947, *1,* 443–447.

Lorion, R. P. Socioeconomic status and traditional treatment approaches reconsidered. *Psychological Bulletin,* 1973, *79,* 263–270.

Lorion, R. P. Patient and therapist variables in the treatment of low income patients. *Psychological Bulletin,* 1974, *81,* 344–354.

Lorr, M., McNair, D. M., Michaux, W. W., & Raskin, A. Frequency of treatment and change in psychotherapy. *Journal of Abnormal and Social Psychology,* 1964, *64,* 281–292.

Lowy, F. H., Wintrob, R. M., Borwick, B., Garmaise, G., & King, H. O. A follow-up study of emergency psychiatric patients and their families. *Comprehensive Psychiatry*, 1971, *12*, 36–47.

Luborsky, L., Chandler, M., Auerbach, A. H., Cohen, J., & Bachrach, H. M. Factors influencing the outcome of psychotherapy: A review of quantitative research. *Psychological Bulletin*, 1971, *75*, 145–185.

Luborsky, L., Singer, B., & Luborsky, L. Comparative studies of psychotherapies. *Archives of General Psychiatry*, 1975, *32*, 995–1008.

Malan, D. H. *A study of brief psychotherapy*. London: Tavistock Publications, 1963.

Malan, D. H. The outcome problem in psychotherapy research. *Archives of General Psychiatry*, 1973, *29*, 719–729.

Malan, D. H. *The frontier of brief psychotherapy*. New York: Plenum, 1976a.

Malan, D. H. *Toward the validation of dynamic psychotherapy: A replication*. New York: Plenum, 1976b.

Mann, J. *Time-limited psychotherapy*. Cambridge: Harvard University Press, 1973.

Maris, R. & Connor, H. E., Jr. Do crisis services work: A follow-up of a psychiatric outpatient sample. *Journal of Health and Social Behavior*, 1973, *14*, 311–322.

McGuire, M. The process of short-term insight psychotherapy, I. *Journal of Nervous and Mental Disease*, 1965a, *141*, 89–94.

McGuire, M. T. The process of short-term insight psychotherapy, II: Content, expectations, and structure. *Journal of Nervous and Mental Disease*, 1965b, *141*, 219–230.

McGuire, M. T. The instruction nature of short-term insight psychotherapy. *American Journal of Psychotherapy*, 1968, *22*, 219–231.

McGuire, M. T., & Sifneos, P. E. Problem solving in psychotherapy. *Psychiatric Quarterly*, 1970, *44*, 667–673.

Meltzoff, J., & Kornreich, M. *Research in psychotherapy*. New York: Atherton, 1970.

Merrill, S., & Cary, G. L. Dream analysis in brief psychotherapy. *American Journal of Psychotherapy*, 1975, *29*, 185–193.

Meyer, E., Spiro, H. R., Slaughter, R., Pollack, I. W., Weingartner, H., & Novey, S. Contractually time-limited psychotherapy in an outpatient psychosomatic clinic. *American Journal of Psychiatry*, 1967, Supplement, *124*, 57–68.

Miller, W. B. A psychiatric emergency service and some treatment concepts. *American Journal of Psychiatry*, 1968, *124*, 924–933.

Mintz, J. What is "success" in psychotherapy? *Journal of Abnormal Psychology*, 1972, *80*, 11–19.

Mitchell, K. R., & Orr, F. E. Note on treatment of heterosexual anxiety using short-term massed desensitization. *Psychological Reports*, 1974, *35*, 1093–1094.

Moleski, R., & Tosi, D. J. Comparative psychotherapy: Rational-emotive versus systematic desensitization in the treatment of stuttering. *Journal of Consulting Psychology*, 1976, *44*, 309–311.

Morley, W. E. Treatment of the patient in crisis. *Western Medicine*, 1965, *3*, 77.

Muench, G. A. An investigation of the efficacy of time-limited psychotherapy. *Journal of Counseling Psychology*, 1965, *12*, 294–299.

Muench, G. A., & Schumacher, R. A clinical experiment with rotational time limited psychotherapy. *Psychotherapy: Theory, Research and Practice*, 1968, *5*, 81–84.

Nash, E. H., Hoehn-Saric, R., Battle, C. C., Stone, A. R., Imber, S. D., & Frank, J. D. Systematic preparation of patients for short-term psychotherapy: II. Relation to characteristics of patient, therapist and psychotherapeutic process. Presented at American Psychiatric Association meeting, Los Angeles, California, May 1964. Also *Journal of Nervous and Mental Disease*, 1965, *140*, 374–383.

Nichols, M. P. Outcome of brief cathartic psychotherapy. *Journal of Consulting and Clinical Psychology*, 1974, *42*, 403–410.

Nichols, M. P., & Reifler, C. B. The study of brief psychotherapy in a college health setting. *Journal of the American College Health Association*, 1973, *22*, 128–133.

Nigl, A. J. Effects of presenting symptom and therapist orientation on treatment outcome. A follow-up study of brief therapy with college students. *Journal of the American College Health Association*, 1976, *24* (4), 203–207.

Normand, W. C., Fensterheim, H., Tannenbaum, G., & Sager, C. J. The acceptance of the psychiatric walk-in clinic in a highly deprived community. *American Journal of Psychiatry*, 1963, *120*, 533–539.

Oberman, E. The use of time limited relationship therapy with borderline patients. *Smith College Studies in Social Work*, 1967, *37*, 124–141.

Parad, H. J. The use of time limited crisis intervention on community mental health programming. *Social Service Review*, 1966, *40*, 275–282.

Parad, H. J. *Crisis intervention: Selected readings*. New York: Family Service Association of America, 1967.

Parad, H. J., & Parad, L. J. A study of crisis-oriented planned short-term treatment: Parts I and II. *Social Casework*, 1968, *49*, 418–426.

Pascal, G. R., & Zax, M. Psychotherapeutics: Success or failure? *Journal of Consulting Psychology*, 1956, *20*, 325–331.

Patterson, V., Levene, H., & Breger, L. Treatment and training outcomes with two time-limited therapies. *Archives of General Psychiatry*, 1971, *25*, 161–167.

Patterson, V., & O'Sullivan, M. Three perspectives on brief psychotherapy. *American Journal of Psychotherapy*, 1974, *28*, 265–277.

Paul, G. L. *Insight versus desensitization in psychotherapy*. Stanford: Stanford University Press, 1966.

Paul, G. L. Insight versus desensitization in psychotherapy two years after termination. *Journal of Consulting Psychology*, 1967, *31*, 333–348.

Perlman, H. H. In quest of coping. *Social Casework*, 1975, *56*, 213–225.

Phillips, E. L., & Johnston, M. H. S. Theoretical and clinical aspects of short-term, parent-child psychotherapy. *Psychiatry*, 1954, *7*, 267–275.

Phillips, E. L., & Weiner, D. N. *Short-term psychotherapy and structural behavior change*. New York: McGraw-Hill, 1966.

Prugh, D. G., & Brody, B. Brief relationship therapy in

the military setting. *American Journal of Ortho-psychiatry*, 1946, *16*, 707–721.

Pumpian-Mindlin, E. Consideration in the selection of patients for short-term therapy. *American Journal of Psychotherapy*, 1953, *7*, 641–652.

Reid, W. J. A test of a task-centered approach. *Social Work*, 1975, *20*, 3–9.

Richardson, F. C., & Suinn, R. M. Effects of two short-term desensitization methods in the treatment of test anxiety. *Journal of Counseling Psychology*, 1974, *21*, 457–458.

Robinson, C., Reich, L., Pion, G., Dee, C., Delaney, J. & Hale, R. W. The office management of sexual problems: Brief therapy approaches. *Journal of Reproductive Medicine*, 1975, *15*, 127–144.

Rockwell, W. J., Moorman, J. C.., Hawkins, D., & Musante, G . Individual vs. group: Brief therapy outcome in a university mental health service. *Journal of the American College Health Association*, 1976, *24*, 186–190.

Rogers, L. S. Drop out rates of psychotherapy in government aided mental hygiene clinics. *Journal of Clinical Psychology*, 1960, *16*, 89–92.

Rosenbaum, C. P. Events of early therapy and brief therapy. *Archives of General Psychiatry*, 1964, *10*, 506–512.

Rosenbaum, M., Friedlander, J., & Kaplan S. M. Evaluation of results of psychotherapy. *Psychosomatic Medicine*, 1956, *18*, 113–132.

Rosenthal, D., & Frank, J. The fate of psychiatric clinic outpatients assigned to psychotherapy. *Journal of Nervous and Mental Disease*, 1958, *127*, 330–343.

Rosenthal, H. R. Emergency psychotherapy: A crucial need. *Psychoanalytic Review*, 1965, *52*, 446.

Roth, I., Rhudick, P. J., Shaskan, D. A., Slobin, M. S., Wilkinson, A. E., & Young, H. Long term effects on psychotherapy of initial treatment conditions. *Journal of Psychiatric Research*, 1964, *2*, 283–297.

Roth, R. M., Berenbaum, H. L., & Garfield, S. J. Massed time-limit therapy. *Psychotherapy: Theory, Research and Practice*, 1969, *6*, 54–56.

Rubinstein, E. & Lorr, M. A comparison of terminators and remainers in outpatient psychotherapy. *Journal of Clinical Psychology*, 1956, *12*, 345–349.

Rusk, T. N. Opportunity and technique in crisis psychiatry. *Comprehensive Psychiatry*, 1971, *12*, 249–263.

Rusk, T. N., & Gerner, R. H. A study of the process of emergency psychotherapy. *American Journal of Psychiatry*, 1972, *128*, 882–885.

Saltzman, C., Luetgert, M. J., Roth C. H., Creaser, J., & Howard, L. Formation of a therapeutic relationship: Experiences during the initial phase of psychotherapy as predictors of treatment duration and outcome. *Journal of Consulting and Clinical Psychology*, 1976, *44*, 546–555.

Sarvis, M. A., Dewees, M. S., & Johnston, R. F. A concept of ego-oriented psychotherapy. *Psychiatry*, 1958, *22*, 277–287.

Saul, L. J. On the value of one or two interviews. *Psychoanalytic Quarterly*, 1951, *20*, 613–615.

Schoenberg, B., & Carr, A. C. An investigation of criteria for brief psychotherapy of neurodermatitis. *Psychosomatic Medicine*, 1963, *25*, 253–263.

Schonfield, J., Stone, A. R., Hoehn-Saric, R., Imber, S.

D., & Pande, S. K. Patient-therapist convergence and measures of improvement in short-term psychotherapy. *Psychotherapy: Theory, Research and Practice*, 1969, *6*, 267–272.

Seitz, P. F. D. Dynamically oriented brief psychotherapy: Psychocutaneous excoriation syndromes. *Psychosomatic Medicine*, 1953, *15*, 200–242.

Semrad, E. V., Binstock, W. A., & White, B. Brief psychotherapy. *American Journal of Psychotherapy*. 1966, *20*, 576–596.

Shlien, J. M. Research notes from here and there. Time-limited psychotherapy: An experimental investigation of practical values and theoretical implications. *Journal of Counseling Psychology*, 1957, *4*, 318–323.

Shlien, J. M. Cross-theoretical criteria in time-limited therapy. *6th International Congress of Psychotherapy*, 1964, 118–126.

Shlien, J. M., Mosak, H. H., & Dreikurs, R. Effects of time limits: A comparison of two psychotherapies. *Journal of Counseling Psychology*, 1962, *9*, 31–34.

Sifneos, P. E. *Short-term psychotherapy and emotional crisis.* Cambridge, Mass.: Harvard University Press, 1972.

Sifneos, P. E. Evaluating the results of short-term anxiety provoking psychotherapy. *Psychotherapy and Psychosomatics*, 1975, *25*, 217–220.

Sindberg, R. M. A fifteen-year follow-up study of community guidance clinic clients. *Community Mental Health Journal*, 1970, *6*, 319–324.

Sloane, R. B., Cristol, A. H., Pepernik, M. C., & Staples, F. R. Role preparation and expectation of improvement in psychotherapy. *Journal of Nervous and Mental Disease*, 1970, *150*, 18–26.

Sloane, R. B., Staples, F. R., Cristol, A. H., & Yorkston, N. J. Short-term analytically-oriented psychotherapy versus behavior therapy. *American Journal of Psychiatry*, 1975, *132*, 373–377.

Sloane, R. B., Staples, F. R., Cristol, A. H., Yorkston, N. J., & Whipple, K. *Psychotherapy versus behavior therapy.* Cambridge, Mass.: Harvard University Press, 1975.

Sloane, R. B., Staples, F. R., Cristol, A. H., Yorkston, N. J., & Whipple, K. Patient characteristics and outcome in psychotherapy and behavior therapy. *Journal of Consulting and Clinical Psychology*, 1976, *44*, 330–339.

Small, L. *The briefer psychotherapies.* New York: Brunner/Mazel, 1971.

Small, L. Crisis therapy: Theory and method. In G. D. Goldman and D. S. Milman (Eds.), *Innovations in psychotherapy.* Springfield, Ill.: Charles C Thomas, 1972.

Socarides, C. W. On the usefulness of extremely brief psychoanalytic contacts. *Psychoanalytic Review*, 1954, *41*, 340–346.

Spoerl, R. H. Abstract: Single session psychotherapy. *Diseases of the Nervous System*, 1975, *36*, 283–285.

Stampfl, T. G., & Levis, D. J. Essentials of implosive therapy: A learning theory based psychodynamic behavioral therapy. *Journal of Abnormal Psychology*, 1967, *72*, 496–503.

Staples, F. R., & Sloane, R. B. The relation of speech patterns in psychotherapy to empathic ability, responsiveness to approval and disapproval. *Diseases of the Nervous System,* 1970, *31,* 100–104.

Staples, F. R., & Sloane, R. B. Truax factors, speech characteristics, and therapeutic outcome. *Journal of Nervous and Mental Disease,* 1976, *163,* 135–140.

Staples, F. R., Sloane, R. D., Whipple, K., Cristol, A. H., & Yorkston, N. Process and outcome in psychotherapy and behavior therapy. *Journal of Consulting and Clinical Psychology,* 1976, *44,* 340–350.

Stein, C. Hypnotic projection in brief psychotherapy. *American Journal of Clinical Hypnosis,* 1972, *14,* 143–155.

Stein, C. Brief hypnotherapy for conversion cephalgia (repression headache). *American Journal of Clinical Hypnosis,* 1975, *17,* 198–201.

Stein, H., Murdaugh, J. M., & MacLeod, J. A. As reported anon., in Emotional reaction to illness responds to brief psychotherapy. *Frontiers of Hospital Psychiatry,* 1967, *4,* 15.

Stekel, W. *Technique of analytical psychotherapy.* London: Bodley Head, 1950.

Stewart, H. Six-months, fixed-term, once weekly psychotherapy: A report on 20 cases with follow-ups. *British Journal of Psychiatry,* 1972, *121,* 425–435.

Stone, A. R., Frank, J. D., Hoehn-Saric, R., Imber, S. D., & Nash, E. H. Some situational factors associated with response to psychotherapy. *American Journal of Orthopsychiatry,* 1965, *35,* 682–687.

Stone, A. R., Frank, J. D., Nash, E., & Imber, S. D. An intensive five-year follow-up study of treated psychiatric outpatients. *Journal of Nervous and Mental Disease,* 1961, *133,* 410–422.

Stone, L. Psychoanalysis and brief psychotherapy. *Psychoanalytic Quarterly,* 1951, *20,* 215–236.

Straker, M. Brief psychotherapy in an outpatient clinic: Evolution and evaluation. *American Journal of Psychiatry,* 1966, *124,* 39–45.

Strassi, I., & Messer, S. B. Psychotherapy with patients from lower socioeconomic groups. *American Journal of Psychiatry,* 1976, *30,* 29–40.

Strong, S. Social psychological approach to psychotherapy research. In S. L. Garfield and A. E. Bergin (Eds.), *Handbook of psychotherapy* (Rev. ed.) New York: John Wiley, 1978.

Strupp, H. H. A multidimensional analysis of technique in brief psychotherapy. *Psychiatry,* 1957, *20,* 387–397.

Strupp, H. H. On the basic ingredients of psychotherapy. *Journal of Consulting and Clinical Psychology,* 1973, *41,* 1–8.

Strupp, H. H., & Bloxom. A. Preparing lower-class patients for group psychotherapy: Development and evaluation of a role-induction film. *Journal of Consulting and Clinical Psychology,* 1973, *41,* 373–384.

Strupp, H. H., Hadley, S. W., & Gomes-Schwartz, B. *Psychotherapy for better or worse: An analysis of the problem of negative effects.* New York: Jason Aronson, in press (Manuscript, 1977).

Suinn, R. M., Edie, C. A., & Spinelli, P. R. Accelerated massed desensitization: Innovation in short-term treatment. *Behavior Therapy,* 1970, *1,* 303–311.

Swartz, J. Time-limited brief psychotherapy. *Seminars in*

Psychiatry I, 1969, *4,* 380–388.

Terhune, W. B. Phobic syndrome: Study of 86 patients with phobic reactions. *Archives of Neurology and Psychiatry,* 1949, *62,* 162–172.

Terhune, W. B. Brief psychotherapy with executives in industry. *Progress in Psychotherapy,* 1960, *5,* 132–139.

Uhlenhuth, E., & Duncan, D. Subjective change in psychoneurotic outpatients with medical student therapists. II. Some preliminary determinants of change. *Archives of General Psychiatry,* 1968, *18,* 532–540.

Ursano, R. J., & Dressler, D. M. Brief vs. long term psychotherapy: A treatment decision. *Journal of Nervous and Mental Disease,* 1974, *159,* 164–171.

Visher, J. S. Brief psychotherapy in a mental hygiene clinic. *American Journal of Psychotherapy,* 1959, *13,* 331–342.

Walsh, T. A. People in crisis: An experimental group. *Community Mental Health Journal,* 1974, *10,* 3–8.

Waltzer, H., Hankoff, L. D., Englehardt, D. M., & Kaufman, I. C. Emergency psychiatric treatment in a receiving hospital. *Mental Hospitals,* 1963, *14,* 595–600.

Warren, N. C., & Rice, L. N. Structuring and stabilizing of psychotherapy for low prognosis clients. *Journal of Consulting and Clinical Psychology,* 1972, *39,* 173–181.

Watson, J. B., & Rayner, P. Conditioned emotional reactions. *Journal of Experimental Psychology,* 1920, *3,* 1–14.

Wattie, B. Evaluating short term casework in a family agency. *Social Casework,* 1973, *54,* 609–616.

Wayne, G. J. How long? An approach to reducing the duration of inpatient treatment. In G. J. Wayne and R. R. Koegler (Eds.), *Emergency psychiatry and brief therapy.* Boston: Little, Brown, 1966.

Weitz, L. J., Abramowitz, S. I., Steger, J. A., Calabria, F. M., Conable, M., & Yarus, G. Number of sessions and client-judged outcome: The more the better? *Psychotherapy: Theory, Research and Practice,* 1975, *12,* 337–340.

White, A. M., Fichtenbaum, L., & Dollard, J. Measurement of what the patient learns from psychotherapy. *Journal of Nervous and Mental Disease,* 1969, *149,* 281–293.

Whittington, H. G. Transference in brief psychotherapy: Experience in a college psychiatric clinic. *Psychiatric Quarterly,* 1962, *36,* 503–518.

Wilkins, W. Expectancy of therapeutic gain: An empirical and conceptual critique. *Journal of Consulting and Clinical Psychology,* 1973, *46,* 69–77.

Williams, W. V. Crisis intervention: Effects of crisis intervention on family survivors of sudden death situations. *Community Mental Health Journal,* 1976, *12,* 128–136.

Wolberg, L. R. Methodology in short term therapy. *American Journal of Psychiatry,* 1965, *122,* 135–140.

Wolberg, L. R. (Ed.) *Short-term psychotherapy.* New York: Grune and Stratton, 1965.

Wolkon, G. H. Crisis theory, the application for treatment, and dependency. *Comprehensive Psychiatry,* 1972, *13,* 459–464.

Wolpe, J. Experimental neurosis as learned behavior.

British Journal of Psychology, 1952, *43,* 243–268.

Wolpe, J. *Psychotherapy by reciprocal inhibition.* Stanford: Stanford University Press, 1958.

Wolpe, J., & Lazarus, A. A. *Behavior therapy techniques.* Oxford: Pergamon Press, 1966.

Yalom, I. D., Hovts, P. S., Newell, G., & Rand, K. H. Preparation for patients for group therapy. *Archives*

of General Psychiatry, 1967, *17,* 416–427.

Zitrin, C. M., Klein, D. F., & Lindeman, C. Comparison of short-term treatment regimens in phobic patients: A preliminary report. Proceedings of the *American Psychopathological Association,* 1976, *64,* 233–250.

20

EXPERIENTIAL GROUP RESEARCH: CURRENT PERSPECTIVES

RICHARD L. BEDNAR

University of Kentucky

THEODORE J. KAUL

Ohio State University

An expression of personal perspective and sentiment seems an appropriate way to introduce a project of this nature. When we began this review, we were both disposed by temperament and training to value traditional experimental science as a means of understanding human behavior and group treatments. Although our loyality to these traditions remains unchanged, we have acquired a more vivid appreciation of the conceptual prerequisites for knowledge advancement. After reading hundreds of reports and thousands of pages, we are left with the paradoxical, yet undeniable, impression that the discipline is more aware of subtle points of research design than some of the fundamental issues plaguing the theory and practice of group work. This limited perspective often results in research that is internally sound but conceptually empty. We submit that the discipline can no longer disregard the intimate relationship among conceptual relevancy, methodological adequacy, and research saliency. Without improvement in the conceptual origins of the research, there is little hope that even the most impeccable methodologies can offer useful recommendations to theory development or clinical practice. On the other hand, without further methodological improvements in the research, the most fruitful conceptual issues cannot be approached. Although rarely explicit, this position suggests a recognition of the symbiotic relationship between research and practice. We intend to emphasize this reciprocal relationship in our analysis and review of contemporary group research.

Any thoughtful analysis of the group treatment research must not lose sight of two related facts. The first is the incredible complexity of the group phenomenon. Maintaining experimental control of critical variables becomes more difficult as the number of participants increases. When these variables are interpersonal ones, the control problems increase at a factorial rate. Combined with other ecological problems inherent in the group setting, it is not difficult to recognize the explosion of methodological and logistical problems that face an investigator. The second fact to be remembered is the relatively primitive state of theoretical development obvious in the area of group treatment. In light of these circumstances, we have tried to avoid gratuitous praise or condemnation in our analysis but, instead, have tried to emphasize what we perceive to be the realities facing those concerned with group research and practice.

Although more specific criteria by which research was selected for inclusion will be indicated in the appropriate subsections of this chapter, several arbitrary decisions should be noted now. The first is that group treatment has been defined quite broadly. As Lieberman (1976) has noted, many of the defining boundaries of allegedly different group orientations seem to reflect professional peculiarities and semantic imprecision more than substantive differences. Even so, some characteristics of the literature sample should be noted. To be considered for inclusion, reports needed more to recommend them than the mere presence of group meetings. Inclusion required that we judge the processes involved in group development to be an integral part of the treatment. That is, we considered only treatments that appeared to involve a developing social microcosm, social learning based on feedback and consensual validation, and the opportunity for group participants to be involved in both the helper and helpee roles. Thus, for example, group desensitization studies were not included unless there appeared to be some special circumstances present. Likewise, family therapy studies were excluded as being too narrow for our purposes. Finally, there was a decision to emphasize the more therapeutic applications of groups at the expense of topics such as educational and vocational counseling.

OUTCOME STUDIES

Professional and ethical considerations require that outcome research be of primary importance to public service professions. Unfortunately, systems

of psychological help giving are notorious for fads, movements of near missionary zeal, and unsubstantiated claims. Well-meaning practitioners have subjected their clientele to treatment regimens such as flogging, cold water immersion, imprisonment, and unrelenting psychological abuse. Each of these treatments has had positive therapeutic effects attributed to it in the literature of its day, and some continue to be found in contemporary use. It is, or will be, only through carefully controlled outcome investigations that such reprehensible treatments have achieved their rightful place in the therapeutic museum. It is only through a careful and dispassionate evaluation of the consequences of its accepted treatments that a profession can make legitimate claims for social acceptability.

A conscientious review of the group outcome literature requires an analysis of appropriate conceptual issues, methodological concerns, and collective implications. Such an undertaking with a body of research as polymorphous as this one is an admittedly ambitious objective. Fortunately, space limitations obviate any nondiscriminatory attempt to meet such a goal. Accordingly, we will introduce this section with a brief discussion of several methodological problems of fundamental importance in group research. This will be followed by a review of selected outcome studies that will vary with respect to the specificity of the treatment variables identified. On the basis of these considerations, we will present some tentative implications for clinical practice.

Methodological Problems

Not surprisingly, investigations of group treatment phenomena present several unique methodological concerns. The experimental integrity of this body of research could be compromised by the effects of several pervasive artifacts. One problem seldom acknowledged lies in the specification of the appropriate elements for statistical error terms. This seems as much a conceptual problem as a statistical one. Most investigators have defined error variance in terms of individual deviations from the grand mean, a definition involving two assumptions that may be unwarranted in group research. The first of these is that differences within groups constitute the only conceptually significant error variance; the second is that the appropriate degrees of freedom for error should be based on the number of subjects within treatment groups instead of on the number of experimental treatment groups. Both of these assumptions may not be appropriate in some group treatment research. It seems reasonable to assume that group treatments may involve two sources of conceptually significant error variance instead of one. Of course, the traditional accounting for individual variations within treatment groups is one contributor to experimental error. But, in addition, another source of error may arise when interaction patterns unique to specific groups are confounded with the primary treatment variable and are presumed to represent pure treatment effects. In short, error variance in group research may be a function of differences within treatment groups and between them as well. Groups may be expected to respond differentially to similar treatments as a consequence of the unique developmental ecology of each group, and in many studies this should be considered as experimental error. The standard controls for such situational variability, randomization and replication, may be prohibitively expensive and practically impossible. Nevertheless, if the idiosyncratic differences between groups cannot be controlled, systematic overestimations of treatment effects may result. In the absence of multiple group designs, significant treatment effects can always be attributed in part to the unintended, unrecognized, and perhaps unwelcomed variations in a group's development. If factors unique to different groups mediate or cause therapeutic changes independently of the specific treatment factors operating, these effects belong in the error term for most single-treatment, group outcome studies. Consequently, one should interpret the bulk of the existing research as the descriptive, $N = 1$ variety.

A second methodological concern is the sensitization effects of pretesting, although this concern is not limited to group treatment research. Particularly vulnerable to these effects are the pre-posttest experimental-control group designs. An example should illustrate the point sufficiently. Responding to studies in which significant effects were reported for both experimental and control groups (Treppa & Fricke, 1972; Young & Jacobson, 1970),

Kroeker (1974) employed a Solomon four-group design to isolate the effects of pretesting. The data indicated that the testing interacted significantly with experimental treatment groups, client variables, and outcome measures. Given the frequency with which similar results have been found in different research domains, the implication for group research is that such effects must be controlled for by the addition of appropriate control groups.

Finally, placebo and expectancy effects have implications for virtually all of the group outcome literature. Although not uncommon in any research on interpersonal influence, these phenomena may be especially confounding in group research. Considering the high levels of emotional expression, interpersonal activity, and encouragement to disclose that are so common in therapeutic groups, it should not be surprising to find nonspecific effects arising from situational arousal and enthusiasm. As a case in point, McCardel and Murray (1974) compared the effects of three different group experiences with those of a plausible attention placebo condition and a no-contact control group. Their results indicated that the effects of the group experiences were virtually indistinguishable from those of the placebo group, although they were significantly different from the no-contact control group. These findings suggest that the favorable outcomes of much group research might be accounted for by nonspecific placebo and expectancy effects. Again, given the similarity of these findings with those in other related areas, the implication for investigators is the addition of plausible placebo groups as well as the standard no-contact control group.

Outcome Studies

The literature included in this section was selected and organized on the basis of several considerations. Testimonials and case study reports were excluded because of the limitations inherent in such data. Quantitative reports were generally excluded if: (1) the primary treatment effects were estimated from pre- to posttesting without comparable estimations for a no-treatment control group; (2) the basic data analyses were based on simple difference scores, or were comprised of excessive nonorthogonal pairwise comparisons; and (3) there was nonrandom assignment of subjects to treatment and control conditions, or inappropriately matched samples. Even though these constraints have excluded the bulk of the potential literature, their application may mitigate some inferential error.

This group of studies shares a common characteristic. In each case, group treatment is represented in its most generic form without experimental specification or variation. Important uncontrolled sources of variance include group composition, leadership style, and the frequency, intensity, and duration of group sessions. Consequently, it is impossible to specify the essential treatment processes involved in the investigations beyond the fact that they apparently were given in a group context. Despite these limitations, these studies may contribute to the identification of some of the effects of selected group treatments. They are summarized in the first section of Table 20-1.

As a means of illustrating the methods and findings of this research, we have elected to present one of the better studies in some detail. Diamond and Shapiro (1973) examined the effects of encounter group experiences on participants' locus of control. They reported both an initial study and a replication. The methodologies were similar in both parts, except that experienced professionals led the groups in the initial study, and advanced graduate students served as leaders in the replication phase. In each phase, 30 graduate student volunteers, matched for age, sex, and training experience, were randomly assigned to one of three encounter groups. A similarly matched group of nine students served as the no-treatment control. All subjects were given the Rotter Internal-External Locus of Control Scale (Rotter, 1966) prior to the first group meeting, but their scores and the experimental hypotheses were not revealed to the group leaders. The instrument was administered a second time following eight 2-hour sessions and one 10-hour marathon session over an 11-week period.

Analyses of variance indicated no initial differences on locus of control for the groups. Repeated measures analyses indicated a significant change toward greater internality for the three encounter groups in the initial study, but did not suggest a similar change among no-treatment control members. Similarly, the three experimental groups in the replication phase showed results in the same direction, although at a reduced level of statistical significance. Again, the no-treatment controls failed to manifest similar changes. In view of the care involved in demonstrating the groups' equivalence, and the relative sophistication of the dependent measure, these data provide some indication of a dimension of change associated with group participation. It must be noted again, however, that the specific treatment processes were not identified in this or similar reports. As a result, the sources contributing to these results cannot be identified inasmuch as they could be a function of features idiosyncratic to the treatment or the data set.

The methods and results of additional outcome investigations are summarized in the first part of Table 20-1. All of these studies, selected from a pool of several dozen published reports, are similar in that the treatment condition is a relatively unspecified group process. Inspection of these summaries suggests some findings that warrant particular mention. For example, the studies of Jew, Clanon, and Mattocks (1972) and Redfering (1973) report surprisingly favorable immediate and long-term effects with notoriously difficult treatment populations. Furthermore, two of the six studies with posttreatment follow-up data detected additional positive changes at follow-up, suggesting the presence of "sleeper" effects (Foulds & Hannigan, 1976; Jacobson & Smith, 1972). Finally, of these six follow-up studies, three indicated that early treatment effects persisted into the follow-up period to a degree unmatched by the no-treatment controls.

The remaining literature will not be summarized in any detail because of the overall similarity of these studies in design and outcome (Arbes & Hubbell, 1973; Cooper, 1972b; Dies & Sadowsky, 1974; Felton & Biggs, 1972; Felton & Davidson, 1973; Fromme et al., 1974; Kaye, 1973; Shapiro & Diamond, 1972; Stanton, 1975). The conceptual significance of this research lies in its contribution to identifying some dimensions of change associated with group participation and the effectiveness of selected group experiences. An overview of results indicates that a variety of human characteristics have been found to be significantly affected by group experiences. Methods of measurement have included psychometric assessment, independent ratings, and self-reports. Intrapsychic, interpersonal, and group phenomena have been measured. A more detailed analysis of specific treatment dimensions associated with participation in groups like these can be found in the reviews of Smith (1975b) and Kilman and Sotile (in press).

Finally, it should be noted that these studies provide evidence for the legitimacy of selected group treatment forms. Even though specific causal factors may not be evidenced, some of this research shows genuine creativity, thoughtfulness, and sophistication. The utility of such shotgun studies has probably reached the point of diminishing returns, however. Most of the benefits of such research have been achieved and valuable professional resources can be better used in the search for specific treatment factors that account for the outcomes of group psychological treatments.

Specific Treatments

In this group of investigations relatively more specific treatment dimensions have been specified and related to therapeutic outcomes. While the arbitrary nature of the classification will become obvious, it is difficult to exaggerate the importance of studies of this type. They have the potential to result in greater conceptual precision, more powerful experimental manipulations, and an identifiable empirical foundation on which to base responsible clinical practice and theoretical development. Two such studies (among those summarized in the second section of Table 20-1) will be reviewed in greater detail.

McLachlan (1972) investigated the relationship of leader-client match on conceptual level to therapeutic benefits of group experience. Conceptual level was defined as a bipolar dimension with conceptual dependence and independence as the anchor points. Presumably, the appropriate therapeutic environment for conceptually dependent group members would involve a consistent, well-organized environment in which role expectations are easily recognized. Conversely, group members at the conceptually independent end of the scale would presumably find minimal normative pressure and increasing opportunities for self-differentiation more therapeutic.

The group participants were 92 alcoholic inpatients. Prior to the treatment itself, they all went through a 1-week detoxification period. Then a paragraph completion test was given to assess conceptual level. The five group leaders and their nurse coleaders also completed the measure of conceptual level. Fifty-three patients were classified as dependent conceptual level and 39 as independent conceptual level. These classes were then divided on the basis of the leader's conceptual level. The actual group treatment consisted of 26 hours of contact time over a 3-week period.

Therapeutic change was evaluated on a factor-analyzed scale derived from leader and member judgments of improvement. The factors were labeled patient-rated improvement, staff-rated improvement, and improved adjustment. Analysis of the data revealed a striking and highly significant interaction effect on patient-rated improvement, a function of differential and more desirable therapeutic response of members appropriately matched with leaders on conceptual level. Even though these results cannot be interpreted to indicate that the effects are solely attributable to conceptual level matching, they provide valuable guidance in the search for variables that enhance the effects of group treatment. And their value is not compromised by the fact that the primary independent variable has little historical background in group treatment theory.

Another study of interest was reported by Abramowitz and Jackson (1974), who investigated the differential effects of "here-and-now" versus "there-and-then" therapist interpretations in group therapy. Clients appropriate for group treatment were identified from a college student population and randomly assigned to one of four groups: (1) the here-and-now group, which emphasized the importance of in-group feelings and behavior; (2) the then-and-there group, which emphasized the historical antecedents of current affect; (3) a mixed group, which allowed the features of both interpretations; and (4) an attention placebo group, which involved problem-centered discussions with a leader who withheld clinical interpretations. Role manipulation checks indicate that these groups functioned as designed.

Analysis of the outcome indicators, which included a broad range of psychometric and self-report measures, indicated a tendency for more

TABLE 20-1 Outcome Studies

Author	Type of Group	Leader	Participants
General studies			
Diamond and Shapiro (1973)	Encounter groups	Experienced professionals (replication with graduate)	Graduate student volunteers
Foulds and Guinan (1973)	Marathon	Experienced professionals	College student volunteers
Foulds and Hannigan (1974)	Psychomotor groups	Experienced professional	College student volunteers
Foulds and Hannigan (1976)	Marathon	Experienced professionals	College student volunteers
Haven and Wood (1970)	Group therapy	Psychologist and chaplain	Psychiatric patients
Hewitt and Kraft (1973)	Encounter groups	Not given	Volunteers
Jacobson and Smith (1972)	Encounter groups	With college group, little training; with adult group, experienced professional	College students and adult volunteers
Jew, Clanon, and Mattocks (1972)	Group therapy	Psychiatrists, psychologists, counselors	Psychiatric prisoners
Redfering (1973)	Group counseling	Not given	Institutionalized delinquents

Experimental Conditions	Dependent Variables	Results
E: 2 hours weekly for 8 weeks, plus one 10-hour marathon C: No contact	Locus of control	E significant increase in internality; no significant change for C. Experienced leaders may achieve greater movement
E: 24-hour marathon C: no contact	Affect scale	E increased significantly on self, others, self and others scales; no significant change for C
E: 4 hours weekly for 8 weeks, follow-up at 6 months C: no contact, not followed	Affect scale	E increased significantly on self, others, self and others scales postgroup and at follow-up; no significant change for C at 8 weeks
E: 24-hour marathon C: no contact	POI	E showed significant positive changes on 10 of 12 self-actualization scales that generally persisted at 6 months; no significant change for C at posttest
E: 2 hours weekly of group therapy C: no group or individual therapy	Readmission within 12 months	No significant differences between E and C on readmission
E: two-day encounter group C: no group, but did attend a party together	Self-ratings and observer ratings of openness and self-liking	E rated selves higher on openness and self-liking; C did not No significant differences in observer ratings.
E: college, weekend encounter for growth E: adult, weekend encounter for job relations and growth C: college students not contacted	FIRO-B	Both E showed general positive changes in interpersonal orientation, although college students tended to show more than working adults. Some changes not found at posttest were noted at 2-month follow-up
E: average of 8 hours group therapy per month C: no group therapy	Recidivism	E showed significantly less recidivism at 1-year follow-up, but not at 2- or 4-year follow-up
E: unspecified group counseling C: no group counseling	Semantic differential (evaluative factor)	E significantly more positive than C on father, mother, self evaluations at 12-month follow-up. E more likely to have been released

TABLE 20-1 (*continued*)

Author	Type of Group	Leader	Participants
Shapiro and Diamond (1972)	Encounter groups	Experienced professionals	Graduate student volunteers
Treppa and Fricke (1972)	Marathon	Graduate student	College student volunteers
Uhlemann and Weigel (in press)	Marathon	Not given	College student volunteers
Vernallis, Shipper, Butler and Tomlinson (1970)	Saturation group therapy	Professionals	Psychiatric patients
Weissman, Goldschmid, Gordon, and Feinberg (1972)	Encounter groups	Audiotape	College student volunteers

Specific treatments

Interpersonal influences

Beutler, Jobe, and Elkins (1974)	Group therapy	Experienced professionals	College student outpatients and psychiatric inpatients
Jeske (1973)	Group therapy	Counseling center staff	College student self-referrals
Lieberman, Yalom, and Miles (1973)	Encounter groups	Experienced professionals	College student volunteers
Peretz and Glaser (1974)	Drug education workshops	Professional staff	High school students, drug counselors, social workers, teachers

Experimental Conditions	Dependent Variables	Results
E: 2 hours weekly for 8 weeks, plus one 10-hour marathon C: no contact	Stanford Hypnotiza-bility Scale	E increased significantly, C did not. Greater increases when group empha-sized interpersonal instead of intrapersonal problems
E: weekend marathon encounter group C: no contact	MMPI POI ICL	No significant differences between groups at two-day and 6-week follow-up. Both E and C showed some positive change
E; 17-hour marathon C: no contact	Behavior ratings	E showed greater movement toward desired behavior, although both changed.
E: 15 hours weekly for 16 consecutive weekends C: no group therapy	MMPI Incomplete sentences Social adjust-ment report Symptom rating	E improvement greater than C on MMPI, adjustment, and symptoms at post-treatment; E improvement greater than C on all dependent measures at 6-month follow-up
E: 3 hours weekly for 5 weeks (PEER tape) C: no contact	FIRO-B Semantic differential Art scale	E showed increased self-ideal congruence, self-direction, and creativity
Group leader attitudes were either within or outside the patient's latitude of acceptance. Therapy lasted 3 months	Patient therapist attitude similarity	Patient-therapist attitude dis-similarity was significantly associated with greater patient attitude change Therapist attitude acceptability was associated with greater patient satisfaction
Correlational analysis of frequency of iden-tification with other group members and therapeutic outcome	Self-report of identifi-cation MMPI	Strong positive relationship between the frequency of identification and favorable change on MMPI
Different group approaches, leadership styles, and no-treat-ment controls	Behavioral observations Self-reports Psychometric evaluations	Leadership styles differentially associated with client improvement and deterioration
Correlational analysis of changes in values toward those of the professional staff	Value scale	Participants showed significant shifts in value orientation toward that of the staff. Most influenced values were "honesty, courage, help-fulness"

TABLE 20-1 *(continued)*

Author	Type of Group	Leader	Participants
Group process dimensions			
Levin and Kurtz (1974)	Human relations training	Advanced graduate students	Graduate students enrolled in a group counseling course
Pollack (1971)	Sensitivity training groups	Graduate students	College student volunteers
Roback (1972)	Group therapy	Advanced graduate student	Psychiatric inpatients

Comparative studies

Author	Purpose	Participants
Hanson and Sander (1973)	Compare group versus individual counseling effects on realism of vocational choice	High school students
Jesness (1975)	Compare group transactional analysis versus individual behavior modifications	Adjudicated delinquents
Meichenbaum, Gilmore, and Fedoravicius (1971)	Compare immediate and long-term effects of group therapy versus desensitization for speech anxiety	College student volunteers

Experimental Conditions	Dependent Variables	Results
Structured groups featuring exercises versus unstructured groups featuring an interactive mode	Group opinion questionnaire	Significantly more favorable perceptions of the group experience with the structured format
Homogeneous versus heterogeneous groups	FIRO-B Self-report of satisfaction	Heterogeneous group composition associated with more favorable change on FIRO B. Initial greater satisfaction with homogeneous groups dissipated with time; heterogeneous groups showed greatest gains in satisfaction
Insight-oriented, interaction-oriented, and mixed groups	Behavioral rating scales MMPI Symptom check list Adjective checklist	Mixed orientation groups showed more consistent indications of improvement than did the insight, inter-action, or placebo groups

Experimental Conditions	Dependent Variables	Result
Unrealistically high or low vocational realism; individual, group, or no counseling	Counselor's rating of vocational choice	No significant main effects. Significant interaction suggests that group counseling more effective with unrealistically high choice, individual counseling with unrealistically low choice
Group TA, individual behavior modification, comparison groups	Personality inventory Behavior checklist Recidivism	Group treatment was associated with more favorable outcomes on psychological measures, behavior treatment on behavioral measures. No difference between groups on recidivism, but both were superior to the comparison group
Insight-oriented group therapy, group desensitization, insight and desensitization, placebo control	Behavioral ratings Self-report	Insight and desensitization group was significantly more effective on all measures. No differences between insight only and desensitization only. Differences persisted at 3-month follow-up

TABLE 20-1 *(continued)*

Author	Purpose	Participants
Mitchell and Ng (1973)	Compare individual and combined effects of group counseling, desensitization, and no treatment on academic achievement of test-anxious students	College student volunteers
Mordock, Ellis, and Greenstone (1969)	Compare group versus individual therapy effects on sociometric choices of delinquents	Institutionalized delinquents
Smith and Evans (1971)	Compare group versus individual counseling effects on vocational development	College student volunteers and self-referrals
Tavormina (1975)	Compare the effects of group participation versus operant training with mothers of retarded children	Volunteer mothers of retarded children

Note: E=treatment group; C=control group.

favorable group experiences to be associated with participation in the mixed group and less favorable experiences to be associated with the here-and-now group. Again, although equivocal in many important respects, these results provide important guidance for speculations about central therapeutic processes. They most certainly suggest some directions for additional research.

Although the studies of McLachlan and of Abramowitz and Jackson differ markedly with respect to the sources of therapeutic influence investigated, they are similar in that they represent important contributions to the understanding of how group treatments may affect participants. Additional reports have been summarized in the second section

of Table 20-1. These reports are diverse, but are organized so as to assist in the identification of substantive implications. The categories chosen are: (1) interpersonal influence dimensions, (2) group process dimensions, and (3) comparative studies.

Perusal of the studies summarized in Table 20-1 suggests two disparate conclusions. On the one hand, they represent generally useful contributions to the knowledge base of group psychological treatment. Many are quite sophisticated in their procedures and analyses. In aggregate, they provide further justification of group treatment and a stimulus to further research. Although firm conclusions must await replications and extensions of these investigations, they provide some basis on

Experimental Conditions	Dependent Variables	Results
Group counseling, desensitization, desensitization followed by group counseling, group counseling and desensitization mixed, no-contact control	Study habits survey Grade average Achievement scores Test-anxiety scale	Group counseling combined with desensitization (serially or mixed) led to improved study habits and reduced test anxiety. Desensitization alone led to reduced test anxiety
Group therapy, individual therapy	Sociometric choices for work, social, and rejection	Work choices given, received, and reciprocated were most favorable in group therapy members. No differences between groups on social or rejection
Group counseling, individual counseling no contact control	Vocational decision checklist Counseling rating form	Group treatment significantly more favorable on vocational development measures. Individual treatment was superior to the control group. No differences among groups on counseling ratings
Reflective group participation (discussion of problems), operant training procedures (use of rewards with children), no-treatment control	Attitude survey Problem checklist Behavioral observations	Both treatment groups were significantly more effective than the control on behavioral, attitudinal and self-report measures. A general superiority for the operant training method was noted

which professionals might make treatment decisions in some cases. For all of these reasons, such studies are to be praised.

On the other hand, this literature suggests a second conclusion about what is not being studied. Many of the primary and unique variables of group treatment are not being subjected to empirical test. Three noteworthy sources of information on the mechanisms of groups are Corsini and Rosenberg (1955), Hill (1957), and Yalom (1975). A reading of these works suggests that there is some commonality in the identification of variables presumed to be central curative factors in group treatments. These forces include, among others: (1) corrective recapitulation of the primary family group, (2) in-

terpersonal learning, (3) imitative behavior, (4) altruism, (5) universality, and (6) feelings of belongingness. Cumulatively, these factors may be subsummed within three higher-order concepts. First, group members may improve as a consequence of learning based on their participation in, and evaluation of, a developing social microcosm. Second, psychological growth may result from social learning processes based on interpersonal feedback and consensual validation. And third, individuals may profit from the reciprocal opportunities to be both helpers and helpees in group settings. With a few obvious exceptions, the contemporary group research is devoid of any vigorous effort to test these assertions. The potential utility of concepts derived in other areas to the understanding of group treatment phenomena is undeniable. Still, an empirical analysis of concepts indigenous to group work seems relevant as well. The relatively primitive state of the indigenous concepts presents obvious tactical problems to the experimenter. But without a sustained effort designed to test their validity, the likelihood of any integrated understanding of the uniqueness of group treatments seems low. Of course, these are not mutually exclusive facts. Continued investigations of the utility of borrowed concepts seems warranted, but so does a similar commitment of energy to these commonly held beliefs about the curative forces relatively unique to group processes.

Marathon Group Treatment

There has been a substantial interest in the use of marathon approaches to group treatment. No precise distinction has been drawn between marathons and other group treatments, but it is generally agreed that marathon sessions last from 6 to 48 hours or more. The rationale for the value of the marathon approach seems straightforward; people pretend and defend less as they become more and more fatigued. Advocates of the marathon approach argue that the typical 1 to 3 hours of group meetings do not provide sufficient time for the erosion of social facades. Additionally, they assert that as a member's store of available energy is depleted, that member becomes more apt to show his or her true feelings, act more transparently, and attempt novel modes of behavior. Finally, they state that merely removing an individual from the typical environment may make learning occur more readily.

The critics of marathon techniques have remained unpersuaded by these arguments. They have wondered why, if someone is too tired to pretend, they are not also too tired to practice new behaviors or engage themselves constructively with other members. They have asked why one might assume that new learnings would transfer from the specific marathon setting to the more typical world of the member. Finally, the critics have asked whether changes elicited under such conditions would persist.

Some of these issues are of fundamental impor-

tance in the theory and practice of group work. Because of this, it is unfortunate that so many investigations had to be eliminated from this review for methodological shortcomings that could easily have been corrected. The most common failure was the absense of a comparable group treatment offered over an extended period of time. Conclusions relevant to the conceptual issues involved in this area require comparisons between spaced and massed group treatments. Investigations in which marathon participants were compared with no-treatment controls have been included with the generic outcome literature.

One of the better studies warrants discussion as an illustration of the research methods and results in this area of study. Bare and Mitchell (1972) compared the effects of sensitivity groups offered under three different time patterns. A time-extended condition consisted of 30 hours of group meetings over a 10-week period. The marathon condition consisted of 24 hours of continuous group involvement. The mixed condition consisted of 10 hours of massed treatment, followed by five weekly 2-hour sessions, and ending with another 10-hour session. A fourth group of subjects was given no treatment. Ten experienced group facilitators were selected as leaders. The group participants were 165 mature adults voluntarily seeking a personal growth experience. Individuals who had been receiving therapy within the previous 2 years were excluded from the sample. Members were assigned to the different groups in a modified random fashion. Pretreatment analysis indicated that all groups were similar with respect to age, sex, marital status, occupation, and personality.

Individualized goals were determined for each participant on the basis of information gathered prior to the commencement of the groups. Problem areas were identified that could be rated in behavioral terms. These dimensions were compiled on a behavior change rating sheet and were used as the criteria for assessing the effects of the treatments. Individualized behavior ratings were completed by the group leader, two randomly selected group members, two outside raters closely associated with the target person, and the participant. Ratings were taken immediately following the group's conclusion and again at a 3-month follow-up period. Bare and Mitchell were able to obtain a remarkable 92 percent return at their 3-month follow-up.

Analysis of these data indicated several interesting conclusions. First, participants in the three group treatment conditions showed significantly more behavior change at the conclusion of the group than the control subjects did. Second, this differential result tended to persist at the 3-month follow-up. And third, the effects of spaced, massed, or mixed time patterns were minimal. Although the findings were not significant at the follow-up period, trends in the data suggested that there was less change associated with massed training than for the other two conditions. Assuming that the combination of massed and time-extended conditions was merely a modified form of time-extended treatment, the authors suggested that time-extended treatment seemed to be more facilitative of therapeutic change.

Several additional studies have reported results that fail to support the assertion that marathon treatment enhances the effects of group processes. The counseling center staff at the University of Massachusetts (1972) compared three types of sensitivity groups with an untreated control group. The sensitivity groups were time-extended, marathon, and a no-treatment control condition to test the effects of group participation on self-perceptions and interpersonal behavior. Both the time-extended and marathon groups showed greater positive change than the no-treatment control group, although these differences had dissipated at an 8-week follow-up. Finally, Ross, McReynolds, and Berzins (1974) reported the results of a study comparing marathon treatment with daily group therapy for a small sample of hospitalized narcotic addicts. Both forms of treatment were associated with reductions on the MMPI neurotic triad and increased internal locus of control. The group given the marathon treatment, however, showed a more socially desirable modification in attitudes toward criminal life.

Although there are occasions when proving the null hypothesis is a worthwhile exercise, this is not one of them. Clearly, the assertion that marathon treatment formats enchance the efficacy of group treatments has not been substantiated. That issue

must be resolved through additional empirical effort. There seems to be little point in debating the practical implications of these results, because their value lies in their heuristic impact more than in their substantive conclusions. Any inferences based on the information to date are suspect because of variations between the data sets with regard to leadership variables, client variables, and outcome measures, among others. Answers, if any, will come from multifactorial designs based on multidimensional models of group processes.

Person X Treatment Interaction Studies

Investigations into the interaction of person variables and treatment factors appear to recognize, at least implicitly, some potential limitations in traditional research designs. A complete analysis of this topic is beyond the scope of this chapter, but a thoughtful and provocative presentation can be found in Cronbach (1975). Briefly, if one assumes that events do not occur capriciously, but that they have antecedent causes, two inferences about experimental variance may follow. First, inconsistencies in the literature may not represent inadequate experimental manipulations, faulty control conditions, or sampling error, but may instead represent higher-order interactions among unknown factors. For example, Jones and Medvene (1975) found that group members' initial levels of ego strength interacted with gains in self-actualization from a marathon group experience, while Kimball and Gelso (1974) found no interaction for these two variables. Of course, these differences may be attributable to inconsistencies in experimental manipulations, differences in experimental control, or sampling errors. Alternatively, they may not be inconsistencies at all but veridical representations of a somewhat confounded reality. Further research might be able to demonstrate that knowable characteristics of the samples (e.g., different genetic attributes, environmental variations) account for the apparent inconsistencies with which one group might respond differentially than another to a similar treatment.

A second inference about experimental variation has to do with the choice of the term "error" to modify the noun variance in statistical analysis. Beyond the special meaning of the term in statistical analysis, this may not be the most salubrious choice of labels. Of course, there probably is some error in any investigation. It seems wise to assume, nevertheless, that the bulk of the variance in the statistical error term is merely uncontrolled individual differences. To the extent that this is the case, they may indicate theoretically and pragmatically important factors. The degree to which it is not the case seems most likely answerable through systematic empirical effort.

Another way of saying this is that characteristics of the person can, and most likely will, interact with characteristics of treatments to produce differential effects. Such a statement is a reaffirmation of the inadequacy of the uniformity assumption (Kiesler, 1966). Person X treatment interaction studies should yield information relevant to the question of what kinds of treatments, given by whom, under what conditions, and to what kinds of people eventuate in what kinds of therapeutic outcomes? Although almost any group study could be relevant to this topic, we have summarized a few that have treated person X treatment interactions more specifically. These are presented in Table 20-2.

TABLE 20-2 Person by

Author	Purpose	Participants
Abramowitz, Abramowitz, Roback, and Jackson (1974)	Identify differential effects of directive and nondirective group orientation on members who differ on locus of control	College student volunteers
Abramowitz and Abramowitz (1974)	Compare the effects of insight and interaction group therapy with persons who differ on psychological mindedness	College student volunteers
Jones and Medvene (1975)	Determine the immediate and long-term effects of a marathon group experience on high-, medium-, and low-ego strength participants	College student volunteers
Kilmann, Albert, and Sotile (1975)	Identify differential effects of directive and nondirective group orientation on members who differ on locus of control	College student volunteers
Kimball and Gelso (1974)	Determine the immediate and long-term effects of a marathon group experience on high- and low-ego strength members	College student volunteers

Some potentially interesting inferences may be drawn from the studies in Table 20-2. For example, the Abramowitz et al. (1974) study, and the Kilman et al. (1975) study both suggest that persons with higher levels of internal locus of control may respond more favorably to nondirective or less structured group experiences, at least under some conditions. This suggestion may be modified, however, by the report of Kilman and Howell (1974), not summarized, that persons with higher levels of internality are better therapeutic risks than high externals, regardless of structure consid-

erations. Additionally, the finding of Abramowitz and Abramowitz (1974) that more psychologically minded participants profited more from insight-oriented group therapy than from interaction-oriented therapy may have implications for clinical practice with persons of this nature.

Whether these findings are stable or are themselves representative of more complex interactions cannot be determined on the basis of the available evidence. It could be that they are as much a function of therapist $\times$ treatment or measurement modality $\times$ participant effects as they are of person

Treatment Interaction Studies

Experimental Conditions	Dependent Variables	Results
Structured (directive) or unstructured group treatment. Internal or external locus of control members	Personal control Trait anxiety Self-esteem	High internal locus of control members responded more favorably to the nondirective group approach; high externals responded more favorably to the directive approach
Insight oriented group or interaction oriented group. Psychological mindedness scores of members	Personal control Trait anxiety Self-esteem	Members high on psychological mindedness responded more favorably to insight-oriented groups
Marathon group experience versus no group. Measures of ego strength	POI	Members with initially high levels of ego strength showed the greatest gains in self-actualization after the group experience. These effects had dissipated after 6 weeks
Marathon or time-extended group treatment. Structured (directive) or unstructured group orientation	POI	Data suggested the following rank order of treatment combinations: Internals—unstructured treatments Externals—structured treatments Externals—unstructured treatments Internals—structured treatments
Marathon group experience versus no group. Measures of ego strength	POI	Group participation was associated with gains in self-actualization. Initial levels of ego strength were unrelated to changes in self-actualization

× treatment ones. Continued work in this area is warranted, although it may be more appropriate to treat the person variables as correlational ones and employ mixed model designs instead of continuing to treat them factorially.

Leader Characteristics

Despite the nearly universal agreement that leader characteristics are important determinants of group processes and outcomes, the literature does not reflect much empirical interest in the topic. Lieberman (1976) seemed to reach the same conclusion in his review. Briefly, he reported that there is little empirical basis on which to decide whether experienced leaders are more effective than novices, and whether differential levels of leader skills can reliably be associated with outcomes. He found some research relating the leader's role to outcome indicators, but the relationships seem ambiguous. Refer to Lieberman's excellent review for a more detailed description of these studies.

Premature Terminations and Casualties

These phenomena represent the inefficiencies and tragedies of group treatment. Even though often treated synonymously in the literature, they are perhaps best considered as separate, related categories. Not all persons who leave their groups merit the label of casualty. Some, although not harmed by the group experience, may leave because the group is not meeting their needs because of their own inappropriate expectations, or because of the insensitivity of the leader. Perhaps the term premature termination should be reserved for those for whom group treatment is deemed appropriate, who are not harmed in any discernible way, but who withdraw before their treatment has progressed sufficiently to warrant describing their experience as successful or harmful.

However common they are in the clinical lore, few investigations of premature terminations have appeared in the empirical literature. This is paradoxical, since such cases represent a possible waste of time, energy, and resources for both therapist and client. It is rendered more understandable, however, by reflecting on the methodological problems involved. Among the most basic of these would be the adequate operational definition of each case and the reactivity inherent in following up those who leave their groups.

Four investigations of premature terminations are summarized in Table 20-3. In each case, leaving the group against the therapist's advice defined premature termination. Even though confounded, this probably represents the most appropriate definition in most cases. Two common factors, expectations and personality, appear in these reports. Grotjahn (1972), in a retrospective analysis of those who left groups he led, suggested that they were less motivated for the treatment and tended to fear confrontation from other members of the group or from the leader. Additionally, he found that several terminated because they were becoming psychotic; however, these may be more appropriately classified as casualties if the genesis of their decompensation can be attributed to the group treatment. Similarly, Caine, Wijesinghe, and Wood (1973) reported that premature terminators had less favorable expectations toward the group as indicated by a pretreatment administration of a treatment expectancies questionnaire. Personality differences between premature terminators and those who remained were reported by Sethna and Harrington (1971), who found that those diagnosed as "hysterics" were significantly more likely to leave treatment than those classified as "obsessives." Caine et al. (1973) reported that terminators were less introspective than remainers. Conversely, Koran and Costell (1973) found no differences between their terminators and remainers on several demographic variables, HIM-B scales, or the FIRO-B interchange compatibility scale. Since there may be little overlap among the different instruments used in these studies, the results may not be incompatible.

The two reports of dropouts in Table 20-3 defined their phenomenon differently than those in the premature termination studies. Both Lieberman, Yalom, and Miles (1973) and Rosenzweig and Folman (1974) defined dropouts temporally, without reference to the patient's psychological status. These studies show some similarities with the premature termination studies, however, in that both found that dropouts may hold different expectations about different aspects of group treatment as well as about the treatment in general (e.g., fear of group's attack, one's own anger, or self-disclosure, and less sophisticated concept of therapy). Additionally, if one wishes to consider empathy as a personality variable, the findings of Rosenzweig and Folman suggest that dropouts also differ on that dimension.

Conclusions in the absence of more definitive research are questionable, but these investigations do indicate two *caveats* to the group therapist. First, prospective members should be screened to eliminate those for whom the group represents an unlikely treatment match. Second, the therapist's time is probably well spent in discovering and shaping the expectations of the individual members. Where it is inappropriate to the general concept of group treatment or to some specific aspects of a particular method, the participant's expectation should be treated before therapy commences. For a more thorough discussion of the relationships between expectancies and treatment, we recommend the review by Baekeland and Lundwall (1975).

Whereas dropouts and premature terminations may represent futile efforts and unrealized opportunities, casualties represent a misapplication of a group treatment. There is nearly universal agreement that group treatments may result in casualties among some participants. And there is little debate regarding the necessity for identifying the frequency and sources of these casualties. There is a heated debate, however, about the meaning of the data presented in response to the need. A primary reason for this dispute is that much of the information offered is impressionistic and fortified with passion. Even where the evidence is relatively objective, it is subject to divergent interpretation. While most of the casualty literature seems preoccupied with meeting the need for useful evidence, our analysis suggests that not only are the important questions unanswered, they may not have been asked in ways amenable to answer within the canons of scientific knowledge. Here again, this regrettable state of events may be ascribed to definitional and methodological deficiencies.

The fundamental question in casualty research is not whether they occur or with what frequency. The fundamental question is, "What is a casualty?" Only when that question has been answered can we anticipate progress toward solving the important questions of frequency and causality.

At present, there is excessive latitude in the range of interpretations that can be drawn from observed changes in a group member's behavior.

Two examples can help to make this point. Batchelder and Hardy (1968) defined a casualty as one expressing negative feelings about his or her experiences in a sensitivity or development laboratory. Considering the emphasis such groups place on the open and honest expression of affect, this is a remarkably inclusive definition. Conversely, some have argued that psychotic experiences may constitute examples of important personal growth for some individuals (Laing, 1967), a definition so exclusive that it robs the term casualty of any consensual meaning. In the absense of systematic efforts at differentiating stresses that accompany psychological growth from those which do not, the implication that decompensation can be construed as therapeutic must be actively opposed.

The concept of casualty has no absolute meaning in group treatment. It can be defined only in a multidimensional context. This context should be empirically instead of impressionistically based, essential instead of artifactual. The recent literature may contribute to such a definition and suggests several dimensions of interest. These include the purpose of the treatment, member and leader characteristics, and the measurement perspective employed. A summary of some recent research is shown in Table 20-3.

Recognizing the sacrifice of fidelity implicit in such summaries, several possible inferences are possible. Perhaps the most basic is that many participants have been observed under extremely varied conditions. Most of the data are drawn from sensitivity and encounter groups, but the formats have varied from structured human relations labs to unspecified marathons. The leaders, where specified, range from experienced behavioral scientists to relatively untrained novices. Participants include college students who participate for class credit and established business and professional people. Similarly, the data base and operational definitions employed show a wide latitude. Given the remarkable variation among the components of the investigations and the fact that there are so many uncontrolled sources of error in the studies, it is reasonable to anticipate substantial variation in the results.

While the range of casualty rates is rather great (0 to 8 percent), perhaps the most striking feature of the aggregate data is that they tend to be consis-

TABLE 20-3   Premature Termination

Author	Type of Group	Leader	Participants
Premature terminations			
Caine, Wijesinghe, and Wood (1973)	Psychoanalytic therapy groups	Unspecified clinic staff	130 consecutive admissions assigned to group therapy or to individual behavior therapy
Grotjan (1972)	Group therapy	Author	122 inpatients, outpatients, therapists, and hospital staff
Koran and Costell (1973)	Group therapy	First-year psychiatric residents	87 psychiatric outpatients, mostly middle and upper socioeconomic class
Lieberman, Yalom, and Miles (1973)	Various types of group therapy	Experienced practitioners of each type of therapy	206 college students
Rosenzweig and Folman (1974)	Nondirective	Experienced professionals	26 screened inpatients
Sethna and Harrington (1971)	Psychoanalytic therapy groups	Not given	94 psychiatric inpatients
Casualties			
Cooper (1972)	T-groups	Not given	College student volunteers
Kane, Wallace and Lipton (1971)	T-groups	Psychologists, ministers, psychiatrists, and others	Unknown. Population was all participants in T-groups; sampled 191 neuropsychiatrists

Definition	Results
Leaving the group before at least 9 months of therapy	Terminators had less favorable expectations toward group therapy and were less introspective than remainers
Leaving the group against therapist's advice	Terminators were judged less motivated, were becoming psychotic, or feared confrontation
Leaving the group against therapist's advice	Terminators (18 percent) were not significantly different from remainers on HIM-B, FIRO-B interchange compatibility, demographic, or rated cohesiveness of the group
(1) Attending less than half of the group meetings; (2) missing the final two meetings. In neither case are casualties included	(1) 15 percent dropouts; (2) 17 percent dropouts. Reasons given for dropping out were concern about group's attack, fear of own anger, fear of self-disclosure, and desire for more intimacy from the group
Leaving group before the seventeenth week.	Therapists rated terminators (50 percent) as less empathic, forming poorer therapeutic relationships, having less positive feeling and sophistication of therapy concept than remainers
Leaving the group against therapist's advice	41 percent terminated prematurely; 65 percent of those classified as hysterics, and 30 percent of those classified as obsessives
Increased number of visits to health service for any reason	No difference between group members and a comparison group with no group experience
Emotional disturbance consequential to group participation, diagnosed by psychiatrists	91 persons needed help (proportion indeterminate)

TABLE 20-3 *(continued)*

Author	Type of Group	Leader	Participants
Lieberman, Yalom, and Miles (1973)	Various types of group therapy	Experienced practitioners of each type therapy	206 college students
Mintz (1969)	Marathons	Experienced professionals	80 drawn from a larger sample
Posthuma and Posthuma (1973)	Encounter groups, placebo group, human relations class control group	Experienced, B-type "providers"	24 encounter group members from a church, 23 placebo control members
Reddy (1970)	T-groups; individual therapy and no-treatment control groups	Experienced NTL for T-groups; psychologists for individual therapy	32 college student volunteers in T-groups; 10 self-referred clients; 19 controls
Ross, Kligfield, and Whitman (1971)	T-groups	Not given	2900, of whom 1750 participated in structured management groups
Smith (1975a)	Residential human-relations training labs	Not given	94 mixed professionals, mostly teachers and social workers

tently low. For example, Mintz (1969) reported a 2 percent casualty rate among marathon participants, Ross, Kligfield, and Whitman (1971) estimated less than 1 percent casualties from T-groups, and Smith (1975a) found no instances of casualties when he followed his human relations laboratory participants for 5 months. These results are similar to those reported in surveys by Batchelder and Hardy (1968) and the National Training Laboratory (cited in Hartley, Roback, and Abramowitz, 1976), both of which reported casualty rates of less than 1 percent in training laboratories, and Rogers (1967), who reported a similar rate among alumni of his own groups. Deferring for the moment the 8 percent casualty rate reported by Lieberman, Yalom, and Miles (1973), several explanations are offered for this casualty low. It may be that they are the product of insensitive instruments or investigators, which would contribute to artificially conservative estimates. Or perhaps group treatments are remarkably safe, apparently more so than almost any other active intervention. Still another explanation is that group casualties tend to be a function of relatively specific psychonoxious influences that, when operating, are quite potent.

There is little direct evidence as to the validity of any of these explanations. Useful data would be provided by studies that included at least several of the following characteristics: (1) some commonality

Definition	Results
Increased distress or maladaptive defense lasting 8 months or more and deemed caused by the group	8 percent casualties; another 8 percent judged to be "negative changers"
Self-report of anxiety or depression lasting "several weeks"	2 percent casualties
Self-report of behavior change, judged as overt and negative by experts	No significant differences among groups at posttest or at 6-month follow-up
TSCS scales	T-group members gained more on number of deviant signs. All other comparisons were non-significant
Psychiatrists' assessment of decompensation from group	Less than 1 percent casualties overall and in the management groups
Ratings as considerably hurt by self or three other members.	12 percent "suspect following treatment," none at 5-month follow-up

in the definition and measurement of casualties; (2) use of measures specifically designed to assess decompensation at different levels of development; (3) relevant base rate data from no-treatment and placebo control groups; (4) follow-up assessments; (5) better, or at least known, relationships among the different measurement perspectives; and (6) an independent assessment of casualties.

Cooper (1972a) argued that the negative effects of treatment could appear in physical as well as psychological ways. He followed volunteer participants in a T-group and compared their use of the university health service with that of a matched group of nonvolunteers. Although confounded with volunteering, he found no differences be-

tween the two groups. Reddy (1970) compared the changes in TSCS scales for T-group volunteers, counseling service group therapy clients, and a control group of introductory psychology students. He found that the T-group participants increased significantly more on number of deviant signs, although again one cannot tell if the result is due to relevant treatment effects, greater willingness to acknowledge unusual ideas, or the incomparability of the groups. Finally, Posthuma and Posthuma (1973), in a relatively well-controlled study, compared the effects of encounter group participation with those of a no-treatment and a placebo control condition. The participants were middle-aged and of middle or upper socioeconomic levels. The Behavior Change Index (created by the authors) was given at the end of the treatment and again at a 6-month follow-up. Their results indicated significantly more positive changes associated with the encounter treatment than with the control conditions, even though these had dissipated at the 6-month follow-up. More important to this discussion are the results relevant to negative treatment effects. One or more negative changes were reported for 33 percent of the encounter group and no-treatment controls and for 24 percent of the placebo control participants immediately following the treatments. At the follow-up, the rate for the encounter group remained at 33 percent, but the placebo group had increased to 48 percent and the no-treatment controls to 52 percent. None of these differences within or between groups was statistically significant. If the control groups were valid, these data suggest that some negative change is common in encounter groups, but that such change may not indicate a casualty *qua* casualty.

In the absence of replications and extensions of these studies, aggregate inferences should be viewed as speculative at best. Given this, some common referents occur in the literature, including the psychological characteristics of the group members and leaders and the stylistic factors of the leader.

A truism of the casualty literature is that persons with psychological disturbances prior to group treatment are more likely to manifest deterioration than those not so afflicted (Lieberman et al., 1973; Reddy, 1970). Such findings offer little surprise value, but they do reaffirm the necessity for continuous screening of group members.

A second truism of casualty research is that personality and leadership style factors may influence the likelihood of negative changes. The major work of Lieberman et al. (1973) indicates that some group leaders apparently were unaware of casualties in their groups (defined by participants' and expert judges' evaluations). They also suggested that higher rates were associated with two leadership styles: the energizer and the laissez-faire. Although this may represent the most ambitious empirical inquiry into leader-oriented correlates of casualties, the results are of limited generality for two primary reasons. First, leadership styles were confounded with individual leaders, and there is no way to assess leader behavior by participant characteristic interactions. Second, group leaders were selected from a restricted geographical area that may have attracted group leaders with precisely the personality characteristics (charismatic) that were associated with casualties. A conservative inference would be that leaders must monitor their style on the basis of the members' needs.

Some Preliminary Conclusions

An overview of the group treatment outcome research suggests some preliminary conclusions, *ceteris paribus*. Accumulated evidence indicates that group treatments have been more effective than no treatment, than placebo or nonspecific treatments, or than other recognized psychological treatments, at least under some circumstances. This evidence has been gathered under a variety of conditions, from a wide range of individuals, and in many different ways. Although it may not be the best question to ask, there is a large body of research that indicates that group treatments "work." This conclusion must be qualified, however, since it is empirically and intuitively obvious that not all groups have had uniformly beneficial results. We have seen nonrejections of the null hypothesis in the research, and evidence of casualties as well. In addition, there is little reason to believe that the practices and practitioners sampled in the published literature are representative of the larger population. The conclusion must be qualified on other grounds as well; that is, group treatments have been shown to be somewhat *effective* in helping people achieve more positive and perhaps more healthy evaluations of themselves and others. These improvements are most frequently reported on measures reflecting self-concept assessment, attitude change, and positive personality developments. In spite of the apparent diversity of these measures, it seems most appropriate to view these measures as reflecting a nonspecific factor of improvement based on more favorable subjective evaluations that may or may not be accompanied by observable behavior changes. In spite of the general nature of reported changes, the follow-up literature is clearly encouraging in that the available evidence suggests that some treatment effects persist over time.

Evidence regarding the comparative effectiveness of group treatments is unclear. Even though various group treatments have been reported to be more effective than various other types of psychological treatment, it would be inappropriate to conclude that these differences are a function of group treatment processes alone. In virtually all comparative studies differential outcomes are confounded with factors such as treatment populations, personality characteristics of therapists, outcome measures, and treatment goals. While it is encouraging to see group treatments compare favorably to other forms of psychological treatment, there is still limited information suggesting the differential effects or superiority of any type of group treatment.

Statements about why these treatments elicit therapeutic benefits from some participants seem premature. Causal statements about the curative forces operating in the group context, the circumstances under which they may be brought to bear, or the form in which they may be expressed cannot be supported on the basis of the available literature. We suggest that this unhappy state of affairs can be traced to the fact that many of the central questions have not been asked or, if they have been asked, they have not been posed in a way that permits powerful tests.

There is reason to believe that progress will be made, however. The studies discussed in the "Specific Treatments" and "Person X Treatment Interaction Studies" sections seem to reflect a more sophisticated approach to the empirical analysis of important group phenomena. The viability of responsible group treatment may rest on the replication and extension of investigations that identity specific treatment factors and on the development of matching procedures that consider treatment x person interaction patterns.

PROCESS STUDIES

Considering the criticisms leveled at much of the outcome literature, the relevance of systematic investigations of group process phenomena seems apparent. Such inquiries into the ecological characteristics of therapeutic groups offer the potential for empirical definition of several important group variables. Among these are group structure, cohesion, self-disclosure, and feedback. Each of these factors has been proposed to account for significant proportions of the outcome variance in group work. As we will see, scientific scrutiny has treated some more favorably than others.

Group Structure

In an earlier review, Bednar and Lawlis (1971) noted that pregroup training seemed to hold particular promise for group work. Since then, 18 empirical investigations and several theoretical articles have been published that combine to define group structure and its effects more precisely. They suggest a break from the traditional view, which has seen structure and ambiguity as orthogonal to one another.

Historically, ambiguity has occupied a position of theoretical pre-eminence in systems of interpersonal influence. In individual therapies it has been alleged to enhace transference, facilitate access to learned conditions of worth, and encourage client self-direction. In group treatments ambiguity is said to foster an atmosphere appropriate to the particular group, lead to the expression of problem behaviors, and provide the stimulus for self-exploration and behavior change. In each instance, the underlying rationale for the therapeutic function of ambiguity has had its origin in theories of personality and psychopathology more than in those specific to group work. These beliefs may be valid in some cases, but there is ample reason to doubt their ubiquity. For example, after reviewing substantial literature on the effects of task clarity and structure on human performance, Bednar and Lee (1976) suggested that ambiguity and lack of clarity tend to be associated with increased anxiety, and diminished productivity and learning in a variety of settings.

The effects of structure in the early phases of group treatment were considered in a model presented by Bednar, Melnick, and Kaul (1974). This model proposes that levels of risk and responsibility most conducive to group development can be regulated by the appropriate manipulation of structure variables. Arguing that higher structure increases the likelihood of risk taking by group members without encumbering them with full responsibility for the consequences of these actions, the model suggests that group development proceeds through the following developmental phases: (1) initial ambiguity; (2) increased structure; (3) increased risk taking; (4) development of group cohesion; and (5) increased personal responsibility. The model does not advocate structured group treatment, but attempts to delineate the appropriate function of structure in the initiation of constructive group interactions. Table 20-4 summarizes the experimental work relevant to the model and to other practical issues involved in considerations of structure in group treatments.

These studies are generally superior to those reviewed by Bednar and Lawlis (1971). The research designs are more sophisticated in that: (1) there is a greater use of appropriate control groups; (2) factorial designs crossing treatment variables with theoretically relevant personality dimensions are more common, (3) the research questions are often stated with greater specificity, and (4) there is an increased equivalence between the conceptual and operational definitions of important variables. Nevertheless, there are several design limitations common to these studies,; the most notable may be the absence of follow-up assessments and a continued, although diminished, semantic imprecision.

Inspection of the experimental conditions summarized in Table 20-4 reveals that essentially three processes have been employed to prepare clients for groups. These are role-induction interviews and information dissemination, vicarious behavioral training, and direct practice of target behaviors. These procedures have varied with respect to the timing of their presentation. The specific content conveyed in these procedures also has varied, emphasizing different types of target behaviors, role expectancies, and implied or explicit demand characteristics. These different experimental conditions are apparently unrelated to similar variations in treatment effects. Virtually all of these treatment combinations have been associated with significant and constructive effects. Finally, college students have been studied more often than any other population. However, lower-class clients, hospital patients, and outpatient college students have shown appreciably similar positive responses to the same treatment conditions.

Inspection of the findings in Table 20-4 suggests some conceptually interesting and potentially useful observations stemming from the different investigations. For example, one important dimension along which structure can vary is the degree to which behavioral demands are implied or explicit. Nine different investigations employed a factorial design in which some variation of structure was crossed with a theoretically relevant personality variable. Five of these nine studies (Abramowitz, Abramowitz, Roback, & Jackson, 1974; Bednar & Lee, 1976; D'Augelli & Chinsky, 1974; Evensen & Bednar, 1976; Kilman, Albert, & Sotile, 1975) reported significant structure X personality interaction effects. In each of these studies the subjects with personality characteristic (I-E scores, risk-taking disposition, current level of interpersonal skills) most indicative of higher levels of interpersonal functioning responded more favorably to the lower structure demands, at least on some dependent measures. Conversely, the less adequate participants seemed to respond more favorably to higher demand conditions on some variables. In the absence of additional replications and extensions of these findings, the interpretation just suggested must be considered with caution, eventhough the research points to the value of clarifying the differential effects of structure and person variables.

In addition, two studies (Crews & Melnick, 1976; DeJulio, Bentley & Cockayne, 1976) reported that structure imposed early in the group was related to initially high levels of group performance, but that these effects dissipated with time. In both cases, groups initiated with low structure eventually developed levels of interpersonal functioning equal to that of those initiated under conditions of high structure, which may suggest that practitioners and researchers must conceptualize structure within a developmental context. In addition, these results provide a consistent, although tentative, basis for differential decisions about the utility of structure in long- or short-term groups. Short-term workshops and marathons may profit from the judicious application of structure; long-term groups may or may not.

We have not conveyed the detailed information that helps to provide an understanding of the psychological dimensions involved in the treatments, the dependent measures, or the power of treatment effects. To mitigate this, we have chosen to summarize one study in greater detail.

Evensen and Bednar (1976) employed a randomized design with a 2×4 factorial arrangement of conditions in an investigation of the effects of pregroup structure. They included two levels of risk taking (high and low) and four levels of pregroup preparation. The preparation involved taped instructions and behavioral practice prior to beginning a relatively unstructured interpersonal relations workshop. The cognitive structure condition consisted of an audiotape that informed the participants why sharing personal feelings was an effective method for becoming more intimately acquainted; it instructed them to express those feelings openly and immediately. The behavioral practice condition consisted of taped instructions describing activities that the participants were to try. These activities, designed to provide practice in self disclosure and feedback, included sharing information about themselves with a partner. There was a condition that combined the cognitive and behavioral structures, and a minimal structure condition in which participants were merely told that the purpose of the workshop was to become more closely acquainted.

Participants' risk-taking disposition was measured by the scale developed by Jackson, Hourany, and Vidmar (1971), with high and low risk taking operationally defined as falling one-half standard deviation from the group mean. This technique significantly separated the two groups, which were then randomly assigned to structure conditions. No pregroup differences in risk taking were found across the structure conditions.

Three classes of dependent variables were employed to assess the treatment effects. Group behavior was measured with the Hill Interaction Matrix (Hill, 1965). Ratings were made from audiotapes of the groups by a trained, experienced rater who was blind to both the experimental conditions and hypotheses. Later, reliability, defined as correct quadrant location, was 96 percent on a sample of 80 ratings repeated 2 months later. Self-disclosure and feedback were rated on the Perceived Depth of Interaction Scale (PDIS) developed for this investigation. The PDIS was a self-report instrument consisting of 10 five-point items;

five represented the greatest amount of the quality being judged. Self-ratings were summed to provide a single index of interaction. The PDIS showed significant internal consistency and correlated significantly with the weighted Hill Interaction Matrix (HIM) measure. Group cohesion was assessed by the Gross Cohesion Scale (Gross, 1957), a seven-item self-report instrument that provides an unidimensional index of cohesion.

Results of this investigation suggested that both risk-taking disposition and structure influenced the participants' performance in the workshops. Specifically, high levels of risk taking were related to higher levels of interpersonal communication (on the HIM), group cohesion (on the Gross Cohesion Scale), and perceived depth of interaction (on the PDIS). In addition, the behavioral structure, alone and in combination with the cognitive structure, seemed to facilitate performance in the workshops as measured by the three dependent variables.

Perhaps more importantly, however, was the pattern of person by treatment interactions found. A significant risk X structure interaction was found for each dependent variable. Further analysis of these suggested that they were largely attributable to the differential effects of behavioral structure on high and low risk taking participants. In each case the pregroup behavioral practice was most productive with the high risk taking participants. The high risk takers also showed the highest levels of communication, cohesion, and perceived self-disclosure and feedback. Conversely, the low risk takers had the lowest levels of these qualities. When combined with the cognitive structure treatment, an essentially similar, although less pronounced, pattern of results appeared.

Although this study is subject to the criticisms of a restricted sample, a relatively small N, and at least one dependent variable of questionable stability, it does combine with other research to suggest several methodological and practical recommendations. They warrant the tentative assumption that different levels of structure may have powerful effects on group development, especially in the earlier stages. The precise nature of the effects cannot be specified, but additional research into the development of groups' ecologies seems indicated. Such research must consider the nature of the participants and their expectations, the nature of the

TABLE 20-4   Group

Name	Purpose	Experimental Conditions
Abramowitz, Abramowitz, Roback, and Jackson (1974)	Investigate the effects of directive and nondirective group therapy on internal-external locus of control subjects	1. Relatively directive group 2. Relatively nondirective group 3. Internal-external locus of control group participants
Anchor, Vojtisek, and Patterson (1973)	Investigate the effects of initial group structuring on the group behavior of high- and low-anxiety subjects	1. Specific cognitive instructions to self-disclosure 2. Placebo control 3. High- and low-anxiety group participants
Bednar and Battersby (1976)	Investigate effects of pregroup cognitive structure on early group development	Factorial arrangement of treatments ($2 \times 2 \times 2$) including: 1. Behavioral instructions 2. Goal instructions 3. Persuasive explanation
Crews and Melnick (1976)	Investigate effects of initial and delayed structure and social avoidance on short- and long-term outcomes	Factorial arrangement of treatments (2×3) including: 1. Early group structure 2. Delayed group structure 3. No structure 4. Social anxiety and avoidance
D'Augelli and Chinsky (1974)	Investigate the effects of interpersonal skills and pregroup training on meaningful group participation	Cognitive instruction Cognitive instructions and behavioral practice Placebo control

Structure Studies

Population	Dependent Variables	Major Findings
College outpatients	Expectations for successful life Social alienation scale Feelings of guilt and shame State-trait anxiety inventory Client self-report	Subjects in group more closely matched for their locus of control orientation generally showed a more favorable response to group treatment This was particularly true for internally orientated clients
Hospitalized patients	Group process ratings	High-anxiety subjects talked more in both treatment conditions
College students	Behavior ratings Group cohesion Attitudes toward groups	Specific behavioral instructions associated with more productive group behavior, more favorable attitudes, and higher levels of group cohesion.
College students	Group behavior Group cohesion Attitudes toward group situational anxiety	Early group structure associated with increased self-disclosure as well as higher levels of anxiety. The effects of structure dissipated over time
College students	Group process ratings	Subjects receiving any type of meaningful pretraining engaged in high levels of interpersonal communications Cognitive pretraining was associated with the highest levels of pretraining; this was particularly true of interpersonally skilled subjects

TABLE 20-4 *(continued)*

Name	Purpose	Experimental Conditions
DeJulio, Bentley, and Cockayne (1976)	Investigate the effects of high and low initial structure on short- and long-term group development	1. Audiotaped instructions and examples of desired behaviors at first group meeting 2. Comparable groups without audiotape instruction
Evensen and Bednar (1976)	Investigate the effects of specific pregroup cognitive and behavioral structure and risk-taking disposition on early group development	Factorial arrangement of treatments (2×4) including: 1. Cognitive structure 2. Behavioral structure 3. Cognitive and behavioral structure 4. Minimal structure 5. Risk-taking disposition
Lee and Bednar (1976)	Investigate effects of group structure, risk-taking disposition, and sex on early group development	Factorial arrangement of treatments ($3 \times 2 \times 3 \times 2$) including: 1. Group structure 2. Risk-taking disposition 3. Sex 4. Behavioral tasks
Strupp and Bloxom (1973)	Investigate the effects of pregroup role induction procedures on lower-class patients	Groups introduced to group treatment by: 1. Role induction film 2. Role induction interview 3. Control film

Population	Dependent Variables	Major Findings
College students	Observational group behavior Self-closure questionnaire Self-esteem scale Personal orientation inventory	The high structure started at higher levels of group interaction, but moved toward less productive interaction over time. Low-structure groups began at lower levels of interactions but moved to high levels of group functioning over time
College students	Group behavior Self reports Group cohesion	Risk X structure interaction variables with the high risk-behavioral structure conditions associated with highest levels of group performance on all variables and low risk-behavioral structure lowest performance on most variables
College students	Group behavior Attitudes toward group Group cohesion	Risk X structure interaction with high structure most beneficial for low risk-taking subjects Experimental conditions associated with highest levels of interpersonal communications generally had lowest levels of group cohesion
Lower-class outpatients	Rating of improvement Satisfaction with treatment Symptom discomfort Role expectancies Motivation for treatment in therapy behavior	The two role induction procedures were associated with more favorable therapy experiences, and on several measures the role induction film was superior to the control film

TABLE 20-4 (continued)

Name	Purpose	Experimental Conditions
Warren and Rice (1972)	Investigate the effects of outside therapy structuring on group participation style and attrition	1. Therapy and out of group structuring and stabilization 2. Therapy and out of group stabilization interviews 3. Therapy only
Whalen (1969)	Investigate the effects of pregroup instructions and modeling on early group interactions	Factorial arrangement of treatments (2×2) including: 1. Film model and detailed instructions 2. Detailed instructions only 3. Film model and minimal instructions 4. Minimal instructions only
Zarle and Willis (1975)	Investigate the effects of pregroup stress management techniques on client deterioration from encounter groups	Induced-affect training Induced-affect training and encounter group Induced-affect training only

treatment offered, and the measurement modality employed. These studies also suggest that additional work is needed in the operational definition of ambiguity, probably from the perspectives of both participants and observers. Finally, they call into question an uncritical adherence to theoretical models developed under conditions that may not apply to group treatments.

Cohesion

The concept of group cohesion is ubiquitous in group treatment theory. It is asserted to be a prime therapeutic ingredient in groups, and successes and failures are often attributed to it. Despite this, relatively little research has been published that systematically manipulates variables that are believed to affect cohesion. The research that has been published has led to less consistency of results and interpretation than one would wish. In short, there is little cohesion in the cohesion research.

There seem to be several fundamental sources for this apparent confusion regarding group cohesion and its role in determining the outcomes of group treatments. First, and probably most important, there is little cognitive substance to the concept. It is used to describe and explain many phenomena generally and few specifically. The ingredients of cohesion, when specification is attemp-

TABLE 20-4 *(continued)*

Population	Dependent Variables	Major Findings
Low prognosis college center clientele	Group process analysis Therapist-rated changes Q-sort Group sessions attended	Out of therapy structure and stabilization interview associated with lower attrition, improved group participation, and more perceived personal change
College students	Ratings of observable behavior	Film model and detailed instructions associated with more interpersonal openness
College students	Eysenck Personality Inventory	Group participants not receiving induced affect training showed significant increase on Neuroticism scales whereas group members receiving such training demonstrate significant increases on the Extraversion scale

ted, are often referred to inconsistently and are rarely discussed systematically. The consequence of this is that one cannot divine a consensual definition of the phenomenon. Second, the psychometric properties of cohesion scales typically leave a great deal to be desired. Most scales have few items, reflect limited content domains, are scored on the basis of face validity considerations, and have disappointing reliabilities and validities. Third, authors tend not to recognize (or at least acknowledge) the lack of equivalence between the conceptual and operational definitions they use in studies of cohesion. For example, the same scale is likely to be used in assessing cohesion in different studies

where the conceptual definition may range from attraction to the group as a whole, attraction for peers in the group, liking for the group leader, agreement with the group's goals, or some other aspect of the psychological environment within the group. These conceptual definitions clearly are not necessarily identical.

An understanding of the reasons for this lack of consensual definition may be adduced from common features of those employed. Cohesion is most often defined as a continuous bipolar phenomenon. Again, it may be operationalized as the self-report of attraction to the group as a whole, the individual members of the group, or the specific group function. Cohesion is rarely considered to be a function of some combination of these (and other) dimensions. And, when discussed, these phenomena are often described in terms that can most charitably be called jargon (e.g., friendliness, solidarity, togetherness, groupness). Related to this problem is the fact that many discussions and investigations of cohesion treat it as though it were a relatively stable state. Whether this is the empirical case cannot be discovered, of course, unless one assumes that it is not a state, but a process. Logic and experience suggest that cohesion is a developmental process within groups, and that it is often unstable, subject to situational fluctuations, and multidimensional. It seems likely that these dimensions may be orthogonal to one another and that the research that will be valued in the future will treat cohesion as a complex, changing, relativistic phenomenon. Even further, we suggest that the term be dropped from the empirical vocabulary and that more representative alternatives be found.

Despite the conceptual state of the art, several investigations worthy of note have been located. Two studies suggested methods by which group cohesion might be affected. Ribner (1974) assigned college students to groups of four on the basis of their self-disclosure scores. Groups were either homogeneous or heterogeneous in self-disclosure. In half of the groups, contracts for increased self-disclosure were used; in the other half, no contract was used. Results indicated that the contract to self-disclose enhanced attraction to the group as a whole, but decreased liking for the other group members. In addition, homogeneous groups of high disclosers showed greater liking for other members and attraction to the group than did mixed groups or those homogeneous with low disclosers. Liberman (1971) reported that the therapist could influence the level of cohesion in a therapy group by the systematic application of social reinforcement (specifically, prompts and rewards), and that members of such groups were more likely to show positive therapeutic changes than members of comparison groups.

The developmental nature of cohesion was studied by Dies and Hess (1971). Male narcotic abusers were assigned to either one 12-hour

marathon group or to a therapy group that met for 1 hour per day for 12 consecutive days. Analysis of tape recordings, semantic differential scales, and performance on a prisoner's dilemma game following the treatment indicated that cohesiveness increased with time in both types of group treatment. In addition, their data suggested that there was generally greater cohesion in the marathon groups than in the therapy groups. However, cohesion as a developmental phenomenon was called into question by a correlational study reported by Costell and Koran (1972). In this investigation, outpatients were given the FIRO-B Interchange Compatibility scale, the HIM-B, and a cohesiveness questionnaire after the first and twelfth group therapy sessions. The results indicated that cohesiveness remained essentially stable from the first to twelfth sessions, and that neither the FIRO or HIM data seemed related to the cohesiveness measure. The threats to the external validity of these studies seem apparent, but they do not obviate the possibility that the results are compatible and that the differences are an artifact of group composition, situational factors, or some other unknown variables.

Two developments provide a basis for cautious optimism when considering the future of the cohesion concept. The first is that social and organizational psychologists have presented a series of reports on the topic. The social psychologists (Anderson, Linder, & Lopes, 1973; Good & Nelson, 1973; Lott & Lott, 1965) generally define cohesion as attraction or attractiveness; by such a definition they offer an inferential bridge to the great body of research on that variable. The organizational psychologists (O'Keefe, Kernaghan, & Rubenstein, 1975; Stinson & Hellebrandt, 1972; Stogdill, 1972) offer more specific definitions of cohesion and seek relatively objective correlates of differential levels of cohesion. Direct translation of the results of these studies to group treatments is, of course, unwarranted. Nevertheless, it seems likely that hypotheses and paradigms may transfer to the therapeutic setting.

A second cause of optimism is that several interesting measurement approaches have appeared in the recent literature. These provide relatively clear conceptual definitions of cohesiveness and seem to be more psychometrically sound than many instruments that have been employed previously. Perhaps the most promising of these (in a specific setting) is the Group Atmosphere Scale (Silbergeld, Koenig, Manderscheid, Meeker, & Hornung, 1975). The Group Atmosphere Scale (GAS) was designed to measure the psychosocial environment in outpatient therapy; it is comprised of 12 subscales. Based on the self-reports of 149 participants in 17 different therapy groups, Silbergeld et al. found that they could reliably describe cohesiveness as a function of six subscales (spontaniety, support, affiliation, involvement, insight, and clarity), that long-term therapy groups showed greater cohesion than either long-term counseling or short-term intervention groups, that more cohesive groups scored lower on their Submission subscale, and that stable differences between more and less cohesive groups could be found on the I IIM and on self-reports of communication and anxiety in the group. Replications and extensions with the GAS will be needed before the limits of its utility can be determined, but the scale seems promising. In addition, two factor analyses of group process variables support the contention that cohesion is a multidimensional phenomenon, although neither has lead to a psychometric instrument at this time (Hagstrom & Selvin, 1965; Heckel, Holmes, & Rosecrans, 1971).

In conclusion, we suggest that editors refuse any research that fails to specify the meaning of cohesion, assesses it in vague and obscure ways, and does not indicate the equivalence between their conceptual and operational definitions. Such research is counterproductive and leads to a noncohesive body of literature.

Self-Disclosure

The value of personal self-disclosure in group processes has been subject to scathing criticism and enthusiastic praise as a factor central to successful treatment. Since these views are presented with equal conviction, the question facing a serious reviewer is to determine whether the issues are genuine or *ignus fatuous*. It seems to us that the clinical and empirical implications of self-disclosure for group work are subject to several sources of confusion that come from the conceptual limitations of the concept. These problems are seldom acknowledged in the experimental or theoretical literature.

The most commonly employed conceptual definition of self-disclosure has been that of Jourard (1971), who described it as, ". . . my communication of my private world to you in a language that you clearly understand." This definition, although existentially attractive, does not sufficiently differentiate, describe, or define the diversity of phenomena that may be involved in the process of personal self-disclosure. It is essentially a process definition in which the psychological relevance of the content is attributed secondary importance. If such a definition were ever adequate to an empirically based approach to group therapy, the accumulating evidence calls its utility into serious question at this time. This evidence suggests that self-disclosure is best considered in multidimensional terms and not as a unitary factor.

Perhaps the most pervasive inadequacy of the common definition is its implicit assumption that self-disclosure is a phenomenon that can or cannot occur, that it is a volitional aspect of interpersonal communication. A cursory review of the research in human communication should convince even the most fanatic adherent that this assumption is invalid. If one makes the reasonable assumption that all behavior (not only speech) communicates information to another person (Cherry, 1966) and the equally reasonable assumption that behavior has no opposite, one is lead to conclude that self-disclosure occurs constantly. Similar reasoning lead Watzlawick, Beavin, and Jackson (1967) to assert:

if it is accepted that all behavior in an interactional situation . . . is communication, it follows that no matter how one may try, one cannot not communicate. Activity or inactivity, words or silence, all have message value; they influence others and these others, in turn, cannot not respond to these communications and are themselves communicating. (pp. 48–49)

It seems, then, that self-disclosure is ubiquitous to any human interaction, including that in groups. The person seeking admission to an encounter group is disclosing information about his or her belief system, as is the therapist offering such treatment. Similarly, the leader observing the reticent member makes inferences about that person's internal states. And the leader who insists on being referred to by title is disclosing information to the members of the group. The point is this; demographic variables, titles, modes of dress and speech, and environmental phenomena possess informational value to human beings.

Secondary to the notion that disclosure must occur, consideration must be given to parameters of the disclosures such as positive or negative valence of content and affect expressed, intensity, sources, and aims of the communication, and the interactions among all of these variables. A clinically relevant and experimentally adequate conceptualization of self-disclosure must reflect the complexity of the group situation and the complexity of the disclosure process itself. These would seem to be the minimum conditions for any useful considerations of self-disclosure. Many of these dimensions are researchable by employing relatively straightforward factorial designs in which verbal and nonverbal, positive and negative, leader and member, high and low emotional intensity, early and late in the group development, and so forth, are controlled. But only a series of well-executed and clearly reported empirical efforts can contribute to any stable understanding of their singular and cumulative effects.

Within this context, the recent research may suggest tentative hypotheses about the meaning and implications of self-disclosure. A subset of this work is included in Table 20-5. Perusal of the results reported in this table suggests that, for leaders, higher levels of self-disclosure may be correlated with being perceived as more friendly and helpful (Dies, 1973; May & Thompson, 1973; Strassberg, Roback, Anchor, & Abramowitz, 1975), but that the relationship between self-disclosure and member perceptions of the leader's mental health may be positive (May & Thompson, 1973) or negative (Weigel, Dinges, Dyer, & Staumfjord, 1972). That the latter contradiction may be a function of content dimensions in the disclosures, an uncontrolled variable in many reports, is suggested by the report of Dies, Cohen, and Pines (1973),

who found that therapist transparency was evaluated differentially as a function of context. With respect to the self-disclosures of group participants, higher levels may be associated with a more positive self-concept (Bean & Houston, in press); greater reciprocal attraction (Kahn & Rudestam, 1971; Weigel, Dinges, Dyer, & Straumfjord, 1972); moderate, as opposed to high, levels of approval dependency (Anchor, Vojtisek, & Berger, 1972); ecological considerations such as the disclosures of other participants (Strassberg, Gabel, & Anchor, in press); and an explicit contract to disclose (Ribner, 1974), although in the latter study the contract enhanced only the frequency and depth of member disclosures, but not the level of intimacy. Finally, the amount of member self-disclosure may be negatively associated with desirable therapeutic outcomes, at least with some populations (Strassberg et al., 1975).

The specific methodological difficulties that threaten the internal and external validity of these investigations need not be enumerated. The definitional differences among them mandate the most conservative interpretation of their results. At best, they may be considered as contributing to a more thorough understanding of the several dimensions of disclosure and at worst as throwing more fatuous in the conceptual fire. Practitioners would probably be well advised to assume that disclosing will not prove to be a panacea but may, under conditions as yet unknown, contribute to individual psychological growth.

Feedback

Although it would require no cognitive stretching to consider feedback as a special instance of self-disclosure, we have elected to treat it separately here. It has been commonly accepted that the exchange of personal impressions among individuals committed to candid and responsible communication may constitute one of the most powerful facets of group treatment. It may be that this assumption has its genesis in a reaction to a general societal tendency to respond to others with the socially appropriate comment rather than the experientially veridical one. For whatever reasons, however, feedback has emerged as one of the central therapeutic variables in groups. Some writers have even suggested that people participate in small learning groups to fulfill a personal need for feedback:

> the demand for and popularity of laboratory training today betray an important flaw in our society, namely, the lack of adequate and trustworthy mechanisms of feedback built into our social institutions. Bosses cannot talk to or level with employees, wives with husbands, children with parents, students with teachers, and so forth. (Schein & Bennis, 1965, p. 41)

If feedback is an important therapeutic element in group treatment, it is also an important criterion against which to judge the developmental process of groups. The ability of groups to offer and receive feedback in a healthy, relatively comfortable style may be indicative of substantial disinhibition and new emotional and behavioral learning. This might be reflected in: (1) disconfirmation of unrealistic expectations, especially those associated with interpersonal frankness; (2) increased ability to perceive and learn directly from the consequences of one's actions; and (3) the acquisition of new, more adaptive, interpersonal behaviors. If the assumptions about feedback are correct, one would anticipate that more effectiveness with it should be correlated with positive outcomes as well.

Despite the consensus as to the learning value of feedback, there is a fundamental lack of clarity regarding some basic considerations related to its definition and application. The most frequently used definitions emphasize the exchange of information and perceptions in a manner judged to be genuine. This type of definition, like so many others in group work, is far too simple to accommodate the complexity of the phenomena that it supposedly represents. Some considerations relevant to the role and effects of feedback involve the differential effects of: (1) positive versus negative information, (2) behavioral versus motivational feedback, (3) individual versus consensual reports, (4) timing and sequencing of the information, (5) source and credibility of the information, and (6) interaction of all of these variables with each other. In addition, consideration must be given to the long- and short-term impact of the feedback, its therapeutic effects,

its vicarious influence, and its effect on group development. This list could be expanded without effort, but it should suffice to demonstrate the complexity of the empirical problem.

Our review of the current research (Table 20-5), suggests that this may be another area in which the degree of conviction surpasses the empirical base. Nevertheless, some systematic research has been published; most noteworthy is that of Jacobs, Jacobs, and their colleagues, which speaks to some of these issues and adumbrates the potentially complex resolutions that may be necessary. For example, four studies reported that positive feedback, in general, was perceived as more desirable by recipients than negative feedback (Jacobs et al., 1974; Jacobs, Jacobs, Feldman, & Cavior, 1973; Jacobs, Jacobs, Gatz, & Schaible, 1973; Schaible & Jacobs, 1975). In the first of these studies, feedback was delivered anonymously; in the others the source was known to the recipient. In all but the Schaible and Jacobs study, positive feedback was also perceived as more credible and influential (although, even here, positive feedback was judged to elicit "better effects" than negative feedback). More specifically, positive behavioral feedback was attributed the highest credibility of all types provided (Jacobs et al., 1974), but emotional feedback was generally found to have less impact on group members than either behavioral or mixed feedback (Jacobs et al., 1974). Finally, in an important test of some theoretical predictions, Jacobs, Jacobs, Gatz, and Schaible (1973) found that negative feedback followed by positive feedback led to the greatest acceptance of the information by the participants. This was taken to support the position of Miles (1958) and Stoller (1968), who suggested that early confrontation through negative feedback may "unfreeze" the individual through disconfirmation of the self-concept or, perhaps, altering expectations. Such impact is presumed to have motivational effects that, in turn, enhance the likelihood of learning new behaviors and new modes of interpreting one's own behavior.

The generality of these results cannot be determined on the basis of the available data. Each of the studies cited has involved only college student samples, the conditions under which the data were

TABLE 20-5   Self-Disclosure

Author	Purpose	Participants
Self-disclosure		
Anchor, Vojtisek, and Berger (1972)	Identify the degree to which social desirability is a predictor of self-disclosure in groups	Psychiatric patients
Bean and Houston (unpublished manuscript)	Determine the relationship between self-concept and personal self-disclosure over time in an encounter group	College students
Dies (1973)	Investigate the relationship between leader self-disclosure and evaluation by group members	College students
May and Thompson (1973)	Determine the relationship between leader self-disclosure and perceived ⋅ mental health and helpfulness	College students
Ribner (1974)	Identify the effects of an explicit contract for self-disclosure on early group cohesion	College students
Strassberg, Gabel, and Anchor (in press)	Determine if self-disclosing statements are associated with other self-disclosure	Young adults
Strassberg, Roback, Anchor, and Abramowitz (1975)	Study the relationship of therapist core conditions, patient self-disclosure, and therapeutic outcome	Psychiatric patients
Weigel, Dinges, Dyer, and Straumfjord (1972)	Investigate the relationship between self-disclosure, mental health, and liking ratings	Outpatient college students

Conditions	Dependent Measures	Results
Identified high, medium, and low social desirability members; rated frequency of their self-disclosures in a 40-minute group meeting	Behavioral ratings of self-disclosing comments	High approval dependent patients avoided self-disclosing; moderate approval dependent patients disclosed most frequently
Self-concept measure taken prior to group meeting; rated self-disclosure four times over 1 14-week period	Member's rated self-disclosure. Rated by leader, member, and group	Low self-concept members disclosed less frequently in the early meetings. At the end of the group, they were disclosing as frequently as high self-concept members
Factor analysis of a therapist orientation scale completed by members of 10 therapy groups	Therapist orientation scales	More-disclosing leaders were judged as more friendly, helpful, trusting, intimate, facilitating, and disclosing. A positive relationship was found between time in treatment and favorability of attitudes toward therapist disclosure
Correlational analysis of ratings of self-disclosure, mental health, and helpfulness, taken from members of six encounter groups	Group member perceptions rating scales	Significant positive relationships were found for leader self-disclosure, mental health, and helpfulness ratings. These were unrelated to members' rated self-disclosure
Contract to self-disclose versus no contract	Cohesion questionnaire, ratings of self-disclosure	Contract condition members were significantly higher on frequency and depth of self-disclosure, and rated group cohesiveness
Members participated in a group, and their interactions were rated on a self-disclosure scale	Not available	A significant reciprocal relationship between self-disclosing statements was found
Dichotomized patient sample on the basis of perceived quality of therapeutic relationship and related this to frequency of self-disclosure and outcome	Relationship inventory, MMPI, symptom checklist, and adjustment scales	Patients who viewed their therapist more positively disclosed significantly more often. Less disclosing patients showed more favorable therapeutic outcomes
Correlational analysis of member and leader ratings of self-disclosure, mental health, and liking	Not available	Positive relationships were found between liking and self-disclosure among members. Negative correlation between members' ratings of leader disclosure and mental health

TABLE 20-5 (continued)

Author	Purpose	Participants
Feedback		
Jacobs, Jacobs, Cavior, and Burke (1974)	Study the effects of anonymous emotional and behavioral feedback in a brief encounter group	College students
Jacobs, Jacobs, Feldman, and Cavior (1973)	Determine the effects of positive and negative emotional or behavioral feedback in a brief encounter group	College students
Jacobs, Jacobs, Gatz, and Schaible (1973)	Study the credibility and desirability of different kinds of feedback in a brief encounter group	College students
Schaible and Jacobs (1975)	Study the effects of order and valence of feedback in a brief encounter group	College students

gathered were rather limited (e.g., in the Jacobs et al. 1974 study, feedback was limited to a list of statements prepared by the experimenters), and none of the groups in these studies would be considered as therapeutic in the more restrictive sense of the word. Finally, the differential impact of leader versus member feedback has not been explicated. Despite these limitations, the direction taken by Jacobs, Jacobs, and their associates is commendable. Their work has a programmatic nature all too uncommon in group research. Sacrificing some bandwidth in the interest of increasing the fidelity of their results offers the opportunity for a clearer understanding of the phenomena. Additional laboratory replications and extensions to the clinical setting are clearly in order, but these can now be founded on a reasonable empirical base.

Some Preliminary Conclusions

As was the case with the outcome literature, an overview of the process research suggests some preliminary conclusions, again *ceteris paribus*. The group structure dimension that seemed to hold such promise (Bednar & Lawlis, 1971) has evoked a substantial amount of systematic attention. Although unqualified implications of this research for clinical practice are premature, some tentative suggestions seem warranted. It seems reasonably clear that the perceptions, expectations, and beliefs that a group member holds about the treatment

Conditions	Dependent Measures	Results
Type and valence of anonymous feedback; emotional or behavioral, positive or negative	Cohesion questionnaire, judged improvement in relationship skills, perceived accuracy, and credibility of feedback	Positive feedback was perceived as more credible, desirable, and influential. Positive emotional feedback was associated with greater cohesiveness. Positive behavioral feedback was rated as most credible
Type and valence of feedback positive, negative or mixed, and emotional or behavioral	Adjective checklist, cohesion questionnaire, self-reported evaluation of feedback	Positive feedback was judged more credible, desirable, and influential. Negative behavioral feedback judged more credible than negative emotional feedback. Emotional feedback given lowest impact ratings
Delivery sequences of positive and negative feedback; negative followed by positive, positive followed by negative, mixed sequence	Cohesion questionnaire, perceived accuracy and desirability of feedback, adjective checklist	Negative followed by positive feedback was rated highest on acceptability. Positive feedback tends to be perceived as more believable and desirable than negative
Delivery sequences of feedback; positive followed by negative, negative followed by positive, no feedback followed by positive or negative	Cohesion questionnaire, rated accuracy and desirability of feedback	Positive feedback rated as more acceptable and desirable. Positive followed by negative feedback was rated more credible and desirable than negative followed by positive

can have an immediate influence on his or her experience in the group. That these phenomena can affect early group development seems clearly demonstrated, although the long-term and outcome implications of these effects remain to be explicated. The precise parameters of influence that structure may have are also unclear, although they seem stable over somewhat different participant populations. The concept of structure reflected in the research is probably narrower than that concept applied in the clinical setting. Further research is needed to clarify the implications of this limitation but, for now, the group leader should give careful consideration to structural dimensions.

The research on group cohesion is unclear.

Considering the importance of the concept to group treatments, this is unfortunate. Perhaps the safest implication to be drawn from the current cohesion research is that it seems to be a multidimensional phenomenon and a developmental one. Rated cohesiveness of groups can be manipulated experimentally, but the process and outcome effects that might be consequential to such manipulations are ambiguous. Some promising measurement technologies have been developed, which should assist in specification of the concept of cohesion.

The quality of the research on self-disclosure and feedback surpasses the quality of the concepts. Here again, some adumbration of the dimensions and effects of these important notions can be noted, but implications for practice are limited. Both phenomena can be manipulated in predictable ways. The research reviewed here, along with that reviewed by Cozby (1973), suggests that self-disclosure begets self-disclosure. That is, the frequency of disclosing statements can be affected by modeling, contracting, and perhaps "demanding" them. While some of the effects of the disclosures may be therapeutic, it is not clear that their impact will be limited to positive dimensions. The same situation exists with respect to the literature reviewed that deals with feedback in the group. Although some promising systematic work has been noted, the only stable conclusion that one can draw presently is that people prefer positive feedback to negative feedback in group situations.

CONCLUDING COMMENTS

Serious investigations of group treatments have increased at a geometric rate. It is reasonable to anticipate that such concerted effort on the part of so many would lead to clearly discernible progress. One would expect that the fundamental phenomena have been identified and elaborated, that a systematic integration of the phenomena would be apparent, and that the areas of ambiguity would be amenable to empirical attack.

At one level, a review of the contemporary literature does not support the conclusion that these reasonable expectations have been met. In an absolute sense, the basic concepts and propositions of group psychological treatment are remarkable in their ambiguity. This lack of clarity is manifest when authors employ the same term to denote two or more distinct phenomena and, conversely, when different terms are used to label identical events. When intelligent and well-trained investigators cannot agree on the meaning of basic terms, it is not surprising that the aggregate value of their work may be compromised. Nor is it surprising that this aggregate is resistant to integration and translation to clinical practice. Even though individual researchers have controlled for many sources of variance, conceptual imprecision has unnecessarily limited the value of much of the contemporary re-

search. Evidence of a fact in isolation is important to scientific progress. But even if all the individual facts are undeniable, without an integrating conceptual framework, they carry no more thematic power than a telephone directory. We concur with the most ardent critics of group treatment research who have pointed to the methodological shortcomings of many investigations in this area. Nevertheless, we again submit that the absence of methodological rigor is only part of the problem. Equally important are the inadequacies of the conceptual origins of the research. Those involved in group research can no longer disregard the intimate relationship between conceptual adequacy, methodological precision, and research saliency. Without a sound conceptual base, even the most impeccable methods have limited value. Without rigorous methodology, the most fruitful conceptual issues cannot be approached.

In another context, however, clearly discernible improvements in quality and apparent relevance can be noted. The need for conceptual precision is more and more recognized, and the data base necessary for meeting that need may be developing. The foundations of potentially useful models are beginning to appear in the literature. At a minimum, the sources of some of the current deficiencies in knowledge can be identified. Such developments suggest that there may be justification for some cautious optimism about the future scientific respectability of group treatment. Additionally, unless the group literature represents an epidemic of Type I error, it is safe to conclude that selected group treatments are useful, even though our knowledge about the limits of the usefulness are embarrassingly limited.

It is conceivable and eminently reasonable to many that the practice of group treatment is more relevant and subtle than the research. Improvement in the conceptual foundation of research may require persuading carefully selected practitioners to invest the necessary energy into translating their group experiences into more precise conceptual descriptions. Liberman, Yalom, and Miles (1973) may have approximated this approach when they asked selected exemplars of different orientations to "do their thing" in the laboratory. In any event, if researchers and practitioners cannot communicate more effectively than they have, we may find two autonomous groups attesting an interest in the same phenomena.

Perhaps the major dilemma of this area of research was summarized by John Steinbeck when he described the intellectual provisioning of an expedition he once took. The story emphasizes the perspectives of two people observing a certain fish, the Mexican sierra. One, taking a sample from a formalin solution, describes the fish as having a certain number of spines in its dorsal fin. This observation, made under carefully controlled laboratory conditions, is as undeniable as any single fact in science. Another person hooks the fish, fights it, lands it, and eats it. This person observes the fish's strength, color, smell, and taste and, in addition, experiences something of the interaction of the fish and himself.

> *There is no reason why either approach should be inaccurate. Spine count description need not suffer because another approach is also used. Perhaps out of the two approaches, we thought, there might emerge a picture more complete and even more accurate than either alone could produce. (Steinbeck, 1958, pp. 3–4)*

Our review has convinced us that a meaningful empirical assault on the essential phenomena of group work must await the development of more precise, comprehensive, and relevant descriptions that preserve the essentials of the very phenomena we hope to investigate. Much, although clearly not all, of the research we have reviewed is of the spine count variety. This is not meant perjoratively; the work is necessary and can be important. Nevertheless, scientifically minded practitioners must also participate more intensively. Perhaps an integration of the two approaches will lead to a more complete and even more accurate picture than either approach could produce alone.

REFERENCES

Abramowitz, S. I., & Abramowitz, C. V. Psychological-mindedness and benefit from insight-oriented group therapy. *Archives of General Psychiatry*, 1974, *30*, 610–615.

Abramowitz, C. V., Abramowitz, S. I., Roback, H. B., & Jackson, C. Differential effectiveness of directive and nondirective group therapies as a function of client internal-external control. *Journal of Consulting and Clinical Psychology*, 1974, *42*, 849–853.

Abramowitz, S. I., & Jackson, C. Comparative effectiveness of there-and-then versus here-and-now therapist interpretations in group-psychotherapy. *Journal of Counseling Psychology*, 1974, *21*, 288–293.

Anchor, K. N., Vojtisek, J. E., & Berger, S. E. Social desirability as a predictor of self-disclosure in groups. *Psychotherapy: Theory, Research and Practice*, 1972, *9*, 261–264.

Anchor, K. N., Vojtisek, J. E. & Patterson, R. L. Trait anxiety, initial structuring and self-disclosure in groups of schizophrenic patients. *Psychotherapy: Theory, Research, and Practice*, 1973, *10*, 151–158.

Anderson, N. H., Linder, R., & Lopes, L. L. Integration theory applied to judgements of group attractiveness. *Journal of Personality and Social Psychology*, 1973, *26*, 400–408.

Arbes, B. H., & Hubbell, R. N. Packaged impact: A structured communication skills workshop. *Journal of Counseling Psychology*, 1973, *20*, 332–337.

Baekeland, F., & Lundwall, L. Dropping out of treatment: A critical review. *Psychological Bulletin*, 1975, *82*, 738–783.

Bare, C. E., & Mitchell, R. R. Experimental evaluation of sensitivity training. *Journal of Applied Behavioral Science*, 1972, *8*, 263–276.

Batchelder, R. L., & Hardy, J. M. *Using sensitivity training and the laboratory method: An organizational case study in the development of human resources.* New York: Association Press, 1968.

Bean, B. N., & Houston, B. K. Self-concept and self-disclosure in encounter groups. Unpublished manuscript, University of Kansas.

Bednar, R. L., & Battersby, C. The effects of specific cognitive structure on early group development. *Journal of Applied Behavioral Sciences*, 1976, *12*, 513–522.

Bednar, R. L., & Lawlis, F. Empirical research in group psychotherapy. In A. E. Bergin and S. L. Garfield (Eds.), *Handbook of psychotherapy and behavior change.* New York: Wiley, 1971.

Bednar, R. L., & Lee, F. A theoretical and impirical review of structure and ambiguity in systems of interpersonal influence. Unpublished manuscript, Department of Psychology, University of Kentucky, Lexington, Kentucky, 1976.

Bednar, R. L., Melnick, J., & Kaul, T. Risk, responsibility and structure: A conceptual framework for initiating group counseling and psychotherapy. *Journal of Counseling Psychology*, 1974, *21*, 31–37.

Beutler, L. E., Jobe, A. M., & Elkins, D. Outcomes in group psychotherapy: Using persuasion theory to increase treatment efficiency. *Journal of Consulting and Clinical Psychology*, 1974, *42*, 547–553.

Caine, T. M., Wijesinghe, B., & Wood, R. R. Personality and psychiatric treatment expectancies. *British Journal of Psychiatry*, 1973, *122*, 87–88.

Cherry, C. *On human communication: A review, a sur-*

vey and a criticism. (2nd ed.) Cambridge, Mass: MIT Press, 1966.

Cooper, C. L. An attempt to assess the psychologically disturbing effects of T-group training. British Journal of Social and Clinical Psychology, 1972a, 11, 342–345.

Cooper, C. L. Coping with life stress after sensitivity training. Psychological Reports, 1972b, 31, 602.

Corsini, R. J., & Rosenberg, B. Mechanisms of group psychotherapy: Process and dynamics. Journal of Abnormal and Social Psychology, 1955, 51, 406–411.

Costell, R. M., & Koran, L. M. Compatibility and cohesiveness in group psychotherapy. Journal of Nervous and Mental Disease, 1972, 155, 99–104.

Counseling Center Staff, University of Massachusetts. The effects of three types of sensitivity groups on changes in measures of self-actualization. Journal of Counseling Psychology, 1972, 19, 253–254.

Cozby, P. C. Self-disclosure: A literature review. Psychological Bulletin, 1973, 79, 73–91.

Crews, C., & Melnick, J. The use of initial and delayed structure in facilitating group development. Journal of Counseling Psychology, 1976, 23, 92–98.

Cronbach, L. Beyond the two disciplines of scientific psychology. American Psychologist, 1975, 30, 116–127.

D'Augelli, A. R., & Chinsky, J. M. Interpersonal skills and pretraining: Implications for the use of group procedures for interpersonal learning and for the selection of nonprofessional mental health workers. Journal of Consulting and Clinical Psychology, 1974, 42, 65–72.

DeJulio, R. S., Bentley, A. N., & Cockayne. The effect of pregroup norm setting of an encounter group interaction. Unpublished manuscript, S.U.N.Y. at Geneseo, Geneseo, N.Y., 1976.

Diamond, M. J., & Shapiro, J. L. Changes in locus of control as a function of encounter group experiences: A study and replication. Journal of Abnormal Psychology, 1973, 82, 514–518.

Dies, R. R. Group therapists self-disclosure: An evaluation by clients. Journal of Counseling Psychology, 1973, 20, 344–348.

Dies, R. R., Cohen, L., & Pines, S. Content considerations in group therapist self-disclosures. Proceedings of the 81st Annual Convention of the American Psychological Convention, 1973, 8, 481–482.

Dies, R. R., & Hess, A. An experimental investigation of cohesiveness in marathon and conventional group psychotherapy. Journal of Abnormal Psychology, 1971, 77, 258–262.

Dies, R. R., & Sadowsky, R. A brief encounter group experience and social relationships in a dormitory. Journal of Counseling Psychology, 1974, 21, 112–115.

Evensen, P., & Bednar, R. L. The effects of specific cognitive and behavioral structure on early growth development. Unpublished manuscript, Department of Psychology, University of Kentucky, Lexington, Kentucky, 1976.

Felton, G. S., & Biggs, B. E. Teaching internalization behavior to collegiate low achievers in group psychotherapy. Psychotherapy: Theory, Research

and Practice, 1972, 9, 281–283.

Felton, G. S., & Davidson, H. R. Group counseling can work in the classroom. Academic Therapy, 1973, 8, 461–468.

Foulds, M. L., & Guinan, J. F. Marathon group: Changes in ratings of self and others. Psychotherapy: Theory, Research and Practice, 1973, 10, 30–32.

Foulds, M. L., & Hannigan, P. S. Effects of psychomotor group therapy on ratings of self and others. Psychotherapy: Theory, Research and Practice, 1974, 11, 351–353.

Foulds, M. L., & Hannigan, P. S. Effects of gestalt marathon workshops on measured self-actualization: A replication and follow-up study. Journal of Counseling Psychology, 1976, 23, 60–65.

Fromme, D. K., Whisenant, W. F., & Susky, H. H. Group modification of affective verbalizations. Journal of Consulting and Clinical Psychology, 1974, 42, 866–871.

Good, L. R., & Nelsen, D. A. Effects of person-group and intragroup attitude similarity on perceived group attractiveness and cohesiveness: II. Psychological Reports, 1973, 33, 551–560.

Gross, E. F. Empirical study of the concept of cohesiveness and compatability. Unpublished honors thesis. Department of Social Relations, Harvard University, 1957. Cited by W. C. Schutz, And the Interpersonal Underworld. Palo Alto, Calif.: Science and Behavior Books, Inc., 1970.

Grotjahn, M. Learning from dropout patients: A clinical view of patients who discontinued group psychotherapy. International Journal of Group Psychotherapy, 1972, 22, 306–319.

Hagstrom, W. O., & Selvin, H. C. Two dimensions of cohesiveness in small groups. Sociometry, 1965, 28, 30–43.

Hanson, J. T., & Sander, D. C. Differential effects of individual and group-counseling on realism of vocational choice. Journal of Counseling Psychology, 1973, 20, 541–544.

Hartley, D., Roback, H., & Abramowitz, S. Deterioration effects in encounter groups. American Psychologist, 1976, 31, 247–255.

Haven, G. A., & Wood, B. S. The effectiveness of eclectic group psychotherapy in reducing recidivism in hospitalized patients. Psychotherapy: Theory, Research and Practice, 1970, 7, 153–154.

Heckel, R., Holmes, G., & Rosecrans, C. A factor analytic study of process variables in group therapy. Journal of Clinical Psychology, 1971, 17, 146–150.

Heitler, J. Preparation of lower-class patients for expressive group psychotherapy. Journal of Consulting and Clinical Psychology, 1973, 41, 251–260.

Hewitt, J., & Kraft, M. Effects of an encounter group experience on self-perception and interpersonal relations. Journal of Consulting and Clinical Psychology, 1973, 40, 162.

Hill, W. F. Analysis of interviews of group therapists. Provo Papers 1, 1957.

Hill, W. F. Hill interaction matrix. Los Angeles: University of Southern California Youth Study Center, 1965.

Jackson, D. N., Hourany, L., & Vidmar, N. J. A four-dimensional interpretation of risk-taking. (Research

Bulletin No. 185.) London, Canada: The University of Western Ontario, 1971.

Jacobs, A., Jacobs, M., Cavior, N., & Burke, J. Anonymous feedback: Credibility and desirability of structured emotional and behavioral feedback delivered in groups. *Journal of Counseling Psychology*, 1974, *21*, 106–111.

Jacobs, M., Jacobs, A., Feldman, G., & Cavior, N. Feedback II—The credibility gap: Delivery of positive and negative emotional and behavioral feedback in groups. *Journal of Consulting and Clinical Psychology*, 1973, *41*, 215–223.

Jacobs, M., Jacobs, A., Gatz, M., & Schaible, T. Credibility and desirability of positive and negative structured feedback in groups. *Journal of Consulting and Clinical Psychology*, 1973, *40*, 244–252.

Jacobson, E. A., & Smith, S. J. Effect of weekend encounter group experience upon interpersonal orientations. *Journal of Consulting and Clinical Psychology*, 1972, *38*, 403–410.

Jeske, J. O. Identification and therapeutic effectiveness in group therapy. *Journal of Counseling Psychology*, 1973, *20*, 528–530.

Jesness, C. F. Comparative effectiveness of behavior modification and transactional analysis programs for delinquents. *Journal of Consulting and Clinical Psychology*, 1975, *43*, 758–779.

Jew, C. C., Clanon, T. L., & Mattocks, A. L. The effectiveness of group psychotherapy in a correctional institution. *American Journal of Psychiatry*, 1972, *129*, 602–605.

Jones, D., & Medvene, A. Self-actualization effects of a marathon growth group. *Journal of Counseling Psychology*, 1975, *22*, 39–43.

Jourard, S. M. *The transparent self.* Princeton, N.J.: Van Nostrand Rheinhold, 1971.

Kahn, M. H., & Rudestam, K. E. The relationship between liking and perceived self-disclosure in small groups. *Journal of Psychology*, 1971, *78*, 81–85.

Kane, F. J., Wallace, C. D., & Lipton, M. A. Emotional disturbance related to T-group experience. *American Journal of Psychiatry*, 1971, *127*, 954–957.

Kaye, J. D. Group interaction and interpersonal learning. *Small Group Behavior*, 1973, *4*, 424–448.

Kiesler, D. J. Some myths of psychotherapy research and the search for a paradigm. *Psychological Bulletin*, 1966, *65*, 110–136.

Kilmann, P. R., Albert, B. M., & Sotile, W. M. The relationship between locus of control, structure of therapy, and outcome. *Journal of Consulting and Clinical Psychology*, 1975, *43*, 588.

Kilmann, P. R., & Howell, R. J. The relationship between structure of marathon group therapy, locus of control, and outcome. *Journal of Consulting and Clinical Psychology*, 1974, *42*, 912.

Kilmann, P. R., & Sotile, W. The marathon-encounter group: A review of the outcome literature. *Psychological Bulletin* (in press).

Kimball, R., & Gelso, C. J. Self-actualization in a marathon growth group: Do the strong get stronger? *Journal of Counseling Psychology*, 1974, *21*, 32–42.

Koran, L. M., & Costell, R. M. Early termination from group psychotherapy. *International Journal of*

Group Psychotherapy, 1973, *23*, 346–359.

Kroeker, L. L. Pretesting as a confounding variable in evaluating an encounter group. *Journal of Counseling Psychology*, 1974, *21*, 548–552.

Laing, R. *The politics of experience.* New York: Ballantine, 1967.

Lee, F., & Bednar, R. L. Effects of group structure and risk taking disposition on group behavior, attitudes, and atmosphere. *Journal of Counseling Psychology*, 1976.

Levin, E. M., & Kurtz, R. R. Structured and nonstructured human relations training. *Journal of Counseling Psychology*, 1974, *21*, 526–531.

Lieberman, M. A. Change induction in small groups. *Annual Review of Psychology*, 1976, *27*, 217–250.

Lieberman, M. A., Yalom, I. D., & Miles, M. B. *Encounter groups: First facts.* New York: Basic Books, 1973.

Liberman, R. Reinforcement of cohesiveness in group therapy. *Archives of General Psychiatry*, 1971, *25*, 168–177.

Lott, A. J., & Lott, B. E. Group cohesiveness as interpersonal attraction: A review of relationships with antecedent and consequent variables. *Psychological Bulletin*, 1965, *64*, 259–309.

May, O. P., & Thompson, C. L. Perceived levels of self-disclosure, mental health, and helpfulness of group leaders. *Journal of Counseling Psychology*, 1973, *20*, 349–352.

McCardel, J., & Murray, E. J. Nonspecific factors in weekend encounter groups. *Journal of Consulting and Clinical Psychology*, 1974, *42*, 337–345.

McLachlan, J. F. Benefit from group therapy as a function of patient-therapist match on a conceptual level. *Psychotherapy: Theory, Research and Practice*, 1972, *9*, 317–323.

Meichenbaum, D. H., Gilmore, J. B., & Fedoravicius, A. Group insight versus group desensitization in treating speech anxiety. *Journal of Consulting and Clinical Psychology*, 1971, *36*, 410–421.

Miles, M. B. *Factors influencing response to feedback in human relations training.* New York: Horace Mann-Lincoln Institute of School Experimentation, Teachers College, Columbia University, 1958.

Mintz, E. Marathon groups: A preliminary evaluation. *Journal of Contemporary Psychotherapy*, 1969, *1*, 91–94.

Mitchell, K. R., & Ng, K. T. Effects of group counseling and behavior therapy on the academic achievement of test-anxious students. *Journal of Counseling Psychology*, 1973, *19*, 491–497.

Mordock, J. B., Ellis, M. H., & Greenstone, J. L. The effects of group and individual therapy on sociometric choice of disturbed, institutionalized adolescents. *International Journal of Group Psychotherapy*, 1969, *19*, 510–517.

O'Brien, C. P., Hamm, K. B., Ray, B. A., Pierce, J. F., Luborsky, L., & Mintz, J. Group vs. individual psychotherapy with schizophrenics. *Archives of General Psychiatry*, 1972, *27*, 474–478.

O'Keefe, R. D., Kernaghan, J. A., & Rubenstein, A. H. Group cohesiveness: A factor in the adoption of innovations among scientific work groups. *Small Group Behavior*, 1975, *6*, 282–292.

Peretz, M., & Glaser, F. B. Value change in drug education: The role of encounter groups. *The International Journal of the Addictions,* 1974, *9,* 637–652.

Pollack, H. B. Change in homogeneous and heterogeneous sensitivity training groups. *Journal of Consulting and Clinical Psychology,* 1971, *37,* 60–66.

Posthuma, A. B., & Posthuma, B. W. Some observations on encounter group casualties. *Journal of Applied Behavioral Science,* 1973, *9,* 595–608.

Reddy, W. B. Sensitivity training or group psychotherapy: The need for adequate screening. *International Journal of Group Psychotherapy,* 1970, *20,* 366–371.

Redfering, D. L. Durability of effects of group counseling with institutionalized delinquent females. *Journal of Abnormal Psychology,* 1973, *82,* 85–86.

Ribner, N. G. Effects of an explicit group contract on self-disclosure and group cohesiveness. *Journal of Counseling Psychology,* 1974, *21,* 116–120.

Roback, H. B. Experimental comparison of outcomes in insight- and non-insight-oriented therapy groups. *Journal of Consulting and Clinical Psychology,* 1972, *38,* 411–417.

Rogers, C. R. The process of the basic encounter group. In J. F. T. Bugental (Ed.), *Challenges of humanistic psychology.* New York: McGraw-Hill, 1967.

Rosenzweig, S. P., & Folman, R. Patient and therapist variables affecting premature termination in group psychotherapy. *Psychotherapy: Theory, Research and Practice,* 1974, *11,* 76–79.

Ross, W. D., Kligfield, M., & Whitman, R. W. Psychiatrists, patients, and sensitivity groups. *Archives of General Psychiatry,* 1971, *25,* 178–180.

Ross, W. D., McReynolds, W., & Berzins, J. Effectiveness of marathon group psychotherapy with hospitalized female narcotics addicts. *Psychological Reports,* 1974, *34,* 611–616.

Rotter, J. B. Generalized expectancies for internal vs. external control of reinforcement. *Psychological Monographs,* 1966, *80* (1, Whole No. 609).

Schaible, T., & Jacobs, A. Feedback III: Sequence effects; enhancement of feedback acceptance and group attractiveness by manipulation of the sequence and valence of feedback. *Small Group Behavior,* 1975, *6,* 151–173.

Schein, E. H., & Bennis, W. G. *Personal and organizational change through group methods: The laboratory approach.* New York: Wiley, 1965.

Sethna, E. R., & Harrington, J. A. A study of patients who lapsed from group psychotherapy. *British Journal of Psychiatry,* 1971, *119,* 59–69.

Shapiro, J. L., & Diamond, M. J. Increases in hypnotizability as a function of encounter group training: Some confirming evidence. *Journal of Abnormal Psychology,* 1972, *79,* 112–115.

Silbergeld, S., Koenig, G., Manderscheid, R., Meeker, B., & Hornung, C. Assessment of environment-therapy systems: The group atmosphere scale. *Journal of Consulting and Clinical Psychology,* 1975, *43,* 460–469.

Smith, P. B. Are there adverse effects of sensitivity training? *Journal of Humanistic Psychology,* 1975a, *15,* 29–47.

Smith, P. B. Controlled studies of the outcome of sensitivity training. *Psychological Bulletin,* 1975b, *82,* 597–622.

Smith, R. D., & Evans, J. R. Comparison of experimental group guidance and individual–counseling as facilitators of vocational development. *Journal of Counseling Psychology,* 1973, *20,* 202–208.

Smith, R. J. A closer look at encounter therapies. *International Journal of Group Psychotherapy,* 1970, *20,* 192–209.

Stanton, H. E. Change in self-insight during an intensive group experience. *Small Group Behavior,* 1975, *6,* 487–493.

Steinbeck, J. *The Log From the Sea of Cortez.* London: William Heinemann Ltd., 1958.

Stinson, J., & Hellebrandt, E. Group cohesiveness, productivity, and strength of formal leadership. *Journal of Social Psychology,* 1972, *87,* 99–105.

Stogdill, R. Group productivity, drive and cohesiveness. *Organizational Behavior and Human Performance,* 1972, *8,* 26–43.

Stoller, F. H. Marathon group therapy. In G. M. Gazda (Ed.), *Innovations to group psychotherapy.* Springfield, Ill.: Charles C Thomas, 1968.

Strassberg, D. S., Gabel, H., & Anchor, K. N. Patterns of self-disclosure in parent discussion groups. *Small Group Behavior* (in press).

Strassberg, D. S., Roback, H. B., Anchor, K. N., & Abramowitz, S. I. Self-disclosure in group therapy with schizophrenics. *Archives of General Psychiatry,* 1975, *32,* 1259–1261.

Strupp, H., & Bloxom, A. Preparing lower-class patients for group psychotherapy: Development and evaluation of a role-induction film. *Journal of Consulting and Clinical Psychology,* 1973, *41,* 373–384.

Tavormina, J. B. Relative effectiveness of behavioral and reflective group counseling with parents of mentally retarded children. *Journal of Consulting and Clinical Psychology,* 1975, *43,* 22–31.

Treppa, J. A., & Fricke, L. Effects of a marathon experience. *Journal of Counseling Psychology,* 1972, *19,* 466–467.

Uhlemann, M. R., & Weigel, R. G. Behavior change outcomes of marathon group treatment. *Small Group Behavior* (in press).

Vernallis, F. F,, Shipper, J. C., Butler, D. C., & Tomlinson, T. M. Saturation group psychotherapy in a weekend clinic: An outcome study. *Psychotherapy: Theory, Research and Practice,* 1970, *7,* 144–152.

Warren, N. C., & Rice, L. N. Structure and stabilizing of psychotherapy for low-prognosis clients. *Journal of Consulting and Clinical Psychology,* 1972, *39,* 173–181.

Watzlawick, P., Beavin, J., & Jackson, D. *Progmatics of human communication: A study of interaction patterns, pathologies and paradoxes.* New York: W. W. Norton, 1967.

Weigel, R. G., Dinges, N., Dyer, R., & Straumfjord, A. A. Perceived self-disclosure, mental health, and who is liked in group treatment. *Journal of Counseling Psychology,* 1972, *19,* 47–52.

Weissman, H., Goldschmid, M., Gordon, R., & Feinberg, H. Changes in self-regard, creativity and interpersonal behavior as a function of audio-tape encounter-group experiences. *Psychological Reports,* 1972, *31,* 975–981.

Whalen, C. Effects of a model and instructions of group verbal behaviors. *Journal of Consulting and Clinical*

Psychology, 1969, *33,* 509—521.

Yalom, I. *The theory and practice of group psychotherapy.* New York: Basic Books, 1975.

Young, E., & Jacobson, L. Effects of time-extended marathon group experiences on personality charac-teristics. *Journal of Counseling Psychology,* 1970, *17,* 247—251

Zarle, T., & Willis, S. A pregroup training technique for encounter group stress. *Journal of Counseling Psychology,* 1975, *22,* 49—53.

21

RESEARCH ON MARITAL AND FAMILY THERAPY: PROGRESS, PERSPECTIVE, AND PROSPECT[1]

ALAN S. GURMAN

University of Wisconsin Medical School

DAVID P. KNISKERN

University of Cincinnati College of Medicine

In the last few decades marital-family therapy has become an accepted method of treatment for a variety of mental health problems. Although it is impossible to determine accurately the number of therapists who work with couples and families, it is clear from the recent explosion in the number of conferences, workshops, books, and journals[2] dealing with marital-family therapy that the number is large and rapidly increasing. An exact survey of current practice is prevented by the difficulty of defining precisely or consensually what marital-family therapy is. There are few licensing boards and no standard educational requirements or recognized national organizations.[3] Even the issue of

[1]We would like to thank James Framo, David Keith, Roger Knudson, David Olson, Gerald Patterson, David Rice, M. Duncan Stanton, Robert Weiss, and Richard Wells for their useful feedback on an earlier draft of this chapter. We also extend our warmest thanks to Sally Opgenorth, Judy Koseki, and Dee Jones whose indefatigability converted our idiosyncratic scratchings into consensually understandable sentences, paragraphs, and tables.

[2]With the exception of the *Family Coordinator* and *Journal of Marriage and the Family,* all the relevant jour-

nals have begun within the last 15 years and most within the last 5 years: *Family Process* (1963); *Journal of Family Counseling* (1973); *Family Therapy* (1974); *Journal of Marriage and Family Counseling* (1975); *Journal of Sex and Marital Therapy* (1975); *Journal of Sex Education and Therapy* (1975); *International Journal of Family Therapy* (1978); *Journal of Divorce* (1978); *Alternative Life-Styles* (1978).

[3]Although several states do now have licensing boards, there are still no unified sets of training procedures and experiences that lead to certification as a marital-family

whether marital and family therapy should be taught and practiced together has been fraught with controversy.

In this chapter we will discuss the treatment of marriages and families as variations of the same therapeutic process and as being based on the same theoretical foundations. We have made no distinction between "therapy" and "counseling," since we feel that the application of such labels reflects habits developed in training rather than real differences in orientation or technique.

Marital and family therapies did not begin with the advancement of a new theory or method of practice by a single founder, as did psychoanalysis. They developed slowly, through the work of many individuals in many disciplines. The history of marital-family therapy is, in reality, two parallel histories; one describes the changes that have taken place in technique and treatment structure, and the other concerns the changing ways in which social scientists have viewed behavioral pathology. Although the two developed simultaneously, they did not develop together (Olson, 1970). Marital-family therapy, it has been said, "has not developed because of a theory; it appears that people were struggling to find a theory to fit practice" (Haley, 1971, p. 4).

The conceptual history of marital-family therapy has primarily been a history of family therapy. Marital therapy adopted much of family theory long after the establishment of marital therapy as a strategy of intervention. Despite the overlap in theory, marital theorists tend to use more sociologic concepts, while family theory is frequently couched in psychoanalytic terms.

The history of marital-family therapy as a perspective for viewing abnormal behavior has been one of gradual steps leading from a focus on the individual patient's psyche (Freud), to a focus on the patient's interaction with the environment (Meyer, Adler, Sullivan, Fromm-Reichmann), and culminating recently in a conception of the individual's behavior as functional for a marital or family system (Bertalanffy, 1966; Minuchin, 1974).

Couples were treated together as early as 1932 in England (Olson, 1970). It is difficult to determine who first saw family members together in therapy but, by the early 1950s, marital-family therapy was being practiced by a widely divergent group of therapists; it emerged as a movement in the middle of the 1950s, when pioneers heard of each other's work and began to communicate and to publish their ideas. Family therapy developed primarily through work with severely disturbed individuals with whom other types of intervention had been unsuccessful. This focus on extreme forms of pathology has continued, although family therapists have adapted family therapy for use with all types of troubled families. Marital therapy, on the other hand, began working with some of the least severe problems in living and has only recently been applied to more extreme forms of pathology. The marriage *counseling* movement is unique in that it was formed largely because of demand from couples in conflict rather than at the initiative of therapists. Recently the histories of marital-family therapy in theory and in practice have converged. It has become acceptable practice to see families as units, and a rationale exists behind the treatment process. Variations of the basic marital-family treatment format also have emerged in the last decade: crisis intervention, multiple-family therapy, multiple-impact therapy, couples groups, and so forth.

This proliferation of techniques has resulted in the fragmentation of the marital-family movement into "schools" of family therapy, typically focused around a single well-known therapist (e.g., Murray Bowen, Virginia Satir, Don Jackson, Nathan Ackerman, Carl Whitaker). This is particularly the case in family therapy, where the leaders have been unusually charismatic. Each school has developed its own language and techniques and often disparages the proponents of other schools. In the last few years behaviorally oriented therapists have developed family interventions. Behavioral family therapy shares a great deal with other forms of family therapy, although it has developed from a very different tradition.

Marital-family therapy is presently a widely diverse and growing field. It includes therapists from

therapist. Even the American Association of Marriage and Family Counselors (AAMFC), while conferring a certificate of clinical competence, does not include a large number of active marital-family therapists.

many professions, has no unified theory, and few techniques are specific to it. *Family therapy is unified only in a belief that relationships are of at least as much importance in the behavior and experience of people as are unconscious intrapsychic events.* Consumers of mental health services have apparently shared this belief for some time. In an extensive survey by Gurin, Veroff, and Feld (1960), it was found that 42 percent of all people who had sought professional help for psychological problems viewed the nature of their problems as marital, and another 17 percent viewed their problems as pertaining to other family relationships. Similarly, Parad and Parad (1968a) surveyed 54 agencies of the Family Service Association of America and found that while the modal therapeutic contact was the individual interview, over 75 percent of clients' presenting problems had been described as either "interactive" (37 percent) or "problem posed by another family member" (39 percent) (Parad & Parad, 1968b).

RESEARCH ON MARITAL AND FAMILY THERAPY: PROGRESS AND PERSPECTIVE

History of Research in the Field

Despite the substantive and varied theoretical and clinical ancestry of marital-family therapy, its empirical offspring is still in its infancy. Only 17 years ago Parloff (1961), echoing the sentiments of Hollis (1950), Sletto (1950), Mudd (1957), and Matarazzo (1965), noted that:

> The relevant literature is vast, yet very little of it would be classed by the rigorous investigator as research. Most of the contributors to the area have been clinician-naturalists who, having perhaps a Freud-like vision of themselves, have made salutory advances from observations to conclusions with a maximum of vigor and a minimum of rigor. (p. 445)

Even in the current decade Olson (1970), Goodman (1973), and Winter (1971), reviewing the status of family therapy as science, found little basis for increased optimism. The almost complete absence, until recently, of objective study in the field can be accounted for by three interdependent historical forces. First, the autonomy and unconnectedness of the several independent professional disciplines actively committed to family study (i.e., psychiatry, clinical psychology, social work, family sociology, and the ministry), while offering the potential for useful cross-fertilization, resulted in what Olson (1970) aptly described as the "parallel, but unrelated, developments of marital and family therapy." These developments included the use of differing explanatory frameworks and languages, differing value structures regarding family life and the treatment of dysfunctional families, and early clinical experience with vastly different populations. Second, as Gurman (1971, p. 184) has noted, marital-family therapy was "born in psychiatric (child-guidance) and social work (family service agencies) treatment settings; psychology, typically the discipline most active in psychotherapy research, has hardly made an impact (on the field)." Gurman's observation about the salience of clinical psychology's relative absence from the field of marital therapy is perhaps even more relevant in the case of family therapy which, despite having an early impetus from a psychologist (Bell, 1975), has been primarily populated by psychiatrists and social workers (Stanton, 1975b). Indeed, there is little doubt that Nathan Ackerman deserves the title, "founding father of family therapy." Finally, a general devaluing of the very notion of treating family systems directly, deriving from the psychoanalytic *Zeitgeist* of the first half of this century, and a related devaluing of psychological treatment by nonphysicians, hardly helped to facilitate interprofessional collaboration.

In the last half decade, however, enough substantive empirical study of marital and family therapy had emerged to allow the appearance of several critical reviews of the research literature (Beck, 1975; Gurman, 1971, 1973a, 1973b, 1975a, 1975c; Kniskern, 1975; Lebedun, 1970; Wells, Dilkes, & Trivelli, 1972). These reviews concurred in their cautious optimism about the efficacy of marital and family therapy and found marital-family therapy's gross improvement rates to be surprisingly similar to those reported for individual therapy (Bergin, 1971). The repeated observations in these reviews of the continuing need for controlled investigation, multidimensional change measures, treatment specificity, and the usual rebuke of researchers for common methodological failures continues even in very recent reviews of behavioral marital-family therapy (Greer & D'Zurilla, 1975; Gurman & Kniskern, 1978a; Jacobson & Martin, 1976; Patterson, Weiss, & Hops, 1976; Weiss & Margolin, 1977).

Scope of the Present Review

We do not find as bleak a picture of research in this area at this time, as will become evident shortly. By soliciting relevant reports, many of which were unpublished, from several hundred colleagues in the field[4] and intensively pursuing numerous leads for existing but often obscure research, we have been able to locate over 200 relevant studies, thus far exceeding the scope of previous reviews.

We will critically examine studies reporting gross improvement rates and comparative and controlled studies of both behavioral and nonbehavioral marital and family therapy and will consider the increasing evidence of deterioration in such treatments. Following an analysis of factors influencing therapy outcomes and an assessment of the outcomes of marital-family therapy for a few selected clinical populations, we will examine two other focal strategies, enrichment programs and divorce therapy.

Because of the large amount of data to be considered, we will focus primarily on trends and patterns emerging from our analyses and will pay detailed attention to single studies only when they highlight critical methodological issues, show particular theoretical or clinical relevance, or represent the work of important major research groups. The final section will offer some recommendations for further study and point to some implications for training and practice. Throughout the chapter we will offer our clinical perspective on the meaning of our findings, not to proselytize, but to give some life to numbers.

[4]Space does not allow our thanking by name the dozens of colleagues who have encouraged this chapter and routed relevant data our way, but special appreciation is extended to James Alexander, Dorothy Beck, Chad Emrick, John Gottman, Bernard Guerney, Neil Jacobson, Gerald Patterson, Jack Santa-Barbara, Robert Weiss, Ferdinand Van der Veen, and Richard Wells.

Since this chapter's clinical subject matter overlaps that of others in this volume (Barrett et al., Ross, Marks), it is important to define the boundaries of what we consider to be studies of marital and family therapy. We have chosen to review all available studies in which treatment is explicitly focused on altering the interaction between or among family members, whether in same-generation (husband-wife, child-child) relationships, cross-generation (parent-child) relationships, or both, regardless of who is the "identified patient." Thus, for example, studies as diverse as individual therapy for marital problems and operant child-management training programs for parents are included, since they constitute the treatment of family *relationships*. Analogous interventions focused entirely on changing the behavior of one individual and not administered in a family relationship context (e.g., operant extinction of a child's phobia by a therapist) are thus excluded. Although we recognize that treatments such as individual play therapy for children and even adult individual therapy not focused on family relationships certainly have powerful consequences for marital and family interaction (Fisher & Mendell, 1958; Fox, 1968; Hurvitz, 1967; Kohl, 1962; Sager, Gundlach, Kremer, Lenz, & Royce, 1968), the intent of such therapies does not emphasize change in such relationships.

Evaluating the Adequacy of Outcome Studies

For each controlled or comparative study in the tables that follow, we have indicated a design quality rating based on the following criteria (quality "points" achievable are noted in parentheses).

1. *Controlled assignment to treatment conditions:* random assignment, matching of total groups or matching in pairs (5).

2. *Pre-postmeasurement of change:* it is not uncommon (Gurman, 1973b; Wells et al., 1972) for family therapy research to use postevaluations only (5).

3. *No contamination of major independent variables:* this includes therapists' experience level, number of therapists per treat-

ment condition, and *relevant* therapeutic competence (e.g., a psychoanalyst using behavior therapy for the first time offers a poor test of the power of a behavioral method) (5).

4. *Appropriate statistical analysis* (1).

5. *Follow-up:* none (0), 1 to 3 months (1/2), 3 months or more (1).

6. *Treatments equally valued:* tremendous biases are often engendered for both therapists and patients when this criterion is not met (1).

7. *Treatment carried out as described or expected:* clear evidence (1), presumptive evidence (1/2).

8. *Multiple change indices* used (1).

9. *Multiple vantage points* used in assessing outcome (1).

10. *Outcome not limited to change in the "identified patient":* this criterion is perhaps uniquely required in marital/family therapy (1).

11. *Data on other concurrent treatment:* evidence of none or, if present, of its equivalence across groups (1); mention of such treatment without documentation of amount or equivalence (1/2).

12. *Equal treatment length* in comparative studies (1).

13. *Outcome assessment allows for both positive and negative change* (1).

14. *Therapist-investigator nonequivalence:* earlier reviews (Gurman, 1973b) had found the two to be the same person in about 75 percent of the studies examined (1).

Criterion scores were: 0 to 10, poor; 10 1/2 to 15, fair; 15 1/2 to 20, good; and 20 1/2 to 26, very good. Except where explicitly noted, real patients were studied.

THE OUTCOMES OF NONBEHAVIORAL MARITAL-FAMILY THERAPY

Just as there exist indefatigable translators and syncretists in individual psychotherapy who argue, for example, that psychodynamic therapy is "really" the unsystematic application of learning principles (Wolpe & Rachman, 1960), or that behavioral techniques work because of unconscious symbolic experience (Birk & Brinkley-Birk, 1974; Feather & Rhoads, 1972; Silverman et al., 1974) so, too, do many family therapists (Haley, 1969; Whitaker, 1975) insist that individual therapy "really" amounts to inefficient family therapy of a subsystem. For such therapists family therapy is better defined by the therapist's conceptualization of psychopathology than by who is present in the consultation room. Even within the family field, there is a division of opinion as to what is and is not family therapy, and whether (and under what conditions) treatment should directly involve two (or more) generations, or be limited to one generation. Indeed, there are many "family" therapists who either focus on the marital dyad (Framo, 1976) or conceive of that dyad as being the core family subsystem requiring change (Satir, 1967). As we noted earlier, marital and family therapy have had rather independent geneses, and there are, in fact, many therapists who work almost exclusively with the husband-wife pair or who work predominantly with the entire nuclear family or extended family network system (Speck & Attneave, 1973).

Our position is that marital therapy, when conducted with a couple who have children, is not a unique treatment format, but represents one subtype of family therapy. Even when a couple in treatment is childless, we conceive of therapy as involving the resolution of subtle but salient *interfamily* conflict (Boszormenyi-Nagy & Spark, 1973; Dicks, 1967; Whitaker, 1975) as well as interpersonal and intrapersonal conflict. We are specifying our biases about this issue lest the format of our research review imply a different stance. That is, we will evaluate marital and family therapy research semiindependently for two reasons: (1) we believe it is in keeping with current labeling practices in the field, and (2) such a separation will facilitate the examination of the large amount of data to be considered in this chapter. Within each of the major domains of our review (e.g., gross improvement rates), we will discuss both marital and family therapy before proceeding to the next domain (e.g., comparative studies). In effect, we are reviewing here four bodies of research, i.e., behavioral and non-behavioral marital therapy and family therapy.

Improvement Rates in Marital-Family Therapy

Even though it has become methodologically unfashionable in most areas of psychotherapy research to consider gross rates of improvement as being of any real value (Bergin, 1971; Luborsky et al., 1975), we believe that a thorough accounting of such data in the marital-family field is necessary here because previous reviews (Beck, 1975; Gurman, 1973b, 1975a, 1975c; Kniskern, 1975; Wells et al., 1972) did not include all relevant studies existing at the time of their publication and have examined less than half of the currently available studies. Moreover, such an analysis allows a crude yet heuristically useful comparison with the gross treatment effects of other types of psychotherapy and will serve as the first step in our unfolding analysis of the results of comparative and controlled studies of outcome.

Tables 21-1 and 21-2 summarize the results of 77 studies of marital ($N = 36$) and family ($N = 41$) therapy reporting gross improvement rates. We have generally recorded these results as they appeared in the original reports, but have attempted to clarify issues of sampling bias, unclear findings, and the like, in the footnotes of these tables. Approximately three-quarters of these studies have appeared since 1965. A mixture of client types and problems is represented by these data, with a majority of both marital (89 percent) and family (74 percent) therapies carried out in outpatient settings. Most of the marital studies dealt with couples with undifferentiated difficulties (communication and intimacy problems, dependency and autonomy conflict, etc.). The presenting spouses' diagnosis (most couples therapy begins with one symptomatic partner seeking help) is quite unclear in most of these studies. Many more clearly delineated diagnoses are represented among the

identified patients in the family studies (e.g., phobias, anorexia nervosa, delinquency, psychosis, drug addiction, and alcoholism).

Although the family studies typically used either inexperienced therapists or a combination of inexperienced and experienced therapists, most of the marital studies used experienced clinicians. Two-thirds of the treatments in the studies in Tables 21-1 and 21-2 were of relatively brief duration (i.e., 1 to 20 sessions), yet in only two (Reid & Shyne, 1969; Wattie, 1973) was therapy time-limited.[5] Among the inpatient and day hospital family studies, treatment always involved a combination of approaches [e.g., occupational and recreational therapy, nonfamily group therapy, or individual (identified patient) therapy]; the primary focus and effort, however, was placed on conjoint family therapy. Outpatient family therapy was predominantly conjoint but, at times, included a small number of other types of sessions. The marital studies were generally much more consistent in terms of with whom and in what format treatment sessions were conducted (e.g., conjointly versus individually). Cotherapy was not uncommon to either group of studies, yet most therapy was conducted by a single therapist, and the therapist samples were usually small.

Outcome was based on measures varying from highly objective (e.g., weight gain) to highly subjective (e.g., satisfaction with treatment) and included the full range of rating sources. The modal study can be characterized as using only one evaluative perspective, usually that of the therapist or client(s), and a single change index; among the marital studies, this was a global measure of change or marital satisfaction; among the family studies, it was either identified patient (IP) behavior or symptomatology or overall family functioning.

Some interesting trends, largely consistent with those of comparative and controlled studies to be described shortly, emerge from these studies. In

[5]Here we are arbitrarily defining the criteria for long- and short-term therapy. Other cutoffs (cf: Table 21-1, footnote a) might yield a different assessment of the length of a given treatment. For example, Minuchin et al.'s (1975) treatment of anorexia averaged about 6 months, defined here as "long"; obviously this is quite brief compared to traditional individual treatment of this disorder (Rosman, 1977).

contrast to the results of conjoint, conjoint group, and collaborative-concurrent[6] marital therapies, all of which seem to produce positive change in about two-thirds of patients and all of which involve both spouses in treatment in some manner, individual therapy for marital problems yields improvement in only less than half (48 percent) of its consumers. Our clinical bias and that of others (Fox, 1968; Hurvitz, 1967; Kohl, 1962) is that these data reflect reality and not a systematic sampling bias. Most of the individual therapy studies were conducted in social worker-staffed family service agencies, and there is some evidence that social worker family therapists may underestimate their own effectiveness, in contrast to psychiatrists and psychologists (Santa-Barbara et al., 1975). Still, therapist outcome ratings were used in only two individual therapy studies and were used as the sole change criterion in only one study. Despite recent theoretical arguments (Smith & Hepworth, 1967) in favor of individual therapy for marital problems, as clinicians we are persuaded by the meaningfulness of the data in Table 20-1. Moreover, we will shortly present data on the increasing evidence of disproportionate rates of patient worsening as a result of individual marital therapy.

Overall, *the four major forms of nonbehavioral marital therapy appear to produce beneficial effects in 61 percent of cases and, with individual marital therapy studies excluded, positive effects occur in 65 percent of the treatments, essentially the same gross improvement rates that have been noted for nonmarital individual therapy* (Bergin, 1971).

The results of family therapy are presented in Table 21-2 in terms of who was the identified patient: about half involved child- or adolescent-identified patients, and about half involved adult IPs (identified patients). Collapsing the child and adolescent IP studies and comparing them to the adult studies (and excluding "mixed IP" studies), we find similar rates of change: child-adolescent

[6]In conjoint therapy, both partners are treated together by the same therapist(s); in conjoint groups, couples are similarly seen as a dyad; in concurrent therapy, spouses are treated separately by the same therapist; in collaborative therapy, spouses are treated separately by different therapists who communicate with each other about treatment.

improved, 71 percent; not improved, 29 percent; adult improved, 65 percent; and not improved, 35 percent. These results are, not surprisingly, essentially the same as those across all four IP categories (73 percent improved, 27 percent not improved), since these studies account for most of the patients studied. These figures are strikingly reminiscent of the results usually reported for individual therapy (Bergin, 1971).

The following treatment setting-based improvement rates were found: outpatient—76 percent improved, 24 percent not improved; day hospital—59 percent improved, 41 percent not improved; inpatient—74 percent improved, 26 percent not improved. All the day hospital studies and most of the inpatient studies dealt with adult IPs, so that the effects of IP developmental level and treatment setting on outcome cannot be disentangled from these gross outcome data. It is not surprising that day hospital family therapy has the lowest improvement rate, since the majority of IPs in this setting tend to be chronic and marginally compensated schizophrenics, patients suffering from major affective disorders and long-standing hysterical and borderline personality disorders; in short, they are the most intractable adult consumers of psychotherapy. Given the prognostic pessimism usually elicited among professional therapists who work with such patients, the 59 percent improvement rate for family therapy is probably high compared to the results of other treatment strategies. Still, day hospital settings are far more likely to offer a melange of professional interventions, so that teasing out the unique contribution to outcome of family therapy is far more difficult here than in other treatment settings. Similarly, the impressive improvement rate for family therapy in inpatient settings must be tempered by a recognition of the fact that since most of the IPs in these cases were acutely disturbed, one would expect a high rate of spontaneous IP symptomatic recovery, which is characteristic of this population. Given the relatively brief treatment courses for these families, however, we are impressed that important changes in family system functioning also occurred.

The foregoing results of marital and family therapy may be faulted by some on the basis that most of the outcome criteria were based on patient

TABLE 21-1 Improvement Rates in Studies of the Four Major Forms of Marital Therapy

Author	Treatment Length;[a] Setting[b]	Outcome Criteria (Source)[c]	Patient N[d]	Outcome at Termination[e]		
				Improved	No Change	Worse[f]
Conjoint Therapy						
Becker (1963)	Long; IP	Marital relationship; wife change (T)	7	6	1	NR
Bellville et al. (1969)	Moderate; OPC	Marital satisfaction (T)	44	26	18	NR
Brandreth and Pike (1967)	Short; FSC	Marital relationship; focal problem (H,W,T)	50	31	17[g]	2[g]
Carroll et al. (1963)	Long; OPC	Global improvement (T)	6	4	2	NR
Fitzgerald (1969)	Long; PP	Marriage quality (T)	57[h]	37	20	NR
Gurman (1973c)	Moderate; OPC	Marriage quality (H,W,T)	12	9	3	0
Reding et al. (1967)	Short; OPC	Marriage quality (H,W,T)	10	9	1	0
Wattie (1973)	Long and short; FSC	Overall improvement (H,W)	75[i]	61	14	NR
Total			261	70 percent (183/261)	29 percent (76/261)	1 percent (2/261)

Individual Therapy

Study	Design; Setting	Outcome measure	N			
Ballard and Mudd (1957)	NR; FSC	Marital satisfaction (P,T)	54	30[j]	24	NR
Burton and Kaplan (1968)	x̄ NR; OPC	Global improvement (P)	23	10	13	NR
Fanshel (1958)	NR; FSC	Marital relationship (T)	90	25	58	7
Hepworth and Smith (1972)	Moderate; FSC	Goal achievement (J)	24	12	12	0
Hollis (1949)	NR; FSC	Wife improvement (J)	96	44	52	NR
Most (1964)	Short; FSC	Marital satisfaction (P)	20	16	NR	4
Reid and Shyne (1969)	Short and Long; FSC	Presenting problems (J)	48[k] / 51[k]	31 / 28	13 / 11	4 / 12
Total			406	48 percent (196/406)	45 percent (183/406)	7 percent (27/406)

Conjoint Group Therapy

Study	Design; Setting	Outcome measure	N			
Alkire and Brunse (1974)	Short; VA-OPC	Self-concept (P)	10	4	0	6
Boyd and Bolen (1970)	NR; OPC	H Gambling (O); marital relationship (T)	8[l]	7	1	0
Burton and Kaplan (1968)	x̄ NR; OPC	Alcoholic and nonalcoholic spouse change (P)	80	61	19	NR
Cadogan (1973)	Moderate; OPC	Alcoholic's drinking (P)	20	13	7	0
Corder et al. (1972)	Short; IP	Alcoholic's drinking (P, significant others)	19	15	4	NR
Furmansky (1976)	Moderate; OPC	H drinking behavior (P)	3	1	2	0
Gallant et al. (1970)	NR; OPC	Alcoholic's drinking (O); marital relationship (T)	118	53	65	NR
Hardcastle (1972)	Short; OPC	Therapy work styles (J)	7[m]	3	2	2

TABLE 21-1 (continued)

Author	Treatment Length;[a] Setting[b]	Outcome Criteria (Source)[c]	Patient N[d]	Outcome at Termination[e]		
				Improved	No Change	Worse[t]
Conjoint Group Therapy						
Hooper et al. (1968)	Long; OPC	Global change (J)	10	8	2	NR
Linden et al. (1968)	NR; OPC	Marital relationship (T)	11	10	1	NR
Loescher (1970)	Short; OPC	Alcoholic's drinking (P); global marital change (T)	28	22	2	4
Maizlish and Hurley (1963)	Moderate; CGC	Attitudes regarding self, spouse, children (P)	32	26	6	NR
Smith (1967)[n]	NR: IP	Alcoholic H drinking (H.W.T)	15	11	4	NR
Steinglass et al. (1975)	Short; IP	Global rating (P)	10	10	NR	NR
Targow and Zweber (1969)	Long; OPC	Global rating (P)	26[o]	16	5	5
Total			397	66 percent (260/397)	30 percent (120/397)	4 percent (17/397)
Concurrent and Collaborative Therapy: Individual and Group						
Burton and Kaplan (1968)	x̄ NR; OPC	Global change (P)	121	72	49	NR
Dicks (1967)[p]	Moderate; PP	Marriage quality (T)	35[q]	24	11	0
Ewing et al. (1961)	Long; OPC	Alcoholic H drinking (P)	11	8	3	NR
Gliedman (1957); Gliedman et al. (1956)	Moderate; OPC	Alcoholic H drinking (P); Material interaction (P)	9	2	7	0

Hixenbaugh (1931)	NR; CC		77	47	30	0
Preston et al. (1953)	NR; OPC	Reconciliation (O) Global change (J)	211	137	63	11
Total			464	63 percent (290/464)	35 percent (163/464)	2 percent (11/464)
Grand total			1528	61 percent (929/1528)	35 percent (542/1528)	4 percent (57/1528)

Note: NR = not reported. Data on behavioral therapies are reported elsewhere in this chapter.

a Short = 1 to 10 sessions; moderate = 11 to 20 sessions; long = 21 or more sessions.

b CC = conciliation court; CGC = child guidance center; FSC = family service center or family counseling center; IP = inpatient; OPC = outpatient clinic; PP = private practice; VA = Veterans Administration.

c T = therapist; P = patient; H = husband; W = wife; J = nonparticipant judge or interviewer; O = objective records not requiring trained observation.

d Number of couples or individuals (subjects), depending on criteria used or number of spouses per dyad treated.

e "Improved" includes very much, good deal, and somewhat improved; "no change" includes little improved and no change.

f Entries of zero here are of two types: (1) those clearly specified in the original report as having no deteriorated cases and (2) our determination that, on the basis of the data or other evidence provided by the original authors, but without their explicit statement, all study cases could be reasonably assigned to one of the other two outcome categories.

g The authors report five cases to have had an "uncertain" outcome: (1) improved on one but not both criteria, (2) minimal change marked by extreme conflict at intake, or (3) an *increase* in conflict. We have thus entered one-third of these five cases as "worse," and two-thirds as "no change."

h Fitzgerald reported 37/49 "involved" couples as improved; we consider the eight couples who terminated for unspecified reasons before the fourth session ("uninvolved") to have been treatment failures; thus, the present improvement rates and those in the original report differ.

i Based on 75 mail questionnaire returns of 184 sent. The authors document, however, that this response rate was not affected by client satisfaction with treatment.

j The same single outcome criterion was rated by patients and therapists; the means of these ratings were entered here.

k Outcome was also rated by therapists. These ratings are not included here because they were based (for reasons not apparent in the original report) on a different (larger) N and, therefore, are not directly comparable to the judges' ratings (ratings were very similar: brief therapy—34 improved, 14 no change, 5 worse; open-ended therapy—26 improved, 20 no change, 8 worse. The N (=99) used here is the same as that reported in other literature reviews (Beck, 1975).

l Outcome entries represent the present authors' averaging within change categories across two criteria.

m Four couples were in this therapy group, but data were presented for only seven patients.

n Follow-up reported in Smith (1969).

o Original sample contained 30 patients, but usable follow-up questionnaires were returned by only 26.

p Fifteen couples also had four-way joint interviews interspersed during treatment.

q Of Dicks' 36 couples, one had left the country and could not be followed up; this case is thus excluded here.

r Twenty-four clients reported as still in counseling at the time of the report were excluded from analysis by us.

TABLE 21-2 Improvement Rates in Studies of Family Therapy

Author	Treatment Length;[a] Setting[b]	Outcome Criteria (Source)[c]	Patient N	Outcome at Termination[d]		
				Improved	No Change	Worse[e]
		Child as Identified Patient				
Guerney and Stover (1971)	Long; OPC	Identified patient functioning (T)	68	51	17[f]	0
Kaffman (1963)	Short; OPC	Identified patient and family functioning (T)	29	25	4	0
Kaswan and Love (1969)	Short; OPC	School interaction (J)	14	12	2	NR
Minuchin et al. (1975)	Long; OPC	Identified patient symptoms (O,J)	23[g]	23	0	0
Postner et al. (1971)	Long; OPC	Family interaction (J)	9	5	4	NR
Safer (1966)	Short; OPC	Identified patient symptoms (F)	23[h]	18	5	NR
Schreiber (1966)	Moderate; OPC	Symptoms and family communications (T)	72	36	36[i]	NR
Sigal et al. (1967)	Moderate; OPC	Family interaction (J)	19	14	5	NR
Skynner (1974)	Short; OPC	Family functioning (F)	26	12	14	NR
Spiegel and Sperber (1967)	Short; OPC	Identified patient return to school (PAR)	19	16	3	NR
	Short; OPC	Identified patient symptoms (PAR)	7	7	0	0
Total			370	68 percent (254/370)	32 percent (116/370)	0 percent (0/370)

Adolescent as Identified Patient

Alexander et al. (1976)	Short; OPC	Patient and family functioning (T)	21	12	9	NR
Baird (1973)	Short; OPC	Family interpersonal behavior (T)	4	3	1	0
Burks and Serrano (1965)	Short; IP	Goal attainment (T)	20	15	5	NR
Coughlin and Wimberger (1968)	Long; OPC	Family functioning (T)	10	8	1	1
Donner and Gamson (1968)	Moderate; OPC	Identified patient symptoms (T)	30	20	10	NR
Evans et al. (1971)	Moderate; IP	Identified patient functioning (S)	50	46	4	NR
Ives et al. (1975)	Short; OPC	Goal attainment (T)	8	4[j]	4[j]	NR
MacGregor (1962); MacGregor et al. (1964)	Short;[k] OPC	Family and identified patient functioning (T)	62	49	13	NR
Minuchin et al. (1967)	Long; IP	Family and identified patient functioning (T)	12	7	5	NR
Total			217	75 percent (164/217)	25 percent (52/217)	0 percent (1/217)

Adult as Identified Patient

Abroms et al. (1971)	Short; IP	Symptom checklist (S)	100	86	14	NR
Bowen (1961)	Long; IP	Family functioning (T)	7	3	4	NR
	Long; OPC	Family functioning (T)	7	5	2	NR
Esterson et al. (1965)	Moderate; IP	Hospital and work adjustment (O)	42	35	7	NR
Gartner et al. (1975)	Moderate; DH	Family functioning (T)	91	51	33	7

TABLE 21-2 *(continued)*

Author	Treatment Length [a] Setting [b]	Outcome Criteria (Source) [c]	Patient N	Outcome at Termination [d]		
				Improved	No Change	Worse [e]
Adult as Identified Patient						
Greenberg et al. (1964)	Long; IP	Family relationship (T)	13	8	5[l]	NR
Hendricks (1971)	Long; IP	Addicted identified patient discharge status (O)	85	35	50	NR
Lee and Mayerson (1973)	Short; IP	Identified patient functioning (P)	7	7	0	0
Meeks and Kelly (1970)	Long; DH	Identified patient drinking (F)	5	5	0	0
Pittman et al. (1968)	Short; OPC	Identified patient return to work (O)	5	5	0	0
Stanton and Todd (1976)	Short; OPC	Identified patient heroin in urine and work (O)	15	13	2	0
Zwerling and Mendelsohn (1965)	Long; DH	Identified patient discharge status (S)	98	58	40	NR
Total			475	65 percent (311/475)	33 percent (157/475)	2 percent (7/475)
Mixed Type of Identified Patients						
Amdur et al. (1969)	Moderate; IP	Identified patient weight gain (O)	10	8	2	0
Freeman et al. (1964)	Moderate; OPC	Family functioning (T)	13	11	1	1
Jackson and Weakland (1961)	Long; OPC	Identified patient functioning (T)	18	15	3	0[m]

Study	Treatment[a]	Outcome measure	N	Improved[d]	No change[d]	Worse[d]
Laqueur et al. (1964)	Long; IP	Family functioning (T)[n]	80	62	18	NR
Rosman et al. (1976)	Long; OPC[o]	Identified patient weight gain (O)	53	47	6[p]	NR
Santa-Barbara (1975)[q]	Short; OPC	Presenting problem (F)	189	160	22	7
Shapiro and Harris (1976)	Long; OPC	Family functioning (T, SUP)	7	7	0	0
Weakland et al. (1974)	Short; OPC	Goal attainment (F)	97	70	26	1
Total			467	81 percent (380/467)	17 percent (78/467)	2 percent (9/467)
Grand total			1529	73 percent (1109/1529)	26 percent (403/1529)	1 percent (17/1529)

Note: NR = not reported. Data on behavioral therapies reported elsewhere in this chapter.

a Short = 1 to 10 sessions outpatient or less than 6 weeks inpatient; moderate = 11 to 20 sessions outpatient or 6 to 12 weeks inpatient; long = 21 sessions or more outpatient or 12 weeks or more inpatient.

b IP = inpatient; OPC = outpatient clinic; DH = day hospital.

c T = therapist; P = patient; F = family; PAR = parents; S = ward staff; J = nonparticipant judge or interviewer; O = objective records not requiring trained observation; S = supervisor.

d "Improved" includes very much, good deal, and somewhat improved; no change includes little improved, no change, and no change or worse.

e Entries of zero here are of two types: (1) those clearly specified in the original report as having no deteriorated cases and (2) our determination that, on the basis of the data or other evidence provided by the original authors, but without their explicit statement, all study cases could be reasonably assigned to one of the other two outcome categories.

f All 17 of these patients dropped the program prior to completion.

g Anorectic patients are reported on in Rosman et al. (1976).

h Six other treated families were not included in the analysis because change was judged to be unrelated to therapy.

i Includes 13 families who did not continue treatment to postassessment.

j Improvement was arbitrarily set at a level of 50 percent of goals attained.

k Treatment was intense 2½-day involvement with family (multiple-impact therapy).

l Includes two "uncertain."

m One sibling and two mothers were judged to have become worse.

n Patients reported 67 percent improvement, 21 percent "doubtful," and 12 percent "negative."

o Some patients had a short period of hospitalization.

p Includes three families who terminated after two or three sessions.

q Sample includes many patients previously reported on (Santa-Barbara et al., 1975; Woodward et al., 1975; etc.).

and therapist reports. This argument typically invokes the observation that other criteria (e.g., judges' ratings and objective indices) often show lower improvement rates than participants' evaluations do. Although this is factually true, the implication in this argument is that the latter types of criteria are, ipso facto, superior to participants' judgments of change because patients and therapists, having a personal investment in improvement, are "biased" in their assessments. In fact, as Fiske (1975, 1977) has argued in two outstanding scholarly works, there is little reason to expect that outcome ratings from different vantage points should agree with one another. Instead, they represent distinctive perspectives that are not reducible to one another. For example, Mintz (1977) provides a substantive argument for the unique perspective provided by the psychotherapist in assessing therapeutic change.

Clearly the most impressive results among all the foregoing studies have emerged from the Philadelphia Child Guidance Clinic (PCGC) group, who have reported the outcomes of a clearly delineated, highly teachable system of "Structural Family Therapy" (Minuchin, 1974) with anorexics, asthmatics, diabetics (Minuchin et al., 1975; Rosman et al., 1976), and heroin addicts (Stanton & Todd, 1976). Control groups have been used in only one (Stanton & Todd, 1976) of the PCGC studies. Still, the seriousness, even life-threatening, nature of the psychosomatic disorders studied in the uncontrolled investigations and the use of highly objective change measures (e.g., weight gain, blood sugar levels, respiratory functioning) constitute, to us, compelling evidence of major clinical changes in conditions universally acknowledged to have extremely poor prognoses untreated or treated by standard medical regiments (Bruch, 1971). Even more strikingly, the improvements noted at termination (91 percent for these three studies) have endured at several months' to several years' follow-up, despite the fact that many of these patients had failed to respond to other earlier treatments. The most serious deficits in these studies of a "systems intervention" has been that *system* changes have been examined in only one of the PCGC studies (Stanton & Todd, 1976) and that the effective treatment components (e.g., family

therapy, behavior modification) in the structural therapy for these disorders have not been identified.

Deterioration in Nonbehavioral Marital-Family Therapy

So far we have not discussed the issue of patient or marital-family system worsening as a result of therapy. It must be noted that the "improved," "no change," and "worse" designations in Tables 21-1 and 21-2 are obviously not comparable across studies, since they reflect different criteria, rating perspectives, and so on. Furthermore, some studies either did not include a "worse" category or lumped "no change" and "worse" together, so that the apparent rates of deterioration noted in those tables are clearly biased *against* finding evidence for the phenomenon. Table 21-3 summarizes the reported rates of deterioration in studies of nonbehavioral marital-family therapy. Among those 36 studies that reported or allowed a determination of patient worsening, nearly half (15, or 42 percent) found evidence for deterioration. Because of the methodological shortcomings of these studies noted in this section, it is impossible to speak of "true" deterioration rates or to specify differential deterioration rates as a function of patient type. On the whole, nonetheless, it appears that 5 to 10 percent of patients or of marital or family relationships worsen as the result of treatment. Gurman and Kniskern (1976, 1978b) offer a more detailed description of the studies that provide this evidence. Criteria on which deterioration was demonstrated ranged from suicide, delinquent recidivism, increased alcohol intake, and worsening of presenting problems to broader measures such as lowered self-concept, lowered marital satisfaction, and global ratings of change. Most striking is the fact that when conjoint, conjoint group, and concurrent-collaborative marital therapies are considered together, the rate of deterioration is only half of that resulting from individual marital therapy (i.e., 5.6 percent versus 11.6 percent). *In conjunction with the unimpressive improvement rate noted earlier for individual marital therapy, there appears to be little empirical basis for its continued practice.* With the atypical study of Alkire and Brunse (1974) excluded, the rate of patient worsening in conjoint

TABLE 21-3 Deterioration Rates in Studies of Nonbehavioral Marital and Family Therapy

Therapy Type/ Setting	Number of Studies Reporting Improvement Rates	Number of Studies with "Worse" Category	Number of Studies Reporting Deterioration	Percent of Studies with "Worse" Category Reporting Deterioration	Deterioration Rate Across Studies with "Worse" Category, Percent
Marital Therapy					
Conjoint	8	3 (37 percent)	1	33	2.7 (2/72)
Individual	7	5 (71 percent)	4	80	11.6 (27/233)
Group	15	7 (47 percent)	4	57	16.6 (17/102)
Concurrent/ collaborative	6	4 (67 percent)	1	25	3.3 (11/332)
Total	36	19 (53 percent)	10	53	7.7 (57/739)
Family Therapy					
Inpatient	11	2 (18 percent)	0	0	0 (0/17)
Outpatient	27	13 (48 percent)	4	29	2.1 (10/485)
Day hospital	3	2 (67 percent)	1	50	7.3 (7/96)
Total	41	17 (43 percent)	5	29	2.8 (17/598)
Grand total	77	36 (47 percent)	15	42	5.4 (74/1337)

group therapy is reduced somewhat to 12 percent. Still, this seems to be an unduly high rate of worsening. No evidence exists that might explain this finding, but we would speculate on clinical grounds that deteriorated individuals or couples may be the products of the scapegoating process that occurs almost routinely in group situations.

Essentially nothing is known about family therapy deterioration with IP inpatients or day hospital patients. The extremely low deterioration rate in outpatient family therapy (2.1 percent) is based largely on studies involving an adolescent or child IP. These results are reassuringly consistent with those of Abramowitz (1976), who found very little evidence of deterioration in 42 studies of group therapy with children. Elsewhere, we offer some tentative hypotheses to account for these converging data (Gurman & Kniskern, 1976, 1978b), yet we suspect that since much of the existing research on family therapy has been done by people who strongly endorse family therapy, there has been a subtle bias against viewing cases as having deteriorated. We will review the evidence regarding factors influencing deterioration and will consider deterioration in behavioral marital-family therapy later in this chapter.

Comparative Studies of Marital-Family Therapy

In the preceding section we presented some straightforward comparisons of different types of nonbehavioral couples and family therapy based on gross improvement rates. We now turn to the body of research that has directly compared different types of marital-family therapy with each other and with other therapeutic interventions. Although few of the existing comparative studies used truly superior research designs, nearly half (21/46) of the studies described in Tables 21-4 and 21-5 earned "good" or "very good" design quality ratings and several others (11/46) were at least "fair." Some readers may object to our mixing of good and poor quality studies in the summary of Table 21-4 and in our concluding comment at the end of this section, but we believe this approach is justifiable on several grounds: (1) the results of the "poor" studies are entirely consistent with those of better quality, in keeping with the similar trend found by Bergin (1971) in individual psychotherapy research; (2) the results of these comparative studies are completely in line with both the gross improvement results of marital therapy (Table 21-1) and the results of controlled marital outcome studies (Table 21-6), almost all of which were of superior design quality; this fact seems to imply the consistency and power of an underlying, converging clinical phenomenon that overrides issues of the design quality of individual studies; (3) as Glass (1976) has persuasively argued, arbitrarily discarding studies that fail to meet particular design requirements or eliminating studies that employ outcome measures that a reviewer dislikes is "wasteful of significant data that, though ambiguous when they stand alone, can be informative when viewed in the context of dozens of other studies" (pp. 23–24). Thus, in keeping with Gottman's (this volume) admonition, we are not equating evidence from well-designed studies with evidence from poor studies.

Worthy of historical note is the fact that 82 per-

cent of the studies in Tables 21-4 and 21-5 have appeared since 1970; this signals a recent quantum increase in research sophistication in the field from the studies discussed in the preceding section.

As with the reports of single-group studies, most of the comparative family studies used relatively inexperienced therapists, while the majority of marital studies used experienced clinicians. In both cases outcome ratings tended to be more adequate than in the single-group studies. Most assessed change from several vantage points and/or used multiple criteria. The comparative family work, unfortunately, was limited somewhat by the sole use of IP change measures in 11 out of 20 studies. In general, the marital studies did not share this design weakness in that only 3 out of 25 limited outcome measures to the IP; the other 22 included either system or relationship measures only or both IP and system measures.

The results of comparative marital studies (Table 21-4) are noticeably consistent with the results of single-group studies discussed earlier. Conjoint marital therapy and conjoint group marital therapy emerge nearly unscathed, superior to alternative treatments in 70 percent of the comparisons and inferior in only 5 percent. Interestingly, in all six direct comparisons of these two therapy formats, no outcome differences were found. An important direction for further study will involve an empirical determination of the types of couples for whom each of these therapies is indicated. At the moment, only very speculative criteria are used in this differential assessment process (e.g., Framo, 1973; Grunebaum, Christ & Neiberg, 1976; Gurman, 1971). Moreover, it will be important to determine whether the group nature of group couples therapy or the conjoint treatment format itself accounts for its efficacy.

Concurrent and collaborative marital therapies have received scant attention (Burton & Kaplan, 1968; Cookerly, 1973, 1974, 1976) and, as Gurman (1973a) recently documented, are clearly on the wane in clinical practice. The comparative outcomes of these treatment strategies do not appear to support their regeneration as independent treatment approaches. Still, it will be of real clinical value to determine the conditions under which a combination of individual and conjoint sessions throughout treatment or of selective individual sessions in a predominantly conjoint therapy may enhance the outcomes of conjoint therapy alone.

The low rate of positive outcomes and high rate of deterioration as a result of individual marital therapy noted earlier are not contravened by the results of the comparative studies in Table 21-4. In fact, individual treatment emerges superior to other therapies in only 10 percent of the comparisons and superior to conjoint or conjoint group therapy in only 5 percent. In sum, *we believe these data are persuasive enough to question routinely the value of individual therapy for marital problems. The burden of empirically demonstrating the utility or advantages of such treatment rests now on its advocates.* In contrast to Luborsky et al.'s (1975) conclusions about the comparative efficacy of individual psychotherapies, the dodo bird's verdict here is, "Everyone has *not* won, and only some must have prizes."

As can be seen in Table 21-5, *every study to date that has compared family therapy with other types of treatment has shown family therapy to be equal or superior.* The comparisons have involved family therapy and either individual therapy (Abroms et al., 1971; Budman & Shapiro, 1976; Evans et al., 1971; Ewing, 1975; Johnson, 1971; Love et al., 1972; Pittman et al., 1968; Wellisch et al., 1976) or "services as usual," such as hospitalization of the IP (Langsley et al., 1969; Rittenhouse, 1970), standard probation programs for delinquents (Dezen & Borstein, 1975), traditional parent counseling (Love et al., 1972), or standard methadone programs (Stanton & Todd, 1976), or inpatient programs (Hendricks, 1971) for drug addiction. Specifically, family therapy has emerged superior in 10 out of 14 such comparisons, although it should be noted that the changes achieved were at times of questionable real-life utility [e.g., Love et al.'s (1972) children "significantly" improved their school grades from "C−" to "C" on the average].

The often cited results of the family crisis therapy project of Langsley et al. (1968, 1969), partially replicated by Rittenhouse (1970), deserve mention both because of the ambitiousness of that project and because of frequent misinterpretation of its design. An unusually large sample (150 experimental,

150 control) of acutely disturbed IPs for whom hospitalization and conventional inpatient treatment had been recommended was randomly assigned to either this standard intervention or to short-term, family-centered crisis therapy (CT). CT was clearly superior to hospitalization in terms of both length and frequency of IP readmissions (but not social adjustment) and was able to avert instead of simply delay hospitalization, but it is unclear whether the short-term nature of the intervention, its crisis orientation, or the use of a family focus was most responsible for its comparative effectiveness. As is true of most of the studies in Tables 21-4 and 21-5 the Langsley project did not include a control group, since the hospitalized patients received a variety of (nonfamily) psychotherapies in addition to the usual hospital regimen. Still, one would be hard pressed to have created a true control group given the intensity of the IPs' acute emotional crises. While we agree with Fox (1976) that "avoiding hospitalization for 150 seriously disturbed individuals is no mean acccomplishment" (p. 502), we cannot concur with Wells et al.'s (1972) classification of this project as an "adequate study," particularly since Wells et al. themselves cite the omission of a control group as evidence of inadequacy and suggest at least one design change that could have rendered the "control" group more nearly untreated. In addition, Langsley et al. (1968, 1969) confounded hospitalization versus nonhospitalization with family therapy versus other psychotherapies. Moreover, in the absence of proper controls, the rehospitalization results may have merely reflected a design artifact instead of a treatment effect. It seems appropriate to conclude simply that no outcome differences were established.

In one of the most impressive comparative studies to date, Wellisch et al. (1976) compared family therapy and individual therapy in the treatment of adolescent inpatients. Mixed yet generally better results on a variety of self-report and observational measures were found following family therapy. At the 3-month follow-up, no family-treated adolescent had been rehospitalized, while 43 percent of the individually treated adolescents had been rehospitalized. These results suggest that the questionable Langsley et al. (1968, 1969) find-

TABLE 21-4 Outcomes of Comparative Studies of Marital Therapy

Author	Treatments Compared (Setting)[a]	Outcome Criteria (Source)[b]	Outcome (Design Quality)
Beck and Jones (1973)	Short-term; open-ended Conjoint; individual (FSC)	Overall change (P,T) Overall change (P,T)	No difference Conjoint superior[c]
Burton and Kaplan (1968)	Group: individual individual; concurrent (OPC)	Global self-change (P) Global self-change (P)	Group superior Concurrent superior (poor)
Cookerly (1973)	Group and "interview" concurrent, conjoint, and Individual (OPC)	Marital status (O); quality of outcome status (J)	Conjoint and conjoint group superior (poor)
Cookerly (1974, 1976)[d]	Concurrent, conjoint, and group (OPC)	Individual, personalsocial, and marital adjustment (P)	Concurrent superior on individual pathology; Conjoint and conjoint group superior on marital; no difference in social (good)
Cookerly (1976)[e]	Group and "interview" concurrent, conjoint, and Individual (OPC)	Marital, social, and personal adjustment (P)	Conjoint and conjoint group superior in marital adjustment (poor)
Cookerly (1976)[f]	Group and "interview" concurrent, conjoint, and individual (OPC)	Divorce rate 1 to 3 years posttherapy (O); marital status satisfaction (P)	Lowest divorce rates and most satisfaction in conjoint (37 percent) and conjoint group (40 percent) (poor)
Corder et al. (1972)	Conjoint group; individual group (IP)	Alcoholic spouse's drinking (6-month follow-up)	Conjoint group superior (fair)
Davenport et al. (1975)	Group: individual; community care (MF)	Rehospitalization (O); marital status (O); social functioning (P)	Group superior (fair)
Freeman et al. (1969)	Conjoint; group; individual[g] (OPC)	Marital relationship; division of responsibility (P,T)	No differences (poor)

Study	Treatment	Outcome measures	Results
Friedman (1975)	Conjoint; drug therapy (OPC)	Depression of identification point (P,J); family role performance and marital relationship (P)	Marital therapy superior for marital relationship; drug superior for depressive symptoms (good)
Graham (1968)	Conjoint; conjoint and individual (CC)	Positive references to spouse (J); reconciliation (O); interpersonal dominance and affiliation (P)	Conjoint superior (good)
Hepworth and Smith (1972)	Individual; conjoint and individual[h] (FSC)	Achievements of goals (J)	No difference (poor)
Hickman and Baldwin (1970)	Conjoint; programmed communication training (CC)	Reconciliation (O); marital relationship (P)	Conjoint superior (Very good)
Macon (1975)	Conjoint; conjoint group (FSC)	Communication (P); self-esteem (P); problem-solving skill (P); spouse-image (P)	No difference (fair)
Matanovich (1970)	Encounter group tapes; Individual and Conjoint (CC)	Reconciliation (O); interpersonal dominance and affiliation (P); rating of helpfulness (P)	No difference on any criteria (Very good)
Mayadas and Duehn (1977)	Communication modeling (CM); CM plus video feedback (CMV); Verbal counseling (VC) (OPC)	Five problematic communication behaviors (O)	CMV>CM>VC (Very good)
Mezydlo et al. (1973)	Parish pastoral counseling; "office" priests; lay therapists (all Conjoint) (Catholic FSC)	Target complaints (P)	Office outcome>lay> parish (poor)
Pierce (1973)	Communication training; group (OPC)	Communication skill and self-exploration (J)	Communication training superior (fair)
Reid and Shyne (1969)	Conjoint; individual brief; open-ended (FSC)	Presenting problem (T,J) Presenting problem (T,J)	No difference; brief superior on some dimensions (good)
Smith (1967)	Conjoint group; individual group (IP)	Alcoholic spouse's drinking (H,W,T)	Conjoint group superior (fair)

TABLE 21-4 *(continued)*

Author	Treatments Compared (Setting) [a]	Outcome Criteria (Source) [b]	Outcome (Design Quality)
Swan (1972)	Communication training; eclectic conjoint (CC)	Level of conflict (J)	No differences (good)
Valle and Marinelli (1975)	Communication training; group (PP)	Facilitative skill (J) Marital relationship (P) Individual functioning (P)	Communication training superior (fair)
Wattie (1973)	Short-term; open-ended (FSC)	Marital congruence (P) Global change (P,T,J)	Short-term superior on husband change only (good)
Wells et al. (1975b)	Communication training; conjoint[i] (FSC)	Marital adjustment (P) Dyadic empathy and warmth (P)	No difference at termination; conjoint superior at 3-month follow-up (fair)
Ziegler (1973)	Long group; intensive group (OPC)	CPI and Omnibus Personality Inventory (P)	No clear difference; long had more intense change, intensive, wider range of changes (good)

Summary

Conjoint		Individual		Group	
Conjoint superior	16	Individual superior	2	Group superior	15
Tie	10	Tie	5	Tie	8
Others superior	0	Others superior	12	Others superior	2
Conjoint superior	4	Individual superior	1	Group superior	0
Tie	2	Tie	1	Tie	6
Individual superior	0	Group superior	9	Conjoint superior	0

Conjoint and group (combined) superior	31
Tie	11
All others superior	2

Note: Comparative studies of behavior therapy are reported elsewhere in this chapter.

a FSC = family service center or family counseling centers; OPC = outpatient clinic; CC = conciliation court; PP = private practice; MF = medical facility; IP = inpatient.

b P = patient; T = therapist; J = judge or trained observer; O = objective indices not based on behavioral observation.

c This major national census study examined comparative treatment modalities as at most a secondary (and probably a tertiary) goal; thus, the standards of experimental research are probably not appropriately applied here; hence, we have omitted a design quality rating.

d The author's 1974 report included data only on MMPI changes; his 1976 report included these data plus the other criteria noted. Both reports used the same sample and are, therefore, combined here.

e "Outcome" was actually based on client's "immediate attitudes" toward the helpfulness of sessions and was based on postsession responses for each therapy session over a 4-month period.

f All of Cookerly's studies, two of which (1973, 1974) had been previously reported, were reported in his 1976 paper.

g Although these were the predominant treatment forms, an indeterminable number of study patients were involved in an indeterminable mixture of treatments.

h While the authors describe this study as one comparing individual and conjoint therapy, it is, in fact one of individual versus conjoint *plus* individual therapy: in the "conjoint" condition, averaging 26 sessions per case, 41 percent (11 sessions) were held with wives alone, 31 percent (eight sessions) with husbands alone, and only 28 percent (seven sessions) conjointly.

i Actually, due to clinical necessity, several of the conjoint couples also receive some communication training, although not in groups; although the initial intent was for the conjoint condition to be "behaviorally oriented" (Wells et al., 1975b, p. 1), this treatment clearly emerged as quite eclectic.

TABLE 21-5 Comparative Studies of Family Therapy Outcome

Author	Treatments Compared (Setting)[a]	Outcome Criteria (Source)[b]	Results (Design Quality)
Abroms et al. (1971)	Family;[c] Individual (IP)	Identified patient symptoms at discharge (S)	Family improved 86 percent; individual improved 81 percent (poor)
Alexander and Parsons (1973)	Family behavioral-system; client-centered family; eclectic-dynamic family (OPC)	Identified patient recidivism at 18 months (O)	Behavioral systems = 26 percent recidivism; client-centered = 47 percent; eclectic-dynamic = 73 percent (good)
Bernal and Margolin (1976)	Behavioral parent counseling (BT) Client-centered parent counseling (CG) (OPC)	1. Child's verbal abuse (O) 2. Deviant child behavior (O) 3. Targeted child behavior (Par) 4. Parental attitudes toward child (Par) 5. Satisfaction with therapy (Par)	No differences within or between groups on criteria 1 and 2; no difference between groups on 3, but both showed change; partial superiority for CC on 4; BT superior on 5 (good)
Budman and Shapiro (1976)	Individual;[d] Family[d] Individual terminators;[e] Family terminators[e] (OPC)	Identified patient functioning at 4½-month follow-up (Par,P) Identified patient functioning at 4½-month follow-up (Par,P)	No difference in reported functioning Individual terminators were more positive in reports of patient functioning[f] (poor)
Dezen and Borstein (1975)	E_1 = probation with family therapy E_2 = probation services as usual (OPC)	Identified patient recidivism at 6 months (O) Identified patient symptomatology (Par) Parental overinvolvement (Par) Report of parental behavior (C)	Family probation superior on symptom measure only (fair)
Evans et al. (1971)	Conjoint;[g] individual (IP)	Identified patient symptomatology (S) Return to work (O)	Conjoint superior to individual on both measures (poor)

Study	Treatment	Measure	Results
Ewing (1975)	Crisis intervention; psycho-dynamic child guidance (OPC)	Patient functioning (M)	Crisis equal to child guidance in one-tenth treatment time (poor)
Finol (1973)	Guided videotaped feedback; guided audiotaped feedback; discussion (OPC)	Positive and negative comments toward patient (O)	Videotape superior to audiotape on one measure and to discussion on one measure (good)
Gould and Glick (1976)	Conjoint family; conjoint and multiple family; no family therapy (family unavailable); no family therapy (family available) (IP)	Severity of illness (S), Psychiatric function (S), Role function (IP, Fam.), Employment (S.O.)	On all measures, conjoint> conjoint and multiple> no family therapy (family available)>no family therapy (family unavailable) (fair)
Hendricks (1971)	Multifamily group counseling (MFG), Standard inpatient treatment (IP Addiction Treatment Center)	Continued discharge (outpatient) status at 1-year follow-up (O)	41 percent of MFG patients remained outpts. versus 21 percent for standard addiction treatment (fair)
Jansma (1971)	Conjoint family; multiple family (OPC)	Family adjustment (Fam.), Family congruence (Fam.), Family satisfaction (Fam.), Marital satisfaction (Par)	Multiple superior to conjoint on 7 out of 9 measures (good)
Johnson (1971)	Conjoint family; nonfamily treatment (OPC)	Patterns of communication (O)	Conjoint superior to individual on 8 out of 9 measures (good)
Klein et al.[h] (1975)	E_1=family behavioral-system; E_2=client-centered family groups; E_3=eclectic-dynamic family (OPC)	Sibling court contracts in 3 years (O)	Behavioral-systems = 20 percent; client-centered = 59 percent; eclectic-dynamic = 63 percent (good)
Langsley et al. (1969)	E_1=family crisis intervention (Home); E_2=hospital treatment as usual	Rates of rehospitalization (O), Social adjustment inventory (Family)	Family superior to hospital in length and frequency of readmissions; no difference on adjustment (good)

TABLE 21-5 *(continued)*

Author	Treatment Compared (Setting)[a]	Outcome Criteria (Source)[b]	Results (Design Quality)
Love et al.[l] (1972)	Family-oriented videotape feedback of interaction; individual child psychotherapy; parent counseling (OPC)	Identified patient school interaction ratings (J) and grades (O)	Feedback = parent counseling individual therapy on grades; all treatments improved interaction (good)
Pittman et al. (1968)	E_1 = conjoint family crisis intervention E_2 = individual long term (OPC)	Return to work (O)	Conjoint superior to individual (poor)
Rittenhouse (1970)	Family therapy (home); hospital treatment (IP)	Overall improvement (P) Identified patient readmissions (O); family pathology (F); community functioning (S.O.)	Family superior to hospital on patient improvement and re-admissions; no difference on family or community (good)
Sigal et al. (1976)	Psychodynamically oriented conjoint; early terminators from conjoint treatment (OPC)	Identified patient presenting symptomatology at 4 years from termination (Family); Identified patient new problems (Family); Level of family functioning (Family);	Early terminators had fewer new problems; no differences on other measures[k] (fair)
Stanton and Todd (1976)	Structural family therapy; standard methadone treatment (OPC)	IP heroin use (O) IP work and school adjustment (F)	Family therapy superior to usual heroin addiction treatment (very good)
Trankina (1975)	Traditional child guidance; crisis family therapy (OPC)	Family satisfaction and adjustment (Par) Family life quality (Par) Child behavior (Par) Overall improvement (S, Par)	Crisis therapy superior on criteria 4, with fewer dropouts and in less time (fair)

| Wellisch et al. (1976) | Conjoint family; individual problem oriented (IP) | Rehospitalization (Family); Identified patient return to work or school (Family); Family interaction (J) | Conjoint superior on all measures except family interaction (good) |

[a] OPC = outpatient clinic; IP = inpatient.

[b] S = staff; Fam = family; O = objective indices; J = judge or trained observer; par = Parents; P = patient; S.O. = significant other; C = children; M = mother.

[c] Inpatient families were treated with a variety of individual, group and conjoint family therapy.

[d] Patients or families attending four or more sessions of therapy.

[e] Terminators are those patients or families who attended from 1 to 3 sessions.

[f] Family terminators reported two identified patients had deteriorated; no reports of deterioration in individual terminators.

[g] Treatment as usual in this setting included individual sessions in all cases and often included medication and ECT.

[h] Data is based on follow-up of siblings of identified patients reported on in previous study (Alexander & Parsons, 1973).

[i] Treatment as usual included individual and group psychotherapy, milieu therapy, and medication.

[j] Some of these subjects reported in Kaswan and Love (1969).

[k] There was a strong trend for long-term-treatment families to report better family functioning.

ings may have relfected the benefits of family therapy over other approaches and not the mere superiority of nonhospitalization to hospitalization. Unfortunately, Wellisch et al. provide no assessment of the need for rehospitalization within the two treatment groups.

Although few of the comparative marital or family studies used appropriate control groups (Alexander & Parsons, 1973; Friedman, 1975; Hickman & Baldwin, 1970; Jansma, 1971; Klein et al., 1975; Matanovich, 1970), we are, nonetheless, impressed by the convergence of results from both groups of studies. There have now appeared 30 comparisons of nonbehavioral marital and family therapy with individual or group therapy of the IP. In 22 (73 percent) of these, marital-family treatment emerged superior, with no differences found in seven studies. Moreover, this trend emerges irrespective of whether one includes or excludes the comparative studies rated "poor." We interpret these results as reasonably acceptable evidence that *when one member of a family system or one dyadic relationship within the family present themselves for treatment with problems involving family living, then marital-family therapy represents a more effective general treatment strategy than does individual therapy.* Given the division of opinion within the family field noted earlier with regard to who should be treated in systems therapy, a most important issue that must be addressed in future research involves identification of the conditions under which two-generational (parents and children) and one-generational (marital dyad) therapies maximize outcomes for both the IP and the system as a whole. To date, not a single study has addressed this matter of major theoretical and practical significance.

Controlled Studies of Outcome

The appearance of controlled studies of nonbehavioral marital-family therapy is also an extremely recent phenomenon: 19 of the 22 (86 percent) studies summarized in Tables 21-6 and 21-7 have appeared since 1970. Not included in Table 21-6 are a handful of controlled marital therapy outcome studies that were seriously marred by the use of inappropriate control groups, such as volunteer Ss not seeking treatment (Kind, 1968; Kuhn, 1973a, 1973b; Wattie, 1973) or Ss seeking entirely different, medical (obstetrical) services (Most, 1964), and several single-group studies reporting significant pre-post improvement but lacking a control group altogether (Beutler, 1971; Greene et al., 1975; Gurman, 1975b; McLellan & Stieper, 1971; Rice et al., 1972; Vansteenwegen, 1974, 1976; Verhulst & Vansteenwegen, 1974; Wells et al., 1975a).

In all, there have been 15 comparisons of the outcomes of nonbehavioral marital therapies with untreated control groups and 14 such comparisons of nonbehavioral family therapies. In addition, the studies of Alexander and Parsons (1973) and Klein et al. (1975) included "behavioral-systems" treatments.

The marital therapies (Table 21-6) emerge as superior to control groups in two-thirds (10/15) of the comparisons, with conjoint therapy and communication training programs (which are obviously also conjoint) emerging with the best "box scores." Again, collapsing all the conjoint interventions (conjoint, group, and communication training), we find such treatments superior to controls in 9 out of 12 comparisons, with two showing a "tie" and one (Alkire & Brunse, 1974) finding treatment worse than no treatment. This latter study did not assess the effects of group couples therapy per se, but demonstrated the impact of video feedback in couples groups with whom such feedback had not been a routine part of treatment.

Despite the obvious deficiency of a lack of follow-up in all these marital studies, the fact that predominantly positive outcomes were obtained in treatment that lasted, on the average, only nine sessions, suggests to us that nonbehavioral couples therapies produce real clinical changes beyond those occurring naturalistically.

Among the controlled nonbehavioral family studies, treatment emerges superior to no treatment in 8 out of 16 comparisons. While Knight (1974) found a program of Parent Effectiveness Training (P.E.T.) to produce no positive effects and even some deterioration beyond that occurring in the control group, we do not consider P.E.T. to constitute family therapy as it is typically practiced by professional psychotherapists. In fact, P.E.T. is usually offered to nonclinical parents as an educational rather than therapeutic experience. Its relevance to the treatment of significant clinical problems is called into question by the results of the Knight study. Among the remaining 15 comparisons with untreated groups, the Klein et al. (1975) study actually represents an extension of the Alexander and Parsons (1973) work, examining recidivism rates of the siblings of the juvenile delinquent IPs in the original study. Thus, we view Klein et al.'s study as supplying an additional index of change to the original Alexander and Parsons (1973) study, but not as a separate treatment study itself. With these qualifications and clarifications, nonbehavioral family therapy has yielded results superior to those of no treatment in 8 out of 13 comparisons, with five finding no difference.

In sum, Tables 21-6 and 21-7 show nonbehavioral marital and family therapies to be superior to no treatment in 18 out of 31 comparisons; 11 show a "tie," and two nonrepresentative studies (Alkire & Brunse, 1974; Knight, 1974) showing treatment to be worse than no treatment. Although these results obviously leave unaddressed important issues (to be considered later in this chapter) such as the matching of particular therapeutic strategies with specific clinical problems in family life, they do represent the first published, comprehensive summary of data basically quite favorable to nonbehavioral marital-family psychotherapies. While we recognize the methodological limitations of many of the gross improvement studies (Tables 21-1 and 21-2) and comparative studies (Tables 21-4 and 21-5) cited earlier, we believe that the consistent and converging trends in these groups of studies and in the controlled studies offer reasonable evidence of the salience of nonbehavioral marital and family therapies. Moreover, largely positive results emerge on the basis of a wide variety of criteria, on change measures from a number of evaluative perspectives, for many types of marital and family problems, from therapy conducted by clinicians of all the major therapeutic disciplines, and in therapy carried out in a number of treatment settings. Significantly, still generally lacking is research that allows the specifi-

cation of treatment interventions for well-defined populations and problems.

RESEARCH ON BEHAVIORAL MARITAL-FAMILY THERAPY

In the last decade behavior therapists have paid increasing attention to problems in family living. In fact, sufficient work has accumulated to prompt the appearance of many reviews of behavioral assessment and treatment programs (Greer & D'Zurilla, 1975; Gurman & Kniskern, 1978a; Jacob, 1976; Jacobson & Martin, 1976; Olson, 1972; Patterson, 1971; Patterson et al., 1976; Weiss & Margolin, 1977; Williams, 1975). Our analysis of behavioral marital-family therapy will be limited to single-group and multiple-group controlled and uncontrolled investigations. We will not describe or attempt to summarize the plethora of $N = 1$ papers that have appeared, whether anecdotal (Baird & Redfering, 1975; Eisler & Hersen, 1973; Fensterheim, 1972; Friedman, 1972; Lazarus, 1968; Liberman, 1970; Perlman & Bender, 1975; Rappaport & Harrell, 1972; Rosen & Schnapp, 1974) or experimental (Axelrod et al., 1975; Blechman, Olson & Hellman, 1976; Carter & Thomas, 1973a, 1973b; Eisler & Hersen, 1972; Eisler et al., 1974; Goldiamond, 1965; Goldstein, 1975, 1976; Hickok & Komechak, 1974; Miller & Hersen, 1976; Patterson & Hops, 1972; Wieman et al., 1974; Weiss, 1975a) in nature. These studies typically represent *demonstrations* of successful application of technique rather than *investigations* of outcome. While we do not believe that the world of psychotherapy is easily or meaningfully divided into "non-behavioral" and "behavioral" camps, (see, e.g., Wachtel, 1977) we are discussing social learning approaches to the treatment of family systems separately here because the large body of empirical work recently emerging from that orientation is sufficiently conceptually integrated to be deserving of independent examination.

Social Learning View of Marital-Family Conflict

The core of the social learning conceptualization of marital and family conflict involves Thibaut and

TABLE 21-6 Controlled Studies of Marital Therapy Outcome

Author	Treatment (s); (Treatment Length);[a] Setting[b]	Outcome Criteria (Source)[c]	Results (Design Quality)
Alkire and Brunse (1974)	Videotape feedback in ongoing groups (short); VA-OPC	Self-concept (P) Marital casualties (divorce, separation, suicide) (P)	More casualties and more *decreased* self-concept in treated groups (good)
Cadogan (1973)	Conjoint group (moderate); OPC	1. Drinking behavior (P) 2. Marital communication (P) 3. Acceptance and trust (P)	Treatment>control on criterion 1, not on 2 and 3 (very good)
Cardillo (1971)	Conjoint communication training (short); OPC	1. Self-concept (P) 2. Interpersonal perception method (P) 3. Helpfulness of therapy (P)	Treatment>control on all measures (very good)
Cassidy (1973)	Conjoint communication training (short); PP	1. Communication (P) 2. Target behaviors (P) 3. Attitude toward spouse (P)	Treatment>control on all measures (very good)
Christensen (1974)	Conjoint communication training (short); OPC	1. Self-esteem (P) 2. Decision making (J) 3. Choice fulfillment (P)	Treatment>control on some measures of criterion 1, and on 2; no difference on 3 (very good)
Friedman (1975)	Conjoint (moderate); OPC	1. Two psychiatric rating scales (J) 2. Global change (J) 3. Symptom ratings (P) 4. Family role performance (P) 5. Marital relationship (P)	Treatment>control on most measures (very good)
Graham (1968)	Conjoint; conjoint plus individual (short); CC	1. Reconciliations (O) 2. Positive references to spouse (O) 3. Dominance and affiliation (P)	Conjoint>control on criterion 1 only; conjoint plus individual = control on all criteria (good)

Study	Treatment	Criteria	Results
Griffin (1967)	Individual (short); FSC (wives)	1. Perception of self (P) 2. Perception of spouse (P)	Treatment>control on both measures (good)
Hickman and Baldwin (1970)	Conjoint; programmed communication training (short) CC	1. Reconciliation (O) 2. Attitude toward marriage (P)	Conjoint>control on both criteria; programmed = control (very good)
Matanovich (1970)	Encounter tapes[d] (moderate); conjoint plus individual (short); CC	1. Reconciliation (O) 2. Dominance and affiliation (P)	Encounter tapes>control on criterion 1; conjoint plus individual = control on both criteria (very good)
Pierce (1973)	Communication training; conjoint group (long); OPC	1. Communication skill (J) 2. Self-exploration (J)	Treatment I>control on both criteria; treatment II = control on both criteria (fair)

Summary

Conjoint>control	3	Individual>control	1
No difference	0	No difference	0
Conjoint<control	0	Individual<control	0
Group>control	1	Communication training >control	5
No difference	1	No difference	1
Group<control	1	Communication training <control	0

Conjoint plus individual >control	0		
No difference	2		
Conjoint plus individual <control	0		
Total		Treatment>control	10
		No difference	4
		Treatment<control	1

a Short = 1 to 10 sessions; moderate = 11 to 20 sessions; long = 21 or more sessions.

b CC = conciliation court; FSC = family service or counseling center; OPC = outpatient clinic; PP = private practice; VA = veterans administration.

c J = trained judge or interviewer; O = objective records; P = patient.

d Although this treatment was carried out in a group setting, the report emphasizes within-dyad encounters instead of group process, so that in the summary the study is classified as communication training, not group therapy.

TABLE 21-7 Controlled Studies of Family Therapy Outcome

Author	Treatment(s) (Treatment Length);[a] Setting[b]	Outcome Criteria (Source)[c]	Results (Design Quality)
Alexander and Parsons (1973)	Behavioral-systems; (short); client-centered (short); eclectic-dynamic (moderate); OPC	Identified patient recidivism at 18 months (O)	Behavioral system superior to control. Client-centered and eclectic-dynamic = control (good)
Beal and Duckro (1977)	Conjoint (short); juvenile court	Termination of court hearing or referral to noncourt agencies versus appearance before court (O)	17 percent of treated IPs appeared in court versus 35 percent of untreated cases ($p < .05$) (fair)
Garrigan and Bambrick (1975)	Conjoint (short); school	1. Family adjustment (P) 2. Behavior symptoms (teach) 3. IP self-concept (P) 4. Family relationships (P)	Treatment superior to control on family adjustment only (good)
Garrigan and Bambrick (1977)	Conjoint (short); school for emotionally disturbed children and adolescents	1. Family adjustment (Par) 2. Marital facilitative conditions (F) 3. IP self-concept (P) 4. Family members' state-trait anxiety (F) 5. IP symptoms (Par)	Treatment superior to control on Par rating of family adjustment, on two out of four facilitative conditions and on IP symptoms; no difference on criteria 3 and 4 (very good)
Jansma (1971)	Multiple (?); conjoint (?); OPC	1. Family adjustment (F,T) 2. Family congruence (F,T) 3. Family satisfaction (F,T) 4. Marital adjustment (F,T)	Multiple superior to control on eight out of nine measures. Conjoint family superior to control on one out of nine measures (?)

Study	Treatment	Measures	Results
Katz et al. (1975)	Conjoint (short); OPC	Family interaction (J)	Treatment superior to control on appropriate topic changes; no difference in speech clarity or humor (very good)
Klein et al.[d] (1975)	Behavioral-systems (short); client-centered (short); eclectic-dynamic (moderate); OPC	Sibling recidivism at 3 years (O)	Behavioral-systems superior to control; client-centered and eclectic-dynamic = control (good)
Knight (1974)	Parent effectiveness training (short); OPC	1. Frequency of enuresis (Par) 2. Anxiety (Par) 3. Interpersonal distance (F)	No significant positive effects, some deterioration in female identified patients and parents (?)
Reiter and Kilmann (1975)	Mothers' groups (short); OPC	1. Marital integration (PAR) 2. Verbal interchanges (J) 3. Child symptoms (Par) 4. Family congruence (Par)	Treatment superior to control on measures 1 to 3 (very good)
Stanton and Todd (1976)	Conjoint (moderate); OPC	Identified patient heroin use (O); identified patient work and school adjustment (F)	Therapy superior to attention placebo and no treatment group on both measures (very good)
Stover and Guerney (1967)	Filial therapy (mothers' groups) (short); OPC	1. Mothers' reflective and directive statements (J) 2. Child's playroom behavior (J)	Treatment superior to control on measure 1. no difference on measure 2 (very good)

TABLE 21-7 *(continued)*

Author	Treatment(s) (Treatment Length); [a] Setting [b]	Outcome Criteria (Source) [c]	Results (Design Quality)
Child/adolescent IP therapy>control	6	Adult/family IP>control	2
No difference	6	No difference	1
Child/adolescent IP therapy<control	1	Adult/family IP<control	0
	Total		
		Family therapy>control	8
		No difference	7
		Family therapy<control	1

Summary

[a] Short = 1 to 10 sessions; moderate = 11 to 20 sessions; long = 21 or more sessions.
[b] OPC = outpatient clinic.
[c] O = objective records; P = patient; Par = parents; F = family; Teach = teachers; J = trained judge; T = therapist.
[d] Same families as reported on in Alexander and Parsons (1973).

850

Kelley's (1959) exchange theory model of social psychological interaction in which individuals strive to maximize "rewards" while minimizing "costs." In this model social behavior in a given relationship is maintained by a high ratio of rewards to costs and by the perception that alternative relationships offer fewer comparative rewards and more costs (comparison level of alternatives). The potential for marital and family conflict exists either when optimal behavior-maintaining contingencies do not exist or when faulty behavior change efforts are implemented. In this context, two social reinforcement mechanisms, *coercion* and *reciprocity,* are operative (Patterson & Hops, 1972). Coercion describes an interaction in which both persons provide aversive stimuli that control the behavior of the other person, with negative reinforcement resulting from the termination of this state of affairs, thus maintaining the behavior of both people. Reciprocity describes an exchange in which two people reinforce each other at an equitable rate, with positive reinforcers maintaining the behavior of both.

The social learning position also asserts that, as Lederer and Jackson (1968) phrased it, "nastiness begets nastiness"; that is, the use of aversive stimulation in interpersonal relationships tends to produce reciprocal behavior in the second person. Research has confirmed both that the family member who "gives" the highest rate of aversive stimulation also "receives" the highest rate (Reid, 1967) and that distressed couples can be differentiated from nondistressed couples by the mean rates with which aversive stimuli are exchanged (Birchler & Webb, 1975; Birchler et al., 1972; Birchler et al., 1975; Weiss et al., 1973; Wills et al., 1974), but a recent study by Gottman et al. (1976) found only minimal support for the view that distressed marriages are characterized by less positive or more negative reciprocity than nondistressed marriages. The latter results are more consistent with the difficulty in obtaining consistent differences across studies between distressed and nondistressed families (Jacob, 1975) on other types of indices. In addition, a good deal of research has noted that people in distressed family relationships have poor problem-solving skills (e.g., Vincent et al., 1975; Weiss et al., 1973). Thus, the general goals of behavioral marriage therapy are to increase the rate of rewarding interaction, decrease the rate of aversive interaction, and teach concrete conflict-resolution and problem-solving strategies and skills.

Marital Treatment Strategies

To this end, several variations of the same treatment theme have developed (Azrin et al., 1973; Rappaport & Harrell, 1972; Stuart, 1969a, 1969b, 1976); the Oregon Marital Studies Program, led by Robert Weiss, has emerged as the primary research center for behavioral couples therapy. Their 10-session assessment-intervention package begins with a two-session assessment phase focusing on home tracking of behavior, laboratory sessions for taping problem-solving skills, and so on. Clients are routinely called at home every night to collect home observation data. The assessment instruments used typically include the Locke-Wallace (1959) *Marital Adjustment Scale,* the *Areas of Change Scale* (Birchler & Webb, 1975) the *Marital Activities Inventory,* and the *Marital Status Inventory* (Weiss & Cerreto, 1975). The *Spouse Observation Checklist* (SOC) (Weiss, 1975b) is the central patient self-report instrument. It contains a "universal checklist" of "Pleases" (Ps) and "Displeases" (Ds), defined as behaviors of the spouse that the respondent finds pleasing and displeasing. Both instrumental and affectional Ps and Ds are recorded from 12 categories believed to be important for marital exchanges (communication, companionship, self and spouse independence, etc.). Several studies have tentatively supported the validity of the SOC as an assessment instrument (Weiss et al., 1973; Wills et al., 1974).

Finally, the Oregon group has developed a complex *Marital Interaction Coding System* (MICS) (Hops et al., 1971) based on Patterson et al.'s (1969) family interaction coding system. The MICS categories allow assessment of problem-solving statements, positive and negative responses, and nonverbal communication-facilitating and impeding behaviors. Trained observers score interaction in 30-second intervals from videotapes of couples' interactions. Some tentative validation data for the MICS are now available (Birchler et al., 1975; Patterson et al., 1975; Royce & Weiss, 1975; Vincent et al., 1975; Weiss et al., 1973), although it must be recognized that the scoring categories were determined a priori. It has not yet been demonstrated that behaviors defined as "positive" do, in fact, lead to effective problem solving, nor is it clear whether some behaviors are more salient for conflict resolution than others.

Formal intervention begins in session three and contains six modules: (1) *pinpointing contingencies* relevant to a specific problem; (2) *communication skills training,* utilizing cotherapist modeling, behavior rehearsal, and videotape feedback; (3) *conflict resolution* training; (4) formation of *utility matrices* (i.e., the generation of a "menu" of potential rewards and penalties to be used contingently in contracting); (5) *negotiation and contracting,* utilizing parallel and independent "good faith" contracts (Weiss et al., 1974); and (6) *termination and maintenance,* in which therapist stimulus control over contracting, and the like, is faded.

The Outcomes of Behavioral Marriage Therapy

A comprehensive summary of both analog and naturalistic group-design studies of behavioral marital therapy is presented in Tables 21-8 and 21-9. Treatments were almost always of brief duration, with a mean treatment length of nine sessions for the naturalistic studies. Change criteria, predictably, rely far more heavily on observers' ratings than in nonbehavioral studies, and patient self-report of both global and behaviorally specific changes are quite common. *What is conspicuous by its absence from studies of behavioral marriage therapy is the evaluative perspective of the therapist: in none of the analog studies or the controlled or comparative naturalistic studies was the therapist's judgment of outcome solicited. It is as if the implicit message were that despite the therapist's assumed expertise as a change-agent, he or she offers no uniquely valuable perspective in assessing clinical change!* A variety of therapist experience levels is represented in these studies with over half experienced.

Among the eight controlled analog studies (Table 21-8), only two (Fisher, 1974; Roberts, 1975) yielded results that clearly demonstrate the superiority of behavior therapy to no treatment and, among the five controlled comparative studies, only one (Fisher, 1974) found behavioral

couples therapy's effects to surpass those of alternative interventions. The comparative naturalistic studies offer a more positive picture; six out of seven comparisons favor behavioral therapy (Crowe, 1973, 1976; Jacobson, 1977b; Liberman et al., 1976; Margolin, 1976; Mayadas & Duehn, 1977; McLean et al., 1973). There does not yet exist even one controlled comparative study of behavioral couples therapy with real clients involved in severely disturbed relationships. Moreover, there have been only four controlled studies of behavior therapy with couples convincingly (Jacobson, 1977a; Turkewitz & O'Leary, 1976) or nearly convincingly (Jacobson, 1977b; Tsoi-Hoshmand, 1976) demonstrated to be in relatively severely disturbed relationships, although several uncontrolled studies (Crowe, 1973, 1974; Liberman et al., 1976; Margolin, 1976; McLean et al., 1973; Stuart, 1976; Weiss et al., 1973) have dealt with moderately or severely distressed relationships. Tsoi-Hoshmand's study, in which couples were recruited from both clinics and nonclinic college campus sources, contained both truly distressed couples and some seeking to "make their relationship *more* rewarding" (Tsoi-Hoshmand, 1976, p. 183, emphasis added). Moreover, subjects were recruited from different geographical locations (Hawaii and Mississippi) with different ethnic representation, and were not randomly assigned to treatment conditions. In addition, the use of a "normal" nonhelp-seeking control group was inappropriate.

Jacobson (1977a) also studied couples solicited for research purposes, but his report offers very persuasive evidence of the severity of problems experienced by his couples. This study and a more recent study by the same author (Jacobson, 1977b) were near-replications of the Oregon treatment package and, to date, offer the most convincing data on the utility of the modular approach. Jacobson (1977a) randomly assigned five couples to treatment and five couples to a minimal treatment, waiting-list control group. Presenting both between-group and replicated single-subject data, he found significant improvement on both MICS and Locke-Wallace scores, both of which were maintained at a 12-month follow-up. Jacobson's (1977b) second study used a larger sample and found both *quid pro quo* and good faith contracting modes superior to both a nonspecific control treatment and a waiting-list control group. The immediate clinical relevance of this study is questionable, however, in that all the behavioral change measures (MICS) were based on couples' problem-solving behavior while dealing with *hypothetical* marital problems (from an inventory) and actual but *minor* problems in their own relationship.

Summing across both analog and naturalistic studies, we find behavioral couples' interventions superior to control conditions in 7 of 11 studies and superior to alternative treatments in 8 of 16 comparisons. We believe that these results offer suggestive evidence of the efficacy of this type of treatment (Gurman & Kniskern, 1978a). Interestingly, this 64 percent rate of superiorty to control conditions is virtually identical with the 66 percent rate (10/15 studies) of nonbehavioral couples therapy noted earlier. Evidence of the efficacy of behavioral marriage therapy, however, is somewhat less persuasive than is the existing research on nonbehavioral treatment because of too frequent use of nonclinical analog demonstrations with minimally distressed couples. In addition, (1) an insufficient number of group-design studies and the use of very small therapist and patient samples; (2) the essential lack of replication (except for the work of Jacobson, 1977a, 1977b) of the Oregon work researchers outside that center; and (3) infrequent follow-up further limit the persuasiveness of this research. Elsewhere we (Gurman, 1975d; Gurman, 1978; Gurman & Knudson, 1978, in press) and others (Tsoi-Hoshmand, 1975) have discussed several major theoretical and practical constraints in this type of therapy. We also question the usefulness and meaningfulness of outcome measures that are so reactive to the very nature of behavioral treatment and treatment goals (e.g., tracking of Ps and Ds serving as both a change *strategy* and a change *measure*), rendering them very sensitive to demand characteristics. Moreover, the overlapping patients in several reports of the Oregon group Patterson et al., 1972, 1975; Weiss et al., 1973), which actually examined only 20 couples yet appear at first to have studied 30 (see Table 21-8, footnote 1), make it difficult at times to track the results of specific studies, and missing data from the Oregon group (Patterson et al., 1972) are not explained. While the assessment instruments developed at the Oregon program are shown to be somewhat problematic, it is clear that this group has thus far contributed more to the development of theoretically grounded change measures than any other workers in the marital field, although they can be faulted somewhat on straightforwardly operant grounds (Glisson, 1976; Gurman, 1978). Their efforts to include both objective and traditional self-report measures is especially commendable.

Finally, as Jacobson and Martin (1976) emphasize in their excellent review of this area, there is currently insufficient evidence regarding the relative contribution to outcome of the multiple components (Jacobson, 1977b; Liberman et al., 1976; Margolin, 1976; Tsoi-Hoshmand, 1976) of behavioral couples therapy (e.g., communication training, contracting-negotiation skill training, therapist modeling) to influence clinical practice significantly. This, of course, is equally true of the nonbehavioral marital therapies. Issues such as the types of contracts used (Weiss et al., 1974) and with what types of couples (Jacobson & Martin, 1976), the relative power of single versus simultaneous multiple-contract behavioral exchanges, the relative effectiveness of one versus two therapists, and modifications of the Oregon program for use in treatment centers lacking expensive videotape equipment, research assistants for scoring interactions, and the like, must be addressed if Oregon-type treatment intervention is to have more widespread applicability. Despite these problems and issues, it is unquestionably clear that no researchers have devoted more time and sophisticated effort to empirically studying their clinical work with couples than those at the Oregon Marital Studies Program and their followers (Jacobson, 1977a, 1977b).

Family Treatment Strategies
Behavioral intervention with families derives from the same social learning propositions as behavioral couples therapy (Patterson, 1976), but it differs in some procedural aspects. Unlike marriage therapy, which is always conducted conjointly, *in most*

TABLE 21-8 Analog Group-Design Studies of Behavioral Marital Therapy

Author	Interventions (Treatment Length)[a]	Outcome Criteria (Source)[b]	Results (Design Quality)
Becking (1973)	I. Discrimination training of adaptive and maladaptive problem solving (Short) II. Control[c]	Problem-solving behavior[d] (J) Pleases and displeases daily (C)	No difference on either criterion (very good)
Cotton (1976)	I. Behavioral-exchange training II. Communication training III. Attention-placebo[e]	1. Silence (J) 2. Talk time equality (J) 3. Frequency and duration simultaneous speech (J) 4. Spontaneous agreement (J) 5. Shoice fulfillment (J) 6. Decision time (J) 7. Marital adjustment (C) 8. Marital conflict (C)	Treatment II superior to I and III on criterion 3 only[f] (very good)
Epstein and Jackson (1976)	I. Assertive communication training II. Fostering of "interaction insight" III. Control (Short)	11 verbal behavior communication categories (J) Perceived spouse empathy, congruence, and unconditional positive regard (C)	Treatment I > treatment II and control on "assertive requests"; both treatments > control for "disagreements"; no difference on other measures (very good)
Fisher (1974)	I. Operant group II. Adlerian group III. Control (moderate)	1. Prediction of spouse responses (C) 2. Rated helpfulness (C) 3. Empathy (C)	Treatment I superior to treatment II on criteria 1 and 3 (good)

Study	Treatment	Measures	Results
Follingstad et al. (1976)	Training in (marital) behavior principles, communication training, contracting skills (short)	1. Marital satisfaction (C) 2. Stuart Pre-counseling Inventory (C) 3. Self-monitored positive comments (C) 4. Multiple in-home behavior counts (O)	Significant change on 1,3 and on 8/12 behaviors recorded; temporal order of communications training and contracting showed no difference (very good)
Goldstein (1971)	Frequency counts of H behavior; positive reinforcement of H behavior[g] (moderate)	Change in target behavior (C)	Significant change for 8/10 clients; maintained by 6/7 at 3 to 7-month follow-up (fair)
Goldstein and Francis (1969)	(As above)[g]	(As above)	Significant change for 5/5 clients (fair)
Harrell and Guerney (1976)	I. Training in problem identification, solution-generation, and behavioral exchanges over *mutual* problems II. Control (moderate)	1. Conflict negotiation skill (J) 2. Problem management (C) 3. Marital adjustment (C) 4. Acceptance and trust (C) 5. Marital satisfaction (C) 6. Relationship change (C) 7. Positive and negative verbal behaviors (J)	Significant change on only 3/6 steps of criterion 1; no change on criteria 2 to 6; significant decrease on negative verbal behavior (very good)
McIntosh (1975)	I. Behavioral-exchange negotiation training II. Carkhuff model communication training III. Client-centered (NR)	Communication (C) Marital adjustment (C) Introversion-extroversion (C) Stability-instability (C)	No significant change in any treatment or in control group (fair)
Roberts (1975)	I. Conjoint behavioral-exchange negotiation training (short) II. Control	Marital adjustment (C) Relationship change (C) Workshop evaluation (C) Taylor-Johnson Temperament Analysis (C)	Behavioral program superior to control groups (very good)

TABLE 21-8 *(continued)*

Author	Interventions (Treatment Length) [a]	Outcome Criteria (Source) [b]	Results (Design Quality)
Venema (1976)	I. Behavioral-exchange training II. Communication training III. I plus II (NR)	Marital adjustment (C) Relationship change (C) Communication (C) Taylor-Johnson Temperament Analysis (C) Pleases and displeases (C)	Minimal change in any program; combined superior overall (good)
Welch and Goldstein (1972)	I. Reinforcement lecture and charting positive behavior or lecture only; paired with reinforcement or no reinforcement for lab task (i.e., four treatments) (Short) II. Control[h]	Marital adjustment (C)[i]	All treatments had significant change on adjustment; reinforcement lecture plus charting plus task reinforcement superior (poor)
Wieman (1973)	I. Reciprocal reinforcement therapy II. Conjugal relationship modification (short) III. Control	1. Marital adjustment (C) 2. Expressive and responsive skill (treatment II) (J) 3. Positive statements about spouse (treatment 1) (C) 4. Target behaviors (C)	Both treatments had significant change, maintained at 10-week follow-up; no difference between treatments (very good)

Note: NR = not reported.

a Short = 1 to 10 sessions; moderate = 11 to 20 sessions. No control group used unless indicated.

b C = client; J = trained judge.

c It is not clear from the available report what constituted the eight sessions of the "control" condition; we infer that it was some form of attention-placebo group instead of a true no-treatment group.

d Based on four "levels" of problem-solving behavior, varying in terms of "desirability." No differences were found for any level.

e While the author describes treatment III as a placebo, our reading of the nature of what actually occurred in this group (e.g., leader facilitation of member-member interaction and meaning clarification leads us to conclude that it was, in fact, a nondirective, supportive style of intervention instead of an inert experience.

f While the author considered increases in the frequency and duration of simultaneous speech (i.e., interruptions) to be a positive change, the research evidence on this matter is inconclusive. Moreover, all interruptions are not equivalent (e.g., interruption to attack a spouse versus interruption to seek clarification).

g In actuality, few of the husband behaviors targeted by wives for change were of the sort or import that typically characterize distressed marriages to the extent of seeking professional help (dropping soiled clothing on the bedroom floor, husband's failure to eat three meals a day, etc.).

h Of couples asked to participate, only 62, or 11 percent, returned preintervention questionnaires and two out of these stated their inability to participate in the laboratory tasks. Of the remaining 60 couples, 28 were lost, for unspecified reasons, to attrition. Eight of these "dropouts," who completed both pre- and posttests but "were unable to participate in the other parts of the experiment," came to constitute groups, which necessitated reassignment of couples (p. 7) to treatment conditions different from their initial assignments; the randomization procedure and the constitution of the control group were both devastatingly flawed.

i Although data were collected for two of the treatment groups on daily pleasing behaviors (and their outcomes), the authors unfortunately did not analyze these data for pre-postchange, but examined their frequency as a correlate of general marital satisfaction ($r = .50$, $p > .05$, pretest; $r = .66$, $p > .01$, posttest).

857

TABLE 21-9 Results of Naturalistic Studies of Behavioral Marital Therapy

Author		Interventions (Treatment Length)[a]	Outcome Criteria (Source)[b]	Results (Design Quality)
		Uncontrolled Single-Group Studies (**A**) and Controlled and Comparative Studies (**B**)		
Azrin et al. (1973)	**(A)**	Treatment I: "catharsis counseling" (CC)[c] followed by Treatment II: "reciprocity counseling" (RC): negotiation and informal contracting (N = 12)[d] (moderate)	Marital Happiness Scale (P)	No change in CC; 23/24 spouses (p > .005) reported greater happiness at termination, 21/24 at 1-month follow-up
Knox (1973)		Operant reinforcement of desired spouse behavior and self-administered aversion consequences; followed by *quid pro quo* exchanges (N = 10) (NR)	Follow-up (6 to 12 months) questionnaire (P)	8/10 couples moderately happy or better
Patterson et al. (1972)		P and D spouse observation; pinpointing and discriminating training; communication training behavioral utilities; contract negotiation (N = 10)[e] (short)	MICS scores (J) Spouse-recorded in-vivo Ps and Ds (P)	Significant change on 5/29 MICS scores for H, 4/29 for W; significant increase in Ps for W and decrease in Ds for H; nonsignificant increase in H Ps (p < .10); 3/18 spouses showed P *decreases* and 3/16 showed D *increases*
Patterson et al. (1975)		As above (N = 10)[f]	MICS scores collapsed into "facilitating" and "disrupting" behaviors (J)	Significant change on both measures; both partners in one couple clearly deteriorated, 3/18 other spouses deteriorated on one measure

Stuart (1969b)[g]	Token reinforcement of recorded target behaviors (N = 5) (short)	Frequency of sex, amount of conversation, marital satisfaction (all P)	Clinically significant changes on all criteria, maintained at at 24 to 52-week follow-up
Stuart (1976)	Operant-interpersonal therapy (N = 190)[h] (short)	Achievement of behavior change objectives (T) Marital status and commitment at follow-up (P)	81 percent of cases, both spouses reached behavioral objectives; 77 percent both showed increase commitment; only five divorces at 1-year follow-up; 16 at 5 years
Thomlinson (1974)	Monitoring reinforcement and exchange of desired spouse behavior; behavioral rehearsal and role-playing (N = 8) (short)	Target behavior changes (P) Global evaluation of changes in marriage (P)	Significant increases on targets; very positive global ratings at 5-week follow-up
Weiss et al. (1973)	Study I:[j] as in Patterson et al., 1972 (N = 5) (short)	MICS scores (J) Spouse-recorded Ps and Ds (P)	Significant increases in Ps; D changes ns (missing data); 8/29 MICS scores changed significantly, 2 in "wrong" direction: "accept responsibility" decreased, "complain-criticize" increased
	Study II: as above (N = 5)	1. MICS (collapsed to six categories) (J) 2. Ps and Ds (P) 3. Marital adjustment (P) 4. Willingness-to-change scale (P) 5. Marital Activities Inventory (P)	Significant change on all MICS categories and Ps and Ds; at 3 to 6-month follow-up, significant change on criteria 3 and 5; 3/5 couples clearly improved, 1 clearly deteriorated; 1 showed no change
(B) Crowe (1973, 1974)[k]	I. Directive-behavioral (DB) II. Interpretive-systems (IS) III. Supportive-nondirective (SN)[l] (total N = 42) (short)	1. Marital adjustment 2. Sexual adjustment 3. General adjustment 4. Target complaints 5. Neurotc symptoms (all P,J) 6. Global change (P)	DB>SN on criteria 2, 3, 4, and 6; IS>SN on 1 and 6; SN>IS on 5 (good)

TABLE 21-9 *(continued)*

Author	Interventions (Treatment Length)[a]	Outcome Criteria (Source)[b]	Results (Design Quality)
Jacobson (1977a)	I. Problem-solving training, communication training, contracting ($N = 5$)[m] II. Control ($N = 5$) (short)	Marital adjustment (P) Positive and negative problem-solving behavior (MICS) (J)	Significant improvement on all measures; maintained at 12-month follow-up[n] (good)
Jacobson (1977b)	I. Behavioral *quid pro quo* (QPQ) ($N = 9$) II. Behavioral good faith group (GF) ($N = 8$) III. Nonspecific control group (NS) ($N = 7$) IV. Wait controls (WL) ($N = 6$)	1. Positive verbal behavior (O) 2. Negative verbal behavior (O) 3. Marital adjustment (P) 4. Marital happiness (P)	QPQ and GF both showed significant changes compared to WL and were superior to NS on criteria 1 to 3; overall no difference between outcomes of QPQ and GF (very good)
Liberman et al. (1976)	I. Behavioral Group[o] (including communication training, behavior rehearsal, contracting) ($N = 4$) II. Interaction-insight group;[q] ($N = 5$) (moderate)[p]	1. Marital adjustment (P) 2. Marital activities (P) 3. Willingness to change (P) 4. Daily pleases (P) 5. In-session looks, smiles, touches (J) 6. MICS (six levels) (J) 7. Global rating (P)	Equal improvement for both treatments on criteria 1, 3, and 7; no change for either on 2 and 4; behavioral superior on 5 and 6; evidence of deterioration for behavioral on 2 and 4; for insight on one measure of criterion 2 (fair)
Margolin (1976)	I. Behavioral ($N = 9$) II. Behavioral-cognitive ($N = 9$) III. Nondirective ($N = 9$) (short)	1. Marital adjustment (P) 2. Daily pleases (P) 3. Daily displeases (P) 4. Positive communication behaviors—MICS (J) 5. Negative communication behaviors—MICS (J)	Significant change for all treatments on criteria 3 and 5; treatment I superior on criterion 1; behavioral treatments both superior on criteria 2 and 4; II superior to I on criterion 4 (very good)

Mayadas and Duehn (1977)	I. Communication modeling (CM) II. CM plus video feedback (CMV) III. Verbal counseling (VC) (total $N = 30$) (short)	Five problematic communication behaviors (O)	CM changed 3 out of 5 behaviors, CMV changed 5 out of 5, VC changed 1 out of 5 (very good)
McLean et al. (1973)	I. Behavioral contracting, feedback, etc. ($N = 10$) II. Mixed: combining drug therapy and/or group therapy or GP monitoring; depressed spouse only treated ($N = 10$) (I short, II mixed)	Symptomatic behavior (P) Mood (P) Negative verbal actions and reactions between spouses (J)	Conjoint therapy superior on all measures (good)
Tsoi-Hoshmand[q] (1976)	I. Negotiation, communication training, etc. ($N = 10$) II. No-treatment wait control ($N = 4$) III. Normal control ($N = 6$)	1. Caring (P) 2. Marital satisfaction (P) 3. Learning-in-therapy (J)	Significant change on all measures; demonstrated incremental treatment effects (fair)
Turkewitz and O'Leary (1976)	I. Communication training (CT) ($N = 10$) II. Behavioral exchange negotiation training (BT) ($N = 10$) III. Control ($N = 10$) (short)	1. Communication (P) 2. Marital target problems (P) 3. Desired spouse behavior change (P) 4. Individual problems (P) 5. Marital adjustment (P)	Both treatments superior to control on criteria 1 to 4; BT superior with young couples, CT superior with older couples (very good)
Turner (1972)	Increase positive behavior versus increase positive and decrease negative × cotherapists versus single therapist (i.e., four conditions) ($N = 10$ per cell)[r]	Positive and negative statements checked from inventory regarding marriage and spouse (P)	"Positive only" increased (minimal) positive statements/ maintained pretreatment level and decreased negative statements; "positive-negative" decreased on both measure (good)

See p. 862 for explanatory comments for Table 21-9.

TABLE 21-9 (*continued*)

Note: NR = not reported.

[a] Short = 1 to 10 sessions; moderate = 11 to 20 sessions. No control group unless indicated.

[b] Judge = trained judge; P = patient; T = therapist.

[c] "Catharsis counseling" was actually intended as a placebo procedure, yet its description ("The only point at which the therapist interrupted communication was when the clients were becoming physically angry with each other.") makes it questionable whether clients could have accepted its credibility as psychotherapy.

[d] The sample's representativeness of outpatient clinic couples is questionable in that some (number unspecified) couples were obtained through a mail solicitation consisting "of a one-page notice sent to those students listed in the college mailing list of married students" (Azrin et al., 1973, p. 368).

[e] Five of these couples were also reported on in Weiss et al. (1973), described below. The reports do not allow a determination of which of the Patterson et al. (1975) couples appeared in the Weiss et al. paper.

[f] Some of the couples reported on here also appear in Weiss et al. (1973).

[g] Four of these five couples were also reported on in Stuart (1969a).

[h] Of the first 200 couples followed up by Stuart, three did not provide scoreable responses and seven did not initially agree to the treatment contract.

[i] In addition, in 87 percent of the couples at least one spouse met behavior change objectives, and in 84 percent there was increased commitment in at least one spouse.

[j] These couples were contained in the *N* of 10 in Patterson et al. (1972). As in footnote h, the reports do not allow a determination of which of the Patterson et al. (1972) couples appeared in the Weiss et al. report. In summary, although the total *N* in Patterson et al. (1972, 1975) and Weiss et al. (1973) would appear, from the table, to be 30, our reading is that only 20 couples were studied in the three reports.

[k] Based on preliminary data analyses; follow-up results were not available at the time this chapter was being prepared.

[l] Although Crowe refers to this as a "control procedure," it is clear from his reports that it should be more accurately considered a nondirective comparison treatment; thus this study is not though to be a controlled (in the sense of minimal or no-treatment) investigation.

[m] Although the couples were recruited through newspaper ads and, therefore, are not completely representative of couples who themselves initiate help seeking at clinics, Jacobson's data make it quite convincing that these couples had severely disturbed relationships.

[n] Jacobson also conducted within-couple, experimental, multiple-baseline analyses.

[o] Three therapists per group, a rather unusual arrangement.

[p] Although number of sessions were equal, the behavioral group actually received (Liberman et al., 1976, p. 27) 15 to 45 minutes more per session than the insight group, or approximately 4 hours more.

[q] While all couples studied were "within the clinical range" (unspecified) on the dependent measures at pretreatment, the clinical representativeness of these couples is suspect in that while some (number unspecified) were referred by professional practitioners, others were solicited on the basis of "learning how to make their relationship more rewarding." Moreover, the report does not indicate whether the distribution across experimental conditions (no random assignment) skewed treatment—expecting versus enrichment-expecting couples into one or more of the treatment groups.

[r] Results presented here based on preliminary (and incomplete) data analysis for the cotherapist conditions (positive only versus positive plus negative) only, for 11 couples (6 positive, 5 positive plus negative).

studies of behavioral family therapy the children were not seen at all during intervention sessions. Bilateral behavioral exchange contracts form a core element of couples therapy and are often used in adolescent-problem families (Parsons & Alexander, 1973; Stuart & Tripodi, 1973), yet they are rarely used in cases of child IPs. *A child may "negotiate" which reinforcers and contingencies may be applied to change his or her behavior, but behavioral family therapy, unlike marital therapy, does not allow the possibility that a child may choose not to participate in family members' behavior change efforts.* Thus, the goal of changing parental behavior [use of more effective social/nonsocial reinforcers for prosocial behavior; use of effective punishment (i.e., reinforcement withdrawal) for coercive behaviors] *in order to change the child's behavior* bespeaks a very different philosophical "set" than is present in behavioral marriage therapy. At a metalevel, "coercion" and "reciprocity" are equivalent in the fundamental sense that both are forms of control (Gurman & Knudson, 1978, in press); it can be argued that training parents to adopt the latter approach represents a technical but not a conceptual shift in their manner of relating to children. Although behavioral family therapists do acknowledge that problem children are both the "victims *and* architects of a coercive system" (Patterson, 1976) and do, in fact, shape their parents' behavior, the IP-child is, nonetheless, regarded as the "deviant" family member (Patterson, 1971, p. 761), and the overriding goal of such therapy is to "retrain the *child*" (Patterson, 1971, p. 754, emphasis added). This certainly represents a tremendously different perspective from that shared by nonbehavioral family therapists who, instead of seeing the child's "deviant" behavior as primarily reflecting parental cognitive learning (skill) deficits, view it as functional for the family as a system (Minuchin, 1974) and argue that the system often is invested in the "deviant child's" *not* changing. Not surprisingly, outcome measures in behavioral family studies are typically based on parents' or observers' frequency counts of prosocial and "deviant" child behavior. Measures of family interaction at a systematic level were never used, and even therapist or IP evaluations of change are also rare. Only one study (Ar-

nold et al., 1975) has examined the effects of behavioral intervention on the behavior of the IP child's siblings.

These issues are not of mere theoretical interest, but also involve important clinical and empirical considerations. Psychotherapeutic intervention should be based on what is determined to be "the problem." And behavioral family therapists, while acknowledging the presence of parenting skill deficits, nevertheless seem ultimately to define the child's behavior as "the problem." In fact, using the Patterson group's (Arnold et al., 1975; Patterson, 1974a, 1974b; Skindrud, 1973) own criterion of .45 deviant (aggressive) child responses per minute as the upper limit of the normal range, 12 of the 27 IP children in one of Patterson's (1974b) major recent summaries of his work fell within the normal range at baseline! Furthermore, most of the IPs show deviant behavior rates no higher than their non-IP siblings (Arnold et al., 1975; Patterson, 1974a, 1974b). A recent study conducted independently of the Oregon group similarly found (two-thirds of treated) target children to have compliance levels comparable to those of children not identified as manifesting problematic behavior. The family system's "choice" of an IP, then, often says more about parental perceptual processes than it says about a given child's behavior per se. Such findings highlight the "capricious quality of the deviancy labeling process" (Arnold et al., 1975) implied in the finding of Oltmanns et al. (1976) of consistent negative correlations between marital adjustment and the severity of children's behavior problems. Levitt (1971) has argued that treatment for many childhood problems may have been unnecessary, a conclusion supported by Shepherd et al.'s (1966) finding that

> *referral to a child-guidance clinic is related chiefly to parental reactions. The mothers of clinic-children were more apt to be anxious, depressed and easily upset by stress; they were less able to cope with their children, more apt to discuss their problems and to seek advice. (p. 47)*

Moreover, Patterson (1975) himself concedes, in a footnote, that *just focusing upon child management skills would be sufficient treatment for only about a third of the disrupted families encountered. Many of them require additional skills training in the resolution of severe marital conflicts, depression, and a variety of other problems.* This being the case one can hardly say that training in child management is a sufficient condition for effective treatment (p. 290, emphasis added)

Thus, while the change criterion of "deviant" child behavior is consistent with a social learning model of therapy, it is clearly insufficient for assessing change in the family as a system and in specific dyads within the family (e.g., husband-wife), the clinical importance of which behaviorists have acknowledged recently. Consistent with Patterson's (1975) comment noted above is the recent finding of Reisinger et al. (1976) that mothers with marital difficulties were less able to demonstrate generalization of behavioral management techniques with their children than mothers who did not report such problems. Similar results have been reported by Cole and Morrow (1976).

Behavioral family intervention is understandably, then, educationally and training oriented and almost always of short to moderate length. In most of the studies in Tables 21-10 and 21-11 therapists were inexperienced but very well supervised. The results of the majority of these studies show positive change in parents' reports of change in the IP. Data from observers are also generally positive for targeted behaviors, but demonstrate only marginal ($p < .07$; Patterson, 1974a) positive change for nontargeted deviant behavior. Moreover, improvement was rarely shown to generalize from home to other settings such as the school (Skindrud, 1973), and positive changes at termination of treatment frequently decreased at follow-up. These latter trends are consistent with a recent review of the results of operant clinical intervention reported by Keeley, Shemberg, and Carbonell (1976). They examined 146 operant studies published in three major behavioral journals from 1972 to 1973 to determine whether clinically applied operant research produced lasting, generalizable changes beyond short-term behavioral management. Their analysis convincingly demonstrated the power of

operant methods to manage behaviors under highly controlled stimulus conditions. More provocatively, however, they found a virtual absence of data confirming the endurance and generalization of change to unprogrammed settings. Consistent with our discussion of the labeling of "deviant" child behavior above, Karoly and Rosenthal (1977) have concluded, "Perhaps a treatment package directed at reprogramming the *perceptions. . .* of parents in combination with systematic parent training would yield an even more powerful intervention tool. . ." (emphasis added).

Behavioral family studies are also characterized by a high rate of patient attrition (Patterson, 1974a, 1974b, 43 percent; Weathers & Liberman, 1975, 66 percent) due to treatment dropouts and refusals to be followed up even by families involved in many of the most successful treatment cases (Patterson, 1976, personal communication). Thus, most of the families studied were highly selected and showed only a low to moderate degree of disturbance.

The studies summarized in Table 21-11 show behavioral family intervention to have been superior to no-treatment controls in all five studies of this type and superior to alternative treatments (e.g., client-centered family therapy, avoidance conditioning for alcoholism) in five out of six existing comparisons. In several of the best-designed studies in this group (Alexander & Parsons, 1973; Klein et al., 1975; Malouf & Alexander, 1974), however, it is doubtful that interventions can be considered to have been uniformly "behavioral" by conventional standards. Much of the important Utah group's work with juvenile delinquent families deviated from predominantly operant interventions alone and involved many of the same types of treatment strategies common to "nonbehavioral" family therapies [modeling and prompting of "clear communication of substance *and* feelings" (Alexander & Barton, 1976, p. 178, emphasis added), focusing on family "themes" as well as on discrete behaviors, etc.]. Although the Alexander group has clearly provided some of the best outcome research in the family field, generalization from their generally impressive results (see Table 21-11) may be limited by the facts that their IPs were relatively soft delinquents and their sample was heavily (70 percent) represented by Mormons, who emphasize and usually have stronger family ties than many other groups. Still, while effective therapy is effective therapy, it seems debatable whether the Utah group's work is more accurately viewed, categorically, as closer to the behavioral (operant) tradition or to some nonbehavioral family therapies [e.g., the Structural Family Therapy of Minuchin (1974) or the communication process-oriented therapy of Satir (1967)]. In fact, it is probably a combination of all three influences.

Deterioration in Behavioral Marital-Family Therapy

There is increasing evidence that, not unlike other systems approaches or individual (Bergin, 1971; Lambert et al., 1977) and group (Bednar & Lawlis, 1971) approaches, behavioral marital-family interventions also produce deterioration, or, as Strupp et al. (1976) refer to them, "negative effects." Gurman and Kniskern (1976, 1978b) provide a detailed description of six marital (Liberman et al., 1976; Patterson et al., 1972, 1975; Turner, 1972; Weiss et al., 1973, Studies I and II) and eight family (Arnold et al., 1975; Eyberg & Johnson, 1974; Ferber et al., 1974; Johnson et al., in press; Patterson, 1974a, 1974b; Stuart & Tripodi, 1973; Thomas & Walter, 1973; Walter & Gilmore, 1973) behavior therapy studies that show reasonable to undeniable evidence of worsening as a result of treatment. Rates of negative effects in behavioral marital-family therapy appear to be at least as high and probably higher than those *reported* in studies of nonbehavioral therapies. While only one of these studies was controlled (Walter & Gilmore, 1973), the most important observation is that *in almost every one of these 14 studies deterioration occurred on criteria most central to and valued by behavior therapists,* such as, daily marital Ps and Ds (Liberman et al., 1976; Patterson et al., 1972; Weiss et al., 1973, Study II), positive and negative verbal and nonverbal communication behaviors (Patterson et al., 1975; Weiss et al., 1973, Study I), shared marital time (Liberman et al., 1976), deviant response rates of the child or adolescent IP (Eyberg & Johnson, 1974; Ferber et al., 1974; Johnson et al., in press; Patterson, 1974a, 1974b; Stuart & Tripodi, 1973), or in other family members (Arnold et al., 1975; Thomas & Walter, 1973). It is also interesting that deterioration in behavioral family therapy occurred far more often on trained observer measures than on parents' measures.

Although positive changes also occurred on some criteria in most of these studies, these data suggest that, while not standing alone, behavior therapists, too, are quite humanly fallible. Moreover, behavioral techniques may be not only inappropriate (Salzinger, Feldman, & Portnoy, 1970) but also harmful to some couples and families.

FACTORS INFLUENCING MARITAL-FAMILY THERAPY OUTCOME

It is not sufficient merely to evaluate the relative effectiveness of various marital-family treatments. In this section we summarize the existing evidence on the influence of therapist, patient, and treatment variables on therapeutic outcome in both behavioral and nonbehavioral treatments.

Therapist Factors

Therapist factors affecting outcome in individual treatment have received a great deal of attention over the years; this is evident in the recent volume by Gurman and Razin (1977), which is devoted entirely to this subject. Considerably less attention has been paid to these variables in the marital-family field.

Experience Level

Even though data are limited in this area, more positive outcomes do seem to accrue to experienced than to inexperienced therapists. Freeman et al. (1969) and Griffin (1967) both found more positive outcomes for experienced marital therapists. Roberts (1975) found significantly better results for graduate student marriage therapists than for either experienced or novice paraprofessional therapists. It is not clear, however, whether graduate student status may have reflected greater expertise rather than more clinical experience per se. Schreiber (1966) found that caseworkers with previous group therapy experience had less difficulty in family therapy than therapists who lacked

TABLE 21-10 Analog Group-Design Studies of Behavioral and Filial Family Therapy

Author	Interventions (Treatment Length)[a]	Outcome Criteria (Source)[b]	Results (Design Quality)
Blechman and Olson (1975a)	Family behavioral contract game (short)	On-task and off-task problem-solving behavior (J)	Intervention significantly reduced off-task behavior and increased on-task behavior[c](?)[d]
Blechman and Olson (1975b)	Family behavioral contract game (short)	On-task behavior (J) Off-task behavior (J) Devereux ratings (M) Family activities (M)	Treatment increased on-task behavior and decreased off-task behavior during intervention.[e] Devereux ratings moved to normal; no difference in family activities (?)[d]
Corson (1975)	Charting of deviant behavior and systematic rewards and punishments (long)	Spankings (Par)	Reduction in spanking frequency for all families (poor)
Coufal (1975)	Parent-adolescent relationship development (PARD);[f] Relationship improvement program (RIP)[g] No treatment control (NT); (moderate)	Specific communication patterns (M,D) General communication patterns (M,D) General relationship (M,D)	PARD significantly improved pairs on all measures relative to RIP and NT. RIP significantly improved pairs on all measures (very good)
Ginsberg (1971)	Parent-adolescent relationship development (PARD)[f] (short)	Specific communication patterns (F,sons) General communication patterns (F,sons) General relationship (F,sons) Self-perception (F,sons)	PARD significantly improved pairs on all measures (very good)

Study	Treatment	Measures	Results
Guzzetta (1976)	Modeling, role-playing, social reinforcement (short)	Role-played parental empathy toward child (J)	Treated parents more empathic than controls; inclusion of children (teenagers) did not add to transfer of training (very good)
Hardcastle (1977)	Mother-child behavioral-communication groups (short) No treatment control	1. Family satisfaction (Par) 2. Positive responses (J) 3. Negative responses (J) 4. Patient symptoms (J) 5. Family congruence (Par) 6. Family integration (Par)	Treatment superior to control on 3/5 measures (1, 2, 6) and significantly reduced 4 (very good)
Martin (1975)	Behavioral (short) No treatment control	Problem frequency (Par)	Treated families reported significantly less problem behavior at termination and 6-month follow-up (good)
O'Dell et al. (1976)	Behavior management skills workshop, preceded by: 1. Didactic training in behavior principles 2. Placebo pretraining 3. No pretraining (short)	1. Behavior modification skills (J) 2. Attitudes toward children (Par) 3. Home implementation of skills (Par) 4. Involvement in training (O)	No differences among training conditions except no pretraining possibly superior on criterion 3 (very good)
Peed et al. (1977)	Operant management skills training (short) No treatment control	1. Parent behavior (O) 2. Child compliance (Par) 3. Parental attitude toward target child (Par)	Treatment superior to control on criteria 1 and 2 and on 3 of 8 categories of criterion 3 (very good)
Rose (1974)	Group training in operant management skills for parents (short)	Deviant behavior of identified patient (Par)	76 percent (44/58) of families successfully modified at least one problem behavior (poor)

TABLE 21-10 (continued)

Author	Interventions (Treatment Length) [a]	Outcome Criteria (Source) [b]	Results (Design Quality)
Vogelsong (1975)	Parent-adolescent relationship development (PARD); [f] Relationship improvement program (RIP); No-treatment control; (moderate) [h]	Specific communication patterns (M,D); General communication patterns (M,D); General relationship (M,D)	PARD superior on specific and general communication patterns and two of five measures of general relationship (very good)

[a] Short = 1 to 10 sessions; moderate = 11 to 20 sessions; long = 21 or more sessions.

[b] J = judge or trained observer; M = mother; D = daughter; F = father; Par = parents.

[c] During reversal period levels of on-task behavior returned to baseline levels.

[d] This study used an A-B-A (reversal) design and cannot be evaluated on usual criteria.

[e] During reversal period level of on-task behavior decrease but remained significantly higher than baseline; during reversal period level of off-task behavior returned to baseline.

[f] PART was a structured, communication skills program based on the principles of filial therapy.

[g] RIP was a general discussion program that focused on relationship issues.

[h] One half of patients wore telephones following intervention to "boost" effects in both PARD and RIP groups.

TABLE 21-11 Results of Naturalistic Studies of Behavioral Family Therapy

Author	Interventions (Treatment Length)[a]	Outcome Criteria (Source)[b]	Results (Design Quality)
		Uncontrolled Single-Group Studies	
Alexander et al. (1976)	Behavioral-systems (short)	Identified patient and family functioning (T)	12/21 improved; 9/21 no change
Arnold et al.[c] (1975)	Operant management skills training for parents (short)	Total deviant responses per minute[d] (J)	Siblings significantly reduced aggressive behavior at termination and follow-up[e]
Ferber et al.[f] (1974)	Operant management skills training for parents (short)	Maladaptive behavior per minute (J) Compliance to commands (J) Global change in identified patient (Par)	Short-term success in 3/7 families. At 1-year follow-up only one success
Johnson et al. (1975)	Operant management skills training for parents (moderate)	Global change in identified patient (Par) Targeted deviant behavior in home (J, Par) Overall deviant behavior in home (J) Deviant behavior in school (J)	Significant change in parent perception, some in targeted deviant behavior (J); none in overall deviant behavior; deterioration in school behavior of identified patients[g]
Johnson et al. (in press)	Operant management skills training for parents (moderate)	Adjective checklist rating child (Par) Deviant behavior (Par) Audiotape deviant child behavior (J) Audiotape deviant parent behavior (J)	Parents' reports all positive; tapes: positive change in 3/5 families

869

TABLE 21-11 *(continued)*

Author	Interventions (Treatment Length)[a]	Outcome Criteria (Source)[b]	Results (Design Quality)
	Uncontrolled Single-Group Studies		
Johnson and Cristensen (1975)[h]	Contingency contracting for parents (moderate)	Identified patient deviant behavior in home (Par, J) Adjective checklist rating child (Par)	Parents rated 21/22 of identified patients improved; home observation: 41 percent of the cases reduced deviant behavior and 48 percent targeted deviant behavior by 30 percent[i,j]
O'Leary et al. (1973)	Operant management skills training[k,l] (moderate)	Identified patient referral problems (Par, T)	Parents: 90 percent (63/70) of the identified patients improved. Therapists: 87.1 percent (61/70) improved[m]
Patterson (1974a)[n]	Operant management skills training for parents (short)	Identified patient deviant behavior (Par, J)	Parents report significant reductions in deviant behavior; judges assessed 14 children as positively changed, 6 as negatively changed, and 7 as not changing[o,p]
Skindrud[q] (1973)	Operant management skills training for parents (short)	Identified patient deviant behavior in school (J)	No significant difference in school behavior
Stuart and Tripodi (1973)	Behavioral contracting (moderate)	Identified patient behavior in home, school (Par, O)	No difference in results due to treatment length; 18 pre-postcomparisons, 10 in positive direction, 8 in negative direction

Study	Treatment	Criteria	Results
Thomas and Walter (1973)	Operant management skills training (moderate)	Successful modification of presenting problem (Par) Change in nontargeted behavior (F)	45/48[r] problems modified; in 26 reports of nontargeted behavior, only 13 changed (10 positive and 3 negative)

Controlled and Comparative Studies

Study	Treatment	Criteria	Results
Alexander[x] and Parsons[s] (1973)	Short-term behavior therapy (BT) $N = 46$ (short) Client-centered group (CC) $N = 19$ (short) Dynamic-eclectic (DE) $N = 11$ (moderate) Controls (NT) $N = 10$	Recidivism rates at 18-month follow-up (O)	Recidivism rates: BT = 26 percent CC = 47 percent DE = 73 percent NT = 50 percent (good)
Bernal and Margolin (1976)	Behavioral (parent) counseling (BT) $N = 9$ (short) Client-centered parent counseling (CC) $N = 9$ (short) Wait controls ($N = ?$)[t]	1. Child's verbal abuse (O) 2. Deviant child behavior (O) 3. Targeted child behavior (Par) 4. Parental attitudes toward child (Par) 5. Satisfaction with therapy (Par)	No differences within or between groups on criteria 1 and 2; no differences between groups on 3, but both showed change; partial superiority for CC on 4; BT superior on 5 (good)
Christensen (1976)	Individual operant management skill training (I) Group operant management skill training (G) Self-instructional training (SI)	1. Parental attitude toward child (Par) 2. Parental attitude toward treatment (Par) 3. Observed target behaviors (Par) 4. Family interaction (O)	No difference on criterion 1; no difference between I and G treatments on any criteria; both superior to SI (very good)

TABLE 21-11 *(continued)*

Author	Interventions (Treatment Length)[a]	Outcome Criteria (Source)[b]	Results (Design Quality)
	Controlled and Comparative Studies		
Hedberg and Campbell (1974)	Systematic desensitization (SD) N = 15 Covert sensitization (CS) N = 15 Avoidance conditioning (AC) N = 4[t] Behavioral family counseling (BFC) N = 15 (moderate)	Goal attainment (F, T)	Goal attained: SD = 67 percent CS = 40 percent AC = 0 percent BFC = 74 percent (Fair)
Karoly and Rosenthal[u] (1977)	Operant management skills training for parents (BT) N = 9 (short) Controls (NT) N = 8	Parental perception of family cohesion, conflict, and control (Par) Child target behaviors (Par, O)	BT superior to NT on cohesion only and on both target behavior measures at termination and 1-month follow-up (very good)
Klein et al. (1975)	Behavioral family system (short) N = 46	Sibling recidivism at 3 years[v]	Treatment superior to control (good)
Malouf and Alexander[w] (1974)	Behavioral family systems (short) N = 45	Identified patient recidivism at 18 months	Family superior to control (good)
Martin (1967)	Reinforcement of appropriate interaction by therapist (BT) N = 2 (short) Controls (NT) N = 2	Problem checklist (Teach) Frequent blaming statements (J)	BT superior to NT on both measures (good)
Parsons and Alexander (1973)	Token economy and problem-solving training (BT) N = 20 (short) Placebo-control (PC) N = 10 (short) No treatment control (NC) N = 10	Silence, simultaneous speech, and distribution of verbalization (J) Agreement in expected behavior change (F) Spontaneous agreement (F)	BT superior to PC and NC on three interaction measures. no change on two content measures (very good)
Walter and Gilmore (1973)	I. Operant management skills training for parents (BT)	Deviant behavior in identified patient (J)	

| Wiltz and Patterson (1974) | $N = 6$ (short)
II. Attention-placebo control (AP) $N = 6$ (short) | Symptom checklist (Par)
Parent command behavior (J) | ior in home; BT superior to AP in reducing symptoms; no differences in frequency of commands (very good) |
| | Operant management skills training for parents (BT)
$N = 6$ (short)
Waiting-list control (NT) $N = 6$ | Deviant behavior in identified patient (J) | BT superior to NT in reducing targeting behaviors; no significant reduction in nontargeting deviant behavior (good) |

a Short = 1 to 10 sessions; moderate = 11 to 20 sessions; long = 21 or more sessions.

b J = judge or trained observer; T = therapist; Par = parents; F = family; O = objective records; Teach = teachers.

c Results based on siblings of identified patients from same sample of families as in Patterson (1974a, 1974b).

d Although this study is based on behavior of the 55 siblings over 3 years of age, of the 27 referred children, the data are presented as family mean rates of sibling deviance.

e In 11 families the average sibling's rate of deviant behavior dropped by 30 percent by termination, 6 had increased 30 percent by termination.

f Attempted replication of Patterson group's work.

g Seven of the 15 families did not complete baseline or termination data.

h Included in this sample are the 17 families reported on by Eyberg and Johnson (1974). Sixty-five families were referred for treatment. Of these 24 were seen as inappropriate for treatment, 14 were terminated after baseline but before treatment, 5 were terminated during treatment. Sample of 22 represents 34 percent of initial sample.

i Only 14 families were willing to participate in the 3-month follow-up; consequently data are impossible to interpret.

j Eyberg and Johnson (1974) reporting on 17 out of 22 of these cases reported that 15 out of 17 families increased deviant behavior on at least one of three criteria.

k With older children, families were seen as a unit. With younger children, only parents were seen in therapy.

l Treatment also occasionally included shaping, systematic desensitization, and suggestion.

m Specific problems were rated at 77 percent (134/174) improved by parents and 80.5 percent (140/174) improved by therapists.

n Some or all of the cases were reported on in other articles: Patterson (1974a, and 1974b), Patterson (1975), Patterson (1976), Patterson et al. (1968), Patterson and Reid (1973), Reid and Hendricks (1973).

o Eight families dropped after baseline but before treatment.

p Follow-up data at 6 months (available on only 19 families) were similar to results at termination.

q Reports cn four subjects from Patterson (1974a)

r Does not include 12 cases of premature termination.

s The behavioral treatment group in this study includes all patients reported on in Parsons and Alexander (1973).

t Control group data were being collected but had not been analyzed at the time of this report.

u Eight of twelve patients referred to (AC) dropped the program by the third session.

v Originally reported in Rosenthal (1976).

w Siblings of delinquent IPs reported on by Alexander and Parsons (1973).

x Replication of Alexander and Parsons (1973) with new therapists; used same control data.

such experience. Inexperienced therapists also appeared to have a higher rate of one session dropouts (Shellow et al., 1963). On the other hand, Shellow et al. (1963) found that beyond one session there were no treatment differences attributed to therapist experience level, and Santa-Barbara et al. (1975) also found no relationship between experience as a clinician and family therapy outcome. In almost all these studies, experience levels are questionably categorized (Auerbach & Johnson, 1977) [e.g., Roberts' (1975) "experienced" graduate student therapists]. Furthermore, no one has yet examined the question of the possible differential predictive power of experience as a psychotherapist versus experience as a marital/family therapist. The two are not equivalent.

Three independent studies at the University of Wisconsin have highlighted some interesting issues regarding the experience levels of *cotherapists.* Gurman (1974) found a significant *negative* relationship between cotherapist experience level *differences* and couples therapy outcome, as measured by changes in husband-wife attitudinal convergence. In a later report on the same sample, Gurman (1975b) also found a negative relationship between cotherapist experience difference and pre-postchanges in spouses' ratings of their partners' empathy, warmth, and genuineness. Rice et al. (1972) compared cotherapists' ratings of couples therapy outcome in three therapist pairings, experienced-experienced, inexperienced-inexperienced, and experienced-inexperienced (E-IE). While the ANOVA was not significant, the E-IE group reported the worst outcomes. The meaningfulness of this result was buttressed by Rice et al.'s finding a significant negative relationship between outcome and cotherapist's "felt competition" and a significant positive relationship between outcome and "candidness of postsession talks" by the cotherapists. The implication from these three studies is that experience differences between cotherapists may interfere with maximizing the outcomes of marital and, presumably, family therapy.

Cotherapy

Although cotherapy is widely espoused among marital-family therapists as offering unique advan-

tages over single-therapist treatment, this assumption has never been directly tested in a study of therapy outcome. Indirect evidence based on comparisons of gross improvement rates summed across studies of marital therapy for these two formats has yielded results of no practical difference (Gurman, 1973b), although cotherapists appear to be especially useful in couples' groups (Gurman, 1975a). Consistent with this analysis is Shellow et al.'s (1963) finding that the number of therapists had no effect on the frequency of one-session dropouts from family therapy. Finally, Rice et al. (1976) studied the self-reported therapy "styles" (Rice et al., 1972; Rice et al., 1974) of married (M) (to each other) and nonmarried (NM) (to each other) cotherapists. Results indicated that, in general, M cotherapists, and particularly experienced M cotherapists, were significantly more alike in self-described in-therapy behavior than NM cotherapists. Rice et al. (1976) discussed these results in terms of couple-cotherapist matching and argued that a cotherapist "united front" may have disadvantages in some therapy situations, although similarity of goals (Rice et al., 1972) seems, understandably, not to weaken treatment effects, but to heighten them. Whether heterosexual versus same-sex cotherapy teams offer special advantages in specific clinical situations remains to be investigated.

Gender

The McMaster group in Hamilton, Ontario reports male therapists to have better family therapy outcome than female therapists on the basis of both therapist (Santa-Barbara, 1975) and patient (Woodward et al., 1977) outcome ratings, but not on the basis of objective indices. These results are undoubtedly contaminated by the clear hierarchical therapist prestige structure in Canada. Beck and Jones (1973) found male counselors both more able than female counselors to get husbands involved in counseling and more able to keep husbands in treatment; thus also produced better outcomes in terms of husband change. Similarly, female clients terminated earlier with male than with female counselors. Given some evidence of therapists' bias in favor of traditional marital relationships (Magnus, 1976), the types of analyses in

Beck and Jones' (1973) work should be included in future studies of couples therapy.

Therapist Relationship Skill

The ability of the therapist to establish a positive relationship with his or her clients, long a central issue of individual therapy, receives the most consistent support as an important outcome-related therapist factor in marital-family therapy. Therapist empathy, warmth, and genuineness, the "client-centered triad," appear to be very important in keeping families in treatment beyond the first interview (Shapiro, 1974; Shapiro & Budman, 1973; Waxenberg, 1973). Waxenberg (1973) found that while white family therapists as a group offered higher levels of empathy to white than to nonwhite families, nonwhite families were as likely as white families to remain in treatment when offered high levels of these "facilitative conditions." Shapiro and Budman (1973) found that while empathy was more salient for keeping clients in individual therapy than in family therapy, more active family therapists had fewer dropouts than did less active therapists. Apparently, families respond more positively in initial sessions to expressions of therapist involvement (i.e., activity) than to expressions of mere understanding. Hollis (1968a), using a verbal interaction typology developed earlier (Hollis, 1967, 1968b), found that caseworkers who used more reflective comments instead of directive and ventilative comments in the initial joint couples interview had lower rates of discontinuance. In particular, efforts to promote understanding prematurely in a way that aroused too high a level of client anxiety had clear negative effects on couples returning for further interviews. In a similar vein, Postner et al. (1971), using a process coding scheme developed at the Jewish General Hospital in Montreal for studying verbal interaction in family therapy (Guttman et al., 1971, 1972a, & 1972b; Sigal et al., 1967, 1973; Spector et al., 1970), examined the effects of therapist drive (D) statements (stimulating interaction, information gathering, giving support) and interpretation (I) statements (clarifying motivation, labeling unconscious motivation). They found that three-quarters of the families of therapists with low D/I ratios dropped out of treatment and that a high therapist D/I ratio

early in treatment was predictive of good outcome. Apparently a low D/I style early in therapy may be experienced as too confrontative and thus may increase both premature termination and the chances of poor outcome. The therapist's ability to model meaning clarification (Jones, 1969) and positive perceptions of family members (Graham, 1968) and to facilitate family members' depth of experiencing (De Chenne, 1973) also seem to be important relationship-related skills for marital-family therapists. Apparently *it is important for the marital-family therapist to be active and to provide some structure to early interviews, but not to assault family defenses too quickly.* Of course, as Framo (1975) points out, a family can drop out or prematurely terminate for reasons that have nothing to do with the way therapy was conducted.

Beyond keeping families in treatment, there is evidence that the quality of therapist-patient relationship, as assessed by trained judges (Thomlinson, 1974), clients (Beck & Jones, 1973; Burton & Kaplan, 1968; Mezydlo et al., 1973), and supervisors (Alexander et al., 1976) is positively related to treatment outcome. The most impressive demonstration in this regard has been offered by Alexander et al. (1976). Having demonstrated (Alexander & Parsons, 1973; Klein et al., 1975) that their behavioral-systems family therapy was superior to two alternative treatment types and to no treatment for juvenile delinquent families, Alexander et al. examined the effects on outcome of "structuring" (directiveness, clarity, self-confidence) and "relationship" (warmth, affect-behavior integration, humor) skills. Although structuring skill discriminated between two levels of poor outcome, only relationship skill was able to discriminate between good and very good outcome. The two sets of skills accounted for 60 percent of the outcome variance, and relationship skill accounted for 44.6 percent of the total variance. Thus, *a reasonable mastery of technical skills may be sufficient to prevent worsening or maintain pretreatment functioning, but more refined therapist relationship skills seem necessary to yield truly positive outcomes in marital-family therapy. Moreover, a minimal level of empathic ability is probably needed just to complete therapeutic tasks in the most behavioral of such therapies* (Thomlinson, 1974). All this evidence seems to negate the recent comment by Edwin Thomas to the effect that, "What is needed in marriage counseling is not more kindness or empathy but a special technology" (Koch & Koch, 1976, p. 38). Since relationship skills appear to be fundamental ingredients of good outcome, regardless of the theoretical orientation of marital-family therapists, it will be important to determine which therapist factors are unique to different therapeutic systems and which are held in common (Sundland, 1977).

Patient Factors

Severity and Chronicity of Disorder
While the weight of evidence (Guerney & Stover, 1971; Shapiro, 1974; Shellow et al., 1963; Slipp et al., 1974) suggests that severity of family disturbance has no predictable effect on family continuance in therapy, severity and chronicity of the IP, whether as an individual (Gartner et al., 1975; Zwerling & Mendelsohn, 1965) or as a dyad (Beck & Jones, 1973; Fitzgerald, 1969), appears to be negatively related to treatment outcome, although null findings in this area also exist (Guerney & Stover, 1971; Wattie, 1973). Shellow et al.'s (1963) interesting finding that premature termination was more likely when the presenting problem was intergenerational than when it was "neutral" (e.g., school achievement) again suggests the need for family therapists to avoid frontal attacks on family defenses early in treatment (Guttman, 1973; Hollis, 1968a).

Identified Patient (IP) Diagnosis
Many studies of family therapy outcome do not report results as a function of IP diagnosis, and few studies of marital therapy do so. Of the 1414 family cases in Table 21-2, 855 could be identified as having a specific diagnosis and 488 out of the 1528 cases in Table 21-1 were identifiable as alcoholic IPs. Improvement rates for these diagnostic categories are indicated in the accompanying chart (top, next column).

In the only comparative study of improvement rates in alcoholic marriages, Burton and Kaplan (1968) found conjoint group therapy (75 percent) superior to both concurrent therapy (60 percent)

	N	Improved
Neurotic and Other nonpsychotic	241	69
Psychotic	306	68
Behavior problem	202	64
Anorexia and psychosomatic	86	91
Substance abuse	20	90
Alcoholism	488	60

and individual therapy (43 percent). Moreover, we found an improvement rate of 65 percent for eight conjoint group therapy studies (see Table 21-1). This result and the 60 percent improvement rate noted above for all marital therapies together compare favorably with the results of other psychological treatments for alcoholism at the end of therapy (Emrick, 1975; Emrick et al., 1977).

Among family therapies, more success has been demonstrated with "physical" problems such as anorexia and drug abuse. This may be due to the specific applicability of family interventions to these problems, which have not been very responsive to nonfamily methods. The treatment applied to these problems, structural family therapy (Minuchin, 1974), is more specific than most family therapies, and the outcome measures used (e.g., weight gain) are more objective than the most commonly used indices for change in other family therapies. Indeed, it is striking that family therapy has shown its greatest efficacy when improvement criteria have been most objective. The fact that specific techniques have been developed successfully for specific, relatively homogeneous populations should spur the development of additional problem-specific marital-family therapies in the future (see also the section on sex therapy, which follows).

These family improvement data, even though they lump child, adolescent, and adult cases, parallel the summary findings of Levitt (1957, 1963, 1971) for child psychotherapy. This parallel is even more striking when it is recalled that about two-thirds of the studies described in Table 21-2 involved child and adolescent IPs. While our analysis concurs with Levitt's finding that the poorest child-adolescent outcomes occur among "acting-out behavior problems" such as aggressive behavior and juvenile delinquency, the results of the Alexander group at Utah (Alexander & Parsons, 1973; Klein et al., 1975; Maloaf & Alexander, 1974; Parsons & Alexander, 1973) with delinquents, demonstrate that focal family intervention strategies can be developed to deal with very recalcitrant nonadult problems. *Special problems clearly require special solutions.*

Sexual Dysfunction

The treatment results for therapy of sexual dysfunction reported by Masters and Johnson (1970) signaled the start of remarkable progress in the field. Despite the current widespread use of sex therapies and the proliferation of training programs, sophisticated research in the area has not been abundant (Kaplan, 1974). The modeling of two leaders in the field (Hartman & Fithian, 1972), in the comment, "We are loath to report statistical success rates. We are not interested in developing a numbers game where centers such as ours will enter into a kind of spurious competition based on numbers" (p. 204) has hardly helped.

Most published research on treatment outcomes has suffered from (1) lack of clarity about patient selection; (2) imprecise diagnoses of sexual dysfunctions and patients; (3) failure to control for chronicity of dysfunction or marital adjustment; (4) confounding of specific disorders × the use of dual-therapist team versus single-therapist treatment; and (5) uncontrolled (and unreported) therapist experience levels. Despite these methodological problems, a remarkably consistent picture emerges with regard to cure rates for the major sexual dysfunctions. Typical success rates are: primary orgasmic dysfunction, 90 percent; secondary orgasmic dysfunction, 50 percent or less; premature ejaculation, 90 percent; primary erectile failure, 50 percent; secondary erectile failure, 75 percent. Using Masters and Johnson's (1970) criterion that the female partner be satisfied in at least 50 percent of coital encounters, the improvement rates for primary orgasmic dysfunction are striking. Success for secondary orgasmic dysfunction seems to be heightened by the addition of conjoint couples therapy (Kinder & Blakeney, 1976). Laughren and Kass (1975) reviewed the literature and found an overall improvement rate for *in-vivo*

desensitization of sexual dysfunction (all types) to be 78 percent and for systematic desensitization, 75 percent. Negative changes are rarely reported, although they do seem to exist (Powell et al., 1974).

The typical success rates are impressive for some of the major disorders, but a number of crucial issues remain to be examined. Among these, we consider the following to be the most important: (1) the effects of dysfunction chronicity and marital adjustment on outcome; (2) tying outcomes to more precise diagnostic categories; (3) the matching of dual teams versus single therapists for specific disorders; (4) the presumed advantage of additional marital therapy in cases of secondary orgasmic dysfunction, and the ideal timing of this therapy (i.e., before or concomitant with sex therapy); (5) the effects of massed versus spaced practice for specific disorders (LoPiccolo, 1976); (6) the adjunctive use of programs in sex education, assertiveness training, and so on; (7) the indications for and against treatment in a conjoint couples format versus individual treatment versus a group setting; and (8) assessment of change as a result of sex therapy beyond symptomatic improvement (e.g., Wallace & Barbach, 1974). Kinder and Blakeney (1976), in agreement with Fordney-Settlage (1975), sum it up aptly: "There seems to be general agreement that sex therapy works . . . but why and when are questions yet to be answered" (p. 1).

Quality of Family Interaction and Adaptive Skill
Couples and families appear more likely to continue in treatment and not cancel therapy appointments if spouses are both low in authoritarianism (Slipp et al., 1974), more open to disagreement (Kressel & Slipp, 1975), less coercive and competitive (Santa-Barbara & Epstein, 1974), and less traditional in their roles (Kressel & Slipp, 1975). The probability of a positive outcome seems to be increased when couples do not enter into strong coalitions against the therapist in the first session (O'Connor, 1974), and when families have an employed father (Woodward et al., 1975) and mothers who are not exploitative in social relationships (MacGregor, 1962) and are good decision makers (Bowen, 1961). Pretherapy levels of couples' hostility (Mudd et al., 1950) and mutual

facilitative conditions (Gurman, 1975b) are unrelated to outcome. The relevance of low authoritarianism and coerciveness, less traditional role structure, and nonexploitativeness may manifest itself in Beutler's (1971) and Gurman's (1974) finding that spouse-spouse attitude convergence over the course of therapy was not only positively related to outcome, but also that this dyadic convergence was more highly correlated with change than was spouse-therapist attitudinal convergence. In a related finding, Sigal et al. (1967) reported that low change in family interaction levels was predictive of poor outcome.

Miller and Gottlieb (1974) found that while fathers' personalities had no effect on child-family behavior therapy outcome, mothers' personalities accounted for 80 percent of the outcome variance. Guerney and Stover (1971) failed to confirm the importance of the mother's personality.

Family Constellation and Family Members' Ages

Two studies have found family constellation related to therapy outcome (Woodward et al., 1975, single parent versus intact family; Zwerling & Mendelsohn, 1965, married versus single, female, day hospital IP), but the weight of evidence suggests that neither family constellation (Gartner et al., 1975; Stuart & Tripodi, 1973; Woodward et al., 1975) nor family size (Guerney & Stover, 1971; Wattie, 1973; Woodward et al., 1975) are good predictors of treatment results. Although Woodward et al. (1975) found better outcomes among 6 to 11-year-old IPs than among 12 to 16-year-olds, the majority of evidence shows neither IP age, ages of other family members (Freeman et al., 1969; Guerney & Stover, 1971; Gurman, 1973c; Slipp et al., 1974; Woodward et al., 1975), nor IP birth order (Slipp et al., 1974; Woodward et al., 1975) to be predictive of either marital-family therapy outcomes or of continuation in treatment.

Gurman (1973c) and Freeman et al. (1969) found no relationship between length of couples' marriage and outcome, but Wattie (1973) found that the best outcomes were obtained by couples married 13 to 16 years, a period of lessening dependency of young children. These results may imply that as children become more autonomous in a conflicted marriage, parental anxiety levels increase and provide a stimulus for change. Turkewitz and O'Leary (1976) found behavioral couples therapy superior to communication training with younger ($\bar{x}$ age = 29 years) couples and the reverse with older ($\bar{x}$ age = 42 years) couples.

Demographic Variables
Few studies have examined outcome as a function of family SES, and the results are mixed (Guerney & Stover, 1971; Slipp et al., 1974; Wattie, 1973). Although parental educational level is unrelated to outcome in filial therapy (Guerney & Stover, 1971), lower SES-level parents appear to make better use of direct information and advice, while higher SES-level parents respond more favorably to therapy in which their own autonomy and problem-solving skills are employed (Love et al., 1972). Two marital studies (Freeman et al., 1969; Wattie, 1973) have found husband-wife education level *differences* (the husband usually the more educated) to be related positively to marriage therapy outcome. In addition, Wattie found less improvement in husbands when wives were more educated. These results may imply that the probability of good treatment outcome is decreased the more threatened the husband feels.

Treatment Factors

Treatment Length
Only the study by Reid and Shyne (1969) has found time-limited couples therapy to produce better outcomes than "continuing service" [i.e., open-ended treatment (8 versus 26 sessions)]. Beck and Jones (1973), Ziegler (1973), and Wattie (1973) found no differences between these treatment formats, and Freemen et al. (1969), Stuart and Tripodi (1973), and Dicks (1967) found no relationship between therapy length and treatment results. It should be noted, however, that Stuart and Tripodi compared three relatively brief treatments involving 7.5, 11, and 16.5 hours of therapeutic contact. Only Gurman (1973c) has found a low, but positive, relationship between these two variables in couples therapy. Interestingly, Wattie (1973) did find much more improvement in the husbands of her couples in short-term instead of in open-ended therapy. Perhaps being less threatened by ambiguity about treatment conditions and having a job to be done, as it were, is

more consonant with many males' approaches to interpersonal conflict and change. This possibility is supported by Ehrenkranz' (1967) finding that husbands in open-ended therapy participated less actively and were more present oriented than past oriented compared to their wives. In sum, *the evidence to date suggests that time-limited marital-family therapy is not inferior to open-ended treatment.*

Which Family Members Are Involved in Treatment?

We have already presented the striking comparative improvement rates involved when both instead of just one spouse is involved in marital therapy. The results of studies directly addressing this issue also strongly favor this pattern (Beck & Jones, 1973; Ewing et al., 1961; Freeman et al., 1969; Smith, 1967, 1969), although Reid and Shyne (1969) and Hepworth and Smith (1972) found no difference between these conditions. In Hepworth and Smith's study, which purportedly compared conjoint and individual therapies, these treatment formats were, in fact, overlapping; in the "conjoint" condition 72 percent of the sessions were held with one or the other spouse alone. Again, it appears clear that the involvement of both spouses in treatment greatly enhances the probability of a positive therapeutic outcome. In addition, while there appears to be a questionable amount of generalization of salutory treatment effects from successful child treatment to change in marital discord (Oltmanns et al., 1976), there may be significant generalization from successful marital treatment to child-related target problems (Turkewitz & O'Leary, 1976).

In family therapy, involvement of the father, traditionally the "missing link" in child guidance clinics (Parad & Parad, 1968a), has a very strong influence on both the family's continuing in treatment after the first session (Shapiro & Budman, 1973) and on their improvement (Love et al., 1972). Moreover, family therapy outcome is likely to be better when the therapist talks more to the father then to the mother (Postner et al., 1971). In fact, merely having the family of an inpatient available may be a good prognostic sign, whether the family is actually seen or not (Gould & Glick, 1976)! In a related vein, Levitt (1971), in his review

of research on child therapy, cites three studies as offering evidence with regard to the question of outcome as a function of treatment focus and concludes that these studies support a specific order of treatment effectiveness in terms of focus (most effective—mother and father or both and child; least effective—child alone). Each of these studies suffered severe limitations, however, and require cautious evaluation. Gluck et al. (1964) reported on the outcome of therapy for 55 cases in terms of IP symptoms. Forty-three of these patients were boys between the ages of 3 and 7 years, which seriously limits the generalizability of the findings. Moreover, almost one-third of the responses made by families were scored "unrateable," casting doubts on the adequacy of the authors' assessment strategy. Levitt (1971) also inaccurately cites the report of Lessing and Schilling (1966) as a study of therapy effectiveness when, in fact, the data represented "status of IP at close," not therapeutic improvement. The third study (D'Angelo & Walsh, 1967) is not comparable because the data are reported as mean change scores instead of as percentages of improvement.

Even though we believe that the evidence reviewed earlier in this chapter strongly confirms the superiority of treatment involving several family members over that limited to the child IP, the empirical support for Levitt's argument is revealed to be quite weak.

The Use of Apparatus-Based Interventions

In the past few years two major apparatus-based approaches, videotape feedback and electromechanical signaling systems, have been used more and more in marital-family therapy. Having established that the reliability of videotape observations was as high as for live observations of certain nonverbal dyadic behavior (Eisler et al., 1973a), Eisler et al. (1973b), in an analog study, compared the effects of videotape feedback alone, focused instructions and a combination of the two on eye contact and smiling behavior, and found the combined condition superior. Assessing the effects of similar interventions on more complex levels of interpersonal perception, Edelson and Seidman (1975) found videotape playback plus verbal feedback superior to verbal feedback alone in an analog game-playing situation. Studies with real patients have found videotape feedback superior to audio feedback or discussion in changing parents' behavior (Finol, 1973) and equal to parent counseling and superior to individual child therapy in changing children's behavior (Love et al., 1972). The Alkire and Brunse (1974) study of the effects of videotape feedback in an ongoing couples group demonstrated powerful negative effects on both individuals and relationships and should serve to caution clinicians about the manner in which video feedback is used. In all of these last three studies therapists directed and faciliated discussion, but did not attempt to persuade or influence. It seems likely that videotape feedback can have genuine impact in family therapy, both for better and for worse. Given the assumption that psychotherapy, especially of systems, leads to change by altering the way individuals see themselves in interaction with others, *videotape feedback may offer a useful adjunct to primary treatment interventions, but its independent use to effect change is questionable.* A direct controlled comparison of video feedback with marital or family therapy has yet to be attempted, although Mayadas and Duehn's (1977) study suggests that video feedback in combination with modeling may be superior to verbal couples counseling in shaping specific verbal communication behaviors. Ben-Ami (1976), however, found videotape instruction less facilitative of family members' intake interview behavior than modeling.

The modification of couples' verbal behavior through automated and computer-assisted signaling systems for corrective feedback and instructions has been reported by Thomas and his associates (Carter & Thomas, 1973a, 1973b; Thomas et al., 1970, 1972, 1974). In efforts to transform complex verbal communication into simpler, more specific response units, Thomas et al. developed the Signal System for the Assessment and Modification of Behavior (SAM). SAM consists of units through which spouses can send and receive communication signals to and from each other and to and from a therapist by pressing buttons, and a unit by which the therapist can monitor client communications and signal clients. The system has been used mainly for assessment purposes, but analog studies aimed at changing couples' verbal behavior have also been reported (Carter & Thomas, 1973a, 1973b).

The clinical utility of SAM is yet to be demonstrated.

Two Other Focal Approaches

In this section we will briefly summarize the work to date on two focal intervention programs in the marital/family field that in the last few years have received increasing attention and assumed greater importance among practitioners.

Marital and Family Enrichment Programs

Recently there has been more and more energy devoted to preventive work with couples and families, most of which is subsumed under the attractive rubric of "enrichment." These programs attempt to offer growth-inducing experiences to couples and families whose interactions are basically sound but who wish to make these relationships even more satisfying. Comprehensive chronicles of the history of both marital (Mace & Mace, 1976; Otto, 1975) and family (L'Abate, 1974) programs have recently appeared. Almost all such programs focus on enhancing communication skills, broadening and deepening the emotional and/or sexual lives of couples and families, and reinforcing existing strengths. The majority of enrichment programs have been in the marital and premarital area, and several well-organized programs with national sponsorship now exist. As of 1975, about 180,000 couples had participated in enrichment programs in the United States (Otto, 1975).

Gurman and Kniskern (1977) recently critically reviewed the research on marital and premarital enrichment groups. We will not concentrate here on studies of family enrichment programs because they are few in number and their outcomes are quite consistant with those in the marital area (Coufal, 1975; Ginsberg, 1971; Vogelsong, 1975). Gurman and Kniskern's review of 29 studies, 23 of which were controlled, revealed the following trends: (1) 84 percent of criterion measures were based on participants' self-reports, and the majority of studies used self-reports as the sole change indices; (2) about 60 percent of the criterion measures from all studies showed positive change on overall marital satisfaction and adjustment, relationship skills, and individual personality variables; (3) program results were superior to no treatment in 23 out of 34 (67 percent) comparisons, with 11 "ties"; (4) follow-up, occurring in only four studies, showed only moderate maintenance of gains; (5) the Minnesota Couples Communication Program (Miller et al., 1976a, 1976b) and the Conjugal Relationship Modification Program (Rappaport, 1976) received the strongest empirical support, showing intervention superior to controls in every instance; (6) behavioral-exchange programs did not fare especially well, showing superiority to controls in only two out of six comparisons, with four producing "ties."

Gurman and Kniskern (1977) concluded that the evidence on the outcomes of marital enrichment programs required a cautious estimation of its efficacy due to several important methodological shortcomings in the literature, especially the frequent use of questionable criteria or a narrow range of criteria, lack of follow-up, insufficient inclusion of attention-placebo groups, and failure even to test the notion that program effects generalized to the family system as a whole. In conclusion, Gurman and Kniskern suggested six important empirical issues that needed to be addressed before the implementation of such programs, however well intentioned, outstrip evidence for their effectiveness: (1) durability and (2) generalizability of enrichment-induced change; (3) range of potential participants; (4) developmental "timing" of these programs; (5) demonstration of change through nonparticipant rating sources; and (6) elucidation of salient change-inducing components.

Divorce Counseling/Therapy

Divorce is increasingly less likely to be regarded as an evil. The women's movement, the recent cultural emphasis on personal growth, the weakening of traditional religious ties, and interest in non-monogamous life-styles have removed at least some of the stigma once attached to divorce. Psychotherapists have become involved in the divorce process only very recently and, among the social sciences, the area has largely been the province of sociologists (Goode, 1956; Sussman & Cogswell, 1972). That divorce counseling/therapy is now seen as a subspecialty interest and practice within the helping professions signals a near-revolutionary change in that in the historically oldest discipline of marriage *counseling* divorce was basically frowned on. The goal of counseling was to *improve* the marriage, a euphemism for "saving" it, not to explore, understand, and *perhaps* change it. In fact, a recent best-selling tradebook (Koch & Koch, 1976) on marital-family therapy still conveys this anachronistic assumption in its title, *The Marriage Savers*.

The goals of divorce therapy typically involve aiding the divorced or separated partner to deal with his or her loss, working through ambivalence, and fostering autonomy and self-esteem as a separate person. It should be pointed out that the fact of *divorce does not serve as a useful criterion of the effectiveness of marital therapy without taking into account the goals tailored to a given couple's needs. Conciliation is not equivalent to reconciliation, nor does divorce necessarily constitute evidence of ineffective therapy.*

A few useful clinical papers on the topic have appeared (Brown, 1976; Fisher, 1973; Framo, 1974; Toomim, 1972), but relatively little empirical study has followed. Four subareas have received attention: structured separation with counseling, reconciliation (court) counseling, postdivorce counseling, and the effects of different marital therapies on postdivorce adjustment.

Toomim (1972) describes a humanistically oriented program of "structured separation with counseling" in which married couples in therapy continue to meet conjointly and individually with their therapist during a 3-month period in which they live apart and make no permanent financial, property, or child custody arrangements. At the end of this period, the couple chooses whether to live together permanently, live together on a time-limited trial basis, finalize their separation, or commit themselves to a second period of structured separation. In a 1-year follow-up of 18 couples seen in her private practice, Toomim reports that 6 reinstated their marriage and 12 were divorced. Moreover, 23 of the 24 divorced individuals felt they had "gained equilibrium as single people by the end of the time they agreed to finalize their separation" (p. 310).

Greene et al. (1973) employed a "transient structured distance" (TSD) strategy, differing from

Toomim's (1972) approach in that the marital partners do not live apart; instead, one spouse becomes a "boarder" in his or her own house. TSD is used in the majority of cases to aid clarification of the marital relationship (29 percent) or to assess readiness for separation of divorce (16 percent). The authors report that divorce occurred in 44 percent of 73 TSD arrangements, compared to Toomim's (1972) 66 percent, and that at follow-up of up to several years 23 percent of the couples were "incompatible" but together, and 33 percent were noticeably improved or "reequilibrated" following a situational marital crisis.

Landgraf (1973) examined the effects of voluntary separation during pastoral marriage counseling. He concluded that, among others, several positive changes occurred: improvement in personal maintenance and work-related behavior, extended ranges of social interaction, and less "avoidance-oriented" behavior. At the same time, suffering was not absent; many clients reported increased anxiety, heightened mistrust of people in general, identity diffusion, and the like. Since this study examined changes during, not after, separation, it is possible that most of these "negative" changes represented positive changes in the process of living and developing more individual coping resources.

Three well-designed controlled studies have examined the effects of various conciliation court counseling formats on couples' reconciliation. Graham (1968) found brief conjoint counseling to be superior to a combination of brief conjoint and individual counseling on the reconciliation criterion, with only conjoint counseling superior to randomly assigned controls. No differences were found on other criteria (positive references to spouse, dominance, and affiliation scores). Hickman and Baldwin (1970) found more change in attitudes toward spouse and a higher frequency of reconciliation accruing to couples receiving 8 hours of communication- and problem-centered counseling than to those receiving audiotape-based communication training. Counseling outcomes surpassed those of controls on both criteria. Finally, Matanovich (1970) compared the effectiveness of group meetings using encounter tapes with brief problem-centered counseling. Counseling outcomes were not superior to controls on either change measure (reconciliation, dominance, and affiliation), while the encounter-tape intervention surpassed counseling on the reconciliation criterion.

The only postdivorce counseling study to date compared the effects of a single 2-hour, problem-solving conjoint counseling session with standard litigation processes for couples contesting visitation stipulations. Margolin (1973) randomly assigned 150 such couples to these two interventions and served as the counselor for all 75 counseled couples. In all cases the mother had been granted legal custody of the child(ren). Seventy-three of the 75 counseled couples reached a visitation plan agreement; only one control couple independently formulated a plan prior to their court appearance ($p < .001$). In addition, only nine of the counseled couples returned to Superior Court because of visitation quarrels in a 4-month follow-up, compared to 59 of the 75 control couples ($p < .001$). Counseled couples also reported greater satisfaction than controls on a number of issues involving quality of the fathers' visits, effects of their decision on children, and the like.

Finally, Cookerly's (1976) massive follow-up study of 773 former marriage counseling clients seen in six different treatment formats (see Table 21-4) found that while conjoint therapies produced the best overall outcomes, the individual interview format was ranked second for clients who eventually divorced, with conjoint sessions ranking sixth for these clients. Thus, despite the poor showing of individual marital therapy in general discussed earlier in this chapter, Cookerly's data suggest that the individual format may be more successful than conjoint therapy in divorce situations. One must bear in mind that the counseling studied was not divorce counseling. But, in an indirect way, Cookerly's data support the belief of most divorce counselors that individual sessions offer maximal opportunities to achieve the primary goal of divorce counseling: the growth of an autonomous and self-esteeming individual. These goals, of course, are probably not different from those of conjoint couples therapy (Gurman & Knudson, 1978, in press).

Divorce counseling offers the potential for some very exciting research on family crises and disorganization with important potential benefit for both the children and parents of divorce. The power of divorce counseling in the context of a total family instead of a marital dyad alone is yet to be investigated.

RESEARCH ON MARITAL AND FAMILY THERAPY: PROSPECT

Implications for Practice and Training

The number of formal training opportunities in the marital-family field is rapidly increasing (Beal, 1976; Stanton, 1975a). A variety of general training issues have been discussed at length (Erickson, 1973; Napier & Whitaker, 1973; Shapiro, 1975a, 1975b) and several training models have been broadly described (Ard, 1973; Bodin, 1969a; Cleghorn & Levin, 1973; Dell et al., 1977; Epstein & Levin, 1973; Ferber & Mendelsohn, 1969; Haley, 1974; Stier & Goldenberg, 1975), yet only three detailed accounts of specific teaching strategies have appeared (Birchler, 1975; Bodin, 1969b; Perlmutter et al., 1967). These articles offer much thought-provoking material and raise most of the central training issues of which we are aware; they do not require reiteration here.

We are unaware of any empirical study of either the process or outcomes of training programs or approaches in the field. Not unlike the area of individual psychotherapy training (Garfield, 1977), there now exists no evidence that training experiences in marital-family therapy in fact increase the effectiveness of clinicians. In order to offer some beginning empirical bases for clinical work, we will briefly summarize the implications for both training and practice that seem to follow reasonably from our preceeding review and analysis of research in the marital-family therapy field.

1. *Individual therapy for marital problems is a very ineffective treatment strategy and one that appears to produce more negative effects than alternative approaches.* Individual treatment may be useful in some situations (e.g., divorce counseling), but its general value remains to be demonstrated. Therapy that combines individual and con-

joint sessions may also be indicated in some clinical situations, but there is presently an insufficient empirical basis on which to make such differential decisions. Training programs would do well not to endorse the individual therapy model for the treatment of marital problems, although it is probably true that marital-family therapists need to have a basic mastery of individual therapy in order to be effective systems therapists.

2. *Couples benefit most from treatment when both partners are involved in therapy, especially when they are seen conjointly.* The relative advantages of conjoint interview versus conjoint group therapy, however, remain unspecified.

3. *Family therapy appears to be at least as effective and possibly more effective than individual therapy for a wide variety of problems, both apparent "individual" difficulties and more obvious family conflicts.* Choosing between these two approaches for "individual" problems will, and probably should, continue to reflect the biases and training of individual practitioners.

4. *For certain clinical goals and problems* (e.g., decreasing hospitalization rates for some chronic and acute inpatients, treating anorexia, many childhood behavior problems, juvenile delinquency and sexual dysfunction), *systems therapies offer the treatments of choice. Specific effective treatment programs and strategies exist for some of these problems and should be taught in any training program in marital-family therapy.*

5. *Behavioral marital and family therapies, while offering testable models and relatively precise intervention packages, currently offer insufficient research support to justify the training of neophyte therapists in this framework alone.* Moreover, several technical components of the behavioral paradigm are not unique to it, but exist in common with avowedly "nonbehavioral" marital-family therapies. Nonbehavioral therapies, of course, also lack a sufficient

evidential base to support "single-system" training.

6. *Short-term and time-limited therapies appear to be at least as effective as treatment of longer drration; moreover, most of the positive results of openended therapy were achieved in less than 5 months.* Goal-oriented and problem-centered training experiences constitute an important aspect of teaching beginning family therapists.

7. *Several marital and family "enrichment" programs appear to have real promise as useful preventative strategies in family living.* Practitioners and trainee therapists should acquaint themselves with one or more of these models in order to expand their potential range of therapeutic impact beyond family systems in serious trouble.

8. Analogous to the outcome gains in having both spouses involved in marriage therapy, *the father, long the absent family member in child-oriented treatment, plays a major role in the efficacy of family therapy initiated because of a child or adolescent IP. The wisdom of the traditional mother and child guidance model of practice and training is questionable.* Researchers should note Woodward et al.'s (1977) recent finding that it is far more difficult to obtain follow-up data from fathers than from mothers who have been in family therapy.

9. *Deterioration appears to be as common in marital-family therapy as it is in individual psychotherapies.* Although only a few of the salient factors in producing negative effects have been tentatively identified, *it appears that therapist variables and patient-therapist interaction account for negative effects far more often than patient factors alone. Furthermore, therapist factors that contribute to both improvement and deterioration in individual psychotherapy are equally powerful in the treatment of relationships.*

10. *Therapist relationship skills have major impact on the outcome of marital-family treatment regardless of the "school" orientation of the clinician. Training programs must foster both conceptual-technical skills and relationship skills in their beginning family therapists.*

In a young field already unduly burdened by theoretical and technical polemicism, it would seem unwise to fuel the flames of clinical antagonism and one-upmanship with empirical data that, as we have shown, are lacking in many respects. Thus, the above practical implications are offered as tentatively supported working guidelines, not as final scientific truths. Indeed, we would be disheartened if clinicians were to begin to cite the preceding review as incontrovertible evidence for personally cherished beliefs or to justify personal therapeutic prejudices. Empirical research is not sacrosanct but, in our view, offers one important epistemology that must be articulated with the intuitively rich knowledge of the clinician. *The reification of critical literature reviews is no more productive than the reification of unsubstantiated clinical speculation.*

Implications for Research

As Rubin and Mitchell (1976) have recently documented in their program of couples research, the process of research and counseling may often merge. In this final section we will offer some suggestions in response to a series of interrelated issues involved in assessing change in marital and family therapy: (1) what familial *units* should be assessed; (2) by what *measures* and on what *factors* should these units be assessed; and (3) from what *perspective(s)* should these units and factors be assessed? Since marital and family therapies are neither primarily nor solely concerned with change in a collection of individuals, as in group therapy, the evaluation of therapeutic outcomes clearly cannot be satisfactorily accomplished by using traditional measures of individual change alone. Thus, assessment of therapeutic change cannot be meaningfully carried out by an additive process of mere summing across individual family members. Such an approach is also seriously limited by focusing on individual symptomatic improvement in a modality in which such improvement is viewed, at most, as a secondary goal. A recent survey of family therapists (GAP, 1970) found that symptomatic improvement was viewed as a primary goal by only

23 percent of those surveyed and ranked seventh among "primary goals with all families," following improved communication (85 percent), autonomy and individuation (56 percent), empathy (56 percent), leadersiip flexibility (34 percent), role agreement (32 percent), and reduced conflict (23 percent).

What Units Should be Assessed?

Since marital-family therapy as it is most frequently practiced seeks to improve the functioning of all family members and their intrafamily interactions, it is imperative that change be routinely assessed at the individual, dyadic, and system levels. Obviously, the number of possible loci of change rapidly increases as the system size increases (e.g., in a four-member family there are four individuals, six dyads, four triads, and one family system). Since it will often not be practical to measure change in all possible family subunits, priorities must be established to guide the selection of subunits to be assessed. We propose a tentative model, shown in Table 21-12, that we believe provides these needed guidelines.

We assert that family units I, II, and III, the identified patient, the marriage, and the total system, which in some cases is equivalent to the marriage, are the minimal units for assessment and must be examined in any marital/family therapy outcome study, regardless of the family constellation or treatment context. Units IV to VII represent other family units on two dimensions: same versus other generation relative to the identified patient, and individual versus relationship functioning. These four family units are listed in order of their importance for the assessment of change in marital/family therapy from unit IV, which we consider most important, to unit VII, which we consider least important. Although we recognize that other therapists and researchers may question our decision, we have based our schema for priorities on the belief that dysfunctional families have strong morphostatic characteristics that will tend to negate system change and that could produce symptoms in other family members and relationships.

We would argue that a higher level of positive change has occurred when improvement is evidenced in systematic (total family) or relationship (dyadic) interactions than when it is evidenced in individuals alone. This is true whether the individual is the identified patient, an individual of the same generation as the identified patient, or an individual of the cross-generation relative to the identified patient. In addition, more positive change can be said to have occurred when improvement is noted on a total system level than on a single relationship level which, in turn, reflects more profound change than that achieved by any single individual or even series of individuals. Thus, a low level of family flexibility, adaptability, and change is manifest when symptomatic behavior decreases in the identified patient and appears in another individual of the same generation (family unit IV). Change is "better" when such a shift occurs either across generations in another individual (family unit V) or, better yet, in a relationship (family units VI and VII).

In a sense, then, it is "better" for deterioration to occur at a total system level than on a single relationship level which, in turn, is "better deterioration" than that lodged in any one individual. Deterioration in any family subunit, of course, is undesirable, but removal of a single individual or a single relationship from the system-regulating "scapegoat" position and the emergence of symptomatic behavior at a different level of interactional experience may be necessary in order for the total treatment unit to acknowledge the dysfunctional nature of the marital or family *system*. Our schema is designed to insure that the worst sort of deterioration will be the most likely to be detected. Deterioration in families must be assessed before therapy termination so that steps can be taken to return these deteriorated units to a healthier level of functioning. Since the overwhelming majority of studies reviewed in this chapter were of short duration, it is quite possible that some proportion of the cases of deterioration in marital-family therapy that we have documented (Gurman & Kniskern, 1976, 1978b) may, in fact, have reflected such an intermediate stage of the therapeutic process. If therapy had been of longer duration, some of these couples and families might have "worked through" this intermediate stage to an improved level of functioning. In this context, it should be clear that *in marital-family therapy, deterioration is not necessarily the opposite of improvement.* Empirical study of the endurance of therapy-induced deterio-

TABLE 21-12 A Priority Sequence for Assessing Therapeutic Change in Couples and Families

Treatment Context and Family Constellation

Familial Unit of Assessment	FAMILY THERAPY I: Child as Identified Patient		FAMILY THERAPY II: Parent as Identified Patient	MARITAL THERAPY: Spouse/Parent as Identified Patient	
	Family With More Than One Child	One-Child Family		Marriage with Child(ren)	Childless Marriage
I. Identified patient (IP)	IP child	IP child	IP parent	IP spouse	IP spouse
II. Marriage	Marriage	Marriage	Marriage	Marriage	Marriage
III. Total system	Family	Family	Family	Family	(Marriage)
IV. Same generation of IP: individual	IP's siblings	—	Non-IP spouse	Non-IP spouse	= Non-IP spouse
V. Cross-generation of IP: individual	Each parent	Each parent	Each child	Each child	—
VI. Same generation of IP: relationship	IP child and non-IP child(ren)	—	(Marriage)	(Marriage)	(Marriage)
VII. Cross-generation of IP: relationship	Parents and IP child: child 1 = IP	Parents and IP child	Child(ren) and IP parent	(Parents and child(ren), i.e., Family)	—
	Parents and non-IP child(ren)	(Parents and IP child)	Children and non-IP parent	(As above)	—

Note: Parentheses indicate that this familial unit has already been accounted for at earlier level of assessment priority. Blank spaces indicate that assessment of this familial unit is logically impossible.

ration in couples and families would be of major theoretical and practical value.

What Variables Should Be Studied and What Measures Should Be Used?

Individual therapy researchers have investigated the outcomes of treatment on the basis of literally hundreds of different criteria with relatively little collaborative effort (Strupp & Bergin, 1969). Although the wisdom and practicality of large-scale collaborative studies is questionable (Bergin & Strupp, 1970), there does seem to be at least some agreement as to what measures should constitute a "core battery" in studies of individual psychotherapy (Waskow & Parloff, 1975). No such minimal battery, which would allow useful comparisons among divergent treatment studies, has yet been recommended in the marital-family field. A recent survey (GAP, 1970) of family therapists implied a reasonable degree of preferential consensus about therapists' primary treatment goals, but we are not very optimistic about the probability, in the near future, of achieving agreement about which measures might comprise a core battery in this field. Our pessimism has four bases. First, within the family field we see most contributors as still embroiled in intense proselytizing campaigns, with more allegiance paid to charismatic personalities than to a common goal of empirical scrutiny. Second, systems-oriented therapies have clearly made a major impact on the conceptualization and treatment of psychopathology, but the struggles of family approaches to be accepted by the therapeutic community at large, even recently described as a "war" (McDermott & Char, 1974), may not allow sophisticated scientific examination within the boundaries of the family field until the boundary battles without the field are resolved or at least tempered. Third, even if researchers and clinicians could agree on the core dimensions requiring assessment, as implied in the GAP report, there are major practical problems to be encountered in selecting the measures for these dimensions. Among the more than 100 instruments and scales for the assessment of marital and family interaction recently categorized by Cromwell et al. (1976), many require either extensive or expensive apparatus, tremendous investments of time in their administration, or both. Moreover, the reliability

and validity of most of these instruments have not yet been demonstrated, although a few, such as van der Veen's Family Concept Test (1960), which is firmly rooted in research on the self-concept and has already been used in several dozen studies of family process and family treatment, do stand out on both conceptual and methodological criteria. Such a critical review would fill at least one volume and is obviously beyond the scope of this chapter. Several excellent sources on family interaction research (Framo, 1965; Jacob, 1975; Riskin & Faunce, 1972) and catalogs of family instrumentation (Cromwell et al., 1976; Straus, 1969) now exist. For the near future, the researcher in this field is advised to consult these materials in selecting measures to assess the constructs relevant to a particular study. Finally, it must be remembered that there is at best only moderate agreement among family therapists or between family therapists and the families they treat as to the nature and dimensions of healthy family functioning.

Still, it is clear to us that one of the most serious deficiencies in the family field is that researchers, with the possible exception of behavioral marital therapists, have failed to develop useful and valid measures of most of the core theoretical constructs (e.g., "pseudomutuality," "enmeshment," "collusion," "trianguation") that have become reified among clinicians. *Before spawning dozens of instruments to assess newly emerging dimensions of marital and family interactions, it would be more useful for researchers, in active collaboration with clinicians, to begin to operationalize the salient dimensions of the major theories of marital-family therapy that have already had a tremendous influence on thousands of practitioners. Moreover, measures need to be used that are not only conceptually sound, but that are also meaningful to clinicians and families, lest family therapy researchers evolve a "system" unto themselves that is divorced from clinical application.*

From What Perspective Should Change Be Assessed?

It is more and more recognized that it is difficult in assessing therapeutic change to achieve consensual agreement on outcome measures deriving from different sources or perspectives. For example, therapists' judgments about both the process

(Gurman, 1977) and outcome (Mintz, 1977) of psychotherapy can be routinely expected to show only low correlation with the views of patients and external judges. Fiske (1975) has argued persuasively that since a source of data is not a measuring instrument, attempts to eliminate disagreement among sources and reduce what earlier had been considered error variance are futile. Fiske (1975, p. 20) argues:

A source of data yields observations from a distinctive role providing distinctive experience. When an observer representing a source makes judgments about the complex variables of interest to current psychotherapeutic theory, he is actually processing his own experience. . . . Nearly exact agreement can be obtained only from inanimate measuring instruments or from observers functioning like instruments.

Fiske also notes (p. 23) that, "instead of seeking to minimize (differences in perceptions), researchers should seek to identify the unique components of the perceptions and judgments from each source."

In studying the treatment of relationships, researchers must attend to the unique perceptions of both "insiders" and "outsiders" (Cromwell, et al., 1976; Olson, 1974) of the family system. Olson (1974) considers an "insider" to be "a person in a relationship who is able to provide information on both his own feelings and behavior and his perceptions of the other's with whom he has a relationship," while an "outsider" is a person "who serves as a participant or external observer of interaction between other individuals." We view the reporter's frame of reference somewhat differently from Olson, in that we do not consider the marital/family therapist to be an observer (i.e., an "outsider"). Framo (1965), noting the necessity of family dynamics researchers to acquaint themselves with family treatment, concluded that "It will be hard for anyone who has seen families under the emotional impact of treatment to ever again do family research in the traditional ways. For the first time he will be viewing the family where it lives emotionally. . ." (p. 455). The family therapist does not ultimately remain within the family system, but during the process of treatment he or she is at times as

much a part of the family dynamics as is any member of the family being helped (Minuchin, 1974; Whitaker, 1975). Thus, although the family therapist is only temporarily an "insider" of the *family* system, he or she is always an "insider" of the *treatment* system.

We suggest that in deciding on the perspective from which change in marital/family therapy should be assessed, researchers must consider two dimensions: the perceiver's insideness-outsideness relative to the *treatment system* and the degree of inference involved in making a given judgment. In decreasing order of insideness, we see the following potential evaluative sources: family members, therapist(s), therapy supervisors, significant others, trained judges making inferential assessments (e.g., family members' individuation), objective observers recording noninferential public events (e.g., smiles, self-reference statements), and computers and machines doing likewise (e.g., voice-activated apparatus to record speech duration).

The degree of inference involved in a given judgment increases from simple behavior counts (Level I), to nonbehavioral self-report (Level II), to nonbehavioral reports of "self in relationship to others" (and vice versa) (Level III), to system properties and individual psychodynamics (Level IV). Not all levels are meaningfully or economically assessed by all possible sources. For example, Level IV variables are best judged by the therapist providing treatment or by expert professional judges, Level III variables by family members, Level II variables by family members and/or expert judges (e.g., TAT responses and interpretation), and Level I variables by objective observers or machines. It is obviously much more difficult to measure validly and reliably Level IV variables than variables at Levels I, II, and III.

Marital and family therapy clearly increases the number of potential perspectives from which change may be evaluated, perspectives that, as noted above, will often produce differing evaluations of therapy-induced change. Research that assesses change in several family members and subsystems from multiple perspectives will produce a matrix of outcomes instead of a single index of change. Moreover, developmental considerations in terms of the marital and family life cycle will affect the ways in which family members view both their therapy experience and their therapeutic changes. The interpretive complexity of data generated in this way is likely to be great; we believe that such a matrix will be more representative of "true change" and will ultimately be of increased value to both clinicians and theoreticians.

CODA

We would like to add a final note on the implications of thinking in family systems terms for research on individual psychotherapy. Not unlike others before us (Fisher & Mendell, 1958; Fox, 1968; Hurvitz, 1967; Kohl, 1962; Sager et al., 1968), we assert that a research view of change in individual psychotherapy that ignores the familial or marital context and consequences of individual change is probably incomplete and clinically misleading, if not myopic. When we (Gurman & Kniskern, 1976) first suggested this notion at a national meeting on psychotherapy research, one of our colleagues who is both an active clinician and researcher of psychotherapy provocatively commented that to implement this view, in the face of the complexities already facing individual therapy researchers, would "throw the whole field into chaos." We doubt that such a dramatic consequence would ensue but, despite the consequences, we do strongly believe that our position reflects clinical reality. About two decades ago, family therapists began to challenge the assumptions of individually oriented therapists. It is fitting that family therapy *researchers* now begin to question some of the views of *their* forebears.

REFERENCES

Abramowitz, C. V. The effectiveness of group psychotherapy with children. *Archives of General Psychiatry*, 1976, *33*, 320–326.

Abroms, G., Fellner, C., & Whitaker, C. The family enters the hospital. *American Journal of Psychiatry*, 1971, *127*, 99–105.

Alexander, J., & Barton, C. Behavioral systems therapy with delinquent families. In D. H. L. Olson (Ed.), *Treating relationships*. Lake Mills, Ia.: Graphic, 1976.

Alexander, J., Barton, C., Schiavo, R. S., & Parsons, B. V. Systems-behavioral intervention with families of delinquents: Therapist characteristics, family behavior and outcome. *Journal of Consulting and Clinical Psychology*, 1976, *44*, 656–664.

Alexander, J., & Parsons, B. Short-term behavioral intervention with delinquent families: Impact on family process and recidivism. *Journal of Abnormal Psychology*, 1973, *81*, 219–225.

Alkire, A. A., & Brunse, A. J. Impact and possible casualty from videotape feedback in marital therapy. *Journal of Consulting and Clinical Psychology*, 1974, *42*, 203–210.

Amdur, M., Tucker, G., Detre, T., & Markus, K. Anorexia nervosa: An interactional study. *Journal of Nervous and Mental Disease*, 1969, *148*, 559–566.

Ard, B. Providing clinical supervision for marriage counselors: A model for supervisor and supervisee. *Family Coordinator*, 1973, *22*, 91–97.

Arnold, J. E., Levine, A. G., & Patterson, G. R. Changes in sibling behavior following family intervention. *Journal of Consulting and Clinical Psychology*, 1975, *43*, 683–688.

Auerbach, A., & Johnson, M. Research on the therapist's level of experience. In A. Gurman and A. Razin (Eds.) *Effective psychotherapy: A handbook of research*. New York: Pergamon, 1977.

Axelrod, S., Brander, M., Cole, B., Dougherty, P., Crystal, J., & Hammer, T. Use of behavior modification procedures in marital situations by nonprofessionals. Paper presented at the meeting of the Association for the Advancement of Behavior Therapy, San Francisco, December 1975.

Azrin, N. H., Naster, B. J., & Jones, R. Reciprocity counseling: A rapid learning-based procedure for marital counseling. *Behavior Research and Therapy*, 1973, *11*, 365–382.

Baird, J. P. Changes in patterns of interpersonal behavior among family members following brief family-therapy. (Doctoral dissertation, Columbia University, New York, 1972.) *Dissertation Abstracts International*, 1973, *34*, 404B.

Baird, E., & Redfering, D. L. Behavior modification in marriage counseling. *Journal of Family Counseling*, 1975, *3*, 59–64.

Ballard, R. G., & Mudd, E. H. Some theoretical and practical problems in evaluating effectiveness of counseling. *Social Casework*, 1957, *38*, 533–538.

Beal, D., & Duckro, P. Family counseling as an alternative to legal action for the juvenile status offender. *Journal of Marriage and Family Counseling*, 1977, *3*, 77–81.

Beal, E. W. Current trends in the training of family therapists. *American Journal of Psychiatry*, 1976, *133*, 137–141.

Beck, D. F. Research findings on the outcomes of marital counseling. *Social Casework*, 1975, *56*, 153–181.

Beck, D. F., & Jones, M. A. *Progress on family problems: A nationwide study of clients' and counselors' views on family agency services*. New York: Family Service Association of America, 1973.

Becker, J. "Good premorbid" schizophrenic wives and their husbands. *Family Process*, 1963, *2*, 34–51.

Becking, E. P. Pretraining effects on maladaptive marital behavior within a behavior modification approach.

(Doctoral dissertation, California School of Professional Psychology, San Francisco, 1972.) *Dissertation Abstracts International,* 1973, *33,* 5007B.

Bednar, R. L., & Lawlis, G. F. Empirical research in group psychotherapy. In A. E. Bergin and S. L. Garfield (Eds.), *Handbook of psychotherapy and behavior change.* New York: Wiley, 1971.

Bell, J. E. *Family therapy.* New York: Jason Aronson, 1975.

Bellville, T. P., Raths, O. N., & Belleville, C. J. Conjoint marriage therapy with a husband-and-wife team. *American Journal of Orthopsychiatry,* 1969, *39,* 473–483.

Ben-Ami, U. The effects of pretreatment training on certain intake interview behaviors of family members. *Dissertation Abstracts International,* 1976, *37,* 3060–3061B.

Bergin, A. E. The evaluation of therapeutic outcomes. In A. E. Bergin and S. L. Garfield (Eds.), *Handbook of psychotherapy and behavior change.* New York: Wiley, 1971.

Bergin, A. E., & Strupp, H. H. New directions in psychotherapy research. *Journal of Abnormal Psychology,* 1970, *76,* 13–26.

Bernal, M. E., & Margolin, G. Outcome of intervention strategies for discipline problem children. Paper presented at the Association for the Advancement of Behavior Therapy, New York, December 1976.

Bertalanffy, L. General systems theory and psychiatry. In S. Arieti (Ed.), *American handbook of psychiatry.* Vol. III. New York: Basic Books, 1966.

Beutler, L. E. Attitude similarity in marital therapy. *Journal of Consulting and Clinical Psychology,* 1971, *37,* 298–301.

Birchler, G. R. Live supervision and instant feedback in marriage and family therapy. *Journal of Marriage and Family Counseling,* 1975, *1,* 331–342.

Birchler, G. R., & Webb, L. A social learning formulation of discriminating interaction behaviors in happy and unhappy marriages. Paper presented at the Southwest Psychological Association, Houston, April 1975.

Birchler, G. R., Weiss, R. L., & Vincent, J. P. A multidimensional analysis of social reinforcement exchange between maritally distressed and nondistressed spouse and stranger dyads. *Journal of Personality and Social Psychology,* 1975, *31,* 349–360.

Birchler, G. R., Weiss, R. L., & Wampler, L. D. Differential patterns of social reinforcement as a function of degree of marital distress and level of intimacy. Paper presented at the Western Psychological Association, Portland, April 1972.

Birk, L., & Brinkley-Birk, A. W. Psychoanalysis and behavior therapy. *American Journal of Psychiatry,* 1974, *131,* 499–509.

Blechman, E. A., & Olson, D. H. L. Stimulus control over family problem solving behavior. Paper presented at the Eastern Psychological Association, New York, 1975.

Blechman, E. A., & Olson, D. H. L. The family contract game: Description and effectivness. In D. H. L. Olson (Ed.), *Treating relationships.* Lake Mills, Ia.: Graphic, 1976.

Blechman, E. A., Olson, D. H. L., & Hellman, I. Stimulus control over family problem-solving behavior: The family contract game. *Behavior Therapy,* 1976, *7,* 686–692.

Bodin, A. Family therapy training literature—a brief guide. *Family Process,* 1969a, *8,* 272–297.

Bodin, A. Videotape applications in training family therapists. *Journal of Nervous and Mental Disease,* 1969b, *148,* 251–261.

Boszormenyi-Nagy, I., & Spark, G. M. *Invisible loyalities.* New York: Harper & Row, 1973.

Bowen, M. The family as the unit of study and treatment. *American Journal of Orthopsychiatry,* 1961, *31,* 40–60.

Boyd, W. H., & Bolen, D. W. The compulsive gambler and spouse in group psychotherapy. *International Journal of Group Psychotherapy,* 1970, *20,* 77–90.

Brandreth, A., & Pike, R. Assessment of marriage counseling in a small family agency. *Social Work,* 1967, *12,* 34–39.

Brown, E. M. Divorce counseling. In D.H.L. Olson (Ed.), *Treating relationships.* Lake Mills, Ia.: Graphic, 1976.

Bruch, H. Death in anorexia nervosa. *Psychosomatic Medicine,* 1971, *33,* 135–144.

Budman, S., & Shapiro, R. Patients' evaluations of successful outcome in family and individual therapy. Unpublished manuscript, University of Rochester Medical School, 1976.

Burton, G., & Kaplan, H. M. Group counseling in conflicted marriages where alcoholism is present: Clients' evaluation of effectiveness. *Journal of Marriage and the Family,* 1968, *30,* 74–79.

Burks, H., & Serrano, A. The use of family therapy and brief hospitalization. *Diseases of the Nervous System,* 1965, *26,* 804–806.

Cadogan, D. A. Marital group therapy in the treatment of alcoholism. *Quarterly Journal of Studies on Alcoholism,* 1973, *34,* 1187–1194.

Cardillo, J. P. Effects of teaching communication roles on interpersonal perception and self-concept in disturbed marriages. *Proceedings, 79th Annual Convention of the American Psychological Association,* 1971, 441–442.

Carroll, E. J., Cambor, C. G., Leopold, J. V., Miller, M. D., & Reis, W. J. Psychotherapy of marital couples. *Family Process,* 1963, *2,* 25–33.

Carter, R. D. & Thomas, E. J. A case application of a signaling system (SAM) to the assessment and modification of selected problems of marital communication. *Behavior Therapy,* 1973a, *4,* 629–645.

Carter, R. D., & Thomas, E. J. Modification of problematic marital communication using corrective feedback and instruction. *Behavior Therapy,* 1973b, *4,* 100–109.

Cassidy, M. J. Communication training for marital pairs. Unpublished doctoral dissertation, University of California, Los Angeles, 1973.

Christensen, A. Cost effectiveness in behavioral family therapy. *Dissertation Abstracts International,* 1976, *37,* 3066B.

Christensen, D. J. The effects of intramarriage self-esteem and decision making on a structured marriage counseling program emphasizing interspouse supportiveness. *Dissertation Abstracts International,* 1974, *35,* 3141A.

Cleghorn, J. M., & Levin, S. Training family therapists by setting learning objectives. *American Journal of Orthopsychiatry,* 1973, *43,* 439–446.

Cole, C., & Morrow, W. R. Refractory parent behaviors in behavior modification training groups. *Psychotherapy,* 1976, *13,* 162–169.

Cookerly, J. R. The outcome of the six major forms of marriage counseling: A pilot study. *Journal of Marriage and the Family,* 1973, *35,* 608–611.

Cookerly, J. R. The reduction of psychopathology as measured by the MMPI clinical scales in three forms of marriage counseling. *Journal of Marriage and the Family,* 1974, *36,* 332–335.

Cookerly, J. R. Evaluating different approaches to marriage counseling. In D. H. L. Olson (Ed.), *Treating relationships.* Lake Mills, Ia.: Graphic, 1976.

Corder, B. F., Corder, R. F., & Laidlaw, N. D. An intensive program for alcoholics and their wives. *Quarterly Journal of Studies on Alcoholism,* 1972, *33,* 1144–1146.

Corson, J. A. Families as mutual control systems: Optimization by systematization of reinforcement. In E. J. Mash, L. A. Hamerlynck, and L. C. Handy (Eds.), *Behavior modification and families.* New York: Brunner/Mazel, 1975.

Cotton, M. C. A systems approach to marital training evaluation. Unpublished doctoral dissertation, Texas Tech University, 1976.

Coufal, J. D. Preventive-therapeutic programs for mothers and adolescent daughters: Skills training versus discussion methods. Unpublished doctoral dissertation, Pennsylvania State University, 1975.

Coughlin, F., & Wimberger, H. Group family therapy. *Family Process,* 1968, *7,* 37–50.

Cromwell, R., Olson, D., & Fournier, D. Diagnosis and evaluation in marital and family counseling. In D. H. L. Olson (Ed.), *Treating relationships.* Lake Mills, Ia.: Graphic, 1976.

Crowe, M. J. Conjoint marital therapy: Advice or interpretation? *Journal of Psychosomatic Research,* 1973, *17,* 309–315.

Crowe, M. J. *Conjoint marital therapy: advice or interpretation?* Unpublished data, Institute of Psychiatry, University of London, 1974.

D'Angelo, R., & Walsh, J. F. An evaluation of various therapy approaches with lower socio-economic group children. *Journal of Psychology,* 1967, *67,* 59–64.

Davenport, Y. B., Ebert, M. H., Adland, M. L., & Goodwin, F. W. Lithium prophylaxis: The married couples group. Paper presented at the meeting of the American Psychiatric Association, Anaheim, California, 1975.

De Chenne, T. K. Experiential facilitaton in conjoint marriage counseling. *Psychotherapy,* 1973, *10,* 212–214.

Dell, P. F., Sheely, M. D., Pulliam, G. P., & Goolishian, H. A. Family therapy process in a family therapy seminar. *Journal of Marriage and Family Counseling,* 1977, *3,* 43–48.

Dezen, A. E., & Borstein, I. J. The effects of family sys-

tems interventions on juvenile delinquents and their families by probation officers. Unpublished manuscript, Institute for Juvenile Research, Chicago, 1975.

Dicks, H. V. *Marital tensions.* New York: Basic Books, 1967.

Donner, J., & Gamson, A. Experience with multifamily, time-limited, outpatient groups at a community psychiatric clinic. *Psychiatry,* 1968, *31,* 126–137.

Edelson, R. I., & Seidman, E. Use of videotaped feedback in altering interpersonal perceptions of married couples: A therapy analogue. *Journal of Consulting and Clinical Psychology,* 1975, *43,* 244–250.

Ehrenkranz, S. M. A study of joint interviewing in the treatment of marital problems: Part II. *Social Casework,* 1967, *48,* 570–574.

Eisler, R. M., & Hersen, M. Some considerations in the measurement and modification of marital interaction. Paper presented at the Association for the Advancement of Behavior. Therapy, New York, October 1972.

Eisler, R. M., & Hersen, M. Behavioral techniques in family-oriented crisis intervention. *Archives of General Psychiatry,* 1973, *28,* 111–115.

Eisler, R. M., Hersen, M., & Agras, W. S. Effects of videotape and instructional feedback on nonverbal martal interaction: An analog study. *Behavior Therapy,* 1973, *4,* 551–558. (a)

Eisler, R. M., Hersen, M., & Agras, W. S. Videotape: A method for the controlled observation of nonverbal interpersonal behavior. *Behavior Therapy,* 1973, *4,* 420–425. (b)

Eisler, R. M., Miller, P. M., Hersen, M., & Alford, H. Effects of assertive training on marital interaction. *Archives of General Psychiatry,* 1974, *30,* 643–649.

Emrick, C. D. A review of psychologically oriented treatment of alcoholism. II. The relative effectiveness of different treatment approaches and the effectiveness of treatment versus no treatment. *Journal of Studies on Alcoholism,* 1975, *36,* 88–108.

Emrick, C. D., Lassen, C. L., & Edwards, M. T. Nonprofessional peers as therapeutic agents. In A. Gurman and A. Razin (Eds.), *Effective psychotherapy: A handbook of research.* New York: Pergamon, 1977.

Epstein, N., & Jackson, E. An outcome study of short-term communication training with married couples. Paper presented at the Eastern Psychological Association, New York, April 1976.

Epstein, N. B., & Levin, S. Training for family therapy within a faculty of medicine. *Canadian Psychiatric Association Journal,* 1973, *18,* 203–208.

Erickson, G. Teaching family therapy. *Journal of Education for Social Work,* 1973, *9,* 9–15.

Esterson, A., Cooper, D., & Laing, R. Results of family-oriented therapy with hospitalized schizophrenics. *British Medical Journal,* 1965, *2,* 1462–1465.

Evans, H., Chagoya, L., & Rakoff, V. Devision-making as to the choice of family therapy in an adolescent in-patient setting. *Family Process,* 1971, *10,* 97–110.

Ewing, C. P. Family crisis intervention and traditional child guidance: A comparison of outcomes and factors related to success in treatment. (Doctoral Dissertation, Cornell University, 1975.) *Dissertation Abstracts International,* 1976, *36,* 4686B.

Ewing, J. A., Long, V., & Wenzel, G. G. Concurrent group psychotherapy of alcoholic patients and their wives. *Internationl Journal of Group Psychotherapy,* 1961, *11,* 329–338.

Eyberg, S. M., & Johnson, S. M. Multiple assessment of behavior modification with families: Effects of contingency contracting and order of treated problems. *Journal of Consulting and Clinical Psychology,* 1974, *42,* 599–606.

Fanshel, D. *An overview of one agency's casework operations.* Pittsburgh: Family and Children's Service, 1958.

Feather, B. W., & Rhoads, J. M. Psychodynamic behavior therapy. I. Theory and rationale. *Archives of General Psychiatry,* 1972, *26,* 496–502.

Fensterheim, H. Assertive methods and marital problems. In R. Rubin, H. Fensterheim, J. Henderson, and L. Ullmann (Eds.), *Advances in behavior therapy.* New York: Academic Press, 1972.

Ferber, A., & Mendelsohn, M. Training for family therapy. *Family Process,* 1969, *8,* 25–32.

Ferber, H., Keeley, S., & Shemberg, K. Training parents in behavior modification: Outcome of and problems encountered in a program after Patterson's work. *Behavior Therapy,* 1974, *5,* 415–419.

Finol, G. J. The influence of three methods of interpersonal process recall upon parental verbal interaction with a mentally retarded child using short-term family psychotherapy. (Doctoral dissertation, University of Pittsburgh, 1973.) *Dissertation Abstracts International,* 1973, *34,* 1274B.

Fisher, E. O. A guide to divorce counseling. *Family Coordinator,* 1973, *22,* 291–297.

Fisher, R. E. The effect of two group counseling methods on perceptual congruence in married pairs. (Doctoral dissertation, University of Hawaii, 1973.) *Dissertation Abstracts International,* 1974, *35,* 885A.

Fisher, S., & Mendell, D. The spread of psychotherapeutic effects from the patient to his family group. *Psychiatry,* 1958, *21,* 133–140.

Fiske, D. W. A source of data is not a measuring instrument. *Journal of Abnormal Psychology,* 1975, *84,* 20–23.

Fiske, D. W. Methodological issues in research on the psychotherapist. In A. S. Gurman and A. M. Razin (Eds.), *Effective psychotherapy: A handbook of research.* New York: Pergamon, 1977.

Fitzgerald, R. V. Conjoint marital psychotherapy: An outcome and follow-up study. *Family Process,* 1969, *8,* 260–271.

Follingstad, D. R., Haynes, S. N., & Sullivan, J. Assessment of the components of a behavioral marital intervention program. Paper presented at the Association for the Advancement of Behavior Therapy, New York, December 1976.

Fordney-Settlage, D. S. Heterosexual dysfunction: Evaluation of treatment procedures. *Archives of Sexual Behavior,* 1975, *4,* 367–387.

Fox, R. The effect of psychotherapy on the spouse. *Family Process,* 1968, *7,* 7–16.

Fox, R. Family therapy. In I. Weiner (Ed.), *Clinical methods in psychology.* New York: Wiley, 1976.

Framo, J. L. Systematic research on family dynamics. In I. Boszormenyi-Nagy and J. Framo (Eds.), *Intensive family therapy.* New York: Harper and Row, 1965.

Framo, J. L. Marriage therapy in a couples group. In D. Bloch (Eds.), *Techniques of family therapy: A primer.* New York: Grune & Stratton, 1973.

Framo, J. L. Divorce therapy. Paper presented at the National Council on Family Relations, St. Louis, October 1974.

Framo, J. L. Personal reflections of a family therapist. *Journal of Marriage and Family Counseling,* 1975, *1,* 15–28.

Framo, J. L. Family of origin as a therapeutic resource for adults in marital and family therapy: You can and should go home again. *Family Process,* 1976, *15,* 193–210.

Freeman, S. J. J., Leavens, E. J., & McCulloch, D. J. Factors associated with success or failure in marital counseling. *Family Coordinator,* 1969, *18,* 125–128.

Freeman, V., Klein, A., & Rubenstein, F. *Final report family study project.* Pittsburgh, Pa.: Allegheny General Hospital, 1964.

Friedman, A. S. Interaction of drug therapy with marital therapy in depressive patients. *Archives of General Psychiatry,* 1975, *32,* 619–637.

Friedman, P. M. Personalistic family and marital therapy. In A. Lazarus (Ed.), *Clinical behavior therapy.* New York: Brunner/Mazel, 1972.

Furmansky, B. S. A comparison of alcoholics' group therapy: with and without their spouses. Unpublished manuscript, University of Colorado Medical Center, 1976.

Gallant, P. M., Rich, A., Bey, E., & Terranova, L. Group psychotherapy with married couples: A successful technique in New Orleans alcoholism clinic patients. *Journal of Louisiana State Medical Society,* 1970, *122,* 41–44.

Garfield, S. L. Research on the training of professional psychotherapists. In A. Gurman and A. Razin (Eds.), *Effective psychotherapy: A handbook of research.* New York: Pergamon, 1977.

Garrigan, J., & Bambrick, A. Short term family therapy with emotionally disturbed children. *Journal of Marriage and Family Counseling,* 1975, *1,* 379–385.

Garrigan, J., & Bambrick, A. Family therapy for disturbed children: Some experimental results in special education. *Journal of Marriage and Family Counseling,* 1977, *3,* 83–93.

Gartner, R., Fulmer, R., Weinshel, M., Goldklank, S., & Bresnihan, W. A retrospective study of the effects of family constellation on the course of family therapy. Paper presented at the Society for Psychotherapy Research, Boston, 1975.

Ginsberg, B. G. Parent-adolescent relationship development: A therapeutic and preventative mental health program. Unpublished doctoral dissertation, Pennsylvania State University, 1971.

Glass, G. V. Meta-analysis of psychotherapy outcome studies. Paper presented at the Society for Psychotherapy Research, San Diego, June 1976.

Gliedman, L. H. Concurrent and combined group treatment of chronic alcoholics and their wives. *Interna-*

tional Journal of Group Psychotherapy, 1957, 7, 414–424.

Gliedman, L. H., Rosenthal, D., Frank, J. D., & Nash, H. T. Group therapy of alcoholics with concurrent group meetings of their wives. *Quarterly Journal of Studies on Alcoholism,* 1956, 17, 655–670.

Glisson, D. H. A review of behavioral marital counseling: Has practice tuned out theory? *Psychological Record,* 1976, 26, 95–104.

Gluck, M. R., Tanner, M. M., Sullivan, D. F., & Erickson, P. A. Follow-up evaluation of 55 child guidance cases. *Behavior Research and Therapy,* 1964, 2, 131–134.

Goldiamond, I. Self-control procedures in personal behavior problems. *Psychological Reports,* 1965, 17, 851–868.

Goldstein, M. K. Behavior rate change in marriages: Training wives to modify husbands' behavior. (Doctoral dissertation, Cornell University, 1971.) *Dissertation Abstracts International,* 1971, 32, 559B.

Goldstein, M. K. The behavioral re-creation of love: Not doin' what comes naturally. Paper presented at the Association for the Advancement of Behavior Therapy, San Francisco, December 1975.

Goldstein, M. K. Increasing positive behaviors in married couples. In J. D. Krumboltz and C. E. Thoresen (Eds.), *Counseling methods.* New York: Holt, Rinehart & Winston, 1976.

Goldstein, M. K., & Francis, B. Behavior modification of husbands by wives. Paper presented at the National Council on Family Relations, Washington, D.C., October 1969.

Goode, W. J. *After divorce.* New York: Macmillan, 1956.

Goodman, E. S. Marriage counseling as science: Some research considerations. *Family Coordinator,* 1973, 22, 111–116.

Gottman, J., Notarius, C., Markman, H., Bank, S., & Yoppi, B. Behavior exchange theory and marital decision-making. *Journal of Personality and Social Psychology,* 1976, 34, 14–23.

Gould, E., & Glick, I. Families, family therapy and schizophrenia in an impatient setting: A one year follow-up. Unpublished manuscript, Langley Porter Neuro-psychiatric Institute, 1976.

Graham, J. A. The effect of the use of counselor positive responses to positive perceptions of mate in marriage counseling. *Dissertation Abstracts International,* 1968, 28, 3504A.

Greenberg, I., Glick, I., Match, S., & Riback, S. Family therapy: Indications and rationale. *Archives of General Psychiatry,* 1964, 10, 7–24.

Greene, B. L., Lee, R. R., & Lustig, N. Transient structured distance as a maneuver in marital therapy. *Family Coordinator,* 1973, 22, 15–22.

Greene, B. L., Lee, R. R. & Lustig, N. Treatment of marital disharmony where one spouse has a primary affective disorder (manic depressive illness): I. General overview—100 couples. *Journal of Marriage and Family Counseling,* 1975, 1, 39–50.

Greer, S. E., & D'Zurilla, T. J. Behavioral approaches to marital discord and conflict. *Journal of Marriage and Family Counseling,* 1975, 1, 299–315.

Griffin, R. W. Change in perception of marital relationship as related to marriage counseling. *Dissertation Abstracts International,* 1967, 27, 3956A.*

Group for the Advancement of Psychiatry (GAP). *Treatment of families in conflict.* New York: Science House, 1970.

Grunebaum, H., Christ, J., & Neiberg, N. Diagnosis and treatment planning for couples. *International Journal of Group Psychotherapy,* 1969, 19, 185–202.

Guerney, B., & Stover, L. *Filial therapy.* Unpublished paper, Pennsylvania State University, 1971.

Gurin, E., Veroff, J., & Feld, S. *Americans view their mental health.* New York: Basic Books, 1960.

Gurman, A. S. Group marital therapy: Clinical and empirical implications for outcome research. *International Journal of Group Psychotherapy,* 1971, 21, 174–189.

Gurman, A. S. Marital therapy: Emerging trends in research and practice. *Family Process,* 1973a, 12, 45–54.

Gurman, A. S. The effects and effectiveness of marital therapy: A review of outcome research. *Family Process,* 1973b, 12, 145–170.

Gurman, A. S. Therapist, patient and treatment factors influencing the outcome of marital therapy. Unpublished data, University of Wisconsin Medical School, 1973c.

Gurman, A. S. Attitude change in marital cotherapy. *Journal of Family Counseling,* 1974 2, 50–54.

Gurman, A. S. Some therapeutic implications of marital therapy research. In A. S. Gurman and D. G. Rice (Eds.), *Couples in conflict: New directions in marital therapy.* New York: Aronson, 1975a.

Gurman, A. S. Couples' facilitative communication skill as a dimension of marital therapy outcome. *Journal of Marriage and Family Counseling,* 1975b, 1, 163–174.

Gurman, A. S. Evaluating the outcomes of marital therapy. Paper presented at the Society for Psychotherapy Research, Boston, June 1975c.

Gurman, A. S. Limitations and misuses of behavioral-exchange programs in couples therapy. Paper presented at the Association for the Advancement of Behavior Therapy, San Francisco, December 1975d.

Gurman, A. S. The patient's perception of the therapeutic relationship. In A. Gurman and A. Razin (Eds.), *Effective psychotherapy: A handbook of research.* New York: Pergamon, 1977.

Gurman, A. S. Contemporary marital therapies: A critique and comparative analysis of psychoanalytic, systems and behavioral approaches. In T. Paolino and B. McCrady (Eds.), *Marriage and marital disorders from different perspectives.* New York: Brunner/Mazel, 1978.

Gurman, A. S., & Kniskern, D. P. Deterioration in marital and family therapy: empirical and conceptual issues. Paper presented at the Society for Psychotherapy Research, San Diego, June 1976.

Gurman, A. S., & Kniskern, D. P. Behavioral marriage therapy: II. Empirical perspective. *Family Process,* 1978a, in press.

Gurman, A. S., & Kniskern, D. P. Deterioration in marital and family therapy: empirical, clinical and conceptual issues. *Family Process,* 1978b, 17, 3–20.

Gurman, A. S., & Kniskern, D. P. Enriching research on

marital enrichment programs. *Journal of Marriage and Family Counseling,* 1977, *3,* 3–11.

Gurman, A. S., & Knudson, R. M. Behavioral marriage therapy: I. A psychodynamic-systems critique and reconsideration. *Family Process,* 1978, in press.

Gurman, A. S., & Razin, A. M. *Effective psychotherapy: A handbook of research.* New York: Pergamon, 1977.

Guttman, H. A. A contraindication for family therapy: The prepsychotic or postpsychotic young adult and his parents. *Archives of General Psychiatry,* 1973, *2,* 352–355.

Guttman, H. A., Sigal, J. J., & Chagoya, L. Time-unit coding from the audio-taped interview: A simple method of coding therapy behavior. *Journal of Clinical Psychology,* 1972, *28,* 112–114.

Guttman, H. A., Spector, R. M., Sigal, J. J., Rakoff, V., & Epstein, N. B. Reliability of coding affecting communication in family therapy sessions: Problems of measurement and interpretation. *Journal of Consulting and Clinical Psychology,* 1971, *37,* 397–402.

Guttman, H. A., Spector, R. M., Sigal, J. J., Epstein, N. B., & Rakoff, V. Coding of affective expression in family therapy. *American Journal of Psychotherapy,* 1972, *26,* 185–194.

Guzzetta, R. A. Acquisition and transfer of empathy by the parents of early adolescents through structured learning training. *Journal of Counseling Psychology,* 1976, *23,* 449–453.

Haley, J. An editor's farewell. *Family Process,* 1969, *8,* 149–158.

Haley, J. *Changing families.* New York: Grune & Stratton, 1971.

Haley J. Fourteen ways to fail as a teacher of family therapy. *Family Therapy,* 1974, *1,* 1–8.

Hardcastle, D. R. Measuring effectiveness in group marital counseling. *Family Coordinator,* 1972, *21,* 213–218.

Hardcastle, D. R. A mother-child, multiple family counseling program: Procedures and results. *Family Process,* 1977, *16,* 67–74.

Harrell, J., & Guerney, B. Training married couples in conflict negotiation skills. In D. H. L. Olson (Ed.), *Treating relationships.* Lake Mills, Ia.: Graphic, 1976.

Hartman, W. E., & Fithian, M. A. *Treatment of sexual dysfunction.* Long Beach, Calif.: Center for Marital and Sexual Studies, 1972.

Hedberg, A. G., & Campbell, L. A comparison of four behavioral treatments of alcoholism. *Journal of Behavior Therapy and Psychiatry,* 1974, *5,* 251–256.

Hendricks, W. J. Use of multifamily counseling groups in treatment of male narcotic addicts. *International Journal of Group Psychotherapy,* 1971, *21,* 84–90.

Hepworth, D. H., & Smith, V. G. Partner participation and outcomes in marriage counseling. Unpublished manuscript, University of Utah, 1972.

Hickman, M. E., & Baldwin, B. A. Use of programmed instruction to improve communication in marriage. *Family Coordinator,* 1970, *20,* 121–125.

Hickok, J. E., & Komechak, M. G. Behavior modification in marital conflict: A case report. *Family Process,* 1974, *13,* 111–119.

Hixenbaugh, E. R. Reconciliation of marital maladjustment: An analysis of 101 cases. *Social Forces,* 1931, *10,* 230–236.

Hollis, F. *Women in marital conflict: A casework study.* New York: Family Service Association of America, 1949.

Hollis, F. Evaluating marriage counseling. *Marriage and Family Living,* 1950, *12,* 37–38.

Hollis, F. The coding and application of a typology of casework treatment. *Social Casework,* 1967, *48,* 489–497.

Hollis, F. Continuance and discontinuance in marital counseling and some observations on joint interviews. *Social Casework,* 1968a, *49,* 167–174.

Hollis, F. A profile of early interviews in marital counseling. *Social Casework,* 1968b, *49,* 35–43.

Hooper, D., Sheldon, A., & Koumans, A. J. R. A study of group psychotherapy in married couples. *International Journal of Social Psychiatry,* 1968, *15,* 57–68.

Hops, H., Wills, T. A., Patterson, G. R., & Weiss, R. L. Marital interaction coding system. Unpublished manuscript, University of Oregon, 1971.

Hurvitz, N. Marital problems following psychotherapy with one spouse. *Journal of Consulting Psychology,* 1967, *31,* 38–47.

Ives, P., Schwall, R., & Henderson, M. The effectiveness of short-term multidimensional family intervention in working with families with adolescent problems. Unpublished Masters' thesis, Catholic University of America, 1975.

Jackson, D., & Weakland, J. Conjoint family therapy: Some considerations on theory, technique and results. *Psychiatry,* 1961, *24,* 30–45.

Jacob, T. Family interaction in disturbed and normal families: A methodological and substantive review. *Psychological Bulletin,* 1975, *82,* 33–65.

Jacob, T. Assessment of marital dysfunction. In M. Hersen and A. Bellack (Eds.), *Behavioral assessment: A handbook.* New York: Pergamon, 1976.

Jacobson, N. S. Problem-solving and contingency contracting in the treatment of marital discord. *Journal of Consulting and Clinical Psychology,* 1977, *45,* 92–100.

Jacobson, N. S. Specific and non-specific factors in the effectiveness of a behavioral approach to marital discord. *Journal of Consulting and Clinical Psychology,* 1978, in press.

Jacobson, N. S., & Martin, B. Behavioral marriage therapy: Current status. *Psychological Bulletin,* 1976, *83,* 540–556.

Jansma, T. J. Multiple vs. individual family-therapy: Its effects on family concepts. Unpublished doctoral dissertation, Illinois Institute of Technology, 1971.

Johnson, S. M., Bolstad, O. D., & Lobitz, G. K. Generalization and contrast phenomena in behavior modification with children. In E. J. Nash, L. A. Hamerlynck, and L. C. Handy (Eds.), *Behavior modification and families.* New York: Brunner/Mazel, 1975.

Johnson, S. M., & Christensen, A. Multiple criteria follow-up of behavior modification with families. *Journal of Abnormal Psychology,* 1975, *3,* 135–154.

Johnson, S., Christensen, A., & Bellamy, T. Evaluation of family interventions through unobtrusive audio recordings: Experience in bugging children. *Journal of Applied Behavior Analysis,* in press.

Johnson, T. M. Effects of family therapy on patterns of verbal interchange in disturbed families. Unpublished doctoral dissertation, Fuller Theological Seminary, 1971.

Jones, B. S. Functions of meaning clarification by therapists in a psychotherapy group. (Doctoral dissertation, University of Colorado, 1968.) *Dissertation Abstracts International,* 1969, *29,* 3706A.

Kaffman, M. Short-term family therapy. *Family Process,* 1963, *2,* 216–234.

Kaplan, H. S. *The new sex therapy.* New York: Brunner/Mazel, 1974.

Karoly, P., & Rosenthal, M. Training parents in behavior modification: Effects on perceptions of family interactions and deviant child behavior. *Behavior Therapy,* 1977, *8,* 406–410.

Kaswan, J., & Love, L. Confrontation as a method of psychological intervention. *Journal of Nervous and Mental Disease,* 1969, *148,* 224–237.

Katz, A., Krasinski, M., Philip, E., & Wieser, C. Change in interactions as a measure of effectiveness in short term family therapy. *Family Therapy,* 1975, *2,* 31–56.

Keeley, S., Shemberg, K., & Carbonell, J. Operant clinical intervention: Behavior management or beyond? Where are the data? *Behavior Therapy,* 1976, *7,* 292–305.

Kind, J. The relationship of communication efficiency to marital happiness and an evaluation of short-term training in interpersonal communication with married couples. *Dissertation Abstracts International,* 1968, *29,* 1173B.

Kinder, B. N., & Blakeney, P. Treatment of sexual dysfunction: A review of outcome studies. Unpublished manuscript, University of Texas Medical Branch, 1976.

Klein, N., Alexander, J., & Parsons, B. Impact of family systems intervention on recidivism and sibling delinquency: A study of primary prevention. Paper presented at the Western Psychological Association, Sacramento, 1975.

Knight, N. A. The effects of changes in family interpersonal relationships on the behavior of eneuretic children and their parents. (Doctoral dissertation, University of Hawaii, 1974.) *Dissertation Abstracts International,* 1975, *36,* 783A.

Kniskern, D. P. Research prospects and perspectives in family therapy. Paper presented at the Society for Psychotherapy Research, Boston, June 1975.

Knox, D. Behavior contracts in marriage counseling. *Journal of Family Counseling,* 1973, *1,* 22–28.

Koch, J., & Koch, L. *The marriage savers.* New York: Coward, McCann & Geoghegan, 1976.

Kohl, R. N., Pathologic reactions of marital partners to improvement of patients. *American Journal of Psychiatry, 1962, 118,* 1036–1041.

Kressel, K., & Slipp, S. Perceptions of marriage related to engagement in conjoint therapy. *Journal of Marriage and Family Counseling,* 1975, *1,* 367–377.

Kuhn, J. R. Effectiveness of marriage counseling as measured by change in self-concept. In P. Popenoe (Ed.), *Techniques of marriage and family counseling.* Vol. II. Los Angeles: American Institute of Fam-

ily Relations, 1973a.

Kuhn, J. R. *Marriage counseling: Fact or fallacy?* Hollywood, Calif.: Newcastle, 1973b.

L'Abate, L. Family enrichment programs. *Journal of Family Counseling,* 1974, *2,* 32–44.

Lambert, J., Bergin, A., & Collins, J. Therapist-induced deterioration in psychotherapy. In A. Gurman and A. Razin (Eds.), *Effective psychotherapy: A handbook of research.* New York: Pergamon, 1977.

Landgraf, J. R. The impact of therapeutic marital separation on spouses in pastoral marriage counseling. (Doctoral dissertation, school of Theology at Claremont.) *Dissertation Abstracts International,* 1973, *33,* 5021B.

Langsley, D., Flomenhaft, K., & Machotka, P. Follow-up evaluation of family crisis therapy. *American Journal of Orthopsychiatry,* 1969, *39,* 753–759.

Langsley, D., Pittman, F., Machotka, P., & Flomenhaft, K. Family crisis therapy-results and implications. *Family Process,* 1968, *7,* 145–158.

Laqueur, H., Laburt, H., & Morong, E. Multiple family therapy: Further developments. *International Journal of Social Psychiatry,* 1964, Congress Issue, 70–80.

Laughren, T., & Kass, D. Desensitization of sexual dysfunction: The present status. In A. Gurman and D. Rice (Eds.), *Couples in conflict.* New York: Aronson, 1975.

Lazarus, A. A. Behavior therapy and marriage counseling. *Journal of the Society for Psychosomatic Dentistry and Medicine,* 1968, *15,* 49–56.

Lebedun, M. Measuring movement in group marital counseling. *Social Casework,* 1970, *51,* 35–43.

Lederer, W. J., & Jackson, D. D. *Mirages of marriage.* New York: Norton, 1968.

Lee, A. R., & Mayerson, S. Inpatient individual and family therapy of acute schizophrenia patients without drugs. Unpublished manuscript, Emanuel Mental Health Center, Turlock, California, 1973.

Lessing, E. E., & Schilling, F. H. Relationship between treatment selection variables and treatment outcome in a child guidance clinic: An application of data-processing methods. *Journal of the American Academy of Child Psychiatry,* 1966, *5,* 313–348.

Levitt, E. E. The results of psychotherapy with children: An evaluation. *Journal of Consulting Psychology,* 1957, *21,* 189–196.

Levitt, E. E. Psychotherapy with children: A further evaluation. *Behavior Research and Therapy,* 1963, *1,* 45–51.

Levitt, E. E. Research on psychotherapy with children. In A. E. Bergin and S. L. Garfield (Eds.), *Handbook of psychotherapy and behavior change.* New York: Wiley, 1971.

Liberman, R. P. Behavioral approaches to family and couple therapy. *American Journal of Orthopsychiatry,* 1970, *40,* 106–118.

Liberman, R. P., Levine, J., Wheeler, E., Sanders, N., & Wallace, C. Experimental evaluation of marital group therapy: Behavioral vs. interaction-insight formats. *Acta Psychiatrica Scandinavica,* Supplement, 1976.

Linden, M. E., Goodwin, H. M., & Resnik, H. Group psychotherapy of couples in marriage counseling. *International Journal of Group Psychotherapy,*

1968, *18*, 313–324.

Locke, H. J., & Wallace, K. M. Short marital adjustment and prediction tests: Their reliability and validity. *Marriage and Family Living,* 1959, *21,* 251–255.

Loescher, D. A. Time limited group therapy for alcoholic marriages. *Medical Ecology and Clinical Research,* 1970, *3,* 30–32.

LoPiccolo, J. Personal communication, February 6, 1976.

Love L. R., Kaswan, J., & Bugental, D. E. Differential effectiveness of three clinical interventions for different socioeconomic groupings. *Journal of Consulting and Clinical Psychology,* 1972, *39,* 347–360.

Luborsky, L., Singer, B., & Luborsky, L. Comparative studies of psychotherapies: Is it true that "Everyone has won and all must have prizes?" *Archives of General Psychiatry,* 1975, *32,* 995–1008.

MacGregor, R. Multiple impact psychotherapy with families. *Family Process,* 1962, *1,* 15–29.

MacGregor, R., Ritchie, A., Serrano, A., Schuster, F. P., McDonald, E. C., & Goolishian, H. A. *Multiple impact therapy with families.* New York: McGraw-Hill, 1964.

Mace, D., & Mace, V. Marriage enrichment—a preventive group approach for couples. In D. H. L. Olson (Ed.), *Treating relationships.* Lake Mills, Ia.: Graphic, 1976.

Macon, L. B. A comparative study of two approaches to the treatment of marital dysfunction. (Doctoral dissertation, University of Southern California, 1975.) *Dissertation Abstracts International,* 1975, *36,* 4026–4027A.

Magnus, E. C. Measurement of counselor bias (sex-role stereotyping) in assessment of marital couples with traditional and non-traditional interaction patterns. (Doctoral dissertation, University of Georgia, 1975.) *Dissertation Abstracts International,* 1976, *36,* 2635A.

Maizlish, I. L., & Hurley, J. R. Attitude changes of husbands and wives in time-limited group psychotherapy. *Psychiatric Quarterly Supplement,* 1963, *37,* 230–249.

Malouf, R., & Alexander, J. Family crisis intervention: A model and technique of training. In R. E. Hardy and J. G. Cull (Eds.), *Therapeutic needs of the family.* Springfield, Ill.: Charles C Thomas, 1974.

Margolin, F.M. An approach to resolution of visitation disputes post-divorce: short-term counseling. Unpublished doctoral dissertation, United States International University, 1973.

Margolin, G. A comparison of marital interventions: behavioral, behavioral-cognitive and non-directive. Paper presented at the Western Psychological Association, Los Angeles, April 1976.

Martin, B. Family interaction associated with child disturbance: Assessment and modification. *Psychotherapy,* 1967, *4,* 30–36.

Martin, B. Brief family intervention: Effectiveness and the importance of including father. Paper presented at the Conference on Social Learning in the Family, Eugene, Oregon, 1975.

Masters, W. H., & Johnson, V. E. *Human sexual inadequacy.* Boston: Little-Brown, 1970.

Matanovich, J. P. The effects of short-term group counseling upon positive perceptions of mate in marital counseling. *Dissertation Abstracts International,* 1970, *31,* 2688A.

Mattarazzo, J. Psychotherapeutic processes. *Annual Review of Psychology,* 1965, *16,* 181–224.

Mayadas, N. S., & Duehn, W. D. Stimulus-modeling (SM) videotape for marital counseling: Method and application. *Journal of Marriage and Family Counseling,* 1977, *3,* 35–42.

McClellan, T. A., & Stieper, D. R. A structured approach to group marriage counseling. *Mental Hygiene,* 1971, *55,* 77–84.

McDermott, J. R., Jr., & Char, W. F. The undeclared war between child and family therapy. *Journal of the American Academy of Child Psychiatry,* 1974, *13,* 422–436.

McIntosh, D. M. A comparison of the effects of highly structured, partially structured, and non-structured human relations training for married couples on the dependent variables of communication, marital adjustment, and personal adjustment. (Doctoral dissertation, North Texas State University, 1975.) *Dissertation Abstracts International,* 1975, *36,* 2636–2637A.

McLean, P. D., Ogston, K., & Grauer, L. A behavioral approach to the treatment of depression. *Journal of Behavior Therapy and Experimental Psychiatry,* 1973, *4,* 323–330.

Meeks, D., & Kelly, C. Family therapy with the families of recovering alcoholics. *Quarterly Journal of Studies on Alcohol,* 1970, *31,* 399–413.

Mezydlo, L., Wauck, L. A., & Foley, J. M. The clergy as marriage counselors: A service revisited. *Journal of Religion & Health,* 1973, *22,* 278–288.

Miller, W. H., & Gottlieb, F. Predicting behavioral treatment outcome in disturbed children: A preliminary report of the responsivity index of parents. *Behavior Therapy,* 1974, *5,* 210–214.

Miller, P. M., & Hersen, M. Modification of marital interaction patterns between an alcoholic and his wife. In J. D. Krumboltz and C. E. Thoresnn (Eds.), *Behavioral counseling methods.* New York: Holt, Rinehart & Winston, 1976.

Miller, S., Nunally, E. W., & Wackman, D. B. A communication training program for couples. *Social Casework,* 1976a, *57,* 9–18.

Miller, S., Nunnally, E. W., & Wackman, D. B. Minnesota Couples Communication Program (MCCP): Premarital and marital groups. In D. H. L. Olson (Ed.), *Treating relationships.* Lake Mills, Ia.: Graphic, 1976b.

Mintz, J. The role of the therapist in assessing psychotherapy outcome. In A. Gurman and A. Razin (Eds.), *Effective psychotherapy: A handbook of research.* New York: Pergamon, 1977.

Minuchin, S. *Families and family therapy.* Cambridge, Mass.: Harvard University Press, 1974.

Minuchin, S., Baker, L., Rosman, B., Liebman, R., Milman, L., & Todd, T. A conceptual model of psychosomatic illness in children. *Archives of General Psychiatry,* 1975, *32,* 1031–1038.

Minuchin, S., Montalvo, B., Guerney, B., Rosman, B., & Schumer, F. *Families of the slums.* New York: Basic Books, 1967.

Most, E. Measuring change in marital satisfaction. *Social Work*, 1964, *9*, 64–70.

Mudd, E. H. Knowns and unknowns in marriage counseling research. *Marriage and Family Living*, 1957, *19*, 75–81.

Mudd, E. H., Froscher, H. B., Preston, M. G., & Peltz, W. L. Survey of a research project in marriage counseling. *Marriage and Family Living*, 1950, *12*, 59–62.

Napier, A. Y., & Whitaker, C. A. Problems of the beginning family therapist. *Seminars in Psychiatry*, 1973, *5*, 229–242.

O'Connor, P. A. Coalition formation in conjoint marriage counseling. (Doctoral dissertation, University of Southern California, 1974.) *Dissertation Abstracts International*, 1975, *35*, 4717–4718A.

O'Dell, S. L., Flynn, J. M., & Benlolo, L. T. A comparison of parent training techniques in child behavior modification. Paper presented at the Association for the Advancement of Behavior Therapy, New York, December 1976.

O'Leary, K., Turkewitz, H., & Taffel, S. Parent and therapist evaluation of behavior therapy in a child psychologil clinic. *Journal of Consulting and Clinical Psychology*, 1973, *41*, 279–283.

Oltmanns, T. F., Broderick, J. E., & O'Leary, K. D. Marital adjustment and the efficacy of behavior therapy with children. Paper presented at the Association for the Advancement of Behavior Therapy, New York, December 1976.

Olson, D. H. Marital and family therapy: Integrative review and critique. *Journal of Marriage and the Family*, 1970, *32*, 501–538.

Olson, D. H. Review and critique of behavior modification research with couples and families: Or, are frequency counts all that count? Paper presented at the Association for the Advancement of Behavior Therapy, New York, October 1972.

Olson, D. H. Insiders and outsiders view of relationships: Research stategies. Paper presented at the Symposium on Close Relationships, University of Massachusetts, 1974.

Otto, H. A. Marriage and family enrichment programs in North America—report and analysis. *Family Coordinator*, 1975, *24*, 137–142.

Parad, H. J., & Parad, L. G. A study of crises-oriented planned short-term treatment. Part I. *Social Casework*, 1968a, *49*, 346–355.

Parad, L. G., & Parad, H. J. A study of crises-oriented planned short-term treatment. Part II. *Social Casework*, 1968b, *49*, 418–426.

Parloff, M. B. The family in psychotherapy. *Archives of General Psychiatry*, 1961, *4*, 445–451.

Parsons, B. V., & Alexander, J. F. Short term family intervention: A therapy outcome study. *Journal of Consulting and Clinical Psychology*, 1973, *41*, 195–201.

Patterson, G. R. Behavioral intervention procedures in the classroom and in the home. In A. E. Bergin and S. L. Garfield (Eds.), *Handbook of psychotherapy and behavior change*. New York: Wiley, 1971.

Patterson, G. R. Interventions for boys with conduct problems: Multiple settings, treatments, and criteria. *Journal of Consulting and Clinical Psychology*, 1974a, *42*, 471–481.

Patterson, G. R. Retraining of aggressive boys by their parents: Review of recent literature and follow-up evaluation. *Canadian Psychiatric Association Journal*, 1974b, *19*, 142–161.

Patterson, G. R. The aggressive child: Victim and architect of a coercive system. In E. J. Mash, L. A. Hamerlynck, and L. C. Handy (Eds.), *Behavior modification and families*. New York: Brunner/Mazel, *1975*.

Patterson, G. R. Parents and teachers as change agents: A social learning approach. In D. H. L. Olson (Ed.), *Treating relationships*. Lake, Mills, Ia.: Graphic, 1976.

Patterson, G. R., & Hops, H. Coercion: A game for two: Intervention techniques for marital conflict. In R. Ulrich and P. Mountjoy (Eds.), *The experimental analyses of social behavior*. New York: Appleton-Century-Crofts, 1972.

Patterson, G. R., Hops, H., & Weiss, R. L. A social learning approach to reducing rates of marital conflict. Paper presented at the Association for the Advancement of Behavior Therapy, New York, October 1972.

Patterson, G. R., Hops, H., & Weiss, R. L. Interpersonal skills training for couples in early stages of conflict. *Journal of Marriage and the Family*, 1975, *37*, 29–303.

Patterson, G., Ray, R., & Shaw, D. Direct intervention in families of deviant children. *Oregon Research Institute Research Bulletin*, 1968, *8*(9).

Patterson, G. R., Ray, R., Shaw, D., & Cobb, J. Manual for coding family interactions. Unpublished manuscript, University of Oregon, 1969.

Patterson, G., & Reid, J. Intervention for families of aggressive boys: A replication study. *Behavior Research and Therapy*, 1973, *11*, 383–394.

Patterson, G., Reid, J., Jones, R., & Conger, R. A social learning approach to family intervention. Vol. 1. *Families with aggressive children*. Eugene, Oreg.: Castalia, 1975.

Patterson, G. R., Weiss, R. L., & Hops, H. Training of marital skills. In H. Leitenberg (Ed.), *Handbook of behavior modification and behavior therapy*. New York: Prentice-Hall, 1976.

Peed, S., Roberts, M., & Forehand, R. Evaluation of the effectiveness of a standardized parent training program in altering the interaction of mothers and their non-compliant children. *Behavior Modification*, 1977, *1*, 323–350.

Perlman, L. M., & Bender, S. S. Operant reinforcement with structural family therapy in treating anorexia nervosa. *Journal of Family Counseling*, 1975, *3*, 38–46.

Perlmutter, M., Loeb, G. D., O'Hara, G., & Higbie, I. Family diagnosis and therapy using videotape playback. *American Journal of Orthopsychiatry*, 1967, *37*, 900–905.

Pierce, R. M. Training in interpersonal communication skills with the partners of deteriorated marriages. *Family Coordinator*, 1973, *22*, 223–227.

Ptttman, F., Langsley, D., & DeYoung, C. Work and school phobias: A family approach to treatment. *American Journal of Psychiatry*, 1968, *124*, 1535–1541.

Postner, R., Guttman, H., Sigal, H., Epstein, N., & Rakoff, V. Process and outcome in conjoint family therapy. *Family Process*, 1971, *10*, 451–473.

Powell, L., Blakeney, P., Croft, H., & Pulliam, G. Rapid treatment approach to human sexual inadequacy. *American Journal of Obstetrics and Gynecology*, 1974, *119*, 89–97.

Preston, M. G., Mudd, E. H., & Froscher, H. B. Factors affecting movement in casework. *Social Casework*, 1953, *34*, 103–111.

Rappaport, A. F. Conjugal relationship enhancement program. In D. H. L. Olson (Ed.), *Treating relationships*. Lake Mills, Ia.: Graphic, 1976.

Rappaport, A. F., & Harrell, J. A behavioral exchange model for marital counseling. *Family Coordinator*, 1972, *22*, 203–212.

Reding, G. R., Charles, L. A., & Hoffman, M. B. Treatment of the couple by a couple II. Conceptual framework, case presentation, and follow-up study. *British Journal of Medical Psychology*, 1967, *40*, 243–251.

Reid, J. Reciprocity and family interaction. Unpublished doctoral dissertation, University of Oregon, 1967.

Reid, J., & Hendriks, A. Preliminary analysis of the effectiveness of direct home intervention for the treatment of predelinquent boys who steal. In L. Hamerlynck, L. Handy, and E. Mash (Eds.), *Behavior change: Methodology, concepts and practice*. Champaign, Ill.: Research Press, 1973.

Reid, W. J., & Shyne, A. W. *Brief and extended casework*. New York: Columbia University Press, 1969.

Reisinger, J. J., Frangia, G. W., & Hoffman, E. H. Toddler management training: Generalization and marital status. *Journal of Behavior Therapy and Experimental Psychiatry*, 1976, *7*, 335–340.

Reiter, G. F., & Kilmann, P. R. Mothers as family change agents. *Journal of Counseling Psychology*, 1975, *22*, 61–65.

Rice, D. G., Fey, W. F., & Kepecs, J. G. Therapist experience and "style" as factors in co-therapy. *Family Process*, 1972, *11*, 1–12.

Rice, D. G., Gurman, A. S., & Razin, A. M. Therapist sex, "style" and theoretical orientation. *Journal of Nervous and Mental Disease*, 1974, *159*, 413–421.

Rice, D. G., Razin, A. M., & Gurman, A. S. Spouses as co-therapists: "Style" variables and implications for patient-therapist matching. *Journal of Marriage and Family Counseling*, 1976, *2*, 55–62.

Riskin, J. M., & Faunce, E. E. An evaluative review of family interaction research. *Family Process*, 1972, *11*, 365–455.

Rittenhouse, J. Endurance of effect: Family unit treatment compared to identified patient treatment. *Proceedings, 78th Annual Convention of the American Psychological Association*, 1970, 535–536.

Roberts, P. V. The effects on marital satisfaction of brief training in behavioral exchange negotiation mediated by differentially experienced trainers. (Doctoral dissertation, Fuller Theological Seminary, 1974.) *Dissertation Abstracts International*, 1975, *36*, 457B.

Rose, S. Group training of parents as behavior modifiers. *Social Work*, 1974, *19*, 156–162.

Rosen, R. C., & Schnapp, B. J. The use of a specific behavioral technique (thought-stopping) in the context of conjoint couples therapy: A case report. *Behavior Therapy*, 1974, *5*, 261–264.

Rosenthal, M. Effects of parent training groups on behavior change in target children: Durability, generalization and patterns of family interaction. (Doctoral dissertation, University of Cincinnati, 1975.) *Dissertation Abstracts International*, 1976, *36*, 4706–4707B.

Rosman, B. Symptom change and family change as outcome measures in family research. Paper presented at the American Orthopsychiatric Association, New York, April 1977.

Rosman, B., Minuchin, S., Liebman, R., & Baker, L. Impact and outcome of family therapy in anorexia nervosa. Manuscript submitted for publication, 1976.

Royce, W. S., & Weiss, R. L. Behavioral cues in the judgment of the marital satisfaction: A linear regression analysis. *Journal of Consulting and Clinical Psychology*, 1975, *43*, 816–824.

Rubin, Z., & Mitchell, C. Couples research as couples counseling: Some unintended effects of studying close relationships. *American Psychologist*, 1976, *31*, 17–25.

Safer, D. Family therapy for children with behavioral disorders. *Family Process*, 1966, *5*, 243–255.

Sager, C. J., Gundlach; R., Kremer, M., Lenz, R., & Royce, J. R. The married in treatment: Effects of psychoanalysis on the marital state. *Archives of General Psychiatry*. 1968, *19*, 205–217.

Salzinger, K., Feldman, R. S., & Portnoy, S. Training parents of brain-injured children in the use of operant conditioning procedures. *Behavior Therapy*, 1970, *1*, 4–32.

Santa-Barbara, J. The role of goal attainment scaling in the evaluation of family therapy outcome. Paper presented at the Goal Attainment Scaling Conference, Minneapolis, 1975.

Santa-Barbara, J., & Epstein, N. Conflict behavior in clinical families: Preasymptotic interactions and stable outcomes. *Behavioral Science*, 1974, *19*, 100–110.

Santa-Barbara, J., Woodward, C., Levin, D., Goodman, J., & Epstein, N. The relationship between therapists' characteristics and outcome variables in family therapy. Paper presented at the Canadian Psychiatric Association, Banff, Alberta, 1975.

Satir, V. *Conjoint family therapy*. Palo Alto, Calif.: Science and Behavior Books, 1967.

Schreiber, L. Evaluation of family group treatment in a family agency. *Family Process*, 1966, *5*, 21–29.

Shapiro, R. Therapist attitudes and premature termination in family and individual therapy. *Journal of Nervous and Mental Disease*, 1974, *159*, 101–107.

Shapiro, R. Problems in teaching family therapy. *Professional Psychology*, 1975a, *6*, 41–44.

Shapiro, R. Some implications of training psychiatric nurses in family therapy. *Journal of Marriage and Family Counseling*, 1975b, *1*, 323–330.

Shapiro, R., & Budman, S. Defection, termination, and continuation in family and individual therapy. *Family Process*, 1973, *12*, 55–67.

Shapiro, R., & Harris, R. Family therapy in treatment of the deaf: A case report. *Family Process,* 1976, *15,* 83–96.

Shellow, R., Brown, B., & Osberg, J. Family group therapy in retrospect: Four years and sixty families. *Family Process,* 1963, *2,* 52–67.

Shepherd, M., Oppenheim, A., & Mitchell, S. Childhood behavior disorders and the child guidance clinic: An epidemiological study. *Journal of Child Psychology and Psychiatry,* 1966, *7,* 39–52.

Sigal, J., Barrs, C., & Doubilet, A. Problems in measuring the success of family therapy in a common clinical setting: Impasse and solutions. *Family Process,* 1976, *15,* 225–233.

Sigal, J., Guttman, H., Chagoya, L., & Lasry, J. Predictibility of family therapists' behavior. *Canadian Psychiatric Association Journal,* 1973, *18,* 199–202.

Sigal, J., Rakoff, V., & Epstein, N. Indications of therapeutic outcome in conjoint family therapy. *Family Process,* 1967, *6,* 215–226.

Silverman, L. H., Frank, S. G., & Dachinger, P. A. A psychoanalytic reinterpretation of the effectiveness of systematic desensitization: Experimental data bearing on the role of merging fantasies. *Journal of Abnormal Psychology,* 1974, *83,* 313–318.

Skindrud, K. Generalization of treatment effects from home to school settings. *Oregon Research Institute Research Bulletin,* 1973, *14,*(15).

Skynner, A. School phobia: A reappraisal. *British Medical Journal,* 1974, *47,* 1–15.

Sletto, R. F. What is significant for research in marriage counseling? *Marriage and Family Living,* 1950, *12,* 130–132.

Slipp, S., Ellis, S., & Kressel, K. Factors associated with engagement in family therapy. *Family Process,* 1974, *13,* 413–427.

Smith, C. G. Marital influences on treatment outcome in alcoholism. *Journal of the Irish Medical Association,* 1967, *60,* 433–434.

Smith, C. G. Alcoholics: Their treatment and their wives. *British Journal of Psychiatry,* 1969, *115,* 1039–1042.

Smith, C. G., & Hepworth, D. H. Marriage counseling with one marital partner: Rationale and clinical implications. *Social Casework,* 1967, *48,* 352–359.

Speck, R. V., & Attneave, C. L. *Family networks.* New York: Pantheon, 1973.

Spector, R., Guttman, H., Sigal, J., Rakoff, V. & Epstein, N. Time sampling in family therapy sessions. *Psychotherapy,* 1970, *7,* 37–40.

Spiegel, D., & Sperber, Z. Clinical experiment in short-term family therapy. *American Journal of Orthopsychiatry,* 1967, *37,* 278–279.

Stanton, M. D. Family therapy training: Academic and internship opportunities for psychologists. *Family Process,* 1975a, *14,* 433–439.

Stanton, M. D. Psychology and family therapy. *Professional Psychology,* 1975b, *6* 45–49.

Stanton, M. D., & Todd, T. C. Structural family therapy with heroin addicts: Some outcome data. Paper presented at the Society for Psychotherapy Research, San Diego, June 1976.

Steinglass, P., Davis, D. I., & Berenson, D. In-hospital treatment of alcoholic couples. Paper presented at the American Psychiatric Association, Anaheim, California, 1975.

Stier, S., & Goldenberg, I. Training issues in family therapy. *Journal of Marriage and Family Counseling,* 1975, *1,* 63–68.

Straus, M. A. *Family measurement techniques.* Minneapolis: University of Minnesota Press, 1969.

Stover, L., & Guerney, B. The efficacy of training procedures for mothers in filial therapy. *Psychotherapy,* 1967, *4,* 110–115.

Strupp, H. H., & Bergin, A. E. Some empirical and conceptual bases for coordinated research in psychotherapy. *International Journal of Psychiatry,* 1969, *7,* 18–90.

Strupp, H. H., Hadley, S. W., Gomes, B., & Armstrong, S. Negative effects in psychotherapy: A review of clinical and theoretical issues together with recommendations for a program of research. Unpublished manuscript, Vanderbilt University, 1976.

Stuart, R. B. Operant-interpersonal treatment for marital discord. *Journal of Consulting and Clinical Psychology,* 1969a, *33,* 675–682.

Stuart, R. B. Token reinforcement in marital treatment. In R. D. Rubin and C. M. Franks (Eds.), *Advances in behavior therapy, 1968.* New York: Academic Press, 1969b.

Stuart, R. B. An operant interpersonal program for couples. In D. H. L. Olson (Ed.), *Treating relationships.* Lake Mills, Ia.: Graphic, 1976.

Stuart, R. B., & Tripodi, T. Experimental evaluation of three time-constrained behavioral treatments for predelinquents and delinquents. In R. Rubin, J. Brady, and J. Henderson (Eds.), *Advances in behavior therapy.* New York: Academic Press 1973.

Sundland, D. Theoretical orientations of psychotherapists. In A. S. Gurman and A. M. Razin (Eds.), *Effective psychotherapy: A handbook of research.* New York: Pergamon, 1977.

Sussman, M. B., & Cogswell, B. E. The meaning of variant and experimental marriage styles and family forms in the 1970's. *Family Coordinator,* 1972, *21,* 375–381.

Swan, R. W. Differential counseling approaches to conflict reduction in the marital dyad. (Doctoral dissertation, Arizona State University, 1972.) *Dissertation Abstracts International,* 1972, *32,* 6629B.

Targow, J. G., & Zweber, R. V. Participants' reactions to treatment in a married couples' group. *International Journal of Group Psychotherapy,* 1969, *19,* 221–225.

Thibaut, J. W., & Kelley, H. H. *The social psychology of groups.* New York: Wiley, 1959.

Thomas, E. J., Carter, R. D., Gambrill, E. D., & Butterfield, W. H. A signal system for the assessment and modification of behavior (SAM). *Behavior Therapy,* 1970, *1,* 255–259.

Thomas, E. J., & Walter, C. L. Guidelines for behavioral practice in the open community agency: Procedure and evaluation. *Behavior Research and Therapy,* 1973, *11,* 193–205.

Thomas, E. J., Walter, C. L., & O'Flaherty, K. Assessment and modification of marital verbal behavior using a computer-assisted signal system (CASAM).

Paper presented at the Association for the Advancement of Behavior Therapy, New York, October 1972.

Thomas E. J., Walter, C. L., & O'Flaherty, K. Computer-assisted assessment and modification: Possibilities and illustrative data. *Social Service Review*, 1974, *48*, 170–183.

Thomlinson, R. J. A behavioral model for social work intervention with the marital dyad. (Doctoral dissertation, University of Toronto, 1973.) *Dissertation Abstracts International*, 1974, *35*, 1227A.

Toomim, M. K. Structured separation with counseling: A therapeutic approach for couples in conflict. *Family Process*, 1972, *11*, 299–310.

Trankina, F. J. Aggressive and withdrawn children as related to family perception and outcome of different treatment methods. Unpublished doctoral dissertation, University of Arizona, 1975.

Tsoi-Hoshmand, L. The limits of *quid pro quo* in couple therapy. *Family Coordinator*, 1975, *24*, 51–54.

Tsoi-Hoshmand, L. Marital therapy: An integrative behavioral-learning model. *Journal of Marriage and Family Counseling*, 1976, *2*, 179–191.

Turkewitz, H., & O'Leary, K. D. Communication and behavioral marital therapy: An outcome study. Paper presented at the Association for the Advancement of Behavior Therapy, New York, December 1776.

Turner, A. J. Couple and group treatment of marital discord: An experiment. Paper presented at theAssociation for the Advancement of Behavior Therapy, New York, October 1972.

Valle, S. K., & Marinelli, R. P. Training in human relations skills as a preferred mode of treatment for married couples. *Journal of Marriage and Family Counseling*, 1975, *1*, 359–365.

van der Veen, F. The family concept Q sort. Unpublished manuscript, Dane County Guidance Center, Madison, Wisconsin, 1960. (Available through Institute for Juvenile Research, Chicago).

Vansteenwegen, A. Het communicatiecentrum voor echtparen te Lovenjoel-Leuven: On dery olk naar de resultaten van het dril weken durend therapieprogramma. *Bevolking en Gezin*, 1974, *1*, 105–12..

Vansteenwegen, A. Changes in the perception of basic relational attitudes by couple therapy. Ppper presented at the Society for Psychotherapy Research, San Diego, July 1976.

Venema, H. B. Marriage enrichment: A comparison of the behavioral exchange negotiation and communication models. Doctoral dissertation, Fuller Theological Seminar, 1975.

Verhulst, J., & Vansteenwegen, A. Werking, ideoligie en doelmatigheid van een experimented therapeutisch programma: Het communicatiecentrum vor echtparen te Lovenjoel. *Tijdschrift Voor Psychiatrie*, 1974, *16*, 139–151.

Vincent, J. P., Weiss, R. L., & Birchler, G. R. A behavioral analysis of problem-solving in distressed and nondistressed married and stranger dyads. *Behavior Therapy*, 1975, *6*, 475–487.

Vogelsong, E. L. Preventive-therapeutic programs for mothers and adolescents daughters: A follow-up of relationship enhancement versus discussion and

booster versus no booster methods. Unpublished doctoral dissertation, Pennsylvania State University, 1975.

Wachtel, P. L. *Psychoanalysis and behavior therapy: Toward an integration.* New York: Basic Books, 1977.

Wallace D. H., & Barbach, L. G. Preorgasmic group treatment. *Journal of Sex and Marital Therapy*, 1974, *1*, 146–154.

Walter, H. I., & Gilmore, S. K. Placebo versus social learning effects in parent training procedures designed to alter the behavior of aggressive boys. *Behavior Therapy*, 1973, *4*, 361–377.

Waskow, I. E., & Parloff, M. B. *Psychotherapy change measures.* Washington, D.C.: National Institute of Mental Health, 1975.

Wattie, B. Evaluating short-term casework in a family agency. *Social Casework*, 1973, *54*, 609–616.

Waxenberg, B. R. Therapists' empathy, regard and genuineness as factors in staying in or dropping out of short-term, time-limited family therapy. (Doctoral dissertation, New York, New York University, 1973.) *Dissertation Abstracts International*, 1973, *34*, 1288B.

Weakland, J., Fisch, R., Watzlawick, P., & Bodin, A. Brief therapy: Focused problem resolution. *Family Process*, 1974, *13*, 141–168.

Weathers, L., & Liberman, R. Contingency contracting with families of delinquent adolescents. *Behavior Therapy*, 1975, *6*, 356–366.

Weiss, R. L. Contracts, cognition and change: A behavioral approach to marriage therapy. *Counseling Psychologist*, 1975a, *5*, 15–26.

Weiss, R. L. Spouse observation checklist. Unpublished manuscript, University of Oregon, 1975b.

Weiss, R. L., Birchler, G. R., & Vincent, J. P. Contractual models for negotiation training in marital dyads. *Journal of Marriage and the Family*, 1974, *36*, 321–330.

Weiss, R. L., & Cerreto, M. Marital status inventory: Steps to divorce. Unpublished manuscript, University of Oregon, 1975.

Weiss, R. L., Hops, H., & Patterson, G. R. A framework for conceptualizing marital conflict, a technology for altering it, some data from evaluating it. In L. A. Hamerlynck, L. C. Handy, and E. J. Mash (Eds.), *Behavior change: methodology, concepts and practice.* Champaign, Ill.: Research Press, 1973.

Weiss, R. L., & Margolin, G. Marital conflict and accord. In A. R. Ciminero, K. D. Calhoun and H. E. Adams (Eds.), *Handbook for behavioral assessment.* New York: Wiley, 1977.

Welch, J. C., III, & Goldstein, M. D. The differential effects of operant-interpersonal intervention. Unpublished manuscript, University of Florida, 1972.

Wellisch, D., Vincent, J., & Ro-Trock, G. Family therapy versus individual therapy: A study of adolescents and their parents. In D. H. L. Olson (Ed.), *Treating relationships.* Lake Mills, Ia.: Graphic, 1976.

Wells, R. A., Dilkes, T., & Trivelli, N. The results of family therapy: A critical review of the literature. *Family Process*, 1972, *7*, 189–207.

Wells, R. A., Figurel, J. A., & McNamee, P. Group facilitative training with conflicted marital couples. In A. S.

Gurman and D. G. Rice (Eds.), *Couples in conflict: New directions in marital therapy.* New York: Aronson, 1975. (a)

Wells, R. A., Figurel, J. A., & McNamee, P. Group and conjoint marital therapy: A comparative study. Unpublished manuscript, University of Pittsburgh, 1975. (b)

Whitaker, C. A. A family therapist looks at marital therapy. In A. Gurman and D. Rice (Eds.), *Couples in conflict: New directions in marital therapy.* New York: Aronson, 1975.

Wieman, R. J. Conjugal relationship modification and reciprocal reinforcement: A comparison of treatments for marital discord. Unpublished doctoral dissertation, Pennsylvania State University, 1973.

Wieman, R. J., Shoulder,, D. I., & Farr, J. H. Reciprocal reinforcement in marital therapy. *Journal of Behavior Therapy and Experimental Psychiatry,* 1974, *5,* 291–295.

Wiltz, N. A., & Patterson, G. R. An evaluation of parent training procedures designed to alter inappropriate aggressive behavior of boys. *Behavior Therapy,* 1974, *5,* 215–221.

Williams, A. M. The development of marital therapy as an emerging behavioral science. Unpublished paper, Uniersity of Florida, 1975.

Wills, T. A., Weiss, R. L., & Patterson, G. R. A behavioral analysis of the determinants of marital satisfaction. *Journal of Consulting and Clinical Psychology,* 1974, *42,* 802–811.

Winter, W. D. Family therapy: Research and theory. In C. D. Spielberger (Ed.), *Current topics in clinical and community psychology.* Vol. 3. New York: Academic Press, 1971.

Wolpe, J., & Rachman, S. Psychoanalytic evidence: A critique based on Freud's case of Little Hans. *Journal of Nervous and Mental Disease,* 1960, *131,* 135.

Woodward, C., Santa-Barbara, J., Levin, S., Epstein, N., & Streiner, D. The McMaster family therapy outcome study: III. Client and treatment characteristics significantly contributing to clinical outcomes. Paper presented at the American Orthopsychiatric Association, New York, April 1977.

Woodward, C., Santa-Barbara, J., Levin, S., Goodman, J., Streiner, D., & Epstein, N. Client and therapist characteristics related to family therapy outcome: Closure and follow-up evaluation. Paper presented at the Society for Psychotherapy Research, Boston, 1975.

Ziegler, J. S. A comparison of the effect of two forms of group psychotherapy on the treatment of marital discord. (Doctoral dissertation, University of Pittsburgh, 1972.) *Dissertation Abstracts International,* 1973, *34,* 143–144A.

Zwerling, I., & Mendelsohn, M. Initial family reactions to hospitalization. *Family Process,* 1965, *4,* 50–63.

22

RESEARCH ON PSYCHOTHERAPY AND BEHAVIOR CHANGE WITH THE DISADVANTAGED: PAST, PRESENT, AND FUTURE DIRECTIONS[1]

RAYMOND P. LORION

Temple University

For nearly three decades, interest in serving the mental health needs of the poor and the black has focused more on describing problems than on proposing and, particularly, evaluating solutions. In general, assessments of the mental health delivery system's ability and willingness to respond to the socioemotional needs of the low-income and minority segments of society have been negative and pessimistic. Racial and socioeconomic parameters appeared to be insurmountable barriers to providing effective psychotherapeutic intervention. Paradoxically, these very parameters related epidemiologically to unacceptably high incidence and prevalence levels of psychopathology.

[1] I wish to express my deepest appreciation to Janet Cahill for her invaluable and tireless assistance throughout the preparation of this chapter. I also thank Mary McVeigh and Lennis Mond for their dedicated typing of this manuscript.

Thus, those most in need appeared to be least served, and the system appeared to be at an impasse with a significant portion of its constituency.

Fortunately, however, not all clinicians and researchers accepted as "fact" the "sense" of the literature. Many professionals have identified and implemented the treatment implications derivable from descriptions of prior difficulties in responding to the needs of the disadvantaged. For example, some investigators have assessed systematically the therapeutic impact of modifying "traditional" approaches to reflect disadvantaged life-styles. Others have developed and evaluated alternative service delivery strategies. Still others have proposed, without formally assessing, a variety of innovative treatment approaches. Gradually, we have accumulated a knowledge base from which the salient aspects of disadvantaged life-styles can be studied and reflected in appropriate service delivery strategies. Although it is clear that much work remains to be done, the earlier pessimism appears unwarranted.

In approaching the preparation of this chapter, I must admit to some initial reservations. I was concerned about the relative balance of available clinical-anecdotal versus empirical reports. Would sufficient "hard data" be available to justify valid conclusions about the current state of the art? Would this chapter add another pessimistic note to an already depressing tune? Fortunately, the past decade has been fruitful for the professionals involved in the area of psychotherapy research. Readers of this volume have undoubtedly been impressed by the increased methodological sophistication evidenced, for example, in the chapters on therapeutic outcomes (Chapter 5), client variables (Chapter 6), therapist variables (Chapter 7), and treatment process studies (Chapter 8). We are learning which questions to ask and which procedures are necessary to answer them. We have available a vastly expanded array of treatment alternatives (see Parts III, IV, and V of this volume). Although not yet prescriptively based, the mental health system now appears to have the tools and impetus required to reach that ultimate goal. Specifically in relation to the disadvantaged, we can begin to apply, as systematically as possible, procedures that have been identified as *generally* effective with these individuals.

The goal of this chapter, therefore, is to review alternative pretreatment and treatment approaches that are of demonstrated effectiveness with the disadvantaged segments of the population. It should be evident to the clinically minded reader that genuine treatment options do exist. The materials presented, however, should also provide convincing evidence of the need to invest significantly more financial and professional resources into systematic research in this area. We have made progress, but it is far too limited. For example, we still know embarrassingly little about the life-styles, family patterns, and psychosocial resources of the disadvantaged, yet we are responsible for resolving their emotional difficulties. We have yet to identify the differential effectiveness of available treatment alternatives and thus cannot systematically select from among them. Our community-minded colleagues speak of "prevention" without a clear understanding of what to prevent or what individual and environmental parameters to maximize.

THE DISADVANTAGED GROUPS

Prior to any discussion of therapeutic strategies, subgroups subsumed under the global label "the disadvantaged" should be operationally defined. This term typically refers to the "poor" who have the fewest economic, educational, and cultural resources. Since minority group members, especially blacks, are disproportionately represented among the poor, they are typically included among the disadvantaged. For the purposes of this discussion, the "disadvantaged" will also refer to the "working class." Although they generally live under less financial pressure than the poor, the working class has historically shared the poor's difficulty in obtaining and remaining in psychotherapy (Hollingshead & Redlich, 1958). Thus, this chapter will focus on the poor, minority group members, and the working class.

The business of mental health is to facilitate individual adaptation and adjustment to sources of psychological conflict. To do so, however, requires an appreciation of the conditions under which the conflict evolved and is maintained (Green, 1946). To ignore the cultural and practical realities of the individual's existence in selecting a treatment strategy is shortsighted if it results in premature termination (Lorion, 1973) or, more seriously, in attempts by patients to implement solutions that are perceived in their environment as unacceptable. Although obvious, this point has been regularly ignored in attempts to provide mental health services to the disadvantaged (Allen, 1970a, 1970b; Chess, Clark, & Thomas, 1953; Deane, 1961; Fishman & McCormack, 1969; Savitz, 1952; Schneiderman, 1965). By birth or occupation, mental health professionals belong to the middle- and upper-income groups and must guard continuously against the formulation of ethnocentric judgments about the needs and resources of poor and working-class patients. It is important that our treatment goals and procedures relate to *their* lives. Middle-class solutions may not apply to the working class, just as working-class solutions may be equally inappropriate for the poor.

In his methodological discussion of psychotherapy research, Kiesler (1971) describes three "uniformity" myths that permeate studies of the major variables of the psychotherapy paradigm— patient, therapist, and outcome are each considered as homogeneous entities. The acceptance of any of these assumptions results in naive and prescriptively limited research designs. The patient myth is most immediately relevant. Previous global considerations of the "lower class" have ignored or underemphasized the extensive heterogeneity of that category (Hollingshead & Redlich,1958; Lorion, 1973). Yet differentiations among the lower-class subgroups relate significantly to the definition of their needs and treatment responsiveness (Lorion, 1974b, 1975). The following section briefly summarizes some of these distinguishing characteristics.

In reviewing this material, the reader is advised to guard against a second-level uniformity myth. Significant heterogeneity exists both *across* and *within* each of the disadvantaged subgroups. The characteristics presented are no more than rough guidelines based largely on clinical observations and not on empirical (be it psychological, sociological, or anthropological) data.

The Index of Social Position

The most widely used instrument for determining socioeconomic status (SES) in psychotherapy research has been the Hollingshead Index of Social Position developed for the New Haven community study (Hollingshead & Redlich, 1958). Originally, this Index defined class status in terms of area of residence, occupation, and educational level. A later revision excluded the residency variable in order to maximize the Index's generalizability across communities (Hollingshead, 1957); a relation of .97 between the two forms has been reported (Myers & Bean, 1968). The Hollingshead Index identifies five SES levels ranging from Class I, the highest, to Class V, the lowest. Table 22-1 summarizes the major defining characteristics of each group. Although designed in the 1950s, the Index serves as a useful methodology for assessing relative social standing. It must, however, be rec-

ognized that the profound educational, economic, and social changes of the past two decades— changes effecting, for the most part, the disadvantaged—are nor reflected in the Index's classificatory schema.

The members of Classes IV and V make up the disadvantaged subgroups. Both are typically engaged in manual occupations, relatively uninvolved in the upper-income group's "prestige race," and tend to live in informal, comfortable relationships with others (Gans, 1962; Miller & Riessman, 1969). Their similarities, however, should not overshadow their differences.

The Poor

It is important to recognize that poverty is primarily an economic instead of a psychological state. Federal economic guidelines are used to define poverty and to assess its numbers. In 1974, the Poverty Line, the government's estimate of the minimal purchasing power necessary for the survival of a family of four, was set at $5300. This amount allows for the acquisition of the barest essentials under ideal conditions (i.e., in the absence of unexpected financial crises and reflecting judicious budgeting). Although the proportion of individuals existing below that level has decreased significantly in the last 50 years, nearly 10 percent of the population, more than 20 million people, are included within this conservatively defined category (Perlman, 1976). The demographic characteristics of the poor, include the following:

> The incidence of poverty is high among the lesser educated, blacks, women, children, older people, the unemployed and nonworkers. These demographic characteristics often operate in combination to strengthen subgroup poverty rates. For example, while the incidence of poverty is closely related inversely to educational level, the tendency is most pronounced for blacks who drop out of high school. (Perlman, 1976, p. 38)

Thus, the "poor" are a highly diverse group including unskilled, irregularly and never employed white and nonwhite men and women, migrant farm workers, ghetto dwellers, tenant farmers, and

TABLE 22-1 Occupational, Educational, and Familial Characteristics of Five Socioeconomic Status Levels

Class	Occupational Level	Educational Level	Family Structure
I	Salaried positions in policymaking executive level; private-practice professionals	Professional degrees; A.B. level and beyond	Modal nuclear family of parents and children, with stability encouraged
II	Salaried positions in business and professions; minor professionals included	A.B. level or partial college	Modal nuclear family of parents and children, with stability encouraged
III	"Middle-class" administrative, clerical, sales, technical, and semiprofessional positions	High school diploma	Modal nuclear family of parents and children, with stability encouraged
IV	"Working-class" skilled and semi-skilled manual occupations in unionized trades and industries	High school or technical school diploma with some below tenth grade	Modal nuclear family often three generations, instability more common than I to III
V	"Poor" semiskilled and unskilled manual occupations nonunionized with irregular employment	High school diploma infrequent with many not completing eighth grade	Modal nuclear family extended to three to four generations; divorce, separation, and instability common

Note: The socioeconomic status levels are referenced in Hollingshead and Redlich (1958). Table from Lorion (1973).

drifters (Riessman, Cohen, & Pearl, 1964). Typically, they have little if any job security, are the least educated, live in the worst sections of the community, and have little access to local recreational opportunities. Health and other human services must be obtained from public facilities, often under personally depressing and degrading circumstances (Feagin, 1975).

The psychological consequences of their economic limits are multiple and, not surprisingly, negative. Gladwin (1967) describes poverty in terms of four characteristics, it involves being *poor, despised, incompetent,* and *powerless.*

Being poor defines the economic limits of one's existence and the patterns of one's daily behavior. Without adequate financial resources and reserves, the life of the poor is characterized by an endless series of crises. Available finances must be used immediately for only the most pressing needs. Typically, only small purchases can be made. Unanticipated expenditures require the sacrifice of a necessity. Without regular or sufficient income, financial planning, budgeting, and attempts to save money for future purchases are improbable and unrealistic (Richards, 1966).

The poor perceive themselves and are perceived

by the larger society as despicable. Some discussions of the poor, for example, debate the relative merits of the "deserving" and "undeserving" or "respectable" and "degraded" poor (Sarbin, 1970). The "undeserving" and "degraded" are poor who participate in a "culture of poverty" (Lewis, 1966). They are perceived and see themselves as disinherited and "not included in the collectivity that makes up the *real* society of *real* people" (Rainwater, 1970, p. 9). They are described as lazy, shiftless, and impulse-ridden, and they are perceived as in some way responsible for their poverty (Feagin, 1975; Gladwin, 1967). In every way, their existence is inconsistent with the basic American ideal (i.e., the achievement of success through self-effort). Viewed in this way, they become objects of pity or scorn (McKinney, Lorion, & Zax, 1976). Not surprisingly, the poor are not oblivious to the perceptions and attitudes of others. Indeed, they tend to share some of these very attitudes. They come to perceive themselves in similarly negative terms and are discouraged by what they see in themselves. Understandably, they attempt, whenever possible, to avoid situations in which these views are reinforced.

A third characteristic of many of the poor is *incompetence*. A central element of poverty is its persistence. Regardless of what one does, all too often the state of poverty defies attempts to overcome it. Gladwin (1967) presents poverty as a series of cycles each beginning and ending with poverty:

> being poor means eating poor food and living in unsanitary housing which means having poor health, which means missing a lot of work or school, or perhaps being handicapped or not strong enough to handle the heavy manual work which is often the only kind available, and thus being unemployed much of the time, and so being poor. (p. 77)

Finally, an aspect of poverty extensively discussed in the mental health literature is its sense of *hopelessness*. Alinsky (1967), Haggstrom (1964), Lewis (1967), and others have described the poor as helpless and unable to influence the forces that govern their existence. Their lack of unionization restricts their economic bargaining power and denies them an important political voice. Members of the other social classes can complain when they feel they have been wronged, can criticize inadequate services, and can compare prices when purchasing goods. Dependent on the social agencies or merchants willing to provide credit, goods, and services, the poor must be cautious in voicing their demands and criticisms. Confidence in one's abilities is limited when employment is uncertain at best and wages barely (if at all) compensate for discontinued welfare funds. Thus, employment provides little release from the binds that restrain them. This is shockingly illustrated in the lives of migrant farm workers whose daily wage denies them the minimal resources necessary to escape that way of life (Shotwell, 1961; Wright, 1966). The snares of poverty are clearly visible in interactions with migrant children who voice no optimism for their future (Coles, 1970).

Opportunities for developing mastery and experiencing its potential anxiety-reducing function are rare indeed in the lives of the poor (Cohen, 1964). Wherever they turn, their helplessness and dependency are reinforced as they interact with yet another person or agency making decisions about where, how, and under what conditions they will live, work, and rear their children. It is with traces of these characteristics that they approach (often reluctantly) the mental health system.

The Working Class

Given their educational background, occupational skills, unionization, and participation in the American economy, the working class does not share the crisis reactive existence of the poor (Miller, 1964). Their lives emphasize independence in contrast to the forced dependency of poverty. Miller and Riessman (1969) echo numerous authors in their description of the essential characteristics of the regularly employed American worker:

> he is traditional, "old fashioned," somewhat religious, and patriarchal. The worker likes discipline, structure, order, organization, and directive, definite (strong) leadership, although he does not see such strong leadership in opposition to human, warm, informal, personal qual-

ities. Despite the inadequacy of his education, he is able to build abstractions, but he does so in a slow, physical fashion. He reads ineffectively, is poorly informed in many areas, and is often quite suggestible, although interestingly enough he is frequently suspicious of "talk" and "new fangled ideas." (p. 104)

The working class is often described as very family centered. They tend to value the relationships and cooperation that exist in large extended families (Komarovsky, 1967). Although they seek a comfortable life-style, they do not share the status and prestige goals of the upper-income groups. Their values are often person centered, and their emphasis is more on "getting by" than "getting ahead." Their own educational limitations do not reduce their educational ambitions for their children. Although they respect many social institutions, members of the working class tend to feel isolated from and uncomfortable with most of the agencies that serve them. This includes the schools as well as medical and psychiatric facilities. In dealing with such institutions:

workers like the specific action, the clear action, the understood result. What can be seen and felt is more likely to be real and true in the worker's perspectives which are therefore likely to be limited. The pragmatic orientation of workers does not encourage them to see abstract ideas as useful. (Miller & Riessman, 1969, p. 109)

Socioeconomic parameters are not alone, however, in determining the life-styles of the working class. As noted earlier, its members are family centered, and many retain firm ties to their ethnic origins. The relevance of ethnic variables to the definition of working class life-styles is persuasively discussed by Greeley (1969), who emphasizes the need for social scientists to appreciate the reality of cultural pluralism in our nation. Many individuals, particularly in the working class, identify not only as Americans but as, for example, Italian-Americans or Afro-Americans. Ethnic groups throughout the country provide psychological and social supports to their members. Participation in these groups involves more than racial, religious, national, or geographic characteristics. Most important, "it involves conscious and unconscious processes that fulfill a deep psychological need for security, identity and a sense of historical continuity" (Giordano, 1973, p. 11; 1976).

The relevance of ethnicity to the delivery of mental health services is effectively presented in a monograph by Giordano (1973). His review provides an informative analysis of ethnic factors for the design and delivery of mental health services. Furthermore, he outlines directions for further research on ethnicity. Although not without methodological problems (Lorion, 1976), such investigations can have a significant payoff in extending our understanding of the disadvantaged subcultures.

Age, Race, Sex, and Mental Health

In attempting to provide for the needs of the disadvantaged class, we must be sensitive to parameters other than economics and education. The stresses and environmental resources that relate to an individual's adjustment are also a function of age, race, and sex. These variables interact singly or in combination with SES parameters to define the limits of an individual's existence. What little information we may have acquired in the past about the psychological impact of these parameters must now be reconsidered given ongoing social assaults against ageism, racism, and sexism. Undoubtedly, the 1970s are an era in which various movements— black power, women's liberation, gray power, welfare rights, "silent majority"—have significantly influenced the lives and adjustment potential of the disadvantaged groups discussed in this chapter. Space does not permit even a cursory review of age, sex, and race as correlates of mental health adjustment, but mental health professionals, clinicians, and researchers must become knowledgeable about the mental health impact of these parameters. Interested readers are referred to Carp (1972), Kimmel (1974) and Neugarten (1968) for recent discussions of aging and retirement; see Billingsley (1968), Clark (1965), Coles (1967), Grier and Cobbs (1968), Jones (1971), Moynihan (1965), Serrano and Gibson (1973), Thomas and Sillen (1972), Thornton and Carter (1975), and Watson (1973) for discussion of minority experience; and see Chesler (1972), Franks and Burtle (1974), Maccoby and Jacklin (1974), Rainwater,

Coleman, and Handel (1959), and Seifer (1973) for discussions of the impact of sex and the women's movement on mental health and working-class life-styles.

Until we have available a knowledge base adequate to define the relative weighting of SES, race, sex, and age to an individual's mental health status and responsiveness to alternative intervention strategies, we must guard against overemphasizing any of these parameters. The needs of black patients, for example, may reflect their response to a life of discrimination (Thomas & Sillen, 1972) or their experiences among the poorest and most deprived segments of the population (Lorion, 1975; Perlman, 1976). Similarly, while the women's movement has markedly effected the lives of working-class women in some ways (Seifer, 1973), Siassi's (1974) data suggest that:

> any effort by mental health professionals (how-ever well meaning) to portray the woman of lower-class as oppressed by her male counter-part would at best appear a dubious moral en-terprise. If those efforts are misguided, positive harm may be done to the well-being of the very persons whom the professionals would help. . . .(p. 389)

Faced with such discrepancies, mental health professionals might be tempted to rely on stereotypic views of the disadvantaged. To do so would be self-defeating. As noted earlier, available information provides guideposts with which to evaluate and explore the parameters of a patient's needs and resources. Appreciation of these major variables should enable the sensitive clinician to "fill in the spaces" and hear the patient's message. Such a recommendation may seem trite. However, data to be presented later will establish the relevance to treatment effectiveness of sensitizing the therapist to relevant background information.

MENTAL HEALTH AND THE DISADVANTAGED—PAST OBSTACLES

This section summarizes the major obstacles that have hampered effective mental health treatment of the disadvantaged. Portions of this material have

been considered in Chapter 6 by Garfield, and in Chapter 7 by Parloff, Waskow, and Wolfe and elsewhere (Lorion, 1973, 1974a, 1975; Sanua, 1966) and will not be treated at length. A brief review is necessary, however, to provide the foundation on which the reader can critically evaluate the alternative treatment approaches to be discussed subsequently. The findings presented focus on four major topics.

1. The existence of an imbalance between the mental health needs of the disadvantaged and the availability of appropriate services.

2. The inconsistency among treatment acceptance, attrition, and outcome data.

3. The relevance of patient attitudes and expectations to the design and evaluation of treatment approaches.

4. The relevance of therapist attitudes and expectations to the design and evaluation of treatment approaches.

The Needs of the Disadvantaged

To date, the results of epidemiological surveys have consistently supported the conclusion that the relative distribution of psychological disorders in the population is inversely related to SES. Members of the low-income and minority groups have significantly higher incidence and prevalence rates of psychopathology than their upper-income counterparts.

The now classic New Haven study provided early evidence of this trend. In this survey of case records, Hollingshead and Redlich (1958) compared the number of treated cases from each socioeconomic level relative to each level's proportional representation in the general population; they observed highly significant SES differences in their data. Individuals from Classes I to IV were underrepresented in the patient population; the percentages of Class V patients (the poor) was twice that expected. Systematic analyses of the demographic characteristics of available case records revealed that:

- SES related to patient status for both men and women.
- SES related to patient status at all age levels

except in the adolescent and early adult years.
• SES relationships were roughly comparable for whites and nonwhites.
• SES relationships were comparable across marital status categories.
• SES relationships were comparable for Protestants, Catholics, and Jews.

The generalizability of these findings to the nonpsychiatric population was demonstrated in an equally classic interview of midtown Manhattan residents (Srole, Langer, Michael, Opler, & Rennie, 1962). Interview material was evaluated by independent psychiatrists who rated symptomatic evidence blind and assigned respondents to one of six categories of emotional well-being. No SES differences were observed in the "mild" and "moderate" adjustment categories. Highly significant differences, however, were observed in the two extreme groups. Upper-income individuals were significantly overrepresented in the "Well" category; lower-income individuals were significantly overrepresented in the "impaired" category.

Other epidemiological data support these conclusions. Dohrenwend and Dohrenwend (1969), critically evaluating 44 studies of SES and dysfunction, found consistent links between SES and psychopathology in 80 percent of them. The highest rates of disorder repeatedly occurred in the lowest SES groups. A careful analysis of reported findings indicated that the gap between the *lowest* SES groups and *all other* SES groups was significant for prevalence rates of disorder.

Thus, available epidemiological data are best summarized by Fried (1969).

The evidence is unambiguous and powerful that the lowest social classes have the highest rates of severe psychiatric disorder in our society. Regardless of the measures employed for estimating severe psychiatric disorder and social class, regardless of the region or the date of study, and regardless of the method of study, the great majority of results all point clearly and strongly to the fact that the lowest social class has by far the greatest incidence of psychoses. (p. 113)

Several points about these findings are noteworthy. First, it appears that a valid phenomenon (i.e.,

the relatively higher rate of emotional disorders among the lowest SES groups) has been identified. Second, it is important to recognize that the needs of the poor differ from those of other segments of society. Although they are in need, the working class do not experience the same kind and extent of disorders as the poor. This distinction should be reflected in the design of service delivery approaches. Third, unfortunately, the preponderance of reported epidemiological data assigns individuals to nosological categories. It would be valuable for mental health planners to have available systematic behavioral descriptions of the specific adaptive and maladaptive patterns characteristic of the disadvantaged subgroups. Although rarely obtained, such observational findings could provide important insights into the etiology, manifestation, and maintenance of maladjusted solutions to environmental pressures.

The Availability of Psychotherapy

In a recent review of psychotherapy acceptance and attrition data, I concluded that SES correlated significantly with assignment to and the duration of treatment (Lorion, 1973). In general, low-income status contraindicates individual psychotherapy as an intervention. The relevance of these findings to the mental health system is underlined by the fact that these results were drawn from the records of public clinics in which the ability to pay was supposedly *not* a treatment prerequisite. An extended analysis of this problem is presented by Garfield (Chapter 6).

SES variables appeared to be more critical determinants of treatment disposition than presenting symptoms. Evidence for this conclusion has been reported from Veterans' Administration clinics (Bailey, Warshaw, & Eichler, 1960; Imber, Nash, & Stone, 1955), from the New York Psychiatric Institute (Budner, Esecover, & Malitz, 1964), and from the University of Chicago Medical School (Heine & Trosman, 1960). Additionally, among low SES applicants presenting comparable symptoms, unemployment (Yamamoto & Goin, 1966) and minority group membership (Yamamoto, James, Bloombaum, & Hattem, 1967) were further impediments to therapy assignment. In general, therefore, patients from the low-income groups were either not accepted into treatment or, when accepted, were referred to medication clinics. These trends are continuing today (D'Angelo & Walsh, 1967; Jackson, Berkowitz, & Farley, 1974; Krebs, 1971; Kurtz, Weech, & Dizenhuz, 1970; Lee, Gianturco, & Eisdorfer, 1974; Rosenblatt & Mayer, 1972; Sue, McKinney, Allen, & Hall, 1974; Tischler, Henisz, Myers, & Boswell, 1975a, 1975b).

It appears that low SES patients assigned to individual psychotherapy were disproportionately treated by inexperienced therapists (Hollingshead & Redlich, 1958; Sanua, 1966; Schaffer & Myers, 1954; Sue, McKinney, Allen, & Hall, 1974). Little systematic verification of this trend is available in the mental health literature. Supportive evidence, however, is provided by the fact that in the overwhelming majority of the studies on low SES experiences in psychotherapy, low-income patients were seen almost exclusively by psychiatric residents, medical students, or psychology or social work interns. Senior staff members involved in these studies treated primarily middle-and upper-income patients (Lorion, 1973, 1974a).

SES and Treatment Outcome

An important and admittedly somewhat surprising conclusion of the earlier review was the observation that SES correlated negatively with psychotherapy acceptance and attrition rates but not with available treatment outcome data (Lorion, 1973). Katz, Lorr, and Rubinstein (1958), for example, found no SES differences among "successful" patients; all SES levels were represented among patients completing treatment. Evidence of the seeming independence of outcome and social status charateristics is provided by the reports of Brill and Storrow (1960), Coles, Branch, and Allison (1962), and Rosenthal and Frank (1958). Suggestions have even appeared that low-income patients remaining in treatment beyond 3 months may be more highly motivated for and responsive to psychotherapy than their upper-income counterparts (Albronda, Dean, & Starkweather, 1964; Frank, 1961). Finally, Lerner (1972) provides carefully documented evidence of the potential efficacy of dynamic psychotherapy with low-income minority patients. Her report summarizes a very detailed study that demonstrates the positive impact of therapy (as measured by patient, therapist, and behavioral ratings) with ghetto residents.

These outcome findings do not, of course, indicate that *all* low-income patients can be successfully treated with traditional psychotherapies. They merely demonstrate the invalidity of assuming that the disadvantaged cannot respond to this method. They also make evident the need to replicate and extend the few studies demonstrating the responsiveness of low-income applicants to traditional procedures. Segments of the disadvantaged population responsive to these methods must be identified and procedures designed to maximize their continuation in treatment. Simultaneously, those segments of the disadvantaged unable to benefit from these procedures must also be identified and provided with alternative psychotherapy and behavior change methods.

Therapists Attitudes Toward the Disadvantaged

It appears that negative, outcome-related events involve treatment parameters—acceptance, assignment, and continuation—that occur early in the therapeutic process. Given this fact, it seems reasonable to assess carefully the status of participants at that point in treatment. Numerous authors have questioned the extent to which therapists from the middle- and upper-income groups can empathize with the needs and experiences of the disadvantaged (Chess, Clark, & Thomas, 1953; Green, 1946; Grey, 1969; Lerner, 1972; Lorion, 1974a; Ryan, 1969; Savitz, 1952). Schneiderman (1965), for example, argues that without knowledge of the patient's situational limits and resources, therapists have little basis on which to assess accurately the patient's problem-solving potential or treatment response. Fishman (1969) suggests that in some cases therapy for cooperative ghetto residents may result in an increased awareness of their economic and social handicaps. Under such circumstance,, withdrawal from therapy might be adaptive. In response to these issues, Prince (1969) has questioned whether these early treatment problems do not, in fact, reflect therapist instead of patient variables. Consideration of reported assessment of therapists attitudes suggest that there is some merit to this concern.

Interviews during the 1950s regularly presented therapists as uncomfortable with disadvantaged patients. Some therapists in the New Haven study reported that collaboration with the disadvantaged was hopeless because of these patients' hostility and suspicion (Hollingshead & Redlich, 1958; Schaffer & Myers, 1954). Psychiatric residents reported difficulties in relating empathetically to patients "inappropriate" for approved therapeutic procedures (Auld & Myers, 1954; Kaplan, Kurtz, & Clements, 1968) and who *merely* sought symptomatic relief (Brill & Storrow, 1960). Some therapists disapproved of the sexual and aggressive behavior patterns of the poor; they found middle- and even working-class patients more acceptable and understandable than the poor (Myers & Roberts, 1959; Redlich, Hollingshead, & Bellis, 1955). Others responded negatively to the crude language, violent outbursts, and apathetic treatment response that they associated with the poor (Affleck & Garfield, 1961). In fact, some psychiatric residents were supported in their reluctance to treat the poor by staff members who described such efforts as "a waste of time" (Baum, Felzer, D'Zmura, & Shumaker, 1966). Attempts to research systematically the impact of therapeutic procedures on the poor have failed at times because treatment participants—therapists and patients—would not continue what they experienced as a highly unsatisfying relationship.

Unfortunately, the methodologies used to collect such attitude data do not permit systematic replication. Typically, overall impressions are reported without indications of the generalizability of these feelings across the professional population. Rarely are interview or questionnaire schedules made available; the extent to which observed findings reflect instrument biases cannot be estimated. Few, if any, reports present information about the respondents' prior clinical experience with the disadvantaged. Thus, reported attitudes may reflect the results of many or few actual treatment contacts. They may also simply reflect knowledge of prior data about disadvantaged therapy experiences. If so, such attitudes contribute to a self-fulfilling prophecy (Heine & Trosman, 1960; Meltzoff & Kornreich, 1970).

The relevance of negative therapists attitudes to treatment outcome has been amply demonstrated (see Chapter 7). Parloff (1961) reports that the therapist's perception of a patient relates significantly to the quality of the therapeutic relationship. Van der Veen (1965) and Moos and Clemes

(1967) have shown that the therapist's reaction to a patient relates significantly to observed treatment behaviors. Although they did not assess therapists attitudes directly, White, Fichtenbaum, and Dollard (1964) and later Levitt (1966) found that patients who terminated treatment early experienced significantly more and longer periods of silence during their initial interviews than remainers did. That negative feeling toward the patient may have contributed to the therapist's willingness to allow silent periods to continue cannot be discounted. Recent studies have demonstrated that therapists' attitudes relate significantly to the quality of direct (Didato, 1971) and indirect (Schoenfeld, Lyerly, & Miller, 1971) mental health services provided to the disadvantaged.

Research on therapist treatment expectations also confirms the importance of understanding the pretreatment views of the service provider (Frank, 1961). In an early study, Affleck and Garfield (1961) observed a highly significant and positive correlation between the therapists' prognostic expectations and the duration of treatment. McNair, Lorr, and Callahan (1963) reported that the therapists' perception of patient motivation for change was the variable most predictive of subsequent treatment outcome.

For more than a decade, Goldstein has been a major contributor to the systematic study of the role of therapist expectations in the treatment process. The results of his early research suggest strongly that therapists' pretreatment expectations are more important to treatment outcome than those of the patient (Goldstein, 1960a, 1960b, 1962a, 1962b, 1966a, 1966b; Heller & Goldstein, 1961). Although these studies did not focus directly on SES variables, Goldstein's work is of obvious importance to the area. If, as his data suggest, therapist expectations are critical to the treatment process, their etiology and the means by which they are communicated to the patient must be identified. In an analog study using clinical psychology graduate students as therapists and a single filmed intake interview as the therapy situation, Goldstein (1971) observed that therapists' ratings of patient attractiveness, treatment prognosis, and acceptability were significantly and negatively influenced by diagnostic and motivational descriptions. These "therapists" responded stereotypically to "patients" being seen for a first intake session. Given their training status, the probability that "therapists" response patterns reflected extended clinical experiences with "unacceptable patients" seems low. Perhaps their reactions were the consequence of attitudes brought into or reinforced in training. Goldstein's analog study also provided some insights into the ways in which patients are made aware of their therapists' feelings. Analysis of communications made by therapists during the film revealed that the negative perceptions of the patient and of treatment prognosis were reflected in the quality of therapists' comments. In the face of these results, Goldstein questioned whether, in fact, psychotherapy ends instead of begins with the intake interview. Such a possibility had been raised by Adams and McDonald (1968).

So far, consideration of therapists' attitudes has focused on negative views. Yet not all therapists share such views nor do all low-income patients abruptly terminate treatment. Hiler (1958) reports that therapists perceived as warm by their patients retain in treatment significantly more patients from all SES levels than therapists rated as cold, distant, or passive. Some therapists have expressed a preference for low-income as opposed to middle- and upper-income patients. It appears that such therapists are equally successful with members of all SES groups (Baum et al., 1966; Coles, Branch, & Allison, 1962; McNair, Lorr, & Callahan, 1963). The ability to work with low-income patients seems to be more a function of the therapist's own economic (Baum et al., 1966; Carkhuff & Pierce, 1967; Hiler, 1958; Kandel, 1966) or racial (Carkhuff & Pierce, 1967; Siegel, 1974) background than experience level (Bergin & Garfield, 1971; Lerner, 1972) or treatment approach (Truax & Carkhuff, 1967). Additionally, Carson and Heine (1962) observed that therapists able to work with low-income patients were rated as empathic and objective with all patients. Thus, sufficient data exists to justify the conclusion that therapists' attitudes and expectations significantly influence the impact of treatment for the disadvantaged.

Disadvantaged Attitudes Toward Treatment

Relatively more attention has been focused on identifying the pretreatment attitudes and expectations of disadvantaged patients than of their therapists. Early work in this area consistently reported that the disadvantaged were significantly more negative toward and unsophisticated about mental health services and psychotherapy than their middle- and upper-income counterparts. Although these differences have been recently confirmed directionally, their extent appears to have been markedly reduced.

Observational findings reported during the 1950s suggested that Class IV applicants were uncertain about the appropriateness or efficacy of psychotherapy (Hollingshead & Redlich, 1958) and ashamed of, and frightened by, their need to seek such treatment (Redlich, Hollingshead, & Bellis, 1955). The validity of these conclusions was recently supported on the basis of observed patient behaviors (Myers & Bean, 1968). Other investigators agree that the disadvantaged do not value psychotherapy as an appropriate solution to personal-emotional difficulties (Brill & Storrow, 1960; Gould, 1967; Luborsky, Auerbach, Chandler, Cohen, & Bachrach, 1971; Reiff & Scribner, 1964; Riessman, 1964; Riessman, Cohen, & Pearl, 1964; Schofield, 1964; Wolken, Moriwaki, & Williams, 1973).

Recent studies of patient responses to objective treatment attitude questionnaires, however, question the extent and perhaps even the existence of SES related differences. Kadushin (1969), for example, found few SES related differences among the large sample of clinic applicants completing his extensive questionnaire. Surveying an equally large sample of high school and college students, Fisher and Cohen (1972) found no relationship between social status and mental health attitudes as measured by their experimental measure (Fisher & Turner, 1970). Further research with this scale has demonstrated a similar absence of significant social class differences in clinic samples (Calhoon, Dawes, & Lewis, 1972; Lorion, 1974b). Contrary to conclusions from earlier observational data, Class III, IV, and V white male and female clinic applicants matched on age, religion, and marital status verbalized confidence in the efficacy of their forthcoming treatment, accepted their need for help, perceived little stigma in seeking treatment, and expressed willingness to discuss personal-emotional issues (Lorion, 1974b).

Do these data mean that SES group differences in pretreatment attitudes no longer exist? Not entirely. They may simply reflect the biases of observation versus questionnaire data collection procedures. Observed trends may suggest that such differences have been reduced over the years. They do, however, argue against assuming that all disadvantaged applicants arrive at mental health facilities seeking services for which they have no respect and little desire. They also make evident the need to assess objectively and early in treatment the patient's views of the therapeutic process about to begin.

Patients' expectations about the nature of, and appropriate role behaviors for, psychotherapy significantly influence the course of treatment along a number of dimensions including duration (Garfield & Wolpin, 1963; Lorr & McNair, 1964), attrition rates (Overall & Aronson, 1963), outcome (Lennard & Bernstein, 1960), patient discomfort (Baum & Felzer, 1964), and involvement in the therapeutic process (Kamin & Caughlan, 1963; Levitt, 1966; White, Fichtenbaum, & Dollard, 1964). These data, however, relate to expectations per se and do not reflect directly SES related interactions. As with attitude, it appears that the assessment of the impact of the treatment expectations of the disadvantaged depends, in part, on the methodology used to evaluate them.

In discussions with therapists participating in the New Haven study, Hollingshead and Redlich (1958) observed significant SES differences in patients' understanding of the treatment process. Although members of all SES levels appeared to know little about how therapy works (Baum & Felzer, 1964; Clemes & D'Andrea, 1965; Garfield & Wolpin, 1963; Redlich et al., 1955), the disadvantaged appeared least sophisticated. Auld and Myers (1954), for example, reported that the latter group perceived the therapist as magician, nerve doctor, or mind reader and assumed that psychotherapy would be similar to other forms of medical treatment. Similarly, Schaffer and Myers (1954) concluded that some low-income clients are insulted by the suggestion that their difficulties are emotional and that talking can be of assistance. Furthermore, the most disadvantaged patients were often perceived by their therapists as uncomfortable in treatment, since they believed that the asylum was the only place for the "crazy" (Myers & Roberts, 1959).

A direct psychometric evaluation of low-income treatment expectations was made by Overall and Aronson (1963) in a questionnaire survey of 40 low SES clients. These investigators examined the respondents' views about anticipated therapist behaviors, the relative emphasis on medical versus psychiatric aspects of their problems, and the supportive nature of therapy. Their low-income sample expressed stronger expectations for an active supportive therapist than did a subsequently added middle-class group (Aronson & Overall, 1966). Furthermore, those low SES patients whose expectations were most inaccurate were significantly less likely to return to treatment than their more sophisticated peers were. Although these two combined studies are regularly presented as evidence of the inappropriateness of low-income treatment expectations, serious sampling flaws limit the generalizability of these data. SES levels are confounded with race and religion in such a way that the studies' relevant independent variable cannot be determined.

Two subsequent studies have attempted to overcome these methodological errors. Williams, Lipman, Uhlenhuth, Rickels, Covi, and Mock (1967) asked several hundred clinic applicants to complete the original Overall and Aronson scale. Class V applicants had significantly lower levels of understanding of the treatment process than respondents from *all* other SES levels. Thus, all disadvantaged patients did not share similar pretreatment expectations. Using a modified version of this scale consisting of the items that most strongly discriminated across SES levels in previous studies, Lorion (1974b) found no significant SES differences in 90 white, middle- and low-income applicants. Directionally, however, Class V respondents appeared to understand the least about the process of psychotherapy.

It is possible, perhaps, to review the available data on low-income expectations and argue that whatever differences may have existed in the 1950s are gradually being reduced and will ultimately disappear. Undoubtedly, television, movies, and the popular press have provided much information to the public about the psychotherapy process (Wahl, 1976). As therapists, however, we should not be concerned with evaluating the appropriateness of expectations as a criterion for treatment as much as with understanding and, where necessary, correcting them. Numerous suggestions to this effect have been made over the years. As Lennard and Bernstein (1960) pointed out:

> part of the process of learning about what to communicate in therapy is for the patient to unlearn what he thought he was supposed to talk about and to become sensitive in expectational terms to the requirements of the situation in which he finds himself. (p. 157)

MENTAL HEALTH AND THE DISADVANTAGED—PRESENT APPROACHES

In this section, I will review a variety of intervention strategies that have demonstrated some degree of effectiveness in responding to the needs of the disadvantaged. Thus far, I have provided little evidence that the mental health professions have systematically developed and evaluated effective response alternatives to meet the needs of the low-income segments of the population. The global problem has long been recognized; we must now find solutions. To do so requires that our attention shift from the identification and confirmation of what does not work to the development of strategies that do work. Existing knowledge about past obstacles can contribute significantly to that goal. Additionally, genuine progress in this area depends on the integration of our knowledge about the life-styles of consumers into proposed treatment approaches (Grey, 1969; Heine & Trosman, 1960; Reiff & Scribner, 1964; Riessman, 1964; Riessman et al., 1964; Schneiderman, 1965). Attempts to implement solutions without consideration of background factors has resulted mostly in a succession of unsuccessful new approaches (Levine, 1970; Ruiz & Behrens, 1973).

Although we still do not have at our disposal means for responding prescriptively to all who seek treatment, recent experimental and clinical efforts hold the promise that we will ultimately reach that goal. The strategies to be reviewed do not exhaust the range of alternative treatment approaches now in use with the disadvantaged. Of primary immediate concern is the identification of procedures for which there is available empirical evidence of effectiveness. Treatment strategies that, to date, have been justified primarily with clinical findings will not be discussed here. This is not to suggest that they are without merit, but the extent and limitations of their impact has yet to be demonstrated through systematic means.

Therapist Preparation

Data reviewed already demonstrates the relevance to the course of treatment of the therapists' attitudes toward the disadvantaged. Given this fact, it seems reasonable that attempts to refine treatment approaches for the disadvantaged must, in some way, alter the therapists' potentially negative set at the onset of treatment. Truax and Carhkuff (1967) alert us to the consequences of omitting this step:

> when the therapist pretends to care, pretends to respect, or pretends to understand, he is fooling only himself. The patient may not know why the therapist is "phony" but he can easily detect true warmth from phony and insincere 'professional warmth.' (p. 34)

Thus, procedures must be identified that enable therapists to recognize and resolve their stereotypic views about the poor and the working class. Therapists must begin to perceive disadvantaged patients as potentially responsive to their efforts. This change can result in a reevaluation by therapists of the motivations of the disadvantaged in seeking treatment:

> rather than asking for "less" than he is offered, the working-class and lower-class patient may actually be asking for "more" in the sense that he wants a fuller, more extensive and more permanent relationship than is possible either within the traditional definition of the therapeutic relationship or in terms of what the therapist wishes to enter into. (Miller & Mishler, 1959, p. 288)

Some evidence has been reported to support the treatment implications of therapists' attitude change procedures.

In reviewing the available literature, I found only three studies that examine directly Frank's (1961) assumption that disadvantaged patients would respond more effectively to psychotherapy if therapists were trained to recognize and deal with their attitudes toward such patients. Baum and Felzer (1964) report that more than 65 percent of low-income applicants remained in treatment beyond six sessions when residents were carefully briefed about the life-styles, needs, and expectations of these groups. Throughout the course of treatment, staff conferences dealt openly with therapists' reluctance to work with such patients. As similarities and differences in needs and communication patterns were discussed, Baum and Felzer report that therapists began to recognize and implement changes in previously inflexible treatment approaches. Discussion of actual therapy sessions revealed changes in communication patterns to insure maximum patient understanding of therapists' messages. Care was taken to select analogies carefully. Conscious efforts were made to reinforce the patients' motivation to continue treatment. Bernard (1965) defined therapist's attitudes toward the disadvantaged as a countertransference topic appropriate to supervisory feedback. She reports increases in therapeutic effectiveness among psychiatric residents when supervision dealt openly with their misperceptions and resistance to serving the disadvantaged. Unfortunately, neither Bernard (1965) nor Baum and Felzer (1964) operationally define the criteria used to assess treatment effectiveness, nor do they report any attempt to compare supervised versus unsupervised therapists.

The relative efficacy of modifying or ignoring therapists' pretreatment attitudes toward the disadvantaged was systematically assessed in a recent study by Jacobs, Charles, Jacobs, Weinstein, and Mann (1972). These investigators simultaneously considered the treatment impact of therapist and patient preparation occurring prior to the first treatment session. The results of patient preparation will be discussed in the next section.

In their study, Jacobs et al. (1972) randomly assigned 120 low-income outpatient applicants to one of four experimental conditions.

- "Prepared" patient seen by "prepared" therapist.
- "Nonprepared" patient seen by "prepared" therapist.
- "Nonprepared" patient seen by "nonprepared" therapist.
- "Prepared" patient seen by "nonprepared" therapist.

A total of 24 therapists participated in this study. The study involved a repeated measures design; all psychiatric residents treated patients in each of the four conditions. The therapist preparation, given by the chief resident at the time the case was assigned, consisted of a brief (15 minutes) orientation to low-income life-styles, treatment expectations, and therapeutic problems. This information was incorporated into the regular case assignment procedures used by the chief resident. "Nonprepared" therapists did not discuss SES relevant issues when they met with the chief resident. To insure that the observed findings do not merely reflect the therapists' recognition of the experimental conditions, all therapists were carefully interviewed once the last patient was seen. None gave any evidence suggesting that they were aware of the study's procedures or hypotheses, nor did they recognize any pattern to the chief resident's assignment discussions.

The observed findings demonstrate the merit of including therapist preparation procedures in clinical training and supervision. Treatment effectiveness was assessed using a variety of indices including: treatment duration; the development of a specific treatment plan; and improvement as rated by independent reviewers of case records. After the initial four sessions, therapists retained disadvantaged patients in treatment significantly longer ($p \leq .05$) when prepared than unprepared. They were also significantly more likely to propose a specific treatment plan ($p \leq .05$) and to perceive their patients as improving ($p \leq .05$) when prepared than unprepared. Interestingly, disadvantaged patients seen by unprepared therapists were significantly more likely ($p \leq .05$) to have their psychiatric contact limited to evaluative sessions. On all outcome measures, patients seen in condition 3 (patients and therapists nonprepared) had the least positive experiences. Although nonsignificant, directional differences favoring the prepared patients were observed on attrition rates, the use of medication, and initial evaluation of treatment needs.

Although more refined outcome measures might have been employed, this study demonstrates that significant positive changes can occur in therapists' responses to the disadvantaged using a relatively simple procedure that sensitizes therapists to their disadvantaged patient's needs. Undoubtedly, this study should be replicated and extended. Which therapists did or did not respond to preparation is unknown. Process analyses of actual treatment sessions could provide important insights into the ways in which "preparation" is translated into verbal and nonverbal therapists behaviors. Yet even without these data, it is apparent that the negative self-fulfilling potential of therapists' attitudes and expectations toward the disadvantaged is reversible. Indeed, an even more promising finding reported by Jacobs et al. (1972) is their conclusion that most therapists, regardless of their economic or racial background, can become effective service providers to the disadvantaged.

Patient Preparation

Pretreatment preparation has not been used only with therapists. In fact, the majority of studies in this area have focused primarily on attempts to modify the treatment attitudes and expectations of patients. A variety of procedures to increase patients understanding of the therapeutic process have been reported. Some rely on direct instruction, others on informational interviews, and still others on modeling and role playing. The differential efficacy of these strategies has not been assessed and is as yet unknown. Overall, however, it appears that the majority of patient preparation techniques do significantly improve the mental health treatment experiences of the disadvantaged (Heitler, 1973, 1976).

Assuming that the disadvantaged patient's motivation for therapy could be enhanced early in treatment, Albronda, Dean, and Starkweather (1964) made pretreatment informational interviews available to these patients. Prior to the formal intake session, psychiatric social workers met with patients for one session to aid them in the formulation of specific treatment goals and to clarify the psychotherapeutic process for them. These meetings focused on the specific delineation of the therapist and patient roles. No control subjects (i.e., unprepared) were included in the experimental design. The investigators report significant increases (in comparison to prior case records) in the proportion of applicants who arrived for the formal intake and remained in treatment. Similar findings with a comparable procedure were reported by Baum and Felzer (1964).

Orne and Wender (1968) recommended a socialization procedure to prepare patients for psychoanalytically oriented psychotherapy. Prior to the onset of treatment, the patient participates in an individual clinical interview designed to provide:

- A justification of psychotherapy as an appropriate response to the patient's needs.
- A specific description of the role of the therapist and patient in the treatment process.
- A general overview of the typical course of treatment and of the nature of transference and resistance.

In response to Orne and Wender's (1968) suggestion, investigators at the Phipps Psychiatric Clinic developed the Role Induction Interview (RII) and evaluated its treatment impact in a series of well-designed studies. Hoehn-Saric, Frank, Imber, Nash, Stone, and Battle (1964) report that patients who received the RII behaved more appropriately in therapy than matched controls did. Furthermore, the prepared group responded much more positively to treatment than the controls as assessed by a variety of outcome measures. Significant differences were found on three of these: (1) therapist's ratings of change; (2) patient's rating of change; and (3) a "blind" interviewer's ratings of the patient's social ineffectiveness following treatment.

Careful review of these and related data indicate that an important consequence of utilizing the RII with patients is an increase in the perceived attractiveness of disadvantaged patients for the therapist

(Nash, Hoehn-Saric, Battle, Stone, Imber, & Frank, 1965). Furthermore, it appears that the RIIs can be extended if someone from the patient's environment (e.g., wife, friend, parent) participates in the RII and subsequently supports the therapeutic process (Stone, Imber, & Frank, 1966). The RII's positive contribution to the psychotherapeutic process was validated in a subsequent replication of the Hoehn-Saric et al. (1964) study (Schonfield, Stone, Hoehn-Saric, Imber, & Pande, 1969).

Other attempts to assess the impact of patient preparation have been reported. In a partial replication of the Phipps studies, Sloane, Cristal, Pepernik, and Staples (1970) compared the differential impact of the RII's socialization and faith induction components. Their results demonstrate that the RII's socialization aspects (i.e., role classification) were the major contributor to observed improvements in the course and outcome of treatment. Warren and Rice (1972) agreed with this conclusion in their evaluation of patient preparation *during* the course of treatment. In this study, patients were randomly assigned to one of three conditions: therapy; therapy plus "stabilizating" sessions designed to encourage discussion of transference issues; or therapy plus stabilizing and "structuring" (i.e., socialization) sessions. Significant positive differences were observed for the prepared versus unprepared patients on measures of treatment duration, involvement in the therapeutic process, and improvement as rated by therapists and patients. Warren and Rice's (1972) data demonstrate that structuring contributes significantly to the maintenance of the therapeutic alliance. This finding was also demonstrated in the Jacobs et al. (1972) study described earlier. These investigators demonstrated that prepared disadvantaged patients remained in treatment longer and showed more improvement than matched nonprepared controls.

Since considerable emphasis is often placed on group treatment approaches for the disadvantaged, a number of investigators have applied patient preparation techniques to group members. Using a university population, Yalom, Houts, Newell, and Rand (1967) used a modified version of the Orne and Wender socialization approach. Group members who participated in an initial preparatory session interacted more positively than members of nonprepared groups (Yalom et al., 1967). Heitler (1973) extended these findings by looking specifically at disadvantaged group members in an inpatient setting. He concluded that prepared patients:

> *tended to lower latencies for voluntary participation, to communicate more frequently, spend more clock time communicating, communicate more frequently on a self-initiated basis, to engage in self-exploratory efforts more frequently, and to do so in a greater percentage of their communications. (p. 349)*

Furthermore, the therapist rated prepared patients as more involved, more similar to an ideal group therapy patient, more likely to engage in self-initiated collaborative efforts to explore personal difficulties, and having more hopeful purposes than control patients. These differences were all statistically significant (Heitler, 1976).

Strupp and Bloxom (1973) also studied the effects of patient preparation on group treatment. Their sample consisted of 122 disadvantaged outpatients assigned to one of three conditions: group treatment without preparation, group plus an RII interview, or group plus an RII type film. Significant advantages to prepared patients were observed across a number of dimensions, including motivation toward and understanding of treatment and satisfaction with treatment and with their interpersonal relations. Prepared patients perceived themselves as benefiting more from treatment than the nonprepared controls. Each induction procedure appeared to make a somewhat unique contribution to the observed findings. The interview most effectively imparted specific information about treatment roles to the patient; the film, on the other hand, maximized the patient's motivation to begin and engage in the treatment process.

Given the consistency of reported findings, it appears that some form of pretreatment preparation should be made available to disadvantaged patients. The evidence for the positive impact of preparatory procedures is too overwhelming to ignore. All potential patients cannot and should not be expected to be equally sophisticated about the nature of mental health treatment. Most can, however, be expected to gain therapeutically valuable insights into the treatment process if they are given an opportunity to learn about therapy prior to or early in its inception. Thus, a relatively simple modification of the standard intake to allow for the provision instead of the collection of information promises to increase significantly the availability and potential impact of psychotherapy for the disadvantaged.

It is important, however, to recognize that such similar positive treatment consequences accompany efforts to prepare therapists as well. The differential effect of these two approaches, as already noted, has been considered by Jacobs et al (1972). Although not conclusive, the Jacobs et al (1972) data suggests, and I concur, that the crucial target may be the therapist. Considering the tentativeness of their conclusion, further research is definitely needed to determine the optimal target for treatment preparation (therapist, patient, or both). Future psychotherapy research must also be designed to identify the process mechanisms through which preparatory procedures influence the conduct and outcome of psychotherapy.

Insight-Oriented Approaches

Available data suggest that traditional insight-oriented approaches have not been made available to the low-income segments of the population. It is also true that disadvantaged patients assigned to traditional approaches have, for the most part, been unwilling to remain in that form of treatment. However, on the basis of these facts, one cannot conclude that insight-oriented approaches have not been and cannot be effective with these segments of the population (Lorion, 1973). As indicated earlier, the question of the efficacy of dynamic approaches for the disadvantaged remains unanswered.

I do not intend to suggest that insight-oriented psychotherapy as traditionally presented to middle- and upper-class patients should be made readily available to the disadvantaged. In discussing this question, Freud (1950) recognized the fact that dynamically oriented treatments would have to be altered in ways that recognize and appreciate the realities of low-income life-styles:

one may reasonably expect that at some time or other the conscience of the community will awake and admonish it that the poor man has just as much right to help for his mind as he now has for the surgeons means for saving his life; . . . the task will then arise for us to adapt our techniques to the new conditions. I have no doubt that the validity of our psychological assumptions will impress the uneducated too, that we shall need to find the simplest and most natural expressions for our theoretical doctrines. (p. 400)

In a carefully considered theoretical discussion of treatment approaches for the disadvantaged, Bernard (1971) provides a more contemporary view of this argument.

In the midst of the current whirlwind of innovative and often controversial effort, it seems especially useful to maintain some historical perspective. Otherwise, in reaction against past failures, one risks throwing out the good with the bad, or needlessly wasting the legacy of valid achievement on which one can build, by trying instead to start from scratch. (p. 62)

In seeking to identify effective treatment approaches for the disadvantaged, mental health researchers must not ignore the potential utility of traditional approaches. Instead of simply rejecting insight-oriented approaches as inappropriate for the disadvantaged, it seems reasonable instead to attempt to identify the effective components of these strategies. In this way, the "trappings" can be modified to fit more comfortably into the life-styles of the disadvantaged without significantly altering the primary therapeutic aspects basic to these strategies.

Some evidence of the positive treatment effect for the disadvantaged patients of receiving modified versions of dynamically oriented therapy is available. Gould (1967), for example, states that assembly-line workers responded quite well to his less formal analytic approach. His treatment was offered in a direct, simple manner with minimal emphasis on the social distance between patient and therapist. Early sessions focused on the patient's misconceptions about the nature and goal of mental health treatment (i.e., patient preparation). Whenever possible, psychological jargon was avoided, and everyday language was used to communicate salient concepts to the patient. Gould focused on the patient's concern with specific issues as a means of encouraging discussion of dynamic issues. Gould reports that occasional sessions held by walking in a nearby park greatly facilitated discussions at certain critical points. He also reports that session length was modified in relation to productivity. At times, treatment lasted 20 to 30 minutes; at other times, it lasted the full 50 minutes. Where appropriate, problems were treated at face value and direct advice was offered to the patient. Gould reports that his "flexible" therapeutic approach increased patient comfort and motivation without negatively affecting consideration and resolution of dynamic material.

Unfortunately, Gould did not systematically evaluate his efforts. He reports only *his* impressions of the results of his therapy. Obviously, a more controlled evaluation of this work is necessary. Support for Gould's conclusions, however, is provided by Hacker, Illing, and Bergreen (1965), who report similar improvement in working-class patients participating in analytically oriented therapy. These investigators observed a 50 percent reduction in attrition rates as their therapists responded to patients in an increasingly flexible manner. Yet, without operational definitions of the therapeutic procedures (e.g., what are the specific analytical components and the specific flexible modifications thereof?) and objective measures of their efficacy, these data can only be interpreted suggestively. Ultimate confirmation of these impressionistic reports depends on their replication in a carefully controlled study.

There exists a single systematic evaluation of insight-oriented psychotherapies for ghetto residents. In her excellent book, *Therapy in the Ghetto,* Lerner (1972) reports the results of 5 years of research on outpatient psychotherapy with nontraditional patients. Forty-five patients were seen by 15 different psychotherapists (psychologists and social workers). Of these, eight were highly experienced and seven were relatively less experienced. All the therapists emphasized insight-oriented ap-

proaches in their treatment methods. The 45 patients included 23 black and 22 white outpatients ranging in age from 16 to 57. No specific procedures were used in selecting patients for the study. Outcome measures included a variety of patient and therapist self-description and symptom reduction measures. Additionally, Lerner describes the psychometric development of the Rorschach Psychological Functioning Scale (RPFS). This measure assesses two specific dimensions of adaptive functioning. First, structural soundness relates to the patients gross reality contact, perceptual accuracy, emotional control and integration, and cognitive balance. Second, functional richness refers to the patient's contact with and access to internal processes. This is assessed along two dimensions—affective richness and cognitive richness. Scoring criteria for this measure are discussed in detail in Lerner's book (1972); she reports interrater reliabilities ranging from .65 to .96 for total and subscale scores. Finally, some index of the RPFS's validity is reflected in the fact that it correlated significantly with all major therapist and patient outcome ratings. Thus, it seems that Lerner's primary outcome measure is a viable index of therapeutic effectiveness for these patients.

Of the 30 patients who completed treatment prior to the end of the study (12 of the remaining 15 dropped out of treatment and three were involved in ongoing therapy), 23 showed significant gains in psychological functioning following treatment. No significant racial differences in outcome were observed, nor did same race and cross-racial patient-therapist dyads differ on any measure. These results were suported on the majority of patient and therapist outcome measures used. Lerner emphasizes the extremely significant ($p \leq .005$) relationship found between assessed democratic attitude of the therapist and patient improvement. She interprets this finding as evidence of the fact that democratic or nonauthoritarian attitudes on the part of the therapist:

> Create an ambience which helps clients avail themselves of their own resources, but it may also be that such values make it easier for the very confused and needy people to avail themselves of other gooa things the therapist has to offer, such as warmth, support, ac-

ceptance, protection, understanding, and clarification. (p. 141)

Finally, it should be noted that Lerner's positive results were achieved in less than 9 months and required fewer than 30 sessions. The actual cost per client was somewhere between $200 to $300 for the entire treatment process. Thus, she argues that insight-oriented therapeutic approaches, with understanding and open therapists, are both potentially effective and economically feasible for the disadvantaged. The fact that nearly one-third of her sample (12/45) terminated prematurely underlines, however, the continued importance of developing sensitive procedures of prescriptively matching treatments and patients.

Lerner's excellent study provides a model for future research on insight-oriented approaches with the disadvantaged. Her outcome measures included assessments of both internal and external adjustment parameters of adjustment. Her therapist sample was heterogenious in terms of treatment experience, professional discipline, and race. Although the generalizability of her findings is limited by the size of her patient sample (30), they are clinically and heuristically valuable. Replication and extension of this study with a greater number of patients, more operationally defined treatment approaches and, if possible, direct comparison with other treatment modalities should be carried out as soon as possible. Until that time, the data reviewed in this section, particularly Lerner's results, argue strongly against the arbitrary exclusion of disadvantaged patients from insight-oriented approaches. Obviously, these treatment modalities are appropriate for some disadvantaged clients.

Brief Treatment Approaches

Time-limited therapeutic approaches should be very appropriate for many of the disadvantaged. Not only are their economic and occupational realities inconsistent with long-term treatment (Frank, 1961; Garfield, 1963; McMahon, 1964; Storrow, 1962) but, in fact, most patients remain in treatment for only a brief period as evidenced by reports of *actual* national treatment duration averages. Thirty to sixty percent of psychotherapy patients terminate within the first six sessions, with or without their therapist's consent (Rubenstein &

Lorr, 1956). Fewer than half of over 11,000 patients from 53 clinics remained in treatment beyond eight sessions (Rogers, 1960). For 1966, the National Center for Health Statistics reports an average of fewer than five contacts for almost 1 million patients seen in psychiatric treatment during that year. Thus, median treatment durations range from 3 to 12 sessions and, if only those patients who actually begin treatment are considered, median durations are between five and six sessions (Garfield, 1971). In actual practice, it appears that instead of dropping out in the middle, patients leave treatment at phenomenologically defined end points.

Butcher and Koss (Chapter 19) have already provided a general overview of brief and crisis-oriented psychotherapies. In this section we will consider the relevance of these approaches for the disadvantaged. In earlier analyses of mental health services, Strupp and Bergin (1969) and Urban and Ford (1971) emphasized the importance of developing individualized treatment perscriptions that are realistic and problem oriented. In varying degrees, these goals can be reached using brief psychotherapy approaches. The rationale behind these strategies is clearly described by Barton (1971).

Brief therapists share a commitment to provide something meaningful to all those who seek or should be seeking help, in terms that are acceptable and relevant to the patients. These therapists recognize that they must answer some of the patients needs quickly, and that at times simple, perhaps superficial solutions are more cogent than profound but unduly delayed ones. Simple solutions often have profound preventive consequences. Although the objectives are pragmatic, the therapist need not eschew a dynamic, multifaceted scrutiny of whatever material emerges, selectively sharing with the patient what is germane and useable. (p. 21)

A variety of time-limited approaches have been described for the disadvantaged (Bellak & Small, 1965; Sifneos, 1972; Small, 1971). McMahon (1964), Reiff and Scribner (1964), Riessman (1964), and Schlesinger and James (1969) recommend that time-limited contracts be established immediately to respond directly to presenting symptoms. As these problems are resolved, the therapeutic contract may be renegotiated to deal with more complex intrapsychic difficulties. Evidence of the efficacy of short-term approaches is available (Wolberg, 1967). For example, Avnet (1962) reports that the Group Health Insurance Corporation surveyed 1200 mental health professionals. Following time-limited treatment, 76 percent of their patients were rated as improved. A follow-up study 2 1/2 years later demonstrated that short-term treatment effects continue over time (Avnet, 1965). Unfortunately, the implications of these data are limited by the fact that therapists' ratings defined improvement and there were no control groups included in these studies. Levy (1966) reported similar findings. Only 9 out of 493 patients seen in time-limited treatment (four to six sessions) required any subsequent treatment. Levy interprets their reluctance to seek further treatment as evidence of symptom reduction. Yet, without clear evidence of symptom reduction, the actual impact of brief approaches cannot be assumed. That so few patients sought further treatment may, in fact, reflect the failure of time-limited approaches. Patients may have been reluctant with what they experienced as an unsatisfying treatment.

A more rigorous assessment of brief therapy with the disadvantaged is provided by Koegler and Brill (1967). These investigators compared brief contact therapy with or without medication where indicated, and traditional long-term, insight-oriented psychotherapy. Patients were randomly assigned to treatment conditions and double blind procedures controlled for therapist bias in evaluating the drug treatment. Patients having minimal contact met with their therapist for a limited number of sessions to discuss practical aspects of their problems and to receive medication (or placebos). Koegler and Brill report no differences in symptom reduction between the brief and traditional treatments lasting beyond 6 months. This finding is particularly noteworthy considering the probabilities that disadvantaged patients would remain in treatment for as long as 6 months.

Additional support for time-limited treatment

with the disadvantaged is provided by Goin, Yamamoto, and Silverman (1965) and Yamamoto and Goin (1966). These investigators report that a sizable number of their disadvantaged patients showed noticeable reductions in symptoms following participation in brief, problem-oriented treatment. Since many low-income applicants often fail to arrive for intake, Yamamoto and Goin (1966) scheduled 10 to 15 patients for each 10 therapist hours. At times, several patients were interviewed together in a group intake session. All patients were seen within a few days of contacting the clinic. Some patients responded so well to these streamlined intake procedures that they required no further treatment. Others continued for up to six sessions, during which the therapist participated actively and directly advised the patient. Rapid ongoing access to follow-up clinics was available. Stone and Crowthers (1972) also found significant decreases in dropout rates following the introduction of crisis-oriented, time-limited psychotherapy. These investigators found that blue-collar families utilized psychiatric services much more comfortably and frequently when they were available on a prepaid instead of "fee for service" basis and when they provided direct, immediate problem focusing.

Unfortunately, there presently exist far too few systematic evaluations of short-term treatment approaches with the disadvantaged. Despite this lack, they are being used extensively. The favorable results of these methods seem so clear that it appears that they may become the treatment of choice for disadvantaged patients. This has occurred without careful assessment of their long- and short-term consequences and their optimal prescriptive utility. One cannot, therefore, rule out the possibility that while the disadvantaged are currently receiving more treatment, they are not necessarily receiving more effective treatment.

Behavioral Approaches
In preparing a recent review of behavioral approaches, Krasner (1971) reports that over 4000 studies of this treatment modality have been published. Thus, it is important for the reader to recognize that "behavior therapy" represents a generic term for an assortment of therapeutic procedures differing from traditional expressive psychotherapy

and from each other (modeling, desensitization, aversive psychotherapy, implosion, etc.). Behavioral approaches do, however, share certain characteristics that make them relevant for the disadvantaged. They operate from a conception of psychopathology that allows for a more direct, problem-oriented focus than the dynamic model allows. The behavior therapist does not assume that intrapsychic conflicts must be resolved in order to achieve permanent symptom removal. Thus, a basic match exists between the disadvantaged patients' interest in obtaining direct resolution of their symptoms and the behaviorist's focus on symptom removal (Graziano, 1969).

Evidence of the effectiveness of the behavioral approaches is reviewed in Part III of this volume. Although behavioral approaches initially emphasized the resolution of circumscribed problems such as phobias, ticks, and sexual perversions, recent evidence suggests that they are also appropriate for generalized dysfunctions such as alcholism, addictions, depression, and anxiety reactions (Eysenck, 1972; Krasner, 1971; Lazarus, 1972, 1976).

Unfortunately, few data presently exist that demonstrate the relative effectiveness of behavioral approaches with the working class and the poor. Most recently, Sloane, Staples, Cristol, Yorkston, and Whipple (1975) have completed a well-designed, carefully controlled comparison of traditional expressive and behavior therapies that is also cited in several other chapters in this volume. In this study, 94 patients suffering from moderately severe neuroses and personality disorders were randomly assigned to traditional, behavioral, or a waiting-list control condition. To insure their involvement, control patients were promised therapy within 4 months, were provided with a contact to call in case of crisis, and telephoned irregularly during the 4-month waiting period. At the end of the experimental period, Sloane et al. (1975) observed that all three groups had improved significantly and that the behavioral and traditional therapy groups had improved significantly more than their waiting-list controls. No differences, however, in amount of improvement were found between the therapy groups. At the end of a year, behavior therapy patients were significantly more improved

on reduction of target symptoms than the controls. There was no evidence of symptom substitution in any group. In fact, improvement in target symptoms was accompanied by improvement in other symptoms as well.

The results of the Sloane et al. (1975) study are relevant to this chapter for several reasons. First, their results demonstrate that behavior therapy can be at least as effective as expressive psychotherapy with the problems of typical clinic patients. Second, and perhaps most important, Sloane et al. demonstrate that behavior therapy can effectively serve more heterogenious patient populations than traditional psychotherapies can. In this study, the behavior therapists were equally effective with patients from all socioeconomic backgrounds. Finally, this study exemplifies the level of design sophistication appropriate to the complex issues involved in prescriptive analyses. As will become evident later, the Sloane et al. study closely approximates the "ideal" design.

Marital and Family Approaches

Throughout this chapter I have emphasized the importance of identifying treatment approaches for the disadvantaged that are salient to their lifestyles. Numerous discussions of the working class have stressed the importance of family to the attainment and maintenance of mental health (Gans, 1962; Giordano, 1973; Miller & Mishler, 1959; Miller & Riessman, 1964; Riessman, 1964). Although its composition may differ somewhat, the family is also an important parameter of emotional functioning among the poor and minority groups (Miller & Riessman, 1968; Rainwater, 1966).

More and more often, therefore, the disadvantaged family is perceived as a viable target for mental health services (Chaiklin & Frank, 1973; LaVietes, 1974). Mannino and Shore (1972), for example, report on a program that aims to assist low-income families in their interaction with other social systems. The goals of their "ecologically oriented family intervention" include increases in the family's effectiveness as a unit, and in its capacity to relate to and effectively deal with relevant social systems (e.g., schools, welfare, medical facilities).

Yet low-income families seem hesitant to use

and respond to family services. Rosenblatt and Mayer (1972), for example, reviewed interview data collected from 6200 parents who participated in project ENABLE, a national demonstration program to help socially and economically deprived persons to solve family and neighborhood problems. Black and white women show a marked difference in their willingness to approach professionals for family services. Rosenblatt and Mayer report that 61 percent of white women used professionals as compared to 45 percent of black women. At the same time, the interview data suggest that those least willing to use family services (i.e., blacks and members of the lowest income segment) are most satisfied with the help they receive. These observed satisfaction ratings suggest that increasing the availability and attractiveness of such services can have very positive effects on these segments of the population.

Speer, Fossum, Lippman, Schwartz, and Slocum (1968) support this conclusion in reporting that the major variable on which middle- and low-income families differed in their use of family services was in the number of appointments failed. Class V individuals had significantly more difficulty regularly attending sessions than members of Class III did. They did not differ, however, in terms of continuing in treatment. In a well-designed comparative analysis of child psychotherapy, parent counseling, and "informational feedback," Love, Kaswan, and Bugental (1972) have demonstrated that family-oriented approaches are most effective in serving the needs of the disadvantaged. In this study, a total of 91 referred families who have a child experiencing serious school-related difficulties were assigned to one of three treatment conditions. Additionally, a "nonreferred" control group was used as a "normal" comparison group to provide baseline data on family and school measures. Dependent measures used in this study included school grades, behavioral ratings by objective observers, and ratings of family interaction and communication patterns rated from videotape recordings. The results clearly indicated that parent interventions were significantly more effective in improving their children's performance than child psychotherapy was. Socioeconomic analyses of subjects revealed that the disadvantaged re-

sponded most to procedures that provided direct information and advice. Heinicke (1975) also evaluated the effects of family treatments on the parents of 112 children who were experiencing developmental lags. Consistent with other studies, she found a positive response to family approaches on measured ratings of effectiveness and on specific measures of adjustment.

The general findings reviewed thus far suggest that family oriented approaches can be appropriate for the disadvantaged. However, evidence of their effectiveness is not readily available. Framo (1969) provides a thoughtful anecdotal description of a black ghetto family in treatment. Although he does not evaluate the results of this case objectively, his report provides heuristically valuable insights into problems associated with that approach. Further grist for the subsequent evaluation of family therapy with minority patients is provided in an intriguing conceptual analysis by Sager, Braybo, and Waxenberg (1970). They describe a laboratory exercise in which five black staff members assumed the roles of members of a ghetto family and four distinguished family therapists (Nathan Ackerman, Thomas Brayboy, Robert MacGregor, and Carl Whitaker) individually confronted this "family" in a first interview. The major value of this book lies in its heuristic instead of empirical contribution. Mental health researchers who read this book will identify a variety of meaningful questions that merit immediate and systematic analysis. They will also recognize patient and therapist variables that must be controlled in a methodologically sophisticated study.

A somewhat less subjective evaluation of family therapy with the disadvantaged is provided by Minuchin, Montalvo, Guerney, Rosman, and Schumer, (1967). In their report of an "exploratory" study, the investigators compared 12 ghetto families having a delinquent child with 10 matched "control" families not having a delinquent child on a variety of objective-type family interaction tasks. Following treatment, posttesting was conducted with the experimental families, but not with the control families. In the absence of posttesting for the control group, the reported pre- and post-changes may reflect the impact of the treatment or simply the passage of time. The investigators report that 7 out of the 12 experimental families were judged to be clinically improved on all of the interactional measures after treatment. Although suggestive, these results must be verified in a systematic, methodologically sophisticated way. Wells, Dilkes, and Burckhardt (1976) conclude that this caution holds true for much of the available family therapy research.

If, as Rainwater (1966) suggests, low-income family life is characterized by unstructured marital roles, strategies focusing specifically on improving the marital relationship should also be relevant to the disadvantaged. A fair amount of evidence exists that demonstrates the efficacy of these procedures. In a recent review, Gurman (1973) analyzes 15 studies that meet basic methodological criteria and concludes that across a variety of marital therapy approaches and outcome criteria, more than 66 percent of treated patients improve. The majority of these studies used clinic populations made up primarily of disadvantaged families. Moreover, the average treatment duration was fewer than 20 sessions. Gurman notes that marital therapy, like other therapies (Bergin, 1971), can have deleterious effects on some clients. In roughly 2 percent of the cases treated, the referral problem was worse after treatment. Comparable results are also reported in the most recent survey by Gurman and Kniskern described in Chapter 21 of this volume.

The effectiveness of marital counseling with the disadvantaged is demonstrated by Beck and Jones (1973). Their report summarizes follow-up data (secured by interview or mail questionnaires) on approximately 2000 marital cases served by the Family Service Association of America. Criterion outcome measures included global ratings of patient improvement, indices of change in presenting problem, skills, family relationships, and measures of improvement in specific family members. Independent ratings were secured from counselors and clients in each of these areas. Overall, 60 to 70 percent of the clients returning the questionnaires ($N = 985$) reported improvement across the criterion measures. Beck and Jones attempted to compensate for the absence of a control group by assessing the relationship between change measures and the total number of sessions attended. Patients who had a single marital interview (which the investigators perceive as an approximation of a no-treatment control group) had significantly lower improvement rates than patients attending 2 to 20 sessions.

Further evidence for the efficacy of marital counseling with the disadvantaged is provided in a recent review of outcome studies by Beck (1976). Consideration of eight studies without control groups involving some 500 marital couples demonstrates improvement rates of 65 to 70 percent. Additionally, Beck reports that the combined results of eight studies (mostly reported in dissertation abstracts) that included a control group reveal significantly higher improvement rates in experimental over control subjects. In six of the eight controlled studies, half or more of the outcome measures showed gains that were significant at or above the .05 level. Marital counseling approaches that focused exclusively on improving communication patterns between the marital partners were considered in 12 studies. Nine of these showed statistically significant positive increments on half or more of the measures used to compare treatment and control groups (Beck, 1976).

One of the important findings included in the Beck review is the relatively stronger impact of structured, communication-oriented treatments. A variety of these approaches are reported in a recent work by Olson (1976). Some have been developed specifically with disadvantaged clients; others, although apparently generalizable, have yet to be proven effective generally and specifically with the disadvantaged.

Stuart (1976) describes a behaviorally oriented program to improve communication skills between marital partners. Although a major evaluation of this program used with 750 couples over a 10-year period is still underway, Stuart reports interim findings on 200 couples. In 87 percent of the couples treated, at least one spouse met the initial behavioral objectives; in 81 percent of the cases, those objectives were met by both partners. One year after treatment there were only five divorces; 5 years later, 174 of the 200 couples remained married and reported reasonable satisfaction with the relationship. In view of these preliminary findings, Stuart's operant approach at improving communication skills merits further consideration. Refer to Chapter 21 of this volume for a more extensive analysis of this research and of the work recently reported by Blechman and Olson (1976), who describe a "gamelike" treatment approach for improving the communication and problem-solving skills of family members. Data available thus far suggest the effectiveness of this approach, but they were collected with only a small sample (N = 4) of single-parent families.

Considerably more research will have to be done before the relative benefits and cost of marital and family approaches for disadvantaged clients can be identified. At the present time, we are far too dependent on clinical results and on poorly evaluated results to assume the efficacy of these procedures for the disadvantaged or other segments of society with any degree of certainty. The trend of available findings, however, is consistently positive and suggests that these procedures are worthwhile.

Alternative Manpower Resources

No discussion of psychotherapy with the disadvantaged can be complete without consideration of the alternative, nonprofessional manpower resources utilized more and more with the disadvantaged. Data from three broad areas underlie this "nonprofessional revolution" (Cowen, 1973; Sobey, 1970). First, epidemiological surveys demonstrate an exceedingly high incidence of socioemotional dysfunction in the disadvantaged subgroups. Second, it is clear that in the foreseeable future professional resources will be inadequate to serve those in need of mental health services (Albee, 1959, 1967; Arnhoff, Rubinstein, & Speisman, 1969; Gartner, 1971). Third, it is increasingly clear that even if professional resources were adequate, significant segments of the population, particularly among the disadvantaged, are reluctant to approach formal mental health care givers (Gurin, Veroff, & Feld, 1960; Kadushin, 1969). Thus, the development of additional and alternative manpower resources is a logical step for the mental health system to take.

This chapter will not provide a comprehensive review of the areas in which nonprofessional workers have been used in the delivery of mental health services. There is, however, a substantial body of evidence (some of which is methodologically sound, much of which is based on weak or impressionistic findings) that supports the utilization of alternative manpower sources.

In a recent review of nonprofessional services, Gartner & Riessman (1974) identified three major categories of nonprofessional workers: the traditional hospital-based worker employed in an inpatient setting; the middle-class nonprofessional involved on a voluntary or paid basis in providing services; and the indigenous paraprofessional who is recruited from and works within the local community. Representatives of the last two categories are most relevant to the focus of this chapter.

The best known of the projects utilizing middle-class paraprofessionals in the delivery of mental health services is that developed by Margaret Rioch (1967). In this project, eight middle-class women were selected from among 80 applicants to participate in a 2- year formal training program to become mental health workers. Their training focused on the development of basic psychotherapeutic skills and practicum training. Evaluation of their effectiveness was assessed by outside experts who rated audiotapes (without knowledge of the trainee's status) of trainee interviews with patients. These interviews were rated as of a relatively high professional quality. Symptom reduction measures revealed that 61 percent of the clients seen by the trainees showed some improvement.

Traux (1967) compared lay therapists, clinical psychology graduate students, and experienced therapists in working with chronic hospitalized patients. Evaluating these groups on measures of empathy, warmth, and genuineness, Truax found no significant differences among the groups on the first two; experienced therapists, however, were rated as communicating significantly more genuinely with patients than the other two groups. Overall, Truax concludes that lay therapists made significant contributions to patient improvement across a variety of outcome measures.

The most comprehensive evaluation of nonprofessional performance is reported by Sobey (1970). In her report, she examines the efficacy of more than 10,000 nonprofessionals who were functioning in 185 different NIMH sponsored programs. Her analyses suggest that nonprofessionals are utilized in traditional professional roles (e.g., providing individual and group therapy); in casework; in screening capacities; and in general counseling roles to help peers adjust to their community. Undoubtedly, the number of individuals involved and the variety of functions in which they are employed support Sobey's description of the nonprofessional movement as a "revolution." Testimonials on behalf of the impact of these individuals are available (Cowen, 1973). Summarizing these, Sobey (1970) states:

> An untrained person can develop both skill in observation of symptoms and ability to deliver personal care for the mentally ill. One study project reported that 80 percent of the nonprofessionals trained as practical nurses seemed capable of functioning in therapeutic roles (individual, group, and milieu therapy) in the care of the mentally ill. Where nonprofessionals work with "normal" populations in the community, skills in community organization and reducing the distance between the professional and the community were frequently noted. For innovative roles which nonprofessionals have so often been asked to assume—the teacher-mom, homevisitor, reach-out aide, etc.—the flexibility and spontaneity of nonprofessionals is seen as a primary asset. Generally, nonprofessionals are ready and willing to learn and to undertake more than is expected of them (pp. 177–178)

Unfortunately, however, the majority of data describing their effectiveness evolves from relatively weak or nonexistent research designs (Karlsruher, 1974).

Indigenous paraprofessionals assume an equally varied set of roles (Gartner & Riessman, 1974). Their work ranges from providing escort service, home visits, receiving complaints, and providing mental health information to organizing community meetings, conducting therapy groups, designing aftercare services, and providing supportive psychotherapy to patients. Reiff and Riessman (1965) suggest that the use of indigenous personnel reflects the new concern for the poor and

evolves from the Johnson Administration's War on Poverty. They view the unique quality of the indigenous worker as the fact that he or she is part of the very community in which they serve. Given this, it is assumed that they can establish uniquely therapeutic relationships with clients. Beyond impressionistic and descriptive data, however, there is little hard evidence of the efficacy of their services. In reviewing indigenous roles, Sobey (1970) states:

> It is by now common knowledge that we have romanticized the indigenous worker, and that little hard data is available on the effective employing and training of this type of worker. No evidence exists of the indigenous worker's special knowledge or insight into his fellow man, nor is there evidence that he is necessarily motivated to help his fellow man more than the "socially distant" professional. (p. 187)

> What happens to the indigenous person in the course of the training process? Can he retain assets for which he was originally selected or does he become socially distant like the typical professional? Many considerations need to be spelled out as we inquire into the effective employing and training of indigenous nonprofessionals. (p. 188)

Considering the dearth of conclusive evidence, what justification is there for the continued support of nonprofessional services? I believe that the current state of the art in the evaluation of new manpower resources is similar to that observed in earlier stages of research on psychotherapy. As Cowen (1973) points out, the recency and innovativeness associated with the nonprofessional movement has made it a popular, much replicated phenomena. Individuals involved in its development have depended far too heavily on impressionistic instead of systematic data. Directionally, however, the consistency of reported findings observed across a variety of settings and involving a wide variety of roles cannot be ignored. Nonprofessionals most likely can make an important contribution to the delivery of mental health services for the disadvantaged. Effective utilization of their services, however, depends on information collected in methodologically sophisticated studies.

Thus, available data suggest not a turning away from the nonprofessional "revolution," but a sharpening of the experimental questions asked about nonprofessionals and an increase in the willingness to explore such issues.

RESEARCH ON PSYCHOTHERAPY WITH THE DISADVANTAGED: FUTURE DIRECTIONS

Nonprofessionals have significantly increased the numbers and varieties of services available to the disadvantaged. At this point, however, it is important to demonstrate that the resulting increase in service is synonomous with more *effective* services for these groups.

Undoubtedly, the combined effects of the community mental health centers movement (Bloom, 1977) and the individual efforts of innumerable professionals and nonprofessionals have contributed to the increasing attention being placed on the identification and delivery of mental health services to the disadvantaged. It is apparent that a greater number and variety of services are now available than was previously the case. The range of alternative intervention strategies discussed in this chapter demonstrates the intensity of professional interest in discovering viable resolutions of the previously identified impasse between the mental health system and its low-income constituents. The pessimistic expectations of the past have been replaced by realistically optimistic goals for the future. The accomplishment of these goals, however, depends largely on the attainment of a balance between clinical and empirical efforts. At this time, the contributions of the former far outweigh the latter. As a result, the current proliferation of services exists with little systematic verification of its efficacy. There is no data base from which to select differentially among the available treatment modalities. It is, therefore, essential that future efforts in this area concentrate on systematic evaluations of all aspects of the delivery of services to the disadvantaged.

The dearth of experimental reports on the delivery of mental health services to the disadvantaged is convincingly demonstrated in the statistics reported in Table 22-2. In reviewing the recent mental health literature to identify articles relevant to this chapter, I was struck by the infrequency of their appearance. Systematic consideration of nine professional journals most likely to publish reports in this area revealed that approximately 6 percent of the more than 5000 articles published between 1970 and 1975 focused directly on the delivery of mental health services to the disadvantaged. The percentages of such articles in these journals ranged from 2 to 16 percent. These figures represent the total number of reports—empirical, clinical, and theoretical—appearing during that 6-year period. It is obvious from the data in Table 22-2 that the actual percentages for *empirical* reports are much lower. They decrease even further if the definition of an empirical study is restricted to the reports that include a control group, pre- *and* postmeasures, or follow-up data.

The information in Table 22-2 is purely descriptive. It does not reveal what should or should not be, only what is. In that respect, it is evident that the issues focused on in this chapter have not been high in the priorities of mental health investigators. If the design and implementation of effective, prescriptively oriented treatment modalities is of importance to mental health professionals, a considerable increase in systematic research on the various aspects of that problem must occur.

Such research can concentrate on innumerable topics. Earlier in this chapter I emphasized the importance of responding differentially to the various subgroups that make up the poor, the minority groups, and the working class. Although we now have available general information about these segments of the population, empirically based descriptions of their respective cognitive, affective, and behavioral styles are essential to the development of prescriptive intervention programs. Data reported by Gurin, Veroff, and Feld (1960) reveal that relatively few members of the disadvantaged subgroups perceive mental health professionals as relevant to the alleviation of personal-emotional discomfort. If other formal and informal community resources are used by these groups to resolve psychological difficulties, they must be identified, their procedures must be described, and their impact must be assessed. In this way, the mental health system could complement existing service delivery mechanisms and adopt onto itself the aspects of these "natural" services most relevant to the disadvantaged. Simultaneously, the integration of professional techniques into these community services may maximize their remedial potential. Thus, exploration of existing, informal community resources can contribute to the sharpening and increased relevance of available treatment modalities for the disadvantaged.

Definitions of pathology, deviance, adaptation, and health reflect, of course, relative comparisons between behavioral and affective patterns. The sensitivity of the diagnostic process in assisting us to understand the needs and resources of the disadvantaged is limited, largely by our ignorance of their idiosyncratic life-styles. To obtain further information about such matters, it is essential that we enter into collaborative research efforts with our social science colleagues. The multivariate nature of socioeconomic, racial, and ethnic differences demands that they be studied simultaneously from several perspectives (Lorion, 1976). Initially, efforts in this area will be primarily hypothesis building. Systematic observations within the actual community settings in which the disadvantaged live, work, and recreate must be undertaken. Examples of the kinds of information to be gathered from such efforts are readily available. Despite its age, Gans' (1962) *The Urban Villagers* remains a classic study of the impact of urban renewal (an increasingly salient issue in our cities) on the residents of a Boston working-class community. Imagine the benefits to the design of mental health services for the working class that might have resulted from *in vivo* studies of families affected by serious employment layoffs during the recent recession. The utilization of the skills of the participant observer exemplified in Coles' *Children of Crisis* (1967) and *Uprooted Children* (1970) are appropriate for many of the necessary initial investigations of disadvantaged life-styles. Not only may we gain insights into the patterns of their dysfunctions and the early manifestations of their needs, we may also learn much about their strengths and their resistance to seemingly overwhelming pressures. As a result, we may begin to develop interventions that focus on health and its maintenance instead of pathology.

The attitudes and expectation research discus-

sed earlier should make evident the necessity of systematically assessing these parameters in service providers as well as consumers. Much can be learned if the methodologies of sociology and social psychology are adapted to identify and change the attitudes of participants in mental health services (Goldstein, 1973; Goldstein & Simonson, 1971). For example, it is important to identify strategies that develop within the service providers a willingness to approach and respond, without ethnocentric distortion, to individuals whose lives differ in significant ways from middle-class expectations (Iscoe, 1976). Similarly, we must systematically gain control over the processes involved in undermining a patient's willingness to seek or remain in mental health treatments.

Information acquired from efforts to learn more about the life-styles, needs, and resources of the disadvantaged must ultimately be translated into the design and modification of service delivery procedures. In doing so, mental health researchers must not lose sight of Paul's (1967) rephrasing of the question, "Does treatment X work?" into "*What* treatment, by *whom,* is most effective for *this* individual with *that* specific problem, and under *which* set of circumstances" (p. 111). Without findings of sufficient specificity to fit within that equation, the mental health system is left with procedures general in their application and nonprescriptive in their utility. Given that the treatment of the disadvantaged has in the past been marked by considerable trial and error in attempts to match needs and services, it is important that systematic efforts begin to identify the differential impact of alternative treatment modalities.

By now, the reader has undoubtedly been repeatedly urged to increase the sophistication of experimental questions and procedures. Efforts with the disadvantaged are no less in need of such methodological refinement. Even a cursory discussion of appropriate investigatory strategies for the evaluation of therapeutic approaches is beyond the scope of this chapter. For a further discussion of this topic, refer to Chapter 2 by Gottman and Markman. Obviously, such basic components as operationally defined dependent and independent variables, adequate control groups, pre- and post-measurement using psychometrically sound mea-

TABLE 22-2 Relative frequency of appearance of published reports on the disadvantaged mental health journals, 1970 to 1975.

Journal	Years Counted	Total Articles (TA)	Total Articles on Disadvantaged (DA)	Percent DA/TA	Clinical Articles	Theoretical Articles	Research Articles			
							Total	Control Group	Pre-Post Measure	Follow-up
Journal of Consulting and Clinical Psychology	1970 to 1975	1064	28	3	1	—	27	14	1	1
American Journal of Community Psychology	1973 to 1975	102	114	14	—	2	12	4	3	2
Community Mental Health Journal	1970 to 1975	253	12	5	4	3	5	1	—	—

Journal of Community Psychology	1973 to 1974	163	10	6	1	—	9	3	2	1
Journal of Social Issues	1970 to 1975	273	44	16	—	26	18	3	—	—
Archives of General Psychiatry	1970 to 1975	1050	22	2	2	—	20	6	3	1
American Journal of Orthopsychiatry	1970 to 1975	384	59	15	20	19	20	8	5	1
American Journal of Psychiatry	1970 to 1975	1401	42	3	14	10	18	4	—	—
Social Work	1970 to 1974	383	55	14	8	29	18	1	—	—
Total		5073	286	6	50 (1%)	89 (2%)	147 (3%)	44 (.8%)	17 (.3%)	6 (.1%)

sures, and follow-up assessment are necessary. The exact experimental design depends, of course, on the researcher's resources and the specific investigatory question. In their overview of prescriptive analysis of mental health services, Goldstein and Stein (1976) provide a helpful schematization of alternative psychotherapy research design strategies. Table 22-3 summarizes the questions that can be answered at each level of the Goldstein and Stein hierarchy. It should be evident that as one proceeds to level 4, the complexity of the research increases exponentially, as does the potential for prescriptively viable information. Considering what is presently available, however, research efforts on treatment approaches with the disadvantaged at any of these levels will contribute significantly to our knowledge in this area.

CONCLUSION

It is appropriate to end this chapter with a reassertion of the cautious optimism with which it began. I believe that we have made significant progress during the past decade in our attempts to provide for the mental health needs of the disadvantaged. Viewed from a historical perspective, it is apparent that we have identified the existence of a problem, delineated some of its most salient parameters, and begun to design and, to a limited degree, assess a variety of alternative solutions. Our efforts thus far have been unsystematic and inefficient, but is that not the typical pattern of the early stages of scientific pursuits? As we attempt to provide simple solutions to complex problems, the inadequacy of our knowledge base becomes evident and the limitations of our findings become apparent. Nevertheless, recognition of the parameters involved in the delivery of services to the disadvantaged has increased significantly during the past two decades, and further progress in this area is inevitable. The relative unpopularity of research on the needs and services of the disadvantaged during recent years may reflect the acceptance of earlier pessimism about their appropriateness for, and responsiveness to, the mental health system. Hopefully, the material reviewed in this chapter will contribute to a

TABLE 22-3   Prescriptive Psychotherapies: A Research Hierarchy

Level 1. Nondifferential
    Type 1A: Psychotherapy A for patients X
    Type 1B: Psychotherapist 1 for patients X

Level 2. Unidifferential
    Type 2A: Psychotherapy A versus psychopsychotherapy B for patients X
    Type 2B: Psychotherapist 1 versus psychopsychotherapist 2 for patients X
    Type 2C: Psychotherapy A for patients X versus patients Y

Level 3. Bidifferential
    Type 3A: Psychotherapy A versus psychopsychotherapy B for patients X versus patients Y
    Type 3B: Psychotherapist 1 versus psychopsychotherapist 2 for patients X versus patients Y

Level 4. Tridifferential
    Type 4A: Psychotherapy A versus psychopsychotherapy B for patients X versus patients Y with psychotherapist 1 versus psychotherapist 2

Note: From Goldstein and Stein (1976, p. 21).

renewal of interest in the design and conduct of systematic clinical, observational, and empirical efforts focusing on the mental health of the disadvantaged.

REFERENCES

Adams, P. L., & McDonald, N. F. Clinical cooling out of poor people. *American Journal of Orthopsychiatry,* 1968, *38,* 457–463.

Affleck, D. C., & Garfield, S. L. Predictive judgements of therapists and duration of stay in psychotherapy. *Journal of Clinical Psychology,* 1961, *17,* 134–137.

Albee, G. W. *Mental health manpower trends.* New York: Basic Books, 1959.

Albee, G. W. The relation of conceptual models to manpower needs. In E. L. Cowen, E. A. Gardner, and M. Zax (Eds.), *Emergent approaches to mental health.* New York: Appleton-Century-Crofts, 1967.

Albronda, H. F., Dean, R. L., & Starkweather, J. A. Social class and psychotherapy. *Archives of General Psychiatry,* 1964, *10,* 276–283.

Alinsky, S. D. The poor and the powerful. *Psychiatric Research Reports*, 1967, *21*, 22–28.

Allen, V. L. Theoretical issues in poverty research. *Journal of Social Issues*, 1970a, *26*, 149–167.

Allen, V. L. (Ed.) *Psychological factors in poverty*. Chicago: Markham, 1970b.

Arnhoff, F. N., Rubinstein, E. A., & Speisman, J. C. (Eds.) *Manpower for mental health*. Chicago: Aldine, 1969.

Aronson, H., & Overall, B. Treatment expectations of patients in two social classes. *Social Work*, 1966, *11*, 35–41.

Auld, F., & Myers, J. K. Contributions to a theory for selecting psychotherapy patients. *Journal of Clinical Psychotherapy*, 1954, *10*, 56–60.

Avnet, H. H. *Psychiatric insurance: Financing short-term ambulatory treatment*. New York: Group Health Insurance Co. Inc., 1962.

Avnet, H. H. How effective is short-term therapy? In L. R. Wolberg (Ed.), *Short-term psychotherapy*. New York: Grune & Stratton, 1965.

Bailey, M. A., Warshaw, L., & Eichler, R. M. Patients screened and criteria used for selecting psychotherapy cases in a mental hygiene clinic. *Journal of Nervous and Mental Disease*, 1960, *130*, 72–77.

Barton, H. H. (Ed.) *Brief therapies*. New York: Behavioral Publications, 1971.

Baum, O. E., & Felzer, S. B. Activity in initial interviews with lower-class patients. *Archives of General Psychiatry*, 1964, *10*, 345–353.

Baum, O. E., Felzer, S. B., D'Zmura, T. L., & Shumaker, E. Psychotherapy, dropouts and lower socioeconomic patients. *American Journal of Orthopsychiatry*, 1966, *36*, 629–635.

Beck, D. F. Research findings on the outcomes of marital counseling. In D. H. L. Olson (Ed.), *Treating relationships*. Lake Mills, Ia.: Graphic, 1976.

Beck, D. F., & Jones, M. A. *Progress on family problems: A nationwide study of clients' and counselors' views on family agency services*. New York: Family Service Association of America, 1973.

Bellak, L., & Small, L. *Emergency psychotherapy and brief psychotherapy*. New York: Grune & Stratton, 1965.

Bergin, A. E. The evaluation of therapeutic outcomes. In A. E. Bergin and S. L. Garfield (Eds.), *Handbook of psychotherapy and behavior change: An empirical analysis*. New York: Wiley, 1971.

Bergin, A. E., & Garfield, S. L. *Handbook of psychotherapy and behavior change: An empirical analysis*. New York: Wiley, 1971.

Bernard, V. W. Some principles of dynamic psychiatry in relation to poverty. *American Journal of Psychiatry*, 1965, *122*, 254–267.

Bernard, V. W. Composite remedies for psychosocial problems. *International Psychiatry Clinics*, 1971, *8*, 61–85.

Billingsley, A. *Black families in white America*. Englewood Cliffs, N.J.: Prentice-Hall, 1968.

Blechman, E. A., & Olson, D. H. L. Family contract game: Description and effectiveness. In D. H. L. Olson (Ed.), *Treating relationships*. Lake Mills, Ia.: Graphic, 1976.

Bloom, B. L. *Community mental health: An introduction*. Monterey, Calif.: Brooks Cole, 1977.

Brill, N. Q., & Storrow, H. A. Social class and psychiatric treatment. *Archives of General Psychiatry*, 1960, *3*, 340–344.

Budner, S. S., Escover, H., & Malitz, S. The relationship of social personality, and psychiatric factors to choice of psychiatric therapy. *Comparative Psychiatry*, 1964, *5*, 327–333.

Calhoon, L. G., Dawes, S., & Lewis, P. M. Correlates of attitudes towards help-seeking in outpatients. *Journal of Consulting and Clinical Psychology*, 1972, *38*, 153.

Carkhuff, R. R., & Pierce, R. Differential effects of therapist race and social class upon patient depth of self-exploration in the initial clinical interview. *Journal of Consulting Psychology*, 1967, *31*, 632–634.

Carp, F. M. (Ed.) *Retirement*. New York: Behavioral Publications, 1972.

Carson, R. C., & Heine, R. W. Similarity and success in therapeutic dyads. *Journal of Consulting Psychology*, 1962, *26*, 38–43.

Chaiklin, H., & Frank, C. L. Separation, service delivery and family functioning. *Public Welfare*, Winter 1973, 2–7.

Chesler, P. *Women and madness*. New York: Doubleday, 1972.

Chess, S., Clark, K. B., & Thomas, A. Importance of cultural patterns in psychotherapy. *Psychiatric Quarterly*, 1953, *27*, 102–114.

Clark, K. B. *Dark ghetto*. New York: Harper & Row, 1965.

Clemes, S. R., & D'Andrea, V. J. Patients' anxiety as a function of expectation and degree of initial interview ambiguity. *Journal of Consulting Psychology*, 1965, *29*, 393–404.

Cohen, J. Social work and the culture of poverty. In F. Riessman, J. Cohen, and A. Pearl (Eds.), *Mental health of the poor*. New York: Free Press, 1964.

Coles, N. J., Branch, C. H. H., & Allison, R. B. Some relationships between social class and the practice of dynamic psychotherapy. *American Journal of Psychiatry*, 1962, *118*, 1004–1012.

Coles, R. *Children of crisis: A study of courage and fear*. Boston: Little Brown, 1967.

Coles, R. *Uprooted children*. Pittsburgh: University of Pittsburgh Press, 1970.

Cowen, E. L. Social and community interventions. In P. Mussen and M. Rosenzweig (Eds.), *Annual Review of Psychology*, 1973, *24*, 423–472.

D'Angelo, R. Y., & Walsh, J. F. An evaluation of various therapeutic approaches with lower socioeconomic group children. *Journal of Psychology*, 1967, *67*, 59–64.

Deane, W. N. The culture of the patient: An underestimated dimension in psychotherapy. *International Journal of Social Psychiatry*, 1961, *7*, 181–186.

Didato, S. V. Therapy failure: Pride and/or prejudice of the therapist? *Mental Hygiene*, 1971, *55*, 219–220.

Dohrenwend, B. P., & Dohrenwend, B. S. *Social status and psychological disorder: A causal inquiry*. New York: Wiley, 1969.

Eysenck, H. J. New approaches to mental illness: The

failure of a tradition. In H. Gottesfeld (Ed.), *The critical issues of community mental health.* New York: Behavioral Publications, 1972.

Feagin, J. R. *Subordinating the poor: Welfare and American beliefs.* Englewood Cliffs, N.J.: Prentice-Hall, 1975.

Fisher, E. H., & Cohen, S. L. Demographic correlates of attitudes toward seeking professional psychological help. *Journal of Consulting and Clinical Psychology,* 1972, *39,* 20–24.

Fisher, E. H., & Turner, J., LeB. Orientations to seeking professional help: Development and research utility of an attitude scale, *Journal of Consulting and Clinical Psychology,* 1970, *35,* 75–90.

Fishman, J. R. Poverty, race, and violence. *American Journal of Psychotherapy,* 1969, *23,* 599–607.

Fishman, J. R., & McCormack, J. Mental health without walls: Programs for the ghettos. In J. H. Masserman (Ed.) *Current psychiatric therapies.* Vol. 9. New York: Grune & Stratton, 1969.

Framo, J. L. In-depth family therapy with a black ghetto, intact family. Unpublished manuscript, Temple University, Philadelphia, 1969.

Frank, J. D. Some effects of expectancy and influences in psychotherapy. In J. H. Masserman and J. L. Moreno (Eds.), *Progress in psychotherapy.* Vol. III. New York: Grune & Stratton, 1958.

Frank, J. D. *Persuasion and healing: A comparative study of psychotherapy.* New York: Schocken Books, 1961.

Franks, V., & Burtle, V. *Women in therapy: New psychotherapies for a changing society.* New York: Brunner/Mazel, 1974.

Freud, S. *Collected Papers.* Vol. II. London: Hogarth Press and the Institute of Psychoanalysis, 1950.

Fried, M. Social differences in mental health. In J. Kosa, A. Antonovsky, and I. K. Zola (Eds.), *Poverty and health: A sociological analysis.* Cambridge: Harvard University Press, 1969.

Gans, H. J. *The urban villagers.* New York: Free Press, 1962.

Garfield, S. L. A note on patients' reasons for terminating therapy. *Psychological Reports,* 1963, *13,* 38.

Garfield, S. L. Research on client variables in psychotherapy. In A. E. Bergin and S. L. Garfield (Eds.), *Handbook of psychotherapy and behavior change: An empirical analysis.* New York: Wiley, 1971.

Garfield, S. L., & Wolpin, M. Expectations regarding psychotherapy. *Journal of Nervous and Mental Diseases,* 1963, *137,* 353–362.

Gartner, A. *Paraprofessionals and their performance.* New York: Praeger, 1971.

Gartner, A., & Riessman, F. The performance of paraprofessionals in the mental health field. In G. Caplan (Ed.), *The American handbook of psychiatry.* Vol. II. New York: Basic Books, 1974.

Giordano, J. *Ethnicity and mental health.* New York: National Project on Ethnic America of the American Jewish Committee, 1973.

Giordano, J. Community mental health in a pluralistic society. *International Journal of Mental Health,* 1976, *5,* 5–15.

Gladwin, T. *Poverty U.S.A.* Boston: Little, Brown, 1967.

Goin, M. K., Yamamoto, J., & Silverman, J. Therapy congruent with class linked expectations. *Archives of General Psychiatry,* 1965, *13,* 133–137.

Goldstein, A. P. Patients expectancies and non specific therapy as a basis for (un-) spontaneous remission. *Journal of Clinical Psychology,* 1960a, *16,* 399–403.

Goldstein, A. P. Therapist and client expectation of personality change in psychotherapy. *Journal of Counseling Psychology,* 1960b, *3,* 180–184.

Goldstein, A. P. Participant expectancies in psychotherapy. *Psychiatry,* 1962a, *25,* 72–79.

Goldstein, A. P. *Therapist-patient expectations in psychotherapy.* New York: Pergamon, 1962b.

Goldstein, A. P. Prognostic and role expectancies in psychotherapy. *American Journal of Psychotherapy,* 1966a, *20,* 35–44.

Goldstein, A. P. Psychotherapy research by extrapolation from social psychology. *Journal of Counseling Psychology,* 1966b, *13,* 38–45.

Goldstein, A. P. *Psychotherapeutic attraction.* New York: Pergamon, 1971.

Goldstein, A. P. *Structural learning therapy: Toward a psychotherapy for the poor.* New York: Academic Press, 1973.

Goldstein, A. P., & Simonson, N. R. Social psychological approaches to psychotherapy research. In A. E. Bergin and S. L. Garfield (Eds.), *Handbook of psychotherapy and behavior change: An empirical analysis.* New York: Wiley, 1971.

Goldstein, A. P., & Stein, N. *Prescriptive psychotherapies.* New York: Pergamon, 1976.

Gould, R. E. Dr. Strangeclass: Or how I stopped worrying about the theory and began treating the blue-collar worker. *American Journal of Orthopsychiatry,* 1967, *37,* 78–86.

Graziano, A. M. Clinical innovation and the mental health power structure: A social case history. *American Psychologist,* 1969, *24,* 10–18.

Greeley, A. *Why can't they be like us?* New York: Institute of Human Relations Press, 1969.

Green, A. W. Social values and psychotherapy. *Journal of Personality,* 1946, *14,* 199–228.

Grey, A. L. Social class and the psychiatric patient: A study in composite character. In A. L. Grey (Ed.), *Class and personality in society.* New York: Atherton, 1969.

Grier, W. H., & Cobbs, P. M. *Black rage.* New York: Bantam, 1968.

Gurin, G., Veroff, J., & Feld, S. *Americans view their mental health: A nationwide survey.* New York: Basic Books, 1960.

Gurman, A. S. The effects and effectiveness of marital therapy: A review of outcome research. *Family Process,* 1973, *12,* 145–170.

Hacker, F. J., Illing, H. & Bergreen, S. W. Impact of different social settings on type and effectiveness of psychotherapy. *Psychoanalytic Review,* 1965, *52*(3), 38–49.

Haggstrom, W. C. The power of the poor. In F. Riessman, J. Cohen, and A. Pearl (Eds.), *Mental health of the poor.* New York: Free Press, 1964.

Hatter, J. Racial factors in patient selection. *American Journal of Psychiatry*, 1967, *124*, 630–636.

Heine, R. W., & Trosman, H. Initial expectations of the doctor-patient interaction as a factor in continuance in psychotherapy. *Psychiatry*, 1960, *23*, 275–278.

Heinicke, C. M. Change in child and parent: A social work approach to family intervention. *American Journal of Orthopsychiatry*, 1975, *45*(2), 296–297.

Heitler, J. B. Preparation of lower-class patients for expressive group psychotherapy. *Journal of Consulting and Clinical Psychology*, 1973, *41*, 251–260.

Heitler, J. B. Preparatory techniques in initiating expressive psychotherapy with lower-class, unsophisticated patients. *Psychological Bulletin*, 1976, *83*, 339–352.

Heller, K., & Goldstein, A. P. Client dependency and therapist expectancy as relationship maintaining variables in psychotherapy. *Journal of Consulting Psychology*, 1961, *25*, 371–375.

Hiler, E. W. An analysis of patient-therapist compatibility, *Journal of Consulting Psychology*, 1958, *22*, 341–347.

Hoehn-Saric, R., Frank, J. D., Imber, S. C., Nash, E. H., Stone, A. R., & Battle, C. C. Systematic preparation of patients for psychotherapy: 1. Effects of therapy behavior and outcome. *Journal of Psychiatric Research*, 1964, *2*, 267–281.

Hollingshead, A. B. *Two-factor index of social position.* New Haven, Conn.: Author, 1957.

Hollingshead, A. B., & Redlich, F. C. *Social class and mental illness.* New York: Wiley, 1958.

Imber, S. D., Frank, J. D., Gliedman, L. H., Nash, E. H., & Stone, A. R. Suggestibility, social class, and the acceptance of psychotherapy. *Journal of Clinical Psychology*, 1956, *12*, 341–344.

Imber, S. D., Nash, E. H., & Stone, A. R. Social class and duration of psychotherapy. *Journal of Clinical Psychology*, 1955, *11*, 281–294.

Iscoe, I. Realities and trade-offs in an effective community psychology. Presented at the 84th Annual Convention, American Psychological Association, Washington, D.C., 1976.

Jackson, A. M., Berkowitz, H., & Farley, G. K. Race as a variable affecting the treatment involvement of children. *Journal of Child Psychiatry*, 1974, *13*, 20–31.

Jacobs, D., Charles, E., Jacobs, T., Weinstein, H., & Mann, D. Preparation for treatment of the disadvantaged patient: Effects on disposition and outcome. *American Journal of Orthopsychiatry*, 1972, *42*, 666–674.

Jones, M. J. *Black awareness: A theology of hope.* New York: Abingdon Press, 1971.

Kadushin, C. *Why people go to psychiatrists.* New York: Atherton, 1969.

Kamin, L., & Caughlan, J. Subjective experiences of outpatient psychotherapy. *American Journal of Psychotherapy*, 1963, *17*, 660–668.

Kandel, D. B. Status homophily, social context, and participation in psychotherapy. *American Journal of Sociology*, 1966, *71*, 640–650.

Kaplan, M. L., Kurtz, R. M., & Clements, W. H. Psychiatric residents and lower-class patients: Conflict in

training. *Community Mental Health Journal*, 1968, *4*, 91–97.

Karlsruher, A. E. The nonprofessional as a therapeutic agent. *American Journal of Community Psychology*, 1974, *2*, 61–78.

Katz, M. M., Lorr, M., & Rubinstein, E. A. Remainer patient attributes and their relation to subsequent improvement in psychotherapy. *Journal of Consulting Psychology*, 1958, *22*, 411–413.

Kiesler, D. J. Experimental designs in psychotherapy research. In A. E. Bergin and S. L. Garfield (Eds.), *Psychotherapy and behavior change: An empirical analysis.* New York: Wiley, 1971.

Kimmel, D. C. *Adulthood and aging.* New York: Wiley, 1974.

Koegler, R. R., & Brill, N. Q. *Treatment of psychiatric outpatients.* New York: Appleton-Century-Crofts, 1967.

Komarovsky, M. *Blue-Collar marriages.* New York: Random House, 1967.

Krasner, L. Behavior therapy. In P. Mussen and M. Rosenzweig (Eds.), *Annual Review of Psychology*, 1971, *22*, 483–532.

Krebs, R. L. Some effects of a white institution on black psychiatric outpatients. *American Journal of Orthopsychiatry*, 1971, *41*, 589–596.

Kurtz, R. M., Weech, A. A., & Dizenhuz, I. M. Decision-making as to type of treatment in a child psychiatry clinic. *American Journal of Orthopsychiatry*, 1970, *10*, 795–805.

LaVietes, R. L. Crisis intervention for ghetto children: Contraindications and alternative considerations. *American Journal of Orthopsychiatry*, 1974, *44*, 720–727.

Lazarus, A. A. (Ed.) *Clinical behavior therapy.* New York: Brunner/Mazel, 1972.

Lazarus, A. A. (Ed.) *Multimodal behavior therapy.* New York: Springer Publishing Co., 1976.

Lee, S. H., Gianturco, D. T., & Eisdorfer, C. Community mental health center accessibility. *Archives of General Psychiatry*, 1974, *31*, 335–339.

Lennard, H. L., & Bernstein, A. *The anatomy of psychotherapy: Systems of communication.* New York: Columbia University Press, 1960.

Lerner, B. *Therapy in the ghetto.* Baltimore: John Hopkins University Press, 1972.

Levine, R. A. Consumer participation in planning and evaluation of mental health services. *Social Work*, 1970, *15*, 41–46.

Levitt, E. E. Psychotherapy research and the expectation-reality discrepancy. *Psychotherapy: Theory, Research, and Practice*, 1966, *3*, 163–166.

Levy, R. A. Six-session outpatient therapy. *Hospital and Community Psychiatry*, 1966, *17*, 340–343.

Lewis, H. Syndrome of contemporary urban poverty. *Psychiatric Research Reports*, 1967, *21*, 1–11.

Lewis, O. The culture of poverty. *Scientific American*, 1966, *215*, 19–25.

Lorion, R. P. Socioeconomic status and traditional treatment approaches reconsidered. *Psychological Bulletin*, 1973, *79*, 263–270.

Lorion, R. P. Patient and therapist variables in the treatment of low-income patients. *Psychological Bulletin,* 1974, *81,* 344–354a.

Lorion, R. P. Social class, treatment attitudes, and expectations. *Journal of Consulting and Clinical Psychology,* 1974, *42,* 520b.

Lorion, R. P. Mental health treatment of the low-income groups. *Monograph series on Contemporary Issues of Mental Health,* Bureau of Research and Training—Mental Health, Commonwealth of Pennsylvania, 1975, *1*(2), 1–53.

Lorion, R. P. Ethnicity and mental health: An empirical obstacle course. *International Journal of Mental Health,* 1976, *5,* 16–25.

Lorr, M., & McNair, D. M. Correlates of length of psychotherapy. *Journal of Clinical Psychology,* 1964, *20,* 497–504.

Love, L. R., Kaswan, J., & Bugental, D. E. Differential effectiveness of three clinical interventions for different socioeconomic groupings. *Journal of Consulting and Clinical Psychology,* 1972, *39,* 347–360.

Luborsky, L., Chandler, M., Auerbach, A. H., Cohen, J., & Bachrach, H. M. Factors influencing the outcome of psychotherapy: A review of quantitative research. *Psychological Bulletin,* 1971, *75,* 145–186.

Maccoby, E., & Jacklin, C. *The psychology of sex differences.* Stanford, Calif.: Stanford University Press, 1974.

Mannino, F. V., & Shore, M. F. Ecologically oriented family intervention. *Family Process,* 1972, *11,* 499–505.

McKinney, F., Lorion. R. P., & Zax, M. *Effective behavior and human development.* New York: MacMillan, 1976.

McMahon, J. T. The working-class psychiatric patient: A clinical view. In F. Riessman, J. Cohen, and A. Pearl (Eds.), *Mental health of the poor.* New York: Free Press, 1964.

McNair, D. M., Lorr, M., & Callahan, D. M. Patient and therapist influence on quitting psychotherapy. *Journal of Consulting Psychology,* 1963, *27,* 10–17.

Meltzoff, J., & Kornreich, M. *Research in psychotherapy.* New York: Atherton, 1970.

Miller, S. M. The American lower classes: A typological approach. In F. Riessman, J. Cohen, and A. Pearl (Eds.), *Mental health of the poor.* New York: Free Press, 1964.

Miller, S. M., & Mishler, E. G. Social class, mental illness, and American psychiatry: An expository review. *Millbank Memorial Fund Quarterly,* 1959, *37,* 174–199.

Miller, S. M., & Riessman, F. *Social class and social policy.* New York: Basic Books, 1968.

Miller, S. M., & Riessman, F. The working-class subculture: A new view. In A. L. Grey (Ed.), *Class and personality in society.* New York: Atherton, 1969.

Minuchin, S., Montalvo, B., Guerney, B. G., Rosman, B. L., & Schumer, F. *Families of the slums: An exploration of their structure and treatment.* New York: Basic Books, 1967.

Moos, R. H., & Clemes, S. R. Multivariate study of the patient-therapist system. *Journal of Consulting Psychology,* 1967, *31,* 119–130.

Moynihan, D. P. *The negro family: The case for national action!* Washington, D.C.: U.S. Department of Labor, 1965.

Myers, J. K., & Bean, L. L. *A decade later: A follow-up of social class and mental illness.* New York: Wiley, 1968.

Myers, J. K., & Roberts, B. H. *Family and class dynamics in mental illness.* New York: Wiley, 1959.

Nash, E. H., Hoehn-Saric, R., Battle, C. C., Stone, A. R., Imber, S. D., & Frank, J. D. Systematic preparation of patients for short-term psychotherapy II: Relation to characteristics of patient, therapist and the psychotherapeutic process. *Journal of Nervous and Mental Disease,* 1965, *140,* 374–383.

Neugarten, B. L. (Ed.) *Middle age and aging.* Chicago: University of Chicago Press, 1968.

Nunnally, J. *Popular conceptions of mental health.* New York: Holt, Rinehart & Winston, 1961.

Olson, D. H. L. *Treating relationships.* Lake Mills, Ia: Graphic, 1976.

Orne, M., & Wender, P. Anticipatory socialization for psychotherapy: Method and rationale. *American Journal of Psychiatry,* 1968, *124,* 88–98.

Overall, B., & Aronson, H. Expectations of psychotherapy in patients of lower socioeconomic class. *American Journal of Orthopsychiatry,* 1963, *33,* 421–430.

Parloff, M. B. Therapist-patient relationship and outcome of psychotherapy. *Journal of Consulting Psychology,* 1961, *25,* 29–38.

Paul, G. L. Strategy of outcome research in psychotherapy. *Journal of Consulting Psychology,* 1967, *31,* 109–118.

Perlman, R. *The economics of poverty.* New York: McGraw-Hill, 1976.

Prince, R. Psychotherapy and the chronically poor. In J. C. Finney (Ed.), *Culture change, mental health, and poverty: Essays by Eric Berne (and others).* Lexington: University of Kentucky Press, 1969.

Rainwater, L. Crucible of identity: The negro lower-class family. *Daedalus, Journal of the American Academy of Arts and Sciences,* 1966, *95,* 172–216.

Rainwater, L. Neutralizing the disinherited: Some psychological aspects of understanding the poor. In V. L. Allen (Ed.), *Psychological factors in poverty.* Chicago: Markham, 1970.

Rainwater, L., Coleman, R., & Handel, G. *Workingman's wife.* New York: Oceana Publications, Inc. 1959.

Redlich, F. C., Hollingshead, A. B., & Bellis, E. Social class differences in attitudes towards psychiatry. *American Journal of Orthopsychiatry,* 1955, *25,* 60–70.

Reiff, R., & Riessman, F. The indigenous nonprofessional. *Community Mental Health Journal,* 1965, monograph #1.

Reiff, R., & Scribner, S. Issues in the new national mental health program relating to labor and low-income groups. In F. Riessman, J. Cohen, and A. Pearl (Eds.), *Mental health of the poor.* New York: Free Press, 1964.

Richards, L. G. Consumer practices of the poor. In L. M. Idam (Ed.), *Low income life styles.* Washington, D.C.: Welfare Administration, 1966.

Riessman, F. *New approaches to mental health treatment*

for labor and low-income groups: A survey. New York: National Institute of Labor Education, 1964.

Riessman, F., Cohen J., & Pearl, A. (Eds.) *Mental health of the poor.* New York: Free Press, 1964.

Rioch, M. J. Pilot projects in training mental health counselors. In E. L. Cowen, E. A. Gardner, and M. Zax (Eds.) *Emergent approaches to mental health problems.* New York: Appleton-Century-Crofts, 1967.

Rogers, L. S. Drop-out rates and results of psychotherapy in government aided mental hygiene clinics. *Journal of Clinical Psychology,* 1960, *16,* 89–92.

Rosenblatt, A., & Mayer, J. E. Help-seeking for family problems: A survey of utilization and satisfaction. *American Journal of Psychiatry,* 1972, *128,* 1136–1140.

Rosenthal, D., & Frank, J. D. The fate of psychiatric clinic outpatients assigned to psychotherapy. *Journal of Nervous and Mental Disorders,* 1958, *127,* 330–343.

Rubinstein, E. A., & Lorr, M. A comparison of terminators and remainers in outpatient psychotherapy. *Journal of Clinical Psychology,* 1956, *12,* 345–349.

Ruiz, P., & Behrens, M. Community control in mental health: How far can it go? *Psychiatric Quarterly,* 1973, *47,* 317–324.

Ryan, W. (Ed.) *Distress in the city: Essays on the design and administration of urban mental health services.* Cleveland: Case Western Reserve University Press, 1969.

Sager, C. J., Brayboy, T. L., & Waxenberg, B. R. *Black ghetto family in therapy: A laboratory experience.* New York: Grove Press, 1970.

Sarbin, T. R. The culture of poverty, social identity, and cognitive outcomes. In V. L. Allen (Ed.), *Psychological factors in poverty.* Chicago: Markham, 1970.

Sanua, V. D. Sociocultural aspects of psychotherapy and treatment: A review of the literature. In L. E. Abt and B. F. Riess (Eds.), *Progress in clinical psychology.* New York: Grune & Stratton, 1966.

Savitz, H. A. The cultural background of the patient as part of the physician's armamentarium. *Journal of Abnormal and Social Psychology,* 1952, *47,* 245–254.

Schaffer, L., & Myers, J. K. Psychotherapy and social stratification. *Psychiatry,* 1954, *17,* 83–93.

Schlesinger, B., & James, G. Psychiatry and poverty—A selected review. *Canadian Medical Association Journal,* 1969, *101,* 470–477.

Schneiderman, L. Social class, diagnosis, and treatment. *American Journal of Orthopsychiatry,* 1965, *35,* 99–105.

Schoenfeld, L. S., Lyerly, R. J., & Miller, S. I. We like us: The attitudes of the mental health staff toward other agencies on the Navajo Reservation. *Mental Hygiene,* 1971, *55,* 171–173.

Schofield, W. *Psychotherapy: The purchase of friendship.* Englewood Cliffs, N.J.: Prentice-Hall, 1964.

Schonfield, J., Stone, A. R., Hoehn-Saric, R., Imber, S. R., & Pande, S. K. Patient-therapist convergence and measures of improvement in short-term psychotherapy. *Psychotherapy: Theory, Research, and Practice,* 1969, *6,* 267–272.

Seifer, N. *Absent from the majority: Working class women in America.* New York: National Project on Ethnic America, 1973.

Serrano, A. C., & Gibson, G. Mental health services to the Mexican American community in San Antonio, Texas. *American Journal of Public Health,* 1973, *63,* 1055–1057.

Shotwell, L. R. *The harvesters.* Garden City, N.Y.: Doubleday & Co., 1961.

Siassi, I. Psychotherapy with women and men of lower classes. In V. Franks and V. Burtle Eds.), *Women in therapy: New psychotherapies for a changing society.* New York: Brunner/Mazel, 1974.

Siegel, J. M. A brief review of the effects of race in clinical service interactions. *American Journal of Orthopsychiatry,* 1974, *44,* 555–562.

Sifneos, P. E. *Short-term psychotherapy and emotional crisis.* Cambridge, Mass.: Harvard University Press, 1972.

Sloane, R., Cristol, A., Pepernik, M., & Staples, F. Role preparation and expectancy of improvement in psychotherapy. *Journal of Nervous and Mental Diseases,* 1970, *150,* 18–26.

Sloane, R. B., Staples, F. R., Cristol, A. H., Yorkston, N. J., & Whipple, K. *Psychotherapy versus behavior therapy.* Cambridge, Mass.: Harvard University Press, 1975.

Small, L. *The briefer psychotherapies.* New York: Brunner/Mazel, 1971.

Sobey, F. *The nonprofessional revolution in mental health.* New York: Columbia University Press, 1970.

Speer, D. C., Fossum, M., Lippman, H. S., Schwartz, R., & Slocum, B. A comparison of middle- and lower-class families in treatment at a child guidance clinic. *American Journal of Orthopsychiatry,* 1968, *38,* 814–822.

Srole, L., Langer, T. S., Michael, S. T., Opler, M. K., & Rennie, T. A. C. *Mental health in the metropolis: The midtown Manhattan study.* New York: McGraw-Hill, 1962.

Stone, A. R., Imber, S. D., & Frank, J. D. The role of non-specific factors in short-term psychotherapy. *Australian Journal of Psychology,* 1966, *18,* 210–217.

Stone, J. L., & Crowthers, V. Innovations in program and funding of mental health services for blue-collar families. *American Journal of Psychiatry,* 1972, *128,* 1375–1380.

Storrow, H. A. Psychiatric treatment and the lower-class neurotic patient. *Archives of General Psychiatry,* 1962, *6,* 469–473.

Strupp, H., & Bloxom, A. Preparing lower-class patients for group psychotherapy: Development and evaluation of a role induction film. *Journal of Consulting and Clinical Psychology,* 1973, *41,* 373–384.

Strupp, H. H., & Bergin, A. E. Some empirical and conceptual bases for coordinated research in psychotherapy. *International Journal of Psychiatry,* 1969, *7,* 17–90.

Stuart, R. B. An operant interpersonal program for couples. In D. H. L. Olson (Ed.), *Treating relationships.* Lake Mills, Ia.: Graphic, 1976.

Sue, S., McKinney, H., Allen, D., & Hall, J. Delivery of community mental health services to black and white clients. *Journal of Consulting and Clinical Psychology,* 1974, *42,* 794–801.

Thomas, A., & Sillen, S. *Racism and psychiatry.* New York: Brunner/Mazel, 1972.

Thornton, C. I., & Carter, J. H. Improving mental health services to low-income blacks. *Journal of the National Medical Association,* 1975, *67,* 167–170.

Tischler, G. L., Henisz, J. E., Myers, J. K., & Boswell, P. C. Utilization of mental health services I: Patienthood and the prevalence of symptomatology in the community. *Archives of General Psychiatry,* 1975a, *32,* 411–415.

Tischler, G. L.,, Henisz, J. E., Myers, J. K., & Boswell, P. C. Utilization of mental health services II: Mediators of service allocation. *Archives of General Psychiatry,* 1975b, *32,* 416–418.

Truax, C. B. The training of nonprofessional personnel in therapeutic interpersonal relationships. *American Journal of Public Health,* 1967, *57,* 1778–1791.

Truax, C. B., & Carkhuff, R. R. *Toward effective counseling and psychotherapy.* Chicago: Aldine, 1967.

Urban, H. B., & Ford, D. H. Some historical and conceptual perspectives on psychotherapy and behavior change. In A. E. Bergin and S. L. Garfield (Eds.), *Handbook of psychotherapy and behavior change: An empirical analysis.* New York: Wiley, 1971.

Van der Veen, F. Effects of the therapist and the patient on each other's therapeutic behavior. *Journal of Consulting Psychology,* 1965, *29,* 19–26.

Wahl, O. Six TV myths about mental illness. *T.V. Guide,* 1976, *3/13,* 4–8.

Warren, N. C., & Rice, L. N. Structuring and stabilizing of psychotherapy for low-prognosis clients. *Journal of Consulting and Clinical Psychology,* 1972, *39,* 173–181.

Watson, P. *Psychology and race.* Middlesex, England: Penguin, 1973.

Wells, R. A., Dilkes, T. C., & Burckhardt, N. T. The results of family therapy: A critical review of the literature. In D. H. L. Olson (Ed.), *Treating relationships.* Lake Mills, Ia.: Graphic, 1976.

White, A. M., Fichtenbaum, L., & Dollard, J. Evaluation of silence in initial interviews with psychiatric clinic patients. *Journal of Nervous and Mental Disease,* 1964, *139,* 550–557.

Williams, H. V., Lipman, R. S., Uhlenhuth, E. A., Rickels, K., Covi, L., & Mock, J. Some factors influencing the treatment expectations of anxious neurotic outpatients. *Journal of Nervous and Mental Disease.* 1967, *145,* 208–220.

Wolberg, L. R. *The techniques of psychotherapy part II.* New York: Grune & Stratton, 1967.

Wolkon, G. H., Moriwaki, S., & Williams, K. J. Race and social class as factors in the orientation toward psychotherapy. *Journal of Counseling Psychology,* 1973, *29,* 312–316.

Wright, J. *They harvest despair.* Boston: Beacon Press, 1965.

Yalom, I. D., Houts, P. S., Newell, G., & Rand, K. H. Preparation of patients for group therapy: A controlled study. *Archives of General Psychiatry,* 1967, *17,* 416–427.

Yamamoto, J., & Goin, M. K. Social class factors relevant for psychiatric treatment. *Journal of Nervous and Mental Disease,* 1966, *142,* 332–339.

Yamamoto, J., James, Q. C., Bloombaum, M., & Hattem, J. Racial factors in patient selection. *American Journal of Psychiatry,* 1967, *124,* 630–636.

PART VI

EVALUATING THE TRAINING OF THERAPISTS

23

RESEARCH ON THE TEACHING AND LEARNING OF PSYCHOTHERAPEUTIC SKILLS

RUTH G. MATARAZZO

University of Oregon Health Sciences Center

INTRODUCTION

In the past 10 years, publication in the area of teaching psychotherapy has mushroomed. At the time of my first review of this subject (Matarazzo, Wiens, & Saslow, 1966), the field was aptly characterized by Rogers (1957) as containing "a rarity of research and a plenitude of platitudes." Five years later, it was noted that "this state of affairs has begun to change, apparently in teaching programs of all theoretical persuasions, although progress among them is uneven" (Matarazzo, 1971). At that time, Truax, Carkhuff, and Douds (1964), Truax and Carkhuff (1967), and others had recently initiated their programmatic research on teaching neophyte therapists to provide "facilitative conditions" (i.e., empathy, warmth, unconditional positive regard, and congruence). Ivey and his co-workers (1968) had introduced microcounseling, and they presented preliminary results suggesting its efficacy in teaching some basic aspects of psychotherapeutic skill. Numerous counselor pro-

grams (Demos & Zuwaylif, 1963; Jones, 1963) were presenting evidence of improvement in measures of interviewing skill pre- and postworkshop. Some medical schools were experimenting with new methods of teaching similar skills to medical students and were attempting to evaluate the results. Exponents of behavior modification were teaching behavior modification techniques to the parents and teachers of children with disordered behavior. There was increasing enthusiasm for the use of videotape feedback. As a teaching device, it was beginning to supplant audiotape. Electronic devices, invented earlier, were becoming more popular for communicating with the student-interviewer while he or she was being observed through a one-way screen. To present students with standard stimulus situations, there was experimentation with videotaped, simulated interviews and coached clients. Although none of this research could claim to evaluate the teaching of psychotherapeutic skill at the journeyman level, it was designed to teach several skills presumed to be basic to effective interviewing. Truax and Carkhuff (1967) had underscored the necessity to measure changes (improvement) in the student's behavior subsequent to training and to measure patient improvement as a function of the former. Truax and Carkhuff (1967), Bergin and Solomon (1970), and others developed scales for rating interviewer skills and interviewee behaviors (e.g., depth of self-exploration), which were presumed to be consequent to therapist skill.

Thus, the era of the late 1960s was one of overdue attention to methods of teaching interviewing skill, the means of evaluating that teaching and, to a limited extent, presumed benefit to the patient. It was an era of innovation in all of the above, in applying learning theory and social theory to the teaching process, and in the use of new technologies. This is not to say that the effects were revolutionary, however.

During the past few years, there have been attempts to replicate earlier findings, compare some of the above teaching and evaluation methods with each other, or apply them to new populations. There have been a few excellent critiques of some of the research methods and their theoretical foundations (Blaas & Heck, 1975; Chinsky & Rappaport, 1970; Mintz & Luborsky, 1971; Rappaport & Chinsky, 1972; Resnikoff, 1972). Unfortunately, as a whole, they have not added greatly to our *applied* sophistication, and few important additional innovations have come about. The slow rate of progress is partly due to the great complexity of this research area. That is, we are attempting to measure a combination of conceptual, experiential, and behavioral learning in a constantly shifting, never duplicated stimulus situation. We have poorly defined variables and inadequate measuring instruments that involve subjective judgment and whose use may not be comparable from one study to another. Because of the time-consuming nature of the measurements, the N in each study is likely to be small. Because of the complexity of the behaviors to be learned and the consequent complexity of the teaching program, not *all* aspects of the program are fully described, nor are their effects measured. None of the studies has been faithfully replicated. It is not surprising that *a large aggregate effort has not resulted in a giant step*

forward. This research area is further hampered by our fragmentary knowledge regarding what therapists do that leads to patient improvement along specific dimensions. Consequently, even if we define variables more clearly and increase the efficiency of teaching the defined behaviors, we are not sure that we are selecting the most relevant behaviors. Clearly, what we need most if we are to validate any training program is to study student acquisition of skill, *which is then related to patient improvement.*

It now seems to be generally accepted that post-interview discussion from notes written by the interviewer are of limited value in training. The student-therapist has been found, on each study using this technique, to make significant omissions and distortions, whether consciously or unconsciously (Covner, 1944; Muslin, Burstein. Gedo, and Sadow, 1967). The methods of teaching and supervision currently appearing in the literature and described here primarily involve didactic instruction, supervisor modeling, direct observation of the learner's interviews, (either role played or with real clients), possibly intervention by the supervisor *in-process* with a variant of the "bug in the ear," and postinterview feedback through audio- or videotaping.

A noteworthy aspect of the published research is that it has been done almost exclusively on neophyte therapist-professionals or nonprofessional mental health trainees (e.g., undergraduates, parents, teachers, school counselors). This seems to be due both to the fact that it is easier to define and measure dimensions of basic skill than more subtle ones, and that nonprofessionals are more likely to be trained in sufficiently large groups to enable a study of comparative methods to be conducted. Thus, the most researched type of training is on basic aspects of interviewing skill, such as facilitation of communication and development of a therapeutic relationship, and not on expertise in psychotherapy—a more complex area where the desired behavioral and conceptual skills are more affected by theoretical orientation and personal idiom. Accordingly, there is good reason to suppose that most of the training programs that are reported in the current literature and reviewed here are *not applicable to most graduate programs be-*

yond the first year of practicum training. Professional training programs such as those in psychology, psychiatry, and social work, which presumably teach psychotherapeutic (in contradistinction to interviewing) skills, have thus not benefited greatly from the preponderance of this research.

The majority of the recent literature is clustered about the innovative programs that were emerging in the mid- to late 1960s. These are: (1) the didactic-experiential program described by Truax, Carkhuff, and Douds (1964) and Truax and Carkhuff (1967), aimed at teaching primarily the client-centered, facilitative variables of empathy, unconditional positive regard, warmth, and genuineness, which were proposed earlier by Rogers (1951); (2) Ivey et al.'s (1968) and Ivey's (1971) microcounseling method of teaching specific interviewing skills such as attentiveness, verbal following, minimal activity, accurate reflection, and summarization of feeling; and (3) techniques of teaching behavior modification or operant conditioning skills to nonprofessional trainers (parents, teachers, ward aides, etc.). Little research in this area has been stimulated by the psychoanalytic school, and its training methods appear to be relatively unchanging over the years. Consequently, no attempt will be made to review literature describing those programs.

The remainder of this chapter will attempt to describe and evaluate, for each of these three general approaches, the dimensions of interviewing skill selected for teaching; the methods of teaching these skills, and their apparent effectiveness; the methods of measuring student change; and, where available, the assessment of client benefit. Unfortunately, the latter is rarely known. Two additional brief sections review problems in selection of trainees and special devices used in teaching psychotherapy.

THE CLIENT-CENTERED ORIENTATION

Until recent years, the client-centered group has provided the strongest influence toward making psychotherapy observable, its practice and training techniques and attitudes specifiable, and its results measurable. Rogers and his collaborators were the first to develop brief, well-formulated workshops for the training of psychotherapists and to attempt to measure their effectiveness (Blocksma & Porter, 1947). They specified graded procedures for facilitating the kind of experiential learning that they deemed necessary for the psychotherapist, and they defined the characteristics and behaviors required of the psychotherapist in order to develop a therapeutic relationship and presumably effect patient change. Much current research on the teaching of psychotherapy can be traced to these origins.

Rogers' (1957) graded experiences consisted of the student's (1) listening to tape-recorded interviews of experienced therapists; (2) role-playing therapist with fellow students; (3) observing a series of live demonstrations by the supervisor; (4) participating in group therapy or multiple therapy; (5) conducting individual psychotherapy and recording the interviews for discussion with a facilitative, nondirective supervisor; and (6) personal therapy. Rogers had earlier discarded emphasis on technique (e.g., interpretation), emphasized the attitudinal, relationship aspects of the psychotherapist's behavior (Rogers, 1951), and stated that the student-therapist's learning should take place in a facilitative environment such as the one that the effective therapist provides for his or her patient. He described the "necessary and sufficient" conditions for therapeutic change as the therapist's ability to communicate to the patient *empathic understanding* and *unconditional positive regard* while being *congruent or genuine* as a person. The supervisor must model these behaviors for the student and create a "facilitative" atmosphere for experiential learning (Rogers, 1957).

These facilitative conditions are considered to be universally important in human interaction by the client-centered group. Carkhuff (1967) effectively described this orientation. Both counselors and clients are seen as varying on the same dimensions of interpersonal functioning, with high "therapeutic conditions" being the ingredients of effective living.

Facilitators communicate an accurately empathic understanding of deeper as well as the surface feelings of the second person(s); they are freely and deeply themselves in a nonexploitative relationship; they communicate a very deep respect. . .; and they are helpful in guiding the discussion of personally relevant feelings and experiences in specific and concrete terms.

This is the *reverse* of the client in need of help whose words are unrelated to his or her feelings and, when the responses are genuine to another, they are inclined to be *negative.* He or she has little positive regard for others, and feelings are discussed on an abstract plane. These behaviors are typical of the ineffective person (counselor *or* counselee), and improvement in his or her functioning would take place along the same dimensions. The client-centered programs thus are designed to produce facilitator-therapists who are high on these dimensions.

Research on the Measurement of Client-Centered Constructs and Their Validity

The client-centered group has published a number of research studies suggesting that high therapist conditions in individual psychotherapy, as described above, are associated with constructive patient change, and that the absence of these conditions can lead to deterioration in patient functioning. The research plan in the studies was to have briefly trained judges rate level of therapist "conditions," as reflected in several 2- or 3-minute taped excerpts of each interview. Truax and Carkhuff (1967) reviewed much of this early work. Bergin (1963) also reported that low empathy is related to client deterioration. Truax, Silber, and Carkhuff (1966) reported a beneficial effect of therapist empathy in therapy groups. Bergin and Solomon (1970) found that psychology graduate students' empathy in psychotherapy interviews was related to their general therapeutic competence, as judged by supervisors.

Earlier, Rogers and Truax (1962) reported that degree of self-exploration in the second interview correlated .70 with final case outcome. Anderson (1968) showed that the therapist functioning at high levels of therapeutic conditions could confront clients without decreasing their depth of self-exploration, although confrontations by therapists functioning at lower facilitative levels had a de-

leterious effect on self-exploration ($p < .05$). The high-functioning therapists were found to have a greater tendency to confront patients and, when they did so, confronted them with their *resources.* The lower-functioning therapists tended to confront patients with their *limitations.*

Piaget, Berenson, and Carkhuff (1967) and Holder, Carkhuff, and Berenson (1967) found that high therapist conditions are more important for engendering depth of self-exploration among low-functioning clients than for those patients who are themselves more facilitative. Additionally, Alexik and Carkhuff (1967) and Carkhuff and Alexik (1967) suggested that counselors functioning at high levels are less likely to diminish the therapeutic level of their behavior when interviewing a non-cooperative patient than the low-functioning counselor is. The interviewee was a standard client who later described the counselors and found those functioning at low therapeutic levels to be unimaginative, boring, pedestrian, and perfunctory. Those functioning at high levels were described as stimulating and. exploring; they "left me feeling more hopeful and more courageous."

However, Kratochvil, Aspy, and Carkhuff (1967) found no relationship between therapist "conditions," as usually measured, and depth of client self-exploration; Bergin and Jasper (1969) found global supervisor rating of patient outcome ($n = 24$) unrelated to therapist empathy as rated on the Bergin-Solomon revision of the Truax Accurate Empathy Scale. *Patient* ratings of "feeling understood" correlated positively with patient outcome, as did two measures of therapist behavior from the Barrett-Lennard Relationship Inventory, but these ratings were *not* related to raters' scores on the Truax scale. Bergen and Jasper question the generalizability of Truax' results to nonclient-centered therapy, and later studies (reviewed subsequently) have underscored important methodological problems in much of the research conducted on therapist conditions and their relationship to patient improvement.

Somewhat equivocal results were obtained with another group of nonclient-centered therapists. Four psychiatric residents treated 40 psychiatric outpatients at the Phipps Psychiatric Clinic (Truax, Wargo, Frank, Imber, Battle, Hoehn-Saric, Nash, and Stone, 1966). The most striking result was that the patients who received high ratings of therapeutic conditions were given the most favorable global improvement ratings by *their therapists* ($p < .01$, two-tailed test). The patients' global ratings of their own improvement had a considerably lower although significant correlation with therapeutic conditions ($p < .05$, one-tailed test). Thus, therapists who offered high therapeutic conditions tended to see greater global improvement in their patients, and there was some (relatively meager) evidence to confirm their perception.

A number of investigators have been concerned about the validity and reliability of empathy ratings, and some recent research has suggested caution in accepting earlier results at face value.

Hansen, Moore, and Carkhuff (1968), Burstein and Carkhuff (1968), and Caracena and Vicory (1969) failed to find a relationship between accurate empathy ratings and *client*-perceived empathy. McWhirter (1973) obtained similar results with 45 trainees who interviewed coached clients. Trained judges rated the trainee on the Truax rating scales, and the clients rated the therapist-client relationship on the Barrett-Lennard Relationship Inventory. None of the Truax scales were significantly related to the clients' perceptions of the relationship. McWhirter refers to Shapiro's (1968) finding that many of the important empathy cues are *visual*, whereas these judges, like those in most of the related studies, were rating on the basis of *audiotapes* only. He also suggests that an "objective" outsider may perceive a relationship very differently from the way the involved client does.

Chinsky and Rappaport (1970) and Rappaport and Chinsky (1972) suggest that the AE (accurate empathy) scale may not measure empathy and point out that, in fact, it is more highly correlated with measures of other constructs than it is with alternate measures of "empathy." They point out that Shapiro (1968) found the AE to correlate highly with therapist warmth ($r = .87$), genuineness ($r = .73$), and the semantic differential evaluative dimension of "good-bad." Thus, they assert that a more general therapist quality than empathy is being measured. They point to contradictory results of studies relating AE to outcome, and to Truax et al.'s (1966) study in which it was found that raters gave the same mean AE score to interviewer utterance, with and without knowledge of the associated client statements. Therefore, they claim, the raters must be responding to something other than AE. "How can one assess the accuracy of a therapist's empathy unless there is someone to whom the therapist is responding?" (Chinsky and Rappaport, 1970). They question whether AE can be discriminated as easily as Truax (1967) indicates, and they wonder about its meaning in view of the fact that client ratings of interviewer empathy are unrelated to trained raters' evaluations of AE. They also state that rater reliability has been overestimated through the procedure of a few raters making repeated measurements on a few therapists. They point out that raters cannot help remembering how they rated the therapist earlier, and they tend to strive for consistency.

Mintz and Luborsky (1971), referring to the fact that empathy ratings are similar with and without knowledge of client utterances, state: "Such results suggest that the ratings are not based on the interchange between patient and therapist." They believe that the use of brief segments as rating units precludes valid measurement of relationship variables. They compared segment versus whole interview ratings of "Optimal Empathic Relationship, a dimension describing how good the therapist (and the therapy) is, involving an empathic, skillful focus on feelings, and ideal therapist relationship qualities. . ." (p. 184–185). They found that the "correlational evidence indicated that the dimension actually measured was not the same" in the two conditions and state: "The data of this study suggest that this broad dimension of therapist relationship qualities may be the one major aspect of therapy interaction for which brief segments are *not* appropriate substitutes for whole sessions" (p. 188). They see whole session ratings as describing "therapeutic styles" and as "responsive to the interactional character of therapy in a way that the segment factors are not" (p. 189).

A clue to the high correlation between empathy ratings based on client-therapist interaction and therapist statement alone is provided by Wenegrat (1974). In a factor analysis of ratings of taped interview segments, she found that AE correlated most significantly with the number of therapist statements making specific reference to the client's emotion and to the proportion of total responses referring to emotion. She concludes, in part, that

"AE ratings, as a result, represent verbal indications of therapist assertiveness in dealing with client emotions" (p. 51). She notes that she did not replicate previous research relating AE to number of words spoken by the therapist. However, Hargrove (1974) found that therapists' silence correctly predicted the category of 58 percent of their empathy ratings. The empathy-related silence behaviors were length of therapist delay before responding to the patient's last utterance, therapist noninterrupting behavior, and therapist silence during patient's pause. Thus, apparent listening is associated modestly with ratings of empathy.

Matarazzo and Wiens (in press) have summarized a number of studies relating empathy to temporal measures of interviewer behavior. They conclude that "interviewers who are rated high in level of empathy by judges who listen to randomly selected tape segments are also interviewers who (1) talk more per utterance and per total segment, (2) use total silence (no response) less, (3) speak with a longer reaction time when they do answer their conversational partner, and (4) interrupt the latter less frequently." The above are partly consistent with the findings of Matarazzo, Phillips, Wiens, and Saslow (1965), who did not obtain empathy ratings but measured some temporal aspects of student interviewer behavior pre- and posttraining in an eclectic (nonclient-centered) program. They found a significant increase in reaction time and significant decrease in number of interruptions posttraining. There was a slight but not significant increase in length of single utterance. However, there was a significant decrease in interviewer total talk time (from 19 to 13 percent), a result also obtained by Ivey, et al. (1968). Concurrent with changes in temporal aspects of their behavior, the interviewers decreased their number of "therapist errors" (as rated by the Matarazzo Check List of Therapist Behavior). Thus, increased interviewing experience and training and a decrease in interviewer "errors" are associated with some of the same temporal variables that have been found to be related to empathy. It does seem that numerous measures of interviewer skill are interrelated.

Cochrane (1974) used a therapy analog procedure with response tapes to study the relationship between therapist skill in empathic communication and therapist accuracy of empathic inference as measured by a therapist Q-sort that was "to describe the client as the client saw himself at the time of the interview." She found no relationship ($r = -.32, p < .10$), although this result could be questioned due to the use of a therapy analog and the unknown degree of appropriateness of the Q-sort items and the forced-choice format of the Q-technique.

Blaas and Heck (1975) were concerned with the accuracy or validity of AE ratings. Ten counselor-client interactions, two selected to be at each level of the five-point AE scale, were taped and rated by two groups of judges. One group ($n = 17$) was first given a one-page description of the client, while the other ($n = 14$) had no information about the client. The informed raters were significantly more accurate in their ratings than those who were not informed, and this was particularly true at the higher levels of empathy. Here we have another reminder of the complexity of factors that must be considered when undertaking research in this area.

Wallston and Weetz (1975) found that therapist self-report measures of empathy were unrelated to a behavioral measure of empathy. The measure, however, consisted of responses to videotaped, simulated interview segments instead of real interviews. Hayden (1975) studied the verbal behavior of 20 experienced therapists (4 years or more of posttraining experience) who were rated by peers in regard to effectiveness. He found that the more effective therapists, responding to eight pause points of a taped interview session, were higher in empathy, positive regard, genuineness, experiential instead of weakness confrontation, and use of inner instead of outer focus. There were, obviously, high intercorrelations among these conditions, again suggesting that they are not separate variables, but parts of a more global characteristic.

In an interesting therapy analog study, Johnson (1971) had trained confederates negotiate the financial settlement of a civil law suit with subjects. The confederates were trained to express, singly: warmth of interaction, accuracy of understanding, and the proposal of compromises. Each negotiating session was rated by two independent judges as to whether the confederate was expressing the appropriate attitude. The expression of warmth, as hypothesized, resulted in more favorable attitudes toward the confederate and feelings of trust and being accepted, but did not influence the subjects' willingness to negotiate. Accuracy of understanding produced greater willingness to reach an agreement in negotiations than when the confederate showed inaccurate understanding. And the confederate's proposal of compromises resulted in more agreements. Thus, accuracy of understanding and the proposal of compromises resulted in greater compromise agreements, while warmth increased a positive perception of the relationship. Johnson suggests that "The understanding of the separate effects of these variables in the counseling relationship may facilitate the development of skills specifically aimed at constructively handling different types of problems counselors often face" (p. 216).

In summary, it is necessary to question the results of the client-centered research methods. Their typically inexperienced, briefly trained judges, who were naive to the patients' dynamics, have not been able to rate brief, audiotaped interview segments validly and reliably in a manner that agrees with the patients' ratings of the interaction. Some of the contributory reasons for this are summarized below. The use of multiple responses from a few therapists probably resulted in inflated reliability coefficients on the variables rated. The empathy scale, as frequently used, seems to be related to the total *number* of references to emotion without their necessarily being *accurate* reflections of feeling. Ratings of *brief* interview segments probably do not accurately assess the actual empathic relationship between therapist and client. It seems logical that, in order to make valid ratings, judges need more information about the client than they have been given. Unfortunately, the same research methods were used for many studies, making it necessary to question a large accumulation of research in which these therapeutic dimensions and techniques of measurement have been used. Nonetheless, the training programs developed by this group were innovative and have stimulated new approaches to more efficient and effective teaching of some specific interview dimensions that appear to have promise. They have directed our attention to the advantages of an organized, step-

wise training program, the development of tools for measuring the variables to be taught, and the need for follow-up measurement of both student-therapist and client change. Also, it is apparent that their therapeutic "conditions" continue to be much researched constructs, have some definite behavioral correlates, and are *felt* to be clinically useful.

Research on the Didactic-Experiential Therapist Training Programs

Truax, Carkhuff, and Douds (1964), Truax and Carkhuff (1967), and Carkhuff (1972) added significant refinements to the earlier training procedures of Rogers and carried out ambitious research programs to measure the effectiveness of their training. They charged that most psychotherapy training programs had taught theory and patient psychodynamics instead of how to relate to a patient and conduct psychotherapy.

They were reinforced in the development of their training theory by the research findings of others such as Barrett-Lennard (1962), Feifel and Eells (1963), Kamin and Caughlan (1963), Gardner (1964), Strupp, Wallach, and Wogan (1964), Lorr (1965), and Rice (1965), who found that patients valued the warmth, helpfulness, and human characteristics of the therapist. They also pointed out that therapist warmth and accurate empathy, in turn, had been related to research-based variables such as "depth of patient exploration" and to patient outcome in their own research.

The three central elements of the training program were described as:

> *(1) a therapeutic context in which the supervisor himself provides high levels of therapeutic conditions; (2) highly specific didactic training in the implementation of the therapeutic conditions; and (3) a quasi-group therapy experience where the trainee can explore his own existence, and his individual therapeutic self can emerge. (Truax and Carkhuff, 1967, p. 242)*

More specifically, the steps of the program were described as follows. Students were given extensive reading to do, followed by listening to taped individual psychotherapy sessions to increase their response repertoire. They rated excerpts from these tapes on the scales of "accurate empathy," "nonpossessive warmth," and "genuineness." Subsequently, they practiced making responses to tape-recorded patient statements (especially empathic responses). Outside of class, pairs of students alternated playing "therapist" and "patient" roles in sessions that were recorded, brought to supervisory sessions, and rated on the therapeutic conditions scales. After achieving minimal levels of therapeutic conditions, the students had single interviews with real patients. The interviews were tape-recorded, and samples were played back for rating by the student, his or her peers, and the supervisor. Psychotherapeutic sessions were tape-recorded on a continuing basis, and periodic samples were evaluated in the supervisory session. In the sixth week of the program, quasigroup therapy was initiatedwwith the students, who met for 2-hour sessions once a week. Truax and Carkhuff (1967) state: "Although the experiential content served as a background for the classroom interactions, the experiential qualities came to the foreground in the quasi-group therapy experience, which provided a more concentrated therapeutic encounter" (p. 271). The quasi group therapy consisted of group discussion centered around the trainees' personal or emotional difficulties experienced *in their role as therapists,* and thus was not intended to provide personal psychotherapy for them.

The Truax and Carkhuff (1967) program, therefore, (1) began with a partial theory of the conditions essential to patient behavioral change; (2) included the development and some testing of instruments for measuring those conditions; (3) cited some *research* to indicate that these conditions do foster contructive patient change while their absence is a deterrent to constructive change; and (4) reflected, in its particular training steps, specific attempts to foster the *appropriate attitudes and behaviors* among the students. Truax and Carkhuff also made use of ideas from social learning theory, behavior modification theory, and programmed instruction. For example, the following ideas are from social learning and behavior modification theories:

The major implication of the present tentative analysis is that the therapists or counselors who are high in empathy, warmth, and genuineness are more effective in psychotherapy because they themselves are personally more potent positive reinforcers; and also because they elicit through reciprocal affect a high degree of positive affect in the patient, which increases the level of the patient's positive self-reinforcement, decreases anxiety, and increases the level of positive affect communicated to others, thereby reciprocally increasing the positive affect and positive reinforcement received from others. By contrast, counselors or therapists who are low in communicated accurate empathy, nonpossessive warmth and genuineness are ineffective and produce negative or deteriorative change in the patient because they are noxious stimuli who serve primarily as aversive reinforcers and also because they elicit negative affect in the patient (which increases the level of the patient's negative self-reinforcement, increases the level of negative affect communicated to others, and thus increases reciprocally the negative affect and negative reinforcement received from others. (pp. 161−162)

Some ideas from programmed instruction can be seen in their attempt, as carefully as possible in this complex learning situation, to teach a few relatively simple behaviors at one time, provide immediate feedback, and gradually refine discriminations until a defined level of performance is reached and the student is considered ready for the next learning task. Numbers of investigators have been stimulated to test the effectiveness of this and similar programs, as shown by the continuing number of empirical studies measuring behavior change in student therapists and the aforementioned studies testing the validity of the above constructs. Some of the early investigations of student change with training are described in the following paragraphs. As will be seen, these investigations were followed by more critical later studies showing important flaws in their design and indicating the need for more careful and sophisticated study.

Carkhuff and Truax (1965) evaluated two separate but similar and concurrent training programs. One involved 12 "advanced graduate students"; the other involved five "volunteer but otherwise unselected lay hospital personnel." The classes met twice a week for 2-hour sessions over a 16-week semester. At the end of the semester, six 4-minute excerpts from each student's taped interviews were rated by trained undergraduates for accurate empathy, unconditional positive regard, therapist self-congruence, and client depth of self-exploration. These ratings were compared with ratings of taped excerpts from experienced therapists and from the publicly dispersed tapes of four prominent therapists. The scores tended to rank the groups in the order: experienced therapists, graduate students, lay personnel. However, none of the differences was significant except in regard to the therapist self-congruence dimension. Carkhuff and Truax conclude that during 100 hours of training specifically directed toward variables empirically demonstrated to be necessary for therapist effectiveness, they could bring the performance of students and lay personnel to a level similar to that of experienced therapists (on the client-centered dimensions measured). Berenson, Carkhuff, and Myrus (1966) attempted to measure the effect of different aspects of the integrated, didactic-experiential training program on the functioning of undergraduate college students. Eighteen male and 18 female volunteer students were randomly assigned to: I, the training group proper, which received the total training, including quasigroup therapy; II, the training control group, which received the same program minus the use of the research scales and the quasigroup therapy; and III, a control group, which received no training. Both training groups received 16 hours of training over 8 weeks; Group I had, in addition, 4 hours of group therapy, and Group II had 4 hours of discussion on typical college problems. The students were assessed, pre- and posttraining, in regard to empathy, positive regard, genuineness, concreteness, and degree of self-exploration elicited. These behaviors were assessed by means of ratings of multiple, brief, taped interview segments; inventory reports of standard interviewees as well as significant others; and inventory self-reports. The greatest

gain in interpersonal skill was made by Group I; Group II was intermediate; and the least gain was made by Group III, supporting Berenson et al.'s hypothesis that the total program would have the most effect. Numerous other studies on the didactic-experiential program similar to those described above obtained, for the most part, similar results, but they also have the same shortcomings.

More recently Perry (1975), using the same method of empathy rating, studied the training effects of verbal instruction in empathy followed by a high- or low-empathy modeled interview, or no modeling. She found verbal instruction, alone, to be ineffective. The high-empathy modeling resulted in more and more empathic communication from baseline to the last section of a taped, simulated interview; the negative modeling resulted in decreasingly empathic communication, which underscored the importance of supervisors' skills, as previously reported. (An interesting additional finding was that there was no carryover from trainees' responses in the taped interviews to their behavior in a 15-minute live interview. Again we are reminded that responses in an analog situation may not be indicative of level of skill in an actual interview.) Uhleman, Lea, and Stone (1976) found that the most effective learning took place when didactic instruction preceded modeling, possibly thus directing the learner's attention to the most significant aspects of the model's behavior.

Dowling and Frantz (1975) have added further analog support to previously reported data, indicating that the characteristics of the trainer are important in effecting trainee imitative learning and attitude. (This could be assumed to apply also to the effect of therapist characteristics on the client.) They used eight experimental conditions in which the degree of the leader's facilitative conditions was systematically varied. When the leaders offered high levels of empathy and respect, the subjects imitated significantly more of their attitudes (ethnocentric versus nonethnocentric) than when the leaders offered low levels of the facilitative conditions.

Fry (1973) hypothesized that trainees as well as clients have conditioned anxiety responses to closeness; they consequently used a deconditioning to closeness procedure as part of training for helping skills. The training of the 30 trainees involved role playing and role reversal, with concrete feedback. Measurement of conditions involved rater evaluations of trainee responses to taped stimulus situations and to a 5-minute role-playing session with another trainee. Fry found that both the control and experimental groups benefited from training, but the experimental group benefited significantly more in regard to communicating warmth, empathy, respect, concreteness, and genuineness. He concluded that systematic desensitization is useful when paired with training in order to alleviate the defensiveness of the trainee and enable him or her to move faster to higher levels of interpersonal functioning.

Butler and Hansen (1973) evaluated the effectiveness of a 10-hour, didactic-experiential program, as measured by written responses to tape-recorded standard client statements and oral responses to a tape-recorded standard client. They found a wide discrepancy between the quality of written and oral responses. This was particularly true for their originally lower-functioning students. Gormally and Hill (1974) have offered some methodological guidelines for evaluating the relatively large body of literature surrounding the didactic-experiential training programs. Despite Carkhuff's (1971) description of a typical 100-hour program and his published "programmed text" (Carkhuff, 1972), they point out that many aspects of the training remain unspecified and thus presumed that replication studies may not be measuring equivalent treatments. They point to design inadequacies: the control conditions are often not clearly specified; placebo controls are not used; and placebo groups may not come from the same population as the experimental group.

In addition, as pointed out by Resnikoff (1972), the same rating scales used for training are used to measure outcome, and thus bias results in favor of the experimental group since they, but not the control group, are aware of the rating criteria. Gormally and Hill (1974) question the generalizability of results to real interview situations when the criterion behaviors are measured in artificial situations (i.e., response tapes, written interviews, coached clients). Several studies have suggested

that responses to written or standard client stimuli do not evoke responses from the trainee that are equivalent to his free interview behavior (Butler & Hansen, 1973; Carkhuff, 1969; Gormally, Hill, Gulanick, & McGovern, 1975; Perry, 1975). They also question whether volunteer clients are motivated to engage in self-exploration, and they call for experimental measurement based on the actual criterion (client interview) behaviors and measurement of client benefit.

Gormally and Hill further criticize the extensive utilization of rating scales in the absence of judges who have received standardized training, inasmuch as use of the scales may then vary across studies. Also, since the ratings are not always found to correlate with independent measures (when the latter are used), their implications should be regarded as tentative. Along with other critics, Gormally and Hill point out the high intercorrelations among the scales, their certain lack of independence, and thus our uncertainty regarding what they measure. Furthermore, it seems that the raters' level of functioning, counseling experience, and even sex affect their rating accuracy. These variables have not been controlled, nor have continual checks on reliability been made. Also, the *average* change in a group of trainees is usually the statistic reported, even though *individual* trainee changes are important. Long-term retention of skill has not been measured. Finally, research has indicated that client, therapist, and observer ratings are not highly correlated, and that only *clients'* ratings of therapist-offered conditions correlate consistently with outcome (Kurtz & Grummon, 1972).

In conclusion, there are cogent criticisms of the preceding *research methodology* that should serve as a guide to others who plan to evaluate training programs. The criticisms do not, however, invalidate the fact that the didactic experiential training programs initially made a significant step forward. Some of these studies have at least approximated the definition and measurement of a few important variables that differentiate expert from novice interviewers. The programs were innovative and have stimulated a quantity of research. The research, in turn, has indicated the need for increased rigor and sophistication. Empathy, for example, apparently is not a unitary variable, since it is highly correlated with a number of evaluative, "good-bad" therapist behaviors, at least as it is measured by the Truax scale. There are problems with judges rating the variables as this has been done in most of the studies. We are not justified in assuming that *naive* judges, with *no additional information* regarding the patient and having no standardized training, can accurately rate the therapist variables. It is questionable whether accurate measurements can be made from brief interview excerpts, especially without visual cues. We will have to deal with the fact that observer ratings of therapist conditions are not highly correlated with those of the client and that the client outcome correlates of these ratings are disappointing.

In regard to teaching *method,* we seem to have had more success. For example, it seems justifiable to conclude that supervisor-student relationship and *supervisor modeling* of empathy, warmth, respect, and the like, are important, and that supervisor modeling of low relationship skills is deleterious to student learning. *Explicit definition* of the behaviors to be learned is necessary, followed by practice, preferably in *live* interviews, with feedback by observers who have rated the behaviors in question. Feedback through videotape is useful. Feedback should ideally be obtained from the client. Whether by means of quasigroup therapy or other desensitization technique, deconditioning of therapist anxiety is probably helpful in learning to relate warmly to clients. In short, the client-centered programs have not delivered all that they seemed to promise, but they have made a significant contribution. We cannot assume, however, that their dimensions of therapist skill are unidimensional or equally important with all clients and, most assuredly, we cannot assume that they are the "sufficient conditions" for effective client change.

MICROCOUNSELING

Ivey et al. (1968) developed an ingenious, brief variant of the didactic-experiential program. Their "microcounseling" technique, as originally conceived, focused on teaching specific counseling skills in prepracticum training. They reported three original studies in which they attempted to teach (1) attentiveness (1 hour) and the related concepts of (2) accurate reflection (2) hours), and (3) summarization of feeling (2 hours), respectively. In the study of attentiveness, they divided 38 dormitory counselors into experimental and control groups whose "clients" were 38 paid student volunteers. The experimental procedure was as follows: (1) the student conducted a 5-minute, videotaped interview with the instructions: "Go in and talk with this student; get to know him or her"; (2) the student read the "Attending Behavior Manual"; (3) the student viewed videotaped modeling of attending behavior by effective and less effective counselors, followed by discussion with his or her supervisor; (4) the trainee viewed the initial videotape and was asked to identify his or her own attending behavior; and (5) the student recounseled the same "client" in a second, 5-minute, videotaped interview. As rated by two judges, the experimental students, after 1 hour's training, were significantly higher postinstruction in eye contact and in "verbal following" than the control group, whose members merely conducted two interviews with their clients, with no intervening training. For the experimental group, there was also a significantly greater increase in *client's* ratings on the Semantic Differential Form and the Counselor Effectiveness Scale. Counselor talk time for the experimental group decreased from 47 to 33 percent of the total interview time.

The second (accurate reflection) and third (summarization of feelings) studies were similar, but had an additional 3-minute role-playing session and a third 5-minute interview. (Subjects were beginning counselors from the Department of Psychology, Counseling and Guidance, with 11 and 10 subjects, respectively, for studies 2 and 3.) In each postinterview discussion, the supervisor was careful to reinforce the student's skills. In both the latter studies there were significant increases in the appropriate skill (accurate reflection and accurate summarization, respectively), in *client* ratings, and in the student's self-confidence.

This work was significant in that it defined some widely accepted behaviors of the skilled interviewer, taught them one at a time, gave feedback, repeat trials, and so on, all in a matter of a few hours. The Ivey et al. group has continued to publish on this innovative technique, as have others.

Kelley (1971), teaching the above skills through the microcounseling program to master's degree students in counseling and guidance, compared a supervisor-reinforced group, a self-reinforced group, and a control group. All experimental students read the instructional program, conducted a 20-minute interview, reread the instructional booklet, and listened to (and presumably critiqued) their own audiotape. Only the supervisor-reinforced group reviewed the tape with the supervisor, who attempted to reinforce the appropriate behaviors. This procedure was repeated three times. Posttest data were obtained from a fourth interview, and a control group participated in the posttesting only. Their hypotheses, derived from a study in which Matarazzo, Wiens, and Saslow (1966) found length of utterance, response delay, and the like, related to interviewer skill, were mostly validated. Both groups of microcounseling-trained students made fewer utterances than the controls, spoke with shorter durations, used longer latencies, spoke a smaller percent of interview time, and made fewer interruptions. The supervisor-reinforced group performed significantly better than the self-reinforced group only on the latter two variables. They concluded that the microcounseling paradigm is useful and that, when supervision is not available, self-reinforcement can be utilized.

Elsenrath, Coker, and Martinson (1972) developed an audiotaped program designed to teach students to increase their response delay after an interviewee statement and decrease the length of their own utterances, presumably thus increasing percent of interviewee talk time. Subjects were 41 undergraduate student assistants. Both experimental groups were exposed to the audiotaped program, parts of which required them to respond, received reinforcement from a counselor, and engaged in self-administered reinforcement. Group 1 then conducted an audiotaped interview on the same day, and Group 2 conducted the interview 7 to 10 days later. A control group was not exposed to the audiotaped program. Both treatment groups had longer response delays, used less of the total talk time, and made fewer interruptions. They also

facilitated greater interviewee verbalization. There seemed to be no difference between the two experimental groups, suggesting that the briefly trained skills were retained, at least over that period of time.

An unusually carefully designed study by Moreland, Ivey, and Phillips (1973) compared the learning of 12 medical students who were given 6 weeks of microcounseling training with that of 12 students who were given "equivalent" interview training. The trainees were taught, in groups of four, by either an advanced psychiatric resident or a faculty member. The five microcounseling skills were taught, one per day, by reading a manual, watching a videotaped model demonstrate the selected skill, conducting a videotaped interview, and observing the playback with supervisor reinforcement and critique. The comparison subjects were observed conducting interviews, without preselected, specific behavioral instructions, and were given verbal feedback by their instructors in regard to asking more open questions, attending more to feelings, and so on. Pre- and posttraining interviews were videotaped and rated by two judges who categorized the utterances into microcounseling categories, such as open-ended question and reflection of feeling, and "other." In a later viewing of the tapes, the raters also classified each utterance as good, fair, or poor on the Matarazzo Check List of Therapist Behavior (Matarazzo, Phillips, Wiens, & Saslow, 1965). From pre- to posttest, the microcounseling subjects demonstrated some improvement on all six interviewer skills and, on the attending and reflection of feeling measures, they were significantly better than the alternate group. In addition to the improvement in ratings on variables where they might be presumed to have an edge, the microcounseling subjects more than doubled their percent of "good" statements on the Matarazzo Check List of Therapist Behavior, while the comparison group showed no change. Furthermore, they showed a significantly greater decrease in the category of "poor" statements than the other subjects did. The microcounseling students rated their instructors as more effective than the comparison group did. Moreland et al. hypothesize that this was due to the "characteristics of the training method rather than to the qualities of the particular teachers.'' They also concluded that the microcounseling trainees improved in overall skill instead of in only the specific areas of coaching, inasmuch as they improved on the above independently derived scale.

Canada (1973) taught state employment service interviewers to use openend leads in order to presumably increase average length of interviewee utterance and percent of client talk time. Pre- and posttests were a 20-minute interview with a coached client. One experimental group received cleverly contrived immediate reinforcement of open-end questions by means of a light and a later video recall exercise. The second group had an audio recall exercise approximately one day later. The immediate feedback-video recall group had superior posttest scores on percent of client talk time and average length of client response. It is unfortunate that the effects of immediate versus delayed feedback and video versus audio recall were confounded, but those who train counselors should consider both variables.

Two micromodels were compared by Boyd (1973). Both groups had approximately 3 1/2 hours of training, which included reading the Counselor Verbal Response Manual (Boyd, 1971) and engaging in simulation-modeling exercises. Half of the group then received recall interrogation supervision (Kagan et al., 1967) on one of the pretraining interviews, while the other half received behavioral supervision (Boyd, 1971) in which the supervisor used verbal reinforcement, behavioral rehearsal, modeling, and direct suggestion. A second group had an additional practice interview and 48 hours of learning integration time. Microtraining, regardless of model, was found to improve interviewer performance on all four dimensions of the Counselor Verbal Response Scale (Kagan et al., 1967), and behavioral supervision was more effective than recall interrogation.

Authier and Gustafson (1975) conducted another study comparing the effectiveness of microcounseling training with and without supervision. They taught the six skills of the original microcounseling program: attending behavior, "minimal encourages to talk"; "open invitation to talk"; reflec-

tion of feeling; paraphrasing; and summarization. In contrast to other studies, their results showed that the microtraining was ineffective in both supervised and unsupervised conditions. They hypothesize that their negative results may have been due to poor motivation among their paraprofessional counselors who worked in a drug treatment unit, and they also question whether the skills are as appropriate for interviewing a drug patient population as for interviewing psychiatric patients.

Toukmanian and Rennie (1975) compared the effectiveness of microcounseling training and human relations training with a population of 24 undergraduate students. Microcounseling training focused on counselor attending, verbal following, minimal activity, reflection of feeling, and open inquiry. The human relations training, in accordance with the Truax and Carkhuff model, taught accurate empathy, genuineness, respect, concreteness, self-disclosure, confrontation, and immediacy of relationship. They state that "The instructional techniques of human relations training and microcounseling differ in three major ways . . . the former uses two training phases . . . discrimination training . . . and communication training (whereas) . . . microcounseling . . . uses role playing as its focal point of training." Second, human relations training uses audiotape recordings, whereas microtraining uses videotape. Third, human relations training uses objective ratings of communication level, whereas microtraining uses joint interviewer-supervisor videotape analysis as feedback. On posttest, both training groups were significantly better than the controls on empathy score, and the microtraining group was significantly superior to the human relations training group. Both of the latter made significant improvement on the three communication categories (increase in open invitation to talk and decrease in closed inquiry, interpretation, and advice). There were no further significant differences between the two training groups. Toukmanian and Rennie hypothesize that the greater improvement in empathy score for the microcounseling trainees reflects the greater amount of *practice* given in microcounseling training (instead of an initial period of discrimination training only, as in human relations training). They also believe that videotape is a more effective training medium than audiotape. They call for further investigation of the relative effectiveness of the separate training components.

In summary, there have been numerous studies, some well designed and others less so, that indicate that microcounseling skills can be taught effectively and in a relatively small number of teaching hours to appropriately selected students. To me, the important contribution of microcounseling is that, like the client-centered programs, it has defined what is to be taught; devised appropriate, research-based teaching methods; and used measurement, feedback, and reinforcement of skills. One particular strength of the program lies in its teaching of *well-defined behavioral variables* that seem relatively easy to judge validly and reliably. An open-ended question should be easier to describe, model, and judge than degree of empathy. A proponent of client-centered therapy might insist that empathy is a more significant, necessary, or potent variable, but this has yet to be proved. Importantly, objective, easily taught skills (speech latency, number of interruptions, etc.) seem to correlate with subjective client-centered variables such as empathy. We thus may hope eventually to find more bridges between the relatively objective and subjective aspects of interview behavior.

Another strength of microcounseling measurement and feedback is that, for the most part, whole, brief interviews are used as units instead of the few-minute excerpts used by the didactic-experiential group. The use of videotape feedback and rating is undoubtedly superior to the use of audiotape because *all* the cues, not just selected ones, can be taken into account.

It would probably be pointless to add to the research that has been done in an attempt to measure the relative teaching efficiency of the two related types of programs; obviously they both are, in most instances, effective teaching methods. What seems to emerge from the research is the not surprising finding that carefully programmed teaching methods are superior to those that are more loosely conducted. If the goal behaviors are clearly defined and the teaching methods are appropriately chosen and implemented, the program must be more effective than one in which less precision

has been used. *However, neither program has gone beyond the teaching of basic skills to neophyte therapists. The teaching of more advanced therapists remains a less well-charted area.*

TEACHING THE TECHNIQUES OF BEHAVIOR MODIFICATION

When the first edition of this chapter was being written approximately 8 years ago, the research of those using variables derived from the client-centered orientation was the most innovative and exciting. As of this writing, there is excitement among the behavior modifiers.

By now, operant conditioning and desensitization (classical conditioning) are widely accepted forms of treatment for populations that have been relatively nonamenable to the more traditional forms of psychotherapy (e.g., autistic and retarded children and chronic psychotic adults) and for removal of specific disturbing behaviors and symptoms related to the autonomic nervous system. Considerable research has been conducted on teaching parents and other environmental agents to modify the nonconforming or otherwise disturbing behaviors of children, in the home or at school, through operant conditioning.

There is justification for concluding that operant conditioning, appropriately conceived and applied, is an effective means of shaping behavior, increasing the number of desired responses, and decreasing or eliminating the behaviors targeted for extinction. Numerous studies testify to the improvement of child behavior, including Wahler et al. (1965), Patterson, Cobb, and Ray (1970), Patterson and Reid (1973), Wiltz (1969); Hanf (1967); and Eyberg and Johnson (1974). (See also Chapters 14 and 15.)

In this orientation, a therapist is anyone who uses systematic methods of modifying the behavior of the targeted individual. The approach emphasizes the specification of observable child or adult patient behaviors, the environmental stimuli that are reinforcing them, and the frequency of their occurrence. It is then possible to state what (parent or other) therapist behaviors should be effective in altering the pattern of reinforcement, whether or not the therapist emitted these behaviors, and what changes occurred in the trainee's responses. Thus it is possible to measure both how well the therapist has learned to perform as the supervisor recommends and how effective that performance is in increasing or decreasing the targeted behaviors.

Perhaps largely because the therapists or trainers have been lay individuals, there has been somewhat more complete specification of training programs, follow-up measurement of the trainer's acquired skill, and measurement of the trainer's efficacy in producing the desired changes in the behavior of the trainee. The psychologist's role is usually that of consultant, programming the environment and teaching the principles of behavior modification to other therapist-trainers.

Parent-Child Behavior Modification

Holland (1970) has presented an excellent, detailed interview guide for the professional to use in designing a program to be administered by the parent. This outline emphasizes the importance of careful, preliminary "diagnostic" work. He states that "only with patient and repeated observations of the behavior and the environmental conditions within which the behavior occurs will the necessary clarity of the determinants emerge." He also carefully covers the setting of goals, steps toward the goals, selection of positive and negative reinforcers, and use of the principles of reinforcement and extinction. This would appear to be an eminently useful "how-to" guide, although it would obviously be only part of the didactic background material for a total training program designed for professional supervisors of lay therapists. He does not provide information regarding how it may have been used as part of a training program.

Reisinger, Ora, and Frangia (1976) present a review of behavior therapy research with parents having a child-trainee under age 12. Much of the early research consisted of single case studies, but more recent replications have involved larger Ns. It has been found (Salzinger et al., 1970) that behavior modification training is considerably less effective with less educated parents, although Jacobson, Bushnell, and Risley (1968) found that, by altering their approach, they were able to effect changes in lower-class mothers' child-rearing strategies. Didactic presentation alone (Ray, 1965) has, not surprisingly, been found to be less than optimally effective in parent training (just as with the training of student-professionals).

Relatively few authors have included a full description of their training programs, but the idea of didactic presentation of background principles, demonstration or modeling, and observed practice with feedback seem to be well accepted. Glowgower and Sloop (1976) compared the performance of mothers who were taught the principles of behavior modification, followed by training to change specific target behaviors, with the performance of mothers who were trained only to change target behaviors. They found that the broadly trained mothers dealt better with a wide range of behavior problems and showed better maintenance of skill. The broadly trained mothers initiated more successful home projects, improved in playing with their children, and were more effective in giving commands and obtaining compliance. There was a tendency for them to continue to show improvement at follow-up, while the more specifically trained group showed a decrement in score for home behavior change projects at the 5-month follow-up. This result is important in suggesting that broad training may enable auxiliary therapists to apply their skills appropriately in other problem situations and continue to use their knowledge in the absence of the trainer. The question of generalization of skill and its maintenance continue to concern investigators and clinicians using parent-trainers.

Salzinger, Feldman, and Portnoy (1970) taught the parents (primarily mothers) of 15 brain-injured children "the uses of operant conditioning principles for functionally analyzing behavior and for designing and carrying out behavior modification programs for their own children." They trained the parents to make observational recordings of their own child's problem behaviors and all the consequent events. Parents were required to read an operant conditioning manual and take an examination on it; parent reading comprehension was measured; a series of lectures and discussions on conditioning were presented; and specific, individual programs were worked out with the parents. Parents continued to record child behavior on their observation forms and meet with the trainers for approximately 8 months. Records were mailed in during weeks when no appointment was held, unclear points were discussed, and errors were corrected and returned. At the end, they were asked to fill out a final evaluation form. Salzinger et al. found that all parents who reported carrying out the program as designed (four parents) showed "considerable or complete success." Limited success was achieved by the parents who only partially followed the program (four parents), and those who did not carry out the program or made serious mistakes in carrying it out reported no change (seven parents). Thus it seems that a major obstacle to the use of parent-therapists lies in the problem of motivating them. Salzinger et al. point out that their program was essentially instructional and not training in nature. They presumed that many of their parents would have benefited from a "controlled learning environment set up in homes under supervision" (p. 22) and that with some parents "direct manipulation of the parent-child interaction will probably be necessary for as long as it takes to alter the parents' behavior in an appropriate way and until the corresponding changes in the children prove sufficiently reinforcing to sustain the parents' efforts" (p. 23). The successful parents generally had more education and better reading ability, and they showed better comprehension on the reading test. Salzinger et al. conclude that "we would undoubtedly do better to apply to the parents' behavior the same kind of analysis that we applied to their children's behavior. Parents' no less than their children's behavior is subject to reinforcement contingencies. . . ."

Eyberg and Matarazzo (1975) compared the effectiveness of five didactic behavior modification training sessions for mothers with five individual mother-child training sessions. The children were speech-delayed and were enrolled in a summer workshop designed to stimulate speech and teach the mothers improved parenting skills. The didactic group used a semiprogrammed text (Becker, 1971) with home assignments that were discussed in weekly class meetings. The individually trained mothers were taught and then observed through a one-way screen while performing with their chil-

dren a modification of the standard tasks developed by Hanf (1967). They had guided, real-life rehearsal of appropriate behavior designed to build a positive relationship and to obtain compliance from their children, and they were given immediate feedback following observation. Approximately the same amount of time was expended per mother (1½-hour group meetings versus 20-minute individual mother-child sessions). Although both groups improved, during posttreatment observation sessions the individually trained mothers showed a significantly greater increase in praise and significantly greater decrease in critical statements, and the like, than the group treatment mothers. The individually trained mothers also indicated significantly greater satisfaction with the program. It was concluded that possibly individual, invivo training, practice, and feedback is a more efficacious use of professional time than parent group training. Walter and Gilmore (1973) studied 12 families who had a child with severe out-of-control behavior. Those in the placebo group received attention and encouragement but no behavior modification training, and the child's deviant behavior did not improve. Those in the experimental group read the Patterson and Gullion (1968) programmed text and were examined on the principles. They were then taught how to specify and collect data, daily telephone contact was made, and weekly parent group sessions were held that utilized role playing, modeling, and didactic instruction. Family observations by trained observers disclosed a 61 percent decrease in targeted behavior for the treatment group. This was in agreement with parental reports of a decrease in symptoms.

Ferber, Keeley, and Shemberg (1974), using the Patterson procedure, were unable to duplicate the highly positive results reported in studies such as the preceding one. They reported difficulty in observing the target behaviors at home because the families felt restrained by the presence of the experimenters. They also felt that the "coded" behaviors did not adequately reflect the nature and severity of the total family difficulties. In addition, the changes that did occur tended to dissipate by the time of follow-up. As Patterson, Cobb, and Ray (1973) have indicated, some families may require that treatment be extended over a long period of time. *Severity* of the problem behavior is also likely to be an important factor.

Nay (1975) compared the effectiveness of several methods of teaching time-out procedures to parents. With an unusually large N of 77 mothers, he compared written and oral didactic instruction, videotaped modeling, and modeling coupled with role playing each aspect of time-out. As measured by a questionnaire, all training techniques were equally useful, but assessment through response in a simulated situation suggested that the modeling and modeling plus role-playing groups performed better than either of the didactic groups. Thus, again, method of measuring learning is important. Eyberg and Johnson (1974) found that observation of parent-child behavior yielded less evidence of treatment effect than parent-collected data and parent attitude change. They recommend using multiple methods of assessment.

Rinn, Vernon, and Wise (1975) present evaluation data on 1100 parents who took a course in Positive Parent Training, where they were instructed in the principles of applied operant learning. The parents paid a $30 enrollment fee, $10 of which was refundable for the contingent group if they satisfied all requirements for attendance and performance. Homework was assigned, and completion was required for admittance to class. Home observation data and parent report forms were the criteria of improvement. After session 5, 92 percent reported much improvement, 3 percent reported moderate improvement, and 5 percent were not improved. This is an unusually high percentage of reported success, for reasons that are not clear. The contingent (money refund) group attended more sessions and completed more projects than the noncontingent group, indicating the importance of external contingencies for trainers as well as trainees. Also, middle-income parents attended more classes and were more successful than lower-income parents.

Parents have been trained to treat their own autistic children. Kozloff (1973) describes training parents to interrupt the destructive cycle of parent-child interaction and begin a cycle of increased positive reinforcement. He reports great increments in parental skill and improvement in child behavior.

An unanswered question is how to select and train parents who can be expected to be reasonably competent and also ethical in working with their children, who have no safeguards. Behavior modification techniques can indeed be misapplied, to the detriment of the trainee.

Behavior Modification Programs in the Classroom and Hospital

Token economies and other behavior modification programs have been established in the classroom, on hospital wards, and in penal institutions. However, the training process is usually informal; it involves reading material and the use of previously "trained" assistants to help the teacher put the program into action. Cotler et al. (1972) report moderately good results in improving student-clients' study behavior in this manner, but found that both teacher and students tended to return to their old behaviors when the specific program was not in effect. It seemed necessary to continue to reinforce the trainer and the trainee in order to keep the program going. Difficulty in getting hospital aides to maintain their "therapeutic" behaviors has been reported (Katz, Johnson, & Gelfand, 1972), although contingent monetary bonuses increased the frequency of their reinforcing behaviors.

Johnson, Katz, and Gelfand (1972) report training undergraduate practicum and work-study students to do behavior modification training with hospitalized psychiatric patients. The program consisted of assigned reading material followed by a quiz, and supervision by a graduate student. A well-planned, 6-week summer workshop for 36 teachers is described by Kubany, Sloggett, and Ogata (1972). The first 2½ weeks included instruction on principles of behavior modification by means of reading, lecture, discussion, and movies. The second half of the program incorporated modeling, with the student-observer coding the behaviors of the student-model and being checked for reliability of coding; roles were then reversed, and there was feedback to the model regarding his or her performance. It was an imaginative and ambitious program, and it is unfortunate that no baseline or follow-up data were collected.

Levine and Tilker (1974) describe their approach to training therapists in a behavioral orientation to psychotherapy. They see behavior therapy as differing from nonbehavioral models in the degree of specificity required of the therapist. Thus, "Congruent with a behavioral orientation, supervision is conceived of as the changing of specific response patterns in the neophyte therapist so that he will be able to assist his client in effecting the mutually desired and agreed upon changes in behavior" (p. 182). After the student has learned the principles of academic psychology, they propose gradual exposure to clinical intervention through the following steps.

1. The first step is nonparticipatory observation, where the student can learn the skill of listening without the necessity for formulating a response.

2. The next step is role playing, which is especially helpful for learning information-gathering skills in a situation where the student can receive feedback immediately. Levine and Tilker recommend reinstituting role playing "at all stages of supervision for correction of inappropriate responses as well as for the specific teaching of new techniques."

3. The third step involves the student's sitting in on an interview, followed by a supervisory session in which the interview is discussed. This stage apparently consists initially of the trainee's sitting in while the supervisor takes major responsibility; they then reverse roles. Levine and Tilker believe this is the single best teaching method, because the supervisor and trainee each obtain a clear picture of the other's functioning, and the supervisor can also step in to demonstrate, as necessary.

4. The next step consists of using a "bug in the ear," enabling *in vivo* instruction and feedback. However, Levine and Tilker caution the supervisor not to give too many instructions, which would be interruptive.

5. More advanced supervision is continued through audiovisual tapes, which have the disadvantage of slightly delayed feedback,

but do provide a complete review of interview behaviors and verbal content.

Levine and Tilker make the cogent points that "whatever techniques exist to help clients can potentially be used to help trainees" and that "The single most effective technique that a supervisor has is to provide the trainee with direct, unambiguous feedback about the trainee's functioning along with alternative ways the issue can be handled." They obviously have some stimulating thoughts on the matter of training for interview skill, but apparently have not submitted them to research measurement.

Bond (1974) presents a strong case for behavior therapy and the fact that *diagnosis* is a more important aspect of treatment in this approach than it is in either the client-centered or psychoanalytic models. He says that "behavior therapists, in using the S-O-R model, focus on the specific organism-environment interactions which are problematic for the client in everyday life" (p. 124). Thus, one of the most important goals of (professional) training is that of "behavioral analysis, which involves a careful description of the target behaviors that the client wishes to modify, along with the relevant aspects of environments where these occur." Kanfer and Saslow (1969) state that the goal of the behavioral analysis is the choice of the most appropriate treatment. This may include systematic desensitization, assertive training, aversive conditioning, or the use of an operant technique. Bond states that "Behavior therapy's greater specificity encourages a more active strategy of attempting to influence behavior, which permits a relatively immediate check on the success or failure of the strategy." He believes that the more complete specification of patient goals enables more adequate evaluation of progress toward them. This can aid the supervisor in evaluating the skill of a trainee.

The programs planned for parents in behavior modification have dealt with various aspects of therapeutic intervention training more adequately than any other kind of program so far described in the literature. The behavior modification programs have focused on defining the goal behaviors of the (parent) trainer and those of the (child) trainee, manipulating the sources of motivation for both, comparing training methods, and using both observational measurement of improvement in the child-patient and measurement of parent satisfaction with outcome. This approach to therapy and therapist training is made possible by the ordinarily observable and delimited nature of the chief complaint (e.g. noncompliance) and the environmental variables that are maintaining it. Also important is the programs' well-formulated theoretical base, which determines the choice of specific intervention procedures.

Authors of several studies have noted where a training program has succeeded or failed, analyzed the probable reasons for failure, and systematically altered either the training procedures, the teaching methods, the motivation of the trainee, or the reinforcing stimuli (time-out, reward by preferred activities, praise, etc.). Although other kinds of therapeutic skills do not lend themselves as easily to such objective measurement, we should be able to make progress in this regard. Perhaps the discriminative stimuli and the reinforcing stimuli for us, as supervisors, have not been sufficiently salient for doing so. We do not have to train students in the brief time period that may be all that can be devoted to a single family, and thus we can be less intense. The student's shortcomings in more complex therapeutic situations are not so easily pinpointed. His therapeutic effect on the patient is often not known by the supervisor, and the student may not always complain about lack of results; in fact, the student may be motivated to try to hide any training deficiencies from the supervisor.

Loeber and Weisman (1975) state that "Behavior modification programs usually put heavy emphasis on environmental variables, but, remarkably enough, little attention has been paid to the analysis and control of that class of environmental variables comprising the responses emitted by therapists and trainers. . ." (p. 660). Some behavior modifiers have recognized the need to classify and measure the responses of trainers, using rating scales and checklists. It has been noted that the supervisor-therapist relationship has an aspect of similarity to the therapist-patient relationship in that guiding interpersonal behavior change is the task of the teacher in both instances. It would thus be reasonable to ask, Do supervisors reinforce students, reliably, on a contingent basis? Do they reinforce therapeutically effective responses or, perhaps, reward dependent or other supervisor-reinforcing behaviors? Do we pay more attention to ineffective than to effective behaviors, taking the latter for granted? How do we select the important "target" behaviors to be modified, and are they the most fundamental "error" behaviors or merely ones that are most distressing to the supervisor? If the trainee is oppositional, how should that be handled? It is sometimes observed that supervisors approach trainees more frequently when they show evidence of some kinds of incompetence instead of competence. Alternatively, some less competent students emit behaviors that are likely to "turn off" supervisors when, in fact, the student needs more and not less supervisor attention. Berberich (1971) has shown that improvement in patient response is a powerful therapist reinforcer. By the same token, the most outstanding and socially skillful students sometimes receive the most supervisor attention, although they need it less. The least active student, who emits less behavior, fewer socially reinforcing responses, and less evidence of improved performance, probably often receives the least attention of all.

The supervisor-therapist relationship has an aspect of similarity to the therapist-patient relationship in that guided behavior change is the task of the teacher in both instances. The similarity can be seen more easily in the behavioral approaches where the "patient" is not considered emotionally "ill" but as a "normal" individual who has behavioral excesses or deficits, or maladaptive behaviors that need reshaping.

SELECTION OF STUDENTS FOR PSYCHOTHERAPY TRAINING

There is a common belief that some personality attributes are desirable in therapists and render a trainee more easily trained. Selection programs so far have been disappointing, however, and no well-defined personality variables have been satisfactorily measured and related to performance. As Garfield (1977) concluded ". . . the criteria used to designate psychotherapeutic requisites are global, non-operationally defined, unsystematically appraised in most instances, and lacking in research designed to appraise their importance."

So far we can probably safely say that psychological good health, flexibility, open-mindedness, positive attitudes toward people, and interpersonal skill are associated with success as a psychotherapist. These desirable characteristics, of course, are presumably associated with success in any endeavor in which human interaction is a large component. Lack of these attributes, or personality disturbance, is very likely to hinder the student's growth as a therapist. Whitely et al. (1967) found that the best students were better therapists at the beginning of a 1-year course than were the poorest students at the end of the course. They described a "small, tenacious minority with whom supervision was ineffectual." Intelligence, among this already select group, was found not to be related to empathic ability. However, in relatively unselected populations, such as the parent groups used in behavior modification programs, intelligence and socioeconomic class have been related to success (Salzinger et al., 1970; Rinn et al., 1975).

It is true that some trainees will learn to be adequate therapists far more easily than others, and that poor lifelong habits of relating are a liability for the learner. However, we are left with an embarrassing lack of definable, measurable selection criteria that have been proven to select the best candidates for training. Holt and Luborsky (1958) found little differentiation between the personality characteristics of psychiatrists and "the kind of man one might hope to encounter in any profession and who might be expected to do well in almost any kind of work." Kelly and Goldberg (1959) conducted a large and similarly disappointing study of the characteristics that differentiate therapists from other psychologists. Selection remains a concern of those who train both professional and nonprofessional therapists inasmuch as it has been shown that some are either ineffectual or may induce actual client deterioration (Truax & Carkhuff, 1967). In addition, poorly selected behavior modification trainees have the potential to use behavior modification techniques in an antitherapeutic manner with children or incarcerated adult trainees who do not have freedom of choice and may have no advocates.

SPECIAL DEVICES FOR TEACHING AND EVALUATION OF TEACHING EFFECTIVENESS

Rogers' use of electrical recordings, over 30 years ago, was a major breakthrough in first exposing the psychotherapeutic relationship to direct observation and measurement. The importance of this step can hardly be overestimated, as demonstrated by evidence of the omission and distortion of interview material that is presented for conference discussion by the student-therapist from memory. The one-way screen was a second breakthrough in exposing new dimensions of the therapeutic process to observation.

Videotape and motion pictures have been used for demonstration or modeling purposes in numerous studies previously cited. Strupp and Jenkins (1963) were the first to develop sound motion pictures of therapy interviews with film stops at critical junctures where the viewer is asked for a response. They produced these filmed interviews in order to permit direct comparison of interviewer responses to the same stimulus situation while maximizing the degree of realism. Numerous others have copied this technique as a means of measuring the effects of training. Strupp (as well as other authors) has mentioned awareness of the technique's shortcomings, especially that of lacking true *interaction* between the film patient and the therapist-viewer. This seems to be a fairly serious shortcoming, as evidenced by numerous studies, cited above, in which student responses to standard tapes were unrelated to their level of skill demonstrated in live interview (Carkhuff, 1969; Gormally et al., 1974; Perry, 1975). This result has turned up with sufficient frequency and magnitude to render the use of responses to either audio- or videotapes questionable as a sole criterion measure of therapeutic skill, although they may be useful in the early stages of learning to interview.

Videotape has provided a major breakthrough in psychotherapy training because of its potential for fairly immediate, complete feedback to the student. It is widely used, with and without supervisor reinforcement, and has been reported to be an effective teaching instrument, particularly by the microcounseling group. Indications are that its usefulness is enhanced by the supervisor, but that it is efficacious also with solitary review by the trainee (Kelley, 1971).

Harmatz (1975) reports using a two-channel stereo tape-recorder to record supervisor comments at the appropriate moments of the interview. He feels that the supervisor responds more usefully, having "the full impact of all the cues available in the situation." He recommends this procedure both for "time efficiency and the qualitative aspects of supervision," inasmuch as the students are given "a more realistic view of what the more experienced clinician is thinking when an event actually occurs in the treatment process." Videotape as a means of feedback has the aforementioned disadvantage of being delayed. It also can be a relatively inefficient use of time if one must go through most of the tape to find critical junctures.

Korner and Brown (1962) developed a device called the Mechanical Third ear, which allows the supervisor to make comments to the student during the course of an interview that are unheard by the interviewee. The supervisor speaks into a microphone from behind a one-way screen, and the student receives the message through a small hearing device. Ward (1960, 1962) developed a more sophisticated device (electronic preceptoring) that allows reception through a small radio receiver and obviates the necessity for an extended cord. He reports that students prefer the supervisor to react only at important junctures and with formulations of dynamics, leaving the specific dialog to the interviewer. Gordon (1975) describes a similar device, which can be constructed for $34 to $44, does not require wiring the room, and consequently is more mobile. The price comparison is indeed favorable; the commercially obtained units cost several hundred dollars.

Although the above described "bugs in the ear" open the possibility for improved and timely communication between teacher and student, there have been no carefully devised programs to measure the supervisors' presumably increased teaching effectiveness with their use. However, the immediacy of feedback is beneficial in itself. Also, the "bug" allows the student to immediately interrupt ineffectual behaviors and substitute increasing approximations to therapeutically skillful behavior, with on-the-spot shaping and reinforcement from the supervisor. Probably the "bug" is used more with supervision of advanced students. Since there is little reported research on the teaching of advanced psychotherapeutic skill, this would account for the infrequency of reference to its use. However, among its devotees, the "bug" is considered an indispensible teaching device.

CONCLUSIONS

It is no longer possible to draw together all of the burgeoning research in this area, but most of it has been stimulated by only three broad, theoretically based programs; the client-centered, didactic-experiential program; the microcounseling program (which is conceptually related to the former); and the behavior modification paradigm. There is a considerable similarity of teaching method used in the preponderance of the studies: initial didactic teaching, followed by modeling, role playing, observed practice with immediate feedback, and audio/video taping with replay and feedback. Some studies have concerned themselves with the effectiveness of one combination of methods as compared with another, and some with one experimental group versus less systematically taught controls. Most of the experimental methods seem to produce treatment groups that are superior to the controls. Usually there have been equivocal or less dramatic results in comparing one experimental group to another, as long as the variables to be taught were clearly defined, the appropriate behaviors practiced, and feedback given the trainee regarding the adequacy of his or her performance. Differences between one set of techniques and another, significant at the .05 or .01 level of confidence, do not seem to have practical importance.

Teaching *method* for interviewing skill now seems to be less problematic than the questions of *what* to teach, how best to define and measure skill acquisition, whether the skills are retained over long periods, and whether they are beneficial to the client. However, with regard to what interviewing skills to teach, there seems to be convergence among programs on at least a few *basic* measured variables. (It should be emphasized that these programs have not even attempted to measure more subtle, psychotherapeutic, conceptual skills and appropriate flexibility of response.) The therapist should be warm and reinforcing, attentive and understanding, should encourage the client to do most of the talking, should demonstrate good listening ability, and should be genuine, emphasize the client's assets, and encourage discussion of the specific. A longer list could probably be constructed, but these few are immediately obvious from the general tenor of the research cited here. Varying terms are used, and some are more behaviorally defined, thus being easier to measure and, by implication, easier to teach.

The question of *how* to teach psychotherapy seems not to be greatly different from the matter of how to teach other complex behavioral skills. The research cited has been useful in pointing out the need for clearly stated objectives, progressive stages of learning, measurement of achievement, and feedback to the student. We continue to come back to the question of *what* are effective ingredients of psychotherapy and, therefore, at what point is a student adequately trained. The relatively simple "facilitation of communication" skills of microcounseling and the "relationship" variables of the client-centered group seem to be a necessary foundation for psychotherapy, but it is unlikely that they are sufficient for optimal client benefit. As one example, the therapist also must possess certain kinds of information or understanding that he or she can impart to the patient (sex information, communication skills for marital and social success, understanding of vocational difficulties and opportunities, awareness of the signs of an impending decompensation, etc.). The therapist needs skill in confronting and reassuring the patient. Defining these additional skills is a current concern of licensing and diplomate boards and peer review systems. In my opinion, research could now more profitably move on to these areas.

In any case, there are a number of previously encountered methodological problems that should be kept in mind by those doing research in this area so that past research inadequacies are not repeated. Some that appear particularly important are the following.

It is difficult to define and measure accurately relatively nonbehavioral variables such as accurate empathy and warmth. If they are important therapeutic dimensions, they should be broken down into more easily measured behavioral components such as response delay, length of utterance, number of references to client emotion, and so forth. The judges should be well informed and trained, they should go through a defined training program, and their accuracy should be checked periodically. They should be given as much background information on the client as possible to help insure the validity of their ratings. It is preferable for ratings to be made on large interview segments or whole interviews instead of on brief multiple segments. It is necessary to know the relationship of judges' ratings to patient satisfaction.

There is no demonstrated, valid criterion measure of training benefit other than therapist behavior in a live interview. Responses to tape segments and coached clients have their place in an early stage of a training program, but there is serious question as to whether they are correlated with advanced skill in live interviewing. Until this has been shown, the researcher who demonstrates learner skill improvement in this artificial situation has not proved that real-life behavioral skills have been developed.

It would be desirable to know the motivation of the trainee group; are they presumably highly motivated students working for a degree or diploma of some kind, or are they individuals whose on-the-job skills presumably are being enhanced, whether or not they chose to undertake training for increased interviewing skill? Similarly, are the patients necessarily motivated or are they a captive population? Motivation is particularly difficult to assess in group training, where individual performance is not regularly observed and closely assessed. This seems to be a significant problem in training parent or other groups for behavior modification skills.

Perhaps the most important procedure to be included is that of obtaining feedback from the ultimate recipient of the training product—the patient. Patient satisfaction, patient rating of therapist qualities, and patient outcome remain the final proof of the pudding.

REFERENCES

Alexik, M., & Carkhuff, R. R. The effects of the experimental manipulation of client self-exploration by high-and low-functioning therapists. *Journal of Clinical Psychology,* 1967, *23,* 210–212.

Anderson, S. C. Effects of confrontation by high-and low-functioning therapists. *Journal of Counseling Psychology,* 1968, *15,* 411–416.

Authier, J., & Gustafson, K. Application of supervised and nonsupervised microcounseling paradigms in the training of paraprofessionals. *Journal of Counseling Psychology,* 1975, *22,* 74–78.

Barrett-Lennard, G. T. Dimensions of therapist response as causal factors in therapeutic change. *Psychological Monographs: General and Applied,* 1962, *76,* No. (43) (Whole No. 562).

Becker, W. C. *Parents are teachers, a child management program.* Champaign, Ill.: Research Press, 1971.

Berberich, J. P. Do the child's responses shape the teaching behavior of adults? *Journal of Experimental Research in Personality,* 1971, *5,* 92–97.

Berenson, B. G., Carkhuff, R. R., & Myrus, P. The interpersonal functioning and training of college students. *Journal of Counseling Psychology,* 1966, *13,* 441–446.

Bergin, A. E. The effects of psychotherapy: Negative results revisited. *Journal of Counseling Psychology,* 1963, *10,* 244–250.

Bergin, A. E., & Jasper, L. G. Correlates of empathy in psychotherapy: A replication. *Journal of Abnormal Psychology,* 1969, *74,* 477–481.

Bergin, A. E., & Solomon, S. Personality and performance correlates of empathic understanding in psychotherapy. In T. Tomlinson and J. Hart (Eds.), *New directions in client-centered therapy.* Boston: Houghton-Mifflin, 1970.

Blaas, C. D., & Heck, E. J. Accuracy of accurate empathy ratings. *Journal of Counseling Psychology,* 1975, *22,* 243–246.

Blocksma, D. D., & Porter, E. H., Jr. A short-term training program in client-centered counseling. *Journal of Counseling Psychology,* 1947, *11,* 55–60.

Bond, J. A. Behavior therapy, learning theory and scientific method. *Psychotherapy: Theory, Research and Practice,* 1974, *11,* 118–132.

Boyd, J. D., II. The construction of a microcounseling training model and the assessment of its effectiveness in teaching a cognitively flexible set of verbal response behaviors to neophyte counselors. Doctoral dissertation, Ohio State University, 1971. Ann Arbor, Michigan University Microfilms No. 72–4428, 225.

Boyd, J. D., II. Microcounseling for a verbal response set: Differential effects of two micromodels and two methods of supervision. *Journal of Counseling Psychology,* 1973, *20,* 97–98.

Burstein, J., & Carkhuff, R. Objective therapist and client ratings of therapist offered facilitative conditions of moderate to low functioning therapists. *Journal of Clinical Psychology,* 1968, *24,* 240–249.

Butler, E., & Hansen, J. Facilitative training: Acquisition, retention and modes of assessment. *Journal of Counseling Psychology,* 1973, *20,* 60–65.

Canada, R. M. Immediate reinforcement vs. delayed reinforcement in teaching a basic interview technique. *Journal of Counseling Psychology,* 1973, *20,* 395–398.

Caracena, P., & Vicory, J. Correlates of phenomenological and judged empathy. *Journal of Consulting Psychology,* 1969, *16,* 510–515.

Carkhuff, R. R. Toward a comprehensive model of facilitative inter-personal processes. *Journal of Counseling Psychology,* 1967, *14,* 67–72.

Carkhuff, R. R. *Helping and human relations. A primer for lay and professional helpers. Vol. I, Selection and training.* New York: Holt, Rinehart and Winston, 1969.

Carkhuff, R. R. *The development of human resources.* New York: Holt, Rinehart and Winston, 1971.

Carkhuff, R. R. *The art of helping.* Amherst, Mass.: Human Resource Development Press, 1972.

Carkhuff, R. R., & Alexik, M. Effect of client depth of self-exploration upon high-and low-functioning counselors. *Journal of Counseling Psychology,* 1967, *14,* 350–355.

Carkhuff, R. R., & Truax, C. B. Training in counseling and psychotherapy: An evaluation of an integrated didactic and experiential approach. *Journal of Consulting Psychology,* 1965, *29,* 333–336.

Chinsky, J. M., & Rappaport, J. Brief critique of the meaning and reliability of "accurate empathy" ratings. *Psychological Bulletin,* 1970, *73,* 379–382.

Cochrane, C. T. Development of a measure of empathic communication. *Psychotherapy: Theory, Research and Practice,* 1974, *11,* 41–47.

Cotler, S. B., Applegate, G., King, L. W., & Kristal, S. Establishing a token economy program in a state hospital classroom: A lesson in training student and teacher. *Behavior Therapy,* 1972, *3,* 209–222.

Covner, B. J. Studies in phonographic recordings of verbal material: III. The completeness and accuracy of counseling interview reports. *Journal of General Psychology,* 1944, *30,* 181–203.

Demos, G. D., & Zuwaylif, F. H. Counselor movement as a result of an intensive six-week training program in counseling. *Personnel and Guidance Journal* 1963, *42,* 125–128.

Dowling, T. H., & Frantz, T. The influence of facilitative relationship on imitative learning. *Journal of Counseling Psychology,* 1975, *22,* 259–263.

Elsenrath, D. E., Coker, D. L., & Martinson, W. D. Microteaching interviewing skills. *Journal of Counseling Psychology,* 1972, *19,* 150–155.

Eyberg, S. M., & Johnson, S. M. Multiple assessment of behavior modification with families: Effects of contingency contracting and order of treated problems. *Journal of Consulting and Clinical Psychology,* 1974, *42,* 594–606.

Eyberg, S. M., & Matarazzo, R. G. Efficiency in teaching child management skills: Individual parent-child interaction versus parent group didactic training.

Paper presented at the meeting of the Western Psychological Association, Sacramento, April 1975.

Feifel, H., & Eells, J. Patients and therapists assess the same psychotherapy. *Journal of Consulting Psychology*, 1963, *27*, 310–318.

Ferber, H., Keeley, S. M., & Shemberg, K. M. Training parents in behavior modification: Outcome of and problems encountered in a program after Patterson's work. *Behavior Therapy*, 1974, *5*, 415–419.

Fry, P. S. Effects of desensitization treatment on core condition training. *Journal of Counseling Psychology*, 1973, *20*, 214–219.

Gardner, G. G. The psychotherapeutic relationship. *Psychological Bulletin*, 1964, *61*, 426–437.

Garfield, S. L. Research on the training of professional psychotherapists. In H. Gurman and A. Razin (Eds.), *The therapist's contribution to effective psychotherapy: Empirical assessment*. New York: Pergamon, 1977.

Glowgower, F., & Sloop, E. W. Two strategies of group training of parents as effective behavior modifiers. *Behavior Therapy*, 1976, *7*, 177–184.

Gordon, D. A. A mobile, wireless "bug-in-the-ear" communication system for training and therapy. *Behavior Therapy*, 1975, *6*, 130–132.

Gormally, J., & Hill, C. E. Guidelines for research on Carkhuff's training model. *Journal of Counseling Psychology*, 1974, *21*, 539–547.

Gormally, J., Hill, C. E., Gulanick, N., & McGovern, T. The persistence of communications skills for undergraduate and graduate trainees. *Journal of Clinical Psychology*, 1975, *31*, 369–372.

Hanf, C. Modification of maternal controlling behaviors during mother-child interactions in standardized laboratory situations. Paper presented at first NW meeting of the Association for Advancement of the Behavior Therapies, University of Washington Medical School, November 1967.

Hansen, J., Moore, G., & Carkhuff, R. The differential relationships of objective and client perceptions of counseling. *Journal of Clinical Psychology*, 1968, *24*, 244–246.

Hargrove, D. S. Verbal interaction analysis of empathic and nonempathic responses of therapists. *Journal of Consulting and Clinical Psychology*, 1974, *42*, 305.

Harmatz, M. G. Two-channel recording in the supervision of psychotherapy. *Professional Psychology*, 1975, *6*, 478–480.

Hayden, B. Verbal and therapeutic styles of experienced therapists who differ in peer-rated therapist effectiveness. *Journal of Counseling Psychology*, 1975, *22*, 384–389.

Holder, T., Carkhuff, R. R., & Berenson, B. G. Differential effects of the manipulation of therapeutic conditions upon high-and low-functioning clients. *Journal of Counseling Psychology*, 1967, *14*, 63–66.

Holland, C. J. An interview guide for behavioral counseling with parents. *Behavior Therapy*, 1970, *1*, 70–79.

Holt, R. R., & Luborsky, L. *Personality patterns of psychiatrists*. New York: Basic Books, 1958.

Ivey, A. E. *Microcounseling: Innovations in interviewing training*. Springfield, Ill.: Charles C Thomas, 1971.

Ivey, A. E., Normington, C. J.., Miller, D. C., Merrill, W. H., & Haase, R. F. Microcounseling and attending behavior: An approach to prepracticum counselor training. *Journal of Counseling Psychology*, Monograph Supplement, 1968, *15* (5), Pp. 1–12.

Jacobson, J., Bushnell, D., & Risley, T. Switching requirements in a headstart classroom. *Journal of Applied Behavior Analysis*, 1969, *2*, 43–47.

Johnson, C. A., Katz, R. C., & Gelfand, S. Undergraduates as behavioral technicians on an adult token economy ward. *Behavior Therapy*, 1972, *3*, 589–592.

Johnson, D. W. Effects of warmth of interaction, accuracy of understanding, and the proposal of compromises on listeners' behavior. *Journal of Counseling Psychology*, 1971, *18*, 207–216.

Jones, V. Attitude changes in an NDEA Institute. *Personnel and Guidance Journal*, 1963, *42*, 387–392.

Kagan, N., Krathwohl, D., Goldberg, A., Campbell, R. J., Schankle, P. G., Greenberg, B. S., Danish, S. J., Resnickoff, A., Bowes, J., & Bandy, S. B. *Studies in human interaction: Interpersonal process recall simulated by videotape*. East Lansing: Michigan State University Educational Publication Services, College of Education, 1967.

Kamin, I., & Caughlan, J. Patients report the subjective experience of out-patient psychotherapy: A follow-up study. *American Journal of Psychotherapy*, 1963, *17*, 660–668.

Kanfer, F., & Saslow, G. Behavior diagnosis. In C. M. Franks (Ed.), *Behavior therapy*. New York: McGraw-Hill, 1969.

Katz, R. C., Johnson, C. A., & Gelfand, S. Modifying the dispensing of reinforcers: Some implications for behavior modification with hospitalized patients. *Behavior Therapy*, 1972, *3*, 579–583.

Kelley, J. D. Reinforcement in microcounseling. *Journal of Counseling Psychology*, 1971, *18*, 268–272.

Kelly, L., & Goldberg, L. R. Correlates of later performance and specialization in psychology: *Psychological Monographs*, 1959, *73* (whole No. 482).

Korner, I. N., & Brown, W. H. The mechanical third ear. *Journal of Consulting Psychology*, 1962, *16*, 81–84.

Kozloff, M. A. *Reaching the autistic child: A parent training program*. Champaign, Ill.: Research Press, 1973.

Kratochvil, D., Aspy, D., & Carkhuff, R. R. The differential effects of absolute level and direction of growth in counselor functioning upon client level of functioning. *Journal of Clinical Psychology*, 1967, *23*, 216–217.

Kubany, E. S., Sloggett, B. B., & Ogata, R. Training teachers in the classroom application of learning principles. In R. G. Tharp (Chairman), *Community intervention: A behavioral approach*. Symposium presented at the meeting of the American Psychological Association, Honolulu, September 1972.

Kurtz, R., & Grummon, D. Different approaches to the measurement of therapist empathy and their relationship to therapy outcomes. *Journal of Consulting and Clinical Psychology*, 1972, *39*, 106–116.

Levine, F. M., & Tilker, H. A. A behavior modification approach to supervision of psychotherapy. *Psychotherapy: Theory, Research and Practice*,

1974, *11,* 182–188.

Loeber, R., & Weisman, R. G. Contingencies of therapist and trainer performance: A review. *Psychological Bulletin,* 1975, *82,* 660–688.

Lorr, M. Client perception of therapists: A study of the therapeutic relation. *Journal of Consulting Psychology,* 1965, *29,* 146–149.

Matarazzo, J. D., & Wiens, A. N. Speech correlates of empathy and outcome. *Behavior Modification* (in press).

Matarazzo, R. G. The systematic study of learning psychotherapy skills. In A. E. Bergin and S. L. Garfield (Eds.), *Handbook of psychotherapy and behavior change.* New York: Wiley, 1971. Pp. 895–924.

Matarazzo, R. G., Phillips, J. S., Wiens, A. N., & Saslow, G. Learning the art of interviewing: A study of what beginning students do and their pattern of change. *Psychotherapy: Theory, Research and Practice,* 1965, *2,* 49–60.

Matarazzo, R. G., Wiens, A. N., & Saslow, G. Experimentation in the teaching and learning of psychotherapy skills. In L. A. Gottschalk and A. Auerbach (Eds.), *Methods of research in psychotherapy.* New York: Appleton-Century Crofts, 1966. Pp. 597–635.

McWhirter, J. J. Two measures of the facilitative conditions: A correlation study. *Journal of Counseling Psychology,* 1973, *20,* 317–320.

Mintz, J., & Luborsky, L. Segments versus whole sessions: Which is the better unit for psychotherapy process research? *Journal of Abnormal Psychology,* 1971, *78,* 180–191.

Moreland, J. R., Ivey, A. E., & Phillips, J. S. An evaluation of microcounseling as an interviewer training tool. *Journal of Consulting and Clinical Psychology,* 1973, *41,* 294–300.

Muslin, H. L., Burstein, A. G., Gedo, J. E., & Sadow, L. Research on the supervisory process I. Supervisor's appraisal of the interview data. *Archives of General Psychiatry,* 1967, *16,* 427–431.

Nay, W. R. A systematic comparison of instructional techniques for parents. *Behavior Therapy,* 1975, *6,* 14–21.

Patterson, G. R., Cobb, J. A., & Ray, R. S. A social engineering technology for retraining the families of aggressive boys. In H. E. Adams and I. P. Unikel (Eds.), *Issues and trends in behavior therapy.* Springfield, Ill.: Charles C Thomas, 1973. Pp. 193–210.

Patterson, G. R., & Gullion, M. E. *Living with children: New methods for parents and teachers.* Champaign, Ill.: Research Press, 1968.

Patterson, G. R., & Reid, J. B. Intervention for families of aggressive boys: A replication study. *Behavior Research and Therapy,* 1973, *11,* 383–394.

Perry, M. A. Modeling and instructions in training for counselor empathy. *Journal of Counseling Psychology,* 1975, *22,* 173–179.

Piaget, G. W., Berenson, B. G., & Carkhuff, R. R. Differential effects of the manipulation of therapeutic conditions by high-and moderate-functioning therapists upon high-and low-functioning clients. *Journal of Consulting Psychology,* 1967, *31,* 481–486.

Rappaport, J., & Chinsky, J. M. Accurate empathy: Confusion of a construct. *Psychological Bulletin,* 1972, *77,* 400–404.

Ray, R. S. The training of mothers of a typical child in the use of behavior modification techniques. Unpublished master's thesis, University of Oregon, 1965.

Reisinger, J. J., Ora, J. P., & Frangia, G. W. Parents as change agents for their children: A review. *Journal of Community Psychology,* 1976, *4,* 103–123.

Resnikoff, A Critique of the human resource development model from the viewpoint of rigor. *The Counseling Psychologist,* 1972, *3,* 46–55.

Rice, L. N. Therapists' style of participation and case outcome. *Journal of Consulting Psychology,* 1965, *29,* 155 160.

Rinn, R. C., Vernon, J. C., & Wise, M. J. Training parents of behaviorally-disordered children in groups: A three years' program evaluation. *Behavior Therapy,* 1975, *6,* 378–387.

Rogers, C. R. *Client-centered therapy.* Boston: Houghton Mifflin, 1951.

Rogers, C. R. The necessary and sufficient conditions of therapeutic personality change. *Journal of Consulting Psychology,* 1957, *21,* 95–103.

Rogers, C. R., & Truax, C. B. The relationship between patient intrapersonal exploration in the first sampling interview and the final outcome criterion. *Brief Research Reports,* Wisconsin Psychiatric Institute, University of Wisconsin, 1962, *73.*

Salzinger, K. Feldman, R. S., & Portnoy, S. Training parents of brain injured children in the use of operant conditioning procedures. *Behavior Therapy,* 1970, *1,* 4–32.

Shapiro, J. G. Relationship between expert and neophyte ratings of therapeutic conditions. *Journal of Consulting and Clinical Psychology,* 1968, *32,* 87–89.

Strupp, H. H., & Jenkins, J. J. The development of six sound motion picture simulating psychotherapeutic situations. *Journal of Nervous and Mental Disease,* 1963, *136,* 317–328.

Strupp, H. H., Wallach, M. S., & Wogan, M. Psychotherapy experience in retrospect: Questionnaire survey for former patients and their therapists. *Psychological Monographs: General and Applied,* 1964, *78*(11) (Whole No. 588).

Toukmanian, S. G., & Rennie, D. L. Microcounseling versus human relations training: Relative effectiveness with undergraduate trainees. *Journal of Counseling Psychology,* 1975, *22,* 345–352.

Truax, C. B., & Carkhuff, R. R. *Toward effective counseling and psychotherapy: Training and practice.* Chicago: Aldine, 1967.

Truax, C. B., Carkhuff, R. R., & Douds, J. Toward an integration of the didactic and experiential approaches to training in counseling and psychotherapy. *Journal of Counseling Psychology,* 1964, *11,* 240–247.

Truax, C. B., Silber, L. D., & Carkhuff, R. R. Accurate empathy, nonpossessive warmth, genuineness and therapeutic outcome in lay group counseling. Unpublished manuscript, University of Arkansas, 1966.

Truax, C. B., Wargo, D. G., Frank, J. D., Imber, S. D., Battle, C. C., Hoehn-Saric, R., Nash, E. H., &

Stone, A. R. Therapist empathy, genuineness, and warmth and patient therapeutic outcome. *Journal of Consulting Psychology,* 1966, *30,* 395–401.

Uhleman, M. R., Lea, G. W., & Stone, G. L. Effects of instructions and modeling on trainees low in interpersonal-communications skills. *Journal of Counseling Psychology,* 1976, *23,* 509–513.

Wahler, G., Winkel, G. H., Peterson, R. F., & Morrison, D. C. Mothers as behavior therapists for their own children. *Behavior Research and Therapy,* 1965, *3,* 113–124.

Wallston, K. A., & Weetz, L. J. Measurement of the core dimensions of helping. *Journal of Counseling Psychology,* 1975, *22,* 567–569.

Walter, H. I., & Gilmore, S. K. Placebo versus social learning effects in parent training procedures designed to alter the behavior of aggressive boys. *Behavior Therapy,* 1973, *4,* 361–377.

Ward, C. H. An electronic aide for teaching interviewing techniques. *Archives of General Psychiatry,* 1960, *3,* 357–358.

Ward, C. H. Electronic preceptoring in teaching beginning psychotherapy. *Journal of Medical Education,* 1962, *37,* 1128–1129.

Wenegrat, A. A factor analytic study of the Truax accurate empathy scale. *Psychotherapy: Theory, Research and Practice,* 1974, *11,* 48–51.

Whitely, J. M., Sprinthall, M. A., Mosher, R. L., & Donaghy, R. T. Selection and evaluation of counselor effectiveness. *Journal of Counseling Psychology,* 1967, *14,* 226–234.

Wiltz, N. A., Jr. Modification of behaviors of deviant boys through parent participation in a group technique. Unpublished doctoral dissertation, University of Oregon, 1969.

AUTHOR INDEX

SUBJECT INDEX